LET US KNOW WHAT YOU THINK

In order to produce a directory that will serve you best, we ask that you take the time to fill out this short questionnaire. Thank you for your continued support and please feel free to photocopy this form or attach additional sheets.

Is this the first time you have purchased the *Conservation Directory*?   ❏ Yes   ❏ No

If no, how long have you been purchasing the *Conservation Directory*? _____

How would you categorize yourself? (check one)
❏ Environmental Professional
❏ College or University Library
❏ Career Center
❏ Public Library
❏ Environmental Activist
❏ Business or Corporation
❏ Environmental Lawyer
❏ Conservation Organization
❏ Educator
❏ Student
❏ Scientist
❏ Other _____

What resources would you like to see added to the *Conservation Directory*?

_____

What would you like to see removed from the *Conservation Directory*?

_____

Are you pleased with the format of the *2000 Conservation Directory*?   ❏ Yes   ❏ No

If no, what suggestions do you have for the future organization of the *Conservation Directory* _____

_____

Which index is most useful to you?
❏ Geographic Index
❏ Staff Name Index
❏ Keyword Index
❏ Organization Name Index
❏ I do not use the indices

If organization listings contained less information would the directory be as useful?   ❏Yes ❏No

Would you be interested in purchasing the *Conservation Directory* on CD-ROM?   ❏Yes ❏No

Would you be interested in an online version of the *Conservation Directory*?   ❏Yes ❏No

Additional Comments can be made on the back of this sheet

**MAIL TO: NATIONAL WILDLIFE FEDERATION
ATTN: CONSERVATION DIRECTORY
8925 LEESBURG PIKE; VIENNA, VA 22184
FAX: 703-790-4468**

There are forms in the back of this book for information updates and to suggest new organizations

2000 CONSERVATION DIRECTORY

45TH EDITION

A Guide To Worldwide
Environmental Organizations

Rue E. Gordon, *Editor*

Martha Riecks-Tracey, *Assistant Editor*

Published annually by the
National Wildlife Federation®

NATIONAL WILDLIFE FEDERATION
8925 Leesburg Pike•Vienna•Virginia 22184-0001
www.nwf.org

The mission of the National Wildlife Federation is to educate, inspire, and assist individuals and organizations of diverse cultures to conserve wildlife and other natural resources, and to protect the Earth's environment in order to achieve a peaceful, equitable, and sustainable future.

Printed on recycled paper containing a minimum of 20% post consumer fiber. The balance is pre-consumer fiber.

Copyright© 2000, National Wildlife Federation®
Library of Congress Catalog Card Number 70-10646
ISSN 0069-9 11X
ISBN 1-55821-945-5
The Library of Congress-in-Publication Data is available on file.

> The *Conservation Directory* is published as a public service. Organizations are included on the basis of their stated objectives and other information provided. Inclusion does not imply confirmation of the information nor does it imply any endorsement of the organizations listed by the National Wildlife Federation.

The *Conservation Directory* may be purchased by calling The Lyons Press at 800-836-0510.

If you have any general questions about the *Conservation Directory*, please call 703-790-4000.

LETTER FROM THE EDITORS

To Our Loyal Subscribers:

Even in the midst of the information age, new addresses, changing area codes and shifting internet addresses can make contacting any organization a challenge. So once again, we have done the difficult work for you, tracking down new information for almost every group listed to provide you with the updated 45th edition of the *Conservation Directory*.

We try to improve every edition to make the *Conservation Directory* the most complete and comprehensive directory of environmental organizations and agencies available. Thanks to the help of the Academy for Education Development, the *2000 Conservation Directory* contains many new listings of environmental organizations throughout the world. Other improvements include an expanded Conservation Information Resources section, additional new Non-Governmental Organization listings with a focus on native plant societies, and more fax numbers, e-mail addresses and websites than ever before.

While we have tried to make the information listed in the Directory as accurate as possible, you might still encounter a few errors. We apologize for these mistakes that often arise from circumstances beyond our control, such as elections or other changes that occur after our printing date. For organizations listed in the Directory, an update form is provided at the back of the book--we need your help to produce an accurate directory.

As always, we welcome any comments you have on this edition of the Directory, as well as any further suggestions you may have as to how we can make the Directory even better. A short questionnaire is included in the front of the book for you to complete if you are interested. Thank you.

Sincerely,

Rue E. Gordon
Editor and Coordinator

Martha Riecks-Tracey
Assistant Editor

National Wildlife Federation Executive Staff

Mark Van Putten, *President & Chief Executive Officer*
Eileen Morgan Johnson, *General Counsel*
Lawrence J. Amon, *Vice President for Finance and Administration & Chief Financial Officer*
Natalie S. Waugh, *Senior Vice President, Constituent Programs*
R. Montgomery Fischer, *Vice President & Coordinator, Conservation Programs*

Vice Presidents: Barbara J. Bramble, Robert S. Ertter, J. Scott Feierabend, John H. Giesecke, Philip B. Kavits, Jaime Berman Matyas, Susan Rieff, Steven J. Shimberg, James L. Stofan, Bob Strohm, Carolyn Waldron
Chief Information Technology Officer: Kenneth Herman

National Wildlife Productions: Christopher N. Palmer, *President & CEO*

Past President: Jay D. Hair

Editorial Staff

Rue S. Gordon
Editor/Project Coordinator

James L. Stofan
Vice President, Educational Outreach

Martha Riecks-Tracey
Assistant Editor

Susan B. Weil
Director, Community-Based Education

Furey Design/Kathleen Furey
CoverDesign

Cover Photo Credits

Front Cover Background: Fahkahatchee Strand of Big Cypress Swamp in Florida by Lynn M. Stone
Front Cover: Great Blue Heron by Alan and Sandy Carey
Back Cover: Florida Panther by Lynn M. Stone

TABLE OF CONTENTS

Introduction

Acknowledgements

User's Guide

National Wildlife Federation

National Wildlife Federation Affiliate Organizations

1998 National Conservation Achievement Awards

1999 Goldman Environmental Awards

About the Cover

U. S. CONGRESS, COMMITTEES, AND SUBCOMMITTEES 1

U. S. FEDERAL AND INTERNATIONAL GOVERNMENT AGENCIES 7
Includes Departments of the Executive Branch, Independent Agencies, Commissions, Canadian Federal Government Agencies, and other International Government Agencies

STATE AND PROVINCIAL GOVERNMENT AGENCIES 38
Includes U.S. State and Canadian Provincial Government Agencies

NON-GOVERNMENTAL ORGANIZATIONS 130
Includes United States and International Organizations not affiliated with government agencies

EDUCATIONAL INSTITUTIONS 362
Colleges and universities with conservation and environmental studies programs

CONSERVATION INFORMATION RESOURCES 397
Fish and Wildlife Commissioners and Directors 397
State Agency Coordinators for Environmental Education 399
Sources of Audio-Visual Materials 401
Periodicals and Directories 402
Environmental Databases and Services 406
Natural Heritage Programs 413

FEDERALLY PROTECTED AREAS 418
Bureau of Land Management Districts 418
National Estuarine Research Reserves 421
National Forests 422
National Grasslands 426
National Marine Sanctuaries 426
National Parks 427
National Seashores 428
National Wildlife Refuges 429

INDICES
ORGANIZATION NAME INDEX 439
KEYWORD INDEX 460
STAFF NAME INDEX 527
GEOGRAPHIC INDEX 568

INTRODUCTION

This is the forty-fifth edition of the National Wildlife Federation's *Conservation Directory*. It has been published every year since 1955. The first Directory listed National Wildlife Federation state affiliate organizations and was expanded in 1960 to include other conservation organizations. The Directory now lists U.S. and state government agencies, international, national, regional organizations and commissions, international government agencies and non-governmental organizations from around the world. The Directory has over 3,000 entries, an expansion of more than 100 new organizations from the previous edition. It also includes the winners of the 1999 Goldman Environmental Prize and the National Wildlife Federation's 1998 Conservation Achievement Awards.

Listings include:

- United States Congressional Members, Committees, and Subcommittees
- Federal Government Agencies (United States, Canada and International)
- State and Provincial Government Agencies (United States and Canada)
- Non-Governmental Organizations (United States, Canadian and International)
- Educational Institutions (colleges and universities with Conservation Programs)
- Conservation Information Resources (Periodicals, Sources of Audio-Visual Materials and Databases)
- Federally Protected Conservation Areas (National Parks, Seashores, Grasslands and Wildlife Refuges)
- And more essential and useful information.

ACKNOWLEDGEMENTS

We would like to take the time to thank the many people who have taken part in the production of this book. It is an enormous undertaking each year, and one that would be impossible without the help and support of our colleagues. Their advice and assistance throughout production is the only way we have been able to bring you this extraordinary resource. From the beautiful cover featuring the Everglades to the wisely organized information on its pages, these people have allowed us to once again bring to the public the best directory of conservation organizations. Thanks to all who made it possible to produce a quality publication.

Many thanks to **Kay Lybrand**, Staff Assistant for Communications; **Tim McLean**, Senior Editor for Communications; **Malia Hale**, Legislative Representative; **Kris Thoemke** and **Brad Nunley**, Everglades Project Office; **Peter Frederick**, Assistant Research Professor of Wildlife Ecology at the University of Florida, **Kathleen Furey**, Cover Designer; and **Sharon Levy,** our dedicated librarian. Their tiresome dedication and contributions to the publication of the Directory are greatly appreciated. Without the help of our **Information Systems** staff, it would have been impossible to produce this Directory. And we would like to thank all NWF Staff, especially the **Educational Outreach Department**, for their input, suggestions and support.

Perhaps most important are the many thanks that go to all of the organizations listed and to the individuals involved for their cooperation in providing the information that was included in this Directory. We commend all of these organizations for their continuing work to protect and defend our natural world.

Rue E. Gordon, Editor and Coordinator
Conservation Directory
National Wildlife Federation
8925 Leesburg Pike
Vienna, VA 22184-0001

USERS GUIDE

The Conservation Directory is divided into three parts:

• Part One: Introduction

The introduction provides information about the Directory and other National Wildlife Federation programs. This section also features the winners of the National Conservation Achievement Awards and the Goldman Environmental Prize, addresses of NWF Affiliates and the Table of Contents. The Table of Contents is an excellent resource for beginning a search, listing all section headings with corresponding page numbers.

• Part Two: Descriptive Listings

Entries are arranged alphabetically according to sections:

- *U.S. Congress, Committees, and Subcommittees*
- *U.S. Federal and International Government Agencies:* consists of executive branch organizations, independent government agencies, Commissions and international Government Agencies.
- *State and Provincial Government Agencies:* consists of state agencies that deal with conservation issues, organized by state.
- *Non-Governmental Organizations:* consists of American and international organizations that are not affiliated with any government agency whose mission is to help protect, preserve and defend the natural world. Listed in alphabetical order.
- *Educational Institutions:* consists of colleges and universities with conservation programs and research centers, organized by state.
- *Conservation Information Resources:* includes Fish and Wildlife Commissioners and Directors, state agency Environmental Education Coordinators, periodicals and directories, sources of audio-visual materials, Natural Heritage Programs and environmental databases.
- *Federally Protected Areas:* consists of National Forests, National Marine Sanctuaries, National Estuarine Research Reserves, National Parks, National Seashores, National Grasslands, Bureau of Land Management Districts and National Wildlife Refuges.

National Wildlife Federation Affiliates are listed in the Non-Governmental Organizations section. Governors are listed first for each state in the State Government Section. All entries include name, address, phone and fax number, e-mail and internet address, founding date, membership, senior staff by name and title and description of the organization's primary goals and mission as provided by the organizations.

• Part Three: Indices

Organization Index

This is a quick and easy way to locate an organization. The index includes the name of every organization included in the Directory in alphabetical order with the corresponding page number.

Keyword Index

This useful reference tool lists various subject areas and gives the name of those organizations whose work is related to that keyword. Index citations contain page numbers.

Staff Name Index

The *Conservation Directory* is very helpful if you know the name of an individual involved with an organization but do not know the specific name of the organization. This index lists all individuals cited in Directory listings. Each citation contains the individual's name and page numbers where it appears.

Geographic Index

This index lists agencies and organizations by geographic regions. It is a great way to locate organizations that can be found in a certain state or province.

THE NATIONAL WILDLIFE FEDERATION is the nation's largest member-supported conservation organization, working with individuals, communities, organizations, businesses, and governments to protect wildlife, wild places, and the environment upon which we all depend. Through our grass-roots members, 46 state affiliate organizations, and 11 field offices nationwide, we work with people from all walks of life to conserve wildlife and other natural resources. Our common-sense approach to environmental protection balances the demands of a healthy economy with the need for a healthy environment, ensuring a brighter future for people and wildlife everywhere.

THE MISSION of NWF is to educate, inspire and assist individuals and organizations of diverse cultures to conserve wildlife and other natural resources and to protect the Earth's environment in order to achieve a peaceful, equitable and sustainable future.

WHAT WE DO: NWF focuses its conservation efforts on **Endangered Habitats, Water Quality, Land Stewardship, Wetlands,** and **Sustainable Communities**, pursuing a diverse range of educational outreach and grass-roots advocacy initiatives to safeguard wildlife and wild places. Representative programs within these areas include:

ENDANGERED HABITATS
- Conservation Funding
- Climate Change & Wildlife
- Keep the Wild Alive® Campaign
- Salmon & Habitat Conservation Plans
- Takings & Private Property
- International Endangered Species
- Grizzly Bear Recovery

WATER QUALITY
- Saving Our Watersheds
- Protecting Great Lakes Watersheds from Toxics
- Preventing the Loss or Degradation of Coastlines
- Texas Water Quality and Environmental Flows

LAND STEWARDSHIP
- Northern Forest Restoration
- Wildlife on the Prairie

SUSTAINABLE COMMUNITIES
- Trade & Environment
- Finance & Environment
- Floodplain Management
- Population & Environment
- Proctor Creek Watershed

WETLANDS
- Everglades Restoration
- National Wetlands Protection
- Alaska Wetlands Watch
- Lower Mississippi River Basin
- Texas Coastal Wetlands Study
- Copper River Delta

EDUCATIONAL PROGRAMS: NWF offers the following educational programs that reach thousands of people of all ages, teaching them about nature and wildlife and their importance to human survival.

- **ANIMAL TRACKS®** is an environmental education program that trains elementary and middle school teachers. The program offers both on-line and printed conservation education materials to assist teachers.
- **BACKYARD WILDLIFE HABITAT™** is a program that encourages people to plan and maintain their gardens with the needs of wildlife in mind. Since 1973, NWF has officially certified over 25,000 Backyard Wildlife Habitats. NWF also promotes a **SCHOOLYARD HABITATS®** project to assist and recognize school communities in creating and using habitat-based learning areas on school grounds.
- **CAMPUS ECOLOGY®** assists students, faculty, and administrators in transforming colleges and universities into learning and teaching models of environmental sustainability by providing factual resources, organizing tools, one-on-one consultation, and training clinics.
- **EARTH TOMORROW®** is a conservation leadership education program for high-school aged students. The program is currently piloted in Detroit through the NWF Great Lakes Natural Resource Center.
- **EARTHSAVERS®** is a club program for children (ages 6-13) who care about the Earth and want to help.
- **NATURELINK®** programs encourage youth, teens and families in personal discovery of nature through hands-on learning in the outdoors. NatureLink day and weekend events, camps for youth and teens and week-long family summits build awareness and appreciation of the natural world, develop outdoor skills and encourage children and adults to take action to help the earth.
- **NATIONAL WILDLIFE WEEK,** celebrated each April, is a program that brings free conservation curriculum materials to more than 620,000 educators who reach more than 20 million students.

NATIONAL WILDLIFE PRODUCTIONS (NWP) is the not-for-profit television, film, and multimedia arm of the National Wildlife Federation. NWP's mission is to produce films, television programs and other media that entertain people while opening their eyes to the importance of conserving natural resources for the needs of both people and wildlife. NWP produces NWF documentaries for TBS Superstation, Animal Planet, the Outdoor Life Network, and public television. NWP also produces giant-screen films for large-format theaters.

NWF PUBLICATIONS include award-winning magazines that celebrate wildlife in all its wondrous diversity. *National Wildlife®* and *International Wildlife®* use riveting text and captivating images to educate readers about conservation issues and to explore the latest discoveries affecting the natural world. *Ranger Rick®* for children ages 7 to 12, and *Your Big Backyard®* for kids ages 3 to 6, combine colorful photographs, funny drawings and exciting stories to turn readers on to nature, outdoor adventure, and helping the environment. *Wild Animal Baby*™ for ages 12 months to 3 years, is a board book magazine that helps parents introduce the wonders of the natural world to their children through the use of baby animal photos, creative shape matching, simple stories, fun fingerplays and an online parent guide.

NATIONAL WILDLIFE FEDERATION REGIONAL AND PROJECT OFFICES

- **Headquarters** in Vienna, Virginia; Phone 703-790-4000
- **Alaska Project Office** in Anchorage, Alaska; Phone: 907-258-4800
- **California Natural Resource Center** in San Diego, California; opening February 2000
- **Everglades Project Office** in Naples, Florida; Phone: 941-643-4111
- **Great Lakes Natural Resource Center** in Ann Arbor, Michigan; Phone: 734-769-3351
- **Gulf States Natural Resource Center** in Austin, Texas; Phone: 512-476-9805
- **Northeastern Natural Resource Center** in Montpelier, Vermont; Phone: 802-229-0650
- **Northern Rockies Project Office** in Missoula, Montana; Phone: 406-721-6705
- **Northwestern Natural Resource Center** in Seattle, Washington; opening January 2000
- **Office of Federal and International Affairs (OFIA)** in Washington, DC; Phone: 202-797-6800
- **Rocky Mountain Natural Resource Center** in Boulder, Colorado; Phone: 303-786-8001
- **Southeastern Natural Resource Center** in Atlanta, Georgia; Phone: 404-876-8733

Detailed descriptions of these offices can be found in their listings in the Non-Governmental Organization Section

NWF AFFILIATES

National Wildlife Federation Affiliates are autonomous, statewide organizations that support the purposes and objectives of the National Wildlife Federation. Each affiliate is governed by its own board of directors and develops its own membership on a local level. Affiliates provide NWF with an organized grassroots network nationwide. The elected delegates from the state affiliates determine the conservation policy for NWF through a resolution process at the NWF Annual Meeting. The delegates also elect NWF's Chair, Vice Chairs, and 13 Regional Directors. Detailed descriptions can be found in the Non-Governmental Organization section.

ALABAMA WILDLIFE FEDERATION
46 Commerce St., Montgomery, AL 86104
Phone: 334-832-9453; fax: 334-832-9454
E-mail: alabamawf@mindspring.com
Web site: www.alawild.org

WILDLIFE FEDERATION OF ALASKA
750 West Second Ave., Suite 200
Anchorage, AK 99501-2121
Phone: 907-274-3388; fax: 907-258-4811
E-mail: wfa@micronet.net
Web site: www.micronet.net/users/~wfa/default.html

ARIZONA WILDLIFE FEDERATION
644 N. Country Club, Suite E
Mesa, AZ 85201-4991
Phone: 480-644-0077; fax: 480-644-0078
E-mail: awf@primenet.com
Web site: www.primenet.com/~awf

ARKANSAS WILDLIFE FEDERATION
7509 Cantrell Rd., # 104
Little Rock, AR 72207
Phone: 50l-663-7255; fax: 501-664-7397

PLANNING AND CONSERVATION LEAGUE
926 J Street, Suite 612
Sacramento, CA 95814
Phone: 916-444-8726; fax: 916-448-1789
E-mail: pclmail@pcl.org; Web site: www.pcl.org

COLORADO WILDLIFE FEDERATION
445 Union Blvd., #302; Lakewood, CO 80228
Phone: 303-987-0400; fax: 303-987-0200
E-mail: cwfed@aol.com
Web site: www.coloradowildlife.org

CONNECTICUT FOREST AND PARK ASSOCIATION, INC.
Middlefield, 16 Meriden Rd.
Rockfall, CT 06481-2961
Phone: 860-346-2372; fax: 860-347-7463
E-mail: conn.forest.assoc@asnet.net
Web site: www.ctwoodlands.org

DELAWARE NATURE SOCIETY
P.O. Box 700; Hockessin, DE 19707
Phone: 302-239-2334; fax: 302-239-2473
E-mail: Ashland@DCA.net
Web site: www.dca.net/naturesociety

FLORIDA WILDLIFE FEDERATION
P.O. Box 6870
Tallahassee, FL 32314-6870
Phone: 850-656-7113; fax: 850-942-4431
E-mail: wildfed@aol.com;
Web site: www.fwf.usf.edu

GEORGIA WILDLIFE FEDERATION
1930 Iris Dr.
Conyers, GA 30094-5046
Phone: 770-929-3350; fax: 770-929-3534
E-mail: gwf@gwf.org; Web site: www.gwf.org

CONSERVATION COUNCIL FOR HAWAII
PMB-203, 111 E. Puainako St., Ste. 585
Hilo, HI 96720
Phone: 808-236-2234; Fax: 808-247-2551
Web site: www.planet-hawaii.com/~cch

IDAHO WILDLIFE FEDERATION
P.O. Box 6426; Boise, ID 83707
Phone: 208-342-7055; fax: 208-342-7097
E-mail: iwfboi@cyberhighway.net
Web site: www.idahowildlife.org

INDIANA WILDLIFE FEDERATION
950 North Rangeline Rd., Ste. A
Carmel, IN 46032-1315
Phone: 800-347-3445; fax: 317-571-1223
E-mail: iwf@indy.net

IOWA WILDLIFE FEDERATION
3125 Douglas, #103
Des Moines, IA 50310
Phone: 515-279-0655

KANSAS WILDLIFE FEDERATION
4840 W. 15th St.
Lawrence, KS 66049-3876
Phone: 785-843-7786; fax: 785-843-7555
E-mail: KWF@kswildlife.org; Web site: www.kswildlife.org

LEAGUE OF KENTUCKY SPORTSMEN, INC.
P.O. Box 406
Ft. Thomas, KY 41001
Phone/fax: 606- 635-8896;
E-mail: ksportsmen@hotmail.com; Web site: www.loks.org

LOUISIANA WILDLIFE FEDERATION, INC.
P.O. Box 65239
Baton Rouge, LA 70896-5239
Phone: 225-344-6707; fax: 225-344-6707
E-mail: lawildfed@aol.com

NATURAL RESOURCES COUNCIL OF MAINE
3 Wade Street
Augusta, ME 04330
Phone: 207-622-3101; fax: 207-622-4343
E-mail: nrcm@nrcm.org; Web site: www.nrcm.org/

ENVIRONMENTAL LEAGUE OF MASSACHUSETTS
3 Joy St.; Boston, MA 02108
617-742-2553; fax: 617-742-9656
E-mail: elm@environmentalleague.org
Web site: www.environmentalleague.org

MICHIGAN UNITED CONSERVATION CLUBS, INC.
2101 Wood S.
Lansing, MI 48912-3728
Phone: 517-371-1041; fax: 517-371-1505
E-mail: mucc@mucc.org; Web site: www.mucc.org

MINNESOTA CONSERVATION FEDERATION
551 S. Snelling Ave., #B
St. Paul, MN 55116-1525
Phone/fax: 6l2-690-3077
E-mail: mncf@mtn.org

MISSISSIPPI WILDLIFE FEDERATION
P.O. Box 1814
Jackson, MS 39215-1814
Phone: 601- 420-2100; fax: 601-420-2060
E-mail: mwf@netdoor.com:

CONSERVATION FEDERATION OF MISSOURI
728 W. Main St.
Jefferson City, MO 65101-1159
Phone: 573-634-2322; fax: 573-634-8205
E-mail: modfed@sockets.net; Web site: www.confedmo.com

MONTANA WILDLIFE FEDERATION
P.O. Box 1175
Helena, MT 59624-1175
Phone: 406-449-7604; fax: 406- 449-8946
E-mail: mwf@mtwf.org; Web site: www.montanawildlife.com

NEBRASKA WILDLIFE FEDERATION, INC.
P.O. Box 81437
Lincoln, NE 68501-1437
Phone/fax: 402- 994-2001
E-mail: dh43048@novix.net

NEVADA WILDLIFE FEDERATION
P.O. Box 71238
Reno, NV 89570
Phone: 702-645-5423; Fax: 702-885-0405
E-mail: dupree@pyramid.net; Web site: www.nvwf.org

NEW HAMPSHIRE WILDLIFE FEDERATION
P.O. Box 239
Concord, NH 03302
Phone: 603-224-5953; fax: 603-228-4614
E-mail: nhwf@aol.com; Web site: www.nhwf.org

NEW MEXICO WILDLIFE FEDERATION
3240-A Juan Tabo NE, Ste. 204
Albuquerque, NM 87111
Phone: 505-299-5404

ENVIRONMENTAL ADVOCATES
353 Hamilton St.
Albany, NY 12210
Phone: 518-462-5526; fax: 518-427-0381
E-mail: info@envadocates.org; Web site: www.envadvocates.org

NORTH CAROLINA WILDLIFE FEDERATION
Box 10626
Raleigh, NC 27605
Phone: 919-833-1923; fax: 919-829-1192
Web site: www.ncwildlifefed.org

NORTH DAKOTA WILDLIFE FEDERATION
P.O. Box 7248
Bismarck, ND 58507-7248
Phone: 701-222-2557; fax: 701-222-0334
E-mail: ndwf@gcentral.com

LEAGUE OF OHIO SPORTSMEN
3953 Indianola Ave.
Columbus, OH 43214
Phone: 614-268-9924

OKLAHOMA WILDLIFE FEDERATION
P.O. Box 60126
Oklahoma City, OK 73146-0126
Phone: 405-524-7009; fax: 405-521-9270
E-mail: owf@nstar.net

PENNSYLVANIA FEDERATION OF SPORTSMEN'S CLUBS
2426 N. Second St.
Harrisburg, PA 17110
Phone: 717-232-3480; fax: 717-231-3524
E-mail: pawild@paonline.com; Web site: www.pfsc.org

ENVIRONMENT COUNCIL OF RHODE ISLAND
P.O. Box 9061
Providence, RI 02940
Phone: 401-621-8048; fax: 401-331-5266
E-mail: ecri@studentweb.providence.edu

SOUTH CAROLINA WILDLIFE FEDERATION
2711 Middleburg Dr., Ste. 104
Columbia, SC 29204
Phone: 803-256-0670; fax: 803-256-0690
E-mail: angela@scwf.org; Web site: www.scwf.org

SOUTH DAKOTA WILDLIFE FEDERATION
P.O. Box 7075
Pierre, SD 57501
Phone/fax: 605-224-7524
E-mail: sdwf@cam-walnet.com; Web site: www.sdwf.org

TENNESSEE CONSERVATION LEAGUE
300 Orlando Ave.
Nashville, TN 37209-3257
Phone: 615-353-1133; fax: 615-353-0083
E-mail: conserve.tcl@nashville.com

TEXAS COMMITTEE ON NATURAL RESOURCES
1301 South IH-35, Ste. 301
Austin, TX 78741
Phone: 512-441-1122
E-mail: tconr@eden.com; Web site: www.eden.com/tconr

UTAH WILDLIFE FEDERATION
Box 526367
Salt Lake City, UT 84152-6367
Phone: 801-487-1946; fax: 801-486-0611

VERMONT NATURAL RESOURCES COUNCIL
9 Bailey Ave.
Montpelier, VT 05602
Phone: 802-223-2328; fax: 802-223-0287
E-mail: VNRC@together.net; Web site: www.VNRC.org

VIRGIN ISLANDS CONSERVATION SOCIETY, INC.
Arawak Bldg., Suite 3, Gallows Bay
Christiansted, VI 00820
Phone: 340-773-1989; fax: 340-773-7545
E-mail: sea@viaccess.net; Web site: www.ecani.com/environassoc

WASHINGTON WILDLIFE FEDERATION
P.O Box 1966
Olympia, WA 98507-1966
Phone: 360-705-1903
Web site: www.washingtonwildlife.org

WEST VIRGINIA WILDLIFE FEDERATION, INC.
P.O. Box 275
Paden City, WV 26159
Phone: 304-782-3685
E-mail: pleinbach@aol.com

WISCONSIN WILDLIFE FEDERATION, INC.
242 Keoller Ave.
Oshkosh, WI 54901
Phone: 920-235-9136; fax: 920-235-6030
E-mail: wiwf@execpc.com; Web site: www.easy-axcess.com/wwf

WYOMING WILDLIFE FEDERATION
P.O. Box 106
Cheyenne, WY 82003
Phone: 307-637-5433; fax: 307-637-6629
E-mail: admin@wyomingwildlife.org
Web site: www.wyomingwildlife.org

1998 NATIONAL CONSERVATION ACHIEVEMENT AWARDS

Established in 1965, the National Conservation Achievement Awards are presented annually by the National Wildlife Federation to recognize people and organizations whose work has helped to safeguard wildlife and our natural resources. Recipients, who are chosen through a nomination process, represent a wide variety of ongoing environmental work. The 1998 awards were presented at the 1999 NWF Annual Meeting, in the following categories: *Conservationist of the Year, Affiliate of the Year, Communications, Corporate Leadership, Education, Government, International, Legal/Legislative, Organization, Science, Youth and Special Achievement.*

RECIPIENTS:

Conservationist of the Year
SYLVIA EARLE
President, Deep Ocean Exploration and Research
12812 Skyline Blvd., Oakland, CA 94619
One of the world's leading authorities on oceans and marine life, Sylvia Earle has become the most eloquent spokesperson for the protection of these fragile and endangered ecosystems. She has traveled to more than 60 countries to speak, develop ocean policy and perform research, focusing on the ecology of marine ecosystems, particularly marine plants, and on the development of technology for access and research in the deep sea. Earle has become our ambassador to the ocean, helping educate an entire generation about the health of the oceans and the sustainability of life on earth, while raising awareness of the impact of our actions on the future of the planet.

Affiliate of the Year
NATURAL RESOURCES COUNCIL OF MAINE
271 State Street
Augusta, ME 04330
With four decades of conservation work under its belt, the NRCM has experienced a banner year in its effort to protect and restore Maine's waters and other resources. Most notably, NRCM enjoyed an unprecedented victory in its 10-year struggle to remove the Edwards Dam in Augusta. The dam's removal will reopen an upstream passageway for nine migratory fish and restore access to 17 miles of prime spawning habitat. The continuing efforts of this outstanding organization have helped restore valuable habitat and protect natural resources that comprise a natural treasure in Maine and beyond.

Communications
ROCKY BARKER
Environmental Reporter, Idaho Statesman
1200 North Curtis, Boise, ID 83706
As a journalist and author, Rocky Barker has redefined the environmental beat for newspapers in the West and has contributed enormously to the public's understanding of natural resource issues. Barker's award winning, three-part series on the need to remove four dams on the lower Snake River in Idaho and eastern Washington as part of a salmon recovery effort legitimized what many Idaho readers previously considered a radical environmental proposal. Through his intelligent and balanced reporting, Barker has made dam removal a much-addressed issue throughout his state and the nation.

Corporate Leadership
NATIVE & NATURE
Jim Hills, President
1333 North Oracle, Tucson, AZ 85705

Since its inception in 1984, Native & Nature has been merchandising sustainably-harvested products in its client stores and catalog and has promoted collaborations between businesses, non-profit organizations and native tribes to conserve both wildlife and traditional ecological knowledge. Co-owner Jim Hills has pioneered a bio-regional approach to merchandising, clustering ecologically-related products to reinforce his customers' understanding of environmental principles and explaining their cultural and ecological significance. Native & Nature exemplifies what businesses can do locally and profitably to benefit an ecosystem and enrich cultures.

Education
MAUREEN AUSTIN
Executive Director, CHIRP for Garden Wildlife, Inc.
P.O. Box 532, Alpine, CA 91903

As coordinator for the "Sage and Songbirds" project and director of CHIRP (Center to Help Instill Respect and Preservation for Garden Wildlife), Maureen Austin uses her boundless enthusiasm and dedication to teach and encourage people throughout the town of Alpine, California to garden for wildlife. Speaking to local clubs and organizations about planting organic herb gardens to attract wildlife and trying to re-teach a generation of over-zealous pesticide users, Austin was a driving force behind the transformation of Alpine into the first officially recognized Community Wildlife Habitat.

Government
WELLINGTON E. WEBB
Mayor of Denver, CO
City and County Building, Room 350
Denver, CO 80202

Mayor since 1991, Wellington E. Webb has been a driving force in Denver's urban regeneration, tackling the city's most crippling environmental problems and transforming Denver into an ecological model for the country. As Mayor, he has readily addressed pressing environmental issues, working to curb urban sprawl and encourage sustainable growth, reduce energy use throughout the city, supporting wildlife habitats, expanding parks and combating climate change on the local level through Denver's CO_2 Reduction Plan. Mayor Webb's most notable initiative, the $45 million South Platte River Project, has helped turn a filthy, neglected river into a thriving setting for wildlife, recreation and education.

International
DR. HIROSHI HASEGAWA
Associate Professor of Biology, Toho University
Faculty of Science, Biology Department
Miyama, Funabashi, Chiba, 274 JAPAN

For more than 20 years, ornithologist Hiroshi Hasegawa has been a key figure in one of the most extraordinary wildlife recoveries of all time. The short-tailed albatross, the largest sea bird of the Northern Hemisphere, which was once considered extinct, has miraculously returned to the Pacific skies, thanks to Hasegawa's tireless research and conservation efforts. His efforts are marked by a spiritual respect for the species, and the conviction that humans must correct mistakes of the past and preserve the diversity of life for future generations.

Legal/Legislative
JOHN ADAMS
President, Natural Resources Defense Council
40 West 20th Street, New York, NY 10011

As chief executive of the Natural Resources Defense Council (NRDC) for nearly 30 years, John Adams has developed one of the most respected and powerful environmental organizations in the world, and has become a central figure in the environmental public interest community. Under Adams' leadership, NRDC has helped build the legal structure that established the earliest protection of our natural resources, and which remains our most powerful conservation tool today, including landmark legislation like the National Environmental Policy Act, the Clean Air and Clean Water Acts.

Organization
PARTNERS FOR WILDLIFE
California University of Pennsylvania
Department of Biological and Environmental Sciences
California, PA 15419

A consortium of wildlife groups, environmental organizations, state agencies, a local university, and volunteer landowners, Partners for Wildlife demonstrates what can be achieved when diverse groups work together towards the common cause of conservation. Their most ambitious and successful program has been the Farmland Habitat Restoration Project, initiated in 1993 to encourage area farmers to provide for the needs of wildlife and to help improve the quality of water and wetlands. Partners for Wildlife is a unique organization that has been immensely successful in protecting natural resources and restoring wildlife habitat and populations throughout Pennsylvania.

Science
DR. DAVID MECH
Senior Scientist, U.S. Geological Survey
1992 Folwell Avenue, St. Paul, MN 55108

Dr. David Mech is considered the world's leading authority on the wolf, and perhaps more than any other person, has been responsible for a major change in human attitudes toward this most misunderstood predator. His work, which has resulted in hundreds of scientific articles, books and films, has reached and influenced hundreds of thousands of people around the globe. His outstanding achievements in wolf research and education have advanced the field of wildlife biology and have demonstrated that knowledge is the key to successful conservation.

Youth
NEY FROG PROJECT STUDENTS
Minnesota New Country School
115 North Main Street, Le Sueur, MN 56058

In August of 1995, a nature studies class was hiking through Minnesota's Ney Woods, catching frogs, when they made a grim discovery: half of the frogs that they caught had gruesome deformities on their back legs. This chance discovery by a dozen students at the Minnesota New Country School in Le Sueur has led to a nationwide recognition of the growing problem of amphibian deformities, and has sparked a mass effort to find the cause, and a solution. The Ney Frog Project, has students working with scientists, lawmakers and media to determine the extent of the problem, examine possible causes, raise money for research and spread the word.

Special Achievement
EARTH MINISTRY
Rev. James Mulligan, Executive Director
1305 NE 47th Street, Seattle, WA 98105

A new movement is gaining momentum in the Pacific Northwest and across the country, as people of all religions increasingly recognize their moral responsibility to care for the

earth. Earth Ministry is at the forefront of this movement, creating programs that incorporate environmental and religious themes, working to educate a diverse public and demonstrating that faith and environmental stewardship go hand in hand.

1999 GOLDMAN ENVIRONMENTAL PRIZE

The Goldman Environmental Prize is the world's largest prize program honoring grassroots environmentalists. Founded in 1990 by Richard and Rhoda Goldman, the Prize awards $125,000 annually to six environmental heroes from each of the inhabited continental regions. Nominated by a network of internationally known environmental organizations and a confidential panel of environmental experts, recipients are chosen for their sustained and important environmental achievements. The Prize seeks to offer these environmental heroes the recognition, visibility, and credibility their efforts deserve. For further information on the awards and past recipients, please call 415-788-9090 or e-mail gef@igc.apc.org. Additional information and extended biographies can be obtained at the Goldman Prize Web site (www.goldmanprize.org/).

1999 RECIPIENTS:

SAMUEL NGUIFFO
Cameroon, Africa

Samuel Nguiffo has struggled tirelessly to stop the liquidation of the world's second largest contiguous rainforest for short-term profit. As a lawyer and founder of the Center for Environment and Development, Nguiffo has worked to inform forest-dwelling peoples, including Pygmies, of their legal rights to manage their traditional lands. He is also at the forefront of an international effort to ensure that the Chad/Cameroon oil pipeline does not bring about large scale forest destruction, marine pollution and social dislocation.

KA HSAW WA
Burma, Asia

Ka Hsaw Wa is a young man from the Karen ethnic minority who has undergone torture and risked deaths in opposition to the environmental and human rights policies of a brutal military government. Fleeing Rangoon, he went to live in the forests near the Thai border, where he discovered extensive abuses taking place in the regions inhabited by Burmese. He has documented thousands of cases of forced labor, execution, rape and confiscation of property carried out by the military in support of a pipeline project by a consortium including U.S.-based UNOCAL and the French Total petroleum companies. This information has formed the basis of a precedent-setting lawsuit in U.S. court.

MICHAL KRAVCIK
Slovakia, Europe

Michal Kravcik is a hydrologist who succeeded in galvanizing community participation to stop a proposed large dam, an environmentally destructive project that was conceived in the Communist era of central planning. Using democratic principals, he presented effective alternatives that included the creation of small dams, decentralization of water management authority and restoration of agricultural land. Kravcik helped reinvigorate the local economy by introducing sustainable development projects and has successfully encouraged increased voter population in the country.

JACQUI KATONA & YVONNE MARGARULA
Australia, Island Nations

Jacqui Katona and Yvonne Margarula are two Aboriginal women who have led a massive national campaign to prevent the mining of Jabiluka, one of the world's largest uranium deposits. Located on land that is traditionally owned by the Mirrar people, Jabiluka is surrounded by the country's largest national park, Kakadu, a World Heritage site known for its cultural significance and rich biodiversity. Mining operations, which have been delayed due to the campaign, would release long-lasting radioactive tailings into the park. Katona and Margarula have initiated a process which may lead to the park's designation as a World Heritage site "in danger."

BERNARD MARTIN
Canada, North America

Bernard Martin is a fourth generation fisher who advocated reduced fishing quotas after seeing first-hand that factory trawlers were decimating the once abundant species in the Grand Banks cod fishery. The call was not heeded and in 1992, the fishery closed, abruptly throwing 30,000 Newfoundlanders, including Martin, out of work. Determined that the disaster not be repeated, Martin co-founded FORCE: Fishers Organized for the Revitalization of Communities and Ecosystems. He has traveled extensively throughout Canada and around the world, educating the general public and working with fellow fishers to develop strategies to protect the earth's over-burdened oceans.

JORGE VARELA
Honduras, South/Central America

Jorge Varela has promoted a model of shrimping that respects fragile resources in the Gulf of Fonseca where commercial shrimp farms have proliferated in recent years (largely due to demand from North America) and have led to the clearing of coastal mangrove forests, the poisoning of estuaries and the loss of common fishing grounds. Varela is co-founder of CODEFFAGOLF, an organization of gulf residents that has succeeded in securing two consecutive moratoriums on the expansion of shrimp farming, is bringing 107,000 hectares of wetlands under protection and is sustaining relief efforts in the aftermath of Hurricane Mitch's devastation.

ABOUT THE COVER

THE FRONT COVER of the *2000 Conservation Directory* features a Great Blue Heron, overlaid upon a picture of the Fakahatchee Strand of the Big Cypress Swamp, part of the Florida Everglades. The cypress and palm forest of the Fakahatchee Strand contains the largest concentration and variety of orchids in North America and is a refuge for many other rare plant and animal species. A State Preserve, the Strand is located on the western tip of southern Florida.

The Great Blue Heron is a common wading bird around four feet tall that nests and feeds in the mangrove swamps of the Everglades. Between 400 to 800 Great Blue Herons nest in the Everglades yearly, with the numbers increasing during the winter months with migrating birds. While the current Great Blue Heron population is at a stable level, the continued success of herons depends on the health of the Everglades ecosystem. If the decline of this fragile ecosystem is not halted, herons and the many other birds and animals that still flourish in the Everglades might become threatened species in a not-so-distant future.

ON THE BACK COVER rests a Florida Panther, perhaps the rarest and most elusive native animal of the region. A subspecies of mountain lion adapted to the subtropical environment of Florida, Panthers are usually found in pinelands, hardwood hammocks and mixed swamp forests throughout the Everglades. Solitary animals that require large tracts of secluded territory, panthers are able swimmers with keen eyesight and a strong sense of smell. With an estimated wild population of only 30 to 50 animals, panthers are threatened by further habitat loss, collisions with cars, the detrimental effects of inbreeding and high levels of mercury in their prey.

THE ENDANGERED EVERGLADES:

The Greater Everglades Ecosystem stretches from just north of Lake Okeechobee near Orlando to the Florida Bay at the Gulf of Mexico by the Florida Keys, encompassing 18,000 square miles. Over the past 100 years, man has ditched, diked and drained the swamps, prairies and forests that make up the Everglades to make room for agricultural expansion and a sprawling population. These practices have reduced the heart of the Everglades, the great sawgrass marshes south of Lake Okeechobee, to less than half of its original size of 8 million acres.

As people altered the Everglades, wildlife suffered. The population of wading birds nesting in the everglades decreased by 93 percent since the 1930's. Sixty-eight threatened and endangered species, including the wood stork, the West Indian Manatee and the Florida Panther, live in the Everglades, where they are under constant, increasing pressure from a loss of quality habitat.

Over fifty years ago, Congress enacted the Central & South Florida Project (C&SF), a multipurpose plan designed to deter flooding and provide water for people and agriculture. The C&SF project facilitated construction of 1,000 miles of canals, 720 miles of levees and 200 water control structures in an effort to control where and when fresh water would flow through the Everglades. The results of this project have been disastrous to the health of the Everglades. Instead of allowing water to slowly filter through the Everglades, an average of 1.7 billion gallons of water flows into the Atlantic Ocean and Gulf of Mexico. Not only does this cause problems for the estuaries receiving these massive amounts of freshwater, it contributes to periodic water shortages and salt water intrusion of well fields that supply water to the six million people who live in south Florida.

Drinking water supplies are also threatened by Florida's rapidly growing population, as new development encroaches onto what is left of the Everglades. The paving-over of wetlands has reduced the amount of water that filters into underground aquifers, resulting in decreasing water supplies for more people, while wildlife suffers from the urbanization of vital habitat areas.

Human development and the disrupted water cycle have created many other problems in the ecosystem:

Water Pollution: Nutrients, originating from farms and dairies, "overfertilize" the Everglades and encourage the growth of cattails in places where sawgrass should dominate, changing the entire ecology of the Everglades. Sulfur applied to sugar cane fields appears to be reacting with mercury in the soils to form dangerously high levels of methylmercury, a toxic pollutant. One million acres of the Everglades are under a health advisory for mercury contamination and as scientists collect more samples, other pollutants are being detected.

Non-native Species: Exotic species infest over 1.5 million acres of the Everglades. These non-native species lack natural population controls and expand rapidly in the Everglades where they displace native plants and animals.

Salinity Changes. The altered flow of freshwater to Florida Bay has changed the Bay's historic salinity regime. Current periods of increasing salinity, along with other factors, appear to be the cause of a massive die-off of seagrass in Florida Bay.

THE EVERGLADES RESTUDY

What remains of the Everglades cannot last much longer if these destructive patterns do not change. The widely acknowledged fact that the Everglades ecosystem is in danger of collapse has promoted a massive effort to restore the Everglades. On July 1, 1999, the U.S. Army Corps of Engineers, supported by nine of the nation's largest conservation organizations, including the National Wildlife Federation, presented a comprehensive Everglades Restoration plan to Congress. This plan, referred to as the Everglades Restudy, is one of the largest environmental restoration efforts ever initiated.

The Restudy is essentially a blueprint to save the Everglades by removing destructive man-made water controls and re-establishing the natural flow of water through the Everglades ecosystem. Over the next 20 years, the Restudy would remove barriers to natural overland water flow; build a new storage areas to capture and hold much of the freshwater currently dumped in the ocean and gulf; restore wetlands to treat agricultural and urban runoff water; engineer wastewater reuse facilities to increase the amount of available water; maintain water levels to prevent saltwater intrusion into drinking water supplies; and alter water management at Lake Okeechobee to improve water quality in downstream rivers and coastal estuaries.

This ambitious plan is the crucial first step in the restoration and revival of the Everglades. The Restudy's estimated cost of $8 billion over 20 years, breaks down to $400 million dollars per year, to be split 50-50 by the State of Florida and the Federal Government. That means, per person, the restoration of this national treasure would cost only $1.50 per year--the cost of a slice of pizza. Congress will consider legislation to launch this great restoration effort in Spring, 2000.

WHAT YOU CAN DO:

- **Write your senators and representative and encourage them to support Everglades restoration**.
- **Join the National Wildlife Federation's Everglades Activist Network.**
  Members receive email alerts and updates on current issues affecting Everglades restoration.
  To sign up, send your name, address and fax number to Everglades Project; NWF; 1400 16th St., N.W.; Washington, D.C. 20036 or email this information to hale@nwf.org

For more information about the Everglades and the work of the NWF to restore and preserve this unique ecosystem, contact the National Wildlife Federation's Everglades Project Office; 5051 Castello Drive, #240; Naples, FL 34103; 941-643-4111 or visit www.nwf.org/everglades. To learn more about the C&SF project and the Restudy, visit the project's official web page at www.restudy.org/.

U.S. CONGRESS, COMMITTEES, AND SUBCOMMITTEES

UNITED STATES CONGRESSIONAL MEMEBERS

Listings are by state, with Senators first, then Representatives by District. One may contact a Senator by writing to: The Honorable _____, U.S. Senate, Washington, DC 20510. E-mail addresses are available at www.senate.gov. One may contact a member of the House of Representatives by writing: The Honorable _____, U.S. House of Representatives, Washington, DC 20515. E-mail addresses and district information are available at www.house.gov. **NOTE: Listings as of October, 1999.** Contact the Clerk for changes: House: (D): (202, 225-7330), (R): (202, 225-7350); Senate: (D): (202, 224-4691), (R): (202, 224-6391). The White House Office address is: 1600 Pennsylvania Ave., NW, Washington, DC 20500 (202, 456-1414; E-mail: president@whitehouse.gov; Web site: www.whitehouse.gov).

President of the United States: WILLIAM J. CLINTON
Vice President of the United States: ALBERT GORE, JR.

ALABAMA

Senators: JEFF SESSIONS; RICHARD C. SHELBY
Representatives: 1st, SONNY CALLAHAN; 2nd, TERRY EVERETT; 3rd, BOB RILEY; 4th, ROBERT ADERHOLT; 5th, ROBERT E. CRAMER, JR.; 6th, SPENCER BACHUS; 7th, EARL HILLIARD

ALASKA

Senators: TED STEVENS; FRANK H. MURKOWSKI
Representative: At-Large, DON YOUNG

ARIZONA

Senators: JON KYL; JOHN McCAIN
Representatives: 1st, MATT SALMON; 2nd, ED PASTER; 3rd, BOB STUMP; 4th, JOHN SHADEGG; 5th, JIM KOLBE; 6th, J.D. HAYWORTH

ARKANSAS

Senators: BLANCHE LAMBERT LINCOLN; TIM HUTCHINSON
Representatives: 1st, MARION BERRY; 2nd, VIC SNYDER; 3rd, ASA HUTCHINSON; 4th, JAY DICKEY

CALIFORNIA

Senators: DIANNE FEINSTEIN; BARBARA BOXER
Representatives: 1st, MIKE THOMPSON; 2nd, WALLY HERGER; 3rd, DOUGLAS OSE; 4th, JOHN DOOLITTLE 5th, ROBERT T. MATSUI; 6th, LYNN WOOLSEY; 7th, GEORGE MILLER; 8th, NANCY PELOSI; 9th, BARBARA LEE; 10th, ELLEN TAUSCHER; 11th, RICHARD POMBO; 12th, TOM LANTOS; 13th, FORTNEY STARK; 14th, ANNE ESHOO; 15th, TOM CAMPBELL; 16th, ZOE LOFGREN; 17th, SAM FARR; 18th, GARY CONDIT; 19th, GEORGE RADANOVICH; 20th, CALVIN DOOLEY; 21st, BILL THOMAS; 22nd, LOIS CAPPS; 23rd, ELTON GALLEGLY; 24th, BRAD SHERMAN; 25th, HOWARD McKEON; 26th, HOWARD L. BERMAN; 27th, JAMES ROGAN; 28th, DAVID DREIER; 29th, HENRY A. WAXMAN; 30th, XAVIER BECERRA; 31st, MATTHEW G. MARTINEZ; 32nd, JULIAN C. DIXON; 33rd, LUCILLE ROYBAL-ALLARD; 34th, GRACE NAPOLITANO; 35th, MAXINE WATERS; 36th, STEVEN KUYKENDALL; 37th, J. M. McDONALD; 38th, STEVE HORN; 39th, EDWARD ROYCE; 40th, JERRY LEWIS; 41st, GARY MILLER; 42nd, Vacant; 43rd, KEN CALVERT; 44th, MARY BONO; 45th, DANA ROHRABACHER; 46th, LORETTA SANCHEZ; 47th, CHRISTOPHER COX; 48th, RON PACKARD; 49th, BRIAN BILBRAY; 50th, BOB FILNER; 51st, RANDY CUNNINGHAM; 52nd, DUNCAN HUNTER

COLORADO

Senators: WAYNE ALLARD; BEN N. CAMPBELL
Representatives: 1st, DIANA DeGETTE; 2nd, MARK UDALL; 3rd, SCOTT McINNIS; 4th, ROBERT SCHAFFER; 5th, JOEL HEFLEY; 6th, TOM TANCREDO

CONNECTICUT

Senators: JOE I. LIEBERMAN; CHRISTOPHER J. DODD
Representatives: 1st, JOHN LARSON; 2nd, SAM GEJDENSON; 3rd, ROSA L. DeLAURO; 4th, CHRISTOPHER SHAYS; 5th, JAMES MALONEY; 6th, NANCY L. JOHNSON

DELAWARE

Senators: WILLIAM V. ROTH, JR.; JOSEPH R. BIDEN, JR.
Representative: At-Large, MICHAEL CASTLE

FLORIDA

Senators: CONNIE MACK; BOB GRAHAM
Representatives: 1st, JOE SCARBOROUGH; 2nd, ALLEN BOYD; 3rd, CORRINE BROWN; 4th, TILLIE FOWLER; 5th, KAREN THURMAN; 6th, CLIFFORD STEARNS; 7th, JOHN MICA; 8th, BILL McCOLLUM; 9th, MICHAEL BILIRAKIS; 10th, BILL YOUNG; 11th, JIM DAVIS; 12th, CHARLES CANADY; 13th, DAN MILLER; 14th, PORTER J. GOSS; 15th, DAVE WELDON; 16th, MARK FOLEY; 17th, CARRIE MEEK; 18th, ILEANA ROS-LEHTINEN; 19th, ROBERT WEXLER; 20th, PETER DEUTSCH; 21th, LINCOLN DIAZ-BALART; 22nd, E. CLAY SHAW, JR.; 23rd, ALCEE HASTINGS

GEORGIA

Senators: MAX CLELAND; PAUL COVERDELL
Representatives: 1st, JACK KINGSTON; 2nd, SANFORD BISHOP; 3rd, MICHAEL COLLINS; 4th, CYNTHIA McKINNEY; 5th, JOHN LEWIS; 6th, JOHNNY ISAKSON; 7th, BOB BARR; 8th, SAXBY CHAMBLISS; 9th, NATHAN DEAL; 10th, CHARLIE NORWOOD; 11th, JOHN LINDER

HAWAII

Senators: DANIEL K. INOUYE; DANIEL K. AKAKA
Representatives: 1st, NEIL ABERCROMBIE; 2nd, PATSY T. MINK

U.S. CONGRESS, COMMITTEES AND SUBCOMMITTEES

IDAHO

Senators: LARRY E. CRAIG; MICHAEL D. CRAPO
Representatives: 1st, HELEN CHENOWETH; 2nd, MIKE

ILLINOIS

Senators: PETER G. FITZGERALD; RICHARD DURBIN
Representatives: 1st, BOBBY RUSH; 2nd, JESSE JACKSON, JR.; 3rd, WILLIAM LIPINSKI; 4th, LUIS GUTIERREZ; 5th, ROD BLAGOJEVICH; 6th, HENRY J. HYDE; 7th, DANNY DAVIS; 8th, PHILIP M. CRANE; 9th, JANICE SCHAKOWSKY; 10th, JOHN PORTER; 11th, JERRY WELLER; 12th, JERRY COSTELLO; 13th, JUDY BIGGERT; 14th, DENNIS HASTERT; 15th, THOMAS W. EWING; 16th, DONALD MANZULLO; 17th, LANE EVANS; 18th, RAY LaHOOD; 19th, DAVID PHELPS; 20th, JOHN SHIMKUS

INDIANA

Senators: EVAN BAYH; RICHARD G. LUGAR
Representatives: 1st, PETER J. VISCLOSKY; 2nd, DAVID McINTOSH; 3rd, TIM ROEMER; 4th, MARK SOUDER; 5th, STEVE BUYER; 6th, DAN BURTON; 7th, EDWARD PEASE; 8th, JOHN HOSTETTLER; 9th, BARON HILL; 10th, JULIA CARSON

IOWA

Senators: CHUCK GRASSLEY; TOM HARKIN
Representatives: 1st, JIM LEACH; 2nd, JIM NUSSLE; 3rd, LEONARD BOSWELL; 4th, GREG GANSKE; 5th, TOM LATHAM

KANSAS

Senators: SAM BROWNBACK; PAT ROBERTS
Representatives: 1st, JERRY MORAN; 2nd, JIM RYUN; 3rd, DENNIS MOORE; 4th, TODD TIAHRT

KENTUCKY

Senators: JIM BUNNING; MITCH McCONNELL
Representatives: 1st, EDWARD WHITFIELD; 2nd, RON LEWIS; 3rd, ANNE NORTHUP; 4th, KENNETH LUCAS; 5th, HAROLD ROGERS; 6th, ERNEST FLETCHER

LOUISIANA

Senators: JOHN B. BREAUX; MARY LANDRIEU
Representatives: 1st, DAVID VITTER; 2nd, WILLIAM J. JEFFERSON; 3rd, W.J. TAUZIN; 4th, JIM McCRERY; 5th, JOHN COOKSEY; 6th, RICHARD H. BAKER; 7th, CHRISTOPHER JOHN

MAINE

Senators: SUSAN MARGARET COLLINS; OLYMPIA SNOWE
Representatives: 1st, THOMAS ALLEN; 2nd, JOHN BALDACCI

MARYLAND

Senators: PAUL S. SARBANES; BARBARA A. MIKULSKI
Representatives: 1st, WAYNE T. GILCHREST; 2nd, ROBERT EHRLICH; 3rd, BENJAMIN L. CARDIN; 4th, ALBERT WYNN; 5th, STENY H. HOYER; 6th, ROSCOE BARTLETT; 7th, ELIJAH CUMMINGS; 8th, CONSTANCE MORELLA

MASSACHUSETTS

Senators: EDWARD M. KENNEDY; JOHN F. KERRY
Representatives: 1st, JOHN W. OLVER; 2nd, RICHARD E. NEAL; 3rd, JAMES McGOVERN; 4th, BARNEY FRANK; 5th, MARTIN MEEHAN; 6th, J.F. TIERNEY; 7th, EDWARD J. MARKEY; 8th, MICHAEL CAPUANO, II; 9th, J. MOAKLEY; 10th, WILLIAM DELAHUNT

MICHIGAN

Senators: SPENCER ABRAHAM; CARL LEVIN
Representatives: 1st, BART STUPAK; 2nd, PETER HOEKSTRA; 3rd, VERNON EHLERS; 4th, DAVE CAMP; 5th, JAMES BARCIA; 6th, FRED UPTON; 7th, NICK SMITH; 8th, DEBBIE STABENOW; 9th, DALE KILDEE; 10th, DAVID BONIOR; 11th, JOSEPH KNOLLENBERG; 12th, SANDER LEVIN; 13th, LYNN RIVERS; 14th, JOHN CONYERS, JR.; 15th, CAROLYN KILPATRICK; 16th, JOHN D. DINGELL

MINNESOTA

Senators: ROD GRAMS; PAUL DAVID WELLSTONE
Representatives: 1st, GIL GUTKNECHT; 2nd, DAVID MINGE; 3rd, JIM RAMSTAD; 4th, BRUCE F. VENTO; 5th, MARTIN SABO; 6th, WILLIAM LUTHER; 7th, COLLIN C. PETERSON; 8th, JAMES L. OBERSTAR

MISSISSIPPI

Senators: TRENT LOTT; THAD COCHRAN
Representatives: 1st, ROGER WICKER; 2nd, BENNIE THOMPSON; 3rd, CHARLES PICKERING; 4th, RONNIE SHAWS; 5th, GENE TAYLOR

MISSOURI

Senators: JOHN ASHCROFT; CHRISTOPHER S. BOND
Representatives: 1st, WILLIAM CLAY; 2nd, JAMES TALENT; 3rd, RICHARD A. GEPHARDT; 4th, IKE SKELTON; 5th, KAREN McCARTHY; 6th, PAT DANNER; 7th, ROY BLUNT; 8th, JO ANN EMERSON; 9th, KENNY HULSHOF

MONTANA

Senators: CONRAD R. BURNS; MAX BAUCUS
Representative: At-Large, RICK HILL

NEBRASKA

Senators: CHUCK HAGEL; J. ROBERT KERREY
Representatives: 1st, DOUG BEREUTER; 2nd, LEE TERRY; 3rd, BILL BARRETT

NEVADA

Senators: RICHARD H. BRYAN; HARRY REID

U.S. CONGRESS, COMMITTEES AND SUBCOMMITTEES

Representatives: 1st, SHELLY BERKLEY; 2nd, JIM GIBBONS

NEW HAMPSHIRE

Senators: ROBERT C. SMITH; JUDD GREGG
Representatives: 1st, JOHN E. SUNUNU; 2nd, CHARLES BASS

NEW JERSEY

Senators: ROBERT TORRICELLI; FRANK R. LAUTENBERG
Representatives: 1st, ROBERT E. ANDREWS; 2nd, FRANK LoBIONDO; 3rd, JIM SAXTON; 4th, CHRISTOPHER SMITH; 5th, MARGE ROUKEMA; 6th, FRANK PALLONE, JR.; 7th, BOB FRANKS; 8th, WILLIAM PASCRELL; 9th, STEVEN ROTHMAN; 10th, DONALD M. PAYNE; 11th, RODNEY FRELINGHUYSEN; 12th, RUSH HOLT; 13th, ROBERT MENENDEZ

NEW MEXICO

Senators: PETE V. DOMENICI; JEFF BINGAMAN
Representatives: 1st, HEATHER WILSON; 2nd, JOE SKEEN; 3rd, THOMAS UDALL

NEW YORK

Senators: DANIEL P. MOYNIHAN; CHARLES E. SCHUMER
Representatives: 1st, MICHAEL FORBES; 2nd, RICK LAZIO; 3rd, PETER KING; 4th, CAROLYN McCARTHY; 5th, GARY L. ACKERMAN; 6th, GREGORY MEEK; 7th, JOSEPH CROWLEY; 8th, JERROLD NADLER; 9th, ANTHONY WEINER; 10th, EDOLPHUS TOWNS; 11th, MAJOR R. OWENS; 12th, NYDIA VELAZQUEZ; 13th, VITO FOSSELLA; 14th, CAROLYN MALONEY; 15th, CHARLES B. RANGEL; 16th, JOSE SERRANO; 17th, ELIOT L. ENGEL; 18th, NITA M. LOWEY; 19th, SUE KELLY; 20th, BENJAMIN A. GILMAN; 21st, MICHAEL R. McNULTY; 22nd, JOHN SWEENEY; 23rd, SHERWOOD L. BOEHLERT; 24th, JOHN McHUGH; 25th, JAMES T. WALSH; 26th, MAURICE HINCHEY; 27th, THOMAS REYNOLDS; 28th, LOUISE M. SLAUGHTER; 29th, JOHN J. LaFALCE; 30th, JACK QUINN; 31st, AMO HOUGHTON

NORTH CAROLINA

Senators: JESSE HELMS; JOHN EDWARDS
Representatives: 1st, EVA CLAYTON; 2nd, BOB ETHERIDGE; 3rd, WALTER JONES; 4th, DAVID PRICE; 5th, RICHARD BURR; 6th, HOWARD COBLE; 7th, MIKE McINTYRE; 8th, ROBIN HAYES; 9th, SUE MYRICK; 10th, CASS BALLENGER; 11th, CHARLES H. TAYLOR; 12th, MELVIN WATT

NORTH DAKOTA

Senators: KENT CONRAD; BYRON DORGAN
Representative: At-Large, EARL POMEROY

OHIO

Senators: GEORGE V. VOINOVICH; MIKE DeWINE
Representatives: 1st, STEVE CHABOT; 2nd, ROB PORTMAN; 3rd, TONY P. HALL; 4th, MICHAEL G. OXLEY; 5th, PAUL GILLMORE; 6th, TED STRICKLAND; 7th, DAVID L. HOBSON; 8th, JOHN A. BOEHNER; 9th, MARCY KAPTUR; 10th, DENNIS KUCINICH; 11th, STEPHANIE TUBBS JONES; 12th, JOHN R. KASICH; 13th, SHERROD BROWN; 14th, THOMAS C. SAWYER; 15th, DEBORAH PRYCE; 16th, RALPH REGULA; 17th, JAMES A. TRAFICANT, JR.; 18th, BOB NEY; 19th, STEVEN LaTOURETTE

OKLAHOMA

Senators: JAMES INHOFE; DON NICKLES
Representatives: 1st, STEVE LARGENT; 2nd, TOM COBURN; 3rd, WES WATKINS; 4th, J.C. WATTS; 5th, ERNEST ISTOOK; 6th, FRANK LUCAS

OREGON

Senators: GORDON SMITH ; RON WYDEN
Representatives: 1st, DAVID WU; 2nd, GREG WALDEN; 3rd, EARL BLUMENAUER; 4th, PETER A. DeFAZIO; 5th, DARLENE HOOLEY

PENNSYLVANIA

Senators: RICK SANTORUM; ARLEN SPECTER
Representatives: 1st, ROBERT BRADY; 2nd, CHAKA FATTAH; 3rd, ROBERT BORSKI; 4th, RON KLINK; 5th, JOHN PETERSON; 6th, TIM HOLDEN; 7th, CURT WELDON; 8th, JIM GREENWOOD; 9th, BUD SHUSTER; 10th, DONALD SHERWOOD; 11th, PAUL E. KANJORSKI; 12th, JOHN P. MURTHA; 13th, JOSEPH HOEFFEL; 14th, WILLIAM J. COYNE; 15th, PATRICH TOOMEY; 16th, JOSEPH PITTS; 17th, GEORGE W. GEKAS; 18th, MICHAEL DOYLE; 19th, WILLIAM F. GOODLING; 20th, FRANK MASCARA; 21st, PHILIP ENGLISH

RHODE ISLAND

Senators: JACK REED; vacant
Representatives: 1st, PATRICK KENNEDY; 2nd, ROBERT WEYGAND

SOUTH CAROLINA

Senators: STROM THURMOND; ERNEST F. HOLLINGS
Representatives: 1st, MARK SANFORD; 2nd, FLOYD SPENCE; 3rd, LINDSEY GRAHAM; 4th, JAMES DEMINT; 5th, JOHN SPRATT, JR.; 6th, JAMES CLYBURN

SOUTH DAKOTA

Senators: TIM JOHNSON; THOMAS A. DASCHLE
Representative: At-Large, JOHN THUNE

TENNESSEE

Senators: WILLIAM FRIST; FRED THOMPSON
Representatives: 1st, WILLIAM JENKINS; 2nd, JOHN J. DUNCAN, JR; 3rd, ZACH WAMP; 4th, VAN HILLEARY; 5th, BOB CLEMENT; 6th, BART GORDON; 7th, ED BRYANT; 8th, JOHN S. TANNER; 9th, HAROLD FORD, JR.

TEXAS

Senators: KAY B. HUTCHISON; PHIL GRAMM
Representatives: 1st, MAX SANDLIN; 2nd, JIM TURNER; 3rd, SAM JOHNSON; 4th, RALPH M. HALL; 5th, PETE SESSIONS; 6th, JOE BARTON; 7th, BILL ARCHER; 8th, KEVIN BRADY; 9th, NICK

LAMPSON; 10th, LLOYD DOGGETT; 11th, CHET EDWARDS; 12th, KAY GRANGER; 13th, MAC THORNBERRY; 14th, RON PAUL; 15th, RUBEN HINOJOSA; 16th, SILVESTRE REYES; 17th, CHARLES W. STENHOLM; 18th, SHEILA JACKSON-LEE; 19th, LARRY COMBEST; 20th, CHARLIE GONZALEZ; 21st, LAMAR S. SMITH; 22nd, TOM DeLAY; 23rd, HENRY BONILLA; 24th, MARTIN FROST; 25th, KEN BENTSEN; 26th, RICHARD ARMEY; 27th, SOLOMON P. ORTIZ; 28th, CIRO D. RODRIGUEZ; 29th, GENE GREEN; 30th, EDDIE B. JOHNSON

UTAH

Senators: ROBERT BENNETT; ORRIN G. HATCH
Representatives: 1st, JAMES V. HANSEN; 2nd, MERRILL COOK; 3rd, CHRIS CANNON

VERMONT

Senators: JAMES M. JEFFORDS; PATRICK J. LEAHY
Representative: At-Large, BERNIE SANDERS

VIRGINIA

Senators: JOHN WARNER; CHARLES S. ROBB
Representatives: 1st, HERBERT H. BATEMAN; 2nd, OWEN B. PICKETT; 3rd, ROBERT SCOTT; 4th, NORMAN SISISKY; 5th, VIRGIL GOODE; 6th, ROBERT GOODLATTE; 7th, THOMAS J. BLILEY, JR.; 8th, JAMES P. MORAN; 9th, FREDERICK BOUCHER; 10th, FRANK R. WOLF; 11th, THOMAS DAVIS, III

WASHINGTON

Senators: SLADE GORTON; PATTY MURRAY
Representatives: 1st, JAY INSLEE; 2nd, JACK METCALF; 3rd, BRIAN BAIRD; 4th, DOC HASTINGS; 5th, GEORGE NETHERCUTT; 6th, NORMAN D. DICKS; 7th, JIM McDERMOTT; 8th, JENNIFER DUNN; 9th, ADAM SMITH

WEST VIRGINIA

Senators: ROBERT C. BYRD; JOHN D. ROCKEFELLER, IV
Representatives: 1st, ALAN B. MOLLOHAN; 2nd, BOB WISE, JR.; 3rd, NICK J. RAHALL, II

WISCONSIN

Senators: HERBERT KOHL; RUSSELL FEINGOLD
Representatives: 1st, PAUL RYAN; 2nd, TAMMY BALDWIN; 3rd, RON KIND; 4th, JERRY KLECSKA; 5th, THOMAS BARRETT; 6th, THOMAS E. PETRI; 7th, DAVID R. OBEY; 8th, MARK GREEN; 9th, JIM SENSENBRENNER

WYOMING

Senators: CRAIG THOMAS; MICHAEL ENZI
Representative: At-Large, BARBARA CUBIN

DISTRICT OF COLUMBIA

Delegate At-Large: ELEANOR HOLMES NORTON

GUAM

Delegate At-Large: ROBERT A. UNDERWOOD

PUERTO RICO

Resident Commissioner At-Large: CARLOS A. ROMERO-BARCELO

VIRGIN ISLANDS

Delegate At-Large: DONNA M. CHRISTIAN

AMERICAN SAMOA

Delegate At-Large: ENI FALEOMAVAEGA

HOUSE COMMITTEES

HOUSE COMMITTEE ON RESOURCES
Rm. 1324 Longworth House Office Bldg., Washington, DC 20515
Phone: 202-225-2761
Description: Consists of 52 members: Forest reserves and national parks created from the public domain; national parks lands; forfeiture of land grants and alien ownership, including alien ownership of mineral lands; geological survey; interstate compacts relating to apportionment of waters for irrigation purposes; irrigation and reclamation, including water supply for reclamation projects, and easements on public lands for irrigation projects, and acquisition of private lands when necessary to complete irrigation projects; measures relating to the care and management of Indians, including the care and allotment of Indian lands and general and special measures relating to Indian claims; measures (including funding measures) relating generally to the U.S. territories, commonwealths, and successor governments of the Trust Territory of the Pacific Islands, except measures concerning the federal tax system and federal appropriations; military parks and battlefields; national cemeteries administered by the Secretary of the Interior, and parks within the District of Columbia; mineral land laws and claims and entries thereunder; mineral resources of the public lands; mining interests generally; mining schools and experimental stations; petroleum conservation on the public lands and conservation of the radium supply in the U.S.; preservation of prehistoric ruins and objects of interest on the public domain; public lands generally, including entry, easements, and grazing thereon; relations of the U.S. with the Indians and the Indian tribes; regulation of the domestic nuclear energy industry, including regulation of research and development of reactors and nuclear regulatory research. Also special oversight functions with respect to all programs affecting Indians and nonmilitary nuclear energy and research and development, including the disposal of nuclear waste.
Contact(s):
Chair: DON YOUNG
Chief of Staff: LLOYD JONES

HOUSE COMMITTEE ON AGRICULTURE
Rm. 1301, Longworth House Office Bldg., Washington, DC 20515
Phone: 202-225-2171
Founded: 1820
Description: Adulteration of seeds, insect pests, and protection of birds and animals in forest reserves; agriculture generally; agricultural and industrial chemistry; agricultural colleges and experiment stations; agricultural economics and research;

U.S. CONGRESS, COMMITTEES AND SUBCOMMITTEES

agricultural education extension services; agricultural production and marketing and stabilization of prices of agricultural products; animal industry and diseases of animals; crop insurance and soil conservation; dairy industry; entomology and plant quarantine; extension of farm credit and farm security; forestry in general, and forest reserves other than those created from the public domain; human nutrition and home economics; inspection of livestock and meat products; plant industry, soils, and agricultural engineering; rural electrification; commodities exchanges and rural development.
Contact(s):
Chair: LARRY COMBEST
Subcommittees: Department Operations, Oversight, Nutrition and Forestry; General Farm Commodities, Resource Conservation and Credit; Livestock and Horticulture; Risk Management, Research and Specialty Crops.

HOUSE COMMITTEE ON APPROPRIATIONS
Rm. H-218, Capitol Bldg., Washington, DC 20515
Phone: 202-225-2771
Description: Consists of 60 members: Appropriation of the revenue for the support of the government, rescissions of appropriations contained in appropriation acts, and transfers of unexpended balances.
Contact(s):
Chair: BILL YOUNG
Subcommittees: Agriculture, Rural Development, Food and Drug Administration; Commerce, Justice, State, and Judiciary; District of Columbia; Energy and Water Development; Foreign Operations, Export Financing, and Related Programs; Interior; Labor, Health and Human Services, and Education; Legislative; Military Construction; National Security; Transportation; Treasury, Postal Service, and General Government; VA, HUD, and Independent Agencies.

HOUSE COMMITTEE ON COMMERCE
2125 Rayburn House Office Bldg., Washington, DC 20515
Phone: 202-225-2927
Description: Jurisdiction: Interstate and foreign commerce generally; national energy policy generally; measures relating to the exploration, production, storage, supply, marketing, pricing, and regulation of energy resources, including all fossil fuels, solar energy, and other unconventional or renewable energy resources; measures relating to the conservation of energy resources; measures relating to the commercial application of energy technology; measures relating to energy information generally; measures relating to: (A) the generation and marketing of power (except by federally chartered or federal regional power marketing authorities), (B) the reliability and interstate transmission of, and ratemaking for, all power, and (C) the siting of generation facilities (except the installation of interconnections between government waterpower projects); interstate energy compacts; measures relating to general management of the Department of Energy, and the management and all functions of the Federal Energy Regulatory Commission; regulation of interstate and foreign communications; securities and exchanges; consumer affairs and consumer protection; travel and tourism; public health and quarantine; health and health facilities, except health care supported by payroll deductions; and biomedical research and development. The committee shall have the same jurisdiction with respect to regulation of nuclear facilities and of use of nuclear energy as it has with respect to regulation of non-nuclear facilities and of use of non-nuclear energy.
Contact(s):
Chair: THOMAS BLILEY
Chief of Staff: JAMES DERDERIAN
General Counsel: JAMES BARNETTE
Subcommittees: Telecommunications, Trade, and Consumer Protection; Finance and Hazardous Materials; Health and Environment; Energy and Power; Oversight and Investigations.

HOUSE COMMITTEE ON EDUCATION AND THE WORKFORCE
2181 Rayburn House Office Bldg., Washington, DC 20515
Phone: 202-225-4527
Description: Jurisdiction: Measures relating to education or labor generally; child labor; Gallaudet College; Howard University; convict labor and the entry of goods made by convicts into interstate commerce; labor standards; labor statistics; mediation and arbitration of labor disputes; regulation or prevention of importation of foreign laborers under contract; food programs for children in schools; United States Employees' Compensation Commission; vocational rehabilitation; wages and hours of labor; welfare of miners; and work incentive programs.
Contact(s):
Chair: BILL GOODLING
Subcommittees: Elementary, Secondary, and Vocational Education; Postsecondary Education and Training; Labor Standards, Occupational Health and Safety; Labor-Management Relations; Human Resources; and Select Education and Civil Rights.

HOUSE COMMITTEE ON INTERNATIONAL RELATIONS
2170 Rayburn House Office Bldg., Washington, DC 20515
Phone: 202-225-5021
Description: Jurisdiction: Foreign policy; international economic and environmental policy; international conferences and congresses; United Nations organizations; fishing agreements; nuclear export policy.
Contact(s):
Chair: BENJAMIN A. GILMAN
Subcommittees: Africa; Asia and the Pacific; the Western Hemisphere; International Economic Policy and Trade; International Operations and Human Rights.

HOUSE COMMITTEE ON RULES
Rm. H-312, Capitol Bldg., Washington, DC 20515
Phone: 202-225-9191
Description: Consists of 13 members: Grants rules outlining conditions for floor debate on legislation reported by regular standing committees, which includes granting emergency waivers under the Congressional Budget Act of 1974; also has legislative authority to create committees, change the rules of the House, and provide order of business of the House.
Contact(s):
Chair: DAVID DRIER (CA)
Vice Chair: PORTER J. GROSS (FL)

HOUSE COMMITTEE ON TRANSPORTATION AND INFRASTRUCTURE
Rm. 216, Rayburn House Office Bldg., Washington, DC 20515
Phone: 202-225-4472; Fax: 202-226-0921
Description: Consists of 73 members.
Contact(s):
Chairman: BUD SHUSTER
Subcommittees: Coast Guard and Maritime Transportation; Public Buildings and Economic Development; Railroads; Surface Transportation; Water Resources; and Environment.

SENATE COMMITTEES

SENATE COMMITTEE ON AGRICULTURE, NUTRITION, AND FORESTRY
Rm. 328-A, Russell Bldg., Washington, DC 20510
Phone: 202-224-2035
Description: Concerned with agriculture and agricultural commodities; inspection of livestock, meat, and agricultural products; animal industry and diseases; pests and pesticides; agricultural extension services and experiment stations; forestry in general and forest reserves and wilderness areas other than those created from the public domain; agricultural economics and research; human nutrition; home economics; farm credit and farm security; rural development, rural electrification and watersheds; agricultural production, marketing, and stabilization of prices; crop insurance and soil conservation; school nutrition programs; food stamp programs; food from fresh waters; plant industry, soils, and

U.S. CONGRESS, COMMITTEES AND SUBCOMMITTEES

agricultural engineering. Such committee shall also study and review, on a comprehensive basis, matters relating to food, nutrition, and hunger, both in the United States and foreign countries, and rural affairs and report thereon from time to time.
Contact(s):
Chair: RICHARD LUGAR
Chief Clerk: ROBERT STURM
Chief Counsel: DAVID JOHNSON
Minority Staff Director: MARK HALVERSON
Ranking Minority Member: TOM HARKIN
Staff Director: KEITH LUSE
Subcommittees: Production and Price Competitiveness; Marketing, Inspection, and Product Promotion; Forestry, Conservation, and Rural Revitalization; Research, Nutrition, and General Legislation.

SENATE COMMITTEE ON APPROPRIATIONS
SD-128, Capitol Bldg., Washington, DC 20510
Phone: 202-224-3471

Description: Concerned with all proposed legislation, messages, petitions, memorials, and other matters relating to appropriation of the revenue for the support of the federal government.
Contact(s):
Chair: TED STEVENS

SENATE COMMITTEE ON COMMERCE SCIENCE AND TRANSPORTATION
U.S. Senate SD508, Washington, DC 20510
Phone: 202-224-5115

Description: Concerned with interstate commerce; transportation; regulation of interstate common carriers, including railroads, buses, trucks, vessels, pipelines, and civil aviation; merchant marine and navigation; marine and ocean navigation, safety and transportation, including navigational aspects of deepwater ports; Coast Guard; inland waterways, except construction; communications; regulation of consumer products and services, except for credit, financial services, and housing; the Panama Canal, except for maintenance, operation, administration, sanitation, and government, and interoceanic canals generally; standards and measurements; highway safety; science, engineering and technology research, and development and policy; nonmilitary aeronautical and space sciences; transportation and commerce aspects of Outer Continental Shelf lands; marine fisheries; coastal zone management; oceans, weather, and atmospheric activities; sports.
Contact(s):
Chair: JOHN McCAIN
Subcommittees: Aviation; Communications; Consumer Affairs, Foreign Commerce and Tourism; Science, Technology, and Space; Surface Transportation and Merchant Marine; Oceans and Fisheries.

SENATE COMMITTEE ON ENERGY AND NATURAL RESOURCES
Rm. SD-364, Dirksen Bldg., Washington, DC 20510
Phone: 202-224-4971; E-mail: admin@energy.senate.gov

Description: Concerned with the comprehensive study and review of matters relating to energy and resources development. Jursdiction: Coal production, distribution, and utilization; energy policy; energy regulation and conservation; energy related aspects of deepwater ports; energy research and development; extraction of minerals from oceans and Outer Continental Shelf lands; hydroelectric power, irrigation, and reclamation; mining education and research; mining, mineral lands, mining claims, and mineral conservation; national parks, recreation areas, wilderness areas, wild and scenic rivers, historical sites, military parks and battlefields, and on the public domain, preservation of prehistoric ruins and objects of interest; naval petroleum reserves in Alaska; nonmilitary development of nuclear energy; oil and gas production and distribution; public lands and forests, including farming and grazing thereon, and mineral extraction therefrom; solar energy systems; and territorial possessions of the United States, including trusteeships.
Contact(s):
Chair: FRANK MURKOWSKI

SENATE COMMITTEE ON ENVIRONMENT AND PUBLIC WORKS
Rm. SD-410, Dirksen Bldg., Washington, DC 20510
Phone: 202-224-6176

Description: Committee on Environment and Public Works, to which shall be referred all proposed legislation, messages, petitions, memorials, and other matters relating to the following subjects: environmental policy; environmental research and development; ocean dumping; fisheries and wildlife; environmental aspects of Outer Continental Shelf lands; solid waste disposal and recycling; environmental effects of toxic substances, other than pesticides; water resources; flood control and improvements of rivers and harbors, including environmental aspects of deepwater ports; public works, bridges, and dams; water pollution; air pollution; noise pollution; nonmilitary environmental regulation and control of nuclear energy; regional economic development; construction and maintenance of highways; public buildings and improved grounds of the United States generally, including federal buildings in the District of Columbia. Such committee shall also study and review on a comprehensive basis matters relating to environmental protection and resource utilization and conservation, and report thereon from time to time.
Contact(s):
Chair: JOHN H. CHAFEE
Minority Staff Director: J. THOMAS SLITER
Staff Director: JIMMIE POWELL
Subcommittees: Transportation and Infrastructure; Superfund; Waste Control and Risk Assesment; Clean Air, Wetlands, Private Property, and Nuclear Safety; Drinking Water, Fisheries, and Wildlife.

SENATE COMMITTEE ON FOREIGN RELATIONS
Washington, DC 20510-6225
Phone: 202-224-4651

Description: Jurisdiction: Foreign and national security policy; international treaties, conferences, and congresses; World Bank and International Monetary Fund; oceans and international environmental and scientific affairs; humanitarian assistance and hunger; and United Nations and its affiliated organizations.
Contact(s):
Chair: JESSE HELMS
Chair, Subcommittee on African Affairs: BILL FRIST
Chair, Subcommittee on East Asian and Pacific Affairs: CRAIG THOMAS
Chair, Subcommittee on European Affairs: GORDON H. SMITH
Chair, Subcommittee on International Economic Policy, Export and Trade Promotion: CHUCK HAGEL
Chair, Subcommittee on International Operations: ROD GRAMS
Chair, Subcommittee on Near Eastern and South Asian Affairs: SAM BROWNBACK
Chair, Subcommittee on Western Hemisphere, Peace Corps, Narcotics and Terrorism: PAUL COVERDELL
Subcommittees: African Affairs; East Asian and Pacific Affairs; European Affairs; International Economic Policy, Export and Trade Promotion; International Operations; Near Eastern and South Asian Affairs; Western Hemisphere, Peace Corps, Narcotics and Terrorism

SENATE COMMITTEE ON HEALTH, EDUCATION, LABOR, AND PENSIONS
SD-428, Dirksen Bldg., Washington, DC 20510
Phone: 202-224-5375

Contact(s):
Chair: JAMES JEFFORDS
Subcommittees: Aging; Children, Family, Drugs, and Alcoholism; Education, Arts, and Humanities; Employment and Productivity; Handicapped; and Labor.

U.S. FEDERAL AND INTERNATIONAL GOVERNMENT AGENCIES

COMMISSIONS

APPALACHIAN REGIONAL COMMISSION
1666 Connecticut Ave., NW, Washington, DC 20235
Phone: 202-884-7700
Founded: 1965
Description: To promote economic and human development in the 13-state Appalachian region and to provide a framework for joint federal and state efforts. Includes 406 counties in Alabama, Georgia, Kentucky, Maryland, Mississippi, New York, North Carolina, Ohio, Pennsylvania, South Carolina, Tennessee, Virginia and West Virginia.
Contact(s):
Executive Director: TOM HUNTER; Phone: 202-884-7700
Federal Co-Chairman: JESSE L. WHITE JR.; Phone: 202-884-7660
Public Information: MICHAEL KIERNAN; Phone: 202-884-7771
States' Co-Chairman: GOV. CECIL UNDERWOOD
States' Washington Representative: BILL WALKER; Phone: 202-884-7746

ATLANTIC STATES MARINE FISHERIES COMMISSION
1444 Eye St., NW, 6th Fl., Washington, DC 20005
Phone: 202-289-6400; Fax: 202-289-6051; E-mail: Info@asmfc.org; Web site: www.asmfc.org
Founded: 1942
Description: The Commission was established by the Atlantic States Marine Fisheries Compact to promote better utilization of the fisheries, marine and shell of the 15 Atlantic seaboard states, Maine to Florida, through the development of a joint program for the promotion and protection of such fisheries, and by the prevention of physical waste of the fisheries from any cause.
Contact(s):
Chairman: DAVID V.D. BORDEN
Vice Chairman: SUSAN SHIPMAN
Executive Director: JOHN H. DUNNIGAN

COLUMBIA RIVER INTER-TRIBAL FISH COMMISSION
729 NE Oregon, Suite 200, Portland, OR 97232
Phone: 503-238-0667
Founded: 1977
Description: The Commission was formed to return salmon to Columbia basin rivers and to protect the Indian tribes' treaty-reserved fishing rights.
Contact(s):
Executive Director: DON SAMPSON

StreamNet Library
729 NE Oregon St., Suite 190, Portland, OR 97232
Phone: 503-731-1304; Fax: 503-731-1260; E-mail: fishmail@critfc.org; Web site: www.streamnet.org
Description: The StreamNet Library is a cooperative venture of the region's fish and wildlife agencies and tribes and serves these organizations. It is a fisheries and aquatic species library emphasizing management and restoration of the Columbia River salmon and sturgeon, providing data and data services. Open to the public.
Contact(s):
Head Librarian: LENORA OFTERDAHL; E-mail: oftl@critfc.org
Assistant Librarian: LAURIE NOCK; E-mail: nocl@critfc.org
Library Technician: DAVID LIBERTY; E-mail: libd@critfc.org
Keyword(s): Librarians/Information Professionals, Salmon Recovery, Libraries

DELAWARE RIVER BASIN COMMISSION
P.O. Box 7360, West Trenton, NJ 08628
Phone: 609-883-9500; Fax: 609-883-9522; E-mail: drbc@drbc.state.nj.us
Founded: 1961
Description: The Delaware River Basin Compact created the Delaware River Basin Commission to develop and implement plans, policies, and projects relating to the water resources of the Delaware River Basin. The Commission is responsible for adopting and promoting "uniform and coordinated policies for water conservation, control, use, and management in the basin."
Contact(s):
Executive Director: CAROL R. COLLIER
Public Information Officer: CHRISTOPHER M. ROBERTS
Publication(s): *Delaware River Basic Compact; Annual Report; Water Resources Program; Administrative Manual and Water Code*

GREAT LAKES FISHERY COMMISSION
2100 Commonwealth Blvd., Suite 209, Ann Arbor, MI 49105-1563
Phone: 734-662-3209; Fax: 734-741-2010; Web site: www.glfc.org
Description: The 1955 Canada-U.S. Convention on Great Lakes Fisheries established the Commission to advise governments on ways to improve the fisheries, to develop and coordinate fishery research programs, to develop measures and implement programs to manage sea lamprey, and to improve and perpetuate fishery resources.
Contact(s):
Executive Secretary: CHRIS GODDARD
Publication(s): *Economics of Great Lakes Fisheries: A 1985 Assessment; Fish Community Objectives for Lake Superior, The State of Lake Superior in 1992; Fish-Community Objectives for Lake Huron.*

GREAT LAKES INDIAN FISH AND WILDLIFE COMMISSION
P.O. Box 9, Odanah, WI 54861
Phone: 715-682-6619; Fax: 715-682-9294
Founded: 1983
Description: Provide biological, enforcement, and legal services to our member tribes in matters related to off-reservation treaty gathering rights in Wisconsin, Michigan, and Minnesota.
Contact(s):
Chairman of the Board: TOM MAULSON
Deputy Administrator: GERALD DePERRY
Executive Administrator: JAMES H. SCHLENDER
Publication(s): *Masinaigan; Technical reports*

GULF STATES MARINE FISHERIES COMMISSION
P.O. Box 726, Ocean Springs, MS 39566-0726
Phone: 228-875-5912; Fax: 228-875-6604; E-mail: lsimpson@gsmfc.org; Web site: www.gsmfc.org
Founded: 1949
Description: The GSMFC is an interstate compact of the states of Alabama, Florida, Louisiana, Mississippi, and Texas, authorized by the U.S. Congress. The Commission has 15 commissioners. The purpose of the Commission is to promote better utilization of the fisheries, marine, shell and anadromous, of the seaboard of the Gulf of Mexico by cooperative programs for the promotion and protection of such fisheries and the prevention of the physical waste of the fisheries from any cause.
Contact(s):
Chairman: GEORGE SEKUL
Assistant Director: RONALD R. LUKENS
Executive Director: LARRY B. SIMPSON

HELSINKI COMMISSION/ BALTIC MARINE ENVIRONMENT PROTECTION COMMISSION
Katajanokanlaituri 6 B FIN- 00160, Helsinki Finland
Phone: 358-9-6220220; Fax: 358-9-62202239; E-mail: helcom@helcom.fi
Founded: 1980
Description: To protect the marine environment of the Baltic Sea against pollution from all sources.
Contact(s):
Executive Secretary: MIECZYSLAW S. OSTOJSKI
Administrative Officer: RITVA KOSTAKOW-KAMPE
Environment Secretary: KJELL GRIP
Maritime Secretary: ANNE CHRISTINE BRUSENDORFF
Programme Implementation Coordinator: ULRICH KREMSER
Technological Secretary: AIN LÄÄNE

U.S. FEDERAL AND INTERNATIONAL GOVERNMENT AGENCIES - COMMISSIONS

Publication(s): *Baltic Sea Environment Proceedings (BSEP); HELCOM News*

INTER-AMERICAN TROPICAL TUNA COMMISSION
c/o Scripps Institution of Oceanography 8604 La Jolla Shores Dr., La Jolla, CA 92037-1508
Phone: 619-546-7100

Founded: 1949

Description: Charged with the investigation and conservation of the tuna and dolphin resources of the eastern Pacific Ocean. Member nations: U.S., Costa Rica, El Salvador, Ecuador, France, Japan, Mexico, Nicaragua, Panama, Vanuatu and Venezuela. Established by convention between the U.S. and Costa Rica.

Contact(s):
Director: ROBIN L. ALLEN; Phone: 858-546-7019
Editor: WILLIAM H. BAYLIFF; Phone: 858-546-7025
Publication(s): *Bulletin of the Inter-American Tropical Tuna Commission; Annual Report; Special Report of the Inter-American Tropical Tuna Commission*

INTERNATIONAL JOINT COMMISSION
National Headquarters, 1250 23rd St., NW, Suite 100, Washington, DC 20440
Phone: 202-736-9000

Description: Established by the Boundary Waters Treaty of 1909 to prevent and resolve disputes regarding the use of the waters on the U.S.- Canadian Boundary, and to act as an independent advisor on issues referred by both countries. Regional office monitors, evaluates, and reports on compliance with the Great Lakes Water Quality Agreement of November 22, 1978. Commission functions in quasi-judicial, investigative, and coordination capacities.

Contact(s):
Canadian Section Secretary: MURRAY CLAMEN; Phone: 613-995-2984
Director, Regional Office: THOMAS BEHLEN; Phone: 519-257-6700; Fax: 519-257-6740
Public Information Officer: JENNIFER DAY; Phone: 313-226-2170, ext. 6733; Fax: 519-257-6740; E-mail: DayJ@windsor.ijc.org.
Public Information Officer: FRANK BEVACQUA; Phone: 202-736-9024; Fax: 202-736-9015; E-mail: bevacquaf@washington.ijc.org
Publication(s): *Focus*

Canada Office
100 Metcalfe St., 18th Fl., Ottawa, Ontario K1P 5M1
Phone: 613-995-2984

Great Lakes Regional Office
8th Fl. 100 Ouellette Ave., Windsor, Ontario N9A 6T3
Phone: 519-257-6700; Fax: 313-226-2170

INTERNATIONAL PACIFIC HALIBUT COMMISSION
P.O. Box 95009, Seattle, WA 98145-2009
Phone: 206-634-1838; Fax: 206-632-2983

Founded: 1923

Description: Scientific investigation and management of the Pacific halibut resource. Established by a convention between Canada and the United States.

Contact(s):
Director: BRUCE M LEAMAN

INTERNATIONAL WHALING COMMISSION
The Red House 135 Station Rd., Impington, Cambridge+132 CB4 9NP UNITED KINGDOM
Phone: 01223-233971; Fax: 01223-232876; E-mail: iwcoffice@compuserve.com

Founded: 1946

Description: Established under the International Convention for the Regulation of Whaling in 1946 to provide for the conservation of whale stocks and the orderly development of the whaling industry. Member Nations: USA, Antigua and Barbuda, Argentina, Australia, Austria, Brazil, Chile, People's Republic of China, Costa Rica, Denmark, Dominica, Finland, France, Germany, Grenada, India, Ireland, Italy, Japan, Kenya, Republic of Korea, Mexico, Monaco, Netherlands, New Zealand, Norway, Oman, Peru, Russia Federation, Saint Kitts and Nevis, Saint Lucia, Saint Vincent and the Grenadines, Senegal, Solomon Islands, South Africa, Spain, Sweden, Switzerland, United Kingdom and Venezuela.

Contact(s):
Chairman (Ireland): M. CANNY
Executive Officer (Cambridge): M. HARVEY
Secretary (Cambridge): DR. R. GAMBELL
U.S. Commissioner: DR. J. BAKER, U.S. Department of Commerce, Rm. 5128, Herbert C. Hoover Bldg., 14th and Constitution Ave., NW, Washington, DC 20230
Vice Chairman (Sweden): PROF. BO FERNHOLM
Publication(s): *Annual reports of the Commission (including reports and papers of the Scientific Committee); Special Issues Series on specialist cetacean subjects; International Journal of Cetacean Research and Management*

INTERSTATE COMMISSION ON THE POTOMAC RIVER BASIN
6110 Executive Blvd., Suite 300, Rockville, MD 20852-3903
Phone: 301-984-1908

Founded: 1940

Description: Interstate compact, established by Maryland, Pennsylvania, Virginia, West Virginia, and the District of Columbia. Coordinates tabulates, and summarizes existing data on condition of streams in Potomac Watershed; promotes uniform legislation; disseminates information; cooperates in studies; promotes coordination of program in Basin states. Areas of interest are water quality, water supply, and land resources associated with the Potomac and its tributaries.

Contact(s):
Administrative Assistant: SUSAN M. JACKSON
Associate Director of Living Resources: JAMES D. CUMMINS
Associate Director of Water Quality: CARLTON HAYWOOD
Associate Director, Water Resources: DR. ROLAND C. STEINER
Executive Director: JOSEPH K. HOFFMAN
Public Affairs Officer: CURTIS DALPRA
Publication(s): *Potomac Basin Reporter; In the Anacostia Watershed*

MARINE MAMMAL COMMISSION
4340 East-West Highway, Rm. 905, Bethesda, MD 20814
Phone: 301-504-0087; Fax: 301-504-0099; E-mail: firstinitialandlastname@mmc.gov

Founded: 1972

Description: Established by the Marine Mammal Protection Act of 1972, P.L. 92-522, the Marine Mammal Commission, in consultation with its Committee of Scientific Advisors on Marine Mammals, periodically reviews the status of marine mammal populations; manages a research program concerned with their conservation; and develops, reviews, and makes recommendations on federal activities and policies which affect the protection and conservation of marine mammals.

Contact(s):
Executive Director: JOHN R. TWISS JR.
Scientific Program Director: DR. ROBERT J. HOFMAN
Policy and Program Analyst: DAVID W. LAIST
General Counsel: MICHAEL L. GOSLINER
Publication(s): *Annual Report; Research Reports*

MIGRATORY BIRD CONSERVATION COMMISSION
1849 C St., NW (ARL SQ. 622), Washington, DC 20240
Phone: 703-358-1716

Founded: 1929

Description: Considers, passes upon, and fixes the prices for lands recommended by the Secretary of the Interior for purchase or lease by him under the Migratory Bird Conservation Act of February 18, 1929, as amended, as migratory bird refuges in the National Wildlife Refuge System.

Contact(s):
Chairman: BRUCE BABBITT, Secretary of the Interior; Phone: 202-208-7351; Fax: 202-208-6956
Secretary: JEFFERY M. DONAHOE; Phone: 703-358-1716; Fax: 703-358-2223

U.S. FEDERAL AND INTERNATIONAL GOVERNMENT AGENCIES - COMMISSIONS

MINNESOTA-WISCONSIN BOUNDARY AREA COMMISSION
619 2nd St., Hudson, WI 54016
Phone: 651-436-7131; Fax: 715-386-9571; E-mail: mwbac@mwvac.state.wi.us
Founded: 1965
Description: To conduct studies, develop recommendations, and coordinate planning for protection, use, and development in the public interest of lands, river valleys, and waters that form the boundary between Minnesota and Wisconsin, principally on the St. Croix and Mississippi rivers.
Contact(s):
Secretary: JESSIE MESCHIEVITZ
Executive Director: BUCK MALICK
Office Manager: ROSETTA M. HERRICKS
Public Affairs Director: JAMES M. HARRISON

NEW ENGLAND INTERSTATE WATER POLLUTION CONTROL COMMISSION
Boott Mills South, 100 Foot of John St., Lowell, MA 01852-1124
Phone: 978-323-7929
Founded: 1947
Description: The Commission provides a forum for interstate communication on high priority water-related environmental issues; provides training opportunities for state environmental staff and wastewater treatment plant operators; and provides the public with outreach and training materials on a wide range of environmental issues.
Contact(s):
Executive Director: RONALD F. POLTAK
Publication(s): *Water Connection (newsletter); LUSTLine (bulletin on underground storage tanks); Annual Report; NEI Environmental Information Catalog*
Keyword(s): Water Pollution

NORTH AMERICAN WETLANDS CONSERVATION COUNCIL
4401 North Fairfax Dr., Suite 110, Arlington, VA 22203
Phone: 703-358-1784; Fax: 703-358-2282; E-mail: r9arw_nawwo@mail.fws.gov; Web site: www.fws.gov/r9nawwo/nawcahp.html
Founded: 1989
Description: The North American Wetlands Conservation Council encourages public-private partnerships to conserve wetland ecosystems for waterfowl, other migratory birds, fish, and wildlife. Grant projects with a 1-1 match are funded to acquire, restore, and enhance wetlands and associated habitats in Canada, the U.S., and Mexico.
Contact(s):
Coordinator: DAVID A. SMITH
Deputy Executive Officer: STEVE FUNDERBURLS; Phone: 703-358-1784
Publication(s): *North American Wetlands Conservation Act Progress Report for 1994-1995 and 1996-1997; North American Wetlands Conservation Act Grant Application Instructions*
Keyword(s): Aquatic Habitats, Birds, Coasts, Grants, Waterfowl, Wetlands

NORTH PACIFIC ANADROMOUS FISH COMMISSION
Suite 502, 889 W. Pender St., Vancouver, British Columbia V6C 3B2 Canada
Phone: 604-775-5550; Fax: 604-775-5577
Founded: 1993
Description: Established by a Convention between Canada, Japan, Russia, and the U.S. for the conservation of the anadromous fish resources of the North Pacific Ocean.
Contact(s):
Executive Director: VLADIMIR FEDORENKO
President (Japan): F. ULMER
Vice President (Canada): V. IZMAILOV

NORTHEAST ATLANTIC FISHERIES COMMISSION
22 Berners St., London WIP 4DY United Kingdom
Phone: 0207-631-0016; Fax: 0207-636-9225; E-mail: info@neafc.org
Founded: 1980
Description: To promote the conservation and optimum utilization of the fishery resources of the northeast Atlantic, within a framework appropriate to the regime of extended coastal state jurisdiction over fisheries, and to encourage international cooperation and consultation with respect to these resources.
Contact(s):
President: O. TOUGAARD
Vice President: E. LEMCHE
Vice President: V. SOKOLOV
Secretary: SIGMUND ENGESAETER
Publication(s): *Annual Report; Handbook of Basic Texts*

NORTHEASTERN FOREST FIRE PROTECTION COMMISSION
36 Roslyn Ave., Warner, NH 03278-4021
Phone: 603-456-3474
Description: International forest fire protection mutual aid organization composed of three commissioners each from CT, ME, MA, NH, RI, VT, NY and the Canadian Provinces of Quebec, New Brunswick and Nova Scotia plus New England national forests (Green Mountain and While Mountain). Uniform fire organization planning and suppression technique training carried out annually by the members. The Northeastern Interstate Forest Fire Protection Compact is the governing document that established the organization.
Contact(s):
Executive Director: CLARK M. DAVIS, 36 Roslyn Ave., Warner, NH 03278-4021; Phone: 603-456-3474

OHIO RIVER VALLEY WATER SANITATION COMMISSION
5735 Kellogg Ave., Cincinnati, OH 45228-1112
Phone: 513-231-7719
Founded: 1948
Description: An interstate agency representing Illinois, Indiana, Kentucky, New York, Ohio, Pennsylvania, Virginia and West Virginia for control of water pollution in the Ohio River Valley Compact District.
Contact(s):
Chairman (IL): ROY MUNDY JR.
Vice Chairman (IN): VASILIKI KERAMIDA JR
Secretary and Treasurer (NY): DOUGLAS CONROE
Executive Director and Chief Engineer: ALAN H. VICORY JR.
Editor: KRISTI ROSE
Editor: JEANNE JAHNIGEN ISON
Publication(s): *ORSANCO Quality Monitor; Annual Report; publications of general or technical interest, such as Ohio River fish populations, trace chemicals, and monitoring programs.*

PACIFIC SALMON COMMISSION
1155 Robson St., Suite 600, Vancouver, British Columbia V6E 1B5 Canada
Phone: 604-684-8081
Description: Charged with implementation of the Pacific Salmon Treaty signed by Canada and the United States in 1985, the Commission provides regulatory advice and recommendations to the U.S. and Canada relative to their management of salmon originating in one country, but subject to interception by the other. The Commission is also charged with conserving Pacific Salmon stocks in order to achieve optimum production, and dividing salmon harvests so each nation receives benefits equivalent to salmon produced in its waters. Each nation appoints four commissioners and four alternates to serve on the Commission. The Commission is the body through which the U.S. and Canada can work to resolve complex salmon management problems.
Contact(s):
Executive Secretary: DON KOWAL

PACIFIC STATES MARINE FISHERIES COMMISSION
45 SE 82nd Dr., Suite 100, Gladstone, OR 97027-2522
Phone: 503-650-5400; Fax: 503-650-5426
Founded: 1947
Description: The Commission serves the Pacific states of Alaska, California, Idaho, Oregon, and Washington to promote conservation, development, and management of marine and anadromous fisheries

of mutual concern through a coordinated regional approach to fisheries research, monitoring, and utilization. Activities focus on multi-state databases, inter-jurisdiction fishery management plans, marine debris, saving fisheries habitat, and marine mammal/fishery interactions.
Contact(s):
Executive Director: RANDY FISHER

ST. CROIX INTERNATIONAL WATERWAY COMMISSION
Box 610, Calais, ME 04619
Phone: 506-466-7550; Fax: 506-466-7551
Description: A commission of the state of Maine and province of New Brunswick to help implement a cooperative international management plan for the St. Croix River system, which forms 110 miles of the U.S. and Canada border.
Contact(s):
Executive Director: LEE SOCHASKY
Co-Chairman: DON OLMSTEAD
Co-Chairman: KEN GORDON
Publication(s): *Management Plan for the St. Croix International Waterway; Annual Report; St. Croix Heritage Brochure*

SUSQUEHANNA RIVER BASIN COMMISSION
1721 N. Front St., Harrisburg, PA 17102
Phone: 717-238-0422
Description: Conservation and development of water resources and water-related resources in the river basin, comprising parts of Maryland, New York and Pennsylvania.
Contact(s):
Executive Director: PAUL O. SWARTZ, 1721 N. Front St., Harrisburg, PA 17102; Phone: 717-238-0422
Publication(s): *Annual Report; Susquehanna guardian (newsletter)*

UPPER COLORADO RIVER COMMISSION
355 S. 4th East St., Salt Lake City, UT 84111
Phone: 801-531-1150
Founded: 1949
Description: An administrative agency composed of commissioners appointed by the states of the Upper Division of the Colorado River - Colorado, New Mexico, Utah and Wyoming, and by the President of the U.S.
Contact(s):
Chairman: FRANK E. MAYNES, P.O. Drawer 2717, Durango, CO 81501
Executive Director and Secretary: WAYNE E. COOK

EXECUTIVE BRANCH

COUNCIL ON ENVIRONMENTAL QUALITY
722 Jackson Pl., NW, Washington, DC 20503
Phone: 202-456-6224 or 202-395-5750
Founded: 1970
Description: CEQ serves as the source of environmental expertise and policy analysis for the President and other organizations within the Executive Office of the President, and provides for coordination between departments and agencies. It is also charged with implementing statutory or regulatory requirements and programs.
Contact(s):
Chair (Acting): GEORGE T. FRAMPTON JR.
Administrative Officer: CAROLYN MOSLEY
Associate Director for Congressional Relations: JUDY JABLOW
Associate Director for Fisheries and Coastal Issues: SARAH LASKIN
Associate Director for Global Environment: DAVID SANDALOW
Associate Director for Natural Resources: BILL LEARY
Associate Director for Sustainable Development: KEITH LAUGHLIN
Associate Director for Toxics and Environmental Protection: BRAD CAMPBELL
Associate Director for Transportation, Energy and Land Management: LINDA LANCE
Director for Communications: ELLIOT DIRINGER
General Counsel: DINAH BEAR
Special Assistant for Outreach and Communications: NATHAN HURST
Publication(s): *CEQ Annual Report*

ENVIRONMENTAL PROTECTION AGENCY
401 M St., SW, Washington, DC 20460
Phone: 202-260-2090; Web site: www.epa.gov
Description: The Environmental Protection Agency (EPA) was established as an independent agency in the Executive Branch of the U.S. Government, pursuant to Reorganization Plan No. 3 of 1970, effective December 2, 1970. EPA endeavors to achieve systematic control and abatement of pollution, by properly administering and integrating a variety of research, monitoring, standard-setting and enforcement activities.
Contact(s):
Administrator: CAROL BROWNER; Phone: 202-260-4700
Deputy Administrator (Acting): PETER D. ROBERTSON
Associate Administrator for Communications, Education, and Media Relations: LORETTA M. UCELLI; Phone: 202-260-9828
Associate Administrator for Congressional and Intergovernmental Relations: JOSEPH R. CRAPA; Phone: 202-260-5200
Associate Administrator for Reinvention (Acting): JAY BENFORADO; Phone: 202-260-1849
Civil Rights Director: ANN E GOODE
Science Advisory Board Director: DONALD G. BARNES; Phone: 202-260-4125
Small and Disadvantaged Business Utilization Director: JEANETTE L. BROWN; Phone: 202-260-4100
Chief Financial Officer (Acting): SALLYANNE HARPER; Phone: 202-260-1151
Comptroller: W. S. RYAN; Phone: 202-260-9674
General Counsel (Acting): SCOTT C. FULTON; Phone: 202-260-8064
Inspector General (Acting): NIKKI I. TINSLEY; Phone: 202-260-3137

Administration and Resources Management
Contact(s):
Assistant Administrator (Acting): ALVIN M. PESACHOWITZ; Phone: 202-260-4600
Director of Administration and Resources Management, Research Triangle Park, NC: WILLIAM LAXTON; Phone: 919-541-2258
Director of Administration, Cincinnati, OH: WILLIAM M. HENDERSON; Phone: 513-569-7910
Director of Information Resources Management (Acting): MARK DAY; Phone: 202-260-4465
Human Resources and Organizational Services Director: DAVID J. O'CONNOR; Phone: 202-260-4467

Air and Radiation
Contact(s):
Assistant Administrator: ROBERT PERCIASEPE; Phone: 202-260-7400
Deputy Administrator: RICHARD D. WILSON; Phone: 202-260-7400
Air Quality Planning and Standards Director: JOHN S. SEITZ; Phone: 919-541-5504
Atmospheric Programs Director: PAUL M. STOPLMAN; Phone: 202-564-9150
Mobile Sources Director: MARGO T. OGE; Phone: 202-233-7645
Radiation and Indoor Air Director (Acting): LAWRENCE G. WEINSTOCK; Phone: 202-564-9370

Enforcement and Compliance
Contact(s):
Assurance Administrator: STEVEN A. HERMAN; Phone: 202-564-2440
Compliance Director: ELAINE G. STANLEY; Phone: 202-564-2280
Criminal Enforcement, Forensics, and Training Director: EARL E. DEVANEY; Phone: 202-564-2480
Environmental Justice Director (Acting): ROBERT J. KNOX; Phone: 202-564-2515
Federal Activities Director: RICHARD E. SANDERSON; Phone: 202-564-2400
Regulatory Enforcement Director: ERIC V. SCHAFFER; Phone: 202-564-2220

Site Remediation Enforcement Director: BARRY N. BREEN; Phone: 202-564-5110

Policy
Contact(s):
Assistant Administrator: DAVID M. GARDINER; Phone: 202-260-4332
Economy and Environment Director: ALBERT M. MCGARLAND; Phone: 202-260-3354
Program Support and Resource Management Director: PAMELA P STERLING; Phone: 202-260-4335
Regulatory management and Information Director: THOMAS E. KELLY; Phone: 202-260-4335
Sustainable Ecosystems and Communities Director (Acting): LEONARD J. FLECKENSTEIN; Phone: 202-260-4002

Prevention, Pesticides, and Toxic Substances
Contact(s):
Assistant Administrator: LYNN R. GOLDMAN; Phone: 202-260-2902
Pesticide Programs Director: MARCIA E. MULKEY; Phone: 703-305-7090
Pollution Prevention and Toxics Director: WILLIAM H. SANDERS III; Phone: 202-260-3810

Region I (CT, ME, MA, NH, RI, VT)
John F. Kennedy Federal Building, Boston 02203-0001
Phone: 617-918-1111; Web site: www.epa.gov/region01
Contact(s):
Regional Administrator: JOHN P. DEVILLARS; Phone: 617-918-1010

Region II (NJ, NY, PR, VI)
290 Broadway, New York, NY 10007-1866
Phone: 212-637-3000; Web site: www.epa.gov/region02/
Contact(s):
Regional Administrator: JEANNE M. FOX; Phone: 212-637-5000

Region III (DE, DC, MD, PA, VA, WV)
1650 Arch St., Philadelphia, PA 19103
Phone: 215-814-5000; Web site: www.epa.gov/region03/
Contact(s):
Regional Administrator: MICHAEL McCABE; Phone: 215-814-2900

Region IV (AL, FL, GA, KY, MS, NC, SC, TN)
61 Forsyth St., SW, Atlanta, GA 30303
Phone: 404-562-9900; Web site: www.epa.gov/region04
Contact(s):
Regional Administrator: JOHN H. HANKINSON JR.; Phone: 404-562-8357

Region IX (GU, AS, NV, HI, CA, AZ)
75 Hawthorne St., San Francisco, CA 94105
Phone: 415-744-1702; Web site: www.epa.gov/region09/
Contact(s):
Regional Administrator: FELICIA A. MARCUS; Phone: 415-744-1001

Region V (IL, IN, MI, NM, OH, WI)
77 West Jackson Blvd., Chicago, IL 60604-3507
Phone: 312-353-2000; Web site: www.epa.gov/region5/
Contact(s):
Regional Administrator (Acting): DAVID A. ULRICH; Phone: 312-886-3000

Region VI (AR, LA, NM, OK, TX)
Fountain Place, 12th Fl., Suite 1200, 1445 Ross Ave., Dallas, TX 75202-2733
Phone: 214-665-6444; Web site: www.epa.gov/regiono6/
Contact(s):
Regional Administrator: GREGG COOKE; Phone: 214-665-2100

Region VII (IA, KS, MO, NE)
726 Minnesota Ave., Kansas City, KS 66101
Phone: 913-551-7000; Web site: www.epa.gov/region07/

Contact(s):
Regional Administrator: DENNIS D. GRAMS; Phone: 913-551-7006

Region VIII (CO, MT, ND, SD, UT, WY)
999 18th St., Suite 500, Denver, CO 80202-2466
Phone: 303-312-6312; Web site: www.epa.gov/region08/
Contact(s):
Regional Administrator: WILLIAM P. YELLOWTAIL JR.; Phone: 303-312-6308

Region X (WA, OR, ID, AK)
1200 Sixth Ave., Seattle, WA 98101
Phone: 206-553-1200; E-mail: epa-seattle@epamail.epa.gov; Web site: www.epa.gov/region10/
Contact(s):
Regional Administrator: CHARLES C. CLARKE; Phone: 206-553-1234

Research and Development
Contact(s):
Assistant Administrator: HENRY L. LONGEST II; Phone: 202-564-6620
Science Policy Directory: DOROTHY E. PATTON; Phone: 202-564-6705
National Center for Environmental Assessment: WILLIAM H. FARLAND; Phone: 202-564-3322
National Center for Environmental Research and Quality Assurance: PETER W. PREUSS; Phone: 202-564-6825
National Exposure Research Laboratory Director: GARY J. FOLEY Ph.D.; Phone: 919-541-2106
National Health and Environmental Effects Director: LAWERNCE W. REITER Ph.D.; Phone: 919-541-2281
Associate Director for Ecology: GILMAN D. VEITH Ph.D.; Phone: 919-541-2283
Associate Director for Health: HAROLD ZENICH Ph.D.; Phone: 919-541-2283
National Risk Management Research Laboratory Director: TIMOTHY OPPELT; Phone: 513-569-7418

Solid Waste and Emergency Response
Contact(s):
Assistant Administrator (Acting): TIMOTHY FIELDS JR.; Phone: 202-260-4610
Chief Preparedness and Prevention Director: JAMES L. MAKRIS; Phone: 202-260-8600
Emergency and Remedial Response (Superfund/Oil Programs) Director: STEPHEN D. LUFTIG; Phone: 703-603-8960
Solid Waste Director (Acting): ELIZABETH COTSWORTH; Phone: 703-308-8895
Technology Innovation Director: WALTER W. KOVALICK JR.; Phone: 703-603-9910

Water
Contact(s):
Assistant Administrator (Acting): JONHATHAN C. FOX; Phone: 202-260-5700
American Indian Environmental Directory: KATHY GOROSPE; Phone: 202-260-7939
Ground Water and Drinking Water Director: CYNTHIA C. DOUGHERTY; Phone: 202-260-5543
Science and Technology Director: TUDOR T. DAVIES; Phone: 202-260-5400
Wastewater Management Director: MICHAEL B. COOK; Phone: 202-260-5850
Wetlands, Oceans, and Watersheds Director: ROBERT H. WAYLAND III; Phone: 202-260-7166

UNITED STATES DEPARTMENT OF AGRICULTURE
14th St. and Independence Ave., SW, Washington, DC 20250
Phone: 202-720-8732
Founded: 1862

U.S. FEDERAL AND INTERNATIONAL GOVERNMENT AGENCIES - EXECUTIVE BRANCH

Description: Created by Congress to acquire and disperse "useful" information on subjects connected with agriculture in the most general and comprehensive sense of that word, and to procure, propagate, and distribute among the people new and valuable seeds and plants. Today, in addition to managing the national forests and grasslands, USDA manages a variety of research, regulatory, domestic and foreign marketing, food and nutrition, and many other programs.
Contact(s):
Secretary: DAN GLICKMAN; Phone: 202-720-3631
Under Secretary (Acting) for Food Safety: DR. CATHY WOTEKI; Phone: 202-720-7025
Under Secretary (Acting) for Research Education and Economics: MILEY GONZALEZ; Phone: 202-720-5923
Under Secretary for Farm and Foreign Agricultural Services: AUGUST SCHUMACHER; Phone: 202-720-3111
Under Secretary for Food Nutrition and Consumer Services: SHIRLEY WATKINS; Phone: 202-720-7711
Under Secretary for Natural Resources and Environment: JAMES LYONS; Phone: 202-720-7173
Under Secretary for Rural Development: JILL LONG-THOMPSON; Phone: 202-720-4581
Assistant Secretary for Administration: BRAD PITTMAN-EVANS; Phone: 202-720-3291
Assistant Secretary for Congressional Relations: DAVE CARLIN; Phone: 202-720-7095
Assistant Secretary for Marketing and Regulatory Programs: MIKE DUNN; Phone: 202-720-4256
Chief Economist: KEITH COLLINS; Phone: 202-720-4164
Deputy Secretary: RICHARD ROMINGER; Phone: 202-720-6158
Director (Acting) of Communications: TOM AMONTREE; Phone: 202-720-4623

ANIMAL AND PLANT HEALTH INSPECTION SERVICE
U.S. Dept. of Agriculture, P.O. Box 96464, Washington, DC 20090-6464
Contact(s):
Chief of Staff: RICK CERTO
Director of Western Region: MIKE WORTHEN, 12345 W. Alameda Pkwy., Suite 204, Lakewood, CO 80228; Phone: 303-969-6560
Deputy Administrator for International Services: ANGEL CIELO; Phone: 202-720-7021
Deputy Administrator of Animal Damage Control: BOBBY R. ACORD; Phone: 202-720-2054
Deputy Director of Legislative and Public Affairs: LINDA SWACINA; Phone: 202-720-3981
Director of Denver Wildlife Research Center: RICHARD D. CURNOW, P.O. Box 25266, Bldg. 16, Federal Center, Denver, CO 80225-0266; Phone: 303-236-7820
Director of Eastern Region: GARY E. LARSON, Suite 301, 3322 West End Avenue, Nashville, TN 37027; Phone: 615-736-2007
Director of Legislative and Public Affairs: PATRICK COLLINS; Phone: 202-720-2511
Director of Operational Support Staff: ROBERT BOKMA; Phone: 301-734-8892
Director of Trade Support Team: JOHN GREIFER; Phone: 202-720-7677
Administrator: DR. ISI SIDDIQUI; Phone: 202-720-3668
Assistant Director for Executive Correspondence: LYNN QUARLES; Phone: 301-734-7776
Assistant Director for Public Affairs: RICK McNANEY; Phone: 301-734-7799
Associate Deputy Administrator for International Services: CARL CASTLETON; Phone: 202-720-7021
Associate Deputy Administrator of Animal Damage Control: WILLIAM H. CLAY; Phone: 202-720-2054
Associate Deputy Administrator of International Services: DAN SHEESLEY; Phone: 202-720-7593
Freedom of Information Act Officer: MICHAEL MARQUIS; Phone: 301-734-8296
Publication(s): *Careers in APHIS*

Animal Care
Description: Investigates and prosecutes violations of federal laws governing the movement of animals and plants between states or into and out of the United States and regulates the humane care and treatment of warmblooded animals used for purposes of research or exhibition, for sale as pets at the wholesale level, or transported in commerce.
Contact(s):
Acting Deputy Administrator for Regulatory Enforcement and Animal Care: RON DEHAVEN; Phone: 301-734-4980
Assistant Deputy Administrator (Acting) for Animal Care: WM. RON COOK; Phone: 301-734-4981

Animal Care Eastern Regional Office
2568A Riva Rd., Suite 302, Annapolis, MD 21401-7400
Contact(s):
Regional Director: ELIZABETH GOLDENTYER; Phone: 410-571-8692

Animal Care Regional Central Office
501 Felix St., Bldg. 11, Ft. Worth, TX 76115
Contact(s):
Regional Director: WALTER A. CHRISTENSEN

Animal Care Western Regional Office
9580 Micron Ave., Suite. J, Sacramento, CA 95827-2623
Contact(s):
Regional Director: ROBERT M. GIBBONS; Phone: 916-857-6205

International Services Central America, Caribbean & Panama Office
USDA-APHIS-IS, American Embassy, Guatemala, Unit 3319, APO 34024-3319
Phone: 011-502-331-2036
Contact(s):
Assistant Director of Operational Support: MARY NEAL; Phone: 301-734-8261
Associate Deputy Administrator: CHARLES SCHWALBE; Phone: 202-720-4441
Chief Operations Officer for Biological Assessment and Taxonomic Support: REBECCA BECH; Phone: 301-734-8896
Deputy Administrator (Acting) for Plant Protection and Quarantine: AL ELDER; Phone: 202-720-5601
Director of Central Region: ROBERT L. WILLIAMSON, 3505 Boca Chica Blvd, Suite 360, Brownsville, TX 78521-4065; Phone: 210-504-4150
Director of National Biological Control Institute: MICHAEL J. ORAZE; Phone: 301-734-4329
Director of Northeastern Region: PAUL EGGERT, Blason II, 1st Fl., 505 S. Lenola Rd., Moorestown, NJ 08057; Phone: 609-968-4960
Director of Southeastern: JERRY FOWLER, 3505 25th Ave., Bldg. 1, North Gulfport, MS 39501; Phone: 601-863-1813
Director of Western Region: JAMES R. REYNOLDS, 9580 Micron Ave., Suite 1, Sacramento, CA 95827; Phone: 916-857-6065
Phytosanitary Issues Management Team: ROBERT SPAIDE; Phone: 301-734-8262
Program Coordinator of Boll Weevil: GARY CUNNINGHAM; Phone: 301-734-8676
Regional Director: FAROUK HAMDY

International Services Europe, Africa, Russia, Near East Office
USDA-APHIS-IS FAS-USEU, PSC 82, Box 002, APO 09724
Phone: 011-322-508-2762
Contact(s):
Regional Director: ALEX B. THIERMANN

International Services Mexico Office
USDA-APHIS-IS, P.O. Box 3087, Laredo, TX 78044
Phone: 011-525-520-6892
Contact(s):
Regional Director: PETER FERNANDEZ

U.S. FEDERAL AND INTERNATIONAL GOVERNMENT AGENCIES - EXECUTIVE BRANCH

International Services Screwworm Eradication Program Office
USDA-APHIS-IS, P.O. Box 3087, Laredo, TX 78044
Phone: 011-525-520-4222
Contact(s):
Regional Director: JOHN WYSS

International Services South America Office: USDA/APHSIS
American Embassy Santiago, Unit 4113, APO, NY 34033
Phone: 011-562-638-1989
Contact(s):
Regional Director: JAMES MACKLEY

International Services Asia and Pacific Office
USDA-APHIS-IS, Unit 66, 4700 River Rd., Riverdale, MD 20737
Phone: 301-734-8292
Contact(s):
Regional Director: ROBERT T. TANAKA

Plant Protection and Quarantine
Description: Regulates the importation of plants, plant products, and animal products from foreign countries. Regulates the movement of such products between U.S. possessions and the mainland and the importation and interstate movement of plant pests. Inspects and certifies plants and plant products for export. Administers cooperative programs with states to control and eradicate insects, diseases, weeds, and nematodes of economic importance. Enforces the Convention on International Trade in Endangered Species of Flora and Fauna (CITES) for plants.

Regulatory Enforcement Eastern Regional Office
2568A Riva Rd., Suite 302, Annapolis, MD 21401-7400
Contact(s):
Regional Director: JOHN S. KINSELLA

Veterinary Services
Description: Regulates the importation of animals, animal semen, embryos, and animal products from foreign countries and the interstate movement of animals. Inspects and certifies animals for export. Administers cooperative federal-state programs to control and eradicate animal pests and diseases. Provides laboratory support for animal health programs and diagnostic referral assistance for private and state laboratories.
Contact(s):
Chief of Foreign Animal Disease Diagnostic Laboratory: ALFONSO TORRES, P.O. Box 848, Greenport Long Island, NY 11844-0848; Phone: 516-323-2506
Chief of Veterinary Services National Center for Import and Export: GARY S. COLGROVE; Phone: 301-734-6954
Deputy Administrator for Veterinary Services: JOAN M. ARNOLDI; Phone: 202-720-5193
Director (Acting) of Veterinary Services Operations Support Staff: RICHARD L. RISSLER; Phone: 301-734-8097
Director of Central Region: RUBE HARRINGTON, 100 W. Pioneer Pkwy., Suite. 100, Arlington, TX 76010; Phone: 817-885-7850
Director of National Veterinary Services Laboratories: JAMES PEARSON, P.O. Box 844, 1800 Dayton Rd., Ames, IA 50010; Phone: 515-239-8301
Director of Northern Region: WILLIAM W. BUISCH, One Winners Cir., Suite. 100, Albany, NY 12203; Phone: 518-453-0103
Director of Southeastern Region: CHESTER GIPSON, 501 E. Polk St., Suite 880, Tampa, FL 33602-3945; Phone: 813-228-2952
Director of Western Region: ROBERT M. NERVIG, 384 Inverness Dr. S., Englewood, CO 80112; Phone: 303-784-6201
National Animal Health Programs Staff: MICHAEL GILSDORF; Phone: 301-734-6954
Veterinary Services Brucellosis Eradication Staff: GRANVILLE H. FRYE; Phone: 301-734-8711
Veterinary Services Emergency Programs: JOSEPH ANNELLI; Phone: 301-734-7767
Veterinary Services Trade Negotiator for National Center for Import and Export: ROBERT F. KAHRS; Phone: 301-734-3294

ECONOMIC RESEARCH SERVICE
1800 M St., NW, Washington, DC 20036
Phone: 202-694-5050; Fax: 202-694-5757; E-mail: service@econ.ag.gov.; Web site: www.ecm.ag.gov
Description: Provides a program of agricultural, economic, and social research and analysis, statistical programs, technical consultation, planning assistance, and associated services. Conducts research and staff work relating to natural resources and environmental quality, including supplies, uses, and projected future requirements for land and water; effects of environmental quality improvement measures on agricultural production and agricultural resource use; achievement of environmental goals in rural areas; ownership and control of land and water resources; methods for natural resource planning; and evaluation of natural resource plans and projects.
Contact(s):
Administrator: SUSAN OFFUTT
Director of Information Services Division (Acting): FRED HOFF
Director of Publication Services Branch: ADRIE CUSTER
Director of Resource Economics Division: KITTY SMITH
Publication(s): *Various research monographs on natural resources use, pest control, agricultural inputs, conservation, food, rural issues, commodities, and U.S. trade.*

FARM SERVICE AGENCY (FSA), FORMERLY AGRICULTURAL STABILIZATION AND CONSERVATION SERVICE
USDA, FSA, CEPA, STOP 0513, 1400 Independence Ave., SW, Washington, DC 20250-0513
Phone: 202-720-6221
Description: Administers the following: Conservation Reserve Program, Emergency Conservation Program, various commodity loan programs, production flexibility contracts, and various farm loan and disaster assistance programs.
Contact(s):
Director, Conservation and Environmental Programs: ROBERT STEPHENSON
Administrator: KEITH KELLY
Deputy Administrator for Farm Loan Programs: CAROLYN COOKSIE
Deputy Administrator for Farm Programs: LARRY MITCHELL
Director of Price Support Division: GRADY BILBERRY
Director of Production, Emergencies and Compliance Divison: DIANE SHARP
Director of Public Affairs: TADE SULLIVAN

NATURAL RESOURCES CONSERVATION SERVICE (formerly Soil Conservation Service)
USDA, 14th and Independence Ave., SW, P.O. Box 2890, Washington, DC 20013
Phone: 202-720-3210
Founded: 1935
Description: NRCS has national responsibility for helping America's farmers, ranchers, and other private landowners develop and carry out voluntary efforts to conserve and protect our natural resources. NRCS is the technical delivery arm for conservation of the United States Department of Agriculture. It provides technical assistance and conservation programs through a unique partnership with America's soil and water conservation districts and state conservation agencies.
Contact(s):
Director, Conservation Communications Staff: DAVID C. WHITE, Rm. 6121-s, Washington, DC 20013; Phone: 202-720-3210; Fax: 202-720-1564; E-mail: dave.white@usda.gov
Program Assistant: JOYCE HAWKINS, Rm. 6121-s, Washington, DC 20013; Phone: 202-720-3210; Fax: 202-720-1564; E-mail: joyce.hawkins@usda.gov
AK Public Affairs Spcialist: VACANT, 949 E. 36th Ave., Suite 400, Achorage, AK 99508-4362; Phone: 907-271-2424; Fax: 907-271-3951
AL Public Affairs Specialist: JOAN LOVE SMITH, 665 Opelika Rd., Auburn, AL 36830-0311; Phone: 334-887-4530; Fax: 334-887-4551; E-mail: joan.smith@al.nrcs.usda.gov

AR Public Affairs Specialist: SONJA S. CODERRE, Federal Office Bldg., Rm. 5404, 700 W. Capitol Ave., Little Rock, AR 72201-3228; Phone: 501-301-3133; Fax: 501-301-3189; E-mail: scoderre@ar.usda.gov

AZ Public Affairs Specialist: MARY ANN MCQUINN, 3003 N. Central Ave., Suite 800, Phoenix, AZ 85012-2945; Phone: 602-280-8778; Fax: 602-280-8809; E-mail: mmcquinn@az.nrcs.usda.gov

CA Public Affairs Specialist: ANITA BROWN, 2121-C 2nd St., Suite 102, Davis, CA 95616-5475; Phone: 530-792-5644; Fax: 530-792-5791; E-mail: anita.brown@ca.usda.gov

CO Public Affairs Specialist: PETRA BARNES, 655 Parfet St., Rm. E 200C, Lakewood, CO 80215-5517; Phone: 303-236-2886, ext. 216; Fax: 303-236-2896; E-mail: pbarnes@co.nrcs.usda.gov

CT Public Affairs Specialist (Acting): CAROLYN MILLER, 16 Professional Park Rd., Storrs, CT 06268-1299; Phone: 860-487-4029; Fax: 860-487-4054; E-mail: cmiller@ct.nrcs.usda.gov

DE Public Affairs Specialist: PAUL PETRICHENKO, 1203 College Park Dr., Suite 101, Dover, DE 19904-8713; Phone: 302-678-4178; Fax: 302-678-0843; E-mail: ppetrichencko@de.nrcs.usda.gov

FL Public Affairs Specialist: DOROTHY STALEY, 2614 NW, 43rd St., Gainesville, FL 32606-6611; Phone: 352-338-9565; Fax: 352-338-9574; E-mail: dstaley@fl.nrcs.usda.gov

GA Public Affairs Specialist: JODY CHRISTIANSEN, Federal Bldg., Box 13, 355 E. Hancock Ave., Athens, GA 30601-2769; Phone: 706-546-2114; Fax: 706-546-2275; E-mail: jody@ga.nrcs.usda.gov

HI Public Affairs Specialist: LYNN HOWELL, 300 Ala Moana Blvd., Rm. 4316, Honolulu, HI 96850-0002; Phone: 808-541-2600, ext. 110; Fax: 808-541-2652; E-mail: lhowell@hi.nrcs.usda.gov

IA Public Affairs Specialist: LYNN BETTS, 693 Federal Bldg., 210 Walnut St., Des Moines, IA 50309-2180; Phone: 515-284-4262; Fax: 515-284-4394; E-mail: lynn.betts@ia.nrcs.usda.gov

ID Public Affairs Specialist: SHARON NORRIS, 3244 Elder St., Rm 124, Boise, ID 83705-4711; Phone: 208-378-5725; Fax: 208-378-5735; E-mail: snorris@id.nrcs.usda.gov

IL Public Affairs Specialist: PAIGE MITCHELL BUCK, 1902 Fox Dr., Champaign, IL 61820-7335; Phone: 217-398-5273; Fax: 217-398-5310; E-mail: paige.mitchell@il.nrcs.usda.gov

IN Public Affairs Specialist: MICHAEL MCGOVERN, 6013 Lakeside Blvd., Indianapolis, IN 46278-2933; Phone: 317-290-3222, ext. 324; Fax: 317-290-3225; E-mail: mmcgover@in.nrcs.usda.gov

KS Public Affairs Specialist: MARY SCHAFFER, 760 S. Broadway, Salina, KS 67401; Phone: 785-823-4571; Fax: 785-823-4540; E-mail: mary.shaffer@ks.nrcs.usda.gov

KY Public Affairs Specialist: LOIS JACKSON, 771 Corporate Dr., Suite 110, Lexington, KY 40503-5479; Phone: 606-224-7372; Fax: 606-224-7399; E-mail: ljackson@kystate.ky.nrcs.usda.gov

LA Public Affairs Specialist: HERB BOURQUE, 3737 Government St., Alexandria, LA 71302-3727; Phone: 318-473-7762; Fax: 318-473-7682; E-mail: hbourque@laso2.la.nrcs.usda.gov

MA Public Affairs Specialist: WENDI KROLL, 451 West St., Amherst, MA 01002-2995; Phone: 413-253-4351; Fax: 413-253-4375; E-mail: wkroll@ma.nrcs.usda.gov

MD Public Affairs Specialist: CAROL HOLLINGSWORTH, John Hanson Business Center, 339 Busch's Frontage Rd., Suite 30, Annapolis, MD 21401-5534; Phone: 410-757-0861, ext.313; Fax: 410-757-0687; E-mail: carol.hollingsworth@md.usda.gov

ME Public Affairs Specialist: ELAINE TREMBLE, 5 Godfrey Dr., Orono, ME 04473; Phone: 207-866-7241; Fax: 207-866-7262; E-mail: etremble@me.nrcs.usda.gov

MI Public Affairs Specialist: CHRISTINA COULON, 1405 S. Harrison Rd., Rm. 101, East Lansing, MI 48823-5243; Phone: 517-337-6701; Fax: 517-337-6905; E-mail: ccoulon@miso.mi.nrcs.usda.gov

MN Public Affairs Specialist: SYLVIA RAINFORD, 600 Farm Credit Services Bldg., 375 Jackson St., St. Paul, MN 55101-1854; Phone: 612-602-7859; Fax: 612-602-7914; E-mail: str@mn.nrcs.usda.gov

MO Public Affairs Specialist: NORM KLOPFENSTEIN, Parkade Center, Suite 250, 601 Business Loop, 70 West, Columbia, MO 65203-2546; Phone: 573-876-0911; Fax: 573-876-0913; E-mail: normk@mo.nrcs.usda.gov

MS Public Affairs Specialist: JEANINE MAY, Federal Bldg., Suite 1321, 100 W. Capitol St., Jackson, MS 39269-1399; Phone: 601-965-4337; Fax: 601-965-4536; E-mail: jbm@ms.nrcs.usda.gov

MT Public Affairs Specialist: LORI VALDEZ, Federal Bldg., Rm. 443, 10 E. Babcock St., Bozeman, MT 59715-4704; Phone: 406-587-6842; Fax: 406-587-6761; E-mail: lvaladez@mt.nrcs.usda.gov

NC Public Affairs Specialist: ANDREW SMITH, 4405 Bland Rd., Suite 205, Raleigh, NC 27609-6293; Phone: 919-873-2107; Fax: 919-873-2156; E-mail: asmith@nc.nrcs.usda.gov

ND Public Affairs Specialist: ARLENE DEUTSCHER, Federal Bldg., 220 E. Rosser Ave., Rm. 278, 220 E. Rosser Ave., Bismarck, ND 58502-1458; Phone: 701-250-4768; Fax: 701-250-4778; E-mail: ajd@nd.nrcs.usda.gov

NE Public Affairs Specialist: PAT MCGRANE, Federal Bldg., Rm. 152, 100 Centennial Mall, N., Lincoln, NE 68508-3866; Phone: 402-437-5328; Fax: 402-437-5327; E-mail: pat.mcgrane@ne.usda.gov

NH Public Affairs Specialist: ALYSSA ALDRICH, Federal Bldg., 2 Madbury Rd., Durham, NH 03824; Phone: 603-868-7581; Fax: 603-868-5301; E-mail: aaldrich@nh.nrcs.usda.gov

NJ Public Affairs Specialist: IRENE LIEBERMAN, 1370 Hamilton St., Somerset, NJ 08873-3157; Phone: 732-246-1171, ext.124; Fax: 732-246-2358; E-mail: ilieberman@nj.nrcs.usda.gov

NM Public Affairs Specialist: vacant , 6200 Jefferson St., NE, Suite 305, Albuquerque, NM 87109-3734; Phone: 505-761-4404; Fax: 505-761-4463

NV Public Affairs Specialist: LIZ WARNER, 5301 Langley Ln., Bldg. F, Suite 201, Reno, NV 89511; Phone: 775-784-5288; Fax: 702-784-5939; E-mail: ewarner@nv.nrcs.usda.gov

NY Public Affairs Specialist: VACANT, 441 S. Salina St., Suite 354, Syracuse, NY 13202-2450; Phone: 315-477-6524; Fax: 315-477-6550; E-mail: kathy.carpenter@ny.nrcs.usda.gov

OH Public Affairs Specialist: LATAWNYA DIA, 200 North High St., Rm., Columbus, OH 43215-2748; Phone: 614-469-6962; Fax: 614-469-2083; E-mail: l atawnya.dia@oh.nrcs.usda.gov

OK Public Affairs Specialist: DWAIN PHILLIPS, 100 USDA Agriculture Center Bldg., Suite 203, Stillwater, OK 74074-2624; Phone: 405-742-1243; Fax: 405-742-1201; E-mail: dwain.phillip@ok.usda.gov

OR Public Affairs Specialist: GAYLE NORMAN, 101 SW Main Street, Suite 1300, Portland, OR 97204-3221; Phone: 503-414-3236; Fax: 503-414-3101; E-mail: gnorman@or.nrcs.usda.gov

PA Public Affairs Specialist: STACY MITCHELL, One Credit Union Pl., Suite 340, Harrisburg, PA 17110-2993; Phone: 717-237-2208; Fax: 717-237-2238; E-mail: smitchell@pa.nrcs.usda.gov

PAC BAS Public Affairs Specialist: MARIE C. MUNDHEIM; Phone: 671-472-7490, ext. 21; Fax: 671-472-7298; E-mail: pacbas@ite.net

Puerto Rico Public Affairs Specialist: BECKY FRATICELLI, IBM Bldg., 6th Fl., 654 Munoz Rivera Ave., Hato Rey, PR 00918-7013; Phone: 787-766-5206, ext. 236; Fax: 787-766-5987; E-mail: becky@pr.nrcs.usda.gov

RI Public Affairs Specialist: VACANT, 60 Quaker Ln., Suite 46, Warwick, RI 02886-0111; Phone: 401-828-1300; Fax: 401-828-0433; E-mail: jcomerford@ri.nrcs.usda.gov

SC Public Affairs Specialist: PERDITA BELK, Strom Thurmond Federal Bldg., 1835 Assembly St., Rm. 950, Columbia, SC 29201-2489; Phone: 803-765-5402; Fax: 803-253-3670; E-mail: pbelk@sc.nrcs.usda.gov

SD Public Affairs Specialist: JOYCE WATKINS, 200 4th St., SW, Federal Bldg., Huron, SD 57350-2475; Phone: 605-352-1228; Fax: 605-352-1261; E-mail: joyce.watkins@sdso1.sd.nrcs.usda.gov

TN Public Affairs Specialist: LARRY BLICK, 675 U.S. Courthouse, 801 Broadway St., Nashville, TN 37203-3878; Phone: 615-736-5490; Fax: 615-736-7764; E-mail: lblick@tn.nrcs.usda.gov

U.S. FEDERAL AND INTERNATIONAL GOVERNMENT AGENCIES - EXECUTIVE BRANCH

TX Public Affairs Specialist: HAROLD BRYANT, W.R. Poage Federal Bldg., 101 S. Main St., Temple, TX 76501-7682; Phone: 254-742-9811; Fax: 254-742-9819; E-mail: hbryant@tx.nrcs.usda.gov

UT Public Affairs Specialist: RON NICHOLS, Wallace F. Bennett.FB, 125 South State Street, Rm. 4402, Salt Lake City, UT 84138-0350; Phone: 801-524-4556; Fax: 801-524-4403; E-mail: rnichols@ut.nrcs.usda.gov

VA Public Affairs Specialist: PAT PAUL, Culpeper Bldg, 1606 Santa Rosa Rd., Suite 209, Richmond, VA 23229-5014; Phone: 804-287-1681; Fax: 804-287-1737; E-mail: ppaul@va.nrcs.usda.gov

VT Public Affairs Specialist: ANNE HILLARD, 69 Union St., Winooski, VT 05404-1999; Phone: 802-951-6796; Fax: 802-951-6327; E-mail: ahillard@vt.nrcs.usda.gov

WA Public Affairs Specialist: CHIRS BIEKER, Rock Pointe Tower 2, Suite 450, West 316 Boone Ave., Spokane, WA 99201-2348; Phone: 509-323-2912; Fax: 509-323-2909; E-mail: cbieker@wa.nrcs.usda.gov

WI Public Affairs Specialist: RENAE ANDERSON, 6515 Watts Rd., Suite 200, Madison, WI 53719-2726; Phone: 608-276-8732; Fax: 608-276-5890; E-mail: randerso@wi.nrcs.usda.gov

WV Public Affairs Specialist: PEG REESE, 75 High St., Rm. 301, Morgantown, WV 26505; Phone: 304-291-4152, ext. 168; Fax: 304-291-4628; E-mail: preese@wv.nrcs.usda.gov

WY Public Affairs Specialist: NANCY ATKINSON, Federal Office Bldg., 100 East B St., Room 3124, Casper, WY 82601; Phone: 307-261-6482; Fax: 307-261-6490; E-mail: nla@wy.nrcs.usda.gov

RESEARCH EDUCATION AND ECONOMICS
Rm. 217-W, 1400 Independence Ave., SW, Washington, DC 20250
Phone: 202-720-5923
Contact(s):
Under Secretary: I. MILEY GONZALEZ
Deputy Under Secretary: EILEEN KENNEDY; Phone: 202-720-8885

Agricultural Research Service
REE, Washington, DC 20250
Description: Conducts research in natural resources, plant sciences, animal sciences, food sciences and human nutrition.
Contact(s):
Deputy Administrator (NPS): K. DARWIN MURRELL; Phone: 301-504-5084
Administrator: FLOYD P. HORN; Phone: 202-720-3656
Associate Administrator: EDWARD KNIPLING; Phone: 202-720-3658
Associate Deputy Administrator for Animal Production, Product Value, and Safety (NPS): CAIRD REXROAD; Phone: 301-504-7050
Associate Deputy Administrator for Crop Production, Product Value, and Safety (NPS): JUDITH ST. JOHN; Phone: 301-504-6252
Associate Deputy Administrator for Natural Resources and Sustainable Agricultural Systems (NPS): ALLEN DEDRICK; Phone: 301-504-7987

ARS Beltsville Office: USDA
Rm. 223, B-003 BARC-West, Beltsville, MD 20705
Phone: 301-504-6078
Contact(s):
Area Director: PHYLLIS E. JOHNSON

ARS Mid South Office: USDA
P.O. Box 225, Stoneville, MS 38776
Phone: 601-686-5265
Contact(s):
Area Director: THOMAS J. ARMY

ARS Midwest Office: USDA
1815 N. University St., Peoria, IL 61604
Phone: 309-681-6602
Contact(s):
Area Director ARS North Atlantic Office: USDA
600 E. Mermaid Ln., Wynmoor, PA 19038
Phone: 215-233-6593; Fax: 215-233-6719
Contact(s):
Area Director: WILDA MARTINEZ

ARS Northern Plains Office: USDA
1201 Oakridge Rd., Suite 150, Fort Collins, CO 80525
Phone: 970-229-5557
Contact(s):
Area Director: WILBERT BLACKBURN

ARS Pacific West Office: USDA
800 Buchanan St., Albany, CA 94710
Phone: 510-559-6060
Contact(s):
Area Director: A. A. BETSCHART

ARS South Atlantic Office: USDA
Russell Agr. Res. Center, P.O. Box 5677, College Station Rd., Athens, GA 30604-5677
Phone: 706-546-3311
Contact(s):
Area Director: ROGER BREEZE

ARS Southern Plains Office: USDA
7607 Eastmark Dr., Suite 230, College Station, TX 77840
Phone: 409-260-9346
Contact(s):
Area Director: CHARLES ONSTAD

Cooperative State Research, Education, and Extension Service
Washington, DC 20250
Description: The Cooperative State Research, Education, and Extension Service links the research and education resources and programs of the U.S. Department of Agriculture and works with land-grant institutions in each state, territory, and the District of Columbia.
Contact(s):
Associate Administrator: COLIEN HEFFERAN; Phone: 202-720-7441
Administrator: CHARLES W. LAUGHLIN; Phone: 202-720-4423
Deputy Administrator for Competitive Research Grants and Awards Management: SALLY ROCKEY; Phone: 202-401-1761
Deputy Administrator for Families 4-H and Nutrition: ALMA HOBBS; Phone: 401-720-2908
Deputy Administrator for Partnerships: GEORGE COOPER; Phone: 202-720-5623
Deputy Administrator for Science and Education Resources Development: JANE COULTER; Phone: 202-720-3377
Deputy Administrator of Plant and Animal Systems: EDWARD M. WILSON; Phone: 202-401-4329

CSREES-Natural Resources and Environment
Rm. 802, Aerospace Center, Mail Stop 2210, 1400 Independence Ave., SW, Washington, DC 20250-2210
Phone: 202-401-4555; Fax: 202-401-1706
Description: NRE is the operational staff of the CSREES. NRE is responsible for providing leadership and administering research and educational programs that ensure the efficient use and conservation of the Nation's natural resources and protection of the environment.
Contact(s):
Deputy Administrator: RALPH OTTO; E-mail: rotto@reeusda.gov
Liaison, State Ag. Experiment Station/CSREES National Environment Initiative (SUNEI): CHUCK KRUEGER; Phone: 202-401-6516; E-mail: ckrueger@psu.edu
National Program Leader, Water Quality: CYNTHIA GARMAN-SQUIER; Phone: 202-401-4510; E-mail: cgarmansquier@reeusda.gov
National Program Leader, Accountability and Evaluation: LEON HUNTER; Phone: 202-401-5934; E-mail: lhunter@reeusda.gov
National Program Leader, Chesapeake Bay Program: ANDY WEBER; Phone: 410-267-9875; E-mail: aweber@reeusda.gov
National Program Leader, Environmental Health: JANE DODDS; Phone: 202-401-4044; E-mail: jdodds@reeusda.gov

National Program Leader, Fish and Wildlife: JAMES E. MILLER; Phone: 202-401-6602; E-mail: jmiller@reeusda.gov

National Program Leader, Forestry Biology: CATALINO BLANCHE; Phone: 202-401-4190; E-mail: cblanche@reeusda.gov

National Program Leader, Forestry Management: LARRY BILES; Phone: 202-401-4926; E-mail: ibiles@reeusda.gov

National Program Leader, Housing and Environment: JOE WYSOCKI; Phone: 202-401-4980; E-mail: jwysocki@reeusda.gov

National Program Leader, Soils Science: RAYMOND KNIGHTON; Phone: 202-401-6417; E-mail: knighton@reeusda.gov

National Program Leader, Sustainable Development and Environmental Education: GREG CROSBY; Phone: 202-401-6050; E-mail: gcrosby@reeusda.gov

National Program Leader, Water Quality: TIMOTHY STRICKLAND; Phone: 202-401-5952; E-mail: tstrickland@reeusda.gov

National Program Leader, Water Quality: MAURICE HORTON; Phone: 202-401-4504; E-mail: mhorton@reeusda.gov

National Program Leader, Water Quality and Animal Waste Initiative: MARY ANN ROZUM; Phone: 202-401-4533; E-mail: mrozum@reeusda.gov

National Program Leader, Water Quality and Extension Indian Reservation Program: FRED SWADER; Phone: 202-401-5853; E-mail: fswader@reeusda.gov

National Program Leader, Wood Products: DONALD E. NELSON; Phone: 202-401-6444; E-mail: dnelson@reeusda.gov

UNITED STATES FOREST SERVICE
P.O. Box 96090, Washington, DC 20090-6090
Phone: 202-205-8333; Web site: www.fs.fed.us
Description: Administers National Forests and National Grasslands and is responsible for the management of their resources. Cooperates with federal and state officials in the enforcement of game laws on the National Forests and in the development and maintenance of wildlife resources; cooperates with the state and private owners in the application of sound forest management practices, in protection of forest lands against fire, insects, diseases, and in the distribution of planting stock. Conducts research in the entire field of forestry and wildland management.
Contact(s):
Chief: MIKE DOMBECK; Phone: 202-205-1661
Director of Office Communications: GEORGE D. LENNON; Phone: 202-205-8333
Civil Rights Director (Acting): THELMA FLOYD; Phone: 202-205-1585
Law Enforcement and Investigations: BILL WASLEY; Phone: 703-605-4690
International Programs: VALDIS MEZAINIS; Phone: 202-205-1650
Chief Financial Officer: VINCETTE GOERL; Phone: 202-205-1784
Deputy Operations: CLYDE THOMPSON; Phone: 202-205-1707
Deputy Operations Programs and Legislation: RONALD STEWART; Phone: 202-205-1663
Deputy Research and Development: ROBERT LEWIS; Phone: 202-205-1665
Chief Operating Officer: PHIL JANIK; Phone: 202-205-1661
Associate Deputy Research and Development: BARBARA WEBER; Phone: 202-205-1702
Deputy National Forest System: JIM FURNISH; Phone: 202-205-1523
Associate Deputy National Forest System: GLORIA MANNING; Phone: 202-205-1465
Associate Deputy National Forest System: PAUL BROUHA; Phone: 202-205-1465
Associate Deputy Programs and Legislation: SANDRA KEY; Phone: 202-205-1071
Deputy State and Private Forestry: JANICE McDOUGLE; Phone: 202-205-4657
Assistant Deputy State and Private Forestry: LARRY PAYNE; Phone: 202-205-1602
Associate Deputy State and Private Forestry (Acting): ROBIN L. THOMPSON; Phone: 202-205-1331
Associate Chief for Natural Resources: HILDA DIAZ-SOLTERO; Phone: 202-205-1491

Alaska Region 10
709 W. 9th St., P.O. Box 21628, Juneau, AK 99802-1628
Phone: 907-586-8863
Contact(s):
Regional Forester: RICK CABLES

Eastern Region 9
310 W. Wisconsin Ave., Suite 500, Milwaukee, WI 53203
Phone: 414-297-3600
Contact(s):
Regional Forester: ROBERT T. JACOBS

Forest Products Laboratory Station
One Gifford Pinchot Dr., Madison, WI 53705-2398
Phone: 608-231-9200
Contact(s):
Director: THOMAS E. HAMILTON

Intermountain Region 4
Federal Office Bldg. 324, 25th St., Ogden, UT 84401
Phone: 801-625-5605
Contact(s):
Regional Forester: JACK A. BLACKWELL

North Central Forest Experiment Station
1992 Folwell Ave., St. Paul, MN 55108
Phone: 612-649-5249
Contact(s):
Director: LINDA R. DONOGHUE

Northeastern Area State and Private Forestry
100 Matsonford Rd., 5 Radnor Corporate Center, Suite 200, Radnor, PA 19087-4585
Phone: 610-975-4139
Contact(s):
Area Director: MICHAEL T. RAINS

Northeastern Research Station
100 Matsonford Rd., 5 Ranor Corporate Center, Suite 200, Radnor, PA 19087-4585
Phone: 610-975-4017
Contact(s):
Director: BOV B EAV

Northern Region 1
200 E. Broadway, P.O. Box 7669, Missoula, MT 59807
Phone: 406-329-3316
Contact(s):
Regional Forester: DALE BOSWORTH

Pacific Northwest Region 6
333 SW 1st Ave., P.O. Box 3523, Portland, OR 97208
Phone: 503-808-2200
Contact(s):
Regional Forester (Acting): NANCY GRAYBEAL

Pacific Northwest Research Station
333 SW 1st Ave., P.O. Box 3890, Portland, OR 97208-3890
Phone: 503-808-2100
Contact(s):
Director: THOMAS J. MILLS

Pacific Southwest Region 5
Mare Island, 1323 Club Dr., Vallejo, CA 94592
Phone: 707-562-9000
Contact(s):
Regional Forester (Acting): BRADLEY E. POWELL

Pacific Southwest Research Station
800 Buchanan St., West Annex Building, Albany, CA 94710-0011
Phone: 510-559-6310
Contact(s):
Director: HAL SALWASSER

U.S. FEDERAL AND INTERNATIONAL GOVERNMENT AGENCIES - EXECUTIVE BRANCH

Rocky Mountain Region 2
P.O. Box 25127, Lakewood, CO 80225
Phone: 303-275-5450
Contact(s):
Regional Forester: LYLE LAVERTY

Rocky Mountain Research Station
240 W. Prospect St., Ft. Collins, CO 80526-2098
Phone: 970-498-1126
Contact(s):
Director: DENVER P. BURNS

Southern Region 8
1720 Peachtree Rd., NW, Suite 760, Atlanta, GA 30367
Phone: 404-347-4178
Contact(s):
Regional Forester: ELIZABETH ESTILL

Southern Research Station
P.O. Box 2680, Asheville, NC 28802
Phone: 704-257-4300
Contact(s):
Director: PETER J. ROUSSOPOULOS

Southwestern Region 3
517 Gold Ave., SW, Albuquerque, NM 87102
Phone: 505-476-3300
Contact(s):
Regional Forester: ELEANOR S. TOWNS

UNITED STATES DEPARTMENT OF COMMERCE
Herbert C. Hoover Bldg., Rm. 5610, 15th St. and Constitution Ave., NW, Washington, DC 20230
Phone: 202-219-3605; Web site: www.doc.gov
Description: The Department of Commerce promotes job creation, economic growth, sustainable development, and improved living standards for all Americans, by working in partnership with business, universities, communities, and workers.
Contact(s):
Secretary: WILLIAM M. DALEY; Phone: 202-482-2112
Deputy Secretary: ROBERT L. MALLETT

ECONOMIC DEVELOPMENT ADMINISTRATION
Department of Commerce, Herbert C. Hoover Bldg., Rm. 7800, 14th St. and Constitution Ave., NW, Washington, DC 20230
Phone: 202-482-5081
Description: Conducts programs to help stimulate private enterprise and create permanent jobs in economically distressed areas of the Nation. Provides public works grants and planning and technical assistance in areas with high unemployment or low median family income.
Contact(s):
Assistant Secretary: PHILLIP A. SINGERMAN; Phone: 202-482-5081; Fax: 202-273-4781; E-mail: Psingerm@doc.gov

NATIONAL OCEANIC AND ATMOSPHERIC ADMINISTRATION
Department of Commerce, Herbert C. Hoover Bldg., Rm. 5128, 14th and Constitution Ave., NW, Washington, DC 20230
Phone: 202-482-3384
Founded: 1970
Description: NOAA was created within the Department of Commerce to promote global environmental stewardship and to describe and predict changes in the Earth's environment. NOAA conducts oceanic and atmospheric research; maintains environmental databases and disseminates environmental information products; manages living marine resources and the marine environment; and operates environmental satellites, ships, aircraft, and buoys. NOAA provides the environmental information, science, technology, and resource management expertise necessary for our nation to build a future sustained by both environmental stewardship and economic growth.
Contact(s):
Assistant Secretary: TERRY D. GARCIA; Phone: 202-482-3567
Deputy Under Secretary: SCOTT B. GUDES; Phone: 202-482-4569
Under Secretary: DR. D. JAMES BAKER; Phone: 202-482-3436

National Environmental Satellite, Data, and Information Service
Federal Bldg. #4, Rm. 2069, Suitland and Silver Hill Roads, Suitland, MD 20746
Phone: 301-457-5115
Description: Manages satellites which observe the natural variability of the global Earth systems - the ocean, atmosphere, features of the solid earth, and the near-space system.
Contact(s):
Assistant Administrator: GREGORY W. WITHEE; Phone: 301-457-5115301-457-5115

National Marine Fisheries Service
Silver Spring Metro Center 3, 1315 East-West Hwy., Silver Spring, MD 20910
Phone: 301-713-2239
Description: Provides management, research, and services for the protection and rational use of living marine resources for their aesthetic, economic, and recreational value. Determines the consequences of the natural environment and human activities on living marine resources and provides knowledge and services to achieve efficient and judicious domestic and international management, use, and conservation of the resources.
Contact(s):
Assistant Administrator: PENELOPE DALTON; Phone: 301-713-2239

National Ocean Service
Rm. 13609, 1305 East-West Highway, Silver Spring, MD 20910
Phone: 301-713-3074
Description: Administers the National Geodetic Survey, Nautical and Aeronautical Charting, National Estuarine Research Reserves, National Marine Sanctuaries, Coastal Zone Management, Marine Assessments and Coastal Ocean Programs.
Contact(s):
Assistant Administrator: NANCY FOSTER Ph.D.; Phone: 301-713-3074
Public Affairs Officer: DAN DEWELL; Phone: 301-713-3070

National Weather Service
Silver Spring Metro Center 2, 1325 East-West Hwy., Silver Spring, MD 20910
Phone: 301-713-0689
Description: Observes, describes, and predicts the natural variability of the atmosphere, and to some extent, the ocean and the earth, in order to protect life and property and enhance the national economy.
Contact(s):
Deputy Assistant Administrator for Modernization: LOUIS J. BOEZI; Phone: 301-713-0397
Deputy Assistant Administrator for Operations: DR. SUSAN ZEVIN; Phone: 301-713-0711
Director and Assistant Administrator for Weather Service: DR. JOHN J. KELLY JR.
Director of National Centers for Environmental Prediction: DR. RONALD D. McPHERSON; Phone: 301-713-8016
Director of National Data Buoy Center: DR. JERRY C. McCALL; Phone: 601-688-2800
Director of National Hurricane Center: DR. ROBERT BURPEE; Phone: 305-229-4470
Director of Severe Storm Forecast Center: FREDERICK P. OSTBY; Phone: 816-426-5922
National Weather Service Alaska Region: RICHARD J. HUTCHEON; Phone: 907-271-5136
National Weather Service Central Region: RICHARD P. AUGULIS; Phone: 816-426-5400
National Weather Service Eastern Region: JOHN FORSING; Phone: 516-244-0100
National Weather Service Pacific Region: RICHARD H. HAGEMEYER; Phone: 808-541-1641
National Weather Service Western Region: DR. THOMAS D. POTTER; Phone: 801-524-5122

Public Affairs Officer of Weather: RANDEE EXTER; Phone: 301-713-0622
Southern Region: HARRY S. HASSEL; Phone: 817-334-2651

Office of Global Program
1100 Wayne Ave., Suite 1210, Silver Spring, MD 20910
Phone: 301-427-2089; Fax: 301-427-2073
Description: Provides the primary focus for coordination with national and international scientific communities in the areas of global warming, Tropical Oceans and Global Atmosphere Project, and worldwide climate research.
Contact(s):
Director: DR. J. MICHAEL HALL; Phone: 301-427-2089

Office of Oceanic and Atmospheric Research
Silver Spring Metro Center 3, 1315 East-West Hwy., Silver Spring, MD 20910
Phone: 301-713-2458
Description: Conducts environmental research in the oceans, atmosphere, and space. Administers the National Sea Grant College Program, which provides grants to academic institutions for research, education, and advisory/extension services in the marine environment.
Contact(s):
Assistant Administrator: DAVID L. EVANS
Deputy Assistant Administrator: LOUISA KOCH
Director of Environmental Research Laboratories: DR. JAMES L. RASMUSSEN; Phone: 301-713-2458
Director of National Sea Grant College Program of Extension Service (Acting): RONALD C. BAIRD; Phone: 301-713-2448
Director of National Undersea Research Program: DR. BARBARA MOORE; Phone: 301-713-2427
Public Affairs Officer: DANE KONOP; Phone: 301-713-2483
Resource Management: MARYANN WHITCOMB; Phone: 301-713-2454

UNITED STATES DEPARTMENT OF DEFENSE
The Pentagon, Office of the Secretary, 3400 Defense Pentagon, Washington, DC 20301-3400
Web site: www.denir.asd.mil
Description: Responsible for the security of the U.S. by establishing policies and procedures relating to national defense. The Department of Defense conducts programs to prevent pollution, enhance the environment, and conserve the natural and cultural resources on military lands.
Contact(s):
Deputy Secretary: JOHN J. HAMRE
Secretary: WILLIAM COHEN; Phone: 703-695-5261
Director of Administration Management: DAVID D. COOKE
Director of Conservation: L. PETER BOICE; Phone: 703-604-0524; Fax: 703-607-4237; E-mail: boicepl@acq.osd.mil
Publication(s): Natural Resources in the Department of Defense; Cultural Resources in the Department of Defense; Legacy Resource Management Program Report to Congress; DOD Commanders' Guide to Biodiversity; Coral Reef Conservation Guide for Military; Chesapeake Bay Watershed Access Guide

UNITED STATES DEPARTMENT OF EDUCATION
400 Maryland Ave., SW, Washington, DC 20202-0498
Phone: 1-800-USA-LEARN; Web site: www.ed.gov
Contact(s):
Deputy Secretary: MARSHALL SMITH
Secretary: RICHARD W. RILEY; Phone: 202-401-3000
Executive Secretariat Director: PHILIP S. LINK
Assistant Secretary of Civil Rights: NORMA V. CANTU; Phone: 202-401-1000
Assistant Secretary of Educational Research and Improvement: SHARON ROBINSON; Phone: 202-219-1385
Assistant Secretary of Elementary and Secondary Education and Deputy Assistant Secretary (Acting): JUDITH JOHNSON
Assistant Secretary of Human Resources and Administration: ROD McCOWAN
Assistant Secretary of Intergovernmental and Interagency Affairs (Designee): MARIO MORENO
Assistant Secretary of Legislation and Congressional Affairs: KAY L. CASSTEVENS
Assistant Secretary of Office of Adult and Vocational Education: AGUSTA KAPPNER
Assistant Secretary of Postsecondary Education (Acting): CLAUDIO R. PRIETO; Phone: 202-708-5547
Assistant Secretary of Special Education and Rehabilitative Services: JUDITH HEUMANN; Phone: 202-205-5465
Chief Financial Officer of Management and Budget/Services: DON WURTZ
Chief of Staff: BILLY WEBSTER
Director (Acting) of Bilingual Education and Minority Languages Affairs: EUGENE GARCIA
Director of Policy and Planning: ALAN L. GINSBURG
Director of Public Affairs: DAVID FRANK; Phone: 202-401-3026
General Counsel: JANNIENNE S. STUDLEY; Phone: 202-401-6000
Inspector General: JAMES B. THOMAS JR.

UNITED STATES DEPARTMENT OF ENERGY
Forrestal Bldg., 1000 Independence Ave., SW, Washington, DC 20585
Phone: 202-586-5000; Web site: www.doe.gov
Description: Provides the framework for a comprehensive and balanced national energy strategy through the coordination and administration of the energy functions of the federal government. The department is responsible for research, development, and demonstration of energy technology; the marketing of federal power; energy conservation programs; the nuclear weapons program; energy regulatory programs; and a central energy data collection and analysis program. Established by the Department of Energy Organization Action: 1977.
Contact(s):
Secretary: BILL RICHARDSON; Phone: 202-586-6210
Assistant Secretary of Environment, Safety and Health (Acting): PETER N. BRUSH; Phone: 202-586-5430
Assistant Secretary of Environmental Restoration and Waste Management (Acting): JAMES M. OWENDOFS; Phone: 202-586-7710
Assistant Secretary of Fossil Energy (Acting): ROBERT S. KRIPOWITCZ; Phone: 202-586-5506
Administrator of Energy Information Administration: JAY E. HAKES; Phone: 202-586-4361
Assistant Secretary of Congressional and Intergovernmental Affairs: JOHN M. ANGELL, III; Phone: 202-586-5450
Assistant Secretary of Energy Efficiency and Renewable Energy: DAN W. REICHER; Phone: 202-586-9220
Director of Office of Public Affairs: BROOK D. ANDERSON; Phone: 202-586-5823
Publication(s): National Energy Strategy; National Energy Strategy: One Year Later; Report to the Congress of the United States: Limiting New Greenhouse Gas Emissions in the United States; Assessment of Costs and Benefits of Flexible and Alternative Fuel Use in the United States Transportation Sector

CARBON DIOXIDE INFORMATION ANALYSIS CENTER
Oak Ridge National Laboratory, P.O. Box 2008 MS-6335, Oak Ridge, TN 37831-6335
Phone: 423-574-0390; Web site: cdiac.esd.ornl.gov
Founded: 1982
Description: The Carbon Dioxide Information Analysis Center (CDIAC) provides data and information support for the United States Department of Energy's global change research program and makes these data and information products available to a multidisciplinary community of researchers, policymakers, and educators at no cost.
Contact(s):
Director: ROBERT M. CUSHMAN; Phone: 423-574-4791
User Services: SONJA B. JONES; Phone: 423-574-3645
Publication(s): Trends Online; CDIAC Communications

FEDERAL ENERGY REGULATORY COMMISSION
888 First St., NE, Washington, DC 20426

U.S. FEDERAL AND INTERNATIONAL GOVERNMENT AGENCIES - EXECUTIVE BRANCH

Phone: 202-208-1088; Web site: www.ferc.fed.us
Founded: 1977
Description: The Federal Energy Regulatory Commission regulates the interstate aspects of the electric power and natural gas industries and establishes rates for transporting oil by pipeline. The Commission issues and enforces licenses for construction and operation of nonfederal hydroelectric power projects. The FERC also advises federal agencies on the merits of proposed federal multiple-purpose water development projects.
Contact(s):
Secretary: DAVID P. BOERGERS; Phone: 202-208-0400
Chair: JAMES HOECKER; Phone: 202-208-0000
Chief Administrative Law Judge: CURTIS J. WAGNER JR.; Phone: 202-219-2500
Chief Information Officer (Acting): THOMAS R. HERLIHY; Phone: 202-208-1055
Commissioner: CURTIS L. HERBERT JR.; Phone: 202-208-0601
Commissioner: WILLIAM L. MASSEY; Phone: 202-208-0366
Commissioner: VICKY A. BAILEY; Phone: 202-208-0388
Commissioner: LINDA K. BREATHITT; Phone: 202-208-0377
Director and Chief Financial Officer of Finance, Accounting, and Operations: THOMAS R. HERLIHY; Phone: 202-208-0300
Director of Economic Policy: RICHARD P. O'NEILL; Phone: 202-208-0100
Director of Electric Power Regulation: SHELTON M. CANNON; Phone: 202-208-1200
Director of Hydropower Licensing: CAROL L. SAMPSON; Phone: 202-219-2700
Director of Office of Administrative Litigation: VIRGINIA STRASSER; Phone: 202-219-2600
Director of Office of External Affairs: REBECCA F. SCHAFFER; Phone: 202-208-0004
Director of Pipeline Regulation: KEVIN P. MADDEN; Phone: 202-208-0700
General Counsel: DOUGLAS W. SMITH; Phone: 202-208-1000

UNITED STATES DEPARTMENT OF HEALTH AND HUMAN SERVICES

200 Independence Ave., SW, Washington, DC 20201
Web site: www.hhs.gov
Description: The Department of Health and Human Services is the United States government's principal agency for protecting the health of all Americans and providing essential human services, especially for those who are least able to help themselves.
Contact(s):
Secretary: DONNA SHALALA; Phone: 202-690-7000
Deputy Secretary: KEVIN THURM; Phone: 202-690-6133
Assistant Deputy Secretary for Health: NEIL STILLMAN; Phone: 202-690-7694
Administration for Aging: WILLIAM F. BENSON; Phone: 202-401-4634
Administration for Children and Families: OLIVIA GOLDEN; Phone: 202-401-2337
Administrator of Health Care Financing Administration: BRUCE C. VLADECK; Phone: 202-690-6726
Assistant Secretary for Legislation: RICHARD TARPLIN; Phone: 202-690-7627
Assistant Secretary for Management and Budget (Acting): JOHN J. CALLAHAN; Phone: 202-690-6396
Assistant Secretary for Planning and Evaluation: DR. MARGARET HAMBURG; Phone: 202-690-7858
Assistant Secretary for Public Affairs (Acting): MELISSA SKOLFIELD; Phone: 202-690-7850
Chief of Staff: WILLIAM CORR; Phone: 202-690-7431
Counselor to the Secretary: ANN ROSEWATER; Phone: 202-690-8157
Office of Civil Rights: DENNIS W. HAYASHI; Phone: 202-619-0403
Office of Consumer Affairs: LESLIE BYRNE; Phone: 202-565-0040
Office of Inspector General: JUNE G. BROWN; Phone: 202-619-3148
Office of the General Counsel: HARRIET S. RABB; Phone: 202-690-7741

FOOD AND DRUG ADMINISTRATION

5600 Fishers Ln., Rockville, MD 20857
Phone: 410-433-1544; Web site: www.fda.gov
Description: Protects the health of American consumers by enforcing federal laws which require that foods must be safe, pure and wholesome; human and veterinary drugs, biologies and therapeutic devices must be safe and effective; cosmetics and radiation-emitting products must be harmless; and that all these products must be honestly and informatively labeled and packaged.
Contact(s):
Director: D. BRUCE BURLINGTON; Phone: 410-443-4690
Director: RICHARD H. TESKE; Phone: 410-594-1740
Director: BERNARD A. SCHWETZ; Phone: 501-543-7517
Director: GERALD F. MEYER; Phone: 410-443-2894
Director: DR. FRED R. SHANK; Phone: 202-205-4850
Director: KATHRYN C. ZOON; Phone: 410-496-3556
Director: DR. MARY ANN DANELLO; Phone: 410-443-1565
Associate Commissioner for Consumer Affairs: R. ALEXANDER GRANT; Phone: 410-443-5006
Associate Commissioner for Health Affairs: DR. STUART L. NIGHTINGALE; Phone: 410-433-6143
Associate Commissioner for Legislative Affairs: DIANNE E. THOMPSON; Phone: 410-443-3793
Associate Commissioner for Management and Operations: SHARON SMITH HOLSTON; Phone: 410-443-3370
Associate Commissioner for Planning and Evaluation: PAUL L. COPPINGER; Phone: 410-433-4230
Associate Commissioner for Public Affairs: JAMES A. O'HARA, III; Phone: 410-443-1130
Associate Commissioner for Regulatory Affairs: RONALD G. CHESEMORE; Phone: 410-433-1594
Chief Counsel for Office of General Counsel: MARY JANE PORTER; Phone: 410-443-4370
Deputy Commissioner for External Affairs: CAROL SCHEMAN; Phone: 410-443-2400
Deputy Commissioner for Management and Systems: MARY JO VEVERKA; Phone: 410-443-1263
Deputy Commissioner for Operations: JANE HENNEY; Phone: 410-433-2400
Deputy Commissioner for Policy: MICHAEL R. TAYLOR; Phone: 410-443-2854
Director of AIDS Coordination Staff: DR. RANDOLPH WYKOFF
Director of Office of Biotechnology: DR. HENRY MILLER; Phone: 410-443-7573
Director of Office of Equal Employment and Civil Rights: ROSAMELIA de la ROCHA; Phone: 410-443-5541
Director of Office of Executive Operations: JOSEPH A. LEVITT; Phone: 410-443-5004
Director of Office of Orphan Products Development: DR. MARLENE HAFFNER
Director of Press Relations for Staff of Office of Public Affairs: BETSY ADAMS; Phone: 410-443-4177
Ombudsman: AMANDA PEDERSEN; Phone: 410-443-1306
Special Assistant to the Commissioner for Program Policy: JACK W. MARTIN; Phone: 410-443-6776

UNITED STATES DEPARTMENT OF HOUSING AND URBAN DEVELOPMENT

HUD Bldg., 451 7th St., SW, Washington, DC 20410
Phone: 202-755-5111; Web site: www.hud.gov
Contact(s):
Secretary: ANDREW M. CUOMO; Phone: 202-708-0417
Assistant Deputy Secretary for Field Policy and Management (Acting): MARY MADDEN; Phone: 202-708-2426
Assistant Secretary for Community Planning and Development: CARDELL COOPER; Phone: 202-708-0123
Assistant Secretary for Public and Indian Housing: HAROLD LUCAS; Phone: 202-708-0950
Assistant Secretary of Housing FHA Commissioner: BILL APGAR; Phone: 202-708-3600

Deputy Assistant Secretary for Research, Evaluation and Monitoring: XAVIER de-SOUZA BRIGGS; Phone: 202-708-1600
Deputy Chief of Staff for Policy and Programs: JACQUIE LAWING; Phone: 202-708-2236
General Deputy Assistant Secretary for Administration: JOSEPH SMITH; Phone: 202-708-0940
Inspector General: SUSAN GAFFNEY; Phone: 202-708-0430

UNITED STATES DEPARTMENT OF JUSTICE
Environment and Natural Resources Division, Rm. 2143, 10th St. and Constitution Ave., NW, Washington, DC 20530
Phone: 202-514-2701

Description: The Environment and Natural Resources Division handles litigation involving American's pollution control laws; central resources laws, the protection and enhancement of the American environment and wildlife resources; the acquisition, administration, and disposition of public land, water, and mineral resources; and the safeguarding of Indian rights and property.

Contact(s):
Attorney General: JANET RENO; Phone: 202-514-2001
Appellate Section Chief: JAMES KILBOURNE; Phone: 202-514-2748
Assistant Attorney General: LOIS J. SCHIFFER; Phone: 202-514-2701
Deputy Assistant Attorney General: EILEEN SOBECK; Phone: 202-514-0943
Deputy Assistant Attorney General: JAMES F. SIMON; Phone: 202-514-3370
Deputy Assistant Attorney General: JOHN CRUDEN; Phone: 202-514-2718
Environmental Crimes Section Chief: STEVEN SOLOW; Phone: 202-272-9877
Environmental Defense Section Chief: LETITIA J. GRISHAW; Phone: 202-514-2219
Environmental Enforcement Section Chief: JOEL GROSS; Phone: 202-514-1604
Executive Officer: ROBERT BRUFFY; Phone: 202-616-3147
General Litigation Section Chief: WILLIAM M. COHEN; Phone: 202-305-0440
Indian Resources Section Chief: JAMES J. CLEAR; Phone: 202-305-0259
Land Acquisition Section Chief: VIRGINIA P. BUTLER; Phone: 202-305-0316
Policy of Legislation and Special Litigation Section Chief: PAULINE H. MILIUS; Phone: 202-514-2586
Principal Deputy Assistant Attorney General: PETER D. COPPELMAN; Phone: 202-514-4760
Wildlife and Marine Resources Section Chief: JEAN E. WILLIAMS; Phone: 202-305-0228

UNITED STATES DEPARTMENT OF LABOR
200 Constitution Ave., NW, Washington, DC 20210
Phone: 202-219-5000; Web site: www.dol.gov

Contact(s):
Secretary: ALEXIS M. HERMAN; Phone: 202-693-6000
Deputy Secretary (Acting): EDWARD B. MONTGOMERY; Phone: 202-693-6002
Mine Safety and Health Administrator: J. DAVITT McATEER; Phone: 703-235-1385

JOB CORPS
Department of Labor, Employment and Training Administration, Frances Perkins Bldg., 200 Constitution Ave., NW, Washington, DC 20210
Phone: 202-219-8550

Description: Authorized by the Job Training Partnership Act, the program includes conservation centers known as Civilian Conservation Centers, located primarily in rural areas and operated for the Department of Labor by the departments of Agriculture and Interior conservation agencies. In addition to providing training and other assistance to young people, the programs of work experience, training, and remedial education are focused upon activities to conserve, develop, or manage public resources or public recreational areas or to assist in developing community projects in the public interest.

Contact(s):
Director: MARY H. SILVA; Phone: 202-219-8550

MINE SAFETY AND HEALTH ADMINISTRATION
Department of Labor, Ballston Tower 3, 4015 Wilson Blvd., Arlington, VA 22203
Phone: 703-235-1452

Description: Objectives are to administer the Federal Mine Safety and Health Act, thereby promoting safety and health in the mining industry, preventing disasters, and protecting the health and safety of the nation's miners.

Contact(s):
Assistant Secretary: J. DAVITT McATEER; Phone: 703-235-1385
Deputy Assistant Secretary: MARVIN NICHOLS; Phone: 703-235-2600
Administrator of Coal Mine Health and Safety: ROBERT ELAM; Phone: 703-235-9423
Administrator of Metal and Nonmetal Mine Health and Safety: EARNEST C. LEASTER JR.; Phone: 703-235-1565
Director of Administration and Management: PATRICIA SILVEY; Phone: 703-235-1383
Director of Educational Policy and Development: JEFFREY DUNCAN; Phone: 703-235-1515
Office of Congressional and Legislative Affairs: SYLVIA MILANESE; Phone: 703-235-1392
Office of Information and Public Affairs Acting Director: HAL GLASSMAN; Phone: 703-235-1452
Office of Standards of Regulations and Variances of Director: CAROL JONES; Phone: 703-235-1910

UNITED STATES DEPARTMENT OF STATE
Main State Department Bldg., 2201 C St., NW, Washington, DC 20520
Phone: 202-647-4000; Fax: 202-736-7720

Contact(s):
Secretary: MADELEINE ALBRIGHT
Acting Under Secretary for Global Affairs: C. WENDY SHERMAN

BUREAU OF OCEANS AND INTERNATIONAL ENVIRONMENTAL AND SCIENTIFIC AFFAIRS
Department of State, 2201 C St., NW, Washington, DC 20520

Description: OES has the principal responsibility for formulating and implementing U.S. policies for oceans, environmental, scientific, and technological aspects of U.S. relations with other governmental and multilateral institutions. The Bureau's activities cover a broad range of foreign policy issues relating to environment, pollution, tropical forests, biological diversity, wildlife, oceans policy, fisheries, global climate change, atmospheric ozone-depletion, space, and advanced technologies.

Contact(s):
Assistant Secretary (Acting): MELINDA L. KIMBLE; Phone: 202-647-1554
Deputy Assistant Secretary of Environment and Development (OES/E): RAFE POMERANCE; Phone: 202-647-2232
Deputy Assistant Secretary of Oceans, Fisheries and Space (OES/O): MARY BETH WEST; Phone: 202-647-2396
Executive Assistant/Executive Director of Administration: STEPHANIE KINNEY; Phone: 202-647-3622
Office of Ecology and Terrestrial Conservation (OES/ETC) Director: MARY MCLEAD; Phone: 202-647-2418
Office of Emerging Infectious Diseases (OES/EID) Director: NANCY CARTER FOSTER; Phone: 202-647-2435
Office of Environment Policy (OES/ENV) Director: MICHAEL D. MTELITS; Phone: 202-647-9266
Office of Global Change (OES/EGC) Director: DANIEL A. REIFSNYDER; Phone: 202-647-4069
Office of Marine Conservation (OES/OMC) Director: DAVID A. BALTON; Phone: 202-647-2335
Office of Oceans Affairs (OES/OA) Director: R. TUCKER SCULLY; Phone: 202-647-3262

Office of Science and Environmental Initiative (OES/SCI) Director: LESLIE GERSON; Phone: 202-647-3625
Office of Space and Advanced Technology (OES/SAT) Director: RALPH BRAIBANTI; Phone: 202-647-2433
Principle Department Assisting Secretary: MELINDA L. KIMBLE
Special Negotiator: AMB. MARK HAMBLEY
U.S. Man and the Biosphere Program (MAB) Director: ROGER E. SOLES; Phone: 703-235-2948

UNITED STATES MAN AND THE BIOSPHERE PROGRAM (U.S. MAB)

U.S. MAB Secretariat, OES/ETC/MAB SA-44C, 1st Fl. Dept. of State, Washington, DC 20522-4401
E-mail: mabres@aol.com; Web site: www.usmab.org

Description: The mission of the United States Man and the Biosphere Program (U.S. MAB) is to explore, demonstrate, promote, and encourage harmonious relationships between people and their environments, building on the MAB network of Biosphere Reserves and interdisciplinary research. The long-term goal of the U.S. MAB Program is to contribute to achieving a sustainable society early in the 21st century. The MAB mission and long-term goal will be implemented, in the U.S. and internationally, through public-private partnerships and interdisciplinary research, experimentation, education, and information exchange on options by which societies can achieve sustainability.

Contact(s):
Chairman of U.S. MAB National Committee: DAVID HALES
Executive Director of U.S. MAB: DR. ROGER E. SOLES; Phone: 202-776-8318
Publication(s): *U.S. MAB Bulletin; research reports from U.S. MAB; proceedings of symposia, conferences, and workshops; directories and bibliographies*

UNITED STATES DEPARTMENT OF THE AIR FORCE

Environmental Division, HQ USAF/ILEV, 1260 Air Force Pentagon, Washington, DC 20330-1260

Description: A comprehensive natural resources conservation program focusing on fish and wildlife management, forestry, outdoor recreation, and soil and water conservation has been conducted on Air Force lands since the mid-1950's. Current policy requires all installations with significant land and water resources to develop integrated natural resource management plans as part of the base comprehensive planning process.

Air Force Center for Environmental Excellence
3207 North Rd., Brooks AFB, TX 78235-5363
Phone: 210-536-3334
Contact(s):
Chief, Consultant Division, Environmental Conservation and Planning (AFCEE/ECC): EDWARD J. BAKUNAS

Air Force Civil Engineering Support Agency
139 Barnes Dr., Tyndall AFB, FL 32403-5319
Phone: 904-283-6465
Contact(s):
Management Agronomist (AFCESA/CEM): WAYNE FORDHAM

Bird Aircraft Strike Hazard (BASH) Team
9700 Avenue G, Bldg. 24499, Kirtland AFB, NM 87117-5671
Phone: 505-846-5674
Contact(s):
Chief, BASH Team (HQ AFSA/SEFW): MAJ. PETER WINDLER

Office of the Civil Engineer
1260 Air Force Pentagon, Washington, DC 20330-1260
Phone: 703-604-0632
Contact(s):
Chief of Cultural Resources Team (AF/ILEVP): STEPHANIE STEVENSON; Phone: 703-604-0551
Chief of Environmental Division (AF/ILEV): COL. BRIAN MILLER; Phone: 703-604-0650
Chief of Environmental Planning (AF/ILEVP): LYNN ENGELMAN; Phone: 703-607-0221
Chief of Natural Resources Team (AF/ILEVP): J. DOUGLAS RIPLEY; Phone: 703-604-0632

MAJOR AIR COMMANDS

Air Combat Command
129 Andrews St., Suite 102, Langley AFB, VA 23665-2769
Phone: 757-764-9338
Contact(s):
Natural Resources Manager (HQ ACC/CEVA): ROY BARKER

Air Education and Training Command
266 F St., West, Bldg. 901, Randolph AFB, TX 78150-4321
Phone: 210-652-3959
Contact(s):
Natural Resources Manager (HQ AETC/CEV): CARL W. LAHSHER

Air Force Base Conversion Agency (AFBCA)
Contact(s):
Conservation Manger (HQ AFBCA/EV): JERRY CLEAVER, 1700 N. Moore St., Suite 2300, Arlington, VA 22209-2802; Phone: 703-696-5536

Air Force District of Washington
3700 Brookley Ave., Washington, DC 20332
Phone: 202-767-8600
Contact(s):
Chief of Environmental Planning Branch (HQ 11WG/CEV): MARK DICKERSON

Air Force Material Command
4225 Logistics Ave., Suite 8, Wright Patterson, OH 45433-5747
Phone: 937-656-1409
Contact(s):
Natural Resource Manager (HQ AFRES/CEVP): MICHAEL CORNELIUS

Air Force Reserves (AFRES)
155 2nd St., Robins AFB, GA 31098-1635
Phone: 912-327-1072
Contact(s):
Natural Resource Manager (HQ AFRES/CEVP): THOMAS PILCHER

Air Force Space Command (AFSPC)
150 Vandenberg St., Suite 1105, Peterson AFB, CO 80914-4150
Phone: 719-554-9915
Contact(s):
Natural Resources Manager (HQ AFSPC/CEVP): STAN ROGERS

Air Force Special Operations Command HQ/AFSOC/CEV
100 Bartley St., Suite 218E, Hurlburt Field, FL 32544-5273
Phone: 850-884-2260
Contact(s):
Natural Resource Manager and Entomologist: MICHAEL APPLEGATE; Phone: 904-884-2260

Air Mobility Command (AMC)
507 A St., Scott AFB, IL 62225-5022
Phone: 618-256-5764
Contact(s):
Natural Resources Manager (HQ AMC/CEVP): WILLIAM J. SUMMERS

Air National Guard (ANG)
3500 Fetchet Ave., Andrews AFB, MD 20331-5157
Phone: 301-836-8798
Contact(s):
Natural Resources Manager (HQ ANG/CEVP): PAT RICHERSON

Pacific Air Forces (PACAF)
25 E St., Suite D-306, Hickman AFB, HI 96853-5412

Phone: 808-449-9695
Contact(s):
Natural Resources Manager (HQ PACAF/CEVEP): ARTHUR BUCKMAN

U.S. Air Force Academy
8120 Edgerton Dr., Suite 40, USAF Academy, CO 80840-2400
Phone: 719-333-3336
Contact(s):
Natural Resource Manager (HQ USAFA/CEVP): DANA GREEN

U.S. Air Forces Europe (USAFE)
Unit 3050, Box 10, Ramstein AB/APO AE 09094 Germany
Phone: 011-49-6371-47-6382
Contact(s):
Natural Resources Manager (HQ USAFE/CEV): DAVID DENTINO

MAJOR U.S. INSTALLATIONS

Alaskan Remote Sites (611 Support Group)
Contact(s):
Natural Resources Manager: GENE AUGUSTINE; Phone: 907-552-0788

Altus AFB, OK
Contact(s):
Natural Resources Manager: JIM BELLON; Phone: 405-481-7606

Anderson AFB, Guam
Contact(s):
Natural Resources Manager: HEIDI HIRSH; Phone: 671-366-2549

Andrews AFB, MD
Contact(s):
Natural Resources Manager: BRIAN LAFLAMME; Phone: 301-981-2348

Arnold AFB, TN
Contact(s):
Natural Resources Manager: MARK MORAN; Phone: 615-454-4066

Avon Park AFB, FL
Contact(s):
Chief of Conservation Programs: PAUL EBERSBACH; Phone: 914-452-4119 ext. 301

Barksdale AFB, LA
Contact(s):
Natural Resources Manager: BRUCE HOLLAND; Phone: 318-456-1981

Beale AFB, CA
Contact(s):
Natural Resources Manager: KRISTEN CHRISTOPHERSON; Phone: 530-634-2643

Bolling AFB, Washington, DC
Contact(s):
Natural Resources Manager: FIORAVANTE GAETANO; Phone: 202-767-8603

Brooks AFB, TX
Contact(s):
Natural Resources Manager: HAMID KAMALPOUR; Phone: 210-536-6703

Cannon AFB, NM
Contact(s):
Natural Resources Manager: RICK CROW; Phone: 505-784-6383

Charleston AFB, SC
Contact(s):
Natural Resource Manager: AL URRUTIA; Phone: 843-963-4978

Columbus AFB, MS
Contact(s):
Natural Resources Manager: LT. CHIN SU; Phone: 601-434-7958

Davis-Monthan AFB, AZ
Contact(s):
Natural Resources Manager: GWEN LISA; Phone: 520-228-3215

Dover AFB, DE
Contact(s):
Natural Resources Manager: MILTON BECK; Phone: 302-677-6850

Dyess AFB, TX
Contact(s):
Natural Resources Manager: DON PITTS; Phone: 915-696-5619

Edwards AFB, CA
Contact(s):
Natural Resources Manager: MARK HAGAN; Phone: 805-277-1418

Eglin AFB, FL
Contact(s):
Natural Resources Manager: RICK MCWHITE; Phone: 850-882-4164

Eielson AFB, AK
Contact(s):
Natural Resources Manager: GERALD VON RUEDEN; Phone: 907-377-4210

Ellsworth AFB, SD
Contact(s):
Natural Resources Manager: CHRIS LEONARD; Phone: 605-385-6629

Elmendorf AFB, AK
Contact(s):
Natural Resources Manager: ALAN RICHMOND; Phone: 907-552-2282

F.E. Warren AFB, WY
Contact(s):
Natural Resources Manager: TOM SMITH; Phone: 307-773-4357

Fairchild, AFB, AK
Contact(s):
Natural Resources Manager: GERALD JOHNSON; Phone: 509-247-2313

Goodfellow AFB, TX
Contact(s):
Natural Resources Manager: LYNDAL FISHER; Phone: 915-657-3470

Grand Forks AFB, ND
Contact(s):
Natural Resources Manager: WAYNE C. KOOP; Phone: 701-747-4590

Hanscom AFB, MA
Contact(s):
Natural Resources Manager: DON MORRIS; Phone: 615-377-4667

Hickam AFB, HI
Contact(s):
Natural Resources Manager: LT. DAWN WAGNER; Phone: 808-449-1584/ext. 205

Hill AFB, UT
Contact(s):
Natural Resources Manager: MARCUS BLOOD; Phone: 801-777-4618

U.S. FEDERAL AND INTERNATIONAL GOVERNMENT AGENCIES - EXECUTIVE BRANCH

Holloman AFB, NM
Contact(s):
Natural Resources Manager: HILDY REISER; Phone: 505-475-3931

Hurlburt Field, FL
Contact(s):
Natural Resources Manager: PHILIP PRUIT; Phone: 850-884-4651

Keesler AFB, MS
Contact(s):
Natural Resources Manager: MARGARET SARTAR; Phone: 505-844-2489

Kelly AFB, TX
Contact(s):
Natural Resources Manager: RUSS REAN; Phone: 210-925-3100/ext. 215

Kirtland AFB, NM
Contact(s):
Natural Resources Manager: BOB DOW; Phone: 505-846-6857

Lackland AFB, TX
Contact(s):
Natural Resources Manager: GABRIEL GONZALES; Phone: 512-671-4843

Langley AFB, VA
Contact(s):
Natural Resources Manager: PATSY KERR; Phone: 757-764-1090

Laughlin AFB, TX
Contact(s):
Natural Resources Manager: JIM TAYON; Phone: 830-298-4298

Little Rock AFB, AR
Contact(s):
Natural Resources Manager: JAMES POPHAM; Phone: 501-988-6809

Luke AFB (and the Barry M. Goldwater AFR), AZ
Contact(s):
Chief of Conservation Programs: ROBERT BARRY; Phone: 602-856-3823, ext. 242

MacDill AFB, FL
Contact(s):
Natural Resources Manager, Vacant; Phone: 813-828-2567

Malmstrom AFB, MT
Contact(s):
Natural Resources Manager: TIM NEU; Phone: 406-731-6437

Maxwell AFB, AL
Contact(s):
Natural Resources Manager: DENNIS TATES; Phone: 334-953-3892

McChord AFB, WA
Contact(s):
Natural Resources Manager: CHERY L. DUNNING; Phone: 253-984-3913

McClellan AFB, CA
Contact(s):
Natural Resources Manager: MARCELO GARCIA; Phone: 919-643-1742

McConnell AFB, KS
Contact(s):
Natural Resources Manager: JAY ZIMMERMAN; Phone: 316-652-3927

McGuire AFB, NJ
Contact(s):
Natural Resources Manager: KING MAK; Phone: 609-724-2096

Moody AFB, GA
Contact(s):
Natural Resources Manager: TIMOTHY BOTTOMLEY; Phone: 912-257-4980

Mountain Home AFB, ID
Contact(s):
Natural Resources Manager: NATHAN ROWLAND; Phone: 208-828-4297

Nellis AFB, NV (and Nellis Air Force Range)
Contact(s):
Natural Resources Manager: ERIC WATKINS; Phone: 702-652-3173

New Boston AFB, NH
Contact(s):
Natural Resources Manager: STEPHEN NAJJAR; Phone: 603-471-2426

Offut AFB, NE
Contact(s):
Natural Resource Manager: GENE SVENSEN; Phone: 402-232-5891

Patrick AFB, FL
Contact(s):
Natural Resources Manager: CLAY GORDON; Phone: 407-494-2905

Peterson AFB, CO
Contact(s):
Natural Resources Manager: DAN RODRIGUEZ; Phone: 719-556-1459

Pope AFB, SC
Contact(s):
Natural Resources Manager: PAUL HANDS; Phone: 910-394-1633

Randolph AFB, TX
Contact(s):
Natural Resources Manager: JOHN WILDIE; Phone: 512-652-4668

Scott AFB, IL
Contact(s):
Natural Resources Manager: WILLIAM CALVERT; Phone: 618-256-2092

Seymour Johnson AFB (and Dare County AFR) NC
Contact(s):
Natural Resources Manager: BRIAN HENDERSON; Phone: 919-736-6501

Shaw AFB, SC
Contact(s):
Natural Resources Manager: TERRY MADEWELL; Phone: 803-668-9977

Sheppard AFB, TX
Contact(s):
Natural Resources Manager: TIM HUNTER; Phone: 940-283-5698

Shriever AFB, CO
Contact(s):
Natural Resources Manager: RALPH MITCHELL; Phone: 719-567-2075

Tinker AFB, OK
Contact(s):
Natural Resources Manager: JOHN KRUPOVAGE; Phone: 405-734-3259

Travis AFB, CA
Contact(s):
Natural Resources Manager: ROBERT HOLMES; Phone: 707-424-3897

Tyndall AFB, FL
Contact(s):
Natural Resources Manager: BOB BATES; Phone: 850-283-2641

Vance AFB, OK
Contact(s):
Natural Resources Manager: SHANNON ELLEDGE; Phone: 580-249-6244

Vandenberg AFB, CA
Contact(s):
Natural Resources Manager: ALLAN NAYDOL; Phone: 805-734-8232/ext.69687

Whiteman AFB, MO
Contact(s):
Natural Resources Manager: LT. HENRY; Phone: 660-687-1227

Wright-Patterson AFB, OH
Contact(s):
Natural Resources Planner: TERRI LUCAS; Phone: 937-257-5535/Ext. 262

UNITED STATES DEPARTMENT OF THE ARMY
Pentagon, Washington, DC 20310
Contact(s):
Deputy Assistant Secretary of the Army (Environment of Safety of and Occupational Health): RAYMOND J. FATZ; Phone: 703-695-7824
Assistant for Environmental Quality: PHIL HUBER; Phone: 703-614-9555

ASSISTANT CHIEF OF STAFF FOR INSTALLATION MANAGEMENT, OFFICE OF THE DIRECTOR OF ENVIRONMENTAL PROGRAMS, AND CONSERVATION TEAM
Attn: DAIM-ED-N, 600 Army Pentagon, Washington, DC 20310-0600
Description: Natural and cultural resources professionals are responsible for the management of approximately 12 million acres of land on Army military installations. Management objectives include: Compliance with environmental laws, conservation and protection of resources, support to the military mission uses of the land, and contributions to programs which support the public needs. Resources managed include: Land, forest, wildlife, soils, vegetation and historical and archaeological sites.
Contact(s):
Conservation Team Leader: VIC DIERSING; Phone: 703-696-8913
Cultural Resources Specialist: CHUCK WRIGHT; Phone: 703-693-0675
Natural Resource Specialist: BILL WOODSON; Phone: 703-693-0678
Natural Resources Specialist: DAVID BOOKER; Phone: 703-693-0673

ARMY TRAINING AND DOCTRINE COMMAND
Department of the Army, HQ TRADOC, ATBO-SE, Environmental Division, Fort Monroe, VA 23651
Description: Manages conservation programs for 2 million acres at 16 Army installations nationwide. It also provides for compliance with federal, state, and local environmental regulations.
Contact(s):
Conservation and Analysis Branch: SHAWN HOLSINGER; Phone: 757-727-3045
General/Technical Libraries of HQ TRADOC (ATBO-NT) of Director: FRANCES DOYLE, Ft. Monroe, VA 23651
Natural Resources Specialist: ROBERT ANDERSON; Phone: 757-727-2077
NEPA Consultant: JOHN ESSON; Phone: 757-727-3335
NEPA Consultant: JIM WHITE; Phone: 757-727-5896
NEPA Consultant: DR. JACK DAMRON; Phone: 757-727-4135
Publication(s): *Historic Preservation Sourcebook; Army Leader's Guide to NEPA; Endangered Species Law Sourcebook*

ENGINEER RESEARCH AND DEVELOPMENT CENTER/CONSTRUCTION ENGINEERING RESEARCH LABORATORIES CERL
P.O. Box 9005, Champaign, IL 61826-9005
Phone: 217-352-6511
Founded: 1969
Description: CERL conducts research on infrastructure and environmental problems facing the operations of military facilities. CERL also conducts research on innovative materials and engineering procedures; energy reduction measures and equipment; management systems; air and water pollution; environmental compliance; and natural resource management.
Contact(s):
Director: DR. MICHAEL O'CONNOR
Champaign Public Affairs: DANA FINNEY
Publication(s): *CERL Abstracts; Index to Publications; The Cutting Edge*

HEADQUARTERS, U.S. ARMY TRAINING AND DOCTRINE COMMAND
ATBO-SE, Fort Monroe, VA 23651
Contact(s):
Agronomist of Fort Dix: ROGER SMITH; Phone: 609-562-2040
Agronomist of Fort Leonard Wood: MARVIN MYERS; Phone: 314-596-0871
Agronomist of Fort Rucker: DELARIE PARMER; Phone: 205-255-9363
Agronomist of Health Services Command, Academy of Health Sciences: WILLIAM PITTMAN; Phone: 512-221-4411
Agronomist of Schofield Barracks: PATRICK CHING; Phone: 808-655-6383
Agronomist of U.S. Army Military District of Washington: JAMES MURPHY; Phone: 202-696-3815
Agronomist of U.S. Military Academy, Natural Resources Branch: ROBERT JONES; Phone: 914-938-3467
Archeologist: DR. MARIE COTTRELL; Phone: 804-727-2389
Archeologist of Fort Bliss: PAUL LUKOWSKI; Phone: 915-568-6999
Archeologist of Fort Bliss: GLEN DeGARMO; Phone: 915-568-5140
Biological Tech./Game Warden of Fort Sill: KEVIN McCURDY; Phone: 405-351-4324
Biologist of DA Headquarters: JAMES McCRACKEN; Phone: 803-751-4622
Biologist of Fort Lee: JAMES LOEWEN; Phone: 804-734-5080
Chief (Acting) of Environmental and Natural Resources Division of Fort Belvoir: DOROTHY KEOUGH; Phone: 703-806-4007
Chief Environment Branch of Fort Chaffee: BOB COLEMAN; Phone: 501-484-2516
Chief Environmental Management Division of Fort Knox: AL FREELAND; Phone: 502-624-3629
Chief Natural Resources Manager of Fort Benning: CHARLES FORD; Phone: 706-544-7319
Chief Natural Resources Section of Fort Chaffee: JERRY STURDY; Phone: 501-484-2231
Chief of Environment of Fort Benjamin Harrison: THOMAS SHAFER; Phone: 317-549-5386
Chief of Environmental and Natural Resources of Fort Gordon: STEVE WILLARD; Phone: 706-791-2403
Chief of Environmental Resources Management of Army National Guard Bureau: LTC. ROBERT McGUIRE; Phone: 703-756-5794
Chief of Natural Resources of DA Headquarters: MARK DUTTON; Phone: 803-751-4103
Chief of Natural Resources of U.S. Military Academy, Natural Resources Branch: JOE DESCHENES; Phone: 914-938-2314
Chief of Natural/Environmental Resources of Fort Sill: GENE STOUT; Phone: 405-351-4324
Director of Environment of Fort McClellan: RON LEVY; Phone: 205-848-3539
Ecologist of Fort Bliss: KEVIN VON FINGER; Phone: 915-568-7031

U.S. FEDERAL AND INTERNATIONAL GOVERNMENT AGENCIES - EXECUTIVE BRANCH

Entomologist: DONALD TEIG; Phone: 804-727-2366
Entomologist of Fort Benning: CHRIS DUNN; Phone: 706-545-3224
Entomologist of Fort Eustis: JOHN SCHENCK; Phone: 804-878-2585
Entomologist of Fort Rucker: ROBERT TURNBOW; Phone: 205-255-3710
Entomologist of Headquarters of U.S. Army Pacific: STUART HAYASHI; Phone: 808-438-2180
Entomologist of U.S. Army Military District of Washington: JOE TARNOPOL; Phone: 202-475-1003
Environmental Officer of U.S. Army Military District of Washington: EDNA BARBER; Phone: 202-696-3815
Environmental Protection Specialist of Fort Greely: JOYCE BEELMAN; Phone: 907-451-2141
Environmental Protection Specialist of Fort Greely: BRAD FRISTOE; Phone: 907-451-2159
Environmental Protection Specialist of Fort Greely: DOUG DASHER; Phone: 907-451-2172
Environmental Protection Specialist of Headquarters of U.S. Army Pacific: LAWRENCE HIRAI; Phone: 808-438-8997
Environmental Protection Specialist of Schofield Barracks: MARK SALLEY; Phone: 808-656-2878
Environmental Specialist of Fort Richardson: BILL QUIRK; Phone: 907-384-3021
Fish and Wildlife Administrator of Fort Sill: GLEN WAMPLER; Phone: 405-442-8111
Forester of Fort Belvoir: MIKE HUDSON; Phone: 703-806-4007
Forester of Fort Benning: JACK GREENLEE; Phone: 706-544-7319
Forester of Fort Eustis: TONY RIZZIO; Phone: 804-878-4152
Forester of Fort Gordon: ALLEN BRASWELL; Phone: 706-791-2327
Forester of Fort Knox: DAVE APSLEY; Phone: 502-624-8147
Forester of Fort Leavenworth: MATT NOWAK; Phone: 913-684-2749
Forester of Fort Leonard Wood: STEVE THURMAN; Phone: 314-596-0871
Forester of Fort McClellan: BILL GARLAND; Phone: 205-848-3758
Forester of Fort Rucker: BOB SHUFFIELD; Phone: 205-255-9368
Forester of Information Systems Command: JOHN MILLER; Phone: 602-533-7083
Forester of Military Traffic Management Command, Military Ocean Terminal: HERSHEL GAW; Phone: 919-457-8292
Natural Resources Manager of Army National Guard Bureau: MARK IMLAY; Phone: 703-756-5794
Natural Resources Manager of Camp Atterbury: RONALD MOORE; Phone: 812-526-1250
Natural Resources Manager of Navajo Depot Activity: SSG. DON HACK; Phone: 602-774-7161 ext. 274
Natural Resources Specialist: BOB ANDERSON; Phone: 804-727-2077
Natural Resources Specialist of Fort Chaffee: WAYNE JOHNDROWN; Phone: 501-484-2231
Natural Resources Specialist of Fort McClellan: LUTHER OWEN; Phone: 205-848-5663
Natural Resources Team of U.S. Army Environmental Center: JERRY WILLIAMSON; Phone: 410-612-6833
Natural Resources Team of U.S. Army Environmental Center: SCOTT BELFIT; Phone: 410-612-6831
Natural Resources Team of U.S. Army Environmental Center: ERIC SEABORN; Phone: 410-612-6833
Natural Resources Team of U.S. Army Environmental Center: PAMELA KLINGER; Phone: 410-612-6832
Natural Resources Team of U.S. Army Environmental Center: WILLIAM HERB; Phone: 410-671-1234
Natural Resources Team of U.S. Army Environmental Center: BOB DECKER; Phone: 410-612-6831
Natural Resources Team of U.S. Army Environmental Center: STEVE SEKSCIENSKI; Phone: 410-612-6832
Wildlife Biologist of DA Headquarters: BILL GATES; Phone: 803-751-4793
Wildlife Biologist of Fort Benning: ROBERT KING; Phone: 706-544-7319
Wildlife Biologist of Fort Chaffee: CLARK REAMES; Phone: 501-484-2231
Wildlife Biologist of Fort Dix: ROGER MEYERS; Phone: 609-562-2040
Wildlife Biologist of Fort Gordon: KENNETH BOYD; Phone: 706-791-2403
Wildlife Biologist of Fort Leonard Wood: TOM GLUECK; Phone: 314-596-0871
Wildlife Biologist of Fort Richardson: WILLIAM GOSSWEILER; Phone: 907-384-3017
Wildlife Biologist of Information Systems Command: SHERIDAN STONE; Phone: 602-538-7340
Wildlife Biologist Tech. of Fort Knox: DONALD SHEROAN; Phone: 502-624-7373

HQ ARMY MATERIAL COMMAND
Alexandria, VA 22333-0001
Contact(s):
Agronomist of Red River Army Depot (Texas): TOM COLEMAN; Phone: 903-334-2385
Agronomist of U.S. Army Research Laboratory (Maryland): BOB WARDWELL; Phone: 301-394-1060
Archeologist of White Sands Missile Range (New Mexico): ROBERT BURTON; Phone: 505-678-8731
Chief of Conservation and Preservation of Dugway Proving Ground (Utah): JOHN MARTIN; Phone: 801-831-2986
Entomologist of U.S. Army Aberdeen Proving Ground Support Activities (Maryland): ABDUL SHIEK; Phone: 410-278-3303
Environmental Protection Specialist of U.S. Army Aberdeen Proving Ground Support Activities (Maryland): STEVE WAMPLER, Directorate of Safety Health and Environment, ; Phone: 410-671-4843
Environmental Protection Specialist of U.S. Army Aberdeen Proving Ground Support Activities (Maryland): TIMOTHY McNAMARA, Directorate of Safety Health and Environment, ; Phone: 410-278-5622
Forester of Anniston Army Depot (Alabama): WILLIAM BURNS; Phone: 205-235-4217
Forester of Red River Army Depot (Texas): TERRY RUTH; Phone: 903-334-2379
Forester of Redstone Arsenal Support Activity (Alabama): JESSE HORTON; Phone: 205-876-3122
Forester of U.S. Army Aberdeen Proving Ground Support Activities (Maryland): ROGER STOFLET; Phone: 410-278-4915
Forester, Chief LM of Red River Army Depot (Texas): BENNIE MURRAY; Phone: 903-334-2379
Forester, Installations and Services Activity (Illinois): TOM VORAC; Phone: 309-782-4062
Land Manager of Blue-Grass Army Depot: MS. BILLYE HASLETT; Phone: 606-625-6669
Natural Resources Manager of Jefferson Proving Ground (Indiana): KEN KNOUF; Phone: 812-273-7436
Natural Resources Manager of Letterkenny Army Depot (Ohio): RANDY QUINN; Phone: 717-267-8438
Natural Resources Manager of Savanna Army Depot (Illinois): BOB SPEAKER; Phone: 815-273-8533
Natural Resources Specialist, Installations and Services Activity (Illinois): RICHARD CLEWELL; Phone: 309-782-8252
Project Engineer of Tooele Army Depot (Utah): MASON WALKER; Phone: 801-833-2891
Wildlife Biologist of U.S. Army Aberdeen Proving Ground Support Activities (Maryland): JAMES POTTIE; Phone: 410-278-6772
Wildlife Biologist of U.S. Army Aberdeen Proving Ground Support Activities (Maryland): JAMES BAILEY; Phone: 410-278-6748
Wildlife Biologist of White Sands Missile Range (New Mexico): DAISAN TAYLOR; Phone: 505-678-6140
Wildlife Biologist of White Sands Missile Range (New Mexico): PATRICK MORROW; Phone: 505-678-7095
Wildlife Biologist of Yuma Proving Ground (Arizona): VALERIE MORRILL; Phone: 602-328-2244
Wildlife Biologist of Yuma Proving Ground (Arizona): JUNIOR KERNS; Phone: 602-328-2148

U.S. ARMY CORPS OF ENGINEERS
20 Massachusetts Ave., NW, Washington, DC 20314-1000

Description: The mission of the Corps of Engineers is to provide quality, responsive engineering and environmental services to the nation. The Corps plans, designs, builds, and operates water resources and other civil works projects. The Corps designs and manages the construction of military facilities and activities for the Army and Air Force and provides design and construction management support for other defense and federal agencies. In addition to military and civilian engineers, the Corps has a diverse workforce of biologists, geologists, hydrologists, natural resource managers and other professionals.

Contact(s):
Chief of Engineers: LT. GEN. JOE N. BALLARD; Phone: 202-761-0001
Chief, Environmental Compliance: JAMES E. WOLCOTT; Phone: 202-761-0200
Chief, Natural Resources: DARRELL L. LEWIS; Phone: 202-761-0247
Chief, Office of Environmental Policy: DR. ROBERT F. SOOTS JR.; Phone: 703-428-6491
Chief, Public Affairs: COL. ROBERT N. MIRELSON; Phone: 202-761-0010
Chief, Regulatory: JOHN STUDT; Phone: 202-761-1785
Cultural Resources Coordinator: PAUL D. RUBENSTEIN; Phone: 202-761-1257
Deputy Chief of Engineers: MAJ. GEN. ALBERT J. GENETTI JR.; Phone: 202-761-0002
Director of Civil Works: MAJ. GEN RUSSEL FUHRMAN; Phone: 202-761-0099
Endangered Species/NEPA Coordinator: JOHN BELLINGER; Phone: 202-761-0166
Executive Secretary, Environmental Advisory Board: LLOYD SAUNDERS; Phone: 202-761-8731
Fish and Wildlife Coordinator: TIMOTHY R. TOPLISEK; Phone: 202-761-1789

U.S. Army Cold Regions Research and Engineering Laboratory
72 Lyme Rd., Hanover, NH 03755-1290
Phone: 603-646-4386

U.S. Army Construction Engineering Research Laboratories
P.O. Box 9005, Champaign, IL 61826-9005
Phone: 217-373-6714

U.S. Army Corps of Engineers Water Resources Support Center
7701 Telegraph Road, Alexandria, VA 22315-3868
Phone: 703-428-7250

U.S. Army Engineer District, Alaska
P.O. Box 898, Anchorage, AK 99506-0898
Phone: 907-753-2520

U.S. Army Engineer District, Albuquerque
4101 Jefferson Plaza NE, Albuquerque, NM 87109
Phone: 505-342-3171

U.S. Army Engineer District, Baltimore
P.O. Box 1715, Baltimore, MD 21203-1715
Phone: 410-962-2809

U.S. Army Engineer District, Buffalo
1766 Niagara Street, Buffalo, NY 14207-3199
Phone: 716-879-4200

U.S. Army Engineer District, Charleston
P.O. Box 919, Charleston, SC 29401-0919
Phone: 803-727-4201

U.S. Army Engineer District, Chicago
111 N. Canal Street, Suite 600, Chicago, IL 60606-7206
Phone: 312-353-6400

U.S. Army Engineer District, Detroit
P.O. Box 1027, Detroit, MI 48231-1027
Phone: 313-226-4680

U.S. Army Engineer District, Fort Worth
P.O. Box 17300, Forth Worth, TX 76102-0300
Phone: 817-978-2196

U.S. Army Engineer District, Galveston
Jadwin Building, 2000 Fort Point Road, Galveston, TX 77550
Phone: 409-766-3049

U.S. Army Engineer District, Honolulu
Building 230, Fort Shafter, HI 96858-5440
Phone: 808-438-9862

U.S. Army Engineer District, Huntington
502 8th Street, Huntington, WV 25701-2070
Phone: 304-529-5453

U.S. Army Engineer District, Jacksonville
P.O. Box 4970, Jacksonville, FL 32232-0019
Phone: 904-232-2235

U.S. Army Engineer District, Kansas City
601 E. 12th Street, Kansas City, MO 64106-2896
Phone: 816-983-5241

U.S. Army Engineer District, Little Rock
P.O. Box 867, Little Rock, AR 72203-0867
Phone: 501-324-5551

U.S. Army Engineer District, Los Angeles
P.O. Box 2711, Los Angeles, CA 90053-2325
Phone: 213-452-3921

U.S. Army Engineer District, Louisville
P.O. Box 59, Louisville, KY 40201-0059
Phone: 502-582-5736

U.S. Army Engineer District, Memphis
167 N. Main Street, Room B202, Memphis, TN 38103-1894
Phone: 901-544-3348

U.S. Army Engineer District, Mobile
P.O. Box 2288, Mobile, AL 36628-0001
Phone: 334-690-2505

U.S. Army Engineer District, Nashville
P.O. Box 1070, Nashville, TN 37202-1070
Phone: 615-736-7161

U.S. Army Engineer District, New England
696 Virginia Rd., Concord, MA 01742-2751
Phone: 978-318-8237

U.S. Army Engineer District, New Orleans
P.O. Box 60167, New Orleans, LA 70160-0267
Phone: 504-862-2201

U.S. Army Engineer District, New York
Jacob K. Javits Federal Building, 26 Federal Plaza, New York, NY 10278-0090
Phone: 212-264-5818

U.S. Army Engineer District, Norfolk
803 Front Street, Norfolk, VA 23510-1096
Phone: 757-441-7606

U.S. Army Engineer District, Philadelphia
Wanamaker Building, 100 Penn Square East, Philadelphia, PA 19107-3390
Phone: 215-656-6500

U.S. Army Engineer District, Pittsburgh
Rm. 1828, William S. Moorhead Federal Building, 1000 Liberty Avenue, Pittsburgh, PA 15222-4186
Phone: 412-395-7501

U.S. FEDERAL AND INTERNATIONAL GOVERNMENT AGENCIES - EXECUTIVE BRANCH

U.S. Army Engineer District, Portland
P.O. Box 2946, Portland, OR 97208-2946
Phone: 503-808-4510

U.S. Army Engineer District, Rock Island
P.O. Box 2004, Rock Island, IL 61204-2004
Phone: 309-794-5900

U.S. Army Engineer District, Sacramento
1325 J Street, Sacramento, CA 95814-2922
Phone: 916-557-7461

U.S. Army Engineer District, San Francisco
333 Market Street, San Francisco, CA 94105-2195
Phone: 415-977-8658

U.S. Army Engineer District, Savannah
P.O. Box 889, Savannah, GA 31402-0889
Phone: 912-652-5279

U.S. Army Engineer District, Seattle
P.O. Box 3755, Seattle, WA 98124-3755
Phone: 206-764-3769

U.S. Army Engineer District, St. Louis
1222 Spruce Street, St. Louis, MO 63103-2833
Phone: 314-331-8010

U.S. Army Engineer District, St. Paul
Army Corps of Engineers Center, 190 East 5th Street, St. Paul, MN 55101-1638
Phone: 612-290-5201

U.S. Army Engineer District, Tulsa
P.O. Box 61, Tulsa, OK 74121-0061
Phone: 918-669-7366

U.S. Army Engineer District, Vicksburg
4155 Clay Street, Vicksburg, MS 39180-3435
Phone: 601-631-5052

U.S. Army Engineer District, Walla Walla
201 North 3rd Avenue, Walla Walla, WA 99362-1876
Phone: 509-527-7020

U.S. Army Engineer District, Wilmington
P.O. Box 1890, Wilmington, NC 28402-1890
Phone: 910-251-4626

U.S. Army Engineer Division, Great Lakes and Ohio
Regional Headquarters, P.O. Box 1159, Cincinnati, OH 45201-1159
Phone: 513-684-3010

U.S. Army Engineer Division, Great Lakes and Ohio River
Regional Headquarters, 111 North Canal Street, Chicago, IL 60606-7205
Phone: 312-353-6317

U.S. Army Engineer Division, Mississippi Valley
P.O. Box 80, Vicksburg, MS 39181-0080
Phone: 601-634-5757

U.S. Army Engineer Division, North Atlantic
Fort Hamilton Military Community, General Lee Ave., Guilding 302, Brooklyn, NY 11252
Phone: 718-491-8707

U.S. Army Engineer Division, Northwestern
Regional Headquarters, 12565 West Center Road, Omaha, NE 68144-3869
Phone: 401-697-2600
Regional Headquarters, P.O. Box 2870, Portland, OR 97208-2870
Phone: 503-808-3710

U.S. Army Engineer Division, Pacific Ocean
Building 230, Fort Shafter, HI 96858-5440
Phone: 808-438-9862

U.S. Army Engineer Division, South Atlantic
Room 322, 77 Forsyth St., SW, Atlanta, GA 30303-3490
Phone: 404-331-7444

U.S. Army Engineer Division, South Pacific
333 Market Street, San Francisco, CA 94105-2195
Phone: 415-977-8221

U.S. Army Engineer Division, Southwestern
1114 Commerce Street, Dallas, TX 75242-0216
Phone: 214-767-2510

U.S. Army Engineer Waterways Experiment Station
3909 Halls Ferry Road, Vicksburg, MS 39180-6199
Phone: 601-634-2504

U.S. Army Topographic Engineering Center
7701 Telegraph Rd., Alexandria, VA 22315-3864
Phone: 703-428-6634

U.S. ARMY FORCES COMMAND
Forester, HQ FORSCOM, Attn: AFPI-ENE, Fort McPherson, GA 30330-1062
Phone: 404-464-5762; Fax: 404-669-7827; E-mail: cannons@forscom.army.mil
Contact(s):
Forester: STUART M. CANNON
Wildlife Biologist: DR. ALBERT E. BIVINGS; E-mail: bivingsb@forscom.army.mil

U.S. MILITARY ACADEMY

Natural Resources Branch
DHPW, West Point, NY 10996-1592
Phone: 914-938-2314; Fax: 914-938-2324
Contact(s):
Branch Chief and Forester: JOE DESCHENES
Fish and Wildlife Biologist: JAMES BEEMER
ITAM Program Manager: CATHERINE COLEMAN; Phone: 914-938-5453
Agronomist: ROBERT JONES; Phone: 914-938-6789

UNITED STATES DEPARTMENT OF THE INTERIOR
Interior Bldg., 1849 C St., NW, Washington, DC 20240
Phone: 202-208-3100; Web site: www.doi.gov
Description: The mission of the Department of the Interior is to protect and provide access to our Nation's natural and cultural heritage and honor our trust responsibilities to tribes.
Contact(s):
Secretary: BRUCE BABBITT; Phone: 202-208-7351
Chief of Staff: ANNE SHIELDS
Inspector General: EARL DEVANEY
Assistant Secretary of Budget and Finance: ROBERT L. LAMB
Assistant Secretary of Fish of Wildlife of and Parks: DONALD J. BARRY
Assistant Secretary of Indian Affairs: KEVIN GOVER
Assistant Secretary of Land and Minerals Management (Acting): SYLVIA BACA
Assistant Secretary of Policy of Management of and Budget: M. JOHN BERRY
Assistant Secretary of Water and Science: PATRICIA BENEKE
Associate Solicitor of General Law: KAREN SPRECHER-KEATING
Associate Solicitor of Indian Affairs: DERRILL JORDAN
Associate Solicitor of Land and Water Resources: DALE PONTIUS
Associate Solicitor of Parks and Wildlife: RENEE STONE
Commissioner of Bureau of Reclamation: ELUID L. MARTINEZ
Deputy Commissioner of Bureau of Indian Affairs: HILDA MANUEL
Director of Geological Survey: CHARLES GROAT
Director of Minerals Management Service: WALT ROSENBUSCH
Director of National Business Center: TIMOTHY G. VIGOTSKY

U.S. FEDERAL AND INTERNATIONAL GOVERNMENT AGENCIES - EXECUTIVE BRANCH

Director of National Park Service: ROBERT G. STANTON
Director of Office of Communications: MICHAEL GAULDIN
Director of Office of Congressional and Legislative Affairs: LENNA AOKI
Director of Office of Hearings and Appeals: BOB BAUM
Director of Office of Policy Analysis: JAMES PIPKEN
Director of Office of Surface Mining Reclamation and Enforcement: KATHERINE KARPAN
Director of United States Fish and Wildlife Service: JAMIE RAPPAPORT CLARK

BUREAU OF INDIAN AFFAIRS
1849 C St., NW, Washington, DC 20240
Phone: 202-208-5116
Founded: 1824
Description: An agency charged with carrying out the major portion of the trust responsibility of the United States to Indian tribes. This trust includes the protection and enhancement of Indian lands and the conservation and development of natural resources, including fish, wildlife, and outdoor recreation resources.
Contact(s):
Assistant Secretary: KEVIN GOVER; Phone: 202-208-7163
Deputy Commissioner: HILDA A. MANUEL; Phone: 202-208-5116
Director of Office of Trust Responsibilities: TERRY VIRDEN; Phone: 202-208-5831
Chief of Branch of Fish, Wildlife and Recreation: GARY L. RANKEL; Phone: 202-208-4088

BUREAU OF LAND MANAGEMENT
Office of Public Affairs, 1849 C. St., NW, LS-406, Washington, DC 20240
Phone: 202-208-3801; Web site: www.blm.gov
Founded: 1946
Description: Administers the public lands which are located primarily in the Western states and which amount to about 48 percent over 272 million acres of all federally owned lands. These lands and resources are managed under multiple-use principles, including outdoor recreation, fish and wildlife production, livestock grazing, timber, industrial development, watershed protection, and onshore mineral production. BLM districts and managers are listed in the Federally Protected Areas section.
Contact(s):
Deputy Director: TOM FRY
Assistant Director of Business and Fiscal Services: BOB DOYLE; Phone: 202-208-4864
Assistant Director of Communications: LARRY FINFER; Phone: 202-208-6913
Assistant Director of Human Resources: WARREN JOHNSON; Phone: 202-501-6723
Assistant Director of Information Resources Management: GAYLE GORDON
Assistant Director of Minerals, Realty, & Resource Protection: CARSON CULP; Phone: 202-208-4201
Assistant Director of Renewable Resources & Planning: HENRI BISSON; Phone: 202-208-4896
Environmental (NEPA) Issues: CAROL MacDONALD; Phone: 202-452-5111

National Applied Resource Center
Denver Federal Center, Bldg. 50, Denver, CO 80225
Phone: 303-236-6454
Contact(s):
Director: LEE BARKOW
AK State Director: FRANCIS R. CHERRY, 222 W. 7th Ave., #13, Anchorage, AK 99513; Phone: 907-271-5076
AZ State Director: DENISE MEREDITH, 222 North Central Avenue, Phoenix, AZ 85004; Phone: 602-417-9500
CA Associate State Director: ALFRED WRIGHT, 28 Cottage Way, Rm. W-1824, Sacramento, CA 95825; Phone: 916-978-4600
CO State Director: ANN MORGAN, 2850 Youngfield St., Lakewood, CO 80215; Phone: 303-239-3700
Eastern States Director: W. HORD TIPTON, 7450 Boston Blvd., Springfield, VA 22153; Phone: 703-440-1700
ID State Director: MARTHA G. HAHN, 1387 S. Vinnell Way, Boise, ID 83709-1657; Phone: 208-373-4001
MT State Director: LARRY E. HAMILTON, 5001 Southgate Dr., Billings, MT 59101; Phone: 406-896-5012
NM State Director: WILLIAM CALKINS, 1474 Rodeo Rd., Santa Fe, NM 87504; Phone: 505-438-7501
NV State Director: ROBERT ABBEY, 1340 Financial Blvd, Reno, NV 89502-7147; Phone: 702-861-6590
OR State Director: ELAINE ZIELINSKI, 1515 SW 5th Ave., Portland, OR 97208; Phone: 503-952-6024
UT State Director: G. WILLIAM LAMB, 324 S. State St., Suite 301, Salt Lake City, UT 84145-0155; Phone: 801-539-4010
WY State Director: AL PIERSON, 5353 Yellowstone Rd., Cheyenne, WY 82003; Phone: 307-775-6001

National Office of Fire and Aviation
National Interagency Fire Center, 3833 S. Development Ave., Boise, ID 83705
Phone: 208-387-5512; Fax: 208-387-5797
Contact(s):
Director: LESTER ROSENKRANCE

BUREAU OF RECLAMATION
U.S. Department of the Interior 1849 C St., NW, Washington, DC 20240
Description: The Bureau of Reclamation was created by the Reclamation Act of 1902 to reclaim arid lands in the 17 Western states. This has been accomplished by the development of a system of works for the storage, diversion, and development of water. Reclamation's future role entails a shift in emphasis from development to total resource management and more effective use of existing facilities. Nonstructural means of meeting future water and power needs is now being emphasized.
Contact(s):
Commissioner: ELUID L. MARTINEZ; Phone: 202-208-4157
Chief of Staff: STEVEN RICHARDSON; Phone: 202-208-4292
Chief of Public Affairs Division: PAUL BLEDSOE; Phone: 202-208-4662
Director of Operations: STEPHEN MAGNUSSEN; Phone: 202-208-4082

Denver Office
Bldg. 67, Denver Federal Center, P.O. Box 25007, Denver, CO 80225
Contact(s):
Deputy Director of Office of Policy: WAYNE O. DEASON; Phone: 303-445-2781
Director of Human Resources: DAVID MONTOYA; Phone: 303-445-2670
Director of Management Services: KATHY GORDON; Phone: 303-445-3002
Director of Reclamation Service Center: NEAL STESSMAN; Phone: 303-445-2692

Great Plains Region
P.O. Box 36900, Billings, MT 59107-6900
Phone: 406-247-7600
Contact(s):
Director: MARYANNE BACH
Director of Public Affairs Officer: RODNEY J. OTTENBREIT; Phone: 406-657-7608
Environmental Specialist: JOHN BOEHMKE; Phone: 406-247-7715

Lower Colorado Region
P.O. Box 61470, Boulder City, NV 89006-1470
Phone: 702-293-8411
Contact(s):
Director: BOB JOHNSON
Director of Public Affairs Officer: BOB WALSH

Mid Pacific Region
Federal Office Bldg., 2800 Cottage Way, Sacramento, CA 95825
Phone: 916-978-5000

U.S. FEDERAL AND INTERNATIONAL GOVERNMENT AGENCIES - EXECUTIVE BRANCH

Contact(s):
Director (Acting): KIRK RODGERS

Pacific Northwest Region
1150 N. Curtis Rd., Suite 100, Boise, ID 83706-1234
Phone: 208-378-5012
Contact(s):
Director: BILL MacDONALD

Upper Colorado Region
125 South State St., Rm. 6107, Salt Lake City, UT 84138
Phone: 801-524-3600
Contact(s):
Regional Director: CHARLES CALHOUN
Chief of Environmental Resources Group: CHRISTINE KARAS; Phone: 801-524-3679
Public Affairs Officer: BARRY WIRTH; Phone: 801-524-3774

NATIONAL PARK SERVICE
U.S. Department of the Interior, 1849 C St., NW, Washington, DC 20240
Phone: 202-208-6843; Web site: www.nps.gov
Description: Administers 1, 378 parks, monuments, and other administrative classifications of national significance for their recreational, historical, and natural values. Manages landmarks programs for natural and historic properties; coordinates Wild and Scenic Rivers System and National Trail System; administers study and grants programs. A listing of National Parks can be found in the Federally Protected Areas section.
Contact(s):
Chief of Office of Public Affairs: DAVID BARNA; Phone: 202-208-6843
Deputy Director: DENIS GALVIN; Phone: 202-208-3818
Deputy Director: JACQUELINE LOWEY; Phone: 202-208-6741
Associate Director of Budget and Administration: SUE MASICA; Phone: 202-208-6953
Associate Director of Cultural Resources: KATE STEVENSON; Phone: 202-208-7625
Associate Director of Natural Resources: MICHAEL SOUKUP; Phone: 202-208-3884
Associate Director of Park Operations: MAUREEN FINNERTY; Phone: 202-208-5651
Associate Director of Professional Services: BILL SHADDOX; Phone: 202-208-3264
Office of Legislative and Congressional Affairs: KITTY ROBERTS; Phone: 202-208-5656
Comptroller: C. BRUCE SHEAFFER; Phone: 202-208-4566
Director: ROBERT G. STANTON; Phone: 202-208-6843
Alaska Regional Director: ROBERT BARBEE, 2525 Gambell St., Rm. 107, Anchorage, AK 99503-2892; Phone: 907-257-2687
Intermountain Regional Director: JOHN E. COOK, 12795 Alameda Parkway, Denver, CO 80225; Phone: 303-969-2500
Midwest Regional Director: WILLIAM SCHENK, 1709 Jackson St., Omaha, NE 68102; Phone: 402-221-3471
National Capital Regional Director: TERRY CARLSTROM, 1100 Ohio Dr., SW, Washington, DC 20242; Phone: 202-619-7256
Northeast Region Director: MARIE RUST, U.S. Customs House, 5th Fl., 200 Chestnut St., Philadelphia, PA 19106; Phone: 215-597-7013
Pacific West Regional Director: JOHN REYNOLDS, 600 Harrison St., Suite 600, San Francisco, CA 94107; Phone: 415-427-1300
Southeast Regional Director: JERRY BELSON, 100 Alabama St., SW, Atlanta Federal Center, Atlanta, GA 30303; Phone: 404-562-3100

OFFICE OF SURFACE MINING RECLAMATION AND ENFORCEMENT
Department of Interior, Interior South Bldg., 1951 Constitution Ave., NW, Washington, DC 20240
Phone: 202-208-2719
Description: Established by the Surface Mining Control and Reclamation Act of 1977 to administer the nationwide program to protect society and the environment from adverse effects of coal mining operations, to establish national standards for regulating the surface environmental effects of coal mining, to support state implementation of such regulatory programs and to promote reclamation of abandoned mine lands.
Contact(s):
Chief of Staff: MARGY WHITE; Phone: 202-208-4006
Director: KATHY KARPAN; Phone: 202-208-4006
Assistant Director of Finance and Administration: ROBERT EWING; Phone: 202-208-2560
Assistant Director of Program Support: MARY JOSIE BLANCHARD; Phone: 202-208-4264
Office of Communications: NANCY SMITH; Phone: 202-208-2565

UNITED STATES FISH AND WILDLIFE SERVICE
Department of Interior, 1849 C. St., Rm. 3012, Washington, DC 20240
Phone: 202-208-5634; Web site: www.fws.gov
Description: Effective July 1, 1974, an act of Congress (Public Law 93-271, April 22, 1974 renamed the Bureau of Sport Fisheries and Wildlife, the United States Fish and Wildlife Service, under the Assistant Secretary for Fish and Wildlife and Parks. The Service is the lead federal agency in the conservation of the nation's migratory birds, threatened and endangered species, certain marine mammals, and sport fishing. The Service administers fish and wildlife restoration grant programs to state governments, provides technical assistance to state and foreign governments, serves as lead federal agency in international conventions on wildlife conservation and operates a program of public affairs and education to enhance the public's understanding and appreciation of America's fish and wildlife resources.
Contact(s):
Director: JAMIE RAPPAPORT CLARK; Phone: 202-208-4717
Deputy Director: JOHN G. ROGERS JR.; Phone: 202-208-4545
Assistant Director of Administration: PAUL W. HENNE; Phone: 202-208-4888
Assistant Director of Ecological Services: GARY FRAZER; Phone: 202-208-4646
Assistant Director of External Affairs: THOMAS O. MELIUS; Phone: 202-208-4500
Assistant Director of Fisheries: CATHLEEN SHORT; Phone: 202-208-6394
Assistant Director of International Affairs: MARSHALL JONES; Phone: 202-208-6393
Assistant of Refuges and Wildlife: DANIEL M. ASHE; Phone: 202-208-5333
Chief of Division of Contracting and General Services: JUANITA B. WILLIAMS; Phone: 703-358-1901
Chief of Division of Endangered Species: NANCY GLOMAN; Phone: 703-358-2171
Chief of Division of Engineering: PAUL J. CAMP; Phone: 303-275-2300
Chief of Division of Environmental Contaminants: EVERETT WILSON; Phone: 703-358-2148
Chief of Division of Finance: DAVID HOLLAND; Phone: 703-358-1742
Chief of Division of Fish and Wildlife Management Assistance: HANNIBAL BOLTON; Phone: 703-358-1718
Chief of Division of Habitat Conservation: BENJAMIN TUGGLE; Phone: 703-358-2161
Chief of Division of Information Resources Management: WILLIAM T. BROOKS; Phone: 703-358-1729
Chief of Division of Law Enforcement: KEVIN ADAMS; Phone: 703-358-1949
Chief of Division of National Fish Hatcheries: WILLIAM KNAPP; Phone: 703-358-1715
Chief of Division of Personnel Management: KENT BAUM; Phone: 202-208-6104
Chief of Division of Realty: JEFFERY M. DONAHOE; Phone: 703-358-1713
Chief of Division of Refuge: JIM KURTH; Phone: 703-358-1744
Chief of FWS Finance Center: ARTHUR FORD, Denver Federal Center, P.O. Box 25207, Denver, CO 80225-0207

Chief of Office for Human Resources: JEROME BUTLER; Phone: 202-208-3195
Chief of Office of Congressional and Legislative Services: ALEXANDRA PITTS; Phone: 202-208-5403
Chief of Office of Federal Aid: ROBERT LANGE; Phone: 703-358-2156
Chief of Office of International Affairs: HERBERT A. RAFFAELE; Phone: 703-358-1754
Chief of Office of Management Authority: KENNETH B. STANSELL; Phone: 703-358-2093
Chief of Office of Migratory Bird Management: JON ANDREW; Phone: 703-358-1714
Chief of Office of Public Affairs: MEGAN DURHAM; Phone: 202-208-4131
Program Manager of Federal Duck Stamp Program: ROBERT C. LESINO; Phone: 202-208-4354

Alaska Regional Office 7
1011 E. Tudor Rd., Anchorage, AK 99503
Contact(s):
Regional Director: DAVID B. ALLEN; Phone: 907-786-3542

California-Nevada Operations
2800 Cottage Way, Rm. W-2606, Sacramento, CA 95825
Phone: 916-414-6464; Fax: 916-414-6486
Contact(s):
Manager: MICHAEL J. SPEAR

Delaware Estuary Project
R.R. 1 Box 146-A, Smyrna, DE 19977
Phone: 302-653-9152
Description: The Delaware Estuary Project was established to coordinate, complement, and support existing U.S. Fish and Wildlife Service programs, focusing on important natural resource issues in the Delaware River watershed. The office provides technical assistance to the EPA's National Estuary Program for the Delaware Bay and Delaware's Inland Bays Estuary programs (started in 1988.

Great Lakes-Big Rivers Regional Office 3
1 Federal Dr., Federal Bldg., Fort Snelling, MN 55111
Contact(s):
Regional Director: WILLIAM F. HARTWIG; Phone: 612-713-5301
Deputy Regional Director: MARVIN E. MORIARTY; Phone: 612-713-5304
Assistant Regional Director of External Affairs: SUSAN DREIBAND; Phone: 612-713-5310

Mountain-Prairie Regional Office 6
134 Union Blvd., P.O. Box 25486, Denver, CO 80225
Contact(s):
Regional Director: RALPH MORGENWECK; Phone: 303-236-7920
Regional Director of External Affairs: TERRY SEXSON; Phone: 303-236-7905; Fax: 303-236-3815

National Conservation Training Center
Rt. 1 Box 166, Shepherdstown, WV 25443
Phone: 304-876-1600/304-876-7200; Fax: 304-876-7218
Description: The mission of the Center is to advance conservation of fish, wildlife, and their habitats through leadership in conservation education for the public, training for the conservation and resource management community, and fostering alliances among diverse interest.
Contact(s):
Chief, Division of Training: TODD JONES; Phone: 304-876-7431
Director: JOHN R. LEMON; Phone: 304-876-7263
Deputy Director: MONA WOMACK; Phone: 304-876-7263

National Fish and Wildlife Forensics Laboratory
1490 East Main St., Ashland, OR 97520
Phone: 503-482-4191; Fax: 503-482-4989
Description: The mission of the Laboratory is to provide forensic crime lab, support for wildlife law enforcement investigations at the federal, state, and international levels.
Contact(s):
Director: KEN GODDARD

Northeast Regional Office 5
300 Westgate Center Dr., Hadley, MA 01035
Phone: 413-253-8200
Contact(s):
Regional Director: RONALD E. LAMBERTSON; Phone: 413-253-8300

Pacific Regional Office 1
Eastside Federal Complex, 911 NE 11th Ave., Portland, OR 97232-4181
Contact(s):
Regional Director: ANN BADGLEY; Phone: 503-231-6828
Chief Officer of Public Affairs: JOAN JEWETT; Phone: 503-231-6121

Southeast Regional Office 4
1875 Century Blvd., Atlanta, GA 30345
Contact(s):
Regional Director: SAM HAMILTON; Phone: 404-679-4000

Southwest Regional Office 2
500 Gold Ave., SW, Rm. 3018, Albuquerque, NM 87102
Contact(s):
Regional Director: NANCY KAUFMAN; Phone: 505-248-6282
Assistant Director of External Affairs: TOM BAUER; Phone: 505-248-6911; Fax: 404-248-6915

UNITED STATES GEOLOGICAL SURVEY
USGS National Center, 12201 Sunrise Valley Dr., Reston, VA 20192
Phone: 703-648-4000; Web site: www.usgs.gov
Founded: 1879
Description: The Geological Survey works in cooperation with more than 2,000 organizations across the country to provide reliable, impartial, scientific information to resource managers, planners, and other customers.
Contact(s):
Director: CHARLES G. GROAT; Phone: 703-648-7411
Senior Advisor to the Director: AMY HOLLEY; Phone: 703-648-4410
Chief, Office of Equal Opportunity: S. KAYE COOK; Phone: 703-648-7770
Chief, Office of External Affairs: BARBARA WAINMAN; Phone: 703-648-4460
Chief, Office of Personnel: ROBERT W. HOSENFELD; Phone: 703-648-7442
Chief, Office of Program and Planning Coordination: ANNE E. KINSINGER; Phone: 703-648-4451
Chief, Office of Program Support: JAMES C. LEUPOLD; Phone: 703-648-7200
Chief, Program Operations Office: MARTIN ECKES; Phone: 703-648-4430
Public Affairs Officer: TRUDY P. HARLOW; Phone: 703-648-4483
Senior Advisor, Science Applications: JAMES F. DEVINE; Phone: 703-648-4423
Congressional Liaison Officer: TIMOTHY J. WEST; Phone: 703-648-4455
Associate Director for Biology: DENNIS B. FENN; Phone: 703-648-4050
Associate Director for Geology: P. PATRICK LEAHY; Phone: 703-648-6600
Associate Director for Mapping: RICHARD E. WITMER; Phone: 703-648-5747
Associate Director for Programs: BARBARA J. RYAN; Phone: 703-648-7413
Associate Director for Water: ROBERT M. HIRSCH; Phone: 703-648-5215
Associate Director of Operations: BARBARA RYAN; Phone: 703-648-7413
Central Regional Director: THOMAS J. CASADEVALL, Denver Federal Center, Mail Stop 150, Denver, CO 80225; Phone: 303-236-5900/ext. 303

U.S. FEDERAL AND INTERNATIONAL GOVERNMENT AGENCIES - EXECUTIVE BRANCH

Eastern Regional Director: BONNIE A. McGREGOR, 1700 Leetown Rd., Kearneysville, WV 25430; Phone: 703-648-5166
Western Regional Director: JOHN D. BUFFINGTON, 909 First Ave., 8th Fl., Seattle, WA 98104; Phone: 206-220-4600

Biological Resources Division
12201 Sunrise Valley Dr., MS-300, Reston, VA 20192
Phone: 703-648-4050

Description: The Biological Resources Division works with others to provide the scientific understanding and technologies needed to manage the Nation's biological resources.
Contact(s):
Chief Biologist: DENNIS B. FENN; Phone: 703-648-4050
Deputy Chief Biologist for Science: SUSAN D. HASELTINE; Phone: 703-648-4060
Chief of International Affairs: WILLIAM GREGG; Phone: 703-648-4067
Central Regional Chief Biologist: DR. J. LARRY LUDKE, Central Regional Office, Denver Federal Center, P.O. Box 25046, Bldg. 20, Mailstop 300, Denver, CO 80225-0046; Phone: 303-236-2730/222
Eastern Regional Chief Biologist: DR. A. WILLIAM PALMISANO, Eastern Regional Office, 1700 Leetown Rd., Kearneysville, WV 25430; Phone: 304-724-4500

UNITED STATES DEPARTMENT OF THE NAVY
1000 Navy Pentagon, Department of the Navy, Washington, DC 20350-1000
Web site: www.navy.mil

Description: The mission of the Navy is to maintain, train, and equip combat-ready Naval forces capable of winning wars, deterring aggression and maintaining freedom of the seas.
Contact(s):
Secretary: HON. RICHARD DANZIG
Undersecretary: HON. JERRY MACARTHUR HULTIN

U.S. MARINE CORPS
Headquarters, U.S. Marine Corps, 2 Navy Annex, Washington, DC 20380-4775
Phone: 703-695-8332

Description: The Marine Corps, as America's premier crisis response force, trains as it fights. Accordingly, Marine Corps cultural and natural resources managers provide and maintain a variety of landscapes to support military training, while protecting and preserving the cultural and natural resources the American people cherish for their intrinsic value.
Contact(s):
Head of Natural Resources Section: JIM OMANS; Phone: 703-695-8232

Marine Corps Installations
Contact(s):
MCAGCC Twentynine Plams, CA: Head of Natural Resources Branch: ROY MADDEN; Phone: 619-830-5719
MCAS Beufort, SC: Head of Environmental Management Department: ALICE HOWARD; Phone: 803-522-7370
MCAS Cherry Point, NC: Head of Environmental Department: MAJOR MARK BRANNAN
MCAS Yuma, AZ: Head of Natural Resources Branch: RON PEARCE; Phone: 802-341-3318
MCB Camp Lejeune, NC: Head of Environmental Management Department: BOB WARREN; Phone: 910-451-5003
MCB Camp Pendleton, CA: Head of Environmental Management Department: LUPE ARMAS; Phone: 619-725-3561
MCCDC Quantico, VA: Head of Environmental Management Department: BRUCE FRIZZELL; Phone: 703-640-4030
MCLB Albany, GA: Head of Environmental Management Department: JERRY PALMER; Phone: 912-439-6261
MCLB Barstow, CA: Head of Environmental Management Department: JACK STORMO; Phone: 619-577-6111
MCRD Parris Island, SC: Head of Environmental Management Department: JOHNSIE NABORS; Phone: 803-525-2779

UNITED STATES DEPARTMENT OF TRANSPORTATION
Office of Public Affairs, Nassif Bldg., 400 7th St., SW, Washington, DC 20590
Phone: 202-366-4000; Web site: www.dot.gov
Founded: 1967

Description: Composed of these main elements: The United States Coast Guard, Federal Aviation Administration, Federal Highway Administration, Federal Railroad Administration, Maritime Administration, St. Lawrence Seaway Development Corporation, National Highway Traffic Safety Administration, Federal Transit Administration, and Research and Special Programs Administration. Major objectives are to develop and improve a coordinated national transportation system consistent with other national objectives, such as environmental protection, and to stimulate technological advances in the industry, preserving the nation's free enterprise transportation network.
Contact(s):
Secretary: RODNEY SLATER; Phone: 202-366-1111
Deputy Secretary: MORTIMER L. DOWNEY; Phone: 202-366-2222
Assistant to the Secretary and Director of Public Affairs: WILLIAM SCHULZ
Publication(s): *Public Roads (Federal Highway Administration); Merchant Vessels of the United States (United States Coast Guard)*

FEDERAL AVIATION ADMINISTRATION
FOB 10A 800 Independence Ave., SW, Washington, DC 20591
Phone: 202-267-3484

Description: Charged with regulating air commerce to foster aviation safety; promoting civil aviation and a national system of airports; achieving efficient use of navigable airspace; and developing and operating a common system of air traffic control and air navigation for both civilian and military aircraft.
Contact(s):
Administrator: JANE GARVEY; Phone: 202-267-3111

FEDERAL HIGHWAY ADMINISTRATION
Attn: Executive Director, Washington Headquarters, 400 7th St., SW, Washington, DC 20590

Description: Charged with carrying out the Department of the Transportation responsibilities concerned with the highway mode of land transport, including intermodal connections, has the primary missions of ensuring the safety of the motor carrier industry and that the Nation's highway transportation system is safe, economic, and efficient with respect to the movement of people and goods, while giving full consideration to the highway's impact on the environment and social and economic conditions.
Contact(s):
Administrator: KENNETH R. WYKLE; Phone: 202-366-0650
Deputy Administrator: GLORIA J. JEFF; Phone: 202-366-2240
Executive Director: ANTHONY R. KANE; Phone: 202-366-2242
Chief Counsel: KAREN E. SKELTON; Phone: 202-366-0740
Director, Office of Administration: GEORGE S. MOORE; Phone: 202-366-0604
Director, Office of Civil Rights: EDWARD W. MORRIS JR.; Phone: 202-366-0693
Director, Office of corporate Management: FRED J. HEMPEL; Phone: 202-366-9393
Director, Office of Policy: WALTER L. SUTTON; Phone: 202-366-0585
Director, Office of Professional Development: JOSEPH S. TOOLE; Phone: 703-235-0519
Director, Office of Public Affairs: GAIL R. SHIBLEY; Phone: 202-366-0660
Director, Office of Research, Development, and Technology: DENNIS C. JUDYCKI; Phone: 202-493-3165
Program Manager, Office of Federal Lands: ARTHUR E. HAMILTON; Phone: 202-366-9494
Program Manager, Office of Infrastructure: VINCENT F. SCHIMMOLER; Phone: 202-366-0371
Program Manager, Office of Motor Carrier and Highway Safety: JULIE A. CIRILLO; Phone: 202-366-2519

Program Manager, Office of Operations: CHRISTINE M. JOHNSON; Phone: 202-366-0408
Program Manager, Office of Planning and Environment: CYNTHIA L. BURBANK; Phone: 202-366-0342
Keyword(s): Engineering, Historic Preservation, Planning Management, Transportation

FEDERAL RAILROAD ADMINISTRATION
400 7th St., SW, Stop 5, Washington, DC 20590
Phone: 202-366-4000
Founded: 1967
Description: The FRA promulgates and enforces rail safety regulations, administers financial assistance programs for designated railroads, conducts research and development in support of improved railroad safety and national rail transportation policy, as well as monitors rail passenger service nationwide, and consolidates government support of rail transportation activities.
Contact(s):
Administrator: JOLENE M. MOLITORIS
Chief Counsel: S. MARK LINDSEY
Associate Administrator for Safety: GEORGE GAVALLA
Director of Office Public Affairs: PAMELA BARRY

FEDERAL TRANSIT ADMINISTRATION
400 7th St., SW, Washington, DC 20590
Phone: 202-366-4043
Description: Seeks to improve the environmental standards of American cities through grant programs which extend and modernize existing urban mass transit equipment and facilities and which study, develop, and test new equipment and concepts in urban mass transit applications and operations.
Contact(s):
Administrator of Office of the Administrator: GORDON J. LINTON; Phone: 202-366-4040
Associate Administrator for Planning: CHARLOTTE M. ADAMS; Phone: 202-366-4033
Associate Administrator for Program Management: HIRAM J. WALKER; Phone: 202-366-4020
Deputy Associate Administrator: JANET L. SAHAJ; Phone: 202-366-4020
Associate Administrator for Research Demonstration and Innovation: EDWARD L. THOMAS; Phone: 202-366-4052
Deputy Associate Administrator: A. M. YEN; Phone: 202-366-4991
Associate Administrator for Administration: DORRIE Y. ALDRICH; Phone: 202-366-4007
Deputy Associate Administrator: TIMOTHY B. WOLGAST; Phone: 202-366-4007
Deputy Administrator of Office of Administration: NURIA FERNANDEZ; Phone: 202-366-4325
Director, Office of Public Affairs: BRUCE C. FRAME; Phone: 202-366-4319
Executive Information, Office of Public Affairs: MARY KNAPP; Phone: 202-366-9788
Chief Counsel: PATRICK W. REILLY; Phone: 202-366-4063
Deputy Chief Counsel: GREGORY B. MCBRIDE; Phone: 202-366-4063
Director, Office of Civil Rights: AURTHER ANDREW LOPEZ; Phone: 202-366-4018
Associate Administrator for Budget and Policy: MICHAEL A. WINTER; Phone: 202-366-4050
Deputy Associate Administrator: JOHN W. SPENCER; Phone: 202-366-1691
Keyword(s): Transportation

NATIONAL HIGHWAY TRAFFIC SAFETY ADMINISTRATION
Nassif Bldg., 400 7th St., SW, Washington, DC 20590
Phone: 202-366-9550
Contact(s):
Deputy Director: PHILIP R. RECHT; Phone: 202-366-2775
Executive Director: DONALD C. BISCHOFF; Phone: 202-366-2111
Administrator: RICARDO MARTINEZ; Phone: 202-366-1836
Associate Administrator for Administration (Acting): HERMAN L. SIMMS; Phone: 202-366-1788
Associate Administrator for Plans and Policy: WILLIAM WALSH; Phone: 202-366-2550
Associate Administrator for Research and Development: RAYMOND OWINGS; Phone: 202-366-1537
Associate Administrator for Safety Assurance: KENNETH WEINSTEIN; Phone: 202-366-9700
Associate Administrator for Safety Performance Standards: L. ROBERT SHELTON; Phone: 202-366-1810
Associate Administrator for Traffic Safety Programs (Acting): JAMES NICHOLS; Phone: 202-366-1755
Chief Counsel: FRANK SEALES JR.; Phone: 202-366-9511

SAINT LAWRENCE SEAWAY DEVELOPMENT CORPORATION
U.S. Department of Transportation, 400 7th St. SW, Suite 5424, Washington, DC 20590
Phone: 202-366-0091
Contact(s):
Administrator: ALBERT S. JACQUEZ; Phone: 202-366-0091
Deputy Director of Office of Congressional and Public Affairs: DENNIS E. DEUSCHL, P.O. Box 44090, Washington, DC 20026-4090; Phone: 202-366-0110

UNITED STATES COAST GUARD
2100 2nd St., SW, Washington, DC 20593-0001
Phone: 202-267-2229
Contact(s):
Chief of Staff: TIMOTHY W. JOSIAH; Phone: 202-267-1642

UNITED STATES DEPARTMENT OF TREASURY
1500 Pennsylvania Ave., NW, Washington, DC 20220
Phone: 202-622-2000; Fax: 202-622-6415; Web site: www.ustreas.gov
Description: The basic functions of the Department of the Treasury include: economic and fiscal policy; government accounting, cash, and debt management; international economic policy; and enforcement of customs and trade laws.
Contact(s):
Secretary: LAWRENCE H. SUMMERS; Phone: 202-622-2000
Deputy Secretary: STUART E. EIZENSTAT

U.S. CUSTOMS SERVICE
Headquarters, 1300 Pennsylvania Ave., NW, RRB-6-4A, Washington, DC 20229
Phone: 202-927-1770; Fax: 202-927-1393
Description: The United States Customs Service is responsible for the enforcement of the U.S. laws regarding the importation and exportation of injurious and endangered species.
Contact(s):
Commissioner: RAYMOND W. KELLY
Assistant Commissioner for Office of Field Operations, Rm. 5-5C: CHARLES W. WINWOOD; Phone: 202-927-0100
Assistant Commissioner for Office of Investigations, Rm. 6-5E: BONNI G. TISCHLER; Phone: 202-927-1600
Special Agent in Charge: GARY W. WAUGH, Detroit, MI 48226-2568
Special Agent in Charge: JOHN HENSLEY, Terminal Island, CA 90731
Special Agent in Charge: EDWARD W. LOGAN, San Diego, CA 92101
Special Agent In Charge: CHARLIE SIMONSEN, San Francisco, CA 94111
Special Agent in Charge: KEN KILROY, Seattle, WA 98104-1048
Special Agent in Charge: GARY HILLBERRY, Denver, CO 80112-5131
Special Agent in Charge: ALLAN DOODY, Baltimore, MD 21202
Special Agent in Charge: JEREMIAH J. SULLIVAN, Buffalo, NY 14202
Special Agent in Charge: LEONARD C. LINDHEIM, San Antonio, TX 78216
Special Agent in Charge (Acting): AWILDA VILLAFANE, 555 E. River Rd., Tucson, AZ 85704
Special Agent in Charge (Acting): BEN DEVANE, Atlanta, GA 30354

U.S. FEDERAL AND INTERNATIONAL GOVERNMENT AGENCIES - INDEPENDENT AGENCIES

Special Agent in Charge (Acting): FRANK FIGUEROA, Miami, FL 33166
Special Agent in Charge (Acting): BRUCE MURRAY, Tampa, FL 33607
Special Agent in Charge (Acting): BOBBY FERNANDEZ, Old San Juan, PR 00901
Special Agent in Charge (Acting): MARVIN WALKER, New York, NY 10048-0945
Special Agent in Charge (Acting): JOE WEBBER, El Paso, TX 79925
Special Agent in Charge (Acting): JAMES LEWIS, Chicago, IL 60607

East Texas CMC
2323 S. Shepard St., Suite 1200, Houston, TX 77019
Phone: 713-313-2843
Contact(s):
Director: JOHN BABB

Gulf CMC
423 Canal St., Rm. 337, New Orleans, LA 70130
Phone: 504-670-2404
Contact(s):
Director: PATRICIA DUFFY

Mid America CMC
610 S. Canal St., Suite 900, Chicago, IL 60607
Phone: 312-983-9100
Contact(s):
Director: GARNET FEE

New York CMC
6 World Trade Center, Rm. 716, New York, NY 10048
Phone: 212-637-7900
Contact(s):
Director (Acting): GEORGE HEAVEY

North Atlantic CMC
10 Causeway St., Rm. 801, Boston, MA 02222
Phone: 617-565-6210
Contact(s):
Director: PHILIP SPAYD

Southeast
909 SE 1st Ave., Miami, FL 33131
Phone: 305-536-5283
Contact(s):
Director: HOWARD COOPERMAN

South Pacific CMC
One World Trade Center, P.O. Box 32639, Long Beach, CA 90832
Phone: 562-980-3100
Contact(s):
Director: AUDREY ADAMS

INDEPENDENT AGENCIES

ADVISORY COUNCIL ON HISTORIC PRESERVATION
1100 Pennsylvania Ave., NW, #809, The Old Post Office Bldg., Washington, DC 20004
Phone: 202-606-8503
Description: An independent federal agency, the Council is the primary policy advisor to the President and Congress on historic preservation matters and guides, and other federal agencies to ensure their actions do not result in unnecessary harm to the nation's historic properties. The Council was established by the National Historic Preservation Act of 1966, is made up of the heads of seven federal departments whose actions regularly affect historic properties; eight members, a governor and a mayor appointed by the President; and representatives of the National Trust for Historic Preservation and the National Conference of State Historic Preservation Officers. The Council is supported by a small professional staff. Offices are in Washington, DC and Denver.
Contact(s):
Executive Director: JOHN FOWLER
Keyword(s): Environmental Preservation, Public Health Protection, Solid Waste Management, Toxic Substances

GENERAL SERVICES ADMINISTRATION
GSA Bldg., 1800 F St., NW, Washington, DC 20405
Phone: 202-501-1231
Description: Concerned with the conveyance of surplus real property for wildlife conservation purposes to the Secretary of Interior or to a state, pursuant to Public Law 537, 80th Congress.
Contact(s):
Administrator: DAVID BARRAM
Director of Program Development and Outreach: RONALD L. RICE; Phone: 202-501-0052
Director of Redeployment Services Division/Property Disposal Division: JOHN Q. MARTIN; Phone: 202-501-4671

NATIONAL SCIENCE FOUNDATION
4201 Wilson Blvd., Arlington, VA 22230
Phone: 703-306-1234
Founded: 1950
Description: Responsible for the support of science and engineering research and the development of science education programs. Policy is set by the National Science Board, which is composed of 24 part-time members appointed by the President, with the consent of the Senate, and includes the Director of the Foundation.
Contact(s):
Deputy Director: DR. JOSEPH BORDOGNA; Phone: 703-306-1000
Director: DR. RITA COLWELL; Phone: 703-306-1000
Chairman of National Science Board: DR. EAMON A. KELLY; Phone: 703-306-2000
Director of Office of Legislative and Public Affairs: JULIA A. MOORE; Phone: 703-306-1070
Head Librarian: STEPHANIE BIANCHI; Phone: 703-306-0658
Publication(s): *Guide to Programs; Grant Proposal Guide; NSF in a Changing World: The National Science Foundation Strategic Plan; Where Discoveries Begin*
Keyword(s): Ecological Education

NATIONAL TRANSPORTATION SAFETY BOARD
490 L'Enfant Plaza East, SW, Washington, DC 20594
Phone: 202-314-6000
Description: The Safety Board is an independent federal accident investigation agency. The Board's mission is to determine the "probable cause" of transportation accidents and to formulate safety recommendations to improve transportation safety.
Contact(s):
Chairman: JAMES HALL
Vice Chairman: ROBERT T. FRANCIS II
Chief Financial Officer: CRAIG KELLER
Director of Office of General Counsel: RON BATTOCCHI
Director of Office of Government, Public, and Family Affairs: JAMIE FINCH
Managing Director: PETER GOELZ

NUCLEAR REGULATORY COMMISSION
Washington, DC 20555
Phone: 301-415-7000
Founded: 1975
Description: Five-member commission responsible for regulating all commercial uses of nuclear energy to, protect the health and safety of the public and the environment.
Contact(s):
Deputy Director: THEMIS P. SPEIS; Phone: 301-415-6802
Deputy Director: ROGER A. FORTUNA; Phone: 301-415-3476
Deputy Director: DENWOOD F. ROSS; Phone: 301-415-7473
Deputy Director: ELIZABETH A. HAYDEN; Phone: 301-415-8200
Deputy Director: JAMES F. McDERMOTT; Phone: 301-415-7516
Deputy Director: MALCOLM R. KNAPP; Phone: 301-415-8468
Executive Director: JOHN T. LARKINS; Phone: 301-415-7360

Executive Director: JOHN T. LARKINS; Phone: 301-415-7360
Director: PAUL H. LOHAUS; Phone: 301-415-2326
Director: BRIAN K. GRIMES; Phone: 301-415-1193
Associate Director: LINDA E. PORTNER; Phone: 301-415-1776
Associate Director of Contract, Security, F01 and Publications: EDWARD L. HALMAN; Phone: 301-415-7305
Associate Director of Facilities and Property Management: MICHAEL L. SPRINGER; Phone: 301-415-8080
Associate Director of Office of Administration: PATRICIA G. NORRY; Phone: 301-415-7443
Associate Director of Projects: ROY P. ZIMMERMAN; Phone: 301-415-1284
Associate Director, Insp. and Tech. Review: ASHOK C. THADANI; Phone: 301-415-1274
Associate General Counsel for Hearing, Enforcement, and Administration: STEPHEN G. BURNS; Phone: 301-415-1740
Chairman: SHIRLEY ANN JACKSON; Phone: 301-415-1820
Chairman of Advisory Committee on Nuclear Waste: MARTIN J. STEINDLER; Phone: 301- 415-7360
Chief Administrative Judge and Chairman of Atomic Safety and Licensing Board Panel: B. PAUL COTTER JR.; Phone: 301-415-7450
Commissioner: KENNETH C. ROGERS; Phone: 301-415-1855
Commissioner: GRETA J. DIRUS; Phone: 301-415-1820
Deputy: ARTHUR B. BEACH; Phone: 708-829-9658
Deputy: LUIS A. REYES; Phone: 404-331-5610
Deputy: WILLIAM F. KANE; Phone: 610-337-5340
Deputy: SAMUEL J. COLLINS; Phone: 817-860-8226
Deputy Chief Administrative Judge: FREDERICK J. SHON; Phone: 301-415-7468
Deputy Chief Financial Officer/Controller: RONALD M. SCROGGINS; Phone: 301-415-7501;
Deputy Controller: JESSE L. FUNCHES; Phone: 301-415-7322
Deputy Director (Acting): ASHOK C. HADAN; Phone: 301-415-1272
Deputy Director of Division of Reactor Programs: THOMAS T. MARTIAN; Phone: 301-415-1199
Deputy Director of Licensing Support Systems Administrator: ARNOLD E. LEVIN; Phone: 301-415-7458
Deputy Director of Office of State Programs: RICHARD L. BANGART; Phone: 301-415-3340
Deputy Executive Director for Nuclear Materials, Safety, Safeguards, and Operations Support: HUGH L. THOMPSON JR.; Phone: 301-504-1713
Deputy Executive Director for Nuclear Reactor Regulation, Regional Operations and Research: JAMES L. MILHOAN; Phone: 301-415-1705
Deputy General Counsel: MARTIN G. MALSCH; Phone: 301-415-1740
Director (Acting) of Office of Commission Appellate Adjudication: JOHN F. CORDES JR.; Phone: 301-415-1600
Director (Acting) of Office of Nuclear Reactor Regulation: FRANK MIRAGLIA; Phone: 301-415-1270
Director of Division of Engineering: BRIAN SHERON; Phone: 301-415-2722
Director of Division of Engineering Technology: LAWRENCE C. SHAO; Phone: 301-415-5678
Director of Division of Fuel Cycle Safety and Safeguards: ELIZABETH Q. TENEYCK; Phone: 301-415-7212
Director of Division of Industrial and Medical Nuclear Safety: DONALD A. COOL; Phone: 301-415-7197
Director of Division of Inspection and Support Programs: FRANCIS P. GILLESPIE; Phone: 301-415-1275
Director of Division of Reactor Controls and Human Factors: BRUCE A. BOGER; Phone: 301-415-1004
Director of Division of Regulatory Applications: BILL M. MORRIS; Phone: 301-415-6207
Director of Division of Systems Safety and Analysis: GARY M. HOLAHAN; Phone: 301-415-2884
Director of Division of Systems Technology: M. WAYNE HODGES; Phone: 301-415-5728
Director of Division of Waste Management: JOHN T. GREEVES; Phone: 301-415-7358
Director of Financial Management, Procurement, and Administration Staff: LLOYD J. DONNELLY; Phone: 301-415-5828
Director of Incident Response Division: FRANK CONGEL; Phone: 301-415-7476
Director of Office for Analysis and Evaluation of Operational Data: EDWARD L. JORDAN; Phone: 301-415-7472
Director of Office of Congressional Affairs: DENNIS K. RATHBUN; Phone: 301-415-1776
Director of Office of Enforcement: JAMES LIEBERMAN; Phone: 301-415-2741
Director of Office of Information Resources Management: GERALD F. CRANFORD; Phone: 301-415-7585
Director of Office of International Programs: CARLTON R. STOIBER; Phone: 301-415-1780
Director of Office of Investigations: GUY P. CAPUTO; Phone: 301-415-2373
Director of Office of Nuclear Material Safety and Safeguards: CARL J. PAPERIELLO; Phone: 301-415-7800
Director of Office of Nuclear Regulatory Research: DAVID L. MORRISON; Phone: 301-415-6641;
Director of Office of Personnel: PAUL E. BIRD; Phone: 301-415-7516
Director of Office of Public Affairs: WILLIAM M. BEECHER; Phone: 301-415-8200
Director of Office of Small Business and Civil Rights: IRENE LITTLE; Phone: 301-415-7380
Director of Program Management, Policy Development, and Analysis Staff: JOHN J. LINEHAN; Phone: 301-415-7780
Director of Safety Programs Division: C. E. ROSSI; Phone: 301-415-7499
Director of Spent Fuel Project Office: WILLIAM D. TRAVERS; Phone: 301-415-8500
Director of Technical Training Division: KENNETH A. RAGLIN; Phone: 423-855-6500
Executive Director for Operations: JAMES M. TAYLOR; Phone: 301-415-1700
General Counsel: KAREN D. CYR; Phone: 301-415-1743
Inspector General: HUBERT BELL; Phone: 301-415-5930
Licensing and Regulation: WILLIAM J. OLMSTEAD; Phone: 301-415-1740
Regional Administrator, Region 1: HUBERT J. MILLER, 475 Allendale Rd., King of Prussia, PA 19406-1415; Phone: 610-337-5299
Regional Administrator, Region 2: STEWART D. EBNETER, 101 Marietta St., Suite. 2900, Atlanta, GA 30323-0199; Phone: 404-331-5500
Regional Administrator, Region 3: ARTHUR B. BEACH, 801 Warrenville Rd., Lisle, IL 60532-4351; Phone: 708-829-9500
Regional Administrator, Region 4: LEONARD J. CALLAN, 611 Ryan Plaza Dr., Suite 4000, Arlington, TX 76011-8064; Phone: 817-860-8225
Secretary of the Commission: JOHN C. HOYLE; Phone: 301-415-1969
Vice Chairman: PAUL W. POMEROY; Phone: 301-415-7360
Vice Chairman: ROBERT L. SEALE; Phone: 301-415-7360
Keyword(s): Energy

PEACE CORPS
1111 20th St., NW, Washington, DC 20526
Phone: 202-692-2100; Web site: www.peacecorps.gov
Founded: 1961
Description: The Peace Corps was established by President John F. Kennedy to promote world peace and friendship. Since 1961, more than 155,000 Americans have joined the Peace Corps and have served in 134 countries around the world. The Peace Corps has three goals: to provide volunteers who contribute to the social, economic, and human development of interested countries; to promote a better understanding of Americans among the people whom Peace Corps volunteers serve; and to strengthen Americans' understanding of the other peoples and cultures--to help bring the world back home.
Contact(s):
Deputy Director: CHARLES BAQUET III; Phone: 202-692-2100

U.S. FEDERAL AND INTERNATIONAL GOVERNMENT AGENCIES - INTERNATIONAL

Publication(s): *Peace Corps Times, The*

TENNESSEE VALLEY AUTHORITY
400 W. Summit Hill Dr., Knoxville, TN 37902
Phone: 423-632-2101
Founded: 1933
Description: TVA was created by an Act of Congress for the regional development of the Tennessee Valley region in Tennessee, Kentucky, Mississippi, Alabama, Virginia, Georgia, and North Carolina. In 1964, TVA opened Land Between The Lakes as a national demonstration project for outdoor recreation, environmental education, and resource management.
Contact(s):
Chairman of the Board: CRAVEN CROWELL
Chief Administrative Officer: NORMAN A. ZIGROSSI
President and Chief Operating Officer: OSWALD J. ZERINGUE
Senior Vice President and General Counsel: EDWARD S. CHRISTENBURY
Senior Vice President for Strategic Initiatives: PEYTON T. HARRISTON JR.
Executive Vice President and Chief Financial Officer: DAVID N. SMITH
Executive Vice President of River System Operations and Environment: KATHRYN J. JACKSON
Executive Vice President, Customer Service and Marketing: MARK O. MEDFORD
Executive Vice President, Fossil Power Group: JOSEPH R. BYNUM
Executive Vice President, Transmission/Power Supply Group: WILLIAM TERRY BOSTON
Executive Vice President/Chief Officer and Nuclear Officer of TVA Nuclear: JOHN A. SCALICE
Publication(s): *RiverPulse; Recreation on TVA Lakes;* various others on different subjects

Knoxville and Chattanooga Corporate Library
400 W. Summit Hill Dr., ET PC, Knoxville, TN 37902-1499
Phone: 423-632-3464; Fax: 423-632-4475

Muscle Shoals Technical Library
CTR 1E, Muscle Shoals, AL 35660
Phone: 205-386-2417; Fax: 205-386-2453

INTERNATIONAL

CANADIAN WILDLIFE SERVICE
3rd Fl., Place Vincent Massey, 351 St. Joseph Blvd., Hull, Quebec K1A 0H3 Canada
Contact(s):
Director General: DAVID BRACKETT; Phone: 819-997-1301; Fax: 819-953-7177

ECOSYSTEM AND ENVIRONMENTAL RESOURCES DIRECTORATE
6th Fl., Place Vincent Massey, 351 St. Joseph Blvd., Hull, Quebec K1A 0H3 Canada
Contact(s):
Director General: JENNIFER MOORE; Phone: 819-997-5674; Fax: 819-994-2541

ECOSYSTEM SCIENCE DIRECTORATE
7th Fl., Place Vincent Massey, 351 St. Joseph Blvd., Hull, Quebec K1A 0H3 Canada
Contact(s):
Director General: KEN SATO; Phone: 819-953-9307; Fax: 819-994-2724

CONSERVATION COUNCIL OF WESTERN AUSTRALIA
2 Delhi St., West Perth, West Australia 6000 Australia
Phone: 08-9420-7266; Fax: 08-9420-7273
Description: To promote the cause of conservation and environmentalism throughout the state of Western Australia; and to serve as a liaison to other bodies dealing with conservation and environmental issues.
Contact(s):
Contact: RACHEL SIEWERT

DEPARTMENT FOR ENVIRONMENT, HERITAGE AND ABORIGINAL AFFAIRS
Level 9, Chesser House, 91-97 Grenfell Street, Adelaide 5000 Australia
Phone: 08-8204-9322; Fax: 08-8204-9321
Contact(s):
Chief Executive: JOHN SCANLON

DEPARTMENT OF CANADIAN HERITAGE

CORPORATE SERVICE
Contact(s):
Assistant Deputy Minister: PETER HOMULAS; Phone: 819-994-3046

DEPARTMENT OF FISHERIES AND OCEANS
200 Kent St., Ottawa, Ontario K1A 0E6
Phone: 613-993-0999;TDD: 613-941-6517; Fax: 613-990-1866; Web site: www.dfo-mpo-gc-ca
Description: Fisheries and Oceans Canada is responsible for policies and programs in support of Canada's economic, ecological, and scientific interests in oceans and inland water; and for safe, effective and environmentally sound marine services responsive to the needs of Canadian in a global economy.
Contact(s):
Minister: HERB DHALIWAL; Phone: 613-992-3474
Deputy Minister: WAYNE WOUTERS; Phone: 613-993-2200

Canadian Coast Guard
Contact(s):
Deputy Commissioner: B. ELLIOTT; Phone: 613-998-1570
Assistant Deputy Minister, Marine Services/Commissioner: JOHN ADAMS; Phone: 613-998-1571
Director General: Marine Navigation Services: J. MURRAY; Phone: 613-990-5608
Director General: Program, Planning and Coordination: S. SHIRREFF; Phone: 613-998-1440
Director General: Rescue, Safety and Environmental Response: A. O' TOOLE; Phone: 613-990-3110
Director General: Technical and Operational Services: JACQUES CLAVELLE; Phone: 613-998-1638

Communications
Contact(s):
Director General: PAUL SCHUBERT; Phone: 613-993-0989

Corporate Services
Contact(s):
Assistant Deputy Minister: CAROL BEAL; Phone: 613-993-0868
Director General: Finance and Administration: DAVID BICKERTON; Phone: 613-993-2664
Director General: Human Resources: PAT NAPOLI; Phone: 613-990-0022
Director General: Information Management and Technology Services: GRETA BOSSENMAIER; Phone: 613-993-2051
Director General: Small Craft Harbours: ROBERT BERGERON; Phone: 613-993-1937

Fisheries and Management
Contact(s):
Assistant Deputy Minister: PAT CHAMUT; Phone: 613-990-9864
Director General: Aboriginal Affairs: SHARON ASHLEY; Phone: 613-991-0180
Director General: Conservation and Protection: DAVID BEVAN; Phone: 613-990-6012
Director General: International: EARL WISEMAN; Phone: 613-993-1873

Director General: Program Planning and Coordination: DAVID BALFOUR; Phone: 613-993-2574
Director General: Resource Management: JACQUE ROBICHAUD; Phone: 613-990-0189

Legal Services
Contact(s):
General Counsel: LILIANA LONGO; Phone: 613-990-8326

Oceans
Contact(s):
Assistant Deputy Minister: MATTHEW KING; Phone: 613-993-0850
Director General: Habitat Management and Environmental Science: GERRY SWANSON; Phone: 613-991-1280
Director General: Oceans Directorate: DANIEL McDOUGALL; Phone: 613-990-0001

Policy
Contact(s):
Assistant Deputy Minister: LISEANNE FORAND; Phone: 613-993-1808
Director General: Aquaculture Restructuring and Adjustment: DAVID RIDEOUT; Phone: 613-993-1914
Director General: Economic and Policy Analysis: LORI RIDGEWAY; Phone: 613-993-1914
Director General: Policy, Coordination, and Liaison: G. BEAUPRE; Phone: 613-990-0007
Director General: Strategic Priorities and Planning: MIKE ALEXANDER; Phone: 613-990-0146

Science
Contact(s):
Assistant Deputy Minister: JOHN DAVIS; Phone: 613-990-5123
Director General: Fisheries and Oceans Science: WILLIAM DOUBLEDAY; Phone: 613-990-0271
Director General: Hydrography: TONY O'CONNOR; Phone: 613-995-4413
Director General: Program Planning and Coordination: BRIAN WILSON; Phone: 613-990-0149

ENVIRONMENTAL CONSERVATION SERVICE
15th Fl., Place Vincent Massey, 351 St. Joseph Blvd., Hull, Quebec K1A OH3 Canada
Description: In Environmental Conservation Service (ECS) our goal is to ensure that future generations of Canadians inherit a natural environment as rich as the one we enjoy today. We work with many partners--individual Canadians, environmental and community groups, Aboriginal peoples, industry, other levels of government, and international organizations. We provide information on the natural environment to Canadians.
Contact(s):
Assistant Deputy Minister: KAREN BROWN; Phone: 819-997-2161; Fax: 819-997-1541
Director General: KEN SATO

ATLANTIC REGION ENVIRONMENT CANADA
63 E. Main St., Box 1590, Sackville, New Brunswick E0A 3C0 Canada
Phone: 506-364-5044; Fax: 506-364-5062
Contact(s):
Regional Director: GEORGE FINNEY

ONTARIO REGION ENVIRONMENT CANADA
4905 Dufferin St., Dawnsview, Ontario M3H 5T4 Canada
Phone: 416-739-5839; Fax: 416-739-5845
Contact(s):
Regional Director: SIMON LLEWELLYN

PACIFIC AND YUKON REGION: ENVIRONMENT CANADA
Suite 700, 1200 West 73rd Ave., Vancouver, British Columbia V4K-6H9 Canada
Phone: 604-664-4065; Fax: 604-664-4068
Contact(s):
Regional Director (Acting): LESLIE CHURCHLAND

PRAIRIE AND NORTHERN REGION
Canadian Wildlife Service; Environment Canada, Rm. 200, Twin Atria Bldg. #2, 4999-98th Ave., Edmonton, Alberta T6B 2X3 Canada
Phone: 780-951-8853; Fax: 780-495-2615
Contact(s):
Regional Director: GERALD McKEATING

QUEBEC REGION ENVIRONMENT CANADA
Canadian Wildlife Service, 1141 Route de l'Eglise, P.O. Box 10100, 9th Floor, Sainte-Foy, Quebec G1V 4H5 Canada
Phone: 418-648-2543; Fax: 418-649-6575
Contact(s):
Director: ISABELLE RINGUET

ENVIRONMENTAL PROTECTION SERVICE
Place Vincent Massey, 351 Blvd. St. Joseph, Hull, Quebec, Ontario K1A 0H3 Canada
Description: Purpose is to formulate and take action to meet threats to environment arising through adverse impacts of human activities. Priority responsibilities include toxic chemicals, acid rain ozone depletion, urban smog, and the ongoing management of concerns such as hazardous wastes.
Contact(s):
Assistant Deputy Minister: H. A. CLARKE; Phone: 819-997-1575
Assistant Director General of Regulatory Affairs and Program Integration: J. MOORE; Phone: 819-997-5674
Chief of Operations: B. SCHACKER; Phone: 819-953-1706
Director General of Special Projects: G. ALLARD; Phone: 819-994-3408
Director of Finance and Administration Branch: D. BOWIE; Phone: 819-997-3391
Director of Personnel Branch: C. LANGLOIS; Phone: 819-953-1183
Executive Assistant: C. GRAHAM; Phone: 819-997-1575

AIR POLLUTION PREVENTION DIRECTORATE
Contact(s):
Assistant Director of Transboundary Air Issues Branch: WAYNE DRAPER; Phone: 819-953-8441; Fax: 819-953-9547
Director General: D. EGAR, Place Vincent Massey, 11e et., 351, Blvd., St. Joseph Hull, Quebec K1A 0H3 Canada; Phone: 819-997-1298; Fax: 819-953-9547
Director of Global Air Issues Branch: A. MacKENZIE; Phone: 819-994-1924; Fax: 819-994-0549

ENVIRONMENTAL TECHNOLOGY ADVANCEMENT DIRECTORATE
Contact(s):
Director General: ED NORRENA; Phone: 819-953-3160; Fax: 819-953-9029

NATIONAL PROGRAMS DIRECTORATE
Contact(s):
Assistant Director General: R. BOULDEN; Phone: 819-997-2019; Fax: 819-997-0086
Assistant Director of Environmental Assessment: B. STACEY; Phone: 819-953-1690
Director of Environmental Emergencies: M. TAYLOR; Phone: 819-953-0607
Director of Office of Enforcement: D. KIMMETT; Phone: 819-953-1523; Fax: 819-997-0086

TOXICS POLLUTION PREVENTION DIRECTORATE
Contact(s):
Director General: V. SHANTORA, Place Vincent Massey, 11e et., 351, Blvd., St. Joseph Hull, Quebec K1A 0H3 Canada; Phone: 819-953-1114; Fax: 819-953-5371
Director of Commercial Chemicals Evaluation Branch: J. BUCCINI; Phone: 819-997-1499; Fax: 819-953-4936
Director of Hazardous Waste Management Branch: G. CORNWALL; Phone: 819-953-1712; Fax: 819-953-7643
Director of National Office of Pollution Prevention: J. RIORDAN; Phone: 819-953-3353; Fax: 819-953-7970

EGYPTIAN ENVIRONMENTAL AFFAIRS AGENCY
30, Misr Helwan St., Maadi, Cairo Egypt
Phone: 02-525-6442; Fax: 02-525-6451
Contact(s):
H.E. Minister: NADIA M. EBEID
DR. NIRVANA KHADR; Phone: 02-525-6447
Publication(s): *Annual Report; EAS, National Workplan and Law*

INSTITUTO NACIONAL DE BIODIVERSIDAD (INBIO)
Apdo. #22-3100, Santo Domingo Costa Rica
Phone: 506-244-0690; Fax: 506-244-2816; E-mail: askinbio@quercus.inbio.ac.cr
Founded: 1989
Description: INBIO is conducting a biodiversity inventory in Costa Rica's protected areas. Through this knowledge, society will be able to appreciate and value the resources contained in the wildlands, and use this information in a sustainable manner.
Contact(s):
Deputy Director: DR. ALFIO PIVA
Biodiversity Education: SONIA ROJAS
Biodiversity Garden: NATALIA ZAMORA
Biodiversity Inventory: CARLOS MARIO RODRIGUEZ
Biodiversity Prospecting Coordinator: DR. NICOLAS MATEO
Communication: ANA GLENA VALDEZ
Director General: DR. RODRIGO GAMEZ
Information Management Coordinator: DR. ERIC MATA
Publications: MARIA LOURDES GONZOLEZ
Publication(s): *Biodiversity Prospecting; Biodiversidad de Costa Rica: Lecturas para Ecoturistas; Guia de Aves de Costa Rica; Mariposas Heliconius de Costa Rica.*

MINISTRY OF THE ENVIRONMENT OF THE CZECH REPUBLIC
Vrsovicka 65, 100 10 Prague 10 Czech Republic
Phone: 420-2-6712-2769; Fax: 420-2-6731-0370; E-mail: roudna@env.cz
Contact(s):
Chairman: DR. PETER ROTH; Phone: 420-2-67122041; Fax: 420-2-67311096; E-mail: roth@env.cz
Minister: MILENA ROUDNA; Phone: 420-2-67122769; Fax: 420-2-67310307; E-mail: roudna@env.cz

ENVIRONMENTAL COMMISSION
Academy of Sciences of The Czech Republic, Narodni 3, 11720 Praha 1 Czech Republic
Phone: 420-2-2420538; Fax: 420-2-24220944
Contact(s):
Secretary: MILOS KUZVART; E-mail: petr.kuzvart@enc.cz

NATURAL RESOURCES CANADA, CANADIAN FOREST SERVICE
580 Booth St., Ottawa, Ontario K1A 0E4 Canada
Web site: www.NRCan.gc.ca/cfs
Description: CFS promotes sustainable development of Canada's forests and competitiveness of the Canadian forest sector for the well-being of present and future generations of Canadians. The CFS also establishes links with other non-governmental organizations to better address issues such as international trade, market access and the sustainable management of forests world-wide.
Contact(s):
Deputy Minister: JEAN C. McLOSKEY; Phone: 613-992-3456; Fax: 613-992-3828
Minister: ANNE McLELLAN; Phone: 613-996-2007; Fax: 613-996-4516
Assistant Deputy Minister of Canadian Forest Service: YVAN HARDY; Phone: 613-947-7400; Fax: 613-947-7395
Director General: GERRIT VAN RAALTE, P.O. Box 4000, Regent St., Fredericton, New Brunswick E3B 5P7 Canada; Phone: 506-452-3508; Fax: 506-452-3140
Director General: NORMAND LAFRENIERE, 1055 du P.E.P.S. St., P.O. Box 3800, Sainte-Foy, Quebec G1V-4C7 Canada; Phone: 418-648-3957; Fax: 418-648-7317
Director General: ED KONDO, P.O. Box 490, 1219 Queen St. East, Sault Ste. Marie, Ontario P6A 5M7 Canada; Phone: 705-949-9461/Ext. 2039; Fax: 705-759-5714
Director General: BOYD CASE, 5320 122 St., Edmonton, Alberta T6H 3S5 Canada; Phone: 403-435-7202; Fax: 403-435-7396
Director General: PAUL ADDISON, 506 West Burnside Rd., Victoria, British Columbia V8Z 1M5 Canada; Phone: 604-363-0608; Fax: 604-363-6088
Director General for Industry, Economics and Programs Branch (IEPB): DOUG KETCHESON; Phone: 613-947-9052; Fax: 613-947-9038
Director General of Policy, Planning and International Affairs Branch (PPIAB): JACQUES CARETTE; Phone: 613-947-9100; Fax: 613-947-9038
Director General of Science Branch: GORDON MILLER; Phone: 613-947-8984; Fax: 613-947-9090
Director of Communications and Executive Services: SYLVIE LETELLIER; Phone: 613-947-7404; Fax: 613-947-7396
Manager of Sector Human Resources Unit: SYLVIA FREHNER; Phone: 613-947-7386; Fax: 613-947-7409

UNITED NATIONS RESEARCH INSTITUTE FOR SOCIAL DEVELOPMENT (UNRISD)
Palais des Nations, CH 1211, Geneva 10 Switzerland
Phone: 41-22-798-8400, 798-5850; Fax: 41-22-740-0791; E-mail: info@UNRISD.org; Web site: www.unrisd.org
Founded: 1963
Description: UNRISD is an autonomous agency that researches the social dimensions of contemporary development problems. The Institute provides governments, development agencies, grassroots organizations, and scholars with a better understanding of how development policies and processes of economic, social, and environmental change affect different social groups. UNRISD promotes original research and strengthens research capacity in developing countries.
Contact(s):
Director: DHARAM GHAI
Publication(s): *UNRISD News; The Challenge of Peace; Focus on Integrating Gender into The Politics of Development; Discussion Papers; Occasional Papers; Briefing Papers; Conference Reports; Monographs; Co-publications.*
Keyword(s): Agriculture, Biodiversity, Conservation of Protected Areas, Developing Countries, Environment, Fisheries, Forest Management, Internships, Land Use Planning, Research, Rural Development, Sustainable Development

STATE AND PROVINCIAL GOVERNMENT AGENCIES

UNITED STATES

ALABAMA

GOVERNOR OF ALABAMA: DONALD SIEGELMAN
State Capitol, 600 Dexter Ave., Montgomery, AL 36130
Phone: 334-242-7100

ALABAMA COOPERATIVE EXTENSION SYSTEM
109 Duncan Hall, Auburn, AL 36849-5612
Phone: 334-844-4444; Web site: www.aces.edu/
Founded: 1914
Description: The extension system (Alabama A&M and Auburn Universities), through its statewide network of County Extension Offices, conducts informal education programs using research-based knowledge and techniques. Programs are offered in agriculture and forestry profitability; developing, conserving and managing natural resources; enhancing family and individual well being; developing human resources; and community development.
Contact(s):
Extension Director: STEPHEN B. JONES; E-mail: sjones@acesag.auburn.edu
Assistant Director/Family Programs: MARTHA R. JOHNSON, ACES, 107-A Duncan Hall, Auburn University, AL 36849; Phone: 334-844-5540; E-mail: mjohnson@acesag.auburn.edu
Communications Specialist, Publications: CAROLYN A. WHATLEY, ACES, 122 Duncan Hall Annex, Auburn University, AL 36849; Phone: 334-844-5690; E-mail: cwhatley@acesag.auburn.edu
Extension Wildlife Specialist: JAMES ARMSTRONG, Dept. of Zoology and Wildlife Science, 331 Funchess Hall, Auburn University, AL 36849; Phone: 334-844-9233; Fax: 334-844-0234
Publication(s): *Contact Extension Communications*
Keyword(s): Agriculture, Fisheries, Forests and Forestry, Gardening and Horticulture, Wildlife Management

ALABAMA COOPERATIVE FISH AND WILDLIFE RESEARCH UNIT (USDI)
331 Funchess Hall, Auburn University, Auburn, AL 36849
Phone: 334-844-4796
Founded: 1935
Description: The unit is sponsored by the Biological Resources Division, U.S. Geological Survey; Alabama Department of Conservation and Natural Resources, Division of Game and Fish; Auburn University; and the Wildlife Management Institute. Fish and wildlife research, graduate education and technical assistance are the unit's primary purposes.
Contact(s):
Leader: DR. JAMES B. GRAND
Assistant Leader of Fisheries: DR. ELISE R. IRWIN
Assistant Leader of Wildlife: DR. MICHAEL S. MITCHELL
Keyword(s): Biodiversity, Endangered and Threatened Species, Fisheries, Wildlife and Wildlife Habitat, Wildlife Management

ALABAMA DEPARTMENT OF AGRICULTURE AND INDUSTRIES
The Richard Beard Bldg., P.O. Box 3336, Montgomery, AL 36109-0336
Phone: 334-240-7171
Description: The Alabama Department of Agriculture and Industries is responsible for enforcing the laws of Alabama relating to agriculture. It also works to provide agribusiness assistance such as marketing, loan mediation, and trade information. The department strives to ensure consumer safety and to promote all of Alabama agriculture.
Contact(s):
Commissioner: CHARLES BISHOP

ALABAMA DEPARTMENT OF CONSERVATION AND NATURAL RESOURCES
64 N. Union St., Montgomery, AL 36130
Phone: 334-242-3486; Fax: 334-242-3489
Contact(s):
Assistant Commissioner: BOB MACRORY; Phone: 334-242-3487
Chief of Accounting: SUSAN MIMS; Phone: 334-242-3260
Chief of Engineering: TERRY BOYD; Phone: 334-242-3476
Chief of Film and Video Section: DENNIS HOLT, P.O. Box 278, Pelham, AL 35124; Phone: 205-663-7938
Chief of Information: DAN BROTHERS; Phone: 334-242-3151/800-262-3151
Chief of Personnel and Payroll: JEFF GREENE; Phone: 334-242-3502
Commissioner: JAMES D. MARTIN; Phone: 334-242-3486
Director of Division of Game and Fish: CHARLES D. KELLEY; Phone: 334-242-3465
Director of Division of Marine Police: WILLIAM B. GARNER; Phone: 334-242-3673
Director of Division of Marine Resources: R. VERNON MINTON, P.O. Box 189, Dauphin Island, AL 36528; Phone: 334-861-2882
Director of Division of State Lands: JAMES H. GRIGGS; Phone: 334-242-3484
Director of Division of State Parks (Acting): DON COOLEY; Phone: 334-242-3334
Editor: CINDY THOMPSON; Phone: 334-242-3151/1-800-262-3151; Fax: 334-242-1880
Property Inventory Manager: JOHN F. DAVIS; Phone: 334-242-2574
Publication(s): *Outdoor Alabama*

ALABAMA DEPARTMENT OF ECONOMIC AND COMMUNITY AFFAIRS, COASTAL PROGRAMS (ADECA)
1208 Main St., Daphne, AL 36526
Phone: 334-626-0042; Fax: 334-626-3503; E-mail: ala-coastal@surf.nos.noaa.gov
Founded: 1979
Description: The program goal of the Alabama Coastal Area Management Program is to protect and, where possible, enhance or restore Alabama's coastal resources for this and succeeding generations.
Contact(s):
Chief: GIL GILDER; Phone: 334-242-5502
Manager: PHILLIP HINESLEY; Phone: 334-626-0042; Fax: 334-626-3503; E-mail: phinesley@surf.nos.noaa.gov
Publication(s): *Alabama's Coastal Connection; Research Roundup; Various Program Brochures*
Keyword(s): Coasts, Conservation, Planning Management

ALABAMA DEPARTMENT OF ENVIRONMENTAL MANAGEMENT
P.O. Box 301463, Montgomery, AL 36130-1463
Phone: 205-271-7700; Fax: 205-271-7950
Founded: 1982
Description: To respond in an efficient, comprehensive, and coordinated manner to environmental problems, thereby assuring a safe, healthful and productive environment. Encompasses water quality, public water supply, underground injection control, solid waste, hazardous waste, air pollution control, well water standards, operator certification and coastal area functions.
Contact(s):
Director: JAMES W. WARR
Deputy Director: MARILYN ELLIOTT
Office of General Counsel: OLIVIA JENKINS
Staff of Air Division: RON GORE
Staff of Field Operations: STEVE JENKINS
Staff of Land Division: GERALD HARDY
Staff of Office of Education and Outreach: JIM MOORE
Staff of Permits and Services: JOHN POOLE
Staff of Public Affairs: CLARK BRUNER
Staff of Water Division: CHARLES HORN
Publication(s): *Environmental Update*

Keyword(s): Air Quality and Pollution, Coasts, Solid Waste Management, Water Pollution Management, Wetlands

ALABAMA FORESTRY COMMISSION
513 Madison Ave., Montgomery, AL 36130
Phone: 334-240-9300; Fax: 334-240-9390
Description: The FC was created by the 1969 session of the Alabama Legislature and is charged by law to protect, conserve and increase the timber and forest resources of the state. A seven-member board is the policymaking body of the Commission. The State Forester is Chief Administrative Officer. Fire prevention and suppression, educational programs and materials and free forest management assistance are some of the services offered to the general public.
Contact(s):
Chairman: JAMES D. SPEARS
Assistant State Forester: RICHARD H. CUMBIE; Phone: 334-240-9367
Director of Administration Division: JOHN C. KUMMEL; Phone: 334-240-9333
Director of Forest Programs Division: DAVID FREDERICK; Phone: 334-240-9335
Editor: KIM GILLILAND; Phone: 334-240-9355
State Forester: TIMOTHY C. BOYCE; Phone: 334-240-9304
Publication(s): *Alabama's TREASURED Forests*
Keyword(s): Environmental and Conservation Education, Forest Management, Forests and Forestry, Renewable Resources, Sustainable Development, Urban Forestry

ALABAMA SEA GRANT PROGRAM
Mississippi and Alabama Sea Grant Consortium, Caylor Bldg., Gulf Coast Research Lab., P.O. Box 7000, Ocean Springs, AL 39566-7000
Phone: 228-875-9341; Fax: 228-875-0528
Contact(s):
Director: BARRY A. COSTA-PIERCE; E-mail: b.costapierce@usm.edu
Coordinator and Extension Marine Specialist: DR. RICHARD K. WALLACE, Alabama Sea Grant Extension Program: 4170 Commanders Dr., Mobile, AL 36615; Phone: 334-438-5690; Fax: 334-438-5670

ALABAMA SOIL AND WATER CONSERVATION COMMITTEE
Exe. Dir., P.O. Box 304800, Montgomery, AL 36130
Contact(s):
Chair: MICKY SMITH, Rt. 1, Box 85A, Emelle, AL 35459; Phone: 205-652-7459/205-652-3438
Executive Director: STEPHEN M. CAUTHEN, P.O. Box 304800, Montgomery, AL 36130-4800; Phone: 334-242-2681; Fax: 334-242-0551; E-mail: scauthen@dsmd.dsmd.state.al.us

ALASKA

GOVERNOR OF ALASKA: TONY KNOWLES
P.O. Box 110001, Juneau, AK 99811-0001
Phone: 907-465-3500

ALASKA COOPERATIVE FISH AND WILDLIFE RESEARCH UNIT
209 Irving I Bldg., P.O. Box 757020, University of Alaska Fairbanks, Fairbanks, AK 99775-7020
Phone: 907-474-7661
Founded: 1950
Description: Sponsored jointly by the U.S. Geological Service, Alaska Department of Fish and Game, University of Alaska Fairbanks, U.S. Fish and Wildlife Service and Wildlife Management Institute, the Unit conducts graduate education and research programs on the ecology and management of Alaskan fish and wildlife and their habitats.
Contact(s):
Leader: DR. F. JOSEPH MARGRAF
Assistant Leader of Ecology: DR. A. DAVID McGUIRE
Assistant Leader of Fisheries: DR. JACQUELINE D. LAPERRIERE
Assistant Leader of Wildlife: DR. BRAD GRIFFITH
Keyword(s): Aquatic Habitats, Ecology, Fisheries, Wildlife and Wildlife Habitat, Wildlife Management

ALASKA DEPARTMENT OF ENVIRONMENTAL CONSERVATION
410 Willoughby Ave., Juneau, AK 99801-1795
Phone: 907-465-5000
Founded: 1971
Description: Created by the Seventh Alaska Legislature to protect the quality of the state's natural resources and the health and quality of life of its people. The department has broad regulatory authority in the areas of water quality, drinking water, air quality, solid waste disposal, oil spills, subsurface pollution, pesticides, food safety, seafood wholesomeness, sanitation and radiation. The department also has programs for construction of water, sewer and solid waste facilities in Alaskan cities and villages.
Contact(s):
Commissioner: MICHELE BROWN; Phone: 907-465-5065
Deputy Commissioner (Acting): KURT FREDRIKSSON; Phone: 907-465-5065
Director of Division of Administrative Services: BARBARA FRANK; Phone: 907-465-5010
Director of Division of Air and Water Quality: TOM CHAPPLE; Phone: 907-269-7686
Director of Division of Environmental Health: JANICE ADAIR; Phone: 907-269-7644
Director of Division of Facilities Construction and Operations: DAN EASTON; Phone: 907-465-5180
Director of Spill Prevention and Response (Acting): LARRY DIETRICK; Phone: 907-465-5250
Director of Statewide Public Service: MIKE CONWAY; Phone: 907-465-5337
Public Information: CHARLES FEDULLO; Phone: 907-269-3784
Keyword(s): Air Quality and Pollution, Environmental Health, Environmental Planning, Environmental Protection, Public Health Protection, Solid Waste Management, Water Pollution Management, Water Quality

ALASKA DEPARTMENT OF FISH AND GAME
P.O. Box 25526, Juneau, AK 99802
Phone: 907-465-4100
Description: A research and management agency whose mission is to develop and organize its technical, human and fiscal assets to maintain, rehabilitate and enhance the fish and wildlife resources of the state, and to provide for their sustained optimum use consistent with the social, cultural, environmental and economic needs of the public.
Contact(s):
Board of Fisheries Chairman: DR. JOHN R. WHITE, Bering Sea Dental Center, P.O. Box 190, Bethel, AK 99559
Board of Fisheries Vice Chair: DAN J. COFFEY, 207 E. Northern Lights Blvd., Suite 200, Anchorage, AK 99503
Board of Game Chair: LORI QUAKENBUSH, P.O. Box 82391, Fairbanks, AK 99708
Board of Game Vice Chairman: GREG ROCZICKA, P.O. Box513, Bethel, AK 99559
Commissioner: FRANK RUE
Deputy Commissioner: ROBERT BOSWORTH
Deputy Commissioner: DAVID BENTON
Director of Commercial Fisheries Management and Development Division: DOUG MECOM; Phone: 907-465-4210
Director of Division of Administration: KEVIN BROOKS; Phone: 907-465-5999
Director of Division of Sport Fish: KEVIN DELANEY; Phone: 907-465-4180
Director of Division of Subsistence: MARY PETE; Phone: 907-465-4147
Director of Division of Wildlife Conservation: WAYNE REGELIN; Phone: 907-465-4190
Director of Habitat and Restoration Division: KEN TAYLOR; Phone: 907-465-4105

Executive Director of Board of Fish: DIANA COTE; Phone: 907-465-6098
Executive Director of Board of Game: DIANA COTE; Phone: 907-465-6095
Public Communications Section: NANCY LONG; Phone: 907-465-6167
Special Assistant for Legislative Liaison: GERON BRUCE; Phone: 907-465-6143
Keyword(s): Fisheries, Hunting, Renewable Resources, Sport Fishing, Wildlife and Wildlife Habitat

ALASKA DEPARTMENT OF NATURAL RESOURCES
400 Willoughby, 5th Fl., Juneau, AK 99801
Phone: 907-465-2400
Contact(s):
Commissioner: JOHN SHIVELY
Director of Division of Geological and Geophysical Surveys (Acting): MILTON WILTSE, 794 University Ave. Suite 200, Fairbanks, AK 99709-3654; Phone: 907-451-5000
Director of Division of Agriculture: JAY KERTULLA, 1800 Glenn Hwy. Suite 12: P.O. Box 949, Palmer, AK 99645-0949; Phone: 907-745-7200
Director of Division of Land: JANE ANGVIK, 3601 C St. Suite 1122, Anchorage, AK 99503-5947; Phone: 907-269-8503
Director of Division of Mining and Water Management: JULES TILESTON, 3601 C St., Anchorage, AK 99503-5935; Phone: 907-269-8600
Director of Division of Oil and Gas: KEN BOYD, 3601 C St. Suite 1380, Anchorage, AK 99503-5948; Phone: 907-269-8800
Director of Division of Parks and Outdoor Recreation: JIM STRATTON, 3601 C St. Suite 1200, Anchorage, AK 99503-5921; Phone: 907-269-8700
State Forester of Division of Forestry: TOM BOUTIN, 3601 C St. Suite 1030, Anchorage, AK 99503; Phone: 907-269-8463
Keyword(s): Agriculture, Forests and Forestry, Land Use Planning, Public Lands, Renewable Resources

ALASKA DEPARTMENT OF PUBLIC SAFETY
P.O. Box 111200, Juneau, AK 99811
Phone: 907-465-4322
Description: Responsible for enforcing all Fish and Game laws and regulations of the state.
Contact(s):
Commissioner: RONALD L. OTTE
Director of Fish and Wildlife Protection: COL. JOHN D. GLASS
Enforcement Commander: MAJ. JOSEPH S. D'AMICO
Operations Commander: CAPT. ALAN G. CAIN
Keyword(s): Hunting, Resource Law Enforcement, Sport Fishing, Trapping, Wildlife Management

Division of Fish and Wildlife Protection
5700 E. Tudor Rd., Anchorage, AK 99507
Phone: 907-269-5509

ALASKA HEALTH PROJECT
218 East 4th Avenue, Anchorage, AK 99501
Phone: 907-276-2864; Fax: 907-279-3089
Founded: 1980
Description: To provide information and advocacy on occupational and environmental health issues in Alaska, the Pacific Northwest and Canada.
Contact(s):
Executive Director: DANIEL MIDDAUGH
Instructor: R. J. GRYDER
Publication(s): *Involve waste management and worker health, and are inclusive of a 22 edition list.*
Keyword(s): Communications, Engineering, Environmental and Conservation Education, Solid Waste, Training

ALASKA SEA GRANT COLLEGE PROGRAM
University of Alaska, P.O. Box 755040, Fairbanks, AK 99775-5040
Phone: 907-474-7086; Fax: 907-474-6285; E-mail: fnrkd@uaf.edu; Web site: www.uaf.edu/seagrant/
Description: A state/federal partnership administered by the National Oceanic and Atmospheric Administration and the University of Alaska that sponsors and conducts marine research, graduate education, marine industry advisory services and formal and nonformal public education aimed at promoting the wise use and conservation of Alaska's coastal and marine resources.
Contact(s):
Director: RONALD K. DEARBORN; E-mail: fnrkd@uaf.edu
Director of Marine Advisory Program: DONALD E. KRAMER, University of Alaska Carlton Trust Bldg.: Suite 110: 2221 E. Northern Lights Blvd., Anchorage, AK 99508-4140; Phone: 907-274-9691; Fax: 907-277-5242; E-mail: afdek@uaa.alaska.edu
Communications Manager: KURT BYERS, Alaska Sea Grant College Program, University of Alaska: P.O. Box 755040, Fairbanks, AK 99775-5040; Phone: 907-474-6702; E-mail: fnkmb1@uaf.edu
Publications Manager: SUE KELLER, P.O. Box 755040, Fairbanks, AK 99775-5040; Phone: 907-474-6703; E-mail: fnsk@uaf.edu
Publication(s): *Guide to Marine Mammals of Alaska; Management Strategies for Exploited Fish Populations; Biennial Program Report; Sea Week Curriculum Series; posters, videos; free catalog*
Keyword(s): Coasts, Environmental and Conservation Education, Fisheries, Marine Mammals, Oceanography

ALASKA STATE EXTENSION SERVICES
Alaska Cooperative Extension Bldg., P.O. Box 756180, University of Alaska, Fairbanks, AK 99775-6180
Phone: 907-474-7246; Fax: 907-474-6971; Web site: zorba.uafadm.alaska.edu/coop-ext/
Contact(s):
Director (Interim): DR. ANTHONY T. NAKAZAWA; E-mail: anatn@uaa.alaska.edu
Agriculture & Community Development: SARAH McCLELLAN; Phone: 907-452-8251, ext.3248; E-mail: ffsem@uaf.edu
Resource Development Agent: ROBERT F. GORMAN; Phone: 907-747-6065; E-mail: ffrfg@uaf.edu
Land Resources Agent: MICHELE HEBERT; Phone: 907-452-1530; E-mail: ffmah@uaf.edu
Fish and NR Specialist: PETER J. STORTZ, CES/Palmer Research Center, 533 E. Fireweed Ln., Palmer, AK 99645; Phone: 907-746-9459; Fax: 907-746-2677

AMERICAN SAMOA

GOVERNOR OF AMERICAN SAMOA
Executive Office Bldg., Pago Pago, American Samoa 96799
Phone: 011-684-633-4116
Contact(s):
Governor: TAUESE P.F. SUNIA

AMERICAN SAMOA DEPARTMENT OF AGRICULTURE
American Samoa Government, Pago Pago, American Samoa 96799 American Samoa
Phone: 011-684-699-9272; Fax: 011-684-699-4031
Contact(s):
Director: PHILO F. MALUIA

ARIZONA

GOVERNOR OF ARIZONA: JANE DEE HULL
State House, 1700 W. Washington, Phoenix, AZ 85007
Phone: 602-542-4331

ARIZONA COOPERATIVE FISH AND WILDLIFE RESEARCH UNIT (USDI)
Rm. 104, Biological Sciences East, University of Arizona, Tucson, AZ 85721
Phone: 520-621-1959; Fax: 520-621-8801

STATE AND PROVINCIAL GOVERNMENT AGENCIES - ARIZONA

Description: The Unit is a cooperative effort by the U.S. Department of Interior, the Arizona Game and Fish Department, the University of Arizona and the Wildlife Management Institute. The Unit conducts research on fish and wildlife questions for client agencies.
Contact(s):
Leader: O. EUGENE MAUGHAN

ARIZONA DEPARTMENT OF AGRICULTURE
1688 W. Adams, Phoenix, AZ 85007
Phone: 602-542-4373; Fax: 602-542-5420
Description: The ADA regulates and supports Arizona agriculture in a manner that encourages farming, ranching and agribusiness while protecting consumers and natural resources. The ADA provides a number of services to its regulated industry, as well as the general public.
Contact(s):
Director: SHELDON R. JONES; Phone: 602-542-0998

Animal Services Division
1688 W. Adams, Phoenix, AZ 85007
Description: The Animal Services Division is responsible for the protection of livestock from theft and disease and for the regulation of the state's aquaculture, dairy, egg and slaughtering and meat-processing industries.
Contact(s):
Associate Director: JOE LANE; Phone: 602-542-6309

Environmental Services Division
Description: The Environmental Services Division is responsible for regulating the agricultural industry to ensure the safe use of pesticides and to ensure the quality of feed, fertilizer and pesticide formulations.
Contact(s):
Associate Director: JACK D. PETERSON; Phone: 602-542-3579

Integrated Pest Management (IPM)
Contact(s):
Fruit and Vegetable State Standardization and Federal State Grade Inspection (IPM): AL DAVIS
Native Plant Program Manager of IPM: JIM McGINNIS
Non-Program Manager of IPM: DONNA DIAZ
Port of Entry Program Manager of IPM: DIANE PARKER
Survey and Detection Program Manager of IPM: DONNA DIAZ
Keyword(s): Agriculture, Pesticides

Plant Services Division
Phone: 602-542-0996; Fax: 602-542-0999
Description: The Plant Services Division is responsible for enforcement of state plant regulatory statutes, state agricultural industry plants, and plant health service programs.
Contact(s):
Associate Director: JOHN CARAVETTA; Phone: 602-542-0994

ARIZONA DEPARTMENT OF ENVIRONMENTAL QUALITY
3033 N. Central Ave., Phoenix, AZ 85012
Phone: 602-207-2300
Founded: 1987
Description: The Arizona Department of Environmental Quality shall preserve, protect, and enhance the environment and the public health, and shall be a leader in the development of public policy to maintain and improve the quality of Arizona's air, land, and water resources.
Contact(s):
Acting Deputy Director: CHARLES MATTHEWSON; Phone: 602-207-2204
Director: JACQUELIN E. SCHAFER; Phone: 602-207-2203
Director of Administration Division: JOHN F. TIMKO
Director of Air Quality Division: NANCY C. WRONA; Phone: 602-207-2308
Director of Waste Programs Division: JEAN A. CALHOUN; Phone: 602-207-2381
Director of Water Quality Division: KAREN L. SMITH; Phone: 602-207-2306
Keyword(s): Air Quality and Pollution, Environmental and Conservation Education, Environmental Protection, Pollution Prevention, Solid Waste Management, Toxic Substances, Water Pollution, Water Quality

ARIZONA GAME AND FISH DEPARTMENT
2221 W. Greenway Rd., Phoenix, AZ 85023-4312
Phone: 602-942-3000
Description: The mission of the Arizona Game and Fish Department is to conserve, enhance and restore Arizona's diverse wildlife resources and habitats through aggressive protection and management programs, and to provide wildlife resources and safe watercraft and off-highway vehicle recreation for the enjoyment, appreciation and use by present and future generations.
Contact(s):
Deputy Director: STEVE FERRELL
Director: DUANE L. SHROUFE
Administrative Officer: G. PATRICK O'BRIEN
Assistant Director of Field Operations Division: MIKE SENN
Assistant Director of Information and Education Division: DAVE DAUGHTRY
Assistant Director of Special Services Division: JIM BURTON
Assistant Director of Wildlife Management Division: BRUCE TAUBERT
Commissioner Chair: WILLIAM BERLAT
Funds and Contracts: ALAN SILVERBERG
Heritage Program Coordinator: ROBIN BECK
Personnel Manager: DIANA A. SHAFFER
Publications Editor: CAROL SEAY-GREENEY
Regional Coordinator: HEIDI VASILOFF
Publication(s): *Arizona Wildlife Views*
Keyword(s): Environmental and Conservation Education, Nongame Wildlife, Sport Fishing, Wildlife and Wildlife Habitat, Wildlife Management

ARIZONA GEOLOGICAL SURVEY
416 W. Congress St., Suite 100, Tucson, AZ 85701
Phone: 520-770-3500
Founded: 1881
Description: Develops, maintains, and disseminates information related to the geologic framework, geological hazards and limitations and mineral and energy resources. Provides staff support for the Arizona Oil and Gas Conservation Commission, which regulates the drilling and production of oil, gas, geothermal, carbon dioxide and helium resources.
Contact(s):
Director and State Geologist: DR. LARRY D. FELLOWS; Phone: 520-770-3500
Publication(s): *Arizona Geology; circulars; special papers; bulletins; maps; open-file reports; miscellaneous maps; contributed maps and reports; digital information; Down-To-Earth*
Keyword(s): Energy, Engineering, Environmental and Conservation Education, Geology, Land Use Planning, Mineral Resources, Public Information, Research, Water Resources

ARIZONA LAND DEPARTMENT
1616 W. Adams St., Phoenix, AZ 85007
Phone: 602-542-4621; Fax: 602-542-2590
Founded: 1915
Description: The purpose of the Arizona State Land Department is to manage 9.4 million acres of Trust lands, through leasing and sale, in order to generate revenue for 14 state institutions. Resource protection and preservation is an integral part of trust land management.
Contact(s):
Commissioner of State Land: J. DENNIS WELLS
Deputy Commissioner of State Land: MICHAEL E. ANABLE
Director of Administration and Resource Analysis Division: LYNN LARSON; Phone: 602-542-4621
Director of Fire Management Division: KIRK ROWDABAUGH; Phone: 602-255-4059
Director of Forestry Division: T. MIKE HART; Phone: 602-542-4627

Director of Natural Resources Division: ROBERT E. YOUNT; Phone: 602-542-4625
Director of Operations Division: RICHARD B. OXFORD; Phone: 602-542-4602
Director of Planning and Land Disposition Division: BILL FOSTER; Phone: 602-542-1704
NRCD Administrator: BILL WARSKOW; Phone: 602-542-2699; Fax: 602-524-4688; E-mail: wwarskow@lnd.state.az.us
Keyword(s): Land Use Planning, Public Lands, Renewable Resources, Sustainable Development, Water Resources

ARIZONA STATE EXTENSION SERVICES
University of Arizona, P.O. Box 210036, Tucson, AZ 85721-0036
Phone: 520-621-7205; Fax: 520-621-1314; Web site: ag.arizona.edu/extension/
Contact(s):
Associate Dean and Director of Cooperative Extension: DR. JAMES A. CHRISTENSON; Phone: 520-621-7209; E-mail: jimc@ag.arizona.edu
Associate Director, Programs: DEBORAH YOUNG; Phone: 520-621-5308; E-mail: djyoung@ag.arizona.edu
Assistant Director, 4-H: BILL PETERSON; Phone: 520-621-3623; E-mail: bpeters@ag.arizona.edu
Aquaculture Specialist: KEVIN FITZSIMMONS, Soil, Water, and Environmental Science, P.O. Box 210038, University of Arizona, Tucson, AZ 85721; Phone: 520-626-3324; E-mail: kevfitz@ag.arizona.edu
Natural Resources Specialist, Wildlife: LARRY SULLIVAN, School of Renewable Natural Resources: College of Agriculture, P.O. Box 210043, University of Arizona, Tucson, AZ 85721; Phone: 520-621-7998; Fax: 520-621-8801; E-mail: sullivan@ag.arizona.edu
Range Management and Forest Resources Program Chair: DR. GEORGE RUYLE, School of Renewable Natural Resources: College of Agriculture, P.O. Box 210043, University of Arizona, Tucson, AZ 85721; Phone: 520-621-1384; E-mail: gruyle@ag.arizona.edu
Watershed Management Specialist: DR. RICHARD HAWKINS, School of Renewable Natural Resources: College of Agriculture, P.O. Box 210043, University of Arizona, Tucson, AZ 85721; Phone: 520-621-7273; E-mail: rhawkins@ag.arizona.edu

ARIZONA STATE PARKS BOARD
1300 W. Washington Ave., Phoenix, AZ 85007
Phone: 602-542-4174; Fax: 602-542-4188; Web Site: www.pr.state.az.us
Founded: 1957
Description: The purposes and objectives of the Arizona State Parks Board are to select, acquire, preserve, establish and maintain areas of natural features, scenic beauty, historical and scientific interest, zoos and botanical gardens, for the education, pleasure, recreation and health of the people.
Contact(s):
Executive Director: KENNETH E. TRAVOUS
Chairperson: SHERI GRAHAM
Public Information Officer: ELLEN BILBREY; Phone: 602-542-1996
Publication(s): *Arizona Rivers and Streams Guide; Arizona State Trails Guides; Arizona Wildlife Viewing Guides; Access Arizona (disabled/seniors)*
Keyword(s): Botanical Gardens, Cultural Preservation, Natural Areas, Nongame Wildlife, Outdoor Recreation

ARKANSAS

GOVERNOR OF ARKANSAS: MIKE HUCKABEE
250 State Capitol, Little Rock, AR 72201
Phone: 501-682-2345

ARKANSAS COOPERATIVE RESEARCH UNIT
Department of Interior, U.S. Geological Survey, Biological Sciences SCEN 617, University of Arkansas, Fayetteville, AR 72701
Phone: 501-575-6709; Fax: 501-575-3330
Founded: 1988
Description: Primary purpose is field research, graduate research training in fisheries and wildlife resources, technical assistance and extension activities. Areas of research include habitat selection, life history and demographics, ecology, animal behavior and fisheries and wildlife biology.
Contact(s):
Unit Leader: DR. DAVID G. KREMENTZ
Keyword(s): Ecology, Fisheries, Research, Wildlife and Wildlife Habitat, Wildlife Management

ARKANSAS DEPARTMENT OF PARKS AND TOURISM
One Capitol Mall, Little Rock, AR 72201
Phone: 501-682-7777; Fax: 501-682-1364
Description: Develop, maintain and operate 50 state parks and four museums; advertise and promote all the state's recreation and travel potentials; provide information to attract retirees and others wanting to relocate; and assist communities in establishing local litter prevention and recycling projects.
Contact(s):
Executive Director: RICHARD W. DAVIES; Phone: 501-682-2535
Director of Administration: R. L. CARGILE; Phone: 501-682-2039
Director of Great River Road Division: NANCY CLARK; Phone: 501-682-1120
Director of Historical Resources and Museum Services Section: PATRICIA M. MURPHY; Phone: 501-682-3603
Director of History Commission: DR. JOHN L. FERGUSON; Phone: 501-682-6900
Director of Parks Division: GREG BUTTS; Phone: 501-682-7743
Director of Tourism Division: JOE DAVID RICE; Phone: 501-682-1088
Keep Arkansas Beautiful: ROBERT PHELPS; Phone: 501-682-3507
Outdoor Recreation Grants: BRYAN KELLAR; Phone: 501-682-1301
Keyword(s): Cultural Preservation, Environmental and Conservation Education, Environmental Preservation, Historic Preservation, Outdoor Recreation

ARKANSAS GAME AND FISH COMMISSION
#2 Natural Resources Dr., Little Rock, AR 72205
Phone: 501-223-6300
Founded: 1915
Description: The mission of the Arkansas Game and Fish Commission is to wisely manage the fish and wildlife resources of Arkansas while providing maximum enjoyment for the people.
Contact(s):
Chairman: WITT STEPHENS JR.; Phone: 501-748-2411
Director: STEVE N. WILSON; Phone: 501-223-6305; Fax: 501-223-6448; E-mail: snw001@agfc.state.ar.us
Assistant Director: SCOTT HENDERSON; Phone: 501-223-6309; Fax: 501-223-6448; E-mail: shenderson@agfc.state.ar.us
Assistant Director: SCOTT C. YAICH; Phone: 501-223-6307; Fax: 501-223-6448; E-mail: syaich@agfc.state.ar.us
Chief of Computer Services: BILL ROBINSON; Phone: 501-223-6368
Chief of Educational Services: REBECCA PATTERSON; Phone: 501-223-6370
Chief of Enforcement: LOREN HITCHCOCK; Phone: 501-223-6384
Chief of Fiscal Services: RAY SEBREN; Phone: 501-223-6341
Chief of Fisheries Management: ALLEN CARTER; Phone: 501-223-6371
Chief of Human Resources: MARY GRACE SMITH; Phone: 501-223-6317
Chief of Wildlife Management: DONNY HARRIS; Phone: 501-223-6359
Editor: KEITH SUTTON; Phone: 501-223-6406
Editor: JIM SPENCER; Phone: 501-223-6336
Legal Counsel: JIM GOOHART; Phone: 501-223-6327
Operational Services: BILL WHITE; Phone: 501-223-6355

STATE AND PROVINCIAL GOVERNMENT AGENCIES - ARKANSAS

Public Affairs Coordinator: STEPHEN R. WILSON; Phone: 501-223-6408
Publication(s): *Arkansas Game and Fish Magazine; Arkansas Outdoors Newsletter; Explore Arkansas*

ARKANSAS STATE EXTENSION SERVICES
P.O. Box 391, Little Rock, AR 72203
Web Site: www.uaex.edu/

Description: An off-campus education organization with faculty and offices in each county with the basic mission to disseminate and encourage the application of research-generated knowledge and leadership techniques to individuals, families, and communities. The county faculty is backed by subject matter specialists and their research counterparts.
Contact(s):
Chair, Department of Aquaculture and Fisheries: CAROLE R. ENGLE, 1890 Research and Extension: UAPB: Box 4990, Pine Bluff, AR 71611; Phone: 501-543-8537; E-mail: engle_c@vx4500.uapb.edu
Associate Vice President for Agriculture-Extension: DAVID E. FOSTER; Phone: 501-671-2001; E-mail: dfoster@uaex.edu
Dean of School of Forestry: BOB BLACKMON, University of Arkansas-Monticello, P.O. Box 3468, Monticello, AR 71665; Phone: 870-460-1049; E-mail: blackmon@uamont.edu
Section Leader--Environmental and Natural Resources: TOM L. RILEY JR.; Phone: 501-671-2080; E-mail: triley@uaex.edu
Extension Fisheries Specialist: H. STEVEN KILLIAN, 405 Suite A: Highway 65+82, Lake Village, AR 71653; Phone: 870-265-8055; E-mail: skillian@uaexsun.uaex.edu
Extension Fisheries Specialist: NATHAN M. STONE, P.O. Box 4966: UAPB, Pine Bluff, AR 71611; Phone: 870-543-8141; E-mail: stone_n@vx4500.uapb.edu
Extension Fisheries Specialist: DAVID HEIKES, P.O. Box 4912: UAPB, Pine Bluff, AR 71611; Phone: 870-543-8537; E-mail: heikes_d@vx4500.uapb.edu
Extension Fisheries Specialist: JOSEPH MARET, P.O. Drawer D, Lonoke, AR 72086; Phone: 501-676-3124; E-mail: jmaret@lonoke.uaex.edu
Extension Forester: FRANK A. ROTH II, Rt. 3 Box 258, Hope, AR 71801; Phone: 501-777-1549; E-mail: froth@uaex.edu
Extension Forester: TAMARA L. WALKINGSTICK; Phone: 501-671-2346; E-mail: walkingstick@uaex.edu
Environmental Management Specialist of Agriculture: MICHAEL B. DANIELS; Phone: 501-671-2281; E-mail: mdaniels@uaex.edu
Extension Specialist, Waste Management: SUZANNE SMITH HIRREL; Phone: 501-671-2288; E-mail: shirrel@uaex.edu
Extension Specialist, Wildlife: REBECCA STOUT MCPEAKE; Phone: 501-671-2285; Fax: 501-671-2185; E-mail: rstout@uaex.edu
Assistant Extension Specialist, Environmental Education: LESLIE GALL, #1, Four-H Way, Little Rock, AR 72211; Phone: 501-821-4444; E-mail: lgall@uaex.edu
Assistant Extension Specialist, Natural Resources: BILL KINKAID, P.O. Box 4966, Pine Bluff, AR 71611; Phone: 870-543-8530; E-mail: wkinkaid@uaex.edu
Assistant Extension Specialist, Natural Resources: CAROL GUFFEY, P.O. Box 3468, Monticello, AR 71656; Phone: 870-460-1052; E-mail: guffey@uamont.edu
Assistant Extension Specialist, Natural Resources and Fire Ant Management: KELLY LOFTIN; Phone: 501-671-2361; E-mail: kloftin@uaex.edu
Assistant Extension Specialist, Wildlife: REX R. ROBERG; Phone: 501-671-2334; E-mail: rrobert@uaex.edu
Extension Assistant Specialist Natural Resources and Fire Ant Management: DONNA R. SHANKLIN, P.O. Box 3468, Monticello, AR 71655; Phone: 870-460-1893; E-mail: shanklin@uamont.edu
Assistant Professor: ANDREW GOODWIN, P.O. Box 4990: UAPB, Pine Bluff, AR 71611; Phone: 870-543-8150; E-mail: goodwin@seark.net
Associate Professor--Economics: DR. RICHARD KLUENDER, P.O. Box 3468, UAM, Monticello, AR 71656; Phone: 870-460-1949; E-mail: kluender@uamont.edu

Natural Resources Instructor: LUCY MORELAND, #1, Four-H Way, Little Rock, AR 72211; Phone: 501-821-4444; E-mail: lmoreland@uaex.edu
Keyword(s): Agriculture, Forests and Forestry, Gardening and Horticulture, Renewable Resources, Wildlife and Wildlife Habitat

DEPARTMENT OF ENVIRONMENTAL QUALITY (ARKANSAS)
8001 National Dr., P.O. Box 8913, Little Rock, AR 72219-8913
Phone: 501-682-0744; Web site: www.adeq.state.ar.us
Founded: 1949
Description: To prevent, abate, and control all types of pollution and maintain the state's natural environment.
Contact(s):
Chairman: THOMAS SCHUECK
Director: RANDALL MATHIS
Deputy Director: LARRY WILSON
Deputy Director: JIM SHIRRELL
Administrator of Management Services: DR. ED MORRIS
Chief of Air Division: KEITH MICHAELS
Chief of Computer Services Division: ROBERT GAGE
Chief of Construction Assistance Division: MIKE CHANDLER
Chief of Customer Service Division: JAMES GILSON
Chief of Environmental Preservation Division: GREGG PATTERSON
Chief of Fiscal Division: ROBIN MORRISSEY
Chief of Hazardous Waste Division: MIKE BATES
Chief of Legal Division: AL ECKERT
Chief of Mining Division: FLOYD DURHAM
Chief of Regulated Storage Tank Division: JIM SHELL
Chief of Solid Waste Division: DENNIS BURKS
Chief of Technical Services Division: RICHARD CASSAT
Chief of Water Division: CHUCK BENNETT
Vice Chairman: JULIA PECK MOBLEY
Publication(s): *Arkansas Waste Line*
Keyword(s): Air Quality and Pollution, Ecology, Environmental Protection, Solid Waste, Water Pollution

FORESTRY COMMISSION (ARKANSAS)
3821 W. Roosevelt Rd., Little Rock, AR 72204-6395
Phone: 501-296-1940; Fax: 501-296-1949
Description: To prevent and suppress forest fires; control forest insects and diseases; grow and distribute forest planting stock; and collect and disseminate information concerning growth, utilization and renewal of forests.
Contact(s):
Baucum Nursery: ALAN MURRAY; Phone: 501-907-2485
Commission Chairman: TOM R. CURTNER
Deputy State Forester: ROBERT J. McFARLAND
Fire Control: JOHN V. BURTON
Fiscal Department: BOB C. CHAPMAN
Forest Management: LARRY NANEE
Information and Education: JAMES E. GRANT JR.
State Forester: JOHN T. SHANNON
Keyword(s): Forests and Forestry

NATURAL AND SCENIC RIVERS COMMISSION (ARKANSAS)
1500 Tower Bldg., 323 Center St., Little Rock, AR 72201
Phone: 501-324-9159; Fax: 501-324-9154; E-mail: info@dah.state.ar.us
Founded: 1979
Description: The purpose of the Natural and Scenic Rivers Commission is to prepare surveys and recommendations to the governor and the legislature for the preservation of selected rivers in the state of Arkansas possessing outstanding natural, scenic, educational, geological, recreational, historic, fish and wildlife, scientific and cultural values of great present and future benefit to the people.
Contact(s):
Director: JANE JONES
Publication(s): *Arkansas Landowners Guide to Stream Bank Management; Arkansas Floater's Kit; Arkansas River - Resource in Criis - What Are the Limits? How Do We Share? (Poster 28 x 40)*

Keyword(s): Environmental and Conservation Education, Environmental Planning, Rivers, Water Pollution Management, Water Resources

NATURAL HERITAGE COMMISSION (ARKANSAS)
1500 Tower Bldg., 323 Center St., Little Rock, AR 72201
Phone: 501-324-9619; Fax: 501-324-9618; Web site: www.heritage.state.ar.us/nhc
Founded: 1973
Description: Responsible for system of natural areas; acquires and holds both lands and interests in land; maintains a registry of natural areas in other ownerships; maintains a Heritage Inventory System and environmental review and information sharing program; and defends natural areas from adverse influences.
Contact(s):
Chairman: RAYMOND ABRAMSON
Deputy Director: MINA MARSH; E-mail: mina@dah.state.ar.us
Executive Director: HAROLD K. GRIMMETT; E-mail:
    harold@dah.state.ar.us
Chief of Research: TOM FOTI; E-mail: tom@dah.state.ar.us
Coordinator of Environmental Applications: WILLIAM M.
    SHEPHERD; E-mail: bills@dah.state.ar.us
Coordinator of Stewardship: JOHN BENEKE; E-mail:
    johnb@dah.state.ar.us
Keyword(s): Biodiversity, Endangered and Threatened Species, Environmental Preservation, Land Purchase, Natural Areas, Rivers, Sustainable Ecosystems

PINE BLUFF COOPERATIVE FISHERY RESEARCH PROJECT
USGS-BRG-University of Arkansas,, Ag. Exp. Station, 1200 N. University, P.O. Box 4005, Pine Bluff, AR 71611
Phone: 501-543-8165
Description: The Pine Bluff Cooperative Fishery Research Project is a cooperative educational effort between the U. S. Geological Survey-Biological Resources Division, Cooperative Research Units Division and the University of Arkansas - Pine Bluff. The project provides undergraduate training in fisheries science and biology and conducts research on environmental problems, fisheries and related topics.
Contact(s):
Project Leader: DR. STEVE LOCHMANN
Keyword(s): Endangered and Threatened Species, Environmental and Conservation Education, Environmental Law, Environmental Protection, Fisheries, Research, Rivers

STATE PLANT BOARD (ARKANSAS)
1 Natural Resources Dr., P.O. Box 1069, Little Rock, AR 72203
Phone: 501-225-1598
Contact(s):
Director: GERALD KING
Assistant Director: DARRYL LITTLE
Keyword(s): Native Plants

CALIFORNIA

GOVERNOR OF CALIFORNIA: GRAY DAVIS
State Capitol, Sacramento, CA 95814
Phone: 916-445-2841

CALIFORNIA COOPERATIVE FISHERY RESEARCH UNIT (USGS)
Fisheries Department, Humboldt State University, Arcata, CA 95521
Phone: 707-826-3268
Contact(s):
Leader: DR. WALTER G. DUFFY
Assistant Leader: DR. MARGARET WILZBACH
Senior Advisory Scientist: DR. KENNETH CUMMINS
National Media Relations Specialist for USGS/BRD: CATHERINE HAECKER

CALIFORNIA DEPARTMENT OF EDUCATION
Office of Environmental Education
721 Capitol Mall, P.O. Box 944272, Sacramento, CA 94244-2720
Founded: 1970
Description: The California Department of Education provides technical assistance and curriculum leadership in environmental education for counties and schools in California. The department offers an annual competitive grant program and provides curriculum and other publications related to environmental education in California.
Contact(s):
Environmental Education Consultant: BILL ANDREWS; Phone: 916-657-5374; Fax: 916-657-3682
Publication(s): *Endangered Species Resource Guide; Environmental Education Compendia on Air Quality, Energy Resources, Human Communities, Integrated Waste Management, Natural Communities, and Water Resources; A Child's Place in the Environment; Greatest Hits of Environmental Education*
Keyword(s): Air Quality and Pollution, Endangered and Threatened Species, Environmental and Conservation Education, Scholarships and Grants, Education

CALIFORNIA ENVIRONMENTAL PROTECTION AGENCY
555 Capitol Mall, Suite 525, Sacramento, CA 95814
Founded: 1991
Description: The Secretary for Environmental Protection, a member of the Governor's Cabinet, serves as the Governor's principal advisor on environmental protection issues and oversees the activities of the Air Resources Board, Water Resources Control Board, Integrated Waste Management Board, the Department of Toxic Substances Control, the Office of Environmental Health Hazard Assessment and the Department of Pesticide Regulation.
Contact(s):
Secretary: WINSTON H. HICKOX; Phone: 916-445-3846
Deputy Secretary of Law Enforcement and Counsel (Acting): LISA BROWN; Phone: 916-327-2064
Deputy Secretary of Policy Development: ENRIQUE G. FARIAS; Phone: 916-324-8124
Director of Communications: JAMES SPAGNOLE; Phone: 916-324-9670
Director of Legislative (Acting): PATTY ZWARTS; Phone: 916-322-7315
Undersecretary: C. BRIAN HADDIX

California Air Resources Board
P.O. Box 2815, Sacramento, CA 95812
Phone: 916-322-2990
Founded: 1968
Description: The California Air Resources Board is responsible for the adoption and enforcement of the state's ambient air quality standards, rules, and regulations for the control of vehicular air pollution and toxic air contaminants throughout the state. Oversees the efforts of 34 air pollution control districts that regulate emissions from industrial facilities. Studies the causes of air pollution and evaluates its effort upon human, plant, and animal life. The Board is comprised of 11 members.
Contact(s):
Chairman: ALAN C. LLOYD
Administrative Services Division Chief: LARRY MORRIS; Phone: 916-322-8198
Assistant Executive Officer: LYNN TERRY; Phone: 916-322-2739
Chief Deputy Executive Officer: TOM CACKETTE; Phone: 916-322-2892
Compliance Division Chief: JAMES J. MORGESTER; Phone: 916-322-6022
Deputy Executive Officer: MICHAEL SCHEIBLE; Phone: 916-322-2890
Executive Officer: MICHAEL P. KENNY; Phone: 916-445-4383
Legislative Office Chief: RON OGLESBY; Phone: 916-322-2896
Mobile Source Division Chief: BOB CROSS; Phone: 818-575-6820

STATE AND PROVINCIAL GOVERNMENT AGENCIES - CALIFORNIA

Monitoring and Laboratory Division Chief: WILLIAM V. LOSCUTOFF; Phone: 916-445-3742
Office of Legal Affairs, General Counsel: KATHLEEN WALSH; Phone: 916-322-2884
Office of Ombudsman, Chief: JIM SCHONING; Phone: 916-323-6791
Public Information Officer: JERRY MARTIN; Phone: 916-322-2990
Research Division Chief: DR. JOHN R. HOLMES; Phone: 916-445-0753
Stationary Source Division Chief: PETER D. VENTURINI; Phone: 916-445-0650
Technical Support Division Chief: TERRY W. McGUIRE; Phone: 916-322-5350

Department of Pesticide Regulation
830 K. St., Exec Office, Rm 307, Sacramento, CA 95814-3510
Phone: 916-445-4300
Description: The Department of Pesticide Regulation regulates all aspects of pesticides sales and use, recognizing the need to control pests, while protecting public health and the environment and fostering reduced-risk pest management strategies.
Contact(s):
Director: PAUL HELLIKER; Phone: 916-445-4000
Keyword(s): Air Quality and Pollution, Pesticides, Solid Waste Management, Toxic Substances, Water Pollution Management

Department of Toxic Substances Control
400 P St., 4th Fl., Sacramento, CA 95814
Phone: 916-323-9723
Description: Responsible for overseeing the cleanup of hazardous waste sites; monitoring and regulatory management of hazardous waste transportation, treatment, storage and disposal; and promotion of hazardous waste reduction in California.
Contact(s):
Director: EDWIN LOWRY
Deputy Director: BOB BORZEUERI; Phone: 916-322-0449

Integrated Waste Management Board, CIWMB
8800 Cal Center Dr., Sacramento, CA 95826
Founded: 1990
Description: The CIWMB is comprised of six members; four appointed by the governor and two by the legislature. CIWMB's goal is to protect the public's health and safety and the environment through waste prevention, waste diversion, and safe waste processing and disposal. Also, minimizing waste generation and disposal in California while facilitating the development of industries that use recyclable materials, will be realized by establishing sustainable markets for recyclable materials, reducing reliance on land disposal, and effectively educating the public.
Contact(s):
Chairman: DAN E. EATON
Executive Director: RALPH CHANDLER; Phone: 916-255-2296

Office of Environmental Health Hazard Assessment
301 Capital Mall, Rm. 205, Sacramento, CA 95815-4327
Phone: 916-324-7572
Description: The Office of Environmental Health Hazard Assessment is charged with assessing human health risks posed by chemicals in the environment. The office is also the lead agency for implementation of the Safe Drinking Water and Toxic Enforcement Act of 1986 (Proposition 65).
Contact(s):
Director: DR. JOAN E. DENTON

Water Resources Control Board
901 P St., P.O. Box 100, Sacramento, CA 95812-0100
Phone: 916-657-1247
Description: To protect water quality and allocate water rights. These objectives are achieved through two action programs: water quality and water rights.
Contact(s):
Chairman: JAMES M. STUBCHAER
Deputy Director: DALE CLAYPOOLE
Executive Director: WALT PETTIT

Regional Executive Officer of the Central Coast Region: ROGER BRIGGS; Phone: 805-549-3147
Regional Executive Officer of the Central Valley Region: GARY CARLTON; Phone: 916-255-3000
Regional Executive Officer of the Colorado River Basin Region: PHIL GRUENBERG; Phone: 619-346-7491
Regional Executive Officer of the Lahonton Region: HAROLD SINGER; Phone: 916-542-5400
Regional Executive Officer of the Los Angeles Region: DENNIS DICKERSON; Phone: 213-266-7500
Regional Executive Officer of the North Coast Region: LEE MICHLIN; Phone: 707-576-2220
Regional Executive Officer of the San Diego Region: JOHN ROBERTUS; Phone: 619-467-2952
Regional Executive Officer of the San Francisco bay Region: LORETTA BARSAMILAN; Phone: 510-286-1255
Regional Executive Officer of the Santa Ana Region: GERALD THIBEAULT; Phone: 909-782-4130

CALIFORNIA SEA GRANT COLLEGE SYSTEM
California Sea Grant College, University of California, 9500 Gilman Dr., La Jolla, CA 92093-0232
Phone: 619-534-4440; Fax: 858-534-2231; E-mail: caseagrant@ucsd.edu; Web site: www-csgc.ucsd.edu/
Description: A multi-university program of marine research, extension services, and education that contributes to the growing body of knowledge about coastal and oceanic resources and helps solve contemporary problems in the marine sphere.
Contact(s):
Interim Director: CLINTON WINANT
Coordinator of Sea Grant Extension Program: DR. CHRISTOPHER DEWEES, Cooperative Extension: University of California, Davis, CA 95616; Phone: 530-752-1497
Director of USC Sea Grant Program: DR. LINDA DUGUAY, University of Southern California: University Park, Los Angeles, CA 90089-0373; Phone: 213-740-1961; Fax: 213-740-5936; E-mail: seagrant@mizar.usc.edu
Leader of USC Sea Grant Marine Advisory Program and Associate Director of USC Sea Grant Program: JUDY LEMUS Ph.D., USC Sea Grant Program Marine Advisory Service: University of Southern California: University Park, Los Angeles, CA 90089-0373; Phone: 213-740-1965; Fax: 213-740-5936
Publication(s): *Sea Grant in Brief*
Keyword(s): Biotechnology, Coasts, Fisheries, Water Resources, Wetlands

CALIFORNIA STATE EXTENSION SERVICES
Cooperative Extension and Agricultural Experiment Station, University of California, 1111 Franklin St., 6th Fl., Oakland, CA 94607-5200
Phone: 415-987-0060; Web site: danr.ucop.edu/regional.htm
Contact(s):
Vice President: W. R. GOMES, Agricultural and Natural Resources, Director AES & CE; Phone: 415-987-0060
Associate Vice President and Associate Director AES & EC: HENRY J. VAUX JR.; Phone: 415-987-0026
Regional Director, Central Coast and South: SUSAN LAUGHLIN, 125 Highlander Hall, University of California, Riverside, CA 92521; Phone: 714-787-3321
Regional Director, Central Valley: LINDA MANTON, Kearney Agricultural Center, 9240 S. Riverbend Ave., Parlier, CA 93648; Phone: 209-891-2566
Regional Director, North Coast and Mountain: NICELMA J. KING, University of California, Davis, CA 95616; Phone: 916-754-8509
Assistant Vice President, Programs and Assistant Director AES & State Leader CE: LANNY LUND
Dean: MICHAEL T. CLEGG, College of Natural and Agricultural Sciences; Associate Director: AES & CE: University of California, Riverside, CA 92521; Phone: 714-787-3101
Dean: BENNIE OSBURN, Veterinary Medicine, University of California, Davis, CA 95616; Phone: 916-752-1360

STATE AND PROVINCIAL GOVERNMENT AGENCIES - CALIFORNIA

Dean: NEAL VAN ALFEN, College of Agricultural and Environmental Sciences, Associate Director of AES Programs, University of California, Davis, CA 95616; Phone: 916-752-1605
Dean: GORDON C. RAUSSER, College of Natural Resources: Associate Director: AES & CE: University of California, Berkeley, CA 94720; Phone: 15-642-7171
Wildlife Specialist: E. LEE FITZHUGH, Wildlife and Conservation Biology, University of California, 1 Shields Ave., Davis, CA 95616-8751; Phone: 530-752-1496; Fax: 530-752-4154

CALIFORNIA STATE LANDS COMMISSION
100 Howe Ave., Suite 100, South, Sacramento, CA 95825-8202
Phone: 916-574-1800
Description: Jurisdiction over and management responsibility for state-owned sovereign and legislatively granted lands. Handles related land leases, exchanges, and associated transactions. Conducts oil, gas, geothermal, and leasing of other mineral on state-owned lands. Related activities include boundary and ownership determination, granted lands administration, and maintaining land information systems.
Contact(s):
Executive Officer: PAUL D. THAYER
Legislative Liaison: WILLIAM V. MORRISON
Chief Counsel: JACK RUMP; Phone: 916-574-1850
Chief, Environmental Planning and Management Division: DWIGHT E. SANDERS; Phone: 916-574-1890
Chief, Land Management Division: ROBERT L. LYNCH; Phone: 916-574-1940
Chief, Marine Facilities Division: GARY L. GREGORY, 330 Golden Shore, Suite 210, Long Beach, CA 90802
Chief, Mineral Resources Division: PAUL MOUNT, 200 Oceangate, 12th Fl., Long Beach, CA 90802; Phone: 562-590-5205
Executive Officer: ROBERT C. HIGHT; Phone: 916-574-1800
Lieutenant Governor: CRUZ M. BUSTAMANTE
State Controller: KATHLEEN CONNELL
State Director of Finance: B. TIMOTHY GAGE
Keyword(s): Public Lands

DEPARTMENT OF FOOD AND AGRICULTURE (CALIFORNIA)
P.O. Box 942871, 1220 N St., Sacramento, CA 94271-0001
Phone: 916-654-0466
Description: To assure public health, safety, and welfare; protects agriculture by administering, directing and enforcing the state's agricultural laws and regulations.
Contact(s):
Secretary: ANN M. VENEMAN; Phone: 916-654-0433
Chief Counsel: FRANCINE KAMMEYER; Phone: 916-654-1393
Deputy Secretary: DARRELL GUENSLER; Phone: 916-654-0321
Director of Animal Industry: RICHARD BREITMEYER; Phone: 916-654-0881
Director of Fairs and Expositions: SHARON JENSEN; Phone: 916-263-2952
Director of Inspection Services: ROBERT WYNN; Phone: 916-654-0792
Director of Marketing Services: KELLY KRUG; Phone: 916-654-1240
Director of Measurement Standards: BARBARA BLOCH; Phone: 916-229-3000
Director of Plant Industry: ISI SIDDIQUI; Phone: 916-654-0317
Legislative Director: GREG HARNER; Phone: 916-654-0326
Policy and Planning Assistant Secretary: NITA VAIL; Phone: 916-653-7643
Public Affairs Assistant Secretary: KEVIN HERGLOTZ; Phone: 916-654-0462
Undersecretary: A. J. YATES; Phone: 916-654-0321

GOVERNOR'S OFFICE OF PLANNING AND RESEARCH (CALIFORNIA)
1400 10th St., P.O. Box 3044, Sacramento, CA 95812-3044
Phone: 916-322-2318
Founded: 1970
Description: Primary areas of concentration are the development of environmental and related land use goals and policies; growth management; evaluation of state plans and programs; and preparation of statewide environmental goals and policies statements.
Contact(s):
Director: LORETTA LYNCH
State Clearinghouse Senior Planner: TERRY ROBERTS; Phone: 916-445-0613
Keyword(s): Environmental Planning, Geography, Land Use Planning, Planning Management, Population Growth

RESOURCES AGENCY, THE
1416 9th St., Rm. 1311, Sacramento, CA 95814
Phone: 916-653-5656
Description: Responsible for ensuring an adequate and properly balanced management of government functions related to California's natural environment.
Contact(s):
Assistant Secretary of Administration and Finance: DON WALLACE
Assistant Secretary of Conservation Programs: DEBBIE DRAKE
Deputy Assistant of Communications: SANTANA GARCIA
Deputy Secretary for Legislative Affairs: JULIE MacDONALD
Deputy Secretary for Operations: JIM YOUNGSON
General Counsel: MAUREEN GORSEN
Secretary of Resources: DOUGLAS P. WHEELER
Under Secretary of Resources: MICHAEL A. MANTELL

California Coastal Commission
45 Fremont St., Suites 1900 and 2000, San Francisco, CA 94105-2219
Phone: 415-904-5200; Fax: 415-904-5400
Description: Coastal management agency that carries out mandated policies on coastal conservation and development through regulation and planning programs. These policies deal with public access to the coast, coastal recreation, the California marine environment, coastal land resources and coastal development of various types, including power plant and other energy installation.
Contact(s):
Chief Counsel: RALPH FAUST
Chief Deputy Director: SUSAN HANSCH
Chief of Administrative Services Division: LANE YEE
Deputy Director for Energy, Ocean Resources and Water Quality: JAIME KOOSER
Deputy Director for North Coast District: STEVE SCHOLL
Executive Director: PETER DOUGLAS
Public Education and Activities Coordinator: CHRISTIANE PARRY

California Coastal Conservancy
1330 Broadway, Suite 1100, Oakland, CA 94612
Phone: 510-286-1015; Fax: 510-286-0470
Description: A state agency using planning, land-use conflict resolution, acquisition, and development techniques in the restoration, enhancement, and preservation of coastal resources. Program areas include agricultural preservation, lot consolidation, urban waterfront restoration, coastal resource enhancement, the reservation of significant resource sites, provision of public access, and assistance to nonprofit organizations.
Contact(s):
Executive Officer: BILL AHERN
Publication(s): *Coast and Ocean*

California Conservation Corps
1719 24th St., Sacramento, CA 95814
Phone: 916-445-0307
Founded: 1976
Description: The CCC was created with a dual mission: the employment and development of the state's youth, and the protection and enhancement of California's natural resources. Some 42 million hours of public service conservation work and emergency assistance have been provided by the Corps in its twenty years of existence.
Contact(s):
Director: AL ARAMBURU

STATE AND PROVINCIAL GOVERNMENT AGENCIES - CALIFORNIA

Deputy Director of External Affairs: JOHN COLEMAN
Deputy Director of Program Support: KAREN MEYRELES
Regional Deputy Director: WALT HUGHES
Regional Deputy Director: PAUL CARRILLO
Regional Deputy Director: TOM POWERS
Regional Deputy Director: STEW OGBURN
Special Assistant to the Director: CRAIG MILLER

California Energy Commission
1516 9th St., Sacramento, CA 95814
Phone: 916-654-4287; Fax: 916-654-4420
Founded: 1975
Description: To ensure continuation of a reliable and affordable supply of energy for California at a level consistent with the state's needs.
Contact(s):
Chairman: CHARLES R. IMBRECHT; Phone: 916-654-5000
Deputy Director (Acting) of Administrative Services: CYNTHIA HOBSON; Phone: 916-654-5204; Fax: 916-654-4423
Deputy Director of Energy Efficiency Division: ROSS DETER; Phone: 916-654-5013; Fax: 916-654-4304
Deputy Director of Energy Facilities Siting and Environmental Protection Division: ROBERT L. THERKELSEN; Phone: 916-654-3924; Fax: 916-654-3882
Deputy Director of Energy Forecasting Resource Assessment Division: DAN NIX; Phone: 916-654-4861; Fax: 916-654-4559
Deputy Director of Energy Technology Division: NANCY DELLER; Phone: 916-654-4628; Fax: 916-654-4676
Executive Director (Acting): KENT SMITH; Phone: 916-654-4996
Vice Chair: DAVID A. ROHY; Phone: 916-654-4930
Vice Chair: JANANNE SHARPLESS; Phone: 916-654-5036
Vice Chair: SALLY RAKOW; Phone: 916-654-3992

California Water Commission
1416 9th St., Rm. 1148, Sacramento, CA 95814
Phone: 916-653-5958; Fax: 916-653-9745
Founded: 1913
Description: Serves as a policy advisory body to the Director of Water Resources on matters within the Department's jurisdiction and coordinates state and local views on federal appropriations for water projects in California. The commission also conducts public hearings and investigations statewide for the department and provides an open forum for interested citizens to voice their opinion on water development issues.
Contact(s):
Executive Officer: RAYMOND E. BARSCH
Keyword(s): Fisheries, Flood Control, Rivers, Water Resources, Watersheds, Wetlands

Colorado River Board of California
770 Fairmont Ave., Suite 100, Glendale, CA 91203-1035
Phone: 818-543-4676
Founded: 1937
Description: The board was established to represent California, its agencies, and citizens in matters concerning the water and power resources provided by the Colorado River and its tributaries. Working with federal and state agencies, Congress, courts, and other Colorado River Basin states, the board analyzes engineering, legal, and economic matters concerning the use of Colorado River resources within the United States.
Contact(s):
Executive Director: GERALD R. ZIMMERMAN

Department of Boating and Waterways
1629 S St., Sacramento, CA 95814
Phone: 916-445-6281; Fax: 916-327-7250
Description: Makes loans to public agencies and small businesses for small craft harbor development and grants to public agencies for boat-launching facilities, floating restrooms, and vessel waste disposal equipment; licenses yacht and ship brokers and for-hire vessel operators; conducts programs of boating safety, education, and regulation; and grants funds to local entities for boating law enforcement activities. Participates with the Corps of Engineers and local agencies in the construction of beach erosion control projects, assists local jurisdictions in obtaining the greatest benefits available from federal beach erosion programs, and conducts an aquatic pest control program in the Sacramento-San Joaquin Delta.
Contact(s):
Interim Director: CARLTON D. MOORE
Chief of Administrative Services Division: DEBRA DeVERTER; Phone: 916-263-08421
Chief of Boating Facilities Division: DON WALTZ; Phone: 916-263-8122
Chief of Boating Operations Division: DOLORES FARRELL; Phone: 916-262-8181
Keyword(s): Coasts, Grants, Lakes, Oceanography, Outdoor Recreation

Department of Conservation
801 K St., MS 24-01, Sacramento, CA 95814
Phone: 916-322-1080; Fax: 916-445-0732
Description: The mission of the department is to protect health and safety, ensure environmental quality, and support the state's long-term economic viability in the use of California's land and mineral resources.
Contact(s):
Deputy Director: PAT MEEHAN
Chief Deputy Director: STEVE ARTHUR

Department of Fish and Game
1416 9th St., Sacramento, CA 95814
Phone: 916-653-7664; Fax: 916-653-1856
Description: Responsible for the protection and management of fish and wildlife and threatened native plants in California. Enforces the laws pertaining to fish and game and threatened native plants enacted by the legislature and the regulations of the Fish and Game Commission.
Contact(s):
Chief Deputy Director: RYAN BRODDRICK; Phone: 916-653-7556
Deputy Director of Administration: R. A. BERNHEIMER; Phone: 916-653-4633
Deputy Director of Habitat Conservation Division: RON REMPE.REMPEL; Phone: 916-653-1070
Deputy Director of Wildlife and Inland Fisheries Division: TERRY MANSFIELD; Phone: 916-653-6184
Chief, Central Valley Bay-Delta: PERRY HERRGESELL; Phone: 209-948-7800
Chief, Conservation Education & Enforcement: RICH ELLIOTT; Phone: 916-653-4094
Chief, Fisheries Programs: GENE FLEMING; Phone: 916-653-4280
Chief, Habitat Conservation Planning: SUSAN COCHRANE; Phone: 916-653-4875
Chief, Lands & Facilities: RON PELZMAN; Phone: 916-653-4899
Chief, Water & Aquatic Habitat Conservation: JIM STEELE; Phone: 916-653-2459
Chief, Watershed Restoration: TIM FARLEY; Phone: 916-653-6194
Chief, Wildlife and Habitat Data Analysis: JANINE STENBACK
Chief, Wildlife Programs: DAVE ZEZULAK; Phone: 916-653-7203
General Counsel (Acting): ANN MALCOLM; Phone: 916-654-3821
Director: ROBERT C. HIGHT; Phone: 916-653-7667
Administrator for Spill Prevention and Response Division (Acting): GARY GREGORY; Phone: 916-445-9338
Intergovernmental Affairs Representative: L. B. BOYDSTUN; Phone: 916-653-3136
Legislative Representative: JULIE E. OLTMANN; Phone: 916-653-5581

Department of Forestry and Fire Protection
1416 9th St., P.O. Box 944246, Sacramento, CA 94244-2460
Phone: 916-653-5121
Description: The department protects the people of California from fires, responds to emergencies, and protects and enhances forest, range, and watershed values providing social, economic, and environmental benefits to rural and urban citizens.
Contact(s):
Director: ANDREA E. TUTTLE; Phone: 916-653-7772

Chief Deputy Director: WOODY K. ALLSHOUSE; Phone: 916-653-4175
Deputy Director, Fire Protection: JAMES E. OWEN; Phone: 916-653-9424
Deputy Director, Resource Management: ROSS JOHNSON; Phone: 916-653-4298

Department of Parks and Recreation
1416 9th St., P.O. Box 942896, Sacramento, CA 94296-0001
Phone: 916-653-8380
Description: Responsible for the acquisition, preservation, development, interpretation, and operation of the state park system; also responsible for the administration of grants for recreation to local government and for development of the California Outdoor Recreation Resources Plan.
Contact(s):
Director: RUSTY AREIAS
Chief Deputy Director: MARY WRIGHT
Chief Deputy Director of Administration: DENZIL VERARDO; Phone: 916-653-0528
Chief Deputy Director of Park Stewardship: KEN JONES; Phone: 916-653-8288
Chief of Environmental Design Division: ROBERT D. CATES; Phone: 916-653-7475
Chief of Northern Division: JOHN KNOTT; Phone: 916-657-4042
Chief of Park Services Division: BILL BERRY; Phone: 916-653-2021
Chief of Resource Management Division: RICHARD G. RAYBURN; Phone: 916-653-6745
Chief of Southern Division: DICK TROY; Phone: 916-657-4042
Deputy Director of Historic Preservation Office (Acting): DAN ABEYTA; Phone: 916-653-6624
Deputy Director of Legislation: CINDY SHAMROCK; Phone: 916-653-6887
Deputy Director of Marketing and Revenue Generation: LEZLIE PUGLIA
Deputy Director of Off Highway Motor Vehicle Recreation (Acting): CARL DRAKE; Phone: 916-324-4442
Human Resources: RAY ANN WATSON; Phone: 916-653-9990
Legal Office: TIM LAFRANCHI; Phone: 916-653-6884
Keyword(s): Outdoor Recreation

Department of Water Resources
1416 9th St., P.O. Box 942836, Sacramento, CA 94236-0001
Phone: 916-653-5791
Description: To manage the water resources of California in cooperation with other agencies, to benefit the state's people, and to protect, restore, and enhance the natural and human environments.
Contact(s):
Director: THOMAS M. HANNIGAN; Phone: 916-653-7007
Deputy Director: STEPHEN L. KASHIWADA; Phone: 916-653-7092
Chief Deputy Director: STEVE MACAULAY; Phone: 916-653-6055
Chief Counsel: SUSAN N. WEBER; Phone: 916-653-6186
Assistant Director of Legislation: L. LUCINDA CHIPPONERI; Phone: 196-653-0488
District Chief of Central: KARL P. WINKLER; Phone: 916-227-7550
District Chief of San Joanquin: LOUIS A. BECK; Phone: 209-445-5222
District Chief of Southern: CHARLES R. WHITE; Phone: 818-543-4600
Division of Engineering: LES HARDER; Phone: 916-653-3927
Division of Fiscal Services: CHESTER M. WINN; Phone: 916-653-4413
Division of Flood Management: GEORGE QUALLEY; Phone: 916-653-7572
Division of Land and Right of Way: FRANK CONTI; Phone: 916-653-7891
Division of Management Services: LINDA GAGE; Phone: 916-653-6743
Division of Planning and Local Assistance: WILLIAM J. BENNETT, 1020 9th St., Sacramento, CA 95814; Phone: 916-327-1646
Division of Safety of Dams: STEVE VERIGIN; Phone: 916-445-7606
Environmental Services Office: RANDALL L. BROWN, 3252 S St., Sacramento, CA 95816; Phone: 916-227-7531
Office of Water Education: PETE WEISSER; Phone: 196-653-7431
State Water Project Planning Office: KATHY KELLY; Phone: 916-653-1099

Fish and Game Commission
1416 9th St., Rm. 1320, P.O. Box 944209, Sacramento, CA 94244-2090
Phone: 916-653-4899
Founded: 1870
Description: Adopts fish, game, and plant regulations as authorized by the Fish and Game Code and sets policies for the Department of Fish and Game.
Contact(s):
President: MIKE CHRISMAN
Executive Director: ROBERT R. TREANOR

Native American Heritage Commission
915 Capitol Mall, Rm. 364, Sacramento, CA 95814
Phone: 916-653-4082
Contact(s):
Executive Secretary: LARRY MYERS

San Francisco Bay Conservation and Development Commission
30 Van Ness Ave., Suite 2011, San Francisco, CA 94102
Phone: 415-557-3686
Founded: 1965
Description: To implement a planning and regulatory program designed to conserve and use beneficially the environmental, economic, social, and aesthetic values of San Francisco Bay through carefully considered and democratically determined policies. Composed of 27 commissioners, representing the public and state, federal, and local governmental agencies.
Contact(s):
Chairman: ROBERT TUFTS
Deputy Director: STEVE McADAM
Executive Director: WILL TRAVIS
Chief Planner: JEFFRY BLANCHFIELD

State Reclamation Board
1416 9th St., Rm. 1601, Sacramento, CA 95814
Phone: 916-653-5434; Fax: 916-653-5805
Founded: 1911
Description: Agency provides flood protection along the Sacramento and San Joaquin Rivers and their tributaries by planning, constructing, operating, and maintaining flood control projects in cooperation with local, state, and federal agencies, and by implementing nonstructural flood control measures.
Contact(s):
President: BARBARA LeVAKE
Vice President: FRANCES MIZUNO
Secretary: BRENDA JAHNS-SOUTHWICK
General Manager: PETER D. RABBON

Wildlife Conservation Board
1807 13th St., Suite 103, Sacramento, CA 95814-7117
Phone: 916-445-8448; Fax: 916-323-0280
Founded: 1947
Description: In concert with the Department of Fish and Game, the board authorizes the acquisition, restoration, and enhancement of land and water for wildlife conservation and related recreational purposes. The board also administers the Inland Wetlands Conservation Program and the California Riparian Habitat Conservation Program to protect, restore, and enhance wetland and riparian habitats.
Contact(s):
Executive Director: W. JOHN SCHMIDT
Assistant Executive Director of Development Program: GEORGIA LIPPHARDT
Assistant Executive Director of Land Acquisition: JAMES V. SARRO

COLORADO

GOVERNOR OF COLORADO: BILL OWENS
136 State Capitol, Denver, CO 80203
Phone: 303-866-2471

COLORADO COOPERATIVE FISH AND WILDLIFE RESEARCH UNIT (USDI)
201 Wagar Bldg., Dept. of Fishery and Wildlife Biology, Colorado State University, Ft. Collins, CO 80523-1484
Phone: 970-491-5396
Founded: 1947
Description: Offers expertise and training facilities in fish and wildlife population ecology, aquatic habitat analysis, conservation biology, sampling and analysis theory, and biostatistics.
Contact(s):
Assistant Leader: DR. KENNETH P. BURNHAM
Assistant Leader: DR. ERIC P. BERGERSEN
Leader: DR. DAVID R. ANDERSON
Keyword(s): Birds, Endangered and Threatened Species, Fish Wildlife Management, Fisheries, Nongame Wildlife, Whirling Disease

COLORADO DEPARTMENT OF AGRICULTURE
700 Kipling St., Suite 4000, Lakewood, CO 80215
Phone: 303-239-4100
Founded: 1949
Description: Strives to meet the increasingly complex needs of agriculture through work on marketing problems, technological changes in pest and insect control, and rapidly changing patterns in crop and livestock operations.
Contact(s):
Brand Commissioner of Board of Stock Inspection Division: GARY SHOUN
Commission Chairman: MAX L. HARPER
Commissioner: DON AMENT
Deputy Commissioner: ROBERT G. McLAVEY
Director of Animal Industry Division: DR. JERRY BOHLENDER DVM
Director of Division of Inspection and Consumer Services: RONALD TURNER
Director of Markets Development Division: JIM RUBINGH
Director of Plant Industry Division: JOHN GERHARDT
Resource Analyst: DAVID CARLSON
Keyword(s): Agriculture, Environmental and Conservation Education, Pesticides, Public Lands, Toxicology

COLORADO DEPARTMENT OF EDUCATION
201 E. Colfax Ave., State Office Bldg., Denver, CO 80203
Phone: 303-866-6787; Fax: 303-866-6836
Description: Conservation Education Services, jointly with the Colorado Division of Wildlife.
Contact(s):
Environmental Education Consultant: DON HOLLUMS; Phone: 303-866-6787; E-mail: hollums_d@cde.state.co.us
Keyword(s): Environmental and Conservation Education, Environmental Ethics, Pollution Prevention, Urban Environment, Wildlife and Wildlife Habitat, Schoolyard Habitats

COLORADO DEPARTMENT OF NATURAL RESOURCES
1313 Sherman, Rm. 718, Denver, CO 80203
Phone: 303-866-3311; Fax: 303-866-2115
Founded: 1968
Description: Responsible for mineral and energy, land, water, wildlife, and park resources management for the state. Also responsible for major environmental conservation and management programs.
Contact(s):
Deputy Director: BILL DALEY
Deputy Director: RONALD W. CATTANY
Executive Director: GREG WALCHER
Human Resources Director: CINDY HORIUCHI

Colorado Geologic Survey
1313 Sherman St., Rm. 715, Denver, CO 80203
Phone: 303-866-2611; Fax: 303-866-2461
Contact(s):
State Geologist: VICKI COWART

Division of Minerals and Geology
1313 Sherman St., Rm. 215, Denver, CO 80203
Phone: 303-866-3567; Fax: 303-832-8106
Contact(s):
Director: MICHAEL B. LONG

Division of Parks and Outdoor Recreation
1313 Sherman St., Rm. 618, Denver, CO 80203
Phone: 303-866-3437; Fax: 303-866-3206
Contact(s):
Director: LAURIE MATHEWS

Division of Water Resources
1313 Sherman St., Rm. 818, Denver, CO 80203
Phone: 303-866-3581; Fax: 303-866-3589
Contact(s):
State Engineer: HAROLD SIMPSON

Division of Wildlife
6060 Broadway, Denver, CO 80216
Phone: 303-297-1192; Fax: 303-294-0894
Contact(s):
Director: JOHN MUMMA

Oil and Gas Conservation Commission
1120 Lincoln St., Suite 801, Denver, CO 80203
Phone: 303-894-2100; Fax: 303-894-2109
Contact(s):
Director: RICHARD GRIEBLING

Soil Conservation Board
1313 Sherman St., Rm. 219, Denver, CO 80203-2243
Phone: 303-866-3351; Fax: 303-832-8106

State Board of Land
1313 Sherman St., Rm. 620, Denver, CO 80203
Phone: 303-866-3454; Fax: 303-866-3152
Contact(s):
Director: CHARLES BEDFORD

Water Conservation Board
1313 Sherman St., Rm. 721, Denver, CO 80203
Phone: 303-866-3441; Fax: 303-866-4474
Contact(s):
Director: PETER EVANS
Keyword(s): Environmental and Conservation Education, Outdoor Recreation, Public Lands, Water Resources, Wildlife Management

COLORADO DEPARTMENT OF PUBLIC HEALTH AND ENVIRONMENT
4300 Cherry Creek Dr., S., Denver, CO 80246-1530
Phone: 303-692-2000
Description: The Colorado Department of Public Health and Environment has the responsibility for improving and protecting the health and environment for Colorado's citizens by: assuring a healthy working and living environment, protecting people against exposure to diseases, establishing preventive health services and providing a quality environment through air, waste, water, radiation and other environmental protection activities.
Contact(s):
Executive Director: JANE E. NORTON

COLORADO STATE FOREST SERVICE
Forestry Bldg., Colorado State University, Ft. Collins, CO 80523-5060
Phone: 970-491-6303; Fax: 970-491-7736
Founded: 1885

Description: The mission of the State Forest Service is to achieve stewardship of Colorado's environment through forestry outreach and service.
Contact(s):
Assistant State Forester: BILL WILCOX
State Forester: JAMES E. HUBBARD
Community Forestry: PHIL HOEFER
Conservation Education: BOB STURTEVANT
Forest Management: PHIL SCHWOLERT
Wildfire Protection: RICH HOMANN
Keyword(s): Environmental and Conservation Education, Forests and Forestry, Land Use Planning, Sustainable Ecosystems, Urban Forestry

COLORADO STATE UNIVERSITY COOPERATIVE EXTENSION
1 Administration Bldg., Colorado State University, Ft. Collins, CO 80523
Phone: 970-491-6281; Fax: 970-491-6208; Web site: www.colostate.edu/Depts/CoopExt/
Founded: 1914
Description: A branch of Colorado State University. Conducts statewide noncredit educational programs off campus.
Contact(s):
Director of Cooperative Extension: MILAN A. REWERTS; E-mail: mrewerts@coop.ext.colostate.edu
Associate Director of Programs: DR. MARY McPHAIL GRAY; E-mail: gray@coop.ext.colostate.edu
Extension Agent-Natural Resources: SHELLEY STANLEY, 15200 W. Sixth Ave., Golden, CO 80401; Phone: 303-271-6620
Extension Wildlife Specialist: Animal Damage Control: DR. WILLIAM F. ANDELT, Dept. of Fishery and Wildlife Biology: 109 Wagar: Colorado State University, Ft. Collins, CO 80523; Phone: 970-491-7093
Extension Wildlife Specialist: Wildlife Management: DR. DELWIN E. BENSON, Dept. of Fishery and Wildlife Biology: 109 Wagar: Colorado State University, Ft. Collins, CO 80523; Phone: 970-491-6411; Fax: 970-491-5091
Keyword(s): Agriculture, Biotechnology, Environmental and Conservation Education, Gardening and Horticulture, Health and Nutrition, Hunting, Outdoor Recreation, Pesticides, Precision Farming, Renewable Resources, Rural Development, Solid Waste Management, Sustainable Development, Sustainable Ecosystems, Urban Environment

GOVERNOR'S OFFICE OF ENERGY, MANAGEMENT, AND CONSERVATION (COLORADO)
1675 Broadway, Suite 1300, Denver, CO 80202-4613
Phone: 303-620-4292; E-mail: oec@csn.net; Web site: www.state.co.us/oec/
Founded: 1977
Description: OEC's mission includes leading the citizens of Colorado by promoting the efficient use of energy and resources. OEC develops, implements, and monitors energy conservation programs and offers services for individuals, community organizations, institutions, businesses and government. Those services are designed to reduce energy consumption and increase awareness of the environmental, economic and personal benefit to efficient energy use.
Contact(s):
Director: RICK GRICE
Publication(s): *Recycle Colorado Bulletin*
Keyword(s): Environmental and Conservation Education, Renewable Resources, Solar Energy, Solid Waste Management, Composting

CONNECTICUT

GOVERNOR OF CONNECTICUT: JOHN G. ROWLAND
210 Capitol Ave., Hartford, CT 06106
Phone: 800-406-1527

CONNECTICUT COUNCIL ON ENVIRONMENTAL QUALITY
79 Elm Street, Hartford, CT 6106
Phone: 860-424-4000; Fax: 860-424-4070; E-mail: karl.wagener@po.state.ct.us
Founded: 1971
Description: Prepares annual reports to the Governor on the status of Connecticut's environment; receives and investigates citizen complaints pertaining to the environment; and reviews environmental assessments of construction activities of state agencies. The council is composed of nine appointed members who serve without compensation.
Contact(s):
Chairman: DONAL C. O'BRIEN JR.
Executive Director: KARL J. WAGENER
Publication(s): *Environmental Quality in Connecticut (Annual Report)*
Keyword(s): Environment, Environmental Planning, Environmental Protection, Land Use Planning

CONNECTICUT DEPARTMENT OF AGRICULTURE
765 Asylum Ave., Hartford, CT 06105
Phone: 860-713-2503
Contact(s):
Deputy Commissioner: BRUCE H. GRESCZYK
Commissioner: SHIRLEY FERRIS
Deputy Director: Marketing and Technology: FRANK A. INTINO; Phone: 860-713-2503
Deputy Director: Regulation and Inspection: GABRIEL F. MOQUIN; Phone: 860-713-2508
Director: Administration: DAWN L. CASSADA; Phone: 860-713-2502
Director: Aquaculture Division: JOHN VOLK, P.O. Box 97, Milford, CT 06460; Phone: 203-874-2855
Director: Farmland Preservation: JOSEPH J. DIPPEL; Phone: 860-713-2511
Director: Marketing and Technology: ROBERT R. PELLEGRINO; Phone: 860-713-2503
Director: Personnel: EMILIE M. ANDREWS; Phone: 860-713-2501
Director: Regulation and Inspection: DR. BRUCE A. SHERMAN; Phone: 860-713-2504
Executive Director: Connecticut Marketing Authority: DAVID CAREY, 101 Reserve Rd., Hartford, CT 06106; Phone: 860-566-3699

CONNECTICUT DEPARTMENT OF ENVIRONMENTAL PROTECTION
79 Elm St., Hartford, CT 06106-5127
Description: Created by the Connecticut General Assembly to conserve, protect, and improve the state's environment and to manage the basic resources of air, water, and land for the benefit of present and future generations.
Contact(s):
Assistant Commissioner, Air, Water and Waste: JANE STAHL; Phone: 860-424-3009
Assistant Commissioner, Environmental Conservation: DAVID K. LEFF; Phone: 860-424-3005
Chief: Bureau of Air Management: CARMINE N. DIBATTISTA; Phone: 860-424-3026
Chief: Bureau of Natural Resources: EDWARD C. PARKER; Phone: 860-424-3010
Chief: Bureau of Outdoor Recreation: RICHARD K. CLIFFORD; Phone: 860-424-3014
Chief: Bureau of Waste Management: RICHARD J. BARLOW; Phone: 860-424-3021
Chief: Bureau of Water Management: ROBERT L. SMITH; Phone: 860-424-3704
Commissioner: ARTHUR J. ROCQUE JR; Phone: 860-424-3001
Director: Communications: Education: and Publications: MICHELE SULLIVAN; Phone: 860-424-4100
Director: Fisheries Division: ERNEST E. BECKWITH; Phone: 860-424-3474
Director: Forestry Division: DONALD H. SMITH; Phone: 860-424-3630

STATE AND PROVINCIAL GOVERNMENT AGENCIES - DELAWARE

Director: Land Acquisition and Management: CHARLES J. REED; Phone: 860-424-3016
Director: Law Enforcement Division: GEORGE J. BARONE JR.; Phone: 860-424-3012
Director: Natural Resources Center: STEVEN O. FISH; Phone: 860-424-3642
Director: Parks Division: PAMELA A. ADAMS; Phone: 860-424-3200
Director: Wildlife Division: DALE W. MAY; Phone: 860-424-3011
Staff: DALE MAY; Phone: 860-424-3011
Publication(s): *Connecticut Wildlife*

CONNECTICUT SEA GRANT
Sea Grant College Program, University of Connecticut, 1084 Shennecossett Rd., Groton, CT 06430-6097
Phone: 860-405-9110; Fax: 860-405-9109; Web site: www.ucc.uconn.edu/~wwwsgo/
Contact(s):
Director: EDWARD C. MONAHAN; E-mail: sgoadm01@uconnvm.uconn.edu

UNIVERSITY OF CONNECTICUT COOPERATIVE EXTENSION
College of Agriculture and Natural Resources, Box U-66, 1376 Storrs Rd., University of Connecticut, Storrs, CT 06269-4066
E-mail: bwilbur@canr1.cag.uconn.edu; Web site: www.lib.uconn.edu/CANR/ces/
Description: Natural resource components include forest management, forest stewardship, urban forestry, water resources, and wildlife management.
Contact(s):
Extension Educator: Forest Management: STEPHEN BRODERICK, 139 Wolf Den Rd., Brooklyn, CT 06234; Phone: 860-774-9600
Extension Specialist: Water Resources: DR. GLENN WARNER, Natural Resources Management and Engineering: Box U-87: University of Connecticut, Storrs, CT 06269-4087; Phone: 860-486-2840
Extension Specialist: Wildlife and Director, Wildlife Conservation Research Center: DR. JOHN S. BARCLAY, Natural Resources Management and Engineering: Box U-87: University of Connecticut, Storrs, CT 06269-4087; Phone: 860-486-0143; Fax: 860-486-5875
Program Leader: Marine Advisory Program: NORMAN BENDER, University of CT-MAS: 1084 Shennecossett Rd., Groton, CT 06340-6097; Phone: 860-445-8664
State Climatologist: DR. DAVID R. MILLER, Natural Resources Management and Engineering: Box U-87: University of Connecticut, Storrs, CT 06269-4087; Phone: 860-486-2840

DELAWARE

GOVERNOR OF DELAWARE: THOMAS R. CARPER
Tatnall Bldg., William Penn St., Dover, DE 19901
Phone: 302-739-4101

DELAWARE DEPARTMENT OF AGRICULTURE
2320 S. DuPont Highway, Dover, DE 19901-5515
Phone: 302-739-4811; Fax: 302-697-4463
Description: The DDA works to provide mandated services which protect the health and welfare of Delaware consumers and to advertise those services; to promote the sound utilization of resources, especially agricultural lands; and to advance the economic viability of the food, fiber, and agricultural industries of Delaware.
Contact(s):
Secretary: JOHN F. TARBURTON: JR.
Agriculture Compliance Laboratory: TERESA CRENSHAW
Community Relations Officer: ANNE FITZGERALD
Deputy Secretary: SUSAN STUCHLIK-EDWARDS
Executive Assistant: BRUCE R. WALTON
Keyword(s): Agriculture, Forests and Forestry, Land Use Planning, Pesticides, Urban Forestry

DELAWARE DEPARTMENT OF NATURAL RESOURCES AND ENVIRONMENTAL CONTROL
89 Kings Highway, Dover, DE 19901
Phone: 302-739-4403; Fax: 302-739-6242
Founded: 1970
Description: The mission of the Delaware Department of Natural Resources and Environmental Control is to protect and manage the state's natural resources, protect public health and safety, provide quality outdoor recreation and to serve and educate the citizens of Delaware to promote the wise use, conservation and enhancement of Delaware's environment.
Contact(s):
Secretary: NICHOLAS A. DIPASQUALE
Executive Assistant: DAVID SMALL
Editor, DNREC News: MELINDA CARL; Phone: 302-739-4506
Editor, Outdoor Delaware: KATHLEEN JAMISON; Phone: 302-739-4506
Publication(s): *Outdoor Delaware, DNREC News*
Keyword(s): Air Quality and Pollution, Beaches, Environmental and Conservation Education, Soil Conservation, Waste Management, Water Quality, Wildlife Management

Division of Air and Waste Management
89 Kings Hwy., P.O. Box 1401, Dover, DE 19903
Contact(s):
Director: DENISE FERGUSON-SOUTHARD; Phone: 302-739-4764
Administrator: Air Resources: DARRYL TYLER; Phone: 302-739-4791
Manager: Hazardous Wastes: NANCY MARKER; Phone: 302-739-3689
Manager: Solid Waste: JAMIE RUTHERFORD; Phone: 302-739-3820
Manager: Underground Storage Tanks: KATHLEEN STILLER; Phone: 302-323-4588
Manager: Site Investigation and Remediation: N. V. RAMAN; Phone: 302-323-4540
Administrator Enforcement: MAJOR WILLIAM HILL; Phone: 302-739-5072

Division of Fish and Wildlife
89 Kings Hwy., P.O. Box 1401, Dover, DE 19903
Contact(s):
Director: ANDREW T. MANUS; Phone: 302-739-5295
Administrator: Enforcement: MAJ. JAMES GRAYBEAL; Phone: 302-739-3440
Administrator: Fisheries: CHARLES A. LESSER; Phone: 302-739-3441
Administrator: Wildlife: H. LLOYD ALEXANDER JR.; Phone: 302-739-5297
Federal Aid Coordinator and Senior Planner: LYNN HERMAN; Phone: 302-739-5296
Manager: Acquisitions: PHIL CARPENTER; Phone: 302-739-3441
Manager: Construction: LACY NICHOLS; Phone: 302-739-3441

Division of Parks and Recreation
Contact(s):
Director: CHARLES SALKIN; Phone: 302-739-4401
Manager: Cultural & Recreation Services: JAMES O'NEILL; Phone: 302-739-4413
Manager: Park Operations: CLYDE SHIPMAN; Phone: 302-739-4406
Manager: Planning, Preservation and Development: MARK R. CHURA; Phone: 302-739-5285

Division of Soil and Water Conservation
Phone: 302-739-4411; Fax: 302-739-6724
Contact(s):
Director: JOHN A. HUGHES; E-mail: jhughes@dnrec.state.de.us
Administrator: Delaware Coastal Management Program: SARAH COOKSEY; Phone: 302-739-3451
Administrator: Shoreline and Waterway Management: ROBERT D. HENRY

Keyword(s): Air Quality and Pollution, Environmental and Conservation Education, Soil Conservation, Water Pollution Management, Wildlife Management

Division of Water Resources
Contact(s):
Director: KEVIN DONNELLY; Phone: 302-739-4860
Manager: Wetlands and Subaqueous Lands: WILLIAM F. MOYER; Phone: 302-739-4691
Manager: Watershed Assessment: JOHN SCHNEIDER; Phone: 302-739-4590
Manager: Ground Water Discharges: RODNEY WYATT; Phone: 302-739-4761
Manager: Water Supply: STEWART LOVELL; Phone: 302-739-4793
Manager: Surface Water Discharges: PEDER HANSEN; Phone: 302-739-5731
Administrator: Environmental Services: SERGIO HUERTA

DELAWARE GEOLOGICAL SURVEY
DGS Bldg., University of Delaware, Newark, DE 19716
Phone: 302-831-2833; Fax: 302-831-3579; E-mail: DGS@mvs.udel.edu
Founded: 1951
Description: The survey was formed to study the geology, water, and other earth resources of Delaware; also to prepare reports, maps, and otherwise disseminate its findings, and to provide assistance in its area to other agencies and individuals.
Contact(s):
Associate Director: JOHN H. TALLEY
Librarian: DOROTHY C. WINDISH
State Geologist and Director: ROBERT R. JORDAN
Keyword(s): Geology, Research, Water Resources

DELAWARE SEA GRANT PROGRAM
University of Delaware, Newark, DE 19716-3501
Phone: 302-831-2841; Fax: 302-831-4389; Web site: www.ocean.udel.edu/seagrant/
Contact(s):
Director: DR. CAROLYN THOROUGHGOOD; E-mail: C.Thoroughgood@mvs.udel.edu
Executive Director: DAVID McCARREN; Phone: 302-831-8255

DELAWARE SOLID WASTE AUTHORITY
1128 S. Bradford St., P.O. Box 455, Dover, DE 19903
Phone: 302-739-5361; Fax: 302-739-4287; Web site: www.dswa.com
Founded: 1975
Description: To define, develop, and implement cost-effective plans and programs for solid waste management which best serve Delaware and protect our public health and environment.
Contact(s):
Chief Executive Officer (P.E., DEE): N. C. VASUKI
Chief of Administrative/ Services Officer (P.E.): THOMAS E. HOUSKA II
Chief Operating Officer (P.E., DEE): PASQUALE S. CANZANO
Publication(s): *Statewide Solid Waste Management Plan and Executive Summary; Great Waste Mystery Curriculum, The; Marketing Research Findings and Executive Summary; Trash Tracks (DSWA Newsletter)*
Keyword(s): Environmental and Conservation Education, Environmental Planning, Public Health Protection, Research, Solid Waste Management

DELAWARE STATE EXTENSION SERVICE
Delaware Cooperative Extension, Townsend Hall, University of Delaware, Newark, DE 19717-1303
Phone: 302-831-2504; Fax: 302-831-6758; Web site: bluehen.ags.udel.edu/deces/
Contact(s):
Dean, College of Agricultural Sciences and Director, Agricultural Experiment Station: DR. JOHN C. NYE; Phone: 302-831-2501; E-mail: nye@udel.edu
Associate Dean for Extension and Outreach: DR. PATRICIA S. BARBER; E-mail: pbarber@udel.edu
Aquaculture Specialist: JOHN W. EWART, University of Delaware Aquac. Research Center, 700 Pilottown Rd., Lewes, DE 19958; Phone: 302-645-4060; Fax: 302-645-4007
Keyword(s): Agriculture, Conservation Tillage, Energy Conservation, Engineering, Environmental and Conservation Education, Environmental Protection, Flowers, Plants, and Trees, Forest Management, Gardening and Horticulture, Health and Nutrition, Insects and Butterflies, Land Use Planning, Pesticides, Precision Farming, Public Health Protection

DISTRICT OF COLUMBIA

DEPARTMENT OF PUBLIC WORKS
2000 14th St., NW, Washington, DC 20009
Phone: 202-645-7044
Contact(s):
Director: VANESSA BURNS
Keyword(s): Pedestrian Environment, Solid Waste, Transportation, Urban Environment, Water Pollution

DISTRICT OF COLUMBIA DEPARTMENT OF HEALTH

Environmental Health Administration, Watershed Protection Division
2100 Martin Luther King Jr. Ave., SE, Suite 203, Washington, DC 20020
Phone: 202-645-6623
Contact(s):
Program Manager: DR. HAMID KARIMI

DISTRICT OF COLUMBIA STATE EXTENSION SERVICES
University of the District of Columbia, 4200 Connecticut Ave. N.W., Suite 3009, Washington, DC 20008
Phone: 202-274-7115; Web site: www.udc.edu/www/misc/land_grant.html
Contact(s):
Director of Cooperative Extension Service: DR. LILLIE MONROE-LORD
State Specialist: Agriculture and Natural Resources: DR. MOHAMED KAHN

FLORIDA

GOVERNOR OF FLORIDA: JEB BUSH
State Capitol, Tallahassee, FL 32399-0001
Phone: 850-488-2272

FLORIDA COOPERATIVE FISH AND WILDLIFE RESEARCH UNIT (USDI)
P.O. Box 110450, 117 Newins-Ziegler Hall, University of Florida, Gainesville, FL 32611-0450
Founded: 1979
Description: Established by cooperative agreement among the National Biological Survey, Florida Game and Fresh Water Fish Commission, and the University of Florida. Primary purpose is research, graduate education, and extension activities integrating fish and wildlife ecology and management in Florida's unique ecosystems, particularly wetlands.
Contact(s):
Assistant Unit Leader of Fisheries:
Assistant Unit Leader: Wildlife: DR. H. FRANKLIN PERCIVAL
Unit Leader: DR. WILEY M. KITCHENS
Keyword(s): Aquatic Habitats, Biodiversity, Endangered and Threatened Species, Reptiles and Amphibians, Wetlands

FLORIDA DEPARTMENT OF AGRICULTURE AND CONSUMER SERVICES
The Capitol, PL10, Tallahassee, FL 32399-0800
Contact(s):
Commissioner: BOB CRAWFORD; Phone: 850-488-3022

STATE AND PROVINCIAL GOVERNMENT AGENCIES - FLORIDA

Division of Forestry
Founded: 1927
Description: To protect and manage Florida's forest resources through a stewardship ethic to assure these resources will be available for future generations. Current number of employees: 1,100.
Contact(s):
Assistant Director: MIKE C. LONG; Phone: 850-414-9967
Director: L. EARL PETERSON; Phone: 850-922-0135
Chief of Fire Control: LARRY F. WOOD; Phone: 850-488-6595
Chief of Forest Management: C. CHARLES MAYNARD; Phone: 850-488-6611
Chief of Planning and Support Services: ROBERT B. McDONALD; Phone: 850-414-0843
Chief: Field Operations: RAYMOND K. GEIGER; Phone: 850-414-9969

Office of Agricultural Water Policy
Suite C, Administration Bldg., 3125 Conner Blvd., Tallahassee, FL 32399-1650
Phone: 850-488-6249
Description: Provides administrative, legislative, and promotional assistance to 63 Soil and Water Conservation Districts in Florida.
Contact(s):
Director: CHUCK ALLER
Soil and Water Conservation Administrator: JOHN C. FOLKS; Phone: 850-488-6249

Soil and Water Conservation Council
Contact(s):
Chair: RICHARD MACHEK, 17 NW 16th St., Delray Beach, FL 33444
SWC Administrator: CLEGG HOOKS, 3125 Conner Blvd., Suite C, Conner Bldg., Tallahassee, FL 32399; Phone: 850-488-6249; Fax: 850-921-2153

FLORIDA DEPARTMENT OF ENVIRONMENTAL PROTECTION
3900 Commonwealth Blvd., Tallahassee, FL 32399-3000
Contact(s):
Secretary: VIRGINIA B. WETHERELL; Phone: 904-488-1554/904-488-4805
Communications Director: CATHERINE ARNOLD; Phone: 904-488-1073
Deputy Secretary: KIRBY GREEN III; Phone: 904-488-7131
Director for Air Resources Management Division: HOWARD RHODES; Phone: 850-488-0114
Director for Division of Administrative and Technical Services: NEVIN SMITH; Phone: 850-488-2955
Director for Division of Administrative Services: MYRA WILLIAMS; Phone: 850-488-0878
Director for Division of Law Enforcement: MICKEY WATSON; Phone: 850-488-5600
Director for Division of Recreation and Parks: FRAN MAINELLA; Phone: 850-488-6131
Director for Division of State Lands: PETE MALLISON; Phone: 850-488-2725
Director for Division of Waste Management: JOHN M. RUDDELL; Phone: 850-487-3299
Director for Division of Water Facilities: MIMI DREW; Phone: 852-487-1855
Director for Ecosystem Management Division: PAM McVETY; Phone: 850-488-7454
Director for Marine Resources Division: ED CONKLIN; Phone: 850-488-6058
General Counsel: PERRY ODOM; Phone: 904-488-9735
General Counsel: PERRY ODOM; Phone: 850-488-9730
Inspector General: PINKY HALL; Phone: 904-488-2287
Special Assistant: MOLLIE PALMER; Phone: 904-488-1554

Air Resources Management Division
3900 Commonwealth Blvd., Tallahassee, FL 32399
Contact(s):
Staff: HOWARD RHODES; Phone: 904-488-0114
Staff of Air Monitoring and Assessment: DOTTY DILTZ; Phone: 904-488-6140
Staff of Air Regulation: CLAIR FANCY; Phone: 904-488-1344

Beaches and Shores Division
3900 Commonwealth Blvd., Tallahassee, FL 32399-3000
Contact(s):
Staff: KIRBY GREEN; Phone: 904-487-4469
Staff of Coastal Data Acquisition: HAROLD BEAN; Phone: 904-487-4471
Staff of Coastal Engineering and Regulation: AL DEVEREAUX; Phone: 904-488-3181
Staff of Beach Management: LONNIE RYDER; Phone: 904-487-1262

Ecosytem Management Division
Contact(s):
Ecosytem Planning and Coordination: ZRNIE BARNETT; Phone: 904-487-4892
Executive Coordinator: PAM McVETY; Phone: 904-488-7454
Staff of Environmental Education: JIM LEWIS; Phone: 904-488-7326/9334
Staff of Intergovernmental Programs: DEBBIE PAZZISH; Phone: 904-487-2231
Staff of Water Policy/SWIM: JANET LLEWELLYZ; Phone: 904-488-0784

Environmental Resource Permitting Division
Contact(s):
Staff: JEREMY CRAFT; Phone: 904-488-3177
Staff of Surface Water Management: ; Phone: 904-488-6221

Law Enforcement Division
Contact(s):
Staff: MICKEY WATSON; Phone: 904-488-5757
Staff of Coastal Protection: DEBBIE PREBBLE; Phone: 904-487-2974
Staff of Vessel Titling and Registration: ELAYNE HUEBNER; Phone: 904-488-1195
Staff of Technical Services: HENRY NASH; Phone: 904-488-5600

Legislative and Cabinet Affairs Division
Contact(s):
Executive Services Director: NEVIN SMITH; Phone: 904-488-2955
Staff: DIANE HADI; Phone: 904-487-2916
Staff of General Services: JOHN CHERRY; Phone: 904-488-1309
Staff of Information Systems: JOHN WILLMOTT; Phone: 904-488-0892
Staff of Administrative Services: MYRA WILLIAMS; Phone: 904-488-8587
Staff of Budget: JAMIE DELOACH; Phone: 904-488-8587
Staff of Finance and Accounting: JACK DULL; Phone: 904-488-1093
Staff of Human Resource Services: ALYCE PARMER; Phone: 904-488-2996
Staff of Laboratories: JERRY BROOKS; Phone: 904-488-2790
Staff of Management Systems: MANNY MUNOZ; Phone: 904-922-4146
Staff of Quality Assurance: SYLVIA LABIE; Phone: 904-488-2796
Staff of Systems Support: RICK MITCHELL; Phone: 904-488-4883/904-487-1841

Marine Resource Division
Contact(s):
Staff: ED CONKLIN; Phone: 904-488-6058
Staff of Fisheries Management and Assistance: VIRGINIA VAIL; Phone: 904-922-4340
Staff of Florida Marine Research Institute (St. Petersburg): KEN HADDAD; Phone: 813-896-8626
Staff of Marine Resources Regulation and Development: DAVID HELL; Phone: 904-488-5471
Staff of Protected Species Management: PAT ROSE; Phone: 904-922-3456
Staff of Sanctuaries and Research Reserves: DANNY RILEY; Phone: 904-488-3456

Recreation and Parks division
Contact(s):
Staff: FRAN MAINELLA; Phone: 904-488-6131
Staff of Aquatic Plant Management: TOM BROWN; Phone: 904-488-5631
Staff of Design and Construction Division: MIKE BULLOCK; Phone: 904-488-2191
Staff of Geology: WALTER SCHMIDT; Phone: 904-488-4191
Staff of Local Recreational Services: DON GERTEISEN; Phone: 904-488-7896
Staff of Mine Reclamation: JOE BAKKER; Phone: 904-488-8217
Staff of Natural and Cultural Resources: DANA BRYANT; Phone: 904-488-8666
Staff of Operational Services: JOHN BAUST; Phone: 904-488-3300
Staff of Park Planning: ALBERT GREGORY; Phone: 904-488-2200

State Lands Division
Contact(s):
Deputy Director of Land Acquisition: DIANA DARTLAND; Phone: 904-488-3797
Staff: PETE MALLISON; Phone: 904-488-2725
Staff of Appraisal: JOHN SANTANGINI; Phone: 904-488-9025
Staff of Conservation and Recreation Lands Program (CARL): GREG BROCK; Phone: 904-487-1750
Staff of Land Acquisition: ED KUESTER; Phone: 904-488-2351
Staff of Land Management Services: DAN CRABB; Phone: 904-488-2291
Staff of Submerged Lands and Preserves: MIKE ASHEY; Phone: 904-488-2297
Staff of Survey and Mapping: TERRY WILKINSON; Phone: 904-488-2427

Waste Management Division
Contact(s):
Staff: JOHN RUDDELL; Phone: 904-487-3299
Staff of Solid and Hazardous Waste: BILL HINKLEY; Phone: 904-488-0300
Staff of Waste Cleanup: DOUG JONES; Phone: 904-488-0190

Water Facilities Division
Contact(s):
Staff: MIMI DREW; Phone: 904-487-1855
Staff of Drinking Water and Ground Water Resources: MARY WILLIAMS; Phone: 904-488-3601
Staff of Local Government Wastewater Financial Assistance: DON BERRYHILL; Phone: 904-488-8163
Staff of Water Facilities Planning and Regulation: RICHARD DREW; Phone: 904-487-0563

FLORIDA FISH AND WILDLIFE CONSERVATION COMMISSION
620 S. Meridian St., Tallahassee, FL 32399-1600
Phone: 850-487-3796; Web site: www.state.fl.us/fwc/
Contact(s):
Assistant Executive Director: VICTOR J. HELLER; Phone: 850-488-3084
General Counsel: JAMES V. ANTISTA; Phone: 850-487-1764
Executive Director: DR. ALLAN L. EGBERT; Phone: 850-487-3796
Director: Division of Administrative Services: SANDRA PORTER; Phone: 850-488-6551
Director: Division of Freshwater Fisheries: EDWIN J. MOYER; Phone: 850-488-0331
Director: Division of Law Enforcement: ROBERT L. EDWARDS; Phone: 850-488-6251
Director: Division of Marine Fisheries: DR. RUSSELL S. NELSON; Phone: 850-487-0554
Director: Division of Wildlife: FRANK MONTALBANO III; Phone: 850-488-3831
Director: Office of Environmental Services: BRAD HARTMAN; Phone: 850-488-6662
Director: Office of Informational Services: L. ROSS MORRELL; Phone: 850-488-4676
Editor: DICK SUBLETTE; Phone: 850-488-5564
Publication(s): FLORIDA WILDLIFE
Keyword(s): Aquatic Habitats, Birds, Endangered and Threatened Species, Environment, Fisheries, Hunting, Lakes, Outdoor Recreation, Sport Fishing, Wildlife and Wildlife Habitat, Wildlife Management

FLORIDA SEA GRANT COLLEGE
Florida Sea Grant College Program, P.O. Box 110400, University of Florida, Gainesville, FL 32611-0400
Phone: 352-392-5870; Fax: 352-392-5113; Web site: gnv.ifas.ufl.edu/~seaweb/homepage/fsg.htm
Description: A statewide university-based program of coastal and ocean research, education, and public service to enhance productivity, conservation, and long-term use and management of marine systems and resources.
Contact(s):
Director: Florida Sea Grant College Program: DR. JAMES C. CATO; E-mail: jcc@gnv.ifas.ufl.edu
Associate Director: Florida Sea Grant College Program: DR. WILLIAM SEAMAN; E-mail: seaman@gnv.ifas.ufl.edu
Assistant Dean and Coordinator: Sea Grant Extension Program: DR. MARION L. CLARKE, P.O. Box 110405, University of Florida, Gainesville, FL 32611-0405; Phone: 352-392-1837; E-mail: mlc@gnv.ifas.ufl.edu
Publication(s): Fathom Magazine; Florida Sea Grant SGEB-5; listing of various publications available
Keyword(s): Coasts, Environmental and Conservation Education, Fisheries

FLORIDA STATE COOPERATIVE EXTENSION SERVICE
1038 McCarty Hall, P.O. Box 110210, University of Florida, Gainesville, FL 32611-0210
Phone: 352-392-1761; Web site: www.ifas.ufl.edu/WWW/AGATOR/HTM/CES.HTM
Contact(s):
Dean of Extension: DR. CHRISTINE T. WADDILL, 1038 McCarty Hall, P.O. Box 110210, University of Florida, Gainesville, FL 32611-0210
Director of Energy Extension Service (Acting): PIERCE H. JONES, Box 110570, 102 Rogers Hall, University of Florida, Gainesville, FL 32611-0570; Phone: 352-392-8074; Fax: 352-392-4092; E-mail: ez@agen.ufl.edu
Assistant Extension Scientist, Wildlife: WILLIAM H. KERN, Pinellas County Extension Office, 12175 125th St. North, Largo, FL 33774-3695; Phone: 813-582-2100; Fax: 813-582-2149; E-mail: whk@gnv.ifas.ufl.edu
Wildlife Agent: JOESPH M. SCHAEFER, Univ. of Florida, Wildlife Ecology and Conservation, P.O. Box 110430, Gainesville, FL 32611-0430; Phone: 352-846-0568; Fax: 352-392-6984
Keyword(s): Environmental and Conservation Education, Fisheries, Forests and Forestry, Lakes, Wildlife Management

FLORIDA STATE DEPARTMENT OF HEALTH
State Health Office, 2020 Capital Circle SE, BIN # AOO, Tallahassee, FL 32399-1701
Phone: 904-487-2945; Fax: 850-410-1375
Contact(s):
Deputy State Health Officer for Prevention and Control Programs: RICHARD G. HUNTER; Phone: 850-487-2945
Division Director of Environmental Health: SHARON HEBER; Phone: 850-488-6811
Environmental Hazards: ROGER INMAN; Phone: 850-488-3385
Environmental Programs: BART BIBLER; Phone: 850-488-4070
Environmental Programs: ERIC GRIMM; Phone: 850-487-0004
Epidemiology Programs, Chief (Acting): RUSSELL MARDON; Phone: 850-488-3370
Keyword(s): Public Health Protection, Toxic Substances, Toxicology

LEE COUNTY PARKS AND RECREATION SERVICES
Regional Park Program Office, 7330 Gladiolus Dr., Fort Myers, FL 33908
Phone: 941-432-2004; Fax: 941-432-2032; Web site:www.lee.county.com
Founded: 1990

STATE AND PROVINCIAL GOVERNMENT AGENCIES - GEORGIA

Description: To promote and develop environmental awareness in Southwest Florida by conducting educational programs which teach ecological concepts and outdoor skills, and by coordinating informational events which alert citizens and community leaders of environmental concerns.
Contact(s):
Environmental Educator: JOHN KISEDA; E-mail: kisedajb@leegov.com
Interpretive Naturalist: MARY RUDE; E-mail: rudeme@leegov.com
Outdoor Recreation Specialist: NANCY MacPHEE; E-mail: macpheen@leegov.com
Publication(s): *Elements Newsletter; Explorers Companion Brochure*
Keyword(s): Biodiversity, Birds, Conservation of Protected Areas, EcoAction, Endangered and Threatened Species, Energy Conservation, Environmental and Conservation Education, Environmental Preservation, Environmental Protection, Land Preservation, Nature Preservation, Outdoor Recreation, Public Lands, Wetlands, Wildlife and Wildlife Habitat

MARINE LABORATORY (FLORIDA)
Florida State University, Rt. 1, Box 219A, Sopchoppy, FL 32358
Phone: 904-697-4095; Fax: 904-697-4098
Description: Includes studies on the biology, chemistry, and geology of coastal communities, physical oceanography of near-shore waters, aquatic and terrestrial ecosystems, and aquaculture.
Contact(s):
Director: NANCY H. MARCUS
Keyword(s): Aquatic Habitats, Biology, Coasts, Fisheries, Oceanography

SOUTH FLORIDA WATER MANAGEMENT DISTRICT
3301 Gun Club Rd., P.O. Box 24680, West Palm Beach, FL 33416-4680
Phone: 561-686-8800; Fax: 561-682-6200
Description: Responsible for local cooperation in the Federal-State Central and Southern Florida flood Control Project. Goals include: Flood control, water supply, water quality, and environmental protection for sixteen counties in south Florida. Additional benefits are preservation of natural conditions in the Everglades, land purchases under Save Our Rivers program and enhancement of wetlands, fish, wildlife, waterfowl and public recreation.
Contact(s):
Executive Director: FRANK FINCH P.E.
Chief of Staff: JAMES BLOUNT
Director for Government Affairs and Communications: MICHAEL SLAYTON
Director for Everglades Construction Project: JOSEPH SCHWEIGART
Deputy Executive Director for Corporate Resources (Acting): TREVOR CAMPBELL
Deputy Executive Director for Water Resource Operations (Acting): JEANNE HALL
Deputy Executive Director for Water Resource Management (Acting): WILLIAM MALONE
Keyword(s): Flood Control, Everglades

SOUTHWEST FLORIDA WATER MANAGEMENT DISTRICT (SWFWMD)
2379 Broad St., U.S. 41 South, Brooksville, FL 34609-6899
Phone: 352-796-7211; Fax: 352-754-6885
Founded: 1961
Description: A governmental agency dedicated to resource protection conservation programs, which are supported through regulatory and nonregulatory initiatives and cooperative funding projects.
Contact(s):
Manager of the Water Resource Projects Section: KATHLEEN E. COATES
Water Resource Analyst Staff and Secretary of the Florida Water Wise Council: KATHY FOLEY

Publication(s): *Fifty Ways to do Your Part; Plant Guide and associated technical bulletins; list of vendors and manufacturers of water conservation devices and services; various residential and commercial water conservation education resources.*
Keyword(s): Environmental and Conservation Education, Environmental Planning, Natural Systems, Rivers, Water Conservation, Water Quality, Water Resources, Wetlands

GEORGIA

GOVERNOR OF GEORGIA: ROY BARNES
203 State Capitol, Atlanta, GA 30334
Phone: 404-656-1776

GEORGIA COOPERATIVE FISH AND WILDLIFE RESEARCH UNIT (USDI)
Warnell School of Forest Resources, University of Georgia, Athens, GA 30602-2152
Phone: 706-542-5260
Founded: 1984
Description: The Unit is supported by the Biological Resources Division, USGS; Georgia Department of Natural Resources; and the Wildlife Management Institute; and the University of Georgia. Fisheries and wildlife research, graduate education and training, technical assistance and extension are the main missions of the Unit.
Contact(s):
Assistant Leader: Wildlife: MICHAEL J. CONROY
Unit Leader: CECIL A. JENNINGS
Keyword(s): Aquatic Habitats, Environmental Preservation, Fisheries, Wildlife and Wildlife Habitat, Wildlife Management

GEORGIA DEPARTMENT OF AGRICULTURE
Agriculture Bldg., 19 Martin Luther King Dr., Capitol Sq., Atlanta, GA 30334
Phone: 404-656-3600
Founded: 1874
Description: The department serves farmers and consumers in the state by verifying and enforcing the accuracy and quality of both products and services in many areas including food products, seed, fertilizers, pesticides, fuel, weights and measures and bedding, and by overseeing the health and well-being of Georgia's livestock, poultry and commercial pet industry.
Contact(s):
Commissioner of Agriculture: TOMMY IRVIN
Assistant Commissioner for Consumer Protection Field Forces: CAMERON SMOAK; Phone: 404-656-3627
Assistant Commissioner for Entomology and Pesticides: RON CONLEY; Phone: 404-656-0437
Assistant Commissioner for Fuel and Measures: BILL TRUBY; Phone: 404-656-3605
Assistant Commissioner for Public Affairs: BRENDA JAMES-GRIFFIN; Phone: 404-656-3689
Assistant Commissioner of Administration: EARL HARRIS; Phone: 404-656-3608
Assistant Commissioner of Animal Industry: DR. LEE MEYERS; Phone: 404-656-3671
Assistant Commissioner of Finance: PHIL KEA; Phone: 404-656-3608
Assistant Commissioner of Marketing: BOBBY HARRIS; Phone: 404-656-3368
Publication(s): *Farmers and Consumers Market Bulletin; Georgia Agricultural Facts; Georgia Poultry Facts;*
Keyword(s): Agriculture, Consumer Protection, Consumer Services, Food Safety, Pesticides

Consumers Services Library
Agriculture Bldg., Rm. 224, Capitol Square, Atlanta, GA 30334
Phone: 404-656-3685; Fax: 404-651-7957

GEORGIA DEPARTMENT OF EDUCATION
1766 Twin Towers E., Atlanta, GA 30334-5040

STATE AND PROVINCIAL GOVERNMENT AGENCIES - GEORGIA

Phone: 404-656-0913
Contact(s):
Science Program Specialist: BOB MOORE

GEORGIA DEPARTMENT OF NATURAL RESOURCES
205 Butler St., SE, East Tower, Atlanta, GA 30334
Phone: 404-656-3500
Contact(s):
Commissioner: LONICE C. BARRETT

Coastal Resources Division
One Conservation Way, Brunswick, GA 31520
Contact(s):
Director: DUANE HARRIS; Phone: 912-264-7218

Environmental Protection Division
Contact(s):
Director: HAROLD REHEIS; Phone: 404-656-4713
Assistant Director: DAVID WORD
Chief: Air Protection Branch: RON METHIER
Chief: Hazardous Waste Branch: JENNIFER KADUCK
Chief: Land Protection Branch: MARK SMITH
Chief: Program Coordination Branch: JIM SETSER
Chief: Water Protection Branch: ALAN HALLUM
Chief: Water Resources Branch: NOLTON JOHNSON

Historic Preservation Division
Contact(s):
Director: RAY LUCE; Phone: 404-656-2840

Parks, Recreation and Historic Sites Division
Contact(s):
Director: BURT WEERTS; Phone: 404-656-2770
Chief: Maintenance and Construction Section: DAVID FREEDMAN
Chief: Parks Operation Section: WAYNE ESCOE

Pollution Prevention Assistance Division
Contact(s):
Director: BOB KERR; Phone: 404-651-5120

Program Support Division
Contact(s):
Director: PAUL BURKHALTER; Phone: 404-656-7559

Wildlife Resources Division
2070 U.S. Highway 278, SE, Social Cir., GA 30025
Phone: 770-918-6400
Contact(s):
Director: DAVID WALLER
Chief: Fisheries Management: MIKE GENNINGS; Phone: 770-918-6406
Chief: Game Management: TODD HOLBROOK; Phone: 770-918-6404
Chief: Law Enforcement: COL. WALT TAYLOR; Phone: 770-918-6408
Chief: Nongame Wildlife/Natural Heritage: MIKE HARRIS; Phone: 770-761-3035

GEORGIA FORESTRY COMMISSION
P.O. Box 819, Macon, GA 31202-0819
Phone: 912-751-3500
Founded: 1925
Description: To foster, improve, and encourage reforestation; to engage in research and other projects for better forestry practices; to inform the public of the values and benefits of forestry; and to detect, prevent, and combat forest fires.
Contact(s):
Deputy Director: WILLIAM R. LAZENBY; Phone: 912-751-3480
Director: J. FRED ALLEN; Phone: 912-751-3480
Board of Commissioner Chairman: JIM L. GILLIS JR.
Chief of Forest Administration: GARLAND NELSON; Phone: 912-751-3464
Chief of Forest Management: LYNN HOOVEN; Phone: 912-751-3458
Chief of Forest Products Utilization, Marketing, and Development: TOMMY LOGGINS; Phone: 912-751-3521
Chief of Forest Protection: ALAN DOZIER; Phone: 912-751-3488
Chief of Information and Education: SHARON DOLLIVER; Phone: 912-751-3530
Chief of Reforestation: JOHNNY BRANAN; Phone: 912-751-3530
Editor: LYNN WALTON; Phone: 912-751-3530
Personnel Officer: RANDALL PERRY; Phone: 404-298-4949
Publication(s): *Georgia Forestry; Wood Using Industries*

GEORGIA SEA GRANT COLLEGE PROGRAM
The University of Georgia, Marine Sciences Bldg. Rm. 220, Athens, GA 30602-3636
Phone: 706-542-5954; Fax: 706-542-3652; Web site: alpha.marsci.uga.edu/gaseagrant.html
Founded: 1971
Description: A part of the National Sea Grant College Program, the Georgia program fosters the sustainable development and environmental stewardship of the nation's marine resources. It is a competitive grant program funding, applied marine research, education, and advisory service projects at universities in Georgia.
Contact(s):
Director: DR. WILLIAM GRAY POTTER; Phone: 706-542-0621
Associate Director: Collections and Public Services: DR. BARABARA WINTERS; Phone: 706-542-0626
Director, Sea Grant College Program: DR. MAC RAWSON JR.; E-mail: mrawson@arches.uga.edu
Leader of Marine Advisory Service Communicator: DAVID BRYANT
Leader: Education Program: DR. WILLIAM HAYES
Leader: Marine Advisory Service: KEITH GATES
Keyword(s): Coasts, Environmental and Conservation Education, Oceanography, Renewable Resources, Sustainable Development

GEORGIA STATE EXTENSION SERVICE
College of Agricultural and Environmental Sciences, 101 Conner Hall, The University of Georgia, Athens, GA 30602-7501
Phone: 706-542-3924; Fax: 706-542-0803; Web site: www.ces.uga.edu/
Contact(s):
Dean and Director: DR. GALE A. BUCHANAN; Phone: 706-542-3924; E-mail: caesdean@arches.uga.edu
Associate Dean for Extension: DR. WILLIAM R. LAMBERT, Cooperative Extension Service, The University of Georgia, Athens, GA 30602-7504; Phone: 706-542-3824; Fax: 706-542-8815; E-mail: blambert@arches.uga.edu
Aquaculture and Fisheries Specialist: DR. GEORGE W. LEWIS; Phone: 706-542-9038
Extension Coordinator for Forest Resources Unit: DR. BEN D. JACKSON; Phone: 706-542-9051
Wildlife Specialist: DR. JEFFERY J. JACKSON, University of Georgia, Warnell School of Forest Resources, Athens, GA 30602-2152; Phone: 706-542-9054; Fax: 706-542-3342

STATE SOIL AND WATER CONSERVATION COMMISSION (GEORGIA)
P.O. Box 8024, Athens, GA 30603
Phone: 706-542-3065
Founded: 1937
Description: Established under the Soil Conservation Districts Act to work with and assist the 40 Soil and Water Conservation Districts and their 370 District Supervisors throughout Georgia.
Contact(s):
Chairman: J. M. PLEMONS; Phone: 706-935-4324
Executive Director: F. GRAHAM LILES JR.; Phone: 706-542-3065; Fax: 706-542-4242
Editor: DAVID BENNETT
Publication(s): *Conservation Commission; Conservation Contact*
Keyword(s): Agriculture, Soil Conservation, Urban Environment, Water Resources, Wetlands

STATE AND PROVINCIAL GOVERNMENT AGENCIES - GUAM

GUAM

GOVERNOR OF GUAM: CARL T.C. GUTIERREZ
Executive Chambers, P.O. Box 2950, Agana, Guam 96932
Phone: 011-671-472-8931

DEPARTMENT OF PARKS AND RECREATION (GUAM)
P.O. Box 2950, Agana, Guam 96910
Phone: 671-475-6296/7; Fax: 671-472-9626
Contact(s):
Deputy Director: FRANKLIN J. GUTIERREZ
Director: A. J. SHELTON
Keyword(s): Historic Preservation, Nature Preservation, Outdoor Recreation

DIVISION OF FORESTRY AND SOIL RESOURCES OF GUAM
192 Dairy Road, Mangilao, Guam 96923
Phone: 671-735-3949; Fax: 671-734-0111
Founded: 1953
Description: The DFSR was formed for the management, protection, and enhancement of the territory's forest and land resources to produce ample amounts of water, wood, fiber, and recreation to benefit the most number of people.
Contact(s):
Chief: DAVID T. LIMTIACO; E-mail: dlimti@ns.gu
Forester I: LOUANN C. GUZMAN; E-mail: lcguzman@ns.gu
Forester I: BELMINA I. SOLIVA; E-mail: bsoliva@ns.gu
Management Forester: RODOLFO L. ANDO; E-mail: rlando@ns.gu
Urban and Community Forester: JOSEPH L.M. ACFALLE; E-mail: jacfalle@ns.gu
Keyword(s): Afforestation, Environmental and Conservation Education, Fire Prevention, Forest Management, Forest Stewardship, Urban Forestry

GUAM COASTAL MANAGEMENT PROGRAM
Bureau of Planning, P.O. Box 2950, Agana, Guam 96932
Phone: 671-472-4201; Fax: 671-477-1812
Founded: 1979
Contact(s):
Administrator: Guam Coastal Management Program: MICHAEL L. HAM
Director: Bureau of Planning: VINCENT P. ARRIOLA
Library Services: Bureau of Planning: Supervisor: SUSAN M. HAM
Publication(s): *Public Television Show: Man, Land, and Sea (Guam only)*; List of publications, posters, and fliers available upon request.
Keyword(s): Coasts, Coral Reefs, Planning Management, Sustainable Development, Sustainable Ecosystems

GUAM COOPERATIVE EXTENSION SERVICE
College of Agriculture and Life Sciences (CALS) Bldg., Rm. 206, University of Guam, 303 University Dr., University of Guam Station, Mangilao, Guam 96923
Phone: 671-735-2000; Fax: 671-734-6842; Web site: uog2.uog.edu/cals/GCE/mission.html
Contact(s):
Dean of CALS and Director of Extension Service and Agricultural Experiment Station: JEFF BARCINAS; Phone: 671-735-2002; E-mail: jbarcina@uog9.uog.edu
Associate Dean, Cooperative Extension (Acting): VICTOR T. ARTERO; Phone: 671-735-2004; E-mail: vartero@uog9.uog.edu
Associate Director of the Agricultural Experiment Station: JOHN W. BROWN; Phone: 671-735-2140; Fax: 671-734-4600; E-mail: gwall@uog9.uog.edu
Extension Assistant: CLARISSA D. SAN NICHOLAS; E-mail: cdsannic@uog9.uog.edu
Aquaculturist: DAVID P. CHRISOTOMO, 303 University Dr., UOG Station, Mangilao, GU 96923; Phone: 671-735-2080; Fax: 706-734-5600

GUAM DEPARTMENT OF AGRICULTURE
192 Dairy Rd., Mangilao, Guam 96923
Phone: 671-734-3941/42/43; Fax: 671-734-6569
Founded: 1950
Description: Charged with responsibility for the conservation and management of Guam's fish, wildlife, soil, and forestry resources, together with development of agricultural and fishery production for food purposes.
Contact(s):
Deputy Director: JOSEPH G. SABLAN
Director: MICHAEL W. KUHLMANN, 192 Dairy Rd., Mangilao, GU 96923; Phone: 671-734-3942; Fax: 671-734-6569

Division of Aquatic and Wildlife Resources
192 Dairy Rd., Mangilao, Guam 96923
Phone: 671-734-3944/45; Fax: 671-734-6570
Contact(s):
Administrative Officer: ALAN G. VAN AKEN
Chief: ROBERT D. ANDERSON

GUAM ENVIRONMENTAL PROTECTION AGENCY
P.O. Box 22439, Guam Main Facility, Barrigada, Guam 96921
Phone: 671-472-8863
Founded: 1973
Description: Activities include: land-use planning; review of environmental impact assessments and environmental protection plans; supervision, planning, and regulation of all new or modified wastewater sources; and the development and protection of potable water supplies; solid and hazardous waste management, pesticides importation, distribution, and use; and air pollution sources. Provide field and laboratory support for the agency's water, air and land regulatory programs.
Contact(s):
Administrative Services Officer Administrative Services: ROSALIE A. LANCERO
Administrator: JESUS T. SALAS
Administrator: Air and Land Programs Division: CONCHITA S.N. TAITANO
Assistant to the Administrator: BEN MACHOL
Board of Directors Chairman: ALBERT W.C. WONG
Board of Directors Vice-Chair: JOSEPHINE B. COAD
Chief Engineer: Water Programs Division: NARCISO G. CUSTODIO P.E.
Chief Planner: Environmental Planning and Review: JORDAN KAYE
Chief: Analysis Section: MILA P. PADOR
Chief: Surveillance: MELVIN B. BORJA
Deputy Administrator:
Director: Air Pollution Control Program: JOAQUIN Q. CRUZ
Director: Drinking Water Program: ANGEL B. MARQUEZ
Director: Pesticides Enforcement Program: VIRGILIO L. OBIAS
Director: Solid and Hazardous Waste Program: FRANCIS P. DAMIAN
Director: Water Pollution Control Program: DOMINGO S. CABUSAO
Director: Water Resources Management Program: MARILOU B. YAMANAKA
Legal Counsel: ELISABETH T. CRUZ
Public Information Officer: GRACE OMEGA GARCES
Special Assistant to the Administrator: MARK PETERSEN
Territorial Hydrogeologist: H. VICTOR WUERCH
Publication(s): *Annual Report*; list available on request.

HAWAII

GOVERNOR OF HAWAII: BENJAMIN CAYETANO
235 S. Beretania St., State Capitol, Honolulu, HI 96813
Phone: 808-586-0034

COLLEGE OF TROPICAL AGRICULTURE AND HUMAN RESOURCES
University of Hawaii, 3050 Maile Way, Honolulu, HI 96822
Phone: 808-956-8131
Founded: 1901
Description: Plan and implement research and extension in agriculture, natural resources, and human resources relevant to Hawaii and the tropics, with emphasis on the Pacific and Asia.

STATE AND PROVINCIAL GOVERNMENT AGENCIES - HAWAII

Contact(s):
Interim Associate Dean and Associate Director for Research: CATHERINE G. CAVALETTO
Publication(s): *Various research and extension*
Keyword(s): Agriculture, Biotechnology, Chemical Pollution Control, Conservation Tillage, Engineering, Environment, Flowers, Plants, and Trees, Gardening and Horticulture, Health and Nutrition, Insects and Butterflies, Landscape Architecture, Pesticides, Public Health Protection, Renewable Resources, Research

DEPARTMENT OF LAND AND NATURAL RESOURCES

Division of Boating and Ocean Recreation (DOBOR
333 Queen Street, Room 300, Honolulu, HI 96813
Phone: 808-587-1963

Division of Water Resource Management,
P.O. Box 621, Honolulu, HI 96809
Phone: 808-587-0215
Contact(s):
Deputy: RAE M. LOUI
Keyword(s): Environmental Protection, Fisheries, Land Preservation, Water Resources, Wildlife Management

DEPARTMENT OF LAND AND NATURAL RESOURCES (HAWAII)
Box 621, Honolulu, HI 96809
Phone: 808-587-0400
Contact(s):
Chairman: Commission on Water Resources Management: MICHAEL D. WILSON
Chairperson: MICHAEL D. WILSON; Phone: 808-587-0041
Deputy to Chairperson: RAE M. LOUI
Deputy to Chairperson: GILBERT S. COLOMA-AGARAN
Manager: Aquaculture Development Program (ADP): JOHN S. CORBIN

Division of Aquatic Resources
1151 Punchbowl St., Honolulu, HI 96813
Phone: 808-587-0100
Contact(s):
Administrator (Acting): WILLIAM DEVICK
Program Manager: Commercial Fisheries Aquaculture Branch: ERIC W. ONIZUICA

Division of Conservation and Resources Enforcement
1151 Punchbowl St., Honolulu, HI 96813
Phone: 808-587-0077
Contact(s):
Administrator (Acting): GARY MONIZ
Manager: Hunter Education Program: WENDELL W.S. KAM; Phone: 808-587-0200

Division of Forestry and Wildlife
1151 Punchbowl St., Honolulu, HI 96813
Phone: 808-587-0166
Contact(s):
Administrator: MICHAEL G. BUCK
Manager: Forestry Program: CARL T. MASAKI

Division of Historic Preservation
33 S. King St., 6th Fl., Honolulu, HI 96809
Contact(s):
Administrator: DON HIBBARD; Phone: 808-587-0045

Division of State Parks
P.O. Box 621, Honolulu, HI 96809
Phone: 808-587-0300
Contact(s):
Administrator: State Parks: RALSTON H. NAGATA

Land Division
P.O. Box 621, Honolulu, HI 96809
Phone: 808-587-0432
Contact(s):
Administrator: DEAN UCHIDA

ENVIRONMENTAL CENTER
Water Resource Research Center, University of HI, 2550 Campus Rd., Honolulu, HI 2550
Phone: 808-956-7361; Fax: 808-956-3980; Web site: www.hawaii.edu/catalog/special-pgms-files/inter-progs.html#es

Founded: 1970
Description: To stimulate, expand, and coordinate education, research, and service efforts of the university related to ecological relationships, natural resources, and environmental quality, with special relation to human needs and social institutions, particularly with regard to the state.
Contact(s):
Director: ROGER FUJIOKA
Associate Environmental Coordinator: JACQUELIN N. MILLER; E-mail: jackiem@hawaii.edu
Environmental Coordinator: JOHN T. HARRISON; E-mail: jth@hawaii.edu
Keyword(s): Environmental and Conservation Education, Environmental Law, Research, Water Quality

HAWAII COOPERATIVE FISHERY RESEARCH UNIT (USDI)
2538 The Mall, University of Hawaii, Honolulu, HI 96822
Phone: 808-956-8350; Fax: 808-956-9812; E-mail: jparrish@zoogate.zoo.hawaii.edu
Description: Activities include research, graduate program teaching, and public service regarding inshore marine and inland waters with emphasis on native fishes and invertebrates.
Contact(s):
Leader: DR. JAMES D. PARRISH
Keyword(s): Aquatic Habitats, Fisheries, Islands, Oceanography, Sustainable Ecosystems

HAWAII DEPARTMENT OF AGRICULTURE
P.O. Box 22159, Honolulu, HI 96823-2159
Description: Promotes the best use of Hawaii's agricultural resources. Concerned with the protection of agricultural lands and water and diversification of the state's agricultural economy. Functions include agricultural planning, agricultural credit, product promotion and market development, plant and animal quarantine, plant and animal disease and pest control, milk control, livestock and market reporting service, commodities grading, pesticide use enforcement, and enforcement of weights and measures standards.
Contact(s):
Chairperson: JAMES NAKATANI; Phone: 808-973-9551
Chief: Administrative Services: ELAINE T. ABE; Phone: 808-973-9606
Deputy to the Chairperson: LETITIA N. UYEHARA; Phone: 808-973-9553
Head: Agricultural Loan Division: DOREEN K. SHISHIDO; Phone: 808-973-9460
Head: Agricultural Resource Management Division: PAUL T. MATSUO; Phone: 808-973-9475
Head: Agriculture Development Division: SAMUEL CAMP; Phone: 808-973-9566
Head: Animal Industry Division: CALVIN W.S. LUM; Phone: 808-483-7111
Head: Plant Industry Division: DR. LYLE WONG; Phone: 808-973-9535
Head: Quality Assurance Division: SAMUEL CAMP; Phone: 808-586-0870

HAWAII DEPARTMENT OF HEALTH
Office of Environmental Quality Control, 235 S. Beretania St., Suite 702, Honolulu, HI 96813
Phone: 808-586-4185
Description: OEQC advises the Governor on environmental quality control matters; implements Hawaii's EIS law; reviews all documents required by Hawaii's EIS process; and informs the public of proposed actions through The Environmental Notice (OEQC Bulletin). The director of OEQC is also responsible for environmental

STATE AND PROVINCIAL GOVERNMENT AGENCIES - IDAHO

education projects, and proposing and encouraging legislation supporting the preservation of environmental resources.
Contact(s):
Director: GENEVIEVE SALMONSON
Publication(s): *A Guidebook for the Hawaii State Environmental Review Process; OEQC Bulletin; Annual Report--Environmental Indicators and Report Card*
Keyword(s): Environmental and Conservation Education, Environmental Law

HAWAII SEA GRANT PROGRAM
University of Hawaii, 2525 Correa Rd., HIG 238, Honolulu, HI 96822
Phone: 808-956-7031; Fax: 808-956-3014; Web site: www.soest.hawaii.edu/SEAGRANT/
Description: The University of Hawaii Sea Grant College Program supports research projects in marine-related areas. Its extension arm has agents and specialists located in Honolulu, Maui, the Big Island of Hawaii, Pohnpei (Federated States of Micronesia) and Saipan Commonwealth of the Northern Mariana Islands). Agents help marine users benefit from the Sea Grant-supported research, especially in the areas of commercial and recreational fishing, aquaculture, marine recreation and tourism development, marine education and conservation.
Contact(s):
Director: Sea Grant College Program: DR. CHARLES HELSLEY; E-mail: sg-dir@soest.hawaii.edu
Director ot Sea Grant Extension Service: BRUCE J. MILLER; Phone: 808-956-8645; Fax: 808-956-2858
Director of Communications Program: PRISCILLA P. BILLIG; Phone: 808-956-2414; Fax: 808-956-2880
Associate Director: ROSE T. PFUND
Aquaculture Extension Agent: RICHARD BAILEY; Phone: 808-956-2873; Fax: 808-956-2858
Aquaculture Extension Specialist: CLYDE TAMARU; Phone: 808-956-2869; Fax: 808-956-2858
Coastal Recreation & Tourism Extension Agent: CHRISTINE WOOLAWAY; Phone: 808-956-2872; Fax: 808-956-2858
Coastal Recreation & Tourism Extension Agent: RAYMOND S. TABATA; Phone: 808-956-2866; Fax: 808-956-2858
Coastal Resource Management Extension Agent: PETER J. RAPPA; Phone: 808-956-2868; Fax: 808-956-2858
Fisheries Extension Agent: ALAN KAM; Phone: 808-956-2865; Fax: 808-956-2858
Fisheries Extension Agent: RICHARD E. BROCK; Phone: 808-956-2859; Fax: 808-956-2858
Hanauma Bay Educational Program Volunteer Coordinator: JEFF KUWABARA; Phone: 808-396-1319; Fax: 808-956-2858
Pacific Region Environmental Education Specialist: ELIZABETH KUMABE; Phone: 808-956-2860; Fax: 808-956-2858
Pacific Region Sustainable Development Agent: ANNE M. ORCUTT-BAILEY; Phone: 808-956-2862; Fax: 808-956-2858

INSTITUTE OF MARINE BIOLOGY
University of Hawaii, P.O. Box 1346, Kaneohe, HI 96744-1346
Phone: 808-236-7401
Description: Concerned with research in tropical marine biology and oceanography with emphasis on coral reef biology, aquaculture, fish endocrinology, and behavior of reef organisms. Provides research facilities for investigations in tropical marine biology. Offers annual summer program in selected topics for graduate students.
Contact(s):
Director: PHILIP HELFRICH

UNIVERSITY OF HAWII COOPERATIVE EXTENSION PROGRAM
College of Tropical Agriculture and Human Resources, Gilmore Hall 202, 3050 Maile Way, Univ. of Hawaii at Manoa, Honolulu, HI 96822
Phone: 808-956-8234; Fax: 808-956-9150; Web site: www2.ctahr.hawaii.edu/extout/extout.asp
Contact(s):
Dean and Director of Cooperative Extension (Interim): DR. H. MICHAEL HARRINGTON; E-mail: ta_dean1@avax.ctahr.hawaii.edu
Associate Dean and Associate Director for Cooperative Extension (Interim): CHAROTTE NAKAMURA; Phone: 808-956-8139; E-mail: ta_hitahr@avax.ctahr.hawaii.edu
Researcher/Fisheries Specialist: RICHARD E. BROCK, Univ. of Hawaii Sea Grant Program, 1000 Pope Rd./MSB 204, Honolulu, HI 96822; Phone: 808-956-2859; Fax: 808-956-2858

WATER RESOURCES RESEARCH CENTER
University of Hawaii, Holmes Hall 283, 2540 Dole St., Honolulu, HI 96822
Phone: 808-956-7847
Founded: 1964
Description: WRRC's mission is to coordinate and conduct research to identify, characterize and quantify water and environmental concerns of the state, the nation and other Pacific Islands and formulate methods for resolving these concerns. WRRC produces reports, national and international journal articles, books, newsletters and project bulletins and organizes seminars, workshops and conferences.
Contact(s):
Director: JAMES E. T. MONCUR
Communications Coordinator: PHILIP S. MORAVCIK
Publication(s): *Technical Report; Technical Memorandum Report; Annual Report; Cooperative Report; Publications List; Project Reports and Special Publications*
Keyword(s): Aquatic Habitats, Oceanography, Public Health Protection, Water Pollution Management, Water Resources

IDAHO

GOVERNOR OF IDAHO
700 West Jefferson, Boise, ID 83720-0034
Phone: 208-334-2100
Contact(s):
Governor: DIRK KEMPTHORNE

DEPARTMENT OF LANDS (IDAHO)
P.O. Box 83720, 954 West Jefferson Street, Boise, ID 83720-0500
Phone: 208-334-0200
Description: The State Board of Land Commissioners is a constitutional board charged with administering the trust under which endowment lands are held. These lands were granted to the state at the time of statehood for the financial support of nine beneficiaries, the largest being the common schools.
Contact(s):
Attorney General: ALAN G. LANCE; Phone: 208-334-2400
Secretary of State: PETE T. CENARRUSA; Phone: 208-334-2300
Secretary to the Board and Director of the Idaho Department of Lands: STANLEY F. HAMILTON; Phone: 208-334-0200
State Board of Land Commissioner President: GOV. DIRK KEMPTHORNE; Phone: 208-334-2100
State Controller: J. D. WILLIAMS; Phone: 208-334-3100
Superintendent of Public Instruction: DR. MARILYN HOWARD; Phone: 208-332-6800

IDAHO COOPERATIVE EXTENSION
University of Idaho, Cooperative Extension, P.O. Box 443163, Moscow, ID 83844-3163
Phone: 208-885-6639; Fax: 208-885-5050; Web site: www.uidaho.edu/ag/extension/
Contact(s):
Associate Dean and Extension Director: DR. LEROY D. LUFT; E-mail: EXTDIR@UIDAHO.EDU
Associate Extension Director (Interim): ARLINDA NAUMAN; Phone: 208-885-5883; E-mail: ANAUMAN@UIDAHO.EDU

Agriculture and Extension Education: LOU RIESENBERG, 1134 W 6th Street, Moscow, ID 83844; Phone: 208-885-6358; E-mail: LRIESENB@UIDAHO.EDU

Extension Forester: RONALD L. MAHONEY, Univ. of Idaho, College of Forestry, Moscow, ID 83844-1140; Phone: 208-885-6356; Fax: 208-885-6226

IDAHO COOPERATIVE FISH AND WILDLIFE RESEARCH UNIT (USDI)

College of Forestry, Wildlife and Range Sciences, University of Idaho, Moscow, ID 83844-1141
Phone: 208-885-6336

Founded: 1963

Description: An interagency organization which conducts research, graduate level training, and extension in the fields of fish, wildlife, and conservation biology.

Contact(s):
Leader: DR. J. MICHAEL SCOTT
Assistant Leader: DR. R. GERALD WRIGHT
Assistant Leader: DR. JAMES L. CONGLETON
Assistant Leader: DR. THEODORE C. BJORNN

Keyword(s): Biodiversity, Birds, Endangered and Threatened Species, Fisheries, Wildlife and Wildlife Habitat

IDAHO DEPARTMENT OF PARKS AND RECREATION

P. O. Box 83720, Boise, ID 83720-0065
Phone: 208-334-4199

Founded: 1965

Description: To formulate and put into execution a long-range program for the acquisition, planning, protection, operation, maintenance, development, and wise use of parks; and to provide state leadership in recreation.

Contact(s):
Director: YVONNE FERRELL
Deputy Director: WILLIAM A. DOKKEN
Chairman of the Board: GLENN E. SHEWMAKER; Phone: 208-736-3608

Keyword(s): Cultural Preservation, Environmental and Conservation Education, Environmental Preservation, Outdoor Recreation, Rivers

IDAHO DEPARTMENT OF WATER RESOURCES

Statehouse, Boise, ID 83720

Description: Administration of State Water Plan and Energy Plan; allocation and planning of water resources and energy programs and projects; permit and license procedures for water rights, dams, and mine tailing impoundment structures, well construction, injection wells, and stream channel alterations.

Contact(s):
Director: KARL J. DREHER; Phone: 208-327-7910
Administrator of Energy Division: ROBERT W. HOPPIE; Phone: 208-327-7910
Administrator of Policy and Planning Division: WAYNE T. HAAS; Phone: 208-327-7910
Administrator of Resources Administration Division: NORMAN C. YOUNG; Phone: 208-327-7910
Chairman of the Board: CLARENCE FARR; Phone: 208-678-8620

Publication(s): *Water and Energy Information Bulletins; Rules; State Water Plan, and Newsletter*

IDAHO FISH AND GAME DEPARTMENT

600 S. Walnut, Box 25, Boise, ID 83707
Phone: 208-334-3700; Fax: 208-334-2114; Web site: www.state.id.us/fishgame

Founded: 1938

Description: To preserve, protect, perpetuate, and manage all wildlife within the state of Idaho; to make and declare such rules and regulations, and to employ personnel necessary to administer and enforce the harvest of wildlife.

Contact(s):
Interim Director: JERRY MALLET; Phone: 208-334-5159
Bureau Chief of Administration: STEPHEN BARTON; Phone: 208-334-3782
Chief of DP Management: BOB ROYCE; Phone: 208-334-3700
Chief of Enforcement: AL NICHOLSON; Phone: 208-334-3736
Chief of Engineering: PHIL JEPPSON; Phone: 208-334-3730
Chief of Fisheries: VIRGIL K. MOORE; Phone: 208-334-3791
Chief of Information and Education: PAT CUDMORE; Phone: 208-334-3746/x257
Chief of Natural Resources Policy: TRACEY TRENT; Phone: 208-334-2595
Chief of Wildlife: STEVE HUFFAKER; Phone: 208-334-2920
Editor: JACK TRUEBLOOD; Phone: 208-334-3746

Publication(s): *Idaho Fish & Game News*

Keyword(s): Environmental and Conservation Education, Fisheries, Hunting, Sport Fishing, Wildlife Management

IDAHO FISH AND WILDLIFE FOUNDATION

P.O. Box 2254, Boise, ID 83701
Phone: 208-334-2648; Fax: 208-334-2148; E-mail: mdugger@idfg.state.id.us

Founded: 1990

Description: To facilitate the organization and funding of natural resource projects: fish, wildlife, habitat, and education. Work with Idaho Department of Fish and Game and other entities to build public and private partnerships for wildlife projects.

Contact(s):
Executive Director: GAYLE VALENTINE

Publication(s): *Steelhead Fishing Economic Survey (1996); Steelhead Fishing Economic Values brochure; Salmon Fishing Economic Survey (1998).*

Keyword(s): Environmental and Conservation Education, Fisheries, Natural Areas, Nature Centers, Wildlife and Wildlife Habitat

IDAHO GEOLOGICAL SURVEY

Morrill Hall, Third Floor, University of Idaho, Moscow, ID 83844-3014
Phone: 208-885-7991

Founded: 1919

Description: The Survey is the lead state agency for the collection, interpretation, and dissemination of all geologic and mineral data for Idaho. Conducts field investigations and laboratory studies; assists in preparation of geologic maps, derivative land-use planning, and geologic hazards maps; provides expertise to individuals and governmental and private groups in planning land use.

Contact(s):
Director: EARL H. BENNETT; Phone: 208-885-7991
Associate Director: KURT L. OTHBERG
Associate Director: ROY M BRECKENRIDGE; Phone: 208-885-7991

IDAHO STATE DEPARTMENT OF AGRICULTURE

P.O. Box 790, Boise, ID 83701
Phone: 208-334-3240

Contact(s):
Director: PATRICK A. TAKASUGI
Division of Agricultural Inspections Administrator: LANE JOLLIFFE; Phone: 208-332-8666
Division of Agricultural Resources, Marketing, and Development: MIKE EVERETT; Phone: 208-332-8531
Division of Animal Industries Administrator: DR. BOB HILLMAN; Phone: 208-332-8541
Division of Plant Industries and Labs Administrator: DR. ROGER R. VEGA; Phone: 208-332-8627

Keyword(s): Agriculture, Biotechnology, Chemical Pollution Control, Endangered and Threatened Species, Land Preservation, Land Use Planning, Pesticides, Public Health Protection, Soil Conservation, Solid Waste Management, Toxic Substances, Water Pollution, Water Quality, Watersheds

IDAHO STATE SOIL CONSERVATION COMMISSION

P.O. Box 790, Boise, ID 83701-0790
Phone: 208-332-8650

Founded: 1939

Description: Coordinates programs and activities of Soil Conservation Districts in Idaho. Concerned with overall leadership and administration of districts in development, wise use, and conservation of soil and water and other closely related resources.

STATE AND PROVINCIAL GOVERNMENT AGENCIES - ILLINOIS

Participates in the National Cooperative Soil Survey Program through employment of soil scientists and has been designated the state water quality management agency for private and state agricultural lands. Administers low-interest loan program for conservation improvements on private and public lands.
Contact(s):
Chairman: GARY GRINDSTAFF, 4074 N. 1750 E., Bahl, ID 83316; Phone: 208-543-5755; Fax: 208-543-5295
Administrator: JERRY NICOLESCU; Phone: 208-332-8649; Fax: 208-334-2386
Keyword(s): Agriculture, Environmental and Conservation Education, Renewable Resources, Soil Conservation, Water Resources

STATE OF IDAHO DIVISION OF ENVIRONMENTAL QUALITY
1410 N. Hilton St., Boise, ID 83706-1255
Phone: 208-373-0502; Fax: 208-373-0417
Description: Administers and directs programs designed to protect and enhance the environment and public health. Emphasis is placed on monitoring, technical assistance and environmental education at the community level. The agency is also responsible for all permitting and permit review functions.
Contact(s):
Chief of Staff: J. R. SANDOVAL; Phone: 208-373-0240
Administrator of Division of Environmental Quality: C. STEPHEN ALLRED; Phone: 208-373-0240
State Air Quality Program Administrator: ORVILLE GREEN; Phone: 208-373-0440
State Waste Program Administrator: KATHERINE KELLY; Phone: 208-373-0502
State Water Quality Program Administrator: DAVID MABE; Phone: 208-373-0502
Publication(s): *Hazardous Waste Report; Drinking Water Report; Goundwater Report; Strategic Plan; State of the Environment Report; Performance Partnership Agreement*
Keyword(s): Air Quality and Pollution, Environmental Planning, Environmental Protection, Water Quality

ILLINOIS

GOVERNOR OF ILLINOIS: GEORGE RYAN
State Capitol, Rm. 207, Springfield, IL 62706
Phone: 217-782-6830/TDD800-526-0884

ILLINOIS DEPARTMENT OF AGRICULTURE
State Fairgrounds, P.O. Box 19281, Springfield, IL 62794-9281
Phone: 217-782-9272
Founded: 1917
Description: The Illinois Department of Agriculture protects and promotes the state's agricultural and natural resources. The agency provides services that benefit consumers, farmers, and agribusinesses.
Contact(s):
Director: BECKY DOYLE
Deputy Director for Natural Resource and Agri-Industry Regulation: CHET BORUFF
Executive Office: Assistant Director: DAVE BENDER
Superintendent for Fairs and Promotions: JIM REYNOLDS
Publication(s): *Illinois Agricultural Guide; Illinois Agricultural Organizations Directory; Illinois Grain and Livestock Market News; Illinois Food Products*
Keyword(s): Agriculture, Land Use Planning, Pesticides, Renewable Resources, Soil Conservation

Soil and Water Conservation Districts Advisory Board
P.O. Box 19281, Springfield, IL 62794-9281
Phone: 217-782-6297; Fax: 217-524-4882
Contact(s):
Bureau Chief: TERRY DONOHUE

ILLINOIS DEPARTMENT OF NATURAL RESOURCES
524 S. 2nd St., Rm. 400 LTP, Springfield, IL 62701-1787
Phone: 217-782-6302
Description: The mission of the Illinois Department of Natural Resources is to promote an understanding and appreciation of the state's natural resources and work with the people of Illinois to protect and manage those resources to ensure a high quality of life for present and future generations.
Contact(s):
Deputy Director: JIM GARNER
Deputy Director: BRUCE CLAY
Director: BRENT MANNING
Chief Fiscal Officer: JOHN BANDY; Phone: 217-785-8552
Chief Legal Counsel: ROBERT LAWLEY; Phone: 217-782-1809
Chief of Law Enforcement Office: TOM WAKOLBINGER; Phone: 217-782-6431
Conservation Foundation Executive Director: JOHN SCHMITT; Phone: 312-814-7237
Director of Law Enforcement Office: LARRY CLOSSON; Phone: 217-782-6431
Director of Legislation and Constituency Services: DIANE HENDREN; Phone: 217-785-0073
Director of Office Mines and Minerals: RICHARD MOTTERSHAW; Phone: 217-782-0031
Director of Office of Administration: KEVIN SRONCE; Phone: 217-782-0179
Director of Office of Capital Development: BRUCE CLARK; Phone: 217-782-1807
Director of Office of Land Management and Education: JERRY BEVERLIN; Phone: 217-782-6752
Director of Public Affairs Office: CAROL KNOWLES; Phone: 217-785-0970
Director of Public Services Office: JIM FULGENZI; Phone: 217-782-7454
Director of Realty and Environmental Planning Office: TOM FLATTERY; Phone: 217-782-7940
Director of Resource Conservation Office: KIRBY COTTRELL; Phone: 217-785-8547
Director of Water Resources Office: DON VONNAHME; Phone: 217-782-2152
Division Manager of Internal Audit Office: BRAD HAMMOND; Phone: 217-785-0853
Equal Employment Opportunity Officer: THERESA CUMMINGS; Phone: 217-785-0067
Publication(s): *Digest of Hunting and Trapping Regulations; Illinois Fishing Information Book; State Park Magazine; Outdoor Illinois Magazine*
Keyword(s): Biodiversity, Biology, Conservation of Protected Areas, Endangered and Threatened Species, Environmental and Conservation Education

ILLINOIS DEPARTMENT OF TRANSPORTATION
2300 S. Dirksen Pkwy., Springfield, IL 62764
Phone: 217-782-5597
Contact(s):
Secretary: KIRK BROWN; Phone: 217-782-6828
Chief of Environment: PETER J. FRANTZ; Phone: 217-782-4770; Fax: 217-524-9356
Chief: Bureau of Design and Environment: WILLIAM T. SUNLEY; Phone: 217-782-7526; Fax: 217-524-0989
Director: Division of Highways: JAMES C. SLIFER; Phone: 217-782-2151; Fax: 217-524-2972
Keyword(s): Transportation

ILLINOIS ENVIRONMENTAL PROTECTION AGENCY
1021 North Grand Ave. E., Springfield, IL 62794-9276
Phone: 217-782-3397; Fax: 217-782-9039
Founded: 1970
Description: Responsible for implementing the environmental program for the state of Illinois. Administers a variety of programs to protect the air, land, and water.
Contact(s):
Deputy Director: WILLIAM SEITH
Director: THOMAS V. SKINNER
Chief: Bureau of Air: BHARAT MATHUR; Phone: 217-785-4140

Chief: Bureau of Land: WILLIAM CHILD; Phone: 217-785-9407
Chief: Bureau of Water: JAMES PARK; Phone: 217-782-1654
Editor: JOAN MURARO; Phone: 217-785-7209
Head Librarian: NANCY SIMPSON, 1021 N. Grand Ave. E., P.O. Box 19276, Springfield, IL 62794-9276; Phone: 217-782-9691
Manager: Public Information: DENNIS McMURRAY
Publication(s): *Digester/Over the Spillway; Environmental Progress*
Keyword(s): Air Quality and Pollution, Environmental Law, Environmental Preservation, Toxic Substances, Water Pollution

ILLINOIS NATURE PRESERVES COMMISSION (INPC)
524 S. Second St., Lincoln Tower Plaza, Springfield, IL 62701-1787
Phone: 217-785-8686
Founded: 1963
Description: The mission of the Illinois Nature Preserves Commission (INPC) is to assist private and public landowners in protecting high quality natural areas and habitats of endangered and threatened species in perpetuity, through voluntary dedication of such lands into the Illinois Nature Preserves System. The commission promotes the preservation of these significant lands, and once dedicated as nature preserves, oversees their stewardship, management, and protection.
Contact(s):
Secretary: JONATHON ELLIS
Director: CAROLYN TAFT GROSBOLL
Chairperson: GUY FREAKER
Deputy Director for Protection: DON McFALL
Deputy Director for Stewardship: RANDY HEIDORN
Legal Counsel: CAROLYN T. GROSBOLL
Vice Chairperson: JOYCE O'KEEFE
Keyword(s): Environmental Preservation, Land Preservation, Nature Preservation

UNIVERSITY OF ILLNOIS EXTENSION
214 Mumford Hall (MC-710), 1301 W. Gregory Dr., Urbana, IL 61801
Phone: 217-333-5900; Fax: 217-244-5403; E-mail: campion@uiuc.edu; Web site: www.extension.uiuc.edu/welcome.html
Contact(s):
Associate Dean: DENNIS R. CAMPION; E-mail: dcampion@uiuc.edu
Assistant Dean, Extension Operations: PATRICIA J. BUCHANAN; E-mail: buchananp@mail.aces.uiuc.edu
Assistant Dean, Extension Program Coordination: JOHN C. VAN ES; E-mail: e-van1@uiuc.edu
Natural Resource Information: RICHARD WARNER, W503 Turner Hall, Urbana, IL 61801; Phone: 217-333-5199; Fax: 217-244-3219

INDIANA

GOVERNOR OF INDIANA: FRANK O'BANNON
Rm. 206, Statehouse, Indianapolis, IN 46204
Phone: 317-232-4567

ILLINOIS-INDIANA SEA GRANT PROGRAM
Purdue University, Department of Forestry and Natural Resources, 1200 Forest Products Bldg., West Lafayette, IN 47907-1200
Phone: 765-494-3573; Fax: 765-496-6026; Web site: ag.ansc.purdue.edu/il-in-sg/
Contact(s):
Director: PHILLIP E. POPE; E-mail: ppope@purdue.edu
Assistant Director: BRIAN MILLER; E-mail: bmiller@fnr.purdue.edu
Communications Coordinator: ROBIN G. GOETTEL; Phone: 217-333-9448; Fax: 217-333-2614; E-mail: goettel@uiuc.edu

INDIANA DEPARTMENT OF ENVIRONMENTAL MANAGEMENT
P.O. Box 6015, Indianapolis, IN 46206
Phone: 317-232-8603

Description: The Indiana Department of Environmental Management is dedicated to conserving, protecting, enhancing, restoring, and managing Indiana's environment. We strive to fairly but vigorously enforce laws and standards; promulgate regulations consistent with the law and public policy; and promote conservation, pollution prevention, and a healthy and sustainable ecosystem. We are committed to making Indiana a cleaner, healthier place to live.
Contact(s):
Acting Assistant Commissioner for Solid and Hazardous Waste: BRUCE PALIN; Phone: 317-232-3210
Assistant Commissioner for Environmental Response: MARY BETH TUOHY; Phone: 317-308-3006
Assistant Commissioner for Office of Pollution Prevention: THOMAS NELTNER; Phone: 317-232-8172
Assistant Commissioner for Water Management: MATHEW RUEFF; Phone: 317-232-8476
Assistant Commissioner of Enforcement: FELICIA GEORGE; Phone: 317-233-5523
Assistant Commissioner Results and Chief Counsel: DAVE HENSEL; Phone: 317-233-0942
Assistant Commissioner: Air Management: JANET McCABE, Phone: 317-233-6861
Commissioner: JOHN M. HAMILTON; Phone: 317-232-8611
Deputy Commissioner for Environmental and Regulatory Affairs: TIMOTHY METHOD; Phone: 317-233-3706
Deputy Commissioner for Operations: CAROLE CASTO BRUBAKER; Phone: 317-232-8180
Director of Business & Legislative Relations: ERICKA SEYDEL; Phone: 317-232-8598
Director of Investigations: LEON GRIFFITH; Phone: 317-232-8128
Director of Media & Communication Services: PETE BLUM; Phone: 317-232-8560
Director of Northcentral Office: JUDY DIOUS THOMANN; Phone: 812-436-2570
Director of Northwest Regional Office: DAVID ROZ MANICH; Phone: 219-881-6712
Director of Planning & Assessment: LARRY WILSON; Phone: 317-233-6645

INDIANA DEPARTMENT OF NATURAL RESOURCES
402 W. Washington St., Rm. W255B, Indianapolis, IN 46204-2748
Phone: 317-232-4200
Description: The DNR administers more than 100 properties throughout Indiana, comprising more than 400,000 acres. The DNR provides recreational opportunities for millions of Hoosiers and out-of-state visitors annually at its state parks, forests, reservoirs, and fish and wildlife areas. The DNR also has wide-ranging responsibilities such as maintaining the Indiana State Museum and more than a dozen historic sites throughout the state; ensuring that coal mining and reclamation of those mines take place in a manner that is in the best interests of the citizens of Indiana, and making sure that proper use is made of, and adequate protection is given to, the state's natural resources such as water, soil, forests, wildlife and historic resources.
Contact(s):
Director: PATRICK R. RALSTON; Phone: 317-232-4020
Chairman: Lands and Cultural Resources Advisory Council: JERRY MILLER; Phone: 317-232-4020
Chairman: Natural Resources Commission: MICHAEL KILEY; Phone: 317-232-4020
Chairman: Water and Resource Regulation Advisory Council: JOSEPH SIENER; Phone: 317-232-4020
Chief Counsel: LORI KAPLAN; Phone: 317-232-4020
Chief Hearings Officer: STEVEN LUCAS; Phone: 317-232-0156
Controller: JAMES VAUGHN; Phone: 317-232-4020
Deputy Director: Bureau of Lands and Cultural Resources: JOHN T. COSTELLO; Phone: 317-232-4020
Deputy Director: Bureau of Mine Reclamation: PAUL EHRET; Phone: 317-232-4020
Deputy Director: Bureau of Water and Resource Regulation: DAVID L. HERBST; Phone: 317-232-4020

STATE AND PROVINCIAL GOVERNMENT AGENCIES - IOWA

Deputy Director: Law Enforcement and Administration: DAVID VICE; Phone: 317-232-4020
Director: Division of Accounting: THOMAS BARTON; Phone: 317-232-4041
Director: Division of Budget and Support Services: RICHARD LEKENS; Phone: 317-232-4036
Director: Division of Fish and Wildlife: GARY DOXTATER; Phone: 317-232-4080
Director: Division of Historic Preservation and Archaeology: DANIEL J. FOGERTY; Phone: 317-232-1646
Director: Division of Human Resources: S. FRANCES MILLER; Phone: 317-232-4031
Director: Division of Internal Audit: JAMES LIVERETT; Phone: 317-232-8092
Director: Division of Land Acquisition: JOHN DAVIS; Phone: 317-232-4050
Director: Division of Law Enforcement: COL. CHARLES; Phone: 317-232-4010
Director: Division of Nature Preserves: JOHN BACONE; Phone: 317-232-4052
Director: Division of Oil and Gas: JIM SLUTZ; Phone: 317-232-4055
Director: Division of Outdoor Recreation (Administers Land and Water Conservation Fund): EMILY KRESS; Phone: 317-232-4070
Director: Division of Public Information and Education: STEPHEN SELLERS; Phone: 317-232-4200
Director: Division of Reclamation: MIKE SPONSLER; Phone: 812-665-2207
Director: Division of Reservoir Management: J. BLAKE TAYLOR; Phone: 317-232-4060
Director: Division of Safety & Training: PHILIP WAGNER; Phone: 317-232-4145
Director: Division of Safety and Training: PHILIP WAGNER; Phone: 317-232-4145
Director: Division of Soil Conservation: HARRY NIKIDES; Phone: 317-233-3880
Director: Division of State Museum and Historical Sites: DR. RICHARD GANTZ; Phone: 317-232-1637
Director: Division of State Parks: GERALD PAGAC; Phone: 317-232-4124
Director: Division of Water: JOHN SIMPSON; Phone: 317-232-4160
Director: Internal Audit: JIM LIVERETT; Phone: 317-232-8092
Director: Management Information Systems: MIKE QUIGLEY; Phone: 317-232-4007
Editor: STEPHEN SELLERS
Head Chief Engineer: Division of Engineering: TOM HOHMAN; Phone: 317-232-4150
State Entomologist Director: Division of Entomology and Plant Pathology: DR. ROBERT WALTZ; Phone: 317-232-4120
State Forester: Head: Division of Forestry: DR. BURNELL FISCHER; Phone: 317-232-4105
Publication(s): *Outdoor Indiana*
Keyword(s): Forests and Forestry, Historic Preservation, Outdoor Recreation, Water Resources, Wildlife Management

Division of Soil Conservation
402 W. Washington St., Rm. W265, Indianapolis, IN 46204-2739
Phone: 317-233-3870; Web site: www.dnr.state.in.us/soilcons/index.htm
Description: The Division's mission is to facilitate the protection, wise use, and enhancement of Indiana's soil and water resources by: coordinating implementation of the state's T-by-2000 soil conservation/water quality protection program and providing assistance to local soil and water conservation districts.
Contact(s):
Director: HARRY S. NIKIDES; Phone: 317-233-3880; Fax: 317-233-3882; E-mail: harry_nikides_at_dnrlan@ima.isd.state.in.us
Chairman of the Board: PETER A. HIPPENSTEEL
Vice Chairman: DAVID L. AVERY
Publication(s): *Indiana Handbook for Erosion Control in Developing Areas*; Topsoil; Lake and River Enhancement Program; Urban Conservation Program; Use of Sand or Pea Gravel in Underwater Beach Construction; Who We Are and What We Do*; Erosion Control for the Home Builder; Wetland Conservation Guidelines; Your Resource Guide to Water Quality; Lakeshore Protection in Indiana* (all publications except those noted with * are available on our website).
Keyword(s): Agriculture, Lakes, Rivers, Soil Conservation, Water Quality

INDIANA GEOLOGICAL SURVEY
Institute of Indiana University, 611 N. Walnut Grove, Bloomington, IN 47405
Phone: 812-855-7636
Founded: 1869
Description: Conducts basic and applied research in geology and disseminates geologic information as published reports and maps; consults with industry, academia, and the public on the geologic makeup, mineral and energy resources, and geologic hazards of the state.
Contact(s):
Assistant Director: JOHN R. HILL; Phone: 812-855-6067
Director and State Geologist: JOHN C. STENMETZ; Phone: 812-855-5067
Keyword(s): Environmental Planning, Geology, Mineral Resources

INDIANA STATE DEPARTMENT OF HEALTH
Two North Meridian St., Indianapolis, IN 46204
Phone: 317-233-7400
Contact(s):
State Health Commissioner: DR. RICHARD D. FELDMAN
Keyword(s): Health and Nutrition, Nuclear/Radiation, Public Health Protection, Toxic Substances, Toxicology

PURDUE UNIVERSITY EXTENSION SERVICES
1140 Agriculture Administration Bldg., Purdue University, West Lafayette, IN 47907-1140
Phone: 888-398-4636 or 765-494-8489; Fax: 765-494-5876; E-mail: extension@aes.purdue.edu; Web site: www.ces.purdue.edu/
Contact(s):
Director, Cooperative Extension Service: DAVID C. PETRITZ; E-mail: david.petritz@ces.purdue.edu
Program Leader, Leadership and Community Development: JANET S. AYRES; Phone: 765-494-4215; E-mail: ayres@agecon.purdue.edu
Program Leader, 4-H/Youth: LINDA CHEZEM; Phone: 765-494-8422; E-mail: lchezem@four-h.purdue.edu
Wildlife Specialist and Sea Grant Coordinator: BRIAN K. MILLER, Purdue Univ., 1159 Forestry Building, West Lafayette, IN 47907-1159; Phone: 765-494-3586; Fax: 765-496-2422

IOWA

GOVERNOR OF IOWA: TOM VILSACK
State Capitol, DesMoines, IA 50319
Phone: 515-281-5211

IOWA ASSOCIATION OF COUNTY CONSERVATION BOARDS
405 SW 3rd, Suite 1, Ankeny, IA 50021
Description: Promotes the objectives of Iowa's County Conservation Boards, board member education, information exchange, legislation, and public awareness.
Contact(s):
President: DAN HEISSEL
Vice President: STEVE LEKWA
Secretary: ANN ADKINS
Executive Secretary: DON BRAZELTON
Publication(s): *Iowa Board Member; IACCB Newsletter; IACCB Legislative Update; Outdoor Adventure Guide (Area Directory); Board Member Handbook*

IOWA COOPERATIVE FISH AND WILDLIFE RESEARCH UNIT
Animal Ecology Department 11 Science Hall II Iowa State University, Ames, IA 50011-3221
Phone: 515-294-3056; Fax: 515-294-5468
Founded: 1932
Contact(s):
Assistant Leader of Fisheries: CLAY L. PIERCE
Assistant Leader of Wildlife: ROLF R. KOFORD
Keyword(s): Biodiversity, Fisheries, Gap Analysis, Research, Sustainable Ecosystems, Wildlife and Wildlife Habitat

IOWA DEPARTMENT OF AGRICULTURE AND LAND STEWARDSHIP

Bureau of Field Services
E. 9th and Grand Ave., Wallace Bldg., Des Moines, IA 50319-0034
Contact(s):
JAMES GILLESPIE; Phone: 515-281-5258

Bureau of Financial Incentive Program
E. 9th and Grand Ave., Wallace Bldg., Des Moines, IA 50319-0034
Contact(s):
WILLIAM McGILL; Phone: 515-281-5851

Bureau of Mines and Minerals
E. 9th and Grand Ave., Wallace Bldg., Des Moines, IA 50319-0034
Contact(s):
KENNETH R. TOW; Phone: 515-281-6142

Bureau of Water Resources
E. 9th and Grand Ave., Wallace Bldg., Des Moines, IA 50319-0034
Contact(s):
DEAN LEMKE; Phone: 515-281-6146

Division of Soil Conservation
Wallace State Office Bldg., Des Moines, IA 50319
Phone: 515-281-5851
Description: Administers soil and water conservation district laws. Allocates state appropriations to 100 soil and water conservation districts for personnel, commissioners' expense, and financial incentives for erosion control and water quality measures. Reviews watershed and RC & D project applications. Oversees erosion control law. Involved with water resources and nonpoint-source pollution control planning. Division licenses mine operations and administers federal surface mining and Abandoned Mine Land Program regulations.
Contact(s):
Director: JAMES B. GULLIFORD; Phone: 515-281-6146; Fax: 515-281-6170; E-mail: jgull@sela.osmre.gov
Assistant Director: KENNETH R. TOW; Phone: 515-281-6142
Chairperson: MARY ANN DRISH, 1373 Spruce Ave., Brighton, IA 52540
Vice Chairperson: RUSSELL BRANDES, 37333 Mahogany Rd., Hancock, IA 51536-4012

IOWA DEPARTMENT OF NATURAL RESOURCES
E. 9th and Grand Ave., Wallace Bldg., Des Moines, IA 50319-0034
Phone: 515-281-5145; Fax: 515-281-8895
Founded: 1986
Description: Established with the merging of the following state agencies: Iowa Conservation Commission, Department of Water, Air and Waste Management; Iowa Geological Survey; and the resources/conservation functions of the Energy Policy Council. The seven-member Natural Resources Commission is a policy and rule-setting authority over the Fish and Wildlife Division, Parks, Recreation, and Preserves Division, and the Forestry Division; the nine-member Environmental Protection Commission is the policy and rule-setting authority over the Environmental Protection Division and the Waste Management Division.
Contact(s):
Director: PAUL W. JOHNSON
Deputy Director: LARRY J. WILSON
Chief of Information-Education Bureau: ROSS HARRISON
Editor of Iowa Conservationist: JULIE HOLMES SPARKS
Environmental Protection Commission Chair: WILLIAM EHM
Natural Resource Commission Chair: JOAN SCHNEIDER
Keyword(s): Air Quality and Pollution, Aquatic Habitats, Birds, Chemical Pollution Control, Conservation of Protected Areas, Endangered and Threatened Species, Energy, Environment, Fisheries, Geology, Hunting, Lakes, Land Purchase, Natural Areas

Administrative Services Division
Des Moines, IA 50319-
Contact(s):
Administrator: LINDA HANSON
Chief of Administrative Support Bureau: SALLY JAGNANDAN
Chief of Budget and Finance Bureau: MARK SLATTERLY
Chief of Construction Services Bureau: BASIL NIMRY
Chief of Land Acquisition and Management Bureau (Acting): LARRY BARTLEMAN
Chief of Licensing Bureau and Data Processing Bureau: JUDY PAWELL

Cooperative North American Shotgunning Education Program
Wallace State Office Bldg., Des Moines, IA 50319
Phone: 515-281-6156; Fax: 503-884-2974
Founded: 1982
Description: The Cooperative North American Shotgunning Program is a research, information, and education program designed to assist wildlife professionals, hunters, and sportsmen in making a successful transition from lead shot to nontoxic shot, as well as educating sportsmen on improving shooting skills and harvest efficiency, thereby reducing wounding losses.
Contact(s):
Chairman: RICHARD BISHOP, Wallace State Bldg., DesMoines, IA 50319; Phone: 515-281-6156
Consultant: TOM ROSTER, 1190 Lynnewood Blvd., KlamathFalls, OR 97601; Phone: 503-884-2974
Contact for Atlantic Flyway: LLOYD ALEXANDER, 89 Kings Highway, P.O. Box 1401, Dover, DE ; Phone: 302-739-5287
Contact for Canadian Wildlife Service: BOB MCLEAN, 17th Fl., Place Vincent Massey, Ottawa, Ontario K1A 0H3 Canada; Phone: 819-997-2957
Contact for Central Flyway: GEORGE VANDEL, 445 E. Capitol, Pierre, SD; Phone: 605-773-3381
Contact for Mississippi Flyway: JOHN SMITH, P.O. Box 180, Jefferson City, MO 65102-0180; Phone: 573-751-4115
Contact for Pacific Flyway: DON CHILDRESS, 1420 E. 6th, Box 20071, Helena, MT 59601; Phone: 406-444-2612
Publication(s): *CONSEP Newsletter; Periodic Ballistics Reports*
Keyword(s): Hunting, Waterfowl, Wildlife Management

Energy and Geological Resources Division
Contact(s):
Administrator: LARRY BEAN
Chief of Energy Bureau: SHARON TAHTINEN
Chief of Geological Survey Bureau: DON KOCH

Environmental Protection Division
Contact(s):
Administrator: MICHAEL VALDE
Chief of Air Quality Bureau: PETE HAMLIN
Chief of Compliance & Enforcement Bureau: MIKE MURPHY
Chief of Land Quality Bureau: JOE OBR
Chief of Water Quality Bureau: JACK RIESSEN

Fish and Wildlife Division
Contact(s):
Administrator: ALLEN FARRIS
Chief of Fisheries Bureau: MARION CONOVER
Chief of Law Enforcement Bureau: LOWELL JOSLIN
Chief of Wildlife Bureau: RICHARD BISHOP
Coordinator of Hunter Safety: SONNY SATRE

STATE AND PROVINCIAL GOVERNMENT AGENCIES - KANSAS

Forests and Prairies Division
Contact(s):
Administrator: MIKE BRANDRUP
Chief of Forestry Services Bureau: JOHN WALKOWIAK
Chief of State Forests Management Bureau: JIM BULMAN

Parks
Contact(s):
Administrator: MIKE CARRIER
Chief of Field Operations Bureau: STEPHEN PENNINGTON
Chief of Program Administration Bureau: ARNIE SOHN

Waste Management Division
Contact(s):
Administrator: ROYA STANLEY
Executive Officer: BRENT LANING

IOWA STATE EXTENSION SERVICES
Attn: Vice Provost of Extension Services, 218 Beardshear Hall, Iowa State University, Ames, IA 50011
Phone: 515-294-6192; Fax: 515-294-4715; E-mail: vpforext@exnet.iastate.edu; Web site: www.exnet.iastate.edu/
Description: ISU Extension is a client-centered organization that provides research-based, unbiased information and education to help people make better decisions in their personal, community, and professional lives.
Contact(s):
Extension Forester: PAUL H. WRAY, 251 Bessey Hall, Iowa State University, Ames, IA 50011; Phone: 515-294-1168
Extension Wildlife Conservationist: JAMES L. PEASE, 103 Science II, Iowa State University, Ames, IA 50011; Phone: 515-294-7429; Fax: 515-294-7874

KANSAS

GOVERNOR OF KANSAS: BILL GRAVES
State Capitol, 2nd Fl., Topeka, KS 66612-1590
Phone: 913-296-3232

KANSAS BIOLOGICAL SURVEY
2041 Constant Ave., Foley Hall, Lawrence, KS 66047-2906
Phone: 785-864-7725; Fax: 785-864-5093
Founded: 1959
Description: A research and development branch of the University of Kansas whose purpose is to survey and inventory the native plants and animals of Kansas, report on its findings, and develop and administer lands for the study and preservation of native animal and plant resources.
Contact(s):
Assistant Director: PAUL M. LIECHTI
Associate Director: DR. FRANK deNOYELLES
Director and State Biologist: DR. EDWARD MARTINKO
Keyword(s): Aquatic Habitats, Biodiversity, Endangered and Threatened Species, Prairies, Sustainable Ecosystems

KANSAS COOPERATIVE FISH AND WILDLIFE RESEARCH UNIT
205 Leasure Hall, Kansas State University, Manhattan, KS 66506-3501
Phone: 785-532-6070; Fax: 785-532-7159; Web site: www.ksu.edu/kscfwru/
Founded: 1991
Contact(s):
Assistant Leader of Fisheries: DR. CHRISTOPHER S. GUY
Assistant Leader of Wildlife: DR. JACK F. CULLY JR.
Leader: DR. PHILIP S. GIPSON

KANSAS DEPARTMENT OF AGRICULTURE
901 S. Kansas Ave., Topeka, KS 66612-1280
Contact(s):
Secretary: ALICE DEVINE
Chief Engineer and Director of Water Resources Division: DAVID L. POPE; Phone: 785-296-3717
Operations Manager for Water Resources Division: STEVE STANKIEWICZ
Water Appropriations Program Manager: TOM HUNTZINGER
Water Management Services Program Manager: MATT SCHERER
Keyword(s): Agriculture, Environmental and Conservation Education, Renewable Resources, Water Resources, Wetlands

KANSAS DEPARTMENT OF WILDLIFE AND PARKS
900 SW Jackson St., Suite 502, Topeka, KS 66612
Phone: 785-296-2281; Fax: 785-296-6953
Description: Charged with the conservation of state wildlife and fishery resources, provision of environmental services and habitat protection, and park development and management. Administers state boating law, hunter education programs, Land and Water Conservation Funds, and other related functions.
Contact(s):
Secretary: STEVEN A. WILLIAMS
Assistant Secretary for Administration: RICHARD KOERTH
Boating Education (Topeka Office): CHERYL SWAYNE
Commissioner Members Chairman: JOHN DYKES; Phone: 913-831-3058
Federal Aid Coordinator: TERRY DENKER
Keyword(s): Agriculture, Aquatic Habitats, Biodiversity, Biology, Birds, Communications, Conservation of Protected Areas, Conservation Tillage, Ecology, Endangered and Threatened Species, Environment, Fisheries, Hunting, Lakes

Region 5
1500 W. 7th, P.O. Box 777, Chanute, KS 66720-0777
Phone: 316-431-0380

Operations Office
512 SE 25th Ave., Pratt, KS 67124-8174
Phone: 316-672-5911
Contact(s):
Administrative Services Division: MIKE THEURER
Assistant Secretary for Operations: ROB MANES
Coordinator of Hunter Education and Fur Harvester Education Sections: WAYNE DOYLE
Coordinator of Wildlife Education Service: ROLAND STEIN
Editor: MIKE MILLER
Fisheries and Wildlife Division: JOE KRAMER
Information and Education: BOB MATHEWS
Parks Division: JEROLD HOVER
Public Information: BOB MATHEWS
Publication(s): *Kansas Wildlife and Parks*
Keyword(s): Fisheries, Outdoor Recreation, Public Lands, Sport Fishing

Region 1
P.O. Box 338, 1426 Hwy 183 Alt., Hays, KS 67601
Phone: 785-628-8614
Publication(s): *Kansas Wildlife and Parks*

Region 2
3300 SW 29th St., Topeka, KS 66614
Phone: 785-273-6740

Region 3
1001 W. McArtor Rd., Dodge City, KS 67801
Phone: 316-227-8609

Region 4
6232 E. 29th St. N, Wichita, KS 67220
Phone: 316-683-8069

KANSAS FOREST SERVICE
2610 Claflin Rd., Manhattan, KS 66502-2798
Phone: 785-532-3300; Fax: 785-532-3305
Description: Provides technical forestry assistance to landowners, wood industries, and communities; conducts a tree distribution program, and a rural fire protection program.
Contact(s):
Conservation Forester: WILLIAM L. LOUCKS

Fire Manager: CASEY McCOY
Rural Forestry Coordinator: ROBERT L. ATCHISON
State Forester: RAYMOND G. ASLIN
Keyword(s): Environmental and Conservation Education, Forest Management, Forests and Forestry, Renewable Resources, Urban Forestry, Water Quality, Water Resources

KANSAS GEOLOGICAL SURVEY
1930 Constant Ave., Campus West, Kansas University, Lawrence, KS 66047
Phone: 785-864-3965
Founded: 1889
Description: Purpose is to research and develop information about minerals, water resources, and geologic hazards of Kansas, and to publish reports on those subjects.
Contact(s):
Deputy Director: WILLIAM E. HARRISON
Chief: Geohydrology: DON WHITTEMORE
Chief: Geologic Investigations: PIETER BERENDSEN
Chief: Mathematical Geology: JOHN C. DAVIS
Chief: Petroleum Research: TIMOTHY CARR
Director and State Geologist: M. LEE ALLISON
Publication(s): *Bulletin; journals; maps; technical series; educational series; public information circulars.*
Keyword(s): Energy, Environmental and Conservation Education, Geology, Water Pollution, Water Resources

KANSAS STATE CONSERVATION COMMISSION
109 SW Ninth St., Suite 500, Topeka, KS 66612-1215
Phone: 785-296-3600; Fax: 785-296-6172; Web site: www.ink.org/public/kscc
Founded: 1937
Description: The SCC administrative responsibility is to provide leadership, direction, and support to the conservation districts, watershed districts, and other special purpose districts for the protection and enhancement of Kansas' natural resources. It administers a total of ten programs: seven are financial assistance programs funded by appropriations from the Special Revenue Fund of the State Water Plan.
Contact(s):
Executive Director: TRACY D. STREETER; Phone: 913-296-3600; Fax: 913-296-6172
Keyword(s): Environmental and Conservation Education, Soil Conservation, Water Pollution, Water Quality, Water Resources, Watersheds, Wetlands

KANSAS STATE DEPARTMENT OF HEALTH AND ENVIRONMENT
Landon State Office Bldg., Rm. 620, Topeka, KS 66612-1290
Description: The Kansas Department of Health and Environment is responsible for administering a diverse collection of programs that enhance public health and state wildlife protection efforts. The path of the department is defined by strengthening programs and developing initiatives on pollutant releases, spill cleanup, air and water quality, water resources, pollution prevention, waste management, and general health and environmental protection.
Contact(s):
Secretary: GARY R. MITCHELL; Phone: 785-296-0461
Director of Division of Health:
Director: Bureau of Environmental Field Services: THERESA HODGES; Phone: 785-296-6603
Director: Bureau of Environmental Health Services: STEVE PAIGE; Phone: 785-296-5600
Director: Bureau of Environmental Remediation: LARRY KNOCHE; Phone: 785-296-1660
Director: Bureau of Waste Management: BILL BIDER
Director: Bureau of Water: KARL MUELDENER; Phone: 785-296-5500
Director: Division of Environment: RON HAMMERSCHMIDT; Phone: 785-296-1535
Director: Office of Public Information: DON BROWN; Phone: 785-296-1529

Keyword(s): Air Quality and Pollution, Environment, Health and Nutrition, Pollution Prevention, Public Health Protection, Solid Waste, Water Quality, Water Resources

KANSAS STATE EXTENSION SERVICES
Wildlife Damage Control, Department of Animal Sciences and Industry, 127 Call Hall, Kansas State University, Manhattan, KS 66506-1600
Phone: 785-532-5734; Fax: 785-532-5681; Web site: www.oznet.ksu.edu/
Founded: 1914
Contact(s):
Extension Specialist: CHARLES D. LEE
Keyword(s): Hunting, Predators, Trapping, Wetlands, Wildlife and Wildlife Habitat, Wildlife Management, Youth Organizations

KANSAS WATER OFFICE
901 S. Kansas Ave., Topeka, KS 66612-1249
Phone: 913-296-3185
Description: State water planning, policy, and coordination agency. Prepares state plan of water resources management; conservation; fish and, wildlife, and recreation and development reviews water laws, and recommends new or amendatory legislation. Administers the state water marketing program.
Contact(s):
Assistant Director: CLARK DUFFY
Director: AL LeDOUX
Keyword(s): Lakes, Planning Management, Rivers, Sustainable Development, Water Resources

KENTUCKY

GOVERNOR OF KENTUCKY: PAUL E. PATTON
State Capitol, 700 Capitol St., Frankfort, KY 40601
Phone: 502-564-2611

KENTUCKY DEPARTMENT OF AGRICULTURE
7th Fl., 500 Mero St., Frankfort, KY 40601
Phone: 502-564-4696
Founded: 1876
Description: The service, regulatory and promotional agency for Kentucky's agriculture industry.
Contact(s):
Commissioner: BILLY RAY SMITH
Director: Division of Communications: MISTIANNA H. BARNES; Phone: 502-564-4696
Editor: STACEY GISH; Phone: 502-746-7030
Publication(s): *Kentucky Agricultural News*
Keyword(s): Agriculture, Environmental and Conservation Education, Pesticides, Soil Conservation, Wetlands

KENTUCKY DEPARTMENT OF FISH AND WILDLIFE RESOURCES
#1 Game Farm Rd., Frankfort, KY 40601
Phone: 1-800-858-1549; Fax: 502-564-6508; E-mail: username%gamefarm%fw%internet@msmail.state.ky.us
Founded: 1944
Description: We are stewards of Kentucky's fish and wildlife resources and their habitats. We manage for the perpetuation of these resources and their use by present and future generations. Through partnerships, we will enhance wildlife diversity and promote sustainable use, including hunting, fishing, boating and other nature-related recreation.
Contact(s):
Commissioner: C. TOM BENNETT
Coordinator of Pittman-Robertson Section: DON WALKER
Coordinator of Sport Fish Restoration Section: JAMES AXON
Deputy Commissioner: THOMAS A. YOUNG
Director of Administrative Services Division: ROBERT M. BATES
Director of Division of Fisheries: PETER W. PFEIFFER
Director of Division of Information and Education: LEE CAROLAN
Director of Division of Law Enforcement: DAVID LOVELESS

STATE AND PROVINCIAL GOVERNMENT AGENCIES - KENTUCKY

Director of Division of Wildlife: ROY GRIMES
Director of Engineering Division: CHARLES BUSH
Director of Public Affairs Division: LYNN GARRISON
District 1 Commissioner: MIKE BOATWRIGHT, 2601 N. 10th St., Paducah, KY 42001
District 2 Commissioner: TOM BAKER, 661 A U.S. 31 W. By-Pass, Bowling Green, KY 42101
District 3 Commissioner: ALLEN K. GAILOR, 730 W. Market, Louisville, KY 40202
District 4 Commissioner: CHARLES BALE, 855 Parkers Grove Rd., Hodgenville, KY 42748
District 5 Commissioner: JAMES RICH, 5975 Taylor Mill Rd., Covington, KY 41015
District 6 Commissioner: FRANK BROWN, 124 Lancaster Ave., Richmond, KY 40475; Fax: 606-624-0820
District 7 Commissioner: DOUG HENSLEY, P.O. Box 480, Hazard, KY 41701; Fax: 606-436-5180
District 8 Commissioner: DR. ROBERT C. WEBB, 45 Webb Circle, Grayson, KY 41143
District 9 Commissioner: DAVID GODBY, P.O. Box 1277, Somerset, KY 42502; Fax: 606-677-0115
Regional Boating Supervisor: DENNIS WATSON, Route 1 Sand Knob, Falls of Rough, KY 40119
Regional Boating Supervisor: STEVE OWENS, 338 Candlelite Drive, Almo, KY 42020
Regional Boating Supervisor: REED SANDERS, 185 Gwinn Island Circle, Danville, KY 40422
Regional Boating Supervisor: K. R. HENDERSON, P.O. Box 131, Clarkson, KY 42726
Regional Law Enforcement Supervisor: GERALD ALEXANDER, 6575 Beech Grove Rd., Farmington, KY 42040
Superintendent of State Game Farm: JOHN AKERS
Publication(s): *Kentucky Wildlife Viewing Guide; Kentucky Afield Magazine; Kentucky Fish; Hunting and Fishing Regulation Guides*
Keyword(s): Biodiversity, Environmental and Conservation Education, Fisheries, Wildlife and Wildlife Habitat

KENTUCKY DEPARTMENT OF PARKS
10th Fl., Capital Plaza Tower, Frankfort, KY 40601
Phone: 502-564-2172
Contact(s):
Commissioner: KENNY RAPIER
Deputy Commissioner: BOB BENDER
Director of Resort Parks: JIM GOODMAN
Director: Rangers: DANNY REED
State Naturalist: CAREY TICHENOR
Keyword(s): Land Preservation, Outdoor Recreation, Public Lands

KENTUCKY GEOLOGICAL SURVEY
228 Mining and Mineral Resources Bldg., University of Kentucky, Lexington, KY 40506-0107
Phone: 606-257-5500
Founded: 1854
Description: Investigates the geology and mineral and water resources of Kentucky and makes this information available to the public. It is a research and service organization.
Contact(s):
Assistant State Geologist for Administration: JOHN D. KIEFER
Assistant State Geologist for Research and Head: Coal and Minerals Section: JAMES C. COBB
Director and State Geologist: DONALD C. HANEY
Head: Computer and Laboratory Services Section: STEVEN J. CORDIVIOLA
Head: Publications Section: DONALD W. HUTCHESON
Head: Stratigraphy and Petroleum Geology Section: JAMES DRAHOVZAL
Head: Water Resources Section: JAMES S. DINGER
Publication(s): *List available on request.*

KENTUCKY SOIL AND WATER CONSERVATION COMMISSION
663 Teton Trail, Frankfort, KY 40601
Contact(s):
Chair: DAVID GERREIN; Phone: 606-623-3960
Director of Division of Conservation: STEPHEN A. COLEMAN; Phone: 502-564-3080; Fax: 502-564-9195; E-mail: coleman@NREPC.NR.STATE.KY.US

KENTUCKY STATE COOPERATIVE EXTENSION SERVICES
S-107 Agricultural Science Bldg. N., University of Kentucky, Lexington, KY 40546-0091
Phone: 606-257-4302; Fax: 606-323-1031; Web site: www.ca.uky.edu/coopext/
Contact(s):
Associate Director of Extension Service: DR. WALTER J. WALLA; E-mail: wwalla@ca.uky.edu
Assistant Extension Director of Agriculture: DR. CURTIS ABSHER, 309 Garrigus Bldg., University of Kentucky, Lexington, KY 40546; Phone: 606-257-1846; E-mail: cabsher@ca.uky.edu
Assistant Director, Rural and Economic Development: RICK MAURER, 500 Garrigus Bldg., University of Kentucky, Lexington, KY 40546-0215; Phone: 606-257-7585; E-mail: rmaurer@ca.uky.edu
Wildlife Specialist: THOMAS G. BARNES, Univ. of Kentucky, Dept. of Forestry, Lexington, KY 40546-0073; Phone: 606-257-8633; Fax: 606-323-1031
Publication(s): *Extension Today*

KENTUCKY STATE NATURE PRESERVES COMMISSION
801 Schenkel Ln., Frankfort, KY 40601
Phone: 502-573-2886; Fax: 502-573-2355; E-mail: STMP:ksnpcemail@mail.state.ky.us; Web site:www.nr.state.ky.us/nrepc/dnr/ksnpc/index.htm
Founded: 1976
Description: KSNP's mission is to protect Kentucky's natural heritage by (1) identifying, acquiring, and managing natural areas that represent the best known occurrences of rare native species, natural communitites, and significant natural features in a statewide nature preserve system; (2) working with others to protect biological diveristy; and (3) educating Kentuckians as to the value and purpose of nature preserves and biodiversity conservation.
Contact(s):
Director: DONALD S. DOTT JR.; Phone: 502-573-2886; Fax: 502-573-2355; E-mail: don.dott@mail.state.ky.us
Chair of Commission: CLARA WHEATLEY; Phone: 502-358-8643
Secretary of Commission: KEN JACKSON; Phone: 606-734-4436

NATURAL RESOURCES AND ENVIRONMENTAL PROTECTION CABINET
5th Fl., Capital Plaza Tower, Frankfort, KY 40601
Phone: 502-564-3350; Fax: 502-564-3354
Contact(s):
Secretary: JAMES BICKFORD
Deputy Secretary: BRUCE WILLIAMS
General Counsel: Office of Legal Services: BARBARA FOSTER; Phone: 502-564-5576; Fax: 502-564-6131

Department for Environmental Protection
14 Reilly Rd., Frankfort, KY 40601
Phone: 502-564-2150; Fax: 502-564-9245
Contact(s):
Commissioner: ROBERT W. LOGAN
Deputy Commissioner: RALPH COLLINS
Director: Division for Air Quality: JOHN E. HORNBACK; Phone: 502-573-3382; Fax: 502-573-3787
Director: Division of Environmental Services: WILLIAM E. DAVIS; Phone: 502-564-6120; Fax: 502-564-8930
Director: Division of Waste Management: ROBERT DANIELL; Phone: 502-564-6716; Fax: 502-564-4049
Director: Division of Water: JACK A. WILSON; Phone: 502-564-3410; Fax: 502-564-4245

Department for Natural Resources
663 Teton Trail, Frankfort, KY 40601
Phone: 502-564-2184; Fax: 502-564-6193
Contact(s):
Commissioner: HUGH N. ARCHER

Director: Division of Conservation: STEVE COLEMAN; Phone: 502-564-3080; Fax: 502-564-7484
Director: Division of Energy: JOHN STAPLETON; Phone: 502-564-7192; Fax: 502-564-7484
Director: Division of Forestry: MARK MATUSZEWSKI; Phone: 502-564-4496; Fax: 502-564-6553

Department for Surface Mining Reclamation and Enforcement
#2 Hudson Hollow, Frankfort, KY 40601
Phone: 502-564-6940; Fax: 502-564-5698
Contact(s):
Commissioner: CARL CAMPBELL
Deputy Commissioner: ALLEN LUTTRELL
Director: Division of Abandoned Lands: STEPHEN HOHMANN; Phone: 502-564-2141; Fax: 502-564-6544
Director: Division of Field Services: MARK THOMPSON; Phone: 502-564-2340; Fax: 502-564-5848
Director: Division of Permits: VICKI PETTUS; Phone: 502-564-2320; Fax: 502-564-6764

Environmental Quality Commission
14 Reilly Rd., Frankfort, KY 40601
Phone: 502-564-2150; Fax: 502-567-4245
Contact(s):
Chair: ALOMA DEW
Executive Director: LESLIE COLE

Nature Preserves Commission
801 Schenkel Ln., Frankfort, KY 40601
Phone: 502-573-2886; Fax: 502-573-2355
Contact(s):
Chairman: CLARA WHEATLEY
Director: DON S. DOTT; Phone: 502-573-2355

LOUISIANA

GOVERNOR OF LOUISIANA: M. J. FOSTER JR.
State Capitol, P.O. Box 94004, Baton Rouge, LA 70804
Phone: 504-342-7015

LOUISIANA COOPERATIVE FISH AND WILDLIFE RESEARCH UNIT (USDI)
U.S. Geological Survey, School of Forestry, Wildlife and Fisheries, FWF Building, Rm. 124, Louisiana State University, Baton Rouge, LA 70803-6202
Phone: 225-388-4179; Fax: 225-388-4227
Contact(s):
Leader: CHARLES F. BRYAN; Phone: 225-388-4184; E-mail: cbryan@lsu.edu
Assistant Leader: ALAN D. AFTON; Phone: 225-388-4212; E-mail: Aafton@lsu.edu

LOUISIANA DEPARTMENT OF AGRICULTURE AND FORESTRY
P.O. Box 631, Baton Rouge, LA 70821-0631
Phone: 504-922-1234
Contact(s):
Assistant Commissioner: Office of Management and Finance: SKIP RHORER
Deputy Commissioner: BUD COURSON; Phone: 504-922-1238; Fax: 504-922-1253
Commissioner: BOB ODOM

Office of Forestry
P.O. Box 1628, Baton Rouge, LA 70821-1628
Phone: 225-925-4500
Founded: 1944
Description: Charged with: detection and suppression of wildfire on forest lands; providing technical management assistance to forest landowners; and dissemination of materials and information for education of the public. Produces approximately 50 million seedlings annually (pine and hardwood) for Louisiana landowners, operates a 400-acre seed orchard that produces slash and loblolly pine seed that are genetically improved. Actively engaged in promoting urban forestry activities.
Contact(s):
Chairman: BURTON D. WEAVER JR.
Associate State Forester: CYRIL LeJEUNE
Chief: Forest Management: DONALD P. FEDUCCIA; Phone: 225-925-4500
Chief: Forest Protection: LOUIS HEATON III
Chief: Information: Education: and Urban Forestry: JAMES L. CULPEPPER; Phone: 225-925-4500
Chief: Reforestation: CHARLES MATHERNE; Phone: 225-925-4515
State Forester: PAUL D. FREY; Phone: 225-952-8002
Keyword(s): Environmental and Conservation Education, Forest Management, Outdoor Recreation, Renewable Resources, Sustainable Ecosystems, Urban Forestry

Office of Soil and Water Conservation, State Soil and Water Conservation Committee
P.O. Box 3554, Baton Rouge, LA 70821-3554
Phone: 504-922-1269
Founded: 1938
Description: To assist soil and water conservation districts in carrying out their conservation programs, to coordinate activities among districts, and to secure the cooperation and assistance of state and federal agencies in the work of such districts.
Contact(s):
Chairman: PEDRO ANGELLE, 4879 Main Hwy., St. Martinville, LA 70582; Phone: 318-332-2910; Fax: 318-332-6563
Vice Chairman: THAD SPURLOCK
Secretary and Treasurer: A. LEE ALLEE
Executive Director: BRADLEY E. SPICER; Phone: 504-922-1269; Fax: 504-922-2577

LOUISIANA DEPARTMENT OF NATURAL RESOURCES
625 N. 4th St., Baton Rouge, LA 70802
Phone: 225-342-8955; Fax: 224-342-3442; Web site: www.dnr.state.la.us
Contact(s):
Deputy Secretary: JAMES HANCHEY
Secretary: JACK CALDWELL; Phone: 225-342-4503; Fax: 225-342-5861
Undersecretary: ROBERT D. HARPER

Office of Coastal Restoration and Management
Phone: 504-342-1375
Contact(s):
Assistant Secretary: KATHERINE G. VAUGHAN

Office of Conservation
Phone: 504-342-5500
Contact(s):
Commissioner of Conservation: PHILIP N. ASPRODITES

Office of Mineral Resources
Phone: 504-342-4615
Contact(s):
Assistant Secretary: GUS C. RODEMACHER

LOUISIANA DEPARTMENT OF WILDLIFE AND FISHERIES
P.O. Box 98000, Baton Rouge, LA 70898-9000
Phone: 225-765-2800
Founded: 1872
Description: Established as a part of state government to protect, conserve and replenish the natural resources of the state, including wild game and nongame quadrupeds or animals, oysters, fish and other aquatic life.
Contact(s):
Chairman: BILL BUSBICE JR.
Secretary: JAMES H. JENKINS JR.; Phone: 225-765-2623
Administrator: Colonel: Law Enforcement Division: WINTON VIDRINE; Phone: 225-765-2989
Administrator: Fur & Refuge Division: BRANDT SAVIOE; Phone: 225-765-2811

STATE AND PROVINCIAL GOVERNMENT AGENCIES - MAINE

Administrator: Inland Fisheries Division: BENNIE FONTENOT; Phone: 225-765-2330
Administrator: Marine Fisheries Division: KAREN FOOTE; Phone: 225-765-2384
Administrator: Wildlife Division: TOMMY PRICKETT; Phone: 225-765-2346
Assistant Secretary: Office of Fisheries: JOHN ROUSSEL; Phone: 225-765-2801
Assistant Secretary: Office of Wildlife: PHIL BOWMAN; Phone: 225-765-2806
Director and Head: Information and Education Division: DR. LYLE M. SONIAT; Phone: 225-765-2916
Undersecretary: Office of Management and Finance: JAMES L. PATTON; Phone: 225-765-2860
Vice Chairman: DANIEL J. BABIN
Publication(s): *Louisiana Conservationist*
Keyword(s): Fish Wildlife Management, Wildlife and Wildlife Habitat

LOUISIANA GEOLOGICAL SURVEY
P.O. Box G, University Station, Baton Rouge, LA 70893
Web site: www.lgs.lsu.edu
Founded: 1934
Description: The Survey is charged with conducting geologic investigations and preparing technical reports that assist in finding and developing new reserves of natural resources in the state and in protecting the state's environment.
Contact(s):
Director: CHACKO J. JOHN
Keyword(s): Coasts, Energy, Geology, Water Resources, Wetlands

LOUISIANA SEA GRANT COLLEGE PROGRAM
Louisiana State University, Baton Rouge, LA 70803
Phone: 225-388-6710; Fax: 225-388-6331; Web site: www.laseagrant.org/
Founded: 1968
Description: The Louisiana Sea Grant College Program is a research, education, and public service organization supported by federal, state, and private sector funds. The Program provides the knowledge, trained personnel, and public awareness needed to wisely and effectively develop and manage coastal and marine areas and resources in a manner that will assure sustainable economic and societal benefits.
Contact(s):
Assistant Director: MICHAEL M. LIFFMANN
Executive Director: DR. JACK R. VANLOPIK, Louisiana State University, Baton Rouge, LA 70803; Phone: 225-388-6710; Fax: 225-388-6331; E-mail: jvl@lsu.edu
Associate Director: RONALD E. BECKER, Sea Grant College Program, Louisiana State University, Baton Rouge, LA 70803; Phone: 225-388-6345
Communications Coordinator: ELIZABETH B. COLEMAN, Louisiana Sea Grant College Program, Louisiana State University, Baton Rouge, LA 70803; Phone: 225-388-6448/6449
Publication(s): *Coast and Sea: Marine and Coastal Research in Louisiana's Universities (Quarterly Louisiana Coastal Law)*
Keyword(s): Coasts, Environmental and Conservation Education, Renewable Resources, Sustainable Development, Wetlands

LOUISIANA STATE EXTENSION SERVICES
P.O. Box 25100, Baton Rouge, LA 70894-5100
Phone: 225-388-6083 or 504-388-4141; Fax: 504-388-2467; Web site: www.agctr.lsu.edu/wwwac/Ices.html
Contact(s):
Director of Extension Service: DR. JACK L. BAGENT; E-mail: jlngent@agctr.lsu.edu
Assistant Specialist for Forestry: DR. TODD F. SHUPE; Phone: 225-388-4087; Fax: 225-388-2478; E-mail: tshupe@agctr.lsu.edu
Assistant Specialist for Forestry and Wildlife: DR. DONALD P. REED; Phone: 225-388-4087; Fax: 225-388-2478; E-mail: dreed@agctr.lsu.edu
Assistant Specialist for Wetland and Coastal Resources: DR. REX CAFFEY; Phone: 225-388-2266; Fax: 225-388-2478; E-mail: rcaffey@agctr.lsu.edu
Associate Specialist of Aquaculture: DR. CHARLES G. LUTZ; Phone: 225-388-2152; Fax: 225-388-2478; E-mail: glutz@agctr.lsu.edu
Project Leader of Aquaculture: Fisheries: Wetland & Coastal Management and Sea Grant and Specialist for Marine Resource Economics: DR. KENNETH J. ROBERTS; Phone: 225-388-2145; Fax: 225-388-2478; E-mail: kroberts@agctr.lsu.edu
Project Leader of Forestry and Wildlife and Specialist of Wildlife: DR. JAMES F. FOWLER; Phone: 225-388-4087; Fax: 225-388-2478; E-mail: jfowler@agctr.lsu.edu
Specialist for Seafood Technology: DR. MICHAEL W. MOODY; Phone: 225-388-2152; Fax: 225-388-2478; E-mail: mmoody@agctr.lsu.edu
Specialist: Forestry: DR. ROBERT H. MILLS; Phone: 225-388-4087; Fax: 225-388-2478; E-mail: bmills@agctr.lsu.edu

OFFICE OF STATE PARKS, DEPARTMENT OF CULTURE, RECREATION, AND TOURISM
P.O. Box 44426, Baton Rouge, LA 70804
Phone: 225-342-8111 or 1-888-677-1400; E-mail: parks@crt.state.la.us
Founded: 1934
Description: Created to plan, design, construct, operate, and maintain the state's parks, natural areas, recreational facilities, and commemorative sites. Office has 17 parks or recreational areas, 15 commemorative sites, and one preservation area open to the public. The Office is assisted by the Parks and Recreation Commission an advisory board appointed by the Governor.
Contact(s):
Assistant Secretary: DWIGHT LANDRENEAU
Keyword(s): Cultural Preservation, Historic Preservation, Nature Preservation, Outdoor Recreation, Public Lands

STATE OFFICE OF CONSERVATION (LOUISIANA)
P.O. Box 94275, Capitol Sta., Baton Rouge, LA 70804-9275
Phone: 225-342-5540
Description: The State Office of Conservation is an oil and gas regulatory agency.
Contact(s):
Assistant Commissioner: JIM WELSH
Commissioner: PHILIP N. ASPERODITES
Keyword(s): Energy, Engineering, Geology, Pollution Prevention, Transportation

MAINE

GOVERNOR OF MAINE: ANGUS S. KING JR.
State House, Station 1, Augusta, ME 04333
Phone: 207-287-3531

MAINE ATLANTIC SALMON COMMISSION (formerly Maine Atlantic Salmon Authority)
650 State St., Bangor, ME 04401-5654
Phone: 207-941-4449; Fax: 207-941-4443; Web site: www.state.me.us/ASA
Founded: 1948
Description: The Atlantic Salmon Commission was established for the purposes of undertaking research, planning, management, restoration, and propagation of the Atlantic sea run salmon in the state. The Commission has authority to adopt and amend regulations to promote the conservation and propagation of Atlantic salmon in all Maine waters.
Contact(s):
Commissioner of Inland Fisheries and Wildlife: LEE PERRY
Commissioner of Marine Resources: GEORGE LAPOINTE
Keyword(s): Atlantic Salmon, Biology, Endangered and Threatened Species, Fisheries, Rivers, Sport Fishing

MAINE COOPERATIVE FISH AND WILDLIFE RESEARCH UNIT (USDI)
USGS Biological Resources Division, 5755 Nutting Hall, University of Maine, Orono, ME 04469-5755
Phone: 207-581-2870
Founded: 1935
Description: Provide graduate training and research experience in wildlife and fish ecology and management. Supported cooperatively by the University of Maine in Orono, ME, Maine Department of Inland Fisheries and Wildlife, U.S. Geological Survey, and the Wildlife Management Institute.
Contact(s):
Leader: DR. WILLIAM B. KROHN, 258 Nutting Hall, University of Maine, Orono, ME 04469; Phone: 207-581-2870; Fax: 207-581-2858
Assistant Leader: Fisheries: DR. JOHN R. MORING, 310 Murray Hall, University of Maine, Orono, ME 04469; Phone: 207-581-2582
Assistant Leader: Wildlife: CYNTHIA S. LOFTIN, 230 Nutting Hall, University of Maine, Orono, ME 04469; Phone: 207-581-2843; Fax: 207-581-2858
Keyword(s): Aquatic Habitats, Biodiversity, Fisheries, Geographic Information Systems, Wildlife and Wildlife Habitat, Wildlife Management, Wildlife Research, Wetland Habitat

MAINE DEPARTMENT OF AGRICULTURE, FOOD, AND RURAL RESOURCES
Office of Agricultural Natural and Rural Resources, 28 State House Station, Augusta, ME 04333-0028
Contact(s):
Director: PETER N. MOSHER; Phone: 207-287-1132; Fax: 207-287-7548; E-mail: peter.mosher@state.me.us
Commissioner: ROBERT W. SPEAR; Phone: 207-287-3419

MAINE DEPARTMENT OF CONSERVATION
22 State House Station, Augusta, ME 04333-0022
Phone: 207-287-2211
Founded: 1973
Description: To preserve, protect, and enhance the land resources of the State of Maine; to encourage the wise use of the scenic, mineral, and forest resources; to ensure that coordinated planning for the future allocation of lands for recreational, forest production, mining, and other public and private uses is effectively accomplished; and to provide for the effective management of public lands.
Contact(s):
Administrative Assistant: GALE ROSS
Commissioner: RONALD B. LOVAGLIO
Deputy Commissioner: DAWN GALLAGHER
Director of General Services: WILL HARRIS
Director of Public Information: SUSAN BENSON

Land Use Regulation Commission
State House, Station #22, Augusta, ME 04333
Phone: 207-287-2631, In-state toll free 1800-452-8711
Contact(s):
Director: JOHN WILLIAMS
Resource Administrator: ANDREW FISK

Maine Forest Service
22 State House Station, Augusta, ME 04333
Phone: 207-287-2791
Contact(s):
Director: CHUCK GADZIK
Forest Fire Control Supervisor: TOM PARENT
Forest Policy and Management: DON MANSIUS
Resource Administrator: PETER BERINGER
State Entomologist: DAVE STRUBLE

Natural Resource Information & Mapping
22 State House Station, Augusta, ME 04333
Phone: 207-287-2801
Contact(s):
Director, Applied Geology: TOM WEDDLE
Director, Maine Natural Areas: MOLLY DOCHERTY; Phone: 207-287-8045
Director, Resource Date Services: ROBERT TUCKER
State Geologist and Director: ROBERT MARVINNEY

MAINE DEPARTMENT OF CONSERVATION

Bureau of Parks and Lands
22 State House Station, Augusta, ME 04333
Phone: 207-287-3821
Contact(s):
Deputy Director: HERB HARTMAN
Director: TOM MORRISON; Phone: 207-287-3821
Allagash Wilderness Waterway: TIM CAVERLY
Boating Facilities: RICHARD SKINNER
Off-Road Vehicle Program: SCOTT RAMSAY
Planning & Land Use Acquisition: RALPH KNOLL
Resource Administrator: MARLENE BOWMAN

MAINE DEPARTMENT OF ENVIRONMENTAL PROTECTION
State House Station 17, Augusta, ME 04333
Phone: 207-287-7688; Fax: 207-287-7826
Founded: 1972
Description: DEP is charged with the protection and improvement of Maine's natural environment and acting in the best interests of the citizens' health and quality of life.
Contact(s):
Commissioner: EDWARD O. SULLIVAN
Deputy Commissioner: ERIKA MORGAN
Director: Bureau of Air Quality: JAMES BROOKS
Director: Bureau of Land and Water Quality: MARTHA KIRKPATRICK
Director: Bureau of Remediation and Waste Management: ALLAN BALL
Publication(s): *A Citizen's Guide to Lake Watershed Surveys; The Quality of Maine Waters--A Condensed Version on the 1996 Maine Water Quality Assessment; Watershed: An Action Guide to Improving Maine Waters; Planning Guides for Municipalities (series); Issue profiles and fact sheets on a variety of topics*
Keyword(s): Air Quality and Pollution, Environmental Protection, Pollution Prevention, Solid Waste Management, Water Quality

MAINE DEPARTMENT OF INLAND FISHERIES AND WILDLIFE
284 State St., Station #41, Augusta, ME 04333-0041
Phone: 207-287-8000
Founded: 1880
Contact(s):
Chief: Engineering and Realty Division: G. DONALD TAYLOR; Phone: 207-287-5210
Chief: Fishery Research and Management Division: PETER M. BOURQUE; Phone: 207-287-5261
Chief: Wildlife Research and Management Division: G. MARK STADLER; Phone: 207-287-5252
Colonel: Bureau of Warden Service: TIMOTHY PEABODY; Phone: 207-287-2766
Commissioner: LEE E. PERRY; Phone: 207-287-5202
Deputy Commissioner: FREDERICK B. HURLEY JR; Phone: 207-287-3371
Director: Bureau of Administrative Service: RICHARD RECORD; Phone: 207-287-5210
Director: Bureau of Information and Education: DONALD KLEINER; Phone: 207-287-5244
Director: Bureau of Resource Management: KENNETH D. ELOWE; Phone: 207-287-5252
Director: Licensing and Registration Division: VESTA C. BILLING; Phone: 207-287-5225
Rules and Regulations Officer: ANDREA L. ERSKINE; Phone: 207-287-5201
Publication(s): *Maine Fish and Wildlife*
Keyword(s): Endangered and Threatened Species, Fisheries, Hunting, Recreational Boating, Sport Fishing, Wildlife and Wildlife Habitat, Enforcement, Education, Snowmobiling

STATE AND PROVINCIAL GOVERNMENT AGENCIES - MARYLAND

MAINE DEPARTMENT OF MARINE RESOURCES
21 State House Station, Augusta, ME 04333-0021
Phone: 207-624-6550
Founded: 1867
Description: Responsible for research, development, promotion, planning, and enforcement of laws relating to conservation of Maine's marine resources. The department was established to conserve and develop marine and estuarine resources of the state of Maine by conducting and sponsoring scientific research, promoting and developing the Maine commercial fishing industry, and by advising agencies of government concerned with development or activity in coastal waters.
Contact(s):
Chief of Bureau of Marine Patrol: JOSEPH E. FESSENDEN
Commissioner: GEORGE LAPOINTE
Deputy Commissioner: E. PENN ESTABROOK
Director of Bureau of Resource Management: DR. LINDA MERCER, West Boothbay Harbor, ME 04575; Phone: 207-633-9500
Director of Division of Administrative Services: GILBERT M. BILODEAU
Keyword(s): Aquatic Habitats, Ecology, Environmental and Conservation Education, Fisheries, Public Health Protection

MAINE SEA GRANT PROGRAM
5715 Coburn Hall #14, University of Maine, Orono, ME 04469-5715
Phone: 207-581-1435; Fax: 207-581-1426; Web site: www.seagrant.unh.edu/home.htm
Contact(s):
Director, Interim: IAN DAVISON; E-mail: davison@maine.maine.edu
Program Leader, Interim: RON BEARD; Phone: 207-581-1442; E-mail: rbeard@umext.maine.edu
Executive Director, Lobster Institute: ROBERT BAYER; Phone: 207-581-1443; E-mail: rbayer@maine.edu
Extension Associate, Darling Marine Center: DANA MORSE, Clarks Cove, Walpole, ME 04573; Phone: 207-563-3146, ext. 205,; Fax: 207-563-3119; E-mail: dana.l.morse@umit.maine.edu
Finfish Aquaculture Specialist: CHRIS BARTLETT, Marine Technology Center, Washington County Technical College, 16 Deep Cove Road, Eastport, ME 04631-0618; Phone: 207-853-2518; Fax: 207-853-0940; E-mail: chris.bartlett@umit.maine.edu
Keyword(s): Aquatic Habitats, Coasts, Environmental and Conservation Education, Fisheries, Oceanography

UNIVERSITY OF MAINE COOPERATIVE EXTENSION
Attn: Prog. Admin., 5741 Libby Hall, University of Maine, Orono, ME 04469-5741
Phone: 207-581-2902; Fax: 207-581-1387; Web site: www.umext.maine.edu/
Contact(s):
Program Administrator: CATHERINE ELLIOTT
Forestry Specialist: JAMES F. PHILP, 261 Nutting Hall, University of Maine, Orono, ME 04469-5755; Phone: 207-581-2885

MARYLAND

GOVERNOR OF MARYLAND: PARRIS N. GLENDENING
State House, 100 State Cir., Annapolis, MD 21404
Phone: 410-974-3901

DEPARTMENT OF THE ENVIRONMENT
2500 Broening Hwy., Baltimore, MD 21224
Phone: 410-631-3000
Founded: 1987
Description: The Department of the Environment is charged with protection of the state's land, air and water resources, to ensure the long-term protection of public health and quality of life.
Contact(s):
Secretary: JANE T. NISHIDA; Phone: 410-631-3084
Assistant Secretary: ROBERT G. HOYT; Phone: 410-631-4187
Deputy Secretary: ARTHUR W. RAY; Phone: 410-631-3086
Director of Administrative and Employee Services: ALLAN P. JENSEN; Phone: 410-631-3116
Director of Air and Radiation Management Administration: MERRYLIN ZAW-MON; Phone: 410-631-3255
Director of Office of Communications: SUSAN E. WOODS; Phone: 410-631-3172
Director of Technical and Regulatory Services Administration: MICHAEL HAIRE; Phone: 410-631-3680
Director of Waste Management Administration: RICHARD W. COLLINS; Phone: 410-631-3304
Director of Water Management Administration: J. L. HEARN; Phone: 410-631-3567
Librarian: DR. ETTA LYLES; Phone: 410-631-3818
Publication(s): *Regulatory Calendar; Annual Air Quality Data Report; Biennial Water Report; List of Potential Hazardous Waste Sites*
Keyword(s): Air Quality and Pollution, Environmental Protection, Pollution Prevention, Solid Waste Management, Water Pollution

MARYLAND DEPARTMENT OF AGRICULTURE
50 Harry S. Truman Pkwy., Annapolis, MD 21401
Phone: 410-841-5700
Founded: 1972
Description: Created as a cabinet-level state agency, the Department is charged with assisting soil conservation districts to protect state waters from agricultural nonpoint source pollution, overseeing numerous inspection, testing, grading, and marketing programs, mosquito control and gypsy moth control, and forest pest management under various laws. The department also has responsibility for regulatory functions, such as pesticide applicators, weights and measures, nursery inspection, seed and turf regulation, certification; and agricultural chemical and product registration.
Contact(s):
Secretary: HENRY A. VIRTS, D.V.M.; Phone: 410-841-5880
Deputy Secretary: HAGNER R. MISTER; Phone: 410-841-5881
Assistant Secretary: Marketing, Animal Industries and Consumer Services: BRAD POWERS; Phone: 410-841-5782
Assistant Secretary: Office of Plant Industries and Pest Management: DR. CHARLES W. PUFFINBERGER; Phone: 410-841-5870
Assistant Secretary: Office of Resource Conservation: ROYDEN POWELL; Phone: 410-841-5865
Counsel: CRAIG A. NIELSEN; Phone: 410-841-5883
Editor: HAROLD KANAREK
State Veterinarian: DR. ROGER O. OLSON; Phone: 410-841-5810
Publication(s): *List on request.*

Agricultural Commission
50 Harry S. Truman Pkwy., Annapolis, MD 21401
Phone: 410-841-5882
Founded: 1961
Description: Established by law as the Agricultural Advisory Board to the Governor, the Maryland Agricultural Commission was renamed in 1968 and placed within the Department of Agriculture in 1973. The commission formulates and makes proposals for the advancement of Maryland agriculture by serving as an advisory body to the Secretary of Agriculture. Composed of 24 members, one member is the principal administrative officer for agricultural affairs at the University of Maryland; one appointee represents consumer interests and serves a three-year term; the remaining 22 members are appointed for three-year terms by the Governor from nominations submitted by commodity and agricultural organizations.
Contact(s):
Chairman: HENRY PASSI
Executive Director: GILBERT O. BOWLING; Phone: 410-841-5882

State Soil Conservation Committee
50 Harry S. Truman Pkwy., Annapolis, MD 21401
Phone: 410-841-5863
Founded: 1937
Description: Established to organize soil conservation districts and to establish policy, resolve problems to give guidance and assistance to districts. The SSCC membership includes

representatives from the Maryland Departments of Natural Resources, Agriculture, and Environment, Maryland Agricultural Commission, University of Maryland, Maryland Association of Soil Conservation Districts, and five soil conservation district supervisors. The committee is a unit of the Maryland Dept. of Agriculture.
Contact(s):
Chairman: DAVE THOMAS, 203 Middleton Rd., Oakland, MD 21550; Phone: 301-334-3952, ext. 5378
Executive Secretary: LOUISE LAWRENCE; Phone: 410-841-5863; Fax: 410-841-5914
Assistant Secretary: ROYDEN POWELL; Phone: 410-841-5865; Fax: 410-841-5914
Publication(s): *SSCC Reporter Newsletter*
Keyword(s): Agriculture, Environmental and Conservation Education, Fisheries, Pesticides

MARYLAND DEPARTMENT OF NATURAL RESOURCES
Tawes State Office Bldg., Annapolis, MD 21401
Contact(s):
Secretary: JOHN R. GRIFFIN; Phone: 410-260-8101
Deputy Secretary: CAROLYN D. DAVIS; Phone: 410-260-8102
Director: Public Communications Office: LIZ KALINOWSKI; Phone: 410-260-8001
Legislative Officer: Intergovernmental and Community Relations: NITA SETTINA; Phone: 410-260-8110
Principal Counsel: JOSEPH P. GILL; Phone: 410-260-8350

Chesapeake Bay and Watershed Programs
Tawes State Office Bldg., Annapolis, MD 21401
Contact(s):
Assistant Secretary: VERNA E. HARRISON; Phone: 410-260-8116
Chief of Regional Chesapeake Bay Program: CAROLYN WATSON; Phone: 410-260-8729
Director of Chesapeake and Coastal Watershed Administration: DAVID BURKE; Phone: 410-260-8705
Director of Education, Bay Policy, and Growth Management: THERESA PEIRNO; Phone: 410-260-8715
Director of Resource Assessment Service: PAUL MASSICOT; Phone: 410-260-8680

Management Services
Contact(s):
Assistant Secretary: ALLEN W. CARTWRIGHT JR.; Phone: 410-260-8106
Director of Audit and Management Review: STEVE POWELL; Phone: 410-260-8383
Director of Chesapeake Bay Trust: DAVID A. MINGES; Phone: 410-974-2941
Director of Finance and Administrative Services: BONNIE MULIERI; Phone: 410-260-8032
Director of Human Resources Services: KATHRYN MARR; Phone: 410-260-8081
Director of Maryland Environmental Trust: JOHN BERNSTEIN; Phone: 410-514-7900
Keyword(s): Fisheries, Forests and Forestry, Public Lands, Watersheds, Wildlife Management

Public Lands Division
Contact(s):
Assistant Secretary: JAMES W. DUNMYER; Phone: 410-260-8108
Director of Engineering and Construction: ROBERT P. GAUDETTE; Phone: 410-260-8897
Director of Land and Water Conservation: MICHAEL J. NELSON; Phone: 410-260-8446
Director of Program Open Space: H. GRANT DeHART; Phone: 410-260-8425
Director of Resource Planning: GENE PIOTROWSKI; Phone: 410-260-8405
Superintendent of Natural Resources Police: COL. JOHN RHOADS; Phone: 410-260-8881
Superintendent of State Forest and Park Service: COL. RICK BARTON; Phone: 410-260-8186

Resource Management Services
Contact(s):
Assistant Secretary: DR. SARAH J. TAYLOR-ROGERS; Phone: 410-260-8113
Director of Environmental Review: RAY C. DINTAMAN JR.; Phone: 410-260-8331
Director of Fish, Heritage and Wildlife: ERIC C. SCHWAAB; Phone: 410-260-8582
Director of Fisheries: DOROTHY L. LEONARD; Phone: 410-260-8251
Director of Forest Service: JAMES MALLOW; Phone: 410-260-8501
Director of Licensing Registration Services: BRUCE GILMORE; Phone: 410-260-8233
Director of Wildlife and Natural Heritage: JOSH SANDT; Phone: 410-974-3195
Executive Director of Chesapeake Bay Critical Areas Commission: REN SEREY; Phone: 410-974-2426

MARYLAND SEA GRANT COLLEGE
Sea Grant College, University of Maryland, 112 Skinner Hall, College Park, MD 20742-7640
Phone: 301-405-6371; Fax: 301-314-9581; Web site: www.mdsg.umd.edu/
Founded: 1977
Description: Maryland Sea Grant supports marine research, education, and outreach activities, especially in connection with the Chesapeake Bay. It currently supports research at four of the region's marine laboratories, and on the campuses of the University System of Maryland, the Johns Hopkins University and other institutions of higher learning.
Contact(s):
Director: JONATHAN KRAMER; Phone: 301-405-6371; E-mail: kramer@mdsg.umd.edu
Assistant Director: JACK GREER; Phone: 301-405-6377
Publication(s): *Maryland Marine Notes ; Watershed; Maryland Sea Grant Books and Videos*
Keyword(s): Aquatic Habitats, Biotechnology, Environmental and Conservation Education, Fisheries, Oceanography

MARYLAND STATE COOPERATIVE EXTENSION
University of Maryland, 1104 Symons Hall, College Park, MD 20742
Phone: 301-405-2072; Web site: www.agnr.umd.edu/CES/
Contact(s):
Associate Dean and Associate Director of Maryland Cooperative Extension: DR. JAMES WADE, University of Maryland, Cooperative Extension, 1200 Symons Hall, College Park, MD 20742-5565; Phone: 301-405-2907; Fax: 301-405-2963
Dean and Director of Agricultural Experiment Station and Maryland Cooperative Extension: DR. THOMAS A. FRETZ; Fax: 301-314-9146
Coordinator: Sea Grant Extension Program: DR. DOUG LIPTON, University of Maryland, Cooperative Extension, 2218B Symons Hall, College Park, MD 20742; Phone: 301-405-1280
Program Leader and Assistant Director of Agriculture and Natural Resources Program: DR. JAMES HANSON, University of Maryland, Cooperative Extension, 1200 Symons Hall, College Park, MD 20742-5565; Phone: 301-405-7992; Fax: 301-405-2963
Regional Natural Resource Specialist: JONATHAN KAYS, University of Maryland, Cooperative Extension, Western Maryland Research and Education Center, 18330 Keedysville Road, Keedysville, MD 21756; Phone: 301-432-2735, ext. 323; Fax: 301-432-4089
Regional Natural Resource Specialist: BOB TJADEN, University of Maryland, Cooperative Extension, Wye Research and Education Center, P.O. box 169, Queenstown, MD 21658; Phone: 410-827-8056; Fax: 410-827-9039

MARYLAND-NATIONAL CAPITAL PARK AND PLANNING COMMISSION
6611 Kenilworth Ave., Riverdale, MD 20737
Phone: 301-454-1740

STATE AND PROVINCIAL GOVERNMENT AGENCIES - MASSACHUSETTS

Founded: 1927
Description: Established by the General Assembly of the state of Maryland to provide for the orderly development of Montgomery and Prince George's counties; to provide a system of parks to serve the residents of this bi-county region; and to provide recreation programs and services in Prince George's county.
Contact(s):
Chairman: WILLIAM H. HUSSMANN, 8787 Georgia Ave., Silver Spring, MD 20910; Phone: 301-495-4605
Executive Director: TRUDYE MORGAN JOHNSON; Phone: 301-454-1740
Acting Director of Prince George's County Parks and Recreation: MARY WELLS-HARLEY; Phone: 301-699-2582
Director of Montgomery County Department of Parks and Planning: CHARLES LOEHR; Phone: 301-495-4500
Director: Prince George's County Planning: FERN V. PIRET; Phone: 301-952-3595
General Counsel, Legal Department: RICHARD A. ROMINE; Phone: 301-454-1670
Montgomery County Director: Parks: DONALD K. COCHRAN; Phone: 301-495-2500
Secretary-Treasurer, Department of Finance: A. EDWARD NAVARRE; Phone: 301-454-1540
Vice Chairman: ELIZABETH HEWLETT, 14741 Governor Oden Bowie Dr., Upper Marlboro, MD 20772; Phone: 301-952-3560

MASSACHUSETTS

GOVERNOR OF MASSACHUSETTS: ARGEO PAUL CELLUCCI
State House, Rm. 360, Boston, MA 02133
Phone: 617-727-3600

EXECUTIVE OFFICE OF ENVIRONMENTAL AFFAIRS

Division of Fisheries and Wildlife
100 Cambridge St., Rm. 1902, Boston, MA 02202
Contact(s):
Director of Law Enforcement: RICHARD MURRAY, 175 Portland St., Boston, MA 02114; Phone: 617-727-3190
Director: WAYNE F. MacCALLUM; Phone: 617-727-3155
Director of Public Access Board: JACK SHEPPARD, 1440 Soldiers Field Rd, Brighton, MA 02135; Phone: 617-727-1843

EXECUTIVE OFFICE OF ENVIRONMENTAL AFFAIRS (MASSACHUSETTS)
Leverett Saltonstall Bldg., 100 Cambridge St., Rm. 2000, Boston, MA 02202
Phone: 617-660-1100
Description: The cabinet-level environmental agency in the state and includes within the secretariat all state environmental agencies.
Contact(s):
Secretary: BOB DURAND
Director: Coastal Zone Management: TOM SKINNER; Phone: 617-727-9530
Director: Conservation Services: JOEL A. LERNER; Phone: 617-727-1552
Director: Impact Review Unit (MEPA): JAY WICKERSHAM; Phone: 617-727-5830
Under Secretary: Administration & Finance: STEVE BERNARD

Animal Health
Leverett Staltonstall Bldg., 100 Cambridge St., Rm. 2000, Boston, MA 02202
Contact(s):
Program Coordinator: ROBERT BENNETT; Phone: 617-727-3018

Bureau of Land Use
Leverett Staltonstall Bldg., 100 Cambridge St., Rm. 2000, Boston, MA 02202
Contact(s):
Chief: RICHARD HUBBARD; Phone: 617-727-0464

Bureau of Markets
Leverett Staltonstall Bldg., 100 Cambridge St., Rm. 2000, Boston, MA 02202
Contact(s):
Chief: SUSAN BLACK; Phone: 617-727-3000

Bureau of Pesticides
Leverett Staltonstall Bldg., 100 Cambridge St., Rm. 2000, Boston, MA 02202
Contact(s):
Chief: BRAD MITCHELL; Phone: 617-727-7712

Department of Environmental Management
100 Cambridge St., Rm. 1905, Boston, Boston, MA 02202
Phone: 617-727-3163
Contact(s):
Chief of Legal Services: KATE LEWIS; Phone: 617-727-3160
Commissioner: PETER WEBBER
Deputy Commissioner (Acting): Resource Conservation: RICHARD THIBEDEAU; Phone: 617-727-3267
Director of Engineering: RALPH SILVA; Phone: 617-727-3160
Director: Division of Forests and Parks: TODD FREDERICKS; Phone: 617-727-3180

Department of Environmental Protection
One Winter St., Boston, MA 02108
Phone: 617-292-5500
Contact(s):
Assistant Commissioner: Waste Prevention: JAMES COLEMAN; Phone: 617-292-5570
Commissioner: LAUREN A. LISS
Director of Planning and Evaluation: BARBARA KWETZ; Phone: 617-292-5593

Department of Fisheries, Wildlife, and Environmental Law Enforcement
100 Cambridge St., Rm. 1901, Boston, MA 02202
Contact(s):
Assistant Commissioner: BOB AUSTIN
Commissioner: JOHN PHILLIPS; Phone: 617-727-1614
Director: Division of Marine Fisheries: PHILIP G. COATES; Phone: 617-727-3193

Department of Food and Agriculture
100 Cambridge St., Rm. 2103, Boston, MA 02202
Phone: 617-727-3000
Contact(s):
Commissioner: JONATHAN HEALY

Division of Agricultural Development
100 Cambridge St., Rm. 2103, Boston, MA 02202
Contact(s):
Director: JAMES HINES; Phone: 617-727-3018

Division of Regulatory Services
100 Cambridge St., Rm. 2103, Boston, MA 02202
Contact(s):
Director: DAVID SHELDON; Phone: 617-727-3020

Division of Wetlands and Waterways,
One Winter St., Boston, MA 02108
Phone: 617-292-5695
Contact(s):
Director: CHRISTY FOOTE-SMITH

Metropolitan District Commission,
20 Somerset St., Boston, MA 02108
Phone: 617-727-5114
Founded: 1919
Description: Operates and maintains 19 swimming pools, 17 salt water beaches, 3 fresh water beaches, 23 skating rinks, and various other recreational facilities; also maintains a network of parkways and main traffic roadways and a police force for protection of its property and people using its facilities.

Contact(s):
Commissioner: DAVID BALFOUR
Director: Division of Recreation: GARY DOAK; Phone: 617-727-9547
Director: Reservations and Historic Sites Unit: BRIAN BRODERICK; Phone: 617-727-2744

State Commission for Conservation of Soil, Water and Related Resources
Contact(s):
Executive Secretary: THOMAS C. ANDERSON, 100 Cambridge Street, Boston, MA 02202; Phone: 617-727-9800, ext. 232; Fax: 617-727-2630; E-mail: tanderson_EOE@state.ma.us
Contact: THOMAS QUINK, 67 Church Street, Gilbertville, MA 01031-9864; Phone: 413-477-8870

Watershed Division
Contact(s):
Director: JOSEPH McGINN

MASSACHUSETTS COOPERATIVE FISH AND WILDLIFE RESEARCH UNIT (USDI)
Box 34220, Holdsworth Natural Resources Ctr., University of Massachusetts, Amherst, MA 01003-4220
Phone: 413-545-0398
Founded: 1948
Description: Provides graduate training and research experience in fisheries and wildlife research management, ecology, habitat, population dynamics, and management. Supported cooperatively by the University of Massachusetts, Massachusetts Division of Fisheries and Wildlife, Massachusetts Division of Marine Fisheries, the U.S. Department of Interior, U.S.G.S.-BRD, and the Wildlife Management Institute.
Contact(s):
Leader: STEVE DeSTEFANO
Assistant Leader: Fisheries: MARTHA E. MATHER
Assistant Leader: Wildlife: REBECCA FIELD
Keyword(s): Biodiversity, Environmental and Conservation Education, Fisheries, Wildlife and Wildlife Habitat, Wildlife Management

MASSACHUSETTS HIGHWAY DEPARTMENT
10 Park Plaza, Boston, MA 02116
Phone: 617-973-7800
Description: The mission of the Massachusetts Highway Department is to provide a safe, efficient, quality highway system in a cost-effective and environmentally sensitive manner that continuously meets the diverse needs of its users.
Contact(s):
Chief Engineer: THOMAS F. BRODERICK; Phone: 617-973-7830
Commissioner: MATTHEW J. AMORELLO; Phone: 617-973-7800
Deputy Chief Engineer: Construction: DAVID ANDERSON; Phone: 817-973-7491
Deputy Chief Engineer: Environmental Division: GREGORY PRENDERGAST; Phone: 617-973-7484
Deputy Chief Engineer: Highway Engineering: JOHN BLUNDO; Phone: 617-973-7521
Deputy Chief Engineer: Operations: GORDON BROZ; Phone: 617-973-7741
Project Development: KEVIN WALSH; Phone: 617-973-7529
Supervisor: Cultural Resources Unit: JAMES ELLIOTT; Phone: 617-973-7494
Supervisor: Permitting and Regulatory Compliance: LISA RHODES; Phone: 617-973-7582
Supervisor: Wetlands and Water Resources: HENRY BARBARO; Phone: 617-973-7419
Keyword(s): Air Quality, Cultural Preservation, Environment, Hazardous Materials & Waste, Noise, Solid Waste, Transportation, Water Quality, Wetlands

MIT SEA GRANT COLLEGE PROGRAM
E38-330/Kendall Sq., 292 Main St., Cambridge, MA 02139-9910
Phone: 617-253-7131; Fax: 617-258-5730; Web site: web.mit.edu/seagrant/
Contact(s):
Director: CHRYS CHRYSSOSTOMIDIS; E-mail: chrys@deslab.mit.edu

UNIVERSITY OF MASSACHUSETTS EXTENSION
Stockbridge Hall, Box 30099, University of Massachusetts, Amherst, MA 01003
Phone: 413-545-6555; Fax: 413-545-4800; Web site: www.umass.edu/umext/
Contact(s):
Director: JOHN M. GERBER; E-mail: jgerber@umext.umass.edu
Natural Resources and Environmental Conservation Program: ANNA HICKS, Holdsworth Hall, University of Massachusetts, Amherst, MA 01003; Phone: 413-545-4743; Fax: 413-545-4358; E-mail: ahicks@umext.umass.edu
Conservation Specialist: SCOTT D. JACKSON, University of Massachusetts, Department of Forestry and Wildlife Management, Holdsworth Natural Resources Center, Amherst, MA 01003; Phone: 413-545-2665
Keyword(s): Fisheries, Forests and Forestry, Renewable Resources, Sustainable Ecosystems, Urban Forestry

WOODS HOLE OCEANOGRAPHIC INSITITUTION (WHOI) SEA GRANT PROGRAM
Woods Hole Oceanographic Institution, 193 Oyster Pond Rd., MS #2, Woods Hole, MA 02543-1525
Phone: 508-289-2398; Fax: 508-457-2172; E-mail: seagrant@whoi.edu; Web site: www.whoi.edu/seagrant/
Founded: 1973
Description: The WHOI Sea Grant Program supports research, education, and advisory projects to promote the wise use and understanding of ocean and coastal resources for the public benefit. it is part of the National Sea Grant College Program of the National Oceanic and Atmospheric Administration, a network of 29 individual programs located in each of the coastal and Great Lakes states to foster cooperation among government, academia, and industry.
Contact(s):
Director: DR. JUDITH E. McDOWELL; Phone: 508-289-2557; E-mail: jmcdowell@whoi.edu
Communicator: TRACEY I. CRAGO; Phone: 508-289-2665
Fisheries Aquaculture Specialist: DR. DALE F. LEAVITT; Phone: 508-289-2997
Program Assistant: SHERI D. DEROSA; Phone: 508-289-2398
Keyword(s): Aquaculture, Biodiversity, Coasts, Fisheries, Oceanography, Water Pollution

MICHIGAN

GOVERNOR OF MICHIGAN: JOHN ENGLER
State Capitol, P.O. Box 30013, Lansing, MI 48909
Phone: 517-373-3400

MICHIGAN DEPARTMENT OF AGRICULTURE
4th Fl., Ottawa Bldg., P.O. Box 30017, Lansing, MI 48909
Phone: 517-373-1052
Contact(s):
Director: DAN WYANT
Director of Pesticide & Plant Pest Management Division: KEN RAUSCHER; Phone: 517-373-1087
Keyword(s): Agriculture, Biodiversity, Flowers, Plants, and Trees, Pesticides, Soil Conservation

MICHIGAN DEPARTMENT OF COMMUNITY HEALTH
Lewis Cass Bldg., 320 S. Walnut, Lansing, MI 48913
Phone: 517-373-3500
Founded: 1996
Description: The department is responsible for health policy and management of the state's publicly-funded health service systems. It was created by Governor Engler in order to provide a more holistic

approach to health care in Michigan. It is the largest department in Michigan government.
Contact(s):
Director: JAMES K. HAVERMAN JR.
Keyword(s): Public Health Protection

MICHIGAN DEPARTMENT OF ENVIRONMENTAL QUALITY
106 West Allegan St., Hollister Building, 6th Fl., P.O. Box 30473, Lansing, MI 48909-7973
Phone: 517-373-7917; Fax: 517-241-7401; Web site: www.deq.state.mi.us
Founded: 1995
Description: Our mission is to drive improvements in environmental quality for the protection of public health and natural resources to benefit current and future generations. This will be accomplished through effective administration of agency programs, and providing for the use of innovative strategies, while helping to foster a strong and sustainable economy.
Contact(s):
Deputy Director for Operations: GARY R. HUGHES; Phone: 517-241-7394; Fax: 517-241-7401
Deputy Director for Programs and Regulations: ARTHUR R. NASH JR.; Phone: 517-241-7392; Fax: 517-241-7401
Director: RUSSELL J. HARDING; Phone: 517-373-7917
Chief of Financial and Business Services Division: DENNIS FEDEWA; Phone: 517-241-7427; Fax: 517-241-7428
Director of Office of the Great Lakes: G. TRACY MEHAN; Phone: 517-335-4056; Fax: 517-335-4053
Keyword(s): Air Quality and Pollution, Chemical Pollution Control, Coasts, Drinking Water Protection, Environmental and Conservation Education, Environmental Protection, Geology, Lakes, Mining, Pollution Prevention, Solid Waste Management, Toxic Substances, Toxicology, Water Pollution, Water Resources

MICHIGAN DEPARTMENT OF NATURAL RESOURCES
Box 30028, Lansing, MI 48909
Phone: 517-373-1214; Web site: www.dnr.states.mi.us
Founded: 1921
Description: State agency for administration, including enforcement of laws and regulations, regarding the state's natural resources; and for enhancing recreational opportunities and quality. Derived from the Department of Conservation.
Contact(s):
Director: K. L. COOL; Phone: 517-373-2329
Chief of Finance and Operations Service Bureau: ROB ABENT; Phone: 517-373-1750
Chief of Fisheries: KELLY SMITH; Phone: 517-373-1280
Chief of Forest Management: JOHN M. ROBERTSON; Phone: 517-373-1275
Chief of Human Resources: JAMES A. CARTER; Phone: 517-373-1207
Chief of Law Enforcement: HERBERT BURNS; Phone: 517-373-1230
Chief of Office of Internal Audit: THOMAS BENSON; Phone: 517-373-0755
Chief of Parks and Recreation: RODNEY STOKES; Phone: 517-373-9900
Chief of Real Estate: MINDY KOCH; Phone: 517-241-2438
Chief of Wildlife: REBECCA HUMPHRIES; Phone: 517-373-1263
Deputy for Administrative Services: KELLI SOBEL; Phone: 517-373-2425
Deputy for Resource Management: GEORGE E. BURGOYNE JR.; Phone: 517-373-0046
Deputy Upper Peninsula Field Headquarters: JAMES EKDAHL; Phone: 906-228-6561
Equal Opportunity, Litigation and Legal Services: CORDREE McCONNELL; Phone: 517-373-3503
Executive Assistant: GUY GORDON; Phone: 517-373-2329
Executive Secretary to the Natural Resources Commission: TERESA GLODEN; Phone: 517-373-2352
Field and Investigative Studies: GERALD THIEDE; Phone: 517-335-4225
Information and Education (Acting) and Press Secretary: TIM ROBY; Phone: 517-373-1214
Legislative Liaison: CAROL BAMBERY; Phone: 517-373-0023
Mackinac Island State Park Commission: CARL R. NOLD; Phone: 906-847-3328
Keyword(s): Fisheries, Forests and Forestry, Outdoor Recreation, Public Lands, Wildlife Management

MICHIGAN SEA GRANT COLLEGE PROGRAM
University of Michigan, 2200 Bonisteel Blvd., Ann Arbor, MI 48109-2099
Phone: 734-764-1138; Fax: 734-647-0768; Web site: www.engin.umich.edu/seagrant/
Founded: 1969
Description: To promote the understanding and wise use of the Great Lakes through research, education and extension.
Contact(s):
Director: DR. RUSSELL MOLL; Phone: 734-763-1437; E-mail: rmoll@umich.edu
Assistant Director: PEGGY BRITT; Phone: 734-763-1437
Associate Director: DR. WILLIAM W. TAYLOR, College of Ag. and Natural Resources, Michigan State University, 104 Agriculture Hall, East Lansing, MI 48824; Phone: 517-355-0233
Program Leader: Sea Grant Extension: JOHN D. SCHWARTZ, Michigan Sea Grant College Program, Michigan State University, 334 Natural Resources Bldg., East Lansing, MI 48824; Phone: 517-355-9637
Publications Assistant: BROOKE SCELZA; Phone: 734-764-1118
Senior Editor: JOYCE DANIELS; Phone: 734-647-0766

MICHIGAN STATE UNIVERSITY EXTENSION
Bulletin Office, 10-B Agriculture Hall, East Lansing, MI 48824
Phone: 517-355-0240; Fax: 517-355-6473; E-mail: msue@msue.msu.edu; Web site: www.msue.msu.edu/msue/
Description: Helps people improve their lives through an educational process that applies knowledge to critical issues, needs, and opportunities. Publications, instructional videos and microcomputer software are listed in a catalogue (available by writing to the Bulletin Office).
Contact(s):
Associate Vice Provost and Director: DR. ARLEN G. LEHOLM; Phone: 517-355-2308
Assistant Vice Provost and Associate Director: DR. LEAH COX RITCHIE; Phone: 517-355-0265
Interim Assistant Vice Provost and Associate Director: DR. LARRY OLSEN; Phone: 517-355-0118
Associate Professsor: SHARI L. DANN, 9A Natural Resource Bldg., East Lansing, MI 48824; Phone: 517-353-0675; Fax: 517-336-1699
Keyword(s): Agriculture, Forests and Forestry, Pesticides, Water Resources, Wildlife Management

MINNESOTA

GOVERNOR OF MINNESOTA: JESSE VENTURA
130 State Capitol, 75 Constitution Ave., St. Paul, MN 55155
Phone: 612-296-3391

MINNESOTA BOARD OF WATER AND SOIL RESOURCES
One W. Water St., Suite 200, St. Paul, MN 55107
Phone: 651-296-3767
Founded: 1987
Description: Formed under M.S. chapter 103B to develop the capabilities of local governments in resource management. Works most often with soil and water conservation districts, watershed districts, watershed management organizations, and counties. Provides these local governments with financial and technical assistance. Administers programs focusing on erosion control and water quality.
Contact(s):
Chair: KATHLEEN ROER

Director: RONALD D. HARNACK; Fax: 651-297-5615; E-mail: ron.harnack@bwsr.state.mn.us
Publication(s): *Water BillBoard, The; Directory of local governments; various brochures, reports, and fact sheets*
Keyword(s): Conservation Tillage, Erosion Control, Lakes, Land Use Planning, Soil Conservation, Training, Water Resources, Watersheds, Wetlands

MINNESOTA COOPERATIVE FISH AND WILDLIFE RESEARCH UNIT
U.S. Geological Survey, Biological Resources Division, University of Minnesota, Department of Fisheries and Wildlife, 200 Hodson Hall, 1980 Folwell Ave., St. Paul, MN 55108
Phone: 612-624-3421
Founded: 1987
Description: The research mission of the Minnesota Cooperative Fish and Wildlife Research Unit (MNCFWRU) is to address the biological, social, and economic aspects of both game and nongame wildlife and fisheries management in the context of conservation of biological diversity, and integrity and sustainability of ecosystems.
Contact(s):
Assistant Leader: Fisheries: DR. BRUCE C. VONDRACEK
Assistant Leader: Wildlife: DR. DAVID C. FULTON
Librarian: LORALEE KERR, 375 Hodson Hall, 1980 Folwell Ave., St.Paul, MN 55108; Phone: 612-624-9288
Unit Leader: DR. DAVID E. ANDERSEN
Keyword(s): Aquatic Habitats, Fisheries, Nongame Wildlife, Toxicology, Wildlife and Wildlife Habitat

MINNESOTA DEPARTMENT OF AGRICULTURE
90 W. Plato Blvd., St. Paul, MN 55107
Phone: 651-297-2200
Founded: 1919
Description: Enforces laws to protect the public health, promote family farming and marketing of Minnesota farm products, conserve soil and water, and prevent fraud and deception in the manufacture and distribution of foods, animal feeds, fertilizers, pesticides, seeds, and other items.
Contact(s):
Commissioner: GENE HUGOSON
Deputy Commissioner: SHARON CLARK
Assistant Commissioner: PERRY AASNESS
Assistant Commissioner: TOM MASSO
Director of Administrative Services: BECKY LESCHNER; Phone: 651-215-5770
Director of Dairy and Food Inspection: FRED MITCHELL; Phone: 651-296-1590
Director of Grain and Produce Inspection: DALE HEIMERMANN; Phone: 612-341-7190
Director: Agricultural Statistics: MIKE HUNST; Phone: 651-296-3896
Director: Agriculture Certification: JAMES GRYNIEWSKI; Phone: 651-297-2230
Director: Agriculture Finance: JIM BOERBOOM; Phone: 651-297-3557
Director: Agriculture Marketing and Development: GERALD HEIL; Phone: 651-296-1486
Director: Agronomy and Plant Protection: GREG BUZICKY; Phone: 651-297-7121
Director: Information Services: KAREN NELSON; Phone: 651-296-4659
Director: Laboratory Services: WILLIAM KRUEGER; Phone: 651-296-3273
Keyword(s): Agriculture, Biodiversity, Pesticides, Sustainable Development, Water Pollution

MINNESOTA DEPARTMENT OF NATURAL RESOURCES
500 Lafayette Rd., St. Paul, MN 55155-4001
Phone: 612-296-6157
Founded: 1931
Description: The Department of Conservation was renamed the Department of Natural Resources (DNR) in 1971. The DNR's goal is to achieve optimum natural resources planning, protection, and development responsive to public need, consistent with resource potentials, and for the social and economic well-being of both present and future generations.
Contact(s):
Administrator, Bureau of Engineering: JOHN ERNSTER; Phone: 651-296-2119
Administrator, Bureau of Human Resources: MARY O'NEILL; Phone: 651-296-6493
Administrator, Bureau of Licenses: MARGARET WINKEL-LEDIN; Phone: 651-296-4507
Administrator, Bureau of Management Information Services: HENRY MAY; Phone: 651-297-3906
Administrator, Management and Budget Services: PEGGY ADELMANN; Phone: 651-296-8340
Administrator, Bureau of Field Services: NORM KORDELL; Phone: 651-297-3758
Assistant Commissioner, Operations: BRAD MOORE; Phone: 651-296-5229
Chief: Ecological Services Section: LEE PFANNMULLER; Phone: 651-296-2835
Chief: Fisheries Section: RON PAYER; Phone: 651-296-3325
Chief: Wildlife Section: TIM BREMICKER; Phone: 651-296-3344
Commissioner: ALLEN GARBER; Phone: 651-296-2549
Deputy Commissioner: STEVE MORSE; Phone: 651-296-2540
Director: Agricultural Policy: WAYNE EDGERTON; Phone: 651-297-8341
Director: Division of Enforcement: BILL BERNHJELM; Phone: 651-296-4828
Director: Division of Fish and Wildlife: ROGER HOLMES; Phone: 651-297-1308
Director: Division of Forestry: GERALD ROSE; Phone: 651-296-4491
Director: Division of Lands and Minerals: WILLIAM BRICE; Phone: 651-296-4807
Director: Division of Parks and Recreation: WILLIAM MORRISSEY; Phone: 651-296-9223
Director: Division of Waters: KENT LOKKESMOE; Phone: 651-296-4800
Director: Regulatory and Legislative Services: MICHELLE BEEMAN; Phone: 651-296-0915
Director: Trails and Waterways Unit: DENNIS ASMUSSEN; Phone: 651-297-1151
Library Director: COLLEEN MLECOCH; Phone: 651-296-1305
Regional Administrator: PAUL SWENSON; Phone: 218-755-3955
Regional Administrator: JOHN GUENTHER; Phone: 218-327-4455
Regional Administrator: CHERYL HEIDE; Phone: 507-359-6000
Regional Administrator: LARRY NELSON; Phone: 507-285-7418
Regional Administrator: KATHLEEN WALLACE; Phone: 612-772-7900
Publication(s): *Minnesota Conservation Volunteer, The*

MINNESOTA ENVIRONMENTAL QUALITY BOARD
3rd Fl. Centennial Bldg., 658 Cedar St., St. Paul, MN 55155
Phone: 612-296-9027
Founded: 1973
Description: The EQB is Minnesota's principal forum for discussing environmental issues. The EQB provides an opportunity for the public to have direct input into the development of the state's environmental policy. The EQB is an independent decision-making body and is staffed by the Minnesota Office of Strategic and Long Range Planning.
Contact(s):
Executive Director: MICHAEL SULLIVAN
Commissioner: ROD SANDO; Phone: 612-297-1257
Publication(s): *EQB Monitor*
Keyword(s): Energy, Environmental Planning, Sustainable Development, Sustainable Ecosystems, Water Resources

MINNESOTA GEOLOGICAL SURVEY
University of Minnesota, 2642 University Ave., St. Paul, MN 55114
Phone: 612-627-4780
Founded: 1872

Description: Established as a Geological and Natural History Survey, reconstituted in 1911 as the Minnesota Geological Survey to investigate the geology of the state; describe, classify and map the geological formations and mineral and water resources; and investigate all aspects of the geology affecting the environment.
Contact(s):
Director: DAVID L. SOUTHWICK
Associate Director and Chief Geologist: GLENN B. MOREY
Publication(s): List available on request.
Keyword(s): Geology, Water Resources

MINNESOTA POLLUTION CONTROL AGENCY
520 Lafayette Rd., St. Paul, MN 55155
Phone: 612-296-6300
Founded: 1967
Description: Administers the state statutes covering water pollution, air pollution, and solid and hazardous waste control.
Contact(s):
Assistant Commissioner: GORDON WEGWART; Phone: 612-296-7319
Chairman of the Board and Commissioner: CHARLES W. WILLIAMS; Phone: 612-296-7301
Deputy Commissioner: PETER LARSON; Phone: 612-296-7305
Director: Division of Administrative Services: ELAINE JOHNSON; Phone: 612-296-7224
Director: Division of Air Quality: LISA J. THORVIG; Phone: 612-296-7331
Director: Division of Groundwater and Solid Waste: JAMES WARNER; Phone: 612-296-7777
Director: Division of Hazardous Waste: TIMOTHY K. SCHERKENBACH; Phone: 612-297-8502
Director: Division of Water Quality: PATRICIA M. BURKE; Phone: 612-296-7202

Brainerd, MN
1601 Minnesota St., Brainerd, MN 56401
Phone: 218-828-2492
Contact(s):
Director: LARRY SHAW

Detroit Lakes, MN
Lake Avenue Plaza 714 Lake Ave. Suite 220, Detroit Lakes, MN 56501
Phone: 218-847-1519
Contact(s):
Director: JEFF LEWIS

Duluth, MN
Duluth Government Service Center, Rm. 704; 320 W. 2nd St., Duluth, MN 55802
Phone: 218-723-4660
Contact(s):
Director: WAYNE GOLLY

Marshall, MN
700 N. Seventh St., Marshall, MN 56258
Phone: 507-537-7146
Contact(s):
Director: MARK JACOBS

Rochester, MN
2116 Campus Dr. SE, Rochester, MN 55904
Phone: 507-285-7343
Contact(s):
Director: LARRY LANDHERR

MINNESOTA SEA GRANT COLLEGE PROGRAM
Univ. of MN, 208 Washburn Hall, 2305 E. 5th St., Duluth, MN 55812-1445
Phone: 218-726-8710; Fax: 218-726-6556; E-mail: seagr@d.umn.edu; Web site: www.d.umn.edu/seagr/
Description: A statewide program that supports research, outreach, and educational programs related to Lake Superior and Minnesota's inland waters. Research areas include: water quality, fisheries, biotechnology, aquaculture, exotic species and coastal tourism.
Contact(s):
Director: CARL RICHARDS; E-mail: crichard@d.umn.edu
Coodinator, Superior Lakewatch: ELAINE RUZYCKI; Phone: 218-720-4337; Fax: 218-720-4219; E-mail: eruzycki@sage.nrri.umn.edu
Coordinator, Exotic Species Information Center: DOUG JENSEN; Phone: 218-726-8712; E-mail: djensen1@d.umn.edu
Editor: SHARON MOEN; Phone: 218-726-6195; E-mail: smoen@d.umn.edu
Publication(s): Seiche, The Newsletter
Keyword(s): Aquatic Habitats, Biotechnology, Communications, Environment, Fisheries, Lakes, Sustainable Development, Sustainable Ecosystems, Water Pollution, Water Resources, Wildlife Management

MINNESOTA STATE EXTENSION SERVICES
University of Minnesota, 240 Coffey Hall, 1420 Eckles Ave., St. Paul, MN 55108-6070
Phone: 612-625-1915; Fax: 612-625-6227; E-mail: info@mes.umn.edu; Web site: www.mes.umn.edu/
Contact(s):
Dean and Director Extension Service: KATHERINE FENNELLY; Phone: 612-624-2703
Associate Dean and Collegiate Program Leader: STEVEN B. DALEY LAURSEN; Phone: 612-624-9298
Extension Specialist: Aquaculture: ANNE KAPUSCINSKI; Phone: 612-624-3019
Forest Resources Specialist: MELVIN J. BAUGHMAN; Phone: 612-624-0734
Housing Specialist: PATRICK HUELMAN; Phone: 612-624-1286
Public Policy Specialist: STEVEN TAFF; Phone: 612-625-3103
Sea Grant Extension and Fisheries Educator: JEFFREY GUNDERSON
Tourism Educator Specialist: GLENN KREAG
Water Quality Educator Specialist: CYNTHIA HAGLEY
Wildlife Specialist: JAMES R. KITTS; Phone: 612-624-3298
Youth Specialist: STEPHAN CARLSON; Phone: 612-626-1259
Wildlife Specialist: JAMES A. COOPER, 216 Hodson, Univ. of Minesota, St. Paul, MN 55108; Phone: 612-624-1223; Fax: 612-625-5299

MISSISSIPPI

GOVERNOR OF MISSISSIPPI: KIRK FORDICE
P.O. Box 139, Jackson, MS 39205
Phone: 601-359-3151; Fax: 601-359-3741

GULF COAST RESEARCH LABORATORY
P.O. Box 7000, Ocean Springs, MS 39566
Phone: 601-872-4200
Founded: 1947
Description: Conducts research in marine biology, fisheries, geology, chemistry, and oceanography, and conducts an academic program in the marine sciences.
Contact(s):
Assistant Director: Research: WILLIAM W. WALKER
Editor: ROBERT T. VANALLER
Interim Director: ROBERT T. VANALLER
Publication(s): Marine Briefs Newsletter; Gulf Research Reports-Scientific Journal

MISSISSIPPI COOPERATIVE FISH AND WILDLIFE RESEARCH UNIT (USDI)
Mailstop 9691, Mississippi State University, Mississippi State, MS 39762
Phone: 662-325-2643
Founded: 1978
Description: The Unit is sponsored by the U.S.G.S. Biological Resources Division; Mississippi Department of Wildlife, Fisheries, and Parks; Mississippi State University; and the Wildlife

Management Institute. Fisheries and wildlife research, graduate education, technical assistance, and extension are the Unit's main missions.
Contact(s):
Leader: HAROLD L. SCHRAMM JR.
Assistant Leader: Fisheries: L. E. MIRANDA
Assistant Leader: Wildlife: FRANCISCO J. VILELLA
Keyword(s): Endangered and Threatened Species, Fisheries, Nongame Wildlife, Rivers, Sport Fishing

MISSISSIPPI DEPARTMENT OF AGRICULTURE AND COMMERCE
P.O. Box 1609, Jackson, MS 39215-1609
Phone: 601-354-7050
Founded: 1906
Description: The department was created to foster and promote the business of agriculture. Duties include: Regulatory, consumer protection, marketing, and a wide range of service activities.
Contact(s):
Commissioner: DR. LESTER SPELL JR.
Deputy Commissioner: CHRIS SPARKMAN; Phone: 601-359-1138
Director of Administration and Finance: RODNEY SANDERS; Phone: 601-359-1132
Director of Board of Animal Health: DR. JIM WATSON; Phone: 601-359-1170
Director of Consumer Protection: JOHN TILLSON; Phone: 601-359-1148
Director of Farmers Market: BILLY CARTER; Phone: 601-354-6818
Director of Fruit & Vegetable Inspections: DONNIS ROBERSON; Phone: 601-354-6573
Director of Grain Inspection: RALPH HOWELL; Phone: 601-947-4095
Director of Information Systems: UMESH SANJANWALA; Phone: 601-359-1151
Director of Market Development: ROGER BARLOW; Phone: 601-359-1158
Director of Market News: BILLY CARTER; Phone: 601-354-6818
Director of Meat Inspection: DR. ROBERT WEST; Phone: 601-359-1193
Director of National Agricultural Statistics: TOMMY GREGORY; Phone: 601-965-4575
Director of Petroleum: ROBERT LOUYS; Phone: 601-359-1101
Director of Regulatory Services: JULIA McLEMORE; Phone: 601-359-1144
Director of Weights and Measures: RUSSELL ROBBINS; Phone: 601-359-1117
Editor: CLAUDE NASH; Phone: 601-359-1123
Personnel Officer: STELLA CESSNA; Phone: 601-359-1152
Publication(s): *Mississippi Market Bulletin*

MISSISSIPPI DEPARTMENT OF ENVIRONMENTAL QUALITY

Office of Land and Water Resources
Southport Mall, P.O. Box 10631, Jackson, MS 39289
Phone: 601-961-5200
Founded: 1956
Description: Administers Water Use Permitting Act of 1985, the licensing of water well drillers and the 1978 Dam Safety Act; inventories water resources; coordinates water and land resources planning; and conducts reviews of proposed water resources development.
Contact(s):
Head: CHARLES T. BRANCH
Chief: Division of Hydrologic Investigation and Reporting: PATRICIA A. PHILLIPS; Phone: 601-961-5213

Office of Pollution Control
P.O. Box 10385, Jackson, MS 39289-0385
Phone: 601-961-5171
Contact(s):
Head: CHARLES H. CHISOLM

MISSISSIPPI DEPARTMENT OF WILDLIFE, FISHERIES, AND PARKS
P.O. Box 451, Jackson, MS 39205
Phone: 601-362-9212
Description: The purpose of the MDWFP is to manage, conserve, develop, and protect Mississippi's outdoors, state parks, wildlife and marine resources, and their habitats; and to provide continuing recreational, economic, educational, ecological, aesthetic, social and scientific benefits for present and future generations.
Contact(s):
Deputy Administrator: BOB TYLER; Phone: 601-364-2004
Executive Director: DR. SAM POLLES; Phone: 601-364-2000
Executive Assistant: BILL QUISENBERRY; Phone: 601-364-2005
Boating Enforcement: JIMMY LAIRD; Phone: 601-364-2182
Chief: Fisheries: RON GARAVELLI; Phone: 601-364-2202
Chief: Game: BILL THOMASON; Phone: 601-364-2212
Chief: Law Enforcement: RANDALL MILLER; Phone: 601-364-2232
Coordinator: Planning and Policy: TOMMY SHROPSHIRE; Phone: 601-364-2107
Director of Marketing: ELLEN B. MORGAN; Phone: 601-364-2152
Director: Administrative Services: ROBERT COOK; Phone: 601-364-2006
Director: Museum of Natural Science: LIBBY HARTFIELD; Phone: 601-354-7303
Director: Public Information: JIM WALKER; Phone: 601-364-2124
Director: Support Services Division: AL TUCK; Phone: 601-364-2046
Editor: DAVID L. WATTS; Phone: 601-364-2129
Head Librarian: MARY P. STEVENS, Museum of Natural Science, 111 N. Jefferson, Jackson, MS 39202-2897; Phone: 601-354-7303
Hunter Education: STEVE ADCOCK; Phone: 601-364-2192
Outdoor Recreation Grants: MITIZ STUBBS; Phone: 601-364-2156
Publication(s): *Mississippi Outdoors; Mississippi*
Keyword(s): Endangered and Threatened Species, Fisheries, Outdoor Recreation, Wetlands, Wildlife Management

MISSISSIPPI FORESTRY COMMISSION
301 N. Lamar St., Suite 300, Jackson, MS 39201
Phone: 601-359-1386; Fax: 601-359-1349; Web site: www.mfc.state.ms.us
Founded: 1926
Description: Basic duties are forest protection against wildfire, insects, and disease; operation of tree-seedlings nurseries for reforestation; provision of forest resource management assistance to private landowners; and creation of interest in forestry.
Contact(s):
Deputy State Forester Services: JAMES MORDICA
Deputy State Forester: Management Chief: EVERARD BAKER
Deputy State Forester: Protection Chief: WILLIAM LAMBERT
Editor: KENT GRIZZARD
Editor and Education Director: HAROLD ANDERSON
Fiscal Officer: LEZLIN PROCTOR
Information Director: KENT GRIZZARD
State Forester: JAMES L. SLEDGE JR.
Publication(s): *Forestry Forum Magazine;* various forest management brochures
Keyword(s): Environmental and Conservation Education, Forests and Forestry, Public Lands, Renewable Resources, Urban Forestry

MISSISSIPPI SEA GRANT PROGRAM
Mississippi-Alabama Sea Grant Consortium, Caylor Bldg., Gulf Coast Research Laboratory, P.O. Box 7000, Ocean Springs, MS 39566-7000
Phone: 228-875-9341; Fax: 228-875-0528
Contact(s):
Director: BARRY A. COSTA-PIERCE; E-mail: b.costapierce@usm.edu
Extension Marine Specialist: DR. RICHARD K. WALLACE

MISSISSIPPI SOIL AND WATER CONSERVATION COMMISSION
Attn: Public Relations Director, P.O. Box 3005, Jackson, MS 39225

STATE AND PROVINCIAL GOVERNMENT AGENCIES - MISSOURI

Founded: 1938
Description: Originally established as the state agency for the control of soil erosion. Current statutory responsibilities include assistance to local soil and water conservation districts in the areas of water and soil quality projects, qualifications and elections of Commissioners, and administration of programs. Other responsibilities include reviewing and commenting on surface mining reclamation efforts. Also serves as the state resource agency for agricultural nonpoint source pollution issues and projects by assisting individual landowners, operators and other organized groups through demonstrations and educational programs.
Contact(s):
Chairman: ROSS McGEHEE, 176 McGehee Road, Natchez, MS 39120
Executive Director: GALE MARTIN, P.O. Box 23005, Jackson, MS 39225-3005; Phone: 601-354-7645; Fax: 601-354-6628
Public Relations Director: EMMA CERAMI, P.O. Box 23005, Jackson, MS 39225-3005
Publication(s): *Conservation Comments*
Keyword(s): Environmental and Conservation Education, Erosion Control, Nonpoint Source Pollution, Soil Conservation, Water Pollution, Water Quality, Water Resources

MISSISSIPPI STATE DEPARTMENT OF HEALTH
P.O. Box 1700, Jackson, MS 39215-1700
Contact(s):
Director: Division of Epidemiology: DR. MARY CURRIER; Phone: 601-576-7725
Director: Environmental Health: RICK HARRINGTON; Phone: 601-576-7680
State Health Officer: DR. F. E. THOMPSON; Phone: 601-576-7633

MISSISSIPPI STATE EXTENSION SERVICES
Box 9663, Mississippi State, MS 39762
Phone: 662-325-8594; Fax: 662-325-2118; Web site: ext.msstate.edu/
Contact(s):
Director of Extension Service: DR. RONALD A. BROWN; E-mail: brown@ext.msstate.edu
Wildlife Specialist: DEAN STEWART, Box 9690, Mississippi State, MS 39762 601-325-3174; Phone: 601-325-8750
Keyword(s): Environmental and Conservation Education, Fisheries, Forests and Forestry, Wildlife and Wildlife Habitat, Wildlife Management

MISSOURI

GOVERNOR OF MISSOURI: MEL CARNAHAN
State Capitol, P.O. Box 720, Jefferson City, MO 65102
Phone: 573-751-3222

MISSOURI COOPERATIVE FISH AND WILDLIFE RESEARCH UNIT (USDI)
302 Anheuser-Busch Natural Resources Building, Fisheries and Wildlife, University of Missouri, Columbia, MO 65211-7240
Phone: 573-882-3634; Fax: 573-884-5070
Founded: 1985
Description: Established by cooperative agreement among the Biological Resources Division of the U.S. Geological Survey, Missouri Department of Conservation, University of Missouri, and Wildlife Management Institute. Primary purpose is research and graduate student education in wildlife conservation, aquatic ecology, and fisheries management areas.
Contact(s):
Administrative Officer: SANDY CLARK; Phone: 573-882-3634
Assistant Leader: Fisheries: DR. DAVID L. GALAT; Phone: 573-882-9426
Assistant Leader: Wildlife: DR. RONALD D. DROBNEY; Phone: 573-882-9420
Leader: DR. CHARLES F. RABENI; Phone: 573-882-3524
Keyword(s): Fisheries, Rivers, Waterfowl, Wetlands, Wildlife and Wildlife Habitat

MISSOURI DEPARTMENT OF AGRICULTURE
P.O. Box 630, 1616 Missouri Blvd., Jefferson City, MO 65101
Phone: 573-751-4211
Contact(s):
Deputy Director: KYLE VICKERS
Director: JOHN L. SAUNDERS
Public Information Officer: SALLY OXENHANDLER

MISSOURI DEPARTMENT OF CONSERVATION
P.O. Box 180, Jefferson City, MO 65102-0180
Phone: 573-751-4115; Fax: 573-751-4467
Founded: 1937
Description: The department is responsible for the control, management, restoration, conservation and regulation of the bird, fish, game, forestry and all wildlife resources of the state. These responsibilities are met through a wide variety of programs encompassing fish, wildlife, and forest management, regulations and enforcement, conservation education and interpretation, endangered species and policy development.
Contact(s):
Deputy Director: JOHN W. SMITH
Director: JERRY M. CONLEY
Assistant to Director: GERALD E. ROSS
General Counsel: JANE A. SMITH
Internal Auditor: ROBBIE B. BRISCOE
Publication(s): *Missouri Conservationist*

Administrative Services Division
Contact(s):
Administrator: DAVID W. ERICKSON

Design and Development Division
Contact(s):
Administrator: WILLIAM F. LUECKENHOFF

Fisheries Division
Contact(s):
Administrator: NORMAN P. STUCKY

Forestry Division
Contact(s):
Administrator: MARVIN D. BROWN

Human Resources Section
Contact(s):
Chief: DEBORAH L. GOFF

Natural History Section
Contact(s):
Chief: RICHARD H. THOM

Outreach and Education Division
Contact(s):
Administrator: KATHRYN S. LOVE

Protection Division
Contact(s):
Administrator: RONALD L. GLOVER

Wildlife Division
Contact(s):
Administrator: OLIVER A. TORGERSON

MISSOURI DEPARTMENT OF NATURAL RESOURCES
P.O. Box 176, Jefferson City, MO 65102
Phone: 314-751-4422; Fax: 1-800-334-6946
Description: The Missouri Department of Natural Resources is the state resource management agency responsible for addressing environmental and natural resource-related issues. Areas of responsibility include: protecting Missouri's air, land and water resources, enforcing related laws where applicable; managing and maintaining the state's 80 state parks and state historic sites while protecting and promoting Missouri's cultural heritage and recreational opportunities; assisting citizens and government in the area of energy-efficiency management and developing the state's

mineral resources in an environmentally conscious and safe manner.
Contact(s):
Director: STEPHEN M. MAHFOOD, P.O. Box 176, Jefferson City, MO 65102-0176; Phone: 573-751-4732
Deputy Director: JEFF STAAKE; Phone: 573-522-8796
Communications Director: NINA THOMPSON; Phone: 573-751-1010
Director of Division of Administrative Support: GARY HEIMERICKS; Phone: 573-751-7961
Director of Division of Energy: ANITA RANDOLPH; Phone: 573-751-2254
Director of Division of Environmental Quality: JOHN A. YOUNG; Phone: 573-751-0763
Director of Division of State Parks: DOUGLAS EIKEN; Phone: 573-751-9392
Director of Division Geology and Land Survey: DR. JAMES H. WILLIAMS; Phone: 573-368-2102
Director of Environmental Improvement and Energy Resources Authority: THOMAS WELCH, P.O. Box 744, Jefferson City, MO 65102-0176; Phone: 573-751-4919
Eastern Parks District Administrator: DAN PAIGE, 2901 Highway 61, Festus, MO 63028; Phone: 314-937-3697
Jefferson City Regional Office Administrator: ROBERT HENTGES, P.O. Box 176, Jefferson City, MO 65102-0176; Phone: 573-751-2729
Kansas City Regional Office Administrator: JIM MACY, 500 NE Colbern Rd., Lee's Summit, MO 667086-4710; Phone: 816-554-4100
Missouri River District: LARRY JOHNSON, P.O. Box 166, Boonville, MO 65233; Phone: 660-882-8196
North Hills District Administrator: FRANK ST. CLAIR, P.O. Box 314, Brookfield, MO 64628; Phone: 660-258-7496
Northeast Regional Office Administrator: STEVE DECKER, 1709 Prospect Dr., Macon, MO 63552-2602; Phone: 660-385-2129
Northern Missouri Historic District Administrator: JAMES REHARD, P.O. Box 314, Brookfield, MO 64628; Phone: 660-258-7496
Ozarks District Administrator: DENNY BOPP, P.O. Box 951, Lebanon, MO 65536; Phone: 417-532-7361
Southeast Regional Office Administrator: GARY GAINES, 948 Lester St., P.O. Box 1420, Poplar Bluff, MO 63901-1420; Phone: 573-840-9750
Southern Missouri Historic District: GARY WALRATH, 2901 Highway 61, Festus, MO 63028; Phone: 314-937-3697
Southwest Regional Office Administrator: BRUCE MARTIN, 2040 W. Woodland, Springfield, MO 65807-5912; Phone: 471-891-4300
St. Louis Regional Office Administrator: ROBERT ECK, 10805 Sunset Office Dr., St. Louis, MO 63127-1017; Phone: 314-301-7100
Publication(s): *Missouri Resources*
Keyword(s): Energy, Environmental Preservation, Geology, Outdoor Recreation, Public Lands

MISSOURI STATE EXTENSION SERVICES
University of Missouri, 309 University Hall, Columbia, MO 65211
Phone: 573-882-7754; Fax: 573-884-4204; Web site: extension.missouri.edu/
Contact(s):
Director: Extension Service: DR. RONALD J. TURNER
Extension Fish and Wildlife Specialist: ROBERT A. PIERCE II, 302 Natural Resources Bldg., Columbia, MO 65211; Phone: 573-882-4337; Fax: 573-882-5070
Extension Forester: JOHN P. SLUSHER, 203 Natural Resources Bldg., Columbia, MO 65211; Phone: 573-882-4444; Fax: 573-882-1977

MONTANA

GOVERNOR OF MONTANA: MARC RACICOT
P.O. Box 0801, State Capitol, Helena, MT 59620
Phone: 406-444-3111

MONTANA BUREAU OF MINES AND GEOLOGY
Montana Tech of the University of Montana, Butte, MT 59701-8997
Phone: 406-496-4167
Founded: 1919
Description: Established by law to aid the development and wise use of the state's mineral, energy, and groundwater resources by geologic and hydrogeologic studies of their occurrence and potential. Publishes formal reports and maps on Montana geology and groundwater.
Keyword(s): Energy, Geology, Water Resources

MONTANA COOPERATIVE FISHERY RESEARCH UNIT (USDI)
Dept. of Biology, Montana State University, P.O. Box 173460, Bozeman, MT 59717-3460
Phone: 406-994-4549; Fax: 406-994-7479
Contact(s):
Assistant Leader: DR. ALEXANDER ZALE; Phone: 406-994-4549
Leader: DR. ROBERT G. WHITE; Phone: 406-994-3491; E-mail: ubirw@montana.edu
Keyword(s): Aquatic Habitats, Endangered and Threatened Species, Fisheries, Research, Rivers

MONTANA COOPERATIVE WILDLIFE RESEARCH UNIT (USGS/BRD)
University of Montana, Missoula, MT 59812
Phone: 406-243-5372; Fax: 406-243-6064
Founded: 1950
Description: Conducts basic and applied research, trains graduate students in wildlife biology and management, and disseminates information. Research specialties include breeding productivity, nest predation, and habitat use by birds (particularly nongame and waterfowl species) in relation to land use practices, predator populations, and natural variation in the environment.
Contact(s):
Assistant Leader: DR. THOMAS E. MARTIN; E-mail: tmartin@selway.umt.edu
Leader: DR. I. J. BALL; E-mail: ball1@selway.umt.edu
Keyword(s): Birds, Forests and Forestry, Grasslands, Nongame Wildlife, Waterfowl, Wetlands

MONTANA DEPARTMENT OF AGRICULTURE
P.O. Box 200201, Helena, MT 59620-0201
Phone: 406-444-3144
Contact(s):
Director: W. RALPH PECK
Administrator: Agricultural Development Division: WILL KISSINGER; Phone: 406-444-2402
Administrator: Agricultural Sciences Division: GARY L. GINGERY; Phone: 406-444-2944
Keyword(s): Agriculture, Endangered and Threatened Species, Ground Water Protection, Pest Management, Pesticides

MONTANA DEPARTMENT OF FISH, WILDLIFE, AND PARKS
1420 E. 6th, P.O. Box 200701, Helena, MT 59620-0701
Phone: 406-444-3186; Fax: 406-444-4952
Contact(s):
Director: PATRICK J. GRAHAM; Phone: 406-444-3186
Administrator: Administration and Finance: DAVE MOTT; Phone: 406-444-4786
Administrator: Conservation Education: RON AASHEIM; Phone: 406-444-4038
Administrator, Enforcement: BEATA GALDA; Phone: 406-444-5657
Administrator, Parks: DOUG MONGER; Phone: 406-444-3750
Administrator, Wildlife: DON CHILDRESS; Phone: 406-444-2612
Administrator, Fisheries: LARRY PETERMAN; Phone: 406-444-2449
Chief of Operations: RICH CLOUGH; Phone: 406-444-3186
Chief of Staff: CHRISTIAN SMITH; Phone: 406-444-3186
Editor: DAVE BOOKS; Phone: 406-444-2474
Publication(s): *Montana Outdoors*

Keyword(s): Environmental and Conservation Education, Hunting, Outdoor Recreation, Sport Fishing, Wildlife and Wildlife Habitat

MONTANA DEPARTMENT OF NATURAL RESOURCES AND CONSERVATION
1625 11th Ave., P.O. Box 201601, Helena, MT 59620-1601
Phone: 406-444-2074; Fax: 406-444-2684
Founded: 1971
Description: Administers state-owned water projects; plans, regulates, and coordinates the development and use of state school trust, land, and forest resources; wildland fire protection; service forestry; water-right adjudication; floodplain management; supervision, assistance, and coordination for local conservation and grazing districts; and regulation of oil and gas production.
Contact(s):
Director: BUD CLINCH; Phone: 406-444-2074
Administrator for Central Services Division: ANN BAUCHMAN; Phone: 406-444-6734
Administrator: Conservation and Resource Development Division: RAY BECK, 1520 E. 6th Ave., Helena, MT 59620; Phone: 406-444-6667; Fax: 406-444-6721; E-mail: rbeck@mt.gov
Administrator: Forestry Division: DON ARTLEY, 2705 Spurgin Rd., Missoula, MT 59801; Phone: 406-542-4300
Administrator: Oil and Gas Conservation Division: TOM RICHMOND, 2535 St. Johns Ave., Billings, MT 59102; Phone: 406-656-0040
Administrator: Reserved Water Rights Compact Commission: SUSAN COTTINGHAM; Phone: 406-444-6841
Administrator: Trust Land Management Division: JEFF HAGENER; Phone: 406-444-4978
Administrator: Water Resources Division: JACK STULTS, 1520 E. 6th Ave., Helena, MT 59620; Phone: 406-444-6605
Chief Legal Counsel: DONALD D. MacINTYRE; Phone: 406-444-6713
Personnel and EEO Officer: SHANNON KIRBY; Phone: 406-444-4942
Special Projects Coordinator: WAYNE WETZEL; Phone: 406-444-6722
Supervisor and Editor for Information Services: CAROLE MASSMAN; Phone: 406-444-6737
Keyword(s): Agriculture, Soil Conservation, Water Resources, Forestry, Oil and Gas

MONTANA ENVIRONMENTAL QUALITY COUNCIL
State Capitol, P.O. Box 201704, Helena, MT 59620-1704
Phone: 406-444-3742
Contact(s):
Chair: SENATOR WILLIAM CRISMORE
Vice-Chair: REPRESENTATIVE KIM GILLAN
Legislative Environmental Analyst: TODD EVERTS
Keyword(s): Air Quality and Pollution, Environmental Law, Land Use Planning, Water Quality, Water Resources

MONTANA NATURAL HERITAGE PROGRAM
1515 E 6th Ave., Helena, MT 59620-1800
Phone: 406-444-3009; Fax: 406-444-0581; E-mail: mtnhp@nris.state.mt.us; Web site: www.nris.state.mt.us/mtnhp
Founded: 1985
Description: A centralized repository and clearinghouse of information on Montana's biodiversity, emphasizing features and species that are rare, threatened, endangered, or in need of further research.
Contact(s):
Director: SUSAN CRISPIN
Publication(s): *Montana Plant Species of Special Concern; Montana Animal Species of Special Concern; Montana Bird Distribution*
Keyword(s): Zoology

MONTANA STATE EXTENSION SERVICES
Vice Provost and Director of Extension P.O. Box 172230, Montana State University, Bozeman, MT 59717-2230
Phone: 406-994-6647; E-mail: iciad@montana.edu; Web site: extn.msu.montana.edu/

Contact(s):
Extension Wildlife Specialist: JIM KNIGHT, Dept. of Animal and Range Science, Montana State University, Bozeman, MT 59717; Phone: 406-994-5579; Fax: 406-944-5589

NEBRASKA

GOVERNOR OF NEBRASKA: MIKE JOHANNS
P.O. Box 94848, Lincoln, NE 68509
Phone: 402-471-2244; Fax: 402-471-6031

CONSERVATION AND SURVEY DIVISION (NEBRASKA)
University of Nebraska-Lincoln, 113 Nebraska Hall, 901 N. 17th St., Lincoln, NE 68588
Phone: 402-472-3471; Fax: 402-472-4608
Description: CSD, the state geological, water, soil and land cover survey, has state-mandated responsibilities to inventory and investigate geologically related natural resources of the state; to record the results of these investigations; to assist non-profit, private and governmental agencies working to conserve the state's natural resources; to study the geologic history and geography of the state to aid sustainable economic development; and to publish maps, reports and electronic information about these activities.
Contact(s):
Director: MARK S. KUZILA; Phone: 402-472-7537

GAME AND PARKS COMMISSION

Game and Parks Commission
1212 Deer Park Blvd., Omaha, NE 68108
Phone: 402-595-2144

GAME AND PARKS COMMISSION-NEBRASKA

Ak-Sar-Ben Aquarium
21502, W. Hwy. 31, Gretna, NE 68028
Phone: 402-332-3901; Fax: 402-332-5853

NEBRASKA DEPARTMENT OF AGRICULTURE
301 Centennial Mall S., P.O. Box 94947, Lincoln, NE 68509
Phone: 402-471-2341
Contact(s):
Assistant Director: GREG IBACH; Fax: 402-471-6876
Director: MERLYN CARLSON

NEBRASKA DEPARTMENT OF ENVIRONMENTAL QUALITY
Suite 400, The Atrium, 1200 N St., P.O. Box 98922, Lincoln, NE 68509-8922
Phone: 402-471-2186
Founded: 1971
Description: Created by the Nebraska Environmental Protection Act. Administers and enforces rules and regulations, and monitors the quality of the environment in Nebraska.
Contact(s):
Director: MICHAEL LINDER
Deputy Director (Administration) and Hearing Officer, State Environmental Quality Council: TOM LAMBERSON
Deputy Director (Programs): JAY RINGENBERG
Public Information Officer and Publications Editor: BRIAN MCMANUS

Publication(s): *Environmental Update*

NEBRASKA DEPARTMENT OF WATER RESOURCES
State House Station, Box 94676, Lincoln, NE 68509
Phone: 402-471-2363
Description: Administers and enforces the state water laws and all matters pertaining to water rights; measuring and recording the flow of various streams and canals; approving plans and specifications for dam construction; inspection of dams; and registration of wells.
Contact(s):
Deputy Director: ANN SALOMON BLEED
Director: ROGER K. PATTERSON

Legal Counsel: LeROY W. SIEVERS
Permits and Adjudications: SUSAN A. FRANCE
State Hydrologist: ANN SALOMON BLEED
Publication(s): *Channels Newsletter; Biennial Report; Hydrographic Report*
Keyword(s): Engineering, Lakes, Rivers, Water Resources

NEBRASKA GAME AND PARKS COMMISSION
2200 N. 33rd St., P.O. Box 30370, Lincoln, NE 68503-0370
Phone: 402-471-0641; Web site: www.ngpc.state.ne.us.
Description: The commission has sole charge of state parks, game and fish, and all things pertaining thereto; boating; and administration of the Land and Water Conservation Fund.
Contact(s):
Assistant Director: KIRK NELSON; Phone: 402-471-5537; E-mail: knelson@ngpc.state.ne.us
Assistant Director: ROGER KUHN; Phone: 402-471-5512
Assistant Director: NOELYN ISOM; Phone: 402-471-5537; E-mail: bisom@ngpc.state.ne.us
Chair: THOMAS O'NEILL JR.
Director: REX AMACK; Phone: 402-471-5539; E-mail: ramack@ngpc.state.ne.us
Administrator: Engineering: JIM SHEFFIELD; Phone: 402-471-5557; E-mail: jsheff@ngpc.state.ne.us
Administrator: Administration: MARK BROHMAN; Phone: 402-471-5537; E-mail: mbrohman@ngpc.state.ne.us
Administrator: Budget and Fiscal: LARRY WITT; Phone: 402-471-5523; E-mail: lwitt@ngpc.state.ne.us
Administrator: Central Regional Parks Manager: JAMES CARNEY; Phone: 402-471-5547; E-mail: jcarney@ngpc.state.ne.us
Administrator: Fisheries: DON GABELHOUSE JR.; Phone: 402-471-5515; E-mail: gabel@ngpc.state.ne.us
Administrator: Information and Education: PAUL HORTON; Phone: 402-471-5481; E-mail: phorton@ngpc.state.ne.us
Administrator: Law Enforcement: TED BLUME; Phone: 402-471-5533; E-mail: tblume@ngpc.state.ne.us
Administrator: Operations and Construction: EARL JOHNSON; Phone: 402-471-5525
Administrator: Parks: JAMES FULLER; Phone: 402-471-5550; E-mail: jfuller@ngpc.state.ne.us
Administrator: Planning and Development: DUANE WESTERHOLT; Phone: 402-471-5511; E-mail: dwester@ngpc.state.ne.us
Administrator: Realty: BRUCE SACKETT; Phone: 402-471-5536; E-mail: bsackett@ngpc.state.ne.us
Administrator: Wildlife: JAMES DOUGLAS; Phone: 402-471-5411; E-mail: jdouglas@ngpc.state.ne.us
Editor: DON CUNNINGHAM
Librarian: BARBARA VOELTZ, 2200 N 33rd St., P.O. Box 30370, Lincoln, NE 68503; Phone: 402-471-5587; Fax: 402-471-5528; E-mail: bvoeltz@ngpc.state.ne.us
Western Regional Parks Manager: STEVE KEMPER; Phone: 308-665-2900
Publication(s): *Nebraskaland Magazine*

NEBRASKA NATURAL RESOURCES COMMISSION
301 Centennial Mall S., 4th Fl., P.O. Box 94876, Lincoln, NE 68509-4876
Phone: 402-471-2081
Founded: 1937
Description: The state agency responsible for comprehensive water resources planning, flood plain management, administration of state financial assistance for water resources, flood control, and soil and water conservation. It also has advisory and administrative responsibility for Natural Resources Districts throughout the state.
Contact(s):
Director: DAYLE E. WILLIAMSON; Phone: 402-471-2081; Fax: 402-471-3132; E-mail: daylew@nrcdec.nrc.state.ne.us
Chairperson: WAYNE DAVIS, HC 70, Box 29, Hay Springs, NE 69347; Phone: 308-327-2766
Publication(s): *Nebraska Resources*
Keyword(s): Environmental and Conservation Education, Planning Management, Rivers, Soil Conservation, Water Resources

NEBRASKA STATE EXTENSION SERVICES
211 Agricultural Hall, University of Nebraska, Lincoln, NE 68583-0703
Phone: 402-472-2966; Web site: ianrwww.unl.edu/ianr/coopext/coopext.htm
Contact(s):
Dean and Director of Cooperative Extension (Interim): ELBERT C. DICKEY; E-mail: edickey1@unl.edu
Dept. Head, Agricultural Leadership, Education and Communication: EARL B. RUSSELL, 300 Agricultural Hall, University of Nebraska, Lincoln, NE 68583-07098; Phone: 402-472-2807; Fax: 402-472-5863; E-mail: erussell2@unl.edu
Director, Center for Rural Community Revitalization and Development: JOHN ALLEN, 58C H.C. Filley Hall, University of Nebraska, Lincoln, NE 68583-0947; Phone: 402-472-8012; Fax: 402-472-0688; E-mail: jallen1@unl.edu
Vertebrate Pest Specialist: SCOTT E. HYGNSTROM, 202 Natural Resources Hall, University of Nebraska, Lincoln, NE 68583-0819; Phone: 402-472-6822; Fax: 402-472-2964
Keyword(s): Agriculture, Environmental and Conservation Education, Renewable Resources, Rural Development, Sustainable Ecosystems, Wildlife and Wildlife Habitat

NEVADA

GOVERNOR OF NEVADA: KENNY GUINN
State Capitol, Carson City, NV 89710
Phone: 702-687-5670

NEVADA BUREAU OF MINES AND GEOLOGY
Mail Stop 178, University of Nevada, Reno, NV 89557-0088
Phone: 775-784-6691
Description: Conducts research on Nevada geology and mineral resources. Collects and disseminates information (including published maps and reports) on Nevada geology, mineral resources, base maps and aerial photos.
Contact(s):
Director and State Geologist: JONATHAN G. PRICE
Keyword(s): Geography, Geology, Land Use Planning, Public Lands, Water Resources

NEVADA DEPARTMENT OF AGRICULTURE
350 Capitol Hill Ave., Reno, NV 89502-2923
Phone: 775-688-1180; Fax: 775-688-1178
Contact(s):
Director: PAUL J. IVERSON
Administrator and State Veterinarian, Division of Animal Industry: DR. DAVID THAIN
Administrator, Division of Plant Industry: ROBERT GRONOWSKI

NEVADA DEPARTMENT OF CONSERVATION AND NATURAL RESOURCES
Capitol Complex, 123 W. Nye Ln., Carson City, NV 89706-0818
Phone: 775-687-4360
Contact(s):
Assistant Director: FREEMAN K. JOHNSON
Executive Secretary: COLLEEN M. MURPHY
Director: PETER G. MORROS
Administrator and State Land Registrar and Administrator of Conservation Districts Division: PAMELA B. WILCOX; Phone: 775-687-4363
Administrator: Division of Environmental Protection: ALLEN BIAGGI; Phone: 775-687-4670
Administrator: Division of State Parks: WAYNE PEROCK; Phone: 775-687-4384
Administrator: Division of Water Planning: NAOMI DUERR; Phone: 775-687-3600
Administrator: Division of Wildlife: TERRY CRAWFORTH; Phone: 775-688-1500
Program Manager: Nevada Natural Heritage: GLENN CLEMMER; Phone: 775-687-4245

State Engineer: Division of Water Resources: R. MICHAEL TURNIPSEED; Phone: 775-687-4278
State Forester: Division of Forestry: ROY W. TRENOWETH; Phone: 775-684-2500

NEVADA DIVISION OF WILDLIFE
1100 Valley Rd., Reno, NV 89512
Phone: 775-688-1500; Fax: 775-688-1595
Description: A regulatory and policymaking body, administering laws, regulations, and policies. Mission is the protection, propagation, restoring, introduction, transplanting, and management of wildlife throughout the state.
Contact(s):
Administrator: TERRY R. CRAWFORTH
Board of Wildlife Commissioner Chairman: BILL BRADLEY
Board of Wildlife Commissioner Vice Chairman: BOYD SPRATLING
Chief, Conservation Education: DAVID K. RICE
Chief, Enforcement: THOMAS ATKINSON
Chief, Fisheries: GENE WELLER
Chief, Game: GREGG TANNER

NEVADA NATURAL HERITAGE PROGRAM
1550 E. College Parkway, Suite 145, Carson City, NV 89706-7921
Phone: 775-687-4245; Fax: 775-687-1288; Web site: www.state.nv.us/nvnhp/
Founded: 1986
Description: The program represents an ongoing effort to collect and standardize data on Nevada's sensitive biodiversity and share this information with developers, researchers, and decision-makers for environmentally wise planning.
Contact(s):
Program Manager: GLENN CLEMMER
Publication(s): *Nevada's Sensitive Species List; Scorecard-Highest Priority Conservation Sites; Endangered, Threatened, and Sensitive Vascular Plants of Nevada*
Keyword(s): , Biodiversity, Conservation, Conservation of Protected Areas, Endangered and Threatened Species, Sensitive Species

NEVADA COOPERATIVE EXTENSION
University of Nevada, 2345 Red Rock St., Suite 100, Las Vegas, NV 89146
Phone: 702-251-7531; Fax: 702-222-3100
Contact(s):
Assistant Director: JANET USINGER-LESQUEREUX; Phone: 702-251-7531
Central Area Agronomy and Range Specialist: JASON DAVIDSON, Fallon, NV ; Phone: 702-428-0212
Director: KAREN HINTON
State Range Specialist and Riparian Scientist: SHERMAN SWANSON, 1000 Valley Rd., Reno, NV 89512; Phone: 702-784-4057; Fax: 702-784-4583
State Water Specialist: MARK WALKER; Phone: 702-784-1938
Western Area Natural Resources Specialist: ED SMITH; Phone: 702-782-9960
Western Area Water Specialist: JOHN COBOURN; Phone: 702-832-4150
Keyword(s): Renewable Resources, Sustainable Ecosystems, Water Resources

NEW HAMPSHIRE

GOVERNOR OF NEW HAMPSHIRE: JEANNE SHAHEEN
State House, Rm. 208, Concord, NH 03301
Phone: 603-271-2121

COUNCIL ON RESOURCES AND DEVELOPMENT
c/o Office of State Planning, 2 1/2 Beacon St., Concord, NH 03301
Phone: 603-271-2155
Founded: 1963
Description: The ten members on the council represent the state's development and resource agencies. The council conducts studies and presents recommendations concerning problems in the fields of environmental protection, natural resources and growth management; consults with, negotiates with, and obtains information from other state and federal agencies; offers guidance and recommendations to the Governor and Council or the General Court; recommends disposition or lease of state-owned surplus real property; and resolves differences or conflicts concerning development, resource management and the implementation of the state policy.
Contact(s):
Chairman: JEFFREY H. TAYLOR

DEPARTMENT OF RESOURCES AND ECONOMIC DEVELOPMENT
P.O. Box 1856, 172 Pembroke Rd., Concord, NH 03302-1856
Contact(s):
Chief of Bureau of Off-Highway Recreational Vehicles: PAUL GRAY; Phone: 603-271-3254
Commissioner: GEORGE BALD; Phone: 603-271-2411
Director of Division of Economic Development: STUART ARNETT; Phone: 603-271-2341
Director of Division of Forests and Lands: PHILIP A. BRYCE; Phone: 603-271-2214
Director of Division of Parks: RICHARD McLEOD; Phone: 603-271-3556
Urban Forester of Urban Forestry Center: J. B. CULLEN; Phone: 603-431-6774

MAINE/NEW HAMPSHIRE SEA GRANT PROGRAM
Kingman Farm, University of New Hampshire, Durham, NH 03824-3512
Phone: 603-749-1565; Fax: 603-743-3997; Web site: www.seagrant.unh.edu/home.htm
Contact(s):
Director: ANN C. BUCKLIN; Phone: 603-862-0122; E-mail: acb@cisunix.unh.edu
Associate Director and Program Leader: BRIAN DOYLE; E-mail: brian.doyle@unh.edu
Coordinator, Communications: STEVE ADAMS; E-mail: steve.adams@unh.edu
Editor/Information Specialist: MARIE POLK; E-mail: marie.polk@unh.edu
Keyword(s): Aquatic Habitats, Coasts, Environmental and Conservation Education, Fisheries, Marine Mammals, Oceanography, Renewable Resources, Research, Sea Grass, Sport Fishing, Sustainable Development, Sustainable Ecosystems, Water Pollution, Wetlands

NEW HAMPSHIRE DEPARTMENT OF AGRICULTURE, MARKETS, AND FOOD
P.O. Box 2042, Concord, NH 03302-2042
Founded: 1913
Description: The department is responsible for a broad range of activities, including protecting the environment, food safety, market integrity, animal and plant health, and the economic security of the New Hampshire agricultural industry.
Contact(s):
Commissioner: STEPHEN H. TAYLOR; Phone: 603-271-3551; Fax: 603-271-1109
Publication(s): *Weekly Market Bulletin*
Keyword(s): Agriculture, Environmental Justice, Land Protection, Rural Development, Sustainable Development

State Conservation Committee
P.O. Box 2042, Concord, NH 03302-2042
Phone: 603-271-3551
Founded: 1945
Description: The SCC consists of twelve members. Six members represent state agencies, five are appointed, and one represents the NH Association of Conservation Commissions. Duties are to offer assistance to supervisors of the ten conservation districts, keep

supervisors of each district informed of other district activities, and coordinate the conservation of New Hampshire activities.
Contact(s):
Chair: PETER BLAKEMAN, P.O. Box 4, North Sutton, NH 03260; Phone: 603-927-4163; Fax: 603-224-8260
Coordinator: JOANNA PELLERIN, 118 North Rd., Brentwood, NH 03833-6614; Phone: 603-679-2790; Fax: 603-679-2860
Coordinator: Representing (NPS): ERIC WILLIAMS
Member: MARJORY SWOPE; Phone: 603-224-7867
Member: ROBERT VARNEY; Phone: 603-271-2358
Member: GEORGE BALD; Phone: 603-271-2214
Member: STEPHEN H. TAYLOR; Phone: 603-271-3551
Member: DR. WILLIAM MAUTZ; Phone: 603-862-1450
Member: DR. JOHN PIKE; Phone: 603-862-1520
Keyword(s): Agriculture, Environmental and Conservation Education, Soil Conservation, Water Resources, Wetlands

NEW HAMPSHIRE DEPARTMENT OF ENVIRONMENTAL SERVICES
6 Hazen Dr., P.O. Box 95, Concord, NH 03302-0095
Phone: 603-271-3503
Founded: 1987
Description: The DES is a result of a legislatively-mandated state environmental agency. The DES consists of three divisions: Water Division; Waste Management Division; and Air Resources Division.
Contact(s):
Assistant Commissioner: G. DANA BISBEE
Commissioner: ROBERT W. VARNEY
Director of Air Resources Division: KENNETH A. COLBURN, 64 N. Main St., Caller Box 2033, Concord, NH 03302; Phone: 603-271-1370; Fax: 603-271-1381
Director of Waste Management Division: DR. PHILIP J. O'BRIEN; Phone: 603-271-2900; Fax: 603-271-2456
Director of Water Division: HARRY T. STEWART; Phone: 603-271-3503; Fax: 603-271-2982
Keyword(s): Air Quality and Pollution, Solid Waste, Water Pollution, Water Resources, Wetlands

NEW HAMPSHIRE FISH AND GAME DEPARTMENT
2 Hazen Dr., Concord, NH 03301
Phone: 603-271-3422; Fax: 603-271-1438
Contact(s):
Commission Chairman: RICHARD MOQUIN
Commission Vice Chairman: ELLIS HATCH
Commissioner Secretary: JIM JONES
Executive Director: WAYNE E. VETTER
Business Administrator: RICHARD N. CUNNINGHAM
Chief: Access and Engineering Division: JOHN S. BOWYER JR.
Chief: Inland Fisheries: STEPHEN G. PERRY
Chief: Law Enforcement Division: COL. RONALD ALIE
Chief: Marine Fisheries Division: JOHN I. NELSON JR.
Chief: Public Affairs Division: JUDY STOKES
Chief: Wildlife Division: STEVEN J. WEBER
Keyword(s): Biology, Endangered and Threatened Species, Environmental and Conservation Education, Fisheries, Hunting, Internships, Nongame Wildlife, Sport Fishing, Trapping, Wildlife Management

NEW HAMPSHIRE NATURAL HERITAGE INVENTORY
P.O. Box 1856, Concord, NH 03302-1856
Phone: 603-271-3623; Fax: 603-271-2629
Founded: 1987
Description: New Hampshire Natural Heritage Inventory is responsible for finding, tracking, and providing information about the state's rare species and exemplary ecosystems.
Contact(s):
Coordinator: DAVID VAN LUVEN
Publication(s): *List of New Hampshire's Rare Plant Species; List of New Hampshire's Rare Animal Species; Checklist of New Hampshire's Vascular Plants*
Keyword(s): Biodiversity, Biology, Ecology, Endangered and Threatened Species, Flowers, Plants, and Trees, Terrestrial Habitats

UNIVERSITY OF NEW HAMPSHIRE COOPERATIVE EXTENSION
59 College Rd., Taylor Hall, Durham, NH 03824-2618
Web site: ceinfo.unh.edu/
Founded: 1925 (Forestry Program)
Description: The natural resource components include Forest Stewardship, Community Forestry, Rural Economic Well-Being, Agriculture and Natural Resource Conservation Education.
Contact(s):
Dean and Director of UNH Cooperative Extension: DR. JOHN PIKE, UNH, 59 College Rd., Taylor Hall, Durham, NH 03824-3587; Phone: 603-862-1520
Extension Specialist: Water Resources: FRANK S. MITCHELL, UNH Cooperative Extension, 55 College Rd., Pettee Hall, Durham, NH 03824-3599; Phone: 603-862-1067
Extension Specialist: Water Resources Lakes Lay Monitoring Program: JEFFREY SCHLOSS, UNH, 55 College Rd., Pettee Hall, Durham, NH 03824-3599; Phone: 603-862-3848
Forest Stewardship Coordinator: KAREN BENNETT, UNH Cooperative Extension, 55 College Rd., Pettee Hall, Durham, NH 03824-3599; Phone: 603-862-2512
Program Leader: Forestry/Wildlife: ROBERT LEE EDMONDS; Phone: 603-862-2619
Wildlife Specialist: ELLEN SNYDER, UNH Cooperative Extension, 55 College Rd., Pettee Hall, Durham, NH 03824-3599; Phone: 603-862-3594; Fax: 603-862-2157
Keyword(s): Environmental and Conservation Education, Forests and Forestry, Lakes, Land Use Planning, Open Spaces, Urban Forestry, Water Resources, Wildlife and Wildlife Habitat

NEW JERSEY

GOVERNOR OF NEW JERSEY: CHRISTINE T. WHITMAN
State House, 125 W. State St., Office of the Governor, CN-001, Trenton, NJ 08625
Phone: 609-292-6000

NEW JERSEY DEPARTMENT OF AGRICULTURE
CN 330, Trenton, NJ 08625
Contact(s):
Assistant Secretary: SAMUEL GARRISON; Phone: 609-292-5530
Chief of Staff: CAROL SHIPP; Phone: 609-633-7794
Coordinator of Soil and Water Conservation Services: SAMUEL R. RACE; Phone: 609-292-5540
Director of Division of Administration: JOHN J. GALLAGHER JR.; Phone: 609-292-6931
Director of Division of Animal Health: DR. ERNEST ZIRKLE; Phone: 609-292-3965
Director of Division of Dairy and Commodity Regulation: DHUN B. PATEL; Phone: 609-292-5575
Director of Division of Markets: DR. H. VANCE YOUNG; Phone: 609-292-5536
Director of Division of Plant Industry: ROBERT J. BALAAM; Phone: 609-292-5441
Director of Division of Rural Resources: GEORGE HORZEPA; Phone: 609-292-5532
Executive Director of State Agriculture Development Committee: GREGORY ROMANO; Phone: 609-984-2504
Keyword(s): Agriculture

State Soil and Conservation Committee
P.O. Box 330, Trenton, NJ 08625
Phone: 609-292-5540
Founded: 1937
Description: A unit of state government administered by the state Dept. of Agriculture. Responsible for conservation of soil resources and control and prevention of soil erosion and nonpoint source pollution, prevention of damage by floodwater or sediment, and conservation of water for agricultural purposes. Provides direction, leadership, standards, rules, funding, and administrative assistance; coordinates local district conservation programs; and is interagency with 12 members.

STATE AND PROVINCIAL GOVERNMENT AGENCIES - NEW JERSEY

Contact(s):
Chairman: ARTHUR R. BROWN JR.; Phone: 609-292-3976; Fax: 609-292-3978
Executive Secretary: SAMUEL R. RACE; Phone: 609-292-5540; Fax: 609-633-7229; E-mail: agurace@ag.state.nj.us
Publication(s): *On Land and Water; Standards for Soil Erosion and Sediment Control in New Jersey*
Keyword(s): Agriculture, Renewable Resources, Soil Conservation, Urban Environment, Water Pollution, Water Quality, Water Resources, Watersheds

NEW JERSEY DEPARTMENT OF ENVIRONMENTAL PROTECTION
401 E. State St., P. O. 402, Trenton, NJ 08625-0402
Phone: 609-292-2885
Contact(s):
Assistant Commissioner: Policy and Planning: BOB TUDOR; Phone: 609-292-1254
Assistant Commissioner: Enforcement: MARLEN DOOLEY; Phone: 609-984-3285
Assistant Commissioner: Environmental Regulation: GARY SONDERMEYER; Phone: 609-292-2795
Assistant Commissioner: Land Use Management: RAY CANTOR, 401 E. State St., P.O. Box 439; Phone: 609-292-2178
Assistant Commissioner: Management and Budget: RONALD TUMINSKI; Phone: 609-292-2916
Assistant Commissioner: Natural and Historic Resources: JIM HALL; Phone: 609-292-3541
Assistant Commissioner: Site Remediation: RICHARD GIMELLO; Phone: 609-292-1250
Commissioner: ROBERT C. SHINN JR.
Deputy Commissioner: JUDY JENGO; Phone: 609-292-9661
Deputy Commissioner: MARK SMITH; Phone: 609-292-2885
Director: Communications: PETER PAGE; Phone: 609-777-1344
Director: Division of Science and Research: LESLIE McGEORGE; Phone: 609-984-6070
Editor: DENISE MIKICS; Phone: 609-777-4182
Publication(s): *New Jersey Outdoors*

Division of Fish, Game, and Wildlife
P.O. Box 400, Trenton, NJ 08625-0400
Phone: 609-292-2965
Contact(s):
Director: ROBERT L. McDOWELL; Phone: 609-292-9410
Assistant Director: Central Services: ROBERT ITCHMONEY; Phone: 609-292-0891
Chief: Bureau of Marine Fisheries: TOM McCLOY; Phone: 609-984-5546
Chief: Freshwater Fisheries: ROBERT SOLDWEDEL; Phone: 609-292-8642
Chief: Lands Management: TONY PETRONGOLO; Phone: 609-292-1599
Chief: Law Enforcement: ROB WINKEL; Phone: 609-292-9430
Chief: Shell Fisheries: JIM JOSEPH; Phone: 609-984-5546
Chief: Wildlife Education: DAVID CHANDA; Phone: 609-292-9450
Chief: Wildlife Management: FRED CARLSON; Phone: 609-292-6685
Chief, Endangered and Nongame Species Program: LARRY NILES; Phone: 609-292-9101

Division of Parks and Forestry
P.O. Box 404, Trenton, NJ 08625-0404
Phone: 609-292-2733
Contact(s):
Deputy Director: CARL R. NORDSTROM; Phone: 609-292-5990
Director: GREGORY A. MARSHALL
Administrator: Office of Historic Preservation: DOROTHY P. GUZZO; Phone: 609-984-0176
Assistant Director: State Park Service: JAMES BARRESI; Phone: 609-292-2530
Assistant Director: State Park Service: RICHARD F. BARKER; Phone: 609-292-2772

Chief: Bureau of Forest Fire Management and State Fire Warden: DAVID B. HARRISON; Phone: 609-292-2977
Chief: Bureau of Forest Management: State Forester: LES ALPAUGH; Phone: 609-292-2531
Communications Coordinator: AMY CRADICK; Phone: 609-984-1423
Education Coordinator: FRANK GALLAGHER; Phone: 609-292-8190

Division of Publicly Funded Site Remediation
401 E. State St., P.O. Box 402, Trenton, NJ 08625-0402
Phone: 609-984-2902
Contact(s):
Director: ANTHONY J. FARRO

Division of Solid and Hazardous Waste
P.O. Box 414, Trenton, NJ 08625-0414
Phone: 609-984-6880
Contact(s):
Director: JOHN CASRER

Geological Survey
P.O. Box 427, Trenton, NJ 08625-0427
Phone: 609-292-1185; Fax: 609-633-1004;
Web site: www.state.nj.us/dep.njgs
Founded: 1835
Description: Formed to study, evaluate and prepare maps and reports on New Jersey's resources. In addition to a geologic map and information on the mineral industry and water resources, the survey provides geologic and ground water reports, geologic and topographic maps, ground water monitoring, and other resource information.
Contact(s):
Chief of Bureau of Geology and Topography: RICHARD DALTON; Phone: 609-292-2576
Chief of Bureau of Ground Water Resource Evaluation: KARL MUESSIG; Phone: 609-984-6587
Editor: THOMAS SECKLER; Phone: 609-292-2576
State Geologist: HAIG KASABACH; Phone: 609-292-1185
Keyword(s): Geology, Water Resources

Green Acres and Recreation Program
P.O. Box 412, Trenton, NJ 08625-0412
Phone: 609-984-0500
Contact(s):
Administrator: THOMAS WELLS
Chief of Compliance: JEANNE DONLON; Phone: 609-984-0631
Chief of Office of Natural Resource Damages: MARTIN J. McHUGH; Phone: 609-984-5475
Chief of Outdoor Recreation Planning: ROBERT STOKES; Phone: 609-984-0495
Deputy Administrator: DENNIS DAVIDSON; Phone: 609-984-0555

NEW JERSEY PINELANDS COMMISSION
P.O Box 7, New Lisbon, NJ 08064
Phone: 609-894-7300; Fax: 606-894-7330; E-mail: info@njpines.state.nj.us; Web site: www.state.nj.us/pinelands/
Founded: 1979
Description: State planning and regulatory agency with jurisdiction over land use and development in the million-acre Pinelands national reserve; 53 municipalities in the state Pinelands area have and revise local master plans and zoning ordinances to incorporate standards of regional conservation plan.
Contact(s):
Chairman: DANIEL L. KELLEHER
Executive Director: TERRENCE D. MOORE
Assistant Director of Development Review and Enforcement: WILLIAM F. HARRISON
Assistant Director of Planning and Management: JOHN C. STOKES
Editor of Publications: NANCY SOPER; E-mail: info@njpines.state.nj.us
Educational Coordinator: BETSY CARPENTER
Publication(s): *Pinelander, The Newsletter;* a list of reports and studies is available upon request.

Keyword(s): Environmental Preservation, Land Use Planning, Planning Management, Sustainable Ecosystems, Water Resources

NEW JERSEY SEA GRANT COLLEGE PROGRAM
New Jersey Marine Sciences Consortium, Bldg. 22, Fort Hancock, NJ 07732
Phone: 908-872-1300; Fax: 732-872-9573; Web site: www.njmsc.org/seagrant.htm
Description: The New Jersey Marine Sciences Consortium is an alliance of 29 institutions from New Jersey, New York and Pennsylvania formed for the purposes of conducting sponsored research in marine and coastal sciences, technology development through group action; and assembling material resources which lie beyond the capabilities of the individual member institutions. The consortium manages the Sea Grant College Program and the Sea Grant Extension Program.
Contact(s):
Director: MICHAEL P. WEINSTEIN; E-mail: mikew@njmsc.org
Associate Sea Grant Director/Sea Grant Extension Director: ELEANOR A. BOCHENEK; E-mail: Eleanor@njmsc.org

NEW JERSEY STATE EXTENSION SERVICES
Rutgers Cooperative Extension, 88 Lipman Dr., New Brunswick, NJ 08901-8525
Phone: 732-932-9306
Contact(s):
Director: ZANE R. HELSEL
Specialist in Forest Resources: DR. MARK C. VODAK, Rutgers, The State University, Cook College, P.O. Box 231, New Brunswick, NJ 08903; Phone: 732-932-8993
Keyword(s): Agriculture, Gardening and Horticulture, Pesticides, Solid Waste Management, Youth Organizations

NEW MEXICO

GOVERNOR OF NEW MEXICO: GARY JOHNSON
State Capitol, Suite 400, Santa Fe, NM 087503
Phone: 505-827-3000

ENERGY, MINERALS, AND NATURAL RESOURCES DEPARTMENT
2040 Pacheco St., Santa Fe, NM 87505
Phone: 505-827-5950
Description: As the steward for New Mexico's natural resources, the department seeks to preserve the unique natural beauty of New Mexico and to facilitate the beneficial development and use of its resources in an environmentally responsible manner.
Contact(s):
Cabinet Secretary: JENNIFER SALISBURY, 2040 S. Pacheco, Santa Fe, NM 87505; Phone: 505-827-5950

Administrative Services Division
2040 Pacheco St., Santa Fe, NM 87505
Phone: 505-827-5925
Description: Provides clerical, record keeping, and administrative support to the department in the areas of personnel, budget, procurement and contracting, and administration of federal and state grants.
Contact(s):
Director: JIM FIRKINS
Keyword(s): Energy, Environmental and Conservation Education, Environmental Preservation, Outdoor Recreation, Renewable Resources

Energy Conservation and Management Division
Villagra Bldg., 408 Galisteo St., Santa Fe, NM 87505
Phone: 505-827-5900
Description: Administers state and federally funded energy conservation and alternative energy technology programs to state agencies, political subdivisions, regional organizations, nonprofit community service agencies, and New Mexico energy consumers, by providing engineering and technical assistance, and informational, financial, and programmatic support.
Contact(s):
Director: DIANE CARON

Forestry and Resources Conservation Division
Villagra Bldg., 408 Galisteo St., Santa Fe, NM 87501
Phone: 505-827-5830
Description: Provides management and protection of New Mexico's renewable forest, rangeland, soil and water resources through professional forest, pest, fire and land management; provides law enforcement and administration, public education in conservation; and supports to enhance the environment and quality of resources to protect jobs and maintain social and economic benefits.
Contact(s):
State Forester: TOBY MARTINEZ

Mining and Minerals Division
2040 Pacheco St., Santa Fe, NM 87505
Phone: 505-827-5970
Description: Provides for the study, development, and optimum production of the mineral and energy resources within the state; the reduction of hazards associated with these processes consistent with the conservation of these resources; the protection of public health, safety, and the environment, and the economic well-being of the citizens.
Contact(s):
Director: KATHLEEN GARLAND

Oil Conservation Division
2040 S. Pacheco St., Santa Fe, NM 87505
Phone: 505-827-7131
Description: Regulates and sets standards for operations related to the drilling and production of crude oil, natural gas, and geothermal resources and promotes the development and conservation of these resources while ensuring the prevention of waste and protection. Cares for the prevention of loss and contamination of freshwater supplies.
Contact(s):
Director: BILL LeMAY

State Parks and Recreation Division
2040 S. Pacheco St., Santa Fe, NM 87505
Phone: 505-827-7465
Description: Provides and cares for the recreational resources, facilities, and opportunities, and promotes user safety on recreational land and water to benefit and enrich the lives of New Mexico residents and visitors alike.
Contact(s):
Director: TOM TRUJILLO

NEW MEXICO BUREAU OF MINES AND MINERAL RESOURCES
Campus Station, Socorro, NM 87801
Phone: 505-835-5420; Fax: 505-835-6333
Founded: 1927
Description: Charged with investigating and reporting on all types of mineral resources and the geology of the state, including environmental geology, water resources, and geological hazards; responsible for conducting applied research on all aspects of geology and mineral resources.
Contact(s):
Director and State Geologist: DR. PETER SCHOLLE; Phone: 505-835-5302
Editor: DR. JANE LOVE
Environmental Geologist: DR. MICHAEL WHITWORTH; Phone: 505-835-5921
Environmental Geologist: DR. BRUCE ALLEN; Phone: 505-255-0317
Environmental Geologist: DR. DAVID W. LOVE; Phone: 505-835-5146
Manager of Geological Extension Service: SUSAN WELCH; Phone: 505-835-5112
Publication(s): *Bulletins; Circulars; Memoirs; Ground Water Reports; Geologic Maps; New Mexico Geology; Lite Geology;*

STATE AND PROVINCIAL GOVERNMENT AGENCIES - NEW MEXICO

Scenic Trips to the Geologic Past; Databases on CD-ROM and home page
Keyword(s): Chemistry, Energy, Geology, Natural History, Water Resources

Geological Information Center Library
Campus Station, Socorro, NM 87801
Phone: 505-835-5145; Fax: 505-835-6333; Web site: www.geoinfo.nmt.edu/
Keyword(s): Librarians/Information Professionals

NEW MEXICO COOPERATIVE FISH AND WILDLIFE RESEARCH UNIT
P.O. Box 30003, MSC 4901, New Mexico State University, Las Cruces, NM 88003-0003
Phone: 505-646-6053
Founded: 1988
Description: Supported cooperatively by the U.S.G.S. Biological Resources Division, New Mexico State University, New Mexico Department of Game and Fish and the Wildlife Management Institute, the New Mexico Fish and Wildlife Research Unit's primary purpose is research on management and conservation of fish and wildlife species and graduate research training in fisheries and wildlife resources.
Contact(s):
Leader: BRUCE C. THOMPSON
Assistant Leader for Fisheries: COLLEEN A. CALDWELL
Keyword(s): Aquatic Habitats, Arid Lands, Conservation Planning, Endangered and Threatened Species, Toxic Substances, Wildlife and Wildlife Habitat

NEW MEXICO DEPARTMENT OF AGRICULTURE
MSC 3189, P.O. Box 30005, Las Cruces, NM 88003-8005
Founded: 1955
Description: Organized to protect state agriculture from importation of plant diseases and insects and help control those that gain entrance; to ensure products offered for sale meet quality standards as advertised and labeled; maintain inspection of agricultural products for interstate shipping; laboratory analyses of animal diseases and deaths on fee basis; promote state agricultural commodities; provide market news; and conduct consumer and producer service activities designated by law.
Contact(s):
Assistant Director: JEFF M. WITTE; Phone: 505-646-3007
Director and Secretary: FRANK A. DUBOIS; Phone: 505-646-3007
Director of Agricultural and Environmental Services Division: LARRY DOMINGUEZ; Phone: 505-646-3208
Director of Agricultural Programs and Resources Division: RONALD J. WHITE; Phone: 505-646-2642
Director of Marketing and Development Division: EDWARD AVALOS; Phone: 505-646-4929
Director of Standards and Consumer Services Division: GARY WEST; Phone: 505-646-1616
Director of Veterinary Diagnostic Services: DR. RICHARD LaROCK; Phone: 505-841-2576
Head of Public Relations: LANA DICKSON; Phone: 505-646-3008
State Chemist of Laboratory: RICK JANECKA; Phone: 505-646-3318
State Seed Analyst of Laboratory: RICHARD KOCHEVAR; Phone: 505-646-3407
Publication(s): *Biennial Report; New Mexico Agricultural Statistics*

NEW MEXICO DEPARTMENT OF GAME AND FISH
P.O. Box 25112, Santa Fe, NM 87504
Phone: 505-827-7911
Description: The State Game Commission and the Game and Fish Department are administratively attached to the Energy, Minerals, and Natural Resources Department. The responsibility of the State Game Commission is to develop policy for the Game and Fish Department.
Contact(s):
Director: JERRY MARACCHINI, P.O. Box 25112, Santa Fe, NM 87504; Phone: 505-827-7899
Assistant Director of Field Operations: LARRY BELL; Phone: 505-827-7899
Assistant Director of Resource Divisions: SCOTT BROWN; Phone: 505-827-7899
Assistant Director of Administrative Services and Information Systems Services: ROBERTA SALAZAR-HENRY; Phone: 505-827-7899
Cabinet Secretary of Energy, Minerals, and Natural Resources: JENNIFER SALISBURY; Phone: 505-827-5950
Chairman of State Game Commission: BILL BRININSTOOL
Chief of Administrative Services (Acting): LYDIA DURAN; Phone: 505-827-7920
Chief of Conservation Services: TOD STEVENSON; Phone: 505-827-7882
Chief of Public Affairs: LUKE SHELBY; Phone: 505-827-7911
Chief of Fish Management: JACK KELLY; Phone: 505-827-7905
Chief of Law Enforcement: JOHN MILES; Phone: 505-827-7934
Chief of Wildlife Division: BARRY HALE; Phone: 505-827-7885

Albuquerque NM Office
3481 Midway Pl. NE, Albuquerque, NM 87109
Phone: 505-841-8881
Contact(s):
Chief: GLENN CASE

Las Cruces NM Office
566 N. Telshor Blvd., Las Cruces, NM 88011
Phone: 505-522-9796
Contact(s):
Chief: STEVE HENRY

Raton NM Office
P.O. Box 1145, 215 York Canyon Rd., Raton, NM 87740
Phone: 505-445-2311
Contact(s):
Chief: JOANNA LACKEY

Roswell NM Office
1912 West 2nd St., Roswell, NM 88201
Phone: 505-624-6135
Contact(s):
Chief: ROY HAYES

NEW MEXICO ENVIRONMENT DEPARTMENT
1190 Saint Francis Dr., P.O. Box 26110, Santa Fe, NM 87502
Description: To preserve, protect, and perpetuate New Mexico's environment for present and future generations.
Contact(s):
Secretary: MARK E. WEIDLER; Phone: 505-827-2855
Chief of Department of Energy Oversight Bureau: JOHN PARKER; Phone: 505-827-4252
Chief of Solid Waste Bureau: ERALD SILVA; Phone: 505-827-0197
Chief of Air Quality Bureau: CECILIA WILLIAMS; Phone: 505-827-0042
Chief of Ground Water Protection and Remediation Bureau: MARCY LEAVITT; Phone: 505-827-2919
Chief of Hazardous & Radioactive Materials Bureau: BENITO GARCIA; Phone: 505-827-4358
Chief of Occupational Health and Safety Bureau: SAM ROGERS; Phone: 505-827-2877
Chief of Program Support Bureau: CLIFF HAWLEY; Phone: 505-827-2844
Chief of Underground Storage Tank Bureau: DAVID DURAN; Phone: 505-827-2932
Director of Administrative Services Division: ROBERT MENKE; Phone: 505-827-2774
Director of Environmental Protection Division: PETER MAGGIORE; Phone: 505-827-2855
Director of Field Operations Division: TITO MADRID; Phone: 505-827-2855
Director of Water and Waste Management Division: NATHAN ("ED") KELLY; Phone: 505-827-2855
Manager of District II: JAMES BEARZI; Phone: 505-474-4405
Manager of District III: KEN SMITH; Phone: 505-524-6300

Manager of District IV: GARY McCASLIN; Phone: 505-624-6046

NEW MEXICO SOIL AND WATER CONSERVATION COMMISSION
Chair, 11 McMillen Rd., Silver City, NM 88061
Contact(s):
Chair: DUTSON HUNT, 11 McMillen Rd., Silver City, NM 88061; Phone: 505-535-2420; Fax: 505-388-0376
Acting Bureau Chief: JEFF LEWIS, 530 S. Melendres, Las Cruces, NM 88005; Phone: 505-524-6210; Fax: 505-524-6211

NEW MEXICO STATE EXTENSION SERVICES
Box 30003, Campus Box 3AG, NM State University, Las Cruces, NM 88003
Phone: 505-646-3748; Web site: www.cahe.nmsu.edu/ces/
Contact(s):
Extension Department Head of Animal Resources: RON PARKER, Box 3AE, NM State University, Las Cruces, NM 88003; Phone: 505-646-1709
Extension Department Head of Plant Sciences: RON BYFORD, Box 3AE, NM State University, Las Cruces, NM 88003; Phone: 505-646-2458
Extension Range Management Specialist: CHRIS ALLISON, Box 3AE, NM State University, Las Cruces, NM 88003; Phone: 505-646-1944
Extension Wildlife Specialist: JON BOREN, Box 3AE, NM State University, Las Cruces, NM 88003; Phone: 505-646-1164; Fax: 505-646-1281
Interim Associate Dean and Director CES: BILLY DICTSON, NM State University, Box 3AE, Las Cruces, NM 88003; Phone: 505-646-3015
Interim Dean and Chief Administrative Officer: JERRY G. SCHICKEDANZ

STATE ENGINEER OFFICE/INTERSTATE STREAM COMMISSION
Bataan Memorial Bldg., P.O. Box 25102, Santa Fe, NM 87504
Phone: 505-827-6175; Fax: 505-827-6188
Description: Administration, development, protection, and conservation of the water resources of the state of New Mexico.
Contact(s):
Chairman: J. PHELPS WHITE III, P.O. Box 874, Roswell, NM 88202-0874; Phone: 505-662-5701; Fax: 505-625-0227
Chief of Technical Division: DONALD T. LOPEZ
Chief of Water Rights Division: PAUL SAAVEDRA
General Counsel of Legal Services Division: TED APODACA
Interstate Stream Engineer: NORMAN GAUME; Phone: 505-827-6160; Fax: 505-827-6188
Librarian: BARBARA AUSTIN, State Engineer Office Library, P.O. Box 25102, Bataan Memorial Bldg., Santa Fe, NM 87504; Phone: 505-827-6187; Fax: 505-827-6188
State Engineer and Secretary: THOMAS C. TURNEY; Phone: 505-827-6160
Vice Chairman: TRACY SEIDMAN HEPHNER, P.O. Box 277, Wagon Mound, NM 87752; Phone: 505-666-2497
Publication(s): *Water Line*
Keyword(s): Water Resources

NEW YORK

GOVERNOR OF NEW YORK: GEORGE E. PATAKI
State Capitol, 138 Eagle St., Albany, NY 12224
Phone: 518-474-7516

ADIRONDACK PARK AGENCY
P.O. Box 99, Ray Brook, NY 12977
Phone: 518-891-4050
Founded: 1971
Description: Created by state law and charged with developing a state Land Master Plan for the 40% of the park that is public land and a Private Land Use and Development Plan for the private lands within the six-million-acre Adirondack Park. The agency also administers the state's Wild, Scenic, and Recreational Rivers System Act for private lands within the park and the state's Freshwater Wetlands Act for both state and private lands within the park. The agency also operates two Adirondack Park Visitor Interpretive centers (nature education and tourism information centers) at Paul Smiths and Newcomb, which are open year-round.
Contact(s):
Chairman: RICHARD LEFEBVRE
Deputy Director: KARYN B. RICHARDS
Executive Director: DANIEL T. FITTS
Director of Interpretive Programs: SANDRA BUREAU
Director of Planning: JOHN BANTA
Director of Regulatory Programs: WILLIAM J. CURRAN
Publication(s): *Adirondack Park, Land Use Planning for the Adirondack Park, Annual Report, The*; publications list available upon request.
Keyword(s): Environmental and Conservation Education, Lakes, Land Use Planning, Rivers, Wetlands

ENVIRONMENTAL PROTECTION BUREAU
Department of Law, State of New York, 120 Broadway, New York City, NY 10271
Description: Institutes legal actions on behalf of the people of the state in cases involving air and water pollution, protection of wildlife, waste site remediation, and protection of scenic and natural resources. Has responsibility for enforcement of laws protecting endangered species of wildlife, as well as public nuisance actions to restrain pollution and other environmental damage.
Contact(s):
Assistant Attorney General in Charge: WILLIAM HELMER; Phone: 518-474-8096
Environmental Engineer: PETER SKINNER; Phone: 518-474-2432

NEW YORK COOPERATIVE FISH AND WILDLIFE RESEARCH UNIT
Department of Natural Resources, Fernow Hall, Cornell University, Ithaca, NY 14853
Phone: 607-255-2839
Founded: 1961 (Wildlife Unit), 1963 (Fisheries Unit), 1984 Combined.
Description: Primary purpose is field and laboratory research on management and conservation of a variety of fish and wildlife species, and graduate research training in fisheries and wildlife resources. Supported cooperatively by U.S. Geological Survey, Cornell University, New York State Department of Environmental Conservation, and the Wildlife Management Institute.
Contact(s):
Assistant Leader of Fisheries: DR. MARK B. BAIN; Phone: 607-255-2840
Assistant Leader of Wildlife: DR. RICHARD A. MALECKI; Phone: 607-255-2836
Leader: DR. MILO E. RICHMOND; Phone: 607-255-2151; E-mail: MER6@cornell.edu

NEW YORK DEPARTMENT OF AGRICULTURE AND MARKETS
1 Winners Cir., Albany, NY 12235
Phone: 518-457-3880
Founded: 1884
Description: Promotes and regulates production, manufacturing, marketing, storing, and distribution of food. Supervises quality of plant materials, health of animals, and regulates dogs. Also, represents agricultural interests before NY Public Service Commission on siting of transmission lines and power plants.
Contact(s):
Commissioner: DONALD R. DAVIDSEN
Director of Division of Agricultural Protection and Support Services: KIM T. BLOT
Director of Division of Plant Industry: ROBERT MUNGARI
Public Information Officer: PETE GREGG
Keyword(s): Agriculture, Biotechnology, Flowers, Plants, and Trees, Pesticides, Soil Conservation

STATE AND PROVINCIAL GOVERNMENT AGENCIES - NEW YORK

State Soil and Water Conservation Committee
Contact(s):
Chair: PHILIP GRIFFEN, 28 Spook Hollow Rd., Stillwater, NY 12170; Phone: 518-664-5038
Director: JOHN WILDEMAN; Phone: 518-457-3738; Fax: 518-457-1204

NEW YORK DEPARTMENT OF ENVIRONMENTAL CONSERVATION
50 Wolf Rd., Albany, NY 12233
Founded: 1970
Description: The mission of the New York State Department of Environmental Conservation is to conserve, improve and protect its natural resources and environment, and control water, land and air pollution, in order to enhance the health, safety and welfare of the people of the state and their overall economic and social well-being.
Contact(s):
Commissioner: JOHN P. CAHILL; Phone: 518-457-1162
Executive Deputy Commissioner: GAVIN DONOHUE; Phone: 518-457-2390
Special Assistant to the Commissioner: LINDA FRICK; Phone: 518-457-0904
Adirondacks: JOHN KELLY; Phone: 518-623-3671
Assistant Commissioner for Administrative Services: SUSAN TALUTO; Phone: 518-457-6533
Assistant Commissioner for Office of Bond Act: JOHN MCKEON; Phone: 518-457-6558
Assistant Commissioner for the Office of Public Protection: JAMES TUFTEY; Phone: 518-457-0331
Assistant Commissioner of Office of Hearings and Mediation Services: JAMES FERREIRA; Phone: 518-457-3468
Assistant Commissioner of Office of Science and Technology: S. T. RAO; Phone: 518-457-3200
Deputy Commissioner for Natural Resources: PETER DUNCAN; Phone: 518-457-0975
Deputy Commissioner for Water Quality and Environmental Remediation: ERIN CROTTY; Phone: 518-457-1415
Deputy Commissioner Air and Waste Management: CARL JOHNSON
Environmental Facilities Corporation: TERRY AGRISS; Phone: 518-457-4222
Fresh Kills: PAUL GALLAY; Phone: 718-482-4949
General Counsel: FRANK BIFERA; Phone: 518-457-4415
Hudson River: FRAN DUNWELL; Phone: 914-256-3017
Legislative Counsel: STEPHEN BOBARAKIS; Phone: 518-457-2239
Marine Resources: GORDON COLVIN; Phone: 516-444-0430
Natural Resources Planning: FRANCIS SHEEHAN; Phone: 518-457-4208
Salmon River: FRAN VERDOLIVA; Phone: 315-298-7605
Special Projects: JIM AUSTIN; Phone: 518-457-6610
Special Projects: TOM KUNKEL; Phone: 518-457-6610
Publication(s): *Environmental Notice Bulletin*

Division of Air Resources
50 Wolf Rd., Albany, NY 12233
Contact(s):
Director: ROBERT WARLAND; Phone: 518-457-7230

Division of Environmental Enforcement
Contact(s):
Director: CHARLES SULLIVAN; Phone: 518-457-4348

Division of Environmental Permits
Contact(s):
Director: JEFFREY SAMA; Phone: 518-457-7424

Division of Environmental Remediation
Contact(s):
Director: MICHAEL O'TOOLE; Phone: 518-457-5861

Division of Fish, Wildlife and Marine Resources
Contact(s):
Director: GERRY BARNHART; Phone: 518-457-5690

Division of Forest Protection & Fire Management
Contact(s):
Director (Acting): THOMAS RINALDI; Phone: 518-457-5740

Division of Information Services
Contact(s):
Director (Acting): WILLIAM BERNASKI; Phone: 518-457-6367

Division of Lands and Forests
Contact(s):
Director: FRANK DUNSTAN; Phone: 518-457-2475

Division of Law Enforcement
Contact(s):
Director (Acting): DAVE EGELSTON; Phone: 518-457-5681

Division of Legal Affairs
Contact(s):
Director: ALISON SMITH; Phone: 518-457-3551

Division of Management and Budget
Contact(s):
Director: RICHARD K. RANDLES; Phone: 518-457-1141

Division of Mineral Resources
Contact(s):
Director: GREGORY SOVAS; Phone: 518-457-9337

Division of Operations
Contact(s):
Director: ROBERT BARSHIELD; Phone: 518-457-6310

Division of Public Affairs and Education
Contact(s):
Director: LAUREL REMUS; Phone: 518-457-0840

Division of Solid & Hazardous Materials
Contact(s):
Director: STEPHEN HAMMOND; Phone: 518-457-6934

Division of Water
Contact(s):
Director: N. G. KAUL; Phone: 518-457-6674

Press Office
Contact(s):
Public Information Officer: JENNIFER POST

Regional Directors
Contact(s):
Region 1: RAYMOND COWEN III, Bldg. 40, State University of New York, Stony Brook, NY 11794; Phone: 516-444-0345
Region 2: MARY ELLEN KRIS, Hunters Point Plaza, Long Island City, NY 11101; Phone: 718-482-4900
Region 3: MARC MORAN, 21 S. Putt Corners Rd., New Paltz, NY 12561; Phone: 914-256-3005
Region 4: STEVE SCHASSLER, 11 North Westcott Road, Schenectady, NY 12306; Phone: 518-357-2068
Region 5: STUART BUCHANAN, Route 86, P.O. Box 296, Ray Brook, NY 12977; Phone: 518-897-1211
Region 6: SANDY LEBARRON, 317 Washington Street, Watertown, NY 13204; Phone: 315-785-2239
Region 7: KENNETH LYNCH, 615 Erie Blvd., W, Syracuse, NY 13204; Phone: 315-426-7400
Region 8: JOHN HICKS, 6274 E. Avon-Lima Road, Avon, NY 14414; Phone: 716-226-2466
Region 9: GERALD MIKOL, 270 Michigan Avenue, Buffalo, NY 14203; Phone: 716-851-7200

NEW YORK DEPARTMENT OF HEALTH
Tower Bldg., Empire State Plaza, Albany, NY 12237
Contact(s):
Director of Center for Environmental Health (P.E.): RONALD TRAMMONTANO; Phone: 518-458-6400

NEW YORK GEOLOGICAL SURVEY AND STATE MUSEUM
Cultural Education Center, Albany, NY 12230
Phone: 518-474-5816; Fax: 518-486-3696; E-mail: rfakundi@mail.nysed.gov

Founded: 1836

Description: The Geological Survey and State Museum serves as a clearinghouse for information concerning bedrock and surficial geology within the state. The survey conducts regular mapping projects and investigations in basic, environmental, and applied geology and publishes maps and reports of investigations.

Contact(s):
Engineering and Environmental Geology, Geologic Information-Open File: ROBERT H. FICKIES; Phone: 518-474-5810
Oil and Gas Office Director: RICHARD NYAHAY; Phone: 518-486-2161
State Geologist and Chief Scientist: ROBERT H. FAKUNDINY

Publication(s): *New York State Geogram; publications list of the New York State Geological Survey*

Keyword(s): Coasts, Energy, Geology, Land Use Planning, Museum, Water Resources

NEW YORK SEA GRANT
121 Discovery Hall, SUNY at Stony Brook, Stony Brook, NY 11794-5001
Phone: 516-632-6905; Fax: 516-632-6917; E-mail: NYSeaGrant@notes.cc.sunysb.edu; Web site: www.seagrant.sunysb.edu/

Founded: 1971

Description: A cooperative program of the State University of New York and Cornell University fostering the wise use and development of coastal resources through research grants, extension advisory services, education, training, and informational materials.

Contact(s):
Director: DR. JACK S. MATTICE; E-mail: jmattice@ccmail.sunysb.edu
Assistant Director: CORNELIA G. SCHLENK
Associate Director and Program Leader: DALE BAKER, New York Sea Grant, 348 Roberts Hall, Cornell University, Ithaca, NY 14853-4203; Phone: 607-255-2832
Communicator: BARBARA A. BRANCA; Phone: 516-632-6956
Assistant Communicator: PAUL FOCAZIO; Phone: 516-632-6910
Fiscal Officer of New York Sea Grant: STEFANIE MASSUCCI
Great Lakes Program Coordinator: DAVID WHITE, New York Sea Grant, 101 Rich Hall, SUNY College at Oswego, Oswego, NY 13126-3599; Phone: 315-341-3042
Marine Program Coordinator: ROBERT KENT, New York Sea Grant, Cornell University Lab, 3059 Sound Ave., Riverhead, NY 11901-1098; Phone: 516-727-3910

Keyword(s): Coasts, Environmental and Conservation Education, Research, Scholarships and Grants, Water Resources

NEW YORK STATE COOPERATIVE EXTENSION
New York State College of Agriculture and Life Sciences, and Human Ecology, 365 Roberts Hall, Cornell University, Ithaca, NY 14853-4203
Phone: 607-255-2237; Web site: www.cce.cornell.edu/

Contact(s):
Agriculture: R. DAVID SMITH
Chairman/Department Extension Leader: DR. JAMES P. LASSOIE, Department of Natural Resources, 118 Fernow Hall, Cornell University, Ithaca, NY 14853-3001; Phone: 607-255-2810
Director of Cooperative Extension: DR. D. MERRILL EWERT
Environmental/Conservation Youth Education: DR. MARIANNE E. KRASNY, Associate Professor, Dept. of Natural Resources, 16 Fernow Hall, Cornell University, Ithaca, NY 14853-3001; Phone: 607-255-2827
Forestry Resource Management: DR. PETER J. SMALLIDGE, Sr. Extension Associate, Dept. of Natural Resources, 116 Fernow Hall, Cornell University, Ithaca, NY 14853-3001; Phone: 607-255-4696
Forestry/Wildlife: GARY R. GOFF, Extension Associate/Director Master Forest Owners/COVERTS Volunteer Program, Dept. of Natural Resources, 104 Fernow Hall, Cornell University, Ithaca, NY 14853-3001; Phone: 607-255-2824
Human Dimensions Research Unit: TOMMY L. BROWN, Sr. Res. Assoc., Dept. of Natural Resources, 122B Fernow Hall, Cornell University, Ithaca, NY 14853-3001; Phone: 607-255-7695
Protected Area Planning and Management: DR. DAVID W. GROSS, Sr. Extension Associate & Environmental Program Leader, Department of Natural Resources, 112 Fernow Hall, Cornell University, Ithaca, NY 14853-3001; Phone: 607-255-2825
Sportfishing and Aquatic Resources Education (SAREP): STEVE BROWN, Director, Extension Associate, Dept. of Natural Resources, 120 Fernow Hall, Cornell University, Ithaca, NY 14853-3001; Phone: 607-255-9370
Wetlands: DR. REBECCA L. SCHNEIDER, Assistant Professor, Dept. of Natural Resources, 122C Fernow Hall, Cornell University, Ithaca, NY 14853-3001; Phone: 607-255-2110
Wildlife Management: DR. PAUL CURTIS, Sr. Extension Associate, Dept. of Natural Resources, 114 Fernow Hall, Cornell University, Ithaca, NY 14853-3001; Phone: 607-255-2835; Fax: 607-255-2815

Keyword(s): Agriculture, Environmental and Conservation Education, Fisheries, Forest Management, Planning Management, Renewable Resources, Solid Waste Management, Sustainable Ecosystems, Water Resources, Wetlands, Wildlife Management

NEW YORK STATE FISH AND WILDLIFE MANAGEMENT BOARD
50 Wolf Rd, Albany, NY 12233

Founded: 1957

Description: Membership composed of sportsmen, landowners, and local government representatives. State and regional boards advise the Department of Environmental Conservation in programs designed to improve resource management by landowners and increase public access to private lands.

Contact(s):
Chairman: EMORY GREEN, 519 Rte 247, Rushville, NY 14544; Phone: 716-554-3362
Secretary: RANDALL STUMVOLL, 50 Wolf Rd., Albany, NY 12233; Phone: 518-457-4480
Vice Chairman: LEWIS NAGY JR., RTE 1, Box 271-A1, Glenfield, NY 13343; Phone: 315-376-3389

Keyword(s): Hunting, Outdoor Recreation, Public Lands, Water Resources, Wildlife and Wildlife Habitat

Region 3
2 Ridgeway, Goshen, NY 10924
Phone: 914-294-9360
Contact(s):
Board Chairman: RUDY VALLET

Region 4
Milford, NY 13807
Phone: 607-286-7601
Contact(s):
Board Chairman: DEANE WINSOR

Region 5
Letsonville Rd., Paradox, NY 12858
Phone: 518-585-7250
Contact(s):
Board Chairman: DON SAGE

Region 6
81 Miner St., Canton, NY 13617
Phone: 315-386-8345
Contact(s):
Board Chairman: EVERETT QUACKENBUSH

Region 7
2365 Olanco Rd., Marietta, NY 13110
Phone: 315-636-8891
Contact(s):
Board Chairman: CRAIG TRYON

STATE AND PROVINCIAL GOVERNMENT AGENCIES - NORTH CAROLINA

Region 8
947 NYS Rt. 96, Waterloo, NY 13165
Phone: 315-539-2820
Contact(s):
Board Chairman: JOHN ANDREWS

Region 9
7915 State Rd., Eden, NY 14057
Phone: 716-992-9668
Contact(s):
Board Chairman: JIM AGLE

NEW YORK STATE OFFICE OF PARKS, RECREATION AND HISTORIC PRESERVATION
The Governor Nelson A. Rockefeller Empire State Plaza, Agency Bldg. 1, Albany, NY 12238
Phone: 518-474-0456, TDD 518-486-1899; Fax: 518-474-4492
Description: Administers and operates 151 parks, park preserves, and recreational facilities, three arboretums, and 35 historic sites throughout the state; administers 15 heritage areas in partnership with local communities. Acquires and protects public lands and open space; coordinates athletic programs; develops environmental interpretive programs; maintains a field services bureau which oversees historic resources and National Historic Register entries; administers boating and snowmobiling laws.
Contact(s):
Chief Counsel: MEGAN LESSER LEVINE; Phone: 518-474-0447
Commissioner: BERNADETTE CASTRO; Phone: 518-474-0443
Deputy Commissioner for Administration: NANCY PALUMBO; Phone: 518-474-0430
Deputy Commissioner for Historic Preservation: WINTHROP J. ALDRICH; Phone: 518-473-5385
Deputy Commissioner for Land Management: ALBERT E. CACCESE; Phone: 518-474-0402
Deputy Commissioner for Operations, New York City/Long Island: EDWARD F. WANKEL; Phone: 516-669-1000
Deputy Commissioner for Operations, Saratoga/Taconic/Palisades: JULIA S. STOKES; Phone: 518-584-2000
Director of Communications: BRIAN R. VATTIMO; Phone: 518-486-1868
Director of Law Enforcement: TIMOTHY H. COWIN; Phone: 518-474-0402
Director of Marine, Coastal, and Legislative Program Development: DOMINIC JACANGELO; Phone: 518-474-7336
Publication(s): *New York State Operated Parks; Historic Sites and Their Programs; Exploring New York's Past; New York State Boater's Guide; New York State Boat Launching Sites*
Keyword(s): Cultural Preservation, Environmental and Conservation Education, Environmental Preservation, Historic Preservation, Outdoor Recreation

OFFICE OF ENERGY EFFICIENCY AND ENVIRONMENT
New York State Dept. of Public Service, 3 Empire State Plaza, Albany, NY 12223
Phone: 518-474-1677; Fax: 518-474-5026
Founded: 1970
Description: The Office of Energy Efficiency and Environment provides staff support in developing and administering policies that assure appropriate consideration of energy efficiency and environmental protection in utility regulation, management, and restructuring. The office also plays a major role in the development of systems and procedures necessary to introduce retail competition in the state.
Contact(s):
Director: DR. LAURENCE B. DEWITT; Phone: 518-474-1677
Keyword(s): Acid Rain, Energy, Environmental Planning, Land Use Planning, Renewable Resources

TUG HILL COMMISSION
317 Washington St., Watertown, NY 13601
Phone: 315-785-2380; Fax: 315-785-2574; E-mail: tughill@tughill.org
Founded: 1972
Description: The Tug Hill Commission is a nonregulatory state agency charged with helping local governments, organizations, and citizens shape the future of this rural, 2,100 square mile region, especially its environment and economy.
Contact(s):
Executive Director: ROBERT QUINN
Publication(s): *Headwaters; Tug Hill Program, The; Cooperative Rural Planning; Issue Paper series*
Keyword(s): Environmental Planning, Historic Preservation, Outdoor Recreation, Planning Management, Rural Development

NORTH CAROLINA

GOVERNOR OF NORTH CAROLINA: JAMES B. HUNT JR.
State Capitol, 116 W. Jones St., Raleigh, NC 27603-8001
Phone: 919-733-4240

NORTH CAROLINA DEPARTMENT OF ENVIRONMENT AND NATURAL RESOURCES
P.O. Box 27687, Raleigh, NC 27611
Phone: 919-733-4984
Contact(s):
Secretary: WAYNE McDEVITT; Phone: 919-715-4101
Assistant Secretary for Environment: BILL HOLMAN; Phone: 919-715-4141
Director of Division of Water Resources: JOHN MORRIS; Phone: 919-733-4064
Director of Coastal Management: DONNA MOFFITT; Phone: 919-733-2293
Director of Division of Marine Fisheries: PRESTON PATE; Phone: 919-726-7021
Director of Division of Radiation Protection: MEL FRYE; Phone: 919-571-4141
Director of Division of Solid Waste Management: BILL MEYER; Phone: 919-733-4996
Director of Environmental Water Quality: PRESTON HOWARD; Phone: 919-733-7015
Director of Forest Resources: STANFORD M. ADAMS; Phone: 919-733-2162
Director of Museum of Natural Sciences: DR. BETSY BENNETT; Phone: 919-733-7450
Director of North Carolina Aquariums: RHETT WHITE; Phone: 919-733-2290
Director of Office of Environmental Education: ANNE TAYLOR; Phone: 919-733-0711
Director of Office of Pollution Prevention and Environmental Assistance: GARY HUNT; Phone: 919-715-4100
Director of Public Affairs: DON REUTER; Phone: 919-715-4112
Director of Soil and Water Conservation: DEWEY BOTTS; Phone: 919-733-2302
Director of State Parks and Recreation: DR. PHIL McKNELLY; Phone: 919-733-4181
Director of Zoological Park: DR. DAVID JONES; Phone: 910-879-7102
Executive Director of Wildlife Resources Commission: CHARLES R. FULLWOOD, JR.; Phone: 919-733-3391
Land Resources Staff: CHARLES GARDNER; Phone: 919-733-3833
Librarian: FIONA CLEM

NORTH CAROLINA COOPERATIVE EXTENSION SERVICE
North Carolina State University, Box 7602, Raleigh, NC 27695
Phone: 919-515-2811; Fax: 919-515-3135; Web site: www.ces.ncsu.edu/
Contact(s):
Director of Extension Service: DR. JON F. ORT
Assistant Director and State Program Leader: DR. ROGER CRICKENBERGER, NCSU, Box 7602, Raleigh, NC 27695-7602; Phone: 919-515-3252; Fax: 919-515-5950
Aquaculture Specialist: HARRY V. DANIELS, Vernon James Research and Extension Center, 207 Research Station Rd., Plymouth, NC 27962; Phone: 919-793-4428

Aquaculture Specialist: THOMAS M. LOSORDO, Box 7646, North Carolina State University, Raleigh, NC 29695; Phone: 919-515-7587

Extension Aquaculture Specialist: RONALD G. HODSON, Sea Grant, Box 8605, North Carolina State University, Raleigh, NC 27695; Phone: 919-515-2454

Extension Fisheries Specialist: JAMES A. RICE, Box 7617, North Carolina State University, Raleigh, NC 27695; Phone: 919-515-4592

Extension Trout Specialist: JEFFREY M. HINSHAW, Research and Extension Center, Box 9628, 2016 Fanning Bridge Rd., Fletcher, NC 28732-9216; Phone: 704-684-3562

Extension Wildlife Specialist: CHRIS MOORMAN, North Carolina State University, Box 8003, Raleigh, NC 27695; Phone: 919-515-5578; Fax: 919-515-6883

Forestry Specialist and Extension Leader: CRAIG R. McKINLEY, North Carolina State University, Box 8003, Raleigh, NC 27695; Phone: 919-515-5576; Fax: 919-515-6883

Wildlife Specialist and Extension Leader: PETER T. BROMLEY, Zoology Dept., Box 7646, North Carolina State University, Raleigh, NC 27695; Phone: 919-515-7587; Fax: 919-515-4592

Keyword(s): Agriculture, Environmental and Conservation Education, Fisheries, Wildlife Management, Youth Organizations

NORTH CAROLINA COOPERATIVE FISH AND WILDLIFE RESEARCH UNIT (USDI)
Box 7617, 4105 Gardner Hall, North Carolina State University, Raleigh, NC 27695
Phone: 919-515-2631

NORTH CAROLINA DEPARTMENT OF AGRICULTURE
P.O. Box 27647, Raleigh, NC 27611
Contact(s):
Commissioner: JAMES A. GRAHAM; Phone: 919-733-7125
Agronomic Services Staff: DR. RICHARD REICH; Phone: 919-733-2556
Aquaculture & Natural Resources Staff: TOM ELLIS; Phone: 919-733-7125
Food and Drug Protection Staff: BRUCE WILLIAMS; Phone: 919-733-7366
Legal Staff: DAVID McLEOD; Phone: 919-733-7125
Pesticide Disposal Staff: WILLIAM McCLELLAND; Phone: 919-733-7366
Pesticide Section Staff: JOHN SMITH; Phone: 919-733-3556
Plant Conservation Program Staff: CECIL FROST; Phone: 919-733-3610
Plant Industry Division Staff: BILL DICKERSON; Phone: 919-733-3930
Public Affairs Staff: JIM KNIGHT; Phone: 919-733-4216
Research Stations Staff: PAT KELLEY; Phone: 919-733-3236
Structural Pest Staff: CARL FALCO; Phone: 919-733-6100
Veterinary Services Staff: DR. ANDREW MIXSON; Phone: 919-733-7601

Keyword(s): Agriculture, Health and Nutrition, Pesticides, Soil Conservation

NORTH CAROLINA DEPARTMENT OF ENVIRONMENT AND NATURAL RESOURCES

State Soil and Water Conservation Commission
1614 Mail Service Center, Raleigh, NC 27699-1614
Phone: 919-733-2302
Founded: 1937
Description: A unit of state government administered by the Division of Soil and Water Conservation in the Department of Environment and Natural Resources. To organize soil and water conservation districts; grant funds for operations, technical assistance, and the NC Agriculture Cost-Share Program for Nonpoint Source Pollution Control--a water quality program; provide for control of soil erosion and improvement of water quality; accept PL566 Small Watershed applications. Support staff provided through the Division of Soil and Water Conservation Commission.

Contact(s):
Chairman: JAMES FERGUSON, 11571 Betsy Gap Rd., Clyde, NC 28721; Phone: 704-627-6458
Director: DAVID S. VOGEL; Phone: 919-715-6097; Fax: 919-715-3559; E-mail: David.Vogel@ncmail.net

NORTH CAROLINA SEA GRANT PROGRAM
Box 8605, 100B 1911 Bldg., North Carolina State University, Raleigh, NC 27695-8605
Phone: 919-515-2454; Fax: 919-515-7095; Web site: www2.ncsu.edu/sea_grant/seagrant.html
Contact(s):
Director: DR. RONALD G. HODSON; E-mail: ronald_hodson@ncsu.edu
Associate Director: STEVEN G. OLSON
Keyword(s): Aquaculture, Aquatic Habitats, Aquatic Species, Coasts, Ecotourism, Estuaries, Fisheries, Harmful Algal Blooms, Oceanography, Seafood Technology, Water Pollution, Water Quality, Coastal Construction and Erosion

NORTH CAROLINA WILDLIFE RESOURCES COMMISSION
Mailing Address: 1701 Mail Service Center, Raleigh, NC 27699-1701
Phone: 919-733-3391; Fax: 919-733-7083
Founded: 1947
Description: The commission has the function, purpose, and duty to manage, restore, develop, cultivate, conserve, protect, and regulate the wildlife resources of the state, and to administer the laws relating to boating, hunting, fishing, and other wildlife resources, including nongame.
Contact(s):
Commission Chairman: JOHN E. PECHMANN; Phone: 910-483-0107
Assistant Director: RICHARD B. HAMILTON
Commission Vice Chairman: WES SEEGARS; Phone: 919-735-8211
Executive Director: CHARLES R. FULLWOOD
Chief of Division of Administrative Services: CECILIA F. EDGAR; Phone: 919-733-3391
Chief of Division of Conservation Education: A. SIDNEY BAYNES; Phone: 919-733-7123
Chief of Division of Enforcement: COL. ROGER W. LeQUIRE; Phone: 919-733-7191
Chief of Division of Inland Fisheries: FRED HARRIS; Phone: 919-733-3633
Chief of Division of Wildlife Management: DAVID T. COBB; Phone: 919-733-7291
Division of Engineering Services: GORDON MYERS; Phone: 919-715-3155
Head of Personnel Section: CAROL A. BATKER; Phone: 919-733-2241
Publications Coordinator and Editor: LARRY S. EARLEY; Phone: 919-733-7123
Publication(s): *Wildlife in North Carolina*
Keyword(s): Fisheries, Hunting, Nongame Wildlife, Wildlife and Wildlife Habitat, Wildlife Management

NORTH DAKOTA

GOVERNOR OF NORTH DAKOTA: EDWARD T. SCHAFER
State Capitol, 600 E. Blvd. Ave., Bismarck, ND 58505-0001
Phone: 701-328-2200

INSTITUTE FOR ECOLOGICAL STUDIES
P.O. Box 7110, University of North Dakota, Grand Forks, ND 58202
Phone: 701-777-2851
Founded: 1965
Description: A nonprofit university research center devoted to ecology, policy analysis and environmental biology. A interdisciplinary staff composed of university faculty, biologists, and associates conducts basic and applied research centering in the

STATE AND PROVINCIAL GOVERNMENT AGENCIES - NORTH DAKOTA

upper Midwest, and provides technical services for government, corporate agencies and the public.
Contact(s):
Interim Director: RICHARD CRAWFORD
Publication(s): *Contributions; research reports*
Keyword(s): Biodiversity, Endangered and Threatened Species, Environmental and Conservation Education, Wetlands, Wildlife and Wildlife Habitat

NORTH DAKOTA DEPARTMENT OF AGRICULTURE
600 E. Blvd. Ave., Department 602, Bismarck, ND 58505-0020
Web site: www.state.nd.us/agr
Description: The North Dakota Department of Agriculture is the regulating and licensing agency for the agricultural industry in North Dakota.
Contact(s):
Commissioner: ROGER JOHNSON; Phone: 701-328-2231; Fax: 701-328-4567; E-mail: rojohnso@state.nd.us

NORTH DAKOTA DEPARTMEL OF HEALTH
600 East Blvd. Ave., Bismarck, ND 58505-0200
Description: State pollution control programs.
Contact(s):
Chief Environmental Health Section: FRANCIS SCHWINDT, P.O. Box 5520, Bismarck, ND 58506-5520; Phone: 701-328-5150; Fax: 701-328-5200
Director of Division of Environmental Engineering: DANA K. MOUNT, P.O. Box 5520, Bismarck, ND 58506-5520; Phone: 701-328-5188; Fax: 701-328-5200
Director of Division of Municipal Facilities: JACK LONG, P.O. Box 5520, Bismarck, ND 58506-5520; Phone: 701-328-5211; Fax: 701-328-5200
Director of Division of Waste Management: NEIL KNATTERUD, P.O. Box 5520, Bismarck, ND 58506-5520; Phone: 701-328-5166; Fax: 701-328-5200
Director of Division of Water Quality: DENNIS FEWLESS, P.O. Box 5520, Bismarck, ND 58506-5520; Phone: 701-328-5210; Fax: 701-328-5200
State Health Officer: MURRAY SAGSVEEN; Phone: 701-328-2372; Fax: 701-328-4727
Keyword(s): Air Quality and Pollution, Environmental Justice, Public Health Protection, Solid Waste Management, Water Quality

NORTH DAKOTA GAME AND FISH DEPARTMENT
100 N. Bismarck Expressway, Bismarck, ND 58501
Phone: 701-328-6300; Fax: 701-328-6352
Contact(s):
Deputy Director: ROGER ROSTVET
Director: DEAN C. HILDEBRAND
Chief of Administrative Services: PAUL SCHADEWALD
Chief of Enforcement: RAY GOETZ
Chief of Fisheries: TERRY STEINWAND
Chief of Information and Education: TED UPGREN
Chief of Natural Resources: MIKE McKENNA
Chief of Wildlife: RANDY KREIL
Editor: HAROLD UMBER
Publication(s): *North Dakota Outdoors*
Keyword(s): Environmental and Conservation Education, Hunting, Nongame Wildlife, Sport Fishing, Wildlife Management

NORTH DAKOTA GEOLOGICAL SURVEY
600 E. Blvd., Bismarck, ND 58505-0840
Phone: 701-328-8000
Founded: 1895
Description: Responsible for collecting and disseminating geologic information.
Contact(s):
State Geologist: JOHN P. BLUEMLE
Publication(s): *NDGS Newsletter*
Keyword(s): Energy, Environmental Preservation, Geology, Land Use Planning, Water Pollution

NORTH DAKOTA PARKS AND RECREATION DEPARTMENT
1835 Bismarck Expressway, Bismarck, ND 58504

Phone: 701-328-5357
Founded: 1993
Description: Plan and coordinate government programs encouraging the full development and preservation of existing and future parks, outdoor recreation areas, nature preserves, rare plant and animal species, and unique natural communities.
Contact(s):
Director: DOUG PRCHAL
Coordinator of Nature Preserve/Natural Heritage Programs: KATHY DUTTENHEFNER
Coordinator of Planning and Natural Resources: JESSE HANSON
Publication(s): *Discover Newspaper*
Keyword(s): Biodiversity, Environmental Preservation, Historic Preservation, Land Preservation, Nature Preservation

NORTH DAKOTA STATE EXTENSION SERVICE
North Dakota State University, Box 5437, Fargo, ND 58105-5437
Phone: 701-231-7173; Fax: 701-231-8520; Web site: www.ext.nodak.edu/
Contact(s):
Director, Extension Service: DR. SHARON ANDERSON; E-mail: ext-dir@ndsuext.nodak.edu
Director, North Dakota Agricultural Experiment Station: DR. COLE GUSTAFSON, NDSU, Box 5655, Fargo, ND 58105-5655; Phone: 701-231-7655; Fax: 701-231-8520; E-mail: exp-dir@ndsuext.nodak.edu
Natural Resource Information: KEVIN K. SEDIVEC, NDSU, P.O. Box 5053, Fargo, ND 58105; Phone: 701-652-2951

NORTH DAKOTA STATE FOREST SERVICE
307 First St. E., Bottineau, ND 58318-1100
Phone: 701-228-5422
Founded: 1891
Description: Mission Statement: Caring for, protecting, and improving forest resources for future generations.
Contact(s):
Centennial Trees Coordinator: THOMAS CLAEYS; Phone: 701-228-5486; Fax: 701-228-5448
Community Forestry Coordinator: W. L. JACKSON BIRD, 1511 E. Interstate Ave., Bismarck, ND 58501; Phone: 701-328-9945; Fax: 701-250-4454
Fire Management Coordinator: MAURE SAND, 1511 E. Interstate Ave., Bismarck, ND 58501; Phone: 701-328-9946; Fax: 701-250-4454
Information and Education Coordinator: GLENDA FAUSKE; Phone: 701-228-5446
Staff Forester: THOMAS BERG; Phone: 701-228-5483
State Forester: LARRY KOTCHMAN; Phone: 701-228-5422
Towner Nursery Manager: ROY LAFRAMBOISE, 878 Nursery Rd., Towner, ND 58788; Phone: 701-537-5636; Fax: 701-537-5680
Publication(s): *Prairie Forester, The*
Keyword(s): Environmental and Conservation Education, Flowers, Plants, and Trees, Forests and Forestry, Public Lands, Urban Forestry

NORTH DAKOTA STATE SOIL CONSERVATION COMMITTEE
4023 North State St., Suite 30, Bismarck, ND 58501-0620
Phone: 701-328-3725; Fax: 701-328-5123
Founded: 1937
Description: To organize soil conservation districts and provide for control and prevention of soil erosion; represent the state in soil conservation matters; accept P.L. 566 Small Watershed applications and, assign planning priority; and administer the Surface Mining Reports Law; and soil conservation technician grants program.
Contact(s):
Chairperson: MARVIN HALVERSON
Soil Conservation Coordinator: SCOTT HOCHHALTER; E-mail: shochhal@ndsuext.nodak.edu
Keyword(s): Agriculture, Environmental and Conservation Education, Pesticides, Soil Conservation, Wetlands

NORTH DAKOTA WATER COMMISSION
900 E. Blvd., Bismarck, ND 58505-0850

Phone: 701-328-2750; Fax: 701-328-3696
Contact(s):
Secretary and State Engineer: DAVID A. SPRYNCZYNATYK

OHIO

GOVERNOR OF OHIO: ROBERT TAFT
State House, 77 S. High St., 30th Fl., Columbus, OH 43266
Phone: 614-466-3555

ENVIRONMENTAL REVIEW APPEALS COMMISSION
236 E. Town St., Rm. 300, Columbus, OH 43215
Phone: 614-466-8950
Description: The Environmental Review Appeals Commission is an administrative commission designed to review the actions of the Ohio EPA, State Fire Marshal, and the various county boards of health charged with environmental jurisdiction in order to determine that the agencies' actions have been reasonable and lawful.
Contact(s):
Chairman: TONI E. MULRANE
Vice Chairman: JULIANNA F. BULL
Member: MARIA J. ARMSTRONG
Executive Secretary: MARY J. OXLEY

OHIO DEPARTMENT OF AGRICULTURE
8995 E. Main Street, Reynoldsburg, OH 43068
Phone: 614-466-2732
Contact(s):
Director: FRED L. DAILEY
Communication Director: MARK ANTHONY; Phone: 614-752-4505

OHIO DEPARTMENT OF NATURAL RESOURCES
Fountain Square, Columbus, OH 43224
Phone: 614-265-6565
Founded: 1949
Description: The mission of the Ohio Department of Natural Resources is to provide for the preservation, conservation, utilization and enjoyment of our natural resources through the wise management, careful planning, efficient and effective delivery of services, and the collection and dissemination of data and information needed for environmental protection and natural resource management decisions. We recognize that these actions impact the social, recreational, and economic well-being of our citizens and that education is the key to the realization of an environmental ethic and the preservation of our natural and cultural heritage.
Contact(s):
Director: SAMUEL W. SPECK; Phone: 614-265-6875
Assistant Director: J. WILLIAM MOODY; Phone: 614-265-6877
Deputy Director: LORI WATIKER; Phone: 614-265-6845
Deputy Director: RON KOLBASH; Phone: 614-265-6875
Deputy Director: SCOTT ZODY; Phone: 614-265-6845
Acting Chief of Division of Engineering: JOEL REED; Phone: 614-265-6948
Chief of Division of Civilian Conservation: SALLY PROUTY; Phone: 614-265-6423
Chief of Division of Forestry: RONALD ABRAHAM; Phone: 614-265-6694
Chief of Division of Geological Survey: THOMAS BERG; Phone: 614-265-6576
Chief of Division of Mines and Reclamation (Acting): RUSS SCHOLL; Phone: 614-265-6633
Chief of Division of Natural Areas and Preserves (Acting): STUART LEWIS; Phone: 614-265-6453
Chief of Division of Oil and Gas: TOM TUGNED; Phone: 614-265-6917
Chief of Division of Parks and Recreation: DAN WEST; Phone: 614-265-6561
Chief of Division of Real Estate and Land Management: WAYNE WARREN; Phone: 614-265-6395
Chief of Division of Soil and Water Conservation: LAWRENCE VANCE; Phone: 614-265-6610; Fax: 614-262-2064; E-mail: larry.vance@dnr.ohio.gov.us
Chief of Division of Water: JIM MORRIS; Phone: 614-265-6717
Chief of Division of Watercraft: JEFF HOEDT; Phone: 614-265-6480
Chief of Division of Wildlife: MICHAEL BUDZIK; Phone: 614-265-6300
Chief of Office of Human Resources: PETER KING; Phone: 614-265-6859
Chief of Office of Marketing Services: NANCY MANACKE; Phone: 614-265-6787
Chief of Office of Recycling and Litter Prevention: MICHAEL CANFIELD; Phone: 614-265-6333
Keyword(s): Forests and Forestry, Outdoor Recreation, Soil Conservation, Water Resources, Wildlife Management

OHIO ENVIRONMENTAL PROTECTION AGENCY
Lazarus Government Center, 122 S. Front St., P.O. Box 1049, Columbus, OH 43216-1049
Phone: 614-644-3020
Founded: 1972
Description: State regulatory agency with jurisdiction covering air, waste water, drinking water, hazardous waste, and land pollution control; maintains central office in Columbus and has five district offices.
Contact(s):
Director: CHRISTOPHER JONES; Phone: 614-644-2782
Assistant Director: JENNIFER TIELL; Phone: 614-644-2782
Deputy Director of Administration: JOHN CHILDS; Phone: 614-644-2339
Deputy Director of Legal Affairs: JOSEPH KONCELIK; Phone: 614-644-2782
Deputy Director of Policy: PATRICIA MADIGAN; Phone: 614-644-2782
Chief of Division of Air Pollution Control: ROBERT HODANBOSI; Phone: 614-644-2270
Chief of Division of Drinking and Ground Waters: MICHAEL BAKER; Phone: 614-644-2752
Chief of Division of Emergency and Remedial Response: CINDY HAFNER; Phone: 614-644-2924
Chief of Division of Environmental and Financial Assistance: GREG SMITH; Phone: 614-644-2798
Chief of Division of Environmental Services: GERRY IOANNIDES; Phone: 614-644-4231
Chief of Division of Hazardous Waste Management: MICHAEL SAVAGE; Phone: 614-644-2917
Chief of Division of Solid and Infectious Waste: BARBARA BRDICKA; Phone: 614-644-2621
Chief of Division of Surface Water: LISA MORRIS; Phone: 614-644-2001
Chief of Office of Environmental Education: CAROLYN WATKINS; Phone: 614-644-2873
Chief of Office of Pollution Prevention: MIKE KELLEY; Phone: 614-644-3467
Chief of Public Interest Center: CAROL HESTER; Phone: 614-644-2166
Keyword(s): Air Quality and Pollution, Environmental and Conservation Education, Solid Waste, Water Pollution, Wetlands

OHIO OFFICE OF ENERGY EFFICIENCY
77 S. High St., 26th Fl., Columbus, OH 43215
Phone: 614-466-6797; Fax: 614-466-1864; E-mail: sward@odod.state.oh.us; Web site: www.odod.ohio.gov/cdd/oee
Founded: 1979
Description: The Office of Energy Efficiency, Ohio's state energy office, develops policies and programs that use energy efficiency and renewable energy to enhance economic benefits and better Ohio's environment.
Contact(s):
Chief: SARA WARD; E-mail: sward@odod.state.oh.us
Assistant Chief: DAWN SMITH; E-mail: dsmith@odod.state.oh.us

Residential Programs: TIM LENAHAN; Phone: 614-466-8434; E-mail: tlenahan@odod.state.oh.us
Commercial/Industrial Programs: BILL MANZ; Phone: 614-466-7429; E-mail: wmanz@odod.state.oh.us
Education Programs: STJEPAN VLAHOVICH; Phone: 614-466-0545; E-mail: svlahovich@odod.state.oh.us
Publication(s): *Ohio's Home Weatherization Assistance Program: An Independent Evaluation; Ohio's Home Weatherization Assistance Program (brochure); 1999 Energy Efficiency Bookmark Contest Winners*
Keyword(s): Air Quality, Consumer Services, Energy, Energy Conservation, Green Building, Healthy Home, Renewable Resources, Solar Energy, Sustainable Energy, Transportation, Energy Efficiency

OHIO SEA GRANT COLLEGE PROGRAM
1314 Kinnear Rd., Rm. 1541, Columbus, OH 43212-1194
Phone: 614-292-8949; Fax: 614-292-4364; Web site:www.sg.ohio-state.edu/
Description: The Ohio Sea Grant College Program is dedicated to the goal of promoting the understanding and management, development, utilization, and conservation of ocean, coastal, and Great Lakes resources, specifically Lake Erie, through research, education, outreach, and communications. The program is administrated by Ohio State University. Stone Laboratory is Ohio's biological field station located on Gibraltar Island at Put-in-Bay, Ohio.
Contact(s):
Director: DR. JEFFREY M. REUTTER; E-mail: reutter.1@osu.edu
Assistant Director and Communications Coordinator: KAREN T. RICKER; E-mail: ricker.15@osu.edu
Publication(s): *Twine Line (bi-monthly newsletter)*
Keyword(s): Aquatic Habitats, Aquatic Species, Environmental and Conservation Education, Fisheries, Lakes, Research, Toxicology, Water Pollution

OHIO STATE EXTENSION SERVICES
Ohio State University Extension, 2 Agricultural Administration Bldg., 2120 Fyffe Rd., Columbus, OH 43210
Phone: 614-292-4067; Fax: 614-688-3807; E-mail: smith.150@osu.edu; Web site: www.ag.ohio-state.edu/
Description: To help people improve their lives through an educational process using scientific knowledge focused on identified issues and needs.
Contact(s):
Director: KEITH SMITH; E-mail: smith.150@osu.edu
Director of School of Natural Resources: GARY MULLINS, Ohio State University, 210 Kottman Hall, 2021 Coffey Rd., Columbus, OH 43210; Phone: 614-292-2265; Fax: 614-292-7432; E-mail: mullins.2@osu.edu
Associate Director of Environmental Education: DR. ROBERT ROTH, School of Natural Resources, 207 Kottman Hall, 2021 Coffey Rd., Columbus, OH 43210; Phone: 614-292-2265; Fax: 614-292-7432; E-mail: Roth.3@osu.edu
Extension Specialist of Natural Resources: ERIK NORLAND, School of Natural Resources, 2021 Coffey Rd., Columbus, OH 43210; Phone: 614-292-6544; Fax: 614-292-7432; E-mail: norland.1@osu.edu

OKLAHOMA

GOVERNOR OF OKLAHOMA: FRANK KEATING
State Capitol Bldg., Suite 212, Oklahoma City, OK 73105
Phone: 405-521-2342

DEPARTMENT OF WILDLIFE CONSERVATION
1801 N. Lincoln, P.O. Box 53465, Oklahoma City, OK 73152
Phone: 405-521-3851; Fax: 405-521-6535
Founded: 1909
Contact(s):
Director: GREG D. DUFFY; Phone: 405-521-4660
Chief of Fisheries: KIM ERICKSON; Phone: 405-521-3721
Chief of Game: RICHARD HATCHER; Phone: 405-521-2739
Chief of Information-Education: DAVID WARREN; Phone: 405-521-3855
Chief of Law Enforcement: JOHN STREICH; Phone: 405-521-3719
Commission Chairman: WM. H. CRAWFORD
Commission Vice Chairman: HARLAND STONECIPHER
Commissioner Secretary: MARK PATTON
Editor: NELS RODEFELD; Phone: 405-521-4635
Employee Services and Communications Staff: HANK STOKES; Phone: 405-232-1569
Employee Services Property Staff: KEN RYEL; Phone: 405-521-4600
Fiscal Services Coordinator: ROBERT TAYLOR; Phone: 405-521-4665
Human Resources Staff: MELINDA STURGESS; Phone: 405-521-4640
Natural Resources Section Staff: RON SUTTLES; Phone: 405-521-4616
Publication(s): *Outdoor Oklahoma*
Keyword(s): Aquatic Habitats, Endangered and Threatened Species, Environmental and Conservation Education, Hunting, Sport Fishing

OKLAHOMA BIOLOGICAL SURVEY
111 E. Chesapeake St., University of Oklahoma, Norman, OK 73019
Phone: 405-325-4034; Fax: 405-325-7702
Founded: 1927
Description: State office and organized research unit of university. Acquires information on biological resources and natural areas, conducts research on natural biota, jointly maintains Bebb Herbarium, has responsibility for Oklahoma Natural Heritage Inventory, and provides training for students. Jointly operates Oklahoma Fishery Research Laboratory with Oklahoma Department of Wildlife Conservation.
Contact(s):
Director: CARYN C. VAUGHN; Phone: 405-325-4034; E-mail: cvaughn@ou.edu
Coordinator of Oklahoma Natural Heritage Inventory: BRUCE HOAGLAND; Phone: 405-325-1985; E-mail: bhoagland@ou.edu
Curator of Bebb Herbarium: MIA MOLVRAY; Phone: 405-325-6443; E-mail: mmolvray@ou.edu
Executive Director of Sutton Avian Research Center: STEVE K. SHERROD; Phone: 918-336-7778; E-mail: gmsarc@aol.com
Keyword(s): Biodiversity, Biology, Botany, Conservation of Protected Areas, Ecology, Endangered and Threatened Species, Flowers, Plants, and Trees, Geographic Information Systems, Nongame Wildlife, Wildlife and Wildlife Habitat, Zoology

OKLAHOMA COOPERATIVE FISH AND WILDLIFE RESEARCH UNIT (USDI)
404 Life Sciences West Bldg., Oklahoma State University, Stillwater, OK 74078-3051
Phone: 405-744-6342
Contact(s):
Leader: DAVID M. LESLIE JR.
Assistant Leader (Ecology): WILLIAM L. FISHER
Assistant Leader (Fisheries): DANA L. WINKLEMAN
Keyword(s): Endangered and Threatened Species, Fisheries, Nongame Wildlife, Research, Wildlife and Wildlife Habitat

OKLAHOMA DEPARTMENT OF ENVIRONMENTAL QUALITY
1000 NE 10th St., Oklahoma City, OK 73117-1212
Phone: 405-271-8056
Description: The Department of Environmental Quality is dedicated to providing quality service to the people of Oklahoma through comprehensive environmental protection and management programs. Those programs are designed to assist the people of the state in sustaining a clean sound environment and in preserving and enhancing our natural surroundings.
Contact(s):
Executive Director: MARK S. COLEMAN; Phone: 405-271-8056

Deputy Executive Director: STEVEN A. THOMPSON; Phone: 405-271-8056
Director of Air Quality: LARRY BYRUM; Phone: 405-271-5220
Director of Complaints and Local Services: LARRY McKEE; Phone: 405-271-7363
Director of Customer Services: JUDY DUNCAN; Phone: 405-271-1400
Director of Public Information and Education: ELLEN BUSSERT; Phone: 405-271-8056
Director of Support Services: LAWRENCE A. GALES; Phone: 405-271-8062
Director of Waste Management: H.A. Caves; Phone: 405-271-5338
Director of Water Quality: JON CRAIG; Phone: 405-271-5205
General Counsel: BOB KELLOGG; Phone: 405-271-8056
Publication(s): *Clear View; Certified Operator News Letter (Waterworks and Wastewater); Superfund program Sites Status Report; Air Quality Annual Report*
Keyword(s): Air Quality and Pollution, Environmental Protection, Pollution Prevention, Solid Waste Management, Water Quality

OKLAHOMA GEOLOGICAL SURVEY
University of Oklahoma, Sarkeys Energy Center, 100 E. Boyd, Rm. N-131, Norman, OK 73019-0628
Phone: 405-325-3031; Web site: www.ou.edu/special/ogs-pttc
Founded: 1908
Description: To investigate and disseminate information on the geology of the state, with special reference to mineral resources and environmental issues. Investigations include: geologic mapping, evaluation of metallic and nonmetallic mineral deposits, and studies of earthquakes, groundwater, and fossil fuels, plus basic research and environmental studies.
Contact(s):
Director: CHARLES J. MANKIN
Associate Director: KENNETH S. JOHNSON
Librarian: CLAREN KIDD, 100 E. Boyd, Rm. 220, Norman, OK 73019-0628
Promotion and Information Specialist: CONNIE G. SMITH
Publication(s): *Oklahoma Geology Notes; bulletins, circulars, guidebooks, geologic map series, educational publications series, hydrologic atlases, special publications.*
Keyword(s): Energy, Environment, Geology, Land Use Planning, Mapping, Water Resources

OKLAHOMA STATE BOARD OF AGRICULTURE
2800 N. Lincoln Blvd., Oklahoma City, OK 73105
Phone: 405-521-3864
Description: The Oklahoma Department of Agriculture is principally a service agency, but it is also a promotional and cooperative agency for segments of agriculture and forestry. Major divisions of the department are forestry, animal industry, legal, plant industry, marketing, water quality, agriculture laboratory, and the federal-state cooperative programs of wildlife services and agricultural statistics.
Contact(s):
Deputy Commissioner: DR. CHARLES FREEMAN; Phone: 405-521-3864/Ext.202
Assistant Commissioner: COY MORSE
Secretary of Agriculture: DENNIS HOWARD
Administration Staff: DAVID LIGON; Phone: 405-521-3864/Ext.220
Director of Agricultural Laboratory: SUE CANNON; Phone: 405-521-3864
Director of Agricultural Statistics: BARRY BLOYD; Phone: 405-525-9226
Director of Animal Industry Services: DR. BURKE HEALEY; Phone: 405-521-3864
Director of Forestry Services: ROGER L. DAVIS; Phone: 405-521-3864
Director of Legal Services: DR MARK NEWMAN; Phone: 403-521-3864 Ext. 344
Director of Market Development 414 Services: RICK MALONEY
Director of Wildlife Services: JOHN E. STEUBER; Phone: 405-521-4039
Information Officer: JACK CARSON; Phone: 405-521-3864/Ext.414
Keyword(s): Agriculture, Environmental Law, Forests and Forestry, Pesticides, Urban Environment

OKLAHOMA STATE CONSERVATION COMMISSION
2800 N. Lincoln Blvd., Suite 160, Oklahoma City, OK 73105
Phone: 405-521-2384; Fax: 405-521-6686; Web site: www.state.ok.us/-conscom
Founded: 1938
Description: To assist and supervise conservation districts in carrying out conservation practices of all renewable natural resources.
Contact(s):
Chairman: ALLEN MOFFAT
Executive Director: MIKE THRALLS
Assistant Director: BEN POLLARD
Director of Abandoned Mine Land Reclamation Program: MIKE KASTL
District Operations Director: DR. DAN A. SEBERT
Information Officer: MARK HARRISON
Interim Director of Water Quality Program: JIM LEACH
Publication(s): *Conservation Conversation Newsletter; Geographic Information Systems Newsletter*
Keyword(s): Abandoned Mine Land Reclamation, Environmental and Conservation Education, Nonpoint Source Pollution, Soil Conservation, Upstream Flood Prevention

OKLAHOMA STATE EXTENSION SERVICES
Oklahoma State University, Rm. 139, Agricultural Hall, Stillwater, OK 74078
Phone: 405-744-5398; Fax: 405-744-5339; Web site: www.okstate.edu/OSU_Ag/oces/
Founded: 1946
Description: Extension Forestry and Wildlife are a unit of the Oklahoma Cooperative Extension Service and the Department of Forestry, Division of Agricultural Sciences and Natural Resources, Oklahoma State University. The Department of Forestry provides accredited education in forest resources management, conducts forestry research through the Oklahoma Agricultural Experiment Station, and brings forest resources education to the citizens of Oklahoma through its extension efforts.
Contact(s):
Director of Cooperative Extension Service: DR. SAM E. CURL
Interim Associate Director of Cooperative Extension Service: DR. D. C. COSTON, Oklahoma State University, Rm. 139, Agricultural Hall, Stillwater, OK 74078; Phone: 405-744-5398
Interim Department Head of Forestry: DR. CHARLES TAVER, Oklahoma State University, Rm. 012, Agricultural Hall, Stillwater, OK 74078; Phone: 405-744-5437/Ext.5284
Assistant Extension Forester and Wildlife Specialist: KENNETH HITCH, Oklahoma State University, Rm. 242, Agricultural Hall, Stillwater, OK 74078; Phone: 405-744-5445
Extension Wildlife Specialist: DR. RONALD MASTERS, Oklahoma State University, Rm. 240, Agricultural Hall, Stillwater, OK 74078; Phone: 405-744-6432/Ext.8065; Fax: 405-744-9693
Publication(s): *Oklahoma Renewable Resources newsletter; Oklahoma Forest Industry bulletin; Natural Resources Speakers Bureau*
Keyword(s): Endangered and Threatened Species, Environmental and Conservation Education, Forests and Forestry, Urban Forestry, Wildlife Management

OKLAHOMA TOURISM AND RECREATION DEPARTMENT
P.O. Box 52002, Capitol Post Office, Oklahoma City, OK 73105-4492
Phone: 405-521-2409
Founded: 1972
Description: To encourage residents and travelers to "Native America" as a vacation destination; and to develop human and natural resources for the purpose of promoting tourism, recreation, wildlife preservation, and environmental conservation. An annual industry conference is held each fall.
Contact(s):
Chief of Operations: DOUG ENEVOLDSEN; Phone: 405-521-4678

STATE AND PROVINCIAL GOVERNMENT AGENCIES - OREGON

Director of Lodges: TOM RICH; Phone: 405-521-3793
Cabinet Secretary and Executive Director: JAYNE JAYROE; Phone: 405-521-2413
Director of State Parks: JOHN RESSMEYER; Phone: 405-521-4291
Division of Administration: DEBBIE SHARP; Phone: 405-521-2471
Division of Human Resources: AMOS MOSES; Phone: 405-522-4523
Division of Planning and Development: KRISTINA S. MAREK; Phone: 405-521-2973
Division of Travel and Tourism: KATHLEEN MARKS; Phone: 405-521-3981
Publisher: JOAN HENDERSON; Phone: 405-521-2496
Publication(s): *Oklahoma Today; Oklahoma Vacation*
Keyword(s): Nature Preservation, Nongame Wildlife, Outdoor Recreation, Public Lands

OKLAHOMA WATER RESOURCES BOARD
3800 N. Classen Blvd., Oklahoma City, OK 73118
Phone: 405-530-8800; Fax: 405-530-8900
Founded: 1957
Description: Promulgates water quality standards for state; lead agency in Clean Lakes Program; investigates pollution complaints; assesses water quality, quantity of groundwater, and stream water; issues permits for water use; administers dam safety, floodplain management programs, and plans for adequate supplies of good quality water for all beneficial uses; updates plans; administers financial assistance programs for water and wastewater systems.
Contact(s):
Chairman: J. ROSS KIRTLEY
Executive Director: DUANE A. SMITH
Assistant to the Director: MICHAEL R. MELTON
Librarian: SUSAN BIRCHFIELD
Publication(s): *Oklahoma Water News*
Keyword(s): Environmental and Conservation Education, Lakes, Rivers, Water Quality, Water Resources

OREGON

GOVERNOR OF OREGON: JOHN A. KITZHABER
254 State Capitol, Salem, OR 97310
Phone: 503-378-3111

DEPARTMENT OF FISH AND WILDLIFE (OREGON)
2501 SW 1st Ave., Portland, OR 97207
Phone: 503-872-5310
Founded: 1975
Description: Responsibilities include management of fish and wildlife resources and regulation of commercial and recreational harvest.
Contact(s):
Director: JIM GREER; Phone: 503-872-5272
Deputy Director: STEVE WILLIAMS; Phone: 503-872-5272
Editor: PAT WRAY; Phone: 541-757-4206
Fish Division Director: DOUG DEHART; Phone: 503-872-5252
Habitat Division Director: KAY BROWN; Phone: 503-872-5255
Head of Realty: WAYNE RAWLINS; Phone: 503-872-5310
Head of Statistical Services: DALE CHRISTENSEN; Phone: 503-872-5267
Human Resources Division Director: CAROL BROWN; Phone: 503-872-5262
Information and Education Division Director: LISA DeBRUYCKERE; Phone: 503-872-5264
Wildlife Division Director: RICHARD BERRY; Phone: 503-872-5260
High Desert Region Director: CHIP DALE; Phone: 541-388-6363
NE Region Director: CRAIG ELY; Phone: 541-963-2138
NW Region Director: CHRIS WHEATON; Phone: 503-657-2000
SW Region Director: BOB MULLEN; Phone: 541-440-3353
Publication(s): *Oregon Wildlife*

DEPARTMENT OF GEOLOGY AND MINERAL INDUSTRIES
800 NE Oregon St., Suite 965, #28, Portland, OR 97232-2162
Phone: 503-731-4100

Contact(s):
Librarian: KLAUS NEVENDORF, 800 NE Oregon St., Suite 965, #28, Portland, OR 97232-2162
State Geologist: DONALD A. HULL
Publication(s): *List available on request from Nature of the Northwest Information Center, Suite 177, 800 NE Oregon St., #5, Portland, OR 97232-2162 503-872-2750, Fax: 503-731-4066*

DEPARTMENT OF TRANSPORTATION (OREGON)
Mgr. Of Env., 1158 Chemeketa St., NE, Salem, OR 97310
Contact(s):
Manager of Environmental Services Section: EB ENGELMANN, Oregon Department of Transportation, 1158 Chemeketa St., NE, Salem, OR 97310; Phone: 503-986-3477
Keyword(s): Engineering, Environment, Environmental Planning, Research, Transportation

OREGON COOPERATIVE FISH AND WILDLIFE RESEARCH UNIT (USDI)
Department of Fisheries and Wildlife, Oregon State University, Corvallis, OR 97331-3803
Phone: 503-737-4531
Description: Research focus on physiological, ecological, and genetic factors affecting production and performance of freshwater fishes. The staff consists of two permanent and two-three other Ph.D., level scientists, as well as graduate students and technicians.
Contact(s):
Assistant Leader: DR. HIRAM W. LI
Leader: DR. CARL B. SCHRECK
Keyword(s): Aquatic Habitats, Biodiversity, Environmental and Conservation Education, Fisheries, Wildlife Disease, Genetics Physiology

OREGON COOPERATIVE FISH AND WILDLIFE RESEARCH UNIT (USDI)
104 Nash Hall, Oregon State University, Corvallis, OR 97331
Phone: 541-737-1938
Contact(s):
Wildlife Assistant Leader: DR. DANIEL D. ROBY
Wildlife Leader: DR. ROBERT G. ANTHONY
Keyword(s): Endangered and Threatened Species, Nongame Wildlife, Raptors, Wildlife and Wildlife Habitat, Wildlife Management, Environmental Contaminants

OREGON DEPARTMENT OF AGRICULTURE
Natural Resources Division, 635 Capitol St., NE, Salem, OR 97310-0110
Founded: 1939 (Department of Agriculture), 1989 (Natural Resources Division)
Description: Supervises the organization and operation of soil and water conservation districts, approves or disapproves all projects, practices, personnel, budgets, contracts, and regulations of Oregon's 45 districts. State administrative agency for nonpoint source water quality programs dealing with agricultural lands. Also responsible for managing the state's field burning weather monitoring program, the native plant species conservation program and the weather modification program.
Contact(s):
Administrator: JOHN MELLOTT; Phone: 503-378-3810; E-mail: jmellott@oda.state.or.us
Advisory Member: ANDREW HASHIMOTO, Department of Agriculture Engineering, Oregon State University, Corvallis, OR 97331-2213; Phone: 503-737-2041
Advisory Member: JACK SAINSBURY, ASCS, 1220 SW 3rd. Ave., 15th Fl., Portland, OR 97204-2880; Phone: 503-326-2741
Advisory Member: BOB GRAHAM, SCS, 1220 SW 3rd Ave., 16th Fl., Portland, OR 97204-2881; Phone: 503-326-2751
Advisory Member: RAY LEDGERWOOD, NACD, NE 1615 Eastgate Blvd., Suite B, Pullman, WA 509-334-1823
Assistant Administrator: CHARLES CRAIG; Phone: 503-378-3810
Soil and Water Conservation Commission Chairman: THOMAS STRAUGHAN, 1421 SW 45th Dr., Pendleton, OR 97801; Phone: 503-278-0218; E-mail: tstraugh@orednet.org

Soil and Water Conservation Commissioner Vice Chairman: JOE BRUMBACH, 4260 Buckhorn Rd., Roseburg, OR 97470; Phone: 503-673-3998
Publication(s): *Oregon Natural Resources Conservation News*

OREGON DEPARTMENT OF ENVIRONMENTAL QUALITY (DEQ)
811 SW 6th Ave., Portland, OR 97204
Phone: 503-229-5696
Founded: 1969
Description: Our mission is to be an active leader in restoring, maintaining, and enhancing the quality of Oregon's air, water, and land.
Contact(s):
Director: LANGDON MARSH; Phone: 503-229-5300
Eastern Region Administrator: STEPHANIE HALLOCK; Phone: 541-338-6146
Laboratory Administrator: RICK GATES; Phone: 503-229-5983
Northwest Region Administrator: NEIL MULLANE; Phone: 503-229-5372
Waste Management Cleanup Administrator: MARY WAHL; Phone: 503-229-5072
Water Quality Administrator: MICHAEL LLEWELYN; Phone: 503-229-5324
Western Region Administrator: STEVE GREENWOOD; Phone: 541-686-7838
Publication(s): *Recycling Newsletter; Beyond Waste; Tankline*
Keyword(s): Air Quality and Pollution, Environmental and Conservation Education, Environmental Cleanup, Solid Waste Management, Water Pollution Management

OREGON DEPARTMENT OF FORESTRY
2600 State St., Salem, OR 97310-1336
Phone: 503-945-7200; Fax: 503-945-7212
Founded: 1911
Description: The department is responsible for fire protection of 15.8 million acres of private and public forests; directs insect and disease management on 11 million acres of state and private forests; manages 789,000 acres of state-owned forests; provides forestry assistance to private forest landowners; enforces other Oregon forest laws; provides forestry information to schools, organizations, and individuals; and advises Governor and State Legislature on forestry matters.
Contact(s):
Assistant State Forester of Administrative Services: CLARK SEELY; Phone: 503-945-7203
Assistant State Forester of Forest Management: RAY CRAIG; Phone: 503-945-7204
Assistant State Forester of Forest Protection: CHARLIE STONE; Phone: 503-945-7205
Assistant State Forester of Resource Policy: ANN HANUS; Phone: 503-945-7206
Deputy State Forester: J. MICHAEL BEYERLE; Phone: 503-945-7202
Director of Fire Prevention: RICK GIBSON; Phone: 503-945-7440
Director of Fire Protection: LANNY QUACKENBUSH; Phone: 503-945-7435
Director of Forestry Assistance: WALLACE RUTLEDGE; Phone: 503-945-7392
Director of Public Affairs: CARY GREENWOOD; Phone: 503-945-7420
Director of State Forest Management: MIKE BORDELON; Phone: 503-945-7348
Eastern Oregon Area Director: CLIFF LIEDTKE, 3501 E 3rd St., Prineville, OR 97754; Phone: 541-447-5658; Fax: 541-447-1469
Northwest Oregon Area Director: ROY WOO, 801 Gales Creek Rd., Forest Grove, OR 97117-1199; Phone: 503-357-2191; Fax: 503-357-4548
Southern Oregon Area Director: DAN SHULTS, 1758 NE Airport Rd., Roseburg, OR 97470-1499; Phone: 541-440-3412; Fax: 541-440-3424
State Board of Forestry Member: DICK BALDWIN, 97 Constantine Pl., Eugene, OR 97405; Phone: 541-344-8519
State Board of Forestry Member: BRAD WITT, 2110 State St., Salem, OR 97301; Phone: 503-585-6320
State Board of Forestry Member: WAYNE KRIEGER, 95702 Skyview Ranch Rd., Gold Beach, OR 97444; Phone: 541-247-7990
State Board of Forestry Member: SAM JOHNSON, 1449 SW Davenport St., Portland, OR 97201; Phone: 503-223-4772
State Board of Forestry Member: JANET NEUMAN, 10015 SW Terwilliger Blvd., Portland, OR 97219; Phone: 503-768-6633
State Board of Forestry Member: HOWARD SOHN, Box 1137, Roseburg, OR 97470; Phone: 541-673-0141
State Board of Forestry Member Chair: DAVID E. GILBERT, P.O. Box 36, Joseph, OR 97846
State Forester: JAMES E. BROWN; Phone: 503-945-7211
Publication(s): *Forest Log, The*
Keyword(s): Endangered and Threatened Species, Fisheries, Forests and Forestry, Urban Forestry

OREGON FISH AND WILDLIFE DIVISION/DEPARTMENT OF STATE POLICE
400 Public Service Bldg., Salem, OR 97310
Phone: 503-378-3720; Fax: 503-363-5475
Description: The Fish and Wildlife Division is charged with the enforcement of fish and game, commercial fish, shellfish, environmental protection laws, and all endangered species laws, rules, and regulations. Also provides general law enforcement services in rural areas. Provides law enforcement services on contract with the Oregon Department of Fish and Wildlife, the Department of Environmental Quality, and the Department of Forestry. Enforcement priorities for fish and wildlife resources cooperatively identified with ODFW.
Contact(s):
Aircraft Supervisor: LT. J. E. HUNSAKER; Phone: 503-378-3720
C & D Director (Captain): LINDSAY A. BALL; Phone: 503-378-3720
District I Supervisor of Portland, OR: LT. K. L. ALLISON; Phone: 503-731-3027
District II Supervisor of Salem, OR: LT. S. R. LANE; Phone: 503-378-2110
District III Supervisor of Medford, OR: LT. S. P. ROSS; Phone: 503-776-6114
District IV Supervisor of Baker City, OR: LT. R. D. SCORBY; Phone: 503-523-5848
Special Investigations Unit Supervisor: SGT. W. D. MARKEE; Phone: 503-378-3387
Staff of Commercial Fisheries: SGT. D. M. CLEARY; Phone: 503-378-3720
Staff of Wildlife: LT. C. K. KOK; Phone: 503-378-3720
Keyword(s): Endangered and Threatened Species, Environmental Law, Fisheries, Hunting, Law Enforcement, Wildlife and Wildlife Habitat

OREGON PARKS AND RECREATION DEPARTMENT
1115 Commercial St., NE, Suite 1, Salem, OR 97301-1002
Phone: 503-378-6305
Founded: 1921
Description: To provide and protect outstanding natural, scenic, cultural, historic, and recreational sites for the enjoyment and education of present and future generations.
Contact(s):
Deputy Director: LAURIE WARNER
Director: BOB MEINEN; Phone: 503-378-5019
Keyword(s): Environmental and Conservation Education, Historic Preservation, Natural Areas, Ocean Conservation, Outdoor Recreation, Rivers

OREGON SEA GRANT PROGRAM
500 Kerr Administration Bldg., Oregon State University, Corvallis, OR 97331-2131
Phone: 541-737-2714; Fax: 503-737-2392; E-mail: sghelp@seagrant.orst.edu; Web site: seagrant.orst.edu/
Description: Oregon Sea Grant takes an integrated approach to addressing the problems and opportunities of Oregon's marine resources through three related primary activities--research,

education, and extension services. Oregon Sea Grant responds to the needs of ocean users.
Contact(s):
Program Director: ROBERT E. MALOUF; E-mail: maloufr@ccmail.orst.edu
Assistant Director for Programs: JAN AUYONG; E-mail: jan.auyong@orst.edu
Extension Program Leader: JAY RASMUSSEN, Hatfield Marine Science Center, 2030 S. Marine Science Dr., Newport, OR 97365; Phone: 541-867-0370; Fax: 541-867-0369; E-mail: jay.rasmussen@hmsc.orst.edu
Assistant Director for Communications: JOSEPH CONE, 402 Kerr Admin. Bldg. OSU, Corvallis, OR 97331-2134; Phone: 541-737-2716; Fax: 541-737-7958; E-mail: joe.cone@orst.edu
Publication(s): *Catalogue available upon request from Sea Grant Communications.*
Keyword(s): Biotechnology, Coasts, Communications, Fisheries, Oceanography

OREGON STATE EXTENSION SERVICES
Oregon State University, 101 Ballard Extension Hall, Corvallis, OR 97331-3604
Phone: 541-737-2713; Fax: 541-737-4423; Web site: www.osu.orst.edu/extension/
Contact(s):
Dean and Director: LYLA HOUGLUM; E-mail: lyla.houglum@orst.edu
Associate Director: PETER BLOOME; E-mail: peter.bloome@orst.edu
Regional Director: DEBORAH MADDY; Phone: 541-737-2711; E-mail: deborah.maddy@orst.edu
Regional Director: MICHAEL STOLTZ; Phone: 541-737-2711; E-mail: michael.stoltz@orst.edu
Extension Program Coordinator, Agriculture: DR. WILLIAM BRAUNWORTH, Stag Hall, Room 138, Oregon State University, Corvallis, OR 97331; Phone: 541-737-4251; Fax: 541-737-3178; E-mail: Bill.Braunworth@orst.edu
Program Leader, Forestry: A. SCOTT REED, 119 Peavy Hall, Oregon State University, Corvallis, OR 97331; Phone: 541-737-3700; Fax: 541-737-3008
Natural Resources Information: W. DANIEL EDGE, 104 Nash Hall, Oregon State University, Corvallis, OR 97331-3803; Phone: 541-737-1953; Fax: 541-737-3590

OREGON WATER RESOURCES DEPARTMENT
158 12th St. NE, Salem, OR 97310
Phone: 503-378-8455; Fax: 503-378-2496; Web site: www.wrd.state.or.us
Description: The Water Resources Department is the steward of the state's water resources. The agency enforces state water laws and policies; promotes actions that restore and protect stream flows and watersheds in order to ensure the long-term sustainability of Oregon's ecosystems, economy, and quality of life; addresses water supply needs; and increases the understanding of the resource and the demands on it.
Contact(s):
Director: MARTHA O. PAGEL; Phone: 503-378-2982
Administrator of Administrative Services Division: BRUCE MOYER; Phone: 503-378-8455
Administrator of Field Services Division: TOM PAUL; Phone: 503-378-8455
Administrator of Technical Services Division: BARRY NORRIS; Phone: 503-378-8455
Administrator of Water Rights and Adjudications: DICK BAILEY; Phone: 503-378-8455

Water Resources Commission
Founded: 1985
Description: The Water Resources Commission was created to oversee policy and all rulemaking activity of the department.
Contact(s):
Chair, Commissioner, West Central Region: NANCY LEONARD; Phone: 541-563-2187
Commissioner, Eastern Region: JIM NAKANO; Phone: 541-889-6823
Commissioner, Eastside at Large: TYLER HANSELL; Phone: 541-567-8939
Commissioner, North Central Region: RON NELSON; Phone: 541-548-6047
Commissioner, Northwest Region: JOHN FREWING; Phone: 503-227-1276
Commissioner, Southwest Region: DAN THORNDIKE; Phone: 541-857-8222
Vice Chair, Commissioner, Westdale at large: MIKE JEWETT; Phone: 541-773-2727
Keyword(s): Planning Management, Rivers, Sustainable Development, Sustainable Ecosystems, Water Resources

STATE MARINE BOARD (OREGON)
P.O. Box 14145, Salem, OR 97309-5065
Phone: 503-378-8587
Contact(s):
Director: PAUL E. DONHEFFNER
Keyword(s): Outdoor Recreation, Recreational Boating, Water Quality

PENNSYLVANIA

GOVERNOR OF PENNSYLVANIA: TOM RIDGE
Rm. 225, Main Capitol Bldg., Harrisburg, PA 17120
Phone: 717-787-2500

CITIZENS ADVISORY COUNCIL TO PENNSYLVANIA DEPARTMENT OF ENVIRONMENTAL PROTECTION
Attn: Executive Director, Rachel Carson State Office Bldg., 5th Fl., P.O. Box 8459, Harrisburg, PA 17105-8459
Phone: 717-787-4527; Fax: 717-772-5748; Web site: www.cac.dep.state.pa.us
Contact(s):
Executive Director: SUSAN M. WILSON
Publication(s): *Annual Report; Regional Report;*
Keyword(s): Environmental Protection, Public Health Protection, Public Participation

PENNSYLVANIA COOPERATIVE FISH AND WILDLIFE RESEARCH UNIT
Merkle Bldg., Pennsylvania State University, University Park, PA 16802
Phone: 814-865-4511
Founded: 1938
Description: Established as a cooperative activity among Pennsylvania State University, Pennsylvania Fish and Boat Commission, Wildlife Management Institute, Pennsylvania Game Commission, and the Department of the Interior. Areas of research are: The effects of natural and manmade forces on aquatic and terrestrial ecosystems, animal-habitat interactions, acid precipitation effects, fish and wildlife management, and health profiles of game animals. Graduate training is also provided.
Contact(s):
Leader: DR. ROBERT F. CARLINE
Assistant Leader for Wildlife: DR. DUANE DIEFENBACH
Publication(s): *Annual Report available on request.*

PENNSYLVANIA DEPARTMENT OF AGRICULTURE
2301 N. Cameron St., Harrisburg, PA 17110-9408
Phone: 717-787-4737
Founded: 1895
Description: The Department of Agriculture was established as an administrative agency of the Executive Department of the Commonwealth. The Secretary of Agriculture is charged with "encouraging and promoting agriculture and related industries throughout the Commonwealth." The Department's mission is accomplished through three major programs: Consumer protection, property protection, and agribusiness development. Three deputies help determine policy, program development and overall

administration. The department provides a full range of services to farmers and consumers from Harrisburg through seven regional offices located around the state.
Contact(s):
Agricultural Development Bureau: CARL MULLER; Phone: 717-783-9944
Comptroller: ROSS E. STARNER; Phone: 717-772-7000
Deputy Secretary of Marketing of Promotion of and Program Services: RUSSELL C. REDDING; Phone: 717-787-3418
Deputy Secretary of Regulatory Programs: CHRISTIAN R. HERR; Phone: 717-787-4626
Deputy Secretary, Administrator: DR. ZOANN PARKER; Phone: 717-783-6985
Director of Administrative Services Bureau: ROBERT KORBONITS; Phone: 717-787-4854
Director of Animal Health and Diagnostic Service: JOHN ENCIC; Phone: 717-783-6677
Director of Dog Law Enforcement Bureau: RICHARD HESS; Phone: 717-787-4833
Director of Farmland Protection Bureau: RAY PICKERING; Phone: 717-783-3167
Director of Food Safety Bureau: LEROY C. CORBIN; Phone: 717-787-4315
Director of Government Donated Food Bureau: BARRY SHUTT; Phone: 717-787-2940
Director of Market Development Bureau: BRAD JONES; Phone: 717-787-6041
Director of Pennsylvania Agricultural Statistics Service: WALLACE EVANS; Phone: 717-787-3904
Director of Pennsylvania State Farm Show Bureau: DENNIS GRUMBINE; Phone: 717-787-5373
Director of Plant Industry Bureau: LYLE FORER; Phone: 717-787-4843
Director of Race Horse Testing Laboratory: DR. CORNELIUS E. UBOH; Phone: 610-436-3501
Director of Ride and Measurement Standards Bureau: CHARLES BRUCKNER; Phone: 717-787-6772
Director of Veterinary Diagnostic Laboratory: DR. FRED ROMMEL; Phone: 717-787-8808
Executive Assistant: GREG PARRISH; Phone: 717-705-2122
Executive Secretary of Pennsylvania Horse Racing Commission: BEN NOLT; Phone: 717-787-1942
Legal Counsel: GERALD OSBURN; Phone: 717-787-8744
Office of Legislation: GWEN BOWER; Phone: 717-772-2854
Office of Policy: MARY BENDER; Phone: 717-783-2058
Press Office Staff: ROBERT BUNTY; Phone: 717-787-5085
Secretary of Agriculture: SAMUEL E. HAYES JR.; Phone: 717-772-2853
Publication(s): *Agriculture News*
Keyword(s): Agriculture, Flowers, Plants, and Trees, Land Preservation, Pesticides, Public Health Protection

Region I
13410 Dunham Rd., Meadville, PA 16335
Phone: 814-332-6890
Contact(s):
Director: GEORGE GREGG

Region II
2542 County Farm Rd., Suite 102, Montowsville, PA 17754-9685
Phone: 570-433-2640
Contact(s):
Director: J. WAYNE YORKS

Region III
Rt. 92 South, P.O. Box C, Tunkhannock, PA 18657
Phone: 570-836-2181
Contact(s):
Director: RUSSELL GUNTON

Region IV
5349 William Flynn Hwy., Gibsonia, PA 15044
Phone: 724-443-1585
Contact(s):
Director: R. EDWIN NEHRIG

Region V
1307 7th St., Cricket Field Plaza, Altoona, PA 16601-4701
Phone: 814-946-7315
Contact(s):
Director: KENNETH MOWRY

Region VI
P.O. Box 419, Summerdale, PA 17093
Phone: 717-787-3400
Contact(s):
Director: WARREN MATHIAS

Region VII
Rt. 113, P.O. Box 300, Creamery, PA 19420
Phone: 610-489-1003
Contact(s):
Director: FRANK STEARNS

State Conservation Commission
2301 N. Cameron St., Harrisburg, PA 17110
Phone: 717-787-8821
Founded: 1945
Description: To establish policy for Pennsylvania's 66 local conservation districts. Programs administered by the commission include: a $2,850,000 annual grant program, which provides funds to conservation districts for the employment of managerial and technical staff; a $5.2 million annual Chesapeake Bay Program, which provides technical and financial assistance to farmers to install soil conservation and nutrient management practices, and a $4,000,000 annual grant program; which provides funds to local municipalities for the maintenance of dirt and gravel roads.
Contact(s):
Chairman: SAMUEL E. HAYES JR.
Executive Secretary: KARL G. BROWN; Fax: 717-705-3778; E-mail: kbrown@agric.state.us
Keyword(s): Agriculture, Environmental and Conservation Education, Soil Conservation

PENNSYLVANIA DEPARTMENT OF CONSERVATION AND NATURAL RESOURCES
P.O. Box 8767, Harrisburg, PA 17105-8767
Phone: 717-787-2869; Fax: 717-705-2832; Web site: www.dcnr.state.pa.us
Founded: 1995
Description: To maintain and preserve state parks; to manage state forest lands to assure their long-term health, sustainability and economic use; to provide information on Pennsylvania's ecological and geologic resources; and to administer grant and technical assistance programs that will benefit river conservation, trails and greenways, local recreation, regional heritage conservation and environmental education programs across Pennsylvania.
Contact(s):
Secretary: JOHN C. OLIVER; Phone: 717-787-2869
Executive Director, Conservation and Natural Resources Advisory Council to DCNR: KURT LEITHOLF, 8th Fl., Rachel Carson State Office Bldg., P.O. Box 8773, Harrisburg, PA 17105-8773; Phone: 717-705-0031
Press Secretary: GRETCHEN LESLIE; Phone: 717-772-9101
Senior Advisor to Secretary: SALLY JUST; Phone: 717-787-2869
Director of Community Relations: GERALYN UMSTEAD; Phone: 717-772-9087
Director of Environmental Education and Information: JOSH FIRST; Phone: 717-705-2862
Director of Policy: FREDERICK G. CARLSON; Phone: 717-772--9087
Director, Bureau of Administrative Services: DANA A. DATRES; Phone: 717-787-2362
Director, Bureau of Facility Design and Construction: EUGENE J. COMOSS; Phone: 717-787-7398
Director, Bureau of Forestry: JAMES R. GRACE; Phone: 717-787-2703

STATE AND PROVINCIAL GOVERNMENT AGENCIES - PENNSYLVANIA

Director, Bureau of Personnel: DENNIS L. FARLEY; Phone: 717-787-5496
Director, Bureau of Recreation and Conservation: LARRY WILLIAMSON; Phone: 717-783-2658
Director, Bureau of State Parks: ROGER FICKES; Phone: 717-787-6640
Director, Bureau of Topographic and Geologic Survey: DONALD M. HOSKINS; Phone: 717-787-2169
Chief Counsel: WILLIAM W. SHAKELY; Phone: 717-772-4171
Deputy Secretary for Administration: KAREN K. DEKLINSKI; Phone: 717-772-9100
Deputy Secretary for Conservation and Engineering Services: RICHARD G. SPRENKLE; Phone: 717-787-9306
Executive Deputy Secretary for Parks and Forestry: JOHN PLONSKI; Phone: 717-772-9104
Legislative Liaison: JOSEPH P. GRACI; Phone: 717-772-9101
Publication(s): *Resource; PA State Park Recreation Guide; Penn's Woods; Become a Conservation Volunteer, Discover DCNR*
Keyword(s): Biodiversity, Conservation of Protected Areas, Environmental and Conservation Education, Forest Management, Geology, Land Preservation, Natural Areas, Outdoor Recreation, State Parks, State Forests, Community Conservation

PENNSYLVANIA DEPARTMENT OF ENVIRONMENTAL PROTECTION

Public Participation Coordinator, 16th Floor, Rachel Carson State Office Bldg., P.O. Box 2063, Harrisburg, PA 17105-2063
Phone: 717-783-7404; E-mail: To DEP staff, use: lastname.firstname@dep.state.pa.us; Web site: www.dep.state.pa.us

Founded: 1971
Description: The Department of Environmental Protection's mission is to protect Pennsylvania's air, land, and water from pollution and to provide for the health and safety of its citizens through a cleaner environment. We will work as partners with individuals, organizations, governments, and businesses to prevent pollution and restore our natural resources.

Contact(s):
Secretary: JAMES M. SEIF; Phone: 717-787-2814
21st Century Environment Commission Executive Director: CAROL COLLIER; Phone: 717-772-4770
Chief Counsel: MICHAEL BEDRIN; Phone: 717-787-4449
Deputy Secretary for Air, Recycling and Radiation Protection: DENISE K. CHAMBERLAIN; Phone: 717-772-2724
Deputy Secretary for Federal/State Relations: DONALD S. WELSH; Phone: 717-783-1566
Deputy Secretary for Field Operations: TERRY R. FABIAN; Phone: 717-787-5028
Deputy Secretary for Management and Technical Services: KENWOOD GIFFHORN; Phone: 717-787-7116
Deputy Secretary for Mineral Resources Management: ROBERT C. DOLENCE; Phone: 717-783-5338
Deputy Secretary for Pollution Prevention and Compliance Assistance: ROBERT J. BASKANIC; Phone: 717-783-0540
Deputy Secretary for Water Management (Acting): ROBERT C. YOWELL; Phone: 717-787-4686
Director (Acting), Bureau of Water Quality Protection: GLENN E. MAURER; Phone: 717-787-2666
Director (Acting), Bureau of Water Supply Management: FREDERICK A. MARROCCO; Phone: 717-787-9035
Director of Environmental Education: HELEN OLENA; Phone: 717-772-1828
Director of Local Government Relations: DON HERSHEY; Phone: 717-787-9580
Director of Program Integration and Effectiveness: KIMBERLY NELSON; Phone: 717-787-9580
Director of Program Operations, Pollution Prevention and Compliance Assistance: MEREDITH L. HILL; Phone: 717-783-0540
Director, Bureau of Abandoned Mine Reclamation: ERNEST F. GIOVANNITTI; Phone: 717-783-2267
Director, Bureau of Air Quality: JAMES M. SALVAGGIO; Phone: 717-787-9702
Director, Bureau of Deep Mine Safety: RICHARD STRICKLER; Phone: 717-787-1376
Director, Bureau of Fiscal Management: RONALD K. FLORY; Phone: 717-787-1319
Director, Bureau of Human Resources (Acting): KAREN MITCHELL; Phone: 717-787-9313
Director, Bureau of Information Services: DARWIN AURAND; Phone: 717-772-5909
Director, Bureau of Investigations: GARY F. NILAND; Phone: 717-787-0453
Director, Bureau of Land Recycling and Waste Management: JAMES P. SNYDER; Phone: 717-783-2388
Director, Bureau of Mining and Reclamation: RODERICK FLETCHER; Phone: 717-787-5103
Director, Bureau of Office Systems and Services: JAMES S. TOOTHAKER; Phone: 717-787-4190
Director, Bureau of Oil and Gas Management: JAMES E. ERB; Phone: 717-772-2199
Director, Bureau of Regulatory Counsel: RICHARD P. MATHER; Phone: 717-787-7060
Director, Bureau of Watershed Conservation: STUART I. GANSELL; Phone: 717-787-5267
Director, Bureau of Waterways Engineering: MICHAEL D. CONWAY; Phone: 717-787-3411
Director, District Mining Operations: JEFFREY D. JARRETT; Phone: 412-942-7283
Director, The Policy Office: BARBARA A. SEXTON; Phone: 717-783-8727
Economic Development Project Coordinator: MICHAEL WOLF; Phone: 717-787-9580
Executive Deputy Secretary: DAVID E. HESS; Phone: 717-772-1856
Legislative Liaison: PAMELA A. WITMER; Phone: 717-783-8303
Office for River Basin Cooperation Executive Director: IRENE B. BROOKS; Phone: 717-772-4785
Press Secretary: CHRISTINA NOVAK; Phone: 717-787-1323
Public Participation Coordinator: CHRISTOPHER ALLEN; Phone: 717-783-7404
Senior Counselor to the Governor: PATRICK J. SOLANO; Phone: 717-783-6387
Publication(s): *PA Geology; Annual Report of Mining Activities; PA DER Publications*
Keyword(s): Environmental Preservation, Public Health Protection

PENNSYLVANIA FISH AND BOAT COMMISSION

P.O. Box 67000, Harrisburg, PA 17106-7000
Phone: 717-657-4518

Founded: 1866
Description: To conduct and support public education and information efforts related to aquatic resource protection, improvement, and management programs, and enhance public understanding of the wise and safe use of our fishing and boating resources.

Contact(s):
President: DONALD K. ANDERSON
Vice President: TED KEIR
Executive Director: PETER A. COLANGELO; Phone: 717-657-4515
Art Director: TED R. WALKE; Phone: 717-564-6846
Deputy Executive Director/Chief Counsel: DENNIS T. GUISE; Phone: 717-657-4525
Director of Bureau of Administration Services: WASYL J. POLISCHUK, JR.; Phone: 717-657-4522
Director of Bureau of Boating and Education: JOHN F. SIMMONS; Phone: 717-657-4538
Director of Bureau of Engineering and Development: JAMES A. YOUNG; Phone: 814-359-5152
Director of Bureau of Fisheries: DELANO R. GRAFF; Phone: 814-359-5169
Director of Bureau of Law Enforcement: THOMAS J. KAMERZEL; Phone: 717-657-4542
Editor: ARTHUR J. MICHAELS; Phone: 717-657-4520
Legislative Liaison: JOSEPH A. GREENE; Phone: 717-657-4517
Planning Coordinator: THOMAS P. FORD; Phone: 717-657-4394

Publication(s): *Pennsylvania Angler and Boater*
Keyword(s): Aquatic Habitats, Environmental and Conservation Education, Fisheries, Outdoor Recreation, Sport Fishing

Region 1 Northwest
11528 State Highway 98, Meadville, PA 16335
Phone: 814-337-0444
Contact(s):
Law Enforcement Supervisor: GARY E. DEIGER

Region 2 Southwest
236 Lake Rd., Somerset, PA 15501-1644
Phone: 814-445-8974
Contact(s):
Law Enforcement Supervisor: EMIL SVETAHOR

Region 3 Northeast
P.O. Box 88, Sweet Valley, PA 18656-0008
Phone: 717-477-5717
Contact(s):
Law Enforcement Supervisor: KERRY L. MESSERLE

Region IV Southeast
Box 8, Elm, PA 17521-0008
Phone: 717-626-0228
Contact(s):
Law Enforcement Supervisor: JEFFREY S. BRIDI

Region V North Central
P. O. Box 187, Fishing Creek Rd., Lamar, PA 16848-0187
Phone: 717-726-6056
Contact(s):
Law Enforcement Supervisor: PAUL F. SWANSON

Region VI South Central
1704 Pine Rd., Newville, PA 17241-9544
Phone: 717-486-7087
Contact(s):
Law Enforcement Supervisor: WILLIAM E. HARTLE

PENNSYLVANIA FOREST STEWARDSHIP PROGRAM
DCNR, Bureau of Forestry, P.O. Box 8552, Harrisburg, PA 17105-8552
Phone: 717-787-2106
Founded: 1990
Description: To educate Pennsylvania forest landowners and citizens about the importance of sound forest management and the need to conserve our forest resources for future generations through wise use today. Works in conjunction with the Stewardship Incentive Program, which provides cost-share assistance to landowner's forest management practices.
Contact(s):
Director: DR. JAMES GRACE
Program Coordinator: GENE ODATO
Publication(s): *Forest Stewardship Bulletin Series (forest management information) for landowners: Pennsylvania Forest Stewardship-Our Link to the Past, Our Legacy for the Future; Sources of Information and Guidance for Forest Stewards; Teaching Youth About Forest Stewardship*
Keyword(s): Biodiversity, Forests and Forestry, Sustainable Ecosystems, Water Resources, Wildlife and Wildlife Habitat

PENNSYLVANIA GAME COMMISSION
2001 Elmerton Ave., Harrisburg, PA 17110-9797
Phone: 717-787-4250; Fax: 717-772-0542
Founded: 1895
Contact(s):
Deputy Executive Director: MICHAEL W. SCHMIT; Phone: 717-787-3633
President: VERNON K. SHAFFER
Vice President: DR. NICHOLS SPOCK
Secretary: SAMUEL J. DUNKLE
Executive Director: VERNON R. ROSS; Phone: 717-787-3633
Associate Editor: ROBERT D'ANGELO; Phone: 717-787-3745
Chief of Audio-Visual Services Division: JOSEPH OSMAN; Phone: 717-787-1434
Chief of Hunter and Trapper Education Division: KEITH A. SNYDER; Phone: 717-787-7015
Chief of Public Information Division: F. BRUCE WHITMAN; Phone: 717-787-7015
Chief of Publications Division: ROBERT C. MITCHELL; Phone: 717-787-3745
Coordinator of Project Wild: THERESA ALBERICI; Phone: 717-783-4872
Director of Bureau of Administration: THOMAS C. WYLIE; Phone: 717-787-5670
Director of Bureau of Automated Technology Services: ROBERT STRAILEY; Phone: 717-787-4076
Director of Bureau of Information and Education (Acting): J. CARL GRAYBILL, JR.; Phone: 717-787-6286
Director of Bureau of Land Management: GREGORY J. GRABOWICZ; Phone: 717-787-6818
Director of Bureau of Wildlife Management: CALVIN W. DuBROCK; Phone: 717-787-5529
Editor, Pennsylvania Game News: ROBERT C. MITCHELL; Phone: 717-787-3745
Legislative Liaison: WILLIAM D. SCHULTZ; Phone: 717-783-1076
North Central Regional Director: HENRY G. STANKEWICH; Phone: 570-398-4744
Northeast Regional Director: BARRY L. WARNER; Phone: 570-675-1143
Northwest Regional Director: HOWARD L. HARSHAW; Phone: 814-432-3187
Southcentral Regional Director: WILLIS A. SNEATH; Phone: 814-643-1831
Southeast Regional Director: BARRY K. MOORE; Phone: 610-926-3136
Southwest Regional Director: HARRY E. RICHARDS; Phone: 724-238-9523
Publication(s): *Pennsylvania Game News*
Keyword(s): Hunting, Public Lands, Trapping, Wildlife and Wildlife Habitat, Wildlife Management

PENNSYLVANIA STATE EXTENSION SERVICES
217 Agricultural Administration Bldg., Pennsylvania State University, University Park, PA 16802-2600
Phone: 814-863-3438; Web site: www.cas.psu.edu/docs/COEXT/COOPEXT.HTML
Contact(s):
Director of Extension: DR. THEODORE R. ALTER
Associate Director of Extension: DR. DIANE V. BROWN, 217 Agricultural Administration Bldg., Pennsylvania State University, University Park, PA 16802-2600; Phone: 814-863-3438
Pesticides Coordinator: DR. WINAND K. HOCK, 114 Buckhout Laboratory, Pennsylvania State University, University Park, PA 16802; Phone: 814-863-0263
Wildlife Resource Specialist: DR. MARGARET BRITTINGHAM, 320 Forest Resources Lab., Pennsylvania State University, University Park, PA 16802; Phone: 814-863-8442; Fax: 814-863-7193

PUERTO RICO

GOVERNOR OF PUERTO RICO: PEDRO J. ROSSELLO
La Fortaleza, P.O. Box 82, San Juan, PR 00901
Phone: 787-721-7000

COMITE DESPERTAR CIDRENO
Box 1714, Cidra, PR 00739
Phone: 787-739-5492
Founded: 1987
Description: Primarily devoted to educate and organize communities in the east-central part of the island to deal with water pollution and wildlife habitat. Also deals with toxic waste problems.

STATE AND PROVINCIAL GOVERNMENT AGENCIES - RHODE ISLAND

Contact(s):
President: OLGA I. RODRIGUEZ BERRIOS
Secretary: VIVIAN MORALES SANTIAGO
Treasurer: JUANITA GARCIA
Publication(s): *Despertar Cidreno*
Keyword(s): Air Quality and Pollution, Endangered and Threatened Species, Environment, Lakes, Urban Environment

PUERTO RICO DEPARTMENT OF AGRICULTURE
Box 10163, Santurce, PR 00908-1163
Phone: 809-721-2120; Fax: 809-722-0291
Contact(s):
Executive Secretary: BRENDA ECHEVARRIA MARRERO

PUERTO RICO DEPARTMENT OF NATURAL AND ENVIRONMENTAL RESOURCES
P.O. Box 5887, Puerta de Tierra Sta., San Juan, PR 00906
Phone: 809-724-8774/809; Fax: 723-3090
Founded: 1973
Description: To develop, protect, manage, evaluate, and administer the natural resources of Puerto Rico; and to derive maximum public benefits.
Contact(s):
Secretary: PEDRO A. GELABERT; Phone: 809-723-3090
Keyword(s): Biodiversity, Environmental and Conservation Education, Fisheries, Forests and Forestry, Land Purchase

PUERTO RICO SEA GRANT PROGRAM
Marine Education Program, A. ORTIZ-SOTOMAYOR, Coordinator, Marine Education Center, Humacao University College, HUC Station, Humacao, PR 00791-4300
Phone: 787-850-9360; Fax: 787-850-0710; Web site: gnv.ifas.ufl.edu/~seaweb/homepage/upr.htm
Founded: 1985
Description: Promote marine education activities among pre-college teachers and students. Facilitate interdisciplinary teaching and learning experience using the marine environment as a resource.
Contact(s):
Director of UPR Sea Grant College Program: DR. MANUEL VALDEZ-PIZZINI; E-mail: ma_valdes@rumac.upr.clu
Keyword(s): Aquatic Habitats, Biodiversity, Coasts, Coral Reefs, EcoAction, Endangered and Threatened Species, Environmental and Conservation Education, Fisheries, Geology, Islands, Mangrove Habitats, Marine Mammals, Natural Areas, Oceanography

PUERTO RICO STATE EXTENSION SERVICES
Puerto Rico Agricultural Extension Service, P.O. Box 9031, Mayaguez, PR 00681-9031
Phone: 787-833-2665; Fax: 787-265-4130
Founded: 1934
Description: The Cooperative Extension Service helps people improve their lives through an educational process that uses scientific knowledge focused on issues and needs. It is a dynamic, ever-changing organization pledged to meet the country's needs for research, knowlege, and educational programs that will enable people to make practical decisions that can improve their lives.
Contact(s):
Associate Dean and Subdirector: PEDRO RODRIGUEZ, University of Puerto Rico, Mayaguez, PR 00681
Dean and Director: DR. RAFAEL F. DAVILA, University of Puerto Rico, Mayaguez, PR 00681; Phone: 787-832-4040
Specialist Agricultural Programs: RAFAEL OLMEDA
Specialist of i/c 4-H Clubs and Youth: SANTIAGO ARIAS
Specialist of i/c CRD Program: RAMON L. TORRES
Specialist of i/c Home Economics and Nutrition: TERESA NIEVES
Publication(s): *Related to Agriculture, Home Economics, Leadership, and Community Development*
Keyword(s): Agriculture, Environmental and Conservation Education, Health and Nutrition, Soil Conservation, Youth Organizations

SOIL CONSERVATION COMMITTEE OF PUERTO RICO
P.O. Box 10163, Santurce, PR 00908
Phone: 787-725-3040
Contact(s):
Secretary of Agriculture: DR. MIGUEL MUNOZ; Phone: 787-721-2120; Fax: 787-722-2283
Executive Secretary: BRENDA ECHEVARRIA MARRERO; Phone: 787-725-3040; Fax: 787-723-8512

RHODE ISLAND

GOVERNOR OF RHODE ISLAND: LINCOLN ALMOND
State House, Providence, RI 02903
Phone: 401-222-2080

DEPARTMENT OF ENVIRONMENTAL MANAGEMENT (RHODE ISLAND)
235 Promenade St., Providence, RI 02908
Phone: 401-222-2774
Description: The Department of Environmental Management's top priorities include the preservation and protection of the environmental quality of Rhode Island. Air pollution, water pollution, and waste disposal problems are handled by the DEM. The DEM develops, administers, and enforces programs designed to preserve and manage Rhode Island's forests, parks, farms, wildlife, fisheries, and coastline. DEM is also responsible for providing, on the average, 750 full-time jobs for the people of Rhode Island.
Contact(s):
Director: JAN H. REITSMA, 235 Promenade St., Providence, RI 02908; Phone: 401-222-2771
Assistant Director of Water Resources: ALICIA M. GOOD, 235 Promenade St., Providence, RI 02908; Phone: 401-222-3961
Associate Director for Natural Resource Management (DEM): MALCOLM J. GRANT, 235 Promenade St., Providence, RI 02908; Phone: 401-222-6605
Associate Director for Planning and Administration: FREDERICK J. VINCENT, 235 Promenade St., Providence, RI 02908; Phone: 401-222-2776
Associate Director for Water Quality Management (DEM): EDWARD S. SZYMANSKI, 235 Promenade St., Providence, RI 02908; Phone: 401-222-3961
Associate Director of Bureau of Environmental Protection: JAMES FESTER, 235 Promenade St., Providence, RI 02908; Phone: 401-222-2234
Chief Hearing Officer of Administrative Adjudication: KATHLEEN LANPHEAR, 235 Promenade, Providence, RI 02908; Phone: 401-222-1357
Chief of Agriculture: KENNETH AYERS, 83 Park St., Providence, RI 02903; Phone: 401-222-2781
Chief of Air Resources: STEPHEN MAJKUT, 235 Promenade St., Providence, RI 02908; Phone: 401-222-2808
Chief of Coastal Resources (Acting): JAMES T. BEATTIE, 83 Park St., Providence, RI 02903; Phone: 401-222-3429
Chief of Criminal Investigation Office: MARTIN A. CAPPELLI, 235 Promenade St., Providence, RI 02908; Phone: 401-222-6768
Chief of Enforcement: STEVEN HALL, 83 Park St., Providence, RI 02903; Phone: 401-222-2284
Chief of Fish and Wildlife: JOHN STOLGITIS, Stedman Government Center, Wakefield, RI 02879; Phone: 401-222-3075
Chief of Forest Environment: THOMAS DUPREE, R.F.D. #2 Box 851, NorthScituate, RI 02859; Phone: 401-222-1414
Chief of Management Services: GLENN MILLER, 235 Promenade St., Providence, RI 02908; Phone: 401-222-6825
Chief of Office of Human Resources: MELANIE MARCACCIO, 235 Promenade St., Providence, RI 02908; Phone: 401-222-2774
Chief of Parks and Recreation: LARRY MOURADJIAN, 2321 Hartford Ave., Johnston, RI 02919; Phone: 401-222-2632
Chief of Permitting: RUSSELL J. CHATEAUNEUF, 235 Promenade St., Providence, RI 02908; Phone: 401-222-2306
Chief of Planning and Development: ROBERT SUTTON, 235 Promenade St., Providence, RI 02908; Phone: 401-222-2776
Chief of Strategic Planning and Policy: JANET KELLER, 235 Promenade St., Providence, RI 02908; Phone: 401-277-3434

Chief of Technical and Customer Assistance: RONALD GAGNON, 291 Promenade St., Providence, RI 02908; Phone: 401-277-2797
Chief of Waste Management: TERRENCE GRAY, 235 Promenade St., Providence, RI 02908; Phone: 401-277-2797
Chief of Watershed and Standards: SUSAN BUNDY, 235 Promenade St., Providence, RI 02908
Compliance and Inspection: DEAN ALBRO, 235 Promenade St., Providence, RI 02908; Phone: 401-277-6820

DEPARTMENT OF TRANSPORTATION (RHODE ISLAND)
Two Capitol Hill, Providence, RI 02903
Phone: 401-277-2481
Description: To provide a safe, efficient, effective, and environmentally responsible intermodal transportation system that supports economic development and improves our quality of life.
Contact(s):
Director: WILLIAM F. BUNDY
Keyword(s): Engineering, Transportation

RHODE ISLAND COOPERATIVE EXTENSION SERVICE
Woodward Hall, University of Rhode Island, Kingston, RI 02881
Phone: 401-874-2900; Fax: 401-874-2259
Contact(s):
Director (Interim) and Community Economic Development Leader: HOWARD FOSTER; Phone: 401-874-2599
Aquaculture and Fisheries Leader: JOSEPH DeALTERIS; Phone: 401-874-5333; Fax: 401-789-8930; E-mail: joede@uriacc.uri.edu
Natural Resources Leader: ART GOLD; Phone: 401-874-2903; Fax: 401-874-4561; E-mail: agold@uriacc.uri.edu
Community Revitalization and Economic Development Specialist: DAVID ABEDON, University of Rhode Island, Rodman Hall, Kingston, RI 02881; Phone: 401-792-2981; Fax: 401-792-4395; E-mail: david@uriacc.uri.edu
Keyword(s): Agriculture, Pesticides, Water Pollution Management, Water Resources, Wetlands

RHODE ISLAND SEA GRANT
University of RI, Graduate School of Oceanography, S. Ferry Rd., Narragansett, RI 02882-1197
Phone: 401-874-6800; Fax: 401-789-8340; E-mail: allard@gso.uri.edu; Web site: seagrant.gso.uri.edu/riseagrant/
Contact(s):
Director: SCOTT W. NIXON; E-mail: snixon@gsosun1.gso.uri.edu

RHODE ISLAND STATE CONSERVATION COMMITTEE
Chair, Sosnowski Farm, P.O. Box 722, W. Kingston, RI 02892
Contact(s):
Chair: HON. SUSNA. SOSNOWSKI, Sosnowski Farm, P.O. Box 722, W. Kington, RI 02892; Phone: 401-783-7704; E-mail: senmike@uriacc.uri.edu

STATE WATER RESOURCES BOARD (RHODE ISLAND)
265 Melrose St., Providence, RI 02907
Phone: 401-277-2217; Fax: 401-277-4707
Founded: 1967
Description: The Water Resources Board is the key agency in water-supply planning, financing, regulation, and development. The Board also plans for the future water needs of cities and towns.
Contact(s):
Chairman: DANIEL SCHATZ
General Manager and Secretary and Treasurer: M. PAUL SAMS
Vice Chairman: MAURICE TRUDEAU
Publication(s): *RI Public Water Supply; RI Fish and Wildlife; RI Industrial Water; RI Legal and Legislative Aspects of Water Supply*
Keyword(s): Land Use Planning, Public Health Protection, Renewable Resources, Water Quality, Water Resources

SOUTH CAROLINA

GOVERNOR OF SOUTH CAROLINA: JIM HODGES
P.O. Box 11829, Columbia, SC 29211
Phone: 803-734-9400

CLEMSON UNIVERSITY EXTENSION SERVICE
Clemson University, Clemson, SC 29634-0310
Phone: 864-656-3382
Contact(s):
Director of Extension Service: DANIEL B. SMITH, 103 Barre Hall, Clemson University, Clemson, SC 29634-0310; Phone: 864-656-3382; E-mail: DBSMITH@clemson.edu
Director of School of Natural Resources: DR. ALLEN DUNN, 130 Lehotsky Hall, Clemson University, Clemson, SC 29634; Phone: 864-656-3215; E-mail: ADUNN@clemson.edu
Extension Entomologist: DR. P. M. HORTON, 111 Long Hall, Clemson University, Clemson, SC 29634-0365; Phone: 864-656-3113; E-mail: MHORTON@clemson.edu
Extension Fish Specialist: JOHN R. SWEENEY, Department Head of Aquaculture, Fisheries, and Wildlife, Lehotsky Hall, Clemson University, Clemson, SC 29634-0362; Phone: 864-656-3117; E-mail: JSWNY@clemson.edu
Extension Forester: DR. LARRY NELSON, 272-E Lehotsky Hall, Clemson University, Clemson, SC 29634-1003; Phone: 864-656-4866; E-mail: LNELSON@clemson.edu
Extension Wildlife Specialist: DR. GREG YARROW; Phone: 864-656-7370; E-mail: GYARROW@clemson.edu

DEPARTMENT OF INTERIOR, U.S.G.S/B.R.D, SOUTH CAROLINA COOPERATIVE FISH AND WILDLIFE RESEARCH UNIT
G27 Lehotsky Hall, Clemson University, Clemson, SC 29634
Phone: 864-656-0168
Founded: 1988
Description: The Unit conducts ecological research of importance to its cooperators, i.e., the Department of Interior, Clemson University, and the state of South Carolina. Its mission also involves training of graduate students in fish and wildlife biology and related fields.
Contact(s):
Assistant Leader of Fisheries: J. JEFFERY ISELY
Assistant Leader of Wildlife: CRAIG R. ALLEN
Unit Leader: DAVID L. OTIS
Keyword(s): Birds, Endangered and Threatened Species, Fisheries, Hunting, Landscape Ecology, Nongame Wildlife, Research, Sport Fishing, Wetlands, Wildlife and Wildlife Habitat, Wildlife Management

DEPARTMENT OF PARKS, RECREATION AND TOURISM
Edgar A. Brown Bldg., 1205 Pendleton St., Columbia, SC 29201
Phone: 803-734-1700
Contact(s):
Director: WILLIAM R. JENNINGS
Agency Spokesperson: LOUIS A. FONTANA
Deputy Director: RONALD R. CARTER
Director of Business Development Office: TONI T. NANCE
Director of Division of Marketing: R. MOKE MCGOWAN
Director of Division of Parks and Recreation: CHARLES W. HARRISON
Director of Division of Tourism Development: ISABEL HILL
Director of Finance Office: MANDY KIBLER
Director of Heritage Tourism Development Office: CURT COTTLE
Director of Information Technology: DAVID M. ELWART
Director of Internal Operations: ROGER DEATON
Director of Marketing Office: TERRI L. COWLING
Director of New Market Development: ROBERT G. LIMING
Director of Office of Recreation, Planning, and Engineering: BETH McCLURE
Director of Sales Office: AMY DUFFY
Director of State Park Service: VAN A. STICKLES

STATE AND PROVINCIAL GOVERNMENT AGENCIES - SOUTH CAROLINA

FORESTRY COMMISSION (SOUTH CAROLINA)
Box 21707, Columbia, SC 29221-1707
Phone: 803-896-8800; E-mail: jrich@forestry.state.sc.us
Founded: 1927
Description: Provides basic forest fire protection on all state and private forest lands in South Carolina; assists landowners in proper management and utilization of forest lands; promotes forest fire prevention and other forestry practices through an information and education program; and operates forest tree nursery, seed orchards, and state forests.
Contact(s):
State Forester: J. HUGH RYAN; Phone: 803-896-8800
Executive Assistant to State Forester: JUDY J. WESTON; Phone: 803-896-8875
Deputy State Forester: BILL BOYKIN; Phone: 803-896-8832
Commission Chairman: ED MUCKENFUSS, P.O. Box 1950, Summerville, SC 29484; Phone: 843-871-5000
Commission Vice Chairman: GEORGE E. CALLAWAY, 308 Fuller St., Manning, SC 29102; Phone: 803-435-8133
Technical Assistant to the State Forester: C. DEAN CARSON; Phone: 803-896-8822
Director of Field Operations Support: TIM ADAMS; Phone: 803-896-8802
Director of Administration Division: JOE RICHBOURG; Phone: 803-896-8858
Coastal Regional Forester: CECIL CAMPBELL; Phone: 843-538-3708
Pee Dee Regional Forester: STEVE SCOTT; Phone: 843-662-5571
Piedmont Regional Forester: CHARLES RAMSEY; Phone: 803-276-0205
Keyword(s): Environmental and Conservation Education, Forests and Forestry, Rural Development, Urban Forestry, Wetlands

SOUTH CAROLINA DEPARTMENT OF AGRICULTURE
Wade Hampton Office Bldg., P.O. Box 11280, Columbia, SC 29211
Phone: 803-734-2210
Founded: 1904
Description: Administers more than 30 state laws relating to agriculture and the consumer. Represents the farmer in national, regional, and state policy matters and is involved in local and international programs of commodity promotion. Enforces regulatory programs affecting the consumer on a statewide basis.
Contact(s):
Executive Assistant to the Commissioner: KAY RIKE
Commissioner: D. LESLIE TINDAL
Administrative Manager: DANIEL P. BREAZEALE SR.
Assistant Commissioner of Consumer Services: CAROL FULMER
Assistant Commissioner of Executive Affairs: DAVID L. TOMPKINS
Assistant Commissioner of Laboratory Services: WILLIAM BROOKS
Director of Agribusiness Development: LARRY BOYLESTON
Director of Market Services: DICK JESSE
Director of Marketing and Promotions: WAYNE MACK
Director of Public Information: BECKY J. WALTON
Editor: CARLA BRAY
Publication(s): *South Carolina Market Bulletin, The*
Keyword(s): Agriculture, Chemistry, Gardening and Horticulture, Wetlands

SOUTH CAROLINA DEPARTMENT OF HEALTH AND ENVIRONMENTAL CONTROL
J. Marion Sims Bldg., 2600 Bull St., Columbia, SC 29201
Contact(s):
Bureau of Air Quality: JAMES A. JOY III; Phone: 803-734-4750
Commissioner: DOUGLAS E. BRYANT; Phone: 803-734-4880
Deputy Commissioner of Environmental Quality Control Office: R. LEWIS SHAW; Phone: 803-734-5360
Publication(s): *A General Guide to Environmental Permitting in South Carolina*
Keyword(s): Air Quality and Pollution, Public Health Protection, Solid Waste Management, Toxic Substances, Water Resources

Office of Ocean and Coastal Resource Management (OCRM)
Suite 400, 1362 McMillan Ave., Charleston, SC 29405
Phone: 803-744-5838; Fax: 803-744-5847
Description: OCRM is a division of South Carolina's Department of Health and Environmental Control. OCRM has the dual responsibility of protecting the coastal environment while promoting responsible development within the eight coastal counties.
Contact(s):
Bureau Chief: CHRISTOPHER L. BROOKS
Director of Permitting: STEVE MOORE
Director of Planning: STEVE SNYDER
Publication(s): *Carolina Currents; Legislature Update*
Keyword(s): Coasts, Environmental Law, Environmental Planning, Environmental Preservation, Wetlands

SOUTH CAROLINA DEPARTMENT OF NATURAL RESOURCES
Rembert C. Dennis Bldg., P.O. Box 167, Columbia, SC 29202
Phone: 803-734-3888
Founded: 1994
Description: The Department was created by Act 181 of 1993 to provide for the conservation, management, utilization, and protection of the state's natural resources. It also administers the state's Heritage Trust Program for significant natural areas and historical sites. Five state agencies combined July 1, 1994, to form the SC Dept. of Natural Resources: the former Wildlife and Marine Resources Dept.; SC Geological Survey; Migratory Waterfowl Committee; and the non-regulatory portions of the Water Resources Commission and the Land Resources Conservation Commission.
Contact(s):
Director: DR. PAUL A. SANDIFER; Phone: 803-734-4007
Associate Director: CARY D. CHAMBLEE; Phone: 803-734-9102
Board Chairman: DR. JOAB M. LESESNE; Phone: 864-597-4010
Deputy Director of Administrative Services Division: JOHN B. REEVES; Phone: 803-734-3883
Deputy Director of Conservation Education and Communications Division: PRESCOTT S. BAINES; Phone: 803-734-3948
Deputy Director of Land, Water and Conservation Division: ALFRED H. VANG, 1201 Main St., Suite 1100, Columbia, SC 29201; Phone: 803-737-0800
Deputy Director of Marine Resources Division: DR. JOHN V. MIGLARESE, P.O. Box 12559, Charleston, SC 29422-2559; Phone: 843-762-5000
Deputy Director of Natural Resources Law Enforcement Division: COL. ALVIN WRIGHT; Phone: 803-734-4021
Deputy Director of Wildlife and Freshwater Fisheries Division: WILLIAM S. McTEER; Phone: 803-734-3889
Director Emeritus: DR. JAMES A. TIMMERMAN JR.; Phone: 803-798-2858
Publication(s): *South Carolina Wildlife; Resource, The; South Carolina Geology; South Carolina Weekly Climate Summary*
Keyword(s): Endangered and Threatened Species, Fisheries, Hunting, Natural Areas, Wildlife Management

SOUTH CAROLINA ENERGY OFFICE
1201 Main St., Suite 820, Columbia, SC 29201
Phone: 803-737-8030; Fax: 803-737-9846; Web site: www.state.sc.us/energy/
Description: The SC Energy Office is responsible for the statewide promotion of energy conservation and cost effective use of new energy sources.
Contact(s):
Director: MITCH PERKINS
Public Information Coordinator: RENEE DAGGERHART; E-mail: rdaggerhart@drd.state.sc.us
Publication(s): *Energy Connection Newsletter, The; $aving Money in Your Manufactured Home Through Energy Efficiency--A Guide for South Carolinians; How to Reduce Your Energy Costs--A Guide for Business, Industry, Government, and Institutions; Energy Savers; The Energy Factbook; The Annual Fuel Economy Guide; Improving the Efficiency of your Duct System.*
Keyword(s): Energy, Renewable Resources, Solar Energy, Solid Waste, Transportation

SOUTH CAROLINA SEA GRANT CONSORTIUM
287 Meeting St., Charleston, SC 29401
Phone: 843-727-2078; Fax: 843-727-2080; Web site:www.csc.noaa.gov/SCSeaGrant/
Description: A University-based state agency that supports research, education and outreach to conserve coastal and marine reserves and provide economic opportunities for the cities of South Carolina and the region.
Contact(s):
Executive Director: M. RICHARD DEVOE; E-mail: devoemr@musc.edu
Assistant Director: ELAINE KNIGHT; E-mail: knightel@musc.edu
Director of Communications: LINDA BLACKWELL; E-mail: blackwlj@musc.edu
Extension Program Leader: BOB BACON; E-mail: baconrh@musc.edu
Publication(s): *Coastal Heritage; Inside SeaGrant; extension materials; marine education publications and slide presentations; aquaculture handbooks; coastal hazard information.*
Keyword(s): Fisheries, Oceanography, Sustainable Development, Sustainable Ecosystems, Wetlands

SOUTH DAKOTA

GOVERNOR OF SOUTH DAKOTA: WILLIAM J. JANKLOW
500 E. Capitol, Pierre, SD 57501
Phone: 605-773-3212

BOARD OF MINERALS AND ENVIRONMENT
Department of Environment and Natural Resources, 523 E. Capitol Avenue, Pierre, SD 57501
Founded: 1981
Description: The Board of Minerals and Environment promulgates rules and issues permits in the areas of air quality, solid waste, hazardous waste, mineral exploration and mining, and oil and gas exploration and production.
Contact(s):
Secretary of the Department: NETTIE H. MYERS; Phone: 605-773-5559

SOUTH DAKOTA COOPERATIVE FISH AND WILDLIFE RESEARCH UNIT (USDI)
Department of Wildlife and Fisheries Sciences, South Dakota State University, Brookings, SD 57007
Phone: 605-688-6121; Fax: 605-688-4515; E-mail: charles-berry@sdstate.edu
Description: Conducts fish and wildlife research and provides training for fishery and wildlife biologists. Cooperating Agents: South Dakota Department of Game, Fish and Parks, South Dakota State University, U.S. Geological Survey, U.S.D.I., Wildlife Management Institute.
Contact(s):
Assistant Leader for Fisheries: STEVEN R. CHIPPS
Assistant Leader for Wildlife: KENNETH F. HIGGINS
Leader: CHARLES R. BERRY JR.
Publication(s): *Annual Report*
Keyword(s): Endangered and Threatened Species, Fisheries, Grasslands, Prairies, Rivers, Wetlands

SOUTH DAKOTA DEPARTMENT OF AGRICULTURE
523 E. Capitol, Foss Bldg., Pierre, SD 57501-3182
Phone: 605-773-5425
Contact(s):
Secretary: DARRELL CRUEA
State Forester: RAYMOND A. SOWERS; Phone: 605-773-3623

Division of Resource Conservation and Forestry
523 E. Capitol Ave., Pierre, SD 57501-3182
Contact(s):
Director: RAYMON D.A. SOWERS; Phone: 605-773-3623

State Conservation Commission
523 E. Capitol Ave., Pierre, SD 57501-3182
Phone: 605-773-3623
Contact(s):
Chairman: BILL KEIRY

SOUTH DAKOTA DEPARTMENT OF ENVIRONMENT AND NATURAL RESOURCES
523 E. Capitol, Joe Foss Office Bldg., Pierre, SD 57501
Phone: 605-773-3151; Fax: 605-773-6035; Web site: www.state.sd.us.denr
Description: To provide environmental and natural resources assessment, financial assistance, and regulation in a customer service orientated manner which provides protection of public health, conservation of natural resources, preservation of the environment, and promotes economic development.
Contact(s):
Secretary: NETTIE H. MYERS
Director of Division of Environmental Services: STEVE PIRNER; Phone: 605-773-3153
Director of Division of Financial and Technical Assistance: DAVID TEMPLETON; Phone: 605-773-4216
Keyword(s): Air Quality and Pollution, Chemical Pollution Control, Environment, Environmental Protection, Grants, Lakes, Mining, Solid Waste, Solid Waste Management, Toxic Substances, Water Pollution, Water Quality, Water Resources, Watersheds

SOUTH DAKOTA GAME, FISH, AND PARKS DEPARTMENT
523 East Capitol, Pierre, SD 57501-3182
Phone: 605-773-3387
Contact(s):
Secretary: JOHN COOPER; Phone: 605-773-3387
Boating and Hunting Safety: WILLIAM SHATTUCK; Phone: 605-773-4506
Communications Manager: SCOTT CARBONNEAU; Phone: 605-773-3485
Director of Administration Division: KEN ANDERSON; Phone: 605-773-3396
Director of Custer State Park Division: ROLLIE NOEM; Phone: 605-255-4515
Director of Parks and Recreation Division: DOUG HOFER; Phone: 605-773-3391
Director of Wildlife Division: DOUG HANSEN; Phone: 605-773-3381
Editor: BRUCE COONROD; Phone: 605-773-3485
Federal Aid Manager: WAYNE WINTER; Phone: 605-773-6228
Operations Assistant Director of Wildlife Division: EMMETT KEYSER; Phone: 605-773-4607
Specialist of Enforcement: RONALD CATLIN; Phone: 605-773-4505
Specialist of Environmental Review: JOHN KIRK; Phone: 605-773-4501
Specialist of Game: RON FOWLER; Phone: 605-773-4193
Specialist of Habitat: DAVE McGUIGAN; Phone: 605-773-4194
Staff Specialist of Fisheries: DENNIS UNKENHOLZ; Phone: 605-773-4508
Technical Services Assistant Director of Wildlife Division: GEORGE VANDEL; Phone: 605-773-4192
Turn in Poachers (TIPs) Training Coordinator: ROBERT SCHUURMANS; Phone: 605-773-5906
Publication(s): *South Dakota Conservation Digest*
Keyword(s): Aquatic Habitats, Fisheries, Outdoor Recreation, Terrestrial Habitats, Wildlife and Wildlife Habitat

SOUTH DAKOTA STATE EXTENSION SERVICES
South Dakota State University, AgH, P.O. Box 2207D, Brookings, SD 57007
Phone: 605-688-4792; Web site: www.abs.sdstate.edu/CES/index2.htm
Contact(s):
Director of Cooperative Extension Service: LARRY J. TIDEMANN
Extension Range Management Specialist: JAMES R. JOHNSON, West River Ag. Center, South Dakota State University, 1905 Paza Blvd., Rapid City, SD 55702-9302; Phone: 605-394-9302

STATE AND PROVINCIAL GOVERNMENT AGENCIES - TENNESSEE

Range Management Specialist: SCOTT KRONBERG, Animal & Range Sciences Dept., P.O. Box 2170, South Dakota State University, Brookings, SD 57007; Phone: 605-688-5412
Range Management Specialist: PATRICIA S. JOHNSON, West River Ag. Center, South Dakota State University, 1905 Plaza Blvd., Rapid City, SD 57702-9302
Keyword(s): Agriculture, Environmental and Conservation Education, Pesticides, Renewable Resources, Water Resources

TENNESSEE

GOVERNOR OF TENNESSEE: DON SUNDQUIST
State Capitol, 1st Fl., Nashville, TN 37423-0001
Phone: 615-741-2001

DEPARTMENT OF ENVIRONMENT AND CONSERVATION (TENNESSEE)
401 Church St., Nashville, TN 37243
Phone: 615-532-0109
Description: To plan, promote, protect, and conserve this state's natural, cultural, recreational, and historical resources and to enforce environmental laws and regulations that protect the state's land and water.
Contact(s):
Commissioner: MILTON H. HAMILTON JR.; Phone: 615-532-0109
Director of Air Pollution Control: TRACY CARTER; Phone: 615-532-0554
Director of Geology: RON ZURAWSKI; Phone: 615-532-1500
Director of Groundwater Protection: KENT TAYLOR; Phone: 615-532-0762
Director of Historical Commission: HERBERT HARPER; Phone: 615-532-1550
Director of Indian Affairs: TOYE HEAPE; Phone: 615-532-0745
Director of Land Reclamation: TIM EAGLE; Phone: 615-594-6203
Director of Natural Heritage Division: REGGIE REEVES; Phone: 615-532-0434
Director of Radiological Health: MIKE MOBLEY; Phone: 615-532-0364
Director of Recreation Resources: JOYCE HOYLE; Phone: 615-742-6521
Director of Solid Waste Management: MIKE APPLE; Phone: 615-532-0780
Director of Superfund: JIM HAYNES; Phone: 615-532-0900
Director of Underground Storage Tanks: JOHN WALTON; Phone: 615-532-0945
Director of Water Pollution Control: PAUL DAVIS; Phone: 615-532-0625
Director of Water Supply: DAVID DRAUGHON; Phone: 615-532-0191
Asst. Commissioner for Conservation: TOM CALLERY; Phone: 615-532-0208
Asst. Commissioner for Environment: WAYNE SCHARBER; Phone: 615-532-0225
Asst. Commissioner for Marketing: PAM INMAN; Phone: 615-532-0263
Asst. Commissioner for State Parks: WALTER BUTLER; Phone: 615-532-0001
Environmental Policy Office: Phone: 615-532-8545
General Counsel: JOE SANDERS; Phone: 615-532-0131
Public Information Officer: KIM OLSON; Phone: 615-532-0288
State Archaeologist of Archaeology Division: NICK FIELDER; Phone: 615-741-1588

TENNESSEE AGRICULTURAL EXTENSION SERVICES
P.O. Box 1071, Knoxville, TN 37901-1071
Phone: 423-974-7114; Fax: 423-974-1068; Web site: www.utextension.utk.edu/
Contact(s):
Dean of Extension Service: DR. BILLY G. HICKS; E-mail: bghicks@utk.edu
General Fish and Wildlife Specialist: DR. THOMAS K. HILL; Phone: 423-974-7164; Fax: 423-974-4714; E-mail: tkhill@utk.edu
General Wildlife Specialist: DR. CRAIG HARPER; Phone: 423-974-7346; Fax: 423-974-4714; E-mail: charper@utk.edu

TENNESSEE COOPERATIVE FISHERY RESEARCH UNIT (USDI)
Tennessee Technological University, Box 5114, Cookeville, TN 38505
Phone: 615-372-3032/3094
Contact(s):
Leader: DR. JAMES B. LAYZER
Keyword(s): Fisheries

TENNESSEE DEPARTMENT OF AGRICULTURE
P.O. Box 40627, Melrose Station, Ellington Agricultural Center, Nashville, TN 37204
Phone: 615-360-0103
Contact(s):
Commissioner: DAN WHEELER

State Soil Conservation Committee
Ellington Agriculture Center, P.O. Box 40627, Nashville, TN 37204
Phone: 615-360-0108
Contact(s):
Chair: BARRY LAKE, P.O. Box 107, Hickory Valley, TN 38042; Phone: 901-764-2909
Executive Secretary: JIM NANCE; Phone: 615-360-0108
Keyword(s): Agriculture, Environmental and Conservation Education, Pollution Prevention, Soil Conservation, Water Quality

WILDLIFE RESOURCES AGENCY
P.O. Box 40747, Ellington Agricultural Center, Nashville, TN 37204
Phone: 615-781-6500
Founded: 1949
Description: Created to have full and exclusive jurisdiction of the duties and functions relating to wildlife and boating and to the management, protection, propagation, and conservation of wildlife, including hunting and fishing.
Contact(s):
Executive Director: GARY T. MYERS; Phone: 615-781-6552
Assistant Director of Field Operations: RON FOX; Phone: 615-781-6557
Assistant Director of Staff Operations: ALLEN S. GEBHARDT; Phone: 615-781-6555
Chief of Administrative Services Division: KEN TARKINGTON; Phone: 615-781-6512
Chief of Boating Division: ED CARTER; Phone: 615-781-6682
Chief of Engineering Division: LES HAUN; Phone: 615-781-6545
Chief of Environmental Division: DAVID McKINNEY; Phone: 615-781-6643
Chief of Fish Management Division: BILL REEVES; Phone: 615-781-6575
Chief of Information & Education: DAVE WOODWARD; Phone: 615-781-6502
Chief of Law Enforcement Division: BOB HARMON; Phone: 615-781-6580
Chief of Management Systems: LOY FULFORD; Phone: 615-781-6528
Chief of Personnel: JIM DILLARD; Phone: 615-781-6594
Chief of Planning and Federal Aid: CLIFTON J. WHITEHEAD; Phone: 615-781-6599
Chief of Real Estate and Forestry Division: JOHN GREGORY; Phone: 615-781-6560
Chief of Wildlife Management Division: LARRY MARCUM; Phone: 615-781-6610
Commission Chairman: JOHN SMOLKO
Commission Vice Chairman: EARL BENTZ
Editor: DAVE WOODWARD; Phone: 615-781-6502
Education Supervisor: NORMAN BATES; Phone: 615-781-6538
General Counsel: L. BROOKS GARLAND; Phone: 615-781-6606
Manager of Nongame/Endangered Species: BOB HATCHER; Phone: 615-781-6670
Regional Manager of Cumberland Plateau (Region III): CLARENCE COFFEY; Phone: 931-484-9571

Regional Manager of East Tennessee (Region IV): BOB RIPLEY; Phone: 615-587-7037
Regional Manager of Middle Tennessee (Region II): STEVE PATRICK; Phone: 615-781-6622
Regional Manager of West Tennessee (Region I): GARY COOK; Phone: 901-423-5725
Publication(s): *Tennessee Wildlife*
Keyword(s): Endangered and Threatened Species, Hunting, Nongame Wildlife, Sport Fishing, Wildlife Management

TEXAS

GOVERNOR OF TEXAS: GEORGE W. BUSH
P.O. Box 12428, Austin, TX 78711
Phone: 512-463-2000

BUREAU OF ECONOMIC GEOLOGY
University of Texas at Austin, University Station, Box X, Austin, TX 78713-7508
Phone: 512-471-1534
Founded: 1909
Description: Functions as a state geological survey. Program includes basic research; application of geology to resources, conservation, and engineering problems; and publication of varied reports and maps. Maintains an extensive environmental mapping program.
Contact(s):
Director: W. L. FISHER
Associate Director for Administration: D. C. RATCLIFF
Publication(s): *Publications, University of Texas Report of Investigations; geological circulars; special publications; environmental geologic atlases; Geological Atlas of Texas; geological quadrangle maps; guidebooks; handbooks; annual reports; mineral resource circula*
Keyword(s): Energy, Geology, Water Resources

GUADALUPE-BLANCO RIVER AUTHORITY
933 East Court, Seguin, TX 78155
Phone: 830-379-5822; Fax: 830-379-9718
Founded: 1935
Description: Responsibility to develop, conserve, and protect the water resources within a ten-county statutory district and to aid in the prevention of soil erosion and flooding. Actively engaged in water supply, irrigation, hydroelectric power generation, water and wastewater treatment, and outdoor recreation operations.
Contact(s):
Chief Engineer: THOMAS D. HILL
Deputy General Manager: FRED BLUMBERG
Director of Accounting and Finance: ALVIN SCHUERG
Director of Project Development: DAVID WELSCH
Director of Water Quality: DEBBIE MAGIN
General Manager: W. E. WEST JR.
Manager of Communications and Education: JUDY GARDNER
Manager of Utility Operations: JOHN SMITH
Manager of Water Resources Operations: BRYAN SEROLD

TEXAS AGRICULTURAL EXTENSION SERVICE
Texas A&M University, College Station, TX 77843-7101
Phone: 409-845-4747; Fax: 409-862-1637; Web site: agextension.tamu.edu/
Contact(s):
Director of Extension Service: EDWARD A. HILER
Associate Department Head and Extension Program Leader: DR. C. WAYNE HANSELKA, Rangeland Ecology and Management, Rt. 2 Box 589, Corpus Christi, TX 78406-9704; Phone: 361-265-9203; Fax: 361-265-9434; E-mail: c-hanselka@tamu.edu
Associate Department Head and Extension Program Leader: DR. DONNY W. STEINBACH, Department of Wildlife and Fisheries Sciences, 111 Nagle Hall, Texas A&M University, College Station, TX 77843; Phone: 409-845-7471; Fax: 409-845-7103; E-mail: d-steinbach@tamu.edu
Associate Department Head and Extension Program Leader: ALAN D. DREESEN, Department of Forest Science, 4390 FM 1488, Conroe, TX 77384-3905; Phone: 409-273-2120; Fax: 409-273-5233; E-mail: a-dreesen@tamu.edu
Associate Director for Agriculture Sciences: DR. B. L. HARRIS, Texas A&M University, College Station, TX 77843-7101; Phone: 409-862-3932; Fax: 409-845-9542; E-mail: b-harris4@tamu.edu
Keyword(s): Agriculture, Environmental and Conservation Education, Forests and Forestry, Renewable Resources, Sustainable Development

TEXAS COOPERATIVE FISH AND WILDLIFE RESEARCH UNIT
Texas Tech. University, Lubbock, TX 79409-2120
Phone: 806-742-2851; Fax: 806-742-2946; E-mail: nparker@ttu.edu; Web site: www.tcru.ttu.edu/tcru
Founded: 1988
Description: To conduct research, train graduate students, and provide technical assistance in the maintenance and management of fish and wildlife biodiversity, bioinformatics, wetland ecology, molecular (genetic) biology, aquatic and wildlife ecology, general and reproductive physiology, and fish culture using the technical expertise of three federal staff members and collaborators.
Contact(s):
Leader: NICK C. PARKER
Assistant Leader of Fisheries: REYNALDO PATINO
Keyword(s): Agriculture, Biodiversity, Biotechnology, Environment, Fisheries, Bioinformatics

TEXAS DEPARTMENT OF AGRICULTURE
P.O. Box 12847, Austin, TX 78711
Phone: 512-463-7476; Fax: 512-463-1104; Web site: www.agr.state.tx.us
Founded: 1904
Description: Our mission is to make Texas the nation's leader in agriculture while providing efficient and extraordinary service.
Contact(s):
Commissioner: SUSAN COMBS
Deputy Commissioner: MARTIN A. HUBERT
Special Assistant of Producer Relations: D. MATT BROCKMAN
Assistant Commissioner, Field Operations: DANNY PRESNAL
Assistant Commissioner, Communications: ALLEN SPEICE
Assistant Commissioner, Administrative Services: RAETTE HEARNE; Fax: 512-463-7582
Assistant Commissioner, Pesticide Division: DONNIE DIPPEL; Fax: 512-475-1618
Assistant Commissioner, Regulatory Division: WALDO MORGAN; Fax: 512-463-8225
Assistant Commissioner, Marketing and Promotion: DELANE CAESER; Fax: 512-463-7843
Assistant Commissioner, Finance & Agribusiness: LEE DEVINEY; Fax: 512-475-1762

TEXAS DEPARTMENT OF HEALTH
1100 W. 49th St., Austin, TX 78756
Phone: 512-458-7111
Founded: 1879
Description: The Department of Health was created to protect and promote the health of the people of Texas.
Contact(s):
Deputy Commissioner of Public Health Sciences and Quality: DEBRA STABENO; Phone: 512-458-7437
Commissioner of Health: DR. WILLIAM R. ARCHER
Associate Commissioner of Environmental and Consumer Health: JOSEPH FULLER; Phone: 512-458-7541
Chief of Bureau of Environmental Health (P.E.): JOHN JACOBI; Phone: 512-834-6640
Director of Seafood Safety Division: KIRK WILES; Phone: 512-719-0215
Keyword(s): Health and Nutrition, Nuclear/Radiation, Toxic Substances, Toxicology

TEXAS FOREST SERVICE
301 Tarrow, Suite 364, College Station, TX 77840-7896

STATE AND PROVINCIAL GOVERNMENT AGENCIES - TEXAS

Phone: 409-458-6600
Founded: 1915
Description: To encourage and aid private landowners to practice multiple-use forestry; to protect private forest land against wildfire, insects, and diseases; and to inform the public of the contribution that forests make.
Contact(s):
Associate Director for Administration: TOM G. BOGGUS
Director: JAMES B. HULL
Associate Director of Forest Resource Development: EDWIN H. BARRON; Phone: 409-458-6650
Associate Director of Forest Resources Protection: BOBBY R. YOUNG; Phone: 409-639-8100
Head of Forest Products Department: I. DEWAYNE WELDON; Phone: 409-639-8180
Regional Forester of Northern Region: ERNEST H. SMITH, P.O. Box 3527, Longview, TX 75606-3527; Phone: 903-234-2829
Regional Forester of Southern Region: WILLIAM E. OATES, 1825 Sycamore, Huntsville, TX 77340; Phone: 409-435-0852
Regional Forester of West Texas: ROBERT F. FEWIN, Rt. 3 Box 216, Lubbock, TX 79401; Phone: 806-746-5801
Keyword(s): Flowers, Plants, and Trees, Forest Management, Forests and Forestry, Public Lands, Renewable Resources, Urban Forestry, Water Quality

TEXAS GENERAL LAND OFFICE
Stephen F. Austin State Office Bldg., 1700 N. Congress Ave., Austin, TX 78701-1495
Phone: 512-463-5001
Description: Serves as the custodian of approximately 20.5 million acres of state-owned land including 4.25 million acres of submerged coastal land. Responsibilities include: protecting state land from unlawful use; managing special projects which protects the state's natural resources; and providing the public with information pertaining to the state's land resources.
Contact(s):
Commissioner: DAVID DEWHURST; Phone: 512-463-5256
Deputy Commissioner, Resource Management: ANDREW NEBLETT
Keyword(s): Coasts, Public Lands

TEXAS PARKS AND WILDLIFE DEPARTMENT
4200 Smith School Rd., Austin, TX 78744
Phone: 512-389-4800
Description: The agency manages and conserves natural and cultural resources of Texas for the use and enjoyment of future generations.
Contact(s):
Executive Director: ANDREW SANSOM; Phone: 512-389-4802
Chief Financial Officer: JAYNA BURGDORF; Phone: 512-389-4420
Chief of Staff: GENE MCCARTY; Phone: 512-389-4651
Chief Operating Officer: ROBERT L. COOK; Phone: 512-389-4976
Commission Chairman: LEE M. BASS
Commission Vice Chairman: RICHARD HEATH
Director of Coastal Fisheries: HAL OSBURN; Phone: 512-389-4862
Director of Communications: LYDIA SALDANA; Phone: 512-389-4994
Director of Human Resources: ANNETTE DOMINGUEZ; Phone: 512-389-4809
Director of Infrastructure: DAN PATTON; Phone: 512-389-4995
Director of Inland Fisheries: PHIL DUROCHER; Phone: 512-389-8110
Director of Law Enforcement: JIM ROBERTSON; Phone: 512-389-4845
Director of Resource Protection: LARRY McKINNEY; Phone: 512-389-4864
Director of State Parks: WALTER D. DABNEY; Phone: 512-389-4874
Director of Wildlife: GARY GRAHAM; Phone: 512-389-4971
Editor, Texas Parks and Wildlife Magazine: SUSAN EBERT; Phone: 512-912-7000
Media and News Coordinator: TOM HARVEY; Phone: 512-389-4453
Publication(s): *Texas Parks and Wildlife Magazine*

TEXAS SEA GRANT PROGRAM
Sea Grant College Program, Texas A&M University, 1716 Briarcrest, S-702, Bryan, TX 77802
Phone: 409-845-3854; Fax: 409-845-7525; Web site: texas-sea-grant.tamu.edu/
Contact(s):
Director: ROBERT R. STICKNEY; E-mail: stickne@unix.tamu.edu
Associate Director, Marine Information Service: AMY BROUSSARD, 1716 Briarcrest, Suite 603, Bryan, TX 77802; Phone: 409-862-3767; Fax: 409-862-3786; E-mail: abrouss@unix.tamu.edu
Marine Advisory Service Program Coordinator (Acting): RUSSELL MIGET, Texas A&M University, Natural Resources Center, 6300 Ocean Dr., Suite 2800, Corpus Christi, TX 78412; Phone: 512-980-3460; Fax: 512-980-3465; E-mail: rmiget@falcon.tamucc.edu
Editor, Texas Shores Magazine: JIM HINEY, 1716 Briarcrest, Suite 603, Bryan, TX 77802; Phone: 409-862-3773; Fax: 409-862-3786; E-mail: bohiney@unix.tamu.edu
Publication(s): *Texas Shores; Marine Education*
Keyword(s): Agriculture, Aquatic Habitats, Biology, Coasts, Communications, Conservation of Protected Areas, Coral Reefs, Ecology, Endangered and Threatened Species, Environment, Environmental and Conservation Education, Environmental Ethics, Environmental Law, Environmental Planning, Environmental Preservation

TEXAS STATE SOIL AND WATER CONSERVATION BOARD
P.O. Box 658, Temple, TX 76503-0658
Phone: 254-773-2250
Description: The Texas State Soil and Water Conservation Board is a state agency established to administer and carry out Texas' soil and water conservation law. The Board is charged with the responsibility of administering and coordinating Texas' soil and water conservation program with the state's 216 local soil and water conservation districts. The Board is also the agency responsible for planning, implementing, and managing programs and practices for abating agricultural and silvicultural nonpoint source pollution within Texas.
Contact(s):
Executive Director: ROBERT G. BUCKLEY, 311 N. 5th St., Temple, TX 76501-3107; Fax: 254-773-3311
Keyword(s): Agriculture, Environmental and Conservation Education, Renewable Resources, Soil Conservation, Water Resources

TEXAS WATER DEVELOPMENT BOARD
1700 N. Congress, Austin, TX 78701
Phone: 512-463-7847
Founded: 1957
Description: Texas Water Development Board provides loans to local governments for water supply projects; water quality projects, including wastewater treatment, municipal solid waste management, and nonpoint source pollution control; agricultural water conservation projects; and flood control projects. Provides water-related research and planning and agricultural water conservation funding.
Contact(s):
Chairman: WILLIAM B. MADDEN
Border Project Management Division: FERNANDO ESCARCEGA; Phone: 512-475-2070
Deputy Executive Administrator for Office of Project Finance and Construction Assistance: J. KEVIN WARD; Phone: 512-463-0991
Deputy Executive Administrator for Planning: TOMMY KNOWLES; Phone: 512-463-8043
Director of Water Resources Information: RODDY SEEKINS; Phone: 512-463-8043
Executive Administrator: CRAIG D. PEDERSEN; Phone: 512-463-7850
General Counsel: SUZANNE SCHWARTZ; Phone: 512-463-7981
Northern Project Management Division: GEORGE GREEN; Phone: 512-463-7853

Special Assistant for Intergovernmental and External Customer Relations: LEONARD OLSON; Phone: 512-463-7931
Texas Natural Resource Information System: CHARLES PALMER; Phone: 512-475-8402
Vice Chairman: NOE FERNANDEZ
Publication(s): *Water For Texas - Today and Tomorrow; Texas Water Facts;* ground water reports since 1957; bay and estuary reports since 1967
Keyword(s): Aquatic Habitats, Environmental and Conservation Education, Planning Management, Rivers, Water Resources

UTAH

GOVERNOR OF UTAH: MIKE LEAVITT
210 State Capitol, Salt Lake City, UT 84114
Phone: 801-538-1000

UTAH COOPERATIVE FISH AND WILDLIFE RESEARCH UNIT (USDI-USGS-BRD-CRU)
College of Natural Resources, Utah State University, Logan, UT 84322-5210
Phone: 435-797-2509/2509
Founded: 1935 (Wildlife), 1962 (Fisheries), 1985 (combined)
Description: The unit conducts research and training in all aspects of fishery and wildlife biology and management.
Contact(s):
Assistant Leader of Wildlife: DR. THOMAS C. EDWARDS, JR.; Phone: 435-797-2509
Financial Assistant: ESTHER BIESINGER; Phone: 435-797-2558
Leader: DR. JOHN A. BISSONETTE; Phone: 435-797-2511
Keyword(s): Aquatic Habitats, Biodiversity, Birds, Ecology, Endangered and Threatened Species, Fisheries, Landscape Analysis, Mammals, Nongame Wildlife, Predators, Renewable Resources, Sport Fishing, Terrestrial Habitats, Wildlife and Wildlife Habitat

UTAH DEPARTMENT OF AGRICULTURE
350 N. Redwood Rd., Salt Lake City, UT 84116
Phone: 801-538-7100; Fax: 801-538-7126
Contact(s):
Commissioner: MILES FERRY
Deputy Commissioner: VAN BURGESS
Director of Administrative Services: RENEE MATSUURA
Director of Marketing: RANDY PARKER
Director of Plant Industry: G. RICHARD WILSON
Information Officer: EL SHAFFER
Staff of Agricultural Development and Conservation: JAMES CHRISTENSEN
Staff of Food and Dairy: KYLE STEPHENS
Staff of Weights and State Chemist: AHMAD SALARI
State Veterinarian: DR. MICHAEL MARSHALL

UTAH DEPARTMENT OF HEALTH
P.O. Box 144102, Salt Lake City, UT 84116-4102
Phone: 801-538-6101
Contact(s):
Executive Director: ROD BETIT
Department of Health Public Information Officer: ROSS MARTIN; Phone: 801-538-6339
Keyword(s): Biotechnology, Health and Nutrition, Public Health Protection, Toxic Substances, Toxicology

UTAH GEOLOGICAL SURVEY
1594 W. North Temple, Suite 3110, P.O. Box 146100, Salt Lake City, UT 84114-6100
Phone: 801-537-3300; Fax: 801-537-3400
Contact(s):
Director (Acting): KIMM HARTY

UTAH STATE DEPARTMENT OF NATURAL RESOURCES
1594 W. North Temple, Suite 3710, P.O. Box 145610, Salt Lake City, UT 84114-5610
Phone: 801-538-7200; Fax: 801-538-7315
Contact(s):
Deputy Director: MARTY OTT
Deputy Director: SHERM HOSKINS
Executive Director: KATHLEEN CLARKE
Assistant Director: DARIN BIRD

Division of Forestry, Fire and State Lands
1594 W. North Temple, Suite 3520, P.O. Box 145703, Salt Lake City, UT 84114-5703
Phone: 801-538-5555; Fax: 801-533-4111
Description: Legislation enacted July 1994 dissolved the Division and Board of State Lands and Forestry and created the Division of Sovereign Lands and Forestry, and the Sovereign Lands and Forestry Advisory Council. Division and council names were legislatively changed to Division of Forestry, Fire and State Lands and Forestry, Fire and State Lands Advisory Council in July 1995.
Contact(s):
State Forester and Director: ARTHUR W. DUFAULT
Strategic Planner: KARL KAPPE

Division of Oil, Gas and Mining
1594 W. North Temple, Suite 1210, P.O. Box 145801, Salt Lake City, UT 84114-5801
Phone: 801-538-5340; Fax: 801-359-3940
Contact(s):
Director: LOWELL BRAXTON

Division of Parks and Recreation
1594 W. North Temple, Suite 116, P.O. Box 146001, Salt Lake City, UT 84114-6001
Phone: 801-538-7220; Fax: 801-538-7378
Contact(s):
Deputy Director: MARY TULLIUS
Deputy Director: DAVE MORROW
Director: COURTLAND NELSON
Boating Coordinator: TED WOOLLEY
Chief of Law Enforcement: JAY CHRISTIANSON; Phone: 801-538-7326
Park Planning Manager: TERRY GREEN; Phone: 801-538-7346
Regional Manager of Northeast: DENNIS WEAVER; Phone: 801-533-5127
Regional Manager of Northwest: JIM HARLAND; Phone: 435-649-9109
Regional Manager of Southeast: TIM SMITH; Phone: 435-259-3750
Regional Manager of Southwest: GORDON TOPHAM; Phone: 435-586-4497

Division of Water Resources
1594 W. North Temple, Suite 310, P.O. Box 146201, Salt Lake City, UT 84114-6201
Phone: 801-538-7230; Fax: 801-538-7279
Contact(s):
Director: D. LARRY ANDERSON

Division of Water Rights
1594 W. North Temple, Suite 220, P.O. Box 146300, Salt Lake City, UT 84114-6300
Phone: 801-538-7240; Fax: 801-538-7467
Contact(s):
State Engineer and Director: ROBERT L. MORGAN
Assistant State Engineer: JERRY OLDS
Assistant State Engineer: KENT JONES
Assistant State Engineer: LEE H. SIM
Assistant State Engineer: RICHARD HALL

Division of Wildlife Resources
1594 W. North Temple, Suite 2110, P.O. Box 146301, Salt Lake City, UT 84114-6301
Phone: 801-538-4700; Fax: 801-538-4709
Contact(s):
Assistant Director: MAX G. MORGAN
Assistant Director: KEVIN CONWAY
Director: JOHN KIMBALL

STATE AND PROVINCIAL GOVERNMENT AGENCIES - VERMONT

Chair: BRENDA FREEMAN
Board Member: BRENDA FREEMAN
Board Member: J. COLIN ALLAN
Board Member: CONNIE BROOKS
Board Member: B. CURTIS DASTRUP
Board Member: RICK E. DANVIR
Board Member: RAYMOND V. HEATON
Supervisor of Central Region: JORDAN PEDERSEN, 115 N. Main St., Springfield, UT 84663; Phone: 435-489-5678; Fax: 435-489-7000
Supervisor of Northeast Region: WALT DONALDSON, 152 E. 100 N., Vernal, UT 84078; Phone: 435-789-3103; Fax: 435-789-8343
Supervisor of Northern Region: ROBERT HASENYAGER, 515 E. 5300 S., Ogden, UT 84405; Phone: 435-476-2740; Fax: 435-479-4010
Supervisor of Southeastern Region: MILES MORETTI, 475 W. Price River Dr., Suite C, Price, UT 84501; Phone: 435-636-0260; Fax: 435-637-7361
Supervisor of Southern Region: JIM GUYMON, P.O. Box 606, Cedar City, UT 84721; Phone: 435-865-6100; Fax: 435-586-2457

Office of Energy and Resource Planning
1594 W. North Temple, Suite 3610, P.O. Box 146480, Salt Lake City, UT 84114-6480
Phone: 801-538-5428; Fax: 801-521-0657
Contact(s):
Director: JEFFREY S. BURKS

UTAH STATE EXTENSION SERVICES
College of Natural Resources, 4900 Old Main Hall, Utah State University, Logan, UT 84322-4900
Phone: 801-797-2201; Web site: www.ext.usu.edu/
Contact(s):
Dean: DR. F. E. BUSTY; Phone: 801-797-2445
Vice President for Extension and Continuing Education: DR. ROBERT L. GILLILAND
Animal Damage Management Extension Specialist: DR. ROBERT SCHMIDT; Phone: 801-797-2459
Assistant Dean for Extension and Administration: DR. CHARLES W. GAY; Phone: 801-797-2445
Extension Fish and Wildlife Specialist: DR. TERRY A. MESSMER; Phone: 801-797-2459
Extension Forester: DR. MIKE KUHNS; Phone: 801-797-4056
Extension Outdoor Recreation and Tourism Specialist: DR. STEPHEN W. BURR; Phone: 801-797-2530
Extension Range Specialist: DR. G. ALLEN RASMUSSEN; Phone: 801-797-2469
Extension Range Specialist: DR. ROGER E. BANNER; Phone: 801-797-2472
Utah Geographic Alliance: DR. CLIFFORD B. CRAIG; Phone: 801-797-1790
Water Quality Extension Specialist: NANCY MESNER; Phone: 801-797-2465
Keyword(s): Forests and Forestry, Public Lands, Renewable Resources, Water Resources, Wetlands

UTAH STATE SOIL CONSERVATION COMMISSION
350 N. Redwood Rd., Salt Lake City, UT 84116
Phone: 801-538-7120
Founded: 1938
Description: Assists Utah's 39 soil conservation districts (SCD) in encouraging land operators to implement measures and practices; to prevent soil deterioration; restore depleted soil; prevent flood damage; improve irrigation water efficiency; and to encourage nonpoint water pollution control programs. The commission has 12 members; 5 ex-officio and 7 governor-appointed SCD members with their alternates.
Contact(s):
Chairman: MILES FERRY
Executive: K. N. JACOBSON

Keyword(s): Agriculture, Environmental and Conservation Education, Renewable Resources, Soil Conservation, Sustainable Development

VERMONT

GOVERNOR OF VERMONT: HOWARD DEAN
Pavilion Office Bldg., Montpelier, VT 05609
Phone: 802-828-3333; Fax: 802-828-3339

AGENCY OF NATURAL RESOURCES
103 S. Main St., Waterbury, VT 05671
Phone: 802-241-3600
Founded: 1970
Description: The Agency's mission is to act as a steward of Vermont's natural resources. We work to manage Vermont's natural systems and to foster public understanding so that the integrity, vitality, and diversity of these natural systems are sustained or restored.
Contact(s):
Secretary: BARBARA G. RIPLEY; Phone: 802-241-3600
Deputy Secretary: JOHN KASSEL; Phone: 802-241-3600
Director of Media and Public Relations: JAMES E. BRESSOR; Phone: 802-241-3600
Director of Planning: STEPHEN B. SEASE; Phone: 802-241-3620
Enforcement: SALVATOR SPINOSA; Phone: 802-241-3820
Executing Special Assistant: BERNARD JOHNSON; Phone: 802-241-3601
General Counsel: MARK SINCLAIR

Department of Environmental Conservation
Waterbury Complex, 10 S., Waterbury, VT 05677
Contact(s):
Commissioner: CANUTE PALMASSE; Phone: 802-241-3800
Director of Air Quality: RICHARD A. VALENTINETTI; Phone: 802-241-3840
Director of Environmental Assistance: RICHARD PHILLIPS
Director of Facilities: LARRY FITCH; Phone: 802-241-3737
Director of Waste Management: P. HOWARD FLANDERS; Phone: 802-241-3888
Director of Wastewater: MARILYN DAVIS; Phone: 802-241-3822
Director of Water Quality: WALLACE McLEAN; Phone: 802-241-3770
Director of Water Supply: JAY RUTHERFORD; Phone: 802-241-3400

Department of Fish and Wildlife
103 S. Main, 10 South, Waterbury, VT 05671-0501
Phone: 802-241-3700
Contact(s):
Business Manager: SANDY BARTON
Chair of Fish and Wildlife Board: MONTGOMERY MOORE
Commissioner: ALLEN ELSER
Director of Fisheries: TIM HESS
Director of Law Enforcement: ROGER WHITCOMB
Director of Operations: ANGELO INCERPI
Director of Wildlife: RON REGAN
Information and Education: JOHN HALL
Keyword(s): Air Quality and Pollution, Fisheries, Solid Waste Management, Water Resources

Department of Forests, Parks, and Recreation
Commissioner's Office, 103 South Main St., Waterbury, VT 05671
Phone: 802-241-3670
Contact(s):
Chief of Forest Resource Management: M. BRIAN STONE
Chief of Forest Resource Protection: H. BRENTON TEILLON
Chief of Park Operations: CRAIG WHIPPLE
Commissioner: CONRAD MOTYKA
Director of Forests: DAVID STEVENS; Phone: 802-241-3678
Director of State Parks: LARRY SIMINO; Phone: 802-241-3655

State Naturalist: CHARLES JOHNSON

Environmental Board
East State St., Montpelier, VT 05602
Phone: 802-828-3309
Contact(s):
Chairman: JOHN EWING
General Counsel: GEORGE GAY

Vermont Geological Survey
103 S. Main St., Center Bldg., Waterbury, VT 05671-0301
Phone: 802-241-3496; Fax: 802-241-3281; Web site: www.anr.state.vt.us/geology/vgshmpg.htm
Founded: 1844
Description: The Vermont Geological Survey encompasses two divisions. The State Geologist provides surveys of the geology, mineral resources, topography and geological information services to citizens, industry, and state and federal agencies. The Radioactive Waste Management Program manages the disposal of low-level radioactive waste generated in Vermont.
Contact(s):
State Geologist: LAWRENCE R. BECKER
Publication(s): *Price list sent upon request or visit the web site.*
Keyword(s): Communications, Environmental Preservation, Geology, Nuclear/Radiation, Toxic Substances

UNIVERSITY OF VERMONT EXTENSION
601 Main St., Burlington, VT 05401-3439
Phone: 802-656-2990; Web site: ctr.uvm.edu/ext
Founded: 1914
Description: UVM Extension is a system of informal education, bringing research information in a practical form to Vermont residents. Extension with the specific expertise of our state university meets the needs of agriculture, communities, families and youth. Programs are specifically focused on natural resource conservation, sustainable agriculture and rural development, health care in rural areas, resource distribution in communities, and the contemporary stresses on the American family.
Contact(s):
Director: LAWRENCE K. FORCIER
Director of Sustainable Agriculture Center: VERN GRUBINGER; Phone: 802-257-7967
Family and Community Resource and Economic Development: LOIS FREY; Phone: 802-223-2389
Family and Community Resource and Economic Development: CATHERINE HALBRENDT; Phone: 802-656-0291
Natural Resources and Environmental Management: DOUG LANTAGNE; Phone: 802-524-6501
Nutrition, Food Safety, and Health: DALE STEEN; Phone: 802-748-8177
Nutrition, Food Safety, and Health: ROBERT TYZBIR; Phone: 802-656-3374
Program Leader of Agriculture: NEIL PELSUE; Phone: 802-257-7967
Program Leader of Agriculture: ALAN GOTLIEB; Phone: 802-656-0474
Extension Forester: THOM J. McEVOY, School of Natural Resources, 345 Aiken Center, Burlington, VT 05405; Phone: 802-656-2913; Fax: 802-656-8683
Keyword(s): Acid Rain, Health and Nutrition, Research, Sustainable Development, Youth Organizations

Publications Office
Communications and Technology Resources, Agricultural Engineering Bldg., Burlington, VT 05405-0004
Phone: 802-656-0301

VERMONT DEPARTMENT OF AGRICULTURE, FOOD, AND MARKETS
116 State St., Drawer 20, Montpelier, VT 05620-2901
Phone: 802-828-2500
Founded: 1908
Contact(s):
Business Manager of Administrative Services: RUDOLPH POLLI; Phone: 802-828-3567
Commissioner: LEON C. GRAVES; Phone: 802-828-2430
Deputy Commissioner of Administration: KENNETH BECKER
Director of Plant Industry of Laboratories of and Consumer Assurance: PHILIP R. BENEDICT; Phone: 802-828-2431
State Veterinarian: DR. SAMUEL HUTCHINS; Phone: 802-828-2421
Publication(s): *Agriview; list available on request.*

Natural Resources Conservation Council
116 State St., Montpelier, VT 05620-2901
Description: The Conservation Council is the administrative body for the 14 conservation districts in Vermont. The goal of conservation districts is to ensure the wise use, protection and enhancement of Vermont soil, water, and related natural resources; to foster public awareness and appreciation of the need for conservation; and to advance the concept that we are all stewards of the living earth.
Contact(s):
Executive Secretary: JON W. ANDERSON; Phone: 802-828-3529
Chairperson: TOM BUSHY, 116 State St., Montpelier, VT 05620-2901
Keyword(s): Agriculture, Environmental and Conservation Education, Environmental Preservation, Soil Conservation, Water Pollution

State Conservation Commission
Contact(s):
Chair: THOMAS BUSHEY; Phone: 802-985-2048; Fax: 802-951-6327
Executive Secretary: JON W. ANDERSON; Phone: 802-828-3529; Fax: 802-828-2361; E-mail: jwa@agr.state.vt.us

VERMONT DEPARTMENT OF HEALTH
P.O. Box 70, 108 Cherry St., Burlington, VT 05402
Phone: 802-863-7280
Contact(s):
Commissioner: DR. JAN K. CARNEY; Phone: 802-863-7280
Director of Health Protection: LARRY CRIST; Phone: 802-863-7223
Keyword(s): Air Quality and Pollution, Health and Nutrition, Pesticides, Toxic Substances, Toxicology

VIRGIN ISLANDS

GOVERNOR OF THE VIRGIN ISLANDS: CHARLES W. TURNBULL
Government House, Charlotte Amalie, St.Thomas, VI 00802
Phone: 340-774-0001

DEPARTMENT OF PLANNING AND NATURAL RESOURCES
Suite 231, Nisky Center, St. Thomas, VI 00803
Phone: 809-774-3320
Founded: 1970
Description: Responsible for: Fish and wildlife; trees, vegetation and water resources; air and water pollution control; flood control; sewers and sewage disposal; culture and the arts; libraries and museums; minerals and other natural resources; historical preservation; submerged lands; earth change permits; and oil spill prevention and control.
Contact(s):
Commissioner: DEAN C. PLASKETT ESQ.
Chief of Wildlife Bureau: DAVID NELLIS
Director of Coastal Zone Management: JANICE D. HODGE
Director of Environmental Enforcement Division: LUCIA ROBERTS
Director of Environmental Protection Division: HOLLIS GRIFFIN
Director of Fish and Wildlife Division: BARBARA KOJIS; Phone: 809-775-6762
Publication(s): *Annual Report; Zone Management Notes (CZM Notes); Blue Book; Proceedings - Fisheries in Crisis Conference (Division of Fish and Wildlife; Wildlife Plant booklet; Natural History*

STATE AND PROVINCIAL GOVERNMENT AGENCIES - VIRGINIA

Atlas to the Cays of the Virgin Islands; Species Technical Bulletin (Bureau
Keyword(s): Aquatic Habitats, Birds, Endangered and Threatened Species, Environmental and Conservation Education, Mammals

Division of Fish and Wildlife
6291 Estate Nazareth, 101, St. Thomas, VI 00802
Phone: 340-775-6762; Fax: 340-775-3972
Contact(s):
Director: DR. BARBARA KOJIS; E-mail: bkojis@hotmail.com

VIRGIN ISLANDS COOPERATIVE EXTENSION SERVICE
University of Virgin Islands, R.R. #2 Box 10,000, Kingshill, St. Croix, VI 00850
Phone: 340-692-4080; Fax: 340-692-4085; Web site: rps.uvi.edu/CES/
Contact(s):
Director of CES: KWAME N. GARCIA SR.
Director of Agricultural Experiment Station: JAMES RAKOCY, University of VI, RR2, Box 10,000, Kingshill, VI 00850; Phone: 340-692-4031; Fax: 340-692-4035
Coordinator, Integrated Pest Management of Pesticide Impact Assessment Program Liaison: DR. JOZEF KEULARTS
Program Leader of Agriculture and Natural Resources: CLINTON GEORGE

VIRGIN ISLANDS SOIL AND WATER CONSERVATION DIVISION
Contact(s):
Commissioner: HENRY SCHUSTER JR.; Phone: 809-778-0997

VIRGINIA

GOVERNOR OF VIRGINIA: JAMES S. GILMORE II
State Capitol, Richmond, VA 23219
Phone: 804-786-2211
Contact(s):
Secretary of Natural Resources: JOHN PAUL WOODLEY JR.; Phone: 804-786-0044
Deputy Secretary of Natural Resources: RONALD P. HAMM; Phone: 804-786-0044

DEPARTMENT OF FORESTRY
P.O. Box 3758, Fontaine Research Park, 900 Natural Resources Drive, Charlottesville, VA 22903-0758
Phone: 804-977-6555; Fax: 804-296-2369
Founded: 1914
Description: The mission of the Department of Forestry is to protect and develop healthy, sustainable forest resources for Virginians. The Department assists private landowners with the management and protection of forest resources. We also provide at-cost seedlings for reforestation of the state's forestlands, and management of public state forests and other state public forest lands.
Contact(s):
Deputy State Forester: BETTINA K. RING
Fiscal Director: FAYE E. DiFAZIO
Human Resources Director: ELLIE WHINNERY
State Forester: JAMES W. GARNER
Team Leader for Forest Management: JAMES D. STARR
Team Leader for General Services: RONALD S. JENKINS
Team Leader for Information Technology: JAMES A. COPONY
Team Leader for Resource Information: TIMOTHY C. TIGNER
Team Leader for Resource Protection: GREGORY L. SANDERS

MARINE RESOURCES COMMISSION (VIRGINIA)
P.O. Box 756, Newport News, VA 23607
Phone: 757-247-2200
Founded: 1875
Description: This state agency holds regulatory jurisdiction over all commercial and sports fishing, marine fish, marine shellfish, and marine organisms in the tidal waters of Virginia. Holds permit jurisdiction on all projects involving use of state-owned submerged lands and authority over use or development in vegetated and non-vegetated tidal wetlands and coastal primary sand dunes.
Contact(s):
Chief of Administration and Finance: ROBERT D. CRAFT
Chief of Conservation and Replenishment: JIM WESSON
Chief of Fisheries Management: JACK G. TRAVELSTEAD
Chief of Law Enforcement: STEVEN G. BOWMAN
Chief of Management Information Systems: ERIK J. BARTH
Chief, Habitat Management: ROBERT W. GRABB
Commissioner: WILLIAM A. PRUITT
Publication(s): *Virginia Landings Bulletin*

NORTHERN VIRGINIA REGIONAL PARK AUTHORITY
5400 Ox Rd., Fairfax Station, VA 22039
Phone: 703-352-5900; Fax: 703-273-0905
Founded: 1959
Description: To preserve open and wooded areas and provide outdoor recreation to meet the needs of a growing population.
Contact(s):
Chairman: WALTER L. MESS
Executive Director: DAVID C. HOBSON
Publication(s): *Discover Your Regional Parks; Calendar of Events; Policy Plan; Washington and Old Dominion Railroad Regional Park Trail Guide*
Keyword(s): Botanical Gardens, Environmental and Conservation Education, Environmental Preservation, Flowers, Plants, and Trees, Outdoor Recreation

VIRGINIA COOPERATIVE FISH AND WILDLIFE RESEARCH UNIT (USDI)
106 Cheatham Hall, Virginia Polytechnic Institute and State University, Blacksburg, VA 24061
Phone: 540-231-5927
Founded: 1935
Description: Founded for training graduate students in fisheries and wildlife; with teaching and extension in fisheries and wildlife biology. Cooperatively supported by the Biological Resources Division of U.S.G.S., Department of Game and Inland Fisheries, and Virginia Polytechnic Institute and State University.
Contact(s):
Assistant Leader: DR. PAUL L. ANGERMEIER; Phone: 540-231-4501
Assistant Leader: DR. MICHAEL R. VAUGHAN; Phone: 540-231-5046
Leader: DR. RICHARD J. NEVES
Publication(s): *Annual reports; journal articles; research publications.*
Keyword(s): Aquatic Habitats, Endangered and Threatened Species, Fisheries, Wildlife and Wildlife Habitat, Wildlife Management

VIRGINIA DEPARTMENT OF AGRICULTURE AND CONSUMER SERVICES
P.O. Box 1163, Richmond, VA 23209
Phone: 804-786-3501; Fax: 804-371-2945
Founded: 1877
Description: To promote the economic growth and development of Virginia agriculture, encourage environmental stewardship, and provide consumer protection. Thirteen-member board appointed by Governor.
Contact(s):
Department Commissioner: J. CARLTON COURTER III; Phone: 804-786-3501
Director of Communication: ELAINE J. LIDHOLM; Phone: 804-786-7686
Director of Policy Planning and Research: ROY E. SEWARD; Phone: 804-786-3535
Editor: ELAINE J. LIDHOLM
Manager of Pesticides Services: DR. MARVIN A. LAWSON; Phone: 804-371-6558
Publication(s): *Bulletin*
Keyword(s): Agriculture, Endangered and Threatened Species, Pesticides

STATE AND PROVINCIAL GOVERNMENT AGENCIES - VIRGINIA

VIRGINIA DEPARTMENT OF CONSERVATION AND RECREATION
203 Governor St., Suite 302, Richmond, VA 23219
Phone: 804-786-6124
Description: The Department's mission is to conserve, protect, enhance, and advocate wise use of Virginia's natural, recreational, and scenic resources in order to maintain and improve the quality of life for present and future generations. The Department is responsible for administrative support of various state collegial bodies including: The Board of Conservation and Recreation, the Virginia Cave Board, the Virginia Soil and Water Conservation Board, the Breaks Interstate Park Commission, the Conservation and Development of Public Beaches Board, Chippokes Plantation Farm Foundation, Virginia State Parks Foundation, Virginia Land Conservation Foundation and 17 state Scenic River Boards and Committees.
Contact(s):
Director: DAVID G. BRICKLEY; Phone: 804-786-2123
Chief Deputy (Acting): LEON E. APP
Administrative Staff Specialist: LINDA J. COX
Conservation & Development Programs Supervisor: DAVID C. DOWLING

Board of Conservation and Recreation
203 Governor St., Suite 302, Richmond, VA 23219
Contact(s):
Chairman: W. BRUCE WINGO, 203 Governor St., Suite 302, Richmond, VA 23219

Breaks Interstate Park Commission
203 Governor St., Suite 302, Richmond, VA 23219
Contact(s):
Chairman: JACK C. SYKES, 101 Summitt Drive, Pikesville, KY 41501; Phone: 606-432-1447
Advisor: JOSEPH ELTON

Chippokes Plantation Farm Foundation
203 Governor St., Suite 302, Richmond, VA 23209
Contact(s):
Chairman: FREDERICK M. QUAYLE, Member, Senate of Virginia, 3808 Poplar Hill Road, Chesapeake, VA 23321
Advisor: KATHERINE R. WRIGHT

Conservation and Development of Public Beaches Board
203 Governor St., Suite 302, Richmond, VA 23209
Contact(s):
Chairman: DONALD O. CAMPEN JR., 7603 Hillside Avenue, Richmond, VA 23229
Advisor: CARLTON LEE HILL

Division of Administration
203 Governor St., Suite 302, Richmond, VA 23219
Contact(s):
Director: WILLIAM E. PRICE, 203 Governor St, Suite 204, Richmond, VA 23219; Phone: 804-786-0001
Director of ADP: DONALD H. BRYNE
Director of Finance: TIMOTHY BISHTON
Director of Human Resources: KAREN CAREY

Division of Dam Safety
203 Governor St., Suite 302, Richmond, VA 23219
Contact(s):
Director: JOSEPH S. HAUGH, 203 Governor Street, Suite 423, Richmond, VA 23219; Phone: 804-786-1369

Division of Natural Heritage
203 Governor St., Suite 302, Richmond, VA 23219
Contact(s):
Director: THOMAS L. SMITH, 217 Governor St., 3rd Floor, Richmond, VA 23219; Phone: 804-786-7951

Division of Planning and Recreation Resources
203 Governor St., Suite 302, Richmond, VA 23219
Phone: 804-786-1119
Contact(s):
Director: JOHN R. DAVY

Division of Soil and Water Conservation
203 N. Governor St., Suite 206, Richmond, VA 23219
Phone: 804-786-6523
Contact(s):
Director: JACK E. FRYE; E-mail: dordswc@erols.com

Division of State Parks
Contact(s):
Director: JOSEPH ELTON, 203 Governor St., Suite 306, Richmond, VA 23219; Phone: 804-786-4375

Virginia Cave Board
Contact(s):
Chairman: BILL KEITH, Rt. 1 Box 17, Cleveland, VA 24225
Advisor: LAWRENCE R. SMITH

Virginia Soil and Water Conservation Board
Contact(s):
Chairman: CHARLES E. HORN, 203 Governor St., Suite 206, Richmond, VA 23219; Phone: 804-786-2064
Advisor: JACK E. FRYE

VIRGINIA DEPARTMENT OF ENVIRONMENTAL QUALITY
629 E. Main St., Richmond, VA 23219
Phone: 804-698-4442
Founded: 1993
Description: The Department of Environmental Quality strives to provide efficient, cost-effective services that promote a proper balance between environmental improvement and economic vitality.
Contact(s):
Director: DENNIS H. TREACY
Environmental Education Coordinator: ANN REGN
Keyword(s): Air Quality and Pollution, Environment, Solid Waste Management, Water Resources

VIRGINIA DEPARTMENT OF GAME AND INLAND FISHERIES
4010 W. Broad St., P.O. Box 11104, Richmond, VA 23230
Phone: 804-367-1000; E-mail: dgifweb@dgif.state.va.us; Web site: www.dgif.state.va.us
Description: To provide for the management, conservation, restoration, and enhancement of the Commonwealth's fish and wildlife resources. The department also provides boat registration and titling services and boating law administration and enforcement; as well as providing public informational and educational services related to wildlife resources and recreational boating
Contact(s):
Director of Administration: RAYMOND E. DAVIS; Phone: 804-367-2387; E-mail: rdavis@dgif.state.va.us
Director: WILLIAM L. WOODFIN JR.; Phone: 804-367-9231; Fax: 804-367-0405; E-mail: bwoodfin@dgif.state.va.us
Boating Law Administrator: CHARLES A. SLEDD; Phone: 804-367-6481; E-mail: csledd@dgif.state.va.us
Capital Outlay Program Manager: PHIL LOWNES; Phone: 804-367-1253; E-mail: plownes@dgif.state.va.us
Director of Boating Division: LARRY G. HART; Phone: 804-367-1295; E-mail: lhart@dgif.state.va.us
Director of Fisheries Division: GARY F. MARTEL; Phone: 804-367-0509; E-mail: gmartel@dgif.state.va.us
Director of Human Resources: LARRY HARIZANOFF; Phone: 804-367-8195; E-mail: lharizanoff@dgif.state.va.us
Director of Hunter Safety: TERRY BRADBERY; Phone: 804-367-8704; E-mail: tbradbery@dgif.state.va.us
Director of Information Management Systems: VIRGIL E. KOPF; Phone: 804-367-0787; E-mail: vkopf@dgif.state.va.us
Director of Law Enforcement Division: JEFFREY A. UERZ; Phone: 804-367-0776; E-mail: juerz@dgif.state.va.us
Director of Program Development: CHARLES A. SLEDD; Phone: 804-367-6481; E-mail: csledd@dgif.state.va.us
Director of Wildlife Diversity Division: DAVID K. WHITEHURST; Phone: 804-367-4335; E-mail: dwhitehurst@dgif.state.va.us

STATE AND PROVINCIAL GOVERNMENT AGENCIES - VIRGINIA

Director of Wildlife Division: ROBERT W. DUNCAN; Phone: 804-367-9588; E-mail: rduncan@dgif.state.va.us
Editor: LEE WALKER; E-mail: lwalker@dgif.state.va.us
Federal Aid Coordinator of Fisheries: FRED D. LECKIE; Phone: 804-367-8629; E-mail: fleckie@dgif.state.va.us
Federal Aid Coordinator of Wildlife: RICK BUSCH; Phone: 804-367-1215; E-mail: rbusch@dgif.state.va.us
Media Relations Coordinator: JULIA DIXON SMITH; Phone: 804-367-0991; E-mail: jsmith@dgif.state.va.us
Publication(s): *Virginia Wildlife*

Region I
5806 Mooretown Rd., Williamsburg, VA 23188
Phone: 757-253-7072

Region II (Lynchburg)
910 Thomas Jefferson Rd., Forest, VA 24551-9223
Phone: 804-525-7522

Region III
1796 Highway Sixteen, Marion, VA 24354
Phone: 540-783-4860

Region IV (Staunton)
P.O. Box 996, Verona, VA 24482
Phone: 540-248-9360

Region V
1320 Belman Rd., Fredericksburg, VA 22401
Phone: 540-899-4169

VIRGINIA DEPARTMENT OF HEALTH
Commissioner's Office, Suite 214, Main St. Station, 1500 E. Main St., Richmond, VA 23219
Phone: 804-786-3561
Founded: 1872
Description: The Department carries out protective and preventive public health services for all citizens of the Commonwealth and provides public health care services to the indigent.
Contact(s):
Commissioner (M.D., M.P.H.): ANNE PETERSON
Deputy Commissioner of Administration: HELEN TARANTINO
Publication(s): *Virginia's Health*

VIRGINIA DEPARTMENT OF MINES, MINERALS AND ENERGY
Ninth St. Office Bldg., 8th Fl., 202 N. Ninth St., Richmond, VA 23219
Phone: 804-692-3200; Fax: 804-692-3237
Founded: 1985
Description: The department is committed to enhancing the development and conservation of energy and mineral resources in a safe and environmentally sound manner in order to support a more productive economy in Virginia.
Contact(s):
Director: O. GENE DISHNER

Division of Energy
Description: The Division of Energy promotes the efficient use and conservation of energy and the use of alternative energy sources.
Contact(s):
Director: STEPHEN A. WALZ, Ninth St. Office Bldg., 8th Fl., 202 N. Ninth St., Richmond, VA 23219; Phone: 540-692-3211

Division of Gas and Oil
Description: The Division of Gas and Oil regulates the operation and reclamation of gas and oil extractions.
Contact(s):
Director: TOM FULMER, P.O. Box 1416, Abingdon, VA 24212; Phone: 540-676-5423

Division of Mined Land Reclamation
Drawer 900, Big Stone Gap, VA 24219
Phone: 540-523-8100

Description: The Division of Mined Land Reclamation regulates the operation of coal surface-mining activities, enforces the reclamation laws and regulations, and administers financial resources for reclaiming abandoned coal mining sites.

Division of Mineral Mining
Description: The Division of Mineral Mining regulates the operation of non-coal mining activities for environmental protection and worker safety.
Contact(s):
Director: CONRAD T. SPANGLER III, P.O. Box 3727, Charlottesville, VA 22903; Phone: 804-951-6310

Division of Mineral Resources
Description: The Division of Mineral Resources provides information on Virginia's geology, mineral resources, and physical and cultural features
Contact(s):
State Geologist: STANLEY S. JOHNSON, Box 3667, Charlottesville, VA 22903; Phone: 804-951-6350

VIRGINIA DEPARTMENT OF MINES, MINERALS, AND ENERGY

Division of Mines
Description: The Division of Mines enforces the coal mining laws of the Commonwealth to promote the safety and health of coal miners.
Contact(s):
Chief: FRANK A. LINKOUS, P.O. Drawer 900, Big Stone Gap, VA 24219; Phone: 540-523-8100

VIRGINIA MUSEUM OF NATURAL HISTORY
1001 Douglas Ave., Martinsville, VA 24112
Phone: 540-666-8600; Fax: 540-632-6487
Founded: 1988
Description: Preserves, studies, and interprets Virginia's natural and cultural heritage through a statewide system of museum facilities, research sites and educational programs. The museum has more than eleven million specimens in collections.
Contact(s):
Executive Director: STEPHEN J. PIKE; E-mail: spike@ngocomm.net
Staff: DR. JUDY WINSTON; Phone: 540-666-8609; E-mail: jwinston@vmnh.org
Publication(s): *Virginia Explorer, The; VMNH Newsletter; Books; Scientific Publication Series; Children's Activity Books*
Keyword(s): Biodiversity, Endangered and Threatened Species, Environmental and Conservation Education, Geology, Museum, Research

VIRGINIA OUTDOORS FOUNDATION
203 Governor St., Suite 317, Richmond, VA 23219
Phone: 804-225-2147; Fax: 804-371-4810
Description: To preserve Virginia's natural scenic, historic, scientific, open space, and recreational areas by means of private philanthropy. The Foundation accepts gifts of cash, stock, real property, or open spaces easements to achieve its purpose.
Contact(s):
Chairman: PAUL G. ZILUCA
Executive Director: TAMARA VANCE
Keyword(s): Conservation of Protected Areas, Land Preservation, Open Space

VIRGINIA SEA GRANT PROGRAM
Virginia Graduate Marine Science Consortium, 170 Rugby Rd., Madison House, University of Virginia, Charlottesville, VA 22903
Phone: 804-924-5965; Fax: 804-982-3694; Web site: www.virginia.edu/virginia-sea-grant/
Contact(s):
Director: DR. WILLIAM L. RICKARDS; E-mail: rickards@virginia.edu
Staff of Marine Advisory Program: DR. WILLIAM DuPAUL, Virginia Institute of Marine Science, Gloucester Point, VA 23062; Phone: 804-684-7163
Keyword(s): Aquatic Habitats, Coasts, Environmental and Conservation Education, Renewable Resources, Wetlands

VIRGINIA STATE EXTENSION SERVICES
Virginia Polytechnic Institute and State University, Blacksburg, VA 24061-0402
Phone: 540-231-5299; Web site: www.ext.vt.edu/
Contact(s):
Extension Aquaculture Specialist: BRIAN L. NERRIE, Virginia State University, P.O. Box 9081, Petersburg, VA 23806; Phone: 804-524-5903
Extension Fisheries Specialist: DR. LOUIS A. HELFRICH, Department of Fisheries and Wildlife Sciences, Virginia Polytechnic Institute and State University, Blacksburg, VA 24061-0321; Phone: 540-231-5059
Extension Wildlife Specialist: DR. JAMES A. PARKHURST, Department of Fisheries & Wildlife Sciences, Virginia Polytechnic Institute and State University, Blacksburg, VA 24061-0321; Phone: 540-231-9283; Fax: 540-231-7265
Extension Wildlife Specialist: DR. GERALD H. CROSS, Department of Fisheries and Wildlife Sciences, Virginia Polytechnic Institute and State University, Blacksburg, VA 24061-0321; Phone: 540-231-8844
Interim Director of Cooperative Extension: J. DAVID BARRETT
Project Leader of Forestry and Wildlife Extension: DR. JAMES E. JOHNSON, College of Natural Resources, Virginia Polytechnic Institute and State University, Blacksburg, VA 24061-0324; Phone: 540-231-7679
Sea Grant Extension Seafood Technologist: DR. GEORGE J. FLICK JR., Dept. of Food Science and Technology, Virginia Polytechnic Institute and State University, Blacksburg, VA 24061-0418; Phone: 540-231-6965

WASHINGTON

GOVERNOR OF WASHINGTON: GARY LOCKE
Legislative Bldg., P.O. Box 40002, Olympia, WA 98504-0002
Phone: 360-902-4111

COLUMBIA RIVER GORGE COMMISSION
P.O. Box 730, White Salmon, WA 98672
Phone: 509-493-3323; Fax: 509-493-2229
Description: Established by the states of Oregon and Washington to implement the Columbia River Gorge National Scenic Area Act by developing a regional management plan, in cooperation with the U.S. Forest Service. The commission is composed of three members from Oregon, three from Washington, and one from each of the six local Gorge counties. A Secretary of Agriculture appointee is a thirteenth nonvoting member. Purpose of the National Scenic Area Act is to protect and enhance scenic, natural, cultural, and recreation resources, while encouraging economic development within 13 established urban areas.
Contact(s):
Chairman: ANNE SQUIER
Interim Executive Director: CLAIRE A. PUCHY
Vice Chairman: BUD QUINN
Keyword(s): Environmental Planning, Land Use Planning, Natural Areas, Outdoor Recreation, Wildlife and Wildlife Habitat

DEPARTMENT OF FISH AND WILDLIFE (WASHINGTON)
600 Capitol Way, N., Olympia, WA 98501-1091
Phone: 360-902-2200; Fax: 360-902-2947
Founded: 1933
Contact(s):
Deputy Director: DIRK BRAZIL; Phone: 360-902-2232
Director: DR. BERNARD SHANKS; Phone: 360-902-2225
Assistant Director of Administrative Services: DAVE BRITTELL; Phone: 360-902-2206
Assistant Director of Enforcement Program: RON SWATFIGURE; Phone: 360-902-2927
Assistant Director of Fish Management Program: BRUCE CRAWFORD; Phone: 360-902-2325
Assistant Director of Habitat and Lands Services Program: ELYSE KANE; Phone: 360-902-2402
Assistant Director of Wildlife Management Program: DAVE BRITTELL; Phone: 360-902-2504
Regional Director: SARA LABORDE, 48 B Devonshire Rd., Montesona, WA 98563; Phone: 206-249-6522
Regional Director: LEE VAN TUSSENBROOK, 5405 NE Hazel Dell, Vancouver, WA 98663; Phone: 206-696-6211
Regional Director: BOB EVERITT, 16018 Mill Creek Blvd., Mill Creek, WA 98012; Phone: 425-775-1311
Regional Director: DALE BAMBRICK, 1701 S. 24th Ave., Yakima, WA 98902-5720; Phone: 509-575-2740
Regional Director: JEFF TAYER, 1550 Alder St., NW, Ephrata, WA 98823; Phone: 509-754-4624
Regional Director: BRUCE SMITH, 8702 N. Division St., Spokane, WA 99218; Phone: 509-456-4082
Regional Director: MIKE KUTTEL, 600 Capital Way N., Olympia, WA 98501-1091; Phone: 360-902-2804
Keyword(s): Aquatic Habitats, Endangered and Threatened Species, Hunting, Sport Fishing, Wildlife and Wildlife Habitat

INTERAGENCY COMMITTEE FOR OUTDOOR RECREATION (IAC)
1111 Washington St., SE, P.O. Box 40917, Olympia, WA 98504-0917
Phone: 360-902-3000
Founded: 1965
Description: IAC administers grants and technical assistance programs for public recreation, open space, and conservation projects in Washington state. The agency assists local, state, federal, and nonprofit organizations in planning, acquiring, and developing recreation resources. IAC also writes the state's outdoor recreation and open space plan, as well as plans on trails and non-highway off-road vehicle recreation.
Contact(s):
Special Assistant to the Director: JIM FOX; Phone: 360-902-3021
Director: LAURA ECKERT JOHNSON; Phone: 360-902-3000
Assistant Director of Management Services: DEBRA WILHELMI; Phone: 360-902-3005
Manager of Applied Planning: GREGORY W. LOVELADY; Phone: 360-902-3008
Manager of Project Services: ERIC JOHNSON; Phone: 360-902-3015
Keyword(s): Environmental Preservation, Land Purchase, Land Use Planning, Outdoor Recreation, Public Lands

STATE PARKS AND RECREATION COMMISSION (WASHINGTON)
7150 Cleanwater Ln., P.O. Box 42650, Olympia, WA 98504-2650
Founded: 1912
Description: To acquire, develop, improve, and maintain state parks and recreation areas. Involvement includes but is not limited to state parks, seashore conservation, water and boating safety, snowmobile safety and natural and historic heritage interpretation.
Contact(s):
Deputy Director: FRANK BOTELER; Phone: 360-902-8502
Director: CLEVE PINNIX; Phone: 360-902-8501
Administrator of Public Affairs: SUSAN ZEMEK; Phone: 360-902-8562
Assistant Director of Administrative Services: RITA COOPER; Phone: 360-902-8525
Assistant Director of Operations: KATHY SMITH; Phone: 360-902-8594
Assistant Director of Resources Development: LARRY FAIRLEIGH; Phone: 360-902-8642
Chief Engineer: TOM BOYER; Phone: 360-902-8616
Chief of Boating Programs: JIM FRENCH; Phone: 360-902-8515
Chief of Budget Services: BETHANY MILLER; Phone: 360-902-8532
Chief of Employee Services: JUDY JOHNSON; Phone: 360-902-8568
Chief of Environmental Coordination: BILL JOLLY; Phone: 360-902-8636
Chief of Fiscal Services: SANDY REES; Phone: 360-902-8575

STATE AND PROVINCIAL GOVERNMENT AGENCIES - WASHINGTON

Chief of Information Processing: ART BROWN; Phone: 360-902-8585
Chief of Natural Resource Management: DAN INGMAN; Phone: 360-902-8592
Chief of Parks Maintenance: PAUL GEORGE; Phone: 360-902-8540
Chief of Programs Management: JAMES HORAN; Phone: 360-902-8580
Chief of Research and Long Range Planning: WILLIAM C. JOLLY; Phone: 360-902-8641
Chief of Site Planning: BILL KOSS; Phone: 360-902-8629
Chief of Visitor Protection and Law Enforcement: BILL GANSBERG; Phone: 360-902-8598
Chief of Visitor Services: PAM McCONKEY; Phone: 360-902-8595
Contracts Specialist: WAYNE McLAUGHLIN; Phone: 360-902-8599
Legislative Liaison: REX DERR; Phone: 306-902-8504
Keyword(s): Cultural Preservation, Nature Preservation, Open Space, Outdoor Recreation, Public Lands

Eastern Region
Contact(s):
Staff (Acting): JIM HARRIS, 2201 N. Duncan Dr., Wenatchee, WA 98801; Phone: 509-662-0420

Northwest Region
Contact(s):
Staff: TERRY DORAN, P.O. Box 487, Burlington, WA 98801-1007; Phone: 360-755-9231

Puget Sound Region
Contact(s):
Staff: DON SIMMONS, 1602 29th St., SE, Auburn, WA 98002; Phone: 206-931-3907

Southwest Region
Contact(s):
Staff: PAUL MALMBERG, 11838 Tilley Rd., S., Olympia, WA 98512-9167; Phone: 360-753-7143

WASHINGTON COOPERATIVE FISH AND WILDLIFE RESEARCH UNIT (USDI)
U.S. Geological Survey, School of Fisheries, Box 357980, University of Washington, Seattle, WA 98195
Phone: 206-543-6475; Fax: 206-616-9012
Founded: 1988
Description: The goals of the WCFWRU are: (1) conduct research in support of the Department of the Interior and Washington State; (2) train graduate students in fisheries and wildlife science through research support and by teaching; and (3) disseminate research results to the scientific community, management agencies and the general public.
Contact(s):
Assistant Leader of Wildlife: GLENN R. VanBLARICOM
Leader: CHRISTIAN E. GRUE
Keyword(s): Aquatic Habitats, Biodiversity, Fisheries, Toxicology, Wildlife and Wildlife Habitat

WASHINGTON DEPARTMENT OF AGRICULTURE
P.O. Box 42560, Olympia, WA 98504-2560
Phone: 360-902-1800; Web site: www.wa.gov/agr
Contact(s):
Deputy Director: BILL BROOKRESON; Phone: 360-902-1810
Director: JIM JESERNIG; Phone: 360-902-1801
Assistant Director of Agency Operations: KELLY GWIN; Phone: 360-902-1978
Assistant Director of Commodity Inspection: BOB GORE; Phone: 360-902-1827
Assistant Director of Consumer and Producer Protection Division: JULIE SANDBERG; Phone: 360-902-1850
Assistant Director of Food Safety and Animal Health Division: CANDACE JACOBS; Phone: 360-902-1888
Assistant Director of Laboratory Services: MARY M. TOOHEY; Phone: 360-902-1907
Assistant Director of Pesticide Management Division: BOB ARRINGTON; Phone: 360-902-2011
Information Officer: LINDA WARING; Phone: 360-902-1815
State Veterinarian: DR. ROBERT MEAD; Phone: 360-902-1881
Keyword(s): Agriculture, Pesticides

WASHINGTON DEPARTMENT OF ECOLOGY
P.O. Box 47600, Olympia, WA 98504-7600
Phone: 360-407-6000
Founded: 1970
Description: Charged with programs of air quality control, water pollution control, solid waste management, management of water resources, hazardous waste management, reduction, and cleanup, shoreline management, coastal zone management, and State Environmental Policy Act (SEPA).
Contact(s):
Deputy Director: DAN SILVER; Phone: 360-407-7011
Director: TOM FITZSIMMONS; Phone: 360-407-7001
Administrative Services Manager: CAROL FLESKES; Phone: 360-407-7012
Assistant Director of Legislative & Intergovernmental Relations: BILL ALKIRE; Phone: 360-407-7003
Attorney General of Office of Attorney General: DAVID MEARS; Phone: 360-459-6158
Chief Financial Officer: NANCY STEVENSON; Phone: 360-407-7005
Librarian: PHYLLIS SHAFER; Phone: 206-407-6150

Central Regional Office
Contact(s):
Staff: POLLY ZEHM; Phone: 509-457-7120

Eastern Regional Office
Contact(s):
Staff: TONY GROVER; Phone: 509-456-6149

Northwest Regional Office
Contact(s):
Staff: RAY HELLWIG; Phone: 425-649-7010

Southwest Regional Office
Contact(s):
Staff: SUE MAUERMANN; Phone: 360-407-6307

WASHINGTON DEPARTMENT OF NATURAL RESOURCES
P.O. Box 47001, Olympia, WA 98504-7001
Phone: 360-902-1000
Contact(s):
Commissioner of Public Lands: JENNIFER M. BELCHER; Phone: 360-902-1004
Communications: SUE ZEMEK; Phone: 360-902-1023
Department Supervisor: CHARLES BAUM; Phone: 360-902-1034
Deputy Commissioner: KALEEN COTTINGHAM; Phone: 360-902-1003
Executive Assistant: MICHELLE BENTON; Phone: 360-902-1004
Geology Library Manager: CONNIE MANSON; Phone: 360-902-1472
Manager of Agricultural Resources Division (Acting): BILL BOYUM; Phone: 360-902-1130
Manager of Aquatic Resources Division: MARIA VICTORIA PEELER; Phone: 360-902-1100
Manager of Employee Services Division: JUDI BRUNNER; Phone: 360-902-1150
Manager of Engineering Division: TONY IFIE; Phone: 360-920-1200
Manager of Financial Management Division: LOREN STERN; Phone: 360-902-1250
Manager of Forest Practices Division: CATHERINE ELLIOTT; Phone: 360-902-1400
Manager of Forest Resources Division: MICHAEL PEREZ-GIBSON; Phone: 360-902-1340
Manager of Geology and Earth Resources Division: RAY LASMANIS; Phone: 360-902-1450
Manager of Information Technology Division: AL BLOOMBERG; Phone: 360-902-1500
Manager of Resource Protection Division: RANDY ACKER; Phone: 360-902-1300

Manager of Resources Planning and Asset Management Division: JOY KENISTON-LONGRIE; Phone: 360-902-1600
Publication(s): *DNR News*

Central Region
Contact(s):
Staff: HOWARD THRONSON; Phone: 360-748-2383

Northeast Region
Contact(s):
Staff: STEVE MEACHAM; Phone: 509-684-7474

Northwest Region
Contact(s):
Staff: BILL WALLACE; Phone: 360-856-3500

Olympic Region
Contact(s):
Staff: TOM ROBINSON; Phone: 360-374-6131

South Puget Sound Region
Contact(s):
Staff: BONNIE BUNNING; Phone: 360-825-1631

Southeast Region
Contact(s):
Staff: BILL BOYUM; Phone: 509-925-8510

Southwest Region
Contact(s):
Staff: RICK COOPER; Phone: 360-577-2025

WASHINGTON NATURAL HERITAGE PROGRAM
Forest Resources Division, Dept. of Natural Resources, Olympia, WA 98504-7016
Phone: 360-902-1682; Fax: 360-902-1783; Web site: www.wa.gov/dnr/htdocs/fr/nhp/wanhp.html
Founded: 1978
Description: Identify and evaluate native ecosystems and species, set conservation priorities, provide information to protect these irreplaceable resources for the benefit of current and future generations.
Contact(s):
Program Manager (Acting) and Botanist: JOHN GAMON; Phone: 360-902-1661
Publication(s): *State of Washington Natural Heritage Plan; Endangered, Threatened, and Sensitive Vascular Plants of Washington with working list of Rare Non-vascular Species*
Keyword(s): Biodiversity, Botany, Zoology

WASHINGTON SEA GRANT PROGRAM
3716 Brooklyn Ave., NE, Seattle, WA 98105-6716
Phone: 206-543-6600; Fax: 206-685-0380; E-mail: seagrant@u.washington.edu; Web site: www.wsg.washington.edu/
Description: Since 1968, Washington Sea Grant Program has supported research, advisory, and communication activities for the benefit of marine resources, users, and communities. It is part of a national network of universities meeting the changing environmental and economic needs of people in our coastal and Great Lakes regions.
Contact(s):
Director: LOUIE S. ECHOLS; E-mail: echols@u.washington.edu
Assistant Director of Advisory Services: MICHAEL S. SPRANGER, Marine Advisory Services, University of Washington, 3716 Brooklyn Ave., NE, Seattle, WA 98105; Phone: 206-685-9261
Assistant Director: ANDREA COPPING; Phone: 206-685-8209
Communications Manager: NANCY BLANTON; Phone: 206-685-9215
Publications Coordinator/Web Master: SUSAN COOK; Phone: 206-685-2606; Fax: 206-685-0380
Senior Program Associate: MEGAN BAILIFF; Phone: 206-685-1108
Publication(s): *El Niño North: Niño Effects in the Eastern Subarctic Pacific Ocean; Ocean Ecology of North Pacific Salmonids; Guide to Manila Clam Culture in Washington; Shape and Form of Puget Sound, The*
Keyword(s): Biotechnology, Fisheries, Oceanography, Sustainable Development, Wetlands

WASHINGTON STATE CONSERVATION COMMISSION
P.O. Box 47721, Olympia, WA 98504-7721
Phone: 206-407-6200; Fax: 206-407-6215
Founded: 1939
Description: Assists, guides, and coordinates the programs of 48 conservation districts and encourages the cooperation and collaboration of the federal, state, regional, interstate, and local public agencies which assist them; keeps the public informed of renewable natural resource conservation activities.
Contact(s):
Chair: RONALD JURIS, P.O. Box 157, Bickleton, WA 98322-0157
Executive Director: STEVEN R. MEYER; Phone: 206-407-6201; Fax: 360-407-6215; E-mail: smey461@ecy.wa.gov
Central WA Field Representative: CHUCK BAGLEY; Phone: 509-664-3154; Fax: 509-665-3366
Eastern WA Field Representative: WILLIAM C. BROUGHTON; Phone: 509-397-4740; Fax: 509-397-4921
Grants Officer: ROBERT P. BOTTMAN; Phone: 360-407-6204
Puget Sound Field Representative: STU TREFRY; Phone: 360-407-6211
Keyword(s): Agriculture, Environmental and Conservation Education, Renewable Resources, Soil Conservation, Water Resources

WASHINGTON STATE EXTENSION SERVICES
Washington State University, P.O. Box 646230, Pullman, WA 99164
Phone: 509-335-2933; Web site: ext.wsu.edu/
Description: Washington State University Cooperative Extension helps people develop leadership skills and use research-based knowledge to improve their economic status and quality of life.
Contact(s):
Associate Dean and Associate Director of Extension Services: MICHAEL J. TATE
Program Leader: EDWARD B. ADAMS, Washington State University Cooperative Extension, 668 N. Riverpoint Blvd., Box B, Spokane, WA 99202-1662; Phone: 509-358-7960; Fax: 509-358-7900; E-mail: adamse@wsu.edu
Extension Forester: DAVID M. BAUMGARTNER, Department of Natural Resource Sciences, P.O. Box 646410, Washington State University, Pullman, WA 99164-6410; Phone: 509-335-2964
Extension Forester: DONALD P. HANLEY, College of Forest Resources, University of Washington, Box 352100, Seattle, WA 98195-2100; Phone: 206-685-4960
Extension Naturalist: JOHN H. MUNN, Washington State University CES, 600 128th St., SE, Everett, WA 98208; Phone: 425-388-2400; Fax: 425-338-3994
Extension Urban and Community Horticulture (Interim): SHEILA GRAY, Washington State University, 207 4th Ave. N., Kelso, WA 98262-4124; Phone: 360-577-3014
Keyword(s): Agriculture, Environmental and Conservation Education, Forests and Forestry, Renewable Resources, Sustainable Ecosystems

WASHINGTON STATE OFFICE OF ENVIRONMENTAL EDUCATION
Office of Superintendent of Public Instruction, 2800 NE 200th St., Seattle, WA 98155-1418
Phone: 206-365-3893; Web site: cisl.ospi.wednet.edu/cisl/enved/envedtoc.html
Description: To provide curriculum resources and training for teachers in environmental education, and to evaluate these programs pursuant to improving content and effectiveness. The office is responsible for E.E. program coordination and cooperation as it applies to K-12 public school programs and to state mandate requiring E.E. integrated into the K-12 curriculum.

Contact(s):
Administrative Assistant: MICHELE HALFHILL
State Supervisor of Environmental Education: TONY ANGELL
Publication(s): *Clean Water, Streams and Fish: A Holistic View of Watersheds; Energy Food & You; Puget Sound Habitats Teachers Guide and Charts; Closing the Achievement Gap: Using the Environment as an Integrating Context for Learning; Tools for Understanding: Focus on Environmental Education*
Keyword(s): Environmental and Conservation Education, Solid Waste Management, Sustainable Ecosystems, Water Pollution Management, Wildlife and Wildlife Habitat

WEST VIRGINIA

GOVERNOR OF WEST VIRGINIA: CECIL UNDERWOOD
State Capitol Complex, Charleston, WV 25305-0370
Phone: 304-558-2000

WEST VIRGINIA BUREAU OF ENVIRONMENT
Division of Environmental Protection, #10, McJunkin Rd., Nitro, WV 25143-2546
Phone: 304-759-0515
Founded: 1991
Description: The Division of Environmental Protection is charged with the protection of West Virginia's environment through the regulation and administration of the state's abandoned mine lands, air quality, mining & reclamation, oil & gas, waste management, and water resources programs.
Contact(s):
Director: MICHAEL P. MIANO
Chief Communications Officer: ANDY GALLAGHER; Phone: 304-759-0515
Chief of Administration: RANDY HUFFMAN; Phone: 304-759-0515
Chief of Air Quality: JOHN JOHNSTON; Phone: 304-558-4022
Chief of Legal Services: BILL ADAMS; Phone: 304-558-9160
Chief of Mining & Reclamation: JOHN AILES; Phone: 304-759-0510
Chief of Oil & Gas: TED STREIT; Phone: 304-759-0514
Chief of Waste Management: B. F. SMITH; Phone: 304-558-5929
Chief of Water Resources: BARBARA S. TAYLOR; Phone: 304-558-2107

WEST VIRGINIA COOPERATIVE FISH AND WILDLIFE RESEARCH UNIT
Division of Forestry, West Virginia University, P.O. Box 6125, Morgantown, WV 26506-6125
Phone: 304-293-3794, ext. 2430
Description: A cooperative research and graduate education organization sponsored by the Biological Resources Division of USGS, West Virginia Division of Natural Resources, West Virginia University, and Wildlife Management Institute. The role of the unit is to conduct natural resources research of state, regional, or national scope, and to train graduate-level researchers in natural resources.
Contact(s):
Assistant Leader: Wildlife: DR. PETRA BOHALL WOOD
Unit Leader: Fisheries: DR. PATRICIA MAZIK
Keyword(s): Aquatic Habitats, Fisheries, Nongame Wildlife, Rivers, Toxicology, Wildlife and Wildlife Habitat

WEST VIRGINIA DEPARTMENT OF AGRICULTURE
State Capitol, Rm. M-28, Charleston, WV 25305
Phone: 304-558-3550; Fax: 304-558-0451
Contact(s):
Assistant Commissioner: JANET L. FISHER
Commissioner: GUS R. DOUGLASS
Deputy Commissioner: DAVID E. MILLER
Director of Plant Industries Division: DR. CHARLES C. COFFMAN
Keyword(s): Agriculture, Pesticides, Public Health Protection, Soil Conservation, Water Resources

West Virginia Soil Conservation Agency
Contact(s):
Executive Director: LANCE TABOR; Phone: 304-558-2204; Fax: 304-558-1635; E-mail: taborl@wvlc.wvnet.edu

WEST VIRGINIA DIVISION OF NATURAL RESOURCES
1900 Kanawha Blvd. E., Charleston, WV 25305
Phone: 304-558-2754; Fax: 304-558-3147
Founded: 1933
Description: The Division's objective is to provide a comprehensive program for the exploration, conservation, development, protection, enjoyment, and use of the natural resources of the state of West Virginia. The commission was the forerunner of the Department of Natural Resources, created by the legislature in 1961 and modified to the Division of Natural Resources in 1993.
Contact(s):
Deputy Director: TONY POLITINO
Executive Secretary: HARRY F. PRICE; Phone: 304-558-3315
Director: JOHN B. RADER
Assistant Chief in charge of Biometrics and Planning: WALT KORDEK; Phone: 304-637-0245
Assistant Chief in charge of Coldwater Fisheries: MICHAEL V. SHINGLETON; Phone: 304-637-0245
Assistant Chief in charge of Game Management: PAUL R. JOHANSEN; Phone: 304-558-2771
Assistant Chief in charge of Special Projects: DONALD P. PHARES; Phone: 304-637-0245
Assistant Chief in charge of Warmwater Fisheries: BERT E. PIERCE; Phone: 304-558-2771
Chief of Law Enforcement: JAMES D. FIELDS; Phone: 304-558-2784
Chief of Parks & Recreation: CORDIE HUDKINS; Phone: 304-558-2764
Chief of Wildlife Resources: BERNARD F. DOWLER; Phone: 304-558-2771
Conservation Education/Litter Control: EMILY J. FLEMING; Phone: 304-558-3370
Deputy Chief, Law Enforcement: W. B. DANIEL; Phone: 304-558-2784
Deputy Chief, Parks and Recreation: KEN CAPLINGER; Phone: 304-558-2764
Deputy Chief, Wildlife Resources: GORDON C. ROBERTSON; Phone: 304-558-2771
District I Commissioner: DR. CHARLES P. CAPITO, Suite #3 2619 Pennsylvania Ave., Weirton, WV 36062; Phone: 304-723-3355
District I Commissioner: JEFFREY S. BOWERS, HC 70 Box 40 A, Sugar Grove, WV 26815; Phone: 304-358-3333
District II Commissioner: CARL E. GAINER, P.O. Box 670, Richwood, WV 26261; Phone: 304-846-6247
District Ii Commissioner: CHARLES R. HOOTEN, 1570 Summit Drive, Charleston, WV 25302; Phone: 304-346-0521
District II Commissioner: CARL FRISCHKORN, 1234 Upper Ridgeway Rd., Charleston, WV 25314; Phone: 304-926-9036
District II Commissioner: DR. THOMAS R. HOMAN, 1410 Bedford Rd., Charleston, WV 25314; Phone: 304-346-3330
Editor: ARNOUT HYDE JR.; Phone: 304-558-9152
Public Information Officer: HOY MURPHY; Phone: 304-558-3380
Real Estate Management: JAMES JONES; Phone: 304-558-3225; Fax: 304-558-3680
Publication(s): *Wonderful West Virginia*
Keyword(s): Aquatic Habitats, Hunting, Nongame Wildlife, Sport Fishing, Wildlife Management

WEST VIRGINIA GEOLOGICAL AND ECONOMIC SURVEY
Box 879, Morgantown, WV 26507-0879
Phone: 304-594-2331; Fax: 304-594-2575
Founded: 1897
Description: Charged with the responsibility of examining all geological formations and physical features of the state with particular emphasis on their economic importance, utilization, and conservation and preparing reports and maps of the geology and natural resources of West Virginia.

STATE AND PROVINCIAL GOVERNMENT AGENCIES - WISCONSIN

Contact(s):
Associate State Geologist and Deputy Director: CARL J. SMITH; Phone: 304-594-2331
Deputy Director of Finance and Administration: JOHN D. MAY
Director and State Geologist: LARRY D. WOODFORK; Phone: 304-594-2331; E-mail: woodfork@geoserv.wvnet.edu
Editor: CHUCK GOVER; Phone: 304-594-2331
Program Manager for Administration: GLORIA J. ROWAN
Program Manager for Coal: NICK FEDORKO III
Program Manager for Geologic Date: MARY C. BEHLING
Program Manager for Oil and Gas: KATHERINE LEE AVARY
Program Manager for Publications and Graphics Section: CHARLES H. GOVER
Program Manager for Service: STEVEN W. McCLELLAND
Publication(s): *Bulletins; reports of investigations; circulars; coal-geology bulletins; environmental geology bulletins; mineral resources series; river basin bulletins; basic data reports; county geologic reports; educational series; state park bulletins; field trip guide.*

WEST VIRGINIA STATE EXTENSION SERVICE
West Virginia University, 817 Knapp Hall, Morgantown, WV 26506
Phone: 304-293-5691; Web site: www.wvu.edu/~exten/
Contact(s):
Director, Center for Agricultural and Natural Resources Development: DR. RICHARD ZIMMERMAN, West Virginia University, 2080 Agricultural Science Bldg., P.O. Box 6108, Morgantown, WV 26506-6108; Phone: 304-293-6131; E-mail: rzimmerm@wvu.edu
Associate Director, Center for Agriculture and Natural Resources Development: EDMOND B. COLLINS, West Virginia University, 2078 Agricultural Sciences Bldg., P.O. Box 6108, Morgantown, WV 26506-6108; Phone: 304-293-6131; E-mail: ecollin2@wvu.edu
Associate Provost for Extension and Public Service: DR. LAWRENCE S. COTE, West Virginia University, 817 Knapp Hall, P.O. Box 6031, Morgantown, WV 26506-6125; Phone: 304-293-5691; E-mail: lcote@wvu.edu
Extension Specialist, Land Reclamation: DR. JEFFREY G. SKOUSEN, West Virginia University, 1106 Agricultural Science Bldg., Morgantown, WV 26506-6108; Phone: 304-293-6131; E-mail: jskousen@wvu.edu
Extension Specialist, Nutrient Management: THOMAS J. BASDEN, West Virginia University, 1058 Agricultural Sciences Bldg., P.O. Box 6108, Morgantown, WV 26506-6108; Phone: 304-293-6131; E-mail: tbasden2@wvu.edu
Extension Specialist, Soil and Water Resources: DR. D. K. BHUMBLA, West Virginia University, 1072 Agricultural Sciences Bldg., P.O. Box 6108, Morgantown, WV 26506-6108; Phone: 304-293-6131; E-mail: dbhumbla@wvu.edu
Extension Specialist, Wildlife: WILLIAM GRAFTON, West Virginia University, 311-B Percival Hall, P.O Box 6125, Morgantown, WV 26506-6125; Phone: 304-293-4797/Ext.2493; Fax: 304-293-7553; E-mail: wgrafton@wvu.edu
Keyword(s): Agriculture, Forests and Forestry, Pesticides, Renewable Resources, Water Resources

WISCONSIN

GOVERNOR OF WISCONSIN: TOMMY G. THOMPSON
State Capitol, Madison, WI 53707
Phone: 608-266-1212

WISCONSIN CONSERVATION CORPS
30 W. Mifflin, Suite 406, Madison, WI 53703-2558
Phone: 608-266-7730
Founded: 1983
Description: The WCC provides work experience and personal development opportunities to young adults, ages 18-25, and valuable conservation and other services to Wisconsin communities. Approximately 550 corps members annually work at four dozen rotating project sites throughout the state. Government agencies and nonprofit organizations are eligible to apply for WCC assistance.
Contact(s):
Executive Director: LAURA DEGOLIER
Publication(s): *On Corps! Newsletter; Biennial Report*
Keyword(s): Environmental and Conservation Education, Fisheries, Forests and Forestry, Outdoor Recreation, Water Resources

WISCONSIN COOPERATIVE FISHERY RESEARCH UNIT (USDI)
College of Natural Resources, University of Wisconsin, Stevens Point, WI 54481
Phone: 715-346-2178
Description: Interagency organization on the federal, state, and university levels. It carries out research, training, and extension in biology and management of freshwater fishery resources.
Contact(s):
Leader: DR. MICHAEL A. BOZEK
Keyword(s): Aquatic Habitats, Fisheries, Lakes, Rivers, Sport Fishing

WISCONSIN COOPERATIVE WILDLIFE RESEARCH UNIT (USDI)
USGS, Department of Wildlife Ecology, 204 Russell Laboratories, University of Wisconsin, Madison, WI 53706-1598
Phone: 608-263-6882
Contact(s):
Leader: DR. DONALD H. RUSCH

WISCONSIN DEPARTMENT OF AGRICULTURE TRADE AND CONSUMER PROTECTION

Land and Water Resources Bureau
2811 Agriculture Dr., P.O. Box 8911, Madison, WI 53708-8911
Phone: 608-224-4620
Description: Responsible for administering state soil and water conservation and farmland preservation programs.
Contact(s):
Bureau Director: DAVID JELINSKI; Phone: 608-224-4621; Fax: 608-224-4615
Secretary: BEN BRANCEL
Keyword(s): Environment, Environmental Preservation, Land Preservation, Land Use Planning, Rural Development, Soil Conservation, Water Quality, Water Resources, Watersheds, Wetlands

WISCONSIN DEPARTMENT OF NATURAL RESOURCES
Box 7921, Madison, WI 53707
Phone: 608-266-2621
Description: Responsibilities include: fisheries, wildlife, forest, parks management, endangered resources protection, forest fire control, air and water pollution control, solid and hazardous waste management, mining regulation, enforcement of conservation and environmental laws, flood plain and shoreland zoning, water management and regulation, lake rehabilitation, and long-range planning in the broad fields of outdoor recreation and natural resources.
Contact(s):
Secretary: GEORGE E. MEYER; Phone: 608-266-2121
Deputy Secretary: DARRELL L. BAZZELL; Phone: 608-266-2252
Administrator of Administration and Technology Division: FRANCIS M. FENNESSY; Phone: 608-264-6133
Administrator of Air and Waste Division: JAY C. HOCHMUTH; Phone: 608-267-9521
Administrator of Customer Assistance and External Relations Division: CRAIG L. KARR; Phone: 608-266-5896
Administrator of Enforcement and Science Division: DAVID J. MEIER; Phone: 608-266-0015
Administrator of Land Division: STEVEN W. MILLER; Phone: 608-266-5782
Administrator of Water Division: SUSAN L. SYLVESTER; Phone: 608-266-1099
Bureau of Cooperative Environmental Assistance: LYNDA M. WIESE; Phone: 608-267-3125

STATE AND PROVINCIAL GOVERNMENT AGENCIES - WISCONSIN

Bureau of Enterprise Information Technology and Applications: SHARON L. MICHEL; Phone: 608-266-7547
Bureau of Watershed Management: ALLEN K. SHEA; Phone: 608-267-2759
Deputy Administrator of Air and Waste Division: MARY JO KOPECKY; Phone: 608-261-8448
Deputy Administrator of Bureau of Water: BRUCE J. BAKER; Phone: 608-266-1902
Director of Bureau of Administrative and Field Services: MARTIN M. HENERT; Phone: 608-266-9980
Director of Bureau of Air Management: LLOYD L. EAGAN; Phone: 608-266-0603
Director of Bureau of Communication and Education: LAUREL J. STEFFES; Phone: 608-266-8109
Director of Bureau of Community Financial Assistance: KATHRYN A. CURTNER; Phone: 608-266-0860
Director of Bureau of Drinking Water and Ground Water: ROBERT M. KRILL; Phone: 608-267-7651
Director of Bureau of Endangered Resources: STAN DRUCKENMILLER; Phone: 608-226-2136
Director of Bureau of Facilities and Lands: ROBERT W. RODEN; Phone: 608-266-2197
Director of Bureau of Finance: HERBERT M. ZIMMERMAN; Phone: 608-266-0062
Director of Bureau of Forestry: GENE FRANCISCO; Phone: 608-266-0842
Director of Bureau of Human Resources: DEBRA K. MARTINELLI; Phone: 608-266-2048
Director of Bureau of Integrated Science Services: JAMES T. ADDIS; Phone: 608-266-0837
Director of Bureau of Law Enforcement: THOMAS L. HARELSON; Phone: 608-266-1115
Director of Bureau of Legal Services: JAMES A. KURTZ; Phone: 608-266-3695
Director of Bureau of Management and Budget: JOSEPH P. POLASEK; Phone: 608-266-2794
Director of Bureau of Management and Habitat Protection: MICHAEL D. STAGGS; Phone: 608-267-0796
Director of Bureau of Remediation and Redevelopment: MARK F. GIESFELDT; Phone: 608-267-7562
Director of Bureau of Waste Management: SUZANNE BANGERT; Phone: 608-266-0014
Director of Bureau of Wildlife Management: THOMAS M. HAUGE; Phone: 608-266-2193
Director of Customer Service and Licensing: MARILYN A. DAVIS; Phone: 608-267-7799
Director of Parks and Recreation: SUSAN C. BLACK; Phone: 608-266-2185
Natural Resources Board Chairman: TRYGVE A. SOLBERG; Phone: 715-356-7711
Natural Resources Board Secretary: JAMES TIEFENTHALER JR.; Phone: 414-513-1111
Natural Resources Board Vice-Chair: NEAL SCHNEIDER; Phone: 608-754-4444
Northeast Regional Director: WILLIAM SELBIG, P.O. Box 10448, Green Bay, WI 54307; Phone: 920-492-5815
Northern Regional Director: WILLIAM H. SMITH, 810 W. Maple Street, Spooner, WI 54801; Phone: 715-635-4010
South Central Regional Director: RUTHE BADGER, 3911 Fish Hatchery Road, Madison, WI 53711; Phone: 608-275-3260
Southeast Regional Director: GLORIA L. McCUTCHEON, P.O. Box 12436, Milwaukee, WI 53212; Phone: 414-263-8510
West Central Regional Director: SCOTT HUMRICKHOUSE, P.O. Box 4001, Eau Claire, WI 54702; Phone: 715-839-3711
Editor, WI Natural Resources Magazine: LARRY SPERLING, Box 7921, Madison, WI 53707; Phone: 608-356-7711
Librarian: ERIN E. BAGGOTT; Phone: 608-267-7592
Publication(s): *WI Natural Resources Magazine*
Keyword(s): Air Quality and Pollution, Endangered Resources, Forests and Forestry
Land Management, Outdoor Recreation, Solid Waste, Water Resources

WISCONSIN DEPARTMENT OF PUBLIC INSTRUCTION
125 S. Webster St., P.O. Box 7841, Madison, WI 53707-7841
Phone: 800-441-4563; Fax: 608-267-9110
Description: A state government agency that promotes environmental education in public schools and supervises teacher preparation programs. Conducts workshops, and provides consultant services to elementary and secondary schools, colleges and universities. Produces publications to aid in program development.
Contact(s):
Environmental Education Consultant: SUE GRADY; Phone: 608-266-2364
Publication(s): *A Guide to Curriculum Planning in Environmental Education;* "Wisconsin's Model Academic Standards for Environmental Education"
Keyword(s): Environmental and Conservation Education

WISCONSIN ENVIRONMENTAL EDUCATION BOARD (WEEB)
P.O. Box 7841, Madison, WI 53707-7841
Phone: 608-266-3155
Founded: 1990
Description: Grants board providing $200,000 annually to environmental education (EE) initiative projects within the state of Wisconsin, with a maximum grant of $20,000 per project. The board priorities are further development of previously funded WEEB projects.
Contact(s):
Chairperson: JACK FINSER
Program Assistant: RON RUECKERT
Publication(s): *Annual Report; Grant Application*
Keyword(s): Environmental and Conservation Education, Scholarships and Grants

WISCONSIN GEOLOGICAL AND NATURAL HISTORY SURVEY
University of Wisconsin Extension, 3817 Mineral Point Rd., Madison, WI 53705
Phone: 608-262-1705
Founded: 1897
Description: Created by the legislature, with the responsibility to survey the state's geology, mineral, water, soil, plant, animal, and climate resources, and to coordinate topographic mapping.
Contact(s):
Assistant Director: RONALD HENNINGS; Phone: 608-263-7395
Budgeting Specialist: KATHLEEN ZWETTLER; Phone: 608-262-9418
State Geologist and Director: JAMES ROBERTSON; Phone: 608-263-7384
Keyword(s): Geology, Natural History, Soil Conservation, Water Resources

WISCONSIN SEA GRANT INSTITUTE
Attn: Director, UW Sea Grant Institute, 1975 Willow Dr., Fl. 2, Madison, WI 53706-1177
Phone: 608-262-0905; Fax: 608-262-0591; Web site: www.seagrant.wisc.edu/
Founded: 1968
Description: The University of Wisconsin Sea Grant Institute is a statewide program of basic and applied research, education, and technology transfer dedicated to the wise stewardship and sustainable use of Great Lakes and ocean resources.
Contact(s):
Director: DR. ANDERS W. ANDREN; E-mail: awandren@seagrant.wisc.edu
Assistant Director for Administration and Information Technology: MARY LOU REEB; Phone: 608-263-3296; E-mail: mlreeb@seagrant.wisc.edu
Assistant Director of Advisory Services: ALLEN H. MILLER; Phone: 608-262-0644; E-mail: ahmiller@seagrant.wisc.edu
Assistant Director of Communications: STEPHEN WITTMAN; Phone: 608-263-5371; E-mail: swittman@seagrant.wisc.edu
Keyword(s): Aquatic Habitats, Biotechnology, Fisheries, Lakes, Water Pollution

WISCONSIN STATE EXTENSION SERVICES
University of Wisconsin Extension, 432 N. Lake St., Madison, WI 53706
Phone: 608-263-2775
Contact(s):
Dean and Director of Cooperative Extension: DR. CARL O'CONNOR
Extension Forester: DR. BILL KLASE, A113 Russell Laboratories, University of Wisconsin; 1630 Linden Dr., Madison, WI 53706; Phone: 608-262-0134
Extension Wildlife Specialist: DR. ROBERT L. RUFF, 226 Russell Laboratories, University of Wisconsin; 1630 Linden Dr., Madison, WI 53706; Phone: 608-263-2071
Extension Wood Processing Specialist: TOM SCHOCKLY, 120 Russell Labs; 1630 Linden Dr., Madison, WI 53706; Phone: 608-262-3455
Statewide Program Leader: DR. PATRICK WALSH, Community, Natural Resource and Economic Development, University of Wisconsin-Extension, Rm. 625, 432 N. Lake St., Madison, WI 53706; Phone: 608-262-1748
Wildlife Specialist: DR. SCOTT CRAVEN, Kemp Natural Resources Station, 801 Kemp Woods Rd., Woodruff, WI 54568; Phone: 715-356-9070; Fax: 608-262-6099

WYOMING

GOVERNOR OF WYOMING: JIM GERINGER
State Capitol Bldg., Rm. 124, Cheyenne, WY 82002
Phone: 307-777-7434

DEPARTMENT OF COMMERCE
Division of Economic and Community Development, Energy Section1st Floor, Herschler Bldg., Cheyenne, WY 82002
Phone: 307-777-7284; Fax: 307-777-5840
Founded: 1985
Description: To promote the enhancement of domestic fossil energy resources, as well as the production of sustainable/renewable energy, while fostering the conservation of current energy resources.
Contact(s):
Executive Director: JOHN F. NUNLEY III
Publication(s): *Wyoming Minerals Yearbook; Wyoming Recycling Directory*

ENVIRONMENTAL QUALITY DEPARTMENT
122 W. 25th St., Herschler Bldg., Cheyenne, WY 82002
Phone: 307-777-7937
Founded: 1973
Description: Established to plan the development, use, reclamation, preservation, and enhancement of the air, land, and water resources of the state.
Contact(s):
Director: DENNIS HEMMER; Phone: 307-777-7938
Administrator of Abandoned Mine Land: EVON GREEN; Phone: 307-777-6145
Administrator of Air Quality: DAN OLSON; Phone: 307-777-7391
Administrator of Land Quality: RICHARD CHANCELLOR; Phone: 307-777-7756
Administrator of Management Services: JAMES UZZELL; Phone: 307-777-7937
Administrator of Water Quality: GARY BEACH; Phone: 307-777-7781
Manager of Solid Waste Program: DAVID A. FINLEY; Phone: 307-777-7752

INDUSTRIAL SITING DIVISION/DEPARTMENT OF ENVIRONMENTAL QUALITY
State of Wyoming, 3rd Fl, E Herschler Bldg., Cheyenne, WY 82002
Phone: 307-777-4369; E-mail: VFORSE@missc.state.wy.us; Web site: www.DEQ.state.wy.us
Founded: 1975
Description: Administers the Wyoming Industrial Development Information and Siting Act, which deals with the social, economic, and environmental impacts of large-scale industrial development. Responsibilities consist of investigating, reviewing, processing, and serving notice of permit applications.
Contact(s):
Administrator: GARY G. BEACH; Phone: 307-777-7369

STATE FORESTRY DIVISION (WYOMING)
1100 W. 22nd St., Cheyenne, WY 82002
Phone: 307-777-7586; Fax: 307-637-8726
Founded: 1952
Description: Has direction of all forestry matters within the jurisdiction of the state of Wyoming; manages of state-owned forest land; coordinates fire protection on twenty-nine million acres of state and private rural lands; assists landowners and communities in proper management of woody vegetation and forested lands; and provides forestry information to schools, organizations and individuals.
Contact(s):
Assistant State Forester of Fire Management: RAY A. WEIDENHAFT
Assistant State Forester of Forest Management: HOWARD C. PICKERD
Deputy State Forester: DANIEL J. PERKO
State Forester: THOMAS W. OSTERMANN
Publication(s): *Wyoming State Forest Resource Program; Wyoming's Forest Wealth; Wyoming State Forest Resource Program (Executive Summary)*
Keyword(s): Diseases, Flowers, Plants, and Trees, Forests and Forestry, Insects and Butterflies, Renewable Resources, Urban Forestry, Wildlife Management

WYOMING COOPERATIVE FISH AND WILDLIFE RESEARCH UNIT (USDI)
University of Wyoming, Box 3166, Biological Sciences Bldg., Rm. 419, Laramie, WY 82071
Phone: 307-766-5415; Fax: 307-766-5400
Founded: 1980
Description: Conducts research under auspices of the USGS Biological Resources Division and Wyoming Game and Fish Department in the northern Rocky Mountain region.
Contact(s):
Leader: DR. STANLEY H. ANDERSON
Assistant Leader of Fisheries: DR. WAYNE A. HUBERT
Assistant Leader of Wildlife: DR. FRED G. LINDZEY
Keyword(s): Endangered and Threatened Species, Fisheries, Nongame Wildlife, Wildlife and Wildlife Habitat, Wildlife Management

WYOMING DEPARTMENT OF AGRICULTURE
2219 Carey Ave., Cheyenne, WY 82002
Phone: 307-777-7321; Fax: 307-777-6593
Contact(s):
Deputy Director: JIM SCHWARTZ; Phone: 307-777-6591
Director: RON MICHELI; Phone: 307-777-6569; Fax: 307-777-6593; E-mail: rmiche@missc.state.wy.us
Natural Resource and Policy Manager: GRANT STUMBOUGH; Phone: 307-777-6579

WYOMING DEPARTMENT OF COMMERCE

Division of State Parks and Historic Sites
1st Floor, Herschler Bldg, Cheyenne, WY 82002
Phone: 307-777-6323
Founded: 1967
Description: Responsible for administering the state parks, state recreation areas, historic sites, petroglyph site, archaeological site, markers and monuments, snowmobile program, and state trails program.
Contact(s):
Assistant Administrator: LARRY HOOTMAN; Phone: 307-777-6025
Director of Division of State Parks and Historic Sites: GARY THORSON; Phone: 307-777-6324; Fax: 307-777-6472

STATE AND PROVINCIAL GOVERNMENT AGENCIES - ALBERTA

Keyword(s): Historic Preservation, Land Preservation, Nature Preservation, Outdoor Recreation, Public Lands

WYOMING GAME AND FISH DEPARTMENT
5400 Bishop Blvd., Cheyenne, WY 82006
Phone: 307-777-4600; Fax: 307-777-4610
Founded: 1939
Description: To provide an adequate and flexible system for the control, propagation, management, protection, and regulation of Wyoming wildlife for the public interest.
Contact(s):
Deputy Director: BILL WICHERS
Deputy Director: STEVE FACCIANI
Director: JOHN BAUGHMAN
Chief of Fiscal Division: LARRY GABRIELE; Phone: 307-777-4516
Chief of Fish Division: MIKE STONE; Phone: 307-777-4559
Chief of Wildlife Division: JAY LAWSON; Phone: 307-777-4579
District Wildlife Supervisor: SCOTT TALBOTT, 3030 Energy Ln., Suite 100, Casper, WY 82604; Phone: 307-473-3400
District Wildlife Supervisor: KENT SCHMIDLIN, 260 Buena Vista, Lander, WY 82520; Phone: 307-332-2688
District Wildlife Supervisor: GREGG ARTHUR, 528 S. Adams, Laramie, WY 82070; Phone: 307-745-4046
District Wildlife Supervisor: STEVE DeCECCO, 351 Astle, GreenRiver, WY 82935; Phone: 307-875-3223
District Wildlife Supervisor: GARY SHORMA, Box 6249, Sheridan, WY 82801; Phone: 307-672-7418
District Wildlife Supervisor: GARY BROWN, 2820 State Highway 120, Cody, WY 82414; Phone: 307-527-7125
District Wildlife Supervisor: BERNIE HOLZ, Box 67, Jackson, WY 83001; Phone: 307-733-2321
Special Assistant for Policy: LARRY KRUCKENBERG; Phone: 307-777-4539
Publication(s): *Wyoming Wildlife (800-548-9453)*
Keyword(s): Environmental and Conservation Education, Fisheries, Hunting, Nongame Wildlife, Wildlife and Wildlife Habitat

WYOMING STATE BOARD OF LAND COMMISSIONERS
Herschler Bldg., Cheyenne, WY 82002
Phone: 307-777-7331; Fax: 307-777-5400
Contact(s):
Chairman: JIM GERINGER
Secretary: STEPHAN REYNOLDS
Keyword(s): Environment, Land Preservation, Public Lands, Renewable Resources

WYOMING STATE EXTENSION SERVICES
University Station, Box 3354, Laramie, WY 82071
Phone: 307-766-5124; Fax: 307-766-3998
Contact(s):
Director and Associate Dean: GLEN WHIPPLE; E-mail: glen@uwyo.edu
Interim Director: BARB FARMER; Phone: 307-766-3702
Associate Director: STEVE AAGARD; Phone: 307-766-5170
Associate Director: RUTH WILSON; Phone: 307-766-3567
Publication(s): *Journal articles; scientific abstracts; science monographs; research journals; bulletins; 4-H publications; regional publications*
Keyword(s): Agriculture, Environmental and Conservation Education, Sustainable Development, Water Resources, Wildlife Management

WYOMING STATE GEOLOGICAL SURVEY
Box 3008, Laramie, WY 82071
Phone: 307-766-2286; Fax: 307-766-2605; E-mail: wsgs@wsgs.uwyo.edu; sales@wsgs.uwyo.edu
Founded: 1933
Description: Activities include surface and subsurface geologic mapping; mineral, rock, and fossil investigations; natural resource and natural hazards investigations; and assistance in resources development.
Contact(s):
Coal Geologist: ROBERT M. LYMAN
Editor: RICHARD W. JONES
Geologic Hazards Geologist: JAMES C. CASE
Geologic Mapping Geologist: ALAN J. VERPLOEG
Industrial Minerals Geologist: RAY E. HARRIS
Petroleum Geologist: RODNEY H. DeBRUIN
Senior Economic Geologist of Metals and Precious Stones: W. DAN HAUSEL
State Geologist: GARY B. GLASS; E-mail: gglass@wsgs.uwyo.edu
Publication(s): *Memoirs; bulletins; reports of investigations; public information circulars; quarterly newsletter (Wyoming Geo-notes); list of publications sent on request.*
Keyword(s): Energy, Geology, Land Use Planning, Mineral Resources

INTERNATIONAL

TANZANIA COASTAL MANAGEMENT PARTNERSHIP
Henile Sellasie St., P.O. Box 71886, Dar Es Salaam Tanzania
Phone: +255+51-667589; Fax: 668611; E-mail: gluhikula@epog.or.tz
Description: Integrated coastal management policy process in Tanzania.
Contact(s):
Contact: G. LUHIKULA
Keyword(s): Coasts

CANADA

ALBERTA

ALBERTA DEPARTMENT OF ENVIRONMENTAL PROTECTION
Main Fl., Petroleum Plaza, North Tower, 9945-108 St., Edmonton, Alberta T5K296 Canada
Phone: 403-427-7381
Founded: 1992
Description: The Department of Environmental Protection is responsible for protecting, enhancing, and ensuring the wise use of Alberta's environment. The services within the department work cooperatively to meet the needs of Albertans by protecting wildlife, forests, parks, and other natural resources through enforcement of provincial legislation and ensuring the sustainable management of all these resources.
Contact(s):
Information Centre: Phone: 403-944-0313
Library: Phone: 409-427-587; Fax: 403-422-0170
Minister: TY LUND; Phone: 403-427-2391
Publication(s): *State of Environment Report; Annual Regulation Guides to Sportfishing, Hunting, and Trapping; Timber Supply Report; State of Alberta's Wildlife Report*

Communications Division
9th Floor, Petroleum Plaza, S. Tower, 9945-108 St., Edmonton, Alberta T5K 2C6 Canada
Contact(s):
Director: BOB SCOTT; Phone: 403-427-8636

Corporate Management Service
9th Floor, Petroleum Plaza, S. Tower, 9945-108 St., Edmonton, Alberta T5K 2C6 Canada

Environmental Service
Contact(s):
Assistant Deputy Minister: DOUG TUPPER; Phone: 403-427-6247

Land and Forest Service
Contact(s):
Assistant Deputy Minister: CLIFF HENDERSON; Phone: 403-427-3542

Natural Resources Service
Contact(s):
Deputy Minister: MORLEY BARRET; Phone: 403-427-6749

BRITISH COLUMBIA

MINISTRY OF ENVIRONMENT, LANDS, AND PARKS
P.O. Box 9339, Victoria, British Columbia V8W 9M1 Canada
Phone: 604-387-9422
Description: The Ministry of Environment's mission is to provide leadership in building environmental principles into day-to-day decisions of governments, corporations, and private individuals; to monitor and report on the state of the environment, and to ensure that defensible environmental standards are set and complied with; and to manage natural habitats, fish, wildlife, and water resources for ecological diversity and the economic and recreational opportunities they provide.
Contact(s):
Deputy Minister: DEREK THOMPSON; Phone: 250-387-5429
Assistant Deputy Minister for Wildlife, Habitat, and Enforcement: JIM WALKER; Phone: 250-356-0139
Assistant Deputy Minister, Corporate Services: GREG KOYL; Phone: 250-387-9888
Assistant Deputy Minister, Headquarters Division: DON FAST; Phone: 250-387-1280
Assistant Deputy Minister, Parks Division: DENIS O'GORMAN; Phone: 250-387-9997
Assistant Deputy Minister, Regions Division: JON O'RIORDAN; Phone: 250-387-9877
Minster: HON. JOAN SAWICKI; Phone: 250-387-1187
Director of Resource Stewardship Branch: ROD DAVIS; Phone: 250-356-7725
Director of Resources Inventory Branch: JIM MATTISON; Phone: 250-387-1112
Director of Wildlife: DOUG DRYDEN; Phone: 250-387-9731

MINISTRY OF FISHERIES
3rd Floor, 780 Blanshard St., Victoria, British Columbia V8V 1X4 Canada
Contact(s):
Director of Recreational Fisheries: JAMIE ALLEY; Phone: 250-387-9711
Minister: HON. DENNIS STREIFEL; Phone: 250-356-2735

MINISTRY OF SMALL BUSINESS TOURISM AND CULTURE
P.O. Box 9805, Stn. Prov. Govt., 1405 Douglas St., Victoria, British Columbia V8W 9W1 Canada
Contact(s):
Assistant Deputy Minister: Culture, Recreation, Heritage & Sport Division: DAVID RICHARDSON, P.O. Box 9817, Stn. Prov. Govt., 5th Floor, 800 Johson Street, Victoria, British Columbia V8W 9W3 Canada; Phone: 250-387-0106
Assistant Deputy Minister: Culture, Recreation, Heritage & Sport Division: DAVID RICHARDSON, P.O. Box 9804, Stn. Prov. Govt., 4th Floor, 1405 Douglas Street, Victoria, British Columbia V8W 9W1 Canada; Phone: 250-356-7363
Assistant Deputy Minister: Management Services Division: RHONDA HUNTER, P.O. Box 9802, Stn. Prov. Govt., 2nd Floor, 1405 Douglas Street, Victoria, British Columbia V8W 9W1 Canada; Phone: 250-356-1680
Assistant Deputy Minister: Government Agents, Small Business and Co-operatives Division: DEBORAH GEORGE, P.O. Box 9804, Stn. Prov. Govt., 4th Floor, 1405 Douglas St., Victoria, British Columbia V8W 9W1; Phone: 250-356-7363
Chief Executive Officer, Royal British Columbia Museum: BILL BARKLEY, P.O. Box 9815, Stn. Prov. Govt., 675 Belleville St., Victoria, British Columbia V8W 9W5 Canada; Phone: 250-387-3685
Deputy Minister: LYN TAIT, P.O. Box 9805 Stn. Prov. Govt., Victoria, British Columbia V8W 9W1 Canada; Phone: 250-356-2175
Director, British Columbia Film Commission: PETER MITCHELL, 601 West Cordova St., Vancouver, British Columbia V6B 1G1; Phone: 604-660-2732
Executive Director: Tourism and Corporate Policy Division: LYNELLE SPRING, P.O. Box 9806, Stn. Prov. Govt., 5th Floor, 1405 Douglas St., Victoria, British Columbia V8W 9W1 Canada; Phone: 250-387-8002
Minister: IAN G. WADDEL, Rm. 322, Parliament Buildings, Victoria, British Columbia V8V 1X4 Canada; Phone: 250-387-1683
President and Chief Executive Officer, Tourism British Columbia: ROD HARRIS, P.O. Box 9830, Stn. Prov. Govt., 300 - 1803 Douglas St., Victoria, British Columbia V8W 9W5 Canada; Phone: 250-356-2026

MANITOBA

DEPARTMENT OF INDUSTRY, TRADE AND TOURISM
Travel Manitoba, Department RHO, 7th Fl., 155 Carlton St., Winnipeg, Manitoba R3C3H8 Canada
Phone: 204-945-3777/ext. RHO/1800-665-0040/ext.RHO; Fax: 204-945-2302; Web site:www.travelmanitoba.com
Description: Coordinates visits to Manitoba by travel and outdoor editors; produces and distributes travel and outdoor literature and films.
Contact(s):
Assistant Deputy Minister of Tourism and Business Development: LORETTA CLARKE; Phone: 204-945-4204
Director of Marketing: STATIA ELLIOT; Phone: 204-945-6777
Marketing Consultant: COLETTE FONTAINE; Phone: 204-945-4045

MANITOBA DEPARTMENT OF NATURAL RESOURCES
Rm. 333, Legislative Bldg., Winnipeg, Manitoba R3C0V8 Canada
Phone: 204-945-3730
Description: The purpose of Manitoba Natural Resources is to encourage wise use of Manitoba's natural resources and preserve them for future generations.
Contact(s):
Minister: HON. J. GLEN CUMMINGS
Special Assistant to the Minister: PETER CONNELLY; Phone: 204-945-1206
Assistant Deputy Minister: HARVEY BOYLE, Box 80,200 Saulteaux, Winnipeg; Phone: 204-945-4842
Assistant Deputy Minister: DR. MERLIN SHOESMITH, Box 80, 200 Saulteaux Cres., Winnipeg, Manitoba R3J 3W3 Canada; Phone: 204-945-6829
Deputy Minister: DAVID TOMASSON, Rm. 327, Legislative Bldg., Winnipeg, Manitoba R3C 0V8 Canada; Phone: 204-945-3785
Director of Financial Services: PETER J. LOCKETT, Box 85,200 Saulteaux, Winnipeg, Manitoba, Canada; Phone: 204-945-4187
Director of Fisheries Branch: JOE O'CONNOR, Box 20, 200 Saulteaux Cres., Winnipeg, Manitoba R3J 3W3 Canada; Phone: 204-945-7814
Director of Forestry: GORD JONES, Box 70, 200, Saulteaux Cres., Winnipeg, Manitoba R3J 3W3 Canada; Phone: 204-945-7998
Director of Headquarters Operations: WAYNE FISHER, Box 44, 200 Saulteaux Cres., Winnipeg, Manitoba R3J 3W3 Canada; Phone: 204-945-6647
Director of Human Resources: LORRAINE METZ, 500-326 Broadway WPG MB, R3C 0S5 Canada; Phone: 204-945-2810
Director of Lands Branch: HARLEY JONASSON, 123 Main St., W., Box 20000, Neepawa, Manitoba R0J 1H0 Canada; Phone: 204-476-3441
Director of Parks and Natural Areas: C. GORDON PROUSE, Box 50, 200 Saulteax Cres., Winnipeg, Manitoba R3J 3W3 Canada; Phone: 204-945-4362
Director of Policy Coordination: BLAIR McTAVISH, Box 38, 200 Saulteaux Cres., Winnipeg, Manitoba R3J 3W3 Canada; Phone: 204-945-6658

STATE AND PROVINCIAL GOVERNMENT AGENCIES - NEW BRUNSWICK

Director of Resource Information Systems: KERRY POOLE, Box 90, 200 Saulteaux Cres., Winnipeg, Manitoba R3J 3W3 Canada; Phone: 204-945-2929

Director of Surveys and Mapping: WAYNE LEEMAN, 1007 Century St., Winnipeg, Manitoba R3H 0W4 Canada; Phone: 204-945-0011

Director of Water Resources Branch: STEVEN TOPPING, Box 11 200 Saulteaux, Winnipeg, Manitoba R3E 3J5 Canada; Phone: 204-945-7488

Director of Wildlife: BRIAN GILLESPIE, Box 24, 200 Salteaux Cres., Winnipeg, Manitoba R3J 3W3 Canada; Phone: 204-945-7761

Executive Director of Land Information Centre: JACK SCHREUDER, 1007 Century St., Winnipeg, Manitoba R3H 0W4 Canada; Phone: 204-945-6613

Executive Director of Management Services: W. J. PODOLSKY, Box 85,200 Saulteaux, Winnipeg, Manitoba R3J 3W3 Canada; Phone: 204-945-4056

Central Region
Box 6000, Gimli, Manitoba R0C1B0 Canada
Phone: 204-642-6096
Contact(s):
Regional Director: WORTH HAYDEN
Regional Superintendent: SYD ROBAK

Eastern Region
Box 4000, Lac du Bonnet, Manitoba R0E1A0 Canada
Phone: 204-345-1433
Contact(s):
Regional Director: BOB ENNS
Regional Superintendent: BOB CAMERON

Northeastern Region
Box 28, 59 Elizabeth Rd., Thompson, Manitoba R8N1X4 Canada
Phone: 204-677-6628
Contact(s):
Regional Director: DON COOK
Regional Superintendent: STEVE KEARNEY

Northwestern Region
Box 2550, 3rd St. and Ross Ave., The Pas, Manitoba R9A1M4 Canada
Phone: 204-627-8261
Contact(s):
Regional Director: ALBERT D. KING
Regional Superintendent: ROB DEAN

Western Region
Box 488, 340-9th St., Brandon, Manitoba R7A5Z4 Canada
Phone: 204-726-6299
Contact(s):
Regional Director: BOB WOOLEY
Regional Superintendent: BLAIR BASTIAN

NEW BRUNSWICK

NEW BRUNSWICK DEPARTMENT OF NATURAL RESOURCES AND ENERGY
P.O. Box 6000, Fredericton, New Brunswick E3B5H1 Canada
Contact(s):
Deputy Minister: DAVID MACFARLANE; Phone: 506-453-2501
Executive Director of Fish and Wildlife: DR. ARNOLD H. BOER, P.O. Box 6000, Fredericton, New Brunswick E3B 5H1 Canada; Phone: 506-453-2440
Minister: HON. JEANNOT VOLPÉ; Phone: 506-453-2510

NEWFOUNDLAND

NEWFOUNDLAND DEPARTMENT OF FOREST RESOURCES AND AGRIFOODS
P.O. Box 8700, St. John's, Newfoundland A1B4J6 Canada
Contact(s):
Assistant Deputy Minister: MUHAMMAD NAZIR; Phone: 709-729-2704
Deputy Minister: ROBERT SMART; Phone: 709-729-4720
Minister: HON. KEVIN AYLWARD; Phone: 709-729-4715

Ecosystem Health Division
P.O. Box 8700, St. John's, Newfoundland A1B4J6 Canada
Contact(s):
Director: D. FONG; Phone: 709-729-1804
Senior Biologist (Endangered Species): J. BRAZIL; Phone: 709-729-3773
Senior Biologist (Environmental/Land Use): C. BUTLER; Phone: 709-729-2543

Inland Fish and Wildlife Division
Bldg. 810, Pleasantville, P.O. Box 8700, St. John's, Newfoundland A1B4J6 Canada
Description: Objective is to maintain diverse and abundant wildlife populations and wildlife habitat; provide for the safe and sustainable use of wildlife, both consumptive and nonconsumptive; and help create a social environment conducive to effective wildlife conservation.
Contact(s):
Director: J. HANCOCK; Phone: 709-729-2817
Chief of Inland Fish: K. CURNEW; Phone: 709-729-2540
Chief of Research and Inventory: S. MAHONEY; Phone: 709-729-3593
Chief of Wildlife Management Planning: M. CAHILL; Phone: 709-729-2548
Manager of Conservation Services: J. BLAKE; Phone: 709-729-3509
Manager of Salmonier Nature Park and Environmental Education: R. JARVIS; Phone: 709-729-6974
Senior Biologist (Inland Fish): M. VanZYLL de JONG; Phone: 709-729-4306
Senior Biologist (Small Game/Fur): M. McGRATH; Phone: 709-729-0748
Supervisor of Administration: L. CROKE; Phone: 709-729-2636
Supervisor of Licencing: R. GULLIVER; Phone: 709-729-2630
Publication(s): *Newfoundland and Labrador Hunting and Trapping Guide; Trappers Guide; Newfoundland and Labrador Hunter Education Manual (student and instructor editions); Trapper's Update; Endangered Species Poster and brochure series*

Legislation and Compliance Division
P.O. Box 8700, St. John's, Newfoundland A1B 4J6 Canada
Contact(s):
Director: R. WHITTEN; Phone: 709-729-2647

Regional Offices
Contact(s):
Eastern Director (Gander): E. BLACKMORE; Phone: 709-256-1451
Labrador Director (Goose Bay): K. COLBERT; Phone: 709-896-3405
Regional Comliance Manager: R. TRASK; Phone: 709-256-1461
Regional Compliance Manager: D. LeBOUBON; Phone: 709-896-2541
Regional Compliance Manager: M. PARSONS; Phone: 709-637-2918
Regional Ecologist: L. SOPER; Phone: 709-637-2399
Western Director (Corner Brook): A. MASTERS; Phone: 709-637-2370

NORTHWEST TERRITORIES

DEPARTMENT OF RESOURCES, WILDLIFE AND ECONOMIC DEVELOPMENT, GOVERNMENT OF THE NORTHWEST TERRITORIES
Scotia Centre Box 21, 600 5102 - 50 Ave., Yellowknife, Northwest Territories X1A3S8 Canada
Description: Has broad responsibility for wildlife and fisheries environmental protection, forest management, parks and tourism, trade and investment, and minerals, oil, and gas in the Northwest Territories, and provides assistance to people dependent on these resources to harvest wildlife in a manner which will ensure continued availability of the resource.
Contact(s):
Minister: STEPHEN KAKFWI; Phone: 867-669-2366; Fax: 867-873-0169
Deputy Minister: JOSEPH HANDLEY; Phone: 867-920-8048; Fax: 867-873-0563
Assistant Deputy Minister of Resources and Economic Development: DOUG DOAN; Phone: 867-873-7115; Fax: 867-873-0114
Assistant Deputy Minister, West: ROBERT BAILEY; Phone: 867-920-6389; Fax: 867-873-0114
Director of Community Economic Development Services: GERRY LEPRIEUR; Phone: 867-873-7838; Fax: 867-873-0434
Director of Corporate Service: JIM KENNEDY; Phone: 867-873-7532; Fax: 867-920-2756
Director of Diamond Projects: MARTIN IRVING; Phone: 867-920-3125; Fax: 867-873-0254
Director of Environmental Protection: EMERY PAQUIN; Phone: 867-873-7654; Fax: 867-873-0221
Director of Forest Management: BEATRICE LEPINE, Box 7, Fort Smith, Northwest Territories X0E 0P0 Canada; Phone: 867-872-770; Fax: 867-872-2077
Director of Minerals, Oil and Gas: DOUG MATTHEWS; Phone: 867-920-3222; Fax: 867-920-0254
Director of Parks and Tourism: ROBIN REILLY; Phone: 867-873-7902; Fax: 867-873-0163
Director of Policy and Legislation: KATHRYN EMMETT; Phone: 867-920-8046; Fax: 867-873-0114
Director of Trade and Investment: OTTO OLAH; Phone: 867-873-7361; Fax: 867-920-0101
Director of Wildlife and Fisheries: DOUG STEWART; Phone: 867-920-8064; Fax: 867-873-0293
Librarian: ALISON WELCH, NWT Resources, Wildlife and Economic Development Library, Scotia Centre 5th Floor, 600 5102 - 50 Ave., Yellowknife, NT X1A 3S8 Canada; Phone: 867-920-8606/867- 873-0293
Regional Superintendent for Deh Cho: PAUL KRAFT, Box 240, Fort Simpson, NT X0E0N0 Canada; Phone: 879-695-2231; Fax: 897-695-2442
Regional Superintendent for Inuvik: RON MORRISON, Bag 1, Inuvik, NT X0E0T0 Canada; Phone: 879-777-7286; Fax: 879-777-7238
Regional Superintendent for North Slave: LARRY ADAMSON, Box 2668, Yellowknife, NT X1A2P9 Canada; Phone: 879-920-6134; Fax: 879-873-6230
Regional Superintendent for Sahtu: CELINA STROEDER, Box 130, Normal Wells, NT X0E 0V0 Canada; Phone: 879-587-2310; Fax: 879-587-2204
Regional Superintendent for South Slave: LLOYD JONES, Box 390, Fort Smith, NT X0E 0P0 Canada; Phone: 867-872-4242; Fax: 879-872-4250
Publication(s): *Safety in Bear Country; Summary of Hunting Regulations; NWT Explorers Guide; NWT Wildlife Sketches; Sport Fishing Guide*

NOVA SCOTIA

NOVA SCOTIA DEPARTMENT OF FISHERIES AND AQUACULTURE
P.O. Box 2223, Halifax, Nova Scotia B3J3C4 Canada
Phone: 902-424-4560
Description: The Department is involved in almost all aspects of the province's fishing industry. It has significant input into some of the policies and programs legislated and administered by the federal government, which has jurisdiction over much of the fishery. The department has jurisdictional responsibility for developing and regulating aquaculture and freshwater recreational fisheries. It is also responsible for the licensing and inspection of fish processing plants. The department provides training, marketing, and loan assistance to the industry. Department goals include conservation development and enhancement of renewable fisheries resources for the benefit of all Nova Scotians.
Contact(s):
Deputy Minister: PETER UNDERWOOD; Phone: 902-424-0300
Director of Aquaculture: LEO MUISE; Phone: 902-424-3664
Director of Inland Fisheries: MURRAY HILL; Phone: 902-485-7021
Director of Loan Board: JIM SARTY; Phone: 902-424-0312
Director of Marketing: JANIS RAYMOND; Phone: 902-424-0330
Director of Policy, Planning and Coastal Resources: GREG ROACH; Phone: 902-424-0348
Director of Technology and Inspection: DAVE HANSEN; Phone: 902-424-0337
Director of Training & Field Services: BARB RILEY; Phone: 902-424-0328
Minister: KEITH COLWELL; Phone: 902-424-8953

NOVA SCOTIA DEPARTMENT OF NATURAL RESOURCES
P.O. Box 698, Halifax, Nova Scotia B3J2T9 Canada
Phone: 902-424-5935
Description: Charged with the administration of the Wildlife Act, Endangered Species Act and various other statutes. Inherent in the legislation and incumbent upon the Department are responsibilities pertaining to the productivity of the forests generally, the supply of forest products, the conservation of wildlife, the development of mineral resources, the administration of Crown Lands, and the enhancement of recreational areas.
Contact(s):
Minister: ERNIE FAGE; Phone: 902-424-4037
Deputy Minister: DANIEL J. GRAHAM; Phone: 902-424-4121
Publication(s): *Nature's Resources; Nova Scotia Trappers Newsletter*

Corporate Service Unit
Contact(s):
Director of Finance: FRANK DUNN; Phone: 902-424-3288
Information Officer: SUSAN MADER ZINCK; Phone: 902-424-2354

Land Services Branch
Contact(s):
Executive Director: ROSALAND PINFORD; Phone: 902-424-4267
Director Land Administration: JO-ANNE HIMMELMAN; Phone: 902-424-4267

Regional Services Branch
Contact(s):
Executive Director: BRIAN GILBERT; Phone: 902-424-3949
Director of Crown Lands Management: DAN EIDT; Phone: 902-424-7594
Director of Extension Services: BILL SMITH; Phone: 902-424-4445
Director of Private Lands Management: ARDEN WHIDDEN; Phone: 902-424-5703
Manager of Enforcement: JOHN MOMBOURQUETTE; Phone: 902-424-5254

Renewable Resources Branch
Contact(s):
Executive Director: ED MacAULAY; Phone: 902-424-4103
Director of Forestry: NANCY McINNIS LEEK, P.O. Box 68, Truro, Nova Scotia B2N 5B8 Canada; Phone: 902-893-5749
Director of Parks and Recreation: GREG HAVERSTOCK, R.R. #1, Belmont, Colchester County, Nova Scotia B0M 1C0 Canada; Phone: 902-662-3030; Fax: 902-662-2160

STATE AND PROVINCIAL GOVERNMENT AGENCIES - ONTARIO

Director of Wildlife: BARRY C. SABEAN, 136 Exhibition St., Kentville, Nova Scotia B4N 4E5 Canada; Phone: 902-679-6139; Fax: 902-679-6176

Supervisor of Wildlife Parks: BERT VISSERS, P.O. Box 299, Shubenacadie, Nova Scotia B0N 2H0 Canada; Phone: 902-758-2040

ONTARIO

MINISTRY OF NATURAL RESOURCES

Algonquin Forestry Authority
84-6 Isabella St., Huntsville, Ontario K8A5S5 Canada
Phone: 613-735-0173
Contact(s):
General Manager: B. A. CONNELLY

Corporate Services Division
Description: This division facilitates the delivery of ministry programs by providing leadership, strategic advice, and responsive results-oriented services to ministry clients. These services include business planning, audit and evaluation, financial, administrative, legal, and human resources. The division also develops corporate and administrative policies and gives advice on standards, guidelines, planning, and management. It is the primary liaison with the central agencies of government for corporate policy and the functions associated with the Chief Administrative Officer.
Contact(s):
Director of Corporate Affairs Branch: LARRY DOUGLAS; Phone: 416-314-1923
Director of Finance and Administration Branch: JOHN KENRICH; Phone: 705-755-2505
Director of Human Resources Branch: GEORGE ROSS; Phone: 705-755-3131
Director of Legal Services Branch: BARRY JONES; Phone: 416-314-2002

Field Services Division
Description: Delivering resource management programs for Ontario's fisheries, wildlife, forests and provincial lands is the responsibility of this division. It is also responsible for the Aviation, Flood, and Fire Management Branch and the Provincial Enforcement Section. The division's structure is highly decentralized with three regional offices, 25 district offices, and 17 area offices located across the province.
Contact(s):
Director of Aviation, Flood, and Fire Management: JACK McFADDEN; Phone: 705-945-5937
Director of Northwest Region: MIKE WILLICK; Phone: 807-475-1264
Director of South Central Region: DICK HUNTER; Phone: 705-755-3235
Manager of Enforcement Section: GUY WINTERON; Phone: 705-755-1750

Fish and Wildlife Branch
300 Water St., P.O. Box 7000, Peterborough, Ontario K9J8M5 Canada
Contact(s):
Director: ANDREW HOUSER; Phone: 705-755-1909
Manager of Fisheries: EVAN THOMAS; Phone: 705-755-1906
Manager of Wildlife: JIM YOUNG; Phone: 705-755-1925

Natural Resource Management Division
Description: The division is responsible for ensuring that natural resource programs are responsive to the needs of Ontarians and consistent with the ministry's vision of sustainable development and its mission of ecological sustainability. Its mandate covers lands, waters, forests, fish, wildlife, and parks, and includes fish hatcheries, tree nurseries, and the management of the Great Lakes.
Contact(s):
Director of Fish and Wildlife Branch: ANDREW HOUSER; Phone: 705-755-1909
Director of Forest Management Branch: BILL THORNTON; Phone: 705-945-6660
Director of Land Use Planning Branch: DAVE WATTON; Phone: 705-755-2369
Director of Lands and Natural Heritage Branch: BOB BEECHER; Phone: 705-755-1212
Director of Ontario Parks: NORM RICHARDS; Phone: 705-755-1702

Northeast Region
Ontario Government Complex, Highway 101 East, P.O. Bag 3020, South Porcupine, Ontario P0N 1HO Canada
Phone: 705-235-1153
Contact(s):
Regional Director: BOB GALLOWAY

Northwest Region
Ontario Government Bldg., P.O. Box 5000, 435 James St., South, Thunder Bay, Ontario P7C5G6 Canada
Phone: 807-475-1261
Contact(s):
Regional Director: MIKE WILLICH

Ontario
Toronto, Ontario M7A1W3 Canada
Description: The ministry's business plan establishes the following as MNR's core businesses: natural resource management; Crown land management; public safety and enforcement; parks and protected areas; and geographic information. In pursuing these core businesses, the ministry contributes to the environmental, social, and economic well being of Ontario through the biological features of provincial interest, and protects human life, the resource base, and physical property from the threats of forest fires, floods, and erosion.
Contact(s):
Assistant Deputy Minister for Corporate Services: PATRICIA E. MALCOLMSON; Phone: 416-314-1897
Assistant Deputy Minister for Field Services: CAMERON D. CLARK; Phone: 807-475-1438
Assistant Deputy Minister for Natural Resource Management: GAIL BEGGS; Phone: 416-314-6131
Assistant Deputy Minister for Science and Information Resources: DR. DAVID BALSILLIE; Phone: 416-314-1528
Commissioner of Mining and Lands: RUSSELL YURKOW, 700 Bay St., 24th Fl., Toronto, Ontario M5G1Z6 Canada; Phone: 416-314-2323
Deputy Minister: RON VRANCART; Phone: 416-314-2150
Director of Communications Services: JOHN McHUGH; Phone: 416-314-2119
Director of Communications Services Branch: JOAN KRANTZBERG; Phone: 416-314-2119
Minister: HON. CHRIS HODGSON; Phone: 416-314-2301
Parliamentary Assistant: TED CHUDLEIGH; Phone: 416-314-2193

Science and Information Resources Division
Description: Provides the ministry with leadership in the development and application of scientific knowledge, information management, and information technology. The division also plays a lead role in the provision of land-related information.
Contact(s):
Associate Director of Zimbabwe Natural Resource Management: COLLIN TURNPENNY; Phone: 416-314-1550
Director of Information Management and Systems Branch: GLENN HOLDER; Phone: 705-755-2139
Director of Information Technology Services Branch: DES McKEE; Phone: 705-755-1401
Director of Science Development and Transfer Branch: JIM MacLEAN; Phone: 705-755-1565

South Central Region
P.O. Box 9000, Brendale Square, Huntsville, Ontario P0A1K0 Canada
Phone: 705-789-9611
Contact(s):
Regional Director: ALLAN STEWART

NIAGARA ESCARPMENT COMMISSION
232 Guelph St., Georgetown, Ontario L7G4B1 Canada
Phone: 905-877-5191
Founded: 1973
Description: Maintains the Niagara Escarpment and land in its vicinity substantially as a continuous natural environment, and ensures that only such development occurs as is compatible with that natural environment. The commission was established under the Niagara Escarpment Planning and Development Act. In 1990, the Niagra Escarpment was designated a World Biosphere Reserve.
Contact(s):
Chair: DON SCOTT
Director: FRANK SHAW
Manager of Development Control: KEITH C. JORDAN
Manager of Public Affairs: RICHARD MURZIN
Public Affairs Officer: SUSAN POWELL

PRINCE EDWARD ISLAND

PRINCE EDWARD ISLAND DEPARTMENT OF TECHNOLOGY AND ENVIRONMENT
P.O. Box 2000, Charlottetown, Prince Edward Island C1A7N8 Canada
Description: To work with individuals, businesses, groups and communities to protect, enhance and enjoy in a sustainable way the province's environment and natural resources.
Contact(s):
Minister: HON. MITCH MURPHY; Phone: 902-368-4863
Deputy Minister: BILL OROST; Phone: 902-368-5340
Director of Fish and Wildlife Division: ARTHUR SMITH; Phone: 902-368-6083
Firearm Safety Coordinator: CLARE J. BIRCH; Phone: 902-368-4686
Habitat and Natural Areas Biologist: ROSEMARY CURLEY; Phone: 902-368-4807
Head of Investigations and Enforcement: GERALD MacDOUGALL; Phone: 902-368-4808
Waterfowl and Furbearer Biologist: RANDALL DIBBLEE; Phone: 902-368-4666
Publication(s): *Tracks in the Snow; Patterns of the Pond; Wildlife Policy; The Bald Eagle in Prince Edward Island; Our Land and Water*

QUEBEC

DEPARTMENT OF ENVIRONMENT AND WILDLIFE (QUEBEC)
Edifice Marie-Guyart, 675, Blvd. Rene-Levesque Est, Quebec City, Quebec G1R5V7 Canada
Contact(s):
Assistant Deputy Minister for Sustainable Development: SUZANNE GIGUERE; Phone: 418-521-3860
Assistant Deputy Minister of Operations: NORMAN D. CARRIER; Phone: 418-521-3860
Assistant Deputy Minister of Recreation of Environment: DENYS JEAN; Phone: 418-521-3860
Assistant Deputy Minister of Wildlife and Natural Heritage: GEORGE ARSENAULT; Phone: 418-521-3860
Departmental Secretary: HERVE BOLDUC; Phone: 418-521-3860
Deputy Minister: DIANE GAUDET; Phone: 418-521-3860
Director General of Administration: ANDRE TAILLON; Phone: 418-521-3860
Director of Institutional Affairs and Communications: LUCIEN BEAUMONT; Phone: 418-521-3823
Director of Intergovernmental and Native Affairs: LUC POIRIER; Phone: 418-521-3828
Director of Quebec Aquarium: ANDRE MARTEL; Phone: 418-659-5266
Director of Quebec Parks: LUC BERTHIAUME; Phone: 418-644-9393
Director of Wildlife Territories, Regulations and Permits: CLAUDETTE BLAIS; Phone: 418-643-7674
Interim Director of Quebec Zoo: ANDRE MARTEL; Phone: 418-622-0313
Minister: PAUL BEGIN; Phone: 418-521-3911

SASKATCHEWAN

SASKATCHEWAN ENVIRONMENT AND RESOURCE MANAGEMENT
3211 Albert St., Regina, Saskatchewan S4S5W6 Canada
Founded: 1930
Description: To manage, enhance, and protect Saskatchewan's natural and environmental resources - fish, forests, parks, lands, wildlife, air and water for conservation, recreation, social, and economic purposes, all to be sustained for future generations.
Contact(s):
Minister: HON. LORNE SCOTT, 361 Legislative Bldg., Regina, Saskatchewan S4S 0B3 Canada; Phone: 306-787-0393
Deputy Minister: STUART KRAMER; Phone: 306-787-2930
Director of Communication Services: RICK BATES; Phone: 306-787-0114
Publication(s): *State of the Environment Report; Annual Reports*

Corporate Services
3211 Albert St., Regina, Saskatchewan S4S 5W6 Canada
Contact(s):
Executive Director of Corporate Services: LYNN TULLOCH; Phone: 306-787-1176
Corporate Development: SUE MITTEN; Phone: 306-787-2336
Corporate Development: AL PARENTEAU; Phone: 306-787-8449
Corporate Development: DAVE TULLOCH; Phone: 306-787-1095
Director of Information Management: MIKE DUMELIE; Phone: 306-787-3194
Director of Service Bureau: DONNA KELLSEY; Phone: 306-787-6121
Publication(s): *State of the Environment Report; Annual Reports*

East Boreal EcoRegion
Box 3003, Prince Albert, Saskatchewan S6V6G1 Canada
Phone: 306-953-2899
Contact(s):
Regional Director: RON ERICKSON

Enforcement and Compliance Branch
Contact(s):
Regional Director: DAVE HARVEY, Box 3003, Prince Albert, Saskatchewan S6V 6G1 Canada; Phone: 306-953-2993

Fire Management and Forest Protection Branch
Contact(s):
Regional Director: MURDOCH CARRIERRE, Box 3003, Prince Albert, Saskatchewan S6V 6G1 Canada; Phone: 306-953-2206

Grassland EcoRegion
350 Cheadle St. W., Swift Current, Saskatchewan S9H4G3 Canada
Phone: 306-778-8527
Contact(s):
Regional Director: SYD BARBER

Operations
Contact(s):
Assistant Deputy Minister: DAVE PHILLIPS; Phone: 306-787-9079
Director of Regional Services: HUGH HUNT; Phone: 306-787-9117

Parkland EcoRegion
112 Research Dr., Saskatoon, Saskatchewan S7K2H6 Canada
Phone: 306-933-6249
Contact(s):
Regional Director: MERV SWANSON

Policy and Assessment
Contact(s):
Executive Director: RON ZUKOWSKY; Phone: 306-787-6285
Director of Environmental Assessment Branch: LARRY LECHNER; Phone: 306-787-5786
Director of Policy and Legislation: LYNDA LANGFORD; Phone: 306-787-6868
Public Involvment and Aboriginal Affairs: Phone: 306-787-7803

Programs
Contact(s):
Assistant Deputy Minister: BOB RUGGLES; Phone: 306-787-5419
Director of Environmental Protection Branch: JOE MULDOON; Phone: 306-787-6178
Director of Fish and Wildlife Branch: DENNIS SHERRATT; Phone: 306-787-2309
Director of Forest Ecosystems Branch: AL WILLCOCKS, Box 3003, Prince Albert, Saskatchewan S6V 6G1 Canada; Phone: 306-953-2486
Director of Parks and Special Places Branch: DON MacAULAY; Phone: 306-787-2846
Director of Water Management: ED DEAN; Phone: 306-787-7812
Director of Sustainable Land Management Branch: DOUG MAZUR; Phone: 306-787-7024
Director of Economic Development Branch: SHELLY VANDERMEY; Phone: 306-787-5482
Director of Saskatchewan Wetland Conservation Corporation: BOB CARLES, 101-2022 Cornwall St., Regina, Saskatchewan S4P 2K5 Canada; Phone: 306-787-0779

Shield EcoRegion
Box 5000, La Ronge, Saskatchewan S0J1L0 Canada
Phone: 306-425-4231
Contact(s):
Regional Director: JOHN SCHISLER

West Boreal EcoRegion
201-2nd St. W, Meadow Lake, Saskatchewan S9X1C7 Canada
Phone: 306-236-7540
Contact(s):
Regional Director: TOM HARRISON

YUKON TERRITORY

DEPARTMENT OF RENEWABLE RESOURCES
Box 2703, Whitehorse, Yukon Territory Y1A 2C6 Canada
Contact(s):
Acting Assistant Deputy Minister: JIM CONNELL; Phone: 402-667-8955
Acting Director of Fish and Wildlife: DON TOEWS; Phone: 403-667-5715
Acting Director of Policy and Planning: KARYN ARMOUR; Phone: 403-667-5634
Deputy Minister: BILL OPPEN; Phone: 403-667-5460
Director of Agriculture: DAVE BECKMAN; Phone: 403-667-5838
Director of Environmental Protection and Assessment: JOE BALLANTYNE; Phone: 403-667-8177
Director of Finance and Administration: STAN MARINOSKE; Phone: 403-667-5197
Director of Parks and Outdoor Recreation: JIM MCINTYRE; Phone: 403-667-5261

NON-GOVERNMENTAL ORGANIZATIONS

20/20 VISION
1828 Jefferson Pl., NW, Washington, DC 20036
Phone: 202-833-2020; Fax: 202-833-5307; E-mail: cari-ann@2020vision.org; Web Site: www.2020vision.org
Founded: 1986; Membership: 10,000
Scope: National
Description: Vision is a nonprofit grassroots organization dedicated to protecting the environment and promoting peace through lobbying and citizen education and activism.
Contact(s):
Executive Director: JAMES K. WYERMAN; E-mail: Jwyerman@2020vision.org
Legislative Director: LAURA KRIV; E-mail: laura@2020vision.org
Outreach Coordinator: NATALIE HILDT; E-mail: natalie@2020vision.org
Program Coordinator: CARI ANN LaGRASSA; E-mail: cari-ann@2020vision.org
Publication(s): *Legislative Update; Action Alert Postcards; Tools for Activists Fact Sheets*
Keyword(s): EcoAction, Environmental and Humanitarian Education

A

A. E. HOWELL WILDLIFE CONSERVATION CENTER
HCR #61, Box 6, N. Amity, ME 04471-9601
Phone: 207-532-6880; Fax: 207-532-0910
Founded: 1981; Membership: 225
Scope: National
Description: The A.E.H.W.C.C., Inc. and Spruce Acres Refuge have combined to provide a 65+ acre Refuge Rehabilitation center for people from all the world to enjoy. The Conservation Center is a nonprofit organization established for the purpose of preserving our natural resources and providing educational programs to all people to encourage proper wildlife and natural resource management.
Contact(s):
Vice President: PENNY KERN
Chairman of the Board: MAXIM LANGSTAFF
Founder/President/Wildlife Rehabilitator: ARTHUR E. HOWELL JR.
Secretary and Treasurer: DOROTHY HOWELL
Publication(s): *Membership and Features; If You Care Please Leave Them There; Coyotes in Maine; Trees - Walk The Nature Trails; Planet Earth; American Wetlands*
Keyword(s): Environmental and Conservation Education, Mammals, Raptors, Wetlands, Wildlife Rehabilitation

A.B. ENVIRONMENTAL EDUCATION CENTER
Oglebay Institute, Oglebay Park, Wheeling, WV 26003
Phone: 304-242-6855; Fax: 304-242-4203
Scope: Statewide
Description: Oglebay Institute operates a variety of programs: Resident nature summer camps for adults and children; Ecotourism Club; resident environmental education programs; children's day camping; special workshops and weekends; exhibits; school programs; and also the A.B. Brooks Environmental Education Center and Speidel Observatory.
Contact(s):
Associate Director of Environmental Education: TISH SHERRIN
Associate Director of Environmental Education: JENNIFER SHELBURNE
Associate Director of Environmental Education: JEFF DONAHUE
Director of Nature and Environmental Education: FORD H. PARKER
Keyword(s): Aquatic Habitats, Fisheries, Renewable Resources, Water Pollution Management, Wetlands

ABUNDANT LIFE SEED FOUNDATION
P.O. Box 772, 930 Lawrence, Port Townsend, WA 98368
Phone: 360-385-5660; Fax: 360-385-7455; E-mail: abundant@olypen.com
Founded: 1975; Membership: 1,200
Scope: National
Description: Abundant Life Seed Foundation is a nonprofit, tax-exempt organization that propagates and preserves seeds of Northwest native plants and heritage (non-hybrid) vegetables, herbs, and flowers. The Foundation conducts the distribution of seeds (and related books) via a mail-order catalog. Also operates the World Seed Fund, donating seed internationally to those in need, both in the United States and internationally.
Contact(s):
President: CINDI BITTLE
Manager: ALETA ANDERSON
Secretary and Treasurer: DAVE DAVISON
Publication(s): *Seed and Book Catalog; Seed Midden*
Keyword(s): Agriculture, Endangered and Threatened Species, Flowers, Plants, and Trees, Gardening and Horticulture, Native Plants

ACADEMY FOR EDUCATIONAL DEVELOPMENT
1825 Connecticut Ave., Washington, DC 20009
Phone: 202-884-8000; Fax: 202-884-8997; E-mail: greencom@aed.org; Web Site: www.aed.org
Founded: 1961
Scope: International
Description: A domestic and international development organization with a multi-million dollar environmental education, communication, environmental health population agenda working in over 25 countries.
Contact(s):
Senior Vice-President: GREGORY NIBLETT; E-mail: niblett@aed.org
Executive Vice-President: WILLIAM SMITH; Phone: 202-884-8750; Fax: 202-884-8752; E-mail: bsmith@aed.org
Director: BRIAN A. DAY; Phone: 202-884-8897; E-mail: bday@aed.org
Latin America Director: RICHARD J. BASSI; Phone: 202-884-8898; E-mail: rbassi@aed.org
Publication(s): *Human Native: Starting with Behavior; What Works*
Keyword(s): Agriculture, Air Quality, Asia Water Environment, Biodiversity, Communications, Conservation, Coral Reefs, Drinking Water Protection, Ecotourism, Environmental and Conservation Education, International Conservation, Natural Resource Conservation, Recycling, Women in the Environment

ACRES LAND TRUST
2000 N. Wells St., Fort Wayne, IN 46808-2474
Phone: 219-422-1004; Fax: 219-422-1004; Web Site: www.acres-land-trust.org
Founded: 1960; Membership: 850
Scope: Statewide
Description: A nonprofit organization dedicated to the acquisition and permanent preservation of natural areas in northeastern Indiana. Conducts a guided field-trip program for children and adults. Organizes canoe trips, concerts and festivals for the membership and the public. Administers 40 nature preserves totaling more than 2,600 acres.
Contact(s):
Executive Director: CAROLYN MCNAGNY
President: JAMES D. HADDOCK
Vice President: THEODORE H. HEEMSTRA
Vice President: SAM SCHWARTZ
Vice President: ROBERT C. WEBER
Treasurer: RICHARD E. WALKER
Publication(s): *Acres Quarterly; Acres Brochure; Field*
Keyword(s): Biodiversity, Endangered and Threatened Species, Environmental and Conservation Education, Land Preservation, Wetlands

ACTION FOR NATURE, INC.
2269 Chestnut St., Suite 263, San Francisco, CA 94123
Phone: 415-421-2640; Fax: 415-922-5717; E-mail: action@dnai.com; Web Site: www.actionfornature.org
Scope: National
Description: Action for Nature was organized to foster respect and affection for nature through personal environmental initiatives. AFN

is a clearing-house and catalyst for personal action projects and publicizes young peoples' successful environmental initiatives through a newsletter and publication of a book of some of their stories.
Contact(s):
President: EVELYN BALLARD DE GHETALDI
Secretary: MARY MURRAY GRIFFIN-JONES
Treasurer: DAVID YAMAKAWA
Publication(s): *Acting for Nature (book)*
Keyword(s): Youth Organizations, Environmental Communication

ADIRONDACK COUNCIL, THE
P.O. Box D-2, Elizabethtown, NY 12932
Phone: 518-873-2240; Fax: 518-873-6675
Founded: 1975; Membership: 18,000
Scope: Statewide
Description: A nonprofit environmental organization working for protection and preservation of the six million acre Adirondack Park. Programs include monitoring and influencing state programs in the park, helping to promote understanding of the park and the need to protect its very special character, and supporting and advancing positive programs to enhance the park and benefit its people.
Contact(s):
Chairman: DAVID SKOVRON
Secretary: DEAN COOK
Treasurer: CURTIS WELLING
Executive Director: TIMOTHY BURKE
Vice Chairman: DAVID BRONSTON
Vice Chairman: THOMAS D. THACHER II
Publication(s): *Adirondack Council Newsletter; Adirondack Wildguide: A Natural History of The Adirondack Park; State of the Park*
Keyword(s): Acid Rain, Land Use Planning, Open Space, Sustainable Development, Wildlife and Wildlife Habitat

ADIRONDACK MOUNTAIN CLUB, INC., THE
814 Goggins Rd., Lake George, NY 12845-4117
Phone: 518-668-4447; Fax: 518-668-3746; E-mail: adkinfo@adk.org; Web Site: www.adk.org
Founded: 1922; Membership: 30,000+
Scope: Statewide
Description: The Adirondack Mountain Club is dedicated to the protection and responsible recreational use of the New York State Forest Preserve, parks, and other wild lands and waters. The Club is a member-directed organization committed to public service and stewardship. ADK employs a balanced approach to outdoor recreation, advocacy, environmental education, and natural resource conservation. ADK has 26 chapters in NY and NJ.
Contact(s):
President: TERRY SEXTON
Executive Director: JO A. BENTON; Phone: 518-668-4447
Deputy Executive Director for Public and Legal Affairs: NEIL WOODWORTH; Phone: 518-449-3870; E-mail: nwoodworth@global2000.net
Editor: NEAL BURDICK, 35 Woods Dr., Canton, NY 13617
North Country Director of Facilities: JOHN MILLION
North Country Director of Field Programs: TIMOTHY TIERNEY
Publication(s): *Adirondac Magazine; Guides and maps to Adirondack and Catskill Trails; Adirondack Canoe Waters: North Flow, South and West Flow, Western and Central New York State; Adirondack cultural and literary history information; Climbing, skiing and mountain biking guides*
Keyword(s): Bicycle, Conservation of Protected Areas, Environmental and Conservation Education, Environmental Preservation, Environmental Protection, Forest Management, Land Preservation, Natural Areas, Natural History, Nongame Wildlife, Outdoor Recreation, Public Lands, Trail, Wilderness, Wildlands Management

ADIRONDACK NATURE CONSERVANCY/ADIRONDACK LAND TRUST, INC.
P.O. Box 65, Keene Valley, NY 12943
Phone: 518-576-2082
Founded: 1984
Scope: Statewide
Description: The Adirondack Nature Conservancy and Adirondack Land Trust are separate land conservation organizations that have acted in partnership since 1988, coordinating programs and staff. The Adirondack Nature Conservancy protects the plants, animals, and natural communities that represent the diversity of life in the Adirondacks by protecting the lands and waters they need to survive.
Contact(s):
Chairman: EDWARD McNEIL, 108 Burlingame Rd., Syracuse, NY 13202-1604
Secretary: FRANCISCA IRWIN, Rt. 1 Box 80, Essex, NY 12936
Treasurer: MEREDITH PRIME, Heather Hill, Lake Placid, NY 12946
Executive Director: TIMOTHY L. BARNETT
Publication(s): *Developing a Land Conservation Strategy: A Handbook for Land Trusts (1987)*
Keyword(s): Agriculture, Forests and Forestry, Land Preservation, Open Space, Sustainable Development

ADKINS ARBORETUM
P.O. Box 100, Ridgely, MD 21660
Phone: 410-634-2847; Fax: 410-634-2878; E-mail: ealtman@shore.intercom.net; Web Site: www.bluecrab.org/adkins
Founded: 1979; Membership: 203
Scope: Statewide
Description: Adkins Arboretum is dedicated to the appreciation, understanding and stewardship of the indigenous, non-tidal plant communities of the Central Delmarva Peninsula. It strives to maintain a divers and dynamic living collection that is authentic, engaging and a model for land management. As a significant cultural, education, scientific and recreational resource, the Arboretum fosters civic pride, encourages public dialogue and contributes to the economic vitality of the region.
Contact(s):
President: DEBBY BENNET; Phone: 410-479-1343, ext. 152; Fax: 410-479-1443
Vice President: K. MARC TEFFEAU; Phone: 410-827-8056; Fax: 410-827-9059
Secretary: CAROL STOCKLEY; Phone: 410-479-1750
Treasurer: JOHN ATWOOD; Phone: 410-822-4032
Executive Director: ELLIE ALTMAN; Phone: 410-634-2847; Fax: 410-634-2878; E-mail: ealtman@shore.intercom.net
Publication(s): *Native Seed*
Keyword(s): Biodiversity, Conservation of Protected Areas, Ecology, Endangered and Threatened Species, Environmental and Conservation Education, Flowers, Plants, and Trees, Landscape Architecture, Wetlands, Wildlife and Wildlife Habitat, Native Plants

ADOPT-A-STREAM FOUNDATION, THE
600-128th St., SE, Everett, WA 98208-6353
Phone: 425-316-8592; Fax: 425-338-1423; E-mail: aasf@streamkeeper.org; Web Site: www.streamkeeper.org
Founded: 1985
Scope: National
Description: Adopt-A-Stream Foundation's mission is to empower people to become stewards of watersheds, wetlands, and streams. The Foundation's long term goal is to ensure that all streams are adopted by watershed residents. The current focus is in the Pacific Northwest. The Foundation conducts "Streamkeeper" workshops that train volunteers and students of all ages to conduct watershed inventories, monitor small streams and other educational programming.
Contact(s):
Vice President: JIM ROWLEY
Secretary: DAN CROUSE
Treasurer: GRANT WOODFIELD
Executive Director: TOM MURDOCH
Board President: DARRYL WILLIAMS
Publication(s): *Adopting a Stream: A Northwest Handbook; Adopting a Wetland: A Northwest Guide; A Streamkeeper's Field Guide: Watershed Inventory and Stream Monitoring Methods;*

Streamlines; Video: *The Streamkeeper*, featuring Bill Nye "The Science Guy."
Keyword(s): Aquatic Habitats, Environmental and Conservation Education, Environmental Planning, Environmental Preservation, Environmental Protection, Fisheries, Lakes, Land Use Planning, Nature Preservation, Nongame Wildlife, Open Space, Raptors, Reptiles and Amphibians, Rivers, Urban Environment

AFRICAN WILDLIFE FOUNDATION
1400 16th St., NW, Suite 120, Washington, DC 20036
Phone: 202-939-3333; Fax: 202-939-3332; E-mail: awfwash@igc.apc.com; Web Site: www.awf.org
Scope: International
Description: The African Wildlife Foundation recognizes that the wildlife and wild lands of Africa have no equal. We work with people-our supporters worldwide and our partners in Africa-to craft and deliver creative solutions for the long-term wellbeing of Africa's remarkable species, habitats, and the people who depend upon them.
Contact(s):
President: R. MICHAEL WRIGHT
Vice President for Program: PATRICK J. BERGIN
Secretary: JANE W. GASTON
Treasurer: HENRY P. MCINTOSH IV
Assistant Treasurer: BARBARA DiPIETRO
Chairman of the Board: STUART T. SAUNDERS JR
Vice Chair of the Board: DAVID CHALLINOR
Publication(s): *African Wildlife News*
Keyword(s): Conservation of Protected Areas, Endangered and Threatened Species, International Conservation, Sustainable Development, Wildlife and Wildlife Habitat

AFRICAN WILDLIFE NEWS SERVICE
P.O. Box 546, Olympia, WA 98507-0546
Phone: 360-459-8862; Fax: 360-459-8771; E-mail: awnews@aol.com; Web Site: www.africanwildlife.org
Founded: 1990
Scope: International
Description: AWNS is a nonprofit, tax-exempt news agency dedicated to reporting the latest news and information on African wildlife.
Contact(s):
President: STEPHEN R. MISHKIN
Vice President: HANK KLEIN
Secretary: PAULA J. SCHWEICH
Treasurer: STEPHEN R. MISHKIN
Editor: STEPHEN R. MISHKIN
Publication(s): *African Wildlife Update*
Keyword(s): Conservation of Protected Areas, Endangered and Threatened Species, International Conservation, Wildlife and Wildlife Habitat, Wildlife Management

AIR AND WASTE MANAGEMENT ASSOCIATION
One Gateway Center, 3rd Fl., Pittsburgh, PA 15222
Phone: 412-232-3444; Fax: 412-232-3450
Founded: 1907; Membership: 13,000
Scope: National
Description: The Air and Waste Management Association is a nonprofit, technical, and environmental association that provides a neutral forum for discussing all sides of an environmental issue. The Association encourages environmental technology development, facilitates technology transfer, and improves environmental management and education. As a leading forum for discussing diverse views on environmental issues, it challenges leaders, professionals, and citizens worldwide to use dialogue for improving the quality of decisions affecting our environment.
Contact(s):
President: PAUL KING
Secretary: DENNIS MITCHELL
Treasurer: DOUGLAS BISSET
1st Vice President: ROBERT E. HALL
Immediate Past President: WILLIAM C. ZEGEL
Publication(s): *Journal of the Air & Waste Management Association*; other publications include proceedings of specialty conferences and symposia, prints and videotapes; *EM*; *A&WMA News*, monthly newsletter
Keyword(s): Air Quality and Pollution, Engineering, Environmental Law, Greenhouse Effect/Global Warming, Solid Waste Management

ALABAMA ASSOCIATION OF SOIL AND WATER CONSERVATION DISTRICTS
Attn: Executive Director, P.O. Box 304800, Montgomery, AL 36130-4800
Scope: Statewide
Contact(s):
President: GEORGE ROBERTSON JR., 2181 County Rd. 22, Waverly, AL 36879; Phone: 334-887-6070; Fax: 334-826-8219
1st Vice President: JAKE HARPER, Rt. 1 Box 468, Camden, AL 36726; Phone: 334-682-4463
2nd Vice President: TERRY POAGUE, 3716 Clause Fleahop Rd., Tallahassee, AL 36078; Phone: 334-567-6183
Board Member: CHARLES A. HOLMES, Rt 1 Box 212, Marion, AL 36756; Phone: 334-683-6869; Fax: 334-583-6869
Secretary/Treasurer: CHARLES W. RITTENOUR JR., 1144 Meriwether Rd., Pike Road, AL 36064; Phone: 334-284-5320
Keyword(s): Conservation Districts

ALABAMA B.A.S.S. CHAPTER FEDERATION
ATTN: President, P.O. Box 190, Notasulga, AL 36866
Scope: Statewide
Description: An organization of Bassmaster chapters, affiliated with the Bass Anglers Sportsman Society, organized to fight pollution, assist state and national conservation agencies in their efforts, and teach the young people of our country good conservation practices. Dedicated to the realistic conservation of our water resources.
Contact(s):
President: AL REDDING; Phone: 334-257-1177; Fax: 334-257-4665; E-mail: alred@auburn.campus.cwix.net
Conservation Director (Acting): BOBBY KNOWLES, 16241 Hagler Mill Drive, Northport, AL 35475; Phone: 205-339-9900

ALABAMA ENVIRONMENTAL COUNCIL
2717 7th Ave. S., Suite 207, Birmingham, AL 35233
Phone: 205-322-3126; Fax: 205-324-3784
Founded: 1967; Membership: 1,500 individuals, 40 organizations
Scope: Statewide
Description: Dedicated to the preservation of Alabama's environment on all fronts: air, water, land, and wildlife.
Contact(s):
President: JEFF deGRAFFENREID
Director of Recycling: KEITH JOHNS
Publication(s): *State News*
Keyword(s): Endangered and Threatened Species, Environmental and Conservation Education, Forests and Forestry, Recycling, Solid Waste, Water Pollution

ALABAMA NATURAL HERITAGE PROGRAM
The Nature Conservancy, 1500 E. Fairview Ave., Montgomery, AL 36106
Phone: 334-834-4519; Fax: 334-834-5439; E-mail: alnhp@wsnet.com; Web Site: www.heritage.tnc.org/nhp/usal/
Founded: 1989
Scope: Regional
Description: The mission of the Alabama Natural Heritage program is to provide the best available scientific information on the biological diversity of Alabama, guide conservation action and promote sound stewardship practices within the state and throughout the Southeast.
Contact(s):
Executive Director, Alabama Chapter of The Nature Conservancy: KATHY FREELAND; Phone: 205-251-1155; Fax: 205-251-4444
Director: JAREL HILTON
Publication(s): *Natural Heritage News*; *Inventory List of Rare Threatened and Endangered Plants, Animals, and Natural Communities of Alabama*

NON-GOVERNMENTAL ORGANIZATIONS - A

Keyword(s): Biodiversity, Conservation, Conservation of Protected Areas, Endangered and Threatened Species, Land Use Planning, Natural Areas, Natural History, Nature Preservation

ALABAMA WATERFOWL ASSOCIATION, INC. (AWA)
P.O. Box 67, Guntersville, AL 35768
Phone: 205-259-2509
Founded: 1987; Membership: 1,276
Scope: Statewide
Description: To protect, enhance, and create wetlands habitat for all wildlife species and other human values; and to enhance waterfowl population and protect our hunting heritage in Alabama.
Contact(s):
Executive Director: GARY BENEFIELD, P.O. Box 67, Guntersville, AL 35976; Phone: 205-593-7712
Chief Executive Officer: JERRY D. DAVIS, 1346 County Rd. 11, Scottsboro, AL 35768; Phone: 205-259-2509
Executive Treasurer: ROGER CROUCH, P.O. Box 67, Guntersville, AL 35976
Publication(s): *Wetlands and Waterfowl News*
Keyword(s): Historic Preservation, Hunting, Waterfowl, Wetlands, Wildlife and Wildlife Habitat

ALABAMA WILDFLOWER SOCIETY, THE
606 India Rd., Opelika, AL 36801
Phone: 334-745-2494; Fax: 334-749-5200; E-mail: deancar@auburn.edu; Web Site: www.auburn.edu/~deancar
Founded: 1971; Membership: 500+
Scope: Statewide
Description: The society promotes knowledge, appreciation, use of native plants, preserves and propagates rare native plants, preserves areas of significant native flora, and provides scholarships.
Contact(s):
President: VIRGINIA LUSK; Phone: 205-988-0299; E-mail: ginny1@bellsouth.net
Vice President: SHIRLEY FIFIELD; Phone: 334-277-2070; E-mail: rgfifi@aol.com
Board Member: CAROLINE R. DEAN
Editor: GEORGE WOOD; Phone: 205-339-2541
Publication(s): *Newsletter of the Alabama Wildflower Society; Wildflower Brochure*
Keyword(s): Conservation Biology, Conservation of Protected Areas, Endangered and Threatened Species, Scholarships, Wildflowers, Native Plants

ALABAMA WILDLIFE FEDERATION
46 Commerce St., Montgomery, AL 86104
Phone: 334-832-9453; Fax: 334-832-9454; E-mail: alabamawf@mindspring.com; Web Site: www.alawild.org
Founded: 1935
Scope: Statewide
Description: A representative statewide organization affiliated with the National Wildlife Federation, dedicated to the protection and enhancement of wildlife and its habitat through public education and government interaction.
Contact(s):
President: BO STARKE
Executive Director, Alternative Representative: TIM GOTHARD
Editor: APRIL LUPARDUS
Representative: REBECCA PRICHETT
Publication(s): *Alabama Wildlife*

ALASKA ASSOCIATION OF SOIL AND WATER CONSERVATION DISTRICTS
ATTN: President, P.O. Box 2376, Kodiak, AK 99615
Scope: Statewide
Contact(s):
President, Board Member: OMAR STRATMAN, P.O. Box 2376, Kodiak, AK 99615; Phone: 907-486-5578; Fax: 907-486-5578
1st Vice President: SHIRLEY SCHOLLENBERG, HC 67 Box 250, Anchor Point, AK 99556; Phone: 907-567-3467
2nd Vice President: MERIBETH CRICK, P.O. Box 56505, North Pole, AK 56505; Phone: 907-488-2215
Secretary-Treasurer: MEG BURGETT, P.O. Box 874554, Wasilla, AK 99687; Phone: 907-373-0885
Alternate Board Member: MIKE CARLSON, P.O. Box 953, Delta Junction, AK 99737; Phone: 907-895-4819
Project Coordinator: DOUG WITTE, 351 W. Parks Hwy #101, Wasilla, AK 99645; Phone: 907-373-7923; Fax: 907-373-7192
Keyword(s): Conservation Districts

ALASKA AUDUBON SOCIETY
308 G. St., Suite 217, Anchorage, AK 99501
Phone: 907-276-7034; Fax: 907-276-5069; E-mail: jschoen@audubon.org
Membership: 2,400
Scope: Statewide
Description: The Alaska Audubon Society applies sound science and common sense to protect birds, other wildlife, and their habitats in Alaska. The staff works in cooperation with five local chapters to create a culture of conservation and an environmental ethic that supports a healthy, sustainable economy and a quality of life in harmony with Alaska's natural environment.
Contact(s):
Executive Director: DR. STANLEY E. SENNER
Office Manager/Education Coordinator: CATHERINE DENNERLEIN
Senior Scientist: DR. JOHN W. SCHOEN
Keyword(s): Biodiversity, Biology, Birds, Conservation of Protected Areas, Endangered and Threatened Species, Environmental and Conservation Education, Forest Management, Nature Preservation, Predators, Public Lands, Sustainable Ecosystems, Wetlands, Wildlands, Wildlife and Wildlife Habitat

ALASKA CENTER FOR THE ENVIRONMENT
519 W. 8th, Suite 201, Anchorage, AK 99501
Phone: 907-274-3621; Fax: 907-274-8733; E-mail: akcenter@alaska.net
Founded: 1971
Scope: Statewide
Description: Nonprofit organization that functions as an advocacy and citizen organizing facility for Alaskan environmental activities. With a professional staff of twelve and a corps of volunteers, the center conducts policy analyses and encourages grassroots activism to conserve and protect Alaska's natural resources, particularly its wildlands.
Contact(s):
Executive Director: JEFF RICHARDSON
Alaska Rainforest Campaign Grassroots Organizer: SCOTT ANAYA
Director of Alaska Rainforest Issues: KAREN BUTTON
Director of Issues and State Lands Director: CLIFF EAMES
Director of Trailside Discovery Camp: TOM BUREK; Phone: 907-274-5437
Director of Transportation Project: CHERYL RICHARDSON
Director of Valley ACE: DORI McDANNOLD, 642 S. Alaska St., Suite 201, Palmer, AK 99645; Phone: 907-745-8223; Fax: 907-745-8223
Financial Director and Officer Manager: JENNY NORRIS
Membership Director and Volunteer Coordinator: PATTY BLISS
Project Coordinator of Potter Marsh Watershed: RANDY VIRGIN
Keyword(s): Natural Resource Conservation, Wildlands

ALASKA CONSERVATION ALLIANCE
750 West 2nd Ave., Suite 109, Anchorage, AK 99501
Phone: 907-258-6171; Fax: 907-258-6177; E-mail: unite@akvoice.org
Founded: 1997
Scope: National
Description: An alliance dedicated to strengthening environmental organizations and empowering individuals to protect Alaska's environment through public education, training, advocacy, communication, and strategy development, all with respect for communities and human dignity.
Contact(s):
President: CLAIRE HOLLAND

NON-GOVERNMENTAL ORGANIZATIONS - A

Secretary: MICHELLE WILSON
Treasurer: BETH CARLSON
Executive Director: KAY BROWN
Field Organizer: PAULA PHILLIPS
Radio Program Coordinator: MARLO SHEDLOCK
Keyword(s): Air Quality and Pollution, Ancient Forests, Aquatic Habitats, Chemical Pollution Control, Cultural Preservation, EcoAction, Environment, Environmental and Conservation Education, Environmental Justice, Environmental Protection, Sustainable Development, Wetlands, Wilderness, Wildlife Protection

ALASKA CONSERVATION FOUNDATION
750 W. 2nd Ave., Suite 104, Anchorage, AK 99501-2167
Phone: 907-276-1917; Fax: 907-274-4145; E-mail: acfinfo@akcf.org
Scope: Statewide
Description: A community foundation providing grants for environmental conservation in Alaska. It is not a membership organization. It lists its donors as "Circle of Friends."
Contact(s):
Chair: MATT KIRCHOFF
Executive Director: DEBORAH WILLIAMS
Honorary Chair: JIMMY CARTER
Secretary and Treasurer: PEG TILESTON
Vice Chair of Alaska Trustees: CINDY ADAMS
Vice Chair of National Trustees: DAVID ROCKEFELLER JR.
Publication(s): *Alaska Conservation Directory; Dispatch; Annual Report; Grant Guidelines*
Keyword(s): Fisheries, Forests and Forestry, Sustainable Ecosystems, Water Resources, Wildlife and Wildlife Habitat

ALASKA CONSERVATION VOICE
750 West 2nd Ave., Suite 109, Anchorage, AK 99501
Phone: 907-258-6171; Fax: 907-258-6177; E-mail: unite@akvoice.org
Founded: 1997
Scope: Statewide
Description: An organization dedicated to protecting Alaska's environment through public education and advocacy in the Alaska state legislature, Congress and other forums.
Contact(s):
President: SHANNON O'FALLON
Secretary: CLAIRE HOLLAND
Treasurer: BETH CARLSON
Executive Director: KAY BROWN
Field Organizer: PAULA PHILLIPS
Program Coordinator: MARLO SHEDLOCK
Keyword(s): Air Quality and Pollution, Ancient Forests, Aquatic Habitats, Chemical Pollution Control, Cultural Preservation, EcoAction, Environment, Environmental and Conservation Education, Environmental Justice, Environmental Protection, Sustainable Development, Wetlands, Wilderness, Wildlife Protection

ALASKA NATURAL HISTORY ASSOCIATION
750 West Second Ave., Suite 100, Anchorage, AK 99501-2167
Phone: 907-274-8440; Fax: 907-274-8343; E-mail: charles_money@nps.gov; Web Site: www.alaskanha.org
Founded: 1959; Membership: 1,500
Scope: Statewide
Description: The Alaska Natural History Association is dedicated to enhancing the understanding and conservation of Alaska's natural and cultural resources by providing educational materials and services.
Contact(s):
Executive Director: CHARLES MONEY
Keyword(s): Arctic, Cultural Preservation, Environmental and Conservation Education, Natural History, Natural Resource Conservation, Environmental Education Curriculum

ALASKA NATURAL RESOURCE AND OUTDOOR EDUCATION ASSOCIATION
P.O. Box 110536, Anchorage, AK 99511-0536
Web site: www.sfos.alaska.edu:8000/ANROE/ANROE_home.html
Founded: 1983; Membership: 85
Scope: Statewide
Description: ANROE is a statewide network of K-12 school teachers, state and federal agency staff, university faculty and staff, students, and other concerned citizens united to promote the development, delivery, and implementation of educational efforts that help people of all ages learn about and appreciate Alaska's natural resources.
Contact(s):
President: LAUREL DEVANEY; Phone: 907-456-0558; Fax: 907-456-0454; E-mail: laurel_devaney@fws.gov
Publication(s): *Flyways, Pathways, and Waterways (newsletter); ANROE Guide to Natural Resource Education Materials (catalog)*
Keyword(s): Environmental and Conservation Education, Natural History, Training

ALASKA RAINFOREST CAMPAIGN
406 G St., #209, Anchorage, AK 99501
Phone: 907-222-2552; Fax: 907-222-2598; E-mail: info@akrain.org; Web Site: www.akrain.org
Founded: 1992; Membership: 14,000 in Alaska/2 million nationwide
Scope: Statewide/National
Description: Alaska Rainforest Campaign is a coalition of Alaska-based and national environmental organizations working to protect the coastal old-growth rainforests of Alaska, especially the Tongass and Chugach National Forests.
Contact(s):
Director of Washington, DC Office: MATTHEW ZENCEY, 320 Fourth St., NE, Washington, DC 20002; Phone: 202-544-0475; Fax: 202-544-5197
National Field Director: CORRIE BOSMAN
Keyword(s): Rainforests

ALASKA WILDLIFE ALLIANCE, THE
P.O. Box 202022, Anchorage, AK 99520
Phone: 907-277-0897; Fax: 907-277-7423; E-mail: awa@alaska.net
Founded: 1978
Scope: Statewide
Description: The Alliance is a nonprofit organization whose mission is the protection of Alaska's natural wildlife and habitat diversity for its intrinsic value as well as for the benefit of present and future generations.
Contact(s):
Executive Director: DR. PAUL JOSLIN
Associate Director: KAREN DEATHERAGE

ALBERTA FISH AND GAME ASSOCIATION, THE
6924-104 St., Edmonton, Alberta T6H 2L7 Canada
Phone: 780-437-2342; Fax: 780-438-6872; E-mail: office@afga.org
Founded: 1908; Membership: 15,000
Scope: Statewide
Description: To promote through education, lobbying, and programs the conservation and utilization of fish and wildlife, and to protect and enhance the habitat they depend upon.
Contact(s):
President: DAVE POWELL
Editor: KEVIN ROLFE
Executive Vice President: RON HOUSER
Publication(s): *Outdoor Edge, The*
Keyword(s): Fish Wildlife Management

ALBERTA TRAPPERS ASSOCIATION
#2 9919-106 St., Westlock, Alberta T7P 2K1 Canada
Phone: 780-349-6626
Founded: 1974; Membership: 1,500
Scope: Statewide
Description: Cooperates with all trappers associations and government agencies for a sensible conservation program.
Contact(s):
President: TED GANSKE, Box 6038, Bonnyville, Alberta T9N 2G7 Canada; Phone: 780-826-5026

NON-GOVERNMENTAL ORGANIZATIONS - A

1st Vice President: MARC MCOUAT, Box 1898, High Level, Alberta T0H 1Z0 Canada; Phone: 780-926-2756
2nd Vice President: WILMA BEHRENS, Box 6123, Edson, Alberta T7E 1T6 Canada; Phone: 780-723-2209
Editor: TED GANSKE
Editor and Executive Manager: LUISE VALENTINE
Publication(s): *Alberta Trapper, The*

ALBERTA WILDERNESS ASSOCIATION
Box 6398, Station D, Calgary, Alberta T2P 2E1 Canada
Phone: 403-283-2025; Fax: 403-270-2743; E-mail: awa@web.net
Founded: 1968; Membership: 2,500
Scope: Statewide
Description: A province-wide, non-profit, charitable organization with a mission to be an advocate for wild Alberta through awareness and action, and functioning on the values of eco-centredness, integrity, respectfulness, participation, tenacity, and passion. The AWA promotes sound ideas and policies for wilderness conservation, fosters appreciation and enjoyment of wilderness, and works with government, industry, organizations and individuals to encourage careful management of Alberta's natural lands and waters.
Contact(s):
President: GLENDA HANNA
Vice President: JENNIFER KLIMEK
Vice President: PETER SHERRINGTON
Secretary: COLIN YOUNG
Administrator: GLENDA HOLST
Conservation Director: DIANNE PACHAL
Editor: WENDY ADAMS
Editor: SHIRLEY BRAY
Past President: CLIFF WALLIS
Volunteer Coordinator: LEE TYMCHUK
Publication(s): *Wild Lands Advocate; Eastern Slopes Wildlands: Our Living Heritage; Landscapes of Southern Alberta; Wild Alberta- Our Last Best Hopes; Willmore Wilderness Park;* list of other publications upon request.
Keyword(s): Conservation of Protected Areas, Endangered and Threatened Species, Environmental Preservation, Nature Preservation, Public Lands, Wilderness, Wildlands, Wildlife and Wildlife Habitat

ALDO LEOPOLD FOUNDATION, INC.
E12919 Levee Rd., P.O. Box 77, Baraboo, WI 53913-0077
Phone: 608-355-0279; Fax: 608-356-7309; E-mail: leopold@baraboo.com; Web Site: www.aldoleopold.org
Founded: 1982
Scope: National
Description: The mission is to promote harmony between people and land. Activities include restoration, research, education, maintaining photographic archives, and acting as a clearinghouse for information about Aldo Leopold. The nonprofit organization was founded by the children of Aldo Leopold.
Contact(s):
Chairman: ESTELLA B. LEOPOLD
Executive Director: WELLINGTON HUFFAKER; E-mail: leopoldbh@baraboo.com
Administrative Assistant: TERESA SEAROCK; E-mail: leopoldts@baraboo.com
Publication(s): *Leopold Outlook, The; Notes from the*
Keyword(s): Ecology, Environmental and Conservation Education, Environmental Ethics, Land Conservation, Land Management, Prairies, Restoration, Training, Native Plants

ALLIANCE FOR THE CHESAPEAKE BAY
P.O. Box 1981, Richmond, VA 23218
Phone: 804-775-0951
Founded: 1971; Membership: 80 organizations and 900 individuals
Scope: Statewide
Description: To build, maintain, and serve the partnership among the general public, the private sector, and the government that is essential for establishing and sustaining policy, programs, and the political will to preserve and restore the resources of the Chesapeake Bay.
Contact(s):
President: JOHN T. KAUFFMAN; Phone: 610-774-5043
Secretary: TERRY HARWOOD; Phone: 301-380-3106
Treasurer: MICHAEL MARINO; Phone: 410-347-6201
Executive Director: FRANCES FLANIGAN, 6600 York Rd. Suite 100, Baltimore, MD 21212; Phone: 410-377-6270
Vice-President, Maryland: JOSEPH A. TIERNAN; Phone: 410-234-5328
Vice-President, Pennsylvania: WALTER L. POMEROY; Phone: 717-763-4985
Vice-President, Virginia: SUSAN TAYLOR HANSEN; Phone: 757-397-3481
Publication(s): *Bay Journal*
Keyword(s): Environment, Environmental and Conservation Education, Environmental Protection, Fisheries, Pollution Prevention, Population Growth, Rivers, Sustainable Development, Toxic Substances, Water Pollution, Water Quality, Water Resources, Watersheds, Wetlands

Baltimore Office
6600 York Rd., Suite 100, Baltimore, MD 21212
Phone: 410-377-6270; Fax: 410-377-7144
Scope: Statewide
Keyword(s): Environmental and Conservation Education, Rivers, Water Pollution, Water Quality, Wetlands

CRIS Office
P.O. Box 1981, Richmond, VA 23218
Phone: 800-662-CRIS
Scope: Statewide

Harrisburg Office
225 Pine St., Harrisburg, PA 17101
Phone: 717-236-8825; Fax: 717-236-9019
Scope: Statewide

AMANAKA'A AMAZON NETWORK
60 E. 13th St., 5th Fl., New York, NY 10003
Phone: 212-253-9502; Fax: 212-253-9507
Founded: 1990
Scope: National
Description: The Amanaka's Amazon Network is a nonprofit environmental and social justice organization. Amanaka'a serves as a liaison between the peoples of the Amazon and their allies in the U.S. We work to educate the American public about the Amazon Rainforest and its peoples, and support grassroots organizations in the Amazon.
Contact(s):
President: ZEZE WEISS
Vice President: JOHN FRIEDE
Secretary: CHRISTINE HALVORSON
Executive Director (Acting): CHRISTINE HALVORSON
Publication(s): *Letters from the Amazon;* series of booklets by people of the Amazon; *Amanaka'a Update*
Keyword(s): Cultural Preservation, Environmental Protection, Human Rights, Indigenous People, Rainforests, Sustainable Development

AMERICA THE BEAUTIFUL FUND
1730 K. St., NW, Suite 1002, Washington, DC 20006
Phone: 202-638-1649
Founded: 1965
Scope: National
Description: America the Beautiful Fund gives recognition, technical support, small seed grants, gifts of free seeds and national recognition awards to volunteers and community groups to initiate new local action projects improving the quality of the environment, including design, land preservation, local food production, arts, historical and cultural preservation, and horticultural therapy.

Contact(s):
President: NANINE BILSKI, 1730 K St. Suite 1002, Washington, DC 20006
Vice President: KAY LAUTMAN, 1730 Rhode Island Ave., NW, Suite 700, Washington, DC 20036
Vice President: JEAN WALLACE DOUGLAS, 4733 Woodway Ln., NW, Washington, DC 20016
Secretary: PENNY PAGANO, 4701 Berkley Terr., NW, Washington, DC 20007
Treasurer: SUSAN ANDERSON, 235 Mason Dr., Manhasset, NY 11030
Chairman of the Board: THOMAS FARRELL, First Chicago, 153 W 51 St., New York, NY 10019
Publication(s): Old Glory; Better Times; The Green Earth Guide
Keyword(s): Agriculture, Biodiversity, Botanical Gardens, Conservation of Protected Areas, Conservation Tillage, Cultural Preservation, Culture, Ecology, Environmental and Conservation Education, Flowers, Plants, and Trees, Gardening and Horticulture, Grants, Health and Nutrition, Historic Preservation

AMERICAN ALLIANCE FOR HEALTH PHYSICAL EDUCATION AND RECREATION AND DANCE
1900 Association Dr., Reston, VA 22091
Phone: 703-476-3400
Membership: 30,000
Scope: National
Description: A voluntary professional organization for educators in the fields of physical education, sports and athletics, dance, health and safety, recreation, and outdoor and environmental education. Its purpose is the improvement of education through such professional services as consultation, periodicals and special publications, conferences and workshops, leadership development, determination of standards, and research.
Contact(s):
President: CAROL V. PERSSON, Westfield State College, Westfield, MA 01086
District Representative: MARY-MARGARET McHUGH, Illinois Benedictine College, 5700 College Rd., Lisle, IL 60532
District Representative: WILLIAM J. VINCENT, Department of Kinesiology, California State University, 18111 Nordhoff St., Northridge, CA 91330
District Representative: HELEN CHREST, Box 179, East Helena, MT 59635
District Representative: KATHY KINDERFATHER, 15 E. Jackson Rd., Webster Groves, MO 63119
District Representative: GLENN ROSWAL, Department of HPER, Jacksonville State University, Jacksonville, FL 32265
District Representative: JIM AGLI, PE Department, Southern Connecticut State University, New Haven, CT 06515
Editor: FRAN ROWAN
Executive Vice President: A. GILSON BROWN
President Elect: QUENTINE CHRISTIAN, 7000 Quill Leaf Cove, Austin, TX 78750
Publication(s): Journal of Physical Education, Recreation and Dance; Health Education; AAHPERD Update; Strategies

AMERICAN ASSOCIATION FOR LEISURE AND RECREATION (AALR)
1900 Association Dr., Reston, VA 20191
Phone: 703-476-3472
Founded: 1939; Membership: 3,000
Scope: National
Description: The AALR was formed to promote school, community, and national leisure and recreation programs; to communicate to society the importance of intelligent use of leisure time; and to provide for those working or interested in recreation and leisure the opportunity to network and to join together for mutual strength and benefit.
Contact(s):
President: RANDY SWEDBURG, Concordia University, 7141 Sherbrooke W., Montreal, Quebec H4B 1R6 Canada; Phone: 514-848-3331; Fax: 514-848-4200
Past President: DONNA THOMPSON, University of Northern Iowa, School of HPELS, National Program for Playground Safety, 209 WRC, Cedar Falls, IA 50614-0241; Phone: 800-554-7529; Fax: 319-273-7308
President Elect: DALE ADKINS, Western Illinois University, Dept. of RPTA, 400 Currens Hall, 1 University Circle, Macomb, IL 61455; Phone: 309-298-1584; Fax: 309-298-2967; E-mail: KD-Adkins1@wiu.edu
Representative to the Board of Governors: NORMAN GILCHREST, Baylor University, HHPR Dept., Box 97313, Waco, TX 76798-7313; Phone: 254-710-3505; Fax: 254-710-3527; E-mail: buddy_gilchrest@baylor.edu
Publication(s): Leisure Today; AALReporter
Keyword(s): Family Recreation, Leisure, Outdoor Recreation

AMERICAN ASSOCIATION FOR THE ADVANCEMENT OF SCIENCE
1200 New York Ave., NW, Washington, DC 20005
Phone: 202-326-6400
Founded: 1848; Membership: 140,000
Scope: National
Description: Objectives are to further the work of scientists, to facilitate cooperation among them, to foster scientific freedom and responsibility, to improve the effectiveness of science in the promotion of human welfare, and to increase public understanding and appreciation of the importance and promise of the methods of science in human progress.
Contact(s):
President: M. R. GREENWOOD
Treasurer: WILLIAM T. GOLDEN; Phone: 212-425-0333
Chairman of the Board: RITA COLWELL
Editor-in-Chief: FLOYD E. BLOOM; Phone: 202-326-6505
Executive Officer: RICHARD S. NICHOLSON; Phone: 202-326-6639
Publication(s): Science; Science Books and Films, Science's Next Wave
Keyword(s): Biodiversity, Biology, Communications, Greenhouse Effect/Global Warming, Population Growth

AMERICAN ASSOCIATION OF BOTANICAL GARDENS AND ARBORETA, INC.
351 Longwood Rd., Kennett Square, PA 19348
Phone: 610-925-2500
Founded: 1940; Membership: 2,400
Scope: National
Description: AABGA is a nonprofit, membership organization serving North American botanical gardens, arboreta, and their professional staffs.
Contact(s):
President: ERIC TSCHANZ, President and Executive Director of Powell Gardens, 1609 NW U.S. Hwy 50, Kingsville, MO 64061
Vice-President: MARY PAT MATHESON, Director of Red Butte Garden and Arboretum, University of Utah, 18A deTrobriand St., Salt Lake City, UT 84113-5044
Secretary: KATHLEEN SOCOLOFSKY, Director of UC Davis Arboretum, One Shields Ave., Davis, CA 95616
Treasurer: RICHARD V. PIACENTINI, Executive Director of Phipps Conservatory and Botanical Gardens, One Schenley Park, Pittsburgh, PA 15213-3830
Executive Director: CARLA PASTORE
Director of Publications: VICKI MATTERN
Past President: GERALD T. DONNELLY, Executive Director of the Moton Arboretum, 4100 Illinois Rte. 53, Lisle, IL 60532-1293
Publication(s): Public Garden, The; AABGA Newsletter
Keyword(s): Botanical Gardens, Flowers, Plants, and Trees, Gardening and Horticulture, Internships

AMERICAN ASSOCIATION OF FIELD BOTANISTS
P.O. Box 23542, Chattanooga, TN 37422
Founded: 1983; Membership: 200
Scope: National
Description: The American Association of Field Botanists is an organization of amateur and professional botanists dedicated to the protection of native plants and the preservation of their natural

NON-GOVERNMENTAL ORGANIZATIONS - A

habitats, the exchange of information necessary to understand and maintain biodiversity, and the education of the public regarding threatened and endangered flora.
Contact(s):
President: CHARLES L. WILSON, 4201 Gann Store Rd., Hixson, TN 37343; Phone: 423-875-9625
Secretary: JOYCE S. MERRITT, 327 Guild Dr., Chattanooga, TN 37421
Treasurer: KURT A. EMMANUELE, Baylor School, Box 1337, Chattanooga, TN 37401
Publication(s): *American Association of Field Botanists Newsletter*
Keyword(s): Biodiversity, Conservation of Protected Areas, Ecology, Endangered and Threatened Species, Flowers, Plants, and Trees

AMERICAN ASSOCIATION OF ZOO KEEPERS, INC.
Administrative Offices, 635 SW Gage Blvd., Topeka, KS 66606
Phone: 785-273-1980; Fax: 785-273-1980
Founded: 1967; Membership: 2,800
Scope: National
Description: An international nonprofit organization of animal keepers and other persons interested in quality animal care and in promoting animal keeping as a profession. Chapters are active at zoos throughout North America. Promotes continuing education for keepers, national and international conservation projects, keeper-initiated zoo research, and educational publications.
Contact(s):
Administrative Secretary of Administrative Offices: BARBARA MANSPEAKER
Board of Directors: JAN REED-SMITH, John Ball Zoo, 1300 W. Fulton St., Grand Rapids, MI 49504; Phone: 616-336-4301
Board of Directors: DAVID LUCE, Oklahoma City Zoological Park, 2101 NE 50th St., Oklahoma City, OK 73111; Phone: 405-424-3344
Board of Directors: LUCY SEGERSON, NC Zoo, 4401 Zoo Parkway, Asheboro, NC 27203-9416; Phone: 910-879-7672
Board of Directors: MARILYN COLE, Box 335, Pickering, Ontario L1V 2R6 Canada; Phone: 905-683-2116
Board of Directors: DIANE CALLAWAY, Omaha's Henry Doorly Zoo, 3702 S. 10th St., Omaha, NE 68107; Phone: 402-733-8401
Board of Directors: JACQUE BLESSINGTON, Kansas City Zoological Gardens, 6700 Zoo Dr., Kansas City, MO ; Phone: 816-871-5700
Board of Directors: SCOTT M. WRIGHT, Cleveland Metroparks Zoo, 3900 Brookside Park Dr., Cleveland, OH 44109; Phone: 216-661-6500
Editor: SUSAN CHAN
Executive Director of the Board: ED HANSEN, c/o AAZK Inc., 635 SW Gage Blvd., Topeka, KS 66606-2066; Phone: 785-273-1980
President of the Board: RIC URBAN, Houston Zoological Gardens, 1513 N. MacGregor Way, Houston, TX 77030; Phone: 713-284-8303
Publication(s): *Animal Keepers' Forum; Diet Notebook and Mammals vol. 1; Handbook of Zoonotic Diseases; Crisis Management Resource Notebook*
Keyword(s): Conservation of Protected Areas, Endangered and Threatened Species, International Conservation, Natural History, Wildlife Management, Zoological Parks, Zoology

AMERICAN BASS ASSOCIATION, INC.
P.O Box 896, Gate City, VA 24251-0896
Phone: 540-386-2109; E-mail: aba@mounet.com
Founded: 1985; Membership: 20,000
Scope: National
Description: A nonprofit, tax-exempt national association dedicated to protecting and enhancing America's fishery resources; to promoting bass fishing as a major sport; and to teaching young people the fun of fishing and instilling in them an appreciation of the life-giving waters of America.
Contact(s):
President: BOB BARKER
Secretary: JOHN KEEGAN, 104 S. Cove Rd., Williamsburg, VA 23188; Phone: 757-564-0825
Director: AUDREY BARNETT, 1201 Bohmen, Pubelo, CO 81006
Director: WAYNE J. HOOD, 2909 N. Bayshore Dr., LaCrosse, WI 54603
Director-At-Large: ED METZGER, 710 Edgewater Dr., Inverness, FL 34450
Director of Eastern Region: PAUL NOECHEL, Rt. 2 Box 270, Lost Creek, WV 26385
Director of Northeast Region: JOHN COWAN, 235 Ridgeview, Weare, NH 03281
Keyword(s): Fish Wildlife Management, Sport Fishing, Water Quality, Fish

AMERICAN BASS ASSOCIATION OF CONNECTICUT, THE
Attn: President, 7 Banquo Brae Rd., Brookfield Center, CT 06804
Scope: Statewide
Contact(s):
President: JIM BALL; Phone: 203-775-1954

AMERICAN BASS ASSOCIATION OF EASTERN PENNSYLVANIA/ NEW JERSEY, THE
Attn: President, 1943 3rd. St., Langhorn, PA 19047
Scope: Statewide
Contact(s):
President: ED HARGRAVES; Phone: 215-752-8491

AMERICAN BASS ASSOCIATION OF KENTUCKY, THE
3301 Hardeman Dr., Ashland, KY 41101
Scope: Statewide
Contact(s):
President: MARK BAYES; Phone: 606-324-4894

AMERICAN BASS ASSOCIATION OF LAKE ERIE REGION, THE (Western PA and Western NY)
c/o Tournament Director, 2228 S. Neshannock Rd., W. Middlesex, PA 16159
Scope: Statewide
Contact(s):
Tournament Director: JOHN GEIWITZ; Phone: 412-347-0151

AMERICAN BASS ASSOCIATION OF MAINE, THE
Attn: President, 450 Back Brooke Rd., Monroe, ME 04951
Scope: Statewide
Contact(s):
President: BUTCH GREEN; Phone: 207-525-3001

AMERICAN BASS ASSOCIATION OF MARYLAND, THE
Attn: President, 622 Powhattan Beach Rd., Pasadena, MD 21122
Founded: 1987
Scope: Statewide
Contact(s):
President: CLANCY THORN JR.; Phone: 410-255-0499
Publication(s): *Maryland ABA News*
Keyword(s): Environmental Preservation, Fisheries, Sport Fishing, Water Resources, Youth Organizations

AMERICAN BASS ASSOCIATION OF MASSACHUSETTS, THE
Attn: President; 10 Winter Ave., Clinton, MA 01510
Scope: Statewide
Contact(s):
President: DAVE T. SULLIVAN; Phone: 508-368-7521

AMERICAN BASS ASSOCIATION OF NEW HAMPSHIRE, THE
Attn: President, 235 Ridgeview Rd., Weare, NH 03281
Scope: Statewide
Description: An organization of the individual members and bass fishing clubs, affiliated with the American Bass Association, Inc., dedicated to protecting and enhancing the state's fishery resources; to promote the sport of bass fishing; and to teach youngsters the fun of fishing and instill in them an appreciation of the life-giving waters of America.

Contact(s):
President: JOHN COWAN; Phone: 603-529-2642

AMERICAN BASS ASSOCIATION OF VIRGINIA, THE
c/o President, 4718 Hunt Ridge Rd., Roanoke, VA 24012
Scope: Statewide
Contact(s):
President: MIKE FOSBRE; Phone: 540-977-3116

AMERICAN BASS ASSOCIATION OF WEST VIRGINIA, THE
Attn: President, P.O. Box 235, West Milford, WV 26451
Scope: Statewide
Contact(s):
President: PAUL NOECHEL; Phone: 304-745-4961
Keyword(s): Environmental and Conservation Education, Internships, Natural History, Outdoor Recreation

AMERICAN BASS ASSOCIATION OF WISCONSIN, THE
c/o President, 2215 Greenbay St., LaCrosse, WI 54601
Scope: Statewide
Contact(s):
President: PAM LEHMANN; Phone: 608-784-8181

AMERICAN BIRD CONSERVANCY
1250 24th St., NW, Suite 400, Washington, DC 20037
Phone: 202-778-9666; Fax: 202-778-9778; E-mail: abc@abcbirds.org
Founded: 1994
Scope: National
Description: American Bird Conservancy (ABC), is a U.S. based, nonprofit, membership organization dedicated to the conservation of wild birds and their habitats throughout the Americas. ABC supports the Partners in Flight initiative through the magazine Bird Conservation and programs such as the Important Bird Areas Program.
Contact(s):
Chairman: HOWARD P. BROKAW
President: DR. GEORGE H. FENWICK
Vice Chair: CYNTHIA LENHART
Vice President of Government Relations: GERALD WINEGRAD
Vice President of Membership Development: MERRIE MORRISON
Vice President of Conservation: DR. DAVID PASHLEY
Director of Cats Indoors Campaign: LINDA WINTER
Director of Important Bird Areas: DR. ROBERT CHIPLEY
Director of Pesticides and Birds Campaign: KELLEY TUCKER
Director of Program Development: MIKE PARR
Publication(s): *Bird Conservation*
Keyword(s): Birds, Conservation of Protected Areas, Endangered and Threatened Species, Environmental Planning, International Conservation

AMERICAN BIRDING ASSOCIATION
P.O. Box 6599, Colorado Springs, CO 80934
Phone: 719-578-1614
Founded: 1969; Membership: 22,000
Scope: National
Description: The American Birding Association provides leadership to field birders by increasing their knowledge, skills, and enjoyment of birding. The ABA supports the interests of birders of all ages and experience and actively encourages the conservation of birds and their habitats.
Contact(s):
President: ALLAN R. KEITH
Vice President: WAYNE R. PETERSEN
Secretary: BLAKE MAYBANK
Treasurer: GERARD ZIARNO
Executive Director: PAUL GREEN
Editor: PAUL BAICICH
Editor: MATT PELIKAN
Publication(s): *Birding; Winging It; Field Notes; ABA Checklist; ABA/Lane Series of Birdfinding Guides (15 titles); Volunteer Directory; Membership Directory*
Keyword(s): Biodiversity, Birds, Environmental and Conservation Education, Outdoor Recreation, Wildlife and Wildlife Habitat

AMERICAN CAMPING ASSOCIATION, INC.
5000 State Rd. 67N, Martinsville, IN 46151
Phone: 765-342-8456; E-mail: aca@aca-camps.org; Web Site: www.acacamps.org/
Founded: 1910; Membership: 5,600
Scope: National
Description: The American Camping Association is a national community of camp professionals dedicated to enriching the lives of children and adults through camp experience. ACA recognizes the camp experience as a significant contributor to positive child and youth development. It is the only organization that accredits all types of camps based on 300 standards for health, safety and program quality.
Contact(s):
President: RODGER POPKIN
Director of Public Relations: BOB SCHULTZ
Executive Vice President: PEG SMITH
Publication(s): *Camping Magazine; Guide to Accredited Camps; various camp-related publications*
Keyword(s): Environmental and Conservation Education, Health and Nutrition, Internships, Outdoor Recreation, Youth Organizations

AMERICAN CANAL SOCIETY, INC.
840 Rinks Ln., Savannah, TN 38372-6774
Founded: 1972; Membership: 900
Scope: National
Description: A nonprofit organization dedicated to historic canal research, preservation, and canal parks.
Contact(s):
President: TERRY K. WOODS, 6939 Eastham Circle, Canton, OH 44708
Editor: DAVID ROSS
Secretary and Treasurer: CHARLES W. DERR, 117 Main St., Freemansburg, PA 18017; Phone: 610-691-0956
Publication(s): *American Canals (Quarterly Bulletin), American Canal Guides #1, #2, #3, #4, #5; Best From American Canals #1, #2, #3, #4 #5, #6, #7, #8*
Keyword(s): Cultural Preservation

AMERICAN CAVE CONSERVATION ASSOCIATION
119 E. Main St., P.O. Box 409, Horse Cave, KY 42749
Phone: 502-786-1466
Founded: 1977
Scope: National
Description: The ACCA is a national organization formed to conserve caves and karstlands, and other resources associated with them. Primary objectives are to provide information, technical assistance, and public education and management training programs; and operation of the American Cave and Karst Center, a national environmental education center and museum.
Contact(s):
President: ROY POWERS JR.; Phone: 540-546-5386
Vice President: TOM ALEY; Phone: 417-785-4289
Executive Director: DAVID G. FOSTER; Phone: 502-786-1466
Publication(s): *American Caves Magazine*
Keyword(s): Cave, Endangered and Threatened Species, Environmental and Conservation Education, Geology, Land Use Planning, Museum, Water Resources

AMERICAN CETACEAN SOCIETY
P.O. Box 1391, San Pedro, CA 90733-0391
Phone: 310-548-6279; Fax: 310-548-6950; E-mail: acs@pobox.com; Web Site: www.acsonline.org
Founded: 1967; Membership: 1,200
Scope: National
Description: A nonprofit organization that works in the areas of conservation, education, and research to protect marine mammals, especially whales, dolphins, and porpoises, and the oceans they live in.
Publication(s): *Whalewatcher: Journal of the American Cetacean Society; Spyhopper; ACS National Newsletter*

NON-GOVERNMENTAL ORGANIZATIONS - A

Keyword(s): Aquatic Habitats, Endangered and Threatened Species, Environmental and Conservation Education, Marine Mammals, Wildlife and Wildlife Habitat

AMERICAN CHESTNUT FOUNDATION, THE
469 Main St., P.O. Box 4044, Bennington, VT 05201-4044
Phone: 802-447-0110; Fax: 802-447-3712; E-mail: chestnut@acf.org; Web Site: www.chestnut.acf.org
Founded: 1983; Membership: 2,800
Scope: National
Description: Funded by private contributions, the purpose of The American Chestnut Foundation is to promote the preservation and restoration of the American chestnut, an important wildlife and timber tree killed by a blight early in the Twentieth Century; to operate two research breeding farms in Meadowview, VA; to provide grants for cutting edge research; and to identify surviving trees and establish satellite research plantings.
Contact(s):
President: L. L. COULTER, P.O. Box 365, Central Lake, MI 49622
Secretary: DR. DENNIS FULBRIGHT, Dept. of Botany and Plant Pathology, 166 Plant Biology, Michigan State University, E.Lansing, MI 48824
Treasurer: DR. WILLIAM MacDONALD, College of Agriculture and Forestry, West Virginia University, P.O. Box 6057, Morgantown, WV 26506
Development Director: TAMMY L. CARPENTER, 469 Main St., P.O. Box 4044, Bennington, VT 05201-4044
Membership Director: KELLY GRUNDMAN, 469 Main St., P.O. Box 4044, Bennington, VT 05201-4044
Vice President of Development: FORREST MACGREGOR, TACF Asheville Office, 46 Haywood St., Suite 213, Ashevill, NC 28801
Vice President of Science: DR. J. HILL CRADDOCK, U of TN - Chattanooga, 615 McCallie Ave, Chattanooga, TN 37403-2598
Publication(s): *Bark, The; Journal of The American Chestnut Foundation*
Keyword(s): Biodiversity, Endangered and Threatened Species, Flowers, Plants, and Trees, Wildlife and Wildlife Habitat

AMERICAN CONSERVATION ASSOCIATION, INC.
1200 New York Ave., NW, Suite 400, Washington, DC 20005
Phone: 202-289-2431; Fax: 202-289-1396
Founded: 1958
Scope: National
Description: A non-membership nonprofit, educational and scientific organization formed to advance knowledge and understanding of conservation, and to preserve and develop natural resources for public use.
Contact(s):
President: LAURANCE ROCKEFELLER
Secretary: R. SCOTT GREATHEAD
Treasurer: CARMEN REYES
Executive Director: CHARLES CLUSEN
Founder Honorary Trustee: LAURANCE S. ROCKEFELLER
Keyword(s): Air Quality and Pollution, Coasts, Environmental Law, Outdoor Recreation, Urban Environment

New York Office
30 Rockefeller Plaza, Rm. 5402, New York, NY 10112
Phone: 212-649-5822
Scope: National

AMERICAN COUNCIL FOR AN ENERGY-EFFICIENT ECONOMY
1001 Connecticut Ave., NW, #801, Washington, DC 20036
Phone: 202-429-8873; Fax: 202-429-2248; E-mail: ace3pubs@ix.netcom.com; Web Site: aceee.org
Founded: 1980
Scope: National
Description: Advancing energy efficiency as a means of promoting both economic prosperity and environmental protection. ACEEE conducts technical and policy assessments; advises governments and utilities; publishes books, conference proceedings and reports; organizes conferences and workshops; and informs consumers.
Contact(s):
Deputy Director: STEVE NADEL; Phone: 202-429-8873; Fax: 202-429-2248
President: CARL BLUMSTEIN; Phone: 202-429-8873; Fax: 202-429-2248
Executive Director: HOWARD GELLER; Phone: 202-429-8873; Fax: 202-429-2248
Publication(s): *Consumer Guide to Home Energy Savings: Guide to Energy-Efficient Office Equipment; Transportation and Energy: Strategies for a Sustainable Transportation System; Using Consensus Building to Improve Utility Reulation; Energy Innovations: A Prosperous Path to a Clean Environment; Green Guide to Cars and Trucks*
Keyword(s): Energy, Pollution Prevention, Transportation, Energy Efficiency, Utility Restructuring

AMERICAN FARMLAND TRUST
1200 18th St., NW, Suite 800, Washington, DC 20036
Phone: 202-331-7300; E-mail: info@farmland.org
Founded: 1980; Membership: 39,000
Scope: National
Description: AFT is a nonprofit conservation organization working to stop the loss of productive farmland and to promote farming practices that lead to a healthy environment. Its programs include public education, technical assistance, policy development, and direct farmland-protection projects.
Contact(s):
President: RALPH E. GROSSI
Assistant Vice-President of Field Programs: ROBERT WAGNER
Chairman of the Board: WILLIAM K. REILLY
Controller: SHARON PHENNEGER
Director for Farmland Advisory Services: JULIA FREEDGOOD
Director of Center for Agriculture in the Environment: DR. ANN SORENSEN
Director of Farms: BRYAN PETRUCCI
Director of Land Protection: DENNIS BIDWELL
Director of Public Education: BERNADINE PRINCE
Executive Committee of the Board Chairman: ALFRED H. TAYLOR JR.
Senior Vice President for Public Policy: EDWARD THOMPSON JR.
Vice Chairman of the Board: EDWARD H. HARTE
Vice-President for Marketing: JIMMY DAUKAS
Vice-President for Programs: TIM WARMAN
Publication(s): *Your Land Is Your Legacy (1997); Saving American Farmland: What Works (1997); Farming on the Edge II (1997); Living on the Edge: The Costs and Risks of Scatter Development (1998); Sharing the Responsibility: What Agricultural Landowners Think About Property Rights, Government Regulation, and the Environment (1998); American Farmland (Quarterly Magazine); Investing in the Future of Agriculture (1997); A Landscape of Choice: Strategies for Improving Patterns of Community Growth (1998); Smart Growth Versus Sprawl in California (1999)*
Keyword(s): Agriculture, Environmental and Conservation Education, Land Purchase, Land Use Planning, Wetlands

AMERICAN FEDERATION OF MINERALOGICAL SOCIETIES
Central Office, P.O. Box 26523, Oklahoma City, OK 73126-0523
Founded: 1945; Membership: 56,000
Scope: National
Description: To promote popular interest and education in the various earth sciences, in particular, the subjects of geology, mineralogy, paleontology, lapidary and other related subjects, and to sponsor and provide means of coordinating the work and efforts of all persons and groups interested therein; to sponsor and encourage the formation and international development of societies and regional federations, and by and through such means to strive toward greater international goodwill and fellowship.
Contact(s):
President: LEWIS ELROD, 2699 Lascassas Pike, Murfreesboro, TN 37230
Secretary: DAN McLENNAN, P.O. Box 26523, Oklahoma City, OK 73126-0523

Treasurer: TOBY COZENS, 4401 SW Hill St., Seattle, WA 98116-1924
Editor: MEL ALBRIGHT, Rt. 3 Box 8500, Bartlesville, OK 74003
Publication(s): *American Federation Newsletter; AFMS Safety Manual; AFMS Uniform Rules booklets*
Keyword(s): Environmental Preservation, Public Lands, Wilderness

AMERICAN FISHERIES SOCIETY
Headquarters, 5410 Grosvenor Ln., Suite 110, Bethesda, MD 20814
Phone: 301-897-8616; Fax: 301-897-8096; E-mail: main@fisheries.org; Web Site: www.fisheries.org
Founded: 1870; Membership: 9,200
Scope: National
Description: A professional society to promote the conservation, development, and wise utilization of fisheries, both recreational and commercial.
Contact(s):
President: CHRISTINE M. MOFFITT, Dept. of Fish & Wildlife Resources, University of Indiana, Moscow, ID 83844; Phone: 208-885-7047; Fax: 208-885-9080; E-mail: cmoffitt@uidaho.edu
President-Elect: CARL V. BURGER, USFWS Abernathy Tech Center, 1440 Abernathy Rd., Longview, WA 98632; Phone: 360-425-6072; Fax: 360-636-1855; E-mail: carl_v_burger@mail.fws.gov
1st Vice-President: KENNETH L. BEAL, 1 Blackburn Dr., Glouester, MA 01930; Phone: 978-281-9267; Fax: 978-281-9117; E-mail: ken.beal@noaa.gov
2nd Vice-President: FRED HARRIS, NC Wildlife Red. Comm., 1721 Mail Service Center, Raleigh, NC 27699-1721; Phone: 919-733-3633; Fax: 919-715-7643; E-mail: HarrisFa@mail.wildlife.state.nc.us
Past President: ROBERT F. CARLINE, 113 Merkle Bldg., University Park, PA 16802; Phone: 814-865-5611; Fax: 814-863-4710; E-mail: F7u@psu.edu
Executive Director: GHASSAN N. RASSAM
Director of Administration and Finance: BETSY FRITZ
Publication(s): *Transactions of the American Fisheries Society; North American Journal of Fisheries Management; Progressive Fish-Culturist, The Journal of Aquatic Animal Health, Fisheries*
Keyword(s): Aquatic Habitats, Fisheries, Renewable Resources, Water Pollution, Water Pollution Management, Wetlands, Professional Organization

Bioengineering Section
1646 Jeannette Pl., Bainbridge Island, WA 98110
Phone: 206-842-8195; Fax: 206-842-8195
Scope: National
Contact(s):
President: WAYNE J. DALEY; E-mail: wjd1163@aol.com

Canadian Aquatic Resources Section
2204 Main Mall, Univ. BC, Vancouver, British Columbia V6T 1Z4 Canada
Phone: 604-222-6753; Fax: 604-660-1849
Scope: National
Contact(s):
President: BRUCE R. WARD; E-mail: Bruce.Ward@gems8.gov.bc.ca

Computer User Section
Dept. of Natural Sciences, MS Valley State Univ., Itta Bena, MS 38941
Phone: 601-254-3383; Fax: 601-254-3668
Scope: National
Contact(s):
President: MICHAEL D. PORTER; E-mail: mdporter@cypress.mcsr.olemiss.edu

Early Life History
NOAA - National Marine Fisheries Service, The Beaufort Laboratory, 101 Pivers Island Rd., Beaufort, NC 28526
Phone: 252-728-8727; Fax: 252-728-8747
Scope: National
Contact(s):
President: JEFF GOVONI; E-mail: jgovoni@hatteras.bea.nmfs.gov

Education Section
Dept. of Fish and Wildlife, MI State University, East Lansing, MI 48824
Phone: 517-353-3373; Fax: 517-432-1699
Scope: National
Contact(s):
President: THOMAS G. COON; E-mail: coontg@pilot.msu.edu

Equal Opportunities Section
4020 N. New Jersey, Indianapolis, IN 46205
Phone: 371-233-5468; Fax: 317-233-3882
Scope: National
Contact(s):
President: GWEN WHITE; E-mail: gwhite@dnr.state.in.us

Estuaries Section
NOAA/NMFS F/HP4 Off., Hab. Prot., 1315 East-West Highway, Silver Spring, MD 20910-3282
Phone: 301-713-2319; Fax: 301-713-1043
Scope: National
Contact(s):
President: STEPHEN M. WASTE; E-mail: stephen.waste@noaa.gov

Fish Culture Section
Fisheries Research Lab, Southern IL Univ., Carbondale, IL 62901-6511
Phone: 618-453-2890; Fax: 618-536-7761
Scope: National
Contact(s):
President: CHRISTOPHER KOHLER; E-mail: ckohler@siu.edu

Fish Health Section
CA State Univ., Dept. of Biological Sciences, Hayward, CA 94542
Phone: 510-881-3422; Fax: 510-888-4747
Scope: National
Contact(s):
President: BEVERLY A. DIXON; E-mail: bdixon@csuhayward.edu

Fisheries Administrators Section
CO Division Wildlife, 6060 N. Broadway, Denver, CO 80216
Phone: 303-291-7362; Fax: 303-294-0874
Scope: National
Contact(s):
President: ROBIN F. KNOX; E-mail: robin.knox@state.co.us

Fisheries History Section
8200 Pine Cross, Ann Arbor, MI 48103
Phone: 734-426-2975; Fax: 734-426-2975
Scope: National
Contact(s):
President: CARLOS FETTEROLF

Fisheries Law Section
1271 Quaker Hill Dr., Alexandria, VA 22314
Phone: 703-461-9201; Fax: 703-461-9290
Scope: National
Contact(s):
President: DAVID L. ALLISON; E-mail: dallison@msn.com

Fisheries Management Section
OK Fish Res Lab, 500 E. Constellation, Norman, OK 73072
Phone: 405-325-7288; Fax: 405-325-7631
Scope: National
Contact(s):
President: JEFF C. BOXRUCKER; E-mail: jboxrucker@aol.com

Genetics Section
4302 Underwood St., University Park, MD 20782
Phone: 301-864-2553

NON-GOVERNMENTAL ORGANIZATIONS - A

Scope: National
Contact(s):
President: JOHN M. EPIFANIO; E-mail: jepifan@atlas.vcu.edu

International Fisheries Section
4408 Santa Clara Ct., Fairfax, VA 22030
Phone: 202-205-0878; Fax: 202-205-1054
Scope: National
Contact(s):
President: GLEN K. CONTRERAS; E-mail: gaygle@aol.com

Introduced Fish Section
Lee Co. Hyacinth Control, P.O. Box 60005, Fort Myers, FL 33906
Phone: 813-694-5844; Fax: 813-694-5844
Scope: National
Contact(s):
President: JOHN R. CASSANI; E-mail: jcassani@peganet.com

Marine Fisheries Section
Hatfield Marine Science Center, Oregon State University, 2030 Marine Sciences Dr., Newport, OR 97365
Phone: 541-867-0135; Fax: 541-867-0138
Scope: National
Contact(s):
President: STEVEN BERKELEY; E-mail: Steve.Berkeley@HMSC.ORST.EDU

Native People Fisheries Section
USFWS, 4401 N. Fairfax Dr., Suite 840, Arlington, VA 22203
Phone: 703-358-1718; Fax: 703-358-2044
Scope: National
Contact(s):
President: HANNIBAL BOLTON; E-mail: hannibal_bolton@fws.gov

North Central Division
USGS-BRD-ECRC, 4200 New Haven Rd., Columbia, MO 65201-9634
Phone: 573-875-5399; Fax: 573-876-1896
Scope: National
Contact(s):
President: PAM HAVERLAND; E-mail: pamela_haverland@usgs.gov

Northeastern Division
Dept. of Natural Resources, 122A Fernow Hall, Cornell Univ., Ithaca, NY 14853
Phone: 607-255-2822; Fax: 607-255-0349
Scope: National
Contact(s):
President: BARBARA KNUTH; E-mail: bak3@cornell.edu

Physiology Section
Dept. Animal Science, 2357 Main Mall, Suite 208, Univ. BC, Vancouver, British Columbia V6T 1Z4 Canada
Phone: 604-822-6846; Fax: 604-822-4400
Scope: National
Contact(s):
President: GEORGE K. IWAMA; E-mail: giwama@unixg.ubc.ca

Socioeconomics Section
P.O. Box 1102X0, Univ. of Florida, Gainesville, FL 32611
Phone: 352-392-4991; Fax: 352-392-3646
Scope: National
Contact(s):
President: CHARLES M. ADAMS; E-mail: adams@fred.ifas.ufl.edu

Southern Division
35450 Highland Dr., Eustis, FL 32726
Phone: 352-742-6438; Fax: 352-742-6461
Scope: National
Contact(s):
President: MARTY HALE; E-mail: halem@gfc.state.fl.us

Water Quality Section
Dynamac, 200 SW 35th St., Corvallis, OR 97333
Phone: 541-754-4516; Fax: 541-754-4716
Scope: National
Contact(s):
President: ROBERT M. HUGHES; E-mail: hughesb@mail.cor.epa.gov

Western Division
Dept. of Fish & Game, WHDAB, 1807-13th St., Suite 202, Sacramento, CA 95814
Phone: 916-327-0712; Fax: 916-324-0475
Scope: National
Contact(s):
President: KEN HASHAGEN; E-mail: khashage@hq.dfg.ca.gov

AMERICAN FISHERIES SOCIETY, ALABAMA CHAPTER
Attn: President, Alabama Chapter, 3355 Audubon Rd., Montgomery, AL 36106-2404
Founded: 1991
Scope: Statewide
Contact(s):
President: GREGORY M. LEIN; Phone: 334-844-9318; E-mail: glein@acesag.auburn.edu

AMERICAN FISHERIES SOCIETY, ALASKA CHAPTER
Attn: President, P.O. Box 20686, Juneau, AK 99802
Founded: 1973
Scope: Statewide
Contact(s):
President: CINDY A. HARTMANN; Phone: 907-586-7585; Fax: 907-586-7014; E-mail: cindy.hartmann@noaa.gov

AMERICAN FISHERIES SOCIETY, ARIZONA-NEW MEXICO CHAPTER
Attn: President, 3500 S. Lake Mary Rd., Flagstaff, AZ 86001
Founded: 1967
Scope: Statewide
Contact(s):
President: SCOTT J. REGER; Phone: 520-774-5045; Fax: 520-779-1825; E-mail: sreger@gf.state.az.us

AMERICAN FISHERIES SOCIETY, ARKANSAS CHAPTER
Attn: President, 102 NE 2nd St., Bryant, AR 72022
Founded: 1986
Scope: Statewide
Contact(s):
President: BRAIN K. WAGNER; Phone: 501-847-3611; Fax: 501-847-1869; E-mail: bkwagner@agfc.state.ar.us

AMERICAN FISHERIES SOCIETY, ATLANTIC INTERNATIONAL CHAPTER
Attn: President, Kleinschmidt Association, 75 Main St., Pittsfield, ME 04967
Founded: 1975
Scope: Regional
Contact(s):
President: BRANDON H. KULIK; Phone: 207-487-3328; Fax: 207-487-3124; E-mail: kulik@kassociates.com

AMERICAN FISHERIES SOCIETY, AUBURN UNIVERSITY CHAPTER
Attn: President, 203 Swingle Hall, Auburn University, AL 36840
Founded: 1974
Scope: Statewide
Contact(s):
President: JOE STEWIG; Phone: 334-844-4767; Fax: 334-844-9208; E-mail: jstewig@scesag.auburn.edu

AMERICAN FISHERIES SOCIETY, BONNEVILLE CHAPTER
Attn: President, P.O. Box 305, Dutch John, UT 84023
Phone: 801-789-3103
Founded: 1963
Scope: Statewide

Contact(s):
President: ROGER W. SCHNEIDERVIN; Phone: 801-885-3249; E-mail: nrdwr.rschneid@state.ut.us
Publication(s): *Quarterly newsletter; bulletins*

AMERICAN FISHERIES SOCIETY, CALIFORNIA-NEVADA CHAPTER
Attn: President, 300 Plum St., #25, Capitola, CA 95010
Founded: 1963
Scope: Regional
Contact(s):
President: PATRICK J. COULSTON; Phone: 831-649-2882; Fax: 831-649-2894; E-mail: pcoulsto@dfg.hq.ca.gov

AMERICAN FISHERIES SOCIETY, COLLEGE OF ENVIRONMENTAL SCIENCE AND FORESTRY CHAPTER
Attn: President, 146 Redfield Pl., Syracuse, NY 13210
Founded: 1975
Scope: Statewide
Contact(s):
President: PATRICIA THOMPSON; Phone: 315-472-0488; E-mail: pfthom01@mailbox.syr.edu

AMERICAN FISHERIES SOCIETY, COLORADO-WYOMING CHAPTER
Attn: President, Box 1078, Pinedale, WY 82941
Founded: 1966
Scope: Statewide
Contact(s):
President: RONALD REMMICK; Phone: 307-367-4353; Fax: 307-367-4403; E-mail: rremmi@missc.state.wy.us

AMERICAN FISHERIES SOCIETY, DAKOTA CHAPTER
Attn: President, Dept. of Biology, Box 9019, University of North Dakota, Grand Forks, ND 58202
Founded: 1964
Scope: Statewide
Contact(s):
President: STEVEN W. KELSCH; Phone: 701-777-2621; Fax: 701-777-2623; E-mail: kelsch@plains.nodak.edu
Publication(s): *ARI News Bulletin*

AMERICAN FISHERIES SOCIETY, FLORIDA CHAPTER
Attn: President, 5920 1st St., SW, Vero Beach, FL 32968
Founded: 1981
Scope: Statewide
Contact(s):
President: R. GRANT GILMORE; Phone: 561-465-2400; Fax: 561-468-0757; E-mail: rggilmorej@aol.com

AMERICAN FISHERIES SOCIETY, GEORGIA CHAPTER
Attn: President, GA DNR Albany Fisheries, 2024 Newton Rd., Albany, GA 31701-3576
Founded: 1985
Scope: Statewide
Contact(s):
President: MATTHEW E. THOMAS; Phone: 912-430-4256; Fax: 912-430-5110; E-mail: matt_thomas@mail.dnr.state.ga.us

AMERICAN FISHERIES SOCIETY, GREATER PORTLAND, OR CHAPTER
Attn: President, 4997 Pettejohn Rd. S, Salem, OR 97302
Founded: 1962
Scope: Statewide
Contact(s):
President: ROLAND G. MONTAGNE; Phone: 503-731-7518; Fax: 503-731-7080; E-mail: montar@portptld.com
Publication(s): *Audubon Warbler; Urban Naturalist, The; Familiar Birds of the Northwest; Protecting a Vanishing Ecosystem - The Ancient Forests of the Pacific Northwest*

AMERICAN FISHERIES SOCIETY, HAWAII CHAPTER
Attn: President, 7 Waterfront Plaza, Suite 400, 500 Ala Moana Blvd., Honolulu, HI 96813
Founded: 1982
Scope: Statewide
Contact(s):
President: PAUL K. BIENFANG; Phone: 808-836-3424; Fax: 808-537-1307; E-mail: bienfang@ceatech.com

AMERICAN FISHERIES SOCIETY, HUMBOLDT CHAPTER
Attn: President, HSU Dept. Fisheries, Arcata, CA 95521
Founded: 1973
Scope: Local Region
Contact(s):
President: KRISTINE BRENNEMAN; Phone: 707-826-3955; Fax: 707-826-4060; E-mail: kjb@axe.humboldt.edu

AMERICAN FISHERIES SOCIETY, IDAHO CHAPTER
Attn: President, 2250 W. Buckhorn Ct., Eagle, ID 83616
Founded: 1963
Scope: Statewide
Contact(s):
President: CINDY WILLIAMS; Phone: 208-939-8697; Fax: 208-939-4086; E-mail: cdwill@cyberhighway.net

AMERICAN FISHERIES SOCIETY, ILLINOIS CHAPTER
Attn: President, Max McGraw Wildlife Fdn., P.O. Box 9, Dundee, IL 30118
Founded: 1963
Scope: Statewide
Contact(s):
President: VICTOR J. SANTUCCI; Phone: 847-695-4610; Fax: 847-741-8157; E-mail: Vsantuc@ix.netcom.com

AMERICAN FISHERIES SOCIETY, INDIANA CHAPTER
Attn: President, Asherwood Environmental Science Center, 7496 State Rd. 124, Wabash, IN 46992
Founded: 1970
Scope: Statewide
Contact(s):
President: JERRY SWEETEN; Phone: 219-563-8148; Fax: 219-563-7276; E-mail: jsweeten@netusa1.net

AMERICAN FISHERIES SOCIETY, IOWA CHAPTER
Attn: President, Wildlife Research Station, 1436 255th St., Boone, IA 50036
Founded: 1969
Scope: Statewide
Contact(s):
President: RICHARD H. MCWILLIAMS; Phone: 515-432-2823; Fax: 515-432-2835; E-mail: fishmgt@opencomine.com

AMERICAN FISHERIES SOCIETY, KANSAS CHAPTER
Attn: President, KS Dept. of Wildlife & Parks, P.O. Box 1525, Emporia, KS 66801-1525
Founded: 1975
Scope: Statewide
Contact(s):
President: RANDALL D. SCHULTZ; Phone: 316-342-0658; Fax: 316-342-6248; E-mail: randys@wp.state.ks.us

AMERICAN FISHERIES SOCIETY, KENTUCKY CHAPTER
Attn: President, Eastern Fisheries District, 2744 Lake Rd., Prestonburg, KY 41653
Founded: 1990
Scope: Statewide
Contact(s):
President: KEVIN J. FREY; Phone: 606-886-1537

AMERICAN FISHERIES SOCIETY, LOUISIANA CHAPTER
Attn: President, LA Dept. of Wildlife and Fisheries, P.O. Box 98000, Baton Rouge, LA 70898
Founded: 1979
Scope: Statewide
Contact(s):
President: RICK A. KASPRZAK; Phone: 225-765-2375

NON-GOVERNMENTAL ORGANIZATIONS - A

AMERICAN FISHERIES SOCIETY, MICHIGAN CHAPTER
Attn: President, 484 Cherry Creek Rd., Marquette, MI 49855
Founded: 1973
Scope: Statewide
Contact(s):
President: JAMES W. PECK; Phone: 906-249-1611; E-mail: peckjw@state.mi.us

AMERICAN FISHERIES SOCIETY, MID-ATLANTIC CHAPTER
Attn: President, DE State University, 1200 N. Dupont Hwy., Dover, DE 19901
Founded: 1983
Scope: Statewide
Contact(s):
President: BERNARD R. PETROSKY; Phone: 302-739-5179; Fax: 302-739-4997; E-mail: bpetrosk@dsc.edu

AMERICAN FISHERIES SOCIETY, MID-CANADA CHAPTER
Attn: President, 19 Acadia Bay, Winnipeg, Manitoba R3T 3J1 Canada
Founded: 1986
Scope: National
Contact(s):
President: ARTHUR J. DERKSEN; Phone: 204-945-7791; Fax: 204-948-2308; E-mail: aderksen@nr.gov.mb.ca

AMERICAN FISHERIES SOCIETY, MINNESOTA CHAPTER
Attn: President, 4593 Hay Creek Rd. SW, Fort Ripley, MN 56449
Founded: 1967
Scope: Statewide
Contact(s):
President: PAUL J. RADOMSKI; Phone: 218-828-2246; Fax: 218-828-6022; E-mail: paul.radomski@dnr.state.mn.us

AMERICAN FISHERIES SOCIETY, MISSISSIPPI CHAPTER
Attn: President, Dept. of Biology, University of Mississippi, University, MS 38677
Founded: 1975
Scope: Statewide
Contact(s):
President: GLENN PARSONS; Phone: 601-232-7479; Fax: 601-232-5144; E-mail: bygrp@olemiss.edu

AMERICAN FISHERIES SOCIETY, MISSOURI CHAPTER
c/o President, MO Dept. of Conservation, 1110 S. College Ave., Columbia, MO 65201
Founded: 1963
Scope: Statewide
Contact(s):
President: STEVEN A. FISCHER; Phone: 573-882-9880; Fax: 573-882-4517; E-mail: fischs@mail.conservation.state.mo.us

AMERICAN FISHERIES SOCIETY, MONTANA CHAPTER
Attn: President, MT State University, Dept. of Biology, Bozeman, MT 59717
Founded: 1998
Scope: Statewide
Contact(s):
President: THOMAS E. MCMAHON; Phone: 406-994-2492; Fax: 406-994-7479; E-mail: ubitm@montana.edu

AMERICAN FISHERIES SOCIETY, NEBRASKA CHAPTER
Attn: President, 333 S. 4th St., Columbus, NE 68601
Founded: 1969; Membership: 60
Scope: Statewide
Contact(s):
President: MICHAEL P. GUTZMER; Phone: 402-563-5754; Fax: 402-563-5168; E-mail: mpgutz@nppd.net

AMERICAN FISHERIES SOCIETY, NEW MEXICO STATE UNIVERSITY STUDENT CHAPTER
Attn: President, 505 W. Griggs, Apt. A6, Las Cruces, NM 88005
Founded: 1972
Scope: Statewide
Contact(s):
President: JESSYCA LUCERO; Phone: 505-647-1860; E-mail: jeslucer@nmsu.edu

AMERICAN FISHERIES SOCIETY, NEW YORK CHAPTER
Attn: President, 130 Genesis Court, Owego, NY 13827
Founded: 1968
Scope: Statewide
Contact(s):
President: ALLEN PETERSON; Phone: 607-762-4753; Fax: 607-762-4005; E-mail: ampeterson@nyseg.com

AMERICAN FISHERIES SOCIETY, NORTH CAROLINA CHAPTER
Attn: President, c/o Duke Power Co., 13339 Hagers Ferry Rd., Huntersville, NC 28078
Founded: 1990
Scope: Statewide
Contact(s):
President: DAVID J. COUGHLAN; Phone: 704-875-5236; Fax: 704-875-5032; E-mail: djcoughl@duke-energy.com

AMERICAN FISHERIES SOCIETY, NORTH PACIFIC INTERNATIONAL CHAPTER
Attn: President, c/o WA Dept. of Fish and Wildlife, P.O. Box 43149, Olympia, WA 98504
Founded: 1978
Scope: National
Contact(s):
President: KURT L. FRESH; Phone: 360-902-2756; Fax: 360-902-2980; E-mail: freshklf@dfw.wa.gov

AMERICAN FISHERIES SOCIETY, NORTHWESTERN ONTARIO CHAPTER
Attn: Presdent, c/o CNFER, 955 Oliver Rd., Lakehead University, Thunder Bay, Ontario P7B 5E1 Canada
Founded: 1979
Scope: National
Contact(s):
President: ROBERT KUSHNERIUK; Phone: 807-343-4036; Fax: 807-343-4001; E-mail: Rob.Kushneriuk@mnr.gov.on.ca

AMERICAN FISHERIES SOCIETY, OHIO CHAPTER
Attn: President, c/o Ohio DNR, 10517 Canal Rd. SE, Hebron, OH 43025
Founded: 1974
Scope: Statewide
Contact(s):
President: MICHAEL E. COSTELLO; Phone: 614-265-6349; Fax: 614-262-1143; E-mail: mike.costello@dnr.state.oh.us

AMERICAN FISHERIES SOCIETY, OKLAHOMA CHAPTER
Attn: President, Rt. 1, Box 520, Bryon, OK 73722
Founded: 1968
Scope: Statewide
Contact(s):
President: JULIA MATLOCK; Phone: 580-474-2663; Fax: 580-474-2664; E-mail: byronfsh@socencom.net

AMERICAN FISHERIES SOCIETY, OREGON CHAPTER
Attn: President, 2910 NW Miller Ln., Albany, OR 97321
Founded: 1964
Scope: Statewide
Contact(s):
President: TIMOTHY S. HARDIN; Phone: 541-926-2262; Fax: 541-926-1230; E-mail: hardint@peak.org

AMERICAN FISHERIES SOCIETY, PENNSYLVANIA CHAPTER
Attn: President, 513 Hillside Ave., State College, PA 16803
Founded: 1969
Scope: Statewide

Contact(s):
President: R. SCOTT CARNEY; Phone: 814-355-4837; E-mail: scarney@lazerlink.com
Publication(s): *ACP Drummer*

AMERICAN FISHERIES SOCIETY, POTOMAC CHAPTER
Attn: President, 305 Hillsboro Dr., Silver Spring, MD 20902
Founded: 1976
Scope: Statewide
Contact(s):
President: WILLIAM D. CHAPPELL; Phone: 301-713-2341; Fax: 301-713-0596; E-mail: william.chappell@noaa.gov

AMERICAN FISHERIES SOCIETY, SOUTH CAROLINA CHAPTER
Attn: President, c/o SCWMRD, P.O. Box 4496, Rock Hill, SC 29732
Founded: 1982
Scope: Statewide
Contact(s):
President: RICHARD W. CHRISTIE; Phone: 803-366-7024; Fax: 803-366-1672; E-mail: dchristie@infoave.net

AMERICAN FISHERIES SOCIETY, SOUTHERN NEW ENGLAND CHAPTER
Attn: President, c/o NMFS NE Fish Center, 166 Water St., Woods Hole, MA 02543-1097
Founded: 1967
Scope: Statewide
Contact(s):
President: JOHN F. KOCIK; Phone: 508-495-2207; Fax: 508-495-2393; E-mail: jkocik@whsun1.wh.whoi.edu

AMERICAN FISHERIES SOCIETY, SOUTHERN ONTARIO CHAPTER
Attn: President, c/o MTO Environmental Section, 1201 Wilson Ave., Downsview, Ontario M2M 1J8 Canada
Founded: 1988
Scope: National
Contact(s):
President: CYNTHIA J.A. MITTON-WALKER; Phone: 416-235-5230; Fax: 416-235-4940; E-mail: mitton@mto.gov.on.ca

AMERICAN FISHERIES SOCIETY, TENNESSEE CHAPTER
Attn: President, c/o TN Tech, Dept. of Biology, Wildlife and Fish Science, Cookeville, TN 38505
Founded: 1977
Scope: Statewide
Contact(s):
President: DR. S. BRADFORD COOK; Phone: 931-372-3194; E-mail: sbc5959@tntech.edu

AMERICAN FISHERIES SOCIETY, TEXAS A&M CHAPTER
Attn: President, c/o Texas A&M Wildlife and Fisheries Science, 210 Nagle Hall, College Station, TX 77843-2258
Founded: 1969
Scope: Statewide
Contact(s):
President: BRIAN HEALY; Phone: 409-847-9335; E-mail: bhealy@tamu.edu

AMERICAN FISHERIES SOCIETY, TEXAS CHAPTER
Attn: President, c/o Texas Parks and Wildlife Division, 4200 Smith School Rd., Austin, TX 78744
Founded: 1976
Scope: Statewide
Contact(s):
President: PAUL HAMMERSCHMIDT; Phone: 512-389-4862; Fax: 512-389-4388; E-mail: paul.hammerschmidt@tpwd.state.tx.us

AMERICAN FISHERIES SOCIETY, TIDEWATER CHAPTER
Attn: President, c/o VA Institute of Marine Science, Gloucester Point, VA 23062
Phone: 919-328-6718
Founded: 1986
Scope: Statewide
Contact(s):
President: JOHN E. OLNEY SR.; Phone: 804-642-7334; Fax: 804-642-7097; E-mail: olney@vims.edu

AMERICAN FISHERIES SOCIETY, UNIVERSITY OF WYOMING STUDENT CHAPTER
Attn: President, P.O. Box 3166, Laramie, WY 82071-3166
Scope: Statewide
Contact(s):
President: NATHAN P. NIBBELINK; Phone: 307-766-2426; Fax: 307-766-5625; E-mail: nathan@uwyo.edu

AMERICAN FISHERIES SOCIETY, VIRGINIA CHAPTER
Attn: President, c/o Dept. of Fisheries and Wildlife, Virginia Tech, Blacksburg, VA 24060-0321
Founded: 1990
Scope: Statewide
Contact(s):
President: STEVE L. MCMULLIN; Phone: 540-231-8847; Fax: 540-231-7580; E-mail: smcmulli@vt.edu

AMERICAN FISHERIES SOCIETY, VIRGINIA TECH CHAPTER
Attn: President, 101 Cheatham Hall, Blacksburg, VA 24061
Founded: 1972
Scope: Statewide
Contact(s):
President: TIMOTHY COPELAND; Phone: 540-231-3329; Fax: 540-231-7580; E-mail: tcopelan@vt.edu
Publication(s): *Lab Notes*

AMERICAN FISHERIES SOCIETY, WEST VIRGINIA CHAPTER
Attn: President, P.O. Box 67, Elkins, WV 26241
Founded: 1989
Scope: Statewide
Contact(s):
President: MICHAEL V. SHINGLETON; Phone: 304-637-0245; Fax: 304-637-0250; E-mail: mshingleton@dnr.state.wv.us

AMERICAN FISHERIES SOCIETY, WISCONSIN CHAPTER
Attn: President, c/o College of Natural Resources, University of Wisconsin, Stevens Point, WI 54481
Founded: 1972
Scope: Statewide
Contact(s):
President: MICHAEL J. HANSEN; Phone: 715-346-3420; Fax: 715-346-3624; E-mail: mhansen@uwsp.edu
Publication(s): *CNRA Report, The; Wisconsin Roadsides*

AMERICAN FOREST FOUNDATION
1111 19th St., NW, Suite 780, Washington, DC 20036
Phone: 202-463-2462
Founded: 1981
Scope: National
Description: American Forest Foundation conducts charitable education and research programs. AFF supports American Tree Farm System -- 71,000 private landowners managing 95 million acres of forests -- and Project Learning Tree (PLT), award-winning pre K-12 environmental education curriculum and training program, active in U.S. and abroad. Nongrantmaking.
Contact(s):
President: LAURENCE D. WISEMAN
Vice President of American Tree Farm System: ROBERT SIMPSON
Vice President of Project Learning Tree: KATHY McGLAUFLIN
Publication(s): *Tree Farmer Magazine; PLT Branch*
Keyword(s): Communications, Environmental and Conservation Education, Forests and Forestry, Renewable Resources

AMERICAN FORESTS (formerly American Forestry Association)
P.O. Box 2000, Washington, DC 20013
Phone: 202-955-4500; Fax: 202-955-4588; E-mail: member@amfor.org; Web Site: www.americanforests.org
Founded: 1875

Scope: National
Description: Building on its rich history as the oldest national citizens' conservation organization in the U.S. and conservation movement pioneer, American Forests has several programs to address today's environmental challenges: Global ReLeaf 2000, the Urban Forest Center and the Forest Policy Center.
Contact(s):
Executive Director: DEBORAH GANGLOFF
Board Chair: JONATHAN SILVER
Treasurer: RICHARD PORTERFIELD
Senior Vice President for Development: RICHARD J. CROUSE
Vice President of Communications: DANIEL C. SMITH
Vice President of Forest Policy Center: GERALD J. GRAY
Vice President of Urban Forest Center: GARY MOLL
Editor: MICHELLE ROBBINS
Famous & Historic Tree Nursery: JEFF MEYER; Phone: 904-765-0727
Field Representative: JANE WESTENBERGER
Field Representative: ZANE G. SMITH JR.
Field Representative: BOB SKIERA
Southeast Region Coordinator: STACEY MANDELL; Phone: 305-372-6555
Publication(s): *American Forests (quarterly magazine)*
Keyword(s): Environmental and Conservation Education, Forests and Forestry, Greenhouse Effect/Global Warming, Outdoor Recreation, Public Lands, Trees, Urban Forestry

AMERICAN GEOGRAPHICAL SOCIETY
120 Wall St., Suite 100, New York, NY 10005-3904
Phone: 212-422-5456; Fax: 212-422-5480; E-mail: amgeosoc@earthlink.net
Founded: 1851
Scope: National
Description: The AGS has sponsored research projects field work, and educational travel, held symposia and lectures, and published scientific and popular books, periodicals, and maps. Its publications bring accurate, up-to-date information on man and the land to more than 8,000 fellows and subscribers in over 100 countries.
Contact(s):
Chair: JOHN E. GOULD
President: DONALD LLOYD-JONES
Secretary: JOHN R. MATHER
Treasurer: JOHN J. McCABE
Executive Director: MARY LYNNE BIRD
Chair Emeritus: RICHARD H. NOLTE
Editor: PAUL STARRS, Geographical Review Dept. Geography, University of Neveda-Reno, Reno, NV 89557
Editor, Focus and Around the World: HILARY LAMBERT HOPPER, Dept. of Geography, University of Kentucky, Lexington, KY 40506
Editor, *Ubique*: PETER G. LEWIS
Publication(s): *Geographical Review; Focus; Ubique, Around the World Program*
Keyword(s): Environmental and Conservation Education, Greenhouse Effect/Global Warming, Land Use Planning, Sustainable Development, Urban Environment

AMERICAN GEOLOGICAL INSTITUTE
4220 King St., Alexandria, VA 22302-1502
Phone: 703-379-2480; Fax: 703-379-7563; E-mail: agi@agi.web.org
Founded: 1948
Scope: National
Description: AGI provides information services for earth scientists to be an advocate for the interests of the earth-science community; plays a major role in strengthening earth-science education; and increases public awareness of the role that earth sciences play in mankind's use of resources and interaction with the environment.
Contact(s):
Executive Director: DR. MARCUS E. MILLING
Publication(s): *Geotimes; Bibliography and Index of Geology; Glossary of Geology; Directory of Geoscience Departments*
Keyword(s): Geology

AMERICAN GROUND WATER TRUST
P.O. Box 1796, 16 Centre St., Concord, NH 03301
Phone: 603-228-5444; Fax: 603-228-6557; E-mail: agwtHQ@aol.com; Web Site: www.agwt.org
Founded: 1987
Scope: National
Description: The American Ground Water Trust is an independent nonprofit, membership organization which promotes public awareness of the environmental and economic importance of ground water through public education programs. The Trust promotes opportunity, cooperation, and action among individuals, groups, and organizations throughout America.
Contact(s):
Chairman: RANDY LYNE
Secretary: CHRIS CATANIA
Treasurer: MIKE LALLY
Executive Director: ANDREW W. STONE
Vice Chair: SAM DANIELS
Publication(s): *Ground Water information pamphlets; Ground Water and Wetlands in the United States; Ground Water Basics (video), Education Poster, Wellowner newsletter; Water Well Basics (video)*
Keyword(s): Environmental and Conservation Education, Geology, Ground Water Protection, Scholarships and Grants, Water Pollution, Water Resources

AMERICAN HIKING SOCIETY
1422 Fenwick Ln., Silver Spring, MD 20910
Phone: 301-565-6704; Web Site: www.americanhiking.org
Founded: 1976
Scope: National
Description: American Hiking Society (AHS) is a recreation-based conservation organization dedicated to establishing, protecting and maintaining foot trails in America. AHS is comprised of over 120 member trail clubs and 10,000 individual members, represents half a million outdoors-people and serves as the voice of the American hiker. AHS effectively lobbies to encourage funding for trails and promotes volunteerism in trail building and maintenance.
Contact(s):
President: DAVID LILLARD
Vice-President: MARY MARGARET SLOAN
Membership/marketing: SALLY GRIMES
Development: CHRIS CHESAK
Editor, American Hiker: CHRIS REITER
Publication(s): *American Hiker; Pathways Across America; Helping Out in the Outdoors*
Keyword(s): Environmental and Conservation Education, Forests and Forestry, Land Use Planning, Outdoor Recreation, Public Lands, Trail

AMERICAN HORSE PROTECTION ASSOCIATION
1000 29th St., NW, Suite T-100, Washington, DC 20007
Phone: 202-965-0500
Founded: 1966
Scope: National
Description: A national nonprofit, tax-exempt organization dedicated entirely to the welfare of horses, both wild and domestic. Works for the enforcement of all humane legislation for both wild and domestic horses.
Contact(s):
Vice President: MICHELE RYDELL
Executive Director: ROBIN C. LOHNES
President and Chairman of the Board of Directors: NANCY G. HARGRAVE
Secretary and Treasurer: NANCY A. MURRAY
Publication(s): *Newsletter; Special Bulletins*
Keyword(s): Environmental Law, Land Use Planning, Mammals, Public Lands, Wildlife Management

AMERICAN HUMANE ASSOCIATION
63 Inverness Dr. East, Englewood, CO 80112
Phone: 303-792-9900; Web Site: www.americanhumane.org
Founded: 1877

Scope: **National**
Description: AHA provides training and resources to 6,500 animal care and control agencies in the US and Canada; ensures the humane treatment of animals in movies and TV productions; serves as a national coordinator of emergency animal relief during natural disasters and works on legislation to protect animals.
Contact(s):
President: ROBERT F.X. HART
Director of Communications: JACK SPARKS
Director of Shelter Programs: CONNIE HOWARD
Director of Humane Education: MICHAEL KAUFMANN
Publication(s): *Shoptalk; Protecting Animals*
Keyword(s): Animal Welfare

AMERICAN INSTITUTE OF BIOLOGICAL SCIENCES
1444 I St., NW, Washington, DC 20005
Phone: 202-628-1500; Fax: 202-628-1509
Founded: 1947; Membership: 8,000
Scope: **National**
Description: A national organization for biology and biologists, combining an individual membership organization with the federation principle. Operates educational, advisory, liaison, informational, publication and editorial programs to serve biologists, promote unity and effectiveness of effort, and apply knowledge of biology to human welfare.
Contact(s):
President: DR. GARY BARRETT, Inst. Of Ecology, Univ. of GA, Athens, GA 30602-2202; Phone: 706-542-2968; Fax: 706-542-4819; E-mail: gbarrett@sparrow.ecology.uga.edu
Executive Director: DR. RICHARD O'GRADY
Editor: DR. REBECCA CHASAN
Immediate Past President: DR. FRANCES C. JAMES, Dept. of Biological Sciences, FL State Univ., Tallahassee, FL 32306; Phone: 850-644-2217; Fax: 850-644-9829; E-mail: james@bio.fsu.edu
President-elect: DR. GREGORY J. ANDERSON, Ecology & Evolutionary Bio., University of CT, Storrs, CT 06269-3043; Phone: 860-486-4555; Fax: 860-486-6364/4320; E-mail: ander@uconnvm.uconn.edu
Secretary and Treasurer: DR. JANE BROCKMANN, Professor of Zoology, University of Fl, Gainesville, FL 32611-8525; Phone: 352-392-1297; Fax: 352-392-3704; E-mail: hjb@zoo.ufl.edu
Publication(s): *BioScience*
Keyword(s): Biology, Grants, Sustainable Ecosystems, Zoology

AMERICAN INSTITUTE OF FISHERY RESEARCH BIOLOGISTS
c/o Dr. Gary Sakagawa, National Marine Fisheries Service, Southwest Fisheries Science Center, P.O. Box 271, La Jolla, CA 92038-0271
Founded: 1957; Membership: 1,200
Scope: **National**
Description: The Institute was founded to advance the science of fishery biology and to promote conservation and proper use of fishery resources. It serves that goal primarily by being concerned with the professional development and performance of its members, and recognition of their competence and achievement.
Contact(s):
President: DR. GARY SAKAGAWA
Secretary: DR. BARBARA E. WARKENTINE, SUNY-Maritime College, Science Dept., 6 Pennyfield Ave, Ft. Schuyler, Bronx, NY 10465-4198; Phone: 206-543-1101
Treasurer: DR. JOSEPH W. RACHLIN, Dept. Of Biological Sciences, Lehman College of CUNY, 250 Bedford Park Blvd., W., Bronx, NY 10468-1589
Editor: DR. GENE R. HUNTSMAN, 205 Blades Rd., Havelock, NC 28523; Phone: 704-274-7773
Publication(s): *Briefs*
Keyword(s): Aquatic Habitats, Biology, Fisheries, Renewable Resources, Professional Organization

AMERICAN LAND CONSERVANCY
456 Montgomery St., Suite 1450, San Francisco, CA 94104
Phone: 415-403-3850; Fax: 415-403-3856; E-mail: alc@econet.org; Web Site: www.alcnet.org
Founded: 1990
Scope: **National**
Description: To preserve land for this and future generations; in particular, to preserve its scientific, historic, educational, ecological, geological, recreational, agricultural, and scenic features, and its native plant and animal life or biotic community.
Contact(s):
President: HARRIET BURGESS
Publication(s): *American Land Conservancy Newsletter; Statement of Opportunity Brochure; Fifty Wildflowers of Bear Valley*
Keyword(s): Coasts, Deserts, Forests and Forestry, Land Purchase, Public Lands

AMERICAN LANDS (formerly Western Ancient Forest Campaign)
726 7th St., SE, Washington, DC 20003
Phone: 202-547-9400; Fax: 202-547-9213; E-mail: wafcdc@AmericanLands.org
Founded: 1991
Scope: **National**
Description: The mission of American Lands is the protection and recovery of North American native forest, grassland, and aquatic ecosystems; the preservation of biological diversity; the restoration of watershed integrity; and the promotion of environmental justice in connection with these goals. This mission is accomplished by strengthening grassroots conservation networks; providing advocacy services and other assistance to local conservation groups; and helping to improve communications and coordination among these groups and other societal institutions.
Contact(s):
President: RANDI SPIVAK, K-2 Communications, 880 Apollo St. Suite 239, El Segundo, CA 90245; Phone: 310-563-2610
Treasurer: CHUCK WILLER, Coast Range Association, P.O. Box 2250, Corvallis, OR 97339; Phone: 541-758-0255
Executive Director: JIM JONTZ; Phone: 202-547-9095
Campaign Coordinator: STEVE HOLMER; Phone: 202-547-9105
Publication(s): *Report from Washington*
Keyword(s): Aquatic Habitats, Forests and Forestry, Public Lands

AMERICAN LEAGUE OF ANGLERS AND BOATERS
1225 New York Ave., NW, #450, Washington, DC 20005
Phone: 202-682-9530; Fax: 202-682-9529
Founded: 1985
Scope: **National**
Description: ALAB was formed to be a vigilant patron of the Sport Fishing and Boating Enhancement Act (PL 98-369 and the Aquatic Resources Trust Fund created by the Act. Composed of more than 30 organizations, ALAB is dedicated to this pioneering user-pays legislation which provides some $330 million annually in funding for U.S. Coast Guard recreational boating programs and in matching grants to the states for sportfish research and enhancement, as well as wetlands conservation, boating safety, and boating access improvements. Membership in ALAB is open to nonprofit organizations, businesses, corporations, and individuals seeking improvement in the scope and health of the nation's aquatic resources and expansions of opportunities for responsible utilization by the fishing and boating public.
Contact(s):
Treasurer: GEORGE STEWART; Phone: 302-678-9143
Co-chair: VERONICA FLOYD; Phone: 703-960-2223
Co-chair: DERRICK CRANDALL; Phone: 202-682-9530
Immediate Past Chair: PAUL BROUHA; Phone: 301-897-8616
Keyword(s): Fisheries, Outdoor Recreation, Sport Fishing, Water Resources

AMERICAN LITTORAL SOCIETY
Headquarters, Sandy Hook, Highlands, NJ 07732
Phone: 201-291-0055
Founded: 1961; Membership: 8,000
Scope: **National**

Description: A national organization of professionals and amateurs interested in the study and conservation of coastal habitat, barrier beaches, wetlands, estuaries, and near-shore waters, and their fish, shellfish, bird, and mammal resources. Publishes scientific and popular material. Conducts field trips, dive and study expeditions, and a fish tag-and-release program. Special activities for scuba divers.
Contact(s):
President: MICHAEL HUBER
Vice President: FRANK STEIMLE
Secretary: ANGELA CRISTINI
Treasurer: SHELDON ABRAMS
Executive Director: D. W. BENNETT
Publication(s): *Underwater Naturalist; Coastal Reporter*
Keyword(s): Aquatic Habitats, Coasts, Coral Reefs, Fisheries, Wetlands

Coral Reef Conservation Center Office
2809 Bird Ave., Suite 162, Miami, FL 33160
Phone: 305-358-4600
Scope: National
Contact(s):
Head: ALEXANDER STONE

Delaware Riverkeeper Crossing
P.O. Box 326, Washington Crossing, PA 18977
Phone: 215-369-1188
Scope: National
Contact(s):
Contact: MAYA VAN ROSSUM

New York Office
28 West 9th Rd., Broad Channel, NY 11693
Phone: 718-634-6467; Web Site: Scope: National
Contact(s):
Contact: DONALD RIEPE; E-mail: DonRiepe@AOL.com
Editor: BARBARA TOBORG
New York State Beach Cleanup Coordinator: BARBARA COHEN; E-mail: ALSBEACH@AOL.com
Publication(s): *Littorally Speaking* (newsletter)
Keyword(s): Coasts

AMERICAN LIVESTOCK BREEDS CONSERVANCY
P.O. Box 477, 15 Hillsboro, Pittsboro, NC 27312
Phone: 919-542-5704
Founded: 1977; Membership: 4,000
Scope: National
Description: ALBC is a nonprofit membership organization working to protect genetic diversity in domestic animals through the conservation of nearly 100 rare breeds of livestock and poultry in America. ALBC does research on breed status and characteristics, operates a gene bank to preserve genetic materials for the future, and provides technical support on conservation breeding and animal use in sustainable, diversified agriculture.
Contact(s):
Chair: CLAUDE HUGHES
Secretary: DARWIN KELSEY
Treasurer: THOMAS WALVOORD
Executive Director: DR. DONALD BIXBY
Technical Coordinator: PHILLIP SPONENBERG
Vice Chair: JEFF BUMP
Publication(s): *ALBC News; Taking Stock: The North American Livestock Census; A Conservation Breeding Handbook; A Rare Breeds Album of American Livestock; Birds of a Feather: Saving Rare Turkeys from Extinction*
Keyword(s): Agriculture, Biodiversity, Endangered and Threatened Species, Historic Preservation, Sustainable Development

AMERICAN LUNG ASSOCIATION
1740 Broadway, New York, NY 10019-4374
Phone: 212-315-8700
Founded: 1904
Scope: National
Description: Formerly known as the National Tuberculosis and Respiratory Disease Association. The American Lung Association is a voluntary agency concerned with the conquest of lung disease and the promotion of lung health, which includes preventing and controlling air pollution. National Air Conservation Commission and local and state air conservation committees work with citizenry and other groups for effective air pollution control. Informational material available from national, state, and local lung associations.
Contact(s):
Director of National Health Programs: RONALD WHITE; Phone: 202-785-3355
Editor: ROBERT A. KLOCKE
Managing Director: JOHN R. GARRISON; Phone: 212-315-8701
Publication(s): *American Journal of Respiratory and Critical Care Medicine; American Journal of Respiratory Cell and Molecular Biology*
Keyword(s): Air Quality and Pollution

AMERICAN MUSEUM OF NATURAL HISTORY
Central Park West at 79th St., New York, NY 10024
Phone: 212-769-5000
Founded: 1869; Membership: 515,000
Scope: National
Description: Conducts research in anthropology, astronomy, entomology, herpetology, ichthyology, invertebrates, mammalogy, earth and planetary sciences, ornithology, and vertebrate and invertebrate paleontology using museum collections and field studies. Publishes scientific and popular material. Instructs the public, especially its over three million yearly visitors, in natural sciences, including living and extinct animals, ecological relationships, evolution of earth and life, development of human cultures, and astronomy.
Contact(s):
President: ELLEN V. FUTTER; Phone: 212-769-5997
Publication(s): *Natural History; Bulletin of the American Museum of Natural History; American Museum Novitates; Anthropological Papers of the American Museum of Natural History; Micropaleontology Press; Curator*
Keyword(s): Biodiversity, Endangered and Threatened Species, Geology, Natural History, Zoology

AMERICAN NATURE STUDY SOCIETY
c/o PEEC, R.D. Box 1010, Dingmans Ferry, PA 18328
Founded: 1908; Membership: 800
Scope: National
Description: Promotes environmental education and avocation by conducting meetings, workshops and field excursions, producing and distributing publications, and contributing to publications of other agencies; cooperates with organizations with allied interests, and, through membership in Alliance for Environmental Education, encourages members to contribute consultant services; assists in training nature lay leaders.
Contact(s):
President: STEVE MELCHER, 103 Kreag Rd., Fairport, NY 14450-363; Phone: 716-425-1059
Secretary: BETTY McKNIGHT, R.D. 3, Trumansburg, NY 14886
Treasurer: PAUL SPECTOR, Holden Arboretum, 9500 Sperry Rd., mentor, OH 44094; Phone: 216-256-1110
Editor: JANET HAWKES, 1420 Tanghannock Blvd., Ithaca, NY 14850; Phone: 607-273-6260
Editor: FLORENCE MAURO, PEEC, R.D. 2 Box 1010, Dingmans Ferry, PA 18328; Phone: 717-828-2319
Recording Secretary: FLO MAURO, PEEC, R.D. 2 Box 1010, Dingmans Ferry, PA 18328; Phone: 717-828-2319
Publication(s): *ANSS Newsletter; Nature Study, A Journal of Environmental Education and Interpretation*
Keyword(s): Environmental and Conservation Education, Natural History, Outdoor Recreation, Urban Environment, Youth Organizations

AMERICAN OCEANS CAMPAIGN
Headquarters, 725 Arizona Ave., Suite 102, Santa Monica, CA 90401

Phone: 310-576-6162; Fax: 310-576-6170; E-mail: aoc@earthlink.net; Web Site: www.americanoceans.org
Founded: 1987; Membership: 22,000
Scope: National
Description: The wellbeing and sustainability of the Earth is dependent upon healthy oceans. The mission of American Oceans Campaign is to safeguard the vitality of the oceans and our coastal waters. AOC is committed to scientific information in advocating for sound public policy. We are equally committed to developing partnerships with all entities interested in protecting the environment. AOC seeks to ensure healthy sources of food and coastal recreation as well as to protect the ocean's grandeur for future generations.
Contact(s):
President: TED DANSON
Vice President: ANNETT WOLF
Treasurer: BARBARA KOHN
Executive Director: DAVID YOUNKMAN
Board Chair: JERRY KRAMER
Publication(s): *Splash; Estuaries on the Edge: The Vital Link Between Land and Sea; Chemical Contaminant Release Into the Santa Monica Bay: A Pilot Study; Drainage to the Oceans: The Effects of Stormwater Pollution on Coastal Waters*
Keyword(s): Aquatic Habitats, Beaches, Coasts, Estuaries, Fisheries, Marine Protected Areas, Pollution Prevention, Public Health Protection, Water Pollution, Water Quality

Washington, DC Office
600 Pennsylvania Ave., SE, Suite 210, Washington, DC 20005
Phone: 202-544-3526; Fax: 202-544-5625; E-mail: aocdc@wizard.net
Scope: National

AMERICAN ORNITHOLOGISTS' UNION
National Museum of Natural History, MRC-116, Smithsonian Institution, Washington, DC 20560-0116
Phone: 202-357-2051; Fax: 202-633-8084; E-mail: aou@nmnh.si.edu
Founded: 1883; Membership: 4,000
Scope: National
Description: Aims to advance ornithological science through its publications, annual meetings, committees, and membership.
Contact(s):
President: FRANK GILL, National Audubon Society, 700 Broadway, New York, NY 10003; Phone: 212-979-3074
Vice President: MARY V. McDONALD, Lewis Science Center 129, University of Central Arkansas, Conway, AR 72035; Phone: 501-450-5924
Secretary: M. ROSS LEIN, Dept. of Biology, University of Calgary, 2500 University Dr., NW, Calgary, Alberta T2N 1N4 Canada
Treasurer: FRED SHELDON, Museum of Natural Science, Louisiana State University, Baton Rouge, LA 70803; Phone: 504-388-2855; Fax: 504-388-3075
Chairman of the Conservation Committee: STEVEN BEISSINGER, Director of Ecosystem Science, 151 Hilgard Hall #3110, University of California, Berkeley, CA 94720-3110; Phone: 313-763-5945
Editor: THOMAS MARTIN, The Auk Editorial Office, Montana Cooperative Research Unit, NS 205, University of Montana, Missoula, MT 59812
Mongraphs Editor: DAVID WIEDENFELD, Sutton Avian Research Center, P.O. Box 2007, Bartlesville, OK 74005
Newsletter Editor: CHERYL TRINE, 3889 E. Valley View, Berrien Springs, MI 49103; Phone: 508-224-6521
President-Elect: JOHN FITZPATRICK, Cornell Laboratory of Ornithology, 159 Sapsucker Rd., Ithica, NY 14850
Publication(s): *Auk; Ornithological Monographs; Ornithological Newsletter*
Keyword(s): Birds

AMERICAN PIE (PUBLIC INFORMATION ON THE ENVIRONMENT)
124 High St., P.O. Box 340, South Glastonbury, CT 06073
Phone: 1-800-320-APIE; Fax: 860-633-5090; E-mail: info@americanpie.org; Web Site: www.AmericanPIE.org
Founded: 1993; Membership: 405
Scope: National
Description: American PIE is a 501(c)(3 nonprofit group serving the nation with a 1-800 Environmental Information Line. The organization offers action programs and uniquely accessible assistance to people who have environmental questions and concerns in a wide variety of subject areas ranging from drinking water safety to wetlands preservation. Trained staff answer the information line Monday-Friday, 8:30 - 5:00 Eastern time.
Contact(s):
Director: LAWRENCE R. BACON, 36 Carriage Dr., Farmington, CT 06032; Phone: 860-674-8442
President and Secretary: TONI BENNETT EASTERSON
Vice President and Treasurer: BRAD EASTERSON; Phone: 860-633-9786
Publication(s): *American PIE*
Keyword(s): Communications, EcoAction, Environmental and Conservation Education, Environmental Justice, Pesticides

AMERICAN PLANNING ASSOCIATION
1776 Massachusetts Ave., NW, Washington, DC 20036
Phone: 202-872-0611; Fax: 202-872-0643
Founded: 1909; Membership: 29,000
Scope: National
Description: Provides informational services, education, and research in city and regional planning. Includes the American Institute of Certified Planners who set professional and ethical standards and participates in the accreditation of planning degree programs. Forty-six chapters include all of the states. Sixteen divisions address planning specialties and provide placement services and studies.
Contact(s):
President: ERIC DAMIAN KELLEY
Executive Director: FRANK SO; Phone: 202-872-0611
Editor: SYLVIA LEWIS
Immediate Past President: SAM CASELLA
Secretary and Treasurer: JAMES SHELBY
Publication(s): *PLANNING Magazine; Journal of The American Planning Association; Land Use Law and Zoning Digest; Environment and Development Newsletter*
Keyword(s): Environmental Law, Environmental Planning, Land Use Planning, Planning Management, Urban Environment

AMERICAN RECREATION COALITION
1225 New York Ave., NW, #450, Washington, DC 20005
Phone: 202-682-9530; Fax: 202-682-9529
Founded: 1979
Scope: National
Description: ARC is a national nonprofit, tax-exempt federation of more than 125 recreation-related trade associations, corporations, and enthusiasts' organizations that provides a unified voice for American recreation interests to ensure their full participation in government policy-making on such issues as energy and public lands and waters management. ARC also initiates and supports partnerships between public and private recreation providers and conducts meetings, seminars, and activities to improve public awareness of recreation opportunities.
Contact(s):
Chairman: DAVID J. HUMPHREYS, RVIA, 1896 Preston White Dr., Reston, VA 22090; Phone: 703-620-6003
President: DERRICK A. CRANDALL
Vice President of Member Services: CATHERINE A. AHERN

AMERICAN RESOURCES GROUP
374 Maple Ave. E.; Suite 310, Vienna, VA 22180
Phone: 703-255-2700
Founded: 1981
Scope: National
Description: A conservation service organization engaged in education, monitoring, research, and related activities to promote the wise use of America's forest resources. Provides forestry,

NON-GOVERNMENTAL ORGANIZATIONS - A

environmental inventory, conservation support services, and land acquisition assistance to conservation organizations, public agencies, and landowners. Programs include: Land Conservation Fund of America (land acquisition), National Forestry Network (referrals), National Historic Lookout Register, American Woodlands (demonstration forests and conservation easements), and National Forestry Association Forest Practice Certification.
Contact(s):
President: DR. KEITH A. ARGOW
Executive Secretary: NANCY GABRIEL
Vice President of Forestry: LOREN LARSON
Editor: DR. KEITH A. ARGOW
Green Tag Forestry Certification: DAVID EDSON; Phone: 202-827-4456
Northeast Representative of National Historic Lookout Register: BOB SPEAR; Phone: 973-209-7897
Northwest Representative of National Historic Lookout Register: RAY KRESEK; Phone: 509-466-9171
Publication(s): *Conservation News Digest*
Keyword(s): Forests and Forestry, Land Purchase, Public Lands, Renewable Resources

AMERICAN RIVERS (formerly American Rivers Conservation Council)
1025 Vermont Ave., NW, Suite 720, Washington, DC 20005
Phone: 202-347-7550; Fax: 202-347-9240; E-mail: amrivers@amrivers.org; Web Site: www.amrivers.org
Founded: 1973
Scope: National
Description: America's leading river conservation organization. Preserves and restores America's river systems and fosters a river stewardship ethic. River conservation goals focused on protecting wild rivers, restoring hometown rivers, and repairing big rivers. Conservation programs in wild/nationally significant rivers, hydropower reform, urban rivers, and floodplains. Three-part strategy: develop and demonstrate community-based solutions to protect and restore rivers; communicate river values and build a diverse nationwide constituency for river conservation; and advocate reform of national policies and practices to foster river health and restore river values.
Contact(s):
President: REBECCA R. WODDER
Vice-President for Conservation: ANN MILLS
Vice-President for Resource Development: PAT APPEL
Chair, Board of Directors: WHITNEY HATCH
Chair of Scientific and Technical Advisory Committee: DR. J. DAVID ALLAN
Director of Floodplain Programs: SCOTT FABER
Senior Director of Dam Programs: MARGARET BOWMAN
Director of River Restoration Finance: BETSY OTTO
Policy Director of Hydropower Programs: ANDREW FAHLUND
Communications Associate: AMY SOUERS
Conseration Outreach Coordinator: SUZY MCDOWELL
Manager, Membership Services: BEA KELLER
Mississippi River Regional Representative: JEFF STEIN
Missouri River Regional Representative: CHAD SMITH
Publication(s): *American Rivers Newsletter; America's Most Endangered Rivers (Annual Report); Mississippi Monitor; Missouri Monitor; In Harm's Way: The Costs of Floodplain Development; Voyage of Recovery: Restoring the Rivers of Lewis and Clark*
Keyword(s): Conservation, Dams, Environmental and Conservation Education, Riparian Restoration, Rivers, Water Resources, Watersheds, Wetlands, Salmon Recovery, Hydropower Relicensing

Maine Field Office
4-R Fundy Rd., Falmouth, ME 04105
Phone: 207-781-8364; Fax: 207-781-8369; E-mail: sbrooke@amrivers.org
Scope: Regional
Contact(s):
Office Director: STEVE BROOKE

Montana Field Office
215 Woodland Estates, Great Falls, MT 59404
Phone: 406-454-2076; Fax: 406-454-2530; E-mail: mablers@amrivers.org
Scope: Regional
Contact(s):
Office Director: MARK ALBERS

Nebraska Field Office
650 J St., Suite 400, Lincoln, NE 68508
Phone: 402-477-7910; Fax: 402-477-2565; E-mail: csmith@amrivers.org
Scope: Regional

Northwest Regional Office
150 Nickerson St., Suite 311, Seattle, WA 98109
Phone: 206-213-0330; Fax: 206-213-0334; E-mail: arnw@amrivers.org
Scope: Regional
Contact(s):
Office Director: KATHERINE RANSEL
Northwest Director of Hydropower Programs: ROB MASONIS

Quad Cities Field Office
326 W. Third St., Suite 714, Davenport, IA 52801
Phone: 319-884-4481; Fax: 319-884-4511; E-mail: jstein@amrivers.org
Scope: Regional

Southwest Regional Office
4120 N. 20th St., Suite G, Phoenix, AZ 85016
Phone: 602-234-3946; Fax: 602-234-2217; E-mail: arsw@amrivers.org
Scope: Regional
Contact(s):
Office Director: MARY ORTON
Senior Conservation Associate: MINDY SCHLIMGEN-WILSON

AMERICAN SOCIETY FOR ENVIRONMENTAL HISTORY
701 Vickers Ave., Durham, NC 27701
Phone: 919-682-9319
Founded: 1976; Membership: 1,000
Scope: National
Description: A nonprofit international society that seeks understanding of human ecology through the perspectives of history and the humanities.
Contact(s):
President: DONALD J. PISANI, Department of History, University of Oklahoma-Missouri, Normal, OK 73019; Phone: 405-325-6001
Vice President: JEFFREY STINE, National Museum of American History, Smithsonian Institute, Washington, DC 20560; Phone: 202-357-2058
Secretary: LISA MIGHETTO, Historical Research Associates, 119 Pine St., Suite 207, Seattle, WA 98101
Treasurer: GAIL EVANS, 427 Grant St., Silverton, OR 97381
Book Review Editor: MARK HARVEY, Department of History, North Dakota State University, Su Station, P.O. Box 5075, Fargo, ND 58105-5075
Editor: HAL K. ROTHMAN, Department of History, University of Nevada-Las Vegas, Las Vegas, NV 89154; Phone: 702-739-3349
Publication(s): *Environmental History; newsletter*
Keyword(s): Environmental and Conservation Education, Environmental Law, Natural History, Public Lands, Water Resources

AMERICAN SOCIETY OF ICHTHYOLOGISTS AND HERPETOLOGISTS
Attn: Secretary, Grice Marine Laboratory, University of Charleston SC, Charleston, SC 29412
WWW: http://www.utexas.edu/depts/asih/
Founded: 1913; Membership: 3,500
Scope: International
Description: To advance the scientific study of fishes, amphibians, and reptiles.

Contact(s):
President: ROBERT C. CASHNER, Dept. of Biological Sciences, University of New Orleans, New Orleans, LA 70148
Secretary: ROBERT KARL JOHNSON, Grice Marine Laboratory, University of Charleston SC, Charleston, SC 29412; Phone: 843-406-4017; E-mail: johnsonr@cofc.edu
Treasurer: LARRY M. PAGE, Center for Biodiversity, Illinois Natural History Survey, 607 E. Peabody, Champaign, IL 61820; Phone: 217-333-6847
Chairperson of Committee on Environmental Quality: GENE S. HELFMAN, Institute of Ecology, 711 Biological Sciences Building, University of Georgia, Athens, GA 30602; Phone: 407-393-3331; E-mail: helfman@sparc.ecology.uga.edu
Editor: MICHAEL E. DOUGLAS, Department of Zoology, Arizona State University, Tempe, AZ 85287-1501; Phone: 602-965-1752
Publication(s): *Copeia; ASIH Special Publications*
Keyword(s): Aquatic Habitats, Biology, Endangered and Threatened Species, Reptiles and Amphibians, Zoology, Fish

AMERICAN SOCIETY OF INTERNATIONAL LAW/WILDLIFE INTEREST GROUP
PMB 805, 2124 Kittredge St., Berkeley, CA 94704
Phone: 510-310-3733; Fax: 510-251-2203; E-mail: asilwildlife@pacbell.net; Web Site: www.eelink.net/~dsilwildlife
Founded: 1984
Scope: International
Description: The ASIL and WIG works to improve the effectiveness of international wildlife treaty regimes and national legislation that implements such regimes.
Contact(s):
Co-chairman: WILLIAM C. BURNS; E-mail: JIWLP@earthling.net
Publication(s): *Journal of International Wildlife Law and*
Keyword(s): Environmental Law, Environmental Legislation, International Trade and Environment, International Wildlife, International Environmental Law, Wildlife Protection

AMERICAN SOCIETY OF LANDSCAPE ARCHITECTS
636 Eye St., NW, Washington, DC 20001-3736
Phone: 202-686-ASLA
Founded: 1899; Membership: 12,500
Scope: National
Description: ASLA is a professional organization representing the landscape architecture profession in the United States. Landscape architecture, comprehensive by definition, is the art and science of analysis, planning, design, management, preservation, and rehabilitation of the land. ASLA works on issues such as land use planning, sustainable communities, transportation, public open space, and water conservation. The mission of ASLA is the advancement of the art and science of landscape architecture by leading and informing the public, by serving members, and by leading the profession in achieving quality in the natural and built environments.
Contact(s):
Director of Public Affairs: JIM TOLLIVER
Editor: ANNE POWELL
Executive Vice-President: PETER KIRSCH
Publication(s): *Landscape Architecture Magazine; Landscape Architecture News Digest (LAND)*
Keyword(s): Land Use Planning, Landscape Architecture, Open Space, Public Lands, Urban Environment

AMERICAN SOCIETY OF LIMNOLOGY AND OCEANOGRAPHY
Attn: Helen Schneider Lemay, 5400 Bosque Blvd., Suite #680, Waco, TX 76710-4446
Phone: 254-399-9635; Fax: 254-776-3767; E-mail: business@aslo.org; Web Site: www.aslo.org/
Founded: 1936; Membership: 3,700
Scope: National
Description: To promote the advancement of the various aquatic science disciplines through scientific and technical symposia, colloquia and meetings; promotion of scientific research; discussion, publication and education; and conducting special programs in response to community interest.
Contact(s):
President: THOMAS C. MALONE, Horn Point Lab., U. of MD Ctr. For Env. Sci., P.O. Box 775, Cambridge, MD 21613; Phone: 410-221-8406; Fax: 410-221-8473; E-mail: malone@hpl.umces.edu
Secretary: ASIT MAZUMDER, Dept. of Biology, University of Victoria, P.O. Box 3020, Stn. CSC, Victoria, BC VSW 3N5 Canada; Phone: 250-472-4789; Fax: 250-721-7120; E-mail: mazumder@uvic.ca
Treasurer: RUSSELL A. MOLL, MI Sea Grant Program, U. of MI, 2200 Bonisteel Blvd., Ann Arbor, MI 48109-2099; Phone: 734-763-1437; Fax: 734-647-0768; E-mail: rmoll@umich.edu
Executive Director: SUSAN C. WEILER
Editor-in-Chief: EVERETT J. FEE, 343 Lady MacDonald Crescent, Canmore, ALBERTA T1W 1H5 Canada; Phone: 403-609-2456; Fax: 403-609-2400; E-mail: efee@telusplanet.net
President-elect: WILLIAM M. LEWIS JR., Rm. 318, CIRES, Main Campus, U. of CO, Boulder, CO 80309-0334; Phone: 303-492-6378; Fax: 303-492-0928; E-mail: lewis@spot.colorado.edu
Publication(s): *Limnology and Oceanography; Bulletin*
Keyword(s): Lakes, Ocean Conservation, Rivers, Streams, Wetlands

AMERICAN SOCIETY OF MAMMALOGISTS
ATTN: President American Society of Mammalogists, Dept. Of Biology, Texas Tech Univesity, Lubbock, TX 79409
Founded: 1919; Membership: 3,600
Scope: National
Description: Encourages research and learning in all phases of mammalogy and by holding annual meetings for presentation and discussion of the results of research dealing with mammals, through issuing periodicals and other publications, and by giving advice on matters pertaining to mammals, particularly conservation issues.
Contact(s):
President: ROBERT J. BAKER, Department of Biology, Texas Tech. University, Lubbock, TX 79409; Phone: 806-742-2702
1st Vice President: ALICIA V. LINZEY, Department of Biology, Indiana University of Pennsylvania, Indiana, PA 15705; Phone: 412-357-2352
2nd Vice President: SARAH B. GEORGE, Utah Museum of Natural History, University of Utah, Salt Lake City, UT 84112; Phone: 801-581-4889
Chairman of Committee on Conservation of Land Mammals: GORDON L. KIRKLAND JR., The Vertebrate Museum, Shippensburg University, Shippensburg, PA 17257
Chairman of Committee on Legislation and Regulations: WINSTON P. SMITH, Southern Forest Experimental Station, S. Hardwoods Laboratory, P.O. Box 227, Stoneville, MS 38776
Chairman of Committee on Marine Mammals: JOHN E. HAYNING, Natural History Museum of Los Angles CA, 900 Exposition Blvd., Los Angles, CA 90007; Phone: 213-746-2999
Managing Editor: TROY L. BEST, Department of Zoology, 331 Funchess Hall, Auburn University, AL 36849; Phone: 205-844-9260
Secretary and Treasurer: H. DUANE SMITH, Department of Zoology, Brigham Young University, Provo, UT 84602; Phone: 801-378-2492
Publication(s): *Journal of Mammalogy; Mammalian Species; Special Publications of American Society of Mammalogists*
Keyword(s): Endangered and Threatened Species, International Conservation, Mammals, Marine Mammals, Nongame Wildlife

AMERICAN SPORTFISHING ASSOCIATION
1033 North Fairfax St., Suite 200, Alexandria, VA 22314
Phone: 703-519-9691; Fax: 703-519-1872; E-mail: info@asafishing.org; Web Site: www.asafishing.org
Founded: 1994; Membership: 500
Scope: National
Description: ASA is a nonprofit industry association working to ensure healthy and sustainable fisheries resources and increase

NON-GOVERNMENTAL ORGANIZATIONS - A

sportfishing participation through education, conservation, promotion, and marketing.
Contact(s):
Chairman: MARK MASTERSON
President and CEO: MIKE HAYDEN
Publication(s): *American Sportfishing*

AMERICAN WATER RESOURCES ASSOCIATION
4 West Federal St., PO Box 1626, Middleburg, VA 20118-1626
Phone: 540-687-8390; Fax: 540-687-8395; E-mail: awrahq@aol.com; Web Site: www.awra.org
Founded: 1964; Membership: 3,500
Scope: National
Description: A nonprofit scientific organization which advances water resources research, planning, development, and management; establishes a common meeting ground for engineers and physical, biological, and social scientists concerned with water resources; disseminates information in the field of water resources policy, science, and technology through the publication of a scientific journal newsletter and symposium proceedings. Two specialty conferences/symposia and one Annual Conference on Water Resources are held each year.
Contact(s):
President: JANET L. BOWERS
Secretary and Treasurer: ISABEL GONZALEZ-JETTINGHOFF
Editor: CHRISTOPHER LANT
Editor: N. EARL SPANGENBERG
Executive Vice President: KENNETH D. REID
President Elect: JOHN S. GROUNDS III
Publication(s): *Journal of the American Water Resources Assiciation; Symposium Proceedings; Water Resources IMPACT*
Keyword(s): Environmental and Conservation Education, Renewable Resources, Rivers, Water Resources, Wetlands

AMERICAN WATER WORKS ASSOCIATION (AWWA)
6666 W. Quincy Ave., Denver, CO 80235
Phone: 303-794-7711; Fax: 303-795-1440; Web Sites: www.waterwiser.org and www.awwa.org
Founded: 1881; Membership: 56,000
Scope: National
Description: The AWWA advances the science, technology, consumer awareness management, government policies, and water use efficiencies related to public drinking water.
Contact(s):
Executive Director: JACK W. HOFFBUHR
Deputy Executive Director: ROBERT C. RENNER
Deputy Executive Director of Government Affairs Division: JOHN H. SULLIVAN, 1401 New York Ave. NW, Suite 640, Washington, DC 20005; Phone: 202-628-8303
Publication(s): *Main Stream; AWWA Journal; Opflow; WaterWiser - The Water Efficiency Clearinghouse (an on-line Internet Resource (http://www.waterwiser.org)*
Keyword(s): Planning Management, Pollution Prevention, Public Health Protection, Water Quality, Water Resources

AMERICAN WHITEWATER
1430 Fenwick Ln., Silver Spring, MD 20910
Phone: 301-589-9453; Fax: 301-589-6121; Web Site: www.awa.org
Founded: 1957; Membership: 8,000
Scope: National
Description: American Whitewater's mission is to conserve and restore America's whitewater resources and enhance opportunities to enjoy them safely. This is achieved by means of conservation, river access, education, safety and event programs.
Contact(s):
President: RIC ALESCH; Phone: 303-987-6724; E-mail: ralesch@world.att.net
Vice-President: RISA CALLAWAY; Phone: 864-306-9920; E-mail: risashi@mindspring.com
Executive Director: RICHARD BOWERS; E-mail: RichB@amwhitewater.org
Executive Assistant: SAM MCLAMB; E-mail: Sam@amwhitewater.org
Publication(s): *American Whitewater Journal*
Keyword(s): Rivers

AMERICAN WILDLANDS
6551 S. Revere Parkway, Suite 160, Englewood, CO 80111
Phone: 303-649-1211; Fax: 303-649-1221
Founded: 1977; Membership: 2,800
Scope: Regional
Description: A nonprofit conservation organization dedicated to ecologically sustainable use and protection of America's wildland resources in the Rocky Mountains West, including wilderness, wetlands, rangelands, free-flowing rivers, wildlife and fisheries, and forests.
Contact(s):
President: SALLY A. RANNEY
Executive Director: JEFF LARMER
Executive Editor: CLIFTON MERRITT
Secretary and Treasurer: CLIFTON MORRITT
Vice Chairman: WILLIAM CUNNINGHAM
Publication(s): *On The Wild Side; Forest Activist Green Papers; Policy Reports*
Keyword(s): Biodiversity, Forests and Forestry, Public Lands, Wildlands, Wildlife and Wildlife Habitat

AMERICAN WILDLIFE RESEARCH FOUNDATION, INC.
P.O. Box 902, Hartsdale, NY 10530-0902
Phone: 914-761-2653; Fax: 914-761-2653
Founded: 1911; Membership: 51
Scope: International
Description: AWRF uses the interest income of its funds to support research of wildlife and its habitats. Its mission is to enhance fish and wildlife resources and their habitats through research, education and conservation, ensuring that present and future generations can continue to use and enjoy them.
Contact(s):
President: PETER ROEMER; Phone: 914-677-8393; Fax: 914-677-9013
Vice President: STUART L. FREE; Phone: 518-861-5357; Fax: 518-452-6392
Secretary: WILLIAM M. SCHWERD; Phone: 518-885-8995; Fax: 518-885-9078
Treasurer: ROGER H. COLE; Phone: 914-761-2653; Fax: 518-761-2653
Contact for Moon Library at Syracuse University, College of ESF: DR. MAURICE M. ALEXANDER; Phone: 315-492-0032
Publication(s): *Newsletter*
Keyword(s): Grants, Research

AMERICAN ZOO AND AQUARIUM ASSOCIATION (AZA)
8403 Colesville Rd, Suite 710, Silver Spring, MD 20910
Phone: 301-562-0777; Fax: 301-562-0888
Founded: 1924; Membership: 6,200
Scope: National
Description: Dedicated to the improvement of modern, professionally-managed zoological parks and aquariums through conservation, public education, scientific research, and membership services. Administers scientifically-managed captive breeding and field conservation programs for 134 threatened and endangered species through its Species Survival Plan Program.
Contact(s):
President: RICHARD LATTIS
Deputy Director and Director of Government Affairs: KRISTIN VEHRS
Director of Conservation and Science: DR. MICHAEL HUTCHINS
Director of Conservation Education: DR. BRUCE CARR
Director of Development and Marketing: ROBERT RAMIN
Director of Finance and Administration: LAURA BENSON
Director of Public Affairs: JANE BALLENTINE
Executive Director: SYDNEY J. BUTLER

Publication(s): COMMUNIQUE; AZ A Membership Directory; Annual Report on Conservation and Science; Annual and Regional Conference Proceedings
Keyword(s): Aquariums, Endangered and Threatened Species, International Conservation, Wildlife Management, Zoological Parks

AMERICANS FOR THE ENVIRONMENT
1400 16th St., NW, Box 24, Washington, DC 20036-2266
Phone: 202-797-6665; Fax: 202-797-6563; E-mail: afedc@AforE.org; Web Site: www.AforE.org
Founded: 1982
Scope: National
Description: Americans for the Environment is a nonpartisan educational organization.
Contact(s):
Board of Directors Chair: STELLA KOCH
Board of Directors Member: JERALD WHITE
Board of Directors Member: JOHN ECHEVERRIA
Board of Directors Member: BETTY SPENCE
Board of Directors Member: CHUCK PAQUETTE
Board of Directors Member: JOY OAKES
Board of Directors Member: ROY HOAGLAND
Board of Directors Member: JONI BOSH
Board of Directors Member: MONTE BELOTE
Board of Directors Member: JOHANNAH BARRY
Board of Directors President: ROY MORGAN
Board of Directors Secretary: TENSIE WHELAN
Board of Directors Treasurer: ALICE WALKER
Board of Directors Vice-Chair: CONNIE MAHER
Publication(s): *Lobbying Strategies; Opposition to Conservation Ballot Measures; Permissible Political Activities; Political Agenda of the "Wise Use" Movement, The; Taking the Initiative*
Keyword(s): Environment

ANACOSTIA WATERSHED SOCIETY
The George Washington House, 4302 Baltimore Ave., Bladensburg, MD 20710
Phone: 301-699-6204; Fax: 301-699-3317; E-mail: robert@anacostiaws.org; Web Site: www.anacostiaws.org
Founded: 1989; Membership: 1000
Scope: Regional
Description: The Anacostia Watershed Society provides opportunities for volunteers to take part in local environmental restoration projects; and provides advocacy for environmental equity issues in the Anacostia-Washington region.
Contact(s):
President: ROBERT E. BOONE
Secretary: JOHN PERHONIS
Treasurer: DAVID TIBBETTS
Executive Director: JAMES CONNOLLY
Publication(s): *Voice of the River*
Keyword(s): Environmental Protection, Pollution Prevention, Rivers, Water Pollution, Watersheds

ANCIENT FOREST INTERNATIONAL
P.O. Box 1850, Redway, CA 95560
Phone: 707-923-3015; Fax: 707-923-3015
Founded: 1989
Scope: National
Description: An alliance of conservationists dedicated to helping preserve, study, and increase awareness of the Earth's few still-intact forest ecosystems, while providing habitat continuity through the creation of corridors. Old-growth forests of southern Chile, highland Mexico, Ecuador, and the north Pacific coast are current projects. Work is also underway to document the distribution of ancient rainforests worldwide and to promote their preservation.
Contact(s):
President: RICK KLEIN
Secretary: SUZELLE HUNT
Treasurer: ROSE MADRONE
Publication(s): *News of Old Growth; Chile's Native Forest: An Overview*
Keyword(s): Biodiversity, Endangered and Threatened Species, Forests and Forestry, International Conservation, Land Purchase

ANGLERS FOR CLEAN WATER
P.O. Box 17900, Montgomery, AL 36141
Phone: 205-272-9530
Founded: 1970
Scope: National
Description: A nonprofit organization dedicated to educating the American public on the conditions of pollution nationwide and to the danger of the failure to halt the pollution of the streams, rivers, and lakes of the United States and to promote, educate, and inform the American public of the need for conservation of our water and fisheries resources.
Contact(s):
President: HELEN SEVIER
Communications: ANN LEWIS
Conservation Director: BRUCE SHUPP
Editor: MATT VINCENT
Finance: KARL DABBS
Publication(s): *Living Waters*
Keyword(s): Aquatic Habitats, Communications, Environmental and Conservation Education, Fisheries, Water Resources

ANIMAL PROTECTION INSTITUTE
P.O. Box 22505, 2831 Fruitridge Rd., Sacramento, CA 95822
Phone: 916-731-5521; Fax: 916-731-4467; E-mail: onlineapi@aol.com; Web Site: www.api4animals.org
Founded: 1968; Membership: 80,000
Scope: National
Description: The Animal Protection Institute is a national animal advocacy nonprofit organization dedicated to protecting animals against abuse through enforcement and legislative actions, investigations, advocacy campaigns, crisis intervention, public awareness, and education. Specific areas of concern are wildlife protection and habitat conservation, companion animals, marine mammals, domestic and farm animals, animals used in research, and humane education.
Contact(s):
Executive Director: ALAN BERGER
Chairman of the Board: DUF FISCHER
Creative Services: BARBARA TUGAEFF
Editor: GIL LAMONT
Program Director: DENA JONES
Publication(s): *Animal Issues*
Keyword(s): Endangered and Threatened Species, Hunting, Mammals, Marine Mammals, Nongame Wildlife, Predators, Public Lands, Trapping, Wildlife and Wildlife Habitat

ANIMAL WELFARE INSTITUTE
P.O. Box 3650, Washington, DC 20007
Phone: 202-337-2332; Fax: 202-338-9478; Web Site: www.animalwelfare.com
Founded: 1951; Membership: 15,000
Scope: National
Description: Active in improvement of conditions for laboratory animals and reducing the numbers used in research, protection of endangered species, Save the Whales campaign, ending use of steel jaw traps, stopping imports of wild birds for the pet trade, and humane education. Albert Schweitzer award is presented for outstanding contributions to animal welfare.
Contact(s):
President: CHRISTINE STEVENS; Phone: 202-337-2332
Vice President: CYNTHIA WILSON
Secretary: FREEBORN JEWETT
Treasurer: FRED HUTCHISON
Executive Director: CATHY LISS; Phone: 202-337-2332
Editor: CHRISTINE STEVENS
Executive Secretary: LYNNE HUTCHISON
Farm Animal Consultant: DIANE HALVERSON
International Coordinator: BEN WHITE
Laboratory Animal Consultant: VIKTOR REINHARDT D.M.V., PH.D.
Mail Order Secretary: NELL NAUGHTON

NON-GOVERNMENTAL ORGANIZATIONS - A

Publications Coordinator: KELLY HANSEN; Phone: 202-337-2332
Research Associate: ADAM ROBERTS; Phone: 202-337-2332
Publication(s): *Animal Welfare Institute Quarterly; Animals and Their Legal Rights; Endangered Species Handbook; Alternative Traps*
Keyword(s): Endangered and Threatened Species, International Conservation, Mammals, Marine Mammals, Trapping

ANTARCTICA PROJECT
P.O. Box 76920, Washington, DC 20013
Phone: 202-234-2480; Fax: 202-234-2482; E-mail: antarctica@igc.org
Founded: 1982
Scope: National
Description: Works to preserve Antarctica by monitoring all activities to ensure minimal environmental impact and consulting with key users of Antarctica, including scientists, tourists, governments. Conducts legal and policy research and analysis; produces educational materials; focuses international scientific community on globally-significant research. Secretariat to Antarctic and Southern Ocean Coalition (ASOC), composed of 240 conservation groups in 50 nations.
Contact(s):
Director: BETH CLARK
Counsel: JIM BARNES
Publication(s): *ECO Newspaper (ASOC); Antarctica Project (Quarterly Newsletter); publications and educational resources list on request*
Keyword(s): Biodiversity, Conservation of Protected Areas, International Conservation, Wilderness

APPALACHIAN MOUNTAIN CLUB
5 Joy St., Boston, MA 02108
Phone: 617-523-0636; Fax: 617-523-0722
Founded: 1876; Membership: 83,800
Scope: Regional
Description: The AMC pursues a far-reaching conservation agenda while encouraging responsible recreation, based on the philosophy that successful, long-term conservation depends on firsthand experience and enjoyment of the natural environment. Areas of focus: Northern Forest, Sterling Forest, White Mountain N.F., NY and NJ Highlands, Berkshire and Taconics Region, Delaware Water Gap National Recreation Area, and Acadia National Park. Expertise: Conservation policy, advocacy; land, trail, river and greenway stewardship; environmental research, education, guidebook and outdoor leadership publishing.
Contact(s):
Deputy Director: WALTER GRAFF; Phone: 603-466-2721
President: JENNIFER HUNTINGTON
Executive Director: ANDREW J. FALENDER
Conservation Director: TOM STEINBACH; Phone: 617-523-0655/ext.358
Director of Conservation Programs: KEVIN KNOBLOCH; Phone: 617-523-0655/ext.365
Research Director: DR. KENNETH KIMBALL; Phone: 603-466-2721
Publication(s): *Appalachia Journal; AMC Outdoors; AMC guidebooks and maps*
Keyword(s): Air Quality and Pollution, Environmental and Conservation Education, Outdoor Recreation, Public Lands, Rivers, Trail

APPALACHIAN TRAIL CONFERENCE
P.O. Box 807, Harpers Ferry, WV 25425-0807
Phone: 304-535-6331; Fax: 304-535-2667
Founded: 1925; Membership: 29,000
Scope: National
Description: Coordinates preservation and management of the Appalachian Trail, a 2,160 mile footpath and protective corridor generally following the crest of the Appalachian Mountains from Maine to Georgia. Prepares and distributes trail guidebooks and other user information.
Contact(s):
Chair: DAVID B. FIELD, 191 Emerson Mill Rd., Hampden, ME 04444; Phone: 207-862-3674
Secretary: MARIANNE J. SKEEN, 553 N. Superior Ave., Decatur, GA 30033; Phone: 404-633-1486
Treasurer: KENNARD HONICK, 1800 Second St., Suite 810, Sarasota, FL 34236; Phone: 941-366-3944
Executive Director: DAVID N. STARTZELL
Editor and Director of Public Affairs: BRIAN B. KING
Vice Chair: BRIAN T. FITZGERALD, 55 Ward Hill Rd., South Duxbury, VT 05660; Phone: 802-496-7094
Vice Chair: JAMES HUTCHINGS, 551 Windridge Parkway, Hardy, VA 24101; Phone: 540-427-4536
Vice Chair: THYRA C. SPERRY, 740 Oak Hill Dr., Boiling Springs, PA 17007-9624; Phone: 717-258-5261
Publication(s): *Appalachian Trailway News; Register, The; Trail Lands; Inside ATC*
Keyword(s): Endangered and Threatened Species, Environmental and Conservation Education, Historic Preservation, Land Purchase, Outdoor Recreation, Trail

ARCHAEOLOGICAL CONSERVANCY
5301 Central Ave., NE, Suite 1218, Albuquerque, NM 87108
Phone: 505-266-1540
Founded: 1979
Scope: National
Description: National nonprofit membership organization dedicated to the permanent preservation of the most significant archaeological sites in the United States, usually through acquisition. Cooperates with government, universities, museums, and private conservation organizations to acquire lands for permanent archaeological preserves.
Contact(s):
President: MARK MICHEL
Chairman of the Board: EARL GADBERY
Eastern Regional Director: ROB CRISELL, 1307 S. Glebe Rd., Arlington, VA 22204; Phone: 703-979-4410
Midwest Regional Office Director: PAUL GARDNER, 74 E. Jeffrey Pl., Columbus, OH 43214; Phone: 614-267-1100
Southeastern Regional Office Director: ALAN GRUBER, 5997 Cedar Crest Rd., Acworth, GA 30101; Phone: 770-975-4344
Southwest Regional Office Director: JAMES B. WALKER, 5301 Central Ave. NE, Suite 1218, Albuquerque, NM 87108; Phone: 505-266-1540
Western Regional Office Director: LYNN DUNBAR, 1217 23rd St., Sacramento, CA 95816-4917; Phone: 916-448-1892
Publication(s): *American Archaeology*
Keyword(s): Cultural Preservation, Historic Preservation, Land Purchase

ARCHBOLD BIOLOGICAL STATION
P.O. Box 2057, Lake Placid, FL 33862-2057
Phone: 941-465-2571; Fax: 941-699-1297; E-mail: archbold@archbold-station.org
Founded: 1941
Scope: Statewide
Description: The Station is an independent, nonprofit facility devoted to long-term ecological research and conservation. Primary focus is on organisms, including many endangered species, and environments of the unique Lake Wales Ridge and adjacent Florida.
Contact(s):
Executive Director: DR. HILARY SWAIN
Assistant Director for Agro-Ecology: DR. PATRICK BOLEN
Education Coordinator: NANCY DEYRUP
Internship Coordinator: DIANNE CUMMINGS
Librarian: FRED LOHRER
Publication(s): *Biennial Report*
Keyword(s): Ecology, Endangered and Threatened Species, Environmental and Conservation Education, Environmental Preservation, Research

ARCHERY MANUFACTURERS AND MERCHANTS ORGANIZATION (AMO)
4131 NW 28th Lane #7, Gainesville, FL 32606
Phone: 352-377-8262; Fax: 352-375-3961; Web Site: www.amo-archery.org
Founded: 1953; Membership: 500
Scope: National
Contact(s):
Director of Member Services: PAT WISEMAN SNIDER
Marketing Director: DOUG ENGH
President and CEO: DICK LATTIMER
Publication(s): *AMO Newsletter*
Keyword(s): Hunting, Outdoor Recreation, Wildlife and Wildlife Habitat, Wildlife Management, Youth Organizations

ARCTIC INSTITUTE OF NORTH AMERICA
University Library Tower, 2500 University Dr., NW, Calgary, Alberta T2N 1N4 Canada
Phone: 403-220-7515
Founded: 1945; Membership: 2,200
Scope: National
Description: A nonprofit research organization dedicated to acquisition, interpretation, and dissemination of knowledge of the polar regions. Sponsors research by its thirty research associates.
Contact(s):
Executive Director: MICHAEL ROBINSON
Business Manager: ANNE NAIL
Chair of the Canadian Board of Directors: ROSES MARIE KARNES
Chairman of the AINA USA Board of Governors: CARL BENSON
Editor: KAREN McCULLOUGH
Publication(s): *Arctic Journal*
Keyword(s): Arctic

ARIZONA ASSOCIATION OF CONSERVATION DISTRICTS
Attn: Executive Director, 3003 N. Central Ave., Suite 800, Phoenix, AZ 85012
Scope: Statewide
Contact(s):
Executive Director: MARCAREO HERRERA; Phone: 602-280-8803; Fax: 602-280-8779
President and Board Member: SHARON REID, Rt. 1 Box 49-C, St. David, AZ 85630; Phone: 520-586-3347
1st Vice President: FRANK MARTINEZ, Box 1152, Parker, AZ 85344; Phone: 520-669-8459
Secretary/Treasurer: JOHNNY LAVIN, HC 1 Box 760, Benson, AZ 83602; Phone: 520-212-3211; Fax: 520-384-2735
Vice President: ROBERT AHKEAH, P.O. Box 550, Shiprock, NM 87420; Phone: 505-368-5430
Keyword(s): Conservation Districts

ARIZONA B.A.S.S. CHAPTER FEDERATION
Attn: President, 34130 North 10th St., Phoenix, AZ 85027
Phone: 602-434-9199
Scope: Statewide
Description: An organization of Bassmaster chapters, affiliated with the Bass Anglers Sportsman Society, organized to fight pollution, assist state and national conservation agencies in their efforts, and teach the young people of our country good conservation practices. Dedicated to the realistic conservation of our water resources.
Contact(s):
President: MIKE SEGELKE
Conservation Director: DAVE COHEN, 839 S. Westwood #266, Mesa, AZ 85210; Phone: 602-962-9009

ARIZONA WILDLIFE FEDERATION
644 N. Country Club Dr., Suite E, Mesa, AZ 85201-4991
Phone: 480-644-0077; Fax: 480-644-0078; E-mail: awf@primenet.com; Web Site: www.primenet.com/~awf
Founded: 1923
Scope: Statewide

Description: A representative statewide organization, affiliated with the National Wildlife Federation, dedicated to the protection and enhancement of wildlife and its habitat through public education and government interaction.
Contact(s):
President: DAVID MORRIS
Representative: JOHN CALKINS
Editor: STEVE GALIZIOLLI
Alternative Representative: ACE PETERSON
Publication(s): *Arizona Wildlife News*

ARKANSAS ASSOCIATION OF CONSERVATION DISTRICTS
Attn: Exec. Vice President, 101 E. Capitol, Ste. 350, Little Rock, AR 72201
Scope: Statewide
Contact(s):
President: DON R. MITCHELL, Box 8004 State Line Plaza, Texarkana, AR 75502; Phone: 870-773-1061; Fax: 870-774-0409
1st Vice President: PAUL MAYFIELD, 783 Rio Vista Rd., Bald Knob, AR 72010; Phone: 501-724-5932; E-mail: mayfield@IPA.Net
2nd Vice President: BILL RAINWATER, P.O. Box 2245, Jonesboro, AR 72401; Phone: 870-935-1624
Executive Vice President: JOHNNY BELEW; Phone: 501-682-2915; Fax: 501-682-3991
Secretary/Treasurer: ROY MAHLER, Rt. 2 Box 130, Elkins, AR 72727; Phone: 501-643-3385
Keyword(s): Conservation Districts

ARKANSAS B.A.S.S. CHAPTER FEDERATION
Attn: President, Rt. 1 Box 225L, Branch, AR 72928
Phone: 501-635-5951
Scope: Statewide
Description: An organization of Bassmaster chapters, affiliated with the Bass Anglers Sportsman Society, organized to fight pollution, assist state and national conservation agencies in their efforts, and teach the young people of our country good conservation practices. Dedicated to the realistic conservation of our water resources.
Contact(s):
President: GENE CARSON
Conservation Director: BOB WEST, 153 SR 333, Russellville, AR 72801; Phone: 501-967-5486

ARKANSAS ENVIRONMENTAL EDUCATION ASSOCIATION
P.O. Box 210, Hackett, AR 72937
Phone: 501-638-7151; Fax: 501-638-7123; E-mail: arkenved@aol.com
Founded: 1995; Membership: 100
Scope: Statewide
Description: The Association promotes environmental education and supports the work of environmental educators in Arkansas.
Contact(s):
President: ROBERT McAFEE
Secretary: CONSTANCE GWINN; Phone: 501-756-5583, ext. 232; E-mail: cqwinn@crg.org
Treasurer and President Elect: SUZANNE SMITH HIRREL; Phone: 501-671-2288; Fax: 501-671-2185; E-mail: shirrel@vavaex.edu
Publication(s): *Natural State, The; Membership Directory, EE Resource Directory*
Keyword(s): Environmental and Conservation Education, Education

ARKANSAS WILDLIFE FEDERATION
7509 Cantrell Rd., #104, Little Rock, AR 72207
Phone: 501-663-7255; Fax: 501-664-7397
Founded: 1936
Scope: Statewide
Description: A representative statewide organization, affiliated with the National Wildlife Federation, dedicated to the protection and enhancement of wildlife and its habitat through public education and government interaction.
Contact(s):
President: JIMMY REYNOLDS
Executive Director: TERRY HORTON
Representative: JIM WOOD

NON-GOVERNMENTAL ORGANIZATIONS - A

Editor: BOB APPLE
Alternative Representative: STEVE DUZAN
Publication(s): *Arkansas Out of Doors*

ARLINGTON OUTDOOR EDUCATION ASSOCIATION, INC.
P.O. Box 5646, Arlington, VA 22205
Phone: 540-347-2258
Founded: 1967; Membership: 1,200
Scope: Local Region
Description: AOEA's Outdoor Lab annually provides approximately 9,000 northern Virginia school children, in grades kindergarten through twelve, with enriching environmental and educational opportunities in a natural setting. In addition to daily classes during the school year, the lab conducts camps during the summer and astronomical observatory sessions throughout the year.
Contact(s):
President: CATHERINE REISING-JONES
Vice President: KATHLEEN DRENNAN
Secretary: AIMEE HILL
Treasurer: SCOTT SMITH
Editor: KATHLEEN DRENNAN; Phone: 703-525-6284
Lab Director: NEIL HEINEKAMP
Keyword(s): Aquatic Habitats, Environmental and Conservation Education, Environmental Protection, Fisheries, Land Preservation

ASSOCIATION FOR CONSERVATION INFORMATION, INC.
Attn: President, New Hampshire Fish and Game Department, 2 Hazen Dr., Concord, NH 33301
Founded: 1938
Scope: National
Description: Facilitates free exchange of ideas, materials, techniques, experiences, and procedures bearing on conservation information and education and establishes media furthering such exchange; promotes public understanding of basic conservation principles; informs states, territories, and provinces that do not have conservation education programs of their desirability and assists them in setting up conservation education, information and public relations programs.
Contact(s):
President: JUDY STOKES, New Hampshire Fish and Game Department, 2 Hazen Dr., Concord, NH 3301; Phone: 603-271-3211
Vice President: DAVID WARREN, Oklahoma Dept. of Wildlife Conservation, 1801 N. Lincoln, Oklahoma City, OK 73105; Phone: 405-521-3855
Secretary: JOAN GUILFOYLE, Region 3, US Fish & Wildlife Service, 1 Federal Dr., Federal Bldg., Fort Snelling, MN 55111; Phone: 612-725-3519
Treasurer: DAVID K. RICE, Nevada Department of Conservation and Natural Resources, P.O. Box 10678, Reno, NE 89520; Phone: 702-688-1550
Balance Wheel Editor: GARY THOMAS, Illinois Department of Conservation, 524 S. Second St., Springfield, IL 62701-1787; Phone: 217-782-7454
Immediate Past President: CHRIS CHAFFIN, Idaho Department of Fish and Game, P.O. Box 25, Boise, ID 83707; Phone: 208-334-3746
Publication(s): *Balance Wheel, The*
Keyword(s): Environmental and Conservation Education

ASSOCIATION FOR FISH AND WILDLIFE ENFORCEMENT TRAINING
Attn: President Alberta Fish and Wildlife, Main Fl. N. Tower, Petroleum Plaza 9945 - 108 St., Edmonton, Alberta T5K 2G6 Canada
Scope: National
Description: The goal of the association is to promote and enhance professional standards of training in fish and wildlife enforcement. The objectives are: to promote officer safety and a safer working environment; exchange training information; promote law enforcement research and development; to encourage cost-effective training programs; to act as a repository for catalogue agency training personnel and materials; and to host annual workshop to facilitate the exchange of training information. Open to Canadian and United States agencies.
Contact(s):
President: CHUCK MOORE, Nova Scotia Dept. of Natural Resources, P.O. Box 698, Halifax, Nova Scotia B3J 2T9; Phone: 902-424-8925; E-mail: cmoore@gov.ns.ca
Vice President: GARY BERLIN, Colorado Division of Wildlife, 6060 Broadway, Denver, CO 80216; Phone: 303-291-7211; E-mail: gary.berlin@state.co.us
Secretary: DAVE WINDSOR, Indiana Dept. of Natural Resources, 402 W. Washington St., Indianapolis, IN 46204; Phone: 317-232-4014; E-mail: dwinsor@dnr.state.in.us
Treasurer: JACK HARRIGAN, Manitoba Natural Resources, Legislative Bldg., Winnipeg, Manitoba R3C 0V8; Phone: 204-945-6005; E-mail: jharrigan@nr.gov.mb.ca
Keyword(s): Law Enforcement, Resource Law Enforcement, Wildlife Management

ASSOCIATION FOR THE PROTECTION OF THE ADIRONDACKS, THE
P.O. Box 951, Schenectady, NY 12301
Phone: 518-377-1452; Fax: 518-377-1452
Founded: 1901; Membership: 1,500
Scope: Statewide
Description: To protect the natural character of the state forest preserve lands in the Adirondacks and Catskills as water-holding and regulating forests which serve as a home for wildlife and as wilderness recreation areas, and to protect and enhance the natural resources of the Adirondack Park.
Contact(s):
President: THOMAS L. COBB, Box 454, Bear Mountain State Park, Bear Mountain, NY 10911
Vice President: HARVEY M. KELSEY JR.
Vice President: CLAIRE L BARNETT
Vice President: PAUL M. BRAY
Secretary: MARYDE KING
Treasurer: DAVID NEWHOUSE
Executive Director: DAVID H. GIBSON
Keyword(s): Biodiversity, Lakes, Land Use Planning, Public Lands, Sustainable Development

ASSOCIATION OF AMERICAN GEOGRAPHERS
1710 16th St., NW, Washington, DC 20009-3198
Phone: 202-234-1450; E-mail: gaia@aag.org; Web Site: www.aag.org
Founded: 1904; Membership: 7,000
Scope: National
Description: To further professional investigations in geography and encourage the application of geographic findings in education, government, and business.
Contact(s):
President: WILLIAM L. GRAF, Dept. of Geography, AZ State University, Box 870104, Tempe, AZ 85286; Phone: 602-965-7533; E-mail: graf@asu.edu
Vice President: REGINALD G. GOLLEDGE, Dept. of Geography, University of CA, Santa Barbara, CA 93106-4060; Phone: 805-893-2731
Secretary: RICHARD A. MARSTON, Geography & Recreation Dept., University of WY, Laramie, WY 82071-3371; Phone: 307-766-3311; E-mail: marston@uwyo.edu
Treasurer: LIZBETH A. PYLE, Institutional Analysis & Planning, P.O. Box 6710, WV University, Morgantown, WV 26506-6710; Phone: 304-293-7664/4906; E-mail: lpyle@wvu.edu
Executive Director: RONALD F. ABLER
Editor of AAG Journal: JOHN PAUL JONES III, University of KY, Dept. of Geography, Lexington, KY 40506-0027; Phone: 606-257-6950
Editor of Newsletter: LINDA BRADSHAW
Past President: PATRICIA GOBER, Dept. of Geography, AZ State University, Box 870104, Tempe, AZ 85287-0104; Phone: 602-965-7533; E-mail: gober@asu.edu
Publication(s): *The Annals; Professional Geographer, The; AAG Newsletter*

Keyword(s): Agriculture, Geography, Land Use Planning, Urban Environment, Water Resources

ASSOCIATION OF AVIAN VETERINARIANS
Central Office, P.O. Box 811720, Boca Raton, FL 33481
Phone: 561-393-8901; Fax: 561-393-8902
Founded: 1980; Membership: 3,600
Scope: International
Description: The Association of Avian Veterinarians is a nonprofit international organization dedicated to advancing and promoting avian medicine and stewardship.
Contact(s):
President: GLENN H. OLSEN, Patuxent Environmental Science Center, 11510 American Holly Dr., Laurel, MD 20708
Coordinator of Publications: CATHY LYONS, Library AAV Publications Office, P.O. Box 618372, Orlando, FL 32861; Phone: 407-521-6401
Immediate Past President: DR. SUSAN E. OROSZ, Avian University of Tennesee, Department Comp. Animal Medicine, Knoxville, TN 37923
President-Elect: JERRY LABONDE, Avian and Exotic Animal Hospital, 6900 S. Holly Cir., Englewood, CO 80112
Publication(s): *Journal of the Association of Avian Veterinarians: Advancing and Promoting Avian Medicine and Stewardship; 1980-1996 Proceedings of the Annual Conference*
Keyword(s): Birds, Endangered and Threatened Species, Environmental and Conservation Education, International Conservation, Wildlife Rehabilitation

ASSOCIATION OF CONSERVATION ENGINEERS
Attn: President, IL Dept. of Nuclear Safety, 1035 Outer Park Dr., Springfield, IL 62704
Founded: 1961; Membership: 200
Scope: National
Description: To encourage and broaden the educational, social, and economic interests of conservation engineering practices; to promote recognition of the importance of sound engineering practices in fish, wildlife, and recreation development; to enable each member to take advantage of the experience of other states.
Contact(s):
President: GARY McCANDLESS, IL Dept. of Nuclear Safety, 1035 Outer Park Dr., Springfield, IL 62704; Phone: 217-782-1329; Fax: 217-524-6417
Secretary and Treasurer: JIM PRICE, AR Game & Fish Commission, #2 Natural Resources Dr., Little Rock, AR 72205; Phone: 501-219-4306; Fax: 501-219-4315
Publication(s): *A.C.E. Newsletter; handbook; conference proceedings; informational brochure*
Keyword(s): Engineering, Environmental and Conservation Education, Outdoor Recreation, Water Resources, Wildlife and Wildlife Habitat

ASSOCIATION OF CONSULTING FORESTERS OF AMERICA
732 North Washington St., Suite 4-A, Alexandria, VA 22314-1921
Phone: 703-548-0990; Fax: 703-548-6395; E-mail: DIRECTOR@acf-foresters.com; Web Site: www.acf-foresters.com
Founded: 1948; Membership: 550
Scope: National
Description: The Association of Consulting Foresters of America, Inc. represents interests of private consulting foresters. Administers a continuing education program, enforces a code of ethics, and promotes use of private consulting foresters.
Contact(s):
President: WILLIAM C. HUMPHRIES JR.
Administrative Director: LYNN C. WILSON
Gulf Director: J. MARVIN TAYLOR
Northern Director: WILLIAM M. STEIGERWALDT
Past President: RONALD E. STUNTZNER
President-Elect: DAVID C. PARKER
Southern Director: GERALD W. FRAZIER
Western Director: GEORGE D. GENTRY
Publication(s): *Consultant, The; Membership Specialization Directory*
Keyword(s): Environmental and Conservation Education, Forests and Forestry, Renewable Resources, Wildlife and Wildlife Habitat, Wildlife Management, Professional Organization

ASSOCIATION OF FIELD ORNITHOLOGISTS
Attn: President, Inst. For Field Ornithology, Univ. of ME at Machias, 9 O'Brien Ave., Machias, ME 04654
Founded: 1922
Scope: National
Description: To promote the study of birds in their natural habitats throughout the new world and dissemination of the information obtained from this study.
Contact(s):
President: CHARLES D. DUNCAN, Inst. For Field Ornithology, Univ. of ME at Machias, Machias, ME 04654; Phone: 207-255-1358; E-mail: cduncan@acad.umm.maine.edu
Vice President: JEROME A. JACKSON, Dept. of Biology, MS State Univ., P.O. Box GY, Mississippi State, MS 39762; Phone: 601-325-3210; E-mail: picus@ra.msstate.edu
Secretary: RUSS McCLAIN, Department of Biology, University of Memphis Memphis, Memphis, TN 38152; Phone: 901-678-2581; E-mail: wrmcclain@msuvxi.memphis.edu
Treasurer: GEORGE B. MOCK, P.O. Box 393, Mattapoisett, MA 02739; Phone: 508-758-4408; E-mail: gmock@nyclubricants.com
Editor: DR. C. RAY CHANDLER, Dept. of Bio., GA Southern Univ., Statesboro, GA 30460-8042; Phone: 912-681-5657; E-mail: chandler@gasou.edu
Publication(s): *Journal of Field Ornithology*
Keyword(s): Biology, Birds, Conservation Biology, Research

ASSOCIATION OF GREAT LAKES OUTDOOR WRITERS
109 N. Broadway, P.O. Box 354, Hartington, NE 67839
Phone: 402-254-3266
Founded: 1957; Membership: 320
Scope: Regional
Description: A nonprofit professional association of outdoor communicators dedicated to perpetuate the great outdoors through the judicious use of the written and spoken word.
Contact(s):
Chairman of the Board: MARTIN JARANOWSKI, P.O. Box 604, Glenwood, IN 60425; Phone: 765-629-2493
President: PEGGY BOEHMER, P.O. Box 96, Goose Lake, IA 52750; Phone: 319-242-3046
Vice President: MIKE SEELING, 13608 Rt. 176, Woodstock, IL 60098; Phone: 815-337-0112
Secretary/Treasurer: BILL CHAFFEE, P.O. Box 125, Laurens, IA 52570; Phone: 712-845-4541
Executive Director: GARY HOWEY
Editor: BOB SCHMIDT, 5016 Argyle, Chicago, IL 60630; Phone: 773-283-7871
Publication(s): *AGLOW Horizons*
Keyword(s): Environmental Communication

ASSOCIATION OF MIDWEST FISH AND GAME LAW ENFORCEMENT OFFICERS
Attn: Executive Secretary, CO Div. of Wildlife, Law Enforcement Section, 6060 Broadway, Denver, CO 80216
Phone: 303-291-7216; E-mail: dave.croonquist@state.co.us
Founded: 1944
Scope: International
Description: To promote law enforcement cooperation among members, develop efficient cooperative law enforcement practices, establish a medium for disseminating information relating to illegal game law practices, devise legislative or regulatory changes for improving and standardizing law enforcement, and encourage the highest possible standards and practices of law enforcement among member organizations in the United States and Canada.
Contact(s):
Executive Secretary: DAVE CROONQUIST

Keyword(s): Environmental Law, Fisheries, Outdoor Recreation, Renewable Resources, Wildlife Management

ASSOCIATION OF NEW JERSEY ENVIRONMENTAL COMMISSIONS

P.O. Box 157, Mendham, NJ 07945
Phone: 973-539-7547; Fax: 973-539-7713; E-mail: anjec@aol.com; Web Site: www.anjec.org

Founded: 1969; Membership: 2,100
Scope: Statewide
Description: Private, nonprofit environmental organization serving the state's municipal environmental commissions, environmental organizations, and individual members by providing training programs, publications, research, reference, and liaison services.
Contact(s):
President: GARY SZELC
Executive Director: SALLY DUDLEY
Director of ANJEC Resource Center (Library): JAMIE MAURER
Publication(s): *ANJEC Report; Environmental Manual for Municipal Officials; Freshwater Wetlands Protection in New Jersey: A Manual for Local Officials; Keeping Our Garden State Green: A Local Government Guide for Greenway and Open Space Planning; Environmental Commissioner's Handbook; Directory of Environmental Consultants,* serving New Jersey Area
Keyword(s): Environmental Preservation, Environmental Protection, Open Space, Pollution Prevention, Rural Development, Sustainable Development, Training, Water Quality, Water Resources, Watersheds

ASSOCIATION OF STATE AND TERRITORIAL HEALTH OFFICIALS

1275 K St., NW, Suite 800, Washington, DC 20005
Phone: 202-371-9090; Fax: 202-371-9797

Founded: 1941
Scope: National
Description: ASTHO represents the directors of public health in each of the 50 states, the District of Columbia, and the U.S. Territories. Its purpose is to formulate and influence through collective action the establishment of sound national public health policy. ASTHO also assists and serves state health agencies in the development and implementation of state programs and policies in advancing the public health and prevention of disease.
Contact(s):
President: PATRICIA A. NOLAN MD, MPH; Phone: 401-222-2231
Executive Vice President: GEORGE E. HARDY JR.,MD,MPH
Publication(s): *Tobacco-Free Press; Environmental Health News; Astho Report*
Keyword(s): Communications, Environment, Health and Nutrition, Public Health Protection

ATLANTIC CENTER FOR THE ENVIRONMENT

Headquarters, 55 S. Main St., Ipswich, MA 01938-2396
Phone: 978-356-0038; Fax: 978-356-7322; Web Site: www.qlf.org

Scope: Regional
Description: A regional community-based conservation organization promoting public involvement in resource management through year-round education, policy, and research programs in Atlantic Canada, Eastern Quebec, and New England (the Atlantic Region). As a technical assistance resource for local private and public agencies, the Atlantic Center provides resource assessments, conservation planning and strategy, policy analysis, and information services. It conducts many of its programs through an intern work force, which it recruits from colleges and universities across North America. The Atlantic Center also facilitates the exchange of ideas between its region and others. It has an active exchange program with organizations in Latin America and the Caribbean, the Middle East, and Europe. The Atlantic Center is a division of the Quebec-Labrador Foundation.
Contact(s):
President: LAWRENCE B. MORRIS
Administrative Assistant: LINDA R. MITTON
President of QLF Canada: KATHLEEN A. BLANCHARD
Vice President for International Programs: JESSICA BROWN
Vice President of Operations: THOMAS F. HORN
Publication(s): *Compass*
Keyword(s): Environmental and Conservation Education, International Conservation, Internships, Scholarships and Grants, Sustainable Development

New England Office
P.O. Box 217, Montpelier, VT 05602
Phone: 802-229-0707; Fax: 802-229-1603
Scope: Regional
Contact(s):
Vice President: THOMAS F. HORN

QLF Canada Office
1253 McGill College Ave., Suite 680, Montreal, Quebec H3B 2Y5 Canada
Phone: 514-395-6020; Fax: 514-395-4505
Scope: Regional

ATLANTIC SALMON FEDERATION

International Headquarters, P.O. Box 429, St. Andrews, New Brunswick E0G 2X0 Canada
Phone: 506-529-4581; Fax: 506-529-4438; E-mail: asf@nbnet.nb.ca

Founded: 1982; Membership: 40,000
Scope: International
Description: The largest international nonprofit organization dedicated to the preservation and wise management of the Atlantic salmon and its habitat. It was established upon consolidation of two leading salmon organizations, The Atlantic Salmon Association and The International Atlantic Salmon Foundation. ASF programs are directed toward research, conservation, education, and international cooperation. The Federation supports a network of regional groupings of local salmon conservation and other organizations which address a variety of salmon issues. ASF is totally dependent on contributions from individuals, foundations, and corporations in Canada, the United States, and overseas. Membership inquiries are welcomed.
Contact(s):
President: BILL TAYLOR
Chairman of Canada (Montreal) Office: JOHN HOUGHTON, 1253, av. McGill College, bureau 680, Montreal, Quebec H3B 2Y5 Canada; Phone: 514-871-9660
Chairman of New York Office: DONALD C. O'BRIEN JR., Milbank, Tweed, Hadley, and McCloy, One Chase Manhattan Plaza, 54th Floor, New York, NY 10005-1413; Phone: 212-530-5818
Controller: BILL MALLORY
Director, U.S. Programs: ANDREW GOODE
Editor: JIM GOURLAY, P.O. Box 429, St. Andrews, New Brunswick E0G2X0 Canada; Phone: 506-529-4581
Executive Director of Communications and Public Policy: SUE SCOTT
Executive Director, Development: ROBERT BEATTY
Vice President-Research and Environment: DR. FREDERICK WHORISKEY
Publication(s): *Atlantic Salmon Journal, The*
Keyword(s): Atlantic Salmon, Endangered and Threatened Species, Research, Wildlife and Wildlife Habitat, Wildlife Management, Salmon Recovery

ATLANTIC STATES LEGAL FOUNDATION

658 W. Onondaga St., Syracuse, NY 13204-3757
Phone: 315-475-1170; E-mail: aslf@igc.apc.org

Founded: 1982; Membership: 8,250
Scope: National
Description: Atlantic States Legal Foundation, Inc., enforces environmental laws, engages in public education, conducts research and promotes environmental justice for the economically disadvantaged and people of color.
Contact(s):
President: SAMUEL H. SAGE
Executive Director: LOUCHES POWELL JR.
Research Associate: THEODORE NEWMAN

Staff Attorney: SEAN P. LYNCH
Publication(s): *Quarterly newsletter*
Keyword(s): Chemical Pollution Control, Developing Countries, Environmental and Conservation Education, Environmental Justice, Environmental Law, Lakes, Mining, People of Color in the Environment, Pollution Prevention, Public Health Protection, Renewable Resources, Solid Waste Management, Sustainable Development, Sustainable Ecosystems, Urban Environment

AUDUBON COUNCIL OF CONNECTICUT
c/o Audubon Center in Greenwich, 613 Riversville Rd., Greenwich, CT 06831
Phone: 203-629-1248
Founded: 1967; Membership: 24,000
Scope: Statewide
Description: The Audubon Council of Connecticut is a coalition of 16 chapters and affiliates of the National Audubon Society in Connecticut, representing close to 10,000 residents. The Council recognize humankind's dependence on the natural environment and appreciates the beauty and wondrous diversity of the natural world. The mission of the Council is, therefore, to protect and restore biodiversity in our state and on our planet.
Contact(s):
President: JANE-KERIN MOFFOT, 98 Valley Rd., #12, Cos Cob, CT 06807; Phone: 203-629-1248
Keyword(s): Birds, Environment, Natural Areas

AUDUBON COUNCIL OF ILLINOIS
Attn: President, 1631 N. Evergreen, Arlington Heights, IL 60004
Founded: 1973
Scope: Statewide
Description: Composed of representatives of 13 National Audubon Society chapters in Illinois, the Council's purpose is to coordinate efforts of the chapters on statewide environmental issues.
Contact(s):
President: BOB LIPPOLD, 1631 N. Evergreen, Arlington Heights, IL 60004; Phone: 847-870-0337
Vice President: MARIANNE HAHN, 18429 Gottschalk Ave., Homewood, IL 60430; Phone: 708-799-0249
Secretary: JILL VENSKUS, 109 W. Traube Ave., Downers Grove, IL 60515; Phone: 630-963-9258
Treasurer: MARY BLACKMORE, 9024 W. Grove Rd., Forreston, IL 61030; Phone: 815-938-3204
Keyword(s): Biodiversity, Birds, Environmental Preservation, Wetlands, Wildlife and Wildlife Habitat

AUDUBON INTERNATIONAL
Headquarters, 46 Rarick Rd., Selkirk, NY 12158
Phone: 518-767-9051; Fax: 518-767-9076; Web Site: www.audubonint1.org
Founded: 1897; Membership: 2,500+ properties/395,534 associate members
Scope: International
Description: Audubon International is a nonprofit environmental organization that specializes in sustainable natural resource management. The mission of Audubon International is to improve the quality of life and the environment through research, education, and conservation assistance.
Contact(s):
Business Manager: PAULA DONNELLY
Director of Environmental Education: JEAN MACKAY
Director of Environmental Planning: DR. MILES SMART; Phone: 919-380-9640
Director of Research: DR. LAWRENCE WOOLBRIGHT; Phone: 518-783-2440
Director of Sustainable Development Demonstration: NANCY RICHARDSON; Phone: 502-869-9419
Executive Assistant: MARY L. JACK
MIS: ERIC DODSON
President and CEO: RONALD G. DODSON
Publication(s): *ACSS Field Notes; Stewardship News; Landscape Restoration Handbook; Principles for Sustainable Resource Management; A Guide to Environmental Stewardship on the Golf Course*
Keyword(s): Biodiversity, Birds, Environmental and Conservation Education, Environmental Planning, Land Use Planning, Nongame Wildlife, Renewable Resources, Research, Sustainable Development, Water Quality, Wildlife and Wildlife Habitat

AUDUBON NATURALIST SOCIETY OF THE CENTRAL ATLANTIC STATES
8940 Jones Mill Rd., Chevy Chase, MD 20815
Phone: 301-652-9188; Fax: 301-951-7179; E-mail: hq@audubonnaturalist.org; Web Site: www.audubonnaturalist.org
Founded: 1897; Membership: 11,000
Scope: Regional
Description: One of the original independent Audubon societies active in environmental education, conservation issues, sanctuaries, and natural science studies in the greater Washington metropolitan area for 100 years. The ANS is headquartered at Woodend, a 40-acre Nature Preserve in suburban Maryland.
Contact(s):
President: JEFF SMITH
Vice President: STAN SHETLER Ph.D.
Treasurer: KATHLENN MALLOY
Executive Director: MIKE NELSON
Director of Conservation: NEAL FITZPATRICK
Director of Education: JANE HUFF
Director of Finance: MURIEL ROBINSON
Editor: LESLIE CRONIN
Publication(s): *Naturalist News*
Keyword(s): Birds, Environmental and Conservation Education, Natural History, Nature Preservation, Sustainable Development, Water Quality

AUDUBON OF KANSAS (formerly Kansas Audubon Council)
813 Juniper Dr., Manhattan, KS 66502
Phone: 785-537-4385; E-mail: rklataske@hotmail.com
Founded: 1974; Membership: 5,000
Scope: Statewide
Description: A statewide nonprofit organization working in partnership with eleven local Audubon chapters, a Board of Trustees and other members. Established in 1974, leadership was expanded in 1999 to establish Audubon of Kansas as a broad-based alliance to promote appreciation and stewardship of the natural ecosystems of Kansas, with special emphasis on conservation of prairies, grassland birds and other wildlife.
Contact(s):
Board of Trustees, Chairman: WILLIAM R. BROWNING M.D., 205 W. Main, Madison, KS 66806
Vice Chairman: RICHARD G. TUCKER, P.O. Box 875, Parsons, KS 67357
Secretary: PATRICIA MARLETT, 4406 W. 11th, Wichita, KS 67212
Treasurer: CAROL CUMBERLAND, 1106 Gretchen, Wichita, KS 67206
Executive Director: RON KLATASKE
Keyword(s): Birds, Conservation, Environmental and Conservation Education, Grasslands, Prairies, Wildlife and Wildlife Habitat

AUDUBON SOCIETY OF MISSOURI
Attn: President, 1001 SW 19th, Blue Springs, MO 64015
Phone: Rare Bird Hotline: 573-445-9115
Founded: 1901
Scope: Statewide
Description: A nonprofit statewide society affiliated with National Audubon Society. Dedicated to the preservation and protection of birds and all wildlife forms and habitat; to educate citizenry toward appreciation of the natural world; and to work for wise conservation practices related to people and wildlife.
Contact(s):
President: MIKE BECK; Phone: 816-229-6811
Vice President: SUSAN HAZELWOOD, 3005 Chapel Hill Rd., Columbus, MO 65203; Phone: 573-445-9925

NON-GOVERNMENTAL ORGANIZATIONS - B

Secretary: SUSAN DORNFELD, 700 S. Weller, Springfield, MO 65208; Phone: 417-831-9702
Treasurer: JEAN GRAEBNER, 1800 S. Roby Farm Rd., Rocheport, MO 65279; Phone: 314-698-2855
Hotline Coordinator: JERRY & EDGE WADE, 1221 Bradshaw Ave., Columbia, MO 65203-0807; Phone: 573-445-6697
Publication(s): *Bluebird, The; Annotated Checklist of the Birds of Missouri; Guide to the Birding Areas of Missouri, A*
Keyword(s): Birds, Environmental and Conservation Education, Natural History, Wildlife and Wildlife Habitat

AUDUBON SOCIETY OF NEW HAMPSHIRE
3 Silk Farm Rd., Concord, NH 03301-8200
Phone: 603-224-9909
Founded: 1914; Membership: 7,000
Scope: Statewide
Description: Independent statewide nonprofit organization dedicated to the preservation, understanding, and appreciation of New Hampshire's wildlife and other natural resources.
Contact(s):
President: RICHARD MOORE
Secretary: LARRY SUNDERLAND, RFD 1 Box 179, Hillsboro, NH 03244
Treasurer: KIRK LEONI, 224 Reservoir Rd., Weare, NH 03281
Chair of the Board of Trustees: TOM BURACK, Sheehan, Phinney, Bass, and Green, 1000 Elm St., Manchester, NH 03105-3701
Director for Membership: JENNIFER FOX
Director of Education: SCOTT FITZPATRICK
Director of Environmental Affairs: JULIAN ZELAZNY
Director of Loon Preservation Committee: HARRY VOGEL
Vice Chairperson: SYLVIA BATES, Rt. 1, Box 313, Ashland, NH 03217
Vice President for Conservation: RICHARD COOK
Keyword(s): Wildlife and Wildlife Habitat

AUDUBON SOCIETY OF PORTLAND
5151 NW Cornell Rd., Portland, OR 97210
Phone: 503-292-6855; Fax: 503-292-1021; E-mail: general@audubon-pdx.org
Founded: 1902; Membership: 7,500
Scope: Local
Description: The Audubon Society of Portland promotes the enjoyment, understanding and protection of native birds, other wildlife and their habitats, focusing on the local community and the Pacific Northwest.
Contact(s):
President: MARLI LINTNER
Vice President: KAHLER MARTINSON
Secretary: SCOTT LUKENS
Treasurer: MARY CHRISTENSEN
Executive Director: DAVE ESHBAUGH
Director of Conservation: PAUL KETCHAM
Publication(s): *Audubon Warbler*
Keyword(s): Ancient Forests, Birds, Conservation, Endangered and Threatened Species, Environmental and Conservation Education, Environmental Protection, Natural History, Outdoor Recreation, Sustainable Development, Urban Environment, Wetlands, Wildlife Rehabilitation

AUDUBON SOCIETY OF RHODE ISLAND
12 Sanderson Rd., Smithfield, RI 02917-2600
Phone: 401-949-5454; Fax: 401-949-5788; E-mail: audubon_ri@ids.net
Founded: 1897; Membership: 4,500
Scope: Statewide
Description: To focus attention on critical natural resource problems, provide leadership when conservation action is necessary, carry out a broad program of public conservation education, and preserve examples of unique natural areas and native wildlife habitat.
Contact(s):
President: SAMUEL H. HALLOWELL JR.
Secretary: DR. JOSEPH D. DIMASE
Treasurer: FRANK SCIUTO
Executive Director: LEE C. SCHISLER JR.
1st Vice President: A. MAX KOHLENBERG
2nd Vice President: DOUGLAS L. KRAUS
Director of Properties and Acquisitions: LAWRENCE TAFT
Editor: KEN WEBER
Membership Secretary: DORIS THORPE
Publication(s): *Audubon Society of Rhode Island Report; Checklist of Rhode Island Birds; Fields Notes of Rhode Island Birds*
Keyword(s): Air Quality and Pollution, Birds, Coasts, Conservation of Protected Areas, Endangered and Threatened Species, Environment, Environmental and Conservation Education, Environmental Preservation, Fisheries, Flowers, Plants, and Trees, Insects and Butterflies, Land Preservation, Open Space, Wildlife Management

AUDUBON SOCIETY OF WESTERN PENNSYLVANIA
Beechwood Farms Nature Reserve, 614 Dorseyville Rd., Pittsburgh, PA 15238-1618
Phone: 412-963-6100; Fax: 412-963-6761
Founded: 1916; Membership: 5,500
Scope: Local
Description: The mission of the Audubon Society of Western Pennsylvania is to inspire and educate people of southwestern Pennsylvania to be respectful and responsible stewards of the natural world.
Contact(s):
President: CAROLYN SANFORD
Vice President: DANFORTH FALES
Secretary: MARIAN CROSSMAN
Treasurer: JIM WILKINSON
Publication(s): *Bulletin; Seasoning; Teacher Guide*
Keyword(s): Birds, Environmental and Conservation Education, Flowers, Plants, and Trees, Insects and Butterflies, Mammals, Natural History, Raptors, Reptiles and Amphibians, Waterfowl, Wildlife and Wildlife Habitat

AVSC INTERNATIONAL
79 Madison Ave., New York, NY 10016
Phone: 212-561-8000; Fax: 212-779-9439; E-mail: info@avsc.org; Web Site: www.avsc.org
Founded: 1943; Membership: 5,500
Scope: National
Description: A nonprofit family planning and reproductive health organization. To ensure through education, research, and service, that men and women everywhere have access to reproductive health care, including safe contraception. Special expertise in the areas of female sterilization, vasectomy, postpartum contraceptive care, post-abortion contraceptive care, and reproductive health programs for men.
Contact(s):
Chair: LYMAN B. BRAINERD JR.
President: DR. AMY E. POLLACK
Chief of Operations and Vice President: TERRENCE W. JEZOWSKI
Director of Programs: LYNN BAKAMJIAN
Medical Director and Vice President: DR. VANNESSA COUINS
Publication(s): *AVSC News*
Keyword(s): Family Planning, Health and Nutrition, Population Growth

B

BAMA BACKPADDLERS ASSOCIATION
307 Madison Pl., Trussville, AL 35173
E-mail: backpaddler@mindspring.com; Web Site: backpaddler.home.mindspring.com/bba/
Founded: 1978; Membership: 150+
Scope: Statewide
Description: Dedicated to promoting recreation, conservation, education and safety on Alabama's waterways.
Contact(s):
President: PAM BRADY

Trip Coordinator: MIKE COWAN
Treasurer: NANCY CATE
Newsletter: RENEE CLARK; E-mail: kayakbba@aol.com
Conservation: JENNIFER TAYLOR; Phone: 205-951-0320; E-mail: jentay@uab.edu
Publication(s): *As the Eddy Turns*
Keyword(s): Conservation, Dams, Development, Local Resource Conservation, Outdoor Recreation, Protecting Special Places, Rivers, Water Pollution, Water Quality, Water Resources

BARRIER ISLAND TRUST, INC.
P.O. Box 37310, Tallahassee, FL 32315
Founded: 1989; Membership: 200
Scope: Statewide
Description: To preserve the natural resources of Florida's barrier islands, initially focusing on Dog Island and Apalachicola Bay, hold and manage barrier island property to preserve it in its natural state, promote research on barrier island ecology and translate research into educational programs and effective policies for protection of barrier islands.
Contact(s):
Board of Trustee Chair: GUY SMITH IV, 352 North St., Greenwich, CT 06830; Phone: 203-629-1264
Board of Trustee President: LEROY COLLINS III, 16 Davis Blvd. #12, Tampa, FL 33606; Phone: 813-259-9484
Board of Trustee Treasurer: MITCHELL SMITH, P.O. Box 1912, Albany, GA 31702
Board of Trustee Vice President: DIANNE MELLON, 1515 Country Club, Tallahassee, FL 32301; Phone: 850-877-3942
Keyword(s): Coasts, Islands, Land Preservation, Land Protection

BASS ANGLERS SPORTSMAN SOCIETY (B.A.S.S, INC.)
5845 Carmichael Rd., Montgomery, AL 36117
Phone: 334-272-9530; Web Site: www.bassmasters.com
Founded: 1968
Scope: National
Description: Organized to fight pollution, assist state and national conservation agencies in their efforts, and teach the young people of our country good conservation practices. Dedicated to the realistic conservation of our water resources.
Contact(s):
Chairman and CEO: HELEN SEVIER
National Conservation Director: BRUCE SHUPP
National Federation Director: DON K. CORKRAN
Publication(s): *Bassmaster Magazine; Guns & Gear; B.A.S.S. Times; Fishing Tackle Retailer; Television Show: The Bassmasters*
Keyword(s): Conservation, Sport Fishing, Water Pollution, Water Resources

BAT CONSERVATION INTERNATIONAL
P.O. Box 162603, Austin, TX 78716
Phone: 512-327-9721; Web Site: www.batcon.org
Founded: 1982; Membership: 14,000
Scope: International
Description: A nonprofit organization with members in 60 countries. BCI's purpose is to document and publicize the values and conservation needs of bats, to promote bat conservation projects, and to assist with management initiatives worldwide.
Contact(s):
Chairman: MICHAEL L. COOK
Secretary: MRS. JOHN C. PHILLIPS
Treasurer: MARK RITTER
Founder and Executive Director: DR. MERLIN D. TUTTLE
Publication(s): *BATS(quarterly)*
Keyword(s): Biodiversity, Biology, Ecology, Endangered and Threatened Species, Environment, Environmental and Conservation Education, International Conservation, Mammals, Nongame Wildlife, Research, Scholarships, Wildlife and Wildlife Habitat, Bats

BERKSHIRE-LITCHFIELD ENVIRONMENTAL COUNCIL, INC.
P.O. Box 552, Lakeville, CT 06039
Phone: 203-435-2004
Founded: 1970; Membership: 1,000
Scope: Statewide
Description: Primarily concerned with energy, invasive transportation, and land use issues in the southern Berkshires and Litchfield Hills. Offers public programs and environmental education for all ages.
Contact(s):
President: STARLING W. CHILDS; Phone: 203-542-5569
Vice President: NIC OSBORN
Secretary: ELLERY W. SINCLAIR
Treasurer: PETER DOLAN
Executive Director: JUDY ISACOFF THOMAS
Counsel: WILLIAM F. MORRILL
Publication(s): *BLEC News*
Keyword(s): Agriculture, Biodiversity, Environmental and Conservation Education, Environmental Preservation, Wilderness

BEYOND PESTICIDES/NATIONAL COALITION AGAINST THE MISUSE OF PESTICIDES
701 E St. SE Suite 200, Washington, DC 20003
Phone: 202-543-5450; E-mail: ncamp@ncamp.org; Web Site: www.ncamp.org
Founded: 1981
Scope: National
Description: Nonprofit membership organization committed to assisting individuals, organizations, and communities with useful information on pesticides and their alternatives. NCAMP's information clearinghouse provides material on a wide range of both agricultural and urban issues concerning protection of children, workers' safety, food safety, lawn care safety, groundwater problems, and alternatives to pesticides, as well as legislation.
Contact(s):
Executive Director: JAY FELDMAN
Editor: JAY FELDMAN
President Board of Directors: ALLEN SPALT
Publication(s): *Pesticides and You Newsletter (Quarterly); NCAMP's Technical Report (Monthly); Poison Poles: Their Toxic Trial and the Safer Alternatives; Safety at Home: A Guide to the Hazards of Lawn and Garden Pesticides and Safer Ways to Manage Pests; Unnecessary Risks: The Benefit Side of the Pesticides Risk-Benefit Equation; The Schooling of State Pesticide Laws*
Keyword(s): Agriculture, Environment, Insects and Butterflies, Pesticides, Toxicology

BIG BEND NATURAL HISTORY ASSOCIATION
P.O. Box 196, Big Bend National Park, TX 79834
Phone: 915-477-2236
Founded: 1956; Membership: 559
Scope: Nationwide
Description: A private nonprofit organization whose main objectives are to facilitate popular interpretation of the scenic, scientific and historical values of Big Bend, and to encourage research related to those values. To accomplish these goals, the association is authorized by the National Park Service to publish, print, or otherwise provide books, maps, and illustrative material on the Big Bend region and to sponsor a Big Bend seminar program.
Contact(s):
Chairman: ROB DUNAGAN; Phone: 915-336-5274
Executive Director: MIKE BOREN
Editor: THOMAS VANDENBERG
Publication(s): *Big Bend Paisano*
Keyword(s): Environmental and Conservation Education, Flowers, Plants, and Trees, Gardening and Horticulture, National Parks, Natural Areas, Nature Preservation

BILLFISH FOUNDATION, THE
2419 E. Commercial Blvd., Suite 303, Ft. Lauderdale, FL 33308
Phone: 954-938-0150/800-438-8247; Fax: 954-938-5311
Scope: International
Description: The Billfish Foundation is a nonprofit organization dedicated to the conservation of billfish worldwide through scientific research, education, and advocacy. Through scientific, economic and conservation decisions provided through research, TBF strives for sound and constructive measures to recover overfished stocks.

NON-GOVERNMENTAL ORGANIZATIONS - B

Contact(s):
Chairman of Trustees: WINTHROP P. ROCKEFELLER
Executive Director: ELLEN PEEL
President of Trustees and Vice Chairman: MEL M. IMMERGUT
Vice Chairman of Trustees: RALPH VICENTE
Treasurer of Trustees: BOBBY JONES
Publication(s): *TBF News; Billfish; Spearfish*
Keyword(s): Billfish, Environmental and Conservation Education, Fisheries, International Conservation, Research, Sport Fishing, Migration

BIO-INTEGRAL RESOURCE CENTER
P.O. Box 7414, Berkeley, CA 94707
Phone: 510-524-2567
Founded: 1979; Membership: 5,000
Scope: National
Description: A nonprofit educational organization dedicated to providing information on least-toxic pest control.
Contact(s):
Executive Director: LAURIE SWIADON
Executive Director and Managing Editor of Publications: WILLIAM QUARLES
Business Manager: JENNIFER BATES
Publication(s): *IPM Practitioner, The; Common Sense Pest Control; Least-toxic Pest Management for Fleas, Termites, Cockroaches, Raccoons, Ticks, and more*
Keyword(s): Agriculture, Gardening and Horticulture, Insects and Butterflies, Pesticides, Urban Environment

BIODIVERSITY LEGAL FOUNDATION
P.O. Box 278, Louisville, CO 80027
Phone: 303-926-7606; E-mail: blfrog@aol.com
Founded: 1991; Membership: 1,400
Scope: National
Description: The Biodiversity Legal Foundation is a nonprofit, science-based tax-exempt organization dedicated to the preservation of all native plants, animals, and naturally functioning ecosystems. Through educational, administrative, and legal actions, we endeavor to encourage improved public attitudes for all living things.
Contact(s):
President: EDWARD W. MUDD JR.
Vice President: ROGER CANDEE
Director: JASPER CARLTON
Secretary and Treasurer: JOYCE HUDSON
Publication(s): *Administrative and Legal Update; How You Can Help Rare and Endangered Species within the Framework of Existing Conservation Law; Guidelines for the Preparation of Species Status Reviews and Species Conservation Assessments; Guide to Ecosystem Management*
Keyword(s): Biodiversity, Endangered and Threatened Species, Environmental Law, Fisheries, Nongame Wildlife, Prairies, Predators, Public Lands, Sustainable Ecosystems, Wildlife and Wildlife Habitat

BIOMASS USERS NETWORK
383 Franklin St., Bloomfield, NJ 07003
Phone: 201-680-9100
Founded: 1985; Membership: 51 countries
Scope: International
Description: To advance rural economic development in Third World countries in an environmentally sound manner, through the innovative production and efficient use of biomass resources.
Contact(s):
Chairman: DAVID MAZAMBANI
Publication(s): *Network News*
Keyword(s): Energy, Flowers, Plants, and Trees, Forests and Forestry, Soil Conservation, Sustainable Development

BIRDLIFE INTERNATIONAL
Canada Nature Federation,1 Nicholas St., Ste. 606, Ottawa, Ontario KIN 7B7 Canada
Phone: 613-562-3447; Fax: 613-562-3371; E-mail: cnf@cnf.ca; Web Site: www.magna.cal~cnfgen

Scope: National
Description: Protection of birds and their habitats in Canada, in their winter quarters in North and South America, and off Canada's coasts are among major concerns.
Contact(s):
Contact: MICHAEL BRADSTREET, Bird Studies Canada, Box 160, Port Rowan, Ontario N0E 1M0 Canada; Phone: 519-586-3531; Fax: 519-586-3532
Contact: CAROLINE SCHULTZ
Keyword(s): Birds, Conservation of Protected Areas, Endangered and Threatened Species, Environmental Preservation, International Conservation, Nature Preservation, Wildlife and Wildlife Habitat

BLUEBIRDS ACROSS VERMONT PROJECT
255 Sherman Hollow Rd., Hungtinton, VT 05462
Phone: 802-434-3068
Founded: 1987; Membership: 800
Scope: Statewide
Description: A project of the Vermont Audubon Council and Green Mountain Audubon, Bluebirds Across Vermont (BAV) was formed to help restore native eastern bluebird populations. BAV promotes the proper placement of correctly built nestboxes by informed citizens who monitor them throughout the nesting season and send the data to BAV for yearly compilation.
Contact(s):
Contact: MARK LaBARR

BOONE AND CROCKETT CLUB
Old Milwaukee Depot, 250 Station Dr., Missoula, MT 59801
Phone: 406-542-1888; Fax: 406-542-0784; E-mail: bcclub@boone-crockett.org; Web Site: www.boone-crockett.org
Founded: 1887
Scope: National
Description: A 501 (c) (3) organization. Established by Theodore Roosevelt and other concerned sportsmen to promote hunting ethics, foster the concept of Fair Chase, and help establish wildlife conservation practices which led to the recovery of big game animals in North America. The Club documents the records of North American big game and exhibits its National Collection of Heads and Horns in Cody, WY.
Contact(s):
President: DANIEL A. PEDROTTI; Phone: 512-884-2443
Secretary: GILBERT ADAMS; Phone: 409-835-3000
Treasurer: JOSEPH A. OSTERVICH; Phone: 608-486-2341
Communications Committee: GEORGE A. BETTAS; Phone: 509-335-4531
Conservation Committee: THOMAS D. PRUE; Phone: 541-276-4246
Director of North American Big Game Records: JACK RENEAU; Phone: 406-542-1888
Ethics Committee: WILLIAM O. BARRETT; Phone: 210-829-7831
Museum Committee: FREDERICK J. KING; Phone: 406-994-2654
Records of North American Big Game Committee: C. RANDALL BYERS; Phone: 208-885-7341
Publication(s): *FAIR CHASE; Records of North American Big Game; Records of North American Elk and Mule Deer; An American Crusade for Wildlife; Records of North American Whitetail Deer; Return of Royalty*
Keyword(s): Environmental and Conservation Education, Hunting, Public Lands, Scholarships and Grants, Wildlife and Wildlife Habitat

BOONE AND CROCKETT FOUNDATION
Old Milwaukee Depot, 250 Station Dr., Missoula, MT 59801
Phone: 406-542-1888; Fax: 406-542-0784; E-mail: bcclub@boone-crockett.org; Web Site: www.boone-crockett.org
Scope: National
Description: The BCF owns and operates the 6,000 acre Theodore Roosevelt Memorial Ranch near Dupuyer, MT, as a working cattle ranch for research, education and demonstration. BCF supports natural resource conservation research, education, and

demonstration primarily through the Boone and Crockett wildlife conservation program in conjunction with the University of Montana.
Contact(s):
President: DANIEL A. PEDROTTI; Phone: 512-884-2443
Secretary: GILBERT ADAMS; Phone: 409-835-3000
Treasurer: JOSEPH A. OSTERVICH; Phone: 608-486-2341
Conservation Education Program Manger: LISA FLOWERS; Phone: 406-466-2078
Professor of Wildlife Conservation: JACK WARD THOMAS; Phone: 406-243-5566
TRMR Manager: ROBERT K. PEEBLES; Phone: 406-472-3380
Keyword(s): Hunting, Renewable Resources, Sustainable Development, Sustainable Ecosystems, Wildlife and Wildlife Habitat

BORDER ECOLOGY PROJECT (BEP)
Drawer CP, Bisbee, AZ 85603
Phone: 520-432-7456; Fax: 520-432-7473; E-mail: bep@primenet.com
Founded: 1983
Scope: National
Description: BEP advocates for solutions to environmental problems along the U.S./Mexico border. Areas of focus include Right-to-Know, environmental pollution, international trade, mining, hazardous materials trucking, and bi-national environmental health issues including lupus.
Contact(s):
Director: DICK KAMP
Coordinator: A. CAROLINE HOTALING
Publication(s): *Environmental and Health Conditions in the Interior of Mexico: Options for Transnational Safeguards; Environmental Protection within the Mexican Mining Sector and the Impact of the World Bank Loan #3359*
Keyword(s): Air Quality and Pollution, Rivers, Solid Waste Management, Toxic Substances, Water Pollution Management

BOTANICAL CLUB OF WISCONSIN
c/o Wisconsin Academy of Science, Arts, and Letters, 1922 University Ave., Madison, WI 53705
Phone: 608-262-5489; Fax: 608-265-2993; E-mail: jpbennet@facstaff.wisc.edu
Founded: 1969; Membership: 185
Scope: Statewide
Description: Botanical Club of Wisconsin promotes preservation of Wisconsin's native plants and educates the public as to the value of plants. The Club also fosters research on plant biology and provides a means for fellowship and information exchange.
Contact(s):
President: EMMET J. JUDZIEWICZ; Phone: 920-842-4620
Vice President: JAMES P. BENNETT
Secretary: JUNE DOBBERPUHL; Phone: 608-267-5037; Fax: 608-266-2925
Treasurer: EDWARD N. GLOVER; Phone: 608-437-4578
Publication(s): *Wisconsin Flora; The Bulletin of the Botanical Club of Wisconsin*
Keyword(s): Environmental and Conservation Education, Flowers, Plants, and Trees, Nature Preservation

BOTANICAL SOCIETY OF WESTERN PENNSYLVANIA
5837 Nicholson St., Pittsburgh, PA 15217-2309
Phone: 412-521-9425; E-mail: yoree@sgi.net; Web Site: www.home.kiski.net//~speedy/b1.html
Membership: 200
Scope: Local
Description: Botanical Society of Western Pennsylvania brings together those who are interested in botany and encourages the study of botany and knowledge of plants.
Contact(s):
President: DR. MARY JOY HAYWOOD; Phone: 412-578-6175
Secretary: LOREE SPEEDY
Treasurer: WALTER GARDILL; Phone: 412-364-5308
Publication(s): *Wildflowers*
Keyword(s): Conservation, Environmental and Conservation Education, Flowers, Plants, and Trees, Gardening and Horticulture

BOUNTY INFORMATION SERVICE (WILDLIFE)
4849 E. St. Charles Rd., Columbia, MO 65201
Phone: 573-474-6967; E-mail: claun01@mail.coin.missouri.edu
Founded: 1966
Scope: National
Description: Promotes the removal of bounties in North America by publishing Bounty News and studies of the bounty system and by coordinating activities and legal aspects.
Contact(s):
Director and Editor: H. CHARLES LAUN
Publication(s): *Bounty News; A Guide to the Removal of Bounties*
Keyword(s): Environmental and Conservation Education, Mammals, Trapping, Wildlife and Wildlife Habitat, Wildlife Management

BOY SCOUTS OF AMERICA
National Office, P.O. Box 152079, 1325 West Walnut Hill Ln., Irving, TX 75015-2079
Phone: 214-580-2000
Founded: 1910
Scope: National
Description: Boy Scouts of America (BSA) was chartered by Congress in 1916 to provide an educational program for boys and young adults that builds character and develops responsibility, citizenship, and personal fitness. Community groups with goals compatible with BSA receive national charters to use the Scouting program as part of their own youth work.
Contact(s):
President: EDWARD E. WHITACRE JR.
Treasurer: JOHN C. CUSHMAN
Assistant Treasurer: FRANCIS H. OLMSTEAD JR
Chief Scout Executive: JERE B. RATCLIFFE
Conservation Director: DAVID R. BATES
Regional Executive: ROY L. WILLIAMS, P.O. Box 22019, Tempe, AZ 85285-2019; Phone: 602-752-7000
Regional Executive: RAYMOND L. BLACKWELL, P.O. Box 3085, Naperville, IL 60566-7085; Phone: 630-983-6730
Regional Executive: PARVIN L. BISHOP, P.O. Box 440728, Kennesaw, GA 30144; Phone: 770-421-1601
Regional Executive of Northeast Region: KENNETH L. CONNELLY, P.O. Box 268, Jamesburg, NJ 08831-0268; Phone: 609-655-9600
Keyword(s): Environmental and Conservation Education, Outdoor Recreation, Youth Organizations

BRANDYWINE CONSERVANCY, INC.
P.O. Box 141, Chadds Ford, PA 19317
Phone: 610-388-2700; Fax: 610-388-1575
Founded: 1967; Membership: 4,200
Scope: Regional
Description: A nonprofit organization providing model land use and environmental regulations for Pennsylvania municipalities. Brandywine Conservancy provides land, water resources and historic site conservation and management assistance to landowners and conservation organizations, primarily in southeastern Pennsylvania and northern Delaware.
Contact(s):
Chairman: GEORGE A. WEYMOUTH
Executive Director: JAMES H. DUFF
Director of Environmental Management Center: KATHRYN A. SATERSON
Associate Director of Design (Environmental Management Center): JOHN SNOOK
Associate Director of Municipal Assistance (Environmental Management Center): WESLEY R. HORNER
Associate of Director of Land Stewardship (Environmental Management Center): DAVID D. SHIELDS
Public Relations: HALSEY SPRUANCE
Publication(s): *Catalyst; Environmental Currents; Environmental Management Handbook*
Keyword(s): Environmental Protection, Land Conservation, Land Use Planning, Pollution Prevention, Water Resources, Wetlands

NON-GOVERNMENTAL ORGANIZATIONS - C

BRITISH COLUMBIA FIELD ORNITHOLOGISTS
P.O. Box 8059, Victoria, British Columbia V8W 3R7 Canada
Founded: 1991; Membership: 250
Scope: Statewide
Description: To promote the study and enjoyment of birds in British Columbia; to disseminate knowledge and appreciation of birds by means of publications; to foster cooperation between amateur and professional ornithologists; and to promote conservation of birds and their habitats.
Contact(s):
President: TONY GREENFIELD, P.O. Box 319, Sechelt, British Columbia V0N 3A0 Canada; Phone: 250-885-5539
Vice President: BRYAN GATES, 3085 Uplands Rd., Victoria, British Columbia V8R 6B3 Canada; Phone: 250-598-7789
Treasurer: JIM FLICZUK, 3614-1507 Queensbury Ave., Victoria, British Columbia V8P 5M5 Canada; Phone: 250-656-8066
Editor: MARILYN BUHLER, 1132 Loenholm Rd., Victoria, British Columbia V8Z 2Z6 Canada; Phone: 250-744-2521
Editor: ANDY BUHLER, 1132 Loenholm Rd., Victoria, British Columbia V8Z 2Z6 Canada; Phone: 250-744-2521
Editor: MARTIN K. McNICHOLL, 4735 Canada Way, Burnaby, British Columbia V5G 1L3 Canada; Phone: 250-294-9333
Publication(s): *British Columbia Birds (journal); BC Birding (newsletter)*
Keyword(s): Birds

BRITISH COLUMBIA WATERFOWL SOCIETY, THE
5191 Robertson Rd., Delta, British Columbia V4K 3N2 Canada
Phone: 604-946-6980
Membership: 2,426
Scope: Statewide
Description: The organization was set in 1963 on federal land leased for 30 years to be opened to the public as a bird viewing area at the mouth of the Fraser River, which supports one of the largest wintering populations of waterfowl in Canada. The organization attempts to promote awareness of all parts of the environment.
Contact(s):
President: KEN HALL
Vice President: JOHN BOWLES
Secretary: VARRI JOHNSON
Treasurer: JAMES MORRISON
Manager: JOHN IRELAND
Publication(s): *Marsh Notes; BirdCheck List*

BROOKS BIRD CLUB INC., THE
P.O. Box 4077, Wheeling, WV 26003
Founded: 1932; Membership: 1,000
Scope: National
Description: A nonprofit organization formed to encourage the study and conservation of birds and other phases of natural history. Members in thirty-eight states, Canada and eight foreign countries. Named in honor of A.B. Brooks, naturalist.
Contact(s):
President: JAMES BULLARD, P.O. Box 137, Ashton, MD 20861
Vice President: FRED MCCULLOUGH
Secretary: VIRGINIA CRONENBERGER, Rt. 1 Box 37, Petroleum, WV 26161
Treasurer: GERALD A. DEVAUL, 17 Mozart Rd., Wheeling, WV 26003
Administrator: CARL A. SLATER, 57290 Mehlmen Rd., Bellaire, OH 43906
Immediate Past President: TOM FOX, Route L Box 420, Millstone, WV 25261
Mail-Bag Editor: WILLIAM MURRAY, P.O. Box 944, New Cumberland, WV 26047
Membership Chairman: CAROLYN CONRAD, 423 Warwood Ave., Wheeling, WV 26003
President-Elect: CINDY ELLIS, 103A Oakwood Estates, Scott Depot, WV 25560
Redstart-Editor: DR. A. R. BUCKELEW JR., Box J, Bethany, WV 26032
Publication(s): *Redstart, The; Mail Bag, The*

Keyword(s): Birds, Environmental and Conservation Education, Flowers, Plants, and Trees, Nature Preservation, Wildlife and Wildlife Habitat

BROTHERHOOD OF THE JUNGLE COCK, INC., THE
P.O. Box 576, Glen Burnie, MD 21061
Scope: National
Description: Seeks to teach youth the true meaning of conservation. Primary interest is the preservation of American game fishes, placing great emphasis on adult responsibility of personal instruction along those lines.
Contact(s):
President: GUS DAY
Secretary: EDWARD T. LITTLE, 6623 Kenwood Ave., Baltimore, MD 21237; Phone: 401-682-4631
Treasurer: M. H. DAY, 706 Orchard Way, Silver Spring, MD 20904
1st Vice President: WILLIAM SIMMS
Administrator: BOSLEY WRIGHT; Phone: 410-761-7727
Keyword(s): Endangered and Threatened Species, Environmental and Conservation Education, Fisheries, Water Pollution, Youth Organizations

C

CADDO LAKE INSTITUTE, INC.
P.O. Box 2710, Aspen, CO 81612
Phone: 970-925-2710; Fax: 970-923-4245; E-mail: ornitzb2@aol.com
Scope: National
Description: A non-profit organization whose purpose is environmental awareness. The program director is based near Caddo Lake, Texas. The director will coordinate college programs. Students are paid a stipend to collect samples and return to the student's laboratory for analysis; will also give seminars at secondary schools, all to promote environmental awareness.
Contact(s):
President: DWIGHT SHELLMAN; E-mail: 72007.165@compuserve.com
Vice President: SARA KNEIPP; Phone: 903-938-3545; Fax: 903-938-3545; E-mail: sjkneipp@aol.com
Publication(s): *Caddo Lake Institute Update*
Keyword(s): Ecology, Internships, Watersheds, Wetlands, Wildlife and Wildlife Habitat, Youth Organizations

CALIFORNIA ACADEMY OF SCIENCES
Golden Gate Park, San Francisco, CA 94118
Phone: 415-221-5100
Founded: 1853; Membership: 24,000
Scope: Statewide
Description: The Academy of Sciences' goal is the exploration and interpretation of natural history. Maintains research collections and operates a museum-aquarium-planetarium complex to which one and one-half million visitors come each year.
Contact(s):
Director: DR. PATRICK KOCIOLEK
Board of Trustees Chairman: W. RICHARD BINGHAM
Vice Chairman: SANDRA LINDER
Vice Chairman: MERVIN G. MORRIS
Vice-President: DR. JOHN S. PEARSE
Secretary: MARTHA KROPF
Publication(s): *Academy Newsletter; California Wild; Proceedings; Occasional Papers*
Keyword(s): Aquariums, Environment, Museum, Natural History, Nature Preservation, Reptiles and Amphibians, Research

California Academy of Sciences Library
Golden Gate Park, San Francisco, CA 94118
Phone: 415-750-7102, 415-750-7361; Fax: 415-750-7106; E-mail: library@calacademy.org; Web Site: www.calacademy.org
Scope: Statewide
Description: Non-circulating, closed-stack collection open to the public. Reference requests accepted by mail, phone, fax or e-mail.

Interlibrary loan requests accepted. Library holdings included in OCLC, University of CA MELVYL on-line catalog and CA Union List of Periodicals.
Contact(s):
Librarian: ANNE MARIE MALLEY
Keyword(s): Librarians/Information Professionals, Libraries

CALIFORNIA ASSOCIATION OF RESOURCE CONSERVATION DISTRICTS
Attn: President, 8158 Panorama Trail, Inyokern, CA 93527
Scope: Statewide
Contact(s):
President: DONNA THOMAS; Phone: 760-377-4525; Fax: 760-377-4525
Vice President: JOHN SCHRAMEL, 681 Main St., Greenville, CA 95947; Phone: 530-284-7954; Fax: 530-284-6211
Executive Director: TOM WEHRI, 801 K St. Suite 1318, Sacramento, CA 95814; Phone: 916-447-7237; Fax: 916-447-2532; E-mail: carcd@ns.net
Secretary-Treasurer: ROBERT BEEGLE, 3911 Yellowstone Ln., El Dorado, CA 95762; Phone: 916-852-6691; Fax: 916-852-6693
Board Member: CHUCK PRITCHARD, 9765 Carrisa Highway, Santa Margarita, CA 93453; Phone: 805-475-2386; Fax: 805-475-2533
Keyword(s): Conservation Districts

CALIFORNIA B.A.S.S. CHAPTER FEDERATION
Attn: President, 8437 Jonquil Way, Citrus Heights, CA 95610
Scope: Statewide
Description: An organization of Bassmaster chapters, affiliated with the Bass Anglers Sportsman Society, organized to fight pollution, assist state and national conservation agencies in their efforts, and teach the young people of our country good conservation practice. Dedicated to the realistic conservation of our water resources.
Contact(s):
President: RODGER STEGALL; Phone: 916-726-7241

CALIFORNIA NATIVE PLANT SOCIETY, THE
1722 J St., Suite 17, Sacramento, CA 95814
Phone: 916-447-2677; Fax: 916-447-2727; E-mail: cnps@cnps.org; Web site: www.cnps.org
Founded: 1965; Membership: 10,000
Scope: Statewide
Description: A statewide nonprofit organization of amateurs and professionals with a common interest in California's native plants. The society, working through its local chapters, seeks to increase understanding of California's native flora and to preserve the rich resource for future generations. Membership is open to all.
Contact(s):
President: JACOB SIGG; Phone: 415-731-3028
Executive Director: ALLEN BARNES
Editor and Vice President of Publications: JOYCE HAWLEY
Legal Advisor: SANDY MCCOY
Vice President for Chapter Relations: BERTHA MCKINLEY
Publication(s): *Fremontia; Bulletin; Conservation & Management of Rare and Endangered Plants; Terrestrial Vegetation of California; California's Changing Landscape; Inventory of Rare and Endangered Vascular Plants of California; Flora of San Bruno Mountain; Plant Communities of Marin County; Flowering Plants of Santa Monica Mountains; Chapter Newsletters*
Keyword(s): Biodiversity, Endangered and Threatened Species, Environmental and Conservation Education, Environmental Preservation, Wetlands, Native Plants

CALIFORNIA TRAPPERS ASSOCIATION
Attn: Executive Secretary, 99 Poinsettia Gardens Dr., Ventura, CA 93004
Phone: 805-647-8903; Fax: 805-647-9970
Founded: 1969; Incorporated: 1973; Membership: 420
Scope: Statewide
Description: Dedicated to the encouragement of conservation, enhancement, and scientific management of all our natural resources, especially furbearing mammals. Promotes state and federal wildlife projects through volunteer skilled labor and financial contributions. Gives $500 to $1,000 grants each year to college students studying furbearing mammals.
Contact(s):
President: KEITH CARLY, P.O. Box 73, Elk Creek, CA 95939; Phone: 916-968-5038
Vice President: JOHN CLARK, 907 Holmes Flat Rd., Red Crest, CA 95569; Phone: 707-722-4259
Treasurer: TOM LAUSTALOT, 18907 Indian Creek Rd., Fort Jones, CA 96032; Phone: 916-468-2228
Executive Secretary: DONALD L. STEHSEL
Lobbyist: KATHY LYNCH; Phone: 916-537-7169
Publication(s): *Fur Facts; Legislative Alerts*
Keyword(s): Biology, Endangered and Threatened Species, Environmental and Conservation Education, Environmental Ethics, Environmental Planning, Environmental Preservation, Environmental Protection, Predators, Renewable Resources, Scholarships and Grants, Trapping, Wetlands, Wilderness, Wildlands, Wildlife and Wildlife Habitat

CALIFORNIA TROUT, INC.
870 Market St., #859, San Francisco, CA 94102
Phone: 415-392-8887
Founded: 1970; Membership: 5,000 individuals
Scope: Statewide
Description: Statewide organization of anglers dedicated to protection and restoration of wild trout, native steelhead, and their waters in California, and to the creation of high-quality angling adventures for the public to enjoy. Motto: "Keeper of the Streams."
Contact(s):
Executive Director: MARK BERGSTROM
Board Chairman: BILL HOOPER
Marketing Communications Director: MELISSA MILLER
Publication(s): *Streamkeepers Log*
Keyword(s): Fisheries, Forests and Forestry, Outdoor Recreation, Sport Fishing, Trout, Water Conservation, Hydropower Relicensing

CALIFORNIA WATERFOWL ASSOCIATION
4630 Northgate Blvd., Suite 150, Sacramento, CA 95834
Phone: 916-648-1406; Fax: 916-648-1665
Founded: 1945
Scope: Statewide
Description: A statewide nonprofit, public benefit corporation, whose principal objectives are the conservation, protection, and enhancement of California's waterfowl resources and the waterfowling opportunities which they provide. The association directly represents the interests of over 13,000 sportsmen and conservationists throughout the state and indirectly represents the interests of other Californians who are concerned with and benefit from these unique resources.
Contact(s):
President: DR. ROBERT MCLANDRESS
Chairman of the Board: BOB BELL
Director of Waterfowl Programs: GREG YARRIS
Director of Wetland Programs: DAVE PATTERSON
Directo of Government Affairs: BILL GAINES
Director of Communications/Education: BECKY EASTER
Director of Development: JON ROTH
Publication(s): *California Waterfowl Magazine; Sprig Tales Newsletter*
Keyword(s): Environmental and Conservation Education, Habitat Conservation, Hunting, Water Resources, Waterfowl, Wetlands

CALIFORNIA WILDLIFE DEFENDERS
P.O. Box 2025, Hollywood, CA 90078
Phone: 213-663-1856
Scope: Statewide
Description: A nonprofit association working to eradicate prejudice towards predator animals, especially coyotes. Responsible for the discontinuation of the removal and destruction of wildlife policies in the city of Los Angeles, halting the use of leghold traps there and author of an ordinance enacted in several California cities banning the feeding of coyotes in order to limit exacerbation of urban coyote problems.

NON-GOVERNMENTAL ORGANIZATIONS - C

Contact(s):
Director: LILA BROOKS
Associate: JESSICA GATES
Associate: ALBERTA BURKE
Associate: DR. SUZANNE ULMAN
Publication(s): *Wildlife Alerts; How to Coexist with Urban Wildlife* (brochure)
Keyword(s): Nature Preservation, Nongame Wildlife, Predators, Trapping, Wildlife and Wildlife Habitat, Wildlife Management, Wildlife Rehabilitation

CALIFORNIA WILDLIFE FEDERATION
P.O. Box 1527, Sacramento, CA 95812-1527
Phone: 916-441-7563
Founded: 1952; Membership: 8,600 individuals
Scope: Statewide
Description: A nonprofit statewide organization of councils, clubs, and individual members dedicated to promote the conservation, enhancement, scientific management, and wise use of all our natural resources.
Contact(s):
President: RANDY WALKER, 4908 Sunset Dr,, Fresno, CA 93704; Phone: 559-225-9003
Vice President: TIM LEBLANC, P.O. Box 1343, Lake Arrowhead, CA 92352; Phone: 909-336-1048
Treasurer: C. M. STARR III, 2105 Westhaven Ave., Bakersfield, CA 93304; Phone: 661-835-8337
Editor: CHERI FULLER
Publication(s): *California Wildlife*
Keyword(s): Biodiversity, Endangered and Threatened Species, Fisheries, Hunting, Wildlife and Wildlife Habitat

CALIFORNIA, FOREST LANDOWNERS OF
980 9th St., Suite 1600, Sacramento, CA 95814
Phone: 916-972-0273; Fax: 916-971-1504
Founded: 1974; Membership: 1,000
Scope: Statewide
Description: A statewide organization affiliated with the National Woodland Owners Association that provides educational programs, information services, and legislative representation to families who own forest land for long-term investment, recreational, and conservation reasons.
Contact(s):
President: PETER PARKER
1st Vice President: LEN LINDSTRAND JR.
2nd Vice President: ALLEN EDWARDS
Secretary: RON ADAMS
Treasurer: JIM CHAPIN
Executive Director and Editor: DANIEL M. WELDON
Publication(s): *Forest Landowner*
Keyword(s): Forests and Forestry

CALIFORNIANS FOR POPULATION STABILIZATION (CAPS)
3440 Wilshire Blvd., #1006, Los Angeles, CA 90010
Phone: 213-387-6454; E-mail: caps@cap-s.org; Web Site: www.cap-s.org
Founded: 1986; Membership: 3,000
Scope: Statewide
Description: CAPS is a nonprofit membership organization dedicated to stabilizing population in California to protect and preserve the state's environment, ecology, and resources. CAPS believes overpopulation is the ultimate environmental threat. Activities include: public education, media campaigns, public policy research and advocacy, and grassroots organizing.
Contact(s):
Executive Director: DANIELLE ELLIOTT
Publication(s): *CAPS Data Reports; CAPS NEWSLETTERS; action alerts; brochures and fact sheets*
Keyword(s): Environmental Preservation, Land Preservation, Land Use Planning, Open Space, Population Growth

CAMP FIRE BOYS AND GIRLS
4601 Madison Ave., Kansas City, MO 64112
Phone: 816-756-1950; E-mail: info@campfire.org; Web Site: www.campfire.org
Founded: 1910; Membership: 629,000
Scope: National
Description: Open to boys and girls from birth to 21 years of age, without regard to race, creed, ethnic origin, sex, or income level. Provides a program of informal education that focuses on developing skills in interpersonal relationships, decision-making, leadership, creativity, citizenship, community service, and individual growth.
Contact(s):
Director of Program Services and Expansion: SANDI SHAW
National Executive Director and CEO: STEWART J. SMITH
National President: GRETCHEN L. BIENEMAN
Keyword(s): Air Quality and Pollution, Endangered and Threatened Species, Environmental and Conservation Education, Health and Nutrition, Outdoor Recreation

CAMP FIRE CLUB OF AMERICA, THE
230 Campfire Rd., Chappaqua, NY 10514
Phone: 914-941-0199; Fax: 914-923-0977
Founded: 1897
Scope: National
Description: Works to preserve forests and woodland; to protect and conserve the wildlife of our country; and to sponsor and support all reasonable measures to the end that present and future generations may continue to enjoy advantages and benefits of life outdoors.
Contact(s):
President: SCOTT T. SUTTON
Chairman of Committee on Conservation of Forests and Wildlife: LEONARD J. VALLENDER
Deputy Chairman of Committee on Conservation of Forests and Wildlife: EUGENE McCARDLE
Editor: STEVE BURNETT
Secretary of Committee on Conservation of Forests and Wildlife: THOMAS F. QUIRK
Publication(s): *Backlog, The*
Keyword(s): Forests and Forestry, Hunting, Sport Fishing, Wildlife and Wildlife Habitat, Wildlife Management

CAMP FIRE CONSERVATION FUND
230 Camp Fire Rd., Chappaqua, NY 10514
Phone: 914-941-9681
Founded: 1977
Scope: National
Description: A tax-exempt membership organization, dedicated to the preservation of wildlife and its habitat to coordinate the efforts of sportsmen's and conservation organizations; to inform the general public and governmental agencies with regard to intelligent use of our natural resources; and to support and promote conservation research.
Contact(s):
President: GEORGE R. LAMB
Secretary: HENRY F. AYRES JR.
Treasurer: MOTTELL D. PEEK
Keyword(s): Endangered and Threatened Species, Environmental and Conservation Education, Scholarships and Grants, Wildlife and Wildlife Habitat, Wildlife Management

CAMPAIGN FOR A PROSPEROUS GEORGIA
1083 Austin Ave., NE, Atlanta, GA 30307
Phone: 404-659-5675; Fax: 404-659-5676
Founded: 1983; Membership: 300
Scope: Statewide
Description: CPG is a nonprofit statewide organization protects the environment and improves the economy by changing the way energy is produced and consumed in Georgia through public education and advocacy.
Contact(s):
President: CAROL ANN DALTON
Vice President: NA`TAKI OSBORNE
Secretary: SUSAN ABRAMSON

Treasurer: MIKI DAVIS
Publication(s): *Plugging In; technical reports*
Keyword(s): Air Quality and Pollution, Energy, Sustainable Development

CANADA-UNITED STATES ENVIRONMENTAL COUNCIL (United States Office)
1101 14th St., NW, Suite 1400, Washington, DC 20005
Phone: 202-682-9400/243; Fax: 202-682-1331
Founded: 1974
Scope: International
Description: Non-governmental organization sponsored by Canadian and American conservation and environmental groups. Established to facilitate interchange of information and cooperative action on questions of concern in the two nations.
Contact(s):
Coordinating Committee Co-Chairman: JAMES G. DEANE, Defenders of Wildlife, 1101 14th St. NW, Suite 1400, Washington, DC 20005; Phone: 202-682-9400/ext.243; Fax: 202-682-1334
Coordinating Committee Co-Chairman: JULIE GELFAND, Canadian Nature Federation, Suite 606, 1 Nicholas St., Ottawa, Ontario K1N 7B7 Canada; Phone: 613-562-3447; Fax: 613-562-3371
Keyword(s): Air Quality and Pollution, Endangered and Threatened Species, Public Lands, Wildlife and Wildlife Habitat, Wildlife Management

CANADIAN ARCTIC RESOURCES COMMITTEE, INC.
7 Hinton Ave. N., Suite 200, Ottawa, Ontario K1Y 4P1 Canada
Phone: 613-759-4284; Fax: 613-722-3318
Founded: 1971
Scope: National
Description: To ensure that important social, environmental, and economic ramifications of northern development are studied and analyzed before major decisions relating to northern Canada are made; to exchange information and viewpoints among the public, government, and industry; to develop better perspectives on options available; and to inform the public.
Contact(s):
Executive Director: JOHN PATRICK CRUMP
Chairperson: ALEXANDER HUNTER
Publication(s): *Northern Perspectives Member's Update; list of books on request.*
Keyword(s): Arctic, Urban and Rural Development

CANADIAN COOPERATIVE WILDLIFE HEALTH CENTRE
Dept. of Veterinary Pathology, WCVM, Univ. of Saskatchewan, 52 Campus Dr., Saskatoon, Saskatchewan S7N 5B4 Canada
Phone: 306-966-5099/800-567-2033; Fax: 306-966-7439; E-mail: ccwhc@sask.usask.ca
Founded: 1992
Scope: National
Description: The Canadian Cooperative Wildlife Health Centre is a national organization that provides diagnosis of disease, investigation of disease outbreaks, information, education, and consultation to wildlife managers, veterinarians, and members of the public on matters pertaining to the health of free-living wild animals in Canada.
Contact(s):
Co-Director: G. A. WOBESER; Phone: 306-966-7310
Co-Director: F. A. LEIGHTON; Phone: 306-966-7281
Contact for Atlantic Region: DR. PIERRE-YVES DAOUST; Phone: 902-566-0667
Contact for Ontario Region: DR. I. BARKER; Phone: 519-823-8800/4616
Contact for Quebec Region: DR. DANIEL MARTINEAU; Phone: 514-773-8521
Contact for West and North Region: DR. TRENT BOLLINGER; Phone: 306-966-5099
Publication(s): *Wildlife Health Centre Newsletter; Bulletin du Centre de la Sante de la Faune; Wildlife Disease Investigation Manual; Directory of Wildlife Health Expertise*
Keyword(s): Birds, Mammals, Reptiles and Amphibians, Research, Wildlife Disease

CANADIAN ENVIRONMENTAL LAW ASSOCIATION
517 College St., Suite 401, Toronto, Ontario M6G 4A2 Canada
Phone: 416-960-2284; Fax: 416-960-9392; E-mail: cela@web.net; Web Site: www.web.net/cela
Founded: 1970
Scope: National
Description: Nonprofit, independent, public-interest legal group formed to use current environmental laws to protect the environment, and to promote better environmental legislation throughout Canada.
Contact(s):
Executive Director: PAUL MULDOON
Communications Coordinator: DAVID MCLARNMCLAREN
Coordinator: SARAH MILLER
Counsel: THERESA MCLENAGHAN
Counsel: RAMANI NADARAJAH
Counsel: RICHARD LINDGREN
Director of International Programs: MICHELLE SWENARCHUK
Librarian: LISA MCSHANE
Researcher: KATHY COOPER
Publication(s): *Newsletter; Intervenor, The*
Keyword(s): Environmental Law

CANADIAN FEDERATION OF HUMANE SOCIETIES
30 Concourse Gate, Suite 102, Nepean, Ontario K2E 7V7 Canada
Phone: 613-224-8072; Fax: 613-723-0252; E-mail: cfhs@storm.ca; Web Site: www.cfhs.ca
Founded: 1957; Membership: 45
Scope: National
Description: CFHS is a national body comprised of animal welfare organizations and individuals whose purpose is to promote compassion and humane treatment for all animals.
Contact(s):
President: J. JOY RIPLEY
Executive Director: FRANCES RODENBURG
Editor: FRANCES RODENBURG
Editor: STEPHANIE BROWN
Publication(s): *Caring for Animals; Animal Welfare in Focus; The Humane Educator*
Keyword(s): Agriculture, Endangered and Threatened Species, Fisheries, Marine Mammals, Trapping, Wildlife and Wildlife Habitat, Wildlife Management, Animal Welfare

CANADIAN FORESTRY ASSOCIATION
185 Somerset St., W., Suite 203, Ottawa, Ontario K2P 0J2 Canada
Phone: 613-232-1815; Fax: 613-232-4210; E-mail: cfa@cyberus.ca
Founded: 1900
Scope: National
Description: The Canadian Forestry Association is a federation of self-governing Provincial Forestry Associations across Canada. It is non-governmental and non-industrial. Its purpose is to develop public understanding and cooperation in the wise use, conservation, and sustainable development of Canada's forests and related resources of land, water, and wildlife.
Contact(s):
President: SUSAN GESNER
Immediate Past President: IVAN BALENOVIC
Vice President: BARRY WAITO
Publication(s): *Forest Forum; Proceedings of National Forest Congress 1992; National Forest Education Resources Catalogue; Proceedings: Canadian Urban Forests Conference*
Keyword(s): Forests and Forestry

CANADIAN INSTITUTE FOR ENVIRONMENTAL LAW AND POLICY (CIELAP)
517 College St., Suite 400, Toronto, Ontario M6G 4A2 Canada
Phone: 416-923-3529; Fax: 416-923-5949
Founded: 1970

NON-GOVERNMENTAL ORGANIZATIONS - C

Scope: National
Description: CIELAP is an independent, not-for-profit research and education institute providing environmental law and policy analysis. CIELAP provides leadership in the development of environmental law and policy which promotes the public interest and the principles of sustainability, including the protection of the health and well-being of present and future generations, and of the natural environment.
Contact(s):
President: DAVID POWELL
Executive Director: ANNE MITCHELL
Secretary and Treasurer: MURRAY KLIPPENSTEIN
Publication(s): *Environment on Trial: A Guide to Ontario Environmental Law and Policy; A Carbon Dioxide Strategy for Ontario: A Discussion paper; Ontario's Environment and the "Common Sense Revolution"; Hazardous Waste Management in Ontario: A Report and Recommendation; Electricity Competition and Clean Air*
Keyword(s): Environmental Law

CANADIAN INSTITUTE OF FORESTRY/INSTITUT FORESTIER DU CANADA
151 Slater St., Suite 606, Ottawa, Ontario K1P 5H3 Canada
Phone: 613-234-2242; Fax: 613-234-6181
Founded: 1908; **Membership:** 2,400
Scope: National
Description: Our mission is to advance the stewardship of Canada's forest resources through leadership, professional competence and public awareness. Our membership includes foresters, forest technicians, academics, scientists and others with a professional interest in Forestry. CIF/IFC represents the largest professional voice for forestry in Canada.
Contact(s):
President: BRUCE FERGUSON, 1218 Royal Drive, Peterborough, ON K9H 6R4 Canada; Phone: 705-755-3209; Fax: 705-755-3292
Executive Director: ROXANNE M. COMEAU, 151 Slater St., Suite 606, Ottawa, Ontario K1P 5H3 Canada; Phone: 613-234-2242; Fax: 613-234-6181; E-mail: cif@cif-ifc.org
Past President: EVELYNN WRANGLER, Alberta Environmental Protection, Lands & Forest Service, 9th floor, 9920-108 St., Edmonton, AB T5K 2M4 Canada; Phone: 780-422-4599; Fax: 780-427-0085; E-mail: evelynne.wrangler@gov.ab.ca
Publication(s): *The Forestry Chronicle*
Keyword(s): Forests and Forestry, Professional Organization

CANADIAN NATIONAL SPORTSMEN'S SHOWS
703 Evans Ave., Suite 202, Toronto, Ontario M9C 5E9 Canada
Phone: 416-695-0311; Fax: 416-695-0381
Founded: 1948
Scope: National
Description: A national corporation presenting outdoor shows and events. Products relate to fishing, hiking, camping, boating, skiing, and the consumer shows are produced from Vancouver to Quebec City. All net proceeds are distributed to projects that encourage Canadians to appreciate, enjoy, and protect Canada's outdoor heritage.
Contact(s):
Chairman: WALTER G. OSTER
Executive **Keyword(s):** Outdoor Recreation

CANADIAN NATURE FEDERATION
1 Nicholas St., Suite 520, Ottawa, Ontario K1N 7B7 Canada
Phone: 613-562-3447; Fax: 613-562-3371
Founded: 1971
Scope: Statewide
Description: Canada's national naturalists' organization promotes protection of nature, its diversity and the processes that sustain it. The Federation was formed from the Canadian Audubon Society, the CNF represents over 150 affiliated conservation groups and 40,000 individual supporters across the country.
Contact(s):
President: CLIFF WALLIS
Executive Director: JULIE GELFAND; Phone: 613-562-3447
Director of Conservation Programs: CAROLINE SCHULTZ
Editor: BARBARA STEVENSON
Publication(s): *Nature Canada Magazine; Nature Alert*

CANADIAN PARKS AND WILDERNESS SOCIETY
880 Wellington St., Suite 506, Ottawa, Ontario K1R 6K7 Canada
Phone: 613-569-7226; Fax: 613-569-7098; E-mail: info@cpaws.org; Web Site: www.cpaws.org
Founded: 1963
Scope: National
Description: A national, nonprofit advocacy organization dedicated to the protection of wilderness areas and the preservation and proper stewardship of Canada's national and provincial parks.
Contact(s):
President: DAVID THOMSON
Executive Director: MARY GRANSKOU
Manager of Membership Services: CLAYTON FORREST
Publication(s): *Wilderness Activist, The*
Keyword(s): National Parks, Wilderness

CANADIAN SOCIETY OF ENVIRONMENTAL BIOLOGISTS
P.O. Box 962, Station F, Toronto, Ontario M4Y 2N9 Canada
Founded: 1959
Scope: National
Description: A Canada-wide society of environmental biologists whose primary goals are: the conservation of the natural resources of Canada; the prudent management of these resources so as to minimize adverse environmental effects; the interchange of ideas among environmental biologists; and maintaining high professional standards in education, research, and management related to natural resources and the environment.
Contact(s):
President: SEAN SHARPE
Publication(s): *Canadian Society of Environmental Biologists Newsletter*
Keyword(s): Biology, Professional Organization

CANADIAN WILDLIFE FEDERATION
2740 Queensview Dr., Ottawa, Ontario K2B 1A2 Canada
Phone: 613-721-2286; Fax: 613-721-2902
Founded: 1961; **Membership:** 250,000
Scope: National
Description: To foster understanding of natural processes so that people may live in harmony with the land and its resources for the long-term benefit and enrichment of society; to maintain a substantial program of information and education based on ecological principles; and to conduct or sponsor research and scientific investigation.
Contact(s):
President: YVES JEAN
Secretary: PAT DOYLE
Treasurer: NICHOLAS LAURIN
1st Vice President: NESTOR ROMANIUK
2nd Vice President: DERREK STANLEY
3rd Vice President: BOB BARTON
Executive Vice President: COLIN MAXWELL
Past President: CARL SHIER
Publication(s): *Wildlife Update; Canadian Wildlife; Wild Magazine; Your Big Backyard; Biosphere; You Can Do It*

CANVASBACK SOCIETY
P.O. Box 101, Gates Mills, OH 44040
Founded: 1975
Scope: National
Description: A nonprofit, tax-exempt organization established to conserve, restore, and promote the increase of the canvasback species of duck on the North American continent.
Contact(s):
Chairman of the Board: KEITH C. RUSSELL
President and Treasurer: OAKLEY V. ANDREWS; Phone: 216-621-0200
Keyword(s): Renewable Resources, Water Pollution Management, Water Resources, Waterfowl, Wetlands

CARIBBEAN CONSERVATION CORPORATION
P.O. Box 2866, Gainesville, FL 32602
Phone: 904-373-6441; Fax: 904-375-2449
Scope: International
Description: A nonprofit international membership organization founded in 1959 to support research and conservation of marine turtles in the Caribbean and throughout the world. In addition to conservation activities, it operates a research station at Tortuguero, Costa Rica--the site of the largest green turtle nesting colony in the Caribbean Sea--and maintains a semi-natural impoundment for sea turtles on Great Inagua Island in the Bahamas.
Contact(s):
President: ANTHONY D. KNERR, 891 Park Ave., New York, NY 10021
Secretary: CAROLINE P. MAYNARD, 219 Hudson St., Pelham Manor, NY 10803
Executive Director: DAVID CARR
Chairman of the Board of Directors: L. CLAY, 24 Federal St., Boston, MA 02110
Editor: SUSAN MARYNOWSKI
Publication(s): *Velador*

CARIBBEAN NATURAL RESOURCES INSTITUTE
St. Lucia Office, P.O. Box VF 383 New Dock Rd., Vieux Fort, St. Lucia West Indies
Phone: 758-454-6060; Fax: 758-454-5188; E-mail: canari@candw.lc
Founded: 1986
Scope: National
Description: To create avenues for the equitable participation and effective collaboration of Caribbean communities and institutions in managing the use of natural resources critical to development.
Contact(s):
Executive Director: YVES RENARD
Board of Directors Chair: DR. CAROL JAMES
Publication(s): *Caribbean Moss Bulletin; Community and the Environment: Lessons from the Caribbean; Canari Guidelines Series*
Keyword(s): Coral Reefs, Mangrove Habitats, Rural Development, Sustainable Development, Training, Forestry

CAROLINA BIRD CLUB, INC.
P.O. Box 29555, Raleigh, NC 27626-0555
Founded: 1937; Membership: 1,100
Scope: Statewide
Description: A nonprofit, educational ornithological organization to promote bird study and conservation. Affiliated local chapters.
Contact(s):
President: LEN PARDUE, 16th Circle, Asheville, NC 28801
Editor: CLYDE SMITH JR., 2615 Wells Ave., Raleigh, NC 27608; Phone: 919-781-2637
Editor: BOB WOOD, 2421 Owl Circle, West Columbia, NC 29169
Headquarters Secretary: TULLIE HOYLE JOHNSON, Raleigh, NC 27626; Phone: 919-733-7450
Publication(s): *Chat, The; CBC Newsletter*
Keyword(s): Birds

CARRYING CAPACITY NETWORK
2000 P St., NW, Suite 240, Washington, DC 20036-5915
Phone: 202-296-4548; Fax: 202-296-4609; E-mail: ccn@us.net; Web Site: www.carryingcapacity.org
Founded: 1989; Membership: 20,000
Scope: National
Description: CCN is a nonprofit network which mobilizes many diverse individuals and groups to meet the critical challenges facing our nation with solid information and analysis, effective advocacy tools, and targeted solutions. CCN's action-oriented initiatives focus on achieving national revitalization, population stabilization, immigration limitation, resource conservation, and economic sustainability.
Contact(s):
President of the Board: DAVID F. DURHAM
Vice President: VIRGINIA ABERNETHY
Associate Director: KATHLEEN MCNEILLY
Secretary and Treasurer: K. R. HAMMOND
Publication(s): *Network Bulletin; FOCUS*
Keyword(s): Agriculture, Environment, Population Growth, Renewable Resources, Sustainable Development, Wilderness

CASCADIA RESEARCH
218 1/2 W. 4th Ave., Olympia, WA 98501
Phone: 206-943-7325
Founded: 1979
Scope: National
Description: A nonprofit, tax-exempt organization established to conduct scientific research and education related to marine mammals and birds. Primary funding for research projects comes from federal and state agencies and environmental groups.
Contact(s):
President: GRETCHEN STEIGER
Vice President: JAMES CUBBAGE
Secretary and Treasurer: JOHN CALAMBOKIDIS
Keyword(s): Birds, Endangered and Threatened Species, Marine Mammals, Nongame Wildlife, Water Pollution

CATSKILL CENTER FOR CONSERVATION AND DEVELOPMENT, INC., THE
Route 28, Arkville, NY 12406-0504
Phone: 914-586-2611; Fax: 914-586-3044; E-mail: cccd@catskill.net; Web Site: www.catskillcenter.org
Founded: 1969; Membership: 4,000
Scope: Statewide
Description: The Catskill Center is a non-for-profit membership organization concerned with increasing public awareness of and involvement with issues affecting human communities and the natural environment of the Catskill Mountain Region. Its activities emphasize environmental education and regional planning advocacy, as well as development and support of programs relating to historic preservation, sustainable economic development and regional arts and culture in the Catskill.
Contact(s):
President: GEDDY SVEIKAUSKAS
Executive Director: DARLENE DOWNING
Secretary: H. CLAUDE SHOSTAL
Treasurer: HELEN K. CHASE
Publication(s): *Catskill Center News; Successful Catskill Communities; Catskill Environmental Monograph; Summary Guide to the Terms of the Watershed Agreement*
Keyword(s): Alternative Agriculture, Culture, Environmental and Conservation Education, Land Protection, Natural Resource Conservation, Rural Development, Sustainable Development

CATSKILL FOREST ASSOCIATION
P.O. Box 336, Arkville, NY 12406
Phone: 914-586-3054; Fax: 914-586-4071
Founded: 1982; Membership: 275
Scope: Local
Description: Advocates of quality forest management practices to improve the health of the forest and prevent threats to the forest ecosystem, the Catskill Forest Association is an independent nonprofit regional organization that supports forest conservation efforts in the Catskill Mountains through the promotion of forest stewardship by landowners, foresters, timber harvesters, and the general public.
Contact(s):
President: JERRY GOTSCH
Vice President: DOUGLAS MURPHY
Secretary and Treasurer: ART ROTMAN
Executive Director: RICHARD D. SLOMAN
Publication(s): *CFA News*
Keyword(s): Biodiversity, Environmental and Conservation Education, Forests and Forestry, Sustainable Development, Sustainable Ecosystems

CAVE RESEARCH FOUNDATION
P.O. Box 126, Loiusville, KY 40201-0126
Phone: 502-637-2030
Founded: 1957

NON-GOVERNMENTAL ORGANIZATIONS - C

Scope: National
Description: The Foundation is a nonprofit organization that supports and promotes research, interpretation, and conservation activities in caves and karst areas. Permanent field operations are maintained within Mammoth Cave National Park, Carlsbad Caverns National Park, Sequoia and Kings Canyon National Parks, and Lava Beds National Monument. Approximately 800 joint-venturers participate in program.
Contact(s):
President: PHILIP DIBLASI; Phone: 502-852-6724; Fax: 502-852-6725; E-mail: pjdibl01@home.louisville.edu
Secretary: JOHN TINSLEY III; Phone: 415-327-2368
Treasurer: PAUL CANNALEY; Phone: 317-862-5618
Editor: RICHARD ZOPF, 1112 Xenia Ave., Yellow Springs, OH 45378-1101
Editor: PATRICIA KAMBESIS, 3473 Regalwoods Dr., Doraville, GA 30340
Publication(s): *Annual Report; CRF Newsletter; Cave* **Keyword(s):** Environmental Preservation, Geology, Historic Preservation, Public Lands, Scholarships and Grants

CENTER FOR BIOLOGICAL DIVERSITY
P.O. Box 710, Tuscon, AZ 85702-0710
Phone: 520-623-5252; Fax: 520-623-9797; E-mail: swcbd@sw-center.org; Web Site: www.sw-center.org
Founded: 1989; *Membership:* 5,200
Scope: Regional
Description: The Southwest Center for Biological Diversity uses a combination of scientific research, public education, and strategic litigation to defend the forests, rivers and deserts of western North America.
Contact(s):
Conservation Chair: DR. ROBIN SILVER; Phone: 602-246-4170; Fax: 602-249-2576; E-mail: rsilver@sw-center.org
President and Executive Director: KIERAN SUCKLING; E-mail: ksuckling@sw-center.org
Publication(s): *Action Alerts of the SW Center For Biologival Diversity*
Keyword(s): Biodiversity, Deserts, Endangered and Threatened Species, Forest Management, Mining, Public Lands, Watersheds

CENTER FOR CHESAPEAKE COMMUNITIES
209 West St., Suite 201, Annapolis, MD 21401
Phone: 410-267-8595; Fax: 410-267-8597; E-mail: shall@chesapeakecommunities.org; Web Site: www.chesapeakecommunities.org
Founded: 1997
Scope: Regional
Description: A nonprofit, independent organization dedicated to assisting local governments in the Chesapeake Bay watershed in their environmental restoration and protection initiatives.
Contact(s):
Executive Director: GARY C. ALLEN; E-mail: gallen@chesapeakecommunities.org
Keyword(s): Environment, Environmental and Conservation Education, Environmental Planning, Environmental Preservation, Environmental Protection, Land Management, Land Use Planning, Nonpoint Source Pollution, Sustainability

CENTER FOR ENVIRONMENT
1336 Bay Ave., Annapolis, DC 21403
Founded: 1985
Scope: National
Description: A nonprofit public interest organization dedicated to protecting the environment, enhancing the human ecology, and working to ensure the efficient use of natural resources. CE's secondary mission is to provide opportunities for blacks and other minorities to participate in the environmental movement. Major areas of concern are: Air quality and pollution, water resources and pollution, energy, renewable resources, toxic substances, Africa and Third World environment, land use, internships, and urban environment.
Contact(s):
Chairman: CHARLES STEPHENSON
President: NORRIS McDONALD; Phone: 202-879-3183
Treasurer: JANNIE PITTMAN
Publication(s): *African American Environmentalist; A complete list of (CE)2's publications is available upon request.*

CENTER FOR ENVIRONMENTAL EDUCATION
c/o Antioch New England, 40 Avon St., Keene, NY 03431
Phone: 603-355-3251; Fax: 603-357-0781; E-mail: cee@antiochne.edu; Web Site: www.cee-ane.org
Founded: 1989; *Membership:* 5,000
Scope: National
Description: A nonprofit environmental education resource center housing one of the nation's most comprehensive collections of environmental education materials. The library has over 10,000 materials--books, videos, curricula and resources that can be accessed in person, by phone, fax, or through the Web site.
Contact(s):
Co-Executive Director: CINDY THOMASHOW
Co-Executive Director: DAVID SOBEL
Founder: JAYNI CHASE
Publication(s): *Grapevine Newsletter; Blueprint for a Green School*
Keyword(s): Environmental and Conservation Education, Internships, Youth Organizations

CENTER FOR ENVIRONMENTAL INFORMATION
55 St. Paul St., Rochester, NY 14604-1314
Phone: 716-262-2870; Fax: 716-262-4156; Web Site: www.rochesterenvironment.org
Founded: 1974
Scope: National
Description: Provides on-call reference and referral and current awareness and educational services to scientists, educators, government agency staff, policymakers, business and industry managers and interested citizens. Sponsors conferences and seminars.
Contact(s):
Executive Director: WILLIAM R. WAGNER
Editor: DR. FREDERICK M. O'HARA JR., P.O. Box 4273, Oak Ridge, TN 37831; Phone: 423-482-1447
Publication(s): *Global Climate Change Digest; Proceedings of Annual Conferences;*
Keyword(s): Acid Rain, Communications, Energy, Environmental and Conservation Education, Greenhouse Effect/Global Warming

CENTER FOR ENVIRONMENTAL PHILOSOPHY
EESAT Bldg., Rm. 370, Corner of Ave. C and Mulberry, University of North Texas, P.O. Box 310980, Denton, TX 76203-0980
Phone: 940-565-2727; Fax: 940-565-4439; E-mail: ee@unt.edu; Web Site: www.cep.unt.edu
Founded: 1980
Scope: National
Description: A nonprofit, tax-deductible organization. The Center promotes research and instruction in environmental ethics and its application in environmental policy and decision-making. The Center works with governmental and environmental organizations on conferences, workshops, and other educational projects.
Contact(s):
Vice President: J. BAIRD CALLICOTT, Dept. of Philosophy, Univ. of North TX, P.O. Box 310920, Denton, TX 76203-0920; Phone: 940-565-2255; Fax: 940-565-4448; E-mail: callicott@unt.edu
Executive Director: JAN DICKSON, Center for Environmental Philosophy, Univ. of North TX, P.O. Box 310980, Denton, TX 76203-0980; Phone: 940-565-2727; Fax: 940-565-4439; E-mail: jdickson@unt.edu
President, Editor and Publisher: EUGENE C. HARGROVE, Center for Environmental Philosophy, Univ. of North TX, P.O. Box 310980, Denton, TX 76203-0980; Phone: 940-565-2727; Fax: 940-565-4439; E-mail: hargrove@unt.edu
Secretary and Treasurer: MAX OELSCHLAEGER, Dept. Humanities, Arts & Religion, Northern Arizona, P.O. Box 6031,

Flagstaff, AZ 86011-6031; Phone: 520-523-0389; E-mail: Max.Oelschlaeger@Nau.edu
Publication(s): *Environmental Ethics: An Interdisciplinary Journal Dedicated to the Philosophical Aspects of Environmental Problems*
Keyword(s): Environmental Ethics, Wilderness

CENTER FOR ENVIRONMENTAL STUDY
Grand Rapids Community College, 143 Bostwick NE, Grand Rapids, MI 49503
Phone: 616-234-3935; Fax: 616-234-3936; E-mail: ces1@iserv.net; Web Site: www.cesmi.org/
Founded: 1969
Scope: National
Description: The Center for Environmental Study, a 501C (3) organization, has served its community as an independent, science-based environmental education and research authority. It provides curricula and conducts professional development workshops on a variety of subjects ranging from water and air quality to tropical forest and Great Lakes issues.
Contact(s):
Executive Director: DR. RICK SULLIVAN
Board Chair: JOHN K. MARTIN
Founder: PETER M. WEGE
Publication(s): *Mahogany: A Research Bibliography of Swietenia; Field Guide to Ecosystems and Habitats of the Great Lakes Region (in prep.); The Great Lakes - An Interactive CD-ROM Game for grade 3--adult*
Keyword(s): Air Quality and Pollution, Communications, Ecology, Environmental and Conservation Education, Watersheds, Wildlife and Wildlife Habitat, Youth Organizations

CENTER FOR HEALTH, ENVIRONMENT, AND JUSTICE
P.O. Box 6806, Falls Church, VA 22040-6806
Phone: 703-237-2249; Fax: 703-237-8389; E-mail: CCHW@essential.org; Web Site: www.essential.org/cchw or www.hoharm.org
Founded: 1981
Scope: National
Description: CHEJ provides assistance to more than 8,000 grassroots citizens groups fighting for environmental justice. CHEJ is a nonprofit organization dedicated to helping people nationwide by providing one-on-one assistance and information on how to organize politically, scientifically, and legally to prevent or clean up environmental disasters. Founded by Lois Marie Gibbs.
Contact(s):
Executive Director: LOIS MARIE GIBBS
Publication(s): *Everyone's Backyard; catalog of how-to guide books; Environmental Health Monthly; Dioxin Digest*
Keyword(s): Internships, People of Color in the Environment, Scholarships and Grants, Toxic Substances, Women in the Environment

CENTER FOR INDEPENDENT SOCIAL RESEARCH
Department of Environmental Sociology, 14 Vine, St. Petersburg 197002 Russia
Phone: 812-234-50-18; E-mail: centre@indepsocres.org
Founded: 1994; Membership: 45
Scope: International
Description: Environmental non-governmental management and accountability research collection of best sustainability practices in St. Petersburg region.
Contact(s):
Director: VICTOR VORONKOV
Publication(s): *Towards a Sustainable Future; Environmental Activism in Russia and the U.S.; Ecology of the Neva River: Ecological Movement in Russia*
Keyword(s): Sustainability

CENTER FOR INTERNATIONAL ENVIRONMENTAL LAW (CIEL)
1367 Connecticut Ave., NW, Suite 300, Washington, DC 20036-1860
Phone: 202-785-8700; Fax: 202-785-8701; E-mail: cielus@igc.apc.org; Web Site: www.econet.apc.org/ciel/
Founded: 1989
Scope: International
Description: The CIEL is a public interest environmental law organization founded to focus the energy and experience of the public interest environmental law movement on reforming international environmental law and institutions, and on forging stronger and more meaningful connection between the top down diplomatic approach of international law, and the bottom up participatory approach that has been the hallmark of the public interest environmental law movement.
Contact(s):
President: DURWOOD J. ZAELKE
Executive Director: DAVID B. HUNTER
Publication(s): *International Environmental Law and Policy; Biodiversity in the Seas: Implementing the Convention on Biological Diversity in Marine and Coastal Habitats; A Citizen's Guide to the World Bank Inspection Panel; Trade and the Environment: Law, Economics, and Policy; Carbon Conservation: Climate Change, Forests and the Clear Development Mechanism; a complete list of CIEL's publications is available upon request on CIEL's home page.*
Keyword(s): Biodiversity, Environmental and Conservation Education, Environmental Law, Greenhouse Effect/Global Warming, International Trade and Environment, International Environmental Law

CENTER FOR MARINE CONSERVATION
1725 DeSales St., NW, Suite 600, Washington, DC 20036
Phone: 202-429-5609; Fax: 202-872-0619; E-mail: cmc@dccmc.org; Web Site: www.cmc-ocean.org
Founded: 1972; Membership: 120,000
Scope: National
Description: A nonprofit, scientific organization dedicated to protecting marine wildlife and its habitats, and to conserving coastal and ocean resources. The center's programs are conducted in five major areas: Fisheries and Wildlife Conservation, Ecosystem Protection, Biodiversity Conservation, International Initiatives, Citizen Monitoring, and Outreach. Program efforts focus on research, policy analysis, education, and public information and involvement.
Contact(s):
President: ROGER E. McMANUS
Chairman of the Board: E.U. CURTIS BOHLEN
Director of Constituency Development: DAVID DIXON
Director of Ecosystems Programs: JACK SOBEL
Director of the Chesapeake Region: SEBA SHEAVLEY, 1432 Great Neck Rd., Virginia Beach, VA 23454; Phone: 757-496-0920
Director of the Gulf Coast Region, (acting): KIM DAVIS, One Beach Dr. SE, #304, St. Petersburg, FL 33701; Phone: 727-895-2188
Director of the Pacific Coast Region: WARNER CHABOT, 580 Market St., Suite 550, San Francisco, CA 94104; Phone: 415-391-6204
Director of the Alaska Region: KRIS BALLIET, 425 G. St., Anchorage, AK ; Phone: 907-258-9922
Director of Citizen Outreach and Monitoring Program: EMILY MORGAN
Director of Marine Conservation Wildlife Program: NINA YOUNG
Vice-President for Communications and Marketing, (acting): ROSE BIERCE
Vice-President for Development: DAVID KNIGHT
Vice-President for Finance and Administration: PETER JONES
Vice-President for Marine Wildlife Conservation and General Counsel: WILLIAM ROBERT IRVIN
Publication(s): *Marine Conservation News; Coastal Connection; International Coastal Cleanup Report; list of additional publications on request.*
Keyword(s): Biodiversity, Conservation of Protected Areas, Coral Reefs, Ecology, Endangered and Threatened Species, Environmental and Conservation Education, Fisheries, International Conservation, Marine Mammals, Pollution Prevention, Sustainable Ecosystems, Water Pollution, Watersheds, Wildlife Management, Cleanup

CENTER FOR PLANT CONSERVATION
P.O. Box 299, St. Louis, MO 63166

NON-GOVERNMENTAL ORGANIZATIONS - C

Phone: 314-577-9450; Fax: 314-577-9465; E-mail: cpc@mobot.org; Web Site: www.mobot.org/cpc
Scope: National
Description: A national network of 28 botanical gardens and arboreta dedicated to the conservation and study of rare and endangered U.S. plants. The Center establishes conservation collections of endangered species in regional gardens and seed banks as a resource for conservation and research efforts: The National Collection of Endangered Plants.
Contact(s):
Executive Director: DR. BRIEN A. MEILLEUR
Publication(s): *Plant Conservation (newsletter); Plant Conservation Directory; Restoring Diversity; Guidelines for the Manangent of Orthodox Seeds, Plants in Peril*
Keyword(s): Biodiversity, Botanical Gardens, Endangered and Threatened Species, Environment, Environmental and Conservation Education, Environmental Preservation, Flowers, Plants, and Trees

CENTER FOR RESOURCE ECONOMICS
Island Press, 1718 Connecticut Ave., NW, Suite 300, Washington, DC 20009
Phone: 202-232-7933; E-mail: info@islandpress.org
Founded: 1978
Scope: National
Description: The Center for Resource Economics is a nonprofit organization that develops, publishes, markets and disseminates books and other information products essential for solving local and global environmental problems and planning for the future.
Contact(s):
President and Publisher: CHARLES SAVITT; Phone: 202-232-7933
VP of Finances and CFO: CHERI LEVY; Phone: 202-232-7933
VP/Assoc. Publisher: DAN SAYRE; Phone: 202-232-7933
Editor, Shearwater Books: JONATHON COBB; Phone: 914-631-7088
Marketing Director: SAMUEL DORRANCE; Phone: 202-232-7933
Publication(s): *Island Press Book Distribution Center: Box 7, Covelo, CA 954281-800-828-1302; 707-983-6432; FAX: 707-983-6414*
Keyword(s): Biodiversity, Energy, Sustainable Development, Sustainable Ecosystems, Wetlands

CENTER FOR RESOURCEFUL BUILDING TECHNOLOGY
P.O. Box 100, Missoula, MT 59806
Phone: 406-549-7678; Fax: 406-549-4100; E-mail: crbt@montana.com; Web Site: www.montana.com/crbt
Founded: 1990
Scope: National
Description: The Center for Resourceful Building Technology (CRBT) is a non-profit corporation dedicated to promoting environmentally responsible practices in construction. Its mission is to serve as both catalyst and facilitator in encouraging building technologies that realize a sustainable and efficient use of resources.
Contact(s):
Chair: TIM MELLGREN, 151 Fairway Dr., Missoula, MT 59801; Phone: 406-728-6711
Founder: STEVE LOKEN, 2605 Lincoln Hills Dr., Missoula, MT 59802; Phone: 406-728-1412
Research Director: TRACY MUMMA
Technical Director: DALE McCORMICK
Publication(s): *Guide to Resource Efficient Building Elements; Recraft 90 Handbook; Affordable Resource Efficiency: Reducing Construction and Demolition Waste; Building Our Children's Future*
Keyword(s): Environmental and Conservation Education, Environmental Preservation, Forests and Forestry, Renewable Resources, Sustainable Development

CENTER FOR SCIENCE IN THE PUBLIC INTEREST
1875 Connecticut Ave., NW, Suite 300, Washington, DC 20009
Phone: 202-332-9110; Fax: 202-265-4954; E-mail: cspi@cspinet.org; Web Site: www.cspinet.org
Founded: 1971; Membership: 1,000,000
Scope: National
Description: National consumer advocacy organization that focuses on health, nutrition, and alcohol issues. CSPI informs the public of its findings through a variety of publications, press releases, speeches, media appearances, and initiates legal actions. The Center has an intern program throughout the year.
Contact(s):
Executive Director: DR. MICHAEL F. JACOBSON
Publication(s): *Nutrition Action Healthletter; reports, posters, books, and video*
Keyword(s): Agriculture, Health and Nutrition, Internships, Pesticides, Toxicology

CENTER FOR THE STUDY OF TROPICAL BIRDS, INC. (Administrative Office)
218 Conway, San Antonio, TX 78209-1716
Phone: 210-828-5306/1-800-858-CSTB; Fax: 210-828-9732; E-mail: CSTBInc1@aol.com
Founded: 1987
Scope: International
Description: A nonprofit organization devoted to the conservation of tropical bird life through cooperative programs of scientific research, conservation and education. Current projects include raising palms to save cracids in El Cielo Biosphere Reserve in Tamaulipas, Mexico; Development of avi-tourism in Zapata, Texas and release of endangered Red Siskins on the Bocas Islands of Trinidad (www.lfpt.rwthaachen.de/~ckr/carduelan/red-trini.html), in addition to field studies on Singing Quail, Bearded Wood partridges and other birds along the Rio Grande in Texas and NE Mexico.
Contact(s):
Treasurer: MICHAEL GARTSIDE
Director: JACK CLINTON EITNIEAR
Mexico Program Coordinator: ALVARO ARAGON TAPIA
Keyword(s): Birds, Endangered and Threatened Species, Grants, International Conservation, Nongame Wildlife, Raptors, Research, Wildlife and Wildlife Habitat, Wildlife Management

CENTER FOR THE STUDY OF TROPICAL BIRDS, INC. (Field Office)
22 Cesar Lopez De Lara Y Carranza No. 553, Fovissste, Ciudad Victoria C.P. 87020 Mexico
Phone: 13-16-09-52
Scope: International

CENTER FOR WATERSHED PROTECTION
8391 Main St., Ellicott, MD 21043
Phone: 410-461-8323; Fax: 410-461-8324; E-mail: mrrunoff@pipeline.com; Web Site: www.pipeline.coml~mrrunoff
Founded: 1992
Scope: National
Description: CWP is dedicated to new cooperative ways of protecting and restoring watersheds.
Contact(s):
Administrative Director: 10 HYE YEONG KWON
Executive Director: THOMAS R. SCHUELER
Principal Engineer: dc RICHARD A. CLAYTON
Publication(s): *Watershed Protection Techniques; Site Planning for Urban Stream Protection; Environmental Indicators to Assess Stormwater Control Programs and Practices*
Keyword(s): Environmental Planning, Land Use Planning, Urban Environment, Water Pollution Management, Watersheds

CENTER FOR WILDLIFE LAW
Institute of Public Law at University of New Mexico School of Law, 1117 Stanford NE, Albuquerque, NM 87131
Phone: 505-277-8695; Fax: 505-277-5483; Web Site: ipl.unm.edu/cwl
Founded: 1990
Scope: National
Description: Through projects, publications, conferences, and training programs, the Center provides wildlife law and policy analysis and other educational information to legal and non-legal communities. The Center also conducts a unique law-related wildlife education program. Staff have expertise in wildlife and

environmental law and policy, biology, education, geographic information systems, publishing.
Contact(s):
Director: RUTH S. MUSGRAVE
Publication(s): *Wildlife Law News Quarterly; Federal Wildlife Laws Handbook with Related Laws; State Wildlife Laws Handbook; Wild Friends: Kids Bringing People Together on Wildife Issues; The Status of Poaching in the U.S.; Wild News*

CENTRAL OHIO ANGLERS AND HUNTERS CLUB
P.O. Box 28224, Columbus, OH 43228
Scope: Statewide
Description: Promotion of conservation and conservation education in all their phases, with a particular reference to land, air, and water; to promote good fellowship and good citizenship; to inculcate regard for the rights of others and respect for the obedience to law; to support a safe and effective conservation program for and by the state and nation.
Contact(s):
President: DAN SWEET, 1460 Windham Rd., Columbus, OH 43220; Phone: 614-442-1244
Vice President: DOUG EAKINS, 767 Larri Ct., W. Jefferson, OH 43162; Phone: 614-879-7757
Treasurer: GREG HOLBEN, 372 Madison Dr., N., W. Jefferson, OH 43162; Phone: 614-879-5958
Secretary: JAMES STURGILL, 782 Bernese Ct., Reynoldsburg, OH 43068; Phone: 740-863-4481
Keyword(s): Conservation, Hunting, Sport Fishing

CENTRO de INFORMACION, INVESTIGACION y EDUCACION SOCIAL (CIIES)
RR-9, Buzon 1722, San Juan, PR 00926-9736
Phone: 787-292-0620; Fax: 787-760-0496
Founded: 1989
Scope: Statewide
Description: CIIES was founded as a part of Servicios Cientificos y Tecnicos, a nonprofit organization dealing with natural resources, environmental health, and safety issues. It provides services in the form of seminars, workshops, and a resource center to students, teachers, journalists, communities, and workers.
Contact(s):
Secretary: JOSE SEPULVEDA
Treasurer: MARIA VILCHES
Director: DR. NEFTALI GARCIA MARTINEZ
Keyword(s): Biodiversity, Environmental and Conservation Education, Environmental Justice, Habitat Conservation, Pollution Prevention

CETACEAN SOCIETY INTERNATIONAL
P.O. Box 953, Georgetown, CT 06829
Phone: 203-431-1606; Fax: 203-431-1606; E-mail: 71322.1637@compuserve.com; Web Site: elfi.com/csihome.html
Founded: 1974; Membership: 500
Scope: International
Description: CSI is dedicated to the preservation and protection of all cetaceans (whales, dolphins, and porpoises) and the marine environment on a global basis. CSI is an all-volunteer, nonprofit conservation education and research organization with representatives in over 21 countries.
Contact(s):
President: WILLIAM W. ROSSITER, 21 Laurel Hill Rd., Ridgefield, CT 06877; Phone: 203-544-8902; E-mail: william_rossiter@compuserve.com
Vice President: BARBARA KILPATRICK, 15 Wood Pond Rd., West Hartford, CT 06107; Phone: 860-561-0187
Secretary: MARTHA FITZGERALD, 120 Retreat Ave. C-3, Hartford, CT 06106; Phone: 860-246-3143
Treasurer: ROBERT VICTOR, 57 Crossroads Ln., Glastonbury, CT 06033; E-mail: rfvictor@juno.com
Director Emeritus: DR. ROBBINS BARSTOW, 190 Stillwold Dr., Wethersfield, CT 06109; Phone: 860-563-2565; E-mail: robbinsb@aol.com
Publication(s): *Whales Alive (newsletter); Meet the Great Ones (book, English and Spanish); Several education packages.*
Keyword(s): Endangered and Threatened Species, Environmental Protection, International Conservation, Marine Mammals, Research

CHARLES A. AND ANNE MORROW LINDBERGH FOUNDATION, THE
2150 Third Ave. N, Suite 310, Anoka, MN 55303
Phone: 612-576-1596; Fax: 612-576-1664; E-mail: lindbergh@lsd.net
Founded: 1977
Scope: National
Description: The Charles A. and Anne Morrow Lindbergh Foundation is a nonprofit organization, advancing Charles and Anne Morrow Lindbergh's vision of a balance between technological progress and environmental preservation by offering Lindbergh Grants to individuals for research and educational projects which will further this balance, presenting the Lindbergh Award for extraordinary contributions to the balance, and sponsoring other projects and programs. Associate membership information is available by writing the Foundation office.
Contact(s):
President: REEVE LINDBERGH
Vice President: CLARE HALLWARD
Vice President and Chairman of Award Selection and Lecture Committee: KRISTINA LINDBERGH
Secretary: JAMES W. LLOYD
Treasurer: CHARLES J. KELLY JR.
Executive Director: MARLENE WHITE
Chairperson of Grants Selection Committee: CLARE HALLWARD
Editor: KELLEY WELF
Publication(s): *Charles A. and Anne Morrow Lindbergh Foundation Newsletter, The*
Keyword(s): Agriculture, Environmental Preservation, Research Grants, Sustainable Development, Water Resources, Wildlife and Wildlife Habitat

CHELONIA INSTITUTE
P.O. Box 9174, Arlington, VA 22209
Phone: 703-516-2600
Founded: 1977
Scope: National
Description: A private operating foundation with ecological concerns focused primarily on the conservation of marine turtles. The Institute undertakes a broad range of programs including technical publications, land acquisition, and so on, and works cooperatively with other organizations.
Contact(s):
Assistant Director: MARY W. TRULAND
Director and Trustee: ROBERT W. TRULAND
Program Director: DR. PETER PRITCHARD

CHESAPEAKE BAY FOUNDATION, INC.
Headquarters, 162 Prince George St., Annapolis, MD 21401
Phone: 410-268-8816; Web Site: www.savethebay.cbf.org
Founded: 1966; Membership: 80,000
Scope: National
Description: A nonprofit membership organization established to promote the environmental protection and restoration of Chesapeake Bay and its full watershed. CBF operates programs in environmental education and environmental protection and restoration.
Contact(s):
Chairman: WAYNE A. MILLS
President: WILLIAM C. BAKER
Vice President for Education: DONALD R. BAUGH
Vice President for Public Affairs: MICHAEL SHULTZ
Vice President for Resource Protection and Restoration: MICHAEL HIRSHFIELD
Publication(s): *Save the Bay; Megalops; Grassroots* **Keyword(s):** Environmental and Conservation Education, Environmental Protection, Restoration, Watersheds

NON-GOVERNMENTAL ORGANIZATIONS - C

CHESAPEAKE BAY FOUNDATION, INC. (Maryland Office)
111 Annapolis St., Annapolis, MD 21401
Phone: 410-268-8833; Fax: 410-280-3513
Founded: 1967; Membership: 80,000
Scope: Statewide
Description: The Chesapeake Bay Foundation's Maryland office conducts activities of the foundation specific to the state of Maryland and operates field offices in southern Maryland and Delaware.
Contact(s):
Executive Director: THERESA PIERNO
Keyword(s): Aquatic Habitats, Environmental and Conservation Education, Environmental Justice, Land Use Planning, Renewable Resources

CHESAPEAKE BAY FOUNDATION, INC. (Pennsylvania Office)
The Old Waterworks Bldg., 614 N. Front St., Suite G, Harrisburg, PA 17101
Phone: 717-234-5550; Fax: 717-234-9632
Founded: 1966; Membership: 83,000
Scope: Statewide
Description: The Foundation conducts activities and programs specific to the Commonwealth of Pennsylvania.
Contact(s):
Executive Director: JOLENE CHINCHILLI
Publication(s): *Fresh Air; Recycling Roll Call; Council in Action; Environmentalists for Public Transit Newsletter*
Keyword(s): Air Quality and Pollution, Energy, Solid Waste, Transportation

CHESAPEAKE BAY FOUNDATION, INC. (Virginia Office)
1001 E. Main St., Heritage Bldg., Suite 710, Richmond, VA 23219
Phone: 804-780-1392; Fax: 804-648-4011
Founded: 1967
Scope: Statewide
Description: The Chesapeake Bay Foundation conducts activities of the foundation in the Commonwealth of Virginia and operates field offices in Norfolk and Tappahannock, Virginia.
Contact(s):
Assistant Director: ROY HOAGLAND
Executive Director: JOSEPH MAROON
Keyword(s): Birds, Environmental and Conservation Education, Environmental Protection, Nature Preservation, Water Quality

CHESAPEAKE FARMS
7319 Remington Dr., Chestertown, MD 21620
Phone: 410-778-8400
Founded: 1956
Scope: National
Description: Operated by Dupont Agricultural Products to demonstrate, research, and promote sustainable farming and wildlife management practices. Provides a forum for exploring agricultural issues and interactions between environmental and economic sustainability. Agricultural project conducted by coalition of Dupont, universities, government and private organizations. Wildlife research conducted through graduate fellows.
Contact(s):
Manager: MARK C. CONNER

CHESAPEAKE WILDLIFE HERITAGE (CWH)
P.O. Box 1745, Easton, MD 21601
Phone: 410-822-5100; Fax: 410-822-4016; E-mail: info@cheswildlife.org; Web Site: www.cheswildlife.org
Founded: 1980; Membership: 750
Scope: Regional
Description: A private, nonprofit conservation group working with private and public landowners to restore and protect wildlife habitat in the Chesapeake Bay watershed. CWH constructs and manages wetlands, warm season grass and wildflower meadows, nesting structures, marshes, and woodlands. CWH advises on and carries out sustainable farming techniques in order to benefit the Chesapeake Bay and its wildlife. CWH also conducts ecological research on plants and migratory birds.

Contact(s):
Board of Directors President: LARRY ALBRIGHT
Habitat Ecologist: MICHAEL ROBIN HAGGIE
Habitat Ecologist: JOHN E. GERBER
Secretary of Public Relations: DEBBIE COLLISON
Keyword(s): Wildlife and Wildlife Habitat

CHICAGO HERPETOLOGICAL SOCIETY
2060 N. Clark St., Chicago, IL 60614
Phone: 312-281-1800
Founded: 1966; Membership: 1,957
Scope: Statewide
Description: The Chicago Herpetological Society is a group of reptile and amphibian enthusiasts. Its goals are education, conservation, and the advancement of herpetology.
Contact(s):
President: STEVE SPITZER, 1939 W Lunt Ave., Chicago, IL 60626; Phone: 773-262-1847
Vice President: JACK SCHOENFELDER, c/o Ivy Tech College, 2401 Valley Dr., Valparaiso, IN 46383; Phone: 219-929-1525
Treasurer: GARY FOGEL, 4108 N. Damen Ave., Chicago, IL 60618; Phone: 312-935-6938
Publication(s): *Bulletin of the Chicago Herpetological* **Keyword(s):** Biology, Environmental and Conservation Education, Reptiles and Amphibians, Scholarships and Grants, Zoology

CHIHUAHUAN DESERT RESEARCH INSTITUTE
P.O. Box 905, Ft. Davis, TX 79734
Founded: 1974
Scope: National
Description: Nonprofit organization formed to promote human understanding and appreciation of the Chihuahuan Desert through scientific research and public education. Current studies include life history related studies, systematic zoology, systematic botany, desert ecology, anthropology, archeology, geology, and theoretical ecology.
Contact(s):
President: ROB DUNAGAN
Vice President: JAMES F. SCUDDAY
Secretary: THOMAS BRUNNER
Treasurer: LARRY BRYANT
Executive Director: DENNIS J. MILLER
Publication(s): *CDRI Contributions; Chihuahuan Desert Discovery, The; Chihuahaun Newsbriefs*
Keyword(s): Biology, Deserts, Endangered and Threatened Species, Geology, Natural History

CHINA REGION LAKES ALLIANCE
RR 1, Box 970, South China, ME 04358
Phone: 207-445-5021; Fax: 207-445-3208
Founded: 1994
Scope: Local
Description: To protect and improve water quality in 3 culturally eutrophic Maine lakes, (China Lake, Threemile Pond and Webber Pond) and to benefit our local economy through integrated watershed management.
Contact(s):
President: DANIEL J. DUBORD; Phone: 207-872-2743; Fax: 207-872-2962
Executive Director: REBECCA MANTHEY
Publication(s): *Walk for a Rainy Day: What You Can Do For Your Camp Road; Vegetative Buffer Strips; Starting a Local Youth Conservation Corps*
Keyword(s): Environmental and Conservation Education, Environmental Planning, Lakes, Pollution Prevention, Water Pollution, Water Quality, Water Resources, Watersheds

CHLORINE-FREE PAPER CONSORTIUM (CPC)
1411 Ellis Ave., Ashland, WI 54806
Phone: 715-682-1847; Fax: 715-682-1308; E-mail: mail@clfree.org; Web Site: www.clfree.org
Scope: National
Description: The CPC aims to reduce the use of chlorinated substances in the paper-making process by informing people about

the effects of chlorine by-products and facilitating communication between buyers and sellers of chlorine-free paper products. A project of Northland College and the National Wildlife Federation.
Contact(s):
Executive Coordinator: JEFFERY M. HUXMANN; E-mail: huxmann@clfree.org
Publication(s): *Brochure*
Keyword(s): Chemical Pollution Control, Hazardous Materials & Waste, Health and Nutrition, International Trade and Environment, Pollution Prevention, Research, Toxic Reduction, Toxic Substances, Water Pollution Management, Water Quality

CHRISTINA CONSERVANCY, INC.
P.O. Box 1680, Wilmington, DE 19899-1680
Phone: 302-984-3801
Scope: Statewide
Description: The purpose of the Christina Conservancy, Inc. is to preserve, protect, and urge the wise use of the Christina River.
Contact(s):
President: EDWARD W. COOCH JR.
Keyword(s): Rivers

CINCINNATI NATURE CENTER
4949 Tealtown Rd., Milford, OH 45150-9752
Phone: 513-831-1711; Fax: 513-831-8052
Founded: 1965; Membership: 5,500
Scope: Local Region
Description: A private, non-profit organization consiting of a nature preserve and two working farms which provide environmental, natural history and agricultural education for the Greater Cincinnati area.
Contact(s):
Chairman of the Board: THOMAS C. RINK
President/Executive Director: WILLIAM H. HOPPLE III
Education Director: CONNIE BROCKMAN; Phone: 513-965-4891
Publication(s): *Newsleaf (newsletter)*
Keyword(s): Agriculture, Ecology, Environmental and Conservation Education, Internships, Interpretation, Natural History, Nature Centers, Professional Development.

CIRCUMPOLAR CONSERVATION UNION
900 17th St., NW, 3rd Fl., Washington, DC 20006-2596
Phone: 202-429-7440; Fax: 202-429-7444; E-mail: circumpolar@igc.apc.org; Web Site: www.circumpolar.org
Founded: 1993
Scope: National
Description: Circumpolar Conservation Union is a public interest initiative dedicated to protecting the ecological and cultural integrity of the Arctic for present and future generations. CCU works nationally and internationally through policy advocacy, public education, and by building links among diverse constituencies, to achieve comprehensive legal protection for the Arctic.
Contact(s):
Executive Director: EVELYN M. HURWICH
Keyword(s): Arctic, Environmental Law, Indigenous People, Sustainable Development

CITIZENS ALLIANCE FOR SAVING THE ATMOSPHERE AND THE EARTH (CASA)
1-3-17-711 Tanimachi, Chuo-ku, Osaka 540-0012 Japan
Phone: 81-6-941-3745; Fax: 81-6-941-5699; E-mail: casa@netplus.ne.jp; Web Site: www.netplus.ne.jp/-casa/
Founded: 1988
Scope: International
Description: CASA is committed to preserving both the local and global environment through solidarity with both Japanese and international environmental NGO's. CASA is composed of 50 NGO's and about 500 individuals, such as scientists, teachers, lawyers, farmers, grassroots activitists, artists, consumer group leaders, and others.
Contact(s):
Executive Director: YUJI NISHI
Managing Director: MITSUTOSHI HAYAKAWA
Representative Director: TSUNETOSHI YAMAMURA
Publication(s): *CASA Letter (Japanese)*

CITIZENS NATURAL RESOURCES ASSOCIATION OF WISCONSIN, INC.
Attn: President, 3805 Paunack St., Madison, WI 53711
Phone: 608-231-9721
Founded: 1951
Scope: Statewide
Description: To protect Wisconsin's natural resources through education, legislation, and the courts. The CNRA initiated and sponsored the action that resulted in the banning of DDT in Wisconsin and two years later in the United States. Recently, the CNRA has been concentrating on protecting and restoring native vegetation along Wisconsin's roads.
Contact(s):
President: KIRA HENSCHEL
Vice President: LORRIE OTTO, 9701 N. Lake Dr., Milwaukee, WI 53217; Phone: 414-352-0734
Secretary: LAURA ALLHANDS, N 5908 S. Center Rd., Beaver Dam, WI 53916; Phone: 920-885-9598
Treasurer: CHARLES STURM, J-1233 Mayfair Rd. Suite 125, Milwaukee, WI 53226
Editor: JAN SCALPONE, 2033 Menominee Dr., Oshkosh, WI 54901; Phone: 920-231-0063
Membership Chair: LOUISE COUMBE, 1028 Elmwood Ave., Oshkosh, WI 54901
Publication(s): *CNRA Report, The; Wisconsin Roadsides*

CITIZENS' NUCLEAR INFORMATION CENTER
1-58-15-3F Higashi-Nakano, Nakano-ku, Tokyo 164-0003 Japan
Phone: 81-3-5330-9520; Fax: 81-3-5330-9530
Founded: 1975
Scope: International
Description: A nonprofit organization to collect and provide the public a broad range of information on nuclear power issues, and cooperate with individuals and other organizations concerned with nuclear proliferation in Japan and around the world. Information includes the Japanese government policy of plutonium utilization, effects of radioactive contamination, nuclear power plant accidents, economics, and other impacts on the local communities caused by construction of nuclear power plants.
Contact(s):
Co-Director: HIDEYUKI BAN
International Relations Officer: GAIA HOERNER
Publication(s): *Citizens' Nuclear Information Center Report (Japanese); Nuke Info Tokyo (English)*
Keyword(s): Nuclear Energy

CLEAN OCEAN ACTION

Main Office
P.O. Box 505, Sandy Hook, NJ 07732
Phone: 732-872-0111; Fax: 732-872-8041; E-mail: cleanocean@monmouth.com; Web Site: www.cleanoceanaction.org
Founded: 1984
Scope: Regional
Description: A broad-based coalition of 175 conservation, fishing, diving, boating, real estate, student, and civic groups; over 300 businesses; and thousands of citizens concerned with the degraded waters off the New York and New Jersey coasts. COA uses education, research, and citizen action to pressure public officials to enact and enforce protective laws for our marine resources. Programs include: storm drain stenciling; regulatory reviews; contaminated sediments; and non-point source pollution.
Contact(s):
President: DERY BENNETT
Vice President: WILLIAM FEINBERG
Secretary: PAT SCHNEIDER
Treasurer: BEN FOREST
Executive Director: CINDY ZIPF
Publication(s): *Ocean Advocate*

NON-GOVERNMENTAL ORGANIZATIONS - C

Keyword(s): Coasts, Contaminated Sediments, Nonpoint Source Pollution, Water Pollution

Mid-Coast Office
P.O. Box 1303, Tuckerton, NJ 08087
Phone: 609-294-8040; Fax: 609-294-8044; E-mail: MMaxCOA@aol.com
Scope: Local Region

South Jersey Office
P.O. Box 1098, Wildwood, NJ 08260
Phone: 609-729-7262; Fax: 609-729-3383; E-mail: AATotah@aol.com
Scope: Local Region

CLEAN WATER ACTION
4455 Connecticut Ave., NW, Suite A300, Washington, DC 20008-2328
Phone: 202-895-0420; Fax: 202-895-0438; E-mail: cleanwater@essential.org; Web Site: www.cleanwateraction.org
Scope: National
Description: The national citizen's organization working full-time for clean safe water at an affordable cost, control of toxic chemicals, and protection of our natural resources.
Contact(s):
Development Associate: JIM PIERCE

CLEAN WATER FUND
4455 Connecticut Ave., NW, Suite A 300, Washington, DC 20008
Phone: 202-895-0420; Fax: 202-895-0438; E-mail: cleanwater@essential.org
Scope: National
Description: Clean Water Fund is a 501 c (3) research, training and educational organization that advances environmental and consumer protection with a special focus on water pollution, toxic hazards, solid waste management, and natural resources.
Contact(s):
Board of Directors, Executive Vice President: DAVID ZWICK
Board of Directors, President: PETER VAN LOCKWOOD
Board of Directors, Treasurer: KATHLEEN ATERNO
Development Associate: JIM PIERCE; Phone: 202-895-0432
Publication(s): *WATER: Riches for Clean Up, Pennies for Prevention, 1993; SOLID WASTE: Expanding Rhode Island's Market with RI War on Waste, 1993; TOXICS: If Its Broke, Fit it, 1993; TOXICS: Toxic Metals in Batteries, 1992*

CLEAN WATER NETWORK, THE
1200 New York Avenue, NW, Suite 400, Washington, DC 20005
Phone: 202-289-2395; Fax: 202-289-1060; E-mail: cleanwaternt@igc.org; Web Site: www.cwn.org
Scope: National
Description: The Clean Water Network is a national alliance of over 1,000 organizations representing environmentalists, commercial fishers, anglers, surfers, family farmers, environmental justice advocates, faith communities, civic associations, boaters, labor unions, and recreational enthusiasts working together for cleaner waters.
Contact(s):
Grassroots Coordinator: AMI GRACE; Phone: 202-289-2421
National Coordinator: KATHY NEMSICK; Phone: 202-289-2395

CLEVELAND MUSEUM OF NATURAL HISTORY, THE
1 Wade Oval Dr., University Cir., Cleveland, OH 44106
Phone: 216-231-4600/x219; Fax: 216-231-5919; E-mail: botany@cmnh.org
Founded: 1920; Membership: 9,000
Scope: Statewide
Description: To instill an understanding of and appreciation for nature and inspire responsibility for conservation and stewardship of natural diversity. The Museum program areas include exhibits, publications, education, collections, research, and natural areas. The Museum owns a system of 22 sanctuaries.
Contact(s):
Director: DR. JAMES KING
Coordinator of Natural Areas: JAMES BISSELL
Publication(s): *Explorer; Kirtlandia*
Keyword(s): Environmental and Conservation Education, Museum, Research

CLIMATE INSTITUTE
333 1/2 Pennsylvania Ave., S.E., Washington, DC 20003
Phone: 202-547-0104; Fax: 202-547-0111
Founded: 1986; Membership: 1,500
Scope: International
Description: Designed to serve as a catalyst for international response and cooperation to address the threats posed by climate change and depletion of the stratospheric ozone layer. The Climate Institute operates as a bridge between scientists and policymakers with the intent of expediting policy responses to the challenges posed by human-induced climate change.
Contact(s):
President: JOHN C. TOPPING JR.; Phone: 202-547-0104, ext. 14
Director of Programs: MICHELE PENA; Phone: 202-547-0104, ext. 13
Publication(s): *Climate Alert; Coping with Climate Change; Forests in a Changing Climate; Climate Change in Asia; Environmental Exodus*
Keyword(s): Coasts, Energy, Sustainable Development, Urban Forestry

COALITION FOR CLEAN AIR
10780 Santa Monica Blvd., #210, Los Angeles, CA 90025
Phone: 310-441-1544
Founded: 1970; Membership: 2,000
Scope: Statewide
Description: A nonprofit, tax-exempt organization dedicated to restoring clean, healthful air to Southern California residents through a combination of efforts including outreach and education, litigation, research, and policy advocacy.
Contact(s):
President: GLADYS MEADE
Vice President: RALPH PERRY
Treasurer: DAVID ALLGOOD
Executive Director: LINDA WAADE
Policy Director: TIM CARMICHAEL
Publication(s): *Clearing the Air*
Keyword(s): Air Quality and Pollution, Environmental Protection, Pollution Prevention

COALITION FOR EDUCATION IN THE OUTDOORS
S.U.N.Y. at Cortland Box 2000, Cortland, NY 13045
Phone: 607-753-4971; Fax: 607-753-5982; E-mail: taproot@cortland.edu
Founded: 1986
Scope: National
Description: The Coalition is composed of more than 100 businesses, institutions, organizations, associations, centers, agencies, and individuals affiliated in support of communicating and networking concerning education in, for and about the outdoors. The Coalition's magazine is a critically acclaimed education resource. The Coalition also conducts a biennial Outdoor Education Research Symposium.
Contact(s):
Executive Coordinator: DR. CHARLES H. YAPLE
Publication(s): *Taproot; Outdoor Education Research Symposium Proceedings*
Keyword(s): Environmental and Conservation Education, Environmental Ethics, Nature Preservation, Outdoor Education, Outdoor Recreation, Wildlands

COALITION FOR NATURAL STREAM VALLEYS, INC.
430 Orchard Rd., Newark, DE 19711-5137
Phone: 302-366-8059
Membership: 50 individuals and 12 organizations

Scope: Regional
Description: The purpose of the Coalition for Natural Stream Valleys, Inc. is to promote the wise use of, and the preservation of natural stream valleys.
Contact(s):
Chairman: ROLAND R. ROTH
Corresponding Secretary: DORTHY P. MILLER

COAST ALLIANCE
600 Pennsylvania Ave., SE, Suite 340, Washington, DC 20003
Phone: 202-546-9554; Fax: 202-546-9609; E-mail: coast@coastalliance.org; Web Site: www.coastalliance.org
Founded: 1979
Scope: National
Description: The Coast Alliance is a nonprofit public interest group dedicated to raising public awareness about our priceless coastal resources. Composed of concerned activists across the United States, the Coast Alliance provides information on activities affecting the nation's four coasts: the Atlantic, Pacific, Gulf of Mexico, and Great Lakes.
Contact(s):
Executive Director: JACQUELINE SAVITZ
Chairperson of the Board: DERY BENNETT
Treasurer and Secretary: TODD MILLER
Vice Chairperson: DAVID MILLER
Publication(s): *And Two If By Sea: Fighting The Attack on America's Coasts; Storm on The Horizon: The National Flood Insurance Program and America's Coasts; Using Common Sense to Protect The Coasts: The Need to Expand The Coastal Barrier Resources System; Getting to the Bottom of It; Pointless Pollution: Preventing Polluted Runoff and Protecting America's Coasts*
Keyword(s): Aquatic Habitats, Coasts, Contaminated Sediments, Development, Environmental and Conservation Education, Land Use Planning, Runoff, Water Pollution

COASTAL CONSERVATION ASSOCIATION
4801 Woodway, Suite 220 West, Houston, TX 77056
Phone: 713-626-4234; Fax: 713-626-5852
Founded: 1977; Membership: 55,000
Scope: National
Description: A national nonprofit corporation organized exclusively for the purpose of promoting and advancing the preservation, conservation, and protection of the marine, animal, and plant life both onshore and offshore along the coastal areas of the United States for the benefit and enjoyment of the general public.
Contact(s):
President: ALEX JERNIGAN
Vice President: GUS SCHRAM III
Chairman of the Board: WALTER W. FONDREN III
Editor: DOUG PIKE
Executive Director of Alabama Regional Office: DAVID DEXTER, 144 Florence Place, Mobile, AL 36607; Phone: 334-478-3474; Fax: 334-476-5214
Executive Director of Connecticut Regional Office: RON DOMURAT, P.O. Box 290224, Wethersfield, CT 06129-0224; Phone: 860-529-7878
Executive Director of Florida Regional Office: TED FORSGREN, 905 East Park Ave., Tallahassee, FL 32301-2646; Phone: 904-224-3474; Fax: 904-224-5199
Executive Director of Georgia Regiona Office: BILL FORD, Varsity Plaza, 11418 Abercorn, Suite C, Savannah, GA 31419; Phone: 912-920-2300; Fax: 912-920-2313
Executive Director of Louisiana Regional Office: JEFF ANGERS, 8281 Goodwood, Suite B1, Baton Rouge, LA 70806; Phone: 504-952-9200; Fax: 504-952-9204
Executive Director of Maine Regional Office: PAT KELIHER, 40 Lafayette St., Yarmouth, ME 04096; Phone: 207-846-1015; Fax: 207-846-1168
Executive Director of Massachusetts Regional Office: DAVID RIMMER, 4 Middle St., Suite 215, Newburyport, MA 01950; Phone: 978-499-4313; Fax: 978-499-4314
Executive Director of New York Regional Office: JOHN MCMURRAY, P.O. Box 1118, West Babylon, NY 11704; Phone: 516-422-4162
Executive Director of North Carolina Regional Office: DICK BRAME, 2030 Eastwood Rd., Suite 3, Wilmington, NC 28403; Phone: 910-256-0083; Fax: 910-256-6040
Executive Director of South Carolina Regional Office: BETH PIERCE, P.O. Box 1823, Mt. Pleasant, SC 29465; Phone: 843-852-7880; Fax: 843-852-9202
Executive Director of Texas Regional Office: KEVIN DANIELS, 4801 Woodway, Suite 220W, Houston, TX 77056; Phone: 713-626-4222; Fax: 713-961-3801
Executive Director of Virginia Regional Office: RICHARD WELTON, 2100 Marina Shores Dr., Suite 108, Virginia Beach, VA 23451; Phone: 757-481-1226; Fax: 757-481-6910
Secretary and Treasurer: DAVID G. CUMMINS
Vice Chairman: WILL OHMSTEDE
Publication(s): *Tide*
Keyword(s): Aquatic Habitats, Coasts, Fisheries, Sport Fishing, Water Quality, Water Resources, Wetlands

COASTAL CONSERVATION ASSOCIATION GEORGIA
P.O. Box 60366, Savannah, GA 31420
Phone: 919-920-2300; Fax: 912-920-2313; E-mail: ccaga@premierweb.net; Web Site: www.ccaga.org
Founded: 1987; Membership: 700
Scope: Statewide
Description: The CCAG promotes conservation through education-- promoting, protecting and enhancing the availability of marine, animal, plant life and other coastal resources for the benefit and enjoyment of the general public.
Contact(s):
Chairman: MARTIN NeSMITH; Phone: 912-739-1744; Fax: 912-739-4889
Vice-Chairman: WILLIAM PHILLIPS; Phone: 912-764-6567; Fax: 912-764-6568; E-mail: ringo@bulloch.com
President, Savannah Chapter: RICHARD COOMER; Phone: 912-691-1929; Fax: 912-356-3837
Executive Director: JOEL E. WILLIAMS JR.; E-mail: joel@reeloutdoor.com
Publication(s): *Tidelines (newsletter)*
Keyword(s): Coasts, Conservation of Protected Areas, Conservation Plannning, Environmental and Conservation Education, Fish Wildlife Management, Fisheries, Marine Conservation, Preservation and Protection, Water Quality

COASTAL GEORGIA CENTER FOR SUSTAINABLE DEVELOPMENT
P.O. Box 598, 202 Broad St., Darien, GA 31305
Phone: 912-437-8160; Fax: 912-437-8163; E-mail: dksusdev@gale.net
Founded: 1997
Scope: Regional
Description: To promote sustainable use, protection, enhancement, and understanding of coastal Georgia's natural, economic, historic, and cultural resources through education, advocacy, technical assistance, and research.
Contact(s):
Executive Director: DAVID KYLER
Publication(s): *Works in Progress; Surface Water Withdrawal and Coastal Economic Issues; Fisheries and Water Resource Permit Issues in the Lower Altamaha and Other Coastal Georgia Rivers*
Keyword(s): Water Quality

COASTAL GEORGIA LAND TRUST, THE
3025 Bull St., #254, Savannah, GA 31405
Phone: 912-231-0507; Fax: 912-233-1143; E-mail: cglt@bellsouth.net
Founded: 1993; Membership: 60
Scope: Regional
Description: The mission of the Coastal Georgia Land Trust, Inc., a nonprofit organization, is to promote the responsible stewardship and preservation of land in coastal Georgia.

NON-GOVERNMENTAL ORGANIZATIONS - C

Contact(s):
President, Board of Directors: JO HICKSON; Phone: 912-236-0845; Fax: 912-236-2225; E-mail: jch_asla@bellsouth.net
Vice President, Board of Directors: ALAN BAILEY; Phone: 912-925-3159; Fax: 912-927-9766; E-mail: acbailey@worldnet.atf.net
Executive Director: MARY A. ELFNER
Keyword(s): Conservation Easements, Habitat Conservation, Historic Preservation, Land Conservation, Land Preservation, Land Protection, Natural Areas, Natural History, Nature Preservation, Open Space, Stewardship, Sustainable Development, Wetlands, Wildlife and Wildlife Habitat, Native Plants

COASTAL SOCIETY, THE
P.O. Box 25408, Alexandria, VA 22313-5408
Phone: 703-768-1599; Fax: 703-768-1598
Founded: 1975
Scope: International
Description: The Coastal Society is an organization of private sector, academic and governmental professionals and students dedicated to actively addressing emerging coastal issues, fostering dialog, forging partnerships and promoting communication and education.
Contact(s):
President: MEGAN D. BAILIFF, University of Washington, Box 355060, Seattle, WA 98105-5060; Phone: 206-685-1108
President Elect: WALTER CLARK, 415 Englewood Ave., Durham, NC 27701
Treasurer: WILLIAM W. HALL, 3635 Fremont Ave. North, #307, Seattle, WA 98103; Phone: 406-442-4002
Secretary: CAMILLE E. COLEY, University of Rhode Island, Kingston, RI ; Phone: 301-713-3155
Past President: MICHAEL K. ORBACH, Nicholas School for the Environment, Duke University, 135 Duke Marine Lab Rd., Beaufort, NC 28516-9720
Executive Director: JUDY TUCKER
Publication(s): *Coastal Society, The Bulletin;* conference proceedings
Keyword(s): Coasts, Environmental and Conservation Education, Sustainable Development, Water Pollution, Wetlands

COLORADO ASSOCIATION OF SOIL CONSERVATION DISTRICTS
Attn: President, 18105 Enoch Rd., Colorado Springs, CO 80930
Scope: Statewide
Contact(s):
President, Alternate Board Member: ROBERT CORDOVA, 18105 Enoch Rd., Colorado Springs, CO 80930; Phone: 719-683-2126
Vice President: JIM ROSSI, P.O. Box 247, Oak Creek, CO 80467; Phone: 970-638-4459
Secretary and Treasurer: LEE CAMPBELL, 1603 Eastlawn Ave., Durango, CO 81301; Phone: 970-247-1496; Fax: 970-385-7910
Board Member: JOHN FREZIERS, 1858 M Rd., Fruita, CO 81521; Phone: 970-858-7165
Executive Director: , 3000 Youngfield St. Suite 163, Lakewood, CO 80215-6545; Phone: 303-232-6242; Fax: 303-232-1624
Executive Assistant: MARY KLEIN, 3000 Youngfield St., Suite 163, Lakewood, CO 80215-6545; Phone: 303-232-6242; Fax: 303-232-1624
Keyword(s): Conservation Districts

COLORADO B.A.S.S. CHAPTER FEDERATION
Attn: President, 4485 Enchanted Circle N., Colorado Springs, CO 80917
Phone: 719-597-2304
Scope: Statewide
Description: An organization of Bassmaster chapters, affiliated with the Bass Anglers Sportsman Society, organized to fight pollution, assist state and national conservation agencies in their efforts, and teach the young people of our country good conservation practices. Dedicated to the realistic conservation of our water resources.
Contact(s):
President: JOHN BENTZ
Conservation Director: PAT SNIDER, 4842 W. 9th St. Rd., Greeley, CO 80634; Phone: 970-353-5375

COLORADO ENVIRONMENTAL COALITION
1536 Wynkoop, #5C, Denver, CO 80202
Phone: 303-534-7066; Fax: 303-534-7063; E-mail: infocec@cecenviro.org; Web Site: www.cecenviro.org
Founded: 1965; Membership: 50 organizations plus 2,300 individuals
Scope: Statewide
Description: The Colorado Environmental Coalition is the grass roots action arm of Colorado's environmental movement. The Coalition coordinates the conservation community and mobilizes citizen constituencies behind environmental campaigns to preserve wilderness, wildlife, and a sustainable way of life.
Contact(s):
President: JOHN POWERS
Executive Director: SUSAN TIXIER; Phone: 303-534-5533; E-mail: sjtix@cecenviro.org
Associate Director: TED FICKES; Phone: 303-534-7066; E-mail: fickes@cecenviro.org
Circuit Rider: TREY BECK; Phone: 303-534-1774; E-mail: trey@cecenviro.org
Field Director: JEFF WIDEN; Phone: 970-385-8509; E-mail: widen@cecenviro.org
Field Organizer: MONICA PIERGROSSI; Phone: 303-534-7492; E-mail: monica@cecenviro.org
Growth Management: LAUREN MARTENS; Phone: 303-534-5798; E-mail: martens@cecenviro.org
Membership Director: JODY KENNEDY; Phone: 303-534-7310; E-mail: jody@cecenviro.org
West Slope Field Organizer: PETE KOLBENSCHLAG, 1000 N 9th St., #29, Grand Junction, CO 81501; Phone: 970-243-0002; E-mail: pete@cecenviro.org
Publication(s): *Colorado Environmental Report; Colorado Environmental Handbook-State of the State; Conservationist's Wilderness Proposal for BLM Lands*
Keyword(s): Environmental Health, Public Lands, Sustainable Development, Wilderness, Wildlife and Wildlife Habitat

COLORADO FORESTRY ASSOCIATION
P.O. Box 270132, Ft. Collins, CO 80527
Phone: 970-491-6303
Founded: 1982; Membership: 650
Scope: Statewide
Description: A statewide organization affiliated with the National Woodland Owners Association, concerned with forest ecology and advocating a forest-perpetuating balance between preservation and harvest of Colorado forests.
Contact(s):
President: C.W. MILLER, Bellvue, CO
Vice President: KEN ASHLEY, Ft. Collins, CO
Secretary: BETTY DAY, Aurora, CO
Treasurer: ED OLMSTED, Northglen, CO
Editor: JOHN ORAM; Phone: 303-477-0552
Publication(s): *Colorado Forestry*
Keyword(s): Forests and Forestry

COLORADO NATURAL HERITAGE PROGRAM
254 General Services Bldg., Colorado State University, Ft. Collins, CO 80523
Phone: 970-491-1309; Fax: 970-491-3349; E-mail: heritage@lamar.colostate.edu; Web Site: www.cnhp.colostate.edu
Founded: 1979
Scope: Statewide
Description: The mission of the Colorado Natural Heritage Program is to preserve the natural diversity of life by contributing the scientific foundation that leads to lasting conservation of Colorado's biological wealth.

Contact(s):
Director: MARY KLEIN; Phone: 970-491-1309; Fax: 970-491-3349; E-mail: heritage@lamar.colostate.edu
Publication(s): *Rare and Imperiled Animals, Plants, and Plant Communities of Colorado; Colorado Rare Plant Guide; Colorado Conservation Status Handbook*
Keyword(s): Biodiversity, Ecology, Land Management, Land Use Planning

COLORADO TRAPPERS ASSOCIATION
P.O. Box 397, Empire, CO 80438
Founded: 1975; Membership: 500
Scope: Statewide
Description: Associate of Fur Takers of America and National Trappers Association. Dedicated to the wise conservation and management of fur-bearing animals, the education of fur harvesters and public about fur-bearer management and the preservation of America's rich heritage in the harvest of wild furs.
Contact(s):
President: AL DAVIDSON, Box 225, Gunnison, CO 81230; Phone: 970-641-4022
Vice President: MARVIN MILLER, 29156 Summit Ranch Dr., Golden, CO 80401; Phone: 303-526-9207
Secretary: DEBRA WATTS, P.O. Box 397, Empire, CO 80438; Phone: 303-569-2551
Treasurer: DEBORAH LINDAHL, 5109 Parkway Cir., W., Ft. Collins, CO 80525; Phone: 970-206-0309
Director of Public Relations: BILL ROGERS, Box 128, Brighton, CO 80601; Phone: 303-659-0773
Director of Publications: MAJ. L. BODDICKER
Editor: MAJ. L. BODDICKER
Publication(s): *Managing Rocky Mountain Furbearers; Fur Marketing and Trappers Supply Handbook*
Keyword(s): Agriculture, Hunting, Predators, Trapping, Wildlife Management

COLORADO WATER CONGRESS
1390 Logan St., Suite 312, Denver, CO 80203
Phone: 303-837-0812; Fax: 303-837-1607
Founded: 1958
Scope: Statewide
Description: To institute and advance programs for the conservation, development, protection, and efficient utilization of the water resources of Colorado.
Contact(s):
President: JIM HOKIT
Vice President: NEIL JAQUET
Executive Director: RICHARD D. MacRAVEY
Publication(s): *Colorado Water Rights; Colorado Water Almanac & Directory; Water Intelligence Report; Water Legal News; Water Legislative Report; Water Research News; Water Special Report; Water Quality News; Colorado Laws Enacted of Interest to Water Users*

COLORADO WILDLIFE FEDERATION
445 Union Blvd., #302, Lakewood, CO 80228-1243
Phone: 303-987-0400; Fax: 303-987-0200; E-mail: cwfed@aol.com; Web Site: www.coloradowildlife.org
Founded: 1952
Scope: Statewide
Description: A representative statewide organization, affiliated with the National Wildlife Federation, dedicated to the protection and enhancement of wildlife and its habitat through public education and government interaction.
Contact(s):
Chair: DENNIS BUECHLER
Executive Director and Editor: DIANE GANSAUER
Alternate Representative: COLLEEN GADD
Publication(s): *Colorado Wildlife*

COLORADO WILDLIFE HERITAGE FOUNDATION
6060 Broadway, Denver, CO 80216
Phone: 303-291-7212
Founded: 1989
Scope: Statewide
Description: The Colorado Wildlife Heritage Foundation has been endorsed by four Colorado governors. The foundation's objectives are threefold: (1) environmental education, (2) habitat acquisition and management, and (3) wildlife research. Where appropriate, the foundation pursues projects with the support and expertise of the Colorado Division of Wildlife.
Contact(s):
President: TERRY COMBS, American Cargo Handling P.O. Box 17594, Denver, CO 80217; Phone: 303-398-2416
Executive Director: EDWARD J. ALEXANDER, Colorado Wildlife Heritage Foundation 6060 Broadway, Denver, CO 80216; Phone: 303-291-7416
Director: CHARLES L. WARREN, 333 Logan St., Denver, CO 80203; Phone: 303-778-7797
Chairman: JAMES COWPERTHWAITE, 378 S. Pontiac Way, Denver, CO 80224; Phone: 303-355-3957
Treasurer: BUCK HUTCHISON, Hutchison Western P.O. Box 1158, Adams City, CO 80022; Phone: 303-287-2826
Secretary: LINDA HAMLIN, 100 Dexter St., Denver, CO 80220; Phone: 303-388-8176
Keyword(s): Endangered and Threatened Species, Environmental and Conservation Education, Land Purchase, Sustainable Ecosystems, Wildlife and Wildlife Habitat

COLUMBIA BASIN FISH AND WILDLIFE AUTHORITY
2501 SW 1st Ave. Suite 200, Portland, OR 97201
Phone: 503-326-7031
Founded: 1982
Scope: Regional
Description: A regional association of all the fish and wildlife agencies (two federal, five state) and Indian tribes (13 in the Columbia River Basin (Idaho, Montana, Oregon, and Washington). Established to coordinate planning and implementation of the fish and wildlife provisions of the Pacific Northwest Electric Power Planning and Conservation Act and for oversight of fish and wildlife resource management under the Fish and Wildlife Coordination Act and other authorities. Current charter: 1987.
Contact(s):
Chairman: ANN BADGLEY, US Fish and Wildlife Service, 911 NE 11th Ave., Portland, OR 97232; Phone: 503-231-6118; Fax: 503-872-2716
Executive Director: DR. BRIAN J. ALLEE; Phone: 503-229-0191; Fax: 503-229-0443; E-mail: brian@cbfwf.org
Fish Passage Center Manager: MICHELE DeHART, 2501 SW 1st Ave., Suite 230, Portland, OR 97201-4752; Phone: 503-230-4288; Fax: 503-230-7559; E-mail: mdehart@fpc.org
Keyword(s): Fish Wildlife Management, Fisheries, Wildlife and Wildlife Habitat, Wildlife Rehabilitation

COMMITTEE FOR NATIONAL ARBOR DAY
Attn: National Chairman, 63 Fitzrandolph Rd., West Orange, NJ 07052
Founded: 1936
Scope: National
Description: To establish a unified national observance date on the last Friday in April.
Contact(s):
National Chairman: HARRY J. BANKER, 63 Fitzrandolph Rd., West Orange, NJ 07052
Honorary National Chairman: MRS. EDWARD H. SCANLON, P.O. Box 38247, Olmsted Falls, OH 44138
Keyword(s): Trees

COMMITTEE FOR THE NATIONAL INSTITUTE FOR THE ENVIRONMENT (CNIE)
1725 K Street NW, Suite 212, Washington, DC 20006
Phone: 202-530-5810; Fax: 202-628-4311; E-mail: cnie@cnie.org; Web Site: www.cnie.org
Founded: 1990
Scope: National
Description: The CNIE is a nonprofit organization of scientists, policymakers, environmentalists, business representatives and other

stakeholders in environmental policy. The CNIE's mission is to improve the scientific basis for making decisions on environmental issues through the creation and successful operation of a National Institute for the Environment. The proposed entity, which would be affiliated with the National Science Foundation, would reform the relationship between science and environmental decision-making by establishing programs for environmental research, assessment, education and training, and a National Library for the Environment.
Contact(s):
Chair: STEPHEN P. HUBBELL, Professor of Botany, University of Georgia, Dept. Of Botany, Athens, GA 30602; Phone: 706-583-0393; Fax: 706-542-1805
Executive Director: PETER D. SAUNDRY
Secretary and Treasurer: A. KARIM AHMED, President, Global Children's Health and Environmental Fund; Phone: 202-789-1201; Fax: 202-789-1206
Vice Chair: HENRY F. HOWE, Professor and Ecology Coordinator, University of Illinois at Chicago, Biological Sciences, (M/C 066), 845 W. Taylor St., Chicago, IL 60607-7060; Phone: 312-996-0666; Fax: 312-996-2017
Publication(s): *A Proposal for a National Institute for the Environment; Federal Environmental Research and Development Programs; Environmental Justice: Breaking New Ground; over 600 Congressional Service Reports and many other resources available through on-line library.*
Keyword(s): Communications, Environmental and Conservation Education, Sustainable Development, Sustainable Ecosystems, Wildlife and Wildlife Habitat, Libraries

COMMITTEE ON AGRICULTURAL SUSTAINABILITY FOR DEVELOPING COUNTRIES
10 G Street, NE, Suite 800, Washington, DC 20002
Phone: 202-729-7600
Founded: 1987
Scope: National
Description: The Committee on Agricultural Sustainability aims to increase support for farmers in developing countries working to improve their living conditions and feed the world's expanding population without destroying the soil and water supplies on which agricultural productivity ultimately depends.
Contact(s):
Chairman: ROBERT O. BLAKE
Keyword(s): Agriculture, Developing Countries, Soil Conservation, Sustainable Development

COMMUNITIES FOR A BETTER ENVIRONMENT
500 Howard St., Suite 506, San Francisco, CA 94105
Phone: 415-243-8373
Founded: 1971; Membership: 15,000
Scope: Statewide
Description: The CBE is a nonprofit, multiracial environmental health organization working to prevent public exposure to toxic chemical pollutants. CBE has over 19 years experience in the California environmental arena. CBE uses science-based research, legal tactics, and organizing strategies to prevent air and water pollution, to eliminate toxic hazards, and to improve the health of the people of California.
Contact(s):
Executive Director: RICHARD TOSHIYUK DRURY
Board President: STEPHANIE PINCETL
Secretary: EVERETT DELANO
Publication(s): *Environmental Review; Oil Rag*
Keyword(s): Air Quality and Pollution, Environmental Justice, Environmental Law, Internships, Water Pollution

COMMUNITY CONSERVATION CONSULTANTS/HOWLERS FOREVER, INC.
50542 Zintz Rd., Rt. 1 Box 96, Gays Mills, WI 54631
Phone: 608-735-4717; Fax: 608-735-4765; E-mail: ccc@mwt.net
Founded: 1989
Scope: National
Description: Specializing in catalyzing of community-based conservation initiatives and designing for their sustainability. Active in Wisconsin, Belize and India. Coordination of volunteers for projects.
Contact(s):
Assistant Director: DR. JONATHAN LYON
Director: DR. ROB HORWICH
Keyword(s): Conservation, Local Resource Conservation

COMMUNITY ENVIRONMENTAL COUNCIL
930 Miramonte Dr., Santa Barbara, CA 93109
Phone: 805-963-0583
Founded: 1970; Membership: 600
Scope: National
Description: CEC's primary goal is to serve as a connecting institution linking government agencies, business and industry, universities and regulatory bodies, environmental organizations, and the community. Using Santa Barbara as its urban laboratory, CEC conducts research and develops local programs in recycling, hazardous waste, sustainable agriculture, and environmental education.
Contact(s):
President: CHARLES ECKBERG, 930 Miramonte Dr., Santa Barbara, CA 93109; Phone: 805-963-0583
Vice President: SUSAN VAN ATTA, 930 Miramonte Dr., Santa Barbara, CA 93209; Phone: 805-963-0583
Secretary: JERRY STURMER, 930 Miramonte Dr., Santa Barbara, CA 93109; Phone: 805-963-0583
Treasurer: BILL ADLER, 930 Miramonte Dr., Santa Barbara, CA 93109; Phone: 805-963-0583
Executive Director: JON CLARK, 930 Miramonte Dr., Santa Barbara, CA 93109; Phone: 805-963-0583
Publication(s): *Gildea Review; Manufacturing with Recyclables; A Question of Responsibility: Recycling Market Development*
Keyword(s): Gardening and Horticulture, Land Use Planning, Solid Waste Management, Sustainable Development, Toxic Substances

COMMUNITY RIGHTS COUNSEL
1726 M St., NW, Suite 703, Washington, DC 20036-4524
Phone: 202-296-6889; Fax: 202-296-6895; E-mail: crc@communityrights.org; Web Site: www.communityrights.org
Founded: 1997
Scope: National
Description: CRC is a public interest law firm defending laws that make our communities healthier, more livable, and socially just.
Contact(s):
Program Director: F. G. COURTNEY
Keyword(s): Endangered and Threatened Species, Environmental Law, Environmental Planning, Land Preservation, Land Use Planning, Open Space, Planning Management, Sustainable Development, Urban Environment, Wetlands

CONCERN, INC.
1794 Columbia Rd. NW, Washington, DC 20009
Phone: 202-328-8160; Fax: 202-387-3378; E-mail: concern@igc.apc.org; Web Site: www.sustainable.org
Founded: 1970
Scope: National
Description: A nonprofit, tax-exempt organization that provides environmental information to individuals and groups. Concern's publications give an overview of the issue and include guidelines to encourage and aid citizen participation in the community and in policy decisions at the local, state, and federal levels of government. Also developing a community sustainability program, including a database on sustainability.
Contact(s):
Chair: BURKS LAPHAM
Executive Director: SUSAN BOYD
Publication(s): *Community Action Guides on Pesticides, Drinking Water, Farmland, Waste, Household Waste, and Global Warming*
Keyword(s): Environmental and Conservation Education, Pesticides, Solid Waste Management, Sustainable Development, Water Resources

CONFEDERATED SALISH AND KOOTENAI TRIBES
P.O. Box 278, Pablo, MT 59855
Phone: 406-675-2700; Fax: 406-675-2806
Scope: Statewide
Description: The 1.25 million acre Flathead Indian Reservation was created in 1855 by the Treaty of the Hellgate as a homeland for the Salish, Kootenai, and Pend d' Oreille Tribes. The constitutional government of the Confederated Salish and Kootenai Tribes was formed in 1934 and approved by the Secretary of the Interior in 1935 to establish a more responsible organization, promote our general welfare, conserve and develop our land and resources, and secure to ourselves and our posterity the power to exercise certain rights of self-government. The Tribal Natural Resources Department includes the divisions of Water, Environmental Protection, Lands, and Fisheries, Wildlife, Recreation, and Conservation. The Tribal Forestry Department is responsible for forest management activities on the Reservation.
Contact(s):
Executive Secretary: JOSEPH E. DUPUIS
Forestry Department Head: RALPH GOODE
Natural Resources Department Head: SAM MORIGEAU
Tribal Chairman: MICHAEL T. PABLO
Publication(s): *Char-Koosta News*
Keyword(s): Cultural Preservation, Environmental Preservation, Land Use Planning, Renewable Resources, Wildlife Management

CONFERENCE OF NATIONAL PARK COOPERATING ASSOCIATIONS
8375 Jumpers Hole Rd. Suite 104, Millersville, MD 21108
Phone: 410-647-9001; Fax: 410-647-9003; E-mail: cnpca@nps.gov
Founded: 1977
Scope: National
Description: CNPCA is the official umbrella organization for nonprofit interpretive associations that operate bookstores and sales areas in national parks and in other federal, state, and municipal vistor centers. The Associations are the single largest contributors of donated funds for the support of education, vistor services, and research activities in our nation's parks ($17 million per year).
Contact(s):
Executive Director: PAULA DEGEN, 8375 Jumpers Hole Rd., Suite 104, Millersville, MD 21108; Phone: 410-647-9001
Publication(s): *Newswire; Exchange, The; Cooperating Association Directory*
Keyword(s): Natural Areas, Outdoor Recreation, Public Lands, Training

CONNECTICUT ASSOCIATION OF SOIL AND WATER CONSERVATION DISTRICTS, INC.
Attn: President, 54 Bare Hill Rd., Goshen, CT 06756
Scope: Statewide
Contact(s):
President: JOHN BREAKELL; Phone: 860-491-2243
Secretary/Treasurer: TONY INCH, 134 Heather Lane, Wilton, CT 06897; Phone: 203-762-9994
Vice President: NORMA O'LEARY, 62 O'Leary Place, Thompson, CT 06277; Phone: 860-923-2969; Fax: 860-923-9554
Keyword(s): Conservation Districts

CONNECTICUT AUDUBON SOCIETY, INC.
118 Oak St., Hartford, CT 06106
Phone: 860-527-8737
Founded: 1898; Membership: 8,500
Scope: Statewide
Description: Dedicated to environmental education to conserve natural resources. Sanctuary acquisition and management, legislative action, and wildlife and natural areas research.
Contact(s):
President: SHERMAN T. KENT; Phone: 860-527-8737
Vice President: PETER KUNKEL
Vice President: BRAD BELISLE
Vice President: BARBARA MILLER
Vice President: JUDITH RICHARDSON
Chairman of the Board: LESLIE CAROTHERS
Director of Development: ALISON OLIVIERI; Phone: 203-254-3315
Director of Environmental Affairs: LISA SANTACROCE; Phone: 860-527-8737
Editor: CATHY O'DONNELL; Phone: 203-254-1092
Teacher/Naturalist: LAURIE PARADIS-BRANT
Teacher/Naturalist: ANN F. GUION
Teacher/Naturalist: KASHA BREAU
Teacher/Naturalist: CHRIS KRUMPERMAN
Teacher/Naturalist: RICHARD JULIAN
Teacher/Naturalist: JEFF WEILER
Teacher/Naturalist: JAMES SIRCH
Vice President of Legal: W. BRADLEY MOREHOUSE
Keyword(s): Environmental and Conservation Education, Environmental Protection, Open Space, Sustainable Development, Wildlife and Wildlife Habitat

CONNECTICUT B.A.S.S. CHAPTER FEDERATION
Attn: President, P.O. Box 763, Killingsworth, CT 06419
Scope: Statewide
Description: An organization of Bassmaster chapters, affiliated with the Bass Anglers Sportsman Society, organized to fight pollution, assist state and national conservation agencies in their efforts, and teach the young people of our country good conservation practices. Dedicated to the realistic conservation of our water resources.
Contact(s):
President: FRED PERRY; Phone: 860-663-3330
Conservation Director: LEE JOHNSON, 155 Candlewood Lake Rd. North, New Milford, CT 06776; Phone: 860-350-1368

CONNECTICUT BOTANICAL SOCIETY
P.O. Box 208104, Yale University Herbarium, 165 Prospect St., New Haven, CT 06520-8104
Founded: 1903; Membership: 300
Scope: Statewide
Description: The Society increases knowledge of the state's flora accumulate and maintains specimens and records for a permanent botanical record. The Society also recommends botanically significant areas for protection and supports scholarly botanical research.
Contact(s):
President: CASPER J. ULTEE; Phone: 860-633-7557; E-mail: casperu@aol.com
Vice President: CAROL LEMMON; Phone: 203-488-7813
Secretary: KAREN SEXTON; Phone: 860-228-4647
Treasurer: EDWARD P. STAUTON; Phone: 203-888-6277
Publication(s): *Newsletter; Yearbook; The Vascular Flora of Southeastern Connecticut*
Keyword(s): Conservation, Endangered and Threatened Species, Environmental Protection, Flowers, Plants, and Trees, Nature Preservation, Wetlands

 CONNECTICUT FOREST AND PARK ASSOCIATION
Middlefield, 16 Meriden Rd., Rockfall, CT 06481-2961
Phone: 860-346-2372; Fax: 860-347-7463; E-mail: conn.forest.assoc@snet.net; Web Site: www.ctwoodlands.org
Scope: Statewide
Description: A representative statewide organization, affiliated with the National Wildlife Federation and the National Woodland Owners Association, dedicated to the protection and enhancement of wildlife and its habitat through public education and government interaction.
Contact(s):
President: RICHARD A. WHITEHOUSE
Executive Director: JOHN E. HIBBARD
Representative: RUTH CUTLER
Alternate Representative and Editor: CAROL E. YOUELL
Publication(s): *Connecticut Woodlands*

CONNECTICUT FUND FOR THE ENVIRONMENT
1032 Chapel St., 3rd Fl., New Haven, CT 06510
Phone: 203-787-0646; Fax: 203-787-0246
Membership: 3,000

Scope: Statewide
Description: CFE is a nonprofit group dedicated to protecting Connecticut's natural resources through legal action, education and scientific investigation.
Contact(s):
President: DR. GORDON GEBALLE
Vice-President: CAMPBELL HUDSON III
Vice-President: MICHAEL KASHGARIAN
Secretary: NANCY FAESY
Treasurer: THOMAS HOLLOWAY
Executive Director: DONALD S. STRAIT
Publication(s): *Newsletter; Fact Sheets; Annual Reports*
Keyword(s): Air Quality and Pollution, Energy, Open Space, Toxic Substances, Water Pollution, Wetlands

CONNECTICUT PUBLIC INTEREST RESEARCH GROUP (Conn PIRG)
41 S. Main, W. Hartford, CT 06107
Phone: 203-233-7554; Fax: 203-233-7574
Founded: 1972; Membership: 31,000
Scope: Statewide
Description: Works for concrete solutions to improve and protect our environment. Engaged in public education, study, and legislative action in many areas of the environment, including water and air pollution and solid waste.
Contact(s):
State Director: DON JACOBSEN
Organizing Director: APRIL CLAXTON
Field Associate: KATIE WHITE
Publication(s): *ConnPIRG Reports*
Keyword(s): Air Quality and Pollution, Endangered and Threatened Species, Solid Waste Management, Toxic Substances, Water Pollution Management

CONNECTICUT RIVER WATERSHED COUNCIL INC.
Headquarters, One Ferry St., Easthampton, MA 01027
Phone: 413-529-9500; Fax: 413-529-9501; E-mail: crwc@crocker.com; Web Site: www.ctriver.org
Founded: 1952; Membership: 2,300
Scope: Regional
Description: A member-supported nonprofit organization, CRWC is a regional voice for improvement and protection of the Connecticut River and water resources throughout the 11,260 square-mile, four-state river basin of Vermont, New Hampshire, Massachusetts, and Connecticut. CRWC participates in relevant environmental and resource allocation issues through its land conservancy, water quality improvement, and watershed stewardship programs. Land conservancy revolving loan fund. Conservation education and research grant fund.
Contact(s):
Chairman: NEIL W. SHERIDAN
Secretary: NANCY ROGERS
Executive Director: TOM MINER
Vice Chair: ERLING HEISTAD
Vice Chair: NANCY ROGERS
Vice Chair: ANDY WIZNER
Publication(s): *Currents and Eddies; Complete Boating Guide to the Connecticut River*
Keyword(s): Environmental Protection, Land Use Planning, Rivers, Water Pollution, Water Quality, Watersheds, Wetlands

CONNECTICUT WATERFOWL ASSOCIATION, INC.
P.O. Box 74, Bozrah, CT 06334-0074
Phone: 860-535-8482
Founded: 1967; Membership: 300
Scope: Statewide
Description: To preserve, reclaim, and enhance wetland and wildlife habitat in the state of Connecticut in a manner that promotes the wise use of our natural resources and the progress of our society.
Contact(s):
President: PATRICIA HOCHMAN, 18 Langworthy Ave., Stonington, CT 06378
Vice President: PAUL ROTHBART, 177 Romulus Rd., Cheshire, CT 06410; Phone: 860-295-9523
Treasurer: PAUL CAPOTOSTO, 23 Beechwood Rd., Oakdale, CT 06370; Phone: 860-642-7239
Publication(s): *Connecticut Waterfowl and Wetlands*
Keyword(s): Environmental and Conservation Education, Waterfowl, Wetlands, Wildlife and Wildlife Habitat, Wildlife Management

CONSERVANCY OF SOUTHWEST FLORIDA, THE
Attn: Director for Marketing and Communications, 1450 Merrihue Dr., Naples, FL 34102-3449
Phone: 941-262-0304; Fax: 941-262-0672; E-mail: home@conservancy.org; Web Site: www.conservancy.org
Founded: 1964; Membership: 5,500
Scope: Local Region
Description: Leading the challenge to protect and sustain Southwest Florida's natural environment through environmental policy, science and education. The Conservancy manages two nature centers, offers learning adventures, rehabilitates injured wildlife, monitors sea turtles and acquires land.
Contact(s):
President and CEO: DAVID E. GUGGENHEIM; E-mail: davidg@conservancy.org
VP, Environmental Policy: MICHAEL SMITH; E-mail: michaels@conservancy.org
Div. Director, Environmental Education: HOLLIS J. GILLESPIE; E-mail: hollisg@conservancy.org
Director, Environmental Science: STEVE BORTONE; E-mail: steveb@conservancy.org
Director, Marketing and Communications: MARAN HILGENDORF; E-mail: maranh@conservancy.org
Publication(s): *Update; Eye on the Issues; Yearbook*
Keyword(s): Biodiversity, Conservation Biology, Endangered and Threatened Species, Environmental and Conservation Education, Internships, Land Preservation, Museum, Nature Centers, Sea Turtles, Wildlife Rehabilitation

CONSERVATION AND RESEARCH FOUNDATION, INC., THE
24 Schillhammer Rd., Jericho, VT 05465
Founded: 1953
Scope: National
Description: To promote the conservation of renewable natural resources; to encourage study and research in the biological sciences; and to deepen understanding of the intricate relationship between man and the environment that supports him.
Contact(s):
President: H. W. VOGELMANN, 24 Schillhammer Rd., Jericho, UT 05405
Secretary: RICHARD H. GOODWIN SR., Box 5264, Connecticut College, New London, CT 06320
Keyword(s): Air Quality and Pollution, Environmental Law, Population Growth, Renewable Resources, Wildlife and Wildlife Habitat

CONSERVATION COUNCIL FOR HAWAII
PMB-203, 111 E. Puainako St., Suite. 585, Hilo, HI 96720
Phone: 808-968-6360; Fax: 808-589-6360; Web Site: www.planet-hawaii.com/~cch
Scope: Statewide
Description: A representative statewide organization, affiliated with the National Wildlife Federation, dedicated to the protection and enhancement of wildlife and its habitat through public education and government interaction.
Contact(s):
Chair, Representative and Editor: KATE SCHUERCH
Executive Director: KAREN BLUE
Alternate Representative: SEAN CASEY
Publication(s): *The Hawai'I Conserver*

CONSERVATION COUNCIL OF NORTH CAROLINA
P.O. Box 12671, Raleigh, NC 27605

Phone: 919-839-0006; Fax: 919-839-0767; E-mail: ccnc@bellsouth.net
Founded: 1968; Membership: 750, 30+ member organizations
Scope: Statewide
Description: To initiate, participate in, and coordinate local, regional, state, and national action in environmental and energy matters and in conservation and environmental education.
Contact(s):
President: RICK JOHNSON, 600 Winding Creek, Carthage, NC 28327
Vice President: JANE SHARP, 307 Granville Rd., Chapel Hill, NC 27514
Coordinator: CARRIE OREN; Phone: 919-839-0006
Editor: MAUREEN SUTTON, 345 N. Page, Southern Pines, NC 28387
Lobbyist: NAT MUND; Phone: 919-839-0020
Publication(s): *Carolina Conservationist Newsletter*
Keyword(s): Air Quality and Pollution, Coasts, Energy, Environmental and Conservation Education, Nuclear/Radiation, Rivers, Solid Waste

CONSERVATION DISTRICTS FOUNDATION INC.
Davis Conservation Library, 408 E. Main, P.O. Box 776, League City, TX 77574-0855
Phone: 281-332-3402; Fax: 281-332-5259
Founded: 1962
Scope: National
Description: Directed by the Conservation Districts Foundation, Inc., an adjunct of the National Association of Conservation Districts. Collects various conservation and environmental education materials. Dedicated to the memory of Waters S. Davis, Past President of NACD.
Contact(s):
Chief Executive Officer: ERNEST SHEA, NACD, 509 Capitol Ct. NE, Washington, DC 20002; Phone: 202-547-6223
Director of Office of Public Affairs: RONALD G. FRANCIS; Phone: 281-332-3402/28; E-mail: ron-francis@nacdnet.org
Keyword(s): Environmental and Conservation Education, Soil Conservation, Water Resources, Wetlands, Wildlife Management, Libraries

CONSERVATION FEDERATION OF MARYLAND/For A Rural Maryland (F.A.R.M.)
P.O. Box 455, Poolesville, MD 20837
Phone: 301-916-3510
Scope: Statewide
Description: The Conservation Federation of Maryland is devoted to the wise use, conservation, aesthetic appreciation, and restoration of wildlife and other natural resources. The Conservation Federation of Maryland was recently merged with For A Rural Maryland to help safeguard the dwindling supply of farmland and open space in the state of Maryland.
Contact(s):
President: DOLOLRES MILMORE, 18801 River Rd., Poolesville, MD 20837
Vice President: CAROLINE TAYLOR GOLDMAN, 15711Hughes Rd., Poolesville, MD 20837
Secretary: CATHY HALL, 17826 Walling Rd., Poolesville, MD 20837
Treasurer: MARILYN EMERY, 9713 Old Spring Dr., Kensington, MD
Keyword(s): Agriculture, Conservation of Protected Areas, Environmental Justice, Land Preservation, Sustainable Development

CONSERVATION FEDERATION OF MISSOURI

728 W. Main St., Jefferson City, MO 65101-1159
Phone: 573-634-2322; Fax: 573-634-8205; E-mail: modfed@sockets.net; Web Site: www.confedmo.com
Scope: Statewide
Description: A representative statewide organization, affiliated with the National Wildlife Federation, dedicated to the protection and enhancement of wildlife and its habitat through public education and government interaction.
Contact(s):
President and Alternative Representative: HOWARD FLEMING
Executive Director: DENNY BALLARD
Representative: ABE PHILLIPS
Editor: CHARLES DAVIDSON
Publication(s): *Missouri Wildlife*

CONSERVATION FORCE
3900 N. Causeway Blvd., Suite 1045, Metairie, LA 70002
Phone: 504-837-1233; Fax: 504-837-1145; E-mail: JJW-NO@worldnet.att.net
Founded: 1997; Membership: 50,125
Scope: International
Description: The force was formed to unify sportsmen's organizations, improve the profile of hunters and further the role and valve of hunting in wildlife conservation as a force.
Contact(s):
President: JOHN J. JACKSON III
Vice President: DR. JAMES TEER; Phone: 409-458-1359; Fax: 409-845-3786
International Vice President: BERTRAND DES CLERS; Phone: 011-33-1565-97755; Fax: 011-33-1565-97756
Publication(s): *Conservation Force Supplement to the Hunting Report*
Keyword(s): Bears, Biodiversity, Conservation, Conservation Plannning, Endangered and Threatened Species, Environmental Law, Fish Wildlife Management, Hunting, Indigenous People, International Conservation, International Wildlife, Legal Advocacy, Sustainability, Wildlife and Wildlife Habitat, Wildlife Management

CONSERVATION FUND, THE
1800 North Kent St., Suite 1120, Arlington, VA 22209
Phone: 703-525-6300; Fax: 703-525-4610
Founded: 1985
Scope: National
Description: The Conservation Fund seeks sustainable conservation solutions for the 21st century, emphasizing the integration of economic and environmental goals. Through land conservation services, demonstration projects, education and community-based activities, the Fund develops innovative measures to conserve land and water. The Fund forges partnerships to protect America's irreplaceable outdoor heritage and a tangible legacy for future generations. Programs: Land Conservation Services, Sustainable Programs, American Land Conservation Program, American Greenways, Freshwater Institute, Conservation Leadership Network, Civil War Battlefield Campaign. Awards: Alexander Calder Conservation Award, Cartledge Award for Excellence in Environmental Education, American Greenways DuPont, American Land Conservation, CF Industries National Watershed, Hastings National Park Leadership awards.
Contact(s):
President: JOHN F. TURNER
Treasurer: HADLAI A. HULL
Secretary: PAMELA GRAY
Chairman: PATRICK F. NOONAN
Vice President, Development: ELIZABETH M. MADISON
Chief Financial Officer: STEVEN F. KNELL
Conservation Leadership Network Liaison: MARK A. BENEDICT
Director of American Greenways Program: EDWARD T. MCMAHON
Director of Civil War Battlefield Program: FRANCES H. KENNEDY
Director of Great Lakes Office: ELIZABETH J. CISAR; Phone: 312-913-9305
Director of Midwest Office: MARGARET A. KOHRING; Phone: 312-913-9459
Director of Montana Office: KIKU A. HANES; Phone: 406-388-9733
Director of Texas Office: DANIEL G. McNAMARA JR.; Phone: 512-477-1712
Director of Vermont Office: NANCY BELL; Phone: 802-492-3368
Editor: MIKE McQUEEN
Senior Vice President and General Counsel: RICHARD L. ERDMANN
Senior Vice President, Real Estate: DAVID M. SUTHERLAND

NON-GOVERNMENTAL ORGANIZATIONS - C

Senior Vice President, Sustainable Programs: LAWRENCE A. SELZER
Vice President, Florida Office: ELIZABETH B. DOWDLE; Phone: 561-624-4925
Vice President, Georgia Office: REX R. BONER; Phone: 770-414-0211
Vice President, Western Regional Office: SYDNEY S. MACY; Phone: 303-444-4369
Publication(s): *Common Ground*
Keyword(s): Environmental and Conservation Education, Land Purchase, Land Use Planning, Training, Water Resources

CONSERVATION INTERNATIONAL
2501 M Street NW, Suite 200, Washington, DC 20037
Phone: 202-429-5660; Fax: 202-887-5188; Web Site: www.conservation.org
Founded: 1987; Membership: 4,000
Scope: International
Description: Conservation International (CI) is a private nonprofit organization dedicated to the preservation of tropical and temperate ecosystems. CI works in partnership with indigenous peoples and with organizations to sustain biological diversity and the ecological processes that support life on earth. CI has programs in Bolivia, Botswana, Brazil, Colombia, Costa Rica, Ecuador, Ghana, Guatemala, Guyana, Indonesia, Madagascar, Mexico, Papua, New Guinea, Panama, Peru, the Philippines, the Solomon Islands, and Suriname.
Contact(s):
President: RUSSELL MITTERMEIER
CEO and Chairman of the Board: PETER SELIGMANN
Keyword(s): Biodiversity, Endangered and Threatened Species, Environmental and Conservation Education, Forests and Forestry, International Conservation

CONSERVATION LAW FOUNDATION (CLF) (Vermont Office)

New England Region
15 E. State St., Suite 4, Montpelier, VT 05602
Phone: 802-223-5992; Fax: 802-223-0060; Web Site: www.clif.org
Scope: Regional

CONSERVATION LAW FOUNDATION, INC. (CLF)
Headquarters, 62 Summer St., Boston, MA 02110
Phone: 617-350-0990; Web Site: www.clf.org
Founded: 1966; Membership: 10,000
Scope: Regional
Description: CLF is a nonprofit, member-supported environmental law organization dedicated to improving resource management, environmental protection, and public health in New England. Work includes: Energy and water conservation, environmental health, transportation planning, water resources protection, land preservation, and marine resources protection.
Contact(s):
President: DOUGLAS I. FOY
Treasurer: EUGENE H. CLAPP
Chairman of the Board: CHARLES C. CABOT JR.
Vice Chairman of the Board: PAULA W. GOLD
Vice Chairman of the Board: JOHN M. TEAL
Publication(s): *Take Back Your Streets (community transportation planning); Power to Spare I&II (energy conservation opportunities in New England); A Silent and Costly Epidemic (costs of childhood lead poisoning); TROUBLED WATERS (report on the environmental health of Casco Bay); Annual Report; Journal: Conservation Matters; Handbood of Local Pesticide Regulations for Massachusetts; Rim of the Gulf (estuaries as valuable natural resources); The Effects of Fishing Gear on the Seafloor of New England*
Keyword(s): Air Quality and Pollution, Energy, Environmental Law, Transportation, Water Pollution
   Main Office, 120 Tillson Ave., Rockland, ME 04841
   Phone: 207-594-8107
Scope: National

CONSERVATION TECHNOLOGY INFORMATION CENTER
1220 Potter Dr., Rm. 170, West Lafayette, IN 47906-1383
Phone: 765-494-9555; Fax: 765-494-5969
Founded: 1982; Membership: 70 Corporate, 34 Institutional, 7 Government Agencies, 20,000 individuals
Scope: National
Description: Conservation Technology Information Center (CTIC) is a nonprofit information and data transfer center. The national Center promotes environmentally and economically beneficial agricultural decision-making by: producing and circulating information, data, and contacts, coordinating national initiatives, and sponsoring interactive meetings and conferences. The Center is supported by members and participating governmental agencies.
Contact(s):
Executive Director: JOHN HASSELL; E-mail: hassell@ctic.purdue.edu
Chair, Board of Directors: PAUL KINDINGER, 11701 Boman Dr., Ste. 110, St. Louis, MO 63146; Phone: 314-567-6655; Fax: 314-567-6808
Natural Resources Specialist: DAN TOWERY; E-mail: towery@ctic.purdue.edu
Project Manager: KAROL KEPPY
Water Quality Specialist: LYN KIRSHNER; E-mail: kirschner@ctic.purdue.edu
Publication(s): *CTIC Partners Newsletter; Conservation Tillage: A Checklist for U.S. Farmers; Watershed Management; Nonpoint Source Water Quality Contacts Directory*
Keyword(s): Conservation Tillage, Precision Farming, Water Quality, Watersheds

CONSERVATION TREATY SUPPORT FUND
3705 Cardiff Rd., Chevy Chase, MD 20815
Phone: 301-654-3150; Fax: 301-652-6390; E-mail: ctsf@conservationtreaty.org; Web Site: www.conservationtreaty.org
Founded: 1986
Scope: International
Description: CTSF provides direct support to major inter-governmental treaties, including CITES (the endangered species treaty), the wetlands and the migratory species treaty, through fund-raising and education.
Contact(s):
President: GEORGE A. FURNESS JR.; Phone: 301-652-6390; Fax: 301-652-6390
Vice President: FREDERICK E. MORRIS; Phone: 703-683-8512; Fax: 703-683-4622
Secretary: FAITH T. CAMPBELL; Phone: 202-861-2242; Fax: 202-861-4622
Treasurer: LAWRENCE N. MASON; Phone: 703-241-8896; Fax: 703-241-8896
Publication(s): *CITES Endangered Species Book; CITES Video (also Wetlands Video); Caribbean Buyer Beware Poster "Wild Treasures of the Caribbean"; "Treasures of Wetlands" Poster; Bateman prints and posters*
Keyword(s): Biodiversity, Habitat Conservation, International Conservation, Wetlands, Wildlife and Wildlife Habitat

CONSERVATION TRUST OF PUERTO RICO
P.O. Box 9023554, 155 Tetuan St., Old San Juan, PR 00902-3554
Phone: 787-722-5834; E-mail: FIDEICOMISO@fideicomiso.org; Web Site: www.fideicomiso.org
Founded: 1970
Scope: Statewide
Description: A private nonprofit institution created by the Governor of Puerto Rico and the U.S. Secretary of the Interior to preserve and enhance Puerto Rico's natural beauty and resources, primarily through land acquisition. Owns or manages over 14,000 acres representative of the island's major endangered habitats. It educates the public about environmental issues; manages a vast reforestation program; and finances conservation in Caribbean countries via debt-for-nature swaps. Puerto Rico's major conservation organization, the

Trust acts as land acquisition agent for the Commonwealth Department of Natural Resources.
Contact(s):
Chairman: ANTONIO LUIS FERRE
Executive Director: FRANCISCO JAVIER BLANCO
Assistant Executive Director: JOSÉ L. BARRETO
Program and Properties Director: ALEXIS MOLINARES
Keyword(s): Land Protection

COOK INLET KEEPER
P.O. Box 3269, Homer, AK 99603
Phone: 907-235-4068; Fax: 907-235-4069; E-mail: keeper@xy2.net; Web Site: www.xy2/~keeper
Founded: 1995; Membership: 600
Scope: Regional
Description: The mission of Cook Inlet Keeper is to protect the Cook Inlet Watershed and the life it sustains. Keeper relies on environmental monitoring, research, education, and advocacy to give citizens the tools they need to protect water quality.
Contact(s):
President: STEVE KOTEFF; Phone: 907-345-8302; E-mail: koteff@alaska.net
Vice President: LISA THOMAS; Phone: 907-235-4102; Fax: 907-235-4202
Secretary: PAMELA K. MILLER; Phone: 907-276-3337; Fax: 907-222-7715; E-mail: acat@akcf.org
Treasurer: JIM HEMMING; Phone: 907-235-2535; Fax: 907-235-2531
Executive Director: BOB SHAVELSON
Director: BRAD VAN APPEL
Publication(s): *State of the Inlet Report; Cook Inlet Watershed Directory; Cook Inlet GIS Atlas on CD-ROM*
Keyword(s): Environmental Law, Toxic Substances, Water Quality, Watersheds

COOPER ORNITHOLOGICAL SOCIETY
Department of Biology, University of California, Los Angeles, CA 90024-1606
Founded: 1893; Membership: 2,340
Scope: National
Description: Observation and cooperative study of birds; the spread of interest in bird study; the conservation of birds and wildlife in general; the publication of ornithological knowledge.
Contact(s):
President: DR. J. MICHAEL SCOTT, Department of Fish and Wildlife Resources, University of Idaho, Moscow, ID 83844-1141; Phone: 208-885-6960; E-mail: mscott@uidaho.edu
Secretary: DR. EILEEN KIRSCH, BRD/USGS, Upper Mississippi Science Center, P.O. Box 818, LaCrosse, WI 54602; Phone: 608-783-6451 ext226; E-mail: eileen_kirsch@usgs.gov
Treasurer: DR. ERICK CAMPBELL, 2114 NE 90th Ave, Vancouver, WA 98664; Phone: 503-952-6382; E-mail: ecampbel@or.blm.gov
Editor, Studies in Avian Biology: DR. JOHN T. ROTENBERRY, Department of Biology, University of California, Riverside, CA 92521; Phone: 909-787-3953; E-mail: rote@citrus.ucr.edu
Editor, The Condor: DR. WALTER KOENIG, Hastings Natural History Reservation, 38601 E. Carmel Valley Rd., Carmal Valley, CA 93924; Phone: 408-659-5981; E-mail: wicker@uclink.berkeley.edu
President-Elect: DR. GLENN E. WALSBERG, Department of Biology, Arizona State University, Tempe, AZ 85287-1501; Phone: 602-965-3543; E-mail: walsberg@asu.edu
Publication(s): *Condor, The; Studies in Avian Biology*

COOSA RIVER BASIN INITIATIVE
408 Broad St., Rome, GA 30161
Phone: 706-232-2724; E-mail: crbi@roman.net
Founded: 1992; Membership: 160
Scope: Regional
Description: CRBI works to inform and empower citizens so they may become involved with the process of creating a cleaner, healthier, economically viable Coosa River Basin.
Contact(s):
President: RAY KELLY; Phone: 256-779-6299
Vice President: TERRY JENNINGS; Phone: 706-232-0973; E-mail: jennings@roman.net
Education Chair: LESLIE CARROLL; Phone: 706-235-6232; E-mail: blrcarrol@aol.com
Membership Chair: SUSAN CARLSON; Phone: 706-290-0536; E-mail: carlsons@mail.floyd.public.lib.ga.us
Water Monitoring Chair: CHERYL GARNER; Phone: 706-291-1702; E-mail: CGarner32@aol.com
Publication(s): *Main Stream, The*
Keyword(s): Environmental Cleanup, Environmental Legislation, Environmental Protection, Flood Control, Habitat Conservation, Lakes, Preservation and Protection, Restoration, Stewardship, Water Conservation, Water Pollution, Water Quality, Water Resources, Watersheds, Wetlands

CORAL REEF ALLIANCE, THE (CORAL)
64 Shattuck Square, Suite 220, Berkeley, CA 94704
Phone: 510-848-0110; Fax: 510-848-3720; E-mail: coralmail@aol.com; Web Site: www.coral.org/
Founded: 1994; Membership: 3,500
Scope: National
Description: The Coral Reef Alliance is a nonprofit organization that works with divers, government conservation organizations, and others to promote coral reef conservation around the the world. CORAL focuses primarily on helping local communities to establish their own marine protected area. CORAL also sponsors a number of educational programs and publications.
Contact(s):
Executive Director: STEPHEN COLWELL
Director of Education: CARLOS WESLEY
Managing Director: SHAWN REIFSTECK
Publication(s): *Coral News; Coral Reefs - The Vanishing Rainbow*
Keyword(s): Coasts, Conservation of Protected Areas, Coral Reefs, International Conservation

CORNELL LAB OF ORNITHOLOGY
159 Sapsucker Woods Rd., Ithaca, NY 14850
Phone: 607-254-2473; E-mail: www.ornith.cornell.edu
Founded: 1917; Membership: 23,000
Scope: National
Description: A membership institute dedicated to the study, appreciation, and conservation of birds world-wide. The Lab maintains programs in academic research, public education, and citizen involvement. The Lab promotes science to foster understanding about nature and the importance of the earth's biological diversity.
Contact(s):
Associate Director: SCOTT SUTCLIFFE; Phone: 607-254-2424
Associate Editor: LESLIE INTEMANN; Phone: 607-254-2451
Curator of Library of Natural Sounds: GREGORY BUDNEY; Phone: 607-254-2406
Curatorial Associate for Systematics and Collections: KEVIN McGOWAN; Phone: 607-257-8135
Director of Bioacoustics Research Program: CHRISTOPHER CLARK; Phone: 607-254-2405
Director of Bird Population Studies: ANDRE DHONDT; Phone: 607-254-2445
Director of Education Program: RICK BONNEY; Phone: 607-254-2440; E-mail: birdeducation@cornell.edu
Editor: TIM GALLAGHER; Phone: 607-254-2443
Louis Agassiz Fuertes Director: JOHN FITZPATRICK; Phone: 607-254-2410
Publication(s): *Living Bird; Birdscope; Bird Notes*
Keyword(s): Biodiversity, Birds, Environmental and Conservation Education, Natural History, Nongame Wildlife

COUNCIL FOR ENVIRONMENTAL EDUCATION
c/o Josetta Hawthorne, Executive Director, 5555 Morningside Dr., Suite 212, Houston, TX 77005
Phone: 713-520-1936; Fax: 713-520-8008
Founded: 1970

NON-GOVERNMENTAL ORGANIZATIONS - C

Scope: National
Description: The Council for Environmental Education is a nonprofit education organization creating a partnership and network between education and natural resource professionals. CEE cosponsors balanced, non-biased environmental education programs such as Project Learning Tree, Project WILD, Project WILD Aquatic and Project WET. In an effort to encourage more environmental education outreach to urban youth, CEE has launched WET in the City, a community-based water education initiative.
Contact(s):
President: BILL ANDREWS; Phone: 916-657-5374
Executive Director and Director, WET in the City: JOSETTA HAWTHORNE
Project Learning Tree Director: KATHY MCGLAUFLIN, 1111 19TH St., NW, Suite 780, Washington, DC 20036; Phone: 202-436-2468
Project WET Director: DENNIS NELSON, Montana State University, Culbertson Hall, Bozeman, MT 59717; Phone: 406-994-5392
Project WILD Director: DONNA ASBURY, 707 Conservation Ln., Suite 305, Gaithersburg, MD 20878; Phone: 301-527-8900
Keyword(s): Environmental and Conservation Education, Urban Environment

COUNCIL FOR PLANNING AND CONSERVATION
Box 228, Beverly Hills, CA 90213
Phone: 310-276-2685; E-mail: esharris@earthlink.net
Scope: Statewide
Description: Serves as a clearinghouse for information and gives inexperienced groups ready access to advice and assistance. Provides a center through which opportunities for southern California's environmental protection and enhancement may be communicated. Concerns include: air and water quality, water supply, energy options, waste management, land use, transportation, coastal conservation, urban planning and housing.
Contact(s):
Vice President: BETTY H. HARRIS
President and Executive Director: ELLEN STERN HARRIS
Treasurer and Secretary: SAM WEISZ
Keyword(s): Air Quality, Energy, Planning Management, Transportation, Urban and Rural Development, Coastal Construction and Erosion

COUSTEAU SOCIETY, INC., THE
Headquarters, 870 Greenbrier Cir., Suite 402, Chesapeake, VA 23320
Phone: 800-441-4395; Fax: 727-523-2747; E-mail: cousteau@infi.net; Web Sites: www.cousteau.org; dolphinlog.org or cousteausociety.org
Founded: 1973; Membership: 200,000
Scope: International
Description: A nonprofit, membership-supported environmental education organization dedicated to the protection and improvement of the quality of life for present and future generations. Believing that an informed and alerted public can best make the choices that will sustain the water planet, it produces television films, research, books and other publications, exploring relationships between humans and ecosystems.
Contact(s):
President: FRANCINE COUSTEAU
Vice President Finance: ROBERT L. STEELE
Publication(s): *Calypso Log; Dolphin Log*
Keyword(s): Aquatic Species, Environmental and Conservation Education, Marine Conservation, Sustainable Ecosystems, Water Resources

COUSTEAU SOCIETY, INC., THE (France Office)
92 Avenue Kleber, Paris, Paris 75116 France
Phone: 44-34-06-06
Scope: International

CRAIGHEAD ENVIRONMENTAL RESEARCH INSTITUTE
Box 156, Moose, WY 83012
Phone: 307-733-3387
Founded: 1955

Scope: National
Description: A nonprofit professional organization of scientists, dedicated to exploring the cause-and-effect relationships of man and his environment. Activity includes research, education, and conservation, with emphasis on ecological studies and interdisciplinary approach. Originally the Outdoor Recreation Institute. Staff Members: 6.
Contact(s):
President: FRANK C. CRAIGHEAD JR.
Media Director: CHARLES S. CRAIGHEAD; Phone: 307-739-9527
Program Director: FRANK L. CRAIGHEAD
Keyword(s): Raptors, Rivers, Wildlife and Wildlife Habitat

CRAIGHEAD WILDLIFE-WILDLANDS INSTITUTE
5200 Upper Miller Creek Rd., Missoula, MT 59803
Phone: 406-251-3867; Fax: 406-251-5069; E-mail: cwwi@mssl.uswest.net
Founded: 1977
Scope: National
Description: A nonprofit, multidisciplinary research center in the Northern Rockies devoted to field-based ecological discovery and scientific activism. The Institute's mission is to generate new ecological information and concepts, widely communicate these insights, and influence public policy and individual behavior in directions that preserve regional biodiversity.
Contact(s):
Chairman of the Board: DR. JOHN J. CRAIGHEAD, 5125 Orchard Ln., Missoula, MT 59803; Phone: 406-251-3944
Director of Science: DR. JOHN T. HOGG, 194 McCalla Creek Dr., Stevensville, MT 59870; Phone: 406-642-3035
Publication(s): *The Grizzly Bears of Yellowstone: Their Ecology in the Yellowstone Ecosystem 1959-1992 (1995); An Integrated Satellite Technique to Evaluate Grizzly Bear Habitat Use (1997); Mapping Arctic Vegetation in Northwest Alaska Using Landsat MSS Imagery (1988); Hawks in Hand (1997)*
Keyword(s): Biodiversity, Ecology, Endangered and Threatened Species, Predators, Research, Sustainable Ecosystems

CRESTON VALLEY WILDLIFE MANAGEMENT AUTHORITY
P.O. Box 640, Creston, British Columbia V0B 1G0 Canada
Phone: 250-428-3260
Founded: 1968
Scope: Statewide
Description: A unique joint provincial-private agency established in 1968 to conserve, develop, and manage remaining waterfowl habitat in a mountain valley. Broader purpose is to demonstrate cooperative wetland management in action. Operates a 17,000-acre wetland and upland complex, primarily as a waterfowl management area, with public recreation facilities (campground, trails, and visitor center).
Contact(s):
Area Manager: BRIAN G. STUSHNOFF; Phone: 250-428-3260
Chairman of the Management Authority: STEVE BULLOCK; Phone: 250-428-2214
Publication(s): *Creston Valley Wildlife Management Area Annual*

CROSBY ABORETUM, THE, Mississippi State University
P.O. Box 1639, Picayune, MS 39466
Phone: 601-799-2311; Fax: 601-799-2372; E-mail: crosbyar@datastar.net; Web Site: www.crosbyarboretum.org
Founded: 1980; Membership: 700
Scope: Statewide
Description: The main activity of the Arboretum is to preserve, protect and display plants native to the pearl river drainage basin. Additionally, we provide environmental and horticultural research opportunities and offer educational, scientific, and recreational programs.
Contact(s):
President: LYNN GAMMILL; Phone: 601-264-5249; Fax: 601-271-2064
Vice President: ED BLAKE JR.; Phone: 601-544-1935; Fax: 601-544-0003
Secretary: JANE WILDS; Phone: 504-641-7931

Treasurer: STEWART GAMILL III; Phone: 601-264-5246; Fax: 601-271-2064
Senior Curator: BOB BRZUSZEK; Phone: 601-799-2311; Fax: 601-799-2372
Publication(s): *Native Trees for Urban Landscapes*
Keyword(s): Biodiversity, Conservation, Ecology, Environmental and Conservation Education

D

DAWES ARBORETUM, THE
7770 Jacksontown Rd., SE, Newark, OH 43056-9380
Phone: 740-323-2355 / 1-800-44-DAWES; Web Site: www.dawesarb.org
Founded: 1929
Scope: Statewide
Description: A not-for-profit organization that promotes the planting of forest and ornamental trees, and promotes increased love and knowledge of trees, shrubs, and related subjects through over 200 annually-offered classes and programs. The 1,149-acre grounds are open daily from dawn to dusk, free of charge.
Contact(s):
Director: DONALD R. HENDRICKS
Editor: LUKE E. MESSINGER
Horticulturist: MICHAEL E. ECKER
Natural Resource Specialist: TIMOTHY A. MASON
Naturalist and Educator: LORI A. TOTMAN
Researcher: ELAINE G. HENDRICKS
Publication(s): *Dawes Arboretum Newsletter, The*
Keyword(s): Botanical Gardens, Flowers, Plants, and Trees

DEEP-PORTAGE CONSERVATION RESERVE
2197 Nature Center Dr., NW, Hackensack, MN 56452-2431
Phone: 218-682-2325; Fax: 218-682-3121; Web Site: www.deep-portage.org
Founded: 1975
Scope: Statewide
Description: Deep-Portage is a 6,100-acre demonstration working forest with a primary purpose of environmental education. The campus includes dormitories, classrooms, laboratory, theater, interpretive center, natural history museum, and thirty-seven miles of recreational trails. It is owned by Cass County and operated by the Deep-Portage Conservation Foundation, a nonprofit corporation.
Contact(s):
Executive Director: DALE YERGER
Foundation President: CLARENCE WESTIN
Publication(s): *Deep-Portage Log*
Keyword(s): Environmental and Conservation Education, Forests and Forestry, Internships, Water Resources, Wildlife and Wildlife Habitat

DEFENDERS OF WILDLIFE
1101 14th St., NW, Suite 1400, Washington, DC 20005
Phone: 202-682-9400; Fax: 202-682-1331; E-mail: information@defenders.org; Web Site: www.defenders.org
Founded: 1947; Membership: 250,000
Scope: National
Description: Since 1947, Defenders of Wildlife has been one of the nation's most effective advocates for wildlife, endangered species, and habitat. Defenders works to protect and restore native species, habitats, ecosystems, and overall biological diversity. Defenders is a nonprofit, tax-exempt organization, supported by 250,000 members and activists across the country.
Contact(s):
President: RODGER SCHLICKEISEN
Secretary: ANN F. BOREN
Treasurer: ARTHUR C. MARTINEZ
Chairman of the Board: ALAN R. PILKINGTON
Director of Development: MARTHA SCHUMACHER
Director of Habitat Conservation Division: ROBERT DEWEY
Director of Legal Division: WILLIAM J. SNAPE III
Director of Media Relations: JOAN MOODY
Director of Membership: KATE MATHEWS
Director of Science Division: LAURA HOOD
Director of Species Conservation Division: ROBERT M. FERRIS
Director of West Coast: SARA VICKERMAN, 1637 Laurel St., Lake Oswego, OR 97034; Phone: 503-697-3222
Editor: HEIDI RIDGLEY
Editor: JAMES G. DEANE
Editor: MARIA W. CECIL
Regional Representative of Alaska: JOEL BENNETT, 15255 Point Louisa Rd., Juneau, AK 99801; Phone: 907-586-1255
Regional Representative of Arizona: CRAIG MILLER, 6020 S. Camino de la Tierra, Tucson, AZ 85746; Phone: 520-578-9334
Regional Representative of Florida: CHRISTINE SMALL, 31409 Prestwick Ave., Sorrento, FL 32776; Phone: 352-735-6909
Regional Representative of Florida: LAURIE MacDONALD, 103 Wildwood Ln., St. Petersburg, FL 33705; Phone: 813-821-9585
Regional Representative of New Mexico: SUSAN GEORGE, P.O. Box 40046, Albuquerque, NM 87196-0046; Phone: 505-255-5966
Regional Representative of New York: STEVE KENDROT, P.O. Box B2598, Plattsburgh, NY 12901; Phone: 518-563-9307
Regional Representative of Northern Rockies: HANK FISCHER, 1534 Mansfield Ave., Missoula, MT 59801; Phone: 406-549-0761
Regional Representative of Washington: GERRY RING ERICKSON, 2324 NE 103rd St., Seattle, WA 98125-7642; Phone: 206-522-5139/360-427-2887
Vice Chairman: WINSOME McINTOSH
Vice President for Communications: JAMES G. DEANE
Vice President for Operations: CHARLES J. ORASIN
Vice President for Program: MARK SHAFFER
Viewing Guide Program Manager: KATE DAVIES
Publication(s): *DEFENDERS*
Keyword(s): Biodiversity, Endangered and Threatened Species, Environment, Environmental and Conservation Education, Environmental Preservation, Environmental Protection, Nature Preservation, Predators, Wilderness, Wildlife and Wildlife Habitat, Wolves

DELAWARE ASSOCIATION OF CONSERVATION DISTRICTS
Attn: President, 2138 Graves Rd., Hockessin, DE 19707
Founded: 1953
Scope: Statewide
Description: DACD is a voluntary nonprofit alliance that provides a forum for discussion and coordination among the Delaware Conservation Districts as they work to ensure the wise use and treatment of renewable resources.
Contact(s):
President and Board Member: DARIEL RAKESTRAW, 2138 Graves Rd., Hockessin, DE 19707; Phone: 302-239-2969
Alternate Board Member: TERRY PEPPER, 104 Captain Davis Dr., Campden-Wyoming, DE 19934; Phone: 302-697-6176; Fax: 303-736-2040; E-mail: kentcol@aol.com
Staff Assistant: SHIRLEY BOWDEN, P.O. Box 242, Dover, DE 19903-0242; Phone: 302-739-4441, ext. 34; Fax: 302-739-6724; E-mail: sbowden@state.de.us
Vice President: GREG MCCABE, Rd. Box 120A, Selbyville, DE 19975; Phone: 302-436-2171; Fax: 302-436-5597
Keyword(s): Agriculture, Land Use Planning, Soil Conservation, Urban Environment, Water Pollution Management, Conservation Districts

DELAWARE AUDUBON SOCIETY
P.O. Box 1713, Wilmington, DE 19899
Phone: 302-428-3959; E-mail: mail@delawareaudubon.org; Web Site: www.delawareaudubon.org
Membership: 1500
Scope: Statewide
Description: The Delaware Audubon Society promotes an appreciation and understanding of nature to preserve and protect our natural environment and to affirm the necessity for clean air and water and the stewardship of our natural resources.
Keyword(s): Preservation and Protection, Water and Air Quality

NON-GOVERNMENTAL ORGANIZATIONS - D

DELAWARE B.A.S.S. CHAPTER FEDERATION
Attn: President, 3700 South State St., Camden, DE 19934
Scope: Statewide
Description: An organization of Bassmaster chapters, affiliated with the Bass Anglers Sportsman Society, organized to fight pollution, assist state and national conservation agencies in their efforts, and teach the young people of our country good conservation practices. Dedicated to the realistic conservation of our water resources.
Contact(s):
President: JIM FIELDS; Phone: 302-698-9257
Conservation Director: BRUCE COLE, 1311 Simms Woods Rd., Dover, DE 19901; Phone: 302-674-3353

DELAWARE FORESTRY ASSOCIATION
2320 S. DuPont Hwy., Dover, DE 19901
Phone: 302-739-4811
Founded: 1982; Membership: 315
Scope: Statewide
Description: A statewide organization affiliated with the National Woodland Owners Association, dedicated to promote good forest practices and multiple use of private forest lands in Delaware.
Contact(s):
President and Editor: W. ALLEN JONES; Phone: 410-742-3163
Vice President: JIM BENNETT
Publication(s): *DFA Newsletter*
Keyword(s): Forests and Forestry

DELAWARE GREENWAYS, INC.
P.O. Box 2095, Wilmington, DE 19899
Phone: 302-655-7275
Founded: 1989; Membership: 500
Scope: Statewide
Description: Preserve, enhance, and connect the ecological, scenic, historical, cultural, and recreational resources in Delaware.
Contact(s):
Executive Director: GAIL L. VAN GILDER
Assistant Executive Director: TIM PLEMMONS
Director of Fund Development: SARA JANE SPAULDING
Keyword(s): Cultural Preservation, Environmental Preservation, Historic Preservation, Sustainable Development, Transportation

DELAWARE MUSEUM OF NATURAL HISTORY
P.O. Box 3937, Wilmington, DE 19807
Phone: 302-658-9111; Fax: 302-658-2610; Web Site: www.delmnh.org
Founded: 1957; Membership: 630
Scope: Statewide
Description: The Delaware Museum of Natural History exists to excite and inform people about the natural world. The Museum's core purpose is to help develop a caring society that respects and values our planet. The major focus of the Museum is continued leadership in research and collections in malacology and ornithology and the ecology of the Delmarva Peninsula.
Contact(s):
Director: GEOFF HALFPENNY
Editor and Public Relations: STEPHEN REYNOLDS
Librarian and Malacology: DR. TIM PEARCE
Librarian and Ornithology: GENE K. HESS
Publication(s): *Nemouria; Musenews*
Keyword(s): Birds, Museum, Natural History, Research

DELAWARE NATURE SOCIETY
P.O. Box 700, Hockessin, DE 19707-0700
Phone: 302-239-2334; Fax: 302-239-2473; E-mail: Ashland@DCA.net; Web Site: www.dca.net/naturesociety
Founded: 1964; Membership: 8,000
Scope: Statewide
Description: A representative statewide organization, affiliated with the National Wildlife Federation, dedicated to the protection and enhancement of wildlife and its habitat through public education and government interaction.
Contact(s):
President: PETER H. FLINT

Executive Director: MIKE RISKA
Representative: JUNE MacARTOR
Editor: JANICE TAYLOR
Alternative Representative: BERNARD DEMPSEY
Publication(s): *Birds of Delaware; Butterflies of Delmarva*
Keyword(s): Air Quality and Pollution, Endangered and Threatened Species, Environmental and Conservation Education, Natural Areas, Wetlands

DELAWARE WILD LANDS, INC.
315 Main St., P.O. Box 505, Odessa, DE 19730-0505
Phone: 302-378-2736
Founded: 1961
Scope: Statewide
Description: A nonprofit charitable land conservancy actively engaged in acquiring areas on the Delmarva Peninsula for their natural resource values and for educational purposes; presently owns and manages approximately 20,000 acres. Produced two films, "The Endangered Shore" and "Swamp," available on loan or for purchase.
Contact(s):
Executive Director: HOLGER H. HARVEY
Keyword(s): Coasts, Land Purchase, Wetlands, Wildlands

DELMARVA ORNITHOLOGICAL SOCIETY
P.O. Box 4247, Greenville, DE 19807
Founded: 1963; Membership: 320
Scope: Statewide
Description: The purpose of this society shall be the promotion of the study of birds, the advancement and diffusion of ornithological knowledge, and the conservation of birds and their environment.
Contact(s):
President: JOHN P. JANOWSKI, 122 Pine Valley Dr., Middletown, DE 19709; Phone: 302-834-9710
Vice President: JIM WHITE, 3507 Barley Mill Rd., Hockessin, DE 19707; Phone: 302-239-7065
Editor: GENE K. HESS, P.O. Box 3937, Greenville, DE 19807; Phone: 302-378-9357
Editor: KAREN ZEITLER, 1307 Quincy Dr., Green Acres, Wilmington, DE 19803; Phone: 302-478-9173
Publication(s): *Delmarva Ornithologist; DOS Flyer*

DELTA WATERFOWL FOUNDATION
R.R. 1 Box 1, Portage la Prairie, Manitoba R1N 3A1 Canada
Phone: 204-239-1900
Scope: National
Description: Delta Waterfowl's primary mission is to support graduate student training and research on all aspects of waterfowl and wetlands ecology and management. Since 1938, Delta students have produced over 200 graduate theses and 600 scientific publications. In addition to graduate research, Delta is currently involved in several demonstration projects including: Adopt-A-Pothole, a habitat easement program; Hen Houses, predator-resistant nesting structures, Voluntary Restraint, a hunter ethics program and several policy initiatives.
Contact(s):
President: STEPHAN D. BUSCH
Vice President: DANIEL C. HUGES JR.
Secretary: THOMAS P. HUTCHENS
Treasurer: DONALD J. DOUGLAS
Executive Vice President: JONATHAN SCARTH
Keyword(s): Communications, Environmental and Conservation Education, International Conservation, Waterfowl, Wetlands

DELTA WILDLIFE, INC.
P.O. Box 276, Stoneville, MS 38776
Phone: 662-686-3370; Fax: 662-686-3382
Founded: 1990; Membership: 2,000
Scope: Regional
Description: Delta Wildlife is committed to wildlife habitat enhancement, habitat restoration and conservation education in northwest Mississippi.
Contact(s):
Chairman: BILL KENNEDY; Phone: 662-265-5828

Executive Director: TREY COOKE; Phone: 662-686-3370
Publication(s): *Delta Wildlife Magazine*
Keyword(s): Agriculture, Communications, Environmental and Conservation Education, Wetlands, Wildlife and Wildlife Habitat

DESERT FISHES COUNCIL
P.O. Box 337, Bishop, CA 93515
Phone: 760-872-8751
Founded: 1969; Membership: 300
Scope: International
Description: A nationwide and international representation of state, federal, and university scientists and resource specialists and private conservation groups to provide for the exchange and transmittal of information on the status, protection, and management of the endemic fauna and flora of North American desert ecosystems.
Contact(s):
Executive Secretary. EDWIN P. PISTER, Desert Fishes Council, P.O. Box 337, Bishop, CA 93515; Phone: 760-872-8751; E-mail: phildesfish@telis.org
Chairman and Editor: GARY GARRETT, TX Parks and Wildlife, HC 7, Box 62, Ingram, TX 78025; Phone: 830-866-3356; E-mail: gpg@ktc.com
Publication(s): *Proceedings of the Desert Fishes Council*
Keyword(s): Aquatic Habitats, Conservation of Protected Areas, Deserts, Endangered and Threatened Species, Fisheries, Natural Areas, Sustainable Development, Water Resources, Zoology, Native Fish

DESERT RESEARCH FOUNDATION OF NAMIBIA, THE
7 Rossini St., Windhoek Namibia
Phone: +264-61-229-855; E-mail: drfn@org.na
Scope: International
Contact(s):
Contact: MARY SEELY
Publication(s): *Enviroteach Resource Kit*
Keyword(s): Aquatic Habitats, Biodiversity, Endangered and Threatened Species, Environmental and Conservation Education, Habitat Conservation, International Wildlife, Land Management, Nature Study, Sustainable Development, Water Conservation, Zoology, Native Plants

DESERT TORTOISE COUNCIL
P.O. Box 1738, Palm Desert, CA 92261
Phone: 619-431-8449
Founded: 1975
Scope: National
Description: Formed to assure the continued survival of viable populations of the desert tortoise, Gopherus agassizi, which is endemic to Arizona, California, Nevada, and Utah.
Contact(s):
Secretary: ED LaRUE
Treasurer: MARE SAZAKI
Co-Chairman: KATHERINE ZODER
Co-Chairman: DANIEL PATTERSEN
Recording Secretary: ED LaRUE
Keyword(s): Biology, Conservation of Protected Areas, Deserts, Endangered and Threatened Species, Environment, Environmental Protection, Health and Nutrition, Land Preservation, Land Use Planning, Mining, Nature Preservation, Public Lands, Reptiles and Amphibians, Wildlife and Wildlife Habitat

DESERT TORTOISE PRESERVE COMMITTEE, INC.
4067 Mission Inn Ave., Riverside, CA 92501
Phone: 909-683-3872; Fax: 909-683-6949; E-mail: dtpc@pacbell.net; Web Site: www.tortise-tracks.org
Founded: 1974
Scope: Regional
Description: A nonprofit organization formed to promote the welfare of the desert tortoise in the southwestern United States and to manage and establish preserves in the Western Mojave Desert.
Contact(s):
President: BOB BROOKS, 13711 East Gaylin St., Whittier, CA 90601

Executive Director: MICHAEL J. CONNOR Ph.D.
Publication(s): *Newsletter; Tortoise T-R-A-C-K-S*
Keyword(s): Endangered and Threatened Species, Land Purchase, Nongame Wildlife, Wildlife and Wildlife Habitat, Wildlife Management

DISTRICT OF COLUMBIA SOIL AND WATER CONSERVATION DISTRICT
ATTN: Chair, 800 9th St. SW 3rd Fl., Washington, DC 20024
Scope: Statewide
Contact(s):
Chair: THEODORE GORDON; Phone: 202-442-5855; Fax: 202-442-4808
Acting District Manager: ALEXANDER OKECHUKWU, 2100 Martin Luther King Jr. Ave. SE Suite 203, Washington, DC 20020; Phone: 202-645-6059, ext. 3060; Fax: 202-645-6063
Keyword(s): Conservation Districts

DRAGONFLY SOCIETY OF THE AMERICAS, THE
2091 Partridge Ln., Binghamton, NY 13903
Phone: 607-722-4939
Founded: 1989; Membership: 200
Scope: National
Description: The organization is concerned with all factors relevant to the world species assemblage of odonata (Insecta: Dragonflies). We study their systematics, biology, and taxonomy. The organization is also concerned with maintaining and improving the environmental conditions for Odonata through better water quality management, wetlands conservation, and aquatic habitat preservation.
Contact(s):
President: MICHAEL MAY, Dept. Of Entomology, Cook College, Rutgers University, New Brunswick, NJ 08903
Secretary: S.W. DUNKLE, Biology Department, Collin Co. Community College, Plano, TX 75074
Treasurer: J.J. DAIGLE, 2166 Kimberly Ln., Tallahassee, FL 32311
Editor: T.W. DONNELLY, 2091 Partridge Lane, Binghamton, NY 13903
Publication(s): *ARGIA; Bulletin of American Odonatology*
Keyword(s): Aquatic Habitats, Environmental Preservation, Insects and Butterflies, Rivers, Wetlands

DUCKS UNLIMITED CANADA

Oak Hammock Marsh Conservation Centre
One Mallard Way at Hwy. 220, P.O. Box 1160, Stonewall, Manitoba R0C 2Z0 Canada
Phone: 204-467-3000; Fax: 204-467-9028
Founded: 1938
Scope: Nationwide
Description: Ducks Unlimited Canada's mission is to conserve wetlands and associated habitats for the benefit of North America's waterfowl, which in turn provide healthy environments for wildlife and people.
Contact(s):
Chairman of the Board: GEORGE C. REIFEL, Suite 440-1055 W. Hastings St., Vancouver, BC V6E 2E9 Canada; Phone: 604-688-1055
President: G. TOD WRIGHT, Suite 500-1 King St. W., Hamilton, Ontario L8P 1A4 Canada; Phone: 905-523-2353
Vice President: MEL F. BELICH Q.C., 2900, 421-7th Ave. S.W., Calgary, Alberta T2P 4K9 Canada; Phone: 403-231-3910
Secretary: PETER D. CARTON, 115 Ball Crescent, Saskatoon, Saskatchewan S7K 6C9 Canada; Phone: 306-933-3700
Treasurer: RONALD J. HICKS C.A., 302 Laval Crescent, Saskatoon, Saskatchewan S7H 4K8 Canada; Phone: 306-343-4410
Chief Biologist/Canadian Director of the Institute for Wetland and Waterfowl Research: DR. BRIAN T. GRAY
Chief Engineer: R. W. COLEY
Chief Financial Officer: L. J. WARREN
Communications Manager: ROBERT KINDRACHUK
Executive Vice-President: DON A. YOUNG
Human Resources Manager/Corporate Counsel: GARY GOODWIN

NON-GOVERNMENTAL ORGANIZATIONS - D

Manager of Conservation Programs: ROB B. FOWLER
Manager of Education Program: DR. RICK WISHART
National Director of Fundraising, Marketing and Membership: RICHARD L.H. WALKER
Keyword(s): Waterfowl, Wetlands

DUCKS UNLIMITED (Alberta, Canada)
#200, 10720 - 178 St., Edmonton, Alberta T5S 1L3 Canada
Phone: 403-489-2002; Fax: 403-489-1856
Scope: Statewide
Contact(s):
Alberta NAWMP Coordinator: BRETT CALVERLEY
Conservation Programs Biologist: GARY STEWART
Conservation Programs Biologist: LES WETTER, #1, 550-45 St., Red Deer, Alberta T4N 1L1 Canada; Phone: 403-342-1314; Fax: 403-346-1211
Pacific Regional Director: JIM WOHL
Pacific Regional Director: GORDON EDWARDS
Publication(s): *Conservator*

DUCKS UNLIMITED (Nova Scotia, Canada)
P.O. Box 430, #64 Highway 6, Amherst, Nova Scotia B4H 3Z5 Canada
Phone: 902-667-8726; Fax: 902-667-0916
Scope: Statewide
Contact(s):
Senior Biologist: MARK GLOUTNEY; E-mail: m_gloutney@ducks.ca
Senior Engineer: BRIAN MCCULLOUGH; E-mail: b_mccullough@ducks.ca

DUCKS UNLIMITED (Ontario, Canada)
566 Welham Rd., Barrie, Ontario L4N 8Z7 Canada
Phone: 705-721-4444; Fax: 705-721-4999; E-mail: du_barrie@ducks.ca
Scope: Statewide
Contact(s):
Manager Eastern Ontario Field Office: RON MAHER
Manager Western Ontario Field Office: BOB CLAY

DUCKS UNLIMITED (Quebec, Canada)
Suite 260, 710 Bouvier St., Quebec City, Quebec G2J 1C2 Canada
Phone: 418-623-1650
Founded: 1938; Membership: 140,000
Scope: Statewide
Description: Ducks Unlimited Canada is an international, private, non-profit organization dedicated to the conservation of wetlands and associated habitats for the perpetuation of North America's waterfowl, which in turn provide healthy environments for wildlife and people.
Contact(s):
Director of Regional Operations: PATRICK PLANTE
Manager of Field Operations: BERNARD FILION
Publication(s): *Conservator; Conservationniste*

DUCKS UNLIMITED (Saskatchewan Operation, Canada)
P.O. Box 4465, 1606-4th Ave., Regina, Saskatchewan S4P 3W7 Canada
Phone: 306-569-0424; Fax: 306-565-3699
Founded: 1938
Scope: Statewide
Description: A private, nonprofit, conservation organization dedicated to preserving waterfowl by creating and restoring breeding habitat in Canada. This organization is funded by sportsmen of United States and Canada.
Contact(s):
Agricultural Program Specialist: L. R. MOATS
Director of Public Policy: D. A. CHEKAY
Manager of field Operations: TIM THIELE
Publication(s): *Newsletter*

DUCKS UNLIMITED, INC.
Headquarters, One Waterfowl Way, Memphis, TN 38120
Phone: 901-758-3825; Fax: 901-758-3850
Founded: 1937; Membership: 701,000
Scope: National
Description: The mission of Ducks Unlimited is to fulfill the annual life cycle needs of North American waterfowl by protecting, enhancing, restoring, and managing important wetlands and associated uplands. Only those activities which contribute directly toward that end shall be undertaken by Ducks Unlimited, Inc.
Contact(s):
President: JULIUS F. WALL, P.O. Box 226, Clinton, MO 64735; Phone: 660-885-2221
First Vice President: DR. L. J. MAYEUX, P.O. Box 1529, Marksville, LA 71351; Phone: 318-253-9643
Secretary: MICHAEL J. BROOKS, One Branch Place 181-4, St. Louis, MO 63118; Phone: 314-577-7717
Treasurer: W. BRUCE LEWIS, P.O. Box 1344, Natchez, MS 39120; Phone: 601-446-6621
Executive Secretary: BILL R. WILLSEY, One Waterfowl Way, Memphis, TN 38120; Phone: 901-758-3825
Executive Vice President: D. A. YOUNG, One Waterfowl Way, Memphis, TN 38120; Phone: 901-758-3825
Controller: ROBERT D. MIMS
Director of Conservation Policy: FRED ABRAHAM, 1301 Pennsylvania Ave., NW, Suite 402, Washington, D.C. 20004
Director of Database Marketing: BOB DAVIS
Director of Development Atlantic Region: DAVID H. TREVETT
Director of Development Great Plains Region: MIKE BURTON
Director of Development Southern Region: JOHN BELZ
Director of Development Western Region: JIM GLEASON
Director of Field Operations Programs Support: DAN GARDNER Ph.D.
Director of Human Resources and Staff Development: DAVID T. RILEY
Director of Latin American Program: MONSERRAT CARBONELL
Director of Leadership Giving: JONATHAN KRONSBERG
Director of Licensing: STEPHEN TONNING
Director of Marketing: MICHAEL CLEARY
Director of Meetings and Conferences: CLIFFORD J. SCHULTZ
Director of Membership Programs: LINDA SCHOENROCK
Director of Operations Great Lakes/ Altlantic Regional Office: RICHARD B. PIERCE, 331 Metty Dr., Suite 4, Ann Arbor, MI 48103; Phone: 734-623-2000; Fax: 734-623-2035
Director of Operations, Great Plains Regional Office: JEFFREY NELSON, 3502 Franklin Ave., Bismarck, ND 58501; Phone: 701-258-5599; Fax: 701-258-8364
Director of Operations, Southern Regional Office: KENNETH BABCOCK, 193 Business Park Dr., Suite E, Ridgeland, MS 39157-6026; Phone: 601-956-1936; Fax: 601-956-7814
Director of Operations, Western Regional Office: RONALD A. STROMSTAD, 3074 Gold Canal Dr., Rancho Cordova, CA 95670; Phone: 916-852-2000; Fax: 916-852-2200
Senior Group Manager Field Operations/Membership/Administration: JAMES L. WARE
Director of Publishing and Communications: LEE SALBER
Chairman of the Board: GENE M. HENRY, 3472 Orvold Park, McFarland, WI 53558; Phone: 608-838-3648
Chief Biologist: DR. BRUCE BATT
Chief Financial Officer: RANDY L. GRAVES
Contact for Alabama: DOUGLAS N. LASHER, 209 Willow Bend, Wetumpka, AL 36093; Phone: 334-514-0561; Fax: 334-514-0562
Contact for Alaska: JAMES KING, P.O. Box 4073, 1870 N. Kentucky Derby Dr., Palmer, AK 99645; Phone: 907-745-3946; Fax: 907-745-3947
Contact for Arizona: MIKE SHIRE, 5938 E. Corrine Dr., Scottsdale, AZ 85254; Phone: 480-483-6186; Fax: 480-483-9251
Contact for Arkansas: JEFF LAWRENCE, #9, River Drive Estates South, Pangburn, AR 72121; Phone: 501-728-4949; Fax: 501-728-3132
Contact for California: PAUL WOODBURY, 3074 Gold Canal Dr., Rancho Cordova, CA 95670-6116; Phone: 916-852-2000; Fax: 916-852-2200

Contact for Colorado: DR. JOHN L. SCHMIDT, 10923 Legacy Ridge Ct., Westminster, CO 80031; Phone: 303-465-3628; Fax: 303-465-3638
Contact for Connecticut: CRAIG FERRIS, 3 Orange Pippin Rd., Sandy Hook, CT 06482; Phone: 203-426-2466; Fax: 203-426-2733
Contact for Delaware: JOSEPH F. ROWAN, 204 Friendship Dr., Centreville, MD 21617; Phone: 410-758-3145; Fax: 410-758-3998
Contact for Florida: DOUG WILLIAMS, 1862 Jefferson Rd., Tallahassee, FL 32311; Phone: 850-656-0053; Fax: 850-656-1313
Contact for Georgia: DAN DENTON, P.O. Box 870131, Mountain Park Branch, Stone Mountain, GA 30087; Phone: 770-985-5922; Fax: 770-985-4065
Contact for Hawaii: BOB MAZGAJ, 4186 Brooks Rd., Valley Springs, CA 95252; Phone: 209-772-1966; Fax: 209-772-1883
Contact for Idaho: STEVE HALL, 6613 Wright Lane, Nampa, ID 83686; Phone: 208-463-9900; Fax: 208-463-9944
Contact for Illinois: GARY ERICKSON, 31764 North Harris Rd., Libertyville, IL 60048; Phone: 847-223-9426; Fax: 847-223-3437
Contact for Indiana: BRUCE MARHEINE, 2761 E. County Rd., 350 N., Sullivan, IN 47882; Phone: 812-397-2740; Fax: 812-397-5156
Contact for Iowa: ROCK BRIDGES, P.O. Box 223 (UPS-225 W. Main, Lower Level), Lake Mills, IA 50450; Phone: 515-592-3600; Fax: 515-592-3602
Contact for Kansas: TOM MUNICH, 4020 Coachman Rd., Manhattan, KS 66502-8809; Phone: 785-539-6262; Fax: 785-539-6363
Contact for Kentucky: BEN R. BURNLEY, 6887 Old Corydon Rd., Henderson, KY 42420; Phone: 502-836-9507; Fax: 502-826-5949
Contact for Louisiana: EARL D. NORWOOD JR., 109 Frazier Rd., P.O. Box 578, Ruston, LA 71270; Phone: 318-255-6768; Fax: 318-255-2844
Contact for Maine: ERIC GOODENOUGH, HC 72 Box 3800, Ossipee Hill Rd., E., Waterboro, ME 04030; Phone: 207-247-8448; Fax: 207-247-8333
Contact for Maryland: CHIP HEAPS, 136 Goucher Way, Churchville, MD 21028-1218; Phone: 410-399-4093; Fax: 410-734-6247
Contact for Massachusetts: PHILIP D. WARREN, Hill Rd., P.O. Box 488, Alstead, NH 03602; Phone: 603-835-2490; Fax: 603-835-6243
Contact for Michigan: BRET PLASTERS, 16374 Paddock Club Blvd., Linden, MI 48451; Phone: 810-735-6826; Fax: 810-735-6827
Contact for Minnesota: BILL ALLEN, R.R. #2 Box 148, Wabasha, MN 55981; Phone: 651-565-2369
Contact for Mississippi: BILLY JOE CROSS, 193 Business Park, Suite E, Ridgeland, MS 39157-6026; Phone: 601-956-1936; Fax: 601-956-7814
Contact for Missouri: MITCHELL J. ROGERS, P.O. Box 385, 110 1/2 West Jefferson, Clinton, MO 64735; Phone: 660-885-7555; Fax: 660-885-8626
Contact for Montana: STEVE R. BAYLESS, 5225 Collins Dr., Helena, MT 59602; Phone: 406-458-5794; Fax: 406-458-1907
Contact for Nebraska: JOSEPH M. HYLAND, Rt. 9, 9909 South 56th St., Lincoln, NE 68506; Phone: 402-423-8188; Fax: 402-423-3753
Contact for Nevada: DR. JOHN LUDWIG, 1595 Watt St., Reno, NV 89509; Phone: 775-786-1021; Fax: 775-786-0472
Contact for New Hampshire: ERIC GOODENOUGH, HC Box 72, Ossipee Hill Rd., E., Waterboro, ME 04030; Phone: 207-247-8448; Fax: 207-247-8333
Contact for New Jersey: JOSEPH DEMARTINO, 133 Fox Hollow Dr., Lanoka Harbor, NJ 08734; Phone: 609-971-5845; Fax: 609-971-7365
Contact for New Mexico: MIKE SHIRE, 5938 E. Corrine Dr., Scottsdale, AZ 85254; Phone: 480-483-6168; Fax: 480-483-9251
Contact for New York: D. ALLEN STARLING, 4411 Allen's Point, Union Springs, NY 13160; Phone: 315-889-7210; Fax: 315-889-9941
Contact for North Carolina: DONALD J. MANLEY, 25 Scott Pl., Clinton, NC 28328; Phone: 910-592-3898; Fax: 910-590-3000
Contact for North Dakota: CONRAD N. HILLMAN, 3502 Franklin Ave., Bismarck, ND 58501-0761; Phone: 701-258-5599; Fax: 701-258-8364
Contact for Ohio: LARRY HARMON, 341 Deer Trail Rd., Thornville, OH 43076; Phone: 740-323-0703; Fax: 740-323-0793
Contact for Oklahoma: LARRY E. KRAMER, 1700 E. Walking Sky, Edmond, OK 73013; Phone: 405-330-3549; Fax: 405-330-3551
Contact for Oregon: BRENT LAWS, 20555 Dorchester East, Bend, OR 97702; Phone: 541-382-5662; Fax: 541-382-4425
Contact for Pennsylvania: PETER G. BROWN, 217 Pfulgh Rd., Butler, PA 16001; Phone: 724-865-2422; Fax: 724-865-2691
Contact for Rhode Island: CRAIG FERRIS, 3 Orange Pippin Rd., Sandy Hook, CT 06482; Phone: 203-426-2466; Fax: 203-426-2733
Contact for South Carolina: CURTIS WOOTEN, 391 Creole Pl., Mt. Pleasant, SC 29464; Phone: 843-884-5972; Fax: 843-849-6821
Contact for South Dakota: DOUG JONES, 2018 Antelope, Pierre, SD 57501; Phone: 605-224-0563; Fax: 605-224-6447
Contact for Tennessee: JOHN C. KRUZAN, 20 Lock 8 Ln., Carthage, TN 37030; Phone: 615-774-3192; Fax: 615-774-3850
Contact for Texas: JIMMY DUNKS, 7806 Phoenix Pass, Austin, TX 78737; Phone: 512-288-3615; Fax: 512-288-8315
Contact for Utah: PHILLIP WAGNER, 1617 West Galbraith Ln., Kaysville, UT 84037; Phone: 801-546-4619; Fax: 801-359-9457
Contact for Vermont: PHILIP D. WARREN, Hill Rd., P.O. Box 488, Alstead, NH 03602; Phone: 603-835-2490; Fax: 603-835-6243
Contact for Virginia: CHIP HEAPS, 136 Goucher Way, Churchville, MD 21028-1218; Phone: 410-399-4093; Fax: 410-734-6247
Contact for Washington: FRANK R. LOCKARD, 4251 Green Cove, NW, Olympia, WA 98502; Phone: 360-866-0525; Fax: 360-866-5519
Contact for West Virginia: DONNIE L. STACY, HC 37, Box 201, Frankfort, WV 24938; Phone: 304-497-0888; Fax: 304-497-4352
Contact for Wisconsin: BRUCE GRUTHOFF, W8840 E. Jason Dr., Beaver Dam, WI 53916; Phone: 920-887-8972; Fax: 920-887-8865
Contact for Wyoming: BARRY FLOYD, 760 West 54th St., Casper, WY 82601; Phone: 307-472-6980; Fax: 307-472-3130
General Counsel: JAMES FLOOD
Group Manager of Conservation Programs: DR. W. ALAN WENTZ
Group Manager of Publishing and Communications: CHRIS DORSEY
Magazine Editor-in-Chief: TOM FULGHAM
National Director of Conservation: DR. JACK PAYNE
National Director of Development: DELBERT W. CASE
National Director of Field Operations: GARY GOODPASTER
North Atlantic Flyway Vice President: PAUL MAKAREVICH JR.
North Central Flyway Vice President: STEVE TONSO
North Pacific Flyway Vice President: HARLEY HANSEN
Northeast Mississippi Flyway Vice President: DOUG BIECHELE
Northwest Mississippi Flyway Vice President: LOWELL MOHLER
Senior Vice President (Advisory to the President) of Communications: JILL OLSEN
Senior Vice President (Advisory to the President) of Conservation: WICKHAM CORWIN
Senior Vice President (Advisory to the President) of Development: JAMES HULBERT
Senior Vice President (Advisory to the President) of Event Merchandise: WILLIAM COLVIN
Senior Vice President (Advisory to the President) of Membership: BARRY E. WOOD
Senior Vice President (Advisory to the President) of Strategic Planning: JAMES F. DODD III
South Atlantic Flyway Vice President: RICHARD S. JOHNSON

NON-GOVERNMENTAL ORGANIZATIONS - E

South Central Flyway Vice President: MICHAEL SIMPSON
South Mississippi Flyway Vice President: DR. L. J. MAYEUX
South Pacific Flyway Vice President: STEPHEN G. DENKERS
Publication(s): *Ducks Unlimited Magazine; PUDDLER Magazine*

DUCKS UNLIMITED, INC. - WETLANDS AMERICA TRUST INC.
One Waterfowl Way, Memphis, TN 38120
Phone: 901-758-3825
Scope: Regional
Description: A nonprofit trust organized to operate exclusively for charitable, educational, scientific and conservation purposes. The Trust seeks to protect the natural balance of our continent's wetland ecosystems, ensuring the future viability of waterfowl and other wetland wildlife.
Contact(s):
President: JAMES C. KENNEDY
Assistant Secretary: BILL R. WILLSEY
Chief Operating Officer: D. A. YOUNG
Keyword(s): International Conservation, Water Resources, Waterfowl, Wetlands, Wildlife and Wildlife Habitat

E

E-P EDUCATION SERVICES, INC.
15 Brittany Ct., Cheshire, CT 06410
Phone: 203-271-2756; Fax: 203-271-2756
Founded: 1972
Scope: Statewide
Description: A nonprofit group formed to promote environmental and population education in Connecticut and committed to assisting educators in the task of providing quality environmental education for the citizens of our state.
Contact(s):
Vice President: MICHAEL SCHAEFER
Secretary: LINA ANN LAWALL
Treasurer: J. ROBERT BOUCHARD
President and Executive Director: LARRY SCHAEFER
Keyword(s): Environmental and Conservation Education, Land Use Planning, Pesticides, Planning Management, Wetlands

EAGLE NATURE FOUNDATION, LTD.
300 East Hickory, Apple River, IL 61001
Phone: 815-594-2306; Fax: 815-594-2305; E-mail: eaglenature.tni@juno.com
Founded: 1995; Membership: 1,250+
Scope: International
Description: ENF is a nonprofit international organization, which develops and implements habitat preservation strategies, conducts a wide variety of nature education and awareness programs, and engages in and supports bald eagle research.
Contact(s):
President and Executive Director: TERRENCE N. INGRAM
Vice President: EUGENE L. SMALL; Phone: 773-434-8328
Secretary: SUSAN ERTMER; Phone: 815-845-2253
Treasurer: ROBERT TORSBERG; Phone: 815-652-4443
Director: JOSEPH LUKASCYK; Phone: 708-430-0779
Director: JAMES RONNERUD; Phone: 608-776-2755
Director: PHYLLIS SIGAFUS; Phone: 815-594-2518
Publication(s): *Bald Eagle News; Nature News; The Bald Eagle - Our National Symbol*
Keyword(s): Birds, Endangered and Threatened Species, Environmental and Conservation Education, Preservation

EARTH DAY NEW YORK
201 E. 42nd St., #3200, New York, NY 10017
Phone: 212-922-0048; Fax: 212-922-1936; E-mail: earthdayny@aol.com; Web Site: www.home.dti.net/earthday
Founded: 1989
Scope: National
Description: Earth Day New York is a low-overhead, broadly educational nonprofit 501c(3) organization that promotes environmental awareness and solutions through a three-pronged program: 1) involving schools, teachers, and students through the Earth Day Education Program; 2) educating public and private policymakers through conferences; and 3) involving the general public in annual Earth Day events.
Contact(s):
Executive Director and Vice President: PAMELA LIPPE; Phone: 212-922-0048; Fax: 212-922-1936
Chairman: DOUGLAS DURST; Phone: 212-789-1155; Fax: 212-789-1199
President: FRED KENT; Phone: 212-620-5660; Fax: 212-620-3821
Secretary: JIM TRIPP; Phone: 212-505-2100; Fax: 212-505-2375
Treasurer: TIMON MALLOY; Phone: 203-535-5326; Fax: 203-353-5329
Publication(s): *Lessons Learned Four Times Square; Building the Sustainable Economy Conference I Proceedings; Earth Day Education Program 1991-1999*
Keyword(s): Environmental and Conservation Education, Green Building, Internships

EARTH FORCE
1908 Mount Vernon Ave., 2nd Fl., Alexandria, VA 22301
Phone: 703-299--9400; Fax: 703-299-9485; E-mail: earthforce@earthforce.org
Founded: 1993
Scope: National
Description: Earth Force is a national nonprofit environmental organization. Earth Force is dedicated to young people changing their communities and caring for our environment now, while developing life-long habits of active citizenship and environmental stewardship.
Contact(s):
President: THOMAS D. MARTIN
Secretary: F. JOHN HAGELE, 9th Flr., 1515 Market St., Philadelphia, PA 19102; Phone: 212-851-8640
Board of Directors Chair: DOUGLAS FOY; Phone: 617-350-0990; Fax: 617-350-4030
President and Director: TOM D. MARTIN; Phone: 703-519-6867; Fax: 703-299-9485
Vice President for Local Programs: DONNA POWER
Vice President for National Programs: ANNIE BRODY
Publication(s): *Free Campaign Materials for Kids and Educators*
Keyword(s): Environmental and Conservation Education, Youth Organizations

EARTH FOUNDATION
5151 Mitchelldale Suite B-11, Houston, TX 77092
Phone: 713-686-9453
Founded: 1990; Membership: 15,000 Schools
Scope: National
Description: The purpose of Earth Foundation is to empower educators and students to work towards a sustainable economy, just society, and healthy environment. Our focus is on education, fundraising for conservation, and cooperative programs with conservation groups and indigenous organizations working in the race to save the planet.
Contact(s):
Vice President: DONNA LAX-EDISON, 5151 Mitchelldale B11
President and Director: CYNTHIA EVERAGE, 5151 Mitchelldale B11, Houston, TX 77092
Publication(s): *Rainforest Rescue Campaign Teacher* Keyword(s): Biodiversity, Coral Reefs, Endangered and Threatened Species, Environmental and Conservation Education, Environmental Preservation, International Conservation, Land Purchase, Rainforests

EARTH ISLAND INSTITUTE
300 Broadway, Suite 28, San Francisco, CA 94133
Phone: 415-788-3666; Fax: 415-788-7324; E-mail: earthisland@earthisland.org; Web Site: www.earthisland.org
Founded: 1982; Membership: 20,000
Scope: National
Description: Through education and activism, Earth Island Institute counteracts threats to the biological and cultural diversity that

sustains and enriches the global environment. The Institute develops and supports projects that promote the conservation, preservation, and restoration of the Earth. The Institute was founded by David Brower, veteran environmental leader.
Contact(s):
Chair: DAVID R. BROWER
President: BOB WILKINSON
Secretary: MARIA MOYER-ANGUS
Treasurer: TIM RANDS
Executive Director: JOHN A. KNOX
Executive Director: DAVID PHILLIPS
Publication(s): *Earth Island Journal; Paper Locator; Ocean Alert*
Keyword(s): Endangered and Threatened Species, International Conservation, Marine Mammals, Sustainable Development, Urban Environment

EARTH SHARE
3400 International Dr., NW, Suite 2K, Washington, DC 20008
Phone: 1-800-875-3863/202-537-7100; Fax: 202-537-7101;
Web Site: www.earthshare.org
Founded: 1988
Scope: National
Description: Earth Share is a nonprofit, federated fund-raising organization that represents nonprofit environmental and conservation organizations in workplace payroll deduction campaigns nationwide. Funds raised support these organizations' environmental and conservation programs and services. Earth Share also provides educational public service announcements about the environment.
Contact(s):
Chairman: JAY FELDMAN, 701 E St. SE, Washington, DC 20003; Phone: 202-543-5450; Fax: 202-543-4791
President: KALMAN STEIN
Secretary: CHUCK PAQUETTE, 8925 Leesburg Pike, Vienna, VA 22184; Phone: 703-790-4016
Keyword(s): Air Quality and Pollution, Environmental and Conservation Education, Environmental Preservation, Water Resources, Wildlife and Wildlife Habitat

EARTHJUSTICE LEGAL DEFENSE FUND (formerly Sierra Club Legal Defense Fund, Inc.)
Headquarters, 180 Montgomery St., Suite 1400, San Francisco, CA 94104-4209
Phone: 415-627-6700; Fax: 415-627-6740
Scope: National
Description: A nonprofit, tax-deductible public-interest law firm created to bring lawsuits on behalf of environmental and citizens' organizations to protect the environment. As such, provides staff lawyers to initiate legal action. Also engages in administrative proceedings before federal, state, and local agencies, and negotiates settlement agreements whenever possible.
Contact(s):
President: BUCK PARKER
Editor: TOM TURNER
Vice President for Finance and Administration: BRUCE NEIGHBOR
Vice President for Programs: BILL CURTISS
Vice President of Development: STEVE KATZ
Vice President of Human Resources: NANCI PATTERSON
Publication(s): *Annual Report; In Brief (newsletter); Ka Palila (Hawaii newsletter)*
Keyword(s): Air Quality and Pollution, Environmental Law, Forests and Forestry, Public Lands, Wildlife and Wildlife Habitat

California Office
180 Montgomery St., Suite 1400, San Francisco, CA 94104
Phone: 415-627-6700
Scope: National
Contact(s):
Managing Attorney: DEBORAH REAMES
Staff Attorney: PAUL BEACH
Staff Attorney: MIKE SHERWOOD

Florida Office
111 S. Martin Luther King Jr. Blvd., P.O. Box 1329, Tallahassee, FL 32302
Phone: 904-681-0031
Scope: Regional
Contact(s):
Managing Attorney: DAVID G. GUEST
Staff Attorney: ANSLEY SAMSON

Hawaii Office
223 S. King, 4th Fl., Honolulu, HI 96813
Phone: 808-599-2436
Scope: Regional
Contact(s):
Managing Attorney: PAUL ACHITOFF
Staff Attorney: DAVID HENKIN

Louisiana Office
400 Magazine St., 4th Fl., New Orleans, LA 70130
Phone: 504-522-1394
Scope: Regional
Contact(s):
Managing Attorney: NATHALIE WALKER
Staff Attorney: ERIC HUBER

Montana Office
222 E. Main St., Suite 300, Bozeman, MT 59715
Phone: 406-586-9699
Scope: Regional
Contact(s):
Managing Attorney: DOUGLAS L. HONNOLD

Rocky Mountain Office
1631 Glenarm Pl., Suite 300, Denver, CO 80202
Phone: 303-623-9466
Scope: Regional
Contact(s):
Managing Attorney: ROBERT WIYGUL
Staff Attorney: SUSAN DAGGETT

Seattle, Washington Office
705 Second Ave., Suite 203, Seattle, WA 98104
Phone: 206-343-7340
Scope: Regional
Contact(s):
Managing Attorney: PATTI GOLDMAN
Staff Attorney: TODD TRUE

Southeast Alaska Office
325 4th St., Juneau, AK 99801
Phone: 907-586-2751; Fax: 907-463-5891
Scope: Regional
Contact(s):
Managing Attorney: ERIC JORGENSEN
Staff Attorney: THOMAS S. WALDO

Washington, DC Office
1625 Massachusetts Ave., NW, Suite 702, Washington, DC 20036
Phone: 202-667-4500
Scope: Regional
Contact(s):
Managing Attorney: HOWARD FOX
Staff Attorney: DAVID BARON

EARTHLAW
University of Denver, Forbes House, 1714 Poplar St., Denver, CO 80220
Phone: 303-871-6996; Fax: 303-871-6991; E-mail: earthlaw@earthlaw.org; Web Site: www.earthlaw.org
Scope: Regional
Description: Earthlaw's mission is to protect and preserve the West's biodiversity, air, land and water by providing free legal services to grassroots environmental groups and by training new

NON-GOVERNMENTAL ORGANIZATIONS - E

lawyers in the strategy, skills and value of public interest environmental work.
Contact(s):
Executive Director: MARK HUGHES
Keyword(s): Environmental Law

EARTHSCAN
120 Pentonville Rd., London, London N1 9JN United Kingdom
Phone: 0171-278-0433; Fax: 0171-278-1142; E-mail: earthinfo@earthscan.co.uk; Web Site: www.earthscan.co.uk
Scope: National
Description: A publishing house for books addressing environment and development issues in both industrialized countries and the developing world, taking as a starting point the inescapable link between poverty and environmental degradation. All aspects of sustainable development are covered, including international relations, environmental law and institutions, global environmental change, population growth, and the management of resources and economics, as well as social and cultural questions such as the role of women.
Contact(s):
Editor: FRANCES MACDERMOTT
Editor: RUTH COLEMAN
Marketing Executive: CLAIRE BAGNALL
Publishing Director: JONATHAN SINCLAIR WILSON
Keyword(s): Environmental Planning, Population Growth, Sustainable Development, Urban Environment

EARTHSTEWARDS NETWORK
P.O. Box 10697, Bainbridge Island, WA 98110
Phone: 206-842-7986
Founded: 1980; Membership: 1,800
Scope: International
Description: International network for global conflict resolution. Utilizes rainforest reforestation and urban forestry projects to bring together peoples of cultures-in-conflict to work to heal the environment.
Contact(s):
Board President: FLOYD WINSETT
Director of Peace Trees Vietnam: MARTA HATHAWAY
Office Manager: MARSI NAPIER
Publication(s): *Earthstewards Handbook; Warriors of the Heart; Earthstewards Newsletter; Essence Book of Days - 2000; Essence Book of Meditations and Blessings*
Keyword(s): Communications, International Conservation, Urban Forestry, Youth Organizations

EARTHTRUST
25 Kaneohe Bay Dr., Kailua, HI 96734
Phone: 808-254-2866; Fax: 808-254-6409; E-mail: earthtrust@aloha.net; Web Site: www.earthtrust.org
Founded: 1976
Scope: International
Description: Earthtrust is an international nonprofit wildlife conservation organization. It involves small groups of highly capable people, involved with innovative investigations and projects, in partnership with private industry, governments and other environmental groups. Earthtrust is aimed at resolving wildlife crisis situations. Earthtrust's focus is to expose the poaching of endangered species and the sale of endangered whale meat in Asian markets through the use of DNA analysis and the protection of dolphins world-wide.
Contact(s):
President: DONALD WHITE
Keyword(s): Dolphins, Endangered and Threatened Species, Environmental Law, International Conservation, Marine Mammals, Wildlife and Wildlife Habitat

EARTHWATCH INSTITUTE
680 Mt. Auburn St., Box 9104, Watertown, MA 02471-9104
Phone: 617-926-8200 or 1-800-776-0188; Fax: 617-926-8532; E-mail: info@earthwatch.org; Web Site: www.earthwatch.org
Founded: 1971; Membership: 23,000 US/35,000 internationally
Scope: International

Description: Earthwatch is a nonprofit organization that sponsors scientific field research worldwide. It recruits paying volunteers to help field scientists with their research. Volunteers go on short term expeditions to 50 countries and 25 US states.
Contact(s):
President: ROGER BERGEN
Vice President: ANDREW MITCHELL
Chief Financial Officer: STELLA CHAN
Executive Director of Center for Field Research: DR. MARIE STUDER
Publication(s): *Earthwatch Magazine; Earthwatch Expedition Guide; Solutions*
Keyword(s): Biodiversity, Coral Reefs, Cultural Preservation, Endangered and Threatened Species, Environmental and Conservation Education, Flowers, Plants, and Trees, Geology, Grants, International Conservation, Internships, Research, Sustainable Development, Sustainable Ecosystems, Zoology, Volunteering

EAST CENTRAL ILLINOIS FUR TAKERS
R.R. 2, Paxton, IL 60957
Phone: 217-379-4067
Founded: 1974; Membership: 200
Scope: Statewide
Description: State chapter of Fur Takers of America. Helps monitor furbearing wildlife populations in the state and helps conserve this renewable resource.
Contact(s):
President: GREG ANDERSON
Vice President: JIM LIFT
Secretary-Treasurer: MIKE WILSON; Phone: 217-949-5221

EASTERN SHORE LAND CONSERVANCY
P.O. Box 169, Queenstown, MD 21658
Phone: 410-827-9756; Fax: 410-827-9039; E-mail: eslcmain@usa.net
Founded: 1990; Membership: 843
Scope: Statewide
Description: The Eastern Shore Land Conservancy preserves farms, forests and natural areas for future generations, utilizing a variety of voluntary land protection tools that are available to landowners.
Contact(s):
Executive Director: ROBERT J. ETGEN
Publication(s): *Conservancy Update; Preserving Land for Our Future;* fact sheets
Keyword(s): Land Preservation, Land Protection, Natural Areas, Nature Preservation, Open Space

ECODEFENSE
Moskowsky pr. 120-34, Kaliningrad 236006 Russia
Phone: +7-0112-437286; Fax: +7-0112-437286; E-mail: ecodefense@ecodef.koenig.su
Scope: International/Regional
Description: Ecodefense is a non-governmental, nonprofit environmental organization that works to inform and involve more ordinary citizens to environment and social activity through the organizing environmental events and spread of the information.
Contact(s):
Director of the Center for Coordination of Education Project: 9 ALEXANDRA KOROLERA
Editor: dc GALINA RAGOUZINA
Publication(s): *Ecodefense Magazine; Coastwatch Baltic Report; Gamblin House Magazine*
Keyword(s): Camp, Coasts, Communications, Environmental and Conservation Education, National Parks, Networking, Nuclear Energy, Research Grants, Sustainable Agriculture, Training

ECOLOGICAL SOCIETY OF AMERICA, THE
1707 H St., NW, Suite 400, Washington, DC 20006
Phone: 202-833-8773; E-mail: esahq@esa.org
Founded: 1915; Membership: 7,200
Scope: National

Description: The Ecological Society of America is the nation's premier professional society of ecologists. ESA promotes the responsible application of ecological principles to the solution of environmental problems through ESA reports, journals, and expert testimony to Congress. Each summer, ESA convenes a conference featuring the latest findings in ecological research.
Contact(s):
President: DIANA WALL
Executive Director: KATHERINE S. McCARTER
Director for Public Affairs: NADINE LYMN
Publication(s): *Ecology; Ecological Applications; Ecological Monographs; Bulletin of the Ecological Society of America; Conservation Ecology; Issues in Ecology*
Keyword(s): Biodiversity, Biology, Ecology, Ecosystems, Endangered and Threatened Species, Environment, Internships, Wildlife and Wildlife Habitat, Professional Organization, Ecological Education

ECOLOGY CENTER
2530 San Pablo Ave., Berkeley, CA 94702
Phone: 510-548-2220; E-mail: info@ecologycenter.org; Web Site: www.ecologycenter.org
Founded: 1969
Scope: Statewide
Description: A nonprofit organization working to develop a more responsible society by identifying environmentally destructive practices and demonstrating sound alternatives. Programs include an environmental information clearinghouse, library, classes, book and eco-products store, sponsorship of three weekly farmers' markets, and weekly residential curbside recycling service in the city of Berkeley, CA. Primary service area: Greater San Francisco Bay region.
Contact(s):
Editor: LAIRD TOWNSEND
Publication(s): *Terrain*
Keyword(s): Ancient Forests, EcoAction, Endangered and Threatened Species, Environment, Environmental and Conservation Education, Environmental Justice, Gardening and Horticulture, Internships, Land Preservation, People of Color in the Environment, Pesticides, Public Lands, Renewable Resources, Wildlife and Wildlife Habitat, Women in the Environment

ECOTOURISM SOCIETY, THE
P.O. Box 755, North Bennington, VT 05257
Phone: 802-447-2121; Fax: 802-447-2122; E-mail: ecomail@ecotourism.org; Web Site: www.ecotourism.org
Founded: 1990; Membership: 1,400
Scope: International
Description: The Ecotourism Society is an international nonprofit membership organization dedicated to finding the resources and building the expertise to make tourism a viable tool for conservation and sustainable development.
Contact(s):
President: MEGAN EPLER WOOD, P.O. Box 755, North Bennington, VT 05257; Phone: 802-447-2121; Fax: 802-447-2122; E-mail: ecomail@ecotourism.org
Membership and Book Program Director: NICOLE R. RIOTTE
Publication(s): *Ecotourism: A Guide for Planners and Managers Volume I&II; Ecotourism Bibliography; Ecotourism Guidelines for Nature Tour Operators; Ecotourism Society Quarterly Newsletter; Ecolodge Sourcebook for Planners and Developers*
Keyword(s): Biodiversity, Developing Countries, Ecotourism, Environmental and Conservation Education, International Conservation, Outdoor Recreation, Sustainable Development, Tourism, Travel

EDUCATIONAL COMMUNICATIONS, INC.
P.O. Box 351419, Los Angeles, CA 90035
Phone: 310-559-9160; Fax: 310-559-9160; E-mail: ECNP@aol.com; Web Site: home.earthlink.net/~dragonflight/ecoprojects.htm
Founded: 1958
Scope: National
Description: EC creates and promotes educational and scientific projects and programs for the public, focusing on environmental concerns. It founded The Ecology Center of Southern California in 1972; since 1977 has sponsored the award-winning Environmental Directions, a weekly national and international radio series heard in 8 states and on shortwave and internet; and since 1984 has produced three-time Emmy-nominated ECONEWS, a weekly television series broadcast on over 100 cable and PBS outlets nationally. Educational Communications, Inc. is credited with over 400 award-winning programs including "Gem in the Heart of the City," "Wind: Energy for the '90's and Beyond" and "Population Crisis USA." In 1993, started Project Ecotourism, to promote responsible travel and donations overseas.
Contact(s):
Administrative Coordinator: LESLIE LEWIS
Associate Director: ANNA HARLOWE
Executive Producer and Director: NANCY PEARLMAN
Publication(s): *The Compendium Newsletter: A Guide to Ecological Activism; catologs of programs; Directory of Environmental Organizations*
Keyword(s): Communications, Ecotourism, Environmental and Conservation Education, International Conservation, Population Growth, Wildlife and Wildlife Habitat

ELM RESEARCH INSTITUTE
Elm St., P.O. Box 150, Westmoreland, NH 03467
Phone: 603-358-6198; Fax: 603-358-6305; Web Site: www.forelms.org
Founded: 1967; Membership: 2,000
Scope: National
Description: A nonprofit organization which has funded over $1,000,000 in research for the treatment of Dutch elm disease and development of the disease-resistant American Liberty Elm, supplies equipment and information pertaining to elm care and treatment of Dutch elm disease, propagates the American Liberty Elm and distributes it under the auspices of the Johnny Elmseed Project with the assistance of local Boy Scouts and other nonprofit groups. Over 750 nurseries have been established since 1984. ERI provides a free ceremonial tree and commemorative plaque to the first 100 communities which agree to plant 10 more trees in 2000.
Contact(s):
Assistant Director: YVONNE SPALTHOFF
Executive Director: JOHN P. HANSEL
Publication(s): *Specialized Elm Care Information; ELM LEAVES; Data on Elm Injections*
Keyword(s): Endangered and Threatened Species, Flowers, Plants, and Trees, Historic Preservation, Urban Forestry

ELSA WILD ANIMAL APPEAL

Louisiana Chapter
5500 Swift Plant Rd., Lake Charles, LA 70615
Phone: 318-439-8879
Scope: Statewide
Description: Regional branch of ELSA WILD ANIMAL APPEAL; concerned with wildlife matters, educational programs, liaison with other wildlife and governmental groups for the betterment of natural environment and wildlife protection; establishes local volunteer corps to implement programs in conjunction with the Calcasieu Parish Animal Control and Protection Department; and participates in Wildlife Rehabilitation Programs with Heck Haven and Westlake Bird Sanctuary.
Contact(s):
Contact: LAURA LANZA
Keyword(s): Birds, Endangered and Threatened Species, Mammals, Urban Environment, Wildlife Rehabilitation

ENDANGERED SPECIES COALITION
1101 14th St., NW, Suite 1400, Washington, DC 20005
Phone: 202-682-9400; Web Site: www.stopextinction.org
Founded: 1982; Membership: 450 environmental, scientific, and religious organizations
Scope: National

NON-GOVERNMENTAL ORGANIZATIONS - E

Description: The goal of the Coalition is to broaden and mobilize public support for protecting endangered species.
Contact(s):
Executive Director: BROCK EVANS
Publication(s): *Activist Tools; Newsletter*
Keyword(s): Biodiversity, Endangered and Threatened Species, Environmental Law

ENTOMOLOGICAL SOCIETY OF AMERICA
9301 Annapolis Rd., Lanham, MD 20706-3115
Phone: 301-731-4535
Founded: 1889
Scope: National
Description: To promote the scientific study of insects and related arthropods. Specialty sections include systematic behavior, toxicology, bio-genetics, plant protection, medical and veterinary, regulatory and extension, and related scientific disciplines.
Contact(s):
President: DR. SHARRON QUINSENBERRY
Executive Director: JAMES E. OLMES
Past President: DR. CHRISTIAN Y. OSETO
Publication(s): *Annals of the Entomological Society of America; Journal of Economic Entomology; Environmental Entomology; Medical Entomology; American Entomologist; ESA Newsletter; Arthropod Management Tests*
Keyword(s): Agriculture, Biology, Biotechnology, Insects and Butterflies, Zoology

ENVIRONMENT COUNCIL OF RHODE ISLAND
P.O. Box 9061, Providence, RI 02940
Phone: 401-621-8048; Fax: 401-331-5266; E-mail: ecri@studentweb.providence.edu
Scope: Statewide
Description: A representative statewide organization, affiliated with the National Wildlife Federation, dedicated to the protection and enhancement of wildlife and its habitat through public education and government interaction.
Contact(s):
President and Representative: PAUL A. BEAUDETTE
Editor: AIMEE TAVARES
Alternate Representative: LAURA LANDEN
Publication(s): *Audubon Society of Rhode Island Report; Checklist of RI Birds - 1900-1989; Fields Note of RI Birds*
Keyword(s): Birds, Environmental and Conservation Education, Natural History, Renewable Resources, Wildlife and Wildlife Habitat

ENVIRONMENTAL ACTION FUND (EAF)
P.O. Box 22421, Nashville, TN 37202
Phone: 615-385-4389
Founded: 1976
Scope: Statewide
Description: A nonprofit, nonpartisan union of citizen groups joined to preserve and protect Tennessee's natural resources and environmental health. EAF works for strong environmental legislative programs and policies.
Contact(s):
President: MARK MANNER, 2424 Golf Club Ln., Nashville, TN 37215
Secretary: SANDY BIVENS, 3504 General Bates Dr., Nashville, TN 37204
Treasurer: PAUL DAVIS, 5462 Vanderbilt Rd., Old Hickory, TN 37138

ENVIRONMENTAL ADVOCATES
353 Hamilton St., Albany, NY 12210
Phone: 518-462-5526; Fax: 518-427-0381; E-mail: info@envadvocates.org; Web Site: www.enadvocates.org
Founded: 1969
Scope: Statewide
Description: A representative statewide organization, affiliated with the National Wildllife Federation, dedicated to the protection and enhancement of wildlife and its habitat through public education and government interaction.

Contact(s):
President: OAKES AMES
Executive Director: VAL WASHINGTON
Representative: STEVE ALLINGER
Editor: JEFF JONES
Affiliate Representative: CHARLES KRUZANSKY
Publication(s): *The Greensheet*

ENVIRONMENTAL AIR FORCE
22 Rittenhouse Rd., Broomll, PA 19008
Phone: 610-353-1535; Fax: 610-356-5814
Founded: 1989; Membership: 280
Scope: National
Description: A nonprofit membership organization dedicated to providing free aviation services to environmental and conservation groups worldwide. These services are provided through a network of member pilots and include aerial surveys and photography, flying essential observers, etc.
Contact(s):
Executive Director: ALAN M. BRECHER
Publication(s): *Despatches*
Keyword(s): Environmental and Conservation Education, Environmental Preservation, International Conservation, Land Preservation, Wildlife and Wildlife Habitat

ENVIRONMENTAL AND ENERGY STUDY INSTITUTE (EESI)
122 C St., NW, Suite 700, Washington, DC 20001
Phone: 202-628-1400; Fax: 202-628-1825
Founded: 1985
Scope: National
Description: The EESI is dedicated to promoting environmentally sustainable societies. EESI produces credible, timely information, and innovative public policy initiatives that lead to transitions to social and economic patterns that sustain people, the environment, and the natural resources upon which present and future generations depend.
Contact(s):
Chair: RICHARD L. OTTINGER
Executive Director: CAROL WERNER
Director and Senior Fellow of the Sustainable Communities Program: DON GRAY
Director of Energy and Climate Change Program: CAROL WERNER
Publication(s): *Environment and Energy Weekly; Environment and Energy Update; CMAQ Update*
Keyword(s): Energy, Greenhouse Effect/Global Warming, International Conservation, Transportation, Water Resources

ENVIRONMENTAL CAREER CENTER
100 Bridge St., Suite A1, Hampton, VA 23669
Phone: 757-727-7891; Fax: 757-727-7904; E-mail: ecc@visi.net
Founded: 1980
Scope: National
Description: Dedicated to helping people help the environment through internships, career counseling, diversity achievement program, career research, newsletters, and career seminars. Environmental Partnership Program provides paid apprenticeships in natural resources management and environmental protection. Partnerships with environmental employers and universities. Conducts career seminars for professional societies, universities, and agencies.
Contact(s):
Vice President: DR. JOHN E. DAMRON
Secretary: BARBARA ROUTTEN
Treasurer: KESHA A. OLIVER
President and Executive Director: JOHN ESSON
Keyword(s): Environmental and Conservation Education, Internships, People of Color in the Environment, Training

ENVIRONMENTAL CAREERS ORGANIZATION, INC., THE
179 South St., 3rd Fl., Boston, MA 02111
Phone: 617-426-4375; Web Site: www.eco.org
Founded: 1972
Scope: National

Description: ECO protects and enhances the environment through the development of professionals, the promotion of careers and the inspiration of individual action. This is accomplished through placement, career advisement, career products and research and consulting. ECO has three regional offices and an alumni network of over 6,500 individuals.
Contact(s):
President: JOHN R. COOK JR.
Treasurer: JUDITH M. STOCKDALE
Publication(s): *Complete Guide to Environmental Careers, The; Beyond the Green*
Keyword(s): Careers, Internships, People of Color in the Environment

ENVIRONMENTAL CONCERN INC.
210 W. Chew Ave., P.O. Box P, St. Michaels, MD 21663
Phone: 410-745-9620; Fax: 410-745-3517
Founded: 1972
Scope: National
Description: A nonprofit corporation founded for the purpose of researching, developing, and applying the technology and methodologies used in creating, restoring, and preserving wetlands. Environmental Concern focuses on consulting services, supply native wetland plants, the construction of wetlands, wetland horticulture and professional and scholastic educational programs.
Contact(s):
President: EDGAR W. GARBISCH
Vice President: F. ALBERT MCCULLOUGH III
Vice President: JOANNA L. GARBISCH
Secretary and Treasurer: JOANNA L. GARBISCH
Publication(s): *Wetland Journal; Wow! The Wonders of Wetlands; Wetland Planting Guide for the Northeastern United States; Evaluation for Planned Wetlands: A Procedure for Assessing Wetland Functions and a Guide to Functional Design; "A Comprehensive Review of Wetlands Assessment Procedures: A Guide for Wetland Practitioners*
Keyword(s): Environmental and Conservation Education, Gardening and Horticulture, Renewable Resources, Research, Wetlands

ENVIRONMENTAL DEFENSE CENTER, INC.
906 Garden St., Santa Barbara, CA 93101
Phone: 805-963-1622; Fax: 805-962-3152
Founded: 1977
Scope: Statewide
Description: A nonprofit, public-interest environmental law firm providing legal services to citizens' groups and environmental organizations on environmental issues facing California's central coast region since 1977. The Center focuses on a wide range of issues, including oil development, toxic wastes, air and water pollution, species and habitat protection, open space preservation, land use, and coastal access.
Contact(s):
Chairman of the Board: KEN FALSTROM
Chief Counsel: MARC CHYTILO
Counsel: MARC McGINNES
Staff Attorney: JOHN BUSE
Staff Attorney: CAMERON BENSON
Staff Attorney: LINDA KROP
Keyword(s): Environmental Law, Land Use Planning, Water Resources, Wildlife and Wildlife Habitat

ENVIRONMENTAL DEFENSE FUND, INC.
Headquarters, 257 Park Ave., S., New York, NY 10010
Phone: 212-505-2100; Fax: 212-505-2375; Web Site: www.edf.org
Founded: 1967; Membership: 300,000
Scope: National
Description: The Environmental Defense Fund (EDF), headquartered in New York and with five other offices nationwide, is a leading nonprofit, tax-exempt environmental advocacy organization active in a wide range of issues, including protection of the global and regional atmosphere, promotion of environmental health through reduced exposure to toxic chemicals, protecting and restoring biodiversity and critical rivers and wetlands, and restoring the health of our oceans.
Contact(s):
Executive Director: FRED KRUPP; Phone: 212-505-2100
Chairman of the Board of Trustees: JOHN H. WILSON
Deputy Director of Operations: ED BAILEY
Deputy Director of Programs: MARCIA ARONOFF
Editor: JOEL PLAGENZ; Phone: 212-505-2100
General Counsel: JAMES T. TRIPP
International Counsel: ANNIE PETSONK
Legislative Director: ELIZABETH THOMPSON
Strategic Communications Director: STEVE COCHRAN
Publication(s): *EDF Letter*
Keyword(s): Air Quality and Pollution, Aquatic Habitats, Biodiversity, Biotechnology, Chemical Pollution Control, Energy, Fisheries, International Conservation, Pollution Prevention, Transportation, Water Quality, Water Resources, Watersheds, Wetlands

Alliance for Environmental Innovation
6 North Market Bldg., Faneuil Hall Marketplace, Boston, MA 02109
Phone: 617-723-2996; Fax: 617-723-7996
Scope: Regional
Description: The Alliance for Environmental Innovation is a joint project of EDF and The Pew Charitable Trusts.
Contact(s):
Director: JACKIE PRINCE ROBERTS

Capital Office
1875 Connecticut Ave., NW, Washington, DC 20009
Phone: 202-387-3500; Fax: 202-234-6049
Scope: National

North Carolina Office
2500 Blue Ridge Rd., Suite 330, Raleigh, NC 27607
Phone: 919-881-2601; Fax: 919-881-2607
Scope: Regional

Rocky Mountain Office
1405 Arapahoe, Boulder, CO 80302
Phone: 303-440-4901; Fax: 303-440-8052
Scope: Regional

Texas Office
44 East Ave., Austin, TX 78701
Phone: 512-478-5161; Fax: 512-478-8140
Scope: Regional

West Coast Office
5655 College Ave., Oakland, CA 94618
Phone: 510-658-8008; Fax: 510-658-0630
Scope: Regional

ENVIRONMENTAL EDUCATION ASSOCIATES
P.O. Box 1802, San Anselmo, CA 94979-1802
Phone: 415-281-3388; Fax: 415-460-9762; E-mail: weinsoff@ix.netcom.com; Web Site: www.marin.org/NPO/eea/index.html
Founded: 1994
Scope: Statewide
Description: A non-profit organization working in public high schools to provide students with coursework in environmental law and policy with a focus on endangered species, environmental justice and water quality.
Contact(s):
Executive Director: DAVID WEINSOFF; Phone: 415-460-9760; Fax: 415-460-9762
Chair, Board of Directors: DANIEL PRESS; Phone: 831-459-3263; Fax: 831-459-4015; E-mail: dpress@cats.ucsc.edu
Publication(s): *Endangered Species Act: The Case of the Yellow-backed Rat Skunk; Environmental Justice: A Planning Commission*

Hearing to Approve/Deny a Household Hazardous Waste Facility Plan
Keyword(s): Endangered and Threatened Species, Environmental and Conservation Education, Environmental Justice, Environmental Law, Water Quality, Education

ENVIRONMENTAL EDUCATION ASSOCIATION OF ILLINOIS
26893 Carol Ln., Ingleside, IL 60041
Phone: 847-740-2590
Founded: 1970; Membership: 600
Scope: Statewide
Description: Environmental Education Association of Illinois is the only organization in Illinois that makes environmental literacy its primary goal as it strives to instill a sense of community between the native ecosystems and people.
Contact(s):
President: DEB CHAPMAN
President-Elect: KAREN ZUCKERMAN; Phone: 309-697-1325
Secretary: KIM PETZING; Phone: 217-384-4062
Treasurer: DAVE GURITZ; Phone: 847-428-2240
Membership: CURT CARTER, S.I.U.E. Mail Code 6888, Carbondale, IL 62901; Phone: 618-453-1121
Publication(s): *Illinois Environmental Education UPDATE*
Keyword(s): Aquatic Habitats, Environmental and Conservation Education, Flowers, Plants, and Trees, Solid Waste Management, Wildlife and Wildlife Habitat

ENVIRONMENTAL EDUCATION ASSOCIATION OF INDIANA
Attn: President, Richardson Wildlife Sanctuary, 64 West Rd., Dune Acres, Chesterton, IN 46304
Founded: 1969
Scope: Statewide
Description: A statewide, nonprofit organization dedicated to the wise use and management of natural resources through environmental conservation education. Activities include an annual meeting, workshops, teaching materials, exhibits, and youth environmental summit.
Contact(s):
President: JOHN THIELE JR.; Phone: 219-787-8983
Treasurer: DOUG WALDMAN, 11832 Kress Rd., Roanoke, IN 46783; Phone: 317-672-3842
Editor: SAM CARMAN, 5822 E CR 1000N, Pittsboro, IN 46167; Phone: 317-232-4105
Immediate Past President: CATHY MEYER, 119 W 7th, Bloomington, IN 47404; Phone: 812-349-2800
Publication(s): *CREED Newsletter*
Keyword(s): Environmental and Conservation Education, Education

ENVIRONMENTAL EDUCATION ASSOCIATION OF WASHINGTON
P.O. Box 4122, Bellingham, WA 98227
Web site: www.halcyon.com/eeaw/
Scope: Statewide
Description: The EEAW promotes and stimulates the development of effective environmental education in our state's schools and communities. The organization successfully creates an environmentally literate citizenry who practice care and respect for our state's natural environments. EEAW is a strong and vital organization that has successfully positioned environmental education as a resource to improve student learning and achievement, enhance business practices and support sustainable communities.
Contact(s):
President: MICHELE HALFHILL; Phone: 206-365-3893; E-mail: mihalfhill@aol.com
President Elect: MARTY FORTIN; Phone: 360-497-7131; E-mail: fortin@myhome.net
Keyword(s): Environmental and Conservation Education, Education

ENVIRONMENTAL EDUCATION COUNCIL OF OHIO
P.O. Box 2911, Akron, OH 44309-2911
Phone: 330-761-0855; E-mail: ad388@acorn.net
Founded: 1967; Membership: 600
Scope: Statewide
Description: EECO is a statewide organization whose purpose is to promote environmental education which nurtures knowledge, attitudes, and behaviors that foster global stewardship. EECO brings together educators from many settings to provide opportunities to share ideas, materials, and techniques. Members include classroom teachers, naturalists, camp staff, teacher educators, youth leaders, and agency personnel.
Contact(s):
President: HERB BRODA, 426 Oakley Rd., Wooster, OH 44691; Phone: 330-657-2796
Vice President: SUE HENNIS; Phone: 330-345-6771, ext. 226
Secretary: SABIHA DAUDI, 2754 Clifton Rd., Upper Arlington, OH 43221; Phone: 614-481-8483
Treasurer: TIM TAYLOR; Phone: 740-366-3276
Executive Director: TERESA M. MOURAD; Phone: 330-761-0855
Publication(s): *EECO Newsletter; Ohio Sampler: Outdoor and Environmental Education; Directory of Ohio Environmental Education Sites and Resources; Integrating Environmental Education and Science*
Keyword(s): Environmental and Conservation Education, Stewardship, Youth Organizations, Education

ENVIRONMENTAL EDUCATORS OF NORTH CAROLINA (EENC)
P.O. Box 4901, Chapel Hill, NC 27515-4901
Founded: 1990; Membership: over 200
Scope: Statewide
Description: EENC advocates and supports the development and implementation of quality education that promotes responsible environmental decision-making and actions. Sponsors workshops and an annual conference.
Contact(s):
President: SHEILA JONES; Phone: 919-250-1050
Advisor: DEBORAH MILLER; Phone: 919-541-5552
Publication(s): *EENC Networking Directory, EENC Newsletter, EENC Brochure*
Keyword(s): Environmental and Conservation Education, Education

ENVIRONMENTAL ENTERPRISES ASSISTANCE FUND, INC.
1655 N. Fort Meyer Dr., Fifth Fl., Arlington, VA 22209
Phone: 703-522-5928; Fax: 703-522-6450; E-mail: eeaf@igc.apc.org
Founded: 1990
Scope: National
Description: EEAF is a non-profit organization that operates as a venture capital fund; it provides long term risk capital and management assistance to environmentally beneficial businesses in developing countries, where such capital is otherwise unavailable.
Contact(s):
President: BROOKS BROWNE
Vice President: J. D. DOLINER
Senior Vice President: HELEN CHAIKOVSKY
Keyword(s): Agriculture, Biodiversity, Developing Countries, Energy, Energy Conservation, Fisheries, Pollution Prevention, Renewable Resources, Solar Energy, Sustainable Development, Water Pollution

ENVIRONMENTAL FUND FOR GEORGIA
1447 Peachtree St., Suite 502, Atlanta, GA 30309
Phone: 404-873-3173; Fax: 404-873-1284; E-mail: efg@efg.org; Web Site: www.efg.org
Founded: 1993
Scope: Statewide
Description: The Environmental Fund for Georgia is a federation of 22 leading environmental organizations raising funding and awareness through workplace giving campaigns.
Contact(s):
Executive Director: ALICE ROLLS; E-mail: alice@efg.org
Campaign Coordinator: SAMANTHA PUTT; E-mail: sam@efg.org
Keyword(s): Environment, Environmental and Conservation Education, Funding

ENVIRONMENTAL LAW ALLIANCE WORLDWIDE (E-LAW)
U.S. Office: 1877 Garden Ave., Eugene, OR 97403

Phone: 541-687-8454; Fax: 541-687-0535; E-mail: elawus@elaw.org; Web Site: www.elaw.org
Founded: *1989*
Scope: *International*
Description: E-LAW is an international network of public-interest attorneys and scientists dedicated to using law to protect the environment. E-LAW's 24 offices, located around the world exchange vital legal and scientific information. Advocates in more than 50 countries are linked electronically and can call on E-LAW for information to support their environmental protection work.
Contact(s):
Chair: JOHN BONINE, School of Law, University of Oregon, Eugene, OR 97403; Phone: 541-346-3823
President: MICHAEL AXLINE, School of Law, University of Oregon, Eugene, OR 97403; Phone: 541-346-3823
Executive Director: BERN JOHNSON
Publication(s): *E-LAW Update*
Keyword(s): Environmental Law, International Conservation

ENVIRONMENTAL LAW AND POLICY CENTER OF THE MIDWEST
35 East Wacker Dr., Suite 1300, Chicago, IL 60601-2208
Phone: 312-673-6500; Fax: 312-795-3730; E-mail: elpc@elpc.org; Web Site: www.elpc.org
Founded: *1993*
Scope: *Regional*
Description: A nonprofit public interest environmental advocacy organization working to implement sustainable energy strategies, promote innovative transportation approaches, expand and develop green markets and develop sound environmental management practices in Illinois, Indiana, Michigan, Minnesota, Ohio and Wisconsin.
Contact(s):
Executive Director: HOWARD A. LEARNER; E-mail: Hlearner@elpc.org
Director of Communications: MICHAEL TRUPPA; E-mail: Mtruppa@elpc.org
Director of Operations: KEVIN BRUBAKER; E-mail: Kbrubaker@elpc.org
Director of Public Affairs: DEBORAH ANDRACA ANDERSON; E-mail: Daandraca@elpc.org
Publication(s): *Visions, Choosing a Future for Growing Communities; Lake County at the Crossroads No. 2*
Keyword(s): Environmental Law, Environmental Living, Management Plans, Sustainability, Sustainable Energy, Transportation

ENVIRONMENTAL LAW INSTITUTE, THE
1616 P St., NW, Suite 200, Washington, DC 20036
Phone: 202-939-3800; Fax: 202-939-3868; Web Site: www.eli.org
Founded: *1969*
Scope: *National*
Description: The Environmental Law Institute advances environmental protection by improving law, policy and management. ELI researches pressing problems, educates professionals and citizens about the nature of these issues, and convenes all sectors in forging effective solutions.
Contact(s):
President: J. WILLIAM FUTRELL
Chairman of the Board: DONALD STEVER
Director of Communications: STEPHEN R. DUJACK
Head Librarian: LAWRENCE ROSS; Phone: 202-328-5150
Secretary and Treasurer: ROBERT PERCIVAL
Publication(s): *ELR - Environmental Law Reporter, The; National Wetlands Newsletter; The Environmental Forum*
Keyword(s): Biodiversity, Conservation, Environmental Law, Natural Resource Conservation, Sustainable Development, Wetlands, Pollution Control, Federalism, International Environmental Law

ENVIRONMENTAL LEAGUE OF MASSACHUSETTS
3 Joy St., Boston, MA 02108
Phone: 617-742-2553; Fax: 617-742-9656; E-mail: elm@environmentalleague.org; Web Site: www.environmentalleague.org
Scope: *Statewide*
Description: A representative statewide organization, affiliated with the National Wildlife Federation, dedicated to the protection and enhancement of wildlife and its habitat through public education and government interaction.
Contact(s):
President: JAMES GOMES
Chair: RICHARD JOHNSON
President: DON HINCHEY
Representative: STEPHEN LEONARD
Alternate Representative: NANCY SMITH
Affiliate Representative: KEMPER E. EAGLE
Editor: THOMAS W. EVANS
Publication(s): *ELM Bulletin*
Keyword(s): Aquatic Habitats, Fisheries, Renewable Resources, Water Pollution Management, Wetlands

ENVIRONMENTAL MEDIA ASSOCIATION
10780 Santa Monica Blvd., Suite 210, Los Angeles, CA 90025
Phone: 310-446-6244; Fax: 310-446-6255; E-mail: ema@ema1.org; Web Site: www.ema-online.org
Founded: *1989*
Scope: *National*
Description: EMA works to mobilize the entertainment community in a global effort to educate people about environmental problems, and inspire them to act on those problems now.
Contact(s):
Director of Programs and Administration: KELLEY SKUMAUTZ; E-mail: kelley@ema1.org
Director of Special Events: PATIE MALONEY; E-mail: patie@ema1.org
Publication(s): *Green Light*
Keyword(s): Environmental Communication

ENVIRONMENTAL PROTECTION ASSOCIATION OF GHANA
P.O. Box AS 32, Asawasi-Kumasi, Asawasi-Kumasi Ghana
Phone: 0233-051-29950; Fax: 233-51-22537
Founded: *1987;* **Membership:** *220*
Scope: *International*
Description: The Association was established with the major objective of promoting an environmentally clean society and ecologically sustainable development. Association activities have been concentrated on the following: tree planting, afforestation, education, awareness, seminars and workshops, health, women and development, income generation, and rural development.
Contact(s):
Director: F. A. JANTUAH
First Deputy Director: KWABENA ANTWI
Project Manager: JOHN KWADWO OWUSU
Second Deputy Director: F. A. OWUSU
Publication(s): *Annual Report*

ENVIRONMENTAL RESOURCE CENTER (ERC)
411 East Sixth St., P.O. Box 819, Ketchum, ID 83340
Phone: 208-726-4333; Fax: 208-726-1531; E-mail: erc@micron.net
Founded: *1989;* **Membership:** *800*
Scope: *National*
Description: The ERC is a nonprofit organization that provides resources and educational programs to the public about local, regional, and global environmental issues.
Contact(s):
Executive Director: MOLLY GOODYEAR
Publication(s): *Aquila*
Keyword(s): Ecology, Energy Conservation, Environmental and Conservation Education, Internships, Natural History

NON-GOVERNMENTAL ORGANIZATIONS - F

ENVIROSOUTH, INC.
P.O. Box 11468, Montgomery, AL 36111
Phone: 205-277-7050; Fax: 205-277-7080
Founded: 1975
Scope: National
Description: A private nonprofit organization specializing in recycling information and related services for the Southeast Recycling Market Council, and the annual Southeast Recycling Conference and Trade Show.
Contact(s):
President: MARTHA McINNIS; Phone: 205-277-7050
Publication(s): *EnviroSouth Magazine*
Keyword(s): Communications, Environmental and Conservation Education, Natural History, Renewable Resources, Solid Waste Management

EUROPARC FEDERATION
Kroellstrasse 5, D - 94481 Grafenau, 94481 Germany
Phone: 49-8552-96100; Fax: 49-8552-961019; E-mail: office@europarc.org; Web Site: www.europarc.org
Founded: 1973; Membership: 325 member organizations
Scope: International
Description: The EUROPARC Federation (formally known as the Federation of Nature and National Parks of Europe) is a pan-European, not-for-profit, non-governmental organization, which promotes and supports the full range of protected areas in Europe. EUROPARC aims to facilitate the exchange of technical and scientific expertise, information and personnel between parks and reserves. It organizes training and exchange programs, and provides professional advice on the establishment and development of protected areas.
Contact(s):
President: DR. PATRIZIA ROSSI
Director: EVA PONGRATZ
Deputy Director: RACHEL GRAY
Publication(s): *European Bulletin: Nature and National Parks; EUROPARC 1992/1993/1994/1995/1996/1997/1998: Proceedings of the Federation's Annual Conference and General Assembly; Seminar and Workshop Reports on varied issues of protected area management.*
Keyword(s): Conservation of Protected Areas, International Conservation

EUROPEAN ASSOCIATION FOR AQUATIC MAMMALS
P.O. Box 58, 3910AB, Rhenen, The Netherlands
Phone: 31-317-612294
Founded: 1973; Membership: 175
Scope: National
Description: To promote the free exchange of knowledge and to further scientific progress pertaining to the treatment, management, and conservation of aquatic mammals; to provide an organization for the above individuals, to improve practical husbandry; and to advance, by continued study, the basis for maintaining aquatic mammals in captivity.
Contact(s):
President: DR. JOHN R. BAKER
President Elect: GERALDINE LACAVE
Secretary and Treasurer: FRANS J. ENGELSMA
Publication(s): *Aquatic Mammals; Newletters*
Keyword(s): Endangered and Threatened Species, Environmental and Conservation Education, Marine Mammals, Water Pollution Management, Zoological Parks

EUROPEAN CETACEAN SOCIETY
c/o Deutsches Meeresmuseum, Katharinenberg 14, 18439, Stralsund Germany
Phone: 49-3831-265021; Fax: 49-3831-265060; Web Site: web.inter.NL.net/users/J.W.Broekema/ecs
Founded: 1987; Membership: 450
Scope: International
Description: The European Cetacean Society's main focus is to promote and coordinate scientific study and conservation of cetaceans and to gather and disseminate information to members and to the public.
Contact(s):
Chairman: CHRISTINA LOCKYER
Secretary: BEATRICE JANN
Treasurer: ROLAND LICK; E-mail: Rlick2059@aol.com
Editor: PETER EVANS
Publication(s): *European Cetacean Society Newsletter; European Research on Cetaceans*
Keyword(s): Aquatic Species, Biodiversity, Dolphins, Endangered and Threatened Species, Environmental Preservation, Marine Mammals, Natural History, Whales, Wildlife Management

EVERGLADES COORDINATING COUNCIL (ECC)
7901 W. 25 Ct., Hialeah, FL 33106
Phone: 305-248-9924
Founded: 1970; Membership: 14 affiliate organizations
Scope: Statewide
Description: ECC is an umbrella organization of south Florida sports-persons and conservation organizations united in a desire to protect wildlife habitat, assure sound wildlife management practices, and provide for properly regulated outdoor recreational activities.
Contact(s):
President: LEE CHAMBERLAIN, 4251 SW 77th Ave., Davie, FL 33328; Phone: 305-791-8711
Vice President: HAROLD L. JOHNSON, 3701 NW 66th Ave., Miami, FL 33166; Phone: 305-871-1860
Secretary: BARBARA JEAN POWELL, 22951 SW 190th Ave., Miami, FL 33170; Phone: 305-246-1381
Treasurer: DAVE CHARLAND, 3559 NW 52nd St., Ft. Lauderdale, FL 33309; Phone: 305-484-7777
Director: RALPH JOHNSON, 7901 W. 25th Ct., Hialeah, FL 33016; Phone: 305-825-4667
Publication(s): *Newsletter*
Keyword(s): Hunting, Outdoor Recreation, Wetlands, Wildlife and Wildlife Habitat, Wildlife Management, Everglades

F

FAIRFAX AUDUBON SOCIETY
P.O. Box 128, Annandale, VA 22003-0128
Phone: 703-256-6895; Fax: 703-256-2060
Founded: 1980; Membership: 4,500
Scope: Statewide
Description: The Fairfax Audubon Society--a chapter of the National Audubon Society, is committed to the Audubon mission which is to conserve and restore natural ecosystems, focusing on birds and other wildlife, and their habitats.
Contact(s):
President: TISH TYSON, 8641 Mt. Vernon Hwy., Alexandria, VA 22309; Phone: 703-780-0925
Treasurer: DUNCAN LOVE, 9204 Holborn Ave., Anandale, VA 22003; Phone: 703-978-3262
Publication(s): *Potomac Flier*
Keyword(s): Biodiversity, Birds, Conservation of Protected Areas, Ecology, Environmental and Conservation Education, Environmental Planning, Environmental Preservation, Environmental Protection, Natural Areas, Nongame Wildlife, Raptors, Wildlife and Wildlife Habitat

FEDERAL CARTRIDGE COMPANY
900 Ehlen Dr., Anoka, MN 55303
Phone: 612-323-3827; Fax: 612-323-2506
Scope: National
Contact(s):
Conservation Manager: WILLIAM STEVENS
Keyword(s): Hunting, Wildlife Management

FEDERAL WILDLIFE OFFICER'S ASSOCIATION
P.O. Box 5404, Saginaw, WI 48603-0404
Phone: 603-433-0502; Fax: 603-433-0509; Web Site: www.fwoa.org

Scope: National
Description: The Federal Wildlife Officer's Association is an organization dedicated to the protection of wildlife and plants, the enforcement of federal wildlife law, the fostering of cooperation and communication among federal wildlife officers and the perpetuation, enhancement and defense of the wildlife officer profession.
Contact(s):
President: TIMOTHY J. SANTEL; Phone: 217-793-9554; Fax: 217-793-2835
Vice President: CHRISTOPHER E. DOWD; Phone: 617-424-5750; Fax: 617-424-5757
Secretary and Treasurer: JAMES R. GALE; Phone: 517-686-4578; Fax: 517-686-2837
Publication(s): *The Federal Wildlife Officer Newsletter*
Keyword(s): Birds, Endangered and Threatened Species, Environmental and Conservation Education, Environmental Justice, Environmental Protection, Hunting, International Conservation, Law Enforcement, Mammals, Marine Mammals, Nongame Wildlife, Pesticides, Predators, Raptors, Professional Organization

FEDERATION OF ALBERTA NATURALISTS
Box 1472, Edmonton, Alberta T5J 2N5 Canada
Phone: 708-427-8124
Founded: 1970; Membership: 21 Clubs
Scope: Statewide
Description: To increase Albertans' knowledge of natural history; foster creation of new natural history groups; promote natural areas; and provide a forum for discussion and means of taking action on environmental problems of concern to naturalists.
Contact(s):
President: DEREK JOHNSON
Treasurer: PAT CLAYTON
Executive Director: GLEN SEMENCHUK
Editor: BRIAN PARKER
Publication(s): *Alberta Naturalist*
Keyword(s): Birds, Environmental and Conservation Education, Natural History, Nature Preservation, Public Lands

FEDERATION OF ENVIRONMENTAL EDUCATION IN ST. PETERSBURG
Lomonosov St., 11, St. Petersburg 191002 Russia
Phone: 812-110-68-49; Fax: 812-110-68-49; E-mail: fee@mail.spb.org; Web Site: http://spb.org.ru/fee
Founded: 1994
Scope: International
Description: The basis direction of the Federation is culture, education, enlightenment, public health, science, economics, business, and enterprise.
Contact(s):
President: SEZGEI ALEXEEV
Publication(s): *Conception of Environmental Education in St. Petersburg; Environment and Education; Materials of International Conference for Environmental Education*
Keyword(s): Acid Rain, Agriculture, Air Quality and Pollution, Ecology, Ecotourism, Environmental and Conservation Education, Environmental Health, Environmental Planning, Sustainable Development

FEDERATION OF FLY FISHERS
P.O. Box 1595, 502 S. 19th, Suite #1, Bozeman, MT 59771
Phone: 406-585-7592; Fax: 406-585-7596; E-mail: 74504.2605@compuserve.com; Web Site: www.fedflyfishers.org
Founded: 1965
Scope: National
Description: To promote international fly fishing as a most enjoyable and sportsmanlike method of fishing and to preserve all species of fish in all classes of waters through local stream and fisher restoration projects, conservation grants, audiovisual programs, public education, and international committees.
Contact(s):
President: GREG PITTS
Secretary: GARY GRANT
Treasurer: KENT JENNINGS
Contact for Salt Water Committee: RON WINN
Contact for Steelhead Committee: HOWARD JOHNSON
Contact for Warm Water Committee: FRED STEVENSON
IFFC Director: BOB WILTSHIRE, 215 E. Lewis, Livingston, MT 59047; Phone: 406-222-9369
Managing Director: LAUREN BAGLEY
Vice-President of Communications: DAVID HALBLOM
Vice-President of Conservation: VERNE LEHMBERG
Vice-President of Education: SUSAN HALBLOM
Vice-President of Fund Raising: TRACIE MALER
Vice-President of Membership: DENNIS BRAKKE
Publication(s): *Flyfisher, The; Ospre, The; Clubwire, The*
Keyword(s): Environmental and Conservation Education, Environmental Preservation, Fisheries, Sport Fishing

FEDERATION OF NEW YORK STATE BIRD CLUBS, INC.
P.O. Box 440, Loch Sheldrake, NY 12759
Founded: 1947; Membership: 45 clubs, 800 individuals
Scope: Statewide
Description: To further the study of bird life in New York state and to disseminate knowledge thereof, to educate the public on the need for conserving natural resources and to document the ornithology of the state.
Contact(s):
President: MARY ALICE KOENEKE, 362 Nine Mile Point Rd., Oswego, NY 13126; Phone: 315-342-3402
Treasurer: SUE ADAIR, 107 Fox Run Drive, Schenectady, NY 12303; Phone: 518-355-8008
Corresponding Secretary: WILLIAM B. REEVES, 107 Elberta Dr., E. Northport, NY 11731; Phone: 516-499-1688
Editor: PHYLLIS JONES, 9 Hallock Rd., Pond Eddy, NY 12770; Phone: 914-557-6591
Editor: MANNY LEVINE, 585 Mead Terrace, S. Hempstead, NY 11550
Recording Secretary: BARBARA BUTLER, RD2, Box 161, Verbank, NY 12585
Publication(s): *Kingbird, The; New York Birders; Checklist of the Birds of New York State*
Keyword(s): Birds, Wildlife and Wildlife Habitat

FEDERATION OF ONTARIO NATURALISTS
355 Lesmill Rd., Don Mills, Ontario M3B 2W8 Canada
Phone: 416-444-8419; Fax: 416-444-9866; E-mail: info@ontarionature.org; Web Site: www.ontarionature.org
Founded: 1931; Membership: 15,000
Scope: Statewide
Description: Committed to protecting and increasing awareness of Ontario's natural areas and wildlife, and exerts influence to protect our natural environment. Eighty-three federated clubs across Ontario.
Contact(s):
President: JANE TOPPING
Vice President: MARK DORFMAN
Executive Director: RIC STYMMES
Chief Administrative Officer: JEAN LABRECQUE
Director of Conservation: RON REID
Editor: NANCY CLARKE
Publication(s): *Seasons*
Keyword(s): Natural Areas

FEDERATION OF WESTERN OUTDOOR CLUBS
512 Boylston Ave. E., #106, Seattle, WA 98102
Phone: 206-322-3041
Founded: 1932; Membership: 385
Scope: Regional
Description: Established for mutual service and for the promotion of the proper use, enjoyment and protection of America's scenic, wilderness, and outdoor recreation resources. Forty-three affiliated clubs in Alaska, British Columbia, and the western states.
Contact(s):
President: BROCK EVANS, 5449 33rd Ave., NW, Washington, DC 20015

NON-GOVERNMENTAL ORGANIZATIONS - F

Vice President: WINCHELL HAYWARD, 208 Willard N., San Fransico, CA 94118
Secretary: NANCY KROENING, 5615 40th Ave., W, Seattle, WA 98199
Treasurer: MARTIN HUEBNER, 1995 McKinzie Dr., Idaho Falls, ID 83404
Editor: HAZEL WOLF, 512 Boylston Ave., E, #106, Seattle, WA 98102
Publication(s): *Outdoors West*
Keyword(s): Deserts, Environmental and Conservation Education, Forests and Forestry, Outdoor Recreation, Wildlife and Wildlife Habitat

FISH AND WILDLIFE INFORMATION EXCHANGE
203 W. Roanoke St., Blacksburg, VA 24061
Phone: 540-231-7348; Fax: 540-231-7019; E-mail: fwiexchg@vt.edu
Founded: 1984
Scope: National
Description: The FWIE is a clearinghouse and technical assistance center to state and federal fish and wildlife agencies in the area of fish and wildlife databases and computer applications. The FWIE is available to help agencies with biological and administrative information management for application to environmental assessment, planning, extension, research, and education. The FWIE is a unit within the Department of Fisheries and Wildlife Sciences, Virginia Tech.
Contact(s):
Project Leader: JEFFERSON L. WALDON
Keyword(s): Aquatic Habitats, Biodiversity, Birds, Ecology, Endangered and Threatened Species, Fisheries, Insects and Butterflies, Mammals, Nongame Wildlife, Reptiles and Amphibians, Sport Fishing, Terrestrial Habitats, Wildlife and Wildlife Habitat, Wildlife Management

FISH AND WILDLIFE REFERENCE SERVICE
5430 Grosvenor Ln., Bethesda, MD 20814
Phone: 800-582-3421; Fax: 301-564-4059; E-mail: fw9_fa_reference_service@fws.gov
Founded: 1965
Scope: National
Description: A computerized information retrieval system and clearinghouse, providing selected reports on fish and wildlife management. Operated under a contract with the U.S. Fish and Wildlife Service to provide access to reports produced by the Federal Aid in Fish and Wildlife Restoration Program, the Cooperative Fishery and Wildlife Research Units Program, the Endangered Species Grants Program, and the Anadromous sport Fish Conservation Program.
Contact(s):
Editor: GEOFFREY YEADON
Project Leader: PAUL WILSON
Publication(s): *Fish and Wildlife Reference Service (Newsletter)*
Keyword(s): Endangered and Threatened Species, Fisheries, Nongame Wildlife, Wildlife and Wildlife Habitat, Wildlife Management

FISHAMERICA FOUNDATION
1033 N. Fairfax St., Suite 200, Alexandria, VA 22314
Phone: 703-548-6338
Scope: National
Description: FishAmerica Foundation is the conservation arm of the American Sportfishing Association. The Foundation is a nonprofit organization dedicated to enhancing the water quality and fish populations of North America.
Contact(s):
Managing Director: TOM MARSHALL
Keyword(s): Environmental and Conservation Education, Outdoor Recreation, Sport Fishing, Water Pollution, Water Resources

FLORIDA ASSOCIATION OF SOIL AND WATER CONSERVATION DISTRICTS
Attn: President, 16806 NW 40th PL, Newberry, FL 32669
Scope: Statewide
Contact(s):
President: TIM FORD; Phone: 352-472-5462; Fax: 352-472-5435
Executive Director: COURTENAY MCCORMICK, P.O. Box 753, Callahan, FL 32011; Phone: 904-879-3375; Fax: 904-879-2408
1st Vice President: TODD UNDERHILL, 6408 Goldfinch St., Sarastota, FL 34241; Phone: 941-923-3782; Fax: 941-924-3422
2nd Vice President: LYNDA JACOBS, 1811 West Cr. 419, Chulota, FL 32766; Phone: 407-365-6031; Fax: 407-365-5067
Administrative Consultant: SANDY HOWE, 16806 NW 40th Place, Newberry, FL 32669; Phone: 352-472-5462; Fax: 352-472-5435
Board Member: TOM FORD, Rt. 2 Box 1077, Bryceville, FL 32009; Phone: 904-879-1002
Secretary and Treasurer: VIRGINIA MCCALL, P.O. Box 276, Salem, FL 32356; Phone: 850-584-2721; Fax: 850-584-2619
Keyword(s): Conservation Districts

FLORIDA AUDUBON SOCIETY
1331 Palmetto Ave., Suite 110, Winter Park, FL 32789
Founded: 1900; Membership: 35,000
Scope: Statewide
Description: A statewide organization formed to promote public interest, understanding, and protection of Florida wildlife, and of the environment and habitats that support it.
Contact(s):
President: CLAY HENDERSON
Secretary: JANET JACKSON
Treasurer: GARY FROHMAN
Chairman of the Board: HAL TURVILLE, 150 W. Minnehaha Ave., Clermont, FL 34711
Editor: SANDRA BOGAN
Senior Vice President: CHARLES LEE
Vice President of Chapter Relations: LARRY THOMPSON
Vice President, Center for Birds of Prey: RESEE COLLINS
Publication(s): *Florida Naturalist, The*
Keyword(s): Birds, Conservation of Protected Areas, Coral Reefs, Endangered and Threatened Species, Environmental and Conservation Education, Forest Management, Lakes, Land Use Planning, Population Growth, Public Lands, Raptors, Rivers, Sea Grass, Wildlife and Wildlife Habitat

FLORIDA B.A.S.S. CHAPTER FEDERATION
Attn: President, 210- 14th St. NE, Naples, FL 34120
Scope: Statewide
Description: An organization of Bassmaster chapters, affiliated with the Bass Anglers Sportsman Society, organized to fight pollution, assist state and national conservation agencies in their efforts, and teach young people of our good conservation practices. Dedicated to the realistic conservation of our water resources.
Contact(s):
President: GERALD BATTEN; Phone: 941-353-7941

FLORIDA DEFENDERS OF THE ENVIRONMENT, INC. (Home Office)
4424 NW 13 St., Suite C-8, Gainesville, FL 32609
Phone: 352-378-8465; Fax: 352-377-0869; E-mail: fde@bellsouth.net; Web Site: www.fladefenders.org
Scope: Statewide
Description: FDE promotes conservation, restoration, and sustainable use of Florida's natural resources by providing the public and private sector with objective information and analysis developed through a statewide network of volunteer specialists. Guided by the motto "FDE gets the facts," the organization achieves realistic goals by targeting a limited number of complex environmental issues and providing expert scientific analysis, sustained tracking, advocacy, and litigation when necessary.
Contact(s):
President: RICHARD HAMANN ESQ; Phone: 352-392-2237; Fax: 352-392-1457
Vice President: DR. JOE SIRY
Secretary: BRAM D.E. CANTER ESQ
Treasurer: DR. FRANK NORDLIE

Executive Director: ROBIN MITCHELL
Coordinator of Apalachicola River: STEVE LEITMAN
Coordinator of Ocklawaha River: DAVID J. WHITE
Coordinator of Suwannee River: SUSAN VINCE
Coordinator of Suwannee River: BOB SIMONS
Restoration Specialist: KRISTINA JACKSON
Publication(s): *Monitor, The*
Keyword(s): Biodiversity, Environmental Law, Land Use Planning, Rivers, Water Quality, Water Resources, Watersheds, Wildlife and Wildlife Habitat

FLORIDA EXOTIC PEST PLANT COUNCIL
P.O. Box 24680, West Palm Beach, FL 33416
Founded: 1984; Membership: 400
Scope: Statewide
Description: FLEPPC goals are directed toward building public awareness about the serious threat invasive plants pose to native ecosystems, secure funding, and support for control and management of exotic plants, and developing integrated management and control methods.
Contact(s):
Chairperson: ANTONIO J. PERNAS; Phone: 305-242-7846; E-mail: tony_pernas@nps.gov
Secretary: JACKIE SMITH; Phone: 561-791-4720
Treasurer: DAN THAYER; Phone: 561-682-6129; Fax: 561-681-6232
Editor: AMY FERRITER; Phone: 561-682-6097; E-mail: aferriter@sfwmd.gov
Publication(s): *Wildland Weeds; Florida Exotic Pest Plant Council Newsletter*
Keyword(s): Biology, Conservation, Environmental Preservation, Natural Areas, Plants

FLORIDA FORESTRY ASSOCIATION
P.O. Box 1696, Tallahassee, FL 32302
Phone: 904-222-5646; Fax: 904-222-6179
Founded: 1923
Scope: Statewide
Description: Nonprofit, trade-supported organization of industries, businesses, and individuals who encourage the promotion, development and protection of forestry in Florida.
Contact(s):
President: CHARLES THOMPSON
Executive Vice-President and Editor: JEFF DORAN
President-Elect: BOB MOORE
Secretary and Treasurer: HARRY VAN LOOCK, Rt. 3 Box 260, Perry, FL 32347
Publication(s): *Pines and Needles; Florida Forests* **Keyword(s):** Forests and Forestry

FLORIDA NATIVE PLANT SOCIETY
P.O. Box 690278, Vero Beach, FL 32969-0278
Phone: 561-562-1598
Founded: 1980; Membership: 3,400
Scope: Statewide
Description: Promotes preservation, conservation, and restoration of native plants and native plant communities of Florida, and provides information through publications, conferences, workshops and a statewide membership organized by local chapters.
Contact(s):
President: CANDACE WELLER, 1515 Country Club Rd. N., St. Petersburg, FL 33710; Phone: 727-345-4619
Vice President: KIM ZARILLO, 760 Cajeput Cir., Melbourne Village, FL 32904; Phone: 407-727-1713
Vice President: DON SPENCE, P.O. Box 321, Roseland, FL 32957; Phone: 407-589-0319
Treasurer: ROBERT BAREISS, 10301 Bellwood Ave., New Port Richey, FL 34654; Phone: 727-842-3133
Publication(s): *Palmetto, The; Florida's Incredible Wild Edibles; Planning and Planting Your Native Plant Yard; Butterfly Gardening with Florida's Native Plants; Common Grasses of Florida and the Southeast; Big Trees: The Florida Register*

Keyword(s): Biodiversity, Endangered and Threatened Species, Environmental and Conservation Education, Flowers, Plants, and Trees, Natural Areas, Native Plants

FLORIDA ORNITHOLOGICAL SOCIETY
c/o Jim Cox; 1503 Wekewa Nene, Tallahassee, FL 32301
Phone: 850-942-2489; E-mail: necox@nettally.com
Founded: 1072; Membership: 500
Scope: Statewide
Description: To engage in pursuits that advance ornithology in Florida; to facilitate education about birds in the wild; to unite amateurs and professionals on the study of birds in the wild; and to publish a scientific journal and other publications, relevant to the member's common interests.
Contact(s):
President: JIM COX; E-mail: necox@nettally.com
Vice President: ANN SCHNAPF, 7217 N. Ola, Tampa, FL 33604; Phone: 941-643-2249
Secretary: DR. RICHARD L. WEST, 2808 Rabbit Hill Rd., Tallahassee, FL 32312; Phone: 904-386-6371; E-mail: richlwest@aol.com
Treasurer: ERIC STOLEN, Mail Code OYN-2, Kennedy Space Center, FL 32899; Phone: 813-455-8340
Editor: SEAN ROWE, 4845 Rayburn Rd., Coco, FL 32926
Librarian: R. TODD ENGSTROM, Rte 1, Box 678, Tallahassee, FL 32312; Phone: 850-893-4153, ext. 223; E-mail: engstrom@bio.fsu.edu
Publication(s): *Florida Field Naturalist; Florida Ornithological Society Newsletter*
Keyword(s): Birds, Endangered and Threatened Species, Environmental and Conservation Education, Natural History, Nongame Wildlife

FLORIDA PANTHER PROJECT, INC., THE
P.O. Box 19866, Sarasota, FL 34276
Phone: 941-379-2221
Founded: 1993
Scope: Statewide
Description: To assist in the sensible and responsible recovery of the Florida Panther in Florida, by raising funds to purchase environmentally sensitive panther habitat across Florida. Guest speakers available.
Contact(s):
President: WILLIAM SAMUELS, P.O. Box 19866, Sarasota, FL 34276; Phone: 941-379-2221
Executive Director: BOB MILLS, Gifts and Fundraising 4269 Hearthstone Pl., Sarasota, FL 34238; Phone: 941-966-7765
Advisory Board: TIM MALLON, 3715 Felda St., Cocoa, FL 32926; Phone: 407-633-4799
Board of Directors: JUDY CONDA, 6551 Gulfgate Pl., Sarasota, FL 34321; Phone: 941-921-7300
Keyword(s): Endangered and Threatened Species, Environmental and Conservation Education, Land Purchase, Nongame Wildlife, Wildlife and Wildlife Habitat

FLORIDA PUBLIC INTEREST RESEARCH GROUP (Florida PIRG)
704 West Madison St., Tallahassee, FL 32304
Phone: 850-224-3321; E-mail: floridapirg@pirg.org; Web Site: www.pirg.org/floridapirg
Founded: 1981; Membership: 35,000
Scope: Statewide
Description: Florida PIRG is a nonprofit organization committed to researching, educating, organizing, and advocating programs to protect Florida's environment. These programs include preventing offshore drilling, promoting recycling, and other vital issues.
Contact(s):
Executive Director: MARK FERRULO
Publication(s): *Citizen Agenda; Florida PIRG reports*
Keyword(s): Environmental Protection

FLORIDA SPORTSMEN'S CONSERVATION ASSOCIATION
P.O. Box 20051, West Palm Beach, FL 33416-0051
Phone: 561-478-5965

Founded: 1994; Membership: 288
Scope: Statewide
Description: The Florida Sportsmen's Conservation Association promotes conservation, preservation, and propagation of all forms of game wildlife species, nongame wildlife species, and marine life. The Association stimulates a greater interest in any and all legitimate outdoor recreational activities, assures sportsmen that they may continue to use areas for legitimate outdoor recreational activities, works towards the opening of all lands and waters for legitimate outdoor recreational activities, where feasible, and promote the enactment of fair game and fisheries laws and to assist in the enforcement of the laws.
Contact(s):
President: BISHOP WRIGHT, 15439-94th St. N., West Palm Beach, FL 33412; Phone: 561-795-1375
Secretary: KEVIN SMITH, 15856-93rd St. N., West Palm Beach, FL 33412; Phone: 561-795-4112
Treasurer: RICHARD ANDREA, 12334-77th Pl. N., West Palm Beach, FL 33412; Phone: 561-795-1136
1st Vice-President: ROBERT STOSSEL JR., 14241-77th Pl. N., Loxahatchee, FL 33470; Phone: 561-753-7880
2nd Vice-President: MARK DOMBROSKI, 1842 Lynton Cir., Wellington, FL 33414; Phone: 561-793-7200
Publication Director: BRUCE BRITT, 7407 Southern Blvd., West Palm Beach, FL 33413; Phone: 561-688-2553
Keyword(s): Environmental and Conservation Education, Land Use Planning, Outdoor Recreation, Public Lands, Wildlife and Wildlife Habitat

FLORIDA TRAIL ASSOCIATION, INC.
P.O. Box 13708, Gainesville, FL 32604-1708
Phone: 352-378-8823/800-343-1882
Founded: 1964; Membership: 5,500
Scope: Statewide
Description: This association was formed to instill in Floridians and in visitors to Florida an appreciation and a desire to conserve the natural beauty of Florida by all lawful means; to promote the creation of a hiking trail, to be called the Florida Trail, to run the length of the state; and to provide an opportunity for hiking and camping.
Contact(s):
President: RICHARD SCHULER
Secretary: JENNIFER REINOSO
Treasurer: DENNIS NYMARK
1st Vice-President for Administration: DEBORAH STEWART-KENT
2nd Vice-President for Membership: SYLVIA DUNNAM
3rd Vice-President for Trails: FRED SCHILLER
4th Vice-President for Public Relations: KEVIN BUTLER
Publication(s): *Footprint, The*
Keyword(s): Environmental and Conservation Education, Natural Areas, Outdoor Recreation, Pedestrian Environment, Trail

FLORIDA WILDLIFE FEDERATION
P.O. Box 6870, Tallahassee, FL 32314-6870
Phone: 850-656-7113; Fax: 850-942-4431; E-mail: wildfed@aol.com; Web Site: www.fwf.usf.edu/
Founded: 1935
Scope: Statewide
Description: A representative statewide organization, affiliated with the National Wildlife Federation, dedicated to the protection and enhancement of wildlife and its habitat through public education and government interaction.
Contact(s):
President: MANLEY K. FULLER
Chair and Alternative Representative: LYNN ALAN THOMPSON
Representative: VIRGINIA BROCK
Editor: RICHARD FARREN
Publication(s): *Florida Fish and Wildlife News*

FOOD AND AGRICULTURE ORGANIZATION OF THE UNITED NATIONS
Viale delle Terme di Caracalla, Rome 00100 Italy
Phone: 06-57051; Fax: 39-06-5705-3369; Web Site: www.fao.org
Founded: 1945; Membership: 178 (including EC-Member Organization)
Scope: International
Description: To raise levels of nutrition and standards of living, to improve the production and distribution of agricultural products, and to better the conditions of rural populations. FAO has adopted an overriding strategy of integrated sustainable development. All operations are geared to meet basic human needs without compromising those of future generations.
Contact(s):
Director-General: JACQUES DIOUF
Deputy Director-General: D. HARCHARIK
Director of Information Division: CHRISTINA ENGFELDT
Contact for the Sustainable Development Department: H. CARSALADE
Inspector-General: P. G. WILSON
Publication(s): *State of Food and Agriculture; Unasylva; Non-Wood News; Forest Genetic Resources; FAO Aquaculture (newsletter); Document database (www.fao.org/library/dlubin/DlfaodcE.htm); FAO Electronic Journals (www.fao.org/library/dlubin/DleljrnE.htm)*
Keyword(s): Agriculture, Fisheries, Forests and Forestry, Health and Nutrition, Rural Development

FOREST FIRE LOOKOUT ASSOCIATION
374 Maple Ave., E., Suite 310, Vienna, VA 22180
Phone: 703-255-2700; Fax: 703-281-9200; Web Site: www.firelookout.org
Founded: 1990; Membership: 650
Scope: National
Description: A national organization devoted to forest protection through the inventory, maintenance and volunteer staffing of forest fire lookouts and fire towers in the 49 states that have them and throughout the world. Maintains a database of designs and available lookout parts and salvage. Organized into 21 states and regional chapters.
Contact(s):
Chair: KEITH A. ARGOW; Phone: 703-255-2700
Eastern Deputy Chair: MARK HAUGHWOUT; Phone: 802-476-8341
Western Deputy Chair: GARY WEBER; Phone: 207-443-2465
Historian: MICHAEL A. PFEIFFER; Phone: 501-967-4167
Restorations: HENRY ISENBERG; Phone: 508-883-0834
National Historic Lookout Register: NANCY GABRIEL; Phone: 703-255-2700
Publication(s): *Lookout Network*
Keyword(s): Environmental Preservation, Environmental Protection, Forest Management, Forests and Forestry, Historic Preservation, Museum, Preservation and Protection

FOREST HISTORY SOCIETY, INC.
701 Vickers Ave., Durham, NC 27701
Phone: 919-682-9319; Fax: 919-682-2349; E-mail: recluce2@duke.edu
Founded: 1946; Membership: 1,500
Scope: National
Description: A nonprofit educational institution, the Forest History Society is dedicated to the advancement of historical understanding of human interaction with the forest environment--forest industries, forestry, conservation, and other forms of use and appreciation. A membership organization, it sponsors programs in research, publication, archives-library, and professional service.
Contact(s):
Chairman: THOMAS R. DUNLAP
President: STEVE ANDERSON
Editor: HAL ROTHMAN
Librarian: CHERYL OAKES
Publication(s): *Forest History Today; Environmental History*
Keyword(s): Conservation of Protected Areas, Environmental Law, Forests and Forestry, Land Use Planning, Public Lands

FOREST LANDOWNERS ASSOCIATION, INC.
Suite 120, 4 Executive Park, E., P.O. Box 95385, Atlanta, GA 30347
Phone: 404-325-2954; Fax: 404-325-2955

Founded: 1941
Scope: Regional
Description: Nonprofit forestry organization of timberland owners large and small in 17 southern states seeking to give private timberland owners and related interests a greater voice in matters affecting their business.
Contact(s):
President: G. EDWARD MUCKENFUSS
Executive Vice President: STEVE NEWTON
Editor: MATTHEW WORKMAN
Regional Vice President: GUERRY B. DOOLITTLE, Champion International, 9485 Regency Sq. Blvd, Jacksonville, FL 32225-8155
Regional Vice President: L. KEVILLE LARSON, P.O. Box 2143, Mobile, AL 36652
Regional Vice President: C. E. BUSH, 6701 Carmel Road, Suite 404, Charlotte, NC 28226
Regional Vice President: PEGGY CLARK, 1203 Pine St., Arkadelphia, AR 71923
Regional Vice President: Dr. JOHN H. BOWEN, Box 159, Louisville, TN 37777
Publication(s): *Forest Landowner Magazine; Forest Landowner Manual*
Keyword(s): Environmental and Conservation Education, Forests and Forestry, Renewable Resources, Urban Forestry

FOREST SERVICE EMPLOYEES FOR ENVIRONMENTAL ETHICS (FSEEE)
P.O. Box 11615, Eugene, OR 97440
Phone: 541-484-2692; Fax: 541-484-3004; E-mail: afseee@afseee.org; Web Site: www.afseee.org
Founded: 1989; Membership: 13,000
Scope: National
Description: A national nonprofit organization of Forest Service employees, retirees, other resource professionals, and concerned citizens working to change from within the Forest Service's basic management philosophy to a land ethic that ensures ecologically and economically sustainable management.
Contact(s):
President: DAVE IVERSON
Executive Director: ANDY STAHL
Editor: MATT RASMUSSEN
Field Director: BOB DALE
Secretary and Treasurer: CYNTHIA REICHELT
Publication(s): *Forest Magazine*
Keyword(s): Biodiversity, Environmental and Conservation Education, Forests and Forestry, Public Lands, Wildlife and Wildlife Habitat, Professional Organization

FOREST SOCIETY OF MAINE
P.O. Box 775, 115 Franklin St., Bangor, ME 04402
Phone: 207-945-9200; Fax: 207-945-9229
Founded: 1984
Scope: Statewide
Description: A statewide land trust working with landowners on forest land conservation projects that maintain the environmental, recreational and economic values of Maine's forests, primarily through conservation easements.
Contact(s):
Executive Director: ALAN HUTCHINSON; E-mail: alanhfsm@mint.net
Director of Development and Communications: LESLIE HUDSON; E-mail: ljhfsm@mint.net
Keyword(s): Biodiversity, Conservation, Ecosystems, Forest Management, Forest Stewardship, Forests and Forestry, Land Preservation, Land Purchase, Sustainable Ecosystems, Sustainable Resources

FOREST TRUST
P.O. Box 519, Santa Fe, NM 87504-0519
Phone: 505-983-8992; Fax: 505-986-0798; E-mail: forest@theforesttrust.org
Founded: 1984
Scope: National
Description: A nonprofit organization dedicated to protecting the integrity of the forest ecosystem and improving the lives of people in rural communities. The Trust challenges conventional forest management philosophies and provides protection strategies to grassroots environmental organizations, rural communities, and public agencies. The Trust also provides land management services to owners of private lands with significant conservation values and serves as the institutional home for the Forest Stewards Guild.
Contact(s):
Director: HENRY H. CAREY
Accountant: RON DRYDEN
Community Forestry Program: RYAN S. TEMPLE
Development Coordinator: LAURA McCARTHY
Forest Stewards Guild: STEVEN A. HARRINGTON
National Forest Program: SHIRL HARRINGTON
Publication(s): *Forest Trust Quarterly Report; El Cuartonero; Distant Thunder*
Keyword(s): Environmental Preservation, Forests and Forestry, Land Use Planning, Rural Development, Sustainable Development

FOREST WATCH
10 Langdon St., Montpelier, VT 05602
Phone: 802-223-3216; Fax: 802-223-1363; E-mail: JNORTHUP@TOGETHER.NET; Web Site: www.forestwatch.org
Founded: 1994; Membership: 2,000
Scope: Regional
Description: Forest Watch saves and recreates wild forests, reforms public land management, advocates ecological forestry and watches over the forests with a network of citizen volunteers.
Contact(s):
Deputy Director: SUE HIGBY; E-mail: SHIGBY@together.net
Executive Director: JIM NORTHUP
Publication(s): *Visions: A Wild-eyed Look at Forests; State of the Forest Report*
Keyword(s): Ancient Forests, Conservation Biology, Endangered and Threatened Species, Forest Management, Forest Stewardship, Forests and Forestry, Legal Advocacy, National Forests, Natural Areas, Public Lands, Reforestation, Sustainable Ecosystems, Trees, Urban Forestry, Wildlife and Wildlife Habitat

FOSSIL FUELS POLICY ACTION INSTITUTE/ALLIANCE FOR A PAVING MORATORIUM
P.O. Box 4347, Arcata, CA 95518-4347
Phone: 707-826-7775; Fax: 707-822-7007; Web Site: www.tidepool.com/alliance
Founded: 1988; Membership: 1,200
Scope: International
Description: As the founder of the Alliance for a Paving Moratorium, Fossil Fuels Action directs road-fighting and education to address loss of farmland, wilderness, and community. APM unites over 150 groups and businesses in a call for an end to new road construction while promoting alternative transportation and the car-free lifestyle. We envision sustainability, embracing nature and sharing, rejecting the technofix designed to perpetuate status quo economics.
Contact(s):
Board of Directors, Member: RICHARD REGISTER
Board of Directors, Member: LONNIE MAXFIELD
Board of Directors, Member: DEBBIE LUKAS
Board of Directors, President: JAN LUNDBERG
Publication(s): *Auto-Free Times*
Keyword(s): Air Quality and Pollution, Energy, Environmental Planning, Environmental Preservation, Land Use Planning, NAFTA Superhighway, Population Growth, Road Construction, Sustainable Development, Transportation, Urban Environment, Watersheds, Wilderness

FOSSIL FUELS POLICY ACTION INSTITUTE/ALLIANCE FOR A PAVING MORATORIUM (South American Bureau Office)
P.O. Box 1394, Correo Central, Buenos Aires 1000 Argentina
Scope: International

NON-GOVERNMENTAL ORGANIZATIONS - F

Contact(s):
Contact: RAUL H. RIUTOR

FOSSIL RIM WILDLIFE CENTER
P.O. Box 2189, Glen Rose, TX 76043
Phone: 254-897-2960
Founded: 1987
Scope: National
Description: A 2,100-acre wildlife preserve dedicated to the preservation of endangered and rare species with the ultimate goal of returning these species to the wild. Sixty animal species are represented, and Fossil Rim participates in 12 Species Survival Plan programs. Programs include public education, research into the management and propagation of endangered species, training of conservation professionals, and support for the creation of similar efforts around the world.
Contact(s):
Chairman of the Board: M. CHRISTINE JURZYKOWSKI
Chief Operating Officer: CRAIG BRESTRUP; Phone: 254-897-2960x202
Director of Communications: YOLA CARLOUGH; Phone: 254-897-2960x206
Vice President of Conservation: BRUCE A. WILLIAMS; Phone: 254-897-2960x304
Keyword(s): Endangered and Threatened Species, Environmental and Conservation Education, International Conservation, Internships, Sustainable Ecosystems

FOUNDATION FOR NORTH AMERICAN BIG GAME
P.O. Box 2710, Woodbridge, VA 22193
Phone: 703-878-2119
Founded: 1992; Membership: 1,000
Scope: National
Description: A nonprofit membership organization with major objectives of protection and encouragement of sport hunting in North America; education of the general public to the values of sport hunting, both direct and indirect; and the conservation and welfare of the big-game species of the continent.
Contact(s):
President: DON J. KIRN; Phone: 816-761-4351; Fax: 816-761-8737
Vice President: WARREN K. PARKER; Phone: 816-229-8899; Fax: 816-229-5933
Secretary: DON R. MORGAN; Phone: 352-473-2662; Fax: 352-473-2166
Treasurer: E. WAYNE POCIUS; Phone: 215-536-9616; Fax: 215-536-5815
Executive Director: WILLIAM HAROLD NESBITT; Phone: 703-590-4449; Fax: 703-878-2119
Board Member: TAZ RIDLEY; Phone: 913-661-3532; Fax: 913-661-3510
Board Member: EDWARD N. NANNINI; Phone: 916-485-8111; Fax: 916-485-1709
Publication(s): *North American Big Game (quarterly magazine)*
Keyword(s): Environmental and Conservation Education, Hunting, Mammals, Wildlife and Wildlife Habitat, Wildlife Management

FOUNDATION FOR NORTH AMERICAN WILD SHEEP
720 Allen Ave., Cody, WY 82414
Founded: 1977; Membership: 5,000
Scope: National
Description: A nonprofit organization whose purposes are to: promote the management of and safeguard against the extinction of all species of wild sheep native to the continent of North America; promote the protection of the remaining wild sheep populations and their habitat; and promote the re-establishment of wild sheep populations in suitable habitat. The Foundation funds wild sheep research, wildlife studies, improves habitat, finances sheep transplants, and supports hunting and game management policies based on sound, proven principles.
Contact(s):
President: TED SCHUTTE, 5554 180th St., Sibley, IA 51249; Phone: 712-754-3729; Fax: 712-754-3195
1st Vice President: DAVE BULL, 4941 Comanche, Pocatello, ID 83204; Phone: 208-232-3298; Fax: 208-232-6720
2nd Vice President: ROYCE WOOD, 4245 Production Court, N. Las Vegas, NV 89115; Phone: 702-643-3078; Fax: 702-643-7899
Secretary: MATT WOLFE, P.O. Box 309, Kasilof, AK 99610-0309; Phone: 907-262-7058
Treasurer: MIKE BAUMANN, 7436 W. 83rd Way, Arvada, CO 80003-1637; Phone: 303-940-6690; Fax: 303-940-6659
Publication(s): *Wild Sheep*
Keyword(s): Environmental and Conservation Education, Wildlife and Wildlife Habitat, Wildlife Disease, Wildlife Management, Wildlife Rehabilitation

FRANKFURT ZOOLOGICAL SOCIETY--HELP FOR THREATENED WILDLIFE
Alfred-Brehm-Platz 16, Frankfurt D-60316 Germany
Phone: 069-94344644; Fax: 069-439348
Founded: 1858; Membership: 6,000
Scope: International
Description: A private organization that supports wildlife/nature conservation and environmental/conservation education with international, national, and regional projects.
Contact(s):
President: DR. RICHARD FAUST
Projects Officer and Executive Assistant to the President: INGRID KOBERSTEIN
Regional Representative for Eastern Africa: DR. MARKUS BORNER
Publication(s): *Mitteilungen an die Mitglieder*
Keyword(s): Wildlife and Wildlife Habitat, Zoological Parks

FRIENDS OF ACADIA
P.O. Box 725, Bar Harbor, ME 04609
Phone: 207-288-3340; Fax: 207-288-8938; E-mail: stephanie@foa.acadia; Web Site: www.foacadia.org
Founded: 1986; Membership: 2,500
Scope: Statewide
Description: Friends of Acadia is a nonprofit organization providing citizen support in partnership with the National Park Service to preserve and protect Acadia National Park and the communities that surround it.
Contact(s):
President: W. KENT OLSON
Board of Directors Chairman: H. LEE JUDD
Director of Association Conservation: MARLA MAJOR
Director of Conservation: STEPHANIE M. CLEMENT
Director of Operations: EILEEN ST.GERMAIN
Publication(s): *Friends of Acadia Journal*
Keyword(s): Conservation of Protected Areas, Outdoor Recreation, Public Lands

FRIENDS OF ANIMALS INC.
777 Post Rd. Suite 205, Darien, CT 06820
Phone: 203-656-1522; Fax: 203-656-0267; E-mail: foa@igc.org; Web Site: www.friendsofanimals.org
Founded: 1957; Membership: 200,000
Scope: National
Description: An international animal protection organization that works to protect animals from cruelty, abuse, and institutionalized exploitation. FOA's efforts protect and preserve animals and their habitats around the world.
Contact(s):
President and Editor: PRISCILLA FERAL
Secretary and Treasurer: SALLY LEINER-MALANGA
Publication(s): *Act'ionLine*
Keyword(s): Endangered and Threatened Species, Hunting, Marine Mammals, Trapping, Wildlife and Wildlife Habitat

FRIENDS OF DISCOVERY PARK
3801 W. Government Way, Seattle, WA Phone: 206-285-6862
Founded: 1974; Membership: 540
Scope: Statewide
Description: To create and protect an open space of quiet and tranquility where the works of man are minimized. A place which emphasizes its natural environment and to promote the

development of Discovery Park according to a master plan responsive to these goals.
Contact(s):
President: VALERIE CHOLVIN
Vice President: GAYLE PODRABSKY
Secretary/Treasurer: NANCY KROENIG
Publication(s): *Explorer*
Keyword(s): Environmental Planning, Landscape Architecture, Nongame Wildlife, Open Space, Sustainable Ecosystems, Wetlands

FRIENDS OF THE BOUNDARY WATERS WILDERNESS
1313 5th St., SE, Suite 329, Minneapolis, MN 55414
Phone: 612-379-3835; Fax: 612-379-3842; E-mail: kevin@friends-bwca.org; Web Site: www.friends-bwca.org
Founded: 1976; Membership: 4,000
Scope: Statewide
Description: Established to protect and preserve the wilderness character of northeastern Minnesota's million-acre Boundary Waters Canoe Area (BWCA) Wilderness and the surrounding areas in the international Quetico-Superior Ecosystem. Works on wilderness protection, acid rain, forestry issues, water quality, rivers protection, wilderness management, and wildlife species, such as the wolf.
Contact(s):
Secretary: ELIZABETH SCHUNIESING
Treasurer: JEFF EVANS
Chairperson: JON NELSON
Executive Director and Editor: KEVIN PROESCHOLDT
Vice-Chairperson: BECKY ROM
Publication(s): *BWCA Wilderness News*
Keyword(s): Acid Rain, Biodiversity, Endangered and Threatened Species, Forests and Forestry, Water Quality, Wilderness, Wildlands

FRIENDS OF THE EARTH
The Global Bldg., 1025 Vermont Ave., NW, Suite 300, Washington, DC 20005
Phone: 202-783-7400; Fax: 202-783-0444; E-mail: foe@foe.org; Web Site: www.foe.org
Scope: National
Description: A global advocacy organization based in Washington, DC, with 61 international affiliates. Merged with Environmental Policy Institute and the Oceanic Society in 1990. Dedicated to protecting the planet from environmental disaster and preserving biological, cultural, and ethnic diversity. With strong ties to the grassroots in the U.S. and around the world, Friends of the Earth believes individuals and communities must have a voice in environmental policymaking that affects their lives. Fights ozone depletion, global warming, toxic chemical threats, nuclear hazards, groundwater contamination, environmentally unsound international lending policies, and irresponsible corporate practices. Produces the Earth Budget; works to change tax code to support environmentally sustainable policies. Budget is $2.7 million.
Contact(s):
President: BRENT BLACKWELDER
Publication(s): *Friends of the Earth Newsmagazine; Anatomy of a Deal, The Technical and Economic Feasibility of Replacing Methyl Bromide, River of Red Ink; Green Scissors Annual Report*
Keyword(s): Air Quality and Pollution, Environmental Protection, Pesticides, Transportation, Water Quality

Northwest Regional Office (WA, OR, ID)
4512 University Way, NE, Seattle, WA 98105
Phone: 206-633-1661; Fax: 206-633-1935
Scope: National
Contact(s):
Contact: SHAWN CANTRELL

FRIENDS OF THE REEDY RIVER
P.O. Box 9351, Greenville, SC 29604
Phone: 864-255-5009; Fax: 864-288-9262; E-mail: REEDYRIVR@aol.com; Web Site: www.reedyriver.org
Founded: 1993; Membership: 300
Scope: Statewide
Description: FORR is a nonprofit river advocacy group committed to watershed protection and restoration of the Reedy River in upstate South Carolina.
Contact(s):
Executive Director: DR. DAVE HARGETT; Phone: 864-297-3566; E-mail: hargett@prodigy.net
Watershed Coordinator: CAMILLE BUCK; Phone: 864-232-9720; E-mail: reedyrivr@aol.com
Publication(s): *Membership Brochure and Newsletter; NPS Brochure; Padding Guide*
Keyword(s): Conservation Easements, Environmental Protection, Greenways, Habitat Conservation, Nonpoint Source Pollution, Riparian Restoration, Rivers, Runoff, Trail, Watersheds

FRIENDS OF THE RIVER
915 20th St., Sacramento, CA 95814
Phone: 916-442-3155; Fax: 916-442-3396; E-mail: info@friendsoftheriver.org; Web Site: www.friendsoftheriver.org
Founded: 1973; Membership: 6,000
Scope: Statewide
Description: A nonprofit membership organization dedicated to the preservation, protection, and restoration of rivers, streams, and watersheds through public education, citizen activist training and organizing, and expert advocacy to influence public policy.
Contact(s):
Executive Director: BETSY REIFSNIDER
Board of Directors Chair: JIM WHEATON
Editor and Advertising: CHARLIE CASEY
Publication(s): *Headwaters*
Keyword(s): Energy, Environmental and Conservation Education, Outdoor Recreation, Rivers, Water Resources, Watersheds

FRIENDS OF THE SAN JUANS
P.O. Box 1344, Friday Harbor, WA 98250
Phone: 206-378-2319; Fax: 360-378-2324; E-mail: friends@sanjuans.org; Web Site: www.sanjuans.org
Founded: 1979; Membership: 1300
Scope: Regional
Description: To protect to the fullest extent possible the scenic, aesthetic, ecological and sociological qualities, and resources of the San Juan Islands and the Northwest straits marine ecosystem. Promoting long-range planning and monitoring development.
Contact(s):
Executive Director: KEVIN RANKER
Publication(s): *Friends of the San Juan Newsletter*
Keyword(s): Aquatic Habitats, Coasts, Forest Management, Islands, Land Use Planning, Marine Mammals, Oceanography, Sea Grass, Sustainable Development, Shorelines

FRIENDS OF THE SEA OTTER
2150 Garden Rd., B-4, Monterey, CA 93940
Phone: 831-373-2747; Fax: 831-373-2749; Web Site: www.seaotter@seaotters.org
Founded: 1968; Membership: 5,000
Scope: Statewide
Description: A nonprofit organization dedicated to the protection and maintenance of a healthy population of southern sea otters, a threatened species, as well as sea otters throughout their north pacific range, and all sea otter habitat. Encourages research and public education to develop a sound conservation program.
Contact(s):
President: JOHN FISCHER
Vice President: RON STEVENS
Secretary: JEAN MANN MACDONALD
Administrative Assistant: JEAN HALLETT
Attorney: STUART SOMACH; Phone: 916-444-3900
Center Director: CATHY COLE
Executive Director for Education: JEFFERY CALDER
Science Director: JAMES CURLAND
Publication(s): *Otter Raft, The*
Keyword(s): Aquatic Habitats, Biodiversity, Biology, Coasts, Endangered and Threatened Species, Environment, Environmental

and Conservation Education, Fisheries, Mammals, Water Pollution, Otters

FUND FOR ANIMALS INC., THE
200 W. 57th St., New York, NY 10019
Phone: 212-246-2096
Founded: 1967; Membership: 250,000
Scope: National
Description: National nonprofit animal-protection organization whose purpose is to preserve wildlife and promote humane treatment for all animals. Primarily serves as an advocacy group and information and education agency to help domestic and wild animals. The Fund operates four hands-on facilities.
Contact(s):
President: MARIAN PROBST
Executive Vice President: MICHAEL MARKARIAN, 8121 Georgia Ave., Silver Spring, MD 20190
Chief of Legislative Services: CHRISTINE WOLF, 8121 Georgia Ave., Silver Spring, MD 20910
Legal Counsel: EDWARD J. WALSH JR., Vedder, Price, Kaufman, Kammholz, and Day, 805 3rd Ave., New York, NY 10022; Phone: 212-407-7740
Field Officer: CHUCK TRAISI, Manager of Animal Trust Santuary, 18740 Highland Valley Rd., Ramona, CA 92065
Field Officer: CHRIS BYRNE, Manager of Black Beauty Ranch, P.O. Box 367, Murchison, TX 75778
Field Officer: KIMBERLY STURLA, 808 Alamo Dr., Suite 306, Vacaville, CA 95688
Field Officer: MARION STARK, P.O. Box 9029, Albany, NY 12209
Field Officer: ANDREA REED, P.O. Box 11294, Jackson, WY ; Phone: 307-859-8840
Field Officer: JULIE LEWIN, 16 Vera St., West Hartford, CT 06119
Field Officer: VIRGINIA HANDLEY, Fort Mason Center, Rm. 3262, San Francisco, CA 94123; Phone: 415-474-4020
Field Officer: LAURA SIMON, 21 Sperry Rd., Betany, CT 06524; Phone: 203-393-3669
Field Officer: CAROLINE GILBERT, Rt. 2 Box 559, Simponsville, SC 29681; Phone: 803-963-4389
Field Officer: DORIS DIXON, 2841 Colony Rd., Ann Arbor, MI 48104; Phone: 313-971-4632
Field Officer, Manager of Have a Heart Clinic: LIA ALBO, 335 W. 52nd St., New York, NY 10019
Keyword(s): Endangered and Threatened Species, Marine Mammals, Trapping, Wildlife and Wildlife Habitat, Wildlife Rehabilitation

FUNDACION NATURA - COLOMBIA
A. A. 55402, Santa Fe De Bogota, Colombia
Phone: 571-3400569-3400137; Fax: 571-3400124; E-mail: snatura@xolnodo.apc.org
Founded: 1984
Scope: Regional
Description: Fundacion Natura is a Colombian nonprofit, non-governmental organization. It works with other national governmental and non-governmental organizations as well as international partners to attain the required knowledge to design viable conservation strategies that encompass biological, social, political, and economic variables.
Contact(s):
Executive Director: ELSA M. ANGEL
Publication(s): *Annual Report; Tropical Newsletter; Trua Wuandra*

FUTURE FISHERMAN FOUNDATION
1033 N. Fairfax St., Suite 200, Alexandria, VA 22314
Phone: 703-519-9691; Fax: 703-519-1872
Scope: National
Description: The educational arm of the American Sportfishing Association, the Foundation is a nonprofit organization dedicated to promoting participation and education in fishing as well as enhancement and protection of aquatic resources. Develops and coordinates the national program "Hooked On Fishing - Not on Drugs". The Foundation is a national leader in recreational fishing and aquatic resource education and offers student and instructor educational materials.
Contact(s):
President: MIKE HAYDEN
Executive Director: KATHLEEN DRISCOLL MCKEE
Keyword(s): Environmental and Conservation Education, Outdoor Recreation, Sport Fishing, Water Pollution, Water Resources, Youth Organizations

G

GALIANO CONSERVANCY ASSOCIATION
R.R. 1, Porlier Pass Rd., Galiano Island, British Columbia V0N 1P0 Canada
Phone: 250-539-2424; Fax: 250-539-2424; E-mail: galiano_conservancy@gulfislands.com
Founded: 1989; Membership: 300
Scope: Local
Description: The Galiano Conservancy Association is a community-based, regionally-oriented conservation organization and land trust. Its purposes are to preserve, protect, and enhance the quality of the human and natural environment of the area through public education; management, and ownership of conservation land; and research and restoration projects.
Contact(s):
Secretary: ROSE LONGINI; Phone: 250-539-3007; Fax: 250-539-2424
Co-Coordinator: JILLIAN RIDINGTON; Phone: 250-539-3095; Fax: 250-539-3096; E-mail: ridington@gulfislands.com
Coordinator: KEN MILLARD; Phone: 250-539-5878; Fax: 250-539-2424
Publication(s): *Archipelago; Newsletter; Bulletin*
Keyword(s): Aquatic Habitats, Biodiversity, Coasts, Conservation of Protected Areas, Environmental and Conservation Education, Environmental Planning, Fisheries, Forest Management, Islands, Land Preservation, Land Purchase, Land Use Planning, Natural Areas, Pesticides

GAME CONSERVANCY U.S.A. (formerly American Friends of the Game Conservancy)
P.O. Box 8328, Vero Beach, FL 71106
Phone: 561-234-8718; Fax: 561-234-6081
Founded: 1985; Membership: 525
Scope: National
Description: Game Conservancy USA's primary functions are to raise funds to support the research and educational activities of The Game Conservancy Trust in the U.K., to support antipoaching efforts in Tanzania, and to promote beneficial programs that pertain to the conservation of wildlife resources worldwide.
Contact(s):
President: F. WARRINGTON GILLET JR., 159 Via del Lago, Palm Beach, FL 33480; Phone: 407-655-6789; Fax: 407-832-1762
Secretary: WILLIAM E. MURRAY, 200 E. 61st ST. #4-G, New York, NY 10021; Phone: 212-832-23232; Fax: 212-319-5238
Executive Director: GEORGE F. MORRIS, 190 Camelia Ct. N., Vero Beach, FL 32963; Phone: 561-234-8718; Fax: 561-234-6081
Administrative Director: KIMBERLY A. MCMAHON, 365-20th Ave, Vero Beach, FL 32962; Phone: 516-234-8718; Fax: 561-234-6081
Librarian: JAMES LONG, The Game Conservancy Trust Fordingbridge, Hampshire, SP61EF United Kingdom; Phone: 011-44-1425-652381; Fax: 011-44-1425-655848
Publication(s): *American Friends of the Game Conservancy Newsletter*
Keyword(s): Scholarships and Grants, Wildlife and Wildlife Habitat, Wildlife Disease, Wildlife Management, Wildlife Rehabilitation

GAME CONSERVATION INTERNATIONAL (GAME COIN)
4600 Broad Ave., Ft. Worth, TX 76107
Phone: 817-738-5438; Fax: 817-737-2911
Founded: 1967; Membership: 500
Scope: International

Description: A nonprofit organization dedicated to responsible sustainable use of fish and wildlife and preserving the hunting and fishing heritage for future generations. Supports strong educational programs for classrooms and sponsors the state and province Outstanding Hunter Education awards from Mexico to Canada. Its National Junior Wildlife Artist competition encourages high school youngsters to compete for thousands of dollars in prizes under the theme: OUR WILDLIFE HERITAGE: PASS IT ON! Created the 4-H Shooting Competition in Texas that has been copied nationwide.
Contact(s):
President: HARRY TENNISON; Phone: 210-271-0448
Keyword(s): Endangered and Threatened Species, International Conservation, Wildlife and Wildlife Habitat, Wildlife Management

GARDEN CLUB OF AMERICA, THE
14 East 60th St., New York, NY 10022
Phone: 212-753-8287
Founded: 1913
Scope: National
Description: A national nonprofit organization with member clubs from coast to coast and in Hawaii. Its purpose is to stimulate the knowledge and love of gardening, to share the advantages of association by means of educational meetings, conferences, correspondence and publications, and to restore, improve, and protect the quality of the environment through educational programs and action in the fields of conservation and civic improvement.
Contact(s):
President: MRS. FREDERIK C. HANSEN JR
Conservation Chairman: MRS. GEORGE H. DAVIS
Corresponding Secretary: MRS. GARY L. SHORT
Horticulture Chairman: MRS. EDWARD D. DOWLING
National Affairs and Legislation Committee: MRS. WILLIAM P. BOGGESS II
Keyword(s): Endangered and Threatened Species, Environmental and Conservation Education, Flowers, Plants, and Trees, Gardening and Horticulture, Scholarships and Grants

GENERAL FEDERATION OF WOMEN'S CLUBS
1734 N St., NW, Washington, DC 20036
Phone: 202-347-3168; Fax: 202-835-0246; E-mail: gfwc@gfwc.org
Founded: 1890
Scope: National
Description: The General Foundation of Women's Clubs (GFWC) is an international organization of community-based volunteer women's clubs dedicates to community service since 1890. GFWC programs and projects encompass the major issues of our time including literacy, health, preservation of natural resources, abuse prevention, and solid waste management.
Contact(s):
President: MAXINE S. SCARBRO
Treasurer: ROSE M. DITTO
1st Vice President: JUDY LUTZ
2nd Vice President: ERNIE SHRINER
Beautification Program Chair: JOYCE SCHAEFER, Rd #4 Box 32, Seaford, DE 19973
Conservation Department Coordinator: TERRI WOGAN, 5401 E. Marilyn Rd., Scottsdale, AZ 85254
Director of Junior Clubs: BABS CONDON
Editor: NANCY HOFFMAN
President-Elect: SHELBY P. HAMLETT
Program Director: PAT NOLAN
Recording Secretary: JACQUELYN PIERCE
Resource Conservation Program Chair: BARBARA NUNNARI, 13200 Ridge Dr., Rockville, MD 20850
Water Quality Program Chair: NORMA CHESNEY, 1331 Jill Terrace, Homewood, IL 60430
Publication(s): *GFWC CLUBWOMAN*
Keyword(s): Energy, Environmental and Conservation Education, Environmental Preservation, Nature Preservation, Solid Waste Management

GEORGE MIKSCH SUTTON AVIAN RESEARCH CENTER INC.
P.O. Box 2007, Bartlesville, OK 74005
Phone: 918-336-7778; Fax: 918-336-7783; E-mail: gmsarc@aol.com
Founded: 1983
Scope: National
Description: The Sutton Research Center is a non-profit, tax-exempt organization conducting scientific studies, conservation projects and educational programs regarding avian species worldwide. Topics of particular interest include raptor population surveys and studies, bald eagle population monitoring, avian captive breeding and re-introductions, ecological studies of grassland birds including songbirds and game birds, public education projects and cooperative wildlife conservation efforts with landowners.
Contact(s):
Treasurer: HOWARD R. BURMAN
Executive Director: DR. STEVE K. SHERROD
Board Chairman: STEPHEN S. ADAMS
Publication(s): *The Sutton Newsletter*
Keyword(s): Biodiversity, Birds, Conservation of Protected Areas, Endangered and Threatened Species, Environment, Environmental and Conservation Education, Environmental Preservation, Environmental Protection, International Conservation, Nature Preservation, Nongame Wildlife, Prairies, Predators, Raptors, Renewable Resources

GEORGE WRIGHT SOCIETY, THE
P.O. Box 65, Hancock, MI 49930
Phone: 906-487-9722; Fax: 906-487-9405; E-mail: gws@mail.portup.com
Founded: 1980; Membership: 600
Scope: International
Description: The George Wright Society is organized for the purposes of promoting the application of knowledge, fostering communication, improving resource management, and providing information to improve public understanding and appreciation of the basic purposes of natural and cultural parks and equivalent reserves.
Contact(s):
President: RICHARD W. SELLARS, National Park Service, P.O. Box 728, Santa Fe, NM 87504-0728; Phone: 505-988-6020
Executive Director: DAVID HARMON, Hancock Office
Publication(s): *George Wright Forum, The*
Keyword(s): Environmental Preservation, Environmental Protection, Historic Preservation

GEORGIA ASSOCIATION OF CONSERVATION DISTRICT SUPERVISORS
Attn: President, 321 Glenhaven Dr., Milledgeville, GA 31061
Phone: 912-452-2515
Scope: Statewide
Contact(s):
President: RALPH HARRINGTON; Phone: 912-452-2609
Board Member: JOHN H. REDDING, P.O. Box 409, Monroe, GA 30655; Phone: 770-267-5283; Fax: 770-267-0014
President Elect: CARL ELLIOT BRACK, 25 Maple Lane, Carrollton, GA 30117; Phone: 770-214-8501
Secretary and Treasurer: T. LARRY NIX, 3776 Anglin Dr., Gainesville, GA 30507; Phone: 770-534-7890
Keyword(s): Conservation Districts

GEORGIA B.A.S.S. CHAPTER FEDERATION
Attn: President, 11575 Northgate Trail, Roswell, GA 30075
Scope: Statewide
Description: An organization of Bassmaster chapters, affiliated with the Bass Anglers Sportsman Society, organized to fight pollution, assist state and national conservation agencies in their efforts, and teach young people of our country's good conservation practices. Dedicated to the realistic conservation of our water resources.
Contact(s):
President: LARRY S. LEWIS; Phone: 770-993-6597
Conservation Director: SCOTT HENDRICKS, 5131 Maner Rd., Smyrna, GA 30080; Phone: 404-799-2159

NON-GOVERNMENTAL ORGANIZATIONS - G

Publication(s): *Georgia Federation Newsletter; Georgia Outdoor News*

GEORGIA CONSERVANCY, INC., THE
1776 Peachtree St., NW, Suite 400, S., Atlanta, GA 30309
Phone: 404-876-2900; Fax: 404-872-9229
Founded: 1967; Membership: 7,000
Scope: Statewide
Description: The Georgia Conservancy is a nonprofit organization of people dedicated to the responsible stewardship of Georgia's vital natural resources. We strive to balance the demands of social and economic progress with our commitment to protect the environment.
Contact(s):
President: JOHN A. SIBLEY III
Chairman of the Board: JOHN IZARD JR
Secretary: BETTY N. MORI
Treasurer: JAMES E. BOSTIC JR.
Coastal Programs Director: PATRICIA MCINTOSH, 428 Bull St, Savannah, GA 31410; Phone: 912-447-5910; Fax: 912-447-5911
Publication Director: LISA P. PATRICK
Vice President for Education and Advocacy: SUSAN KIDD
Vice President for Planning and Development: ROBERT D. SMULIAN
Publication(s): *Panorama: Highroad Guide to the North Georgia Mountains; Highroad guide to the Georgia Coast and Okefenokee; Stream of Conscience: Natural Solutions for Clean Water; The Hiking Trails of North Georgia; Wetlands: Georgia's Vanishing Treasure; Blueprints for Successful Communities: A Guide to Shaping Living Places*
Keyword(s): Air Quality and Pollution, Chemical Pollution Control, Development, Environment, Environmental Protection, Forest Management, Land Use Planning, Open Space, Pollution Prevention, Renewable Resources, Transportation, Urban Environment, Water Resources, Wetlands, Smart Growth

GEORGIA ENVIRONMENTAL COUNCIL, INC.
P.O. Box 2388, Decatur, GA 30031-2388
Membership: 70+ organizations, 20+ subscribers
Scope: Statewide
Description: A statewide umbrella for organizations interested in environmental protection that seeks to facilitate the exchange of information among member organizations, to provide a forum for discussion of environmental issues of interest to the members, and to monitor state government legislative activities having to do with the environment.
Contact(s):
President: SUSAN VARLAMOFF; Phone: 770-978-0752
Secretary: TONY SCARDACI; Phone: 404-634-6511
Treasurer: TREY GIBBS; Phone: 404-605-0000
Past President: SUSAN WOOTTON; Phone: 770-953-8759
Publication(s): *GEC Monitor; Directory of Environmental Groups in Georgia; Legislative Monitor*
Keyword(s): Environmental and Conservation Education

GEORGIA ENVIRONMENTAL ORGANIZATION, INC (GEO)
3185 Center St., Smyrna, GA 30080-7039
Phone: 404-605-0000; Fax: 404-350-9997; E-mail: geoeco@geoeco.org; Web Site: www.geoeco.org
Founded: 1991; Membership: 2,000
Scope: Statewide
Description: GEO is a non-profit, citizen-oriented organization established to preserve and protect Georgia's environment through education, collaboration, research, planning, legislation, and grassroots organizing. The mission of GEO is to create an ecologically sound, sustainable society by developing and implementing cooperative, long-range policies, plans and programs and by carrying out hands-on projects within local communities.
Contact(s):
Executive Director: DR. OLIN M. IVEY
President, Board of Directors: SUSANNA MACKENZIE EUSTON
Publication(s): *Georgians on Sustainbility; GEOdyssey; In 'My Backyard - A Citizens Guide to Watershed Planning and Protection; RIO-River Inventory for Organizing: Watershed Atlas-Directory; Case Studies for Watershed Protection*
Keyword(s): Environmental and Conservation Education, Sustainable Development

GEORGIA ENVIRONMENTAL POLICY INSTITUTE
380 Meigs St., Athens, GA 30601
Phone: 706-546-7507; Fax: 706-613-7775; E-mail: gepi@ix.netcom.com
Founded: 1993
Scope: Statewide
Description: GEPI helps communities develop proactive strategies for a healthy environment through technical and legal services. The organization's primary focus is on land conservation.
Contact(s):
Chair: LEE CARMON; Phone: 706-369-5650; Fax: 706-369-5792; E-mail: lcarmon@negia.net
Executive Director: HANS NEUHAUSER
Publication(s): *A Landowner's Guide - Conservation Easements for Natural Resources Protection; A Summary of Takings Law; Right Whale News*
Keyword(s): Conservation Easements, Conservation of Protected Areas, Conservation Plannning, Environmental Law, Land Conservation, Land Management, Land Preservation, Land Protection, Land Purchase, Marine Conservation, Natural Areas, Stewardship, Sustainability, Watersheds, Wetlands

GEORGIA FEDERATION OF FOREST OWNERS
3402 Manchester Dr., Waycross, GA 31501
Phone: 912-283-0871
Founded: 1974; Membership: 120
Scope: Statewide
Description: A statewide organization affiliated with the National Woodland Owners Association to perpetuate good forest practices on private woodlands in Georgia including soil and water conservation, wildlife management, reforestation, and utilization of forest products.
Contact(s):
President: PATRICIA MCCARTHY
Executive Director: ARCHIE MCEUEN
Keyword(s): Forests and Forestry

GEORGIA FORESTRY ASSOCIATION, INC.
505 Pinnacle Ct., Norcross, GA 30071-3656
Phone: 770-416-7621; Fax: 770-840-8961; E-mail: info@gfagrow.org; Web Site: www.gfagrow.org
Founded: 1907; Membership: 4,300
Scope: Statewide
Contact(s):
President: MARSHALL THOMAS
Vice President: BILL MILLER
Treasurer: DALE GREENE
Executive Director and Editor: CHRIS BARNEYCASTLE
Publication(s): *Tops; GFA News; Legislative Bulletin*
Keyword(s): Communications, Forests and Forestry, Training, Transportation

GEORGIA TRAPPERS ASSOCIATION
P.O. Box 335, Doerun, GA 31744
Phone: 912-782-5417
Founded: 1979; Membership: 630
Scope: Statewide
Description: An organization of Georgia trappers and friends of trappers, affiliated with Georgia Wildlife Federation and National Trappers Association, organized to protect the rights of trappers to trap, to coordinate a trappers education program with the Georgia Department of Natural Resources and to conserve and protect the natural resources of Georgia.
Contact(s):
President: TOM ETHRIDGE, P.O. Box 335, Doerun, GA 31744
Vice President:
General Organizer: TOMMY KEY, Rt. 2, Newnan, GA 30623
NTA Director: RALPH GOODSON, P.O. Box 4398, Albany, GA 31706

Secretary and Treasurer: GRACE M. CONDER, P.O. Box 474, Brooklet, GA 30415

GEORGIA TRUST FOR HISTORIC PRESERVATION
1516 Peachtree St., NW, Atlanta, GA 30309-2916
Phone: 404-881-9980; Fax: 404-875-2205; E-mail: gatrust@bellsouth.net; Web Site: www.georgiatrust.org
Founded: 1973; Membership: 9,000
Scope: Statewide
Description: The Georgia Trust for Historic Preservation promotes an appreciation of Georgia's diverse historic resources and provides for their protection and use to preserve, enhance and revitalize Georgia's communities.
Contact(s):
President and CEO: GREGORY B. PAXTON; Phone: 404-885-7801; E-mail: gpaxton@georgiatrust.org
Sr. Director of Communications, Membership and Development: GRETA TERRELL; Phone: 404-885-7803; E-mail: gterrell@georgiatrust.org
Communications Manager: SALLY BRANCA; Phone: 404-885-7802; E-mail: sbranca@georgiatrust.org
Publication(s): *The Rambler (bi-monthly newsletter); Window on the Past, Door to Our Future; Neel Reid, Architect (hardcover book by William R. Mitchell, Jr.)*
Keyword(s): Cultural Preservation, Development, Historic Preservation, Internships, Museum, Open Spaces, Pedestrian Environment, Rural Development, Urban Environment, Smart Growth

GEORGIA WILDLIFE FEDERATION
1930 Iris Dr., Conyers, GA 30094-5046
Phone: 770-929-3350; Fax: 770-929-3534; E-mail: gwf@gwf.org; Web Site: www.gwf.org
Founded: 1936
Scope: Statewide
Description: A representative statewide organization, affiliated with the National Wildlife Federation, dedicated to the protection and enhancement of wildlife and its habitat through public education and government interaction.
Contact(s):
Chair and Alternative Representative: JOCELYN MOORE
President and CEO: JERRY McCOLLUM
Executive Vice President and COO: JAMES R. WILSON
Representative: CHARLIE MILLER
Publication(s): *Georgia Wildlife*

GIRL SCOUTS OF THE UNITED STATES OF AMERICA
420 5th Ave., New York, NY 10018-2798
Phone: 212-852-8000
Founded: 1912; Membership: 3 million
Scope: National
Description: The national organization offers an informal education and recreation program designed to help each girl develop her own values and sense of worth as an individual. It provides opportunities for girls to experience, to discover, and to share planned activities that meet their interests. These activities encourage personal development through a wide variety of projects in social action, environmental action, wildlife values education, youth leadership, career exploration and community service.
Contact(s):
President: CONNIE L. MATSUI
Membership and Program Consultant: LAURAINE MERLINI
National Director of Membership and Program Cluster: SHARON WOODS HUSSEY
National Executive Director: MARSHA JOHNSON EVANS
Washington Representative: LaVERNE ALEXANDER, 1025 Connecticut Ave. NW, Suite 309, Washington, DC 20036-5405; Phone: 202-659-3780
Publication(s): *Outdoor Education in Girl Scouting; Earth Matters; Investigaciones divertidas y faciles de la naturaleza y ciencia; Fun and Easy Activities with Nature and Science; Fun and Easy Nature and Science Investigations*
Keyword(s): Environmental and Conservation Education, Outdoor Recreation, Urban Environment, Women in the Environment, Youth Organizations

GLACIER INSTITUTE, THE
P.O. Box 7475, Kalispell, MT 59904
Phone: 406-755-1211; Fax: 406-755-7154; E-mail: glacinst@digisys.net; Web Site: www.digisys.net/glacinst
Founded: 1983
Scope: National
Description: The Glacier Institute serves students of all ages as an educational leader in the Crown of the Continent Ecosystem, emphasizing hands-on, field-based experiences promoting a balanced understanding of the science of ecology and human interaction with the environment.
Contact(s):
President: JODIE JOHNSON
Vice President: DOUG MOREHOUSE
Secretary: SCOTT C. WURSTER
Executive Director: KRISTIN RIPPETO BRUNINGA
Program Director: CARLY HUTT
Program Director: R. J. DEVITT
Keyword(s): Aquatic Habitats, Conservation, Ecology, Geology, Internships, Natural History, Sustainable Ecosystems, Wildlife and Wildlife Habitat

GLOBAL CITIES PROJECT, THE
2962 Fillmore St., San Francisco, CA 94123
Phone: 415-775-0791; Fax: 415-775-4159; E-mail: epc@globalcities.org; Web Site: http://www.globalcities.org
Founded: 1989
Scope: National
Description: The Global Cities Project provides local governments, businesses, and citizens with comprehensive, up-to-date information on local environmental policies and programs, promoting the development of environmentally and economically sound policy at the local level.
Contact(s):
President: WALTER McGUIRE
Chief Financial Officer: COLLEEN McCARTY, 2962 Fillmore St., San Francisco, CA 94123; Phone: 415-775-0791
Publication(s): *Building Sustainable Communities: A Guide for Local Government; Case Studies*
Keyword(s): Air Quality and Pollution, Energy, Energy Conservation, Environment, Land Use Planning, Open Space, Pollution Prevention, Solid Waste Management, Sustainable Development, Transportation, Urban Forestry, Water Quality

GLOBAL ENVIRONMENTAL MANAGEMENT INITIATIVE (GEMI)
818 Connecticut Ave., NW, 2nd Fl., Washington, DC 20006
Phone: 202-296-7449
Founded: 1990; Membership: 27
Scope: National
Description: The Global Environmental Management Initiative (GEMI), an industry-initiated coalition of domestic and multinational Fortune 500 companies, is dedicated to helping businesses achieve environmental, health, and safety excellence. Through the activities of its workgroups, it has generated and distributed concrete tools for industry use in a number of environmental management fields.
Contact(s):
Chairman: ROBERT SHERMAN
Executive Director: STEVEN B. HELLEM
Contact: MARY BETH PARKER
Publication(s): *Total Quality Environmental Management Primer; Corporate Quality and Environmental Management II: Measurements and Communications; Environmental Self-Assessment Program; Benchmarking Primer*
Keyword(s): Communications, Environmental and Conservation Education, International Conservation, Planning Management, Sustainable Development

NON-GOVERNMENTAL ORGANIZATIONS - G

GLOBAL INDUSTRIAL AND SOCIAL PROGRESS RESEARCH INSTITUTE (GISPRI)
3rd Fl., Skousenmitsui Bldg., 2-1-1 Toranomon, Minato-ku, Tokyo 105-0001 Japan
Phone: 81-3-5563-8800; Fax: 81-3-5563-8810; E-mail: info@gispri.or.jp; Web Site: www.gispri.or.jp
Founded: 1988
Scope: International
Description: A nonprofi foundation established to conduct research and submit policy proposals in such areas as resource conservation, global environmental problems, and relationship between industry and economy.
Contact(s):
President: GAISHI HiRAIWA
Executive Director: AKINOBU YASUMOTO
Secretary General: KIYOSHI KAWAMATSU
Publication(s): *GISPRI Newsletter (Japanese); GISPRI (English)*

GOPHER TORTOISE COUNCIL
Florida Museum of Natural History, P.O. Box 117800, University of Florida, Gainesville, FL 32611
Phone: 904-392-1721
Founded: 1978; Membership: 500
Scope: Regional
Description: A nonprofit organization formed to assure the continued survival of viable populations of the gopher tortoise, Gopherus polyphemus, and its associated upland habitat in the southeastern United States.
Contact(s):
Secretary: TERRI STILSON, 2879 Thaxton Dr., #52, Palm Harbor, FL 34684
Treasurer: CHRISTIAN NEWMAN, 3839 NW 67th Pl., Gainesville, FL 32653
Co-Chair: GEORGE HEINRICH, Boyd Hill Nature Park, 1101 Country Club Way S., St. Petersburg, FL 33705
Editor: JOHN JENSEN, Georgia DNR, 116 Rum Creek Dr., Forsyth, GA 31029
Membership Secretary: LORA SMITH
Publication(s): *Tortoise Burrow, The Bulletin*
Keyword(s): Endangered and Threatened Species, Nongame Wildlife, Reptiles and Amphibians, Wildlife and Wildlife Habitat, Wildlife Management

GRAND CANYON TRUST
Headquarters, 2601 N Fort Valley Rd., Flagstaff, AZ 86001
Phone: 520-774-7488; E-mail: info@grandcanyontrust.org
Founded: 1985; Membership: 4,200
Scope: National
Description: The mission of the Grand Canyon is to protect and restore the canyon country of the Colorado Plateau---its spectacular landscapes, flowing rivers, clean air, diversity of plants and animals, and areas of beauty and solitude.
Contact(s):
President: GEOFFREY S. BARNARD; Phone: 520-774-7488
Communication Manager: STEELE WOTKYNS
Director of Conservation Field Programs: BRAD ACK
Director of Conservation Policy: TOM ROBINSON
Director of Development: KATRINA ROGERS
Membership Coordinator: DARCY ALLEN
Utah Conservation Director: BILL HEDDEN
Publication(s): *Colorado Plateau Advocate; Annual Report; Action Alerts*
Keyword(s): National Parks

GRAND CANYON TRUST (Moab, Utah Office)
HC 64, Box 1801, Moab, UT 84532-9610
Phone: 435-259-5284; Fax: 435-259-5348
Scope: Regional

GRAND CANYON TRUST (St. George, UT Office)
199 N. Main St., St. George, UT 84770
Phone: 435-673-8558; Fax: 435-673-8545
Scope: Regional

Contact(s):
Director: JIM MCMAHON
Keyword(s): Land Preservation, Land Use Planning, Public Lands, Sustainable Development, Water Resources

GRASSLAND HERITAGE FOUNDATION
P.O. Box 394, Shawnee Mission, KS 66201
Phone: 913-262-3506
Founded: 1976; Membership: 700
Scope: National
Description: A tax-exempt, nonprofit organization dedicated to prairie preservation and education. We encourage the preservation of all remaining prairies and work to increase public awareness of our prairie heritage.
Contact(s):
President: ANN SIMPSON
Publication(s): *GHF News*

GREAT BEAR FOUNDATION
P.O. Box No. 9383, Missoula, MT 59807
Phone: 406-829-9378; Fax: 406-829-9379
Founded: 1982; Membership: 2,500
Scope: International
Description: A membership-based organization dedicated to protecting all eight species of bears and their habitat. Programs range from supporting scientific research to educational outreach in schools.
Contact(s):
President: CHARLES JONKEL
Publication(s): *Bear News*
Keyword(s): Endangered and Threatened Species, Environmental and Conservation Education, International Conservation, Public Lands, Wildlife and Wildlife Habitat

GREAT LAKES SPORT FISHING COUNCIL
P.O. Box 297, Elmhurst, IL 60126
Phone: 630-941-1351; Fax: 630-941-1196; E-mail: hdqtrs@great-lakes.org; Web Site: www.great-lakes.org
Founded: 1973; Membership: 325,000
Scope: National
Description: A nonprofit confederation of organizations and individuals throughout the Great Lakes states and provinces whose members are concerned with the present and future of sport fishing in the Great Lakes and adjoining waters. The Council, which acts as a clearinghouse for the exchange of information among members, also seeks to protect the Great Lakes against pollution and exploitation by commercial, individual, or other interests. over 100 U.S. and Canadian organizations with a combined membership of more than 325,000 families.
Contact(s):
President: DAN THOMAS
Vice President: ROBERT MITCHELL, 6466 Parkview, Troy, MI 48098; Phone: 810-558-6547; Fax: 810-575-9713
Secretary: MEL BOTH, 3538 S. Whitnall Ave., Milwaukee, WI 53207; Phone: 414-744-8711
Treasurer: TOM COUSTON, 12 W. Schaumburg Rd, Schaumburg, IL 60194; Phone: 847-519-1711
Editor: DAN THOMAS, P.O. Box 297, Elmhurst, IL 60126
Publication(s): *Great Lakes Basin Report*
Keyword(s): Aquatic Habitats, Environmental and Conservation Education, Fisheries, Sport Fishing, Wetlands

GREAT LAKES UNITED
Headquarters, Buffalo State College, Cassety Hall, 1300 Elmwood Ave., Buffalo, NY 14222
Phone: 716-886-0142; Fax: 716-886-0303
Scope: International
Description: An international coalition of environmental, conservation sports, labor, business, and native people organizations, and individuals throughout the eight Great Lakes states and two Canadian Provinces. GLU is dedicated to the protection, conservation, and restoration of the Great Lakes-St. Lawrence River Basin Ecosystem.

Contact(s):
President: JACK MANNO, Great Lakes Research Consortium, 24 Bray Hall, SUNY College of Environmental Science and Forestry, Syracuse, NY 13210; Phone: 315-470-6816; Fax: 315-470-6970; E-mail: jpmanno@mailbox.syr.edu
Vice President: LYNDA LUKASIK, Bay Area Restoration Council; 148 Oakland Dr., Hamilton, Ontario L8E 1B6 Canada; Phone: 905-560-1177; E-mail: llukasik@worldchat.com
Secretary: TIM BROWN, Lake Michigan Federation, 1825 West Wabanasia, Chicago, IL 60622; Phone: 312-554-0900; Fax: 312-554-0193; E-mail: thbrown@delta-institute.org
United States Treasurer: ED MICHAEL, Trout Unlimited, 223 Barberry Road, Highland Park, IL 60035; Phone: 847-831-4159; Fax: 847-831-1035; E-mail: 71750.1477@compuserve.com
Canadian Treasurer: MANFRED KOECHLIN, Bay of Quinte RAP Team, 276 Dufferein Avenue, Belleville, Ontario K8N 3X7 Canada; Phone: 613-962-9492; Fax: 613-962-9492
Publication(s): *Great Lakes United, The; Pollution Prevention Bulletin; GLU Action Updates, occasional reports.*
Keyword(s): Biodiversity, Communications, Conservation of Protected Areas, Environmental Justice, Environmental Protection, Fisheries, International Conservation, Pollution Prevention, Toxic Substances, Water Pollution, Water Quality, Water Resources, Watersheds, Wetlands

Montreal Office/Canada at-Large
460 St. Catherine W., #805, Montreal, Quebec H3B 1A7 Canada
Phone: 514-396-3333; Fax: 514-861-8949; E-mail: sgingras@glu.org
Scope: National
Contact(s):
Director: JANE WILKINS, Sierra Club of Eastern Canada; 699 Bush St., Bel Fountain, Ontario L0N 1B0 Canada; Phone: 519-927-5924; Fax: 519-927-9828
Director: JIM MAHON, Canadian Auto Workers Local 1520; 120 Tufton Pl., London, Ontario N6C 4W9 Canada; Phone: 519-681-3680; Fax: 519-652-0586; E-mail: jimahon@home.com
Director: JULIAN HOLENSTEIN, Environment North; 427 Queen St., Thunder Bay, Ontario P7B 2K3 Canada; Phone: 807-345-7784; E-mail: julian@tbaytel.net
Director: DANIEL GREEN, Societe pour Vaincre la Pollution; C.P. 65 Place D'Armes, Montreal, Quebec H2Y 3E9 Canada; Phone: 514-844-5477; Fax: 514-844-1446; E-mail: greentox@total.net
Director: LILIANE COTNOIR, Front Common Quebecois pour une Gestion Ecologique des Dechets; 2025 A Masson #001, Montreal, Quebec H2H 2P7 Canada; Phone: 514-396-2286; Fax: 514-396-9041; E-mail: cotnoirl@mlink.net

GREAT OUTDOORS CONSERVANCY, THE
4311 Manatee Ave., West, Suite 210, Bradenton, FL 34209-3948
Phone: 941-708-3456; Fax: 941-708-3535; E-mail: conserve@TheGreatOutdoors.org; Web Site: www.TheGreatOutdoors.org
Founded: 1998; Membership: 525 (four chapters)
Scope: National
Description: The conservancy is a nonprofit national marketing, fundraising, and educational organization for land conservation and expands wild, natural, scenic and recreational areas in the United States by the acquisition of land for the benefit of wildlife and the public's enjoyment for generations to come.
Contact(s):
President: BILL LaMEE; E-mail: BlaMee@TheGreatOutdoors.org
Publication(s): *Partnerships in Preservation*
Keyword(s): Conservation Easements, Environmental and Conservation Education, Land Conservation, Land Management, Land Preservation, Land Protection, Land Purchase, Mountain Ecosystems, Open Space, Outdoor Education, Public Access, Watersheds, Wilderness, Wildlife and Wildlife Habitat

GREAT PLAINS NATIVE PLANT SOCIETY
P.O. Box 461, Hot Springs, SD 57747
Phone: 605-745-3397; Fax: 605-745-3397
Founded: 1984
Scope: Regional
Description: Promotes the protection and study of native plants of the Great Plains through the formation of a Botanic Garden, an annual seed exchange, field trips and newsletter.
Contact(s):
President: CYNTHIA REED
Vice-President: DR. RONALD WEEDON
Publication(s): *Plains Plants*
Keyword(s): Botanical Gardens, Botany, Flowers, Plants, and Trees, Gardening and Horticulture, Grasslands, Great Plains, Wildflowers, Native Plants

GREAT SMOKY MOUNTAINS INSTITUTE AT TREMONT
9275 Tremont Rd., Townsend, TN 37882
Phone: 423-448-6709; Fax: 423-448-9250; E-mail: gsmit@smokiesnha.org; Web Site: www.nps.gov/grsm/tremont.htm
Founded: 1969
Scope: Statewide
Description: A residential environmental education center in the Great Smoky Mountains National Parks. Programs promote awareness, appreciation, and stewardship of national parks and are offered for children and adults.
Contact(s):
Chairman: TOM TAYLOR; Phone: 800-721-6064; Fax: 423-982-6583
Secretary: JOHN MINCEY; Phone: 803-635-3561; Fax: 803-635-3561
Treasurer: HARTWELL HERRING; Phone: 423-974-1755; Fax: 423-974-4631
Executive Director: TERRY MADDOX
Director: KEN VOORHIS; Phone: 423-448-6709; Fax: 423-448-9250; E-mail: ken@smokiesnha.org
Publication(s): *Connecting People and Nature; Trees of the Smokies; Hiking Guide to the Smokies*
Keyword(s): Environmental and Conservation Education, National Parks, Natural History

GREATER YELLOWSTONE COALITION
P.O. Box 1874 13 S. Willson, Bozeman, MT 59771
Phone: 406-586-1593; Fax: 406-586-0851; E-mail: gyc@greatyellowstone.org; Web Site: www.greatyellowstone.org
Founded: 1983; Membership: 7,500
Scope: National
Description: A nonprofit, tax-exempt organization to preserve and protect the Greater Yellowstone Ecosystem and its unique quality of life by enhancing the ecosystem concept, raising the national public consciousness about the Greater Yellowstone Ecosystem, and combining the political effectiveness of the coalition's 7,500 individual members and more than 120 national and regional member organizations.
Contact(s):
President: DWIGHT MINTON
Vice President: RUTH SHEA
Executive Director: MIKE CLARK
Editor: JON CATTON
Secretary and Treasurer: ROBERT KEITH
Publication(s): *Greater Yellowstone Report; Greater Yellowstone Today; Annual Report; EcoAction Alerts*
Keyword(s): Endangered and Threatened Species, Forests and Forestry, Private Land Development, Public Lands, Wildlife and Wildlife Habitat, Wildlife Management

GREEN (GLOBAL RIVERS ENVIRONMENTAL EDUCATION NETWORK)
1908 Mt. Vernon Ave., Second Fl., Alexandria, VA 22301
Phone: 703-299-9400; Fax: 703-299-9485; E-mail: green@earthforce.org

NON-GOVERNMENTAL ORGANIZATIONS - G

Founded: 1989
Scope: National
Description: The Global Rivers Environmental Education Network (GREEN) seeks to improve education through a global network that promotes watershed stewardship.
Contact(s):
President: THOMAS MARTIN; Phone: 703-519-6867
Vice President of National Programs: VINCE MELDRUM; Phone: 703-519-6864
Founder: WILLIAM STAPP, University of Michigan, 2050 Delaware Ave., Ann Arbor, MI 48104
Publication(s): *Field Manual for Water Quality Monitoring; Investigating Streams and Rivers; Sourcebook for Watershed Education; Environmental Education for Empowerment*
Keyword(s): Biology, Environment, Environmental and Conservation Education, Environmental Preservation, Environmental Protection, Inquiry Based Education, Pollution Prevention, Rivers, Water Pollution, Water Quality, Water Resources, Watersheds, Wetlands

GREEN MOUNTAIN AUDUBON SOCIETY
255 Sherman Hollow Rd., Huntington, VT 05462
Phone: 802-434-3068; E-mail: audubonmtn@aol.com
Founded: 1962; Membership: 2,000
Scope: Statewide
Description: Green Mountain Audubon Society is a chapter of the National Audubon Society. The Society operates nature center and wildlife sanctuary areas in Huntington, Shelburne, and Popasquash Island in Lake Champlain. The Nature Center offers environmental education programs for visitors and local schools year-around.
Contact(s):
Board President: SHIRLEY JOHNSON
Keyword(s): Environmental and Conservation Education, Nature Centers

GREEN MOUNTAIN CLUB INC., THE
4711 Waterbury-Stowe Rd., Waterbury Center, VT 05677
Phone: 802-244-7037; Fax: 802-244-5867
Founded: 1910; Membership: 8,000
Scope: National
Description: The mission of the GMC is to make Vermont mountains play a larger part in the life of the people by protecting and maintaining the Long Trail System and fostering, through education, the stewardship of Vermont's hiking trails and mountains. The Club operates field programs and publishes guidebooks, maps, and educational materials in its efforts to maintain and protect the 440-mile Long Trail system. It is the advocate group for hiking in Vermont.
Contact(s):
President: ROLF ANDERSON, Rt. 242 Box 1010-G, Montgomery Center, VT 05471; Phone: 802-326-4789
Vice President: MARTY LAWTHERS, 4 Hillside Dr., Peru, NY 12927
Secretary: RICHARD WINDISH, 16 Forest St., Brattleboro, VT 05301
Treasurer: WALTER POMROY, Box 280, Johnson, VT 05606
Executive Director: BEN ROSE
Publication(s): *Long Trail News, The Long Trail Guide; Day Hiker's Guide to Vermont; Long Trail End-to-Ender's Guide; Green Mountain Adventure, Vermont's Long Trail*
Keyword(s): Environmental and Conservation Education, Internships, Natural History, Outdoor Recreation, Trail

GREEN PARTY USA
P.O. Box 1134, Lawrence, MA 01842
Phone: 978-682-4353; Fax: 978-682-4353-call first; E-mail: gpusa@igc.org; Web Site: www.greens.org/gpusa
Founded: 1984
Scope: National
Contact(s):
Clearinghouse Coordinator: TAMARA TREJO; E-mail: gpusa@igc.org
Coordinating Committee Member: JOHN STITH; E-mail: stithgreens@hotmail.com
Coordinating Committee Member: STARLENE RANKIN; E-mail: starlene@igstate.edu
Coordinating Committee Member: ADAM BERG; E-mail: AMBerg@juno.com
Keyword(s): Air Quality and Pollution, Environmental Justice, Nuclear/Radiation, Sustainable Development, Water Quality, Politics and Government

GREEN SEAL
1001 Connecticut Ave., NW, Suite 827, Washington, DC 20036
Phone: 202-872-6400; Fax: 202-872-4324
Founded: 1989
Scope: National
Description: Green Seal helps organizations and individuals make environmentally responsible choices in their purchases. It develops environmental standards and tests products against these standards, identifying those products that are environmentally responsible through the award of an environmental "seal of approval." The Environmental Partners Program helps businesses develop green procurement plans through buying guides and monthly reports on green products.
Contact(s):
President: ARTHUR WEISSMAN
Chair of the Board: BRYAN THOMLISON; Phone: 609-737-8841
Publication(s): *Environmental Criteria and Standards; Catalog of Green Seal-Certified Products; Campus Green Buying Guide; Office Green Buying Guide; Monthly Choose Green Reports; Greening Your Property (A buying guide for hotels and motels)*
Keyword(s): Air Quality and Pollution, Energy, Environmental and Conservation Education, Renewable Resources, Sustainable Development

GREENPEACE, INC.
1436 U St., NW, Washington, DC 20009
Phone: 202-462-1177
Founded: 1971; Membership: 420,000
Scope: National
Description: A nonprofit organization dedicated to preserving the earth and the life it supports through nonviolent direct action, lobbying, public education, and research. Greenpeace seeks to protect biodiversity in all its forms; prevents pollution and abuse of the earth's ocean, land, air, and fresh water; end all nuclear threats; and promotes peace, global disarmament, and nonviolence.
Contact(s):
Executive Director: KRISTEN ENGBERG
Biodiversity and Ocean Ecology Campaign Coordinator: SUSAN SABELLA
Climate: KALEE KREIDER
Director of Communications: ADLAI AMOR
Director of Development: JULIE CRUDELE
Editor-in-Chief: DAVID BARRE
National Campaigns Director: LYNN THORP
Toxins and Energy: BILL WALSH
Publication(s): *Greenpeace Quarterly (magazine)*
Keyword(s): Energy, Fisheries, Greenhouse Effect/Global Warming, Nuclear/Radiation, Toxic Substances

GROUNDWATER FOUNDATION, THE
P.O. Box 22558, Lincoln, NE 68542-2558
Phone: 402-434-2740, 1-800-858-4844; Fax: 402-434-2742; E-mail: info@groundwater.org; Web Site: www.groundwater.org
Founded: 1985; Membership: 4,000
Scope: National
Description: The Groundwater Foundation is a nonprofit foundation dedicated to educating the public about conservation and management of groundwater. The Foundation is a clearinghouse for general groundwater information, sponsors the Nebraska Children Groundwater Festival, and coordinates the "Groundwater Guardian", a national community recognition program.
Contact(s):
President: SUSAN SEACREST
Groundwater Guardian Program Director: RACHAEL HERPEL
Youth Programs Director: CHAD FOUST

Publication(s): *Aquifer, The; Groundwater Catalog*
Keyword(s): Environmental and Conservation Education, Ground Water Protection, Pollution Prevention, Water Resources

GULF OF MEXICO FISHERY MANAGEMENT COUNCIL
The Commons at Rivergate, Suite 1000; 3018 U.S. Highway 301 North, Tampa, FL 33619-2266
Phone: 813-228-2815; Fax: 813-225-7015; E-mail: wayne.swingle@gulfcouncil.org
Founded: 1976; Membership: 21
Scope: National
Description: The Gulf Council is responsible for developing and monitoring fishery management plans to provide for the best use of the fishery resources in the federal waters of Gulf of Mexico.
Contact(s):
Executive Director: WAYNE E. SWINGLE
Keyword(s): Fisheries

H

H. JOHN HEINZ III CENTER FOR SCIENCE, ECONOMICS, AND THE ENVIRONMENT
1001 Pennsylvania Ave., NW, Suite 735, South, Washington, DC 20004
Phone: 202-737-6307; Fax: 202-737-6410; E-mail: info@heinzctr.org; Web Site: www.heinzctr.org
Founded: 1995
Scope: National
Description: The H. John Heinz III Center is a nonprofit institution dedicated to improving the scientific and economic foundation of environmental policy. The Center's mission is to collaboratively identify emerging environmental issues, conduct related scientific research and economic analyses, and create and disseminate nonpartisan policy options for solving environmental problems.
Contact(s):
Board of Trustees Chair: JOHN SAWHILL
Senior Fellow and President: WILLIAM J. MERRELL
Senior Fellow and Senior Vice President: MARY HOPE KATSOUROS
Senior Fellow and Vice President for Research: ROBERT FRIEDMAN
Keyword(s): Coasts, Environmental Protection, Fisheries, Research

HARDWOOD FOREST FOUNDATION
P.O. Box 34518, Memphis, TN 38184-0518
Phone: 901-377-1818; Fax: 901-382-6419
Founded: 1989; Membership: 400
Scope: National
Description: The Hardwood Forest Foundation is a public, nonprofit organization dedicated to supporting research and education about North American hardwood forests. The main programs focus on distributing factual information about forest management and forest-related issues in the form of video tapes, computer programs, and publications to elementary and high schools.
Contact(s):
President: NORMAN MURRAY
Executive Vice President: PAUL HOUGHLAND JR.
Keyword(s): Forest Management

HAWAII ASSOCIATION OF CONSERVATION DISTRICTS
Attn: President, P.O. Box 1170, Waiuku, HI 96793
Founded: 1939; Membership: 2,200
Scope: Statewide
Description: For better understanding, appreciation, and conservation of Hawaii's native wildlife resources, especially its unique and endangered bird species and their associated ecosystems.
Contact(s):
President: DAVID NORBRIGA; Phone: 808-244-7951; Fax: 808-244-4108
Executive Director: MIKE TULANG, 919 Ala Moana Blvd. Rm. 309, Honolulu, HI 96814; Phone: 808-586-4389; Fax: 808-586-4300
1st Vice President: JOLOYCE KAIA, P.O. Box 404, Hana, HI 96713; Phone: 808-248-7725
Alternate Board Member: TED INOUYE, P.O. Box 278, Hanamaulu, HI 96715; Phone: 808-245-3027
Alternate Board Member: VALERIE MENDES, 1100 Alakea St. #1200, Honolulu, HI 96813; Phone: 808-531-8181
Keyword(s): Conservation Districts

HAWAII AUDUBON SOCIETY
850 Richards Street, #505, Honolulu, HI 96813-4709
Phone: 808-528-1432; Fax: 808-537-5294; E-mail: hiaudsoc@pixi.com
Founded: 1939; Membership: 1,800
Scope: Statewide
Description: For better understanding, appreciation, and conservation of Hawaii's native wildlife resources, especially its unique and endangered bird species and their associated ecosystems.
Contact(s):
President: WENDY JOHNSON
Vice President: JOHN T. HARRISON
Recording Secretary: SHARON REILLY
Publication(s): *Elepaio (Journal); Hawaii's Birds; Voice of Hawaii's Birds (cassette tapes); checklists; field card checklist; Map-Treasures of O'ahu*
Keyword(s): Aquatic Habitats, Biodiversity, Birds, Conservation of Protected Areas, Endangered and Threatened Species, Environmental and Conservation Education, Environmental Preservation, Islands, Natural Areas, Nongame Wildlife, Public Lands, Wildlife and Wildlife Habitat

HAWAII NATURE CENTER
2131 Makiki Heights Dr., Honolulu, HI 96822
Phone: 808-955-0100; Fax: 808-955-0116
Founded: 1981; Membership: 2,000
Scope: Statewide
Description: The Hawaii Nature Center promotes wise stewardship of the Islands through environmental education programs for school children and the general public. School programs focus on full-day, hands-on field adventures; community programs include adult interpretive hikes, family nature adventures and customized excursions for scouts, senior citizens and other special groups. The Iao Valley Interactive Science Arcade includes hands-on exhibits of native flora, fauna and streamlife for residents and visitors to Maui. Field sites on Oahu and Maui.
Contact(s):
Education Director: DIANA KING
Keyword(s): Aquatic Habitats, Biodiversity, Birds, Ecology, Endangered and Threatened Species, Environment, Environmental and Conservation Education, Insects and Butterflies, Interpretive Center, Natural History, Nature Centers, Rainforests, Terrestrial Habitats, Wetlands

HAWAII SOCIETY OF AMERICAN FORESTERS
1151 Punchbowl St., Rm. 323, Honolulu, HI 96813
Founded: 1970
Scope: Statewide
Description: A nonprofit, tax-exempted organization working on environmental issues facing the state of Hawaii. Concerned with land use, native forests, water pollution, pesticides, coastal issues, and over-development.
Contact(s):
Chairperson: KARL DALLA ROSA; Phone: 808-522-8233
Past Chair: NICK DUDLEY; Phone: 808-487-5561
Secretary and Treasurer: KATIE S. FRIDAY; Phone: 808-935-6292
Keyword(s): Biodiversity, Endangered and Threatened Species, Forests and Forestry, Islands, Sustainable Development

HAWAIIAN BOTANICAL SOCIETY
c/o Botany Dept., University of Hawaii, 3190 Maile Way, Honolulu, HI 96822
Phone: 808-956-8072/ 683-0274
Founded: 1924; Membership: 200
Scope: Statewide

NON-GOVERNMENTAL ORGANIZATIONS - H

Description: Objectives of society are: to advance the science of botany in all of its applications; To encourage research in botany in all of its phases; to promote the botanical welfare of its members; and to develop the spirit of good fellowship and cooperation in botanical matters. The Society is particularly interested in the preservation of the Hawaiian flora.
Contact(s):
President: MINDY WILKINSON
Vice President: ALVIN YOSHINAGA
Secretary: LEILANI DURAND
Treasurer: RON FENSTEMACHER
Editor: CLIFFORD MORDEN
Publication(s): Newsletter of the Hawaiian Botanical

HAWK AND OWL TRUST, THE
c/o Zoological Society of London, Regent's Park, London, NW1 4RY United Kingdom
Phone: 0181-450-0662; Fax: 0181-450-0662
Founded: 1969
Scope: National
Description: The Hawk and Owl Trust works for the conservation and appreciation of wild birds of prey and their habitats through projects which involve practical research, creative conservation, and imaginative education. Current projects include: Barn Owl Conservation Network; Operation Raptor Link; Farmland, Riverside and Forestry Link Scheme; Habitat Link. Its National Conservation and Education Centre is situated in Buckinghamshire
Contact(s):
Chairman: BARBARA HANDLEY
President: THE RIGHT HONORABLE THE EARL OF SHAFTESBURY
Director of Conservation and Research: COLIN SHAWYER
Press and Public Relations: BARBARA HALL
Vice Chairman: ROBIN REES-WEBBE
Publication(s): The Raptor (journal/annual report); newsletters: Peregrine, Network Newslink, Adopt a Box
Keyword(s): Birds, Environment, Environmental and Conservation Education, Raptors, Wildlife and Wildlife Habitat

HAWK MIGRATION ASSOCIATION OF NORTH AMERICA
Attn: Treasurer, R.R. 2 Box 301-A, New Ringgold, PA 17960
Founded: 1974; Membership: 1,000
Scope: National
Description: A nonprofit organization whose purpose is to advance the knowledge of bird-of-prey migration across the continent, to monitor raptor populations as an indicator of environmental health, to study further the behavior of raptors, and to contribute to greater public understanding of birds of prey.
Contact(s):
Chair: WILLIAM H. BARNARD, Norwich University, Biology Department, Northfield, VT 05663; Phone: 802-485-2342
Secretary: WILLIAM J. GALLAGHER, P.O. Box 822, Boonton, NJ 07005-0822; Phone: 973-335-0674
Treasurer: DOUGLAS WOOD, R.R. 2, Box 301-A, New Ringgold, PA 17960
Publication(s): Hawk Migration Studies
Keyword(s): Raptors

HAWK MOUNTAIN SANCTUARY ASSOCIATION
1700 Hawk Mountain Rd., Kempton, PA 19529
Phone: 610-756-6961; Fax: 610-756-4468; Web Site: www.hawkmountain.org
Founded: 1934; Membership: 10,000
Scope: International
Description: The Association is a nonprofit organization devoted to the conservation of birds of prey worldwide and a greater understanding of the central Appalachian environment. A full-time staff assisted by interns and volunteers, carries out coordinated programs in education, research, monitoring, and sanctuary management. A visitor center is open year-round, and the 2,400-acre Sanctuary is maintained as a high-quality natural area with trails open to the public.
Contact(s):
Chairman: CLIFFORD L. JONES
Treasurer: JOHN B. BEINECKE
Executive Director: CYNTHIA R. LENHART
Research Director: KEITH L. BILDSTEIN
Publication(s): Hawk Mountain News; Mountain and the Migration, The; Hawks Aloft; World Atlas of Raptor Migration
Keyword(s): Birds, Mountain Ecosystems, Nongame Wildlife, Raptors, Migration

HAWKWATCH INTERNATIONAL, INC.
1800 South West Temple, Suite A226-1, Salt Lake City, UT 84115
Phone: 801-484-6808801-484-6808; Fax: 801-484-6810; E-mail: hwi@hawkwatch.org; Web Site: www.hawkwatch.org
Founded: 1986; Membership: 3,000
Scope: International
Description: HawkWatch International is a nonprofit organization promoting healthy and sustainable populations of hawks, eagles, falcons and other raptors through high quality science, education and conservation programs.
Contact(s):
Executive Director: HOWARD GROSS; Phone: 801-484-6502; E-mail: hgross@hawkwatch.org
Science Director: DR. JEFF SMITH; Phone: 801-484-6758; E-mail: jsmith@hawkwatch.org
Associate Director: MARTI OUELLETTE; Phone: 801-484-6758; E-mail: mouellette@hawkwatch.org
Chair: DAWN SEBESTA PHD, 2466 Meadows Dr., Park City, UT 84060-7032; Phone: 435-649-3024; E-mail: stoney@pcfastnet.com
Treasurer: BENITA PULINS CPA,MBA, C/O Pricewaterhouse Coopers LLP, 36 S. State St., Suite 1700, Salt Lake City, UT 84111; Phone: 801-537-5227; E-mail: benita.r.pulins@us.pwcglobal.com
Secretary: MARLENE FORD, 2798 East 2880 South, Salt Lake City, UT 84109-2029; Phone: 801-467-8057; E-mail: tabby@slkc.uswest.net
Publication(s): Raptorwatch
Keyword(s): Birds, Endangered and Threatened Species, Environmental and Conservation Education, Raptors, Wildlife and Wildlife Habitat

HEADLANDS INSTITUTE
Golden Gate National Recreation Area Bldg. 1033, Sausalito, CA 94965
Phone: 415-332-5771; Fax: 415-332-5784
Founded: 1979; Membership: 8,000
Scope: National
Description: To create sustained global environmental stewardship through educational adventures in nature's classroom.
Contact(s):
Chairman: DAVID JAY FLOOD
Executive Director: BRUCE A. TRUITT
Keyword(s): Environmental and Conservation Education, International Conservation, Natural History, Sustainable Development, Urban Environment

HENRY A. WALLACE INSTITUTE FOR ALTERNATIVE AGRICULTURE (HAWIAA)
9200 Edmonston Rd., Suite 117, Greenbelt, MD 20770-1551
Phone: 301-441-8777; Fax: 301-220-0164; E-mail: hawiaa@access.digex.net; Web Site: www.hawiaa.org
Founded: 1983
Scope: National
Description: HAWIAA is a nonprofit, membership research and education organization established to encourage and facilitate adoption of resource-conserving, low-cost, environmentally sound, and economically viable farming systems.
Contact(s):
Executive Director: GARTH YOUNGBERG
Policy Studies Program Director: DAVID E. ERVIN
Keyword(s): Agriculture, Research, Sustainable Agriculture

NON-GOVERNMENTAL ORGANIZATIONS - H

HIGH DESERT MUSEUM, THE
59800 S. Highway 97, Bend, OR 97702-7963
Phone: 503-382-4754
Founded: 1974; Membership: 5,300
Scope: National
Description: Created to broaden the knowledge and understanding of the natural and cultural history and resources of the high desert country for the purpose of promoting thoughtful decision-making that will sustain the region's natural and cultural heritage. It is a "living," participation-oriented museum that focuses on the Intermountain West -- portions of eight Western states and the Canadian province of British Columbia. Opened to the public in 1982.
Contact(s):
Chairman of the Board of Trustees: MICHAEL HOLLERN
Director of Education: KATHLEEN RONNING
Editor and Communications Director: JACK COOPER
Native Heritage Curator: VIVIAN ADAMS
President (Acting): JERRY N. MOORE
Vice President of Development: WILLIAM A. REICHARDT
Western Heritage Curator: ROBERT BOYD
Publication(s): *High Desert Quarterly; Sagebrush Legacy*
Keyword(s): Cultural Preservation, Deserts, Environmental and Conservation Education, Natural History, Wildlife and Wildlife Habitat

HIMALAYAN WILDLIFE FOUNDATION
Centre One, House 1, Street 15, Islamabad F 7/2 Pakistan
Phone: 92-51-276113; Fax: 92-51-824484; E-mail: vzakaria@hbp.sdnpk.undp.org
Founded: 1993
Scope: International
Description: HWF is a nonprofit, non-governmental organization dedicated to safeguarding the biodiversity of Pakistan's Northern areas. The efforts of HWF have included: involving local communities in the conservation process, coordinating protection and park management activities with the local administration and wildlife department.
Contact(s):
Contact: DR. ANIS UR RAHMAN
Coordinator: MUJAHID AHMAD
Keyword(s): Bears, Himalayan Range, National Parks, Wildlife Protection

HOLDEN ARBORETUM, THE
9500 Sperry Rd., Kirtland, OH 44094
Phone: 440-256-1110; Fax: 440-256-1655; E-mail: holden@holdenarb.org
Founded: 1931; Membership: 7,200
Scope: National
Description: The Holden Arboretum's mission is to acquire, maintain and display collections of plants and conserve natural areas for education, scientific inquiry and personal inspiration. The Arboretum develops and maintains documented biological collections, emphasizing woody plants of northeast Ohio; develops improved plants for the landscape through breeding and selection; studies, manages and conserves the natural environment, including the Holden Arboretum lands; and provides diverse learning experiences in horticulture, botany and natural history.
Contact(s):
Executive Director: DR. RICHARD H. MUNSON
Director of Education: PAUL C. SPECTOR
Director of Horticulture: PETER BRISTOL
Director of Research: DR. ROBERT MARQUARD
Head Librarian: NADIA AUFDERHEIDE, Warren H. Corning Library, 9500 Sperry Rd., Kirtland, OH 44094; Phone: 440-256-1110 ext225; Fax: 440-256-5836
Publication(s): *Arboretum Leaves, The; Environmental Thinking and Learning (ETAL)*
Keyword(s): Botanical Gardens, Ecology, Environmental and Conservation Education, Flowers, Plants, and Trees, Gardening and Horticulture, Natural History

HOLLY SOCIETY OF AMERICA, INC.
11318 W. Murdock, Wichita, KS 67212-6609
Founded: 1947; Membership: 600
Scope: National
Description: National nonprofit organization dedicated to bringing together persons interested in any phase of holly culture. Collects and disseminates information about holly; studies methods of conservatively cutting and marketing holly; promotes research and hybridization; publishes research papers; and popularizes the use of holly as a landscape material.
Contact(s):
President: BARBARA TAYLOR
Secretary: LINDA R. RICHARDSON
Treasurer: RUTH S. BRADLEY
Administrative Vice President: MICHAEL R. PONTTI
Editor: DR. SANDRA F. MCDONALD, 4302 Chesapeake Ave., Hampton, VA 23699-4638
Executive Vice President: DANIEL C. TURNER
Publication(s): *Holly Society Journal (including the proceedings); H.S.A. Books*

HOOD CANAL LAND TRUST
P.O. Box 861, Belfair, WA 98528
Scope: Local
Description: The Hood Canal Land Trust works to preserve shorelines, wetlands, forests and farmlands crucial to local wildlife, water quality and scenic splendor for future generations. The Land Trust sees preservation as a pathway to saving the special tranquility of life which has long enchanted residents and attracted visitors to the Hood Canal and nearby watersheds. The Land Trust holds 510 Acres under its protection.
Contact(s):
President: GARY PARROTT
Keyword(s): Environmental Preservation, Land Preservation, Water Quality, Waterfowl, Wetlands, Wildlife and Wildlife Habitat

HOOSIER ENVIRONMENTAL COUNCIL
1002 E. Washington St., Suite 300, Indianapolis, IN 46202
Phone: 317-685-8800; Fax: 317-686-4794
Founded: 1983; Membership: 40,000 individual members & 65 group members
Scope: Statewide
Description: To encourage and promote more aggressive environmental regulation and enforcement in the state of Indiana. The Council objectives are as follows: Facilitation of communication between environmental groups and individuals; coordination of action on current environmental issues, educational programs and publications; and representation of the concerns of the membership before administrative officials and regulatory boards/agencies of the state and federal government.
Contact(s):
President: ERIC MAYER, 2020 First Indiana Plaza 135 N. Penn, Indianapolis, IN 46204; Phone: 317-634-7477
Secretary: CHARLOTTE ROBERTSON, 980 N. 400 East, Chesterton, IN 46304
Treasurer: ALICE SCHLOSS, 4525 N. Park Ave., Indianapolis, IN 46205
Executive Director: JEFFREY STANT, 1002 E. Washington St. Suite 300, Indianapolis, IN 46202; Phone: 317-685-8800
Editor: JEFF STANT, 1002 E. Washington St. Suite 300, Indianapolis, IN 46202; Phone: 317-685-8800
Publication(s): *Monitor; Boardwatch*
Keyword(s): Air Quality and Pollution, Biodiversity, Environmental and Conservation Education, Solid Waste Management, Water Quality

HUDSONIA LIMITED
Bard College Field Station, Annandale, NY 12504-0500
Phone: 914-758-7053/7023; Fax: 914-758-7033
Founded: 1981
Scope: National
Description: Hudsonia Limited is a nonprofit, non-advocacy institute for research, education, and technical assistance in the

environmental sciences, focusing on the Hudson River Valley. There are over 25 research associates and other technical personnel. Hudsonia conducts pure and applied research on natural and social-sciences aspects of the environment, produces educational publications, and offers programs for environmental decision makers and natural history courses for a broader audience.
Contact(s):
Executive Director: MELISSA EVERETT; E-mail: everett@bard.edu
Science Director: ERIK KIVIAT; E-mail: kiviat@bard.edu
Staff Botanist: GRETCHEN STEVENS
Publication(s): *News From Hudsonia (quarterly); Guide to Biodiversity in the Hudson River Valley (forthcoming)*
Keyword(s): Aquatic Habitats, Endangered and Threatened Species, Fisheries, Flowers, Plants, and Trees, Ecological Education

HUMAN ECOLOGY ACTION LEAGUE, INC. THE (HEAL)
P.O. Box 29629, Atlanta, GA 30359-0629
Phone: 404-248-1898; Fax: 404-248-0162; E-mail: HEALNatnl@aol.com; Web Site: members.aol.com/HEALNatnl/index.html
Founded: 1977; Membership: 9,000
Scope: National
Description: A nonprofit volunteer organization of people affected by or concerned about environmental conditions that are hazardous to human health. It serves as an information clearinghouse on exposure-related illness; alerts the general public about the potential dangers of chemicals; and encourages healthy lifestyles that minimize potentially hazardous environmental exposures.
Contact(s):
President: MURIEL A. DANDO
Secretary: DR. KENNETH V. KING JR.
Treasurer: LYDIA C. JONES
Editor: DIANE C. THOMAS
Publication(s): *Human Ecologist, The*
Keyword(s): Air Quality and Pollution, Health and Nutrition, Pesticides, Toxic Substances, Urban Environment

HUMANE SOCIETY OF THE UNITED STATES, THE
2100 L St., NW, Washington, DC 20037
Phone: 202-452-1100; Fax: 301-258-3077
Founded: 1954; Membership: 6,200,000
Scope: National
Description: A nonprofit organization dedicated to the protection of animals, both domestic and wild. Professional staff experienced in animal control, cruelty investigation, humane and environmental education, farm animals, federal and state legislative activities, wildlife and habitat protection, and laboratory animal welfare; offer resources to local organizations, government, media, and the general public.
Contact(s):
Secretary: DR. AMY FREEMAN LEE
CFO: G. THOMAS WAITE III
Chairman of the Board: O. J. RAMSEY
Director of The Center for Respect of Life and Environment: DR. RICHARD M. CLUGSTON
Executive Vice President: PATRICIA FORKAN
Library Assistant: SHARON GEIGER, The Joyce Mertz Gilmore Library, HSUS Offices, 700 Professional Dr., Gaithersburg, MD 20879; Phone: 202-452-1100
President of Earthvoice: PAUL G. IRWIN
President, CEO: PAUL G. IRWIN
President, Humane Society International: PAUL G. IRWIN
Senior Vice President of Wildlife: DR. JOHN W. GRANDY
Vice Chairman: DR. DAVID O. WIEBERS
Vice President and General Counsel: ROGER A. KINDLER
Publication(s): *HSUS News; Kind News; Shelter Sense; Kind Teacher;*
Keyword(s): Endangered and Threatened Species, Hunting, Marine Mammals, Trapping, Wildlife and Wildlife Habitat

HUMBOLT FIELD RESEARCH INSTITUTE
Attn: Director, P.O. Box 9, Steuben, ME 04680-0009
Phone: 207-546-2821; Fax: 207-546-3042; E-mail: humboldt@nemaine.com
Founded: 1981
Scope: International
Description: A nonprofit educational and research organization providing advanced and professional training programs in all aspects of natural history (terrestrial, freshwater and marine) and encouraging similar pursuits. Classical natural history training programs are held in Maine and the American Tropics. Ecological restoration seminars are held in a number of cities across the United States and Canada.
Contact(s):
Director: JOERG-HENNER LOTZE
Publication(s): *Northeastern Naturalist (a quarterly, peer-reviewed scientific journal)*
Keyword(s): Biodiversity, Environmental and Conservation Education, Natural History, Restoration, Wetlands

HUMMINGBIRD SOCIETY, THE
Attn: Office of the President, 249 E. Main St., Suite 4, Newark, DE 19711
Phone: 302-369-3699; Fax: 302-369-1816; E-mail: info@hummingbird.org; Web Site: www.hummingbird.org
Founded: 1996; Membership: 1,200
Scope: International
Description: The Hummingbird Society is a nonprofit corporation dedicated solely to hummingbirds, through disseminating information, education, support of scientific research, and protection of habitat.
Contact(s):
President: DR. H. ROSS HAWKINS
Vice President: GARY A. GRIFFITH; Phone: 410-392-4491; E-mail: garygriffith@mail.mris.com
Secretary: FRANCES HAMILTON OATES; Phone: 610-274-0551; E-mail: hamilton@magpage.com
Treasurer: WILLIAM N. BARRY; Phone: 302-239-1797; E-mail: billb@wserve.com
Director: DR. ROBERT L. GELL; Phone: 410-287-1025; E-mail: rgell@ed.cecil.cc.md.us
Publication(s): *The Hummingbird Connection*
Keyword(s): Birds, Conservation, Endangered and Threatened Species, Environmental and Conservation Education, International Conservation, Research

HUNTSMAN MARINE SCIENCE CENTRE
Brandy Cove, St. Andrews, New Brunswick E0G 2X0 Canada
Phone: 506-529-1200; Fax: 506-529-1212; Web Site: www.unb.ca/huntsman
Founded: 1969
Scope: National
Description: The HMSC is a nonprofit organization with a reputation for excellence in coastal and marine science research and education. It is supported by universities, corporations, federal and provincial government agencies, and the public. Located on one of the most biologically active bodies of water in the world, it provides information, research, education, and training opportunities for students, investigators, industry, government and the public.
Contact(s):
Executive Director: JOHN H. ALLEN; Phone: 506-529-1200
Associate Director: MICHAEL D.B. BURT; Phone: 506-529-1200
Board of Directors Chair: DR. PAUL D.N. HEBERT, Chair of Zoology Dept.; University of Guelph, Guelph, Ontario N1G 2W1 Canada
Publication(s): *Huntsman Marine Science News; Seawords; Sea Trek Bulletin; Atlantic Reference Centre Species Identification Series*
Keyword(s): Air Quality and Pollution, Aquaculture, Aquariums, Aquatic Habitats, Biodiversity, Biology, Birds, Coasts, Ecology, Environment, Fisheries, Oceanography, Research, Sustainable Ecosystems, Training

I

IDAHO ASSOCIATION OF SOIL CONSERVATION DISTRICTS
Attn: President, Box 697, Lava Hot Springs, ID 83246
Scope: Statewide
Contact(s):
President, alternate board member: KEVIN KOESTER; Phone: 208-776-5382; Fax: 208-776-5043
Vice President: ALICE WALLACE, 1005 N. 5th Avenue, Sandpoint, ID 83864; Phone: 208-263-0895; Fax: 208-265-8486
Secretary: KYLE HAWLEY, 1180 Lewis Rd., Moscow, ID 83843; Phone: 208-882-1290; Fax: 208-883-4239
Treasurer: ROGER STUTZMAN, 1937-B 400N, Buhl, ID 83316; Phone: 208-543-6824; Fax: 208-543-6824
Executive Director: KENT FOSTER, P.O. Box 2637, Boise, ID 83701; Phone: 208-338-5900; Fax: 208-338-9537
Board Member: ROD ROBISON, 2697 W 6300S, Rexburg, ID 83440; Phone: 208-356-7110; Fax: 208-356-7240
Keyword(s): Conservation Districts

IDAHO B.A.S.S. CHAPTER FEDERATION
Attn: President, 9906 W. Deep Canyon Dr., Star, ID 83669
Scope: Statewide
Description: An organization of Bassmaster chapters, affiliated with the Bass Anglers Sportsman Society, organized to fight pollution, assist state and national conservation agencies in their efforts, and teach the young people of our country good conservation practices. Dedicated to the realistic conservation of our water resources.
Contact(s):
President: ALLAN T. CHANDLER; Phone: 208-286-7138
Conservation Director: STEVE SPICKLEMIER, 3766 S. Rush Creek Place, Boise, ID 83706; Phone: 208-342-5006

IDAHO CONSERVATION LEAGUE
P.O. Box 884, Boise, ID 83701
Phone: 208-345-6933; Fax: 208-344-0344
Founded: 1973; Membership: 2,600
Scope: Statewide
Description: The Idaho Conservation League is Idaho's largest statewide conservation organization. Based on grassroots activism and a professional staff, ICL works to preserve and protect Idaho's wild lands, water and wildlife.
Contact(s):
President: JERRY PAVIA, P.O. Box 912, Bonners Ferry, ID 83805; Phone: 208-267-7374
Vice-President: PAT FORD, 1511 N. 11th St., Boise, ID 83702; Phone: 208-345-9067
Secretary: ROBIN PURCELL, 4731 Eugene, Boise, ID 83702
Treasurer: TOM POMEROY, P.O. Box 1765, Ketchum, ID 83340
Executive Director: RICK JOHNSON; Phone: 208-726-4366
Central Idaho Associate: LINN KINCANNON
Conservation Director: JOHN McCARTHY
North Idaho Associate: LARRY McLAUD
State Affairs Director: SCOTT BROWN
Publication(s): *Idaho Conservation League News; Citizen's Guide to the Legislature*
Keyword(s): Biodiversity, Environmental Preservation, Public Lands, Water Pollution, Wilderness

IDAHO ENVIRONMENTAL COUNCIL
1568 Lola St., Idaho Falls, ID 83402
Scope: Statewide
Description: Founded to coordinate and stimulate the creative ideas, manpower, and financial resources of conservation-minded individuals and organizations; and to provide an increased understanding of modern man's impact upon his environment. Action, the objective, is based on information and research.
Contact(s):
President: ALAN HAUSRATH; Phone: 208-336-4930
Editor: JERRY JAYNE; Phone: 208-523-6692
Vice President for Northern Idaho: DENNIS BAIRD; Phone: 208-882-8289
Vice President for Southeastern Idaho: RALPH MAUGHAN; Phone: 208-233-7091
Publication(s): *IEC Newsletter*

IDAHO FOREST OWNERS ASSOCIATION
P.O. Box 1257, Coeur d'Alene, ID 83816
Phone: 208-762-9303
Founded: 1983; Membership: 300
Scope: Statewide
Description: A statewide organization, affiliated with the National Woodland Owners Association, of forest landowners dedicated to the management, use, and protection of private forest resources in Idaho.
Contact(s):
President: KENNON MCCLINTOCK; Phone: 208-267-7064
Vice President: JIM THOMAS; Phone: 208-245-2758
Secretary: KIRK DAVID; Phone: 208-769-1525
Treasurer: OZZIE OSBORN; Phone: 208-664-3889
Executive Director: AMY GILLETTE
Editor: LORI D. RASOR, 4033 SW Canyon Rd., Portland, OR 97221; Phone: 503-288-1367, ext. 104
Publication(s): *Northwest Woodlands*
Keyword(s): Forests and Forestry

IDAHO WILDLIFE FEDERATION
P.O. Box 6426, Boise, ID 83707
Phone: 208-342-7055; Fax: 208-342-7097; E-mail: iwfboi@cyberhighway.net; Web Site: www.idahowildlife.org
Scope: Statewide
Description: A representative statewide organization, affiliated with the National Wildlife Federation, dedicated to the protection and enhancement of wildlife and its habitat through public education and government interaction.
Contact(s):
President and Representative: JACK FISHER
Executive Director: KENT LAVERTY
Editor: BILL GOODNIGHT
Alternate Representative: JIM KEATING
Publication(s): *Idaho Wildlife News*

ILLINOIS ASSOCIATION OF CONSERVATION DISTRICTS
9313 Bull Valley Rd., Woodstock, IL 60098
Phone: 815-338-7664; Fax: 815-338-2773; E-mail: conserve@Delphi.com
Founded: 1972; Membership: 40
Scope: Statewide
Description: To promote the objectives and activities of the Conservation District of Illinois as set forth in the Illinois Conservation District Act and to cooperate with county, state, federal, and private agencies in resource management.
Contact(s):
President: KEN KONSIS; Phone: 217-442-1691
Vice President: CRAIG HUBERT; Phone: 815-678-4431
Assistant Secretary and Treasurer: KEN FISKE; Phone: 815-338-7664
Secretary and Treasurer: JOHN KREMER; Phone: 815-547-7935
Keyword(s): Cultural Preservation, Endangered and Threatened Species, Environmental and Conservation Education, Land Preservation, Sustainable Ecosystems

ILLINOIS ASSOCIATION OF SOIL AND WATER CONSERVATION DISTRICTS
Attn: President, Rt. 1 Box 680, Greenview, IL 62642
Scope: Statewide
Contact(s):
President: DEBORAH CAVANAUGH-GRANT; Phone: 217-968-5583; Fax: 217-968-5512
Vice President: MARK BESSE, 7341 Sand Rd., Erie, IL 61250; Phone: 309-659-7716; Fax: 309-659-7716
Board Member: TERRY BOGNER, Rt. 1 Box 186, Henry, IL 61537; Phone: 309-364-3478; Fax: 309-364-3802

NON-GOVERNMENTAL ORGANIZATIONS - I

Secretary, Alternative Board Member: JERRY SNODGRASS, 13501 N 1700th Ave., Geneseo, IL 61254; Phone: 309-944-2869; Fax: 309-937-2171
Treasurer: DALE JAHRAUS, Rt. 1 Box 38B, St. Peter, IL 62880; Phone: 618-349-6119
Executive Director: STEVE STALCUP, 2520 Main St., Springfield, IL 62702-1262; Phone: 217-744-3414; Fax: 217-744-3420
Keyword(s): Conservation Districts

ILLINOIS AUDUBON SOCIETY
425 B N. Gilbert St., P.O. Box 2418, Danville, IL 61834
Phone: 217-446-5085; Fax: 217-446-6375
Founded: 1897
Scope: Statewide
Description: The Society is dedicated to the preservation and enjoyment of wildlife and their habitats.
Contact(s):
President: RITA RENWICK, 1508 W. Acres Rd., Joliet, IL 60435
Vice President: DAVID MILLER, 813 N. Center, McHenry, IL 60050
Executive Director and Editor, Cardinal News: MARILYN F. CAMPBELL
Editor, Illinois Audubon: DEBBIE SCOTT NEWMAN
Publication(s): *Illinois Audubon; Cardinal News, The*
Keyword(s): Biodiversity, Birds, Endangered and Threatened Species, Land Preservation, Wildlife and Wildlife Habitat

ILLINOIS B.A.S.S. CHAPTER FEDERATION
Attn: President, 7150 N. University, Peoria, IL 61614
Scope: Statewide
Description: An organization of Bassmaster chapters, affiliated with the Bass Anglers Sportsman Society, organized to fight pollution, assist state and national conservation agencies in their efforts, and to teach the young people of our country good conservation practices. Dedicated to the realistic conservation of our water resources.
Contact(s):
President: JEFF PETERSON; Phone: 309-692-4036
Conservation Director: JOHN GROSS, 2425 Huntington Rd., Springfield, IL 62703; Phone: 217-529-8341(H)/217-529-5411(W)
Publication(s): *Illinois B.A.S.S. Federation Newsletter* inserted in "Midwest Outdoors" magazine

ILLINOIS ENVIRONMENTAL COUNCIL
319 W. Cook St., Springfield, IL 62704
Phone: 217-544-5954; Fax: 217-544-5958; E-mail: iec@eosinc.com
Founded: 1975; Membership: 70 groups plus individual members
Scope: Statewide
Description: Statewide coalition committed to advocating for Illinois laws and policies that promote a healthful environment and conservation of resources. The Illinois Environmental Council Education Fund administers programs of education and outreach for the coalition.
Contact(s):
Board of Directors President: ELEANOR ROEMER
Coordinator for Power Plant Clean-up Project: JOHN THOMPSON; Phone: 618-457-0137
Director of Administration: ELLEN SCHMIDT
Executive Director and Legislative Director: LYNNE PADOVAN
Publication(s): *IEC Bulletin; Action Alerts; Environmental Voting Record*
Keyword(s): Air Quality and Pollution, Pesticides, Solid Waste, Water Resources, Wildlife and Wildlife Habitat, Politics and Government

ILLINOIS NATIVE PLANT SOCIETY
Forest Glen Preserve, 20301 E. 900 N. Rd., Westville, IL 61883
Phone: 217-662-2142; E-mail: ilnps@aol.com; Web Site: www.vccd.org
Founded: 1982; Membership: 450
Scope: Statewide
Description: Dedicated to the preservation, conservation, and study of the native plants and vegetation of Illinois.
Contact(s):
Executive Board: KEN KONSIS
Publication(s): *Erigenia; Harbinger*
Keyword(s): Aquatic Habitats, Biodiversity, Botanical Gardens, Conservation of Protected Areas, Endangered and Threatened Species, Environmental Preservation, Environmental Protection, Flowers, Plants, and Trees, Natural Areas, Prairies, Wetlands, Native Plants

ILLINOIS NATURAL HERITAGE FOUNDATION
320 S. 3rd St., Rockford, IL 61104
Phone: 815-964-6666; Fax: 815-964-6666
Founded: 1982
Scope: Statewide
Description: A nonprofit organization to protect Illinois's native flora and fauna, and to encourage wise stewardship of the natural resources that affect them.
Contact(s):
President: RANDALL VINCENT
Vice President: GARY McINTYRE
Executive Director: ED STIRLING
Land Preservation Specialist: DAVID CLUTTER
Research and Management Specialist: HEATHER SWENSON
Keyword(s): Biodiversity, Endangered and Threatened Species, Environmental Preservation, Native Plants

ILLINOIS PRAIRIE PATH
P.O. Box 1086, Wheaton, IL 60189
Phone: 630-752-0120
Founded: 1963; Membership: 2,000
Scope: Statewide
Description: To preserve natural areas and establish footpaths and other protected areas to be used for scientific, educational, and recreational purposes by the public. Adds trail amenities and promotes development of a 61-mile trail for bicyclists, hikers, and joggers on a former railroad right-of-way spanning DuPage County, extended Jan. 1972 into Kane County to the Fox River, and extended Dec. 1979 4 1/2 miles into Cook County. Incorporated 1965, in 1971 designated part of National Trails System.
Contact(s):
President: DAVID TATE
Secretary: NANCY BECKER
Treasurer: PAUL MOORING
Editor: JEAN MOORING, 295 Abbotsford Ct., Glen Ellyn, IL 60137; Phone: 630-469-4289
Publication(s): *Newsletter; Illinois Prairie Path, The; Trail*
Keyword(s): Bicycle, Environmental and Conservation Education, Environmental Preservation, Outdoor Recreation, Public Lands, Trail, Wildlife and Wildlife Habitat

ILLINOIS WALNUT COUNCIL
Forest Glen Preserve, 20301 E. 900 N. Rd., Westville, IL 61883
Phone: 217-662-2142; E-mail: vccd@soltec.net; Web Site: www.vccd.org
Membership: 130
Scope: Statewide
Description: To promote the growth and use of the black walnut (Juglans nigra, and the education of good forestry practices with concerns toward wildlife and soil erosion.
Contact(s):
President: BOB TRIMBLE, 804 Tyler Court, Monticello, IL 61856
Vice President: WAYNE WILDY, 7718 Wildy Rd., New Athens, IL 62264
Secretary: STEVE FELT, 522 Roberts Ln., Sherrard, IL 61281
Publication(s): *Walnut Council Bulletin; Juglans*
Keyword(s): Forest Management, Pesticides, Renewable Resources, Research, Soil Conservation, Sustainable Development, Trees, Watersheds, Wildlife and Wildlife Habitat

INDIAN CREEK NATURE CENTER
6665 Otis Rd., SE, Cedar Rapids, IA 52403

Phone: 319-362-0664; Fax: 319-362-2876; E-mail: tbnature@aol.com
Founded: 1973; Membership: 900
Scope: Statewide
Description: The Indian Creek Nature Center is dedicated to fostering an appreciation of nature through environmental education and providing a natural facility for education and non-obtrusive recreation.
Contact(s):
President: MARK OGDEN; Phone: 319-366-7641
Executive Director: RICH PATTERSON
Treasurer: DENNIS REDMOND; Phone: 319-366-2163
Publication(s): *Currents*
Keyword(s): Environmental and Conservation Education, Nature Study

INDIANA ASSOCIATION OF SOIL AND WATER CONSERVATION DISTRICTS, INC.
Attn: President, 2840 S SR 9, La Grange, IN 46761-9774
Scope: Statewide
Contact(s):
President: CAREY McKIBBEN; Phone: 219-463-2355
Vice President: STEVE GRABER, 3850 Greenhurst Ct., Auburn, IN 46706-9559; Phone: 219-925-0676
Alternate Board Member: GARRY TOM, 5377 E. 800 N., Syracuse, IN 46567-9548; Phone: 219-834-2416; Fax: 219-834-5636
Secretary: SHERMAN BRYANT, 7343 N 650 E., N. Webster, IN 46555-9332; Phone: 219-834-2496
Treasurer: JIM DROEGE, 1200 Caborn Rd., Mount Bernon, IN 47620-9032; Phone: 812-985-5574
Executive Director: CHRISTA JONES, 225 SE St. Suite 740, Indianapolis, IN 46202; Phone: 317-692-7374; Fax: 317-692-7363; E-mail: iaswcd@indy.net
Board Member: GENE SCHMIDT, 15722 S 400 W, Hanna, IN 46340; Phone: 219-797-5045
Keyword(s): Conservation Districts

INDIANA AUDUBON SOCIETY, INC.
Mary Gray Bird Sanctuary, R.R. 6 Box 163, Connersville, IN 47331
Phone: 317-827-0908; Web Site: www.indianaaudubon.org
Founded: 1898; Membership: 980
Scope: Statewide
Description: Works for the conservation of wildlife, especially birds.
Contact(s):
President: JANE MILLER, 4020 S. Rural, Independence, IN 46227-3865
Vice President: LARRY CARTER, 7496 N. Co. Rd. 2005, Ridgeville, IN 47380-9546
Secretary: DAN LEACH, 2313 S. 30th St., Bedford, IN 47421-5415
Treasurer: CLARE OSKAY, 551 Teton Trail, Indianapolis, IN 46217-3927
Editor: MARY GOUGH, 901 Maplewood Dr., New Castle, IN 47362; Phone: 317-529-5225
Editor: CHARLES E. KELLER, 2505 E. Maynard Dr., Indianapolis, IN 46226; Phone: 317-786-5822
Resident Agent and Manager of Sanctuary Management: DEANNA BARRICKLOW, 3499 S. Bird Sanctuary Rd., Connersville, IN 47331-8721; Phone: 317-825-9788
Keyword(s): Birds, Conservation of Protected Areas, Ecology, Environmental and Conservation Education, Flowers, Plants, and Trees, Insects and Butterflies, Waterfowl

INDIANA B.A.S.S. CHAPTER FEDERATION
Attn: President, 1488 S. Country Rd, 125 W., New Castle, IN 47362
Scope: Statewide
Description: An organization of Bassmaster chapters, affiliated with the Bass Anglers Sportsman Society, organized to fight pollution, assist state and national conservation agencies in their efforts, and teach the young people of our country good conservation practices. Dedicated to the realistic conservation of our water resources.
Contact(s):
President: ELDON CRABTREE; Phone: 765-529-6106
Conservation Director: PAUL HOLLABAUGH, 1415 Cherokee Rd., Ft. Wayne, IN 46808; Phone: 219-483-0525

INDIANA FORESTRY AND WOODLAND OWNERS ASSOCIATION
5578 South 500 W., Atlanta, IN 46031-9363
Phone: 317-758-4735
Founded: 1977; Membership: 1,100
Scope: Statewide
Description: A statewide organization affiliated with the National Woodland Owners Association, providing leadership and programs to advance forestry in Indiana.
Contact(s):
President: ROBERT KOENIG
1st Vice President: THOMAS MOEHL
2nd Vice President: ALAN J. BOLENBAUGH
Secretary: WILLIAM SIGMAN
Treasurer: WARREN BAIRD
Editor: JAN MYERS; Phone: 317-583-2422
Forestry Educational Foundation: PETE HALSTEAD
Publication(s): *Leaves and Limbs*
Keyword(s): Forests and Forestry

INDIANA NATIVE PLANT AND WILDFLOWER SOCIETY
6106 Kingsley Dr., Indianapolis, IN 46220
Phone: 317-253-3863; E-mail: rai38@aol.com; Web Site: www.inpaws.org
Founded: 1993; Membership: 550
Scope: Statewide
Description: To promote the appreciation, preservation, conservation, utilization and scientific study of the flora native to Indiana; and to educate the public about the values, beauty, diversity, and environmental importance of indigenous vegetation.
Contact(s):
President: RUTH ANN INGRAHAM; Phone: 317-253-3863
Vice President: KEVIN TUNGESVICK; Phone: 317-354-2775
Treasurer: JEAN VIETOR; Phone: 317-823-1542
Corresponding Secretary: ROGER HEDGE; Phone: 317-232-4052
Recording Secretary: CAROLYN BRYSON; Phone: 317-873-4205
Publication(s): *Indiana Native Plant and Wildflower Society News*
Keyword(s): Biodiversity, Flowers, Plants, and Trees, Nature Preservation, Prairies, Sustainable Ecosystems

INDIANA STATE TRAPPERS ASSOCIATION, INC.
Attn: President, 828 Elm St., Huntington, IN 46750
Founded: 1961; Membership: 265
Scope: Statewide
Description: A statewide organization dedicated to the conservation, restoration, and wise use of wildlife and other renewable natural resources. Provides public education concerning the role of trapping in the management of wildlife.
Contact(s):
President: KEN BROSMAN, 828 Elm St., Huntington, IN 46750; Phone: 812-939-3215
Vice President: JERRY MILLER, R.R. 1 21 N. 300 W., Bluffton, IN 46714
Director: NELSON TEETERS, R.R. 1 Box 140A, West Union, IN 60180
Director: JOHN DREIMAN, R.R. 1 Box 179, Monroe City, IN 47557
Director: ROBERT COATS, R.R. 1 Box 300, Portland, IN 47371
Secretary and Treasurer: KAREN MOSS, R.R. 1 Box 57, Clay City, IN 47841; Phone: 219-369-1573

INDIANA WILDLIFE FEDERATION
950 N. Rangeline Rd., Suite A, Carmel, IN 46032-1315
Phone: 800-347-3445; Fax: 317-571-1223; E-mail: iwf@indy.net
Scope: Statewide
Description: A representative statewide organization, affiliated with the National Wildlife Federation, dedicated to the protection and

enhancement of wildlife and its habitat through public education and government interaction.
Contact(s):
President and Alternative Representative: CHARLES O'NEILL
Executive Director: PAULA YEAGER
Representative: DWIGHT SHELTON
Editor: MICKEY KOEHLER
Publication(s): *Hoosier Conservation*

INFORM, INC.
120 Wall St., 16th Fl., New York, NY 10005
Phone: 212-361-2400; Fax: 212-361-2412; E-mail: inform@informinc.org; Web Site: www.informinc.org
Founded: 1973; Membership: 1,000
Scope: National
Description: A nonprofit tax-exempt environmental research and education organization that identifies and reports on practical solutions for problems in municipal solid waste, chemical hazards, air quality, and alternative vehicle fuels, with an emphasis on pollution prevention and waste reduction.
Contact(s):
President: JOANNA D. UNDERWOOD
Chairman of the Board: CHARLES A. MORAN
Director of Research: DR. NEVIN COHEN
Publication(s): *INFORM Reports (Newsletter); China at the Crossroads; Gearing up for Hydrogen; Building for the Future; Tracking Toxic Chemicals; Rethinking Resources*
Keyword(s): Air Quality and Pollution, Energy, Solid Waste Management, Toxic Substances, Transportation

INITIATIVE FOR SOCIAL ACTION AND RENEWAL IN EURASIA
1601 Connecticut Ave., NW, Suite 301, Washington, DC 20009
Phone: 202-387-3034; Fax: 202-667-3291; E-mail: postmaster@isar.org; Web Site: www.isar.org
Founded: 1983; Membership: 500
Scope: International
Description: ISAR promotes citizens participation and the development of the NGO sector in the former Soviet Union by supporting community activists and grassroots groups.
Contact(s):
Executive Director: ELIZA KLOSE; E-mail: eliza@isar.org
Publication(s): *Give and Take; ISAR in Focus*
Keyword(s): Environmental and Conservation Education, Grants, International Conservation, Training, Women in the Environment

INLAND BIRD BANDING ASSOCIATION
R.D. 2 Box 26, Wisner, NE 68791
Phone: 402-529-6679
Founded: 1922
Scope: National
Description: Promotes cooperation among its members and other organizations, with state, federal, or other officials or individuals engaged in bird banding or other scientific work with birds; informs the public of the purposes and results secured by banding.
Contact(s):
President: JOHN J. FLORA, 3636 Williams, Dearborn, MI 48124
Secretary: CAROL RUDY, W. 3866 Hwy. H, Chilton, WI 53084
Treasurer: C. HOLMES SMITH, 6305 Cumberland Rd. SW, Sherrodsville, OH 44675
Editor: WILLETTA LUESHEN, R. 2 Box 26, Wisner, NE 68791
Editor: DAN KRAMER, 3451 Co. Rd. 256, Victory, OH 43464
Membership Secretary: AL VALENTINE, 17403 Oakington Ct., Dallas, TX 75252
Publication(s): *North American Bird Bander; Inland Bird Banding Newsletter*

INSTITUTE AND SCHOOL FOR ENVIRONMENT AND NATURAL RESOURCES, University of Wyoming (IENR and SENR)
P.O. Box 3971, Laramie, WY 82071
Phone: 307-766-5080; Fax: 307-766-5099; E-mail: ienr@uwyo.edu; Web Site: www.uwyo.edu/enr/
Founded: 1994; Membership: 43 Member Board of Directors
Scope: Nationwide
Description: Current projects include workshops on ESA and NEPA, reports on Brucellosis in the Greater Yellowstone Area, and an open spaces initiatives in Grand Teton National Park
Contact(s):
Assistant Director: KELLY COLLINI
Director: DR. HAROLD BERGMAN; Phone: 307-766-5677
Keyword(s): Endangered and Threatened Species, Open Spaces

INSTITUTE FOR CIVIC INITIATIVES SUPPORT
Chayanova St., 4-13, Moscow Russia
Phone: 7-095-251-7617; Fax: 7-095-251-7617; E-mail: clearh@glasnet.ru
Founded: 1993
Scope: International
Description: The Institute supports civic initiatives through information, publications, training, grant-making programs, and environmental education projects.
Contact(s):
Director: BOGDAN MILA
Publication(s): *Information Bulletin for Environmental NGO's; Strength of Movement; Seeds for Democracy Report*
Keyword(s): Communications, Environmental and Conservation Education, Grants, Networking, Training

INSTITUTE FOR CONSERVATION LEADERSHIP
6930 Carroll Ave. Suite 420, Takoma Park, MD 20912
Phone: 301-270-2900; Fax: 301-270-0610; E-mail: ici@ici.org
Scope: National
Description: The mission of the Institute is to train and empower volunteer leaders and to build volunteer institutions that protect and conserve the earth's environment. Services offered include training and technical assistance for nonprofit organizations and leaders in organizational development, fundraising, board development, volunteer recruitment, strategic planning, and related topics. Services also include meeting facilitation, coalition development, and network building.
Contact(s):
Executive Director: DIANNE RUSSELL
Administrative Assistant: ROSE WILLIAMS
Associate Director: BAIRD STRAUGHAN
Office Manager: CHIQUITA EDWARDS
Project Manager: PETER LANE
Keyword(s): Communications, Environment, Pollution Prevention, Training

INSTITUTE FOR EARTH EDUCATION, THE
Cedar Cove, Greenville, WV 24945
Phone: 304-832-6404; Fax: 304-832-6077; E-mail: iee1@aol.com; Web Site: www.eartheducation.org
Founded: 1974; Membership: 2,000
Scope: National
Description: The Institute for Earth Education develops and disseminates focused educational programs to promote an understanding of, appreciation for, and harmony with the earth's natural systems and communities. The Institute conducts workshops, provides a seasonal journal, hosts an international conference, supports local and international branches, and publishes numerous books and program materials.
Contact(s):
Chair: STEVE VAN MATRE
Executive Staff Chair: BILL WEILER
International Internship Coordinator: FRAN BIRES
International Membership Services Coordinator: LAURIE FARBER
International Program Coordinator: BRUCE JOHNSON
International Training Coordinator: MIKE MAYER
Publication(s): *Talking Leaves Journal; Earth Education Sourcebook; Earth Education: A New Beginning; Earthkeepers; Earth Speaks, The; Sunship III*
Keyword(s): Ecology, Environmental and Conservation Education, Environmental Preservation, International Conservation, Internships

INSTITUTE OF ECOSYSTEM STUDIES
Mary Flagler Cary Arboretum, Box AB, Millbrook, NY 12545-0129

Phone: 914-677-5343; Fax: 914-677-5976; Web Site: www.ecostudies.org
Scope: International
Description: Devoted to the understanding of ecosystem structure and function. The program focus is on disturbance and recovery of northern temperate ecosystems. Education and research interests include wildlife management, bio-geochemistry, landscape ecology, aquatic ecology, plant-animal interactions, microbial ecology, forest ecology, chemical ecology, and air and water quality.
Contact(s):
Director: DR. GENE E. LIKENS
Administrator: JOSEPH S. WARNER
Animal Ecologist: DR. RICHARD S. OSTFELD
Aquatic Ecologist: DR. STUART E.G. FINDLAY
Aquatic Ecologist: DR. MICHAEL L. PACE
Aquatic Microbiologist: DR. JONATHAN J. COLE
Bio-geochemist: DR. NINA M. CARACO
Ecologist: DR. CLIVE G. JONES
Educational Research and Development Specialist: DR. KATHLEEN HOGAN; Phone: 914-677-5359
Forest Ecologist: DR. KATHLEEN C. WEATHERS
Forest Ecologist: DR. CHARLES D. CANHAM
Freshwater Ecologist: DR. DAVID L. STRAYER
Head of Education: DR. ALAN R. BERKOWITZ; Phone: 914-677-5359
Librarian: ANNETTE R. FRANK
Microbial Ecologist: DR. PETER M. GROFFMAN
Plant Ecologist: DR. STEWARD T.A. PICKETT
Plant Ecologist: DR. GARY M. LOVETT
Wildlife Biologist and Manager: RAYMOND J. WINCHCOMBE; Phone: 914-677-9818
Publication(s): *Newsletter; Occasional Publications*
Keyword(s): Acid Rain, Air Quality and Pollution, Ecology, Environmental and Conservation Education, Ecological Education

INSTITUTO BRASIL DE EDUCACAO AMBIENTAL
Rua Visconde de Ouro Preto, 5/7 Andor, Rio de Janeiro 22250-120 Brasil
Phone: 55-21-554-8811; Fax: 55-21-554-8811; E-mail: instbrasil@openlink.com.br
Founded: 1997
Scope: International
Description: It works with environmental education, integrating it to teacher's daily practices. The network involves 57 different institutions in Brasil.
Contact(s):
Executive Director: VERA RODRIGUES
Publication(s): *Muda o Mundo, Raimundo; Rodamundo*
Keyword(s): Environmental and Conservation Education, Training

INTERFAITH COUNCIL FOR THE PROTECTION OF ANIMALS AND NATURE INC. (ICPAN)
3691 Tuxedo Rd. NW, Atlanta, GA 30305
Phone: 404-814-1371
Founded: 1980; Membership: 3,000
Scope: National
Description: Composed of people of all faiths, ICPAN works to promote conservation and environmental and humane education, mainly within the religious community. We try to make religious leaders, institutions, and the general public aware of our moral spiritual obligations, as emphasized in the Bible, to protect animals and the natural environment.
Contact(s):
Chairman: JOHN A. HOYT, 2100 L St. NW, Washington, DC 20037; Phone: 202-452-1100
President: LEWIS G. REGENSTEIN, 3691 Tuxedo Rd. NW, Atlanta, GA 30327; Phone: 404-814-1371
Director: PAUL G. IRWIN, 2100 L St. NW, Washington, DC 20037; Phone: 202-452-1100
Publication(s): *Replenish the Earth: The Teachings of the World's Religions on Protecting Animals and Nature; Replenish the Earth: A Booklet on The Bible's Message of Conservation and Kindness to Animals; Cleaning up America the Poisoned: How to Survive our Polluted Society*
Keyword(s): Endangered and Threatened Species, Environmental and Conservation Education, International Conservation, Sustainable Development, Wildlife and Wildlife Habitat

INTERNATIONAL ASSOCIATION FOR BEAR RESEARCH AND MANAGEMENT
c/o Bernie Peyton, 2841 Forest Ave., Berkley, CA 94705
Fax: 510-549-3116; E-mail: ucumari@aol.com
Founded: 1968
Scope: International
Description: A professional organization of biologists, animal or land managers, and private citizens with an interest or involvement in bear research and management. The Association encourages and reports research and management by various agencies or university research groups, sponsors the tri-annual International Conference on Bear Research and Management, publishes the proceedings of the conference, and sponsors or aids a world network of regional bear workshops, groups, and committees, and the IUCN Bear Group.
Contact(s):
President: BRUCE MCLELLAN, British Columbia Service Research Branch, RPO #3 Box 9158, Relestoke, Bristish Columbia V0E 3K0 Canada; Fax: 250-837-7626; E-mail: bruce.mclellan@gems9.gov.bc.ca
Vice President: KATE KENDALL, Glacier Science Center, Glacier National Park, West Glacier, MT 59936-0128; Fax: 406-888-7990; E-mail: katherine_kendall@usgs.gov
Secretary: BERNIE PEYTON
Treasurer: GORDON WARBURTON, North Carolina Wildlife Resource Commission, 4470 Hidden View Loop, Marion, NC 28752; Fax: 828-652-8170; E-mail: warburg@mail.wildlife.state.nc.us
Publication(s): *Ursus, formerly Bears: Their Biology and Management (Conference Proceedings); International Bear News (Quarterly Newsletter)*
Keyword(s): Bears, Biology, Endangered and Threatened Species, Land Use Planning, Public Lands, Wildlife Management

INTERNATIONAL ASSOCIATION FOR ENVIRONMENTAL HYDROLOGY (IAEH)
P.O. Box 35324, San Antonio, TX 78235
Phone: 210-344-5418; Fax: 210-344-9941; E-mail: hydroweb@mail.org; Web Site: www.hydroweb.com
Founded: 1991; Membership: 500
Scope: International
Description: IAEH works to foster a global interchange of ideas, approaches, and technologies for environmental cleanup and protection of fresh water resources and pollution prevention; to place special focus on approaches to cleanup, prevention, and protection that are practical in less affluent countries; to further the development of environmentally sound solutions that are realistic from the economic standpoint; to seek solutions to cleanup, pollution prevention, and environmental protection; and to place pollution cleanup and prevention in the context of broader water resource and environmental issues.
Contact(s):
President: DR. ROGER W. PEEBLES, 308 Montfort Dr., San Antonio, TX 78216; Phone: 210-344-5418
Publication(s): *Journal of Environmental Hydrology; Environmental Hydrology Report Software: HYDROKIT, a two-CD-ROM set with over 60 popular groundwater and surface water modeling programs*
Keyword(s): Developing Countries, Environment, Environmental and Conservation Education, International Conservation, Pollution Prevention, Water Pollution, Water Resources

INTERNATIONAL ASSOCIATION OF FISH AND WILDLIFE AGENCIES
444 North Capitol St., NW Suite 544, Washington, DC 20001
Phone: 202-624-7890; Fax: 202-624-7891; Web Site: www.sso.org/iafwa
Scope: International

NON-GOVERNMENTAL ORGANIZATIONS - I

Description: Association of states or territories of the United States, provinces of Canada, the Commonwealth of Puerto Rico, the United States Government, the Dominion Government of Canada, and governments of countries located in the western hemisphere, as well as individual associate members whose principal objective is conservation, protection, and management of wildlife and related natural resources.
Contact(s):
Executive Committee Chair: ROBERT McDOWELL, Director, New Jersey Division of Fish, Game and Wildlife, P.O. Box 400, Trenton, NJ 08625-0300
Executive Committee Vice Chair: ARNOLD BOER, Executive Director of Fish and Wildlife, NEW Brunswick Department of Natural Resources and Energy, P.O. Box 6000, Fredericton, New Brunswick E3B 5H1 Canada
President: DAVID J. WALLER, Director, Wildlife Resources Division, Georgia Department of Natural Resources, 2070 U.S. Highway 278, SE, Social Circle, GA 30025
Executive Vice President: R. MAX PETERSON
Vice President: PATRICK GRAHAM, Director, Montana Department of Fish, Wildlife and Parks, 1420 E. 6th, P.O. Box 200701, Helena, MT 59620-0701
Secretary and Treasurer: C. THOMAS BENNETT, Kentucky Department of Fish and Wildlife Resources, One Game Farm Rd., Frankfort, KY 40601
International Resource Director: DONALD E. MacLAUCHLAN
Legislative Director: GARY J. TAYLOR
Resource Director: BOB MILES
Wildlife Diversity Director: NAOMI EDELSON
Annual Proceedings Editor: WM. HAROLD NESBITT
Executive Committee Member: ALLAN L. EGBERT
Executive Committee Member: JOHN BAUGHMAN
Executive Committee Member: STEVEN A. WILLIAMS
Executive Committee Member: G. BRENT MANNING
Executive Committee Member: ANDREW T. MANUS
Executive Committee Member: GEORGE E. MEYER
Executive Committee Member (Past President): ROGER M. HOLMES
Fur Resources Committee Project Coordinator: SAMARA TRUSSO
Legal Counsel: PAUL A. LENZINI
NAWMP Coordinator: LEN UGARENKO
Sportfish and Wildlife Restoration Outreach Project Manager and Newsletter Editor: MARY JANE WILLIAMSON
Publication(s): *Newsletter; Annual Proceedings*

INTERNATIONAL ASSOCIATION OF NATURAL RESOURCE PILOTS
200 Patrick St., SW, Vienna, VA 22180-6703
Phone: 703-560-1271
Membership: 200
Scope: International
Description: Performs aviation and aircrew conservation-related responsibilities for federal and state game and fish divisions and departments of natural resources throughout the U.S. and for their counterparts in the Canadian provinces. Additional membership includes a variety of aviation-oriented corporations and advanced technological suppliers of equipment used in the performance of the aviation missions.
Contact(s):
President: DAVE YOUNKIN, Colorado Division of Wildlife, 1200 Gregory Rd., Fort Collins, CO 80524; Phone: 970-484-2836; E-mail: dave.younkin@state.co.us
Vice President: PAUL D. ANDERSON; Phone: 701-328-6613; E-mail: panderson@state.nd.us
Secretary: JIM BREDY, U.S. Fish and Wildlife Service, P.O. Box 1461, Cedar Crest, NM 87008; Phone: 505-248-6630; E-mail: jim_bredy@fws.gov
Treasurer and Librarian: JOHN C. CLEM, Ohio Division of Wildlife, 9740 Briarwood Dr., Plain City, OH 43064; Phone: 614-873-4163; E-mail: john_clem@compuserve.com
Past President: JACK KEATON, Ohio Department of Transportation, 13618 Woods Opossum Road, Mt. Sterling, OH 43143; Phone: 614-793-5050; E-mail: skyking33@juno.com
Newsletter Editor: PETE HOBSTETTER, Ohio Department of Transportation, 2829 W. Granville Rd., Columbus, OH 43085; Phone: 614-793-5088; E-mail: MAG10@prodigy.net
Public Affairs Officer: FRANCIS SATTERLEE, 200 Patrick St., SW, Vienna, VA 22180; Phone: 703-560-1271
Publication(s): *Conservation Aviation*
Keyword(s): Agriculture, Biodiversity, Birds, Chemical Pollution Control, Conservation of Protected Areas, Endangered and Threatened Species, Environmental Law, Environmental Planning, Fisheries, Forest Management, Hunting, Lakes, Land Use Planning, Natural Areas, Nongame Wildlife

INTERNATIONAL ASSOCIATION OF WILDLAND FIRE (formerly Fire Research Institute)
E. 8109 Bratt Rd., Fairfield, WA 99012
Phone: 509-523-4003; Fax: 509-523-5001; E-mail: greenlee@cet.com; Web Site: www.wildfiremagazine.com
Founded: 1991; Membership: 1,500
Scope: International
Description: The International Association of Wildland Fire was organized to promote a fuller understanding of wildland fire. The Association is built on the belief that an understanding of this dynamic natural force is vital for natural resource management, firefighter safety, and harmonious interactions between people and their environment.
Contact(s):
President: MIKE DEGROSKY; Phone: 307-543-0949
Executive Director: JASON GREENLEE; Phone: 509-283-2397
Editor: MIKE WEBER; Phone: 403-435-7210
Publication(s): *International Directory of Wildland Fire; International Bibliography of Wildland Fire; International Journal of Wildland Fire; Wildfire Magazine; Current Titles in Wildland Fire*
Keyword(s): Ecology, Endangered and Threatened Species, Forests and Forestry, Terrestrial Habitats, Wildlands

INTERNATIONAL BICYCLE FUND
4887 Columbia Dr. S., Seattle, WA 98108-1919
Phone: 206-767-0848; E-mail: ibike@ibike.org; Web Site: www.ibike.org
Founded: 1983
Scope: International
Description: The International Bicycle Fund's programs fall into the areas of transportation planning, sustainable economic development, safety education, and promoting international understanding. Within these programs we address issues of the environment, energy policy, public health, appropriate technology, land use patterns, sustainable systems, resource conservation, and employment generation. IBF coordinates and cooperates with organizations and individuals worldwide. IBF is a nonprofit organization.
Contact(s):
President: DAVID MOZER
Publication(s): *IBF News*
Keyword(s): Environmental and Conservation Education, Land Use Planning, Pedestrian Environment, Sustainable Development, Transportation

INTERNATIONAL CENTER FOR EARTH CONCERNS
2162 Baldwin Rd., Ojai, CA 93023
Phone: 805-649-3535; Fax: 805-649-1757
Founded: 1994
Scope: International
Description: The ICEC involves people with nature by fostering their appreciation of the natural world through environmental education and training.
Contact(s):
Chairman: JOHN TAFT
President: PAUL IRWIN
Secretary: RICK GOULD
Publication(s): *Earth Pulse*
Keyword(s): Botanical Gardens, Ecology, Environmental and Conservation Education, Environmental Protection

INTERNATIONAL CENTER FOR GIBBON STUDIES
P.O. Box 800249, Santa Clarita, CA 91380
Phone: 661-296-2737; Fax: 661-296-1237; E-mail: GIBBONCNTR@AOL.COM

Founded: 1977
Scope: International

Description: The International Center for Gibbon Studies ensures the preservation and propagation and a safe haven for all gibbon species living in the wild and in captivity; supports ongoing field conservation projects; and educates the public about the importance of this species and saving their natural habitat.

Contact(s):
Acting Director of Research: DR. BJORN MERKER, Institute for Biomusicology, Mid Sweden, Ostersund, S-83125 Sweden
Assistant Director of Research: DR. ELAINE BAKER, Department of Psychology, Marshall University, Huntington, WV 25755
Board of Directors President, Facility Director, and Chairman of the Board: ALAN MOOTNICK, P.O. Box 800249, Santa Clarita, CA 91380; Phone: 661-296-2737
Board of Directors Vice President: DR. GERI-ANN GALANTI, 2906 Ocean Ave., Venice, CA 90291; Phone: 310-827-0937
Director of Education and Conservation: DR. LORI SHEERAN, California State University at Fullerton, ; Phone: 714-773-2765

Keyword(s): Environmental and Conservation Education, Research, Training, Wildlife Management, Zoology

INTERNATIONAL CENTER FOR TROPICAL ECOLOGY
The University of Missouri at St. Louis, R224 Research Bldg., 8001 Natural Bridge Rd., St. Louis, MO 63121-4499
Phone: 314-516-5219; Fax: 314-516-6233; Web Site: ecology.umsl.edu/~biology/icte/

Founded: 1990
Scope: International

Description: The ICTE is one of the premier institutes in the United States for the study of tropical biology and conservation. The Center's three primary missions include the training of graduate students in the vital areas of tropical ecology and conservation, the education of undergraduates about the importance of these areas, and involvement of the community in educational activities with respect to issues related to conservation and biodiversity.

Contact(s):
Secretary: BERNADETTE DALTON; Phone: 314-516-6203; Fax: 314-516-6233; E-mail: bdalton@umsl.edu
Associate Director: DR. PATRICK OSBORNE; Phone: 314-516-5219; Fax: 314-516-6233; E-mail: posborne@jinx.umsl.edu
Director: DR. BETTE LOISELLE; Phone: 314-516-6224; Fax: 314-516-6233; E-mail: loiselle@jinx.umsl.edu

Keyword(s): Biodiversity, Ecology, Tropical Biodiversity and Conservation

INTERNATIONAL CENTRE FOR CONSERVATION EDUCATION
Greenfield House, Guiting Power, Cheltenham GL54 5TZ United Kingdom
Phone: 144-1242-674839; Fax: 144-1242-674839; E-mail: maikcec@aol.com

Founded: 1984
Scope: International

Description: ICCE works to promote a greater understanding of global environmental issues and sustainable development.

Contact(s):
Director: MARK N. BOULTON, Greenfield House Guiting Power, Cheltenham, GL545TZ United Kingdom; Phone: 144-1242-674839

Publication(s): *Environmental Audio-Visual Materials; Annual Review; Environmental Education Resources; Organise International Training Programmes in Environmental Education.*

Keyword(s): Biodiversity, Communications, Environmental and Conservation Education, International Conservation, Sustainable Development

INTERNATIONAL COUNCIL OF ENVIRONMENTAL LAW
D-53175, Bonn, Godesberger A22ee, Adenaueralle 108-112 Germany
Phone: 49-228-2692-240; Fax: 49228/2692-252

Founded: 1969
Scope: International

Description: A nonprofit, non-governmental international organization with elected membership, structured in ten regions worldwide, for the purpose of exchange of information on international environmental law, policy, and administration and mutual assistance among members.

Contact(s):
Editor: MARLENE JAHNKE, Ireland
Executive Governor: DR ABDULBAR AL-GAIN, Saudi Arabia
Executive Governor: DR W. E. BURHENNE, Germany

Publication(s): *Environmental Policy and Law; ICEL References to Environmental Policy and Law Literature; Directory of Members; International Environmental Soft Law; International Environmental Law; Conservation in Development*

Keyword(s): Environmental Law, International Conservation

INTERNATIONAL CRANE FOUNDATION
E-11376 Shady Ln. Rd. P.O. Box 447, Baraboo, WI 53913-0447
Phone: 608-356-9462; E-mail: cranes@savingcranes.org; Web Site: www.savingcranes.org

Founded: 1973; Membership: 7,000
Scope: International

Description: Preservation of cranes through research, conservation, captive propagation, restocking, field ecology, and public education.

Contact(s):
Deputy Director: JAMES HARRIS
Director: GEORGE ARCHIBALD
Assistant to the Director: SUSAN FINN
Conservation Coordinator: CLAIRE MIRANDE
Curator of Birds: SCOTT SWENGEL
Deputy Director of Finance and Administration: PETER MURRAY
Development: ROBERT HALLAM
Field Ecologist: JEB BARZEN
Librarian: BETSY DIDRICKSON, The Ron Sauey Memorial Library For Bird Conservation, E-11376 Shady Lane Rd., P.O. Box 447, Baraboo, WI 53913-0447; Phone: 608-356-9462
Site Manager: DAVID CHESKY

Publication(s): *ICF Bugle, The (Quarterly Magazine); Proceedings of the 7th N. American Crane Workshop, 1997; Reflections: The Story of Cranes*

Keyword(s): Birds, Endangered and Threatened Species, Environmental and Conservation Education, International Conservation, Wetlands

INTERNATIONAL ECOLOGY SOCIETY (IES)
1471 Barclay St., St. Paul, MN 55106-1405
Phone: 612-579-7008

Founded: 1975; Membership: 6,000
Scope: International

Description: One hundred percent volunteer-staffed, nonprofit international organization dedicated to the protection of the environment and the encouragement of better understanding of all life forms.

Contact(s):
Vice President: GEORGE E. JOHNSON
Contact (Dakota): MAGGIE WARREN, Hermosa, SD
North East Representative: BINA ROBINSON, Box 26, Swain, NY 14884-0026
President and Publisher: R. J. F. KRAMER

Publication(s): *Eco-Humane Letter; Sunrise (neighborhood news); Action Alerts*

Keyword(s): Endangered and Threatened Species, Marine Mammals, Trapping, Wildlife and Wildlife Habitat, Wildlife Management

INTERNATIONAL EROSION CONTROL ASSOCIATION (IECA)
P.O. Box 4904, Steamboat Springs, CO 80477
Phone: 970-879-3010; Fax: 970-879-8563

Founded: 1972; Membership: 1,900

NON-GOVERNMENTAL ORGANIZATIONS - I

Scope: International
Description: To provide opportunities for the worldwide exchange of information and economic methods of erosion control.
Contact(s):
Executive Director: BEN NORTHCUTT
Publication(s): *Proceedings of Annual Conference; Membership Directory; Products and Services Directory; bi-monthy magazine, quarterly newsletter, IECA Resource Catalog, IECA compilations*
Keyword(s): Engineering, Environmental and Conservation Education, International Conservation, Soil Conservation, Water Pollution

INTERNATIONAL FUND FOR ANIMAL WELFARE
411 Main St., Yarmouth Port, MA 02675
Phone: 508-362-4944; Web Site: www.wfaw.org
Founded: 1969; Membership: 1.7 million
Scope: International
Description: An international nonprofit, tax-exempt organization in the U.S. dedicated to the protection of wild and domestic animals and their habitats. IFAW's goals are pursued through a strategic plan consisting of three distinct program areas: Commercial Expoitation and Trade of Wild Animals, Animals in Crisis and Distress, and Habitat for Animals.
Contact(s):
Chief Executive Officer: FRED O'REGAN
Founder: BRIAN D. DAVIES

Australian Office
P.O. BOX 322, Helensburg, New South Wales 2058 Australia
Scope: International
Contact(s):
Contact: SALLY WILSON

Belgium Office
50 Rue du Taciturne, 1040 Brussels, Belgium
Scope: International
Contact(s):
Contact: STANLEY JOHNSON

French Office
BP 78 51170, Fismes, France
Scope: International
Contact(s):
Contact: CHANTAL DERTY

German Office
Postfach 55 04 67 D-22564, Hamburg, Germany
Scope: International
Contact(s):
Contact: TOM MARTENS

Holland Office
Sterrenweg 3B, 2651 HZ Berkel en Rodenrijs, Holland
Scope: International
Contact(s):
Office Manager: JETTY TAK

Hong Kong Office
P.O. Box 82 Sai Kung PO, Kowloon, Kowloon China
Scope: International
Contact(s):
Contact: JILL ROBINSON

Italian Office
Via Bocca di Leone 36-Int 4, Rome 187 Italy
Scope: International
Contact(s):
Contact: WALTER CAPORALE

Philippines Office
14 East Maya, Phil-Am Homes, Quezon City 1100 Phillipines
Scope: International
Contact(s):
Contact: MEL ALIPIO

Russian Office
Apt. 84, Protochniy Pereulok 11, Moscow 21099 Russia
Scope: International
Contact(s):
Contact: MASHA VORONTSOVA

South African Office
P.O. Box 2587, Rivonia, 2128 South Africa
Scope: International
Contact(s):
Contact: DAVID BARRITT

United Kingdom
Warren Court Park Rd., Crownborough, E.Sussex TN6 2QH United Kingdom
Scope: International
Contact(s):
Director: CINDY MILBURN

INTERNATIONAL GAME FISH ASSOCIATION
300 Gulf Stream Way, Dania Beach, FL 33004
Phone: 954-927-2628; Fax: 954-924-4299; E-mail: IGFAHQ@aol.com
Founded: 1939
Scope: International
Description: A nonprofit, tax-deductible organization which maintains and promotes ethical international angling regulations and compiles world game fish records for saltwater, freshwater, and fly fishing. Also represents and informs recreational fishermen regarding research, conservation, and legislative developments related to their sport. Encourages and supports game fish tagging programs and other scientific data collection efforts. There are over 250 international representatives and 1,000 affiliated fishing clubs.
Contact(s):
Chairman: GEORGE C. MATTHEWS
Vice Chairman: JOHN W. ANDERSON II
President: MICHAEL LEECH
Secretary: ROY E. NAFTZGER
Treasurer: MICHAEL LEVITT
Publication(s): *World Record Game Fishes; International Angler, The; Rule Book for Freshwater, Saltwater and Fly Fishing*
Keyword(s): Fisheries, Sport Fishing

INTERNATIONAL HUNTER EDUCATION ASSOCIATION
PO. Box 490, Wellington, CO 80549
Phone: 970-568-7954; Fax: 970-568-7955; E-mail: ihea@webaccess.net; Web Site: ihea.com
Membership: 65,000
Scope: International
Description: To provide leadership and establish standards in the development of hunters to be safe, responsible, knowledgeable, and involved.
Contact(s):
President: CAPT. ED TYER
Vice President: TIM LAWHERN
Vice President: PHIL HAUGHIAN
Vice President: TONY BURTT
Secretary: MAC LANG
Treasurer: ALAN HIERONYMOUS
Executive Vice-President: DR. DAVID M. KNOTTS
Instructor Board Member: RICHARD McQUILLAN
Instructor Board Member: ED AUGUSTINE
Instructor Board Member: JOHN PANIO JR.
President Elect: LES SMITH
Publication(s): *Hunter Education Journal; Hunter Education Student Guide*
Keyword(s): Environmental and Conservation Education, Hunting, Outdoor Recreation, Training, Wildlife Management

INTERNATIONAL INSTITUTE FOR ENERGY CONSERVATION
750 1st St., Suite 940 NE, Washington, DC 20002
Phone: 202-842-3388; Fax: 202-842-1565; E-mail: iiec@iiec.org
Founded: 1984

Scope: International
Description: A nonprofit organization established to accelerate the global adoption of energy-efficiency policies, technologies, and practices to enable economically and ecologically sustainable development.
Contact(s):
Director: STEWART BOYLE
Director: STEVE HALL
Director: TERRY KRAFT OLIVER
Chairman of the Board: JOHN C. FOX
Executive Director and President: RUSSELL STURM
Publication(s): *E-Notes; Integrated Transport Management and Development, Opportunities for the U.S. Energy Efficiency Industry in Chile; Global Energy Efficiency Initiative Sustainable Energy Guide*
Keyword(s): Energy, Greenhouse Effect/Global Warming, International Conservation, Sustainable Development, Transportation

INTERNATIONAL MARINE MAMMAL PROJECT, THE
Earth Island Institute, 300 Broadway, Suite 28, San Francisco, CA 94133
Phone: 415-788-3666I/1-888-DOLPHIN; Fax: 415-788-7324; E-mail: marinemammal@earthisland.org
Founded: 1982; Membership: 35,000
Scope: International
Description: IMMP is a nonprofit research, education, and monitoring project of Earth Island Institute. IMMP is committed to ending dolphin mortality caused by the U.S. and international tuna industries, stopping the use of drift nets, and promoting sustainable fishing practices. In addition, IMMP aims to halt commercial whaling worldwide and ban live capture and display of marine mammals.
Contact(s):
Executive Director: DAVID PHILLIPS
Publication(s): *Earth Island Journal; Ocean Alert*
Keyword(s): Aquariums, Aquatic Habitats, Biodiversity, Dolphins, Endangered and Threatened Species, Environmental and Conservation Education, Environmental Law, Fisheries, International Conservation, Internships, Mammals, Marine Mammals, Nature Preservation, Wildlife and Wildlife Habitat

INTERNATIONAL MARITIME ORGANIZATION
4 Albert Embankment, London SE1 7SR United Kingdom
Phone: 0171-735-7611; Fax: 0717-857-3210; E-mail: info@imo.org; Web Site: www.imo.org
Founded: 1959; Membership: 156
Scope: International
Description: To improve maritime safety and to prevent marine pollution from ships, through the adoption of international conventions, protocols, codes, and recommendations.
Contact(s):
Secretary-General: WILLIAM A. O'NEIL
Publication(s): *IMO News*
Keyword(s): Environmental Law, Greenhouse Effect/Global Warming, Sustainable Development, Transportation, Water Pollution Management

INTERNATIONAL OCEANOGRAPHIC FOUNDATION
University of Miami, Rosenstiel School of Marine & Atmosphere Science, 4600 Rickenbacker Causeway Virginia Key, Miami, FL 33149
Phone: 305-361-4061
Founded: 1953; Membership: 55,000
Scope: International
Description: Nonprofit foundation organized to encourage the extension of human knowledge by scientific study and exploration of the oceans in all their aspects and to acquaint and educate the general public concerning the vital role of the oceans to all life on this planet.
Contact(s):
President: EDWARD T. FOOTE II
Vice President: DAVID A. LIEBERMAN
Vice President: OTIS BROWN
Vice President: LUIS GLASER
Secretary: LOURDES LaPAZ, 400 SE 2nd Ave., 4th Fl., Miami, FL 33131; Phone: 305-375-8498; Fax: 305-375-9188
Treasurer: DIANE M. COOK
Keyword(s): Environmental and Conservation Education, Fisheries, Marine Mammals, Oceanography, Outdoor Recreation

INTERNATIONAL OSPREY FOUNDATION INC., THE
P.O. Box 250, Sanibel, FL 33957
Phone: 941-472-1862
Founded: 1981; Membership: 300
Scope: International
Description: A nonprofit organization dedicated to studying the problem of restoring osprey numbers to a stable population, making recommendations to enhance the continued survival of the osprey and initiating educational programs. Yearly grant of up to $1000.00 given for graduate work. Work relating to all raptors is acceptable, but osprey study is given priority.
Contact(s):
President: DAVID LOVELAND
Vice President: ANNE MITCHELL
Secretary and Treasurer: INGE GLISSMAN
Publication(s): *TIOF Newsletter - one International NL - one 'local' NL*
Keyword(s): Birds, International Wildlife, Nongame Wildlife, Raptors, Wildlife Management

INTERNATIONAL PLANT PROPAGATION SOCIETY, INC., THE
Washington Park Arboretum, 2300 Arboretum Dr., Seattle, WA 98112
Phone: 206-543-8602; Fax: 206-527-2796
Founded: 1950; Membership: 3,200
Scope: International
Description: The Society was founded to seek and share information on plant propagation. The Sociey has nine regional chapters, three in USA and Canada, Australia, New Zealand, Great Britain and Ireland, Scandinavian, Japan and Southern Africa and holds area meetings in Latin America.
Contact(s):
Executive Secretary and Treasurer: JOHN A. WOTT
Publication(s): *Annual Proceedings of all regional meetings and papers; regional newsletters of meetings for members*
Keyword(s): Flowers, Plants, and Trees, Plant Propagation, Urban Environment, Urban Forestry

INTERNATIONAL PRIMATE PROTECTION LEAGUE
P.O. Box 766, Summerville, SC 29484
Phone: 843-871-2280; Fax: 843-871-7988; E-mail: ippl@awod.com; Web Site: www.ippl.org/
Founded: 1973; Membership: 16,000
Scope: International
Description: A nonprofit international organization devoted to the conservation and protection of non-human primates. There are branches in the United States, United Kingdom and field representatives in 32 countries.
Contact(s):
Secretary: MARJORIE DOGGETT, 1 Toh Heights, 507802 Singapore
Treasurer: DIANE WALTERS
Chairperson: DR. SHIRLEY McGREAL
Publication(s): *International Primate Protection League News (IPPI News)*
Keyword(s): Endangered and Threatened Species, Forests and Forestry, International Conservation, Mammals, Wildlife Rehabilitation

INTERNATIONAL RIVERS NETWORK (IRN)
1847 Berkeley Way, Berkeley, CA 94703
Phone: 510-848-1155; Fax: 510-848-1008; E-mail: irn@irn.org; Web Site: www.irn.org
Founded: 1986; Membership: 1,600
Scope: International
Description: IRN supports local communities working to protect their rivers and watersheds. We work to halt destructive river

development projects and encourage equitable and sustainable methods of meeting needs for water, energy and flood management. Members include environmentalists, engineers, hydrologists, human rights activists, and academics who are committed to the study and defense of rivers and riverine communities.
Contact(s):
President: PHIL WILLIAMS
Director: JULIETTE MAJOT
Africa Campaigns: LORI POTTINGER
Assistant to Executive Director: ANNIE OVCAMINS
Campaign Director: PATRICK McCULLY
Editor: LORI POTTINAER
Library Coordinator: YVONNE CUELLAR
Office Operations: PETRA YEE
South America Campaigns: GLENN SWITKES
Publication(s): *World Rivers Review; special briefings; action alerts; working papers*
Keyword(s): Development, Flood Control, Rivers

INTERNATIONAL SNOW LEOPARD TRUST
4649 Sunnyside Ave., N., Suite 325, Seattle, WA 98103
Phone: 206-632-2421; Fax: 206-632-3967; E-mail: islt@serv.net
Founded: 1981; Membership: 1400
Scope: International
Description: A nonprofit organization dedicated to the conservation of the endangered snow leopard and its mountain habitat through a balanced approach that considers the needs of the local people and the environment; and provides workshops, field training, equipment, publications, conservation education programs, and a centralized database for organizing and disseminating information.
Contact(s):
President: CHARLIE MORSE
Vice President: LEWIS MACFARLANE
Treasurer: STEVEN KEARSLEY
Executive Director: ANNE EDGERTON; Phone: 206-632-2421
Chair and Founder: HELEN FREEMAN
Keyword(s): Biodiversity, Endangered and Threatened Species, Environmental and Conservation Education, International Conservation, Sustainable Ecosystems

INTERNATIONAL SOCIETY FOR ECOLOGICAL ECONOMICS
1313 Dolly Madison Blvd., #402, McLean, VA 22101
Phone: 703-790-1745; E-mail: ISEE@igc.com
Founded: 1988; Membership: 1,600
Scope: International
Description: ISEE actively encourages the integration of the study and the management of ecology and economics in order to achieve an ecologically and economically sustainable world.
Contact(s):
President of Board of Directors: RICHARD NORGARRD
Publication(s): *Ecological Economics*
Keyword(s): Biodiversity, Environmental Planning, Sustainable Development, Sustainable Ecosystems

INTERNATIONAL SOCIETY FOR ENDANGERED CATS (ISEC)
3070 Riverside Dr., Suite 160, Columbus, OH 43221
Phone: 614-487-8760; Fax: 614-487-8769
Founded: 1988; Membership: 600
Scope: International
Description: ISEC's purpose is to raise awareness of the plight of endangered wild cats, and thereby prevent their extinction. ISEC offers conservation education programs, collects and disseminates information about wild cats, and supports specific conservation projects around the world. Member IUCN
Contact(s):
President: BILL SIMPSON, 3070 Riverside Dr., Suite 160, Columbus, OH 43221
Executive Director: PATRICIA CURRIE, 196 W. Central, Delaware, OH 43015; Phone: 740-369-9794
Publication(s): *Cat Tales*
Keyword(s): Endangered and Threatened Species, Environmental and Conservation Education, International Conservation, Wild Cats, Wildlife and Wildlife Habitat

INTERNATIONAL SOCIETY FOR ENVIRONMENTAL ETHICS
Department of Philosophy, University of Windsor, Windsor, Ontario N9B 3P4 Canada
Phone: 519-253-4232
Founded: 1990; Membership: 650
Scope: International
Description: The International Society for Environmental Ethics' main purpose is to promote the critical analysis of ethical issues related to the natural environment, to further and support philosophical and scientific meetings and conferences nationally and internationally, and to provide material and media aids suitable for teaching environmental philosophy and environmental ethics.
Contact(s):
President: MARK SAGOFF, Director of Institute for Philosophy and Public Policy, University of Maryland, Baltimore, MD 20742
Vice President: J. BAIRD CALLICOTT, Philosophy Department, University of Wisconsin at Stevens Point, Stevens Point, WI 54481
Secretary: DR. LAURA WESTRA, University of Windsor, Windsor, Ontario N9B 3P4 Canada; Phone: 519-253-4232
Treasurer: EDWARD HETTINGER, College of Charleston, Charleston, SC 29424
Publication(s): *International Society for Environmental Ethics Newsletter*

INTERNATIONAL SOCIETY FOR THE PRESERVATION OF THE TROPICAL RAINFOREST, THE
3931 Camino De La Cumbre, Sherman Oaks, CA 91423
Phone: 818-788-2002; Fax: 818-990-3333
Founded: 1984; Membership: 12,000
Scope: International
Description: The International Society for the Preservation of the Tropical Rainforest is dedicated to the global conservation of tropical forest resources through the promotion of park implementation, sustainable agriculture, and timber harvesting.
Contact(s):
Director: EDWARD ASNER, 3931 Camino De La Cumbre, Sherman Oaks, CA 91423; Phone: 818-788-2002
President and Director: ARNOLD NEWMAN, 3931 Camino De La Cumbre, Sherman Oaks, CA 91423; Phone: 818-788-2002
Vice President and Director: ROXANNE KREMER, 3931 Camino De La Cumbre, Sherman Oaks, CA 91423; Phone: 818-788-2002
Publication(s): *Tropical Rainforest: A World Survey of Our Most Valuable and Endangered Habitat (with a blueprint for survival); Amazon Hotline*
Keyword(s): Biodiversity, Cultural Preservation, Endangered and Threatened Species, Environmental Preservation, Greenhouse Effect/Global Warming

INTERNATIONAL SOCIETY OF ARBORICULTURE
P.O. Box 3129, Champaign, IL 61826-3129
Phone: 217-355-9411; Fax: 217-355-9516
Founded: 1924; Membership: 10,500
Scope: International
Description: To promote and improve the care and preservation of shade and ornamental trees through research and education.
Contact(s):
President: AL CHERRY, Horsham, PA
Vice President: DR. GARY WATSON, Lisle, IL
Executive Director: BILL KRUIDENIER
Editor: DEREK VANNICE, P.O. Box GG, Savoy, IL 61874
Editor: DR. ROBERT MILLER, College of Natural Resources, University of Wisconsin/Stevens Point, Stevens Point, WI 54481
President-Elect: DR. DAN NEELY, Scott City, MO
Publication(s): *Journal of Arboriculture; Arborist News; Valuation of Landscape Trees, Shrubs, and Other Plants; Planting Tree and Shrubs; Publication listings to include "A Photographic Guide for Evaluation of Hazard Trees in Urban Areas"; " Arborist Certificate*

Guide"; VHS Video Tapes on Construction Damage to Trees on Wooded Lots

INTERNATIONAL SOCIETY OF TROPICAL FORESTERS, INC.
5400 Grosvenor Ln., Bethesda, MD 20814
Phone: 301-897-8720; Fax: 301-897-3690; E-mail: istfi@igc.apc.org
Founded: 1950; Membership: 2,000
Scope: International
Description: A nonprofit organization founded with the objective of providing an information exchange for members involved in the management, protection, and wise use of tropical forests.
Contact(s):
President: WARREN T. DOOLITTLE, USA
Vice President: NAPOLEON VERGATA, Philippines
Director of Africa: B. M. TAZL, Gambia
Director of Asia: NAPOLEON VERGATA, Philippines
Director of Latin America: RODOLFO SALAZAR, Costa Rica
Director at Large: JEFFERY BURLEY, United Kingdom
Director at Large: CHUM LAI, Philippines
Director at Large: JOHN E.D. FOX, Australia
Editor: FRANK H. WADSWORTH
Publication(s): *ISTF News; ISTF Noticizs*
Keyword(s): Biodiversity, Forest Management, International Conservation, Renewable Resources, Sustainable Ecosystems, Urban Forestry

INTERNATIONAL SONORAN DESERT ALLIANCE
201 Esperanza Ave., P.O. Box 687, Ajo, AZ 85321
Phone: 520-387-6823; Fax: 520-387-5626
Founded: 1992; Membership: 673
Scope: International
Description: The purpose of the International Sonoran Desert Alliance is to promote environmentally sustainable and culturally sound economic development while protecting the natural and tri-cultural heritage of the western Sonoran Desert.
Contact(s):
President: JOSEPH JOAQUIN
Vice President: MANUEL GONZALEZ
Vice President: GRACIELA BARAJAS
Secretary: KENIA CASTAÑEDA
Treasurer: SUE N. TOUT
Executive Director: REYNALDO CANTU
Keyword(s): Cultural Preservation, Deserts, International Conservation, People of Color in the Environment, Sustainable Development

INTERNATIONAL UNION FOR CONSERVATION OF NATURE AND NATURAL RESOURCES (IUCN) THE WORLD CONSERVATION UNION
Headquarters, Rue Mauverney 28, CH-1196, Gland Switzerland
Phone: 022.9990001; Web Site: www.iucn.org
Founded: 1948
Scope: International
Description: An independent body to promote scientifically-based action for the conservation of nature and to ensure that development is sustainable and provides a lasting improvement in the quality of life for people all over the world. Eight hundred eighty voting members in 138 countries; 73 states, 107 government agencies, and 623 non-governmental organizations. Also 35 non-voting affiliate members. Maintains a global network of more than 6,000 scientists and professionals organized into six commissions.
Contact(s):
President: YOLANDA N. KAKABADSE
Treasurer: CLAES DE DARDEL
Chairman for Species Survival Commission (SSC) (Canada): DAVID BRACKETT
Chairman of Commission on Ecosystem Management (United Kingdom): EDWARD MALTBY
Chairman of Commission on Education and Communication (The Netherlands): DR. FRITZ HESSELINK
Chairman of Commission on Environmental Economic and Social Policy (United Kingdom): DR. TARIQ J. BUNURI
Chairman of Commission on Environmental Law (CEL) (US): PROF. NICHOLAS ROBINSON
Chairman of Commission on Protected Areas (WCPPA) (United Kingdom): PROF. ADRIAN PHILLIPS
Chairman of the Bureau (Eduador): SRA YOLANDA N. KAKABADSE
Director General (Germany): MARIETTA R. VON BIBERSTEIN KOCH-WESER
Director of Biodiversity Policy Coordination Division: JEFFREY A. McNEELY
Director of Finance: MARIA GRAZIA IURI
Director of Global Programme (Switzerland): PATRICK DUGAN
Publication(s): *World Conservation Bulletin; Red Data Books (describing threatened species of mammals, amphibia and reptilia, invertebrates and plants); United Nations List of National Parks and Protected Areas; Books on conservation and development, land and freshwater animals, marine and coastal ecology and management, national parks and other protected areas, and regional conservation; Environmental Policy and Law Papers; World Conservation Strategy: Living Resource Conservation for Sustainable Development; Caring for the Earth--A Strategy for Sustainable Living; A Pocket Guide to IUCN.*
Keyword(s): Conservation, Developing Countries, Development, Sustainable Development

Bangladesh Country Office
House #13, Road 3, Dhanmond, RIA 1205, Dhaka 1205 Bangladesh
Scope: International
Contact(s):
Head: ANWARUL ISLAM

Botswana Country Office
Private Bag 00300, Gaborone Botswana
Scope: International
Contact(s):
Country Representative: RUUD JANSEN

Burkina Country Fasso Office
01 BP 3133, 515 Rue Agostino Neto, Ouagadougou 01, Ouagadougou 01 Burkina Fasso
Scope: International
Contact(s):
Country Representative: MICHEL KOUDA

Canada Country Office
380 St. Antoine St. W., Office 3200, Montreal, Quebec H2Y 3X7 Canada
Scope: International
Contact(s):
Head: MALCOLM MERCER

Environmental Law Centre
Adenauerallee 214, Bonn 53113 Germany
Scope: International
Contact(s):
Head: CHARLES DI LEVA

Guinea-Bissau Country Office
Apartado 23, 1031 Bissau Guinea-Bissau
Scope: International
Contact(s):
Chef de Mission: DR. NELSON GOMES DIAS

Lao People's Democratic Republic Country Office
P.O. Box 4340, 15 Fa Ngum Rd., Vientiane, Lao People's Democratic Republic
Scope: International
Contact(s):
Country Representative: STUART CHAPE

NON-GOVERNMENTAL ORGANIZATIONS - I

Mali Country Office
BP 1567, Bamako Mali
Scope: International
Contact(s):
Chef de Mission: MOCTAR TRAORE

Mozambique Country Office
971 Rue Armando Tivane, Maputo, Mozambique
Scope: International
Contact(s):
Country Representative: EBENIZARIO CHONGUICA

Nepal Country Office
P.O. Box 3923, Lalitpur, Dhobighat, Kathmandu Nepal
Scope: International
Contact(s):
Country Representative: DR. AMBIKA ADHIKARI

Niger Country Office
BP 10933, Niamey, Niger, West Africa
Scope: International
Contact(s):
Country Representative: M. M. MAMANE

P.O. Box 11536
Hatfield, Pretoria 0028 South Africa
Scope: International
Contact(s):
SALIEM FAKIR

Pakistan Country Office
1 Bath Island Rd., Karachi 75530 Pakistan
Scope: International
Contact(s):
Country Representative: ABAN MARKER KABRAJI

Regional Office for Eastern Africa
P.O. Box 68200, Mukoma Rd., Langata, Nairobi Kenya
Scope: International
Contact(s):
Regional Representative: ELDAD TUKAHIRWA

Regional Office for Europe
Marienhof, Bredaseweg 387, 5037 LD, Tilburg Netherlands
Scope: International
Contact(s):
Regional Director (interim): ELIZABETH HOPKINS
European Program Coordinator: ZBIGNIEW KARPOWICZ

Regional Office for Meso America
Apartado 0146-2150, Moravia, San Jose, Costa Rica
Scope: International
Contact(s):
Regional Director: DR. ENRIQUE LAHMANN

Regional Office for South America
Casilla Postal 17-17-626, Avenida Atahualpa 955 y Republica Edificio Digicom Piso 4, Quito Ecuador
Scope: International
Contact(s):
Regional Representative: DR. ROBERTO FRANCO

Regional Office for Southern Africa (ROSA)
P.O. Box 745, Harare, Zimbabwe
Scope: International
Contact(s):
Regional Representative: YEMI KATERERE

Regional Office for West Africa
BP 1618, Quagadougou 01 Burkina Faso
Scope: International
Contact(s):
Regional Representative: IBRAHIM THIAW

Regional Office of South and Southeast Asia
P.O. Box 4, 302 Outreach Bldg., AIT, Klong Luang, Pathumthani 12120 Thailand
Scope: International
Contact(s):
Head: DR. MOHAMMED ZAKIR HUSSAIN

Regonal Office for Central Africa
B.P. 5506, c/o IUCN Project Office DHA, Yaounde, Cameroon
Scope: International
Contact(s):
Coordinator for Central Africa: ASSITOU NDINGA

Senegal Country Office
BP 3215 Ave. Bourguiba x rue 3, Castors, Dakar Senegal
Scope: International
Contact(s):
Chef de Mission: ABDOULAYE KANE

Sri Lanka Country Office
48 Vajira Ln., Colombo 5 Sri Lanka
Scope: International
Contact(s):
Country Representative: SHIRANEE YASARATNE

Subregional Office for Central Europe
U1 Narbutta 40/21, Warsaw 02-541 Poland
Scope: International
Contact(s):
Head: DR. ZENON TEDERKO

Subregional Office for the Commonwealth of Independent States
P.O. Box 265, Moscow 1254755 Russian
Scope: International
Contact(s):
Head: VLADIMIR MOSHKALO

U.S. Office, Washington, DC
1630 Connecticut Ave., NW, Washington, DC 20009
Phone: 202-387-4826; Fax: 202-387-4823; E-mail: postmaster@iucnus.org; Web Site: www.iucn.org
Scope: International

Uganda Country Office
P.O. Box 10950, Plot 39 Acacia Ave., Kampala, Uganda
Scope: International
Contact(s):
Country Representative: ALEX MUHWEEZI

Vietnam Country Office
P.O. Box 60, International Post Office, 13, Tran Hung Dao, Hanoi, Vietnam
Scope: International
Contact(s):
Country Representative: NGUYEN MINH THONG

Zambia Country Office
Asco Bldg., Private Bag W, 356 Luanshya Rd., Plot No 5116, Lusaka, Zambia
Scope: International
Contact(s):
Country Representative: SALLY LINDA MULALA

INTERNATIONAL WILD WATERFOWL ASSOCIATION
5614 River Styx Rd., Medina, OH 44256
Founded: 1958; Membership: 500
Scope: International
Description: Works toward protection, conservation, and reproduction of any species of wild waterfowl considered in danger of eventual extinction; encourages breeding of well-known and rare species in captivity. Established Avicultural Hall of Fame. Sponsors annual conference and gives grants in field.

Contact(s):
President: WALTER B. STURGEON JR., 7 James Farm, Durham, NH 03824; Phone: 603-659-5442
Secretary: NANCY COLLINS, 5614 River Styx Rd., Medina, OH 44256; Phone: 216-725-8782
Treasurer: WILLIAM R. LOWE, 3010 Shady Ln., Billings, MT 59102; Phone: 406-245-6119
1st Vice President: EDWARD ASPER, Vice President of Sea World, 7007 Sea World Dr., Orlando, FL 32821; Phone: 407-351-3600
2nd Vice President: PAUL DYE, 10114 54th Pl. NE, Everett, WA 98205; Phone: 206-342-8346
Publication(s): *IWWA Newsletter*
Keyword(s): Endangered and Threatened Species, International Conservation, Scholarships and Grants, Waterfowl, Wildlife and Wildlife Habitat

INTERNATIONAL WILDERNESS LEADERSHIP (WILD) FOUNDATION
P.O. Box 1380, Ojai, CA 93024
E-mail: info@wild.org
Founded: 1974; Membership: 5,000
Scope: International
Description: The International Wilderness Leadership Foundation is dedicated to protecting wilderness and wildlife, providing environmental experience and training and promoting the correct use of wildlands worldwide.
Contact(s):
Chairman: ROBERT BARON, 350 Indiana St., Golden, CO 80401
President: VANCE G. MARTIN; Phone: 805-640-0390
Treasurer: MICHAEL SWEATMAN, Rt. 1, P.O. Box 659 1503, Waterbury, VT 05672; Phone: 802-244-8981
Vice President of Science and Education: DR. JOHN HENDEE, College of Forestry, University of Idaho, Moscow, ID 83843; Phone: 208-885-2267
Publication(s): *Leaf Newsletter, The; Wilderness Management; For the Conservation of Earth; Wilderness, the Way Ahead; Arctic Wilderness; International Journal of Wilderness*
Keyword(s): Environmental and Conservation Education, International Conservation, Wilderness, Wildlands

INTERNATIONAL WILDLIFE COALITION (IWC) AND THE WHALE ADOPTION PROJECT
70 E. Falmouth Highway, E. Falmouth, MA 02536
Phone: 508-548-8328; Fax: 508-548-8542; Web Site: www.iwc.org
Founded: 1984; Membership: 275,000
Scope: International
Description: IWC is a nonprofit, tax-exempt organization dedicated to preserving wildlife and their habitats. As an internationally recognized non-governmental organization, IWC's achievements have been accomplished through grassroots advocacy, activism, research, and education efforts. IWC's Whale Adoption Project protects and researches marine mammals.
Contact(s):
President: DANIEL MORAST, 70 E. Falmouth Highway, E. Falmouth, MA 02536; Phone: 508-548-8328; Fax: 508-548-8542; E-mail: dmorast@iwc.org
Vice President: STEPHEN BEST, P.O. Box 988, Shelburne, Ontario L0N1S0 Canada; Phone: 519-925-3440; Fax: 519-925-2003; E-mail: sbest@iwc.org
Brazil Project Coordinator: JOSE TRUDA PALAZZO JR., P.O. Box 5087, Florianopolis, S.C. 88040-970 Brazil; Phone: 55-482-340021; Fax: 55-482-341580; E-mail: BRAZILIAN_WILDLIFE@zaz.com.br
Canada Director: ANNE DONCASTER, P.O. Box 340, Carling, Ontario P0B1J0 Canada; Phone: 705-765-6341; Fax: 705-765-6435; E-mail: adncstr@muskoka.com
Canada Project Director: DR. RONALD ORENSTEIN, 130 Adelaide St. West, Suite 1940, Toronto, Ontario M5H3P5 Canada; Phone: 905-820-7886; Fax: 905-569-0116; E-mail: ornstn@inforamp.net
Sri Lanka Representative: DR. HIRAN JAYEWARDENE, 218/1 Bauddhaloka Mawatha, Colombo 7, Sri Lanka; Phone: 94-1-580236; Fax: 94-1-580236
United Kingdom Director: CHARLES WARTENBERG, 141A, High St., Edenbridge, Kent TN85AX England; Phone: 44-1732-86695; Fax: 44-1732-866995
Vice-President of Programs: DONNA HART, P.O. Box 138, Elsberry, MO 63343; Phone: 314-898-5600; Fax: 314-898-5411; E-mail: dlhart@inlink.com
Publication(s): *WhaleWatch; Wildlife Watch; Whales of the World Teacher's Kit; Wildlife and You and What You Can Do To Help*
Keyword(s): Endangered and Threatened Species, International Conservation, Mammals, Marine Mammals, Whales, Wildlife and Wildlife Habitat

INTERNATIONAL WILDLIFE REHABILITATION COUNCIL (IWRC)
4437 Central Pl., Suite B-4, Suisun, CA 94585-1633
Phone: 707-864-1761/Wildlife Care Referral Line 707-864-1762; Fax: 707-864-3106; E-mail: iwrc@inreach.com; Web Site: www.iwrc-online.org
Founded: 1972; Membership: 1,800
Scope: International
Description: IWRC is a membership-supported organization dedicated to the care and rehabilitation of injured and orphaned wildlife and their eventual return into the wild. Committed to the training and education of wildlife rehabilitators, with a goal towards professionalism and expertise in the field.
Contact(s):
President: MARGE GIBSON
Vice President: SUSAN HECKLY
Secretary/Treasurer: LEE THEISEN-WATT
Executive Director: MARY REYNOLDS
Publication(s): *Journal of Wildlife Rehabilitation; Basic Wildlife Rehabilitation; Minimum Standards and Accreditation; Current Protocol for Treatment of Oil Contaminated Birds; other publications and catalog available.*
Keyword(s): Biology, Natural History, Wildlife and Wildlife Habitat, Wildlife Disease, Wildlife Rehabilitation

INTERNATIONAL WOLF CENTER (Administrative Offices)
5930 Brooklyn Blvd., #204, Minneapolis, MN 55429
Phone: 612-560-7374; Fax: 612-560-7368
Scope: International

INTERNATIONAL WOLF CENTER (Educational Services)
1396 Highway 169, Ely, MN 55731
Phone: 218-365-4695; Fax: 218-365-3318; E-mail: wolfinfo@wolf.org; Web Site: www.wolf.org
Founded: 1985; Membership: 9,000+
Scope: International
Description: The International Wolf Center supports the survival of the wolf around the world by teaching about its life, its associations with other species and its dynamic relationship to humans.
Contact(s):
Chair: NANCY JO TUBBS
Secretary: ROLF PETERSON
Treasurer: PAUL ANDERSON
Executive Director: WALTER M. MEDWID
Information Resources Coordinator: LINDA AYLSWORTH
Vice Chair: DR. L. DAVID MECH
Publication(s): *International Wolf Magazine; Guidelines for Gray Wolf Management; various educational pamphlets*
Keyword(s): Endangered and Threatened Species, Environmental and Conservation Education, International Conservation, Mammals, Wildlife and Wildlife Habitat, Wildlife Management, Wolves

INTERPRETATION CANADA
c/o Kerry Wood Nature Centre, 6300-45 Ave., Red Deer, Ontario T4N 3M4 Canada
Founded: 1973; Membership: 625
Scope: National
Description: Interpretation Canada is dedicated to raising public awareness, understanding, and appreciation for Canada's natural and cultural heritage, provides training, networking, and advocacy

NON-GOVERNMENTAL ORGANIZATIONS - I

for interpreters, and promotes the role of interpretation in fields such as conservation, education, recreation, and tourism.
Contact(s):
Chairperson: ANN FINLAYSON, 782 E. Kings Rd., North Vancouver, BC V1K 1E3 Canada; Phone: 604-987-8653; Fax: 604-987-8629; E-mail: annfinlayson@bc.sympatico.ca
Member Services: JIM ROBERTSON, Kerrywood Nature Centre, 6300-45 Ave., Red Deer, Alberta T4N 3M4 403-346-2010 Canada; Phone: 403-347-2590; E-mail: kwnc@supernet.ab.ca
Publication(s): *Interpscan - national journal; regional newsletters from Northwest Territories, British Columbia, Alberta, Ontario, and Atlantic region; annual membership directory*
Keyword(s): Culture, Interpretation, Training

INTERTRIBAL BISON COOPERATIVE (ITBC)
1560 Concourse Dr., Rapid City, SD 57703
Phone: 605-394-9730; Fax: 605-394-7742; E-mail: itbc@enetis.net
Founded: 1991; Membership: 47 Tribes, Honorary & Associate
Scope: National
Description: The ITBC is dedicated to the restoration of buffalo to Indian lands in a manner which is compatible with the cultural practices and spiritual beliefs of the respective tribes.
Contact(s):
President: LOUIS LAROSE, Winnebago Tribe of NE, Rte 1, Box 15, Winnebago, NE 68071; Phone: 402-878-2711
Vice President: CARL A. TSOSIE, Picuris Pueblo, P.O. Box 127, Penasco, NM 87553; Phone: 505-587-2519
Secretary: ARTHUR DENNY JR., Rt. 2 Box 163, Niobrara, NE 68760; Phone: 402-857-2302
Treasurer: RICHARD ARCHULETA, Taos Pueblo, P.O. Box 3164, Taos, NM 87571; Phone: 505-758-3883
Executive Director: TIMOTHY WAPATO
Publication(s): *Buffalo Tracks*
Keyword(s): Cultural Preservation, Land Preservation, Prairies, Sustainable Development, Wildlife and Wildlife Habitat

IOWA ACADEMY OF SCIENCE
University of Northern Iowa, Cedar Falls, IA 50614-0508
Phone: 319-273-2021; Fax: 319-273-2807
Founded: 1875; Membership: 1,275
Scope: Statewide
Description: To further the work of scientists, facilitate cooperation among them, and increase public understanding and appreciation of the importance and promise of the methods of science in human progress. A conservation section meets each year as part of an annual convention submitting papers dealing with all conservation happenings.
Contact(s):
President: NEIL BERSTEIN, Biology Dept., Mt. Mercy College, 1330 Elmhurst, Cedar Rapids, IA 52402
Executive Director and Manager Editor: DAVID V. MCCALLEY
President-Elect: DARREL HOFF, Dept. of Physics, Luther College, Decorah, IA 52101
Publication(s): *Journal of the Iowa Academy of Science; Iowa Science Teachers Newsletter; IAS Bulletin*
Keyword(s): Environmental and Conservation Education

IOWA ASSOCIATION OF NATURALISTS
R.R. 1 Box 53, Guthrie Center, IA 50115
Phone: 515-747-8383
Founded: 1978; Membership: 120
Scope: Statewide
Description: Organization of persons interested in promoting the development of skills and education within the art of interpreting the natural and cultural environment. Members representing county, state, federal, and private conservation education agencies, organizations, and facilities.
Contact(s):
President of the Board: TODD VON EHWEGAN, Cerro Gordo County Conservation Board 3501 Lime Creek Rd., Mason City, IA 50401
Secretary of the Board: SANDY FULCHER, Black Hawk County Conservation Board, 657 Reserve Dr., Cedar Falls, IA 50613; Phone: 319-277-2187
Treasurer of the Board: JOEL VAN ROEKEL, Warren County Conservation Board 1565 118th Ave., Indianola, IA 50125; Phone: 515-961-6169
Vice President of the Board: STEVE MARTIN, Butler County Conservation Board, Henry Woods State Park, 28727 Timber Rd., Clarkville, IA 50619; Phone: 319-278-1130
Workshop Coordinator: BRUCE VOIGHTS, Wright County Conservation Board, 1720 O'Brien Ave., Clarion, IA 50525; Phone: 515-532-3185
Keyword(s): Environmental and Conservation Education, Interpretation

IOWA ASSOCIATION OF SOIL AND WATER CONSERVATION DISTRICT COMMISSIONERS
Attn: President, 1152 160th St., Gladbrook, IA 50131
Scope: Statewide
Contact(s):
President, Board Member: DAN BRUENE; Phone: 515-473-2338; Fax: 515-473-2455
Vice President: WILLIAM BENNETT, 4331 Dove Rd., Elgin, IA 82141-9526; Phone: 319-426-5695; Fax: 319-426-5695
Secretary: BERNIE BOLTON, 38995 Honeysuckle Rd., Oakland, IA 52560-9686; Phone: 712-482-3386; Fax: 712-482-3386
Treasurer: ART RALSTON, 2629 200th St., Moville, IA 51039-8036; Phone: 712-873-3719
Executive Director: JILL KNAPP, 3829 71st St., Ste. A, Urbandale, IA 50322; Phone: 515-278-5362; Fax: 515-278-5362
Keyword(s): Conservation Districts

IOWA AUDUBON
P.O. Box 71174, Grinnell, IA 50325
Phone: 515-267-0701; E-mail: p2eph@audubon.org
Scope: Statewide
Description: The state office of the National Audubon Society supporting the 12 Audubon groups in Iowa. Iowa Audubon's mission is to promote the enjoyment, protection and restoration of Iowa's natural ecosystems with a focus on birds, other wildlife and their habitats.
Contact(s):
Executive Director: PAUL ZEPH
Keyword(s): Biodiversity, Birds, Environmental and Conservation Education, Environmental Protection, Restoration, Wildlife and Wildlife Habitat

IOWA B.A.S.S. CHAPTER FEDERATION
Attn: President, 3282 Midway, Marion, IA 52302
Scope: Statewide
Description: An organization of Bassmaster chapters, affiliated with the Bass Anglers Sportsman Society, organized to fight pollution, assist state and national conservation agencies in their efforts, and teach the young people of our country good conservation practices. Dedicated to the realistic conservation of our water resources.
Contact(s):
President: TOM BOWLER; Phone: 319-393-1481

IOWA CONSERVATION EDUCATION COUNCIL, INC.
c/o Conservation Education Center, Rt. 1, Box 53, Guthrie Center, IA 50115
Phone: 515-747-8383
Founded: 1958; Membership: 800
Scope: Statewide
Description: To encourage and lead the development and practice of a widespread and effective conservation education program in Iowa.
Contact(s):
Bookkeeper: DOROTHY PIMLOTT, 205 I Ave., Nevada, IA 50319; Phone: 515-281-3146
Chairperson: STACEY SNYDER NEWBROUGH, P.O. Box 210, Tripoli, IA 50676
Editor: NANCY GESKE, 2400 Timberland, Ames, IA 50010; Phone: 515-292-2981

Editor: JOEL GESKE, 2400 Timberland, Ames, IA 50010; Phone: 515-292-2981
Vice Chairperson: MARILYN IRWIN, 2046 F Ave., Perry, IA 50220; Phone: 515-465-4755
Vice Chairperson: KATHY McKEE, 1002 Prairie, Gutherie Center, IA 50115; Phone: 515-747-3771
Vice Chairperson: CRAIG ZOELLNER, 500 College Dr., Mason City, IA 50401; Phone: 515-421-4319

IOWA ENVIRONMENTAL COUNCIL
711 E. Locust St., Des Moines, IA 50309
Phone: 515-244-1194; Fax: 515-244-7856; E-mail: iecmail@earthweshare.org; Web Site: www.earthweshare.org
Founded: 1994; Membership: 60 organizations, 700 individuals, 8 cooperators
Scope: Statewide
Description: The Iowa Environmental Council is an alliance of diverse organizations and individuals working with all Iowans to protect our natural environment. We seek a sustainable future through shaping public policy, research and education, coalition-building, and advocacy.
Contact(s):
President: DENNIS KEENEY
Vice President: DAVID HURD
Secretary: GAIL BARELS
Treasurer: MARK ACKELSON
Executive Director: LINDA D. APPELGATE
Publication(s): *Iowa Environmental Quarterly; News Bulletin; Legislative Action*
Keyword(s): Agriculture, Biodiversity, Pesticides, Water Quality

IOWA NATIVE PLANT SOCIETY
Botany Department, Iowa State University, Ames, IA 50011-1020
Phone: 515-294-9499; Fax: 515-294-1337
Founded: 1995; Membership: 175
Scope: Statewide
Description: Iowa Native Plant Society is an organization of amateurs and professionals who are interested in the scientific, educational, cultural aspects, preservation, and conservation of Iowa's native plants.
Contact(s):
President: ED FREESE
Vice President: FRED CRANE; Phone: 515-279-8440
Secretary and Treasurer: MARY BROWN; Phone: 319-338-3875
Publication(s): *Iowa Native Plant Society Newsletter*
Keyword(s): Biodiversity, Conservation, Endangered and Threatened Species, Environmental and Conservation Education, Environmental Preservation, Flowers, Plants, and Trees, Prairies, Wetlands, Native Plants

IOWA NATURAL HERITAGE FOUNDATION
Attn: Communications Coordinator, Insurance Exchange Bldg., Suite 444, 505 Fifth Ave., Des Moines, IA 50309
Phone: 515-288-1846; Fax: 515-288-0137; E-mail: info@inhf.org; Web Site: www.inhf.org
Founded: 1979; Membership: 5,000
Scope: Statewide
Description: An independent, statewide, nonprofit organization founded by business and community leaders to involve the private sector in protecting Iowa's natural resources. Program emphasis on land protection, landowner education, resource planning, wetland restoration and rail-trail development in Iowa.
Contact(s):
Chairman: BARB MACGREGOR
Vice Chairman: MIKE LAMAIR
President: MARK C. ACKELSON
Secretary: RICHARD E. RAMSAY
Treasurer: MICHAEL E. RILEY
Communications Coordinator: CATHY ENGSTROM
Director of Development and Communications: ANITA O'GARA
Director of Finance: LAURA McVAY
Director of Land Projects: BRUCE MOUNTAIN
Director of Land Stewardship: JOE MCGOVERN
Director of Trails and Greenways: LISA HEIN
Publication(s): *Iowa Natural Heritage; The Landowner's Options; Enjoy Iowa's Recreation Trails Guidebook*
Keyword(s): Conservation of Protected Areas, Endangered and Threatened Species, Flowers, Plants, and Trees, Internships, Land Preservation, Natural Areas, Nature Preservation, Outdoor Recreation, Prairies, Rivers, Sustainable Development, Trail, Wetlands, Wildlands, Wildlife and Wildlife Habitat

IOWA PRAIRIE NETWORK
6736 Laural, Omaha, NE 68104
Phone: 402-571-6230; Fax: 402-571-6230; E-mail: pollockg@top.net; Web Site: www.netins.net/showcase/bluestem/1pnapp.htm
Founded: 1990; Membership: 300
Scope: Statewide
Description: The Iowa Prairie Network is dedicated to protecting Iowa prairie heritage.
Contact(s):
President: GLENN POLLOCK
Vice President: CINDY HILDEBRAND
Treasurer: CAROLE KERN; Phone: 319-273-2813
Director: DAVID HANSEN; Phone: 515-357-3665
Publication(s): *IPN News; Native Prairie Management Guide; A Prairie Bibliography*
Keyword(s): Prairies

IOWA TRAILS COUNCIL
P.O. Box 131, Center Point, IA 52213-0131
Phone: 319-849-1844
Founded: 1983; Membership: 1,200
Scope: Statewide
Description: A membership nonprofit organization primarily active in the Midwest, but with membership in over one-half the states and in several foreign countries. Primary purpose is to acquire and convert former railroad rights-of-way into recreational trails.
Contact(s):
Chairman: ELDON L. COLTON, 716 Oakland Rd. NE, Cedar Rapids, IA 52402
Secretary/Treasurer and Executive Director: TOM F. NEENAN, P.O. Box 131, Center Point, IA 52213-0131; Phone: 319-849-1844
Vice Chairman: DR. DAVID LYON, 116 10th Ave. S., Mt. Vernon, IA 52314; Phone: 319-895-8240
Publication(s): *Trails Advocate (bi-monthly mini magazine); Bicycle Trails of Iowa (128 page color illustrated book)*
Keyword(s): Bicycle, Environmental Preservation, Land Preservation, Land Use Planning, Nature Preservation, Outdoor Recreation, Trail, Transportation

IOWA TRAPPERS ASSOCIATION, INC.
c/o Anna Marie Scalf, 123 N. Madison Ave., Ottumwa, IA 52501
Phone: 515-682-3937
Founded: 1950; Membership: 2,000
Scope: Statewide
Description: A nonprofit organization that works to continue the wise use and harvest of Iowa's renewable resource of fur-bearing animals. Cooperates with all recognized conservation agencies, law enforcement agencies, and legislative committees, and provides input on the benefits and necessity of trapping.
Contact(s):
President: TOM WALTERS, 1723 20th St., Bettendorf, IA 52722-3829; Phone: 319-359-6949
Vice President: JAMES L. STAUFFER, 29602 202nd St., Clarksville, IA 50619-9801; Phone: 319-278-4004
Secretary: CHRIS GRILLOT, 2769 110th Ave., Wheatland, IA 52777; Phone: 319-374-1074
Treasurer: ANNA MARIE SCALF, 123 N. Madison Ave., Ottumwa, IA 52501; Phone: 515-682-3937
Editor: PAUL WAIT, 700 E. State St., Iola, WI 54990; Phone: 715-445-2214
Publication(s): *Trapper and Predator Caller, The*

NON-GOVERNMENTAL ORGANIZATIONS - I

Keyword(s): Environmental and Conservation Education, Outdoor Recreation, Trapping, Wildlife and Wildlife Habitat, Wildlife Management

IOWA WILDLIFE FEDERATION
3125 Douglas, #103, Des Moines, IA 50310
Phone: 515-279-0655
Scope: Statewide
Description: A representative statewide organization, affiliated with the National Wildlife Federation, dedicated to the protection and enhancement of wildlife and its habitat through public education and government interaction.
Contact(s):
President: JOE WILKINSON
Representative: DOUG THOMPSON
Editor: MIKE HODGES
Alternate Representative: LOREN FORBES

IOWA WILDLIFE REHABILITATORS ASSOCIATION
1005 Harken Hill Dr., P.O. Box 217, Osceola, IA 50036
Phone: 515-342-2783
Founded: 1986; Membership: 50
Scope: Statewide
Description: A nonprofit organization established to disseminate information pertaining to wildlife rehabilitation and medicine to veterinarians, rehabilitators, naturalists and others; to communicate and cooperate with environmental/conservation organizations; and to encourage the public to become more aware of the earth and its wild creatures. This is done through newsletters, educational material, state and regional conferences, and presentations.
Contact(s):
President: MARLENE EHRESMAN; Phone: 515-296-2995
Vice President: HEATHER BLEVINS; Phone: 515-277-7745
Secretary: WENDY VAN DeWALLE; Phone: 515-964-9592
Treasurer: BETH BROWN; Phone: 515-342-2783
Publication(s): *newsletters, educational materials*
Keyword(s): Wildlife Rehabilitation

IOWA WOMEN IN NATURAL RESOURCES
P.O. Box 20083, Des Moines, IA 50320-0083
Founded: 1988; Membership: 150
Scope: Statewide
Description: A nonprofit organization dedicated to providing professional development to individuals interested in all natural resource careers by promoting communication among professionals, encouraging girls and women to consider natural resource careers, conducting outdoor skills workshops, providing networking and support systems for women working in natural resources and providing career enhancement training.
Contact(s):
President: KATHY SHANNON; Phone: 515-432-8391; Fax: 515-433-9624
Vice President: LAURA SURBER; Phone: 515-961-6169
Secretary: JOLI VOLLERS; Phone: 712-548-3303
Treasurer: THERESA MINAYA; Phone: 712-258-0838
Publication(s): *IWINR News; IWINR Membership Directory*
Keyword(s): Environment, Training, Women in the Environment

IOWA WOODLAND OWNERS ASSOCIATION
2735 14th Ave., Marion, IA 52302-1848
Phone: 515-233-1161
Founded: 1987; Membership: 450
Scope: Statewide
Description: A statewide organization affiliated with the National Woodland Owners Association, organized to advance good forestry on the 1.5 million acres of timberland owned by 28,000 non-industrial private landowners in Iowa.
Contact(s):
President: AL MANNING
Vice President: TOM WOODRUFF
Secretary and Editor: E. O. FRYE; Phone: 319-377-2540
Treasurer: JOANNE MENSINGER; Phone: 319-259-1160
Publication(s): *Timber Talk*
Keyword(s): Forests and Forestry

ISLAND CONSERVATION EFFORT
90 Edgewater Dr. #901, Coral Gables, FL 33133
Phone: 305-666-5381; Fax: 305-663-9941
Founded: 1988; Membership: 200
Scope: International
Description: Island Conservation Effort is dedicated to the preservation of island natural resources, fauna, and habitats on which their preservation depends. We promote conservation, education, and research to obtain necessary data to support conservation measures.
Contact(s):
President: MARTHA WALSH-McGEHEE, 90 Edgewater Dr. #901, Coral Gables, FL 33133; Phone: 305-666-5381; E-mail: tropbird@gate.net
Vice President: MICHELLE PUGH, P.O. Box 4254, Christiansted, St. Croix 00820 US Virgin Islands; Phone: 340-773-7030; E-mail: divexp@viaccess.net
Secretary and Treasurer: DR. ROSEMARIE GNAM, 13 East Rosemont Ave., Alexandria, VA 22301; Phone: 703-739-9803
Keyword(s): Birds, Coral Reefs, Endangered and Threatened Species, Environmental and Conservation Education, Islands, Research

ISLAND INSTITUTE, THE
410 Main St., Rockland, ME 04841
Phone: 207-594-9209; Fax: 207-594-9314; Web Site: www.islandinstitute.org
Founded: 1983; Membership: 5,000
Scope: National
Description: Private, nonprofit organization dedicated to sustaining island and coastal communities through community initiatives, publications, resource management, science and marine research.
Contact(s):
Chairman: HORACE A. HILDRETH JR.; Phone: 207-774-5981
President: PHILIP W. CONKLING; Phone: 207-594-9209
Vice President: PETER RALSTON; Phone: 207-594-9209
Chief Operating Officer: JOSEE SHELLEY CPA; Phone: 207-594-9209
Marine Resources Director: BILL MACDONALD; Phone: 207-594-9209
Managing Editor: DAVID PLATT; Phone: 207-594-9209
Publication(s): *Island Journal; Working Waterfront; Gulf of Maine Environmental Atlas; Islands in Time*
Keyword(s): Cultural Preservation, Fisheries, Islands, Sustainable Development

ISLAND RESOURCES FOUNDATION
Headquarters, 1718 P St., NW, Suite T-4, Washington, DC 20036
Phone: 202-265-9712; Fax: 202-232-0748; E-mail: irf@irf.org; Web Site: www.irf.org
Founded: 1972
Scope: International
Description: An independent center for the study of island systems, dedicated to improved resources management, comprehensive development planning, the conservation of cultural, physical, and natural resources of islands.
Contact(s):
Chairman: DR. EDWARD L. TOWLE
Secretary: CHARLES W. CONSOLVO
Treasurer: JUDITH A. TOWLE
President and Executive Director: BRUCE G. POTTER
Vice Chairman: HENRY U. WHEATLEY
Keyword(s): Coasts, International Conservation, Islands, Land Use Planning, Water Resources

Eastern Caribbean Biodiversity Program Office
P.O. Box 2103, St. Johns, St. Johns Antigua, West Indies
Phone: 268-463-7740; Fax: 268-463-7740; E-mail: klindsay@irf.org
Scope: Regional

ISSAQUAH ALPS TRAILS CLUB (I.A.T.C.)
P.O. Box 351, Issaquah, WA 98027

Phone: 206-328-0480
Founded: 1979; Membership: 3,500
Scope: Local
Description: A nonprofit membership organization established to preserve and promote trails and open space in the area east of Seattle along the I-90 highway corridor from Lake Washington to the Cascades, primarily in the area known as the "Issaquah Alps."
Contact(s):
President: BARBARA JOHNSON
Vice President: KEN KONIGSMARK
Secretary: DIANA BANNER
Treasurer: STEVEN J. DREW
Chairman of the Board: HARVEY MANNING
Publication(s): *Washington State We're In The; Targeting Tomorrow - Washington's Economy Adjusts to the 90's; Speaking of Ground Water; Washington State Public Port Districts*
Keyword(s): Air Quality and Pollution, Energy, Planning Management, Solid Waste, Wetlands

IZAAK WALTON LEAGUE OF AMERICA ENDOWMENT
3185 Dubuque St., NE, Iowa City, IA 52240
Phone: 319-351-7037
Founded: 1943
Scope: National
Description: Organized to help rebuild Outdoor America by the acquisition for governmental agencies of unique natural areas for the use of future generations. Members of the Izaak Walton League of America.
Contact(s):
President: WENDELL P. HALEY, 1840 NE 92nd Ave., Portland, OR 97220; Phone: 503-253-9749
Vice President: DR. LARRY C. SMITH, 1611 Alderman Dr., Greensboro, NC 27408; Phone: 336-834-0018
Secretary: CHARLES L. ELDRIDGE, 2008 74th St., Des Moines, IA 50322; Phone: 515-244-0932
Treasurer: WILLIAM D. WEBER, 6357 W. Encantado Ct., Rockford, MI 49341; Phone: 616-456-8691; Fax: 616-456-1915
Executive Secretary: ROBERT C. RUSSELL
Honorary President: HOWARD S. WHITE, P.O. Box 527, Havana, IL 62644; Phone: 309-543-4391
Keyword(s): Acid Rain, Environmental and Conservation Education, Fisheries, Hunting, Natural Areas, Outdoor Recreation

IZAAK WALTON LEAGUE OF AMERICA, INC., THE
Headquarters, 707 Conservation Ln., Gaithersburg, MD 20878-2983
Phone: 301-548-0150; Fax: 301-548-0146; Web Site: www.iwla.org
Membership: 50,000
Scope: National
Description: Promotes means and opportunities for educating the public to conserve, maintain, protect, and restore the soil, forest, water, air, and other natural resources of the U.S. and promotes the enjoyment and wholesome utilization of those resources.
Contact(s):
President: DONALD FERRIS
Vice President: STAN ADAMS
Secretary: GEORGIA C. TOWNSEND
Treasurer: CHARLES WILES
Executive Director: PAUL HANSEN
Chairman of the Executive Board: TIMOTHY W. REID
Conservation Director: JIM MOSHER
Director of Midwest Office: WILLIAM GRANT, 1619 Dayton Ave., Suite 202, St. Paul, MN 55104; Phone: 651-649-1446; Fax: 651-649-1494
Editor and Media Director: ZACHARY HOSKINS
Publication(s): *Outdoor America; League Leader*
Keyword(s): Environmental Protection, Hunting, Outdoor Ethics, Public Lands, Sustainability, Water Quality, Wildlife Management

Alaska Division
P.O. Box 670650, Chugiak, AK 99567
Scope: Statewide
Contact(s):
President: THOMAS CARTER; Phone: 907-333-0243

California Division
c/o President, 3619 West 227th Pl., Torrance, CA 90505-2660
Phone: 604-688-1055
Founded: 1938
Scope: Statewide
Contact(s):
President: ANDREW D. KISSNER; Phone: 310-791-0793

Colorado Division
Attn: President, 1314 Margo Ln., Colorado Spring, CO 80909-3064
Scope: Statewide
Contact(s):
President: NELSON BURTON; Phone: 719-473-0700
Secretary: AMY MILLER, 513 Strachan Dr., Fort Collins, CO 80525-2130; Phone: 970-223-5379

Florida Division
Attn: President, 700 Biltmore Way, Apt. 407, Coral Gables, FL 33134
Scope: Statewide
Contact(s):
President: JUANITA GREENE
Secretary: PAMELA PIERCE, P.O. Box 236, Homestead, FL 33090-0236; Phone: 305-451-0993

Illinois Division
Attn: President, P.O. Box 80, Kewane, IL 61443-0080
Scope: Statewide
Contact(s):
President: JACK KAISER; Phone: 309-853-4338
Secretary: MARSHA JOHNSON, 1512 45th St., Moline, IL 61265-3544; Phone: 309-797-8255

Indiana Division
Attn: President, 2173 Pennsylvania St., Portage, IN 46368-2444
Scope: Statewide
Contact(s):
President: CHARLES SIAR; Phone: 219-762-4876
Secretary: BOBBY SCHROADER, 418 N. Harvey St., Griffith, IN 46319-2116; Phone: 219-924-2343
Editor: JAMES DANIELS
Publication(s): *Hoosier Waltonian, The*

Iowa Division
821 E. Walnut, Suite 130, Des Moines, IA 50309
Phone: 515-271-5657
Scope: Statewide
Contact(s):
President: DOYLE ADAMS, 707 N. 7th St., Indianola, IA 50125-1430; Phone: 515-961-6004

Maryland Division
Attn: Secretary, 14110 Clopper Rd., Boyds, MD 20841-9721
Phone: 301-972-1627
Scope: Statewide
Contact(s):
Vice-President: GEROGIA C. TOWNSEND, 406 Leighton Ave., Silver Spring, MD 20901; Phone: 301-588-8335
Secretary: THOMAS W. FISHER; Phone: 301-972-1627

Michigan Division
c/o President, 55 Kenton SE, Grand Rapids, MI 49548
Scope: Statewide
Contact(s):
President: DAN SPALINK; Phone: 616-281-3026
Secretary: ROBERT STEGMIER, 5285 Windmill Dr. NE, Rockford, MI 49341-9311; Phone: 616-866-4769

NON-GOVERNMENTAL ORGANIZATIONS - J

Minnesota Division
555 Park St., #140, St. Paul, MN 55103
Phone: 651-221-0215
Scope: Statewide
Contact(s):
President: GARY SCHVARTZ, 100 Shady Ave, Owatonna, MN 55060-3144; Phone: 507-451-6676
Secretary: STEVE MCNAUGHTEN, 60 Aspen Highland Pl., NE, Owatonna, MN 55060; Phone: 507-4513513

Nebraska Division
Attn: President, 3017 Midway Rd., Grand Island, NE 68803-2436
Scope: Statewide
Contact(s):
President: ROGER METTENBRINK; Phone: 308-384-0656
Secretary: LURLIE CAMPBELL, 17125 Sodtown Rd., Ravenna, NE 68869; Phone: 308-452-3800

New York Division
c/o President, 3826 Lane Rd., Cazenovia, NY 13035
Phone: 315-655-3375
Scope: Statewide
Contact(s):
President: MATT WEBBER; Phone: 315-655-3375
Secretary: WARREN GILES, 118 Clinton St., Penn Yan, NY 14527-1701; Phone: 315-536-4249

Ohio Division
Attn: Secretary, 953 Greenwood Ave., Hamilton, OH 45011-1817
Scope: Statewide
Contact(s):
President: KEVIN FLOWERS, 6793 Midnight Sun Dr., Mainville, OH 45039; Phone: 513-697-6100
Secretary: YVONNE HAYES; Phone: 513-863-8018

Oregon Division
Attn: President, 329 SE 29th Ave., Portland, OR 97214
Founded: 1930
Scope: Statewide
Description: To protect, perpetuate, and strive for renewal of Oregon's natural resources, including the air, soil, woods, waters, and wildlife; to promote means and opportunities for education of the public in respect to such resources and the enjoyment and utilization thereof.
Contact(s):
President: JEANNE NORTON; Phone: 503-235-7634
Secretary: CORAL TORLEY, 1820 NW Woodland Dr., Corvallis, OR 97330-1019; Phone: 541-752-0114

Pennsylvania Division
Attn: President, 100 1st Ave., Red Lion, PA 17356-1610
Scope: Statewide
Contact(s):
President: PAUL L. WILSON; Phone: 717-246-2748
Secretary: MARTHA SHAFFER, P.O. Box 35, Loganville, PA 17342-0035; Phone: 717-428-2883
Keyword(s): Land Preservation, Land Purchase, Land Use Planning, Natural Areas

South Dakota Division
Attn: President, 798 11th St., SW, Watertown, SD 57350-3060
Scope: Statewide
Contact(s):
President: CHARLES CLAYTON; Phone: 605-352-2598
Secretary: SIDNEY WAGNER, JR., 367 Lakeshore Dr., McCook, SD 57046-4002; Phone: 605-232-4511

Virginia Division
Attn: President, 5235 Richardson Dr., Fairfax, VA 22032-3930
Scope: Statewide
Contact(s):
President: BIRTRUN KIDWELL JR.; Phone: 703-232-6563
Secretary: JEANNE M. KLING, 6110 Occoquan Forst Drive, Manassas, VA 20112-3018
Publication(s): *PEC Newsreporter*; Periodic books and special reports.

Washington Division
Attn: President, 400 95th Ave. NE, Bellevue, WA 98004-1359
Scope: Statewide
Contact(s):
President: RONNI McGLENN; Phone: 425-455-1986
Secretary: GORDON PETERSON, 3806 N 24th, Tacoma, WA 98406-5313; Phone: 253-761-8758

West Virginia Division
c/o President, P.O. Box 921, Shepherdstown, WV 25443-0921
Scope: Statewide
Contact(s):
President: C. FREDERICK FORD; Phone: 304-876-2457
Secretary: MARION MEADE, P.O. Box 2600, Elkins, WV 26241-2600; Phone: 304-636-7978

Wisconsin Division
Attn: President, 5316 Forest Cir., N, Stevens Point, WI 54481-5605
Scope: Statewide
Contact(s):
President: ROBERT ELLIKER; Phone: 715-344-1803
Secretary: GERALD J. ERNST, 811 4th St., Plover, WI 54467-2253; Phone: 715-344-4668
Publication(s): *Wisconsin Rivers*; Periodic Action Alerts and News Bulletins
Keyword(s): Environmental and Conservation Education, Rivers, Water Quality, Water Resources, Watersheds

Wyoming Division
Attn: President, 1072 Empinado, Laramie, WY 82070
Phone: 307-742-2785
Scope: Statewide
Contact(s):
President: RAYMOND G. JACQUOT; Phone: 307-742-2785
Publication(s): *Powder River Breaks*
Keyword(s): Agriculture, Energy, Environment, Solid Waste Management, Water Resources

J

J.N. (DING) DARLING FOUNDATION
785 Crandon Blvd #1206, Key Biscayne, FL 33149
Phone: 305-361-9788; Fax: 305-361-9789; E-mail: kipkoss@compuserve.com
Founded: 1962
Scope: National
Description: A nonprofit organization formed to continue the ideals and work of pioneer conservationist "Ding" Darling, with an emphasis on conservation education. The Foundation has no paid staff. With all services, including legal and accounting, provided by its trustees, the Foundation is able to funnel 100% of contributed funds into selected projects.
Contact(s):
President of Board of Trustees and Chairman of Executive Committee: CHRISTOPHER D. KOSS
Keyword(s): Environmental and Conservation Education, Water Resources, Waterfowl, Wildlife and Wildlife Habitat

JACK H. BERRYMAN INSTITUTE FOR WILDLIFE DAMAGE MANAGEMENT
Department of Fisheries and Wildlife, Utah State University, Logan, UT 84322-5210
Phone: 435-797-2436
Scope: National
Description: The Jack H. Berryman Institute is a national non-profit organization that is centered at Utah State University. It engages in

research, education, and extension activities aimed at resolving human and wildlife conflicts, enhancing the positive aspects of wildlife, and increasing human tolerance of wildlife problems.

JACK MINER MIGRATORY BIRD FOUNDATION, INC.
P.O. Box 39, Kingsville, Ontario N9Y 2E8 Canada
Phone: 519-733-4034 or 877-289-8328 (toll free); E-mail: info@jackminer.com; Web Site: www.jackminer.com
Founded: 1904
Scope: Statewide
Description: A nonprofit (501(c)3) foundation inc. in both the U.S. and Canada. This sanctuary and its founder, Jack Miner, have become internationally known as one of the earliest efforts in waterfowl conservation. Often referred to as "The Father of Conservation", Jack Miner pioneered the tagging of waterfowl in 1909. The sanctuary is open year round to the public with no admission fee.
Contact(s):
Vice President: EDNA MINER
Secretary: MARILYN HAGENIERS
President and Treasurer: KIRK W. MINER
Keyword(s): Birds, Nature Centers, Waterfowl

JACKSON HOLE CONSERVATION ALLIANCE
P.O. Box 2728, Jackson, WY 83001
Phone: 307-733-9417; Fax: 307-733-9008; E-mail: jhca@wyoming.com; Web Site: www.jhalliance.com
Founded: 1979; Membership: 1,750
Scope: Local Region
Description: The Alliance is a nonprofit organization dedicated to responsible land stewardship in Jackson Hole, Wyoming, to ensure that human activities are in harmony with the area's irreplaceable wildlife, scenic and other natural resources.
Contact(s):
President: KARLA PENDEXTER; Phone: 307-739-1729
Vice President: DAVID HARDIE; Phone: 307-733-8018
Vice President: LESLIE PETERSON; Phone: 307-733-2016
Secretary: JEAN BARASH; Phone: 307-739-8669
Treasurer: EDMUND A. DONNAN JR.; Phone: 307-733-3278
Executive Director: DR. FRANZ J. CAMENZIND
Program Director: PAMELA LICHTMAN
Publication(s): *Alliance News, The; Mosquito Abatement Program in teton County, Wyoming, The; Welcome to the Neighborhood*
Keyword(s): Biodiversity, Conservation, Endangered and Threatened Species, Environment, Fisheries, Forest Management, Land Use Planning, Open Space, Wilderness, Wildlife and Wildlife Habitat

JACKSON HOLE LAND TRUST
P.O. Box 2897, Jackson, WY 83001
Phone: 307-733-4707
Founded: 1980
Scope: Statewide
Description: A private, nonprofit land conservation organization which works to preserve open space and the scenic, ranching, and wildlife values of Jackson Hole by assisting landowners who wish to protect their land in perpetuity. Not a membership organization.
Contact(s):
President: ALLAN TESSLER
First Vice President: TANIA EVANS
Second Vice President: MICHAEL CARUSO
Secretary: JOHN KREMER
Treasurer: MIA JENSEN
Executive Director: LESLIE MATTSON
Publication(s): *Land Trust Newsletter*
Keyword(s): Agriculture, Land Preservation, Land Purchase, Open Space, Wildlife and Wildlife Habitat

JACKSON HOLE PRESERVE, NC.
30 Rockefeller Plaza, Rm. 5600, New York, NY 10112
Phone: 212-649-5819
Founded: 1940
Scope: National

Description: Nonprofit, charitable, and educational organization, established to conserve areas of outstanding primitive grandeur and natural beauty and to provide facilities for their use and enjoyment by the public.
Contact(s):
President: GEORGE R. LAMB
Secretary: ANTONIA M. GRUMBACH
Treasurer: CARMEN REYES
Chairman of the Board: LAURANCE S. ROCKEFELLER
Vice Chairman of the Board: CLAYTON W. FRYE JR.

JANE GOODALL INSTITUTE, THE
P.O. Box 14890, Silver Spring, MD 20911
Phone: 301-565-0086/1-800-592-JANE; Fax: 301-565-3188; E-mail: JGIinformation@janegoodall.org; Web Site: www.janegoodall.org
Founded: 1977; Membership: 17,000
Scope: International
Description: The Jane Goodall Institute is an international organization dedicated to the conservation and understanding of wildlife, particularly chimpanzees, and to promoting environmental education, reforestation, and humanitarianism worldwide.
Contact(s):
Executive Director: STEWART HUDSON; E-mail: shudson@janegoodall.org
Director of Communications: CARRIE SCHLUTER; E-mail: jgicommunications@janegoodall.org
Director of Roots and Shoots: JEANNE MCCARTY; E-mail: j.mccarty@janegoodall.org
Deputy Director of Project Development: GARY NORTH; E-mail: GWNJHU@aol.com
Publication(s): *Annual JGI World Report; Semi-annual Roots and Shoots Network; ChimpanZOO Newsletter*
Keyword(s): Reforestation, Wildlife and Wildlife Habitat, Environmental and Humanitarian Education, Animal Welfare, Wildlife Research, Chimpanzees

JAPAN WILDLIFE RESEARCH CENTER (JWRC)
Yushima 2-29-3, Bunkyo-ku, Tokyo 113 Japan
Phone: 81-3-3813-8806; Fax: 81-3-3813-8958; E-mail: mkomoda@jwrc.or.jp
Founded: 1978
Scope: International
Description: JWRC has carried out research works and has accumulated data on nature of Japan and developed techniques for research and management of wildlife and its habitat. JWRC is also trying to contribute to the conservation of nature through fact finding and accumulation of basic data.
Contact(s):
President: YASUYUKI OSHIMA
Executive Director: KAZUHIRO YAMASE
Keyword(s): Wildlife Management, Wildlife Research

JOHN INSKEEP ENVIRONMENTAL LEARNING CENTER
19600 S. Molalla Ave., Oregon City, OR 97045
Phone: 503-657-6958 ext2351; E-mail: elc@clackamas.cc.or.us
Founded: 1972
Scope: Statewide
Description: A source of teacher training and community education on environmental education topics, focusing on urban watershed issues. Located on a restored industrial site featuring buildings made from salvaged and recycled materials.
Contact(s):
Director: JOHN LeCAVALIER
Keyword(s): Environmental and Conservation Education, Recycling, Watersheds

NON-GOVERNMENTAL ORGANIZATIONS - K

K

KANSAS ACADEMY OF SCIENCE
Attn: President, Division of Biological Sciences, Emporia State University, Emporia, KS 66901
Founded: 1868; Membership: 500
Scope: Statewide
Description: A nonprofit organization to increase, diffuse, and promote knowledge in various departments of science; interest young people in science and encourage them to consider science as their profession; aid the improvement of science teaching; and aid in development of the state's economic growth.
Contact(s):
President: KAREN DeBRES, Department of Geography Kansas State University, Manhattan, KS 66506; Phone: 913-532-6727
Secretary: PIETER BERENDSEN, Kansas Geological Survey University of Kansas, Lawrence, KS 66047; Phone: 913-864-4991
Editor: DAN MERRIAM, Kansas Geological Survey University of Kansas, Lawrence, KS 66047; Phone: 913-864-4991
President-Elect: DAVID K. SAUNDERS, Division of Biological Sciences Emporia State University, Emporia, KS 66901; Phone: 316-341-5610
Publication(s): *Transactions of the Kansas Academy of Science*
Keyword(s): Biology, Chemistry, Geography, Geology, Natural History

KANSAS ADVISORY COUNCIL FOR ENVIRONMENTAL EDUCATION
Attn: President, 1005 Merchants Tower, Topeka, KS 66612
Founded: 1969
Scope: Statewide
Description: Organized to promote and support effective environmental education in order to enhance awareness, knowledge, and concern about the environment among the citizens of Kansas. The advisory council is made up of representatives of over 180 public and private organizations, institutions, business organizations, and individuals.
Contact(s):
President and Council Member: CLARK DUFFY, 1005 Merchants Tower, Topeka, KS 66612; Phone: 913-234-0589
Vice President: CAROL WILLIAMSON, 1209 Willow Dr., Olathe, KS 66061; Phone: 913-764-6036
Secretary: CONNIE ELDERS, 455 N. Main 11th Fl., Wichita, KS 67202; Phone: 316-264-8323
Treasurer: RUTH GENNRICH, Museum of Natural History University of Kansas, Lawrence, KS 66045-2454; Phone: 913-864-4173
Publication(s): *KACEE News*

KANSAS ASSOCIATION FOR CONSERVATION AND ENVIRONMENTAL EDUCATION
2610 Claflin Rd., Manhattan, KS 66502-2743
Phone: 785-532-3314; Fax: 785-532-3305; E-mail: jstrick@oz.oznet.ksu.edu
Founded: 1969; Membership: 130 organizations/120 individuals
Scope: Statewide
Description: Kansas Association for Conservation and Environmental Education was organized to promote and support effective conservation and environmental education in Kansas. The Association is made up of over 200 public and private organizations and individuals.
Contact(s):
Assistant Director: LAURA DOWNEY; Phone: 785-532-3322
President: DEE TURNER; Phone: 785-296-1036; Fax: 785-296-6172; E-mail: dturner@scc.state.ks.us
Vice President: CINDY FORD; Phone: 316-235-4728; Fax: 316-235-4194; E-mail: cford@pittstate.edu
Treasurer: CLARK DUFFY; Phone: 785-296-3185; Fax: 785-296-0878
Executive Director: JOHN STRICKLER
Publication(s): *KACEE NEWS; Annual Report; Workshop Brochure*
Keyword(s): Environment, Environmental and Conservation Education

KANSAS ASSOCIATION OF CONSERVATION DISTRICTS
Attn: President, Rt. 1 Box 110, Glen Elder, KS 67446
Scope: Statewide
Contact(s):
President, Alternate Board Member: CARL JORDAN; Phone: 785-545-3361; Fax: 785-545-3659
Vice President: SANDRA JONES, 5160 E Rd 17, Johnson, KS 67855; Phone: 316-492-6495; Fax: 316-492-2772
Executive Director: RICHARD G. JONES, 522 Winn Rd., Salina, KS 67401-3668; Phone: 785-827-5847; Fax: 785-827-7784
Board Member: DON PAXSON, P.O. Box 487, Penokee, KS 67659; Phone: 785-421-2480; Fax: 785-421-5662
Secretary-Treasurer: DON REZAC, 12350 Ranch Rd., Emmett, KS 66422; Phone: 785-535-2961; Fax: 785-457-2868
Keyword(s): Conservation Districts

KANSAS B.A.S.S. CHAPTER FEDERATION
Attn: President, P.O. Box 330, Alba, MO 64830
Scope: Statewide
Description: An organization of Bassmaster chapters, affiliated with the Bass Anglers Sportsman Society, organized to fight pollution, assist state and national conservation agencies in their efforts, and teach the young people of our country good conservation practices. Dedicated to the realistic conservation of our water resources.
Contact(s):
President: JON STEWART; Phone: 417-525-4940
Conservation Director: KIM HUEY, 9914 North Plum, Hutchinson, KS 67502; Phone: 316-662-1638

KANSAS HERPETOLOGICAL SOCIETY
University of Kansas Natural History Museum, Dyche Hall, Lawrence, KS 66045
Founded: 1974; Membership: 250
Scope: Statewide
Description: The Kansas Herpetological Society is a nonprofit organization designed to encourage education and dissemination of scientific information through the facilities of the Society; and to encourage conservation of wildlife in general and of amphibians and reptiles in Kansas in particular.
Contact(s):
Editor: ERIC RUNDQUIST, Animal Care Unit, B054 Malott, University of Kansas, Lawrence, KS 66045
Treasurer: KAREN TOEPFER, 303 W. 39th St., Hays, KS 67601; Phone: 785-628-1437
Publication(s): *Kansas Herpetological Society Newsletter*
Keyword(s): Ecology, Environmental and Conservation Education, Natural History, Nongame Wildlife, Reptiles and Amphibians

KANSAS NATURAL RESOURCE COUNCIL
P.O. Box 2635, Topeka, KS 66601
WWW: http://home.kscable.com/levelspace/KNRC.htm
Founded: 1981; Membership: 500
Scope: Statewide
Description: Environmental advocacy including public education, lobbying, and litigation.
Contact(s):
President: JOAN VIBERT, 1981 Indiana, Ottawa, KS 66067; Phone: 785-746-8885; E-mail: windwalker@computer.services.com
Director: CHARLES BENJAMIN, 401 Boulder St., Lawrence, KS 66049; Phone: 785-841-5902; E-mail: knrcsierra@cjnetworks.com
Publication(s): *KNRC Journal; Weekly Legislative Updates*
Keyword(s): Agriculture, Energy, Environmental Legislation, Prairies, Rivers, Water Resources

KANSAS ORNITHOLOGICAL SOCIETY
Attn: President, P.O. Box 395, Wilson, KS 67490
Founded: 1949; Membership: 430
Scope: Statewide
Description: Formed to promote the study of ornithology, to advance the members in ornithological science, to promote conservation, and the appreciation of birds by the general public.

Contact(s):
President: GREG FARLEY, Ft. Hays State University, Hays, KS 67601; Phone: 785-628-5965
Vice President: JOHN SCHUKMAN, 14207 Robin Rd., Leavenworth, KS 66048; Phone: 913-727-5141
Treasurer: EDWIN MILLER, 218 Bermuda Dr., Independence, KS 67301; Phone: 316-331-6295
Business Manager: JAMES BARNES, 1425 S. Wichita St., Wichita, KS 67213; Phone: 316-265-4059
Corresponding Secretary: KAREN GANOUNG, 2 NW 120th Rd., Hoisington, KS 67544; Phone: 316-653-2123
Editor: CHUCK OTTE, 613 Tamerisk, Junction City, KS 66441-3359; Phone: 785-238-8800
Editor: MAX C. THOMPSON, 1729 East 11th St., Winfield, KS 67156; Phone: 316-221-1856
Membership Coordinator: SUSAN BARNES, 1425 S. Wichita St., Wichita, KS 67213; Phone: 316-265-4059
Publication(s): *K.O.S. Bulletin; Horned Lark, The*
Keyword(s): Birds, Endangered and Threatened Species, Environmental and Conservation Education, Raptors, Wildlife and Wildlife Habitat

KANSAS WILDFLOWER SOCIETY
R.L. McGregor Herbarium, 2045 Constant Ave., Lawrence, KS 66047-3729
Phone: 785-864-3453; Fax: 785-864-5093
Founded: 1978; Membership: 300
Scope: Statewide
Description: The Society provides educational materials and sponsors activities to promote the conservation and cultivation of the native plants of Kansas.
Contact(s):
President: DWIGHT R. PLATT; Phone: 316-283-2500; Fax: 316-284-5286
Secretary: CYNTHIA FORD; Phone: 316-235-4726
Treasurer: SISTER PATRICIA M. STANLEY; Phone: 316-689-4070; E-mail: wichitacsj@feist.com
Agent: CRAIG C. FREEMAN
Publication(s): *KWS Newsletter*
Keyword(s): Conservation, Flowers, Plants, and Trees, Prairies, Native Plants

KANSAS WILDLIFE FEDERATION
4840 W. 15th St., Lawrence, KS 66049
Phone: 785-843-7786; Fax: 785-843-7555; E-mail: KWF@kswildlife.org; Web Site: www.kswildlife.org
Scope: Statewide
Description: A representative statewide organization, affiliated with the National Wildlife Federation, dedicated to the protection and enhancement of wildlife and its habitat through public education and government interaction.
Contact(s):
President and Representative: STEVEN SORENSEN
Editor: STEVE MILANO
Alternate Representative: CARL SORENSEN

KANSAS WILDSCAPE FOUNDATION
P.O. Box 4029, Lawrence, KS 66046
Phone: 785-843-9453; Fax: 785-843-6379; E-mail: kansaswild@aol.com
Founded: 1991; Membership: 650
Scope: Statewide
Description: The Kansas Wildscape Foundation is dedicated to conserving and perpetuating the land, wild species, and the rich beauty of Kansas for the use and enjoyment of all. Wildscape is a public/private partnership with the Kansas Department of Wildlife and Parks.
Contact(s):
President: JIM HUNTINGTON
Vice President: GENE ARGO, Midwest Energy, Inc., 1330 Canterbury Rd., Hays, KS 67601; Phone: 785-625-1402
Vice President: BILL HAWES, RR #2, Box 210, Smith Center, KS 66967
Vice President: ROBERT L. RING, P.O. Box 4067, Wichita, KS 67204; Phone: 316-838-9093
Secretary: BOB BEACHY, P.O. Box 134446, Kansas City, MO 64199-3446
Treasurer: CHARLIE BECKER, 1321 Wakarusa Dr., Lawrence, KS 66049
Executive Director: HARLAND PRIDDLE
Director of Member Services and Administration: JENEE ROSS ARMBRISTER
Keyword(s): Land Preservation, Wetlands, Wildlife and Wildlife Habitat, Youth Organizations

KEEP AMERICA BEAUTIFUL, INC.
1010 Washington Blvd., 7th Fl., Stamford, CT 06901
Phone: 203-323-8987
Founded: 1953
Scope: National
Description: A national nonprofit public education organization dedicated to litter prevention and improved waste handling practices in American communities. Keep America Beautiful trains and certifies communities into the Keep America Beautiful System, a behavior-based approach to improved waste handling.
Contact(s):
President: G. RAYMOND EMPSON
Chairman of the Board: MELINDA M. SWEET
Senior Vice President of Development and Environmental Programming: SUSANNE WOODS
Vice Chairman of the Board: JOHN F. BARD
Publication(s): *Network News*
Keyword(s): Communications, Environmental and Conservation Education, Environmental Preservation, Public Lands, Solid Waste Management

KEEP FLORIDA BEAUTIFUL, INC.
2615 N. Monroe St., Suite 200, Tallahassee, FL 32303-4027
Phone: 850-385-1528; Fax: 850-385-4020; Web Site: www.keepflbeautiful.org
Founded: 1991
Scope: Statewide
Description: KFB's mission is to empower individuals to take greater responsibility for their community environment.
Contact(s):
Executive Director: FRANK WALPER
Chairman, Board of Directors: CHARLES O. HINSON III
Keyword(s): Aquatic Habitats, Communications, Environmental Preservation, Renewable Resources, Solid Waste Management

KENTUCKY ACADEMY OF SCIENCE
Attn: President, Dept. of Biology, Campbellsville University, Campbelsville, KY 42718
Founded: 1914; Membership: 612
Scope: Statewide
Description: To encourage scientific research, promote the diffusion of scientific knowledge, and unify the scientific interests of Kentucky.
Contact(s):
President: GORDON K. WEDDLE, Dept. of Biology, Campbellsville University, Campbellsville, KY 42718; Phone: 270-789-5238; Fax: 270-789-5170
President-Elect: BLAINE FERRELL, Dept. of Biology, Western Kentucky University, Bowling Green, KY 42101; Phone: 270-745-5999
Vice President: RON ROSEN, Dept. of Biology, Berea College, Berea, KY 40403; Phone: 606-986-9341, ext. 6318; Fax: 606-986-4506
Secretary: STEPHANIE DEW, Dept. of Biology, Centre College, Danville, KY 40422; Phone: 606-238-5316
Treasurer: WILLIAM E. HOUSTON, Dept. of Biology, Western Kentucky University, Bowling Green, KY 42103; Phone: 270-745-2031; Fax: 502-745-6471
Editor: JOHN W. THIERET, Dept. of Biological Sciences, Northern Kentucky University, Highland Heights, KY 41099; Phone: 606-572-6390; Fax: 606-572-5639

Publication(s): *Journal of the Kentucky Academy of Science*
Keyword(s): Research

KENTUCKY ASSOCIATION FOR ENVIRONMENTAL EDUCATION (KAEE)
Blackacre Nature Preserve, 3200 Tucker Station Rd., Jeffersontown, KY 40299
Phone: 502-473-3437
Scope: Statewide
Description: Organized to promote and support formal and nonformal environmental education programs throughout the state. Promotes information sharing, research, and development of EE programs and activities. Annually sponsors a three-day conference.
Contact(s):
President: DR. JOE BAUST, Center for Environmental Education, Murray State University, Murray, KY 42071; Phone: 270-762-2595; E-mail: joe.baust@coe.murraystate.edu
Executive Director: KAREN P. REAGOR, P.O. Box 176055, Covington, KY 41017; Phone: 606-578-0312; E-mail: KPReagor@aol.com
Publication(s): *Newsletter; E.E. Resource Guide; Earth Day Handbook*
Keyword(s): Environmental and Conservation Education

KENTUCKY ASSOCIATION OF CONSERVATION DISTRICTS
Attn: President, 1299 Lillies Ferry Rd., Winchester, KY 40391
Scope: Statewide
Contact(s):
President, Alternate Board Member: JOHN E. CHISM; Phone: 606-744-8909; Fax: 502-564-9195
Vice President: PATRICK M. HENDERSON, Rt. 1 Box 146, Irvington, KY 40146; Phone: 502-547-6206; Fax: 502-564-9195
Board Member: JAMES LACY, 300 Sanfield Rd., Campton, KY 41301; Phone: 606-662-4161; Fax: 606-668-7033
Secretary-Treasurer: KEVIN JEFFRIES, 1503 E. Hwy. 22, Crestwood, KY 40014; Phone: 502-222-9877; Fax: 502-222-0046
Keyword(s): Conservation Districts

KENTUCKY AUDUBON COUNCIL
Attn: President, 16509 Bradbe Rd., Fisherville, KY 40023
Founded: 1971
Scope: Statewide
Description: A statewide Audubon Council for the seven key chapters of the National Audubon Society. Works to promote, foster, and encourage the conservation and preservation of all wildlife, plants, soils, water, air, and other natural resources for the benefit of all people.
Contact(s):
President: JEFF FRANK, 16509 Bradbe Rd., Fisherville, KY 40023; Phone: 502-266-7181
Vice President: JOAN NOEL, 645 Foxfire Dr., Elizabethtown, KY 42701
Secretary: MAGGIE SELVIDGE, 904 North Dr., Hopkinsville, KY 42240; Phone: 502-886-8078
Treasurer: BERTHA M. TIMMEL, 3604 Graham Rd., Louisville, KY 40207; Phone: 502-893-5601

KENTUCKY B.A.S.S. CHAPTER FEDERATION
Attn: President, 562 N. Saint Gregory Church, Coxs Creek, KY 40013
Scope: Statewide
Description: An organization of Bassmaster chapters, affiliated with the Bass Anglers Sportsman Society, organized to fight pollution, assist state and national conservation agencies in their efforts, and teach the young people of our country good conservation practices. Dedicated to the realistic conservation of our water resources.
Contact(s):
President: STEVEN TAYLOR; Phone: 502-331-9656

KENTUCKY RESOURCES COUNCIL
P.O. Box 1070, Frankfort, KY 40602
Phone: 502-875-2428; Fax: 502-875-2845; E-mail: fitzkrc@aol.com
Scope: Statewide
Description: The KRC is a nonprofit, membership-based statewide organization dedicated to the conservation and prudent use of Kentucky's natural resources. The Council is comprised of Kentuckians from all walks of life: Urban dwellers and rural residents, farmers, river recreationists, and conservationists. This broad-based membership shares a common concern with the impact of mineral extraction, natural resource development, and economic development on our homes, health, and quality of life.
Contact(s):
Director: TOM FITZGERALD
Keyword(s): Environmental Law, Environmental Protection, Toxic Substances, Water Pollution Management

KENTUCKY WOODLAND OWNERS ASSOCIATION
3395 Upper Tug Fork Rd., Alexandria, KY 41001
Phone: 606-635-7826
Founded: 1991; Membership: 350
Scope: Statewide
Description: A statewide nonprofit organization, affiliated with the National Woodland Owners Association, organized to promote good forest stewardship, circulate information on timber marketing, and encourage private property responsibility among woodland owners throughout the Commonwealth of Kentucky.
Contact(s):
President and Editor: DON GIRTON
Secretary: PASCHAL PHILLIPS
Treasurer: HERB LLOYD
Publication(s): *Kentucky Woodlands*
Keyword(s): Forests and Forestry

KENTUCKY-TENNESSEE SOCIETY OF AMERICAN FORESTERS
1080 Iroquois Dr., Mt. Sterling, KY 40353
Scope: Statewide
Description: K-T SAF is the Kentucky-Tennessee section of the Society of American Foresters, and carries out the policies and programs of SAF within these two states. See the Society of American Foresters listing for more information.
Contact(s):
Chair: RICK WILCOX; Phone: 606-745-3156
Chair-Elect: DAVE WALTERS, 6209 Foothills Dr., Mufreesboro, TN 37129; Phone: 615-837-5470
Secretary and Treasurer: GRANT CURRY, 610 Trus Joist Lane, Chavies, KY 41727; Phone: 606-436-8787; E-mail: -
Publication(s): *KT-SAF Newsletter*
Keyword(s): Environmental Planning, Renewable Resources, Urban Forestry

KEYSTONE CENTER, THE
1628 Saints John Rd., Keystone, CO 80435
Phone: 970-513-5800; Fax: 970-262-0152; Web Site: www.keystone.org
Founded: 1975
Scope: National
Description: A nonprofit center for environmental dispute resolution, mediation, and facilitation. Conducts national policy dialogues on environmental, energy, natural resources, health, and science/technology issues; assists in environmental decision making and regulatory negotiations; provides environmental mediation services; provides training and organizational development services in environmental conflict resolution.
Contact(s):
Chairman: PAUL TEBO
President: KATHY PROSSER
Publication(s): *Consensus; Discovery*
Keyword(s): Biotechnology, Energy, Environmental and Conservation Education, Health and Nutrition, Natural Resource Conservation

KIDS FOR SAVING EARTH WORLDWIDE
P.O. Box 421118, Minneapolis, MN 55442
Phone: 612-559-1234; Fax: 612-559-6980; E-mail: kseww@aol.com; Web Site: www.kidsforsavingearth.org/
Founded: 1989

Scope: National
Description: KSEW's mission is to educate and empower children to help to protect the Earth's environment by providing free educational materials to kids, schools, and organizations through the KSE Network. Curriculum guides are also available.
Contact(s):
President and Director: TESSA HILL
Publication(s): *List available upon request.*
Keyword(s): Air Quality and Pollution, Aquatic Habitats, Conservation of Protected Areas, Endangered and Threatened Species, Energy Conservation, Environment, Environmental and Conservation Education, Environmental Preservation, Environmental Protection, Flowers, Plants, and Trees, International Conservation, Land Preservation, Nature Preservation, Pollution Prevention, Youth Organizations

KODIAK BROWN BEAR TRUST
11930 Circle Dr., Anchorage, AK 99516
Phone: 907-345-2939
Founded: 1981
Scope: National
Description: The Kodiak Brown Bear Trust is an Alaska-based nonprofit wildlife conservation trust whose mission is to support conservation of the majestic Kodiak brown bear through funding of habitat protection, research and public education.
Contact(s):
Chairman: DAVE CLINE
Executive Director: TIM RICHARDSON, 6707 Old Stage Rd., North Bethesda, MD 20852-4329; Phone: 301-770-6496
Keyword(s): Research, Wildlife and Wildlife Habitat, Wildlife Protection

L

LADY BIRD JOHNSON WILDFLOWER CENTER
4801 La Crosse Ave., Austin, TX 78739
Phone: 512-292-4200; Web Site:
Founded: 1982; Membership: 19,000
Scope: National
Description: The Lady Bird Johnson Wildflower Center's purpose is to educate people about the environmental necessity, economic value, and natural beauty of native plants. The Wildflower Center, a nonprofit organization, serves North America by promoting the preservation and use of native plants through education programs, information dissemination, and by example.
Contact(s):
Communications Director: KAREN BASSETT
Executive Directory: ROBERT G. BREUNIG Ph.D.
Founders: LADY BIRD JOHNSON and HELEN HAYES
Public Programs Manager and Senior Botanist: FLO OXLEY
Senior Horticulturist: DENISE DELANEY
Publication(s): *Native Plants magazine*
Keyword(s): Endangered and Threatened Species, Environmental and Conservation Education, Flowers, Plants, and Trees, Landscape Architecture, Trees, Wildflowers

LAKE ERIE CLEAN-UP COMMITTEE, INC.
Attn: President, 29789 Fort Rd., Rockwood, MI 48173
Founded: 1959
Scope: National
Description: The LECC's mission is to stop pollution of Lake Erie and of all freshwater lakes and streams; to inform the public of the need for greater pollution controls; to prevent the return to the methods of the past; and to encourage industry to do more research. Our Great Lakes are a fragile part of our ecosystem and we must continue to protect them. Membership includes representatives of Michigan and Ohio citizen groups.
Contact(s):
President: LEONARD MANNAUSA, 29789 Fort Rd., Rockwood, MI 48173; Phone: 313-379-3891
Secretary: RICHARD G. MICKA, 47 E. Elm, Monroe, MI 48162; Phone: 313-242-0909
Treasurer: JEROME C. FALWELL, 30251 Worth, Gibraltor, MI 48173
Keyword(s): Coasts, Remedial Action Plans, Water Pollution Management, Water Resources, Waterfowl, Wetlands

LAKE MICHIGAN FEDERATION
220 S. State St., Suite 2108, Chicago, IL 60604
Phone: 312-939-0838; Fax: 312-939-2708; E-mail: lmf001@aol.com; Web Site: www.lakemichigan.org
Founded: 1970
Scope: National
Description: A coalition of citizens and citizen organizations in Wisconsin, Illinois, Indiana, and Michigan dedicated to protecting Lake Michigan through community action and research. Supported by foundation and corporate grants, membership and contributions.
Contact(s):
Treasurer: ARTHUR MARTIN
Executive Director: CAMERON DAVIS
Board of Directors President: ELLEN PARTRIDGE
Publication(s): *Lake Michigan Monitor; A Citizen's Action Guide; A Citizen's Guide to Cleaning Up Contaminated Sediments (book); Wetlands and Water Quality: A Citizen's Guide.*
Keyword(s): EcoAction, Environment, Habitat Conservation, Lakes, Pollution Prevention, Protecting Special Places, Water Pollution, Watersheds

LAKE SUPERIOR GREENS
P.O. Box 1144, Superior, WI 54880
Phone: 715-392-5782; Fax: 715-394-6856
Founded: 1991; Membership: 100
Scope: National
Description: Lake Superior Greens is a grassroots group joined to other Green groups in our dedication to a more sustainable lifestyle and a healthy planet. We are active locally as well as on a state, national, and international basis, recognizing that all issues are interrelated.
Contact(s):
Contact: ROSIE SEYMOUR, 1606 N. 18th St., Superior, WI 54880; Phone: 715-395-0494
Contact: JOHN SCHRAUFNAGEL, 1506 N. 19th, Superior, WI 54880; Phone: 715-394-6660
Contact: BOB BROWNE, 422 Fisher Ogden, Superior, WI 54880; Phone: 715-394-6235
Steering Committee: JAN CONLEY, 2406 Hughitt, Superior, WI 54880; Phone: 715-392-5782
Publication(s): *monthly newsletter*
Keyword(s): Pesticides, Sustainability, Toxic Substances, Water Quality, Wetlands

LAND BETWEEN THE LAKES ASSOCIATION
Land Between The Lakes, 100 Van Morgan Dr., Golden Pond, KY 42211-9001
Phone: 502-924-2088
Founded: 1983; Membership: 3,000
Scope: National
Description: A private nonprofit membership organization supporting and promoting Tennessee Valley Authority's Land Between The Lakes, a 170,000-acre national demonstration in natural resource management, environmental education, and recreation.
Contact(s):
Chairman: AUSTIN CARROLL, General Manager, Hopkinsville Electric System, P.O. Box 544, Hopkinsville, KY 42240; Phone: 502-887-4210
President: CHARLES MATHENY
Director: GAYE LUBER
Keyword(s): Cultural Preservation, Environmental and Conservation Education, Lakes, Natural Areas, Prairies, Public Lands

LAND TRUST ALLIANCE, THE
1319 F St., NW, Suite 501, Washington, DC 20004
Phone: 202-638-4725; Fax: 202-638-4730; Web Site: www.lta.org

NON-GOVERNMENTAL ORGANIZATIONS - L

Founded: 1982; Membership: 2,100
Scope: National
Description: Provides training, technical assistance and publications for local and regional land trusts to increase their skills and strengthen the land trust movement; fosters public policies that further land trusts' goals; sponsors the National Land Trust Rally; and builds awareness among a broad constituency of the consequences of diminishing land resources and the role of land trusts in saving land.
Contact(s):
Chairman: JAMES J. ESPY
President: JEAN W. HOCKER
Vice-President for Programs: ANDREW ZEPP
Secretary: CONSTANCE BEST
Treasurer: DAVID HARTWELL
Vice-Chair: JOHN TURNER
Vice-President of Development: JOHN CHAPPELL
Vice-President of Operations: PHIL JONES
Publication(s): *Exchange; Conservation Easement Handbook; Appraising Easements; Federal Tax Law of Conservation Easements; Starting a Land Trust; National Directory of Conservation Land Trusts; Conservation Easement Stewardship Guide*
Keyword(s): Conservation Easements, Environmental and Conservation Education, Environmental Law, Environmental Preservation, Land Conservation, Land Protection, Land Purchase, Land Use Planning

LAND WATCH MONTEREY COUNTY
Box 908, Monterey, CA 93942
Phone: 831-375-3752; Fax: 831-375-8466; E-mail: LANDWATCH@MCLW.ORG; Web Site: www.LANDWATCH.ORG
Founded: 1997; Membership: 800
Scope: Regional
Description: Land Watch is committed to fundamental land use reform and works to build public support for better land use policies at the local, regional, and state level.
Contact(s):
Executive Director: GARY A. PATTON; Phone: 831-375-7396; E-mail: GAPATTON@MCLW.ORG
Publication(s): *State of Monterey County; Update*
Keyword(s): Environment, Environmental and Conservation Education, Environmental Planning, Environmental Preservation, Environmental Protection, Land Management, Land Preservation, Land Protection, Land Use Planning, Protecting Special Places, Transportation, Urban Environment

LEAGUE OF CONSERVATION VOTERS
1920 L St., NW, Suite 800, Washington, DC 20036
Phone: 202-785-8683; Fax: 202-835-0491; E-mail: lcv@lcv.org; Web Site: www.lcv.org
Founded: 1970; Membership: 25,000
Scope: National
Description: The LCV is the national, bipartisan political action arm of the environmental movement. LCV works to elect pro-environment candidates to Congress; publishes the National Environmental Scorecard, which rates members of Congress on key environmental votes; raises funds for campaigns through its Political Action Committee and Earthlist; and is governed by a Board of Directors made up of leaders from major national environmental organizations.
Contact(s):
Chair: THEODORE ROOSEVELT IV
President: DEB CALLAHAN
Secretary: WADE GREENE
Treasurer: WINSOME McINTOSH
Executive Director, Educational Fund: BETH SULLIVAN
Chief Financial Officer: ANNE SAER
Publication(s): *National Environmental Scorecard; Presidential Scorecard; LCV Insider Newsletter.*
Keyword(s): Conservation, Politics and Government

LEAGUE OF ENVIRONMENTAL JOURNALISTS
P.O. Box 1062, Accra Ghana
Phone: 233-21-221--849; Fax: 233-21-310-028; E-mail: lejcec@ghana.com
Founded: 1991
Scope: International
Description: To mobilize journalists and the mass media for the affective and meaningful coverage of the environment.
Contact(s):
President: MIKE ANANA
Vice President: ISABELLA GYAN
Treasurer: ELLIOT O. ANSAH
Publication(s): *Covering the Environment, A Guide Book on the Environmental Journalism in developing countries*
Keyword(s): Biodiversity, Conservation of Protected Areas, Dams, Developing Countries, Endangered and Threatened Species, Environmental and Conservation Education, International Trade and Environment, Sustainable Energy, Waste Management

LEAGUE OF KENTUCKY SPORTSMEN, INC.
P.O. Box 406, Ft. Thomas, KY 41001
Phone: 606-635-8896; Fax: 606-635-8896; E-mail: ksportsmen@hotmail.com; Web Site: www.loks.org
Scope: Statewide
Description: A representative statewide organization, affiliated with the National Wildlife Federation, dedicated to the protection and enhancement of wildlife and its habitat through public education and government interaction.
Contact(s):
President and Alternative Representative: FRED KIRSCH
Representative: LINDA SAUNDERS
Publication(s): *Kentucky Sportsman, The*

LEAGUE OF OHIO SPORTSMEN
3953 Indianola Ave., Columbus, OH 43214
Phone: 614-268-9924
Scope: Statewide
Description: A representative statewide organization, affiliated with the National Wildlife Federation, dedicated to the protection and enhancement of wildlife and its habitat through public education and government interaction.
Contact(s):
President: DON SEEDORF
Representative: MARILYN M. LIEB
Alternate Representative: GEORGE LYNCH

LEAGUE OF WOMEN VOTERS OF IOWA
P.O. Box 93775, Des Moines, IA 50393-3775
Founded: 1920; Membership: 750
Scope: Statewide
Description: A nonpartisan organization of local chapters and members-at-large, affiliated with the League of Women Voters of the U.S., whose purpose is to promote political responsibility through informed and active participation of citizens in government and to act on selected governmental issues. We promote and support management, preservation, and conservation of our natural resources.
Contact(s):
President: GAIL QUINN; Phone: 515-684-8094
Vice President: MYRNA LOEHRLEIN; Phone: 319-365-3199
Environmental Coordinator: JUDIE HOFFMAN; Phone: 515-292-2660
Publication(s): *Iowa Voter; Legislative Newsletter*
Keyword(s): Air Quality and Pollution, Chemical Pollution Control, Energy Conservation, Environmental Protection, Land Use Planning, Pollution Prevention, Soil Conservation, Solid Waste Management, Water Quality, Politics and Government

LEAGUE OF WOMEN VOTERS OF THE U.S.
1730 M St. NW, Washington, DC 20036
Phone: 202-429-1965; Fax: 202-429-0854
Founded: 1920; Membership: 100,000
Scope: National

Description: Nonpartisan organization of 100,000 members located in all 50 states, the District of Columbia, Hong Kong, and the Virgin Islands, working to promote political responsibility through informed and active participation of citizens in government. Takes political action on water and air quality, solid and hazardous waste management, land use, and energy. The League of Women Voters Education Fund carries out educational projects, publishes materials, and arranges conferences on water and energy issues.
Contact(s):
President: CAROLYN JEFFERSON JENKINS
Executive Director: JANE GRUENEBAUM
Editor: MONICA SULLIVAN
Program Manager of Water Resources: ELANA COHEN
Program Manager, Energy Resources: SHARON LLOYD-O'CONNOR
Publication(s): *National Voter, The*
Keyword(s): Communications, Energy, Environmental and Conservation Education, Water Resources

LEAGUE OF WOMEN VOTERS OF WASHINGTON
1411 4th Ave., Bldg., #803, Seattle, WA Phone: 206-622-8961
Membership: 2,218
Scope: Statewide
Description: The League of Women Voters is a nonpartisan political organization that encourages the informed and active participation of citizens in government and influences public policy through education and advocacy. Any citizen over 18 may become a voting member.
Contact(s):
President: ELIZABETH PIERINI
Vice President: KAREN DURHAM
Vice President: JEAN WELLS
Secretary: BETSY GREENE
Treasurer: MYRA HOWREY
Publication(s): *The State We're In; Washington; Targeting Tomorrow - Washington's Economy Adjusts to the 90's; Speaking of Ground Water; Washington State Public Port Districts; Public Assistance as Social Policy; Higher Education in Washington State; Gun Control in Washington; Direct Democracy: The Initiative/Referendum Process in Washington State; Washington's Dynamic Forests*
Keyword(s): Forests and Forestry, Outdoor Recreation, Public Lands, Rivers, Wildlife and Wildlife Habitat

LEAGUE TO SAVE LAKE TAHOE
955 Emerald Bay Rd., South Lake Tahoe, CA 96150
Phone: 530-541-5388; Web Site: www.KeepTahoeBlue.com
Founded: 1957; Membership: 4,800
Scope: National
Description: A private, nonprofit corporation dedicated to preserving the environmental balance, scenic beauty, and recreational opportunities of the Lake Tahoe Basin.
Contact(s):
President: WILLIAM A. CALLENDER
Vice President: ADOLPHUS ANDREWS JR.
Vice President: CHARLES MCLEOD
Vice President: TOM MERTENS
Secretary: STEFFI MOOERS
Treasurer: WILLIAM R. MARKEN, 680 Milverton Rd., Los Altos, CA 94022
Executive Director: ROCHELLE NASON
Publication(s): *Keep Tahoe Blue*
Keyword(s): Environmental and Conservation Education, Environmental Preservation, Lakes, Land Use Planning, Water Pollution

LEARNING FOR ENVIRONMENTAL ACTION PROGRAMME (LEAP)
OISE/UT, Rm. 7-184, 252 Bloor St. W., Toronto, Ontario M5S 1V6
Phone: 416-923-6641, ext. 2367; Fax: 416-926-4749
Founded: 1990
Scope: International
Description: LEAP is an international program that develops and supports environmental adult education through research, community programs, workshops, seminars and policy work.
Contact(s):
International Coordinator: DARLENE CLOVER; E-mail: dclover@oise.utoronto.ca
Publication(s): *Case Studies in Environmental Adult and Popular Education; The Nature of Transformation: Environmental Adult and Popular Education; Pachamara (International Newsletter)*
Keyword(s): Environmental and Conservation Education, Environmental Justice, Environmental Literacy, Networking, Overconsumption, Public Participation, Research, Women in the Environment, Environmental Communication, Education

LEGACY INTERNATIONAL
1020 Legacy Drive, Bedford, VA 24523
WWW: www.legacyintl.org
Founded: 1979
Scope: National
Description: Legacy International is a nonprofit, private voluntary organization serving public and private organizations facing the need to manage change. Legacy's expertise and experience bring about practical designs. Creative and innovative projects use interdisciplinary teams, extended networks, public and private partnerships, and citizen exchanges. Legacy has achieved international recognition for its accomplishments in environmentally sound development, conflict resolution, curriculum design, and leadership training.
Contact(s):
President: J. E. RASH, Rt. 4 Box 265, Bedford, VA 24523; Phone: 703-297-5982
Executive Director: DR. IRA KAUFMAN, 128 N. Fayette St., Alexandria, VA 22314; Phone: 703-549-3630
Publication(s): *Legacy World*
Keyword(s): Environmental and Conservation Education, Environmental Planning, Planning Management, Sustainable Development, Youth Organizations

LEGAL ENVIRONMENTAL ASSISTANCE FOUNDATION INC. (LEAF)
1114 Thomasville Rd., Suite E, Tallahassee, FL 32303-6290
Phone: 850-681-2591; E-mail: leaf@lewisweb.net; Web Site: www.lewisweb.net/leaf
Founded: 1979
Scope: National
Description: LEAF is a charitable public-interest environmental law firm that protects human health from pollution. We provide legal and technical assistance to citizens and grassroots organizations in Florida, Georgia, and Alabama. LEAF is a membership organization and provides assistance and services free of charge.
Contact(s):
Chairman: LARRY THOMPSON
President: B. SUZI RUHL
Vice President: DAVID LUDDER
Vice President: CYNTHIA VALENCIC
Secretary: VICTOR JOHNSON
Treasurer: ROBERT WEBB
Publication(s): *LEAF BRIEFS; various educational documents. Citizens may write for a publications list.*
Keyword(s): Energy, Energy Conservation, Environmental Justice, Environmental Law, Environmental Protection, Pesticides, Pollution Prevention, Rivers, Solar Energy, Water Pollution

LIFE OF THE LAND
76 North King St., Suite 203, Honolulu, HI 96817
Phone: 808-533-3454; Fax: 808-533-0993
Membership: 1,000
Scope: Statewide
Description: To preserve and protect the life of the land through promoting sustainable energy and land use policies and to promote open government through research, education, advocacy and, when necessary, litigation.

NON-GOVERNMENTAL ORGANIZATIONS - L

Contact(s):
President: GUY NAKAMOTO
Vice President: ART MORI
Administrator: HENRY Q CURTIS
Keyword(s): Land Use Planning, Sustainable Energy

LIGHTHAWK
The Presidio of San Francisco, PO Box 29231, San Francisco, CA 94129-0231
Phone: 415-561-6250; Fax: 415-561-6251; E-mail: sfo@lighthawk.org; Web Site: www.lighthawk.org
Founded: 1979
Scope: International
Description: LightHawk's mission is to use aerial education and advocacy, harnessing the power of flight, to defend the environment. LightHawk's staff and volunteer pilots conduct aerial missions with key decision-makers, media representatives, community leaders and conservation groups, illuminating critical environmental concerns by flying over and into lands otherwise inaccessible. LightHawk operates regional programs in the Pacific Northwest, British Columbia, California, the Rocky Mountains, Mexico and Central America.
Contact(s):
President: JOHN WYLDE
Secretary: SUSAN JORDAN
Treasurer: MICHAEL AZEEZ
Executive Director (Acting): LES WELSH
Publication(s): *Lighthawk Newsletter; Intercom; Air*
Keyword(s): Ancient Forests, Aquatic Habitats, Biodiversity, Birds, Coasts, Conservation of Protected Areas, Endangered and Threatened Species, Environment, Environmental and Conservation Education, Environmental Planning, Environmental Preservation, Environmental Protection, Forest Management, Geography

Northern Rocky Mountain Field Office
31845 Frontage Rd., Bozeman, MT 59715
Phone: 406-586-8572; Fax: 406-585-7835; E-mail: sarahd@lighthawk.org
Scope: Regional
Contact(s):
Program Coordinator: SARAH DEOPSCINE
Currents

Northwest Field Office
2915 E. Madison St., Suite 306, Seattle, WA 98112
Phone: 206-860-2832; Fax: 206-860-2836; E-mail: jennyl@lighthawk.org
Scope: Regional
Contact(s):
Director of Flight Operations: KEMP HIATT
Executive Director (Acting): LES WELSH
NW Regional Director: AMY SCHLACHTENHAUFEN

Southern Rocky Mountain Field Office
303 Unit F AABC, Aspen, CO 81611
Phone: 970-925-6987; Fax: 970-925-2701; E-mail: micheleg@lighthawk.org
Scope: Regional
Contact(s):
Associate Executive Director: BRUCE GORDON

LONG LIVE THE KINGS
19435 184th Pl., NE, Woodinville, WA 98072
Phone: 206-788-6023
Founded: 1985
Scope: Regional
Description: To rebuild wild salmon populations in specific Northwest Rivers and to enhance their habitat. We are supported by foundations, corporations, individuals, Indian tribes, and fishing and environmental organizations. We are not a membership group.
Contact(s):
Executive Director: JOHN A. SAYRE
Chairman of the Board: JIM YOUNGREN
Publication(s): *Long Live the Kings Newsletter*

Keyword(s): Aquatic Habitats, Endangered and Threatened Species, Fisheries, Rivers, Water Resources

LOUISIANA ASSOCIATION OF CONSERVATION DISTRICTS
Attn: President, 663 Holmes Rd., Keatchie, LA 71046
Scope: Statewide
Contact(s):
President: JERRY HOLMES, 663 Holmes Rd., Keatchie, LA 71046; Phone: 318-933-5375; Fax: 318-872-3178
Boad Member: JOHN COMPTON, 6267 Moss Side Ln., Baton Rouge, LA 70808; Phone: 225-766-7979
Secretary/Treasurer and Board Member: CHARLES DUPUY, 313 N. Monroe St, Ste #4, Marksville, LA 71351; Phone: 318-253-7603; Fax: 318-253-8890
Vice-President, Board Member: JOHN WOODWARD, 1902 Savanne Rd., Houma, LA 70360; Phone: 504-879-3528; Fax: 504-876-5267
Keyword(s): Conservation Districts

LOUISIANA AUDUBON COUNCIL
355 Napoleon St., Baton Rouge, LA 70802-5955
Phone: 225-346-8761
Founded: 1989
Scope: Statewide
Description: To implement the Audubon cause in Louisiana on issues of statewide concern; coordinate activities among the Audubon chapters in Louisiana; and advocate on behalf of birds, wildlife and their habitat.
Contact(s):
President: DORIS FALKENHEINER
Vice-President: ESTHER BOYKIN
Secretary: ANDREA MATTISON
Treasurer: CLYDE MATTISON
Keyword(s): Birds, Endangered and Threatened Species, Nongame Wildlife, Wetlands, Wildlife and Wildlife Habitat

LOUISIANA B.A.S.S. CHAPTER FEDERATION
Attn: President, 603 Terri Dr., Luling, LA 70070
Scope: Statewide
Description: An organization of Bassmaster chapters, affiliated with the Bass Anglers Sportsman Society, organized to fight pollution, assist state and national conservation agencies in their efforts, and teach the young people of our country good conservation practices. Dedicated to the realistic conservation of our water resources.
Contact(s):
President: KEVIN GAUBERT; Phone: 504-785-9069
Conservation Director: WILL COURTNEY, 4548 Chelsea Dr., Baton Rouge, LA 70809; Phone: 504-923-1908

LOUISIANA FORESTRY ASSOCIATION
P.O. Drawer 5067, Alexandria, LA 71307
Phone: 318-443-2558
Founded: 1947; Membership: 2,300
Scope: Statewide
Description: Trade-supported association whose purpose is the conservation of the state's forest land and the promotion of the products and services derived therefrom.
Contact(s):
President: DON POWELL
Executive Director: CHARLES A. VANDERSTEEN
1st Vice President: TOM RHODES
2nd Vice President: JOHN BARR
3rd Vice President: ROBIN RICHERSON
Treasurer: FRANK FOOTE
Staff Forester: CLYDE M. TODD
Publication(s): *Forests and People*
Keyword(s): Forests and Forestry, Research, Scholarships and Grants, Training, Wildlife and Wildlife Habitat

LOUISIANA WILDLIFE FEDERATION, INC.
P.O. Box 65239, Baton Rouge, LA 70896-5239
Phone: 504-344-6707; Fax: 504-344-6707; E-mail: lawildfed@aol.com
Scope: Statewide

Description: A representative statewide organization, affiliated with the National Wildlife Federation, dedicated to the protection and enhancement of wildlife and its habitat through public education and government interaction.
Contact(s):
President and Alternative Representative: KATHY WASCOM
Executive Director and Editor: RANDY P. LANCTOT
Representative: EDGAR F. VEILLON
Publication(s): *Louisiana Wildlife Federation*

LOWER MISSISSIPPI RIVER CONSERVATION COMMITTEE
2524 S. Frontage Rd. Suite C, Vicksburg, MS 39180-5269
Phone: 601-629-6602; Fax: 601-636-9541; E-mail: rf4r_lmrcc@fws.gov
Scope: Regional
Description: The Committee provides an organizational structure and forum for coordinating and facilitating cooperative activities involving the natural resources of the Lower Mississippi River. Also encourages sustainable use of Lower Mississippi River natural resources for long-term environmental, social, and economic benefits.
Contact(s):
Chairman: JIM WISE, Water Division, AR Dept. of Environmental Quality, 8001 National Dr., P.O. Box 8913, Little Rock, AR 72219-8913; Phone: 501-682-0744; Fax: 501-682-0910; E-mail: WISE@ADEQ.STATE.AR.US
Coordinator: RON NASSAR, 2524 S. Frontage Rd., Ste. C, Vicksburg, MS 39180-5269; Phone: 601-629-6602
Publication(s): *LMRCC Newsletter, The*
Keyword(s): Fisheries, Land Use Planning, Rivers, Sustainable Ecosystems, Water Quality

LVIV REGIONAL INSTITUTE OF EDUCATION
18A Ohiyenko St., Lviv 79007 Ukraine
Phone: 380-322-724-752; Fax: 380-322-728-073; E-mail: lonmio@lonmio.lviv.ua
Founded: 1992
Scope: Regional
Description: Provides updated scientific and methodological information on different disciplines to the schools of Lviv region as well as postgraduate training for school teachers.
Contact(s):
Senior Researcher: OLEH HARASEWYCH; E-mail: oharasew@lonmio.lviv.ua
Publication(s): *English through Environmental Education*
Keyword(s): Communications, Environmental and Conservation Education, Environmental Ethics, Environmental Living, Outdoor Education, Research Grants, Scholarships and Grants, Sustainability, Water Pollution Management, Environmental Education Curriculum

M

MACBRIDE RAPTOR PROJECT
W.H., KCC, 6301 Kirkwood Blvd., SW, Cedar Rapids, IA 52406
Phone: 319-398-5495
Founded: 1985
Scope: Statewide
Description: The Macbride Raptor Project is devoted to the preservation of Iowa's birds of prey and their natural habitats through rehabilitation of sick or injured raptors, education of the public to the role of raptors in our environment, and research on various aspects of raptor biology.
Contact(s):
Director: JODEANE CANCILLA
Veterinarian: DR. ARLIN KARSTEN
Volunteer Coordinator: KATHY KELLY
Publication(s): *Raptor Review*
Keyword(s): Raptors, Wildlife Rehabilitation

MAGIC
P.O. Box 5894, Stanford, CA 94309
Phone: 650-323-7333; Fax: 650-323-4232; E-mail: magic@ecomagic.org; Web Site: www.ecomagic.org
Founded: 1979; Membership: 200
Scope: Statewide
Description: Magic's programs apply methods and principles of ecology to clarify values, improve health, increase cooperation, and steward the environment. Activities include lectures and seminars about the nature of value; life-planning workshops, swim, run, and hatha yoga instruction; mentoring, community organizing, habitat enhancement, water and land, resource planning; neighborhood design and publishing.
Contact(s):
President: ROBIN BAYER; E-mail: robin@ecomagic.org
Treasurer: DAVID SCHROM; E-mail: david@ecomagic.org
Publication(s): *Oak Regeneration on Stanford Lands; Liveable City; Human Ecology, A Science for Living Well*
Keyword(s): EcoAction, Ecology, Environmental and Conservation Education, Health and Nutrition, Sustainable Ecosystems, Urban Environment, Water Resources, Wildlife and Wildlife Habitat

MAINE ASSOCIATION OF CONSERVATION COMMISSIONS (MACC)
P.O. Box 702, Bath, ME 04330
Founded: 1969; Membership: 80 commissions
Scope: Statewide
Description: A membership organization whose objectives are twofold: to assist Maine municipalities in establishing conservation commissions; to assist the existing 200+ conservation commissions through technical assistance and educational programs.
Contact(s):
President: MIKE CLINE
Executive Director: BOB CUMMINGS
Publication(s): *Grass Roots*
Keyword(s): Environmental and Conservation Education, Environmental Planning, Environmental Protection, Solid Waste, Water Resources

MAINE ASSOCIATION OF CONSERVATION DISTRICTS
Attn: President, 2467 Exeter Rd., Exeter, ME 04435-3107
Scope: Statewide
Contact(s):
President, Alternate Board Member: NEIL CRANE; Phone: 207-379-2641; Fax: 207-379-2644
Vice President: JOHN A. HEMOND, 46 N. Verreill Rd, Minot, ME 04258; Phone: 207-345-5333
Secretary: LARRY MacDONALD, Box 1187, Greenville, ME 04441; Phone: 207-695-2639
Treasurer: FRED HARDY, 879 Weeks Mill Rd., New Sharon, ME 04955; Phone: 207-778-4320
Executive Director: WILLIAM BELL, P.O. Box 228, Augusta, ME 04330; Phone: 207-622-4443; Fax: 207-623-3748; E-mail: newengag@mint.net
Board Member: RAYMOND HARRIS, Rt. 1 Box 8396, Washburn, ME 04786; Phone: 207-764-3217
Keyword(s): Conservation Districts

MAINE AUDUBON SOCIETY
22 Gilsland Farm Rd., P.O. Box 6009, Falmouth, ME 04105
Phone: 207-781-2330; E-mail: maineaudubon@maineaudubon.org; Web Site: www.maineaudubon.org
Founded: 1843; Membership: 6,500
Scope: Statewide
Description: Dedicated to the protection, conservation, and enhancement of Maine's ecosystems through the promotion of individual understanding and actions. Programs focusing on forest conservation, endangered and threatened species protection, wildlife and wildlife habitats, grassroots activism, environmental education, and school curriculum enhancement. Nature day camp, field trip and world tour program, store and 13 sanctuaries.
Contact(s):
Executive Director: THOMAS A. URQUHART
Editor: JOHN LOVELL

Publication(s): *Habitat: Journal of the Maine Audubon*
Keyword(s): Coasts, Endangered and Threatened Species, Environmental and Conservation Education, Forests and Forestry, Natural History

MAINE B.A.S.S. CHAPTER FEDERATION
Attn: President, R.R. 1 Box 332, Hollis Center, ME 04042
Scope: Statewide
Description: An organization of Bassmaster chapters, affiliated with the Bass Anglers Sportsman Society, organized to fight pollution, assist state and national conservation agencies in their efforts, and teach young people of our country good conservation practices. Dedicated to the realistic conservation of our water resources.
Contact(s):
President: ERIC LOW; Phone: 207-929-8553
Conservation Director: NORM MOULTON, R.R. 1 Box 103D, Ellsworth, ME 04605; Phone: 207-667-6913; E-mail: bassme@midmaine.com
Publication(s): *Federation Guide*

MAINE COAST HERITAGE TRUST
169 Park Row, Brunswick, ME 04011
Phone: 207-729-7366; Fax: 207-729-6863
Founded: 1970
Scope: Statewide
Description: To protect land that is essential to the character of Maine, in particular its coastline and islands. Provides free advisory services on open-space protection to landowners, town officials, state and federal agencies, land trusts, and other private conservation organizations.
Contact(s):
Chairman: HAROLD E. WOODSUM JR.
President: JAMES J. ESPY JR.
Treasurer: JOHN M. ROBINSON
Editor: CHRIS HAMILTON
Publication(s): *Conservation Options, A Guide For Maine Landowners; Directory of Maine Land Conservation Trusts; Annual Report; Maine Heritage; Technical Bulletins*
Keyword(s): Coasts, Islands, Land Preservation, Natural Areas, Open Space

MAINE ENVIRONMENTAL EDUCATION ASSOCIATION, INC.
485 Chewonki Neck Rd., Wiscasset, ME 04578
Phone: 207-882-7323
Founded: 1981; Membership: 225
Scope: Statewide
Description: The Maine Environmental Education Association (MEEA) Facilitates and promotes environmental education in Maine through the sharing of ideas, resources, information and cooperative programs among educators, organizations and concerned individuals. MEEA offers a newsletter, annual conference, Environmental Educator of the Year award and Teacher Mine Grants.
Contact(s):
President: DOT LAMSON
Secretary: TOM MULLIN, Maine Project Learning Tree, P.O. Box 344, Augusta, ME 04332; Phone: 207-626-7990
Treasurer: PAUL ARTHUR
Publication(s): *Connections*
Keyword(s): Environmental and Conservation Education, Natural History, Education

MAINE, SMALL WOODLAND OWNERS ASSOCIATION OF,
153 Hospital St., P.O. Box 836, Augusta, ME 04332
Phone: 207-626-0005
Founded: 1975; Membership: 1,500
Scope: Statewide
Description: A statewide nonprofit organization, affiliated with the National Woodland Owners Association, which pursues better understandings, skills, and directions in small woodland ownership/management under integrated use objectives.
Contact(s):
President: EVERETT TOWLE; Phone: 207-929-6481
Vice President: ANCYL THURSTON; Phone: 207-623-9147
Secretary: CARL VAN HUSEN; Phone: 207-696-3665
Treasurer: RICHARD PIERCE; Phone: 207-562-7042
Editor and Executive Director: JEFFREY ROMANO
Publication(s): *SWOAM News*
Keyword(s): Forests and Forestry

MANASOTA-88
5314 Bay State Rd., Palmetto, FL 34221
Scope: Statewide
Contact(s):
Chairman: GLORIA RAINS; Phone: 813-722-7413
Editor: GLORIA RAINS
Vice-Chairman: MRS. LAURENCE QUY, Bradenton, FL 34209; Phone: 941-792-5509
Vice-Chairman: REBECCA EGER, 324 W. Royal Flamingo Dr., Sarasota, FL 33578; Phone: 813-366-1765
Keyword(s): Biodiversity, Environmental Law, Nuclear/Radiation, Sustainable Ecosystems, Toxic Substances

MANITOBA NATURALISTS SOCIETY
401-63 Albert St., Winnipeg, Manitoba R3B 1G4 Canada
Phone: 204-943-9029
Founded: 1920; Membership: 1,500
Scope: Statewide
Description: Fosters an awareness and appreciation of the natural environment and an understanding of humanity's place therein; and sponsors lectures, workshops, field trips on natural history topics, and recreational outings that are environmentally friendly.
Contact(s):
President: JACK DUBOIS; Phone: 204-261-1966
Secretary: FRANK PENNER; Phone: 204-667-1513
Executive Director: HERTA GUDAUSKAS; Phone: 204-943-9029
Publication(s): *Bulletin; Manitoba's Tall Grass Prairie: A Field Guide to an Endangered Space; The Birds of Southeastern Manitoba; Wings Along Winnipeg; The Wild Plants of Birds Hill Park*
Keyword(s): Natural History, Outdoor Recreation

MANITOBA WILDLIFE FEDERATION
70 Stevenson Rd., Winnipeg, Manitoba R3H 0W7 Canada
Phone: 204-633-5967; Fax: 204-632-5200
Founded: 1944; Membership: 14,000
Scope: Statewide
Description: Promotes conservation, safety, and good sportsmanship. Manages the Habitat Trust Fund which secures critical land to ensure habitat for wildlife. Protects the interests of anglers and hunters.
Contact(s):
President: RANDY WALKER
Secretary: DARLENE GARNHAM
Past President: LARRY THIESSEN
Publication(s): *Wildlife Crusader/Outdoor Edge*
Keyword(s): Wildlife and Wildlife Habitat

MANOMET CENTER FOR CONSERVATION SCIENCES
81 Stage Point Rd. P.O. Box 1770, Manomet, MA 02345
Phone: 508-224-6521; Fax: 508-224-9220; Web Site: www.manomet.org
Founded: 1969; Membership: 3,000
Scope: National
Description: Manomet is a non-profit conservation research institute dedicated to promoting informed conservation policy and natural resource management through applied research. At study sites throughout the Americas, Manomet scientists and volunteers monitor migrant songbird and shorebird populations, identify critical wetlands habitats, design fisheries conservation and management strategies, and develop plans for sustainable management of temperate and tropical forest ecosystems. Manomet's environmental education program serves as the interpretive link between our research work and the information needs of the public. Manomet is membership supported.
Contact(s):
Chair: MRS JEPTHA H. WADE
Director of Programs: DR. KATHARINE C. PARSONS
Office Manager: JENNIE ROBBINS; E-mail: jrobbins@manomet.org

President and Director: LINDA E. LEDDY
Keyword(s): Biodiversity, Birds, Coasts, Ecology, Endangered and Threatened Species, Environment, Fisheries, Forest Management, Internships, Land Use Planning, Natural Areas, Nongame Wildlife, Pesticides, Research

MARIN CONSERVATION LEAGUE
55 Mitchell Blvd., Suite 21, San Rafael, CA 94903
Phone: 415-472-6170
Founded: 1934; Membership: 4,000
Scope: Statewide
Description: The Marin Conservation League has worked to preserve and protect the natural assets of Marin County. The league works on all issues affecting the county environment, seeking partnerships with diverse groups to influence public policy and educate citizens and decision makers in understanding critical issues and options.
Contact(s):
President: KATHY LOWREY
Secretary: ROBERT BERNER
Treasurer: LAWRENCE SMITH
Executive Director: JERRY EDELBROCK
1st Vice President: DON NEUBACHER
2nd Vice President: JEAN STARKWEATHER
Education Coordinator: ANITA FRANZI
Publication(s): *MCL News*
Keyword(s): Agriculture, Environmental and Conservation Education, Environmental Preservation, Land Use Planning, Public Lands

MARINE CONSERVATION BIOLOGY INSTITUTE
Headquarters, 15806 NE 47th Ct., Redmond, WA 98052-5208
Phone: 425-883-8914; Fax: 425-883-3017; E-mail: caroline@mcbi.org; Web Site: www.mcbi.org
Founded: 1996
Scope: National
Description: MCBI is a nonprofit, non-partisan, tax-exempt organization dedicated to advancing the multidisciplinary science of marine conservation biology. MCBI helps scientists to generate information that arms people with knowledge crucial for informed decision-making.
Contact(s):
President: DR. ELLIOTT A. NORSE
Program Director: AMY MATHEWS-AMOS, 205 Edgewood St., Arlington, VA 22201; Phone: 8703-276-1434; Fax: 703-276-1528; E-mail: amymcbi@mcbi.org
Keyword(s): Biodiversity, Marine Protected Areas, Seabed Disturbance

MARINE ENVIRONMENTAL RESEARCH INSTITUTE (MERI)
772 W. End Ave., New York, NY 10025
Phone: 212-864-6285; Fax: 212-864-1470; E-mail: meri@interport.net
Founded: 1990; Membership: 400
Scope: National
Description: MERI is a nonprofit organization dedicated to protecting the health and biodiversity of the marine environment. MERI's programs are international in scope and include direct field research, environmental and conservation education, training, and collaboration with the world's scientific community. MERI strives to address the problems of global marine pollution, endangered species and habitat degradation, and environmental emergencies affecting marine life.
Contact(s):
Chairman: DR. LEMUEL A. EVANS, 3536 Paintwater Pl., Las Vegas, NV 89129-7338
President: DR. SUSAN D. SHAW, P.O. Box 179, Brooklin, ME 04616
Vice President: SUZANNE B. HOPKINS, 15200 Old York Road, Monkton, MD 21111
Secretary: JOAN F. KOVEN, Astrolabe Inc., 4812 V St. NW, Washington, DC 20007
Treasurer: PAMELA STACEY

Resource Center Director: ELIZABETH PETTERSON, MERI Resource Center, Main St., P.O. Box 300, Brooklin, ME 04616; Phone: 207-359-8078; Fax: 207-359-8079; E-mail: meri@downeast.net
Publication(s): *MERI News; MERI Resource Center News; research publications*
Keyword(s): Biodiversity, Endangered and Threatened Species, Environmental and Conservation Education, Marine Mammals

MARINE MAMMAL CENTER, THE
Marin Headlands, Golden Gate National Recreation Area (GGNRA, Sausalito, CA 94965
Phone: 415-289-7325
Founded: 1975; Membership: 35,000
Scope: National
Description: The Marine Mammal Center is a nonprofit organization licensed to rescue and rehabilitate sick, injured, and orphaned marine mammals that strand along the northern and central California coast. Information derived from routine medical treatment is shared with scientists worldwide. Through education programs, the Center promotes public awareness of the ocean environment among over 100,000 visitors annually.
Contact(s):
Chair: JERRY GIBBONS, 130 Battery Street, Suite 330, San Francisco, CA 94111; Phone: 415-291-4999
Treasurer: SHELDON WOLFE, Steefel, Levitt, & Weiss, One Embarcadero Center, 30th Fl., San Francisco, CA 94111-3784; Phone: 415-788-0900
Executive Director: MARGARET BURKS
Publication(s): *Release, The; Annual Report; various scientific papers.*
Keyword(s): Environmental and Conservation Education, Marine Mammals, Wildlife Disease, Wildlife Rehabilitation

MARINE TECHNOLOGY SOCIETY
1828 L St., NW, Suite 906, Washington, DC 20036-5104
Phone: 202-775-5966
Founded: 1963; Membership: 2,500
Scope: International
Description: An ocean-oriented, multidisciplinary, international professional society, formed to encourage the development of the technology, education, operational expertise, and public awareness needed to advance man's capability to work effectively in all ocean areas and depths.
Contact(s):
President: NORMAN B. ESTABROOK
Executive Director: JUDITH T. KRAUTHAMER
Managing Editor: MELLISSA CORLEY
Publication(s): *Marine Technology Society Journal; MTS Newsletter Currents; various proceedings*
Keyword(s): Engineering, Oceanography, Water Resources

MARYLAND ASSOCIATION OF CONSERVATION DISTRICTS
Attn: President, 14919 Roxbury Rd., P.O. Box 189, Gleneig, MD 21737
Scope: Statewide
Contact(s):
President and Alternative Board Member: MARTHA CLARK; Phone: 410-531-3455
Vice President: ROBERT FITZGERALD, 27570 Fitzgerald Rd., Princess Anne, MD 21853; Phone: 410-651-3701
Secretary: ROBERT ZIEHM, 9025 Chevrolet Dr., Ste J, Ellicott City, MD 21042; Phone: 410-465-3180
Executive Director: LYNNE HOOT, 53 Slama Rd., Edgewater, MD 21037; Phone: 410-956-5771; Fax: 410-956-0161
Alternate Board Member: GEORGE LECHLIDER, 24110 Laytonsville Rd., Gaithersburg, MD 20882; Phone: 301-253-1501
Treasurer and Council Member: DONALD SPICKLER, 14854 Hicksville Rd., Clear Spring, MD 21722; Phone: 301-842-2534; Fax: 301-842-2534; E-mail: dspick@erols.com
Keyword(s): Conservation Districts

NON-GOVERNMENTAL ORGANIZATIONS - M

MARYLAND B.A.S.S. CHAPTER FEDERATION
Attn: President, 14520 National Pike, Clear Spring, MD 21722
Scope: Statewide
Description: An organization of Bassmaster chapters, affiliated with the Bass Anglers Sportsman Society, organized to fight pollution, assist state and national conservation agencies in their efforts, and teach the young people of our country good conservation practices. Dedicated to the realistic conservation of our water resources.
Contact(s):
President: BUTCH WARD; Phone: 301-842-3200
Conservation Director: BILL SHEPARD, 1508 Dover Ct., Glen Burnie, MD 21061; Phone: 703-305-1807; E-mail: shepdeal@erols.com
Publication(s): *Maryland State Federation Update*

MARYLAND FORESTS ASSOCIATION
P.O. Box 599, Grantsville, MD 21536
Phone: 301-895-5369; Fax: 301-895-5369; E-mail: mfa@hereintown.net; Web Site: mdforests.org
Membership: 525
Scope: Statewide
Description: A nonprofit 501c (3) citizens organization for people interested in trees, forests, related natural resources, and forestry. To promote the maintenance of a healthy and productive forestland base to enhance the economic, environmental, and social well-being of all who live in the state.
Contact(s):
President: PETER A. ALEXANDER
Vice President: TONLY DIPAOLO
Vice President: GEORGE GILMORE
Vice President: JOHN H. COLTON
Executive Director: KARIN E. MILLER
Secretary and Treasurer: RICHARD STANFIELD
Publication(s): *Crosscut, The; MFA Legislative Update*
Keyword(s): Environment, Environmental and Conservation Education, Forests and Forestry, Renewable Resources, Sustainable Ecosystems

MARYLAND NATIVE PLANT SOCIETY
P.O. Box 4877, Silver Spring, MD 20914
WWW: www.geocities.com.rainforest/vines/2996
Founded: 1990; Membership: 1,000
Scope: Statewide
Description: MNPS is a nonprofit organization that uses education, research, and community service to foster awareness and appreciation for Maryland's native flora and habitats, leading to their conservation.
Contact(s):
President: RODERICK HOYT SIMMONS; Phone: 703-256-7671
Vice President: LOUIS ARONICA; Phone: 202-722-1081
Secretary: SAMUEL JONES; Phone: 410-838-7950
Treasurer: CHARMANE TRUESDELL; Phone: 301-470-4462
Director: MARC IMLAY; Phone: 301-283-0808
Publication(s): *Native News*
Keyword(s): Biodiversity, Native Plants

MARYLAND ORNITHOLOGICAL SOCIETY, INC.
Cylburn Mansion, 4915 Greenspring Ave., Baltimore, MD 21209
Phone: 410-244-0032
Founded: 1945; Membership: 2,400
Scope: Statewide
Description: Nonprofit statewide organization of 16 chapters. Aims to promote the knowledge, protection, and conservation of wildlife and natural resources; to foster appreciation of the natural environment; to establish educational and scientific projects to inform and enrich the public; and to record, evaluate, and publish observations of bird life in Maryland.
Contact(s):
President: ROBERT RINEER, 8326 Philadelphia Rd., Baltimore, MD 21237; Phone: 410-391-8499
Vice President: NORM SAUNDERS, 1261 Cavendish Rd., Colesville, MD 20905; Phone: 301-989-9035
Secretary: SYBIL WILLIAMS, 2000 Baltimore Rd. #A24, Rockville, MD 20851; Phone: 301-762-0560
Treasurer: JEFF METTER, 1301 N. Rolling Rd., Catonsville, MD 21228; Phone: 410-788-4877
Editor: CHANDLER S. ROBBINS, Patuxent Wildlife Research Center, Laurel, MD 20811; Phone: 301-498-0281
Publication(s): *Maryland Birdlife; Maryland Yellowthroat,*
Keyword(s): Birds, Environmental and Conservation Education, Natural History, Wildlife and Wildlife Habitat

MASSACHUSETTS ASSOCIATION OF CONSERVATION COMMISSIONS (MACC)
10 Juniper Rd., Belmont, MA 02478
Phone: 617-489-3930
Founded: 1961; Membership: 3,200
Scope: Statewide
Description: Protects wetlands and open space through education and advocacy.
Contact(s):
President: GREGOR I. McGREGOR
Secretary: DONALD MacIVER
Executive Director: DR. SALLY A. ZIELINSKI
1st Vice President: GEORGE A. HALL
2nd Vice President: INGEBORG HEGEMAN
3rd Vice President: HELEN D. BETHELL
Publication(s): *Environmental Handbook for Massachusetts Conservation Commissioners, 1991 Edition; Newsletter of the Association for members of conservation commissions, government agencies, educational institutions, and environmental organizations*
Keyword(s): Environmental and Conservation Education, Environmental Preservation, Land Purchase, Public Lands, Wetlands

MASSACHUSETTS ASSOCIATION OF CONSERVATION DISTRICTS
Attn: President, 25 Shore Rd., Bourne, MA 02532
Scope: Statewide
Contact(s):
President, Alternate Board Member: PEGGY FANTOZZI PACHECO, 25 Shore Rd., Bourne, MA 02532; Phone: 508-759-4363; Fax: 508-759-4363
Vice President: ED HIMLAN, P.O. Box 577, Leaminister, MA 01453; Phone: 978-534-0379; Fax: 978-534-1329
Secretary: ANNE MERRIAM, 157 State Rd E, Westminster, MA 01473; Phone: 978-874-2432
Treasurer: DONALD LAMBERT, 178 Moulton Hill Rd, Monson, MA 01057; Phone: 413-267-4837
Board Member: THOMAS QUINK, 67 Church St., Gilbertville, MA 01031-9864; Phone: 413-477-8870; Fax: 413-477-8870

MASSACHUSETTS AUDUBON SOCIETY, INC.
208 S. Great Rd., Lincoln, MA 01773
Phone: 781-259-9500; Fax: 781-259-8899
Founded: 1896; Membership: 64,000
Scope: Statewide
Description: A nonprofit organization committed to the protection of the environment for people and wildlife. One of the oldest conservation organizations in the world and the largest in New England. Owns and protects 28,000 acres with 13 wildlife sanctuaries across Massachusetts. Programming priorities: conservation, education and advocacy.
Contact(s):
President: LAURA JOHNSON
Secretary: ALYNN D. HARVEY
Board of Directors Chairman: LEE SPELKE
Editor: JOHN HANSON MITCHELL
Publication(s): *Sanctuary*
Keyword(s): Biodiversity, Birds, Ecology, Environment, Environmental Protection, Land Preservation, Natural History, Wildlife and Wildlife Habitat

MASSACHUSETTS B.A.S.S. CHAPTER FEDERATION
Attn: President 52 Elm St., Clinton, MA 01510
Scope: Statewide

Description: An organization of Bassmaster chapters, affiliated with the Bass Anglers Sportsman Society, organized to fight pollution, assist state and national conservation agencies in their efforts, and teach young people of our country good conservation practices. Dedicated to the realistic conservation of our water resources.
Contact(s):
President: JIM MARINO; Phone: 978-365-6987
Conservation Director: DEAN PERCIVAL, 396 Green St., Northboro, MA 01532; Phone: 508-366-2030; E-mail: mail@whiznet.com

MASSACHUSETTS ENVIRONMENTAL EDUCATION SOCIETY
Box 105, 290 Turnpike Rd., Westboro, MA 01581
Phone: 978-779-6382
Founded: 1977; Membership: 325
Scope: Statewide
Description: Massachusetts Environmental Education Society is a professional organization dedicated to the promotion of environmental education in Massachusetts. Members include teachers, naturalists, youth group leaders, education consultants, agencies and organizations. Annual conference is held for professional development.
Contact(s):
President: DAWN SATHER
Vice President: MIKE DATTILIO
Secretary: JENNIFER WIEST
Treasurer: CAREY BUTTFIELD
Publication(s): *MEES Observer*
Keyword(s): Environment, Environmental and Conservation Education, Professional Development, Training, Professional Organization

MASSACHUSETTS FORESTRY ASSOCIATION
P.O. Box 1096, Belchertown, MA 01007-1096
Phone: 413-323-7326
Founded: 1970; Membership: 1,100
Scope: Statewide
Description: A voluntary nonprofit association, affiliated with the National Woodland Owners Association; dedicated to conservation, stewardship, and advocacy of the forestland of Massachusetts. An educational organization offering information, workshops, conferences, publications, and professional assistance. Begun in 1970 as the Massachusetts Land League, changed to present name in 1986.
Contact(s):
President: MARY ELLEN LEES
Vice President: HUGH PUTNAM JR.
Executive Director: GREGORY COX
Editor: GREGORY COX
Secretary and Treasurer: TIM FOWLER
Publication(s): *Woodland Steward, The*
Keyword(s): Forests and Forestry

MASSACHUSETTS TRAPPER'S ASSOCIATION, INC.
155 Williams Rd., Concord, MA 01742
Phone: 508-369-5065
Founded: 1950
Scope: Statewide
Description: Objectives are to develop leadership for the advancement of the interests of the trapper and the fur industry, and to promote sound management for the conservation of furbearing animals.
Contact(s):
President: WILLIAM ANDRADE, 8 Williams St., Bedford, MA 01730; Phone: 617-275-1809
Secretary: IRENE HAYES, 155 Williams Rd., Concord, MA 01742; Phone: 508-369-5065
Treasurer: LINDA SILKONIS, 71 Great Rd., Maynard, MA 01754-2027; Phone: 617-246-2136
Public Relations: TOM HAYES, 155 Williams Rd., Concord, MA 01742; Phone: 508-369-5065
Publication(s): *Fur Ever*
Keyword(s): Mammals, Trapping, Wetlands, Wildlife and Wildlife Habitat, Wildlife Management

MATTS (MID-ATLANTIC TURTLE AND TORTOISE SOCIETY, INC.)
2914 E. Joppa Rd., #103, Baltimore, MD 21234-3031
Phone: 410-882-2769; Fax: 410-882-0839; E-mail: gpokmd@bigfoot.com; Web Site: www.matts.herptiles.com
Founded: 1997; Membership: 200
Scope: National
Description: A nonprofit organization dedicated to promoting the study of Mid-Atlantic chelonian natural history, responsible herpetoculture, and conservation of habitat.
Contact(s):
President: GREGORY POKRYWKA
Vice President: BRIAN McLAREN; Phone: 301-384-7444; E-mail: brianCRCC@aol.com
Secretary: DR. DONALD KEEFER; Phone: 410-561-1668; E-mail: keefercham@aol.com
Publication(s): *Terrapin Tales, The*
Keyword(s): Conservation, Natural History, Zoology, Herpetoculture, Herpetology, Turtles, Tortoises

MAX McGRAW WILDLIFE FOUNDATION
P.O. Box 9, Dundee, IL 60118
Phone: 847-741-8000; Fax: 847-741-8157; E-mail: mcgrawwild@aol.com
Founded: 1962
Scope: National
Description: Conducts wildlife and fisheries research and management and conservation education projects; cooperates with other conservation agencies and institutions.
Contact(s):
President: FREDERICK G. ACKER
Vice President: RICHARD T. SCHROEDER
Vice President: SCOTT M. ELROD
Treasurer: TIMOTHY N. THOELECKE
Director of Research: JOHN D. THOMPSON
Secretary and Executive Director: STANLEY W. KOENIG
Publication(s): *Descriptive brochure; Wildlife Management Notes Series; Annual Research Report*
Keyword(s): Biodiversity, Biology, Birds, Conservation Tillage, Endangered and Threatened Species, Environmental and Conservation Education, Environmental Preservation, Fisheries, Hunting, Internships, Land Use Planning, Mammals, Natural Areas, Nature Preservation, Nongame Wildlife

MERCK FOREST AND FARMLAND CENTER, INC.
Rt. 315, Box 86, Rupert, VT 05768
Phone: 802-394-7836; Fax: 802-394-2519; E-mail: merck@vermontel.com; Web Site: www.merckforest.org
Scope: Statewide
Description: Over 3,100 acres of field, farm, and forest open year-round to the public in the heart of the Taconic range in southwestern Vermont. Outdoor and environmental education experiences for individuals, families, and organized groups. Over 28 miles of trails, 65-acre organic demonstration farm, camping cabins and sites, a solar-powered visitor center and sustainable forestry information.
Contact(s):
President: ALAN CALFEE
Director: RICHARD THOMPSON TUCKER
Keyword(s): Environmental and Conservation Education, Forests and Forestry, Solar Energy

MICHIGAN ASSOCIATION OF CONSERVATION DISTRICTS
Attn: President, 14302, OP Ave. E., Climax, MI 49034
Scope: Statewide
Contact(s):
President and Board Member: LARRY LEACH; Phone: 616-746-4648; Fax: 616-746-4393
Vice President: JOE SLATER, 6780 Brunswick Rd, Holton, MI 49425; Phone: 616-821-2843
Executive Director: MARILYN SHY, 101 S. Main P.O. Box 539, Lake City, MI 49651; Phone: 616-839-3360; Fax: 616-839-3361; E-mail: mdistricts@aol.com

NON-GOVERNMENTAL ORGANIZATIONS - M

Administrative Assistant: CAROL BOGARD, 101 S. Main, P.O. Box 539, Lake City, MI 49651; Phone: 616-839-3360; Fax: 616-839-3361
Secretary and Treasurer, Alternate Board Member: RODNEY DRAGICEVICH, 29396 Heritage Lane, Paw Paw, MI 49079; Phone: 616-375-3005
Keyword(s): Conservation Districts

MICHIGAN AUDUBON SOCIETY
6011 W. St. Joseph, Suite 403, P.O. Box 80527, Lansing, MI 48908-0527
Phone: 517-886-9144; Fax: 517-886-9466; E-mail: mas@voyager.net; Web Site: mas.mi.audubon.org
Founded: 1904; Membership: 10,000
Scope: Statewide
Description: The Michigan Audubon Society works to protect the Great Lakes ecosystem for people and wildlife. The society conducts scientific research, educates, and advocates for the protection of species and habitats through five major centers, three affiliate organizations, forty-six chapters, and sanctuaries totaling over 5,000 acres of land.
Contact(s):
President: GARY SIEGRIST, 11772 Trist Rd., Grass Lake, MI 49240
Secretary: LARRY UHSIE, 19057 12 Mile Rd., Battle Creek, MI 49014
Treasurer: CHARLES MACDONALD, 945 Tihart, Okemos, MI 48864
1st Vice President: LORETTA GOLD, 143 Lillie Ave., Battle Creek, MI 49015
2nd Vice President: HAROLD PROWSE, P.O. Box 336, Metamora, MI 48455
Business Manager: EILEEN SCAMEHORN
Editor-in-Chief: JULIE CRAVES
Editor-in-Chief: DAVID WORTHINGTON
Publication(s): *Jack-Pine Warbler; Michigan Birds & Natural History*
Keyword(s): Birds, EcoAction, Environmental and Conservation Education, Land Preservation

MICHIGAN B.A.S.S. CHAPTER FEDERATION
Attn: President, 1010 S. West Ave., Jackson, MI 49203
Scope: Statewide
Description: An organization of Bassmaster chapters, affiliated with the Bass Anglers Sportsman Society, organized to fight pollution, assist state and national conservation agencies in their efforts, and teach the young people of our country good conservation practice. Dedicated to the realistic conservation of our water resources.
Contact(s):
President: JIM RICE; Phone: 517-789-1008
Conservation Director: RON SPITLER, 2710 Browning Dr., Lake Orion, MI 48360; Phone: 248-391-4393

MICHIGAN ENVIRONMENTAL COUNCIL
119 Pere Marquette, Lansing, MI 48912
Phone: 517-487-9539; Fax: 917-487-9541; E-mail: mlenvcouncil@igc.apc.org
Founded: 1980
Scope: Statewide
Description: A statewide coalition of 37 citizen environmental and conservation organizations united to protect and enhance Michigan's human and natural environment and to ensure its sustainability. The Council acts through networking, advocacy, education, and research.
Contact(s):
Chairman: ELIZABETH HARRIS, E. Michigan Environmental Action Council 21220 W. 14 Mile Rd., Bloomfield Township, MI 48301-4000; Phone: 313-258-5188
Executive Director: CAROL K. MISSELDINE
Secretary (At-Large Board Member): JOEL HUNT
Vice Chair: ALISON HORTON
Vice Chair: ALICE AUSTIN; Phone: 517-663-2400
Publication(s): *Michigan Environmental Report; Land: Michigan's Promise, Michigan's Future; Groundwater at Risk: A Citizen's Guide*
Keyword(s): Communications, Energy, Land Use Planning, Pollution Prevention, Urban Environment

MICHIGAN FORESTS ASSOCIATION
1558 Barrington St., Ann Arbor, MI 48103-5603
Phone: 734-913-9167
Founded: 1951; Membership: 1,100
Scope: Statewide
Description: A statewide organization affiliated with the National Woodland Owners Association, with concern for the full spectrum of forest activity, enterprise, development, and conservation in Michigan.
Contact(s):
President: GORDON TERRY
Vice President: RUTH J. DAKE
Treasurer: ALLAN KERTON
Executive Director: McCLAIN SMITH
Editor: DON INGLE, P.O. Box 78, Baldwin, MI 48103
Editor: McCLAIN SMITH
Publication(s): *MFA Leaves; Michigan Forests*
Keyword(s): Forests and Forestry

MICHIGAN LAND USE INSTITUTE
P.O. Box 228, Benzonia, MI 49016
Phone: 616-882-4723; Fax: 616-882-7350; E-mail: mlui@traverse.com; Web Site: www.mlui.org
Founded: 1995; Membership: 1,100
Scope: Statewide
Description: Michigan Land Use Institute is a nonprofit environmental economic policy research organization focused on reforming land use policy and curbing sprawl.
Contact(s):
Treasurer: RICHARD HITCHINGHAM
Executive Director: KEITH SCHNEIDER
Managing Director: HANS VOSS
Publication(s): *Great Lakes Bulletin; Rivers at Risk; Benzie County Wetlands - A Resource Worth Protecting*
Keyword(s): Environment, Environmental and Conservation Education, Environmental Protection

MICHIGAN NATURAL AREAS COUNCIL
University of Michigan, Botanical Gardens, 1800 N. Dixboro Rd., Ann Arbor, MI 48105
E-mail: mnac@cyberspace.org; Web Site: www.cyberspace.org/~mnacl
Founded: 1947; Membership: 150
Scope: Statewide
Description: The Michigan Natural Areas Council promotes the preservation of outstanding natural areas, prepares reports based on field investigations, and serves as an informed-citizens advisory on such matters.
Contact(s):
Chair: DR. SYLVIA M. TAYLOR, 10353 Judd Rd., Willis, MI 48191; Phone: 313-461-9390; E-mail: smtaylot@umich.edu
Treasurer: CHRISTOPHER L. GRAHAM, 725 Peninsula Ct., Ann Arbor, MI 48105; E-mail: kfdh64@prodigy.com
Editor: ROBERT GRESE
Vice Chair: ROBERT GRESE, 1512 Carlton, Ann Arbor, MI 48103; E-mail: bgrese@umich.edu
Publication(s): *Michigan Natural Areas News and Views (natural areas, endangered species, and relevant conservation news*
Keyword(s): Endangered and Threatened Species, Flowers, Plants, and Trees, Islands, Nature Preservation, Prairies, Wilderness

MICHIGAN NATURE ASSOCIATION
7981 Beard Rd., Box 102, Avoca, MI 48006-0102
Phone: 313-324-2626
Founded: 1952; Membership: 1,400
Scope: Statewide
Description: Purpose is to acquire and maintain nature sanctuaries that contain examples of Michigan's original flora and fauna. Holds title to 149 properties totaling 7,702 acres in 52 counties of Michigan. MNA lands contain 206 of Michigan's endangered, threatened, and of special concern species. Available to public for nature education and appreciation.

Contact(s):
President: KAREN WEINGARDEN; Phone: 810-546-5429
Editor: BERTHA DAUBENDIEK, Box 102, Avoca, MI 48006
Executive Secretary and Treasurer: BERTHA DAUBENDIEK; Phone: 810-324-2626
Publication(s): *Members' Newsletter; MNA Nature Sanctuary Guidebook 7th edition, 1993; MNA--In Retrospect: A Celebration of 28 Years of Preserving Michigan's Wild and Rare Natural Lands 1960-1988; Walking Paths in Keweenaw; In Our Trust (1990-91, 30-minute Wildlife Video)*
Keyword(s): Birds, Endangered and Threatened Species, Flowers, Plants, and Trees, Insects and Butterflies, Land Preservation, Land Purchase, Mammals, Natural Areas, Natural History, Nature Preservation, Nongame Wildlife, Prairies, Reptiles and Amphibians, Wetlands, Wildlife and Wildlife Habitat

MICHIGAN UNITED CONSERVATION CLUBS, INC.

2101 Wood St., Lansing, MI 48912-3728
Phone: 517-371-1041; Fax: 517-371-1505; E-mail: mucc@mucc.org; Web Site: www.mucc.org
Scope: Statewide
Description: A representative statewide organization, affiliated with the National Wildlife Federation, dedicated to the protection and enhancement of wildlife and its habitat through public education and government interaction.
Contact(s):
President: WILLIAM WHIPPEN
Executive Director: JIM GOODHEART
Representative: ARTHUR DITTMAR
Editor: DENNIS KNICKERBOCKER
Alternate Representative: JAMES CAMPBELL
Publication(s): *Michigan Out-of-Doors*

MICHIGAN WILDLIFE HABITAT FOUNDATION
6425 S. Pennsylvania, Suite 9, Lansing, MI 48911
Phone: 517-882-3110; Fax: 517-882-3687
Founded: 1982; Membership: 2,500
Scope: Statewide
Description: The Michigan Wildlife Habitat Foundation is a nonprofit membership organization, which restores and improves wildlife habitat through cost-effective projects. We want future generations to enjoy the same world of natural experiences we do today.
Contact(s):
President: DR. KEITH GROTY
Chairman: MICHAEL DePOLO
Executive Director: DENNIS FIJALKOWSKI
Publication(s): *Wildlife Volunteer, The*
Keyword(s): Aquatic Habitats, Renewable Resources, Terrestrial Habitats, Wetlands, Wildlife and Wildlife Habitat

MID-ATLANTIC COUNCIL OF WATERSHED ASSOCIATIONS
12 Morris Rd., Ambler, PA 19002
Scope: National
Description: Promotes the exchange of ideas on citizen watershed association activities and advises any group wishing to start a new watershed association.
Contact(s):
President: LORAH HOPKINS, 960 Old Mill Rd., Wyomissing, PA 19610; Phone: 215-372-3916
Secretary: ROBERT STRUBLE JR., Brandywine Valley Association, Inc. 1760 Unionville-Wawaset Rd., West Chester, PA 19382; Phone: 215-793-1090
Treasurer: DAVID FROCHLICH, Wissahickon Valley Watershed Associatoin, 12 Morris Rd., Ambler, PA 19002; Phone: 215-646-8866
Keyword(s): Environmental and Conservation Education, Land Use Planning, Rivers, Water Pollution, Water Resources, Watersheds

MID-ATLANTIC FISHERY MANAGEMENT COUNCIL
300 S. New St. Rm. 2115, Dover, DE 19904
Phone: 302-674-2331; Fax: 302-674-5399
Founded: 1976
Scope: National
Description: Mid-Atlantic Fishery Management Council is one of eight regional fishery management councils established to carry out provisions of Magnuson-Stevens Fishery Conservation and Management Act. The Council is charged with responsibility to prepare fishery management plans and amendments to such plans for implementation by the Secretary of Commerce.
Contact(s):
Chairman: DR. JAMES GILFORD, College of Marine Studies, University of Delaware, Newark, DE 19711; Phone: 302-831-2650
Executive Director: DANIEL T. FURLONG, MAFMC, 300 S. New St., Rm. 2115, Dover, DE 19901; Phone: 302-674-2331
Publication(s): *Newsletter*
Keyword(s): Fisheries, Marine Mammals, Wetlands, Marine Fisheries

MINERAL POLICY CENTER
1612 K St., NW, Suite 808, Washington, DC 20006
Phone: 202-887-1872; Fax: 202-887-1875
Founded: 1988; Membership: 2,500
Scope: National
Description: MPC is a national environmental membership organization. The Center is a research, education, and advocacy organization dedicated to cleaning up and preventing pollution from mining. The Center works for common sense environmental reform of mineral policy. The Center produces educational materials on mining impact, offers training for and works closely with, citizens groups affected by mining damage.
Contact(s):
President: STEPHEN D'ESPOSITO
Board of Director: THOMAS A. TROYER
Board of Director: KARIN P. SHELDON
Board of Director: SHARON K. BENJAMIN
Board of Directors Chairman: J. MICHAEL MCCLOSKEY
Reform Campaign Director: ALAN SEPTOFF
Communication Director: SUSAN A BRACKETT
Vice President for Operations: VALERIE KEELS
Publication(s): *MPC News; Mining Conservation Directory; Canary Calls; Mine Wire*
Keyword(s): Environmental Law, Mineral Resources, Mining, Public Lands, Solid Waste, Toxic Substances, Water Pollution

MINNESOTA ASSOCIATION OF SOIL AND WATER CONSERVATION DISTRICTS
Attn: President, 50066 County 43 Blvd., Pine Island, MN 55963
Scope: Statewide
Contact(s):
President: OWEN KNUTSON, 50066 County 43 Blvd., Pine Island, MN 55963; Phone: 507-356-8781; Fax: 507-732-7651; E-mail: knutsona@philbred.com
Vice President: RICHARD ZUPP, Rt. 4 Box 139, Pipestone, MN 56164; Phone: 507-825-3024
Secretary-Treasurer: SCOTT HOESE, 5520 Polk Ave., Mayer, MN 55360; Phone: 612-657-2223
Executive Director: LEANN BUCK, 790 Cleveland Ave. S. Suite 216, St. Paul, MN 55116; Phone: 612-690-9028; Fax: 612-690-9065; E-mail: lbuck@pioneerplanet.infi.net
Keyword(s): Conservation Districts

MINNESOTA B.A.S.S. CHAPTER FEDERATION
Attn: President, P.O.B. 225, Howard Lake, MN 55349
Scope: Statewide
Description: An organization of Bassmaster chapters, affiliated with the Bass Anglers Sportsman Society, organized to fight pollution, assist state and national conservation agencies in their efforts, and teach the young people of our country good conservation practices. Dedicated to the realistic conservation of our water resources.
Contact(s):
President: JAY GREEN; Phone: 612-339-5609
Conservation Director: JOHN SCHNEIDER, 2865 Matilda St., Roseville, MN 55113; Phone: 651-653-6810

NON-GOVERNMENTAL ORGANIZATIONS - M

MINNESOTA CENTER FOR ENVIRONMENTAL ADVOCACY (MCEA)
26 E. Exchange St., Suite 206, St. Paul, MN 55101-2264
Phone: 651-223-5969
Founded: 1974; Membership: 800
Scope: Statewide
Description: The Minnesota Center for Environmental Advocacy is a nonprofit organization that uses law, science, and research to protect Minnesota's natural resources, wildlife, and the health of its people.
Contact(s):
Chair: ANGUS M. VAUGHAN
Secretary: STEVEN M. HOFFMAN
Treasurer: GAYLE PETERSON
Executive Director: PETER H. BACHMAN
Vice Chair: ROBERT G. DUNN
Publication(s): *Advocacy Update*
Keyword(s): Air Quality and Pollution, Feedlots and Pollution, Legal Advocacy, Pesticides, Toxic Reduction, Water Quality

MINNESOTA CONSERVATION FEDERATION
551 S. Snelling Ave., #B, St. Paul, MN 55116-1525
Phone: 612-690-3077; Fax: 612-690-3077; E-mail: mncf@mtn.org
Scope: Statewide
Description: A representative statewide organization, affiliated with the National Wildlife Federation, dedicated to the protection and enhancement of wildlife and its habitat through public education and government interaction.
Contact(s):
President and Representative: GORDY MEYER
Alternate Representative: CHRIS VOKATY
Editor: BARB PRINDLE
Publication(s): *Minnesota Out-of-Doors*

MINNESOTA FORESTRY ASSOCIATION
P.O. Box 496, Grand Rapids, MN 55744
Phone: 218-326-3000
Membership: 1,200
Scope: Statewide
Description: A nonprofit organization, affiliated with the National Woodland Owners Association, dedicated to promoting the high potential advantages of intensive scientific management of forests, woodlots, and other renewable resources.
Contact(s):
President: JAMES LEMMERMAN; Phone: 218-624-3847
Vice-President: DAVID PARENT; Phone: 612-753-1619
Secretary: PHIL BRADLEY; Phone: 218-724-0401
Treasurer: RICHARD KNOLL; Phone: 320-983-2480
Executive Director and Editor: TERRANCE WEBER
Publication(s): *Minnesota Better Forests*
Keyword(s): Forests and Forestry

MINNESOTA GROUND WATER ASSOCIATION
4779 126th St., N., White Bear Lake, MN 55110-5910
Founded: 1981; Membership: 500
Scope: Statewide
Description: MGWA's mission is to advocate the wise use and protection of gound water, and to provide education to the users of Minnesota's ground water.
Contact(s):
President: JAMES LUNDY; Phone: 651-296-7822; Fax: 651-297-8676; E-mail: jm.lundy@pca.state.mn.us
Treasurer: LEE TROTTA; Phone: 651-638-3160; Fax: 651-638-3226; E-mail: trottaLC@usfilter.com
Advertising Manager: LEIGH HARROD; Phone: 651-474-8678; E-mail: mn_homebase@worldnet.att.net
Business Manager: DR. JEANETTE LEETE; Phone: 651-426-6122; Fax: 651-426-5449
Editor: TOM CLARK; Phone: 651-296-8580; Fax: 651-297-7709; E-mail: tom.p.clark@pca.state.mn.us
Secretary and Membership: JAN FALTEISEK; Phone: 651-296-3877; Fax: 651-296-0445; E-mail: jan.falteisek@dnr.state.mn.us
Past President: JAMES PIEGAT; Phone: 612-470-6075
Publication(s): *Minnesota Ground Water Association Newsletter; Minnesota Ground Water Association Directory*
Keyword(s): Environmental and Conservation Education, Environmental Planning, Environmental Preservation, Ground Water Protection

MINNESOTA HERPETOLOGICAL SOCIETY (James Ford Bell Museum of Natural History)
10 Church St., SE, University of Minnesota, Minneapolis, MN 55455-0104
Phone: 612-624-7065
Founded: 1981; Membership: 350
Scope: Statewide
Description: A nonprofit organization chartered for the conservation and preservation of reptiles and amphibians, through the education of members and the public.
Publication(s): *MHS Newsletter*
Keyword(s): Endangered and Threatened Species, Environmental and Conservation Education, Nature Preservation, Nongame Wildlife, Reptiles and Amphibians

MINNESOTA NATIVE PLANT SOCIETY
220 Biological Sciences Center, 1445 Gortner Ave., University of Minnesota, St. Paul, MN 55108
E-mail: ceumb@stolaf.edu; Web Site: www.stolaf.edu/depts/biology/mnps
Founded: 1982; Membership: 306
Scope: Statewide
Description: A nonprofit organization dedicated to education about native Minnesota flora and to its preservation and conservation. Activities include monthly meetings, summer field trips, sponsorship of symposia and publication of a regular newsletter.
Publication(s): *Minnesota Plant Press*
Keyword(s): Biodiversity, Endangered and Threatened Species, Environmental and Conservation Education, Environmental Preservation, Prairies, Native Plants

MINNESOTA ORNITHOLOGISTS' UNION
James Ford Bell Museum of Natural History, 10 Church St. SE, University of Minnesota, Minneapolis, MN 55455
Founded: 1937; Membership: 1,400
Scope: Statewide
Description: Statewide organization contributing to scientific knowledge through bird observations; stimulating public interest in birds; and working to preserve bird life and bird habitat.
Contact(s):
President: ANN KESSEN, 31145 Gensis Ave., Stacy, MN 55079
Treasurer: MARK CITSAY, 210 Mariner Way, Bayport, MN 55003
Editor: ANTHONY HERTZEL, 8461 Pleasant View Dr., Mounds View, MN 55112
Editor: JIM WILLIAMS, 5239 Cranberry Lane, Webster, WI 54893
Membership Secretary: ELIZABETH BELL, 5868 Pioneer Rd., St. Paul Park, MN 55071
Recording Secretary: AL BATT, RR 1, Box 56A, Hartland, MN 56042
Publication(s): *Loon, The; Minnesota Birder*
Keyword(s): Biology, Birds, Geography, Nongame Wildlife, Waterfowl

MINNESOTA PARKS AND TRAILS COUNCIL
26 Exchange St. E, Suite 314, St. Paul, MN 55101-2294
Phone: 615-281-0508
Founded: 1954; Membership: 1,100
Scope: Statewide
Description: The mission of the Council is to further the establishment, development, and enhancement of parks and trails within the state of Minnesota, and to encourage their prudent use and protection.
Contact(s):
President: ELEANOR WINSTON

Vice President: MARK STROBEL
Vice President: JEFF OLSON
Vice President: JOHN LEINEN JR.
Secretary: ALAN RUVELSON JR.
Treasurer: MICHAEL PRICHARD
Executive Director: DORIAN GRILLEY
Publication(s): *Newsletter*
Keyword(s): Environmental and Conservation Education, Environmental Preservation, Land Purchase, Outdoor Recreation, Public Lands, Trail

MINNESOTA WILDLIFE HERITAGE FOUNDATION, INC.
5701 Normandale Rd., Suite 325, Minneapolis, MN 55424
Phone: 612-925-1923
Scope: Statewide
Description: Formed to promote the idea of charitable giving for conservation purposes and to assist people in making charitable donations of property for wildlife habitat.
Contact(s):
President: JAMES MADY, 7338 Frontier Trail, Chanhassen, MN 55317
Secretary and Legal Counsel: LAURENCE F. KOLL, 633 Sunset Ln., Mendota Heights, MN 55118; Phone: 612-291-9155
Vice President and Director: HUGH C. PRICE, 4424 Dunham Dr., Edina, MN 55435; Phone: 612-925-2486

MINNESOTA WINGS SOCIETY, INC.
P.O. Box 11323, Minneapolis, MN 55411
Phone: 612-588-2966
Founded: 1978; Membership: 200
Scope: Statewide
Description: To present a program to high school students called "Sight and Save Wildlife Management." This program helps students and enables them to improve wildlife habitat around some of the species they see every day.
Contact(s):
President: THURMAN TUCKER, 1321 N. Irving Ave., Minneapolis, MN 55411; Phone: 612-588-2466
Vice President: DAVID DONNA, 4200 IDS Center, 80 S. 8th St., Minneapolis, MN 55402; Phone: 612-371-3211
Secretary: MARTIN HANSON, 1530 Quinlan Ave., So., St. Croix Beach, MN 55043; Phone: 612-436-8242
Treasurer: JIM McLELLAN, 10273Yellow Cir. Dr., Minnetonka, MN 55343; Phone: 612-933-2263
Publication(s): *Wings (newsletter*
Keyword(s): Birds, Environmental and Conservation Education, Land Preservation, Wildlife and Wildlife Habitat, Wildlife Management

MISSISSIPPI ASSOCIATION OF CONSERVATION DISTRICTS, INC.
Attn: President, P.O. Box 998, Pascagoula, MS 39568-0988
Scope: Statewide
Contact(s):
Board Member: DARYL BURNEY, P.O. Box 603, Coffeeville, MS 38922; Phone: 601-675-2703; Fax: 601-675-2786
President: BENNY GOFF; Phone: 228-769-3070; Fax: 228-769-3005
1st Vice President: MARC CURTIS, P.O. Box 958, Leland, MS 38756; Phone: 601-686-2321
2nd Vice President: JACK WINSTEAD, 5337 Lawrence Rd., Lawrence, MS 39336
Secretary and Treasurer: GALE MARTIN, P.O. Box 23005, Jackson, MS 39225-3005; Phone: 601-354-7645; Fax: 601-354-6628
Keyword(s): Conservation Districts

MISSISSIPPI B.A.S.S. CHAPTER FEDERATION
Attn: President, 1518 W. Clayton, Greenwood, MS 38930
Scope: Statewide
Description: An organization of Bassmaster chapters, affiliated with the Bass Anglers Sportsman Society, organized to fight pollution, assist state and national conservation agencies in their efforts, and teach the young people of our country good conservation practices. Dedicated to the realistic conservation of our water resources.
Contact(s):
President: HARVEY CHERRY; Phone: 601-455-6477
Conservation Director: JOHN HAMILTON, 404 Meadowlane, Aberdeen, MS 39730; Phone: 601-369-8290

MISSISSIPPI INTERSTATE COOPERATIVE RESOURCE ASSOCIATION
P.O. Box 774, Bettendorf, IA 52722-0774
Phone: 309-793-5811
Founded: 1989; Membership: 160
Scope: National
Description: An interstate organization of 28 state departments of conservation and natural resources working in collaboration with federal agencies, Native American tribes, and other interests to improve the conservation, development, management, and utilization of interjurisdictional fishery resources in the Mississippi River basin through improved coordination and communication among the responsible management entities.
Contact(s):
Chairman: BILL REEVES, Tennessee Wildlife Resources Agency, P.O. Box 40747, Ellington Agricultural Center, Nashville, TN 37204
Coordinator and Executive Secretary: JERRY L. RASMUSSEN, P.O. Box 774, Bettendorf, IA 52722-0774
Vice Chairman: NORM STUCKY, Missouri Dept. of Conservation, P.O. Box 180, Jefferson City, MO 65102-0180
Publication(s): *River Crossings; Other Periodic Reports*
Keyword(s): Endangered and Threatened Species, Fisheries, Rivers, Sport Fishing, Water Resources

MISSISSIPPI NATIVE PLANT SOCIETY
P.O. Box 357, Stoneville, MS 38776-0357
Founded: 1981; Membership: 300
Scope: Statewide
Description: The Mississippi Native Plant Society promotes the study and use of native and naturalized species of Mississippi, their use in landscaping, the appreciation of natural ecological communities of the state, and the conservation or preservation of these species, habitats and plant associations, using the principles of conservation biology and ecosystem management.
Contact(s):
Editor: LYNN LIBOUS-BAILEY
Secretary and Treasurer: DEBORA MANN, 114 Auburn Dr., Clinton, MS 39056-6002; Phone: 601-974-1415
Publication(s): *Mississippi Native Plants*
Keyword(s): Environmental and Conservation Education, Flowers, Plants, and Trees, Landscape Architecture, Natural History, Native Plants

MISSISSIPPI RIVER BASIN ALLIANCE
2105 First Ave., South, Suite 301, Minneapolis, MN 55404
Phone: 612-870-3441; Fax: 612-870-4846; E-mail: mrbaoffice@mrba.org; Web Site: www.mrba.org/mrba
Founded: 1992; Membership: 125
Scope: Regional
Description: To protect and restore the ecological, economic, cultural, historical, and recreational resources in the Basin, and to eliminate barriers of race, class and economic status which divide us in the quest to achieve these purposes.
Contact(s):
Executive Director: TIMOTHY SULLIVAN
President: BILL REDDING, Sierra Club, Midwest Office, 214 N. Henry St, Suite 203, Madison, WI 53703; Phone: 608-257-4994
Vice President: WILLIE FORRENOT S, Louisiana Attorney General's Office, 301 Main St., 12th Floor, Baton Rouge, LA 70801-1916; Phone: 225-342-7894
Secretary: MICHELLE THELEN, C.U.R.E., 405 N. 8th St., Montevideo, MN 56265; Phone: 320-269-9326
Treasurer: JOHN THOMAS, 2316 Powderhorn Ln., Boulder, CO 80303; Phone: 303-773-5248
Publication(s): *Alliance Newsletter; Mississippi River Basin Directory*

NON-GOVERNMENTAL ORGANIZATIONS - M

Keyword(s): Greenways, Navigation, People of Color in the Environment, Rivers, Water Quality, Wetlands

MISSISSIPPI WILDLIFE FEDERATION
P.O. Box 1814, Jackson, MS 39215-1814
Phone: 601-420-2100; Fax: 601-420-2060; E-mail: mwf@netdoor.com
Scope: Statewide
Description: A representative statewide organization, affiliated with the National Wildlife Federation, dedicated to the protection and enhancement of wildlife and its habitat through public education and government interaction.
Contact(s):
President: JOHN HARVEY
Executive Director: MARLA SPEED
Representative: RAMON CALLAHAN
Editor: ALAN HUFFMAN
Alternate Representative: BOB FAIRBANK
Publication(s): *Mississippi Wildlife*

MISSOURI ASSOCIATION OF SOIL AND WATER CONSERVATION DISTRICTS
Attn: President, 15201 Hwy. M, Chillicothe, MO 64601
Scope: Statewide
Contact(s):
President and Board Member: STEVE HOPPER; Phone: 660-639-2575
Vice President, Alternate Board Member: SAM BRUCE GRAVES SR., Rt. 2 Box 7, Tarkio, MO 64491; Phone: 660-736-4368
Treasurer: DAVID DIX, P.O. Box 756, Eminence, MO 65466; Phone: 573-226-3787
Executive Secretary: PEGGY LEMONS, 1209 Biscayne Dr., Jefferson City, MO 65109; Phone: 573-893-5188; Fax: 573-893-7328; E-mail: peggy@mojefferso.fsc.usda.gov
Keyword(s): Conservation Districts

MISSOURI AUDUBON COUNCIL
619 Norris Dr., Jefferson City, MO 65109
Phone: 314-635-6018
Membership: 9,000
Scope: Statewide
Description: A statewide council composed of delegates from 14 National Audubon chapters and the Audubon Society of Missouri. Formed to coordinate efforts on various conservation and environmental issues in Missouri. Advised and assisted by the National Audubon Society.
Contact(s):
Chairperson: KAREN UHLENHUTH, 3714 E. Roanoke Dr., Kansas City, MO 64111; Phone: 816-561-1371
Keyword(s): Biodiversity, Birds, Endangered and Threatened Species, Environment, Water Quality

MISSOURI B.A.S.S. CHAPTER FEDERATION
Attn: President, 29 Eagles Way Ln., Lakes St. Louis, MO 63367
Scope: Statewide
Description: An organization of Bassmaster chapters, affiliated with the Bass Anglers Sportsman Society, organized to fight pollution, assist state and national conservation agencies in their efforts, and teach the young people of our country good conservation practices. Dedicated to the realistic conservation of our water resources.
Contact(s):
President: RON HAUSER; Phone: 314-561-1139; E-mail: hausers@inlink.com
Conservation Director: JIM NOAH, 916 SE 5th St. Terrace, Lee's Summit, MO 64063; Phone: 816-524-8360; E-mail: jimnoah@compuserve.com

MISSOURI FOREST PRODUCTS ASSOCIATION
611 E. Capitol Ave., Suite One, Jefferson City, MO 65101
Phone: 573-634-3252; Fax: 573-636-2591; E-mail: info@mfpanews.org; Web Site: www.mfpanews.org
Founded: 1970; Membership: 350
Scope: Statewide
Description: The Missouri Forest Products Association is a non-profit organization committed to promoting closer working relationships among the wood products industry and the conservation and wise use of natural resources.
Contact(s):
Executive Director: CORY T. RIDENHOUR; E-mail: cory@mfpanews.org
President: RICHARD LANDERS
President-Elect: JON SMITH
Publication(s): *MFPA News; Professional Timber*
Keyword(s): Conservation, Conservation Planning, Environmental Ethics, Forest Management, Forest Stewardship, Forests and Forestry, Internships, Sustainable Resources, Training, Trees, Urban Forestry

MISSOURI NATIVE PLANT SOCIETY
P.O. Box 20073, St. Louis, MO 63144-0073
Phone: 314-894-9021; E-mail: jahar@stlnet.com; Web Site: www.missouri.edu/~umo_herb/monps
Founded: 1979; Membership: 350
Scope: Statewide
Description: To promote the enjoyment, preservation, conservation, restoration, and study of the flora native to Missouri; to educate the public about the values of the beauty, diversity and environmental importance of indigenous vegetation; and to publish related information.
Contact(s):
President: JACK H. HARRIS
Vice President: SUE HOLLIS; Phone: 816-561-9419
Secretary: LYNDA RICHARDS; Phone: 573-364-8567
Treasurer: DONNA KENNEDY; Phone: 636-256-7578
Editor: PAT HARRIS; Phone: 314-894-9021
Editor: GEORGE YATSKIEVYCH; Phone: 314-577-9522
Publication(s): *Missouriensis; Petal Pusher*
Keyword(s): Biodiversity, Endangered and Threatened Species, Environment, Environmental Preservation, Environmental Protection, Flowers, Plants, and Trees, Forest Management, Gardening and Horticulture, Natural Areas, Natural History, Nature Preservation, Prairies, Public Lands, Wildlands, Native Plants

MISSOURI PRAIRIE FOUNDATION
P.O. Box 200, Columbia, MO 65205
Fax: 573-442-0260; E-mail: gfreeman@mail.com.missouri.edu
Founded: 1966
Scope: Statewide
Description: A nonprofit citizens' group organized to ensure the preservation of native prairie along with associated plant and animal life by acquisition, management protection, control, and perpetuation of the prairie; to carry on educational programs; and to provide scientific research relative to native prairie.
Contact(s):
President: GEORGE D. NICHOLS; Phone: 417-682-8768
Vice President: DR. ELIZABETH A. GARRETT; Phone: 573-446-3778
Secretary: RUSSELL RUNGE; Phone: 573-581-8754
Treasurer: JOHN R. CLINE; Phone: 314-581-6566
Advisor to the Board: D. M. CHRISTIESEN
Editor: CAROL DAVIT, c/o MDC, P.O. Box 180, Jefferson City, MO 65102; Phone: 573-751-4115, ext. 874
Publication(s): *Missouri Prairie Journal*
Keyword(s): Biodiversity, Conservation of Protected Areas, Endangered and Threatened Species, Environmental and Conservation Education, Land Preservation, Land Purchase, Prairies, Native Plants

MONITOR INTERNATIONAL
154 Quiet Waters Pl., Annapolis, MD 21403
Phone: 410-268-5155; Fax: 410-268-8788; E-mail: info@monitorinternational.org; Web Site: www.monitorinternational.org
Founded: 1978
Scope: International

Description: Monitor International is a nonprofit corporation, conserves biological diversity and cultural heritage, and promotes environmentally sustainable development or marine and freshwater ecosystems throughout the world.
Contact(s):
President: DAVID READ BARKER
Vice President: LISA BORRE
Secretary: JOHN DOLAN
Treasurer: RICHARD TOBIN
Board of Trustees Chairman: MILTON M. KAUFMANN
Publication(s): *Sustainable Development; Success Stories; Lake Toba-Lake Champlain Exchange*
Keyword(s): Coasts, Developing Countries, Lakes, Sustainable Development

MONO LAKE COMMITTEE
P.O. Box 29, Lee Vining, CA 93541
Phone: 760-647-6595
Founded: 1978; Membership: 18,000
Scope: Statewide
Description: The Mono Lake Committee is a nonprofit citizens' group dedicated to protecting and restoring the Mono Basin ecosystem; educating the public about Mono Lake and the impacts on the environment of excessive water use; and promoting cooperative solutions that protect Mono Lake and meet real water needs without transferring environmental problems to other areas.
Contact(s):
Chair: ED MANNING
Chair: SALLY GAINES
Secretary: TOM SOTO
Executive Director: FRANCIS SPIVY-WEBER; Phone: 310-316-0041
Editor: ARYA DEGENHARDT
Editor: GEOFFREY McQUILKIN
Publication(s): *Mono Lake Newsletter; Mono Lake Guidebook; Plants of the Mono Basin; Geology of the Mono Basin; South Tufa: A Self-guided Walking Tour of Mono Lake*
Keyword(s): Birds, Lakes, Sustainable Development, Water Resources, Wetlands

MONTANA ASSOCIATION OF CONSERVATION DISTRICTS
Attn: President, P.O. Box 21, Ekalaka, MT 59324
Phone: 406-443-5711
Scope: Statewide
Contact(s):
Board Member: DENNIS DeVRIES, P.O. Box 562, Polson, MT 59860; Phone: 406-883-6848; Fax: 406-883-2356; E-mail: ddvsb@digisys.net
President, Alternative Board Member: LUTHER WATERLAND, P.O. Box 21, Ekalaka, MT 59324; Phone: 406-775-6347
Vice President: TOM STELLING, 5 Rocky Roof Rd., Ft. Shaw, MT 59443; Phone: 406-264-5879; Fax: 406-264-5630
Treasurer: DALE MARXER, 654 Millegan Rd., Great Falls, MT 59405; Phone: 406-866-3259
Administrative Assistant: JAN McINERNEY, 501 N. Sanders, Suite 2, Helena, MT 59601; Phone: 406-443-5711; Fax: 406-443-0174
Executive Vice President: MIKE VOLESKY, 501 N. Sanders, Suite 2, Helena, MT 59601; Phone: 406-443-5711; Fax: 406-449-0174; E-mail: macd@mt.net
Keyword(s): Conservation Districts

MONTANA AUDUBON
P.O. Box 595, Helena, MT 59624
Phone: 406-443-3949; E-mail: mtaudubon@mcn.net
Founded: 1976
Scope: Statewide
Description: The statewide organization of the nine National Audubon Society chapters in Montana. Montana Audubon is involved in education, research, conservation, and public advocacy on issues affecting Montana's birds, wildlife, and other natural heritage. We enable Montana's 3,000 Audubon members to work together for the Audubon cause.
Contact(s):
President: HOWARD STRAUSE, 1917 W. Hill Pl., Great Falls, MT 59404; Phone: 406-727-7516
Vice President: DOROTHY POULSEN, 42 Olive, Helena, MT 59601; Phone: 406-449-7129
Secretary: CHUCK CARLSON, P.O. Box 227, Ft. Peck, MT 59223; Phone: 406-526-3245
Treasurer: BILL BALLARD, 5120 Larch Av., Missoula, MT 59802; Phone: 406-549-5097
Executive Director: JANET ELLIS
Keyword(s): Biodiversity, Birds, Land Use Planning, Wetlands

MONTANA B.A.S.S. CHAPTER FEDERATION
Attn: President, 221 Garland St., Kalispell, MT 59901
Scope: Statewide
Description: An organization of Bassmaster chapters, affiliated with the Bass Anglers Sportsman Society, organized to fight pollution, assist state and national conservation agencies in their efforts, and teach the young people of our country good conservation practice. Dedicated to the realistic conservation of our water resources.
Contact(s):
President: STEVE McGUIRE; Phone: 406-752-8400

MONTANA ENVIRONMENTAL INFORMATION CENTER
P.O. Box 1184, Helena, MT 59624
Phone: 406-443-2520; Fax: 406-443-2507; E-mail: meic@meic.org
Founded: 1973; Membership: 4,000
Scope: Statewide
Description: Overall purpose is to protect and restore Montana's natural environment. Educates and mobilizes citizens on Montana environmental issues to press for wise decisions at local, state, and federal levels. Priority issues include: Water quality, solid waste, hardrock mining, hazardous waste, environmental policy, air quality, land use planning, toxic chemicals, and energy conservation.
Contact(s):
Executive Director: JIM JENSEN
Board of Directors President: JOHN RAY
Board of Directors Vice President: HARVEY BJORNLIE
Publication(s): *Down to Earth; Capitol Monitor; Blackfoot Activist*
Keyword(s): Air Quality, Energy, Land Use Planning, Mining, Solid Waste Management, Toxic Substances, Water Quality

MONTANA FOREST OWNERS ASSOCIATION
17975 Ryan's Ln., Evaro, MT 59802
Phone: 406-726-3787; Fax: 406-549-2287
Scope: Statewide
Description: A statewide organization affiliated with the National Woodland Owners Association, dedicated to the careful use and active enjoyment of private forest lands in Montana. Goals are achieved through active forestry education programs, public communications, networking, and political advocacy.
Contact(s):
President: THORN LIECHTY
Vice President: PETER KOLB
Vice President: TOM CASTLES
Secretary: KAREN LIECHTY
Treasurer: JIM HAVILAND
Publication(s): *Big Sky NIPF-TY Notes*
Keyword(s): Forests and Forestry

MONTANA LAND RELIANCE
P.O. Box 355, Helena, MT 59624-0355
Phone: 406-443-7027; E-mail: mtland.mt.net
Scope: Statewide
Description: A private nonprofit land trust protecting and conserving ecologically and agriculturally significant land in Montana, as well as sharing knowledge of voluntary, private-sector land conservation techniques. Pioneering ways to assure a legacy of responsibly managed private land.
Contact(s):
President: DUDE TYLER, 418 S. Yellowstone, Livingston, MT 59047
Vice President: ROY O'CONNOR, 5015 Larch Ave., Missoula, MT 59802

NON-GOVERNMENTAL ORGANIZATIONS - M

Eastern Manager: CHRISTOPHER MONTAGUE, P.O. Box 171, Billings, MT 59103-0171; Phone: 406-259-1382; E-mail: mlr@mcn.net
Glacier/Flathead Regional Office: AMY EATON, P.O. Box 460, Bigfork, MT 59911-0460; Phone: 406-837-2178; E-mail: mlrnw@digisys.net
Secretary and Treasurer: GEORGE OLSEN, Galusha, Higgens & Galusha, Box 1699, Helena, MT 59624-1699
Publication(s): *Annual Report; Montana Spaces; Better Trout Habitat; Tax Implications of Donated Conservation Easements: An Introduction to Conservation Easements; A Guide to Planned Giving: Creation of a Conservation Legacy*
Keyword(s): Agriculture, Environment, Environmental Protection, Fisheries, Forest Management, Land Preservation, Natural Areas, Nature Preservation, Open Space, Rivers, Water Resources, Watersheds, Wetlands, Wildlife and Wildlife Habitat

MONTANA WILDERNESS ASSOCIATION
P.O. Box 635, Helena, MT 59624
Phone: 406-443-7350; Fax: 406-443-0750; E-mail: mwa@wildmontana.org; Web Site: www.wildmontana.org
Founded: 1958; Membership: 3,300
Scope: Statewide
Description: A nonprofit membership organization dedicated to the preservation and proper management of Montana's wild lands, including designated and de facto wilderness areas, national parks, national forests, wildlife refuges, and BLM lands in Montana. The Montana Wilderness Association has five chapter affiliates and four field offices.
Contact(s):
President: DENNIS TIGHE; Phone: 406-761-5463
Vice President: KEN SINAY; Phone: 406-586-1155
Director: BOB DECKER
Education Director: SUSAN MILES BRYAN
Program Director: JOHN GATCHELL
Publication(s): *Wild Montana; Wilderness Walks Program*
Keyword(s): Biodiversity, Forests and Forestry, Public Lands, Sustainable Ecosystems, Wilderness, Wildlife and Wildlife Habitat

MONTANA WILDLIFE FEDERATION
P.O. Box 1175, Helena, MT 59624-1175
Phone: 406-449-7604; Fax: 406-449-8946; E-mail: mwf@mtwf.org; Web Site: www.montanawildlife.com
Scope: Statewide
Description: A representative statewide organization, affiliated with the National Wildlife Federation, dedicated to the protection and enhancement of wildlife and its habitat through public education and government interaction.
Contact(s):
President and Alternative Representative: JOSH TURNER
Representative: KATHY HADLEY
Publication(s): *Montana Wildlife*

MOTE MARINE LABORATORY
1600 Ken Thompson Parkway, Sarasota, FL 34236
Phone: 941-388-4441; Fax: 941-388-4312; E-mail: info@mote.org
Founded: 1955; Membership: 4,000
Scope: National
Description: MML is an independent, nonprofit research organization dedicated to excellence in marine and environmental sciences. Since its inception, the laboratory's primary missions have been the pursuit of excellence in scientific research and the dissemination of information to the scientific community as well to the general public. MML operates a public aquarium, the Arthur Vining Davis Library and a marine science education and long distance learning program.
Contact(s):
Chairman: FREDERICK M. DERR, 1600 Ken Thompson Pkwy, Sarasota, FL 34236
President: WILLIAM R. MOTE, 1600 Ken Thompson Pkwy, Sarasota, FL 34236
Secretary: J. ROBERT LONG, 1486 Hillview Dr., Sarasota, FL 34239
Treasurer: ROBERT R. NELSON, 1600 Ken Thompson Pkwy, Sarasota, FL 34236
Executive Director: DR. KUMAR MAHADEVAN, 1600 Ken Thompson Pkwy., Sarasota, FL 34236
Vice Chairman: FREDERICK M. DERR, 1600 Ken Thonpson Pkwy, Sarasota, FL 34236
Publication(s): *Mote News; Views from Mote; Mote Marine Laboratory Collected Papers (list upon request)*
Keyword(s): Aquaculture, Aquariums, Biology, Chemistry, Dolphins, Endangered and Threatened Species, Environmental and Conservation Education, Fisheries, Manatees, Sea Turtles

MOUNT GRACE LAND CONSERVATION TRUST
137 N. Main St., New Salem, MA 01355
Phone: 978-544-7170; Fax: 978-544-3877; E-mail: mtgrace@shaysnet.com
Founded: 1987; Membership: 500
Scope: Local
Description: Mount Grace Land Conservation Trust is dedicated to the protection of forests, agricultural land, and other open space in North Central Massachusetts. In 12 years, Mount Grace Land Conservation Trust has permanently protected 11,000 acres in 90 separate projects.
Contact(s):
President/Executive Director: SHAUN BENNETT
Keyword(s): Agriculture, Conservation of Protected Areas, Forest Management, Nature Preservation, Open Space, Stewardship, Wildlife and Wildlife Habitat

MOUNT SHASTA AREA AUDUBON SOCIETY
P.O. Box 530, Mount Shasta, CA 96067
Phone: 916-842-2537
Founded: 1971; Membership: 124
Scope: Statewide
Description: Protects, enhances, and enjoys the natural environment of the Mount Shasta region, including its birds, wildlife, forests, mountains, meadows, and waters.
Contact(s):
President: BETTE KOERNER
Secretary: WILLO BALFREY, 2934 Nighthawk Ln., Weed, CA 96094; Phone: 916-938-2342
Editor: MIKE HAUPTMAN; Phone: 916-842-2537
Publication(s): *Endeavor*

MOUNTAIN CONSERVATION TRUST OF GEORGIA, INC.
104 N. Main St., Suite B3, Jasper, GA 30143
Phone: 706-692-4077; Fax: 706-692-4077; E-mail: mctg@mindspring.com
Founded: 1994; Membership: 360
Scope: Local Region
Description: Dedicated to the permanent conservation of the natural resources and scenic beauty of the mountains and foothills of north Georgia through land protection, partnerships and education.
Contact(s):
Executive Director: BARBARA DECKER Ph.D.
President: GARY REECE; Phone: 706-692-2424
Keyword(s): Environmental and Conservation Education, Land Protection, Watersheds, Wildlife and Wildlife Habitat

MOUNTAIN LION FOUNDATION
P.O. Box 1896, Sacramento, CA 95812
Phone: 916-442-2666; Fax: 916-442-2871; E-mail: MLF@mountainlion.org
Founded: 1986; Membership: 30,000
Scope: Statewide
Description: The Mountain Lion Foundation is a nonprofit conservation and education organization dedicated to protecting wildlife and their habitat throughout California.
Contact(s):
President: KATHY FLETCHER
Vice President: JOSEPH HURWITZ

Secretary: SHARON CAVALLO
Treasurer: TOBY COOPER
Executive Director: LYNN SADLER; Phone: 916-442-2666
Director of Conservation Programs: TOM MARTENS
Director of Education: CAITLIN RIVERS
Legal Program Director: J. WILLIAM YEATES
Publication(s): *Mountain Lion Update; Cougar: The American Lion; Preserving Cougar Country; Crimes Against the Wild: Poaching in California*
Keyword(s): Biodiversity, Conservation of Protected Areas, Endangered and Threatened Species, Environmental Law, Hunting, Land Preservation, Mammals, Nongame Wildlife, Predators, Wildlife and Wildlife Habitat, Wildlife Management

MOUNTAINEERS, THE (Conservation Division)
300 3rd Ave., W., Seattle, WA 98119
Phone: 206-284-6310
Founded: *1906;* **Membership:** *15,000*
Scope: *Regional*
Description: The Mountaineers provides opportunities for outdoor recreation and training to its members and strives to protect the environment through community outreach, education, and political action.
Contact(s):
President: BILL MAXWELL
Executive Director: STEVE COSTIE
Conservation Coordinator: JOHAN HELLMAN
Publication(s): *numerous titles published by Mountaineers Books*
Keyword(s): Coasts, Outdoor Recreation, Public Lands, Rivers, Wilderness, Wildlife and Wildlife Habitat

MULE DEER FOUNDATION, THE
1005 Terminal Way, Suite 170, Reno, NV 89502
Phone: 775-322-6558; Fax: 775-322-3421
Founded: *1988;* **Membership:** *6,400*
Scope: *National*
Description: The Mule Deer Foundation is a wildlife conservation organization that focuses on mule deer and their subspecies for habitat improvement.
Contact(s):
Chairman: KELLY SMITH, 63570 Johnson Rd., Bend, OR 97701; Phone: 541-382-7969
President: WILLIAM I. MORRILL Ph.D.
Publication(s): *Mule Deer*
Keyword(s): Environmental and Conservation Education, Hunting, Outdoor Recreation, Wildlife and Wildlife Habitat, Wildlife Management

MUSKIES, INC.
2301 7th St. N., Fargo, ND 58102
Phone: 701-239-9540
Founded: *1966;* **Membership:** *6,864*
Scope: *National*
Description: A nonprofit organization dedicated to establishing hatcheries and introducing the Muskellunge into suitable waters, abating water pollution, promoting a high quality muskellunge sport fishery, supporting selected conservation practices, promoting muskellunge research, disseminating muskellunge information, maintaining records of habits, growth, and range, and promoting good fellowship and sportsmanship.
Contact(s):
President: JIM SMITH, 1299 S. Carson Way, Aurora, CO 80012; Phone: 303-745-0630
President: STEVE BUDNIK, 5751 Monticello Way, Madison, WI 53719; Phone: 608-271-2872
Secretary: MIKE BRANDT, R.R. #7, Hayward, WI 54843; Phone: 715-462-3563
Treasurer: DAN RILEY, 3031 14th Avenue S., Moorhead, MN 56560; Phone: 218-236-8160
1st Vice President: SMOKEY SWENSON, 4023 Girard Avenue, Minneapolis, MN 55412; Phone: 612-522-9744
2nd Vice President: PAUL FRAMSTEAD, 7079 S. Uinta Street, Englewood, CO 80112; Phone: 303-694-3287
Administrative Secretary: PAT JOHNSON, 2301 7th St. N., Fargo, ND 58102; Phone: 701-239-9540
Editor: KEITH OGDEN, Rt. 1 Box 185, Cavalier, ND 58220; Phone: 701-265-8023
Publication(s): *Muskie*
Keyword(s): Lakes, Outdoor Recreation, Sport Fishing, Water Resources, Wildlife Management

N

NATIONAL 4-H COUNCIL
7100 Connecticut Ave., Chevy Chase, MD 20815-4999
WWW: www.fourhcouncil.edu
Founded: *1976*
Scope: *National*
Description: The National 4-H Council is a youth development organization fostering innovation and shared learning. An Environmental Stewardship program engages youth and adults to work as partners in developing creative, community-based solutions to environmental challenges. We also provide science-based educational materials that promote critical thinking skills and youth action grants.
Contact(s):
Project Coordinator: DAVID CARRIER; Fax: 301-961-2894; E-mail: carrier@fourhcouncil.edu
Project Director: KASHYAP CHOKSI; Fax: 301-961-2894; E-mail: choksi@fourhcouncil.edu
Publication(s): *Monthly e-mail update; environmental education materials on biotechnology, energy, transportation, food issues, endangered species and water quality*
Keyword(s): Biotechnology, Energy, Environmental and Conservation Education, Pesticides, Renewable Resources, Sustainable Development, Transportation, Wildlife and Wildlife Habitat, Youth Organizations

NATIONAL ARBOR DAY FOUNDATION
100 Arbor Ave., Nebraska City, NE 68410
Phone: 402-474-5655; Fax: 402-474-0820
Founded: *1971;* **Membership:** *1,000,000*
Scope: *National*
Description: A nonprofit, membership organization, sponsors Trees for America, Arbor Day, Tree City USA, Conservation Trees and Rain Forest Rescue educational programs. The Foundation publishes "Arbor Day National Poster Contest" and other instructional units for grade schools.
Contact(s):
Chair: TONY DORRELL
Vice Chair: PRESTON COLE, 211 N. 12th St., Lincoln, NE 68508
Honorary Trustee and Chairman: STEWART UDALL
President: JOHN ROSENOW
Information Director: GARY BRIENZO
Program Director: MARY YAGER, 211 N. 12th St., Lincoln, NE 68508
Editor: DR. JAMES R. FAZIO
Publication(s): *Arbor Day; Tree City USA Bulletin; Conservation Trees (booklet); Celebrate Arbor Day (booklet); Library of Trees*
Keyword(s): Environmental and Conservation Education, Flowers, Plants, and Trees, Forests and Forestry, Soil Conservation, Trees, Urban Forestry

NATIONAL ASSOCIATION FOR INTERPRETATION
P.O. Box 2246, Fort Collins, CO 80522
Phone: 970-484-8283/1-888-900-8283; Web Site: ww.interpnet.com
Founded: *1954;* **Membership:** *3,600*
Scope: *International*
Description: A nonprofit professional organization, employed by agencies and organizations concerned with natural and cultural resources, conservation, management and with the interpretation of the natural and historical environment.

NON-GOVERNMENTAL ORGANIZATIONS - N

Contact(s):
President: CEM BASMAN, So. Illinois University, Dept. of Forestry, Carbondale, IL 62901-4411; Phone: 618-453-7476; Fax: 618-453-7475; E-mail: cbasman@siu.edu
Executive Director: DR. TIM MERRIMAN, P.O. Box 2246, Fort Collins, CO 80522; Phone: 970-484-8283; Fax: 970-484-8179; E-mail: naiexec@aol.com
Editor: NANCY NICHOLS, Communication Director of NAI, P.O. Box 2246, Fort Collins, CO 80522; Phone: 970-484-8283; E-mail: naicom@aol.com
Publication(s): *Legacy; NAI News; Jobs in Interpretation; Journal of Interpretation Research; El Intérprete and Investigaciones en Interpretación*
Keyword(s): Communications, Environmental and Conservation Education, Internships, Interpretation, Natural History, Professional Organization

NATIONAL ASSOCIATION OF BIOLOGY TEACHERS
11250 Roger Bacon Dr., #19, Reston, VA 20190-5202
Phone: 703-471-1134 or 800-406-0775; Fax: 703-435-5582; E-mail: nabter@aol.com; Web Site: www.nabt.org
Founded: 1938; Membership: 7,500
Scope: National
Description: The only national association specifically organized to assist teachers in the improvement of biology/life science teaching. NABT offers teachers an opportunity to develop professionally through its journal, annual convention, summer workshops, and other publication programs.
Contact(s):
President: RICHARD D. STOREY, Chair, Dept. of Biology, The Colorado College, Colorado Springs, CO 80903; Phone: 719-389-6406; E-mail: rstorey@coloradocollege.edu
Executive Director: DR. WAYNE W. CARLEY, NABT, 11250 Roger Bacon Drive, #19, Reston, VA 20190-5202; Phone: 703-471-1134 or 800-406-0775; E-mail: nabt31@bellatlantic.net
Editor: RANDY MOORE, College of Arts & Sciences, University of Louisville, Louisville, KY 40292; Phone: 502-852-6490; E-mail: r0moor01@homer.louisville.edu
Managing Editor: CHRISTINE CHANTRY, NABT, 11250 Roger Bacon Drive, #19, Reston, VA 20190-5202; Phone: 703-471-1134 or 800-406-0775
Secretary and Treasurer: CATHERINE WILCOXSON, 2833 Douglas Dr., Fremont, NE 68025; E-mail: catherine.wilcoxson@nau.edu
Past President: VIVIAN LEE WARD, Access Excellence-Genentech, Inc., Mail Stop 16B, 460 Point San Bruno Blvd., South San Francisco, CA 94080; Phone: 650-225-8750; E-mail: vlward@gene.com
Publication(s): *American Biology Teacher, The; News and Views; The Monograph Series*
Keyword(s): Biology, Biotechnology, Environmental and Conservation Education, Zoology

NATIONAL ASSOCIATION OF CONSERVATION DISTRICTS
Headquarters, 509 Capitol Ct., NE, Washington, DC 20002
Phone: 202-547-6223; Fax: 202-547-6450; E-mail: info@nacdnet.org; Web Site: www.nacdnet.org
Founded: 1946
Scope: National
Description: A nonprofit organization serving as the national instrument of its membership - 3,000 local districts and 54 state and territorial associations. Conservation districts, local subdivisions of state government, work to promote the conservation, wise use and orderly development of land, water, forests, wildlife, and related natural resources.
Contact(s):
President: RUDY RICE, 8310 State Rte 14, DuQoin, IL 62832-9741; Phone: 618-542-4102; Fax: 618-542-3966
1st Vice President: J. READ SMITH, 11751 Lancaster Rd., St. John, WA 99171-9723; Phone: 509-648-3922; Fax: 509-648-3293
2nd Vice President: GARY MAST, 6055 CR 203 Rte 4, Millersburg, OH 44654; Phone: 330-674-6278; Fax: 330-674-3690
Secretary/Treasurer: TIM REICH, 1007 Kingsbury St., Belle Fourche, SD 57717; Phone: 605-892-4366
Chief Executive Officer: ERNEST C. SHEA; Phone: 202-547-6223; Fax: 202-547-6450
Director of National Wetlands Conservation Alliance: GENE WHITAKER
Director of Programs: EUGENE LAMB
Government Affairs/Communications Specialist: LAURA MCNICHOL
Capacity Center Contact: RAY LEDGERWOD, NE 1615 Eastgate Blvd., Suite B, Pullman, WA 99163; Phone: 509-334-1823; Fax: 509-334-3453
Director of Government Affairs: DAVID GAGNER
Director of Operations: BOB DOUCETTE
Director of Development/Membership: KAREN MCKAY
Director of Leadership Services, North: DEBRA A. BOGAR, 9150 W. Jewell Ave Ste 111, Lakewood, CO 80232-6469; Phone: 303-988-1893; Fax: 303-988-1896
Director of Leadership Services, South: ROBERT TOOLE, 4617 Cahaan Creek Rd., Edmond, OK 73034; Phone: 405-359-9011; Fax: 405-359-9047
Director of Meeting and Convention Services: BOB RASCHKE, 9150 W. Jewell Ave Ste 102, Lakewood, CO 80232-6469; Phone: 303-988-1810; Fax: 303-988-1896
Director of NACD Policy Center: BILL HORVATH, 1052 Main St. Ste 204, Stevens Point, Wi 54481-2895; Phone: 715-341-1022; Fax: 715-341-1023
Publication(s): *Tuesday Letter; District Leader, The; America's Conservation Districts; Guide to Conservation Careers; Environmental Film Service Catalogue; Service Center Catalogue; other conservation-related informational and educational publications*
Keyword(s): Agriculture, Environmental and Conservation Education, Soil Conservation, Urban Environment, Water Pollution, Conservation Districts

League City Office
P.O. Box 855, League City, TX 77574
Phone: 281-332-3402, Order: 1-800-825-5547; Fax: 281-332-5259
Scope: National
Contact(s):
Catalog Sales Representative: BECKY CORTEZ
Office of Public Affairs Director: RONALD G. FRANCIS
Office of Public Affairs Education Specialist: WENDY REISTLE
Office of Public Affairs Members Communications Specialist: BETH DETHLEFSEN
Service Center Director of Association and Administrative Services: S. JEFF WINTERS
Service Center Production Manager: MAXINE MATHIS

NATIONAL ASSOCIATION OF ENVIRONMENTAL PROFESSIONALS, THE (National Office)
6524 Ramoth Dr., Jacksonville, FL 32226-3202
Phone: 904-251-9900; Fax: 904-251-9901; E-mail: naep@ilnk.com; Web Site: www.naep.org
Founded: 1975; Membership: 2,000
Scope: National
Description: NAEP is the professional association of the environmental professions, dedicated to the promotion of ethical practice, technical competency, and professional standards in the environmental field and recognition of the environmental profession since 1975.
Keyword(s): Air Quality and Pollution, Energy, Environmental Planning, Solid Waste Management, Water Resources, Professional Organization

NATIONAL ASSOCIATION OF RECREATION RESOURCE PLANNERS
c/o Tim Bradle, Treasurer, Texas Parks & Wildlife Dept., 4200 Smith School Rd., Austin, SC 78744-3291
Phone: 512-912-7109; Fax: 512-707-2742
Scope: National
Description: A nonprofit organization involved in the exchange of recreation resource planning information among federal, state and

regional agencies. Participates in national recreation concerns, promotes improvements in the state-of-the-art of recreation planning and professionalism among its members and acts as an advocate for conservation and recreation opportunities for the future.
Contact(s):
President: GORDON KIMBALL, Minnesota
Vice President: ROBERT SAMMON, New Hampshire
Treasurer: TIM BRADLE, Texas
Publication(s): *NARRP Newsletter*
Keyword(s): Land Use Planning, Open Space, Outdoor Recreation, Planning Management, Public Lands

NATIONAL ASSOCIATION OF SERVICE AND CONSERVATION CORPS (NASCC)
666 11th St., NW, Suite 1000, Washington, DC 20001
Phone: 202-737-6272; Fax: 202-737-6277; E-mail: nascc@nascc.org; Web Site: www.nascc.org
Founded: 1985; Membership: 180
Scope: National
Description: NASCC unites and supports youth corps as a permanent strategy for achieving the nation's youth development, community service, and environmental restoration goals. NASCC serves as an advocate, central reference point, and source of assistance for the growing number of state and local youth corps around the country.
Contact(s):
President: KATHLEEN SELZ
Vice President, Field Services: HARRY BRUELL
Vice President, Government Relations and Public Affairs: ANDREW MOORE
Director for Member Services: LESLIE WILKOFF
Publication(s): *Youth Corps Profiles; Youth Corps Resource Book; Corpsmember Wellness Guide; Urban Waterways Restoration Training Manual*
Keyword(s): Environmental and Conservation Education, People of Color in the Environment, Riparian Restoration, Trail, Training, Urban Environment, Youth Organizations

NATIONAL ASSOCIATION OF STATE DEPARTMENTS OF AGRICULTURE
1156 15th St., NW, Suite 1020, Washington, DC 20005
Phone: 202-296-9680; Fax: 202-296-9686; E-mail: nasda@patriot.net; Web Site: www.nasda-hq.org
Scope: National
Description: The National Association of State Departments of Agriculture (NASDA) is a nonprofit, nonpartisan association of public officials comprised of the executive heads of the fifty State Departments of Agriculture and those from territories of Puerto Rico, Guam, American Samoa, and the Virgin Islands. NASDA's mission is to support and promote the American agriculture industry, while protecting consumers and the environment, through the development, implementation, and communication of sound policy and programs.
Contact(s):
Chief Executive Officer: RICHARD W. KIRCHHOFF
Publication(s): *NASDA News (weekly); Ag In Perspective (quarterly)*
Keyword(s): Agriculture, Biotechnology, Conservation of Protected Areas, Conservation Tillage, Environmental Protection, Health and Nutrition, Pesticides, Precision Farming, Public Farming, Public Lands, Rural Development, Water Pollution, Water Quality, Water Resources, Wetlands

NATIONAL ASSOCIATION OF STATE FORESTERS
NASF Executive Director: BILL IMBERGAMO 444 N. Capitol St. NW Suite 540, Washington, DC 20001
Phone: 202-624-5415; E-mail: nasf@sso.org; Web Site: www.stateforesters.org
Scope: National
Description: Members are state foresters or equivalent officials whose agencies are the legally-constituted authorities for public forestry work within the states. In cooperation with federal agencies, private organizations, and individuals, NASF promotes sound forest management on public and private lands.
Contact(s):
President: STAN ADAMS, NC Div. of Forest Resources, P.O. Box 29581, Raleigh, NC 27626-0581; Phone: 919-733-2162, ext. 202
Vice President: CONNIE MOTYKA, VT Dept. of Forest, Parks and Recreation, 103 S. Main St., Waterbury, VT 05671-0601; Phone: 802-241-3670
Treasurer: LARRY KOTCHMAN, ND Forest Service, 307 First St., Bottineau, ND 58318-1100; Phone: 701-228-5422
NASF Executive Director: BILL IMBERGAMO
Northeastern Area Regional Representative: JIM MALLOW, MD Forest Service, Dept. of Natural Resources, Tawes State Office Bldg., 580 Taylor Ave., E-1, Annapolis, MD 21401; Phone: 410-260-8501
Southern Group Regional Representative: KEN ARNEY, TN Dept. of Agriculture, Div. Of Forestry, P.O. Box 40627, Melrose Station, Nashville, TN 37204; Phone: 615-837-5520
Western Council Regional Representative: TOBY MARTINEZ, NM Forestry Div., P.O. Box 1948, Santa Fe, NM 87504-1948; Phone: 505-827-5830
Publication(s): *NASF Washington Update*
Keyword(s): Forests and Forestry, Public Lands, Soil Conservation, Urban Forestry, Water Resources, Professional Organization

NATIONAL ASSOCIATION OF STATE OUTDOOR RECREATION LIAISON OFFICERS
Attn: President, Administrator for Division of Customer Assistance and External Relations, Dept. of Natural Resources, P.O. Box 7921, Madison, WI 53707
Founded: 1967
Scope: National
Description: An organization of 56 gubernatorial-appointed state and territorial officials working with the National Park Service and the Department of the Interior to strengthen the nation's total outdoor recreation program. Represents state and local interests in administration of the Land and Water Conservation Fund Program, which provides money for acquisition and development of recreation land and facilities.
Contact(s):
President: CRAIG L. KARR, Administrator for Division of Customer Assistance and External Relations, Department of Natural Resources, P.O. Box 7921, Madison, WI 53707; Phone: 608-266-5896
Vice President: COURTLAND C. NELSON, Director of Division of Parks and Recreation, P.O. Box 146001, Salt Lake City, UT 84114-6001; Phone: 801-538-7362
Secretary: CHARLES A. SALKIN, Director of Division of Parks and Recreation, 89 Kings Hwy, Dover, DE 19901; Phone: 302-739-4401
Executive Director: NEY C. LANDRUM, 126 Mill Branch Rd., Tallahassee, FL 32312; Phone: 850-893-4959
Keyword(s): Land Purchase, Outdoor Recreation, Planning Management

NATIONAL ASSOCIATION OF STATE PARK DIRECTORS
Attn: Executive Director, 9894 E. Holden Pl., Tucson, AZ 85748
Founded: 1962; Membership: 50
Scope: National
Description: Works to unite the states on a common ground for the development of park systems to meet the intensive public demand for out-of-doors recreational opportunities; to promote the exchange of ideas regarding the development of state park systems; to encourage and develop professional leadership; and to expand and improve park policies and practices.
Contact(s):
President: KENNETH E. TRAVOUS, Executive Director of Arizona State Parks, 1300 W. Washington, Phoenix, AZ 85007
Executive Director: GLEN ALEXANDER, 9894 E. Holden Pl., Tucson, AZ 85748
Secretary and Treasurer: YVONNE FERRELL, Director, Dept. of Parks & Rec., PO Box 83720-0065, Boise, ID 83720-00665

Keyword(s): Environmental and Conservation Education, Land Purchase, Land Use Planning, Outdoor Recreation, Public Lands, Professional Organization

NATIONAL ASSOCIATION OF UNIVERSITY FISHERIES AND WILDLIFE PROGRAMS
ATTN: President, Department of Animal Ecology, Iowa State University, Ames, IA 50011-3221
Founded: 1991
Scope: National
Description: Meets annually at the North American Wildlife and Natural Resources Conference. The purpose is to foster improved communications among members and between other agencies, organizations, and the general public in order to provide a unified voice for academic fisheries and wildlife programs.
Contact(s):
President: CHARLES G. SCALET, Department of Wildlife and Fisheries Sciences, South Dakota State University, Brookings, SD 57007-1696; Phone: 605-688-6121
President-Elect: BRUCE W. MENZEL, Department of Animal Ecology, Iowa State University, Ames, IA 50011-3221; Phone: 515-294-7419
Secretary and Treasurer: ERIK FRITZELL, Department of Fisheries and Wildlife, Oregon State University, Corvallis, OR 97331; Phone: 541-737-2910
Keyword(s): Environmental and Conservation Education, Fisheries, Wildlife and Wildlife Habitat

NATIONAL AUDUBON SOCIETY
Headquarters, 700 Broadway, New York, NY 10003-9501
Phone: 212-979-3000
Founded: 1905; Membership: 550,000
Scope: International
Description: Solid Science, policy research, lobbying, citizen science and action, and education -- these are the tools used by the Audubon Society to protect the land and habitat that are critical to our health and the health of the planet. With the support of 550,000 members (in addition to the 500,000 elementary school students in the Audubon Adventures Program) and an extensive chapter network in the United States and Latin America, Audubon draws on the enthusiasm and power of the grassroots to save our threatened ecosystems.
Contact(s):
Chairman of the Board: DONAL C. O'BRIEN JR.; Fax: 212-353-0377
President and CEO: JOHN FLICKER
Editor-in-chief Audubon Magazine: LISA GOSSELIN
Senior Vice-President of Development: CAROL ANN MAY
Senior Vice-President of Field Operations and Sanctuaries: GLENN E. OLSON
Senior Vice-President of Marketing and Communications: CLARE TULLY
Senior Vice-President of Operations: JAMES A. CUNNINGHAM
Senior Vice-President of Public Policy and Campaigns: DANIEL BEARD
Senior Vice-President of Science: FRANK GILL
Vice-President of Membership: CELIA TENNENBAUM
Vice-President of Publishing: JAMES FISHMAN
Vice-President/Controller: CAROLE J. MCNAMARA
Publication(s): *Audubon; Audubon Field Notes; Audubon Adventures*
Keyword(s): Birds

Everglades Campaign Office
444 Brickell Ave., Suite 850, Miami, FL 33131
Phone: 305-371-6399; Fax: 305-371-6398
Scope: Regional
Contact(s):
Director: STUART STRAHL
Human Population and Resource Use Director: PATRICIA WAAK, 4150 Darley Ave., Suite 7, Boulder, CO 80303; Phone: 303-499-5155; Fax: 303-499-0286
Keyword(s): Everglades

Project Puffin
159 Sapsucker Woods Rd., Ithaca, NY 14850
Scope: Regional
Contact(s):
Director: STEPHEN KRESS

Scully Science Center
306 S. Bay Ave., Islip, NY 11751
Phone: 516-277-4289; Fax: 516-581-5268
Scope: Regional
Contact(s):
Director: DR. CARL SAFINA

Tavernier Science Center
115 Indian Mound Tr., Tavernier, FL 33070
Phone: 305-852-5092; Fax: 305-852-4889
Scope: Regional
Contact(s):
Coordinator: JEROME LORENZ

Washington, D.C. Office
1901 Pennsylvania Ave., NW, Suite 1100, Washington, DC 20006
Phone: 202-861-2242; Fax: 202-861-4290
Scope: Regional
Contact(s):
DAN BEARD

NATIONAL AUDUBON SOCIETY, LIVING OCEANS PROGRAM
550 South Bay Ave., Islip, NY 11751
Phone: 516-859-3032; Fax: 516-581-5268; E-mail: mlee@audubon.org; Web Site: www.audubon.org/campaign/10
Founded: 1993; Membership: 4,000
Scope: National
Description: Living Oceans is the marine conservation program of National Audubon Society. The program is dedicated to reversing the mismanagement of marine fisheries which has led to the depletion of marine wildlife, and to restore the health of our marine environment and coastal habitats.
Contact(s):
Assistant Director: MERCEDES LEE; Phone: 516-224-3669
Director: DR. CARL SAFINA
Staff Scientist: DR. MERRY CAMHI; Phone: 516-581-2927
Publication(s): *Living Oceans News; Audubon Guide to Seafood*
Keyword(s): Marine Conservation, Ocean Conservation

NATIONAL AVIARY
Allegheny Commons West, Pittsburgh, PA 15212-5248
Phone: 412-323-7235; Fax: 412-321-4364; E-mail: info@aviary.org; Web Site: www.aviary.org
Founded: 1952; Membership: 1,750
Scope: National
Description: The National Aviary works to inspire respect for nature through the appreciation of birds. Travel the world at the National Aviary and visit over 500 exotic and endangered birds in natural habitats.
Contact(s):
Executive Director: DAYTON BAKER
Publication(s): *Bird Calls*
Keyword(s): Biodiversity, Birds, Botanical Gardens, Conservation, Endangered and Threatened Species, Environmental and Conservation Education, Flowers, Plants, and Trees, Raptors, Wildlife and Wildlife Habitat, Zoology

NATIONAL BIRD-FEEDING SOCIETY
P.O. Box 23, Northbrook, IL 60065-0023
Phone: 847-272-0135; E-mail: feedbirds@aol.com
Founded: 1989; Membership: 15,000
Scope: National
Description: The National Bird-Feeding Society works to make feeding of wild birds better for birds as well as for people. The Society also works to encourage suitable feeding and nesting habitats for backyard birds to thrive; sponsors education and research on backyard birds; and helps people learn more ways to

attract and care for birds, to share bird-feeding experiences, observations, and to help the environment through the backyard.
Contact(s):
Executive Director: SUE WELLS
Chairman Emeritus: DONALD STOKES
Chairman of Board of **Publication(s):** *The Bird's-Eye reView*
Keyword(s): Birds, Conservation of Protected Areas, Environment, Flowers, Plants, and Trees, Research

NATIONAL BOATING FEDERATION
P.O. Box 4111, Annapolis, MD 21403
Phone: 410-626-8566
Founded: 1966; Membership: 2 million
Scope: National
Description: National, all-volunteer, non-profit boating organization consisting principally of regional or special interest boating organizations and yacht clubs. Activities include monitoring federal legislation and rule-making as they affect recreational boating. The NBF promotes the interests of those who use boats for cruising, water skiing, fishing, and other water sports.
Contact(s):
President: ROBERT DAVID, 70 Garfield Lane, West Dennis, MA 02670-2321; Phone: 508-394-5670; Fax: 508-394-7236
Vice-President: ROGER K. BROWN, 111 S. View Court, Shore Acres, NJ 08723-7520; Phone: 732-236-3516; Fax: 732-477-0071
Secretary and Treasurer: WILLIAM A. HEIDER, 1114 Appletree Lane, Erie, PA 16509-3917; Phone: 814-825-3011; Fax: 814-825-5284
Public Relations and Editor: JILL ANDRICK, P.O. Boxk 211, Salem, OR 97308-0211; Phone: 503-580-0769
Past President: WILLIAM D. MITCHELSON, 9483 N. Fairway Cr., Milwaukee, WI 53217-1316; Phone: 414-352-0967
Publication(s): *The LOOKOUT; Recreational Boating News and Legislative Issues*
Keyword(s): Coasts, Lakes, Outdoor Recreation, Rivers, Water Pollution

NATIONAL COALITION FOR MARINE CONSERVATION
3 W. Market St., Leesburg, VA 20176
Phone: 703-777-0037; Fax: 703-777-1107
Founded: 1973
Scope: National
Description: A nonprofit, privately-supported organization devoted exclusively to the conservation of ocean fish and the protection of their environment. Promotes public awareness of marine conservation issues and stimulates the formulation of responsible public policy.
Contact(s):
President and Editor: KEN HINMAN
Chairman of the Board: CHRISTOPHER M. WELD, One Post Office Square 24th Fl., Boston, MA 02109; Phone: 617-338-2909
Director of Communication and Development: CHRISTINE WILKINS
Publication(s): *Marine Bulletin*
Keyword(s): Coasts, Environmental and Conservation Education, Fisheries, Sport Fishing, Wetlands

NATIONAL COUNCIL FOR GEOGRAPHIC EDUCATION
16A Leonard Hall, Indiana University of Pennsylvania, Indiana, PA 15705
Phone: 412-357-6290
Founded: 1915; Membership: 4,000
Scope: National
Description: To promote and advance geographic and environmental education in the public schools and colleges of the U.S. and Canada.
Contact(s):
President: JAMES F. PETERSON
Secretary: SANDRA MATHER
Executive Director: RUTH I. SHIREY
Editor: JONATHAN LEIB, Department of Geography, Florida State University, Tallahassee, FL 32306-4016
Vice President of Curriculum and Instruction: ROBERT BEDNARZ

Vice President of Finance: CELESTE FRASER
Vice President of Publications and Products: GARY ELBOW
Publication(s): *Journal of Geography; Water In the Global Environment; list of other publications available upon request.*
Keyword(s): Environmental and Conservation Education

NATIONAL COUNCIL OF STATE GARDEN CLUBS, INC.
4401 Magnolia Ave., St. Louis, MO 63110
Phone: 314-776-7574; Fax: 314-776-5108
Founded: 1929; Membership: 243,597/8,858 clubs
Scope: National
Description: Coordinates and furthers the interests and activities of the State Federations of Garden Clubs and aids in the protection and conservation of natural resources; protects civic beauty and encourages the improvement of roadsides and parks; encourages and assists in establishing and maintaining botanical gardens and horticultural centers; and advances the arts of gardening and landscape design, and study of horticulture.
Contact(s):
President: DEEN DAY SMITH, 4725 Peachtree Corners Circle, Suite 300, Norcross, GA 30092-2599
1st Vice President: LOIS DUPRE SHUSTER, Seven Springs, Champion, PA 15622-9801
2nd Vice President: JUNE P. WOOD, 7000 Seminole Rd., NE, Albuquerque, NM 87110-2739
Corresponding Secretary: MARVINA W. NORTHCUTT, 505 Wood Valley Dr. SW, Marietta, GA 30064-3349
Treasurer: SUSAN GOODYEAR SLIVKEN, 4613 37th Ave., Rock Island, IL 61201-7108
Executive Director: FRAN MANTLER
Conservation/Natural Resources Wildlife/Endangered Species Chairperson and "Backyard Habitats for Wildlife": MARION B. HILBAID, 2902 Greenridge Rd., Orange Park, FL 32073-6412; Phone: 904-264-6619; Fax: 904-264-2440; E-mail: marionh@bellsouth.net
Editor: SUSAN DAVIDSON, 102 S. Elm St., St. Louis, MO 63119; Fax: 314-968-1664; E-mail: susand4@juno.com
Publication(s): *National Gardener, The*
Keyword(s): Gardening and Horticulture, Natural Resource Conservation

NATIONAL EDUCATION ASSOCIATION
1201 16th St., NW, Washington, DC 20036
Phone: 202-833-4000
Founded: 1857; Membership: 2,000,000
Scope: National
Description: Works to elevate the character and advance the interests of the teaching profession and to promote the cause of education in the U.S.
Contact(s):
President: ROBERT F. CHASE
Vice President: REG WEAVER
Executive Director: DON CAMERON
Secretary and Treasurer: DENNIS VAN ROEKEL

NATIONAL ENVIRONMENTAL HEALTH ASSOCIATION
720 S. Colorado Blvd., S. Tower, Suite 970, Denver, CO 80246-1925
Phone: 303-756-9090; Fax: 303-691-9490; E-mail: staff@neha.org; Web Site: www.neha.org
Founded: 1937; Membership: 5,000
Scope: National
Description: NEHA is a member nonprofit organization that offers a wide variety of educational credentialing and advancement opportunities for people involved or interested in environmental health issues. It is the largest society of environmental health practitioners in the nation today, numbering almost 5,000 members and growing.
Contact(s):
Executive Director: NELSON E. FABIAN
Publication(s): *Journal of Environmental Health; Self Paced Learning Modules; Environment News Digest; various books, manuals, etc.*

Keyword(s): Air Quality and Pollution, Environmental Health, Food Safety, Solid Waste, Toxic Substances, Water Pollution, Water Resources

NATIONAL FARMERS UNION
11900E. Cornell Ave., Aurora, CO 80014-3194
Phone: 303-337-5500
Founded: 1902
Scope: National
Description: Believes that the soil, water, forest and other natural resources of the nation should be used and conserved in a manner to pass these resources on undiminished to future generations and that publicly and privately owned land and resources should be administered in the interest of all the public.
Contact(s):
President: LELAND H. SWENSON
Vice President: CHARLES NASH
Editor: MARILYN WENTZ, 11900 E. Cornell Ave., Aurora, CO 80014-3194; Phone: 303-337-5500
Treasurer/Secretary: DAVID CARTER
Vice President of Legislative Services: LARRY MITCHELL, 400 Virginia Ave. SW, Suite 710, Washington, DC 20024; Phone: 202-554-1600
Publication(s): *National Farmers Union News*
Keyword(s): Agriculture, Environmental Law, Health and Nutrition, Renewable Resources, Soil Conservation

NATIONAL FFA ORGANIZATION
P.O. Box 15160, National FFA Center, Alexandria, VA 22309
Phone: 703-360-3600
Founded: 1928
Scope: National
Description: The FFA is a national organization of high school agriculture students in public secondary schools. Congress granted the organization a federal charter in 1950, making it an integral part of the high school agriculture program. Major aims are to provide activities that will stimulate students to higher achievement in the study of production agriculture, agriscience, agribusiness, and agrimarketing, and give them opportunities through student-planned programs for leadership and self-development.
Contact(s):
Executive Secretary: C. COLEMAN HARRIS; Phone: 703-360-3600
Advisor: DR. LARRY D. CASE; Phone: 703-360-3600
Publication(s): *FFA New Horizons Magazine, The; FFA Advisor Publication; Update Newsletter*
Keyword(s): Agriculture, Biotechnology, Gardening and Horticulture, Renewable Resources, Youth Organizations

NATIONAL FIELD ARCHERY ASSOCIATION
31407 Outer I-10, Redlands, CA 92373
Phone: 1-800-811-2331 909-794-2133
Membership: 20,000
Scope: National
Description: A nonprofit national membership headquarters for all archers.
Contact(s):
President: WALTER RUEGER, 122 Stanton Ave., Ripon, WI 54971
Bowhunting Committee Chairman: TIM ATWOOD, 3175 Racine, Riverside, CA 92503
Editor: ARLYNE RHODE
Executive Secretary: MARIHELEN ROGERS
Publication(s): *Archery Magazine*
Keyword(s): Hunting, Scholarships and Grants, Sport Fishing, Youth Organizations

NATIONAL FISH AND WILDLIFE FOUNDATION
1120 Connecticut Ave., NW, Suite 900, Washington, DC 20036
Phone: 202-857-0166; Fax: 202-857-0162; E-mail: info@nfwf.org
Founded: 1984
Scope: National
Description: A national nonprofit grant-making and grant-seeking organization dedicated to the conservation of natural resources -- fish, wildlife, and plants. NFWF was established by Congress to leverage federally, appropriated funds by forging public and private partnerships which result in conservation activities that pinpoint and solve root causes of environmental problems.
Contact(s):
Deputy Director: ALEX ECHOLS
Executive Director: AMOS S. ENO
Chairman of the Board: MAGALEN O. BRYANT
Chief Financial Officer: GINETTE RING
Director of Conservation Education Initiative: TOM KELSCH
Director of Conservation Policy: LORRAINE HOWERTON
Director of Conservation Programs: WHITNEY C. TILT
Director of Development and Marketing: ANNE WALTON
Director of Fisheries, Conservation and Management Initiative: JERRY CLARK
Director of Neotropical Migratory Bird Conservation Program: PETER W. STANGEL
Director of Wetlands and Private Lands: MOIRA MCDONALD
Director of Wildlife and Habitat Initiative: GARY KANIA
Keyword(s): Birds, Endangered and Threatened Species, Environmental and Conservation Education, Fisheries, Wildlife and Wildlife Habitat

NATIONAL FLYWAY COUNCIL
South Dakota Game Fish and Parks, 523 E. Capitol, Pierre, SD 57501
Scope: National
Contact(s):
Chairman: GEORGE VANDEL, South Dakota Game, Fish, and Parks Department, 523 E. Capitol, Pierre, SD 57501

Atlantic Flyway Office
Division of Fish and Wildlife Department of Environmental Conservation 50 Wolf Rd., Albany, NY 12233
Phone: 518-457-5690
Scope: Regional
Contact(s):
Chairman: KENNETH WICH

Central Flyway Office
Kansas Department of Wildlife and Parks Rt. 2 Box 54A, Pratt, KS 67124
Scope: Regional
Contact(s):
Chairman: JOE KRAMER

Mississippi Flyway Office
Section of Wildlife Natural Resources, 500 Lafayette Rd., St. Paul, MN 55155
Scope: Regional
Contact(s):
Chairman: ROGER HOLMES

NATIONAL FOREST FOUNDATION
1099 14th St., NW, Suite 5600W, Washington, DC 20005
Phone: 202-501-2473; Fax: 202-219-6585; E-mail: 1.girard@if.arctic.com
Founded: 1993
Scope: National
Description: The National Forest Foundation supports the U.S. Forest Service in its management, protection and use of the nation's forest lands by increasing awareness and appreciation to further the purposes of the National Forest System, including support for research and cooperative programs, and by raising private funds to better protect and nurture forest lands.
Contact(s):
Acting President: TERRY AUSTIN
Assistant Vice President for Conservation Programs: KENNETH GALLIK
Chief Financial Officer: BRENDA A. JONES
Events Coordinator: JULIA LAM
Vice President for Membership: CINDA JONES
Publication(s): *Forest Leader*

Keyword(s): Environmental and Conservation Education, Forests and Forestry, Outdoor Recreation, Public Lands, Wildlife and Wildlife Habitat

NATIONAL FORESTRY ASSOCIATION
374 Maple Ave., E., Suite 310, Vienna, VA 22180
Phone: 703-255-2300; Fax: 703-281-9200
Founded: 1981; Membership: 42,000
Scope: National
Description: A nationwide advocate of sustainable forestry on private and public lands. Programs include the National Forestry Network, Green Tag Forestry, the American Hardwood Management Advisory Board and the National Historic Lookout Register.
Contact(s):
President: KEITH A. ARGOW; E-mail: nwoa@mindspring.com
Staff Forester: LOREN LARSON
National Historic Lookout Register: NANCY GABRIEL
Hardwood Management Advisory Board: ARLYN PERKEY; Phone: 304-285-1523
Editor: ERIC A. JOHNSON; Phone: 315-369-3078
Publication(s): *Forestry Advantage, The*
Keyword(s): Conservation of Protected Areas, Forest Management, Forests and Forestry, Renewable Resources, Sustainable Resources, Green Certification

NATIONAL FOUNDATION TO PROTECT AMERICA'S EAGLES (Save The Eagle)
P.O. Box 120206, Nashville, TN 37212
Phone: 615-847-4171
Founded: 1985
Scope: National
Description: Dedicated to saving, restoring, and protecting America's endangered national symbol, the Bald Eagle, and preserving America's wildlife, waterways, forests, natural resources, ecosystems, and environment.
Contact(s):
Vice President: BOBBY J. HALLIBURTON
Secretary: STEVEN C. COMPTON
Treasurer: JULIETTE INGRAM
President and CEO: AL LOUIS CECERE, P.O. Box 120206, Nashville, TN 37212
Publication(s): *American Eagle News*

NATIONAL GARDENING ASSOCIATION
180 Flynn Ave., Burlington, VT 5401
Phone: 802-863-1308; Fax: 802-863-5962
Founded: 1972; Membership: 200,000
Scope: National
Description: The mission of the National Gardening Association is to sustain the essential values of life and community, renewing the fundamental links between people, plants, and the earth. Through gardening, we promote environmental responsibility, advance multidisciplinary learning and scientific literacy, and create partnerships that restore and enhance communities.
Contact(s):
President: DAVID E. ELS
Administrative Coordinator of GrowLab: JIM FLINT
Assistant Treasurer and CFO: A. WILLIAM MILLER II
Associate Director of Education: EVE PRANIS
Board of Directors Vice-Chair: JAMES SCHASSER
Director of Advertising: LARRY SOMMERS
Director of Circulation: BETSY BRADBURY
Director of Development: RETTA HUTTLINGER
Director of Education Programs: DOUGLAS HARRIS
Editor-in-Chief: MICHAEL MacCASKEY
Horticulturist: CHARLIE NARDOZZI
Managing Editor: DAN HICKEY
Market Research: BRUCE BUTTERFIELD
Senior Editor: JACK RUTTLE
Publication(s): *National Gardening Magazine; Guide to Kids Gardening; Community Garden Book, The; National Gardening Survey; Gardening; Gardening Video Series; GrowLab: A Complete Guide to Gardening in the Classroom; Ruth Page's Gardening Journal; GROWLAB: Activities for*
Keyword(s): Environmental and Conservation Education, Flowers, Plants, and Trees, Gardening and Horticulture, Youth Organizations

NATIONAL GEOGRAPHIC SOCIETY
1145 17th St., NW, Washington, DC 20036
Phone: 202-857-7000; Web Site: nationalgeographic.com
Founded: 1888; Membership: 10,000,000
Scope: International
Description: For the increase and diffusion of geographic knowledge.
Contact(s):
President and CEO: JOHN M. FAHEY JR.
Chairman of the Board: GILBERT M. GROSVENOR
Editor of National Geographic: WILLIAM L. ALLEN
Senior Vice President and Chief Financial Officer: CHRISTOPHER A. LIEDEL
Senior Vice President: NINA HOFFMAN
Senior Vice President: TERRENCE B. ADAMSON
Senior Vice President: ROBERT B. SIMS
Vice Chairman of the Board: REG MURPHY
Publication(s): *National Geographic; National Geographic World Magazine (for children); National Geographic Traveler; Books; Atlases; Maps; Globes; Filmstrips; Documentary Films; Classroom Materials; National Geographic Adventure Magazine; National Geographic Channel*
Keyword(s): Environmental and Conservation Education, Geography, Natural History, Oceanography, Public Lands

NATIONAL GRANGE, THE
1616 H St., NW, Washington, DC 20006-4999
Phone: 202-628-3507; Web Site: www.nationalgrange.org
Founded: 1867; Membership: 300,000
Scope: National
Description: Rural family service organization with special interests in community service and agriculture.
Contact(s):
Secretary: SHIRLEY LAWSON, 120 Wilson Ave., Rumford, RI 02916; Phone: 401-434-1491
Executive Committee Chairman: ROBERT CLARK; Phone: 360-683-4431
Executive Committee Secretary: A. R. HENNINGER; Phone: 815-544-4522
Legislative Director: LEROY WATSON, Washington D.C. Office
Master: KERMIT W. RICHARDSON, Washington DC Office
Publication(s): *View From The Hill; Grange Today*
Keyword(s): Agriculture, Environmental Law, Land Use Planning, Soil Conservation, Transportation

NATIONAL GROUND WATER ASSOCIATION, THE
601 Dempsey Rd., Westerville, OH 43081
Phone: 1-800-551-7379/614-898-7791; Fax: 614-898-7786; Web Site: www.ngwa.org
Founded: 1948
Scope: National
Description: The NGWA is the world's leading organization committed to the study of the occurrence, development, and protection of ground water. The Association annually sponsors educational programs dealing with a wide variety of water issues, including toxic substances, solid waste, and water pollution. Operates on-line data bases at Web Site.
Contact(s):
Executive Director: KEVIN McCRAY
Information: SANDY MASTERS, National Ground Water Information Center, 601 Dempsey Dr., Westerville, OH 43081
Publication(s): *Water Well Journal; Ground Water Monitoring and Remediation; Journal of Ground Water*
Keyword(s): Environmental and Conservation Education, Geology, Water Pollution, Water Resources

NATIONAL HUNTERS ASSOCIATION, INC.
P.O. Box 820, Knightdale, NC 27545
Phone: 919-365-7157

NON-GOVERNMENTAL ORGANIZATIONS - N

Founded: 1976
Scope: National
Description: The National Hunters Association, Inc. was incorporated under the laws of NC to protect your hunting rights in the U.S. and around the world. Dedicated to hunter safety, the preservation of the rights of the individual sportsman to pursue the sport of hunting and the preservation of an adequate supply of game for the sportsman to hunt -- now and in the future.
Contact(s):
President: D. V. SMITH
Vice President: JIM HUNTER
Secretary and Treasurer: FAYE M. SMITH
Publication(s): *NHA Newsletter*
Keyword(s): Environmental and Conservation Education, Hunting, Trapping, Youth Organizations

NATIONAL MILITARY FISH AND WILDLIFE ASSOCIATION
12428 Pinecrest Ln., Newburg, MD 20664
Founded: 1983; Membership: 700
Scope: National
Description: A nonprofit organization established to promote professional natural resources management on over 25.5 million acres of United States Department of Defense lands worldwide. Membership is comprised primarily of professional Department of Defense natural resources personnel.
Contact(s):
President: MARK HAGAN, AFFTC/EMXC, Edwards Air Force Base, CA 93524-1103; Phone: 661-277-1418
Vice President: DON PITTS, 7 CES/CEVA, Dyess Air Force Base, TX 79607; Phone: 915-696-5664
Director-At-Large: PAT WALSH, 347 WG, DET 1, OLA/CEVN, Avon Park AFR, FL 33825; Phone: 941-452-4254
Director-At-Large: JIM BAILY, STEAP-SH-ER, APG, MD 21005-5001; Phone: 410-278-6748
Secretary and Treasurer: TAMMY CONKLE, MCAS MIRAMAR, San Diego, CA 92145-2103; Phone: 619-577-6498
Eastern Regional Director: SCOTT SMITH, Dare County AF Range, Manteo, NC 27954; Phone: 919-722-1001
Eastern Regional Director: JAMES BEEMER, USMA, West Point, NY 10996-1592; Phone: 914-938-2314
Western Regional Director: RHYS EVANS, MCAGCC, Twenty-nine Palms, CA 92278-8110; Phone: 760-830-7396
Western Regional Director: WADE EAKLE, USAED South Pacific, San Francisco, CA 94105-2197; Phone: 415-977-8030
Editor of Newsletter: RICHARD BUNN, AFZC-ECM-NR, Fort Carson, CO 80913-5000; Phone: 719-576-8074
President-Elect: DAVE TAZIK, ATTN: CEWES-EN, Vicksburg, MS 39180-6199
Publication(s): *Fish and Wildlife News*
Keyword(s): Biodiversity, Fisheries, Land Use Planning, Public Lands, Wildlife and Wildlife Habitat, Professional Organization

NATIONAL NETWORK OF FOREST PRACTITIONERS
P.O. Box 487, Santa Fe, NM 87504
Phone: 505-995-0000; Fax: 505-986-0798; E-mail: danl@nnfp.org; Web Site: www.nnfp.org
Founded: 1990; Membership: 200
Scope: National
Description: The National Network of Forest Practitioners is a grassroots alliance of rural people, organizations and businesses finding practical ways to integrate economic development, environmental protection and social justice.
Contact(s):
Executive Director: DANIEL MARKHAM
Director of Projects: THOMAS BENDLER, 29 Temple Pl., 2nd Floor, Boston, MA 02111; Phone: 617-338-7821; Fax: 617-422-0881; E-mail: tbrendler@igc.org
Publication(s): *Practitioner (newsletter); Directory; Engaging Communities in the Research Process*
Keyword(s): Environmental Justice, Environmental Protection, Forest Stewardship, Forests and Forestry, Indigenous People, Natural Resource Conservation, Reforestation, Research, Rural Development, Sustainable Development

NATIONAL ORGANIZATION FOR RIVERS (NORS)
P.O. Box 6847, Colorado Springs, CO 80934
Phone: 719-579-8759
Founded: 1979; Membership: 10,000
Scope: National
Description: A nonprofit organization dedicated to education about whitewater river sports, including kayaking, rafting, and canoeing; to preserving rivers; and to protecting river access rights of the general public.
Contact(s):
President: GARY LACY
Vice President: BEN HARDING
Board Member: EARL PERRY
Board Member: FLETCHER ANDERSON
Editor: GREG MOORE
Membership Director: MARY McCURDY
Secretary, Treasurer, and Executive Director: ERIC LEAPER
Publication(s): *Currents*

NATIONAL PARK FOUNDATION
1101 17th St., NW, Suite 1102, Washington, DC 20036
Phone: 202-785-4500; Fax: 202-785-3539; Web Site: NATIONALPARKS.ORG
Founded: 1967
Scope: National
Description: The National Park Foundation is the official nonprofit partner of the National Park Service. Created by Congress in 1967, the Foundation raises support from corporations, foundations, and individuals to preserve and enhance America's National Parks. Over the past five years, the National Park Foundation has raised more than $42 million in direct support for the National Parks.
Contact(s):
Chairman: BRUCE BABBITT
President: JAMES D. MADDY
Secretary: ROBERT G. STANTON
Treasurer: CLAUDIA SCHECHTER
Executive Vice President: JILL NICOLL
Vice Chairman: B. KENNETH WEST
Publication(s): *Complete Guide to America's National Parks, The;*
Keyword(s): Cultural Preservation, Environmental and Conservation Education, Historic Preservation, National Parks, Nature Preservation, Outdoor Recreation, Public Lands

NATIONAL PARK TRUST
415 2nd St., NE, Suite 210, Washington, DC 20002
Phone: 202-548-0500; Fax: 202-548-0595; E-mail: Nptrust@aol.com; Web Site: www.parktrust.org
Founded: 1983
Scope: National
Description: The private nonprofit land conservancy dedicated exclusively to protecting resources within and around parklands and other natural and historic properties. The Trust is the only private citizen group recognized by Congress to own and manage, in cooperation with the National Park Service, a unit of the National Park System, The Tallgrass Prairie National Preserve, established in 1996. The Trust has acquired land in over 40 other parks units and finished 4 parks.
Contact(s):
President: PAUL C. PRITCHARD
Vice President: DAVINDER KHANNA
Secretary: WILLIAM BROWNELL
Treasurer: FRED MEYER
Chairman of the Board of Trustee: STEPHAN MILLER
Development Director: SUSAN HAWLEY
Publication(s): *NPT News, newsletter*
Keyword(s): Historic Preservation, Land Purchase, National Parks, Public Lands, Wildlife and Wildlife Habitat

NATIONAL PARKS AND CONSERVATION ASSOCIATION (NPCA)
Headquarters, 1776 Massachusetts Ave., NW, Washington, DC 20036

Phone: 202-223-6722; Fax: 202-659-0650; E-mail: natparks@aol.com; Web Site: www.npca.org
Founded: 1919; Membership: 500,000
Scope: National
Description: A private nonprofit citizen organization, dedicated solely to preserving, protecting, and enhancing the U.S. National Park System. As a "watchdog" group, NPCA has been an advocate as well as a constructive critic of the National Park Service. NPCA has focused on the health of the entire system, from specific sites and programs to the processes of planning, management, and evaluation.
Contact(s):
Vice President: CAROL ATEN
Secretary: JENNIFER B. ROBERTSON
Director of Communications: JEROME UHER
Vice-President of Development: JESSIE BRINKLEY
Vice-President of Conservation Policy: WILLIAM J. CHANDLER
Vice-President of Membership: TERRY L. VINES
Publication(s): *National Parks; ParkWatcher*
Keyword(s): Cultural Preservation, Land Preservation, National Parks, Public Lands

Alaska Regional Office
329 F St., Suite 208, Anchorage, AK 99501
Phone: 907-277-6722; Fax: 907-277-6723; E-mail: CHIPNPCA@aol.com
Scope: Regional
Contact(s):
Director: CHIP DENNERLEIN

Heartland Regional Office
P.O. Box 25354, Woodbury, MN 55125-5354
Phone: 612-735-8008; E-mail: LORINPCA@aol.com
Scope: Regional
Contact(s):
Director: LORI NELSON

Northeast Regional Office
P.O. Box 382372, Cambridge, MA 02238-0354
Phone: 617-354-8940; E-mail: EILEENNPCA@aol.com
Scope: Regional
Contact(s):
Director: EILEEN WOODFORD

Pacific Regional Office
P.O. Box 1289, Oakland, CA 94604
Phone: 510-839-9922; Fax: 510-839-9926; E-mail: BRIANNPCA@aol.com
Scope: Regional
Contact(s):
Director: BRIAN HUSE

Rocky Mountain Regional Office
100 Eagle Lake Dr., Fort Collins, CO 80524
Phone: 970-493-2545; Fax: 970-493-2527; E-mail: mpeterson@npca.org
Scope: Regional
Contact(s):
Director: MARK PETERSON

Southeast Regional Office
P.O. Box 930, Norris, TN 37828
Phone: 423-494-7008; Fax: 423-494-0426; E-mail: DONNPCA@aol.com
Scope: Regional
Contact(s):
Director: DON BARGER

Southwest Regional Office
823 Gold Ave., SW, Albuquerque, NM 87102
Phone: 505-247-1221; Fax: 505-247-1222; E-mail: DAVENPCA@aol.com
Scope: Regional

Contact(s):
Director: DAVID SIMON

NATIONAL RECREATION AND PARK ASSOCIATION
22377 Belmont Ridge Rd., Ashburn, VA 20148
Phone: 703-858-0784; Fax: 703-858-0794
Membership: 23,500
Scope: National
Description: A national nonprofit service, education, and research organization dedicated to the improvement of park and recreation leadership, programs, and facilities. The Association attempts to build public understanding that leisure programs and environments are indispensable to the well-being of a nation and its citizens.
Contact(s):
Secretary: ALICE CONKEY
Executive Director: R. DEAN TICE
Chairman of the Board: ERIC O'BRIEN
Chairman of the Executive Committee and President: CHRIS JARVI
Coordinator of Friends of Parks and Recreation: SUZANNE MATHIS
Director of Public Policy: BARRY TINDALL
Great Lakes Regional Director: WALTER JOHNSON, 650 W. Higgins, Hoffman Estates, IL 60195; Phone: 708-843-7529
Northeast Regional Director: KATHY SPANGLER, Recreation and Park Assoc., 22377 Belmont Ridge Road, Ashburn, VA 20148; Phone: 703-858-0784
Pacific Regional Director: PAMELA EARLE, 350 S. 333rd St., #103, Federal Way, WA 98003; Phone: 206-661-2265
Southeast Regional Director: W. TOM MARTIN, JR, 1285 Parker Rd., Conyers, GA 30207; Phone: 404-760-1668
Vice Chairman: RIP WILKENSON, Baton Rouge, LA
Western Regional Director: DICK HORTON, CO; Phone: 719-632-7031
Publication(s): *Parks and Recreation Magazine; Journal of Leisure Research; Therapeutic Recreation Journal; Recreation and Parks Law Reporter; Park Practice Program; Dateline: NRPA*

NATIONAL RESEARCH COUNCIL
2101 Constitution Ave., NW, Washington, DC 20418
Phone: 202-334-2000
Founded: 1916
Scope: National
Description: An independent advisor to the federal government on scientific and technical questions of national importance. Jointly administered by the National Academies of Sciences and Engineering and the Institute of Medicine.
Contact(s):
Chairman: DR. BRUCE M. ALBERTS
Chief Operating Officer: SUZANNE H. WOOLSEY
Director of Office of News and Public Information: SUSAN TURNER-LOWE VINES
Publication(s): *Catalogue available upon request.*

NATIONAL RIFLE ASSOCIATION OF AMERICA
Headquarters, 11250 Waples Mill Rd., Fairfax, VA 22030
Phone: 703-267-1000; Fax: 703-267-3909
Founded: 1871; Membership: 2,800,000
Scope: National
Description: A nonprofit organization dedicated to protect and defend the Constitution of the United States, especially the right to possess and use firearms for recreation and personal protection; to promote public safety, law and order, and the national defense; and to train members of law enforcement agencies, the military, and private citizens of good repute in marksmanship and the safe handling and efficient use of small arms.
Contact(s):
President: CHARLTON HESTON
Secretary: EDWARD J. LAND JR.
Treasurer: WILSON H. PHILLIPS JR.
1st Vice President: KAYNE B. ROBINSON
2nd Vice President: SANDRA S. FROMAN
Assistant Manager of Hunter Services: JANICE E. TAYLOR; Phone: 703-267-1523

NON-GOVERNMENTAL ORGANIZATIONS - N

Credentials Program Coordinator for Training: KAREN DRUMMOND; Phone: 703-267-1481
Director of Conservation, Wildlife and Natural Resources Division: SUSAN LAMSON; Phone: 703-267-1541
Director of Education and Training Division: WILLIAM J. POOLE JR.; Phone: 703-267-1414
Executive Director of General Operations: CRAIG D. SANDLER
Executive Vice President: WAYNE R. LAPIERRE JR.
Instructor and Coach Trainer for Training: HOWARD H. MOODY; Phone: 703-267-1401
Manager for Training: CHARLES MITCHELL; Phone: 703-267-1431
Manager for Youth Programs: MATTHEW SZRAMOSKI; Phone: 703-267-1596
Manager of Hunter Services: ROBERT L. DAVIS JR.; Phone: 703-267-1522
Program Assistant of Hunter Services: MONTEY S. EMBREY; Phone: 703-267-1503
Program Coordinator of Hunter Services: BRITT J. FORD; Phone: 703-267-1516
Wildlife Management Specialist of Hunter Services (ECHO): BILLY R. TEMPLETON; Phone: 703-267-1501
Publication(s): *American Rifleman, American Hunter, American Guardian & Insights*
Keyword(s): Hunting, Outdoor Recreation, Wildlife and Wildlife Habitat, Youth Organizations

NATIONAL SCIENCE TEACHERS ASSOCIATION
1840 Wilson Blvd., Arlington, VA 22201
Phone: 703-243-7100; Fax: 703-243-7177; Web Site: www.nsta.org
Founded: 1944; Membership: 53,000
Scope: National
Description: NSTA is the world's largest organization committed to improving science education at all levels - preschool through college. NSTA's membership includes science teachers, science supervisors, administrators, scientists, business and industry representatives and others involved in science education.
Contact(s):
President: EMMA WALTON; Phone: 703-243-7100/907-274-7033
Executive Director: GERALD F. WHEELER; Phone: 703-312-9254
Editor: JOAN McSHANE
President-Elect: ARTHUR EISENKRAFT; Phone: 703-243-7100/914-241-6043
Publication(s): *Science and Children; Science Scope; The Science Teacher; Journal of College Science Teaching; NSTA Reports!; Quantum; Dragonfly*
Keyword(s): Environmental and Conservation Education

NATIONAL SHOOTING SPORTS FOUNDATION, INC.
Flintlock Ridge Office Center, 11 Mile Hill Rd., Newtown, CT 06470-2359
Phone: 203-426-1320; Fax: 203-426-1087; E-mail: info@nssf.org; Web Site: www.nssf.org
Founded: 1960
Scope: National
Description: Nonprofit educational, trade-supported association sponsors a wide variety of programs to create a better understanding of and a more active participation in the shooting sports and in practical conservation.
Contact(s):
President and CEO: ROBERT T. DELFAY
Executive Director: DOUGLAS PAINTER
Director of Conservation Partnerships: CHRIS CHAFFIN
Director of Research and Information Services: LARRY FERENCE
Editorial Director: BILL BRASSARD
National Coordinator of STEP OUTSIDE: JODI DiCAMILLO
Vice-President of Finance and Administration: NANCY COBURN
Keyword(s): Environmental and Conservation Education, Hunting, Outdoor Recreation, Renewable Resources, Wildlife and Wildlife Habitat

NATIONAL SPELEOLOGICAL SOCIETY, INC.
2813 Cave Ave., Huntsville, AL 35810-4431
E-mail: nss@caves.org; Web Site: www.caves.org
Founded: 1941; Membership: 12,000
Scope: National
Description: A nonprofit membership organization dedicated to the exploration, study, and conservation of America's caves and caverns, related features, and the ecology of caves.
Contact(s):
President: FRED L. WEFER, P.O. Box 47, McDowell, VA 24458-0047; Phone: 540-396-3543
Conservation Chairman: DAVID JAGNOW, 1300 Iris St., Apt. 103, Los Alamos, NM 87544-3140; Phone: 505-662-0553; E-mail: djagnow@roadrunner.com
International Secretary: JOHN LEE MOSES, 15807 River Roads Dr., Houston, TX 77079-5041; Phone: 281-597-1494
Publication(s): *NSS News; Journal of Cave and Karst Studies; publishers of speleological books*
Keyword(s): Biology, Endangered and Threatened Species, Environmental and Conservation Education, Geology

NATIONAL TRAPPERS ASSOCIATION, INC.
P.O. Box 3667, Bloomington, IL 61702
Phone: 309-829-2422; Fax: 309-829-7615
Founded: 1959
Scope: National
Description: A national trappers organization dedicated to promoting sound conservation legislation; to conserving the nation's natural resources; to helping implement environmental education programs; and to promoting a continued annual fur-bearer harvest as a necessary wildlife management tool.
Contact(s):
President: DAVE SOLLMAN, RR 1, Box 391-1, Heltonsville, IN 47436; Phone: 812-834-5334; Fax: 812-834-5334
Vice President: JOHN H. BECHTEL III, 164 Wheatland Dr., Gettysburg, PA 17325; Phone: 717-337-0734; Fax: 717-337-0734
Conservation Director: LAWRENCE KLINE, 1373 Ironwood St., Woodbridge, VA 22191; Phone: 703-494-8995; Fax: 703-494-8995
Editor and Advertising Manager: TOM KRAUSE, P.O. Box 513, Riverton, WY 82501; Phone: 307-856-3830; Fax: 307-857-2993; E-mail: tkrause@wyoming.com
General Organizer: ROYL SCHOONOVER, P.O. Box 308, Westminster, VT 05158-0308; Phone: 802-722-9062; Fax: 802-722-9062
Publication(s): *American Trapper*
Keyword(s): Renewable Resources, Sustainable Development; Trapping, Wildlife and Wildlife Habitat, Wildlife Management

NATIONAL TREE TRUST
1120 G St., NW, Suite 770, Washington, DC 20005
Phone: 202-628-8733; Fax: 202-628-8735; Web Site: www.nationaltreetrust.org
Founded: 1990
Scope: National
Description: The National Tree Trust serves as a catalyst for local volunteer and community service groups in growing, planting, and maintaining trees in rural communities, urban areas, and along the nation's highways. NTT mobilizes volunteer groups, promotes public awareness, provides educational and tree planting grants, and unites civic and corporate institutions in support of public land tree plantings.
Contact(s):
Executive Director: GEORGE L. CATES, Major General, USMC (Ret.)
Publication(s): *National Tree Trust News, The*
Keyword(s): Environment, Environmental and Conservation Education, Forests and Forestry, Public Lands, Urban Forestry

NATIONAL TRUST FOR HISTORIC PRESERVATION
Headquarters, 1785 Massachusetts Ave., NW, Washington, DC 20036
Phone: 202-588-6000
Founded: 1949; Membership: 250,000

Scope: National
Description: Private nonprofit membership organization chartered by Congress to encourage the public to participate in the preservation of America's historic and cultural heritage through advocacy, education, technical assistance, financial aid to nonprofit groups, and demonstration programs.
Contact(s):
President: RICHARD MOE
Publication(s): *Historic Preservation News; Historic Preservation Magazine; Preservation Law Reporter; Historic Preservation Forum*
Keyword(s): Environmental and Conservation Education, Historic Preservation, Land Use Planning, Renewable Resources, Urban Environment

Mid Atlantic
One Penn Center at Suburban Station, Suite 1520, 1617 John F. Kennedy Blvd., Philadelphia, PA 19144
Phone: 215-568-8162
Scope: Regional
Contact(s):
Director: PATRICIA WILSON

Midwest Office
53 W. Jackson Blvd., Suite 1135, Chicago, IL 60604
Phone: 312-939-5547
Scope: Regional
Contact(s):
Director: TIM TURNER

Mountains and Plains
511 16th St., Suite 700, Denver, CO 80202
Phone: 303-623-1504
Scope: Regional
Contact(s):
Director: BARBARA PAHL

Northeast Office
7 Faneuil Hall Marketplace, 5th Fl., Boston, MA 02109
Phone: 617-523-0885
Scope: Regional
Contact(s):
Director: WENDY NICHOLAS

Southern Office
456 King St., Charleston, SC 29403
Phone: 803-722-8552
Scope: Regional
Contact(s):
Director: SUSAN KIDD

Texas and New Mexico Offices
500 Main St., Suite 606, Fort Worth, TX 76102
Phone: 817-332-4398
Scope: Regional
Contact(s):
Director: ELIZABETH WILLIS

Western
One Sutter St., Suite 707, San Francisco, CA 94104
Phone: 419-956-0610
Scope: Regional
Contact(s):
Director: KATHRYN BURNS

NATIONAL WATER RESOURCES ASSOCIATION
3800 N. Fairfax Dr., Suite #4, Arlington, VA 22203
Phone: 703-524-1544; Fax: 703-524-1548; E-mail: nwra@erols.com; Web Site: www.nwrs.org
Scope: National
Description: Promotes development, conservation and management of the water resources of 17 western state associations, including cities, counties, conservation districts, and individual members.
Contact(s):
President: DEWITT MOSS, 269-B S. 300E, Jerome, ID 83338
Executive Vice President: THOMAS F. DONNELLY
Publication(s): *National Waterline; Water Writes; Water Report*
Keyword(s): Agriculture, Endangered and Threatened Species, Nonpoint Source Pollution, Water Pollution, Water Resources, Wetlands

NATIONAL WATERSHED COALITION
9304 Lundy Ct., Burke, VA 22015
Phone: 703-455-6886; Fax: 703-455-6888; E-mail: jwpeterson@erols.com
Founded: 1989
Scope: National
Description: The NWC is a nonprofit coalition made up of national, regional, state, and local organizations, associations, and individuals, that advocate dealing with natural resources problems and issues using the watershed as the planning and implementation unit.
Contact(s):
Chair: W. R. HAMM
Vice Chair: CARRY SMITH
Secretary: D. SEBERT
Executive Director: JOHN W. PETERSON
Publication(s): *Watershed News*

NATIONAL WATERWAYS CONFERENCE INC.
1130 17th St., NW, Washington, DC 20036-4676
Phone: 202-296-4415
Founded: 1960; *Membership:* 500
Scope: National
Description: To promote a better understanding of the public value of water resource and water transportation programs and to show their importance to the total environment.
Contact(s):
Chairman: CRAIG E. PHILIP, Pres. Of Ingram Barge Co., P.O. Box 23049, Nashville, TN 37202-3049; Phone: 615-298-8223
Vice-Chairman: FRED C. RASKIN, Pres. and CEO of Eastern Enterprises, Inc., 9 Riverside Rd., Weston, MA 02493-2214; Phone: 781-647-2300
Secretary: MICHAEL J. TOOHEY, Director of Federal Government Relations, Ashland, Inc., 601 Pennsylvania Ave., NW, #540-N, Washington, DC 20004; Phone: 202-223-8290
Treasurer: SCOTT ROBINSON, Port Director of Muskogee City-County Port Authority, 4901 Harold Scoggins Dr., Muskogee, OK 74403; Phone: 918-682-7886
President and Editor: HARRY N. COOK
Publication(s): *Newsletter*
Keyword(s): Coasts, Energy, Rivers, Water Resources

NATIONAL WHISTLEBLOWER CENTER
National Whistleblower Legal Defense and Education Fund, 3238 P. St., NW, Washington, DC 20007
Phone: 202-342-1902; Fax: 202-342-6984; E-mail: whistle@whistleblowers.org; Web Site: www.whistleblowers.org
Founded: 1988
Scope: National
Description: The Fund is the only public interest law firm dedicated to enforcing and enhancing the legal protections of employees who blow the whistle on significant violations of law, environmental protection, nuclear safety, and first amendment rights. The Fund provides legal advice, resources, and referrals for counsel to whistleblowers nationwide and conducts seminars and other outreach activities.
Contact(s):
Chairperson: STEPHEN M. KOHN; Phone: 202-342-6980
Publication(s): *Whistleblower News; Law Reporter*
Keyword(s): Environmental Ethics, Environmental Justice, Environmental Law, Training

NATIONAL WILD TURKEY FEDERATION, CANADA, INC., THE
c/o Kevin Townsend, Regional Director, 75 Mill St., Wroxeter, Ontario N0G 2X0 Canada

Phone: 519-335-6893; Fax: 519-335-6050; E-mail: ontrdkt@wcl.on.ca
Founded: 1998
Scope: International
Description: A non-profit organization dedicated to the wise conservation and management of the North American Wild Turkey and protecting the turkey hunting tradition. Supports annual research grants program.
Contact(s):
President: RUSS DAVIES
Vice-President: RANDY ROLOSON
Secretary/Treasurer: JACK PLAYNE
CEO/Executive Vice-President: ROB KECK
Vice-President for Conservation Programs: JAMES EARL KENNAMER Ph.D.
Keyword(s): Conservation, Hunting, Research Grants

NATIONAL WILD TURKEY FEDERATION, INC., THE
770 Augusta Rd., P.O. Box 530, Edgefield, SC 29824-0530
Phone: 803-637-3106; Fax: 803-637-0034; E-mail: nwtf@nwtf.net; Web Site: www.nwtf.org
Founded: 1973; Membership: 211,000
Scope: International
Description: A nonprofit organization dedicated to the wise conservation and management of the North American Wild Turkey and protecting the turkey hunting tradition. Comprised of 1,300 state and local affiliates. Supports annual research grants program.
Contact(s):
CEO/Executive Vice President: ROB KECK
Chief Operating Officer: CARL BROWN
Vice President for Conservation Programs: JAMES EARL KENNAMER Ph.D.
Chief Financial Officer: JAMES SPARKS
Director of Communications: TAMMY BRISTOW
Director of Development: DONNA LEGGETT
Publication(s): *Turkey Call Magazine; Caller, The; JAKES Magazine; Women in the Outdoors Magazine*
Keyword(s): Forests and Forestry, Hunting, Public Lands, Research Grants, Wildlife Management, Women in the Environment

NATIONAL WILDLIFE FEDERATION
Headquarters, 8925 Leesburg Pike, Vienna, VA 22184-0001
Phone: 703-790-4000; Fax: 703-442-7332; Web Site: www.nwf.org
Founded: 1936; Membership: 4 million+
Scope: National/International
Description: A nonprofit organization whose mission is to educate, inspire, and assist individuals and organizations of diverse cultures to conserve wildlife and other natural resources and to protect the Earth's environment in order to achieve a peaceful, equitable, and sustainable future. NOTE. Any correspondence for a member of the Board of Directors of the National Wildlife Federation should be directed to the National Wildlife Federation mailing address or fax number.
Contact(s):
Chair of the Board: PAULA J. DEL GIUDICE
Vice Chair of Central Region: BECKY SCHEIBELHUT
Vice Chair of Eastern Region: EDWARD CLARK, JR.
Vice Chair of Western Region: BRYAN PRITCHETT
Immediate Past Chair: GERALD BARBER
Past Chair: THOMAS L. WARREN
Director-At-Large: VIRGINIA P. ALLERY
Director-At-Large: RICHARD J. BALDES
Director-At-Large: JUDITH ESPINOSA
Director-At-Large: TOM GONZALES
Director-At-Large: MARY C. HARRIS
Director-At-Large: STANLEY A. MOBERLY
Director-At-Large: RODOLFO OGARRIO
Director-At-Large: JOHN S. RAINEY
Director-At-Large: JEROME C. RINGO
Regional Director of Region 1 (CT, MA, ME, NH, RI, VT): STEPHEN E. PETRON
Regional Director of Region 2 (DC, DE, MD, NJ, NY, PA): CHARLES BROWN, JR.
Regional Director of Region 3 (NC, SC, VA, WV): HARMON SHADE
Regional Director of Region 4 (AL, FL, GA, MS, PR, VI): J. STEPHEN O'HARA, JR.
Regional Director of Region 5 (AR, KY, MO, TN), Vacant
Regional Director of Region 6 (IL, IN, OH): DAN DEEB
Regional Director of Region 7 (MI, MN, WI): JAMES BALDOCK
Regional Director of Region 8 (LA, OK, TX): EARL B. MATTHEW
Regional Director of Region 9 (IA, KS, NE, ND, SD): SPENCER TOMB
Regional Director of Region 10 (AZ, CO, NM, UT): CHARLES E. OLMSTED, III
Regional Director of Region 11 (AK, OR, WA): ALLEN W. GUISINGER
Regional Director of Region 12 (CA, HI, NV, Guam): STEVEN L. MONTGOMERY
Regional Director of Region 13 (ID, MT, WY): JO LYN REEVES
President and Chief Executive Officer: MARK VAN PUTTEN
General Counsel: EILEEN MORGAN JOHNSON
Vice President for Finance and Administration and Chief Financial Officer: LAWRENCE J. AMON
Senior Vice President, Constituent Programs: NATALIE S. WAUGH
Vice President and Coordinator, Conservation Programs: R. MONTGOMERY FISCHER
Vice President: BARBARA J. BRAMBLE
Vice President: ROBERT S. ERTTER
Vice President: J. SCOTT FEIERABEND
Vice President: JOHN H. GIESECKE
Vice President: PHILIP B. KAVITS
Vice President: JAIME BERMAN MATYAS
Vice President: SUSAN RIEFF
Vice President: STEVEN J. SHIMBERG
Vice President: JAMES L. STOFAN
Vice President: BOB D. STROHM
Vice President: CAROLYN WALDON
Chief Information Technology Officer: KENNETH HERMAN
President and Chief Executive Officer of National Wildlife Productions: CHRISTOPHER N. PALMER
Past President: JAY D. HAIR
Editor of Conservation Directory: RUE E. GORDON
Editor of International Wildlife: JONATHAN FISHER
Editor of National Wildlife: MARK WEXLER
Editor of Ranger Rick: GERALD BISHOP
Editor of Your Big Backyard and Wild Animal Baby: DONNA JOHNSON
Publication(s): *National Wildlife; International Wildlife; Ranger Rick; Conservation Directory; Your Big Backyard; EnviroAction; Ecodemia; NatureScope; National Wildlife Week; Animal Tracks; EarthSavers; Wild Animal Baby*
Keyword(s): Endangered and Threatened Species, International Conservation, Land Preservation, Sustainable Development, Water Quality, Wetlands, Everglades

Alaska Project Office
750 W. Second Ave., Suite 200, Anchorage, AK 99501
Phone: 907-258-4800; Fax: 907-258-4811
Scope: Regional
Description: The Alaska Project Office specializes in wetlands protection. The staff use litigation, education, and other tools to protect Alaska's incomparable wetlands resources.
Contact(s):
Director: TONY TURRINI; E-mail: turrini@nwf.org

Everglades Project Office
5051 Castello Dr., Suite 240, Naples, FL 34103
Phone: 941-643-4111; Fax: 941-643-5130
Scope: Regional
Description: The Everglades Project Office specializes in conserving and protecting the Big Cypress Watershed region of the Everglades. Advocating conservation-based land use planning, staff engages policy and decision-makers at the federal,

state, and local level and uses litigation and educational programs to influence management, legal, and legislative issues effecting the Everglades.
Contact(s):
Director (Acting): KRIS THOEMKE; E-mail: thoemke@nwf.org

Great Lakes Natural Resource Center
506 E. Liberty, Ann Arbor, MI 48104-2210
Phone: 734-769-3351; Fax: 734-769-1449;
Scope: Regional
Description: The National Wildlife Federation's Great Lakes Natural Resource Center unites people throughout the eight-state Great Lakes region, the U.S. and Canada to protect the world's greatest freshwater seas and the surrounding ecosystem. The Center's staff of scientists, educators, lawyers, and organizers work with citizens and activists to end the toxic pollution and habitat destruction that threaten the health of wildlife, fish, and people in the Great Lakes region.
Contact(s):
Director: TIM EDER; E-mail: eder@nwf.org

Gulf States Natural Resource Center
44 East Ave., Suite 200, Austin, TX 78701
Phone: 512-476-9805; Fax: 512-476-9810
Scope: Regional
Description: The Gulf States Natural Resource Center is working to protect threatened rivers and important wetlands in the region and to restore polluted watersheds. The Center also promotes NWF's educational programs by working with schools and other organizations.
Contact(s):
Director: SUSAN KADERKA; E-mail: kaderka@nwf.org

Northeast Natural Resource Center
58 State St., Montpelier, VT 05602
Phone: 802-229-0650; Fax: 802-229-4532;
Scope: Regional
Description: The Northeast Natural Resource Center represents NWF on a local and regional basis and works with state-based affiliates and like-minded organizations to protect our valuable woods, water, and wildlife resources across New England. Applying common-sense programs in education, advocacy and research, our goals are to provide conservation leadership and protection for wildlife.
Contact(s):
Director: ERIC PALOLA; E-mail: palola@nwf.org

Northern Rockies Project Office
240 N. Higgins, Suite 2, Missoula, MT 59802
Phone: 406-721-6705; Fax: 406-721-6714
Scope: Regional
Description: The Northern Rockies Project Office focuses on safeguarding the ecosystems of our national forests and other public lands important to wildlife and people.
Contact(s):
Director: THOMAS M. FRANCE; E-mail: france@nwf.org

Office of Federal and International Affairs
1400 16th St., NW, Suite 501, Washington, DC 20036
Phone: 202-797-6800; Fax: 202-797-6646
Scope: National/International
Description: Advocates NWF's position on important issues affecting the national and international communities. It provides technical, scientific and legal support to state affiliates and field offices on selected issues. The International Program works with the U.S. Congress, international lending organizations, select Federal agencies and non-governmental organizations (foreign and domestic) to promote conservation advocacy in support of biologically sound, socially equitable and economically viable sustainable development. The National Program advocates the Federation's position before all three branches of government and works cooperatively with the private sector to achieve mutually desired goals.

Contact(s):
Legislative Director: JIM LYON; E-mail: lyon@nwf.org

Rocky Mountain Natural Resource Center
2260 Baseline Rd., Suite 100, Boulder, CO 80302
Phone: 303-786-8001; Fax: 303-786-8911
Scope: Regional
Description: The Rocky Mountain Natural Resource Center is dedicated to the conservation of wildlife and natural resources on public and private lands throughout the Rocky Mountains and Plains States. Center staff are working to restore biological diversity on millions of acres of native grasslands, to promote the restoration of water quality in our streams and rivers, and to promote the restoration of bison populations residing in Yellowstone National Park to lands throughout their historic range.
Contact(s):
Director: CATHERINE SCALES JOHNSON; E-mail: JohnsonC@nwf.org

Southeastern Natural Resource Center
1330 West Peachtree St., Suite 475, Atlanta, GA 30309
Phone: 404-876-8733; Fax: 404-892-1744
Scope: Regional
Description: The Southeastern Natural Resource Center in Atlanta forges links between people and the environment, promoting sustainable practices to enhance the quality of life in our communities for people and wildlife. For example, NWF leads the Proctor Creek Watershed Action to clean up and revitalize one of Atlanta's most polluted watersheds, and is protecting wetlands like the Greater Okefenokee Ecosystem.
Contact(s):
Director: ANDREW SCHOCK; E-mail: schock@nwf.org

California Project Office
Opening February 2000
San Diego, CA
Scope: Regional

Northwestern Natural Resource Center
Opening January 2000
Seattle, WA
Scope: Regional

NATIONAL WILDLIFE FEDERATION ENDOWMENT, INC.
8925 Leesburg Pike, Vienna, VA 22184-0001
Phone: 703-790-4000
Scope: National
Description: Established to support the conservation education and resource management programs of the National Wildlife Federation. Gifts and bequests are invested, and income is transferred to the National Wildlife Federation.
Contact(s):
Secretary: EILEEN MORGAN JOHNSON
Treasurer: LAWRENCE J. AMON
Assistant Secretary: NATALIE WAUGH
Board of Trustee: RAYMOND L. GOLDEN
Board of Trustee: MARY C. HARRIS

Board of Trustee: JAMES L. CARROLL
Board of Trustee and Ex-Officio: PAULA J. DEL GIUDICE
Board of Trustee Vice Chair: ALLEN W. GUISINGER
Chairman and Trustee: JOHN S. RAINEY

NATIONAL WILDLIFE PRODUCTIONS, INC.
8925 Leesburg Pike, Vienna, VA 22184
Phone: 703-790-4077; Fax: 703-790-4076; E-mail: nwp@nwf.org; Web site: www.nwf.org/nwp/

Scope: National
Description: National Wildlife Productions is the television, film, and multimedia arm of the National Wildlife Federation (NWF). The goal of NWP is to fulfill NWF's conservation mission by creating and producing television and mass-media projects, including children's television programs, documentaries, large format films, feature films, TV movies, and interactive multimedia programs.
Contact(s):
President and Chief Executive Officer: CHRISTOPHER PALMER
Chairman: MARK VAN PUTTEN
Secretary: EILEEN MORGAN JOHNSON
Treasurer: LAWRENCE J. AMON

NATIONAL WILDLIFE REFUGE ASSOCIATION
1776 Massachusetts Ave., NW, Suite 200, Washington, DC 20036
Phone: 202-296-9729; Fax: 202-296-6030; E-mail: nwra@refugenet.org; Web Site: www.refugenet.org
Founded: 1975
Scope: National
Description: The NWRA is the only national membership, nonprofit organization dedicated solely to protecting and preserving the National Wildlife Refuge System and to increasing public understanding and appreciation of it. Our mission is to preserve and enhance the integrity of the nation's largest network of lands and waters set aside primarily for the benefit of wildlife. Membership open to interested persons, organizations and institutions.
Contact(s):
President: DAVID TOBIN; Phone: 202-296-9729; E-mail: nwra_david@refugenet.org
Administration: MICHAEL MORAN
Director, Field Services and Communications: KATE MALLECK; E-mail: nwra_kate@refugenet.org
Friends Initiative Consultant: BEVERLY HEINZE-LACEY, c/o Parker River NWR, 261 Northern Blvd., Newburport, MA 01950; Phone: 978-465-4178; Fax: 978-465-2807; E-mail: Vice President of Development and Membership: ELLEN CROTEAU; E-mail: nwra_ellen@refugenet.org
Publication(s): *Flyer (Quarterly); Friends Flyer (Quarterly); Taking Flight - An Introduction to building refuge friends organizations, Annual Refuge Friends Group Directory, Annual National Wildlife Refugees Calendar*
Keyword(s): Conservation of Protected Areas, Environmental Preservation, Environmental Protection, Public Lands, Wildlife and Wildlife Habitat

NATIONAL WILDLIFE REHABILITATORS ASSOCIATION
14 N. 7th Ave., St. Cloud, MN 56303
Phone: 320-259-4086
Founded: 1982
Scope: National
Description: A nonprofit membership organization committed to promoting and improving the integrity and professionalism of wildlife rehabilitation and contributing to the preservation of natural ecosystems. The Organization disseminates information, provides training, and encourages networking through a quarterly journal, an annual membership directory, reviewed publications, annual symposia, and active committees for standards, wildlife medicine, education, awards, and grants.
Contact(s):
President: ELAINE M. THRUNE; Phone: 320-255-4911
Vice President: MICHAEL COX
Secretary: ERICA A. MILLER DVM
Treasurer: MARTHA POKRAS
Editor: DR. DANEIL R. LUDWIG, P.O. Box 2339, Glen Ellyn, IL 60138
Editor: BEA ORENDORFF, P.O. Box 245, Butler, KY 41006
Publication(s): *Wildlife Rehabilitation annual volumes; Principles of Wildlife Rehabilitation; Training Opportunities in Wildlife Rehabilitation; Minimum Standards for Wildlife Rehabilitation; NWRA Quarterly Journal*
Keyword(s): Birds, Environmental and Conservation Education, Mammals, Wildlife and Wildlife Habitat, Wildlife Rehabilitation

NATIONAL WOODLAND OWNERS ASSOCIATION
374 Maple Ave., E., Suite 310, Vienna, VA 22180
Phone: 703-255-2700; Fax: 703-281-9200; E-mail: nwoa@mindspring.com
Founded: 1983; *Membership:* 43,000/ 31 state affiliates
Scope: National
Description: A nationwide association of woodland owners united to foster good stewardship of their non-industrial private forest lands. Working together with cooperating and affiliated state woodland owners and forestry associations, the Association is a voice for private landowners on forestry, wildlife, and resource conservation issues. Sponsors the American Federation of Forest and Woodland Owner Associations.
Contact(s):
President: KEITH A. ARGOW
Vice-President, Midwest Region: WARREN BAIRD
Vice-President, Northeast Region: JILL CORNELL
Vice-President, South Region: DON GIRTON
Vice-President, Western Region: NELS HANSON
Executive Committee Chair: BERT UDELL
Canadian Federation of Woodlot Owners: PETER DeMARSH; Phone: 509-
Editor, National Woodlands: ERIC A. JOHNSON; Phone: 315-369-3078
Editor, Woodland Report: KEITH A. ARGOW
Publication(s): *National Woodlands Magazine, Woodland Report (newsletter)*
Keyword(s): Forests and Forestry

NATIVE AMERICAN FISH AND WILDLIFE SOCIETY (NAFWS)
750 Burbank St., Broomfield, CO 80020
Phone: 303-466-1725; Fax: 303-466-5414
Founded: 1982; *Membership:* 1,500
Scope: National
Description: The Native American Fish and Wildlife Society is a nonprofit organization serving the needs of fish, wildlife, and natural resources on Tribal lands across the United States, including Alaska. The Society membership is comprised of approximately 1,500 professional and technical personnel associated with Native American natural resource programs. One hundred thirty seven federally-recognized tribes represent the Society, and many federal agencies rely on the Society's expertise and established network.
Contact(s):
President: ARTHUR BLAZER
Vice President: RANDY NOKA
Executive Director: KEN Q. POYNTER
Secretary and Treasurer: CAMERON MARTINEZ
Technical Director: PATRICK DURHAM
Publication(s): *From the Eagle's Nest*
Keyword(s): Cultural Preservation, Environmental Planning, Fisheries, Forests and Forestry, Wildlife Management

NATIVE PLANT SOCIETY OF NORTHEASTERN OHIO
2651 Kerwick, University Heights, OH 44118
Phone: 216-371-4454
Founded: 1982; *Membership:* 100
Scope: Statewide
Description: The Native Plant Society of Northeastern Ohio educates about, views, protects and preserves native plants, trees, and shrubs.
Contact(s):
President and Editor: TOM SAMPLINER; Phone: 216-371-4454
Vice President: GEORGE WILDER; Phone: 216-932-3351
Secretary: BRIAN GILBERT; Phone: 216-486-8765
Treasurer: JUDY BRADT-BARNHART; Phone: 440-548-2414
Publication(s): *On the Fringe*
Keyword(s): Ancient Forests, Aquatic Habitats, Botanical Gardens, Conservation, Endangered and Threatened Species, Flowers, Plants, and Trees, Prairies, Wetlands, Native Plants

NATIVE PLANT SOCIETY OF OREGON
P.O. Box 902, Eugene, OR 97440
WWW: www.npsoregon.org/

Founded: 1961; Membership: 919
Scope: Statewide
Description: The Native Plant Society of Oregon is a nonprofit statewide organization. The Society is dedicated to the enjoyment, conservation, and study of Oregon's native vegetation.
Contact(s):
President: BRUCE NEWHOUSE; Phone: 541-343-2364; E-mail: newhouse@efu.org
Vice-President/Treasurer: MICHAEL McKEAG; Phone: 503-642-3965
Secretary: RHODA LOVE; Phone: 541-345-6241
Publication(s): *Bulletin of the Native Plant Society of Oregon; Conservation and Management of Native Plants and Fungi; Proceedings from a Conference of the Native Plant of Oregon; KALMIOPSIS: Journal of the Native Plant Society of Oregon*
Keyword(s): Biodiversity, Conservation, Endangered and Threatened Species, Environmental Protection, Native Plants

NATIVE PLANT SOCIETY OF TEXAS
P.O. Box 891, Georgetown, TX 78627
Phone: 512-238-0695; Fax: 512-238-0703; E-mail: dtucker@io.com
Founded: 1980; Membership: 2,000
Scope: Statewide
Description: A nonprofit organization dedicated to the education and promotion of conservation, preservation, and utilization of the native plants and the plant habitats of Texas.
Contact(s):
President: BOBBY PEISER, 102 Tyler Terrace, San Angelo, TX 76905; Phone: 915-651-7992; E-mail: nopeiser@wcc.net
President-Elect: GEORGIA PRAKASH, 1905 William Brewster, Irving, TX 75061; Phone: 972-259-2020; E-mail: prakash2@airmail.net
Coordinator: DANA TUCKER; Phone: 512-238-0695
Botanical Advisor: CHESTER M. ROWELL JR, P.O. Box 817, Marfa, TX 79863; Phone: 915-729-3421
Publication(s): *Native Plant Society of Texas News*
Keyword(s): Native Plants

NATIVE PRAIRIES ASSOCIATION OF TEXAS
3503 Lafayette Ave., Austin, TX 78722
Phone: 512-476-1663; Fax: 512-476-1663; E-mail: buzzandlee@sprintmail.com
Membership: 200
Scope: National
Description: Native Prairies Association of Texas is dedicated to conservation and restoration of native prairies, through education, research, public awareness, agency cooperation, management, restoration, and acquisitions.
Contact(s):
President: JAMES ALDERSON; Phone: 258-742-9888; Fax: 254-298-1273
Vice President: GENE HEINEMANN; Phone: 512-337-0618
Secretary: LEE STONE
Treasurer: PAUL McCYNSKI; Phone: 254-896-5534
Publication(s): *Prairie Dog, The*
Keyword(s): Conservation Easements, Prairies, Restoration

NATURAL AREAS ASSOCIATION
P.O. Box 1504, Bend, OR 97709
Phone: 541-317-0199; Fax: 541-317-0140; E-mail: naa@natareas.org
Founded: 1980; Membership: 2,200
Scope: International
Description: A nonprofit organization of professional and active volunteers in natural area identification, preservation, protection, management, and research. Provides a medium of exchange and coordination to advance the understanding and appreciation of natural areas and natural diversity.
Contact(s):
President: HARRY R. TYLER JR., Maine State Planning Office, 184 State St., State House Station 38, Augusta, ME 04333; Phone: 207-287-1489; Fax: 207-287-7379; E-mail: hank.tyler@state.me.us
Vice President: CARL BECKER, Natural Heritage Division, Illinois Dept. of Natural Resources, 524 Second St., Springfield, IL 62701-1787; Phone: 217-785-8774; Fax: 217-785-8277; E-mail: cbecker@dnrmail.state.il.us
Secretary: PEG KOHRING, P.O. Box 506, Sawyer, MI 49125; Phone: 312-913-9459; Fax: 312-913-9523; E-mail: Pkohring@aol.com
Treasurer: SAM PEARSALL, 1307 Chaney Rd, Raleigh, NC 27606; Phone: 919-403-8558; Fax: 919-403-0379; E-mail: spearsall@tnc.org
Executive Director: REID SCHULLER, P.O. Box 1504, Bend, OR 97709; Phone: 541-317-0199; Fax: 541-317-0140; E-mail: naa@natareas.org
Journal Editor: CHUCK WILLIAMS, Biology Dept., Clarion University, Clarion, PA 16214; Phone: 814-226-1936; Fax: 814-226-2731; E-mail: cwilliams@mail.clarion.edu
Publication(s): *Natural Areas Journal, Natural Area News*
Keyword(s): Biodiversity, Conservation of Protected Areas, Endangered and Threatened Species, Land Preservation, Natural Areas, Nature Preservation, Nongame Wildlife, Wildlands

NATURAL HISTORY SOCIETY OF MARYLAND, INC., THE
2643 N. Charles St., Baltimore, MD 21218-4590
Phone: 410-235-6116
Founded: 1929; Membership: 300
Scope: Statewide
Description: A nonprofit membership organization formed to promote the appreciation of natural history through education, research, and publication--thereby fostering stewardship of natural and cultural resources. The Society maintains a museum of Maryland objects and a library, and bestows the Edmund B. Fladung Award to recognize persons exemplifying the society's goals.
Contact(s):
President: DONNELL E. REDMAN
Vice President: JOSEPH MCSHARRY
Treasurer: RICHARD LEADER
Board of Trustees Chairman: CHARLES A. DAVIS
Editor: JOSEPH McSHARRY
Editor: ARNOLD NORDEN
Editor: HERBERT S. HARRIS JR.
Editor: DONNER E. REDMAN
Librarian: C. HAVEN KOLB
Recording Secretary: WILLIAM F. SEIP
Publication(s): *Bulletin of the Maryland Herpetological Society; The Maryland Naturalist; News and Views; Proceedings of the Natural History Society of Maryland*
Keyword(s): Birds, Flowers, Plants, and Trees, Insects and Butterflies, Mammals, Natural History, Reptiles and Amphibians

NATURAL LAND INSTITUTE
320 S. 3rd St., Rockford, IL 61104
Phone: 815-964-6666; Fax: 815-964-6661; E-mail: nli@aol.com
Founded: 1958; Membership: 650
Scope: Statewide
Description: A nonprofit organization dedicated to preserving natural areas and natural diversity through a comprehensive program of land protection, stewardship, research, education, and advocacy.
Contact(s):
President: RANDALL G. VINCENT
Vice President: GARY McINTYRE
Secretary: BRUCE ROSS-SHANNON
Treasurer: RUSSELL JOHANSSON
Executive Director: EDWIN W. STIRLING
Natural Resources Manager: JILL KENNAY
Publication(s): *Land and Nature; Boone and Winnebago Regional Greenways Plan*
Keyword(s): Aquatic Habitats, Biodiversity, Birds, Conservation of Protected Areas, Ecology, Endangered and Threatened Species, Environmental Planning, Environmental Preservation, Environmental

Protection, Land Preservation, Land Purchase, Land Use Planning, Natural Areas, Watersheds

NATURAL LANDS TRUST, INC.
Hildacy Farm, 1031 Palmers Mill Rd., Media, PA 19063
Phone: 610-353-5587; Fax: 610-353-0517
Founded: 1961; Membership: 1,100
Scope: Regional
Description: Natural Lands Trust is a regional land trust dedicated to working with people to conserve land in the Philadelphia metropolitan region and other nearby areas of environmental concern by acquiring and managing preserve properties, accepting conservation easements, and encouraging and supporting the conservation efforts of landowners, communities, government agencies, and other nonprofit organizations.
Contact(s):
President: PHILIP S. WALLIS
Board of Trustees Chairman: DOUGLAS C. WALKER
Vice-President for Conservation Planning: RANDALL G. ARENDT
Vice-President of Finance and Administration: JILL A. BEMIS
Vice-President of Landowner Stewardship: PETER J. SMYRL
Publication(s): *Nature Lands*

NATURAL RESOURCES COUNCIL OF AMERICA
1025 Thomas Jefferson St. NW Suite 109, Washington, DC 20007-5291
Phone: 202-333-0411; Fax: 202-333-0412
Founded: 1946; Membership: 83
Scope: National
Description: An association of nonprofit environmental and conservation organizations dedicated to the protection, conservation, and responsible management of the nation's natural resources. The Council coordinates cooperative efforts between its members, government agencies, private citizens, and businesses. The Council also administers the Conservation Round Table Luncheon series, an annual Conservation Community Banquet and Awards program and publishes a bimonthly newsletter.
Contact(s):
Executive Director: ANDREA J. YANK
Keyword(s): Fisheries, Forests and Forestry, Public Lands, Water Resources, Wildlife and Wildlife Habitat

NATURAL RESOURCES COUNCIL OF MAINE
3 Wade St., Augusta, ME 04330
Phone: 207-622-3101; Fax: 207-622-4343; E-mail: nrcm@nrcm.org; Web Site: www.nrcm.org
Scope: Statewide
Description: A representative statewide organization, affiliated with the National Wildlife Federation, dedicated to the protection and enhancement of wildlife and its habitat through public education and government interaction.
Contact(s):
President: ELLEN BAUM
Executive Director and Alternative Representative: EVERETT B. CARSON
Representative: PAUL LIEBOW
Editor: LESLIE E. HAHN
Publication(s): *Maine Environment*

NATURAL RESOURCES DEFENSE COUNCIL, INC.
Headquarters, 40 W. 20th St., New York, NY 10011
Phone: 212-727-2700; E-mail: nrdcinfo@nrdc.org; Web Site: www.nrdc.org
Founded: 1970; Membership: 400,000
Scope: National
Description: Nonprofit membership organization dedicated to protecting America's endangered natural resources and to improving the quality of the human environment. Combines interdisciplinary legal and scientific approach in crafting innovative solutions, monitoring government agencies, bringing legal action and disseminating citizen information. Areas of concentration: air and water pollution, global warming, nuclear safety, land use, urban environment, pollution prevention, ecosystem management, wilderness and wildlife protection, international environment, Alaska, energy efficiency, forestry and ocean and fisheries protection.
Contact(s):
Executive Director: JOHN H. ADAMS; Phone: 212-727-2700
Chairman of the Board: FREDERICK A. SCHWARZ JR.; Phone: 212-727-2700
Editor: DANA FOLEY
Editor: KATHRIN LASSILA
Publication(s): *Amicus Journal, The; A complete list of NRDC's books and reports is available upon request.*

Los Angeles, California Office
6310 San Vicente Blvd., Suite 250, Los Angeles, CA 90048
Phone: 213-934-6900
Scope: National

San Francisco, California Office
71 Stevenson St., #1825, San Francisco, CA Phone: 415-777-0220
Scope: National

Washington, D.C. Office
1200 New York Ave., NW, Ste. 400, Washington, DC 20005
Phone: 202-289-6868
Scope: National

NATURAL RESOURCES INFORMATION COUNCIL
Anne Hedrich Science & Technology Library, 3100 Old Main Hill, Logan, UT 84322-3100
Phone: 435-797-2165; Fax: 435-797-7475; E-mail: annhed@cc.usu.edu; Web Site: www.usu.edu/~cnr/quinney/nrichome.html
Founded: 1991; Membership: 25
Scope: National
Description: Federal, state, provincial, academic and special research librarians and information specialists from U.S. and Canada who facilitate the exchange of information on sustainable natural resources. Goals are to build a network of resource people to collect and disseminate information on sustainable natural resources and to provide continuing education.
Contact(s):
Membership: ANNE HEDRICH; Phone: 435-797-2165; Fax: 435-797-7475; E-mail: annhed@cc.usu.edu
Treasurer: BARBARA VOELTZ; E-mail: bvoeltz@ngpc.state.ne.us
Publication(s): *Fish and Game Natural Resource Library Survey, Annual Newsletter*
Keyword(s): Natural History, Natural Science, Sustainability, Sustainable Resources, Librarians/Information Professionals

NATURAL SCIENCE FOR YOUTH FOUNDATION
130 Azalea Dr., Roswell, GA 30075
Phone: 404-594-9367
Scope: National
Description: Provides counseling to community groups in the planning and development of environmental and natural science centers, museums, and native animal parks which are designed particularly to meet the needs and interests of children and young people. Conducts an annual conference as part of its widespread effort to promote professional excellence in environmental and natural science centers and museums.
Contact(s):
President: CHARLES S. COCHRANE
Secretary: GEORGINE PINDAR
Treasurer: JOHN L. HAMMAKER
Founder and President Emeritus: JOHN RIPLEY FORBES
Publications Director: OWEN D. WINTERS
Publication(s): *Directory of Natural Science Centers; Natural Science Center News; Opportunities Jobs Bulletin*
Keyword(s): Environmental and Conservation Education, Natural History, Outdoor Recreation, Wildlife Rehabilitation, Youth Organizations

NATURE CONSERVANCY OF CANADA, THE
110 Eglinton Ave., W., Suite 400, Toronto, Ontario M4R 1A3 Canada
Phone: 416-932-3202 or 1-800-465-0029; Fax: 416-932-3208; E-mail: nature@natureconservancy.ca; Web Site: www.natureconservancy.ca

Founded: 1962
Scope: National
Description: The Nature Conservancy of Canada is the only national charity dedicated to preserving ecologically significant areas, places of special beauty and education interest through outright purchase, donations and conservation agreements.
Contact(s):
Chairman: TED BOSWELL
Executive Director: JOHN LOUNDS
Director of Development: JOHN W. HOCHSTADT
Publication(s): *Annual Report; Ark, The*
Keyword(s): Land Preservation, Land Purchase

NATURE CONSERVANCY, THE
Headquarters, 4245 North Fairfax Dr., Arlington, VA 22208
Phone: 703-841-5300; Fax: 703-841-1283; Web Site: www.tnc.org

Founded: 1951; Membership: 1,021,000
Scope: International
Description: International nonprofit membership organization committed to preserving biological diversity by protecting natural lands, and the life they harbor; cooperates with educational institutions, public and private conservation agencies. Works with states through "natural heritage programs" to identify ecologically significant natural areas. Manages a system of over 1,600 nature sanctuaries nationwide.
Contact(s):
President: JOHN C. SAWHILL
Chairman of the Board: SAM JOHNSON
Chief Conservation Officer: BILL WEEKS
Chief Operations Officer: STEVE HOWELL
Communications: DAVID WILLIAMSON
Conservation Science: DEBORAH JENSEN
Development and Marketing: GRACE VANCE
Domestic Conservation: GREG ROW
General Counsel: MIKE DENNIS
Government Relations: MAGGIE COON
Human Resources Business Services: DIANE GOSTING
Human Resources Field Services: JOY GADDY
Administration: RAY CULTER
Editor-in-Chief: RON GEATZ
International Conservation: ALEXANDER WATSON
Membership: DONNA CHEREL
Publication(s): *Nature Conservancy Magazine, The*
Keyword(s): Biodiversity, Endangered and Threatened Species, International Conservation, Land Purchase, Wildlife and Wildlife Habitat

Eastern Division Office
Lee Park, Suite 470, 1100 E. Hector St., Conshohocken, PA 19428
Phone: 610-834-1323
Scope: Regional
Contact(s):
Vice President: LAURA JOHNSON, 201 Devonshire St., 5th Fl., Boston, MA 02110; Phone: 617-542-1908
Editor-in-Chief: RON GEATZ
Executive Editor: MARK CHEATER
Hawaii Director: REX JOHNSON; Phone: 808-537-4508
Keyword(s): Biodiversity, Endangered and Threatened Species, International Conservation, Land Purchase, Wildlife and Wildlife Habitat

Great Plains Division
1313 5th St., SE, Suite 320, Minneapolis, MN 55414
Phone: 612-331-0750
Scope: Regional
Contact(s):
Vice President: ROBERT MCKIM

Mid-Atlantic Division Office
4011 University Dr., Suite 201, Durham, NC 27707
Phone: 919-403-8558
Scope: Regional
Contact(s):
Vice President: KATHERINE SKINNER

Midwest Division Office
6375 Riverside Dr., Suite 50, Dublin, OH 43017
Phone: 614-717-2770
Scope: Regional
Contact(s):
Vice President: DAVID WEEKES

Northeast Division Office
159 Waterman St., Providence, RI 02906
Phone: 401-751-2521
Scope: Regional
Contact(s):
Vice President: JOHN COOK

Northwest & Hawaii Division Office
217 Pine St., Suite 1100, Seattle, WA 98101
Phone: 206-343-4344
Scope: Regional
Contact(s):
Vice President: ELLIOT MARKS

Rocky Mountain Division Office
117 E. Mountain Ave., #201, Fort Collins, CO 80524
Phone: 970-484-2886
Scope: Regional
Contact(s):
Vice President: BRUCE RUNNELS

South Central Division Office
P.O. Box 1440, San Antonia, TX 78295-1440
Phone: 210-224-8774
Scope: Regional
Contact(s):
Vice President: ROBERT POTTS

Southeast Division Office
222 S. Westmonte Dr., Suite 300, Altamonte Springs, FL 32714
Phone: 407-682-3664
Scope: Regional
Contact(s):
Vice-President: ROBERT BENEDICK

Western Division Office
201 Mission St., 4th Fl., San Francisco, CA 94105
Phone: 415-777-0487
Scope: Regional
Contact(s):
Vice President: STEVE MCCORMICK

NATURE CONSERVANCY, THE, ALABAMA CHAPTER
2821 C 2nd Ave., Birmingham, AL 35233
Phone: 205-251-1155
Scope: Statewide

NATURE CONSERVANCY, THE, ALASKA CHAPTER
421 W. First Ave., #200, Anchorage, AK 99501
Phone: 907-276-3133
Scope: Statewide

NATURE CONSERVANCY, THE, ARIZONA CHAPTER
300 E. University Blvd., #230, Tuscon, AZ 85705
Phone: 520-622-3861
Scope: Statewide

NON-GOVERNMENTAL ORGANIZATIONS - N

NATURE CONSERVANCY, THE, ARKANSAS CHAPTER
601 N. University Ave., Little Rock, AR 72205
Phone: 501-663-6699
Scope: Statewide

NATURE CONSERVANCY, THE, ASIA/PACIFIC PROGRAM
1116 Smith St., #201, Honolulu, HI 96817
Phone: 808-537-4508
Scope: International

NATURE CONSERVANCY, THE, CALIFORNIA CHAPTER
201 Mission St. 4th Fl., San Francisco, CA 94105
Phone: 415-777-0487
Scope: Statewide
Contact(s):
Contact: STEVE McCORMICK

NATURE CONSERVANCY, THE, COLORADO CHAPTER
1244 Pine St., 4th Fl., Boulder, CO 80302
Phone: 303-444-2950
Scope: Statewide

NATURE CONSERVANCY, THE, CONNECTICUT CHAPTER
55 High St., Middletown, CT 06457
Phone: 860-344-0716
Scope: Statewide

NATURE CONSERVANCY, THE, DELAWARE CHAPTER
260 Chapman Rd., #210D, Newark, DE 19702
Phone: 302-369-4144
Scope: Statewide

NATURE CONSERVANCY, THE, EASTERN NEW YORK CHAPTER
200 Broadway, 3rd Floor, Troy, NY 12180
Phone: 518-272-0195
Scope: Local Region

NATURE CONSERVANCY, THE, FLORIDA CHAPTER
222 S. Westmonte Dr. Suite 300, Altamonte Springs, FL 32714
Phone: 407-682-3664
Scope: Statewide

NATURE CONSERVANCY, THE, GEORGIA CHAPTER
1330 W. Peachtree St., #410, Atlanta, VA 30309-2904
Phone: 404-873-6946; Fax: 404-873-6984
Scope: Statewide

NATURE CONSERVANCY, THE, HAWAII CHAPTER
1116 Smith St., #201, Honolulu, HI 96817
Phone: 808-537-4508
Scope: Statewide

NATURE CONSERVANCY, THE, IDAHO CHAPTER
P.O. Box 165, Sun Valley, ID 83353
Phone: 208-726-3007
Scope: Statewide

NATURE CONSERVANCY, THE, ILLINOIS CHAPTER
8 S. Michigan Ave., #900, Chicago, IL 60603
Phone: 312-346-8166
Scope: Statewide

NATURE CONSERVANCY, THE, INDIANA CHAPTER
1330 W. 38th St., Indianapolis, IN 46208
Phone: 317-923-7547
Scope: Statewide

NATURE CONSERVANCY, THE, IOWA CHAPTER
108 3rd St., Suite 300, Des Moines, IA 50309-4758
Phone: 515-244-5044
Scope: Statewide

NATURE CONSERVANCY, THE, KANSAS CHAPTER
820 S.E. Quincy, #301, Topeka, KS 66612-1158
Phone: 785-233-4400
Scope: Statewide

NATURE CONSERVANCY, THE, KENTUCKY CHAPTER
642 W. Main St., Lexington, KY 40508
Phone: 606-259-9655
Scope: Statewide

NATURE CONSERVANCY, THE, LATIN AMERICA AND CARRIBBEAN DIVISION
4245 N. Fairfax Dr., Suite 100, Arlington, VA 22203
Phone: 703-841-5300
Scope: International

NATURE CONSERVANCY, THE, LOUISIANA CHAPTER
P.O. Box 4125, Baton Rouge, LA 70821
Phone: 225-338-1040
Scope: Statewide

NATURE CONSERVANCY, THE, MAINE CHAPTER
14 Maine St., #401, Brunswick, ME 04011
Phone: 207-729-5181
Scope: Statewide

NATURE CONSERVANCY, THE, MARYLAND/D.C. CHAPTER
2 Wisconsin Cir., #300, Chevy Chase, MD 20815
Phone: 301-656-8673
Scope: Statewide

NATURE CONSERVANCY, THE, MASSACHUSETTS CHAPTER
70 Milk St., #300, Boston, MA 02109
Phone: 617-423-2545
Scope: Statewide

NATURE CONSERVANCY, THE, MICHIGAN CHAPTER
2840 E. Grand River, #5, East Lansing, MI 48823
Phone: 517-332-1741
Scope: Statewide

NATURE CONSERVANCY, THE, MINNESOTA CHAPTER
1313 Fifth St., SE, #320, Minneapolis, MN 55414
Phone: 612-331-0750
Scope: Statewide

NATURE CONSERVANCY, THE, MISSISSIPPI CHAPTER
6400 Lakeover Rd., Suite C, Jackson, MS 39213
Phone: 601-713-3355
Scope: Statewide

NATURE CONSERVANCY, THE, MISSOURI CHAPTER
2800 S. Brentwood Blvd., St. Louis, MO 63144
Phone: 314-968-1105
Scope: Statewide

NATURE CONSERVANCY, THE, MONTANA CHAPTER
32 South Ewing, Helena, MT 59601
Phone: 406-443-0303
Scope: Statewide

NATURE CONSERVANCY, THE, NEBRASKA CHAPTER
1722 St. Mary's Ave., #403, Omaha, NE 68102
Phone: 402-342-0282
Scope: Statewide

NATURE CONSERVANCY, THE, NEVADA CHAPTER
1771 E. Flamingo, #111B, Las Vegas, NV 89119
Phone: 702-737-8744
Scope: Statewide

NATURE CONSERVANCY, THE, NEW HAMPSHIRE CHAPTER
2 1/2 Beacon St., #6, Concord, NH 03301
Phone: 603-224-5853
Scope: Statewide

NATURE CONSERVANCY, THE, NEW JERSEY CHAPTER
200 Pottersville Rd., Chester, NJ 07930
Phone: 908-879-7262
Scope: Statewide

NATURE CONSERVANCY, THE, NEW MEXICO CHAPTER
212 E. Marcy, #200, Santa Fe, NM 87501
Phone: 505-988-3867
Scope: Statewide

NATURE CONSERVANCY, THE, NEW YORK ADIRONDACK CHAPTER
P.O. Box 65, Route 73, Keene Valley, NY 12943
Phone: 518-576-2082
Scope: Local Region

NATURE CONSERVANCY, THE, NEW YORK CENTRAL/WESTERN CHAPTER
339 East Ave., Suite 300, Rochester, NY 14604
Phone: 716-546-8030
Scope: Local Region

NATURE CONSERVANCY, THE, NEW YORK CITY CHAPTER
570 Seventh Ave., #601, New York, NY 10018
Phone: 212-997-1880
Scope: Local Region

NATURE CONSERVANCY, THE, NEW YORK LONG ISLAND CHAPTER
250 Lawrence Hill Rd., Cold Spring Harbor, NY 11724
Phone: 516-367-3225
Scope: Local Region

NATURE CONSERVANCY, THE, NEW YORK LOWER HUDSON CHAPTER
41 S. Moger Ave., Mt. Kisco, NY 10549
Phone: 914-244-3271
Scope: Local Region

NATURE CONSERVANCY, THE, NEW YORK SOUTH FORK/SHELTER ISLAND CHAPTER
P.O. Box 5125, E. Hampton, NY 11937
Phone: 516-329-7689
Scope: Local Region

NATURE CONSERVANCY, THE, NORTH CAROLINA CHAPTER
4011 Univeristy Dr., #201, Durham, NC 27707
Phone: 919-403-8558
Scope: Statewide

NATURE CONSERVANCY, THE, NORTH DAKOTA CHAPTER
2000 Schafer St., Suite B, Bismarck, ND 58501
Phone: 701-222-8464
Scope: Statewide

NATURE CONSERVANCY, THE, OHIO CHAPTER
6375 Riverside Dr., #50, Dublin, OH 43017
Phone: 614-717-2770
Scope: Statewide

NATURE CONSERVANCY, THE, OKLAHOMA CHAPTER
23 West Fourth, #200, Tulsa, OK 74103
Phone: 918-585-1117
Scope: Statewide

NATURE CONSERVANCY, THE, OREGON CHAPTER
821 SE 14th Ave., Portland, OR 97214
Phone: 503-230-1221
Scope: Statewide

NATURE CONSERVANCY, THE, PENNSYLVANIA CHAPTER
1100 E. Hector St., #470, Conshohocken, PA 19428
Phone: 610-834-1323
Scope: Statewide

NATURE CONSERVANCY, THE, RHODE ISLAND CHAPTER
159 Waterman St., Providence, RI 02906
Phone: 401-331-7110
Scope: Statewide

NATURE CONSERVANCY, THE, SOUTH CAROLINA CHAPTER
P.O. Box 5475, Columbia, SC 29250
Phone: 803-254-9049
Scope: Statewide

NATURE CONSERVANCY, THE, SOUTH DAKOTA CHAPTER
1000 West Ave. N., Suite 100, Sioux Falls, SD 57104
Phone: 605-331-0619
Scope: Statewide

NATURE CONSERVANCY, THE, TENNESSEE CHAPTER
50 Vantage Way, #250, Nashville, TN 37228
Phone: 615-255-0303
Scope: Statewide

NATURE CONSERVANCY, THE, TEXAS CHAPTER
P.O. Box 1440, San Antonio, TX 78295-1440
Phone: 210-224-8774
Scope: Statewide

NATURE CONSERVANCY, THE, UTAH CHAPTER
559 E. South Temple, Salt Lake City, UT 84102
Phone: 801-531-0999
Scope: Statewide

NATURE CONSERVANCY, THE, VERMONT CHAPTER
27 State. St., Montpelier, VT 05602
Phone: 802-229-4425
Scope: Statewide

NATURE CONSERVANCY, THE, VIRGIN ISLANDS CHAPTER
148 Norre Gade, 2nd Fl., Charlotte Amalie, VI 00802
Phone: 809-774-7633
Scope: Statewide

NATURE CONSERVANCY, THE, VIRGINIA CHAPTER
1233-A Cedars Ct., Charlottesville, VA 22903
Phone: 804-295-6106
Scope: Statewide

NATURE CONSERVANCY, THE, WASHINGTON CHAPTER
217 Pine St., #1100, Seattle, WA 98101
Phone: 206-343-4344
Scope: Statewide

NATURE CONSERVANCY, THE, WEST VIRGINIA CHAPTER
723 Kanawha Blvd. E., #500, Charleston, WV 25301
Phone: 304-345-4350
Scope: Statewide

NATURE CONSERVANCY, THE, WISCONSIN CHAPTER
633 W. Main St., Madison, WI 53703
Phone: 608-251-8140
Scope: Statewide

NATURE CONSERVANCY, THE, WYOMING CHAPTER
258 Main St., #200, Lander, WY 82520
Phone: 307-332-2971
Scope: Statewide

NATURE CONSERVATION SOCIETY OF JAPAN, THE (NACS-J)
Nihon-Shizen-Hogo-Kyokai, Yamaji Saubauncho Bldg. 3F, 5-24 Sanbancho, Chiyoda Ku, Tokyo 102 Japan
Phone: 81-3-3265-0521; Fax: 81-3-3265-0527
Founded: 1951; Membership: 20,000
Scope: International
Description: A nonprofit, membership conservation organization devoted to promoting conservation, research, and education concerning the natural areas and wildlife in Japan, and also a

recently launched international project to support biodiversity in developing countries.
Contact(s):
President: MAKOTO NUMATA
Director General: KIYOSHI OKUTOMI
Publication(s): *Nature Conservation (Japanese); Red List of Plant Species in Japan (Japanese); Red List of Plant Communities in Japan (Japanese)*

NATURE SASKATCHEWAN
Attn: Administration Coordinator, 206-1860 Lorne St., Regina, Saskatchewan S4P 2L7 Canada
Phone: 306-780-9273; Fax: 306-780-9263; E-mail: nature.sask@unibase.com; Web Site: www.unibase.com/~naturesk
Founded: 1947; Membership: 2,000
Scope: Statewide
Description: Nature Saskatchewan is the largest non-profit nature organization in the province, committed to preserving our natural environment. We operate a nature bookshop, offer ecological tours, own nature sanctuaries, and support conservation and research activities and nature education.
Contact(s):
Honorary President: MARY GILLILAND
President: DIANA BIZECKI ROBSON
Secretary: MICHELLE WILLIAMSON
Treasurer: DALE HJERTAAS
1st Vice-President: JENNIFER NEUDORF
2nd Vice-President: WILLIAM SARJEANT
Director of Administration: RUBY LaFAYETTE
Director of Conservation: ATTILA CHANADY
Director of Education: GREG FENTY
Director of Member Services: ROBERT WARNOCK
Director of Research: DIETHER PESCHKEN
Member-at-Large: PETER GRIFFITHS
Member-at-Large: PAULE HJERTAAS
Past President: KATHLEEN DONAUER
Publication(s): *Blue Jay; Nature Views; special publication*
Keyword(s): Aquatic Habitats, Biodiversity, Birds, Conservation of Protected Areas, Ecology, Endangered and Threatened Species, Environment, Environmental Law, Flowers, Plants, and Trees, Insects and Butterflies, Land Preservation, Mammals, Natural Areas, Natural History

NEBRASKA ASSOCIATION OF RESOURCE DISTRICTS
601 South 12th St., Suite 201, Lincoln, NE 68508
Phone: 402-471-7670; Fax: 402-471-7677; E-mail: nard@nrcdec.nrc.state.ne.us
Scope: Statewide
Contact(s):
President: CLINT JOHANNES, 326 Road K, Richland, NE 68601; Phone: 402-352-5640; Fax: 402-563-4272
Vice President: PETE RUBIN, 416 Bellvue North, Bellvue, NE 68005; Phone: 402-7337369
Executive Director: DEAN EDSON, 601 S. 12th St., Suite 201, Lincoln, NE 68508; Phone: 402-471-7674; Fax: 402-471-7677
Secretary/Treasurer: ORUIL GIGSTAD, RR 1 Box 54, Syracuse, NE 68446; Phone: 402-269-3267
Keyword(s): Natural Resource Conservation, Conservation Districts

NEBRASKA AUDUBON COUNCIL
11649, Burt St. #11, Omaha, NE 68154
Phone: 402-493-0373
Founded: 1985; Membership: 3,750
Scope: Statewide
Description: A statewide council of representatives of the eight National Audubon Society chapters in Nebraska. The Council's purpose is to coordinate efforts of the chapters on statewide environmental issues and advocate protection, preservation, and wise use of our soil, water, plants, and wildlife.
Contact(s):
President: ALICE RUMERY, 3911 Ave. E., Kearney, NE 68847; Phone: 308-237-3358
Treasurer: IONE WERTHMAN, 11649 Burt St., #11, Omaha, NE 68154; Phone: 402-493-0373
Legislative Coordinator: DAVID SANDS, The Apothecary, Suite 217, 140 N. 8th St., Lincoln, NE 68508; Phone: 402-475-1177

NEBRASKA B.A.S.S. CHAPTER FEDERATION
Attn: President, 1518 Kozy Dr., Columbus, NE 68601
Scope: Statewide
Description: An organization of Bassmaster chapters, affiliated with the Bass Anglers Sportsman Society, organized to fight pollution, assist state and national conservation agencies in their efforts, and teach the young people of our country good conservation practices. Dedicated to the realistic conservation of our water resources.
Contact(s):
President: JOE CITTA JR.; Phone: 402-563-2297
Conservation Director: TOM BOYD, 1610 S. Blaine, Grand Island, NE 68803; Phone: 308-382-8357

NEBRASKA ORNITHOLOGISTS' UNION, INC. (University of Nebraska State Museum)
W436 Nebraska Hall, Lincoln, NE 68588-0514
Phone: 402-472-8366
Founded: 1899; Membership: 250
Scope: Statewide
Description: To promote the study of ornithology in Nebraska by both professionals and amateurs; to publish the results of independent studies; and to promote the passage and enforcement of judicious laws for bird protection.
Contact(s):
Vice President: LANNY RANDOLPH, 50374 24th Rd., Gibbon, NE 68840-9654; Phone: 308-468-5057
Secretary: ROBIN HARDING, 50374 24th Rd., Gibbon, NE 68840-9654; Phone: 308-468-5057
Treasurer: SUE AMIOTTE, 11 City Dam Rd., Chasron, NE 69337; Phone: 308-432-3783
Director: ALICE KENITZ, 190648 County Rd. 22, Gering, NE 69341; Phone: 308-436-2959
Director: MARK BROGIE, 508 Seeley, Box 316, Creighton, NE 68729; Phone: 402-358-5675
Director: TOM LABEDZ, 724 Glenarbor Cir., Lincoln, NE 68512; Phone: 402-423-1384
Librarian: MARY LOU PRITCHARD, 6325 O St. #515, Lincoln, NE 68510-2246
President and Newsletter Editor: BETTY ALLEN, 9628 Emmet St., Omaha, NE 68134
Publication(s): *Nebraska Bird Review, The*
Keyword(s): Birds

NEBRASKA WILDLIFE FEDERATION, INC.
P.O. Box 81437, Lincoln, NE 68501-1437
Phone: 402-994-2001; Fax: 402-994-2001; E-mail: dh43048@navix.net
Founded: 1970
Scope: Statewide
Description: A representative statewide organization, affiliated with the National Wildlife Federation, dedicated to the protection and enhancement of wildlife and its habitat through public education and government interaction.
Contact(s):
President: DAVID KOUKOL
Executive Director and Editor: DUANE HOVORKA
Representative: GENE OGLESBY
Alternative Representative: DAN LUDWIG
Publication(s): *Prairie Blade*

NEVADA ASSOCIATION OF CONSERVATION DISTRICTS
Attn: President, HC 65 Box 11, Carlin, NV 89822-9701
Scope: Statewide
Contact(s):
President, Alternative Board Member: PATSY TOMERA; Phone: 775-754-2333
Executive Director: MYRNA WOLFE, 2002 Idaho St., Elko, NV 89801; Phone: 775-738-8431; Fax: 775-738-7229

Board Member: JOE SICKING, 1550 Cushman Rd., Fallon, NV 89406; Phone: 775-423-5216; Fax: 775-738-7229
Keyword(s): Conservation Districts

NEVADA WILDLIFE FEDERATION
P.O. Box 71238, Reno, NV 89570
Phone: 702-645-5423; Fax: 702-885-0405; E-mail: dupree@pyramid.net; Web Site: www.nvwf.org
Scope: Statewide
Description: A representative statewide organization, affiliated with the National Wildlife Federation, dedicated to the protection and enhancement of wildlife and its habitat through public education and government interaction.
Contact(s):
President: FRANK MAXWELL
Representative: GALE DuPREE
Editor: ED JORGENSEN
Alternative Representative: JEANIE COLE
Publication(s): *Nevada Wildlife*

NEVIS HISTORICAL AND CONSERVATION SOCIETY
P.O. Box 563, Charlestown, St. Kitts and Nevis
Phone: 869-469-5786; Fax: 869-469-0274
Founded: 1980; Membership: 500
Scope: National
Description: To foster the conservation of the natural, historic, and cultural aspects of Nevis and its surrounding waters by educational programs, publishing projects, and other awareness endeavors.
Contact(s):
President: LYRA RICHARDS; Phone: 869-469-2164,(W)869-469-5565/5796/1451
Vice President: CALVIN HOWELL; Phone: 869-469-1347
Secretary: EDRISE FELLOWS; Phone: 869-469-2147
Treasurer: JEFFIFER LOWREY
Publication(s): *Nevis Historical and Conservation Society Newsletter; FCO News; Nevis Environmentalist*
Keyword(s): Cultural Preservation, Environmental and Conservation Education, Historic Preservation, Nature Preservation, Sustainable Development

NEW BRUNSWICK WILDLIFE FEDERATION
Box 1066, Moncton, New Brunswick E1C 8P2 Canada
Phone: 506-859-1240
Founded: 1924
Scope: Statewide
Description: Promotes the wise use of renewable natural resources, with prime emphasis on education of the young. Affiliated with the Canadian Wildlife Federation.
Contact(s):
President: RICHARD DEBOW
Keyword(s): Environmental and Conservation Education

NEW ENGLAND ASSOCIATION OF ENVIRONMENTAL BIOLOGISTS (NEAEB)
60 Westview St., Lexington, MA 02173
Phone: 617-860-4300
Founded: 1976
Scope: Regional
Description: A professional society of environmental scientists, engineers and planners from industry and state and federal agencies in the northeast, working to coordinate and enhance environmental programs in each state. The organization advances technical information on environmental research, planning and management and evaluates the effectiveness of environmental regulations for protection of water quality.
Contact(s):
Executive Committee: ERNEST PIZZUTO
Information Officer: DAVID MCDONALD, EPA 60 Westview St., Lexington, MA 02421; Phone: 781-860-4609
Keyword(s): Professional Organization

NEW ENGLAND COALITION FOR SUSTAINABLE POPULATION (NECSP)
P.O. Box 194, Sullivan, NH 03445
Phone: 603-847-9798; E-mail: d9cat@cheshire.net
Founded: 1996; Membership: 50 organizations and individuals
Scope: Regional
Description: NECSP is a network of organizations and individuals committed to achieving a sustainable human population at the local, state, regional, national and global levels.
Contact(s):
Coordinator: ANNIE FAULKNER
Publication(s): *NECSP News (quarterly newsletter)*
Keyword(s): Family Planning, Habitat Conservation, Networking, Overconsumption, Population Growth, Reproductive Rights, Sustainability, Sprawl

NEW ENGLAND NATURAL RESOURCES CENTER
Box 44, Wayland, MA 01778
Phone: 508-358-2261
Founded: 1970; Membership: 15
Scope: National
Description: A nonprofit trust organized to provide a focal point for discussion and resolution of regional natural resource and environmental issues.
Contact(s):
Chairman: PERRY HAGENSTEIN, Box 44, Wayland, MA 01778
Vice Chairman: RUSSELL L. BRENNEMAN, Murtha, Cullina, Richter & Pinney, 101 Pearl St., Hartford, CT 06102
Keyword(s): Communications, Renewable Resources

NEW ENGLAND WILD FLOWER SOCIETY, INC.
180 Hemeway Rd., Framingham, MA 01701-2699
Phone: 508-877-7630; Fax: 508-877-3658; E-mail: newfs@newfs.org; Web Site: www.newfs.org/
Founded: 1900; Membership: 5,000
Scope: National
Description: The New England Wild Flower Society is a nonprofit organization that promotes the conservation of temperate North American plants through conservation and research, education, horticulture and habitat preservation.
Contact(s):
President: MOLLY BEARD
Vice President: POLLY PIERCE
Secretary: DANA N. JOST
Treasurer: LALOR BURDICK
Executive Director: DAVID L. DeKING
Publication(s): *New England Wild Flower - Journal and Program Events; New England Wild Flower - Conservation Notes of New England Wild Flower Society; Garden in the Woods Trail guide, Annual Seed and book Catalogue, Botanical Clubs and Native Plant Societies of the U.S. and Canada*
Keyword(s): Botanical Gardens, Conservation, Endangered and Threatened Species, Environmental and Conservation Education, Gardening and Horticulture, Natural History, Native Plants

NEW HAMPSHIRE ASSOCIATION OF CONSERVATION COMMISSIONS
54 Portsmouth St., Concord, NH 03301
Phone: 603-224-7867
Founded: 1970; Membership: 188 municipalities in NH/1,300 conservation commissioners
Scope: Statewide
Description: A nonprofit organization whose purpose is to foster conservation and wise use of NH's natural resources and to assist and facilitate communication and cooperation among the state's 200 conservation commissions.
Contact(s):
President: DIANE EADIE
Vice President: KATHERINE METZGER
Secretary: PETER BAKER
Treasurer: JAMES MEIKLEJOHN
Executive Director and Editor: MARJORY M. SWOPE
Publication(s): *NH Conservation News; Handbook for Municipal Conservation Commissions in New Hampshire; Legislative Updates*
Keyword(s): Conservation, Environmental Law, Environmental Preservation, Land Use Planning, Water Resources, Wetlands

NON-GOVERNMENTAL ORGANIZATIONS - N

NEW HAMPSHIRE ASSOCIATION OF CONSERVATION DISTRICTS
Attn: President, P.O. Box 404, Sunappe, NH 03782
Scope: Statewide
Contact(s):
President: ROBERT L. WARD, P.O. Box 404, Sunapee, NH 03782; Phone: 603-763-5425; Fax: 603-763-4194
1st Vice President: KITTY MILLER, 56 Concord Rd., Lee, NH 03824; Phone: 603-868-5217; Fax: 603-743-3667
2nd Vice President: CALVIN J. PERKINS, 68 Isacc Perkins Rd., Lyme, NH 03768; Phone: 603-795-2584; Fax: 603-743-3477
Administrator: JOAN RICHARDSON, 73 Main St., P.O. Box 533, Conway, NH 03818-0533; Phone: 603-447-2771; Fax: 603-447-8945
Board Member: JOHN HODSDON, 85 Daniel Webster Hwy., Meredith, NH 03253; Phone: 603-279-6126; Fax: 603-528-8783
Secretary and Treasurer: STANELY GRIMES, 529 Buck St., Pembroke, NH 03275; Phone: 603-485-9326; Fax: 603-233-6030
Keyword(s): Conservation Districts

NEW HAMPSHIRE B.A.S.S. CHAPTER FEDERATION
Attn: President, 98 Chase Rd., Londonderry, NH 03053
Scope: Statewide
Description: An organization of Bassmaster chapters, affiliated with the Bass Anglers Sportsman Society, organized to fight pollution, assist state and national conservation agencies in their efforts, and teach the young people of our country good conservation practices. Dedicated to the realistic conservation of our water resources.
Contact(s):
President: DICK FRUCI; Phone: 603-434-6759
Conservation Director: A. J. DISILVA, P.O.B. 923, North Conway, NH 03860; Phone: 603-356-2220

NEW HAMPSHIRE LAKES ASSOCIATION
7 South State St., Concord, NH 03301
Phone: 603-226-0299; Fax: 603-224-9442; E-mail: info@nhlakes.org; Web Site: www.nhlakes.org
Founded: 1992; Membership: 2,100 individuals, 165 associations
Scope: Statewide
Description: The New Hampshire Lakes Association is a nonprofit education and advocacy organization dedicated to protecting and preserving New Hampshire's lakes for the responsible and equitable enjoyment of everyone. The NHLA provides assistance to individuals and lake associations throughout New Hampshire.
Contact(s):
Executive Director: NANCY CHRISTIE; E-mail: nchristie@nhlakes.org
Publication(s): *Lakeside (quarterly magazine), Educational Brochures*
Keyword(s): Aquatic Habitats, Environment, Environmental and Conservation Education, Environmental Planning, Environmental Protection, Lakes, Land Use Planning, Open Space, Outdoor Recreation, Water Quality, Watersheds

NEW HAMPSHIRE TIMBERLAND OWNERS ASSOCIATION
54 Portsmouth St., Concord, NH 03301
Phone: 603-224-9699; Fax: 603-225-5898
Founded: 1911; Membership: 1,400
Scope: Statewide
Description: A statewide organization affiliated with the National Woodland Owners Association, dedicated to the promotion of wise forest management and the protection of forestry interests in New Hampshire.
Contact(s):
President: KEVIN EVANS
Secretary: SARAH SMITH
Treasurer: TED TICHY
Executive Director: ERIC W. KINGSLEY
Editor: PATRICK D. HACKLEY
President-Elect: BOB BERTI

Publications: TIMBER CRIER
Keyword(s): Forests and Forestry

NEW HAMPSHIRE WILDLIFE FEDERATION
P.O. Box 239, Concord, NH 03302
Phone: 603-224-5953; Fax: 603-228-4614; E-mail: nhwf@aol.com; Web Site: www.nhwf.org
Scope: Statewide
Description: A representative statewide organization, affiliated with the National Wildlife Federation, dedicated to the protection and enhancement of wildlife and its habitat through public education and government interaction.
Contact(s):
Executive Director: DARREL COVELL
Representative: JOHN MONSON
Vice President: RUSSELL KOTT
Editor: MARGARET LANE
Publication(s): *New Hampshire Wildlife*

NEW JERSEY AGRICULTURAL SOCIETY
P.O. Box 331, Trenton, NJ 08625
Phone: 609-394-7766
Founded: 1781; Membership: 1,100
Scope: Statewide
Description: The Society has continually worked to educate the public and promote agriculture in New Jersey. The Society is charitable, nonprofit, and conducts numerous educational programs about agriculture's vital role in the economy of New Jersey.
Contact(s):
President: EARL F. ERVEY
Vice President: PAMELA MOUNT
Secretary and Treasurer: ARTHUR R. BROWN JR.
Assistant Secretary and Treasurer: RICHARD NIEUWENHUIS
Editor: JONI ELLIOTT
Publication(s): *Harbinger; Garden View*
Keyword(s): Agriculture

NEW JERSEY ASSOCIATION OF CONSERVATION DISTRICTS
Attn: 234 Chapel Heights Rd., Sewell, NJ 08080
Scope: Statewide
Contact(s):
President: JAY KANDLE; Phone: 609-589-7916
Secretary, Alternative Board Member: EDWARD DIPOLVERE, 53 Cubberly Rd., Trenton, NJ 08690; Phone: 609-586-2684
Treasurer: ALLEN D. CARTER, P.O. Box 403, Tuckahoe, NJ 08250; Phone: 609-628-2466
1st Vice President: CLIFFORD R. LUNDIN, 8 Skytop Rd., Andover, NJ 07821; Phone: 973-398-2511
2nd Vice President: KENNETH B. MARSH, 534 Hanford Place, Westfield, NJ 07909; Phone: 908-233-4528
Board Member: KENNETH ROEHRICH, 451 Schooley's Mountain Rd., Hackettstown, NJ 07840; Phone: 908-852-5787
Keyword(s): Conservation Districts

NEW JERSEY AUDUBON SOCIETY
P.O. Box 126, 9 Hardscrabble Rd., Bernardsville, NJ 07924
Phone: 908-204-8998
Founded: 1897; Membership: 16,000
Scope: Statewide
Description: Fosters environmental awareness and a conservation ethic among New Jersey citizens; protects New Jersey's birds, mammals, other animals, and plants, especially endangered and threatened species; and promotes preservation of New Jersey's valuable natural habitats.
Contact(s):
Board Chairperson: CHARLES F. WEST
Cape May Bird Observatory: Northwood Center, 701 E. Lake Dr., P.O. Box 3, Cape May Point, NJ 08212; Phone: 609-884-2736
Director for Nature Center of Cape May: GRETCHEN FERRANTE, 1600 Delaware Ave., Cape May, NJ 08204; Phone: 609-898-8848
Director of Lorrimer Sanctuary: GORDON SCHULTZE, P.O. Box 125, 790 Ewing Ave., Franklin Lakes, NJ 07417; Phone: 201-891-2185

Director of Owl Haven Nature Center: PETE BACINSKI, 250 Route 522, P.O. Box 26, Tennent, NJ 07763; Phone: 732-780-7007
Director of Rancocas Nature Center: KARL ANDERSON, 794 Rancocas Rd., Mt. Holly, NJ 08060; Phone: 609-261-2495
Director of Weis Ecology Center: KARLA RISDON, 150 Snake Den Rd., Ringwood, NJ 07456; Phone: 973-835-2160
President and CEO: THOMAS J. GILMORE
Vice President for Conservation: RICHARD KANE
Vice President for Education: PATRICIA KANE, Sherman and Hoffman Sanctuaries, 111 Hardscrabble Rd., P.O. Box 693, Bernardsville, NJ 07924; Phone: 908-766-5787
Vice President of Natural History Information: PETER DUNNE, Cape May Bird Observatory, Center for Research and education, 600 Rt. 47 N., Cape May Court House, NJ 08210; Phone: 609-861-0700
Keyword(s): Environmental and Conservation Education, Land Preservation, Natural History

NEW JERSEY B.A.S.S. CHAPTER FEDERATION
Attn: President, 77 Kenvil Ave., Succasunna, NJ 07876
Scope: Statewide
Description: An organization of Bassmaster chapters, affiliated with the Bass Anglers Sportsman Society, organized to fight pollution, assist state and national conservation agencies in their efforts, and teach the young people of our country good conservation practices. Dedicated to the realistic conservation of our water resources.
Contact(s):
President: TONY GOING; Phone: 973-584-9387
Conservation Director: JOHN TURNEY, 13 Pumpkin Hill Rd., Warwick, NY 10990; Phone: 914-986-0669

NEW JERSEY CONSERVATION FOUNDATION
Bamboo Brook, 170 Longview Rd., Far Hills, NJ 07931
Phone: 908-234-1225; Fax: 908-234-1189; Web Site: www.eclipse.net/~njcf
Founded: 1960; Membership: 6,400
Scope: Statewide
Description: A nonprofit membership organization concerned with environmental education issues related to land use and open-space acquisition and preservation through use of its revolving land fund. Formed from the Great Swamp Committee of the North American Wildlife Foundation.
Contact(s):
President: C. LAWRENCE KELLER
Secretary: PETER B. MOORE
Treasurer: LANGDON PALMER
Executive Director: DAVID F. MOORE
1st Vice President: HOPE E. ROBERTSON
2nd Vice President: CYNTHIA KELLOGG
Counsel: JAMES P. WYSE
Editor: PATRICIA J. BAXTER
Publication(s): *New Jersey Conservation; New Jersey Highlands, The: Treasures at Risk; Greenways to the Arthurkill; Charting a Course for the Delaware Bay Watershed*
Keyword(s): Agriculture, Biodiversity, Environmental and Conservation Education, Environmental Planning, Land Preservation, Land Purchase, Land Use Planning, Natural Areas, Nature Preservation, Open Space, Public Lands, Sustainable Development, Sustainable Ecosystems, Urban Environment, Watersheds

NEW JERSEY ENVIRONMENTAL LOBBY
204 W. State St., Trenton, NJ 08608
Phone: 609-396-3774; Fax: 609-396-4521
Founded: 1969; Membership: 1,000 individuals and 150 local and statewide environmental organizations
Scope: Statewide
Description: To advocate for legislation and regulation that is protective and preservative of both the natural and the built environment with a view, always, of protecting human health for all citizens and future generations. Conversely, we oppose those laws and regulations that are detrimental to the above.
Contact(s):
President: ANNE POOLE, 43 Four Mile Rd., Pemberton, NJ 08068; Phone: 609-894-4113
Vice President: KIM KAISER, 40 E. Valley Brook Rd., Long Valley, NJ 07853
Secretary: MARK HERZBERG, 24 Clinton Pl., Metuchen, NJ 08840; Phone: 908-494-4883
Treasurer: AL KENT, 39 Crystal Ave., West Orange, NJ 07052; Phone: 201-731-6546
Publication(s): *NJ Environmental Lobby News; periodic special reports*
Keyword(s): Air Quality and Pollution, Energy, Land Use Planning, Sustainable Development, Transportation

NEW JERSEY FORESTRY ASSOCIATION
1628 Prospect St., Trenton, NJ 08638
Phone: 609-771-8301
Founded: 1975; Membership: 900
Scope: Statewide
Description: A statewide organization affiliated with the National Woodland Owners Association. Formed to encourage the scientific management and perpetuation of woodlands in New Jersey.
Contact(s):
President: THOMAS F. BULLOCK; Phone: 609-696-5300
Vice President: GEORGE H. PIERSON; Phone: 609-737-0489
Executive Secretary and Editor: RON SHEAY
Editor: RICHARD F. WEST
Publication(s): *New Jersey Woodlands*
Keyword(s): Forests and Forestry

NEW MEXICO ASSOCIATION OF CONSERVATION DISTRICTS
Attn: President, P.O. Box 344, Carlsbad, NM 88220
Scope: Statewide
Contact(s):
President: TOM TOWNSEND; Phone: 505-885-3925; Fax: 505-887-5700
Alternate Board Member: JOE PAUL LACK JR., P.O. Box 274, Hatch, NM 97937; Phone: 505-267-1016; Fax: 505-267-1234
Vice President: BRIAN GREENE, Rt. 1 Box 22, Mountainair, NM 87036; Phone: 505-849-1080; Fax: 505-847-0615
Treasurer: LEEDRUE HYATT, 8410 Flying U Rd., NE, Deming, NM 88030; Phone: 505-546-9694; Fax: 505-546-3265
Baord Member: DENNIS SHUGART, 1801 Monte Vista, Dalhart, TX 79022; Phone: 806-249-6633; Fax: 505-374-2970
Executive Director: DEBBIE HUGHES, 163 Trail Canyon Rd., Carlsbad, NM 88220; Phone: 505-981-2400; Fax: 505-981-2422
Keyword(s): Conservation Districts

NEW MEXICO B.A.S.S. CHAPTER FEDERATION
Attn: President, 164 Monte Rey South, Los Alamos, NM 87544
Scope: Statewide
Description: An organization of Bassmaster chapters, affiliated with the Bass Anglers Sportsman Society, organized to fight pollution, assist state and national conservation agencies in their efforts, and teach the young people of our nation good conservation practices. Dedicated to the realistic conservation of our water resources.
Contact(s):
President: LARRY KNECHT; Phone: 505-672-3536
Conservation Director: RON GILWORTH, P.O. Box 717, Socorro, NM 87801; Phone: 505-835-1200
Publication(s): *New Mexico B.A.S.S. Federation Newsletter "BigMouth"*

NEW MEXICO ENVIRONMENTAL LAW CENTER
1405 Luisa St. Suite 5, Santa Fe, NM 87505
Phone: 505-989-9022; Fax: 505-989-3769
Founded: 1987; Membership: 1,000
Scope: Statewide
Description: The New Mexico Environmental Law Center is a nonprofit, public interest law firm. The Law Center is the only New Mexico organization that provides free legal services for the preservation of the state's natural resources and protection of its citizens against environmental hazards. The Law Center represents

grassroots organizations, individuals, and other environmental groups in site-specific efforts; participates in statewide and federal legislative advocacy; and provides public education.
Contact(s):
Executive Director: DOUGLAS MEIKLEJOHN
Keyword(s): Environmental Law

NEW MEXICO WILDLIFE FEDERATION
3240-A Juan Tabo NE, Suite 204, Albuquerque, NM 87111
Phone: 505-299-5404
Scope: Statewide
Description: A representative statewide organization, affiliated with the National Wildlife Federation, dedicated to the protection and enhancement of wildlife and its habitat through public education and government interaction.
Contact(s):
President and Alternative Representative: CHUCK EASTON
Representative and Editor: MARY REED
Publication(s): *New Mexico Wildlife Federation Newsletter*

NEW YORK ASSOCIATION OF CONSERVATION DISTRICTS, INC.
Attn: President, 6947 Macomber Rd., Oakfield, NY 14125
Scope: Statewide
Contact(s):
President: HARRY KELSEY; Phone: 716-948-5788
Vice President: JOE GERGELA, P.O. Box 341, Center Moriches, NY 11934; Phone: 516-727-3777
Secretary: CARL SEYMOUR, 242 Grange Hall Rd., Schuylerville, NY 12871; Phone: 518-695-9249
Treasurer: WILLIAM CHAMBERLAIN, Box 487, Henderson Harbor, NY 13651; Phone: 315-938-7106
Executive Vice President: ANITA CARTIN, 1 Winners Cir., Albany, NY 12235; Phone: 518-457-7229; Fax: 518-457-2716
Keyword(s): Conservation Districts

NEW YORK B.A.S.S. CHAPTER FEDERATION
Attn: President, 274 N. Goodman St., Rochester, NY 14607
Scope: Statewide
Description: An organization of Bassmaster chapters, affiliated with the Bass Anglers Sportsman Society, organized to fight pollution, assist state and national conservation agencies in their efforts, and teach the young people of our country good conservation practices. Dedicated to the realistic conservation of our water resources.
Contact(s):
President: SCOTT KELLER; Phone: 716-266-2083
Conservation Director: SCOTT FRANCK, R.D. 2 Box 2073, Gilchrist Hill Rd., Hartford, NY 12838; Phone: 518-632-5232

NEW YORK FOREST OWNERS ASSOCIATION, INC.
P.O. Box 180, Fairport, NY 14450
Phone: 716-377-6060
Founded: 1962; Membership: 1,800
Scope: Statewide
Description: A statewide organization, affiliated with the National Woodland Owners Association, organized to unite the 500,000 owners of 11 million acres of forest land in New York in encouraging the wise management of private woodland resources in New York State by promoting, protecting, representing, and serving the interests of woodland owners.
Contact(s):
President: RONALD PEDERSON; Phone: 518-753-4336
Treasurer: DON WAGNER; Phone: 315-733-7391
Administrator: DEBORAH GILL; Phone: 716-377-6060
Editor: MARY BETH MALMSHEIMER; Phone: 315-497-1078
Publication(s): *Forest Owner*
Keyword(s): Forests and Forestry

NEW YORK PUBLIC INTEREST RESEARCH GROUP (NYPIRG
Main Office, 9 Murray St., 3rd Fl., New York, NY 10007
Phone: 212-349-6460; Fax: 212-349-7474
Founded: 1973; Membership: 80,000
Scope: Statewide
Description: The NYPIRG is a nonprofit, nonpartisan research group established and directed by New York state college students. Staff lawyers, researchers, and advocates work with students and other citizens developing citizenship skills and shaping public policy on environmental preservation, good government, and consumer issues.
Contact(s):
Executive Director: CHRIS MEYER
Chairperson: MICHAEL LIVERMORE
Publication(s): *NYPIRG Agenda; NYC Council Watch; Get the Lead Out*
Keyword(s): Environmental Justice, Pesticides, Solid Waste Management, Toxic Substances, Transportation

NEW YORK TURTLE AND TORTOISE SOCIETY
P.O. Box 878, Orange, NY 07051
Phone: 212-459-4803
Founded: 1970; Membership: 2,100
Scope: National
Description: The Society is dedicated to the conservation and preservation of habitat, and the promotion of proper husbandry and captive propagation of turtles. Education of members and the public is a key goal. Events held in the NYC area include a seminar, field trips, and show.
Contact(s):
President: SUZANNE DOHM
Vice President: ALLEN FOUST
Secretary: RITA DEVINE
Editor of Proceedings: JIM VAN ABBEMG
Membership: JOAN FRUMKIES
Treasurer of Wildlife Rehabilitation: LORI CRANER
Publication(s): *Plastron Papers; Journal of the New York Turtle and Tortoise Society; NYTTS; NewsNotes*
Keyword(s): Environmental and Conservation Education, Nongame Wildlife, Reptiles and Amphibians, Wildlife Rehabilitation, Zoology

NEW YORK-NEW JERSEY TRAIL CONFERENCE INC.
232 Madison Ave., New York, NY 10016
Phone: 212-685-9699
Founded: 1920; Membership: 10,000
Scope: Regional
Description: A nonprofit organization which coordinates the efforts of hiking and outdoor groups in New York and New Jersey to build and maintain over 1,300 miles of foot trails and whose purpose is to protect and conserve open space, wildlife, and places of natural beauty and interest.
Contact(s):
President: H. NEIL ZIMMERMAN
Vice President: GARY HAUGLAND
Secretary: DANIEL CHAZIN
Executive Director: JoANN DOLAN
Chairman of Trails Council: GARY HAUGLAND
Publication(s): *Trail Walker; New York Walk Book; New Jersey Walk Book; Guide to the Appalachian Trail in New York and New Jersey; Guide To The Long Path; Catskill Trails Map Set; Hiking the Catskills; Iron Mine Trails; Delaware Water Gap National Recreation Area Hiking Guide; Health Hints for Hikers; Circuit Hikes; Harriman Trails Guide; Scenes and Walks in the Northern Shawongunks; several map sets.*
Keyword(s): Land Preservation, Natural Areas, Open Space, Outdoor Recreation, Trail

NEWFOUNDLAND LABRADOR WILDLIFE FEDERATION
Attn: President, 67 Commonwealth Ave., Mount Pearl, Newfoundland A1N1W7 Canada
Phone: 709-364-8415
Membership: 900 - 24 Affiliated Clubs 5300 members
Scope: Statewide
Contact(s):
President: GORDON COOPER, 67 Commonwealth Ave., Mount Pearl, Newfoundland A1N 1W7 Canada; Phone: 709-368-6180
Secretary: FRANCES CLEARY, 14 Fairhaven Pl., St. John's, Newfoundland A1E 4S1 Canada; Phone: 709-335-2226

Keyword(s): Acid Rain, Air Quality and Pollution, Ancient Forests, Aquatic Habitats, Biodiversity, Birds, Ecology, Environmental Ethics, Forest Management, Lakes, Mammals, Nongame Wildlife, Solid Waste Management, Trapping, Wildlife and Wildlife Habitat

NIPPON ECOLOGY NETWORK
Ecology Center Bldg., 3 Fukuromachi, Shinjukku-ku, Tokyo 162 Japan
Phone: 81-3-5228-3344; Fax: 81-3-5228-6040; Web Site: www.venture-web.or.jp/ecoland
Scope: International
Description: NEN is currently involved in many aspects of environment, agriculture, and food safety issues. Among NEN operations are: Radish boya, an organic and natural food home delivery system servicing over 55,000 homes; the Japan Ecology Center, an information center; Atopikko Chikyu no ko, a network of medical advisors and the allergy afflicted; and the Tree Free Club, an organization that promotes the use of alternatives to tree-based papers and manages the Tree Free Fund; the promotion and sales of water purification system and the Green Marketing Institute, an environmental marketing consultation and research firm.
Contact(s):
Chairman: MICHIAKI TOKUE
Publication(s): *Kurashi-no-ki (Environmental Lifestyle Magazine, Japanese); Japan Ecology Center News*

NORTH AMERICAN ASSOCIATION FOR ENVIRONMENTAL EDUCATION
Headquarters, 1825 Connecticut Ave., NW, Suite 800, Washington, DC 20009-5708
Phone: 202-884-8912; Fax: 202-884-8455; E-mail: csmith409@aol.com; Web Site: www.naaee.org
Founded: 1971
Scope: National
Description: NAAEE is dedicated to promoting environmental education and supporting the work of environmental educators in North America and around the world. NAAEE is made up of students and professionals who have thought seriously about how individuals become literate concerning environmental issues and about how to prepare people to work together towards resolving environmental problems.
Contact(s):
President: JUDY BRAUS
Treasurer: JAMES ELDER
Executive Director: EDWARD J. McCREA
Publication(s): *Environmental Communicator; Annual Conference Proceedings; NAAEE Directory of Environmental Educators and others*
Keyword(s): Communications, Environment, Environmental and Conservation Education, Environmental Literacy, International Conservation, Networking, Professional Development, Training, Urban Environment

Conference, Publications and Membership Office
410 Tarvin Rd., Rock Spring, GA 30739
Phone: 706-764-2926; Fax: 706-764-2094
Scope: National

NORTH AMERICAN BENTHOLOGICAL SOCIETY
c/o Allen Marketing and Management, P.O. Box 1897, Lawrence, KS 66044-8897
Founded: 1953; Membership: 1,950
Scope: National
Description: The Society is an international scientific organization whose purpose is to promote better understanding of the biotic communities of lake and stream bottoms and their role in aquatic ecosystems. The Society provides media for disseminating results of scientific investigations and other information to aquatic biologists and to the scientific community at large.
Contact(s):
President: NANCY B. GRIMM; Phone: 602-965-4735
Secretary: DONNA GIBERSON; Phone: 902-566-0797
Treasurer: KIM H. HAAG; Phone: 813-243-5800
Editor: DR. DONALD W. WEBB, Illinois Natural History Survey, 607 E. Peabody St., Champaign, IL 61820
Editor: DR. STEVE CANTON, Chadwick and Associates Inc., 5575 S. Sycamore St., Suite 101, Littleton, CO 80120
Editor: DAVID M. ROSENBERG, Freshwater Institute, 501 University Crescent, Winnipeg, MB R3T 2N6 Canada
Publication(s): *Journal of the North American Benthological Society; Bulletin of the North American Benthological Society; Current and Selected Bibliography of Benthic Biology*
Keyword(s): Aquatic Habitats, Biology, Lakes, Streams

NORTH AMERICAN BLUEBIRD SOCIETY
P.O. Box 74, Darlington, WI 53530-0074
Phone: 608-329-6403; Fax: 608-329-7057; E-mail: nabluebird@aol.com; Web Site: www.nabluebirdsociety.org
Founded: 1978; Membership: 3,500
Scope: International
Description: The North American Bluebird Society, a non-profit conservation, education and research organization, promotes the recovery of bluebirds and other native, cavity-nesting species. On-going research, educational material development, including two slide programs, outreach initiatives through the NABS Speakers Bureau and a comprehensive web site on blue-birding, address issues related to bluebirds and other native cavity-nesting bird species.
Contact(s):
President: RAY HARRIS, Box 2650, Pincher Creek, AB T0K 1W0 Canada
Vice President: DOUG LeVASSEUR, 20680 Township Rd. #120, Senecaville, OH 43780-9707
Treasurer: CHUCK FINLEY, RR Box 241-c, Nebraska City, NE 68410
Co-Executive Director: JOHN IVANKO, P.O. Box 74, Darlingten, WI 53530
Co-Executive Director: LISA KIVIRIST, P.O. Box 74, Darlingten, WI 53530
Editor: JIM WILLIAMS, 5239 Cranberry Ln., Webster, WI 54893
Recording Secretary: ARLENE RIPLEY, 3513 Smithville Dr., Dunkirk, MD 20754
Vice President of Community Relations: CAROL McDANIEL, 14953 Highway 23, Darlington, WI 53530
Publication(s): *Bluebird Magazine (formerly Sialia)*
Keyword(s): Birds

NORTH AMERICAN BUTTERFLY ASSOCIATION
4 Delaware Rd., Morristown, NJ 07960
Phone: 973-285-0907; Fax: 973-285-0936; E-mail: naba@naba.org; Web Site: www.naba.org
Founded: 1993; Membership: 3,000
Scope: International
Description: NABA promotes public enjoyment and conservation of butterflies, encouraging non-consumption activities such as butterfly watching, gardening and photography.
Contact(s):
President: JEFFREY GLASSBERG
Vice-President: ANN SWENGEL
Webmaster: JIM SPRINGER; E-mail: springer@naba.org
Publication(s): *American Butterflies; Butterfly Garden News; NABA 4th of July Butterfly Count Report*
Keyword(s): Biodiversity, Conservation, Ecotourism, Endangered and Threatened Species, Environmental and Conservation Education, Gardening and Horticulture, Insects and Butterflies, Interpretive Center, Outdoor Recreation

NORTH AMERICAN COALITION ON RELIGION AND ECOLOGY (NACRE)
5 Thomas Cir., NW, Washington, DC 20005
Founded: 1989; Membership: 6,300
Scope: National
Description: NACRE is an ecumenical and interfaith environmental organization designed to help the North American religious community enter into the environmental movement in the 1990s and

to help environmental organizations and the wider society become aware and act upon these same ethical values.
Contact(s):
Chairman of the Board: BRUCE ANDERSON
President and CEO: DR. DONALD B. CONROY
Secretary and Treasurer: DR. CAROLYN M. GUTOWSKI
Publication(s): *ECO-Letter*
Keyword(s): Biodiversity, International Conservation, Renewable Resources, Urban Environment

NORTH AMERICAN CRANE WORKING GROUP
7030 Kilgor Rd., Gibbon, NE 68840
Phone: 308-233-5576
Founded: 1988
Scope: National
Description: An organization of professional biologists, aviculturists, land managers, and other interested individuals dedicated to the conservation of cranes and their habitats in North America.
Contact(s):
President: SCOTT HEREFORD, Mississippi Crane Refuge, 7200 Crane Ln., Gauthier, MS 39553
Vice President: WENDY BROWN, 1208 Claire Ct. NW, Albuquerque, NM 87104
Secretary: STEPHEN A. NESBITT, 4005 S. Main St., Gainesville, FL 32601
Treasurer: GARY R. LINGLE, 7030 Kilgor Rd., Gibbon, NE 68840; Phone: 308-233-5576
Editor: JANE NICOLICH, R.R. 2 Box 264A, Laurel, MD 20708
Publication(s): *Unison Call, The*
Keyword(s): Biodiversity, Birds, Endangered and Threatened Species, Wetlands, Wildlife and Wildlife Habitat

NORTH AMERICAN FALCONERS ASSOCIATION
Attn: President, Rt. 1, Box 82A, Ellinwood, KS 67526-9801
Founded: 1962
Scope: National
Description: A nonprofit fraternal organization with the following purposes: improve and encourage competency in the practice of falconry; urge recognition of falconry as a legal field sport; and promote scientific study, conservation, and welfare of birds of prey with an appreciation of their value in nature.
Contact(s):
President: DR. J. TIMOTHY KIMMEL, Rt. 1, Box 82A, Ellinwood, KS 67526-9801
Treasurer: SUE CECCHINI, 7220 Burgess Rd., Colorado Springs, CO 80908
Corresponding Secretary: ROBERT H. GLASS, 33 Tanager Ln., Robbinville, NJ 08691
Editor: SUE CECCHINI, 7220 Burgess Rd., Colorado Springs, CO 80908
Editor: DAN CECCHINI JR., 7220 Burgess Rd., Colorado Springs, CO 80908; Phone: 303-495-4506
Editor: WILLISTON SHOR, 318 Montford Ave., Mill Valley, CA 94941
Publication(s): *Hawk Chalk (quarterly); Journal (annual)*
Keyword(s): Conservation, Hunting, Raptors

NORTH AMERICAN FISHING CLUB
12301 Whitewater Dr., Suite 260, Minnetonka, MN 55343
Phone: 612-988-7401; Fax: 612-936-9755; E-mail: fishingclub@pclink.com
Founded: 1988; Membership: 500,000
Scope: International
Description: The North American Fishing Club is a membership organization dedicated to enhancing the fishing skills and enjoyment of anglers. The NAFC is the largest association of multi-species anglers in North America.
Contact(s):
President: STEVEN F. BURKE
Executive Director: STEVE PENNAZ
Publication(s): *North American Fisherman*
Keyword(s): Aquatic Habitats, Fisheries, Lakes, Sport Fishing

NORTH AMERICAN GAMEBIRD ASSOCIATION, INC.
1214 Brooks Ave., Raleigh, SC 27607
Phone: 919-782-6758; Fax: 919-515-7070; E-mail: gamebird@naga.org
Founded: 1932; Membership: 1,600
Scope: National
Description: To promote educational work and develop interest in game bird breeding and hunting preserves (nonprofit); to afford a means of cooperation with the federal and state governments in all matters of concern to the industry; and to encourage study of the sciences connected with the live production, preparation for markets, and marketing of game bird eggs and game birds.
Contact(s):
President: ROYD HATT, Box 134, Green River, UT 84525; Phone: 801-564-3224
Executive Director: DR. GARY S. DAVIS, 1214 Brooks Ave., Raleigh, NC 27607; Phone: 919-782-6758 or 919-515-5403
Publication(s): *Wildlife Harvest Magazine; Membership Directory; Game Bird Propagation Book; List of Hunting Resort Members.*
Keyword(s): Birds, Hunting, Waterfowl, Wildlife and Wildlife Habitat, Wildlife Management

NORTH AMERICAN LOON FUND
6 Lily Pond Rd., Gilford, NH 03246
Phone: 603-528-4711
Founded: 1979
Scope: National
Description: A nonprofit organization established to sponsor loon conservation, public education, and scientific research projects across the U.S. and Canada. Sponsors annual grant program, and organizes annual research conference.
Contact(s):
Chairman: JORDAN S. PROUTY
Treasurer: ELLEN BARTH
Executive Director: LINDA OBARA
Clerk: GUY A. SWENSON
Publication(s): *Loon Call Newsletter; Annotated Bibliography of the Loons, Gaviidae; Educational poster and resource directory*
Keyword(s): Endangered and Threatened Species, Lakes, Nongame Wildlife, Scholarships and Grants, Wildlife and Wildlife Habitat

NORTH AMERICAN NATIVE FISHES ASSOCIATION
123 W. Mt. Airy Ave., Philadelphia, PA 19119
Founded: 1972; Membership: 450
Scope: National
Description: Membership includes ichthyologists, students, sportsmen, amateur naturalists, and aquarists who seek to promote the study, research, and conservation of North American native fishes. Goals are to promote the restoration and protection of habitat and to distribute information about native fishes.
Contact(s):
President: RAYMOND S. KATULA
Vice President: PHILIP NIXON
Treasurer: ROBERT E. SCHMIDT
Secretary and Editor: BRUCE GEBHARDT; Phone: 215-247-0384
Publication(s): *American Currents Magazine*
Keyword(s): Aquatic Habitats, Endangered and Threatened Species, Fisheries, Nongame Wildlife

NORTH AMERICAN WILDLIFE PARK FOUNDATION, INC.
Battle Ground, IN 47920
Phone: 765-567-2265; E-mail: wolfpark@dcwi.com; Web Site: www.wolfpark.org
Founded: 1972; Membership: 1,500
Scope: National
Description: A nonprofit organization which operates a Wolf Park; provides continuous behavior research programs; offers lectures and a teaching program, as well as four Wolf Behavior seminars per year; monitors legislation on predators; and provides research opportunities for scientists and students.

Contact(s):
Assistant Treasurer and Assistant Secretary: ALBERT W. ZIMMERMANN, Suite 418, 3320 N. Meridian St., Indianapolis, IN 46204
President, Treasurer, and Editor: DR. ERICH KLINGHAMMER, Battle Ground, IN 47920
Publication(s): *Wolf Park News*

NORTH AMERICAN WOLF SOCIETY
850 37th St., Boulder, CO 80303
Founded: 1973
Scope: National
Description: Nonprofit, tax-exempt volunteer organization dedicated to the wise stewardship of the wolf and other wild canids found in North America. Produces educational materials appropriate to all age levels, as well as an annual summary of wolf recovery and management activities in North America.
Contact(s):
President:
Publication(s): *yearly summaries*
Keyword(s): Endangered and Threatened Species, Environmental and Conservation Education, Wildlife and Wildlife Habitat, Wildlife Management

NORTH ATLANTIC SALMON CONSERVATION ORGANIZATION
11 Rutland Square, Edinburgh, EH1 2AS United Kingdom
Phone: 131-228-2551; Fax: 131-228-4384; E-mail: hq@nasco.org.uk; Web Site: www.nasco.org.uk
Founded: 1984
Scope: International
Description: NASCO is an intergovernmental organization established to contribute to the conservation, restoration, enhancement, and rational management of salmon stocks in the North Atlantic Ocean through international cooperation. The member parties are: Canada, Denmark (in respect to the Faroe Islands and Greenland), the European Union, Iceland, Norway, the Russian Federation, and the USA.
Contact(s):
Secretary: DR. M.L. WINDSOR
Publication(s): *Biennial reports on the activities of the organization; Ten Year Review of the Activities of the North Atlantic Salmon Conservation Organization; annual reports of the meetings of the Council and Commissions; handbook of basic texts*
Keyword(s): Acid Rain, Fisheries, Greenhouse Effect/Global Warming, International Conservation, North Atlantic Salmon, Salmon Recovery

NORTH CAROLINA ASSOCIATION OF SOIL AND WATER CONSERVATION DISTRICTS
Attn: President, 1713 NE 55W, Coats, NC 27521
Scope: Statewide
Contact(s):
President: JEFF TURLINGTON; Phone: 910-897-6788
1st Vice President: FRANKLIN WILLIAMS, 7530 S NC 41, Wallace, NC 28466; Phone: 910-285-7409
2nd Vice President: JAMES HOLLIFIELD, P.O. Box 475, Bostic, NC 28018; Phone: 828-245-4565; Fax: 828-287-4817
President: EDDIE STROUP, 11416 Timber Ridge Rd., Charlotte, NC 28213; Phone: 704-596-8394; Fax: 704-336-3486
Secretary: VASTINE MITCHELL, 505 W. 34th St., Lumberton, NC 28358; Phone: 910-738-5672; Fax: 910-739-8306
Treasurer: BRUCE WHITFIELD, 5968 Gordonton Rd., Hurdle Mills, NC 27541; Phone: 336-599-0917; Fax: 336-599-6516
Board Member: WADE CARRIGAN, 1245 Oak Ridge Rd., Mooresville, NC 28115; Phone: 704-663-1236; Fax: 704-873-1712
Alternate Board Member: JOHN FINCH, 5958 West NC 97, Spring Hope, NC 27882; Phone: 252-478-7230; Fax: 252-459-9850
Keyword(s): Conservation Districts

NORTH CAROLINA B.A.S.S. CHAPTER FEDERATION
Attn: President, 403 Red Wood Ct., Lenoir, NC 28645
Scope: Statewide
Description: An organization of Bassmaster chapters, affiliated with the Bass Anglers Sportsman Society, organized to fight pollution, assist state and national conservation agencies in their efforts and teach the young people of our country good conservation practices. Dedicated to the realistic conservation of our water resources.
Contact(s):
President: ED CANNON; Phone: 828-728-8550

NORTH CAROLINA BEACH BUGGY ASSOCIATION, INC.
Box 940, Manteo, NC 27954
Phone: 252-473-4880; E-mail: otrbksnc@erols.com; Web Site: www.ncbba.org
Membership: 4,414
Scope: Statewide
Description: NCBBA is an organization dedicated to preserving natural resources and coastal areas of North Carolina. Its purpose is to unite in an organization all persons interested in the natural beach resources of the Outer Banks of North Carolina and elsewhere, and establish a Code of Ethics of beach behavior to which each member must subscribe to uphold.
Contact(s):
President: W. JAMES KEENE, 23134 Homestead Lane, Franklin, VA 23851; Phone: 757-562-2554
Vice President: TOM BURKE, 2512 S. Virginia Dare Trl., Nags Head, NC 27959
Secretary: SHARON NEWBOLD, 600 S. Memorial Drive, Kill Devil Hills, NC 27948; Phone: 252-480-2453
Treasurer: BRENDA OUTLAW, P.O. Box 940, Manteo, NC 27954; Phone: 252-473-4880; Fax: brendaoutlaw@hotmail.com
Editor: JOHN NEWBOLD
Publication(s): *NCBBA News, The*
Keyword(s): Coasts, Endangered and Threatened Species, Fisheries, Outdoor Recreation, Sport Fishing

NORTH CAROLINA COALITION, INC.
P.O. Box 122, Franklin, NC 28744
Phone: 828-369-7877; Fax: 828-369-7877; E-mail: rivers@dnet.net; Web Site: www.geocities.com/Yosemite.Cabin/8968
Founded: 1998; Membership: 62
Scope: Statewide
Description: The coalition promotes conservation, protection and enhancement of watersheds and rivers; encourages founding and growth of local organizations devoted to those ends through information sharing and cooperation.
Contact(s):
Executive Director: PEG JONES
Keyword(s): Air Quality and Pollution, Conservation, Dams, Drinking Water Protection, Resource Law Enforcement, Rivers, Runoff, Streams, Upstream Flood Prevention, Urban and Rural Development, Water and Air Quality, Water Pollution, Watersheds, Wildlife and Wildlife Habitat

NORTH CAROLINA COASTAL FEDERATION, INC.
Attn: Amanda Lail, 3609 Highway 24 (Ocean), Newport, NC 28570
Phone: 252-393-8185; Fax: 252-393-7508; E-mail: nccf@nccoast.org; Web Site: www.nccoast.org
Founded: 1982; Membership: 5,000
Scope: Statewide
Description: The Coastal Federation focuses on the twenty coastal counties in North Carolina, with citizens working together for a healthy coast..
Contact(s):
Executive Director: TODD MILLER
Director of Development: SALLY STEELE
Director of Education: TED WILGIS
Publication(s): *Coastal Review; State of Coast Report; Sound Advice*
Keyword(s): Environmental and Conservation Education, Estuaries, Land Use Planning, Water Quality

NORTH CAROLINA FORESTRY ASSOCIATION
1600 Glenwood Ave., Suite I, Raleigh, NC 27608-2355

Phone: 919-834-3943 / 1-800-231-7723 NC only; Fax: 919-832-6188
Founded: 1911; Membership: 2,450
Scope: Statewide
Description: The North Carolina Forestry Association promotes and protects the long-term health and productivity of the forest ecosystem to enhance the environment and economy of North Carolina.
Contact(s):
President: ED KESSLER, Bunn Hardwoods, P.O. Box 188, Bunn, NC 27508
Executive Vice President: ROBERT W. SLOCUM JR., 1600 Glenwood Ave., Suite I, Raleigh, NC 27608-2355; Phone: 919-834-3943
President-Elect: DAN OWENS, Georgia-Pacific Corp., P.O. Box 1536, Wendell, NC 27591
Publication(s): *TreeLine*
Keyword(s): Communications, Environmental and Conservation Education, Forests and Forestry, Renewable Resources

NORTH CAROLINA HERPETOLOGICAL SOCIETY
Attn: President, Three Lakes Nature Center and Aquarium, 400 Sausiluta Dr., Richmond, VA 23227
Founded: 1978
Scope: Statewide
Description: A nonprofit group formed to promote an interest in and to educate members and the general public concerning the ecological importance and conservation of reptiles and amphibians.
Contact(s):
President: TOM THORP; Phone: 804-261-8230; E-mail: tt-threelakes@juno.com
Vice President: DAN LOCKWOOD, 112 E. Skyhawk Dr., Cary, NC 27513; Phone: 919-460-3504; E-mail: ddlockwood@email.msn.com
Secretary: JOE ZAWADOWSKI, 503 Valley Dr., Durham, NC 27704; Phone: 919-684-6062; E-mail: Joe_Zawadowski@bba.mc.duke.edu
Treasurer: DAN DOMBROWSKI, NC State Museum of Natural Sciences, P.O. Box 29555, Raleigh, NC 27626-0555; Phone: 919-733-7450, ext. 504; E-mail: dan_dombrowski@mail.enr.state.nc.us
Editor: JEFF BEANE, 4433 Graham Newton Rd., Raleigh, NC 27606; Phone: 919-733-7450, ext 754; E-mail: jeff_beane@mail.enr.state.nc.us
Advisor: ALVIN BRASWELL, 1208 Buffaloe Rd., Garner, NC 27529; Phone: 919-733-7450, ext 751; E-mail: alvin_braswell@mail.enr.state.nc.us
Publication(s): *NC HERPS*
Keyword(s): Reptiles and Amphibians

NORTH CAROLINA RECREATION AND PARK SOCIETY, INC.
883 Washington St., Raleigh, NC 27605
Phone: 919-832-5868; Fax: 919-832-3323
Founded: 1944; Membership: 2,300
Scope: Statewide
Description: A nonprofit organization formed to promote the wise use of leisure and intelligent development of the state's recreation resources. An affiliate of The National Recreation and Park Association.
Contact(s):
President: BUTCH KISIAH, Asheville Parks and Recreation, P.O. Box 7148, Asheville, NC 28802; Phone: 828-259-5800; Fax: 828-259-5606
Executive Director: MIKE WATERS, 883 Washington St., Raleigh, NC 27605
Editor: KARLA HENDERSON, UNC-Chapel Hill, LSRA Curriculum, Campus Box 3185, Evergreen House, Chapel Hill, NC 27599-3185; Phone: 919-962-1222; Fax: 919-962-1223
Publication(s): *North Carolina Recreation and Park Review; NCRPS News*
Keyword(s): Environmental Preservation, Open Space, Outdoor Recreation, Youth Organizations

NORTH CAROLINA WILD FLOWER PRESERVATION SOCIETY
c/o NC Botanical Garden, CB #3375, Totten Center, UNC-CH, Chapel Hill, NC 27599-3375
Fax: 336-370-8172; Web Site: www.ncwildflower.org/ or
Founded: 1951; Membership: 320
Scope: Statewide
Description: A non-profit organization dedicated to the enjoyment and conservation of native plants and their habitats through education, protection and propagation.
Contact(s):
President: CHARLOTTE PATTERSON; Phone: 336-643-4656
Vice-President: ALICE ZAWADZKI; Phone: 919-834-4172; E-mail: alice_zawadzki@mail.agr.state.nc.us
Recording Secretary: EVELYN CALDWELL; Phone: 919-851-5780
Corresponding Secretary: CARLA OLDHAM; Phone: 919-932-3311
Editor: CRAIG MORETZ; Phone: 919-563-1795
Publication(s): *NC Wild Flower Preservation Society Newsletter; NC Native Plant Propagation Handbook*
Keyword(s): Botanical Gardens, Botany, Endangered and Threatened Species, Habitat Conservation, Plant Propagation, Research Grants, Stewardship, Sustainable Ecosystems, Wildflowers, Native Plants

NORTH CAROLINA WILDLIFE FEDERATION
Box 10626, Raleigh, NC 27605
Phone: 919-833-1923; Fax: 919-829-1192; Web Site: www.ncwildlifefed.org
Scope: Statewide
Description: A representative statewide organization, affiliated with the National Wildlife Federation, dedicated to the protection and enhancement of wildlife and its habitat through public education and government interaction.
Contact(s):
President and Alternative Representative: DALE MOSTELLER
Executive Director: DOCK KORNEGAY
Representative: CHUCK RICE
Editor: EDDIE NICKENS
Publication(s): *Friend Of Wildlife*

NORTH CASCADES CONSERVATION COUNCIL
P.O. Box 95980, Seattle, WA 98145-2980
Phone: 206-282-1644; Fax: 206-684-1379; E-mail: steveB@premier.net
Founded: 1957; Membership: 500
Scope: Regional
Description: The Council seeks to protect and preserve the North Cascades' scenic, scientific, recreational, educational, wildlife, and wilderness values from the Columbia River to the US-Canadian border in the state of Washington.
Contact(s):
Chairman: PATRICK D. GOLDSWORTHY; Phone: 206-282-1644
President: MARC BARDSLEY; E-mail: steveb@premier1.net
Vice President: CHARLES EHLERT
Secretary: PHIL ZALESKY
Treasurer: THOMAS H. BRUCKER
Publication(s): *Wild Cascades, The*
Keyword(s): Ancient Forests, Biodiversity, Conservation of Protected Areas, Environmental Preservation, Environmental Protection, Fisheries, Forest Management, Lakes, Land Preservation, Land Use Planning, Mining, Natural Areas, Nature Preservation, Outdoor Recreation

NORTH DAKOTA ASSOCIATION OF SOIL CONSERVATION DISTRICTS
Attn: President, P.O. Box 267, Crosby, ND 58703
Scope: Statewide
Contact(s):
President: RONALD D. JACOBSON; Phone: 701-965-6165; Fax: 701-965-4337
Vice-President: RODNEY HICKLE, 1631 28th Ave., SW, Center, ND 58530; Phone: 701-794-3342

Executive Vice-President: GARY PUPPE, P.O. Box 1601, 3310 University Dr., Bismarck, ND 58502-1601; Phone: 701-223-8518; Fax: 701-223-1291
Keyword(s): Conservation Districts

NORTH DAKOTA NATURAL SCIENCE SOCIETY
Division of Biological Sciences, Box 4050, Emporia, KS 66801
Phone: 316-341-5623; Web Site: www.emporia.edu/s/www/biosci/pn/pn.htm
Founded: 1967; Membership: 350
Scope: Regional
Description: Dedicated to the observation, recording, study, and preservation of all aspects of the natural history of the Great Plains.
Contact(s):
President: DR. JANE AUSTIN, Northern Prairie Wildlife Research Center, Jamestown, ND 58401
Editor: DR. ELMER FINCK, Div. Of Biological Sciences, Box 4050, Emporia, KS 66801
Publication(s): *Prairie Naturalist, The*
Keyword(s): Fisheries, Great Plains, Natural History, Nongame Wildlife, Prairies, Wildlife and Wildlife Habitat

NORTH DAKOTA WILDLIFE FEDERATION, INC.
P.O. Box 7248, Bismarck, ND 58507-7248
Phone: 701-222-2557; Fax: 701-222-0334; E-mail: ndwf@gcentral.com
Scope: Statewide
Description: A representative statewide organization, affiliated with the National Wildlife Federation, dedicated to the protection and enhancement of wildlife and its habitat through public education and government interaction.
Contact(s):
President and Alternative Representative: ART MIELKE
Representative: JAMES BOLEY
Editor: LARRY CRAWFORD
Publication(s): *Flickertales*

NORTHCOAST ENVIRONMENTAL CENTER
879 Ninth St., Arcata, CA 95521
Phone: 707-822-6918; Fax: 707-822-0827; E-mail: nec@igc.apc.org
Founded: 1971; Membership: 4,500
Scope: Regional
Description: A tax-exempt educational organization dedicated to illuminating the relationships between humankind and the biosphere. The Center provides environmental information and referral services for northwestern California and Southwestern Oregon and operates a library open to the public.
Contact(s):
Director: TIM McKAY
Editor: SID DOMINITZ
Office Manager: CONNIE STEWART
Librarian: STAN LARSON
Librarian: GAIL SELLSTROM
Publication(s): *Econews*
Keyword(s): Ancient Forests, Biodiversity, Endangered and Threatened Species, Environmental Protection, Forests and Forestry, Public Lands, Watersheds, Wilderness, Libraries

NORTHEAST ASSOCIATION OF FISH AND WILDLIFE RESOURCE AGENCIES
Attn: President, Director of Div. Of Fish & Wildlife, DNR and Environmental Control, 89 Kings Hwy., Dover, NJ 19901
Scope: Regional
Description: Consists of heads of fish and game agencies in 11 northeastern states, Canadian Maritime Provinces, Newfoundland, Ontario, and Quebec. Meets at least yearly to review progress, consider mutual problems, coordinate programs on a regional basis, and promote sound fish and game management programs.
Contact(s):
President: ANDREW MARCUS, Director of Division of Fish & Wildlife, DNR and Environmental Control, 89 Kings Hwy, Dover, DE 19901; Phone: 302-739-5295; Fax: 302-739-6157

Vice President: EDWARD PARKER, Chief of Connecticut Bureau of Natural Resources, 79 Elm Street, Hartford, CT 06106-5127; Phone: 860-424-3061; Fax: 860-424-4070

NORTHEAST CONSERVATION LAW ENFORCEMENT CHIEFS' ASSOCIATION (CLECA)
Attn: Secretary, RI Dept. of Environmental Management, 83 Park St., Providence, PA 02908
Phone: 401-277-2284
Scope: Regional
Contact(s):
President: COL. RONALD ALIE, Chief. New Hampshire Fish and Game Dept., Law Enforcement Division, 2 Hazen Dr., Concord, NH 033301; Phone: 603-271-3127; Fax: 603-271-1438
Vice Presidents: THOMAS J. KAMERZEL, Dir., Bureau of Law Enforcement, Pennsylvania Fish and Boat Commission, P.O. Box 67000, Harrisburg, PA 17106-7000; Phone: 717-567-4542; Fax: 717-657-4033
Secretary and Treasurer: THOMAS GREENE
Keyword(s): Law Enforcement, Professional Organization

NORTHEAST SUSTAINABLE ENERGY ASSOCIATION
50 Miles St., Greenfield, MA 01301
Phone: 413-774-6051; Fax: 413-774-6053; E-mail: nesea@nesea.org; Web Site: www.nesea.org
Founded: 1974; Membership: 1,200
Scope: Regional
Description: The Northeast Sustainable Energy Association (NESEA) aims to strengthen the economy and lessen our impact on the environment by bringing sustainable energy into everyday use. Through its programs and activities, NESEA offers an alternative vision of responsible energy use and works with policymakers, industry, educators, students, and the general public to make this vision a reality.
Contact(s):
Secretary: NANCY SCHALCH
Treasurer: PAUL ELDRENKAMP
Board of Directors Chair: ED SMELOFF
Executive Director: THOMAS THOMPSON; E-mail: tthompson@nesea.org
Associate Director, Director of Operations: FRANK TRIPOLI; E-mail: tripoli@hotmail.com
Director of Education: CHRIS MASON; E-mail: cmason@nesea.org
Director of Energy Park: SANDY THOMAS; E-mail: sthomas@nesea.org
Director of Transportation Programs: NANCY HAZARD; E-mail: nhazard@nesea.org
Manager of Building Program: JONATHON TAUER; E-mail: jtauer@nesea.org
Publication(s): *Northeast Sun; Getting Around Without Gasoline; Totally Tree-mendous Activities*
Keyword(s): Environmental and Conservation Education, Solar Energy, Sustainable Buildings, Sustainable Energy, Transportation

NORTHEAST WILDLIFE ADMINISTRATORS ASSOCIATION
c/o Gary Parsons, Bureau of Wildlife, Division of Fish, Wildlife and Marine Resources, 50 Wolf Rd., Rm. 562, Albany, NY 12233-4754
Phone: 518-457-3730; Fax: 518-457-0691
Founded: 1983
Scope: National
Description: Members include the wildlife management program administrators of the northeast U.S. state and eastern Canadian provincial fish and wildlife agencies. The goal of NEWAA is to coordinate and facilitate the work of regional technical wildlife management committees to promote sound wildlife management programs and to exchange ideas, methods, and approaches to administrative and operational problems in wildlife management.
Contact(s):
Chairman: GARY PARSONS; E-mail: gxparson@gw.dec.state.ny.us
Keyword(s): Endangered and Threatened Species, Hunting, Nongame Wildlife, Wildlife and Wildlife Habitat, Wildlife Management, Professional Organization

NON-GOVERNMENTAL ORGANIZATIONS - N

NORTHERN ALASKA ENVIRONMENTAL CENTER
218 Driveway St., Fairbanks, AK 99701-2806
Phone: 907-452-5021; Fax: 907-452-3100; E-mail: naec@mosquitonet.com; Web Site: http://www.mosquitonet.com/~naec
Founded: 1971; Membership: 1,300
Scope: Statewide
Description: The Northern Alaska Environmental Center works to protect some of the wildest country left in North America -- the vast Interior and Arctic regions of Alaska -- through education, advocacy, grassroots organizing, and sheer perseverance. The Northern Center's priorities are to protect Alaska's Arctic from oil drilling; promote ecologically sound, sustainable management of Alaska's boreal forests; defend wild rivers from mining pollution and roads; and encourage better environmental understanding, particularly by our youth.
Contact(s):
President: PAM GROVES
Vice President: CLARICE DUKEMINIER
Secretary: LINDA DEFOLIART
Treasurer: MARGARET EAGLETON
Executive Director: SYLVIA WARD
Boreal Forest Campaign Coordinator: NANCY FRESCO
Communications and Membership Director: BETH CAISSIE
Wilderness Campaign Coordinator: DEB MOORE
Publication(s): *Northern Line, The; Arctic Action; Boreal Briefs; Conservation Abstracts*
Keyword(s): Arctic, Environmental and Conservation Education, Forest Management, Natural Areas, Public Lands, Rivers, Sustainable Ecosystems, Taiga, Tundra, Water Quality, Wilderness, Wildlands

NORTHERN PLAINS RESOURCE COUNCIL
2401 Montana Ave., #200, Billings, MT 59101-2336
Phone: 406-248-1154
Founded: 1972; Membership: 3,000
Scope: National
Description: NPRC is a grassroots citizens' organization of farmers, ranchers, townspeople, and other conservationists. NPRC works on natural resource and agricultural issues to promote sustainable economic development, and to maintain Montana's unique rural quality of life. NPRC is dedicated to family agriculture and to stewardship of air, land, and water.
Contact(s):
Chair: JERRY SIKORSKI
Secretary: NELLIE ISRAEL
Treasurer: BARBARA VARNES
Research Coordinator: TED LANGE
Staff Director: TERESA ERICKSON
Vice Chair: DENA HOFF
Publication(s): *Plains Truth, The; Reclaiming the Wealth (A Citizens' Guide to Hard Rock Mining in Montana); Legislative Bulletin*
Keyword(s): Agriculture, Air Quality and Pollution, Energy, Mining, Solid Waste Management, Water Quality

NORTHWEST ATLANTIC FISHERIES ORGANIZATION (NAFO)
P.O. Box 638, Dartmouth, Nova Scotia B2Y 3Y9 Canada
Phone: 902-468-5590; Fax: 902-468-5538
Founded: 1979
Scope: International
Description: Works for the optimum utilization, rational management, and conservation of the fishery resources of the convention area in the Northwest Atlantic. Contracting Parties: Bulgaria, Canada, Cuba, Denmark for the Faroes and Greenland, Estonia, European Union, France (for St. Pierre and Miquelon), Iceland, Japan, Korea, Latvia, Lithuania, Norway, Poland, Romania, Russia and the USA.
Contact(s):
Executive Secretary: LEONARD I. CHEPEL
Assistant Executive Secretary: T. AMARATUNGA
Fisheries Commission Chairman: P. GULLESTAD, Norway
Fisheries Commission Vice Chairman: D. SWANSON
General Council, Vice Chairman:
President of NAFO and Chairman of General Council: A. RODIN, Russia
Scientific Council Chairman: H. P. CORNUS, EU
Scientific Council Vice-Chairman: W. B. BRODIE, Canada
Publication(s): *Annual Report; Journal of Northwest Atlantic Fishery Science; Statistical Bulletin; Scientific Council Studies; Sampling Yearbook; List of Fishing Vessels; Index of Meeting Documents*
Keyword(s): Biology, Fisheries, International Conservation, Oceanography

NORTHWEST COALITION FOR ALTERNATIVES TO PESTICIDES
P.O. Box 1393, Eugene, OR 97440
Phone: 541-334-5044; Fax: 541-344-6923; E-mail: info@pesticide.org; Web Site: www.pesticide.org
Founded: 1977
Scope: Regional
Description: The Northwest Coalition for Alternatives to Pesticides works to protect people and the environment by advancing healthy solutions to pest problems.
Contact(s):
Executive Director: NORMA GRIER; E-mail: ngrier@pesticide.org
Information Services Coordinator: POLLYANNA LIND
Program Associate: NEVA HASSANEIN Ph.D.; E-mail: neva@pesticides.org
Program Associate: BECKY RILEY; E-mail: briley@pesticides.org
Program Associate: KAREN MURPHY; E-mail: kmurphy@pesticide.org
Editor: CAROLINE COX; E-mail: ccox@pesticide.org
Publication(s): *Journal of Pesticide Reform; Diminishing Returns: Salmon Decline and Pesticides; Pesticides and Children*
Keyword(s): Agriculture, Alternative Agriculture, Pest Management, Pesticides, Toxicology

NORTHWEST ECOSYSTEM ALLIANCE
1421 Cornwall Ave., Suite 201, Bellingham, WA 98225
Phone: 360-671-9950; Fax: 360-671-8429; E-mail: nwea@ecosystem.org; Web Site: ecosystem.org
Founded: 1989; Membership: 6,000
Scope: Regional
Description: The Northwest Ecosystem Alliance protects and restores wildlands in the Pacific Northwest and supports such efforts in British Columbia. The Alliance bridges science and advocacy, working with activists, policymakers, and the public to conserve our natural heritage.
Contact(s):
President: EMILY BARNETT
Secretary: JEFFREY JON BODE
Treasurer: TOM CAMPION
Executive Director: MITCH FRIEDMAN
Publication(s): *Northwest Conservation: News and Priorities; Wild Salmon and Trout Action Plan: Of Wolves and Washington; Cascadia Wild: Protecting an International Ecosystem; Conservation Biology and National Forest Management in the Inland Northwest: A Handbook for Activists*
Keyword(s): Ancient Forests, Biodiversity, Conservation of Protected Areas, Ecology, Endangered and Threatened Species, Environment, Forest Management, Internships, Nature Preservation, Predators, Raptors, Reptiles and Amphibians, Sustainable Ecosystems, Trapping, Wildlife and Wildlife Habitat

NORTHWEST ENVIRONMENT WATCH
1402 3rd Ave. #1127, Seattle, WA 98101
Phone: 206-447-1880; Fax: 206-447-2270; E-mail: new@northwestwatch.org; Web Site: www.northwestwatch.org
Founded: 1993; Membership: 1,500
Scope: Regional
Description: NEW's mission is to foster sustainability in the Pacific Northwest. NEW provides citizens with intelligence reports on the latest findings from the natural and social sciences, and guides them in creating a sustainable economy.

Contact(s):
Executive Director: ALAN DURNING
Office Manager: RHEA CONNORS
Research Director: JOHN RYAN
Publication(s): *State of the Northwest; This Place on Earth; The Car and The City; Stuff, Misplaced Blame*
Keyword(s): Population Growth, Sustainable Development, Transportation

NORTHWEST INTERPRETIVE ASSOCIATION
909 1st Ave., Suite 630, Seattle, WA 98104
Phone: 206-220-4140
Founded: 1974
Scope: Regional
Description: The Association supports interpretation and education on public lands administered by the National Park Service, U.S. Forest Service, and other agencies in the Pacific Northwest. Proceeds from the sale of interpretive publications are donated to these agencies to educate visitors in the area's natural and cultural history.
Contact(s):
Executive Director: MARY QUACKENBUSH
Chairman of the Board: JIM TORRENCE
Vice Chairman: TOM SCRIBNER
Keyword(s): Cultural Preservation, Environmental and Conservation Education, Natural History, Outdoor Recreation, Wilderness

NORTHWEST RESOURCE INFORMATION CENTER
2811 W. State St., P.O. Box 427, Eagle, ID 83616
Phone: 208-939-0714; Fax: 208-939-7263
Founded: 1976
Scope: National
Description: NRIC promotes through research, public education, technology transfer, and litigation the concept that ecological diversity and environmental quality are synonymous with long-term economic productivity and quality of life.
Contact(s):
Executive Director: ED CHANEY, 2811 W. State St., Eagle, ID 83616; Phone: 208-939-8731
Keyword(s): Environmental Protection, International Conservation, Sustainable Development, Sustainable Ecosystems, Watersheds

NOVA SCOTIA FEDERATION OF ANGLERS AND HUNTERS
P.O. Box 654, Halifax, Nova Scotia B3J 2T3 Canada
Phone: 902-423-6793; Fax: 902-423-6793; E-mail: NSWF@chebucto.ns.ca
Founded: 1930; Membership: 6,500
Scope: Statewide
Description: Affiliated with the Canadian Wildlife Federation and the National Coalition of Provincial and Territorial Wildlife Federations. Aims to unite all conservation organizations in Nova Scotia, fosters appreciation of wildlife and habitat, promotes fish and game management, seeks enactment and enforcement of laws necessary for environmental controls as well as conservation of wildlife resources.
Contact(s):
President: RANNIE GILLIS
Executive Director: A. J. RODGERS

NOVA SCOTIA FORESTRY ASSOCIATION
P.O. Box 1113, Truro, Nova Scotia B2N 5G9 Canada
Phone: 902-893-4653; Fax: 902-893-1197
Founded: 1959
Scope: Statewide
Description: The Nova Scotia Forestry Association is a nonprofit, charitable organization dedicated to promoting the wise use and management of our forest resources through education programs for youth. Programs emphasize the importance of being good stewards of our natural resources.
Contact(s):
President: TIM ROCK
Executive Director: DEBBIE TOTTEN
Keyword(s): Environmental and Conservation Education, Forest Management, Pollution Prevention

NW ENERGY COALITION
219 First Ave., So., Suite 100, Seattle, WA 98104
Phone: 206-621-0094; Fax: 206-621-0097; E-mail: nwec@nwenergy.org; Web Site: www.nwenergy.org
Founded: 1981
Scope: National
Description: NWEC is a region-wide coalition of public interest groups and progressive utilities. The energy coalition works for a clean, affordable energy policy for the Pacific Northwest and British Columbia. The Coalition advocates for energy conservation and renewable resources, wild salmon, and low income/consumer protection.
Contact(s):
Chairman: DEB SMITH
Director: SARA PATTON
Publication(s): *NW Energy Coalition Report; Energy Activist; Plugging People into Power;*
Keyword(s): Energy, Fisheries, Renewable Resources, Solar Energy, Salmon Recovery

O

OCEAN VOICE INTERNATIONAL
P.O. Box 37026 3332 McCarthy Rd., Ottawa, Ontario K1V 0W0 Canada
Phone: 613-990-8819; Fax: 613-521-4205
Founded: 1987; Membership: 150
Scope: National
Description: To conserve the diversity of marine life, protect and restore marine ecosystems and ecological services, enhance the quality of life and equity of benefits for coastal peoples, and promote ecologically sustainable harvest of marine resources.
Contact(s):
President: DR. DON E. McALLISTER, P.O. Box 37026, 3332 McCarthy Rd., Ottawa, Ontario K1V 0W0 Canada; Phone: 613-264-8986
Secretary: KATJA RODRIGUEZ, 370 Metcalfe St., Apt. 712, Ottawa, Ontario K2P 159 Canada
Treasurer: PHYLLIS KOFMEL, 409 Huron Ave. S., Ottawa, Ontario K1Y 0X2 Canada; Phone: 613-729-1893
Publication(s): *Sea Wind; Save Our Coral Reefs; How Green is Your School?; Green School Biodiversity Booklet, The Status of the World Ocean and its Biodiversity; Global Freshwater Biodiversity; Striving for the Integrity of Freshwater Ecosystems*
Keyword(s): Aquatic Habitats, Biodiversity, Coral Reefs, Developing Countries, International Conservation

OHIO ACADEMY OF SCIENCE, THE
1500 W. 3rd Ave., Suite 223, Columbus, OH 43212-2817
Phone: 614-488-2228; E-mail: oas@iwaynet.net
Founded: 1891; Membership: 2,000
Scope: Statewide
Description: A nonprofit organization designed to stimulate interest in the sciences, to promote research, to improve instruction in the sciences, to disseminate scientific knowledge, and to recognize high achievement in attaining these objectives.
Contact(s):
President: SPENCER E. REAMES, Benjamin Logan HS, 6609 St. Rt. 47 E., Bellefontaine, OH 43311; Phone: 937-592-1666
Secretary: DR. RONALD L. STUCKEY, Ohio State University, Museum of Biological Diversity, 1315 Kinnear Ave., Columbus, OH 43212-1192; Phone: 614-292-6095
Treasurer: DR. MICHAEL HERSCHLER
Editor: DR. THOMAS W. SCHMIDLIN, Kent State University, Department of Geography, Kent, OH 44242; Phone: 330-672-4632
Executive Officer: LYNN EDWARD ELFNER
Publication(s): *Ohio Journal of Science, The; Ohio Academy of Science Newsletter*

NON-GOVERNMENTAL ORGANIZATIONS - O

Keyword(s): Biotechnology, Communications, Environmental and Conservation Education, Youth Organizations, Ecological Education

OHIO ALLIANCE FOR THE ENVIRONMENT
1500 West Third Ave., Columbus, OH 43212
Phone: 614-487-9957; Fax: 614-487-9957; Web Site: www.ohioalliance.org
Founded: 1977
Scope: Statewide
Description: A statewide nonprofit organization established to provide leadership in resolving environmental conflicts and to promote and support adult environmental education in Ohio. The Alliance is a non-advocacy organization working to establish channels of communication among diverse groups with environmental concerns and to provide balanced environmental information through conferences, publications, roundtable discussions, and seminars.
Contact(s):
President: JANE TAFT, Community Outreach Manager, Lafarge Corporation, P.O. Box 160, Paulding, OH 45879-0160; Phone: 419-399-4861, ext. 234; Fax: 419-399-2459; E-mail: amfdjt@bright.net
Vice President: JIM SWANEY Ph.D., Dept. of Economics, Wright State Univ., 3640 Colonel Glenn Hwy., Dayton, OH 45435; Phone: 937-775-2769; Fax: 937-775-3545; E-mail: jswaney@nova.wright.edu
Secretary: SUSAN COVEY, Facilitator and Trainer, 58 Olentangy St., P.O. Box 82249, Columbus, OH 43202-2249; Phone: 614-571-8705; Fax: 614-261-0163; E-mail: scovey@iwaynet.net
Treasurer: LISA NOVOSAT-GRADERT ESQ., Brouse and McDowell, 500 First National Tower, Akron, OH 44308-1471; Phone: 330-535-5711; Fax: 330-253-8601; E-mail: lngradert@browse.com
Executive Director: IRENE PROBASCO; E-mail: probasco@ohioalliance.org
Editor: JANE HAYNES, Natural Resources Specialist, League of Women Voters of Ohio Education Fund, 17 South High St.., Columbus, OH 43215; Phone: 614-469-1505; Fax: 614-469-7918; E-mail: sjhaynes@juno.com
Publication(s): *Focus on the Issue; OAE Newsletter*
Keyword(s): Communications, Environmental and Conservation Education

OHIO AUDUBON COUNCIL, INC.
121 Larchmont Rd., Springfield, OH 45503
Founded: 1969; Membership: 20,000
Scope: Statewide
Description: Associated with the National Audubon Society. Works to promote, foster, and encourage the conservation and preservation of all wildlife, plants, soil, water, air, and other natural resources for the benefit of all citizens. 20 chapters, two affiliates.
Contact(s):
President: JOYCE PELZ, Greater Akron AS, 560 Surfside Drive, Akron, OH 44319; Phone: 330-645-0953
Vice President: PETE PRECARIO, Columbus AS, 524 Blenheim Road, Columbus, OH 43214; Phone: 614-262-0050
Secretary: DOROTHY KOONTZ, Firelands AS, 740 Chestnut Lane, Huron, OH 44839; Phone: 216-433-2883
Treasurer: ALAN DOLAN, Canton AS, P.O. Box 935, Massillon, OH 44648; Phone: 330-832-2491
Past President: MIKE COOGAN, Dayton AS, 2477 W. Alex-Bell Rd., Dayton, OH 45459-1187; Phone: 513-643-1726
Keyword(s): Birds, Endangered and Threatened Species, Environmental and Conservation Education, Wetlands, Wildlife and Wildlife Habitat

OHIO B.A.S.S. CHAPTER FEDERATION
ATTN: President, 376 N. Dorset, Troy, OH 45373
Scope: Statewide
Description: An organization of Bassmaster chapters, affiliated with the Bass Anglers Sportsman Society, organized to fight pollution, assist state and national conservation agencies in their efforts, and teach the young people of our country good conservation practices. Dedicated to the realistic conservation of our water resources.
Contact(s):
President: DENNIS BECKER; Phone: 937-335-2078
Conservation Director: JIM DOSS, 43 Portsmouth Rd., Gallipolis, OH 45631; Phone: 740-446-9810

OHIO BIOLOGICAL SURVEY
1315 Kinnear Rd., Columbus, OH 43212-1192
Phone: 614-292-9645
Founded: 1912
Scope: Regional
Description: An inter-institutional organization of 106 colleges, universities, museums and other organizations in Ohio, ten other states and the province of Ontario. Produces and disseminates scientific and technical information concerning the flora and fauna of the Ohio environment, and larger areas of which Ohio is an integral part.
Contact(s):
Executive Director: DR. BRIAN J. ARMITAGE
Chairman of the Advisory Board: DR. TERRY D. KEISER, Ohio Northern University
Editor: VEDA M. CAFAZZO
Publication(s): *Bulletins; Miscellaneous Publications; Notes; Informative Publications*
Keyword(s): Biodiversity, Endangered and Threatened Species, Environmental and Conservation Education, Flowers, Plants, and Trees, Natural History, Nature Preservation

OHIO ENERGY PROJECT
7099 Huntley Rd., Columbus, OH 43229
Phone: 614-785-1717; Fax: 614-785-1731; E-mail: ohenergy@infinet.com; Web Site: www.ohioenergy.org
Founded: 1984; Membership: 625
Scope: Statewide
Description: A nonprofit organization promoting energy education, efficiency and conservation, youth leadership development, using a fun hands on multi-dimensional, Inter-disciplinary approach and a "kids teaching kids" philosophy.
Contact(s):
Executive Director: SHAUNI NIX
Director: RICH SMITH
Education Coordinator: ELAINE BARNES
Finance Manager: JUDITH ELEKES
Publication(s): *Energy Source, The*
Keyword(s): Energy, Energy Conservation, Environmental and Conservation Education, Scholarships, Youth Organizations, Youth Leadership

OHIO ENVIRONMENTAL COUNCIL, INC.
Suite 201, 1207 Grandview Ave., Columbus, OH 43212
Phone: 614-487-7506
Founded: 1969
Scope: Statewide
Description: The Ohio Environmental Council is a statewide organization providing resources for local environmental organizations across Ohio. The OEC promotes improved environmental quality in the state through advocacy, research, education and collaborative efforts.
Contact(s):
President: PAT HAMMEL, 217 E. Patterson, Columbus, OH 43202; Phone: 614-487-6954; Fax: 614-487-8506; E-mail: phammel@ocsea.org
Vice-President: VIRGINIA AVENI, 1600 Clubside Rd., Lynhurst, OH 44124; Phone: 216-443-3716; Fax: 216-443-3737; E-mail: cpc@planning.co.cuyahoga.oh.us
Secretary: ANTHONY J. CELEBREZZE III, 253 H. E. Kossuth, Columbu, OH 43206; Phone: 614-644-7613; Fax: 614-446-4120(call first)
Treasurer: BRUCE CORNETT, Green Environmental Coalition, Box 266, Yellow Springs, OH 45387; Phone: 937-767-5000; Fax: 937-767-8587/9041; E-mail: bcornett@greenlink.org
Executive Director: VICKI LEE DEISNER

Publication(s): *Ohio Environmental Report Newsletter; Green Pages* (listing of Ohio environmental groups and resources; variety of other publications on critical environmental issues for Ohio
Keyword(s): Air Quality and Pollution, Energy, Environmental and Conservation Education, Environmental Justice, Lakes, Pollution Prevention, Sustainable Development, Sustainable Ecosystems, Toxic Substances, Water Pollution, Water Quality, Water Resources, Watersheds, Factory Farms

OHIO FEDERATION OF SOIL AND WATER CONSERVATION DISTRICTS
Attn: President, 21199 SR 4, Marysville, OH 43040
Scope: Statewide
Contact(s):
President, Alternate Board Member: STEVE ROBINSON; Phone: 937-644-0452; Fax: 937-644-0452
Vice President: DAVID LINKHART, 1782 Fawcett Rd., Xenia, OH 45385-9458; Phone: 937-376-5731; Fax: 937-376-5731
Board Member: ROBERT CARROLL, 660 Spruce St., Wauseon, OH 43567; Phone: 419-335-3239; Fax: 419-337-4787
Secretary-Treasurer: THOMAS REINNGER, 12055 Lick Rd., Cinncinnati, OH 45251; Phone: 513-851-9672
Keyword(s): Conservation Districts

OHIO FORESTRY ASSOCIATION, INC., THE
1335 Dublin Rd., Suite 203D, Columbus, OH 43215
Phone: 614-486-6767
Founded: 1903; Membership: 1,500
Scope: Statewide
Description: A statewide organization, affiliated with the National Woodland Owners Association, organized to promote the welfare of the people and private enterprise of Ohio by improving, through education, the wise management of Ohio's forest resource. Sponsors annual forestry camp for youths 14-19; assists schools' conservation activities and education; and coordinates American Tree Farm Program in Ohio.
Contact(s):
Chairman: GARY KASTER
President: EUGENE WATTERS
1st Vice-President: MELVIN J. YODER
Secretary, Editor and Executive Director: JIM LEE; Phone: 614-486-6767
Past Chairman: JOHN V. SCHMIDT
Publication(s): *Ohio Woodlands*
Keyword(s): Camp, Forests and Forestry

OHIO NATIVE PLANT SOCIETY
6 Louise Dr., Chagrin Falls, OH 44022
Phone: 440-338-6622
Founded: 1982; Membership: 1,000
Scope: Statewide
Description: The Ohio Native Plant Society is dedicated to preservation, conservation and education concerning all native plants of Ohio.
Contact(s):
Executive Secretary: A. K. MALMQUIST
Keyword(s): Botanical Gardens, Botany, Environmental and Conservation Education, Flowers, Plants, and Trees, Wildflowers, Native Plants

OKLAHOMA ACADEMY OF SCIENCE
P.O. Box 701915, Tulsa, OK 74170-1915
Phone: 918-495-6944
Founded: 1909; Membership: 705 members, 60 libraries
Scope: Statewide
Description: To stimulate scientific research; to promote fraternal relationship among those engaged in scientific work in Oklahoma; to diffuse among the citizens of the state a knowledge of the various departments of science; and to investigate and make known the material, education, and other resources of the state.
Contact(s):
President: CONSTANCE E.S. TAYLOR, Department of Biology, Southeastern Oklahoma State University, Durant, OK 74701; Phone: 405-924-0121
Editor: FRANKLIN R. LEACH, Department of Biochemistry Oklahoma State University, Stillwater, OK 74078-0454; Phone: 405-744-6206
Executive Secretary and Treasurer: EDWARD N. NELSON, Department of Biology Oral Roberts University, Tulsa, OK 74171; Phone: 918-495-6944
President-Elect: RONALD J. TYRL, Department of Botany Oklahoma State University, Stillwater, OK 74078; Phone: 405-744-9558
Recording Secretary: CHARLES M. MATHER, Biology Department University of Sciences and Arts of Oklahoma, P.O. Box 82517, Chickasha, OK 73018; Phone: 405-224-3140
Publication(s): *Proceedings-Oklahoma Academy of Science; Annals-Oklahoma Academy of Science; Transactions-Oklahoma Junior Academy of Science; CAS Newsletter*
Keyword(s): Environmental and Conservation Education, Natural History, Research, Training, Wildlife and Wildlife Habitat

OKLAHOMA ASSOCIATION OF CONSERVATION DISTRICTS
Attn: President, P.O. Box 107, Chelsea, OK 74016-0107
Scope: Statewide
Contact(s):
President, Alternate Board Member: CAROL GAUNT, Rt. 5 Box 244, Weatherford, OK 73096-8815; Phone: 405-772-5107
Vice President: RICK JEANS, Rt 1 Box 184, Tonkawa, OK 74653; Phone: 405-628-2223
Vice President: MATT GARD, Rt. 1, Box 16, Fairview, OK 73737-9621; Phone: 580-438-2320
Vice President: MARK MOEHLE, 1601 Shadow Court, Edmond, OK 73013-2683; Phone: 405-340-8884; Fax: 405-842-8744
Secretary: CHRISTY KIMBLE, Oklahoma County CD, 1120 NW 63rd STE G101, Oklahoma City, OK 73116; Phone: 405-848-1933; Fax: 405-842-8744
Treasurer: WAYNE SMITH, 506 N. Pennsylvania, Mangum, OK 73554-3036; Phone: 405-782-3575; Fax: 405-782-3581
Board Member: BILLY WILSON, P.O. Box 208, Kinta, OK 74552-0208; Phone: 918-768-3542; E-mail: bwilson@cwis.net
Past President: GEORGE FRALEY, P.O. Box 107, Chelsea, OK 74016-0107; Phone: 918-789-2511; Fax: 918-789-2835
Keyword(s): Conservation

OKLAHOMA AUDUBON COUNCIL
1728 S. Quaker, Tulsa, OK 74120
Phone: 918-592-1614
Founded: 1987; Membership: 4,000
Scope: Statewide
Description: A statewide council of representatives of the eight National Audubon Society chapters in Oklahoma. The council coordinates the efforts of the chapters on statewide environmental issues, and advocates protection, preservation, and wise use of soil, water, plants, and wildlife.
Contact(s):
President: SUE WOODWARD, 1728 S. Quaker, Tulsa, OK 74120; Phone: 918-592-1614
Treasurer: JOHN KENNINGTON, 11224 S. 83rd E. Ave., Bixby, OK 74008; Phone: 918-369-3923

OKLAHOMA B.A.S.S. CHAPTER FEDERATION
Attn: President, 2300 E. Coleman Rd., Ponca City, OK 74604
Scope: Statewide
Description: An organization of Bassmaster chapters, affiliated the with Bass Anglers Sportsman Society, organized to fight pollution, assist state and national conservation agencies in their efforts, and teach the young people of our country good conservation practices. Dedicated to the realistic conservation of our water resources.
Contact(s):
President: ROBERT CARTLIDGE; Phone: 580-765-0165
Conservation Director: DON LINDER, 2409 Cardinal, Ponca City, OK 74604; Phone: 580-762-3301
Publication(s): *Scissortail, The; Bulletin of the Oklahoma Ornithological Society, The; Oklahoma B.A.S.S. Federation Newsletter*

OKLAHOMA NATIVE PLANT SOCIETY
c/o Tulsa Garden Center, 2435 S. Peoria, Tulsa, OK 74114
Phone: 405-872-9652; Fax: 405-872-8361; E-mail: onps@aol.com; Web Site: www.telepath.com/chadcox/onps.html
Founded: 1986; Membership: 375
Scope: Statewide
Description: Oklahoma Native Plant Society encourages the study, protection, propagation, appreciation, and use of Oklahoma's native plants.
Contact(s):
President: DR. SHEILA STRAWN; Phone: 405-733-0864
Vice President: TINA JULICH; Phone: 405-598-6742
Secretary: CLAIRE MILLER; Phone: 918-743-3149
Treasurer: JUDY JORDAN; Phone: 405-321-1611
Publication(s): *Gaillardia, The; Native Plant Selection Guide for Oklahoma Woody Plants*
Keyword(s): Biodiversity, Conservation, Ecology, Endangered and Threatened Species, Environmental Protection, Flowers, Plants, and Trees, Natural Areas, Prairies, Public Lands, Rivers, Rural Development, Terrestrial Habitats, Wetlands, Wilderness, Native Plants

OKLAHOMA ORNITHOLOGICAL SOCIETY
Attn: Buiness Manager, 1701 W. Will Rogers, Claremore, OK 74017
Phone: 918-343-7706
Founded: 1950; Membership: 600
Scope: Statewide
Description: Affiliated with National Audubon Society and the Oklahoma Wildlife Federation. Dedicated to the observation, study, and conservation of birds in Oklahoma.
Contact(s):
President: JUNE KETCHUM, HCR 70, Box 156, Ardmore, OK 73401
Secretary: MICHAEL BAY, Dept. Biology, East Central state Univ., Ada, OK 74820
Treasurer: MARTY KAMP, 6422 s. Indianapolis Pl., Tulsa, OK 74136
Business Manager: KEITH W. MARTIN, Rogers Univ., 1701 W. Will Rogers, Claremore, OK 74017
Editor: JACK D. TYLER, Biology Dept., Cameron State University, Lawton, OK 73501
Editor: BONNIE GALL, Rt. 1, Box 515F, Bartlesville, OK 74006

OKLAHOMA WILDLIFE FEDERATION
P.O. Box 60126, Oklahoma City, OK 73118
Phone: 405-524-7009; Fax: 405-521-9270; E-mail: owf@nstar.net
Scope: Statewide
Description: A representative statewide organization, affiliated with the National Wildlife Federation, dedicated to the protection and enhancement of wildlife and its habitat through public education and government interaction.
Contact(s):
President: PAUL PURSER JR.
Executive Officer: MARGARET RUFF
Representative: J. MICHAEL ENTZ
Editor: LANCE MEEK
Alternate Representative: ROYCE MEEK
Publication(s): *Outdoor News*

OKLAHOMA WOODLAND OWNERS ASSOCIATION
2657 S. Trenton, Tulsa, OK 74114-2727
Phone: 918-569-4287
Membership: 754
Scope: Statewide
Description: A statewide organization affiliated with the National Woodland Owners Association to advance forest management skills of Oklahoma woodland owners. Other objectives are to promote education and networking, provide timber marketing, and to monitor and act upon legislation.
Contact(s):
President and Editor: PATT NELSON
1st Vice-President: MILES SCHULZE
Secretary: JOHN AHERN
Treasurer: AL REITER
Publication(s): *Oklahoma Woodlands*
Keyword(s): Forests and Forestry

OLYMPIC PARK ASSOCIATES
13245 40th Ave., NE, Seattle, WA 98125-4617
Phone: 206-364-3933; Web Site: www.halcyon.com/rdpayne/opa.html
Founded: 1948; Membership: 400
Scope: Local
Description: Dedicated to preservation of the integrity and wilderness of Olympic National Park and surrounding areas, as well as supporting wild land and wildlife habitat protection elsewhere in the nation. Currently working on restoration of the Elwha River ecosystem, elimination of exotic species from Olympic National Park and restoration and protection of salmon spawning areas.
Contact(s):
President: POLLY DYER; Phone: 206-364-3933
Vice President: TIM McNULTY; Phone: 360-681-2480
Secretary: PHILIP ZALESKY; Phone: 425-337-2479
Treasurer: JOHN W. ANDERSON; Phone: 206-523-5043
Editor: SALLY W. SOEST; Phone: 206-860-2865
Publication(s): *Voice of the Wild Olympics*
Keyword(s): National Parks, Wilderness, Native Plants, Salmon Recovery

OLYMPIC PARK INSTITUTE
111 Barnes Point Rd., Port Angeles, WA 98363
Phone: 360-928-3720; Fax: 360-928-3046; E-mail: opi@yni.org; Web Site: www.yni.org/opi
Founded: 1987
Scope: National
Description: Mission is to inspire personal connection to the natural world and responsible actions to sustain it. OPI provides residential field science programs in Olympic National Park for adults, families and K-12 classrooms. Elderhostel and field seminar programs are also available. Programs introduce themes of ecology, sustainability and stewardship.
Contact(s):
Chairman: TERRY MIX, Seafirst Bank, P.O. Box 3977, Seattle, WA 98124; Phone: 206-358-7651
Executive Director: MAITLAND PEET, 111 Barnes Point Rd., Port Angeles, WA 98363; Phone: 360-938-3720
Keyword(s): Ancient Forests, Biodiversity, Biology, Birds, Coasts, Conservation of Protected Areas, Cultural Preservation, Ecology, Endangered and Threatened Species, Energy, Environment, Environmental Protection, Fisheries, National Parks, Environmental Education Curriculum

ONTARIO FEDERATION OF ANGLERS AND HUNTERS, INC., THE
4601 Guthrie Dr., Box 2800, Peterborough, Ontario K9J 8L5 Canada
Phone: 705-748-6324; Fax: 705-748-9577; E-mail: ofah@kawartha.com
Founded: 1928; Membership: 81,000
Scope: Statewide
Description: Purpose is to conserve Ontario's natural resources and promote ethical angling and hunting practices.
Contact(s):
President: RUSSELL PIPER
Treasurer: FRANK WICK
Executive Vice President: RICK MORGAN
Editor: MARK HOLMES
Publication(s): *Call of the Loon; Hunter Education News; Canadian Fishing and Hunting Trade News; Angler and Hunter Hotline*

ONTARIO FORESTRY ASSOCIATION
307--200 Consumers Rd., Toronto, Ontario M2J 4R4 Canada

Phone: 416-493-4565; Fax: 416-493-4608; E-mail: forestry@oforest.on.ca; Web Site: www.oforest.on.ca
Founded: 1949; Membership: 1,500+
Scope: Statewide
Description: Ontario Forestry Association works to raise awareness and understanding of all aspects of Ontario's forests and to develop commitment to stewardship of forest ecosystems. Programs include: Envirothon, Community Woodland Steward Initiative, Consultant Registry, Land use and forest management, forestry publicity and historical data.
Contact(s):
President: C. WALKER-GAYLE
1st Vice President: ANNE KOVEN
2nd Vice President: ALEX RIGSBY
Editor: J. D. COATS
Executive Vice President: ERIK TURK RPF
Publication(s): *Ontario Forest Products Marketing Bulletin; OFA newsletter*
Keyword(s): Forest Management, Forests and Forestry, Forestry

OPENLANDS PROJECT
25 E. Washington St., Suite 1650, Chicago, IL 60604
Phone: 312-427-4256; Fax: 312-427-6251; E-mail: openlands@aol.com; Web Site: www.openlands.org
Scope: Local
Description: A private, nonprofit organization, Openlands Project was founded in 1963 to protect, enhance and expand land and water--to provide a healthy environment and a more livable place for all people of the region. Openlands preserves open space through land acquisition, greenways, watershed planning and restoration, urban greening initiates, advocacy and technical assistance.
Contact(s):
President: TONY DEAN
Secretary: JANIS NOTZ
Treasurer: J. TIMOTHY RITCHIE
Executive Director: GERALD W. ADELMANN
Greenways Director: DERS ANDERSON
Urban Greening Director: GLENDA DANIEL
Publication(s): *Openlander; Annual Report; Under Pressure: Land Consumption in the Chicago Region*
Keyword(s): Environmental Preservation, Land Purchase, Land Use Planning, Urban Environment, Watersheds

OREGON ASSOCIATION OF CONSERVATION DISTRICTS
Attn: President, 2524 Mitchell Butte Rd., Nyssa, OR 97913
Scope: Statewide
Contact(s):
President and Board Member: MIKE BARLOW, 2524 Mitchell Butte Rd., Nyssa, OR 97913; Phone: 541-372-2886; Fax: 541-889-4304
1st Vice-President, Alternate Board Member: DON LUCAS, HC 60 Box 4000, Lakeview, OR 97630; Phone: 541-947-2482; Fax: 541-947-5854; E-mail: donald_lucas@yahoo.comdonald_lucas@yahoo.com
2nd Vice President: JOHN MCDONALD, 30730 SW Simpson Rd, Cornelius, OR 97113; Phone: 503-640-2841; Fax: 503-648-9606
Executive Director: KEVIN CAMPBELL, 1200 Court St., NE, Suite 302, Salem, OR 97301; Phone: 503-566-3475; Fax: 503-373-2353
Secretary/Treasurer: STAN CHRISTENSEN, 16350 Delashmutt Ln., McMinnville, OR 97128; Phone: 503-472-6307
Keyword(s): Conservation Districts

OREGON B.A.S.S. CHAPTER FEDERATION
Attn: President, 8399 SW Wilson St., Wilsonville, OR 97070
Scope: Statewide
Description: An organization of Bassmaster chapters, affiliated with Bass Anglers Sportsman Society, organized to fight pollution, assist state and national conservation agencies in their efforts, and teach the young people of our country good conservation practices. Dedicated to the realistic conservation of our water resources.
Contact(s):
President: GARY YEXLEY; Phone: 503-682-6810
Conservation Director: CHUCK LANG, 4775 Gardner Rd., SE, Salem, OR 97302; Phone: 503-588-1920
Publication(s): *EarthWatch Oregon*
Keyword(s): Air Quality and Pollution, Land Use Planning, Transportation, Water Quality, Water Resources

OREGON ENVIRONMENTAL COUNCIL
520 SW 6th, #940, Portland, OR 97204-1535
Phone: 503-222-1963; Fax: 506-222-1405; E-mail: oec@orcouncil.org
Founded: 1968; Membership: 40 organizations, 2,000 individuals
Scope: Statewide
Description: Oregon Environmental Council is a nonprofit organization whose mission is to restore and protect Oregon's clean water and air now and for future generations. OEC brings Oregonians together to create and promote socially just and economically sound environmental policies.
Contact(s):
President: ANN WHEELER-BARTOL
Vice President: ED MCNAMARA
Executive Director: JEFF ALLEN
Secretary and Treasurer: RANDY POZDENA
Publication(s): *EarthWatch Oregon*
Keyword(s): Air Quality and Pollution, Environmental Justice, Pesticides, Pollution Prevention, Rivers, Transportation, Water Pollution, Water Quality

OREGON NATURAL RESOURCES COUNCIL
5828 N. Greeley Avenue, Portland, OR 97217
Phone: 503-283-6343; Fax: 503-283-0756
Founded: 1972; Membership: 3,500 individuals
Scope: Statewide
Description: A nonprofit, state-wide organization to aggressively protect and restore Oregon's wildlands, wildlife, and waters as an enduring legacy, and dedicated to permanently protect public forest lands and protect and restore critical habitat for native species.
Contact(s):
President: JANE BECKWITH
President: JIM MIDDAUGH
Executive Director: REGNA MERRITT; E-mail: rm@onrc.org
Advocacy Director: TIM LILLEBO, 16 NW Kansas, Bend, OR 97701; Phone: 541-382-2616; Fax: 503-385-3370; E-mail: tl@onrc.org
Conservation Director: KEN RAIT; E-mail: kr@onrc.org
Director of Finance, Administration and Development: SUSAN KEROSKY; E-mail: sk@onrc.org
Grassroots Coordinator: ERIN MADDEN; E-mail: em@onrc.org
Southern Oregon Field Rep.: WENDELL WOOD, 943 Lakeshore Drive, Klamath Falls, OR 97601; Phone: 541-885-4886; Fax: 541-885-4887; E-mail: ww@onrc.org
Western Oregon Field Rep.: DOUG HEIKEN, P.O. Box 11648, Eugene, OR 97440; Phone: 541-344-0675; Fax: 541-343-0996; E-mail: onrcdoug@efn.org
Publication(s): *Wild Oregon*
Keyword(s): Ancient Forests, Conservation of Protected Areas, Environmental Preservation, Environmental Protection, Natural Areas, Public Lands, Watersheds, Wilderness, Wildlands

OREGON SMALL WOODLANDS ASSOCIATION
P.O. Box 3079, Salem, OR 97302-0079
Phone: 503-588-1813
Founded: 1967; Membership: 3,500
Scope: Statewide
Description: A statewide organization affiliated with the National Woodland Owners Association, dedicated to the protection, management, use and enhancement of Oregon's forest resources.
Contact(s):
President: JOHN ROUNDS; Phone: 541-447-1342
Executive Director: DENNY MILES
1st Vice-President: BILL ARSENAULT; Phone: 541-584-2272
2nd Vice-President: GARY SPRINGER; Phone: 541-757-8665

2nd Vice-President: SARA LEIMAN; Phone: 541-847-5590
2nd Vice-President: LYNN BREESE; Phone: 541-447-6762
2nd Vice-President: JOHN POPPINO; Phone: 503-653-1678
Editor: LORI D. RASOR; Phone: 503-228-3624
Publication(s): *Northwest Woodlands, Update Newsletter*
Keyword(s): Environmental and Conservation Education, Forests and Forestry, Renewable Resources

OREGON SOCIETY OF AMERICAN FORESTERS
4033 SW Canyon Rd., Portland, OR 97221
Phone: 503-224-8046; Fax: 503-226-2515
Founded: 1900; Membership: 1,450
Scope: Statewide
Description: The mission of the society is to advance the science, education, technology, and practice of forestry; enhance its members' competency and professionalism; and use the knowledge and skills of the profession to benefit society.
Contact(s):
Chair: JULIE STANGELL, 41909 Deerhorn Rd., Springfield, OR 97478
Chair-Elect ('99): BLAIR MOODY, 564 Burgandy Circle, Medford, OR 97504
Manager and Editor: LORI RASOR, 4033 SW Canyon Rd., Portland, OR 97221; Phone: 503-224-8046

OREGON TROUT, INC.
117 SW Nuito Parkway, Portland, OR 97204-3512
Phone: 503-222-9091; Fax: 503-222-9187; E-mail: info@ortrout.org; Web Site: www.ortrout.org
Scope: Statewide
Description: An Oregon-based organization focused on the protection and restoration of native fish and their ecosystems.
Contact(s):
Executive Director: GEOFF PAMPUSH
Conservation Director: JIM MYRON
Publication(s): *Riverkeeper*
Keyword(s): Habitat Conservation, Wildlife and Wildlife Habitat, Native Fish

OREGON WILDLIFE HERITAGE FOUNDATION
P.O. Box 30406, Portland, OR 97294-3406
Phone: 503-255-6059; Fax: 503-255-6467
Founded: 1981
Scope: Statewide
Description: The Oregon Wildlife Heritage Foundation is a nonprofit, tax-exempt foundation incorporated under the laws of the state of Oregon. It has a 501(c(3 determination under the I.R.S. code. It receives grants and contributions to be used to fund selected projects beneficial to the fish and wildlife resources of Oregon and the people who enjoy them.
Contact(s):
President: KIM MacCOLL JR.
Vice President: MARCIA HARTMAN
Secretary: CHARLES LILLEY
Treasurer: NELSON RUTHERFORD
Executive Director: ROD BROBRCK
Director Emeiritus and Editor: ALLAN L. KELLY
Keyword(s): Wildlife and Wildlife Habitat

ORGANIZATION FOR BAT CONSERVATION
1553 Haslett Rd., Haslett, MI 48840
Phone: 517-339-5200; Fax: 517-339-5618; E-mail: obcbats@aol.com; Web Site: www.batconservation.org
Founded: 1990; Membership: 3,250
Scope: International
Description: One of the only international non-profit organizations dedicated to bat conservation. This mission is fulfilled through education and habitat preservation.
Contact(s):
Executive Director: KIM WILLIAMS; Phone: 517-339-5200, ext. 9
Director: ROB MIES
Director of Operations: DENISE TOMLINSON; Phone: 517-339-5481
Publication(s): *Understanding Bats; Bats: The True Story (video); Simple Guide to Bat House Designs*
Keyword(s): Conservation, Endangered and Threatened Species, Habitat Conservation, International Conservation, Interpretation, Rehabilitation, Zoological Parks, Bats

ORGANIZATION OF WILDLIFE PLANNERS
1900 Kanawha Blvd. E., Charleston, WV 25305
Phone: 304-558-2771
Founded: 1978
Scope: National
Description: A nonprofit, tax-exempt organization comprised of professional state and federal fish and wildlife resource planners, natural resources educators, professional conservationists, and associated interests dedicated to improving, through education and training, the quality of state-level resources management and planning. The focus of the organization is on developing the necessary tools and skills to conduct effective planned management systems.
Contact(s):
President: DAN ZEKOR, Missouri Department of Conservation, P.O. Box 180, Jefferson City, MO 65102
Treasurer: ARTHUR M. JOHNSEN, New York Department of Environmental Conservation, Rt. 10, Stamford, NY 12167
1st Past President: TOMMY SHROPSHIRE, Mississippi Department of Wildlife, Fisheries, and Parks, P.O. Box 451, Jackson, MS 39205
2nd Past President: THOMAS WASSON, Ohio Division of Wildlife, 1840 Belcher Dr., Columbus, OH 43224-1329
Editor: SHERRY CROUCH, Arizona Game & Fish Department, 2221 West Greenway, Phoenix, AZ 85023
President-Elect: LARRY D. CARTEE, South Carolina Department of Natural Resources, P.O. Box 167, Columbia, SC 29202
Publication(s): *Tomorrow's Management, Newsletter*
Keyword(s): Planning Management

ORNITHOLOGICAL COUNCIL
1725 K St., NW, Suite 212, Washington, DC 20006-1401
Phone: 202-530-5810; Fax: 202-628-4311; E-mail: oc@cnie.org; Web Site: www.nmnh.si.edu/BIRDNET
Founded: 1992; Membership: 10 scientific societies/7,000 ornithologists
Scope: National
Description: The Council provides impartial scientific information about birds for sound decisions, policies, or management actions; links the scientific community with public and private decision-makers; informs ornithologists of actions that affect birds or the study of birds; and speaks for scientific ornithology when the study of birds might be affected. Web site contains links to ornithological scientific societies.
Contact(s):
Chair: DR. DAVID E. BLOCKSTEIN
Executive Director: ELLEN PAUL, 3713 Chevy Chase Lake Drive, Apt 3, Chevy Chase, MD 20815; Phone: 301-986-8568; Fax: 301-986-5205; E-mail: epaul@dclink.com
Publication(s): *Ornithological Newsletter; Use of Wild Birds in Research; Bird Issue Briefs; recent ornithological literature on-line, Grants and Awards in Ornithology*
Keyword(s): Biology, Birds, Environmental and Conservation Education, Raptors, Research Grants, Waterfowl

OUTDOOR CIRCLE, THE
1314 S. King, #306, Honolulu, HI 96814
Phone: 808-593-0300; Fax: 808-593-0525; E-mail: mail@outdoorcircle.org; Web Site: www.outdoorcircle.org
Founded: 1912
Scope: Statewide
Description: A nonprofit organization whose purpose is to work for and develop a more beautiful state, freeing it from disfigurement, conserving and developing its natural beauty, and cooperating in educational and other efforts towards preservation of open spaces, parklands, recycling, and antilitter.

Contact(s):
President: CAROL HENDRICKS
Treasurer: MARY FLEMING
1st Vice President: PAULA RESS
Chief Executive Officer: MARY STEINER
Publication(s): *Keep Hawaii Green; Pua Nani: Hawaii is a Garden; Majesty: Exceptional Trees of Hawaii; Majesty II; Exceptional Trees of Hawaii, The; Trees and Flowers of the Hawaiian Islands; Our Familiar Island Trees*
Keyword(s): Beautification, Land Preservation, Natural Areas, Open Space, Public Lands, Trees, Urban Forestry

OUTDOOR RECREATION COUNCIL OF BRITISH COLUMBIA
334 - 1367 W. Broadway, Vancouver, British Columbia V6H 4A9 Canada
Phone: 604-737-3058; E-mail: orcbc@istar.ca; Web Site: home.istar.ca/~orcbc/
Founded: *1976*
Scope: *Statewide*
Description: The ORC of BC is a nonprofit society formed to serve as a mechanism independent from government, through which the interests and activities of groups organized on a provincial basis concerned with outdoor recreation, education, and conservation can be coordinated and represented to government, industry, and the public.
Contact(s):
Chair: DOUG LEAVERS
Executive Director: NORMA WILSON
Director: DON GRIFFITHS
Director: BEVERLY FELSKE
Director: JOHN CAMPBELL
Director: WAYNE BOURQUE
Secretary and Treasurer: GEORGEEN GOTT-JANZEN
Publication(s): *Outdoor Report*
Keyword(s): Conservation of Protected Areas, Land Use Planning, Outdoor Recreation, Research, Rivers, Wilderness

OUTDOOR WRITERS ASSOCIATION OF AMERICA, INC.
27 Ft. Missoula Rd, Ste. 1, Missoula, MT 59804-7200
Phone: 406-728-7434
Founded: *1927; Membership: 2,000*
Scope: *National*
Description: We strive to improve ourselves in the art and media of our craft and to increase our knowledge and understanding in supporting the conservation of our natural resources. To this end we pledge ourselves to maintain the highest ethical standards in the exercise of our craft.
Contact(s):
Chairman of the Board: TOM WHARTON, 1024 Ramona Ave., Salt Lake City, UT 84105; Phone: 801-237-2039
Executive Director: STEVE WAGNER
Vice President: JIM CASADA, 1250 Yorkdale Dr., Rock Hill, SC 29730
1st Vice-President: CLIFF SHELBY, HCR 64, Box 522, Flippin, AR 72634; Phone: 870-453-8337
2nd Vice-President: BILL MONROE, 14292 S. Forsythe Rd., Oregon City, OR 97045; Phone: 888-222-8231
3rd Vice-President: LAURIE LEE DOVEY, 160 White Pines Dr., Alpharetta, GA 30004; Phone: 770-475-3793
Editor: KEVIN RHOADES
Publication(s): *Outdoors Unlimited*
Keyword(s): Communications, Environmental and Conservation Education, Outdoor Recreation, Wildlife and Wildlife Habitat

OZARK SOCIETY, THE
P.O. Box 2914, Little Rock, AR 72203
Founded: *1962; Membership: 1,000*
Scope: *Statewide*
Description: To promote the knowledge and enjoyment of the scenic and scientific resources, particularly free-flowing streams, wilderness areas, and unique natural areas of the Ozark-Ouachita mountain region, and to help protect those resources for present and future generations.

Contact(s):
President: STEWART NOLAND
Publication(s): *Pack and Paddle, The*
Keyword(s): Natural Areas, Wilderness

OZARKS RESOURCE CENTER
P.O. Box 1198, Ava, MO 65608
Phone: 417-683-6245; E-mail: jlorrain@goin.missouri.org
Founded: *1978; Membership: 1,750*
Scope: *National*
Description: The Center provides research, education, technical assistance, and dissemination of information on renewable resources-based technology, sustainable agriculture, environmentally responsible practices, sustainable community economic development, and self-reliance for the family, farm, community, Ozarks, and other bio-regions.
Contact(s):
President: DONNA JONES, RR 1 Box 68A-1, Dora, MO 65637; Phone: 417-261-2518
Vice President: CORLISS SCHAFFER, HCR 64 Box 221, West Plains, MO 65775; Phone: 417-257-0670
Secretary: KATHI TRANTHAM, 7969 County Rd. 3010, West Plains, MO 65775; Phone: 417-256-6518
Treasurer: DENISE VAUGHN, Rt. 3 Box 200, Mtn. View, MO 65548; Phone: 417-256-6518
Executive Director: JANICE LORRAIN, Rt. 1 Box 393, Ava, MO 65608; Phone: 417-683-5049
Publication(s): *Broadcaster, The (newsletter); Talking Oak Leaves (newsletter)*
Keyword(s): Cultural Preservation, Environmental and Conservation Education, Environmental Preservation, Rural Development, Sustainable Development

OZONE ACTION
1700 Connecticut Ave., NW, 3rd Fl., Washington, DC 20009
Phone: 202-265-6738; Fax: 202-986-6041; E-mail: ozone_action@ozone.org; Web site: www.ozone.org
Founded: *1992*
Scope: *National*
Description: Ozone Action educates the public about threats from ozone depletion and human-induced climate change. Ozone Action investigates and publicizes attempts to weaken our global environmental protections and exposes attempts by industry to distort public debate.
Contact(s):
President: JOHN PASSACANTANDO
Board Chair: KEVIN SWEENEY
Publication(s): *Ozone Action News; Ties That Blind; Black Market CFC Reports; Climate Change Current Effects Summaries*
Keyword(s): Greenhouse Effect/Global Warming, Ozone Depletion

P

PACIFIC BASIN ASSOCIATION OF SOIL AND WATER CONSERVATION DISTRICTS
Attn: President, P.O. Box 12596, Tamuning, Guam 96931
Scope: *Statewide*
Contact(s):
President: FELIX QUAN; Phone: 671-632-7114; Fax: 671-632-7114
Secretary-Treasurer: ESTANISLAO HOCOG, P.O. Box 12, Tinian MP, GU 96952; Phone: 670-433-0690; Fax: 670-433-3152
Vice President: PATRICK CALVO, P.O. Box 2795, Saipan, MP 96950; Phone: 670-234-6120; Fax: 670-235-6122
Keyword(s): Conservation Districts

PACIFIC FISHERY MANAGEMENT COUNCIL
2130 SW 5th Ave., Suite 224, Portland, OR 97201
Phone: 503-326-6352; Fax: 503-326-6831; Web Site: www.pcouncil.org
Scope: *National*
Description: Nonprofit organization established by the Magnuson-Stevens Fishery Conservation and Management Act of 1976.

Develops management plans for fisheries off the coasts of Washington, Oregon, and California. Fourteen voting and five nonvoting members, of which nine are appointed by the Secretary of Commerce. Members include state and federal fishery agency managers, knowledgeable citizens and a tribal representative.
Contact(s):
Executive Director: LAWRENCE D. SIX
Administrative Officer: JOHN S. RHOTON
Economic Analysis Coordinator: JAMES L. SEGER
Fishery Management Coordinator, Marine: JAMES W. GLOCK
Fishery Management Coordinator, Salmon: JOHN COON
Keyword(s): Aquatic Habitats, Fisheries, Renewable Resources, Sport Fishing

PACIFIC INSTITUTE FOR STUDIES IN DEVELOPMENT, ENVIRONMENT, AND SECURITY
654 13th St., Oakland, CA 94612
Phone: 510-251-1600; Fax: 510-251-2203; E-mail: pistaff@pacinst.org; Web Site: www.pacinst.org
Founded: 1987
Scope: International
Description: The institute is a policy research organization that focuses on the interface of security, development and environmental protection issues. Areas of focus include climate change and water.
Contact(s):
Executive Director: PETER GLEICK; E-mail: pgleick@pipeline.com
Director of Communications: WILLIAM C. BURNS; E-mail: wburns@pacinst.org
Publication(s): *Pacific Institute Report; Global Change; Occasional papers and reports on an ongoing basis.*
Keyword(s): Asia Water Environment, Dams, Developing Countries, Development, Drinking Water Protection, Environmental and Conservation Education, Greenhouse Effect/Global Warming, Ground Water Protection, International Conservation, Internships, Local Resource Conservation, Ozone Depletion, Sustainable Development, Sustainable Ecosystems, Water Conservation

PACIFIC NORTHWEST TRAIL ASSOCIATION
13595 Avon Allen Rd., Mount Vernon, WA 98273
Phone: 306-424-0407
Founded: 1977; Membership: 300
Scope: National
Description: The PNTA was formed to promote the development of a continuous foot and horse trail from the Continental Divide at Glacier National Park to the Pacific Ocean at Olympic National Park. The PNTA encourages land use and conservation education through exposure to the historic and natural diversity of the Pacific Northwest.
Contact(s):
Chair: Duane Melcher; Phone: 306-424-0407
Publication(s): *Nor'wester; Pacific Northwest Trail, The, a guidebook to the 1,100 mile PNT (available on diskette); Blanchard Hill and Chuckanut Mountain Map*
Keyword(s): Environmental and Conservation Education, Internships, Outdoor Recreation, Pedestrian Environment, Public Lands

PACIFIC RIVERS COUNCIL
P.O. Box 10798, Eugene, OR 97440
Phone: 541-345-0119; Fax: 541-345-0710
Founded: 1987; Membership: 1,200
Scope: National
Description: The purpose of the Pacific Rivers Council is to protect and restore rivers, their watersheds and native aquatic species.
Contact(s):
Executive Director: TRYG SLETTELAND
Conservation Director: DAVID BAYLES
Publication(s): *Entering the Watershed; Freeflow; various briefing books and reports*
Keyword(s): Biodiversity, Fisheries, Public Lands, Rivers, Watersheds, Native Fish

PACIFIC SEABIRD GROUP
Box 179, 4505 University Way, NE, Seattle, WA 98105
Founded: 1972; Membership: 415
Scope: International
Description: An international organization to promote the knowledge, study and conservation of Pacific seabirds.
Contact(s):
Chair: ALAN BURGER, Dept. of Biology, Univ. of Victoria, Victoria, CANADA V8W 3N5; Phone: 250-721-7127; Fax: 250-721-7120
Secretary: KATHY KULETZ, USFWS, 1011 East Tudor Rd., Anchorage, AK 99503; Phone: 907-786-3453; Fax: 907-786-3641
Treasurer: JAN HODDER, Oregon Institute of Marine Bio., Univ. of Oregon, Charleston, OR 97420; Phone: 541-888-2581/ext. 215; Fax: 541-888-3240
Chair-Elect: ED MURPHY, Institute of Arctic Biology, Univ. of Alaska Fairbanks, Fairbanks, AK 99712-0180; Phone: 907-474-7154; Fax: 907-474-6967
Editor: STEVEN M. SPEICH, 4720 N. Oeste Pl., Tucson, AZ 85749; Phone: 520-760-2110; Fax: 520-760-0228
Publication(s): *Pacific Seabird Group Bulletin*
Keyword(s): Birds, Endangered and Threatened Species, Environmental and Conservation Education, Wildlife and Wildlife Habitat, Zoology

PACIFIC WHALE FOUNDATION
101 N. Kihei Rd., Kihei, HI 96753
Phone: 808-879-8860; Fax: 808-879-2615
Founded: 1980
Scope: National
Description: A nonprofit tax-exempt 501(c)(3) organization dedicated to saving whales, dolphins and their ocean habitats through marine research, public education and marine conservation. Pacific Whale Foundation actively studies whales, dolphins and coral reef communities throughout the Pacific to ensure their survival and recovery. The award-winning Ocean Outreach Program educates people about marine conservation through Research Internships, school programs, an Adopt-a-Whale program, and an Adopt-a-Dolphin program.
Contact(s):
President: GREGORY D. KAUFMAN
Vice President: DR. PAUL H. FORESTELL
Editor: ANNE RILLERO
Secretary and Treasurer: DIXIE BONGOLAN
Publication(s): *Fin and Fluke; Soundings; Whalewatch News; Maui Outdoor Adventure*
Keyword(s): Aquatic Habitats, Dolphins, Endangered and Threatened Species, Environmental and Conservation Education, Internships, Marine Mammals, Whales

PANOS INSTITUTE, THE
1701 K St., NW, 11 Fl., Washington, DC 20036
Phone: 202-223-7940; Fax: 202-223-7947
Founded: 1986
Scope: International
Description: The Panos Institute consists of three autonomous nonprofit, non-governmental organizations located in London, Paris and Washington, DC, working to raise public understanding of sustainable development issues. The Washington, DC institute focuses its work on Latin America, the Caribbean and the United States.
Contact(s):
Secretary: DIANE McGLYNN
Treasurer: JACOB SCHERR
Board of Directors Chair: WILLIAM D. CARMICHAEL
Vice President and Executive Director: MELANIE BETH OLIVIERO
Publication(s): *We Speak For Ourselves; SIDAmerica; Eco-Reports; From Information to Education*
Keyword(s): Communications, Environmental and Conservation Education, Internships, Population Growth, Sustainable Development

PARTNERS IN PARKS
4916 Butterworth Pl. NW, Washington, DC 20016

Phone: 202-364-7244; Fax: 202-364-7246; E-mail: partpark@cqi.com
Founded: 1988
Scope: National
Description: A nonprofit organization that encourages, promotes, and establishes professional level partnerships between national park and other public land managers and those who would contribute their time and skills to studying, protecting, and interpreting natural and cultural features.
Contact(s):
President: SARAH G. BISHOP
Secretary and Treasurer: DAVID A. KIKEL
Keyword(s): Conservation of Protected Areas, Cultural Preservation, Natural Areas, Nature Preservation, Public Lands, Research

PAWS/OLYMPIC WILDLIFE RESCUE
1393 Mox-Chehaus Rd., McCleary, WA 98557
Phone: 360-495-3337
Scope: Statewide
Description: Olympic Wildlife Rescue is a nonprofit, tax-exempt organization dedicated to the care of injured, orphaned, and ill northwest wildlife. We operate a licensed wildlife rehabilitation center in McCleary, Washington (about 20 miles west of Olympia).
Contact(s):
President: GARY BANKERS
Vice President: SHAWN NEWMAN
Secretary: PAT PRINGLE
Treasurer: CAROL CHATWOOD
Director: JEANNE WASSERMAN
Publication(s): *Ptarmigan Ptales*
Keyword(s): Environmental and Conservation Education, Outdoor Recreation, Renewable Resources, Wilderness, Wildlife and Wildlife Habitat, Wildlife Rehabilitation

PENNSYLVANIA ASSOCIATION OF CONSERVATION DISTRICT DIRECTORS, INC.
Attn: President, 534 Kennedy Rd., Airville, PA 17032
Scope: Statewide
Contact(s):
President, Alternate Board Member: PATRICIA SUECK, 534 Kennedy Rd., Airville, PA 17032; Phone: 717-862-3486; Fax: 717-862-3486
Secretary: RONALD ROHALL, P.O. Box 27, Rector, PA 15677; Phone: 412-238-4973
Treasurer: CLOYD E. BRENNEMAN, 103 Courthouse, Mercer, PA 16137; Phone: 412-662-3800
Executive Director: SUSAN FOX, 225 Pine St., Harrisburg, PA 17101; Phone: 717-236-1006; Fax: 717-236-6410
1st Vice President: FRANKLIN LONG JR, Rd. 1 Box 441, Tyrone, PA 16886; Phone: 814-648-4838
2nd Vice President: MURRAY LAITE, 512 Electric Ave, Lewistown, PA 17044; Phone: 717-248-6733
Board Member: ROBERT WAGNER, 373 Scott Rd., Quarryville, PA 17566; Phone: 717-529-2831; Fax: 717-529-2155

PENNSYLVANIA AUDUBON SOCIETY
100 Wildwood Way, Harrisburg, PA 17110
Phone: 717-763-4985; Fax: 717-763-4981; E-mail: painquiries@audubon.org
Founded: 1987; Membership: 27,000
Scope: Statewide
Description: The Pennsylvania Audubon Society promotes and encourages the conservation and protection of our natural resources through public education, communication with public officials, and sponsorship of programs to help children and adults become aware of their relationship to the environment.
Contact(s):
President: CARMEN SANTASANIA, 1410 Charles St., State College, PA 16801; Phone: 814-359-5760
Secretary: MARIAN CROSSMAN, 6 Tussey Circle, Pittsburgh, PA 15237; Phone: 412-366-3339
Treasurer: LEIGH ALTADONNA, 161 Greenwood Ave., Wyncote, PA 15834; Phone: 215-886-0656
Executive Director: CINDY ADAMS DUNN
Publication(s): *Quarterly Newsletter; Population&Habitat Newsletter; Pennsylvania Sonbirds - a K-12 Teacher's Guide; Important Bird Areas of Pennsylvania Report; Audubon Protecting Animals Through Habitat; Project Mayfly; Wetlands Action Guide*
Keyword(s): Birds, Environmental and Conservation Education, Natural History, Outdoor Recreation, Wetlands, Wildlife and Wildlife Habitat

PENNSYLVANIA B.A.S.S. CHAPTER FEDERATION, INC.
Attn: President, 769 N. Cottage Rd., Mercer, PA 16137
Scope: Statewide
Description: An organization of Bassmaster chapters, affiliated with the Bass Anglers Sportsman Society, organized to fight pollution, assist state and national conservation agencies in their efforts, and teach the young people of our country good conservation practices. Dedicated to the realistic conservation of our water resources.
Contact(s):
President: MIKE DUNKERLEY; Phone: 412-475-2422
Conservation Director: BILL REICHERT, 51 N. 4th St., Cressona, PA 17929; Phone: 717-385-2122

PENNSYLVANIA CITIZENS ADVISORY COUNCIL TO DEPARTMENT OF ENVIRONMENTAL PROTECTION
13th Fl., RCSOB P.O. Box 8459, Harrisburg, PA 17105-8459
Phone: 717-787-4527
Scope: Statewide
Description: Created by Act 275 of the PA General Assembly, 1971.
Contact(s):
Executive Director: SUSAN M. WILSON
Administrative Assistant: STEPHANIE MIOFF
Chairperson: JOLENE CHINCHILLI
Vice Chairperson: DAVID STRONG
Keyword(s): Air Resources, Public Participation, Waste Resources, Water Resources

PENNSYLVANIA ENVIRONMENTAL COUNCIL, INC. (PEC)
117 S. 17th St., 23rd Fl., Philadelphia, PA 19103-5022
Phone: 215-563-0250/1-800-322-9214 in PA
Founded: 1969; Membership: 2,500
Scope: Statewide
Description: Private nonprofit statewide membership organization devoted to the protection and improvement of Pennsylvania's environment through education, advocacy and consensus building. PEC brings together nonprofits, government agencies, businesses and citizens to develop environmental policy, take action on environmental issues and work for effective environmental legislation, regulation and enforcement.
Contact(s):
President and CEO: ANDREW S. MCELWAINE
Senior Vice President and COO: ANDREW W. JOHNSON
Regional Director of Southeastern Office: PATRICK STARR
Regional Director of Western PA Office: DAVITT WOODWELL
Regional Director of Community Planning, Western PA Office: ANNA BRIENICH
Regional Director of Northeastern PA Office: ELLEN ALAIMO
Vice President and Director of French Creek Project: BRIAN HILL
Publication(s): *Environmental Forum Newsletter; PA Legislative Updates; Guiding Growth; Building Better Communities and Preserving our Countryside; Environmental Advisory Council Handbook; Transit-Oriented Development Handbook; Urban Vacant Land Handbook; Environmental Advisory Council Handbook; Creating Connections: The Pennsylvania Greenways and Trails How-To Manual; A Watershed Primer for Pennsylvania: A Collection of Essays on Watershed Issues*
Keyword(s): Environmental Legislation, Greenways, Sustainable Development, Watersheds

NON-GOVERNMENTAL ORGANIZATIONS - P

PENNSYLVANIA FEDERATION OF SPORTSMEN'S CLUBS
2426 N. Second St., Harrisburg, PA 17110
Phone: 717-232-3480; Fax: 717-231-3524; E-mail: pawild@paonline.com; Web Site: www.pfsc.org
Scope: Statewide
Description: A representative statewide organization, affiliated with the National Wildlife Federation, dedicated to the protection and enhancement of wildlife and its habitat through public education and government interaction.
Contact(s):
President: RAY MARTIN
Representative: MARK HENRY
Editor: DAVE WOLF
Alternate Representative: ED ZYGMUT

PENNSYLVANIA FORESTRY ASSOCIATION, THE
56 E. Main St., Mechanicsburg, PA 17055
Phone: 717-766-5371
Founded: 1886; Membership: 1,700
Scope: Statewide
Description: An independent nonprofit conservation organization, affiliated with the National Woodland Owners Association dedicated to environmental improvement and wise use of natural resources in Pennsylvania. Membership includes a cross section of all groups and individuals interested in true conservation.
Contact(s):
President: SCOTT KURTZMAN; Phone: 717-225-4711
Vice-President: GEORGE FREEMAN
Secretary: WILLIAM S. CORLETT; Phone: 717-737-7118
Treasurer: JOHN BEVERLY; Phone: 717-787-2039
Editor: JAN ZINN; Phone: 717-632-1648
Publication(s): *Pennsylvania Recreation and Parks*
Keyword(s): Environmental and Conservation Education, Forests and Forestry, Outdoor Recreation, Public Lands, Youth Organizations

PENNSYLVANIA RECREATION AND PARK SOCIETY, INC.
1315 W. College Ave., Suite 200, State College, PA 16801-2776
Phone: 814-234-4272; Fax: 814-234-5276
Founded: 1935; Membership: 1,700
Scope: Statewide
Description: To promote quality recreation and park opportunities for all the citizens of the Commonwealth of Pennsylvania by actively involving professionals and citizens in recreation, park, and conservation programs, by fostering and maintaining high standards of professional qualifications and ethics, and by providing quality educational opportunities.
Contact(s):
President: CARMEN S. WILLIAMS, Director, West Shore Recreation & Leisure Services, P.O. Box 442, New Cumberland, PA 17070-0442; Phone: 717-938-8525
Secretary: ROBERT J. GROW, Park Maintenance Superintendent, Bucks County Parks & Recreation, 901 E. Bridgetown Pike, Langhorne, PA 19047-1564; Phone: 215-757-0571
Treasurer: WILLIAM E. ROSEVEAR, Park Manager, PA Bureau of State Parks, 1100 Pine Grove Rd., Gardners, PA 17324-7174; Phone: 717-486-7174; Fax: 717-486-4961
Executive Director: ROBERT D. GRIFFITH
Editor: VANYLA S. TIERNEY, Recreation Planner, DCNR-Bureau of State Parks, P.O. Box 1519, Mechanicsburgh, PA 17055-9019; Phone: 717-783-2654
President-Elect: R. BRUCE MCFATE, Park Manager, Caledonia State Park, 40 Rocky Mtn. Rd., Fayetteville, PA 17222-9610; Phone: 717-352-2161
Publication(s): *Pennsylvania Recreation and Parks*
Keyword(s): Environmental and Conservation Education, Flowers, Plants, and Trees, Pesticides, Solid Waste, Water Pollution

PENNSYLVANIA RESOURCES COUNCIL, INC., (formerly PA Roadside Council)
3606 Providence Rd., Newtown Square, PA 19073
Phone: 610-353-1555; Fax: 610-353-6257; Web Site: www.prc.org
Founded: 1939
Scope: Statewide
Description: The Pennsylvania Resources Council (PRC) is recognized nationally for its expertise in recycling, waste reduction and litter control. PRC produces educational materials, as well as seminars and conferences for citizens, municipalities, civic groups and corporations. PRC also sponsors the nation's only environmental shopping hotline (1-800-Go-To-PRC). Open to the public, PRC's environmental living center has exhibits and workshops to show the impact of lifestyle choices on the environment.
Contact(s):
President: JOAN BATORY; Phone: 610-344-6257
Vice President: HOWARD WEIN; Phone: 412-392-2128
Vice President: TIM WILLIAMS; Phone: 717-234-4067
Vice President: RICHARD BAPST; Phone: 215-984-7113
Publication(s): *PEEC Seasons; All About Recycling; Environmental Living Up Date; PRC Newsletter*
Keyword(s): Beautification, Environmental and Conservation Education, Environmental Living, Healthy Home, Litter, Natural History, Nature Study, Outdoor Recreation, Pollution Prevention, Recycling, Waste Management, Wildlife and Wildlife Habitat

PEOPLE FOR PUGET SOUND
Headquarters, 1402 Third Ave., #1200, Seattle, WA 98101
Phone: 206-382-7007; Fax: 206-382-7006; E-mail: people@pugetsound.org; Web Site: www.pugetsound.org
Founded: 1991; Membership: 10,000
Scope: National
Description: People for Puget Sound works to protect and restore the imperiled marine and estuarine ecosystems of Puget Sound and the Northwest Straits.
Contact(s):
President of the Board of Directors: KATE JANEWAY
Executive Director: KATHY FLETCHER
Habitat Director: JACQUES WHITE
Field Director: PAM JOHNSON
Communications Director: DOUG SCOTT
Education Coordinator: STEPHANIE RAYMOND
Publication(s): *Sound & Straits* (quarterly newsletter); *Orcas in the Balance* (documentary video); *Habifacts* (newsletter); *Kids Sound* (quarterly newsletter for children)
Keyword(s): Environmental and Conservation Education, Estuaries, Marine Conservation, Marine Protected Areas, Water Quality, Volunteering, Salmon Recovery, Oil Spill Response

North Sound Office
300 S. First St., #207, Mt. Vernon, WA 98273
Phone: 306-336-1931; Fax: 360-336-5422; E-mail: northsound@pugetsound.org
Scope: Local Region
Contact(s):
Director: MIKE SATO

South Sound Office
1063 Capitol Way S., #206, Olympia, WA 98507
Phone: 360-754-9177; Fax: 360-786-5054; E-mail: southsound@pugetsound.org
Scope: Local Region
Contact(s):
Director: BRUCE WISHART

PEOPLE'S FORUM 2001, JAPAN
Maruko Bld. 3F, 1-20-6 Higashiueno, Taitou-ku, Tokyo 110-0015 Japan
Phone: 81-3-3834-2436; Fax: 81-3-3834-2406; E-mail: pf2001jp@jca.ax.apc.org
Scope: International
Description: People's Forum 2001, Japan is an NGO network of national environmental NGO's, CBO's, and individuals being active to bring about sustainable society. The Forum's task is to serve as a clearing house, as well as to provide a framework of activities for the

members. The Forum's activities include research, education, publication, and policy dialogues with different sectors to alter current economic and political systems to be ecologically and socially sustainable.
Contact(s):
Director: TOMOKO SAKUMA

PEREGRINE FUND, THE
5666 W. Flying Hawk Ln., Boise, ID 83709
Phone: 208-362-3716; Fax: 208-362-2376; E-mail: tpf@peregrinefund.org; Web Site: www.peregrinefund.org
Founded: 1970
Scope: National
Description: The Peregrine Fund works nationally and internationally to conserve biological diversity and enhance environmental health by working with birds through management and conservation of species and their habitat, and through education and scientific investigation. Although best known nationally for species restoration, they have assisted on conservation projects in over 40 countries.
Contact(s):
President and CEO: DR. WILLIAM A. BURNHAM
Vice President: JEFFREY R. CILEK
Vice President: J. PETER JENNY
Chairman of Board: HENRY M. PAULSON, JR
Vice Chairman of the Board: D. JAMES NELSON
Secretary: RONALD C. YANKE
Treasurer: PAXSON H. OFFIELD
Publication(s): *The Peregrine Fund Newsletter; Annual Report; Operation Report; progress reports*
Keyword(s): Birds, Endangered and Threatened Species, International Conservation, Raptors, Wildlife Management

PHEASANTS FOREVER, INC.
1783 Buerkle Circle, St. Paul, MN 55110
Phone: 651-773-2000
Founded: 1982; Membership: 86,000 members and 525 chapters
Scope: National
Description: Pheasants Forever, Inc. is a nonprofit conservation organization formed in response to the continued decline of ring-necked pheasants. The mission of Pheasants Forever is to protect and to enhance pheasant and other upland wildlife populations through habitat improvement, public awareness and education programs, and land management policy refinement.
Contact(s):
Chairman: GEORGE A. WILSON
Chief Executive Officer: JEFFERY S. FINDEN
Secretary: ROBERT P. LARSON
Treasurer: RICHARD O. HANOUSEK
Senior Vice President and Chief Financial Officer: HOWARD K. VINCENT
Director of Development and Public Affairs: JOSEPH J. DUGGAN
Director of Governmental Affairs: DAVID E. NOMSEN, 2101 Ridgewood Dr., Alexandria, MN 56308; Phone: 612-763-6103
Senior Regional Wildlife Biologist: JAMES B. WOOLEY JR., 1205 Ilion Ave., Chariton, IA 50049; Phone: 515-774-2238
Editor: MARK HERWIG
Regional Field Representative: MATTHEW B. O'CONNOR, 2880 Thunder Rd., Hopkinton, IA 52237; Phone: 319-926-2357
Regional Representative: JEFF GASKA, W. 9947 Ghost Hill Rd., Beaver Dam, WI 53916; Phone: 920-927-3579
Regional Representative: THOMAS R. KIRSCHENMANN, 420 Dawn Ave., Danville, IL 61832; Phone: 217-446-2958
Regional Representative: KEITH BRUS, 5995 W. Little Portage Rd., Pt. Clinton, OH 43452; Phone: 419-732-7149
Regional Representative: KENNETH E. SOLOMON, 557 Utah Ave. SE, Huron, SD 57350; Phone: 605-352-5268
Regional Representative: PETER S. BERTHELSEN, 101 Alexander Ave., Elba, NE 68835; Phone: 308-754-5339
Regional Representative: MATTHEW HOLLAND, 679 W. River Dr., New London, MN 56273; Phone: 320-354-4373
Regional Representative: BARTH V. CROUCH, 1625 E. Beloit Ave., Salina, KS 67401; Phone: 913-823-9427
Regional Representative: MIKE PARKER, 117 Wilson St., De Witt, MI 48820; Phone: 517-668-1033
Publication(s): *Pheasants Forever*
Keyword(s): Agriculture, Birds, Environmental and Conservation Education, Hunting, Wildlife and Wildlife Habitat

PHYSICIANS FOR SOCIAL RESPONSIBILITY
1101 14th St. NW 7th Floor, Washington, DC 20005
Phone: 202-898-0150
Founded: 1961; Membership: 15,000
Scope: National
Description: Promotes arms reduction, international cooperation to protect the environment, and education and programs aimed at reducing violence.
Contact(s):
President: DR. PETER WILK
Executive Director: DR. ROBERT K. MUSIL
Publication(s): *Monitor; PSR Reports.*
Keyword(s): Environmental Health, Nuclear/Radiation, Pesticides, Toxic Substances, Gun Violence Prevention, Nuclear Abolition

PIEDMONT ENVIRONMENTAL COUNCIL
P.O. Box 460, Warrenton, VA 20188
Phone: 540-347-2334; Fax: 540-349-9003
Founded: 1972
Scope: Statewide
Description: A nonprofit organization formed to conserve natural resources and the pastoral landscape of a nine-county region of the Northern Virginia Piedmont. Public education and services to public officials and citizens, covering: land use; farmland retention; open space conservation; historic preservation; rural transportation policy; and rural planning legislation. Active statewide and federally on rural conservation issues.
Contact(s):
Chairman: EVE D. FOUT
President: CHRISTOPHER G. MILLER
Vice Chairman: JOHN BIRDSALL
Publication(s): *Potomac Appalachian; various topographical maps and hiking guidebooks*
Keyword(s): Environmental Preservation, Land Purchase, Outdoor Recreation, Pedestrian Environment, Public Lands

PINCHOT INSTITUTE FOR CONSERVATION
1616 P St. NW Suite 100, Washington, DC 20036
Phone: 202-797-6580; Fax: 202-797-6583; E-mail: alsample@pinchot.org
Founded: 1963
Scope: National
Description: The Pinchot Institute for Conservation is an independent nonprofit organization established to advance forest conservation thought, policy, and action. Serves as a bridge between the scientific and policymaking communities, providing timely, objective policy research, facilitation, leadership, training, and environmental education on issues relating to the protection and sustainable management of forests.
Contact(s):
Chair: JACKSON F. ENO
President: V. ALARIC SAMPLE
Secretary: MARY COULOMBE
Treasurer: JOHN FRY
Director of Grey Towers National Historic Landmark: EDGAR B. BRANNON, P.O. Box 188, Milford, PA 18337; Phone: 570-296-9630; Fax: 570-296-9675
Vice Chair: DENNIS LeMASTER
Publication(s): *The Pinchot Letter; Grey Towers Press books; numerous policy reports, discussion papers and lecture series.*
Keyword(s): Forests and Forestry, Planning Management, Public Lands, Research, Sustainable Ecosystems

PITTSBURGH HERPETOLOGICAL SOCIETY, THE
c/o The Pittsburgh Zoo, One Wild Pl., Pittsburgh, PA 15206

NON-GOVERNMENTAL ORGANIZATIONS - P

Phone: 412-361-0835; Fax: 412-361-2718; E-mail: phs@trfn.clpgh.org; Web Site: www.trfn.clpgh.org/phs
Founded: 1993; Membership: 258
Scope: National
Description: The society is dedicated to fostering an appreciation of all reptiles and amphibians through husbandry, conservation, and education.
Contact(s):
Co-founder: DOLLY ELLERBROCK; E-mail: diguana@bellatlantic.net
Publication(s): *Pittsburgh Herpetological Society Newsletter, The*
Keyword(s): Conservation, Conservation of Protected Areas, Conservation Plannning, Outdoor Education, Reptiles and Amphibians, Streams, Water Quality

PLANNED PARENTHOOD FEDERATION OF AMERICA, INC.
810 Seventh Ave., New York, NY 10019
Phone: 212-541-7800; Web Site: www.plannedparenthood.org
Founded: 1916
Scope: National
Description: Planned Parenthood Federation of America (PPFA) is a federation of 132 not-for-profit affiliates operating nearly 900 medically-supervised health centers nationwide. Planned Parenthood centers provide a wide range of services--including family planning counseling, contraception, prenatal care, adoption referrals, abortion services, cancer screening, testing and treatment for HIV/AIDS, and other sexually transmitted infections, and sexuality education--to nearly five million men and women each year. For the Planned Parenthood center nearest you, call 1-800-230-PLAN.
Contact(s):
President: GLORIA FELDT
Secretary: ALFRED POINDEXTER III, MD
Treasurer: BARBARA SINGHAUS
Chairperson: MARY SHALLENBERGER
Chief Operating Officer: JOHN ROMO
Librarian: SUSAN PICHLER, Katherine Dexter McCormick Library, 810 Seventh Ave., New York, NY 10019; Phone: 212-261-4637
Vice Chairperson: ALFREDO VIGIL MD
Keyword(s): Family Planning, Health and Nutrition, Population Growth, Reproductive Rights

PLANNING AND CONSERVATION LEAGUE
926 J St., Suite 612, Sacramento, CA 95814
Phone: 916-444-8726; Fax: 916-448-1789; E-mail: pclmail@pcl.org; Web Site: www.pcl.org
Founded: 1965; Membership: 10,000
Scope: Statewide
Description: A representative statewide organization, affiliated with the National Wildlife Federation, dedicated to the protection and enhancement of wildlife and its habitat through public education and government interaction.
Contact(s):
President: SAGE SWEETWOOD
Executive Director, Editor and Alternative Representative: GERALD MERAL
Representative: DAN FROST
Publication(s): *California Today*

POCONO ENVIRONMENTAL EDUCATION CENTER
R.R. 2 Box 1010, Dingmans Ferry, PA 18328
Phone: 717-828-2319; Fax: 717-828-9695; E-mail: peec@ptd.net; Web Site: www.peec.org
Founded: 1986
Scope: Statewide
Description: The Pocono Environmental Education Center (PEEC) advances environmental awareness, knowledge, and skills through education, in order that those who inhabit and will inherit the planet may better understand the complexities of natural and human-designed environments.
Contact(s):
Assistant Director: THOMAS SHIMALLA
President: JOHN PADALINO; E-mail: jack.peec@oal.com

Director: FLORENCE MAURO
Associate Director: PAUL F. BRANDWEIN

POLLUTION PROBE FOUNDATION
12 Madison Ave., Toronto, Ontario M5R 2S1 Canada
Phone: 416-926-1907; Fax: 416-926-1601; E-mail: pprobe@pollutionprobe.org; Web Site: www.pollutionprobe.org
Founded: 1969; Membership: 10,000
Scope: National
Description: Pollution Probe is a Canadian nonprofit organization that exists to define environmental problems through research; to promote understanding through education; and to press for practical solutions through advocacy.
Contact(s):
Executive Director: KEN OGILVIE; Phone: 416-926-1907 ext231
Chairman of Pollution Probe Foundation: EDWARD BABIN
Publication(s): *Canadian Green Consumer Guide, The; Canadian Junior Green Guide, The; Kitchen Handbook, An Environmental Guide; Profit from Pollution Prevention: A Guide to Waste Reduction and Recycling in Canada*

POPE AND YOUNG CLUB
15 E. 2nd St., P.O. Box 548, Chatfield, MN 55923
Phone: 507-867-4144; Fax: 507-867-4144; E-mail: pyclub@isl.net
Founded: 1961; Membership: 3,500
Scope: National
Description: A North American bow hunting and wildlife conservation organization dedicated to the promotion and protection of our bow hunting heritage and North America's wildlife.
Contact(s):
President: G. FRED ASBELL
Treasurer: DONALD ACE MORGAN
Executive Secretary: GLENN E. HISEY
First Vice President: M. R. JAMES

POPULATION ACTION INTERNATIONAL
1120 19th St., NW, Suite 550, Washington, DC 20036
Phone: 202-659-1833
Founded: 1965
Scope: International
Description: Develops worldwide support for international population and voluntary family planning programs through public education, policy analysis, and liaison with international leaders and organizations.
Contact(s):
President: AMY COEN
Secretary: PHYLLIS T. PIOTROW
Treasurer: SCOTT SPANGLER
Vice President, Communications: SALLY ETHELSTON
Vice President, Development: CAROL WALL
Vice President, Human Resources: PAT SINGLETARY
Vice President, International Advocacy: MERCEDES MAS DE XAXAS
Vice President, Public Policy: TERRI BARTLETT
Vice President, Research: ROBERT ENGELMAN
Publication(s): *Population briefing sheets; country status reports; legislative and policy updates; annual report of activities; studies of population-environment linkages*
Keyword(s): Environment, Health and Nutrition, Population Growth, Renewable Resources, Sustainable Development

POPULATION COMMUNICATIONS INTERNATIONAL
777 United Nations Plaza 7C, New York, NY 10017
Phone: 212-687-3366; Fax: 212-661-4188; E-mail: pci@together.org
Founded: 1985; Membership: 10,000
Scope: International
Description: PCI works through mass media and non-governmental organizations to promote elevation of women's status, use of family planning, and small family norms. PCI's social-content soap operas in developing countries are locally researched and produced and weave social themes into long-term script development for radio and television dramas. In the United States PCI also works with

broadcasters and NGOs. Currently PCI is collaborating with NWF to develop an environmental/human sexuality soap opera for U.S. audiences.
Contact(s):
President: DAVID J. ANDREWS
Publication(s): *Member News; Global Intersections*
Keyword(s): Communications, Population Growth, Environmental Communication

POPULATION INSTITUTE, THE
107 Second St., NE, Washington, DC 20002
Phone: 202-544-3300; Fax: 202-544-0068; E-mail: web@populationinstitute.org
Founded: 1969
Scope: National
Description: To enlist and motivate key leadership groups to participate in the effort to bring population growth into balance with resources by means consistent with human dignity and freedom. Works in communications and with mass membership organizations, educational leaders, and policy leaders.
Contact(s):
President: WERNER FORNOS; Phone: 202-544-3300
Secretary: STEPHEN KEESE
Treasurer: JOYCE W. CRAMER
Chairperson of the Board: BETTYE WARD
Vice Chairperson: SARAH G. EPSTEIN
Publication(s): *POPLINE - World Population News Service; Annual Report; Towards The 21st Century (Monograph Series)*
Keyword(s): Air Quality and Pollution, Developing Countries, Environment, Internships, Population Growth, Water Resources

POPULATION REFERENCE BUREAU, INC.
1875 Connecticut Ave., NW, #520, Washington, DC 20009
Phone: 202-483-1100
Founded: 1929; Membership: 4,000
Scope: National
Description: PRB is a nonprofit educational organization which provides timely and objective information on U.S. and international population trends and their implications.
Contact(s):
President: PETER DONALDSON
Chair of the Board: MONTAGUE YUDELMAN
Director of Communications: ELLEN CARNEVALE
Librarian: ZUALI MALSAWMA
Senior Demographer: CARL HAUB
Publication(s): *Population Bulletin; PRB Reports on America; Population Today; World and U.S. Population Data Sheets, teaching kits on population topics; list available on request.*
Keyword(s): Communications, Environmental and Conservation Education, Geography, Population Growth, Sustainable Development

POPULATION-ENVIRONMENT BALANCE, INC.
2000 P St., NW, Suite 210, Washington, DC 20036-5915
Phone: 202-955-5700; Fax: 202-955-6161; E-mail: uspop@balance.org; Web Site: www.balance.org
Founded: 1973; Membership: 10,000
Scope: National
Description: Population-Environment Balance is a grassroots membership organization dedicated to public education regarding the adverse effects of population growth on the environment. "BALANCE" advocates measures that would encourage population stabilization in the U.S.; encourages a responsible immigration policy for the U.S.; and promotes increased funding for contraceptive research and availability. Activities include public education, advocacy, media campaigns, and publications.
Contact(s):
Executive Director: MARIA SEPULVEDA
Chairman of the Board: DR. VIRGINIA ABERNETHY
Publication(s): *Balance Activist; BALANCE data; Action Alerts*
Keyword(s): Air Quality and Pollution, Environment, Population Growth

POTOMAC APPALACHIAN TRAIL CLUB
118 Park St., SE, Vienna, VA 22180
Phone: 703-242-0693; Fax: 703-242-0968; Web Site: patc.net
Founded: 1927; Membership: 6,700
Scope: regional
Description: Maintains 240 miles of the Appalachian Trail from Rock Fish Gap in Virginia to Pine Grove Furnace State Park in Pennsylvania Also maintains an additional 750 miles of trails. Activities include publication of maps and guidebooks, outdoor recreation leadership, construction and maintenance of shelters and cabins and conservation of trail lands through purchase or easements.
Contact(s):
President: WALTER M. SMITH
Treasurer: RICHARD NEWCOMER
Director of Administration: WILSON RILEY
Editor: BIANCA MENEDEZ
General Secretary: WARREN SHARP
Supervisor of Trails: PETER GATJE
Keyword(s): Environmental and Conservation Education, Outdoor Recreation, Trail

POULSBO MARINE SCIENCE CENTER
18743 Front St., NE, P.O. Box 2079, Poulsbo, WA 98370
Phone: 360-779-5549; Fax: 360-779-8960
Founded: 1968
Scope: Regional
Description: The Marine Science Center works to meet the science education needs of public citizens and of students and teachers nationally, regionally, and locally. Hands-on environmental education is at the heart of its mission and is reflected in direct instruction from its facility on Washington's State's Liberty Bay, part of the Puget Sound.
Contact(s):
SCOTT
Director: MICHELLE BENEDICT
Marine Society of the Pacific Northwest, President: MIKE
Keyword(s): Marine Conservation, Nature Centers, Oceanography

POWDER RIVER BASIN RESOURCE COUNCIL
P.O. Box 1178, Douglas, WY 82633
Phone: 307-358-5002; Fax: 307-358-6771
Founded: 1973; Membership: 600
Scope: Statewide
Description: Nonprofit grassroots organization whose major purpose is to help Wyoming people work to prevent and alleviate environmental and rural problems. Major issues include: Coal mining, water development, toxics, wastes, energy conservation, agriculture, and accountable government.
Contact(s):
Chair: WILLIS GEER
Treasurer: MARILYN DAVIDSON
Keyword(s): Mining, Toxic Substances, Water Resources

PRAIRIE CLUB, THE
203 N. Wabash, Suite 1620, Chicago, IL 60601
Phone: 312-899-1539; Fax: 312-899-1541
Founded: 1911; Membership: 800
Scope: National
Description: Organized for the promotion of outdoor recreation in the form of walks, outings, camping, and canoeing; the establishment and maintenance of permanent and temporary camps; and the encouragement of the love of nature.
Contact(s):
President: HERB CARLSON
Executive Director: LORETTA DAVIS
Secretary: ELIZABETH DURKIN
Treasurer: HENRY GRAEF
1st Vice President: JOHN CLANCY
2nd Vice President: LAYTON OLSON
Chairman of Conservation Committee: KAY LINCICOME
Editor: SUSAN MESSER
Publication(s): *The Bulletin*

Keyword(s): Biodiversity, Environmental Preservation, Land Purchase, Outdoor Recreation, Wildlife and Wildlife Habitat

PRAIRIE GROUSE TECHNICAL COUNCIL
Wildlife and Fisheries Sciences Department Texas A&M University, College Station, TX 77843
Phone: 409-845-5777; Fax: 409-845-3786
Membership: 200
Scope: National
Description: Comprises federal, state, and private agency biologists or administrators concerned with the status, research, and management of the prairie-chicken and sharp-tailed grouse in North America.
Contact(s):
Executive Committee: KENNETH GIESEN, 317 W. Prospect, Ft. Collins, CO 80526
Publication(s): *Newsletter and Proceedings*
Keyword(s): Birds, Endangered and Threatened Species, Prairies, Wildlife and Wildlife Habitat, Wildlife Management

PRAIRIE RIVERS NETWORK
809 South 5th, Champaign, IL 61820
Phone: 217-344-2371; Fax: 217-344-2381; E-mail: info@prairierivers.org
Scope: Statewide
Contact(s):
Executive Director: ROB MOORE
Watershed Organizer: MARK MILLER
Publication(s): *Prairie River Notes; Prairie Rivers Directory*
Keyword(s): Water Pollution, Water Quality, River Conservation, Watershed Protection

PRAIRIE RIVERS NETWORK (Formerly Central States Education Center)
809 S. Fifth St., Champaign, IL 61820
Phone: 217-344-2371; Fax: 217-344-2381; E-mail: info@prairierivers.org
Founded: 1968
Scope: Statewide
Description: A statewide river conservation organization working to protect the rivers and streams of Illinois. Organizational and technical assistance is provided to persons and organizations in related activities.
Contact(s):
President: BRUCE M. HANNON; Phone: 217-352-3646
Treasurer: JOHN MCNUSSEN; Phone: 217-398-8531
Executive Director: ROBERT MOORE; E-mail: robmoore@prairierivers.org
Watershed Organizer: MARC MILLER; E-mail: mmiller@prairierivers.org
Publication(s): *Dirty Water, Dirty Business; Rivers*
Keyword(s): Rivers, Water Quality, Water Resources, Watersheds, River Conservation

PREDATOR PROJECT
P.O. Box 6733, Bozeman, MT 59771
Phone: 406-587-3389; Fax: 406-587-3178; E-mail: predproj@avicom.net; Web Site: www.wildrockies.org/predproj
Founded: 1991; Membership: 1000
Scope: National
Description: Since its inception in 1991, Predator Project has worked to conserve and restore ecosystem integrity by protecting predators and their habitats--saving a place for America's predators. We advocate on behalf of over 12 species including: the grizzly bear, wolf, lynx, wolverine, fisher, marten, black-footed ferret, swift fox, burrowing owl, coyote, northern gas hawk, mountain lion, and black bear. Of these, nine are imperiled. We also work on behalf of important prey species, such as prairie dogs, because these animals provide predators with essential food and/or habitat.
Contact(s):
President: SHARON NEGRI
Executive Director: TOM SKEELE
Secretary/Treasurer: JIM STOLTZ
Publication(s): *The Home Range* (quarterly newsletter); *Conservation of Prairie Dog Ecosystems: Learning From the Past to Insure the Prairie Dog's Future; The Wild Bunch; Motorizing Montana's National Forest Trails; At a Crossroads: The wolf and it's place in the Northern Rockies; Roaded Lands, Eroded Habitat: Findings and Implications of the Road Scholars Program 1992-1997*
Keyword(s): Biodiversity, Endangered and Threatened Species, Environmental Protection, Mammals, Nongame Wildlife, Prairies, Predators, Public Lands, Wildlife and Wildlife Habitat, Wildlife Management

PRIORITIES INSTITUTE, THE
P.O. Box 89, Pine, CO 80470-0089
Phone: 303-838-8105; Fax: 303-838-8105; E-mail: mail@priorities.org; Web Site: www.priorities.org
Founded: 1996; Membership: 100
Scope: International
Description: Non-partisan, non-profit research organization focusing on sustainable land use planning, designing car-free eco-cities, international communities, holistic indexing and moral evolution.
Contact(s):
Director/Founder: LOGAN PERKINS; E-mail: logan@priorities.org
Assistant: MELISSA MOON
Publication(s): *Livable Cities; Perspectives and Priorities*
Keyword(s): Environmental and Conservation Education, Environmental Planning, Land Use Planning, Pedestrian Environment, Preservation and Protection, Sustainable Development, Transportation, Urban and Rural Development

PROFESSIONAL BOWHUNTERS SOCIETY
P.O. Box 246, Terrell, NC 28682
Phone: 704-664-2534; Fax: 704-664-2534
Founded: 1963; Membership: 3,000
Scope: National
Description: Created as an organization of dedicated bow hunters interested in promoting a high level of ethics in the taking of wild game with bow and arrow. To provide training for others in safety, shooting skill, and hunting techniques. To practice and promote the wise use of our natural resources and conservation of wildlife.
Contact(s):
President: JIM CHINN, P.O. Box 1315, Hamilton, MT 59840; Phone: 406-363-3816
Vice President: JERRY BRUMM, 8525 Thornapple Lake Rd., Nashville, MI 49073; Phone: 517-852-9340
Council At-Large: TIM REED, P.O. Box 60, Valley Grove, WV 26060; Phone: 304-547-9077
Councilman: DENNIS ALLMAN, 2600 Hill Dr., Morganton, NC 28655; Phone: 704-433-9494
Editor: JACK SMITH
PBS Office: BRENDA KISNER; Phone: 704-664-2534; Fax: 704-664-7471
Secretary and Treasurer: JACK SMITH, P.O. Box 246, Terrell, NC 28682; Phone: 704-664-2534; Fax: 704-664-7471
Senior Councilman: DOUG KERR, R.R. 1, Box 312D, Stoney Lake Rd., Glenfield, NY 13343; Phone: 315-376-8660
Publication(s): *Professional Bowhunter Magazine, The*

PROVINCE OF QUEBEC SOCIETY FOR THE PROTECTION OF BIRDS, INC.
P.O. Box 43, Station B, Montreal, Quebec H3B 3J5 Canada
Phone: 514-637-2141; Fax: 514-939-1048; Web Site: www.minet.ca/~pqspb
Founded: 1917; Membership: 708
Scope: Statewide
Contact(s):
President: BARBARA MacDUFF, 101 Birch Hill, Hudson, Quebec J0P 1J0 Canada; Phone: 450-458-4751
Vice President: BESS MUHLSTOCK, 4807 Jeanne Mance, Montreal, Quebec H2V 4J6 Canada; Phone: 514-274-3810
Vice President: RONALD MUDD, 486 Westhill Ave., Beaconsfield, Quebec H9W 2G3 Canada; Phone: 514-697-7508

Editor: SHEILA ARTHUR, 3804 Royal Ave., Montreal, Quebec H4E
1P1 Canada; Phone: 514-487-4047
Hon. Secretary: KYRA EMO, 140 Irvine Ave., Westmount, Quebec
H3Z 2K2 Canada; Phone: 514-939-9666
Hon. Treasurer: KENNETH THORPE, 5615 Eldridge, Cote St-Luc,
Quebec H4W 2C9 Canada; Phone: 514-483-5031
Publication(s): *Tchebec (Annual Review); Field Check List of Birds in the Montreal Area; Birdfinding in the Montreal Area; The Song Sparrow (monthly newsletter)*
Keyword(s): Birds

PTARMIGANS, THE
P.O. Box 1821, Vancouver, WA 98668
Phone: 206-687-2436/206; Fax: 695-5385
Founded: 1960; Membership: 125
Scope: Statewide
Description: The Ptarmigans were established for the purpose of conducting mountaineering activities in the northwest and in promoting the preservation of the northwest forests, wilderness lands, and mountain scenery. The only membership requirement is a love of the outdoors. Offer a variety of outdoor activities led in an ecologically-minded manner. Help maintain several local trail systems and conduct an annual Basic Climbing School. Visit and observe changes proposed in our northwest forests and mountains. The conservation committee studies issues that affect our outdoor recreation area.
Contact(s):
President: JIM PEDERSEN
1st Vice President: MIKE DIANICH
2nd Vice President: RICHARD CHENOWETH
Secretary: JIM EPLIN
Treasurer: FREDA SHERBURNE
Publication(s): *Preserve Farmlands; A Place in the Islands; Landowner's Guide; Mom's Marsh and Other Fine Places (video)*
Keyword(s): Birds, Environmental and Conservation Education, Environmental Preservation, Islands, Wildlife and Wildlife Habitat

PUBLIC EMPLOYEES FOR ENVIRONMENTAL RESPONSIBILITY (PEER)
2001 S St., NW, Suite 570, Washington, DC 20009
Phone: 202-265-PEER (7337); Fax: 202-265-4192; E-mail: info@peer.org
Founded: 1993
Scope: National
Description: PEER is an alliance of land managers, scientists, biologists, law enforcement officials, and other government professionals dedicated to the protection of the nation's environment. PEER advocates the responsible management of natural resources and promotes environmental ethics, professional integrity and accountability within local, state and federal agencies.
Contact(s):
Executive Director: JEFFREY RUCH
Board Chair: HOWARD WILSHIRE
General Counsel: TODD ROBINS
Administrative Director: ALYSON WALTY
Communications Director: AMANDA CARUFEL
Development Director: EMILY CHARETTE
National Field Director: ROBERT PERKS
Outreach Membership Coordinator: ANN MCCRANIE
Publication(s): *PEEReview; various employee-authored white papers*
Keyword(s): Environmental Ethics, Environmental Protection, Forests and Forestry, Public Lands, Water Resources, Government Accountability

PUBLIC EMPLOYEES FOR ENVIRONMENTAL RESPONSIBILITY (PEER) (West Coast Office)
P.O. Box 30, Hood River, OR 97031
Phone: 541-387-4781; Fax: 541-387-4783
Scope: National

PUBLIC LANDS FOUNDATION
P.O. Box 7226 Arlington, McLean, VA 22207
Phone: 703-790-1988
Founded: 1987
Scope: National
Description: A national, nonprofit, independent advocate to keep the public lands public and for the proper use and protection of the public lands administered by the Bureau of Land Management; implementation of the Federal Land Policy and Management Act (FLPMA); and for professional land management by professional employees.
Contact(s):
President: GEORGE D. LEA; Phone: 703-790-1988
President-Elect: VINCE HECKER; Phone: 301-881-0964
Secretary and Treasurer: VINCE RILEY; Phone: 703-536-7939
Editor: GEORGE D. LEA
Publication(s): *Public Lands Monitor, The*
Keyword(s): Environmental and Conservation Education, Land Use Planning, Public Lands, Renewable Resources, Soil Conservation

PUERTO RICO ASSOCIATION OF SOIL AND WATER CONSERVATION DISTRICTS
Attn: President, P.O. Box 91, Orocovis, PR 00720
Scope: Statewide
Contact(s):
President: PEDRO J. FUENTES, P.O. Box 91, Orocovis, PR 00720; Phone: 787-867-4707
Vice President, Board Member: CARLOS MANTRAS, 1722 Pastemark St., Urb Purple Tree, San Juan, PR 00926; Phone: 787-761-6247
Secretary: HILDA BONILLA, HC 1 Box 8162, Luquillo, PR 00773; Phone: 787-860-0045
Treasurer: NORBERTO COLON, P.O. Box 175, Barranquitas, PR 00794; Phone: 787-857-7965
Administrative Secretary: MIGDALIA RODRIGUEZ, P.O. Box 1225, Casguas, PR 00726; Phone: 787-258-0490; Fax: 787-258-0490
Publication(s): *Verde Luz Newsletter; Puerto Rico Environmental Laws; Puerto Rico Conservation Directory; Puerto Rican Parrot Teacher's Kit, Pablo y Marisol van a la Playa*
Keyword(s): Biodiversity, Coasts, Endangered and Threatened Species, Environmental and Conservation Education, Land Purchase, Wetlands, Conservation Districts

PUERTO RICO CONSERVATION FOUNDATION, THE (PRCF
527 Avenue Andalucia, Suite 75, San Juan, PR 00920-4131
Phone: 787-763-9875; Fax: 787-772-4645; E-mail: fconserv@tld.net; Web Site: www.tld.net/users/fconserv
Founded: 1987
Scope: Statewide
Description: The PRCF is a private nonprofit tax-exempt 501(c)3 organization, dedicated to protecting Puerto Rico's biological biodiversity, focusing on the conservation of threatened and endangered species and other keystone and lesser known species.
Contact(s):
President: JUAN L. RICART
Vice President and Treasurer: ROBERTO E. BIAGGI
Secretary: JOSE A. DUENO
Director: MIGUEL ITURREGUI
Executive Director: ESTHER ROJAS
Publication(s): *Verde Luz Newsletter; Puerto Rico Environmental Laws; Puerto Rico NGOs Directory; Puerto Rican Parrot Teacher's Kit; Pablo y Marisol van Playa; Sea Turtle Kit and various brochures*
Keyword(s): Biodiversity, Conservation, Endangered and Threatened Species, Environmental and Conservation Education, Research

PUGET SOUNDKEEPER ALLIANCE
1415 W. Dravus, Seattle, WA 98119
Phone: 206-286-1309; Fax: 206-286-1082; E-mail: pskeeper@halcyon.com; Web Site: www.halcyon.com/pskeeper
Founded: 1984; Membership: 400
Scope: National

Description: A nonprofit organization whose mission is to serve as stewards for the protection and enhancement of Puget Sound through education, advocacy, monitoring, and celebration.
Contact(s):
President: TOM DILLER, Seattle, WA
Executive Director: ROBERTA M. GUNN, Seattle, WA ; Phone: 206-286-1309
SoundKeeper: B. J. CUMMINGS, Seattle, WA ; Phone: 206-286-1309/1-800-42-PUGET
Treasurer and Secretary: BRAD MCMULLEN
Publication(s): *Sounder*
Keyword(s): Coasts, Environmental and Conservation Education, Environmental Law, Water Pollution, Water Quality

PURPLE MARTIN CONSERVATION ASSOCIATION
Edinboro University of Pennsylvania, Edinboro, PA 16444
Phone: 814-734-4420; Fax: 814-734-5803; E-mail: PMCA@edinboro.edu; Web Site: www.purplemartin.org
Founded: 1987; Membership: 6,500
Scope: International
Description: An international tax-exempt, nonprofit organization dedicated to the conservation of the Purple Martin (Progne subis) species of bird through scientific research, state-of-the-art wildlife management techniques, and public education. The PMCA's scientific staff conducts research on all aspects of martin biology throughout the bird's North, South, and Middle American breeding, wintering, and migratory ranges. The organization functions as a centralized data-gathering and information source on the species, serving both the scientist and the martin enthusiast. Its major mission is educating martin enthusiasts in the proper techniques for managing this human-dependent species.
Contact(s):
Director and Editor: JAMES R. HILL III
Publication(s): *Purple Martin Update*
Keyword(s): Birds, Endangered and Threatened Species, Environmental and Conservation Education, Nongame Wildlife, Wildlife Management

Q

QUAIL UNLIMITED, INC.
31 Quail Run, P.O. Box 610, Edgefield, SC 29824-0610
Phone: 803-637-5731; Fax: 803-637-0037; E-mail: quail@jetbn.net
Founded: 1981; Membership: 50,000
Scope: National
Description: A national nonprofit conservation organization dedicated to improving quail and upland game bird populations through habitat management and research. Organized to re-establish and manage suitable upland game habitat, both public and private lands across the country, and to educate the public to the needs for wildlife habitat management.
Contact(s):
President: STEVE McGHEE, 100 Patterson Circle, Oliver Springs, TN 37840; Phone: 423-574-3685
Administrative Vice President: JERRY W. ALLEN, 1884 Highway 23 West, Edgefield, SC 29824; Phone: 803-637-5877; E-mail: national@qu.org
Director of Chapter Development: TOMMY DEAN, 815 Shawnee Dr., N. Augusta, SC 29841; Phone: 803-637-5731; E-mail: chapterdev@qu.org
Editor: D. KOGON; E-mail: qumag@qu.org
Executive Vice President: JOSEPH R. EVANS, 3012 Sussex Rd., Augusta, GA 30909; Phone: 706-738-0692; E-mail: national@qu.org
National Habitat Coordinator: ROGER WELLS, 868 Road 290, Americus, KS; Phone: 316-443-5834; E-mail: rwells@americusks.net
Director of Agricultural Wildlife Services: DAVID HOWELL, 10364 S. 950 E., Stendal, IN 47585; Phone: 812-536-2272; E-mail: dhowell@psci.net
Great Plains Regional Director: JEFF HODGES, 382 NW Hwy 18, Clinton, MO 64735; Phone: 660-885-7057; Fax: 660-885-7152
Mid-Atlantic Regional Director: WADE TEAGUE, 271 Stevens Church Rd, Goldsboro, NC 27530; Phone: 919-689-3884; Fax: 919-689-2726; E-mail: wadequ@earthlink.net
Midsouth Regional Director: MIKE HANSBROUGH, 10116 Oak Creek Ln., Knoxville, TN 37932; Phone: 423-470-0009; Fax: 423-470-0009; E-mail: mikehans@conc.tds.net
Midwest Regional Director: CHRIS WOLKONOWSKI, 10364 S. 950 E., Stendal, IN 47585; Phone: 812-536-2272; Fax: 812-536-2272; E-mail: cwolk@psci.net
Rocky Mountain Regional Director: HARVEY BRAY, 13 Archway Lane, Pueblo, CO 81005; Phone: 719-561-3825; Fax: 719-561-8977
South Central Regional Director: RANDY GUTHRIE, 2061 Crow Mt. Rd., Russellville, AR 72801; Phone: 501-967-2200; Fax: 501-767-2716; E-mail: rguthrie@cswnet.com
Southeast Regional Director: DANIEL STILLINGER, 31 Quail Run, Edgefield, SC 29824; Phone: 803-637-5731; Fax: 803-637-0037; E-mail: quail1@jetbn.net
Southwest Regional Director: CHIP MARTIN, 1400 L Ave., Anson, TX 79501; Phone: 915-823-3347; Fax: 915-823-3340
Western Regional Director: DICK HALDEMAN, 39455 Black Oak Rd., Temecula, CA 92592; Phone: 909-767-3435; Fax: 909-767-2716; E-mail: quwest@pe.net
Keyword(s): Birds, Wildlife and Wildlife Habitat

QUEBEC WILDLIFE FEDERATION
6780 1st Ave., Bureau 109, Charlesbourg, Quebec G1H 2W8 Canada
Phone: 418-626-6858; Fax: 418-622-6168; E-mail: fede@fqf.qc.ca
Founded: 1945; Membership: 175,000
Scope: Statewide
Contact(s):
Executive Director: ALAIN COSSETTE
President: CLAUDE GAUTHIER
Vice-President: ALAIN GAGNON
Vice-President: MICHEL SAVARD
Vice-President and Secretary: ALAIN BISSON
Vice-President: RODOLPHE LASANE
Biologist: JEAN-PIERRE TREMBLAY
Treasurer: BRUNO PARADIS
Communication Coordinator: MANON GAGNON
Forest Engineer: PATRICK FILIATRAULT
Keyword(s): Hunting, Outdoor Recreation, Public Lands, Renewable Resources, Sport Fishing, Sustainable Development, Training, Waterfowl, Wildlife and Wildlife Habitat, Wildlife Management

R

RACHEL CARSON COUNCIL, INC. (formerly Rachel Carson Trust for the Living Environment Inc.)
8940 Jones Mill Rd., Chevy Chase, MD 20815
Phone: 301-652-1877; Fax: 301-951-7179; E-mail: rccouncil@aol.com; Web Site: members.aol.com/rccouncil/ourpage
Founded: 1965
Scope: National
Description: An international clearinghouse for information on toxic substances, particularly pesticides for both scientists and laymen, distributed by means of publications, conferences, and response to specific questions. Rachel Carson Council is devoted to fostering a sense of wonder and respect toward nature and helping society realize Rachel Carson's vision of a healthy and diverse environment.
Contact(s):
President: DAVID B. McGRATH
Vice President: MARTHA H. TALBOT
Treasurer: FREEBORN G. JEWETT JR.
Executive Director and Secretary: DR. DIANA M. POST
Liaison to the Board: DR. AARON BLAIR

Publication(s): *Basic Guide to Pesticides; Rachel Carson Council News;* books, pamphlets and sheets on specific alternative pest control methods and on pesticides effects; list of current publications available on request.
Keyword(s): Agriculture, Environmental and Conservation Education, Pesticides, Toxic Substances, Water Pollution

RAILS-TO-TRAILS CONSERVANCY
1100 17th S., NW, 10th Fl., Washington, DC 20036
Phone: 202-331-9696; Fax: 202-331-9680
Founded: 1986; Membership: 80,000
Scope: National
Description: The mission of the Rails-to-Trails Conservancy is to enhance America's communities and country sides by converting thousands of miles of abandoned rail corridors, and connecting open space into a nationwide network of public trails.
Contact(s):
President: DAVID BURWELL
Board of Directors Chair: MARK ACKELSON
Board of Directors Treasurer: RICHARD W. ANGLE JR.
Executive Vice President: MARK WOLF-ARMSTRONG
Publication(s): *Trailblazer; Seven-Hundred Great Rail-Trails: A Directory of Multi-Use Paths Created from Abandoned Railroads; Secrets of Successful Rail-Trails: An Acquisition and Organizing Manual for Converting Rails into Trails; Enhancing America's Communities: A Nationwide Survey of The Transportation Enhancements Provisions of ISTEALibrary: (202-331-9696)*
Keyword(s): Environment, Internships, Land Preservation, Outdoor Recreation, Research, Trail

RAINBOW PUSH COALITION
1002 Wisconsin Ave., NW, Washington, DC 20007
Phone: 202-333-5270
Founded: 1984
Scope: National
Description: RPC is a national progressive membership organization committed to public education, empowerment, economic and social justice, and gender and racial equality. The Rainbow Push Coalition has state chapters and a national membership base. The Rainbow Push Coalition addresses such issues as education, voter registration, economic justice, civil rights, environment, labor, and working people's rights.
Contact(s):
Co-chairman of the Board: WILLIE T. BARROW
Co-chairman of the Board: DENNIS RIVERA
President and Founder: REV. JESSE L. JACKSON
Publication(s): *Rainbow Newsletter; Labor Newsletter;* various issue papers, speeches, and briefings; *Rainbow Push Magazine or The Rainbow JaxFax*
Keyword(s): Environmental and Conservation Education, Sustainable Development, Toxic Substances, Urban Environment

RAINFOREST ACTION NETWORK
221 Pine St., Suite 500, San Francisco, CA 94104
Phone: 415-398-4404; Fax: 415-398-2732; E-mail: rainforest@ran.org; Web Site: www.ran.org
Founded: 1985; Membership: 15,000
Scope: National
Description: RAN works nationally and internationally on major campaigns to protect rainforests and defend the rights of indigenous people, using non-violent direct action such as: letter-writing campaigns, boycotts, and demonstrations against corporations and lending agencies contributing to rainforest destruction. RAN also produces educational materials, a teachers' packet, and fact sheets for community organizers.
Contact(s):
President: RANDY HAYES
Executive Director: KELLY QUIRKE
Board Chair: JIM GOLLIN
Board Secretary: DAVID WEIR
Board Treasurer: SCOTT PRICE
Communications Director: MARK WESTLUND
Publications Editor: LAURA FAUTH
Publication(s): *World Rainforest Report; Action Alert; RAG-RAG Rainforest Action Group Newsletter; World Rainforest Week Organizers' Manual*
Keyword(s): Biodiversity, Environmental and Conservation Education, Forests and Forestry, International Conservation, Rainforests

RAINFOREST ALLIANCE
65 Bleecker St., New York, NY 10012
Phone: 212-677-1900; Fax: 212-677-2187; E-mail: canopy@ra.org
Founded: 1986; Membership: 14,000
Scope: International
Description: The Rainforest Alliance is an international nonprofit organization dedicated to the conservation of tropical forests for the benefit of the global community. Its primary mission is to develop and promote economically viable and socially desirable alternatives to the destruction of tropical forests.
Contact(s):
Executive Director: DANIEL R. KATZ
Assistant to the Executive Director: MARGIE AMBROSINO
Associate Director: KARIN KREIDER
Publication(s): *CANOPY, The; Floods of Fortune; Tales from the Jungle; So Fruitful a Fish; Catfish Connection, The*
Keyword(s): Biodiversity, Forests and Forestry, Grants, International Conservation, Rainforests, Sustainable Development

RAINFOREST RELIEF
P.O. Box 150566, Brooklyn, NY 11215
Phone: 718-398-3760; Fax: 718-398-3760; E-mail: relief@igc.org; Web Site: www.enviroweb.org/rainrelief
Founded: 1989; Membership: 250
Scope: National
Description: Rainforest Relief, a nonprofit 501(c)3 organization, works through education and non-violent direct action to end the loss of tropical and temperate rain forests by reducing the demand for products and materials for which rainforests are destroyed. These materials include tropical hardwoods, paper, oil, metals and agricultural products such as bananas, beef, coffee and chocolate.
Contact(s):
President and Director: TIM KEATING
Vice-President: JEFFREY LOCKWOOD
Treasurer: ROSANE BARUFFE
Portland Oregon Chapter, Director: JEFFREY LOCKWOOD, P.O. Box 14232, Portland, OR 97293; Phone: 503-236-3031; E-mail: rainrelief@hotmail.com
Publication(s): *Roots; Raindrops; Rainforest Relief Reports*
Keyword(s): Biodiversity, Cultural Preservation, Environmental and Conservation Education, Forests and Forestry, International Conservation, Overconsumption, Rainforests, Tropical Biodiversity and Conservation

RAINFOREST TRUST, INC., THE
6001 SW 63rd Ave., Miami, FL 33143
Phone: 305-667-2779; Fax: 305-665-0691; E-mail: rforest@rainforesttrust.com; Web Site: www.rainforesttrust.com
Scope: International
Description: The Trust has established a jaguar sanctuary and rainforest preserve in Belize. It also promotes ecotourism and alternative rainforest sustainable agriculture as economically viable alternatives to deforestation, particularly in Jamaica; and promotes programs to educate public school children and farmers about conservation of ecosystems, organic agriculture, and wildlife. The trust has established a second wildlife sanctuary and rainforest preserve in Jamaica.
Contact(s):
Chairman: T. EVELYN HAWKINS; Phone: 305-666-2158
President: BRETT EVELYN ASHMEADE-HAWKINS
Secretary and Treasurer: MARK EVELYN ASHMEADE-HAWKINS
Keyword(s): Agriculture, Ancient Forests, Conservation of Protected Areas, Endangered and Threatened Species, Environmental and Conservation Education, Environmental

Protection, Historic Preservation, Rainforests, Sustainable Ecosystems, Wildlife and Wildlife Habitat

RAPTOR CENTER, THE
University of Minnesota, 1920 Fitch Ave., St. Paul, MN 55108
Phone: 612-624-4745; E-mail: raptor@umn.edu; Web Site: www.raptor.cvm.umn.edu
Founded: 1974; Membership: 4,500
Scope: National
Description: To preserve biological diversity among raptors and other avian species through medical treatment, scientific investigation, education, and management of wild populations.
Contact(s):
Director: PATRICK T. REDIG
Associate Director: RON OSTERBAUER
Board Chair: DEBBIE REYNOLDS
Publication(s): *Raptor Release, The; Medical Management of Birds of Prey; Care and Management of Captive Raptors*
Keyword(s): Birds, Endangered and Threatened Species, Environmental and Conservation Education, Raptors, Wildlife Rehabilitation

RAPTOR EDUCATION FOUNDATION, INC.
P.O. Box 200400, Denver, CO 80220
Phone: 303-680-8500; Fax: 303-680-8502; E-mail: raptor2@usaref.org; Web Site: www.usaref.org
Founded: 1980
Scope: National
Description: A nonprofit, charitable educational organization utilizing non-releasable raptors to promote environmental literacy. Lecturers travel nationwide.
Contact(s):
President and Editor: PETER RESHETNIAK
Vice President: WILLIAM F. GREVE JR.
Vice President: ROBERT P. KOEHLER
Editor: SHERRIE YORK
Secretary: ANNE PRICE
Publication(s): *Talon; Talon Supplement; Eagles, Hawks, Falcons, and Owls of America (a coloring album); Castings (volunteer newsletter)*
Keyword(s): Environmental and Conservation Education, Environmental Preservation, Environmental Protection, Raptors

RAPTOR RESEARCH FOUNDATION, INC.
USGS Forest and Rangeland Ecosystem Science Center, Snake River Field Station, 970 Luck St., Boise, ID 83706
Founded: 1966
Scope: National
Description: A nonprofit corporation formed to stimulate and coordinate the dissemination of information on the biology and management of birds of prey and their habitats. Areas of particular interest include: raptor banding, behavior, captive breeding, conservation, ecology, research techniques, management, migration, population monitoring, pathology, and rehabilitation.
Contact(s):
President: MICHAEL N. KOCHERT; Phone: 208-426-5201; Fax: 208-426-5210; E-mail: mkochert@eagle.idbsu.edu
Vice President: KEITH L. BILDSTEIN, Hawk Mountain Sanctuary, Route 2, Box 191, Kempton, PA 19529; Phone: 910-756-6961; E-mail: bildstein@hawkmountain.org
Secretary: PATRICIA HALL, 436 David Dr. E, Flagstaff, AZ 86001; Phone: 520-526-6222; E-mail: pah@alpine.for.nau.edu
Editor-in-Chief: DR. MARC J. BECHARD, Department of Biology, Boise State University, Boise, ID 83725; Phone: 208-426-3530; E-mail: mbechard@micron.net
Treasurer and Membership Information: JIM FITZPATRICK, Carpenter, St. Croix Valley Nature Center, 12805 St. Croix Tr., Hastings, MN 55033; Phone: 651-437-4359; E-mail: jim@cncstcroix.com
Publication(s): *Journal of Raptor Research; Wingspan; Kettle; (RRF Membership Directory and Handbook - published even-numbered years)*

Keyword(s): Endangered and Threatened Species, Environmental and Conservation Education, Nongame Wildlife, Raptors, Wildlife and Wildlife Habitat

RARE CENTER FOR TROPICAL CONSERVATION
1616 Walnut St., Suite 1010, Philadelphia, PA 19103
Phone: 215-735-3510; Fax: 215-735-3515; E-mail: rare@rarecenter.org
Founded: 1973; Membership: 2,400
Scope: International
Description: RARE Center is a small organization doing innovative work to preserve threatened habitats and ecosystems in Latin America, the Caribbean, and the Pacific. Our programs focus on education and training, habitat protection, and research.
Contact(s):
Chairman: ROGER F. PASQUIER
Vice Chairman: SUSAN M. BABCOCK
President (Acting): BRETT JENKS
Secretary: EMILIE M. PRYOR
Treasurer: SUMNER PINGREE
Director, Conservation Education Program: PAUL J. BUTLER
Director, Ecotourism and Community Development Program: BRETT JENKS
Keyword(s): Environmental and Conservation Education, Environmental Preservation

REEF RELIEF
P.O. Box 430, Key West, FL 33041
Phone: 305-294-3100; Fax: 305-293-9515; Web Site: www.reefrelief.org
Founded: 1989
Scope: National
Description: Reef Relief is a nonprofit membership organization dedicated to preserve and protect Living Coral Reef Ecosystems through local, regional, and global efforts.
Contact(s):
President: MARCI L. ROSE
Secretary: ROBIN ORLANDI
Educational Coordinator: JOEL BIDDLE
First Vice-President: VICTORIA IMPALLOMENI
Founder and Director of Marine Projects: CRAIG QUIROLO
Past President: DR. BRIAN LAPOINTE
Project Coordinator: MICHAEL BLADES
Project Director: DEEVON QUIROLO
Treasurer: PAUL JOHNSON
Publication(s): *Reef Line; Florida's Coral Reef Ecosystem; booklets; flyers Library and Public Educational Facility: Reef Relief Environmental Center and Store, 201 William St., Key West, FL 33040*
Keyword(s): Biodiversity, Coral Reefs, Environmental and Conservation Education, Sustainable Ecosystems, Water Pollution Management

RENEW AMERICA
1200 18th St., NW, Suite 1100, Washington, DC 20036
Phone: 202-721-1545; Fax: 202-467-5780; E-mail: renewamerica@counterpart.org; Web Site: www.crest.org/renew_america
Founded: 1978; Membership: 2,000
Scope: National
Description: Renew America specializes in broad-based environmental program identification, verification, and promotion of positive models for change. By seeking out, promoting and awarding exemplary programs among all sectors, we offer innovative, constructive models to inspire communities and businesses to meet environmental challenges.
Contact(s):
Executive Director: ANNA SLAFER
Publication(s): *Environmental Success Index*
Keyword(s): Environmental and Conservation Education, Sustainability

RENEWABLE ENERGY POLICY PROJECT (REPP)
1612 K St., NW, Suite 410, Washington, DC 20006

Phone: 202-293-2898; Fax: 202-293-5857
Founded: 1995
Scope: National
Description: The Renewable Energy Policy Project (REPP) investigates the emerging relationships among policies, markets and public demand for renewable energy technologies. REPP's mission is to accelerate growth of the renewable energy industry and maximize deployment of renewable energy technology, by providing credible information, insightful analysis and innovative strategies.
Contact(s):
Chairman of the Board of Directors: CARL WINBERG
Executive Director: ROBY ROBERTS
Researach Director: ADAM SERCHUK
Publications and Outreach Manager: MARY KATHRYN CAMPBELL
Keyword(s): Energy, Renewable Resources

RENEWABLE NATURAL RESOURCES FOUNDATION
5430 Grosvenor Ln., Bethesda, MD 20814-2193
Phone: 301-493-9101; Fax: 301-493-6148; E-mail: RNRF@aol.com; Web Site: www.rnrf.org
Founded: 1972
Scope: National
Description: A public, nonprofit, operating foundation. Conducts conferences and symposia on renewable natural resource subjects and public policy alternatives. Developer of the Renewable Natural Resources Center, an office-park complex for natural resource organizations.
Contact(s):
Executive Director: ROBERT D. DAY JD
Chairman of Board of Directors: RICHARD L. DUESTERHAUS
Vice Chairman of the Board: DAVID W. MOODY
Director of Administration and Finance: CHANDRU KRISHNA MBA, CPA
Director of Programs: KRISTEN L. KRAPF MS
Publication(s): *Renewable Resources Journal*
Keyword(s): Environmental and Conservation Education, International Conservation, Land Use Planning, Renewable Resources, Urban Environment

REP AMERICA/REPUBLICANS FOR ENVIRONMENTAL PROTECTION
P.O. Box 7073, Deerfield, IL 60015
Phone: 847-940-0320; Fax: 847-940-0320; Web Site: www.repamerica.org
Founded: 1995
Scope: National
Description: REP aims to resurrect the GOP's conservation tradition and restore natural resource conservation and sound environmental protection as fundamental elements of the Republican Party.
Contact(s):
President: MARTHA A. MARKS Ph.D.; E-mail: martha@repamerica.org
Vice-President: AURIE KRYZUDA
Secretary: JIM DIPESO
Treasurer: SAM BOOHER
Publication(s): *The Green Elephant*
Keyword(s): Biodiversity, Conservation, Endangered and Threatened Species, Environmental Ethics, Environmental Legislation, Environmental Protection, Forest Stewardship, Natural Resource Conservation, Pollution Prevention, Politics and Government

RESOURCE CENTER FOR ENVIRONMENTAL EDUCATION, THE
Okeanskill Prospect, Vladivostok 690106 Russia
Phone: 4232-25-05-66-22-57-63; Fax: 4232-22-57-63; E-mail: liliko@mail.primorye.ru
Founded: 1997
Scope: International
Description: The RCEE is the only center in the Russian far East, dedicated to promoting experiential learning in the fields of environmental education, science, and art for students and teachers.
Contact(s):
Director: LILIA KONDRASHOVA; Phone: +7-4232-42-80-18; Fax: 4232-22-57-63; E-mail: liliko@mail.orimorye.ru
Keyword(s): Camp, Environmental and Conservation Education, Marine Conservation, Networking, Research Grants, Training, Youth Organizations

RESOURCE RENEWAL INSTITUTE, THE
Fort Mason Center Building A, San Francisco, CA 94123
Phone: 415-928-3774; Fax: 415-928-6529; E-mail: info@rri.org
Founded: 1983
Scope: National
Description: The RRI is a national, nonprofit organization advocating state and national comprehensive, integrated environmental strategies (known as Green Plans), modeled on those of the Netherlands and New Zealand. RRI has set up a Global Green Plan Center to act as a clearinghouse for information on Green Plans. For more information, use RRI's e-mail address.
Contact(s):
President: HUEY D. JOHNSON
Executive Director: DANIELLE KRAAIJVANGER
Publication(s): *Saving Cities, Saving Money; The International Green Planner; Green Plans: Greenprint for Sustainability*
Keyword(s): Environmental and Conservation Education, Environmental Planning, Planning Management, Renewable Resources, Sustainable Development, Sustainable Ecosystems

RESOURCE-USE EDUCATION COUNCIL
Attn: Chairman Resource-Use Education Council, Dept. of Environmental Quality, P.O. Box 10009, Richmond, VA 23240-0009
Founded: 1952
Scope: Statewide
Description: A volunteer, nonprofit organization, composed of members of the state and federal government, colleges, and private industry, working to promote the broad principle of environmental education. The Council offers conservation education workshops for educators across Virginia. Scholarships for teachers are available.
Contact(s):
Chairman: ANN REGN, Department of Environmental Quality, P.O. Box 10009, Richmond, VA 23240-0009; Phone: 804-698-4442
Secretary and Treasurer: SUSAN GILLEY, Department of Game and Inland Fisheries, Box 11104, Richmond, VA 23230; Phone: 804-367-1000
Publication(s): *Coldwater Conservationist, The*

RESOURCES FOR THE FUTURE
1616 P St., NW, Washington, DC 20036
Phone: 202-328-5000; Fax: 202-939-3460
Founded: 1952
Scope: National
Description: An independent nonprofit organization that works to advance research and education in the development, conservation, and use of environmental and natural resources. Staff is comprised primarily of economists and policy analysts who research a variety of environmental and natural resource issues.
Contact(s):
President: PAUL R. PORTNEY; Phone: 202-328-5000
Board of Directors Chairman: DARIUS W. GASKINS JR.
Center for Risk Management Director: J. CLARENCE DAVIES III; Phone: 202-328-5093
Director of Development: LESLI CREEDON
Energy and Natural Resources Division Director: MICHAEL TOMAN; Phone: 202-328-5091
Librarian: CHRISTOPHER CLOTWORTHY; Phone: 202-328-5089
Manager of Public Affairs: DAN QUINN; Phone: 202-328-5019
Quality of the Environment Division Director: ALAN KRUPNICK; Phone: 202-328-5059
Vice President of Finance and Administration: EDWARD F. HAND; Phone: 202-328-5029
Publication(s): *Resources*
Keyword(s): Air Quality and Pollution, Biodiversity, Developing Countries, Endangered and Threatened Species, Energy, Energy

NON-GOVERNMENTAL ORGANIZATIONS - R

Conservation, Environment, Environmental Protection, Forest Management, Land Use Planning, Mining, Renewable Resources, Sustainable Development, Transportation

RESPONSIVE MANAGEMENT
P.O. Box 389, Harrisonburg, VA 22801
Phone: 540-432-1888; Fax: 540-432-1892; E-mail: mdduda@rica.net; Web Site: www.responsivemanagement.com
Founded: 1986
Scope: National
Description: Developed to help fish and wildlife organizations understand and work with their constituents. Responsive Management conducts focus group research, telephone and mail surveys, public opinion and attitude research, literature reviews, demographic analysis, and workshops in public opinion polling, marketing, change, communications, dispute resolution, and human dimensions of natural resource management.
Contact(s):
Executive Director: MARK DAMIAN DUDA, P.O. Box 389, Harrisonburg, VA 22801-0389; Phone: 540-432-1888
Publication(s): *Responsive Management Report*
Keyword(s): Communications, Research, Training

RETURNED PEACE CORPS VOLUNTEER FOR ENVIRONMENT AND DEVELOPMENT (RPCV-ED)
P.O. Box 102, Iowa City, IA 52246-0102
Phone: 319-351-3375
Founded: 1991; Membership: 450
Scope: National
Description: The RPCVs-ED was formed to serve as a focal point for action on environment and development issues by Peace Corps alumni and friends.
Contact(s):
Co-chair: KATY HANSEN
Co-chair: MARY STEINMAUS
Editor: SUSAN SINGH, 1762 E. 60th St., Tulsa, OK 74105; Phone: 918-749-7004
Keyword(s): Developing Countries, Environment, Sustainable Development

RHODE ISLAND B.A.S.S. CHAPTER FEDERATION
Attn: President, 64 Oakton St., Woonsocket, RI 02895
Scope: Statewide
Description: An organization of Bassmaster chapters, affiliated with the Bass Anglers Sportsman Society, organized to fight pollution, assist state and national conservation agencies in their efforts, and teach the young people of our country good conservation practices. Dedicated to the realistic conservation of our water resources.
Contact(s):
President: LUCIEN BIBEAULT; Phone: 401-766-7082
Conservation Director: BILL WEIKERT, 156 Ridgewood Rd., Middletown, RI 02842; Phone: 401-846-0512
Publication(s): *Forest Conservationist, The*
Keyword(s): Forests and Forestry

RHODE ISLAND FOREST CONSERVATORS ASSOCIATION
P.O. Box 40328, Providence, RI 02908
Phone: 401-273-8057
Founded: 1989; Membership: 250
Scope: Statewide
Description: A statewide organization affiliated with the National Woodland Owners Association organized to promote stewardship of Rhode Island's wooded lands and watersheds and protect their heritage for future generations.
Contact(s):
President and Editor: MARC J. TREMBLAY
Vice President: ALEX MERRIMIAN
Secretary: MILTON SCHUMACHER
Treasurer: VIRGINIA WARRENDER
Publication(s): *(newsletter)*

RHODE ISLAND STATE ASSOCIATION OF CONSERVATION DISTRICTS
Attn: President, 35 Abbott Run Valley Rd., Cumberland, RI 02864
Scope: Statewide
Contact(s):
President, Board Member: JESSE A. CARPENTER; Phone: 401-762-7346; E-mail: Fahma1@aol.com
Vice President: EMERSON WILDES, Whimshaw Farm, Shaw Rd., Little Compton, RI 02837; Phone: 401-635-2935
Secretary: ROBERT SWANSON, 39 Shannock Hill Rd., Carolina, RI 02812; Phone: 401-364-4069
Treasurer: WILLIAM COLBURN, 5 Pierce Rd., Foster, RI 02825; Phone: 401-397-5989
Publication(s): *Bi-Annual Newsletter; Cultivation Notes 1-16; Wild Plants! (some basic information; other resources and fact sheets)*
Keyword(s): Endangered and Threatened Species, Environmental and Conservation Education, Flowers, Plants, and Trees, Nature Preservation, Terrestrial Habitats, Conservation Districts

RHODE ISLAND WILD PLANT SOCIETY
Box 114, Peace Dale, RI 02883-0114
Founded: 1987; Membership: 600
Scope: Statewide
Description: The Rhode Island Wild Plant Society is a nonprofit conservation organization dedicated to the preservation and protection of Rhode Island's native plants and their habitats. Activities include talks, inventories of local flora, native plant restoration projects and a spring flower show and garden exhibit.
Contact(s):
Executive Director: DEBORAH POOR
President: JULES COHEN, 85 Scrabbletown Rd., N. Kingstown, RI 02852
Publication(s): *RIWPS Newsletter (biannual newsletter)*
Keyword(s): Environmental and Conservation Education, Environmental Preservation, Flowers, Plants, and Trees, Wildflowers, Native Plants

RINCON INSTITUTE, THE
7650 E. Broadway Blvd., Suite 203, Tucson, AZ 85710
Phone: 520-290-0828; Fax: 520-290-0969; E-mail: rincon@sonoran.org
Founded: 1990
Scope: Local Region
Description: The Rincon Institute is a nonprofit organization dedicated to protecting the natural resources of the Rincon Mountain District of Saguaro National Park and the surrounding lands. This goal is accomplished primarily through ecological research, environmental education, natural area protection, private land stewardship and the development of cooperative approaches to resolving land use conflicts.
Contact(s):
Executive Director: LUTHER PROPST
Chairman of the Board: PETER BACKUS
Director of Research: MARK BRIGGS
Outreach Director: MARY VINT
Program Associate: JOSH SCHACHTER
Keyword(s): Conservation of Protected Areas, Ecology, Environmental and Conservation Education, Land Preservation, Land Use Planning, National Parks, Natural Areas, Research, Riparian Restoration, Sustainable Development, Sustainable Ecosystems, Terrestrial Habitats

RIVER ALLIANCE OF WISCONSIN
122 State St., Suite 202, Madison, WI 53703
Phone: 608-257-2424; Fax: 608-251-1655; E-mail: wisrivers@wisconsinrivers.org; Web Site: www.wisconsinrivers.org
Founded: 1993; Membership: 1000
Scope: Statewide
Description: The River Alliance is a nonprofit, nonpartisan citizen advocacy organization for rivers. Our mission is to lead the growing statewide effort to protect, enhance and restore Wisconsin's rivers

and watersheds for their ecological, recreational, aesthetic, and cultural values. Recent program work includes education and information about the impacts of dams on river system health, minimizing ecosystem damage through federal relicensing of hydro dams, and advocacy for selective removal of uneconomical dams for purpose of river restoration.
Contact(s):
Executive Director: TODD L. Ambs
Publication(s): *Wisconsin Rivers (Quarterly); Periodic Action Alerts; News Bulletins and fact Sheets; Canoe (e-mail newsletter)*
Keyword(s): Aquatic Habitats, Dams, Fisheries, Rivers, Water Pollution, Watersheds, Hydropower Relicensing

RIVER FEDERATION
1428 Fenwick Ln., Silver Spring, MD 20910
Phone: 301-589-9454; Fax: 301-589-6121; E-mail: riverfed1@aol.com
Founded: 1981; Membership: 100
Scope: National
Description: River Federation's mission is to work in partnership to conserve and revitalize the nation's rivers. It is a forum for and publishes information on river conservation and revitalization management for river professionals and leaders. It ensures that states are represented in the formulation of national river conservation and revitalization policy. It provides technical communications, planning, and management services to river conservation programs.
Contact(s):
President: DOUGLAS CARTER, Michigan Department of Natural Resources, ; Phone: 517-373-1172; Fax: 517-373-9965
Vice President: EDWARD D. FITE III, Oklahoma Scenic Rivers Commission, ; Phone: 918-456-3281; Fax: 918-456-3281
Executive Director: ROBERT C. HOFFMAN; Phone: 301-589-9454; Fax: 301-589-6121; E-mail: riverfed1@aol.com
Secretary and Treasurer: MOLLY MacGREGOR, Mississippi Headwaters Board; Phone: 218-547-3300; Fax: 218-547-2440
Publication(s): *Institutional Frameworks for Watershed Management Programs (1994); Profiles in River Management; River Federation Newsletter; River Conservation Directory (1990)*
Keyword(s): Land Use Planning, Outdoor Recreation, Planning Management, Rivers, Water Resources

RIVER NETWORK
Headquarters, P.O. Box 8787, 520 SW 6th Ave., Suite 1130, Portland, OR 97204
Phone: 503-241-3506, 1-800-423-6747; Fax: 503-241-9256; E-mail: rivernet@igc.org; Web Site: www.rivernetwork.org
Founded: 1988
Scope: National
Description: River Network supports river advocates at the grassroots, state and regional levels; helps them build effective organizations; and links them together in a national movement to protect and restore America's rivers and watersheds. River Network also works with river conservationists to acquire and conserve riverlands and riparian areas critical for wildlife, fisheries, drinking water, flood plain management, and recreation.
Contact(s):
President: KEN MARGOLIS
Administrative Director: LINDY WALSH
Chairman of Board of Directors: JIM COMPTON
Communications Director: THALIA A. ZEPATOS
Director of Development: BRIGETTE SARABI
Director of Watershed Programs: DON ELDER
Northwest (RLC): SUE DOROFF
Publication(s): *The Watershed Innovators Workshop: Proceedings and The Swift River Principles; How to save a River; River Voices; 1998-1999 River and Watershed Conservation Directory; River Fundraising Alert; Starting Up: A Handbook for New River and Watershed Organizations; Directory of Funding Sources for Grassroots River and Watershed Groups.*
Keyword(s): Land Purchase, Rivers, Watersheds

Eastern Office
4000 Albemarle St., NW, #303, Washington, DC 20016
Phone: 202-364-2550; Fax: 202-364-2520; E-mail: rivernet2@aol.com
Scope: National
Contact(s):
Watershed Program Associate: ALISON COOK

Northern Rockies Office: Riverlands Conservancy Field Office
44 North Last Chance Gulch, #4, Helena, MT 59601
Phone: 406-442-4777; Fax: 406-442-8883
Scope: National
Contact(s):
Contact: HUGH ZACKHEIM
Riverlands Conservancy Director: PHIL WALLIN

RIVER OTTER ALLIANCE, THE
6733 S. Locust Ct., Englewood, CO 80112
Phone: 303-773-2749; Fax: 303-722-7703
Founded: 1990; Membership: 150
Scope: National
Description: The River Otter Alliance promotes the survival of the North American River Otter through education, research, and habitat protection. We support current research and reintroduction programs, monitor abundance and distribution in the United States, and educate through our newsletter on the need to restore and sustain river otter populations.
Contact(s):
President: JUDITH BERG, 4421 S. Parkview Dr., Salt Lake City, UT 84124
Vice-President: DAVID BERG
Secretary: TRACY JOHNSTON, 2715 S. Pierce St., Denver, CO 80227-3531
Treasurer: JOHN MULVIHILL, 6733 S. Locust Ct., Englewood, CO 80112-1007
Publication(s): *River Otter Journal, The*
Keyword(s): Endangered and Threatened Species, Rivers, Trapping, Water Quality, Wildlife Rehabilitation, Otters

RIVERS COUNCIL OF WASHINGTON (formerly Northwest Rivers Council)
509 10th Ave., East, Suite 200, Seattle, WA 98102
Phone: 206-568-1380; Fax: 206-568-1381; E-mail: riverswa@brigadoon.com
Founded: 1984; Membership: 1,000
Scope: Statewide
Description: The mission of the Rivers Council of Washington is to lead an expanding grassroots effort to preserve, enhance, and restore rivers and their watersheds in Washington state for their natural, recreational and cultural values and support compatible efforts of other organizations in the Pacific Northwest.
Contact(s):
President and Chair of Trustees: DOUG NORTH
Vice President: KATE SULLIVAN
Secretary: ANDY HELD
Treasurer: MATT SCOBEL
Executive Director: SCOTT ANDREWS
Publication(s): *Washington Rivers*
Keyword(s): Environmental and Conservation Education, Outdoor Recreation, Rivers, Sustainable Ecosystems, Water Resources, Watersheds

ROCKY MOUNTAIN BIGHORN SOCIETY
P.O. Box 8320, Denver, CO 80201
Founded: 1975; Membership: 1,000
Scope: Statewide
Description: The purpose of the Society is to support the sound management of the Rocky Mountain bighorn sheep and its habitat and to promote the advancement and knowledge of the bighorn.
Contact(s):
President: DENNIS GARDNER, 19114 Silver Ranch Rd., Conifer, CO 80433; Phone: 303-697-4896
Vice President: CLARK KISER, 5580 Lariat Dr., Castle Rock, CO 80401; Phone: 303-660-8597

NON-GOVERNMENTAL ORGANIZATIONS - R

Secretary: DICK TINLIN, 5623 East Long Pl., Englewood, CO 80112; Phone: 303-796-9003
Treasurer: TERRY MARCUM, P.O. Box 866, Edwards, CO 81632; Phone: 970-926-1233
Publication(s): *Bighorn, The; Guide to Sheep Hunting in Colorado*
Keyword(s): Hunting, Trapping, Wildlife and Wildlife Habitat, Wildlife Management, Wildlife Rehabilitation

ROCKY MOUNTAIN ELK FOUNDATION
P.O. Box 8249, Missoula, MT 59807-8249
Phone: 406-523-4500; Fax: 406-523-4550
Founded: 1984; Membership: 110,000
Scope: National
Description: The Foundation's mission is to ensure the future of elk, other wildlife, and their habitat. Projects funded by RMEF include: land protection, habitat enhancement, management, research, conservation education, and hunting heritage.
Contact(s):
Chairman, Board of Directors: PAT GILLIGAN
Vice Chairman, Board of Directors: GEORGE BETTAS
President & CEO: GARY J. WOLFE Ph.D.
Senior Vice President, Finance & Administration/CFO: LARRY PUGH
Senior Vice President, Operations: RON MARCOUX
Senior Vice President of Communication/Public Relations: LANCE SCHELVAN
Vice President of Conservation Programs: ALAN CHRISTENSEN
Vice President of Field Operations/Membership: BILL GEER
Vice President, Legal Affairs/General Counsel: GRANT PARKER
Vice President, Marketing and Planned Giving: DAVID WESLEY
Publication(s): *BUGLE: Journal of Elk Country; Wild Outdoor World (W.O.W.: Kids Conservation Magazine)*
Keyword(s): Environmental and Conservation Education, Hunting, Land Purchase, Open Space, Wildlife and Wildlife Habitat

Intermountain Region Office
1172 S. Oak Leaf Dr., Pueblo West, CO 81007
Scope: Regional
Contact(s):
Regional Director and Contact for CO: MARTY HOLMES; Phone: 719-547-8212
Contact for CO: TOM BROWN; Phone: 303-279-7974
Contact for NM: JOE COKER; Phone: 505-869-0570
Contact for UT: BILL CHRISTENSEN; Phone: 801-254-1922
Contact for WY: DAMIEN MILLER; Phone: 307-332-6084

North-Central Region Office
1320 Canal St., Custer, SD 57730
Scope: Regional
Contact(s):
Regional Director: MIKE MUELLER; Phone: 605-673-2396
Contact for MN and IA: RALPH CINFIO; Phone: 320-203-0932
Contact for ND: LARRY BAESLER; Phone: 605-673-2396
Contact for SD: MIKE MUELLER; Phone: 605-644-2396
Contact for WI: BILL HUNYADI; Phone: 715-769-3559

Northeast Region Office
198 Bennett Rd., Julian, PA 16844
Scope: Regional
Contact(s):
Regional Director: DAVE MESSICS; Phone: 814-353-1667
Contact for DC, DE, MD, NJ, PA: LANCE SCHUL; Phone: 814-343-1807
Contact for ME, NH, VT, NY, CT, MA, RI: DAVE RAGANTESI; Phone: 570-756-3867
Contact for MI and OH: WAYNE BIVANS; Phone: 616-874-9222

Northwest Region Office
9908 Wilbath Ln., Nampa, ID 93686
Scope: Regional
Contact(s):
Regional Director: ART TALSMA; Phone: 208-466-0204
Contact for AK, and Western WA: LLORAN JOHNSON; Phone: 253-539-7651
Contact for Eastern WA: RANCE BLOCK; Phone: 509-226-0388
Contact for MT: KIRK MURPHY; Phone: 406-883-1147
Contact for OR: TOM LYTLE; Phone: 503-362-3062
Contact for Southern ID: ART TALSMA; Phone: 208-466-0204
Contact for Southwest MT and Eastern ID: DAVE TORELL; Phone: 208-528-8914

Pacific Southwest Region Office
P.O. Box 25902, Munds Park, AZ 86017
Scope: Regional
Contact(s):
Contact for AZ: LYLE BUTTON; Phone: 520-714-1774
Contact for Northern CA: MIKE FORD; Phone: 530-842-2021
Contact for NV: TONY KAVALOK; Phone: 775-971-9000
Contact for Southern CA: BILL HARRIS; Phone: 619-486-5601
Regional Director: DAKOTA LIVESAY; Phone: 520-286-1833

South-Central Region Office
1480 8th NE, 186th St., Holt, MO 64048
Scope: Regional
Contact(s):
Regional Director: TERRY CLOUTIER; Phone: 816-320-2681
Contact for IN and IL: DON BLAKELY; Phone: 618-893-4142
Contact for KS and NE: MARK JOHNSON; Phone: 316-672-2201
Contact for MO: DOUG SONNTAG; Phone: 417-581-8062
Contact for OK and East TX: RANDY PORTERFIELD; Phone: 903-677-5740
Contact for West TX: JOE COKER; Phone: 505-869-0570

Southeast Region Office
1323 Robert E. Lee Ln., Brentwood, TN 37027
Scope: Regional
Contact(s):
Regional Director: RON WHITE; Phone: 615-370-0370
Contact for AL, AR, LA, MS: KEVIN BROWN; Phone: 662-690-6681
Contact for GA, FL, NC, SC: DALE NOLAN; Phone: 618-985-2707
Contact for KY, TN, VA, WV: JOHN MECHLER; Phone: 423-609-9593

ROGER TORY PETERSON INSTITUTE
311 Curtis St., Jamestown, NY 14701
Phone: 716-665-2473; Fax: 716-665-3794; E-mail: webmaster@rtpi.org; Web Site: www.rtpi.org
Founded: 1984; Membership: 3,000
Scope: Nationwide
Description: The mission of the Roger Tory Peterson Institute is to create a passion for and knowledge of the natural world in the hearts and minds of children by guiding and inspiring the study of nature in our schools and communities.
Contact(s):
President: JIM BERRY; Phone: 716-665-2473; Fax: 716-665-3794; E-mail: jim@rtpi.org
Director of Development: MIKE LYONS; Phone: 716-665-2473; Fax: 716-665-3794; E-mail: mike@rtpi.org
Director of Education: MARK BALDWIN; Phone: 716-665-2473; Fax: 716-665-3794; E-mail: mark@rtpi.org
Keyword(s): Environment, Environmental and Conservation Education, Natural History, Nature Study, Urban and Rural Development

RUFFED GROUSE SOCIETY, THE
451 McCormick Rd., Coraopolis, PA 15108
Phone: 412-262-4044; E-mail: rgshg@aol.com; Web Site: www.ruffedgrousesociety.org
Founded: 1961; Membership: 23,000
Scope: National
Description: Nonprofit conservation organization dedicated to improving the environment for ruffed grouse, woodcock, and other forest wildlife through maintenance, improvement, and expansion of their habitat. Assists private, industrial, county, state, and federal landholders in forest wildlife habitat improvement programs.
Contact(s):
President: JOE R. IRWIN
Executive Vice President: S. PROSSER MELLON

Vice President: EDWIN H. GOTT JR.
Secretary: GAYLEN J. BYKER
Treasurer: STEPHEN F. QUILL
Executive Director: DR. SAMUEL R. PURSGLOVE
Group Director, Administration and Information Systems: RONALD P. BURKERT
Group Director, Field Services: WILLIAM H. GOUDY; Phone: 570-745-7313
Group Director, Headquaters Services: BRENDA K. OSBORN
Group Director, Publications and Communications: PAUL E. CARSON
Chief Biologist (All Areas): DAN DESSECKER; Phone: 715-234-8302
Regional Biologist (MI, OH): MARK E. BANKER; Phone: 616-829-4797
Regional Director (MD, OH, PA, Washington, DC, VA, Southeastern States): WILLIAM J. KLEIN; Phone: 724-938-3705
Regional Director (MI): DAVID B. MEDEMA; Phone: 616-245-1161
Regional Director (MN, IN): MARK D. FOUTS; Phone: 715-399-2270
Regional Director (NJ, NY, New England): DONNIE W. NICKERSON; Phone: 607-638-5456
Regional Director (WI): PAUL V. CLANTON; Phone: 715-389-1606
Regional Supervisor of Western States: LOUIS S. GEORGE; Phone: 608-788-1786
RGS-Canada Executive Director (All Canada): JIM ABBEY; Phone: 519-842-6027; E-mail: jimabbey@oxford.net
Publication(s): RGS
Keyword(s): Birds, Environmental and Conservation Education, Forests and Forestry, Wildlife and Wildlife Habitat, Wildlife Management

S

SAFARI CLUB INTERNATIONAL
Headquarters, 4800 W. Gates Pass Rd., Tucson, AZ 85745
Phone: 520-620-1220; Fax: 520-622-1205
Founded: 1971; Membership: 33,000
Scope: International
Description: A world-wide charitable organization of hunter-conservationists dedicated to the conservation of wildlife, education of people, service to people in need and the protection of hunters' rights. Sponsors wildlife management research, field projects and works with national and international agencies and governments to promote conservation programs worldwide. Operates two education facilities: the International Wildlife Museum at headquaters and the American Wilderness Leadership School in Jackson, WY.
Contact(s):
President: LAWRENCE S. KATZ
Secretary: GEORGE BANKS
Treasurer: RON SIMMONS
Executive Director: RUDOLPH A. ROSEN
Conventions Director: PAT JOHNSON
Director of Governmental and Conservation Affairs: RICHARD PARSONS
Education Director: DONALD BROWN
Public Relations Director: BILL YOUNG
Publications Director: STEVE COMUS
Publication(s): Safari Magazine; Safari Times; Safari Times Africa; Safari Club; Worldwide Hunting Annual; Record Book of Trophy Animals.
Keyword(s): Endangered and Threatened Species, Environmental and Conservation Education, Hunting, Museum, Wildlife and Wildlife Habitat

Michigan Office
4285 Van Buren, Hudsonville, MI 49426
Founded: 1973; Membership: 200
Scope: Statewide
Description: Goals are to educate the public, especially children, in the realm of conservation as it relates to the hunter. Especially concerned with environmental respect and the preservation of any endangered species.
Contact(s):
President: TERRY BLAUWKAMP; Phone: 616-669-1610
Education: BETTY DYKSTRA; Phone: 616-676-9704
President-Elect: LEN VINING; Phone: 616-698-7440
Program: LANCE NORRIS; Phone: 616-798-3410
Secretary and Treasurer: DENNY ANASTOR; Phone: 616-942-8877

South Africa Office
P.O. Box 10362, Centurion 0046 South Africa
Phone: 27-12/663-8073; Fax: 27-12/663-8075
Scope: National

Washington, DC Office
445-B Carlisle Dr., Herndon, VA 20170
Phone: 703-709-2293; Fax: 703-709-2296
Scope: National

SAFE ENERGY COMMUNICATION COUNCIL
1717 Massachusetts Ave., NW, Suite 106, Washington, DC 20036
Phone: 202-483-8491; Fax: 202-234-9194; Web Site: www.safeenergy.org
Founded: 1980
Scope: National
Description: A coalition of 10 national environmental, safe energy, and public interest media groups. SECC produces broadcast and print ads, studies, commentaries, and graphic editorial services to promote sustainable energy policies and respond to nuclear industry and utility campaigns and helps groups develop media skills.
Contact(s):
President: ANDREW SCHWARTZMAN
Executive Director: SCOTT DENMAN
Administrative Director: SARAH SWEETMAN
Communications Director: LINDA GUNTER
Research Director: CHRISTOPHER MOSER
Publication(s): Power Boosters; MYTHBusters Series; Viewpoint; Enfacts; polls and various energy reports
Keyword(s): Energy, Energy Conservation, Environment, Nuclear Energy, Renewable Resources, Training

SAN JUAN PRESERVATION TRUST, THE
Box 327, Lopez Island, WA 98261
Phone: 360-468-3202; Fax: 360-468-3509; E-mail: sjptrust@rockisland.com; Web Site: www.rockisland.com/~sjptrust/
Founded: 1979; Membership: 1,300
Scope: Statewide
Description: The trust is supported by voluntary contributions from members who support the preservation of wildlife, scenery, and natural heritage of the San Juan Islands of Washington state.
Contact(s):
President: JUDY GILSON MOODY
Vice President: DALE HAZEN
Secretary: BOB DITTMER
Treasurer: MORRIS DALTON
Publication(s): Preserve Farmlands; A Place in the Islands; Landowner's Guide; Mom's Marsh and Other Fine Places (video)
Keyword(s): Islands, Wildlife and Wildlife Habitat

SANIBEL-CAPTIVA CONSERVATION FOUNDATION, INC.
P.O. Box 839, 3333 Sanibel-Captiva Rd., Sanibel, FL 33957
Phone: 941-472-2329; Fax: 941-472-6421; E-mail: sccf@sccf.org; Web Site: www.sccf.org
Founded: 1967
Scope: Statewide
Description: The Sanibel-Captiva Conservation Foundation is a not-for-profit organization dedicated to the preservation of natural resources and wildlife habitat on and around Sanibel and Captiva Islands. Community programs include: Land acquisition, habitat management, landscaping for wildlife, research, education, wildlife assistance, and sea turtle conservation program. The Foundation utilizes the time and talent of over 250 dedicated volunteers.

NON-GOVERNMENTAL ORGANIZATIONS - S

Contact(s):
Executive Director: ERICK LINDBLAD
Business Manager: JEAN BEACH
Education Director: KRISTIE ANDERS
Restoration Ecologist: DAVID CEILLEY
Native Plant Nursery Manager: KATHY BOONE
Publication(s): *Conservation Update; Walk in the Wetlands; Growing Native*
Keyword(s): Environmental and Conservation Education, Habitat Conservation, Islands, Land Management, Land Protection, Wetlands, Wildlife and Wildlife Habitat

SASKATCHEWAN WILDLIFE FEDERATION
444 River St., W., Moose Jaw, Saskatchewan S6H 6J6 Canada
Phone: 306-692-8812; Fax: 306-692-4370
Founded: 1929
Scope: Statewide
Description: Affiliated with the Canadian Wildlife Federation. A nonprofit, citizens' conservation group established for the protection and enhancement of fish and wildlife habitat. One hundred and thirty-seven local branches representing 32,000 members. Includes the Habitat Trust Fund holding title to 15,000 purchased and donated acres, and the Wildlife Tomorrow Program with 400,000 acres under free easement.
Contact(s):
President: JOYCE LORENZ, Box 545, Raymore, Saskatchewan S0A 3JO Canada; Phone: 306-746--4313; Fax: 306-746-5810
Executive Director: ROBERT NOWASAD, 444 River St. W., Moose Jaw, Saskatchewan S6H 6J6 Canada; Phone: 306-692-7772
Land Coordinator: JAMES KROSHUS, 444 River St. W., Moose Jaw, Saskatchewan S6H 6J6 Canada; Phone: 306-693-9022
Officer Manager: SANDRA DEWALD, 444 River St. W., Moose Jaw, Saskatchewan S6H 6J6 Canada; Phone: 306-692-8812
Wildlife Tomorrow Coordinator: CLINT SANBORN, 444 River St. West, Moose Jaw, Saskatchewan S6H 6J6 Canada; Phone: 306-692-3374
Publication(s): *Outdoor Edge*

SAVE AMERICA'S FORESTS
4 Library Ct., SE, Washington, DC 20003
Phone: 202-544-9219
Founded: 1990; Membership: 6,000
Scope: National
Description: A nationwide coalition of grassroots regional and national environmental groups, public interest groups, responsible businesses, and individuals working together to pass strong forest protection legislation in the U.S. Congress.
Contact(s):
Director: CARL ROSS
Co-Director: MARK WINSTEIN
Publication(s): *Save America's Forests Magazine*
Keyword(s): Biodiversity, Forests and Forestry, National Forests, Public Lands, Sustainable Development, Sustainable Ecosystems

SAVE OUR RIVERS, INC.
P.O. Box 122, Franklin, NC 28744
Phone: 828-369-7877; Fax: 828-369-7877; E-mail: rivers@dnet.net
Founded: 1990; Membership: 200
Scope: Statewide
Description: Committed to facilitating active public involvement in decisions concerning our rivers by providing information, initiating programs, encouraging public awareness, promoting coordination of services, activities, resources and opportunities.
Contact(s):
President: PEG JONES
Publication(s): *The Current*
Keyword(s): Conservation, Cultural Preservation, Habitat Conservation, Litter, Riparian Restoration, Rivers, Runoff, Streams, Water Pollution, Watersheds

SAVE SAN FRANCISCO BAY ASSOCIATION
1600 Broadway, Suite 300, Oakland, CA 94612
Phone: 510-452-9261; Fax: 510-452-9266; E-mail: savebay@savesfbay.org; Web Site: http://www.savesfbay.org
Founded: 1961; Membership: 20,000
Scope: Local
Description: Member-supported, non-profit environmental organization dedicated to restoring and protecting San Francisco Bay. We work for the improvement of water quality, adequate fresh water inflow and protection of the Bay's plant, wildlife, fish and human populations and their habitats. Our efforts are focused on public education, collaboration with other organizations, coalition building, litigation, the monitoring of regulatory agencies and input into the legislative process.
Contact(s):
President: NANCY STRAUCH
Vice President: JAKE WARNER
Executive Director: DAVID LEWIS
Editor: PAUL REVIER
Publication(s): *Watershed; information fact sheets*
Keyword(s): Environmental and Conservation Education, Water Pollution, Water Resources, Wetlands, Wildlife and Wildlife Habitat

SAVE THE BAY, INC.
434 Smith St., Providence, RI 02908-3770
Phone: 401-272-3540; Fax: 401-273-7153; Web Site: www.savebay.org
Founded: 1970; Membership: 20,000
Scope: Statewide
Description: Save The Bay is dedicated to restoring and protecting Narragansett Bay--a designated estuary of national significance. As a nonprofit, member-supported environmental organization, Save The Bay works to ensure that the environmental quality of Narragansett Bay and its watershed is restored and protected from the harmful effects of human activity.
Contact(s):
President: KATE KILGUSS
Executive Director: H. CURTIS SPALDING
Editor: JAKE GEORGE
Publication(s): *Bay Bulletin; Backyards on the Bay: A Yard Care Guide for the Coastal Home Owner; Coastal Property and Landscape Management Guidebook*
Keyword(s): Water Pollution Management, Watersheds

SAVE THE DUNES COUNCIL
444 Barker Rd., Michigan City, IN 46360
Phone: 219-879-3937; Fax: 219-872-4875; E-mail: std@savedunes.org; Web Site: www.savedunes.org
Founded: 1952; Membership: 2,000
Scope: National
Description: Dedicated to the preservation of the Indiana Dunes National Lakeshore for public use and enjoyment. Concerned with protecting the ecological values of the dunes region, preserving Lake Michigan, and combating air, water, and hazardous waste pollution. Established by Dorothy Buell.
Contact(s):
Assistant Director: CHARLOTTE J. READ
President: THOMAS SERYNEK, 1000 N. Warrick, Gary, IN 46403; Phone: 219-938-5410
Treasurer: MARK MIHALO, 8 Diana Road, Ogden Dunes, Portage, IN 46368; Phone: 219-763-4871
Executive Director: THOMAS R. ANDERSON
1st Vice President: DOROTHY POTUCEK, 1608 Parkview Ave., Whiting, IN 46394
Editor: CHARLOTTE J. READ
Publication(s): *Challenging the Agency; Newsletter*
Keyword(s): Air Quality and Pollution, Land Preservation, Outdoor Recreation, Public Lands, Water Pollution

Save the Dunes Conservation Fund
444 Barker Rd., Michigan City, IN 46360
Scope: National
Description: Educational and non-lobbying 501c(3) fund to support the goals of the Save the Dunes Council.

Contact(s):
Executive Director: THOMAS R. ANDERSON
Fund Director: SANDRA WILMORE
Keyword(s): Environmental and Conservation Education, Research, Streams, Watersheds

SAVE THE HARBOR/SAVE THE BAY
59 Temple Pl., Suite 304, Boston, MA 02111
Phone: 617-451-2860; Fax: 617-451-0496
Founded: 1986; Membership: 2,000
Scope: Statewide
Description: Save the Harbor/Save the Bay is a nonprofit organization whose mission is to foster a positive vision of Boston Harbor and Massachusetts Bay, and to build a broad-based constituency to promote the restoration and protection of these valuable resources. Services include narrated boat tours of Boston Harbor, discussions of harbor pollution, cleanup projects, history, celebratory events, summer youth program, and a Baywatch Program.
Contact(s):
Chairperson: BETH NICHOLSON
Director of Operations: JODEEN WETHERELL
Director of Policy: CATE DOHERTY
Keyword(s): Environment, Water Pollution, Water Quality, Water Resources, Watersheds

SAVE THE MANATEE CLUB
500 N. Maitland Ave., Maitland, FL 32751
Phone: 407-539-0990; Fax: 407-539-0871; E-mail: education@savethemanatee.org; Web Site: www.savethemanatee.org
Founded: 1981; Membership: 40,000
Scope: National
Description: A national nonprofit organization founded by Governor Bob Graham and singer and songwriter Jimmy Buffett. Objectives are public awareness and education; funding research, rescue, rehabilitation and advocacy and appropriate legal action for the endangered West Indian manatee and its habitat. Funded primarily by the club's Adopt-A-Manatee program.
Contact(s):
Executive Director: JUDITH VALLEE
Co-Chairman: E. F. STALLINGS, P.O. Box 8776, Naples, FL 34101
Co-Chairman: JIMMY BUFFETT, c/o Margaritaville Store, 424A Fleming St., Key West, FL 33040; Phone: 305-296-9089
Communications Director: NANCY SADUSKY
Keyword(s): Endangered and Threatened Species, Environmental and Conservation Education, Mammals, Marine Mammals

SAVE THE SOUND, INC.
185 Magee Ave., Stamford, CT 06902
Phone: 203-327-9786; Fax: 203-967-2677; E-mail: savethesound@snet.net; Web Site: www.savethesound.org
Founded: 1972; Membership: 4,000
Scope: Regional
Description: Save the Sound, Inc. is devoted to protecting, restoring, and appreciating Long Island Sound and its watershed. With a staff of nine full-time employees and additional seasonal employees, STS operates year-round programs in education, research, and advocacy, including Sea Camp, Soundshore Ecology, water quality monitoring, habitat restoration, beach cleanups, and an extensive library.
Contact(s):
Chairman: SHEILA O'NEILL
President: JOHN ATKIN
Secretary: LARRY McGAUGHEY
Treasurer: WILLIAM JESSUP
Chairman Emeritus: ARTHUR GLOWKA
Vice Chairman: LARRY BINGAMAN
Publication(s): *Save the Sound News (Quarterly Newsletter); Water Quality Monitoring: A Guide for Concerned Citizens; Harbor Watch Report (1986-1992); The Sound Connection Curriculum Guide; Long Island Sound Municipal Report Cards*
Keyword(s): Coasts, Environmental and Conservation Education, Environmental Preservation, Restoration, Water Pollution, Wetlands

SAVE THE SOUND, INC. At GARVIES POINT MUSEUM
50 Barry Dr., Glen Cove, NY 11542
Phone: 516-759-2165; Fax: 516-759-0644
Scope: Statewide

SAVE WETLANDS AND BAYS
R.D. 6 Box 98, Millsboro, DE 19966
Phone: 302-945-1317
Founded: 1989; Membership: 230
Scope: Statewide
Description: To protect Delaware's inland bays and fringing marshes from perceived threats.
Contact(s):
Contact: TIL PURNELL

SAVE-THE-REDWOODS LEAGUE
114 Sansome St., Rm. 605, San Francisco, CA 94104
Phone: 415-362-2352
Founded: 1918
Scope: National
Description: Established to rescue from destruction representative areas of our primeval forests; to cooperate with the California Department of Parks and Recreation, the National Park Service, and other agencies in establishing redwood parks and other parks and reservations; to purchase redwood groves by private subscription; to support reforestation and conservation of our forest areas.
Contact(s):
President: RICHARD C. OTTER
Treasurer: FRANK W. WESTWORTH, P.O. Box 44614, San Francisco, CA 94144-0001
Chairman of the Board: BRUCE S. HOWARD
General Counsel: KATE ANDERTON
Secretary and Executive Director (Acting): KATE ANDERTON
Publication(s): *California Redwood Parks and Preserves; Trees, Shrubs and Flowers of the Redwood Region; Redwoods of the Past; Story Told by a Fallen Redwood*
Keyword(s): Forests and Forestry, Land Purchase, Public Lands

SCENIC AMERICA
Headquarters, 801 Pennsylvania Ave., SE, Suite 300, Washington, DC 20003
Phone: 202-543-6200; Fax: 202-543-9130; E-mail: scenic@scenic.org; Web Site: www.scenic.org
Founded: 1978
Scope: National
Description: National membership organization dedicated to preserving and enhancing the scenic character of America's communities and countryside. Provides information and technical assistance on billboard and sign control, scenic byways, tree preservation, highway design, cellular tower siting, and other scenic conservation issues.
Contact(s):
Chair: MADELEINE APPEL
President: MEG MAGUIRE
Vice President for Program Development: RAY FOOTE
Publication(s): *Viewpoints; The Grassroots Advocate; Fighting Billboard Blight: An Action Guide for Citizens and Elected Officials; series of videos and technical bulletins*
Keyword(s): Environmental and Conservation Education, Land Preservation, Land Use Planning, Landscape Architecture, Natural History, Urban Environment

Citizens for a Scenic Florida
505 Wharfside Way, Jacksonville, FL 32207
Phone: 904-396-0037; Fax: 904-398-4647; E-mail: scenicfl@bellsouth.net; Web Site: www.scenicflorida.org
Founded: 1998
Scope: Statewide
Description: Citizens for a Scenic Florida: Preserving Florida's Scenic Heritage.
Publication(s): *Scenic Florida*

NON-GOVERNMENTAL ORGANIZATIONS - S

Keyword(s): Natural Areas

Scenic California
275 5th St., Suite 200, San Francisco, CA 94103
Phone: 415-546-1231; Fax: 415-546-1232; E-mail: gtp@sirius.com
Founded: 1998
Scope: Statewide
Description: Scenic California is dedicated to protecting natural beauty in the environment, preserving and enhancing landscapes and streetscapes, protecting historical and cultural resources, promoting the enhancement of scenic approaches and settings of cities and towns, improving community appearance and fostering the establishment and preservation of scenic roads and viewsheds.
Contact(s):
President: ANN BOREN

Scenic Michigan
P.O. Box 30235, Lansing, MI 48909
Phone: 517-371-1041; Fax: 517-371-1505; E-mail: mtanton@freeway.net; Web Site: www.mucc.org/scenic
Scope: Statewide
Description: Scenic Michigan started under the aegis of Michigan United Conservation Clubs, the largest nonprofit conservation organization in the United States, as a billboard control task force in 1989. The mission of Scenic Michigan is to protect and enhance the appearance and scenic character of Michigan's communities and countryside.
Contact(s):
Environmental Policy Specialist: DANA DEBEL
Executive **Publication(s):** *Scenic Michigan (Newsletter)*

Scenic Missouri
5650A South Sinclair, Columbia, MO 65203
Phone: 573-446-3129; Fax: 573-443-3748; E-mail: scenicmo@tranquility.net; Web Site: www.scenicmissouri.org
Founded: 1993
Scope: Statewide
Description: Scenic Missouri was founded because of a growing concern about the loss of Missouri's scenic heritage. Its mission is to preserve and enhance the scenic beauty of Missouri.
Contact(s):
Executive Director: KARL KRUSE
Publication(s): *Scenic Views*

Scenic North Carolina
P.O. Box 628, Raleigh, NC 27602
Phone: 919-832-3687; Fax: 919-832-3299; E-mail: scenic.nc@worldnet.att.net; Web Site: www.mcis.duke.edu/snc.htm
Scope: Statewide
Description: Our sense of identity as North Carolinians is tied to special places and buildings and views. Each type of landscape has its own kind of beauty, character and uniqueness. Scenic North Carolina is dedicated to preserving and enhancing scenic resources and community appearance in North Carolina.
Contact(s):
Executive Director: DALE McKEEL
Publication(s): *Scenic North Carolina News*

Scenic Texas
1200 Post Oak Blvd., Suite 324, Houston, TX 77056
Phone: 713-629-0481; Fax: 713-629-0485; E-mail: scenicvu@ncosoft.com
Scope: Statewide
Description: The mission of Scenic Texas is to preserve and enhance the scenic character of the visual environment. Scenic Texas has chapters in Houston, Austin, San Antonio, Fort Worth, and Galveston.
Publication(s): *Scenic Views*

SCENIC HUDSON, INC.
9 Vassar St., Poughkeepsie, NY 12601
Phone: 914-473-4440; Fax: 914-473-2648; E-mail: admin@scenichudson.org; Web Site: www.scenichudson.org
Founded: 1963
Scope: Statewide
Description: A nonprofit conservation and environmental organization dedicated to protecting and enhancing the scenic, natural, recreational and historic treasures of the Hudson River Valley. Speakers' Bureau available to the public.
Contact(s):
Chairman: DAVID N. REDDEN; Phone: 914-473-4440
Secretary: ELIZABETH B. PUGH
Treasurer: MARJORIE L. HART
Executive Director: NED SULLIVAN
Editor: MICHELLE TERWILLIGER
Publication(s): *Scenic Hudson News; Signs of the Times (Creative Ideas for Signage; Dealing with Airport Growth; Cooling Tower Report; Understanding Traffic and its Impacts; PCB Dredging Report; Cell Tower Report; Adventure Guide*
Keyword(s): Air Quality and Pollution, Environmental Preservation, Land Preservation, Land Protection, Natural History, Open Space, Rivers, Transportation, Sprawl

SCIENTISTS CENTER FOR ANIMAL WELFARE
7833 Walker Dr., Suite 410, Greenbelt, MD 20770
Phone: 301-345-3500; Fax: 301-345-3503; E-mail: info@scaw.com; Web Site: www.scaw.com
Scope: National
Description: A nonprofit educational organization that promotes the belief that high standards of animal welfare complement the quality of scientific results. SCAW publishes educational material about current issues of animal use in research, testing, and teaching.
Contact(s):
Executive Director: LEE KRULISCH
Keyword(s): Agriculture, Aquariums, Biology, Biotechnology, Birds, Endangered and Threatened Species, Environmental Ethics, Fisheries, Health and Nutrition, Mammals, Marine Mammals, Nongame Wildlife, Public Health Protection, Reptiles and Amphibians, Research

SEA SHEPHERD CONSERVATION SOCIETY
P.O. Box 628, Venice, CA 90294
Phone: 310-301-7325; Fax: 310-574-3161
Founded: 1977; Membership: 28,600
Scope: National
Description: An international direct action marine mammal conservation organization involved in stopping marine mammal slaughters. Special projects include: campaigns against drift net fishing, whaling, the faeroese pilot whale slaughter, and sealing. The Society owns and operates three ships, the Ocean Warrior, the submarine Mirage and the Edward Abbey.
Contact(s):
Editor: PAUL WATSON
Founder: CAPT. PAUL WATSON
Publication(s): *Sea Shepherd Log*
Keyword(s): Endangered and Threatened Species, Environmental and Conservation Education, Fisheries, International Conservation, Marine Mammals

Australia Office
P.O. Box 334, Clifton Hill VIC 3068 Australia
Scope: National

Canada Office
P.O. Box 48446, Vancouver, British Columbia V7X 1A2 Canada
Scope: National

Germany Office/European Community
Postfach 20 05 63, Herne 44635 Germany
Scope: Regional

Great Britain Office
35 Vicarage Grove, London SE5 7LY United Kingdom
Scope: National

Netherlands Office
P.O. Box 97702, 2509 GC The Hague, Netherlands
Scope: National

USA Office
3007 Washington Blvd., #225, Marina del Rey, CA 90292
Phone: 310-301-7325; Fax: 310-574-3161
Scope: National

SEACAMP ASSOCIATION, INC.
1300 Big Pine Ave., Big Pine Key, FL 33043-3336
Phone: 305-872-2331; Fax: 305-872-2555; E-mail: seacampnc@webtv.net; Web Site: www.seacamp.org
Founded: 1964
Scope: International
Description: Non-profit organization encompassing two marine education organizations in the Florida Keys, a summer camp and the school program Newfound Harbor Marine Institute (NHMI). Strong international program with Russia. Member NAAEE.
Contact(s):
Executive Director: IRENE HOOPER
Director of Special Projects: DR. RUSSEL E. BACHERT JR.
Camp Director: GRACE UPSHAW
Director of International Programs: DR. ELENA ISTOMA
Director of NHMI: CHUCK BRANDT
Keyword(s): Camp, Environmental and Conservation Education, Inquiry Based Education, Internships, Mangrove Habitats, Marine Conservation, Nature Study, Ocean Conservation, Outdoor Education, Outdoor Recreation

SEACOAST ANTI-POLLUTION LEAGUE
P.O. Box 1136, Portsmouth, NH 03802
Phone: 603-431-5089
Founded: 1969; Membership: 300
Scope: Statewide
Description: To promote the wise use of natural resources of the seacoast region, and to alert and educate the community and relevant government agencies of threats to the environment. SAPL works to prevent ecological, economic and public health damage from the Seabrook nuclear reactor, the Portsmouth Naval Shipyard and over-development.
Contact(s):
President: DAVIE HILLS
Vice President: MARY METCALF
Secretary: JOHANNA LYONS
Treasurer: JIM HORRIGAN
Executive Director: STEVE HABERMAN
Tag Coordinator: PETER VANDERMARK
Keyword(s): Development, Nuclear/Radiation

SEAPLANE PILOTS ASSOCIATION
421 Aviation Way, Frederick, MD 21701
Phone: 301-695-2083
Founded: 1972; Membership: 7,000
Scope: National
Description: A unit formed to provide seaplane services to agencies and environmental groups involved in forest fire detection, search and rescue, wildlife surveys, pollution patrols, and other related environmental and ecological projects.
Contact(s):
President: . J. J. FREY
Vice President: WALTER WINDUS
Secretary: JERRY POTTER
Executive Director: MICHAEL VOLK
Publication(s): *Water Flying; Water Flying Annual; Water Landing Directory*
Keyword(s): Coasts, Lakes, Outdoor Recreation, Rivers, Water Resources

SHELBURNE FARMS
1611 Harbor Rd., Shelburne, VT 05482
Phone: 802-985-8686; Fax: 802-985-8123; Web Site: www.shelburnefarms.org/
Scope: Regional
Description: Shelburne Farms is a 1,400 acre working farm, national historic site and non-profit environmental education center. Our mission is to cultivate a conservation ethic by teaching and demonstrating stewardship of our natural and agricultural resources.
Contact(s):
President: ALEXANDER S. WEBB; Phone: ext. 16; E-mail: awebb@shelburnefarms.org
VP and Program Director: MEGAN C. CAMP; Phone: ext. 14; E-mail: mcamp@shelburnefarms.org
School Programs Director: JUDY ELSON; Phone: ext. 27; E-mail: jelson@shelburnefarms.org
Publication(s): *Project Seasons; This Lake Alive*
Keyword(s): Agriculture, Environmental and Conservation Education, Forest Stewardship, Historic Preservation, Land Protection, Natural Systems, Stewardship, Sustainable Agriculture, Wetlands, Environmental Education Curriculum

SIERRA CLUB
Headquaters, 85 2nd St., 2nd Fl., San Francisco, CA 94105-3459
Phone: 415-977-5500; Fax: 415-977-5799; E-mail: information@sierraclub.org; Web Site: www.sierraclub.org/
Founded: 1892; Membership: 550,000
Scope: National
Description: To explore, enjoy, and protect the wild places of the earth; to practice and promote the responsible use of the earth's ecosystems and resources; to educate and enlist humanity to protect and restore the quality of the natural and human environment; and to use all lawful means to carry out these objectives. With 65 chapters and 396 groups in North America, the Club's nonprofit program work includes legislation, litigation, public information, publishing, wilderness outings, and conferences. Founded by John Muir.
Contact(s):
President: CHARLES MCGRADY
Vice-President: NICK AUMEN
Secretary: CHARLIE OGLE
Treasurer: ANNE EHRLICH
Fifth Officer: JENNIFER FERENSTEIN
Executive Director: CARL POPE
Associate Executive Director of Conservation and Communications: BRUCE HAMILTON
Communication Director: KIM HADDOW
Director of Conservation Field Services: BOB BINGAMAN
Editor-in-Chief of Sierra: JOAN HAMILTON
Publisher of Books: HELEN SWEETLAND
Publisher of Sierra: ARUN MADAN
Senior Advisor to the Executive Director: GENE COAN
Publication(s): *Sierra; Planet, The; chapter and group newsletters*
Keyword(s): Air Quality and Pollution, Energy, International Conservation, Public Lands, Toxic Substances

Alaska Office
241 E. 5th Ave., #205, Anchorage, AK 99501
Phone: 907-276-4048; Fax: 907-258-6807; E-mail: nw-ak.field@sierraclub.org
Scope: Regional
Contact(s):
Associate Representative: SALLY KABISH, P.O. Box 467, Homer, AK 99603; Phone: 907-235-2896; Fax: 907-235-3720
Senior Alaska Specialist: JACK HESSION

Alaska Rainforest Campaign Office
P.O. Box 467, Homer, AK 99603-0467
Phone: 907-235-2896; Fax: 907-235-3720; E-mail: sally.kabisch@sierraclub.org
Scope: Regional
Keyword(s): Rainforests

Appalachian Field Office
200 N. Glebe Rd., Suite 905, Arlington, VA 22203-3728
Phone: 703-312-0533; Fax: 703-312-0508; E-mail: ap-va.field@sierraclub.org
Scope: Regional

NON-GOVERNMENTAL ORGANIZATIONS - S

Description: DC, DE, GA, MD, NC, SC, TN, VA, WV
Contact(s):
Appalachian Field Director: JOY OAKES

Atlantic Coast Office
P.O. Box 160, Nassau, DE 19969
Phone: 302-664-0627; Fax: 302-644-9712; E-mail: mike.damico@sierraclub.org
Scope: Regional

California/Nevada/Hawaii Office and California Legislative Office
1414 K St., Suite 300, Sacramento, CA 95814-3929
Phone: 916-557-1100; Fax: 916-557-9669; E-mail: ca-nc.field@sierraclub.org
Scope: Regional
Contact(s):
Staff Director: BARBARA BOYLE
State Director: BILL CRAVEN

Canada Office
#1 Nicholas St., Suite 620, Ottawa, Ontario K1N 7B7 Canada
Phone: 613-241-4611; Fax: 613-241-2292; E-mail: sierra.club.canada@sierraclub.org
Scope: Regional
Contact(s):
Executive Director: ELIZABETH MAY

Cleveland Office
Clean Steel Project, 2460 Fairmont Blvd., Suite C, Cleveland, OH 44106-3125
Phone: 216-791-9110; Fax: 216-791-9138; E-mail: mw-oh.field@sierraclub.org
Scope: Regional

Colorado Field Office
2260 Baseline Rd., Suite 105, Boulder, CO 80302-7737
Phone: 303-449-5595; Fax: 303-449-6520; E-mail: sw-co.field@sierraclub.org
Scope: Regional

Columbia Basin Office
2703 Klemgard Rd., Pullman, WA 99163
Phone: 509-332-5173; E-mail: nw-cb.field@sierraclub.org
Scope: Regional

Florida Field Office
475 Central Ave., Suite M-1, St. Petersburg, FL 33701
Phone: 727-824-8813; Fax: 727-824-0936; E-mail: frank.jackalone@sierraclub.org
Scope: Regional

Florida-Miami Field Office
2937 SW 27th Ave., Unit 101, Miami, FL 33133
Phone: 305-476-9898; Fax: 305-476-9414; E-mail: jonathan.ullman@sierraclub.org
Scope: Local Region

Georgia Field Office/Louisiana and Alabama Field Office
1447 Peachtree St. NE, Suite 305, Atlanta, GA 30309-3034
Phone: 404-888-9778; Fax: 404-876-5260; E-mail: ap-ga.field@sierraclub.org
Scope: Regional

Midwest Office
214 N. Henry St., #203, Madison, WI 53703
Phone: 608-257-4994; Fax: 608-257-3513; E-mail: mw-wi.field@sierraclub.org
Scope: Regional
Description: IA, IL, IN, KY, MI, MN, MO, OH, WI
Contact(s):
Associate Representative: BILL REDDING
Regional Representative: BRETT HULSEY
Staff Director: CARL ZICHELLA

Montana Field Office
234 E. Mendenhall St., Bozeman, MT 59715
Phone: 406-582-1281; Fax: 406-582-9504; E-mail: np-mt.field@sierraclub.org
Scope: Regional

New York City Office
116 John St., 31st Fl., New York, NY 10038
Phone: 212-791-9291; Fax: 212-791-0839; E-mail: ne-nyc.field@sierraclub.org
Scope: Regional

Northeast Office
85 Washington St., Saratoga Springs, NY 12866
Phone: 518-587-9166; Fax: 518-583-9062; E-mail: ne-ny@sierraclub.org
Scope: Regional
Description: CT, MA, ME, NH, NJ, NY, PA, RI, VT
Contact(s):
Associate Representative: MARION TRIESTE
Associate Representative: MARK BETTINGER
Staff Director: CHRIS BALLANTYNE

Northern Plains
23 N. Scott St., #27, Sheridan, WY 82801
Phone: 307-672-0425; Fax: 307-674-6187; E-mail: np-wy.field@sierraclub.org
Scope: Regional
Description: KS, MT, NE, ND, SD, WY
Contact(s):
Associate Representative: KIRK KOEPSEL
Senior Regional Staff Director: LARRY MEHLHAFF

Northwest Office
180 Nickerson Ave., Seattle, WA 98109
Phone: 206-378-0114; Fax: 206-378-0034; E-mail: nw-wa.field@sierraclub.org
Scope: Regional
Description: AK, ID, OR, WA
Contact(s):
Associate Representative: JIM YOUNG
Staff Director: BILL ARTHUR

Oakland/San Francisco Bay Area Field Office
85 2nd St., 2nd Fl., San Francisco, CA 94105-3441
Phone: 415-977-5730; Fax: 415-977-5702; E-mail: ca-oa.field@sierraclub.org
Scope: Local Region

Sierra Student Coalition
P.O. Box 2402, Providence, RI 02906-0402
Phone: 401-861-6012; Fax: 401-861-6241; E-mail: sierra.student.coalition@sierraclub.org
Scope: National

Southeast Office
1330 21st Way South, Suite 100, Birmingham, AL 35205
Phone: 205-933-9111; Fax: 205-939-1020; E-mail: se-al.field@sierraclub.org
Scope: Regional
Description: AL, AR, FL, LA, MS, TX
Contact(s):
Grassroots Organizer: JOHN McCOWN
Senior Regional Staff Director: JIM PRICE

Southeast Texas/Arkansas Field Office
54 Chicon St., Austin, TX 78702-5461
Phone: 512-472-9094; Fax: 512-472-8710; E-mail: se-tx.field@sierraclub.org
Scope: Regional

Southern California/Nevada Field Office
3345 Wilshire Blvd., Suite #302, Los Angeles, CA 90010
Phone: 213-387-6528; Fax: 213-387-5383; E-mail:

ca-sc.field@sierraclub.org
Scope: Regional
Contact(s):
Sr. Regional Representative: JIM BLOMQUIST

Southwest Office
812 N. 3rd St., Phoenix, AZ 85004
Phone: 602-254-9330; Fax: 602-258-6533; E-mail: sw-az.field@sierraclub.org
Scope: Regional
Description: AZ, CO, NM, OK, UT
Contact(s):
Staff Director: ROB SMITH

Utah Field Office
2273 S. Highland Dr., Suite 2-D, Salt Lake City, UT 84106-2832
Phone: 801-467-9294; Fax: 801-467-9296; E-mail: sw-ut.field@sierraclub.org
Scope: Regional

Washington, DC Office
408 C St., NE, Washington, DC 20002
Phone: 202-547-1141; Fax: 202-547-6009
Scope: National
Contact(s):
Field Director: BOB BINGAMAN
Legislative Director: DEBBIE SEASE

SIERRA CLUB, ALABAMA CHAPTER
P.O. Box 2862, Tuscaloosa, AL 35403-2862
Phone: 205-333-9153; E-mail: peggie.griffin@sfsierra.sierraclub.org; Web Site: www.sierraclub.org/chapters/al/
Scope: Statewide

SIERRA CLUB, ALASKA CHAPTER
201 Barrow St., Suite 101, Anchorage, AK 99501-2429
Phone: 907-276-8768; Fax: 907-276-4048; E-mail: nw-ak.field@sierraclub.org; Web Site: www.sierraclub.org/chapters/ak/
Scope: Statewide

SIERRA CLUB, ANGELES CHAPTER
3435 Wiltshire Blvd., Suite 320, Los Angeles, CA 90010-1904
Phone: 213-387-4287; E-mail: info@angeleschapter.org; Web Site: angeleschapter.org
Scope: Local Region

SIERRA CLUB, ARKANSAS CHAPTER
P.O. Box 22446, Little Rock, AR 72221-2446
Phone: 501-224-2582; E-mail: davisvh@aristotle.net; Web Site: www.aristotle.net/~sierra/
Scope: Statewide

SIERRA CLUB, ATLANTIC CHAPTER
116 John St., 31 St. Fl., New York, NY 10038-3401
Phone: 212-791-2400; Fax: 212-791-0839; E-mail: atlantic.chapter@sierraclub.org; Web Site: www.sierraclub.org/chapters/ny/
Scope: Statewide

SIERRA CLUB, BRITISH COLUMBIA CHAPTER
576 Johnson St., Victoria, British Columbia V8W 1M3
Phone: 250-386-5255; Fax: 250-386-4453; E-mail: scbc@islandnet.com; Web Site: www.sierraclub.ca/bc/
Scope: Statewide

SIERRA CLUB, CASCADE CHAPTER
8511 15th Ave. NE, Rm. 201, Seattle, WA 98115-3101
Phone: 206-523-2147; Fax: 208-523-2079; E-mail: cascade.chapter@sierraclub.org; Web Site: www.cascadechapter.org/
Scope: Statewide

SIERRA CLUB, CONNECTICUT CHAPTER
118 Oak St., Hartford, CT 06106-1514
Phone: 860-525-2500; Web Site: www.sierraclub.org/chapters/ct/
Scope: Statewide

SIERRA CLUB, CUMBERLAND CAHPTER
259 W. Short St., Lexington, KY 40507-1226
Phone: 806-299-4410; Web Site: www.sierraclub.org/chapters/ky/
Founded: 1968
Scope: Statewide

SIERRA CLUB, DACOTAH CHAPTER
R.R. 1 Box 35, Elmerado, ND 58208
Phone: 701-594-4275; Web Site: www.sierraclub.org/chapters/nd/
Scope: Statewide

SIERRA CLUB, DELAWARE CHAPTER
226 Jeffrey Dr., Middletown, DE 19709-9249
Phone: 302-477-1111; E-mail: delaware.chapter@sierraclub.org; Web Site: members.dca.net/sierrade/
Scope: Statewide

SIERRA CLUB, DELTA CHAPTER
P.O. Box 19469, New Orleans, LA 70179-0469
Phone: 504-836-3062; E-mail: delta.chapter@sierraclub.org; Web Site: www.sierraclub.org/chapters/la/
Scope: Statewide

SIERRA CLUB, EASTERN CANADA CHAPTER
517 College St., Suite 237, Toronto, Ontario M6G 4A2
Phone: 416-960-9606; E-mail: sierraec@interlog.com; Web Site: www.sierraclub.ca/eastern/
Scope: Regional

SIERRA CLUB, FLORIDA CHAPTER
475 Central Ave., Suite M1, St. Petersburg, FL 33701-3817
Phone: 813-824-8813; Fax: 813-824-0936; E-mail: GlenJohn@msn.com; Web Site: www.sierraclub.org/chapters/fl/
Scope: Statewide

SIERRA CLUB, GEORGIA CHAPTER
1447 Peachtree St. NE, Suite 305, Atlanta, GA 30309-3034
Phone: 404-607-1262; Fax: 404-876-5260; E-mail: georgia.chapter@sierraclub.org; Web Site: www.sierraclub.org/chapters/ga/
Scope: Statewide

SIERRA CLUB, GRAND CANYON CHAPTER
812 N. 3rd St., Phoenix, AZ 85004-2020
Phone: 602-253-8633; Web Site: www.sierraclub.org/chapters/az/
Scope: Statewide

SIERRA CLUB, HAWAII CHAPTER
P.O. Box 2577, Honolulu, HI 96803-2577
Phone: 808-538-6816; Fax: 808-537-9019; Web Site: www.hi.sierraclub.org
Scope: Statewide

SIERRA CLUB, HOOSIER CHAPTER
212 W. 10th St., Suite A-335, Indianapolis, IN 46202-3007
Phone: 317-972-1903; E-mail: sierra@netdirect.net; Web Site: hoosier.sierraclub.org/
Scope: Statewide

SIERRA CLUB, ILLINOIS CHAPTER
200 N. Michigan Ave., Suite. 505, Chicago, IL 80601-5908
Phone: 312-251-1680; Fax: 312-251-1780; E-mail: illinois.chapter@sierraclub.org; Web Site: www.sierraclub.org/chapters/il/

NON-GOVERNMENTAL ORGANIZATIONS - S

Scope: Statewide

SIERRA CLUB, IOWA CHAPTER
Thoreau Center, 3500 Kingman Blvd., Des Moines, IA 50311-3798
Phone: 515-277-8868; E-mail: iowa.chapter@sierraclub.org; Web Site: www.sierraclub.org/chapters/ia/
Scope: Statewide

SIERRA CLUB, JOHN MUIR CHAPTER
222 S. Hamilton St., Suite 1, Madison, WI 53703-3201
Phone: 608-256-0565; E-mail: john.muir.chapter@sierraclub.org; Web Site: www.sierraclub.org/chapters/wi/
Scope: Statewide

SIERRA CLUB, KANSAS CHAPTER
13114 W. 125th Terr., Overland Park, KS 66213-2463
Phone: 913-814-0583; E-mail: wildlife1@aol.com; Web Site: www.kssierra.org/
Scope: Statewide

SIERRA CLUB, KERN-KAWEAH CHAPTER
P.O. Box 3357, Bakersfield, CA 93385-3357
Phone: 805-822-4371; E-mail: kern-kaweah.chapter@sierraclub.org; Web Site: www.sierraclub.org/chapters/kernkaweah/
Scope: Local Region

SIERRA CLUB, LOMA PRIETA CHAPTER
3921 E. Bayshore Rd., Suite. 204, Palo Alto, CA 94303-4303
Phone: 650-390-8411; Fax: 650-390-8497; E-mail: loma.prieta.chapter@sierraclub.org; Web Site: www.sierraclub.org/chapters/lomaprieta/
Scope: Local Region

SIERRA CLUB, LONE STAR CHAPTER
54 Chicon St., Austin, TX 78702-5451
Phone: 512-477-1729; Fax: 512-477-8526; E-mail: scls@igc.org; Web Site: www.sierraclub.org/chapters/tx/
Scope: Statewide

SIERRA CLUB, LOS PADRES CHAPTER
P.O. Box 90924, Santa Barbara, CA 93190-0924
Phone: 805-966-6622

SIERRA CLUB, MACKINAC CHAPTER
300 N. Washington Sq., Suite 411, Lansing, MI 48933-1223
Phone: 517-484-2372; Fax: 517-484-3108; E-mail: mackinac.chapter@sierraclub.org; Web Site: www.sierraclub.org/chapters/mi/
Scope: Statewide

SIERRA CLUB, MAINE CHAPTER
One Pleasant St., Portland, ME 04101-3936
Phone: 207-761-5616; Fax: 207-773-8313; E-mail: maine.chapter@sierraclub.org; Web Site: www.sierraclub.org/chapters/me/
Scope: Statewide

SIERRA CLUB, MARYLAND CHAPTER
7338 Baltimore Ave., Suite 101A, College Park, MD 20740-3211
Phone: 301-277-7111; Fax: 301-277-6699; E-mail: maryland.chapter@sfsierra.sierraclub.org; Web Site: www.sierraclub.org/chapters/md/
Scope: Statewide

SIERRA CLUB, MASSACHUSETTS CHAPTER
100 Boylston St., Suite 760, Boston, MA 02116-4610
Phone: 617-423-5775; Fax: 617-423-5858; E-mail: massachusetts.chapter@sierraclub.org; Web Site: members.tripod.com/masssierra/
Scope: Statewide

SIERRA CLUB, MISSISSIPPI CHAPTER
921 N. Congress St., Jackson, MS 39202-2554
Phone: 601-352-1026; Web Site: www.sierraclub.org/chapters/ms/
Scope: Statewide

SIERRA CLUB, MONTANA CHAPTER
415 N. 17th Ave., Bozeman, MT 59715-3109
Phone: 406-587-9782
Scope: Statewide

SIERRA CLUB, MOTHER LODE CHAPTER
1414 K St., Suite 300, Sacramento, CA 95814-3929
Phone: 916-557-1100, ext. 108; Fax: 916-557-9669; E-mail: warren.alford@2xtreme.net; Web Site: www.motherlode.org/
Scope: Statewide

SIERRA CLUB, NEBRASKA CHAPTER
P.O. Box 56, York, NE 68467-0056
Phone: 402-362-3603; E-mail: nebraska.chapter@sierraclub.org; Web Site: www.sierraclub.org/chapters/ne/
Scope: Statewide

SIERRA CLUB, NEW COLUMBIA CHAPTER
709 3rd. St., SW, Washington, DC 20024-3103
Phone: 202-488-0505; Fax: 202-484-1789; E-mail: gwynjones@aol.com; Web Site: www.sierraclub.org/chapters/dc/
Scope: Statewide

SIERRA CLUB, NEW HAMPSHIRE CHAPTER
Three Bicentennial Sq., Concord, NH 03301-4058
Phone: 603-224-8222; Fax: 603-224-5719; E-mail: david.ellenberger@sfsierra.sierraclub.org; Web Site: www.sierraclub.org/chapters/nh/
Scope: Statewide

SIERRA CLUB, NEW JERSEY CHAPTER
57 Mountain Ave., Princeton, NJ 08540-2611
Phone: 609-924-3141
Scope: Statewide

SIERRA CLUB, NORTH CAROLINA CHAPTER
1024 Washington St., Raleigh, NC 27605-1258
Phone: 919-833-8467; E-mail: ncsierra@mindspring.com; Web Site: www.sierraclub-nc.org/
Scope: Statewide

SIERRA CLUB, NORTH STAR CHAPTER (Minnesota)
1313 5th St. SE, Suite 324B, Minneapolis, MN 55414-4504
Phone: 612-379-3853; Fax: 612-379-3855; E-mail: north.star.chapter@sierraclub.org; Web Site: www.northstar.sierraclub.org/
Scope: Statewide

SIERRA CLUB, NORTHERN ROCKIES CHAPTER (Idaho/Washington)
P.O. Box 552, Boise, ID 83701-0552
Phone: 208-384-1023; E-mail:
- northern.rockies.chapter@sierraclub.org; Web Site: www.sierraclub.org/chapters/id/
Scope: Regional

SIERRA CLUB, OHIO CHAPTER
145 N. High St., Suite 409, Columbus, OH 43215-3006
Phone: 614-461-0734; Fax: 614-461-0730; E-mail: ohsc2@igc.apc.org; Web Site: www.sierraclub.org/chapters/oh/
Scope: Statewide

SIERRA CLUB, OKLAHOMA CHAPTER
P.O. Box 60644, Oklahoma City, OK 73146-0644
E-mail: oklahoma.chapter@sierraclub.org; Web Site: www.sierraclub.org/chapters/ok/
Scope: Statewide

NON-GOVERNMENTAL ORGANIZATIONS - S

SIERRA CLUB, OREGON CHAPTER
3701 SE Milwaukie Ave., Suite F, Portland, OR 97202-3835
Phone: 503-238-0442; Fax: 503-238-6281; E-mail: orsierra@spiritone.com; Web Site: www.spiritone.com/~orsierra/
Scope: Statewide

SIERRA CLUB, OZARK CHAPTER (Missouri)
914 N. College St., Suite 1, Columbia, MO 65201-4725
Phone: 573-815-9250; Fax: 573-442-7501; E-mail: ozark.chapter@sierraclub.org; Web Site: www.sierraclub.org/chapters/mo/
Scope: Statewide

SIERRA CLUB, PENNSYLVANIA CHAPTER
600 N. Second St., Box 663, Harrisburg, PA 17108
Phone: 717-232-0101; E-mail: pennsylvania.chapter@sierraclub.org; Web Site: www.sierraclub.org/chapters/pa/
Scope: Statewide

SIERRA CLUB, PRAIRIE CHAPTER (AB, MB, SK)
10511 Saskatchewan Dr., Edmonton, Alberta T6E 4S1
Phone: 780-439-1160; Fax: 780-439-5081; E-mail: prairie@edmonton.freenet.ab.ca; Web Site: www.sierraclub.ca/prairie/
Scope: Regional

SIERRA CLUB, REDWOOD CHAPTER (Northern California)
632 5th St., Santa Rosa, CA 95404-4411
Phone: 707-544-7651; Fax: 707-544-9861; E-mail: heyneedles@aol.com; Web Site: www.monitor.net/redwood/
Scope: Statewide

SIERRA CLUB, RHODE ISLAND CHAPTER
10 Abbott Park Pl., 4th Fl., Providence, RI 02903-3735
Phone: 401-521-4734; Fax: 401-331-5266; E-mail: clear@cyberzone.net; Web Site: www.ultranet.com/~clear/schome.html
Scope: Statewide

SIERRA CLUB, RIO GRANDE CHAPTER (New Mexico/West Texas)
606 Alto St., Santa Fe, NM 87501-2519
Phone: 505-820-0201; E-mail: edenland@earthlink.net; Web Site: www.sierra.nm.org/
Scope: Regional

SIERRA CLUB, ROCKY MOUNTAIN CHAPTER (Colorado)
1410 Grant St., Suite 205 B, Denver, CO 80203-1848
Phone: 303-861-8819; Fax: 303-861-2436; E-mail: rmc-office@juno.com; Web Site: www.rmc.sierraclub.org/
Scope: Statewide

SIERRA CLUB, SAN DIEGO CHAPTER (Sourthern California)
3820 Ray St., San Diego, CA 92104-3623
Phone: 619-299-1743; Fax: 619-299-1742; E-mail: san-diego.chapter@sierraclub.org; Web Site: www.sierraclub.org/chapters/sandiego/
Founded: 1948
Scope: Local Region

SIERRA CLUB, SAN FRANCISCO BAY CHAPTER (Northern California)
2530 San Pablo Ave., Suite 1, Berkeley, CA 94702-2000
Phone: 510-848-0800; Fax: 510-848-3383; E-mail: san-francisco-bay.chapter@sierraclub.org; Web Site: www.sierraclub.org/chapters/sanfranciscobay/nindex.html
Scope: Local Region

SIERRA CLUB, SAN GORGONIO CHAPTER (Southern California)
4079 Mission Inn Ave., Riverside, CA 92501-3204
Phone: 909-684-6203; Fax: 909-684-6172; Web Site: www.sierraclub.org/chapters/sangorgonio/
Scope: Local Region

SIERRA CLUB, SANTA LUCIA CHAPTER
P.O. Box 15755, San Luis Obiapo, CA 93406-5755
Phone: 805-543-8727; E-mail: gfelsman@thegrid.net; Web Site: www.sierraclub.org/chapters/santalucia/
Scope: Local Region

SIERRA CLUB, SOUTH CAROLINA CHAPTER
P.O. Box 2388, 1314 Lincoln St., Suite 211, Columbia, SC 29202
Phone: 803-256-8487; Fax: 803-256-8448; E-mail: scsierra@conterra.com; Web Site: www.microbyte.net/sierra
Founded: 1978
Scope: Statewide

SIERRA CLUB, SOUTH DAKOTA CHAPTER
P.O. Box 1624, Rapid City, SD 57709-1624
Phone: 605-348-1345; Fax: 605-348-1344; E-mail: brademey@rapidnet.com; Web Site: www.sierraclub.org/chapters/sd/
Scope: Statewide

SIERRA CLUB, TEHIPITE CHAPTER (Northern California)
P.O. Box 5396, Fresno, CA 93755-5396
Phone: 209-233-1820; E-mail: Tehipite.Chapter@sierraclub.org; Web Site: www.bigbaldy.com/tehipite/
Scope: Local Region

SIERRA CLUB, TENNESSEE CHAPTER
4641 Villa Green Dr., Nashville, TN 37215-4331
Phone: 615-665-1010; E-mail: tennessee.chapter@sierraclub.org; Web Site: www.sierraclub.org/chapters/tn/
Scope: Statewide

SIERRA CLUB, TOIYABE CHAPTER (Nevada/Eastern California)
P.O. Box 8096, Reno, NV 89507-8096
Phone: 702-323-3162; Web Site: www.sierraclub.org/chapters/nv/
Scope: Statewide

SIERRA CLUB, UTAH CHAPTER
2273 Highland Dr., Suite 2D, Salt Lake City, UT 84106-2832
Phone: 801-467-9297; E-mail: utah.chapter@sierraclub.org; Web Site: www.sierraclub.org/chapters/ut/
Scope: Statewide

SIERRA CLUB, VENTANA CHAPTER (Northern California)
P.O. Box 5667, Carmel, CA 93921-5667
Phone: 831-624-8032; E-mail: ventana@mbay.net; Web Site: www.ventana.org/
Scope: Local Region

SIERRA CLUB, VERMONT CHAPTER
P.O. Box 3154, Burlington, VT 05401-0031
Phone: 802-651-0169; Fax: 888-729-4109; Web Site: www.sierraclub.org/chapters/vt/
Scope: Statewide

SIERRA CLUB, VIRGINIA CHAPTER
Six N. 6th St., Richmond, VA 23219-2419
Phone: 804-225-9113; Fax: 804-225-9114; Web Site: www.sierraclubva.org/
Scope: Statewide

SIERRA CLUB, WEST VIRGINIA CHAPTER
P.O. Box 4142, Morgantown, WV 26504-4142
Phone: 304-363-4006; E-mail: shalom.tazewell@sierraclub.org; Web Site: www.wvsierra.org/
Scope: Statewide

NON-GOVERNMENTAL ORGANIZATIONS - S

SIERRA CLUB, WYOMING CHAPTER
P.O. Box 263, Jackson, WY 83001-0263
Phone: 307-734-0441; E-mail: wyoming.chapter@sierraclub.org; Web Site: www.sierraclub.org/chapters/wy/
Scope: Statewide

SIERRA CLUB FOUNDATION, THE
85 Second St., Suite 750, San Francisco, CA 94105
Phone: 415-995-1780
Founded: 1960
Scope: National
Description: A nonprofit, tax-deductible, public foundation established to finance the educational, literary, and scientific projects of citizen-based groups working on national and international environmental problems. Manages assets in excess of $25 million and over 600 regional or special interest funds principally for charitable conservation purposes. Also manages charitable remainder unitrusts and a pooled income fund with assets over $7.5 million.
Contact(s):
President: ROBERT B. FLINT JR.
Vice President: MARLENE FLUHARTY
Secretary: ROGER W. HERSHEY
Treasurer: RICHARD CELLARIUS
Fifth Officer: MICHAEL LOEB
Executive Director: JOHN DECOOK
Controller: IQBAL PARUPIA
Director of Administration: MARY BETH MCGARRAHAN
Director of Finance: MONA CANNON
Grants Manager: ANDREA MANION
Keyword(s): Environmental and Conservation Education, Environmental Law, Land Use Planning, Public Lands, Urban Environment

SIERRA NEVADA FOREST PROTECTION CAMPAIGN
915 20th St., Sacramento, CA 95814
Phone: 916-442-3155; Fax: 916-442-3396; E-mail: sierra_campaign@friendsoftheriver.org; Web Site: www.sierraforests.org
Founded: 1997
Scope: Regional
Description: The Sierra Nevada Forest Protection Campaign works to protect old growth forests, wildlands and wild rivers in the Sierra Nevada mountain range.
Contact(s):
Director: SCOTT HOFFMAN BLACK
Administrative Assistant: PAMELA FLICK; E-mail: pflick@friendsoftheriver.org
Forest Defense Coordinator: CRAIG THOMAS; E-mail: cthomas@innercite.com
Media Coordinator: LEESA MADDOCK; E-mail: sierra_media@freindsoftheriver.org
Outreach Coordinator: BOB BRISTER; Phone: 559-641-7427; Fax: 559-641-7427; E-mail: sierra_outreach@freindsoftheriver.org
Publication(s): *Stand, The*
Keyword(s): Ancient Forests, Biodiversity, Conservation, Ecosystems, Endangered and Threatened Species, Environmental and Conservation Education, Forests and Forestry, Habitat Conservation, Nature Preservation, Preservation and Protection, Riparian Restoration, Sustainability, Wilderness, Wildlands Management, Wildlife and Wildlife Habitat

SINAPU
2260 Baseline Rd., Suite 203, Boulder, CO 80302
Phone: 303-447-8655; Fax: 303-447-8612; E-mail: sinapu@sinapu.org; Web Site: http://www.sinapu.org/
Founded: 1991; Membership: 1,400
Scope: Statewide
Description: Sinapu, named after the Ute word for wolves, is dedicated to the recovery of native carnivores in the Southern Rocky Mountains and to the restoration of the wild habitat in which all species flourish.
Contact(s):
Program Director: ROB EDWARD
Publication(s): *Southern Rockies Wolf Tracks*
Keyword(s): Ancient Forests, Biodiversity, EcoAction, Ecology, Endangered and Threatened Species, Forest Management, Predators, Public Lands, Wildlands, Wildlife and Wildlife Habitat, Wildlife Management, Wolves

SMITHSONIAN INSTITUTION
1000 Jefferson Dr., SW, Washington, DC 20560
Phone: 202-357-2700, TTY: 202-357-1729
Founded: 1846
Scope: National
Description: An education, museum, and research complex as well as an independent trust instrumentality of the United States, established for the increase and diffusion of knowledge. Mission accomplished by: field investigations; national collections development in arts, history, and science, and their preservation for study, reference, and exhibition; scientific research and publications; programs of national and international cooperative research, conservation, education, and training; answering inquiries from the general public and educational and scientific organizations; long-term loan of selected objects; and sharing of research and educational material on the World Wide Web.
Contact(s):
Secretary: IRA MICHAEL HEYMAN
Provost: J. DENNIS O'CONNOR
Under Secretary: CONSTANCE BERRY NEWMAN; Phone: 202-357-3258
Keyword(s): Ancient Forests, Aquatic Habitats, Biodiversity, Birds, Coral Reefs, Cultural Preservation, Culture, Endangered and Threatened Species, Gardening and Horticulture, Historic Preservation, Insects and Butterflies, Mammals, Marine Mammals, Natural History, Reptiles and Amphibians

National Museum of Natural History
10th St. and Constitution Ave., NW, Washington, DC 20560
Phone: 202-357-2700; Fax: TTY357-1729
Scope: National
Description: A center for the study of humans, plants, animals, fossil organisms, terrestrial and extraterrestrial rocks, and minerals as well as other fields of scientific investigation.
Contact(s):
Director: ROBERT FRI
Chief Scientist of Environmental Research Center: DAVID L. CORRELL, Smithsonian Environmental Research Center, P.O. Box 28, Edgewater, MD 21037; Phone: 301-261-4190

National Zoological Park
3000 Block of Connecticut Ave., NW, Washington, DC 20008
Phone: 202-673-4717/Press: 202-673-4840
Scope: National
Description: Research concentrates on a better understanding of animal behavior and health, particularly endangered species. Through the operation of the zoo's Conservation and Research Center in Front Royal, VA, the NZP is developing a program of animal propagation which will aid in the survival of threatened and endangered species. Undertakes a number of programs overseas to develop new methodology and increase knowledge of species in the wild. The Migratory Bird Center is located at the zoo.
Contact(s):
Director: MICHAEL ROBINSON

Office of Fellowships and Grants
Smithsonian Institution, L'Enfant Plaza, SW, Rm. 7300, Washington, DC 20560
Phone: 202-287-3271
Scope: National
Description: Oversees all Smithsonian fellowships and supports a wide range of research activities. It also provides program and administrative assistance for cooperative teaching arrangements between the Institution and local universities in American history, museum studies, and other areas.

Contact(s):
Director: ROBERTA RUBINOFF

Office of International Relations
Smithsonian Institution, 1100 Jefferson Dr., SW, Rm. 3123, Washington, DC 20560
Phone: 202-357-4795
Scope: National
Description: The Foreign Currency Program supports the research activities of American institutions of higher learning through grants in U.S.-owned local currencies.
Contact(s):
Director: FRANCINE BERKOWITZ

Smithsonian Marine Station at Link Port
5612 Old Dixie Highway, Fort Pierce, FL 34946
Phone: 561-465-6632
Scope: National
Description: Marine studies aim at understanding the ecological function of inland waterways and their relationship to land use policy.
Contact(s):
Director: MARY E. RICE

Smithsonian Press/Smithsonian Productions
470 L'Enfant Plaza, Suite 7100, Washington, DC 20560
Phone: 202-287-3738
Scope: National
Description: Information on history, art, and science research is presented in non-technical style in Smithsonian Institution Research Reports issued four times a year by the Office of Public Affairs (202-357-2627). Smithsonian, the official magazine of the Institution, presents general interest feature articles each month in every subject area of the Smithsonian museums: art, culture, history, science, and technology.
Contact(s):
Director: DANIEL GOODWIN
Director of Communications: DAVID UMANSKY, Arts and Industries Bldg., 900 Jefferson Dr. SW, Rm. 4210, Washington, DC 20560; Phone: 202-357-2627
Editor: DON MOSER, Smithsonian Magazine Arts and Industries, Bldg. 900 Jefferson Dr. SW, RM. 1310C, Washington, DC 20560
Publication(s): *Research in various fields is reported in a continuing series of publications by the Smithsonian Institution Press under the following general headings: Smithsonian contributions to Anthropology, to Astrophysics, Botany, Earth Sciences, Marine Sciences, Paleobiology, Zoology, Air and Space, History and Technology, Folklife and Culture.*

Smithsonian Tropical Research Institute
APO AA, FL 34002-0948
Scope: National
Description: A center for advanced studies in tropical biology. Ecology and evolution of tropical organisms are the primary research interests of the staff. The reserve and laboratories on Barro Colorado Island, as well as marine facilities on both coasts, are available to visiting scientists and students.
Contact(s):
Director: IRA RUBINOFF

SOCIETY FOR ANIMAL PROTECTIVE LEGISLATION
P.O. Box 3719, Georgetown Station, Washington, DC 20007
Phone: 202-337-2334
Founded: 1955
Scope: National
Description: Nonprofit organization which keeps its 7,000 correspondents apprised of current developments in legislation for the protection of animals. Has been instrumental in obtaining enactment of 14 federal laws.
Contact(s):
President: MADELEINE BEMELMANS
Vice President: JOHN F. KULLBERG
Secretary: CHRISTINE STEVENS; Phone: 202-337-2334
Treasurer: ROGER L. STEVENS
Executive Secretary: JOHN GLEIBER; Phone: 202-337-2334
Keyword(s): Endangered and Threatened Species, Mammals, Marine Mammals, Trapping, Wildlife and Wildlife Habitat

SOCIETY FOR CONSERVATION BIOLOGY
Attn: Executive Coordinator, Univ. of Washington, Box 351800, Seattle, WA 98195-1800
Phone: 206-616-4054; Web Site: conbio.rice.edu/scb/
Founded: 1985; Membership: 5,700
Scope: National
Description: A professional society dedicated to providing the scientific information and expertise required to protect the world's biological diversity. Incorporated as a tax-exempt scientific organization, the Society has a board composed of scholars, government personnel, and members of both national and international scientific and conservation organizations.
Contact(s):
President: REED NOSS; Phone: 541-757-0687
Secretary: SARAH REICHARD
Treasurer: STEPHEN R. HUMPHREY; Phone: 352-392-9230
Editor: GARY MEFFE; Phone: 352-846-0557
Executive Coordinator: ALICE BLANDIN; Phone: 206-616-4054; E-mail: conbio@u.washington.edu
Publication(s): *Conservation Biology*
Keyword(s): Biodiversity, Endangered and Threatened Species, Environmental and Conservation Education, International Conservation, Sustainable Development

SOCIETY FOR ECOLOGICAL RESTORATION
1207 Seminole Highway, Suite B, Madison, WI 53711
Phone: 608-262-9547; Fax: 608-265-8557
Founded: 1989; Membership: 2,600
Scope: International
Description: Created to promote the development of ecological restoration both as a discipline and as a model for a healthy relationship with nature, and to raise awareness of the value and limitations of restoration as a conservation strategy.
Contact(s):
Chair: EDITH READ; Phone: 714-751-7373, ext. 2133
Secretary: ERIC HIGGS; Phone: 403-492-5469
Treasurer: DR. WILLIAM HALVORSON; Phone: 520-670-6885
Executive Director: DONALD A. FALK; Phone: 520-626-7201
Editor: WILLIAM NIERING; Phone: 203-447-1911
Vice Chair: GEORGE GANN; Phone: 305-245-6547
Publication(s): *Ecological Restoration; SER News; Restoration Ecology; Proceedings from the Seventh SER Conference, 1995*
Keyword(s): Conservation of Protected Areas, Ecology, Environmental and Conservation Education, Renewable Resources, Restoration, Wildlife Management

SOCIETY FOR INTEGRATIVE AND COMPARTIVE BIOLOGY (formerly AMERICAN SOCIETY OF ZOOLOGISTS)
401 N. Michigan Ave., Chicago, IL 60611-4267
Phone: 800-955-1236 or 312-527-6697; Fax: 312-527-6705; E-mail: sicb@sba.com; Web Site: www.sicb.org
Founded: 1890; Membership: 2,200
Scope: National
Description: The Society for Integrative and Comparative Biology (SICB) is one of the largest and most prestigious professional associations of its kind. SICB is dedicated to promoting the pursuit and public dissemination of important information relating to comparative biology.
Publication(s): *American Zoologist, The*
Keyword(s): Biology, Insects and Butterflies, Mammals, Reptiles and Amphibians, Zoology

SOCIETY FOR MARINE MAMMALOGY, THE
Attn: Secretary, Biological Sciences and Center for Marine Science Research, University of NC at Wilmington, Wilmington, NC 28403
Founded: 1981; Membership: 1,000
Scope: National

NON-GOVERNMENTAL ORGANIZATIONS - S

Description: To promote the educational, scientific, and managerial advancement of marine mammal science; gather and disseminate scientific, technical, and management information, through publications and meetings to members of the society, the public, and public and private institutions; and promote the wise conservation and management of marine mammal resources.
Contact(s):
President: DOUGLAS P. DEMASTER, NMFS-NOAA, 7600 Sand Point Way, NE, Seattle, WA 98115; Phone: 206-526-4047; Fax: 206-526-6615; E-mail: Douglas.Demaster@noaa.gov
President-Elect: DANIEL K. ODELL, Sea World, INC., 7007 Sea World Dr., Orlando, FL 32821-8097
Secretary: D. ANN PABST; Phone: 910-962-7266; Fax: 910-962-4066; E-mail: pbasta@uncwil.edu
Treasurer: JOHN BENGTSON, National Marine Mammal Laboratory, 7600 Sand Point Way, NE, Seattle, WA 98115; Phone: 206-526-4016; Fax: 206-526-6615; E-mail: John.Bengtson@noaa.gov
Awards & Scholarship Committee: CAROL FAIRFIELD, NOAA/NMFS/SEFSC, 1002 Forest Dr., Arnold, MD 21012; Phone: 410-757-7224; E-mail: carol.fairfield@noaa.gov
Committee of Scientific Advisors: STEVEN SWARTZ, National Marine Fisheries Service, 75 Virginia Beach Dr., Miami, FL 33149; Phone: 305-361-4487; Fax: 305-361-4478; E-mail: Steven.Swartz@noaa.gov
Education Committee: EDWARD O. KEITH, Oceanographic Center, Nova Southeastern University, 8000 N. Ocean Dr., Dania, FL 33004; Phone: 954-262-8322; Fax: 954-921-7764; E-mail: edwardok@hpd.nova.edu
Editor: WILLIAM F. PERRIN, Southwest Fisheries Science Center, NMFS, P.O. Box 271, LaJolla, CA 92109; Phone: 619-546-7093; Fax: 619-546-7003; E-mail: wperrin@ucsd.edu
Membership Committee: GLENN R. VANBLARICOM, WA Cooperative Fish & Wildlife Research Unit, Box 357980, University of Washington, Seattle, WA 98195; Phone: 206-543-6475; Fax: 206-616-9012
Scientific Program Committee: PAUL E. NACHTIGALL, Marine Mammal Research Program, Hawaii Institute of Marine Science, University of Hawaii, P.O. Box 1106, Kailua, HI 96734; Phone: 808-247-5297; Fax: 808-247-5831; E-mail: nachtiga@hawaii.edu
Publication(s): *Marine Mammal Science*
Keyword(s): Endangered and Threatened Species, International Conservation, Marine Mammals, Natural History, Wildlife Management

SOCIETY FOR RANGE MANAGEMENT
445 Union St., Suite 230, Lakewood, CO 80228
Phone: 303-986-3309
Founded: 1948; Membership: 4,000
Scope: National
Description: Professional society which promotes understanding of rangeland ecosystems and their management and use for tangible products and intangible values; reports new findings and techniques in range science; promotes public appreciation of rangelands and benefits derived from them; promotes professional development of members.
Contact(s):
President: JOHN MELSIN, 340 N. Minnesota St., Carson City, NV 89703
Executive Vice-President: J. C. WHITTEKIEND; E-mail: srmden@ix.netcom.com
1st Vice-President: JIM O'ROURKE, 61 Country Club Rd., Chadron, NE 69337
Technical Editor: GARY FRASIER, 7820 Stag Hollow Rd., Loveland, CO 80538
Director: GLEN SECRIST, 3818 S. Varian Ave., Boise, ID 83709-4703
Director: JIM LINEBAUGH, 3 Yhvona Dr., Carson City, NV 89706
Director: CAROLYN HHULL-SEIG, 501 E. St. Joseph, Rapid City, SD 57701
Director: PAT SHAVER, 2510 Meadow Ln., Woodburn, OR 97071
Director: ANGELA WILLIAMS, Route 1 Box 108, Paoli, OK 73074
Director: BOB BUDD, Red Canyon Ranch, 350 Red Canyon Rd., Lander, WY 82520
Publication(s): *Journal of Range Management; Rangelands*
Keyword(s): Agriculture, Ecology, Environment, Land Use Planning, Prairies, Public Lands, Renewable Resources, Sustainable Resources, Water Quality, Water Resources, Watersheds, Wetlands, Professional Organization

SOCIETY FOR THE PRESERVATION OF BIRDS OF PREY
P.O. Box 66070, Mar Vista Station, Los Angeles, CA 90066-0070
Phone: 310-840-2322
Founded: 1966
Scope: National
Description: A private charity, non-membership, national association which advocates the strictest possible protection for birds of prey; educates the public about the role of raptors in the ecosystem; opposes lenient harvesting practices and the sale of birds of prey for profit; endorses captive raptor breeding as a conservation technique; and supports the largest collection of literature on birds of prey at any public university or facility. The Society is the only and oldest raptor organization which places emphasis on birds of prey occurring naturally in the wild.
Contact(s):
President and Editor: J. RICHARD HILTON; Phone: 310-636-0072
Publication(s): *Raptor Report, The; Leaflet Series*
Keyword(s): Birds, Endangered and Threatened Species, Falconry, Raptors

SOCIETY FOR THE PROTECTION OF NEW HAMPSHIRE FORESTS
54 Portsmouth St., Concord, NH 03301-5400
Phone: 603-224-9945; Fax: 603-228-0423
Founded: 1901; Membership: 10,000
Scope: Statewide
Description: A voluntary nonprofit organization promoting balanced conservation of New Hampshire's renewable natural resources through land protection, education, advocacy, and forestry.
Contact(s):
President/ Forester: JANE A. DIFLEY
Secretary: PETER POWELL
Chairman of the Board: BEN GAYMAN
Editor and Senior Director, Outreach Programs: RICHARD OBER
Senior Director of Land Conservation: PAUL A. DOSCHER
Publication(s): *Forest Notes*
Keyword(s): Environmental and Conservation Education, Forests and Forestry, Land Purchase, Wildlife and Wildlife Habitat, Wildlife Management

SOCIETY OF AMERICAN FORESTERS
5400 Grosvenor Ln., Bethesda, MD 20814
Phone: 301-897-8720; Fax: 301-897-3690; E-mail: safweb@safnet.org
Founded: 1900; Membership: 18,000
Scope: National
Description: The national organization representing all segments of the forestry profession and the accreditation authority for professional forestry education in the U.S. Objectives are to advance the science, technology, education, and practice of professional forestry and to use the knowledge and skills of the profession to benefit society.
Contact(s):
President: KARL F. WENGER
Vice President: JAMES E. COUFAL
Director of Communications and Marketing Services: LORI GARDNER
Director of Conventions and Meetings: DIANE M. PERL
Director of Finance and Administration: CHARLES N. JACKSON
Director of Resource Policy: LAWRENCE W. HILL
Director of Science and Education: P. GREGORY SMITH
Editorial Director and Director of Publications: REBECCA N. STAEBLER
Executive Vice President: WILLIAM H. BANZHAF

Past President: ROBERT W. BOSWORTH
Past President: HARRY V. WIANT JR.
Publication(s): *Journal of Forestry; Forest Science; Southern Journal of Applied Forestry; Northern Journal of Applied Forestry; Western Journal of Applied Forestry; Forestry Source, The*
Keyword(s): Environmental and Conservation Education, Environmental Law, Forests and Forestry, Public Lands, Renewable Resources

SOCIETY OF TYMPANUCHUS CUPIDO PINNATUS LTD.
Stone Ridge II, Suite 280, N 14 W23777 Stone Ridge Dr., Waukeha, WI 53188-1188
Phone: 414-523-3600; Fax: 414-523-3601; E-mail: mihal@execpc.com
Founded: 1961; Membership: 700
Scope: National
Description: Nonprofit organization dedicated to the preservation of the prairie chicken for all future generations in Wisconsin and all threatened and endangered species native to the state of Wisconsin.
Contact(s):
President: RUSSELL C. SCHALLERT
Vice President: LAWRENCE N. DeLEERS, JR., 4665 Highway Y, Saukville, WI 53080
Vice President: GREGORY SEPTON, Milwaukee Public Museum; 800 W. Wells Street, Milwaukee, WI 53233
Vice President: WILLIAM H. EMORY, Klug and Smith Company, 4425 W. Mitchell, Milwaukee, WI 53214
Secretary: KURT W. REMUS, JR., 3860 N. Port Washington Rd., Milwaukee, WI 53217
Treasurer: GLENN N. GOERGEN, Deloitte and Touche, 250 E. Wisconsin Ave., Milwaukee, WI 53202
Publication(s): *Boom*
Keyword(s): Endangered and Threatened Species, Prairies, Wildlife and Wildlife Habitat, Wildlife Management

SOCIETY OF WETLAND SCIENTISTS
P.O. Box 1897, Lawrence, KS 66044-8897
Phone: 913-843-1221; Fax: 913-843-1274; Web Site: www.sws.org
Founded: 1979; Membership: 4,200
Scope: International
Description: International nonprofit education and charitable society of persons interested in wetland science, technology, and related fields. Encourages educational, scientific, and technological development and advancement in all fields of wetland science. Encourages protection, restoration, and stewardship of wetlands. Student memberships and scholarships available.
Contact(s):
President: DUNCAN PATTEN, Arizona State University, Center for Environmental Studies; Phone: 602-965-2975
Vice President: DONALD CAHOON, National Wetlands Resource Center, 700 Cajundome Blvd., Lafayette, LA 70506; Phone: 318-266-8634
Secretary: JANET KEOUGH, Northern Prairie Science Center, 8711 37th St. SE, Jamestown, ND 58401-7317; Phone: 701-252-5363
Treasurer: BARBARA KLEISS, 197 Skyline, Clinton, MS 39056-5844; Phone: 601-965-4600, ext.5682
Past President: WILLIAM MITSCH, OSU School of Natural Resources, Columbus, OH 43210; Phone: 614-292-9774
Publication(s): *Wetlands; SWS Bulletin*
Keyword(s): Aquatic Habitats, Environmental and Conservation Education, Sustainable Ecosystems, Water Resources, Wetlands

SOIL AND WATER CONSERVATION SOCIETY (formerly Soil Conservation Society of America)
Attn: Deb Happe-vonarb, 7515 NE Ankeny Rd., Ankeny, IA 50021-9764
Phone: 515-289-2331; Fax: 515-289-1227; E-mail: swcs@swcs.org; Web Site: www.swcs.org
Founded: 1945; Membership: 12,000
Scope: National
Description: The Soil and Water Conservation Society is a multidisciplinary membership organization advocating protection, enhancement, and wise use of soil, water, and related natural resources. SWCS programs emphasize the interdependence of natural resources through education, publications, and a network of local chapters throughout the U.S. and Canada. SWCS also manages the World Association of Soil and Water Conservation.
Contact(s):
President: DENNIS PATE, 9644 Quail Ridge, Urbandale, IA 50322; Phone: 515-284-4393; Fax: 515-284-4394
Vice President: ADRIAN ACHTERMANN, 3060 Ardoon Way, Silver Lake, OH 44224; Phone: 330-686-9210; Fax: 330-686-9210
Secretary: HOMER WILKES, 526 Whitegate Dr., Jackson, MS 39206; Phone: 601-965-5205; Fax: 601-965-4940
Treasurer: DANA CHAPMAN, Watershed Agricultural Council, R.R. 1 Box 74, NYS Route 10, Walton, NY 13856; Phone: 607-865-7790; Fax: 607-865-4932
Editor: KELLEY HILTERBRAND
Editor: DEB HAPPE-VONARB
Executive Vice President: CRAIG COX; E-mail: craigcox@swcs.org
Ottawa, Canada Representative: JAMES R. BRUCE
Program Development: CHARLES PERSINGER
Washington, DC Representative: NORMAN A. BERG
Publication(s): *Journal of Soil and Water Conservation; Conservation Voices*
Keyword(s): Agriculture, Conservation Tillage, Environmental and Conservation Education, Environmental Protection, International Conservation, Renewable Resources, Research, Soil Conservation, Sustainable Development, Sustainable Ecosystems, Training, Water Quality, Watersheds, Wetlands, Wildlife and Wildlife Habitat

SONORAN INSTITUTE
7650 E. Broadway Blvd., Suite 203, Tucson, AZ 85710
Phone: 520-290-0828; Fax: 520-290-0969; E-mail: sonoran@sonoran.org; Web Site: www.sonoran.org
Founded: 1990
Scope: National
Description: The mission of the Sonoran Institute is to promote community-based conservation strategies that preserve the ecological integrity of protected lands and at the same time meet the economic aspirations of adjoining landowners and communities. Underlying this mission is the conviction that locally driven and inclusive approaches to conservation produce the most effective results.
Contact(s):
Chairman: FRANK GREGG
Vice-Chair: FRED BOSSELMAN
Secretary/Treasurer: JAKE KITTLE
Associate Director: JOHN SHEPARD
Director of Borderlands Program: STEVE CORNELIUS
Associate Director of Borderlands Program: JOAQUIN MURRIET
Director of Communications: LARA SCHMIT
Director of Land Use Policy: LEE NELLIS
Director of Research: MARK BRIGGS
Executive Director: LUTHER PROPST
Program Associate: JOSH SCHACHTER
Research Associate: SUSAN CULP
Keyword(s): Land Use Planning, Public Lands, Riparian Restoration, Stewardship, Sustainable Development, Community Conservation

Northwest Office
210 S. Wallace St., Suite B3C, Bozeman, MT 59715
Phone: 406-587-7331; Fax: 406-587-2027
Scope: Regional
Contact(s):
Director: RAY RASKER
Program Associate: BEN ALEXANDER
Program Associate: BARB CESTERO

SOUND EXPERIENCE
2310 Washington St., Port Townsend, WA 98368
Phone: 360-379-0438

NON-GOVERNMENTAL ORGANIZATIONS - S

Founded: 1989
Scope: National
Description: Sound Experience involves participants in exploration of Puget Sound from the decks of a traditional sailing ship (the 101' Schooner Adventures). Our mission is protecting Puget Sound through education.
Contact(s):
President: JAN GRAY
Vice President: JAN VULK
Secretary: NIK WORDEN
Treasurer: JANE ISRAEL
Executive Director: JENELL DeMATTEO
Keyword(s): Environmental and Conservation Education, Historic Preservation, Outdoor Recreation, Youth Organizations

SOUTH ATLANTIC FISHERY MANAGEMENT COUNCIL
One Southpark Cir., Suite 306, Charleston, SC 29407-4699
Phone: 843-571-4366; E-mail: safmc@noaa.gov
Founded: 1976
Scope: Regional
Description: Responsible for the conservation and management of fish stocks within the 200-mile limit (federal waters) of the Atlantic off the coasts of North Carolina, South Carolina, Georgia, and Florida.
Contact(s):
Chairman: PETE MOFFITT
Executive Director: ROBERT K. MAHOOD
Publication(s): *South Atlantic Update; Fishery Management Plans*
Keyword(s): Fisheries, Marine Fisheries

SOUTH CAROLINA ASSOCIATION OF CONSERVATION DISTRICTS
Attn: President, P.O. Box 612, Camden, SC 29020
Scope: Statewide
Contact(s):
President, Alternate Board Member: JAMES McLEOD; Phone: 803-432-3516; Fax: 803-425-6749
Vice President: LARRY E. NATES, 112 Luther Dr., Gaston, SC 29053; Phone: 803-755-0319
Secretary: DOROTHY LEE, 202 Indian Trail Rd., Seneca, SC 29672; Phone: 864-888-2925
Treasurer: VENNING MORRISON, 917 State St., West Columbia, SC 29169; Phone: 803-796-9204
Board Member: WALTER B. COUSINS, P.O. Box 622, Newberry, SC 29108; Phone: 803-276-1522; Fax: 803-276-4157
Keyword(s): Conservation Districts

SOUTH CAROLINA B.A.S.S. CHAPTER FEDERATION
Attn: President, 1469 Schurlknight Rd., St. Stephen, SC 29479
Scope: Statewide
Description: An organization of Bassmaster chapters, affiliated with the Bass Anglers Sportsman Society, organized to fight pollution, assist state and national conservation agencies in their efforts, and teach the young people of our country good conservation practices. Dedicated to the realistic conservation of our water resources.
Contact(s):
President: TONY BENNETT; Phone: 803-567-4680
Conservation Director: TOM HUEBLE, 446 Baker Rd., Whitmire, SC 29178; Phone: 803-694-3602
Publication(s): *South Carolina Forestry Journal; South Carolina B.A.S.S. Federation, Inc. Newsletter*
Keyword(s): Forests and Forestry, Land Use Planning, Transportation, Wetlands, Wildlife and Wildlife Habitat

SOUTH CAROLINA COASTAL CONSERVATION LEAGUE
456 King St., P.O. Box 1765, Charleston, SC 29402
Phone: 843-723-8035; Fax: 843-723-8308; E-mail: scccl@charleston.net; Web Site: www.scccl.org
Founded: 1989; Membership: 4,000+
Scope: Regional
Description: SCCCL works to protect our state's coastal resources through programs in land use, forestry, water quality and public education.
Contact(s):
ExCutive Director: DANA BEACH; E-mail: danabeach@scccl.org
Contact for Forestry: JANE LAREAU; E-mail: janel@scccl.org
Contact for H2O: NANCY VINSON; E-mail: nancyv@scccl.org
Contact for Land Use: SAM PASSMORE; E-mail: samp@scccl.org
Publication(s): *Conservation League Newsletter*
Keyword(s): Beaches, Biodiversity, Birds, Environmental and Conservation Education, Environmental Planning, Environmental Preservation, Greenways, Habitat Conservation, Land Management, Land Use Planning, Nonpoint Source Pollution, Urban and Rural Development, Water Quality, Wetlands, Coastal Construction and Erosion

SOUTH CAROLINA ENVIRONMENTAL LAW PROJECT
P.O. Box 1380, Pawleys Island, SC 29585
Phone: 843-527-0078; Fax: 843-527-0540; E-mail: jchanpi@sccoast.net; Web Site: www.scelp.org (under construction)
Founded: 1987
Scope: Statewide
Description: SCELP is a nonprofit organization whose mission is to protect the natural environment of South Carolina by providing legal services and advice to environmental organizations and concerned citizens, and by improving the state's system of environmental regulation.
Contact(s):
President and General Counsel: JAMES S. CHANDLER JR.
Publication(s): *Mountains and Marshes*
Keyword(s): Environmental Law, Environmental Preservation, Environmental Protection, Legal Advocacy, Natural Resource Conservation, Water Quality, Wetlands

SOUTH CAROLINA FORESTRY ASSOCIATION
4901 Broad River Rd., P.O. Box 21303, Columbia, SC 29221
Phone: 803-798-4170
Founded: 1968
Scope: Statewide
Description: A nonprofit educational organization with a membership of timberland owners, wood dealers, wood-using industries, equipment suppliers, and individuals interested in forest conservation and wise use of natural resources.
Contact(s):
President: ROBERT R. SCOTT
Chairman of the Board: WILLIAM P. CATE

SOUTH CAROLINA NATIVE PLANT SOCIETY
P.O. Box 759, Pickens, SC 29671
WWW: www.clemson.edu/scnativeplants
Founded: 1996; Membership: 250
Scope: Statewide
Description: Promotes native plants and plant communities through an education-based agenda. The Society sponsors field trips, symposiums, workshops and lectures. The Society also works with government agencies to assist in seed collection and management.
Contact(s):
President: RICK HUFFMAN; Phone: 864-868-7798; E-mail: rhuffman@innova.net
Vice-President: BILL STRINGER; Phone: 864-656-3527
Publication(s): *Newsletter, Brochure*
Keyword(s): Flowers, Plants, and Trees, Native Plants

SOUTH CAROLINA WILDLIFE FEDERATION
2711 Middleburg Dr., Suite 104, Columbia, SC 29204
Phone: 803-256-0670; Fax: 803-256-0690; E-mail: angela@scwf.org; Web Site: www.scwf.org
Scope: Statewide
Description: A representative statewide organization, affiliated with the National Wildlife Federation, dedicated to the protection and enhancement of wildlife and its habitat through public education and government interaction.
Contact(s):
President and Representative: CHRISTINE P. THOMPSON
Executive Director: ANGELA VINEY
Editor: ROXANNE RHODES
Alternate Representative: JOHN HELMS

Publication(s): *Out of Doors*
Keyword(s): Aquatic Habitats, Fisheries, Renewable Resources, Water Pollution Management, Wetlands

SOUTH DAKOTA ASSOCIATION OF CONSERVATION DISTRICTS
Attn: President, 15074 372nd Ave., Chelsea, SD 57465
Scope: Statewide
Contact(s):
President, Alternate Board Member: HENRY ELSING, 15074 372nd Ave., Chelsea, SD 57465; Phone: 605-887-3337; Fax: 605-887-3337
Vice President: GERALD THADEN, 14321 465th Ave., Marvin, SD 57251-9720; Phone: 605-938-4579
Secretary/Treasurer: JOHN D. MAJERES, RR2 Box 122, Dell Rapids, SD 57022-0208; Phone: 605-428-3090; Fax: 605-988-5773
Executive Secretary: ANGELA EHLERS, 116 N. Euclid, P.O. Box 275, Pierre, SD 57501-0275; Phone: 605-224-0361; Fax: 605-773-4531
Board Member: GENE S. WILLIAMS, P.O. Box 2, Interior, SD 57750-0002; Phone: 605-433-5469; Fax: 605-433-5470; E-mail: gsw111@gwtc.net
Keyword(s): Conservation Districts

SOUTH DAKOTA B.A.S.S. CHAPTER FEDERATION
Attn: President, P.O. Box 266, Winner, SD 57580
Scope: Statewide
Description: An organization of Bassmaster chapters, affiliated with the Bass Anglers Sportsman Society, organized to fight pollution, assist state and national conservation agencies in their efforts, and teach young people of our country good conservation practices. Dedicated to the realistic conservation of our water resources.
Contact(s):
President: CHUCK DOOM; Phone: 605-842-0746
Conservation Director: PHILLIP RISNES, 26643 461st. Ave., Hartford, SD 57033; Phone: 605-332-4755
Publication(s): *South Dakota Bird Notes; Birds of South Dakota, 1991; The South Dakota Breeding Bird Atlas, 1995; B.A.S.S. Federation Newsletter "Dakota Bassin"*
Keyword(s): Birds, Endangered and Threatened Species, Natural History, Raptors, Waterfowl

SOUTH DAKOTA ORNITHOLOGISTS' UNION
P.O. Box 277, Ipswich, SD 57451
Founded: 1949; Membership: 350
Scope: Statewide
Description: To encourage the study of birds in South Dakota and to promote the study of ornithology by more closely uniting the students of this branch of natural science.
Contact(s):
President: DAVID SWANSON, Biology Department University of South Dakota, Vermillion, SD 57069; Phone: 605-624-0203
Vice President: JEFFREY PALMER, 821 NW Fifth St., Madison, SD 57041; Phone: 605-256-9745
Secretary: J. DAVID WILLIAMS; Phone: 605-426-6974
Treasurer: NELDA HOLDEN, 1620 Elmwood Dr., Brookings, SD 57006; Phone: 605-692-8278
Editor: DAN TALLMAN, Box 740, Northern State University, Aberdeen, SD 57401; Phone: 605-226-2255
Publication(s): *South Dakota Bird Notes; Birds of South Dakota (1991); South Dakota Breeding Bird Atlas, The (1995)*
Keyword(s): Agriculture, Air Quality and Pollution, Energy, Solid Waste Management, Water Resources

SOUTH DAKOTA RESOURCES COALITION
P.O. Box 66, Brookings, SD 57006
Phone: 605-697-6675; Fax: 605-697-3028; E-mail: sdrc@brookings.net
Founded: 1972
Scope: Statewide
Description: Seeks to promote the survival and integrity of water, energy, land, wildlife, and air resources, along with justice in their allocation.
Contact(s):
Chair: DAVID NELSON; Phone: 605-693-4893
Vice Chair: KAYE HUNT, P.O. Box 309, Garretson, SD 57030; Phone: 605-594-3558
Secretary: LAWRENCE NOVOTNY; Phone: 605-688-6172
Treasurer: ROBERT ROBY, 4512 Belmont St., Sioux Falls, SD 57102; Phone: 605-371-0743
Editor: SUSAN CORNFORTH; Phone: 605-692-8579
Publication(s): *ECO-Forum*
Keyword(s): Environmental Protection

NON-GOVERNMENTAL ORGANIZATIONS - S

SOUTH DAKOTA WILDLIFE FEDERATION
P.O. Box 7075, Pierre, SD 57501
Phone: 605-224-7524; Fax: 605-224-7524; E-mail: sdwf@cam-walnet.com; Web Site: www.sdwf.org
Scope: Statewide
Description: A representative statewide organization, affiliated with the National Wildlife Federation, dedicated to the protection and enhancement of wildlife and its habitat through public education and government interaction.
Contact(s):
President and Representative: MIKE LARSEN
Executive Director and Editor: CHRIS HESLA
Alternative Representative: CHUCK CLAYTON
Publication(s): *Out of Doors*
Keyword(s): Aquatic Habitats, Fisheries, Renewable Resources, Water Pollution Management, Wetlands

SOUTHEAST ALASKA CONSERVATION COUNCIL (SEACC)
419 6th St., #328, Juneau, AK 99801
Phone: 907-586-6942; Fax: 907-463-3312; E-mail: info@seacc.org
Founded: 1969; Membership: 1,200
Scope: Statewide
Description: SEACC is a coalition of 17 local conservation groups, dedicated to preserving the integrity of Southeast Alaska's magnificent natural environment. Protection of the region's pristine coastal rainforests, abundant fish and wildlife, and outstanding scenery. Provides for a sustainable approach to economic stability, subsistence use areas, recreational opportunities, and a unique way of life.
Contact(s):
President: WAYNE WEIHING, P.O. Box 1193, Wardcove, AK 99928
Vice President: BRUCE BAKER, P.O. Box 211384, Auke Bay, AK 99821
Secretary: JULIE PENN, P.O. Box 22474, Juneau, AK 99802
Treasurer: DANA OWEN, 949 Goldbelt, Juneau, AK 99801
Executive Director: KATYA KIRSCH
Associate Director: BART KOEHLER, P.O. Box 1620, Durango, CO 81302
Conservation Director and Staff Attorney: BUCK LINDEKUGEL
Publication(s): *RAVENCALL; Action Alerts*
Keyword(s): Conservation of Protected Areas, Environment, Fisheries, Forest Management, Internships, Land Use Planning, Outdoor Recreation, Public Lands, Rainforests, Rivers, Sustainable Development, Water Pollution, Water Quality, Watersheds

SOUTHEASTERN ASSOCIATION OF FISH AND WILDLIFE AGENCIES
Attn: President, Commissioner of Kentucky Department of Fish and Wildlife Resources, #1 Game Farm Rd., Frankfort, KY 40601
Scope: Regional
Description: To protect the best interests of the southeastern states by maintaining their right of jurisdiction over their wildlife resources on public and private lands, by supporting or opposing state and federal wildlife legislation, and by making recommendations on federal programs involving aid. Conducts annual conference for the exchange of ideas and research and land management information concerning wildlife and native and fresh water fisheries.
Contact(s):
President: GREG DUFFY, Director, Oklahoma Dept. of Conservation; 1801 North Lincoln, Oklahoma City, OK 73105; Phone: 405-521-4660
Vice President: BILL WOODFIN, Director, Virginia Dept. of Game and Inland Fisheries, 4010 W. Broad St., Richmond, VA 23230; Phone: 804-367-1000
Executive Secretary: ROBERT M. BRANTLY, 8005 Freshwater Farms Rd., Tallahassee, FL 32308; Phone: 850-893-1204
Keyword(s): Biology, Fisheries, Forest Management, Wildlife and Wildlife Habitat, Wildlife Management

SOUTHEASTERN COOPERATIVE WILDLIFE DISEASE STUDY
College of Veterinary Medicine University of Georgia, Athens, GA 30602
Phone: 706-542-1741; Fax: 706-542-5865
Founded: 1957
Scope: Regional
Description: The first regional diagnostic and research service in the U.S. for the specific purpose of investigating wildlife diseases. This joint-state organization currently is sponsored by the Southeastern Association of Fish and Wildlife Agencies; Veterinary Services of APHIS, USDA; and the Biological Resources Division of USDI. Participating states: AL, AR, FL, GA, KY, LA, MD, MO, MS, NC, PR, SC, TN, VA, WV.
Contact(s):
Director: VICTOR F. NETTLES
Publication(s): *SCWDS BRIEFS Newsletter*
Keyword(s): Agriculture, Environmental and Conservation Education, Health and Nutrition, Wildlife Disease, Wildlife Management

SOUTHEASTERN FISHES COUNCIL
c/o Stephen T. Ross, Dept. of Biological Studies, University of Southern Mississippi, Hattiesburg, MS 39406-5018
Scope: National
Description: Objectives are to provide for the pursuit and transmittal of information on the status and protection of southeastern fishes and their habitats, and to promote the perpetuation of rich natural assemblages of fishes and their habitats, as well as the localized unique forms and their habitats.
Contact(s):
Chair: DR. STEPHEN T. ROSS
Secretary: GERRY DINKINS, 3D International Environmental Group, 7039 Maynardville Highway, Knoxville, TN 37830-7976
Treasurer: PEGGY SHUTE, Tennessee Valley Authority, Natural Heritage Progrma, Norris, TN 37820
Editor: DR. FRANK PEZOLD, Department of Biology, Northeast Louisiana State University, Monroe, LA 71209
Past Chair: DR. MELVIN L. WARREN JR.
Publication(s): *Proceedings of the Southeastern Fishes Council*
Keyword(s): Aquatic Habitats, Biodiversity, Conservation of Protected Areas, Endangered and Threatened Species, Fisheries, Natural History, Rivers, Watersheds

SOUTHERN AFRICAN INSTITUTE OF FORESTRY
Postnet, Suite 329, P/Bag X4, Menlo Park, Pretoria 0102 South Africa
Phone: 2712-3481745
Founded: 1967; Membership: 550
Scope: International
Description: Represents professional forestry science at all levels in silviculture, forestry conservation, and timber processing, and disseminates information about forestry inside and outside of the profession.
Contact(s):
President: W. S. OLIVIER
Vice President: P. L. KIME
Secretary: C. VILJOEN
Publicity Officer: DR. D. W. VAN DER ZEL, P.O. Box 1673, Pretoria, 0001 South Africa; Phone: 271-254-59269
Publication(s): *Southern African Forestry Journal; South African Forestry Handbook*
Keyword(s): Forestry

SOUTHERN APPALACHIAN BOTANICAL SOCIETY
Biology Department, 2100 College St., Newberry College, Newberry, SC 29108
Phone: 803-321-5257; Fax: 803-321-5232; E-mail: chorn@newberry.edu
Founded: 1936; Membership: 750
Scope: Regional
Description: A nonprofit organization to disseminate information on the native plants of eastern North America through meetings and publications.

Contact(s):
President: DR. NANCY COILE; Phone: 352-372-3505; E-mail: coilen@doacs.state.fl.us
President-elect: DR. JOE WINSTEAD; Phone: 502-645-6004; E-mail: j.winstead@morehead-st.edu
Secretary and Treasurer: DR. CHARLES HORN; Phone: 803-321-5257; Fax: 803-321-5232; E-mail: chorn@newberry.edu
Past President: DR. DON WINDLER; Phone: 410-830-3034; E-mail: dwindler@towson.edu
Publication(s): *Castanea; Chinquapin*
Keyword(s): Botany, Ecology, Ecosystems, Endangered and Threatened Species, National Forests, Natural History, Research, State Parks, Trees, Wildflowers, Plants, Native Plants

SOUTHERN ENVIRONMENTAL LAW CENTER
201 W. Main St., Suite 14, Charlottesville, VA 22902-5065
Phone: 804-977-4090; Fax: 804-977-1483; E-mail: selcva@selcva.org
Founded: 1985; Membership: 2,000
Scope: National
Description: A regional nonprofit public interest advocacy organization committed to protecting the natural resources of the southeast through direct advocacy in court and before regulatory agencies; through assistance to state and local environmental groups in the region; and through providing regional leadership on key southeastern environmental issues.
Contact(s):
Vice President: TERENCE Y. SIEG
Secretary: MARY RICE
Treasurer: FREDERICK S. MIDDLETON III
Executive Director: FREDERICK S. MIDDLETON III; Phone: 804-977-4090
Board Officers and Chairman of the Board of Trustees: DEADERICK C. MONTAGUE
Communications Coordinator: CATHRYN McCUE; Phone: 804-977-4090
Director of Carolinas Office: LARK HAYES; Phone: 919-967-1450
Publication(s): *Energy 2000: A Blueprint for an Energy Efficient Virginia; Energy Choices: A Primer on Electric Utility Industry Restructuring; Citizen's Guides to Protecting Wetlands in South Carolina, Alabama, and Georgia; Visual Pollution and Sign Control; A Legal Handbook on Billboard Control; Southern Resources (newsletter); Southeast Energy New (newsletter)*
Keyword(s): Acid Rain, Air Quality and Pollution, Coasts, Energy, Energy Conservation, Environmental Law, Forests and Forestry, Land Preservation, Natural Areas, Open Space, Planning Management, Public Lands, Transportation, Water Pollution Management, Wetlands

North Carolina Office
137 E. Franklin St., Suite 404, Chapel Hill, NC 27514-3628
Phone: 919-967-1450; Fax: 919-929-9421; E-mail: selcnc@selcnc.org
Scope: National

SOUTHERN NEW ENGLAND FOREST CONSORTIUM, INC. (SNEFCI)
P.O. Box 760, Chepachet, RI 02816
Phone: 401-568-1610; Fax: 401-568-7874
Founded: 1985
Scope: Regional
Description: SNEFCI promotes wise conservation practices in Southern New England. Our goals are to reduce forest fragmentation, promote stewardship of forest resources, and enhance urban and community forest resources.
Contact(s):
President: THOMAS DuPREE; Phone: 401-277-1414; Fax: 401-647-3590
Vice President: DONALD SMITH; Phone: 860-424-3630; Fax: 860-424-4070
Secretary: GAIL MICHAELS; Phone: 603-868-7694; Fax: 603-868-7604
Treasurer: HANS BERGEY; Phone: 401-821-8746; Fax: 401-821-8746
Executive Director: CHRISTOPHER MODISETTE
Publication(s): *Your Family Land: Legacy or Memory; Your Family Lands: Legacy or Memory: Commonly Asked Questions; Cost of Community Services in Southern New England; Foresters and The Care of Your Land*
Keyword(s): Forest Management, Planning Management, Urban Forestry

SOUTHERN UTAH WILDERNESS ALLIANCE (SUWA)
Headquarters, 1471 S. 1100 E., Salt Lake City, UT 84105-2423
Phone: 801-486-3161
Founded: 1983; Membership: 25,000
Scope: Statewide
Description: SUWA advocates wilderness preservation for qualifying federal public lands in Utah's incomparable canyon country. Through the allied efforts of SUWA's staff, Utah activists, and concerned citizens across the United States, SUWA seeks to give its members and the general public a voice in deciding the fate of America's redrock wilderness.
Contact(s):
Chairman: HANSJORG WYSS
Secretary: JAMES MARTIN
Treasurer: MARK RISTOW
Executive Director: MIKE MATZ
Vice Chairman: TED WILSON
Publication(s): *Quarterly newsletter; bulletins*

Moab Office
P.O. Box 968, Moab, UT 84532-0968
Phone: 801-259-5440
Scope: Statewide

St. George Office
P.O. Box 1726, Cedar City, UT 84721
Scope: Statewide

Washington, DC Office
215 Pennsylvania Ave., SE, Washington, DC 20002
Phone: 202-546-2215
Scope: Statewide

SOUTHFACE ENERGY INSTITUTE
241 Pine St., Atlanta, GA 30308
Phone: 404-872-3549; Fax: 404-872-5009; E-mail: info@southface.org; Web Site: www.southface.org
Founded: 1978; Membership: 350
Scope: Regional
Description: The Southface is a nonprofit organization that promotes the use of sustainable energy and environmental technologies and policies in the building sciences through education, research, and technical assistance.
Contact(s):
President: TILLMAN DOUGLAS; E-mail: tillman@inweb.net
Executive Director: DENNIS CREECH; E-mail: dcreech@southface.org
Publication(s): *The Southface Journal of Energy and Building Technology; A Builder's Guide to Energy Efficient Homes in Georgia; Home Energy Projects*
Keyword(s): Energy Conservation, Environment, Internships, Sustainable Development

SOUTHWEST RESEARCH AND INFORMATION CENTER
P.O. Box 4524, Albuquerque, NM 87106
Phone: 505-346-1455; Fax: 505-346-1459; E-mail: sricdon@earthlink.net; Web Site: www.sric.org
Founded: 1971
Scope: National
Description: SRIC is a nonprofit organization founded to provide timely, accurate information to the public on a broad range of issues related to the environment, human, and natural resources. SRIC's twin objectives are to promote citizen participation and environmental justice, and to protect natural resources.

NON-GOVERNMENTAL ORGANIZATIONS - S

Contact(s):
Vice President: ANNE ALBRINK
Secretary: LALORA CHARLES
Treasurer: WILFRED RAEL
Administrator: DON HANCOCK
Publication(s): *Workbook, The*
Keyword(s): Environmental Justice, Mining, Water Pollution

SPORTSMAN'S ALLIANCE OF MAINE
R.R. 1 Box 1174, Church Hill Rd., Augusta, ME 04330-9749
Phone: 207-622-5503
Founded: 1975; Membership: 13,202
Scope: Statewide
Description: SAM is a statewide nonprofit organization of sportsmen and women dedicated to hunting, fishing, trapping, protection of wildlife habitat, and conservation. Lobbies and works with state agencies on behalf of Maine sportsmen.
Contact(s):
President: EDYE CRONK
Treasurer: RICHARD PARADIS
1st Vice President: JAMES HILLY
2nd Vice President: ROBERT CRAM
Executive Director and Editor: GEORGE A. SMITH
Secretary and Clerk: HERBERT MORSE
Publication(s): *SAM NEWS*

SPORTSMAN'S NETWORK, INC., THE
111 S. Main St., P.O. Box 257, Dry Ridge, KY 41035
Phone: 606-824-6526; Fax: 606-824-0556; E-mail: sportsmen@sportsmansnetwork.org; Web Site: sportsmansnetwork.org
Founded: 1991
Scope: Statewide
Description: The Sportsman's Network is an incorporated statewide nonprofit conservation organization dedicated to educating the public and raising awareness of wildlife conservation through programs which promote controlled hunting, fishing, and other related activities. Also produces "A Moment in Conservation" radio program.
Contact(s):
Vice President: GARY PFERRMAN
Secretary: PAUL COOKENDORFER
Treasurer: WILLIAM A. KREBS
Director of Programs: ORBIN E. SAMPLES III
State Chairman: PETER O. SAMPLES
Keyword(s): Hunting, Land Preservation, Nature Preservation, Rehabilitation, Rivers, Sport Fishing, Training, Trapping, Wetlands, Wildlands, Wildlife and Wildlife Habitat, Wildlife Management

ST. REGIS MOHAWK TRIBE
Environment Division Community Bldg., Hogansburg, NY 13655
Phone: 518-358-5937; Fax: 518-358-6252
Scope: National
Description: To monitor, maintain, and protect the environment of the St. Regis Mohawk Tribe for the prevention of disease and injury to body, mind, and spirit. Participation in hazardous waste remediation, Superfund site cleanups, reservation environmental protection, and air and water quality.
Contact(s):
Akwesasne Library/Cultural Center Librarian: CAROL WHITE
Assistant Director of Environment Division: LES BENEDICT
Director of Environment Division: KEN JOCK
Publication(s): *Iroquois Environmental Newsletter*
Keyword(s): Environmental Protection

STANFORD ENVIRONMENTAL LAW SOCIETY
Stanford Law School, Stanford, CA 94305
Phone: 650-723-4421
Founded: 1969
Scope: Statewide
Description: The Stanford Environmental Law Society is the oldest student organization of its kind in the United States. Its primary function is sponsorship of original research in developing areas of environmental law. The Society relies on contributions, grants, and proceeds from the sale of publications.
Contact(s):
President: ANGELA CHABOT
President: JUGE GREGG
Business Manager: KOL MEDINA
Publication(s): *Stanford Environmental Law Journal; Endangered Species Act, The: A Guide to its Protections and Implementation; Hazardous Waste Disposal Sites; Who Runs the Rivers?*
Keyword(s): Environmental Law, Research

STATE AND TERRITORIAL AIR POLLUTION PROGRAM ADMINISTRATORS AND THE ASSOCIATION OF LOCAL AIR POLLUTION CONTROL OFFICIALS (STAPPA and ALAPCO
444 N. Capitol St.,NW, Suite 307, Washington, DC 20001
Phone: 202-624-7864
Founded: 1980; Membership: STAPPA 55/ALAPCO 210
Scope: National
Description: The national associations of air pollution control agencies in the states, territories, and major metropolitan areas. The associations' members have primary responsibility for ensuring healthy air quality and represent the technical expertise behind the implementation of our nation's air pollution control laws and regulations.
Contact(s):
Executive Director: S. WILLIAM BECKER
Publication(s): *Meeting the 15% Rate of Progress Requirement Under The Clean Air Act: A Menu of Options (1993); <S> Controlling Nitrogen Oxides Under The Clean Air Act: A Menu of Options (1994); Controlling Particulate Matter Under The Clean Air Act: A Menu of Options (1*
Keyword(s): Acid Rain, Air Quality and Pollution, Environment, Greenhouse Effect/Global Warming, Pollution Prevention

STATEWIDE PROGRAM OF ACTION TO CONSERVE OUR ENVIRONMENT (SPACE)
N.H.'s Current Use Coalition, 54 Portsmouth St., Concord, NH 03301
Phone: 603-224-3306
Founded: 1966
Scope: Statewide
Description: A private, nonprofit advocacy coalition of groups dedicated to conserving open space land. S.P.A.C.E.'s work includes advocacy, education, supporting research and working with the state, towns, and individuals on the administration and monitoring of the current use program.
Contact(s):
Chairman: DENNIS D. McKENNEY, 569 N. Bennington Rd., Bennington, NH 03442-4505
Treasurer: KENNETH MARSHALL, 169 N. Main St., Boscawen, NH 03303
Clerk: JOHN BARTO ESQ, Christian Mutual Bldg., 6 Loudon Rd., Concord, NH 03301
Publication(s): *SPACE Newsletter*
Keyword(s): Land Preservation

STEAMBOATERS, THE
P.O. Box 176, Idleyld Park, OR 97447
Phone: 503-496-3003
Founded: 1966; Membership: 400
Scope: National
Description: Formed to preserve, promote, and restore the natural production of wild fish populations, the habitat which sustains them, and the unique aesthetic values of the North Umpqua River for present and future generations.
Contact(s):
President: JIM WATSON; Phone: 541-496-3512; E-mail: samnjim@rosenet.net
Vice President: LEN JANSSEN; Phone: 541-440-9375
Secretary: CHARLIE SPOONER
Treasurer: PAUL MOORE

Keyword(s): Biodiversity, Endangered and Threatened Species, Environmental and Conservation Education, Environmental Law, Planning Management

STOP
130-651 Notre Dame West, Montreal, Quebec H3C 1H9
Canada
Phone: 514-393-9559; Fax: 514-393-9588
Founded: 1970; Membership: 200
Scope: Statewide
Description: Devoted to preserving and improving the quality of the physical and human environment, and to promoting rational utilization of natural resources.
Contact(s):
President: GEORGES HEBERT
Research Director: BRUCE WALKER
Publication(s): *Stop Press*
Keyword(s): Acid Rain, Air Quality and Pollution, Chemical Pollution Control, Environmental and Conservation Education, Solid Waste Management, Toxic Substances, Transportation, Urban Environment, Water Pollution

STRIPERS UNLIMITED, INC.
P.O. Box 3045, S. Attleboro, MA 02703
Phone: 508-226-4007; Fax: 508-226-2031
Founded: 1965; Membership: 500+
Scope: National
Description: Nonprofit organization formed to promote, conserve, and protect striped bass and to protect and restore its environment. Promotes and encourages research on striped bass in order to preserve it as a natural resource and to increase its areas of reproduction. Members in 21 states and two Canadian provinces.
Contact(s):
President: NORMAN WHITTEN, 24 Ellsworth Terr., Lynn, MA 01904
Executive Director and Treasurer: ROBERT B. POND, P.O. Box 3045, S. Attleboro, MA 02703; Phone: 508-226-4007
Executive Secretary and Editor: AVIS E. BOYD, P.O. Box 3166, S. Attleboro, MA 02703; Phone: 508-761-4627
Membership Secretary: CARLEEN PROULX
Publication(s): *Newsletter in North East Woods & Waters, monthly*
Keyword(s): Environmental and Conservation Education, Fisheries, Sport Fishing, Toxic Substances, Water Pollution

STROUD WATER RESEARCH CENTER
970 Spencer Rd., Avondale, PA 19311
Phone: 610-268-2153; Fax: 610-268-0490; Web Site: www.stroudcenter.org
Founded: 1967; Membership: 1,000
Scope: International
Description: The mission of the Stroud Center is to advance the knowledge of river and stream ecosystems through research and education.
Contact(s):
Director: BERNARD W. SWEENEY; E-mail: sweeney@stroudcenter.org
Education Director: JAMES V. MCGONIGLE; E-mail: jmcgonigle@stroudcenter.org
Publication(s): *Upstream (newsletter)*
Keyword(s): Biology, Chemistry, Environmental and Conservation Education, Fieldwork, Outdoor Education, Research, Riparian Restoration, Rivers, Water Pollution, Water Quality, Water Resources, Watersheds

STUDENT CONSERVATION ASSOCIATION, INC.
National Headquarters, Box 550, Charlestown, NH 03603
Phone: 603-543-1700; Fax: 603-543-1828; E-mail: earthwork@sca-inc.org; Web Site: www.sca-inc.org
Founded: 1957; Membership: 24,000
Scope: National
Description: SCA is guided by two premises: high school and college-age volunteers can accomplish a variety of conservation tasks vital to the protection of America's natural resources and the experience gained by these volunteers can significantly impact their education, personal development and career goals.
Contact(s):
President: DALE PENNY
Chair of the Board: EDMUND BARTLETT
Chief Financial Officer: MARK BODIN
Communications: KEVIN HAMILTON
Executive Vice President: VALERIE J. SHAND
Vice President of Development: ROBERT D. HOLLEY
Vice President of Programs: SCOTT C. WEAVER
Founding President: ELIZABETH C. TITUS
Publication(s): *Earth Work, Earth Work Online*
Keyword(s): Careers, Cultural Preservation, Environment, Environmental and Conservation Education, Internships, People of Color in the Environment, Public Lands, Renewable Resources, Youth Organizations

California Office
655 13th St., Suite 304, Oakland, CA 94612
Phone: 510-832-1968
Scope: Regional

Capital Office
1800 N. Kent St., Suite 1260, Arlington, VA 22209
Phone: 703-524-2441
Scope: Regional

Newark Office
P.O. Box 32369, 24 Commerce St., Suite 1430, Newark, NJ 07102
Phone: 973-733-4450
Scope: Regional

Northwest Office
1265 S. Main St., Suite 210, Seattle, WA 98144
Phone: 206-324-4649
Scope: Regional

STUDENT ENVIRONMENTAL ACTION COALITION (SEAC)
P.O. Box 31909, Philadelphia, PA 19104
Phone: 215-222-4711; Fax: 215-222-2896; E-mail: seac@seac.org; Web Site: www.seac.org
Founded: 1988; Membership: 2,000
Scope: National
Description: SEAC is a national student-run and student-led network of progressive organizations and individuals whose aim is to uproot environmental injustices through action and education. We define the environment to include the physical, economical, political, and cultural conditions in which we live. By challenging the power structure that threatens these environmental conditions, SEAC works to create progressive social change on both the local and global levels.
Publication(s): *Threshold*
Keyword(s): Environmental Justice, Social Justice, Solid Waste Management, Wilderness, Youth Organizations

STUDENT PUGWASH USA
815 15th St., NW, Suite 814, Washington, DC 20005
Phone: 202-393-6555; Fax: 202-393-6550; E-mail: spusa@spusa.org
Scope: National
Description: The mission of Student Pugwash USA is to promote the socially responsible application of science and technology in the 21st century. As a student organization, Student Pugwash USA encourages young people to examine the ethical, social, and global implications of science and technology, and to make these concerns a guiding focus of their academic and professional endeavors.
Contact(s):
Executive Director: SANDRA IONNO
Executive Committee Chairman: CONSTANCE PECHURA
Publication(s): *Jobs You Can Live With: Working at the Crossroads of Science, Technology, and Society; Tough Questions; Pugwatch; mindfull: a brainsnack for future leaders with ethical appetites; Global Issues Guidebook*
Keyword(s): Biotechnology, Communications, Energy, Environmental and Conservation Education, Nuclear/Radiation

NON-GOVERNMENTAL ORGANIZATIONS - T

STUDENTS PARTNERSHIP WORLDWIDE
P.O. Box 4892, Nag Pokhari Kathmandu
Phone: 977-1-429051/051/435107; Fax: 434-645-977-1; E-mail: spwnepal@mos.com.np; Web Site: www.spw.org
Scope: International
Description: Youth focus development program working in the field of formal and non-formal education and environmental education in rural government, school of Nepal, and form green club school student group to conserve environmental in their own surroundings.
Contact(s):
Administrative Coordinator: GAURAB RENE
Extension Coordinator: BISHNU BHALTA
Keyword(s): Afforestation, Communications, Conservation, Ecosystems, Environmental Protection, Nature Study, Preservation and Protection, Rural Development, Sustainable Development, Training, Water Pollution, Women in the Environment, Youth Organizations

SUNCOAST SEABIRD SANCTUARY INC.
18328 Gulf Blvd., Indian Shores, FL 33785
Phone: 727-391-6211; Fax: 727-399-2923
Founded: 1972; Membership: 30,000
Scope: National
Description: A private, nonprofit, membership organization dedicated to the rescue, repair, recuperation, and release of healed sick and injured wild birds. The Sanctuary treats and releases over 9,000 birds each year. It provides a safe home for over 600 permanently injured avian species. The Sanctuary is open for visitation every day from 9:00 a.m. till dusk. Guided tours available - free admission.
Contact(s):
Treasurer: HELEN B. HEATH, 18323 Sunset Blvd., Redington Shores, FL 33708; Phone: 727-393-0933
Founder and Director: RALPH T. HEATH JR., 18323 Sunset Blvd., Redington Shores, FL 33708; Phone: 727-391-6211
Publication(s): *Suncoast Seabird Sanctuary Newsletter; S.S.S. Brochure (Blue); If You Find A Baby Bird Book*
Keyword(s): Birds, Endangered and Threatened Species, Environmental and Conservation Education, Waterfowl, Wildlife Rehabilitation

T

TAHOE REGIONAL PLANNING AGENCY
308 Dorla Ct., P.O. Box 1038, Zephyr Cove, NV 89448-1038
Phone: 702-588-4547
Founded: 1969
Scope: National
Description: To establish and implement land use and environmental plans and regulations in the Lake Tahoe Region. Established by Public Law No. 91-148, December 1969, amended by Public Law No. 96-551, December 1980.
Contact(s):
Executive Director: JIM BAETGE
Legal Counsel: JOHN MARSHALL
Legal Counsel: SUSAN SCHOLLEY
Keyword(s): Air Quality and Pollution, Lakes, Land Use Planning, Water Pollution, Wetlands

TALL TIMBERS RESEARCH STATION
13093 Henry Beadel Dr., Tallahassee, FL 32312-9712
Phone: 850-893-4153; Web Site: www.talltimbers.org
Founded: 1958; Membership: 2,100
Scope: International
Description: A nonprofit, tax-exempt scientific and educational organization with a focus on land management, conservation, ecological research, and fire ecology. Information is exchanged in print and on the Internet. Tall Timbers provides publications, seminars, conferences and training programs for land owners and managers, scholars, research scientists, students and concerned citizens.
Contact(s):
Chairman: KATE IRELAND
Secretary: DAPHNE WOODWOOD
Treasurer: LAWTON LANGFORD
Executive Director: LANE GREEN
Librarian: ANN BRUCE, Tall Timbers Library; Fax: 850-668-7781
Research Director: DR. LEONARD A. BRENNAN
Vice Chairperson: WALTER C. SEDGWICK
Publication(s): *Newsletters, annual reports, proceedings, technical reports, and informational bulletins.Services: Literature and data searches, publications and periodicals.*
Keyword(s): Endangered and Threatened Species, Environmental and Conservation Education, Flowers, Plants, and Trees, Wildlife and Wildlife Habitat, Wildlife Management

TALLAHASSEE MUSEUM OF HISTORY AND NATURAL SCIENCE
3945 Museum Dr., Tallahassee, FL 32310
Phone: 850-575-8684; Fax: 850-574-8243; Web Site: www.tallahasseemuseum.org
Founded: 1957; Membership: 5,000
Scope: Statewide
Description: To educate residents and visitors of Tallahassee and the Big Bend area about the region's natural and cultural history, from the beginning of the 19th-century until the present. For this purpose, the museum collects, preserves, and exhibits artifacts and historic buildings, maintains native animals in natural habitats and operates a 19th century farmstead.
Contact(s):
Curator of Animals: MIKE JONES
Curator of Collections and Exhibits: LINDA DEATON
Director of Education: JENNIFER GOLDEN
Director of Institutional Advancement: BETSY BARFIELD
Executive Director/CEO: RUSSELL DAWS
Publication(s): *The Newsletter of The Tallahassee Museum of History and Natural Science*
Keyword(s): Biodiversity, Culture, Endangered and Threatened Species, Environment, Environmental and Conservation Education, Historic Preservation, Mammals, Museum, Natural Areas, Natural History, Nongame Wildlife, Zoological Parks, Zoology

TEENS FOR RECREATION AND ENVIRONMENTAL CONSERVATION (TREC)
Seattle Department of Parks and Recreation, 100 Dexter Ave., N., Seattle, WA 98109-5199
Phone: 206-684-7097; Fax: 206-684-7025; E-mail: robert.warner@CI.Seattle.WA.US; Web Site: www.wawebsites.com/trec
Founded: 1992; Membership: 80 active teen/500-600 teens throughout the community
Scope: Statewide
Description: TREC is an outdoor expedition-level program designed to expose multi-ethnic teens to environmental education, urban conservation, and stewardship, while creating an environment for community leadership and empowerment.
Contact(s):
Contact: ROBERT WARNER

TENNESSEE ASSOCIATION OF CONSERVATION DISTRICTS
Attn: President, 2205 Armour Dr. Rt2, Box 372, Somerville, TN 38068
Scope: Statewide
Contact(s):
President: HARRIS A. ARMOUR III; Phone: 901-465-9684; Fax: 901-465-5608
Vice President: ROY GILLS, 419 Nofattie Rd., Limestone, TN 37615; Phone: 423-257-2305
Executive Director: PHIL CHERRY, 144 Southeast Parkway #210, Franklin, TN 37064; Phone: 615-595-9978, ext. 110; Fax: 615-595-9982
Board Member: JOHN CHARLES WILSON, 560 Orr Rd., Arlington, TN 38002; Phone: 901-867-8289

Secretary-Treasurer: BARRY LAKE, P.O. Box 107, Hickory Valley, TN 38042; Phone: 901-764-2909
Keyword(s): Conservation Districts

TENNESSEE B.A.S.S. CHAPTER FEDERATION
Attn: President, P.O. Box 246, Waverly, TN 37185
Scope: Statewide
Description: An organization of Bassmaster chapters, affiliated with the Bass Anglers Sportsman Society, organized to fight pollution, assist state and national conservation agencies in their efforts, and teach the young people of our country good conservation practices. Dedicated to the realistic conservation of our water resources.
Contact(s):
President: CHARLES MITCHELL; Phone: 931-296-4428
Conservation Director: CHUCK HARGER, 731 Oakland Dr., New Johnsonville, TN 37134; Phone: 931-535-2209
Publication(s): *Chapter Newsletter*
Keyword(s): Aquatic Habitats, Fisheries

TENNESSEE CITIZENS FOR WILDERNESS PLANNING
130 Tabor Rd., Oak Ridge, TN 37830
Phone: 423-482-2153/423-481-0286
Founded: 1966; Membership: 450
Scope: Statewide
Description: Dedicated to achieving and perpetuating protection of natural lands and waters by means of public ownership, legislation, or cooperation with the private sector. Our first focus is the Cumberland and Appalachian regions of East Tennessee, but efforts may extend to the rest of the state and the nation.
Contact(s):
President: JIMMY GROTON, 87 Outer Dr., Oak Ridge, TN 37830; Phone: 423-482-5799
Vice President: ERIC HIRST, 106 Capital Cir., Oak Ridge, TN 37830; Phone: 423-483-1289
Secretary: CHUCK ESTES, 114 Baypath Dr., Oak Ridge, TN 37830; Phone: 423-482-0127
Treasurer: CHARLES KLABUNDE, 219 E. Vanderbilt Dr., Oak Ridge, TN 37830; Phone: 423-483-8055
Executive Director: MARCY REED, 6724 Ball Camp Pike, Knoxville, TN 37931; Phone: 423-691-8807
Editor: LIANE B. RUSSELL, 130 Tabor Rd., Oak Ridge, TN 37830; Phone: 423-482-2153
Publication(s): *TCWP Newsletter*
Keyword(s): Biodiversity, Forest Management, Natural Areas, Nongame Wildlife, Public Lands, Rivers, Water Resources, Watersheds, Wilderness

TENNESSEE CONSERVATION LEAGUE
300 Orlando Ave., Nashville, TN 37209-3257
Phone: 615-353-1133; Fax: 615-353-0083; E-mail: conserve.tcl@nashville.com
Scope: Statewide
Description: A representative statewide organization, affiliated with the National Wildlife Federation, dedicated to the protection and enhancement of wildlife and its habitat through public education and government interaction.
Contact(s):
President and Representative: DICK URBAN
Executive Director: MARTY MARINA
Editor: SUE GARNER
Alternate Representative: MIKE PEARIGEN
Publication(s): *Tennessee Out-of-Doors*

TENNESSEE ENVIRONMENTAL COUNCIL
1700 Hayes St., Suite 101, Nashville, TN 37203
Phone: 615-321-5075; Fax: 615-321-5082; E-mail: tec@nol.com
Founded: 1970; Membership: 44 organizations, 2,200 individuals
Scope: Statewide
Description: A nonprofit coalition working to protect and improve Tennessee's public health, quality of life, and natural heritage. TEC is a 28-year old organization, focused on carrying out the state's environmental policies and regulations on behalf of Tennessee citizens.
Contact(s):
President: PATRICK WILLARD; Phone: 615-297-7243
Secretary: SANDI KURTZ; Phone: 423-892-4403
Treasurer: DR. WILLIAM R. MILLER III; Phone: 931-486-9504
Executive Director: ALAN JONES
Publication(s): *ProTECt*
Keyword(s): Air Quality and Pollution, Chemical Pollution Control, Environment, Environmental Justice, Environmental Protection, Forest Management, Planning Management, Public Health Protection, Solid Waste Management, Sustainable Development, Toxic Substances, Water Pollution

TENNESSEE FORESTRY ASSOCIATION
P.O. Box 290693, Nashville, TN 37229
Phone: 615-883-3832
Founded: 1951
Scope: Statewide
Description: A nonprofit conservation group of about 1300 woodland owners, public and private foresters, educators, and wood using companies, as well as individual citizens and allied businesses, encouraging the development and wise use of Tennessee's forest resources.
Contact(s):
President: WALLACE JOHNSTON
Vice President: STEVE MAVNEY
Vice President: WAYNE TURNER
Vice President: BUSTER JOHNSON
1st Vice President: JOE SAVERY
Keyword(s): Forestry

TENNESSEE WOODLAND OWNERS ASSOCIATION
P.O. Box 1400, Crossville, TN 38557
Phone: 615-484-5535
Founded: 1976; Membership: 80
Scope: Statewide
Description: A statewide organization affiliated with the National Woodland Owners Association to focus on the special needs and concerns of non-industrial private forest owners throughout Tennessee and to promote responsible resource stewardship.
Contact(s):
President: vacant
Secretary/Treasurer: ROBERT HARRISON
Keyword(s): Forests and Forestry

TERRENE INSTITUTE, THE
4 Herbert St., Alexandria, VA 22305
Phone: 703-548-5473; Fax: 703-548-6299; E-mail: terrinst@aol.com; Web Site: www.terrene.org
Founded: 1990
Scope: National
Description: The Terrene Institute is a nonprofit organization that works with corporate, environmental, and government partners to promote innovative and economical solutions for improving environmental quality. Terrene is an environmental education organization that develops conferences, issues forums, and publications that serve both corporate and nonprofit audiences. Terrene's principal work is water issues, including the coordination of American Wetlands Month activities, and nonpoint source water quality. A catalog of Terrene publications is available.
Contact(s):
Executive Vice President: JUDY TAGGART, 4 Herbert St., Alexandria, VA 22305; Phone: 703-548-5473
Publication(s): *Terrene publishes the newsletter "Runoff Report". Ask for catalog of books, posters, and other products.*
Keyword(s): Runoff, Water Resources, Watersheds, Wetlands

TEXAS ASSOCIATION OF SOIL AND WATER CONSERVATION DISTRICTS
Attn: President, 279 Hostetter, New Waverly, TX 77358
Scope: Statewide

NON-GOVERNMENTAL ORGANIZATIONS - T

Contact(s):
President: WAYNE REGISTER; Phone: 713-237-9793; Fax: 713-237-1209
Secretary: BEATRICE E. WHITE, P.O. Box 658, Temple, TX 76503; Phone: 254-778-8741; Fax: 254-773-3311
Secretary-Treasurer: DAYTON ELAM, 600 SW 21st St., Seminole, TX 79360; Phone: 915-758-3504
Vice President, Board Member: JOSE DODIER JR., P.O. Box 13, Zapata, TX 78076; Phone: 956-936-2007
Publication(s): *Big Bend Paisano, The; official park newspaper; Big Bend seminars and sales catalog available on request.*
Keyword(s): Conservation Districts

TEXAS B.A.S.S. CHAPTER FEDERATION
Attn: President, 10301 NW Freeway 302, Houston, TX 77092
Scope: Statewide
Description: An organization of Bassmaster chapters, affiliated with the Bass Anglers Sportsman Society, organized to fight pollution, assist state and national conservation agencies in their efforts, and teach the young people of our country good conservation practices. Dedicated to the realistic conservation of our water resources.
Contact(s):
President: RANDY KINDLER; Phone: 281-807-1625
Conservation Director: ALAN ALLEN, 807 Brazos Suite 311, Austin, TX 78701; Phone: 512-472-2267
Publication(s): *Conservation Progress; Forest Reform Network Newsletter*
Keyword(s): Environmental and Conservation Education, Forests and Forestry, Rivers, Water Resources, Wilderness

TEXAS COMMITTEE ON NATURAL RESOURCES
1301 South IH-35, Suite 301, Austin, TX 78741
Phone: 512-441-1122; E-mail: tconr@eden.com; Web Site: www.eden.com/tconr
Founded: 1968
Scope: Statewide
Description: A representative statewide organization, affiliated with the National Wildlife Federation, dedicated to the protection and enhancement of wildlife and its habitat through public education and government interaction.
Contact(s):
Chairman: DAVID GRAY
Executive Director and Alternate Representative: JANICE BEZANSON
Representative: SUSAN PETERSON
Editor: EDWARD FRITZ

TEXAS FORESTRY ASSOCIATION
P.O. 1488, Lufkin, TX 75902-1488
Phone: 409-632-TREE; Web Site: www.texasforestry.org
Founded: 1914
Scope: Statewide
Description: Private nonprofit statewide organization promoting the conservation, fullest economic development, and utilization of forest and related resources.
Contact(s):
President: TOMMY BURCH, B&W Contractors, Brookeland, TX
Executive Vice President: RONALD H. HUFFORD
Publication(s): *TOES News & Notes*
Keyword(s): Biodiversity, Endangered and Threatened Species, Environmental and Conservation Education, Forests and Forestry, Reforestation, Scholarships and Grants, Sustainability

TEXAS ORGANIZATION FOR ENDANGERED SPECIES
P.O. Box 12773, Austin, TX 78711-2773
Founded: 1972; Membership: 275
Scope: Statewide
Description: A nonprofit statewide organization dedicated to the conservation of endangered, threatened, or rare species and biotic communities of Texas.
Contact(s):
President: GARY VALENTINE; Phone: 254-297-1291
Secretary: DEBORAH HOLLE; Phone: 512-482-5700
Treasurer: C. LEE SHERROD; Phone: 512-328-2430
Chair of Conservation Committee: JASON SINGHURST; Phone: 512-912-7011
Chair of Education Committee: LINDA CAMPBELL; Phone: 512-912-7044
Chair of Natural Resources: PEGGY HOMER; Phone: 512-912-7047
Editor: DAVID LEMKE; Phone: 512-245-2178
Past-President: LEE ANN LINAM; Phone: 512-847-9480
Publication(s): *TOES News & Notes*
Keyword(s): Hunting, Outdoor Recreation, Sustainable Development, Wildlife and Wildlife Habitat, Wildlife Management

TEXAS WILDLIFE ASSOCIATION
1635 NE Loop 410, Suite 108, San Antonio, TX 78209
Phone: 512-826-2904
Founded: 1985; Membership: 5,000
Scope: Statewide
Description: Texas Wildlife Association is a nonprofit corporation, formed to protect and promote the rights of Texas' wildlife managers, land owners, sportsmen, and the state's wildlife resources--especially on private lands.
Contact(s):
President: JAMES L. HAYNE; Phone: 210-226-2161
Vice President: JOSEPH B.C. FITZSIMONS; Phone: 830-876-2754
Secretary: DERRY T. GARDNER; Phone: 512-458-6294
Treasurer: JIMMIE V. THURMOND III; Phone: 210-923-4317
Executive Vice President: DAVID K. LANGFORD; Phone: 210-826-2904
Publication(s): *Texas Wildlife*
Keyword(s): Wildlife Management

THORNE ECOLOGICAL INSTITUTE
5398 Manhattan Cir., Suite 120, Boulder, CO 80303-4239
Phone: 303-499-3647; Fax: 303-499-8340
Founded: 1954
Scope: National
Description: A nonprofit educational institute creating innovative outdoor learning experiences and other educational opportunities that teach stewardship of the earth to children and adults. The Institute offers a variety of environmental education classes to children from the Boulder, Denver area with science-based activities and exciting hands-on lessons.
Contact(s):
Executive Director: PERI CHICKERING
Chairman of the Board: SHAWN MULLIGAN
Founder and President: DR. OAKLEIGH THORNE II
Keyword(s): Camp, Ecology, Environmental and Conservation Education, Fieldwork, Internships, Natural Science, Watersheds, Wetlands, Wildlife and Wildlife Habitat

THREE CIRCLES CENTER FOR MULTICULTURAL ENVIRONMENTAL EDUCATION
P.O. Box 1946, Sausalito, CA 94965
Phone: 415-331-4540; E-mail: circlecenter@igc.apc.org
Founded: 1990
Scope: National
Description: Three Circles Center introduces, encourages, and cultivates multicultural perspectives and values in environmental and outdoor education, recreation, and interpretation.
Contact(s):
Executive Director: RUNNING-GRASS, P.O. Box 1946, Sausalito, CA 94965; Phone: 415-331-4540
Publication(s): *Journal of Multicultural Environmental Education; Perspectives; Monographs; Research Papers*
Keyword(s): Culture, Environment, Environmental and Conservation Education, Justice, Training

THRESHOLD, INC.
International Center for Environmental Renewal, Drawer CU, Bisbee, AZ 85603
Phone: 520-432-7353; E-mail: sactedway.com; Web Site: www.sactedway.com
Founded: 1972
Scope: International

Description: An international center seeking to improve mankind's understanding of and relationship to the environment at five levels: Individual and home, neighborhood, city, bio-region, national, and international. Projects involve environmental research, case studies, planning, education, communication, conferencing, and demonstration activities. Primary focus is on wilderness retreats, vision quests, and awareness training in nature.
Contact(s):
Chairman: JOHN P. MILTON; Phone: 520-432-5814
Vice Chairman: GEORGE A. BINNEY; Phone: 520-398-9163
Secretary, Treasurer and Administrative Officer of Arizona Office: BUD WILSON; Phone: 1-800-294-4795
Director of San Francisco Office: JOHN DIAMANTE; Phone: 415-986-0999
Director of Tucson, Arizona Office: SARAH SHER; Phone: 520-432-7353
Keyword(s): Environmental and Conservation Education, International Conservation, Internships, Land Use Planning, Wilderness, Wildlife and Wildlife Habitat, Vision Quest

TOGETHER FOUNDATION, THE
130 S. Willard St., Burlington, VT 05401
Phone: 802-862-2030
Founded: 1989; Membership: 1,000
Scope: National
Description: To facilitate positive global change by establishing communications and information systems that inventory and integrate the resources and needs of people, projects, and organizations working on environment, sustainable development, and human rights.
Contact(s):
President: ELLA CISNEROS
Vice President: JAMES MacINTYRE
Secretary: ROBIN RUGG
Publication(s): *The Together Foundation Newsletter*
Keyword(s): Communications, Environmental and Conservation Education, Environmental Planning, Sustainable Development

TRAFFIC NORTH AMERICA
c/o World Wildlife Fund, Attn: Director of Program Assistant, 1250 24th St., NW, Washington, DC 20037
Phone: 202-293-4800; Fax: 202-775-8287
Scope: National
Description: Trade Records Analysis of Flora and Fauna in Commerce is a scientific, information-gathering program that monitors the trade in wild animals and plants and the products made from them. It is a program of World Wildlife Fund and is a part of an international network of TRAFFIC offices.
Contact(s):
Director: SIMON HABEL
Director of Program Assistant: HOLLY REED
Program Officer: CHRIS ROBBINS
Senior Program Officer: CRAIG HOOVER
Publication(s): *TRAFFIC USA; Special Reports*
Keyword(s): Birds, Endangered and Threatened Species, Mammals, Wildlife Management

TREAD LIGHTLY! INC.
298 24th St., Suite 325, Ogden, UT 84401
Phone: 801-627-0077 or 800-966-9900
Founded: 1990
Scope: National
Description: Tread Lightly!, Inc. is a nonprofit organization that is an ethical and educational force among outdoor enthusiasts and the industries that serve them. Tread Lightly annually carries out programs designed to instill a proactive, low impact message among enthusiasts, manufacturers, advertising agencies, the media and children of all ages.
Contact(s):
Chairman: ROBERT E. CLEVER, 1919 Torrance Blvd., Torrance, CA 90501-2746; Phone: 310-783-3795
Executive Director: LORI DAVIS
Secretary and Treasurer: DAVID O'DOWD, 221 N. LaSalle St., Chicago, IL 60601-1520; Phone: 312-372-7090
Vice Chairman: PHILIP MILBURN, One Olympic Plaza, Colorado Springs, CO 80909; Phone: 719-578-4717
Publication(s): *Tread Lightly! Trails Newsletter; Guide to Responsible Four-Wheeling; Guide To Responsible Snowmobiling; Guide to Responsible Trail Biking; Guide to Responsible ATV Riding; Guide to Responsible Mountain Biking; Guide to Responsible Personal Watercraft Use; Tread Lightly!'s Leaving a Good Impression Guide*
Keyword(s): Environmental and Conservation Education, Environmental Preservation, International Conservation, Outdoor Recreation

TREEPEOPLE
12601 Mulholland Dr., Beverly Hills, CA 90210
Phone: 818-753-4600; E-mail: treepeople@treepeople.org; Web Site: www.treepeople.org/trees and www.generationearth.com
Founded: 1973; Membership: 20,000
Scope: Statewide
Description: Andy Lipkis and his teenage friends became known as the "TreePeople" when they began planting trees to restore a dying forest. Through innovative education and training programs, TreePeople has involved thousands of students and volunteers in neighborhood renewal and community service throughout southern California. Today, TreePeople is at the forefront of the urban forestry movement, offering sustainable solutions for the urban ecosystem.
Contact(s):
President: ANDY LIPKIS
Director of Forestry Programs: ELEANOR TORRES
Director of Education Program: JEFF HOHENSEE
Publication(s): *Seedling News (member newsletter); The Simple Act of Planting a Tree; Healing Your Neighborhood, Your City and Your world; Second Nature: Adapting L.A.'s Landscape for Sustainable Living*
Keyword(s): Environmental and Conservation Education, Forests and Forestry, Trees, Urban Environment, Urban Forestry, Youth Organizations

TREES ATLANTA
96 Poplar St., NW, Atlanta, GA 30309
Phone: 404-522-4097; Fax: 404-522-6855; E-mail: info@treesatlanta.org; Web Site: www.treesatlanta.org
Founded: 1985; Membership: 2,000
Scope: Statewide
Description: Trees Atlanta is a citizens organization that plants, maintains, and conserves trees in metro Atlanta area and educates the public about the importance of trees.
Contact(s):
Executive Director: MARCIA BANSLEY
Volunteer Coordinator: GREG LEVINE
Publication(s): *Newsletter; Tree Walk Brochure*
Keyword(s): Ecology, Ecosystems, Environment, Environmental Protection, Greenhouse Effect/Global Warming, Stewardship, Trees, Urban Environment, Urban Forestry, Plants

TREES FOR THE FUTURE, INC.
9000 16th St., P.O. Box 7027, Silver Spring, MD 20907
Phone: 301-565-0630; Fax: 301-565-5012; E-mail: info@treesftf.org; Web Site: www.treesftf.org
Founded: 1989; Membership: 6,600
Scope: International
Description: Trees for the Future offers multi-purpose tree seeds, training materials, and technical assistance for requesting communities, institutions and individuals throughout the developing regions of the world. In addition, Trees for the Future creates awareness of the potential threat of Global Climatic Change and the simple, cost-effective solutions of tree-planting to counter the "Global Warming" effect.
Contact(s):
Chairman: DR. JOHN R. MOORE
Executive Director: JULIO NAVARRO-MONZO

President Emeritus: DAVE DEPPNER
Secretary: PATRICIA AIKEN
Treasurer: OSCAR V. GRUSPE
Administrator: DAVID MITZEL
Latin America/Caribbean Coordinator: ERIC SPILDE
Vice Chairman: CELSO MATAAC
Women's and Children's Programs: REMEDIOS G. DEPPNER
Publication(s): *Johnny Apple-Seed News; Technical Papers*
Keyword(s): Agriculture, Air Quality and Pollution, Chemical Pollution Control, Developing Countries, Energy Conservation, Environment, Environmental Planning, Environmental Preservation, Flowers, Plants, and Trees, Greenhouse Effect/Global Warming, International Conservation, Renewable Resources, Rural Development, Sustainable Development

TREES FOR TOMORROW, INC., NATURAL RESOURCES EDUCATION CENTER
P.O. Box 609, Eagle River, WI 54521
Phone: 715-479-6456/1-800-838-9472; Fax: 715-479-2318; E-mail: trees@nnex.net; Web Site: www.treesfortomarrow.com
Founded: 1944
Scope: Statewide
Description: Original purpose to help reforest northern Wisconsin and provide land management assistance; currently an education center which conducts multi-day workshops on the sensible management and use of natural resources. Also sells tree seedlings.
Contact(s):
President: JON SMITH, Louisiana-Pacific Corp., P.O. Box 190, Tomahawk, WI 54487-0190
Director: JIM HOLPERIN
President-elect: FRED SOUBA JR., Consolidated Paper, P.O. Box 8050, Wisconsin Rapids, WI 54495-8050
Keyword(s): Environmental and Conservation Education, Land Management, Trees

TRI-STATE BIRD RESCUE AND RESEARCH, INC.
110 Possum Hollow Rd., Newark, DE 19711
Phone: 302-737-9543; Fax: 302-737-9562
Founded: 1976; Membership: 2,000
Scope: Regional
Description: To study and promote healthy populations of native wildlife by rehabilitation of oiled birds; rehabilitation of injured, diseased, and orphaned birds for release back into the wild; conducting training and education programs for colleagues, peers, and the general public; and conducting medical and biological research consistent with goals of providing for the general well-being of native wildlife.
Contact(s):
President: DR. DAVID D. MOOBERRY, 106 Spottswood Ln., Kennett Square, PA 19348; Phone: 215-444-5495
Vice President: JOHN FRINK, 400 Milton Dr., Wilmington, DE 19802
Secretary: BARBARA DRUDING, 110 Possum Hollow Rd., Newark, DE 19711
Treasurer: MARY ROBINSON, 412 Ribblett Ln., Wilmington, DE 19808; Phone: 302-998-3288
Executive Director: DR. VIRGINIA PIERCE, 110 Possum Hollow Rd., Newark, DE 19711
Contact for Human Resources: JULIE BARTLEY
Publication(s): *Effects of Oil on Wildlife, The; Medical Notes for Rehabilitators; Oiled Bird Rehabilitation; Wildlife and Oil Spills Bulletin; Wildlife and Oil Spills: Rehabilitation, Research, and Contingency Planning*
Keyword(s): Birds, Endangered and Threatened Species, Environmental and Conservation Education, Wildlife Disease, Wildlife Rehabilitation, Oil Spill Response

TROUT UNLIMITED
National Headquarters, 1500 Wilson Blvd., Suite 310, Arlington, VA 22209-2404
Phone: 703-522-0200; Fax: 703-284-9400; E-mail: trout@tu.org; Web Site: http://tu.org
Founded: 1959; Membership: 100,000
Scope: National
Description: A nonprofit, tax-deductible international coldwater fisheries organization dedicated to the conservation, protection, and restoration of coldwater fisheries and their watersheds. Affiliates in Canada, New Zealand, and Australia.
Contact(s):
Chairman of National Resource Board: STEPHEN BORN, 424 Washburn Pl., Madison, WI 53403; Phone: 608-257-6625
Chairman of the Board: OAKLEIGH THORNE
Chief Operating and Financial Officer: KENNETH MENDEZ
Controller: BRUCE APSLEY
Coordinator of TU and FS: DON DUFF
Director of Development: WHIT FOSBURGH
Director of Government Affairs: STEVEN N. MOYER
Director of Public Relations: MAGGIE LOCKWOOD
Director of Resources: JOSEPH McGURRIN
Editor: CHRISTINE ARENA
Editor: PETER RAFLE
Manager of Membership Services: WENDY G. REED
New Zealand Office President: PHIL GATES, U.S. Trade Commission, U.S. Consulate, Private Bag 92022, Auckland, New Zealand
President and Chief Executive Officer: CHARLES F. GAUVIN
Regional Director of Southern Rockies: DAVID NICKUM, 1900 13th St., Ste 101, Boulder, CO 80302; Phone: 303-440-2937; Fax: 303-440-7933
Regional Vice President of Great Lakes: MIKE BROCK, 23410 Beech Rd., Southfield, MI 48034-3482; Phone: 248-356-8195; Fax: 810-592-6098; E-mail: mikebrock@medidone.net
Regional Vice President of Mid-Atlantic: LOU SCHMIDT, Rt. 1 Box 109-A, Bristol, WV 26332-9801; Phone: 304-367-2724; Fax: 304-367-2727; E-mail: lschmidt@lolina.net
Regional Vice President of Midwest: RAY SMITH, 70 N. College Ave., Suite 11, Fayetteville, AR 72701-5337; Phone: 501-521-7011; Fax: 501-443-4333; E-mail: rsmith7011@aol.com
Regional Vice President of New England: DAVID BOWIE, 540 Duck Pond Rd., Westbrook, ME 04092-2510; Phone: 207-854-9978; Fax: 207-770-1211; E-mail: usunmz6m@ibmmail.com
Regional Vice President of Northeast: THOMAS LOPEZZO, 47 Flintlock Dr., Long Valley, NJ 07835-0320; Phone: 973-765-6673; Fax: 973-705-5974; E-mail: 72077.1327@compuserve.com
Regional Vice President of Northern Rockies: KIRK EVENSON, P.O. Box 1525, Great Falls, MT 59403-1525; Phone: 406-454-1384; Fax: 406-761-2610; E-mail: evenson@mch.net
Regional Vice President of Pacific Northwest: K. ROBERT JOHNSON, 14727 SE 145th Pl., Renton, WA 98059-7336; Phone: 425-865-2201; Fax: 425-271-6378; E-mail: kbob@halcyon.com
Regional Vice President of Southeast: KIRK OTEY, 1308 Lexington Ave., Charlotte, NC 28203-4837; Phone: 704-334-3060; Fax: 704-334-0768; E-mail: kskotey@mindspring.com
Regional Vice President of Southern Rockies: JAY ENGEL, 225 County Road 516, Ignacio, CO 81137-9728; Phone: 790-563-6517; Fax: 970-563-9599; E-mail: engelbj@compuserve.com
Regional Vice President of Southwest: STAN GRIFFIN, 27 Dorset Ln., Mill Valley, CA 94941-5203; Phone: 510-528-5390; Fax: 510-528-7880; E-mail: tucalif@ziplink.net
TU and BLM Bring Back The Natives Program Coordinator: DAVID NOLTE, 6322 NW Atkinson Ave., Redmond, OR 97756; Phone: 541-548-FISH; Fax: 541-548-3473; E-mail: dnotte@bend-or.com
Wyoming TU Office Administrator: KATHY BUCHNER, P.O. Box 4069, Jackson, WY 83001; Phone: 307-733-6991; Fax: 307-733-9678; E-mail: kbuchner@wyoming.com
Publication(s): *TROUT magazine; Lines To Leaders; Emerger, The*
Keyword(s): Acid Rain, Aquatic Habitats, Endangered and Threatened Species, Environmental and Conservation Education, Rivers

TROUT UNLIMITED, ALASKA COUNCIL
P.O. Box 3324, Homer, AK 99603-3324
E-mail: tuakjack@pobox.alaska.net
Scope: Statewide

Description: A statewide council with ten active chapters dedicated to the protection and enhancement of the cold water fishery resource.
Contact(s):
Chairman: JACK WILLIS; Phone: (H)907-235-3860

TROUT UNLIMITED, ARIZONA COUNCIL
Arizona Council TU, 77 E. Columbus Ave #200, Phoenix, AZ 85012
Phone: 602-264-5840; E-mail: carm.moehle@azbar.org
Scope: Statewide
Description: A statewide council with four active chapters working for the protection and enhancement of coldwater fishery resources.
Contact(s):
Chairman: CARM MOEHLE

TROUT UNLIMITED, ARKANSAS COUNCIL
784 Texas Way, Fayetteville, AR 72701-4449
Phone: 501-521-0837
Scope: Statewide
Description: A statewide council with 3 active chapters working for the protection and enhancement of coldwater fishery resources.
Contact(s):
Chairman: JOHN HEHR

TROUT UNLIMITED, CALIFORNIA COUNCIL
State Office, 828 San Pablo Ave., Suite 244, Albany, CA 94706
Phone: 510-528-7880
Scope: Statewide
Description: A statewide council with ten active chapters working for the protection and enhancement of coldwater fishery resources.
Contact(s):
Chairman: CHARLES SCHULTZ, 1024 C Los Gamos, San Rafael, CA 94903-2517; Phone: 415-472-5837
Office Director: STAN GRIFFIN; Phone: 510-528-4772; Fax: 510-528-7880

TROUT UNLIMITED, COLORADO COUNCIL
1900 13th, Suite 101, Boulder, CO 80302
Phone: 303-440-2937; Fax: 303-440-7933
Scope: Statewide
Description: A statewide council with 28 active chapters working for the protection and enhancement of coldwater fishery resources.
Contact(s):
Chair: DAVID TAYLOR, 1487 Cross Creek Court, Lafayette, CO 80026-8000; Phone: (H)303-673-9815 (W)800-525-3786; Fax: 303-277-6246; E-mail: dave.taylor@coors.com

TROUT UNLIMITED, CONNECTICUT COUNCIL
654 Cyprus Rd., Newington, CT 06111-5612
Phone: 860-667-2515; E-mail: fraa@fraa.org
Scope: Statewide
Description: A statewide council with nine active chapters working for the protection and enhancement of coldwater fishery resources.
Contact(s):
Chairman: STEVE LEWIS

TROUT UNLIMITED, GEORGIA COUNCIL
Attn: Chairman, 540 Avalon Forest Dr., Lawrenceville, GA 30044-7803
Phone: 770-381-5147; E-mail: gmoran@redmax.com
Scope: Statewide
Description: A statewide council with 14 active chapters working for the protection and enhancement of coldwater fishery resources.
Contact(s):
Chairman: GREG MORAN
Vice Chairman: KEN LOUKO, 2490 Sharondale Dr., NE., Atlanta, GA 30305
Secretary: GENE BARRINGTON, 910 Wood Valley Ct., Cumming, GA 30130; Phone: 770-381-5147
Treasurer: JOE BISHOP, 1640 Powers Ferry Rd., Bldg. 22, Marietta, GA 30067; Phone: 404-933-1919
Environmental Affairs: BILL FOWLER, 3188 Argonne Dr., NE, Atlanta, GA 30305; Phone: 404-231-0898
Membership Director: BOB FOSTER, 5074 Odins Way, Marietta, GA 30067; Phone: 404-992-8789
Resource Director: GARLAND STEWART, 4453 Abingdon Dr., Stone Mountain, GA 30083; Phone: 404-294-0471

TROUT UNLIMITED, IDAHO COUNCIL
Attn: Chairman, P.O. Box AX, McCall, ID 83638-2551
Scope: Statewide
Description: A statewide council with eight active chapters dedicated to the protection and enhancement of the coldwater fishery resource.
Contact(s):
Chairman: ROBERT DUNNAGAN, 57 Maxie Ln., Sandpoint, ID 83864; Phone: 208-263-4433; Fax: 815-346-1400; E-mail: rdunnagan@nidlink.com

TROUT UNLIMITED, ILLINOIS COUNCIL
Attn: Chairman, 2580 Forest View Ave., River Grove, IL 60171-1602
Phone: 312-751-4730; E-mail: jhammon@aol.com or jdhammon@attmail.com
Scope: Statewide
Description: A statewide council with four active chapters working for the protection and enhancement of coldwater fishery resources.
Contact(s):
Chairman: JOSEPH HAMMON

TROUT UNLIMITED, KENTUCKY COUNCIL
Attn: Chairman, 75 Valley Rd., Louisville, KY 40204-1516
Phone: 502-562-0115
Scope: Statewide
Description: A statewide council with three active chapters working for the protection and enhancement of coldwater fishery resources.
Contact(s):
Chairman: STEPHEN WOODRING

TROUT UNLIMITED, MAINE COUNCIL
Attn: President, 16 Mountain St., Camden, ME 04843-1615
Phone: 207-586-5616; E-mail: sva@lincoln.midcoast.com
Scope: Statewide
Description: A statewide council with six active chapters working for the protection and enhancement of coldwater fishery resources.
Contact(s):
Chairman: JEFF REARDON

TROUT UNLIMITED, MARYLAND COUNCIL (Mid-Atlantic)
Attn: President, 3509 Pleasant Plains Dr., Reisterstown, MD 21136-4417
Phone: 410-239-8468; Fax: 410-374-5719; E-mail: tedgodfrey@erols.com
Scope: Statewide
Description: A statewide council with seven active chapters working for the protection and enhancement of coldwater fishery resources.
Contact(s):
Chairman: TED GODFREY

TROUT UNLIMITED, MASSACHUSETTS/RHODE ISLAND COUNCIL
Attn: Chairman, 11 Obeline Dr., North Smithfield, MA 02896-6927
Phone: 860-441-4589; E-mail: frugo@filbaneco.com
Scope: Statewide
Description: A statewide council with 12 active chapters working for the protection and enhancement of coldwater fishery resources.
Contact(s):
Chairman: FRED RUGO

TROUT UNLIMITED, MICHIGAN COUNCIL
Attn: Chairman, 106 Pheasant Run Dr., Troy, MI 48098-1796
Phone: 248-753-1168; Fax: 248-753-1823; E-mail: jjsabina@tir.com
Scope: Statewide

NON-GOVERNMENTAL ORGANIZATIONS - T

Description: A statewide council with 21 active chapters working for the protection and enhancement of coldwater fishery resources.
Contact(s):
Chairman: JOHN SABINA

TROUT UNLIMITED, MINNESOTA COUNCIL
820 Old Crystal Bay Rd., Wayzata, MN 55391-9365
Phone: 612-341-9360; Fax: 612-341-9363
Scope: Statewide
Description: A statewide council with nine active chapters working for the protection and enhancement of coldwater fishery resources.
Contact(s):
Chairman: GEORGE HUST

TROUT UNLIMITED, MONTANA COUNCIL
Attn: Chairman, P.O. Box 1638, Polson, MT 59860
Phone: 406-887-2495
Scope: Statewide
Description: A statewide council with 12 chapters working for the protection and enhancement of coldwater fishery resources.
Contact(s):
Chairman: RIC SMITH
Resource Director: MICHAEL BUSHLY, 2611 5th Ave., S., Great Falls, MT 59405-3023; Phone: 406-7278787; Fax: 406-727-2402; E-mail: mbushly@cmrussell.org

TROUT UNLIMITED, NEVADA COUNCIL
Attn: Chairman, P.O. Box 5882, Spring Creek, NV 89815
Phone: 702-753-4306; Fax: 702-753-4306; E-mail: creekworks@rabbitbrush.com
Scope: Statewide
Description: A statewide council with three active chapters, dedicated to the protection and enhancement of coldwater fishing resources.
Contact(s):
Chairman: MATT HOLFORD

TROUT UNLIMITED, NEW HAMPSHIRE COUNCIL
Attn: Chairman, 9 Sirod Rd., Windham, NH 03087-1401
Phone: 603-896-2236
Scope: Statewide
Description: A statewide council with six active chapters working for the protection and enhancement of coldwater fishery resources.
Contact(s):
Chairman: JAMES NORTON

TROUT UNLIMITED, NEW JERSEY COUNCIL
Attn: Chairman,90-100 Route 206 PMB #122, Stanhope, NJ 07874-3128
Phone: 1-800-524-2784; Fax: 973-691-0441
Scope: Statewide
Description: A statewide council with eight active chapters for the protection and enhancement of coldwater fishery resource.
Contact(s):
Chairman: FREDERICK EGE

TROUT UNLIMITED, NEW YORK COUNCIL
Attn: Chairman, 111 High Point Mountain Rd., West Shokan, NY 12494-5337
Phone: 914-892-8630; E-mail: karwac@ibm.org
Scope: Statewide
Description: A statewide council with 37 active chapters working for the protection and enhancement of coldwater fishery resources.
Contact(s):
Chairman: CHESTER KARWATOWSKI
Publication(s): *Long Casts*

TROUT UNLIMITED, NORTH CAROLINA
Attn: Chairman, 438 Armfield St., Statesville, DC 28677-5702
Phone: 704-878-3560; Fax: 704-878-3464; E-mail: davidstewart@usiway.net
Scope: Statewide
Description: Dedicated to the protection and enhancement of coldwater fishing resources.
Contact(s):
Chairman: DAVID STEWART

TROUT UNLIMITED, NORTH CAROLINA COUNCIL
Attn: Chairman, 135 Tacoma Cir., Asheville, NC 28801-1625
Phone: 704-684-5178; Fax: 704-687-1689
Scope: Statewide
Description: A statewide council with 18 active chapters working for the protection and enhancement of coldwater fishery resource.
Contact(s):
Chairman: KIRK OTEY, 1308 Lexington Ave., Charlotte, NC 28203; Phone: (H) 704-332-8232 (W) 800-432-6268; Fax: 704-375-6425

TROUT UNLIMITED, OHIO COUNCIL
Attn: Chairman, 1487 New Way Dr., Beaver Creek, OH 45434-6925
Phone: 937-426-5757; E-mail: mark.blauvelt@stdreg.com
Scope: Statewide
Description: Dedicated to the protection and enhancement of the coldwater fishery resource.
Contact(s):
President: MARK BLAUVELT

TROUT UNLIMITED, OKLAHOMA COUNCIL
Attn: Chairman, 9528 E. 55th St., Suite A, Tulsa, OK 74145
Phone: 918-822-6633; Fax: 918-627-2383
Scope: Statewide
Description: A statewide council with three active chapters dedicated to the protection and enhancement of coldwater fishing resources.
Contact(s):
Chairman: DALE DEUVALL
Keyword(s): Aquatic Habitats, Fisheries, Renewable Resources, Water Pollution Management, Wetlands

TROUT UNLIMITED, OREGON COUNCIL
Attn: Chairman, 22875,NW Chestnut St., Hillsboro, OR 97124-6545
Phone: 503-844-4519; Fax: 503-844-9929; E-mail: tmilowolf@aol.com
Scope: Statewide
Description: A statewide council with seven active chapters working for the protection and enhancement of the coldwater fishery resource.
Contact(s):
Chairman: THOMAS WOLF

TROUT UNLIMITED, OZARKS COUNCIL (MISSOURI)
2010 Daisy Ln., Jefferson, MO 65109-1810
Phone: 573-751-1039; Fax: 573-634-3096; E-mail: jdwenzlick@juno.com
Scope: Statewide
Description: A statewide council with four active chapters working for the protection and enhancement of coldwater fishery resources.
Contact(s):
Chairman: JOHN WENZLICK

TROUT UNLIMITED, PENNSYLVANIA COUNCIL
Attn: Chairman, RD 1 Box 131B, Spring Mills, PA 16875-9623
Phone: 814-863-7585; Fax: 814-865-9131; E-mail: edb1@psu.edu
Scope: Statewide
Description: A statewide council with 56 active chapters working for the protection and enhancement of the coldwater fishery resource.
Contact(s):
Chairman: EDWARD BELLIS
Publication(s): *TCWA Report*
Keyword(s): Environmental and Conservation Education, Land Use Planning, Water Quality, Watersheds, Wildlife Rehabilitation

TROUT UNLIMITED, SOUTH CAROLINA COUNCIL
Attn: Chairman, 115 Conrad Cir., Columbia, SC 29212-2619

Phone: 803-777-7652; Fax: 803-777-4760; E-mail: malcolmL@gwm.sc.edu
Scope: Statewide
Description: A statewide council with four active chapters working for the protection and enhancement of coldwater fishery resources.
Contact(s):
Chairman: MALCOLM LEAPHART

TROUT UNLIMITED, TENNESSEE COUNCIL
Attn: Chairman, 1326 Lipscomb Dr., Brentwood, TN 37027
Phone: 615-371-9211; E-mail: johns@bwood.com
Scope: Statewide
Description: A statewide council with 10 active chapters working for the protection and enhancement of the coldwater fishery resource.
Contact(s):
Chairman: JOHN SMITHERMAN

TROUT UNLIMITED, UTAH COUNCIL
Attn: Chairman, 1471 E. Canyon Dr., South Weber, UT 84405-9629
Phone: 801-538-7353; Fax: 801-538-7278; E-mail: rwj@utw.com
Scope: Statewide
Description: Dedicated to the protection and enhancement of the coldwater fishery resource.
Contact(s):
Chairman: WES JOHNSON

TROUT UNLIMITED, VERMONT COUNCIL
Attn: Chairman, P.O. Box 163, Island Pond, VT 05846-0163
Phone: 802-334-1674; Fax: 802-334-2991
Scope: Statewide
Description: A statewide council with six chapters working for the protection and enhancement of the coldwater fishery resource.
Contact(s):
Chairman: FRANCIS SMITH

TROUT UNLIMITED, VIRGINIA COUNCIL
Attn: Chairman, 202 Deerfield Ln., Lynchburg, VA 24502-3122
Phone: 804-239-1017; E-mail: dorffly@aol.com
Scope: Statewide
Description: A statewide organization with 16 active chapters working for the protection and enhancement of the coldwater fishery resource.
Contact(s):
Chairman: THOMAS REISDORF

TROUT UNLIMITED, WASHINGTON COUNCIL
Attn: Chairman, 2701 NE 148th Ave., Vancouver, WA 98684-7877
Phone: 360-896-6967; E-mail: ohio12@uswest.net
Scope: Statewide
Description: A statewide council with 31 active chapters working for the protection and enhancement of coldwater fishery resources.
Contact(s):
Chairman: JAMES DERRY
Publication(s): *Trout and Salmon Leader*

TROUT UNLIMITED, WEST VIRGINIA COUNCIL
Attn: Chairman, 180 Oriole Rd., Fraziers Bottom, WV 25082-9724
Phone: 304-937-2214; E-mail: ecrum@aol.com
Scope: Statewide
Description: A statewide council with 8 active chapters working for the protection and enhancement of coldwater fishery resources.
Contact(s):
Chairman: ED CRUM

TROUT UNLIMITED, WISCONSIN COUNCIL
Attn: Chairman, P.O. Box 228, Eau Claire, WI 54702-0228
Phone: 715-831-9568; Fax: 715-831-9568; E-mail: jwelter@discover-net.net
Scope: Statewide
Description: A statewide council with 21 active chapters working for the protection and enhancement of coldwater fishery resources.
Contact(s):
Chairman: JOHN WELTER
Publication(s): *Wisconsin Trout*

TROUT UNLIMITED, WYOMING COUNCIL
Attn: Chairman, P.O. Box 1022, Jackson, WY 83001
Phone: 307-733-1530; E-mail: jbuchner@wyoming.com
Scope: Statewide
Description: A statewide council with 16 active chapters dedicated to the protection and enhancement of the coldwater fishery resource.
Contact(s):
Chairman: JAY BUCHNER
Executive Director: JOHN ZELAZNY, T.U. Wyoming, P.O. Box 4069, Jackson, WY 83001; Phone: 307-733-1486

TRUMPETER SWAN SOCIETY, THE
3800 County Rd. 24, Maple Plain, MN 55359
Phone: 612-476-4663; Fax: 612-476-1514; E-mail: ttss@hennepinparks.org
Founded: 1968; Membership: 500
Scope: International
Description: International scientific and educational organization dedicated to assuring the vitality and welfare of wild Trumpeter Swan populations in North America, and to restoring the species to its original range. The Society promotes research into Trumpeter ecology and management, and provides a framework for exchange of knowledge about the species.
Contact(s):
Executive Director: RUTH E. SHEA, 3346 East 200 N., Rigby, ID 83442
President and Editor: HARVEY K. NELSON, 10515 Kell Ave., Bloomington, MN 55437
Vice President: LARRY GILLETTE
Editor: MADELEINE LINCK
Editor: JANE NOLL WEST
Publication(s): *North American Swans, Bulletin of the Trumpeter Swan Society; Trumpetings; Proceedings and Papers of the 14th Trumpeter Swan Society Conference; Proceedings and Papers of the 15th Trumpeter Swan Society Conference; Proceedings and Papers of the 16th Trumpeter Swan Society Conference*
Keyword(s): Birds, Nongame Wildlife, Waterfowl, Wetlands, Wildlife and Wildlife Habitat

TRUST FOR PUBLIC LAND, THE
Headquarters, National Office, Attn: Public Affairs Assistant, 116 New Montgomery St. 4th Fl., San Francisco, CA 94105
Phone: 415-495-4014/1-800-714-LAND; Fax: 415-495-4103; E-mail: info@tpl.org; Web Site: www.tpl.org
Founded: 1972
Scope: National
Description: TPL specializes in conservation real estate, applying its expertise in negotiations, public finance and law to protect land for public use and enjoyment. TPL has helped protect more than 1 million acres nationwide and has recently launched its Greenprint for Growth campaign to help sprawl-threatened communities protect land as a way to guide development and sustain a healthy economy and a high quality of life.
Contact(s):
President: WILL ROGERS
Executive Vice President: RALPH W. BENSON
Senior Vice President and CFO: ROBERT W. McINTYRE
Vice President: ERNEST COOK, 33 Union St., 4th Fl., Boston, MA 02108; Phone: 617-367-6200
Vice President: KATHY BLAHA, 666 Pennsylvania Ave. SE, Washington, DC 20003; Phone: 202-543-7552
Vice President of External Affairs: JENNIE GERARD
Vice President of Land Transactions: STEPHEN E. THOMPSON, 418 Montezuma, Santa Fe, NM 87501; Phone: 505-988-5922

NON-GOVERNMENTAL ORGANIZATIONS - T

Vice President and Southeast Regional Manager: W. DALE ALLEN, 306 N. Monroe St., Tallahassee, FL 32301-7635; Phone: 904-222-7911
Atlanta Field Office Director: RAND WENTWORTH, 1447 Peachtree St., NE, Suite 601, Atlanta, GA 30309; Phone: 404-873-7306
Mid-Atlantic Regional Manager: ROSE HARVEY, 666 Broadway, New York, NY 10012; Phone: 212-677-7171
New England Regional Manager: WHITNEY HATCH, 33 Union St., 4th Fl., Boston, MA 02108; Phone: 617-367-6200
Northwest Regional Manager: BOWEN BLAIR, Smith Tower, Suite 1510, 506 2nd Ave., Seattle, WA 98104; Phone: 206-587-2447
Southwest Regional Manager: TED HARRISON, 418 Montezuma, Santa Fe, NM 87501; Phone: 505-988-5922
Western Regional Manager: REED HOLDERMAN, 116 New Montgomery, 3rd Fl., San Francisco, CA 94105; Phone: 415-495-5660
Director of Federal Affairs: ALAN FRONT
Director of Public Affairs: SUSAN IVES
Editor: SUSAN IVES
General Counsel: NELSON LEE
Publication(s): *Land and People; Regional newsletters*
Keyword(s): Land Purchase, Open Space, Outdoor Recreation, Watersheds, Wilderness, Smart Growth, Sprawl

TRUST FOR WILDLIFE, INC.
127 Ehrich Rd., Shaftsbury, VT 05262
Phone: 802-447-0746
Founded: 1983
Scope: International
Description: Dedicated to wildlife conservation and education with a focus on wildlife habitats, international partnerships with a focus on Russia, and wildlife rehabilitation with an emphasis on public education.
Contact(s):
President: MARSHAL T. CASE
Secretary: GREGORY SHARP, 225 Reeds Gap Rd., East Northford, CT 6472; Phone: 203-240-6046
Director: LES LINE, P.O. Box 323, Amenia, NY 12501; Phone: 914-373-9135
Director: ED METCALFE, 6373 Vermont Rt 100, Whitingham, VT 05361; Phone: 802-464-0048
Keyword(s): Biodiversity, Communications, Environmental and Conservation Education, International Conservation, Land Preservation, Natural History, Nature Preservation, Wildlife and Wildlife Habitat, Wildlife Rehabilitation, Youth Organizations

TRUSTEES FOR ALASKA
725 Christensen Dr., Suite 4, Anchorage, AK 99501-2101
Phone: 907-276-4244; Fax: 907-276-7110; E-mail: ecolaw@trustees.org; Web Site: www.trustees.org
Founded: 1974; Membership: 1,200
Scope: Statewide
Description: Nonprofit, public-interest, environmental law firm working to ensure that Alaska's unique environmental values are not lost to future generations through irresponsible development or irrational public management. Primarily concerned with protection of Alaska's environment and the wise management of Alaska's resources.
Contact(s):
Chair: KEN ROBERTSON
Secretary: CHRIS ROSE
Treasurer: DAN DICKENSON
Executive Director: ANN L. ROTHE
Litigation Director: PETER VAN TUYN
Staff Attorney: VALERIE BROWN
Staff Attorney: ROBERT RANDALL
Staff Attorney: MICHAEL FRANK
Vice-Chair: MARY McBURNEY
Keyword(s): Environmental Law

TRUSTEES OF RESERVATIONS, THE
572 Essex St., Beverly, MA 01915-1530
Phone: 978-921-1944; Fax: 978-921-1948; E-mail: ttorhq@ttor.org; Web Site: www.thetrustees.org
Founded: 1891; Membership: 21,000
Scope: Statewide
Description: The Trustees of Reservations is the nation's oldest statewide non-profit conservation and preservation organization. TTOR is dedicated to preserving, for public use and enjoyment, properties of exceptional scenic, historic and ecological value in addition to other special places throughout Massachusetts.
Contact(s):
Chairman: ELLIOT SURKIN
President: JANICE HUNT
Secretary: F. SYDNEY SMITHERS
Treasurer: FRANZ COLLOREDO-MANSFELD
Executive Director: FREDERIC WINTHROP
Director of Communications and Marketing: MICHAEL TRIFF
Director of Development: ANN POWELL
Director of Finance and Administration: JOHN MCCRAE
Director of Land Conservation: WESLEY WARD
Director of Planned Giving: SARAH CAROTHERS
Director of Property Management: RICHARD HOWE
Publication(s): *Annual Report; Land Conservation Options: A Guide For Massachusetts Landowners; Newsletter; Reservations Guidebook; Conserving our Common Wealth: A Vision for the Massachusetts Landscape*
Keyword(s): Environmental Protection, Gardening and Horticulture, Historic Preservation, Land Conservation, Nature Preservation, Open Space

TUG HILL TOMORROW LAND TRUST
P.O. Box 6063, Watertown, NY 13601
Phone: 315-785-2382; E-mail: THTomorrow@imcnet.net
Founded: 1990; Membership: 100
Scope: Regional
Description: Tug Hill Tomorrow is a private nonprofit corporation that works to help retain the forests, farms, recreational, and wild lands of the Tug Hill region through education, research, and voluntary land protection.
Contact(s):
Chair: PAUL MILLER, 3825 Miller Rd., Blossvale, NY 13308-9781; Phone: 315-337-4079
Vice Chair: STACEY SMITH, 8978 Church St., Remsen, NY 13438; Phone: 315-896-2814
Secretary/Treasurer: THOMAS J. YOUSEY III, R.D. 1 Box 309, Glenfield, NY 13343; Phone: 315-376-7633
Publication(s): *Greenings; Tug Hill Recreation Guide: A Guide to Cross-Country Skiing, Hiking, Biking, and Fishing; Tug Hill Working Lands; Tug Hill Resource Guide to Educational Programs; Tug Hill Natural History Field Guide*
Keyword(s): Environmental and Conservation Education, Forests and Forestry, Land Preservation, Natural Areas, Open Space

TURTLE CREEK WATERSHED ASSOCIATION, INC.
3001 Meadowbrook Rd., Murrysville, PA 15668-1627
Phone: 724-387-2000; E-mail: GOODFISH@helicon.net; Web Site: www.turtlecreekwatershed.org
Founded: 1969; Membership: 250
Scope: Local Region
Description: The objective of the Turtle Creek Watershed Association, Inc. is to preserve and protect natural resources; educate the community about important environmental issues; monitor and improve water quality; and work with responsible agencies to encourage wise land use planning in the Turtle Creek Watershed.
Contact(s):
President: ROBERT A. MAZIK SR.
Vice President: HENRY HOFFMAN
Secretary: EDWARD FISCHER
Treasurer: A.B. CARL
Executive Director (Temporary): EDWARD FISCHER
Director Emeritus: JAMES TEMPERO
Publication(s): *Conserve; Business Associate; TCWA*

Keyword(s): Endangered and Threatened Species, Environmental and Conservation Education, Environmental Protection, Land Purchase, Rivers, Water Quality, Watersheds, Wildlife and Wildlife Habitat

U

U.S. PUBLIC INTEREST RESEARCH GROUP
218 D St., SE, Washington, DC 20003
Phone: 202-546-9707; Fax: 202-546-2461; E-mail: usping@pirg.org; Web Site: www.pirg.org1
Founded: 1983
Scope: National
Description: U.S. PIRG is the national lobbying office for state PIRGs around the country, representing more than one million members. We conduct independent research and lobby for national environmental and consumer protections.
Contact(s):
Director: GENE KARPINSKI
Publication(s): *Citizen Agenda; A publication list available upon request.*
Keyword(s): Air Quality and Pollution, Chemical Pollution Control, Conservation of Protected Areas, Endangered and Threatened Species, Energy, Energy Conservation, Environment, Environmental Protection, Pollution Prevention, Solid Waste Management, Water Pollution, Wetlands

UNION OF CONCERNED SCIENTISTS
Two Brattle Square, Cambridge, MA 2238
Phone: 617-547-5552; Web Site: www.uscusa.org
Founded: 1969; Membership: 70,000
Scope: National
Description: The Union of Concerned Scientists is a national non-profit working for a cleaner environment and a safer world. UCS is working to encourage preservation of life-sustaining resources, promote energy technologies that are renewable, safe, and cost-effective, promote advanced transportation technologies, encourage sustainable agriculture, and curtail weapons proliferation.
Contact(s):
Chairman: KURT GOTTFRIED
Executive Director: HOWARD RIS JR.
Publication(s): *Newsletter: NUCLEUS; The Gene Exchange; Earthwise; The Consumer's Guide to Effective Environmental Choices; Powerful Solutions: Seven Ways to Switch America to Renewable Electricity; Now or Never: Serious New Plans to Save a Natural Pest Control*
Keyword(s): Agriculture, Biodiversity, Biotechnology, Energy, Environment, Environmental and Conservation Education, Greenhouse Effect/Global Warming, Nuclear Energy, Renewable Resources, Solar Energy, Sustainable Development, Transportation

UNITED NATIONS ENVIRONMENT PROGRAMME
P.O. Box 30552, Nairobi Kenya
Phone: 254--2-623089; Fax: 254-2-623692; E-mail: ipainfo@unep.org; Web Site: www.unep.org
Founded: 1972
Scope: International
Description: The United Nations Environment Programme (UNEP) was established by the U.N. General Assembly to be the environmental conscience of the U.N. system. It assesses the state of the world's environment; environmental management capacity of developing countries; and raises environmental considerations for the social and economic policies and programs of UN agencies. UNEP provides a unique forum to bring countries to the table for negotiations, to build consensus and forge international agreements. In doing so, it makes a particular effort to nurture partnerships with business and industry, the scientific and academic community, non-governmental organizations, community groups, youth, women and sports organizations.
Contact(s):
Deputy Executive Director: SHAFQAT KAKAKHEL
Under Secretary General of the United Nations and Executive Director: KLAUS TOEPFER
Publication(s): *Our Planet Magazine; The Environment in Print; Global Environment Outlook, For Life on Earth (CD-ROM)*
Keyword(s): Air Quality and Pollution, Biodiversity, Biotechnology, Chemical Pollution Control, Coasts, Ecology, Endangered and Threatened Species, Environment, Environmental Ethics, Environmental Law, Environmental Planning, Environmental Protection, International Conservation, Urban Environment, Water Resources

Latin America and Caribbean Region
UNEP-ROLAC (United Nations Environment Programme)
Apdo., Postal 10.793, Mexico, D.F. 11000 Mexico
Phone: 52-5202-4841/6394; Fax: 52-5-202-0950; E-mail: rolac@rolac.unep.mx; Web Site: www.rolac.unep.mx
Scope: International

North America Regional Office
United Nations, Rm. DC2-0803, New York, NY 10017
Phone: 212-963-8210; Fax: 212-963-7341; E-mail: uneprona@un.org
Scope: International
Contact(s):
Director: ADNAN Z. AMIN
Information Officer: JAMES SNIFFEN

UNITED STATES CHAMBER OF COMMERCE
1615 H St., NW, Washington, DC 20062
Phone: 202-659-6000
Founded: 1912
Scope: National
Description: Created to provide business representation on major national issues. Membership includes 3,000 chambers of commerce, 1,200 trade and professional associations, and 215,000 business firms.
Contact(s):
Associate Director (Food Safety, Agriculture): WENDY SAIDI
Associate Director (Regulatory Affairs, Superfund): LOUIS RENJEL
Legislative Assistant (Electricity, Natural Resources): JUDY BROWN
Vice President, Environment and Regulatory Affairs: WILLIAM KOVACS
Keyword(s): Agriculture, Energy, Pollution Control, Trade/Business

UNITED STATES COMMITTEE FOR THE UNITED NATIONS ENVIRONMENT PROGRAMME THE (U.S. and UNEP)
2013 Q St., NW, Washington, DC 20009
Phone: 202-234-3600
Scope: National
Description: A nonprofit support group for the U.N. Environment Programme, U.S. and UNEP generates public awareness of global environmental issues, including ozone layer depletion, the greenhouse effect, and the transport of hazardous chemicals, and UNEP's response to these issues. The organization links UNEP to environmental groups across the U.S.
Contact(s):
President: RICHARD A. HELLMAN
Vice President: MICHAEL D. GRANOFF
Editor: ANN R. ULRICH
Publication(s): *US and UNEP NEWS*
Keyword(s): Agriculture, Endangered and Threatened Species, Environmental and Conservation Education, Greenhouse Effect/Global Warming, International Conservation

UNITED STATES TOURIST COUNCIL
Drawer 1875, Washington, DC 20013-1875
Scope: National
Description: A nonprofit association of conservation-concerned individuals, industries, and institutions who travel or cater to the traveler. Emphasis is on historic and scenic preservation, wilderness and roadside development, ecology through sound planning and education, and support of scientific studies of natural wilderness.

NON-GOVERNMENTAL ORGANIZATIONS - U

Contact(s):
Chairman of Board of Trustees and Executive Director: DR. STANFORD WEST
Keyword(s): Aquatic Habitats, Forests and Forestry, Historic Preservation, International Conservation, Wetlands

UPPER CHATTAHOOCHEE RIVERKEEPER
1900 Emery St., Suite 450, Atlanta, GA 30318
Phone: 404-352-9828; Fax: 404-352-8676; E-mail: rirrkeep@mindspring.com; Web Site: www.chattahoochee.org
Founded: 1994; Membership: 2,300
Scope: Regional
Description: To advocate and secure the protection and stewardship of the Chattahoochee River, its tributaries and watershed using education, research, communication, cooperation, monitoring and legal actions.
Contact(s):
Executive Director: SALLY BETHEA; E-mail: sbethea@mindspring.com
Director of Headwaters Conservation: KATHERINE BAER; Phone: 770-538-2619; Fax: 770-538-2625; E-mail: krivekeeper@mindspring.com
Director of Marketing and Education: DANA POOLE
General Counsel: MICHELLE FRIED; E-mail: mfriverkeeper@mindspring.com
Program Manager for River Basin Protection: MATT KALES; E-mail: mknverkeeper@mindspring.com
Watershed Protection Specialist: ALICE CHANIPAGNE
Publication(s): *River Chat; Stream Chat; Tri-State Coalition Newsletter*
Keyword(s): Environmental and Conservation Education, Research, Rivers, Water Resources, Watershed Protection

UPPER MISSISSIPPI RIVER CONSERVATION COMMITTEE
4469 - 48th Avenue Ct., Rock Island, IL 61201
Phone: 309-793-5800, ext. 522; E-mail: UMRCC@Mississippi-River.com; Web Site: Mississippi-River.com/UMRCC
Founded: 1943
Scope: Regional
Description: Promotes preservation, development, and wise use of the natural and recreational resources of the Upper Mississippi River and formulates policies, plans, and programs for conducting cooperative studies. Members: state conservation departments of Illinois, Iowa, Minnesota, Missouri, and Wisconsin.
Contact(s):
Chairperson: MARY ELLEN VOLLBREECHT, Wisconsin Dept. Of Natural Resources, 101 S. Webster St., Box 7921, Madison, WI 53707; Phone: 608-264-8554
Coordinator: JON DUYVEJONCK; Phone: 309-793-5800, ext. 522
Secretary and Treasurer: KEN BRUMMETT, Missouri Dept. of Conservation, 653 Clinic Rd., Hannibal, MO 63401; Phone: 309-582-5611
Publication(s): *Annual Proceedings; Newsletter; and miscellaneous technical reports*
Keyword(s): Aquatic Habitats, Biology, Fisheries, Rivers, Sustainable Development, Water Quality, Water Resources, Mussels

URBAN HABITAT PROGRAM
P.O. Box 29908, Presidro Station, San Francisco, CA 94129
Phone: 415-561-3333; Fax: 415-561-3334
Founded: 1989
Scope: National
Description: The Urban Habitat Program is a project of Tides Center. Its mission is to build multi-cultural urban environmental leadership for socially-just and sustainable communities in the San Francisco Bay area. Our project areas include transportation, regional land use and social justice, land recycling and brown fields, leadership institute for sustainability and justice, and the goal of ecological literacy, all from an ecological and social justice perspective.
Contact(s):
Director: CARL ANTHONY
Publication(s): *Race, Poverty & the Environment*
Keyword(s): Brown Fields, Cultural Preservation, Environmental Justice, Land Use Planning, People of Color in the Environment, Transportation, Urban Environment

URBAN WILDLIFE RESOURCES
5130 W. Running Brook Rd., Columbia, MD 21044
Phone: 410-997-7161; Fax: 410-997-6849; Web Site: www.erols.com/urbanwildlife
Founded: 1995
Scope: International
Description: Urban Wildlife Resources works to facilitate interaction and cooperation among land managers and planners, biologists, landscape architects, and others in achieving better management of natural resources in urban and urbanizing areas.
Contact(s):
President: DR. LOWELL ADAMS
Publication(s): *Urban Open Space Manager, The*
Keyword(s): Conservation, International Conservation, Open Space, Urban Environment, Urban Forestry, Urban and Rural Development, Wildlife and Wildlife Habitat, Wildlife Management

UTAH ASSOCIATION OF SOIL CONSERVATION DISTRICTS
Attn: President, 403 East Center, Nephi, UT 84648
Scope: Statewide
Contact(s):
President, Alternate Board Member: RANDY GREENHALGH; Phone: 435-623-0845; Fax: 435-623-0845
Vice President: LARRY JOHNSON, P.O. Box 177, Randolph, UT 84064; Phone: 435-793-5625; Fax: 435-793-5625
Executive Vice President: GORDON YOUNKER, 1860 N 100 E, North Logan, UT 84341-2215; Phone: 435-753-6029; Fax: 435-755-2117; E-mail: gordon-yonker@ut.nacdnet.org
Secretary and Treasurer: RICHARD SAUNDERS, 4083 W 12680 S., Payson, UT 84651; Phone: 801-465-2777
Board Member: WILLIAM RIGBY, 1616 N. Main, Centerville, UT 84014; Phone: 801-292-0245; Fax: 801-296-8586
Keyword(s): Conservation Districts

UTAH B.A.S.S. CHAPTER FEDERATION
Attn: President, 3460 Scott Cir., Salt Lake City, UT 84115
Scope: Statewide
Description: An organization of Bassmaster chapters, affiliated with the Bass Anglers Sportsman Society, organized to fight pollution, assist state and national conservation agencies in their efforts, and teach young people of our country good conservation practices. Dedicated to the realistic conservation of our water resources.
Contact(s):
President: GEORGE SOMMER; Phone: 801-487-8711
Conservation Director: WALTER MALDONADO, P.O. Box 482, Green River, UT 84525-0482; Phone: 435-564-8147
Publication(s): *Nature News Notes*
Keyword(s): Environmental and Conservation Education, Natural Areas, Nature Preservation, Nongame Wildlife, Wildlife and Wildlife Habitat

UTAH NATURE STUDY SOCIETY
Attn: President Utah Nature Study Society, 2853 S. 23rd East, Salt Lake City, UT 84109
Founded: 1954
Scope: Statewide
Description: Promotes conservation and nature education through workshops and field trips for members; publicizes conservation problems and issues through meetings and its newsletter. Member of Utah Associated Garden Clubs.
Contact(s):
President: DOROTHY K. PLATT, 2853 S. 23rd East, Salt Lake City, UT 84109
Secretary: MARIA DICKERSON, 323 S. 2nd W., Tooele, UT 84074
Executive Secretary: JEAN WHITE, 377 E. 5300 S., Murray, UT 84107-6019
Editor: CATHERINE QUINN, 1383 S. 300 East, Salt Lake City, UT 84115
Publication(s): *UWA Review*

Keyword(s): Biodiversity, Environmental and Conservation Education, Public Lands, Wilderness, Wildlife Management

UTAH WILDERNESS COALITION
P.O. Box 520974, Salt Lake City, UT 84152-0974
Phone: 801-486-2872; Fax: 801-485-5572
Founded: 1985
Scope: Statewide
Description: Promote and coordinate the preservation of U.S. BLM wildlands in southern and western Utah through public education and the passage of American's Redrock Wilderness Act. The goal includes protection of the remaining wilderness quality public lands under the National Wilderness Preservation System.
Contact(s):
Board Member: WAYNE HOSKISSON, The Sierra Club, 2273 South Highland Drive, Salt Lake City, UT 84106; Phone: 801-467-9294
Board Member: PAM EATON, The Wilderness Society, 7475 Dankin Street, #410, Denver, CO 80221; Phone: 303-650-5818
Board Member: MIKE MATZ, Southern Utah Wilderness Alliance, 1471 S. 1100 E., Salt Lake City, UT 84105; Phone: 801-486-3161
Board Member: JOHN VERANTH, Wasatch Mountain Club, 1390 South 1100 East STE 103, Salt Lake City, UT 84105; Phone: 801-463-9842
Co-Chairperson: BOB BINGAMAN, National Field Director of the Sierra Club, 408 C Street NE, Washington, DC 20002; Phone: 202-547-1141
Co-Chairperson: LARRY YOUNG, 1390 South 1100 East, Salt Lake City, UT 84105; Phone: 801-486-2872
Publication(s): *Wilderness at the Edge*
Keyword(s): Outdoor Recreation, Public Lands, Wilderness

UTAH WILDLIFE FEDERATION
P.O. Box 526367, Salt Lake City, UT 84152-6367
Phone: 801-487-1946; Fax: 801-846-0611
Scope: Statewide
Description: A representative statewide organization, affiliated with the National Wildlife Federation, dedicated to the protection and enhancement of wildlife and its habitat through public education and government interaction.
Contact(s):
Editor: RAY SCHELBLE
Publication(s): *Utah Wildlife News*

UTAH WOODLAND OWNERS COUNCIL
2829 Sleep Hollow Dr., Salt Lake City, UT 84117
Phone: 801-277-1615
Founded: 1997; Membership: 75
Scope: Statewide
Description: A statewide organization affiliated with the National Woodland Owners Association and associated with Utah Farms Bureau, that is working for good forest management practices on the private forest and ranch land in Utah.
Contact(s):
Chairman: RICHARD OLDROYD
Keyword(s): Forests and Forestry

V

VERMONT ASSOCIATION OF CONSERVATION DISTRICTS
Attn: President, 504 Thompson Hill Rd., Weybridge, VT 05753
Scope: Statewide
Contact(s):
President and Board Member: CLAIRE AYER; Phone: 802-545-2142; Fax: 802-545-2142; E-mail: ayer@together.net
Vice President: MARY JEANNE PACKER, RR 2 Box 1371, Poultney, VT 05764; Phone: 802-287-4284; Fax: 802-287-4285
Secretary: MARSHALL REED, HC 32 Box 312, Chittenden, VT 05737; Phone: 802-483-9437; Fax: 802-773-4177
Treasurer: DAVID STEVENS, 1018 Bible Hill Rd., Wells River, VT 05081; Phone: 802-757-2318; Fax: 802-296-3654

Keyword(s): Conservation Districts

VERMONT AUDUBON COUNCIL
65 Millet St., Richmond, VT 05477
Phone: 802-434-4300
Scope: Statewide
Description: A statewide council consisting of eight chapters of the National Audubon Society formed to protect birds, other wildlife and their habitats by promoting a culture of conservation through research, education and advocacy.
Contact(s):
President: WARREN KING, P.O. Box 77, Ripton, VT 05766
Vice President: SEWARD WEBER, R.D. 2, Box 390, Plainfield, VT 05667
Treasurer: SUZANNA LIEPMANN, P.O. Box 112, South Strafford, VT 05070
Keyword(s): Birds, Environmental and Conservation Education, Forests and Forestry, Nongame Wildlife, Planning Management, Wetlands, Wildlife and Wildlife Habitat

VERMONT B.A.S.S. CHAPTER FEDERATION
Attn: President, 19 Pinewood Rd., Montpelier, VT 05602
Scope: Statewide
Description: An organization of Bassmaster chapters, affiliated with the Bass Anglers Sportman Society, organized to fight pollution, assist state and national conservation agencies in their efforts, and teach the young people of our country good conservation practices. Dedicated to the realistic conservation of our water resources.
Contact(s):
President: NORM WHITE; Phone: 802-223-7793
Conservation Director: JIM EDELMAN, 15 John Rowley Rd., Milton, VT 05468; Phone: 802-893-6571
Publication(s): *Vermont Institute of Natural Science; Records of Vermont Birds; Hands on Nature; Atlas of Breeding Birds of Vermont; Waste Away, Annual Report*
Keyword(s): Birds, Endangered and Threatened Species, Environmental and Conservation Education, Natural History, Raptors

VERMONT INSTITUTE OF NATURAL SCIENCE
R.R. 2 Box 532, Woodstock, VT 05091
Phone: 802-457-2779; Fax: 802-457-1053
Founded: 1972; Membership: 5,000
Scope: Statewide
Description: The mission of VINS is to protect Vermont's natural heritage through environmental education and research. Operates VINS Raptor Center, Living Museum of Birds of Prey and VINS Nature Preserve.
Contact(s):
President: DEBORAH GRANQUIST
Vice President: JENEPHER LINGLEBACH
Secretary: DEBORAH SCHOCH
Treasurer: JUDY PETERSON
Executive Director: TIM TRAVER
Education Director: JENNIFER GUARINO
Research Director: CHRISTOPHER RIMMER
Publication(s): *Vermont Institute of Natural Science; Records of Vermont; Hands on Nature; atlas of Breeding Birds of Vermont; Waste Away, Annual Report*
Keyword(s): Agriculture, Environmental and Conservation Education, Forests and Forestry, Land Preservation

VERMONT LAND TRUST
8 Bailey Ave., Montpelier, VT 05602
Phone: 802-223-5234; Fax: 802-223-4223; Web Site: http://www.vlt.org
Founded: 1977; Membership: 4,300
Scope: Statewide
Description: Conserving the productive, recreational, and scenic lands that help give Vermont and its communities their distinctive rural character.
Contact(s):
President: DARBY BRADLEY, 8 Bailey Ave., Montpelier, VT 05602; Phone: 802-223-5234

Vice President for Land Conservation: GIL LIVINGSTON, 8 Bailey Ave., Montpelier, VT 05602; Phone: 802-223-5234
Vice President of Operations: BARBARA WAGNER, 8 Bailey Ave., Montpelier, VT 05602; Phone: 802-223-5234
Publication(s): *Tri-annual newsletters, Annual Report*
Keyword(s): Land Conservation

VERMONT NATURAL RESOURCES COUNCIL
9 Bailey Ave., Montpelier, VT 05602
Phone: 802-223-2328; Fax: 802-223-0287; E-mail: VNRC@together.net; Web Site: www.VNRC.org
Scope: Statewide
Description: A representative statewide organization, affiliated with the National Wildlife Federation, dedicated to the protection and enhancement of wildlife and its habitat through public education and government interaction.
Contact(s):
Chair: MARY ASHCROFT
Executive Director: ELIZABETH COURTNEY
Representative: LEONARD WILSON
Editor: SUE HIGBY
Alternate Representative: STEPHAN HOLMES
Publication(s): *Vermont Environmental Report*

VERMONT STATE-WIDE ENVIRONMENTAL EDUCATION PROGRAMS (SWEEP)
c/o Vermont Natural Resources Council, 9 Bailey Ave., Montpelier, VT 05602
Founded: 1973
Scope: Statewide
Description: SWEEP is a coalition of individuals and organizations promoting environmental education in Vermont. SWEEP's purpose is to foster environmental appreciation and understanding in order to enable Vermonters to make responsible decisions affecting the environment.
Contact(s):
Chair: MARIE LEVESQUE CADUTO, 198 Kerwin Hill Rd., Norwich, VT 05055; Phone: 802-763-8303, ext. 2401
Chair: SUSAN CLARK, 165-A Wood Rd., N. Middlesex, VT 05682; Phone: 802-223-5824
Secretary: LINDA WELLINGS, Shelburne Farms, 1611 Harbor Rd., Shelburne, VT 05482; Phone: 802-985-8686
Treasurer: KAREN SHARPWOLF, Green Mt. Club, 4711 Waterbury-Stowe Rd., Waterbury Center, VT 05677; Phone: 802-244-5867
Publication(s): *SWEEP Newsletter*
Keyword(s): Environmental and Conservation Education

VERMONT WOODLANDS ASSOCIATION
9 Bailey Ave., Montpelier, VT 05602
Phone: 802-584-3333
Scope: Statewide
Description: A statewide organization, affiliated with the National Woodland Owners Association, organized to promote sound forest management throughout Vermont.
Contact(s):
President: ROBERT DARROW M.D.; Phone: 802-773-7144
Vice President: JOHN HEMENWAY; Phone: 802-765-4324
Executive Director: HARRY CHANDLER
Editor: STEPHEN LONG
Editor: VIRGINIA BARLOW
Publication(s): *VTOA Newsletter, Northern Woodlands Magazine*
Keyword(s): Forests and Forestry

VIRGIN ISLANDS CONSERVATION DISTRICT
Attn: President, P.O. Box 1576, Fredericksted, VI 00841
Scope: Statewide
Contact(s):
President and Board Member: HANS LAWAETZ, P.O. Box 1576, Fredericksted, VI 00841; Phone: 340-788-2229; Fax: 340-778-0270
Vice President: JOSEPH SAMUEL, P.O. Box 241, Fredericksted, St. Croix, VI 00841; Phone: 340-772-3168
Alternate Board Member: CEDRICK LEWIS, P.O. Box 303142, St. Thomas, VI 00803; Phone: 340-775-7393
Secretary and Treasurer: ENRICO GASPERI, P.O. Box 895, Christiansted, VI 00824; Phone: 340-773-2386
Publication(s): *Federation Record, The*
Keyword(s): Conservation Districts

VIRGIN ISLANDS CONSERVATION SOCIETY, INC.
Arawak Bldg., Suite 3, Gallows Bay, Christiansted, VI 00820

Phone: 340-773-1989; Fax: 340-773-7545; E-mail: sea@viaccess.net
Founded: 1968
Scope: Statewide
Description: A representative statewide organization, affiliated with the National Wildlife Federation, dedicated to the protection and enhancement of wildlife and its habitat through public education and government interaction.
Contact(s):
President: CARLOS TESITOR
Executive Director, SEA: YVONNE PETERSON
Representative: ELIZABETH GOGGINS
Editor, SEA: EMY THOMAS
Alternate Representative: KEITH RICHARDS
Keyword(s): Agriculture, Coral Reefs, Environmental and Conservation Education, Pollution Prevention, Soil Conservation

VIRGINIA ASSOCIATION OF CONSERVATION DISTRICTS
Attn: President, P.O. Box 127, North, VA 23128
Scope: Statewide
Contact(s):
President: MARILYN W. LAYER, P.O. Box 127, North, VA 23128; Phone: 804-725-4622; Fax: 804-725-4622; E-mail: layer@inna.net
Secretary/Treasurer: ANDREW H. GRANT II, 12615 Norwood Rd., Wingina, VA 24599; Phone: 804-263-8680; Fax: 804-263-4460
Program Coordinator: STEPHANIE MARTIN, 7293 Hanover Green Dr. Ste B101, Mechanicsville, VA 23111; Phone: 804-559-0324; Fax: 804-559-0325
1st Vice President, Alternate Board Member: JOHN R. DIXON, 1228 Rendezous Ln., Bedford, VA 24523; Phone: 540-586-8969; Fax: 540-586-8969
2nd Vice President: DAPHNE W. JAMISON, 290 River Creek Rd., Wirtz, VA 24184; Phone: 540-721-2361; Fax: 540-483-0006; E-mail: Rjam229@aol.com
Board Member: HUDSON REESE, 8125 James D. Hagwood Hwy, Scottsburg, VA 24589; Phone: 804-454-6302; Fax: 804-476-4217
Keyword(s): Conservation Districts

VIRGINIA B.A.S.S. CHAPTER FEDERATION
Attn: President, 113 Lavergne Ln., Virginia Beach, VA 23454
Scope: Statewide
Description: An organization of Bassmaster chapters, affiliated with the Bass Anglers Sportsman Society, organized to fight pollution, assist state and national conservation agencies in their efforts, and teach the young people of our country good conservation practices. Dedicated to the realistic conservation of our water resources.
Contact(s):
President: ROGER FITCHETT; Phone: 757-428-4280
Conservation Director: ED RHODES, 11210 Brewer Rd., Richmond, VA 23233; Phone: 804-360-8922
Publication(s): *VCN News; Environmental Voting Summary; Virginia B.A.S.S. Federation Newsletter "Tightlines"*
Keyword(s): Air Quality and Pollution, Land Use Planning, Water Quality

VIRGINIA CONSERVATION NETWORK
1001 E. Broad St., Suite 410, Richmond, VA 23219
Phone: 804-644-0283; Fax: 804-644-0286
Founded: 1969; Membership: 111 organizations
Scope: Statewide

Description: The Conservation Council of Virginia merged with the Virginia Environmental Network in 1994 to form the Virginia Conservation Network. The Network's member organizations are devoted to advancing a common, environmentally-sound vision for Virginia.
Contact(s):
President: CHRIS MILLER, P.O. Box 460, Warrenton, VA 22186; Phone: 540-347-2334
Vice President: JACK WHITNEY, 318 Kemp Lane, Chesapeake, VA 23325; Phone: 757-473-2000
Treasurer: HYLAN BOYD, 6303 Towanan Rd, Rchmond, VA
Secretary: PATTI JACKSON, P.O. Box 110, Richmond, VA 23218; Phone: 804-730-2898
Publication(s): *1999 Voting Summary*
Keyword(s): Environmental Legislation

VIRGINIA FORESTRY ASSOCIATION
8810B Patterson Ave., Richmond, VA 23229
Phone: 804-741-0836; Fax: 804-741-0838; E-mail: vafa@erols.com
Founded: 1943; Membership: 1,600
Scope: Statewide
Description: An association of landowners and forest industry that promotes stewardship and wise use of forest resources for the economic and environmental benefits of all Virginians.
Contact(s):
President: CROCKETT MORRIS, Waverly, VA
Vice President: DENICE TAPPERO, Hopewell, VA
Treasurer: JOHN CARROLL
Editor: PAUL HOWE
Executive Vice President: PAUL R. HOWE
Past President: RICHARD L. MALM, Franklin, VA
Publication(s): *Bulletin; chapter newsletters; wildflower conservation guidelines; checklists; nursery source list; fact sheets; brochure; invasive alien plant list*
Keyword(s): Endangered and Threatened Species, Environmental and Conservation Education, Flowers, Plants, and Trees, Gardening and Horticulture, Natural Areas

VIRGINIA NATIVE PLANT SOCIETY
Blandy Experimental Farm, 400 Blandy Farm Lane--Unit 2, Boyce, VA 22620
Phone: 540-837-1600; E-mail: vnpsofc@shentel.net; Web Site: www.vnps.org
Founded: 1982; Membership: 2,000
Scope: Statewide
Description: The VNPS and nine chapters throughout Virginia seek further appreciation and conservation of Virginia's wild plants and habitats. Programs emphasize public education, protection of endangered species, habitat preservation, control of invasive alien plants and encouragement of appropriate landscape use of native plants. Includes both amateurs and professionals.
Contact(s):
President: MARIE F. MINOR; Phone: 804-443-5950
Director of Membership: CHARLES SMITH; Phone: 703-361-5125
Treasurer: DR. JOHN FRY; Phone: 540-364-3046
1st Vice President: RICHARD KELLY; Phone: 540-384-7429
2nd Vice President: BEN FITZGERALD
Corresponding Secretary: ELAINE SMITH; Phone: 540-432-6833; Fax: 540-568-3332
Recording Secretary: JUNE GRIFFIN; Phone: 804-296-3219
Director of Botany: DR. STANWYN SHETLER; Phone: 703-430-6523
Director of Conservation: NICKY STAUNTON; Phone: 703-368-9803
Director of Horticulture: NANCY ARRINGTON; Phone: 703-368-9711
Director of Publicity: NANCY HUGO; Phone: 804-798-6364
Director of Registry: BOLEYN DALE; Phone: 804-725-5451
Publication(s): *BULLETIN; Virginia Wildflower of the Year; Nursery Sources to Native Plants; List of Invasive Alien Plants for Virginia; Factsheets on Invasive Alien Plants; List of Recommended Native Plants for Landscaping and Restoration; Chapter Newsletters*
Keyword(s): Botany, Conservation of Protected Areas, Endangered and Threatened Species, Environment, Flowers, Plants, and Trees, Forest Management, Habitat Conservation, Landscape Architecture, Natural Areas, Prairies, Public Lands, Urban Forestry, Watersheds, Wetlands, Native Plants

VIRGINIA SOCIETY OF ORNITHOLOGY
7451 Little River Turnpike, #202, Annandale, VA 22003
Phone: 703-305-7381
Founded: 1929; Membership: 1,000
Scope: Statewide
Description: Dedicated to all aspects of the birds of Virginia, including conservation, field research, education of any interested person or group, and dissemination of all types of information. The VSO coordinates with state agencies and with other private organizations in this mission.
Contact(s):
President: THELMA DALMAS, 1230 Viewmont Dr., Evington, VA 24550; Phone: 804-821-1136
Vice President: LARRY LYNCH, 9430 Tuxford Rd., Richmond, VA 23236; Phone: 804-272-8582
Secretary: LISA HAMILTON, 321 York Ave, Staunton, VA 24401; Phone: 540-885-4808
Treasurer: BARBARA SUE THRASHER, 120 Woodbine Dr., Lynchburg, VA 24502; Phone: 804-239-5850
Publication(s): *Raven, The; VSO Newsletter*
Keyword(s): Birds

W

WASHINGTON ASSOCIATION OF CONSERVATION DISTRICTS
Attn: President, 1301 Crumbaker Rd., Colfax, WA 99111
Scope: Statewide
Contact(s):
President, Alternate Board Member: LARRY COCHRAN; Phone: 509-397-2302; Fax: 509-397-2302
Vice President: COLIN BENNETT, 185 Beebe Rd., Goldendale, WA 98620; Phone: 509-773-5065; Fax: 509-773-5600; E-mail: cbennett@gorge.net
Executive Director: DON STUART, P.O. Box 60055, Shoreline, WA 98160; Phone: 206-546-7690; Fax: 206-546-7740
Board Member: BOB HABERMAN, 771 Hungry Junction Rd., Ellensburg, WA 98926; Phone: 509-925-1713; Fax: 509-925-7730; E-mail: bobhaber@eburg.net
Secretary and Treasurer: MONTE MARTI, 11605 33rd Ct, NE, Lake Stevens, WA 98258; Phone: 425-261-6678; Fax: 425-258-4839
Keyword(s): Conservation Districts

WASHINGTON B.A.S.S. CHAPTER FEDERATION
Attn: President, 16569 162nd Pl., Renton, WA 98058
Scope: Statewide
Description: An organization of Bassmaster chapters, affiliated with the Bass Anglers Sportsman Society, organized to fight pollution, assist state and national conservation agencies in their efforts, and teach the young people of our country good conservation practices. Dedicated to the realistic conservation of our water resources.
Contact(s):
President: JIM OWENS; Phone: 425-271-6569
Conservation Director: DAN PFEIFFER, 4243 E. 29th Ave., Spokane, WA 99223; Phone: 509-495-4416
Keyword(s): Energy, Environmental and Conservation Education, Environmental Preservation, Renewable Resources, Solid Waste

WASHINGTON ENVIRONMENTAL COUNCIL
615 2nd Avenue, #380, Seattle, WA 98104
Phone: 206-622-8103; Fax: 206-622-8113; E-mail: greenwec@aol.com
Founded: 1967; Membership: 3,000
Scope: Statewide
Description: A statewide coalition of 88 member groups and over 3,000 individuals working to protect Washington's forests and wildlife, water and fish, open spaces and quality of life. NEC

NON-GOVERNMENTAL ORGANIZATIONS - W

advocates for the environment at the state legislature, develops environmental policy, educates and involves the public and takes legal action.
Contact(s):
President: DAVE MANN
Vice President: STEVE WHITNEY
Secretary: LAURI AUNAN
Treasurer: JOHN ANDERSON
Executive Director: JOAN CROOKS
Editor: TOM GEIGER
Publication(s): *WEC Voices; Forest Resources News*
Keyword(s): Fish Wildlife Management, Forests and Forestry, Sustainable Development, Water Resources

WASHINGTON FARM FORESTRY ASSOCIATION
P.O. Box 7663, Olympia, WA 98507
Phone: 360-459-0984
Founded: 1944; Membership: 1,250
Scope: Statewide
Description: A statewide organization affiliated with the National Woodland Owners Association, founded to help small woodland owners acquire information on better management of small timber tracts.
Contact(s):
President: CHANDLER NOERENBERG
Vice President: SHERRY FOX
Secretary: BILL and ERIN WOODS
Treasurer: BOB FALKNER
Executive Director and Editor, Landowner News: NELS HANSON; Phone: 360-943-3875
Editor, Northwest Woodlands: LORI D. RASOR, 4033 SW Canyon Rd., Portland, OR 97221; Phone: 503-226-2515
Publication(s): *Northwest Woodlands; Landowner News*
Keyword(s): Environmental and Conservation Education, Environmental Law, Forests and Forestry, Natural History, Scholarships and Grants, Wildlife and Wildlife Habitat

WASHINGTON FOUNDATION FOR THE ENVIRONMENT
P.O. Box 2123, Seattle, WA 98111
E-mail: JudyTurpin@aol.com
Founded: 1979
Scope: Statewide
Description: Dedicated to preserving and enhancing the environmental heritage of Washington state by making small grants to support educational and innovative projects in both the public and private sectors. For grant guidelines, send a message to JudyTurpin@aol.com
Contact(s):
President: BILL JOLLY, 4007 Green Cove, NW, Olympia, WA 98502; Phone: 360-866-9204
Grants Chair: MELANIE ROWLAND, 13742 41st. Ave. NE, Seattle, WA 98125; Phone: 206-526-6537
Vice President: KONRAD LIEGEL, 1103 18th Ave. E., Seattle, WA 98112; Phone: 206-320-8582
Secretary: TRINA WELLMAN, 2611 42nd Ave., W., Seattle, WA 98199; Phone: 206-284-2413
Treasurer: CLEVE PINNIX, 725 Sherman St., Olympia, WA 98502; Phone: 360-943-7836
Keyword(s): Environmental and Conservation Education, Environmental Preservation, Environmental Protection, Grants

WASHINGTON NATIVE PLANT SOCIETY
P.O. Box 28690, Seattle, WA 98118-8690
Phone: 206-323-3336
Founded: 1976; Membership: 1,800
Scope: Statewide
Description: To promote the appreciation and conservation of Washington's native plants and their habitats through study, education, and advocacy.
Contact(s):
President: JOAN FRAZEE, P.O. Box 1082, Leavenworth, WA 98826; Phone: 509-548-2166

Vice President: RICHARD ROBOHM, 963 N. Motor Pl., Seattle, WA 98103; Phone: 206-545-1823
Secretary: TOM JOHNSON, 7742 32nd Ave., Seattle, WA 98115; Phone: 206-525-3176
Treasurer: RICHARD EASTERLY, P.O. Box 4027, Tenino, WA 98589; Phone: 360-264-5644
Publication(s): *Syllabus*
Keyword(s): Outdoor Recreation, Public Lands, Urban Forestry, Wetlands, Youth Organizations, Native Plants

WASHINGTON RECREATION AND PARK ASSOCIATION
350 S. 333rd St., Suite 103, Federal Way, WA 98003
Phone: 253-874-1283; Fax: 253-661-3929
Founded: 1947; Membership: 1,200
Scope: Statewide
Description: Dedicated to enhancing and promoting parks, recreation, and leisure pursuits in Washington state, and plays a vital role in promoting public support for parks and recreation.
Contact(s):
President: JOHN COUCH, P.O. Box 97010, Redmond, WA 98073
Secretary: DENISE NICHOLS, 2301 Fruitvale Blvd., Yakima, WA 98902
Executive Director: LYNN M. DEVOIR CLP, 350 So. 33rd St. #102, Federal Way, WA 98003
President-elect: LARRY OTOS, 1717 S. 13th St., Mount Vernon, WA 98273
Publication(s): *Syllabus*
Keyword(s): Outdoor Recreation

WASHINGTON SOCIETY OF AMERICAN FORESTERS
4033 SW Canyon Rd., Portland, OR 97221
Phone: 503-224-8046
Founded: 1900; Membership: 925 (WA)
Scope: Statewide
Description: Represents the forestry profession in advancing the science, technology, education, and practice of forestry for the benefit of forests, forest managers, and the public.
Contact(s):
Chair: JOCKO BURKS, 3302 Sounview Dr. West, University Place, WA 98466
Chair-Elect ('99): ART SCHICK, 2585 NE Ortis Rd., Poulsbo, WA 98370
Manager/Editor: LORI RASOR, 4033 SW Canyon Rd., Portland, OR 97221

WASHINGTON TOXICS COALITION
4649 Sunnyside Ave., N., Suite 540 East, Seattle, WA 98103
Phone: 206-632-1545; E-mail: info@watoxics.org; Web Site: ww.watoxics.org
Founded: 1981; Membership: 1,500
Scope: Statewide
Description: Works to reduce society's reliance on toxic chemicals through research, education, advocacy, organizing and litigation.
Contact(s):
President: DAVID STITZHAL
Secretary: JENNIFER DOLD
Secretary: DAVE COFFMAN
Treasurer: DON BOLLINGER
Publication(s): *Alternatives; Grow Smart, Grow Safe: A Consumer Guide to Lawn and Garden Products; Trubbling Bubbles: The Case for Replacing Alkylphenol Ethoxylate Surfactants; No Place For Poisons: Reducing Pesticides in School; Home Safe Home (fact sheets); Fact sheets on industry source reduction; Poisons in the Web of Life: The Case for Toxics Reform; Weed Wars: Pesticide Use in Washington Schools*
Keyword(s): Cultural Preservation, Environmental and Conservation Education, Outdoor Recreation, Public Lands, Toxic Reduction, Toxic Substances, Transportation

WASHINGTON TRAILS ASSOCIATION
1305 4th Ave., #512, Seattle, WA 98101-2401
Phone: 206-625-1367
Founded: 1973; Membership: 4,100
Scope: Statewide

Description: Washington Trails Association works to protect and enhance hiking opportunities in Washington state through education, volunteer trail maintenance, advocacy and cooperation with other trail users.
Contact(s):
President: SUSAN ELDERKIN
Executive Director: ELIZABETH LUNNEY
Keyword(s): Environmental and Conservation Education, Natural Areas, Open Space, Outdoor Recreation, Trail, Wildlife and Wildlife Habitat, Wildlife Management, Volunteering

WASHINGTON WILDERNESS COALITION
4649 Sunnyside Ave., N., #242, Seattle, WA 98103
Phone: 206-633-1992; Fax: 206-633-1996; E-mail: wawild@aol.com
Founded: 1979; Membership: 15,000
Scope: Statewide
Description: WWC is a statewide organization of individuals and groups dedicated to preserving wilderness and biodiversity for the benefit of future generations. WWC works to protect and restore wildlands and waters in Washington State through outreach, public education, organizing, and support of grassroots conservation groups.
Contact(s):
President: MARTIN LOESCH
Vice President: MIKE PETERSON
Secretary: CYNDI LEWIS
Treasurer: MICHELLE KINSCH
Executive Director: JOHN LEARY
Canvass Director: PHIL COCHRAN
Field Director: JON OWEN
Membership & Development Coordinator: JULIE HOFFMAN
Publication(s): *Washington Wildfire*
Keyword(s): Biodiversity, Wilderness

WASHINGTON WILDLIFE AND RECREATION COALITION
4001 SW Cloverdale, Seattle, WA 98136-2363
Phone: 206-938-4513; Fax: 206-932-5651
Founded: 1989
Scope: Statewide
Description: The Washington Wildlife and Recreation Coalition was formed in 1989 to promote the acquisition of land for wildlife and outdoor recreation through public education, support of appropriate legislation, and research into outdoor recreation and conservation needs in Washington state. Our long-range goal is to secure state funding for a $450 million, 8-10 year program to acquire and develop parks, trails, water access, wildlife habitat, and natural areas. To date, the state legislature has allocated over $270 million towards that goal.
Contact(s):
Assistant Director: KRISTEN QUIGLEY
President: KENT HULL
Vice President: JOANNE ROBERTS
Vice President: JOHN McGLENN
Secretary: KAREN MUNRO
Treasurer: PETER SCHOLES
Executive Director: JANET WAINWRIGHT
Program Coordinator: LINDSEY AMTMANN
Publication(s): *Land News*
Keyword(s): Land Preservation, Land Purchase, Nature Preservation, Public Lands, Wildlife and Wildlife Habitat

WASHINGTON WILDLIFE FEDERATION
P.O. Box 1966, Olympia, WA 98507-1966
Phone: 360-705-1903; Web Site: www.washingtonwildlife.org
Scope: Statewide
Description: A representative statewide organization, affiliated with the National Wildlife Federation, dedicated to the protection and enhancement of wildlife and its habitat through public education and government interaction.
Contact(s):
President and Alternate Representative: KEN HILTON
Representative: THEA LEVKOVITZ
Keyword(s): Environmental and Conservation Education, Environmental Preservation, Land Purchase, Water Pollution Management, Wetlands

WASHINGTON WILDLIFE HERITAGE FOUNDATION (including Heritage Land Trust
32610 Pacific Highway South, Federal Way, WA 98003
Scope: Statewide
Description: The Foundation is dedicated to fish and wildlife/water and land conservation through resource management, and enhancing habitat and public education, with the involvement, support, and cooperation of both the public and private sector.
Contact(s):
Chairman: BRUCE STUWE, 4727 Crisman Ct., SE, Olympia, WA 98501; Phone: 360-491-9195
Secretary: ROBERT GRIBBLE, 26442 164th SE, Kent, WA 98042; Phone: 253-631-9244
Publication(s): *Land News*
Keyword(s): Land Management, Outdoor Recreation, Wildlife and Wildlife Habitat

WATER ENVIRONMENT FEDERATION
601 Wythe St., Alexandria, VA 22314-1994
Phone: 703-684-2400
Founded: 1928; Membership: 41,000
Scope: International
Description: A nonprofit technical and educational organization with the mission to preserve and enhance the global water environment. Federation members are water quality specialists from around the world, including environmental, civil and chemical engineers, biologists, government officials, treatment plant managers and operators, laboratory technicians, college professors, students, and equipment manufacturers and distributors.
Contact(s):
President: ALBERT W. GOODMAN
Vice President: JAMES H. CLARK
Treasurer: PRAD KHARE
Executive Director: DR. QUINCALEE BROWN
President-Elect: JOE C. STOWE
Publication(s): *Water Environment Research; Water Environment and Technology; WEF Highlights; Operations Forum; Water Environment Regulation Watch; WEF Industrial Wastewater; Watershed and Wet Weather Technical Bulletin;* other titles available on request
Keyword(s): Asia Water Environment, Engineering, Environmental and Conservation Education, Toxic Substances, Water Pollution Management, Water Resources

WATER RESOURCES ASSOCIATION OF THE DELAWARE RIVER BASIN
P.O. Box 867, Valley Forge, PA 19482-0867
Phone: 610-917-0090; Fax: 610-917-0091; E-mail: wradrb@aol.com
Founded: 1959
Scope: National
Description: Nonprofit federation of businesses, industries, academia, government, environmental, and citizen organizations which serves to advise of and advocate the need for adequate water supplies through the orderly conservation, development, and equitable use and reuse of the water and related land resources of the Delaware River Basin.
Contact(s):
Chair: JEREMIAH J. CARDAMONE ESQ
Executive Director: WILLIAM H. PALMER
Keyword(s): Environmental and Conservation Education, Rivers, Water Pollution, Water Resources, Wetlands

WATERLOO-WELLINGTON WILDFLOWER SOCIETY (Formerly the Dogtooth Group)
Botany Dept., University of Guelph, Guelph, Ontario N1G 2W1 Canada
Phone: 519-824-4120, ext. 858; Fax: 519-767-1521; Web Site: www.uoguelph.ca/~botcal/

NON-GOVERNMENTAL ORGANIZATIONS - W

Founded: 1990; Membership: 65
Scope: Local Region
Description: A non-profit organization based in Guelph, Ontario dedicated to the use and protection of native plants in parks, gardens and other open spaces.
Contact(s):
President: CAROLE ANN LACROIX; Phone: 519-824-4120, ext. 8581; E-mail: botcal@uoguelph.ca
Publication(s): *Dogtooth (monthly newsletter)*
Keyword(s): Environmental and Conservation Education, Flowers, Plants, and Trees, Gardening and Horticulture, Nature Preservation, Native Plants

WATERSHED MANAGEMENT COUNCIL
c/o PSRP, U.C. Davis, One Shields Ave., Davis, CA 95616-8688
Phone: 510-273-9066; Fax: 510-530-4640; E-mail: WMC@watershed.org; Web Site: www.watershed.org/wmc
Founded: 1986; Membership: 650
Scope: Regional
Description: The Watershed Management Council is a nonprofit, educational organization dedicated to advancing the art and science of watershed management, with an emphasis on the Western region.
Contact(s):
President: SARI SOMMARSTROM; Phone: 530-467-5783; Fax: 530-467-5733; E-mail: sari@sisqtel.net
President-elect: RICK KATTELMANN; Phone: 760-935-4903
Secretary: JIM BERGMAN; Phone: 530-587-3558
Treasurer: TERRY KAPLAN-HENRY; Phone: 559-784-1500
Publication(s): *Networker, The; Proceedings*
Keyword(s): Land Management, Nonpoint Source Pollution, Rivers, Streams, Water Pollution Management, Watersheds

WELDER WILDLIFE FOUNDATION
P.O. Box 1400, Sinton, TX 78387
Phone: 512-364-2643; Fax: 512-364-2650; E-mail: welderwf@aol.com
Founded: 1954
Scope: National
Description: Established by the will of the late Rob Welder, the Foundation is dedicated to the cause of conservation through research and education in wildlife ecology and management and closely related fields. Operates through a small staff, with research fellowships to graduate students only.
Contact(s):
Director: D. LYNN DRAWE
Assistant Director/Conservation Educator: SELMA N. GLASSCOCK
Assistant Director/Wildlife Biologist: TERRY L. BLANKENSHIP
Keyword(s): Birds, Mammals, Scholarships and Grants, Wildlife and Wildlife Habitat, Wildlife Management

WEST MICHIGAN ENVIRONMENTAL ACTION COUNCIL
1432 Wealthy, SE, Grand Rapids, MI 49506
Phone: 616-451-3051; Fax: 616-451-3054
Founded: 1968; Membership: 700 individuals, 30 organizations
Scope: Local
Description: Provide leadership in environmental protection and preservation in west Michigan and throughout Michigan on issues such as water quality, land use planning and sustainable business. Through the involvement of concerned volunteers, WMEAC has helped landmark environmental legislation and assured application of existing laws.
Contact(s):
President: THOM PETERSON
Executive Director: TOM LEONARD
Publication(s): *Action Issue*
Keyword(s): Air Quality and Pollution, Conservation, Environmental and Conservation Education, Land Use Planning, Sustainability, Waste Management, Water Resources

WEST VIRGINIA ASSOCIATION OF CONSERVATION DISTRICT SUPERVISORS ASSOCIATION, INC.
Attn: President, P.O. Box 711, Gallipolis Ferry, WV 25515
Scope: Statewide
Contact(s):
President, Alternate Board Member: ROBERT BAIRD; Phone: 304-675-6873
Vice President: GERALD MILLER, Box 124, Bolt, WV 25817; Phone: 304-934-7635
Secretary: CLINTON LUCAS, Rt. 1 Box 303-E, West Hamlin, WV 25571; Phone: 304-778-7234
Treasurer: DORIS ASBURY, P.O. Box 35, Liberty, WV 25124; Phone: 304-776-5272; Fax: 304-776-5284
Board Member: LARRY C. SMITH, Rt. 1 Box 543A, Berkeley Springs, WV 25411; Phone: 304-258-2534
Keyword(s): Conservation Districts

WEST VIRGINIA B.A.S.S. CHAPTER FEDERATION
Attn: President, P.O.B. 418, Buckhannon, WV 26201
Scope: Statewide
Description: An organization of Bassmaster chapters, affiliated with the Bass Anglers Sportsman Society, organized to fight pollution, assist state and national conservation agencies in their efforts, and teach the young people of our country good conservation practices. Dedicated to the realistic conservation of our water resources.
Contact(s):
President: JOHN BURDETTE; Phone: 304-472-3600
Conservation Director: JIM SUMMERS, Rt. 1 Box 205, Worthington, WV 26591; Phone: 304-287-7700
Publication(s): *Highlands Voice, The; Monongahela National Forest Hiking Guide, The*
Keyword(s): Forests and Forestry, Public Lands, Rivers, Water Pollution Management, Wilderness

WEST VIRGINIA HIGHLANDS CONSERVANCY
P.O. Box 306, Charleston, WV 25321
Founded: 1967
Scope: Statewide
Description: An organization devoted to the conservation and wise management of West Virginia's natural and historic resources. Active in wilderness preservation, river conservation, public lands management, forestry, mining, air and water quality, water resources management and a wide variety of other environmental and conservation issues.
Contact(s):
President: FRANK YOUNG, Rt. 1 Box 108, Ripley, WV 25271; Phone: 304-372-9329
Treasurer: JACQUELINE HALLINAN, 1120 Swan Rd., Charleston, WV 25314; Phone: 304-345-3718
Secretary: ANDREW MAIER, Rt. 1 Box 27, Hinton, WV 25952; Phone: 304-466-3864
Editor: BILL REED, 350 Bucks Branch, Beckley, WV 25801; Phone: 304-934-5828
Membership Secretary: DAVE SAVILLE, P.O. Box 569, Morgantown, WV 26507; Phone: 304-284-9548
Senior Vice President: JUDY RODD, Rt. 1, Box 178, Moatsville, WV 26405; Phone: 304-265-0018
Vice President of State Affairs: NORM STEENSTRA, 1001 Valley Rd., Charleston, WV 25302; Phone: 304-346-5891
Keyword(s): Mining, Natural Resource Conservation, Water and Air Quality, Water Resources, Wilderness, Forestry

WEST VIRGINIA WILDLIFE FEDERATION, INC.
P.O. Box 275, Paden City, WV 26159
Phone: 304-782-3685; E-mail: pleinbach@aol.com
Scope: Statewide
Description: A representative statewide organization, affiliated with the National Wildlife Federation, dedicated to the protection and enhancement of wildlife and its habitat through public education and government interaction.
Contact(s):
President and Alternate Representative: ART MULLINS
Representative: PAUL JOHANSEN
Editor: PHIL LEINBACH
Publication(s): *West Virginia*

WEST VIRGINIA, WOODLAND OWNERS ASSOCIATION OF
P.O. Box 13695, Sissonville, WV 25360
Phone: 304-594-3648
Founded: 1991; Membership: 425
Scope: Statewide
Description: A statewide organization affiliated with the National Woodland Owners Association that promotes good forestry and sustainable management by non-industrial private owners in West Virginia.
Contact(s):
President: MARK A. BURKE
Vice-President: PAT PLITT
Secretary: EDWARD MURRINER
Treasurer: HOWARD KNOTTS
Editor: DAN KINCAID; Phone: 304-285-1524
Forestry Advisor: BOB WHIPKEY; Phone: 304-558-2788
Publication(s): *West Virginia Woods*
Keyword(s): Forests and Forestry

WESTERN ASSOCIATION OF FISH AND WILDLIFE AGENCIES
Game and Fish Department, 5400 Bishop Blvd., Cheyenne, WY 82006
Scope: Regional
Description: A regional organization including 18 fish and wildlife agencies of 15 states and three Canadian provinces. Meets annually to consider mutual problems and provide a forum for the exchange of information at both administrative and technical levels.
Contact(s):
President: JIM GREER; Phone: 503-872-5272
1st Vice-President: JOHN KIMBALL; Phone: 801-538-4703
2nd Vice-President: JERRY MARACCHINI; Phone: 505-827-7899
Secretary and Treasurer: LARRY KRUCKENBERG, Game and Fish Department, 5400 Bishop Blvd., Cheyenne, WY 82006; Phone: 307-777-4569
Keyword(s): Fish Wildlife Management, Wildlife Management

WESTERN ENVIRONMENTAL LAW CENTER
1216 Lincoln St., Eugene, OR 97401
Phone: 541-485-2471; Fax: 541-485-2457; E-mail: westernlaw@igc.org; Web Site: www.welc.org
Founded: 1993; Membership: 1,500
Scope: Statewide
Description: WELC specializes in environmental law enforcement, working with grassroots citizen groups and Native American tribes to implement our nation's environmental laws. WELC has offices in Eugene, Oregon and Taos, New Mexico.
Contact(s):
President: LORI MADDOX
Vice President: CORRIE YACKULIC
Executive Director: PETER FROST
Litigation Director: MICHAEL AXLINE
Director of Taos Office: GROVE BURNETT; Phone: 505-751-0351; Fax: 505-751-1775; E-mail: law@welctaos.org
Secretary and Treasurer: MARY WOOD
Publication(s): *Defending the West; Biennial Report*
Keyword(s): Air Quality and Pollution, Cultural Preservation, Environmental Law, Forests and Forestry, Mining, Pesticides, Toxic Substances, Water Quality, Wildlife and Wildlife Habitat

WESTERN FORESTRY AND CONSERVATION ASSOCIATION
4033 SW Canyon Rd., Portland, OR 97221
Phone: 503-226-4562; Fax: 503-226-2515; E-mail: richard@westernforestry.org
Founded: 1909
Scope: National
Description: The mission of the WFCA is to promote forest stewardship in western North America. The Association's objectives are to promote the science and practice of forestry, promote the dissemination of forestry research and technical information, and foster cooperation between federal, state, provincial, and private forest agencies.
Contact(s):
President: VINCENT CORRDO
Treasurer: BLAIR HOLMAN
Executive Director: RICHARD ZABEL
Past President: BOB ANDERSON
Keyword(s): Forest Management

WESTERN HEMISPHERE SHOREBIRD RESERVE NETWORK (WHSRN)
c/o Manomet Center for Conservation Services, 81 Stage Point Rd., P.O. Box 1770, Manomet, MA 02345
Phone: 508-224-6521; Fax: 508-224-9220; E-mail: jmcorven@manomet.org; Web Site: www.manomet.org/WHSRN.htm
Founded: 1985; Membership: 140 organizations at 40 sites
Scope: International
Description: As a partnership of Manomet and Wetlands International: the Americas, WHSRN is a voluntary non-regulatory network of 40 critical wetland sites in seven countries which have joined together to study, manage, and promote the sustainable conservation of shorebirds and their habitats for the benefit of the ecosystems and people. WHSRN's strategy promotes a multiple species ecosystem approach to protection of over nine million acres of habitats that are critical staging, nesting, and non-breeding sites of migratory shorebirds, throughout North and South America.
Contact(s):
Director: JIM CORVEN
Publication(s): *WHSRNews; Shorebird Migrations: Fundamentals for Land Managers; Important Shorebird Staging Sites Meeting WHSRN Criteria in the U.S.; The Amazing Migration of Shorebirds (video); Save Our Migratory Shorebirds (curriculum guide and game), Shorebird Atlas; Shorebird Superheros*
Keyword(s): Birds, International Conservation, Sustainable Ecosystems, Wetlands, Wildlife Management, Shorebirds

WESTERN PACIFIC REGIONAL FISHERY MANAGEMENT COUNCIL
1164 Bishop St., Suite 1400, Honolulu, HI 96813
Phone: 808-522-8220; Fax: 808-522-8226
Founded: 1977; Membership: 16
Scope: National
Description: The Council is the policy-making organization for the management of fisheries in and around the EEZs of American Samoa, Guam, Hawaii, and the Northern Mariana Islands, and U.S. possessions in the Pacific Ocean. Council members and members of its advisory bodies: Scientific and Statistical Committee, Plan Teams, and Advisory Panels represent the fishing community, government agencies, and national international fisheries management organizations throughout the region.
Contact(s):
Chairman: JIM D. COOK
Executive Director: KITTY M. SIMONDS
Publication(s): *Pacific Islands Fishery News*
Keyword(s): Commercial Sport Fishing, Fish Wildlife Management, Fisheries, Highly Migratory Species, Islands, Management Plans

WESTERN PENNSYLVANIA CONSERVANCY
209 4th Ave., Pittsburgh, PA 15222
Phone: 412-288-2777; Fax: 412-281-1792; E-mail: wpc@paconserve.org; Web Site: www.paconserve.org/
Founded: 1932; Membership: 25,000
Scope: Local
Description: The Western Pennsylvania Conservancy, working together to save the places we care about, protects natural lands, promotes healthy and attractive communities and preserves Frank Lloyd Wright's masterwork Fallingwater. The Conservancy fosters the integration of ecological protection with economic and social needs while building on the core values of the community and has protected more than 200,000 acres of natural lands in Pennsylvania.
Contact(s):
Chairman: JARVIS B. CECIL
Vice Chairman: E. MICHAEL BOYLE
President and CEO: LARRY J. SCHWEIGER
Executive Vice President and COO: CYNTHIA CARROW
Vice President of Conservation Programs: JACQUELYN BONOMO

Vice President and Director of Fallingwater: LYNDA WAGGONER
Editor and Senior Director of Public Affairs: JULIE LALO
Publication(s): *Conserve; Annual Calendar*
Keyword(s): Conservation of Protected Areas, Endangered and Threatened Species, Gardening and Horticulture, Land Preservation, Sustainable Ecosystems, Urban Environment

WETLAND HABITAT ALLIANCE OF TEXAS
118 E. Hospital, Suite 208, Nacogdoches, TX 75961
Phone: 409-569-9428; Fax: 409-569-6349; E-mail: whatduck@lcc.net
Founded: 1984; Membership: 7,000
Scope: Statewide
Description: A nonprofit organization of conservationists, dedicated to preserving, reclaiming, and enhancing Texas wetland habitat, that promotes the wise use of our natural resources and the progress of our society. Constructs habitat improvement projects on public and private lands, promotes educational programs, performs priority wetland research, and supports legislative conservation efforts.
Contact(s):
Chairman: BRUCE KLINGMAN
Vice President: RICHARD TINSLEY
Treasurer: NEAL JENKINS
Executive Director: JOHN E. FRASIER
Publication(s): *Texas Wetlands*
Keyword(s): Wetlands

WHALE AND DOLPHIN CONSERVATION SOCIETY
Alexander House, James St., West, Bath, Somerset BA1 2BT United Kingdom
Phone: 01225-334511; Fax: 01225-480097; E-mail: campaign@wdcs.org; Web Site: www.wdcs.org
Founded: 1987; Membership: 75,000
Scope: International
Description: The WDCS is dedicated to the conservation, welfare, and appreciation of all species of whale, dolphins and porpoises and their environment.
Contact(s):
Chief Executive: CHRIS STROUD
Director of Conservation: ALSON M. SMITH
Director of Finance: S. DAVIS-HAMILTON
Director of Fundraising: CHRIS VICK
Director of Science: MARK SIMMONDS
Publication(s): *WDCS Magazine; Echo; Orcalog*
Keyword(s): Dolphins, Endangered and Threatened Species, Environmental Protection, Fisheries, Hunting, International Conservation, Marine Mammals, Water Pollution, Wildlife and Wildlife Habitat

WHITE CLAY WATERSHED ASSOCIATION
760 Chambers Rock Rd., Landenberg, PA 19350
Phone: 215-255-4314
Founded: 1965
Scope: Regional
Description: The White Clay Watershed Association is a nonprofit organization devoted to protection and improvement of the environmental quality of the White Clay Creek and valley. The Association works to improve water quality in local streams, conserve open space, woodlands, wetlands and geological features; aid in the preservation of cultural, historical and archaeological sites; increase outdoor recreation opportunities; and conduct educational programs relating to the environment.
Contact(s):
President: JOHN A. MURRAY
Vice President: ROBERT M. STARK
Secretary: CAROL CATANESE
Treasurer: DONNA BUSH
Keyword(s): Cultural Preservation, Environmental Protection, Nature Preservation, Water Quality, Watersheds

WHITETAILS UNLIMITED, INC.
P.O. Box 720, Rhode Island St., Sturgeon Bay, WI 54235
Phone: 414-743-6777
Founded: 1982; Membership: 40,000
Scope: National
Description: Whitetails Unlimited is a national, nonprofit conservation organization. Its purpose is to raise funds in support of education, habitat enhancement, and the preservation of the hunting tradition for the direct benefit of the white-tailed deer and other wildlife species.
Contact(s):
President: JEFFREY B. SCHINKTEN
Executive Director: PETER J. GERL
Chapter Services: KIM MCKINNEY
Field Editor: PETER R. SCHOONMAKER
Field Editor: KEVIN NAZE
Membership Services: CHERYL UECKER
Merchandise: ARLENE PETERSON
National Advisory Board: DANIEL O. TRAINER
National Executive Board: PETER J. GERL
Office Manager: JANET GERL
Production Manager: PETER J. GERL
Production/Design: DENISE DUBICK
Vice President of Finance: WILLIAM E. GERL JR.
Vice President of Marketing: DAVID J. HAWKEY
Publication(s): *Whitetails Unlimited Magazine; WTU Chapter Connections*
Keyword(s): Environmental and Conservation Education, Hunting, Wildlife and Wildlife Habitat, Wildlife Management

WHOOPING CRANE CONSERVATION ASSOCIATION INC.
1393 Henderson Highway, Breaux Bridge, LA Phone: 318-228-7563; Fax: 318-228-7424; E-mail: wcca@excelonline.com
Founded: 1961; Membership: 700
Scope: National
Description: A scientific and educational organization, international in scope, working to prevent the extinction of the whooping crane and save wetland habitats.
Contact(s):
Secretary and Treasurer: MARY L. COURVILLE
Editor: JEROME J. PRATT, 3000 Meadowlark Dr., Sierra Vista, AZ 85635
Publication(s): *Grus Americana*
Keyword(s): Birds, Endangered and Threatened Species, Waterfowl, Wetland Habitat

WILD CANID SURVIVAL AND RESEARCH CENTER
P.O. Box 760, Eureka, MO 63025
Phone: 636-938-5900; Fax: 636-938-6490; E-mail: wolf@spawn.i1.net; Web Site: www.wolfsanctuary.org
Founded: 1971; Membership: 2,000
Scope: National
Description: A nonprofit, conservation organization dedicated to the preservation of wolves and other wild canids through education, research, and captive breeding.
Contact(s):
Chairman: DR. WILLIAM SADLER
Vice-Chair: MARGARET RATZ
Secretary: NINA WARE
Treasurer: KATHRYN STREET
Executive Director: DR. SUE LINDSEY
Publication(s): *Wild Canid Center Review; Wolf Pack* **Keyword(s):** Endangered and Threatened Species, Environmental and Conservation Education, Predators, Reintroduction, Research, Wolves

WILD DOG FOUNDATION, THE
P.O. Box 1603, Mineola, NY 11501-0901
Phone: 516-746-0005; E-mail: SAVEWilddogs@hotMAiL.com; Web Site: www.wilddog.org
Founded: 1996; Membership: 50
Scope: International
Description: The foundation is a conservation and educational group. The foundation promotes wolf restoration to the Adirondack State Park in New York and the Northeast, and deals with less popular predators, mostly wild canines and hyenas. Its flagship species are the African Wild Dog and coyote.

Contact(s):
President: FRANK VINCENTI
Vice President: LEW EGOL
Vice President: HOPE RYDEN
Vice President: PEGGY WEINBERG
Vice President: PAT TRAUB
Vice President: ROBERT BERGHAIER
Publication(s): *Wild*
Keyword(s): Conservation, Endangered and Threatened Species, Environmental and Conservation Education, International Conservation, International Wildlife, Mammals, Predators, Preservation and Protection, Wolves, Wild Dogs, Hyenas

WILD HORSE ORGANIZED ASSISTANCE, INC. (WHOA)
P.O. Box 555, Reno, NV 89504
Phone: 702-323-5908
Founded: 1971; Membership: 12,000
Scope: National
Description: Directs efforts toward the welfare of wild horses and burros; implementation of federal efforts in carrying out terms of the management, protection, and control program for their welfare; student projects pertaining to all phases of our heritage.
Contact(s):
Secretary: BERT LAPPIN; Phone: 702-851-4817
Treasurer: LESLIE JOHNSON; Phone: 702-851-4817
Executive Director and Chairman of the Board: DAWN Y. LAPPIN; Phone: 702-851-4817
Vice Chairman: RUSSELL JOHNSON; Phone: 702-786-7600
Keyword(s): Nongame Wildlife

WILD ONES - NATURAL LANDSCAPERS, LTD
Headquarters, P.O. Box 1274, Appleton, WI 54912-1274
Phone: 877-394-9453 or 920-730-3986; Fax: 920-730-8654; E-mail: woresource@aol.com; Web Site: www.for-wild.org
Founded: 1977; Membership: 2,500 households
Scope: National
Description: Wild Ones is a nonprofit organization seeking to educate and inform members and the public at the plants-roots level and to promote biodiversity and environmental sound practices, thru natural landscaping using native species in developing plant communities.
Contact(s):
President: BRET RAPPAPORT
Vice President: MANDY PLOCH
Secretary: JOE POWELKA
Treasurer: KLAUS WISIOL
Administrative Director: DONNA VANBUECKEN
Publication(s): *Wild Ones Handbook; Wild Ones Journal*
Keyword(s): Ancient Forests, Birds, Conservation, Endangered and Threatened Species, Environmental Ethics, Environmental Preservation, Flowers, Plants, and Trees, Gardening and Horticulture, Grants, Insects and Butterflies, Land Preservation, Natural Areas, Nature Preservation, Native Plants

WILDERNESS EDUCATION ASSOCIATION
W.E.A. Department of Natural Resource Recreation and Tourism Colorado State University, Fort Collins, CO 80523
Phone: 970-223-6252; E-mail: wea@lamar.colostate.edu; Web Site: www.prarienet.org/
Founded: 1977; Membership: 2,500
Scope: National
Description: WEA is a nonprofit membership organization. It promotes national wilderness education and preservation programs by providing for-credit, expedition-based wilderness leadership training programs, developing and publishing state-of-the-art wilderness education publications and training manuals, promoting scholarly research programs, establishing and maintaining national outdoor leadership certification standards, providing support to wildland management agencies to promote wilderness education, and help foster a preservationist land ethic.
Contact(s):
President: DR. DAVID COCKRELL, Department of Human Performance and Leisure Studies, University of Southern Colorado, 2200 Bonforte Blvd., Pueblo, CO 81001-4901; Phone: 719-549-2775; Fax: 719-549-2732
Vice-President: DR. MITCHELL SAKOFS, Outward Bound USA, Rt. 9, R. D. 2, Box 280, Garrison, NY 10524-9757; Phone: 914-424-4000
Secretary: JEFF OLSON, Confidence Learning Center, 6260 Mary Fawcett Memorial Dr., Brainerd, MN 56401; Phone: 218-828-2344
Treasurer: DR. WILLIAM W. FORGEY, One Tower Plaza, 109 E. 89th Ave., Merrillville, IN 46410; Phone: 219-769-6055; Fax: 219-769-6035
Executive Director: DARLA S. DERUITER, WEA Department of Natural Resource Recreation and Tourism, Colorado State University, Fort Collins, CO 80523; Phone: 970-223-6252; Fax: 970-223-6252
Publisher: W. W. NORTON
Publication(s): *WEA Legend; Trustees and Affiliates Briefing System (TABS); The Backcountry Classroom; WEA Affiliate Handbook; New Wilderness Handbook; Wilderness Educator*
Keyword(s): Environmental and Conservation Education, Environmental Preservation, Internships, Outdoor Recreation, Wilderness

WILDERNESS LAND TRUST, THE
4060 Post Canyon Dr., Hood River, OR 97031
Phone: 541-386-9546; Fax: 541-386-9547; E-mail: jon@wildernesstrust.org; Web Site: www.widlernesstrust.org
Founded: 1992; Membership: 800
Scope: National
Description: To facilitate public acquisition of private lands (inholdings) within units of the National Wilderness Preservation System to fulfill the promise of Congress made in The Wilderness Act of 1964 that all generations of Americans will enjoy an enduring resource of wilderness.
Contact(s):
Chairman: JOHN FIELDER, P.O. Box 1261, Englewood, CO 80150; Phone: 303-935-0900
President: JON K. MULFORD
Secretary and Treasurer: ANDY WIESSNER, 811 Potato Patch Dr., Vail, CO 81657; Phone: 303-393-7561
Publication(s): *Wilderness Heritage Newsletter*
Keyword(s): Conservation of Protected Areas, Environmental Protection, Land Preservation, Land Purchase, Wilderness

WILDERNESS SOCIETY, THE
900 17th St., NW, Washington, DC 20006-2596
Phone: 202-833-2300
Founded: 1935; Membership: 300,000
Scope: National
Description: A nonprofit membership organization devoted to preserving wilderness and wildlife, protecting America's prime forests, parks, rivers, and shorelands, and fostering an American land ethic. The Society welcomes membership inquiries, contributions, and bequests.
Contact(s):
Chair: BERT FINGERHUT
President: WILLIAM H. MEADOWS III
Counselor: GAYLORD NELSON
Director of LWCF: SUE GUNN
Director of National Forest Issues: MICHAEL FRANCIS
Director of National Parks and Alaska Issues: ROSE FENNELL
Director of National Wildlife Refuges and Endangered Species Issues: JIM WALTMAN
Program Director of BLM Issues: FRAN HUNT
Regional and State Director: CRAIG GEHRKE, 413 W. Idaho St., Suite 102, Boise, ID 83702; Phone: 208-343-8153
Regional Director: ALLEN SMITH, 430 W. 7th Ave., #210, Anchorage, AK 99501; Phone: 907-272-9453
Regional Director: ROBERT EKEY, 105 W. Main St., Suite E, Bozeman, MT 59715; Phone: 406-586-1600
Regional Director: JAY WATSON, Presidio Bldg. 1016, P.O. Box 29241, San Francisco, CA 94129; Phone: 415-561-6641

NON-GOVERNMENTAL ORGANIZATIONS - W

Regional Director: PAMELA EATON, 7475 Dakin St., Suite 410, Denver, CO 80221; Phone: 303-650-5818
Regional Director: STEVE WHITNEY, 1424 Fourth Ave., Suite 816, Seattle, WA 98101; Phone: 206-624-6430
Regional Director: ROBERT PERSCHEL, 45 Bromfield St., Suite 1101, Boston, MA 02108; Phone: 617-350-8866
Vice President of Communications: SUE LOMENZO
Vice President of Ecology and Economics Research: THOMAS BANCROFT
Vice President of Public Policy: RINDY O'BRIEN
Vice President of Regional Conservation: DARRELL KNUFFKE
Vice President of Resource Development (Acting): STEVE HOWARD
Publication(s): *Wilderness Year, The; Annual: Wilderness America; Newsletter*
Keyword(s): Biodiversity, Forests and Forestry, Public Lands, Sustainable Ecosystems, Wilderness

WILDERNESS WATCH
P.O. Box 9175, Missoula, MT 59807
Phone: 406-542-2048; Fax: 406-542-7714; E-mail: wild@wildernesswatch.org; Web Site: www.wildernesswatch.org
Scope: National
Description: Wilderness Watch is a national, nonprofit, citizen organization dedicated solely to the protection and proper administration of lands within the National Wilderness Preservation System and Wild and Scenic Rivers System. We achieve our goals through the efforts of citizen activists, local chapters, wilderness "adopters", and by working with other local organizations concerned about wilderness and wild river issues.
Contact(s):
Executive Director: GEORGE NICKAS
Publication(s): *Wilderness Watcher*
Keyword(s): Wilderness

WILDFLOWER ASSOCIATION OF MICHIGAN
3825 Farrell Rd., Hastings, SC 49058
Phone: 616-948-2496; Fax: 616-948-2957; E-mail: wam@iserv.net; Web Site: www.iserv.net/~wam
Founded: 1986; Membership: 350
Scope: Statewide
Description: The Wildflower Association of Michigan promotes, coordinates, and participates in education, enjoyment, science, and stewardship of native wildflowers and their habitats.
Contact(s):
President: ROBERT I. WELCH; Phone: 517-483-9675; Fax: 517-483-9619; E-mail: rwelch@lansing.cc.mi.us
Secretary: ESTHER DURNWALD; Phone: 517-647-6010; Fax: 517-647-6072; E-mail: mwf@mvcc.com
Editor: MARJI FULLER; E-mail: marjif@iserv.net
Membership Coordinator: MARILYN CASE; Phone: 616-781-8470; E-mail: mcase15300@aol.com
Publication(s): *Wildflowers; Annual Conference Program*
Keyword(s): Beautification, Botany, Conservation, Endangered and Threatened Species, Environmental and Conservation Education, Grants, Habitat Conservation, Natural Areas, Outdoor Education, Plant Propagation, Prairies, Restoration, Wildflowers, Native Plants

WILDFOWL TRUST OF NORTH AMERICA, INC., THE
P.O. Box 519, Discovery Ln., Grasonville, MD 21638
Phone: 410-827-6694
Founded: 1979; Membership: 600
Scope: National
Description: A nonprofit, tax-exempt organization dedicated to the preservation of wildlife and wetlands through education, conservation, and research. The Trust operates The Horsehead Wetlands Center on its, 500-acre wetland refuge on the Chesapeake Bay's Eastern Shore. The Center provides environmental education programs, a collection of resident waterfowl and raptors in natural habitat settings, a Visitor's Center, trails, and observation blinds and towers. Canoes are available to members.
Contact(s):
President: DR. TORREY C. BROWN
Vice President: WILLIAM STOTT JR.
Executive Director: DR. EDWARD L. DELANEY
Publication(s): *Newsletter*
Keyword(s): Biodiversity, Birds, Environmental and Conservation Education, Research, Wetlands, Wildlife and Wildlife Habitat

WILDLANDS CONSERVANCY
3701 Orchid Pl., Emmaus, PA 18049-1637
Phone: 610-965-4397; E-mail: wildlands@aol.com
Founded: 1973
Scope: Local
Description: A nonprofit, member-supported organization serving eastern Pennsylvania, involved in land and river preservation and environmental education. Wildlands has preserved over 30,000 acres of open space, much of it in cooperation with the Pennsylvania Game Commission. Some of the activities involve the operation of nature preserves and sanctuaries; developing and implementing plans for river conservation and other preservation projects; and the creation of a curriculum (K-College) that teaches responsible watershed stewardship.
Contact(s):
President: PAUL C. WESSEL; Phone: 610-965-4397
Executive Director: THOMAS J. KERR; Phone: 610-965-4397
Keyword(s): Land Preservation, Nature Centers, Rivers, Watersheds, Wildlands

WILDLANDS PROJECT, THE
1955 W Grant Rd., #145, Tucson, AZ 85745-1147
Phone: 520-884-0875; Fax: 520-884-0962; E-mail: wildlands@twp.org; Web Site: www.twp.org
Founded: 1992
Scope: National
Description: The mission of The Wildlands Project is to protect and restore the natural heritage of North America, through the establishment of a connected system of wildlands. TWP coordinates the efforts of regional organizations and individuals in the development of reserve design proposals for a continental vision.
Contact(s):
Chairman: DAVE FOREMAN
President: HARVEY LOCKE
Executive Director: STEVE GATEWOOD; E-mail: SteveG@twp.org
Secretary and Treasurer: DAVID JOHNS
Publication(s): *Wildlands Project, The: Plotting A North American Wilderness Recovery Strategy; Wildlands Project, The: First Thousands Days of the Next Thousand Years; Wild Earth*
Keyword(s): Biodiversity, Conservation of Protected Areas, International Conservation, Wilderness, Wildlands

WILDLIFE ACTION, INC.
P.O. Box 866, Mullins, SC 29574
Phone: 843-464-8473/1-800-753-2264; Fax: 843-464-1914
Founded: 1977; Membership: 14,000
Scope: National
Description: Wildlife Action is a private nonprofit 501(c)3 tax-exempt organization dedicated to the appreciation and enjoyment of our wildlife heritage and to educating the public in the value of protection, restoration, enhancement, and wise use of our natural resources.
Contact(s):
Vice President: TOMMY SIMPSON
Secretary: SANDRA O. BANE
Treasurer: RUSTY RICHARDSON
President and CEO: M. GAULT BEESON JR.
Publication(s): *Wildlife Pride; Wild Things - Our Resource Education Center*
Keyword(s): Environmental and Conservation Education, Environmental Ethics, Environmental Preservation, Outdoor Recreation, Youth Organizations

WILDLIFE CENTER OF VIRGINIA, THE
P.O. Box 1557, Waynesboro, VA 22980-1414

Phone: 540-942-9453; Fax: 540-943-9453; Web Site: www.wildlifecenter.org
Founded: 1982
Scope: International
Description: A nonprofit organization that operates the nation's largest professionally-staffed veterinary teaching and research hospital for native wildlife. Study and documentation of environmental factors that cause injuries, especially pesticide poisoning, are used to monitor environmental and wildlife health trends and support public policy positions. The Center also trains students and professionals from the fields of veterinary medicine, wildlife management and wildlife rehabilitation.
Contact(s):
President: EDWARD E. CLARK JR.
Vice President: SERENA BENSON
Chairman of the Board: ERWIN BOHMFALK
Director of Environmental Education: LISA M. BRISKEY
Director of Veterinary Services: EDWARD J. GENTZ
Publication(s): Handbook of Wildlife Medicine; The Wildlife Center Teacher's Packet; Annual and Mid-year reports, reprints of articles and papers on various topics.
Keyword(s): Birds, Endangered and Threatened Species, Environmental and Conservation Education, Mammals, Nongame Wildlife, Raptors, Wildlife and Wildlife Habitat, Wildlife Disease, Wildlife Rehabilitation

WILDLIFE CONSERVATION SOCIETY
2300 Southern Blvd., Bronx, NY 10460-1099
Phone: 718-220-5100; Fax: 718-733-4460; E-mail: feedback@wcs.org; Web Site: www.wcs.org
Founded: 1895; **Membership:** 100,000
Scope: National
Description: A nonprofit organization which operates an international wildlife and wildlands conservation program with a full-time staff of wildlife biologists conducting field research and training programs around the world. Headquartered in New York City, the Society operates the Bronx Zoo; The New York Aquarium, Central Park Wildlife Center and Tisch Childhood Zoo, Queens Wildlife Center, Prospect Park Wildlife Center, St. Catherine's Island Wildlife Survival Center and a zoological photo library. Education Department offers training programs and curriculum materials globally to teachers K-12.
Contact(s):
Chairman: DAVID T. SCHIFF
President and CEO: CHRISTOPHER SMITH
Senior Vice-President for Development: JENNIFER HERRING
Senior Vice-President for Zoos and Aquariums: RICHARD LATTIS
Senior Vice-President of Education: ANNETTE BERKOVITS;
    Phone: 718-220-5131; E-mail: aberkovits@wcs.org
Senior Vice-President of International Conservation: JOHN ROBINSON
Vice-President -- Strategic Operations: BONNIE SEVY KOEPPEL
Vice-President for Wildlife Health Science: ROBERT COOK
Vice-President of Aquarium Science: LOUIS GARIBALDI
Vice-President of Financial Services: JOHN HOARE
Vice-President--Financial Services: JOHN HOARE
Vice-President--General Counsel: W. B. McKEOWN
Director of Science Resource Center: GEORGE AMATO
Editor-in-Chief: JOAN DOWNS
Librarian: STEVE JOHNSON
Publication(s): Wildlife Conservation; Annual Report
Keyword(s): Aquariums, Endangered and Threatened Species, Environmental and Conservation Education, International Conservation, Wildlife and Wildlife Habitat, Wildlife Management, Zoological Parks, Libraries, Environmental Education Curriculum

WILDLIFE DAMAGE REVIEW (WDR)
P.O. Box 85218, Tucson, AZ 85754
Phone: 520-884-0883; Fax: 520-884-0962; E-mail: wdr@azstarnet.com; Web Site: www.Azstarnet.com/~WDR
Founded: 1991; **Membership:** 3,500
Scope: National
Description: Wildlife Damage Review's mission is to bring much needed public attention to the USDA's Animal Damage Control (ADC) program, renamed Wildlife Services in 1997. This taxpayer supported program traps, snares, poisons, and aerial guns 1-2 million of America's wildlife yearly for private interests. WDR's ultimate goal is to place wildlife management into the hands of those agencies whose vested interest is protection of native diversity and banish management guided by predator prejudice.
Contact(s):
Executive Director: NANCY ZIERENBERG
Publication(s): Special Edition Update; Waste, Fraud, Abuse in the U.S. Animal Damage Control Program; Wildlife Damage Review; Audit of the USDA Animal Damage Control Program; The War on Wildlife (audio CD); Investigating J.F.K. International Airport Gull Hazard Reduction Program.
Keyword(s): Agriculture, Biodiversity, Birds, Chemical Pollution Control, Endangered and Threatened Species, Environmental and Conservation Education, Mammals, Pesticides, Predators, Toxic Substances, Trapping, Wildlife Management

WILDLIFE DISEASE ASSOCIATION
P.O. Box 1897, Lawrence, KS 66044-8897
Founded: 1951; **Membership:** 1,300
Scope: International
Description: An international nonprofit organization of scientists interested in advancing knowledge of the effects of infectious, parasitic, toxic, genetic, and physiologic diseases and environmental factors upon the health and survival of free-living and captive wild animals, and upon their relationships to humans.
Contact(s):
President: DR. ROBERT MCLEAN
Secretary: ELIZABETH HOWERTH
Treasurer: LESLIE UHAZY
Business Manager: IRWIN POLLS
Editor: DR. DANIEL B. PENCE
Publication(s): Journal of Wildlife Diseases; Newsletter
Keyword(s): Biology, Health and Nutrition, Wildlife Disease

WILDLIFE FEDERATION OF ALASKA
750 W. Second Ave., Suite 200, Anchorage, AK 99501-2121

Phone: 907-274-3388; Fax: 907-258-4811; E-mail: wfa@micronet.net; Web Site: www.micronet/users/~wfa/default.html
Founded: 1984
Scope: Statewide
Description: A representative statewide organization, affiliated with the National Wildlife Federation, dedicated to the protection and enhancement of wildlife ands its habitat through public education and government interaction.
Contact(s):
President and Representative: NANCY WAINWRIGHT
Editor: LAURIE FAIRCHILD
Alternate Representative: DEBBIE BANK
Publication(s): Tracks

WILDLIFE FOREVER
10365 West 70th St., Eden Prairie, MN 55344
Phone: 612-833-1522; Fax: 612-833-0804; E-mail: info@wildlifeforever.org; Web Site: www.wildlifeforever.org
Founded: 1987; **Membership:** 65,000
Scope: National
Description: A charitable, nonprofit organization dedicated to preserving America's wildlife heritage through preservation, conservation and management of habitats, plant life, and wildlife. Projects include acquisition, grassroots activities, management, research, education, and ethics for wildlife conservation.
Contact(s):
President: DOUGLAS H. GRANN
Director of Development: ROSS SUBLETT
Director of Marketing: PETE WUEBKER
Publication(s): Cry of the Wild; Wildlife Forever; The First Decade

Keyword(s): Aquatic Habitats, Environment, Environmental and Conservation Education, Fisheries, Flowers, Plants, and Trees, Hunting, Land Purchase, Mammals, Nongame Wildlife, Outdoor Recreation, Public Lands, Raptors, Sport Fishing, Waterfowl

WILDLIFE FOUNDATION OF FLORIDA, INC.
620 S. Meridian St., Tallahassee, FL 32399-1600
Phone: 850-487-3794; Fax: 850-488-6988
Founded: 1994
Scope: Statewide
Description: The mission of the Wildlife Foundation of Florida, Inc. is to provide assistance, funding, and promotional support for the Florida Game and Wildlife Conservation Commission, and in so doing, contribute to the health and well-being of Florida's fish and wildlife resources and their habitats.
Contact(s):
Board of Director: ALLAN L. EGBERT
Board of Director: ROBERT M. BRANTLY
Board of Director: WILLIAM M. BLAKE
Board of Director: GEORGE G. MATTHEWS
Board of Director: LINDA M. BREMER
Board of Director: WILLIAM G. BOSTICK JR.
Board of Director: C. TOM RAINEY
Board of Director: KATE IRELAND
Keyword(s): Fisheries, Hunting, Sport Fishing, Wildlife and Wildlife Habitat, Wildlife Management

WILDLIFE HABITAT CANADA
7 Hinton Ave., North, Suite 200, Ottawa, Ontario K1Y 4P1 Canada
Phone: 613-722-2090; Fax: 613-722-3318; E-mail: receptio@whc.org; Web Site: www.whc.org
Founded: 1984
Scope: National
Description: Wildlife Habitat Canada is a national non-profit organization dedicated to working with private citizens, governments, non-government organizations, and industry to conserve the great variety of wildlife habitats across Canada. The organization develops and implements its own conservation initiatives, such as the Forest Biodiversity Program, but also provides grants for conservation, research, communication and education projects and has a graduate scholarship program.
Contact(s):
Executive Director: DAVID J. NEAVE
Director of Programs: JAMES FORTUNE
Publication(s): *Annual Reports (a list of free publications is contained therein; publications are available upon request.)*
Keyword(s): Agriculture, Biodiversity, Fisheries, Forest Management, Research Grants, Scholarships and Grants, Stewardship, Wetlands, Wildlife and Wildlife Habitat

WILDLIFE HABITAT COUNCIL
1010 Wayne Ave. Suite 920, Silver Spring, MD 20910
Phone: 301-588-8994; Fax: 301-588-4629; E-mail: whc@wildlifehc.org; Web Site: www.wildlifehc.org
Founded: 1987; Membership: 130
Scope: National
Description: A joint effort between the conservation and corporate communities, WHC is an international, nonprofit organization formed to assist corporations in enhancing their lands for the benefit of wildlife. WHC's program includes technical assistance in establishing and maintaining responsible corporate wildlife management practices, environmental mediation, habitat certification, information sharing, employee involvement, and community outreach.
Contact(s):
President: WILLIAM W. HOWARD
Vice President: ROBERT J. JOHNSON
Board of Directors Chairman: DR. CHARLES G. CARSON III
Board of Directors Secretary and Treasurer: HUGH J. DILLINGHAM III
Board of Directors Vice Chair: LAWRENCE A. SELZER
Controller: LAURIE CORAN
Publication(s): *Wildlife Habitat; Registry of Certified and Internationally Accredited Wildlife Habitat Programs; Corporate Homes for Wildlife annual desk calendar*
Keyword(s): Biodiversity, Environmental and Conservation Education, Sustainable Development, Wildlife and Wildlife Habitat, Wildlife Management

WILDLIFE INFORMATION CENTER, INC.
P.O. Box 198, Slatington, PA 18080
Phone: 610-760-8889
Founded: 1986
Scope: National
Description: A nonprofit, member-supported organization whose purpose is to secure and disseminate wildlife conservation, education, recreation, and scientific research information. Programs include: The Kittatinny Raptor Corridor Project and long-term hawk migration field studies at Bake Oven Knob, PA.; in-service teacher training courses and public education; research and preparation of conservation-education papers and reports; maintaining wildlife libraries, photographs, computer databases; and advocating wildlife observation and wildlife tourism. The Center currently is raising funds for the purchase of land for its own wildlife refuge and headquarters.
Contact(s):
President: DAN R. KUNKLE
Secretary: KATHIE ROMANO
Treasurer: MARGARET LIBONATI M.D.
Editor: DAN R. KUNKLE
Publication(s): *Wildlife Conservation Reports; Wildlife Activist; American Hawkwatcher*
Keyword(s): Biodiversity, Birds, Environmental and Conservation Education, Raptors, Wildlife and Wildlife Habitat

WILDLIFE LEGISLATIVE FUND OF AMERICA, THE, AND WILDLIFE CONSERVATION FUND OF AMERICA, THE
801 Kingsmill Parkway, Columbus, OH 43229-1137
Phone: 614-888-4868
Founded: 1978
Scope: National
Description: Companion nonprofit organizations established to protect America's hunting, trapping, and fishing heritage, and the scientific wildlife management practices which support it. The WLFA is the legislative arm. The WCFA is the legal defense, public education, and research arm.
Contact(s):
President: WALTER W. PIDGEON JR
Vice President: RICK STORY
Treasurer: MRS. GILBERT W. HUMPHREY
Chairman of the Board: VINCENT W. SHIEL
Director of National and International Affairs and Washington, D.C. Counsel: WILLIAM P. HORN
Director of Communications: DOUG JEANNERET
Director of State Services: ROBERT T. SEXTON
Director of Field Service: TOM DONNELLY
Vice Chairman: F. ALEX MADDOX JR
Publication(s): *Update*
Keyword(s): Hunting, Sport Fishing, Trapping, Wildlife and Wildlife Habitat, Wildlife Management

WILDLIFE MANAGEMENT INSTITUTE
Suite 801, 1101 14th St., NW, Washington, DC 20005
Phone: 202-371-1808; Fax: 202-408-5059; E-mail: wmihq@aol.com; Web Site: www.wildlifemgt.org/wmi
Scope: National
Description: International nonprofit scientific and educational private membership organization, supported by industries, groups, and individuals, promoting improved professional management of wildlife and other natural resources for the benefit of those resources and North American, including its people.
Contact(s):
Director of Conservation: TERRY Z. RILEY
President: ROLLIN D. SPARROWE
Vice President: RICHARD E. MCCABE

Conservation Policy Specialist: RONALD R. HELINSKI
Finance Manager: CAROL J. PEDDICORD
Midwest Field Representative: VACANT
Northeast Field Representative: SCOT J. WILLIAMSON, R.R. 1, Box 587, Spur Rd., North Stratford, NH 03590; Phone: 603-636-9846; Fax: 603-636-9853; E-mail: wmisw@together.net
Northwest Field Representative: E. CHARLES MESLOW, 8035 NW Oxbow Dr., Corvallis, OR 97330; Phone: 541-752-7205; Fax: 541-753-8772; E-mail: wmicm@aol.com
Partners Program Director: PATRICIA PEACOCK
Senior Scientist: JAMES R. WOEHR
Southeast Field Representative: VACANT
Southwest Field Representative: LEN CARPENTER, 4015 Cheney Dr., Fort Collins, CO 80526; Phone: 970-223-1099; Fax: 970-204-9198; E-mail: lenc@verinet.com
Wildlife Program Coordinator: ROBERT L. BYRNE
Publication(s): *Outdoor News Bulletin; Transactions North American Wildlife and Natural Resources Conference; books and booklets*
Keyword(s): Wildlife Management

WILDLIFE PRESERVATION TRUST INTERNATIONAL, INC.
1520 Locust St., Suite 704, Philadelphia, PA 19102
Phone: 215-731-9770; Fax: 215-731-9766; E-mail: homeoffice@wpti.org; Web Site: www.wpti.org
Founded: 1971; Membership: 3,000
Scope: National
Description: Wildlife Preservation Trust International conserves threatened wild species and their habitats in partnership with local scientists and educators around the world.
Contact(s):
President: THOMAS J. P. McHENRY
Vice President: VIRGINIA C. MARS
Vice President: ALLEN J. MODEL
Secretary: VICTORIA B. MARS
Treasurer: JOHN C. TUTEN JR.
Executive Director: MARY C. PEARL Ph.D.
Director of Administration: JOANNE M. GULLIFER
Director of Conservation Program: FRED W. KOONTZ Ph.D.
Director of Development: PETER WILMERDING
International Field Veterinarian: A. ALONSO AGUIRRE Ph.D.
Publication(s): *On the Edge; Dodo, The; Dodo Dispatch; Wild Times, The; Annual Report*
Keyword(s): Endangered and Threatened Species, Environmental and Conservation Education, Grants, International Conservation, Wildlife and Wildlife Habitat, Wildlife Disease

WILDLIFE SOCIETY, THE
Headquarters, 5410 Grosvenor Ln., Bethesda, MD 20814-2197
Phone: 301-897-9770; Fax: 301-530-2471; E-mail: tws@wildlife.org; Web Site: www.wildlife.org
Founded: 1937; Membership: 9,000
Scope: National
Description: International scientific and educational organization of professionals and students engaged in wildlife research, management, education, and administration. Dedicated to sound stewardship of wildlife resources and the environments upon which wildlife and humans depend; undertakes an active role in preventing human-induced environmental degradation; increases awareness and appreciation of wildlife values; and seeks the highest standards in all activities of the wildlife profession.
Contact(s):
President: NOVA J. SILVY, 210 Nagle Hall, Dept. of Wildlife and Fisheries Science, Texas A&M University, College Station, TX 77843-2258; Phone: 541-737-1954; E-mail: n-silvy@tamu.edu
President-Elect: LEN H. CARPENTER, Wildlife Management Institute, 4015 Cheney Dr., Fort Collins, CO 80526; Phone: 970-223-1099; E-mail: lenc@verinet.com
Vice President: DIANA HALLETT, MO Dept. of Conservation, 1110 College Ave., Columbia, MO 65201; Phone: 573-882-9880; E-mail: halled@mail.conservation.state.mo.us
Past-President: JAMES E. MILLER, USDA-CREES/NRE, AG Box 2210, Rm. 829, Aerospace Center, Washington, DC 20250-2210; Phone: 202-401-6602; E-mail: jmiller@reeusda.gov
Northeast Section Representative: JOHN F. ORGAN, P.O. Box 45, Buckland, MA 01338-0045; Phone: 413-253-8501; E-mail: john_organ@mail.fws.gov
Southeastern Section Representative: ROBERT J. WARREN, Warnell School of Forest Resources, University of Georgia, Athens, GA 30602-2152; Phone: 706-542-6474; E-mail: warren@smokey.forestry.uga.edu
North Central Section Representative: W. DANIEL SVEDARSKY, Northwest Experimental Station, University of Minnesota, ARC Building, Crookston, MN 56716; Phone: 218-281-8129; E-mail: Dsvedars@mail.crk.umn.edu
Central Mountains & Plains Section Representative: GERALD D. KOBRIGER, 225 30th Ave., SW, Dickinson, ND 58601; Phone: 701-227-7431; E-mail: gkobrige@state.nd.us
Southwest Section Representative: ROBERT D. BROWN, Dept. of Wildlife & Fisheries Sciences, 210 Nagle Hall, Texas A&M Univeristy, College Station, TX 77843-2258; Phone: 409-845-1261; E-mail: rdbrown@tamu.edu
Northwest Section Representative: W. DANIEL EDGE, Dept. of Fisheries & Wildlife, Oregon State University, 104 Nash Hall, Corvallis, OR 97331-3803; Phone: 541-737-1953; E-mail: edgew@ucs.orst.edu
Western Section Representative: BRADLEY E. VALENTINE, CA Dept. of Forestry, P.O. Box 670, Santa Rosa, CA 95401; Phone: 707-576-2937; E-mail: brad_valentine@fire.ca.gov
Executive Director: HARRY E. HODGDON
Wildlife Policy Director: THOMAS M. FRANKLIN
Program Director: SANDRA STAPLES-BORTNER, 18214 NE 125th Way, Brush Prairie, WA 98606; Phone: 360-253-4611; E-mail: twsssb@aol.com
Publication(s): *Journal of Wildlife Management, The; Wildlife Monographs; Wildlife Society Bulletin; Wildlifer, The*
Keyword(s): Nongame Wildlife, Renewable Resources, Wildlife and Wildlife Habitat, Wildlife Management

WILDLIFE SOCIETY, ALABAMA CHAPTER
Attn: President, 331 Funchess Hall, Auburn University, Auburn, AL 36830
Scope: Statewide
Contact(s):
President: JAMES B. ARMSTRONG; Phone: 334-844-9233
Secretary and Treasurer: JEFF L. MAKEMSON, 11481 Colonial Dr., Duncanville, AL 35456; Phone: 202-345-3807

WILDLIFE SOCIETY, ALASKA CHAPTER
Attn: President, P.O. Box 72962, Fairbanks, AK 99707
Scope: Statewide
Contact(s):
President: ROGER A. POST, P.O. Box 72962, Fairbanks, AK 99707; Phone: 907-459-7287
President-Elect: GINO DEL FRATE, P.O. Box 1413, Homer, AK 99801; Phone: 907-235-8191
Secretary and Treasurer: ANNE MORKILL, P.O. Box 83381, Fairbanks, AK 99708; Phone: 907-456-0549

WILDLIFE SOCIETY, ALBERTA CHAPTER
Attn: President, Rural Route 4, Sherwood Park, Alberta T8A 3K4 Canada
Scope: Statewide
Contact(s):
President: MIKE DORRANCE
President-Elect: ELSTON H. DZUS, 7204-103 Avenume, Edmonton, AB T6A 0V1 Canada; Phone: 780-453-4109
Secretary and Treasurer: CHRIS C. SHANK, 63 W. Mackay Crescent, Cochrane, AB T0L 0W4 Canada; Phone: 403-932-2388

WILDLIFE SOCIETY, ARIZONA CHAPTER
Attn: President, 130 W. Calle Melendrez, Green Valley, AZ 85614
Scope: Statewide

NON-GOVERNMENTAL ORGANIZATIONS - W

Contact(s):
President: H. REED SANDERSON; Phone: 520-648-6556
President-Elect: BILL BURGER, AZ Game & Fish Dept., 7220 E. University Drive, Mesa, AZ 85296; Phone: 602-981-9400
Treasurer: MARY ANN BENOIT, HC 31, Box 68, Happy Jack, AZ 86024; Phone: 520-527-3640
Corresponding Secretary: KAREN M. SIMMS, Bureau of Land Management, 12661 E. Broadway Blvd., Tucson, AZ 85748; Phone: 520-722-4289
Recording Secretary: MICHAEL T. PRUSS, AZ Game & Fish Dept., 555 W. Greasewood Rd., Tucson, AZ 85745; Phone: 520-628-5376, ext. 143

WILDLIFE SOCIETY, ARKANSAS CHAPTER
Attn: President, P.O. Box 279, Altus, AR 72821-0279
Scope: Statewide
Contact(s):
President: RANDALL B. BULLINGTON; Phone: 501-667-2191
President-Elect: JIM C. BEDNARZ, Dept. of Biological Science, AR State University, P.O. Box 599, State University, AR 72467; Phone: 501-972-3082
Secretary and Treasurer: ALICIA N. LUPKES, 771 Jordan Dr., Monticello, AR 71655; Phone: 870-367-3553

WILDLIFE SOCIETY, CALIFORNIA CENTRAL COAST CHAPTER
Attn: President, USDA Forest Service 6144 Calle Real, Goleta, CA 93117
Scope: Statewide
Contact(s):
President: MAETON FREEL; Phone: 805-681-2764
Vice-President: KEVIN COOPER, USDA Forest Service, 1616 Carlotti Drive, Santa Maria, CA 93117; Phone: 805-681-2764
Secretary: JUSTIN VREELAND, University of California Extension, 2156 Sierra Way, Suite C, San Luis Obispo, CA 93401; Phone: 805-781-5940
Treasurer: MICHAEL T. HANSON, 1203 Madonna Road, San Luis Obispo, CA 93405; Phone: 805-541-0272

WILDLIFE SOCIETY, CALIFORNIA NORTH COAST CHAPTER
Attn: President, Simpson Timber Co., P.O. Box 68, Korbel, CA 95550
Scope: Statewide
Contact(s):
President: LOWELL DILLER, Simpson Timber Co., P.O. Box 68, Korbel, CA 95550; Phone: 707-668-4428
President-Elect: SANDRA VON ARB, 121 S. Cherry Ln., Rio Del, CA 95562; Phone: 707-764-4488
Secretary: TINA L. BARTLETT, 6816 London Dr., Eureka, CA 95503; Phone: 707-441-4865
Treasurer: SCOTT OSBORN, Natural Resources Mgmt. Corp., 1434 3rd St., Eureka, CA 95501; Phone: 707-442-1735

WILDLIFE SOCIETY, COLORADO CHAPTER
Attn: President, 0772 S. Rd. 1E, Monta Vista, CO 81144
Scope: Statewide
Contact(s):
President: KIRK NAVO; Phone: 719-852-4783
President-Elect: TOM POLAR, Colorado Division of Wildlife, 317 W. Prospect St., Fort Collins, CO 80526
Secretary: ROBIN SELL, 810 Taylor Street, Craig, CO 81625; Phone: 970-824-4441
Treasurer: RICHARD R. ROTH, 2597 B 3/4 Rd., Grand Junction, CO 81503-1789; Phone: 719-545-4039

WILDLIFE SOCIETY, FLORIDA CHAPTER
Attn: President, USDA Forest Service, P.O. Box 579, Bristol, FL 32321
Scope: Statewide
Contact(s):
President: SUSAN M. FITZGERALD; Phone: 850-643-2282
Vice President: CAROLYN SEKERAK, P.O. Box 275, Trilby, FL 33593; Phone: 352-669-3153
Secretary and Treasurer: STEPHEN V. ROCKWOOD, 325 Columbus St., Sebastian, FL 32958; Phone: 561-388-4013

WILDLIFE SOCIETY, GEORGIA CHAPTER
Attn: President, D.B. Warnell School of Forest Resources, University of Georgia, Athens, GA 30602-2152
Scope: Statewide
Contact(s):
President: SARAH SCHWEITZER; Phone: 706-542-1150
President-Elect: MARK D. WHITNEY, 2111 US Hwy 278, SE, Social Circle, GA 30025; Phone: 770-918-6416
Secretary and Treasurer: DOUGLAS MICHAEL HOFFMAN, 120 Diamond Dr., Athens, GA 30605; Phone: 706-546-2020

WILDLIFE SOCIETY, HAWAII CHAPTER
40 Kunihi Ln., #221, Kahului, HI 96732
Scope: Statewide
Contact(s):
President: CARRIE L. HAUREZ; Phone: 808-877-1455
President-Elect: FERN P. DUVALL II, 211 Ulana St., Makawao, HI 96768-8034; Phone: 808-871-2929
Secretary: JOY TAMAYOSE, c/o Haleakala National Park, P.O. Box 369, Makawao, HI 96768; Phone: 808-572-4492
Treasurer: DAN MCNULTY-HUFFMAN, 85 Haele Place, Makawao, HI 96768-8053; Phone: 808-572-4491

WILDLIFE SOCIETY, IDAHO CHAPTER
Attn: President, College of Forestry, Wildlife & Range Sciences, University of Idaho, Moscow, ID 83843-1136
Scope: Statewide
Contact(s):
President: KERRY PAUL REESE; Phone: 208-885-6435
Vice-President: ANTHONIE M.A. HOLTHUIJZEN, ID Power Co., Environmental Affairs Dept., Box 70, Boise, ID 83707; Phone: 208-323-8629
Secretary: CHARLES PETERSON, Box 8007, Idaho State University, Pocatello, ID 83209; Phone: 208-236-3922
Treasurer: TONY APA, ID Dept. of Fish & Game, 868 E. Main, Jerome, ID 83204-1819; Phone: 208-324-4359

WILDLIFE SOCIETY, ILLINOIS CHAPTER
Attn: President, Max McGraw Wildlife Foundation, P.O. Box 9, Dundee, IL 60118
Scope: Statewide
Contact(s):
President: JOHN D. THOMPSON; Phone: 847-741-8000
President-Elect: GEORGE FELDHAMER, Dept. of Zoology, Southern Illinois University, Carbondale, IL 62901; Phone: 618-457-8606
Secretary and Treasurer: AARON P. YETTER, IL Natural History Survey, Forbes Biological Station, P.O. Box 590, Havana, IL 62644-0590

WILDLIFE SOCIETY, INDIANA CHAPTER
Attn: President, Dept. of Forestry and Natural Resources, Purdue University, Lafayette, IN 47907
Phone: 765-494-3567
Scope: Statewide
Contact(s):
President: HARMON WEEKS JR.; Phone: 765-494-3567
President-elect: JIM GERBRACHT, IN Dept. of State Parks, Div. Of State Parks and Reservoirs, 402 W. Washington, Room W298, Indianapolis, IN 46204-2745; Phone: 317-232-4124
Secretary and Treasurer: BRIAN FRAWLEY, IN Division of Fish & Wildlife, 3900 Soldiers Home Road, West Lafayette, IN 47906; Phone: 765-463-0032

WILDLIFE SOCIETY, IOWA CHAPTER
Attn: President, 106 W. Wilcoxway, Jefferson, IA 50129
Scope: Statewide
Contact(s):
President: DONALD SIEVERS; Phone: 515-747-8383
President-Elect: DONALD PFEIFFER, 110 Lake Darling Rd., Brighton, IA 52540; Phone: 319-653-4912
Secretary and Treasurer: TODD BOGENSCHUTZ, Wildlife Research Station, 1436 255th St., Boone, IA 50036; Phone: 505-432-2823

NON-GOVERNMENTAL ORGANIZATIONS - W

WILDLIFE SOCIETY, KANSAS CHAPTER
Attn: President, Div. Of Biological Science, Emporia State University, Emporia, KS 66801
Scope: Statewide
Contact(s):
President: ELMER FINCK; Phone: 316-341-5623
President-Elect: M. BRAD MCCORD, P.O. Box 15, Wilson, KS 67490-0015; Phone: 758-658-2588
Secretary-Treasurer: CHARLES LEE, Kansas State University, Room 127, Call Hall, Manhattan, KS 66506-1600; Phone: 785-532-5734

WILDLIFE SOCIETY, KENTUCKY CHAPTER
Attn: President, KY Dept. Fish & Wildlife, #1 Game Farm Rd., Frankfort, KY 40601
Scope: Statewide
Contact(s):
President: ROY GRIMES; Phone: 502-564-4404
President-Elect: CHARLES L. ELLIOTT, Dept. of Biology, Eastern Kentucky University, 521 Lancaster Ave., Richmond, KY 40475-3102; Phone: 606-622-1538
Secretary and Treasurer: DAN ERIC FIGERT; Phone: 501-564-5448

WILDLIFE SOCIETY, LOUISIANA CHAPTER
Attn: President, 5492 Grand Chenier Hwy, Grand Chenier, LA 70643
Scope: Statewide
Contact(s):
President: THOMAS HESS JR.; Phone: 318-538-2165
President-Elect: EDMOND MOUTON LDWF, 2415 Darnall Road, New Iberia, LA 70560; Phone: 318-373-0032
Secretary and Treasurer: CECILIA WALTHER, 4110 Janet Avenue, #6, Baton Rouge, LA 70800; Phone: 504-761-0963

WILDLIFE SOCIETY, MAINE CHAPTER
Attn: Secretary, ME Dept. Inland Fish & Wildlife, P.O. Box 416, Ashland, ME 04732
Scope: Statewide
Contact(s):
President: MARK McCOLLOUGH, ME Inland Fisheries & Wildlife, 650 State Road, Bangor, ME 04401; Phone: 207-941-4475
President-elect: MITSCHKA J. HARTLEY, Dept. Wildlife Ecology, 5755 Nutting Hall, University of Maine, Orono, ME 04467; Phone: 207-581-2939
Secretary-Treasurer: RICHARD T. HOPPE, ME Dept. of Inland Fish & Wildlife, P.O. Box 416, Ashland, ME 04732-0477; Phone: 207-435-3231

WILDLIFE SOCIETY, MANITOBA CHAPTER
Attn:President, Dillion Consulting Ltd., 6 Donald St. S., Winnipeg, Manitoba R3L 0K6 Canada
Scope: Statewide
Contact(s):
President: RHIANNON K.E. CHRISTIE; Phone: 204-475-2382
President-Elect: CORY J. LINDGREN, Box 1160, Stonewall, Manitoba R0C 2Z0 Canada; Phone: 204-467-3000
Secretary and Treasurer: TANYS UHMANN, 1017 Kilkenny Dr., Winnipeg, Manitoba R3T 4K5 Canada; Phone: 204-474-8373

WILDLIFE SOCIETY, MARYLAND-DELAWARE CHAPTER
Attn: President, 1053 Hampton Dr., Crownsville, MD 21032-1315
Scope: Statewide
Contact(s):
President: CAROL BERNSTEIN; Phone: 410-962-3208
Secretary: ELAINE JOHNSON, 12453 Iowa Ave., Nampa, ID 83686-8023
Treasurer: DONALD H. ROHRBACK, 11107 Fort Frederick Rd., Big Pool, MD 21711; Phone: 301-842-3355
President-elect: PHILIP C. NORMAN, 7120 Oakland Mills Rd., Columbia, MD 21046; Phone: 410-313-4724

WILDLIFE SOCIETY, MICHIGAN CHAPTER
Attn: President, 5525 Hayes Tower Rd., Gaylord, MI 49735
Scope: Statewide
Contact(s):
President: BRIAN G. MASTENBROOK
President-Elect: LARRY D. CALDWELL, Biology Dept., Central Michigan University, Mt. Pleasant, MI 48859; Phone: 517-774-3387
Secretary and Treasurer: LORI G. SARGENT, 10832 Fenner Rd., Perry, MI 48872

WILDLIFE SOCIETY, MINNESOTA CHAPTER
Attn: President, 24201 County Rd.10, Bovey, MN 55709
Scope: Statewide
Contact(s):
President: JANET S. BOE; Phone: 218-755-4028
President-Elect: MARTHA J. MINCHAK, 107 N. Maple Ave., Thief River Falls, MN 56701; Phone: 218-681-0946
Secretary and Treasurer: GRETCHEN MEHMEL, P.O. Box 100, Roosevelt, MN 56673-0100; Phone: 218-783-6861

WILDLIFE SOCIETY, MISSISSIPPI CHAPTER
Attn: President, P.O. Box 451, Jackson, MS 39205
Scope: Statewide
Contact(s):
President: MARCUS R. SPENCER; Phone: 601-364-2229
President-Elect: KRISTINA CASSCLES GODWIN, Rt. 1, Box 98, A Hwy 15 S, Ackerman, MS 39735; Phone: 601-285-3264, ext. 15
Secretary and Treasurer: JIMMY D. TAYLOR, 103 W. Bound St., Starkville, MS 39759; Phone: 601-325-3194

WILDLIFE SOCIETY, MISSOURI CHAPTER
Attn: President, 21999 Hwy B, Maitland, MO 64466
Scope: Statewide
Contact(s):
President: R. MARK JACKSON
President-Elect: JOHN H. SCHULZ, Fish & Wildlife Research Center, MO Dept. of Conservation, 1110 S. College Ave., Columbia, MO 65201; Phone: 573-882-9880
Secretary: DENNIS J. BROWNING, 15368 LIV 2386, Chillicothe, MO 64601; Phone: 660-646-6122
Treasurer: JEFF L. HODGES, 382 NW Hwy 18, Clinton, MO 64735; Phone: 660-885-7057

WILDLIFE SOCIETY, MONTANA CHAPTER
Attn: President, 107 Mark Jensen Ln., Polson, MT 59860
Scope: Statewide
Contact(s):
President: DALE BECKER; Phone: 406-675-2700
President-elect: JOHN VORE, MT Fish, Wildlife & Parks, 490 N. Meriden, Kalispell, MT 59901; Phone: 406-751-4588
Secretary and Treasurer: FRANK PICKETT, 40 E. Boadway, Butte, MT 59701; Phone: 406-497-3000

WILDLIFE SOCIETY, NATIONAL CAPITAL CHAPTER
Attn: President, 1801 K St., NW, Suite 203L, Washington, DC 20006
Scope: Statewide
Contact(s):
President: KRISTEN P. LA VINE; Phone: 202-822-8540
Secretary-Treasurer: STEPHANIE L. HUSSEY, P.O. Box 1706, Alexandria, VA 22313; Phone: 703-684-5856

WILDLIFE SOCIETY, NEBRASKA CHAPTER
Attn: President, 2207 Woodbridge Pl., Grand Island, NE 68801
Scope: Statewide
Contact(s):
President: MARK M. CZAPLEWSKI; Phone: 308-385-6282
President-elect: WILLIAM L. VODEHNAL, P.O. Box 342, Basset, NE 68714; Phone: 402-684-2921
Secretary: JUSTIN W. KING, 375 South 7th Ave., Columbus, NE 68601; Phone: 402-563-5088
Treasurer: JEANINE LACKEY, P.O. Box 75, Ceresco, NE 68017; Phone: 402-471-0641

NON-GOVERNMENTAL ORGANIZATIONS - W

WILDLIFE SOCIETY, NEVADA CHAPTER
Attn: President, 4321 Jody Ave., Las Vegas, NV 89120
Scope: Statewide
Contact(s):
President: ROBERT J. TURNER; Phone: 702-458-3969
Secretary and Treasurer: ALAN E. JENNE, P.O. Box 3385, Carson City, NV 89702

WILDLIFE SOCIETY, NEW ENGLAND CHAPTER
Attn: President, Sessions Woods WMA, P.O. Box 1550, Burlington, CT 06013
Scope: National
Contact(s):
President: PAUL REGO; Phone: 860-675-8130
President-Elect: JOHN E. MCDONALD, MA Div. Fish & Wildlife, Field Headquarters, Westborough, MA 01581; Phone: 508-792-7270, ext. 121
Secretary and Treasurer: DAVID P. FULLER, MA Div. Fish & Wildlife, 211 Temple St., West Boylston, MA 01583; Phone: 508-835-3607

WILDLIFE SOCIETY, NEW JERSEY CHAPTER
Attn: President, P.O. Box 34, Oceanville, NJ 08231-0034
Scope: Statewide
Contact(s):
President: TRACY CASSELMAN; Phone: 609-652-1665
Secretary: LAURANCE S. TOROK, 139 George St., Lambertville, NJ 08530-1611; Phone: 609-633-6755
Treasurer: JAMES C. SCIASCA, 4667 McDermott Rd., Bangor, PA 18013; Phone: 908-735-8975

WILDLIFE SOCIETY, NEW MEXICO CHAPTER
Attn: President, 331 Camino de la Tietta, Corrales, NM 87048-8554
Scope: Statewide
Contact(s):
President: GAIL TUNBERG; Phone: 505-842-3151
President-Elect: JAMES R. BIGGS, 10324 Apache NE, Albuquerque, NM 87112; Phone: 505-665-5714
Secretary and Treasurer: DAN SUTCLIFFE, 1898 Quemado, Santa Fe, NM 87505; Phone: 505-473-1436

WILDLIFE SOCIETY, NEW YORK CHAPTER
Wildlife Resources Center, Delmar, NY 12054
Scope: Statewide
Contact(s):
President: MICHAEL J. MATTHEWS, 281 Swift Road, Voorheesville, NY 12186-5031; Phone: 518-429-1662
Secretary: RICHARD B. CHIPMAN, USDA/APHIS/WS, 1930 Route 9, Castleton, NY 12033-9653; Phone: 518-477-4837
Treasurer: JAMES G. DALEY, Clermont St., Albany, NY 12203; Phone: 518-783-5733
Vice-President: CHUCK R. DENTE, 14 Marvin Ave., Demar, NY 12054; Phone: 518-429-1662

WILDLIFE SOCIETY, NORTH CAROLINA CHAPTER
Attn: President, 245 Deepwoods Dr., Marion, NC 28752
Scope: Statewide
Contact(s):
President: GORDON S. WARBURTON; Phone: 828-659-8352
President-Elect: JON HEITSERBERG, 7449 Heartland Drive, Wake Forest, NC 27587; Phone: 919-856-4124
Secretary: MEGAN B. MARTOGLIO, 789 NC Hwy 24-27 East, Troy, NC 27371; Phone: 910-576-6391
Treasurer: CHRIS MCGRATH, 315 Morgan Branch Rd., Leicester, NC 28748; Phone: 828-683-0671

WILDLIFE SOCIETY, NORTH DAKOTA CHAPTER
Attn: President, USFWS, 1500 E. Capital Ave., Bismark, ND 58501
Scope: Statewide
Contact(s):
President: WILLIAM B. BICKNELL; Phone: 701-250-4414
President-Elect: JOHN W. SCHULZ, 517 7th St. S., Devils Lake, ND 58301-3727; Phone: 701-776-5185
Secretary and Treasurer: THERESA OLSON, 4205 38th Ave. NW, Mandan, ND 58554; Phone: 701-250-4242, ext. 3617

WILDLIFE SOCIETY, OHIO CHAPTER
Attn: President, 1535 Marion-Williamsport Rd., Marion, OH 43302
Scope: Statewide
Contact(s):
President: LUTHER T. MILLER; Phone: 740-265-6907
President-Elect: EDWARD LEE SMITH, OSU Ext. E. District Office, 16714 SR 215, Caldwell, OH 43724; Phone: 740-732-2381
Secretary: KENDRA S. WECKER, 107 Glenmont Ave., Columbus, OH 43214; Phone: 614-265-7043
Treasurer: TIM PLAGEMAN, 95-A Lima Ave., Findlay, OH 45840; Phone: 419-424-5000

WILDLIFE SOCIETY, OKLAHOMA CHAPTER
Attn: President, Dept. of Zoology, OK State University, Stillwater, OK 74078
Scope: Statewide
Contact(s):
President: JAMES H. SHAW; Phone: 405-744-5555
President-Elect: MICHAEL D. PORTER, The Noble Foundation, P.O. Box 2180, Ardmore, OK 74078; Phone: 405-223-5810
Secretary: JULIANNE HOAGLAND, 1801 N. Lincoln Blvd., Oklahoma City, OK 73105; Phone: 405-521-4616
Treasurer: JERRY BRABANDER, 10960 S. 241 W. Ave., Sapulpa, OK 74066; Phone: 918-581-7458, ext. 224

WILDLIFE SOCIETY, OREGON CHAPTER
Attn: President, USFWS, 2600 SE 98th, #100, Portland, OR 97266
Scope: Statewide
Contact(s):
President: LAURA TODD; Phone: 503-231-6179
Vice President: DAVID K. KENNEDY, David Evans & Associates, 2828 SW Corbett Ave., Portland, OR 97201; Phone: 503-499-0547
President-Elect: JIM A. THRAILKILL, OR Coop. Wildlife Res. Unit, H.J. Andrews Exper. Forest, P.O. Box 300, Blue River, OR 97413; Phone: 541-822-3359
Vice-President-Elect: DAWN R. KEEGAN, River Source, 212 W. Seventh St., Prineville, OR 97201; Phone: 541-447-8156
Secretary: KATHERINE F. BEAL, U.S. Army Corps of Engineers, P.O. Box 429, Lowell, OR 97452; Phone: 541-937-2131
Treasurer: ED ARNETT, Weyerhauser Company, P.O. Box 275, Springfield, OR 97477; Phone: 541-741-5536
Publication(s): *On Target*

WILDLIFE SOCIETY, PENNSYLVANIA CHAPTER
Attn: President, 415 E. McCormick Ave., State College, PA 16801
Scope: Statewide
Contact(s):
President: SHAYNE HOACHLANDER; Phone: 814-654-8867
President-Elect: MICHELLE SHERBURNE COHEN, 3490 N. Third St., Harrisburg, PA 17110; Phone: 717-232-0593
Secretary: J. MERLIN BENNER, Rural Delivery 1, Box 87, Liverpool, PA 17045; Phone: 717-787-3706
Treasurer: TOM HARDISKY, Rural Route 1, Box 84-D, Loganton, PA 17747-9708; Phone: 717-725-2287

WILDLIFE SOCIETY, SACRAMENTO-SHASTA CHAPTER
Attn: President, W.M. Beaty & Associates, P.O. Box 990898, Redding, CA 96099-0898
Scope: Statewide
Contact(s):
President: ROBERT L. CAREY; Phone: 530-243-2783
Vice-President: CHARLENE A. HALL, 7826 Hamel Ln., Davis, CA 95616

Secretary and Treasurer: LINNEA HALL, Dept. of Biological Sciences, California State University, Sacramento, 6000 J St., Sacramento, CA 95819-6077; Phone: 916-278-6573

WILDLIFE SOCIETY, SAN FRANCISCO BAY AREA CHAPTER
Attn: President, c/o East Bay Regional Park District, 2960 Peralta Oaks Ct., P.O. Box 5318, Oakland, CA 94605-0381
Scope: Statewide
Contact(s):
President: STEVEN BOBZIEN; Phone: 510-635-0138, ext. 2347
President-Elect: JOHN M. BAAS, 210 Maclavey Drive, Martinez, CA 94553; Phone: 510-335-9778
Secretary and Treasurer: TRISH TATARIAN, 1010 Lakeview St., Suite 3A, Petaluma, CA 94952; Phone: 415-896-5900

WILDLIFE SOCIETY, SAN JOAQUIN VALLEY CHAPTER
Attn: President, P.O. Box 9622, Bakersfield, CA 93389
Scope: Statewide
Contact(s):
President: BRIAN CYPHER; Phone: 661-282-3011
President-Elect: SCOTT E. FRAZER, USFWS, P.O. Box 2176, Los Banos, CA 93636-2176; Phone: 209-826-3508
Secretary: GERRIT BUMA, 58371 Ute Tr. Cir., Yucca Valley, CA 92284
Treasurer: CHRISTINE VAN HORN JOB, 3517 Sedona Way, Bakersfield, CA 93309; Phone: 661-834-6781

WILDLIFE SOCIETY, SOUTH CAROLINA CHAPTER
Attn: President-Elect, P.O. Box 167, Columbia, SC 29202
Scope: Statewide
Contact(s):
President: BEN MILLER, 1904 N. Mulberry Drive, Moncks Corner, SC 29461; Phone: 803-899-5780
President-Elect: JUDY BARNES; Phone: 803-734-3609
Secretary and Treasurer: PAUL JOHNS, 2441 Williston Road, Aiken, SC 29802; Phone: 803-725-5337

WILDLIFE SOCIETY, SOUTH DAKOTA CHAPTER
Attn: President, SD Game, Fish, and Parks, 4500 S. Oxbow Ave., Sioux Falls, SD 57106-4114
Scope: Statewide
Contact(s):
President: RON SCHAUER; Phone: 605-362-2700
President-Elect: CARL R. MADSEN, P.O. Box 247, Brookins, SD 57006; Phone: 605-697-2500
Secretary and Treasurer: PAUL F. COUGHLIN, SD Game, Fish & Parks, Box 218, DeSmet, SD 57231; Phone: 605-854-9105

WILDLIFE SOCIETY, SOUTHERN CALIFORNIA CHAPTER
Attn: President, 12551 Hinton Way, Santa Ana, CA 92705
Scope: Statewide
Contact(s):
President: ANNA M. SCHROEDER; Phone: 949-261-5414
Vice-President: BRAD R. BLOOD, 12702 Cowley Ave., Downey, CA 90242; Phone: 626-683-3547
Secretary: KATHLEEN M. KEANE, 5546 E. Parkcrest St., Long Beach, CA 90808; Phone: 310-425-6842
Treasurer: JOHN R. STEPHENSON, 199 Via Del Cerrito, Encinitas, CA 92024; Phone: 619-436-8340

WILDLIFE SOCIETY, TENNESSEE CHAPTER
Attn: President-elect, Dept. of Forestry, Wildlife & Fish, University of Tennessee, P.O. Box 1071, Knoxville, TN 37901
Scope: Statewide
Contact(s):
President: ROBERT WYATT, 1219 Sweet Williams Lane, New Market, TN 37820; Phone: 423-471-0146
President-Elect: DAVID BUEHLER; Phone: 615-781-6610
Secretary and Treasurer: DAVID WHITEHEAD, 172 Steele Road, Vonore, TN 37885; Phone: 423-884-6767

WILDLIFE SOCIETY, TEXAS CHAPTER
Attn: President, 5601 Taylor Ranch Rd., N.W. #422, Albuquerque, NM 87120
Scope: Statewide
Contact(s):
President: PENNY L. BARTNICKI; Phone: 505-248-7465
President-Elect: CLARK ADAMS, College of Agriculture, Wildlife & Fisheries Science, Texas A&M University, College Station, TX 78743-2258; Phone: 409-845-8824
Vice-President: SCOTT E. HENKE, Campus Box 156, Texas A&M University-Kingsville, Kingsville, TX 78363-8202; Phone: 361-593-3689
Secretary: LEE ANN JOHNSON LINAM, 200 Hoots Holler, Wimberly, TX 78676; Phone: 512-847-9480
Treasurer: DON DAVIS, Texas A&M University, College Station, TX 77843-4467; Phone: 409-845-5174

WILDLIFE SOCIETY, UTAH CHAPTER
Attn: President, Bureau of Land Management, 318 N. 100 E., Kanab, UT 84741
Scope: Statewide
Contact(s):
President: HARRY A. BARBER; Phone: 435-644-2672
President-Elect: KATHLEEN M. PAULIN, 1912 E. 1500 North, Vernal, UT 84741
Secretary: LESLIE ROCK, UT Div. Wildlife Resources, 515 E. 5330 Street, Ogden, UT 84405; Phone: 801-476-2740
Treasurer: RANDALL K. THACKER, P.O. Box 337, Altamont, UT 84001; Phone: 435-454-3081

WILDLIFE SOCIETY, VIRGINIA CHAPTER
Attn: President, USDA Forest Service, 110 Southpark Dr., Blacksburg, VA 24060
Scope: Statewide
Contact(s):
President: JESSE L. OVERCASH, USDA Forest Service, 110 Southpark Dr., Blacksburg, VA 24060; Phone: 540-522-4641
Vice-President: JEFFERSON L. WALDON, VPI & SU, Fish & Wildlife Info Exchange, 203 W. Roanoke St., Blacksburg, VA 24061; Phone: 540-231-7348
President-Elect: BRUCE A. LEMMERT, 21 S. Church St., Lovettsville, VA 22080; Phone: 540-822-4219
Secretary: LISA P. SAUSVILLE, VBDGIF, 1320 Belman Rd., Fredricksburg, VA 22401; Phone: 540-899-4169
Treasurer: RALPH M. KEEL, 1232 Geranium Crescent, Virginia Beach, VA 23456; Phone: 757-986-3706

WILDLIFE SOCIETY, WASHINGTON CHAPTER
Attn: President, DNR Forest Stewardship, 1111 Washington St., SE, P.O. Box43155, Olympia, WA 98504-3155
Founded: 1966; Membership: 200
Scope: Statewide
Contact(s):
President: JIM BOTTORFF; Phone: 360-902-2599
Secretary: ANN SPRAGUE, Methow Valley Ranger District, P.O. Box 188, Twisp, WA 98856; Phone: 509-997-2131
Treasurer: CATHERINE RALEY, Forest Sciences Lab, 3625 93rd Ave., S.W., Olympia, WA 98512; Phone: 360-753-7686

WILDLIFE SOCIETY, WEST VIRGINIA CHAPTER
Attn: President, WV DNR-Wildlife, 2006 Robert C. Byrd Dr., Beckley, WV 25801
Scope: Statewide
Contact(s):
President: ROBERT SILVESTER; Phone: 304-256-6947
Vice-President: JIM FREGONARA, WV DNR-Wildlife, P.O. Box 67, Elkins, WV 26241; Phone: 304-637-0245
Secretary-Treasurer: JO WARGO, USFS, P.O. Box 220, Richmond, WV 26261; Phone: 304-846-2695

WILDLIFE SOCIETY, WISCONSIN CHAPTER
Attn: President-Elect, Wisconsin DNR, 3911 Fish Hatchery Rd., Fitchburh, WI 53711
Scope: Statewide

NON-GOVERNMENTAL ORGANIZATIONS - W

Contact(s):
President: MARK S. BOYCE, College of Natural Resources, University of Wisconsin, Stevens Point, WI 54481-3897; Phone: 715-346-3873
President-Elect: MIKE FOY; Phone: 608-273-6275
Secretary and Treasurer: JAMES R. KEIR, DNR Ranger Station, Friendship, WI 53934; Phone: 608-339-4819
Publication(s): *Wisconsin Association for Environmental Education Bulletin;*

WILDLIFE SOCIETY, WYOMING CHAPTER
Attn: President, 260 Buena Vista, Lander, WY 82520
Scope: Statewide
Contact(s):
President: ANDREA CERVOSKI; Phone: 307-332-7723, ext. 232
President-Elect: TOM THORNE, WY Game & Fish Dept., 5400 Bishop Blvd., Cheyenne, WY 82006; Phone: 307-777-4585
Secretary: BRAD PHILLIPS, USFS, 1225 Washington Blvd., Newcastle, WY 82701; Phone: 307-746-2782
Treasurer: TIMOTHY P. THOMAS, WY Game & Fish Dept., P.O. Box 6249, Sheridan, WY 82801; Phone: 307-672-7418

WILDLIFE WAYSTATION
14831 Little Tujunga Canyon Rd., Angeles National Forest, CA 91342-5999
Phone: 818-899-5201
Founded: 1969; Membership: 21,000
Scope: National
Description: A southern California nonprofit refuge providing medical care, refuge, rehabilitation, and placement services for over 4,000 wild and exotic animals annually. Public tours and educational programs available.
Contact(s):
Founder and President: MARTINE COLETTE
Publication(s): *Wildlife Waystation (newsletter); Wild Proofing the Human Habitat (brochure)*
Keyword(s): Endangered and Threatened Species, Environmental and Conservation Education, Mammals, Raptors, Wildlife Rehabilitation

WILSON ORNITHOLOGICAL SOCIETY
Attn: President, Dept. Of Biology, Wheaton College, Norton, MA 02766
Founded: 1888; Membership: 3,170
Scope: National
Description: To advance the science of ornithology and to secure cooperation in measures tending to this end.
Contact(s):
President: JOHN C. KRICHER, Dept. of Biology, Wheaton College, Norton, MA 02766; Phone: 508-285-8200; E-mail: jkricher@wheatonma.edu
First Vice President: WILLIAM E. DAVIS, College of General Studies, 871 Commonwealth Avenue, Boston University, Boston, MA 02215; Phone: 617-353-2886; Fax: 617-353-5868; E-mail: wedavis@bu.edu
Second Vice Presidents: CHARLES R. BLEM, Dept. of Biology, 816 Park Ave./P.O. Box 842012; Virginia Commonwealth University, Richmond, VA 23284-2012; Phone: 804-828-1562; Fax: 804-828-0503; E-mail: cblem@cabell.vcu.edu
Secretary: JOHN A. SMALLWOOD, Dept. of Biology, Montclair State University, Upper Montclair, NJ 07043; Phone: 973-655-5345; Fax: 973-655-7047; E-mail: SMALLWOOD@SATURN.MONTCLAIR.EDU
Treasurer: DORIS J. WATT, Dept. of Biology, Saint Mary's College, Notre Dame, IN 46556-5001; Phone: 219-284-4668; Fax: 219-284-4716; E-mail: DWATT@JADE.SAINTMARYS.EDU
Editor: ROBERT C. BEASON, Dept. of Biology, State University of New York, 1 College Circle, Geneseo, NY 14454; Phone: 716-245-5310; Fax: 716-245-5007; E-mail: wilsonbull@uno.cc.geneseo.edu
Publication(s): *Wilson Bulletin, The*

Keyword(s): Biodiversity, Biology, Birds, Ecology, Environment, Grants, International Conservation, Natural History, Research, Wildlife and Wildlife Habitat, Zoology

WINCHESTER NILO FARMS
Olin Corporation, E. Alton, IL 62024
Phone: 618-258-3133
Scope: National
Contact(s):
Manager: ROGER JONES; Phone: 618-466-0613

WINDSTAR FOUNDATION, THE
2317 Snowmass Creek Rd., Snowmass, CO 81654
Fax: 970-963-1463; E-mail: windstar@rof.net
Founded: 1976
Scope: National
Description: A nonprofit organization co-founded by John Denver and Tom Crum. Windstar works to inspire individuals to make responsible choices and take direct action to achieve a peaceful and environmentally sustainable future.
Contact(s):
Chairman of Board of Trustees: DR. CHERYL CHARLES
Liaison: JEANIE TOMLINSON; Phone: 970-963-5534
Secretary and Treasurer: BETH MILLER
Keyword(s): Environmental and Conservation Education, Sustainability

WISCONSIN ASSOCIATION FOR ENVIRONMENTAL EDUCATION, INC.
Nelson Hall, UWSP, Steven's Point, WI 54481
Phone: 715-346-2796
Founded: 1974; Membership: 450
Scope: Statewide
Description: Promotes environmental education in schools and other institutions and organizations in Wisconsin.
Contact(s):
Chairperson: NANCY PIRAINO
Vice Chairperson: CINDY HALTER
Administrative Assistant: CATHY MCKAY
Publication(s): *WAEE Bulletin; EE News*
Keyword(s): Environmental and Conservation Education, Environmental Law, Lakes, Water Pollution Management, Water Resources, Education

WISCONSIN ASSOCIATION OF LAKES (WAL)
P.O. Box 126, Stevens Point, WI 54481-0126
Phone: 715-346-3424; Fax: 715-346-3436; E-mail: wal@coredcs.com
Founded: 1980; Membership: 287
Scope: Statewide
Description: WAL is a coalition of 287 lake management organizations, as well as hundreds of individual members. The organization is dedicated to the protection of lake ecosystems in Wisconsin. WAL works closely with the Wisconsin Department of Natural Resources and University Extension in the Wisconsin Lakes Partnership.
Contact(s):
President: JIM BURGESS; Phone: 608-257-4443; E-mail: jeburg@aol.com
Secretary: JUDY JOOSS; Phone: 414-877-9301; E-mail: jjooss@techheadnet.com
Treasurer: JOHN SEIBEL; Phone: 715-479-4714; E-mail: jpsmis@nnex.net
Publication(s): *Lake Connection, The*
Keyword(s): Aquatic Habitats, Environmental Preservation, Environmental Protection, Lakes, Land Use Planning, Pollution Prevention, Sustainable Ecosystems, Watersheds, Wetlands

WISCONSIN B.A.S.S. CHAPTER FEDERATION
Attn: President, 6503 Lani Ln., McFarland, WI 53558
Scope: Statewide
Description: An organization of Bassmaster chapters, affiliated with the Bass Anglers Sportsman Society, organized to fight pollution, assist state and national conservation agencies in their efforts, and

teach young people good conservation practices. Dedicated to the realistic conservation of our water resources.
Contact(s):
President: CHUCK ROLFSMEYER; Phone: 608-838-3040
Conservation Director: DON HILDEBRANDT, 2310 N. 6th St., Wausau, WI 54403; Phone: 715-842-3397
Publication(s): *Wisconsin Bass News*

WISCONSIN LAND AND WATER CONSERVATION ASSOCIATION
Attn: President, N2538 Cty Rd., J, Kaukauha, WI 54130
Phone: 608-833-1833; Fax: 608-833-7179; E-mail: wlwca@execpc.com; Web Site: www.execpc.com/~wlwca
Scope: Statewide
Description: Wisconsin Land and Water Conservation Association is a 501(c) (3) non-profit organization representing Wisconsin's 72 county land conservation committees and departments, assisting them with the protection, enhancement and sustainable use of Wisconsin's natural resources, and representing them through education and government interaction.
Contact(s):
President: MARVIN FOX, N2538 Cty Road, J, Kaukauna, WI 54130; Phone: 414-766-3242
Vice President: JOSEPH WISNIEWSKI, 4080 Deerskin Rd., Phelps, WI 54554; Phone: 715-545-2787
Executive Director: BRETT LARSON, One Point Place, Ste 101, Madison, WI 53719-2809; Phone: 608-833-1833; Fax: 608-833-7179
Board Member: ROGER HAHN, 705 Pease St., Augusta, WI 54722; Phone: 715-286-5343
Publication(s): *Thursday Note; Conservation Catalyst*
Keyword(s): Acid Rain, Air Quality, Biodiversity, Biotechnology, Birds, Chemical Pollution Control, Coasts, Communications, Conservation of Protected Areas, Conservation Tillage, EcoAction, Ecology, Endangered and Threatened Species, Energy, Public Lands

WISCONSIN PARK AND RECREATION ASSOCIATION
7000 Greenway, Suite 201, Greendale, WI 53129
Phone: 414-423-1210; Fax: 414-423-1296; E-mail: wpra@execpc.com
Membership: 1,200
Scope: Statewide
Description: A nonprofit organization, affiliated with the National Recreation and Park Association, working with other groups and organizations to achieve the best in park services and recreational opportunities.
Contact(s):
President: PAUL LEUTHOLD, 3805 S. Casper Dr., New Berlin, WI 53151; Phone: 414-797-2443
Editor: STEVE THOMPSON, 7000 Greenway, Suite 201, Greendale, WI 53129; Phone: 414-423-1210
Publication(s): *Badger Birder; Passenger Pigeon*
Keyword(s): Birds, Environment, Environmental and Conservation Education, Environmental Preservation, Environmental Protection

WISCONSIN SOCIETY FOR ORNITHOLOGY, INC., THE
5188 Bittersweet Ln., Oshkosh, WI 54901
Phone: 920-233-1973
Founded: 1939; Membership: 1,200
Scope: Statewide
Description: To stimulate interest in and promote the study of birds in Wisconsin for a better understanding of their biology and basis for their preservation.
Contact(s):
President: SUMNER MATTESON, WDNR, Bureau of Endangered Resources, Box 7921, Madison, WI 53707; Phone: 608-266-1571
Vice President: WILLIAM S. BROOKS, P.O. Box 248, Ripen, WI 54971-0248; Phone: 608-296-2197
Secretary: JANE DENNIS, 138 S. Franklin Ave., Madison, WI 53705-5248; Phone: 608-231-1741
Treasurer: ALEX F. KAILING, W330 N8275 W. Shore Dr., Hartland, WI 53029; Phone: 414-966-1072
Editor: R. TOD HIGHSMITH, 702 Schiller Ct., Madison, WI 53704; Phone: 608-242-1168
Editor: JENNIFER NIELAND, 1066 Harwood Ave., #2, Green Bay, WI 54313; Phone: 414-434-1229
Publicity Chair: BETTIE R. HARRIMAN, 5188 Bittersweet Ln., Oshkosh, WI 54901; Phone: 920-233-1973
Publication(s): *Badger Birder; Passenger Pigeon*
Keyword(s): Birds, Environmental and Conservation Education, Environmental Law, Waterfowl, Wetlands, Wildlife and Wildlife Habitat

WISCONSIN WATERFOWL ASSOCIATION, INC.
P.O. Box 180496, Delafield, WI 53018-0496
Phone: 414-646-5926 or 800-524-8460 (toll free); Fax: 414-646-5949
Founded: 1983; Membership: 7,800
Scope: Statewide
Description: A statewide nonprofit environmental/educational organization that establishes, promotes, assists, and contributes to conservation, restoration, and management of Wisconsin wetlands to perpetuate waterfowl and wildlife. Represents waterfowl enthusiasts via a unified statewide voice on Wisconsin migratory bird hunting regulations and conservation legislation benefiting the protection of wetlands. Educational programs and waterfowl hunting seminars.
Contact(s):
President: JOEL WATSON, W359 N7660 Brown St., Oconomowoc, WI 53066; Phone: 920-474-7635
Vice President: ANNE COOK, 508 E. South St., Beaver Dam, WI 53916; Phone: 920-887-2686
Secretary: BRAD WAGNER, 6318 Walden Way, Madison, WI 53719; Phone: 608-271-4617
Treasurer: ROGER BORD, W2667 Kittie Ct., East Troy, WI 53120; Phone: 414-642-5955
Administrator: KELCY MCCARTHY
Publication(s): *Wisconsin Waterfowl*
Keyword(s): Conservation, Waterfowl, Wetlands

WISCONSIN WILDLIFE FEDERATION
242 Keoller Ave., Oshkosh, WI 54901
Phone: 414-235-9136; Fax: 414-235-6030; E-mail: wiwf@execpc.com;
Web Site: www.easy-axcess.com/wwf
Scope: Statewide
Description: A representative statewide organization, affiliated with the National Wildlife Federation, dedicated to the protection and enhancement of wildlife and its habitat through public education and government interaction.
Contact(s):
President and Alternate Representative: MARTHA KILLISHEK
Representative: RUSSELL HITZ
Editor: DANIEL GRIES
Publication(s): *Wisconservation*
Keyword(s): Aquatic Habitats, Fisheries, Renewable Resources, Water Pollution Management, Wetlands

WISCONSIN WOODLAND OWNERS ASSOCIATION
P.O. Box 285, Stevens Point, WI 54481-0285
Phone: 715-346-4798
Founded: 1979; Membership: 1,900
Scope: Statewide
Description: A statewide organization affiliated with the National Woodland Owners Association, established to advance the interests of woodland owners and the cause of forestry in Wisconsin.
Contact(s):
President: JACK D. EDSON; Phone: 715-878-4331
Vice President: JIM JOHNSON; Phone: 608-271-9718
Secretary: BEVERLY SCHENDEL; Phone: 612-881-7610
Treasurer: DALE LIGHTFUSS; Phone: 920-244-7668
Executive Director: NANCY C. BOZEK
Editor: TIMOTHY EISELE; Phone: 608-233-2904

Publication(s): *Woodland Management*
Keyword(s): Forests and Forestry

WOLF EDUCATION AND RESEARCH CENTER
P.O. Box 917, Boise, ID 83701
Phone: 208-343-2248; Fax: 208-343-1601; E-mail: wolfcenter@rmci.net; Web Site: www.wolfcenter.org
Founded: 1992; Membership: 14,000 plus 80,000 sponsors
Scope: National
Description: The Wolf Education and Research Center is dedicated to providing public information, education, and research concerning endangered species, with an emphasis on the gray wolf, its habitat and ecosystem in the Northern Rocky Mountain region. Our efforts seek to improve public awareness of endangered and threatened species in the area and to develop, in concert with regional cultures and residents, ways to coexist with these species.
Contact(s):
President: LOREN KRONEMAN; Phone: 208-743-1608; Fax: 208-843-7329
Vice President: CLAUDIA AULUM; Phone: 208-788-8557; Fax: 208-788-1171
Secretary: SALLY FARRAR; Phone: 208-336-6562; Fax: 208-384-0540
Executive Director: DAVID DEENEY; Phone: 208-924-6960; Fax: 208-924-6959
Publication(s): *Sawtooth Pack Sponsorship Newsletter; Wild Wolves Sponsorship Newsletter; Wolf Education and Research Center Membership Newsletter*
Keyword(s): Biodiversity, Cultural Preservation, Endangered and Threatened Species, Environmental and Conservation Education, Nature Preservation, Nongame Wildlife, Outdoor Recreation, Predators, Research, Training, Wolves

WOLF FUND, THE
P.O. Box 471, Moose, WY 83012
Phone: 307-733-0740; Fax: 307-733-0962
Founded: 1986
Scope: National
Description: A project of the Center for the Humanities and the Environment. The sole mission of The Wolf Fund is to facilitate the recovery of the gray wolf to Yellowstone National Park. The Wolf Fund maintains an active mailing list. Received 501 (c) (3 status in March of 1990.
Contact(s):
Executive Director: RENEE ASKINS
Publication(s): *Wolf Fund Newsletter, The; Wolf Fund Children's brochure: Wolves, People, and Yellowstone*
Keyword(s): Endangered and Threatened Species, Environmental and Conservation Education, Wildlife and Wildlife Habitat, Wildlife Management, Wildlife Rehabilitation

WOLF HAVEN INTERNATIONAL
3111 Offut Lake Rd., Tenino, WA 98589
Phone: 360-264-4695
Scope: National
Description: The organization's mission is "Working for Wolf Conservation". With the intent on making a difference, all of Wolf Haven's activities have been undergoing changes that seek to strengthen our involvement in research and education.
Contact(s):
President: RICK SCHAEFER
Vice President: ELLEN FORD
Secretary: NANCY JUDGE
Treasurer: GARY BANKERS, 7447 Boston Harbor Rd. NE, Olympia, WA 98506
Executive Director: MAUREEN L. GREELEY
Publication(s): *Wolf Tracks*
Keyword(s): Endangered and Threatened Species

WOMEN'S ENVIRONMENT AND DEVELOPMENT ORGANIZATION (WEDO)
355 Lexington Avenue, 3rd Floor, New York, NY 10017
Phone: 212-973-0325; Fax: 212-973-0335; E-mail: wedo@igc.apc.org; Web Site: http://www.wedo.org
Founded: 1990
Scope: National
Description: On January 27, 1995, Women USA Fund, Inc. changed its name to WEDO. The organization is an international advocacy network actively working to transform society to achieve social, political, economic, and environmental justice for all through the empowerment of women, in all their diversity, and through their equal participation with men in decision-making from grassroots to global arenas.
Contact(s):
President: BELLA ABZUG
Vice President: CHIEF BISI OGUNLEYE
Vice President: JOCELYN DOW
Vice President: THAIS CORRAL
Secretary: MIM KELBER
Treasurer: BROWNIE LEDBETTER
Publication(s): *News and Views* (contact WEDO for a comprehensive list)
Keyword(s): Biotechnology, Environmental and Conservation Education, International Conservation, Population Growth, Renewable Resources

WOMEN'S SHOOTING SPORTS FOUNDATION
4620 Edison Ave., Suite C, Colorado Springs, CO 80915
Phone: 1-800-820-9773
Founded: 1993; Membership: 3,500
Scope: National
Description: The Women's Shooting Sports Foundation is a national, nonprofit membership organization offering an ongoing series of programs to expand shooting opportunities for women.
Contact(s):
Executive Director: SHARI LeGATE
Publication(s): *Outdoors for Women; Women's Resource List, The*
Keyword(s): Hunting, Training, Waterfowl, Women in the Environment

WORLD ASSOCIATION OF GIRL GUIDES AND GIRL SCOUTS (WAGGGS)
World Bureau Olave Centre; 12c Lyndhurst Rd., Hampstead, London NW3-5PQ United Kingdom
Founded: 1928; Membership: 140
Scope: International
Description: WAGGGS is a voluntary worldwide movement open to all girls and young women. Based on spiritual values and dedicated to the education of girls and young women, WAGGGS provides them with opportunities of self-training in the development of character, responsible citizenship, and service in their own and world communities. WAGGGS works for peace by promoting increased understanding between individuals through community, environmental, and international projects.
Contact(s):
Treasurer: CAROL BROWN
Director: LESLEY BULMAN
World Board Chairman: GINNY RADFORD
World Board Vice Chairman: LARAE ORVILLIAN
Publication(s): *Peace Modules; World Issues Series Booklets-Food and Nutrition, AIDS, and Street Children; Our World News; fact sheets on health, environment, food and nutrition*
Keyword(s): Environmental and Conservation Education, Health and Nutrition, Sustainable Development, Training, Women in the Environment, Youth Organizations

WORLD BIRD SANCTUARY (formerly Raptor Rehabilitation and Propagation Project Inc. The)
Box 270270, St. Louis, MO 63127
Phone: 314-938-6193; Fax: 314-938-9464
Founded: 1977; Membership: 1,500
Scope: National
Description: The WBS was established by Walter C. Crawford, Jr. near St. Louis, Missouri. It is a nonprofit, tax-exempt organization whose mission is to preserve the earth's biological diversity and to secure the future of threatened bird species in their natural environments. We work to fulfill that mission through education,

propagation, and rehabilitation. We also have a hands-on internship program.
Contact(s):
President: DR. LEON P. ULLENSVANG
Vice President: SUSAN SEDGWICK-POLING
Secretary: ROBERT J. BRACE
Treasurer: DENNIS V. BREITE
Executive Director: WALTER C. CRAWFORD JR.; Phone: 314-938-6193
Editor: MARION V. ERNST
Publication(s): *Mews News; Methods of Feather Replacement in Birds of Prey; Techniques for Artificial Incubation and Hand-rearing of Raptors; Stress in Captive Birds of Prey*
Keyword(s): Biodiversity, Birds, Endangered and Threatened Species, Environment, Raptors, Wildlife Rehabilitation, Internships

WORLD CONSERVATION MONITORING CENTRE
219 Huntingdon Rd., Cambridge CB3 0DL United Kingdom
Phone: 0123277314; Fax: 1223277722; E-mail: info@wcmc.org.uk; Web Site: www.wcmc.org.uk
Scope: International
Description: The WCMC supports conservation and sustainable development through the provision of information services on issues relating to nature conservation, and through supporting others in the development of their own information management activities. WCMC works in a collaborative manner with a wide range of organizations including three of the foremost global agencies concerned with the environment and nature conservation, IUCN, WWF, and UNEP.
Contact(s):
Chief Executive: DR. MARK COLLINS
Publication(s): *Global Biodiversity: Status of the Earth's living resources; IUCN Red List of Threatened Animals (1996); IUCN Red List of Threatened Plants (1997); Conservation Atlas of Tropical Rainforests; and others*
Keyword(s): Aquatic Habitats, Biodiversity, Birds, Botanical Gardens, Coasts, Conservation of Protected Areas, Coral Reefs, Deserts, Developing Countries, Ecology, Endangered and Threatened Species, Environmental and Conservation Education, Forests and Forestry, International Conservation, Wildlife and Wildlife Habitat

WORLD FORESTRY CENTER
4033 SW Canyon Rd., Portland, OR 97221
Phone: 503-228-1367; Fax: 503-228-4608
Founded: 1966
Scope: National
Description: The World Forestry Center is a nonprofit organization promoting a greater appreciation and understanding of the world's forests and related natural resources. The Center operates a forestry museum adjacent to the Hoyt Arboretum, conference facilities, an international institute, and an 80-acre demonstration forest and outdoor education site. Public tours and classes, school programs, exhibits and special events, conferences, curriculum materials, and publications are available.
Contact(s):
President: DENNIS DYKSTRA
Education Director: RICK ZENN
Publication(s): *Forest Education Program Guide; Branching Out Newsletter*
Keyword(s): Environmental and Conservation Education, Forests and Forestry, International Conservation, Museum, Natural History, Renewable Resources

WORLD PAL (WORLD POPULATION ALLOCATION LIMITED INC.)
52 Stevens St., Suite 1100, White Plains, NY 10606
Phone: 914-684-6539; Fax: 914-684-9607; E-mail: anderson@worldpal.org; Web Site: www.worldpal.org
Scope: National
Description: World Pal is concerned with increasing the awareness that young people have for their environment. World Pal conducts educational awareness programs on the decks of a newly built, four-masted barquetine. The programs are offered in many ports throughout Latin America, from the Rio Grande to Patagonia. While on board, passengers are encouraged to participate in the educational program.
Contact(s):
Executive Director: CAPT. D. C. ANDERSON
Keyword(s): Ecosystems, Environment, Environmental Protection, Population Growth, Sustainable Development

WORLD PARKS ENDOWMENT INC.
1616 P St., NW, #200, Washington, DC 20036
Phone: 202-797-6540; E-mail: worldparks@juno.com; Web Site: www.worldparks.org
Founded: 1988
Scope: International
Description: World Parks Endowment, Inc. is a unique organization that acquires land in the rain forest and other critical sites for biological diversity. It provides funds for park management of tropical rain forests and other ecosystems of great conservation importance, and has developed projects in over 12 countries, including the Sierra de las Minas Biosphere Reserve in Guatemala and the Bilsa Reserve in Ecuador.
Contact(s):
Chairman and President: DANIEL KATZ
Secretary and Executive Director: BYRON SWIFT
Vice President and Treasurer: ROGER PASQUIER
Publication(s): *Annual Report*
Keyword(s): Biodiversity, Land Preservation, Land Purchase, Rainforests, Tropical Biodiversity and Conservation

WORLD PHEASANT ASSOCIATION
P.O. Box 5 Lower Basildon, Reading, Berks RG8 9PF United Kingdom
Phone: 01189-845140; Fax: 01189-843369; E-mail: wpa@gr.apc.org
Founded: 1975
Scope: National
Description: Aims are to develop, promote, and support conservation of all species of the order galliformes with initial emphasis on the family phasianidae.
Contact(s):
Chairman: RICHARD P. HOWARD
President: KEITH HOWMAN
Administrator: NICOLA CHALMERS-WATSON
Editor: DEREK BINGHAM, c/o World Pheasant Association, P.O. Box 5, Lower Basildon, Reading, Berks RG8 9PF United Kingdom
Publication(s): *Annual Review; Newsletters*

WORLD RESOURCES INSTITUTE
10 G St., NE, Washington, DC 20002
Phone: 202-729-7600; Fax: 202-729-7610; Web Site: www.wri.org
Founded: 1982
Scope: National
Description: A policy research center created with funding from the John D. and Catherine T. MacArthur Foundation and others, to help governments, international organizations, the private sector, and others address vital issues of environmental integrity, natural resource management, economic growth, and international security.
Contact(s):
President: JONATHAN LASH
Senior Vice-President/COO: MATTHEW ARNOLD
V.P. for Administration and CFO: MARJORIE BEANE
Publication(s): *Policy Studies Series; Research Report Series; World Resources Report*
Keyword(s): Air Quality and Pollution, Forests and Forestry, Greenhouse Effect/Global Warming, Renewable Resources, Sustainable Development

WORLD SOCIETY FOR THE PROTECTION OF ANIMALS (WSPA)
29 Perkins St. P. O. Box 190, Boston, MA 02130
Phone: 617-522-7000; Fax: 617-522-7077

Founded: 1981
Scope: National
Description: The World Society for the Protection of Animals (WSPA) aims to promote the protection of animals, to prevent cruelty to animals, and to relieve animal suffering in every part of the world. For decades, our tools have been hands-on fieldwork, along with humane education and legislative action as we strive for the humane treatment and safety of animals. WSPA has over 350 member societies in 75 nations that provide support for our many animal protection initiatives.
Contact(s):
President: PAUL G. IRWIN
Vice President: PETER DAVIES
Vice President: HANS PETER HAERING
Secretary: MURDAUGH MADDEN
Treasurer: ROBERT CUMMINGS
Chief Executive: ANDREW DICKSON
International Projects Director: JOHN WALSH
Publication(s): *Animals International; WSPA World; WSPA Campaign News; Annual Report, By-Laws, Policy Statement*
Keyword(s): Endangered and Threatened Species, Mammals, Marine Mammals, Nongame Wildlife, Wildlife Rehabilitation

WORLD WILDLIFE FUND
1250 24th St., NW, Washington, DC 20037
Phone: 202-293-4800; Fax: 202-293-9211
Founded: 1961; Membership: 1.2 million
Scope: International
Description: WWF is the largest private U.S. organization working worldwide to protect wildlife and wildlands--especially in the tropical forests of Latin America, Asia, and Africa. WWF has helped create and protect more than 450 national parks and nature reserves; supports scientific investigations; monitors international trade in wildlife; promotes ecologically- sound development; assists local groups to take the lead in needed conservation projects; and seeks to influence public opinion and the policies of governments and private institutions to promote conservation of the earth's living resources.
Contact(s):
President: KATHRYN S. FULLER
Secretary: ADRIENNE MARS
Treasurer: PAUL F. MILLER JR.
Africa and Madagascar Vice President: HENRI NSANJAMA
Asia, Conservation Finance and Species Conservation Vice President: BRUCE W. BUNTING
Chairman of Board: ROGER W. SANT
Chairman of Executive Committee: EDWARD P. BASS
General Counsel: PATRICIA EWING
Latin America and Caribbean Vice President: TWIG JOHNSON
Managing Vice President for Operations: DEBORAH S. HECHINGER
Marketing, Membership and Communications Vice President: DAVID EVANICH
Senior Vice President: JAMES P. LEAPE
U.S. Conservation and Global Threats Vice President: WILLIAM M. EICHBAUM
Vice President of Research and Development: DIANE W. WOOD
Publication(s): *FOCUS*
Keyword(s): Endangered and Threatened Species, International Conservation, Urban Environment, Wildlife and Wildlife Habitat

WORLD WOMEN IN THE DEFENSE OF THE ENVIRONMENT (WorldWIDE)
1200 18th St., NW, Suite 1100, Washington, DC 20036
Phone: 202- 721-1541; Fax: 202-296-9679; E-mail: ww_info@worldwidenet.org
Founded: 1981
Scope: International
Description: An international organization that seeks to create an environmentally sustainable world through the active participation of women and their communities in environmental protection and in shaping local, national and regional development priorities.
Contact(s):
Executive Director: ANNABELL HERTZ
Keyword(s): Environmental Protection, Sustainable Development, Women in the Environment

WORLDWATCH INSTITUTE
1776 Massachusetts Ave., NW, Washington, DC 20036-1904
Phone: 202-452-1999 Publications 800-555-2028; Fax: 202-296-7365; E-mail: worldwatch@worldwatch.org; Web Site: www.worldwatch.org
Founded: 1974
Scope: International
Description: A nonprofit research organization designed to inform policymakers and the public about emerging global problems and trends and the complex links between the world economy and its environmental support systems. Recent studies have covered issues such as global warming, world water shortages, soil erosion, and the decline in food production compared to population growth, renewable energy, deforestation, transportation, oceans, fisheries, carrying capacity and environmental refugees.
Contact(s):
President: LESTER R. BROWN
Senior Vice President for Research: CHRISTOPHER FLAVIN
Vice President for Research: HILARY FRENCH
Assistant to the President and VP for Special Activities: REAH JANISE KAUFFMAN
Librarian: LORI BROWN
Vice President of Communications: RICHARD C. BELL
Vice President of Operations: JAMES GILLEPSIE
WorldWatch Magazine Editor: ED AYRES
Publication(s): *Worldwatch papers; State of the World; World Watch Magazine; Vital Signs; Environmental Book series; Database Diskette*
Keyword(s): Agriculture, Energy, Population Growth, Renewable Resources, Sustainable Development, Water Resources

WWF JAPAN (WORLD WIDE FUND FOR NATURE JAPAN)
Nihonseimei Akabanebashi Bldg., 3-1-14 Shiba, Minato-Ku, Tokyo 1050-0014 Japan
Phone: 03-3769-1711; Fax: 03-3769-1717
Founded: 1971; Membership: 40,000
Scope: International
Description: WWF Japan is a national organization of WWF - World Wide Fund for Nature - which is one of the world's largest private international conservation organizations.
Contact(s):
Chairperson: HISAKO HATAKEYAMA
Chief Executive Director: MAKOTO HOSHINO
Honorary President: PRINCE AKISHINO
Vice Chairman: TOMIO YOSHIDA
Vice Chairman: MITSUGU KAWAMURA
Publication(s): *WWF News (Japanese); Panda News (Japanese); TRAFFIC Newsletter (Japanese); Environment Education Newsletter (Japanese)*

WYOMING ASSOCIATION OF CONSERVATION DISTRICTS
c/o President, HC 5, Box 106, McFadden, WY 82083
Scope: Statewide
Contact(s):
President: OLIN SIMS; Phone: 307-632-5716; Fax: 307-632-5716
Vice President: VERONICA CANFIELD, P.O. Box 952, Sundance, WY 82729; Phone: 307-283-2062; Fax: 307-283-2170
Board Member: TRACY RENNER, P.O. Box 271, Meeteetse, WY 82433; Phone: 307-868-2355; Fax: 307-868-2470
Executive Director: BOBBI FRANK, 2304 E. 13th St., Cheyenne, WY 82001; Phone: 307-632-5716; Fax: 307-638-4099; E-mail: wacod@trib.com
Keyword(s): Conservation Districts

WYOMING B.A.S.S. CHAPTER FEDERATION
Attn: President, 1008 Rosewood Dr., Rock Springs, WY 82901
Scope: Statewide
Description: An organization of Bassmaster chapters, affiliated with the Bass Anglers Sportsman Society, organized to fight pollution,

assist state and national conservation agencies in their efforts, and teach the young people of our country good conservation practices. Dedicated to the realistic conservation of our water resources.
Contact(s):
President: JOHN WEBER; Phone: 307-362-5863
Conservation Director: DAVID CHANNEL, 317 Winterhawk Dr., Rock Springs, WY 82901; Phone: 307-382-4742

WYOMING NATIVE PLANT SOCIETY
P.O. Box 3452, Laramie, WY 82071
Phone: 307-766-3020; E-mail: clyde@uwyo.edu
Founded: 1981; Membership: 200
Scope: Statewide
Description: The Wyoming Native Plant Society promotes the use and appreciation of the state's native flora through education and supporting research.
Contact(s):
President: JIM OZENBERGER
Vice President: AMY RODERICK
Editor: WALTER FERTIG; Phone: 307-745-3509
Secretary and Treasurer: LAURA WELP
Publication(s): *Castilleja; Landscaping with Wildflowers and Native Plants*
Keyword(s): Endangered and Threatened Species, Flowers, Plants, and Trees, Gardening and Horticulture, Natural Areas, Natural History, Wildlands, Native Plants

WYOMING OUTDOOR COUNCIL
262 Lincoln St., Lander, WY 82520
Phone: 307-332-7031; Fax: 307-332-6899; E-mail: woc@wocnet.org; Web Site: www.wocnet.org
Founded: 1967
Scope: Statewide
Description: A statewide membership organization dedicated to the conservation of Wyoming's natural resources. Promotes sound environmental policy and education of the public for wise decision making. Serves as an active citizen lobby for environmental policies, conducts research, and monitors state and federal agencies.
Contact(s):
President: CHIP RAWLINS, P.O. Box 3482, Larmie, WY 82071
Treasurer: MICHELE BARLOW, 718 S. 5th, Laramie, WY 82070
Executive Director: DAN HEILIG
President-elect: PHIL RIDDLE, 225 Valley View, Lander, WY 82520
Publication(s): *State Legislative Analysis; Frontline Report (newsletter); various reports and alerts*
Keyword(s): Environmental and Conservation Education, Public Lands, Solid Waste, Toxic Substances, Wildlife and Wildlife Habitat, Politics and Government

WYOMING WILDLIFE FEDERATION
P.O. Box 106, Cheyenne, WY 82003
Phone: 307-637-5433; Fax: 307-637-6629; E-mail: admin@wyomingwildlife.org; Web Site: www.wyomingwildlife.org
Scope: Statewide
Description: A representative statewide organization, affiliated with the National Wildlife Federation, dedicated to the protection and enhancement of wildlife and its habitat through public education and government interaction.
Contact(s):
President and Alternate Representative: JIM NARVA
Executive Director: KIM FLOYD
Representative: CRAIG THOMPSON
Editor: KRISTIN SPAN

X

XERCES SOCIETY, THE
4828 SE Hawthorne Blvd., Portland, OR 97215
Phone: 503-232-6639; Fax: 503-233-6794; E-mail: xerces@teleport.com
Founded: 1971; Membership: 7,700
Scope: National
Description: An international nonprofit organization dedicated to invertebrates and the preservation of critical biosystems worldwide. The Society is committed to protecting invertebrates as major components of biological diversity. Emphasis: aquatic invertebrate monitoring to assist in conservation of Pacific Northwest watersheds, butterfly farming in NE Costa Rica, enhancing wild pollinator populations in out-of-play areas of selected Columbia Plateau golf courses, and education through publications.
Contact(s):
President: THOMAS EISNER, Cornell University, Neurobiology and Behavior, W347 Mudd Hall, Ithaca, NY 14853-2702; Phone: 607-255-4464
Vice President: PAUL OPLER, Midcontinent Ecological Science Center, 4512 McMurry Avenue, Ft. Collins, CO 80525; Phone: 970-226-9409
Secretary: ED GROSSWILER, Robertson, Grosswiler, Crown Plaza, Suite 1005, 1500 SW 1st, Portland, OR 97201; Phone: 503-228-3282
Treasurer: KATHERINE JANEWAY, 1932 First Avenue, Suite 510, Seattle, WA 98101; Phone: 206-583-8304
Executive Director: MELODY ALLEN, 4828 SE Hawthorne Blvd., Portland, OR 97215; Phone: 503-232-6639
Editor: MARY TROYCHAK, 4828 SE Hawthorne Blvd., Portland, OR 97215
Publication(s): *Wings: Essays on Invertebrate Conservation (membership magazine); Butterfly Gardening: Creating Summer Magic in Your Garden; Common Names of North American Butterflies, The*
Keyword(s): Biodiversity, Endangered and Threatened Species, Insects and Butterflies

Y

YELLOWSTONE GRIZZLY FOUNDATION (YGF)
P.O. Box 12769, Jackson Hole, CO 83002
Phone: 303-939-8126
Founded: 1986; Membership: 500
Scope: National
Description: The YGF is a nonprofit organization dedicated to the conservation of the threatened grizzly bear and habitat preservation in the Greater Yellowstone Ecosystem. It conducts independent research and draws from that to produce educational materials and programs for both professional and general public audiences.
Contact(s):
President: MARILYN FRENCH, 6675 Upper Cascade Dr., Jackson, WY 83001; Phone: 307-733-8630
Vice President: KAREN SHIRLEY, P.O. Box 3468, Jackson, WY 83001; Phone: 307-733-5311
Secretary: DR. TIMOTHY FLOYD, P.O. Box 3229, Hailey, ID 83333; Phone: 208-726-3968
Treasurer: STEVEN P. FRENCH
Publication(s): *Yellowstone Grizzly Journal*
Keyword(s): Endangered and Threatened Species, Environmental and Conservation Education, Mammals, Wildlife and Wildlife Habitat, Wildlife Management

YMCA EARTH SERVICE CORPS
909 4th Ave., Seattle, WA 98104
Phone: 206-382-5013; E-mail: info@yesc.org; Web Site: www.yesc.org
Founded: 1989
Scope: National
Description: YMCA Earth Service Corps empowers young people to be effective, responsible global citizens by providing opportunities for environmental education and action, leadership development, and international and cross-cultural exchange. Students, working with teachers and the YMCA staff, initiate environmental community service projects, such as tree plantings, water quality monitoring, recycling, and working with younger students.

NON-GOVERNMENTAL ORGANIZATIONS - Z

Contact(s):
National Program Director: KRISTIN JOHNSTAD; Phone: 612-337-3207
Operations and Communications and Development Coordinator: DIANA SMITH; Phone: 206-382-5013 ext.5115
Publication(s): *Only Green World; YMCA Training Guides; Earth Arts for Reflection*
Keyword(s): Environmental and Conservation Education, Environmental Preservation, Urban Environment, Urban Forestry, Youth Organizations

YOSEMITE RESTORATION TRUST
1212 Broadway, Suite 810, Oakland, CA 94612
Phone: 510-763-1403; Fax: 510-208-4435
Founded: 1990
Scope: National
Description: To ensure protection of the natural, scenic, and historic resources of Yosemite National Park and its ecosystems, and to ensure that visitors have the highest quality experience of the park's natural environment.
Contact(s):
President: JANET S. COBB
Vice President: WALTER F. KIESER
Vice President: HAL C. BROWDER
Secretary: JULIE MCDONALD
Treasurer: THOMAS W. GWYN
Publication(s): *Yosemite Viewpoints (Newsletter); special reports on regional transportation, day-use reservations, and housing.*
Keyword(s): National Parks, Nature Preservation, Outdoor Recreation, Rural Development, Transportation, Wilderness

YOUNG ENTOMOLOGISTS' SOCIETY, INC.
6907 W. Grand River Ave., Lansing, MI 48906-9131
Phone: 517-886-0630; E-mail: YESbugs@aol.com; Web Site: members.aol.com/YESbugs/bugclub.html
Founded: 1965; Membership: 750
Scope: National
Description: An international nonprofit organization educates and serves youth and amateur entomologists via publications, programs and the mini-beast Zooseum and Education center; assists in information, talent, scientific literature, and insect specimen exchanges (informational networks); distributes and develops resource materials; and promotes awareness of arthropod importance and the contributions youth and amateur entomologists make to the science of entomology. Founded as Teen International Entomology Group.
Contact(s):
Executive Director: DIANNA K. DUNN; Phone: 517-887-0499
Director of Education: GARY A. DUNN
Publication(s): *Caring for Insect Livestock; Insect World; Flea Market; Insect Study Sourcebook, The; Project B.U.G.S.; Insect Identification Guide*
Keyword(s): Environmental and Conservation Education, Insects and Butterflies, Outdoor Recreation, Youth Organizations, Zoology

YUKON FISH AND GAME ASSOCIATION
P.O. Box 4434, Whitehorse, Yukon Territory Y1A 3T5 Canada
Phone: 403-667-2843
Scope: Statewide
Description: Affiliated with the Canadian Wildlife Federation.

Z

ZERO (REGIONAL ENVIRONMENTAL ORGANIZATION)
158 Fife Ave., Greenwood Park, P.O. Box 5338, Harare Zimbabwe
Phone: 263-4-791333; Fax: 263-4-732858; E-mail: zero@harare.iafrica.com
Founded: 1987
Scope: International
Description: ZERO, a regional environmental organization, is an independent professional, not-for-profit institution dedicated to the development of the rural peoples of southern Africa, especially through the promotion of sustainable management of land resources. ZERO pursues this goal through applied research, policy analysis and influencing national, regional, and international environmental policy making.
Contact(s):
Director: DR. JOSEPH Z. MATOWANYIKA
Chairperson to the Board: DR. YEMI KATERERE
Librarian and Information Officer: J. K. MUTSIGWA
Secretary to the Board: PROF. SAM MOYO
Publication(s): *Books, Working Paper Series, Special Paper Series, and Rural Industries Training Manuals.*
Keyword(s): Developing Countries, Land Management

ZERO POPULATION GROWTH, INC.
1400 16th St., NW, Suite 320, Washington, DC 20036
Phone: 202-332-2200; Fax: 202-332-2302; E-mail: info@zpg.org; Web Site: www.zpg.org
Founded: 1968; Membership: 62000
Scope: National
Description: ZPG is a national nonprofit membership organization that works to educate and motivate Americans to help meet the global population challenge. ZPG mobilizes grassroots support for the adoption of policies and programs necessary to stabilize global population growth.
Contact(s):
President: EDWIN F. LEACH II
Executive Director (Acting): JOHN SEAGER
Policy Counselor: PETER H. KOSTMAYER
Director of Communications: TIM CLINE
Director of Government Relations: BRIAN DIXON
Director of Membership and Development: SUE WOODWARD
Director of Population Education: PAMELA WASSERMAN
Field Director: JAY KELLER
Honorary President: DR. PAUL R. EHRLICH
Political Representative: BRIAN DIXON
Publication(s): *ZPG Reporter; Teachers' PET Term Paper; Action Alerts, Fact sheets, Backgrounders, Media Targets, reports, and promotional brochures*
Keyword(s): Environmental and Conservation Education, Population Growth, Public Health Protection, Renewable Resources, Sustainable Development

ZUNGAROCOCHA RESEARCH CENTER
Iquitos Peru
Web site: www.nvo.com/zungarococha
Founded: 1997
Scope: International
Description: Working to promote both human and wildlife interests in the Peruvian Amazon and provide information to help resolve their conflicts with special attention to acculturation. A permanent facility in collaboration with U.S. and Peruvian institutions for long-term research and training in pure and applied environmental sciences and conservation.
Contact(s):
President: DENISE BACCA, P.O. Box 696, Raton, NM 87740; Phone: 505-445-3603, 18; Fax: 505-445-4101; E-mail: tsi@raton.com
Manager: CARLOS ACOSTA JR., Prospero 652, Iquitos, Peru; Phone: 011-519-423-2648; Fax: 011-519-423-2131
Keyword(s): Biodiversity, Natural Resource Conservation, Rainforests, Research, Tropical Biodiversity and Conservation

EDUCATIONAL INSTITUTIONS

UNITED STATES

ALABAMA

AUBURN UNIVERSITY

Department of Fisheries and Allied Aquacultures
 Swingle Hall, Auburn University, AL 36849
 Phone: 334-844-4786; Fax: 334-844-9208; Web site: www.ag.auburn.edu/dept/faa/
Description: The department sponsors the Southeastern Cooperative Fish Disease Project , providing a fish-kill diagnostic service, training in fish diseases and research on fish diseases to the cooperating member states.
Degrees: B.S., M.S., M.Aq., Ph.D.
Contact(s):
Department Head: DR. JOHN W. JENSEN; E-mail: jjensen@acesag.auburn.edu
Director, International Center for Aquaculture and Aquatic Environments: B. L. DUNCAN Ph.D.; E-mail: bduncan@acesag.auburn.edu
Associate Project Director: DR. JOHN M. GRIZZLE

Department of Biological Sciences
 59 Duggar Dr., Extension Cottage, Auburn University, AL 36849
 Phone: 334-844-4269; Fax: 334-844-5748; Web site: www.auburn.edu/academic/science_math/cosam/docs/
Description: Newly formed from merger of Zoology and Botany departments.
Degrees: B.S., M.S., Ph.D.
Contact(s):
Department Co-Head: DR. MICHAEL C. WOOTEN, 331 Furnchess Hall, Auburn University, AL 36849; Phone: 334-844-4850

School of Forestry and Wildlife
 108 M. White Smith Hall, Auburn University, AL 36849-5418
 Phone: 334-844-1007; Fax: 334-844-1084; Web site: www.forestry.auburn.edu/
Degrees: B.S., M.F., M.S., Ph.D.
Contact(s):
Dean: DR. RICHARD W. BRINKER

ALASKA

UNIVERSITY OF ALASKA AT FAIRBANKS

Department of Biology and Wildlife
 Fairbanks, AK 99775
  Web site: mercury.bio.uaf.edu/
Degrees: B.A., B.S., Ph.D. in Biological Sciences; B.S., M.S., Ph.D. in Wildlife Biology; M.S., Ph.D. in Botany, M.S., Ph.D. in Zoology
Contact(s):
Department of Biology and Wildlife, Head: DR. JOAN BRADDOCK; Phone: 907-474-7671; E-mail: ffjfb@uaf.edu
Institute of Arctic Biology, Interim Director: DR. JAMES S. SEDINGER; Phone: 907-474-7640
Alaska Cooperative Fish and Wildlife Research Unit, Leader: DR. JAMES B. REYNOLDS, 209 Irving, UAF, Fairbanks, AK 99775-7020; Phone: 907-474-7661; Fax: 907-474-6716; E-mail: ffjbr@aurora.alaska.edu

School of Fisheries and Ocean Sciences
 200 O'Neill Building, P.O. Box 757220, Fairbanks, AK 99775-7220
 Phone: 907-474-7824; Fax: 907-474-7204; E-mail: FYSFOS@uaf.edu; Web site: www.sfos.alaska.edu:8000/
Contact(s):
Dean: DR. VERA ALEXANDER

ARIZONA

ARIZONA STATE UNIVERSITY

Center for Environmental Studies
 Box 873211, Arizona State University, Tempe, AZ 85287-1501
 Phone: 480-965-2975; Fax: 480-965-8087; Web site: www.asu.edu/ces or caplter.asu.edu
Description: The Center is involved in the Central Arizona-Phoenix Long Term Ecological Research (CAP LTER) project at Arizona State University, funded by the National Science Foundation and is one of the first urban sites in the LTER network. CAP LTER provides a unique addition to CAP TER research by focusing upon an arid-land ecosystem profoundly influenced, even defined by the presence and activities of humans. Investigations of land-use and ecological consequences in an urban environmental also involves community partners and K-12 schools. Our aim is to understand the changing urban fabric of our arid urban ecosystems and to offer applications to arid cities across the globe.
Contact(s):
Co-Project Director: CHARLES L. REDMAN
Co-Project Director: NANCY GRIMM

NORTHERN ARIZONA UNIVERSITY

College of Arts and Sciences
 NAU Box 5621, Flagstaff, AZ 86011-5621
 Phone: 520-523-2408; Fax: 520-523-0516; E-mail: artsandsciences@nau.edu; Web site: www.nau.edu/artsci/
Description: Department of Biology offers an emphasis in the areas of: Applied Plant Science, Aquatic Biology, Ecology, Cellular and Molecular Biology and Fish and Wildlife Management. Available emphasis areas for Environmental Science: Biology, Chemistry, Applied Geology, Applied Mathematics, Microbiology, Environmental Administration and Policy, Environmental Communications and Environmental Management.
Degrees: B.S. in Environmental Science, Biology, Botany, B.S. Ed. In Biology and Secondary Education
Contact(s):
Director, Center for Environmental Sciences and Education: SCOTT ANDERSON Ph.D., P.O. Box 5694, Flagstaff, AZ 86011-5694; Phone: 520-523-5821; Fax: 520-523-7423; E-mail: Scott.Anderson@nau.edu
Chair, Department of Biological Sciences: DR. LEE C. DRICKAMER; Phone: 520-523-7501; Fax: 520-523-7500; E-mail: Lee.Drickamer@nau.edu

Department of Geography and Public Planning
 Box 15016, Flagstaff, AZ 86011-5016
 Phone: 520-523-2650; Fax: 520-523-1080; Web site: www.geog.nau.edu/
Description: For Public Planning, choice of emphasis in Land Use Planning or Environmental Planning
Degrees: B.S. in Public Planning; M.A. in Rural Development
Contact(s):
Chair, Department of Geography and Public Planning: DR. ROBERT O. CLARK; E-mail: roc@alpine.for.nau.edu

School of Forestry
 Box 15018, Flagstaff, AZ 86011-5018
 Phone: 520-523-3031; Fax: 520-523-1080; Web site: www.for.nau.edu/
Description: Northern Arizona University is in an ideal location for the study of both forestry and recreation. The largest ponderosa pine forest in America, five life zones within fifty miles, recreation and aesthetic areas and extensive wildlife grazing and watershed areas are near Flagstaff.
Degrees: B.S., M.S., Ph.D. in Forestry; B.S. in Park and Recreation Management and Park Ranger Certificate

EDUCATIONAL INSTITUTIONS - ARKANSAS

Contact(s):
Interim Dean: DONALD G. ARGANBRIGHT; E-mail: Donald.G.Arganbright@nau.edu

PRESCOTT COLLEGE

Environmental Studies Program
220 Grove Ave., Prescott, AZ 86301
Phone: 520-778-2090; Fax: 520-776-5137; Web site: www.prescott.edu/rdp/rdp_es.html

Description: The Environmental Studies Program is one of four programs within Prescott College. The program emphasizes experiential and interdisciplinary learning, and focuses on the relationships between the human and non-human worlds and the reciprocal influences each has on the other.
Degrees: B.A.
Contact(s):
Program Coordinator: DR. TIM CREWS

UNIVERSITY OF ARIZONA

Department of Hydrology and Water Resources
122 Harshbarger Bldg. #11, Tucson, AZ Phone: 520-621-5082; Fax: 520-621-1422; E-mail: programs@hwr.arizona.edu; Web site: www.hwr.arizona.edu

Description: The mission of the department is to provide education, research, and service in the fields of hydrology and water resources and to engage in basic and applied research. The department offers comprehensive programs in all areas of surface and subsurface hydrology, water quality, and water resources systems (management, administration, engineering). The department is home to the NSF Science and Technology Center on the Sustainability of Water Resources in Arid Regions, the NASA Southwest Regional Earth Sciences Application Center and the Arizona Research Laboratory for Riparian Studies.
Degrees: B.S., M.S., and Ph.D.
Contact(s):
Academic Advising Coordinator: TERRIE H. THOMPSON; Phone: 520-621-3131
Dean of Libraries: CARLA J. STOFFLE; Phone: 520-621-2101
Department Head: VICTOR R. BAKER; Phone: 520-621-7120
Main Library: ; Phone: 520-621-6441; Fax: 520-621-9722
Undergraduate Coordinator: DONALD R. DAVIS; Phone: 520-621-3801

School of Renewable Natural Resources
325 Biological Sciences East, P.O. Box 210043, Tucson, AZ 85721-0043
Web site: www.srnr.arizona.edu/

Description: The School of Renewable Natural Resources provides instruction, research, and extension in a range of disciplines. The specific academic programs of landscape resources, rangeland and forest resources, watershed resources, and wildlife and fisheries resources provide undergraduate and graduate education. Physical and biological sciences are integrated with socioeconomic and political factors necessary for the conservation, protection, and management of renewable natural resources.
Contact(s):
Associate Director: DR. MALCOM J. ZWOLINSKI; Phone: 520-621-1432
Cooperative Fish and Wildlife Research Unit (U.S. Department of Interior), Leader: DR. O. EUGENE MAUGHAN; Phone: 520-621-1959
Cooperative National Park Resources Studies Unit (U.S. Department of Interior), Leader: DR. WILLIAM HALVORSON; Phone: 520-621-1174
Cooperative Social Sciences Institute (USDA Natural Resources Conservation Service), (M.L.A.), Contact: MICHAEL JOHNSON; Phone: 520-626-4685
Director: DR. C.P. PATRICK REID; Phone: 520-621-7257; Fax: 520-621-8801
Forest Service Cooperative Research Unit (USDA, Rocky Mountain Research Station), Leader: DR. CARL EDMINSTER; Phone: 520-621-2543/970-498-1264
Landscape Studies (B.S., M.S., Ph.D.): DR. D. PHILLIP GUERTIN; Phone: 520-621-1723
Rangeland and Forest Resources, (B.S., M.S., Ph.D.): DR. GEORGE RUYLE; Phone: 520-621-1384
Renewable Natural Resources Studies, (M.S., Ph.D.): DR. MITCHEL MCCLAREN; Phone: 520-621-1673
Watershed Resources Science and Management, (B.S., M.S., Ph.D.): DR. ED DE STEIGUER; Phone: 520-621-3241
Wildlife and Fisheries Resources, (B.S., M.S., Ph.D.): DR. WILLIAM W. SHAW; Phone: 520-621-7265

ARKANSAS

ARKANSAS STATE UNIVERSITY

Department of Biological Science
P. O. Box 1030, State University, AR 72467
Phone: 870-972-3082; Fax: 870-972-3638; Web site: www.csm.astate.edu/~biology/biology.html

Degrees: B.S. in Biology with an emphasis in Botany or Zoology; B.S. in Wildlife Ecology and Management; M.S. in Biology; Ph.D. in Environmental Sciences (multi-disciplinary program).
Contact(s):
Director of Environmental Sciences Program: DR. DAVID HARDING; Phone: 870-972-2007; Fax: 870-972-2638; E-mail: envirsci@navajo.astate.edu

ARKANSAS TECH UNIVERSITY
Russellville, AR 72801
Phone: 501-964-0852; Fax: 501-964-0837; Web site: www.atu.edu
Founded: 1909

Description: Recreation and Park Administration offers five areas of emphasis: Recreation Administration, Therapeutic Recreation, Park Administration, Turf Management and Interpretive Naturalist
Degrees: B.S.
Contact(s):
Head of Biological Sciences: DR. CHARLIE GAGEN; Phone: 501-964-0814; E-mail: charlie.gagen.mail.atu.edu
Fisheries and Wildlife Biology, Director: DR. JOSEPH STOECKEL; Phone: 501-964-0852; E-mail: joe.stoeckel.mail.atu.edu
Recreation and Park Administration, Director: DR. THERESA A. HERRICK, Williamson Hall, Room 100, Russellville, AR 72081; Phone: 501-968-0378; E-mail: rpth@atuvm.atu.edu

UNIVERSITY OF ARKANSAS AT LITTLE ROCK

Department of Biology
2801 S. University Ave., Little Rock, AR 72204
Phone: 501-561-3270; E-mail: biology@ualr.edu; Web site: www.ualr.edu/~biology/

Description: The Environmental Health Sciences Program (www.ualr.edu/~ehsp/) curriculum consists of a common core and a choice from four areas of concentrated study: Environmental quality management; occupational safety and health; environmental planning; and environmental/public health sciences. The Fish and Wildlife Management Program (www.ualr.edu/~biology/programs/wild/) prepares students for conservation biology research and management positions. Meets certification requirements of American Fisheries Society and the Wildlife Society. GIS Applications Laboratory available.
Degrees: B.S.
Contact(s):
Director, Environmental Health Sciences Program: CARL R. STAPLETON; Phone: 501-569-3501; E-mail: crstapleton@ualr.edu
Director, Fisheries & Wildlife Management Program: GARY A. HEIDT; Phone: 501-569-3511; E-mail: gaheidt@ualr.edu

UNIVERSITY OF ARKANSAS AT MONTICELLO

School of Forest Resources/Arkansas Forest Resources Center
Monticello, AR 71656
Phone: 870-460-1052; Fax: 870-460-1092; Web site: www.afrc.uamont.edu/SFR/
Degrees: B.S. in Forestry, B.S. in Wildlife Management, M.S. in Forest Resources
Contact(s):
Dean: DR. BOB BLACKMON

CALIFORNIA

CALIFORNIA POLYTECHNIC STATE UNIVERSITY

College of Architecture and Environmental Design
One Grand Ave., San Luis Obispo, CA 93407
Phone: 805-756-1321; Fax: 805-756-5986; E-mail: CAED@polymail.calpoly.edu; Web site: www.calpoly.edu/~caed/
Degrees: B.L.A., B.S. in City and Regional Planning, M.C.R.P.
Contact(s):
Department Head, Landscape Architecture: WALTER D. BREMER ASLA; E-mail: wbremer@calpoly.edu
Department Head, City and Regional Planning: DR. WILLIAM SIEMBIEDA; Phone: 805-756-1315; E-mail: wsiembie@calpoly.edu

CALIFORNIA STATE UNIVERSITY AT CHICO

Chico, CA 95929-0560
Phone: 530-898-6408; Fax: 530-898-6557; Web site: www.csuchico.edu/
Description: Areas of study include environmental education and interpretation, recreation and natural resource management, parks maintenance and operations, and planning and design.
Degrees: B.S., M.A.
Contact(s):
Chairman, Recreation and Parks Management: DR. DAVID E. SIMCOX; Phone: 530-898-4052; E-mail: dsimcox@oqvax.csuchica.edu
Coordinator, Parks and Natural Resources Management Option: DR. JON HOOPER; Phone: 530-898-5811

CALIFORNIA STATE UNIVERSITY AT FULLERTON

Environmental Studies Program
McCarthy Hall, Fullerton, CA 92834
Phone: 714-278-4872; E-mail: rcalderon@fullerton.edu; Web site: hss.fullerton.edu/envstud/
Founded: 1970
Description: Interdisciplinary graduate program leading to master's degree in environmental sciences, environmental policy and planning or environmental education and communication.
Degrees: M.S.
Contact(s):
Program Director: DR. DENNIS BERG; Phone: 714-278-7044; E-mail: dberg@fullerton.edu

CALIFORNIA STATE UNIVERSITY AT SACRAMENTO

6000 J St., Sacramento, CA 95819
Phone: 916-278-6011; E-mail: infodesk@csus.edu
Description: Biology department offers a concentration in Biological Conservation. Interdisciplinary Environmental Studies program offers a B.A. and the Recreation and Leisure Studies program offers a B.S. or B.A. in Park and Recreation Resource Management.
Contact(s):
Chair, Department of Biological Sciences: DR. LAUREL HEFFERNAN; Phone: 916-278-6535; Fax: 916-278-6993
Advisor, Conservation Biology: C. DAVID VANICEK; Phone: 916-278-6569
Environmental Studies: DR. ANGUS WRIGHT; Phone: 916-278-6620; Fax: 916-278-7582; E-mail: wrighta@csus.edu
Chair, Recreation and Leisure Studies: DR. STEVEN GRAY; E-mail: graysw@csus.edu
Graduate Coordinator, Recreation and Leisure Studies: DR. CARY GOULARD; E-mail: goulardc@hhsserver.hhs.csus.edu

HUMBOLDT STATE UNIVERSITY

College of Natural Resources and Sciences
1 Harpst St., Arcata, CA 95521-8299
Phone: 707-826-3256; Web site: www.humboldt.edu/~cnrs/
Degrees: B.S., M.S.
Contact(s):
Dean: STEVEN A. CARLSON
Chairman, Biological Sciences: DR. TIMOTHY LAWLOR; Phone: 707-826-3246
Chairman, Fisheries: DR. TIM MULLIGAN; Phone: 707-825-5645
Chairman, Forestry: DR. GERALD ALLEN; Phone: 707-826-4243
Chairman, Natural Resources Planning and Interpretation: DR. KEN FULGHAM; Phone: 707-826-4147
Chairman, Oceanography: DR. JEFFRY BORGELD; Phone: 707-826-4147
Chairman, Rangeland Resources and Wildland Soils: DR. KEN FULGHAM; Phone: 707-826-4147
Chairman, Watershed Management: DR. GERALD ALLEN; Phone: 707-826-4243
Chairman, Wildlife: DR. MARK COLWELL; Phone: 707-826-3723
Director, Indian Natural Resources, Sciences, and Engineering Program: RUSSEL BOHAM; Phone: 707-826-4994
Leader, Cooperative Fishery Research Unit: DR. WALTER DUFFY; Phone: 707-826-3268
Project Leader, Experiment Station, Pacific Southwest Forest and Range Station: DR. ROBERT R. ZIEMER; Phone: 707-825-2936

SAN FRANCISCO STATE UNIVERSITY

Wildlands Studies Program
3 Mosswood Cir., Cazadero, CA 95421
Phone: 707-632-5665; E-mail: wildlnds@sonic.net; Web site: wildlandsstudies.com/ws
Founded: 1979
Description: Wildlands Studies offers a year-round series of field study programs in North American and international wilderness locations. Participants join backcountry research teams in a search for answers to important environmental problems concerning wildlife populations and/or wildlands habitats. Participants can earn 3-14 units of university credit.
Contact(s):
Director: CRANDALL BAY; Phone: 707-632-5665

SAN JOSE STATE UNIVERSITY

Department of Environmental Studies
One Washington Sq., San Jose, CA 95192-0115
Phone: 408-924-5450; Fax: 408-924-5477; E-mail: envstdy@email.sjsu.edu; Web site: www.sjsu.edu/depts/EnvStudies/
Founded: 1970
Description: Special interests of the faculty include habitat restoration, environmental impact assessment, energy, water, and forest resource management, human ecology, international development, coastal resource management, solid waste management, and environmental education for teachers. Credit is given for beyond-the-classroom experiences for appropriate Peace Corps Service, Internships programs, Center for Development of Recycling (CDR) and Environmental Resource Center (ERC).
Degrees: B.S., B.A., M.S.
Contact(s):
Department Chairperson: DR. LESTER ROWNTREE

SONOMA STATE UNIVERSITY

Department of Environmental Studies and Planning
1801 E. Cotati Ave., Rohnert Park, CA 94928

EDUCATIONAL INSTITUTIONS - CALIFORNIA

Phone: 707-664-2306; Fax: 707-664-3920; E-mail: ENSP@sonoma.edu; Web site: www.sonoma.edu/ensp/
Description: Interdisciplinary academic program with B.S. and B.A. degrees. Study tracks in environmental education, energy management and design, city and regional planning, water quality, hazardous materials management, and environmental conservation and restoration
Degrees: B.S., B.A.
Contact(s):
Department Chair: JIM STEWART Ph.D.; Phone: 707-664-3144; E-mail: James.Stewart@sonoma.edu

Earth Lab
   1801 E. Cotati Ave., Rohnert Park, CA 94928
   Phone: 707-664-2577; Fax: 707-664-3920; E-mail: EarthLab@sonoma.edu; Web site: www.sonoma.edu/ensp/earthlab.html
Description: The Earthlab is an on-campus demonstration, education, and research center which serves the campus and surrounding communities through programs in environmental education, professional training, teacher workshops, demonstration projects, and scientific research.

STANFORD UNIVERSITY

Center for Conservation Biology
   Stanford, CA 94305-5020
   Phone: 650-723-5924; Web site: http://www.stanford.edu/dept/biology/
***Founded:** 1984*
Description: To develop the science of conservation biology, including its application to solutions for critical conservation problems. The Center conducts scientific and policy research that is building a sound basis for the conservation, management, and restoration of biotic diversity around the world. The overall goal is to develop ways and means for protecting Earth's life support systems and thus enhancing future human well-being.
Contact(s):
President: PROF. PAUL R. EHRLICH

Morrison Institute for Population and Resource Studies
   371 Serra Mall, MC 5020, Stanford, CA 94305-5020
   Phone: 415-723-7518; Fax: 415-725-8244; E-mail: morrison@forsythe.stanford.edu; Web site: www.stanford.edu/group/morrinst/
***Founded:** 1986*
Description: To support research and education in the interconnected global issues of population growth, its effects on the environment, the pressure on natural resources, and the capacity of many nations to achieve sustainable socioeconomic development. Issues are approached through interdisciplinary perspectives of population biology, economics, and social and medical sciences.
Contact(s):
Director: DR. MARCUS W. FELDMAN; Phone: 650-725-1867

UNIVERSITY OF CALIFORNIA AT DAVIS

College of Agriculture and Environmental Science
   One Shields Ave., Davis, CA 95616 - 8571
   Phone: 530-752-3557; Web site: www.aes.ucdavis.edu/
Description: Agricultural research programs and 21 departments.
Degrees: B.S., M.S., Ph.D.
Contact(s):
Chair, Agricultural and Resource Economics: COLIN A. CARTER; Phone: 530-752-1517; Fax: 530-752-5614; E-mail: cacarter@ucdavis.edu
Chair, Entomology: MICHAEL P. PARRELLA Ph.D.; Phone: 530-752-0492; E-mail: mpparrella@ucdavis.edu
Chair, Environmental Design: JO ANN STABB; Phone: 530-752-6809; E-mail: jcstabb@ucdavis.edu
Chair, Environmental Horticulture: D. W. BURGER; Phone: 530-752-0130; Fax: 530-752-1819; E-mail: dwburger@ucdavis.edu
Chair, Environmental Science and Policy: GARY POLIS; Phone: 530-754-8994; Fax: 530-752-3350; E-mail: gapolis@ucdavis.edu
Chair, Environmental Toxicology: MARION G. MILLER; Phone: 530-752-4526; E-mail: mgmiller@ucdavis.edu
Chair, Human and Community Development: LARRY HARPER; Phone: 530-752-3624; E-mail: lharper@ucdavis.edu
Chair, Land, Air and Water Resources: DENNIS E. ROLSTON; Phone: 530-752-2113; Fax: 530-752-1552; E-mail: derolston@ucdavis.edu
Chair, Landscape Architecture: DEAN MACCANNELL; Phone: 530-752-6437; E-mail: edmaccannell@ucdavis.edu
Chair, Nematology: HARRY KAYA; Phone: 530-752-1051; Fax: 530-752-5809; E-mail: hkkaya@ucdavis.edu
Chair, Plant Pathology: JIM MACDONALD; Phone: 530-752-6897; Fax: 530-752-5674; E-mail: jdmacdonald@ucdavis.edu
Chair, Vegetable Crops Program: ARNOLD J. BLOOM; Phone: 530-752-1743; Fax: 530-752-9659; E-mail: ajbloom@ucdavis.edu
Chair, Wildlife, Fish, & Conservation Biology: DEBORAH ELLIOTT-FISK Ph.D.; Phone: 530-752-6586; Fax: 530-752-4514; E-mail: dlelliottfisk@ucdavis.edu
Vice-Chair, Land, Air and Water Resources: ROGER H. SHAW; Phone: 530-752-1822; Fax: 530-752-1552; E-mail: rhshaw@ucdavis.edu
Director, National Institute For Global Environmental Change: RUTH A. RECK; Phone: 530-757-3401; Fax: 530-756-6499; E-mail: rareck@ucdavis.edu

Herbarium
   University of California at Davis, Davis, CA 95616
   Phone: 530-752-1091; Fax: 530-752-5410; E-mail: eadean@ucdavis.edu; Web site: www.aes.ucdavis.edu/search/default.htm
***Founded:** 1923*
Description: The UC Davis Herbarium is the center for research in plant systematics at the University of California, Davis. The Herbarium, of worldwide scope, includes 200,000 specimens. Holdings from California include documentation for many rare and endangered species.
Contact(s):
Director and Curator: ELLEN A. DEAN

UNIVERSITY OF CALIFORNIA AT LOS ANGELES

College of Arts and Letters
   Box 951361, Los Angeles, CA 90095
   Phone: 310-825-4321; Web site: www.college.ucla.edu/
Degrees: B.S., M.A, Ph.D.
Contact(s):
Chair, Department of Atmospheric Sciences: DR. ROGER M. WAKIMOTO; Phone: 310-825-1751
Organismic Biology, Ecology and Evolution: 621 Charles E. Young Dr. S., P.O. Box 951606, Los Angeles, CA 90095-1606; Phone: 310-825-3481; Fax: 310-206-3987; E-mail: nancyp@lifesci.ucla.edu (undergraduate program) or jocelyny@lifesci.ucla.edu (graduate program)

Civil and Environmental Engineering Department
   5731 Boelter Hall, P.O. Box 951593, Los Angeles, CA 90095-1593
   Phone: 310-825-1346; Fax: 310-206-2222; E-mail: deeona@ea.ucla.edu; Web site: www.cee.ucla.edu/
Degrees: B.S., M.S., Ph.D.
Contact(s):
Chair: MICHAEL K. STENSTROM; Phone: 310-825-1408; E-mail: stenstro@seas.ucla.edu

UNIVERSITY OF CALIFORNIA AT RIVERSIDE

Department of Environmental Science
   River, CA 92521
   Phone: 714-787-4551; Web site: envisci.ucr.edu/
***Founded:** 1971*

Description: The Environmental Sciences Program offers four curriculum tracks: Natural Science, Social Science, Environmental Toxicology and Soil Science. Opportunities are available for students to conduct research and to engage in environmental internships. Graduate Degrees available in Soil and Water Science.
Degrees: B.S., B.A., M.S., Ph.D.
Contact(s):
Chair: DR. MARYLYNN VILLINISKI YATES; Phone: 909-787-5488; E-mail: mvyates@mail.ucr.edu

Graduate School of Environmental Science and Engineering
2217 Geology, University of California, Riverside, CA 92521
E-mail: karenh@mail.ucr.edu; Web site: ese.ucr.edu/
Degrees: M.S., Ph.D.

UNIVERSITY OF CALIFORNIA AT SAN DIEGO

Scripps Institution of Oceanography
La Jolla, CA 92093-0208
Phone: 858-534-3206; Fax: 858-534-7889; E-mail: siodept@sio.ucsd.edu; Web site: www-sio.ucsd.edu/
Founded: 1903
Description: A part of the University of California, San Diego, the Scripps Institution of Oceanography is one of the oldest, largest, and most important centers for marine science research and graduate training in the world. The Birch Aquarium serves as the public education center for the institution.
Contact(s):
Director and Vice Chancellor for Marine Sciences: CHARLES F. KENNEL Ph.D.; E-mail: ckennel@ucsd.edu
Chair of the Graduate Department: W. KENDALL MELVILLE Ph.D.; E-mail: gradchr@sio.ucsd.edu

UNIVERSITY OF CALIFORNIA AT SANTA BARBARA

Environmental Studies
Santa Barbara, CA 93106-4170
Phone: 805-893-2968; E-mail: envst_info@envst.ucsb.edu; Web site: ucsbuxa.ucsb.edu/es
Description: The Environmental Studies Program at UCSB remains one of the strongest in terms of student demand and national reputation. The Environmental Studies curriculum is designed to provide students with the scholarly background and intellectual skills necessary to understand complex environmental problems and formulate decisions that are environmentally sound. While the E.S. Program offers both a B.S. and B.A. degree, both majors recognize and stress the importance of understanding the interrelationships between the humanities, social sciences and natural science disciplines within the environment.
Degrees: B.S., B.A.
Contact(s):
Program Chair: JO-ANN SHELTON
Academic Advisor: ERIC ZIMMERMAN

UNIVERSITY OF CALIFORNIA AT SANTA CRUZ

Environmental Studies
Santa Cruz, CA 95064
Phone: 831-459-2634; E-mail: studies@zzyx.ucsc.edu; Web site: zzyx.ucsc.edu/ES/es.html
Degrees: B.A., Ph.D.
Contact(s):
Chairperson: PROF. DAVID GOODMAN

UNIVERSITY OF CALIFORNIA, BERKELEY

Department of Environmental Science, Policy and Management
145 Mulford Hall, Berkeley, CA 94720-3114
Phone: 510-642-6730; Fax: 510-642-4034; E-mail: Undergraduate: espmug@nature.berkeley.edu; Graduate: espmgradproginfo@nature.berkeley.edu; Web site: www.CNR.berkeley.edu/departments/espm/majors/ or nature.berkeley.edu/departments/espm/grad/
Description: The Department has a strong undergraduate program awarding the B.S. degree in Forestry, Resource Management, Molecular Environmental Biology and Conservation and Resource Studies. The graduate degree program (M.S., Ph.D.) integrates the biological, social and physical sciences to provide advanced education in basic and applied environmental sciences, develops critical analytical abilities and fosters the capacity to conduct research on the structure and function of ecosystems through ecosystem levels and their interlocked human social systesms. A Master of Forestry (M.F.) and an M.S. in Range Management are also available.

UNIVERSITY OF SOUTHERN CALIFORNIA

Department of Civil and Environmental Engineering
Los Angeles, CA 90089-2531
Phone: 213-743-7517; E-mail: Emailcivileng@usc.edu; Web site: www.usc.edu
Degrees: B.S., M.S., Ph.D.
Contact(s):
Environmental Social Sciences Program, Dean of the Division: DR. DONALD LEWIS
Chair, Civil and Environmental Engineering Department: DR. L. CARTER WELLFORD

Environmental Studies Program
Science Bldg., Rm. 160, Los Angeles, CA 90089-0740
Phone: 213-740-7770; E-mail: environ@rcf.usc.edu; Web site: www.usc.edu/dept/LAS/enviro/
Description: B.A. combines basic science with the study of social aspects of environmental issues. B.S. combines a concentration in Geology, Biology or Chemistry with social science. The graduate program offers a choice of three concentrations: Global Environmental Issues and Development; Law, Policy and Management; and Environmental Planning and Analysis.
Degrees: B.A., B.S., M.A.
Contact(s):
Director: DR. SHELDON KAMIENIECKI
Advisor/Program Coordinator: JEFF FOSTER

COLORADO

COLORADO MOUNTAIN COLLEGE

Timberline Campus
901 South Hwy 24, Leadville, CO 80461
Phone: 719-486-2015; Fax: 719-486-3212; Web site: www.coloradomtn.edu
Description: Colorado Mountain College is a public two-year community college. The College is fully accredited by the North Central Accrediting Association.
Degrees: Associate Degrees in Wilderness Studies, Outdoor Recreation Leadership and Environmental Technology
Contact(s):
Contact: LINDA ADAMS
Professor of Outdoor Recreational Leadership: KENT CLEMENT
Professor of Biology: EVELYN BOGGS

COLORADO STATE UNIVERSITY

College of Natural Resources
Fort Collins, CO 80523
Phone: 970-491-6675; Fax: 970-491-0279; E-mail: info@cnr.colostate.edu; Web site: www.cnr.colostate.edu
Contact(s):
Dean: DR. A. ALLEN DYER; Phone: 970-491-4997
Assistant Dean: JOYCE BERRY; Phone: 970-491-5405
Cooperative Fish and Wildlife Research Unit, Leader: DR. DAVID ANDERSON; Phone: 970-491-1414
Earth Resources, (B.S., M.S., Ph.D.), Head: DR. JUDITH HANNAH; Phone: 970-491-5662
Fishery and Wildlife Biology, (B.S., M.S., Ph.D.), Head: DR. RANDALL ROBINETTE; Phone: 970-491-5020

EDUCATIONAL INSTITUTIONS - CONNECTICUT

Forest Sciences, (B.S., M.S., M.F., Ph.D.), Head: DR. SUSAN STAFFORD; Phone: 970-491-6911
Natural Resources Ecology Laboratory, Contact: DR. DIANA WALL; Phone: 970-491-1982
Natural Resources Recreation and Tourism, (B.S., M.S., Ph.D.), Head: DR. MICHAEL MANFREDO; Phone: 970-491-6521
Rangeland Ecosystem Science, (B.S., M.S., Ph.D.), Head: DR. DENNIS CHILD; Phone: 970-491-4994

Department of Political Science, Environmental Politics and Policy
Clark Building C-346, Fort Collins, CO 80523
Phone: 970-491-5156; Fax: 970-491-2490; Web site: www.colostate.edu/Depts/PoliSci/grad2.html
Founded: 1975
Description: All Ph.D. students in the program choose Environmental Politics and Policy as one of three sub-fields in political science offered in preparation for their degree. The program prepares doctoral students for university positions and a wide variety of private and public sector careers related to environmental politics and policy.
Degrees: M.A., Ph.D.
Contact(s):
Chair: DR. WAYNE PEAK; E-mail: ebell@vines.colostate.edu
Graduate Coordinator: DIMITRIS STEVIS; E-mail: sksmith@lamar.colostate.edu

UNIVERSITY OF COLORADO

Natural Resources Law Center
Campus Box 401, Boulder, CO 80309-0401
Phone: 303-492-1286; Fax: 303-492-1297; E-mail: nrlc@spot.colorado.edu; Web site: www.colorado.edu/law/NRLC
Description: Conducts research on environmental and natural resources law and policy, including water, public lands, minerals, Indian law, etc. Sponsors conferences and workshops and hosts visiting scholars. Publishes books, research papers, and Resource Law Notes newsletter.
Contact(s):
Director: GARY BRYNER

UNIVERSITY OF COLORADO AT BOULDER

Environmental Center
Campus Box 207, Boulder, CO 80309
Phone: 303-492-8308; Fax: 303-492-1897; E-mail: ecenter@stripe.colorado.edu; Web site: www.colorado.edu/cuenvironmentalcenter
Founded: 1970
Description: The CU Environmental Center is the nation's largest student-run environmental resource center. With over 40 student staff and interns, five permanent staff and 100 volunteers, it is the focal point for efforts to make the Boulder campus more environmentally responsible. Besides giving students applied experience in interdisciplinary environmental problem solving, the center provides direct services to the University community, including award-winning recycling and student bus pass programs and a comprehensive library of environmental books, periodicals and video tapes.
Contact(s):
Director: WILL TOOR

UNIVERSITY OF NORTHERN COLORADO

Department of Biological Sciences
501 20th St., Greeley, CO 80634
Phone: 970-351-2921; Fax: 970-351-2335
Description: The UNC Department of Biological Sciences offers undergraduate and masters degrees in Biology and a Ph.D. in Biology Education, which may emphasize environmental education research.
Contact(s):
Department Chair, Biological Sciences: CURT PETERSON; Phone: 970-351-2923; E-mail: cmpeter@bentley.unco.edu
Department Chair, Environmental Studies: CHARLES OLMSTEAD
Asst. Professor, Biological Sciences: CAROL FORTIN; Phone: 970-351-2510; E-mail: CAFORTI@BENTLEY.UNCO.EDU
Associate Professor, Biological Sciences: GERRY SAUNDRERS

CONNECTICUT

CONNECTICUT COLLEGE
270 Mohegan Ave., New London, CT 06320
Phone: 860-439-5021; Fax: 860-439-2519; Web site: www.conncoll.edu
Description: Environmental Studies has a long and successful history at Connecticut College beginning in 1931 with the establishment of the Connecticut College Arboretum. Since then, a common theme in the program has been to understand the structure and functioning of both natural and managed ecosystems.
Degrees: B.A., B.S., M.S.
Contact(s):
Director, Environmental Studies Program: DR. PETER A. SIVER; Phone: 860-439-2160; Fax: 860-439-2519; E-mail: pasiv@conncoll.edu
Botany Department, Chair: DR. T. PAGE OWEN; Phone: 860-439-2147; E-mail: tpowe@conncoll.edu
Zoology Department, Chair: DR. ROBERT A. ASKINS; Phone: 860-439-2149; Fax: 860-439-2519; E-mail: raask@conncoll.edu
Center for Conservation Biology and Environmental Studies, Director: DR. GLENN D. DREYER; Phone: 860-439-2144; Fax: 860-439-5482; E-mail: gddre@conncoll.edu

SOUTHERN CONNECTICUT STATE UNIVERSITY

Center for the Environment
501 Crescent St. Jennings Hall Rm. 309, New Haven, CT 06515
Phone: 203-392-6600; E-mail: hageman@scsu.ctstateu.edu
Description: The Center for the Environment is an academic center granting graduate and undergraduate degrees in environmental areas, conducting research, and developing epistemological models. An active field study program includes experiences in Costa Rica, South Africa, Madagascar, Ecuador (including the Galapagos Islands) and various sites in the U.S.

UNIVERSITY OF CONNECTICUT

Department of Natural Resources Management and Engineering
Box U-87, 1376 Storrs Road, WBY, Room 308, Storrs, CT 06269-4087
Phone: 203-486-2840; Web site: www.canr.uconn.edu/nrme/
Description: The Department offers degrees in natural resources with emphasis in forestry, fisheries, wildlife, biometeorology, watershed hydrology, remote sensing, soil and water conservation and natural resources engineering.
Degrees: B.S., M.S., Ph.D. in Natural Resources
Contact(s):
Head: DR. DAVID B. SCHROEDER

UNIVERSITY OF NEW HAVEN
300 Orange Ave., West Haven, CT 06516
Phone: 203-932-7101; Fax: 203-933-2036; E-mail: adminfo@charger.newhaven.edu; Web site: www.newhaven.edu/
Contact(s):
Department of Biology and Environmental Science, (B.S., M.S.), Chairman: CHARLES L. VIGUE Ph.D.

YALE UNIVERSITY

School of Forestry and Environmental Studies
205 Prospect St., New Haven, CT 06511

Phone: 203-432-5100; Fax: 203-432-5942; Web site: www.yale.edu/forestry/
Description: The mission of the school is to provide leadership in the science and management of natural resource and environmental systems. The school trains managers for governmental, non-governmental, and corporate institutions, and educates teachers and researchers
Degrees: D.F. & E.S., M.F., M.F.S, M.E.S, Ph.D.

DELAWARE

UNIVERSITY OF DELAWARE

College of Agriculture and Natural Resources
Newark, DE 19717
Phone: 302-831-2501; Web site: http://bluehen.ags.udel.edu/
Description: B.S. in wildlife conservation; M.S. and Ph.D. in entomology and applied ecology
Contact(s):
Department of Entomology and Applied Ecology, Chairperson. DR. JUDITH A. HOUGH-GOLDSTEIN; Phone: 302-831-8889; Fax: 302-831-3651; E-mail: jhough@udel.edu

DISTRICT OF COLUMBIA

GEORGE WASHINGTON UNIVERSITY
2121 I St., NW, Washington, DC 20052
Phone: 202-994-1000; Web site: www.gwu.edu/
Contact(s):
Environmental and Resource Policy, (M.A., Ph.D.), Director: HENRY MERCHANT; Phone: 202-994-7123; Fax: 202-994-6100
Environmental Engineering, (B.S., M.S., D.Sc.), Acting Chair: THEODORE G. TORIDIS, 801 22nd St., Washington, DC 20052; Phone: 202-994-6749; Fax: 202-944-0238; E-mail: toridis@seas.gwu.edu
Environmental Studies, (B.A., B.S., M.S.), Director: HENRY MERCHANT; Phone: 202-994-7118

Law School
2000 H. St., NW, Washington, DC 20052
Phone: 202-994-6260; E-mail: wwww@main.nlc.gwu.edu; Web site: www.law.gwu.edu/
Founded: 1865
Description: Nation's largest graduate and undergraduate environmental law program. Twenty-two environmental courses for J.D. and LL.M. students in addition to land use and other related topics. Emphasizes a practical approach.
Contact(s):
Co-Director: LAURENT R. HOURCLE; Phone: 202-994-4823; E-mail: LHOURCLE@main.nlc.gwu.edu

GEORGETOWN UNIVERSITY

Law Center
600 New Jersey Ave., NW, Washington, DC 20001
Phone: 202-662-9000; E-mail: admis@law.georgetown.edu; Web site: www.law.georgetown.edu/
Contact(s):
Dean: JUDITH C. AREEN

UNIVERSITY OF THE DISTRICT OF COLUMBIA
4200 Connecticut Avenue, NW, Washington, DC 20008
Phone: 202-UDC-4888; Web site: www.udc2.org
Contact(s):
Department of Biological and Environmental Sciences, (A.A.S., B.S.), Acting Chairperson: DR. FREDDIE DIXON, Bldg. 44; Phone: 202-274-7401

FLORIDA

FLORIDA ATLANTIC UNIVERSITY

Pine Jog Environmental Education Center
6301 Summit Blvd., West Palm Beach, FL 33415
Phone: 561-686-6600; Fax: 561-687-4968; Web site: www.fau.edu/divdept/coe/specfac/pinejog.htm
Founded: 1960
Description: Pine Jog is an environmental education center within the College of Education of Florida Atlantic University. The purpose of the Center is to provide environmental education programs which foster an awareness and appreciation of the natural world, promote an understanding of ecological concepts, and instill a sense of stewardship towards the earth and all of its inhabitants.
Contact(s):
Chair, Board of Directors: DONALD MATHIS, Sartory, Mathis, & Beedle, 5840 Corporate Way, West Palm Beach, FL 33407; Phone: 561-683-7500
Executive Director: PATRICIA WELCH; Phone: 561-686-6600

FLORIDA STATE UNIVERSITY
Tallahassee, FL 32306
Phone: 904-644-2525; Web site: www.fsu.edu
Contact(s):
Anthropology, (B.S., M.S., Ph.D.), Chairman: DR. BRUCE T. GRINDAL, Bellamy G-24, Tallahassee, FL 32306-2150; Phone: 850-644-8147; Fax: 850-644-4283; E-mail: bgrindal@mailer.fsu.edu
Biological Science, (B.S., M.S., Ph.D.), Chairman: DR. THOMAS M. ROBERTS, P.O. Box 4340, Tallahassee, FL 32306-4340; Phone: 850-644-3700; Fax: 850-644-9829
Geography (Political Geography and Environmental Studies), (B.S., M.S., Ph.D.), Chairman: DR. PATRICK O'SULLIVAN, P.O. Box 2190, Tallahassee, FL 32306-2190; Phone: 850-644-7175; Fax: 850-644-5913; E-mail: kmcclell@mailer.fsu.edu
Geology, (B.S., M.S., Ph.D.), Chairman: DR. J F. TULL, Carraway Bldg., Tallahassee, FL 32306-4100; Phone: 904-644-1448; Fax: 904-644-4214; E-mail: tull@gly.fsu.edu
Meteorology, (B.S., M.S., Ph.D.), Chairman: DR. DAVID W. STUART, 404 Love Building, Tallahassee, FL 32306-4520; Phone: 850-644-6205; Fax: 850-644-9642; E-mail: stuart@met.fsu.edu
Oceanography, (M.S., Ph.D.), Chairman: DR. WILTON STURGES, 329 OSB, West Call Street, Tallahassee, FL 32306-4320; Phone: 850-644-6700; Fax: 850-644-2581; E-mail: sturges@ocean.fsu.edu

UNIVERSITY OF MIAMI

Rosenstiel School of Marine and Atmospheric Science
4600 Rickenbacker Causeway, Miami, FL 33149
Phone: 305-361-4000; Fax: 305-361-4711; Web site: www.rsmas.miami.edu/
Contact(s):
Dean: DR. OTIS B. BROWN

UNIVERSITY OF FLORIDA

Solar Energy and Energy Conversion Laboratories
237 MEB, Box 116300, Gainesville, FL 32611
Phone: 352-392-0812; Fax: 352-392-1071; E-mail: solar@cimar.me.ufl.edu); Web site: www.me.ufl.edu/SOLAR/
Founded: 1954
Contact(s):
Director: DR. D. YOGI GOSWAMI

School of Forest Resources and Conservation
118 Newins Ziegler Hall P.O. Box 110410, Gainesville, FL 32611-0410
Phone: 352-846-0850; Fax: 352-392-1707; E-mail: sfrc@gnv.ifas.ufl.edu; Web site: aris.sfrc.ufl.edu/Welcome.html
Founded: 1937

EDUCATIONAL INSTITUTIONS - GEORGIA

Description: The school seeks to advance understanding of forests: interactions of their components and environment, their relationships with other ecosystems, and appropriate management practices and conservation strategies. Communicating this knowledge to students, public and other professionals is central to this mission; working together with other disciplines is essential to meeting its challenges.
Degrees: B.S.F.R.C., M.S., M.F.R.C., Ph.D.
Contact(s):
Director: DR. WAYNE H. SMITH
Graduate Programs Coordinator: DR. HENRY L. GHOLZ
Undergraduate Programs Coordinator: DR. GEORGE M. BLAKESLEE

UNIVERSITY OF WEST FLORIDA
11000 University Parkway, Pensacola, FL 32514
Phone: 850-474-2000; Web site: www.uwf.edu/~biology/
Contact(s):
Department of Biology, Chair: DR. JOHN P. RIEHM; E-mail: jriehm@uwf.edu
Institute for Coastal & Estuarine Research, Acting Director: JOE EUGENE LEPO Ph.D.; Phone: 850-474-2079; Fax: 850-474-3496; E-mail: icer@uwf.edu

GEORGIA

EMORY UNIVERSITY
Atlanta, GA 30322
Web site: www.emory.edu/BIOLOGY/
Degrees: B.S., M.S., Ph.D.
Contact(s):
Biology Department, Chair: JOHN C. LUCCHESI
Ecology and Evolution, Professor: CHRIS BECK

GEORGIA INSTITUTE OF TECHNOLOGY
Atlanta, GA 30332-0335
Phone: 404-894-3776; Web site: http://www.gatech.edu/
Contact(s):
Environmental Resources Center, Director: DR. BERND KAHN

UNIVERSITY OF GEORGIA

Daniel B. Warnell School of Forest Resources
Athens, GA 30602-2152
Phone: 706-542-2686; Fax: 706-542-8356; Web site: www.uga.edu/wsfr/
Description: The undergraduate degree (B.S.F.R) offers majors in Forestry, Wildlife, Fisheries and Aquaculture and Forest Environmental Resources. Graduate programs (M.S.,M.F.R., Ph.D.) offers a focus in Wildlife Ecology and Management, Fisheries and Aquaculture and a variety of Forest biology and management fields.
Contact(s):
Dean: DR. ARNETT C. MACE JR.
Cooperative Fish and Wildlife Research Unit, Graduate Program: DR. BRIAN R. CHAPMAN; Phone: 706-542-3929; Fax: 706-542-8356
Undergraduate Program: Phone: 706-542-7995; Fax: 706-542-3293

Marine Institute
Sapelo Island, GA 31327
Phone: 912-485-2125; Web site: Founded: 1953
Description: Concerned with research into the system-ecology, biology, chemistry, and geology of the salt marshes, barrier islands, and near-shore zone of the Georgia coast.
Contact(s):
Director: JAMES J. ALBERTS; E-mail: jalberts@arches.uga.edu
Education Program Specialist: JON O. GARBISCH; E-mail: jgarbisch@peachnet.campuscwix.net

Savannnah River Ecology Laboratory
P.O. Drawer E, Aiken, SC 29802-1030
Phone: 803-725-2473; Fax: 803-725-3309; E-mail: forrest@srel.edu; Web site: www.uga.edu/srel and www.uga.edu/srelherp/
Description: Learning and communicating ecological processes and principles is the mission of the University of Georgia's Savannah River Ecology Laboratory. The Lab accomplishes its mission through research, outreach and education, and service. Research is conducted in wetlands ecology, wildlife ecology and toxicology, and bio-geochemical ecology, including radioecology. Outreach and education activities reach more than 120,000 people annually in Georgia and South Carolina.
Contact(s):
Director: DR. PAUL BERTSCH
Outreach and Education Director: DR. WHIT GIBBONS
Public Relations: ROSEMARY FORREST

HAWAII

UNIVERSITY OF HAWAII

Cooperative Fishery Research Unit
2538 The Mall, Honolulu, HI 96822
Phone: 808-956-8350, 808-956-4708
Contact(s):
Leader: DR. JAMES D. PARRISH

IDAHO

IDAHO STATE UNIVERSITY

Department of Biological Sciences
Box 8007, Pocatello, ID 83209
Fax: 208-236-4570; E-mail: bios@isu.edu; Web site: www.isu.edu/departments/bios/
Description: The Department of Biological Sciences at Idaho State University has high quality degree programs in ecology. Strong basic coursework and original investigations are emphasized at the undergraduate and graduate levels. Habitats available for study range from cold sagebrush deserts to heavily forested areas and includes streams and riparian areas in the Snake River Canyon to its headwaters in Yellowstone National Park.
Contact(s):
Ecology, (B.S., M.S., Ph.D.), Chairman: ROD R. SEELEY Ph.D.; Phone: 208-236-3765; E-mail: seelrodn@isu.edu
Graduate Program Coordinator: MARY E. WATWOOD Ph.D.; Phone: 208-236-3090; E-mail: watwmari@isu.edu

UNIVERSITY OF IDAHO

Alfred W. Bowers Laboratory of Anthropology
Moscow, ID 83844-1114
Phone: 208-885-6754; Fax: 208-885-5878; Web site: www.uidaho.edu/LS/Anth-Lab/
Founded: 1968
Contact(s):
Contact and Research Specialist: DIXIE L. EHRENREICH; E-mail: dixie@uidaho.edu

College of Forestry, Wildlife and Range Sciences
Moscow, ID 83844
Phone: 208-885-2397 or 1-88-88-843246; Fax: 208-885-6226; Web site: www.uidaho.edu/cfwr/
Contact(s):
Dean: DR. CHARLES R. HATCH; Phone: 208-885-6442
Cooperative Park Studies Unit, Leader: DR. GARY MACHLIS; Phone: 208-885-7054
Cooperative Fish and Wildlife Research Unit, Leader: DR. J. MICHAEL SCOTT; Phone: 208-885-6336
Forest Products, (B.S., M.S., Ph.D.), Contact: DR. LEONARD R. JOHNSON; Phone: 208-885-9663
Forest Resources, (B.S., M.S., Ph.D.), Contact: DR. JO ELLEN FORCE; Phone: 208-885-7952
Policy Analysis Group, Contact: DR. JAY O'LAUGHLIN; Phone: 208-885-5776

Range Resources, (B.S., M.S., Ph.D.), Contact: DR. KENDALL JOHNSON; Phone: 208-885-6536
Resource Recreation and Tourism, (B.S., M.S., Ph.D.), Contact: DR. STEVEN HOLLENHORST; Phone: 208-885-7911
Wilderness Research Center, Director: DR. JOHN C. HENDEE; Phone: 208-885-2267

ILLINOIS

BRADLEY UNIVERSITY

Biology Department
    1501 W. Bradley Ave., Peoria, IL 61625
    Phone: 309-677-3020; Web site: www.bradley.edu/academics/las/bio/
Degrees: B.S., B.A., M.S.
Contact(s):
Chairman: JOHN A. DEPINTO
Environmental Biology: BILL MATHIS
Plant Biology: JANET L. GEHRING; E-mail: jgehring@bradley.bradley.edu
Plant Ecology: KELLY MCCONNAUGHAY

EASTERN ILLINOIS UNIVERSITY
    Charleston, IL 61920
    Phone: 217-581-3126; Web site: www.eiu.edu/~biology/
Description: Eastern Illinois University offer an undergraduate degree in Biology, with three options: Teacher Certification, Environmental Biology and Biological Sciences. Within the Biological Sciences, students choose from among 4 concentrations: Biology, Botanical Sciences, Ecology and Systematics, and Cell and Functional Biology. Emphasis is placed upon a fundamental understanding of biology and environmental concerns.
Degrees: B.S., M.S.
Contact(s):
Biological Sciences, (M.S.), Contact: CHARLES COSTA; Phone: 217-581-2520; E-mail: cfcjc@eiu.edu
Environmental Biology Option Coordinator: ROBERT U. FISCHER; Phone: 217-581-2817; E-mail: cfruf@eiu.edu
Biology, Chair: KIPP C. KRUSE; Phone: 217-581-3126; E-mail: cfkck@eiu.edu
Biology Teacher Certificate Option Coordinator: JAMES MCGAUGHEY; Phone: 217-581-2928; E-mail: cfjam@eiu.edu

ILLINOIS STATE UNIVERSITY

Environmental Health Program, Department of Health Sciences
    Campus Box 5220, Normal, IL 61790-5220
    Phone: 309-438-8329; Fax: 309-438-2450; Web site: www.ilstu.edu/
Founded: 1974
Description: Undergraduate education for B.S. in environmental health. Five faculty persons and 165 enrolled students. Four-year undergraduate curriculum accredited by National Environmental Health Science and Protection Accreditation Council. Graduate Education for M.S. in Environmental Health and Safety.
Degrees: B.S., M.S.
Contact(s):
Master's Program Coordinator: THOMAS BIERMA PH.D.
Program Director: SHARRON E. LAFOLLETE PH.D.

SOUTHERN ILLINOIS UNIVERSITY
    Carbondale, IL 62901
    Phone: 618-453-2121; Web site: www.siu.edu
Contact(s):
Cooperative Fisheries Research Lab, (M.S., Ph.D.), Director: DR. CHRISTOPHER C. KOHLER, Mailstop 6511, SIU, Carbondale, IL 62901; Phone: 618-536-7761; E-mail: CKohler@siu.edu
Cooperative Wildlife Research Lab, Director: DR. ALAN WOOLF, Mailstop 6504, SIU, Carbondale, IL 62901; Phone: 618-536-7766; E-mail: awoolf@siu.edu
Forestry, (B.S., M.S.), Chair: DR. JOHN E. PHELPS, Mailstop 4411, SIU, Carbondale, IL 62901; Phone: 618-453-7464; E-mail: jphelps@siu.edu
Plant and Soil Science, (B.S., M.S.), Chair: DR. DONALD J. STUCKY, Mailstop 4415, SIU, Carbondale, IL 62901; Phone: 618-453-2496; E-mail: dstucky@siu.edu
Environmental Studies Program, Director: GEORGE FELDHAMER, Mailstop 6501, SIU, Carbondale, IL 62901; Phone: 618-453-4143; Fax: 618-453-2806; E-mail: feldhamer@zoology.siu.edu

UNIVERSITY OF ILLINOIS AT URBANA-CHAMPAIGN
    Urbana, IL 61801
    Phone: 217-333-1000; Web site: www.uiuc.edu/
Contact(s):
Center for Wildlife Ecology, Illinois Natural History Survey, Director: PATRICK W. BROWN
Civil Engineering, (B.S., M.S., Ph.D.), Head: DAVID E. DANIEL
Geography, (B.S., M.S, Ph.D.), Head: COLIN E. THORN
Integrative Biology (B.A., Ph.D.), Head: SCOTT K. ROBINSON
Landscape Architecture, (B.L.A., M.L.A.), Head: VINCENT J. BELLAFIORE
Natural Resources and Environmental Sciences, (B.S., M.S., Ph.D.), Head: GARY L. ROLFE
Urban and Regional Planning, (B.A., M.U.P., Ph.D.), Head: CHRISTOPHER SILVER

WESTERN ILLINOIS UNIVERSITY

Department of Biological Sciences
    372 Waggoner Hall, Macomb, IL 61455
    Phone: 309-298-1546; Fax: 309-298-2270; E-mail: mibiol@wiu.edu; Web site: www.wiu.edu/users/mibiol/
Description: Office of Aquatic Studies offers courses at the Shedd Aquarium in Chicago
Contact(s):
Fisheries, (B.S., M.S.): DR. LARRY A JAHN; Phone: 309-298-1266; E-mail: LA-Jahn@wiu.edu
Kibbe Life Science Field Station, Director: RICHARD ANDERSON; Phone: 309-298-1553; E-mail: randerson@ccmail.wiu.edu
Office of Aquatic Studies: DR. JEANETTE THOMAS, 6502 34th Ave., Moline, IL 61265; Phone: 309-441-5220; E-mail: mfjat@uxa.ecn.bgu.edu
Wildlife, (B.S., M.S.): DR. THOMAS C. DUNSTAN; Phone: 309-298-1752; E-mail: Thomas_Dunstan@ccmail.wiu.edu

INDIANA

BALL STATE UNIVERSITY

Department of Natural Resources and Environmental Management
    Muncie, IN 47306
    Phone: 765-285-5780; Fax: 765-285-2606; E-mail: nrem@bsu.edu; Web site: www.bsu.edu/nrem
Contact(s):
Departmental Minor in Environmental Management, Advisor: DR. JOHN R. PICHTEL
Departmental Minor in Natural Resources, Advisor: DR. CHARLES O. MORTENSEN
Environmental Interpretation and Outdoor Recreation Management Option, Advisor: DR. CHARLES O. MORTENSEN
Environmental Protection Option, Advisor: DR. THAD GODISH, DR. JOHN PICHTEL, DR. FRED SIEWERT
Interdepartmental Minors in Energy Resources and Environmental Policy, Advisor: DR. JAMES EFLIN
Land Management Option, Advisor: DR. HUGH J. BROWN DR. JAMES EFLIN
Natural Resources and Environmental Management, (B.S., B.A., M.A., M.S.), Chair: DR. CHARLES O. MORTENSEN
Natural Resources Studies Option, Advisor: DR. TIMOTHY F. LYON, DR. PAUL CHANDLER
Occupational and Industrial Hygiene Option, Advisor: DR. THAD GODISH

EDUCATIONAL INSTITUTIONS - IOWA

Teaching Minor in Environmental Studies, Advisor: DR. TIMOTHY F. LYON

INDIANA STATE UNIVERSITY

Department of Biological Sciences
Science Bldg. Rm. 256, Terre Haute, IN 47809
Phone: 812-237-2400; Fax: 812-237-4480; Web site: biology.indstate.edu/dls/
Contact(s):
Ecology and Wildlife, (B.S., M.S., Ph.D): DR. MARION T. JACKSON; E-mail: lsmjack@scifac.indstate.edu

INDIANA UNIVERSITY

School of Public and Environmental Affairs
Bloomington, IN 47405
Phone: 812-855-2457; Fax: 812-855-7802; E-mail: speainfo@indiana.edu; Web site: www.indiana.edu/~speaweb
Founded: 1972
Description: The School of Public Environmental Affairs brings an interdisciplinary approach to the study of the environmental sciences. The focus of the academic programs is to teach techniques that will help graduates preserve and protect the quality of natural resources, identify environmental hazards, and significantly contribute to solutions to enhance quality of life in the world's communities.
Contact(s):
Dean: A. JAMES BARNES
Associate Dean: ROBERT AGRANOFF
Director of Graduate Programs: DAVID JONES
Director of Ph.D. Programs in Public Policy and Public Affairs: LOIS WISE
Director of Undergraduate Programs: FRANK VILARDO

MANCHESTER COLLEGE

Koinonia Environmental and Retreat Center
Box 36, North Manchester, IN 46962
Phone: 219-982-5010; Fax: 219-982-5043; E-mail: bjehrhardt@manchester.edu; Web site: ARES.manchester.edu/academic/koin.html
Founded: 1974
Description: The100-acre facility is used extensively to provide hands-on environmental science education for area students in grades, K-12. A two-story building houses the nature center with many educational displays. The retreat facility will accommodate 32 persons.
Contact(s):
Director: BARBARA J. EHRHARDT

PURDUE UNIVERSITY

Department of Forestry and Natural Resources
1159 Forestry Bldg., West Lafayette, IN
Web site: www.fnr.purdue.edu/
Contact(s):
Department of Forestry and Natural Resources, Head: DR. DENNIS C. LEMASTER; Phone: 765-494-3590; Fax: 765-496-2422
Graduate Program, Director of Graduate Studies: DR. ROBERT K. SWIHART; Phone: 765-494-3621; Fax: 765-496-2422
Undergraduate Programs, Director of Student Services: DR. W. L. MILLS JR.; Phone: 765-494-3575; Fax: 765-496-2422
Fisheries and Aquatic Sciences, (B.S., M.S., Ph.D.):
Forestry, (B.S.F., M.S., Ph.D.):
Natural Resources, (B.S., M.S, Ph.D.):
Wildlife, (B.S., M.S., Ph.D.):
Wood Products Manufacturing Technology, (B.S., M.S., Ph.D.):

IOWA

IOWA STATE UNIVERSITY

College of Agriculture
304 Curtis Hall, Ames, IA 50011-1050
Phone: 515-294-5616; E-mail: edadcock@iastate.edu; Web site: www.ag.iastate.edu/
Contact(s):
Animal Ecology, Fisheries and Wildlife Biology, (B.S., M.S., Ph.D), Chairman: DR. BRUCE W. MENZEL; Phone: 515-294-6148; E-mail: bmenzel@iastate.edu
Forestry, (B.S., M.S., Ph.D.), Chairman: DR. J. MICHAEL KELLY, Department of Forestry, Ames, IA 50011-1021; Phone: 515-294-1166; E-mail: jmkelly@iastate.edu
Horticulture, (B.S., M.S., Ph.D.), Head: DR. MIKE CHAPLIN, Rm. 106B Horticulture Hall, 50011-1100; Phone: 515-294-5893; Fax: 515-294-0730; E-mail: chaplin@iastate.edu

College of Design
Ames, IA 50011
Web site: www.design.iastate.edu/
Contact(s):
Landscape Architecture, (B.L.A., M.L.A.), Chairman: DR. J. TIMOTHY KELLER; E-mail: tkeller@iastate.edu
Community and Regional Planning, (B.S., and graduate degrees), Chair: DR. RIAD G. MAHAYNI; Phone: 515-294-8958; Fax: 515-294-4015; E-mail: rmahayni@iastate.edu

UNIVERSITY OF IOWA
Iowa City, IA 52242
Web site: www.uiowa.edu/
Contact(s):
Civil and Environmental Engineering Program (M.S., Ph.D.), Department Chair: ROBERT ETTEMA, Department Office: 2130 Seamans Center, Iowa City, IA 52242; Phone: 319-335-5647; Fax: 319-335-5660; E-mail: cee@engineering.uiowa.edu
Environmental Health Sciences Research Center, Director: Dr. JAMES A. MERCHANT, 2707 Steindler Bldg., Iowa City, IA 52242; Phone: 319-335-9833; E-mail: james-merchant@uiowa.edu
Environmental Science Program (B.S.): 121 Trowbridge Hall, Iowa City, IA 52242; Phone: 319-335-1818; Fax: 319-335-1821

KANSAS

EMPORIA STATE UNIVERSITY
Emporia, KS 66801
Phone: 316-341-5311; Web site: www.emporia.edu/
Contact(s):
Division of Biological Sciences, Ecology and Wildlife Biology, (B.S., M.S.), Contact: DR. ELMER FINCK

KANSAS STATE UNIVERSITY

Department of Landscape Architecture
302 Seaton Hall, Manhattan, KS 660506-2909
Phone: 785-532-5961; Fax: 785-532-6722; E-mail: la-rcp@ksu.edu; Web site: aalto.arch.ksu.edu/lar/
Degrees: B.L.A., M.L.A., M.A., M.C.R.P.
Contact(s):
Department Head: DR. DAN DONELIN; E-mail: dandon@ksu.edu
Regional and Community Planning, Director: DR. C. A. KEITHLEY; Phone: 785-532-2440; E-mail: cak@ksu.edu

Division of Biology
232 Ackert Hall, Manhatten, KS 66506
Phone: 785-532-6615; Fax: 785-532-6653; Web site: www.ksu.edu/biology/
Contact(s):
Fisheries, (B.S., M.S., Ph.D.), Contact: DR. HAROLD E. KLAASSEN; Phone: 785-532-6654

Konza Prairie Research Natural Area, Contact: DR. DAVID C. HARTNETT; Phone: 785-532-5925
Landscape Architecture, (B.L.A.), Contact: DAN DONELIN; Phone: 785-532-5961
Wildlife (B.S., M.S., Ph.D.), Contact: DR. ROBERT J. ROBEL; Phone: 785-532-6644

College of Agriculture
117 Waters Hall, Manhattan, KS 66506-5506
Phone: 785-532-6151; E-mail: jax1@ksu.edu; Web site: www.ag.ksu.edu/
Contact(s):
Horticulture, Forestry and Recreation Resources, Department Head: DR. THOMAS WARNER, 2021 Throckmorton Plant Science Center, Manhattan, KS 66506; Phone: 785-532-6170; E-mail: twarner@oz.oznet.ksu.edu
Natural Resource Management: DR. TED T. CABLE; Phone: 785-532-1408; E-mail: tcable@oz.oznet.ksu.edu
Department of Agronomy, Head: DR. DAVID B. MENGEL, 2004 Throckmorton Plant Science Center, Manhattan, KS 66506; Phone: 785-532-6101; Fax: 785-532-6094; E-mail: dmengel@bear.agron.ksu.edu
Soil and Water Conservation: DR. MICHEL D. RANSOM; Phone: 785-532-7203; E-mail: mdransom@ksu.edu

Cooperative Fish and Wildlife Research Unit
Leasure Hall, Manhattan, KS 66506-3501
Phone: 785-532-6070; Web site: www.ksu.edu
Description: Provides graduate training and research in fisheries and wildlife biology, research, management, ecology, population dynamics, genetics, and related areas. Supported cooperatively by Kansas State University, The Kansas Department of Wildlife and Parks, the National Biological Service and the Wildlife Management Institute.
Contact(s):
Assistant Leader of Fisheries: DR. CHRISTOPHER S. GUY
Assistant Leader of Wildlife: DR. JACK F. CULLY JR.
Leader: DR. PHILIP S. GIPSON

UNIVERSITY OF KANSAS

Biological Sciences
Haworth Hall, Lawrence, KS 66045
Phone: 785-864-4301; Fax: 785-864-5321; E-mail: iol@www.cc.ukans.edu; Web site: kuhttp.cc.ukans.edu/cwis/units/biol/
Contact(s):
Ecology and Evolutionary Biology, (B.S., M.A., Ph.D.), Chair: THOMAS N. TAYLOR; Phone: 785-864-3625
Experimental and Applied Ecology, with emphasis in aquatic ecology and population biology of small mammals and plants, (M.A., Ph.D.), Director: W. JOHN O'BRIEN; Phone: 785-864-4375
Kansas Applied Remote Sensing Program with emphasis in natural resources management, Director: ED MARTINKO; Phone: 785-864-7770

Environmental Studies Program
Lawrence, KS 66045
E-mail: env-stud@ukans.edu; Web site: www.cc.ukans.edu/~kuesp
Description: Environmental Studies Program offers options in ecology and field biology, environmental policy, environmental impact analysis, environmental health, geology and meterology, water resources, and environmental land-use analysis
Degrees: B.A., B.G.S., B.S.
Contact(s):
Director: STANFORD LOEB ; Phone: 785-842-2059

EDUCATIONAL INSTITUTIONS - KENTUCKY

KENTUCKY

EASTERN KENTUCKY UNIVERSITY
Biological Sciences Department, 521 Lancaster Ave., Richmond, KY 40475-3102
Phone: 606-622-1531; Fax: 606-622-1020; Web site: www.eku.edu
Contact(s):
Applied Ecology (M.S.), Contact: DR. BARBARA RAMEY; Phone: 606-622-1531
Biology--Aquatic Option (B.S.): DR. GUENTER SHUSTER; Phone: 606-622-1531
Biology--Botany Option (B.S.): DR. ROSS CLARK; Phone: 606-622-1531
Environmental Studies (B.S.), Contact: DR. CHARLES ELLIOTT; Phone: 606-622-1531
Lillie Woods Research Natural Area: DR. WILLIAM MARTIN; Phone: 606-622-1476
Wildlife Management (B.S.), Contact: DR. ROBERT FREDERICK; Phone: 606-622-1531

GEORGETOWN COLLEGE

Environmental Science Program
400 E. College St., Georgetown, KY 40324
Phone: 502-863-8088; Web site: www.georgetowncollege.edu/
Description: Environmental Science Degree with tracks in Chemical Science, Biological Science, Chemical-Biological Science and Environmental Policy.
Degrees: B.S.
Contact(s):
Program Coordinator: DR. RICK KOPP; E-mail: rkopp@georgetowncollege.edu

MOREHEAD STATE UNIVERSITY
Morehead, KY 40351
Phone: 606-783-2944; Web site: www.morehead-st.edu/
Contact(s):
Biology, a major in biology (organismal, genetics, microbiology, cell biology, physiology, ecology) is offered (39 semester hours); A minor is also available, (B.S., M.S.): DR. JOE E. WINSTEAD; Phone: 606-783-2944; E-mail: j.winstead@morehead-st.edu
Environmental Science, an area of concentration in environmental science (biology, ecology, environment, environmental planning, wildlife management) is offered (61-62 semester hours) A minor is also available, (B.S.): DR. JOE E. WINSTEAD; Phone: 606-783-2944; E-mail: j.winstead@morehead-st.edu

MURRAY STATE UNIVERSITY
334 Blackburn Science, Murray, KY 42071-0009
Phone: 270-762-2786; Web site: www.murraystate.edu
Contact(s):
Center for Reservoir Research, Contact: DR. DAVID WHITE; Phone: 270-474-2272; E-mail: David.White@murraystate.edu
Department of Biological Sciences, Chairman: DR. TOM J. TIMMONS; E-mail: Tom.Timmons@murraystate.edu
Fisheries, (B.S., M.S.), Contact: DR. TOM J. TIMMONS; Phone: 270-762-6754; E-mail: Tom.Timmons@murraystate.edu
Wildlife, (B.S., M.S.), Contact: DR. STEPHEN B. WHITE; Phone: 270-762-6298; E-mail: Steve.White@murraystate.edu

UNIVERSITY OF KENTUCKY

College of Agriculture
Lexington, KY 40546
Phone: 606-257-7596; Web site: www.uky.edu/
Contact(s):
Forestry, (B.S., M.S., M.S.F.), Chairman: DR. DONALD H. GRAVES
Horticulture, (B.S., M.S.), Chair: DR. DEWAYNE L. INGRAM; Phone: 606-257 1758; E-mail: dingram@ca.uky.edu
Landscape Architecture (B.S.): KAREN GOODLET; Phone: 606-257-7295; E-mail: kgoodlet@ca.uky.edu
Natural Resource Conservation and Management, (B.S.):

EDUCATIONAL INSTITUTIONS - LOUISIANA

UNIVERSITY OF LOUISVILLE
Louisville, KY 40292
Phone: 502-852-6771; Web site: www.louisville.edu/
Description: The Large River Laboratory was established in 1992 to conduct research on river and freshwater systems in Kentucky and surrounding states. Community and population studies of rivers and smaller streams constitute the primary focus of the laboratory.
Contact(s):
Department of Biology: DR. JEFF JACK
Professor: DR. WILLIAM D. PEARSON

LOUISIANA

LOUISIANA STATE UNIVERSITY

School of Forestry, Wildlife and Fisheries
Baton Rouge, LA 70803
Phone: 225-388-4184; Web site:
http://www.coa.lsu.edu/fores/fores.html
Degrees: Fisheries: B.S., M.S., Ph.D.; Wildlife: M.S., Ph.D.;Wildlife and Fisheries Sciences: Ph.D.
Contact(s):

Cooperative Fish and Wildlife Research Unit, Leader: DR. CHARLES F. BRYAN

LOUISIANA TECH UNIVERSITY

School of Forestry
Ruston, LA 71272
Phone: 318-257-4985; Web site: www.ans.latech.edu/forestry-index.html
Description: Located in Louisiana's major forest region, the School of Forestry offers Bachelor of Science degrees in Forestry and Wildlife Conservation. Teaching facilities include a GIS/Remote Sensing Laboratory, a highly trained and diverse faculty and a successful placement record.
Degrees: B.S., B.S.F.
Contact(s):
Director: DR. G. H. WEAVER; E-mail: gweaver@rans.latech.edu
Coordinator of Wildlife Program: DR. JAMES DICKSON; E-mail: jdickson@rans.latech.edu

MCNEESE STATE UNIVERSITY
Lake Charles, LA 70609
Web site: www.mcneese.edu/
Contact(s):
Department of Agriculture, Wildlife Management Professor: BILLY DELANY; Phone: 318-475-5690

NORTHWESTERN STATE UNIVERSITY OF LOUISIANA
Natchitoches, LA 71497
Phone: 318-357-5323; Fax: 318-357-4518; Web site: www.nsula.edu/
Description: To educate students in principles and science of wildlife management; to prepare students for management of natural resources at the professional entry levels; and to provide an emphasis on biodiversity and ecosystems; to orient students toward interpersonal communication
Contact(s):
Biology Sciences, Head: DR. DICK STALLING
Biology/Wildlife Management, (B.S.), Advisor: DR. ARTHUR S. ALLEN; E-mail: allena@alpha.nsula.edu

TULANE UNIVERSITY
New Orleans, LA 70118
Phone: 504-865-5191; Fax: 504-862-8706; E-mail: eebchair@mailhost.tcs.tulane.edu; Web site: www.tulane.edu
Degrees: B.S., M.S., Ph.D.
Contact(s):
Environmental Biology (ecology and systematics), Chairman: DR. DAVID C. HEINS

Law School

Environmental Law Clinic
6329 Freret St., New Orleans, LA 70118-5670
Phone: 504-865-5789; Fax: 504-862-8721; Web site: www.law.tulane.edu/programs/environmental/envirolaw/clinic.htm
Founded: 1989
Description: Provides free legal assistance through its student attorneys to community organizations and indigent persons seeking to protect public health and the environment.
Contact(s):
Director: ROBERT R. KUEHN

Environmental Law Program
Weinmann Hall, Suite 203, New Orleans, LA 70118
Phone: 504-865-5946; Fax: 504-862-8855; E-mail: Ohouck@law.tulane.edu; Web site: www.law.tulane.edu/
Founded: 1981
Description: Environmental law education, research, and advocacy through faculty, staff, JD and graduate student body.
Contact(s):
Director: PROF OLIVER A. HOUCK
Director, Institute of Environmental Law and Policy: JERRY SPEIR

MAINE

COLLEGE OF THE ATLANTIC
105 Eden St., Bar Harbor, ME 04609
Phone: 207-288-5015; Web site: www.coa.edu
Description: The College of the Atlantic is a fully accredited four-year residential college. Students are attracted to its excellent programs in marine biology, environmental studies and ecology, environmental design, public policy, education, and selected humanities. Summer programs in field studies for teachers.
Contact(s):
President: STEVEN KATONA

UNITY COLLEGE
Unity, ME 04988
Phone: 207-948-3131; Web site: www.unity.edu/
Founded: 1966
Description: Unity College is a small, liberal arts college in rural Maine with degree programs specializing in natural resource management and wilderness-based recreation.
Contact(s):
Aquaculture, Contact: A. JIM CHACKO
Arboriculture, Contact: DOUG FOX
Botany and Ecology, Contact: ED BEALS
Conservation Law Enforcement, Contact: LARRY FARNSWORTH
Fisheries, Contact: DAVE POTTER
Park Management, Temporary Contact: TOM MULLINS
Wildlife, Contact: JIM NELSON

UNIVERSITY OF MAINE AT FORT KENT
25 Pleasant St., Fort Kent, ME 04743
Phone: 207-834-7617; Fax: 207-834-7503; Web site: www.umfk.maine.edu/
Description: Located in the heart of Maine's Acadian forest region. Our Bachelor of Science in Environmental Studies degree program provides a solid experiential and academic background to students preparing for careers in education, industry, and public service.
Contact(s):
Environmental Studies, Director: DR. STEVEN SELVA; E-mail: selva@main.maine.edu
President: CHARLES LYONS

UNIVERSITY OF MAINE AT ORONO

College of Natural Sciences, Forestry and Agriculture
Orono, ME 04469
Phone: 207-581-1110; Web site: www.umaine.edu/

Contact(s):
Dean: DR. BRUCE WIERSMA; Phone: 207-581-3202
Cooperative Fish and Wildlife Research Unit, Leader: DR. WILLIAM B. KROHN; Phone: 207-581-2870
Department of Bio-systems Science and Engineering, (B.S., M.E., M.P.S., Ph.D.), Chairman: DR. CHARLES R. WALLACE; Phone: 207-581-2770
Department of Biochemistry, Microbiology and Molecular Biology, (B.A., B.S., M.S., M.P.S., Ph.D.), Chairman: DR. JOHN SINGER; Phone: 207-581-2810
Department of Biological Sciences, (B.A., B.S., M.S., Ph.D.), Chairman: DR. J. MALCOLM SHICK; Phone: 207-581-2551
Department of Food Science and Human Nutrition, Food and Nutrition Sciences, (B.S., M.S., Ph.D.), Chair: DR. RODNEY BUSHWAY; Phone: 207-581-1621
Department of Forest Ecosystem Science, Chairman: DR. WILLIAM LIVINGSTON; Phone: 207-581-2884
Department of Forest Management, (B.S., M.F., M.S., Ph.D.), Chairman: DR. DAVID B. FIELD; Phone: 207-581-2856
Department of Geological Sciences, (B.A., B.S., M.S., Ph.D.), Chair: DR. DANIEL BELKNAP; Phone: 207-581-2152
Department of Plant, Soil, and Environmental Science, (B.S., M.S., Ph.D.), Chairman: DR. IVAN FERNANDEZ; Phone: 207-581-2932
Department of Resource Economics and Policy, (B.S., M.S.), Chairman: DR. GEORGE CRINER; Phone: 207-581-3150
Department of Wildlife Ecology, (B.S., M.S., M.W.C., Ph.D.): DR. JAMES R. GILBERT; Phone: 207-581-2866
Natural Resources Program, (B.S.), Coordinator: MARK ANDERSON; Phone: 207-581-3198

School of Marine Sciences
5741 Libby Hall, Rm. 216A, Orono, ME 04469
Web site: www.umaine.edu/
Degrees: B.S. in Aquaculture, Marine Science; M.S., Ph.D. in Marine Biology, Oceanography; M.S. in Marine Policy
Contact(s):
Chair: DR. BRUCE SIDELL; Phone: 207-581-4381 207-581-4381

MARYLAND

FROSTBURG STATE UNIVERSITY (University of Maryland)

Department of Biology
101 Braddock Rd., Frostburg, MD 21532
Phone: 301-687-4166; Fax: 301-687-3034; Web site: www.fsu.umd.edu
Description: Wildlife and Fisheries Program (B.A, M.A., Ph.D.), Wildlife/Fisheries Biology (M.S.), Applied Ecology; Conservation Biology (M.S.), Biology (B.S., Ph.D.)
Contact(s):
Department Chair: DR. DAVID MORTON; Phone: 301-687-4355; E-mail: dmorton@frostburg.edu.
Appalachian Environmental Laboratory: DR. LOUIS F. PITELKA; Phone: 301-689-3115; E-mail: pitelka@al.umces.edu

JOHNS HOPKINS UNIVERSITY, THE
Baltimore, MD 21218
Phone: 410-516-7092; Web site: www.jhu.edu
Contact(s):
Ecology, (M.A., Ph.D.), Contact: GRACE S. BRUSH
Environmental Chemistry, (M.A., M.S., Ph.D.), Contact: ALAN T. STONE
Environmental Engineering, (M.S.E., Ph.D.), Contact: EDWARD J. BOVVER
Natural Resources, (M.A., M.S., Ph.D.), Contact: M. GORDON WOLMAN

School of Public Health

Pew Environmental Health Commission
111 Market Pl., Suite 850, Baltimore, MD 21202
Phone: 410-659-2690; Fax: 410-659-2699; Web site: pewenvirohealth.jhsph.edu/
Description: The Pew Environmental Health Commission works to strengthen the country's public health system to protect against sickness and disease caused by environmental threats.
Contact(s):
Executive Director: DR. SHELLEY HEARN
Deputy Director: PAUL LOCKE

Center for a Livable Future
615 N. Wolfe St., Suite 1033, Baltimore, MD 21205
Fax: 410-223-1603; E-mail: clf@jhsph.edu; Web site: www.jhsph.edu/environment/
Description: The mission of the Center for a Livable Future is to establish a global resource to develop and disseminate information and to promote policies for the protection of health, the global environment, and our ability to sustain life for future generations.
Contact(s):
Director: ROBERT S. LAWRENCE M.D.; Phone: 410-614-4590; Fax: 410-614-8126; E-mail: rlawrenc@jhsph.edu
Center Coordinator: POLLY WALKER M.D.; Phone: 410-223-1608; E-mail: pwalker@jhsph.edu
Program Director, Henry Spira/GRACE Project on Industrial Animal Production: DAVID R. BRUBAKER Ph.D.; Phone: 410-223-1722; E-mail: dbrubake@jhsph.edu
Project Coordinator, Urban Agriculture: LEO HORRIGAN M.H.S.; Phone: 410-223-1609; E-mail: lhorriga@jhsph.edu

UNIVERSITY OF MARYLAND AT BALTIMORE COUNTY

Department of Biological Sciences
1000 Hilltop Cir., Baltimore, MD 21250
Phone: 410-455-2261; Fax: 410-455-3875; E-mail: ellis@umbc.edu; Web site: www.umbc.edu/biosci/
Description: Ecology and Environmental Biology focus with a strong emphasis on research, scientific approach, faculty contact and extensive lab offerings
Degrees: B.S., B.A., M.S., Ph.D
Contact(s):
Professor and Chair: DR. LASSE LINDAHL; E-mail: lindahl@umbc.edu

UNIVERSITY OF MARYLAND AT COLLEGE PARK

College of Agriculture and Natural Resources
1106 Symons Hall, College Park, MD 20742
Phone: 301-405-1000; Web site:
Contact(s):
Dean: DR. THOMAS FRETZ
Department of Natural Resource Sciences and Landscape Architecture (B.S., B.L.A., M.S., Ph.D.), Chair: DR. RICHARD A. WEISMILLER, Room 2104, Plant Sciences Bldg., College Park, MD 20742; Phone: 301-405-1306; Fax: 301-314-9308; E-mail: rw22@umail.umd.edu
Department of Animal and Avian Sciences (B.S.), Undergraduate Coordinator: DR. GEOFFREY DAHL, Animal Sciences Center, College Park, MD 20742; Phone: 301-405-1373; Fax: 301-314-9059
Department of Animal and Avian Sciences (M.S., Ph.D.), Director: DR. JOSEPH H. SOARES, Animal Sciences Center, College Park, MD 20742; Phone: 301-405-5781; Fax: 301-314-9059; E-mail: advpgrad@deans.umd.edu
Environmental and Resource Policy (B.S.), Agricultural and Resource Economics, Contact: BARBARA BURDICK, 2200A Symons Hall, College Park, MD 20742; Phone: 301-405-1291; Fax: 301-314-9031; E-mail: barbb@arec.umd.edu

Graduate School
College Park, MD 20742-5121

EDUCATIONAL INSTITUTIONS - MASSACHUSETTS

E-mail: grschool@deans.umd.edu; Web site: www.inform.umd.edu/grad/
Contact(s):
Marine-Estuarine-Environmental Sciences (M.S., Ph.D.), Director: DR. KENNETH P. SEBENS, 220 Symons Hall, College Park, MD 20742-5571; Phone: 301-405-6938; Fax: 301-314-4139; E-mail: meesgrad@deans.umd.edu
Plant Biology (M.S., Ph.D.), Director: DR. TODD J. COOKE, 1123 Microbiology Bldg., College Park, MD 20742; Phone: 301-405-6991; Fax: 301-314-9082; E-mail: tc23@umail.umd.edu
Sustainable Development and Conservation Biology (M.S.), Director (Acting): DR. DAVID INOUYE, Department of Biology, College Park, MD 20742; Phone: 301-405-7409; Fax: 301-314-9358; E-mail: consoffc@zool.umd.edu

UNIVERSITY OF MARYLAND AT EASTERN SHORE

Department of Natural Sciences
Carver Hall, Princess Anne, MD 21853
Phone: 301-651-2200; Web site: hawk.umes.edu/sciences/index.html
Description: Environmental Sciences (B.S.), Marine Sciences (B.S., M.S.), Marine, Estuarine, and Environmental Sciences (M.S., Ph.D), Environmental Chemistry (B.S., M.S.)
Contact(s):
Department Chair (Acting): DR. JOESPH OKOH
Coastal Ecology Research Center, Contact: DR. CHARLES HOCUTT
Marine, Estuarine, and Environmental Sciences (M.S., Ph.D), Contact: DR. STEVE REBACH; Phone: 410-651-6013
Environmental Science/Marine Science, Contact: DR. GIAN GUPTA; Phone: 410-651-6030; E-mail: GGUPTA@UMES_BIRD.UMD.EDU

UNIVERSITY OF MARYLAND CENTER FOR ENVIRONMENTAL SCIENCE

P.O. Box 775, Cambridge, MD 21613
Phone: 410-228-9250; Fax: 410-228-3843; Web site: www.cees.edu/
Founded: 1925
Description: UMCES is an institution of the University System of Maryland, with a special mission in multidisciplinary environmental research on Chesapeake Bay, the mid-Atlantic region, and coastal systems around the world.
Contact(s):
President: DR. DONALD F. BOESCH
Horn Point Laboratory, Director and Professor: DR. THOMAS C. MALONE; Phone: 410-228-8200; Fax: 410-476-5490; E-mail: malone@hpl.umces.edu
Chesapeake Biological Laboratory, Director: DR. KENNETH R. TENORE, P.O. Box 38, Solomons, MD 20688; Phone: 410-326-7241; Fax: 410-326-7302; E-mail: tenore@cbl.umces.edu
Appalachian Laboratory, Director: DR. LOUIS F. PITELKA, 301 Braddock Rd., Frostburg State University, Frostburg, MD 21532; Phone: 301-689-3115; Fax: 301-689-8518; E-mail: pitelka@al.umces.edu

MASSACHUSETTS

CLARK UNIVERSITY

International Development Program
950 Main St., Worcester, MA 01610
Phone: 508-793-7201; Fax: 508-793-8820; E-mail: id@clarku.edu; Web site: www.clarku.edu/departments/id/
Founded: 1972
Description: The International Development Program uses a multidisciplinary approach in research and teaching to analyze issues of underdevelopment in Asia, Africa, and Latin America. It draws on faculty from the fields of geography (including GIS), environmental studies, management, anthropology, economics, politics, and history, and serves both U.S. and international students. (B.A. and M.A. degree offered)
Degrees: B.A., M.A.
Contact(s):
International Development Program, Director: DR. BARBARA P. THOMAS-SLAYTER; E-mail: BSLAYTER@clarku.edu
Center for Community-Based Development, Director: DR. RICHARD FORD; E-mail: RFORD@clarku.edu

NORTHEASTERN UNIVERSITY

Biology Department
414 Mugar Life Sciences, Boston, MA 02115
Phone: 617-373-2260; Fax: 617-373-3724; Web site: www.dac.neu.edu/biology/
Contact(s):
Marine Science Center/Marine Biology, (B.S., M.S., Ph.D.), Director: DR. JOSEPH AYERS, East Point, Nahant, MA 01908; Phone: 617-581-7370; E-mail: lobster@neu.edu
Salt Marsh Ecology, (B.S., M.S., Ph.D.), Contact: DR. ERNEST RUBER; Phone: 617-373-4044; E-mail: e.ruber@nunet.neu.edu
Vertebrate Systematics and Ecology (B.S., M.S., Ph.D.): DR. GWILYM S. JONES; Phone: 617-373-2851; E-mail: g.jones@nunet.neu.edu

SCHOOL FOR FIELD STUDIES (Boston University)

16 Broadway, Beverly, MA 01915-4499
Phone: 1-800-989-4435; Fax: 978-927-5127; E-mail: admissions@fieldstudies.org; Web site: www.fieldstudies.org
Founded: 1980
Description: The mission of The School for Field Studies is to provide highly motivated young people from the U.S. and abroad with an excellent practical education in environmental studies, in order that tomorrow's leaders may become more environmentally literate/aware as well as make immediate and future contributions toward the sustainable management of natural resources.
Contact(s):
President: TERRY L. ANDREAS

TUFTS UNIVERSITY

Department of Civil and Environmental Engineering
Anderson Hall, Medford, MA 02155
Phone: 617-627-3211; Fax: 617-627-3994; Web site: www.tufts.edu/
Contact(s):
Environmental Engineering, Contact: LINFIELD C. BROWN; Phone: 617-627-2273; E-mail: lbrown1@tufts.edu
Environmental Geotechnology and Geotechnical Engineering, Contact: CHRISTOPHER SWAN; Phone: 617-627-2212; E-mail: cswan@emerald.tufts.edu
Water Resources, Contact: RICHARD M. VOGEL; Phone: 617-627-4260; E-mail: rvogel@tufts.edu
Hazardous Material Management, Contact: JOHN DURANT; Phone: 617-627-5489; E-mail: jdurant@emerald.tufts.edu

UNIVERSITY OF MASSACHUSETTS

Amherst, MA 01003-4210
Phone: 413-545-2665; Web site: www.umass.edu/
Contact(s):
Department of Natural Resources Conservation, Head: DR. WILLIAM C. MCCOMB
Environmental Sciences, Program Director: DR. GUY R. LANZA; Phone: 413-545-3747
U.S. Forest Service Cooperative Wildlife Research Unit, Leader: DR. RICHARD M. DEGRAAF; Phone: 413-545-0357
U.S. Geological Survey, Massachusetts Cooperative Fish and Wildlife Research Unit, Assistant Leader: DR. MARTHA MATHER; Phone: 413-545-4895
U.S. National Oceanic and Atmospheric Administration Cooperative Education and Researh Program, Director: DR. KEVIN FRIEDLAND; Phone: 413-545-2842

Urban Harbors Institute
100 Morrissey Blvd., Boston, MA 02125-3393
Phone: 617-287-5570; Fax: 617-287-5575; E-mail: urbharbors@umbsky.cc.edu; Web site: www.umb.edu/
Founded: 1989
Description: The Urban Harbors Institute was founded as a center for the study of harbor, coastal and ocean issues. It conducts multidisciplinary research on the policy and management issues affecting the coastal area, with emphasis on the urban waterfront. It also promotes linkages between scientists, government, academic, and business communities to improve decision-making. The institute publishes research, sponsors seminars, conferences, and public forums to disseminate and exchange information.
Contact(s):
Director: RICHARD F. DELANEY
Program Contact: MADELINE WALSH; E-mail: walsh@umbsky.cc.umb.edu

WILLIAMS COLLEGE

Center for Environmental Studies Program
Box 632, Williamstown, MA 01267
Phone: 413-597-2346; Web site: www.williams.edu/
Founded: 1967
Description: The Center for Environmental Studies offers an integrated undergraduate program of studies to liberal arts students in combination with their major discipline. The Center also administers the 2,400 acre Hopkins Memorial Forest, a research and educational facility, as well as the Environmental Science Laboratory and the Matt Cole Memorial Library.
Contact(s):
Director: HENRY W. ART
Hopkins Memorial Forest Manager: ANDREW T. JONES
Program Assistant: RACHEL J. LOUIS

MICHIGAN

CENTRAL MICHIGAN UNIVERSITY
Mt. Pleasant, MI 48859
Web site: www.cmich.edu/
Contact(s):
Conservation Biology (B.S., M.S.), Contact: DR. MICHAEL HAMAS; Phone: 517-774-3185
Fisheries, (B.S., M.S), Contact: DR. DOUGLAS PETERSON; Phone: 517-774-3531
Water Resources (B.S., M.S.), Contact: DR. SCOTT MCNAUGHT; Phone: 517-774-1335
Wildlife, (B.S., M.S.), Contact: DR. JOHN N. KRULL; Phone: 517-774-3412

EASTERN MICHIGAN UNIVERSITY
Ypsilanti, MI 48197
Web site: www.emich.edu/
Contact(s):
Geography and Geology, (B.S., M.S.), Head: MICHAEL KASENOW, 203 Strong Hall, EMU, Ypsilanti, MI 48197; Phone: 734-487-0218; E-mail: geo_kasenow@online.emich.edu
Biology, (B.S., M.S.), Head (Interim): DR. ROBERT NEELY, 316 Mark Jefferson, EMU, Ypsilanti, MI 48197; Phone: 734-487-4242; E-mail: bio_neely@online.emich.edu
Conservation Resource Use, Contact: DR. CATHERINE BACH; Phone: 734-487-0212; E-mail: bio_bach@online.emich.edu
Kresge Environmental Education Center, Director: BEN CZINSKI, 2816 Fish Lake Rd., Lapeer, MI 48446; Phone: 810-667-2350; E-mail: bio_czinski@online.emich.edu

FERRIS STATE UNIVERSITY

College of Allied Health Sciences
200 Ferris Dr., Big Rapids, MI 49307-2740
Phone: 231-591-2313; Fax: 231-591-3788; Web site: www.ferris.edu/htmls/colleges/alliedhe/
Founded: 1964
Description: Educational institution offering B.S. in industrial and environmental health management with options in general environmental health, hazardous materials management, industrial hygiene, and industrial safety.
Degrees: B.S.
Contact(s):
Health Management Department, Head: ELLEN HANELINE; Phone: 231-591-2313; E-mail: Ellen_J_Haneline@ferris.edu

LAKE SUPERIOR STATE UNIVERSITY

School of Natural Sciences
650 W. Easterday Ave, Sault Ste. Marie, MI 49783
Fax: 906-635-2266; Web site: www.lssu.edu
Description: Degrees offered in Biological science, conservation law enforcement, environmental chemistry, environmental science, fisheries/wildlife management and natural resources technology (A.D.).
Degrees: A.D., B.A., B.S.
Contact(s):
Chemistry and Environmental Science, Chair: DR. DAVID MYTON; Phone: 906-635-2431; E-mail: dmyton@gw.lssu.edu
Biology, Chair: DR. BARBARA EVANS; Phone: 906-635-2164; E-mail: bevans@lakers.lssu.edu

MICHIGAN STATE UNIVERSITY

College of Agriculture and Natural Resources
323 Natural Resources Bldg., East Lansing, MI 48824-1222
Phone: 517-355-3421; Fax: 517-353-8994; E-mail: fridgenc@pilot.msu.edu; Web site: www.canr.msu.edu/
Contact(s):
Forestry, (B.S., M.S., Ph.D.), Chairperson: DR. DANIEL E. KEATHLEY; Phone: 517-355-0093; Fax: 517-432-1143; E-mail: keathley@msu.edu
Fisheries and Wildlife, (B.S., M.S., Ph.D.), Chair (Acting): DR. THOMAS COON; Phone: 517-355-4478; Fax: 517-432-1699
Department of Resources Development, (B.S., M.S., Ph.D.), Chair: DR. CYNTHIA FRIDGEN; Phone: 517-355-3421; Fax: 517-353-8994; E-mail: fridgenc@pilot.msu.edu
Park and Recreation Resources, (B.S., M.S., Ph.D.), Chairperson: DR. JOSEPH D. FRIDGEN; Phone: 517-353-5190; Fax: 517-432-3597

MICHIGAN TECHNOLOGICAL UNIVERSITY

School of Forestry and Wood Products
1400 Townsend Dr., Houghton, MI 49931
Phone: 906-487-2454; Fax: 906-487-2915; E-mail: wefrayer@mtu.edu; Web site: forestry.mtu.edu/
Description: Undergraduate concentrations and graduate programs in forest management science, forest biology and ecology, wildlife biology and ecology, and wood science and technology.
Degrees: B.S., M.S., Ph.D.
Contact(s):
Forestry, Dean: W. E. FRAYER

NORTHERN MICHIGAN UNIVERSITY
1401 Presque Isle Ave., Marquette, MI 49855
Phone: 906-227-2700; Web site: www.nmu.edu
Contact(s):
Department of Biology, (B.A., B.S., M.S.), Head: NEIL CUMBERLIDGE, Luther S. West Science Bldg., Rm. 277, Marquette, MI 49855; Phone: 906-227-2310; Fax: 906-227-1063; E-mail: ncumberl@nmu.edu
Department of Geography, Earth Science, Conservation, and Planning, (B.A., B.S.), Head: MICHAEL J. BROADWAY, Luther S. West Science Bldg., Rm. 213, Marquette, MI 49855; Phone: 906-227-2500; Fax: 906-227-1621; E-mail: Mbroadwa@nmu.edu

EDUCATIONAL INSTITUTIONS - MINNESOTA

UNIVERSITY OF MICHIGAN

School of Natural Resources and Environment
Dana Bldg., 430 East University, Ann Arbor, MI 48109-1115
Phone: 313-764-2550; Web site: www.snre.umich.edu/
Contact(s):
Dean: DANIEL A. MAZMANIAN
Landscape Architecture, (M.L.A., B.S., M.S), Concentration Chair: DONNA ERICKSON
Resource Ecology and Management, (B.S., M.S., Ph.D.), Concentration Chair: JAMES S. DIANA
Resource Policy and Behavior, (B.S., M.S., Ph.D.), Concetration Chair: BUNYAN BRYANT

WAYNE STATE UNIVERSITY

Department of Biological Sciences
5047 Gullen Mall, Detroit, MI 48202-3917
Phone: 313-577-2873; E-mail: ccole@biosci.biology.wayne.edu; Web site: biology.biosci.wayne.edu/biology/
Description: Courses offered in such subjects as limnology, ornithology, mammalogy, biogeography, natural history of vertebrates, animal behavior, population genetics, population ecology, microbial ecology, aquatic botany, ecology, advanced ecology, and evolutionary ecology.
Degrees: B.A., B.S., M.S., Ph.D.
Contact(s):
Chairman: JACK LILIEN; Phone: 313-577-2876; E-mail: jlilien@biology.biosci.wayne.edu

WESTERN MICHIGAN UNIVERSITY

Environmental Studies Program
241 Moore Hall, Kalamazoo, MI 49008-5033
Phone: 616-387-2716; Fax: 616-387-4998; Web site: www.wmich.edu/science/docs/esp/esp.html
Description: This undergraduate interdisciplinary program provides intellectual and practical experience that provokes thought about the complex interrelationships between humans, the social and technological systems they develop, and the natural environment. The program encourages students to develop an appreciation for the many elements of planetary health and to devise creative solutions to environmental problems.
Contact(s):
Program Coordinator: MOLLY COLE; E-mail: molly.cole@wmich.edu

MINNESOTA

BEMIDJI STATE UNIVERSITY

Center for Environmental Studies
Bemidji, MN 56601
Phone: 218-755-2000; Web site: http://www.bemidji.msus.edu/
Founded: 1968
Description: The Center for Environmental Studies is a research and teaching unit directed towards understanding our physical, biological, and social environment, and preventing its deterioration. The center conducts laboratory and field studies, both internally and externally funded, and offers baccalaureate and master's degree programs.
Degrees: B.S., M.S.
Contact(s):
Director: STEVEN A. SPIGARELLI; Phone: 218-755-2910; Fax: 218-755-4107; E-mail: saspigarelli@vax1.bemidji.msus.edu

HAMLINE UNIVERSITY

Center for Global Environmental Education
1536 Hewitt Ave., St. Paul, MN 55104-1284
Phone: 651-523-2480; Fax: 651-523-2987; E-mail: cgee@hamline.edu; Web site: cgee.hamline.edu
Founded: 1990
Description: CGEE was founded to nurture greater understanding of the interconnectedness of local and global environments among educators, students, scientists, and citizens.
Contact(s):
Director: TRACY FREDIN; Phone: 651-523-3105; Fax: 651-523-2987; E-mail: tfredin@gw.hamline.edu

ST. CLOUD STATE UNIVERSITY

Environmental and Technological Studies
720 4th Ave. S., St. Cloud, MN 56301
Phone: 320-255-3235; Fax: 320-654-5122; E-mail: ets@condor.stcloudstate.edu; Web site: www.stcloudstate.edu
Description: Linking the human and natural world with programs designed to foster environmental and technological literacy and prepare students who can integrate the interconnections of science, technology, society and the environment through research and assessment.
Contact(s):
Associate Professor: MICHAEL KARIAN; Phone: 320-255-3966

UNIVERSITY OF MINNESOTA AT CROOKSTON
Crookston, MN 56716
Phone: 218-281-8129; Web site: www.crk.umn.edu
Description: Offers a broadly-oriented natural resource major which prepares students for entry-level resource management positions. Practical and field instruction in integrated land management is emphasized leading to a B.S. degree in Natural Resource Management, Park Management, Soil and Water Technology or Natural Resources Law Enforcement.
Degrees: B.S.
Contact(s):
Head: DANIEL SVEDARSKY

UNIVERSITY OF MINNESOTA AT ST. PAUL

College of Natural Resources
2003 Upper Buford Cir., St. Paul, MN 55108
Phone: 612-624-1234; Fax: 612-624-8701; E-mail: info@cnr.umn.edu; Web site: www.cnr.umn.edu/
Founded: 1903
Description: The mission of the College of Natural Resources is to foster a quality environment by contributing to the management, protection, and sustainable use of our natural resources through teaching, research, and outreach.
Degrees: B.S., M.S., Ph.D., D.F.
Contact(s):
Dean of College of Natural Resources: DR. ALFRED D. SULLIVAN
Cooperative Park Studies Unit, Senior Research Associate: DR. DAVE W. LIME; Phone: 612-624-2250
Department of Ecology, Evolution and Behavior, Head: DR. ROBERT W. STERNER, 1987 Upper Buford Cir., St. Paul, MN 55108; Phone: 612-625-6790
Department of Fisheries and Wildlife: DR. IRA R. ADELMAN; Phone: 612-624-3600
Department of Forest Resources, Head: DR. ALAN EK; Phone: 612-624-3400
Department of Wood and Paper Science, Head: DR. JOSEPH G. MASSEY; Phone: 612-624-5200
Conservation Biology Program, Director: DR. DAVID SMITH
Conservation Biology Program, Director: FRANCESCA CUTHBERT; Phone: 612-624-1756
Center for Environmental Learning and Leadership: DR. DORTHY ANDERSON; Phone: 612-624-2721
Center for Natural Resources Policy and Management, Head/Water Resources Science Graduate Program: DR. JIM PERRY; Phone: 612-624-9796
Forestry Library, Librarian: JEAN ALBRECHT, B-50 Natural Resources Administration Bldg., 2003 Upper Buford Cir., St. Paul, MN 55108; Phone: 612-624-3222
Institute for Social Economic and Ecological Sustainability (ISEES): DR. ANNE KAPUSCINSKI; Phone: 612-624-7719

Institute for Sustainable Natural Resource Management: BARBARA COFFIN; Phone: 612-624-4986

Minnesota Cooperative Fish and Wildlife Research Unit, Leader: DR. DAVID E. ANDERSEN; Phone: 612-624-3421

Outreach and Extension, Associate Dean: DR. STEVEN B. DALEYLAURSEN; Phone: 612-624-9298

Student Services Office, Director: BILL K. GANZLIN; Phone: 612-624-6768

Water Resources Center, Director: DR. PATRICK BREZONIK; Phone: 612-624-9282

MISSISSIPPI

MISSISSIPPI STATE UNIVERSITY

College of Forest Resources
Box 9820, Mississippi State, MS 39762
Phone: 662-325-8530; Fax: 601-325-8726; Web site: www.cfr.msstate.edu/

Contact(s):
Dean and Forest and Wildlife Research Center Director: DR. WARREN S. THOMPSON, Box 9680, Mississippi State, 39762; Phone: 601-325-2952; E-mail: wthompson@cfr.msstate.edu

Associate Dean: DR. BOB KARR, Box 9680, Mississippi State, 39762 ; Phone: 601-325-2793; E-mail: bkarr@cfr.msstate.edu

Forestry, (B.S., M.S.), Head: DR. DOUGLAS P. RICHARDS, Box 9681, Mississippi State, 39762; Phone: 601-325-2949; E-mail: drichards@cfr.msstate.edu

Forest Products, (B.S., M.S.), Head: DR. CYNTHIA D. WEST; Phone: 601-325-2119

Wildlife and Fisheries, (B.S., M.S.), Interim Head: DR. BRUCE D. LEOPOLD, MS 39762, Mississippi State, 39762; Phone: 601-325-2619; E-mail: bleopold@cfr.msstate.edu

UNIVERSITY OF SOUTHERN MISSISSIPPI
Hattiesburg, MS 39406
Phone: 601-266-4748; Web site: www.usm.edu/

Contact(s):
Aquatic Biology, (M.S., Ph.D.) and Aquatic Ecology: DR. DAVID BECKETT

Fisheries Biology, (M.S., Ph.D.) and Aquatic Ecology: DR. STEPHEN T. ROSS

Marine Biology, (M.S., Ph.D.), Contact: DR. PATRICIA BIESIOT

Recreation Planning and Resources Management, (B.S., M.S.), Contact: DR. L. CHARLES BURCHELL

Resource Management and Environmental Planning, (B.S., M.S., Ph.D.), Contact: DR. GLENN MATLACK

Zoology, (M.S., Ph.D.), Contact: DR. SUSAN WALLS

MISSOURI

UNIVERSITY OF MISSOURI

The School of Natural Resources
103 Anheuser-Busch Natural Resources Bldg., Columbia, MO 65211-7220
Phone: 573-882-6446; Web site: www.missouri.edu/

Contact(s):
Director: DR. ALBERT R. VOGT

Cooperative Fish and Wildlife Research Unit, Leader: DR. CHARLES RABENI, 302 Anheuser-Busch Natural Resources Bldg., ; Phone: 573-882-3524

Fisheries and Wildlife Department, (B.S., M.S., Ph.D.), Chair: DR. JACK JONES, 302 Anheuser-Busch Natural Resources Bldg., ; Phone: 573-882-3436

Forestry Department, (B.S., M.S., Ph.D.), Chair: DR. CARL SETTERGREN, 302 Anheuser-Busch Natural Resources Bldg., ; Phone: 573-882-2627

Parks, Recreation and Tourism Department, (B.S., M.S.), Chair and Graduate Director: DR. C. RANDALL VESSELL, 105 Anheuser-Busch Natural Resources Bldg.; Phone: 573-882-7088

Soil and Atmospheric Sciences Department, (B.S., M.S., Ph.D.), Chair: DR. R. DAVID HAMMER, 302 Anheuser-Busch Natural Resources Bldg.; Phone: 573-882-6301

WASHINGTON UNIVERSITY

Biology Department
1 Brookings Dr., Campus Box 1137, St. Louis, MO 63110
Phone: 314-935-6860; Fax: 314-935-4432; Web site: www.wustl.edu/

Description: The laboratory is active in applying modern genetic techniques to problems in conservation biology such as conservation forensics (e.g., DNA fingerprinting of elephant tusks), systematics (identifying taxa that are significant evolutionary units), inter- and intraspefic hybridizataion, and genetic management of captive, translocated, and natural populations.

Contact(s):
Department of Biology, Head: DR. RALPH QUATRANO; Phone: 314-935-6868; E-mail: rsq@wustl.edu

MONTANA

MONTANA STATE UNIVERSITY

Department of Biology
Room 310, Lewis Hall, Bozeman, MT 59717
Phone: 406-994-4548; Fax: 406-994-3190; E-mail: biology@montana.edu; Web site: www.montana.edu/wwwbi/

Description: Biology Department offers B.S. in Biology, Biology Teaching, Biomedical Sciences or Fish and Wildlife Management and M.S. and Ph.D. programs with a concentration in Ecology, Conservation Biology, Plant Biology or Neurobiology.

Contact(s):
Department of Biology, Head: DR. ERNEST R. VYSE; E-mail: evyse@montana.edu

Fish and Wildlife Management Program, Coordinator: DR. LYNN R. IRBY; Phone: 406-994-3252; E-mail: ubili@gemini.oscs.montana.edu

College of Agriculture
202 Linfield Hall, P.O. Box 172860, Bozeman, MT 59717
Phone: 406-994-5744; Fax: 406-994-6579; E-mail: agweb@montana.edu; Web site: www.montana.edu/agriculture/College/

Contact(s):
Department of Land Resources and Environmental Sciences,(B.S., M.S., Ph.D.), Head: DR. JEFFERY S. JACOBSON, Leon Johnson Hall, P.O. Box 173120, Bozeman, MT 59717; Phone: 406-994-7060; Fax: 406-994-3933; E-mail: jefj@montana.edu, general information: kathyj@montana.edu

Department of Plant Sciences and Horticulture, Head: DR. NORMAN WEEDEN, 119 AgBioScience Building, Bozeman, MT 59717-3150; Phone: 406-994-4832; Fax: 406-994-7600; E-mail: NWeeden@Montana.edu, general information: Plantsciences@montana.edu

UNIVERSITY OF MONTANA

School of Forestry
Missoula, MT 59812-0576
Phone: 406-243-5521; Fax: 406-243-4845; Web site: www.forestry.umt.edu/

Degrees: Forest Resource Management B.S., M.S., M.E.M., Ph.D.; Recreation Management B.S., M.S., Ph.D.; Range Management B.S., M.S., Ph.D.; Resource Conservation B.S., M.S., Ph.D.; Wildlife Biology B.S., M.S., Ph.D.

Contact(s):
School of Forestry Dean: DR. PERRY J. BROWN; Phone: 406-243-5522

Bolle Center for People and Forests: DR. JAMES BURCHFIELD; Phone: 406-243-6650

EDUCATIONAL INSTITUTIONS - NEBRASKA

Boone and Crockett Wildlife Conservation Program: DR. JACK WARD THOMAS; Phone: 406-243-5566
Inland Northwest Growth and Yield Cooperative: DR. KELSEY MILNER; Phone: 406-243-6653
Institute for Tourism and Recreation Research: DR. NORMA NICKERSON; Phone: 406-243-5686
Mission Oriented Research Program: DR. ROBERT PFISTER; Phone: 406-243-6582
Montana Forest and Conservation Experiment Station, Director: DR. PERRY J. BROWN; Phone: 406-243-5522
Numerical Terradynamic Simulation Group: DR. STEVEN RUNNING; Phone: 406-243-6311
Quantitative Services Group: DR. HANS R. ZUURING; Phone: 406-243-6465
Riparian/Wetland Research Program: DR. PAUL HANSEN; Phone: 406-243-2050
Wilderness Institute: DR. WAYNE FREIMUND; Phone: 406-243-5184
Wildlife Biology Program, Director: DR. DANIEL H. PLETSCHER; Phone: 406-243-5272

School of Law
Missoula, MT 59812-6552
Phone: 406-243-4311; Web site: www.umt.edu/law/
Contact(s):
Dean: E. EDWIN ECK

NEBRASKA

UNIVERSITY OF NEBRASKA

School of Natural Resource Science
303 Biochemistry Hall, Box 830758, Lincoln, NE 68583-0758
Phone: 402-472-9873; Fax: 402-472-4915; E-mail: dsmith3@unl.edu; Web site: www.ianr.unl.edu/snrs/
Contact(s):
Fisheries and Wildlife: RONALD M CASE, 204 Natural Resources Hall, Lincoln, NE 68583; Phone: 402-472-6825; E-mail: rcase@unlinfo.unl.edu
Environmental Studies/Natural Resources: STEVE WALLER, 103 Agriculture Hall, Lincoln, NE 68583-0702; Phone: 402-472-2201
Natural Resource and Environmental Economics: ROSALEE SWARTZ, 204B H.C. Filley Hall, Lincoln, NE 68583-0922; Phone: 402-472-5234; E-mail: agec017@unlvm.unl.edu
Soil Science: BOB SORENSEN, 152 Keim Hall, Lincoln, NE 68583-0914; Phone: 402-472-1507
Range Science: LOWELL MOSER, 352 Keim Hall, Lincoln, NE 68583-0914; Phone: 402-472-1558
Graduate Programs: MARCY TINTERA; Phone: 402-472-6622; E-mail: fofw031@unlvm.unl.edu

NEVADA

UNIVERSITY OF NEVADA AT LAS VEGAS

Environmental Science Program
4505 Maryland Parkway, Box 454030, Las Vegas, NV 89154-4030
Web site: www.unlv.edu/Other_Programs/Environmental_Studies/
Contact(s):
Graduate Program Information: E-mail: neill@ccmail.nevada.edu
Environmental Studies Department, (B.S., B.A., M.S., Ph.D.): DR. JAMES DEACON; E-mail: jdeacon@ccmail.nevada.edu

Water Resources Program
4505 Maryland Pkwy., Las Vegas, NV 89154-4029
Phone: 702-895-3553
Description: The Water Resources Management Graduate Program at the University of Nevada is an interdisciplinary environmental program. The curriculum includes studies in water quality and quantity; surface water and groundwater; and water law, regulation, and management. Offers environmental programs at graduate level.
Contact(s):
Director: DR. DAVID KREAMER; E-mail: kreamerd@nevada.edu

UNIVERSITY OF NEVADA AT RENO
1000 Valley Rd., Reno, NV 89512
Phone: 775-784-4020; Fax: 702-784-4583; Web site: www.unr.edu/
Contact(s):
Conservation Biology, (B.S., M.S., Ph.D.): DR. JOEL BERGER
Department of Environmental and Resource Sciences, Chairman: DR. WATKINS W. MILLER
Environmental Science, (B.S., M.S.): DR. GLENN MILLER
Interdisciplinary Hydrology, (B.S., M.S., Ph.D.): DR. JOHN C. GUITJENS
Natural Resource Management, (B.S., M.S.): DR. DALE JOHNSON
Natural Resource Management, (B.S.,M.S.): DR. ROGER WALKER

NEW HAMPSHIRE

ANTIOCH NEW ENGLAND GRADUATE SCHOOL
40 Avon St., Keene, NH 03431
Phone: 603-357-6265; Fax: 603-357-0718; E-mail: admissions@antiochne.edu; Web site: www.antiochne.edu
Description: Antioch New England Graduate School offers professional training for effective, reflective, environmental leadership. The M.S. Degree in Environmental Studies is a field-oriented program that stresses professional preparation in environmental biology, teaching, communication, administration, policy, and environmental education. Biology and general science teacher certifications are available. The M.S. degree in Resource Management and Administration integrates environmental science, natural resources policy, and administration. The Ph.D Program in Environmental Studies offers an interdisciplinary approach to research in Environmental Education and Environmental Policy.
Contact(s):
Environmental Studies, (Ed.D.): MITCHELL THOMASHOW
Environmental Studies, (M.S.): THOMAS WESSELS
Resource Management, (M.S.): MICHAEL SIMPSON
Resource Management, (M.S.): JOY ACKERMAN

DARTMOUTH COLLEGE

Environmental Studies Program
6182 Steele Hall, Rm. 306, Hanover, NH 03755-3577
Phone: 603-646-2838; Web site:
Founded: 1970
Description: Interdisciplinary academic program providing students with the opportunity to assess the seriousness and complexity of environmental problems and to understand how to search for solutions. Faculty research interests include biological conservation, ecosystem ecology, air pollution, economics, and international environmental governance.
Contact(s):
Chairman: ROSS A. VIRGINIA

KEENE STATE COLLEGE
229 Main St., Keene, NH 03435
Phone: 603-352-1909; Web site: www.keene.edu/
Founded: 1909
Description: A multipurpose, predominantly undergraduate college with a central focus in the liberal arts and sciences. B.S. in Environmental Studies with options in Environmental Policy and Environmental Science or specialization in Environmental Biology, Environmental Chemistry or Environmental Geology
Contact(s):
Program Coordinator: TIM ALLEN; Phone: 603-358-2571; E-mail: tallen@keene.edu

UNIVERSITY OF NEW HAMPSHIRE
Durham, NH 03824
Phone: 603-862-1020; Web site: www.unh.edu/
Contact(s):
Department of Natural Resources, James Hall, Chair: DR. THEODORE E. HOWARD
Environmental Conservation, (B.S.), Program Coordinator: DR. ROBERT T. ECKERT
Forestry, (B.S.) Program Coordinator: DR. RICHARD WEYRICK
Natural Resources, (M.S.), Program Coordinator: DR. RUSSELL CONGALTON
Natural Resources, (Ph.D.), Program Coordinator: DR. JOHN ABER
Soil Science, (B.S.), Program Coordinator: DR. ROBERT HARTER
Water Resources Management, (B.S.), Program Coordinator: DR. WILLIAM MCDOWELL
Wildlife Ecology, (B.S.), Program Coordinator: DR. PETER PEKINS

NEW JERSEY

MONTCLAIR STATE UNIVERSITY
One Normal Ave., Upper Montclair, NJ 07043
Phone: 201-893-5258; Web site: csam.montclair.edu/
Contact(s):
Biology, Chair: DR. BONNIE K. LUSTIGMAN; E-mail: lustigman@saturn.montclair.edu
Earth and Environmental Science, Professor: DR. ROBERT W. TAYLOR; E-mail: taylorr@saturn.montclair.edu

RICHARD STOCKTON COLLEGE
PO Box 195, Pomona, NJ 08240
Phone: 609) 652-4546; Fax: 609-748-5515; E-mail: iaprod573f@vax003.stockton.edu); Web site: www.stockton.edu/
Founded: 1969
Contact(s):
Biology, (B.A., B.S.), Program Coordinator: DR. RICHARD H. COLBY; Phone: 609-652-4355; E-mail: fac131@pollux.stockton.edu
Chemistry, (B.A., B.S.), Program Coordinator: DR. ROGERS BARLATT; E-mail: Barlattr@stockton.edu
Dean and Energy Studies Certificate Program Coordinator: DR. LYNN STILES
Environmental Studies and Geology, (B.A., B.S.), Program Coordinator: DR. MICHAEL D. GELLER; Phone: 609-652-4578
Marine Science, (B.A., B.S.), Program Coordinator: DR. MATTHEW LANDAU; Phone: 609-652-4578; E-mail: mlandau@stockton.edu

ROWAN UNIVERSITY

Pinelands Institute for Natural and Environmental Studies
120-13 Whitesbog Rd., Browns Mills, NJ 08015
Phone: 609-893-1765; Web site: www.rowan.edu/
Contact(s):
Director: GARY PATTERSON
Program Coordinator: MARIA PETER

RUTGERS UNIVERSITY
P.O. Box 231, New Brunswick, NJ 08903
Phone: 201-932-9336; Web site: www.rutgers.edu/
Contact(s):
Environmental Sciences Department, Chair: DR. RONI AVISSAR, 14 College Farm Road, New Brunswick, NJ 08901-8551; Phone: 732-932-9185; Fax: 732-932-8644; E-mail: chair@envsci.rutgers.edu, general information: des@envsci.rutgers.edu
Undergraduate Program Coordinator: DR. ROBERT TATE; Phone: 732-932-9810; E-mail: tate@envsci.rutgers.edu
Graduate Program Director: DR. PETER STROM; Phone: 732-932-8078; E-mail: strom@envsci.rutgers.edu
Agricultural, Food, and Resource Economics Department, Chair: DR. ADESOJI ADELAJA, Cook Office Bldg., 55 Dudley Road, New Brunswick, NJ 08901; Phone: 732-932-9155; Fax: 732-932-8887; E-mail: adelaja@aesop.rutgers.edu
Undergraduate Director: DR. MAURICE HARTLEY; E-mail: hartley@aesop.rutgers.edu
Graduate Director: DR. PETER PARKS; E-mail: parks@aesop.rutgers.edu

NEW MEXICO

NEW MEXICO STATE UNIVERSITY

Department of Fishery and Wildlife Sciences
P.O. Box 30003, Department 4901, Las Cruces, NM 88003
Phone: 505-646-1544; Fax: 505-646-1281; E-mail: natres@nmsu.edu; Web site: leopold.nmsu.edu
Degrees: B.S., M.S.
Contact(s):
Department of Animal and Range Science, (B.S., M.S., Ph.D.), Department Head: DR. BOBBY J. RANKIN; Phone: 505-646-2514

Department of Animal and Range Sciences
Box 30003, Las Cruces, NM 88003
Phone: 1-800-400-1807; Web site: www.nmsu.edu/~dars/
Description: In the Department of Animal and Range Sciences, students can major in animal or range science. The Department also offers pre-veterinary studies. In addition to undergraduate degrees, the Department offers graduate degrees at the Master of Science and Doctor of Philosophy levels. The M.S. or Ph.D. in Animal Science can emphasize nutrition or physiology, and the M.S. or Ph.D. in Range Science students have the option to study in areas including, but not exclusive to, range ecology and watershed management.
Degrees: B.S., M.S., Ph.D.
Contact(s):
Department Head: DR. BOBBY J. RANKIN; Phone: 505-646-5279; E-mail: brankin@nmsu.edu

NEW YORK

ALFRED UNIVERSITY

Division of Environmental Studies
Saxon Dr., Alfred, NY 14802-1205
Phone: 607-871-2634; Fax: 607-871-2697; E-mail: ens@bigvax.alfred.edu; Web site: las.alfred.edu/~ens/
Founded: 1971
Description: The program offers an undergraduate degree in multidisciplinary environmental studies in a liberal arts setting. Students can focus on either natural or social sciences, and many take a second major in biology, geology, political science, economics, etc. The project-oriented program is supervised by fifteen faculty members from different disciplines.
Contact(s):
Chair: DR. MICHELE M. HLUCHY; Phone: 607-871-2838; E-mail: fhluchy@bigvax.alfred.edu

BARD COLLEGE

Graduate School in Environmental Studies
Annandale-on-Hudson, NY 12504-5000
Phone: 914-758-7073; Fax: 914-758-7636; E-mail: gsesinfo@bard.edu; Web site: www.bard.edu
Description: Bard College offers an intensive graduate degree program leading to a Master of Science in Environmental Studies. Students develop an understanding of key ecological and natural concepts and the ability to become effective environmental professionals. Coursework is offered during the summer in two four-week sessions. Students can complete degree requirements, including course and thesis, in three summers. In the year 2001, Bard is launching a master's degree program during the academic

EDUCATIONAL INSTITUTIONS - NEW YORK

year as part of it's new Center for Environmental Policy (CEP). The center is dedicated to teaching, research and public service.

CITY UNIVERSITY OF NEW YORK

College of Staten Island

Environmental Science Masters Program
  6S-310, 2800 Victory Blvd., Staten Island, NY Phone: 718-982-3921; Fax: 718-982-3923; E-mail: oppenheimer@postbox.csi.cuny.edu; Web site: www.library.csi.cuny.edu/dept/as/ces/escpgm.htm
Description: The interdisciplinary masters program in Environmental Science includes ecology, geology, chemistry, environmental engineering, and computer modeling. The objective of the masters program is to expose the students to the scientific principles underlying environmental problems. Research is carried out on wetlands, park planning, air, water and soil pollution, waste disposal, aquatic toxics, environmental epidemiology and risk analysis. Courses are offered in the evenings for full and part time students.
Degrees: M.A.
Contact(s):
Director: DR. JOHN R. OPPENHEIMER

Hunter College
  695 Park Ave., New York, NY 10021
  Web site: www.hunter.cuny.edu
Contact(s):
Department of Geography, affiliated with City University of New York Ph.D program in Earth and Environmental Science, Chairman: PROF. CHARLES A. HEATWOLE; Phone: 212-772-5265; Fax: 212-772-5268
Wexler Library Chief Librarian: LOUISE SHERBY; Phone: 212-772-4146; Fax: 212-772-4142
Energy and Environmental Policy Studies Program: PROF. JEFFERY P. OSLEEB; Phone: 212-772-5413; Fax: 212-772-5268

CORNELL UNIVERSITY

Department of Natural Resources
  118 Fernow Hall, Ithaca, NY 14853
  Phone: 607-255-2821; Fax: 607-255-0349; Web site: www.cals.cornell.edu/
Contact(s):
Chair: DR. JAMES P. LASSOIE; E-mail: jpl4@cornell.edu
Co-Leader, Human Dimensions Research Unit: DR. BARBARA KNUTH; Phone: 607-255-2822; E-mail: bak3@cornell.edu
Cornell Biological Field Station: DR. EDWARD L. MILLS, 900 Shackelton Point Rd., Bridgeport, NY 13030-9750; Phone: 315-633-9243; Fax: 315-633-2358; E-mail: elm5@cornell.edu
Environmental Ethics: DR. RICHARD A. BAER; Phone: 607-255-7797; E-mail: rab12@cornell.edu
Fisheries and Aquatic Sciences: DR. CHARLES C. KRUEGER; Phone: 607-255-2838; Fax: 607-255-1895; E-mail: cck4@cornell.edu
Forest Science: DR. TIMOTHY J. FAHEY; Phone: 607-255-5470; E-mail: tjf5@cornell.edu
Undergraduate Program, Assistant: MARIAN HOVENCAMP; Phone: 607-255-2809; E-mail: mth6@cornell.edu
Plant and Wildlife Inventory: DR. CHARLES R. SMITH; Phone: 607-255-3219; E-mail: crs6@cornell.edu

POLYTECHNIC UNIVERSITY OF NEW YORK

Civil and Environmental Engineering Department
  333 Jay St., Brooklyn, NY 11201
  Phone: 718-260-3220; Web site: www.poly.edu
Description: The Department is engaged in teaching and research in several areas of environmental science and engineering. Masters degrees with environmental focus are offered in civil engineering, environmental engineering, and environmental health science. The Ph.D. is also offered.
Contact(s):
President: DAVID CHANG

RENSSELAER POLYTECHNIC INSTITUTE

Department of Earth and Environmental Sciences
  Jonsson-Rowland Science Center, Rm. 1C25, Troy, NY 12180-3590
  Phone: 518-276-6476; Fax: 518-276-6680; E-mail: ees@rpi.edu; Web site: www.rpi.edu/dept/geo/
Degrees: B.S., M.S.
Contact(s):
Chair: FRANK SPEAR; E-mail: spearf@rpi.edu
Environmental Science, Director: CARL N. McDANIEL

Environmental Management and Policy
  Troy, NY 12180-3590
  Phone: 518-276-6565; E-mail: emap@rpi.edu; Web site: www.rpi.edu/
Description: Rensselaer's EMP program educates students at the masters of science level to undertake a professional role in companies, governmental agencies, and other organizations dealing with environmental and energy matters from a base of technical and managerial knowledge and understanding.
Contact(s):
Director: DR. BRUCE W. PIASECKI

ST. LAWRENCE UNIVERSITY

Environmental Studies Program
  23 Romoda Dr., Canton, NY 13617
  Phone: 315-229-5814; Web site: it.stlawu.edu/~x0rthum/
Founded: 1856
Description: St. Lawrence University is a liberal arts and sciences institution. The institution offers one of the oldest environmental studies programs in the nation. The university is committed to environmentally responsible management practices and comprehensive outdoor education programs.
Degrees: B.S., B.A.
Contact(s):
Environmental Studies Program Director: CAROLYN E. JOHNS; Phone: 315-229-5840; E-mail: cjoh@music.stlawu.edu

STATE UNIVERSITY OF NEW YORK AT CORTLAND
  P.O. Box 2000, Cortland, NY 13045
  Phone: 607-753-2011; Web site: www.cortland.edu/
Contact(s):
Environmental and Outdooor Education, Coordinator: DR. THOMAS PASQUARELLO; Phone: 607-753-5772
Environmental Geology and Environmental Sciences (Concentration for majors in Biology, Geology, Chemistry and Physics), Coordnator: DR. CHRISTOPHER CIRMO; Phone: 607-753-2924; E-mail: cirmoc@cortland.edu

STATE UNIVERSITY OF NEW YORK AT STONY BROOK

Marine Sciences Research Center
  Stony Brook, NY 11794
  Phone: 516-632-8700; Fax: 516-632-8915; Web site: www.msrc.sunysb.edu/
Description: University-wide center to develop marine and atmospheric research, instructional programs and facilities for the State University of New York. Ongoing research projects are directed toward coastal oceanographic processes, marine environmental problems and management, atmospheric sciences and resources management. Among the Center's organized units are the Living marine Resources Institute, the Waste Reduction and Management Institute, the Coastal Ocean Action Strategies Institute, the Institute for Urban Ports and Harbors, the Institute for Planetary and Terrestrial Atmospheres and the Flax Pond Laboratory. Publications of the center include Technical Report Series, Working Report Series; Special Report Series; and a newsletter.

Contact(s):
Dean and Director: MARVIN A. GELLER; Phone: 516-632-8701; E-mail: mgeller@notes.cc.sunysb.edu
Associate Dean: NICHOLAS S. FISHER; Phone: 516-632-8649; E-mail: nfisher@notes.cc.sunysb.edu
Associate Director: W. M. WISE; Phone: 516-632-8656
Graduate Programs: GLENN LOPEZ; Phone: 516-632-8660; E-mail: glopez@notes.cc.sunysb.edu

STATE UNIVERSITY OF NEW YORK COLLEGE OF ENVIRONMENTAL SCIENCE AND FORESTRY

One Forestry Dr., Syracuse, NY 13210-2778
Phone: 315-470-6500; Fax: 315-470-6977; E-mail: esfinfo@esf.edu; graduate information: esfgrad@esf.edu; Web site: www.esf.edu

Founded: 1911
Description: Research has been a hallmark of ESF since its inception. Recent wildlife studies have aimed toward reintroducing lynx and moose to the Adirondack Park; application of molecular biology techniques to identify migrant bird populations; restoration of muskellunge and sturgeon in the St. Lawrence River system; analysis of Flamingo population dynamics in Mexico; tailoring black cherry clones for fast growth and straight limbs; researching willow plantations as a source of biomass energy; cooperating with NASA to analyze polarized-light photographs of Earth; and detailing the effects of acid precipitation on forest ecosystems.
Degrees: A.A.S., B.S., B.L.A., M.S., M.L.A., Ph.D.
Contact(s):
Adirondack Ecological Center, Director: WILLIAM F. PORTER; Phone: 315-470-6798
Cellulose Research Institute, Acting Director: ANATOLE SARKO; Phone: 315-470-6855
Cooperative Park Studies Unit, Director: H. BRIAN UNDERWOOD; Phone: 315-470-6820
Empire State Paper Research Institute, Director: HANNU MAKKONEN; Phone: 315-470-6900
Environmental Institute, Randof G. Park, Director: RICHARD C. SMARDON; Phone: 315-470-6636
Great Lakes Research Consortium, Co-Director: RICHARD C. SMARDON; Phone: 315-470-6816
N.C. Brown Laboratory for Ultrastructure Studies, Director: ROBERT B. HANNA; Phone: 315-470-6880
Polymer Research Institute, Director: ISRAEL CABASSO; Phone: 315-470-4767
Roosevelt Wildlife Station, Director: NEIL H. RINGLER; Phone: 315-470-6770
U.S. Forest Service Unit, Deputy Project Leader: WAYNE ZIPPERER; Phone: 315-448-3201
Faculty of Chemistry, (B.S., M.S., Ph.D.), Chair: JOHN HASSETT; Phone: 315-470-6855
Faculty of Construction Management and Wood Products Engineering, (B.S., M.S., Ph.D.), Chair: GEORGE H. KYANKA; Phone: 315-470-6880
Faculty of Environmental and Forest Biology, (B.S., M.S., Ph.D.), Chair: NEIL H. RINGLER; Phone: 315-470-6743
Faculty of Environmental Resources and Forest Engineering, (B.S., M.S., Ph.D.), Chair: ROBERT H. BROCK JR.; Phone: 315-470-6633
Faculty of Environmental Studies, (B.S., M.S., Ph.D.), Chair: RICHARD C. SMARDON; Phone: 315-470-6636
Faculty of Forestry, (B.S., M.S., Ph.D.), Chair: WILLIAM R. BENTLEY; Phone: 315-470-6536
Faculty of Landscape Architecture, (B.L.A., M.L.A.), Chair: RICHARD HAWKS; Phone: 315-470-6544
Faculty of Paper Science and Engineering, (B.S., M.S., Ph.D.), Chair: LELAND SCHROEDER; Phone: 315-470-6502
Forest Technician Program, (A.A.S.), Director: CHRISTOPHER WESTBROOK; Phone: 315-848-2566

NORTH CAROLINA

APPALACHIAN STATE UNIVERSITY
Boone, NC 28608
Phone: 828-262-2179; Web site: www.appstate.edu
Contact(s):
Department of Biology, Chairperson: DR. VICKI MARTIN; Phone: 828-262-6923; Fax: 828-262-2127; E-mail: martinvj@appstate.edu
Recreation Management Program, Director: DR. KIM SIEGENTHALER; Phone: 828-262-2540
Sustainable Development Minor, Director: DR. JEFF BOYER, 426 Sanford Hall, BOONE, NC 28608; E-mail: boyerjc@appstate.edu

DUKE UNIVERSITY

Nicholas School of the Environment
Box 90328, Durham, NC 27708-0328
Phone: 919-613-8000; Fax: 919-6848741; Web site: www.env.duke.edu
Degrees: M.F., M.E.M., Ph.D., M.S., M.A.
Contact(s):
Dean: DR. NORMAN L. CHRISTENSEN JR.; E-mail: normc@duke.edu
Division of Earth and Ocean Sciences, Chair: DR. JEFFREY A. KARSON; E-mail: jkarson@geo.duke.edu
Coastal Environmental Management and Duke University Marine Laboratory, Director: DR. MICHAEL K. ORBACH; E-mail: mko@mail.duke.edu
Environmental Toxicology: DR. RICHARD T. DI GIULIO; E-mail: richd@duke.edu
Forest Resource Management and Resource Ecology, Economics and Policy: DR. DANIEL D. RICHTER; E-mail: drichter@duke.edu
Water Resources: DR. KENNETH H. RECKHOW; E-mail: reckhow@duke.edu

Organization for Tropical Studies
P.O. Box 90381, Durham, NC 27708-0381
Phone: 919-684-5774; Fax: 919-684-5661; E-mail: nao@acpub.duke.edu; Web site: www.ots.duke.edu/
Founded: 1988
Description: The goal of the Center is to contribute to the alleviation of the world environmental crisis, particularly as it affects the developing countries of the tropics. The CTC works toward this goal through interdisciplinary research into issues of environmental policy relevance, training in environmental management, and dissemination of information.
Contact(s):
Academic Director: NORA BYMUM; E-mail: elb@duke.edu

NORTH CAROLINA STATE UNIVERSITY

College of Agriculture and Life Sciences
Box 7642, Raleigh, NC 27695-7642
Web site: www.cals.ncsu.edu/
Contact(s):
Biological and Agricultural Engineering, (B.S., M.S., M.B.A.E., Ph.D.), Head: DR. JAMES H. YOUNG; Phone: 919-515-6717; Fax: 919-515-7760; E-mail: jim_young@ncsu.edu
Botany, (B.S., M.S., M.L.S., Ph.D.), Head: DR. ERIC DAVIES; Phone: 919-515-2727; E-mail: eric_davies@ncsu.edu
Director of Undergraduate Biology Programs: DR. ROBERT BECKERMAN; Phone: 919-515-9048; E-mail: robert_beckmann@ncsu.edu
Ecology, (M.S.); Environmental Sciences, (B.S.), Coordinator: DR. SAMUEL C. MOZLEY; Phone: 919-515-1981
Soil Science, (B.S., M.S., M.N.R.A., Ph.D.), Head: DR. JOHN L. HAVLIN; Phone: 919-515-2655; E-mail: john_havlin@ncsu.edu
Toxicology, (M.S., M.T., Ph.D.), Head: DR. GARY W. WINSTON; Phone: 919-515-4377; Fax: 919-515-7169; E-mail: gary_winston@ncsu.edu

EDUCATIONAL INSTITUTIONS - NORTH DAKOTA

Zoology, (B.S., M.S., M.L.S., M.W.B., Ph.D.), Head: DR. THURMAN L. GROVE; Phone: 919-515-2741; Fax: 919-515-5327; E-mail: thurman_grove@ncsu.edu

UNIVERSITY OF NORTH CAROLINA AT ASHEVILLE

Environmental Studies Department
CPO 2330, One University Heights, Asheville, NC 28804-8511
Phone: 828-251-6441; Fax: 828-251-6041; E-mail: drobbins@unca.edu; Web site: www.unca.edu/envr_studies/
Founded: 1983
Description: The undergraduate environmental studies curriculum offers degrees options in ecology, pollution control, earth science and natural resource management. There is a required internship program and numerous research opportunities in an environmentally diverse region in areas such as ecology, wetlands restoration, lead and pesticide contamination and waste analysis.
Contact(s):
Contact: DR. RICHARD P. MAAS

UNIVERSITY OF NORTH CAROLINA AT CHAPEL HILL

Chapel Hill, NC 27599-7400
Phone: 919-966-1171; Web site: www.unc.edu
Contact(s):
Environmental Sciences and Engineering, Chairman: DR. WILLIAM H. GLAZE, Environmental Science and Engineering, 105 Miller Hall, Chapel Hill, NC 27599; Phone: 919-966-9917; E-mail: bill_glaze@unc.edu
Air, Radiation, and Industrial Hygiene: DR. RICHARD KAMENS, Environmental Science and Engineering, 115 Rosenau Hall, Chapel Hill, NC 27599; Phone: 919-966-5452; E-mail: kamens@unc.edu
Aquatic and Atmospheric Sciences: DR. RUSSELL F. CHRISTMAN, Environmental Science and Engineering, 164 Rosenau Hall, Chapel Hill, NC 27599; Phone: 919-966-1683; E-mail: russ_christman@unc.edu
Water Resources Engineering: DR. PHILIP C. SINGER, Environmental Science and Engineering, 110 Rosenau Hall, Chapel Hill, NC 27599; Phone: 919-962-3865; E-mail: phil_singer@unc.edu
Environmental Health Sciences: DR. LOUISE M. BALL, Environmental Science and Engineering, 4114E McGavran-Greenberg Hall, Chapel Hill, NC 27599; Phone: 919-966-7306; E-mail: lmball@sph.unc.edu
Institute for Environmental Studies, Director: DR. FREDERIC PFAENDER, Environmental Science and Engineering, 157 Rosenau Hall, Chapel Hill, NC 27599; Phone: 919-966-3842; E-mail: fred_pfaender@unc.edu
Ecology, (M.S., Ph.D.), Chairman: DR. SETH R. REICE, 244 Wilson Hall, Chapel Hill, NC 27599; Phone: 919-962-1375; E-mail: sreice@biomass.bio.unc.edu
Marine Sciences, Chairman: CHRISTOPHER MARTENS, 12-4A Venable Hall, Chapel Hill, NC 27599; Phone: 919-962-0152; E-mail: martens@marine.unc.edu

Environmental Resource Program
CB# 1105 Miller Hall, Chapel Hill, NC 27599
Phone: 919-966-7754; Fax: 919-966-9920
Founded: 1985
Description: The ERP was established to link the resources of the University with the citizens of North Carolina. Since its inception, the ERP has provided information, technical assistance, and training to citizen groups, local governments and school teachers, and has facilitated collaborative decisionmaking about environmental issues. The ERP has five main program areas: environmental education, community outreach and education, collaborative and policy research, Carolina Health and Environment Community Center (CHECC) website and sustainable development.
Contact(s):
Director: DR. FRANCES LYNN
Associate Director: DR. MELVA FARGER OKUN
Research Coordinator: KATHLEEN GRAY

NORTH DAKOTA

NORTH DAKOTA STATE UNIVERSITY
Stevens Hall, Fargo, ND 58105
Phone: 701-231-7087; Fax: 701-231-7149; E-mail: bleier@plains.nodak.edu; Web site: www.ndsu.nodak.edu/zoology/
Description: Wildlife and Fisheries Biology Option in Zoology
Degrees: B.A., B.S., M.S., Ph.D.
Contact(s):
Department Chair: DR. W. J. BLEIER

UNIVERSITY OF NORTH DAKOTA

Biology Department
Grand Forks, ND 58202-9019
Phone: 701-777-2621
Contact(s):
Fishery Research Unit, (B.S., M.S., Ph.D.), Leader: DR. STEVEN KELSCH; E-mail: kelsch@plains.nodak.edu
Wildlife, (B.S., M.S., Ph.D.), Coordinator: DR. RICHARD D. CRAWFORD; E-mail: rcrawfor@badlands.nodak.edu

OHIO

ANTIOCH COLLEGE
Yellow Springs, OH 45387
Phone: 937-767-7331; Fax: 937-767-6323; Web site: www.antioch-college.edu/
Contact(s):
Biology: JILL YAGER; E-mail: jyager@antioch-college.edu
Chemistry: KABUIKA BUTAMINA; E-mail: kbutamina@antioch-college.edu
Geology: PETER TOWNSEND; E-mail: ptownsend@antioch-college.edu
Physics and Solar Energy/Alternative Technology: CHARLES TAYLOR; E-mail: ctaylor@antioch-college.edu

BOWLING GREEN STATE UNIVERSITY
Center for Environmental Programs, Bowling Green, OH 43403
Phone: 419-372-8207; E-mail: rthibau@bgnet.bgsu.edu; Web site: www.bgsu.edu/
Description: Offer undergraduate environmental degree programs in Arts and Sciences, Environmental Policy, and Analysis/Environmental Science)/Health and Human Services.
Contact(s):
Director: ROGER E. THIBAULT; E-mail: rthibau@bgnet.bgsu.edu

HOCKING COLLEGE

School of Natural Resources
3301 Hocking Parkway, Nelsonville, OH 45764
Phone: 740-753-3591; Fax: 740-753-2021; E-mail: admissions@hocking.edu; Web site: www.hocking.edu
Founded: 1969
Description: The mission of our School of Natural Resources is to prepare individuals for careers as technicians in the natural resources profession. Emphasis is placed on basic theory, developing a sustained postive work ethic and the practical application of the development of the competencies required for entry-level positions in recreation, wildlife, forestry, timber harvesting/tree care and a wide variety of land management technology fields.
Degrees: A.D.
Contact(s):
Dean: RUSSELL K. TIPPETT; Phone: 740-753-3591 ext 2317; E-mail: tippet_r@hocking.edu
Fisheries, Biologist: LLOYD D. WRIGHT
Wildlife, Biologist: ALBERT LECOUNT

MIAMI UNIVERSITY
Boyd Hall, Oxford, OH 45056

Phone: 513-529-5811; Fax: 513-529-5814; Web site: www.muohio.edu/
Contact(s):
Architecture, (A.B., M.A.), Chairman: ROBERT A. BENSON
Botany, (A.B., B.S., M.A., Ph.D.), Chairman: DAVID A. FRANCKO
Chemistry, (A.B., B.S., M.S., Ph.D.), Chairman: MICHAEL NOVAK
Geography, (A.B., M.A.) Chairman: JAMES M. RUBENSTEIN
Institute of Environmental Sciences, (M.En.), Director: GENE E. WILLEKE; E-mail: willekge@muohio.edu
Zoology, (A.B., B.S., M.A., M.S., Ph.D.), Chairman: DOUGLAS B. MEIKLE

OBERLIN COLLEGE

Environmental Studies Program
Rice Hall, 10 North Professor Street, Oberlin, OH 44074-1095
Phone: 216-775-8747; Fax: 216-775-8124; E-mail: bev.burgess@oberlin.edu; Web site: www.oberlin.edu/~envs/
Description: An interdisciplinary program that includes 30+ courses across ten departments. Students are required to do significant academic work that spans the sciences, social sciences, and the humanities. The program offers significant off-campus opportunities for students through a Watershed Education Program, a local initiative in sustainable agriculture, and work with the city on energy and development issues.
Contact(s):
Director: DAVID ORR

OHIO STATE UNIVERSITY

School of Natural Resources
2021 Coffey Rd., Columbus, OH 43210
Phone: 614-292-2265
Contact(s):
Cooperative Wildlife and Fishery Research Unit, (B.S., M.S., Ph.D.), Leader: DR. DEANA STOUDER
Cooperative Wildlife and Fishery Research, Assistant Leader: MARTIN STAPANIAN
Department of Landscape Architecture, (B.L.A., M.L.A.):
Department of Zoology, College of Biological Fisheries Biology, (B.S., M.S., Ph.D.): DR. PETER PAPPAS
Interim Director, (B.S., M.S., Ph.D.): DR. GARY W. MULLINS

SHAWNEE STATE UNIVERSITY

Department of Natural Sciences
940 Second St., Portsmouth, OH 45662
Phone: 740-354-3205; Fax: 740-355-2416; Web site: www.shawnee.edu/
Description: B.S. in Natural Science field with minor or certificate in Environmental Studies
Contact(s):
Environmental Certificate Advisor: DR. JEFFREY BAUER; Phone: 740-355-2421; Fax: 740-355-2416; E-mail: jbauer@shawnee.edu

UNIVERSITY OF AKRON

Center for Environmental Studies
215 Crouse Hall, Akron, OH 44325-4102
Phone: 330-972-7991; Fax: 330-972-7611; E-mail: AFOOS@uakron.edu; Web site: www.uakron.edu/envstudies/
Contact(s):
Director (Interim): DR. ANNABELLE FOOS

OKLAHOMA

OKLAHOMA STATE UNIVERSITY
Stillwater, OK 74078
Phone: 405-744-5000; Web site: pio.okstate.edu/
Contact(s):
Cooperative Fish and Wildlife Research Unit, Leader: DR. DAVID M. LESLIE JR., 404 Life Sciences West, ; Phone: 405-744-6342
Department of Botany, (B.S., M.S., Ph.D.), Head: DR. JAMES D. OWNBY; Phone: 405-744-5559
Department of Forestry, (B.S., M.S.), Head: DR. EDWIN L. MILLER; Phone: 405-744-5437
Department of Wildlife/Fisheries/Ecology/Zoology, (B.S., M.S., Ph.D.), Head: DR. JAMES H. SHAW; Phone: 405-744-5555
Environmental Science, (M.S., Ph.D), Program Coordinator: DR. EDWARD T. KNOBBE; Phone: 405-744-9229
Range Management, (B.S., M.S., Ph.D.), Program Coordinator: DR. DAVID M. ENGLE, 477 Ag Hall, Stillwater, OK 74078; Phone: 405-744-6410

OREGON

LEWIS AND CLARK COLLEGE

Law School
0615 S.W. Palatine Hill Rd., Portland, OR 97219
Web site: www.lclark.edu
Description: Strong environmental law training program (Environmental Law Certificate at J.D. level and specialized LL.M. in Environmental and Natural Resources Law); publish journal of Environmental Law; research program in Natural Resources Law Institute (newsletter: NRLI News); conferences and workshops through continuing education program; internships in natural resources; and environmental clinical opportunities.

College of Arts and Sciences
0615 S.W. Palatine Hill Road, Portland, OR 97219
Web site: www.lclark.edu
Description: Undergraduate major in Environmental Studies. Interdisciplinary with participating faculty from all divisions of the college.
Contact(s):
Director of Environmental Studies: DR. EVAN T. WILLIAMS; Phone: 503-768-7699; Fax: 503-768-7369; E-mail: etw@lclark.edu

OREGON STATE UNIVERSITY
Corvallis, OR 97331
Phone: 503-737-0123; Web site: www.osu.orst.edu
Contact(s):
Fisheries and Wildlife, (B.S., M.S., Ph.D.), Head of Wildlife: DR. ERIK K. FRITZELL
Forestry and Forest Recreation, (B.S., M.S., Ph.D.), Acting Dean: DR. BART THIELGES
Rangeland Resources, (B.S., M.S., Ph.D), Head: DR. WILLIAM KRUEGER
Sustainable Forestry Program, Leader of Forestry: DR. STEVEN R. RADOSEVICH
Center for Analysis of Environmental Change, Director: DR. MICHAEL H. UNSWORTH
Consortium on Social Values of Natural Resources, Coordinator of Outdoor Recreation: DR. GEORGE H. STANKEY
Cooperative Fishery and Wildlife Research Unit, Leader: DR. ROBERT G. ANTHONY
Cooperative Fishery and Wildlife Research Unit, Leader: DR. CARL B. SCHRECK

PORTLAND STATE UNIVERSITY

Environmental Sciences and Resources
P.O. Box 751, Portland, OR 97207-0751
Phone: 503-725-4980; Fax: 503-725-3888; E-mail: envir@pdx.edu; Web site: www.esr.pdx.edu
Description: The focus of the program is research on the problems of the environment and resources. The program offers Ph.D. degrees in cooperation with the departments of biology, chemistry, civil engineering, economics, geography, geology, and physics. Master programs include M.S., M.E.M. (Master of Environmental Management), and M.S.T (Master of Science in Teaching).

EDUCATIONAL INSTITUTIONS - PENNSYLVANIA

Bachelor's programs (B.A., B.S.) include tracks in environmental science and environmental policy and management.
Degrees: B.A., B.S., M.S., M.E.M., M.S.T., Ph.D.
Contact(s):
Director: JAMES R. PRATT

SOUTHERN OREGON UNIVERSITY

Environmental Education Program
Ashland, OR 97520
Phone: 541-552-6797; E-mail: janes@sou.edu, jessup@sou.edu; Web site: www.sou.edu/
Founded: 1990
Description: This graduate program grants a Master of Science degree, and provides hands-on learning experiences in conservation biology, interpretive practices, field interpretation, and field studies in southwestern Oregon and elsewhere in the state for students committed to careers in environmental education. Studies are also required in biology and related disciplines of choice to complete the program.
Degrees: M.S.
Contact(s):
Contact: DR. STEWART JANES

TREASURE VALLEY COMMUNITY COLLEGE

Department of Natural Resources
650 College Blvd., Ontario, OR 97914
Phone: 503-889-6493; Web site: www.tvcc.cc.or.us/NatRes/
Description: Offers Associate of Applied Science focusing on Forestry, range management or wildland fire management.
Contact(s):
Professor: JOHN RUSSELL; E-mail: John_Russell@mailman.tvcc.cc.or.us

UNIVERSITY OF OREGON

School of Law
Eugene, OR 97403
Phone: 541-346-3111; Web site: www.law.uoregon.edu/home.html
Contact(s):
Dean: MAURICE J. HOLLAND; E-mail: mholland@law.uoregon.edu
Western Natural Resource Law Clinic, Director: MICHAEL D. AXLINE; E-mail: maxline@law.uoregon.edu

PENNSYLVANIA

CALIFORNIA UNIVERSITY OF PENNSYLVANIA

Biological and Environmental Sciences Department
250 University Ave., California, PA 15419-1394
Phone: 724-938-4200; Fax: 724-938-5743; Web site: www.cup.edu
Contact(s):
Biology, (B.S., M.S.Option), Chair: DR. DAVID BOEHM; Phone: 724-938-4200
Environmental Studies Program Coordinator: DR. ALLAN MILLER; Phone: 724-938-4462; E-mail: miller@cup.edu
Environmental Conservation (Option): DR. THOMAS MOON; Phone: 724-938-4204; E-mail: moon@cup.edu
Environmental Pollution Control (Option): DR. WILLIAM KIMMEL; Phone: 724-938-4213; E-mail: kimmel@cup.edu
Wildlife Biology (Option): DR. WILLIAM GUILIANO; Phone: 724-938-4215; E-mail: giuliano@cup.edu

DREXEL UNIVERSITY

School of Environmental Science, Engineering, and Policy
32nd and Chestnut St., Philadelphia, PA 19104
Phone: 215-895-2266; E-mail: sesep@drexel.edu; Web site: www.drexel.edu/sesep/
Description: Environmental Engineering and Science undergraduate and graduate study is offered by the School of Environmental Science, Engineering, and Policy at Drexel University. Over 25 faculty participate in SESEP programs. Degrees available with specializations in air pollution, environmental assessment, environmental biotechnology, environmental chemistry, environmental health, hazardous and solid waste, subsurface contaminant hydrology, water and wastewater treatment, water resources, environmental risk management and ecology. Programs are offered on a full or part-time basis.
Degrees: B.S., M.S., Ph.D.
Contact(s):
Associate Director: CLAIRE WELTY; Phone: 215-895-2281; E-mail: weltyc@drexel.edu
Director: MICHAEL A. GEALT; Phone: 215-895-2266; E-mail: gealt@drexel.edu

PENNSYLVANIA STATE UNIVERSITY

School of Forest Resources
113 Ferguson Bldg., University Park, PA 16802
Phone: 814-863-7093; Fax: 814-865-3725; Web site: www.sfr.cas.psu.edu
Contact(s):
Director: DR. LARRY A. NIELSEN; Phone: 814-863-7093; E-mail: lan3@psu.edu
Ecology, (M.S., M.E.P.C., M.Eng), Chair: DR. HERSCHEL ELLIOT, 208 Ag Sciences and Industries Bldg.; Phone: 814-865-6942
Environmental Resource Management, (B.S.), Coordinator: DR. LAMARTING HOOD, 208 Ag Sciences and Industries Bldg.; Phone: 814-865-6942
Fisheries and Wildlife Cooperative Research Unit, Leader: DR. ROBERT F. CARLINE, 112A Merkle Bldg.; Phone: 814-865-4511; E-mail: f7u@psu.edu
Forest Resources, (B.S., M.S., Ph.D.), Professor: DR. KIM C. STEINER, 213 Ferguson Bldg.; Phone: 814-865-9351; E-mail: kcs@psu.edu
Wildlife and Fisheries, (B.S., M.S., Ph.D.), Contact: DR. JAY R. STAUFFER JR., 2C Ferguson Bldg.; Phone: 814-865-0645; E-mail: vc5@psu.edu
Wood Products, (B.S., M.S., Ph.D.), Professor: DR. PETER LABOSKY, 309 Forest Resources Laboratory; Phone: 814-865-7423; E-mail: p21@psu.edu

SLIPPERY ROCK UNIVERSITY

Slippery Rock, PA 16057
Phone: 724-738-0512; Web site: www.sru.edu/
Contact(s):
Environmental Education, (B.S., M.Ed.), Coordinator: DR. DAN DZIUBEK; Phone: 724-738-2958
Environmental Science, (B.S.), Program Coordinator: DR. MICHAEL STAPLETON; Phone: 724-738-2495
Environmental Studies, (B.S.), Coordinator: DR. BEVERLY BUCHERT; Phone: 724-738-2389
Institute for the Environment Executive, Committee Chair: DR. DAN DZIUBEK; Phone: 724-738-2958
Park and Resource Management, (B.S., M.S.), Chairman: BRUCE BOLIVER; Phone: 724-738-2068
Pennsylvania Center for Environmental Education, Director: DR. PAULETTE JOHNSON; Phone: 724-738-4555
Sustainable Systems, (M.S.), Coordinator: DR. KAREN KAINER; Phone: 724-738-2622

UNIVERSITY OF PENNSYLVANIA

Graduate School of Fine Arts
119 Meyerson Hall, 210 S. 34th St., Philadelphia, PA 19104-6311
Phone: 215-898-6591; Fax: 215-573-3770; E-mail: jdhunt@pobox.upenn.edu; Web site: www.upenn.edu/gsfa/larp
Degrees: M.L.A., M.R.P.
Contact(s):
Department of Landscape Architecture and Regional Planning, Chairman: JOHN DIXON HUNT

UNIVERSITY OF PITTSBURGH

Biology Department
A234 Langley Hall, Fifth and Ruskin Aves., Pittsburgh, PA 15260
Phone: 412-624-4266; Fax: 412-624-4759; Web site: www.pitt.edu/~biology/

Description: The Biology Department offers a major in Ecology and Evolution, designed to provide the student with a selection of courses covering various aspects of these two fields of biology. The Department operates the Pymatuning Laboratory of Ecology with laboratories and teaching facilities in Northwestern Pennsylvania, offering year-round research opportunities and summer courses.
Degrees: B.S., M.S., Ph.D.
Contact(s):
Department of Biological Sciences, Chairman: DR. DAVID BURGESS; Phone: 412-624-4350; Fax: 412-624-4759
Ecology and Pymatuning Laboratory of Ecology, Director: DR. STEPHEN J. TONSOR, 13142 Hartstown Rd., Linesville, PA 16424; Phone: 814-683-5813; Fax: 814-683-2302; E-mail: tonsor@pitt.edu or ple@toolcity.net

Department of Geology and Planetary Science
321 Engineering Hall, Pittsburgh, PA 15260
Phone: 412-624-8780; Fax: 412-624-3914; E-mail: geology@pop.pitt.edu; Web site: www.geology.pitt.edu

Description: B.A. in Environmental Science based on a strong interdisciplinary framework of courses, co-requisites and a variety of electives in natural and social sciences. B.S. in Environmental Geology also offered.
Degrees: B.A., B.S.
Contact(s):
Advisor: DR. HARDOLD B. ROLLINS
Advisory Board Chair: JAMES V. MAHER

Graduate School of Public Health, Department of Environmental and Occupational Health
260 Kappa Dr., PA 15238
Phone: 412-967-6500; Fax: 412-624-1020; Web site: server1.ceoh.pitt.edu/

Description: The mission of the Department of Environmental and Occupational Health is to reduce the health risks associated with exposure to chemical, physical, and biological agents found in industry and nature. Three degrees and a specialty certificate in risk assessment are offered.
Degrees: M.S., M.P.H. and Ph.D.
Contact(s):
Chairperson: HERBERT S. ROSENKRANZ

WIDENER UNIVERSITY

Department of Civil Engineering
One University Pl., Chester, PA 19013-5792
Phone: 610-499-4042; Fax: 610-499-4059; E-mail: solid.waste@widener.edu; Web site: www.widener.edu/solid.waste

Description: The Department of Civil Engineering at Widener University offers undergraduate and graduate degrees which include courses in water resources, solid waste management, and environmental engineering. Continuing education seminars are taught in solid waste management and recycling. Research and development performed in solid waste and recycling. The department publishes The Journal of Solid Waste Technology and Management.
Contact(s):
Chair: DR. CHARLES L. BARTHOLOMEW
Waste Management Programs, Coordinator: DR. RONALD L. MERSKY
Wolfgram Memorial Library: THERESEA TABORSKY, One University Pl., Chester, PA 19013-5792; Phone: 610-499-4087

WILKES UNIVERSITY

Geo-Environmental Sciences/Engineering Department
Stark Learning Center 441, Wilkes Barre, PA 18766
Phone: 570-408-4610; E-mail: dougalas@wilkes.edu; Web site: wilkes1.wilkes.edu/%7Egse/

Description: The department offers two degree programs. The Environmental Engineering curriculum highlights a balance among the basic areas of water and waste-water engineering, water quality measurement, air pollution measurement and control technology, as well as the more recent demands in the areas of hazardous and solid waste management. The Earth and Environmental Science curriculum requires a concentration of departmental electives that can be used to create an area of specialization such as geology or environmental science.
Contact(s):
Chairman: DALE A. BRUNS; Phone: 717-408-4610; Fax: 717-408-1003; E-mail: dbruns@wilkes.edu

RHODE ISLAND

BROWN UNIVERSITY

Center for Environmental Studies
Box 1943, Providence, RI 02912
Phone: 401-863-3449; Fax: 401-863-3503; Web site: www.brown.edu/departments/environmental_studies

Founded: 1978
Description: The Center for Environmental Studies offers three interdisciplinary degrees (A.B., Sc.B., and M.A.) in environmental problem-solving; coordinates and facilitates environmental efforts within the university community; and collaborates with both state government agencies and community-based groups on projects to improve environmental quality for all Rhode Island residents. All programs aim to integrate teaching, scholarship, and service.
Contact(s):
Director: HAROLD R. WARD; E-mail: Harold_Ward@Brown.Edu
Administrative Manager: PATTI CATON; E-mail: Patti_Caton@Brown.Edu

RHODE ISLAND SCHOOL OF DESIGN

Department of Landscape Architecture
Two College St., Providence, RI 02903
Phone: 401-454-6282; E-mail: ldardept@risd.edu; Web site: www.risd.edu

Description: Graduates depart RISD with the necessary training to work from an informed position, with an environmental ethic, a personal philosophy, their interpretive abilities honed and with creative vision.
Degrees: B.F.A., Dipl. Arch., MLA
Contact(s):
Department Head: DEREK BRADFORD
Undergraduate Department Head: ELIZABETH DEAN HERMANN
Landscape Architecture, (B.L.A., M.L.A.), Head: COLGATE SEARLE

ROGER WILLIAMS UNIVERSITY

One Old Ferry Rd., Bristol, RI 02809
Phone: 401-254-3087; Fax: 401-254-3310; E-mail: mgould@acc.rwu.edu; Web site: www.rwu.edu/

Founded: 1969
Contact(s):
Director, Center for Economic and Environmental Development: MARK GOULD; Phone: 401-254-3087; E-mail: mdg@alpha.rwu.edu

UNIVERSITY OF RHODE ISLAND

Department of Natural Resources Science
Kingston, RI 02881
Phone: 401-874-2495; Fax: 401-874-4561; E-mail: NRS@etal.uri.edu; Web site: www.edc.uri.edu/nrs/

EDUCATIONAL INSTITUTIONS - SOUTH CAROLINA

Description: The teaching mission of the Department of Natural Resources Science is to help students acquire the technical knowledge and practical skills needed to understand and wisely manage natural and disturbed ecosystems and their basic components: soil, water, air and biota. The research mission of the department is to use hypothesis-based methods of scientific inquiry toward development of applicable solutions to environmental problems.
Degrees: B.S., M.S., Ph.D.
Contact(s):
Wildlife Biology and Management/Environmental Science and Management/ Water Resources and Soil Science, Chairman: DR. THOMAS P. HUISBAND

Graduate School of Oceanography and Coastal Resources Center
URI Bay Campus, South Ferry Rd., Narragansett, RI 02882-1197
Phone: 401-874-6246; Fax: 401-874-6889; E-mail: student_info@gso.uri.edu; Web site: www.gso.uri.edu/
Founded: 1972
Description: Dedicated to advancing coastal ecosystem management, nationally and internationally.
Contact(s):
CRC Communications Director: CHIP YOUNG; Phone: 401-874-6630; E-mail: cyoung@gso.uri.edu
Director, RI Sea Grant College Program: SCOTT W. NIXON
Director, URI/NOAA CMER: LAWERNCE J. BUCKLEY

SOUTH CAROLINA

CLEMSON UNIVERSITY

Aquaculture, Fisheries and Wildlife
G08 Lehotsky Hall, Clemson, SC 29634
Phone: 864-656-3117; Web site: http://virtual.clemson.edu/groups/AFW/
Description: The curriculum leading to a B.S. degree provides a solid foundation in basic and applied science, social science, and communication skills. Emphasis areas permit students to broaden their technical knowledge in their chosen career path. Those interested in pursuing a graduate degree program in aquaculture, fisheries, or wildlife management shoud have sound undergraduate training in the biological or related sciences. Programs of study are designed to emphasize relationships between wild animals and their changing environments, or production of aquatic organisms. The graduate program in wildlife biology is accredited by the Southeastern Section of the Wildlife Society.
Degrees: B.S., M.S., Ph.D.
Contact(s):
Chair: DR. JOHN R. SWEENEY

School of the Environment
P.O. Box 340919, Clemson, SC 29634-0919
Phone: 864-656-5567; Fax: 864-656-0672; E-mail: mshrly@clemson.edu; Web site: www.ces.clemson.edu/ees/schintro.html
Description: Made up of the Environmental Engineering and Science Department, the Environmental Toxicology Department, and the Geological Sciences Department administers university-wide Environmental Science and Policy Program.
Contact(s):
Chair of Environmental Engineering and Science; Director of the School of the Environment; Program Coordinator of the Environmental Science and Policy Program: DR. ALAN W. ELZERMAN; Phone: 864-656-5568; E-mail: awlzrmn@clemson.edu
Environmental Toxicology, (M.S., Ph.D.), Chair: DR. JOHN RODGERS; Phone: 864-646-2239
Geological Science, Chair: DR. RICHARD D. WARNER, Box 341908, Clemson, SC 29634; Phone: 864-656-3438; Fax: 864-656-1041; E-mail: wrichar@clemson.edu

Student Services Coordinator: PAM FJELD; Phone: 864-656-1010; E-mail: hpamela@clemson.edu

UNIVERSITY OF SOUTH CAROLINA

Baruch Marine Field Laboratory
P.O. Box 1630, Georgetown, SC 29442
Phone: 843-546-3623; Web site: inlet.geol.sc.edu/
Contact(s):
Resident Director: DR. DENNIS M. ALLEN; Phone: 843-546-3623; E-mail: dallen@belle.baruch.sc.edu

Marine Science Program
Columbia, SC 29208
Phone: 803-777-2692; Fax: 803-777-3935; E-mail: marisci@vm.sc.edu; Web site: marine-science.sc.edu/
Description: The Marine Science Program, in the College of Science and Mathematics at the University of South Carolina, is an interdisciplinary educational program offering curricula which lead to the bachelor of science, master of science, and doctor pf philosophy degrees.
Contact(s):
Marine Science Program, (B.S., M.S., Ph.D.), Director: DR. MADYLYN FLETCHER; Phone: 803-777-5288; E-mail: fletcher@biol.sc.edu

SOUTH DAKOTA

SOUTH DAKOTA STATE UNIVERSITY

Department of Wildlife Fisheries Sciences
P.O. Box 2140B, Brookings, SD 57007-1696
Phone: 605-688-6121; Fax: 605-688-4515; E-mail: jeanne_longieliere@sdstate.edu; Web site: wfs.sdstate.edu/wfsci.htm
Description: Fish and wildlife research, education, and services with emphasis on prairie pothole ecology, fisheries management, wildlife management, and fisheries and wildlife ecology.
Contact(s):
Cooperative Fish and Wildlife Research Unit, Leader: DR. CHARLES R. BERRY
Head: DR. CHARLES G. SCALET
Wildlife and Fisheries Sciences, (B.S., M.S., Ph.D.):

TENNESSEE

MIDDLE TENNESSEE STATE UNIVERSITY

Center for Environment Education
Box 60, Murfreesboro, TN 37132
Phone: 615-898-5449; Fax: 615-898-5920; Web site: www.mtsu.edu/~biol/cee/ceehmpg.html
Description: The Center for Environment Education, an arm of the Biology Department offers a wide variety of offerings on topics related to the environment, including waste reduction and recycling. Workshops for school teachers are offered twice a semester. The center consults with teachers, youth leaders and education organizations in the areas of environmental education, curriculum, teacher training and hands-on learning.
Contact(s):
CINDI SMITH-WALTERS Ph.D.; E-mail: CsmithWA@mtsu.edu
PADGETT KELLY Ph.D.; E-mail: JPKelly@mtsu.edu

TENNESSEE TECHNOLOGICAL UNIVERSITY

Department of Biology
Box 5063, Cookeville, TN 38505
Phone: 615-372-3134; Web site: www.tntech.edu/www/acad/biol/

Contact(s):
Wildlife and Fisheries Science, (B.S., M.S.): DR. DANIEL L. COMBS; E-mail: dlcombs@tntech.edu
Environmental Science, (Ph.D.): DR. DALE ENSOR, P.O. Box 5055, Cookeville, TN 38505; Phone: 931-372-3493; E-mail: densor@tntech.edu

UNIVERSITY OF TENNESSEE AT KNOXVILLE

Department of Forestry, Wildlife and Fisheries
P.O. Box 1071, Knoxville, TN 37901-1071
Phone: 865-974-7126; Fax: 865-974-4714; E-mail: fwf@utkux.utcc.utk.edu; Web site: fwf.ag.utk.edu/
Description: Offer B.S. degree in forestry, forest management concentration, wildland recreation concentration, M.S. in forestry, Thesis and Non-Thesis Option, and B.S. and M.S. degrees in wildlife and fisheries science.
Contact(s):
Professor and Department Head: DR. GEORGE M. HOPPER; E-mail: ghopper@utk.edu
Superintendent, Forestry Experiment Station: RICHARD M. EVANS; E-mail: revans@utk.edu
Associate Department Head, Fisheries: J. LARRY WILSON; E-mail: jlwilson@utk.edu

UNIVERSITY OF TENNESSEE AT MARTIN

School of Agriculture and Human Environment
Martin, TN 38238
Phone: 901-587-7250; Web site: www.utm.edu/departments/agr/agr.shtml
Description: Offers a B.S. degree in natural resources management with concentrations in wildlife biology, environmental management, soil and water conservation, and park and recreation administration.
Degrees: B.S.
Contact(s):
Dean: DR. JIM BYFORD

UNIVERSITY OF THE SOUTH (SEWANEE)

Department of Forestry and Geology
735 University Ave., Sewanee, TN 37383
Phone: 615-598-1479; Web site: www.sewanee.edu/Forestry_Geology/ForestryGeology.html
Description: B.S. in Forestry, B.S. or B.A. in Geology or Natural Resources
Contact(s):
Chairman: PROF STEPHEN SHAVER; Phone: 931-598-1116; E-mail: sshaver@seraph1.sewanee.edu

VANDERBILT UNIVERSITY
Box 1831-Station B, Nashville, TN 37235
Phone: 615-322-2697; Web site: www.vuse.@vanderbilt.edu/ceeinfo/cee.htm
Contact(s):
Environmental Engineering, (B.E., B.S., M.E., M.S., Ph.D.), Chairman: EDWARD L. THACKSTON

TEXAS

RICE UNIVERSITY
6100 Main St., Houston, TX 77251
Phone: 713-527-8101; Web site: www.rice.edu
Contact(s):
Energy and Environmental Systems Institute, (B.A., M.E.S., M.E.E., M.S., Ph.D.), Directory: C. HERB WARD, 6100 Main St., MS 316, Houston, TX 77005; E-mail: eesi@rice.edu
Ecology and Evolutionary Biology Department, (B.S., M.A., Ph.D.), Chair: RONALD L. SASS, 6100 Main St., MS 170, Houston, TX 77005; Phone: 713-527-4919; Fax: 713-285-5232; E-mail: eeb@rice.edu or sass@ruf.rice.edu
Director of Wetland Studies, Ecology Department: FRANK M. FISHER, Houston; Phone: 713-527-5917; E-mail: fisher@rice.edu

School of Architecture
Architecture MS 50; 6100 Main Street, Houston, TX 77005
Phone: 713-527-4864; Fax: 713-285-5277; Web site: www.arch.rice.edu/
Description: Master of Architecture in Urban Design for individuals who already hold a professional degree qualifying them for registration as architects or landscape architects
Contact(s):
Dean: LARS LERUP; E-mail: lars@rice.edu

STEPHEN F. AUSTIN STATE UNIVERSITY

Arthur Temple College of Forestry
Nacogdoches, TX 75962-6109
Phone: 409-468-3301; Fax: 409-468-2489; E-mail: www.environment.sfasu.edu; Web site: www.sfasu.edu
Degrees: Ph.D., D.F.
Contact(s):
Dean: DR. R. SCOTT BEASLEY
Fire Management and Silviculture: DR. BRIAN OSWALD
Forest Eco-Physiology: DR. HANS M. WILLIAMS
Forest Economics: DR. GARY D. KRONRAD
Forest Entomology: DR. DAVID KULHAVY
Forest Hydrology: DR. MINGTEH CHANG
Forest Products: DR. EDWARD DOUGAL
Forest Recreation Management: DR. MICHAEL LEGG
Forest Resources/Wildlife Management: DR. JEFFERY P. DUGUAY
Forest Wildlife Management: DR. R. MONTAGUE WHITING
Forest Wildlife Management: DR. JAMES C. KROLL
GIS/Remote Sensing: DR. PETER SISKA
Interpretation/Conflict Resolution: DR. PAUL H. RISK
Landscape Ecology: DR. DAVID L. KULHAVY
Medicinal Plants: DR. SHIYOU LI
Remote Sensing/Mensuration: DR. DANIEL UNGER
Siviculture/Forest Ecology: DR. MICHAEL FOUNTAIN
Soil Science: DR. KENNETH FARRISH
Urban Forestry: DR. HANS M. WILLIAMS
Water Quality/Forest Hydrology: DR. R. SCOTT BEASLEY

TEXAS A&M UNIVERSITY AT COLLEGE STATION

College of Agriculture and Life Sciences
113 Administration Bldg., College Station, TX 77804-2142
Web site: coals.tamu.edu/
Contact(s):
Forest Science, (B.S., M.S., M.Agr., Ph.D.), Head: DR. TAT SMITH; Phone: 409-845-5000
Institute for Renewable Natural Resources, (B.S., M.Agr.), Director: DR. BOB BROWN; Phone: 409-845-5777
Rangeland Ecology and Management, (B.S., M.S., M.Agr., Ph.D.), Head: DR. BOB WHITSON; Phone: 409-845-5579
Recreation Parks, and Tourism Sciences, (B.S., M.S., M.Agr., Ph.D.), Head: DR. PETER A. WITT; Phone: 409-845-7324
Wildlife and Fisheries Sciences, (B.S., M.S., M.Agr., Ph.D.), Head: DR. BOB BROWN; Phone: 409-845-5777

TEXAS A&M UNIVERSITY AT COMMERCE

Department of Agriculture
Commerce, TX 75429-3011
Phone: 903-886-5350; Fax: 903-886-5990; Web site: www.TAMU-Commerce.edu/coas/agscience/index.html
Founded: 1889
Description: Educational institution offering B.S. and M.S. degrees in agricultural fields and pre-wildlife management programs.
Contact(s):
Department of Agricultural Sciences, Head and Center for Texas Rural Water Studies, Director: DR. DON CAWTHON; E-mail: Don_Cawthon@tamu-commerce.edu

EDUCATIONAL INSTITUTIONS - UTAH

Pre-Wildlife Management, Advisor: DAVID B. CRENSHAW; Phone: 903-886-5329; E-mail: David_Crenshaw@tamu-commerce.edu

TEXAS A&M UNIVERSITY AT KINGSVILLE

Caesar Kleberg Wildlife Research Institute
msc 218, Kingsville, TX 78363
Phone: 361-595-3922; Fax: 361-593-3924; Web site: ckwri.tamuk.edu/

Founded: 1981

Description: A nonprofit institute that emphasizes research on wildlife and range management in Texas. Some work also done in Mexico and Canada. Research specialties include deer, quail, waterfowl, endangered cats, and nongame wildlife.

Contact(s):
Director: DR. FRED C. BRYANT; Phone: 361-593-4025

TEXAS CHRISTIAN UNIVERSITY

Environmental Science Program
P.O. Box 298830, Fort Worth, TX 76129
Phone: 817-921-7271; Fax: 817-921-7789; Web site: www.ensc.tcu.edu/

Degrees: B.S., M.S.

Contact(s):
Director: DR. LEO NEWLAND; E-mail: L.Newland@tcu.edu

TEXAS TECH UNIVERSITY

Lubbock, TX 79409-2125
Phone: 806-742-2841; Fax: 806-742-2280; E-mail: c7wez@ttacs.ttu.edu; Web site: www.rw.ttu.edu/dept/

Contact(s):
Environmental Conservation of Natural Resources, (B.S.):
Range Management, (B.S.):
Range Science, (M.S., Ph.D.):
Wildlife and Fisheries Management, (B.S.):
Wildlife Science and Fisheries Science, (M.S., Ph.D.), Chairman: DR. PHILLIP J. ZWANK

UNIVERSITY OF HOUSTON

Cullen College of Engineering
4800 Calhoun Rd., Houston, TX 77204-4814
Phone: 713-743-4250; Fax: 713-743-4260; Web site: www.egr.uh.edu/CIVE/

Contact(s):
Environmental Engineering Program, (B.S., M.S.) Director: DR. THEODORE G. CLEVELAND; E-mail: Cleveland@UH.EDU

UNIVERSITY OF NORTH TEXAS

Institute of Applied Sciences
NT Box 310559, Denton, TX 76203
Phone: 940-565-2694; Fax: 940-565-4297; Web site: www.ias.unt.edu/

Founded: 1976

Description: An interdisciplinary unit whose primary research activities are oriented towards land and water resources. Research includes aquatic toxicology, surface and groundwater quality, archaelogy, remote sensing, geographic information systems and environmental modeling. In 1998, the institute took on an environmental outreach program that includes the Outdoor Environmental Learning Area (ODELA) and the Sky Theater. Over 200 scientists, support staff, volunteers, graduate and undergraduate students are involved in these activities.

Contact(s):
Aquatic Toxicology and Reservoir Limnology, Director: DR. WILLIAM T. WALLER; Phone: 940-565-2694
Center for Environmental Archaeology, Director: DR. REID FERRING; Phone: 940-565-2694
Center for Environmental Econmics, Director: DR. MIKE NIESWIADOMY; Phone: 940-565-2573
Center for Remote Sensing, Director: DR. SAMUEL F. ATKINSON; Phone: 940-565-2694
Center for Spatial Analysis, Director: DR. ANDY SCHOOLMASTER; Phone: 940-565-2901
Director: DR. KENNETH L DICKSON
Elm Fork Education Center, Coordinator: STEVE SPURGER; Phone: 940-565-2694
Elm Fork Education Center, Coordinator: RUDI THOMPSON; Phone: 940-565-2694
Environmental Chemistry Laboratory, Director: DR. FARIDA SALEH; Phone: 940-565-2694
Environmental Modeling Laboratory, Director: DR. MIGUEL ACEVEDO; Phone: 940-565-2091
Environmental Visualization Laboratory, Director: BRUCE HUNTER; Phone: 940-565-2694
Experimental Stream Director: DR. TOM LAPOINT; Phone: 940-565-2694
Faculty for Environmental Ethics, Coordinator: JAN DICKSON; Phone: 940-565-2727
Faculty for Environmental Philosophy, Executive Director: DR. EUGENE HARGROVE; Phone: 940-565-2266
Graduate Program in Environmental Ethics, (M.A.), Coordinator: DR. EUGENE C. HARGROVE; Phone: 940-565-2266
Graduate Program in Environmental Science, (M.S., Ph.D.), Coordinator: DR. SAMUEL F. ATKINSON; Phone: 940-565-2694
Interdisciplinary Graduate Studies, Dean: DR. SANDRA TERRELL
Planetarium Director: DR. CHRIS LITTLER; Phone: 940-565-2694
Water Research Field Station, Director: DR. JAMES H. KENNEDY; Phone: 940-565-2694
Wetlands Research, Director: DR. ROBERT DOYLE; Phone: 940-565-2694

UTAH

UTAH STATE UNIVERSITY

Berryman Institute for Wildlife Damage Management
Logan, UT 84322-5270
Phone: 435-797-2436; Web site: www.usu.edu/~cnr/fishwild/berry.htm

Founded: 1990

Description: The Jack H. Berryman Institute is a national non-profit organization centered at Utah State University. It engages in research, education, and extension activities aimed at resolving human and wildlife conflicts, enhancing the positive aspects of wildlife, and increasing human tolerance of wildlife problems.

Contact(s):
Director: DR. MICHAEL CONOVER

College of Natural Resources
5200 Old Main Hill, Logan, UT 84322-5200
Phone: 435-797-2445; Fax: 435-797-2443; E-mail: nradvise@cc.usu.edu; Web site: www.cnr.usu.edu/

Description: Forest Resources offers programs in Forest Resources and Ecology, Environmental Studies (B.S. only) and Recreation Resource Management. The Geography Department offers concentrations in many fields including Environmental Education, River Processes and Rural Development/Land Use Planning.

Degrees: B.S., M.S., Ph.D.

Contact(s):
Fisheries and Wildlife Department, Head: RAYMOND D. DUESER; Phone: 435-797-2459; Fax: 435-797-1871; E-mail: dueser@cc.usu.edu or fishnwlf@cc.usu.edu
Conservation Biology Program, Coordinator: GARY E. BELOVSKY; Phone: 435-797-2597; E-mail: belovsky@cc.usu.edu
Department of Forest Resources, Head: TERRY L. SHARIK; Phone: 435-797-3219; Fax: 435-797-4040; E-mail: TLSharik@cc.usu.edu or forestry@cc.usu.edu
Natural Resource Policy Institute, Director: JOANNA ENDTER-WADA

Department of Rangeland Resources, Head: JOHN MALECHEK; Phone: 435-797-2471; E-mail: malechek@cc.usu.edu or rangesci@cc.usu.edu

USU Ecology Center, Director (Acting): MARTYN CALDWELL; Phone: 435-797-2555; E-mail: mmc@cc.usu.edu or ecol@cc.usu.edu

Department of Geography and Earth Resources, Head (Acting): TED J. ALSOP; Phone: 435-797-1790; Fax: 435-797-4048; E-mail: tjalsop@cc.usu.edu

Geography Department M.S. Program, contact: DERRICK J. THOM; Phone: 435-797-1292; E-mail: djthom@cc.usu.edu

VERMONT

JOHNSON STATE COLLEGE
337 College Hill, Johnson, VT 05656-9464
E-mail: jscapply@badger.jsc.vsc.edu; Web site: www.jsc.vsc.edu/
Degrees: B.A. and B.S. in Biology; B.S. Environmental Studies; B.A. Outdoor Education
Contact(s):
Biology: DR. ROBERT GENTER
Ecology: DR. JOHN WRAZEN
Environmental Science and Natural Resources: DR. MARGARET OTTUM
Outdoor Education: DR. KAREN UHLENDORF
Green Chemistry: DR. MARTIN WALKER
Babcock Nature Preserve, Director: DR. JOHN WRAZEN

STERLING COLLEGE
Attn: Director of Admissions, P.O. Box 72, Craftsbury Common, VT 05827-0072
Phone: 802-586-7711; Fax: 802-586-2596; E-mail: admissions@sterlingcollege.edu; Web site: www.sterlingcollege.edu
Founded: 1958
Description: Sterling College offers a B.A. with concentrations in outdoor education and leadership, sustainable agriculture, and wildlands ecology, and management.
Contact(s):
Dean: EDWARD HOUSTON
Director of Admissions: JOHN ZABER
President: JOHN E. WILLIAMSON

UNIVERSITY OF VERMONT

School of Natural Resources
Burlington, VT 05405
Phone: 802-656-4280; Web site: nature.snr.uvm.edu/
Contact(s):
Dean: DR. DONALD H. DEHAYES
Forestry, (B.S., M.S.): DR. CARLTON M. NEWTON
Natural Resources Planning, (M.S.): DR. CARLTON M. NEWTON
Natural Resources, (B.S., Ph.D.): DR. DONALD H. DEHAYES
Recreation Management, (B.S.): DR. ROBERT E. MANNING
Resource Economics, (B.S.): DR. ALPHONSE H. GILBERT
Environmental Sciences Program, (B.S.): DR. ALAN MCINTOSH
Environmental Studies Program, (B.S., B.A.), Interim Director: DR. IAN A. WORLEY
Water Resources and Lake Studies Center, (M.S.), Director: DR. ALAN W. MCINTOSH
Wildlife and Fisheries Biology Program, (B.S., M.S.): DR. DAVID H. HIRTH

VERMONT LAW SCHOOL

Environmental Law Center
Chelsea St., South Royalton, VT 05068
Phone: 802-763-8303; Fax: 802-763-2940; E-mail: elcinfo@vermontlaw.edu; Web site: www.vermontlaw.edu
Description: Vermont Law School's Environmental Law Center offers two master's degrees in Environmental Law. The Master of Studies in Environmental Law is a one-year interdisciplinary program in environmental law, policy, ethics and science designed for graduate students with a range of backgrounds and for law students and lawyers seeking a concentration in Environmental Law. The L.L.M. in Environmental Law is for J.D. graduates seeking to specialize in the practice of environmental law or pursue careers in teaching, research or public policy. The First Nations Environmental Law Program offers fellowships for members of federally recognized Indian tribes who wish to pursue the MSEL Degree, as well as clinical experience for students.
Degrees: M.S.E.L., L.L.M.
Contact(s):
Dean: L. KINVIN WROTH
Director: KARIN P. SHELDON

VIRGIN ISLANDS

UNIVERSITY OF THE VIRGIN ISLANDS

Division of Science and Mathematics
No. 2 John Brewer's Bay, Charlotte Amalie, St. Thomas, VI 00802-9990
Phone: 340-693-1230; Web site: www.uvi.edu/pub-relations/divscima.htm
Degrees: B.A. or B.S. in Marine Biology
Contact(s):
Division of Science and Mathematics, Chair: DR. LYNN ROSENTHAL; Phone: 340-693-1211; Fax: 340-693-1245; E-mail: lrosent@uvi.edu
MacLean Marine Science Center (Acting Director); Biology Coordinator: DR. JAMES F. BATTEY; Phone: 340-693-1381; Fax: 340-693-1385; E-mail: jbattey@uvi.edu

VIRGINIA

COLLEGE OF WILLIAM AND MARY

Virginia Institute of Marine Science/School of Marine Science
P.O. Box 1346, Gloucester Point, VA 23062
Phone: 804-642-7000; Web site: www.vims.edu/
Founded: 1940
Description: A state institution founded for providing research, advisory services, and education for the public and for state and federal agencies responsible for managing marine resources.
Degrees: M.S., Ph.D.
Contact(s):
Dean and Director: L. DONELSON WRIGHT; Phone: 804-684-7103
Biological Sciences, Chair: RICHARD L. WETZEL; Phone: 804-684-7381
Coastal and Ocean Policy, Chair: GENE M. SILBERHORN; Phone: 804-684-7382
Head of Marine Advisory Services: WILLIAM D. DUPAUL; Phone: 804-684-7164
Fisheries Sciences, Chair: J. E. GRAVES; Phone: 804-684-7352
Physical Sciences, Chair: S. A. KUEHL; Phone: 804-684-7118
Environmental Sciences, Chair: M. H. ROBERTS; Phone: 804-684-7260
Director of Research and Advisory Services: E. M. BURRESON; Phone: 804-684-7108

FERRUM COLLEGE
Ferrum, VA 24088
Phone: 540-365-2121; Web site: www.ferrum.edu
Contact(s):
Agriculture, (B.S.): PROF. RON STEPHENS; Phone: 540-365-4360
Biology, (B.S.): DR. BOB R. POHLAD; Phone: 540-365-4367; E-mail: bpohlad@ferrum.edu
Chemistry, (B.S.): PROF. DAVID JOHNSON; Phone: 540-365-4364
Environmental Studies, (B.S.): DR. JOSEPH D. STOGNER; Phone: 540-365-4369

EDUCATIONAL INSTITUTIONS - WASHINGTON

Forestry and Wildlife: DR. MICHAEL MENGAK; Phone: 540-365-4373; E-mail: mmengak@ferrum.edu
Leisure Services, (B.S., B.A.) and Recreation: PROF. KATHY MENGAK; Phone: 540-365-4387; E-mail: kmengak@ferrum.edu
Recreation: DR. DEMPSLY HENSLEY

VIRGINIA POLYTECHNIC INSTITUTE AND STATE UNIVERSITY

College of Natural Resources
Attn: Peggy Quarterman, 324 Cheatham Hall, Blacksburg, VA 24061-0324
Phone: 540-231-5481; Fax: 540-231-7664; E-mail: pquarter@vt.edu; Web site: www.vt.edu

Contact(s):
Center for Environmental and Hazardous Materials Studies, Director: DR. JOHN CAIRNS JR.; Phone: 540-231-7075
Cooperative Fish and Wildlife Unit, Leader: RICHARD J. NEVES; Phone: 540-231-5927; E-mail: mussel@vt.edu
Dean: DR. GREGORY N. BROWN; E-mail: browngn@vt.edu
Department of Fisheries and Wildlife Sciences, (B.S., M.S., Ph.D.), Interm Head: DR. DONALD J. ORTH; Phone: 540-231-5573; E-mail: dorth@vt.edu
Department of Forestry, (B.S., M.S., Ph.D.), Head: DR. HAROLD E. BURKHART; Phone: 540-231-5483; E-mail: burkhart@vt.edu
Department of Wood Science and Forest Products, (B.S., M.S., Ph.D.), Head: DR. GEZA IFJU; Phone: 540-231-8853; E-mail: ifju@vt.edu
U.S. Forest Service Coldwater and Trout Research Unit, Leader: DR. C. ANDREW DOLLOFF; Phone: 540-231-4864; E-mail: adoll@vt.edu

WASHINGTON

ANTIOCH UNIVERSITY SEATTLE

Environment and Community Program
2326 Sixth Ave., Seattle, WA 98121-1814
Phone: 206-441-5352; Fax: 206-441-3307; Web site: www.antiochsea.edu

Founded: est. in 1852; in Seattle since 1975
Description: The E&C program approaches environmental challenges with natural science literacy for professionals in environmental or community development fields. Students gain a clear understanding of the scientific, economic and institutional dimensions of environmental issues. The program publishes the Environment and Community Newsletter.
Degrees: M.A.
Contact(s):
Director: DON COMSTOCK; Phone: 206-441-5352, ext. 5703
Program Coordinator: JONATHAN SCHERCH; Phone: 206-441-5352, ext. 5710; E-mail: scherch@antiochsea.edu
Program Assistant: COURTNEY PUTNAM; Phone: 206-441-5352, ext. 5712; E-mail: cputnam@antiochsea.edu

POULSBO MARINE SCIENCE CENTER
18743 Front St., NE, P.O. Box 2079, Poulsbo, WA 98370
Phone: 360-779-5549; Fax: 360-779-8960

Founded: 1968
Description: The Marine Science Center works to meet the science education needs of public citizens and of students and teachers nationally, regionally, and locally. Hands-on environmental education is at the heart of its mission and is reflected in direct instruction from its facility on Washington's State's Liberty Bay, part of the Puget Sound.
Contact(s):
Director: MICHELLE BENEDICT
Society President: MIKE SCOTT

WASHINGTON STATE UNIVERSITY
Pullman, WA 99164
Web site: www.wsu.edu

Description: WSU has tripartite goals of providing higher education, research, and outreach/service programs relevant to the needs of Washington's citizens. The Department of Natural Resource Sciences (NRS) (http://coopext.cahe.wsu.edu/~nrs/) and Program in Environmental Science and Regional Planning (ESRP) (http://www.sci.wsu.edu/envsci/) are the chief academic units at WSU devoted to understanding, conserving, and managing natural resources, the environments they create, and the values such resources and environments provide to society. Landscape Architecture (L.A.) (http://www.cahe.wsu.edu/~hortla/) offers related programs focused on planning and designing land resources in an environmentally sound manner.
Contact(s):
Environmental Science and Regional Planning, (B.S., M.S., M.R.P., Ph.D.), Chair: WILLIAM BUDD, Washington State University, P.O. Box 644430, Pullman, WA 99164-4430; Phone: 509-335-8536; Fax: 509-335-7636
Horticulture and Landscape Architecture, (B.S., B.L.A.), Chair: CHARLES R. JOHNSON, Washington State University, P. O. Box 646414, 149 Johnson Hall, Pullman, WA 99164-6414; Phone: 509-335-9502; Fax: 509-335-8690
Natural Resource Sciences, (B.S., M.S., Ph.D.), Chair: EDWARD J. DEPUIT, Washington State University, P.O. Box 646410, Pullman, WA 99164-6410; Phone: 509-335-6166; Fax: 509-335-7862

WESTERN WASHINGTON UNIVERSITY

Huxley College of Environmental Studies
Bellingham, WA 98225
Phone: 360-650-3520; E-mail: huxley@cc.wwu.edu; Web site: www.ac.wwu.edu/~huxley/

Founded: 1968
Description: Principally a two-year, upper division and M.S. program; B.A., B.S. in environmental studies; M.S. in environmental science. Also cooperative programs, M.S. in marine and estuarine science and M.A. in political science and environmental studies.
Contact(s):
Dean: DR. BRADLEY F. SMITH; E-mail: bfs@admsec.wwu.edu
Institute for Watershed Studies, Director: DR. ROBIN MATTHEWS; Phone: 360-650-3510; E-mail: rmatthews@wwu.edu
Institute of Environmental Toxicology and Chemistry, Director: DR. WAYNE G. LANDIS; Phone: 360-650-6136; Fax: 360-650-6556; E-mail: landis@cc.wwu.edu
Center for Environmental Science, Director: DR. JOHN T. HARDY; Phone: 360-650-6108; Fax: 360-650-7284; E-mail: jhardy@cc.wwu.edu
Center for Geography and Environmental Social Science, Director: DR. JOHN C. MILES; Phone: 360-650-3284; Fax: 360-650-7702; E-mail: jcmiles@cc.wwu.edu
Shannon Point Marine Center, Director: DR. STEPHEN D SULKIN, 1900 Shannon Point Rd., Anacortes, WA 98221; Phone: 360-293-2188; Fax: 360-293-1083; E-mail: spmc@cc.wwu.edu

WEST VIRGINIA

SHEPHERD COLLEGE

Institute for Environmental Studies
Byrd Center, Shepherdstown, WV 25443
Web site: www.shepherd.wvnet.edu/iesweb/
Description: B.S. in Environmental Studies with focus in physical and biological sciences or resource management.
Contact(s):
Director: DR. ED SNYDER; Phone: 304-876-5227; Fax: 304-876-5028; E-mail: iesweb@shepherd.edu

WEST VIRGINIA UNIVERSITY

College of Agriculture, Forestry and Consumer Sciences
P.O. Box 6108, Morgantown, WV 26506

Phone: 304-293-2395; Fax: 304-293-3740; Web site: www.caf.wvu.edu/

Contact(s):
Division of Forestry, (B.S., M.S., Ph.D.), Director: DR. JOSEPH MCNEEL, P.O. Box 6125, Morgantown, WV 26506-6125; Phone: 304-293-2941; E-mail: jmcneel@wvu.edu
Wildlife and Fisheries Management, (B.S., M.S., Ph.D.), Program Coordinator: DR. ROBERT WHITMORE; Phone: 304-293-2941 ext. 2491; E-mail: u0eae@wvnvm.wvnet.edu
Wood Industries, (B.S.F., M.S., Ph.D.), Program Coordinator: DR. JAMES ARMSTRONG; Phone: 304-293-2941 ext 2486; E-mail: jarmstro@wvu.edu
Recreation and Parks Management, (B.S.R., M.S., Ph.D.), Program Coordinator: DR. STEVE SELIN; Phone: 304-293-2941 ext 2442; E-mail: sselin@wvu.edu
Landscape Architecture (B.S.), Chair: DR. DONALD R. ARMSTRONG; Phone: 304-293-2142 ext. 4489; Fax: 304-293-3752; E-mail: darmstro@wvu.edu
Natural Resource Economics (Ph.D.), Coordinator: DR. TIM T. PHIPPS, P.O. Box 6108, Morgantown, WV; Phone: 304-293-4832; E-mail: tphipps@wvu.edu
Agricultural and Resource Economics, Undergraduate Coordinator: DR. ALAN COLLINS, P.O. Box 6108, Morgantown, WV; Phone: 304-293-4832; E-mail: acollins@wvu.edu
Appalachian Hardwood Center, Director: DR. CURT HASSLER; Phone: 304-293-2941 ext. 2451; E-mail: chassler@wvu.edu

WISCONSIN

NORTHLAND COLLEGE

Sigurd Olson Environmental Institute
Ashland, WI 54806
Phone: 715-682-1223; Fax: 715-682-1218; E-mail: channa@wheeler.northland.edu

Founded: 1972

Description: The Sigurd Olson Environmental Institute was founded at Northland College in 1972 to increase public understanding of the complex relationships between natural and cultural environments in the Lake Superior region and to assist in developing workable solutions to regional environmental problems. The institute seeks to carry out Sigurd Olson's vision by fostering environmental citizenship and educating citizens for a sustainable future.

Contact(s):
Advisory Board Chair: EILEEN LONG
Communications Specialist: LAURENCE WILAND
Environmental Education Specialist: CLAYTON RUSSELL
Executive Director: KENNETH M. BRO
Lake Superior Program Coordinator: JANE SILBERSTEIN
LoonWatch Coordinator: TED GOSTOMSKI
Team Leader: MIKE GARDNER
Officer Manager: CAROLYN HANNA
Timber Wolf Alliance Coordinator: PAM TROXELL
Smart Wood Lake State Program Coordinator: MARCO LOWENSTEIN

ST. NORBERT COLLEGE

Center for International Education
100 Grant St., De Pere, WI 54115-2099
Phone: 920-403-3100; Fax: 920-403-4083; Web site: www.snc.edu/

Founded: 1990

Description: The Center conducts an Annual Global Ecology Series on themes such as the Great Lakes as an endangered resource of North America, Africa and women, population, and international policy-making. Instructional resources and in-service programs are provided for K-1

Contact(s):
Associate Dean for International Studies: DR. JOSEPH D. TULLBANE; Phone: 920-403-3378

UNIVERSITY OF WISCONSIN AT EAU CLAIRE
Eau Claire, WI 54701
Phone: 715-836-4166

Contact(s):
Biology, (B.S., M.S.), Chairman: DR. MICHAEL WEIL
Environmental Science; minor: DR. PAULA KLEINTJES
Geography, (B.S.), Chairman: DR. BRADY FOUST

UNIVERSITY OF WISCONSIN AT GREEN BAY
2420 Nicolet Dr., Green Bay, WI 54311-7001
Phone: 920-465-2000; E-mail: ADMISSNS@UWGB.EDU; Web site: www.uwgb.edu

Description: Natural and Applied Sciences Department offers a bachelor's degree in Environmental Studies. Areas of emphasis focus on Physical Systems and Ecology and Biological Resources. The Department of Public and Environmental Affairs offers a bachelor's degree in Environmental Studies and Planning with an emphasis in public policy or planning. The graduate school offers a M.S. in Environmental Science and Policy with an emphasis in Ecosystems Studies, Resource Management and Environmental Policy and Administration

Contact(s):
Environmental Science, Chair: DR. HALLETT J. HARRIS; Phone: 920-465-2369; Fax: 920-465-2376; E-mail: HARRISH@UWGB.EDU
Department of Public and Environmental Affairs, Chair: DR. DENISE LYNNE SCHEBERLE; Phone: 920-465-2595; E-mail: SCHEBERD@GBMS01.UWGB.EDU
Environmental Science and Policy Program, Associate Dean of Graduate Studies: DR. RONALD D. STIEGLITZ; Phone: 920-465-2123; Fax: 920-465-2718; E-mail: gradstu@uwgb.edu.
Cofrin Arboretum Center for Biodiversity, Director: DR. ROBERT W. HOWE; Phone: 920-465-2272; E-mail: hower@uwgb.edu

UNIVERSITY OF WISCONSIN AT LA CROSSE

College of Science and Allied Health
1725 State St., La Crosse, WI 54601
Web site: perth.uwlax.edu/sah/

Description: Biology, Chemistry and Geography offer B.S. degrees with a concentration in Environmental Science. Biology also offers a concentration in Aquatic Sciences for B.S. and M.S. degrees.

Contact(s):
Aquatic Science Advisor: DR. ROGER J. HARO; Phone: 608-785-6970; E-mail: haro_rj@mail.uwlax.edu
Biology Department/Environmental Science, Contact: DR. ROB TYSER; Phone: 608-785-8238; Fax: 608-785-6959; E-mail: tyser@mail.uwlax.edu
Geography and Earth Science, (B.S.), Chairman: DR. GEORGE HUPPERT; Phone: 608-785-8333; Fax: 608-785-8332; E-mail: huppert@mail.uwlax.edu
Chemistry Department, Chair: DR. BRUCE OSTERBY; Phone: 608-785-8266; Fax: 608-785-8281; E-mail: oster_br@mail.uwlax.edu
River Studies Center, Director: MARK B. SANDHEINRICH; Phone: 608-785-8261; E-mail: sandhein@mail.uwlax.edu

UNIVERSITY OF WISCONSIN AT MADISON

School of Natural Resources
1450 Linden Dr., Rm. 140, Madison, WI 53706-1562
Phone: 608-262-4930

Description: The School of Natural Resources is within the college of Agricultural and Life Sciences. The school offers 13 undergraduate options in natural resources. Graduate instruction is available in many specialized and interdisciplinary areas.

Contact(s):
College Dean: ELTON D. ABERLE
Director, School of Natural Resources: KEVIN MCSWEENEY, 1450 Linden Dr., Rm. 146, Madison, WI 53706; Phone: 608-262-6968

Institute for Environmental Studies (IES)
550 N. Park St., Science Hall, Madison, WI 53706

EDUCATIONAL INSTITUTIONS - WYOMING

Phone: 608-265-5296; Web site: www.ies.wisc.edu/
Description: The IES is an inter-college unit of the University of Wisconsin-Madison that promotes, develops and administers interdisciplinary environmental instruction, research, and public service programs. The Institute offers graduate-level degrees in conservation biology and sustainable development, environmental monitoring, land resources and water resource management; optional graduate curricula in air resources management and energy analysis and policy; and an undergraduate certificate program in environmental studies.
Contact(s):
Director: DR. THOMAS M. YUILL

UNIVERSITY OF WISCONSIN AT STEVENS POINT

College of Natural Resources
Stevens Point, WI 54481
Phone: 715-346-4617; Fax: 715-346-3624; Web site: www.uwsp.edu/acad/cnr/
Description: Located in Central Wisconsin, the College of Natural Resources began in 1946 with the nation's first conservation education major. The College now has over 60 faculty and staff, 1,750 undergraduates and 80 graduate students. The college offers 16 majors and 13 minors.
Contact(s):
Dean: DR. VICTOR D. PHILLIPS
Interim Associate Dean: DR. CHRISTINE THOMAS
Cooperative Fishery Unit, (M.S.), Leader: DR. MICHAEL BOZEK
Environmental Education, (B.S., M.S.): DR. RANDY CHAMPEAU
Forestry, (B.S., M.S.): DR. ROBERT MILLER
Resources Management, (B.S., M.S.): DR. MICHAEL GROSS
Soil Science, (B.S., M.S.): DR. RONALD HENSLER
Water Science, (B.S., M.S.): DR. STAN SZCZYTKO
Wildlife Degrees, (B.S., M.S.): DR. ERIC ANDERSON

WYOMING

UNIVERSITY OF WYOMING
P.O. Box 3166, Laramie, WY 82071
Web site: www.uwyo.edu/
Contact(s):
Department of Zoology and Physiology, Head: DR. NANCY L. STANTON; Phone: 307-766-4207; Fax: 307-766-5625
National Park Service Research Center, Director: DR. HENRY J. HARLOW; Phone: 307-766-4227; Fax: 307-766-5625
Red Buttes Environmental Biology Laboratory, Director: DR. JOSEPH S. MEYER; Phone: 307-766-2017; Fax: 307-766-5625
Wyoming Cooperative Fish and Wildlife Research Unit, Leader: DR. STANLEY H. ANDERSON; Phone: 307-766-5415; Fax: 907-766-5400

CANADA

ALBERTA

UNIVERSITY OF ALBERTA

Faculty of Agriculture, Forestry, and Home Economics
2-14 Agriculture Forestry Centre, Edmonton, Alberta T6G 2P5 Canada
Phone: 780-492-4933/1-800-804-6417 (Western Canada); E-mail: dean.agforhe@ualberta.ca; Web site: www.afhe.ualberta.ca/
Description: Undergraduate Degree Programs: B.Sc. in Agricultural and Food Business Management; Agriculture; Environmental and Conservation Sciences; Forest Business Management; Forestry; Human Ecology; Nutrition and Food Sciences; and Human Ecology/Bachelor of Education. Graduate Degree Programs: M.Sc., M. Ag., M.Eng., Ph.D. in Agricultural Food and Nutritional Science; M.A., MSc., and Ph.D. in Human Ecology; M.Sc., M. Ag., M.F., Ph. D., MBA/MF in Renewable Resources; MSc., MAg., Ph.D., MBA/MAg in Rural Economy.
Contact(s):
Agricultural, Food, and Nutritional Science, Chair: DR. JOHN J. KENNELLY; Phone: 780-492-3239
Human Ecology, Chair: DR. NANCY GIBSON; Phone: 780-492-3883
Renewable Resources, Chair: DR. JIM A. BECK; Phone: 780-492-4413
Rural Economy, Chair: DR. MICHELE VEEMAN; Phone: 780-492-4225

BRITISH COLUMBIA

UNIVERSITY OF BRITISH COLUMBIA
British Columbia
Web site: www.ubc.ca/
Contact(s):
Agricultural Sciences, Dean: PROF. MOURA QUAYLE, 248-2357 Main Mall University Campus, Vancouver, British Columbia V6T 1Z4 Canada
Animal Sciences Department, Contact: DR. D. M. SHACKLETON, 248-2357 Main Mall University Campus, Vancouver, British Columbia V6T 1Z4 Canada
Civil Engineering Department, Head: DR. M. ISAACSON, 2324 Main Mall, Vancouver, British Columbia V6T 1Z4 Canada
Forestry, Dean (Acting): DR. J. MCLEAN, 2424 Main Mall, Vancouver, British Columbia V6T 1Z4 Canada
Geography Department, Head: DR. G. WYNN, 1984 West Mall, Vancouver, British Columbia V6T 1Z5 Canada
Institute for Resources and Environment, Director: DR. L. M. LAVKULICH, Rm. 436E, 2206 E. Mall, Vancouver, British Columbia V6T 1Z3 Canada
Oceanography Department, Head: DR. A. LEWIS, 6270 University Blvd., Vancouver, British Columbia V6T 1Z2 Canada
Westwater Research Centre, Director: DR. M. HEALEY, 1933 W. Mall Annex, Rm. 200, Vancouver, British Columbia V6T 1Z2 Canada
Zoology Department, Head: DR. J. BERGER, 6270 University Blvd., Vancouver, British Columbia V6T 1Z4 Canada

UNIVERSITY OF NORTHERN BRITISH COLUMBIA
3333 University Way, Prince George, British Columbia V2N 4Z9 Canada
Phone: 250-960-5555; Fax: 250-960-5538; Web site: www.unbc.ca
Founded: 1990
Description: UNBC is a research intensive, small university founded in 1990 as "a university in the north, for the north." The faculty of Natural Resources and Environmental Studies develops managers and scientists to effectively meet the demands for natural resources products and services while maintaining a quality environment. Natural Resource Management offers majors in Wildlife and Fisheries, Forestry (accredited by the Canadian Forestry Accreditation Board) and Resource Recreation.
Contact(s):
Natural Resources Management (B.S.): DR. WINIFRED KESSLER; Phone: 250-950-6664; E-mail: winifred@unbc.ca
Resource Based Tourism (B.A.), Environmental Studies (B.A., B.S.), Contact: DR. JEFF ZEIGER; Phone: 250-960-5308; E-mail: zeiger@unbc.ca
Natural Resources and Environmental Studies (M.S., M.A., Ph.D.): Graduate Studies: Phone: 250-960-6336; E-mail: graduate-info@unbc.ca

MANITOBA

UNIVERSITY OF MANITOBA

Faculty of Science
  239 Machray Hall, Winnipeg, Manitoba R3T 2N2 Canada
  Phone: 204-474-8256; Fax: 204-474-7618; Web site: www.umanitoba.ca/faculties/science/

Contact(s):
Botany Department (B.S., M.S., Ph.D.), Head: DR. DAVID PUNTER, 505 Buller Bldg., Winnipeg, Manitoba R3T 2N2 Canada; Phone: 204-474-9813; Fax: 204-474-7604; E-mail: punterd@cc.umanitoba.ca
Environmental Science Program (B.S.), Director: DR. NORMAN R. HUNTER, 231C Machray Hall, Winnipeg, Manitoba R3T 2N2 Canada; Phone: 204-474-9897; Fax: 204-275-3147; E-mail: hunter@ms.umanitoba.ca
Zoology (B.S., M.S., Ph.D), Head: DR. E. HUEBNER, Z320 Duff Roblin Bldg., Winnipeg, Manitoba R3T 2N2 Canada; Phone: 204-474-9245; Fax: 204-474-7588; E-mail: ehuebnr@cc.umanitoba.ca
Natural Resources Institute, Director: DR. SLOBODAN SOMONOVIC
Natural Resources Institute, Associate Director: DR. RICHARD BAYDACK

NEW BRUNSWICK

UNIVERSITY OF NEW BRUNSWICK

Forestry and Environmental Management
  P. O. Box 44555, Fredericton, New Brunswick E3B 6C2 Canada
  Phone: 506-453-4501; Fax: 506-453-3538; E-mail: daug@UNB.ca; Web site: www.unb.ca/departs/forestry/

Description: B.S. in Forest Ecosystem Management or Forest Engineering; Minors include Environmental Science, Wildlife Conservation and Management and Parks and Wilderness.

Contact(s):
Dean: DR. DAVID A. MACLEAN; E-mail: macleand@unb.ca
Assistant Dean and Undergraduate Information: DR. DAVID A. DAUGHARTY; E-mail: daug@unb.ca
Director of Graduate Studies (M.S., Ph.D.): DR. C. H. MENG; E-mail: meng@unb.ca

NOVA SCOTIA

ACADIA UNIVERSITY
  Wolfville, Nova Scotia B0P 1X0 Canada
  Phone: 902-542-2201; Web site: www.acadiau.ca

Founded: 1838

Description: Primarily an undergraduate university, emphasizing a liberal education in a balanced blend of arts, science, and professional studies. Masters degrees are offered in biology, chemistry, computer science, education, english, geology, political science, physiology, and sociology.

Contact(s):
Environmental Chemistry, (B.Sc., Hon., M.Sc.): DAVID A. STILES
Environmental Science (B.Sc., Hon.): DAVID A. STILES
Environmental Geology, (B.Sc., Hon., M.Sc.): ROBERT RAESIDE
Recreation Management, (B.R.M, Hon., Bkin, Hon.): GLYN BISSEX
Wildlife, Fisheries, Aquatic Biology, Marine Ecology, Mammalogy, Animal Behavior, Ornithology, Conservation Biology, Molecular Ecology, Landscape Ecology (B.Sc., Hon.; M.Sc.): SOREN BONDRUP-NIELS

DALHOUSIE UNIVERSITY

School for Resource and Environmental Studies (SRES)
  1312 Robie St., Halifax, Nova Scotia B3H 3J5 Canada
  Phone: 902-494-3632; Fax: 902-494-3728; E-mail: sres@is.dal.ca; Web site: www.mgmt.dal.ca/sres/sres.html

Founded: 1975

Description: Graduate school within the Faculty of Management of Dalhousie University, offering a master of environmental studies (M.E.S.) degree, through a two year program (thesis required). Emphasis of program is on policy and management aspects.

Degrees: M.E.S.

Contact(s):
Director: PETER M. DUINKER Ph.D.

ONTARIO

LAKEHEAD UNIVERSITY

Forestry and Forest Environment
  955 Oliver Rd., Thunder Bay, Ontario P7B 5E1 Canada
  Phone: 807-343-8507; Fax: 807-343-8116; E-mail: mbeck@sky.lakeheadu.ca; Web site: www.lakeheadu.ca/~forwww/forestry.html

Description: B.S. in Forestry or Environmental Studies and M.S. in Forestry

Contact(s):
Environmental Studies: DR. WILLIAM PARKER; E-mail: whparker@flash.lakeheadu.ca
Undergraduate Forestry Programs: DR. GARY MURCHISON; E-mail: Gary.Murchison@lakeheadu.ca
Graduate Forestry Programs: DR. ED SETLIFF; Phone: 807-343-8507; E-mail: Ed.Setliff@lakeheadu.ca

UNIVERSITY OF GUELPH

Ontario Agricultural College
  OAC Dean's Office, Guelph, Ontario N1G 2W1 Canada
  Phone: 519-824-4120; Fax: 519-766-1423; E-mail: oacinfo@oac.uoguelph.ca; Web site: www.oac.uoguelph.ca/

Contact(s):
Environmental Biology (B.S., M.S., Ph.D.), Department Chair: DR. MARK K. SEARS; E-mail: msears@evbhort.uoguelph.ca
Land Resource Science (B.S., M.S., Ph.D.), Department Chair: DR. TERRY GILLESPIE; E-mail: tgillesp@lrs.uoguelph.ca
Rural Planning and Development (M.S., Ph.D.), Director: DR. JOHN E. FITZGIBBON; E-mail: jfitzgib@rpd.uoguelph.ca
Landscape Architecture (B.L.A., M.L.A., M.Sc.L.A.) and LA Community Outreach Centre, Director: DR. MAURICE NELISCHER; E-mail: mnelisch@la.uoguelph.ca
Undergraduate Program Coordinator, LA: DR. NATHAN PERKINS; E-mail: nperkins@la.uoguelph.ca
Arboretum Director: ALAN WATSON; Phone: 519-824-4120, ext. 2356; E-mail: awatson@uoguelph.ca
University of Guelph Insect Collection, Curator: DR. S. A. MARSHALL; E-mail: smarshal@evbhort.uoguelph.ca

UNIVERSITY OF TORONTO

Forestry Department
  33 Willcocks Street, Toronto, Ontario M5S 3B3 Canada
  Phone: 416-978-5751; Fax: 416-978-3834; E-mail: gradprog@forestry.utoronto.ca; Web site: www.forestry.utoronto.ca/

Description: Master of Forest Conservation Program (M.F.C.)

Contact(s):
Dean: DR. RORKE B. BRYAN; E-mail: r.bryan@utoronto.ca
M.F.C. Coordinator: D. BALSILLIE; Phone: 416-978-4638; E-mail: david.balsillie@utoronto.ca

YORK UNIVERSITY

Environmental Studies
  355 Lumbers Bldg. 4700 Keele St., Toronto, Ontario M3J 1P3 Canada
  Phone: 416-736-5252; Fax: 416-736-5679; E-mail: fesinfo@yorku.ca; Web site: www.yorku.ca/faculty/fes

EDUCATIONAL INSTITUTIONS - QUEBEC

Founded: 1968
Description: The faculty of Environmental Studies offers interdisciplinary, flexible, individualized programs at both the undergraduate and graduate levels. FES is committed to a broad definition of environment, offering the opportunity to study natural, built, organizational, and social environments.
Contact(s):
Dean: PETER VICTOR; E-mail: pvictor@yorku.ca
Undergraduate Program Director: RAYMOND A. ROGERS; E-mail: rrogers@yorku.ca
Graduate Program Director: BONNIE KETTEL; E-mail: bkettel@yorku.ca
MES Program Coordinator: BRENT M. RUTHERFORD; E-mail: brentr@yorku.ca
Graduate Planning Programs Coordinator: BARBARA L. RAHDER; E-mail: rahder@yorku.ca

QUEBEC

MCGILL UNIVERSITY

Avian Science and Conservation Centre (ASCC)
21,111 Lakeshore Rd., Ste. Anne de Bellevue, Quebec H9X 3V9 Canada
Phone: 514-398-7760; Fax: 514-398-7990; E-mail: bird@nrs.mcgill.ca; Web site: nrs.mcgill.ca/ascc
Founded: 1974
Description: To promote the study of birds and their conservation, we conduct pure and applied research in the field and laboratory; breed, release and manage endangered species; and train students and interns from all over the world. The Centre publishes a semi-annual newsletter, The Talon.
Degrees: M.Sc., Ph.D.
Contact(s):
Director: DAVID M. BIRD
Curator: IAN RITCHIE; Phone: 514-398-7932; Fax: 514-398-7540; E-mail: ritchie@nrs.mcgill.ca

UNIVERSITE LAVAL
Quebec G1K 7P4 Canada
Phone: 418-656-3333; Web site: www.ulaval.ca/
Contact(s):
Argiculture, (M.S., Ph.D.), Contact: ANDRE GOSSELIN; Phone: 418-656-7234; Fax: 416-656-7856
Forestry, Wood, and Forest Sciences Department, (B.S., M.S., Ph.D.), Contact: MICHEL DESSUREAULT; Phone: 418-656-7128; Fax: 418-656-3177; E-mail: Michel.Dessureault@ffg.ulaval.ca

SASKATCHEWAN

UNIVERSITY OF REGINA

Department of Biology
Regina, Saskatchewan S4S 0A2 Canada
Phone: 306-585-4145; Fax: Fax306-585-4894; Web site: www.uregina.ca/science/biology/index.htm
Contact(s):
Department Head: DR. WILLIAM CHAPCO; Phone: 306-585-4478; E-mail: William.Chapco@uregina.ca
Limnology Laboratory: DR. PETER LEAVITT; Phone: 306-585 4253; E-mail: Leavitt@uregina.ca
Plant Ecology Laboratory: DR. SCOTT WILSON; Phone: 306-585-4287; E-mail: scott.wilson@uregina.ca

UNIVERSITY OF SASKATCHEWAN

College of Agriculture
2D30 - 51 Campus Dr., Saskatoon, Saskatchewan S7N 5A8 Canada
Phone: 306-966-7881; Fax: 306-966-8894; Web site: www.ag.usask.ca/
Contact(s):
Department of Plant Sciences, Head: DR. GRAHAM J. SCOLES, Rm. 4D36 Agriculture Bldg., 51 Campus Dr., Saskatoon, SK S7N 5A8; Phone: 306-966-5855; Fax: 306-966-5015; E-mail: graham.scoles@sask.usask.ca
Department of Soil Science, Head: DR. JIM J. GERMIDA, 5E34.1, Agriculture Building, 51 Campus Dr., Saskatoon, SK S7N 5A8; Phone: 306-966-6836; Fax: 306-966-6881; E-mail: germida@sask.usask.ca

INTERNATIONAL

MUSASHI INSTITUTE OF TECHNOLOGY
3-3-1 Ushikubo-nishi, Tsuzuki-ku, Yokohama 224-0015 Japan
Phone: 0081-45-2600; Fax: 0081-45-2626
Founded: 1938
Description: The University consists of two departments: Civil Engineering and Environmental and Information Studies. Publishes Conservation Biology and Issues on Environment.

SILLMAN UNIVERSITY

Center of Excellence--Coastal Resource Management
Dumaguete City 6200 Philippines
Web site: su.edu.ph
Founded: 1901
Description: Silliman University, with USAID, created an environmental awareness program. Starting with a coastal resource management, it specifically works with the marine laboratory of the university and is currently working on environmental education and environmental communication within the university and in the community through extension programs.
Contact(s):
Researcher: DR. HILCONIDA CALUMPONG; Phone: 63-35-225-2500; E-mail: mlsucrm@mozcom.com
Researcher/Professor: DR. JANET ESTACION; Phone: 63-35-225-2500; E-mail: mlsucrm@mozcom.com
Dean, College of Education: DR. BETSY JOY TAN; Phone: 63-35-225-6711; E-mail: admsucrm@mozcom.com
Researcher/Teacher: ROY OLSEN DE LEON; Phone: 63-35-225-6711; E-mail: admsucrm@mozcom.com
Dean, College of Law/Researcher: MIKHAIL MAXINO ESQ.; Phone: 63-35-225-6711; E-mail: admsucrm@mozcom.com

UNIVERSIDADE FEDERAL DO PARANA

Nimad-Nucle Interdisciplinar de Melo Ambiente e Desenvolvimento
Centro Politechnico, Curitiba Brazil
Phone: 55-041-366-2723; Fax: 55-041-366-2723; E-mail: NIMAD@cce.ufpr.br
Founded: 1989
Description: The objective of the Nucleous e Nimad is interdisciplinary research, teaching and extension directed to natural resource preservation, environmental education and sustainable development promotion.
Contact(s):
EE Coordinator: ZIOLE Z. MALHADAS; Phone: 55-041-252-4461; E-mail: ziolezm@cwb.matrix.com.br
E. Research Coordinator and Research Director: JOSE MILTON ANDRIGUETTO; Phone: 55-041-366-2723; E-mail: nimad@cce.ufpr.br

UNIVERSITY OF BATH

Centre for Research in Education and the Environment (CREE)
Department of Education, Bath BA14 6LP United Kingdom
Phone: 44-122-582-6648; Fax: 44-122-582-6113; E-mail: cree@bath.ac.uk; Web site: www.bath.ac.uk
Founded: 1995
Description: The CREE, based at the University of Bath, carries out research and evaluation studies on environmental and sustainable

education. Edits Environmental Education Research and Assessment and Evaluation in Higher Education.
Contact(s):
Director: DR. WILLIAM SCOTT
DR. ANDREW STABLES
DR. STEPHEN GOUGH
DR. ALAN REID
ELISABETH BARRATT HACKING

UNIVERSITY OF ITO PUNJAB

Institute of Education and Research
New Campus, Lahore 54590 Pakistan
Phone: 92-42-586-4468; Fax: 92-42-586-4004
Description: Environmental Education for Masters students
Contact(s):
Contact: DR. HAFIZ MUHAMMRAD QZBAL; Phone: 42-588-0044; E-mail: hafizm@paknet4.ptc.pk

CONSERVATION INFORMATION RESOURCES

FISH AND WILDLIFE COMMISSIONERS AND DIRECTORS

UNITED STATES

Alabama Division of Game and Fish
64 N. Union St., Montgomery, AL 36130
Director (Acting): CORKY PUGH
Phone: 334-242-3465

Alaska Department of Fish and Game
P.O. Box 25526, Juneau, AK 99802-5526
Commissioner: FRANK RUE
Phone: 907-465-4100

Arizona Game and Fish Department
2221 W. Germany Rd., Phoenix, AZ 85023
Director: DUANE SHROUFE
Phone: 602-942-3000

Arkansas Game and Fish Commission
2 Natural Resources Dr., Little Rock, AR 72205
Director: STEVE N. WILSON
Phone: 501-223-6305

California Department of Fish and Game
P.O. Box 944209, Sacramento, CA 94244-2090
Director: ROBERT C. HIGHT
Phone: 916-653-7664

Colorado Division of Wildlife
6060 Broadway, Denver, CO 80216
Director: JOHN MUMMA
Phone: 303-291-7208

Connecticut Department of Environmental Protection
State Office Bldg. 79 Elm St., Hartford, CT 06106-5127
Deputy Commissioner: THOMAS J. DUDCHIK
Phone: 860-424-3011

DC Dept of Conser and Reg Affairs
Fish Prgm 2100 Martin L. King Ave, SE Suite 203, Washington, DC 20020
Director: IRA PALMER
Phone: 202-645-6064

Delaware Division of Fish and Wildlife
89 Kings Highway, Dover, DE 19903
Director: ANDREW T. MANUS
Phone: 302-739-5295

Div. of Wildlife, Nevada Dept. of Conservation and Nat Resources
1100 Valley Rd., Reno, NV 89512
Administrator: TERRY R. CRAWFORTH
Phone: 702-688-1599

Florida Fish and Wildlife Commission
Farris Bryant Bldg, 620 S. Meridian, Tallahassee, FL 32399-1600
Executive Director: ALLAN L. EGBERT
Phone: 850-488-2975

Georgia Wildlife Resources Division
2070 U.S. Highway 278, SE, Social Circle, GA 30025
Director: DAVID J. WALLER
Phone: 706-577-3020

Guam Department of Agriculture
192 Dairy Rd., Agana, Guam 96910
Director: ANTONIO S. QUITUGUA
Phone: 671-734-3941

Hawaii Department of Land and Natural Resources
P.O. Box 621, Honolulu, HI 96809
Chairman: TIMOTHY JOHNS
Phone: 808-587-0400

Idaho Fish and Game Department
600 S. Walnut, Box 25, Boise, ID 83707
Director (Acting): JERRY MALLET
Phone: 208-334-5159

Illinois Department of Natural Resources
Lincoln Tower Plaza, 524 S. Second St., Springfield, IL 62701-1787
Director: G. BRENT MANNING
Phone: 217-785-0075

Indiana Division of Fish and Wildlife
402 W. Washington St. Rm. W-273, Indianapolis, IN 46204-2212
Director: GARY DOXTATER
Phone: 317-232-4080

Iowa Department of Natural Resources
Wallace State Office Bldg East 9 and Grand Ave, Des Moines, IA 50319-0034
Director: PAUL JOHNSON
Phone: 515-281-5145

Kansas Department of Wildlife and Parks
900 Jackson St., Ste. 502, Topeka, KS 66612-1220
Secretary: STEVE WILLIAMS
Phone: 785-296-2281

Kentucky Department of Fish and Wildlife Resources
#1 Game Farm Rd., Frankfort, KT 40601
Commissioner: C. THOMAS BENNETT
Phone: 502-564-3400

Louisiana Department Wildlife and Fisheries
P.O. Box 98000, Baton Rouge, LA 70898-9000
Secretary: JAMES JENKINS
Phone: 225-765-2623

Maine Department of Inland Fisheries and Wildlife
284 State St., Station #41, Augusta, ME 04333
Commissioner: LEE PERRY
Phone: 207-287-5202

Maryland Department of Natural Resources
Tawas State Office Bldg., Annapolis, MD 21401
Assistant Secretary for Resource Management: SARAH J. TAYLOR-ROGERS
Phone: 410-260-5551

Massachusetts Department of Fisheries
100 Cambridge St., Boston, MA 02202
Director: WAYNE MACCALLUM
Phone: 617-727-3155

Michigan Department of Natural Resources
Stevens T. Mason Bldg., Box 30028, Lansing, MI 48909
Director: K.L. COOL

Phone: 517-373-2329

Minnesota Department of Natural Resources
500 Lafayette Rd., St. Paul, MN 55155-4020
Commissioner: RODNEY W. SANDO
Phone: 651-296-2549

Mississippi Dept of Wildlife, Fisheries and Parks
P.O. Box 451, Jackson, MS 39205
Director: SAM POLLES
Phone: 601-364-2000

Missouri Department of Conservation
2901 W. Truman Blvd. P.O. Box 180, Jefferson City, MO 65102-0180
Director: JERRY M. CONLEY
Phone: 573-751-4115

Montana Department of Fish, Wildlife and Parks
1420 E. Sixth Ave., Helena, MT 59620
Director: PAT GRAHAM
Phone: 406-444-3186

Nebraska Game and Parks Commission
P.O. Box 30370, 2200 N. 33rd, Lincoln, NE 68503
Director: REX AMACK
Phone: 402-471-5539

New Hampshire Fish and Game Department
2 Hazen Dr.,, Concord, NH 03301
Executive Director: WAYNE VETTER
Phone: 603-271-3422

New Jersey Division of Fish, Game and Wildlife
P.O. Box 400, Trenton, NJ 08625-0400
Director: ROBERT MCDOWELL
Phone: 609-292-9410

New Mexico Natural Resources Department
Villagra Bldg. P.O. Box 25112, Santa Fe, NM 87503
Director: JERRY MARACCHINI
Phone: 505-827-7911

New York Department of Environmental Conservation
50 Wolf Rd., Albany, NY 12233
Division of Fish, Wildlife, and Marine Resources: GERRY BARNHART
Phone: 518-457-5690

North Carolina Wildlife Resources Commission
Archdale Bldg. 512 N. Salisbury St., Raleigh, NC 27604-1188
Executive Director: CHARLES FULLWOOD
Phone: 919-733-3391

North Dakota State Game and Fish Department
100 North Bismark Expressway, Bismarck, ND 58510
Commissioner: DEAN HILDEBRAND
Phone: 701-328-6300

Ohio Division of Wildlife
1840 Belcher Dr., Columbus, OH 43224-1329
Chief: MICHAEL J. BUDZIK
Phone: 614-265-6300

Oklahoma Department of Wildlife Conservation
1801 N. Lincoln P.O. Box 53465, Oklahoma City, OK 73152
Director: GREG DUFFY
Phone: 405-521-3851

Oregon Department of Fish and Wildlife
Box 59, Portland, OR 97207
Director: JIM GREER
Phone: 503-872-5410 ext. 401

Pennsylvania Fish and Boat Commission
P.O. Box 67000, Harrisburg, PA 17106-7000
Executive Director: PETE COLANGELO
Phone: 717-657-4515

Pennsylvania Game Commission
2001 Elmerton Ave., Harrisburg, PA 17110-9797
Executive Director: VERNON R. ROSS
Phone: 717-787-3633

Puerto Rico Department of Natural Resources
P.O. Box 9066600 Puerto De Tierra Station, San Juan, PR 00906-6600
Secretary: PEDRO A. GELABERT
Phone: 787-723-3090

Rhode Island Department of Environmental Mgmt.
Stedman Gov. Center 4808 Tower Hill Rd, Wakefield, RI 02879
Chief: JOHN STOLGITIS
Phone: 401-222-3075

South Carolina Department of Natural Resources
Rembert C. Dennis Bldg. Box 167, Columbia, SC 29202
Executive Director: DR. PAUL A. SANDIFER
Phone: 803-734-4007

South Dakota Department of Game, Fish and Parks
Sigurd Anderson Bldg. 523 E. Capitol, Pierre, SD 57501-3182
Secretary: JOHN COOPER
Phone: 605-773-3387

Tennessee Wildlife Resources Agency
Box 40747 Ellington Agr. Center, Nashville, TN 37204
Executive Director: GARY T. MYERS
Phone: 615-781-6552

Texas Parks and Wildlife Department
4200 Smith School Rd., Austin, TX 78744
Executive Director: ANDREW SANSOM
Phone: 512-389-4802

Utah State Division of Wildlife Resources
1594 WN Temple P.O. Box 146301, Salt Lake City, UT 84114-6301
Director: JOHN KIMBALL
Phone: 801-538-4702

Vermont Fish and Game Department
103 S Main St., 10 South, Waterbury, VT 05671-0501
Commissioner: RON REGAN
Phone: 802-241-3730

Virginia Department of Game and Inland Fisheries
4010 W. Broad St. Box 11104, Richmond, VA 23230-1104
Executive Director: WILLIAM L. WOODFIN JR.
Phone: 804-367-9231

Washington Department of Fish and Wildlife
600 Capitol Way North, Olympia, WA 98501-1091
Director: JEFF KOENINGS
Phone: 360-902-2225

CONSERVATION INFORMATION RESOURCES - STATE AGENCY ENVIRONMENTAL EDUCATION COORDINATORS

West Virginia Division of Natural Resources
Wildlife Rescue Section 1900 Kanawha Blvd. E.,
Charleston, WV 25305
Chief: BERNARD DOWLER
Phone: 304-558-2771

Wisconsin Department of Natural Resources
Box 7921, Madison, WI 53707
Secretary: GEORGE E. MEYER
Phone: 608-266-2121

Wyoming Game and Fish Department
5400 Bishop Blvd., Cheyenne, WY 82006
Director: JOHN BAUGHMAN
Phone: 307-777-4601

CANADA

Alberta Department of Forestry Lands and Wildlife
Petroleum Plaza, 9945-108 St., Edmonton, Alberta T5K 2G6
Minister: TY LUND
Phone: 403-427-6733

British Columbia Ministry of Environment, Lands and Parks
Parliament Bldg. P.O. Box 9339 Stn Prov Govt, Victoria, British Columbia V8W 9M1
Director of Wildlife Branch: NANCY BIRCHER
Phone: 250-387-9731

Manitoba Department of Natural Resources
Wildlife Branch, Box 24, 200 Saulteaux Crescent, Winnipeg, Manitoba R3J 3W3
Director: BRIAN GILLESPIE
Phone: 204-945-7761

New Brunswick Department of Natural Resources and Energy
Fish and Wildlife Branch, Centennial Bldg. P.O Box 6000, Fredericton, New Brunswick E3B 5H1
Director: ARNOLD BOER
Phone: 506-453-2433

Newfoundland Department of Natural Resources
Wildlife Division, Newfoundland
Minister: REX GIBBONS
Phone: 709-729-0659

Newfounland Departmnet of Fisheries
P.O. Box 4750, St. John's, Newfoundland A1C 5T7
Director: J. HANCOCK
Phone: 709-737-2817

Northwest Territory Department of Renewable Resources
Box 21, Scotia Center, 5th fl., 5102, 50th Ave., #600, Yellowknife, Northwest Territory X1A 3S8
Director of Wildlife and Fisheries: DOUG STEWART
Phone: 867-920-8064; Fax: 867-873-0293

Nova Scotia Depatment of Natural Resources, Wildlife Division
136 Exhibition St., Kentville, Nova Scotia B4N 4E5
Director: BARRY SABEAN
Phone: 902-679-6139

Ontario Ministry of Natural Resources
Policy Division, 99 Wellesley, Rm. 2327, Witney Block, Queens Park, Toronto, Ontario M7A 1W3
Wildlife Director: ANDREW HOUSER
Phone: 705-755-1909

Prince Edward Island Department of Environmental Resources
11 Kent St. P.O. Box 2000, Charlottetown, Prince Edward Island C1A 798
Minister: HON. BARRY HICKEN
Phone: 902-368-6410

Quebec Ministere Du Loisire
De La Chasse Et De La Peche, 150 est boul, St.-Cyrille, Quebec City, Quebec G1R 4Y1
Director: RENE LESAGE
Phone: 418-644-2823

Saskatchewan Environment and Resource Management
Legislative Bldg. 3211 Albert St., Regina, Saskatchewan S4S 5W6
Director, Fish and Wildlife: DENNIS SHERRATT
Phone: 306-787-2309

Yukon Department Renewable Resources
Wildlife Branch P.O. Box 2703, Whitehorse, Yukon Y1A 2C6
Director of Fish and Wildlife: ARTHUR HOOLE
Phone: 867-667-5715

STATE AGENCY ENVIRONMENTAL EDUCATION COORDINATORS

Alabama: Science Curriculum Development Specialist, ROBERT S. DAVIS, Gordon Persons Bldg., 50 N Ripley St., Montgomery, AL 36104-3833

Alaska: Education Specialist, PEGGY COWAN, 801W. 10th St., Ste.200, Juneau, AK 99801, Phone: 907-465-2826; Fax: 907-465-2713; E-mail: Peggy_Cowan@eed.state.ak.us

Arkansas: Science and Environmental Education Specialist, BILL FULTON, #4 State Capitol Mall, Little Rock, AR 72201-1071, Phone: 501-682-4471; E-mail: bfulton@arkedu.kiz.ar.us

California: Policy and Program Coordination Unit A consultant, Environmental/Conservation Education, BILL ANDREWS, 721 Capitol Mall, P.O. Box 944272, Sacramento, CA 94244-2720, Phone: 916-657-5374; Website: www.cde.ca.gov/cilbranch/oee

Colorado: Consultant, Conservation and Environmental Education Services, DON HOLLUMS, State Office Bldg., 201 E. Colfax, Denver, CO 80203, Phone: 303-866-6787; Fax: 303-866-6836

Connecticut: Science Consultant, STEVE WEINBURG, 165 Capitol Ave., Hartford, CT 06106, Phone: 203-566-6018; E-mail: Steve.weinberg@po.state.ct.us

Delaware: Chief of Environmental Education and Interpretation, LAURIE DRAPER, 89 Kings Highway, P.O. Box 1401, Dover, DE 19903

CONSERVATION INFORMATION RESOURCES - STATE AGENCY ENVIRONMENTAL EDUCATION COORDINATORS

Florida: Director, KATHY ABRAMS, 1311 Paul Russel Rd. Suit 201a, Tallahassee, FL 32301, Phone: 850-487-7900

Georgia: Science Coordinator of K-12, BOB MOORE, 58 Twin Towers East, Atlanta, Ga 30334, Phone: 404-656-0913; Fax: 404-657-7096; E-mail: bmoore@doe.k12.ga.us

Hawaii: Education Specialists-Environmental Education, JOHN W. HAWKINS, 189 Lunalilo Home Rd., 2nd Fl., Honolulu, HI 96825, Phone: 808-395-9252

Idaho: Math/Science Coordinator, PATRICK WHITE, P.O. Box 83720, Boise, ID 83720, Phone: 208-334-2281; Fax: 208-334-2228; E-mail: pwhite@sde.state.id.us

Illinois: Educational Consultant, GWEN POLLOCK, N 242, 100 N. First St., Springfield, IL 62777, Phone: 217-782-2826

Indiana: Science Coordinator, Office of Program Development, LEAH BRICKER, Rm. 229, State House, Indianapolis, IN 46204, Phone: 317-232-9153; Fax: 317-232-9121; E-mail: lbricker@doe.state.in.us

Iowa: Environmental Education Consultant, Curriculum Division, DUANE TOOMSEN, Grimes Office Building, Des Moines, IA 50319, Phone: 515-281-3146

Kansas: Science Consultant, GREG SCHELL, 120 SE 10th, Topeka, KS 66612, Phone: 785-296-8108

Kentucky: Director, JANE WILSON, 663 Tetontral, Frankfort, KY 40601, Phone: 800-882-5271
Science Branch Consultant, CAROL HANLEY, 500 Metro St. 18th fl. Capitol Plaza Tower, Frankfort, KY 40601, Phone: 502-564-2106; Fax: 502-564-9848; E-mail: chanley@kde.state.ky.us

Louisiana: Program Manager, Science and Environmental Education, PAUL A. LONG, P.O. Box 94064, Baton Rouge, LA 70804, Phone: 504-342-6811; E-mail: plong@mail.doe.state.la.us

Maine: Agricultural Education Specialist, DOUG ROBERTSON, 23 State House Station, Augusta, ME 04333, Phone: 207-287-5892

Maryland: Science Specialist, DIANE HOUSEHOLDER, 200 W. Baltimore St., Baltimore, MD 21201, Phone: 410-767-0324

Massachusetts: Statewide Science Coordinator, JOYCE CROCE, 350 Main Street, Malden, MA 02148, Phone: 781-388-3300,ext.300

Michigan: Science Specialist, MOZELL P. LANG, P.O. Box 30008, Lansing, MI 48909, Phone: 517-373-4223; E-mail: mlang@cdp.mde.state.mi.us

Minnesota: Science Specialist, Environmental Education Advisory Board, KATHLEEN LUNGREN, 634a Capitol Square Bldg., St. Paul, MN 55101, Phone: 612-296-4071; Fax: 612-296-3348; E-mail: kathleen.lungren@state.mn.us

Mississippi: Science Specialist, LAURA JONES, P.O. Box 771, Jackson, MS 39205, Phone: 601-359-3778; Fax: 601-359-1818; E-mail: ljones@mde.k12.ms.us

Missouri: Science Consultant, C. J. VARNON, P.O. Box 480, Jefferson, MO 65102, Phone: 573-751-4445; E-mail: cvarnon@mail.dese.state.mo.us

Nebraska: Director, Science Education, JIM WOODLAND, P.O. Box 94987, Lincoln, NE 68509, Phone: 402-471-4329; Fax: 402-472-0117; E-mail: woodland@nde4.nde.state.ne.us

Nevada: Science Education Consultant, RICHARD VINYARD, 700 E. 5th St., Carson City, NV 89701-5096, Phone: 775-681-9186; Fax: 775-687-9118

New Hampshire: Consultant, Science Education, EDWARD J. HENDRY, 101 Pleasant St., Concord, NH 03301, Phone: 603-271-3846

New Jersey: Science Coordinator, DR. BRUCE MARGANOFF, 100 Riverview Plaza, Trenton, NJ 08625, Phone: 609-984-7453; Fax: 609-292-7276

New York: Coordinator, Environmental Education, BARRY W. JAMASON, Education Building Rm. 212EB, Albany, NY 12234

North Carolina: Science Coordinator, WILLIAM TUCCI, Raleigh, NC 27601-2825, Phone: 919-715-1853

North Dakota: Social Studies Coordinator, CURT ERIKSMOEN, Division of Independent Study Box 5036, Fargo, ND 58105-5036, Phone: 701-231-6062

Oklahoma: Science Specialist, MARCIA HICKAMN, Oliver Hodge Building 2500 N. Lincoln, Oklahoma City, OK 73105, Phone: 405-522-3524; Fax: 405-521-6205; E-mail: marcie_hickman@mail.sde.state.ok.us

Oregon: Science Specialist, KATHLEEN HEIDE, 255 Capitol St. NE, Salem, OR 97310-0203, Phone: 503-378-8004,ext. 224; Fax: 503-373-7968; E-mail: kathleen.heide@state.or.us

Pennsylvania: Director, Office of Environmental Education, DR. PATRICIA VATHIS, 333 Market St. 8th Fl., Harrisburg, PA 17126-0333, Phone: 717-783-6994

Rhode Island: Director,Science Instruction, SHIRLEY HENDRIX, 255 Westminster St., Providence, RI 02903, Phone: 401-222-4600,ext.2153; Fax: 401-222-6033

South Carolina: Science and Environmental Education Associate, LINDA D. SINCLAIR, 507 Rutledge Bldg. 1449 Senate St., Columbia, SC 29201, Phone: 803-734-4605; E-mail: lsinclai@sde.state.sc.us

South Dakota: Science Director, JIM HAUCK, Kneip Bldg. 700 Governor's Drive, Pierre, SD 57501, Phone: 605-773-4712

Tennessee: Director, KAREN H. JENKINS, 710 James Robertson Parkway, Nashville, TN 37243-0379, Phone: 615-532-6249; Fax: 615-532-8536; E-mail: kjenkins@mail.state.tn.us

Texas: Environmental Education Coordinator, IRENE PICKHARDT, 1701 W. Congress Ave., Austin, TX 78701, Phone: 512-463-9556

Utah: Science Education Specialist, BRETT D. MOULDING, 250 East 500 S., Salt Lake City, UT 84111, Phone: 801-

538-7791; Fax: 801-538-7521; E-mail: bmouldin@usoe.k12.ut.us

Vermont: Liaison to Environmental Education, TIM FLYNN, 802-828-5129, Fax: tflynn@doe.state.vt.us

Virginia: Science Specialist, DELORES DALTON, P.O. Box 2120, Richmond, VA 23218-2120, Phone: 804-371-0778; Fax: 804-786-5466; E-mail: dudalton@pen.k12.va.us

Washington: Environmental Education Program Supervisor, TONY ANGELL, 2800 NE 200th St., Seattle, WA 98155-1418, Phone: 206-365-3893; Fax: 206-367-4540; E-mail: www.cisl.ospi.wednet.edu/CISL/ENVED/ENVEDTOC.html

West Virginia: State Science Director, PHYLLIS BARNHART, Bldg. 6, Rm. 330, 1900 Kanawha Blvd., East, Charleston, WV 25305-0330, Phone: 304-558-7805; Fax: 304-558-0459; E-mail: pbarnhar@access.K12.wv.us

Wyoming: President, 22 Pheasant Run, Lander, WY 82560, DONN KLESSLHEIM, 2300 Capital Ave., Cheyenne, WY 82002, Phone: 307-332-6518

SOURCES OF AUDIO-VISUAL MATERIALS

American Society of Mammalogists: Mammal Slide Image Library
Division of Biological Sciences
Campus Box 4050 Emporia State Univ., Emporia, KS 66801
Phone: 316-314-5623; Fax: 316-341-5607; E-mail: finckelm@esumail.emporia.edu; Web site: www.emporia.edu/biosci/msl/home.htm
Description: Business Manager: Elmer J Finck
Catalogues available

Audiovisuals for the Environment: International Centre for Conservation Education(ICCE)
Greenfield House, Guiting Power
Cheltenham, Gloosgow GL54 5TZ United Kingdom
Phone: 0451-850777; Fax: 0451-850705
Description: Catalogue of Environmental Audiovisuals available upon request

Berlat Films
1646 West Kimmel Rd., Jackson, MI 49201
Phone: 517-784-6969; Fax: 517-796-2646; E-mail: myrna_berlet@jackson.cc.mi.us
Description: Environmental Education "Great Animals Stories". 20 minute videos on birds and mammals.

Brauer Productions
530 S. Union St., Traverse City, MI (Michigan) 49684
Phone: 616-941-0850; Fax: 616-941-0947; Web site: www.brauer.com
Founded: 1978
Description: Full Service film and video production company serving Traverse City and clients throughout Michigan and the Northwest since 1978.

Bullfrog Films
Oley, PA 19547
Phone: 800-543-FROG (3764); E-mail: bullfrog@econet.org; Web site: www.bullfrogfilms.com
Description: Films and videos rented and sold worldwide to educational institutions. Programs come with study guide, with suggested activities, research topics, debate subjects, and bibliographies. Free catalogues available.

Conservation Education Association: Critical Index of Films on Man and His Environment, The Interstate
19-27 N. Jackson St., Danville, IL 61832

Environmental Media Productions
P.O. Box 1016, Chapel Hill, NC 27514
Phone: 919-933-3003; Fax: 919-942-8785; E-mail: ggerber@envmedia.com
Founded: 1989
Description: Environmental Media designs, produces, and distributes media to support environmental education. Programs are curriculum-based and most are accompanied by teaching guides. Free catalogue available and other educational material.

Environmental Media
Marketing, Disribution and Catalog Sales
P.O. Box 99, Beaufort, SC 29901-099
Phone: 800-ENV-EDUC

Gecko Productions, Inc.
Attn: Director, Natalie Ward, P.O. Box 573, Woods Hole, MA 02543
Phone: 508-548-3313; Fax: 508-548-3317; E-mail: nward@mbl.edu
Founded: 1995
Description: Designs conservation education materials and workshops about marine endangered species and marine protected areas, with emphasis on bringing environmental awareness and cultural understanding to the United States and beyond.

Georgia Department of Natural Resources, Film and Video Unit
205 Butler St., SE, Suite 1354, Atlanta, GA 30334
Phone: 404-657-9851; Fax: 404-651-5871; Web site: www.ganet.org/dnr/parks/video/film.html
Description: ATTN: Circulation Manager. Free loan and sales. Free film catalogue available upon request.

Green Mountain Post Films
P.O. Box 229, Turner Falls, MA 01376
Phone: 413-863-4754; Fax: 413-863-8248; Web site: www.gmpfilms.com
Founded: 1975
Description: A film/video production and distribution company that specializes in media concerning environmental issues.

Green TV
1125 Hayes St., San Francisco, CA 94117
Phone: 415-225-4797; Fax: 415-255-4664; E-mail: fgreen@greentv.org; Web site: www.greentv.org
Founded: 1992
Description: A non-profit video production company specializing in television programming on subjects about human interaction with the natural world. Offers catalog of stock footage of California wildlife, endangered species habitats and the timber industry.

International Film Bureau, Inc.
332 S. Michigan Ave., Chicago, IL 60604
Phone: 312-427-4545; Fax: 312-427-4550
Description: Sales, Rentals; Free Catalogue, 1-800-432-2241

Jere Mossier Productions/Underwater Images
P.O. Box 1415, Hayden, ID 83835
Phone: 208-683-8112; E-mail: mail@jeremossier.com; Web site: www.jeremossier.com
Description: Contracts for producing fisheries, wildlife, and natural history videos.

Media Designs Associates, Inc.
P.O. Box 3189, Boulder, CO 80307
Phone: 303-443-2800/800-228-8854; Fax: 303-443-2882; E-mail: mediades@indra.com; Web site: www.indra.com/mediades
Founded: 1973
Description: Produce and distribute film/video, including laser videodisc and CD-ROM formats. Science education materials produced by themselves and others from NSF, NPS, and West Wind Productions. West Wind specializes in natural history and environmental subjects. Free Catalogues Available.

Montana Fish, Wildlife, and Parks Film Center
1420 E. 6th Ave. P.O. Box 200701, Helena, MT 59620-0701
Phone: 406-444-2426; Fax: 406-444-4952; Web site: fwp.state.mt.us/educat/trunkeddt.htm
Description: Brochure is available upon request.

Neal and Reed Communications, Inc.
169 Belle Forest Cr., Nashville, TN 37221
Phone: 615-662-1946; Fax: 615-662-1995
Description: Produce outreach videos supporting sustainable ecosystems and development, conservation of natural resources, wildlife, and cultural integrity. Specialists in translating complex issues into compelling, motivating communications.

South Carolina Department of Natural Resources, Film Department
P.O. Box 167 or 1000 Assembly St., Columbia, SC 29202
Phone: John Lucas at 803-734-3909
Description: Catalogue Available. Only to groups over 15 people, for South Carolina Residents only.

The Video Project:
200 Estates Drive, Ben Lomond, CA 95005
Phone: 800-475-2638 (1800-4planet); Fax: 831-386-2168; E-mail: videoproject@videoproject.org; Web site: www.videoproject.org/
Description: "Media for a safe and sustainable world." Affordable films and videos on environmental and related issues. The project now offers over 600 programs for sale or rental. Free catalogues available.

U.S. Department of Agriculture Films
Description: Available from film libraries of the 50 state land grant universities. Catalogues available from university film libraries.

U.S. Department of the Interior Films
18th & C St. NW, Washington DC 20240
Description: Catalogue available by writing Office of Public Affairs, U.S. Department of the Interior.

U.S. Forest Service Video Library c/o Audience Planners
5341 Derry Ave. Suite Q, Agoura Hills, CA 91301
Phone: 800-683-8366; Fax: 818-865-1327; Web site: www.r5.fs.fed.us/video
Description: Only cost return postage. Video library and catalogue at web site.

Video Active Productions:
200 Boyden Rd., Canton, NY 13617
Phone: 315-386-8797
Founded: 1985
Description: Part of the movement for environmental justice. Seeking to give a voice to victims, empower potential victims, promote a public dialogue, enhance informed decision making, stimulate local democracy, expose corruption, validate common sense, endorse sustainable development, and reach fronts of problems.

Walkabout Productions, Inc.
632 Harberts Court, Annapolis, MD 21401
Phone: 410-573-1228 or DC Metro area:301-970-2525
Founded: 1975.
Description: Walkabout Productions, Inc., is an EMMY award winning production team that focuses on environment, wildlife, and science documentaries. Filmography is available.

Wildlife Education Program and Design
44781 Bittner Point Rd., Boverly, MN 55709
Phone: 218-245-3049; E-mail: karlyn@uslink.net
Description: A non-profit education organization with slide lectures, Wolf Display, education programs and teachers workshops with "Wolves and Humans" curriculum and a Wolf Learning Stations box of environmental education materials. Nationwide programs available.

Wyoming Game and Fish Department, Video Coordinator
5400 Bishop Blvd, Cheyenne, WY 82002
Phone: 307-777-4630; Fax: 307-777-4610
Description: Catalogue Available

PERIODICALS AND DIRECTORIES

PERIODICALS

Air and Water Pollution Report's Environment Week
951 Pershing Dr., Silver Spring, MD 20910
Phone: 301-587-6300
Weekly-One Year Subscription; One Year - $617.00;

Animals Agenda
P.O. Box 25881, Baltimore, MD 21224
Phone: 410-675-4566; Fax: 410-675-0066; E-mail: office@animalsagenda.org; Web site: www.animalsagenda.org
One Year - $24.00 U.S.;$30.00 Canada/Mexico; $37.00 other foreign;

BioCycle Journal of Composting & Recycling
The J.G. Press, Inc., 419 State Ave., Emmaus, PA 18049
Phone: 610-967-4135

Boating Business
Formula Publication, 447 Spears Rd., Suite 4, Oakville, Ontario L6K 3S7
Phone: 905-842-6591; Fax: 905-842-6843
Editor: Lizanne Madigan

Boston College Environmental Affairs Law Review
Boston College Law School, 885 Centre St., Newton Centre, MA 02159
Quarterly; $23.00-per year;

CONSERVATION INFORMATION RESOURCES - PERIODICALS AND DIRECTORIES

Caretaker Gazette, The
Property Caretaking Opportunities Worldwide, P.O. Box 5887, Carefree, AZ 85377
Phone: 480-488-1970; E-mail: caretaker@uswest.net; Web site: www.angelfire.com/wa/caretaker/
Bimonthly;

Clean Water Report
CJE Associates, 237 Gretna Green Ct., Alexandria, VA 22304
Phone: 703-823-0662; Fax: 703-823-5923
Biweekly; $295.00-per year;

Clearing Magazine
John Inskeep Environmental Learning Center, 19600 S. Molalla Ave., Oregon City, OR 97045
Phone: 503-657-6958,ext.2638; E-mail: clearing@teleport.com
Bimonthly;

Congressional Green Sheets, Inc.
406 E St. SE, Washington, DC 20003
Phone: 202-546-2220; Fax: 202-546-7490; E-mail: wb@greensheets.com; Web site: www.greensheets.com

Container Recycling Report
P.O. Box 10540, Portland, OR 97296
Phone: 503-227-1319; Fax: 503-227-6135
Monthly; $49.00 per year;

E/The Environmental Magazine
P.O. Box 5098, Westport, CT 06881
Phone: 203-854-5559; Fax: 203-866-0602; E-mail: info@emagazine.com; Web site: www.emagazine.com
Six Issues per year; $20 per year; Subscription Department: P.O. Box 2047 Marion, OH 43306;

Ecology Law Quarterly
University of California, Boalt Hall School of Law, Berkeley, CA 94720
Phone: 510-642-0457; Fax: 510-643-9042; E-mail: elq@violet.berkeley.edu
US: $30 per volume/year individuals, $22 per volume/year students, $50 per volume/year institution. $6 per volume/year foreign postage(surface), $32 per volume/year foreign postage(airmail);

Ecology USA
CJE Associates, 237 Gretna Green Ct., Alexandria, VA 22304
Phone: 703-823-0662; Fax: 703-823-5923
Biweekly; $135 per year;

Endangered Species and Wetlands Report
P.O. Box 5393, Takoma Park, MD 20913
Phone: 301-891-3791; Fax: 301-891-3507; E-mail: poplar@crosslink.net; Web site: www.eswr.com
Monthly; $245 a year, discount for new subscribers, qualified non-profit groups, and students; Editor: Steve Davies

Endangered Species Bulletin
Division of Endangered Species, U.S. Fish and Wildlife Service, Washington, DC 20240

Endangered Species Update
School of Natural Resources and Environment, The University of Michigan, Ann Arbor, MI 48109
Phone: 734-763-3243; Fax: 734-936-2195; E-mail: esupdate@umich

Bimonthly; $28 per year (US), $23 for students;

Environment Abstracts Annual
Congressional Information Services, 4520 East-West Hwy., Bethesda, MD 20814
Phone: 800-638-8380 or 301-654-1550; Fax: 301-654-4033
Annually; $495 per year;

Environment Reporter
Bureau of National Affairs, Inc., 1231 25th St., NW, Washington, DC 20037

Environmental Building News
122 Bridge St., Suite 30, Brattleboro, VT 05301
Phone: 802-257-7300 or 800-861-0954; Fax: 802-257-7304; E-mail: ebn@ebuild.com; Web site: www.ebuild.com
11 issues a year; $79 a year. $149 a year for companies with over 24 employees. $30 additional for addressees outside North America. E Build library CD-Rom of all back issues, updated annually, first copy: subscribers $95, non-subscribers $149.; also available: EBN Product Directory of more than 1,200 green building products with model specification language: $89 plus shipping.

Environmental Education Research
Dept. of Education, University of Bath, Bath BA2 7AY
Phone: 44-1225-826648; Fax: 44-1225-826113; E-mail: w.a.h.scott@bath.ac.uk; Web site: www.bath.ac.uk
Academic journal featuring papers on environmental education and education for sustainable development. Co-edited by William Scott, University of Bath.

Environmental Law
Northwestern School of Law; Lewis and Clark College, 10015 SW Terwilliger Blvd., Portland, OR 97219
Phone: 503-768-6700; Fax: 503-768-6671
Quarterly;

Environmental Remediation Technology
Business Publishers, Inc., 8737 Colesville Road, Suite 1100, Silver Spring, MD 20910
Phone: 301-587-6300; Fax: 301-589-8493; Web site: www.bpinews.com
Biweekly; $459 per year (26 issues);

Environmental Science and Technology
American Chemical Society, 1155 16th St. NW, Washington, DC 20036
Phone: 202-872-4582; Fax: 202-872-4582; E-mail: est@acs.org
ACS members: $67; Non-members: $155; Institutions: $973; Students: $50;

Forestry Advantage, The
National Forestry Association, 374 Maple Ave. E., Suite 310, Vienna, VA 22180
Quarterly;

Global Environment Change Report
37 Broadway, Arlington, MA 02174
Phone: 617-648-8700
Twice a month; $457 US and Canada, $557 Foreign;

Harvard Environmental Law Review
Harvard Law School, Cambridge, MA 02138
Phone: 617-495-3110; Fax: 617-496-2148; E-mail: hlselr@hulaw1.harvard.edu

High Country News
Box 1090, Paonia, CO 81428
Phone: 970-527-4898, Subscriptions 800-9051155; Fax: 970-527-4897
Biweekly; $28 per year (individual, school/public libraries) $38 per year (business inst.);
Semi-annually; $28 per year (US). $34 per year (foreign surface mail), $46 per year(foreign air mail);

Industry and Environment Review
United Nations Environment Programme Division of Technology, Industry and Economics (UNEP/TIE), Tour Mirabeau, 39-43 Quai Andre Citroen, 75739 Paris cedex 15
Phone: 33-1-44-37-14-50; Fax: 33-1-44-37-14-74
$45 surface mail, $60 airmail;

International Cleaner Production Information Claeringhouse
United Nations Environment Division of Technology, Industry and Economics (UNEP/TIE), Tour Mirabeau, 39-43 Quai Andre Citroen, 75739 Paris cedex 15
Phone: 33-1-44-37-14-50; Fax: 33-1-44-37-14-74
$50 US;

Land Letter (The Newsletter for Natural Resource Professionals)
Environment and Energy Publishing, LLC, 122 C St., NW, Suite 722, Washington, DC 20001
34 issues/year; $195 introductory rate;

Land Use Law Report
Business Publishers, Inc., 8737 Colesville Rd., Suite 1100, Silver Spring, MD 20910
Phone: 301-587-6300; Fax: 301-589-8493; Web site: www.bpinews.com
Biweekly; $367 per year (includes first class postage);

Landscape Journal
The University of Wisconsin Press, 2537 Daniels St., Madison, WI 53718
Phone: 608-224-3880
Semi-annually; $34 (individual), $92 (institution);

Mother Earth News
49 East 21st St., 11th fl., New York, NY 10010
Phone: 212-260-7210
Bimonthly;

National Boycott News
Institute for Consumer Responsibility (ICR), 3618 Wallingford Ave. N., Seattle, WA 98103
Phone: 206-523-0421; Fax: 206-523-0421

National Environmental Employment Report
Environmental Careers World, 100 Bridge St., Bldg. C, Hampton, VA 23669
Phone: 757-727-7895; Fax: 757-727-7904; E-mail: ecwo@environmental-jobs.com; Web site: www.environmental-jobs.com
Monthly; $19 three issues, $35 six issues, $59 12 issues (individuals), $89 12 issues (universities & organizations), $159 -24 issues.

National Wetlands Newsletter
Environmental Law Institute, 1616 P St. NW, Suite 200, Washington, DC 20036
Phone: 800-433-5120
Bimonthly

National Woodlands Magazine
National Woodland Owners Association, 374 Maple Ave., E, Suite 310, Vienna, VA 22180
Quarterly;

Natural Resources Journal
University of New Mexico School of Law, 1117 Stanford, NE, Albuquerque, NM 87131-1431
Quarterly; $40 ($45 Foreign) per year;

Nuclear Waste News
Business Publishers, Inc., 8737 Colesville Rd., Suite 1100, Silver Spring, MD 20910
Phone: 301-587-6300; Fax: 301-587-1081; Web site: www.bpinews.com
Weekly; $867 per year;

Organic Gardening Magazine
Rodale Press, Inc., 33 E. Minor St., Emmaus, PA 18098
Phone: 610-967-5171; Fax: 610-967-7846
6 issues per year; $19.96;

Outdoor Canada
703 Evans Ave., Suite 202, Toronto, Ontario M9C 5E9
Phone: 416-695-0311; Fax: 416-695-0381

Plastics Recycling Update
P.O. Box 10540, Portland, OR 97296
Phone: 503-227-1319; Fax: 503-227-6135
Monthly; $49 per year;

Pollution Abstracts
Cambridge Scientific Abstracts, 7200 Wisconsin Ave., Bethesda, MD 20814
Phone: 301-961-6700; Fax: 301-961-6720; E-mail: market@csa.com

Preserving Family Land, Book 1: Essential Tax Strategies for the Landowner; Preserving Family Lands. Book 2: More Planning Strategies for the Future
Landowner Planning Center, P.O. Box 2242, Boston, MA 02101
Phone: 617-357-1644

Refuge Reporter
AVOCET TWO, Publisher, Avocet Crossing, Millwood, VA 22646
Phone: 540-837-2152; E-mail: refrep@mnsinc.com; Web site: www.gorp.com/refrep/
Quarterly; $12/year $22/ 2 years;

The Environmental Law Reporter
Environmental Law Institute, 1616 P St. NW Suite 200, Washington, DC 20036
Monthly;

The Game Manager
P.O. Box 1330, West Point, CA 95255
Phone: 209-293-7087; Fax: 209-293-7105
Quarterly; $20 per year;

The Groundwater Newsletter
Water Information Center, Inc., 2525 Arapahoe Ave., Suite E4-910, Boulder, CO 80302
Phone: 303-546-6900; Fax: 303-546-9113
Twice Monthly: U.S. and Canada: 1995-$347; 1996-$347, Overseas: 1995-$377, 1996-$377. Two year subscriptions: U.S.: 1995-$567, 1996-$567. Overseas: 1995-$597, 1996-$597

The Law and the Land
Robinson and Cole, LLP, 280 Trumbull St., Hartford, CT 06103
Phone: 860-275-8200
Quarterly

Tundra Talk Newsletter
Connecticut Caribou Clan, P.O. Box 9344, Bolton, CT 06043
Phone: 860-643-2948; E-mail: captundra@aol.com; Web site: members.aol.com/captundra/TALKNEWSLETTER.html

Virginia Environmental Law Journal
University of Virginia School of Law, Charlottesville, VA 22903
Phone: 804-924-3683; Fax: 804-924-7536; E-mail: acd5t@virginia.edu

Water Newsletter and International Water Report
Water Information Center, Inc., 2525 Arapahoe Ave., Ste. E4-910, Boulder, CO 80302
Phone: 303-391-8799; Fax: 303-294-1239
Monthly; $127 (Domestic & Canada 15% discount-$107.95) $157 (overseas-airmail), Individual issues-$10.58/copy - domestic; $13.08/copy overseas. 2nd copy 9in same envelope)-$50/year; 3rd & 4th copies-$40/year; Two year subscriptions-$216 (domestic); $246 (overseas);

Wild Earth
P.O. Box 455, Richmond, VT 05477
Phone: 802-434-4077; Fax: 802-434-5980; E-mail: info@wild-earth.org; Web site: www.wild-earth.org
Quarterly; Voice for wild nature melding conservation biology and grassroots activism. Covers biodiversity, wilderness protection, land ethics, population problems and more. Editor: Tom Butler; Publisher: Dave Foreman

Wildlife Law News Quarterly
Center for Wildlife Law, School of Law, Institute of Public Law, 1117 Stanford, NE, Albuquerque, NM 87131
Phone: 505-277-5006; Fax: 505-277-7064
$60 one year subscription, $48 student price

Woodland Report (Forestry Newsletter)
National Woodland Owners Association, 374 Maple Ave. E., Suite 310, Vienna, VA 22180
Eight issue/year;

World Environment Report
Business Publishers, Inc., 8737 Colesville Rd., Suite 1100, Silver Spring, MD 20910
Phone: 301-587-6300; Fax: 301-589-8493; Web site: www.bpinews.com
One year (26 issues); $494 per year;

DIRECTORIES

California Environmental Directory: A Guide to Organizations and Resources
California Institute of Public Affairs, P.O. Box 189040, Sacramento, CA 95818
Phone: 916-442-2472; Fax: 916-442-2478; Web site: www.cipahg.org
Regular Price $40. Special price for public, academic, and governmental libraries and for nonprofit public-interest associations ordering on letterhead: $25; Guide to California's state and federal government agencies, universities, major associations and selected agencies concerned with natural resources and the environment.

Congress at Your Fingertips - Congressional Directories
Published by Capital Advantage, P.O. Box 2018, Fairfax, VA 22031
Phone: 703-289-4670 or 800-659-8708 (outside D.C. area); Fax: 703-289-4678
Annually; Single Copy, spiral bound, Standard Version: $13.95 (includes shipping); Provides information on congress members (including photos), key staff, addresses, tips on writing and visiting, congressional schedule and map of office building layout. Free catalog available.

Congressional Staff Directory
CA Staff Directories, Inc., 815 Slaters Ln., Alexandria, VA 22314
Phone: 703-739-0900 or 800-252-1722; Fax: 703-739-0234
Three times a year; $227 - three editions; individual - $89. Also available on diskette and CD-Rom. Contains information concerning Congress: Member contact information, biographies, pictures, office staff, election returns, congressional districts and more.

Directory of Environmental Groups in New England
Environmental Protection Agency, Region 1, REN, John F. Kennedy Federal Bldg., Boston, MA 02203

Directory of Natural Environmental Science Centers
Natural Science for Youth Foundation, 130 Azalea Dr., Roswell, GA 30075
Single Copy: $55 plus $3.50 for postage and handling.; Lists over 1,100 Environmental Science centers throughout the United States, Canada and the Virgin Islands. Provides addresses, phone number, hours, fees, acreage and other special features.

Environmental Grantmaking Foundations Directory
Resources for Global Sustainability, P.O. Box 3665, Cary, NC 27519
Phone: 800-724-1857; Fax: 919-363-9841; E-mail: rgs@environmentalgrants.com; Web site: www.environmentalgrants.com
$100 (print, 1,000 pages) and $110 (CD-Rom). Online Directory to be available in March 2000; Guide to over 800 independent, community and corporate foundations that give environmental grants. Profiles of foundations include contact information, history and philosophy, financial data, sample grants and more. Online directory available March 2000.

Environmental Services Directory for Washington State
P.O. Box 99486, Seattle, WA 98199
Phone: 206-282-2591; Fax: 206-284-6570
A business to business directory of environmental products and information sources covering Washington State's environmental industry.

Federal Staff Directory
CA Staff Directories, Inc., 815 Slaters Ln., Alexandria, VA 22314
Phone: 703-739-0900; Fax: 703-739-0234
Published three times a year; Single Copy; $89 each. Subscription: $227. Also available on CD-Rom and mailing lists; Lists 38,000 Executive Branch Officials by name with contact information and responsibilities from the White House, all departments, regulatory bodies, advisory organizations, agencies and regional offices.

CONSERVATION INFORMATION RESOURCES - DATABASES AND SERVICES

Judicial Staff Directory
CA Staff Directories, 815 Slaters Ln., Alexandria, VA 22314
Phone: 703-739-0900; Fax: 703-739-0234
Single Copy: $89 each. Also available on CD-Rom and mailing lists; Contains listings of all federal courts, judges and staff, including magistrates, court clerks and deputies, probation officers, U.S. Attorneys and U.S. Marshals. Also includes maps of judicial districts, court workload and case statistics.

The New England Environmental Directory (NEED)
8850 O'Brien Creek Rd., Missoula, MT 59801
Phone: 406-543-3359
Biannually; $15; Designed to facilitate access to public agencies, environmental activists and educators and to encourage effective use of environmental education resources.

World Directory of Environmental Organizations
California Institute of Public Affairs in cooperation with the Sierra Club and the IUCN, P.O. Box 189040, Sacramento, CA 95818
Phone: 916-442-2472; Fax: 916-442-2478; Web site: www.cipahq.org
Single Copy $50 plus $2 handling; Describes more than 3,200 organizations in over 200 countries and includes profiles of environmental activities. Also lists key national governmental and non-governmental organizations.

DATABASES AND SERVICES

ABSEARCH
Type: Abstracts and bibliographies
Subject: Wildlife, Ecology, Conservation Biology, Mammalogy, Zoology, Ornithology, Wildfowl, Wetlands, Fisheries, Ichthyology and Herpetology
Language: English
Available Service Through: ABSEARCH, Inc.
Producer: ABSEARCH, Inc.,121 Sweet Ave., Moscow, ID 83843
Phone: 1-800-867-1877; Fax: 208-885-3803; E-mail: absearch@moscow.com; Web site: www.absearch.com
Contact: ABBY L. COLEMEN
Description: ABSEARCH databases include thousands of abstracts and citations from professional research journals in the area of natural resources. The databases are updated as new research becomes available.
Format: CD-ROM and Internet

AGRICOLA
Type: Bibliographic
Subject: Natural Resources, Animal Welfare, Pollution, Pesticides, Land and Water Management
Language: English and over 70 other languages.
Available Service Through: DIALOG, OCLC
Producer: National Agricultural Library, Information Systems Division, 10301 Baltimore Blvd., Beltsville, MD 20705
Phone: 301-504-6813
Contact: DAVID GOLDBERG
Description: Agricola is a database of bibliographic citations covering all aspects of agricultural and food sciences, including natural resources, animal welfare, pollution, pesticides and land and water management. The database has over 3 million records.

AIR AND WATER POLLUTION REPORT
Type: Full Text
Subject: Environmental Law, Air Quality and Pollution, Water Pollution Management, toxic substances.
Language: English
Available Service Through: Newsnet and Predicasts
Producer: Business Publishers, Inc.,951 Pershing Dr., Silver Spring, MD 20910
Phone: 301-587-6300; Fax: 301-587-1081
Contact: DAVID GOELLER
Description: Covers policy regulation and legislation on the Clean Air and Water Acts, global warming research, acid rain , air toxins, indoor air pollutants, and much more, for the regulator and the regulated community.

AQUALINE
Type: Abstracts
Subject: Water Cycle
Language: English
Available Service Through: QUESTEL-ORBIT
Producer: WRc plc,Frankland Rd., Balgrove, Swindon, Wilts SN5 8YF Great Britain
Phone: 01-793-511-711; Fax: 01-793-511-712; E-mail: aqualine@wrcplc.co.uk
Contact: KAREN HUTCHINSON
Description: Aqualine covers the world's literature on the complete hydrological cycle from source to sea, up to and including the continental shelf.

AQUATIC TOXICITY INFORMATION RETRIEVAL (AQUIRE)
Type: Data extract from scientific papers
Subject: Toxicity of chemical substances to aquatic species.
Language: English
Available Service Through: Chemical Information Systems (CIS)
Producer: EPA,Oxford Molecular Group, Inc., Executive Plaza III, Suite 1100, 11350 McCormick Rd., Hunt Valley, MD 21031
Phone: 800-CIS-USER (CIS User Support Group)
Contact: Description: AQUIRE includes more than 129,000 records detailing the effects of chemical substances on aquatic species, including chronic and acute toxicity data.

ARCTIC AND ANTARCTIC REGIONS (Cold Regions)
Type: Bibliographic
Subject: Arctic, Antarctic, Polar Regions, and Cold Regions.
Language: English
Available Service Through: CD-ROM and Internet
Producer: National Information Services Corporation, Wyman Towers, 3100 St. Paul St., Baltimore, MD 21218
Phone: 410-243-0797; Fax: 410-243-0982; E-mail: sales@nisc.com
Contact: Description: Over 826,000+ citations and abstracts from eleven major polar files.

AUSTRALIAN EARTH SCIENCES INFORMATION SYSTEM
Type: Bibliographic
Subject: Environmental protection, pollution, rehabilitation
Language: English
Producer: Australian Mineral Foundation, 63 Conyngham St., Glenside, S.A. 5065 Australia
Phone: 08-83790444: International: 61-8-83790444; E-mail: amf@amf.com.au; Web site: www.anf.com.au/amf
Contact: Information Service Manager
Description: AESIS covers Australian-generated published and unpublished documented material over the full range of the geo sciences. AESIS also covers materials published on continental Australia by non-Australian sources.

Format: CD-ROM, DIALOG File 105

BIOSIS PREVIEWS
Type: Bibliographic
Subject: Botany, Ecology, Environmental Biology, Evolution, Forestry, Horticulture, Plant Physiology, Soil Microbiology, Temperature
Language: English
Available Service Through: OVID Online, Dialog, DIMDI, Data Star, Science and Technology Library Information and Documentation Center, Royal Society of Chemistry, NERAC, Inc., OCLC Online Computer Library Center, Inc.
Producer: BIOSIS, 2100 Arch St., Philadelphia, PA 19103-1399
Phone: 800-523-4806 or 215-587-4800; Fax: 215-587-2016; E-mail: info@mail.biosis.org
Contact: ALAN CLARK
Description: BIOSIS Previews is the online version of the citations found in the printed publications Biological Abstracts and biological Abstracts/RRM. The database contains bibliographic information and abstracts derived from life science source publications.

BIOTECHNOLOGY ABSTRACTS
Language: English
Available Service Through: National Information Services Corp.
Producer: Cambridge Scientific Abstracts, Wydman Towers, 3100 St. Paul St., Baltimore, MD 21218
Phone: 410-243-0797; Fax: 410-243-0982; E-mail: sales@nisc.com
Contact: Description: Database of international literature in molecular biology and genetics, involving agricultural products, plants and animals. Quarterly subscription: $695 (CD-ROM), $975 (Biblioline).
Format: CD-ROM and Biblioline

BUSINESS AND THE ENVIRONMENT
Type: Full text newsletter
Subject: Monthly International coverage of 'green' corporate environmental initiatives, environmental regulations and related topics
Language: English
Available Service Through: hardcopy subscription, access via web site
Producer: Cutter Info. Corp., 37 Broadway, Suite 1, Arlington, MA 02174
Phone: 800-964-5125/617-641-5125
Contact: DENNIS CROWLEY
Description: Subscription includes quarterly Meeting Planner listing of environment-related meetings and conferences worldwide and the ISO 14000 Update, a monthly briefing on the ISO 14000 environmental management standards.

CERCLA INFORMATION SYSTEM (CERCLIS)
Type: Full text
Subject: Superfund Sites
Language: English
Available Service Through: Chemical Information Systems
Producer: EPA, Oxford Molecular Group, Inc., Executive Plaza III, Suite 1100, 11350 McCormick Rd., Hunt Valley, MD 21031
Phone: 800-CIS-USER (CIS User Support Group)
Contact: Description: CERCLIS contains complete public disclosure records from EPA for more than 42,000 US sites proposed or chosen for cleanup under Superfund. It is searchable by name, locale and a variety of methods. Does not include NFRAP sites and PRP.

CHEMICAL EVALUATION SEARCH AND RETRIEVAL SYSTEM (CESARS)
Type: Text and Tabular
Subject: Toxicity of chemicals of concern to the environment
Language: English
Available Service Through: CIS, CCINFOLINE (online), CCINFODISK (CD version)
Producer: Michigan Dept. of Environmental Quality, Surface Water Quality Division, P.O. Box 30273, Lansing, MI 48909
Phone: 517-335-3308
Contact: DENNIS BUSH
Description: Chemicals are evaluated for their toxicity by reviewing the primary literature sources

CHEMICAL HAZARDS INFORMATION SYSTEM (ChemHazIS)
Type: Data extracted from scientific Subject: Toxicity, health, carcinogenicity, chemical-physical properties, transportation, regulations and uses
Language: English
Available Service Through: Chemical Information System
Producer: NTP, Oxford Molecular Group, Inc., Executive Plaza III, Suite 1100, 11350 McCormick Rd., Hunt Valley, MD 210031
Phone: 800-CIS-USER
Contact: Description: ChemHazIS contains over 2,280 chemicals compiled by the National Toxicology Program (NTP). Each record closely resembles a Material Safety Data Sheet (MSDS) format.

CHEMICAL HAZARDS RESPONSE INFORMATION SYSTEM (CHRIS)
Type: Data extracted from scientific Subject: Handling of hazardous materials
Language: English
Available Service Through: Chemical Information System (CIS)
Producer: U.S. Coast Guard, Oxford Molecular Group, Inc., Executive Plaza III, Suite 1100, 11350 McCormick Rd., Hunt Valley, MD 21031
Phone: 800-CIS-USER
Contact: Description: CHRIS is the Coast Guard's principal database for providing information on safe handling of hazardous substances.

COMPUTER-AIDED ENVIRONMENTAL LEGISLATIVE DATA SYSTEM (CELDS)
Type: Abstracts
Subject: Environmental Regulations
Language: English
Producer: Environmental Technical Information System, 611 E. Lorado Taft Dr., #111, Champaign, IL 61820-6921
Phone: 217-333-1369; Fax: 217-244-1717
Contact: ELIZABETH DENNISON
Description: CELDS is an information bank of abstracted federal and state environmental regulations and standards. Abstracts are classified within several environmental sector categories to provide quick access to current regulations.

ECOLINE
Type: Full text, key words
Subject: Acid Rain, Global Warming, Soil Erosion, Environmental Programs
Language: English
Available Service Through: Together Foundation

Producer: Together Foundation and the University of Vermont Environmental Program, 130 S. Willard St., Burlington, VT 05401
Phone: 802-682-2030; Fax: 802-862-1890
Contact: HANS KELLER

ECOLOGY ABSTRACTS
Type: Bibliographic
Subject: Ecology
Language: English
Available Service Through: National Information Services Corporation
Producer: Cambridge Scientific Abstracts, Wyman Towers, 3100 St. Paul St., Baltimore, MD 21218
Phone: 410-243-0797; Fax: 410-243-0982; E-mail: sales@nisc.com
Contact: ROBERT HILTON
Description: Focuses on how organisms of all kinds (microbes, plants and animals) interact with their environments and with other organisms.
Format: CD ROM and online through Dialog, BIOSIS, Life Science Network and BRS.

ECONET
Type: Various Types
Subject: Energy, Environmental Education, Toxic Substances, Sustainable Development, Global Warming, Environmental Justice
Language: English
Available Service Through: Institute for Global Communications
Producer: Institute for Global Communications, P.O. Box 29904, San Francisco, CA 94129-0904
Phone: 415-561-6100; Fax: 415-561-6101; E-mail: econet@igc.apc.org; Web site: www.igc.org
Contact: MICHAEL STEIN
Description: Through the development of communication and information sharing systems, EcoNet seeks to increase collaboration and cooperation between organizations seeking environmental sustainability.

EMERGENCY RELEASE NOTIFICATION SYSTEM (ERNS)
Type: Data extracted from reference
Subject: Notifications of oil and hazardous substances releases and spills
Language: English
Available Service Through: Chemical Information System (CIS)
Producer: EPA, Oxford Molecular Group, Inc., Executive Plaza III, Suite 1100, 11350 McCormick Rd., Hunt Valley, MD 21031
Phone: 800-CIS-USER
Contact: Description: ERNS contains over 231,312 release and spill notifications of oil and/or hazardous substances. It can be used to examine the following categories: transportation accident, equipment failure, operator error, natural phenomenon, dumping and unknown.

ENERGY DESIGN UPDATE
Type: Full Text
Subject: Energy-efficient residential design and construction
Language: English
Available Service Through: Newsnet
Producer: Cutter Information Corp., 37 Broadway, Suite one, Arlington, MA 02174
Phone: 800-964-5118
Contact: KAREN KURR
Description: News and analysis of developments in energy-efficient home construction and practical, hands-on information on the latest building techniques and products.

ENERGY, ECONOMICS AND CLIMATE CHANGE
Type: Full Text
Subject: Economic implications of climate change policies
Language: English
Available Service Through: Newsnet, Predicasts
Producer: Cutter Information Corp., 37 Broadway, Suite one, Arlington, MA 02174
Phone: 800-964-5118
Contact: KAREN KURR
Description: Analyses of latest economic studies and reports pertaining to climate change, legislative updates and utility regulation.

ENTOMOLOGY ABSTRACTS
Language: English
Producer: National Information Services Corp., Suite 6, Wydman Towers, 3100 St. Paul St., Baltimore, MD 21218
Phone: 410-243-0797; Fax: 410-243-0982; E-mail: sales@nisc.com
Contact: Description: Information on geographic distribution, nomenclature, new species and more; 1978-present. Subscription: $1,445 (CD-ROM), $2025 (Biblioline).
Format: CD-ROM and Internet

ENVIROFATE
Type: Data extracted from scientific Subject: Environmental fate of chemicals
Language: English
Available Service Through: Chemical Information Systems
Producer: EPA, Oxford Molecular Group, Inc., Executive Plaza III, Suite 1100, 11350 McCormick Rd., Hunt Valley, MD 21031
Phone: 800-CIS-USER (CIS User Support Group)
Contact: Description: Envirofate deals with the environmental fate or behavior of chemicals released into the environment. It covers a variety of types of data, including more than 15,000 on some 1,300 substances.

ENVIROLINE
Subject: Acid Rain, Environment, Land Use Planning, Population Growth and Transportation
Available Service Through: Dialog
Producer: Congressional Information Service, Inc., 4520 East-West Hwy., Bethesda, MD 20814-3389
Phone: 800-638-8380/301-654-1550; Fax: 301-654-4033
Contact: DIANE KEELY
Description: Publishes indexes, electronic databases and microform collections that provide access to information published by government, private and international sources.

ENVIRONMENT ABSTRACTS
Type: Abstracting and Indexing
Subject: Environment, Air, Water, Noise Pollution, Environmental Law, Wildlife Management, Solid and Toxic Wastes
Language: English
Available Service Through: Dialog, ORBIT, Infoline, ESA-IRS, DIMDI, Data Star, FIZ-TECHNIK, Lexis-Nexis
Producer: Congressional Information Service, Inc., 4520 East-West Hwy., Bethesda, MD 20814-3389
Phone: 301-654-1550
Contact: LARRY SHERIDAN

Description: Abstracts and indexes information from scientific, technical and business journals; conference and symposium proceedings; newsletters; and academic, corporate and government reports.
Format: CD-ROM, microfiche, magnetic tape and printed monthly, quarterly and annual indexes.

ENVIRONMENTAL BIBLIOGRAPHY
Type: Bibliographic, Keywords
Subject: Ecology, Energy, Land Resources, Water Resources, Health
Language: English
Available Service Through: Dialog-file 68, Compuserve (I-Quest), CSA-Environmental Routenet
Producer: International Academy, 5385 Hollister Ave., #210, Santa Barbara, CA 93111
Phone: 805-683-4927; Fax: 805-683-4637; Web site: www.iasb.org
Contact: ELAINE MESSIER
Description: Covers more than 400 scientific and popular journals in social, political and philosophical issues, air, energy, land and water resources, nutrition and health. Author Abstracts, 1997 forward.
Format: also CD ROM

ENVIRONMENTAL RESOURCES TECHNOLOGY (ERTH)
Type: Bibliographic with abstracts
Subject: Petroleum exploration and production
Language: English
Available Service Through: ORBIT-QUESTEL
Producer: Petroleum Abstracts/University of Tulsa, 600 S. College, 101 Harwell, Tulsa, OK 74104-3189
Phone: 918-631-2295/800-247-8678
Contact: DAVID BROWN
Description: A guide to information on ecology and pollution related to petroleum exploration, production and transportation, plus environmental, health and safety topics. Over 47,000 entries updated monthly.
Format: Available in print as E&P Health, Safety and Environment ($185/yr)

FACILITIES INDEX DATA SYSTEM (FINDS)
Type: Reference
Subject: EPA-regulated facilities and sites
Language: English
Available Service Through: Chemical Information Systems
Producer: EPA, Oxford Molecular Group, Inc., Executive Plaza III, Suite 1100, 11350 McCormick Rd., Hunt Valley, MD 21031
Phone: 800-CIS-USER
Contact: Description: FINDS contains several hundred thousand records pertaining to sites and facilities regulated by the EPA. Also contains references to other databases containing information on these sites and facilities.

FISH AND FISHERIES WORLDWIDE
Type: Abstracts and Bibliographic
Subject: Aquaculture, Fish, Fisheries, Marine, Ocean, Water
Language: English
Producer: National Information Services Corp., Wyman Towers, 3100 St. Paul St., Baltimore, MD 21218
Phone: 410-243-0797; Fax: 410-243-0982; E-mail: sales@nisc.com
Contact: Description: Covers the world's literature on fisheries and fish-related topics. Over 109,000 citations are drawn from Fisheries Review, compiled by the U.S. Biological Service, the Fish and Wildlife Reference Service File. Quarterly updates; Subscriptions: $895/yr
Format: CD ROM and internet

FISH AND WILDLIFE REFERENCE SERVICE DATABASE
Type: Bibliographic
Subject: Fisheries, Wildlife and Habitat
Language: English
Available Service Through: U.S. Fish and Wildlife Service web site
Producer: Fish and Wildlife Reference Service, 5430 Grosvenor Ln., #110, Bethesda, MD 20814
Phone: 301-492-6403/800-582-3421; Web site: Fa.r9.fws.gov/r9fwrs/
Contact: PAUL WILSON
Description: Primarily state fish and wildlife agency research reports; some USFWS publications; COOP Unit Theses and dissertations and some USNBS publications.

FLORIDA NATURAL AREAS INVENTORY
Subject: Biodiversity, Endangered and Threatened Species, Natural Areas, Nature Preservation and Wildlife/Wildlife Habitat
1018 Thomasville Rd., Suite 200-C, Tallahassee, FL 32303
Phone: 850-224-8207
Contact: GARY KNIGHT
Description: Information is collected on the status and distribution of natural communities, rare and endangered species of plants and animals and other natural features, then analyzed through an integrated data management system.

GLOBAL ENVIRONMENTAL CHANGE REPORT
Type: Full Text
Subject: Climate Change, Stratospheric Ozone Depletion, Deforestation, Acid Rain
Language: English
Available Service Through: Newsnet, Predicasts
Producer: Cutter Information Corp., 37 Broadway, Arlington, MA 02174
Phone: 800-964-5118
Contact: KAREN KURR
Description: Policy trends, industry actions and scientific findings worldwide on global climate change, noted for its balanced, insightful approach to controversial topics.

GREENNET
Subject: Biodiversity, Environmental/Conservation Education, International Conservation, Waterfowl and Wildlife.
Language: English
Available Service Through: Online Earth Art BBS in Green BBS Door
259 Dorchester Manor Blvd., North Charleston, SC 29420-8108
Phone: 803-552-4389/803-552-2145; Fax: 803-760-2109; E-mail: greennet@earthart.com
Contact: ROBERT B. CHAPMAN
Description: A free international environmental BBS network created to further understanding of important ecological issues now facing the global community. Compiles the International Green BBS list and serves as hub for the Sierra Club BBS network.

GREENWIRE
Language: English
3129 Mt. Vernon Ave., Alexandria, VA 22305
Phone: 703-518-8724; Fax: 703-518-8702; E-mail: greenwire@njdc.com
Contact: DALE CURTIS
Description: Online environmental news service, with a companion online database of more than 30,000 stories.

CONSERVATION INFORMATION RESOURCES - DATABASES AND SERVICES

GROUND WATER MONITOR
Type: Full Text
Subject: Ground water Contamination and Remediation, Waste Management
Language: English
Available Service Through: Newsnet, Predicasts
Producer: Business Publishers Inc., 951 Pershing Dr., Silver Spring, MD 20910-4464
Phone: 301-587-6300; Fax: 301-587-1081
Contact: Description: Complete coverage of state and federal ground water policy and regulation in making new technologies for Remediation of contaminants in ground water.

GROUND WATER NETWORK
Type: Bibliographic database with 78,000 abstracts
Subject: Environmental Protection, Geology, Water Pollution, Management, Water Resources, Water Quality, Rivers, Environmental Law
Language: English
Producer: National Ground Water information Center, 601 Dempsey Rd., Westerville, OH 43081
Phone: 800-551-7379/614-898-7791; Fax: 614-898-7786
Contact: SANDY MASTERS
Description: A fee-based information service conducting literature searches and document delivery. Maintains six databases related to ground water, water treatability, NGWA Certified Ground Water Contractors and U.S. Census on housing and water source information.

H.E.R.M.A.N. (Hierarchial Environmental Retrieval for Management and Networking)
Type: Bibliographic
Subject: Ocean, Shore, Marsh, Waterfowl, Upland Game and Raptor Birds, Bats, Game, Fur Species, Carnivores, Big Game and Marine Mammals
Language: All Languages
Available Service Through: Wildlife Information Service
Producer: Wildlife Information Service, 409 Baca Road, Las Cruces, NM 88005-6021
Phone: 505-527-2547; E-mail: wildlife@greatwhite.com
Contact: JULIE L. MOORE
Description: Contains references and descriptions from 1934 to date. Secondary sources taken from Biological Abstracts, Zoological Record, Wildlife Review, etc.
Format: Diskettes (ASCII-IBM)

HAZARDOUS WASTE NEWS
Type: Full Text
Subject: Environmental Law, Hazardous Waste Management
Language: English
Available Service Through: Newsnet, Predicasts
Producer: Business Publishers, 951 Pershing Dr., Silver Spring, MD 20910-4464
Phone: 301-587-6300; Fax: 301-587-1081
Contact: LOUIS HARRIS
Description: Covers U.S. news, legislation and regulatory issues. RCRA, generation and source reduction, testing and classification, collection, storage and treatment and disposal options.

INDOOR AIR QUALITY UPDATE
Type: Full Text
Subject: Prevention and control of indoor air pollution
Language: English
Available Service Through: Newsnet
Producer: Cutter Information Corp., 37 Broadway, Arlington, MA 02174
Phone: 800-964-5118
Contact: KAREN KURR
Description: Advice on controlling potential pollutant sources, suggestions on building and HVAC design, operation, maintenance, detailed case studies, legislative updates and related issues.

INFORMATION SYSTEM FOR HAZARDOUS ORGANICS IN WATER (ISHOW)
Type: Data extracted from scientific Subject: Environmental fate or behavior of organic chemicals
Language: English
Available Service Through: Chemical Information System (CIS)
Producer: EPA, Oxford Molecular Group, Inc., Executive Plaza III, Suite 1100, 11350 McCormick Rd., Hunt Valley, MD 21031
Phone: 800-CIS-USER (CIS User Support Group)
Contact: Description: ISHOW contains six types of data (melting point, boiling point, partition coefficient, acid dissociation constant, water solubility and vapor pressure) for more than 5,400 chemical substances.

INTER PRESS SERVICE (IPS)/GLOBAL INFORMATION NETWORK)
Type: Full Text
Subject: International with a special focus on developing countries
Language: English and Spanish
Available Service Through: DIALOG, Nexis, Electric Library, NewsBank, Compuserve Newsgrid, Responsive Database Services, Dow Jones Interactive, BBS with IPS Environment Library, Homework Helper Infonautics, Responsive Database Services.
275 Seventh Ave., #1206, New York, NY 10001
Phone: 212-627-0123; Fax: 212-627-6137; E-mail: ipsgin@igc.apc.org
Contact: KATHERINE STAPP
Description: GIN is the distributor of Inter Press Service and other news wires from developing countries with special features on the environment.

IRIS (Integrated Risk Information System)
Type: Data Extracted from Scientific Papers
Subject: Risk assessment of hazardous chemicals
Language: English
Available Service Through: Chemical Information Systems
Producer: EPA, Oxford Molecular Group, Inc., Executive Plaza III, Suite 1100, 11350 McCormick Rd., Hunt Valley, MD 21031
Phone: 800-CIS-USER
Contact: Description: The principal EPA database for assessing potential risk of exposure to hazardous chemical substances. It covers toxicity and carcinogenicity for over 660 substances. Some chemical physical data and regulatory information is also covered.

LAND USE LAW REPORT
Type: Full Text
Subject: Environment, Land Use Planning, Land Preservation
Language: English
Available Service Through: Newsnet and Predicats
Producer: Business Publishers, Inc., 951 Pershing Dr., Silver Spring, MD 20910-4464
Phone: 301-587-6300; Fax: 301-587-1081
Contact: JIM LAWLOR
Description: Covers U.S. news on regulatory issues, legislation, legal decisions and budget proposals affecting land use.

CONSERVATION INFORMATION RESOURCES - DATABASES AND SERVICES

MALLIN
Type: Data extracted from scientific Subject: Chemical-physical properties, fire and health hazards, spill and disposal information, storage and handling information and protective equipment information
Language: English
Available Service Through: Chemical Information Systems
Producer: Mallinckrodt Baker, Inc., Oxford Molecular Group, Inc., Executive Plaza III, Suite 1100, 11350 McCormick Rd., Hunt Valley, MD 21031
Phone: 800-CIS-USER
Contact: Description: Mallin is a collection of Material Safety Data Sheets (MSDS) for over 2,120 chemical substances. Each record of information represents one chemical, prepared in accordance with guidelines issued by the U.S. Occupational Safety and Health Administration.

MARINE OCEANOGRAPHIC AND FRESHWATER RESOURCES
Type: Bibliographic
Subject: Marine, Oceanographic and Freshwater Resources
Language: English
Producer: National Information Services Corp., Wydman Towers, 3100 St. Paul St., Baltimore, MD 21218
Phone: 410-243-0797; Fax: 410-243-0982; E-mail: sales@nisc.com
Contact: Description: Database on marine, oceanographic and related freshwater resources. Coverage of over 949,000 records on international marine and ocean information, as well as information on estuarine and freshwater environments.

MASTER SPECIES FILE, THE
Type: Species Accounts (codes, keywords, text and references)
Subject: Species taxonomy, status, distribution, ecology, Management Practices
Language: English
Producer: Fish and Wildlife Information Exchange, Dept. Of Fisheries and Wildlife, VA Polytechnic Institute, 203 W. Roanoke St., Blacksburg, VA 24060
Phone: 540-231-7348; Fax: 540-231-7019; E-mail: fwiexchg@vt.edu; Web site: fwie.fw.vt.edu
Contact: JEFF WALDON
Description: An archive of species accounts compiled by state and federal fish and wildlife agencies in North America.
Format: online (www)

OIL AND HAZARDOUS MATERIALS TECHNICAL ASSISTANCE DATA SYSTEM (OHM/TADS)
Type: Data extracted from scientific Subject: Handling of hazardous materials
Language: English
Available Service Through: Chemical Information Systems (CIS)
Producer: EPA, Oxford Molecular Group, Inc., Executive Plaza III, Suite 1100, 11350 McCormick Rd., Hunt Valley, MD 21031
Phone: 800-CIS-USERS
Contact: Description: OHM/TADS is the EPA's principal database for providing information on safe handling of hazardous substances.

OIL SPILL INTELLIGENCE REPORT
Type: Full Text
Subject: Oil Spills, Prevention, cleanup and Control
Language: English
Producer: Cutter Information Corp., 37 Broadway, Arlington, MA 02174
Phone: 800-964-5125
Contact: DENNIS CROWLEY
Description: Detailed information on oil spills worldwide and related developments. Customized reports are also available.

OIL SPILL INTELLIGENCE REPORT INTERNATIONAL SPILL DATABASE
Subject: Worldwide oil spills involving 10,000+ gallons
Language: English
Producer: Cutter Information Corp., 37 Broadway, Arlington, MA 02174
Phone: 617-641-5107; Fax: 617-648-8707; E-mail: jwelch@cutter.com
Contact: JEFF WELCH
Description: Lists date, amount, type of oil, damages and more on over 2,500 oil spills that have occurred worldwide. Updated weekly.

OIL SPILL U.S. LAW REPORT
Type: Full Text
Subject: Legislation, litigation, Regulations and Enforcement Actions in the U.S. pertaining to Oil Spills
Language: English
Available Service Through: Newsnet and Predicats
Producer: Cutter Information Corp, 37 Broadway, Arlington, MA 02174
Phone: 800-964-5125
Contact: DENNIS CROWLEY
Description: Details Federal and state oil spill legislation and regulations, litigation and administrative actions, including news and interpretation of the ongoing implementation of the Oil Pollution Act of 1990.

PLANT TOXICITY DATA (PHYTOTOX)
Type: Data Extracted from scientific Subject: Plant toxicity of organic chemicals
Language: English
Available Service Through: Chemical Information System
Producer: University of Oklahoma, Dept. of Botany and Microbiology, Oxford Molecular Group, Inc., Executive Plaza III, Suite 1100, 11350 McCormick Rd., Hunt Valley, MD 21031
Phone: 800-CIS-USER
Contact: Description: PHYTOTOX contains over 70,000 records relating the biological effects of organic chemicals on terrestrial plants. The records of data include information about effects observed in the experiment and bibliographic references to source documents.

POLLUTION ABSTRACTS
Subject: Air, Marine, and Freshwater Pollution
Language: English
Producer: National Information Services Corp, Wydman Towers, 3100 St. Paul St., Baltimore, MD 21218
Phone: 410-243-0797; Fax: 410-243-0982; E-mail: sales@nisc.com
Contact: Description: Information on scientific research and government policies. Also covers journal literature, conference proceedings and hard-to-find documents.

REGISTRY OF TOXIC EFFECTS OF CHEMICAL SUBSTANCES (RTECS)
Type: Data extracted from scientific Subject: Toxicity, Irriation, Mutagenicity, Tumorigenicity, teratogenicity, Carcinogenicity
Language: English

Available Service Through: Chemical Information System (CIS)
Producer: NIOSH, Oxford Molecular Group, Inc., Executive Plaza III, Suite 1100, 11350 McCormick Rd., Hunt Valley, MD 21031
Phone: 800-CIS-USER
Contact: Description: RTECS contains data on more than 135,000 chemical substances.

SIRS RESEARCHER
Type: Full Text
Subject: Earth Science, Physical Science, Life Science, Medical Science, Applied Science, Social Issues and Global Issues
Language: English
Available Service Through: CD-ROM, Tape or online
Producer: SIRS Mandarin, Inc., P.O. Box 2348, Boca Raton, FL 33427-2348
Phone: 800-232-SIRS/561-994-0079
Contact: LINDA MIGNONE
Description: A general reference database containing thousands of full-text articles exploring social, scientific, health, historic, economic, business, political and global issues, searchable by Subject Headings, Topic Browse, or Keyword.
Format: CD ROM, Tape, or online via www

SOILD WASTE REPORT
Type: Full Text
Subject: Environmental Waste
Language: English
Available Service Through: Newsnet and Predicasts
Producer: Business Publishers, Inc., 951 Pershing Dr., Silver Spring, MD 20910-4464
Phone: 301-587-6300; Fax: 301-587-1081
Contact: DAVID R. JONES
Description: Covers general collection, transportation, resource recovery, recycling and ultimate disposal of municipal, commercial, agricultural and non-hazardous industrial refuse.

SOLAR AND RENEWABLE ENERGY OUTLOOK
Type: Full Text
Subject: Solar Energy, Renewable Resources
Language: English
Available Service Through: Newsnet and Predicasts
Producer: Business Publishers, 951 Pershing Dr., Silver Spring, MD 20910-4464
Phone: 301-587-6300; Fax: 301-587-1081
Contact: TODD LEEUWENBURGH
Description: Dedicated exclusively to developments that affect the domestic and international market for a broad range of renewable energy technologies.

TOXIC RELEASE INVENTORY (TRI)
Type: Full Text
Subject: Toxic Chemicals
Language: English
Available Service Through: NLM's TOXNET
Producer: Office of Pollution Prevention and Toxics-EPA, 401 M St., NW, Washington, DC 20460
Phone: 202-260-8387
Contact: RUBY N. BOYA
Description: Mandated by the Emergency Planning and community Right-to-Know Act, TRI contains amounts for over 300 toxic chemicals that facilities release directly to air, water or land or are transported off site.

TOXIC SUBSTANCES CONTROL ACT TEST SUBMISSIONS (TSCATS)
Type: Bibliographic
Subject: Toxicity, Health, Safety, Environmental Fate
Language: English
Available Service Through: Chemical Information System
Producer: EPA, Oxford Molecular Group, Inc., Executive Plaza III, Suite 1100, 11350 McCormick Rd., Hunt Valley, MD 21031
Phone: 800-CIS-USER
Contact: Description: TSCATS contains over 56,000 references to unpublished health, safety, toxicity and environmental fate studies submitted to the EPA. Copies of referenced studies can be ordered through the system.

TOXLINE
Type: Bibliographic
Subject: Toxicology Pollution, Pharmacology, Physiology, Biochemistry
Language: English
Available Service Through: Dialog, DIMDI, STN and Silver Platter.
Producer: BIOSIS, 2001 Market St., Philadelphia, PA 19103-7095
Phone: 800-523-4806/215-587-4847; Fax: 215-587-2016; E-mail: info@mail.biosis.org
Contact: ALAN CLARKE
Description: Biosis is one of five contributors to TOXLINE, an online file containing references to the effects of pollutants, drugs and other chemicals.

U.S. EPA CIVIL ENFORCEMENT DOCKET (DOCKET)
Type: Data extracted from Documents
Subject: Civil judicial cases filed by the Dept. of Justice on behalf of the EPA
Language: English
Available Service Through: Chemical Information System
Producer: EPA, Oxford Molecular Group, Inc., Executive Plaza III, Suite 1100, 11350 McCormick Rd., Hunt Valley, MD 21031
Phone: 800-CIS-USER (CIS User Support Group)
Contact: Description: Contains over 4,200 records of civil lawsuits, compiled by the EPA and updated quarterly.

WASTE MANAGEMENT INFORMATION DATABASE
Type: Full text and Bibliographic
Subject: Solid, Liquid, hazardous and nuclear wastes management; water quality, toxic substances, land reclamation, air pollution and resources recovery
Language: English
Available Service Through: ITTD Network
Producer: International Research and Evaluation, 21098 IRE Control Center, Eagan, MN 55121
Phone: 612-888-9635; Fax: 612-888-9124
Contact: DR. R. DANFORD
Description: Environmental library for the application of knowledge, methods and means.

WATER RESOURCES ABSTRACTS
Type: Abstracts and Bibliographic
Subject: Water Resources, oceans, ground water, fish and marine mammals
Language: English
Producer: National Information Services Corp., Wydman Towers, 3100 St. Paul St., Baltimore, MD 21218
Phone: 410-243-0797; Fax: 410-243-0982; E-mail: sales@nisc.com
Contact: Description: Automated searching of over 334,000 citations and abstracts. Updated quarterly. Year Subscription: $1,265 (CD), $1,895 (Internet)

Format: CD ROM and Internet

WATER RESOURCES WORLDWIDE
Type: Abstracts and Bibliographies
Subject: Water Resources, pollution, waste management, recycling
Language: English
Available Service Through: NISC Discover and BiblioLine
Producer: National Information Services Corp., Wydman Towers, 3100 St. Paul St., Baltimore, MD 21218
Phone: 410-243-0797; Fax: 410-243-0982; E-mail: sales@nisc.com
Contact: Description: Provides 433,000 citations and abstracts from around the world (including WATERLIT, AQUAREF and DELFT HYDRO) and features the WATERLIT thesaurus. Quarterly updates; Subscription: $895 per year.
Format: CD ROM and internet

WILDLIFE WORLDWIDE
Type: Abstracts and Bibliographies
Subject: Wildlife, Endangered Species, Environment and natural resources
Language: English
Producer: National Information Services Corp., Wydman Towers, 3100 St. Paul St., Baltimore, MD 21218
Phone: 410-243-0797; Fax: 410-243-0982; E-mail: sales@nisc.com
Contact: Description: 410,000 records of wildlife databases from the U.S. Biological Services, BIODIC and SWIS database from the Wildlife Information Service. Quarterly updates; $895 yr. subscription.
Format: CD ROM and Internet

WORLD ENVIRONMENT REPORT
Type: Full Text
Subject: Environmental Laws, regulations and environmental business worldwide
Language: English
Available Service Through: Newsnet and Predicasts
Producer: Business Publishers, Inc., 951 Pershing Dr., Silver Spring, MD 20910-4464
Phone: 301-587-6300; Fax: 301-587-1081
Contact: DAVID BOTTORFF
Description: Provides news, information and analysis on international environmental laws and regulations for companies operating abroad.

WORLD ENVIRONMENTAL DIRECTORY
Type: Full Text
Subject: Environmental Resources
Language: English
Available Service Through: Newsnet and Predicasts
Producer: Business Publishers, Inc., 951 Pershing Dr., Silver Spring, MD 20910-4464
Phone: 301-587-6300; Fax: 301-587-1081
Contact: LARRY FISHBEIN
Description: Contains source names and addresses to manufacturers, consultants, federal government, professional organizations, education institutions and more.

NATURAL HERITAGE PROGRAM INFORMATION

NATURAL HERITAGE NETWORK SUPPORT

Association for Biodiversity Information
Director: IRA KIRKHAM
1727 King St., Alexandria, VA 22314
Phone: 703-739-4330; Fax: 703-739-4331

The Nature Conservancy
Conservation Science Division
Director Heritage Operations: TONY WILKINSON
1815 N. Lynn St., Arlington, VA 22209
Phone: 703-841-5300; Fax: 703-841-8796; E-mail: twilkinson@tnc.org

REGIONAL HERITAGE DATA CENTERS

Great Smoky Mounains National Park
Twin Creeks Natural Resources Center
Coordinator and Biologist: JANET ROCK
1314 Cherokee Orchard Rd. Twin Creeks Natural Resources Center, Gatlinburg, TN 37738
Phone: 423-436-1264; Fax: 423-436-5598

Gulf Islands National Seashore
Resource Management Specialist: RILEY HOGGARD
1801 Gulf Breeze Parkway, Gulf Breeze, FL 32561
Phone: 850-934-2617; Fax: 850-932-9654

Mammoth Cave National Park
Division of Science & Resource Management
Natural Resource Data Manager: TERESA LIEBFRIED
Mammoth Cave National Park, P.O. Box 7, Mammoth Cave, KY 42259
Phone: 502-749-2508; Fax: 502-749-2916

National Park Service, South Regional Office
Natural Resource Data Manager: KELLEY WATSON
Atlanta Federal Center, 1924 Bldg. 100 Alabama St., SW,, Atlanta, GA 30303
Phone: 404-562-3113; Fax: 404-562-3201

National Capital Region Conservation Data Canter
C/O C&O Canal National Historical Park, P.O. Box 4, Sharpsburg, MD 21782
Phone: 301-714-2211; Fax: 301-714-2232

Navajo Natural Heritage Program
Navajo Fish & Wildlife Department
Coordinator: JACK MEYER
P.O. Box 1480, Window Rock, AZ 86515
Phone: 520-871-6472; Fax: 520-871-7069; E-mail: jmeyer@tnc.org

TVA Regional Natural Heritage
River Systems Operations and Environment Resource Stewardship
Coordinator: WILLIAM H. REDMOND
TVA, Norris, TN 37828
Phone: 423-632-1593; Fax: 423-632-1795; E-mail: wremond@tva.gov

CANADA-PROVINCIAL PROGRAMS

Alberta Natural Heritage Information Centre
Alberta Environment
Coordinator (Acting): DAN CHAMBERS
2nd Fl., Oxford Pl., 9820 106th St., Edmonton, Alberta T5K 2J6
Phone: 780-427-9706; Fax: 780-427-5980; E-mail: dan.chambers@gov.ab.ca

British Columbia Conservation Data Centre
Ministry of Environment, Land & Parks
Coordinator: ANDREW HARCOMBE
P.O. Box 9344, Station Provincial Gov., Victoria, British Columbia V8W 9M1
Phone: 250-356-0928; Fax: 250-387-2733; E-mail: aharcomb@fwhdept.env.gov.bc.ca

Manitoba Conservation Data Centre
Department of Natural Resources Wildlife Branch
Chief: CAROL SCOTT
Box 24, 200 Saulteaux Crescent, Winipeg, Manitoba R3J 3W3
Phone: 204-945-7743; Fax: 204-945-3077; E-mail: fblovin@nr.gov.mb.ca

Natural Heritage Information Centre
Coordinator: ROB PARRY
P.O. Box 7000, 300 Walter St., 2nd Fl., North Tower, Peterborough, Ontario K9J 8M5
Phone: 705-745-6767; Fax: 705-755-2168; E-mail: parryro@epo.gov.on.ca

Quebec Service De La Conservation Des Especes Menaces
Ministere de l'Environnement
Coordinator: JACQUES PRESCOTT
Direction de la conservation et du patrimoine ecologique
675, boul. Rene-Levesque Est., 10e Etage Boite 21, Quebec G1R 5V7
Phone: 418-521-3907; Fax: 418-646-6169

Saskatchewan Conservation Data Centre
SK Environment & Resource Management
Coordinator: MARLONE KILLABY
3211 Albert St., Regina, Saskatchewan S4S 5W6
Phone: 306-787-7196; Fax: 306-787-7085; E-mail: marlon.killaby.erm@govmail.gov.sk.ca

LATIN AMERICA AND CARIBBEAN PROGRAMS

Centro de Datos para la Conservacion de Bolivia
Executive Director: XIMENA ARAMAYO
Calle Juan Jose Perez, No. 268 1er piso, Casilla 11250, La Paz
Phone: 011-59-12-39-0565; Fax: 011-59-12-37-5371; E-mail: tropico@mail.megalink.com

Centro de Datos para la Conservacion de Colombia
Corporacion Autonoma Regional del Valle del Cauca (CVC)
CDC Coordinator: MARIA ISABEL SALAZAR RAMIREZ
Carrera 56 No. 11-36; Apartado Aereo 2366, Cali
Phone: 339-6671; Fax: 339-6638

Centro de Datos para la Conservacion de Guatemala
Centro de Estudios Conservacionistas (CECON)
Coordinator: OLGA ISABEL VALDEZ RODAS
Universidad de San Carlos, Avenida de la Reforma 0-63, Zona 10, Cuidad de Guatemala 01010
Phone: 331-0904; USA: 011-502; Fax: 34-7664; E-mail: cecon@uvalle.edu.gt

Centro de Datos para la Conservacion de la Naturaleza en Sonora
Instituto del Medioambiente y Desarollo Sostenible de Sonora (Imades)
Coordinator: RAFAEL APAREDES AGUILAR
Reyes y Aguascalientes Esq., Col. San Benito (Antes Escuela Carpio), Hermosillo, Sonora 83241
Phone: 14-32-01; Fax: 14-65-08

Centro de Datos para la Conservacion de Panama
Asociacion Nacional para la Conservacion de la Naturaleza (ANCON)
Director: IVAN A. VALDESPINO
Calle Alberto Navarro, El Cangrego, Apartado Postal 1387, Zona 1, Panama
Phone: 264-8100; USA: 011-507; Fax: 264-2445

Centro de Datos para la conservacion de Paraguay
Sub-Secretaria de Recursos Naturales y Ganaderia
Coordinator: NELIDA RIVAROLA
Presidente Franco y Ayolas Edificio Ayfra, 1er Piso Bloquea cc 3303, Asuncion
Phone: 49-4914; USA: 011-595-21; Fax: 49-5568

Centro de Datos para la conservacion de Peru
Universidad Nacional Agraria La Molina
Director: PEDRO G.VASQUEZ
Facultad de Ciencias Forestales, Apartado 456, Lima 100
Phone: 349-6102; USA: 011-511; Fax: 349-6102; E-mail: cdc@lamolina.edu

Corporacion Centro de Datos para la Conservacion
Executive Director: CARMEN JOSSE
Calle Alfonso de Lamartine e 10-32 y Paris CDLA JIPIJAPA, Quito
Phone: 257-680; USA: 011-593-2; Fax: 245-189; E-mail: cdc@hoy.net

Division de Patrimonio Natural Area de Planificacion de Recusos Integral
Departmento de Recursos Naturales y Ambientales de Puerto Rico
Division Director: MYRIAM GONZALEZ TORRES
P.O. Box 9066600, Puerta de Tierra 00906-6600
Phone: 787-724-8774; Fax: 787-723-4255

Netherlands Antilles Natural Heritage Program
Coordinator: JOHN DE FREITAS
Carmabi Foundation, P.O. Box 2090, Curacao
Phone: 62-4242; USA: 011-599-9; Fax: 62-7680

UNITED STATES NATURAL HERITAGE PROGRAMS

Alabama Natural Heritage Program
Director: JARELL. HILTON
Huntington College, Massey Hall 1500 East Fairview Ave, Montgomery, AL 36106-2148
Phone: 334-834-4519, ext. 21; Fax: 334-834-5439; E-mail: alnhp@wsnet.com

CONSERVATION INFORMATION RESOURCES - NATURAL HERITAGE PROGRAM INFORMATION

Alaska Natural Heritage Program
University of Alaska Anchorage
Interim Director: KEITH BOGGS
707 A St., Anchorage, AK 99501
Phone: 907-257-2780; Fax: 907-257-2789; E-mail: ankwb@vaa.alaska.edu

Arizona Heritage Data Management System
Arizona Game and Fish Department
Coordinator: SABRA S. SCHWARTZ
WM-H 2221 W. Greenway Rd., Phoenix, AZ 85023
Phone: 602-789-3612; Fax: 602-789-3928; E-mail: sschwartz@gf.state.az.us

Arkansas Natural Heritage Commission
Chief of Research: TOM FOTI
Suite 1500, Tower Bldg., 323 Center St., Little Rock, AR 72201
Phone: 501-324-9619; Fax: 501-324-9618; E-mail: tom@dah.state.ar.us

California Natural Heritage Division
Department of Fish and Game, Wildlife and Habitat Analysis Branch
Supervisor: KEN HASHAGEN
1807 13th St., Ste. 202, Sacramento, CA 95814
Phone: 916-322-2493; Fax: 916-324-0475; E-mail: khashage@kirk.dfg.ca.gov

Colorado Natural Heritage Program
Director: MARY KLEIN
College of Natural Resources, Colorado State University, 254 General Services Bilding, Fort Collins, CO 80523
Phone: 970-491-1309; Fax: 970-491-3349; E-mail: mklein@lamar.colostate.edu

Connecticut Natural Diversity Database
Natural Resources Center
Coordinator: NANCY MURRAY
Department of Environmental Protection 79 Elm St., Store Level, Hartford, CT 06106-5127
Phone: 860-424-3540; Fax: 860-424-4058; E-mail: nancy.murray@po.state.ct.us

Delaware Natural Heritage Program
Division of Fish & Wildlife
Coordinator: LYNN BROADDUS
Department of Natural Resources and Environmental Control, 4876 Hay Point Landing Rd., Smyrna, DE 19977
Phone: 302-653-2880; Fax: 302-653-3431; E-mail: lbroaddus@state.de.us

District of Columbia Natural Heritage Program
c/o C&O Canal National Historical Park, P.O. Box 4, Sharpsburg, MD 21782
Phone: 301-714-2211; Fax: 301-714-2232

Florida Natural Areas Inventory
Director: GARY KNIGHT
1018 Thomasville Rd. Suite 200-c, Tallahassee, FL 32303
Phone: 850-224-8207; Fax: 850-681-9364; E-mail: gknight@fnai.org

Georgia Natural Heritage Program
Wildlife Resources Division, Georgia Dept. of Natural Resources
Program Manager: JOHN AMBROSE
2117 U.S. Hwy. 278 SE, Social Circle, GA 30025-4714
Phone: 706-557-3032; Fax: 706-557-3033; E-mail: regina_makomb@mail.dnr.state.ga.us; Website: www.dnr.state.ga.us/dnr/wild/natural.html

Hawaii Natural Heritage Program
The Nature Conservancy of Hawaii
Director: DANIEL ORODENKER
1116 Smith St. Suite 201, Honolulu, HI 96817
Phone: 808-537-4508; Fax: 808-545-2019; E-mail: dorodenker@tnc.org

Idaho Conservation Data Center
Department of Fish & Game
Coordinator: BOB MOSELEY
600 S. Walnut St. Box 25, Boise, ID 83707-0025
Phone: 208-334-3402; Fax: 208-334-2114; E-mail: bmoseley@idfg.state.id.us

Illinois Natural Heritage Division
Department of Resources
Division Chief: CARLBECKER
524 S. 2nd St., Springfield, IL 62701-1787
Phone: 217-785-8774; Fax: 217-785-8277

Indiana Natural Heritage Data Center
Division of Nature Preserves
Coordinator: CLOYCE HEDGE
Department of Natural Resources, 402 West Washington St., Rm. W267, Indianapolis, IN 46204
Phone: 317-232-4052; Fax: 317-233-0133

Iowa Natural Areas Inventory
Department of Natural Resources
Coordinator: DARRYL HOWELL
Wallace State Office Bldg., E. 9th and Grand, 4th Fl., Des Moines, IA 50319-0034
Phone: 515-281-8524; Fax: 515-281-6794

Kansas Natural Heritage Inventory
Kansas Biological Survey
Coordinator/Botanist: CRAIG FREEMAN
University of Kansas. 2041 Constant Ave., Lawrence, KS 66047
Phone: 785-864-3453; Fax: 785-864-5093; E-mail: c-freeman@ukans.edu

Kentucky Natural Heritage Program
Kentucky State Nature Preserves Commission
Director: DONALD S. DOTTJR.
801 Schenkel Ln., Frankfort, KY 40601
Phone: 502-573-2886; Fax: 502-573-2355; E-mail: don.dott@mail.state.ky.us

Louisiana Natural Heritage Program
Department of Wildlife and Fisheries
Coordinator: GARY LESTER
P.O. Box 98000, Baton Rouge, LA 70898
Phone: 225-765-2821; Fax: 225-765-2607

Maine Natural Areas Program
Natural Areas Division, Department of Conservation
Director: MOLLY DOCHERTY
FedEx/UPS: 159 Hospital St.; 93 State House Station, Augusta, ME 04333-0093
Phone: 207-287-8044; Fax: 207-287-8040; E-mail: mnap@state.me.us

Maryland Heritage and Biodiversity Conservation Programs
Department of Natural Resources

Division Director: MIKE SLATTERY
Tawes State Office Bldg., E-1, Annapolis, MD 21401
Phone: 410-260-8540; Fax: 410-260-8595

Massachusetts Natural Heritage & Endangered Species Program
Division of Fisheries & Wildlife
Coordinator: HENRY WOOLSEY
Route 135, Westborough, MA 01581
Phone: 508-792-7270 ext. 200; Fax: 508-792-7275; E-mail: henry.woolsey@state.ma.us

Michigan Natural Features Inventory
Director: JUDITH D. SOULE
P.O. Box 30444, Lansing, MI 48909-7944
Phone: 517-373-1552; Fax: 517-373-6705; E-mail: soulej@state.mi.us

Minnesota Natural Heritage & Nongame Research
Department of Natural Resources
Coordinator: BONITA ELIASON
500 Lafayette Rd., Box 25, St. Paul, MN 55155
Phone: 651-296-2835; Fax: 651-296-1811; E-mail: bonita.eliason@dnr.state.mn.us

Mississippi Natural Heritage Program
Museum of Natural Science
Coordinator (Acting): CHARLES KNIGHT
111 N. Jefferson St., Jackson, MS 39201
Phone: 601-354-7303; Fax: 601-354-7227

Missouri Natural Heritage Database
Missouri Department of Conservation
Heritage Coordinator: DOROTHY BUTLER
P.O. Box 180, (Street:2901 W. Truman Blvd), Jefferson City, MO 65102
Phone: 314-751-4115; Fax: 314-526-5582

Montana Natural Heritage Program
Director: SUE CRISPIN
State Library Bldg., P.O. Box 201800, Helena, MT 59620-1800
Phone: 406-444-3009; Fax: 406-444-0581; E-mail: scrispin@state.mt.us

Nebraska Natural Heritage Program
Game and Parks Commission
Coordinator/Biologist: RICK SCHNEIDER
2200 North 33rd St., P.O. Box 30370, Lincoln, NE 68503
Phone: 402-471-5500; Fax: 402-471-5528

Nevada Natural Heritage Program
Department of Conservation & Natural Resources
Program Manager: GLENN CLEMMER
1550 E. College Parkway, Suite 145, Carson City, NV 89710
Phone: 775-687-4245; Fax: 775-687-1288

New Hampshire Natural Heritage Inventory
Department of Resources & Economic Development
Coordinator: DAVID VANLUVEN
172 Pembroke St., P.O. Box 1856, Concord, NH 03303
Phone: 603-271-3623; Fax: 603-271-2629

New Jersey Natural Heritage Program
Office of Natural Lands Management
Coordinator: TOM BREDEN
22 S. Clinton Ave. CN404; P.O. Box 404, Trenton, NJ 08625
Phone: 609-984-1339; Fax: 609-984-1427; E-mail: tbreden@dep.state.nj.us

New Mexico National Heritage Program
Director/Research Zoologist: PAT MEHLHOP
University of New Mexico, 851 University Blvd., SE, Suite 101, Albuquerque, NM 87131
Phone: 505-272-3545; Fax: 505-272-3544

New York Natural Heritage Program
Department of Environmental Conservation
Director: KATHRYN SCHNEIDER
700 Troy-Schenectady Rd., Latham, NY 12110
Phone: 518-783-3932; Fax: 518-783-3916; E-mail: kschneider@tnc.org

North Carolina Heritage Program
NC Department of Environment, Health and Natural Resources
Division of Parks and Recreation
Coordinator: LINDA PEARSALL
P.O. Box 27687, Raleigh, NC 27611
Phone: 919-733-4181; Fax: 919-715-3085

North Dakota Natural Heritage Inventory
North Dakota Parks and Recreation Department
Coordinator: KATHY DUTTENHEFNER
1835 Bismarck Expressway, Bismarck, ND 58504
Phone: 701-328-5357; Fax: 701-328-5363

Ohio Natural Heritage Data Base
Division of Natural Area and Preserves
Division Chief: GUY DENNY
Department of Natural Resources, 1889 Fountain Square, Bldg. F-1, Columbus, OH 43224-1331
Phone: 614-265-6453; Fax: 614-267-3096

Oklahoma Natural Heritage Inventory
Oklahoma Biological Survey
Coordinator: BRUCE HOAGLAND
111 East Chesapeake St., University of Oklahoma, Norman, OK 73019
Phone: 405-325-1985; Fax: 405-325-7702; E-mail: bhoagland@ou.edu

Oregon Natural Heritage Program
Oregon Field Office
Director: JIMMY KAGAN
The Nature Conservancy, 821 SE 14th Ave., Portland, OR 97214
Phone: 503-731-3070; Fax: 503-230-9639; E-mail: jkagan@tnc.org

Pennsylvania Natural Diversity Inventory PNDI-East
The Nature Conservancy
Heritage Director: ANTHONY DAVIS
34 Airport Dr., Middletown, PA 17057
Phone: 717-948-3962; Fax: 717-948-3957

PNDI-Central
Bureau of Forestry
Environmental Review Coordinator: JEANNE BRENNAN
P.O. Box 8552, Harrisburg, PA 17105
Phone: 717-783-3444; Fax: 717-783-5109

Rhode Island Natural Heritage Program
Department of Environmental Management
Coordinator: RICK ENSER
Division of Planning and Development, 235 Promenade St., 3rd Fl., Providence, RI 02908
Phone: 401-222-2776 ext. 4308; Fax: 401-222-2069

CONSERVATION INFORMATION RESOURCES - NATURAL HERITAGE PROGRAM INFORMATION

South Carolina Heritage Trust
SC Dept. of Natural Resources
Coordinator: STEVE BENNETT
P.O. Box 167, Columbia, SC 29202
Phone: 803-734-3893; Fax: 803-734-3931 (call first)

South Dakota Natural Heritage Data Base
SD Department of Game, Fish & Parks
Acting Coordinator/Botanist: DAVE ODE
523 E. Capitol Ave., Pierre, SD 57501
Phone: 605-773-4227; Fax: 605-773-6245; E-mail: dave.ode@state.sd.us

Tennessee Division of Natural Heritage
Tennessee Department of Environment & Conservation
Heritage Coordinator: SMOOT MAJOR
401 Church St., Life and Casualty Tower, 14th Fl., Nashville, TN 37243
Phone: 615-532-0199; Fax: 615-532-0231

Texas Conservation Data Center
The Nature Conservancy of Texas
Director: DAVID WOLFE
P.O. Box 1440, San Antonio, TX 78295
Phone: 210-224-8774; Fax: 210-228-9805

Utah Natural Heritage Program
Division of Wildlife Resources
Program Coordinator: MIKE CANNING
1594 W. North Temple, Ste. 2110; Box 146301, Salt Lake City, UT 84116-6301
Phone: 801-538-4700; Fax: 801-538-4745; E-mail: nrdwr.mcanning@state.ut.us

Vermont Nongame & Natural Heritage Program
Vermont Fish & Wildlife Department
Program Coordinator: STEVE PARREN
103 S. Main St. 10 S, Waterbury, VT 05671
Phone: 802-241-3700; Fax: 802-241-3295; E-mail: sparren@fwd.anr.state.vt.us

Virginia Division of Natural Heritage
Department of Conservation and Recreation
Division Director: TOM SMITH
217 Governor St., Richmond, VA 23219
Phone: 804-786-7951; Fax: 804-371-2674; E-mail: tos@dcr.state.va.us

Washington Natural Heritage Program
Department of Natural Resources
Program Manager (Acting): JOHN GAMON
P.O. Box 47016; (Street: 1111 Washington St. SE), Olympia, WA 98504
Phone: 360-902-1340; Fax: 360-902-1783; E-mail: john.gamon@wadnr.gov

West Virginia Natural Heritage Program
Department of Natural Resources Operations Center
Coordinator: BRIAN MCDONALD
Ward Rd., P.O. Box 67, Elkins, WV 26241
Phone: 304-637-0245; Fax: 304-637-0250; E-mail: bmcdonald@dnr.state.wv.us

Western Pennsylvania Conservancy
Director: CHARLES BIER
PNDI-West, 209 Fourth Ave., Pittsburgh, PA 15222
Phone: 412-288-2777; Fax: 412-281-1792

Wisconsin Natural Heritage Program
Department of Natural Resources, Endangered Resources
Coordinator: BETTY LES
101 S. Webster St. Box 7921, Madison, WI 53707
Phone: 608-266-7012; Fax: 608-266-2925; E-mail: lesb@mail01.dnr.state.wi.us

Wyoming Natural Diversity Database
Director: WILLIAM REINERS
P.O. Box 3381, Laramie, WY 82071-3381
Phone: 307-766-3023; Fax: 307-766-3026 (call first); E-mail: wndd@uwyo.edu

FEDERALLY PROTECTED AREAS

BUREAU OF LAND MANAGEMENT DISTRICTS

ALASKA: Anchorage District
    Field Manager: THOMAS R. ALEXANDER
    6881 Abbott Loop Rd., Anchorage, AK 99507-2599
    Phone: 907-267-1246; Fax: 907-267-1267
Glennallen District
    Team Leader: CATHIE JENSEN
    P.O. Box 147, Glennallen, AK 99588
    Phone: 907-822-3217; Fax: 907-822- 3120
Northern District
    Manager: DEE RITCHIE
    1150 University Ave., Fairbanks, AK 99709
    Phone: 907-474-2200

ARIZONA: State Office
    222 N. Central Ave., Phoenix, AZ 85004-2203
    Phone: 602-417-9200; Fax: 602-417-9556
Aizona Strip Field Office
    Field Manager: ROGER TAYLOR
    345 E. Riverside Dr., St. George, UT 84790-9000
    Phone: 801-688-3301; Fax: 435-688-3258
Kingman Field Office
    Field Manager: JOHN CHRISTENSEN
    2475 Beverly Ave., Kingman, AZ 86401-3629
    Phone: 520-692-4400; Fax: 520-692-4414
Lake Havasu Field Office
    Field Manager: DON ELLSWORTH
    2610 Sweetwater Ave., Lake Havasu City, AZ 86406-9071
    Phone: 520-505-1200; Fax: 520-505-1208
National Training Center
    9828 N. 31st Ave., Phoenix, AZ 85051-2517
    Phone: 602-906-5500; Fax: 602-906-5555
Phoenix Field Office
    Field Manager: MIKE TAYLOR
    2015 W. Deer Valley Rd., Phoenix, AZ 85027
    Phone: 602-580-5600; Fax: 623-580-5580
Safford Field Office
    Field Manager: WILLIAM CIVISH
    711 S. 14th Ave., Safford, AZ 85546-3321
    Phone: 520-348-4400; Fax: 520-348-4450
San Pedro Project Office
    1763 Paseo San Luis, Sierra Vista, AZ 85635-2240
    Phone: 520-458-3559
Tuscon Field Office
    Field Manager: JESSE JUEN
    12661 E. Broadway, Tucson, AZ 85748-7208
    Phone: 520-722-4289; Fax: 520-751-0948
Yuma Field Office
    Field Manager: GAIL ACHESON
    2555 E. Gila Ridge Rd., Yuma, AZ 85365-2240
    Phone: 520-317-3200; Fax: 520-317-3250

CALIFORNIA: State Office
    State Director (Acting): AL WRIGHT
    2800 Cottage Way, RM W-1834, Sacramento, CA 95825
    Phone: 916-978-4400; Fax: 916-978-4305
Alturas Field Office
    Manager: TIMOTHYJ.BURKE
    708 W. 12th St., Alturas, CA 96101
    Phone: 503-233-4666; Fax: 530-233-5696
Arcata Field Office
    Manager: LYNDA J. ROUSH
    1695 Heindon Rd., Arcata, CA 95521
    Phone: 707-825-2300; Fax: 707-825-2301
Bakersfield District
    Field Manager: RON FELLOWS
    3801 Pegasus Ave., Bakersfield, CA 93308-6837
    Phone: 661-391-6000; Fax: 661-391-6040
Barstow Field Office
    Manager: TIMOTHY M. READ
    2601 Barstow Rd., Barstow, CA 92311
    Phone: 760-252-6000; Fax: 760-252-6099
Bishop Field Office
    Manager: STEVEADDINGTON
    785 N. Main St., Ste E, Bishop, CA 93514
    Phone: 760-872-4881; Fax: 760-872-2894
Eagle Lake Field Office
    Manager: LINDA HANSEN
    2950 Riverside Dr., Susanville, CA 96130
    Phone: 530-257-0456; Fax: 530-257-4831
El Centro Field Office
    Manager: GREG THOMSEN
    1661 S. 4th St., El Centro, CA 92243
    Phone: 760-337-4400; Fax: 760-337-4490
Folsom Field Office
    Manager: DEANE K. SWICKARD
    63 Natoma St., Folsom, CA 95630
    Phone: 916-985-4474; Fax: 916-985-3259
Hollister Field Office
    Manager: ROBERT E. BEEHLER
    20 Hamilton Ct., Hollister, CA 95023
    Phone: (831) 630-5000; Fax: 831-630-5050
Needles Field Office
    Manager: MOLLY BRADY
    101 W. Spikes Rd., Needles, CA 92363
    Phone: 760-326-7000; Fax: 760-326-7099
Palm Springs / South Coast Field Office
    Manager: JAMES KENNA
    690 W. Garnet Ave., P.O. Box 1260, North Palm Springs, CA 92258-1260
    Phone: 760-251-4800; Fax: 760-251-4899
Redding Field Office
    Manager: CHARLES M. SHULTZ
    355 Hemsted Dr., Redding, CA 96002
    Phone: 530-224-2100; Fax: 530-224-2172
Ridgecrest Field Office
    Manager: HECTOR VILLALOBOS
    300 S. Richmond Rd., Ridgecrest,, CA 93555
    Phone: 760-384-5400; Fax: 760-384-5499
Surprise Field Office
    Manager: SUSAN STOKKE
    P.O. Box 460, 602 Cressler St., Cedarville, CA 96104
    Phone: 530-279-6101; Fax: 530-279-2171
Ukiah Field Office
    Manager: RICH BURNS
    2550 N. State St., Ukiah, CA 95482
    Phone: 707-468-4000; Fax: 707-468-4027

COLORADO: State Office
    2850 Youngfield St., Lakewood, CO 80215
    Phone: 303-239-3600; Fax: 303-239-3933
Anasazi Heritage Center
    27501 Hwy. 184, Dolores, CO 81323
    Phone: 970-882-4811; Fax: 970-882-7035
Glenwood Springs Field Office
    Manager: MIKE MOTTICE
    50629 Hwys. 6 & 24; P.O. Box 1009, Glenwood Springs, CO 81602
    Phone: 970-947-2800; Fax: 970-947-2829
Grand Junction Field Office/Northwest
    Manager: CATHERINE ROBERTSON
    2815 H Rd., Grand Junction, CO 81506
    Phone: 907-244-3000; Fax: 970-244-3083
Gunnison Field Office
    Manager: BARRY TOLLEFSON
    216 N. Colorado, Gunnison, CO 81230
    Phone: 970-641-0471; Fax: 970-641-1928

FEDERALLY PROTECTED AREAS - BUREAU OF LAND MANAGEMENT DISTRICTS

Kremmling Field Office
 1116 Park Ave., P.O. Box, Kremmling, CO 80459
 Phone: 970-724-3437; Fax: 970-724-9590
La Jara Field Office
 Manager: CARLOS PINTOS
 15571 County Rd. T5, La Jara, CO 81140
 Phone: 719-274-8971; Fax: 719-274-6301
Little Snake Field Office
 Manager: JOHN HUSBAND
 455 Emerson St., Craig, CO 81625
 Phone: 970-826-5000; Fax: 970-826-5002
Royal Gorge Field Office/Front Range Center
 3170 E. Main St., Canon City, CO 81212
 Phone: 719-269-8500; Fax: 719-269-8599
Saguache Field Office
 Manager: TOM GOODWIN
 46525 Hwy. 114, P.O. Box 67, Saguache, CO 81149
 Phone: 719-655-2547; Fax: 719-655-2502
San Juan Field Office
 Manager: CAL JOYNER
 15 Burnett Ct., Durango, CO 81301
 Phone: 970-247-4874; Fax: 970-385-1375
Uncompahgre Field Office/Southwest Center
 Manager: ALLAN BELT
 2465 S. Townsend Ave., Montrose, CO Phone: 970-240-5300; Fax: 970-240-5367
White River Field Office
 Manager: JOHN MEHLHOFF
 73544 Hwy. 64, Meeker, CO 81641
 Phone: 970-878-3601; Fax: 970-878-5717

IDAHO: State Office
 1387 S. Vinnell Way, Boise, ID 83709-1657
 Phone: 208-373-4000; Fax: 208-373-3904
Bruneau Field Office
 Manager: JENNA WHITLOCK
 3948 Development Ave., Boise, ID 83705-5389
 Phone: 208-384-3300; Fax: 208-384-3493
Burley Field Office
 Manager: THERESA HANLEY
 15 E. 200 South, Burley, ID 83318
 Phone: 208-677-6641; Fax: 208-677-6699
Cascade Field Office
 Manager: JOHN FEND
 3948 Development Ave., Boise, ID 83705-5389
 Phone: 208-384-3300; Fax: 208-384-3493
Challis Field Office
 Manager: RENEE SNYDER
 Hwy. 93, S., / Route 2, Box 610, Salmon, ID 83467
 Phone: 208-756-5400; Fax: 208-756-5436
Coeur D'alene Field Office
 Manager: ERIC THOMPSON
 1808 N. Third St., Coeur D'alene, ID 83814-3407
 Phone: 208-769-5030; Fax: 208-769-5050
Cottonwood Field Office
 Manager: GREG YUNCEVICH
 House 1, Butte Dr. / Route 3, Box 18, Cottonwood, ID 83522-9498
 Phone: 208-962-3245; Fax: 208-962-3275
Idaho Falls Field Office
 Manager: JOE KRAAYENBRINK
 1405 Hollypark Dr., Idaho Falls, ID 83401
 Phone: 208-524-7500; Fax: 208-524-7505
Jarbridge Field Office
 Manager: EDDIE GUERRERRO
 2620 Kimberly Rd., Twin Falls, ID 83301
 Phone: 208-736-2350; Fax: 208-736-2375
Malad Field Office
 Manager (Acting): JEFF STEELE
 138 S. Main, Malad City, ID 83252-1346
 Phone: 208-766-4766; Fax: 208-766-4087
Owyhee Field Office
 Manager: DARYL ALBISTON
 3948 Development Ave., Boise, ID 83705-5389
 Phone: 208-384-3300; Fax: 208-384-3493
Pocatello Field Office
 Manager: JEFF STEELE
 1111 N. 8th Ave., Pocatello, ID 83201
 Phone: 208-236-6860; Fax: 208-234-0246
Salmon Field Office
 Manager: DAVE KROSTING
 Hwy. 93, South / Route 2, Box 610, Salmon, ID 83467
 Phone: 208-756-5400; Fax: 208-756-5436
Shoshone Field Office
 Manager: BILL BAKER
 400 W. F St., P.O. Box 2-B, Shoshone, ID 83352-1522
 Phone: 208) 886-2206; Fax: 208) 886-7317

MISSISSIPPI and EASTERN STATES: Jackson Field Office: Jurisdiction for AL, AR, FL, GA, KY, LA, MI, NC, SC, TN and VA
 Manger: BRUCE DAWSON
 411 Briarwood Dr., Suite 404, Jackson, MS 39206
 Phone: 601-977-5400

MONTANA: Billings Field Office
 Manager: SANDRA BROOKS
 5001 Southgate Dr., Billings, MT 59101
 Phone: 406-896-5013; Fax: 406-896-5301
Butte District
 Manager: MERLE GOOD
 106 N. Parkmont, Butte, MT 59701
 Phone: 406-494-5059; Fax: 406-494-3474
Dillon Field Office
 Manager: SCOTT POWERS
 1005 Selway Dr., Dillon, MT 59725-9431
 Phone: 406-683-2337; Fax: 406-683-2970
Lewistown Field Office
 Manager: DAVID L. MARI
 P.O. Box 1160, Lewistown, MT 59457-1160
 Phone: 406-538-7461; Fax: 406-538-1904
Malta Field Office
 Manager: RICK M. HOTALING
 501 S. 2nd St. E., Malta, MT 59538
 Phone: 406-654-1240; Fax: 406-654-2671
Miles City Field Office
 Manager: TIM MURPHY
 111 Garry Owen Rd., Miles City, MT 59301-0940
 Phone: 406-232-4333; Fax: 406-233-2921
Missoula Field Office
 Manager: NANCY ANDERSON
 3255 Ft. Missoula Rd., Missoula, MT 59804-7293
 Phone: 406-329-3914; Fax: 406-329-3712

MONTANA: State Office for MT, ND and SD
 Director: LARRY E. HAMILTON
 P.O. Box 36800, Billings, MT 59107-6800
 Phone: 406-896-5012; Fax: 406-896-5299

NEVADA: State Office
 P.O. Box 12000, Reno, NV 89520-0006
 Phone: 775-861-6586
Battle Mountain Field Office
 Manager: GERALD M. SMITH
 50 Bastian Rd., Battle Mountain, NV 89820
 Phone: 702-635-4000; Fax: 702-635-4034
Carson City Field Office
 Manager: JOHN O. SINGLAUB
 5665 Morgan Mill Rd., Carson City, NV 89701

Phone: 702-885-6000; Fax: 702-885-6147
Elko Field Office
    Manager: HELEN M. HANKINS
    3900 E. Idaho St., Elko, NV 89801
    Phone: 702-753-0200; Fax: 702-753-0255
Ely Field Office
    Manager: GENE A. KOLKMAN
    702 N. Industrial Way, HC 33, Box 33500, Ely, NV 89301
    Phone: 702-289-1800; Fax: 702-289-1810
Las Vegas Field Office
    Manager: MIKE F. DWYER
    4765 W. Vegas Dr., Las Vegas, NV 89108
    Phone: 702-647-5000; Fax: 702-647-5023
Winnemucca Field Office
    Manager: TERRY REED
    5100 E. Winnemucca Blvd., Winnemucca, NV 89445
    Phone: 702-623-1500; Fax: 702-623-1503

NEW MEXICO: State Office for NM, TX, OK and KS
    Director: MICHELLE CHAVEZ
    P.O. Box 27115, Santa Fe, NM 87502-0115
    Phone: 505-438-7400; Fax: 505-438-7435
Albuquerque Field Office
    435 Montano Rd., NE, Alburquerque, NM 87107
    Phone: 505-761-8700; Fax: 505-761-8911
Carlsbad Field Office
    620 E. Greene St., Carlsbad, NM 88220-6292
    Phone: 505-887-6544; Fax: 505-885-9264
Farmington Field Office
    1235 La Plata Hwy., Suite A, Farmington, NM 87401
    Phone: 505-599-8900; Fax: 505-599-8998
Las Cruces District
    1800 Marquess, Las Cruces, NM 87005-3371
    Phone: 505-525-4300; Fax: 505-525-4412
Roswell District
    2909 W. Second St., Rosewell, NM 88201-2019
    Phone: 505-627-0272; Fax: 505-627-0276
Socorro Field Office
    198 Neel Ave., NW, Socorro, NM 87801-4648
    Phone: 505-835-0412; Fax: 505-835-0223
Taos Field Office
    226 Cruz Alta Rd., Taos, NM 87571-5983
    Phone: 505-758-8851; Fax: 505-758-1620

NORTH DAKOTA: North Dakota Field Office
    Manager: DOUGLAS J. BURGER
    2933 Third Ave., W., West Dickinson, ND 58601-2619
    Phone: 701-225-9148; Fax: 701-227-8510

OKLAHOMA: Tulsa District
    7906 East 33 St., Tulsa, OK 74145-1352
    Phone: 918-621-4100; Fax: 918-621-4130

OREGON: State Office for OR and WA
    1515 SW 5th Ave., Portland, OR 92208-2965
    Phone: 503-952-6002
Burns District
    Manager: TOM DYER
    HC 74-12533, Hwy 20 West, Hines, OR 97738
    Phone: 541-574-4400
Coos Bay Field Office
    Manager: SUE RICHARDSON
    1300 Airport Lane Rd., North Bend, OR 97459
    Phone: 541-756-0100; Fax: 541-751-4303
Eugene Field Office
    2890 Chad Dr., Eugene, OR 97408
    Phone: 541-683-6600; Fax: 541-683-6981
Lakeview Field Offices
    Manager: STEVE ELLIS
    HC10 Box 337, 1300 S. G St, Lakeview, OR 97630
    Phone: 503-947-2177; Fax: 541-947-6399
Medford Field Office
    Manager: RON WENKER
    3040 Biddle Rd., Medford, OR 97504
    Phone: 541-770-2200; Fax: 541-770-2400
Prineville District Field Office
    Manager: JAMES HANCOCK
    P.O. Box 550, Prineville, OR 97754
    Phone: 541-416-6700; Fax: 541-416-6798
Roseburg District
    Manager: CARY OSTERHAUS
    777 NW Garden Valley Blvd., Roseburg, OR 97470
    Phone: 541-440-4930; Fax: 541-440-4948
Salem District Field Office
    Manager: VAN MANNING
    1717 Fabry Rd., SE, Salem, OR 97306
    Phone: 541-375-5646; Fax: 503-375-5622
Vale District
    Manager: JUAN PALMA
    100 Oregon St., Vale, OR 97918
    Phone: 541-473-3144; Fax: 541-473-6213

SOUTH DAKOTA: South Dakota Field Office
    Manager: PATRICK J. GUBBINS
    310 Roundup St., Belle Fourche, SD 57717-1698
    Phone: 605-892-2526; Fax: 605-892-4742

TEXAS: Amarillo Field Office
    801 S. Fillmore St., Ste. 500, Amarillo, TX 79101-3545
    Phone: 806-324-2617; Fax: 806-324-2633

UTAH: State Office
    Director: SALLY WISELY
    324 S. State St., Salt Lake City, UT 84145-0155
    Phone: 801-539-4001
Cedar City District Field Office
    Manager (Acting): ART TATE
    176 East D.L. Sargent Dr, Cedar City, UT 84720
    Phone: 801-865-3053; Fax: 801-865-3058
Fillmore Field Office
    Manager: REX ROWLEY
    35 E. 500 North, Fillmore, UT 84631
    Phone: 435-743-6811
Kanab
    Manager: VERLIN SMITH
    318 N. First East, Kanab, UT 84741
    Phone: 435-644-2672
Moab District Field Office
    Manager: MAGGIE WHITE
    82 E. Dogwood, Moab, UT 84532
    Phone: 435-259-2100
Monticello Field Office
    Manager: KENT WALTER
    435 N. Main, P.O. Box 7, Monticello, UT 84535
    Phone: 435-587-1502
Price Field Office
    Manager: DICK MANUS
    125 S. 600 West, Price, UT 84501
    Phone: 435-636-3601
Richfield District Field Office
    Manager: JERRY GOODMAN
    150 E. 900, N, Richfield, UT 84701
    Phone: 435-896-1523
Salt Lake District
    Manager: GLENN CARPENTER
    2370 S. 2300, W, Salt Lake City, UT 84119
    Phone: 801-977-4300; Fax: 801-997-4397
St. George Field Office
    Manager: JIM CRISP
    345 East Riverside Dr., St. George, UT 84720

FEDERALLY PROTECTED AREAS - NATIONAL ESTUARINE RESEARCH RESERVES

Phone: 435-688-3200
Vernal District
  Manager: DAVE HOWELL
  170 S. 500 St., East, Vernal, UT 84078
  Phone: 801-781-4400; Fax: 801-781-4410

VIRGINIA and EASTERN STATES: Eastern States Office
  State Director: W. HORD TIPTON
  7450 Boston Blvd., Springfield, VA 22153
  Phone: 703-440-1713

WASHINGTON: Spokane District
  1103 N. Fancher, Spokane, WA 99212
  Phone: 509-536-1200; Fax: 509-536-1275

WISCONSIN and EASTERN STATES: Milwaukee Field Office:
  Jurisdiction for CT, DE, IL, IN, IA, ME, MD, MA, MI, MN, MO, NH, NJ, NY, OH, PA, RI, VT, WV and WI
  Manager: JIM DRYDEN
  310 W. Wisconsin Ave., Suite 450, Milwaukee, WI 53203
  Phone: 414-297-4400

WYOMING: State Office for WY and NE
  Director: AL PIERSON
  5353 Yellowstone; P.O. Box 1828, Cheyenne, WY 82003
  Phone: 307-775-6256
Buffalo Field Office
  Manager: DENNIS STENGER
  1425 Fort St., Buffalo, WY 82834-2436
  Phone: 307-684-1100; Fax: 307-684-1122
Casper District
  Manager: JIM MURKIN
  1701 East E St., Casper, WY 82601
  Phone: 307-261-7600; Fax: 307-234-1525
Cody Field Office
  Manager: MIKE BLYMYER
  1002 Blackburn; P.O. Box 518, Cody, WY 82414-0518
  Phone: 307-587-2216; Fax: 307-527-7116
Kemmerer Field Office
  Manager: JEFFREY RAWSON
  312 Highway 189 N., Kemmerer, WY 83101-9710
  Phone: 307-828-4500; Fax: 307-828-4539
Lander Field Office
  Manager: JACK KELLY
  1335 Main; P.O. Box 589, Lander, WY 82520-0589
  Phone: 307-332-8400; Fax: 307-332-8447
Newcastle Field Office
  1101 Washington Blvd., Newcastle, WY 82701-2972
  Phone: 307-746-4453; Fax: 307-746-4840
Pinedale Field Office
  Manager: LESLIE THEISS
  432 E. Mill Street; P.O. Box 768, Pinedale, WY 82941-0768
  Phone: 307-367-5300; Fax: 307-367-5329
Rawlins Field Office
  Manager: KURT KOTTER
  1300 Third St.; P.O. Box 2407, Rawlins, WY 82301-2407
  Phone: 307-328-4200; Fax: 307-328-4224
Rock Springs Field Office
  Manager: STAN McKEE
  280 Highway 191 N., Rock Springs, WY 82901-3448
  Phone: 307-352-0256; Fax: 307-352-0329
Worland Field Office
  Manager: DARRELL BARNES
  S. 23rd St., PO Box 119, Worland, WY 82401-0119
  Phone: 307-347-5100; Fax: 307-347-6195

NATIONAL ESTUARINE RESEARCH RESERVES

ALABAMA: Weeks Bay NERR
  Manager: L. G. ADAMS
  11300 U.S. Highway 98, Fairhope, AL 36532
  Phone: 334-928-9792

CALIFORNIA: Elkhorn Slough NERR
  Managers: STEVE KIMPLE and BECKY CHRISTENSEN
  1700 Elkhorn Slough, Watsonville, CA 95076
  Phone: 408-728-2822
Tijuana River NERR
  Managers: JOANNE KERBAVAZ and PHIL JENKINS
  301 Caspian Way, Imperial Beach, CA 91932
  Phone: 619-575-3613

DELAWARE: Delaware NERR
  Manager: BETSY ARCHER
  Delaware Department of Natural Resources and Environmental Control, 89 Kings Hwy., Dover, DE 1901
  Phone: 302-739-3451

FLORIDA: Apalachicola NERR
  Manager: WOODWARD MILEY
  Department of Environmental Protection, 350 Carroll St., Eastpoint, FL 32328
  Phone: 850-670-4783
Rookery Bay NERR
  Manager: GARY LYTTON
  Department of Environmental Protection, 300 Tower Rd., Naples, FL 34113
  Phone: 941-417-6310

GEORGIA: Sapelo Island NERR
  Manager: BUDDY SULLIVAN
  Georgia Department of Natural Resources, P.O. Box 15, Sapelo Islands, GA 31327
  Phone: 912-485-2251

MAINE: Wells NERR
  Manager: JIM LIST
  342 Landholm Farm Rd., Wells, ME 04090
  Phone: 207-646-1555

MARYLAND: Chesapeake Bay NERR in Maryland
  Manager: KATHY ELLETT
  Department of Natural Resources, Tawes State Office Bldg., B-3, 580 Taylor Ave., Annapolis, MD 21401
  Phone: 410-260-8740

MASSACHUSETTS: Waquoit Bay NERR
  Manager: CHRISTINE GAULT
  Department of Environmental Management, P.O. Box 3092, Waquoit, MA 02536
  Phone: 508-457-0495

NEW HAMPSHIRE: Great Bay NERR
  Manager: PETER WELLENBERGER
  Department of Fish and Game, 225 Main St, Durham, NH 03824
  Phone: 603-868-1095

NEW YORK: Hudson River NERR
  Manager: ELIZABETH BLAIR
  c/o Bard College Field Station, Annandale-on-Hudson, Hudson, NY 12504
  Phone: 914-758-7033

NORTH CAROLINA: North Carolina NERR
  Manager: JOHN TAGGART
  Center for Marine Science Research, University of North Carolina at Willmington, 7205 Wrightsville A, Willmington, NC 28403
  Phone: 919-256-3721

OHIO: Old Woman Creek NERR
  Manager: EUGENE WRIGHT
  2514 Cleveland Rd., East, Huron, OH 44839
  Phone: 419-433-4601

OREGON: South Slough NERR
  Manager: MIKE GRAYBILL
  P.O. Box 5417, Charleston, OR 97420
  Phone: 541-888-5559

PUERTO RICO: Jobos Bay NERR
  Manager: CARMEN GONZALEZ
  Department of Natural Resources, Call Box B, Aquirre, PR 00704
  Phone: 787-853-4617

RHODE ISLAND: Narragansett Bay NERR
  Manager: AL BECK
  Department of Environmental Management, 55 South Reserve Dr., Prudence Island, RI 02872
  Phone: 401-683-6780

SOUTH CAROLINA: ACE Basin NERR
  Manager: MICHAEL McKENZIE
  South Carolina Department of Natural Resources, P.O. Box 12559, Charleston, SC 29412
  Phone: 843-762-5062
North Inlet
  Manager: DENNIS ALLEN
  Winyah Bay NERR, Baruch Marine Field Lab, P.O. Box 1630, Georgetown, SC 29440
  Phone: 809-546-3623

VIRGINIA: Chesapeake Bay NERR in Virginia
  Manager: MAURICE LYNCH
  Virginia Institute of Marine Science, Gloucester Point, VA 23062
  Phone: 804-684-7135

WASHINGTON: Padilla Bay NERR
  Manager: TERRY STEVENS
  1043 Bayview-Edison Rd., Mt. Vernon, WA 98273
  Phone: 360-428-1558

NATIONAL FORESTS

ALABAMA: National Forests in Alabama
  Supervisor: JIM GOODER
  2946 Chestnut St., Montgomery, AL 36107
  Phone: 334-832-4470

ALASKA: Chugach National Forest
  Supervisor: DAVE GIBBONS
  3301 C St., Ste 300, Anchorage, AK 99503-3956
  Phone: 907-271-2525
Tongass-Chatham Area National Forest
  Assistant Supervisor: FRED SALINAS
  204 Siginaka Way, Sitka, AK 99835-7316
  Phone: 907-747-4410
Tongass-Ketchikan Area National Forest
  Supervisor: TOM PUCHLERZ
  Federal Bldg., Ketchikan, AK 99901-6591
  Phone: 907-228-6281
Tongass-Stikine Area National Forest
  Assistant Supervisor: CAROL JORGENSON
  Box 309, Petersburg, AK 99833-0309
  Phone: 907-772-5800

ARIZONA: Apache-Sitgreaves National Forest
  Supervisor: JOHN C. BEDELL
  Federal Bldg., Box 640, Springville, AZ 85938
  Phone: 520-333-4301
Coconino National Forest
  Supervisor: FRED TREVEY
  2323 E. Greenlaw Ln., Flagstaff, AZ 86004
  Phone: 520-527-3600
Coronado National Forest
  Supervisor: JAMES R. ABBOTT
  300 W. Congress, Tucson, AZ 85701
  Phone: 520-635-2681
Kaibab National Forest
  Supervisor: WILLIAM LANNAN
  800 South 6th St., Williams, AZ 86046
  Phone: 520-635-2681
Prescott National Forest
  Supervisor: COY JEMMETT
  344 S. Cortez, Prescott, AZ 86303
  Phone: 520-771-4700
Tonto National Forest
  Supervisor: CHARLES R. BAZAN
  2324 E. McDowell Rd., P.O. Box 5348, Phoenix, AZ 85006
  Phone: 602-225-5200

ARKANSAS: Ouachita National Forest
  Supervisor: ALAN NEWMAN
  Box 1270, Federal Bldg., Hot Springs National Park, AR 71902
  Phone: 501-321-5202
Ozard--St. Francis National Forest
  Supervisor: CHARLES RICHMOND
  605 West Main St., Russeville, AR 72801
  Phone: 501-968-2354

CALIFORNIA: Angeles National Forests
  Supervisor: MIKE ROGERS
  701 N. Santa Anita Ave., Arcadia, CA 91006
  Phone: 626-574-1613
Cleveland National Forest
  Supervisor: ANNE S. FEGE
  10845 Rancho Bernardo Rd., Ste 200, San Diego, CA 92127
  Phone: 619-673-6180
Eldorado National Forest
  Supervisor (Acting): JOHN BERRY
  100 Formi Rd., Placerville, CA 95667
  Phone: 530-622-5061
Inyo National Forest
  Supervisor: JEFFERY BAILEY
  873 N. Main St., Bishop, CA 93514
  Phone: 760-873-2400
Klamath National Forest
  Supervisor (Acting): MICHAEL LEE
  1312 Fairlane Rd., Yreka, CA 96097
  Phone: 530-842-6131
Lake Tahoe Basin Management Unit
  Supervisor (Acting): ED GEE
  870 Emerald Bay Rd., Ste. 1, South Lake Tahoe, CA 96150
  Phone: 530-573-2600
Lassen National Forest
  Supervisor: H. J. SILVERMAN

FEDERALLY PROTECTED AREAS - NATIONAL FORESTS

55 South Sacramento St., Susanville, CA 96130
Phone: 530-257-2151
Los Padres National Forest
   Supervisor: JEANINE DERBY
   6144 Calle Real, Goleta, CA 93117
   Phone: 805-683-6711
Mendocino National Forest
   Supervisor: DANIEL C. CHISHOLM
   825 N. Humboldt Ave., Willows, CA 95988
   Phone: 530-233-5811
Modoc National Forest
   Supervisor: SCOTT CONROY
   800 W. 12th St., Alturas, CA 96101
   Phone: 530-233-5811
Plumas National Forest
   Supervisor: MARK MADRID
   159 Lawrence St., Box 11500, Qunicy, CA 95971
   Phone: 530-283-2050
San Bernardino National Forest
   Supervisor: GENE ZIMMERMAN
   1824 S. Commercenter Cir., San Bernardino, CA 92408
   Phone: 909-383-5588
Sequoia National Forest
   Supervisor: ARTHUR GAFFREY
   900 W. Grand Ave., Porterville, CA 93257
   Phone: 209-784-1500
Shasta-Trinity National Forest
   Supervisor: SHARON HEYWOOD
   2400 Washington Ave., Redding, CA 96001
   Phone: 530-244-2978
Sierra National Forest
   Supervisor: JAMES L. BOYNTON
   1600 Tollhouse Rd., Clovis, CA 93611
   Phone: 209-297-0706
Six Rivers National Forest
   Supervisor: LOU WOLTERING
   1330 Bayshore Way, Eureka, CA 95501
   Phone: 707-442-1721
Stanislaus National Forest
   Supervisor: BEN DELVILLAR
   19777 Greenley Rd., Sonora, CA 95370
   Phone: 209-532-3671
Tahoe National Forest
   Supervisor: STEVE EUBANKS
   631 Coyote St., P.O. Box 6003, Nevada City, CA 95959-6003
   Phone: 530-265-4531

COLORADO: Arapaho and Roosevelt National Forests
   Supervisor: PETER CLARK, JR.
   240 W. Prospect St., Fort Collins, CO 80526
   Phone: 970-498-1110
Grand Mesa, Uncompahgre and Gunnison National Forests
   Supervisor: ROBERT L. STORCH
   2250 Highway 50, Delta, CO 81416
   Phone: 970-874-6600
Pike and San Isabel National Forests
   1920 Valley Dr., Pueblo, CO 81008
   Phone: 719-545-8737
Rio Grande National Forest
   1803 West Highway 160, Monte Vista, CO 81144
   Phone: 719-852-5941
Routt National Forest
   Supervisor: JERRY E. SCHMIDT
   19587 W. US40, Ste 20, Steamboat Springs, CO 80487-9550
   Phone: 970-879-1722
San Juan National Forest
   Supervisor: CALVIN JOYNER
   Federal Bldg., 15 Burhett Court, Durango, CO 81301-3647
   Phone: 970-247-4874
White River National Forest
   Supervisor: MARTHA KETELLE
   Old Federal Bldg., P.O. Box 948, Glenwood Springs, CO 81602
   Phone: 970-945-2521

FLORIDA: National Forests in Forida
   Supervisor: MARSHA KEARNEY
   Woodcrest Office Park, 325 John Knox Rd., Ste F-100, Tallahassee, FL 32303
   Phone: 850-942-9300

GEORGIA: Chattahoochee and Oconee National Forests
   Supervisor: GEORGE G. MARTIN
   1755 Cleveland Hwy., Gainesville, GA 30501
   Phone: 770-536-0541

IDAHO: Boise National Forest
   Supervisor: DAVID D. RITTENHOUSE
   1249 S. Vinnell Way, Ste. 200, Boise, ID 83709
   Phone: 208-373-4100
Caribou-Targhee National Forest
   Supervisor: JERRY B. REESE
   250 S. 4th Ave., Ste 172, Federal Bldg., Pocatello, ID 93201
   Phone: 208-236-7500
Clearwater National Forest
   Supervisor: JAMES L. CASWELL
   12730 Highway 12, Orofino, ID 83544
   Phone: 208-476-4541
Idaho Panhandle National Forests
   Supervisor: DAVID J. WRIGHT
   3815 Schreiber Way, Coeur d'Alene, ID 83814-8863
   Phone: 208-765-7223
Nez-Perce National Forest
   Supervisor: BRUCE BERNHARDT
   Rt. 2, Box 475, McCall, ID 83530
   Phone: 208-983-1950
Payette National Forest
   Supervisor: DAVID F. ALEXANDER
   Forest Service Bldg., Box 1026, McCall, ID 83638
   Phone: 208-634-0700
Salmon-Challis National Forest
   Supervisor: GEORGE MATEJKO
   Forest Service, RR 2, Box 600, Salmon, ID 83467
   Phone: 208-756-5100
Sawtooth National Forest
   Supervisor: WILLIAM P. LEVERE
   2647 Kimberly Rd., East, Twin Falls, ID 83301-7976
   Phone: 208-737-3200

ILLINOIS: Shawnee National Forest
   901 S. Commercial St., Harrisburg, IL 62946
   Phone: 618-253-1000

INDIANA: Hoosier National Forest
   Supervisor: KENNETH G. DAY
   811 Constitution Ave., Beford, IN 47421
   Phone: 812-275-5987

KENTUCKY: Daniel Boone National Forest
   Supervisor: BRADLEY E. POWELL
   1700 Bypass Rd., Winchester, KY 40391
   Phone: 606-745-3100

LOUISIANA: Kisatchie National Forest
   Supervisor: LYNN NEFF

2500 Shreveport Hwy., Pineville, LA 71360
Phone: 318-473-7160

MAINE: White Mountain National Forest
see New Hampshire

MICHIGAN: Hiawatha National Forest
Supervisor: CLYDE N. THOMPSON
2727 N. Lincoln Rd., Escanaba, MI 49829
Phone: 906-786-4062
Huron-Manistee National Forest
1755 S. Mitchell St., Cadillac, MI 49601
Phone: 616-775-2421
Ottawa National Forest
Supervisor: PHYLLIS GREEN
2100 E. Cloverland Dr., Ironwood, MI 49938
Phone: 906-932-1330

MINNESOTA: Chippewa National Forest
Supervisor: LOGAN LEE
Rt. #3, Box 244, Cass Lake, MN 56633
Phone: 218-720-5324
Superior National Forest
Supervisor: JIM SANDERS
8901 Grand Avenue Place, Duluth, MN 55808-1102
Phone: 218-720-5324

MISSISSIPPI: Bienville, Delta, Desoto, Holly Springs, Homochitto, and Tombigbee National Forests
Supervisor: KARL SIDERITS
National Forests in Mississippi, 100 W. Capital St., Ste. 1141, Jackson, MS 39269
Phone: 601-965-4391

MISSOURI: Mark Twain National Forest
Supervisor: RANDY MOORE
410 Fairgrounds Rd., Rolla, MO 65401
Phone: 573-364-4624

MONTANA: Beaverhead--Deerlodge National Forest
420 Barrett St., Dillon, MT 59725-3572
Phone: 406-683-3900
Bitterroot National Forest
Supervisor: RODD RICHARDSON
1801 N. 1st St., Hamilton, MT 59840
Phone: 406-363-7121
Custer National Forest
Supervisor: NANCY CURRIDEN
P.O. Box 50760, Billings, MT 59105
Phone: 406-657-6361
Flathead National Forest
Supervisor: CATHY BARBOULETOS
1935 3rd. Ave., E., Kalispell, MT 59901
Phone: 406-758-5251
Gallatin National Forest
Supervisor: DAVE GARBER
10 E. Babcock Ave., Federal Bldg., Box 130, Bozeman, MT 59771
Phone: 409-587-6702
Helena National Forest
Supervisor: TOM CLIFFORD
2880 Skyway Dr., Helena, MT 59601
Phone: 406-449-5201
Kootenai National Forest
Supervisor: BOB CASTENDA
506 US Highway 2 West, Libby, MT 59923
Phone: 406-293-6211
Lewis and Clark National Forest
Supervisor: RICK PRAUSA
Box 869, 1101 15th St., N., Great Falls, MT 59923
Phone: 406-791-7700
Lolo National Forest
Supervisor: DEBORAH L. R. AUSTIN
Bldg. 24, Ft. Missoula, Missoula, MT 59801
Phone: 406-329-3797

NEBRASKA: Nebraska National Forest
Supervisor: MARY H. PETERSON
125 N. Main St., Chadron, NE 69337
Phone: 308-432-0300

NEVADA: Humboldt--Toiyabe National Forest
Supervisor: GLORIA FLORA
2035 1200 Franklin Way, Sparks, NV 89431
Phone: 775-331-6444

NEW HAMPSHIRE: White Mountain National Forest
Supervisor: RICK CABLES
Federal Bldg. 719 Main St., Box 638, Laconia, NH 03247
Phone: 603-528-8721

NEW MEXICO: Carson National Forest
Supervisor: LEONARD L. LUCERO
Fed. Bldg., 208 Cruz Alta Rd., Box 558, Taos, NM 87571
Phone: 505-758-6200
Cibola National Forest
Supervisor: JEANINE A. DERBY
2113 Osuna Rd. Ne, Ste. A, Albuquerque, NM 87111-1001
Phone: 505-761-4650
Gila National Forest
3005 E. Camino del Bosque, Silber City, NM 88061
Phone: 505-388-8201
Lincoln National Forest
Supervisor: LEE POAGUE
Fed. Bldg., 1101 New York Ave., Alamogordo, NM 88310-6992
Phone: 505-434-7200
Santa Fe National Forest
Supervisor: AL DEFLER
1220 St. Francis Dr., Santa Fe, NM 87504
Phone: 505-988-6940

NORTH CAROLINA: Croatan, Nantahala, Pisgah and Uwharrie National Forests
Supervisor: JOHN RAMEY
P.O. Box 2750, Asheville, NC 28802
Phone: 828-257-4200

OHIO: Wayne National Forest
Supervisor: JOSE ZAMBRANA
219 Columbus Rd., Athens, OH 45701
Phone: 740-592-6644

OREGON: Deschutes National Forest
Supervisor: SALLY COLLINS
1645 Highway 20 East, Bend, OR 97701
Phone: 541-388-2715
Fremont National Forest
Supervisor: CHUCK GRAHAM
524 North G St., Lakeview, OR 97630
Phone: 541-947-2151
Malheur National Forest
Supervisor: MARK BOCHE
139 NE Dayton St., John Day, OR 97845
Phone: 541-575-1731
Mt. Hood National Forest
Supervisor: MIKE EDRINGTON
2955 Division St., Gresham, OR 97030
Phone: 503-666-1700

Ochoco National Forest
Supervisor: TOM SCHMIDT
Box 490, Prineville, OR 97754
Phone: 541-447-6247

Rogue River National Forest
Supervisor: JAMES T. GLADEN
Fed. Bldg., 333 W. 8th St., Box 520, Medford, OR 97501
Phone: 541-776-3600

Siskiyou National Forest
Supervisor: MICHAEL LUNN
Box 440, Grants Pass, OR 97526
Phone: 541-471-6500

Siuslaw National Forest
Box 1148, Corvallis, OR 97339
Phone: 541-750-7000

Umatilla National Forest
Supervisor: JOHN P. KLINE
2517 SW Hailey Ave., Pendleton, OR 97801
Phone: 541-278-3721

Umpqua National Forest
Supervisor: DON OSTBY
Box 1008, Roseburg, OR 97470
Phone: 541-672-6601

Wallowa Whitman National Forests
Supervisor: ROBERT RICHMOND
Box 907, Baker City, OR 97814
Phone: 541-523-6391

Willamette National Forest
Supervisor: DARRELL. KENOPS
Box 10607, Eugene, OR 97440
Phone: 541-465-6521

Winema National Forest
Supervisor: BOB CASTANEDA
2819 Dahlia, Klamath Falls, OR 97601
Phone: 541-883-6714

PENNSYLVANIA: Allegheny National Forest
Supervisor: JOHN E. PALMER
222 Liberty St., Box 847, Warren, PA 16365
Phone: 814-723-5150

PUERTO RICO: Caribbean National Forest
Supervisor: PABLO CRUZ
Call Box 490, Palmer, PR 00721
Phone: 787-888-1810

SOUTH CAROLINA: Francis Marion and Sumter National Forest
Supervisor: JEROME THOMAS
4923 Broad River Rd., Columbia, SC 29212
Phone: 803-561-4000

SOUTH DAKOTA: Black Hills National Forest
Supervisor: JOHN C. TWISS
R.R. 2, Box 200, Custer, SD 57730-9501
Phone: 605-673-2251

TENNESSEE: Cherokee National Forest
Supervisor: ANNE ZIMMERMAN
P.O. Box 2010, Cleveland, TN 37320
Phone: 423-476-9700

TEXAS: Angelia, Davy Crockett, Sabine and Sam Houston National Forest
Supervisor: RONNIE RAUM
National Forest in Texas, Homer Garrison Federal Bldg., 701 N. 1st St., Lufkin, TX 75901
Phone: 409-639-8501

UTAH: Ashley National Forest
Supervisor: BERT KULESZA
355 N. Vernal Ave., Vernal, UT 84078
Phone: 801-789-1181

Dixie National Forest
Supervisor: MARY WAGNER
82 N. 100 E. St., Cedar City, UT 84720-2686
Phone: 435-865-3701

Fishlake National Forest
Supervisor: ROBERT D. MROWKA
115 East 900 North, Richfield, UT 84701
Phone: 435-896-9233

Manti-LaSal National Forest
Supervisor: JANETTE S. KAISER
599 West Price River Dr., Price, UT 84501
Phone: 435-637-2817

Uinta National Forest
Supervisor: PETE KARP
88 West 100 North, Provo, UT 84601
Phone: 801-342-5100

Wasatch-Cache National Forest
Supervisor: BERNIE WEINGARDT
8236 Federal Bldg., 125 S. State St., Salt Lake City, UT 84138
Phone: 801-524-5030

VERMONT: Green Mountain and Finger Lakes National Forest
Supervisor: PAUL BREWSTER
Federal Bldg., 231 N. Main, Rutland, VT 05701-0519
Phone: 802-747-6700

VIRGINIA: George Washington and Jefferson National Forests
Supervisor: BILL DAMON
5162 Valleypointe Pkwy., Roanoke, VA 24019
Phone: 540-265-5100

WASHINGTON: Colville National Forest
Supervisor: ROBERT L. VAUGHT
716 S. Main, Colville, WA 99114
Phone: 509-662-4335

Gifford Pinchot National Forest
Supervisor: TED STUBBLEFIELD
6926 E. 4th Plain Blvd., Vancouver, WA 98668-8944
Phone: 360-891-5000

Mt. Baker-Snoqualmie National Forest
21905 64th Ave. West, Mountlake Terrace, Seattle, WA 98043
Phone: 425-775-4702

Okanogan National Forest
Supervisor: SAM UELGEHR
1240 S. Second, Okanogan, WA 98840
Phone: 509-826-3275

Olympic National Forest
Supervisor: RONALD R. HUMPHREY
1835 Blacklake Blvd., SW, Olympia, WA 98512
Phone: 360-956-2300

Wenatchee National Forest
Supervisor: SONNY O'NEAL
Box 811, Wenatchee, WA 98807
Phone: 509-662-4335

WEST VIRGINIA: Monongahela National Forest
Supervisor: CHUCK MEYERS
USDA Bldg., 200 Sycamore St., Elkins, WV 26241-3962
Phone: 304-636-1800

WISCONSIN: Chequamegon--Nicolet National Forest
Supervisor: D. LYNN ROBERTS
1170 4th Ave., S., Park Falls, WI 54552
Phone: 715-762-2461

WYOMING: Bighorn National Forest
Supervisor: ABIGAIL KIMBELL
1969 S. Sheridam Ave., Sheridan, WY 82801
Phone: 307-672-0751
Bridger-Teton National Forest
Supervisor: TOM PUCHLERZ
Forest Service Bldg., 340 N. Cache, Jackson, WY 83001
Phone: 307-739-5500
Medicine Bow-Routt National Forest
Supervisor: JERRY SCHMIDT
2468 Jackson St., Laramie, WY 82070-6535
Phone: 307-745-2300
Shoshone National Forest
Supervisor: REBECCA AUS
808 Meadow Ln., Cody, WY 82414-4516
Phone: 307-527-6241

NATIONAL GRASSLANDS

CALIFORNIA: Butte Valley National Grassland
Goosewest Ranger District, 37805 Hwy 97, Macdoel, CA 96058
Phone: 530-398-4391

COLORADO: Comanche National Grassland
27162 Hwy. 287, P.O. Box 127, Springfield, CO 81073
Phone: 719-523-6591
Pawnee National Grassland
Director: STEVE CURREY
660 O St., Greenley, CO 80631
Phone: 970-353-5004

IDAHO: Curlew National Grassland
P.O. Box 146, Malad, ID 83252
Phone: 208-7666-4743

KANSAS: Cimmarron National Grassland
242 Hwy. 56 E., P.O. Box 300, Elkhart, KS 67950
Phone: 316-697-4621

NEBRASKA: Oglala National Grassland
16524 Hwy. 385, Chadron, NE 69337
Phone: 308-432-4475

NEW MEXICO: Kiow/Rita Blanca National Grassland
714 Main St., Clayton, NM 88415
Phone: 505-374-9652

NORTH DAKOTA: Little Missouri National Forest, McKenzie Ranger District
Director: LESLEY W. THOMPSON
HC 02, Box 8, Watford City, ND 58854
Phone: 701-842-2393
Little Missouri National Forest, Medora Ranger District
Director: LARRY J. DAWSON
161 21st St. W., Dickinson, ND 58601
Phone: 701-225-5151
Sheyenne National Grassland
Box 946, Lisbon, ND 58054
Phone: 701-683-4342

OKLAHOMA: McClellan Creek/Black Kettle National Grassland
Rt. 1, Box 55B, Cheyenne, OK 73628
Phone: 580-497-2143

OREGON: Crooked River National Forest
Director: BYRON CHENEY
813 SW Hwy 97, Madras, OR 97741
Phone: 541-475-9272

SOUTH DAKOTA: Buffalo Gap National Grassland, Fall River Ranger District
209 N. River, Hot Springs, SD 57747
Phone: 605-745-4107
Buffalo Gap National Grassland, Wall Ranger District / National Grasslands Visitor Center
708 Main St., P.O. Box 425, Wall, SD 57790
Phone: 605-279-2125
Cedar River / Grand River National Grassland
Director: FOREST MORIN
1005 5th Ave. W., P.O. Box 390, Lemmon, SD 57638
Phone: 605-374-3592
Fort Pierre National Grassland
Director: ANTHONY DeTOY
124 South Euclid Ave., P.O. Box 417, Pierre, SD 57501
Phone: 605-224-5517

TEXAS: Lyndon B. Johnson / Caddo National Forest
1400 N. US. 81/287 Hwy., P.O. Box 507, Decatur, TX 76234
Phone: 940-627-5475

WYOMING: Thunder Basin National Grasslands
Director: MALCOLM R. EDWARDS
2250 East Richards, Douglas, WY 82633
Phone: 307-358-4690

NATIONAL MARINE SANCTUARIES

CALIFORNIA: Channel Islands National Marine Sanctuary
Manager: ED CASSANO
113 Harbor Way, Santa Barbara, CA 93109
Phone: 805-568-1582
Cordell Bank National Marine Sanctuary
Manager: EDWARD UEBER
Ft. Mason, Bldg. 201, San Francisco, CA 94123
Phone: 415-561-6622
Gulf of Farallones National Marine Sanctuary
Manager: EDWARD UEBER
Fort Mason Bldg. 201, San Francisco, CA 94123
Phone: 415-561-6622
Monterey Bay National Marine Sanctuary
Manager: WILLIAM J. DOUROS
299 Foam St., Suite D, Monterey, CA 93940
Phone: 831-647-4201

FLORIDA: Florida Keys National Marine Sanctuary
Manager: BILLY CAUSEY
P.O. Box 500368, 5550 Overseas Hwy., Marathon, FL 33050
Phone: 305-743-2437

GEORGIA: Gray's Reef National Marine Sanctuary
Manager: REED BOHNE
10 Ocean Scene Circle, Savannah, GA 31411
Phone: 912-598-2345

HAWAII: Hawaiian Islands Humpback Whale National Sanctuary
Manager: ALLEN TOM
726 South, Kihei, HI 96753
Phone: 808-879-2818

MASSACHUSETTS: Stellwagen Bank National Marine Sanctuary
Manager: BRAD BARR
14 Union St., Plymouth, MA 02360

Phone: 508-747-1691

TEXAS: Flower Garden Banks National Marine Sanctuary
   Manager: SHELLEY DuPUY
   216 W. 26th St., Suite 104, Bryan, TX 77803
   Phone: 409-779-

VIRGINIA: Monitor National Marine Sanctuary
   Manager: JOHN BROADWATER
   c/o the Mariners' Museum, 100 Museum Dr., Newport News, VA 23606
   Phone: 757-599-3122

WASHINGTON: Olympic Coast National Marine Sanctuary
   Manager (Acting): GEORGE GALASSO
   138 W. First St., Port Angeles, WA 98362-2600
   Phone: 360-457-6622

NATIONAL PARKS

ALASKA: Denali National Park
   Superintendent: STEPHEN P. MARTIN
   P.O. Box 74680, Denali Park, AK 99755
   Phone: 907-683-9581
Gates of the Arctic National Park
   Superintendent: DAVID MILLS
   201 First Ave., Doyon Bldg., Fairbanks, AK 99701
   Phone: 907-456-0281
Glacier Bay National Park
   Superintendent: TOMIE LEE
   One Park Rd., Gustavus, AK 99826-0140
   Phone: 907-697-2230
Katmai National Park
   Superintendent: DEB LIGGETT
   One King Salmon Mall, King Salmon, AK 99613
   Phone: 907-246-3305
Kenai Fjords National Park
   Superintendent: ANNE CASTELLINA
   1212 4th Ave., Seward, AK 99664
   Phone: 907-224-3175
Kobuk Valley National Park
   Superintendent: DAVID SPRITES
   P.O. Box 1029, Kotzebue, AK 99752
   Phone: 907-442-3890
Lake Clark National Park
   Superintendent: DEB LIGGETT
   4230 University Dr., Ste. 311, Anchorage, AK 99508
   Phone: 907-271-3751
Wrangell-St. Elias National Park
   Superintendent: JON JARVIS
   P.O.Box 439, Copper Center, AK 99573
   Phone: 907-822-5234

AMERICAN SAMOA: National Park of America Samoa
   Superintendent: CHARLES CRANFIELD
   Pago Pago, American Samoa 96799
   Phone: 684-633-7082

ARIZONA: Grand Canyon National Park
   Superintendent: ROBERT ARNBERGER
   P.O. Box 129, Grand Canyon, AZ 86023
   Phone: 520-638-7945
Petrified Forest National Park
   Superintendent: MICHELLE HELLICKSON
   One Park Rd., Petrified Forest, AZ 86028
   Phone: 520-524-6228

ARKANSAS: Hot Springs National Park
   Superintendent: ROGER GIDDINGS
   P.O. Box 1860, Hot Springs, AR 71902
   Phone: 501-624-3383

CALIFORNIA: Channel Islands National Park
   Superintendent: TIM SETNIKA
   1901 Spinnaker Dr., Ventura, CA 93001
   Phone: 805-658-5700
Death Valley National Park
   Superintendent: RICHARD H. MARTIN
   P.O. Box 579, Death Valley, CA 92328
   Phone: 760-786-2331; Fax: 760-786-3283
Joshua Tree National Park
   Superintendent: ERNEST QUINTANA
   74485 National Park Dr., Twenty-nine Palms, CA 92277
   Phone: 760-367-5500; Fax: 760-367-6392
Lassen Volcanic National Park
   Superintendent: MARILYN PARRIS
   P.O. Box 100, 38050 Hwy 36E, Mineral, CA 96063
   Phone: 530-595-4444
Redwood National Park
   Superintendent: ANDREW RINGGOLD
   1111 Second St., Crescent City, CA 95531
   Phone: 707-464-6101
Sequoia and Kings Canyon National Park
   Superintendent: MICHAEL TOLLEFSON
   47050 Generals Hwy., Three Rivers, CA 93271-9651
   Phone: 559-565-3341
Yosemite National Park
   Superintendent: STANLEY ALBRIGHT
   P.O. Box 577, Administration Bldg., Yosemite National Park, CA 95389
   Phone: 209-372-0200

COLORADO: Mesa Verde National Park
   Superintendent: LARRY WIESE
   P.O. Box 8, Mesa Verde National Park, CO 81330
   Phone: 970-529-4465
Rocky Mountain National Park
   Superintendent: RANDY JONES
   100 Hwy. 36, Estes Park, CO 80517
   Phone: 970-586-1200

FLORIDA: Biscayne National Park
   Superintendent: DICK FROST
   9700 SW 328th St., Homestead, FL 33033
   Phone: 305-230-1144
Dry Tortugas National Park
   Superintendent: RICHARD G. RING
   P.O. Box 6208, Key West, FL 33041
   Phone: 305-242-7700; Fax: 305-242-7711
Everglades National Park
   Superintendent: RICHARD RING
   40001 State Rd. 9336, Homestead, FL 33034
   Phone: 305-242-7700

HAWAII: Haleakala National Park
   Superintendent: DONALD W. REESER
   P.O. Box 369, Makawao, Maui, HI 96768
   Phone: 808-572-9306
Hawaii Volcanoes National Park
   Superintendent: JIM MARTIN
   P.O. Box 52, Hawaii Volcanoes, HI 96718
   Phone: 808-985-6025

IDAHO: Yellowstone National Park, see Wyoming

KENTUCKY: Mammoth Cave National Park
   Superintendent: RONALD SWITZER
   P.O. Box 7, Mammoth Cave, KY 42259
   Phone: 502-758-2254

MAINE: Acadia National Park
Superintendent: PAUL HAERTEL
P.O. Box 177, Bar Harbor, ME 04609
Phone: 207-288-0374

MICHIGAN: Isle Royale National Park
Superintendent: DOUGLAS A. BARNARD
800 E. Lakeshore Dr., Houghton, MI 49931-1895
Phone: 906-482-0986

MINNESOTA: Voyageurs National Park
Superintendent: BARBARA WEST
3131 Hwy. 53, International Falls, MN 56649
Phone: 218-283-9821

MONTANA: Glacier National Park
Superintendent: DAVID MIHALIC
West Glacier, MT 59936
Phone: 406-888-7901
Yellowstone: see Wyoming

NEVADA: Great Basin National Park
Superintendent: REBECCA MILLS
Baker, NV 89311
Phone: 702-234-7331, ext. 202

NEW MEXICO: Carlsbad Caverns National Park
Superintendent: FRANK J. DECKERT
3225 National Park Hwy., Carlsbad, NM 88220
Phone: 505-785-2232

NORTH DAKOTA: Theodore Roosevelt National Park
Superintendent: NOEL POE
P.O. Box 7, 315 2nd Ave., Medora, ND 58645-0007
Phone: 701-623-4466

NORTH CAROLINA: Great Smoky Mountains National Park
see Tennessee

OREGON: Crater Lake National Park
Superintendent: CHUCK LUNDY
P.O. Box 7, Crater Lake, OR 97604
Phone: 541-594-2211

SOUTH DAKOTA: Badlands National Park
Superintendent: WILLIAM SUPERNAUGH
P.O. Box 6, Rt. 240, Interior, SD 57750
Phone: 605-433-5280
Wind Cave National Park
Superintendent: JIM TAYLOR
RR 1, Box 190, Hot Springs, SD 57747-9430
Phone: 605-745-4600

TENNESSEE: Great Smoky Mountains National Park
Superintendent: KAREN WADE
107 Park Headquarters Rd., Gatlinburg, TN 37738
Phone: 423-436-1200

TEXAS: Big Bend National Park
Superintendent: JOSE CISNEROS
P.O. Box 129, Big Bend National Park, TX 79834
Phone: 915-477-1101
Guadalupe Mountains National Park
Superintendent: LARRY HENDERSON
HC 60, Box 400, Salt Flat, TX 79847-9400
Phone: 915-828-3251

UTAH: Arches National Park
Superintendent: WALT DABNEY
P.O. Box 907, Moab, UT 84532-0907
Phone: 435-259-8161
Bryce Canyon National Park
Superintendent: FRED J. FAGERGREN
P.O. Box 17001, Bryce Canyon, UT 84717-0001
Phone: 435-834-5322
Canyonlands National Park
Superintendent: WALTER DABNEY
2282 SW Resource Blvd., Moab, UT 84532-3298
Phone: 801-259-3911
Capitol Reef National Park
Superintendent: ALBERT HENDRICKS
HC 70, Box 15, Torrey, UT 84775-9602
Phone: 435-425-3791
Zion National Park
Superintendent: DON FALVEY
Springdale, UT 84767
Phone: 435-772-3256

VIRGIN ISLANDS: Virgin Islands National Park
Superintendent: RUSSELL BERRY
6310 Estate Nazareth #10, St. Thomas, VI 00802-1102
Phone: 340-775-6238

VIRGINIA: Shenandoah National Park
Superintendent: DOUG MORRIS
3655 US Hwy 211-E, Luray, VA 22835-9036
Phone: 540-999-3400

WASHINGTON: Mount Rainer National Park
Superintendent: WILLIAM BRIGGLE
Tahoma Woods, Star Route, Ashford, WA 98304-9751
Phone: 360-569-2211
North Cascades National Park
Superintendent: BILL PALECK
2105 Hwy. 20, Sedro Woolley, WA 98284-9314
Phone: 360-856-5700
Olympic National Park
Superintendent: DAVID MORRIS
600 E. Park Ave., Port Angeles, WA 98362-6798
Phone: 360-452-4501

WYOMING: Grand Teton National Park
Superintendent: JACK NECKELS
P.O. Drawer 170, Moose, WY 83012-0170
Phone: 307-739-3300
Yellowstone National Park
Superintendent: MICHAEL FINLEY
P.O. Box 168, Yellowstone, WY 82190
Phone: 307-344-7381

NATIONAL SEASHORES

CALIFORNIA: Point Reyes National Seashore
Superintendent: DON NEUBACHER
Point Reyes, CA 94956
Phone: 415-663-8522

FLORIDA: Canaveral National Seashore
Superintendent: ROBERT NEWKIRK
308 Julia St., Titusville, FL 32796-3521
Phone: 407-267-1110
Gulf Islands National Seashore
Superintendent: JERRY A. EUBANKS
1801 Gulf Breeze Pkwy., Gulf Breeze, FL 32561
Phone: 850-934-2604

GEORGIA: Cumberland Island National Seashore
Superintendent: DENNIS DAVIS

FEDERALLY PROTECTED AREAS - NATIONAL WILDILFE REFUGES

P.O. Box 806, Saint Marys, GA 31558
Phone: 912-882-4336

MARYLAND: Assateague Island National Seashore
Superintendent: MARC A. KOENINGS
Rt. 611, 7206 National Seashore Ln., Berlin, MD 21811
Phone: 410-641-1443, ext. 209

MASSACHUSETTS: Cape Cod National Seashore
Superintendent: MARIA BURKS
99 Marconi Site Rd., Wellfleet, MA 02667
Phone: 516-349-3785

NEW YORK: Fire Island National Seashore
Superintendent: CONSTANTINE DILLON
120 Laurel St, Patchogue, NY 11772
Phone: 516-289-4810

NORTH CAROLINA: Cape Hatteras National Seashore
Superintendent: ROBERT REYNOLDS
Rt. 1, Box 675, Manteo, NC 27954
Phone: 252-473-2111
Cape Lookout National Seashore
Superintendent: KARREN BROWN
131 Charles St., Harkers Island, NC 28531
Phone: 252-728-2250

TEXAS: Padre Island National Seashore
Superintendent: JACK WHITWORTH
P.O. Box 181300, Corpus Christi, TX 78480-1300
Phone: 512-949-8173

NATIONAL WILDILFE REFUGES

ALABAMA: Bon Secour
Manager: JANE GRIESS
12295 State Highway 180, Gulf Shores, AL 36542
Phone: 334-540-7720; Fax: 334-540-7301
Choctaw
Manager: DOUGLAS J. BAUMGARTNER
P.O. Box 808, Jackson, AL 36545
Phone: 334-246-3583; Fax: 334-246-5414
Eufaula
Manager: FRANK C. DUKES
509 Old Highway 165, Eufaula, AL 36027
Phone: 334-687-4065; Fax: 334-687-5906
Wheeler (Blowing Wind Cave, Fern Cave, Watercress Darter)
Manager: H. T. STONE
2700 Refuge Hq. Rd., Decatur, AL 35603
Phone: 205-353-7243; Fax: 256-340-9729

ALASKA: Alaska Maritime (Alaska Peninsula Unit, Bering Sea Unit, Chukchi Sea Unit, Gulf of Alaska Unit)
Manager: JOHN L. MARTIN
2355 Kachemak Bay Dr., Ste. 101, Homer, AK 99603-8021
Phone: 907-235-6546; Fax: 907-235-7783
Alaska Peninsula (Becharof)
Manager: DARYL ELONS
P.O. Box 277, King Salmon, AK 99613
Phone: 907-246-3339; Fax: 907-246-6696
Arctic
101 12th Ave., Box 20, Fairbanks, AK 99701
Phone: 907-456-0250; Fax: 907-456-0428
Innoko
Manager: EDWARD S. MERRITT
P.O. Box 69, McGrath, AK 99627
Phone: 907-524-3251; Fax: 907-524-3141
Izembek
Manager: RICHARD POETTER
P.O. Box 127, #1 Izembek Dr., Cold Bay, AK 99571
Phone: 907-532-2445; Fax: 907-532-2549
Kanuti
Manager: TOM EARLY
101 12th Ave., Box 11, Fairbanks, AK 99701
Phone: 907-456-0329; Fax: 907-456-0506
Kenai
Manager: ROBIN WEST
P.O. Box 2139, Ski Hill Rd., Soldotna, AK 99669-2139
Phone: 907-262-7021; Fax: 907-262-3599
Kodiak
Manager: JAY R. BELLINGER
1390 Buskin River Rd., Kodiak, AK 99615
Phone: 907-487-2600; Fax: 907-487-2144
Nowitna (Koyukuk)
Manager: EUGENE WILLIAMS
P.O. Box 287, Galena, AK 99741
Phone: 907-656-1231; Fax: 907-656-1708
Selawik
Manager: LESLIE KERR
P.O. Box 270, Kotzebue, AK 99752
Phone: 907-442-3799; Fax: 907-442-3124
Tetlin
Manager: RICHARD VOSS
P.O. Box 779, Tok, AK 99780
Phone: 907-883-5312; Fax: 907-883-5747
Togiak
Manager: AARON M. ARCHIBERQUE
P.O. Box 270, Dillingham, AK 99576
Phone: 907-842-1063; Fax: 907-842-5402
Yukon Delta
Manager: MICHAEL REARDEN
P.O. Box 346, Bethel, AK 99559
Phone: 907-543-3151; Fax: 907-543-4413
Yukon Flats
Manager: TED HEUER
101 12th Ave., Rm. 264, Fairbanks, AK 99701
Phone: 907-456-0440; Fax: 907-456-0447

ARIZONA: Buenos Aires
Manager: WAYNE SHIFFLETT
P.O. Box 109, Sasabe, AZ 85633
Phone: 502-823-4251; Fax: 520-823-4247
Cabeza Prieta
Manager: DONALD TILLER
1611 N. Second Ave., Ajo, AZ 85321
Phone: 520-387-6483; Fax: 520-387-5359
Imperial
Manager: MITCHELL R. ELLIS
P.O. Box 72217, Yuma, AZ 85365
Phone: 520-783-3371; Fax: 520-783-0652
Kofa
Manager: RAY VARNEY
356 W. First St., Yuma, AZ 85366-6290
Phone: 602-783-7861; Fax: 520-783-8611
Lower Colorado River Complex
Manager: WES MARTIN
P.O. Box D, Yuma, AZ 85364
Phone: 520-343-8112; Fax: 520-343-8320
San Bernardino (Leslie Canyon)
Manager: KEVIN S. COBBLE
P.O. Box 3509, Douglas, AZ 85607
Phone: 520-364-2104; Fax: 520-364-2130

ARKANSAS: Bald Knob
Manager: ROBERT W. ALEXANDER
1439 Coal Chute Rd., Bald Knob, AR 72010
Phone: 501-724-2458; Fax: 501-724-2460
Big Lake

Manager: CLARKE DIRKS
P.O. Box 67, Manila, AR 72442
Phone: 870-564-2429; Fax: 870-564-2573
Cache River
Manager: DENNIS J. WIDNER
Rt. 2, Box 125-T, Augusta, AR 72006
Phone: 501-347-2614; Fax: 501-347-2908
Felsenthal (Overflow, Pond Creek)
Manager: JIM C. JOHNSON
P.O. Box 1157, Crossett, AR 71635
Phone: 870-364-3167; Fax: 870-364-3757
Holla Bend (Logan Cave)
Manager: M. BRUCE BLIHOVDE
Rt. 1, Box 59, Dardanelle, AR 72834-9704
Phone: 501-229-4300; Fax: 501-229-4302
Wapanocca
Manager: GLEN R. MILLER
P.O. Box 279, Turrell, AR 72384
Phone: 870-343-2595; Fax: 870-343-2416
White River
Manager: LARRY E. MALLARD
P.O. Box 308, DeWitt, AR 72042-0308
Phone: 870-946-1468; Fax: 870-946-2591

CALIFORNIA: Hopper Mountain Complex (Hopper Mountain, Battle Creek)
Manager: MARC M. WEITZEL
P.O. Box 5839, Ventura, CA 93005
Phone: 805-644-5158; Fax: 805-644-1732
Humboldt Bay
Manager: KIM A. FORREST
1020 Ranch Rd., Loleta, CA 95551
Phone: 707-733-5406; Fax: 707-733-1946
Kern (Blue Ridge, Pixley)
Manager: DAVID A. HARDT
P.O. Box 670, Delano, CA 93216-0219
Phone: 805-725-2767; Fax: 805-725-6041
Klamath Basin Refuges (Bear Valley, OR; Cear Lake, OR; Lower Klamath, OR & CA; Tule Lake; Upper Klamath, OR; Klamath Forest, OR)
Manager: THOMAS W. STEWART
Rt. 1, Box 74, Tulelake, CA 96134
Phone: 530-667-2231; Fax: 530-667-2231
Modoc
Manager: ANNE MARIE LAROSA
P.O. Box 1610, Alturas, CA 96101
Phone: 530-233-3572; Fax: 530-233-4143
Sacramento (Butte Sink WMA, Colusa, Delevan, North Central Valley, Sacramento River, Sutter, Willow Creek-Lurline WMA)
Manager: GARY W. KRAMER
752 Country Rd., 99W, Willows, CA 95988
Phone: 916-934-2801; Fax: 530-934-7814
San Diego Complex (Tijuana Slough, Sweetwater Marsh, Seal Beach)
Manager: W. DEAN RUNDLE
2736 Loker Ave. W., Suite A, Carlsbad, CA 92008
Phone: 760-930-0168; Fax: 760-930-0168
San Francisco Bay (Antioch Dunes, Don Edwards San Francisco Bay, Ellicott Slough, Farallon, Humbolt Bay, Marin Islands, Salinas River, San Pablo Bay)
Manager: MARGARET T. KOLAR
P.O. Box 524, Newark, CA 94560
Phone: 510-792-0222; Fax: 510-792-5828
San Luis (Grasslands WMA, Kesterson, Merced, San Joaquin River)
Manager: GARY R. ZAHM
P.O. Box 2176, Los Banos, CA 93635-2176
Phone: 209-826-3508; Fax: 209-826-1445
Sonny Bono Salton Sea (Coachella Valley)

Manager: E. CLARK BLOOM
906 W. Sinclair, Calipatria, CA 92233
Phone: 760-348-5278; Fax: 760-348-7245
Stone Lakes
Manager: THOMAS E. HARVEY
2233 Watt Ave., Suite 375, Sacramento, CA 95825-0509
Phone: 916-979-2085; Fax: 916-979-2058

COLORADO: Alamosa NWR (Monte Vista NWR)
Manager: MICHAEL D. BLENDEN
9383 El Rancho Ln., Alamosa, CO 81101-9003
Phone: 719-589-4021; Fax: 719-589-4021
Arapaho (Hutton Lake, Bamforth, Mortenson Lake, Pathfinder)
Manager: GREG LANGER
P.O. Box 457, Walden, CO 80480
Phone: 970-723-8202; Fax: 970-723-8528
Browns Park
Manager: MICHAEL J. BRYANT
1318 Highway 318, Maybell, CO 81640
Phone: 970-365-3613; Fax: 970-365-3614
Rocky Mountain Arsenal
Manager: RAY RAUCH
USF&WS, Bld. 111, Commerce City, CO 80022-1748
Phone: 303-289-0232; Fax: 303-289-0579
Two Ponds
Manager: DANIEL JAMIEL
USF&WS, Bld. 111, Commerce City, CO 80022-1748
Phone: 303-289-0232; Fax: 303-289-0579

DELAWARE: Bombay Hook (Prime Hook NWR)
Manager: PAUL D. DALY
2591 Whitehall Neck Rd., Smyrna, DE 19977
Phone: 302-653-9345; Fax: 302-653-0684
Prime Hook
Manager: GEORGE F. O'SHEA
R.D. 3, Box 195, Milton, DE 19968
Phone: 302-684-8419; Fax: 302-684-8504

FLORIDA: Arthur R. Marshall Loxahatchee NWR (Hope Sound NWR)
Manager: MARK MUSAUS
10216 Lee Rd., Boynton Beach, FL 33437-4796
Phone: 561-732-3684; Fax: 561-369-7190
Chassahowitzka (Crystal River, Egmont Key, Passage Key, Pinellas)
Manager: ELIZABETH SOUHEAVER
1502 S.E. Kings Bay Dr., Crystal River, FL 34429
Phone: 352-563-2088; Fax: 352-795-7961
Florida Panther; Ten Thousand Island
Manager: JIM KRAKOWSKI
3860 Tollgate Blvd., Ste. 300, Naples, FL 34114
Phone: 941-353-8442; Fax: 941-353-8640
Hobe Sound
Manager: RYAN M. NOEL
P.O. Box 645, Hobe Sound, FL 33475-0645
Phone: 561-546-6141
J.N. Ding Darling (Caloosahatchee, Island Bay, Matlacha Pass, Pine Island)
Manager: LOUIS S. HINDSIII
One Wildlife Dr., Sanibel, FL 33957
Phone: 941-472-1100; Fax: 941-472-4061
Lake Woodruff
Manager: HENRY SANSING
P.O. Box 488, DeLeon Springs, FL 32130-0488
Phone: 904-985-4673; Fax: 904-985-0926
Lower Suwannee (Cedar Keys)
Manager: KENNETH L. LITZENBERGER
16450 NW 31st Pl., Chiefland, FL 32626
Phone: 352-493-0238; Fax: 352-493-1935

Merritt Island (Pelican Island, Archie Carr, Lake Wales Ridge, St. Johns)
   Manager: ALBRIGHT R. HIGHT
   P.O. Box 6504, Titusville, FL 32782
   Phone: 407-861-0667; Fax: 407-861-1276
National Key Deer Refuge (Key West, Great White Heron, Crocodile Lake)
   Manager: BARRY W. STIEGLITZ
   P.O. Box 43510, Big Pine Key, Fl 33043-0510
   Phone: 305-872-2239; Fax: 305-872-3675
St. Marks
   Manager: JAMES BURNETT
   P.O. Box 68, St. Marks, FL 32355
   Phone: 850-925-6121; Fax: 850-925-6930
St. Vincent
   Manager: TORRY PEACOCK
   P.O. Box 447, Apalachicola, FL 32329-0447
   Phone: 850-653-8808; Fax: 850-653-9893

GEORGIA: Okefenokee (Banks Lake)
   Manager: MALLORY REEVES
   Rt. 2, Box 3330, Folkston, GA 31537
   Phone: 912-496-7366; Fax: 912-496-3332
Piedmont (Bond Swamp)
   Manager: RONNIE L. SHELL
   718 Juliette Rd., Round Oak, GA 31038
   Phone: 912-986-5441; Fax: 912-986-9646
Savannah Costal Refuges
   Manager: SAM O. DRAKEJR.
   1000 Business Center Dr., Ste. 10, Savannah, GA 31405
   Phone: 912-652-4415; Fax: 912-652-4385

GUAM: Guam
   Manager: ROGER C. DiROSA
   P.O. Box 8134, MOU-3, Dededo, GU 96912
   Phone: 671-355-5096; Fax: 671-355-5098

HAWAII: Hakalau Forest
   Manager: RICHARD C. WASS
   32 K Kincole St, Suite 101, Hilo, HI 96720
   Phone: 808-933-6915; Fax: 808-933-6917
Hawaiian and Pacific Islands NWR Complex
   Manager: JERRY F. LEINECKE
   P.O. Box 50167, Honolulu, HI 96850
   Phone: 808-541-1201; Fax: 808-541-1216
James Campbell NWR and Pearl Harbor NWR
   Manager: DONNA T. STOVALL
   66-590 Kamehameha Hwy., Rm. 2C, Haleiwa, HI 96712
   Phone: 808-637-6330; Fax: 808-637-3578
Johnston Island
   Manager: D. LINDSEY HAYES
   Box 396, APO, AP, HI 96558-0396
   Phone: 808-421-0011; Fax: 808-422-6905
Kealia Pond
   Manager: GLYNNIS T. NAKAI
   P.O. Box 1042, Kihei, HI 96753-1042
   Phone: 808-875-1582; Fax: 808-875-2945
Kilauea Point (Hanalei, Huleia)
   Manager: THOMAS R. ALEXANDER
   P.O. Box 1128, Kiluea, Kauai, Hi 96754-1128
   Phone: 808-828-1413; Fax: 808-828-6634
Midway Atoll
   Manager: ROBERT SHALLENBERGER
   P.O. Box 29460, Midway Island Station #4, Honolulu, HI 96820-1860
   Phone: 808-599-3914
Pacific/Remote Islands Complex (Hawaiian Islands, Baker Island, Howland Island, Jarvis Island, Rose Atoll)
   Manager: DAVID N. JOHNSON
   P.O. Box 50167, Honolulu, HI 96850-5167
   Phone: 808-541-1201; Fax: 808-541-1216

IDAHO: Bear Lake
   Manager: RICHARD R. SJOSTROM
   Box 9, Montpelier, ID 83253
   Phone: 208-847-1757; Fax: 208-847-1319
Camas
   Manager: GERALD L. DEUTSCHER
   2150 E. 2350 N., Hamer, ID 83425
   Phone: 208-662-5423; Fax: 208-662-5525
Deer Flat
   Manager: ELAINE JOHNSON
   13751 Upper Embankment Rd., Nampa, ID 83686
   Phone: 208-467-9278; Fax: 208-467-1019
Grays Lake
   Manager: MICHAEL N. FISHER
   74 Grays Lake Rd., Wayan, ID 83285
   Phone: 208-574-2755; Fax: 208-574-2756
Kootenai
   Manager: DANIEL L. PENNINGTON
   HCR 60, Box 283, Bonners Ferry, ID 83805
   Phone: 208-267-3888; Fax: 208-267-5570
Minidoka
   Manager: MICHAEL R. JOHNSON
   961 E. Minidoka Dam, Rupert, ID 83350
   Phone: 208-436-3589; Fax: 208-436-1570
Oxford Slough WPA
   Manager: TERRELL E. GLADWIN
   1246 Yellowstone Ave., Ste. A-4, Pocatello, ID 83201
   Phone: 208-237-6616; Fax: 208-237-6617
Southeast Idaho Complex
   Manager: RICHARD MUNOZ
   4425 Burley Dr., Ste. A, Chubbuck, ID 83202
   Phone: 208-237-6616; Fax: 208-237-8213

ILLINOIS: Crab Orchard
   Manager: DANIEL W. DOSHIER
   8588 Rt. 148, Marion, Il 62959
   Phone: 618-997-3344; Fax: 618-997-8961
Cypress Creek
   Manager: MARGUERITE HILLS
   137 Rustic Campus Dr., Ullin, IL 62992
   Phone: 618-634-2231; Fax: 618-634-9656
Illinois River National Wildlife and Fish Refuge (Chautauqua, Emiquon, Meredosia)
   Manager: ROSS ADAMS
   19031 E. County Rd. 2105N, Havana, IL 62644
   Phone: 309-535-2290; Fax: 309-535-3023
Mark Twain
   Manager: DICK STEINBACH
   1704 N. 24th St., Quincy, IL 62301
   Phone: 217-224-8580; Fax: 217-224-8583
Mark Twain/Annada District
   Manager: DAVID M. ELLIS
   P.O. Box 88, Annada, MO 63330
   Phone: 314-847-2333; Fax: 314-847-2269
Mark Twain/Brussels District
   Manager: HOWARD PHILLIPS
   HRC, Box 107, Brussels, IL 62013-9711
   Phone: 618-883-2524; Fax: 618-883-2201
Mark Twain/Wapello District
   Manager: KATHLEEN A. MAYCROFT
   10728 County Rd. X-61, Wapello, IA 52653-9477
   Phone: 319-523-6982; Fax: 319-523-6960

INDIANA: Muscatatuck
   Manager: LELAND E. HERZBERGER
   12985 E. U.S. Hwy 50, Seymour, IN 47274
   Phone: 812-522-4352; Fax: 812-522-6826
Patoka River National Wetlands Project

Manager: WILLIAM J. McCOY
510 1/2 W. Morton St., P.O. Box 217, Oakland City, IN 47660
Phone: 812-749-3199; Fax: 812-749-3059

IOWA: De Soto (Boyer Chute NWR)
Manager: GEORGE E. GAGE
1434 316th Ln., Missouri Valley, IA 51555
Phone: 712-642-4121; Fax: 712-642-2877

Neal Smith
Manager: NANCY M. GILBERTSON
P.O. Box 399, Prairie City, IA 50228
Phone: 515-994-3400; Fax: 515-944-3459

Union Slough (Iowa WMD)
Manager: BARRETT L. CHRISTENSEN
1710 360th St., Titonka, IA 50480
Phone: 515-928-2523; Fax: 515-928-2230

KANSAS: Flint Hills (Marais des Cygnes)
Manager: JERREL GAMBLE
P.O. Box 128, 530 W. Maple, Hartford, KS 66854
Phone: 316-392-5553; Fax: 316-392-5554

Kirwin
Manager: WILLIAM H. SCHAFF
R.R. 1, Box 103, Kirwin, KS 67644
Phone: 913-543-6673; Fax: 913-543-5464

Quivira
Manager: DAVE HILLEY
R.R. 3, Box 48A, Stafford, KS 67530
Phone: 316-486-2393; Fax: 316-486-2394

KENTUCKY: Clarks River
Manager: RICHARD HUFFINES
P.O. Box 89, Benton, KY 42025
Phone: 502-527-5770

LOUISIANA: Bayou Cocodrie
Manager: JEROME E. FORD
P.O. Box 1772, Ferriday, LA 71334
Phone: 318-336-7119; Fax: 318-336-5610

Cameron Prairie
Manager: PAUL M. YAKUPZACK
1428 Highway 27, Bell City, LA 70630
Phone: 318-598-2216; Fax: 318-598-2492

Catahoula
Manager: ERIC T. SIPCO
P.O. Drawer Z, Rhinehart, LA 71363-0201
Phone: 318-992-5261; Fax: 318-992-6023

Lacassine
Manager: VICKI C. GRAFE
209 Nature Rd., Lake Arthur, LA 70549
Phone: 318-774-5923; Fax: 318-774-9913

Lake Ophelia (Grand Cole)
Manager: DENNIS SHARP
401 Island Rd., Marksville, LA 71351
Phone: 318-253-4238; Fax: 318-253-7139

Louisiana WMD (Handy Brake)
Manager: JAMES OUCHLEY
1428 Hwy. 143, Farmerville, LA 71241
Phone: 318-726-4400; Fax: 318-726-4667

North Louisiana Wildlife Refuge Complex (D'Arbonne, Upper Ouachita)
Manager: KENNETH O. BUTTS
11372 Hwy 143, Farmerville, LA 71241
Phone: 318-726-4222; Fax: 318-726-4667

Sabine
Manager: CHRIS PEASE
3000 Holly Beach Hwy, Hackberry, LA 70645
Phone: 318-762-3816; Fax: 318-762-3780

Southeast Louisiana Refuges (Bayou Sauvage, Big Branch Marsh, Bogue Chitto, Breton, Delta, Atchafalaya, Shell Keys)
Manager: HOWARD E. POITEVINT
1010 Gause Blvd., Bldg. 936, Slidell, LA 70458
Phone: 504-646-7555; Fax: 504-646-7588

Tensas River
Manager: GEORGE A. CHANDLER JR.
Rt. 2, Box 295, Tallulah, LA 71282
Phone: 318-574-2664; Fax: 318-574-1624

MAINE: Moosehorn
Manager: ROBERT PAYTON
R.R. 1, Box 202, Suite 1, Baring, ME 04694
Phone: 207-454-7161; Fax: 207-454-2550

Petit Manan (Cross Island, Franklin Island, Seal Island, Pond Island MA)
Manager: STAN A. SKUTEK
P.O. Box 279, Millbridge, ME 04658
Phone: 207-546-2124; Fax: 207-546-7805

Rachel Carson
Manager: WARD FEURT
Box 751, Wells, ME 04090
Phone: 207-646-9226; Fax: 207-646-6554

Sunkhaze Meadows (Carlton Pond)
Manager: MARK W. SWEENY
1033 S. Main St., Old Town, ME 04468
Phone: 207-827-6138; Fax: 207-827-6099

MARYLAND: Blackwater (Martin, Susquehanna)
Manager: GLENN A. CAROWAN JR.
2145 Key Wallace Dr., Cambridge, MD 21613
Phone: 410-228-2692; Fax: 410-228-3261

Eastern Neck
Manager: MARTIN C. KAEHNY
1730 Eastern Neck Rd., Rock Hall, MD 21661
Phone: 410-639-7056; Fax: 410-639-2516

Patuxent Research Refuge
Manager: SUSAN R. MCMAHON
12100 Beech Forest Rd., Ste. 4036, Laurel, MD 20708-4036
Phone: 301-497-5580; Fax: 301-497-5765

MASSACHUSETTS: Great Meadows (John Hay, NH, Massasoit, Nantucket, Norman's Long Island, Oxbow, Wapack, NH)
Manager: MANUEL OLIVEIRA
Weir Hill Rd., Sudbury, MA 01776
Phone: 508-443-4661; Fax: 508-443-2898

Monomoy
Manager: SHARON K. WARE
Wikis Way, Morris Island, Chatham, MA 02633
Phone: 508-945-0594; Fax: 508-945-9559

Parker River (Thacher Island)
Manager: JOHN L. FILLIO
161 Northern Blvd., Plum Island, Newburyport, MA 01950
Phone: 508-465-5753; Fax: 508-465-2807

Silvio O. Conte National Wildlife and Fish Refuge
Manager: LAWRENCE A. BANDOLIN
38 Ave. A, Turners Falls, MA 01376
Phone: 413-863-0209; Fax: 413-863-3070

MICHIGAN: Michigan WMD
Manager: JAMES HUDGINS
2651 Coolidge Rd., East Lansing, MI 48823
Phone: 517-351-4230

Seney (Harbor Island, Huron, Kirtland's Warbler WMA)
Manager: MICHAEL G. TANSY
HCR #2, Box 1, Seney, MI 49883
Phone: 906-586-9851; Fax: 906-586-3800

Shiawassee (Michigan Islands, Wyandotte)
  Manager: DOUGLAS G. SPENCER
  6975 Mower Rd., Saginaw, MI 48601
  Phone: 517-777-5930; Fax: 517-777-9200

MINNESOTA: Agassiz
  Manager: MARGARET ANDERSON
  Rt. 1, Box 74, Middle River, MN 56737
  Phone: 218-449-4115; Fax: 218-449-3241
Big Stone
  Manager: RONALD S. COLE
  R.R. Box 25, Odessa, MN 56276
  Phone: 320-273-2191; Fax: 320-273-2231
Detroit Lakes WMD
  Manager: RICK JULIAN
  26624 N. Tower Rd., Detroit Lakes, MN 56501-7959
  Phone: 218-847-4431; Fax: 218-847-4156
Fergus Falls WMD
  Manager: KEVIN J. BRENNAN
  Rt. 1, Box 76, Fergus Falls, MN 56537
  Phone: 218-739-2291; Fax: 218-739-9534
Litchfield WMD
  971 E. Frontage Rd., Litchfield, MN 55355
  Phone: 320-693-2849; Fax: 320-693-2326
Minnesota Valley
  Manager: RICHARD D. SHULTZ
  3815 E. 80th St., Bloomington, MN 55425-1600
  Phone: 612-854-5900; Fax: 612-854-3279
Morris WMD
  Manager: STEVE DELEHANCY
  Rt. 1, Box 877, Morris, MN 56267
  Phone: 612-589-1001; Fax: 612-589-2624
Rice Lake (Mille Lacs)
  Manager: EUGENE C. PATTON
  Rt. 2, Box 67, McGregor, MN 55760
  Phone: 218-768-2402; Fax: 218-768-3040
Sherburne (Crane Meadows)
  Manager: CHARLES W. BLAIR
  17076 293rd Ave., Zimmerman, MN 55398
  Phone: 612-389-3323; Fax: 612-389-3493
Tamarac
  Manager: JAY M. JOHNSON
  35704 County Hwy. 26, Rochert, MN 56578
  Phone: 218-847-2641; Fax: 218-847-9141
Upper Mississippi River W&FR/Winona District
  Manager: JAMES R. FISHER
  51 E. 4th St., Rm. 203, Winona, MN 55987
  Phone: 507-452-4232; Fax: 507-452-0851
Windom WMD
  Manager: STEVEN W. KALLIN
  Rt. 1, Box 273A, Windom, MN 56101
  Phone: 507-831-2220; Fax: 507-831-5524

MISSISSIPPI: Hillside
  1562 Providence Rd., Cruger, MS 35924
  Phone: 662-235-4989; Fax: 662-235-5303
Mississippi Sandhill Crane (Grand Bay)
  Manager: SABRINA KEEN
  7200 Crane Ln., Gautier, MS 39553
  Phone: 601-497-6322; Fax: 601-497-5407
Mississippi WMD (Dahomey, Tallahatchie)
  Manager: STEPHEN W. GARD
  P.O. Box 1070, 16736 Hwy 8 West, Grenada, MS 38902
  Phone: 601-226-8286; Fax: 601-226-8488
Noxubee
  Manager: JIMMY L. TISDALE
  Rt. 1, Box 142, Brooksville, MS 39739
  Phone: 601-323-5548; Fax: 601-323-5806
Panther Swamp
  Manager: W. F. STEVENS
  13695 River Rd., Yazoo City, MS 39194
  Phone: 601-746-5060; Fax: 601-839-2619
St. Catherine Creek
  Manager: JAMES HILL
  P.O. Box 117, Sibley, MS 39165
  Phone: 601-442-6696; Fax: 601-442-8990
Yazoo (Hillside, Mathews Brake, Morgan Brake)
  Manager: TIMOTHY M. WILKINS
  Rt. 1, Box 286, 728 Yazoo Refuge Rd., Hollandale, MS 38748
  Phone: 601-839-2638; Fax: 601-839-2619

MISSOURI: Big Muddy National Wildlife and Fish Refuge
  Manager: TOM BELL
  4200 New Haven Rd., Columbia, MO 65201
  Phone: 573-876-1826; Fax: 573-876-1839
Mingo (Pilot Knob, Ozark Cavefish)
  Manager: GERALD L. CLAWSON
  R.R. 1, Box 103, Puxico, MO 63960
  Phone: 314-222-3589; Fax: 314-222-6343
Squaw Creek
  Manager: RONALD L. BELL
  P.O. Box 158, Mound City, MO 64470
  Phone: 816-442-3187; Fax: 816-442-5248
Swan Lake
  Manager: JOHN GUTHRIE
  Rt. 1, Box 29 A, Sumner, MO 64681
  Phone: 816-856-3323; Fax: 816-856-3687

MONTANA: Benton Lake
  Manager: JAMES E. MCCOLLUM
  922 Bootlegger Trail, Great Falls, MT 59404
  Phone: 406-727-7400; Fax: 406-727-7432
Bowdoin (Black Coulee, Creedman Coulee, Hewitt Lake, Lake Thibadeau)
  Manager: DWAIN M. PRELLWITZ
  HC 65, Box 5700, Malta, MT 59538
  Phone: 406-654-2863; Fax: 406-654-2866
Charles M. Russell (Hailstone, Halfbreed Lake, Lake Mason, UL Bend, War Horse)
  Manager: MIKE HEDRICK
  P.O. Box 110, Lewistown, MT 59457
  Phone: 406-538-8706; Fax: 406-538-7521
Lee Metcalf
  Manager: PATRICK D. GONZLES
  P.O. Box 257, Stevensville, MT 59870
  Phone: 406-777-5552; Fax: 406-777-5542
Medicine Lake (Lamesteer)
  Manager: THEODORE W. GUTZKE
  223 N. Shore Rd., Medicine Lake, MT 59247-9600
  Phone: 406-789-2305; Fax: 406-789-2350
National Bison Range (Nine-pipe, Pablo, Swan River)
  Manager: DAVID S. WISEMAN
  132 Bison Range Rd., Moiese, MT 59824
  Phone: 406-644-2211; Fax: 406-644-2661
Red Rock Lakes
  Manager: DANIEL GOMEZ
  Monida Star Rt., Box 15, Lima, MT 59739
  Phone: 406-276-3536; Fax: 406-276-3538

NEBRASKA: Crescent Lake
  Manager: WILLIAM BEHRENDS
  Phone: 308-762-4893
Crescent Lake/North Platte NWR Complex
  Manager: STEVE KNODA
  P.O. Box 1346, Scottsbluff, NE 69363-1346
  Phone: 308-635-7851; Fax: 308-635-7841
Fort Niobrara/Valentine
  Manager: ROYCE R. HUBER
  HC 14, Box 67, Valentine, NE 69201

Phone: 402-376-3789; Fax: 402-376-3217
Rainwater Basin WMD
    Manager: GENE MACK
    P.O. Box 1686, Kearney, NE 68848
    Phone: 308-236-5015; Fax: 308-236-3899

NEVADA: Ash Meadows
    Manager: ERIC R. HOPSON
    P.O. Box 115, Amargosa Valley, NV 89020
    Phone: 702-372-5435; Fax: 702-372-5436
Desert Complex (Desert Moapa Valley)
    Manager: RICHARD M. BIRGER
    1500 N. Decatur Blvd., Las Vegas, NV 89108
    Phone: 702-646-3401; Fax: 702-646-3812
Pahranagat
    Manager: KEVIN N. SLOAN
    Box 510, Almo, NV 89001
    Phone: 702-725-3417; Fax: 702-725-3389
Ruby Lake
    Manager: KIM D. HANSON
    HC 6, Box 860, Ruby Valley, NV 89833
    Phone: 702-779-2237; Fax: 702-779-2370
Stillwater (Anaho Island, Fallon)
    P.O. Box 1236, Fallon, NV 89407-1236
    Phone: 702-423-5128; Fax: 702-423-0146

NEW HAMPSHIRE: Lake Umbagog
    Manager: PAUL F.CASEY
    Box 240, Errol, NH 03579
    Phone: 603-482-3415; Fax: 603-482-3308

NEW JERSEY: Cape May
    Manager: BRUCE LUEBKE
    24 Kimbles Beach Rd., Cape May Courthouse, NJ 08210-4207
    Phone: 609-463-0994; Fax: 609-463-1667
Edwin B. Forsythe: Barnegat Division
    Manager: JEFFERY KING
    70 Collinstown Rd., P.O. Box 544, Barnegat, NJ 08005
    Phone: 609-698-1378; Fax: 609-698-0109
Edwin B. Forsythe: Brigantine Division
    Manager: TRACY A. CASSELMAN
    P.O. Box 72, Great Creek Rd., Box 72, Oceanville, NJ 08231
    Phone: 609-652-1665; Fax: 609-652-1474
Great Swamp
    Manager: WILLIAM KOCH
    152 Pleasant Plains Rd., Basking Ridge, NJ 07920
    Phone: 201-425-1222; Fax: 201-425-7309
Supawna Meadows
    Manager: TOM WALKER
    197 Lighthouse Rd., Pennsville, NJ 08070
    Phone: 609-935-1487; Fax: 609-935-1198
Wallkill River
    Manager: ELIZABETH A. HERLAND
    1547 County Rt. 565, Sussex, NJ 07461
    Phone: 201-702-7266; Fax: 201-702-7286

NEW MEXICO: Bitter Lake
    Manager: WILLIAM R. RADKE
    P.O. Box 7, Rosewell, NM 88202-0007
    Phone: 505-622-6755; Fax: 505-622-9039
Bosque de Apache
    Manager: PHILIP W. NORTON
    P.O. Box 1246, Socorro, NM 87801
    Phone: 505-835-1828; Fax: 505-835-0314
Las Vegas
    Manager: JOE B. RODRIGUEZJR.
    Rt. 1 Box 399, Las Vegas, NM 87701
    Phone: 505-425-3581; Fax: 505-454-8510
Maxwell
    Manager: JERRY B. FRENCH
    P.O. Box 276, Maxwell, NM 87728
    Phone: 505-375-2331; Fax: 505-375-2332
San Andres
    P.O. Box 756, Las Cruces, NM 88004
    Phone: 505-382-5047; Fax: 505-382-5454
Sevilleta
    Manager: TERRY TADANO
    P.O. Box 1248, Socorro, NM 87801
    Phone: 505-864-4021; Fax: 505-864-7761

NEW YORK: Iroquois
    Manager: BOB LAMOY
    1101 Casey Rd., Alabama, NY 14003
    Phone: 716-948-9154; Fax: 716-948-9538
Long Island Complex (Wetheim, Target Rock, Oyster Bay, Seatuck, Elizabeth A. Morton, Amagansett, Conscience Point)
    Manager: PATRICIA L. MARTINKOVIC
    P.O. Box 21, Shirley, NY 11967
    Phone: 516-286-0485; Fax: 516-286-4003
Montezuma
    Manager: THOMAS M. JASIKOFF
    3395 Rt.5/20 East, Seneca Falls, NY 13148
    Phone: 315-568-5987; Fax: 315-568-8835
St. Lawrence
    127 N. Water St., C/O US Customs House, Ogdensburg, NY 13669
    Phone: 315-393-9002; Fax: 315-393-8570

NORTH CAROLINA: Alligator River (Pea Island)
    Manager: MICHAEL R. BRYANT
    P.O. Box 1969, Manteo, NC 27954
    Phone: 919-473-1131; Fax: 919-473-1668
Mackay Island (Currituck)
    Manager: SUZANNE BAIRD
    P.O. Box 39, Knotts Island, NC 27950
    Phone: 919-429-3100; Fax: 919-429-3185
Mattamuskeet (Cedar Island, Swanquarter)
    Manager: DONALD E. TEMPLE
    Rt. 1, Box N-2, Swan Quarter, NC 27885
    Phone: 919-926-4021; Fax: 919-926-1743
Pee Dee
    Manager: DAN FRISK
    Rt.1, Box 92, Wadesboro, NC 28170
    Phone: 704-694-4424; Fax: 704-694-6570
Pocosin Lakes
    Manager: ELTON J. SAVERY
    3255 Shore Dr., Creswell, NC 27928
    Phone: 919-797-4431; Fax: 919-797-7106
Roanoke River
    Manager: JERRY L. HOLLOMAN
    P.O. Box 430, Windsor, NC 27983
    Phone: 919-794-5326; Fax: 919-794-5338

NORTH DAKOTA: Arrowwood Complex
    Manager: MARK VANIMAN
    7745 11th St. SE, Pingree, ND 58476
    Phone: 701-285-3341; Fax: 701-285-3350
Audubon (Audubon WMD, Camp Lake, Hiddenwood, Lake Ilo, Lake Nettie, Lake Otis, Lost Lake, McLean, Pretty Rock)
    Manager: DAVID G. POTTER
    RR 1, P.O. Box 16, Coleharbor, ND 59531
    Phone: 701-442-5474; Fax: 701-442-5546
Chase Lake
    Manager: MICK ERICKSON
    5924 19th St. SE, Woodworth, ND 58496
    Phone: 701-752-4218; Fax: 701-752-4216
Crosby WMD, Lake Zahl

Manager: TIM KESSLER
P.O. Box 148, Crosby, ND 58730-0148
Phone: 701-965-6488; Fax: 701-965-6487
Des Lacs (Lostwood, Shell Lake, Lostwood WMD)
Manager: FRED G. GIESE
P.O. Box 578, Kenmare, ND 58746-0578
Phone: 701-385-4046; Fax: 701-385-3214
Devils Lake WMD (Brumba, Kellys Slough, Lake Alice, Lake Ardoch, Lambs Lake, Little Goose, Pleasant Lake, Rock Lake, Rose Lake, Silver Lake, Snyder Lake, Stump Lake, Sullys Hill NGP, Wood Lake)
Manager: ROGER HOLLEVOCT
P.O. Box 908, Devil's Lake, ND 58301
Phone: 701-662-8611; Fax: 701-662-8612
J. Clark Salyer (J. Clark Salyer WMD, Buffalo Lake, Cottonwood, Lords Lake, Rabb Lake, School Section Lake, Willow Lake, Wintering River)
Manager: ROBERT L. HOWARD
P.O. Box 66, Upham, ND 58789
Phone: 701-768-2548; Fax: 701-768-2834
Kulm WMD (Boone Hill Creek, Dakota Lake, Lake Patricia, Maple River)
Manager: ROBERT J. VANDEN BERGE
P.O. Box E, Kulm, ND 58456-0170
Phone: 701-647-2866; Fax: 701-647-2221
Long Lake (Long Lake WMD, Florence Lake, Slade, Appert Lake, Canfield Lake, Hutchinson Lake, Lake George, Springwater, Sunburst Lake)
Manager: PAUL C. VAN NINGEN
1200 353rd St. SE, Moffit, ND 58560-9740
Phone: 701-387-4397; Fax: 701-387-4767
Tewaukon (Lake Elsie, Storm Lake, Wild Rice Lake, Tewaukon WMD)
Manager: SANDRA SIEKANICE
9754 143 1/2 Ave. SE, Cayuga, ND 58013
Phone: 701-724-3598; Fax: 701-724-3683
Upper Souris
Manager: DEAN F. KNAUER
17702 212th Ave., NW, Berthold, ND 58718-9666
Phone: 701-468-5467; Fax: 701-468-5600
Valley City WMD
Manager: HARRIS HOISTED
11515 River Rd., Valley City, ND 58072-9619
Phone: 701-845-3466; Fax: 701-845-3482

OHIO: Ottawa (Cedar Point, West Sister Island)
Manager: LARRY D. MARTIN
14000 W. State, Rt. 2, Oak Harbor, OH 43449
Phone: 419-898-0014; Fax: 419-898-7895

OKLAHOMA: Deep Fork
Manager: JON M. BROCK
P.O. Box 816, Okmulgee, OK 74447
Phone: 918-756-0815; Fax: 918-756-0275
Little River (Little Sandy)
Manager: BERLIN A. HECK
P.O. Box 340, Broken Bow, OR 74728
Phone: 405-584-6211; Fax: 405-584-2034
Salt Plains
Manager: RODNEY F. KREY
Rt. 1, Box 76, Jet, OK 73749
Phone: 405-626-4794; Fax: 405-626-4793
Sequoyah (Ozark Plateau)
Manager: STEPHEN L. BERENDZEN
Rt. 1, Box 18A, Vian, OK 74962
Phone: 918-773-5251; Fax: 918-773-5598
Tishomingo
Manager: JOHNNY H. BEALL
Rt. 1, Box 151, Tishomingo, OK 73460
Phone: 405-371-2402; Fax: 405-371-9312

Washita (Optima)
Manager: KENNETH SCHWENDT
Rt. 1, Box 68, Butler, OK 73625
Phone: 405-664-2205; Fax: 405-664-2206
Wichita Mountains Wildlife Refuge
Manager: SAM WALDSTEIN
RR 1, Box 448, Indiahoma, OK 73552
Phone: 405-429-3221; Fax: 405-429-9323

OREGON: Ankeny
Manager: RICHARD J. GUADAGNO
10995 Hwy. 22, Dallas, OR 97338-9343
Phone: 503-623-2749; Fax: 503-623-7812
Hart Mountain National Antelope Refuge
Manager: JENNY BARNETT
P.O. Box 111, Lakeview, OR 97630
Phone: 541-947-3315
Malheur
HC 72, Box 245, Princeton, OR 97721-9505
Phone: 541-493-2612; Fax: 541-493-2405
Mid-Columbia River Complex (Umatilla, Cold Springs, McKay Creek, McNary, Toppenish)
Manager: GARY A. HAGEDORN
P.O. Box 2527, Pasco, OR 99301
Phone: 541-545-8588; Fax: 541-545-8670
Oregon Coastal Refuges (Bandon Marsh, Cape Meares, Nestucca Bay, Oregon Islands, Siletz Bay, Three Arch Rocks)
Manager: ROY W. LOVE
2127 SE OSU Dr., Newport, OR 97365-5258
Phone: 541-867-4550; Fax: 541-867-4551
Sheldon
Manager: MARK A. STRONG
P.O. Box 111, Lakeveiw, OR 97630-0107
Phone: 541-947-3315
Sheldon/Hart Mountain Complex
Manager: MICHAEL L. NUNN
P.O. Box 111, Lakeview, OR 97630
Phone: 541-947-3315; Fax: 541-947-4414
Tualatin River
Manager: RALPH D. WEBBER
16340 SW Beef Bend Rd., Sherwood, OR 97140-8306
Phone: 503-590-5811; Fax: 503-590-6702
Western Oregon Complex (Ankeny, Naskett Slough, Tualatin River, William L. Finley, Brandon Marsh, Cape Meares, Nestucca Bay, Oregon Islands, Siletz Bay, Three Rocks)
Manager: JAMES E. HOUK
26208 Finley Refuge Rd., Corvallis, OR 97333-9533
Phone: 541-757-7236; Fax: 541-757-4450

PENNSYLVANIA: Erie
Manager: THOMAS L. MOUNTAIN
11296 Wood Duck Ln., Guys Mills, PA 16327
Phone: 814-789-3585; Fax: 814-789-2909
John Heinz NWR at Tinicum (Supawna Meadows and Kilcohook Coordination Area)
Manager: RICHARD F. NUGENT
Ste. 104, Scott Plaza 2, Philadelphia, PA 19113
Phone: 610-521-0662; Fax: 610-521-0611

PUERTO RICO: Caribbean Islands Refuges (Cabo Rojo, Desecheo, Laguna Cartagena, Sandy Point, Virgin Islands)
Manager: VAL K. URBAN
P.O. Box 510, Boqueron, PR 00622
Phone: 809-851-7258; Fax: 809-851-7440
Culebra
Manager: TERESA L. TELLEVAST
P.O. Box 190, Culebra, PR 00775
Phone: 787-742-0115

RHODE ISLAND: Ninigret Complex (Block Island, Pettaquamscutt Cove, Sachuest Point, Trustom Pond, Stewart B. McKinney)
  Manager: CHARLES E. HERBERT
  P.O. Box 307, Charlestown, RI 02813
  Phone: 401-364-9124; Fax: 401-364-0170

SOUTH CAROLINA: ACE Basin
  Manager: JAMES D. BROWNING
  P.O. Box 848, Hollywood, SC 29449
  Phone: 803-889-3084; Fax: 803-889-3282
Cape Romain (Santee)
  Manager: GEORGE R. GARRIS
  5801 Hwy. 17 N., Awendaw, SC 29429
  Phone: 843-928-3264; Fax: 843-928-3803
Carolina Sandhills
  Manager: R. SCOTT LANIER
  Rt. 2, Box 100, McBee, SC 29101
  Phone: 803-335-8401; Fax: 803-335-8406

SOUTH DAKOTA: Huron WMD
  Manager: MARK J. HEISINGER
  200 4th St., SW, Rm. 317 Federal Bld., Huron, SD 57350-2470
  Phone: 605-352-5894; Fax: 605-352-6709
Lacreek (Bear Butte)
  Manager: ROLF H. KRAFT
  HC 5, Box 114, Martin, SD 57551
  Phone: 605-685-6508; Fax: 605-685-1173
Lake Andes (Karl E. Mundt)
  Manager: SYLVIA R. PELIZZA
  38627 291st St., Lake Andes, SD 57356
  Phone: 605-487-7603; Fax: 605-487-7604
Madison WMD
  Manager: TOM TORNOW
  P.O. Box 48, Madison, SD 57042
  Phone: 605-256-2974; Fax: 605-256-9432
Sand Lake (Pocasse)
  Manager: JOHN W. KOERNER
  39650 Sand Lake Dr., Columbia, SD 57433
  Phone: 605-885-6320; Fax: 605-885-6401
Waubay
  Manager: DOUGLAS A. LESCHISIN
  RR 1, Box 39, Waubay, SD 57273
  Phone: 605-947-4521; Fax: 605-947-4524
Waubay WMD
  Manager: CONNIE M. MUELLER
  RR 1, Box 39, Waubay, SD 57273
  Phone: 605-947-4521; Fax: 605-947-4524

TENNESSEE: Chickasaw
  Manager: MICHAEL STROEH
  1505 Sandy Bluff Rd., Ripley, TN 38063
  Phone: 901-635-7621; Fax: 901-635-0178
Cross Creeks NWR
  643 Wildlife Rd., Dover, TN 37058
  Phone: 931-232-7477; Fax: 931-232-5958
Hatchie NWR
  Manager: MARVIN L. NICHOLS
  4172 Hwy 76 South, Brownsville, TN 38012-8332
  Phone: 901-772-0501; Fax: 901-772-7839
Lower Hatchie
  Manager: EDWARD RODRIGUEZ
  1505 Sandy Bluff Rd., Ripley, TN 38063
  Phone: 901-635-7621; Fax: 901-635-0178
Reelfoot
  Manager: RANDY COOK
  Fed. Bld. Rm. 129, 309 N. Church St., Dyersburg, TN 38024
  Phone: 901-287-0650; Fax: 901-286-0468
Tennessee
  Manager: JOHN T. TAYLOR
  P.O. Box 849, Paris, TN 38242
  Phone: 901-642-2091; Fax: 901-644-3351

TEXAS: Anahuac (Moody, McFaddin, Texas Point)
  Manager: ANDY LORANGER
  P.O. Box 278, Anahuac, TX 77514
  Phone: 409-267-3337; Fax: 409-267-4314
Aransas
  Manager: J. BRENT GLEZENTANNER
  P.O. Box 100, Austwell, TX 77950
  Phone: 512-286-3559; Fax: 512-286-3722
Attwater Prairie Chicken
  Manager: TERRY A. ROSSIGNOL
  P.O. Box 519, Eagle Lake, TX 77434-0519
  Phone: 409-234-3021; Fax: 409-234-3278
Balcones Canyonlands
  Manager: DEBORAH G. HOLLE
  10711 Burnet Rd., Ste. 201, Austin, TX 78758
  Phone: 512-339-9432; Fax: 512-339-9453
Brazoria (San Bernard, Big Boggy)
  Manager: RONALD G. BISBEE
  1212 N. Velasco, Ste. 200, Angleton, TX 77515-1088
  Phone: 409-849-7771; Fax: 409-849-5118
Buffalo Lake
  Manager: LYNN A. NYMEYER
  P.O. Box 179, Umbarger, TX 79091
  Phone: 806-499-3382
Hagerman
  Manager: JAMES M. WILLIAMS
  6465 Refuge Rd., Sherman, TX 75092
  Phone: 903-786-2826; Fax: 903-786-3327
Laguna Atascosa
  Manager: STEPHEN LABUDA, JR.
  P.O. Box 450, Rio Hondo, TX 78583
  Phone: 210-748-3607; Fax: 210-748-3609
Lower Rio Grande/Santa Anna Complex
  Manager: LARRY DITTO
  Rt. 2, Box 202A, Alamo, TX 78516
  Phone: 210-787-3079; Fax: 210-787-8338
Muleshoe (Grulla, NM)
  Manager: DONALD R. CLAPP
  P.O. Box 549, Muleshoe, TX 79347
  Phone: 806-946-3341; Fax: 806-946-3317
Trinity River
  Manager: STUART J. MARCUS
  P.O. Box 10015, Liberty, TX 77575
  Phone: 409-336-9786; Fax: 409-336-9847

UTAH: Bear River Migratory Bird Refuge
  Manager: ALAN K. TROUT
  58 S. 950 West, Brigham City, UT 84302
  Phone: 801-723-5887; Fax: 435-723-8873
Fish Springs
  Manager: JAY K. BANTA
  P.O. Box 568, Dugway, UT 84022
  Phone: 801-831-5353; Fax: 801-831-5354
Ouray
  266 West 100 North, Ste. 2, Vernal, UT 84078
  Phone: 801-789-0351; Fax: 801-789-4805

VERMONT: Missisquoi
  Manager: ROBERT A. ZELLEY
  P.O. Box 163, Swanton, VT 05488
  Phone: 802-868-4781; Fax: 802-868-2379

VIRGIN ISLANDS: Sandy Point (Green Cay, Buck Island)
  Manager: MICHAEL A. EVANS

3013 Estate Golden Rock, Ste. 167, Christiansted, VI
00820-4355
Phone: 809-773-4554

VIRGINIA: Back Bay (Plum Tree Island)
Manager: JOHN STASKO
4005 Sandpiper Rd., Virginia Beach, VA 23456
Phone: 757-721-2412; Fax: 757-721-6141

Chincoteague (Wallops Island)
Manager: JOHN D. SCHROER
P.O. Box 62, Chincoteague, VA 23336
Phone: 757-336-6122; Fax: 757-336-5273

Eastern Shore of VA (Fisherman Island)
Manager: SUSAN M. RICE
5003 Hallett Circle, Cape Charles, VA 23310
Phone: 757-331-2760; Fax: 757-331-3424

Great Dismal Swamp (Nansemond)
Manager: LLOYD A. CULP, JR.
P.O. Box 349, Suffolk, VA 23434
Phone: 757-986-3705; Fax: 757-986-2353

Potomac River Complex (Mason NecK, Featherstone)
Manager: GREG WEILER
14344 Jefferson Davis Hwy., Woodbridge, VA 22191
Phone: 703-490-4979; Fax: 703-490-5631

Rappahannock River Valley (James River, Presquile)
Manager: HARRY G. BRADY
P.O. Box 189, Prince George, VA 23875
Phone: 804-733-8042

WASHINGTON: Columbia
Manager: ROBERT FLORES
P.O. Drawer E, 735 E. Main St., Othello, WA 99344
Phone: 509-488-2668; Fax: 509-488-0705

Conboy Lake
Manager: HAROLD E. COLE
Box 5, Glenwood, WA 98619-0005
Phone: 509-364-3410; Fax: 509-364-3667

Hanford Complex (Saddle Mountain)
Manager: DAVID E. GOEKE
3520 Port of Benton Rd., Richland, WA 99352
Phone: 509-371-1801; Fax: 509-371-0196

Julia Butler Hansen Refuge for the Columbia White-tailed Deer
Manager: JOEL R. DAVID
P.O. Box 566, Cathlamet, WA 98612-0566
Phone: 509-795-3915; Fax: 360-795-0803

Little Pend Oreille
Manager: LISA LANGELIER
1310 Bear Creek Rd., Colville, WA 99114-9713
Phone: 509-684-8384; Fax: 509-684-8381

Nisqually (Grays Harbor)
Manager: WILLARD B. HESSELBART
100 Brown Farm Rd., Olympia, WA 98516-2302
Phone: 360-753-9467; Fax: 360-534-9302

Pierce (Franz Lake, Steigerwald Lake)
Manager: JEFF W. HOLM
Columbia River Gorge Refuges, 36062 SR 14, Stevenson, WA 98648-9541
Phone: 509-427-5208; Fax: 509-427-4707

Ridgefield
Manager: THOMAS J. MELANSON
P.O. Box 457, Ridgefield, WA 98642-0457
Phone: 509-887-4106; Fax: 360-887-4109

Turnbull
Manager: NANCY J. CURRY
26010 S. Smith Rd., Cheney, WA 99004-9326
Phone: 509-235-4723; Fax: 509-235-4703

Washington Maritime Complex (Copalis, Bungeness, Flattery Rocks, Protection Island, Quillayute Needles, San Juan Islands)
Manager: KEVIN RYAN
33 S. Barr Rd., Port Angeles, WA 38362-9202
Phone: 360-457-8451; Fax: 360-457-9778

Willapa (Lewis and Clark)
Manager: CHARLES E. STENVALL
3888 SR 101, Ilwaco, WA 98624-9707
Phone: 360-484-3482; Fax: 360-484-3109

WEST VIRGINIA: Canaan Valley
Manager: KEVIN DESROBERTS
P.O. Box 1278, Rt. 250 S., Elkins, WV 26241
Phone: 304-637-7312; Fax: 304-636-7824

Ohio River Islands
Manager: JERRY L. WILSON
P.O. Box 1811, Parkersburg, WV 26102-1811
Phone: 304-422-0752; Fax: 304-422-0754

WISCONSIN: Horicon Complex (Fox River, Gravel Island, Green Bay, Leopold WMD)
Manager: PATTI A. MEYERS
W 4279 Headquarters Rd., Mayville, WI 53050
Phone: 920-387-2658; Fax: 920-387-2973

Leopold
Manager: STEVEN J. LENZ
Phone: 920-387-0336; Fax: 920-387-2973

Necedah
Manager: LARRY A. WARGOWSKY
W. 7996 20th St., W., Necedah, WI 54646-7531
Phone: 608-565-2551; Fax: 608-565-3160

St. Croix WMD
Manager: CHET MCCARTY
1764 95th St., New Richmond, WI 54017
Phone: 715-246-7784; Fax: 715-246-4670

Trempealeau
Manager: RICHARD A. FRIETSCHE
W28438 Refuge Rd., Trempealeau, WI 54661
Phone: 608-539-2311; Fax: 608-539-2703

WYOMING: National Elk Refuge
Manager: HARRY REISWIG
675 E. Broadway, P.O. Box C, Jackson, WY 83001
Phone: 307-733-9212; Fax: 307-733-9729

Seedskadee (Cookeville Meadows)
Manager: CAROL DAMBURG
P.O. Box 700, Green River, WY 82935
Phone: 307-875-2187; Fax: 307-875-4425

NATIONAL WILDLIFE REFUGE REGIONAL DIRECTORS

Region 1
PARD, Refuges and Wildlife: CAROLYN BOHAN
911 NE 11th Ave., Eastside Federal Complex, Portland, OR 97232-4181
Phone: 503-231-6214; Fax: 503-231-2364

Region 2
PARD, Refuges and Wildlife: DOM CICCONE
P.O. Box 1306, Albuquerque, NM 87103
Phone: 505-248-7419; Fax: 505-248-6803

Region 3
PARD, Refuges and Wildlife: NITA FULLER
1 Federal Dr., Federal Bldg., Fort Snelling, MN 55111-4056
Phone: 612-713-5401; Fax: 612-713-5288

Region 4
PARD, Refuges and Wildlife: DAVE HEFFERNAN

1875 Century Blvd., NE, Rm. 324, Atlanta, GA 30345
Phone: 404-679-7166; Fax: 404-679-7081

Region 5
PARD, Refuges and Wildlife: TONY LEGER
300 Westgate Center Dr., Hadley, MA 01035-9589
Phone: 413-253-8306; Fax: 413-253-8309

Region 6
PARD, Refuges and Wildlife: KEN MCDERMOND
134 Union Blvd., Lakewood, CO 80228
Phone: 303-236-8145, ext. 638; Fax: 303-236-4792

Region 7
PARD, Refuges and Wildlife: TODD LOGAN
1011 E. Tudor Rd., Anchorage, AK 99503
Phone: 907-786-3545; Fax: 907-786-3640

ORGANIZATION NAME INDEX

20/20 VISION...130
A. E. HOWELL WILDLIFE CONSERVATION CENTER 130
A.B. ENVIRONMENTAL EDUCATION CENTER........................... 130
ABUNDANT LIFE SEED FOUNDATION... 130
ACADEMY FOR EDUCATIONAL DEVELOPMENT 130
ACADIA UNIVERSITY 394
ACRES LAND TRUST.. 130
ACTION FOR NATURE, INC... 130
ADIRONDACK COUNCIL, THE 131
ADIRONDACK MOUNTAIN CLUB, INC., THE 131
ADIRONDACK NATURE CONSERVANCY/ADIRONDACK LAND
   TRUST, INC.. 131
ADIRONDACK PARK AGENCY... 88
ADKINS ARBORETUM... 131
ADOPT-A-STREAM FOUNDATION, THE 131
ADVISORY COUNCIL ON HISTORIC PRESERVATION................. 33
AFRICAN WILDLIFE FOUNDATION.. 132
AFRICAN WILDLIFE NEWS SERVICE.. 132
AGENCY OF NATURAL RESOURCES 111
     Department of Environmental Conservation88, 89, 90, 111, 261,
       291, 398, 416
     Department of Fish and Wildlife 98, 111, 184, 223, 323, 397, 398
     Department of Forests, Parks, and Recreation....................... 111
     Environmental Board 112
     Vermont Geological Survey... 112
AIR AND WASTE MANAGEMENT ASSOCIATION 132
ALABAMA ASSOCIATION OF SOIL AND WATER CONSERVATION
   DISTRICTS 132
ALABAMA B.A.S.S. CHAPTER FEDERATION.............................. 132
ALABAMA COOPERATIVE EXTENSION SYSTEM 38
ALABAMA COOPERATIVE FISH AND WILDLIFE RESEARCH UNIT
   (USDI) 38
ALABAMA DEPARTMENT OF AGRICULTURE AND INDUSTRIES38
ALABAMA DEPARTMENT OF CONSERVATION AND NATURAL
   RESOURCES 38
ALABAMA DEPARTMENT OF ECONOMIC AND COMMUNITY
   AFFAIRS, COASTAL PROGRAMS (ADECA)............................. 38
ALABAMA DEPARTMENT OF ENVIRONMENTAL MANAGEMENT38
ALABAMA ENVIRONMENTAL COUNCIL 132
ALABAMA FORESTRY COMMISSION 39
ALABAMA NATURAL HERITAGE PROGRAM............................. 132
ALABAMA SEA GRANT PROGRAM 39
ALABAMA SOIL AND WATER CONSERVATION COMMITTEE..... 39
ALABAMA WATERFOWL ASSOCIATION, INC. (AWA)................ 133
ALABAMA WILDFLOWER SOCIETY, THE 133
ALABAMA WILDLIFE FEDERATION... 133
ALASKA ASSOCIATION OF SOIL AND WATER CONSERVATION
   DISTRICTS 133
ALASKA AUDUBON SOCIETY 133
ALASKA CENTER FOR THE ENVIRONMENT 133
ALASKA CONSERVATION ALLIANCE 133
ALASKA CONSERVATION FOUNDATION 134
ALASKA CONSERVATION VOICE 134
ALASKA COOPERATIVE FISH AND WILDLIFE RESEARCH UNIT39
ALASKA DEPARTMENT OF ENVIRONMENTAL CONSERVATION39
ALASKA DEPARTMENT OF FISH AND GAME 39
ALASKA DEPARTMENT OF NATURAL RESOURCES 40
ALASKA DEPARTMENT OF PUBLIC SAFETY 40
     Division of Fish and Wildlife Protection 40
ALASKA HEALTH PROJECT.. 40
ALASKA NATURAL HISTORY ASSOCIATION 134
ALASKA NATURAL RESOURCE AND OUTDOOR EDUCATION
   ASSOCIATION 134
ALASKA RAINFOREST CAMPAIGN 134
ALASKA SEA GRANT COLLEGE PROGRAM 40
ALASKA STATE EXTENSION SERVICES 40
ALASKA WILDLIFE ALLIANCE, THE 134
ALBERTA DEPARTMENT OF ENVIRONMENTAL PROTECTION
   123
     Communications Division 105, 123
     Corporate Management Service 123
     Environmental Service41, 48, 52, 54, 67, 87, 94, 97, 106, 123, 405
     Land and Forest Service 123
     Natural Resources Service 124
ALBERTA FISH AND GAME ASSOCIATION, THE....................... 134
ALBERTA TRAPPERS ASSOCIATION 134
ALBERTA WILDERNESS ASSOCIATION.................................... 135
ALDO LEOPOLD FOUNDATION, INC.. 135
ALFRED UNIVERSITY 380
ALLIANCE FOR THE CHESAPEAKE BAY................................... 135
     CRIS Office 135
     Harrisburg Office 135
AMERICA THE BEAUTIFUL FUND.. 135
AMERICAN ALLIANCE FOR HEALTH PHYSICAL EDUCATION AND
   RECREATION AND DANCE 136
AMERICAN ASSOCIATION FOR LEISURE AND RECREATION (AALR)
   136
AMERICAN ASSOCIATION FOR THE ADVANCEMENT OF SCIENCE
   136
AMERICAN ASSOCIATION OF BOTANICAL GARDENS AND
   ARBORETA, INC. 136
AMERICAN ASSOCIATION OF FIELD BOTANISTS..................... 136
AMERICAN ASSOCIATION OF ZOO KEEPERS, INC. 137
AMERICAN BASS ASSOCIATION OF CONNECTICUT, THE 137
AMERICAN BASS ASSOCIATION OF EASTERN PENNSYLVANIA/
   NEW JERSEY, THE.. 137
AMERICAN BASS ASSOCIATION OF KENTUCKY, THE............. 137
AMERICAN BASS ASSOCIATION OF LAKE ERIE REGION, THE
   (Western PA and Western NY) 137
AMERICAN BASS ASSOCIATION OF MAINE, THE 137
AMERICAN BASS ASSOCIATION OF MARYLAND, THE 137
AMERICAN BASS ASSOCIATION OF MASSACHUSETTS, THE 137
AMERICAN BASS ASSOCIATION OF NEW HAMPSHIRE, THE . 137
AMERICAN BASS ASSOCIATION OF VIRGINIA, THE................. 138
AMERICAN BASS ASSOCIATION OF WEST VIRGINIA, THE..... 138
AMERICAN BASS ASSOCIATION OF WISCONSIN, THE........... 138
AMERICAN BASS ASSOCIATION, INC. 137
AMERICAN BIRD CONSERVANCY.. 138
AMERICAN BIRDING ASSOCIATION... 138
AMERICAN CAMPING ASSOCIATION, INC. 138
AMERICAN CANAL SOCIETY, INC.. 138
AMERICAN CAVE CONSERVATION ASSOCIATION................... 138
AMERICAN CETACEAN SOCIETY 138
AMERICAN CHESTNUT FOUNDATION, THE 139
AMERICAN CONSERVATION ASSOCIATION, INC. 139
     New York Office 139, 147, 157
AMERICAN COUNCIL FOR AN ENERGY-EFFICIENT ECONOMY139
AMERICAN FARMLAND TRUST 139
AMERICAN FEDERATION OF MINERALOGICAL SOCIETIES.... 139
AMERICAN FISHERIES SOCIETY 140, 141, 142, 143, 144
     Bioengineering Section 140
     Canadian Aquatic Resources Section 140
     Computer User Section 140
     Early Life History 140
     Education Section 65, 140
     Equal Opportunities Section 140
     Estuaries Section 140
     Fish Culture Section 140
     Fish Health Section 140
     Fisheries Administrators Section 140
     Fisheries History Section 140
     Fisheries Law Section 140
     Fisheries Management Section 140
     Genetics Section 140
     International Fisheries Section... 141
     Introduced Fish Section 141
     Marine Fisheries Section 141
     Native People Fisheries Section 141
     North Central Division 141
     Northeastern Division... 141
     Physiology Section 141
     Socioeconomics Section 141
     Southern Division 48, 141
     Water Quality Section 141
     Western Division 141, 272
AMERICAN FISHERIES SOCIETY, ALABAMA CHAPTER.......... 141
AMERICAN FISHERIES SOCIETY, ALASKA CHAPTER............. 141
AMERICAN FISHERIES SOCIETY, ARIZONA-NEW MEXICO
   CHAPTER 141
AMERICAN FISHERIES SOCIETY, ARKANSAS CHAPTER 141
AMERICAN FISHERIES SOCIETY, ATLANTIC INTERNATIONAL
   CHAPTER 141
AMERICAN FISHERIES SOCIETY, AUBURN UNIVERSITY CHAPTER
   141
AMERICAN FISHERIES SOCIETY, BONNEVILLE CHAPTER ... 141
AMERICAN FISHERIES SOCIETY, CALIFORNIA-NEVADA CHAPTER
   142
AMERICAN FISHERIES SOCIETY, COLLEGE OF ENVIRONMENTAL
   SCIENCE AND FORESTRY CHAPTER.................................. 142

AMERICAN FISHERIES SOCIETY, COLORADO-WYOMING CHAPTER ... 142
AMERICAN FISHERIES SOCIETY, DAKOTA CHAPTER ... 142
AMERICAN FISHERIES SOCIETY, FLORIDA CHAPTER ... 142
AMERICAN FISHERIES SOCIETY, GEORGIA CHAPTER ... 142
AMERICAN FISHERIES SOCIETY, GREATER PORTLAND, OR CHAPTER ... 142
AMERICAN FISHERIES SOCIETY, HAWAII CHAPTER ... 142
AMERICAN FISHERIES SOCIETY, HUMBOLDT CHAPTER ... 142
AMERICAN FISHERIES SOCIETY, IDAHO CHAPTER ... 142
AMERICAN FISHERIES SOCIETY, ILLINOIS CHAPTER ... 142
AMERICAN FISHERIES SOCIETY, INDIANA CHAPTER ... 142
AMERICAN FISHERIES SOCIETY, IOWA CHAPTER ... 142
AMERICAN FISHERIES SOCIETY, KANSAS CHAPTER ... 142
AMERICAN FISHERIES SOCIETY, KENTUCKY CHAPTER ... 142
AMERICAN FISHERIES SOCIETY, LOUISIANA CHAPTER ... 142
AMERICAN FISHERIES SOCIETY, MICHIGAN CHAPTER ... 143
AMERICAN FISHERIES SOCIETY, MID-ATLANTIC CHAPTER ... 143
AMERICAN FISHERIES SOCIETY, MID-CANADA CHAPTER ... 143
AMERICAN FISHERIES SOCIETY, MINNESOTA CHAPTER ... 143
AMERICAN FISHERIES SOCIETY, MISSISSIPPI CHAPTER ... 143
AMERICAN FISHERIES SOCIETY, MISSOURI CHAPTER ... 143
AMERICAN FISHERIES SOCIETY, MONTANA CHAPTER ... 143
AMERICAN FISHERIES SOCIETY, NEBRASKA CHAPTER ... 143
AMERICAN FISHERIES SOCIETY, NEW MEXICO STATE UNIVERSITY STUDENT CHAPTER ... 143
AMERICAN FISHERIES SOCIETY, NEW YORK CHAPTER ... 143
AMERICAN FISHERIES SOCIETY, NORTH CAROLINA CHAPTER 143
AMERICAN FISHERIES SOCIETY, NORTH PACIFIC INTERNATIONAL CHAPTER ... 143
AMERICAN FISHERIES SOCIETY, NORTHWESTERN ONTARIO CHAPTER ... 143
AMERICAN FISHERIES SOCIETY, OHIO CHAPTER ... 143
AMERICAN FISHERIES SOCIETY, OKLAHOMA CHAPTER ... 143
AMERICAN FISHERIES SOCIETY, OREGON CHAPTER ... 143
AMERICAN FISHERIES SOCIETY, PENNSYLVANIA CHAPTER. 143
AMERICAN FISHERIES SOCIETY, POTOMAC CHAPTER ... 144
AMERICAN FISHERIES SOCIETY, SOUTH CAROLINA CHAPTER 144
AMERICAN FISHERIES SOCIETY, SOUTHERN NEW ENGLAND CHAPTER ... 144
AMERICAN FISHERIES SOCIETY, SOUTHERN ONTARIO CHAPTER ... 144
AMERICAN FISHERIES SOCIETY, TENNESSEE CHAPTER ... 144
AMERICAN FISHERIES SOCIETY, TEXAS A&M CHAPTER ... 144
AMERICAN FISHERIES SOCIETY, TEXAS CHAPTER ... 144
AMERICAN FISHERIES SOCIETY, TIDEWATER CHAPTER ... 144
AMERICAN FISHERIES SOCIETY, UNIVERSITY OF WYOMING STUDENT CHAPTER ... 144
AMERICAN FISHERIES SOCIETY, VIRGINIA CHAPTER ... 144
AMERICAN FISHERIES SOCIETY, VIRGINIA TECH CHAPTER ... 144
AMERICAN FISHERIES SOCIETY, WEST VIRGINIA CHAPTER. 144
AMERICAN FISHERIES SOCIETY, WISCONSIN CHAPTER ... 144
AMERICAN FOREST FOUNDATION ... 144
AMERICAN FORESTS (formerly American Forestry Association). 144
AMERICAN GEOGRAPHICAL SOCIETY ... 145
AMERICAN GEOLOGICAL INSTITUTE ... 145
AMERICAN GROUND WATER TRUST ... 145
AMERICAN HIKING SOCIETY ... 145
AMERICAN HORSE PROTECTION ASSOCIATION ... 145
AMERICAN HUMANE ASSOCIATION ... 145
AMERICAN INSTITUTE OF BIOLOGICAL SCIENCES ... 146
AMERICAN INSTITUTE OF FISHERY RESEARCH BIOLOGISTS 146
AMERICAN LAND CONSERVANCY ... 146
AMERICAN LANDS (formerly Western Ancient Forest Campaign) 146
AMERICAN LEAGUE OF ANGLERS AND BOATERS ... 146
AMERICAN LITTORAL SOCIETY ... 146
    Coral Reef Conservation Center Office ... 147
    Delaware Riverkeeper Crossin ... 147
    New York Office ... 139, 147, 157
AMERICAN LIVESTOCK BREEDS CONSERVANCY ... 147
AMERICAN LUNG ASSOCIATION ... 147
AMERICAN MUSEUM OF NATURAL HISTORY ... 147
AMERICAN NATURE STUDY SOCIETY ... 147
AMERICAN OCEANS CAMPAIGN ... 147
    Washington, DC Office ... 134, 148, 192, 308, 314, 324
AMERICAN ORNITHOLOGISTS' UNION ... 148
AMERICAN PIE (PUBLIC INFORMATION ON THE ENVIRONMENT) ... 148
AMERICAN PLANNING ASSOCIATION ... 148
AMERICAN RECREATION COALITION ... 148
AMERICAN RESOURCES GROUP ... 148
AMERICAN RIVERS (formerly American Rivers Conservation Council) ... 149
    Maine Field Office ... 149
    Montana Field Office ... 149, 313
    Nebraska Field Office ... 149
    Northwest Regional Office ... 62, 117, 149, 206
    Quad Cities Field Office ... 149
    Southwest Regional Office ... 30, 80, 117, 149, 153, 264
AMERICAN SAMOA DEPARTMENT OF AGRICULTURE ... 40
AMERICAN SOCIETY FOR ENVIRONMENTAL HISTORY ... 149
AMERICAN SOCIETY OF ICHTHYOLOGISTS AND HERPETOLOGISTS ... 149
AMERICAN SOCIETY OF INTERNATIONAL LAW/WILDLIFE INTEREST GROUP ... 150
AMERICAN SOCIETY OF LANDSCAPE ARCHITECTS ... 150
AMERICAN SOCIETY OF LIMNOLOGY AND OCEANOGRAPHY 150
AMERICAN SOCIETY OF MAMMALOGISTS ... 150
AMERICAN SPORTFISHING ASSOCIATION ... 150
AMERICAN WATER RESOURCES ASSOCIATION ... 151
AMERICAN WATER WORKS ASSOCIATION (AWWA) ... 151
AMERICAN WHITEWATER ... 151
AMERICAN WILDLANDS ... 151
AMERICAN WILDLIFE RESEARCH FOUNDATION, INC. ... 151
AMERICAN ZOO AND AQUARIUM ASSOCIATION (AZA) ... 151
AMERICANS FOR THE ENVIRONMENT ... 152
ANACOSTIA WATERSHED SOCIETY ... 152
ANCIENT FOREST INTERNATIONAL ... 152
ANGLERS FOR CLEAN WATER ... 152
ANIMAL PROTECTION INSTITUTE ... 152
ANIMAL WELFARE INSTITUTE ... 152
ANTARCTICA PROJECT ... 153
ANTIOCH COLLEGE ... 383
ANTIOCH NEW ENGLAND GRADUATE SCHOOL ... 379
ANTIOCH UNIVERSITY SEATTLE ... 391
APPALACHIAN REGIONAL COMMISSION ... 7
APPALACHIAN MOUNTAIN CLUB ... 153
APPALACHIAN STATE UNIVERSITY ... 382
APPALACHIAN TRAIL CONFERENCE ... 153
ARCHAEOLOGICAL CONSERVANCY ... 153
ARCHBOLD BIOLOGICAL STATION ... 153
ARCHERY MANUFACTURERS AND MERCHANTS ORGANIZATION (AMO) ... 154
ARCTIC INSTITUTE OF NORTH AMERICA ... 154
ARIZONA ASSOCIATION OF CONSERVATION DISTRICTS ... 154
ARIZONA B.A.S.S. CHAPTER FEDERATION ... 154
ARIZONA COOPERATIVE FISH AND WILDLIFE RESEARCH UNIT (USDI) ... 40
ARIZONA DEPARTMENT OF AGRICULTURE ... 41
    Animal Services Division ... 41
    Environmental Services Division ... 41, 87
    Integrated Pest Management (IPM) ... 41
    Plant Services Division ... 41
ARIZONA DEPARTMENT OF ENVIRONMENTAL QUALITY ... 41
ARIZONA GAME AND FISH DEPARTMENT ... 41
ARIZONA GEOLOGICAL SURVEY ... 41
ARIZONA LAND DEPARTMENT ... 41
ARIZONA STATE EXTENSION SERVICES ... 42
ARIZONA STATE PARKS BOARD ... 42
ARIZONA STATE UNIVERSITY ... 362
ARIZONA WILDLIFE FEDERATION ... 154
ARKANSAS ASSOCIATION OF CONSERVATION DISTRICTS ... 154
ARKANSAS B.A.S.S. CHAPTER FEDERATION ... 154
ARKANSAS COOPERATIVE RESEARCH UNIT ... 42
ARKANSAS DEPARTMENT OF PARKS AND TOURISM ... 42
ARKANSAS ENVIRONMENTAL EDUCATION ASSOCIATION ... 154
ARKANSAS GAME AND FISH COMMISSION ... 42
ARKANSAS STATE EXTENSION SERVICES ... 43
ARKANSAS STATE UNIVERSITY ... 363
ARKANSAS TECH UNIVERSITY ... 363
ARKANSAS WILDLIFE FEDERATION ... 154
ARLINGTON OUTDOOR EDUCATION ASSOCIATION, INC. ... 155
ASSOCIATION FOR CONSERVATION INFORMATION, INC. ... 155
ASSOCIATION FOR FISH AND WILDLIFE ENFORCEMENT TRAINING ... 155
ASSOCIATION FOR THE PROTECTION OF THE ADIRONDACKS, THE ... 155
ASSOCIATION OF AMERICAN GEOGRAPHERS ... 155
ASSOCIATION OF AVIAN VETERINARIANS ... 156
ASSOCIATION OF CONSERVATION ENGINEERS ... 156

ORGANIZATION NAME INDEX

ASSOCIATION OF CONSULTING FORESTERS OF AMERICA... 156
ASSOCIATION OF FIELD ORNITHOLOGISTS 156
ASSOCIATION OF GREAT LAKES OUTDOOR WRITERS........... 156
ASSOCIATION OF MIDWEST FISH AND GAME LAW ENFORCEMENT OFFICERS... 156
ASSOCIATION OF NEW JERSEY ENVIRONMENTAL COMMISSIONS 157
ASSOCIATION OF STATE AND TERRITORIAL HEALTH OFFICIALS 157
ATLANTIC CENTER FOR THE ENVIRONMENT........................... 157
    New England Office... 157
    QLF Canada Office... 157
ATLANTIC SALMON FEDERATION 157
ATLANTIC STATES LEGAL FOUNDATION.................................. 157
ATLANTIC STATES MARINE FISHERIES COMMISSION 7
AUBURN UNIVERSITY 362
AUDUBON COUNCIL OF CONNECTICUT 158
AUDUBON COUNCIL OF ILLINOIS.. 158
AUDUBON INTERNATIONAL 158
AUDUBON NATURALIST SOCIETY OF THE CENTRAL ATLANTIC STATES 158
AUDUBON OF KANSAS (formerly Kansas Audubon Council)....... 158
AUDUBON SOCIETY OF MISSOURI 158
AUDUBON SOCIETY OF NEW HAMPSHIRE 159
AUDUBON SOCIETY OF PORTLAND 159
AUDUBON SOCIETY OF RHODE ISLAND 159
AUDUBON SOCIETY OF WESTERN PENNSYLVANIA............... 159
AVSC INTERNATIONAL 159
BALL STATE UNIVERSITY 370
BAMA BACKPADDLERS ASSOCIATION..................................... 159
BARD COLLEGE 380
BARRIER ISLAND TRUST, INC... 160
BASS ANGLERS SPORTSMAN SOCIETY (B.A.S.S, INC.)........... 160
BAT CONSERVATION INTERNATIONAL 160
BEMIDJI STATE UNIVERSITY 377
BERKSHIRE-LITCHFIELD ENVIRONMENTAL COUNCIL, INC. ... 160
BEYOND PESTICIDES/NATIONAL COALITION AGAINST THE MISUSE OF PESTICIDES.. 160
BIG BEND NATURAL HISTORY ASSOCIATION 160
BILLFISH FOUNDATION, THE 160
BIODIVERSITY LEGAL FOUNDATION 161
BIO-INTEGRAL RESOURCE CENTER 161
BIOMASS USERS NETWORK... 161
BIRDLIFE INTERNATIONAL 161
BLUEBIRDS ACROSS VERMONT PROJECT 161
BOARD OF MINERALS AND ENVIRONMENT 106
BOONE AND CROCKETT CLUB 161
BOONE AND CROCKETT FOUNDATION 161
BORDER ECOLOGY PROJECT (BEP).. 162
BOTANICAL CLUB OF WISCONSIN... 162
BOTANICAL SOCIETY OF WESTERN PENNSYLVANIA 162
BOUNTY INFORMATION SERVICE (WILDLIFE) 162
BOWLING GREEN STATE UNIVERSITY...................................... 383
BOY SCOUTS OF AMERICA... 162
BRADLEY UNIVERSITY... 370
BRANDYWINE CONSERVANCY, INC... 162
BRITISH COLUMBIA FIELD ORNITHOLOGISTS 163
BRITISH COLUMBIA WATERFOWL SOCIETY, THE................... 163
BROOKS BIRD CLUB INC., THE... 163
BROTHERHOOD OF THE JUNGLE COCK, INC., THE................ 163
BROWN UNIVERSITY... 386
BUREAU OF ECONOMIC GEOLOGY 108
CADDO LAKE INSTITUTE, INC... 163
CALIFORNIA ACADEMY OF SCIENCES 163
    California Academy of Sciences Library............................... 163
CALIFORNIA ASSOCIATION OF RESOURCE CONSERVATION DISTRICTS 164
CALIFORNIA B.A.S.S. CHAPTER FEDERATION 164
CALIFORNIA COOPERATIVE FISHERY RESEARCH UNIT (USGS)44
CALIFORNIA DEPARTMENT OF EDUCATION
    Office of Environmental Education 44, 91, 94, 400
CALIFORNIA ENVIRONMENTAL PROTECTION AGENCY............. 44
    California Air Resources Board.. 44
    Department of Pesticide Regulation.................................. 44, 45
    Department of Toxic Substances Control 44, 45
    Office of Environmental Health Hazard Assessment....... 44, 45
    Water Resources Control Board 44, 45
CALIFORNIA NATIVE PLANT SOCIETY, THE 164
CALIFORNIA POLYTECHNIC STATE UNIVERSITY 364
CALIFORNIA SEA GRANT COLLEGE SYSTEM 45

CALIFORNIA STATE EXTENSION SERVICES............................... 45
CALIFORNIA STATE LANDS COMMISSION 46
CALIFORNIA STATE UNIVERSITY AT CHICO 364
CALIFORNIA STATE UNIVERSITY AT FULLERTON.................. 364
CALIFORNIA STATE UNIVERSITY AT SACRAMENTO............... 364
CALIFORNIA TRAPPERS ASSOCIATION 164
CALIFORNIA TROUT, INC.. 164
CALIFORNIA UNIVERSITY OF PENNSYLVANIA 385
CALIFORNIA WATERFOWL ASSOCIATION 164
CALIFORNIA WILDLIFE DEFENDERS 164
CALIFORNIA WILDLIFE FEDERATION 165
CALIFORNIA, FOREST LANDOWNERS OF 165
CALIFORNIANS FOR POPULATION STABILIZATION (CAPS) ... 165
CAMP FIRE BOYS AND GIRLS 165
CAMP FIRE CLUB OF AMERICA, THE 165
CAMP FIRE CONSERVATION FUND... 165
CAMPAIGN FOR A PROSPEROUS GEORGIA............................ 165
CANADA-UNITED STATES ENVIRONMENTAL COUNCIL (United States Office)... 166
CANADIAN ARCTIC RESOURCES COMMITTEE, INC. 166
CANADIAN COOPERATIVE WILDLIFE HEALTH CENTRE 166
CANADIAN ENVIRONMENTAL LAW ASSOCIATION................. 166
CANADIAN FEDERATION OF HUMANE SOCIETIES 166
CANADIAN FORESTRY ASSOCIATION 166
CANADIAN INSTITUTE FOR ENVIRONMENTAL LAW AND POLICY (CIELAP) 166
CANADIAN INSTITUTE OF FORESTRY/INSTITUT FORESTIER DU CANADA.. 167
CANADIAN NATIONAL SPORTSMEN'S SHOWS....................... 167
CANADIAN NATURE FEDERATION 167
CANADIAN PARKS AND WILDERNESS SOCIETY 167
CANADIAN SOCIETY OF ENVIRONMENTAL BIOLOGISTS 167
CANADIAN WILDLIFE FEDERATION 167
CANADIAN WILDLIFE SERVICE 35
CANVASBACK SOCIETY 167
CARIBBEAN CONSERVATION CORPORATION 168
CARIBBEAN NATURAL RESOURCES INSTITUTE 168
CAROLINA BIRD CLUB, INC. 168
CARRYING CAPACITY NETWORK 168
CASCADIA RESEARCH 168
CATSKILL CENTER FOR CONSERVATION AND DEVELOPMENT, INC., THE 168
CATSKILL FOREST ASSOCIATION 168
CAVE RESEARCH FOUNDATION 168
CENTER FOR BIOLOGICAL DIVERSITY..................................... 169
CENTER FOR CHESAPEAKE COMMUNITIES........................... 169
CENTER FOR ENVIRONMENT 169, 170
CENTER FOR ENVIRONMENTAL EDUCATION 169
CENTER FOR ENVIRONMENTAL INFORMATION 169
CENTER FOR ENVIRONMENTAL PHILOSOPHY 169
CENTER FOR ENVIRONMENTAL STUDY 170
CENTER FOR HEALTH, ENVIRONMENT, AND JUSTICE.......... 170
CENTER FOR INDEPENDENT SOCIAL RESEARCH 170
CENTER FOR INTERNATIONAL ENVIRONMENTAL LAW (CIEL)170
CENTER FOR MARINE CONSERVATION 170
CENTER FOR PLANT CONSERVATION 170
CENTER FOR RESOURCE ECONOMICS 171
CENTER FOR RESOURCEFUL BUILDING TECHNOLOGY 171
CENTER FOR SCIENCE IN THE PUBLIC INTEREST 171
CENTER FOR THE STUDY OF TROPICAL BIRDS, INC. (Field Office) 171
CENTER FOR WATERSHED PROTECTION 171
CENTER FOR WILDLIFE LAW 171
CENTRAL MICHIGAN UNIVERSITY 376
CENTRAL OHIO ANGLERS AND HUNTERS CLUB 172
CENTRO de INFORMACION, INVESTIGACION y EDUCACION SOCIAL (CIIES) 172
CETACEAN SOCIETY INTERNATIONAL 172
CHARLES A. AND ANNE MORROW LINDBERGH FOUNDATION, THE 172
CHELONIA INSTITUTE 172
CHESAPEAKE BAY FOUNDATION, INC. 172, 173
CHESAPEAKE BAY FOUNDATION, INC. (Maryland Office) 173
CHESAPEAKE BAY FOUNDATION, INC. (Pennsylvania Office).. 173
CHESAPEAKE BAY FOUNDATION, INC. (Virginia Office) 173
CHESAPEAKE FARMS 173
CHESAPEAKE WILDLIFE HERITAGE (CWH) 173
CHICAGO HERPETOLOGICAL SOCIETY 173
CHIHUAHUAN DESERT RESEARCH INSTITUTE...................... 173
CHINA REGION LAKES ALLIANCE.. 173

CHLORINE-FREE PAPER CONSORTIUM (CPC) 173
CHRISTINA CONSERVANCY, INC. 174
CINCINNATI NATURE CENTER 174
CIRCUMPOLAR CONSERVATION UNION 174
CITIZENS ADVISORY COUNCIL TO PENNSYLVANIA DEPARTMENT
 OF ENVIRONMENTAL PROTECTION 99
CITIZENS ALLIANCE FOR SAVING THE ATMOSPHERE AND THE
 EARTH (CASA) 174
CITIZENS NATURAL RESOURCES ASSOCIATION OF WISCONSIN,
 INC. 174
CITY UNIVERSITY OF NEW YORK 381
CLARK UNIVERSITY 375
CLEAN OCEAN ACTION
    Main Office 174, 183, 279
    Mid-Coast Office 175
    South Jersey Office 175
CLEAN WATER ACTION 175
CLEAN WATER FUND 175
CLEAN WATER NETWORK, THE 175
CLEMSON UNIVERSITY 104, 387
CLEMSON UNIVERSITY EXTENSION SERVICE 104
CLEVELAND MUSEUM OF NATURAL HISTORY, THE 175
CLIMATE INSTITUTE 175
COALITION FOR CLEAN AIR 175
COALITION FOR EDUCATION IN THE OUTDOORS 175
COALITION FOR NATURAL STREAM VALLEYS, INC. 175
COAST ALLIANCE 176
COASTAL CONSERVATION ASSOCIATION 176
COASTAL CONSERVATION ASSOCIATION GEORGIA 176
COASTAL GEORGIA CENTER FOR SUSTAINABLE DEVELOPMENT
 176
COASTAL GEORGIA LAND TRUST, THE 176
COASTAL SOCIETY, THE 177
COLLEGE OF THE ATLANTIC 373
COLLEGE OF TROPICAL AGRICULTURE AND HUMAN RESOURCES
 57
COLLEGE OF WILLIAM AND MARY 390
COLORADO ASSOCIATION OF SOIL CONSERVATION DISTRICTS
 177
COLORADO B.A.S.S. CHAPTER FEDERATION 177
COLORADO COOPERATIVE FISH AND WILDLIFE RESEARCH UNIT
 (USDI) 49
COLORADO DEPARTMENT OF AGRICULTURE 49
COLORADO DEPARTMENT OF EDUCATION 49
COLORADO DEPARTMENT OF NATURAL RESOURCES 49
    Colorado Geologic Survey 49
    Division of Minerals and Geology 49
    Division of Parks and Outdoor Recreation 40, 49
    Division of Water Resources 49, 52, 83, 91, 110
    Division of Wildlife 39, 49, 54, 67, 82, 92, 94, 110, 398, 417
    Oil and Gas Conservation Commission 41, 49
    Soil Conservation Board 49
    State Board of Land 49, 59
    Water Conservation Board 49, 109
COLORADO DEPARTMENT OF PUBLIC HEALTH AND
 ENVIRONMENT 49
COLORADO ENVIRONMENTAL COALITION 177
COLORADO FORESTRY ASSOCIATION 177
COLORADO MOUNTAIN COLLEGE 366
COLORADO NATURAL HERITAGE PROGRAM 177
COLORADO STATE FOREST SERVICE 49
COLORADO STATE UNIVERSITY 50, 366
COLORADO STATE UNIVERSITY COOPERATIVE EXTENSION ... 50
COLORADO TRAPPERS ASSOCIATION 178
COLORADO WATER CONGRESS 178
COLORADO WILDLIFE FEDERATION 178
COLORADO WILDLIFE HERITAGE FOUNDATION 178
COLUMBIA BASIN FISH AND WILDLIFE AUTHORITY 178
COLUMBIA RIVER GORGE COMMISSION 116
COLUMBIA RIVER INTER-TRIBAL FISH COMMISSION 7
COMITE DESPERTAR CIDREÑO 102
COMMITTEE FOR NATIONAL ARBOR DAY 178
COMMITTEE FOR THE NATIONAL INSTITUTE FOR THE
 ENVIRONMENT (CNIE) 178
COMMITTEE ON AGRICULTURAL SUSTAINABILITY FOR
 DEVELOPING COUNTRIES 179
COMMUNITIES FOR A BETTER ENVIRONMENT 179
COMMUNITY CONSERVATION CONSULTANTS/HOWLERS
 FOREVER, INC. 179
COMMUNITY ENVIRONMENTAL COUNCIL 179
COMMUNITY RIGHTS COUNSEL 179
CONCERN, INC. 179
CONFEDERATED SALISH AND KOOTENAI TRIBES 180
CONFERENCE OF NATIONAL PARK COOPERATING
 ASSOCIATIONS 180
CONNECTICUT ASSOCIATION OF SOIL AND WATER
 CONSERVATION DISTRICTS, INC. 180
CONNECTICUT AUDUBON SOCIETY, INC. 180
CONNECTICUT B.A.S.S. CHAPTER FEDERATION 180
CONNECTICUT BOTANICAL SOCIETY 180
CONNECTICUT COLLEGE 367
CONNECTICUT COUNCIL ON ENVIRONMENTAL QUALITY 50
CONNECTICUT DEPARTMENT OF AGRICULTURE 50
CONNECTICUT DEPARTMENT OF ENVIRONMENTAL PROTECTION
 50
CONNECTICUT FOREST AND PARK ASSOCIATION 180
CONNECTICUT FUND FOR THE ENVIRONMENT 180
CONNECTICUT PUBLIC INTEREST RESEARCH GROUP (Conn
 PIRG) 181
CONNECTICUT RIVER WATERSHED COUNCIL INC. 181
CONNECTICUT SEA GRANT 51
CONNECTICUT WATERFOWL ASSOCIATION, INC. 181
CONSERVANCY OF SOUTHWEST FLORIDA, THE 181
CONSERVATION AND RESEARCH FOUNDATION, INC., THE ... 181
CONSERVATION AND SURVEY DIVISION (NEBRASKA) 81
CONSERVATION COUNCIL FOR HAWAII 181
CONSERVATION COUNCIL OF NORTH CAROLINA 181
CONSERVATION DISTRICTS FOUNDATION INC. 182
CONSERVATION FEDERATION OF MARYLAND/For A Rural Maryland
 (F.A.R.M.) 182
CONSERVATION FEDERATION OF MISSOURI 182
CONSERVATION FORCE 182
CONSERVATION FUND, THE 182
CONSERVATION INTERNATIONAL 183
CONSERVATION LAW FOUNDATION (CLF) (Vermont Office)
    New England Region 183, 335
CONSERVATION LAW FOUNDATION, INC. (CLF) 183
CONSERVATION TECHNOLOGY INFORMATION CENTER 183
CONSERVATION TREATY SUPPORT FUND 183
CONSERVATION TRUST OF PUERTO RICO 183
COOK INLET KEEPER 184
COOPER ORNITHOLOGICAL SOCIETY 184
COOSA RIVER BASIN INITIATIVE 184
CORAL REEF ALLIANCE, THE (CORAL) 184
CORNELL LAB OF ORNITHOLOGY 184
CORNELL UNIVERSITY 381
COUNCIL FOR ENVIRONMENTAL EDUCATION 184
COUNCIL FOR PLANNING AND CONSERVATION 185
COUNCIL ON ENVIRONMENTAL QUALITY 10
COUNCIL ON RESOURCES AND DEVELOPMENT 83
COUSTEAU SOCIETY, INC., THE 185
COUSTEAU SOCIETY, INC., THE (France Office) 185
CRAIGHEAD ENVIRONMENTAL RESEARCH INSTITUTE 185
CRAIGHEAD WILDLIFE-WILDLANDS INSTITUTE 185
CRESTON VALLEY WILDLIFE MANAGEMENT AUTHORITY 185
CROSBY ABORETUM, THE, Mississippi State University 185
DALHOUSIE UNIVERSITY 394
DARTMOUTH COLLEGE 379
DAWES ARBORETUM, THE 186
DEEP-PORTAGE CONSERVATION RESERVE 186
DEFENDERS OF WILDLIFE 186
DELAWARE ASSOCIATION OF CONSERVATION DISTRICTS ... 186
DELAWARE AUDUBON SOCIETY 186
DELAWARE B.A.S.S. CHAPTER FEDERATION 187
DELAWARE DEPARTMENT OF AGRICULTURE 51
DELAWARE DEPARTMENT OF NATURAL RESOURCES AND
 ENVIRONMENTAL CONTROL 51
    Division of Air and Waste Management 51
    Division of Fish and Wildlife 29, 40, 51, 63, 76, 112, 113, 261, 397
    Division of Parks and Recreation .. 51, 76, 94, 104, 110, 258, 416
    Division of Water Resources 49, 52, 83, 91, 110
DELAWARE DEPARTMENT OF NATURAL RESOURCES AND
 ENVIRONMENTAL CONTROL
    Division of Soil and Water Conservation 51, 92, 94, 114
DELAWARE FORESTRY ASSOCIATION 187
DELAWARE GEOLOGICAL SURVEY 52
DELAWARE GREENWAYS, INC. 187
DELAWARE MUSEUM OF NATURAL HISTORY 187
DELAWARE NATURE SOCIETY 187
DELAWARE RIVER BASIN COMMISSION 7

ORGANIZATION NAME INDEX

DELAWARE SEA GRANT PROGRAM 52
DELAWARE SOLID WASTE AUTHORITY 52
DELAWARE STATE EXTENSION SERVICE 52
DELAWARE WILD LANDS, INC. 187
DELMARVA ORNITHOLOGICAL SOCIETY 187
DELTA WATERFOWL FOUNDATION 187
DELTA WILDLIFE, INC. 187
DEPARTMENT FOR ENVIRONMENT, HERITAGE AND ABORIGINAL AFFAIRS 35
DEPARTMENT OF CANADIAN HERITAGE 35
DEPARTMENT OF COMMERCE 122
    NATIONAL OCEANIC AND ATMOSPHERIC ADMINISTRATION 17
DEPARTMENT OF ENVIRONMENT AND CONSERVATION (TENNESSEE) 107
DEPARTMENT OF ENVIRONMENT AND WILDLIFE (QUEBEC) . 128
DEPARTMENT OF ENVIRONMENTAL MANAGEMENT (RHODE ISLAND) 103
DEPARTMENT OF ENVIRONMENTAL QUALITY (ARKANSAS) 43
DEPARTMENT OF FISH AND WILDLIFE (OREGON) 97
DEPARTMENT OF FISH AND WILDLIFE (WASHINGTON) 116
DEPARTMENT OF FISHERIES AND OCEANS 35
DEPARTMENT OF FOOD AND AGRICULTURE (CALIFORNIA) 46
DEPARTMENT OF FORESTRY 113
DEPARTMENT OF GEOLOGY AND MINERAL INDUSTRIES 97
DEPARTMENT OF INDUSTRY, TRADE AND TOURISM 124
DEPARTMENT OF INTERIOR, U.S.G.S/B.R.D, SOUTH CAROLINA COOPERATIVE FISH AND WILDLIFE RESEARCH UNIT 104
DEPARTMENT OF LAND AND NATURAL RESOURCES
    Division of Boating and Ocean Recreation (DOBOR 58
    Division of Water Resource Management, ... 58
DEPARTMENT OF LAND AND NATURAL RESOURCES (HAWAII)58
    Division of Aquatic Resources 58
    Division of Conservation and Resources Enforcement 58
    Division of Forestry and Wildlife 58
    Division of Historic Preservation 58, 63
    Division of State Parks 38, 58, 63, 80, 82, 114, 122
    Land Division 38, 58, 120
DEPARTMENT OF LANDS (IDAHO) 59
DEPARTMENT OF PARKS AND RECREATION (GUAM) 57
DEPARTMENT OF PARKS, RECREATION AND TOURISM 104
DEPARTMENT OF PLANNING AND NATURAL RESOURCES 112
    Division of Fish and Wildlife29, 40, 51, 63, 76, 112, 113, 261, 397
DEPARTMENT OF PUBLIC WORKS 52
DEPARTMENT OF RENEWABLE RESOURCES 129
DEPARTMENT OF RESOURCES AND ECONOMIC DEVELOPMENT 83
DEPARTMENT OF RESOURCES, WILDLIFE AND ECONOMIC DEVELOPMENT, GOVERNMENT OF THE NORTHWEST TERRITORIES 126
DEPARTMENT OF THE ENVIRONMENT 71
DEPARTMENT OF TRANSPORTATION (OREGON) 97
DEPARTMENT OF TRANSPORTATION (RHODE ISLAND) 104
DEPARTMENT OF WILDLIFE CONSERVATION 95
DESERT FISHES COUNCIL 188
DESERT RESEARCH FOUNDATION OF NAMIBIA, THE 188
DESERT TORTOISE COUNCIL 188
DESERT TORTOISE PRESERVE COMMITTEE, INC. 188
DISTRICT OF COLUMBIA DEPARTMENT OF HEALTH
    Environmental Health Administration, Watershed Protection Division 52
DISTRICT OF COLUMBIA SOIL AND WATER CONSERVATION DISTRICT 188
DISTRICT OF COLUMBIA STATE EXTENSION SERVICES 52
DIVISION OF FORESTRY AND SOIL RESOURCES OF GUAM 57
DRAGONFLY SOCIETY OF THE AMERICAS, THE 188
DREXEL UNIVERSITY 385
DUCKS UNLIMITED (Alberta, Canada) 189
DUCKS UNLIMITED (Nova Scotia, Canada) 189
DUCKS UNLIMITED (Ontario, Canada) 189
DUCKS UNLIMITED (Quebec, Canada) 189
DUCKS UNLIMITED (Saskatchewan Operation, Canada) 189
DUCKS UNLIMITED CANADA
    Oak Hammock Marsh Conservation Centre 188
DUCKS UNLIMITED, INC. 189, 191
DUKE UNIVERSITY 382
EAGLE NATURE FOUNDATION, LTD. 191
EARTH DAY NEW YORK 191
EARTH FORCE 191
EARTH FOUNDATION 191

EARTH ISLAND INSTITUTE 191
EARTH SHARE 192
EARTHJUSTICE LEGAL DEFENSE FUND (formerly Sierra Club Legal Defense Fund)
    California Office 192, 326
EARTHJUSTICE LEGAL DEFENSE FUND (formerly Sierra Club Legal Defense Fund, Inc.) 192
    Florida Office 183, 192
    Hawaii Office 192
    Louisiana Office 192
    Montana Office 182, 192
    Rocky Mountain Office 192, 196
    Seattle, Washington Office 192
    Southeast Alaska Office 192
    Washington, DC Office 134, 148, 192, 308, 314, 324
EARTHLAW 192
EARTHSCAN 193
EARTHSTEWARDS NETWORK 193
EARTHTRUST 193
EARTHWATCH INSTITUTE 193
EAST CENTRAL ILLINOIS FUR TAKERS 193
EASTERN ILLINOIS UNIVERSITY 370
EASTERN KENTUCKY UNIVERSITY 372
EASTERN MICHIGAN UNIVERSITY 376
EASTERN SHORE LAND CONSERVANCY 193
ECODEFENSE 193
ECOLOGICAL SOCIETY OF AMERICA, THE 193
ECOLOGY CENTER 194
ECOTOURISM SOCIETY, THE 194
EDUCATIONAL COMMUNICATIONS, INC. 194
EGYPTIAN ENVIRONMENTAL AFFAIRS AGENCY 37
ELM RESEARCH INSTITUTE 194
ELSA WILD ANIMAL APPEAL
    Louisiana Chapter 194
EMORY UNIVERSITY 369
EMPORIA STATE UNIVERSITY 371
ENDANGERED SPECIES COALITION 194
ENERGY, MINERALS, AND NATURAL RESOURCES DEPARTMENT 86
    Administrative Services Division44, 46, 47, 64, 65, 66, 79, 86, 87, 99, 105, 107
    Energy Conservation and Management Division 86
    Forestry and Resources Conservation Division 86
    Mining and Minerals Division 86
    Oil Conservation Division 86
    State Parks and Recreation Division 86
ENTOMOLOGICAL SOCIETY OF AMERICA 195
ENVIRONMENT COUNCIL OF RHODE ISLAND 195
ENVIRONMENTAL ACTION FUND (EAF) 195
ENVIRONMENTAL ADVOCATES 195
ENVIRONMENTAL AIR FORCE 195
ENVIRONMENTAL AND ENERGY STUDY INSTITUTE (EESI) ... 195
ENVIRONMENTAL CAREER CENTER 195
ENVIRONMENTAL CAREERS ORGANIZATION, INC., THE 195
ENVIRONMENTAL CENTER 58
ENVIRONMENTAL CONCERN INC. 196
ENVIRONMENTAL CONSERVATION SERVICE 36
ENVIRONMENTAL DEFENSE CENTER, INC. 196
ENVIRONMENTAL DEFENSE FUND, INC. 196
    Capital Office 196, 326
    North Carolina Office 196, 324
    Rocky Mountain Office 192, 196
    Texas Office 182, 196
    West Coast Office 196
ENVIRONMENTAL EDUCATION ASSOCIATES 196
ENVIRONMENTAL EDUCATION ASSOCIATION OF ILLINOIS ... 197
ENVIRONMENTAL EDUCATION ASSOCIATION OF INDIANA ... 197
ENVIRONMENTAL EDUCATION ASSOCIATION OF WASHINGTON 197
ENVIRONMENTAL EDUCATION COUNCIL OF OHIO 197
ENVIRONMENTAL EDUCATORS OF NORTH CAROLINA (EENC)197
ENVIRONMENTAL ENTERPRISES ASSISTANCE FUND, INC. ... 197
ENVIRONMENTAL FUND FOR GEORGIA 197
ENVIRONMENTAL LAW ALLIANCE WORLDWIDE (E-LAW) 197
ENVIRONMENTAL LAW AND POLICY CENTER OF THE MIDWEST 198
ENVIRONMENTAL LAW INSTITUTE, THE 198
ENVIRONMENTAL LEAGUE OF MASSACHUSETTS 198
ENVIRONMENTAL MEDIA ASSOCIATION 198
ENVIRONMENTAL PROTECTION AGENCY 10

ORGANIZATION NAME INDEX

ENVIRONMENTAL PROTECTION ASSOCIATION OF GHANA ... 198
ENVIRONMENTAL PROTECTION BUREAU 88
ENVIRONMENTAL PROTECTION SERVICE 36
ENVIRONMENTAL QUALITY DEPARTMENT 122
ENVIRONMENTAL RESOURCE CENTER (ERC) 198
ENVIRONMENTAL REVIEW APPEALS COMMISSION 94
ENVIROSOUTH, INC. 199
E-P EDUCATION SERVICES, INC. 191
EUROPARC FEDERATION 199
EUROPEAN ASSOCIATION FOR AQUATIC MAMMALS 199
EUROPEAN CETACEAN SOCIETY 199
EVERGLADES COORDINATING COUNCIL (ECC), ... 199
EXECUTIVE OFFICE OF ENVIRONMENTAL AFFAIRS
    Division of Fisheries and Wildlife 73, 74
EXECUTIVE OFFICE OF ENVIRONMENTAL AFFAIRS
   (MASSACHUSETTS) 73
    Animal Health 13, 73, 78, 84, 100, 117, 140
    Bureau of Land Use 73
    Bureau of Markets 73
    Bureau of Pesticides 73
    Department of Environmental Management62, 73, 103, 416, 421, 422
    Department of Environmental Protection73, 101, 123, 397, 415, 421
    Department of Fisheries, Wildlife, and Environmental Law
      Enforcement 73
    Department of Food and Agriculture 73
    Division of Agricultural Development 73
    Division of Regulatory Services 73
    Division of Wetlands and Waterways, ... 73
    Metropolitan District Commission, ... 73
    State Commission for Conservation of Soil, Water and Related
      Resources 74
    Watershed Division 74
FAIRFAX AUDUBON SOCIETY 199
FEDERAL CARTRIDGE COMPANY 199
FEDERAL WILDLIFE OFFICER'S ASSOCIATION 199
FEDERATION OF ALBERTA NATURALISTS 200
FEDERATION OF ENVIRONMENTAL EDUCATION IN ST.
   PETERSBURG 200
FEDERATION OF FLY FISHERS 200
FEDERATION OF NEW YORK STATE BIRD CLUBS, INC. 200
FEDERATION OF ONTARIO NATURALISTS 200
FEDERATION OF WESTERN OUTDOOR CLUBS 200
FERRIS STATE UNIVERSITY 376
FERRUM COLLEGE 390
FISH AND WILDLIFE INFORMATION EXCHANGE 201
FISH AND WILDLIFE REFERENCE SERVICE 201, 409
FISHAMERICA FOUNDATION 201
FLORIDA ASSOCIATION OF SOIL AND WATER CONSERVATION
   DISTRICTS 201
FLORIDA ATLANTIC UNIVERSITY 368
FLORIDA AUDUBON SOCIETY 201
FLORIDA B.A.S.S. CHAPTER FEDERATION
FLORIDA COOPERATIVE FISH AND WILDLIFE RESEARCH UNIT
   (USDI) 52
FLORIDA DEFENDERS OF THE ENVIRONMENT, INC. (Home Office)
   201
FLORIDA DEPARTMENT OF AGRICULTURE AND CONSUMER
   SERVICES 52
    Division of Forestry . 40, 53, 58, 63, 68, 76, 83, 94, 110, 119, 392
    Office of Agricultural Water Policy 53
    Soil and Water Conservation Council 53
FLORIDA DEPARTMENT OF ENVIRONMENTAL PROTECTION .. 53
    Air Resources Management Division 53
    Beaches and Shores Division 53
    Ecosytem Management Division 53
    Environmental Resource Permitting Division 53
    Law Enforcement Division 51, 53, 68, 84, 105, 107, 114, 284
    Legislative and Cabinet Affairs Division 53
    Marine Resource Division 53
    Recreation and Parks division 54
    State Lands Division 54
    Waste Management Division 54, 64, 65, 84, 87
    Water Facilities Division 54
FLORIDA EXOTIC PEST PLANT COUNCIL 202
FLORIDA FISH AND WILDLIFE CONSERVATION COMMISSION. 54
FLORIDA FORESTRY ASSOCIATION 202
FLORIDA NATIVE PLANT SOCIETY 202
FLORIDA ORNITHOLOGICAL SOCIETY 202
FLORIDA PANTHER PROJECT, INC., THE 202
FLORIDA PUBLIC INTEREST RESEARCH GROUP (Florida PIRG)202
FLORIDA SEA GRANT COLLEGE 54
FLORIDA SPORTSMEN'S CONSERVATION ASSOCIATION 202
FLORIDA STATE COOPERATIVE EXTENSION SERVICE 54
FLORIDA STATE DEPARTMENT OF HEALTH 54
FLORIDA STATE UNIVERSITY 368
FLORIDA TRAIL ASSOCIATION, INC. 203
FLORIDA WILDLIFE FEDERATION 203
FOOD AND AGRICULTURE ORGANIZATION OF THE UNITED
   NATIONS 203
FOREST FIRE LOOKOUT ASSOCIATION 203
FOREST HISTORY SOCIETY, INC. 203
FOREST LANDOWNERS ASSOCIATION, INC. 203
FOREST SERVICE EMPLOYEES FOR ENVIRONMENTAL ETHICS
   (FSEEE) 204
FOREST SOCIETY OF MAINE 204
FOREST TRUST 204
FOREST WATCH 204
FORESTRY COMMISSION (ARKANSAS) 43
FORESTRY COMMISSION (SOUTH CAROLINA) 105
FOSSIL FUELS POLICY ACTION INSTITUTE/ALLIANCE FOR A
   PAVING MORATORIUM 204
FOSSIL FUELS POLICY ACTION INSTITUTE/ALLIANCE FOR A
   PAVING MORATORIUM (South American Bureau Office) 204
FOSSIL RIM WILDLIFE CENTER 205
FOUNDATION FOR NORTH AMERICAN BIG GAME 205
FOUNDATION FOR NORTH AMERICAN WILD SHEEP 205
FRANKFURT ZOOLOGICAL SOCIETY--HELP FOR THREATENED
   WILDLIFE 205
FRIENDS OF ACADIA 205
FRIENDS OF ANIMALS INC. 205
FRIENDS OF DISCOVERY PARK 205
FRIENDS OF THE BOUNDARY WATERS WILDERNESS 206
FRIENDS OF THE EARTH 206
    Northwest Regional Office (WA, OR, ID) 206
FRIENDS OF THE REEDY RIVER 206
FRIENDS OF THE RIVER 206
FRIENDS OF THE SAN JUANS 206
FRIENDS OF THE SEA OTTER 206
FROSTBURG STATE UNIVERSITY (University of Maryland) 374
FUND FOR ANIMALS INC., THE 207
FUNDACION NATURA - COLOMBIA 207
FUTURE FISHERMAN FOUNDATION 207
GALIANO CONSERVANCY ASSOCIATION 207
GAME AND PARKS COMMISSION
   Game and Parks Commission 81, 398, 416
GAME AND PARKS COMMISSION-NEBRASKA
   Ak-Sar-Ben Aquarium 81
GAME CONSERVANCY U.S.A. (formerly American Friends of the
   Game Conservancy) 207
GAME CONSERVATION INTERNATIONAL (GAME COIN) 207
GARDEN CLUB OF AMERICA, THE 208
GENERAL FEDERATION OF WOMEN'S CLUBS 208
GENERAL SERVICES ADMINISTRATION 33
GEORGE MIKSCH SUTTON AVIAN RESEARCH CENTER INC. 208
GEORGE WASHINGTON UNIVERSITY 368
GEORGE WRIGHT SOCIETY, THE 208
GEORGETOWN COLLEGE 372
GEORGIA ASSOCIATION OF CONSERVATION DISTRICT
   SUPERVISORS 208
GEORGIA B.A.S.S. CHAPTER FEDERATION 208
GEORGIA CONSERVANCY, INC., THE 209
GEORGIA COOPERATIVE FISH AND WILDLIFE RESEARCH UNIT
   (USDI) 55
GEORGIA DEPARTMENT OF AGRICULTURE 55
    Consumers Services Library 55
GEORGIA DEPARTMENT OF EDUCATION 55
GEORGIA DEPARTMENT OF NATURAL RESOURCES 56
    Coastal Resources Division 56
    Environmental Protection Division 47, 56, 64, 87, 112
    Historic Preservation Division 56
    Parks, Recreation and Historic Sites Division 56
    Pollution Prevention Assistance Division 56
    Program Support Division 56
    Wildlife Resources Division 56, 223, 397, 415
GEORGIA ENVIRONMENTAL COUNCIL, INC. 209
GEORGIA ENVIRONMENTAL ORGANIZATION, INC (GEO) 209
GEORGIA ENVIRONMENTAL POLICY INSTITUTE 209
GEORGIA FEDERATION OF FOREST OWNERS 209

ORGANIZATION NAME INDEX

GEORGIA FORESTRY ASSOCIATION, INC. 209
GEORGIA FORESTRY COMMISSION 56
GEORGIA INSTITUTE OF TECHNOLOGY 369
GEORGIA SEA GRANT COLLEGE PROGRAM 56
GEORGIA STATE EXTENSION SERVICE 56
GEORGIA TRAPPERS ASSOCIATION 209
GEORGIA TRUST FOR HISTORIC PRESERVATION 210
GEORGIA WILDLIFE FEDERATION 210
GIRL SCOUTS OF THE UNITED STATES OF AMERICA 210
GLACIER INSTITUTE, THE 210
GLOBAL CITIES PROJECT, THE 210
GLOBAL ENVIRONMENTAL MANAGEMENT INITIATIVE (GEMI) 210
GLOBAL INDUSTRIAL AND SOCIAL PROGRESS RESEARCH
  INSTITUTE (GISPRI) 211
GOPHER TORTOISE COUNCIL 211
GOVERNOR OF ALABAMA 38
GOVERNOR OF ALASKA 39
GOVERNOR OF AMERICAN SAMOA 40
GOVERNOR OF ARIZONA 40
GOVERNOR OF ARKANSAS 42
GOVERNOR OF CALIFORNIA 44
GOVERNOR OF COLORADO 49
GOVERNOR OF CONNECTICUT 50
GOVERNOR OF DELAWARE 51
GOVERNOR OF FLORIDA 52
GOVERNOR OF GEORGIA 55
GOVERNOR OF GUAM 57
GOVERNOR OF HAWAII 57
GOVERNOR OF IDAHO 59
GOVERNOR OF ILLINOIS 61
GOVERNOR OF INDIANA 62
GOVERNOR OF IOWA 63
GOVERNOR OF KANSAS 65
GOVERNOR OF KENTUCKY 66
GOVERNOR OF LOUISIANA 68
GOVERNOR OF MAINE 69
GOVERNOR OF MARYLAND 71
GOVERNOR OF MASSACHUSETTS 73
GOVERNOR OF MICHIGAN 74
GOVERNOR OF MINNESOTA 75
GOVERNOR OF MISSISSIPPI 77
GOVERNOR OF MISSOURI 79
GOVERNOR OF MONTANA 80
GOVERNOR OF NEBRASKA 81
GOVERNOR OF NEVADA 82
GOVERNOR OF NEW HAMPSHIRE 83
GOVERNOR OF NEW JERSEY 84
GOVERNOR OF NEW MEXICO 86
GOVERNOR OF NEW YORK 88
GOVERNOR OF NORTH CAROLINA 91
GOVERNOR OF NORTH DAKOTA 92
GOVERNOR OF OHIO 94
GOVERNOR OF OKLAHOMA 95
GOVERNOR OF OREGON 97
GOVERNOR OF PENNSYLVANIA 99
GOVERNOR OF PUERTO RICO 102
GOVERNOR OF RHODE ISLAND 103
GOVERNOR OF SOUTH CAROLINA 104
GOVERNOR OF SOUTH DAKOTA 106
GOVERNOR OF TENNESSEE 107
GOVERNOR OF TEXAS 108
GOVERNOR OF THE VIRGIN ISLANDS 112
GOVERNOR OF UTAH 110
GOVERNOR OF VERMONT 111
GOVERNOR OF VIRGINIA 113
GOVERNOR OF WASHINGTON 116
GOVERNOR OF WEST VIRGINIA 119
GOVERNOR OF WISCONSIN 120
GOVERNOR OF WYOMING 122
GRAND CANYON TRUST 211
GRAND CANYON TRUST (Moab, Utah Office) 211
GRAND CANYON TRUST (St. George, UT Office) 211
GRASSLAND HERITAGE FOUNDATION 211
GREAT BEAR FOUNDATION 211
GREAT LAKES FISHERY COMMISSION 7
GREAT LAKES INDIAN FISH AND WILDLIFE COMMISSION 7
GREAT LAKES SPORT FISHING COUNCIL 211
GREAT LAKES UNITED 211
  Montreal Office/Canada at-Large 212
GREAT OUTDOORS CONSERVANCY, THE 212
GREAT PLAINS NATIVE PLANT SOCIETY 212
GREAT SMOKY MOUNTAINS INSTITUTE AT TREMONT 212
GREATER YELLOWSTONE COALITION 212
GREEN (GLOBAL RIVERS ENVIRONMENTAL EDUCATION
  NETWORK) 212
GREEN MOUNTAIN AUDUBON SOCIETY 213
GREEN MOUNTAIN CLUB INC., THE 213
GREEN PARTY USA 213
GREEN SEAL 213
GREENPEACE, INC. 213
GROUNDWATER FOUNDATION, THE 213
GUADALUPE-BLANCO RIVER AUTHORITY 108
GUAM COASTAL MANAGEMENT PROGRAM 57
GUAM COOPERATIVE EXTENSION SERVICE 57
GUAM DEPARTMENT OF AGRICULTURE 57
  Division of Aquatic and Wildlife Resources 57
GUAM ENVIRONMENTAL PROTECTION AGENCY 57
GULF COAST RESEARCH LABORATORY 77
GULF OF MEXICO FISHERY MANAGEMENT COUNCIL 214
GULF STATES MARINE FISHERIES COMMISSION 7
H. JOHN HEINZ III CENTER FOR SCIENCE, ECONOMICS, AND THE
  ENVIRONMENT 214
HAMLINE UNIVERSITY 377
HARDWOOD FOREST FOUNDATION 214
HAWAII ASSOCIATION OF CONSERVATION DISTRICTS 214
HAWAII AUDUBON SOCIETY 214
HAWAII COOPERATIVE FISHERY RESEARCH UNIT (USDI) 58
HAWAII DEPARTMENT OF AGRICULTURE 58
HAWAII DEPARTMENT OF HEALTH 58
HAWAII NATURE CENTER 214
HAWAII SEA GRANT PROGRAM 59
HAWAII SOCIETY OF AMERICAN FORESTERS 214
HAWAIIAN BOTANICAL SOCIETY 214
HAWK AND OWL TRUST, THE 215
HAWK MIGRATION ASSOCIATION OF NORTH AMERICA 215
HAWK MOUNTAIN SANCTUARY ASSOCIATION 215
HAWKWATCH INTERNATIONAL, INC. 215
HEADLANDS INSTITUTE 215
HELSINKI COMMISSION/ BALTIC MARINE ENVIRONMENT
  PROTECTION COMMISSION 7
HENRY A. WALLACE INSTITUTE FOR ALTERNATIVE
  AGRICULTURE (HAWIAA) 215
HIGH DESERT MUSEUM, THE 216
HIMALAYAN WILDLIFE FOUNDATION 216
HOCKING COLLEGE 383
HOLDEN ARBORETUM, THE 216
HOLLY SOCIETY OF AMERICA, INC. 216
HOOD CANAL LAND TRUST 216
HOOSIER ENVIRONMENTAL COUNCIL 216
HOUSE COMMITTEE ON AGRICULTURE 4
HOUSE COMMITTEE ON APPROPRIATIONS 5
HOUSE COMMITTEE ON COMMERCE 5
HOUSE COMMITTEE ON EDUCATION AND THE WORKFORCE .. 5
HOUSE COMMITTEE ON INTERNATIONAL RELATIONS 5
HOUSE COMMITTEE ON RULES 5
HOUSE COMMITTEE ON TRANSPORTATION AND
  INFRASTRUCTURE 5
HUDSONIA LIMITED 216
HUMAN ECOLOGY ACTION LEAGUE, INC. THE (HEAL) 217
HUMANE SOCIETY OF THE UNITED STATES, THE 217
HUMBOLDT STATE UNIVERSITY 364
HUMBOLT FIELD RESEARCH INSTITUTE 217
HUMMINGBIRD SOCIETY, THE 217
HUNTSMAN MARINE SCIENCE CENTRE 217
IDAHO ASSOCIATION OF SOIL CONSERVATION DISTRICTS .. 218
IDAHO B.A.S.S. CHAPTER FEDERATION 218
IDAHO CONSERVATION LEAGUE 218
IDAHO COOPERATIVE EXTENSION 59
IDAHO COOPERATIVE FISH AND WILDLIFE RESEARCH UNIT
  (USDI) 60
IDAHO DEPARTMENT OF PARKS AND RECREATION 60
IDAHO DEPARTMENT OF WATER RESOURCES 60
IDAHO ENVIRONMENTAL COUNCIL 218
IDAHO FISH AND GAME DEPARTMENT 60
IDAHO FISH AND WILDLIFE FOUNDATION 60
IDAHO FOREST OWNERS ASSOCIATION 218
IDAHO GEOLOGICAL SURVEY 60
IDAHO STATE DEPARTMENT OF AGRICULTURE 60
IDAHO STATE SOIL CONSERVATION COMMISSION 60
IDAHO STATE UNIVERSITY 369

ORGANIZATION NAME INDEX

IDAHO WILDLIFE FEDERATION...218
ILLINOIS ASSOCIATION OF CONSERVATION DISTRICTS........218
ILLINOIS ASSOCIATION OF SOIL AND WATER CONSERVATION
  DISTRICTS...218
ILLINOIS AUDUBON SOCIETY 219
ILLINOIS B.A.S.S. CHAPTER FEDERATION................................219
ILLINOIS DEPARTMENT OF AGRICULTURE 61
  Soil and Water Conservation Districts Advisory Board............61
ILLINOIS DEPARTMENT OF NATURAL RESOURCES 61
ILLINOIS DEPARTMENT OF TRANSPORTATION.......................61
ILLINOIS ENVIRONMENTAL COUNCIL.....................................219
ILLINOIS ENVIRONMENTAL PROTECTION AGENCY................61
ILLINOIS NATIVE PLANT SOCIETY..219
ILLINOIS NATURAL HERITAGE FOUNDATION........................219
ILLINOIS NATURE PRESERVES COMMISSION (INPC) 62
ILLINOIS PRAIRIE PATH 219
ILLINOIS STATE UNIVERSITY 370
ILLINOIS WALNUT COUNCIL..219
ILLINOIS-INDIANA SEA GRANT PROGRAM...............................62
INDIAN CREEK NATURE CENTER...219
INDIANA ASSOCIATION OF SOIL AND WATER CONSERVATION
  DISTRICTS, INC..220
INDIANA AUDUBON SOCIETY, INC..220
INDIANA B.A.S.S. CHAPTER FEDERATION..............................220
INDIANA DEPARTMENT OF ENVIRONMENTAL MANAGEMENT.62
INDIANA DEPARTMENT OF NATURAL RESOURCES 62
  Division of Soil Conservation..63, 64
INDIANA FORESTRY AND WOODLAND OWNERS ASSOCIATION220
INDIANA GEOLOGICAL SURVEY...63
INDIANA NATIVE PLANT AND WILDFLOWER SOCIETY 220
INDIANA STATE DEPARTMENT OF HEALTH 63
INDIANA STATE TRAPPERS ASSOCIATION, INC.....................220
INDIANA STATE UNIVERSITY 371
INDIANA UNIVERSITY 371
INDIANA WILDLIFE FEDERATION...220
INDUSTRIAL SITING DIVISION/DEPARTMENT OF ENVIRONMENTAL
  QUALITY..122
INFORM, INC. 221
INITIATIVE FOR SOCIAL ACTION AND RENEWAL IN EURASIA 221
INLAND BIRD BANDING ASSOCIATION 221
INSTITUTE FOR CIVIC INITIATIVES SUPPORT..........................221
INSTITUTE FOR CONSERVATION LEADERSHIP.......................221
INSTITUTE FOR EARTH EDUCATION, THE...............................221
INSTITUTE FOR ECOLOGICAL STUDIES 92
INSTITUTE OF ECOSYSTEM STUDIES......................................221
INSTITUTE OF MARINE BIOLOGY 59
INSTITUTO BRASIL DE EDUCACAO AMBIENTAL......................222
INSTITUTO NACIONAL DE BIODIVERSIDAD (INBIO)..................37
INTERAGENCY COMMITTEE FOR OUTDOOR RECREATION (IAC)
 116
INTER-AMERICAN TROPICAL TUNA COMMISSION 8
INTERFAITH COUNCIL FOR THE PROTECTION OF ANIMALS AND
  NATURE INC. (ICPAN) 222
INTERNATIONAL ASSOCIATION FOR BEAR RESEARCH AND
  MANAGEMENT 222
INTERNATIONAL ASSOCIATION FOR ENVIRONMENTAL
  HYDROLOGY (IAEH)...222
INTERNATIONAL ASSOCIATION OF FISH AND WILDLIFE AGENCIES
 222
INTERNATIONAL ASSOCIATION OF NATURAL RESOURCE PILOTS
 223
INTERNATIONAL ASSOCIATION OF WILDLAND FIRE (formerly Fire
  Research Institute)..223
INTERNATIONAL BICYCLE FUND...223
INTERNATIONAL CENTER FOR EARTH CONCERNS 223
INTERNATIONAL CENTER FOR GIBBON STUDIES...................224
INTERNATIONAL CENTER FOR TROPICAL ECOLOGY 224
INTERNATIONAL CENTRE FOR CONSERVATION EDUCATION224
INTERNATIONAL COUNCIL OF ENVIRONMENTAL LAW 224
INTERNATIONAL CRANE FOUNDATION 224
INTERNATIONAL ECOLOGY SOCIETY (IES).............................224
INTERNATIONAL EROSION CONTROL ASSOCIATION (IECA)..224
INTERNATIONAL FUND FOR ANIMAL WELFARE 225
  Australian Office..225
  Belgium Office 225
  French Office 225
  German Office 225
  Holland Office 225
  Hong Kong Office 225
  Italian Office...225
  Philippines Office 225
  Russian Office 225
  South African Office 225
  United Kingdom8, 9, 193, 207, 215, 224, 225, 226, 228, 230, 282,
    311, 345, 357, 358, 395, 401
INTERNATIONAL GAME FISH ASSOCIATION............................225
INTERNATIONAL HUNTER EDUCATION ASSOCIATION 225
INTERNATIONAL INSTITUTE FOR ENERGY CONSERVATION. 225
INTERNATIONAL JOINT COMMISSION 8
INTERNATIONAL MARINE MAMMAL PROJECT, THE 226
INTERNATIONAL MARITIME ORGANIZATION 226
INTERNATIONAL OCEANOGRAPHIC FOUNDATION 226
INTERNATIONAL OSPREY FOUNDATION INC., THE..................226
INTERNATIONAL PACIFIC HALIBUT COMMISSION 8
INTERNATIONAL PLANT PROPAGATION SOCIETY, INC., THE 226
INTERNATIONAL PRIMATE PROTECTION LEAGUE..................226
INTERNATIONAL RIVERS NETWORK (IRN)..............................226
INTERNATIONAL SNOW LEOPARD TRUST..............................227
INTERNATIONAL SOCIETY FOR ECOLOGICAL ECONOMICS.. 227
INTERNATIONAL SOCIETY FOR ENDANGERED CATS (ISEC). 227
INTERNATIONAL SOCIETY FOR ENVIRONMENTAL ETHICS ... 227
INTERNATIONAL SOCIETY FOR THE PRESERVATION OF THE
  TROPICAL RAINFOREST, THE 227
INTERNATIONAL SOCIETY OF ARBORICULTURE 227
INTERNATIONAL SOCIETY OF TROPICAL FORESTERS, INC.. 228
INTERNATIONAL SONORAN DESERT ALLIANCE 228
INTERNATIONAL UNION FOR CONSERVATION OF NATURE AND
  NATURAL RESOURCES (IUCN) THE WORLD CONSERVATION
  UNION 228
  Bangladesh Country Office..228
  Botswana Country Office...228
  Burkina Country Fasso Office 228
  Canada Country Office..228
  Environmental Law Centre 228
  Guinea-Bissau Country Office 228
  Lao People's Democratic Republic Country Office.............228
  Mali Country Office..229
  Mozambique Country Office..229
  Nepal Country Office...229
  Niger Country Office..229
  P.O. Box 11536 229
  Pakistan Country Office 229
  Regional Office for Eastern Africa 229
  Regional Office for Europe..229
  Regional Office for Meso America 229
  Regional Office for South America 229
  Regional Office for Southern Africa (ROSA) 229
  Regional Office for West Africa...229
  Regional Office of South and Southeast Asia 229
  Regonal Office for Central Africa 229
  Senegal Country Office...229
  Sri Lanka Country Office...229
  Subregional Office for Central Europe................................229
  Subregional Office for the Commonwealth of Independent States
   229
  U.S. Office, Washington, DC 229
  Uganda Country Office..229
  Vietnam Country Office...229
  Zambia Country Office 229
INTERNATIONAL WHALING COMMISSION 8
INTERNATIONAL WILD WATERFOWL ASSOCIATION...............229
INTERNATIONAL WILDERNESS LEADERSHIP (WILD) FOUNDATION
 230
INTERNATIONAL WILDLIFE COALITION (IWC) AND THE WHALE
  ADOPTION PROJECT...230
INTERNATIONAL WILDLIFE REHABILITATION COUNCIL (IWRC)230
INTERNATIONAL WOLF CENTER (Administrative Offices) 230
INTERNATIONAL WOLF CENTER (Educational Services)..........230
INTERPRETATION CANADA 230
INTERSTATE COMMISSION ON THE POTOMAC RIVER BASIN ... 8
INTERTRIBAL BISON COOPERATIVE (ITBC).............................231
IOWA ACADEMY OF SCIENCE 231
IOWA ASSOCIATION OF COUNTY CONSERVATION BOARDS .. 63
IOWA ASSOCIATION OF NATURALISTS 231
IOWA ASSOCIATION OF SOIL AND WATER CONSERVATION
  DISTRICT COMMISSIONERS..231
IOWA AUDUBON 231
IOWA B.A.S.S. CHAPTER FEDERATION 231
IOWA CONSERVATION EDUCATION COUNCIL, INC................231
IOWA COOPERATIVE FISH AND WILDLIFE RESEARCH UNIT ... 64

ORGANIZATION NAME INDEX

IOWA DEPARTMENT OF AGRICULTURE AND LAND STEWARDSHIP
    Bureau of Field Services 64, 76
    Bureau of Financial Incentive Program 64
    Bureau of Mines and Minerals 64
    Bureau of Water Resources 64
    Division of Soil Conservation 63, 64
IOWA DEPARTMENT OF NATURAL RESOURCES 64
    Administrative Services Division44, 46, 47, 64, 65, 66, 79, 86, 87, 99, 105, 107
    Cooperative North American Shotgunning Education Program64
    Energy and Geological Resources Division 64
    Environmental Protection Division 47, 56, 64, 87, 112
    Fish and Wildlife Division 64, 98, 112, 128
    Forests and Prairies Division 65
    Parks27, 29, 42, 51, 53, 56, 58, 64, 65, 67, 69, 70, 73, 75, 77, 80, 82, 83, 91, 97, 101, 103, 106, 107, 109, 111, 113, 114, 117, 119, 121, 124, 126, 127, 128, 129, 133, 137, 142, 144, 152, 160, 167, 169, 188, 193, 199, 205, 211, 212, 216, 223, 228, 238, 257, 258, 261, 263, 264, 283, 289, 291, 295, 305, 310, 324, 327, 346, 348, 351, 352, 354, 358, 361, 364, 372, 378, 388, 392, 394, 397, 398, 399, 402, 414, 416, 417
    Waste Management Division 54, 64, 65, 84, 87
IOWA ENVIRONMENTAL COUNCIL 232
IOWA NATIVE PLANT SOCIETY 232
IOWA NATURAL HERITAGE FOUNDATION 232
IOWA PRAIRIE NETWORK 232
IOWA STATE EXTENSION SERVICES 65
IOWA STATE UNIVERSITY 371
IOWA TRAILS COUNCIL 232
IOWA TRAPPERS ASSOCIATION, INC. 232
IOWA WILDLIFE FEDERATION 233
IOWA WILDLIFE REHABILITATORS ASSOCIATION 233
IOWA WOMEN IN NATURAL RESOURCES 233
IOWA WOODLAND OWNERS ASSOCIATION 233
ISLAND CONSERVATION EFFORT 233
ISLAND INSTITUTE, THE 233
ISLAND RESOURCES FOUNDATION 233
    Eastern Caribbean Biodiversity Program Office 233
ISSAQUAH ALPS TRAILS CLUB (I.A.T.C.) 233
IZAAK WALTON LEAGUE OF AMERICA ENDOWMENT 234
IZAAK WALTON LEAGUE OF AMERICA, INC., THE 234
    Alaska Division 234
    California Division 234
    Colorado Division 49, 155, 178, 223, 234, 351, 397
    Florida Division 234
    Illinois Division 234
    Indiana Division 234, 397
    Iowa Division 234
    Maryland Division 234
    Michigan Division 234
    Minnesota Division 235
    Nebraska Division 235
    New York Division 235
    Ohio Division 223, 235, 291, 398
    Pennsylvania Division 235
    South Dakota Division 235
    Virginia Division 235, 417
    Washington Division 235
    West Virginia Division 119, 235, 399
    Wisconsin Division 235
J.N. (DING) DARLING FOUNDATION 235
JACK H. BERRYMAN INSTITUTE FOR WILDLIFE DAMAGE MANAGEMENT 235
JACK MINER MIGRATORY BIRD FOUNDATION, INC. 236
JACKSON HOLE CONSERVATION ALLIANCE 236
JACKSON HOLE LAND TRUST 236
JANE GOODALL INSTITUTE, THE 236
JAPAN WILDLIFE RESEARCH CENTER (JWRC) 236
JOHN INSKEEP ENVIRONMENTAL LEARNING CENTER 236
JOHNS HOPKINS UNIVERSITY 374
JOHNS HOPKINS UNIVERSITY, THE 374
JOHNSON STATE COLLEGE 390
KANSAS ACADEMY OF SCIENCE 237
KANSAS ADVISORY COUNCIL FOR ENVIRONMENTAL EDUCATION 237
KANSAS ASSOCIATION FOR CONSERVATION AND ENVIRONMENTAL EDUCATION 237
KANSAS ASSOCIATION OF CONSERVATION DISTRICTS 237
KANSAS B.A.S.S. CHAPTER FEDERATION 237
KANSAS BIOLOGICAL SURVEY 65

KANSAS COOPERATIVE FISH AND WILDLIFE RESEARCH UNIT65
KANSAS DEPARTMENT OF AGRICULTURE 65
KANSAS DEPARTMENT OF WILDLIFE AND PARKS 65
    Operations Office 12, 30, 65, 272
    Region 1 .... 16, 34, 65, 89, 102, 267, 405, 437
    Region 2 .... 17, 34, 65, 89, 102, 267, 437
    Region 3 .... 17, 34, 65, 89, 90, 102, 155, 267, 437
    Region 4 .... 16, 34, 65, 89, 90, 267, 437
    Region 5 .... 65, 89, 90, 267, 438
KANSAS FOREST SERVICE 65
KANSAS GEOLOGICAL SURVEY 66
KANSAS HERPETOLOGICAL SOCIETY 237
KANSAS NATURAL RESOURCE COUNCIL 237
KANSAS ORNITHOLOGICAL SOCIETY 237
KANSAS STATE CONSERVATION COMMISSION 66
KANSAS STATE DEPARTMENT OF HEALTH AND ENVIRONMENT66
KANSAS STATE EXTENSION SERVICES 66
KANSAS STATE UNIVERSITY 371
KANSAS WATER OFFICE 66
KANSAS WILDFLOWER SOCIETY 238
KANSAS WILDLIFE FEDERATION 238
KANSAS WILDSCAPE FOUNDATION 238
KEENE STATE COLLEGE 379
KEEP AMERICA BEAUTIFUL, INC. 238
KEEP FLORIDA BEAUTIFUL, INC. 238
KENTUCKY ACADEMY OF SCIENCE 238
KENTUCKY ASSOCIATION FOR ENVIRONMENTAL EDUCATION (KAEE) 239
KENTUCKY ASSOCIATION OF CONSERVATION DISTRICTS ... 239
KENTUCKY AUDUBON COUNCIL 239
KENTUCKY B.A.S.S. CHAPTER FEDERATION 239
KENTUCKY DEPARTMENT OF AGRICULTURE 66
KENTUCKY DEPARTMENT OF FISH AND WILDLIFE RESOURCES66
KENTUCKY DEPARTMENT OF PARKS 67
KENTUCKY GEOLOGICAL SURVEY 67
KENTUCKY RESOURCES COUNCIL 239
KENTUCKY SOIL AND WATER CONSERVATION COMMISSION 67
KENTUCKY STATE COOPERATIVE EXTENSION SERVICES 67
KENTUCKY STATE NATURE PRESERVES COMMISSION 67
KENTUCKY WOODLAND OWNERS ASSOCIATION 239
KENTUCKY-TENNESSEE SOCIETY OF AMERICAN FORESTERS239
KEYSTONE CENTER, THE 239
KIDS FOR SAVING EARTH WORLDWIDE 239
KODIAK BROWN BEAR TRUST 240
LADY BIRD JOHNSON WILDFLOWER CENTER 240
LAKE ERIE CLEAN-UP COMMITTEE, INC. 240
LAKE MICHIGAN FEDERATION 240
LAKE SUPERIOR GREENS 240
LAKE SUPERIOR STATE UNIVERSITY 376
LAKEHEAD UNIVERSITY 394
LAND BETWEEN THE LAKES ASSOCIATION 240
LAND TRUST ALLIANCE, THE 240
LAND WATCH MONTEREY COUNTY 241
LEAGUE OF CONSERVATION VOTERS 241
LEAGUE OF ENVIRONMENTAL JOURNALISTS 241
LEAGUE OF KENTUCKY SPORTSMEN, INC. 241
LEAGUE OF OHIO SPORTSMEN 241
LEAGUE OF WOMEN VOTERS OF IOWA 241
LEAGUE OF WOMEN VOTERS OF THE U.S. 241
LEAGUE OF WOMEN VOTERS OF WASHINGTON 242
LEAGUE TO SAVE LAKE TAHOE 242
LEARNING FOR ENVIRONMENTAL ACTION PROGRAMME (LEAP) 242
LEE COUNTY PARKS AND RECREATION SERVICES 54
LEGACY INTERNATIONAL 242
LEGAL ENVIRONMENTAL ASSISTANCE FOUNDATION INC. (LEAF) 242
LEWIS AND CLARK COLLEGE 384
LIFE OF THE LAND 242
LIGHTHAWK 243
    Northern Rocky Mountain Field Office 243
    Northwest Field Office 243
    Southern Rocky Mountain Field Office 243
LONG LIVE THE KINGS 243
LOUISIANA ASSOCIATION OF CONSERVATION DISTRICTS ... 243
LOUISIANA AUDUBON COUNCIL 243
LOUISIANA B.A.S.S. CHAPTER FEDERATION 243
LOUISIANA COOPERATIVE FISH AND WILDLIFE RESEARCH UNIT (USDI) 68
LOUISIANA DEPARTMENT OF AGRICULTURE AND FORESTRY68

Office of Forestry 68	MARYLAND-NATIONAL CAPITAL PARK AND PLANNING COMMISSION 72
Office of Soil and Water Conservation, State Soil and Water Conservation Committee 68	MASSACHUSETTS ASSOCIATION OF CONSERVATION COMMISSIONS (MACC) 247
LOUISIANA DEPARTMENT OF NATURAL RESOURCES 68	MASSACHUSETTS ASSOCIATION OF CONSERVATION DISTRICTS 247
Office of Coastal Restoration and Management 68	
Office of Conservation 68, 69	MASSACHUSETTS AUDUBON SOCIETY, INC. 247
Office of Mineral Resources 68	MASSACHUSETTS B.A.S.S. CHAPTER FEDERATION 247
LOUISIANA DEPARTMENT OF WILDLIFE AND FISHERIES 68	MASSACHUSETTS COOPERATIVE FISH AND WILDLIFE RESEARCH UNIT (USDI) 74
LOUISIANA FORESTRY ASSOCIATION 243	
LOUISIANA GEOLOGICAL SURVEY 69	MASSACHUSETTS ENVIRONMENTAL EDUCATION SOCIETY. 248
LOUISIANA SEA GRANT COLLEGE PROGRAM 69	MASSACHUSETTS FORESTRY ASSOCIATION 248
LOUISIANA STATE EXTENSION SERVICES 69	MASSACHUSETTS HIGHWAY DEPARTMENT 74
LOUISIANA STATE UNIVERSITY 373	MASSACHUSETTS TRAPPER'S ASSOCIATION, INC. 248
LOUISIANA TECH UNIVERSITY 373	MATTS (MID-ATLANTIC TURTLE AND TORTOISE SOCIETY, INC.) 248
LOUISIANA WILDLIFE FEDERATION, INC. 243	
LOWER MISSISSIPPI RIVER CONSERVATION COMMITTEE 244	MAX McGRAW WILDLIFE FOUNDATION 248
LVIV REGIONAL INSTITUTE OF EDUCATION 244	MCGILL UNIVERSITY 395
MACBRIDE RAPTOR PROJECT 244	MCNEESE STATE UNIVERSITY 373
MAGIC 244	MERCK FOREST AND FARMLAND CENTER, INC. 248
MAINE ASSOCIATION OF CONSERVATION COMMISSIONS (MACC) 244	MIAMI UNIVERSITY 383
	MICHIGAN ASSOCIATION OF CONSERVATION DISTRICTS 248
MAINE ASSOCIATION OF CONSERVATION DISTRICTS 244	MICHIGAN AUDUBON SOCIETY 249
MAINE ATLANTIC SALMON COMMISSION (formerly Maine Atlantic Salmon Authority) 69	MICHIGAN B.A.S.S. CHAPTER FEDERATION 249
	MICHIGAN DEPARTMENT OF AGRICULTURE 74
MAINE AUDUBON SOCIETY 244	MICHIGAN DEPARTMENT OF COMMUNITY HEALTH 74
MAINE B.A.S.S. CHAPTER FEDERATION 245	MICHIGAN DEPARTMENT OF ENVIRONMENTAL QUALITY 75
MAINE COAST HERITAGE TRUST 245	MICHIGAN DEPARTMENT OF NATURAL RESOURCES 75
MAINE COOPERATIVE FISH AND WILDLIFE RESEARCH UNIT (USDI) 70	MICHIGAN ENVIRONMENTAL COUNCIL 249
	MICHIGAN FORESTS ASSOCIATION 249
MAINE DEPARTMENT OF AGRICULTURE, FOOD, AND RURAL RESOURCES 70	MICHIGAN LAND USE INSTITUTE 249
	MICHIGAN NATURAL AREAS COUNCIL 249
MAINE DEPARTMENT OF CONSERVATION 70	MICHIGAN NATURE ASSOCIATION 249
Maine Forest Service 70	MICHIGAN SEA GRANT COLLEGE PROGRAM 75
Natural Resource Information & Mapping 70	MICHIGAN STATE UNIVERSITY 75, 376
MAINE DEPARTMENT OF ENVIRONMENTAL PROTECTION 70	MICHIGAN STATE UNIVERSITY EXTENSION 75
MAINE DEPARTMENT OF INLAND FISHERIES AND WILDLIFE .. 70	MICHIGAN TECHNOLOGICAL UNIVERSITY 376
MAINE DEPARTMENT OF MARINE RESOURCES 71	MICHIGAN UNITED CONSERVATION CLUBS, INC. 250
MAINE ENVIRONMENTAL EDUCATION ASSOCIATION, INC. 245	MICHIGAN WILDLIFE HABITAT FOUNDATION 250
MAINE SEA GRANT PROGRAM 71	MID-ATLANTIC COUNCIL OF WATERSHED ASSOCIATIONS ... 250
MAINE, SMALL WOODLAND OWNERS ASSOCIATION OF, ... 245	MID-ATLANTIC FISHERY MANAGEMENT COUNCIL 250
MAINE/NEW HAMPSHIRE SEA GRANT PROGRAM 83	MIDDLE TENNESSEE STATE UNIVERSITY 387
MANASOTA-88 245	MIGRATORY BIRD CONSERVATION COMMISSION 8
MANCHESTER COLLEGE 371	MINERAL POLICY CENTER 250
MANITOBA DEPARTMENT OF NATURAL RESOURCES 124	MINISTRY OF ENVIRONMENT, LANDS, AND PARKS 124
Central Region12, 13, 17, 30, 31, 82, 99, 102, 111, 117, 118, 121, 125, 267	MINISTRY OF FISHERIES 124
	MINISTRY OF NATURAL RESOURCES
Eastern Region12, 13, 16, 17, 31, 98, 99, 117, 125, 137, 153, 263, 267	Algonquin Forestry Authority 127
	Corporate Services Division 127
Northeastern Region 12, 125	Field Services Division 99, 127
Northwestern Region 125	Fish and Wildlife Branch 127, 129, 399
Western Region12, 13, 17, 31, 82, 98, 125, 153, 183, 189, 263, 264, 267, 269, 301, 335	Natural Resource Management Division 127
	Northeast Region29, 30, 80, 102, 111, 118, 121, 127, 137, 162, 264, 269, 307
MANITOBA NATURALISTS SOCIETY 245	
MANITOBA WILDLIFE FEDERATION 245	Northwest Region16, 29, 62, 98, 99, 102, 117, 118, 127, 149, 206, 307, 335
MANOMET CENTER FOR CONSERVATION SCIENCES 245	
MARIN CONSERVATION LEAGUE 246	Ontario8, 35, 36, 37, 64, 127, 128, 137, 143, 144, 161, 166, 167, 188, 189, 200, 212, 217, 227, 230, 231, 236, 242, 266, 272, 284, 286, 287, 289, 290, 297, 313, 314, 342, 343, 349, 385, 394, 399, 402, 404, 414
MARINE CONSERVATION BIOLOGY INSTITUTE 246	
MARINE ENVIRONMENTAL RESEARCH INSTITUTE (MERI) 246	
MARINE LABORATORY (FLORIDA) 55	
MARINE MAMMAL CENTER, THE 246	
MARINE MAMMAL COMMISSION 8	Science and Information Resources Division 127
MARINE RESOURCES COMMISSION (VIRGINIA) 113	South Central Region 121, 127, 301
MARINE TECHNOLOGY SOCIETY 246	MINISTRY OF SMALL BUSINESS TOURISM AND CULTURE 124
MARYLAND ASSOCIATION OF CONSERVATION DISTRICTS ... 246	MINISTRY OF THE ENVIRONMENT OF THE CZECH REPUBLIC 37
MARYLAND B.A.S.S. CHAPTER FEDERATION 247	MINNESOTA ASSOCIATION OF SOIL AND WATER CONSERVATION DISTRICTS 250
MARYLAND DEPARTMENT OF AGRICULTURE 71	
Agricultural Commission 71, 72	MINNESOTA B.A.S.S. CHAPTER FEDERATION 250
State Soil Conservation Committee 71, 107	MINNESOTA BOARD OF WATER AND SOIL RESOURCES 75
MARYLAND DEPARTMENT OF NATURAL RESOURCES 72	MINNESOTA CENTER FOR ENVIRONMENTAL ADVOCACY (MCEA) 251
Chesapeake Bay and Watershed Programs 72	
Management Services28, 43, 48, 54, 65, 72, 103, 116, 122, 124, 125	MINNESOTA CONSERVATION FEDERATION 251
	MINNESOTA COOPERATIVE FISH AND WILDLIFE RESEARCH UNIT 76
Public Lands Division 72	
Resource Management Services 72	MINNESOTA DEPARTMENT OF AGRICULTURE 76
MARYLAND FORESTS ASSOCIATION 247	MINNESOTA DEPARTMENT OF NATURAL RESOURCES 76
MARYLAND NATIVE PLANT SOCIETY 247	MINNESOTA ENVIRONMENTAL QUALITY BOARD 76
MARYLAND ORNITHOLOGICAL SOCIETY, INC. 247	MINNESOTA FORESTRY ASSOCIATION 251
MARYLAND SEA GRANT COLLEGE 72	MINNESOTA GEOLOGICAL SURVEY 76
MARYLAND STATE COOPERATIVE EXTENSION 72	MINNESOTA GROUND WATER ASSOCIATION 251

ORGANIZATION NAME INDEX

MINNESOTA HERPETOLOGICAL SOCIETY (James Ford Bell Museum of Natural History) 251
MINNESOTA NATIVE PLANT SOCIETY 251
MINNESOTA ORNITHOLOGISTS' UNION 251
MINNESOTA PARKS AND TRAILS COUNCIL 251
MINNESOTA POLLUTION CONTROL AGENCY 77
    Brainerd, MN 77, 346
    Detroit Lakes, MN 77, 433
    Duluth, MN 77, 424
    Marshall, MN 77
    Rochester, MN 77
MINNESOTA SEA GRANT COLLEGE PROGRAM 77
MINNESOTA STATE EXTENSION SERVICES 77
MINNESOTA WILDLIFE HERITAGE FOUNDATION, INC. 252
MINNESOTA WINGS SOCIETY, INC. 252
MINNESOTA-WISCONSIN BOUNDARY AREA COMMISSION 9
MISSISSIPPI ASSOCIATION OF CONSERVATION DISTRICTS, INC. 252
MISSISSIPPI B.A.S.S. CHAPTER FEDERATION 252
MISSISSIPPI COOPERATIVE FISH AND WILDLIFE RESEARCH UNIT (USDI) 77
MISSISSIPPI DEPARTMENT OF AGRICULTURE AND COMMERCE 78
MISSISSIPPI DEPARTMENT OF ENVIRONMENTAL QUALITY
    Office of Land and Water Resources 78
    Office of Pollution Control 78
MISSISSIPPI DEPARTMENT OF WILDLIFE, FISHERIES, AND PARKS 78
MISSISSIPPI FORESTRY COMMISSION 78
MISSISSIPPI INTERSTATE COOPERATIVE RESOURCE ASSOCIATION 252
MISSISSIPPI NATIVE PLANT SOCIETY 252
MISSISSIPPI RIVER BASIN ALLIANCE 252
MISSISSIPPI SEA GRANT PROGRAM 78
MISSISSIPPI SOIL AND WATER CONSERVATION COMMISSION 78
MISSISSIPPI STATE DEPARTMENT OF HEALTH 79
MISSISSIPPI STATE EXTENSION SERVICES 79
MISSISSIPPI STATE UNIVERSITY 378
MISSISSIPPI WILDLIFE FEDERATION 253
MISSOURI ASSOCIATION OF SOIL AND WATER CONSERVATION DISTRICTS 253
MISSOURI AUDUBON COUNCIL 253
MISSOURI B.A.S.S. CHAPTER FEDERATION 253
MISSOURI COOPERATIVE FISH AND WILDLIFE RESEARCH UNIT (USDI) 79
MISSOURI DEPARTMENT OF AGRICULTURE 79
MISSOURI DEPARTMENT OF CONSERVATION 79
    Administrative Services Division 44, 46, 47, 64, 65, 66, 79, 86, 87, 99, 105, 107
    Design and Development Division 79
    Fisheries Division 47, 50, 69, 79, 84, 105, 114
    Forestry Division 41, 50, 64, 79, 81, 107
    Human Resources Section 79
    Natural History Section 79
    Outreach and Education Division 79
    Protection Division 79, 117
    Wildlife Division 51, 65, 69, 79, 84, 87, 97, 106, 115, 123, 144, 399
MISSOURI DEPARTMENT OF NATURAL RESOURCES 79
MISSOURI FOREST PRODUCTS ASSOCIATION 253
MISSOURI NATIVE PLANT SOCIETY 253
MISSOURI PRAIRIE FOUNDATION 253
MISSOURI STATE EXTENSION SERVICES 80
MIT SEA GRANT COLLEGE PROGRAM 74
MONITOR INTERNATIONAL 253
MONO LAKE COMMITTEE 254
MONTANA ASSOCIATION OF CONSERVATION DISTRICTS 254
MONTANA AUDUBON 254
MONTANA B.A.S.S. CHAPTER FEDERATION 254
MONTANA BUREAU OF MINES AND GEOLOGY 80
MONTANA COOPERATIVE FISHERY RESEARCH UNIT (USDI) .. 80
MONTANA COOPERATIVE WILDLIFE RESEARCH UNIT (USGS/BRD) 80
MONTANA DEPARTMENT OF AGRICULTURE 80
MONTANA DEPARTMENT OF FISH, WILDLIFE, AND PARKS 80
MONTANA DEPARTMENT OF NATURAL RESOURCES AND CONSERVATION 81
MONTANA ENVIRONMENTAL INFORMATION CENTER 254
MONTANA ENVIRONMENTAL QUALITY COUNCIL 81
MONTANA FOREST OWNERS ASSOCIATION 254
MONTANA LAND RELIANCE 254
MONTANA NATURAL HERITAGE PROGRAM 81
MONTANA STATE EXTENSION SERVICES 81
MONTANA STATE UNIVERSITY 378
MONTANA WILDERNESS ASSOCIATION 255
MONTANA WILDLIFE FEDERATION 255
MONTCLAIR STATE UNIVERSITY 380
MOREHEAD STATE UNIVERSITY 372
MOTE MARINE LABORATORY 255
MOUNT GRACE LAND CONSERVATION TRUST 255
MOUNT SHASTA AREA AUDUBON SOCIETY 255
MOUNTAIN CONSERVATION TRUST OF GEORGIA, INC. 255
MOUNTAIN LION FOUNDATION 255
MOUNTAINEERS, THE (Conservation Division) 256
MULE DEER FOUNDATION, THE 256
MURRAY STATE UNIVERSITY 372
MUSASHI INSTITUTE OF TECHNOLOGY 395
MUSKIES, INC. 256
NATIONAL 4-H COUNCIL 256
NATIONAL ARBOR DAY FOUNDATION 256
NATIONAL ASSOCIATION FOR INTERPRETATION 256
NATIONAL ASSOCIATION OF BIOLOGY TEACHERS 257
NATIONAL ASSOCIATION OF CONSERVATION DISTRICTS 257
    League City Office 257
NATIONAL ASSOCIATION OF ENVIRONMENTAL PROFESSIONALS, THE (National Office) 257
NATIONAL ASSOCIATION OF RECREATION RESOURCE PLANNERS 257
NATIONAL ASSOCIATION OF SERVICE AND CONSERVATION CORPS (NASCC) 258
NATIONAL ASSOCIATION OF STATE DEPARTMENTS OF AGRICULTURE 258
NATIONAL ASSOCIATION OF STATE FORESTERS 258
NATIONAL ASSOCIATION OF STATE OUTDOOR RECREATION LIAISON OFFICERS 258
NATIONAL ASSOCIATION OF STATE PARK DIRECTORS 258
NATIONAL ASSOCIATION OF UNIVERSITY FISHERIES AND WILDLIFE PROGRAMS 259
NATIONAL AUDUBON SOCIETY 259
    Everglades Campaign Office 259
    Project Puffin 259
    Scully Science Center 259
    Tavernier Science Center 259
    Washington, D.C. Office 259, 271
NATIONAL AUDUBON SOCIETY, LIVING OCEANS PROGRAM 259
NATIONAL AVIARY 259
NATIONAL BIRD-FEEDING SOCIETY 259
NATIONAL BOATING FEDERATION 260
NATIONAL COALITION FOR MARINE CONSERVATION 260
NATIONAL COUNCIL FOR GEOGRAPHIC EDUCATION 260
NATIONAL COUNCIL OF STATE GARDEN CLUBS, INC. 260
NATIONAL EDUCATION ASSOCIATION 260
NATIONAL ENVIRONMENTAL HEALTH ASSOCIATION 260
NATIONAL FARMERS UNION 261
NATIONAL FFA ORGANIZATION 261
NATIONAL FIELD ARCHERY ASSOCIATION 261
NATIONAL FISH AND WILDLIFE FOUNDATION 261
NATIONAL FLYWAY COUNCIL 261
    Atlantic Flyway Office 261
    Central Flyway Office 261
    Mississippi Flyway Office 261
NATIONAL FOREST FOUNDATION 261
NATIONAL FORESTRY ASSOCIATION 262
NATIONAL FOUNDATION TO PROTECT AMERICA'S EAGLES (Save The Eagle) 262
NATIONAL GARDENING ASSOCIATION 262
NATIONAL GEOGRAPHIC SOCIETY 262
NATIONAL GRANGE, THE 262
NATIONAL GROUND WATER ASSOCIATION, THE 262
NATIONAL HUNTERS ASSOCIATION, INC. 262
NATIONAL MILITARY FISH AND WILDLIFE ASSOCIATION ... 263
NATIONAL NETWORK OF FOREST PRACTITIONERS 263
NATIONAL ORGANIZATION FOR RIVERS (NORS) 263
NATIONAL PARK FOUNDATION 263
NATIONAL PARK TRUST 263
NATIONAL PARKS AND CONSERVATION ASSOCIATION (NPCA) 263
    Alaska Regional Office 30, 264
    Heartland Regional Office 264
    Northeast Regional Office 30, 80, 264
    Pacific Regional Office 30, 264
    Rocky Mountain Regional Office 264
    Southeast Regional Office 30, 80, 264

Southwest Regional Office 30, 80, 117, 149, 153, 264
NATIONAL RECREATION AND PARK ASSOCIATION................264
NATIONAL RESEARCH COUNCIL 264
NATIONAL RIFLE ASSOCIATION OF AMERICA 264
NATIONAL SCIENCE FOUNDATION 33
NATIONAL SCIENCE TEACHERS ASSOCIATION 265
NATIONAL SHOOTING SPORTS FOUNDATION, INC. 265
NATIONAL SPELEOLOGICAL SOCIETY, INC. 265
NATIONAL TRANSPORTATION SAFETY BOARD 33
NATIONAL TRAPPERS ASSOCIATION, INC. 265
NATIONAL TREE TRUST 265
NATIONAL TRUST FOR HISTORIC PRESERVATION 265
    Mid Atlantic 266
    Midwest Office 15, 182, 234, 252, 266, 313
    Mountains and Plains 266, 268
    Northeast Office 266, 313
    Southern Office 266
    Texas and New Mexico Offices 266
    Western5, 6, 12, 13, 17, 28, 31, 35, 72, 82, 83, 98, 125, 131, 136,
        141, 153, 156, 159, 162, 178, 183, 188, 189, 203, 216, 238, 258,
        263, 264, 266, 267, 268, 269, 272, 290, 294, 301, 307, 308, 320,
        335, 343, 344, 350, 385, 393, 417, 435
NATIONAL WATER RESOURCES ASSOCIATION 266
NATIONAL WATERSHED COALITION 266
NATIONAL WATERWAYS CONFERENCE INC. 266
NATIONAL WHISTLEBLOWER CENTER 266
NATIONAL WILD TURKEY FEDERATION, CANADA, INC., THE.266
NATIONAL WILD TURKEY FEDERATION, INC., THE 267
NATIONAL WILDLIFE FEDERATION 267, 268
    Alaska Office (AK, HI)...267
    Everglades Project Office 267
    Gulf States Natural Resource Center (AR, LA, MS, TX).........268
    Northeast Natural Resource Center (CT, MA, ME, NH, RI, VT)268
    Northern Rockies Project Office (ID, MT, WY).......................268
    Office of Federal and International Affairs.............................268
    Rocky Mountain Natural Resource Center (AZ, CO, IA, KS, MO,
        NE, NM, UT) 268
    Southeastern Natural Resource Center (AL, FL, GA, NC, SC, TN,
        VI) 268
NATIONAL WILDLIFE FEDERATION ENDOWMENT, INC. 268
NATIONAL WILDLIFE PRODUCTIONS, INC. 268
NATIONAL WILDLIFE REFUGE ASSOCIATION 269
NATIONAL WILDLIFE REHABILITATORS ASSOCIATION 269
NATIONAL WOODLAND OWNERS ASSOCIATION 269
NATIVE AMERICAN FISH AND WILDLIFE SOCIETY (NAFWS)...269
NATIVE PLANT SOCIETY OF NORTHEASTERN OHIO.............269
NATIVE PLANT SOCIETY OF OREGON 269
NATIVE PLANT SOCIETY OF TEXAS 270
NATIVE PRAIRIES ASSOCIATION OF TEXAS 270
NATURAL AND SCENIC RIVERS COMMISSION (ARKANSAS)....43
NATURAL AREAS ASSOCIATION 270
NATURAL HERITAGE COMMISSION (ARKANSAS)......................44
NATURAL HISTORY SOCIETY OF MARYLAND, INC., THE 270
NATURAL LAND INSTITUTE 270
NATURAL LANDS TRUST, INC. 271
NATURAL RESOURCES AND ENVIRONMENTAL PROTECTION
    CABINET..67
    Department for Environmental Protection 67
    Department for Natural Resources..67
    Department for Surface Mining Reclamation and Enforcement68
    Environmental Quality Commission 68
    Nature Preserves Commission 62, 68, 415
NATURAL RESOURCES CANADA, CANADIAN FOREST SERVICE37
NATURAL RESOURCES COUNCIL OF AMERICA 271
NATURAL RESOURCES COUNCIL OF MAINE 271
NATURAL RESOURCES DEFENSE COUNCIL, INC. 271
    Los Angeles, California Office 271
    San Francisco, California Office 271
    Washington, D.C. Office 259, 271
NATURAL RESOURCES INFORMATION COUNCIL 271
NATURAL SCIENCE FOR YOUTH FOUNDATION......................271
NATURE CONSERVANCY OF CANADA, THE.............................272
NATURE CONSERVANCY, THE 272, 273, 274
    Eastern Division Office 272
    Great Plains Division 272
    Mid-Atlantic Division Office 272
    Midwest Division Office 272
    Northeast Division Office 272
    Northwest & Hawaii Division Office 272
    Rocky Mountain Division Office 272

    South Central Division Office 272
    Southeast Division Office...272
    Western Division Office..272
NATURE CONSERVANCY, THE, ALABAMA CHAPTER.............272
NATURE CONSERVANCY, THE, ALASKA CHAPTER................272
NATURE CONSERVANCY, THE, ARIZONA CHAPTER..............272
NATURE CONSERVANCY, THE, ARKANSAS CHAPTER 273
NATURE CONSERVANCY, THE, ASIA/PACIFIC PROGRAM......273
NATURE CONSERVANCY, THE, CALIFORNIA CHAPTER 273
NATURE CONSERVANCY, THE, COLORADO CHAPTER 273
NATURE CONSERVANCY, THE, CONNECTICUT CHAPTER ...273
NATURE CONSERVANCY, THE, DELAWARE CHAPTER 273
NATURE CONSERVANCY, THE, EASTERN NEW YORK CHAPTER
   273
NATURE CONSERVANCY, THE, FLORIDA CHAPTER 273
NATURE CONSERVANCY, THE, GEORGIA CHAPTER 273
NATURE CONSERVANCY, THE, HAWAII CHAPTER 273
NATURE CONSERVANCY, THE, IDAHO CHAPTER 273
NATURE CONSERVANCY, THE, ILLINOIS CHAPTER 273
NATURE CONSERVANCY, THE, INDIANA CHAPTER 273
NATURE CONSERVANCY, THE, IOWA CHAPTER 273
NATURE CONSERVANCY, THE, KANSAS CHAPTER 273
NATURE CONSERVANCY, THE, KENTUCKY CHAPTER 273
NATURE CONSERVANCY, THE, LATIN AMERICA AND CARRIBBEAN
    DIVISION..273
NATURE CONSERVANCY, THE, LOUISIANA CHAPTER...........273
NATURE CONSERVANCY, THE, MAINE CHAPTER 273
NATURE CONSERVANCY, THE, MARYLAND/D.C. CHAPTER ..273
NATURE CONSERVANCY, THE, MASSACHUSETTS CHAPTER273
NATURE CONSERVANCY, THE, MICHIGAN CHAPTER 273
NATURE CONSERVANCY, THE, MINNESOTA CHAPTER 273
NATURE CONSERVANCY, THE, MISSISSIPPI CHAPTER 273
NATURE CONSERVANCY, THE, MISSOURI CHAPTER 273
NATURE CONSERVANCY, THE, MONTANA CHAPTER............273
NATURE CONSERVANCY, THE, NEBRASKA CHAPTER 273
NATURE CONSERVANCY, THE, NEVADA CHAPTER 273
NATURE CONSERVANCY, THE, NEW HAMPSHIRE CHAPTER 273
NATURE CONSERVANCY, THE, NEW JERSEY CHAPTER 274
NATURE CONSERVANCY, THE, NEW MEXICO CHAPTER 274
NATURE CONSERVANCY, THE, NEW YORK ADIRONDACK
    CHAPTER 274
NATURE CONSERVANCY, THE, NEW YORK CENTRAL/WESTERN
    CHAPTER 274
NATURE CONSERVANCY, THE, NEW YORK CITY CHAPTER..274
NATURE CONSERVANCY, THE, NEW YORK LONG ISLAND
    CHAPTER 274
NATURE CONSERVANCY, THE, NEW YORK LOWER HUDSON
    CHAPTER 274
NATURE CONSERVANCY, THE, NEW YORK SOUTH
    FORK/SHELTER ISLAND CHAPTER 274
NATURE CONSERVANCY, THE, NORTH CAROLINA CHAPTER274
NATURE CONSERVANCY, THE, NORTH DAKOTA CHAPTER ..274
NATURE CONSERVANCY, THE, OKLAHOMA CHAPTER 274
NATURE CONSERVANCY, THE, OREGON CHAPTER 274
NATURE CONSERVANCY, THE, PENNSYLVANIA CHAPTER ...274
NATURE CONSERVANCY, THE, RHODE ISLAND CHAPTER....274
NATURE CONSERVANCY, THE, SOUTH CAROLINA CHAPTER274
NATURE CONSERVANCY, THE, SOUTH DAKOTA CHAPTER ..274
NATURE CONSERVANCY, THE, TENNESSEE CHAPTER 274
NATURE CONSERVANCY, THE, TEXAS CHAPTER 274
NATURE CONSERVANCY, THE, UTAH CHAPTER 274
NATURE CONSERVANCY, THE, VERMONT CHAPTER 274
NATURE CONSERVANCY, THE, VIRGIN ISLANDS CHAPTER..274
NATURE CONSERVANCY, THE, VIRGINIA CHAPTER 274
NATURE CONSERVANCY, THE, WASHINGTON CHAPTER 274
NATURE CONSERVANCY, THE, WEST VIRGINIA CHAPTER ...274
NATURE CONSERVANCY, THE, WISCONSIN CHAPTER 274
NATURE CONSERVANCY, THE, WYOMING CHAPTER............274
NATURE CONSERVATION SOCIETY OF JAPAN, THE (NACS-J)274
NATURE SASKATCHEWAN 275
NEBRASKA ASSOCIATION OF RESOURCE DISTRICTS 275
NEBRASKA AUDUBON COUNCIL 275
NEBRASKA B.A.S.S. CHAPTER FEDERATION 275
NEBRASKA DEPARTMENT OF AGRICULTURE 81
NEBRASKA DEPARTMENT OF ENVIRONMENTAL QUALITY......81
NEBRASKA DEPARTMENT OF WATER RESOURCES................81
NEBRASKA GAME AND PARKS COMMISSION 82
NEBRASKA NATURAL RESOURCES COMMISSION 82
NEBRASKA ORNITHOLOGISTS' UNION, INC. (University of Nebraska
    State Museum) 275

ORGANIZATION NAME INDEX

NEBRASKA STATE EXTENSION SERVICES 82
NEBRASKA WILDLIFE FEDERATION, INC. 275
NEVADA ASSOCIATION OF CONSERVATION DISTRICTS 275
NEVADA BUREAU OF MINES AND GEOLOGY 82
NEVADA DEPARTMENT OF AGRICULTURE 82
NEVADA DEPARTMENT OF CONSERVATION AND NATURAL
 RESOURCES 82
NEVADA DIVISION OF WILDLIFE 83
NEVADA NATURAL HERITAGE PROGRAM 83
NEVADA WILDLIFE FEDERATION 276
NEVIS HISTORICAL AND CONSERVATION SOCIETY 276
NEW BRUNSWICK DEPARTMENT OF NATURAL RESOURCES AND
 ENERGY 125
NEW BRUNSWICK WILDLIFE FEDERATION 276
NEW ENGLAND ASSOCIATION OF ENVIRONMENTAL BIOLOGISTS
 (NEAEB)... 276
NEW ENGLAND COALITION FOR SUSTAINABLE POPULATION
 (NECSP) 276
NEW ENGLAND INTERSTATE WATER POLLUTION CONTROL
 COMMISSION 9
NEW ENGLAND NATURAL RESOURCES CENTER 276
NEW ENGLAND WILD FLOWER SOCIETY, INC. 276
NEW HAMPSHIRE ASSOCIATION OF CONSERVATION
 COMMISSIONS 276
NEW HAMPSHIRE ASSOCIATION OF CONSERVATION DISTRICTS
 277
NEW HAMPSHIRE B.A.S.S. CHAPTER FEDERATION 277
NEW HAMPSHIRE DEPARTMENT OF AGRICULTURE, MARKETS,
 AND FOOD 83
 State Conservation Committee 83
NEW HAMPSHIRE DEPARTMENT OF ENVIRONMENTAL SERVICES
 84
NEW HAMPSHIRE FISH AND GAME DEPARTMENT 84
NEW HAMPSHIRE LAKES ASSOCIATION 277
NEW HAMPSHIRE NATURAL HERITAGE INVENTORY 84
NEW HAMPSHIRE TIMBERLAND OWNERS ASSOCIATION 277
NEW HAMPSHIRE WILDLIFE FEDERATION 277
NEW JERSEY AGRICULTURAL SOCIETY 277
NEW JERSEY ASSOCIATION OF CONSERVATION DISTRICTS277
NEW JERSEY AUDUBON SOCIETY 277
NEW JERSEY B.A.S.S. CHAPTER FEDERATION 278
NEW JERSEY CONSERVATION FOUNDATION 278
NEW JERSEY DEPARTMENT OF AGRICULTURE 84
 State Soil and Conservation Committee 84
NEW JERSEY DEPARTMENT OF ENVIRONMENTAL PROTECTION
 85
 Division of Fish, Game, and Wildlife...................................... 85
 Division of Parks and Forestry.. 85
 Division of Publicly Funded Site Remediation...................... 85
 Division of Solid and Hazardous Waste 85
 Geological Survey27, 30, 38, 42, 44, 64, 68, 70, 76, 77, 79, 85, 88,
   90, 94, 105, 106, 117, 237, 375
 Green Acres and Recreation Program 85
NEW JERSEY ENVIRONMENTAL LOBBY 278
NEW JERSEY FORESTRY ASSOCIATION 278
NEW JERSEY PINELANDS COMMISSION 85
NEW JERSEY SEA GRANT COLLEGE PROGRAM 86
NEW JERSEY STATE EXTENSION SERVICES 86
NEW MEXICO ASSOCIATION OF CONSERVATION DISTRICTS278
NEW MEXICO B.A.S.S. CHAPTER FEDERATION 278
NEW MEXICO BUREAU OF MINES AND MINERAL RESOURCES86
 Geological Information Center Library 87
NEW MEXICO COOPERATIVE FISH AND WILDLIFE RESEARCH
 UNIT 87
NEW MEXICO DEPARTMENT OF AGRICULTURE 87
NEW MEXICO DEPARTMENT OF GAME AND FISH 87
 Albuquerque NM Office 87
 Las Cruces NM Office 87
 Raton NM Office 87
 Roswell NM Office 87
NEW MEXICO ENVIRONMENT DEPARTMENT 87
NEW MEXICO ENVIRONMENTAL LAW CENTER 278
NEW MEXICO SOIL AND WATER CONSERVATION COMMISSION88
NEW MEXICO STATE EXTENSION SERVICES 88
NEW MEXICO STATE UNIVERSITY 380
NEW MEXICO WILDLIFE FEDERATION 279
NEW YORK ASSOCIATION OF CONSERVATION DISTRICTS, INC.
 279
NEW YORK B.A.S.S. CHAPTER FEDERATION 279
NEW YORK COOPERATIVE FISH AND WILDLIFE RESEARCH UNIT
 88
NEW YORK DEPARTMENT OF AGRICULTURE AND MARKETS 88
 State Soil and Water Conservation Committee 89
NEW YORK DEPARTMENT OF ENVIRONMENTAL CONSERVATION
 89
 Division of Air Resources... 89
 Division of Environmental Enforcement................................. 89
 Division of Environmental Permits 89
 Division of Environmental Remediation 89
 Division of Fish, Wildlife and Marine Resources 89, 284
 Division of Forest Protection & Fire Management 89
 Division of Information Services 89
 Division of Lands and Forests 89
 Division of Law Enforcement 29, 53, 54, 63, 66, 89
 Division of Legal Affairs 89
 Division of Management and Budget 89
 Division of Mineral Resources 89, 115
 Division of Operations 89
 Division of Public Affairs and Education 89
 Division of Solid & Hazardous Materials 89
 Division of Water49, 52, 53, 58, 63, 67, 76, 77, 82, 83, 89, 91, 93,
   94, 110
 Press Office 89, 100
 Regional Directors 89
NEW YORK DEPARTMENT OF HEALTH 89
NEW YORK FOREST OWNERS ASSOCIATION, INC. 279
NEW YORK GEOLOGICAL SURVEY AND STATE MUSEUM 90
NEW YORK PUBLIC INTEREST RESEARCH GROUP (NYPIRG 279
NEW YORK SEA GRANT 90
NEW YORK STATE COOPERATIVE EXTENSION 90
NEW YORK STATE FISH AND WILDLIFE MANAGEMENT BOARD90
 Region 3 .... 17, 34, 65, 89, 90, 102, 155, 267, 437
 Region 4 .... 16, 34, 65, 89, 90, 267, 437
 Region 5 .... 65, 89, 90, 267, 438
 Region 6 .... 89, 90, 267, 438
 Region 7 .... 89, 90, 267, 438
 Region 8 .... 17, 89, 91, 267
 Region 9 .... 89, 91, 267
NEW YORK STATE OFFICE OF PARKS, RECREATION AND
 HISTORIC PRESERVATION 91
NEW YORK TURTLE AND TORTOISE SOCIETY 279
NEW YORK-NEW JERSEY TRAIL CONFERENCE INC. 279
NEWFOUNDLAND DEPARTMENT OF FOREST RESOURCES AND
 AGRIFOODS 125
 Ecosystem Health Division 125
 Inland Fish and Wildlife Division 125
 Legislation and Compliance Division 125
 Regional Offices 125
NEWFOUNDLAND LABRADOR WILDLIFE FEDERATION 279
NIAGARA ESCARPMENT COMMISSION 128
NIPPON ECOLOGY NETWORK 280
NORTH CAROLINA DEPARTMENT OF ENVIRONMENT AND
 NATURAL RESOURCES 91
NORTH AMERICAN ASSOCIATION FOR ENVIRONMENTAL
 EDUCATION 280
 Conference, Publications and Membership Office 280
NORTH AMERICAN BENTHOLOGICAL SOCIETY 280
NORTH AMERICAN BLUEBIRD SOCIETY 280
NORTH AMERICAN BUTTERFLY ASSOCIATION 280
NORTH AMERICAN COALITION ON RELIGION AND ECOLOGY
 (NACRE) 280
NORTH AMERICAN CRANE WORKING GROUP 281
NORTH AMERICAN FALCONERS ASSOCIATION 281
NORTH AMERICAN FISHING CLUB 281
NORTH AMERICAN GAMEBIRD ASSOCIATION, INC. 281
NORTH AMERICAN LOON FUND 281
NORTH AMERICAN NATIVE FISHES ASSOCIATION 281
NORTH AMERICAN WETLANDS CONSERVATION COUNCIL 9
NORTH AMERICAN WILDLIFE PARK FOUNDATION, INC. 281
NORTH AMERICAN WOLF SOCIETY 282
NORTH ATLANTIC SALMON CONSERVATION ORGANIZATION282
NORTH CAROLINA ASSOCIATION OF SOIL AND WATER
 CONSERVATION DISTRICTS 282
NORTH CAROLINA B.A.S.S. CHAPTER FEDERATION 282
NORTH CAROLINA BEACH BUGGY ASSOCIATION, INC. 282
NORTH CAROLINA COALITION, INC. 282
NORTH CAROLINA COASTAL FEDERATION, INC. 282
NORTH CAROLINA COOPERATIVE EXTENSION SERVICE 91

ORGANIZATION NAME INDEX

NORTH CAROLINA COOPERATIVE FISH AND WILDLIFE RESEARCH UNIT (USDI) 92
NORTH CAROLINA DEPARTMENT OF AGRICULTURE 92
NORTH CAROLINA DEPARTMENT OF ENVIRONMENT AND NATURAL RESOURCES
    State Soil and Water Conservation Commission 92
NORTH CAROLINA FORESTRY ASSOCIATION 282
NORTH CAROLINA HERPETOLOGICAL SOCIETY 283
NORTH CAROLINA RECREATION AND PARK SOCIETY, INC. .. 283
NORTH CAROLINA SEA GRANT PROGRAM 92
NORTH CAROLINA STATE UNIVERSITY 382
NORTH CAROLINA WILD FLOWER PRESERVATION SOCIETY 283
NORTH CAROLINA WILDLIFE FEDERATION 283
NORTH CAROLINA WILDLIFE RESOURCES COMMISSION 92
NORTH CASCADES CONSERVATION COUNCIL 283
NORTH DAKOTA ASSOCIATION OF SOIL CONSERVATION DISTRICTS 283
NORTH DAKOTA DEPARTMENT OF AGRICULTURE 93
NORTH DAKOTA DEPARTMENT OF HEALTH 93
NORTH DAKOTA GAME AND FISH DEPARTMENT 93
NORTH DAKOTA GEOLOGICAL SURVEY 93
NORTH DAKOTA NATURAL SCIENCE SOCIETY 284
NORTH DAKOTA PARKS AND RECREATION DEPARTMENT 93
NORTH DAKOTA STATE EXTENSION SERVICE 93
NORTH DAKOTA STATE FOREST SERVICE 93
NORTH DAKOTA STATE SOIL CONSERVATION COMMITTEE ... 93
NORTH DAKOTA STATE UNIVERSITY 383
NORTH DAKOTA WATER COMMISSION 93
NORTH DAKOTA WILDLIFE FEDERATION, INC. 284
NORTH PACIFIC ANADROMOUS FISH COMMISSION 9
NORTHCOAST ENVIRONMENTAL CENTER 284
NORTHEAST ASSOCIATION OF FISH AND WILDLIFE RESOURCE AGENCIES 284
NORTHEAST ATLANTIC FISHERIES COMMISSION 9
NORTHEAST CONSERVATION LAW ENFORCEMENT CHIEFS' ASSOCIATION (CLECA) 284
NORTHEAST SUSTAINABLE ENERGY ASSOCIATION 284
NORTHEAST WILDLIFE ADMINISTRATORS ASSOCIATION 284
NORTHEASTERN FOREST FIRE PROTECTION COMMISSION 9
NORTHEASTERN UNIVERSITY 375
NORTHERN ALASKA ENVIRONMENTAL CENTER 285
NORTHERN ARIZONA UNIVERSITY 362
NORTHERN MICHIGAN UNIVERSITY 376
NORTHERN PLAINS RESOURCE COUNCIL 285
NORTHERN VIRGINIA REGIONAL PARK AUTHORITY 113
NORTHLAND COLLEGE 392
NORTHWEST ATLANTIC FISHERIES ORGANIZATION (NAFO) . 285
NORTHWEST COALITION FOR ALTERNATIVES TO PESTICIDES 285
NORTHWEST ECOSYSTEM ALLIANCE 285
NORTHWEST ENVIRONMENT WATCH 285
NORTHWEST INTERPRETIVE ASSOCIATION 286
NORTHWEST RESOURCE INFORMATION CENTER 286
NORTHWESTERN STATE UNIVERSITY OF LOUISIANA 373
NOVA SCOTIA DEPARTMENT OF FISHERIES AND AQUACULTURE 126
NOVA SCOTIA DEPARTMENT OF NATURAL RESOURCES 126
    Corporate Service Unit 126
    Land Services Branch 126
    Regional Services Branch 126
    Renewable Resources Branch 126
NOVA SCOTIA FEDERATION OF ANGLERS AND HUNTERS 286
NOVA SCOTIA FORESTRY ASSOCIATION 286
NUCLEAR REGULATORY COMMISSION 33
NW ENERGY COALITION 286
OBERLIN COLLEGE 384
OCEAN VOICE INTERNATIONAL 286
OFFICE OF ENERGY EFFICIENCY AND ENVIRONMENT 91
OFFICE OF STATE PARKS, DEPARTMENT OF CULTURE, RECREATION, AND TOURISM 69
OHIO ACADEMY OF SCIENCE, THE 286
OHIO ALLIANCE FOR THE ENVIRONMENT 287
OHIO AUDUBON COUNCIL, INC. 287
OHIO B.A.S.S. CHAPTER FEDERATION 287
OHIO BIOLOGICAL SURVEY 287
OHIO DEPARTMENT OF AGRICULTURE 94
OHIO DEPARTMENT OF NATURAL RESOURCES 94
OHIO ENERGY PROJECT 287
OHIO ENVIRONMENTAL COUNCIL, INC. 287
OHIO ENVIRONMENTAL PROTECTION AGENCY 94
OHIO FEDERATION OF SOIL AND WATER CONSERVATION DISTRICTS 288
OHIO FORESTRY ASSOCIATION, INC., THE 288
OHIO NATIVE PLANT SOCIETY 288
OHIO OFFICE OF ENERGY EFFICIENCY 94
OHIO RIVER VALLEY WATER SANITATION COMMISSION 9
OHIO SEA GRANT COLLEGE PROGRAM 95
OHIO STATE EXTENSION SERVICES 95
OHIO STATE UNIVERSITY 384
OKLAHOMA ACADEMY OF SCIENCE 288
OKLAHOMA ASSOCIATION OF CONSERVATION DISTRICTS .. 288
OKLAHOMA AUDUBON COUNCIL 288
OKLAHOMA B.A.S.S. CHAPTER FEDERATION 288
OKLAHOMA BIOLOGICAL SURVEY 95
OKLAHOMA COOPERATIVE FISH AND WILDLIFE RESEARCH UNIT (USDI) 95
OKLAHOMA DEPARTMENT OF ENVIRONMENTAL QUALITY 95
OKLAHOMA GEOLOGICAL SURVEY 96
OKLAHOMA NATIVE PLANT SOCIETY 289
OKLAHOMA ORNITHOLOGICAL SOCIETY 289
OKLAHOMA STATE BOARD OF AGRICULTURE 96
OKLAHOMA STATE CONSERVATION COMMISSION 96
OKLAHOMA STATE EXTENSION SERVICES 96
OKLAHOMA STATE UNIVERSITY 384
OKLAHOMA TOURISM AND RECREATION DEPARTMENT 96
OKLAHOMA WATER RESOURCES BOARD 97
OKLAHOMA WILDLIFE FEDERATION 289
OKLAHOMA WOODLAND OWNERS ASSOCIATION 289
OLYMPIC PARK ASSOCIATES 289
OLYMPIC PARK INSTITUTE 289
ONTARIO FEDERATION OF ANGLERS AND HUNTERS, INC., THE 289
ONTARIO FORESTRY ASSOCIATION 289
OPENLANDS PROJECT 290
OREGON ASSOCIATION OF CONSERVATION DISTRICTS 290
OREGON B.A.S.S. CHAPTER FEDERATION 290
OREGON COOPERATIVE FISH AND WILDLIFE RESEARCH UNIT (USDI) 97
OREGON COOPERATIVE FISH AND WILDLIFE RESEARCH UNIT (USDI) 97
OREGON DEPARTMENT OF AGRICULTURE 97
OREGON DEPARTMENT OF ENVIRONMENTAL QUALITY (DEQ) 98
OREGON DEPARTMENT OF FORESTRY 98
OREGON ENVIRONMENTAL COUNCIL 290
OREGON FISH AND WILDLIFE DIVISION/DEPARTMENT OF STATE POLICE 98
OREGON NATURAL RESOURCES COUNCIL 290
OREGON PARKS AND RECREATION DEPARTMENT 98
OREGON SEA GRANT PROGRAM 98
OREGON SMALL WOODLANDS ASSOCIATION 290
OREGON SOCIETY OF AMERICAN FORESTERS 291
OREGON STATE EXTENSION SERVICES 99
OREGON STATE UNIVERSITY 384
OREGON TROUT, INC. 291
OREGON WATER RESOURCES DEPARTMENT 99
    Water Resources Commission 99, 105
OREGON WILDLIFE HERITAGE FOUNDATION 291
ORGANIZATION FOR BAT CONSERVATION 291
ORGANIZATION OF WILDLIFE PLANNERS 291
ORNITHOLOGICAL COUNCIL 291
OUTDOOR CIRCLE, THE 291
OUTDOOR RECREATION COUNCIL OF BRITISH COLUMBIA .. 292
OUTDOOR WRITERS ASSOCIATION OF AMERICA, INC. 292
OZARK SOCIETY, THE 292
OZARKS RESOURCE CENTER 292
OZONE ACTION 292
PACIFIC BASIN ASSOCIATION OF SOIL AND WATER CONSERVATION DISTRICTS 292
PACIFIC FISHERY MANAGEMENT COUNCIL 292
PACIFIC INSTITUTE FOR STUDIES IN DEVELOPMENT, ENVIRONMENT, AND SECURITY 293
PACIFIC NORTHWEST TRAIL ASSOCIATION 293
PACIFIC RIVERS COUNCIL 293
PACIFIC SALMON COMMISSION 9
PACIFIC SEABIRD GROUP 293
PACIFIC STATES MARINE FISHERIES COMMISSION 9
PACIFIC WHALE FOUNDATION 293
PANOS INSTITUTE, THE 293
PARTNERS IN PARKS 293
PAWS/OLYMPIC WILDLIFE RESCUE 294

ORGANIZATION NAME INDEX

PEACE CORPS 34
PENNSYLVANIA ASSOCIATION OF CONSERVATION DISTRICT
  DIRECTORS, INC. 294
PENNSYLVANIA AUDUBON SOCIETY 294
PENNSYLVANIA B.A.S.S. CHAPTER FEDERATION, INC. 294
PENNSYLVANIA CITIZENS ADVISORY COUNCIL TO DEPARTMENT
  OF ENVIRONMENTAL PROTECTION 294
PENNSYLVANIA COOPERATIVE FISH AND WILDLIFE RESEARCH
  UNIT 99
PENNSYLVANIA DEPARTMENT OF AGRICULTURE 99
  Region I 11, 100, 102, 107, 108, 115
  Region II 11, 100, 107, 108, 115
  Region III 11, 100, 107, 115
  Region IV 11, 100, 102, 108, 115
  Region V 11, 100, 102, 115
  Region VI 11, 100, 102
  Region VII 11, 100
  State Conservation Commission 100, 106, 112
PENNSYLVANIA DEPARTMENT OF CONSERVATION AND NATURAL
  RESOURCES 100
PENNSYLVANIA DEPARTMENT OF ENVIRONMENTAL
  PROTECTION 101
PENNSYLVANIA ENVIRONMENTAL COUNCIL, INC. (PEC) 294
PENNSYLVANIA FEDERATION OF SPORTSMEN'S CLUBS 295
PENNSYLVANIA FISH AND BOAT COMMISSION 101
  Region 1 Northwest 102
  Region 2 Southwest 102
  Region 3 Northeast 102
  Region IV Southeast 102
  Region V North Central 102
  Region VI South Central 102
PENNSYLVANIA FOREST STEWARDSHIP PROGRAM 102
PENNSYLVANIA FORESTRY ASSOCIATION, THE 295
PENNSYLVANIA GAME COMMISSION 102
PENNSYLVANIA RECREATION AND PARK SOCIETY, INC. 295
PENNSYLVANIA RESOURCES COUNCIL, INC., (formerly PA
  Roadside Council) 295
PENNSYLVANIA STATE EXTENSION SERVICES 102
PENNSYLVANIA STATE UNIVERSITY 385
PEOPLE FOR PUGET SOUND 295
  North Sound Office 295
  South Sound Office 295
PEREGRINE FUND, THE 296
PHEASANTS FOREVER, INC. 296
PHYSICIANS FOR SOCIAL RESPONSIBILITY 296
PIEDMONT ENVIRONMENTAL COUNCIL 296
PINCHOT INSTITUTE FOR CONSERVATION 296
PINE BLUFF COOPERATIVE FISHERY RESEARCH PROJECT ... 44
PITTSBURGH HERPETOLOGICAL SOCIETY, THE 296
PLANNED PARENTHOOD FEDERATION OF AMERICA, INC. 297
PLANNING AND CONSERVATION LEAGUE 297
POCONO ENVIRONMENTAL EDUCATION CENTER 297
POLLUTION PROBE FOUNDATION 297
POLYTECHNIC UNIVERSITY OF NEW YORK 381
POPE AND YOUNG CLUB 297
POPULATION ACTION INTERNATIONAL 297
POPULATION COMMUNICATIONS INTERNATIONAL 297
POPULATION INSTITUTE, THE 298
POPULATION REFERENCE BUREAU, INC. 298
POPULATION-ENVIRONMENT BALANCE, INC. 298
PORTLAND STATE UNIVERSITY 384
POTOMAC APPALACHIAN TRAIL CLUB 298
POULSBO MARINE SCIENCE CENTER 298, 391
POWDER RIVER BASIN RESOURCE COUNCIL 298
PRAIRIE CLUB, THE 298
PRAIRIE GROUSE TECHNICAL COUNCIL 299
PRAIRIE RIVERS NETWORK 299
PRAIRIE RIVERS NETWORK (Formerly Central States Education
  Center) 299
PREDATOR PROJECT 299
PRESCOTT COLLEGE 363
PRINCE EDWARD ISLAND DEPARTMENT OF TECHNOLOGY AND
  ENVIRONMENT 128
PRIORITIES INSTITUTE, THE 299
PROFESSIONAL BOWHUNTERS SOCIETY 299
PROVINCE OF QUEBEC SOCIETY FOR THE PROTECTION OF
  BIRDS, INC. 299
PTARMIGANS, THE 300
PUBLIC EMPLOYEES FOR ENVIRONMENTAL RESPONSIBILITY
  (PEER) 300
PUBLIC EMPLOYEES FOR ENVIRONMENTAL RESPONSIBILITY
  (PEER) (West Coast Office) 300
PUBLIC LANDS FOUNDATION 300
PUERTO RICO ASSOCIATION OF SOIL AND WATER
  CONSERVATION DISTRICTS 300
PUERTO RICO CONSERVATION FOUNDATION, THE (PRCF ... 300
PUERTO RICO DEPARTMENT OF AGRICULTURE 103
PUERTO RICO DEPARTMENT OF NATURAL AND ENVIRONMENTAL
  RESOURCES 103
PUERTO RICO SEA GRANT PROGRAM 103
PUERTO RICO STATE EXTENSION SERVICES 103
PUGET SOUNDKEEPER ALLIANCE 300
PURDUE UNIVERSITY 63, 371
PURDUE UNIVERSITY EXTENSION SERVICES 63
PURPLE MARTIN CONSERVATION ASSOCIATION 301
QUAIL UNLIMITED, INC. 301
QUEBEC WILDLIFE FEDERATION 301
RACHEL CARSON COUNCIL, INC. (formerly Rachel Carson Trust for
  the Living Environment Inc.) 301
RAILS-TO-TRAILS CONSERVANCY 302
RAINBOW PUSH COALITION 302
RAINFOREST ACTION NETWORK 302
RAINFOREST ALLIANCE 302
RAINFOREST RELIEF 302
RAINFOREST TRUST, INC., THE 302
RAPTOR CENTER, THE 303
RAPTOR EDUCATION FOUNDATION, INC. 303
RAPTOR RESEARCH FOUNDATION, INC. 303
RARE CENTER FOR TROPICAL CONSERVATION 303
REEF RELIEF 303
RENEW AMERICA 303
RENEWABLE ENERGY POLICY PROJECT (REPP) 303
RENEWABLE NATURAL RESOURCES FOUNDATION 304
RENSSELAER POLYTECHNIC INSTITUTE 381
REP AMERICA/REPUBLICANS FOR ENVIRONMENTAL
  PROTECTION 304
RESOURCE CENTER FOR ENVIRONMENTAL EDUCATION, THE 304
RESOURCE RENEWAL INSTITUTE, THE 304
RESOURCES AGENCY, THE 46
  California Coastal Commission 46
  California Coastal Conservancy 46
  California Conservation Corps 46
  California Energy Commission 47
  California Water Commission 47
  Colorado River Board of California 47
  Department of Boating and Waterways 47
  Department of Conservation 38, 47, 75, 76, 79, 155, 291, 398, 415,
    416, 417
  Department of Fish and Game 39, 47, 48, 60, 155, 397, 415, 421
  Department of Forestry and Fire Protection 47
  Department of Parks and Recreation 48, 310, 327
  Department of Water Resources 48
  Fish and Game Commission 47, 48
  Native American Heritage Commission 48
  San Francisco Bay Conservation and Development Commission 48
  State Reclamation Board 48
  Wildlife Conservation Board 48
RESOURCES FOR THE FUTURE 304
RESOURCE-USE EDUCATION COUNCIL 304
RESPONSIVE MANAGEMENT 305
RETURNED PEACE CORPS VOLUNTEER FOR ENVIRONMENT AND
  DEVELOPMENT (RPCV-ED) 305
RHODE ISLAND B.A.S.S. CHAPTER FEDERATION 305
RHODE ISLAND COOPERATIVE EXTENSION SERVICE 104
RHODE ISLAND FOREST CONSERVATORS ASSOCIATION ... 305
RHODE ISLAND SCHOOL OF DESIGN 386
RHODE ISLAND SEA GRANT 104
RHODE ISLAND STATE ASSOCIATION OF CONSERVATION
  DISTRICTS 305
RHODE ISLAND STATE CONSERVATION COMMITTEE 104
RHODE ISLAND WILD PLANT SOCIETY 305
RICE UNIVERSITY 388
RICHARD STOCKTON COLLEGE 380
RINCON INSTITUTE, THE 305
RIVER ALLIANCE OF WISCONSIN 305
RIVER FEDERATION 306
RIVER NETWORK 306
  Eastern Office 306
  Northern Rockies Office
  Riverlands Conservancy Field Office 306

RIVER OTTER ALLIANCE, THE 306
RIVERS COUNCIL OF WASHINGTON (formerly Northwest Rivers Council) 306
ROCKY MOUNTAIN BIGHORN SOCIETY 306
ROCKY MOUNTAIN ELK FOUNDATION 307
    Intermountain Region Office 307
    North-Central Region Office 307
    Northeast Region Office 307
    Northwest Region Office 307
    Pacific Southwest Region Office 307
    South-Central Region Office 307
    Southeast Region Office 307
ROGER TORY PETERSON INSTITUTE 307
ROGER WILLIAMS UNIVERSITY 386
ROWAN UNIVERSITY 380
RUFFED GROUSE SOCIETY, THE 307
RUTGERS UNIVERSITY 380
SAFARI CLUB INTERNATIONAL 308
    Michigan Office 308
    South Africa Office 308
    Washington, DC Office 134, 148, 192, 308, 314, 324
SAFE ENERGY COMMUNICATION COUNCIL 308
SAN FRANCISCO STATE UNIVERSITY 364
SAN JOSE STATE UNIVERSITY 364
SAN JUAN PRESERVATION TRUST, THE 308
SANIBEL-CAPTIVA CONSERVATION FOUNDATION, INC. .. 308
SASKATCHEWAN ENVIRONMENT AND RESOURCE MANAGEMENT 128
    Corporate Services 35, 124, 127, 128
    East Boreal EcoRegion 128
    Enforcement and Compliance Branch 128
    Fire Management and Forest Protection Branch 128
    Grassland EcoRegion 128
    Operations 5, 6, 12, 13, 16, 17, 19, 21, 28, 29, 30, 32, 34, 35, 36, 38, 39, 40, 41, 42, 46, 47, 51, 53, 55, 62, 65, 74, 75, 76, 80, 82, 87, 91, 96, 101, 104, 105, 106, 107, 108, 111, 116, 117, 124, 128, 157, 159, 186, 189, 190, 196, 198, 205, 227, 241, 243, 250, 257, 259, 265, 272, 284, 291, 307, 310, 339, 342, 348, 359, 361, 413, 417
    Parkland EcoRegion 128
    Policy and Assessment 129
    Programs 5, 10, 11, 12, 13, 16, 17, 20, 22, 23, 30, 31, 32, 33, 34, 37, 38, 39, 41, 42, 45, 46, 47, 50, 53, 54, 57, 75, 81, 87, 88, 91, 93, 95, 99, 100, 103, 112, 114, 116, 117, 129, 131, 139, 146, 147, 149, 153, 157, 159, 164, 166, 167, 170, 171, 174, 175, 179, 182, 183, 189, 190, 191, 192, 194, 196, 198, 205, 209, 211, 212, 213, 230, 240, 241, 244, 245, 256, 257, 261, 262, 265, 267, 284, 286, 289, 290, 304, 306, 307, 312, 319, 325, 326, 330, 331, 335, 340, 344, 349, 369, 371, 379, 382, 383, 385, 386, 387, 393, 394, 395, 401, 407, 415
    Shield EcoRegion 129
    West Boreal EcoRegion 129
SASKATCHEWAN WILDLIFE FEDERATION 309
SAVE AMERICA'S FORESTS 309
SAVE OUR RIVERS, INC. 309
SAVE SAN FRANCISCO BAY ASSOCIATION 309
SAVE THE BAY, INC. 309
SAVE THE DUNES COUNCIL 309
    Save the Dunes Conservation Fund 309
SAVE THE HARBOR/SAVE THE BAY 310
SAVE THE MANATEE CLUB 310
SAVE THE SOUND, INC. 310
SAVE THE SOUND, INC. At GARVIES POINT MUSEUM 310
SAVE WETLANDS AND BAYS 310
SAVE-THE-REDWOODS LEAGUE 310
SCENIC AMERICA 310
    Citizens for a Scenic Florida 310
    Scenic California 311
    Scenic Michigan 311
    Scenic Missouri 311
    Scenic North Carolina 311
    Scenic Texas 311
SCENIC HUDSON, INC. 311
SCHOOL FOR FIELD STUDIES (Boston University) 375
SCIENTISTS CENTER FOR ANIMAL WELFARE 311
SEA SHEPHERD CONSERVATION SOCIETY 311
    Australia Office 311
    Canada Office 8, 311, 313
    Germany Office/European Community 311
    Great Britain Office 311
    Netherlands Office 312
    USA Office 312
SEACAMP ASSOCIATION, INC. 312
SEACOAST ANTI-POLLUTION LEAGUE 312
SEAPLANE PILOTS ASSOCIATION 312
SENATE COMMITTEE ON APPROPRIATIONS 6
SENATE COMMITTEE ON COMMERCE SCIENCE AND TRANSPORTATION 6
SENATE COMMITTEE ON ENERGY AND NATURAL RESOURCES 6
SENATE COMMITTEE ON ENVIRONMENT AND PUBLIC WORKS 6
SENATE COMMITTEE ON FOREIGN RELATIONS 6
SHAWNEE STATE UNIVERSITY 384
SHELBURNE FARMS 312
SHEPHERD COLLEGE 391
SIERRA CLUB 312, 314, 315, 316, 317
    Alaska Office 267, 312
    Alaska Rainforest Campaign Office 312
    Appalachian Field Office 312
    Atlantic Coast Office 313
    California/Nevada/Hawaii Office and California Legislative Office 313
    Canada Office 8, 311, 313
    Cleveland Office 313
    Colorado Field Office 313
    Columbia Basin Office 313
    Florida Field Office 313
    Florida-Miami Field Office 313
    Georgia Field Office/Louisiana and Alabama Field Office 313
    Midwest Office 15, 182, 234, 252, 266, 313
    Montana Field Office 149, 313
    New York City Office 313
    Northeast Office 266, 313
    Northern Plains 15, 313
    Northwest Office 313, 320, 326
    Oakland/San Francisco Bay Area Field Office 313
    Sierra Student Coalition 313
    Southeast Office 313
    Southeast Texas/Arkansas Field Office 313
    Southern California/Nevada Field Office 313
    Southwest Office 314
    Utah Field Office 314
    Washington, DC Office 134, 148, 192, 308, 314, 324
SIERRA CLUB FOUNDATION, THE 317
SIERRA CLUB, ALABAMA CHAPTER 314
SIERRA CLUB, ALASKA CHAPTER 314
SIERRA CLUB, ANGELES CHAPTER 314
SIERRA CLUB, ARKANSAS CHAPTER 314
SIERRA CLUB, ATLANTIC CHAPTER 314
SIERRA CLUB, BRITISH COLUMBIA CHAPTER 314
SIERRA CLUB, CASCADE CHAPTER 314
SIERRA CLUB, CONNECTICUT CHAPTER 314
SIERRA CLUB, CUMBERLAND CAHPTER 314
SIERRA CLUB, DACOTAH CHAPTER 314
SIERRA CLUB, DELAWARE CHAPTER 314
SIERRA CLUB, DELTA CHAPTER 314
SIERRA CLUB, EASTERN CANADA CHAPTER 314
SIERRA CLUB, FLORIDA CHAPTER 314
SIERRA CLUB, GEORGIA CHAPTER 314
SIERRA CLUB, GRAND CANYON CHAPTER 314
SIERRA CLUB, HAWAII CHAPTER 314
SIERRA CLUB, HOOSIER CHAPTER 314
SIERRA CLUB, ILLINOIS CHAPTER 314
SIERRA CLUB, IOWA CHAPTER 315
SIERRA CLUB, JOHN MUIR CHAPTER 315
SIERRA CLUB, KANSAS CHAPTER 315
SIERRA CLUB, KERN-KAWEAH CHAPTER 315
SIERRA CLUB, LOMA PRIETA CHAPTER 315
SIERRA CLUB, LONE STAR CHAPTER 315
SIERRA CLUB, LOS PADRES CHAPTER 315
SIERRA CLUB, MACKINAC CHAPTER 315
SIERRA CLUB, MAINE CHAPTER 315
SIERRA CLUB, MARYLAND CHAPTER 315
SIERRA CLUB, MASSACHUSETTS CHAPTER 315
SIERRA CLUB, MISSISSIPPI CHAPTER 315
SIERRA CLUB, MONTANA CHAPTER 315
SIERRA CLUB, MOTHER LODE CHAPTER 315
SIERRA CLUB, NEBRASKA CHAPTER 315
SIERRA CLUB, NEW COLUMBIA CHAPTER 315
SIERRA CLUB, NEW HAMPSHIRE CHAPTER 315
SIERRA CLUB, NEW JERSEY CHAPTER 315

ORGANIZATION NAME INDEX

SIERRA CLUB, NORTH CAROLINA CHAPTER 315
SIERRA CLUB, NORTH STAR CHAPTER (Minnesota) 315
SIERRA CLUB, NORTHERN ROCKIES CHAPTER (Idaho/Washington)
.... 315
SIERRA CLUB, OHIO CHAPTER 315
SIERRA CLUB, OKLAHOMA CHAPTER 315
SIERRA CLUB, OREGON CHAPTER 316
SIERRA CLUB, OZARK CHAPTER (Missouri) 316
SIERRA CLUB, PENNSYLVANIA CHAPTER 316
SIERRA CLUB, PRAIRIE CHAPTER (AB, MB, SK) 316
SIERRA CLUB, REDWOOD CHAPTER (Northern California) 316
SIERRA CLUB, RHODE ISLAND CHAPTER 316
SIERRA CLUB, RIO GRANDE CHAPTER (New Mexico/West Texas)
.... 316
SIERRA CLUB, ROCKY MOUNTAIN CHAPTER (Colorado) 316
SIERRA CLUB, SAN DIEGO CHAPTER (Southern California) 316
SIERRA CLUB, SAN FRANCISCO BAY CHAPTER (Northern California)
.... 316
SIERRA CLUB, SAN GORGONIO CHAPTER (Southern California)316
SIERRA CLUB, SANTA LUCIA CHAPTER 316
SIERRA CLUB, SOUTH CAROLINA CHAPTER 316
SIERRA CLUB, SOUTH DAKOTA CHAPTER 316
SIERRA CLUB, TEHIPITE CHAPTER (Northern California) 316
SIERRA CLUB, TENNESSEE CHAPTER 316
SIERRA CLUB, TOIYABE CHAPTER (Nevada/Eastern California)316
SIERRA CLUB, UTAH CHAPTER 316
SIERRA CLUB, VENTANA CHAPTER (Northern California) 316
SIERRA CLUB, VERMONT CHAPTER 316
SIERRA CLUB, VIRGINIA CHAPTER 316
SIERRA CLUB, WEST VIRGINIA CHAPTER 316
SIERRA CLUB, WYOMING CHAPTER 317
SIERRA NEVADA FOREST PROTECTION CAMPAIGN 317
SILLMAN UNIVERSITY 395
SINAPU 317
SLIPPERY ROCK UNIVERSITY 385
SMITHSONIAN INSTITUTION 317
    National Museum of Natural History 148, 317
    National Zoological Park 317
    Office of Fellowships and Grants 317
    Office of International Relations 318
    Smithsonian Marine Station at Link Port 318
    Smithsonian Press/Smithsonian Productions 318
    Smithsonian Tropical Research Institute 318
SOCIETY FOR ANIMAL PROTECTIVE LEGISLATION 318
SOCIETY FOR CONSERVATION BIOLOGY 318
SOCIETY FOR ECOLOGICAL RESTORATION 318
SOCIETY FOR INTEGRATIVE AND COMPARTIVE BIOLOGY (formerly AMERICAN SOCIETY OF ZOOLOGISTS) 318
SOCIETY FOR MARINE MAMMALOGY, THE 318
SOCIETY FOR RANGE MANAGEMENT 319
SOCIETY FOR THE PRESERVATION OF BIRDS OF PREY 319
SOCIETY FOR THE PROTECTION OF NEW HAMPSHIRE FORESTS
.... 319
SOCIETY OF AMERICAN FORESTERS 319
SOCIETY OF TYMPANUCHUS CUPIDO PINNATUS LTD 320
SOCIETY OF WETLAND SCIENTISTS 320
SOIL AND WATER CONSERVATION SOCIETY (formerly Soil Conservation Society of America) 320
SOIL CONSERVATION COMMITTEE OF PUERTO RICO 103
SONOMA STATE UNIVERSITY 364
SONORAN INSTITUTE 320
    Northwest Office 313, 320, 326
SOUND EXPERIENCE 320
SOUTH ATLANTIC FISHERY MANAGEMENT COUNCIL 321
SOUTH CAROLINA ASSOCIATION OF CONSERVATION DISTRICTS
.... 321
SOUTH CAROLINA B.A.S.S. CHAPTER FEDERATION 321
SOUTH CAROLINA COASTAL CONSERVATION LEAGUE 321
SOUTH CAROLINA DEPARTMENT OF AGRICULTURE 105
SOUTH CAROLINA DEPARTMENT OF HEALTH AND ENVIRONMENTAL CONTROL 105
    Office of Ocean and Coastal Resource Management (OCRM)105
SOUTH CAROLINA DEPARTMENT OF NATURAL RESOURCES105
SOUTH CAROLINA ENERGY OFFICE 105
SOUTH CAROLINA ENVIRONMENTAL LAW PROJECT 321
SOUTH CAROLINA FORESTRY ASSOCIATION 321
SOUTH CAROLINA NATIVE PLANT SOCIETY 321
SOUTH CAROLINA SEA GRANT CONSORTIUM 106
SOUTH CAROLINA WILDLIFE FEDERATION 321

SOUTH DAKOTA ASSOCIATION OF CONSERVATION DISTRICTS
.... 322
SOUTH DAKOTA B.A.S.S. CHAPTER FEDERATION 322
SOUTH DAKOTA COOPERATIVE FISH AND WILDLIFE RESEARCH UNIT (USDI) 106
SOUTH DAKOTA DEPARTMENT OF AGRICULTURE 106
    Division of Resource Conservation and Forestry 106
    State Conservation Commission 100, 106, 112
SOUTH DAKOTA DEPARTMENT OF ENVIRONMENT AND NATURAL RESOURCES 106
SOUTH DAKOTA GAME, FISH, AND PARKS DEPARTMENT 106
SOUTH DAKOTA ORNITHOLOGISTS' UNION 322
SOUTH DAKOTA RESOURCES COALITION 322
SOUTH DAKOTA STATE EXTENSION SERVICES 106
SOUTH DAKOTA STATE UNIVERSITY 387
SOUTH DAKOTA WILDLIFE FEDERATION 323
SOUTH FLORIDA WATER MANAGEMENT DISTRICT 55
SOUTHEAST ALASKA CONSERVATION COUNCIL (SEACC) 323
SOUTHEASTERN ASSOCIATION OF FISH AND WILDLIFE AGENCIES 323
SOUTHEASTERN COOPERATIVE WILDLIFE DISEASE STUDY 323
SOUTHEASTERN FISHES COUNCIL 323
SOUTHERN AFRICAN INSTITUTE OF FORESTRY 323
SOUTHERN APPALACHIAN BOTANICAL SOCIETY 323
SOUTHERN CONNECTICUT STATE UNIVERSITY 367
SOUTHERN ENVIRONMENTAL LAW CENTER 324
SOUTHERN ILLINOIS UNIVERSITY 370
SOUTHERN NEW ENGLAND FOREST CONSORTIUM, INC. (SNEFCI)
.... 324
SOUTHERN OREGON UNIVERSITY 385
SOUTHERN UTAH WILDERNESS ALLIANCE (SUWA) 324
SOUTHFACE ENERGY INSTITUTE 324
SOUTHWEST FLORIDA WATER MANAGEMENT DISTRICT (SWFWMD) 55
SOUTHWEST RESEARCH AND INFORMATION CENTER 324
ST. CLOUD STATE UNIVERSITY 377
ST. CROIX INTERNATIONAL WATERWAY COMMISSION 10
ST. LAWRENCE UNIVERSITY 381
ST. NORBERT COLLEGE 392
ST. REGIS MOHAWK TRIBE 325
STANFORD ENVIRONMENTAL LAW SOCIETY 325
STANFORD UNIVERSITY 365
STATE ENGINEER OFFICE/INTERSTATE STREAM COMMISSION88
STATE FORESTRY DIVISION (WYOMING) 122
STATE MARINE BOARD (OREGON) 99
STATE OF IDAHO DIVISION OF ENVIRONMENTAL QUALITY 61
STATE OFFICE OF CONSERVATION (LOUISIANA) 69
STATE PARKS AND RECREATION COMMISSION (WASHINGTON)
.... 116
    Eastern Region12, 13, 16, 17, 31, 98, 99, 117, 125, 137, 153, 263, 267
    Northwest Region16, 29, 62, 98, 99, 102, 117, 118, 127, 149, 206, 307, 335
    Puget Sound Region 117
    Southwest Region16, 30, 80, 99, 102, 117, 118, 149, 153, 264, 301, 335, 363
STATE PLANT BOARD (ARKANSAS) 44
STATE SOIL AND WATER CONSERVATION COMMISSION (GEORGIA) 56
STATE UNIVERSITY OF NEW YORK AT CORTLAND 381
STATE UNIVERSITY OF NEW YORK AT STONY BROOK 381
STATE UNIVERSITY OF NEW YORK COLLEGE OF ENVIRONMENTAL SCIENCE AND FORESTRY 382
STATE WATER RESOURCES BOARD (RHODE ISLAND) 104
STATEWIDE PROGRAM OF ACTION TO CONSERVE OUR ENVIRONMENT (SPACE) 325
STEAMBOATERS, THE 325
STEPHEN F. AUSTIN STATE UNIVERSITY 388
STERLING COLLEGE 390
STOP 13, 326
STRIPERS UNLIMITED, INC. 326
STROUD WATER RESEARCH CENTER 326
STUDENT CONSERVATION ASSOCIATION, INC. 326
    California Office 192, 326
    Capital Office 196, 326
    Newark Office 326
    Northwest Office 313, 320, 326
STUDENT ENVIRONMENTAL ACTION COALITION (SEAC) 326
STUDENT PUGWASH USA 326
STUDENTS PARTNERSHIP WORLDWIDE 327

SUNCOAST SEABIRD SANCTUARY INC. 327
SUSQUEHANNA RIVER BASIN COMMISSION 10
TAHOE REGIONAL PLANNING AGENCY 327
TALL TIMBERS RESEARCH STATION 327
TALLAHASSEE MUSEUM OF HISTORY AND NATURAL SCIENCE327
TANZANIA COASTAL MANAGEMENT PARTNERSHIP 123
TEENS FOR RECREATION AND ENVIRONMENTAL CONSERVATION (TREC) 327
TENNESSEE AGRICULTURAL EXTENSION SERVICES............. 107
TENNESSEE ASSOCIATION OF CONSERVATION DISTRICTS. 327
TENNESSEE B.A.S.S. CHAPTER FEDERATION.......................... 328
TENNESSEE CITIZENS FOR WILDERNESS PLANNING 328
TENNESSEE CONSERVATION LEAGUE 328
TENNESSEE COOPERATIVE FISHERY RESEARCH UNIT (USDI)107
TENNESSEE DEPARTMENT OF AGRICULTURE 107
    State Soil Conservation Committee 71, 107
TENNESSEE ENVIRONMENTAL COUNCIL................................. 328
TENNESSEE FORESTRY ASSOCIATION..................................... 328
TENNESSEE TECHNOLOGICAL UNIVERSITY 387
TENNESSEE VALLEY AUTHORITY... 35
TENNESSEE WOODLAND OWNERS ASSOCIATION.................. 328
TERRENE INSTITUTE, THE... 328
TEXAS A&M UNIVERSITY AT COLLEGE STATION 388
TEXAS A&M UNIVERSITY AT COMMERCE 388
TEXAS A&M UNIVERSITY AT KINGSVILLE.................................. 389
TEXAS AGRICULTURAL EXTENSION SERVICE 108
TEXAS ASSOCIATION OF SOIL AND WATER CONSERVATION DISTRICTS 328
TEXAS B.A.S.S. CHAPTER FEDERATION................................... 329
TEXAS CHRISTIAN UNIVERSITY 389
TEXAS COMMITTEE ON NATURAL RESOURCES 329
TEXAS COOPERATIVE FISH AND WILDLIFE RESEARCH UNIT108
TEXAS DEPARTMENT OF AGRICULTURE 108
TEXAS DEPARTMENT OF HEALTH 108
TEXAS FOREST SERVICE 108
TEXAS FORESTRY ASSOCIATION 329
TEXAS GENERAL LAND OFFICE 109
TEXAS ORGANIZATION FOR ENDANGERED SPECIES 329
TEXAS PARKS AND WILDLIFE DEPARTMENT 109
TEXAS SEA GRANT PROGRAM 109
TEXAS STATE SOIL AND WATER CONSERVATION BOARD 109
TEXAS TECH UNIVERSITY... 389
TEXAS WATER DEVELOPMENT BOARD 109
TEXAS WILDLIFE ASSOCIATION 329
THORNE ECOLOGICAL INSTITUTE 329
THREE CIRCLES CENTER FOR MULTICULTURAL ENVIRONMENTAL EDUCATION 329
THRESHOLD, INC... 329
TOGETHER FOUNDATION, THE... 330
TRAFFIC NORTH AMERICA 330
TREAD LIGHTLY! INC.. 330
TREASURE VALLEY COMMUNITY COLLEGE 385
TREEPEOPLE 330
TREES ATLANTA 330
TREES FOR THE FUTURE, INC. 330
TREES FOR TOMORROW, INC., NATURAL RESOURCES EDUCATION CENTER... 331
TRI-STATE BIRD RESCUE AND RESEARCH, INC. 331
TROUT UNLIMITED 331, 332, 333, 334
TROUT UNLIMITED, ALASKA COUNCIL...................................... 331
TROUT UNLIMITED, ARIZONA COUNCIL.................................... 332
TROUT UNLIMITED, ARKANSAS COUNCIL................................ 332
TROUT UNLIMITED, CALIFORNIA COUNCIL.............................. 332
TROUT UNLIMITED, COLORADO COUNCIL............................... 332
TROUT UNLIMITED, CONNECTICUT COUNCIL 332
TROUT UNLIMITED, GEORGIA COUNCIL................................... 332
TROUT UNLIMITED, IDAHO COUNCIL 332
TROUT UNLIMITED, ILLINOIS COUNCIL..................................... 332
TROUT UNLIMITED, KENTUCKY COUNCIL................................ 332
TROUT UNLIMITED, MAINE COUNCIL 332
TROUT UNLIMITED, MARYLAND COUNCIL (Mid-Atlantic) 332
TROUT UNLIMITED, MASSACHUSETTS/RHODE ISLAND COUNCIL 332
TROUT UNLIMITED, MICHIGAN COUNCIL.................................. 332
TROUT UNLIMITED, MINNESOTA COUNCIL.............................. 333
TROUT UNLIMITED, MONTANA COUNCIL.................................. 333
TROUT UNLIMITED, NEW HAMPSHIRE COUNCIL.................... 333
TROUT UNLIMITED, NEW JERSEY COUNCIL 333
TROUT UNLIMITED, NEW YORK COUNCIL 333
TROUT UNLIMITED, NORTH CAROLINA..................................... 333
TROUT UNLIMITED, NORTH CAROLINA COUNCIL................... 333
TROUT UNLIMITED, OHIO COUNCIL... 333
TROUT UNLIMITED, OKLAHOMA COUNCIL............................... 333
TROUT UNLIMITED, OREGON COUNCIL.................................... 333
TROUT UNLIMITED, PENNSYLVANIA COUNCIL 333
TROUT UNLIMITED, SOUTH CAROLINA COUNCIL 333
TROUT UNLIMITED, TENNESSEE COUNCIL 334
TROUT UNLIMITED, UTAH COUNCIL 334
TROUT UNLIMITED, VERMONT COUNCIL 334
TROUT UNLIMITED, VIRGINIA COUNCIL 334
TROUT UNLIMITED, WASHINGTON COUNCIL 334
TROUT UNLIMITED, WEST VIRGINIA COUNCIL 334
TROUT UNLIMITED, WISCONSIN COUNCIL............................... 334
TROUT UNLIMITED, WYOMING COUNCIL 334
TRUMPETER SWAN SOCIETY, THE.. 334
TRUST FOR PUBLIC LAND, THE... 334
TRUST FOR WILDLIFE, INC... 335
TRUSTEES FOR ALASKA.. 335
TRUSTEES OF RESERVATIONS, THE 335
TUFTS UNIVERSITY 375
TUG HILL COMMISSION... 91
TUG HILL TOMORROW LAND TRUST 335
TULANE UNIVERSITY.. 373
TURTLE CREEK WATERSHED ASSOCIATION, INC................... 335
U.S. PUBLIC INTEREST RESEARCH GROUP 336
UINTED STATES DEPARTMENT OF THE AIR FORCE MAJOR U.S. INSTALLATIONS 22
UNION OF CONCERNED SCIENTISTS 336
UNITED NATIONS ENVIRONMENT PROGRAMME.................... 336
    North America Regional Office 336
UNITED NATIONS RESEARCH INSTITUTE FOR SOCIAL DEVELOPMENT (UNRISD).. 37
UNITED STATES DEPARTMENT OF AGRICULTURE RESEARCH EDUCATION AND ECONOMICS........................ 15
UNITED STATES CHAMBER OF COMMERCE 336
UNITED STATES COMMITTEE FOR THE UNITED NATIONS ENVIRONMENT PROGRAMME THE (U.S. and UNEP) 336
UNITED STATES DEPARTMENT OF AGRICULTURE 11
    ANIMAL AND PLANT HEALTH INSPECTION SERVICE......... 12
    ECONOMIC RESEARCH SERVICE 13
    FARM SERVICE AGENCY (FSA), FORMERLY AGRICULTURAL STABILIZATION AND CONSERVATION SERVICE............. 13
    NATURAL RESOURCES CONSERVATION SERVICE (formerly Soil Conservation Service) 13
    RESEARCH EDUCATION AND ECONOMICS......................... 15
    UNITED STATES FOREST SERVICE 16
UNITED STATES DEPARTMENT OF COMMERCE 17
    ECONOMIC DEVELOPMENT ADMINISTRATION................... 17
    NATIONAL OCEANIC AND ATMOSPHERIC ADMINISTRATION 17
UNITED STATES DEPARTMENT OF DEFENSE 18
UNITED STATES DEPARTMENT OF EDUCATION 18
UNITED STATES DEPARTMENT OF ENERGY............................. 18
    CARBON DIOXIDE INFORMATION ANALYSIS CENTER...... 18
    FEDERAL ENERGY REGULATORY COMMISSION 18
UNITED STATES DEPARTMENT OF HEALTH AND HUMAN SERVICES 19
    FOOD AND DRUG ADMINISTRATION 19
UNITED STATES DEPARTMENT OF HOUSING AND URBAN DEVELOPMENT 19
UNITED STATES DEPARTMENT OF JUSTICE............................. 20
UNITED STATES DEPARTMENT OF LABOR................................ 20
    JOB CORPS... 20
    MINE SAFETY AND HEALTH ADMINISTRATION 20
UNITED STATES DEPARTMENT OF STATE 20
    BUREAU OF OCEANS AND INTERNATIONAL ENVIRONMENTAL AND SCIENTIFIC AFFAIRS................. 20
    UNITED STATES MAN AND THE BIOSPHERE PROGRAM (U.S. MAB) 21
UNITED STATES DEPARTMENT OF THE AIR FORCE................ 21
    MAJOR AIR COMMANDS 21
    MAJOR U.S. INSTALLATIONS 22
UNITED STATES DEPARTMENT OF THE ARMY 24
    ARMY TRAINING AND DOCTRINE COMMAND..................... 24
    ENGINEER RESEARCH AND DEVELOPMENT CENTER/CONSTRUCTION ENGINEERING RESEARCH LABORATORIES CERL 24
    HEADQUARTERS, U.S. ARMY TRAINING AND DOCTRINE COMMAND 24
    HQ ARMY MATERIAL COMMAND 25

ORGANIZATION NAME INDEX

U.S. ARMY CORPS OF ENGINEERS 25
U.S. ARMY FORCES COMMAND 27
U.S. MILITARY ACADEMY 27
UNITED STATES DEPARTMENT OF THE INTERIOR 27
   BUREAU OF INDIAN AFFAIRS 28
   BUREAU OF LAND MANAGEMENT 28, 418
   BUREAU OF RECLAMATION 28
   NATIONAL PARK SERVICE 29
   OFFICE OF SURFACE MINING RECLAMATION AND ENFORCEMENT 29
   UNITED STATES FISH AND WILDLIFE SERVICE 29
   UNITED STATES GEOLOGICAL SURVEY 30
UNITED STATES DEPARTMENT OF THE NAVY 31
   U.S. MARINE CORPS 31
UNITED STATES DEPARTMENT OF TRANSPORTATION 31
   FEDERAL AVIATION ADMINISTRATION 31
   FEDERAL HIGHWAY ADMINISTRATION 31
   FEDERAL RAILROAD ADMINISTRATION 32
   FEDERAL TRANSIT ADMINISTRATION 32
   NATIONAL HIGHWAY TRAFFIC SAFETY ADMINISTRATION 32
   SAINT LAWRENCE SEAWAY DEVELOPMENT CORPORATION 32
   UNITED STATES COAST GUARD 32
UNITED STATES DEPARTMENT OF TREASURY 32
   U.S. CUSTOMS SERVICE 32
UNITED STATES TOURIST COUNCIL 336
UNITED STATES TREASURY DEPARTMENT
   U.S. CUSTOMS SERVICE 32
UNITED STSTES DEPARTMENT OF THE AIR FORCE
   MAJOR U.S. INSTALLATIONS 22
UNITY COLLEGE 373
UNIVERSIDADE FEDERAL DO PARANA 395
UNIVERSITE LAVAL 395
UNIVERSITY OF AKRON 384
UNIVERSITY OF ALASKA AT FAIRBANKS 362
UNIVERSITY OF ALBERTA 393
UNIVERSITY OF ARIZONA 363
UNIVERSITY OF ARKANSAS AT LITTLE ROCK 363
UNIVERSITY OF ARKANSAS AT MONTICELLO 364
UNIVERSITY OF BATH 395
UNIVERSITY OF BRITISH COLUMBIA 393
UNIVERSITY OF CALIFORNIA AT DAVIS 365
UNIVERSITY OF CALIFORNIA AT LOS ANGELES 365
UNIVERSITY OF CALIFORNIA AT RIVERSIDE 365
UNIVERSITY OF CALIFORNIA AT SAN DIEGO 366
UNIVERSITY OF CALIFORNIA AT SANTA BARBARA 366
UNIVERSITY OF CALIFORNIA AT SANTA CRUZ 366
UNIVERSITY OF CALIFORNIA, BERKELEY 366
UNIVERSITY OF COLORADO 367
UNIVERSITY OF COLORADO AT BOULDER 367
UNIVERSITY OF CONNECTICUT 51, 367
UNIVERSITY OF CONNECTICUT COOPERATIVE EXTENSION ... 51
UNIVERSITY OF DELAWARE 368
UNIVERSITY OF FLORIDA 368
UNIVERSITY OF GEORGIA 369
UNIVERSITY OF GUELPH 394
UNIVERSITY OF HAWAII 369
UNIVERSITY OF HAWAII COOPERATIVE EXTENSION PROGRAM 59
UNIVERSITY OF HOUSTON 389
UNIVERSITY OF IDAHO 369
UNIVERSITY OF ILLINOIS AT URBANA-CHAMPAIGN 370
UNIVERSITY OF ILLNOIS EXTENSION 62
UNIVERSITY OF IOWA 371
UNIVERSITY OF ITO PUNJAB 396
UNIVERSITY OF KANSAS 372
UNIVERSITY OF KENTUCKY 372
UNIVERSITY OF LOUISVILLE 373
UNIVERSITY OF MAINE AT FORT KENT 373
UNIVERSITY OF MAINE AT ORONO 373
UNIVERSITY OF MAINE COOPERATIVE EXTENSION 71
UNIVERSITY OF MANITOBA 394
UNIVERSITY OF MARYLAND AT BALTIMORE COUNTY .. 374
UNIVERSITY OF MARYLAND AT COLLEGE PARK 374
UNIVERSITY OF MARYLAND AT EASTERN SHORE 375
UNIVERSITY OF MARYLAND CENTER FOR ENVIRONMENTAL SCIENCE 375
UNIVERSITY OF MASSACHUSETTS 74, 375
UNIVERSITY OF MASSACHUSETTS EXTENSION 74
UNIVERSITY OF MICHIGAN 377
UNIVERSITY OF MINNESOTA AT CROOKSTON 377
UNIVERSITY OF MINNESOTA AT ST. PAUL 377
UNIVERSITY OF MISSOURI 378
UNIVERSITY OF MONTANA 378
UNIVERSITY OF NEBRASKA 379
UNIVERSITY OF NEVADA AT LAS VEGAS 379
UNIVERSITY OF NEVADA AT RENO 379
UNIVERSITY OF NEW BRUNSWICK 394
UNIVERSITY OF NEW HAMPSHIRE 84, 380
UNIVERSITY OF NEW HAMPSHIRE COOPERATIVE EXTENSION 84
UNIVERSITY OF NEW HAVEN 367
UNIVERSITY OF NORTH CAROLINA AT ASHEVILLE 383
UNIVERSITY OF NORTH CAROLINA AT CHAPEL HILL .. 383
UNIVERSITY OF NORTH DAKOTA 383
UNIVERSITY OF NORTH TEXAS 389
UNIVERSITY OF NORTHERN BRITISH COLUMBIA 393
UNIVERSITY OF NORTHERN COLORADO 367
UNIVERSITY OF OREGON 385
UNIVERSITY OF PENNSYLVANIA 385
UNIVERSITY OF PITTSBURGH 386
UNIVERSITY OF REGINA 395
UNIVERSITY OF RHODE ISLAND 386
UNIVERSITY OF SASKATCHEWAN 395
UNIVERSITY OF SOUTH CAROLINA 387
UNIVERSITY OF SOUTHERN CALIFORNIA 366
UNIVERSITY OF SOUTHERN MISSISSIPPI 378
UNIVERSITY OF TENNESSEE AT KNOXVILLE 388
UNIVERSITY OF TENNESSEE AT MARTIN 388
UNIVERSITY OF THE DISTRICT OF COLUMBIA 368
UNIVERSITY OF THE SOUTH (SEWANEE) 388
UNIVERSITY OF THE VIRGIN ISLANDS 390
UNIVERSITY OF TORONTO 394
UNIVERSITY OF VERMONT 112, 390
UNIVERSITY OF VERMONT EXTENSION 112
   Publications Office 112, 156
UNIVERSITY OF WEST FLORIDA 369
UNIVERSITY OF WISCONSIN AT EAU CLAIRE 392
UNIVERSITY OF WISCONSIN AT GREEN BAY 392
UNIVERSITY OF WISCONSIN AT LA CROSSE 392
UNIVERSITY OF WISCONSIN AT MADISON 392
UNIVERSITY OF WISCONSIN AT STEVENS POINT 393
UNIVERSITY OF WYOMING 393
UPPER CHATTAHOOCHEE RIVERKEEPER 337
UPPER COLORADO RIVER COMMISSION 10
UPPER MISSISSIPPI RIVER CONSERVATION COMMITTEE 337
URBAN HABITAT PROGRAM 337
URBAN WILDLIFE RESOURCES 337
UTAH ASSOCIATION OF SOIL CONSERVATION DISTRICTS ... 337
UTAH B.A.S.S. CHAPTER FEDERATION 337
UTAH COOPERATIVE FISH AND WILDLIFE RESEARCH UNIT (USDI-USGS-BRD-CRU) 110
UTAH DEPARTMENT OF AGRICULTURE 110
UTAH DEPARTMENT OF HEALTH 110
UTAH GEOLOGICAL SURVEY 110
UTAH NATURE STUDY SOCIETY 337
UTAH STATE DEPARTMENT OF NATURAL RESOURCES 110
   Division of Forestry, Fire and State Lands 110
   Division of Oil, Gas and Mining 110
   Division of Parks and Recreation .. 51, 76, 94, 104, 110, 258, 416
   Division of Water Resources 49, 52, 83, 91, 110
   Division of Water Rights 110
   Division of Wildlife Resources 110, 398, 417
   Office of Energy and Resource Planning 111
UTAH STATE EXTENSION SERVICES 111
UTAH STATE SOIL CONSERVATION COMMISSION 111
UTAH STATE UNIVERSITY 389
UTAH WILDERNESS COALITION 338
UTAH WILDLIFE FEDERATION 338
UTAH WOODLAND OWNERS COUNCIL 338
VANDERBILT UNIVERSITY 388
VERMONT ASSOCIATION OF CONSERVATION DISTRICTS 338
VERMONT AUDUBON COUNCIL 338
VERMONT B.A.S.S. CHAPTER FEDERATION 338
VERMONT DEPARTMENT OF AGRICULTURE, FOOD, AND MARKETS 112
   Natural Resources Conservation Council 112
   State Conservation Commission 100, 106, 112
VERMONT DEPARTMENT OF HEALTH 112
VERMONT INSTITUTE OF NATURAL SCIENCE 338
VERMONT LAND TRUST 338
VERMONT LAW SCHOOL 390

ORGANIZATION NAME INDEX

VERMONT NATURAL RESOURCES COUNCIL 339
VERMONT STATE-WIDE ENVIRONMENTAL EDUCATION
  PROGRAMS (SWEEP) 339
VERMONT WOODLANDS ASSOCIATION 339
VIRGIN ISLANDS CONSERVATION DISTRICT 339
VIRGIN ISLANDS CONSERVATION SOCIETY, INC. 339
VIRGIN ISLANDS COOPERATIVE EXTENSION SERVICE 113
VIRGIN ISLANDS SOIL AND WATER CONSERVATION DIVISION 113
VIRGINIA ASSOCIATION OF CONSERVATION DISTRICTS 339
VIRGINIA B.A.S.S. CHAPTER FEDERATION 339
VIRGINIA CONSERVATION NETWORK 339
VIRGINIA COOPERATIVE FISH AND WILDLIFE RESEARCH UNIT
  (USDI) 113
VIRGINIA DEPARTMENT OF AGRICULTURE AND CONSUMER
  SERVICES 113
VIRGINIA DEPARTMENT OF CONSERVATION AND RECREATION
  114
  Board of Conservation and Recreation 114
  Breaks Interstate Park Commission 114
  Chippokes Plantation Farm Foundation 114
  Conservation and Development of Public Beaches Board 114
  Division of Administration 39, 84, 97, 114
  Division of Dam Safety 114
  Division of Natural Heritage 114, 417
  Division of Planning and Recreation Resources 114
  Division of Soil and Water Conservation 51, 92, 94, 114
  Division of State Parks 38, 58, 63, 80, 82, 114, 122
  Virginia Cave Board 114
  Virginia Soil and Water Conservation Board 114
VIRGINIA DEPARTMENT OF ENVIRONMENTAL QUALITY 114
VIRGINIA DEPARTMENT OF GAME AND INLAND FISHERIES .. 114
  Region I 11, 100, 102, 107, 108, 115
  Region II (Lynchburg) 115
  Region III 11, 100, 107, 115
  Region IV (Staunton) 115
  Region V 11, 100, 102, 115
VIRGINIA DEPARTMENT OF HEALTH 115
VIRGINIA DEPARTMENT OF MINES, MINERALS AND ENERGY 115
  Division of Energy 68, 80, 115
  Division of Gas and Oil 115
  Division of Mined Land Reclamation 115
  Division of Mineral Mining 115
  Division of Mineral Resources 89, 115
VIRGINIA DEPARTMENT OF MINES, MINERALS, AND ENERGY
  Division of Mines 94, 115
VIRGINIA FORESTRY ASSOCIATION 340
VIRGINIA MUSEUM OF NATURAL HISTORY 115
VIRGINIA NATIVE PLANT SOCIETY 340
VIRGINIA OUTDOORS FOUNDATION 115
VIRGINIA POLYTECHNIC INSTITUTE AND STATE UNIVERSITY 391
VIRGINIA SEA GRANT PROGRAM 115
VIRGINIA SOCIETY OF ORNITHOLOGY 340
VIRGINIA STATE EXTENSION SERVICES 116
WASHINGTON ASSOCIATION OF CONSERVATION DISTRICTS 340
WASHINGTON B.A.S.S. CHAPTER FEDERATION 340
WASHINGTON COOPERATIVE FISH AND WILDLIFE RESEARCH
  UNIT (USDI) 117
WASHINGTON DEPARTMENT OF AGRICULTURE 117
WASHINGTON DEPARTMENT OF ECOLOGY 117
  Central Regional Office 31, 117
  Eastern Regional Office 12, 13, 31, 117
  Northwest Regional Office 62, 117, 149, 206
  Southwest Regional Office 30, 80, 117, 149, 153, 264
WASHINGTON DEPARTMENT OF NATURAL RESOURCES 117
  Central Region 12, 13, 17, 30, 31, 82, 99, 102, 111, 117, 118, 121, 125, 267
  Northeast Region 29, 30, 80, 102, 111, 118, 121, 127, 137, 162, 264, 269, 307
  Northwest Region 16, 29, 62, 98, 99, 102, 117, 118, 127, 149, 206, 307, 335
  Olympic Region 118
  South Puget Sound Region 118
  Southeast Region 29, 30, 80, 102, 118, 121, 145, 264, 301, 307, 335
  Southwest Region 16, 30, 80, 99, 102, 117, 118, 149, 153, 264, 301, 335, 363
WASHINGTON ENVIRONMENTAL COUNCIL 340
WASHINGTON FARM FORESTRY ASSOCIATION 341
WASHINGTON FOUNDATION FOR THE ENVIRONMENT 341
WASHINGTON NATIVE PLANT SOCIETY 341
WASHINGTON NATURAL HERITAGE PROGRAM 118
WASHINGTON RECREATION AND PARK ASSOCIATION 341
WASHINGTON SEA GRANT PROGRAM 118
WASHINGTON SOCIETY OF AMERICAN FORESTERS 341
WASHINGTON STATE CONSERVATION COMMISSION 118
WASHINGTON STATE EXTENSION SERVICES 118
WASHINGTON STATE OFFICE OF ENVIRONMENTAL EDUCATION
  118
WASHINGTON STATE UNIVERSITY 391
WASHINGTON TOXICS COALITION 341
WASHINGTON TRAILS ASSOCIATION 341
WASHINGTON UNIVERSITY 378
WASHINGTON WILDERNESS COALITION 342
WASHINGTON WILDLIFE AND RECREATION COALITION 342
WASHINGTON WILDLIFE FEDERATION 342
WASHINGTON WILDLIFE HERITAGE FOUNDATION (including
  Heritage Land Trust 342
WATER ENVIRONMENT FEDERATION 342
WATER RESOURCES ASSOCIATION OF THE DELAWARE RIVER
  BASIN 342
WATER RESOURCES RESEARCH CENTER 59
WATERLOO-WELLINGTON WILDFLOWER SOCIETY (Formerly the
  Dogtooth Group) 342
WATERSHED MANAGEMENT COUNCIL 343
WAYNE STATE UNIVERSITY 377
WELDER WILDLIFE FOUNDATION 343
WEST MICHIGAN ENVIRONMENTAL ACTION COUNCIL 343
WEST VIRGINIA ASSOCIATION OF CONSERVATION DISTRICT
  SUPERVISORS ASSOCIATION, INC. 343
WEST VIRGINIA B.A.S.S. CHAPTER FEDERATION 343
WEST VIRGINIA BUREAU OF ENVIRONMENT 119
WEST VIRGINIA COOPERATIVE FISH AND WILDLIFE RESEARCH
  UNIT 119
WEST VIRGINIA DEPARTMENT OF AGRICULTURE 119
  West Virginia Soil Conservation Agency 119
WEST VIRGINIA DIVISION OF NATURAL RESOURCES 119
WEST VIRGINIA GEOLOGICAL AND ECONOMIC SURVEY 119
WEST VIRGINIA HIGHLANDS CONSERVANCY 343
WEST VIRGINIA STATE EXTENSION SERVICE 120
WEST VIRGINIA UNIVERSITY 391
WEST VIRGINIA WILDLIFE FEDERATION, INC. 343
WEST VIRGINIA, WOODLAND OWNERS ASSOCIATION OF ... 344
WESTERN ASSOCIATION OF FISH AND WILDLIFE AGENCIES 344
WESTERN ENVIRONMENTAL LAW CENTER 344
WESTERN FORESTRY AND CONSERVATION ASSOCIATION . 344
WESTERN HEMISPHERE SHOREBIRD RESERVE NETWORK
  (WHSRN) 344
WESTERN ILLINOIS UNIVERSITY 370
WESTERN MICHIGAN UNIVERSITY 377
WESTERN PACIFIC REGIONAL FISHERY MANAGEMENT COUNCIL
  344
WESTERN PENNSYLVANIA CONSERVANCY 344
WESTERN WASHINGTON UNIVERSITY 391
WETLAND HABITAT ALLIANCE OF TEXAS 345
WHALE AND DOLPHIN CONSERVATION SOCIETY 345
WHITE CLAY WATERSHED ASSOCIATION 345
WHITETAILS UNLIMITED, INC. 345
WHOOPING CRANE CONSERVATION ASSOCIATION INC. 345
WIDENER UNIVERSITY 386
WILD CANID SURVIVAL AND RESEARCH CENTER 345
WILD DOG FOUNDATION, THE 345
WILD HORSE ORGANIZED ASSISTANCE, INC. (WHOA) 346
WILD ONES - NATURAL LANDSCAPERS, LTD 346
WILDERNESS EDUCATION ASSOCIATION 346
WILDERNESS LAND TRUST, THE 346
WILDERNESS SOCIETY, THE 346
WILDERNESS WATCH 347
WILDFLOWER ASSOCIATION OF MICHIGAN 347
WILDFOWL TRUST OF NORTH AMERICA, INC., THE 347
WILDLANDS CONSERVANCY 347
WILDLANDS PROJECT, THE 347
WILDLIFE ACTION, INC. 347
WILDLIFE CENTER OF VIRGINIA, THE 347
WILDLIFE CONSERVATION SOCIETY 348
WILDLIFE DAMAGE REVIEW (WDR) 348
WILDLIFE DISEASE ASSOCIATION 348
WILDLIFE FEDERATION OF ALASKA 348
WILDLIFE FOREVER 348
WILDLIFE FOUNDATION OF FLORIDA, INC. 349
WILDLIFE HABITAT CANADA 349

ORGANIZATION NAME INDEX

WILDLIFE HABITAT COUNCIL 349
WILDLIFE INFORMATION CENTER, INC. 349
WILDLIFE LEGISLATIVE FUND OF AMERICA, THE, AND WILDLIFE CONSERVATION FUND OF AMERICA, THE 349
WILDLIFE MANAGEMENT INSTITUTE 349
WILDLIFE PRESERVATION TRUST INTERNATIONAL, INC. ... 350
WILDLIFE RESOURCES AGENCY 107
WILDLIFE SOCIETY, ALABAMA CHAPTER 350
WILDLIFE SOCIETY, ALASKA CHAPTER 350
WILDLIFE SOCIETY, ALBERTA CHAPTER 350
WILDLIFE SOCIETY, ARIZONA CHAPTER 350
WILDLIFE SOCIETY, ARKANSAS CHAPTER 351
WILDLIFE SOCIETY, CALIFORNIA CENTRAL COAST CHAPTER 351
WILDLIFE SOCIETY, CALIFORNIA NORTH COAST CHAPTER .. 351
WILDLIFE SOCIETY, COLORADO CHAPTER 351
WILDLIFE SOCIETY, FLORIDA CHAPTER 351
WILDLIFE SOCIETY, GEORGIA CHAPTER 351
WILDLIFE SOCIETY, HAWAII CHAPTER 351
WILDLIFE SOCIETY, IDAHO CHAPTER 351
WILDLIFE SOCIETY, ILLINOIS CHAPTER 351
WILDLIFE SOCIETY, INDIANA CHAPTER 351
WILDLIFE SOCIETY, IOWA CHAPTER 351
WILDLIFE SOCIETY, KANSAS CHAPTER 352
WILDLIFE SOCIETY, KENTUCKY CHAPTER 352
WILDLIFE SOCIETY, LOUISIANA CHAPTER 352
WILDLIFE SOCIETY, MAINE CHAPTER 352
WILDLIFE SOCIETY, MANITOBA CHAPTER 352
WILDLIFE SOCIETY, MARYLAND-DELAWARE CHAPTER ... 352
WILDLIFE SOCIETY, MICHIGAN CHAPTER 352
WILDLIFE SOCIETY, MINNESOTA CHAPTER 352
WILDLIFE SOCIETY, MISSISSIPPI CHAPTER 352
WILDLIFE SOCIETY, MISSOURI CHAPTER 352
WILDLIFE SOCIETY, MONTANA CHAPTER 352
WILDLIFE SOCIETY, NATIONAL CAPITAL CHAPTER 352
WILDLIFE SOCIETY, NEBRASKA CHAPTER 352
WILDLIFE SOCIETY, NEVADA CHAPTER 353
WILDLIFE SOCIETY, NEW ENGLAND CHAPTER 353
WILDLIFE SOCIETY, NEW JERSEY CHAPTER 353
WILDLIFE SOCIETY, NEW MEXICO CHAPTER 353
WILDLIFE SOCIETY, NEW YORK CHAPTER 353
WILDLIFE SOCIETY, NORTH CAROLINA CHAPTER 353
WILDLIFE SOCIETY, NORTH DAKOTA CHAPTER 353
WILDLIFE SOCIETY, OHIO CHAPTER 353
WILDLIFE SOCIETY, OKLAHOMA CHAPTER 353
WILDLIFE SOCIETY, OREGON CHAPTER 353
WILDLIFE SOCIETY, PENNSYLVANIA CHAPTER 353
WILDLIFE SOCIETY, SACRAMENTO-SHASTA CHAPTER ... 353
WILDLIFE SOCIETY, SAN FRANCISCO BAY AREA CHAPTER .. 354
WILDLIFE SOCIETY, SAN JOAQUIN VALLEY CHAPTER 354
WILDLIFE SOCIETY, SOUTH CAROLINA CHAPTER 354
WILDLIFE SOCIETY, SOUTH DAKOTA CHAPTER 354
WILDLIFE SOCIETY, SOUTHERN CALIFORNIA CHAPTER . 354
WILDLIFE SOCIETY, TENNESSEE CHAPTER 354
WILDLIFE SOCIETY, TEXAS CHAPTER 354
WILDLIFE SOCIETY, THE 350
WILDLIFE SOCIETY, UTAH CHAPTER 354
WILDLIFE SOCIETY, VIRGINIA CHAPTER 354
WILDLIFE SOCIETY, WASHINGTON CHAPTER 354
WILDLIFE SOCIETY, WEST VIRGINIA CHAPTER 354
WILDLIFE SOCIETY, WISCONSIN CHAPTER 354
WILDLIFE SOCIETY, WYOMING CHAPTER 355
WILDLIFE WAYSTATION 355
WILKES UNIVERSITY 386
WILLIAMS COLLEGE 376
WILSON ORNITHOLOGICAL SOCIETY 355
WINCHESTER NILO FARMS 355
WINDSTAR FOUNDATION, THE 355
WISCONSIN ASSOCIATION FOR ENVIRONMENTAL EDUCATION, INC. 355
WISCONSIN ASSOCIATION OF LAKES (WAL) 355
WISCONSIN B.A.S.S. CHAPTER FEDERATION 355
WISCONSIN CONSERVATION CORPS 120
WISCONSIN COOPERATIVE FISHERY RESEARCH UNIT (USDI) 120
WISCONSIN COOPERATIVE WILDLIFE RESEARCH UNIT (USDI) 120
WISCONSIN DEPARTMENT OF AGRICULTURE TRADE AND CONSUMER PROTECTION
    Land and Water Resources Bureau   120
WISCONSIN DEPARTMENT OF NATURAL RESOURCES 120
WISCONSIN DEPARTMENT OF PUBLIC INSTRUCTION 121
WISCONSIN ENVIRONMENTAL EDUCATION BOARD (WEEB) . 121
WISCONSIN GEOLOGICAL AND NATURAL HISTORY SURVEY 121
WISCONSIN LAND AND WATER CONSERVATION ASSOCIATION 356
WISCONSIN PARK AND RECREATION ASSOCIATION 356
WISCONSIN SEA GRANT INSTITUTE 121
WISCONSIN SOCIETY FOR ORNITHOLOGY, INC., THE 356
WISCONSIN STATE EXTENSION SERVICES 122
WISCONSIN WATERFOWL ASSOCIATION, INC. 356
WISCONSIN WILDLIFE FEDERATION 356
WISCONSIN WOODLAND OWNERS ASSOCIATION 356
WOLF EDUCATION AND RESEARCH CENTER 357
WOLF FUND, THE 357
WOLF HAVEN INTERNATIONAL 357
WOODS HOLE OCEANOGRAPHIC INSITITUTION (WHOI) SEA GRANT PROGRAM 74
WORLD ASSOCIATION OF GIRL GUIDES AND GIRL SCOUTS (WAGGGS) 357
WORLD BIRD SANCTUARY (formerly Raptor Rehabilitation and Propagation Project Inc. The) 357
WORLD CONSERVATION MONITORING CENTRE 358
WORLD FORESTRY CENTER 358
WORLD PAL (WORLD POPULATION ALLOCATION LIMITED INC.) 358
WORLD PARKS ENDOWMENT INC. 358
WORLD PHEASANT ASSOCIATION 358
WORLD RESOURCES INSTITUTE 358
WORLD SOCIETY FOR THE PROTECTION OF ANIMALS (WSPA) 358
WORLD WILDLIFE FUND 359
WORLD WOMEN IN THE DEFENSE OF THE ENVIRONMENT (WorldWIDE) 359
WORLDWATCH INSTITUTE 359
WWF JAPAN (WORLD WIDE FUND FOR NATURE JAPAN) ... 359
WYOMING ASSOCIATION OF CONSERVATION DISTRICTS .. 359
WYOMING B.A.S.S. CHAPTER FEDERATION 359
WYOMING COOPERATIVE FISH AND WILDLIFE RESEARCH UNIT (USDI) 122
WYOMING DEPARTMENT OF AGRICULTURE 122
WYOMING DEPARTMENT OF COMMERCE
    Division of State Parks and Historic Sites 122
WYOMING GAME AND FISH DEPARTMENT 123
WYOMING NATIVE PLANT SOCIETY 360
WYOMING OUTDOOR COUNCIL 360
WYOMING STATE BOARD OF LAND COMMISSIONERS 123
WYOMING STATE EXTENSION SERVICES 123
WYOMING STATE GEOLOGICAL SURVEY 123
WYOMING WILDLIFE FEDERATION 360
XERCES SOCIETY, THE 360
YALE UNIVERSITY 367
YELLOWSTONE GRIZZLY FOUNDATION (YGF) 360
YMCA EARTH SERVICE CORPS 360
YORK UNIVERSITY 394
YOSEMITE RESTORATION TRUST 361
YOUNG ENTOMOLOGISTS' SOCIETY, INC. 361
YUKON FISH AND GAME ASSOCIATION 361
ZERO (REGIONAL ENVIRONMENTAL ORGANIZATION) ... 361
ZERO POPULATION GROWTH, INC. 361
ZUNGAROCOCHA RESEARCH CENTER 361

KEYWORD INDEX

Abandoned Mine Land Reclamation

OKLAHOMA STATE CONSERVATION COMMISSION........... 96

Acid Rain

ADIRONDACK COUNCIL, THE 131
CENTER FOR ENVIRONMENTAL INFORMATION............... 169
FEDERATION OF ENVIRONMENTAL EDUCATION IN ST. PETERSBURG.. 200
FRIENDS OF THE BOUNDARY WATERS WILDERNESS ... 206
INSTITUTE OF ECOSYSTEM STUDIES..................... 221
IZAAK WALTON LEAGUE OF AMERICA ENDOWMENT 234
NEWFOUNDLAND LABRADOR WILDLIFE FEDERATION... 279
NORTH ATLANTIC SALMON CONSERVATION ORGANIZATION 282
OFFICE OF ENERGY EFFICIENCY AND ENVIRONMENT.... 91
SOUTHERN ENVIRONMENTAL LAW CENTER 324
STOP 13, 326
TROUT UNLIMITED 331, 332, 333, 334
UNIVERSITY OF VERMONT EXTENSION 112
WISCONSIN LAND AND WATER CONSERVATION ASSOCIATION 356

Afforestation

DIVISION OF FORESTRY AND SOIL RESOURCES OF GUAM 57
STUDENTS PARTNERSHIP WORLDWIDE 327

Agriculture

ABUNDANT LIFE SEED FOUNDATION 130
ACADEMY FOR EDUCATIONAL DEVELOPMENT............... 130
ADIRONDACK NATURE CONSERVANCY/ADIRONDACK LAND TRUST, INC.................................. 131
ALABAMA COOPERATIVE EXTENSION SYSTEM 38
ALASKA DEPARTMENT OF NATURAL RESOURCES........... 40
AMERICA THE BEAUTIFUL FUND 135
AMERICAN FARMLAND TRUST............................ 139
AMERICAN LIVESTOCK BREEDS CONSERVANCY 147
ARIZONA DEPARTMENT OF AGRICULTURE...................... 41
ARKANSAS STATE EXTENSION SERVICES......................... 43
ASSOCIATION OF AMERICAN GEOGRAPHERS 155
BERKSHIRE-LITCHFIELD ENVIRONMENTAL COUNCIL, INC. 160
BEYOND PESTICIDES/NATIONAL COALITION AGAINST THE MISUSE OF PESTICIDES 160
BIO-INTEGRAL RESOURCE CENTER......................... 161
CANADIAN FEDERATION OF HUMANE SOCIETIES 166
CARRYING CAPACITY NETWORK 168
CENTER FOR SCIENCE IN THE PUBLIC INTEREST 171
CHARLES A. AND ANNE MORROW LINDBERGH FOUNDATION, THE................................... 172
CINCINNATI NATURE CENTER 174
COLLEGE OF TROPICAL AGRICULTURE AND HUMAN RESOURCES.. 57
COLORADO DEPARTMENT OF AGRICULTURE................... 49
COLORADO STATE UNIVERSITY COOPERATIVE EXTENSION.. 50
COLORADO TRAPPERS ASSOCIATION............................. 178
COMMITTEE ON AGRICULTURAL SUSTAINABILITY FOR DEVELOPING COUNTRIES............................ 179
CONSERVATION FEDERATION OF MARYLAND/For A Rural Maryland (F.A.R.M.) 182
DELAWARE ASSOCIATION OF CONSERVATION DISTRICTS 186
DELAWARE DEPARTMENT OF AGRICULTURE 51
DELAWARE STATE EXTENSION SERVICE........................ 52
DELTA WILDLIFE, INC. 187
ENTOMOLOGICAL SOCIETY OF AMERICA...................... 195
ENVIRONMENTAL ENTERPRISES ASSISTANCE FUND, INC. 197
FEDERATION OF ENVIRONMENTAL EDUCATION IN ST. PETERSBURG.. 200
FOOD AND AGRICULTURE ORGANIZATION OF THE UNITED NATIONS... 203
GEORGIA DEPARTMENT OF AGRICULTURE...................... 55
GOVERNOR OF SOUTH CAROLINA 104
HENRY A. WALLACE INSTITUTE FOR ALTERNATIVE AGRICULTURE (HAWIAA) 215
IDAHO STATE DEPARTMENT OF AGRICULTURE 60
IDAHO STATE SOIL CONSERVATION COMMISSION 60
ILLINOIS DEPARTMENT OF AGRICULTURE....................... 61
INDIANA DEPARTMENT OF NATURAL RESOURCES.......... 62
INTERNATIONAL ASSOCIATION OF NATURAL RESOURCE PILOTS... 223
IOWA ENVIRONMENTAL COUNCIL 232
IZAAK WALTON LEAGUE OF AMERICA, INC., THE........... 234
JACKSON HOLE LAND TRUST............................ 236
KANSAS DEPARTMENT OF AGRICULTURE 65
KANSAS DEPARTMENT OF WILDLIFE AND PARKS 65
KANSAS NATURAL RESOURCE COUNCIL 237
KENTUCKY DEPARTMENT OF AGRICULTURE 66
MARIN CONSERVATION LEAGUE 246
MARYLAND DEPARTMENT OF AGRICULTURE 71
MICHIGAN DEPARTMENT OF AGRICULTURE 74
MICHIGAN STATE UNIVERSITY EXTENSION 75
MINNESOTA DEPARTMENT OF AGRICULTURE 76
MONTANA DEPARTMENT OF AGRICULTURE 80
MONTANA DEPARTMENT OF NATURAL RESOURCES AND CONSERVATION................................... 81
MONTANA LAND RELIANCE.............................. 254
MOUNT GRACE LAND CONSERVATION TRUST 255
NATIONAL ASSOCIATION OF CONSERVATION DISTRICTS 257
NATIONAL ASSOCIATION OF STATE DEPARTMENTS OF AGRICULTURE..................................... 258
NATIONAL FARMERS UNION 261
NATIONAL FFA ORGANIZATION 261
NATIONAL GRANGE, THE............................... 262
NATIONAL WATER RESOURCES ASSOCIATION 266
NEBRASKA STATE EXTENSION SERVICES....................... 82
NEW HAMPSHIRE DEPARTMENT OF AGRICULTURE, MARKETS, AND FOOD............................... 83
NEW JERSEY AGRICULTURAL SOCIETY 277
NEW JERSEY CONSERVATION FOUNDATION 278
NEW JERSEY DEPARTMENT OF AGRICULTURE................ 84
NEW JERSEY STATE EXTENSION SERVICES.................... 86
NEW YORK DEPARTMENT OF AGRICULTURE AND MARKETS... 88
NEW YORK STATE COOPERATIVE EXTENSION................. 90
NORTH CAROLINA COOPERATIVE EXTENSION SERVICE 91
NORTH CAROLINA DEPARTMENT OF AGRICULTURE....... 92
NORTH DAKOTA STATE SOIL CONSERVATION COMMITTEE 93
NORTHERN PLAINS RESOURCE COUNCIL 285
NORTHWEST COALITION FOR ALTERNATIVES TO PESTICIDES...................................... 285
OKLAHOMA STATE BOARD OF AGRICULTURE 96
PENNSYLVANIA DEPARTMENT OF AGRICULTURE............ 99
PHEASANTS FOREVER, INC............................. 296
PUERTO RICO STATE EXTENSION SERVICES 103
RACHEL CARSON COUNCIL, INC. (formerly Rachel Carson Trust for the Living Environment Inc.) 301
RAINFOREST TRUST, INC., THE......................... 302
RHODE ISLAND COOPERATIVE EXTENSION SERVICE ... 104
SCIENTISTS CENTER FOR ANIMAL WELFARE 311
SHELBURNE FARMS................................... 312
SOCIETY FOR RANGE MANAGEMENT 319
SOIL AND WATER CONSERVATION SOCIETY (formerly Soil Conservation Society of America)....................... 320
SOUTH CAROLINA DEPARTMENT OF AGRICULTURE 105
SOUTH DAKOTA ORNITHOLOGISTS' UNION 322
SOUTH DAKOTA STATE EXTENSION SERVICES............. 106
SOUTHEASTERN COOPERATIVE WILDLIFE DISEASE STUDY 323
STATE SOIL AND WATER CONSERVATION COMMISSION (GEORGIA).. 56
TENNESSEE DEPARTMENT OF AGRICULTURE 107
TEXAS AGRICULTURAL EXTENSION SERVICE................ 108
TEXAS COOPERATIVE FISH AND WILDLIFE RESEARCH UNIT 108
TEXAS SEA GRANT PROGRAM 109

KEYWORD INDEX - Air Quality

TEXAS STATE SOIL AND WATER CONSERVATION BOARD 109
TREES FOR THE FUTURE, INC. 330
UNION OF CONCERNED SCIENTISTS 336
UNITED STATES CHAMBER OF COMMERCE 336
UNITED STATES COMMITTEE FOR THE UNITED NATIONS ENVIRONMENT PROGRAMME THE (U.S. and UNEP) 336
UTAH STATE SOIL CONSERVATION COMMISSION 111
VERMONT DEPARTMENT OF AGRICULTURE, FOOD, AND MARKETS 112
VERMONT INSTITUTE OF NATURAL SCIENCE 338
VIRGIN ISLANDS CONSERVATION SOCIETY, INC. 339
VIRGINIA DEPARTMENT OF AGRICULTURE AND CONSUMER SERVICES 113
WASHINGTON DEPARTMENT OF AGRICULTURE 117
WASHINGTON STATE CONSERVATION COMMISSION 118
WASHINGTON STATE EXTENSION SERVICES 118
WEST VIRGINIA DEPARTMENT OF AGRICULTURE 119
WEST VIRGINIA STATE EXTENSION SERVICE 120
WILDLIFE DAMAGE REVIEW (WDR) 348
WILDLIFE HABITAT CANADA 349
WORLDWATCH INSTITUTE 359
WYOMING STATE EXTENSION SERVICES 123

Air Quality

ACADEMY FOR EDUCATIONAL DEVELOPMENT 130
COUNCIL FOR PLANNING AND CONSERVATION 185
MASSACHUSETTS HIGHWAY DEPARTMENT 74
MONTANA ENVIRONMENTAL INFORMATION CENTER 254
OHIO OFFICE OF ENERGY EFFICIENCY 94
WISCONSIN LAND AND WATER CONSERVATION ASSOCIATION 356

Air Quality and Pollution

AGENCY OF NATURAL RESOURCES 111
AIR AND WASTE MANAGEMENT ASSOCIATION 132
ALABAMA DEPARTMENT OF ENVIRONMENTAL MANAGEMENT 38
ALASKA CONSERVATION ALLIANCE 133
ALASKA CONSERVATION VOICE 134
ALASKA DEPARTMENT OF ENVIRONMENTAL CONSERVATION 39
AMERICAN CONSERVATION ASSOCIATION, INC. 139
AMERICAN LUNG ASSOCIATION 147
APPALACHIAN MOUNTAIN CLUB 153
ARIZONA DEPARTMENT OF ENVIRONMENTAL QUALITY 41
AUDUBON SOCIETY OF RHODE ISLAND 159
BORDER ECOLOGY PROJECT (BEP) 162
CALIFORNIA DEPARTMENT OF EDUCATION 44
CALIFORNIA ENVIRONMENTAL PROTECTION AGENCY 44
CAMP FIRE BOYS AND GIRLS 165
CAMPAIGN FOR A PROSPEROUS GEORGIA 165
CANADA-UNITED STATES ENVIRONMENTAL COUNCIL (United States Office) 166
CENTER FOR ENVIRONMENTAL STUDY 170
CHESAPEAKE BAY FOUNDATION, INC. (Pennsylvania Office) 173
COALITION FOR CLEAN AIR 175
COMITE DESPERTAR CIDRENO 102
COMMUNITIES FOR A BETTER ENVIRONMENT 179
CONNECTICUT FUND FOR THE ENVIRONMENT 180
CONNECTICUT PUBLIC INTEREST RESEARCH GROUP (Conn PIRG) 181
CONSERVATION AND RESEARCH FOUNDATION, INC., THE 181
CONSERVATION COUNCIL OF NORTH CAROLINA 181
CONSERVATION LAW FOUNDATION, INC. (CLF) 183
DELAWARE DEPARTMENT OF NATURAL RESOURCES AND ENVIRONMENTAL CONTROL 51
DELAWARE NATURE SOCIETY 187
DEPARTMENT OF ENVIRONMENTAL QUALITY (ARKANSAS) 43
DEPARTMENT OF THE ENVIRONMENT 71
EARTH SHARE 192
EARTHJUSTICE LEGAL DEFENSE FUND (formerly Sierra Club Legal Defense Fund, Inc.) 192
ENVIRONMENTAL DEFENSE FUND, INC. 196
FEDERATION OF ENVIRONMENTAL EDUCATION IN ST. PETERSBURG 200
FOSSIL FUELS POLICY ACTION INSTITUTE/ALLIANCE FOR A PAVING MORATORIUM 204
FRIENDS OF THE EARTH 206
GEORGIA CONSERVANCY, INC., THE 209
GLOBAL CITIES PROJECT, THE 210
GREEN PARTY USA 213
GREEN SEAL 213
HOOSIER ENVIRONMENTAL COUNCIL 216
HUMAN ECOLOGY ACTION LEAGUE, INC. THE (HEAL) 217
HUNTSMAN MARINE SCIENCE CENTRE 217
ILLINOIS ENVIRONMENTAL COUNCIL 219
ILLINOIS ENVIRONMENTAL PROTECTION AGENCY 61
INFORM, INC. 221
INSTITUTE OF ECOSYSTEM STUDIES 221
IOWA DEPARTMENT OF NATURAL RESOURCES 64
ISSAQUAH ALPS TRAILS CLUB (I.A.T.C.) 233
KANSAS STATE DEPARTMENT OF HEALTH AND ENVIRONMENT 66
KIDS FOR SAVING EARTH WORLDWIDE 239
LEAGUE OF WOMEN VOTERS OF IOWA 241
MAINE DEPARTMENT OF ENVIRONMENTAL PROTECTION 70
MICHIGAN DEPARTMENT OF ENVIRONMENTAL QUALITY 75
MINNESOTA CENTER FOR ENVIRONMENTAL ADVOCACY (MCEA) 251
MONTANA ENVIRONMENTAL QUALITY COUNCIL 81
NATIONAL ASSOCIATION OF ENVIRONMENTAL PROFESSIONALS, THE (National Office) 257
NATIONAL ENVIRONMENTAL HEALTH ASSOCIATION 260
NEW HAMPSHIRE DEPARTMENT OF ENVIRONMENTAL SERVICES 84
NEW JERSEY ENVIRONMENTAL LOBBY 278
NEWFOUNDLAND LABRADOR WILDLIFE FEDERATION 279
NORTH CAROLINA COALITION, INC. 282
NORTH DAKOTA DEPARTMENT OF HEALTH 93
NORTHERN PLAINS RESOURCE COUNCIL 285
OHIO ENVIRONMENTAL COUNCIL, INC. 287
OHIO ENVIRONMENTAL PROTECTION AGENCY 94
OKLAHOMA DEPARTMENT OF ENVIRONMENTAL QUALITY 95
OREGON B.A.S.S. CHAPTER FEDERATION 290
OREGON DEPARTMENT OF ENVIRONMENTAL QUALITY (DEQ) 98
OREGON ENVIRONMENTAL COUNCIL 290
POPULATION INSTITUTE, THE 298
POPULATION-ENVIRONMENT BALANCE, INC. 298
RESOURCES FOR THE FUTURE 304
SAVE THE DUNES COUNCIL 309
SCENIC HUDSON, INC. 311
SIERRA CLUB 312, 314, 315, 316, 317
SOUTH CAROLINA DEPARTMENT OF HEALTH AND ENVIRONMENTAL CONTROL 105
SOUTH DAKOTA DEPARTMENT OF ENVIRONMENT AND NATURAL RESOURCES 106
SOUTH DAKOTA ORNITHOLOGISTS' UNION 322
SOUTHERN ENVIRONMENTAL LAW CENTER 324
STATE OF IDAHO DIVISION OF ENVIRONMENTAL QUALITY 61
STOP 13, 326
TAHOE REGIONAL PLANNING AGENCY 327
TENNESSEE ENVIRONMENTAL COUNCIL 328
TREES FOR THE FUTURE, INC. 330
U.S. PUBLIC INTEREST RESEARCH GROUP 336
UNITED NATIONS ENVIRONMENT PROGRAMME 336
VERMONT DEPARTMENT OF HEALTH 112
VIRGINIA B.A.S.S. CHAPTER FEDERATION 339
VIRGINIA DEPARTMENT OF ENVIRONMENTAL QUALITY 114
WEST MICHIGAN ENVIRONMENTAL ACTION COUNCIL 343
WESTERN ENVIRONMENTAL LAW CENTER 344
WISCONSIN DEPARTMENT OF NATURAL RESOURCES 120
WORLD RESOURCES INSTITUTE 358

Air Resources

PENNSYLVANIA CITIZENS ADVISORY COUNCIL TO DEPARTMENT OF ENVIRONMENTAL PROTECTION 294

Alternative Agriculture

- CATSKILL CENTER FOR CONSERVATION AND DEVELOPMENT, INC., THE 168
- NORTHWEST COALITION FOR ALTERNATIVES TO PESTICIDES 285

Ancient Forests

- ALASKA CONSERVATION ALLIANCE 133
- ALASKA CONSERVATION VOICE 134
- AUDUBON SOCIETY OF PORTLAND 159
- ECOLOGY CENTER 194
- FOREST WATCH 204
- LIGHTHAWK 243
- NATIVE PLANT SOCIETY OF NORTHEASTERN OHIO 269
- NEWFOUNDLAND LABRADOR WILDLIFE FEDERATION .. 279
- NORTH CASCADES CONSERVATION COUNCIL 283
- NORTHCOAST ENVIRONMENTAL CENTER 284
- NORTHWEST ECOSYSTEM ALLIANCE 285
- OLYMPIC PARK INSTITUTE 289
- OREGON NATURAL RESOURCES COUNCIL 290
- RAINFOREST TRUST, INC., THE 302
- SIERRA NEVADA FOREST PROTECTION CAMPAIGN 317
- SINAPU 317
- SMITHSONIAN INSTITUTION 317
- WILD ONES - NATURAL LANDSCAPERS, LTD 346

Animal Welfare

- AMERICAN HUMANE ASSOCIATION 145
- CANADIAN FEDERATION OF HUMANE SOCIETIES 166
- JANE GOODALL INSTITUTE, THE 236

Aquaculture

- HUNTSMAN MARINE SCIENCE CENTRE 217
- MOTE MARINE LABORATORY 255
- NORTH CAROLINA SEA GRANT PROGRAM 92
- WOODS HOLE OCEANOGRAPHIC INSITITUTION (WHOI) SEA GRANT PROGRAM 74

Aquariums

- AMERICAN ZOO AND AQUARIUM ASSOCIATION (AZA) ... 151
- CALIFORNIA ACADEMY OF SCIENCES 163
- HUNTSMAN MARINE SCIENCE CENTRE 217
- INTERNATIONAL MARINE MAMMAL PROJECT, THE 226
- MOTE MARINE LABORATORY 255
- SCIENTISTS CENTER FOR ANIMAL WELFARE 311
- WILDLIFE CONSERVATION SOCIETY 348

Aquatic Habitats

- A.B. ENVIRONMENTAL EDUCATION CENTER 130
- ADOPT-A-STREAM FOUNDATION, THE 131
- ALASKA CONSERVATION ALLIANCE 133
- ALASKA CONSERVATION VOICE 134
- ALASKA COOPERATIVE FISH AND WILDLIFE RESEARCH UNIT 39
- AMERICAN CETACEAN SOCIETY 138
- AMERICAN FISHERIES SOCIETY 140, 141, 142, 143, 144
- AMERICAN INSTITUTE OF FISHERY RESEARCH BIOLOGISTS 146
- AMERICAN LANDS (formerly Western Ancient Forest Campaign) 146
- AMERICAN LITTORAL SOCIETY 146
- AMERICAN OCEANS CAMPAIGN 147
- AMERICAN SOCIETY OF ICHTHYOLOGISTS AND HERPETOLOGISTS 149
- ANGLERS FOR CLEAN WATER 152
- ARLINGTON OUTDOOR EDUCATION ASSOCIATION, INC. 155
- CHESAPEAKE BAY FOUNDATION, INC. (Maryland Office) .173
- COAST ALLIANCE 176
- COASTAL CONSERVATION ASSOCIATION 176
- DEPARTMENT OF FISH AND WILDLIFE (WASHINGTON) .. 116
- DEPARTMENT OF PLANNING AND NATURAL RESOURCES 112
- DEPARTMENT OF WILDLIFE CONSERVATION 95
- DESERT FISHES COUNCIL 188
- DESERT RESEARCH FOUNDATION OF NAMIBIA, THE 188
- DRAGONFLY SOCIETY OF THE AMERICAS, THE 188
- ENVIRONMENTAL DEFENSE FUND, INC. 196
- ENVIRONMENTAL EDUCATION ASSOCIATION OF ILLINOIS 197
- ENVIRONMENTAL LEAGUE OF MASSACHUSETTS 198
- FISH AND WILDLIFE INFORMATION EXCHANGE 201
- FLORIDA COOPERATIVE FISH AND WILDLIFE RESEARCH UNIT (USDI) 52
- FLORIDA FISH AND WILDLIFE CONSERVATION COMMISSION 54
- FRIENDS OF THE SAN JUANS 206
- FRIENDS OF THE SEA OTTER 206
- GALIANO CONSERVANCY ASSOCIATION 207
- GEORGIA COOPERATIVE FISH AND WILDLIFE RESEARCH UNIT (USDI) 55
- GLACIER INSTITUTE, THE 210
- GREAT LAKES SPORT FISHING COUNCIL 211
- HAWAII AUDUBON SOCIETY 214
- HAWAII COOPERATIVE FISHERY RESEARCH UNIT (USDI) 58
- HAWAII NATURE CENTER 214
- HUDSONIA LIMITED 216
- HUNTSMAN MARINE SCIENCE CENTRE 217
- ILLINOIS NATIVE PLANT SOCIETY 219
- INTERNATIONAL MARINE MAMMAL PROJECT, THE 226
- IOWA DEPARTMENT OF NATURAL RESOURCES 64
- KANSAS BIOLOGICAL SURVEY 65
- KANSAS DEPARTMENT OF WILDLIFE AND PARKS 65
- KEEP FLORIDA BEAUTIFUL, INC. 238
- KIDS FOR SAVING EARTH WORLDWIDE 239
- LIGHTHAWK 243
- LONG LIVE THE KINGS 243
- MAINE COOPERATIVE FISH AND WILDLIFE RESEARCH UNIT (USDI) 70
- MAINE DEPARTMENT OF MARINE RESOURCES 71
- MAINE SEA GRANT PROGRAM 71
- MAINE/NEW HAMPSHIRE SEA GRANT PROGRAM 83
- MARINE LABORATORY (FLORIDA) 55
- MARYLAND SEA GRANT COLLEGE 72
- MICHIGAN WILDLIFE HABITAT FOUNDATION 250
- MINNESOTA COOPERATIVE FISH AND WILDLIFE RESEARCH UNIT 76
- MINNESOTA SEA GRANT COLLEGE PROGRAM 77
- MONTANA COOPERATIVE FISHERY RESEARCH UNIT (USDI) 80
- NATIVE PLANT SOCIETY OF NORTHEASTERN OHIO 269
- NATURAL LAND INSTITUTE 270
- NATURE SASKATCHEWAN 275
- NEW HAMPSHIRE LAKES ASSOCIATION 277
- NEW MEXICO COOPERATIVE FISH AND WILDLIFE RESEARCH UNIT 87
- NEWFOUNDLAND LABRADOR WILDLIFE FEDERATION .. 279
- NORTH AMERICAN BENTHOLOGICAL SOCIETY 280
- NORTH AMERICAN FISHING CLUB 281
- NORTH AMERICAN NATIVE FISHES ASSOCIATION 281
- NORTH CAROLINA SEA GRANT PROGRAM 92
- OCEAN VOICE INTERNATIONAL 286
- OHIO SEA GRANT COLLEGE PROGRAM 95
- OREGON COOPERATIVE FISH AND WILDLIFE RESEARCH UNIT (USDI) 97
- PACIFIC FISHERY MANAGEMENT COUNCIL 292
- PACIFIC WHALE FOUNDATION 293
- PENNSYLVANIA FISH AND BOAT COMMISSION 101
- PUERTO RICO SEA GRANT PROGRAM 103
- RIVER ALLIANCE OF WISCONSIN 305
- SMITHSONIAN INSTITUTION 317
- SOCIETY OF WETLAND SCIENTISTS 320
- SOUTH CAROLINA WILDLIFE FEDERATION 321
- SOUTH DAKOTA GAME, FISH, AND PARKS DEPARTMENT 106
- SOUTH DAKOTA WILDLIFE FEDERATION 323
- SOUTHEASTERN FISHES COUNCIL 323
- TENNESSEE B.A.S.S. CHAPTER FEDERATION 328
- TEXAS SEA GRANT PROGRAM 109
- TEXAS WATER DEVELOPMENT BOARD 109
- TROUT UNLIMITED 331, 332, 333, 334

KEYWORD INDEX - Aquatic Species

TROUT UNLIMITED, OKLAHOMA COUNCIL 333
UNITED STATES TOURIST COUNCIL 336
UPPER MISSISSIPPI RIVER CONSERVATION COMMITTEE
.... 337
UTAH COOPERATIVE FISH AND WILDLIFE RESEARCH UNIT
(USDI-USGS-BRD-CRU) 110
VIRGINIA COOPERATIVE FISH AND WILDLIFE RESEARCH
UNIT (USDI) 113
VIRGINIA SEA GRANT PROGRAM 115
WASHINGTON COOPERATIVE FISH AND WILDLIFE
RESEARCH UNIT (USDI) 117
WATER RESOURCES RESEARCH CENTER 59
WEST VIRGINIA COOPERATIVE FISH AND WILDLIFE
RESEARCH UNIT 119
WEST VIRGINIA DIVISION OF NATURAL RESOURCES 119
WILDLIFE FOREVER 348
WISCONSIN ASSOCIATION OF LAKES (WAL) 355
WISCONSIN COOPERATIVE FISHERY RESEARCH UNIT
(USDI) 120
WISCONSIN SEA GRANT INSTITUTE 121
WISCONSIN WILDLIFE FEDERATION 356
WORLD CONSERVATION MONITORING CENTRE 358

Aquatic Species

COUSTEAU SOCIETY, INC., THE 185
EUROPEAN CETACEAN SOCIETY 199
NORTH CAROLINA SEA GRANT PROGRAM 92
OHIO SEA GRANT COLLEGE PROGRAM 95

Arctic

ALASKA NATURAL HISTORY ASSOCIATION 134
ARCTIC INSTITUTE OF NORTH AMERICA 154
CANADIAN ARCTIC RESOURCES COMMITTEE, INC. 166
CIRCUMPOLAR CONSERVATION UNION 174
NORTHERN ALASKA ENVIRONMENTAL CENTER 285

Arid Lands

NEW MEXICO COOPERATIVE FISH AND WILDLIFE
RESEARCH UNIT 87

Asia Water Environment

ACADEMY FOR EDUCATIONAL DEVELOPMENT 130
PACIFIC INSTITUTE FOR STUDIES IN DEVELOPMENT,
ENVIRONMENT, AND SECURITY 293
WATER ENVIRONMENT FEDERATION 342

Atlantic Salmon

ATLANTIC SALMON FEDERATION 157
MAINE ATLANTIC SALMON COMMISSION (formerly Maine
Atlantic Salmon Authority) 69

Bats

BAT CONSERVATION INTERNATIONAL 160
ORGANIZATION FOR BAT CONSERVATION 291

Beaches

AMERICAN OCEANS CAMPAIGN 147
DELAWARE DEPARTMENT OF NATURAL RESOURCES AND
ENVIRONMENTAL CONTROL 51
SOUTH CAROLINA COASTAL CONSERVATION LEAGUE . 321

Bears

CONSERVATION FORCE 182
HIMALAYAN WILDLIFE FOUNDATION 216
INTERNATIONAL ASSOCIATION FOR BEAR RESEARCH
AND MANAGEMENT 222

Beautification

OUTDOOR CIRCLE, THE 291
PENNSYLVANIA RESOURCES COUNCIL, INC., (formerly PA
Roadside Council) 295
WILDFLOWER ASSOCIATION OF MICHIGAN 347

Bicycle

ADIRONDACK MOUNTAIN CLUB, INC., THE 131
ILLINOIS PRAIRIE PATH 219
IOWA TRAILS COUNCIL 232

Billfish

BILLFISH FOUNDATION, THE 160

Biodiversity

ACADEMY FOR EDUCATIONAL DEVELOPMENT 130
ACRES LAND TRUST 130
ADKINS ARBORETUM 131
ALABAMA COOPERATIVE FISH AND WILDLIFE RESEARCH
UNIT (USDI) 38
ALABAMA NATURAL HERITAGE PROGRAM 132
ALASKA AUDUBON SOCIETY 133
AMERICA THE BEAUTIFUL FUND 135
AMERICAN ASSOCIATION FOR THE ADVANCEMENT OF
SCIENCE 136
AMERICAN ASSOCIATION OF FIELD BOTANISTS 136
AMERICAN BIRDING ASSOCIATION 138
AMERICAN CHESTNUT FOUNDATION, THE 139
AMERICAN LIVESTOCK BREEDS CONSERVANCY 147
AMERICAN MUSEUM OF NATURAL HISTORY 147
AMERICAN WILDLANDS 151
ANCIENT FOREST INTERNATIONAL 152
ANTARCTICA PROJECT 153
ASSOCIATION FOR THE PROTECTION OF THE
ADIRONDACKS, THE 155
AUDUBON COUNCIL OF ILLINOIS 158
AUDUBON INTERNATIONAL 158
BAT CONSERVATION INTERNATIONAL 160
BERKSHIRE-LITCHFIELD ENVIRONMENTAL COUNCIL, INC.
.... 160
BIODIVERSITY LEGAL FOUNDATION 161
CALIFORNIA NATIVE PLANT SOCIETY, THE 164
CALIFORNIA WILDLIFE FEDERATION 165
CATSKILL FOREST ASSOCIATION 168
CENTER FOR BIOLOGICAL DIVERSITY 169
CENTER FOR INTERNATIONAL ENVIRONMENTAL LAW
(CIEL) 170
CENTER FOR MARINE CONSERVATION 170
CENTER FOR PLANT CONSERVATION 170
CENTER FOR RESOURCE ECONOMICS 171
CENTRO de INFORMACION, INVESTIGACION y EDUCACION
SOCIAL (CIIES) 172
COLORADO NATURAL HERITAGE PROGRAM 177
CONSERVANCY OF SOUTHWEST FLORIDA, THE 181
CONSERVATION FORCE 182
CONSERVATION INTERNATIONAL 183
CONSERVATION TREATY SUPPORT FUND 183
CORNELL LAB OF ORNITHOLOGY 184
CRAIGHEAD WILDLIFE-WILDLANDS INSTITUTE 185
CROSBY ABORETUM, THE, Mississippi State University 185
DEFENDERS OF WILDLIFE 186
DESERT RESEARCH FOUNDATION OF NAMIBIA, THE 188
EARTH FOUNDATION 191
EARTHWATCH INSTITUTE 193
ECOLOGICAL SOCIETY OF AMERICA, THE 193
ECOTOURISM SOCIETY, THE 194
ENDANGERED SPECIES COALITION 194
ENVIRONMENTAL DEFENSE FUND, INC. 196
ENVIRONMENTAL ENTERPRISES ASSISTANCE FUND, INC.
.... 197
ENVIRONMENTAL LAW INSTITUTE, THE 198
EUROPEAN CETACEAN SOCIETY 199
FAIRFAX AUDUBON SOCIETY 199
FISH AND WILDLIFE INFORMATION EXCHANGE 201

KEYWORD INDEX - Biodiversity

FLORIDA COOPERATIVE FISH AND WILDLIFE RESEARCH UNIT (USDI) 52
FLORIDA DEFENDERS OF THE ENVIRONMENT, INC. (Home Office) 201
FLORIDA NATIVE PLANT SOCIETY 202
FOREST SERVICE EMPLOYEES FOR ENVIRONMENTAL ETHICS (FSEEE) 204
FOREST SOCIETY OF MAINE 204
FRIENDS OF THE BOUNDARY WATERS WILDERNESS ... 206
FRIENDS OF THE SEA OTTER 206
GALIANO CONSERVANCY ASSOCIATION 207
GEORGE MIKSCH SUTTON AVIAN RESEARCH CENTER INC. 208
GREAT LAKES UNITED 211
HAWAII AUDUBON SOCIETY 214
HAWAII NATURE CENTER 214
HAWAII SOCIETY OF AMERICAN FORESTERS 214
HOOSIER ENVIRONMENTAL COUNCIL 216
HUMBOLT FIELD RESEARCH INSTITUTE 217
HUNTSMAN MARINE SCIENCE CENTRE 217
IDAHO CONSERVATION LEAGUE 218
IDAHO COOPERATIVE FISH AND WILDLIFE RESEARCH UNIT (USDI) 60
ILLINOIS AUDUBON SOCIETY 219
ILLINOIS DEPARTMENT OF NATURAL RESOURCES ... 61
ILLINOIS NATIVE PLANT SOCIETY 219
ILLINOIS NATURAL HERITAGE FOUNDATION 219
INDIANA NATIVE PLANT AND WILDFLOWER SOCIETY ... 220
INSTITUTE FOR ECOLOGICAL STUDIES 92
INTERNATIONAL ASSOCIATION OF NATURAL RESOURCE PILOTS 223
INTERNATIONAL CENTER FOR TROPICAL ECOLOGY ... 224
INTERNATIONAL CENTRE FOR CONSERVATION EDUCATION 224
INTERNATIONAL MARINE MAMMAL PROJECT, THE 226
INTERNATIONAL SNOW LEOPARD TRUST 227
INTERNATIONAL SOCIETY FOR ECOLOGICAL ECONOMICS 227
INTERNATIONAL SOCIETY FOR THE PRESERVATION OF THE TROPICAL RAINFOREST, THE 227
INTERNATIONAL SOCIETY OF TROPICAL FORESTERS, INC. 228
IOWA AUDUBON 231
IOWA COOPERATIVE FISH AND WILDLIFE RESEARCH UNIT 64
IOWA ENVIRONMENTAL COUNCIL 232
IOWA NATIVE PLANT SOCIETY 232
JACKSON HOLE CONSERVATION ALLIANCE 236
KANSAS BIOLOGICAL SURVEY 65
KANSAS DEPARTMENT OF WILDLIFE AND PARKS 65
KENTUCKY DEPARTMENT OF FISH AND WILDLIFE RESOURCES 66
LEAGUE OF ENVIRONMENTAL JOURNALISTS 241
LEE COUNTY PARKS AND RECREATION SERVICES ... 54
LIGHTHAWK 243
MAINE COOPERATIVE FISH AND WILDLIFE RESEARCH UNIT (USDI) 70
MANASOTA-88 245
MANOMET CENTER FOR CONSERVATION SCIENCES ... 245
MARINE CONSERVATION BIOLOGY INSTITUTE 246
MARINE ENVIRONMENTAL RESEARCH INSTITUTE (MERI) 246
MARYLAND NATIVE PLANT SOCIETY 247
MASSACHUSETTS AUDUBON SOCIETY, INC. 247
MASSACHUSETTS COOPERATIVE FISH AND WILDLIFE RESEARCH UNIT (USDI) 74
MAX McGRAW WILDLIFE FOUNDATION 248
MICHIGAN DEPARTMENT OF AGRICULTURE 74
MINNESOTA DEPARTMENT OF AGRICULTURE 76
MINNESOTA NATIVE PLANT SOCIETY 251
MISSOURI AUDUBON COUNCIL 253
MISSOURI NATIVE PLANT SOCIETY 253
MISSOURI PRAIRIE FOUNDATION 253
MONTANA AUDUBON 254
MONTANA WILDERNESS ASSOCIATION 255
MOUNTAIN LION FOUNDATION 255
NATIONAL AVIARY 259
NATIONAL MILITARY FISH AND WILDLIFE ASSOCIATION 263
NATIVE PLANT SOCIETY OF OREGON 269
NATURAL AREAS ASSOCIATION 270

NATURAL HERITAGE COMMISSION (ARKANSAS) 44
NATURAL LAND INSTITUTE 270
NATURE CONSERVANCY, THE 272, 273, 274
NATURE SASKATCHEWAN 275
NEVADA NATURAL HERITAGE PROGRAM 83
NEW HAMPSHIRE NATURAL HERITAGE INVENTORY 84
NEW JERSEY CONSERVATION FOUNDATION 278
NEWFOUNDLAND LABRADOR WILDLIFE FEDERATION ... 279
NORTH AMERICAN BUTTERFLY ASSOCIATION 280
NORTH AMERICAN COALITION ON RELIGION AND ECOLOGY (NACRE) 280
NORTH AMERICAN CRANE WORKING GROUP 281
NORTH CASCADES CONSERVATION COUNCIL 283
NORTH DAKOTA PARKS AND RECREATION DEPARTMENT 93
NORTHCOAST ENVIRONMENTAL CENTER 284
NORTHWEST ECOSYSTEM ALLIANCE 285
OCEAN VOICE INTERNATIONAL 286
OHIO BIOLOGICAL SURVEY 287
OKLAHOMA BIOLOGICAL SURVEY 95
OKLAHOMA NATIVE PLANT SOCIETY 289
OLYMPIC PARK INSTITUTE 289
OREGON COOPERATIVE FISH AND WILDLIFE RESEARCH UNIT (USDI) 97
PACIFIC RIVERS COUNCIL 293
PENNSYLVANIA DEPARTMENT OF CONSERVATION AND NATURAL RESOURCES 100
PENNSYLVANIA FOREST STEWARDSHIP PROGRAM 102
PRAIRIE CLUB, THE 298
PREDATOR PROJECT 299
PUERTO RICO ASSOCIATION OF SOIL AND WATER CONSERVATION DISTRICTS 300
PUERTO RICO CONSERVATION FOUNDATION, THE (PRCF 300
PUERTO RICO DEPARTMENT OF NATURAL AND ENVIRONMENTAL RESOURCES 103
PUERTO RICO SEA GRANT PROGRAM 103
RAINFOREST ACTION NETWORK 302
RAINFOREST ALLIANCE 302
RAINFOREST RELIEF 302
REEF RELIEF 303
REP AMERICA/REPUBLICANS FOR ENVIRONMENTAL PROTECTION 304
RESOURCES FOR THE FUTURE 304
SAVE AMERICA'S FORESTS 309
SIERRA NEVADA FOREST PROTECTION CAMPAIGN 317
SINAPU 317
SMITHSONIAN INSTITUTION 317
SOCIETY FOR CONSERVATION BIOLOGY 318
SOUTH CAROLINA COASTAL CONSERVATION LEAGUE 321
SOUTHEASTERN FISHES COUNCIL 323
STEAMBOATERS, THE 325
TALLAHASSEE MUSEUM OF HISTORY AND NATURAL SCIENCE 327
TENNESSEE CITIZENS FOR WILDERNESS PLANNING 328
TEXAS COOPERATIVE FISH AND WILDLIFE RESEARCH UNIT 108
TEXAS FORESTRY ASSOCIATION 329
TRUST FOR WILDLIFE, INC. 335
UNION OF CONCERNED SCIENTISTS 336
UNITED NATIONS ENVIRONMENT PROGRAMME 336
UTAH COOPERATIVE FISH AND WILDLIFE RESEARCH UNIT (USDI-USGS-BRD-CRU) 110
UTAH NATURE STUDY SOCIETY 337
VIRGINIA MUSEUM OF NATURAL HISTORY 115
WASHINGTON COOPERATIVE FISH AND WILDLIFE RESEARCH UNIT (USDI) 117
WASHINGTON NATURAL HERITAGE PROGRAM 118
WASHINGTON WILDERNESS COALITION 342
WILDERNESS SOCIETY, THE 346
WILDFOWL TRUST OF NORTH AMERICA, INC., THE ... 347
WILDLANDS PROJECT, THE 347
WILDLIFE DAMAGE REVIEW (WDR) 348
WILDLIFE HABITAT CANADA 349
WILDLIFE HABITAT COUNCIL 349
WILDLIFE INFORMATION CENTER, INC. 349
WILSON ORNITHOLOGICAL SOCIETY 355
WISCONSIN LAND AND WATER CONSERVATION ASSOCIATION 356
WOLF EDUCATION AND RESEARCH CENTER 357

KEYWORD INDEX - Bioinformatics

WOODS HOLE OCEANOGRAPHIC INSITITUTION (WHOI)
  SEA GRANT PROGRAM 74
WORLD BIRD SANCTUARY (formerly Raptor Rehabilitation
  and Propagation Project Inc. The) 357
WORLD CONSERVATION MONITORING CENTRE 358
WORLD PARKS ENDOWMENT INC. 358
XERCES SOCIETY, THE 360
ZUNGAROCOCHA RESEARCH CENTER 361

Bioinformatics

TEXAS COOPERATIVE FISH AND WILDLIFE RESEARCH
  UNIT 108

Biology

ALASKA AUDUBON SOCIETY 133
AMERICAN ASSOCIATION FOR THE ADVANCEMENT OF
  SCIENCE 136
AMERICAN INSTITUTE OF BIOLOGICAL SCIENCES 146
AMERICAN INSTITUTE OF FISHERY RESEARCH
  BIOLOGISTS 146
AMERICAN SOCIETY OF ICHTHYOLOGISTS AND
  HERPETOLOGISTS 149
ASSOCIATION OF FIELD ORNITHOLOGISTS 156
BAT CONSERVATION INTERNATIONAL 160
CALIFORNIA TRAPPERS ASSOCIATION 164
CANADIAN SOCIETY OF ENVIRONMENTAL BIOLOGISTS 167
CHICAGO HERPETOLOGICAL SOCIETY 173
CHIHUAHUAN DESERT RESEARCH INSTITUTE 173
DESERT TORTOISE COUNCIL 188
ECOLOGICAL SOCIETY OF AMERICA, THE 193
ENTOMOLOGICAL SOCIETY OF AMERICA 195
FLORIDA EXOTIC PEST PLANT COUNCIL 202
FRIENDS OF THE SEA OTTER 206
GREEN (GLOBAL RIVERS ENVIRONMENTAL EDUCATION
  NETWORK) 212
HUNTSMAN MARINE SCIENCE CENTRE 217
ILLINOIS DEPARTMENT OF NATURAL RESOURCES 61
INTERNATIONAL ASSOCIATION FOR BEAR RESEARCH
  AND MANAGEMENT 222
INTERNATIONAL WILDLIFE REHABILITATION COUNCIL
  (IWRC) 230
KANSAS ACADEMY OF SCIENCE 237
KANSAS DEPARTMENT OF WILDLIFE AND PARKS 65
MAINE ATLANTIC SALMON COMMISSION (formerly Maine
  Atlantic Salmon Authority) 69
MARINE LABORATORY (FLORIDA) 55
MAX McGRAW WILDLIFE FOUNDATION 248
MINNESOTA ORNITHOLOGISTS' UNION 251
MOTE MARINE LABORATORY 255
NATIONAL ASSOCIATION OF BIOLOGY TEACHERS 257
NATIONAL SPELEOLOGICAL SOCIETY, INC. 265
NEW HAMPSHIRE FISH AND GAME DEPARTMENT 84
NEW HAMPSHIRE NATURAL HERITAGE INVENTORY 84
NORTH AMERICAN BENTHOLOGICAL SOCIETY 280
NORTHWEST ATLANTIC FISHERIES ORGANIZATION
  (NAFO) 285
OKLAHOMA BIOLOGICAL SURVEY 95
OLYMPIC PARK INSTITUTE 289
ORNITHOLOGICAL COUNCIL 291
SCIENTISTS CENTER FOR ANIMAL WELFARE 311
SOCIETY FOR INTEGRATIVE AND COMPARTIVE BIOLOGY
  (formerly AMERICAN SOCIETY OF ZOOLOGISTS) 318
SOUTHEASTERN ASSOCIATION OF FISH AND WILDLIFE
  AGENCIES 323
STROUD WATER RESEARCH CENTER 326
TEXAS SEA GRANT PROGRAM 109
UPPER MISSISSIPPI RIVER CONSERVATION COMMITTEE
  337
WILDLIFE DISEASE ASSOCIATION 348
WILSON ORNITHOLOGICAL SOCIETY 355

Biotechnology

CALIFORNIA SEA GRANT COLLEGE SYSTEM 45
COLLEGE OF TROPICAL AGRICULTURE AND HUMAN
  RESOURCES 57
COLORADO STATE UNIVERSITY COOPERATIVE
  EXTENSION 50
ENTOMOLOGICAL SOCIETY OF AMERICA 195
ENVIRONMENTAL DEFENSE FUND, INC. 196
IDAHO STATE DEPARTMENT OF AGRICULTURE 60
KEYSTONE CENTER, THE 239
MARYLAND SEA GRANT COLLEGE 72
MINNESOTA SEA GRANT COLLEGE PROGRAM 77
NATIONAL 4-H COUNCIL 256
NATIONAL ASSOCIATION OF BIOLOGY TEACHERS 257
NATIONAL ASSOCIATION OF STATE DEPARTMENTS OF
  AGRICULTURE 258
NATIONAL FFA ORGANIZATION 261
NEW YORK DEPARTMENT OF AGRICULTURE AND
  MARKETS 88
OHIO ACADEMY OF SCIENCE, THE 286
OREGON SEA GRANT PROGRAM 98
SCIENTISTS CENTER FOR ANIMAL WELFARE 311
STUDENT PUGWASH USA 326
TEXAS COOPERATIVE FISH AND WILDLIFE RESEARCH
  UNIT 108
UNION OF CONCERNED SCIENTISTS 336
UNITED NATIONS ENVIRONMENT PROGRAMME 336
UTAH DEPARTMENT OF HEALTH 110
WASHINGTON SEA GRANT PROGRAM 118
WISCONSIN LAND AND WATER CONSERVATION
  ASSOCIATION 356
WISCONSIN SEA GRANT INSTITUTE 121

Birds

ALASKA AUDUBON SOCIETY 133
AMERICAN BIRD CONSERVANCY 138
AMERICAN BIRDING ASSOCIATION 138
AMERICAN ORNITHOLOGISTS' UNION 148
ASSOCIATION OF AVIAN VETERINARIANS 156
ASSOCIATION OF FIELD ORNITHOLOGISTS 156
AUDUBON COUNCIL OF CONNECTICUT 158
AUDUBON COUNCIL OF ILLINOIS 158
AUDUBON INTERNATIONAL 158
AUDUBON NATURALIST SOCIETY OF THE CENTRAL
  ATLANTIC STATES 158
AUDUBON OF KANSAS (formerly Kansas Audubon Council)
  158
AUDUBON SOCIETY OF MISSOURI 158
AUDUBON SOCIETY OF PORTLAND 159
AUDUBON SOCIETY OF RHODE ISLAND 159
AUDUBON SOCIETY OF WESTERN PENNSYLVANIA 159
BIRDLIFE INTERNATIONAL 161
BRITISH COLUMBIA FIELD ORNITHOLOGISTS 163
BROOKS BIRD CLUB INC., THE 163
CANADIAN COOPERATIVE WILDLIFE HEALTH CENTRE . 166
CAROLINA BIRD CLUB, INC. 168
CASCADIA RESEARCH 168
CHESAPEAKE BAY FOUNDATION, INC. (Virginia Office) ... 173
COLORADO COOPERATIVE FISH AND WILDLIFE
  RESEARCH UNIT (USDI) 49
CORNELL LAB OF ORNITHOLOGY 184
DELAWARE MUSEUM OF NATURAL HISTORY 187
DEPARTMENT OF INTERIOR, U.S.G.S/B.R.D, SOUTH
  CAROLINA COOPERATIVE FISH AND WILDLIFE
  RESEARCH UNIT 104
DEPARTMENT OF PLANNING AND NATURAL RESOURCES
  112
EAGLE NATURE FOUNDATION, LTD. 191
ELSA WILD ANIMAL APPEAL 194
ENVIRONMENT COUNCIL OF RHODE ISLAND 195
FAIRFAX AUDUBON SOCIETY 199
FEDERAL WILDLIFE OFFICER'S ASSOCIATION 199
FEDERATION OF ALBERTA NATURALISTS 200
FEDERATION OF NEW YORK STATE BIRD CLUBS, INC. . 200
FISH AND WILDLIFE INFORMATION EXCHANGE 201
FLORIDA AUDUBON SOCIETY 201
FLORIDA FISH AND WILDLIFE CONSERVATION
  COMMISSION 54
FLORIDA ORNITHOLOGICAL SOCIETY 202
GEORGE MIKSCH SUTTON AVIAN RESEARCH CENTER
  INC. 208
HAWAII AUDUBON SOCIETY 214

Entry	Page
HAWAII NATURE CENTER	214
HAWK AND OWL TRUST, THE	215
HAWK MOUNTAIN SANCTUARY ASSOCIATION	215
HAWKWATCH INTERNATIONAL, INC.	215
HUMMINGBIRD SOCIETY, THE	217
HUNTSMAN MARINE SCIENCE CENTRE	217
IDAHO COOPERATIVE FISH AND WILDLIFE RESEARCH UNIT (USDI)	60
ILLINOIS AUDUBON SOCIETY	219
INDIANA AUDUBON SOCIETY, INC.	220
INTERNATIONAL ASSOCIATION OF NATURAL RESOURCE PILOTS	223
INTERNATIONAL CRANE FOUNDATION	224
INTERNATIONAL OSPREY FOUNDATION INC., THE	226
IOWA AUDUBON	231
IOWA DEPARTMENT OF NATURAL RESOURCES	64
ISLAND CONSERVATION EFFORT	233
JACK MINER MIGRATORY BIRD FOUNDATION, INC.	236
KANSAS DEPARTMENT OF WILDLIFE AND PARKS	65
KANSAS ORNITHOLOGICAL SOCIETY	237
LEE COUNTY PARKS AND RECREATION SERVICES	54
LIGHTHAWK	243
LOUISIANA AUDUBON COUNCIL	243
MANOMET CENTER FOR CONSERVATION SCIENCES	245
MARYLAND ORNITHOLOGICAL SOCIETY, INC.	247
MASSACHUSETTS AUDUBON SOCIETY, INC.	247
MAX McGRAW WILDLIFE FOUNDATION	248
MICHIGAN AUDUBON SOCIETY	249
MICHIGAN NATURE ASSOCIATION	249
MINNESOTA ORNITHOLOGISTS' UNION	251
MINNESOTA WINGS SOCIETY, INC.	252
MISSOURI AUDUBON COUNCIL	253
MONO LAKE COMMITTEE	254
MONTANA AUDUBON	254
MONTANA COOPERATIVE WILDLIFE RESEARCH UNIT (USGS/BRD)	80
NATIONAL AUDUBON SOCIETY	259
NATIONAL AVIARY	259
NATIONAL BIRD-FEEDING SOCIETY	259
NATIONAL FISH AND WILDLIFE FOUNDATION	261
NATIONAL WILDLIFE REHABILITATORS ASSOCIATION	269
NATURAL HISTORY SOCIETY OF MARYLAND, INC., THE	270
NATURAL LAND INSTITUTE	270
NATURE SASKATCHEWAN	275
NEBRASKA ORNITHOLOGISTS' UNION, INC. (University of Nebraska State Museum)	275
NEWFOUNDLAND LABRADOR WILDLIFE FEDERATION	279
NORTH AMERICAN BLUEBIRD SOCIETY	280
NORTH AMERICAN CRANE WORKING GROUP	281
NORTH AMERICAN GAMEBIRD ASSOCIATION, INC.	281
OHIO AUDUBON COUNCIL, INC.	287
OLYMPIC PARK INSTITUTE	289
ORNITHOLOGICAL COUNCIL	291
PACIFIC SEABIRD GROUP	293
PENNSYLVANIA AUDUBON SOCIETY	294
PEREGRINE FUND, THE	296
PHEASANTS FOREVER, INC.	296
PRAIRIE GROUSE TECHNICAL COUNCIL	299
PROVINCE OF QUEBEC SOCIETY FOR THE PROTECTION OF BIRDS, INC.	299
PTARMIGANS, THE	300
PURPLE MARTIN CONSERVATION ASSOCIATION	301
QUAIL UNLIMITED, INC.	301
RAPTOR CENTER, THE	303
RUFFED GROUSE SOCIETY, THE	307
SCIENTISTS CENTER FOR ANIMAL WELFARE	311
SMITHSONIAN INSTITUTION	317
SOCIETY FOR THE PRESERVATION OF BIRDS OF PREY	319
SOUTH CAROLINA COASTAL CONSERVATION LEAGUE	321
SOUTH DAKOTA B.A.S.S. CHAPTER FEDERATION	322
SUNCOAST SEABIRD SANCTUARY INC.	327
TRAFFIC NORTH AMERICA	330
TRI-STATE BIRD RESCUE AND RESEARCH, INC.	331
TRUMPETER SWAN SOCIETY, THE	334
UTAH COOPERATIVE FISH AND WILDLIFE RESEARCH UNIT (USDI-USGS-BRD-CRU)	110
VERMONT AUDUBON COUNCIL	338
VERMONT B.A.S.S. CHAPTER FEDERATION	338
VIRGINIA SOCIETY OF ORNITHOLOGY	340
WELDER WILDLIFE FOUNDATION	343
WESTERN HEMISPHERE SHOREBIRD RESERVE NETWORK (WHSRN)	344
WHOOPING CRANE CONSERVATION ASSOCIATION INC.	345
WILD ONES - NATURAL LANDSCAPERS, LTD	346
WILDFOWL TRUST OF NORTH AMERICA, INC., THE	347
WILDLIFE CENTER OF VIRGINIA, THE	347
WILDLIFE DAMAGE REVIEW (WDR)	348
WILDLIFE INFORMATION CENTER, INC.	349
WILSON ORNITHOLOGICAL SOCIETY	355
WISCONSIN LAND AND WATER CONSERVATION ASSOCIATION	356
WISCONSIN PARK AND RECREATION ASSOCIATION	356
WISCONSIN SOCIETY FOR ORNITHOLOGY, INC., THE	356
WORLD BIRD SANCTUARY (formerly Raptor Rehabilitation and Propagation Project Inc. The)	357
WORLD CONSERVATION MONITORING CENTRE	358

Botanical Gardens

Entry	Page
AMERICA THE BEAUTIFUL FUND	135
AMERICAN ASSOCIATION OF BOTANICAL GARDENS AND ARBORETA, INC.	136
ARIZONA STATE PARKS BOARD	42
CENTER FOR PLANT CONSERVATION	170
DAWES ARBORETUM, THE	186
GREAT PLAINS NATIVE PLANT SOCIETY	212
HOLDEN ARBORETUM, THE	216
ILLINOIS NATIVE PLANT SOCIETY	219
INTERNATIONAL CENTER FOR EARTH CONCERNS	223
NATIONAL AVIARY	259
NATIVE PLANT SOCIETY OF NORTHEASTERN OHIO	269
NEW ENGLAND WILD FLOWER SOCIETY, INC.	276
NORTH CAROLINA WILD FLOWER PRESERVATION SOCIETY	283
NORTHERN VIRGINIA REGIONAL PARK AUTHORITY	113
OHIO NATIVE PLANT SOCIETY	288
WORLD CONSERVATION MONITORING CENTRE	358

Botany

Entry	Page
GREAT PLAINS NATIVE PLANT SOCIETY	212
NORTH CAROLINA WILD FLOWER PRESERVATION SOCIETY	283
OHIO NATIVE PLANT SOCIETY	288
OKLAHOMA BIOLOGICAL SURVEY	95
SOUTHERN APPALACHIAN BOTANICAL SOCIETY	323
VIRGINIA NATIVE PLANT SOCIETY	340
WASHINGTON NATURAL HERITAGE PROGRAM	118
WILDFLOWER ASSOCIATION OF MICHIGAN	347

Brown Fields

Entry	Page
URBAN HABITAT PROGRAM	337

Camp

Entry	Page
ECODEFENSE	193
OHIO FORESTRY ASSOCIATION, INC., THE	288
RESOURCE CENTER FOR ENVIRONMENTAL EDUCATION, THE	304
SEACAMP ASSOCIATION, INC.	312
THORNE ECOLOGICAL INSTITUTE	329

Careers

Entry	Page
ENVIRONMENTAL CAREERS ORGANIZATION, INC., THE	195
STUDENT CONSERVATION ASSOCIATION, INC.	326

Cave

Entry	Page
AMERICAN CAVE CONSERVATION ASSOCIATION	138

Chemical Pollution Control

Entry	Page
ALASKA CONSERVATION ALLIANCE	133

KEYWORD INDEX - Chemistry

ALASKA CONSERVATION VOICE 134
ATLANTIC STATES LEGAL FOUNDATION 157
CHLORINE-FREE PAPER CONSORTIUM (CPC) 173
COLLEGE OF TROPICAL AGRICULTURE AND HUMAN
   RESOURCES 57
ENVIRONMENTAL DEFENSE FUND, INC. 196
GEORGIA CONSERVANCY, INC., THE 209
IDAHO STATE DEPARTMENT OF AGRICULTURE 60
INTERNATIONAL ASSOCIATION OF NATURAL RESOURCE
   PILOTS 223
IOWA DEPARTMENT OF NATURAL RESOURCES 64
LEAGUE OF WOMEN VOTERS OF IOWA 241
MICHIGAN DEPARTMENT OF ENVIRONMENTAL QUALITY 75
SOUTH DAKOTA DEPARTMENT OF ENVIRONMENT AND
   NATURAL RESOURCES 106
STOP 13, 326
TENNESSEE ENVIRONMENTAL COUNCIL 328
TREES FOR THE FUTURE, INC. 330
U.S. PUBLIC INTEREST RESEARCH GROUP 336
UNITED NATIONS ENVIRONMENT PROGRAMME 336
WILDLIFE DAMAGE REVIEW (WDR) 348
WISCONSIN LAND AND WATER CONSERVATION
   ASSOCIATION 356

Chemistry

KANSAS ACADEMY OF SCIENCE 237
MOTE MARINE LABORATORY 255
NEW MEXICO BUREAU OF MINES AND MINERAL
   RESOURCES 86
SOUTH CAROLINA DEPARTMENT OF AGRICULTURE 105
STROUD WATER RESEARCH CENTER 326

Chimpanzees

JANE GOODALL INSTITUTE, THE 236

Cleanup

CENTER FOR MARINE CONSERVATION 170

Coastal Construction and Erosion

COUNCIL FOR PLANNING AND CONSERVATION 185
NORTH CAROLINA SEA GRANT PROGRAM 92
SOUTH CAROLINA COASTAL CONSERVATION LEAGUE. 321

Coasts

ALABAMA DEPARTMENT OF ECONOMIC AND COMMUNITY
   AFFAIRS, COASTAL PROGRAMS (ADECA) 38
ALABAMA DEPARTMENT OF ENVIRONMENTAL
   MANAGEMENT 38
ALASKA SEA GRANT COLLEGE PROGRAM 40
AMERICAN CONSERVATION ASSOCIATION, INC. 139
AMERICAN LAND CONSERVANCY 146
AMERICAN LITTORAL SOCIETY 146
AMERICAN OCEANS CAMPAIGN 147
AUDUBON SOCIETY OF RHODE ISLAND 159
BARRIER ISLAND TRUST, INC. 160
CALIFORNIA SEA GRANT COLLEGE SYSTEM 45
CLEAN OCEAN ACTION 174
CLIMATE INSTITUTE 175
COAST ALLIANCE 176
COASTAL CONSERVATION ASSOCIATION 176
COASTAL CONSERVATION ASSOCIATION GEORGIA 176
COASTAL SOCIETY, THE 177
CONSERVATION COUNCIL OF NORTH CAROLINA 181
CORAL REEF ALLIANCE, THE (CORAL) 184
DELAWARE WILD LANDS, INC. 187
ECODEFENSE 193
FLORIDA SEA GRANT COLLEGE 54
FRIENDS OF THE SAN JUANS 206
FRIENDS OF THE SEA OTTER 206
GALIANO CONSERVANCY ASSOCIATION 207
GEORGIA SEA GRANT COLLEGE PROGRAM 56
GUAM COASTAL MANAGEMENT PROGRAM 57

H. JOHN HEINZ III CENTER FOR SCIENCE, ECONOMICS,
   AND THE ENVIRONMENT 214
HUNTSMAN MARINE SCIENCE CENTRE 217
ISLAND RESOURCES FOUNDATION 233
LAKE ERIE CLEAN-UP COMMITTEE, INC. 240
LIGHTHAWK 243
LOUISIANA GEOLOGICAL SURVEY 69
LOUISIANA SEA GRANT COLLEGE PROGRAM 69
MAINE AUDUBON SOCIETY 244
MAINE COAST HERITAGE TRUST 245
MAINE SEA GRANT PROGRAM 71
MAINE/NEW HAMPSHIRE SEA GRANT PROGRAM 83
MANOMET CENTER FOR CONSERVATION SCIENCES 245
MARINE LABORATORY (FLORIDA) 55
MICHIGAN DEPARTMENT OF ENVIRONMENTAL QUALITY 75
MONITOR INTERNATIONAL 253
MOUNTAINEERS, THE (Conservation Division) 256
NATIONAL BOATING FEDERATION 260
NATIONAL COALITION FOR MARINE CONSERVATION ... 260
NATIONAL WATERWAYS CONFERENCE INC. 266
NEW YORK GEOLOGICAL SURVEY AND STATE MUSEUM 90
NEW YORK SEA GRANT 90
NORTH CAROLINA BEACH BUGGY ASSOCIATION, INC. . 282
NORTH CAROLINA SEA GRANT PROGRAM 92
OLYMPIC PARK INSTITUTE 289
OREGON SEA GRANT PROGRAM 98
PUERTO RICO ASSOCIATION OF SOIL AND WATER
   CONSERVATION DISTRICTS 300
PUERTO RICO SEA GRANT PROGRAM 103
PUGET SOUNDKEEPER ALLIANCE 300
RESOURCES AGENCY, THE 46
SAVE THE SOUND, INC. 310
SEAPLANE PILOTS ASSOCIATION 312
SOUTH CAROLINA DEPARTMENT OF HEALTH AND
   ENVIRONMENTAL CONTROL 105
SOUTHERN ENVIRONMENTAL LAW CENTER 324
TANZANIA COASTAL MANAGEMENT PARTNERSHIP 123
TEXAS GENERAL LAND OFFICE 109
TEXAS SEA GRANT PROGRAM 109
UNITED NATIONS ENVIRONMENT PROGRAMME 336
VIRGINIA SEA GRANT PROGRAM 115
WISCONSIN LAND AND WATER CONSERVATION
   ASSOCIATION 356
WOODS HOLE OCEANOGRAPHIC INSITITUTION (WHOI)
   SEA GRANT PROGRAM 74
WORLD CONSERVATION MONITORING CENTRE 358

Commercial Sport Fishing

WESTERN PACIFIC REGIONAL FISHERY MANAGEMENT
   COUNCIL 344

Communications

ACADEMY FOR EDUCATIONAL DEVELOPMENT 130
AGENCY OF NATURAL RESOURCES 111
ALASKA HEALTH PROJECT 40
AMERICAN ASSOCIATION FOR THE ADVANCEMENT OF
   SCIENCE 136
AMERICAN FOREST FOUNDATION 144
AMERICAN PIE (PUBLIC INFORMATION ON THE
   ENVIRONMENT) 148
ANGLERS FOR CLEAN WATER 152
ASSOCIATION OF STATE AND TERRITORIAL HEALTH
   OFFICIALS 157
CENTER FOR ENVIRONMENTAL INFORMATION 169
CENTER FOR ENVIRONMENTAL STUDY 170
COMMITTEE FOR THE NATIONAL INSTITUTE FOR THE
   ENVIRONMENT (CNIE) 178
DELTA WATERFOWL FOUNDATION 187
DELTA WILDLIFE, INC. 187
EARTHSTEWARDS NETWORK 193
ECODEFENSE 193
EDUCATIONAL COMMUNICATIONS, INC. 194
ENVIROSOUTH, INC. 199
GEORGIA FORESTRY ASSOCIATION, INC. 209
GLOBAL ENVIRONMENTAL MANAGEMENT INITIATIVE
   (GEMI) 210
GREAT LAKES UNITED 211

INSTITUTE FOR CIVIC INITIATIVES SUPPORT 221
INSTITUTE FOR CONSERVATION LEADERSHIP 221
INTERNATIONAL CENTRE FOR CONSERVATION
    EDUCATION 224
KANSAS DEPARTMENT OF WILDLIFE AND PARKS 65
KEEP AMERICA BEAUTIFUL, INC. 238
KEEP FLORIDA BEAUTIFUL, INC. 238
LEAGUE OF WOMEN VOTERS OF THE U.S. 241
LVIV REGIONAL INSTITUTE OF EDUCATION 244
MICHIGAN ENVIRONMENTAL COUNCIL 249
MINNESOTA SEA GRANT COLLEGE PROGRAM 77
NATIONAL ASSOCIATION FOR INTERPRETATION 256
NEW ENGLAND NATURAL RESOURCES CENTER............ 276
NORTH AMERICAN ASSOCIATION FOR ENVIRONMENTAL
    EDUCATION 280
NORTH CAROLINA FORESTRY ASSOCIATION.................. 282
OHIO ACADEMY OF SCIENCE, THE 286
OHIO ALLIANCE FOR THE ENVIRONMENT 287
OREGON SEA GRANT PROGRAM 98
OUTDOOR WRITERS ASSOCIATION OF AMERICA, INC... 292
PANOS INSTITUTE, THE 293
POPULATION COMMUNICATIONS INTERNATIONAL 297
POPULATION REFERENCE BUREAU, INC........................... 298
RESPONSIVE MANAGEMENT 305
STUDENT PUGWASH USA... 326
STUDENTS PARTNERSHIP WORLDWIDE 327
TEXAS SEA GRANT PROGRAM 109
TOGETHER FOUNDATION, THE 330
TRUST FOR WILDLIFE, INC. 335
WISCONSIN LAND AND WATER CONSERVATION
    ASSOCIATION 356

Community Conservation

PENNSYLVANIA DEPARTMENT OF CONSERVATION AND
    NATURAL RESOURCES... 100
SONORAN INSTITUTE... 320

Conservation

ACADEMY FOR EDUCATIONAL DEVELOPMENT................ 130
ALABAMA DEPARTMENT OF ECONOMIC AND COMMUNITY
    AFFAIRS, COASTAL PROGRAMS (ADECA) 38
ALABAMA NATURAL HERITAGE PROGRAM 132
AMERICAN RIVERS (formerly American Rivers Conservation
    Council).. 149
AUDUBON OF KANSAS (formerly Kansas Audubon Council)
    158
AUDUBON SOCIETY OF PORTLAND.................................... 159
BAMA BACKPADDLERS ASSOCIATION 159
BASS ANGLERS SPORTSMAN SOCIETY (B.A.S.S, INC.) .. 160
BOTANICAL SOCIETY OF WESTERN PENNSYLVANIA 162
CENTRAL OHIO ANGLERS AND HUNTERS CLUB 172
COMMUNITY CONSERVATION CONSULTANTS/HOWLERS
    FOREVER, INC. 179
CONNECTICUT BOTANICAL SOCIETY 180
CONSERVATION FORCE 182
CROSBY ABORETUM, THE, Mississippi State University..... 185
ENVIRONMENTAL LAW INSTITUTE, THE............................. 198
FLORIDA EXOTIC PEST PLANT COUNCIL 202
FOREST SOCIETY OF MAINE.. 204
GLACIER INSTITUTE, THE 210
HUMMINGBIRD SOCIETY, THE 217
INTERNATIONAL UNION FOR CONSERVATION OF NATURE
    AND NATURAL RESOURCES (IUCN) THE WORLD
    CONSERVATION UNION 228
IOWA NATIVE PLANT SOCIETY 232
JACKSON HOLE CONSERVATION ALLIANCE 236
KANSAS WILDFLOWER SOCIETY... 238
LEAGUE OF CONSERVATION VOTERS 241
MATTS (MID-ATLANTIC TURTLE AND TORTOISE SOCIETY,
    INC.) 248
MISSOURI FOREST PRODUCTS ASSOCIATION................ 253
NATIONAL AVIARY... 259
NATIONAL WILD TURKEY FEDERATION, CANADA, INC.,
    THE.. 266
NATIVE PLANT SOCIETY OF NORTHEASTERN OHIO....... 269
NATIVE PLANT SOCIETY OF OREGON................................ 269
NEVADA NATURAL HERITAGE PROGRAM........................... 83
NEW ENGLAND WILD FLOWER SOCIETY, INC.................. 276
NEW HAMPSHIRE ASSOCIATION OF CONSERVATION
    COMMISSIONS 276
NORTH AMERICAN BUTTERFLY ASSOCIATION 280
NORTH AMERICAN FALCONERS ASSOCIATION 281
NORTH CAROLINA COALITION, INC. 282
OKLAHOMA ASSOCIATION OF CONSERVATION DISTRICTS
    288
OKLAHOMA NATIVE PLANT SOCIETY 289
ORGANIZATION FOR BAT CONSERVATION 291
PITTSBURGH HERPETOLOGICAL SOCIETY, THE............. 296
PUERTO RICO CONSERVATION FOUNDATION, THE (PRCF
    300
REP AMERICA/REPUBLICANS FOR ENVIRONMENTAL
    PROTECTION 304
SAVE OUR RIVERS, INC. 309
SIERRA NEVADA FOREST PROTECTION CAMPAIGN 317
STUDENTS PARTNERSHIP WORLDWIDE 327
URBAN WILDLIFE RESOURCES 337
WEST MICHIGAN ENVIRONMENTAL ACTION COUNCIL... 343
WILD DOG FOUNDATION, THE... 345
WILD ONES - NATURAL LANDSCAPERS, LTD................... 346
WILDFLOWER ASSOCIATION OF MICHIGAN 347
WISCONSIN WATERFOWL ASSOCIATION, INC................. 356

Conservation Biology

ALABAMA WILDFLOWER SOCIETY, THE............................. 133
ASSOCIATION OF FIELD ORNITHOLOGISTS 156
CONSERVANCY OF SOUTHWEST FLORIDA, THE 181
FOREST WATCH... 204

Conservation Districts

ALABAMA ASSOCIATION OF SOIL AND WATER
    CONSERVATION DISTRICTS 132
ALASKA ASSOCIATION OF SOIL AND WATER
    CONSERVATION DISTRICTS 133
ARIZONA ASSOCIATION OF CONSERVATION DISTRICTS
    154
ARKANSAS ASSOCIATION OF CONSERVATION DISTRICTS
    154
CALIFORNIA ASSOCIATION OF RESOURCE
    CONSERVATION DISTRICTS 164
COLORADO ASSOCIATION OF SOIL CONSERVATION
    DISTRICTS 177
CONNECTICUT ASSOCIATION OF SOIL AND WATER
    CONSERVATION DISTRICTS, INC. 180
DELAWARE ASSOCIATION OF CONSERVATION DISTRICTS
    186
DISTRICT OF COLUMBIA SOIL AND WATER
    CONSERVATION DISTRICT... 188
FLORIDA ASSOCIATION OF SOIL AND WATER
    CONSERVATION DISTRICTS 201
GEORGIA ASSOCIATION OF CONSERVATION DISTRICT
    SUPERVISORS 208
HAWAII ASSOCIATION OF CONSERVATION DISTRICTS . 214
IDAHO ASSOCIATION OF SOIL CONSERVATION DISTRICTS
    218
ILLINOIS ASSOCIATION OF SOIL AND WATER
    CONSERVATION DISTRICTS 218
INDIANA ASSOCIATION OF SOIL AND WATER
    CONSERVATION DISTRICTS, INC. 220
IOWA ASSOCIATION OF SOIL AND WATER CONSERVATION
    DISTRICT COMMISSIONERS 231
KANSAS ASSOCIATION OF CONSERVATION DISTRICTS 237
KENTUCKY ASSOCIATION OF CONSERVATION DISTRICTS
    239
LOUISIANA ASSOCIATION OF CONSERVATION DISTRICTS
    243
MAINE ASSOCIATION OF CONSERVATION DISTRICTS... 244
MARYLAND ASSOCIATION OF CONSERVATION DISTRICTS
    246
MICHIGAN ASSOCIATION OF CONSERVATION DISTRICTS
    248
MINNESOTA ASSOCIATION OF SOIL AND WATER
    CONSERVATION DISTRICTS 250
MISSISSIPPI ASSOCIATION OF CONSERVATION
    DISTRICTS, INC. 252

KEYWORD INDEX - Conservation Easements

MISSOURI ASSOCIATION OF SOIL AND WATER CONSERVATION DISTRICTS..................253
MONTANA ASSOCIATION OF CONSERVATION DISTRICTS 254
NATIONAL ASSOCIATION OF CONSERVATION DISTRICTS 257
NEBRASKA ASSOCIATION OF RESOURCE DISTRICTS ...275
NEVADA ASSOCIATION OF CONSERVATION DISTRICTS 275
NEW HAMPSHIRE ASSOCIATION OF CONSERVATION DISTRICTS..................277
NEW JERSEY ASSOCIATION OF CONSERVATION DISTRICTS..................277
NEW MEXICO ASSOCIATION OF CONSERVATION DISTRICTS..................278
NEW YORK ASSOCIATION OF CONSERVATION DISTRICTS, INC...................279
NORTH CAROLINA ASSOCIATION OF SOIL AND WATER CONSERVATION DISTRICTS..................282
NORTH DAKOTA ASSOCIATION OF SOIL CONSERVATION DISTRICTS..................283
OHIO FEDERATION OF SOIL AND WATER CONSERVATION DISTRICTS..................288
OREGON ASSOCIATION OF CONSERVATION DISTRICTS..................290
PACIFIC BASIN ASSOCIATION OF SOIL AND WATER CONSERVATION DISTRICTS..................292
PUERTO RICO ASSOCIATION OF SOIL AND WATER CONSERVATION DISTRICTS..................300
RHODE ISLAND STATE ASSOCIATION OF CONSERVATION DISTRICTS..................305
SOUTH CAROLINA ASSOCIATION OF CONSERVATION DISTRICTS..................321
SOUTH DAKOTA ASSOCIATION OF CONSERVATION DISTRICTS..................322
TENNESSEE ASSOCIATION OF CONSERVATION DISTRICTS..................327
TEXAS ASSOCIATION OF SOIL AND WATER CONSERVATION DISTRICTS..................328
UTAH ASSOCIATION OF SOIL CONSERVATION DISTRICTS..................337
VERMONT ASSOCIATION OF CONSERVATION DISTRICTS..................338
VIRGIN ISLANDS CONSERVATION DISTRICT..................339
VIRGINIA ASSOCIATION OF CONSERVATION DISTRICTS..................339
WASHINGTON ASSOCIATION OF CONSERVATION DISTRICTS..................340
WEST VIRGINIA ASSOCIATION OF CONSERVATION DISTRICT SUPERVISORS ASSOCIATION, INC..............343
WYOMING ASSOCIATION OF CONSERVATION DISTRICTS..................359

Conservation Easements

COASTAL GEORGIA LAND TRUST, THE..................176
FRIENDS OF THE REEDY RIVER..................206
GEORGIA ENVIRONMENTAL POLICY INSTITUTE..............209
GREAT OUTDOORS CONSERVANCY, THE..................212
LAND TRUST ALLIANCE, THE..................240
NATIVE PRAIRIES ASSOCIATION OF TEXAS..................270

Conservation of Protected Areas

ADIRONDACK MOUNTAIN CLUB, INC., THE..................131
ADKINS ARBORETUM..................131
AFRICAN WILDLIFE FOUNDATION..................132
AFRICAN WILDLIFE NEWS SERVICE..................132
ALABAMA NATURAL HERITAGE PROGRAM..................132
ALABAMA WILDFLOWER SOCIETY, THE..................133
ALASKA AUDUBON SOCIETY..................133
ALBERTA WILDERNESS ASSOCIATION..................135
AMERICA THE BEAUTIFUL FUND..................135
AMERICAN ASSOCIATION OF FIELD BOTANISTS..................136
AMERICAN ASSOCIATION OF ZOO KEEPERS, INC...................137
AMERICAN BIRD CONSERVANCY..................138
ANTARCTICA PROJECT..................153
AUDUBON SOCIETY OF RHODE ISLAND..................159
BIRDLIFE INTERNATIONAL..................161
CENTER FOR MARINE CONSERVATION..................170
COASTAL CONSERVATION ASSOCIATION GEORGIA......176
CONSERVATION FEDERATION OF MARYLAND/For A Rural Maryland (F.A.R.M.)..................182
CORAL REEF ALLIANCE, THE (CORAL)..................184
DESERT FISHES COUNCIL..................188
DESERT TORTOISE COUNCIL..................188
EUROPARC FEDERATION..................199
FAIRFAX AUDUBON SOCIETY..................199
FLORIDA AUDUBON SOCIETY..................201
FOREST HISTORY SOCIETY, INC...................203
FRIENDS OF ACADIA..................205
GALIANO CONSERVANCY ASSOCIATION..................207
GEORGE MIKSCH SUTTON AVIAN RESEARCH CENTER INC...................208
GEORGIA ENVIRONMENTAL POLICY INSTITUTE..............209
GREAT LAKES UNITED..................211
HAWAII AUDUBON SOCIETY..................214
ILLINOIS DEPARTMENT OF NATURAL RESOURCES..........61
ILLINOIS NATIVE PLANT SOCIETY..................219
INDIANA AUDUBON SOCIETY, INC...................220
INTERNATIONAL ASSOCIATION OF NATURAL RESOURCE PILOTS..................223
IOWA DEPARTMENT OF NATURAL RESOURCES..............64
IOWA NATURAL HERITAGE FOUNDATION..................232
KANSAS DEPARTMENT OF WILDLIFE AND PARKS...........65
KIDS FOR SAVING EARTH WORLDWIDE..................239
LEAGUE OF ENVIRONMENTAL JOURNALISTS..................241
LEE COUNTY PARKS AND RECREATION SERVICES.........54
LIGHTHAWK..................243
MISSOURI PRAIRIE FOUNDATION..................253
MOUNT GRACE LAND CONSERVATION TRUST..............255
MOUNTAIN LION FOUNDATION..................255
NATIONAL ASSOCIATION OF STATE DEPARTMENTS OF AGRICULTURE..................258
NATIONAL BIRD-FEEDING SOCIETY..................259
NATIONAL FORESTRY ASSOCIATION..................262
NATIONAL WILDLIFE REFUGE ASSOCIATION..................269
NATURAL AREAS ASSOCIATION..................270
NATURAL LAND INSTITUTE..................270
NATURE SASKATCHEWAN..................275
NEVADA NATURAL HERITAGE PROGRAM..................83
NORTH CASCADES CONSERVATION COUNCIL..............283
NORTHWEST ECOSYSTEM ALLIANCE..................285
OKLAHOMA BIOLOGICAL SURVEY..................95
OLYMPIC PARK INSTITUTE..................289
OREGON NATURAL RESOURCES COUNCIL..................290
OUTDOOR RECREATION COUNCIL OF BRITISH COLUMBIA..................292
PARTNERS IN PARKS..................293
PENNSYLVANIA DEPARTMENT OF CONSERVATION AND NATURAL RESOURCES..................100
PITTSBURGH HERPETOLOGICAL SOCIETY, THE..............296
RAINFOREST TRUST, INC., THE..................302
RINCON INSTITUTE, THE..................305
SOCIETY FOR ECOLOGICAL RESTORATION..................318
SOUTHEAST ALASKA CONSERVATION COUNCIL (SEACC)..................323
SOUTHEASTERN FISHES COUNCIL..................323
TEXAS SEA GRANT PROGRAM..................109
U.S. PUBLIC INTEREST RESEARCH GROUP..................336
VIRGINIA NATIVE PLANT SOCIETY..................340
VIRGINIA OUTDOORS FOUNDATION..................115
WESTERN PENNSYLVANIA CONSERVANCY..................344
WILDERNESS LAND TRUST, THE..................346
WILDLANDS PROJECT, THE..................347
WISCONSIN LAND AND WATER CONSERVATION ASSOCIATION..................356
WORLD CONSERVATION MONITORING CENTRE..........358

Conservation Planning

COASTAL CONSERVATION ASSOCIATION GEORGIA......176
CONSERVATION FORCE..................182
GEORGIA ENVIRONMENTAL POLICY INSTITUTE..............209
MISSOURI FOREST PRODUCTS ASSOCIATION................253
NEW MEXICO COOPERATIVE FISH AND WILDLIFE RESEARCH UNIT..................87
PITTSBURGH HERPETOLOGICAL SOCIETY, THE..............296

Conservation Tillage

AMERICA THE BEAUTIFUL FUND	135
COLLEGE OF TROPICAL AGRICULTURE AND HUMAN RESOURCES	57
CONSERVATION TECHNOLOGY INFORMATION CENTER	183
DELAWARE STATE EXTENSION SERVICE	52
KANSAS DEPARTMENT OF WILDLIFE AND PARKS	65
MAX McGRAW WILDLIFE FOUNDATION	248
MINNESOTA BOARD OF WATER AND SOIL RESOURCES	75
NATIONAL ASSOCIATION OF STATE DEPARTMENTS OF AGRICULTURE	258
SOIL AND WATER CONSERVATION SOCIETY (formerly Soil Conservation Society of America)	320
WISCONSIN LAND AND WATER CONSERVATION ASSOCIATION	356

Consumer Protection

GEORGIA DEPARTMENT OF AGRICULTURE	55

Consumer Services

GEORGIA DEPARTMENT OF AGRICULTURE	55
OHIO OFFICE OF ENERGY EFFICIENCY	94

Contaminated Sediments

CLEAN OCEAN ACTION	174
COAST ALLIANCE	176

Coral Reefs

ACADEMY FOR EDUCATIONAL DEVELOPMENT	130
AMERICAN LITTORAL SOCIETY	146
CARIBBEAN NATURAL RESOURCES INSTITUTE	168
CENTER FOR MARINE CONSERVATION	170
CORAL REEF ALLIANCE, THE (CORAL)	184
EARTH FOUNDATION	191
EARTHWATCH INSTITUTE	193
FLORIDA AUDUBON SOCIETY	201
GUAM COASTAL MANAGEMENT PROGRAM	57
ISLAND CONSERVATION EFFORT	233
OCEAN VOICE INTERNATIONAL	286
PUERTO RICO SEA GRANT PROGRAM	103
REEF RELIEF	303
SMITHSONIAN INSTITUTION	317
TEXAS SEA GRANT PROGRAM	109
VIRGIN ISLANDS CONSERVATION SOCIETY, INC.	339
WORLD CONSERVATION MONITORING CENTRE	358

Cultural Preservation

ALASKA CONSERVATION ALLIANCE	133
ALASKA CONSERVATION VOICE	134
ALASKA NATURAL HISTORY ASSOCIATION	134
AMERICA THE BEAUTIFUL FUND	135
AMERICAN CANAL SOCIETY, THE	138
ARCHAEOLOGICAL CONSERVANCY	153
ARIZONA STATE PARKS BOARD	42
ARKANSAS DEPARTMENT OF PARKS AND TOURISM	42
CONFEDERATED SALISH AND KOOTENAI TRIBES	180
DELAWARE GREENWAYS, INC.	187
EARTHWATCH INSTITUTE	193
GEORGIA TRUST FOR HISTORIC PRESERVATION	210
HIGH DESERT MUSEUM, THE	216
IDAHO DEPARTMENT OF PARKS AND RECREATION	60
ILLINOIS ASSOCIATION OF CONSERVATION DISTRICTS	218
INTERNATIONAL SOCIETY FOR THE PRESERVATION OF THE TROPICAL RAINFOREST, THE	227
INTERNATIONAL SONORAN DESERT ALLIANCE	228
INTERTRIBAL BISON COOPERATIVE (ITBC)	231
ISLAND INSTITUTE, THE	233
LAND BETWEEN THE LAKES ASSOCIATION	240
MASSACHUSETTS HIGHWAY DEPARTMENT	74
NATIONAL PARK FOUNDATION	263
NATIONAL PARKS AND CONSERVATION ASSOCIATION (NPCA)	263
NATIVE AMERICAN FISH AND WILDLIFE SOCIETY (NAFWS)	269
NEVIS HISTORICAL AND CONSERVATION SOCIETY	276
NEW YORK STATE OFFICE OF PARKS, RECREATION AND HISTORIC PRESERVATION	91
NORTHWEST INTERPRETIVE ASSOCIATION	286
OFFICE OF STATE PARKS, DEPARTMENT OF CULTURE, RECREATION, AND TOURISM	69
OLYMPIC PARK INSTITUTE	289
OZARKS RESOURCE CENTER	292
PARTNERS IN PARKS	293
RAINFOREST RELIEF	302
SAVE OUR RIVERS, INC.	309
SMITHSONIAN INSTITUTION	317
STATE PARKS AND RECREATION COMMISSION (WASHINGTON)	116
STUDENT CONSERVATION ASSOCIATION, INC.	326
URBAN HABITAT PROGRAM	337
WASHINGTON TOXICS COALITION	341
WESTERN ENVIRONMENTAL LAW CENTER	344
WHITE CLAY WATERSHED ASSOCIATION	345
WOLF EDUCATION AND RESEARCH CENTER	357

Culture

AMERICA THE BEAUTIFUL FUND	135
CATSKILL CENTER FOR CONSERVATION AND DEVELOPMENT, INC., THE	168
INTERPRETATION CANADA	230
SMITHSONIAN INSTITUTION	317
TALLAHASSEE MUSEUM OF HISTORY AND NATURAL SCIENCE	327
THREE CIRCLES CENTER FOR MULTICULTURAL ENVIRONMENTAL EDUCATION	329

Dams

AMERICAN RIVERS (formerly American Rivers Conservation Council)	149
BAMA BACKPADDLERS ASSOCIATION	159
LEAGUE OF ENVIRONMENTAL JOURNALISTS	241
NORTH CAROLINA COALITION, INC.	282
PACIFIC INSTITUTE FOR STUDIES IN DEVELOPMENT, ENVIRONMENT, AND SECURITY	293
RIVER ALLIANCE OF WISCONSIN	305

Deserts

AMERICAN LAND CONSERVANCY	146
CENTER FOR BIOLOGICAL DIVERSITY	169
CHIHUAHUAN DESERT RESEARCH INSTITUTE	173
DESERT FISHES COUNCIL	188
DESERT TORTOISE COUNCIL	188
FEDERATION OF WESTERN OUTDOOR CLUBS	200
HIGH DESERT MUSEUM, THE	216
INTERNATIONAL SONORAN DESERT ALLIANCE	228
WORLD CONSERVATION MONITORING CENTRE	358

Developing Countries

ATLANTIC STATES LEGAL FOUNDATION	157
COMMITTEE ON AGRICULTURAL SUSTAINABILITY FOR DEVELOPING COUNTRIES	179
ECOTOURISM SOCIETY, THE	194
ENVIRONMENTAL ENTERPRISES ASSISTANCE FUND, INC.	197
INTERNATIONAL ASSOCIATION FOR ENVIRONMENTAL HYDROLOGY (IAEH)	222
INTERNATIONAL UNION FOR CONSERVATION OF NATURE AND NATURAL RESOURCES (IUCN) THE WORLD CONSERVATION UNION	228
LEAGUE OF ENVIRONMENTAL JOURNALISTS	241
MONITOR INTERNATIONAL	253
OCEAN VOICE INTERNATIONAL	286
PACIFIC INSTITUTE FOR STUDIES IN DEVELOPMENT, ENVIRONMENT, AND SECURITY	293

KEYWORD INDEX - Development

POPULATION INSTITUTE, THE 298
RESOURCES FOR THE FUTURE 304
RETURNED PEACE CORPS VOLUNTEER FOR
  ENVIRONMENT AND DEVELOPMENT (RPCV-ED) 305
TREES FOR THE FUTURE, INC. 330
WORLD CONSERVATION MONITORING CENTRE 358
ZERO (REGIONAL ENVIRONMENTAL ORGANIZATION) 361

Development

BAMA BACKPADDLERS ASSOCIATION 159
COAST ALLIANCE 176
GEORGIA CONSERVANCY, INC., THE 209
GEORGIA TRUST FOR HISTORIC PRESERVATION 210
INTERNATIONAL RIVERS NETWORK (IRN) 226
INTERNATIONAL UNION FOR CONSERVATION OF NATURE
  AND NATURAL RESOURCES (IUCN) THE WORLD
  CONSERVATION UNION 228
PACIFIC INSTITUTE FOR STUDIES IN DEVELOPMENT,
  ENVIRONMENT, AND SECURITY 293
SEACOAST ANTI-POLLUTION LEAGUE 312

Diseases

STATE FORESTRY DIVISION (WYOMING) 122

Dolphins

EARTHTRUST 193
EUROPEAN CETACEAN SOCIETY 199
INTERNATIONAL MARINE MAMMAL PROJECT, THE ... 226
MOTE MARINE LABORATORY 255
PACIFIC WHALE FOUNDATION 293
WHALE AND DOLPHIN CONSERVATION SOCIETY 345

Drinking Water Protection

ACADEMY FOR EDUCATIONAL DEVELOPMENT 130
MICHIGAN DEPARTMENT OF ENVIRONMENTAL QUALITY 75
NORTH CAROLINA COALITION, INC. 282
PACIFIC INSTITUTE FOR STUDIES IN DEVELOPMENT,
  ENVIRONMENT, AND SECURITY 293

EcoAction

20/20 VISION 130
ALASKA CONSERVATION ALLIANCE 133
ALASKA CONSERVATION VOICE 134
AMERICAN PIE (PUBLIC INFORMATION ON THE
  ENVIRONMENT) 148
ECOLOGY CENTER 194
LAKE MICHIGAN FEDERATION 240
LEE COUNTY PARKS AND RECREATION SERVICES .. 54
MAGIC 244
MICHIGAN AUDUBON SOCIETY 249
PUERTO RICO SEA GRANT PROGRAM 103
SINAPU 317
WISCONSIN LAND AND WATER CONSERVATION
  ASSOCIATION 356

Ecological Education

ECOLOGICAL SOCIETY OF AMERICA, THE 193
HUDSONIA LIMITED 216
INSTITUTE OF ECOSYSTEM STUDIES 221
OHIO ACADEMY OF SCIENCE, THE 286

Ecology

ADKINS ARBORETUM 131
ALASKA COOPERATIVE FISH AND WILDLIFE RESEARCH
  UNIT 39
ALDO LEOPOLD FOUNDATION, INC. 135
AMERICA THE BEAUTIFUL FUND 135
AMERICAN ASSOCIATION OF FIELD BOTANISTS 136
ARCHBOLD BIOLOGICAL STATION 153

ARKANSAS COOPERATIVE RESEARCH UNIT 42
BAT CONSERVATION INTERNATIONAL 160
CADDO LAKE INSTITUTE, INC. 163
CENTER FOR ENVIRONMENTAL STUDY 170
CENTER FOR MARINE CONSERVATION 170
CINCINNATI NATURE CENTER 174
COLORADO NATURAL HERITAGE PROGRAM 177
CRAIGHEAD WILDLIFE-WILDLANDS INSTITUTE 185
CROSBY ABORETUM, THE, Mississippi State University 185
DEPARTMENT OF ENVIRONMENTAL QUALITY (ARKANSAS)
  43
ECOLOGICAL SOCIETY OF AMERICA, THE 193
ENVIRONMENTAL RESOURCE CENTER (ERC) 198
FAIRFAX AUDUBON SOCIETY 199
FEDERATION OF ENVIRONMENTAL EDUCATION IN ST.
  PETERSBURG 200
FISH AND WILDLIFE INFORMATION EXCHANGE 201
GLACIER INSTITUTE, THE 210
HAWAII NATURE CENTER 214
HOLDEN ARBORETUM, THE 216
HUNTSMAN MARINE SCIENCE CENTRE 217
INDIANA AUDUBON SOCIETY, INC. 220
INSTITUTE FOR EARTH EDUCATION, THE 221
INSTITUTE OF ECOSYSTEM STUDIES 221
INTERNATIONAL ASSOCIATION OF WILDLAND FIRE
  (formerly Fire Research Institute) 223
INTERNATIONAL CENTER FOR EARTH CONCERNS ... 223
INTERNATIONAL CENTER FOR TROPICAL ECOLOGY ... 224
KANSAS DEPARTMENT OF WILDLIFE AND PARKS 65
KANSAS HERPETOLOGICAL SOCIETY 237
MAGIC 244
MAINE DEPARTMENT OF MARINE RESOURCES 71
MANOMET CENTER FOR CONSERVATION SCIENCES 245
MASSACHUSETTS AUDUBON SOCIETY, INC. 247
NATURAL LAND INSTITUTE 270
NATURE SASKATCHEWAN 275
NEW HAMPSHIRE NATURAL HERITAGE INVENTORY 84
NEWFOUNDLAND LABRADOR WILDLIFE FEDERATION .. 279
NORTHWEST ECOSYSTEM ALLIANCE 285
OKLAHOMA BIOLOGICAL SURVEY 95
OKLAHOMA NATIVE PLANT SOCIETY 289
OLYMPIC PARK INSTITUTE 289
RINCON INSTITUTE, THE 305
SINAPU 317
SOCIETY FOR ECOLOGICAL RESTORATION 318
SOCIETY FOR RANGE MANAGEMENT 319
SOUTHERN APPALACHIAN BOTANICAL SOCIETY ... 323
TEXAS SEA GRANT PROGRAM 109
THORNE ECOLOGICAL INSTITUTE 329
TREES ATLANTA 330
UNITED NATIONS ENVIRONMENT PROGRAMME 336
UTAH COOPERATIVE FISH AND WILDLIFE RESEARCH UNIT
  (USDI-USGS-BRD-CRU) 110
WILSON ORNITHOLOGICAL SOCIETY 355
WISCONSIN LAND AND WATER CONSERVATION
  ASSOCIATION 356
WORLD CONSERVATION MONITORING CENTRE ... 358

Ecosystems

ECOLOGICAL SOCIETY OF AMERICA, THE 193
FOREST SOCIETY OF MAINE 204
SIERRA NEVADA FOREST PROTECTION CAMPAIGN 317
SOUTHERN APPALACHIAN BOTANICAL SOCIETY ... 323
STUDENTS PARTNERSHIP WORLDWIDE 327
TREES ATLANTA 330
WORLD PAL (WORLD POPULATION ALLOCATION LIMITED
  INC.) 358

Ecotourism

ACADEMY FOR EDUCATIONAL DEVELOPMENT 130
ECOTOURISM SOCIETY, THE 194
EDUCATIONAL COMMUNICATIONS, INC. 194
FEDERATION OF ENVIRONMENTAL EDUCATION IN ST.
  PETERSBURG 200
NORTH AMERICAN BUTTERFLY ASSOCIATION 280
NORTH CAROLINA SEA GRANT PROGRAM 92

Education

ARKANSAS ENVIRONMENTAL EDUCATION ASSOCIATION 154
CALIFORNIA DEPARTMENT OF EDUCATION 44
ENVIRONMENTAL EDUCATION ASSOCIATES 196
ENVIRONMENTAL EDUCATION ASSOCIATION OF INDIANA 197
ENVIRONMENTAL EDUCATION ASSOCIATION OF WASHINGTON 197
ENVIRONMENTAL EDUCATION COUNCIL OF OHIO 197
ENVIRONMENTAL EDUCATORS OF NORTH CAROLINA (EENC) 197
LEARNING FOR ENVIRONMENTAL ACTION PROGRAMME (LEAP) 242
MAINE DEPARTMENT OF INLAND FISHERIES AND WILDLIFE 70
MAINE ENVIRONMENTAL EDUCATION ASSOCIATION, INC. 245
WISCONSIN ASSOCIATION FOR ENVIRONMENTAL EDUCATION, INC. 355

Endangered and Threatened Species

ABUNDANT LIFE SEED FOUNDATION 130
ACRES LAND TRUST 130
ADKINS ARBORETUM 131
AFRICAN WILDLIFE FOUNDATION 132
AFRICAN WILDLIFE NEWS SERVICE 132
ALABAMA COOPERATIVE FISH AND WILDLIFE RESEARCH UNIT (USDI) 38
ALABAMA ENVIRONMENTAL COUNCIL 132
ALABAMA NATURAL HERITAGE PROGRAM 132
ALABAMA WILDFLOWER SOCIETY, THE 133
ALASKA AUDUBON SOCIETY 133
ALBERTA WILDERNESS ASSOCIATION 135
AMERICAN ASSOCIATION OF FIELD BOTANISTS 136
AMERICAN ASSOCIATION OF ZOO KEEPERS, INC. 137
AMERICAN BIRD CONSERVANCY 138
AMERICAN CAVE CONSERVATION ASSOCIATION 138
AMERICAN CETACEAN SOCIETY 138
AMERICAN CHESTNUT FOUNDATION, THE 139
AMERICAN LIVESTOCK BREEDS CONSERVANCY 147
AMERICAN MUSEUM OF NATURAL HISTORY 147
AMERICAN SOCIETY OF ICHTHYOLOGISTS AND HERPETOLOGISTS 149
AMERICAN SOCIETY OF MAMMALOGISTS 150
AMERICAN ZOO AND AQUARIUM ASSOCIATION (AZA) .. 151
ANCIENT FOREST INTERNATIONAL 152
ANIMAL PROTECTION INSTITUTE 152
ANIMAL WELFARE INSTITUTE 152
APPALACHIAN TRAIL CONFERENCE 153
ARCHBOLD BIOLOGICAL STATION 153
ASSOCIATION OF AVIAN VETERINARIANS 156
ATLANTIC SALMON FEDERATION 157
AUDUBON SOCIETY OF PORTLAND 159
AUDUBON SOCIETY OF RHODE ISLAND 159
BAT CONSERVATION INTERNATIONAL 160
BIODIVERSITY LEGAL FOUNDATION 161
BIRDLIFE INTERNATIONAL 161
BROTHERHOOD OF THE JUNGLE COCK, INC., THE 163
CALIFORNIA DEPARTMENT OF EDUCATION 44
CALIFORNIA NATIVE PLANT SOCIETY, THE 164
CALIFORNIA TRAPPERS ASSOCIATION 164
CALIFORNIA WILDLIFE FEDERATION 165
CAMP FIRE BOYS AND GIRLS 165
CAMP FIRE CONSERVATION FUND 165
CANADA-UNITED STATES ENVIRONMENTAL COUNCIL (United States Office) 166
CANADIAN FEDERATION OF HUMANE SOCIETIES 166
CASCADIA RESEARCH 168
CENTER FOR BIOLOGICAL DIVERSITY 169
CENTER FOR MARINE CONSERVATION 170
CENTER FOR PLANT CONSERVATION 170
CETACEAN SOCIETY INTERNATIONAL 172
CHIHUAHUAN DESERT RESEARCH INSTITUTE 173
COLORADO COOPERATIVE FISH AND WILDLIFE RESEARCH UNIT (USDI) 49
COLORADO WILDLIFE HERITAGE FOUNDATION 178
COMITE DESPERTAR CIDRENO 102
COMMUNITY RIGHTS COUNSEL 179
CONNECTICUT BOTANICAL SOCIETY 180
CONNECTICUT PUBLIC INTEREST RESEARCH GROUP (Conn PIRG) 181
CONSERVANCY OF SOUTHWEST FLORIDA, THE 181
CONSERVATION FORCE 182
CONSERVATION INTERNATIONAL 183
CRAIGHEAD WILDLIFE-WILDLANDS INSTITUTE 185
DEFENDERS OF WILDLIFE 186
DELAWARE NATURE SOCIETY 187
DEPARTMENT OF FISH AND WILDLIFE (WASHINGTON) . 116
DEPARTMENT OF INTERIOR, U.S.G.S/B.R.D, SOUTH CAROLINA COOPERATIVE FISH AND WILDLIFE RESEARCH UNIT 104
DEPARTMENT OF PLANNING AND NATURAL RESOURCES 112
DEPARTMENT OF WILDLIFE CONSERVATION 95
DESERT FISHES COUNCIL 188
DESERT RESEARCH FOUNDATION OF NAMIBIA, THE 188
DESERT TORTOISE COUNCIL 188
DESERT TORTOISE PRESERVE COMMITTEE, INC. 188
EAGLE NATURE FOUNDATION, LTD. 191
EARTH FOUNDATION 191
EARTH ISLAND INSTITUTE 191
EARTHTRUST 193
EARTHWATCH INSTITUTE 193
ECOLOGICAL SOCIETY OF AMERICA, THE 193
ECOLOGY CENTER 194
ELM RESEARCH INSTITUTE 194
ELSA WILD ANIMAL APPEAL 194
ENDANGERED SPECIES COALITION 194
ENVIRONMENTAL EDUCATION ASSOCIATES 196
EUROPEAN ASSOCIATION FOR AQUATIC MAMMALS 199
EUROPEAN CETACEAN SOCIETY 199
FEDERAL WILDLIFE OFFICER'S ASSOCIATION 199
FISH AND WILDLIFE INFORMATION EXCHANGE 201
FISH AND WILDLIFE REFERENCE SERVICE 201, 409
FLORIDA AUDUBON SOCIETY 201
FLORIDA COOPERATIVE FISH AND WILDLIFE RESEARCH UNIT (USDI) 52
FLORIDA FISH AND WILDLIFE CONSERVATION COMMISSION 54
FLORIDA NATIVE PLANT SOCIETY 202
FLORIDA ORNITHOLOGICAL SOCIETY 202
FLORIDA PANTHER PROJECT, INC., THE 202
FOREST WATCH 204
FOSSIL RIM WILDLIFE CENTER 205
FRIENDS OF ANIMALS INC 205
FRIENDS OF THE BOUNDARY WATERS WILDERNESS ... 206
FRIENDS OF THE SEA OTTER 206
FUND FOR ANIMALS INC., THE 207
GAME CONSERVATION INTERNATIONAL (GAME COIN) . 207
GARDEN CLUB OF AMERICA, THE 208
GEORGE MIKSCH SUTTON AVIAN RESEARCH CENTER INC. 208
GOPHER TORTOISE COUNCIL 211
GREAT BEAR FOUNDATION 211
GREATER YELLOWSTONE COALITION 212
HAWAII AUDUBON SOCIETY 214
HAWAII NATURE CENTER 214
HAWAII SOCIETY OF AMERICAN FORESTERS 214
HAWKWATCH INTERNATIONAL, INC. 215
HUDSONIA LIMITED 216
HUMANE SOCIETY OF THE UNITED STATES, THE 217
HUMMINGBIRD SOCIETY, THE 217
IDAHO COOPERATIVE FISH AND WILDLIFE RESEARCH UNIT (USDI) 60
IDAHO STATE DEPARTMENT OF AGRICULTURE 60
ILLINOIS ASSOCIATION OF CONSERVATION DISTRICTS 218
ILLINOIS AUDUBON SOCIETY 219
ILLINOIS DEPARTMENT OF NATURAL RESOURCES 61
ILLINOIS NATIVE PLANT SOCIETY 219
ILLINOIS NATURAL HERITAGE FOUNDATION 219
INSTITUTE FOR ECOLOGICAL STUDIES 92
INTERFAITH COUNCIL FOR THE PROTECTION OF ANIMALS AND NATURE INC. (ICPAN) 222
INTERNATIONAL ASSOCIATION FOR BEAR RESEARCH AND MANAGEMENT 222

KEYWORD INDEX - Endangered and Threatened Species

INTERNATIONAL ASSOCIATION OF NATURAL RESOURCE PILOTS ... 223
INTERNATIONAL ASSOCIATION OF WILDLAND FIRE (formerly Fire Research Institute) ... 223
INTERNATIONAL CRANE FOUNDATION ... 224
INTERNATIONAL ECOLOGY SOCIETY (IES) ... 224
INTERNATIONAL MARINE MAMMAL PROJECT, THE ... 226
INTERNATIONAL PRIMATE PROTECTION LEAGUE ... 226
INTERNATIONAL SNOW LEOPARD TRUST ... 227
INTERNATIONAL SOCIETY FOR ENDANGERED CATS (ISEC) ... 227
INTERNATIONAL SOCIETY FOR THE PRESERVATION OF THE TROPICAL RAINFOREST, THE ... 227
INTERNATIONAL WILD WATERFOWL ASSOCIATION ... 229
INTERNATIONAL WILDLIFE COALITION (IWC) AND THE WHALE ADOPTION PROJECT ... 230
INTERNATIONAL WOLF CENTER (Educational Services) ... 230
IOWA DEPARTMENT OF NATURAL RESOURCES ... 64
IOWA NATIVE PLANT SOCIETY ... 232
IOWA NATURAL HERITAGE FOUNDATION ... 232
ISLAND CONSERVATION EFFORT ... 233
JACKSON HOLE CONSERVATION ALLIANCE ... 236
KANSAS BIOLOGICAL SURVEY ... 65
KANSAS DEPARTMENT OF WILDLIFE AND PARKS ... 65
KANSAS ORNITHOLOGICAL SOCIETY ... 237
KIDS FOR SAVING EARTH WORLDWIDE ... 239
LADY BIRD JOHNSON WILDFLOWER CENTER ... 240
LEAGUE OF ENVIRONMENTAL JOURNALISTS ... 241
LEE COUNTY PARKS AND RECREATION SERVICES ... 54
LIGHTHAWK ... 243
LONG LIVE THE KINGS ... 243
LOUISIANA AUDUBON COUNCIL ... 243
MAINE ATLANTIC SALMON COMMISSION (formerly Maine Atlantic Salmon Authority) ... 69
MAINE AUDUBON SOCIETY ... 244
MAINE DEPARTMENT OF INLAND FISHERIES AND WILDLIFE ... 70
MANOMET CENTER FOR CONSERVATION SCIENCES ... 245
MARINE ENVIRONMENTAL RESEARCH INSTITUTE (MERI) ... 246
MAX McGRAW WILDLIFE FOUNDATION ... 248
MICHIGAN NATURAL AREAS COUNCIL ... 249
MICHIGAN NATURE ASSOCIATION ... 249
MINNESOTA HERPETOLOGICAL SOCIETY (James Ford Bell Museum of Natural History) ... 251
MINNESOTA NATIVE PLANT SOCIETY ... 251
MISSISSIPPI COOPERATIVE FISH AND WILDLIFE RESEARCH UNIT (USDI) ... 77
MISSISSIPPI DEPARTMENT OF WILDLIFE, FISHERIES, AND PARKS ... 78
MISSISSIPPI INTERSTATE COOPERATIVE RESOURCE ASSOCIATION ... 252
MISSOURI AUDUBON COUNCIL ... 253
MISSOURI NATIVE PLANT SOCIETY ... 253
MISSOURI PRAIRIE FOUNDATION ... 253
MONTANA COOPERATIVE FISHERY RESEARCH UNIT (USDI) ... 80
MONTANA DEPARTMENT OF AGRICULTURE ... 80
MOTE MARINE LABORATORY ... 255
MOUNTAIN LION FOUNDATION ... 255
NATIONAL AVIARY ... 259
NATIONAL FISH AND WILDLIFE FOUNDATION ... 261
NATIONAL SPELEOLOGICAL SOCIETY, INC. ... 265
NATIONAL WATER RESOURCES ASSOCIATION ... 266
NATIONAL WILDLIFE FEDERATION ... 267, 268
NATIVE PLANT SOCIETY OF NORTHEASTERN OHIO ... 269
NATIVE PLANT SOCIETY OF OREGON ... 269
NATURAL AREAS ASSOCIATION ... 270
NATURAL HERITAGE COMMISSION (ARKANSAS) ... 44
NATURAL LAND INSTITUTE ... 270
NATURE CONSERVANCY, THE ... 272, 273, 274
NATURE SASKATCHEWAN ... 275
NEVADA NATURAL HERITAGE PROGRAM ... 83
NEW ENGLAND WILD FLOWER SOCIETY, INC. ... 276
NEW HAMPSHIRE FISH AND GAME DEPARTMENT ... 84
NEW HAMPSHIRE NATURAL HERITAGE INVENTORY ... 84
NEW MEXICO COOPERATIVE FISH AND WILDLIFE RESEARCH UNIT ... 87
NORTH AMERICAN BUTTERFLY ASSOCIATION ... 280
NORTH AMERICAN CRANE WORKING GROUP ... 281
NORTH AMERICAN LOON FUND ... 281
NORTH AMERICAN NATIVE FISHES ASSOCIATION ... 281
NORTH AMERICAN WOLF SOCIETY ... 282
NORTH CAROLINA BEACH BUGGY ASSOCIATION, INC. ... 282
NORTH CAROLINA WILD FLOWER PRESERVATION SOCIETY ... 283
NORTHCOAST ENVIRONMENTAL CENTER ... 284
NORTHEAST WILDLIFE ADMINISTRATORS ASSOCIATION ... 284
NORTHWEST ECOSYSTEM ALLIANCE ... 285
OHIO AUDUBON COUNCIL, INC. ... 287
OHIO BIOLOGICAL SURVEY ... 287
OKLAHOMA BIOLOGICAL SURVEY ... 95
OKLAHOMA COOPERATIVE FISH AND WILDLIFE RESEARCH UNIT (USDI) ... 95
OKLAHOMA NATIVE PLANT SOCIETY ... 289
OKLAHOMA STATE EXTENSION SERVICES ... 96
OLYMPIC PARK INSTITUTE ... 289
OREGON COOPERATIVE FISH AND WILDLIFE RESEARCH UNIT (USDI) ... 97
OREGON DEPARTMENT OF FORESTRY ... 98
OREGON FISH AND WILDLIFE DIVISION/DEPARTMENT OF STATE POLICE ... 98
ORGANIZATION FOR BAT CONSERVATION ... 291
PACIFIC SEABIRD GROUP ... 293
PACIFIC WHALE FOUNDATION ... 293
PEREGRINE FUND, THE ... 296
PINE BLUFF COOPERATIVE FISHERY RESEARCH PROJECT ... 44
PRAIRIE GROUSE TECHNICAL COUNCIL ... 299
PREDATOR PROJECT ... 299
PUERTO RICO ASSOCIATION OF SOIL AND WATER CONSERVATION DISTRICTS ... 300
PUERTO RICO CONSERVATION FOUNDATION, THE (PRCF ... 300
PUERTO RICO SEA GRANT PROGRAM ... 103
PURPLE MARTIN CONSERVATION ASSOCIATION ... 301
RAINFOREST TRUST, INC., THE ... 302
RAPTOR CENTER, THE ... 303
RAPTOR RESEARCH FOUNDATION, INC. ... 303
REP AMERICA/REPUBLICANS FOR ENVIRONMENTAL PROTECTION ... 304
RESOURCES FOR THE FUTURE ... 304
RHODE ISLAND STATE ASSOCIATION OF CONSERVATION DISTRICTS ... 305
RIVER OTTER ALLIANCE, THE ... 306
SAFARI CLUB INTERNATIONAL ... 308
SAVE THE MANATEE CLUB ... 310
SCIENTISTS CENTER FOR ANIMAL WELFARE ... 311
SEA SHEPHERD CONSERVATION SOCIETY ... 311
SIERRA NEVADA FOREST PROTECTION CAMPAIGN ... 317
SINAPU ... 317
SMITHSONIAN INSTITUTION ... 317
SOCIETY FOR ANIMAL PROTECTIVE LEGISLATION ... 318
SOCIETY FOR CONSERVATION BIOLOGY ... 318
SOCIETY FOR MARINE MAMMALOGY, THE ... 318
SOCIETY FOR THE PRESERVATION OF BIRDS OF PREY 319
SOCIETY OF TYMPANUCHUS CUPIDO PINNATUS LTD. ... 320
SOUTH CAROLINA DEPARTMENT OF NATURAL RESOURCES ... 105
SOUTH DAKOTA B.A.S.S. CHAPTER FEDERATION ... 322
SOUTH DAKOTA COOPERATIVE FISH AND WILDLIFE RESEARCH UNIT (USDI) ... 106
SOUTHEASTERN FISHES COUNCIL ... 323
SOUTHERN APPALACHIAN BOTANICAL SOCIETY ... 323
STEAMBOATERS, THE ... 325
SUNCOAST SEABIRD SANCTUARY INC. ... 327
TALL TIMBERS RESEARCH STATION ... 327
TALLAHASSEE MUSEUM OF HISTORY AND NATURAL SCIENCE ... 327
TEXAS FORESTRY ASSOCIATION ... 329
TEXAS SEA GRANT PROGRAM ... 109
TRAFFIC NORTH AMERICA ... 330
TRI-STATE BIRD RESCUE AND RESEARCH, INC. ... 331
TROUT UNLIMITED ... 331, 332, 333, 334
TURTLE CREEK WATERSHED ASSOCIATION, INC. ... 335
U.S. PUBLIC INTEREST RESEARCH GROUP ... 336
UNITED NATIONS ENVIRONMENT PROGRAMME ... 336
UNITED STATES COMMITTEE FOR THE UNITED NATIONS ENVIRONMENT PROGRAMME THE (U.S. and UNEP) ... 336

KEYWORD INDEX - Endangered Resources

UTAH COOPERATIVE FISH AND WILDLIFE RESEARCH UNIT (USDI-USGS-BRD-CRU) 110
VERMONT B.A.S.S. CHAPTER FEDERATION 338
VIRGINIA COOPERATIVE FISH AND WILDLIFE RESEARCH UNIT (USDI) 113
VIRGINIA DEPARTMENT OF AGRICULTURE AND CONSUMER SERVICES 113
VIRGINIA FORESTRY ASSOCIATION 340
VIRGINIA MUSEUM OF NATURAL HISTORY 115
VIRGINIA NATIVE PLANT SOCIETY 340
WESTERN PENNSYLVANIA CONSERVANCY 344
WHALE AND DOLPHIN CONSERVATION SOCIETY 345
WHOOPING CRANE CONSERVATION ASSOCIATION INC. 345
WILD CANID SURVIVAL AND RESEARCH CENTER 345
WILD DOG FOUNDATION, THE 345
WILD ONES - NATURAL LANDSCAPERS, LTD 346
WILDFLOWER ASSOCIATION OF MICHIGAN 347
WILDLIFE CENTER OF VIRGINIA, THE 347
WILDLIFE CONSERVATION SOCIETY 348
WILDLIFE DAMAGE REVIEW (WDR) 348
WILDLIFE PRESERVATION TRUST INTERNATIONAL, INC. 350
WILDLIFE RESOURCES AGENCY 107
WILDLIFE WAYSTATION 355
WISCONSIN LAND AND WATER CONSERVATION ASSOCIATION 356
WOLF EDUCATION AND RESEARCH CENTER 357
WOLF FUND, THE 357
WOLF HAVEN INTERNATIONAL 357
WORLD BIRD SANCTUARY (formerly Raptor Rehabilitation and Propagation Project Inc. The) 357
WORLD CONSERVATION MONITORING CENTRE 358
WORLD SOCIETY FOR THE PROTECTION OF ANIMALS (WSPA) 358
WORLD WILDLIFE FUND 359
WYOMING COOPERATIVE FISH AND WILDLIFE RESEARCH UNIT (USDI) 122
WYOMING NATIVE PLANT SOCIETY 360
XERCES SOCIETY, THE 360
YELLOWSTONE GRIZZLY FOUNDATION (YGF) 360

Endangered Resources

WISCONSIN DEPARTMENT OF NATURAL RESOURCES .. 120

Energy

AMERICAN COUNCIL FOR AN ENERGY-EFFICIENT ECONOMY 139
ARIZONA GEOLOGICAL SURVEY 41
BIOMASS USERS NETWORK 161
BUREAU OF ECONOMIC GEOLOGY 108
CAMPAIGN FOR A PROSPEROUS GEORGIA 165
CENTER FOR ENVIRONMENTAL INFORMATION 169
CENTER FOR RESOURCE ECONOMICS 171
CHESAPEAKE BAY FOUNDATION, INC. (Pennsylvania Office) 173
CLIMATE INSTITUTE 175
CONNECTICUT FUND FOR THE ENVIRONMENT 180
CONSERVATION COUNCIL OF NORTH CAROLINA 181
CONSERVATION LAW FOUNDATION, INC. (CLF) 183
COUNCIL FOR PLANNING AND CONSERVATION 185
ENERGY, MINERALS, AND NATURAL RESOURCES DEPARTMENT 86
ENVIRONMENTAL AND ENERGY STUDY INSTITUTE (EESI) 195
ENVIRONMENTAL DEFENSE FUND, INC. 196
ENVIRONMENTAL ENTERPRISES ASSISTANCE FUND, INC. 197
FOSSIL FUELS POLICY ACTION INSTITUTE/ALLIANCE FOR A PAVING MORATORIUM 204
FRIENDS OF THE RIVER 206
GENERAL FEDERATION OF WOMEN'S CLUBS 208
GLOBAL CITIES PROJECT, THE 210
GREEN SEAL 213
GREENPEACE, INC. 213
INFORM, INC. 221

INTERNATIONAL INSTITUTE FOR ENERGY CONSERVATION 225
IOWA DEPARTMENT OF NATURAL RESOURCES 64
ISSAQUAH ALPS TRAILS CLUB (I.A.T.C.) 233
IZAAK WALTON LEAGUE OF AMERICA, INC., THE 234
KANSAS GEOLOGICAL SURVEY 66
KANSAS NATURAL RESOURCE COUNCIL 237
KEYSTONE CENTER, THE 239
LEAGUE OF WOMEN VOTERS OF THE U.S. 241
LEGAL ENVIRONMENTAL ASSISTANCE FOUNDATION INC. (LEAF) 242
LOUISIANA GEOLOGICAL SURVEY 69
MICHIGAN ENVIRONMENTAL COUNCIL 249
MINNESOTA ENVIRONMENTAL QUALITY BOARD 76
MISSOURI DEPARTMENT OF NATURAL RESOURCES 79
MONTANA BUREAU OF MINES AND GEOLOGY 80
MONTANA ENVIRONMENTAL INFORMATION CENTER 254
NATIONAL 4-H COUNCIL 256
NATIONAL ASSOCIATION OF ENVIRONMENTAL PROFESSIONALS, THE (National Office) 257
NATIONAL WATERWAYS CONFERENCE INC. 266
NEW JERSEY ENVIRONMENTAL LOBBY 278
NEW MEXICO BUREAU OF MINES AND MINERAL RESOURCES 86
NEW YORK GEOLOGICAL SURVEY AND STATE MUSEUM 90
NORTH DAKOTA GEOLOGICAL SURVEY 93
NORTHERN PLAINS RESOURCE COUNCIL 285
NW ENERGY COALITION 286
OFFICE OF ENERGY EFFICIENCY AND ENVIRONMENT 91
OHIO ENERGY PROJECT 287
OHIO ENVIRONMENTAL COUNCIL, INC. 287
OHIO OFFICE OF ENERGY EFFICIENCY 94
OKLAHOMA GEOLOGICAL SURVEY 96
OLYMPIC PARK INSTITUTE 289
RENEWABLE ENERGY POLICY PROJECT (REPP) 303
RESOURCES FOR THE FUTURE 304
SAFE ENERGY COMMUNICATION COUNCIL 308
SIERRA CLUB 312, 314, 315, 316, 317
SOUTH CAROLINA ENERGY OFFICE 105
SOUTH DAKOTA ORNITHOLOGISTS' UNION 322
SOUTHERN ENVIRONMENTAL LAW CENTER 324
STATE OFFICE OF CONSERVATION (LOUISIANA) 69
STUDENT PUGWASH USA 326
U.S. PUBLIC INTEREST RESEARCH GROUP 336
UNION OF CONCERNED SCIENTISTS 336
UNITED STATES CHAMBER OF COMMERCE 336
WASHINGTON B.A.S.S. CHAPTER FEDERATION 340
WISCONSIN LAND AND WATER CONSERVATION ASSOCIATION 356
WORLDWATCH INSTITUTE 359
WYOMING STATE GEOLOGICAL SURVEY 123

Energy Conservation

DELAWARE STATE EXTENSION SERVICE 52
ENVIRONMENTAL ENTERPRISES ASSISTANCE FUND, INC. 197
ENVIRONMENTAL RESOURCE CENTER (ERC) 198
GLOBAL CITIES PROJECT, THE 210
KIDS FOR SAVING EARTH WORLDWIDE 239
LEAGUE OF WOMEN VOTERS OF IOWA 241
LEE COUNTY PARKS AND RECREATION SERVICES 54
LEGAL ENVIRONMENTAL ASSISTANCE FOUNDATION INC. (LEAF) 242
OHIO ENERGY PROJECT 287
OHIO OFFICE OF ENERGY EFFICIENCY 94
RESOURCES FOR THE FUTURE 304
SAFE ENERGY COMMUNICATION COUNCIL 308
SOUTHERN ENVIRONMENTAL LAW CENTER 324
SOUTHFACE ENERGY INSTITUTE 324
TREES FOR THE FUTURE, INC. 330
U.S. PUBLIC INTEREST RESEARCH GROUP 336

Energy Efficiency

AMERICAN COUNCIL FOR AN ENERGY-EFFICIENT ECONOMY 139
OHIO OFFICE OF ENERGY EFFICIENCY 94

Enforcement

MAINE DEPARTMENT OF INLAND FISHERIES AND WILDLIFE 70

Engineering

AIR AND WASTE MANAGEMENT ASSOCIATION 132
ALASKA HEALTH PROJECT 40
ARIZONA GEOLOGICAL SURVEY 41
ASSOCIATION OF CONSERVATION ENGINEERS 156
COLLEGE OF TROPICAL AGRICULTURE AND HUMAN RESOURCES 57
DELAWARE STATE EXTENSION SERVICE 52
DEPARTMENT OF TRANSPORTATION (OREGON) 97
DEPARTMENT OF TRANSPORTATION (RHODE ISLAND) . 104
INTERNATIONAL EROSION CONTROL ASSOCIATION (IECA) 224
MARINE TECHNOLOGY SOCIETY 246
NEBRASKA DEPARTMENT OF WATER RESOURCES 81
STATE OFFICE OF CONSERVATION (LOUISIANA) 69
UNITED STATES DEPARTMENT OF TRANSPORTATION 31
WATER ENVIRONMENT FEDERATION 342

Environment

ALASKA CONSERVATION ALLIANCE 133
ALASKA CONSERVATION VOICE 134
ALLIANCE FOR THE CHESAPEAKE BAY 135
AMERICANS FOR THE ENVIRONMENT 152
ASSOCIATION OF STATE AND TERRITORIAL HEALTH OFFICIALS 157
AUDUBON COUNCIL OF CONNECTICUT 158
AUDUBON SOCIETY OF RHODE ISLAND 159
BAT CONSERVATION INTERNATIONAL 160
BEYOND PESTICIDES/NATIONAL COALITION AGAINST THE MISUSE OF PESTICIDES 160
CALIFORNIA ACADEMY OF SCIENCES 163
CARRYING CAPACITY NETWORK 168
CENTER FOR CHESAPEAKE COMMUNITIES 169
CENTER FOR PLANT CONSERVATION 170
COLLEGE OF TROPICAL AGRICULTURE AND HUMAN RESOURCES 57
COMITE DESPERTAR CIDRENO 102
CONNECTICUT COUNCIL ON ENVIRONMENTAL QUALITY 50
DEFENDERS OF WILDLIFE 186
DEPARTMENT OF TRANSPORTATION (OREGON) 97
DESERT TORTOISE COUNCIL 188
ECOLOGICAL SOCIETY OF AMERICA, THE 193
ECOLOGY CENTER 194
ENVIRONMENTAL FUND FOR GEORGIA 197
FLORIDA FISH AND WILDLIFE CONSERVATION COMMISSION 54
FRIENDS OF THE SEA OTTER 206
GEORGE MIKSCH SUTTON AVIAN RESEARCH CENTER INC. 208
GEORGIA CONSERVANCY, INC., THE 209
GLOBAL CITIES PROJECT, THE 210
GREEN (GLOBAL RIVERS ENVIRONMENTAL EDUCATION NETWORK) 212
HAWAII NATURE CENTER 214
HAWK AND OWL TRUST, THE 215
HUNTSMAN MARINE SCIENCE CENTRE 217
INSTITUTE FOR CONSERVATION LEADERSHIP 221
INTERNATIONAL ASSOCIATION FOR ENVIRONMENTAL HYDROLOGY (IAEH) 222
IOWA DEPARTMENT OF NATURAL RESOURCES 64
IOWA WOMEN IN NATURAL RESOURCES 233
IZAAK WALTON LEAGUE OF AMERICA, INC., THE 234
JACKSON HOLE CONSERVATION ALLIANCE 236
KANSAS ASSOCIATION FOR CONSERVATION AND ENVIRONMENTAL EDUCATION 237
KANSAS DEPARTMENT OF WILDLIFE AND PARKS 65
KANSAS STATE DEPARTMENT OF HEALTH AND ENVIRONMENT 66
KIDS FOR SAVING EARTH WORLDWIDE 239
LAKE MICHIGAN FEDERATION 240
LAND WATCH MONTEREY COUNTY 241
LIGHTHAWK 243
MANOMET CENTER FOR CONSERVATION SCIENCES 245
MARYLAND FORESTS ASSOCIATION 247
MASSACHUSETTS AUDUBON SOCIETY, INC. 247
MASSACHUSETTS ENVIRONMENTAL EDUCATION SOCIETY 248
MASSACHUSETTS HIGHWAY DEPARTMENT 74
MICHIGAN LAND USE INSTITUTE 249
MINNESOTA SEA GRANT COLLEGE PROGRAM 77
MISSOURI AUDUBON COUNCIL 253
MISSOURI NATIVE PLANT SOCIETY 253
MONTANA LAND RELIANCE 254
NATIONAL BIRD-FEEDING SOCIETY 259
NATIONAL TREE TRUST 265
NATURE SASKATCHEWAN 275
NEW HAMPSHIRE LAKES ASSOCIATION 277
NORTH AMERICAN ASSOCIATION FOR ENVIRONMENTAL EDUCATION 280
NORTHWEST ECOSYSTEM ALLIANCE 285
OKLAHOMA GEOLOGICAL SURVEY 96
OLYMPIC PARK INSTITUTE 289
POPULATION ACTION INTERNATIONAL 297
POPULATION INSTITUTE, THE 298
POPULATION-ENVIRONMENT BALANCE, INC. 298
RAILS-TO-TRAILS CONSERVANCY 302
RESOURCES FOR THE FUTURE 304
RETURNED PEACE CORPS VOLUNTEER FOR ENVIRONMENT AND DEVELOPMENT (RPCV-ED) 305
ROGER TORY PETERSON INSTITUTE 307
SAFE ENERGY COMMUNICATION COUNCIL 308
SAVE THE HARBOR/SAVE THE BAY 310
SOCIETY FOR RANGE MANAGEMENT 319
SOUTH DAKOTA DEPARTMENT OF ENVIRONMENT AND NATURAL RESOURCES 106
SOUTHEAST ALASKA CONSERVATION COUNCIL (SEACC) 323
SOUTHFACE ENERGY INSTITUTE 324
STUDENT CONSERVATION ASSOCIATION, INC. 326
TALLAHASSEE MUSEUM OF HISTORY AND NATURAL SCIENCE 327
TENNESSEE ENVIRONMENTAL COUNCIL 328
TEXAS COOPERATIVE FISH AND WILDLIFE RESEARCH UNIT 108
TEXAS SEA GRANT PROGRAM 109
THREE CIRCLES CENTER FOR MULTICULTURAL ENVIRONMENTAL EDUCATION 329
TREES ATLANTA 330
TREES FOR THE FUTURE, INC. 330
U.S. PUBLIC INTEREST RESEARCH GROUP 336
UNION OF CONCERNED SCIENTISTS 336
UNITED NATIONS ENVIRONMENT PROGRAMME 336
VIRGINIA DEPARTMENT OF ENVIRONMENTAL QUALITY 114
VIRGINIA NATIVE PLANT SOCIETY 340
WILDLIFE FOREVER 348
WILSON ORNITHOLOGICAL SOCIETY 355
WISCONSIN DEPARTMENT OF AGRICULTURE TRADE AND CONSUMER PROTECTION 120
WISCONSIN PARK AND RECREATION ASSOCIATION 356
WORLD BIRD SANCTUARY (formerly Raptor Rehabilitation and Propagation Project Inc. The) 357
WORLD PAL (WORLD POPULATION ALLOCATION LIMITED INC.) 358
WYOMING STATE BOARD OF LAND COMMISSIONERS ... 123

Environmental and Conservation Education

A. E. HOWELL WILDLIFE CONSERVATION CENTER 130
ACADEMY FOR EDUCATIONAL DEVELOPMENT 130
ACRES LAND TRUST 130
ADIRONDACK MOUNTAIN CLUB, INC., THE 131
ADIRONDACK PARK AGENCY 88
ADKINS ARBORETUM 131
ADOPT-A-STREAM FOUNDATION, THE 131
ALABAMA ENVIRONMENTAL COUNCIL 132
ALABAMA FORESTRY COMMISSION 39
ALASKA AUDUBON SOCIETY 133
ALASKA CONSERVATION ALLIANCE 133
ALASKA CONSERVATION VOICE 134
ALASKA HEALTH PROJECT 40
ALASKA NATURAL HISTORY ASSOCIATION 134

KEYWORD INDEX - Environmental and Conservation Education

ALASKA NATURAL RESOURCE AND OUTDOOR EDUCATION ASSOCIATION 134
ALASKA SEA GRANT COLLEGE PROGRAM 40
ALDO LEOPOLD FOUNDATION, INC. 135
ALLIANCE FOR THE CHESAPEAKE BAY 135
AMERICA THE BEAUTIFUL FUND 135
AMERICAN BASS ASSOCIATION OF WEST VIRGINIA, THE 138
AMERICAN BIRDING ASSOCIATION 138
AMERICAN CAMPING ASSOCIATION, INC. 138
AMERICAN CAVE CONSERVATION ASSOCIATION 138
AMERICAN CETACEAN SOCIETY 138
AMERICAN FARMLAND TRUST 139
AMERICAN FOREST FOUNDATION 144
AMERICAN FORESTS (formerly American Forestry Association) 144
AMERICAN GEOGRAPHICAL SOCIETY 145
AMERICAN GROUND WATER TRUST 145
AMERICAN HIKING SOCIETY 145
AMERICAN NATURE STUDY SOCIETY 147
AMERICAN PIE (PUBLIC INFORMATION ON THE ENVIRONMENT) 148
AMERICAN RIVERS (formerly American Rivers Conservation Council) 149
AMERICAN SOCIETY FOR ENVIRONMENTAL HISTORY ... 149
AMERICAN WATER RESOURCES ASSOCIATION 151
ANGLERS FOR CLEAN WATER 152
APPALACHIAN MOUNTAIN CLUB 153
APPALACHIAN TRAIL CONFERENCE 153
ARCHBOLD BIOLOGICAL STATION 153
ARIZONA DEPARTMENT OF ENVIRONMENTAL QUALITY .. 41
ARIZONA GAME AND FISH DEPARTMENT 41
ARIZONA GEOLOGICAL SURVEY 41
ARKANSAS DEPARTMENT OF PARKS AND TOURISM 42
ARKANSAS ENVIRONMENTAL EDUCATION ASSOCIATION 154
ARLINGTON OUTDOOR EDUCATION ASSOCIATION, INC. 155
ASSOCIATION FOR CONSERVATION INFORMATION, INC. 155
ASSOCIATION OF AVIAN VETERINARIANS 156
ASSOCIATION OF CONSERVATION ENGINEERS 156
ASSOCIATION OF CONSULTING FORESTERS OF AMERICA 156
ATLANTIC CENTER FOR THE ENVIRONMENT 157
ATLANTIC STATES LEGAL FOUNDATION 157
AUDUBON INTERNATIONAL 158
AUDUBON NATURALIST SOCIETY OF THE CENTRAL ATLANTIC STATES 158
AUDUBON OF KANSAS (formerly Kansas Audubon Council) 158
AUDUBON SOCIETY OF MISSOURI 158
AUDUBON SOCIETY OF PORTLAND 159
AUDUBON SOCIETY OF RHODE ISLAND 159
AUDUBON SOCIETY OF WESTERN PENNSYLVANIA 159
BAT CONSERVATION INTERNATIONAL 160
BERKSHIRE-LITCHFIELD ENVIRONMENTAL COUNCIL, INC. 160
BIG BEND NATURAL HISTORY ASSOCIATION 160
BILLFISH FOUNDATION, THE 160
BOONE AND CROCKETT CLUB 161
BOTANICAL CLUB OF WISCONSIN 162
BOTANICAL SOCIETY OF WESTERN PENNSYLVANIA ... 162
BOUNTY INFORMATION SERVICE (WILDLIFE) 162
BOY SCOUTS OF AMERICA 162
BROOKS BIRD CLUB INC., THE 163
BROTHERHOOD OF THE JUNGLE COCK, INC., THE 163
CALIFORNIA DEPARTMENT OF EDUCATION 44
CALIFORNIA NATIVE PLANT SOCIETY, THE 164
CALIFORNIA TRAPPERS ASSOCIATION 164
CALIFORNIA WATERFOWL ASSOCIATION 164
CAMP FIRE BOYS AND GIRLS 165
CAMP FIRE CONSERVATION FUND 165
CATSKILL CENTER FOR CONSERVATION AND DEVELOPMENT, INC., THE 168
CATSKILL FOREST ASSOCIATION 168
CENTER FOR CHESAPEAKE COMMUNITIES 169
CENTER FOR ENVIRONMENTAL EDUCATION 169
CENTER FOR ENVIRONMENTAL INFORMATION 169
CENTER FOR ENVIRONMENTAL STUDY 170
CENTER FOR INTERNATIONAL ENVIRONMENTAL LAW (CIEL) 170
CENTER FOR MARINE CONSERVATION 170
CENTER FOR PLANT CONSERVATION 170
CENTER FOR RESOURCEFUL BUILDING TECHNOLOGY 171
CENTRO de INFORMACION, INVESTIGACION y EDUCACION SOCIAL (CIIES) 172
CHESAPEAKE BAY FOUNDATION, INC. 172, 173
CHESAPEAKE BAY FOUNDATION, INC. (Maryland Office) 173
CHESAPEAKE BAY FOUNDATION, INC. (Virginia Office) ... 173
CHICAGO HERPETOLOGICAL SOCIETY 173
CHINA REGION LAKES ALLIANCE 173
CINCINNATI NATURE CENTER 174
CLEVELAND MUSEUM OF NATURAL HISTORY, THE 175
COALITION FOR EDUCATION IN THE OUTDOORS 175
COAST ALLIANCE 176
COASTAL CONSERVATION ASSOCIATION GEORGIA 176
COASTAL SOCIETY, THE 177
COLORADO DEPARTMENT OF AGRICULTURE 49
COLORADO DEPARTMENT OF EDUCATION 49
COLORADO DEPARTMENT OF NATURAL RESOURCES .. 49
COLORADO STATE FOREST SERVICE 49
COLORADO STATE UNIVERSITY COOPERATIVE EXTENSION 50
COLORADO WILDLIFE HERITAGE FOUNDATION 178
COMMITTEE FOR THE NATIONAL INSTITUTE FOR THE ENVIRONMENT (CNIE) 178
CONCERN, INC. 179
CONNECTICUT AUDUBON SOCIETY, INC. 180
CONNECTICUT WATERFOWL ASSOCIATION, INC. 181
CONSERVANCY OF SOUTHWEST FLORIDA, THE 181
CONSERVATION COUNCIL OF NORTH CAROLINA 181
CONSERVATION DISTRICTS FOUNDATION INC. 182
CONSERVATION FUND, THE 182
CONSERVATION INTERNATIONAL 183
CORNELL LAB OF ORNITHOLOGY 184
COUNCIL FOR ENVIRONMENTAL EDUCATION 184, 237
COUSTEAU SOCIETY, INC., THE 185
CROSBY ABORETUM, THE, Mississippi State University ... 185
DEEP-PORTAGE CONSERVATION RESERVE 186
DEFENDERS OF WILDLIFE 186
DELAWARE DEPARTMENT OF NATURAL RESOURCES AND ENVIRONMENTAL CONTROL 51
DELAWARE NATURE SOCIETY 187
DELAWARE SOLID WASTE AUTHORITY 52
DELAWARE STATE EXTENSION SERVICE 52
DELTA WATERFOWL FOUNDATION 187
DELTA WILDLIFE, INC. 187
DEPARTMENT OF PLANNING AND NATURAL RESOURCES 112
DEPARTMENT OF WILDLIFE CONSERVATION 95
DESERT RESEARCH FOUNDATION OF NAMIBIA, THE ... 188
DIVISION OF FORESTRY AND SOIL RESOURCES OF GUAM 57
EAGLE NATURE FOUNDATION, LTD. 191
EARTH DAY NEW YORK 191
EARTH FORCE 191
EARTH FOUNDATION 191
EARTH SHARE 192
EARTHWATCH INSTITUTE 193
ECODEFENSE 193
ECOLOGY CENTER 194
ECOTOURISM SOCIETY, THE 194
EDUCATIONAL COMMUNICATIONS, INC. 194
ENERGY, MINERALS, AND NATURAL RESOURCES DEPARTMENT 86
ENVIRONMENT COUNCIL OF RHODE ISLAND 195
ENVIRONMENTAL AIR FORCE 195
ENVIRONMENTAL CAREER CENTER 195
ENVIRONMENTAL CENTER 58
ENVIRONMENTAL CONCERN INC. 196
ENVIRONMENTAL EDUCATION ASSOCIATES 196
ENVIRONMENTAL EDUCATION ASSOCIATION OF ILLINOIS 197
ENVIRONMENTAL EDUCATION ASSOCIATION OF INDIANA 197
ENVIRONMENTAL EDUCATION ASSOCIATION OF WASHINGTON 197
ENVIRONMENTAL EDUCATION COUNCIL OF OHIO 197

KEYWORD INDEX - Environmental and Conservation Education

ENVIRONMENTAL EDUCATORS OF NORTH CAROLINA (EENC) 197
ENVIRONMENTAL FUND FOR GEORGIA 197
ENVIRONMENTAL RESOURCE CENTER (ERC) 198
ENVIROSOUTH, INC. 199
E-P EDUCATION SERVICES, INC. 191
EUROPEAN ASSOCIATION FOR AQUATIC MAMMALS 199
FAIRFAX AUDUBON SOCIETY 199
FEDERAL WILDLIFE OFFICER'S ASSOCIATION 199
FEDERATION OF ALBERTA NATURALISTS 200
FEDERATION OF ENVIRONMENTAL EDUCATION IN ST. PETERSBURG 200
FEDERATION OF FLY FISHERS 200
FEDERATION OF WESTERN OUTDOOR CLUBS 200
FISHAMERICA FOUNDATION 201
FLORIDA AUDUBON SOCIETY 201
FLORIDA NATIVE PLANT SOCIETY 202
FLORIDA ORNITHOLOGICAL SOCIETY 202
FLORIDA PANTHER PROJECT, INC., THE 202
FLORIDA SEA GRANT COLLEGE 54
FLORIDA SPORTSMEN'S CONSERVATION ASSOCIATION 202
FLORIDA STATE COOPERATIVE EXTENSION SERVICE 54
FLORIDA TRAIL ASSOCIATION, INC. 203
FOREST LANDOWNERS ASSOCIATION, INC. 203
FOREST SERVICE EMPLOYEES FOR ENVIRONMENTAL ETHICS (FSEEE) 204
FORESTRY COMMISSION (SOUTH CAROLINA) 105
FOSSIL RIM WILDLIFE CENTER 205
FOUNDATION FOR NORTH AMERICAN BIG GAME 205
FOUNDATION FOR NORTH AMERICAN WILD SHEEP 205
FRIENDS OF THE RIVER 206
FRIENDS OF THE SEA OTTER 206
FUTURE FISHERMAN FOUNDATION 207
GALIANO CONSERVANCY ASSOCIATION 207
GARDEN CLUB OF AMERICA, THE 208
GENERAL FEDERATION OF WOMEN'S CLUBS 208
GEORGE MIKSCH SUTTON AVIAN RESEARCH CENTER INC. 208
GEORGIA ENVIRONMENTAL COUNCIL, INC. 209
GEORGIA ENVIRONMENTAL ORGANIZATION, INC (GEO) 209
GEORGIA SEA GRANT COLLEGE PROGRAM 56
GIRL SCOUTS OF THE UNITED STATES OF AMERICA 210
GLOBAL ENVIRONMENTAL MANAGEMENT INITIATIVE (GEMI) 210
GREAT BEAR FOUNDATION 211
GREAT LAKES SPORT FISHING COUNCIL 211
GREAT OUTDOORS CONSERVANCY, THE 212
GREAT SMOKY MOUNTAINS INSTITUTE AT TREMONT ... 212
GREEN (GLOBAL RIVERS ENVIRONMENTAL EDUCATION NETWORK) 212
GREEN MOUNTAIN AUDUBON SOCIETY 213
GREEN MOUNTAIN CLUB INC., THE 213
GREEN SEAL 213
GROUNDWATER FOUNDATION, THE 213
HAWAII AUDUBON SOCIETY 214
HAWAII DEPARTMENT OF HEALTH 58
HAWAII NATURE CENTER 214
HAWK AND OWL TRUST, THE 215
HAWKWATCH INTERNATIONAL, INC. 215
HEADLANDS INSTITUTE 215
HIGH DESERT MUSEUM, THE 216
HOLDEN ARBORETUM, THE 216
HOOSIER ENVIRONMENTAL COUNCIL 216
HUMBOLT FIELD RESEARCH INSTITUTE 217
HUMMINGBIRD SOCIETY, THE 217
IDAHO DEPARTMENT OF PARKS AND RECREATION 60
IDAHO FISH AND GAME DEPARTMENT 60
IDAHO FISH AND WILDLIFE FOUNDATION 60
IDAHO STATE SOIL CONSERVATION COMMISSION 60
ILLINOIS ASSOCIATION OF CONSERVATION DISTRICTS 218
ILLINOIS DEPARTMENT OF NATURAL RESOURCES 61
ILLINOIS PRAIRIE PATH 219
INDIAN CREEK NATURE CENTER 219
INDIANA AUDUBON SOCIETY, INC. 220
INITIATIVE FOR SOCIAL ACTION AND RENEWAL IN EURASIA 221
INSTITUTE FOR CIVIC INITIATIVES SUPPORT 221
INSTITUTE FOR EARTH EDUCATION, THE 221
INSTITUTE FOR ECOLOGICAL STUDIES 92
INSTITUTE OF ECOSYSTEM STUDIES 221
INSTITUTO BRASIL DE EDUCACAO AMBIENTAL 222
INTERFAITH COUNCIL FOR THE PROTECTION OF ANIMALS AND NATURE INC. (ICPAN) 222
INTERNATIONAL ASSOCIATION FOR ENVIRONMENTAL HYDROLOGY (IAEH) 222
INTERNATIONAL BICYCLE FUND 223
INTERNATIONAL CENTER FOR EARTH CONCERNS 223
INTERNATIONAL CENTER FOR GIBBON STUDIES 224
INTERNATIONAL CENTRE FOR CONSERVATION EDUCATION 224
INTERNATIONAL CRANE FOUNDATION 224
INTERNATIONAL EROSION CONTROL ASSOCIATION (IECA) 224
INTERNATIONAL HUNTER EDUCATION ASSOCIATION ... 225
INTERNATIONAL MARINE MAMMAL PROJECT, THE 226
INTERNATIONAL OCEANOGRAPHIC FOUNDATION 226
INTERNATIONAL SNOW LEOPARD TRUST 227
INTERNATIONAL SOCIETY FOR ENDANGERED CATS (ISEC) 227
INTERNATIONAL WILDERNESS LEADERSHIP (WILD) FOUNDATION 230
INTERNATIONAL WOLF CENTER (Educational Services) ... 230
IOWA ACADEMY OF SCIENCE 231
IOWA ASSOCIATION OF NATURALISTS 231
IOWA AUDUBON 231
IOWA NATIVE PLANT SOCIETY 232
IOWA TRAPPERS ASSOCIATION, INC. 232
ISLAND CONSERVATION EFFORT 233
IZAAK WALTON LEAGUE OF AMERICA ENDOWMENT 234
IZAAK WALTON LEAGUE OF AMERICA, INC., THE 234
J.N. (DING) DARLING FOUNDATION 235
JOHN INSKEEP ENVIRONMENTAL LEARNING CENTER .. 236
KANSAS ASSOCIATION FOR CONSERVATION AND ENVIRONMENTAL EDUCATION 237
KANSAS DEPARTMENT OF AGRICULTURE 65
KANSAS FOREST SERVICE 65
KANSAS GEOLOGICAL SURVEY 66
KANSAS HERPETOLOGICAL SOCIETY 237
KANSAS ORNITHOLOGICAL SOCIETY 237
KANSAS STATE CONSERVATION COMMISSION 66
KEEP AMERICA BEAUTIFUL, INC. 238
KENTUCKY ASSOCIATION FOR ENVIRONMENTAL EDUCATION (KAEE) 239
KENTUCKY DEPARTMENT OF AGRICULTURE 66
KENTUCKY DEPARTMENT OF FISH AND WILDLIFE RESOURCES 66
KEYSTONE CENTER, THE 239
KIDS FOR SAVING EARTH WORLDWIDE 239
LADY BIRD JOHNSON WILDFLOWER CENTER 240
LAND BETWEEN THE LAKES ASSOCIATION 240
LAND TRUST ALLIANCE, THE 240
LAND WATCH MONTEREY COUNTY 241
LEAGUE OF ENVIRONMENTAL JOURNALISTS 241
LEAGUE OF WOMEN VOTERS OF THE U.S. 241
LEAGUE TO SAVE LAKE TAHOE 242
LEARNING FOR ENVIRONMENTAL ACTION PROGRAMME (LEAP) 242
LEE COUNTY PARKS AND RECREATION SERVICES 54
LEGACY INTERNATIONAL 242
LIGHTHAWK 243
LOUISIANA DEPARTMENT OF AGRICULTURE AND FORESTRY 68
LOUISIANA SEA GRANT COLLEGE PROGRAM 69
LVIV REGIONAL INSTITUTE OF EDUCATION 244
MAGIC 244
MAINE ASSOCIATION OF CONSERVATION COMMISSIONS (MACC) 244
MAINE AUDUBON SOCIETY 244
MAINE DEPARTMENT OF MARINE RESOURCES 71
MAINE ENVIRONMENTAL EDUCATION ASSOCIATION, INC. 245
MAINE SEA GRANT PROGRAM 71
MAINE/NEW HAMPSHIRE SEA GRANT PROGRAM 83
MARIN CONSERVATION LEAGUE 246
MARINE ENVIRONMENTAL RESEARCH INSTITUTE (MERI) 246
MARINE MAMMAL CENTER, THE 246
MARYLAND DEPARTMENT OF AGRICULTURE 71
MARYLAND FORESTS ASSOCIATION 247

MARYLAND ORNITHOLOGICAL SOCIETY, INC. 247
MARYLAND SEA GRANT COLLEGE 72
MASSACHUSETTS ASSOCIATION OF CONSERVATION
  COMMISSIONS (MACC) 247
MASSACHUSETTS COOPERATIVE FISH AND WILDLIFE
  RESEARCH UNIT (USDI) 74
MASSACHUSETTS ENVIRONMENTAL EDUCATION
  SOCIETY 248
MAX McGRAW WILDLIFE FOUNDATION 248
MERCK FOREST AND FARMLAND CENTER, INC. 248
MICHIGAN AUDUBON SOCIETY 249
MICHIGAN DEPARTMENT OF ENVIRONMENTAL QUALITY 75
MICHIGAN LAND USE INSTITUTE 249
MID-ATLANTIC COUNCIL OF WATERSHED ASSOCIATIONS
  250
MINNESOTA GROUND WATER ASSOCIATION 251
MINNESOTA HERPETOLOGICAL SOCIETY (James Ford Bell
  Museum of Natural History) 251
MINNESOTA NATIVE PLANT SOCIETY 251
MINNESOTA PARKS AND TRAILS COUNCIL 251
MINNESOTA WINGS SOCIETY, INC. 252
MISSISSIPPI FORESTRY COMMISSION 78
MISSISSIPPI NATIVE PLANT SOCIETY 252
MISSISSIPPI SOIL AND WATER CONSERVATION
  COMMISSION 78
MISSISSIPPI STATE EXTENSION SERVICES 79
MISSOURI PRAIRIE FOUNDATION 253
MONTANA DEPARTMENT OF FISH, WILDLIFE, AND PARKS
  80
MOTE MARINE LABORATORY 255
MOUNTAIN CONSERVATION TRUST OF GEORGIA, INC. .. 255
MULE DEER FOUNDATION, THE 256
NATIONAL 4-H COUNCIL 256
NATIONAL ARBOR DAY FOUNDATION 256
NATIONAL ASSOCIATION FOR INTERPRETATION 256
NATIONAL ASSOCIATION OF BIOLOGY TEACHERS 257
NATIONAL ASSOCIATION OF CONSERVATION DISTRICTS
  257
NATIONAL ASSOCIATION OF SERVICE AND
  CONSERVATION CORPS (NASCC) 258
NATIONAL ASSOCIATION OF STATE PARK DIRECTORS. 258
NATIONAL ASSOCIATION OF UNIVERSITY FISHERIES AND
  WILDLIFE PROGRAMS 259
NATIONAL AVIARY 259
NATIONAL COALITION FOR MARINE CONSERVATION 260
NATIONAL COUNCIL FOR GEOGRAPHIC EDUCATION 260
NATIONAL FISH AND WILDLIFE FOUNDATION 261
NATIONAL FOREST FOUNDATION 261
NATIONAL GARDENING ASSOCIATION 262
NATIONAL GEOGRAPHIC SOCIETY 262
NATIONAL GROUND WATER ASSOCIATION, THE 262
NATIONAL HUNTERS ASSOCIATION, INC. 262
NATIONAL PARK FOUNDATION 263
NATIONAL SCIENCE TEACHERS ASSOCIATION 265
NATIONAL SHOOTING SPORTS FOUNDATION, INC. 265
NATIONAL SPELEOLOGICAL SOCIETY, INC. 265
NATIONAL TREE TRUST 265
NATIONAL TRUST FOR HISTORIC PRESERVATION 265
NATIONAL WILDLIFE REHABILITATORS ASSOCIATION ... 269
NATURAL AND SCENIC RIVERS COMMISSION (ARKANSAS)
  43
NATURAL SCIENCE FOR YOUTH FOUNDATION 271
NEBRASKA NATURAL RESOURCES COMMISSION 82
NEBRASKA STATE EXTENSION SERVICES 82
NEVIS HISTORICAL AND CONSERVATION SOCIETY 276
NEW BRUNSWICK WILDLIFE FEDERATION 276
NEW ENGLAND WILD FLOWER SOCIETY, INC. 276
NEW HAMPSHIRE DEPARTMENT OF AGRICULTURE,
  MARKETS, AND FOOD 83
NEW HAMPSHIRE FISH AND GAME DEPARTMENT 84
NEW HAMPSHIRE LAKES ASSOCIATION 277
NEW JERSEY AUDUBON SOCIETY 277
NEW JERSEY CONSERVATION FOUNDATION 278
NEW YORK SEA GRANT 90
NEW YORK STATE COOPERATIVE EXTENSION 90
NEW YORK STATE OFFICE OF PARKS, RECREATION AND
  HISTORIC PRESERVATION 91
NEW YORK TURTLE AND TORTOISE SOCIETY 279
NORTH AMERICAN ASSOCIATION FOR ENVIRONMENTAL
  EDUCATION 280
NORTH AMERICAN BUTTERFLY ASSOCIATION 280
NORTH AMERICAN WOLF SOCIETY 282
NORTH CAROLINA COASTAL FEDERATION, INC. 282
NORTH CAROLINA COOPERATIVE EXTENSION SERVICE 91
NORTH CAROLINA FORESTRY ASSOCIATION 282
NORTH DAKOTA GAME AND FISH DEPARTMENT 93
NORTH DAKOTA STATE FOREST SERVICE 93
NORTH DAKOTA STATE SOIL CONSERVATION COMMITTEE
  93
NORTHEAST SUSTAINABLE ENERGY ASSOCIATION 284
NORTHERN ALASKA ENVIRONMENTAL CENTER 285
NORTHERN VIRGINIA REGIONAL PARK AUTHORITY 113
NORTHWEST INTERPRETIVE ASSOCIATION 286
NOVA SCOTIA FORESTRY ASSOCIATION 286
OHIO ACADEMY OF SCIENCE, THE 286
OHIO ALLIANCE FOR THE ENVIRONMENT 287
OHIO AUDUBON COUNCIL, INC. 287
OHIO BIOLOGICAL SURVEY 287
OHIO ENERGY PROJECT 287
OHIO ENVIRONMENTAL COUNCIL, INC. 287
OHIO ENVIRONMENTAL PROTECTION AGENCY 94
OHIO NATIVE PLANT SOCIETY 288
OHIO SEA GRANT COLLEGE PROGRAM 95
OKLAHOMA ACADEMY OF SCIENCE 288
OKLAHOMA STATE CONSERVATION COMMISSION 96
OKLAHOMA STATE EXTENSION SERVICES 96
OKLAHOMA WATER RESOURCES BOARD 97
OREGON COOPERATIVE FISH AND WILDLIFE RESEARCH
  UNIT (USDI) 97
OREGON DEPARTMENT OF ENVIRONMENTAL QUALITY
  (DEQ) 98
OREGON PARKS AND RECREATION DEPARTMENT 98
OREGON SMALL WOODLANDS ASSOCIATION 290
ORNITHOLOGICAL COUNCIL 291
OUTDOOR WRITERS ASSOCIATION OF AMERICA, INC. . 292
OZARKS RESOURCE CENTER 292
PACIFIC INSTITUTE FOR STUDIES IN DEVELOPMENT,
  ENVIRONMENT, AND SECURITY 293
PACIFIC NORTHWEST TRAIL ASSOCIATION 293
PACIFIC SEABIRD GROUP 293
PACIFIC WHALE FOUNDATION 293
PANOS INSTITUTE, THE 293
PAWS/OLYMPIC WILDLIFE RESCUE 294
PENNSYLVANIA AUDUBON SOCIETY 294
PENNSYLVANIA DEPARTMENT OF AGRICULTURE 99
PENNSYLVANIA DEPARTMENT OF CONSERVATION AND
  NATURAL RESOURCES 100
PENNSYLVANIA FISH AND BOAT COMMISSION 101
PENNSYLVANIA FORESTRY ASSOCIATION, THE 295
PENNSYLVANIA RECREATION AND PARK SOCIETY, INC.
  295
PENNSYLVANIA RESOURCES COUNCIL, INC., (formerly PA
  Roadside Council) 295
PEOPLE FOR PUGET SOUND 295
PHEASANTS FOREVER, INC. 296
PINE BLUFF COOPERATIVE FISHERY RESEARCH
  PROJECT 44
POPULATION REFERENCE BUREAU, INC. 298
POTOMAC APPALACHIAN TRAIL CLUB 298
PRIORITIES INSTITUTE, THE 299
PTARMIGANS, THE 300
PUBLIC LANDS FOUNDATION 300
PUERTO RICO ASSOCIATION OF SOIL AND WATER
  CONSERVATION DISTRICTS 300
PUERTO RICO CONSERVATION FOUNDATION, THE (PRCF
  300
PUERTO RICO DEPARTMENT OF NATURAL AND
  ENVIRONMENTAL RESOURCES 103
PUERTO RICO SEA GRANT PROGRAM 103
PUERTO RICO STATE EXTENSION SERVICES 103
PUGET SOUNDKEEPER ALLIANCE 300
PURPLE MARTIN CONSERVATION ASSOCIATION 301
RACHEL CARSON COUNCIL, INC. (formerly Rachel Carson
  Trust for the Living Environment Inc.) 301
RAINBOW PUSH COALITION 302
RAINFOREST ACTION NETWORK 302
RAINFOREST RELIEF 302
RAINFOREST TRUST, INC., THE 302
RAPTOR CENTER, THE 303
RAPTOR EDUCATION FOUNDATION, INC. 303

KEYWORD INDEX - Environmental and Humanitarian Education

RAPTOR RESEARCH FOUNDATION, INC. 303
RARE CENTER FOR TROPICAL CONSERVATION 303
REEF RELIEF 303
RENEW AMERICA 303
RENEWABLE NATURAL RESOURCES FOUNDATION 304
RESOURCE CENTER FOR ENVIRONMENTAL EDUCATION, THE 304
RESOURCE RENEWAL INSTITUTE, THE 304
RHODE ISLAND STATE ASSOCIATION OF CONSERVATION DISTRICTS 305
RHODE ISLAND WILD PLANT SOCIETY 305
RINCON INSTITUTE, THE 305
RIVERS COUNCIL OF WASHINGTON (formerly Northwest Rivers Council) 306
ROCKY MOUNTAIN ELK FOUNDATION 307
ROGER TORY PETERSON INSTITUTE 307
RUFFED GROUSE SOCIETY, THE 307
SAFARI CLUB INTERNATIONAL 308
SANIBEL-CAPTIVA CONSERVATION FOUNDATION, INC. 308
SAVE SAN FRANCISCO BAY ASSOCIATION 309
SAVE THE DUNES COUNCIL 309
SAVE THE MANATEE CLUB 310
SAVE THE SOUND, INC. 310
SCENIC AMERICA 310
SEA SHEPHERD CONSERVATION SOCIETY 311
SEACAMP ASSOCIATION, INC. 312
SHELBURNE FARMS 312
SIERRA CLUB FOUNDATION, THE 317
SIERRA NEVADA FOREST PROTECTION CAMPAIGN 317
SOCIETY FOR CONSERVATION BIOLOGY 318
SOCIETY FOR ECOLOGICAL RESTORATION 318
SOCIETY FOR THE PROTECTION OF NEW HAMPSHIRE FORESTS 319
SOCIETY OF AMERICAN FORESTERS 291, 319, 341
SOCIETY OF WETLAND SCIENTISTS 320
SOIL AND WATER CONSERVATION SOCIETY (formerly Soil Conservation Society of America) 320
SOUND EXPERIENCE 320
SOUTH CAROLINA COASTAL CONSERVATION LEAGUE. 321
SOUTH DAKOTA STATE EXTENSION SERVICES 106
SOUTHEASTERN COOPERATIVE WILDLIFE DISEASE STUDY 323
SOUTHWEST FLORIDA WATER MANAGEMENT DISTRICT (SWFWMD) 55
STEAMBOATERS, THE 325
STOP 13, 326
STRIPERS UNLIMITED, INC. 326
STROUD WATER RESEARCH CENTER 326
STUDENT CONSERVATION ASSOCIATION, INC. 326
STUDENT PUGWASH USA 326
SUNCOAST SEABIRD SANCTUARY INC. 327
TALL TIMBERS RESEARCH STATION 327
TALLAHASSEE MUSEUM OF HISTORY AND NATURAL SCIENCE 327
TENNESSEE DEPARTMENT OF AGRICULTURE 107
TEXAS AGRICULTURAL EXTENSION SERVICE 108
TEXAS B.A.S.S. CHAPTER FEDERATION 329
TEXAS FORESTRY ASSOCIATION 329
TEXAS SEA GRANT PROGRAM 109
TEXAS STATE SOIL AND WATER CONSERVATION BOARD 109
TEXAS WATER DEVELOPMENT BOARD 109
THORNE ECOLOGICAL INSTITUTE 329
THREE CIRCLES CENTER FOR MULTICULTURAL ENVIRONMENTAL EDUCATION 329
THRESHOLD, INC. 329
TOGETHER FOUNDATION, THE 330
TREAD LIGHTLY! INC. 330
TREEPEOPLE 330
TREES FOR TOMORROW, INC., NATURAL RESOURCES EDUCATION CENTER 331
TRI-STATE BIRD RESCUE AND RESEARCH, INC. 331
TROUT UNLIMITED 331, 332, 333, 334
TROUT UNLIMITED, PENNSYLVANIA COUNCIL 333
TRUST FOR WILDLIFE, INC. 335
TUG HILL TOMORROW LAND TRUST 335
TURTLE CREEK WATERSHED ASSOCIATION, INC. 335
UNION OF CONCERNED SCIENTISTS 336
UNITED STATES COMMITTEE FOR THE UNITED NATIONS ENVIRONMENT PROGRAMME THE (U.S. and UNEP) 336
UNIVERSITY OF NEW HAMPSHIRE COOPERATIVE EXTENSION 84
UPPER CHATTAHOOCHEE RIVERKEEPER 337
UTAH B.A.S.S. CHAPTER FEDERATION 337
UTAH NATURE STUDY SOCIETY 337
UTAH STATE SOIL CONSERVATION COMMISSION 111
VERMONT AUDUBON COUNCIL 338
VERMONT B.A.S.S. CHAPTER FEDERATION 338
VERMONT DEPARTMENT OF AGRICULTURE, FOOD, AND MARKETS 112
VERMONT INSTITUTE OF NATURAL SCIENCE 338
VERMONT STATE-WIDE ENVIRONMENTAL EDUCATION PROGRAMS (SWEEP) 339
VIRGIN ISLANDS CONSERVATION SOCIETY, INC. 339
VIRGINIA FORESTRY ASSOCIATION 340
VIRGINIA MUSEUM OF NATURAL HISTORY 115
VIRGINIA SEA GRANT PROGRAM 115
WASHINGTON B.A.S.S. CHAPTER FEDERATION 340
WASHINGTON FARM FORESTRY ASSOCIATION 341
WASHINGTON FOUNDATION FOR THE ENVIRONMENT .. 341
WASHINGTON STATE CONSERVATION COMMISSION 118
WASHINGTON STATE EXTENSION SERVICES 118
WASHINGTON STATE OFFICE OF ENVIRONMENTAL EDUCATION 118
WASHINGTON TOXICS COALITION 341
WASHINGTON TRAILS ASSOCIATION 341
WASHINGTON WILDLIFE FEDERATION 342
WATER ENVIRONMENT FEDERATION 342
WATER RESOURCES ASSOCIATION OF THE DELAWARE RIVER BASIN 342
WATERLOO-WELLINGTON WILDFLOWER SOCIETY (Formerly the Dogtooth Group) 342
WEST MICHIGAN ENVIRONMENTAL ACTION COUNCIL... 343
WHITETAILS UNLIMITED, INC. 345
WILD CANID SURVIVAL AND RESEARCH CENTER 345
WILD DOG FOUNDATION, THE 345
WILDERNESS EDUCATION ASSOCIATION 346
WILDFLOWER ASSOCIATION OF MICHIGAN 347
WILDFOWL TRUST OF NORTH AMERICA, INC., THE 347
WILDLIFE ACTION, INC. 347
WILDLIFE CENTER OF VIRGINIA, THE 347
WILDLIFE CONSERVATION SOCIETY 348
WILDLIFE DAMAGE REVIEW (WDR) 348
WILDLIFE FOREVER 348
WILDLIFE HABITAT COUNCIL 349
WILDLIFE INFORMATION CENTER, INC. 349
WILDLIFE PRESERVATION TRUST INTERNATIONAL, INC. 350
WILDLIFE WAYSTATION 355
WINDSTAR FOUNDATION, THE 355
WISCONSIN ASSOCIATION FOR ENVIRONMENTAL EDUCATION, INC. 355
WISCONSIN CONSERVATION CORPS 120
WISCONSIN DEPARTMENT OF PUBLIC INSTRUCTION 121
WISCONSIN ENVIRONMENTAL EDUCATION BOARD (WEEB) 121
WISCONSIN PARK AND RECREATION ASSOCIATION 356
WISCONSIN SOCIETY FOR ORNITHOLOGY, INC., THE.... 356
WOLF EDUCATION AND RESEARCH CENTER 357
WOLF FUND, THE 357
WORLD ASSOCIATION OF GIRL GUIDES AND GIRL SCOUTS (WAGGGS) 357
WORLD CONSERVATION MONITORING CENTRE 358
WORLD FORESTRY CENTER 358
WYOMING GAME AND FISH DEPARTMENT 123
WYOMING OUTDOOR COUNCIL 360
WYOMING STATE EXTENSION SERVICES 123
YELLOWSTONE GRIZZLY FOUNDATION (YGF) 360
YMCA EARTH SERVICE CORPS 360
YOUNG ENTOMOLOGISTS' SOCIETY, INC. 361
ZERO POPULATION GROWTH, INC. 361

Environmental and Humanitarian Education

20/20 VISION 130
JANE GOODALL INSTITUTE, THE 236

Environmental Cleanup

COOSA RIVER BASIN INITIATIVE 184
OREGON DEPARTMENT OF ENVIRONMENTAL QUALITY (DEQ) 98

Environmental Communication

ACTION FOR NATURE, INC. 130
ASSOCIATION OF GREAT LAKES OUTDOOR WRITERS .. 156
ENVIRONMENTAL MEDIA ASSOCIATION 198
LEARNING FOR ENVIRONMENTAL ACTION PROGRAMME (LEAP) 242
POPULATION COMMUNICATIONS INTERNATIONAL 297

Environmental Contaminants

OREGON COOPERATIVE FISH AND WILDLIFE RESEARCH UNIT (USDI) 97

Environmental Education Curriculum

ALASKA NATURAL HISTORY ASSOCIATION 134
LVIV REGIONAL INSTITUTE OF EDUCATION 244
OLYMPIC PARK INSTITUTE 289
SHELBURNE FARMS 312
WILDLIFE CONSERVATION SOCIETY 348

Environmental Ethics

ALDO LEOPOLD FOUNDATION, INC. 135
CALIFORNIA TRAPPERS ASSOCIATION 164
CENTER FOR ENVIRONMENTAL PHILOSOPHY 169
COALITION FOR EDUCATION IN THE OUTDOORS 175
COLORADO DEPARTMENT OF EDUCATION 49
LVIV REGIONAL INSTITUTE OF EDUCATION 244
MISSOURI FOREST PRODUCTS ASSOCIATION 253
NATIONAL WHISTLEBLOWER CENTER 266
NEWFOUNDLAND LABRADOR WILDLIFE FEDERATION ... 279
PUBLIC EMPLOYEES FOR ENVIRONMENTAL RESPONSIBILITY (PEER) 300
REP AMERICA/REPUBLICANS FOR ENVIRONMENTAL PROTECTION 304
SCIENTISTS CENTER FOR ANIMAL WELFARE 311
TEXAS SEA GRANT PROGRAM 109
UNITED NATIONS ENVIRONMENT PROGRAMME 336
WILD ONES - NATURAL LANDSCAPERS, LTD 346
WILDLIFE ACTION, INC. 347

Environmental Health

ALASKA DEPARTMENT OF ENVIRONMENTAL CONSERVATION 39
COLORADO ENVIRONMENTAL COALITION 177
FEDERATION OF ENVIRONMENTAL EDUCATION IN ST. PETERSBURG 200
NATIONAL ENVIRONMENTAL HEALTH ASSOCIATION 260
PHYSICIANS FOR SOCIAL RESPONSIBILITY 296

Environmental Justice

ALASKA CONSERVATION ALLIANCE 133
ALASKA CONSERVATION VOICE 134
AMERICAN PIE (PUBLIC INFORMATION ON THE ENVIRONMENT) 148
ATLANTIC STATES LEGAL FOUNDATION 157
CENTRO de INFORMACION, INVESTIGACION y EDUCACION SOCIAL (CIIES) 172
CHESAPEAKE BAY FOUNDATION, INC. (Maryland Office). 173
COMMUNITIES FOR A BETTER ENVIRONMENT 179
CONSERVATION FEDERATION OF MARYLAND/For A Rural Maryland (F.A.R.M.) 182
ECOLOGY CENTER 194
ENVIRONMENTAL EDUCATION ASSOCIATES 196
FEDERAL WILDLIFE OFFICER'S ASSOCIATION 199
GREAT LAKES UNITED 211
GREEN PARTY USA 213
LEARNING FOR ENVIRONMENTAL ACTION PROGRAMME (LEAP) 242
LEGAL ENVIRONMENTAL ASSISTANCE FOUNDATION INC. (LEAF) 242
NATIONAL NETWORK OF FOREST PRACTITIONERS 263
NATIONAL WHISTLEBLOWER CENTER 266
NEW HAMPSHIRE DEPARTMENT OF AGRICULTURE, MARKETS, AND FOOD 83
NEW YORK PUBLIC INTEREST RESEARCH GROUP (NYPIRG) 279
NORTH DAKOTA DEPARTMENT OF HEALTH 93
OHIO ENVIRONMENTAL COUNCIL, INC. 287
OREGON ENVIRONMENTAL COUNCIL 290
SOUTHWEST RESEARCH AND INFORMATION CENTER . 324
STUDENT ENVIRONMENTAL ACTION COALITION (SEAC) 326
TENNESSEE ENVIRONMENTAL COUNCIL 328
URBAN HABITAT PROGRAM 337

Environmental Law

AIR AND WASTE MANAGEMENT ASSOCIATION 132
AMERICAN CONSERVATION ASSOCIATION, INC. 139
AMERICAN HORSE PROTECTION ASSOCIATION 145
AMERICAN PLANNING ASSOCIATION 148
AMERICAN SOCIETY FOR ENVIRONMENTAL HISTORY .. 149
AMERICAN SOCIETY OF INTERNATIONAL LAW/WILDLIFE INTEREST GROUP 150
ASSOCIATION OF MIDWEST FISH AND GAME LAW ENFORCEMENT OFFICERS 156
ATLANTIC STATES LEGAL FOUNDATION 157
BIODIVERSITY LEGAL FOUNDATION 161
CANADIAN ENVIRONMENTAL LAW ASSOCIATION 166
CANADIAN INSTITUTE FOR ENVIRONMENTAL LAW AND POLICY (CIELAP) 166
CENTER FOR INTERNATIONAL ENVIRONMENTAL LAW (CIEL) 170
CIRCUMPOLAR CONSERVATION UNION 174
COMMUNITIES FOR A BETTER ENVIRONMENT 179
COMMUNITY RIGHTS COUNSEL 179
CONSERVATION AND RESEARCH FOUNDATION, INC., THE 181
CONSERVATION FORCE 182
CONSERVATION LAW FOUNDATION, INC. (CLF) 183
COOK INLET KEEPER 184
EARTHJUSTICE LEGAL DEFENSE FUND (formerly Sierra Club Legal Defense Fund, Inc.) 192
EARTHLAW 192
EARTHTRUST 193
ENDANGERED SPECIES COALITION 194
ENVIRONMENTAL CENTER 58
ENVIRONMENTAL DEFENSE CENTER, INC. 196
ENVIRONMENTAL EDUCATION ASSOCIATES 196
ENVIRONMENTAL LAW ALLIANCE WORLDWIDE (E-LAW) 197
ENVIRONMENTAL LAW AND POLICY CENTER OF THE MIDWEST 198
ENVIRONMENTAL LAW INSTITUTE, THE 198
FLORIDA DEFENDERS OF THE ENVIRONMENT, INC. (Home Office) 201
FOREST HISTORY SOCIETY, INC. 203
GEORGIA ENVIRONMENTAL POLICY INSTITUTE 209
GOVERNOR OF SOUTH CAROLINA 104
HAWAII DEPARTMENT OF HEALTH 58
ILLINOIS ENVIRONMENTAL PROTECTION AGENCY 61
INTERNATIONAL ASSOCIATION OF NATURAL RESOURCE PILOTS 223
INTERNATIONAL COUNCIL OF ENVIRONMENTAL LAW ... 224
INTERNATIONAL MARINE MAMMAL PROJECT, THE 226
INTERNATIONAL MARITIME ORGANIZATION 226
KENTUCKY RESOURCES COUNCIL 239
LAND TRUST ALLIANCE, THE 240
LEGAL ENVIRONMENTAL ASSISTANCE FOUNDATION INC. (LEAF) 242
MANASOTA-88 245
MINERAL POLICY CENTER 250
MONTANA ENVIRONMENTAL QUALITY COUNCIL 81
MOUNTAIN LION FOUNDATION 255
NATIONAL FARMERS UNION 261
NATIONAL GRANGE, THE 262

KEYWORD INDEX - Environmental Legislation

NATIONAL WHISTLEBLOWER CENTER 266
NATURE SASKATCHEWAN 275
NEW HAMPSHIRE ASSOCIATION OF CONSERVATION
  COMMISSIONS 276
NEW MEXICO ENVIRONMENTAL LAW CENTER 278
OKLAHOMA STATE BOARD OF AGRICULTURE 96
OREGON FISH AND WILDLIFE DIVISION/DEPARTMENT OF
  STATE POLICE 98
PINE BLUFF COOPERATIVE FISHERY RESEARCH
  PROJECT 44
PUGET SOUNDKEEPER ALLIANCE 300
SIERRA CLUB FOUNDATION, THE 317
SOCIETY OF AMERICAN FORESTERS 291, 319, 341
SOUTH CAROLINA DEPARTMENT OF HEALTH AND
  ENVIRONMENTAL CONTROL 105
SOUTH CAROLINA ENVIRONMENTAL LAW PROJECT 321
SOUTHERN ENVIRONMENTAL LAW CENTER 324
STANFORD ENVIRONMENTAL LAW SOCIETY 325
STEAMBOATERS, THE 325
TEXAS SEA GRANT PROGRAM 109
TRUSTEES FOR ALASKA 335
UNITED NATIONS ENVIRONMENT PROGRAMME 336
WASHINGTON FARM FORESTRY ASSOCIATION 341
WESTERN ENVIRONMENTAL LAW CENTER 344
WISCONSIN ASSOCIATION FOR ENVIRONMENTAL
  EDUCATION, INC. 355
WISCONSIN SOCIETY FOR ORNITHOLOGY, INC., THE 356

Environmental Legislation

AMERICAN SOCIETY OF INTERNATIONAL LAW/WILDLIFE
  INTEREST GROUP 150
COOSA RIVER BASIN INITIATIVE 184
KANSAS NATURAL RESOURCE COUNCIL 237
PENNSYLVANIA ENVIRONMENTAL COUNCIL, INC. (PEC) 294
REP AMERICA/REPUBLICANS FOR ENVIRONMENTAL
  PROTECTION 304
VIRGINIA CONSERVATION NETWORK 339

Environmental Literacy

LEARNING FOR ENVIRONMENTAL ACTION PROGRAMME
  (LEAP) 242
NORTH AMERICAN ASSOCIATION FOR ENVIRONMENTAL
  EDUCATION 280

Environmental Living

ENVIRONMENTAL LAW AND POLICY CENTER OF THE
  MIDWEST 198
LVIV REGIONAL INSTITUTE OF EDUCATION 244
PENNSYLVANIA RESOURCES COUNCIL, INC., (formerly PA
  Roadside Council) 295

Environmental Planning

ADOPT-A-STREAM FOUNDATION, THE 131
ALASKA DEPARTMENT OF ENVIRONMENTAL
  CONSERVATION 39
AMERICAN BIRD CONSERVANCY 138
AMERICAN PLANNING ASSOCIATION 148
AUDUBON INTERNATIONAL 158
CALIFORNIA TRAPPERS ASSOCIATION 164
CENTER FOR CHESAPEAKE COMMUNITIES 169
CENTER FOR WATERSHED PROTECTION 171
CHINA REGION LAKES ALLIANCE 173
COLUMBIA RIVER GORGE COMMISSION 116
COMMUNITY RIGHTS COUNSEL 179
CONNECTICUT COUNCIL ON ENVIRONMENTAL QUALITY 50
DELAWARE SOLID WASTE AUTHORITY 52
DEPARTMENT OF TRANSPORTATION (OREGON) 97
EARTHSCAN 193
FAIRFAX AUDUBON SOCIETY 199
FEDERATION OF ENVIRONMENTAL EDUCATION IN ST.
  PETERSBURG 200
FOSSIL FUELS POLICY ACTION INSTITUTE/ALLIANCE FOR
  A PAVING MORATORIUM 204
FRIENDS OF DISCOVERY PARK 205

GALIANO CONSERVANCY ASSOCIATION 207
INDIANA GEOLOGICAL SURVEY 63
INTERNATIONAL ASSOCIATION OF NATURAL RESOURCE
  PILOTS 223
INTERNATIONAL SOCIETY FOR ECOLOGICAL ECONOMICS
  227
KENTUCKY-TENNESSEE SOCIETY OF AMERICAN
  FORESTERS 239
LAND WATCH MONTEREY COUNTY 241
LEGACY INTERNATIONAL 242
LIGHTHAWK 243
MAINE ASSOCIATION OF CONSERVATION COMMISSIONS
  (MACC) 244
MINNESOTA ENVIRONMENTAL QUALITY BOARD 76
MINNESOTA GROUND WATER ASSOCIATION 251
NATIONAL ASSOCIATION OF ENVIRONMENTAL
  PROFESSIONALS, THE (National Office) 257
NATIVE AMERICAN FISH AND WILDLIFE SOCIETY (NAFWS)
  269
NATURAL AND SCENIC RIVERS COMMISSION (ARKANSAS)
  43
NATURAL LAND INSTITUTE 270
NEW HAMPSHIRE LAKES ASSOCIATION 277
NEW JERSEY CONSERVATION FOUNDATION 278
OFFICE OF ENERGY EFFICIENCY AND ENVIRONMENT 91
PRIORITIES INSTITUTE, THE 299
RESOURCE RENEWAL INSTITUTE, THE 304
SOUTH CAROLINA COASTAL CONSERVATION LEAGUE 321
SOUTH CAROLINA DEPARTMENT OF HEALTH AND
  ENVIRONMENTAL CONTROL 105
SOUTHWEST FLORIDA WATER MANAGEMENT DISTRICT
  (SWFWMD) 55
STATE OF IDAHO DIVISION OF ENVIRONMENTAL QUALITY
  61
TEXAS SEA GRANT PROGRAM 109
TOGETHER FOUNDATION, THE 330
TREES FOR THE FUTURE, INC. 330
TUG HILL COMMISSION 91
UNITED NATIONS ENVIRONMENT PROGRAMME 336

Environmental Preservation

ADIRONDACK MOUNTAIN CLUB, INC., THE 131
ADOPT-A-STREAM FOUNDATION, THE 131
AGENCY OF NATURAL RESOURCES 111
ALBERTA WILDERNESS ASSOCIATION 135
AMERICAN BASS ASSOCIATION OF MARYLAND, THE 137
AMERICAN FEDERATION OF MINERALOGICAL SOCIETIES
  139
ARCHBOLD BIOLOGICAL STATION 153
ARKANSAS DEPARTMENT OF PARKS AND TOURISM 42
ASSOCIATION OF NEW JERSEY ENVIRONMENTAL
  COMMISSIONS 157
AUDUBON COUNCIL OF ILLINOIS 158
AUDUBON SOCIETY OF RHODE ISLAND 159
BERKSHIRE-LITCHFIELD ENVIRONMENTAL COUNCIL, INC.
  160
BIRDLIFE INTERNATIONAL 161
CALIFORNIA NATIVE PLANT SOCIETY, THE 164
CALIFORNIA TRAPPERS ASSOCIATION 164
CALIFORNIANS FOR POPULATION STABILIZATION (CAPS)
  165
CAVE RESEARCH FOUNDATION 168
CENTER FOR CHESAPEAKE COMMUNITIES 169
CENTER FOR PLANT CONSERVATION 170
CENTER FOR RESOURCEFUL BUILDING TECHNOLOGY 171
CHARLES A. AND ANNE MORROW LINDBERGH
  FOUNDATION, THE 172
CONFEDERATED SALISH AND KOOTENAI TRIBES 180
DEFENDERS OF WILDLIFE 186
DELAWARE GREENWAYS, INC. 187
DRAGONFLY SOCIETY OF THE AMERICAS, THE 188
EARTH FOUNDATION 191
EARTH SHARE 192
ENERGY, MINERALS, AND NATURAL RESOURCES
  DEPARTMENT 86
ENVIRONMENTAL AIR FORCE 195
EUROPEAN CETACEAN SOCIETY 199
FAIRFAX AUDUBON SOCIETY 199

KEYWORD INDEX - Environmental Protection

FEDERATION OF FLY FISHERS 200
FLORIDA EXOTIC PEST PLANT COUNCIL 202
FOREST FIRE LOOKOUT ASSOCIATION 203
FOREST TRUST 204
FOSSIL FUELS POLICY ACTION INSTITUTE/ALLIANCE FOR A PAVING MORATORIUM 204
GENERAL FEDERATION OF WOMEN'S CLUBS 208
GEORGE MIKSCH SUTTON AVIAN RESEARCH CENTER INC. 208
GEORGE WRIGHT SOCIETY, THE 208
GEORGIA COOPERATIVE FISH AND WILDLIFE RESEARCH UNIT (USDI) 55
GREEN (GLOBAL RIVERS ENVIRONMENTAL EDUCATION NETWORK) 212
HAWAII AUDUBON SOCIETY 214
HOOD CANAL LAND TRUST 216
IDAHO CONSERVATION LEAGUE 218
IDAHO DEPARTMENT OF PARKS AND RECREATION 60
ILLINOIS ENVIRONMENTAL PROTECTION AGENCY 61
ILLINOIS NATIVE PLANT SOCIETY 219
ILLINOIS NATURAL HERITAGE FOUNDATION 219
ILLINOIS NATURE PRESERVES COMMISSION (INPC) 62
ILLINOIS PRAIRIE PATH 219
INSTITUTE FOR EARTH EDUCATION, THE 221
INTERAGENCY COMMITTEE FOR OUTDOOR RECREATION (IAC) 116
INTERNATIONAL SOCIETY FOR THE PRESERVATION OF THE TROPICAL RAINFOREST, THE 227
IOWA NATIVE PLANT SOCIETY 232
IOWA TRAILS COUNCIL 232
KEEP AMERICA BEAUTIFUL, INC. 238
KEEP FLORIDA BEAUTIFUL, INC. 238
KIDS FOR SAVING EARTH WORLDWIDE 239
LAND TRUST ALLIANCE, THE 240
LAND WATCH MONTEREY COUNTY 241
LEAGUE TO SAVE LAKE TAHOE 242
LEE COUNTY PARKS AND RECREATION SERVICES 54
LIGHTHAWK 243
MARIN CONSERVATION LEAGUE 246
MASSACHUSETTS ASSOCIATION OF CONSERVATION COMMISSIONS (MACC) 247
MAX McGRAW WILDLIFE FOUNDATION 248
MINNESOTA GROUND WATER ASSOCIATION 251
MINNESOTA NATIVE PLANT SOCIETY 251
MINNESOTA PARKS AND TRAILS COUNCIL 251
MISSOURI DEPARTMENT OF NATURAL RESOURCES 79
MISSOURI NATIVE PLANT SOCIETY 253
NATIONAL WILDLIFE REFUGE ASSOCIATION 269
NATURAL HERITAGE COMMISSION (ARKANSAS) 44
NATURAL LAND INSTITUTE 270
NEW HAMPSHIRE ASSOCIATION OF CONSERVATION COMMISSIONS 276
NEW JERSEY PINELANDS COMMISSION 85
NEW YORK STATE OFFICE OF PARKS, RECREATION AND HISTORIC PRESERVATION 91
NORTH CAROLINA RECREATION AND PARK SOCIETY, INC. 283
NORTH CASCADES CONSERVATION COUNCIL 283
NORTH DAKOTA GEOLOGICAL SURVEY 93
NORTH DAKOTA PARKS AND RECREATION DEPARTMENT 93
NORTHERN VIRGINIA REGIONAL PARK AUTHORITY 113
OPENLANDS PROJECT 290
OREGON NATURAL RESOURCES COUNCIL 290
OZARKS RESOURCE CENTER 292
PENNSYLVANIA DEPARTMENT OF ENVIRONMENTAL PROTECTION 101
PIEDMONT ENVIRONMENTAL COUNCIL 296
PRAIRIE CLUB, THE 298
PTARMIGANS, THE 300
RAPTOR EDUCATION FOUNDATION, INC. 303
RARE CENTER FOR TROPICAL CONSERVATION 303
RHODE ISLAND WILD PLANT SOCIETY 305
SAVE THE SOUND, INC. 310
SCENIC HUDSON, INC. 311
SOUTH CAROLINA COASTAL CONSERVATION LEAGUE . 321
SOUTH CAROLINA DEPARTMENT OF HEALTH AND ENVIRONMENTAL CONTROL 105
SOUTH CAROLINA ENVIRONMENTAL LAW PROJECT 321
TEXAS SEA GRANT PROGRAM 109
TREAD LIGHTLY! INC. 330
TREES FOR THE FUTURE, INC. 330
VERMONT DEPARTMENT OF AGRICULTURE, FOOD, AND MARKETS 112
WASHINGTON B.A.S.S. CHAPTER FEDERATION 340
WASHINGTON FOUNDATION FOR THE ENVIRONMENT .. 341
WASHINGTON WILDLIFE FEDERATION 342
WILD ONES - NATURAL LANDSCAPERS, LTD 346
WILDERNESS EDUCATION ASSOCIATION 346
WILDLIFE ACTION, INC. 347
WISCONSIN ASSOCIATION OF LAKES (WAL) 355
WISCONSIN DEPARTMENT OF AGRICULTURE TRADE AND CONSUMER PROTECTION 120
WISCONSIN PARK AND RECREATION ASSOCIATION 356
YMCA EARTH SERVICE CORPS 360

Environmental Protection

ADIRONDACK MOUNTAIN CLUB, INC., THE 131
ADOPT-A-STREAM FOUNDATION, THE 131
ALASKA CONSERVATION ALLIANCE 133
ALASKA CONSERVATION VOICE 134
ALASKA DEPARTMENT OF ENVIRONMENTAL CONSERVATION 39
ALLIANCE FOR THE CHESAPEAKE BAY 135
ANACOSTIA WATERSHED SOCIETY 152
ARIZONA DEPARTMENT OF ENVIRONMENTAL QUALITY . 41
ARLINGTON OUTDOOR EDUCATION ASSOCIATION, INC. 155
ASSOCIATION OF NEW JERSEY ENVIRONMENTAL COMMISSIONS 157
AUDUBON SOCIETY OF PORTLAND 159
BRANDYWINE CONSERVANCY, INC. 162
CALIFORNIA TRAPPERS ASSOCIATION 164
CENTER FOR CHESAPEAKE COMMUNITIES 169
CETACEAN SOCIETY INTERNATIONAL 172
CHESAPEAKE BAY FOUNDATION, INC. 172, 173
CHESAPEAKE BAY FOUNDATION, INC. (Virginia Office) ... 173
CITIZENS ADVISORY COUNCIL TO PENNSYLVANIA DEPARTMENT OF ENVIRONMENTAL PROTECTION 99
COALITION FOR CLEAN AIR 175
CONNECTICUT AUDUBON SOCIETY, INC. 180
CONNECTICUT BOTANICAL SOCIETY 180
CONNECTICUT COUNCIL ON ENVIRONMENTAL QUALITY 50
CONNECTICUT RIVER WATERSHED COUNCIL INC. 181
COOSA RIVER BASIN INITIATIVE 184
DEFENDERS OF WILDLIFE 186
DELAWARE STATE EXTENSION SERVICE 52
DEPARTMENT OF ENVIRONMENTAL QUALITY (ARKANSAS) 43
DEPARTMENT OF LAND AND NATURAL RESOURCES 58
DEPARTMENT OF THE ENVIRONMENT 71
DESERT TORTOISE COUNCIL 188
FAIRFAX AUDUBON SOCIETY 199
FEDERAL WILDLIFE OFFICER'S ASSOCIATION 199
FLORIDA PUBLIC INTEREST RESEARCH GROUP (Florida PIRG) 202
FOREST FIRE LOOKOUT ASSOCIATION 203
FRIENDS OF THE EARTH 206
FRIENDS OF THE REEDY RIVER 206
GEORGE MIKSCH SUTTON AVIAN RESEARCH CENTER INC. 208
GEORGE WRIGHT SOCIETY, THE 208
GEORGIA CONSERVANCY, INC., THE 209
GREAT LAKES UNITED 211
GREEN (GLOBAL RIVERS ENVIRONMENTAL EDUCATION NETWORK) 212
H. JOHN HEINZ III CENTER FOR SCIENCE, ECONOMICS, AND THE ENVIRONMENT 214
ILLINOIS NATIVE PLANT SOCIETY 219
INTERNATIONAL CENTER FOR EARTH CONCERNS 223
IOWA AUDUBON 231
IZAAK WALTON LEAGUE OF AMERICA, INC., THE 234
KENTUCKY RESOURCES COUNCIL 239
KIDS FOR SAVING EARTH WORLDWIDE 239
LAND WATCH MONTEREY COUNTY 241
LEAGUE OF WOMEN VOTERS OF IOWA 241
LEE COUNTY PARKS AND RECREATION SERVICES 54

LEGAL ENVIRONMENTAL ASSISTANCE FOUNDATION INC.
(LEAF) 242
LIGHTHAWK 243
MAINE ASSOCIATION OF CONSERVATION COMMISSIONS
(MACC) 244
MAINE DEPARTMENT OF ENVIRONMENTAL PROTECTION
.... 70
MASSACHUSETTS AUDUBON SOCIETY, INC. 247
MICHIGAN DEPARTMENT OF ENVIRONMENTAL QUALITY 75
MICHIGAN LAND USE INSTITUTE 249
MISSOURI NATIVE PLANT SOCIETY 253
MONTANA LAND RELIANCE 254
NATIONAL ASSOCIATION OF STATE DEPARTMENTS OF
AGRICULTURE 258
NATIONAL NETWORK OF FOREST PRACTITIONERS 263
NATIONAL WILDLIFE REFUGE ASSOCIATION 269
NATIVE PLANT SOCIETY OF OREGON 269
NATURAL LAND INSTITUTE 270
NEW HAMPSHIRE LAKES ASSOCIATION 277
NORTH CASCADES CONSERVATION COUNCIL 283
NORTHCOAST ENVIRONMENTAL CENTER 284
NORTHWEST RESOURCE INFORMATION CENTER 286
OKLAHOMA DEPARTMENT OF ENVIRONMENTAL QUALITY
.... 95
OKLAHOMA NATIVE PLANT SOCIETY 289
OLYMPIC PARK INSTITUTE 289
OREGON NATURAL RESOURCES COUNCIL 290
PINE BLUFF COOPERATIVE FISHERY RESEARCH
PROJECT 44
PREDATOR PROJECT 299
PUBLIC EMPLOYEES FOR ENVIRONMENTAL
RESPONSIBILITY (PEER) 300
RAINFOREST TRUST, INC., THE 302
RAPTOR EDUCATION FOUNDATION, INC. 303
REP AMERICA/REPUBLICANS FOR ENVIRONMENTAL
PROTECTION 304
RESOURCES FOR THE FUTURE 304
SOIL AND WATER CONSERVATION SOCIETY (formerly Soil
Conservation Society of America) 320
SOUTH CAROLINA ENVIRONMENTAL LAW PROJECT 321
SOUTH DAKOTA DEPARTMENT OF ENVIRONMENT AND
NATURAL RESOURCES 106
SOUTH DAKOTA RESOURCES COALITION 322
ST. REGIS MOHAWK TRIBE 325
STATE OF IDAHO DIVISION OF ENVIRONMENTAL QUALITY
.... 61
STUDENTS PARTNERSHIP WORLDWIDE 327
TENNESSEE ENVIRONMENTAL COUNCIL 328
TREES ATLANTA 330
TRUSTEES OF RESERVATIONS, THE 335
TURTLE CREEK WATERSHED ASSOCIATION, INC. 335
U.S. PUBLIC INTEREST RESEARCH GROUP 336
UNITED NATIONS ENVIRONMENT PROGRAMME 336
WASHINGTON FOUNDATION FOR THE ENVIRONMENT .. 341
WHALE AND DOLPHIN CONSERVATION SOCIETY 345
WHITE CLAY WATERSHED ASSOCIATION 345
WILDERNESS LAND TRUST, THE 346
WISCONSIN ASSOCIATION OF LAKES (WAL) 355
WISCONSIN PARK AND RECREATION ASSOCIATION 356
WORLD PAL (WORLD POPULATION ALLOCATION LIMITED
INC.) 358
WORLD WOMEN IN THE DEFENSE OF THE ENVIRONMENT
(WorldWIDE) 359

Erosion Control

MINNESOTA BOARD OF WATER AND SOIL RESOURCES . 75
MISSISSIPPI SOIL AND WATER CONSERVATION
COMMISSION 78

Estuaries

AMERICAN OCEANS CAMPAIGN 147
NORTH CAROLINA COASTAL FEDERATION, INC. 282
NORTH CAROLINA SEA GRANT PROGRAM 92
PEOPLE FOR PUGET SOUND 295

Everglades

EVERGLADES COORDINATING COUNCIL (ECC) 199
NATIONAL AUDUBON SOCIETY 259
NATIONAL WILDLIFE FEDERATION 267, 268
SOUTH FLORIDA WATER MANAGEMENT DISTRICT 55

Factory Farms

OHIO ENVIRONMENTAL COUNCIL, INC. 287

Falconry

SOCIETY FOR THE PRESERVATION OF BIRDS OF PREY 319

Family Planning

AVSC INTERNATIONAL 159
NEW ENGLAND COALITION FOR SUSTAINABLE
POPULATION (NECSP) 276
PLANNED PARENTHOOD FEDERATION OF AMERICA, INC.
.... 297

Family Recreation

AMERICAN ASSOCIATION FOR LEISURE AND RECREATION
(AALR) 136

Federalism

ENVIRONMENTAL LAW INSTITUTE, THE 198

Feedlots and Pollution

MINNESOTA CENTER FOR ENVIRONMENTAL ADVOCACY
(MCEA) 251

Fieldwork

STROUD WATER RESEARCH CENTER 326
THORNE ECOLOGICAL INSTITUTE 329

Fire Prevention

DIVISION OF FORESTRY AND SOIL RESOURCES OF GUAM
.... 57

Fish

AMERICAN BASS ASSOCIATION, INC. 137
AMERICAN SOCIETY OF ICHTHYOLOGISTS AND
HERPETOLOGISTS 149

Fish Wildlife Management

ALBERTA FISH AND GAME ASSOCIATION, THE 134
AMERICAN BASS ASSOCIATION, INC. 137
COASTAL CONSERVATION ASSOCIATION GEORGIA 176
COLORADO COOPERATIVE FISH AND WILDLIFE
RESEARCH UNIT (USDI) 49
COLUMBIA BASIN FISH AND WILDLIFE AUTHORITY 178
CONSERVATION FORCE 182
LOUISIANA DEPARTMENT OF WILDLIFE AND FISHERIES 68
WASHINGTON ENVIRONMENTAL COUNCIL 340
WESTERN ASSOCIATION OF FISH AND WILDLIFE
AGENCIES 344
WESTERN PACIFIC REGIONAL FISHERY MANAGEMENT
COUNCIL 344

Fisheries

A.B. ENVIRONMENTAL EDUCATION CENTER 130
ADOPT-A-STREAM FOUNDATION, THE 131
AGENCY OF NATURAL RESOURCES 111

KEYWORD INDEX - Fisheries

ALABAMA COOPERATIVE EXTENSION SYSTEM 38
ALABAMA COOPERATIVE FISH AND WILDLIFE RESEARCH UNIT (USDI) 38
ALASKA CONSERVATION FOUNDATION 134
ALASKA COOPERATIVE FISH AND WILDLIFE RESEARCH UNIT 39
ALASKA DEPARTMENT OF FISH AND GAME 39
ALASKA SEA GRANT COLLEGE PROGRAM 40
ALLIANCE FOR THE CHESAPEAKE BAY 135
AMERICAN BASS ASSOCIATION OF MARYLAND, THE 137
AMERICAN FISHERIES SOCIETY 140, 141, 142, 143, 144
AMERICAN INSTITUTE OF FISHERY RESEARCH BIOLOGISTS 146
AMERICAN LEAGUE OF ANGLERS AND BOATERS 146
AMERICAN LITTORAL SOCIETY 146
AMERICAN OCEANS CAMPAIGN 147
ANGLERS FOR CLEAN WATER 152
ARKANSAS COOPERATIVE RESEARCH UNIT 42
ARLINGTON OUTDOOR EDUCATION ASSOCIATION, INC. 155
ASSOCIATION OF MIDWEST FISH AND GAME LAW ENFORCEMENT OFFICERS 156
AUDUBON SOCIETY OF RHODE ISLAND 159
BILLFISH FOUNDATION, THE 160
BIODIVERSITY LEGAL FOUNDATION 161
BROTHERHOOD OF THE JUNGLE COCK, INC., THE 163
CALIFORNIA SEA GRANT COLLEGE SYSTEM 45
CALIFORNIA TROUT, INC. 164
CALIFORNIA WILDLIFE FEDERATION 165
CANADIAN FEDERATION OF HUMANE SOCIETIES 166
CENTER FOR MARINE CONSERVATION 170
COASTAL CONSERVATION ASSOCIATION 176
COASTAL CONSERVATION ASSOCIATION GEORGIA 176
COLORADO COOPERATIVE FISH AND WILDLIFE RESEARCH UNIT (USDI) 49
COLUMBIA BASIN FISH AND WILDLIFE AUTHORITY 178
DEPARTMENT OF INTERIOR, U.S.G.S/B.R.D, SOUTH CAROLINA COOPERATIVE FISH AND WILDLIFE RESEARCH UNIT 104
DEPARTMENT OF LAND AND NATURAL RESOURCES 58
DESERT FISHES COUNCIL 188
ENVIRONMENTAL DEFENSE FUND, INC. 196
ENVIRONMENTAL ENTERPRISES ASSISTANCE FUND, INC. 197
ENVIRONMENTAL LEAGUE OF MASSACHUSETTS 198
FEDERATION OF FLY FISHERS 200
FISH AND WILDLIFE INFORMATION EXCHANGE 201
FISH AND WILDLIFE REFERENCE SERVICE 201, 409
FLORIDA FISH AND WILDLIFE CONSERVATION COMMISSION 54
FLORIDA SEA GRANT COLLEGE 54
FLORIDA STATE COOPERATIVE EXTENSION SERVICE 54
FOOD AND AGRICULTURE ORGANIZATION OF THE UNITED NATIONS 203
FRIENDS OF THE SEA OTTER 206
GALIANO CONSERVANCY ASSOCIATION 207
GEORGIA COOPERATIVE FISH AND WILDLIFE RESEARCH UNIT (USDI) 55
GREAT LAKES SPORT FISHING COUNCIL 211
GREAT LAKES UNITED 211
GREENPEACE, INC. 213
GULF OF MEXICO FISHERY MANAGEMENT COUNCIL 214
H. JOHN HEINZ III CENTER FOR SCIENCE, ECONOMICS, AND THE ENVIRONMENT 214
HAWAII COOPERATIVE FISHERY RESEARCH UNIT (USDI)58
HUDSONIA LIMITED 216
HUNTSMAN MARINE SCIENCE CENTRE 217
IDAHO COOPERATIVE FISH AND WILDLIFE RESEARCH UNIT (USDI) 60
IDAHO FISH AND GAME DEPARTMENT 60
IDAHO FISH AND WILDLIFE FOUNDATION 60
INTERNATIONAL ASSOCIATION OF NATURAL RESOURCE PILOTS 223
INTERNATIONAL GAME FISH ASSOCIATION 225
INTERNATIONAL MARINE MAMMAL PROJECT, THE 226
INTERNATIONAL OCEANOGRAPHIC FOUNDATION 226
IOWA COOPERATIVE FISH AND WILDLIFE RESEARCH UNIT 64
IOWA DEPARTMENT OF NATURAL RESOURCES 64
ISLAND INSTITUTE, THE 233
IZAAK WALTON LEAGUE OF AMERICA ENDOWMENT 234
JACKSON HOLE CONSERVATION ALLIANCE 236
KANSAS DEPARTMENT OF WILDLIFE AND PARKS 65
KENTUCKY DEPARTMENT OF FISH AND WILDLIFE RESOURCES 66
LONG LIVE THE KINGS 243
LOWER MISSISSIPPI RIVER CONSERVATION COMMITTEE 244
MAINE ATLANTIC SALMON COMMISSION (formerly Maine Atlantic Salmon Authority) 69
MAINE COOPERATIVE FISH AND WILDLIFE RESEARCH UNIT (USDI) 70
MAINE DEPARTMENT OF INLAND FISHERIES AND WILDLIFE 70
MAINE DEPARTMENT OF MARINE RESOURCES 71
MAINE SEA GRANT PROGRAM 71
MAINE/NEW HAMPSHIRE SEA GRANT PROGRAM 83
MANOMET CENTER FOR CONSERVATION SCIENCES 245
MARINE LABORATORY (FLORIDA) 55
MARYLAND DEPARTMENT OF AGRICULTURE 71
MARYLAND DEPARTMENT OF NATURAL RESOURCES 72
MARYLAND SEA GRANT COLLEGE 72
MASSACHUSETTS COOPERATIVE FISH AND WILDLIFE RESEARCH UNIT (USDI) 74
MAX McGRAW WILDLIFE FOUNDATION 248
MICHIGAN DEPARTMENT OF NATURAL RESOURCES 75
MID-ATLANTIC FISHERY MANAGEMENT COUNCIL 250
MINNESOTA COOPERATIVE FISH AND WILDLIFE RESEARCH UNIT 76
MINNESOTA SEA GRANT COLLEGE PROGRAM 77
MISSISSIPPI COOPERATIVE FISH AND WILDLIFE RESEARCH UNIT (USDI) 77
MISSISSIPPI DEPARTMENT OF WILDLIFE, FISHERIES, AND PARKS 78
MISSISSIPPI INTERSTATE COOPERATIVE RESOURCE ASSOCIATION 252
MISSISSIPPI STATE EXTENSION SERVICES 79
MISSOURI COOPERATIVE FISH AND WILDLIFE RESEARCH UNIT (USDI) 79
MONTANA COOPERATIVE FISHERY RESEARCH UNIT (USDI) 80
MONTANA LAND RELIANCE 254
MOTE MARINE LABORATORY 255
NATIONAL ASSOCIATION OF UNIVERSITY FISHERIES AND WILDLIFE PROGRAMS 259
NATIONAL COALITION FOR MARINE CONSERVATION 260
NATIONAL FISH AND WILDLIFE FOUNDATION 261
NATIONAL MILITARY FISH AND WILDLIFE ASSOCIATION263
NATIVE AMERICAN FISH AND WILDLIFE SOCIETY (NAFWS) 269
NATURAL RESOURCES COUNCIL OF AMERICA 271
NEW HAMPSHIRE FISH AND GAME DEPARTMENT 84
NEW YORK STATE COOPERATIVE EXTENSION 90
NORTH AMERICAN FISHING CLUB 281
NORTH AMERICAN NATIVE FISHES ASSOCIATION 281
NORTH ATLANTIC SALMON CONSERVATION ORGANIZATION 282
NORTH CAROLINA BEACH BUGGY ASSOCIATION, INC. . 282
NORTH CAROLINA COOPERATIVE EXTENSION SERVICE 91
NORTH CAROLINA SEA GRANT PROGRAM 92
NORTH CAROLINA WILDLIFE RESOURCES COMMISSION 92
NORTH CASCADES CONSERVATION COUNCIL 283
NORTH DAKOTA NATURAL SCIENCE SOCIETY 284
NORTHWEST ATLANTIC FISHERIES ORGANIZATION (NAFO) 285
NW ENERGY COALITION 286
OHIO SEA GRANT COLLEGE PROGRAM 95
OKLAHOMA COOPERATIVE FISH AND WILDLIFE RESEARCH UNIT (USDI) 95
OLYMPIC PARK INSTITUTE 289
OREGON COOPERATIVE FISH AND WILDLIFE RESEARCH UNIT (USDI) 97
OREGON DEPARTMENT OF FORESTRY 98
OREGON FISH AND WILDLIFE DIVISION/DEPARTMENT OF STATE POLICE 98
OREGON SEA GRANT PROGRAM 98
PACIFIC FISHERY MANAGEMENT COUNCIL 292
PACIFIC RIVERS COUNCIL 293
PENNSYLVANIA FISH AND BOAT COMMISSION 101

KEYWORD INDEX - Flood Control

PINE BLUFF COOPERATIVE FISHERY RESEARCH PROJECT 44
PUERTO RICO DEPARTMENT OF NATURAL AND ENVIRONMENTAL RESOURCES 103
PUERTO RICO SEA GRANT PROGRAM 103
RESOURCES AGENCY, THE 46
RIVER ALLIANCE OF WISCONSIN 305
SCIENTISTS CENTER FOR ANIMAL WELFARE 311
SEA SHEPHERD CONSERVATION SOCIETY 311
SOUTH ATLANTIC FISHERY MANAGEMENT COUNCIL 321
SOUTH CAROLINA DEPARTMENT OF NATURAL RESOURCES 105
SOUTH CAROLINA SEA GRANT CONSORTIUM 106
SOUTH CAROLINA WILDLIFE FEDERATION 321
SOUTH DAKOTA COOPERATIVE FISH AND WILDLIFE RESEARCH UNIT (USDI) 106
SOUTH DAKOTA GAME, FISH, AND PARKS DEPARTMENT 106
SOUTH DAKOTA WILDLIFE FEDERATION 323
SOUTHEAST ALASKA CONSERVATION COUNCIL (SEACC) 323
SOUTHEASTERN ASSOCIATION OF FISH AND WILDLIFE AGENCIES 323
SOUTHEASTERN FISHES COUNCIL 323
STRIPERS UNLIMITED, INC. 326
TENNESSEE B.A.S.S. CHAPTER FEDERATION 328
TENNESSEE COOPERATIVE FISHERY RESEARCH UNIT (USDI) 107
TEXAS COOPERATIVE FISH AND WILDLIFE RESEARCH UNIT 108
TROUT UNLIMITED, OKLAHOMA COUNCIL 333
UNIVERSITY OF MASSACHUSETTS EXTENSION 74
UPPER MISSISSIPPI RIVER CONSERVATION COMMITTEE 337
UTAH COOPERATIVE FISH AND WILDLIFE RESEARCH UNIT (USDI-USGS-BRD-CRU) 110
VIRGINIA COOPERATIVE FISH AND WILDLIFE RESEARCH UNIT (USDI) 113
WASHINGTON COOPERATIVE FISH AND WILDLIFE RESEARCH UNIT (USDI) 117
WASHINGTON SEA GRANT PROGRAM 118
WEST VIRGINIA COOPERATIVE FISH AND WILDLIFE RESEARCH UNIT 119
WESTERN PACIFIC REGIONAL FISHERY MANAGEMENT COUNCIL 344
WHALE AND DOLPHIN CONSERVATION SOCIETY 345
WILDLIFE FOREVER 348
WILDLIFE FOUNDATION OF FLORIDA, INC. 349
WILDLIFE HABITAT CANADA 349
WISCONSIN CONSERVATION CORPS 120
WISCONSIN COOPERATIVE FISHERY RESEARCH UNIT (USDI) 120
WISCONSIN SEA GRANT INSTITUTE 121
WISCONSIN WILDLIFE FEDERATION 356
WOODS HOLE OCEANOGRAPHIC INSITITUTION (WHOI) SEA GRANT PROGRAM 74
WYOMING COOPERATIVE FISH AND WILDLIFE RESEARCH UNIT (USDI) 122
WYOMING GAME AND FISH DEPARTMENT 123

Flood Control

COOSA RIVER BASIN INITIATIVE 184
INTERNATIONAL RIVERS NETWORK (IRN) 226
RESOURCES AGENCY, THE 46
SOUTH FLORIDA WATER MANAGEMENT DISTRICT 55

Flowers, Plants, and Trees

ABUNDANT LIFE SEED FOUNDATION 130
ADKINS ARBORETUM 131
AMERICA THE BEAUTIFUL FUND 135
AMERICAN ASSOCIATION OF BOTANICAL GARDENS AND ARBORETA, INC. 136
AMERICAN ASSOCIATION OF FIELD BOTANISTS 136
AMERICAN CHESTNUT FOUNDATION, THE 139
AUDUBON SOCIETY OF RHODE ISLAND 159
AUDUBON SOCIETY OF WESTERN PENNSYLVANIA 159
BIG BEND NATURAL HISTORY ASSOCIATION 160
BIOMASS USERS NETWORK 161
BOTANICAL CLUB OF WISCONSIN 162
BOTANICAL SOCIETY OF WESTERN PENNSYLVANIA 162
BROOKS BIRD CLUB INC., THE 163
CENTER FOR PLANT CONSERVATION 170
COLLEGE OF TROPICAL AGRICULTURE AND HUMAN RESOURCES 57
CONNECTICUT BOTANICAL SOCIETY 180
DAWES ARBORETUM, THE 186
DELAWARE STATE EXTENSION SERVICE 52
EARTHWATCH INSTITUTE 193
ELM RESEARCH INSTITUTE 194
ENVIRONMENTAL EDUCATION ASSOCIATION OF ILLINOIS 197
FLORIDA NATIVE PLANT SOCIETY 202
GARDEN CLUB OF AMERICA, THE 208
GREAT PLAINS NATIVE PLANT SOCIETY 212
HOLDEN ARBORETUM, THE 216
HUDSONIA LIMITED 216
ILLINOIS NATIVE PLANT SOCIETY 219
INDIANA AUDUBON SOCIETY, INC. 220
INDIANA NATIVE PLANT AND WILDFLOWER SOCIETY 220
INTERNATIONAL PLANT PROPAGATION SOCIETY, INC., THE 226
IOWA NATIVE PLANT SOCIETY 232
IOWA NATURAL HERITAGE FOUNDATION 232
KANSAS WILDFLOWER SOCIETY 238
KIDS FOR SAVING EARTH WORLDWIDE 239
LADY BIRD JOHNSON WILDFLOWER CENTER 240
MICHIGAN DEPARTMENT OF AGRICULTURE 74
MICHIGAN NATURAL AREAS COUNCIL 249
MICHIGAN NATURE ASSOCIATION 249
MISSISSIPPI NATIVE PLANT SOCIETY 252
MISSOURI NATIVE PLANT SOCIETY 253
NATIONAL ARBOR DAY FOUNDATION 256
NATIONAL AVIARY 259
NATIONAL BIRD-FEEDING SOCIETY 259
NATIONAL GARDENING ASSOCIATION 262
NATIVE PLANT SOCIETY OF NORTHEASTERN OHIO 269
NATURAL HISTORY SOCIETY OF MARYLAND, INC., THE 270
NATURE SASKATCHEWAN 275
NEW HAMPSHIRE NATURAL HERITAGE INVENTORY 84
NEW YORK DEPARTMENT OF AGRICULTURE AND MARKETS 88
NORTH DAKOTA STATE FOREST SERVICE 93
NORTHERN VIRGINIA REGIONAL PARK AUTHORITY 113
OHIO BIOLOGICAL SURVEY 287
OHIO NATIVE PLANT SOCIETY 288
OKLAHOMA BIOLOGICAL SURVEY 95
OKLAHOMA NATIVE PLANT SOCIETY 289
PENNSYLVANIA DEPARTMENT OF AGRICULTURE 99
PENNSYLVANIA RECREATION AND PARK SOCIETY, INC. 295
RHODE ISLAND STATE ASSOCIATION OF CONSERVATION DISTRICTS 305
RHODE ISLAND WILD PLANT SOCIETY 305
SOUTH CAROLINA NATIVE PLANT SOCIETY 321
STATE FORESTRY DIVISION (WYOMING) 122
TALL TIMBERS RESEARCH STATION 327
TEXAS FOREST SERVICE 108
TREES FOR THE FUTURE, INC. 330
VIRGINIA FORESTRY ASSOCIATION 340
VIRGINIA NATIVE PLANT SOCIETY 340
WATERLOO-WELLINGTON WILDFLOWER SOCIETY (Formerly the Dogtooth Group) 342
WILD ONES - NATURAL LANDSCAPERS, LTD 346
WILDLIFE FOREVER 348
WYOMING NATIVE PLANT SOCIETY 360

Food Safety

GEORGIA DEPARTMENT OF AGRICULTURE 55
NATIONAL ENVIRONMENTAL HEALTH ASSOCIATION 260

Forest Management

ADIRONDACK MOUNTAIN CLUB, INC., THE 131
ALABAMA FORESTRY COMMISSION 39
ALASKA AUDUBON SOCIETY 133

CENTER FOR BIOLOGICAL DIVERSITY 169
DELAWARE STATE EXTENSION SERVICE 52
DIVISION OF FORESTRY AND SOIL RESOURCES OF GUAM
 57
FLORIDA AUDUBON SOCIETY 201
FOREST FIRE LOOKOUT ASSOCIATION 203
FOREST SOCIETY OF MAINE 204
FOREST WATCH 204
FRIENDS OF THE SAN JUANS 206
GALIANO CONSERVANCY ASSOCIATION 207
GEORGIA CONSERVANCY, INC., THE 209
HARDWOOD FOREST FOUNDATION 214
ILLINOIS WALNUT COUNCIL 219
INTERNATIONAL ASSOCIATION OF NATURAL RESOURCE
 PILOTS 223
INTERNATIONAL SOCIETY OF TROPICAL FORESTERS, INC.
 228
JACKSON HOLE CONSERVATION ALLIANCE 236
KANSAS FOREST SERVICE 65
LIGHTHAWK 243
LOUISIANA DEPARTMENT OF AGRICULTURE AND
 FORESTRY 68
MANOMET CENTER FOR CONSERVATION SCIENCES 245
MISSOURI FOREST PRODUCTS ASSOCIATION 253
MISSOURI NATIVE PLANT SOCIETY 253
MONTANA LAND RELIANCE 254
MOUNT GRACE LAND CONSERVATION TRUST 255
NATIONAL FORESTRY ASSOCIATION 262
NEW YORK STATE COOPERATIVE EXTENSION 90
NEWFOUNDLAND LABRADOR WILDLIFE FEDERATION ... 279
NORTH CASCADES CONSERVATION COUNCIL 283
NORTHERN ALASKA ENVIRONMENTAL CENTER 285
NORTHWEST ECOSYSTEM ALLIANCE 285
NOVA SCOTIA FORESTRY ASSOCIATION 286
ONTARIO FORESTRY ASSOCIATION 289
PENNSYLVANIA DEPARTMENT OF CONSERVATION AND
 NATURAL RESOURCES 100
RESOURCES FOR THE FUTURE 304
SINAPU
SOUTHEAST ALASKA CONSERVATION COUNCIL (SEACC)
 323
SOUTHEASTERN ASSOCIATION OF FISH AND WILDLIFE
 AGENCIES 323
SOUTHERN NEW ENGLAND FOREST CONSORTIUM, INC.
 (SNEFCI) 324
TENNESSEE CITIZENS FOR WILDERNESS PLANNING 328
TENNESSEE ENVIRONMENTAL COUNCIL 328
TEXAS FOREST SERVICE 108
VIRGINIA NATIVE PLANT SOCIETY 340
WESTERN FORESTRY AND CONSERVATION ASSOCIATION
 344
WILDLIFE HABITAT CANADA 349

Forest Stewardship

DIVISION OF FORESTRY AND SOIL RESOURCES OF GUAM
 57
FOREST SOCIETY OF MAINE 204
FOREST WATCH 204
MISSOURI FOREST PRODUCTS ASSOCIATION 253
NATIONAL NETWORK OF FOREST PRACTITIONERS 263
REP AMERICA/REPUBLICANS FOR ENVIRONMENTAL
 PROTECTION 304
SHELBURNE FARMS 312

Forestry

CARIBBEAN NATURAL RESOURCES INSTITUTE 168
MONTANA DEPARTMENT OF NATURAL RESOURCES AND
 CONSERVATION 81
ONTARIO FORESTRY ASSOCIATION 289
SOUTHERN AFRICAN INSTITUTE OF FORESTRY 323
TENNESSEE FORESTRY ASSOCIATION 328
WEST VIRGINIA HIGHLANDS CONSERVANCY 343

Forests and Forestry

ADIRONDACK NATURE CONSERVANCY/ADIRONDACK
 LAND TRUST, INC. 131
ALABAMA COOPERATIVE EXTENSION SYSTEM 38
ALABAMA ENVIRONMENTAL COUNCIL 132
ALABAMA FORESTRY COMMISSION 39
ALASKA CONSERVATION FOUNDATION 134
ALASKA DEPARTMENT OF NATURAL RESOURCES 40
AMERICAN FOREST FOUNDATION 144
AMERICAN FORESTS (formerly American Forestry
 Association) 144
AMERICAN HIKING SOCIETY 145
AMERICAN LAND CONSERVANCY 146
AMERICAN LANDS (formerly Western Ancient Forest
 Campaign) 146
AMERICAN RESOURCES GROUP 148
AMERICAN WILDLANDS 151
ANCIENT FOREST INTERNATIONAL 152
ARKANSAS STATE EXTENSION SERVICES 43
ASSOCIATION OF CONSULTING FORESTERS OF AMERICA
 156
BIOMASS USERS NETWORK 161
CALIFORNIA TROUT, INC. 164
CALIFORNIA, FOREST LANDOWNERS OF 165
CAMP FIRE CLUB OF AMERICA, THE 165
CANADIAN FORESTRY ASSOCIATION 166
CANADIAN INSTITUTE OF FORESTRY/INSTITUT
 FORESTIER DU CANADA 167
CATSKILL FOREST ASSOCIATION 168
CENTER FOR RESOURCEFUL BUILDING TECHNOLOGY 171
COLORADO FORESTRY ASSOCIATION 177
COLORADO STATE FOREST SERVICE 49
CONSERVATION INTERNATIONAL 183
DEEP-PORTAGE CONSERVATION RESERVE 186
DELAWARE DEPARTMENT OF AGRICULTURE 51
DELAWARE FORESTRY ASSOCIATION 187
EARTHJUSTICE LEGAL DEFENSE FUND (formerly Sierra
 Club Legal Defense Fund, Inc.) 192
FEDERATION OF WESTERN OUTDOOR CLUBS 200
FLORIDA FORESTRY ASSOCIATION 202
FLORIDA STATE COOPERATIVE EXTENSION SERVICE 54
FOOD AND AGRICULTURE ORGANIZATION OF THE UNITED
 NATIONS 203
FOREST FIRE LOOKOUT ASSOCIATION 203
FOREST HISTORY SOCIETY, INC. 203
FOREST LANDOWNERS ASSOCIATION, INC. 203
FOREST SERVICE EMPLOYEES FOR ENVIRONMENTAL
 ETHICS (FSEEE) 204
FOREST SOCIETY OF MAINE 204
FOREST TRUST 204
FOREST WATCH 204
FORESTRY COMMISSION (ARKANSAS) 43
FORESTRY COMMISSION (SOUTH CAROLINA) 105
FRIENDS OF THE BOUNDARY WATERS WILDERNESS ... 206
GEORGIA FEDERATION OF FOREST OWNERS 209
GEORGIA FORESTRY ASSOCIATION, INC. 209
GOVERNOR OF SOUTH CAROLINA 104
GREATER YELLOWSTONE COALITION 212
HAWAII SOCIETY OF AMERICAN FORESTERS 214
IDAHO FOREST OWNERS ASSOCIATION 218
INDIANA DEPARTMENT OF NATURAL RESOURCES 62
INDIANA FORESTRY AND WOODLAND OWNERS
 ASSOCIATION 220
INTERNATIONAL ASSOCIATION OF WILDLAND FIRE
 (formerly Fire Research Institute) 223
INTERNATIONAL PRIMATE PROTECTION LEAGUE 226
IOWA WOODLAND OWNERS ASSOCIATION 233
KANSAS FOREST SERVICE 65
KENTUCKY WOODLAND OWNERS ASSOCIATION 239
LEAGUE OF WOMEN VOTERS OF WASHINGTON 242
LOUISIANA FORESTRY ASSOCIATION 243
MAINE AUDUBON SOCIETY 244
MAINE, SMALL WOODLAND OWNERS ASSOCIATION OF,
 245
MARYLAND DEPARTMENT OF NATURAL RESOURCES 72
MARYLAND FORESTS ASSOCIATION 247
MASSACHUSETTS FORESTRY ASSOCIATION 248
MERCK FOREST AND FARMLAND CENTER, INC. 248
MICHIGAN DEPARTMENT OF NATURAL RESOURCES 75

KEYWORD INDEX - Funding

MICHIGAN FORESTS ASSOCIATION 249
MICHIGAN STATE UNIVERSITY EXTENSION 75
MINNESOTA FORESTRY ASSOCIATION 251
MISSISSIPPI FORESTRY COMMISSION 78
MISSISSIPPI STATE EXTENSION SERVICES 79
MISSOURI FOREST PRODUCTS ASSOCIATION 253
MONTANA COOPERATIVE WILDLIFE RESEARCH UNIT
 (USGS/BRD) 80
MONTANA FOREST OWNERS ASSOCIATION 254
MONTANA WILDERNESS ASSOCIATION 255
NATIONAL ARBOR DAY FOUNDATION 256
NATIONAL ASSOCIATION OF STATE FORESTERS 258
NATIONAL FOREST FOUNDATION 261
NATIONAL FORESTRY ASSOCIATION 262
NATIONAL NETWORK OF FOREST PRACTITIONERS 263
NATIONAL TREE TRUST 265
NATIONAL WILD TURKEY FEDERATION, INC., THE 267
NATIONAL WOODLAND OWNERS ASSOCIATION 269
NATIVE AMERICAN FISH AND WILDLIFE SOCIETY (NAFWS)
 269
NATURAL RESOURCES COUNCIL OF AMERICA 271
NEW HAMPSHIRE TIMBERLAND OWNERS ASSOCIATION
 277
NEW JERSEY FORESTRY ASSOCIATION 278
NEW YORK FOREST OWNERS ASSOCIATION, INC. 279
NORTH CAROLINA FORESTRY ASSOCIATION 282
NORTH DAKOTA STATE FOREST SERVICE 93
NORTHCOAST ENVIRONMENTAL CENTER 284
OHIO DEPARTMENT OF NATURAL RESOURCES 94
OHIO FORESTRY ASSOCIATION, INC., THE 288
OKLAHOMA STATE BOARD OF AGRICULTURE 96
OKLAHOMA STATE EXTENSION SERVICES 96
OKLAHOMA WOODLAND OWNERS ASSOCIATION 289
ONTARIO FORESTRY ASSOCIATION 289
OREGON DEPARTMENT OF FORESTRY 98
OREGON SMALL WOODLANDS ASSOCIATION 290
PENNSYLVANIA FOREST STEWARDSHIP PROGRAM 102
PENNSYLVANIA FORESTRY ASSOCIATION, THE 295
PINCHOT INSTITUTE FOR CONSERVATION 296
PUBLIC EMPLOYEES FOR ENVIRONMENTAL
 RESPONSIBILITY (PEER) 300
PUERTO RICO DEPARTMENT OF NATURAL AND
 ENVIRONMENTAL RESOURCES 103
RAINFOREST ACTION NETWORK 302
RAINFOREST ALLIANCE 302
RAINFOREST RELIEF 302
RHODE ISLAND B.A.S.S. CHAPTER FEDERATION 305
RUFFED GROUSE SOCIETY, THE 307
SAVE AMERICA'S FORESTS 309
SAVE-THE-REDWOODS LEAGUE 310
SIERRA NEVADA FOREST PROTECTION CAMPAIGN 317
SOCIETY FOR THE PROTECTION OF NEW HAMPSHIRE
 FORESTS 319
SOCIETY OF AMERICAN FORESTERS 291, 319, 341
SOUTH CAROLINA B.A.S.S. CHAPTER FEDERATION 321
SOUTHERN ENVIRONMENTAL LAW CENTER 324
STATE FORESTRY DIVISION (WYOMING) 122
TENNESSEE WOODLAND OWNERS ASSOCIATION 328
TEXAS AGRICULTURAL EXTENSION SERVICE 108
TEXAS B.A.S.S. CHAPTER FEDERATION 329
TEXAS FOREST SERVICE 108
TEXAS FORESTRY ASSOCIATION 329
TREEPEOPLE 330
TUG HILL TOMORROW LAND TRUST 335
UNITED STATES TOURIST COUNCIL 336
UNIVERSITY OF MASSACHUSETTS EXTENSION 74
UNIVERSITY OF NEW HAMPSHIRE COOPERATIVE
 EXTENSION 84
UTAH STATE EXTENSION SERVICES 111
UTAH WOODLAND OWNERS COUNCIL 338
VERMONT AUDUBON COUNCIL 338
VERMONT INSTITUTE OF NATURAL SCIENCE 338
VERMONT WOODLANDS ASSOCIATION 339
WASHINGTON ENVIRONMENTAL COUNCIL 340
WASHINGTON FARM FORESTRY ASSOCIATION 341
WASHINGTON STATE EXTENSION SERVICES 118
WEST VIRGINIA B.A.S.S. CHAPTER FEDERATION 343
WEST VIRGINIA STATE EXTENSION SERVICE 120
WEST VIRGINIA, WOODLAND OWNERS ASSOCIATION OF
 344
WESTERN ENVIRONMENTAL LAW CENTER 344
WILDERNESS SOCIETY, THE 346
WISCONSIN CONSERVATION CORPS 120
WISCONSIN DEPARTMENT OF NATURAL RESOURCES . 120
WISCONSIN WOODLAND OWNERS ASSOCIATION 356
WORLD CONSERVATION MONITORING CENTRE 358
WORLD FORESTRY CENTER 358
WORLD RESOURCES INSTITUTE 358

Funding

ENVIRONMENTAL FUND FOR GEORGIA 197

Gap Analysis

IOWA COOPERATIVE FISH AND WILDLIFE RESEARCH UNIT
 64

Gardening and Horticulture

ABUNDANT LIFE SEED FOUNDATION 130
ALABAMA COOPERATIVE EXTENSION SYSTEM 38
AMERICA THE BEAUTIFUL FUND 135
AMERICAN ASSOCIATION OF BOTANICAL GARDENS AND
 ARBORETA, INC. 136
ARKANSAS STATE EXTENSION SERVICES 43
BIG BEND NATURAL HISTORY ASSOCIATION 160
BIO-INTEGRAL RESOURCE CENTER 161
BOTANICAL SOCIETY OF WESTERN PENNSYLVANIA 162
COLLEGE OF TROPICAL AGRICULTURE AND HUMAN
 RESOURCES 57
COLORADO STATE UNIVERSITY COOPERATIVE
 EXTENSION 50
COMMUNITY ENVIRONMENTAL COUNCIL 179
DELAWARE STATE EXTENSION SERVICE 52
ECOLOGY CENTER 194
ENVIRONMENTAL CONCERN INC. 196
GARDEN CLUB OF AMERICA, THE 208
GREAT PLAINS NATIVE PLANT SOCIETY 212
HOLDEN ARBORETUM, THE 216
MISSOURI NATIVE PLANT SOCIETY 253
NATIONAL COUNCIL OF STATE GARDEN CLUBS, INC. .. 260
NATIONAL FFA ORGANIZATION 261
NATIONAL GARDENING ASSOCIATION 262
NEW ENGLAND WILD FLOWER SOCIETY, INC 276
NEW JERSEY STATE EXTENSION SERVICES 86
NORTH AMERICAN BUTTERFLY ASSOCIATION 280
SMITHSONIAN INSTITUTION 317
SOUTH CAROLINA DEPARTMENT OF AGRICULTURE 105
TRUSTEES OF RESERVATIONS, THE 335
VIRGINIA FORESTRY ASSOCIATION 340
WATERLOO-WELLINGTON WILDFLOWER SOCIETY
 (Formerly the Dogtooth Group) 342
WESTERN PENNSYLVANIA CONSERVANCY 344
WILD ONES - NATURAL LANDSCAPERS, LTD 346
WYOMING NATIVE PLANT SOCIETY 360

Genetics

OREGON COOPERATIVE FISH AND WILDLIFE RESEARCH
 UNIT (USDI) 97

Geographic Information Systems

MAINE COOPERATIVE FISH AND WILDLIFE RESEARCH
 UNIT (USDI) 70
OKLAHOMA BIOLOGICAL SURVEY 95

Geography

ASSOCIATION OF AMERICAN GEOGRAPHERS 155
KANSAS ACADEMY OF SCIENCE 237
LIGHTHAWK 243
MINNESOTA ORNITHOLOGISTS' UNION 251
NATIONAL GEOGRAPHIC SOCIETY 262
NEVADA BUREAU OF MINES AND GEOLOGY 82
POPULATION REFERENCE BUREAU, INC. 298

Geology

AGENCY OF NATURAL RESOURCES 111
AMERICAN CAVE CONSERVATION ASSOCIATION 138
AMERICAN GEOLOGICAL INSTITUTE 145
AMERICAN GROUND WATER TRUST 145
AMERICAN MUSEUM OF NATURAL HISTORY 147
ARIZONA GEOLOGICAL SURVEY 41
BUREAU OF ECONOMIC GEOLOGY 108
CAVE RESEARCH FOUNDATION 168
CHIHUAHUAN DESERT RESEARCH INSTITUTE 173
DELAWARE GEOLOGICAL SURVEY 52
EARTHWATCH INSTITUTE 193
GLACIER INSTITUTE, THE 210
INDIANA GEOLOGICAL SURVEY 63
IOWA DEPARTMENT OF NATURAL RESOURCES 64
KANSAS ACADEMY OF SCIENCE 237
KANSAS GEOLOGICAL SURVEY 66
LOUISIANA GEOLOGICAL SURVEY 69
MICHIGAN DEPARTMENT OF ENVIRONMENTAL QUALITY 75
MINNESOTA GEOLOGICAL SURVEY 76
MISSOURI DEPARTMENT OF NATURAL RESOURCES 79
MONTANA BUREAU OF MINES AND GEOLOGY 80
NATIONAL GROUND WATER ASSOCIATION, THE 262
NATIONAL SPELEOLOGICAL SOCIETY, INC. 265
NEVADA BUREAU OF MINES AND GEOLOGY 82
NEW JERSEY DEPARTMENT OF ENVIRONMENTAL
    PROTECTION 85
NEW MEXICO BUREAU OF MINES AND MINERAL
    RESOURCES 86
NEW YORK GEOLOGICAL SURVEY AND STATE MUSEUM 90
NORTH DAKOTA GEOLOGICAL SURVEY 93
OKLAHOMA GEOLOGICAL SURVEY 96
PENNSYLVANIA DEPARTMENT OF CONSERVATION AND
    NATURAL RESOURCES 100
PUERTO RICO SEA GRANT PROGRAM 103
STATE OFFICE OF CONSERVATION (LOUISIANA) 69
VIRGINIA MUSEUM OF NATURAL HISTORY 115
WISCONSIN GEOLOGICAL AND NATURAL HISTORY
    SURVEY 121
WYOMING STATE GEOLOGICAL SURVEY 123

Government Accountability

PUBLIC EMPLOYEES FOR ENVIRONMENTAL
    RESPONSIBILITY (PEER) 300

Grants

AMERICA THE BEAUTIFUL FUND 135
AMERICAN INSTITUTE OF BIOLOGICAL SCIENCES 146
AMERICAN WILDLIFE RESEARCH FOUNDATION, INC. 151
EARTHWATCH INSTITUTE 193
INITIATIVE FOR SOCIAL ACTION AND RENEWAL IN
    EURASIA 221
INSTITUTE FOR CIVIC INITIATIVES SUPPORT 221
RAINFOREST ALLIANCE 302
RESOURCES AGENCY, THE 46
SOUTH DAKOTA DEPARTMENT OF ENVIRONMENT AND
    NATURAL RESOURCES 106
WASHINGTON FOUNDATION FOR THE ENVIRONMENT .. 341
WILD ONES - NATURAL LANDSCAPERS, LTD 346
WILDFLOWER ASSOCIATION OF MICHIGAN 347
WILDLIFE PRESERVATION TRUST INTERNATIONAL, INC.
    350
WILSON ORNITHOLOGICAL SOCIETY 355

Grasslands

AUDUBON OF KANSAS (formerly Kansas Audubon Council)
    158
GREAT PLAINS NATIVE PLANT SOCIETY 212
MONTANA COOPERATIVE WILDLIFE RESEARCH UNIT
    (USGS/BRD) 80
SOUTH DAKOTA COOPERATIVE FISH AND WILDLIFE
    RESEARCH UNIT (USDI) 106

Great Plains

GREAT PLAINS NATIVE PLANT SOCIETY 212
NORTH DAKOTA NATURAL SCIENCE SOCIETY 284

Green Building

EARTH DAY NEW YORK 191
OHIO OFFICE OF ENERGY EFFICIENCY 94

Green Certification

NATIONAL FORESTRY ASSOCIATION 262

Greenhouse Effect/Global Warming

AIR AND WASTE MANAGEMENT ASSOCIATION 132
AMERICAN ASSOCIATION FOR THE ADVANCEMENT OF
    SCIENCE 136
AMERICAN FORESTS (formerly American Forestry
    Association) 144
AMERICAN GEOGRAPHICAL SOCIETY 145
CENTER FOR ENVIRONMENTAL INFORMATION 169
CENTER FOR INTERNATIONAL ENVIRONMENTAL LAW
    (CIEL) 170
ENVIRONMENTAL AND ENERGY STUDY INSTITUTE (EESI)
    195
GREENPEACE, INC. 213
INTERNATIONAL INSTITUTE FOR ENERGY
    CONSERVATION 225
INTERNATIONAL MARITIME ORGANIZATION 226
INTERNATIONAL SOCIETY FOR THE PRESERVATION OF
    THE TROPICAL RAINFOREST, THE 227
NORTH ATLANTIC SALMON CONSERVATION
    ORGANIZATION 282
OZONE ACTION 292
PACIFIC INSTITUTE FOR STUDIES IN DEVELOPMENT,
    ENVIRONMENT, AND SECURITY 293
TREES ATLANTA 330
TREES FOR THE FUTURE, INC. 330
UNION OF CONCERNED SCIENTISTS 336
UNITED STATES COMMITTEE FOR THE UNITED NATIONS
    ENVIRONMENT PROGRAMME THE (U.S. and UNEP) ... 336
WORLD RESOURCES INSTITUTE 358

Greenways

FRIENDS OF THE REEDY RIVER 206
MISSISSIPPI RIVER BASIN ALLIANCE 252
PENNSYLVANIA ENVIRONMENTAL COUNCIL, INC. (PEC) 294
SOUTH CAROLINA COASTAL CONSERVATION LEAGUE 321

Ground Water Protection

AMERICAN GROUND WATER TRUST 145
GROUNDWATER FOUNDATION, THE 213
MINNESOTA GROUND WATER ASSOCIATION 251
MONTANA DEPARTMENT OF AGRICULTURE 80
PACIFIC INSTITUTE FOR STUDIES IN DEVELOPMENT,
    ENVIRONMENT, AND SECURITY 293

Gun Violence Prevention

PHYSICIANS FOR SOCIAL RESPONSIBILITY 296

Habitat Conservation

CALIFORNIA WATERFOWL ASSOCIATION 164
CENTRO de INFORMACION, INVESTIGACION y EDUCACION
    SOCIAL (CIIES) 172
COASTAL GEORGIA LAND TRUST, THE 176
CONSERVATION TREATY SUPPORT FUND 183
COOSA RIVER BASIN INITIATIVE 184
DESERT RESEARCH FOUNDATION OF NAMIBIA, THE 188
FRIENDS OF THE REEDY RIVER 206
LAKE MICHIGAN FEDERATION 240

KEYWORD INDEX - Harmful Algal Blooms

NEW ENGLAND COALITION FOR SUSTAINABLE POPULATION (NECSP) 276
NORTH CAROLINA WILD FLOWER PRESERVATION SOCIETY 283
OREGON TROUT, INC. 291
ORGANIZATION FOR BAT CONSERVATION 291
SANIBEL-CAPTIVA CONSERVATION FOUNDATION, INC. 308
SAVE OUR RIVERS, INC. 309
SIERRA NEVADA FOREST PROTECTION CAMPAIGN 317
SOUTH CAROLINA COASTAL CONSERVATION LEAGUE. 321
VIRGINIA NATIVE PLANT SOCIETY 340
WILDFLOWER ASSOCIATION OF MICHIGAN 347

Harmful Algal Blooms

NORTH CAROLINA SEA GRANT PROGRAM 92

Hazardous Materials & Waste

CHLORINE-FREE PAPER CONSORTIUM (CPC) 173
MASSACHUSETTS HIGHWAY DEPARTMENT 74

Health and Nutrition

AMERICA THE BEAUTIFUL FUND 135
AMERICAN CAMPING ASSOCIATION, INC. 138
ASSOCIATION OF STATE AND TERRITORIAL HEALTH OFFICIALS 157
AVSC INTERNATIONAL 159
CAMP FIRE BOYS AND GIRLS 165
CENTER FOR SCIENCE IN THE PUBLIC INTEREST 171
CHLORINE-FREE PAPER CONSORTIUM (CPC) 173
COLLEGE OF TROPICAL AGRICULTURE AND HUMAN RESOURCES 57
COLORADO STATE UNIVERSITY COOPERATIVE EXTENSION 50
DELAWARE STATE EXTENSION SERVICE 52
DESERT TORTOISE COUNCIL 188
FOOD AND AGRICULTURE ORGANIZATION OF THE UNITED NATIONS 203
HUMAN ECOLOGY ACTION LEAGUE, INC. THE (HEAL) 217
INDIANA STATE DEPARTMENT OF HEALTH 63
KANSAS STATE DEPARTMENT OF HEALTH AND ENVIRONMENT 66
KEYSTONE CENTER, THE 239
MAGIC 244
NATIONAL ASSOCIATION OF STATE DEPARTMENTS OF AGRICULTURE 258
NATIONAL FARMERS UNION 261
NORTH CAROLINA DEPARTMENT OF AGRICULTURE 92
PLANNED PARENTHOOD FEDERATION OF AMERICA, INC. 297
POPULATION ACTION INTERNATIONAL 297
PUERTO RICO STATE EXTENSION SERVICES 103
SCIENTISTS CENTER FOR ANIMAL WELFARE 311
SOUTHEASTERN COOPERATIVE WILDLIFE DISEASE STUDY 323
TEXAS DEPARTMENT OF HEALTH 108
UNIVERSITY OF VERMONT EXTENSION 112
UTAH DEPARTMENT OF HEALTH 110
VERMONT DEPARTMENT OF HEALTH 112
WILDLIFE DISEASE ASSOCIATION 348
WORLD ASSOCIATION OF GIRL GUIDES AND GIRL SCOUTS (WAGGGS) 357

Healthy Home

OHIO OFFICE OF ENERGY EFFICIENCY 94
PENNSYLVANIA RESOURCES COUNCIL, INC., (formerly PA Roadside Council) 295

Herpetoculture

MATTS (MID-ATLANTIC TURTLE AND TORTOISE SOCIETY, INC.) 248

Herpetology

MATTS (MID-ATLANTIC TURTLE AND TORTOISE SOCIETY, INC.) 248

Highly Migratory Species

WESTERN PACIFIC REGIONAL FISHERY MANAGEMENT COUNCIL 344

Himalayan Range

HIMALAYAN WILDLIFE FOUNDATION 216

Historic Preservation

ALABAMA WATERFOWL ASSOCIATION, INC. (AWA) 133
AMERICA THE BEAUTIFUL FUND 135
AMERICAN LIVESTOCK BREEDS CONSERVANCY 147
APPALACHIAN TRAIL CONFERENCE 153
ARCHAEOLOGICAL CONSERVANCY 153
ARKANSAS DEPARTMENT OF PARKS AND TOURISM 42
CAVE RESEARCH FOUNDATION 168
COASTAL GEORGIA LAND TRUST, THE 176
DELAWARE GREENWAYS, INC. 187
DEPARTMENT OF PARKS AND RECREATION (GUAM) 57
ELM RESEARCH INSTITUTE 194
FOREST FIRE LOOKOUT ASSOCIATION 203
GEORGE WRIGHT SOCIETY, THE 208
GEORGIA TRUST FOR HISTORIC PRESERVATION 210
INDIANA DEPARTMENT OF NATURAL RESOURCES 62
NATIONAL PARK FOUNDATION 263
NATIONAL PARK TRUST 263
NATIONAL TRUST FOR HISTORIC PRESERVATION 265
NEVIS HISTORICAL AND CONSERVATION SOCIETY 276
NEW YORK STATE OFFICE OF PARKS, RECREATION AND HISTORIC PRESERVATION 91
NORTH DAKOTA PARKS AND RECREATION DEPARTMENT 93
OFFICE OF STATE PARKS, DEPARTMENT OF CULTURE, RECREATION, AND TOURISM 69
OREGON PARKS AND RECREATION DEPARTMENT 98
RAINFOREST TRUST, INC., THE 302
SHELBURNE FARMS 312
SMITHSONIAN INSTITUTION 317
SOUND EXPERIENCE 320
TALLAHASSEE MUSEUM OF HISTORY AND NATURAL SCIENCE 327
TRUSTEES OF RESERVATIONS, THE 335
TUG HILL COMMISSION 91
UNITED STATES DEPARTMENT OF TRANSPORTATION ... 31
UNITED STATES TOURIST COUNCIL 336
WYOMING DEPARTMENT OF COMMERCE 122

Hunting

ALABAMA WATERFOWL ASSOCIATION, INC. (AWA) 133
ALASKA DEPARTMENT OF FISH AND GAME 39
ALASKA DEPARTMENT OF PUBLIC SAFETY 40
ANIMAL PROTECTION INSTITUTE 152
ARCHERY MANUFACTURERS AND MERCHANTS ORGANIZATION (AMO) 154
BOONE AND CROCKETT CLUB 161
BOONE AND CROCKETT FOUNDATION 161
CALIFORNIA WATERFOWL ASSOCIATION 164
CALIFORNIA WILDLIFE FEDERATION 165
CAMP FIRE CLUB OF AMERICA, THE 165
CENTRAL OHIO ANGLERS AND HUNTERS CLUB 172
COLORADO STATE UNIVERSITY COOPERATIVE EXTENSION 50
COLORADO TRAPPERS ASSOCIATION 178
CONSERVATION FORCE 182
DEPARTMENT OF FISH AND WILDLIFE (WASHINGTON) . 116
DEPARTMENT OF INTERIOR, U.S.G.S/B.R.D, SOUTH CAROLINA COOPERATIVE FISH AND WILDLIFE RESEARCH UNIT 104
DEPARTMENT OF WILDLIFE CONSERVATION 95
EVERGLADES COORDINATING COUNCIL (ECC) 199

FEDERAL CARTRIDGE COMPANY 199
FEDERAL WILDLIFE OFFICER'S ASSOCIATION 199
FLORIDA FISH AND WILDLIFE CONSERVATION
　COMMISSION 54
FOUNDATION FOR NORTH AMERICAN BIG GAME 205
FRIENDS OF ANIMALS INC. 205
HUMANE SOCIETY OF THE UNITED STATES, THE 217
IDAHO FISH AND GAME DEPARTMENT 60
INTERNATIONAL ASSOCIATION OF NATURAL RESOURCE
　PILOTS 223
INTERNATIONAL HUNTER EDUCATION ASSOCIATION ... 225
IOWA DEPARTMENT OF NATURAL RESOURCES 64
IZAAK WALTON LEAGUE OF AMERICA ENDOWMENT 234
IZAAK WALTON LEAGUE OF AMERICA, INC., THE 234
KANSAS DEPARTMENT OF WILDLIFE AND PARKS 65
KANSAS STATE EXTENSION SERVICES 66
MAINE DEPARTMENT OF INLAND FISHERIES AND
　WILDLIFE 70
MAX McGRAW WILDLIFE FOUNDATION 248
MONTANA DEPARTMENT OF FISH, WILDLIFE, AND PARKS
　.. 80
MOUNTAIN LION FOUNDATION 255
MULE DEER FOUNDATION, THE 256
NATIONAL FIELD ARCHERY ASSOCIATION 261
NATIONAL HUNTERS ASSOCIATION, INC. 262
NATIONAL RIFLE ASSOCIATION OF AMERICA 264
NATIONAL SHOOTING SPORTS FOUNDATION, INC. 265
NATIONAL WILD TURKEY FEDERATION, CANADA, INC.,
　THE 266
NATIONAL WILD TURKEY FEDERATION, INC., THE 267
NEW HAMPSHIRE FISH AND GAME DEPARTMENT 84
NEW YORK STATE FISH AND WILDLIFE MANAGEMENT
　BOARD 90
NORTH AMERICAN FALCONERS ASSOCIATION 281
NORTH AMERICAN GAMEBIRD ASSOCIATION, INC. 281
NORTH CAROLINA WILDLIFE RESOURCES COMMISSION 92
NORTH DAKOTA GAME AND FISH DEPARTMENT 93
NORTHEAST WILDLIFE ADMINISTRATORS ASSOCIATION
　.. 284
OREGON FISH AND WILDLIFE DIVISION/DEPARTMENT OF
　STATE POLICE 98
PENNSYLVANIA GAME COMMISSION 102
PHEASANTS FOREVER, INC. 296
QUEBEC WILDLIFE FEDERATION 301
ROCKY MOUNTAIN BIGHORN SOCIETY 306
ROCKY MOUNTAIN ELK FOUNDATION 307
SAFARI CLUB INTERNATIONAL 308
SOUTH CAROLINA DEPARTMENT OF NATURAL
　RESOURCES 105
TEXAS ORGANIZATION FOR ENDANGERED SPECIES 329
WEST VIRGINIA DIVISION OF NATURAL RESOURCES 119
WHALE AND DOLPHIN CONSERVATION SOCIETY 345
WHITETAILS UNLIMITED, INC. 345
WILDLIFE FOREVER 348
WILDLIFE FOUNDATION OF FLORIDA, INC. 349
WILDLIFE LEGISLATIVE FUND OF AMERICA, THE, AND
　WILDLIFE CONSERVATION FUND OF AMERICA, THE .. 349
WILDLIFE RESOURCES AGENCY 107
WYOMING GAME AND FISH DEPARTMENT 123

Hydropower Relicensing

AMERICAN RIVERS (formerly American Rivers Conservation
　Council) 149
CALIFORNIA TROUT, INC. 164
RIVER ALLIANCE OF WISCONSIN 305

Hyenas

WILD DOG FOUNDATION, THE 345

Indigenous People

CIRCUMPOLAR CONSERVATION UNION 174
CONSERVATION FORCE 182
NATIONAL NETWORK OF FOREST PRACTITIONERS 263

Inquiry Based Education

GREEN (GLOBAL RIVERS ENVIRONMENTAL EDUCATION
　NETWORK) 212
SEACAMP ASSOCIATION, INC. 312

Insects and Butterflies

AUDUBON SOCIETY OF RHODE ISLAND 159
AUDUBON SOCIETY OF WESTERN PENNSYLVANIA 159
BEYOND PESTICIDES/NATIONAL COALITION AGAINST THE
　MISUSE OF PESTICIDES 160
BIO-INTEGRAL RESOURCE CENTER 161
COLLEGE OF TROPICAL AGRICULTURE AND HUMAN
　RESOURCES 57
DELAWARE STATE EXTENSION SERVICE 52
DRAGONFLY SOCIETY OF THE AMERICAS, THE 188
ENTOMOLOGICAL SOCIETY OF AMERICA 195
FISH AND WILDLIFE INFORMATION EXCHANGE 201
HAWAII NATURE CENTER 214
INDIANA AUDUBON SOCIETY, INC. 220
MICHIGAN NATURE ASSOCIATION 249
NATURAL HISTORY SOCIETY OF MARYLAND, INC., THE 270
NATURE SASKATCHEWAN 275
NORTH AMERICAN BUTTERFLY ASSOCIATION 280
SMITHSONIAN INSTITUTION 317
SOCIETY FOR INTEGRATIVE AND COMPARTIVE BIOLOGY
　(formerly AMERICAN SOCIETY OF ZOOLOGISTS) 318
STATE FORESTRY DIVISION (WYOMING) 122
WILD ONES - NATURAL LANDSCAPERS, LTD 346
XERCES SOCIETY, THE 360
YOUNG ENTOMOLOGISTS' SOCIETY, INC. 361

International Conservation

ACADEMY FOR EDUCATIONAL DEVELOPMENT 130
AFRICAN WILDLIFE FOUNDATION 132
AFRICAN WILDLIFE NEWS SERVICE 132
AMERICAN ASSOCIATION OF ZOO KEEPERS, INC. 137
AMERICAN BIRD CONSERVANCY 138
AMERICAN SOCIETY OF MAMMALOGISTS 150
AMERICAN ZOO AND AQUARIUM ASSOCIATION (AZA) ... 151
ANCIENT FOREST INTERNATIONAL 152
ANIMAL WELFARE INSTITUTE 152
ANTARCTICA PROJECT 153
ASSOCIATION OF AVIAN VETERINARIANS 156
ATLANTIC CENTER FOR THE ENVIRONMENT 157
BAT CONSERVATION INTERNATIONAL 160
BILLFISH FOUNDATION, THE 160
BIRDLIFE INTERNATIONAL 161
CENTER FOR MARINE CONSERVATION 170
CETACEAN SOCIETY INTERNATIONAL 172
CONSERVATION FORCE 182
CONSERVATION INTERNATIONAL 183
CONSERVATION TREATY SUPPORT FUND 183
CORAL REEF ALLIANCE, THE (CORAL) 184
DELTA WATERFOWL FOUNDATION 187
EARTH FOUNDATION 191
EARTH ISLAND INSTITUTE 191
EARTHSTEWARDS NETWORK 193
EARTHTRUST 193
EARTHWATCH INSTITUTE 193
ECOTOURISM SOCIETY, THE 194
EDUCATIONAL COMMUNICATIONS, INC. 194
ENVIRONMENTAL AIR FORCE 195
ENVIRONMENTAL AND ENERGY STUDY INSTITUTE (EESI)
　.. 195
ENVIRONMENTAL DEFENSE FUND, INC. 196
ENVIRONMENTAL LAW ALLIANCE WORLDWIDE (E-LAW) 197
EUROPARC FEDERATION 199
FEDERAL WILDLIFE OFFICER'S ASSOCIATION 199
FOSSIL RIM WILDLIFE CENTER 205
GAME CONSERVATION INTERNATIONAL (GAME COIN) . 207
GEORGE MIKSCH SUTTON AVIAN RESEARCH CENTER
　INC. 208
GLOBAL ENVIRONMENTAL MANAGEMENT INITIATIVE
　(GEMI) 210
GREAT BEAR FOUNDATION 211
GREAT LAKES UNITED 211

KEYWORD INDEX - International Environmental Law

HEADLANDS INSTITUTE 215
HUMMINGBIRD SOCIETY, THE 217
INITIATIVE FOR SOCIAL ACTION AND RENEWAL IN EURASIA 221
INSTITUTE FOR EARTH EDUCATION, THE 221
INTERFAITH COUNCIL FOR THE PROTECTION OF ANIMALS AND NATURE INC. (ICPAN) 222
INTERNATIONAL ASSOCIATION FOR ENVIRONMENTAL HYDROLOGY (IAEH) 222
INTERNATIONAL CENTRE FOR CONSERVATION EDUCATION 224
INTERNATIONAL COUNCIL OF ENVIRONMENTAL LAW 224
INTERNATIONAL CRANE FOUNDATION 224
INTERNATIONAL EROSION CONTROL ASSOCIATION (IECA) 224
INTERNATIONAL INSTITUTE FOR ENERGY CONSERVATION 225
INTERNATIONAL MARINE MAMMAL PROJECT, THE 226
INTERNATIONAL PRIMATE PROTECTION LEAGUE 226
INTERNATIONAL SNOW LEOPARD TRUST 227
INTERNATIONAL SOCIETY FOR ENDANGERED CATS (ISEC) 227
INTERNATIONAL SOCIETY OF TROPICAL FORESTERS, INC. 228
INTERNATIONAL SONORAN DESERT ALLIANCE 228
INTERNATIONAL WILD WATERFOWL ASSOCIATION 229
INTERNATIONAL WILDERNESS LEADERSHIP (WILD) FOUNDATION 230
INTERNATIONAL WILDLIFE COALITION (IWC) AND THE WHALE ADOPTION PROJECT 230
INTERNATIONAL WOLF CENTER (Educational Services) 230
ISLAND RESOURCES FOUNDATION 233
KIDS FOR SAVING EARTH WORLDWIDE 239
NATIONAL WILDLIFE FEDERATION 267, 268
NATURE CONSERVANCY, THE 272, 273, 274
NORTH AMERICAN ASSOCIATION FOR ENVIRONMENTAL EDUCATION 280
NORTH AMERICAN COALITION ON RELIGION AND ECOLOGY (NACRE) 280
NORTH ATLANTIC SALMON CONSERVATION ORGANIZATION 282
NORTHWEST ATLANTIC FISHERIES ORGANIZATION (NAFO) 285
NORTHWEST RESOURCE INFORMATION CENTER 286
OCEAN VOICE INTERNATIONAL 286
ORGANIZATION FOR BAT CONSERVATION 291
PACIFIC INSTITUTE FOR STUDIES IN DEVELOPMENT, ENVIRONMENT, AND SECURITY 293
PEREGRINE FUND, THE 296
RAINFOREST ACTION NETWORK 302
RAINFOREST ALLIANCE 302
RAINFOREST RELIEF 302
RENEWABLE NATURAL RESOURCES FOUNDATION 304
SEA SHEPHERD CONSERVATION SOCIETY 311
SIERRA CLUB 312, 314, 315, 316, 317
SOCIETY FOR CONSERVATION BIOLOGY 318
SOCIETY FOR MARINE MAMMALOGY, THE 318
SOIL AND WATER CONSERVATION SOCIETY (formerly Soil Conservation Society of America) 320
THRESHOLD, INC. 329
TREAD LIGHTLY! INC. 330
TREES FOR THE FUTURE, INC. 330
TRUST FOR WILDLIFE, INC. 335
UNITED NATIONS ENVIRONMENT PROGRAMME 336
UNITED STATES COMMITTEE FOR THE UNITED NATIONS ENVIRONMENT PROGRAMME THE (U.S. and UNEP) 336
UNITED STATES TOURIST COUNCIL 336
URBAN WILDLIFE RESOURCES 337
WESTERN HEMISPHERE SHOREBIRD RESERVE NETWORK (WHSRN) 344
WHALE AND DOLPHIN CONSERVATION SOCIETY 345
WILD DOG FOUNDATION, THE 345
WILDLANDS PROJECT, THE 347
WILDLIFE CONSERVATION SOCIETY 348
WILDLIFE PRESERVATION TRUST INTERNATIONAL, INC. 350
WILSON ORNITHOLOGICAL SOCIETY 355
WORLD CONSERVATION MONITORING CENTRE 358
WORLD FORESTRY CENTER 358
WORLD WILDLIFE FUND 359

International Environmental Law

AMERICAN SOCIETY OF INTERNATIONAL LAW/WILDLIFE INTEREST GROUP 150
CENTER FOR INTERNATIONAL ENVIRONMENTAL LAW (CIEL) 170
ENVIRONMENTAL LAW INSTITUTE, THE 198

International Trade and Environment

AMERICAN SOCIETY OF INTERNATIONAL LAW/WILDLIFE INTEREST GROUP 150
CENTER FOR INTERNATIONAL ENVIRONMENTAL LAW (CIEL) 170
CHLORINE-FREE PAPER CONSORTIUM (CPC) 173
LEAGUE OF ENVIRONMENTAL JOURNALISTS 241

International Wildlife

AMERICAN SOCIETY OF INTERNATIONAL LAW/WILDLIFE INTEREST GROUP 150
CONSERVATION FORCE 182
DESERT RESEARCH FOUNDATION OF NAMIBIA, THE 188
INTERNATIONAL OSPREY FOUNDATION INC., THE 226
WILD DOG FOUNDATION, THE 345

Internships

AMERICAN ASSOCIATION OF BOTANICAL GARDENS AND ARBORETA, INC. 136
AMERICAN BASS ASSOCIATION OF WEST VIRGINIA, THE 138
AMERICAN CAMPING ASSOCIATION, INC. 138
ATLANTIC CENTER FOR THE ENVIRONMENT 157
CADDO LAKE INSTITUTE, INC. 163
CENTER FOR ENVIRONMENTAL EDUCATION 169
CENTER FOR HEALTH, ENVIRONMENT, AND JUSTICE 170
CENTER FOR SCIENCE IN THE PUBLIC INTEREST 171
CINCINNATI NATURE CENTER 174
COMMUNITIES FOR A BETTER ENVIRONMENT 179
CONSERVANCY OF SOUTHWEST FLORIDA, THE 181
DEEP-PORTAGE CONSERVATION RESERVE 186
EARTH DAY NEW YORK 191
EARTHWATCH INSTITUTE 193
ECOLOGICAL SOCIETY OF AMERICA, THE 193
ECOLOGY CENTER 194
ENVIRONMENTAL CAREER CENTER 195
ENVIRONMENTAL CAREERS ORGANIZATION, INC., THE 195
ENVIRONMENTAL RESOURCE CENTER (ERC) 198
FOSSIL RIM WILDLIFE CENTER 205
GEORGIA TRUST FOR HISTORIC PRESERVATION 210
GLACIER INSTITUTE, THE 210
GREEN MOUNTAIN CLUB INC., THE 213
INSTITUTE FOR EARTH EDUCATION, THE 221
INTERNATIONAL MARINE MAMMAL PROJECT, THE 226
IOWA NATURAL HERITAGE FOUNDATION 232
MANOMET CENTER FOR CONSERVATION SCIENCES 245
MAX McGRAW WILDLIFE FOUNDATION 248
MISSOURI FOREST PRODUCTS ASSOCIATION 253
NATIONAL ASSOCIATION FOR INTERPRETATION 256
NEW HAMPSHIRE FISH AND GAME DEPARTMENT 84
NORTHWEST ECOSYSTEM ALLIANCE 285
PACIFIC INSTITUTE FOR STUDIES IN DEVELOPMENT, ENVIRONMENT, AND SECURITY 293
PACIFIC NORTHWEST TRAIL ASSOCIATION 293
PACIFIC WHALE FOUNDATION 293
PANOS INSTITUTE, THE 293
POPULATION INSTITUTE, THE 298
RAILS-TO-TRAILS CONSERVANCY 302
SEACAMP ASSOCIATION, INC. 312
SOUTHEAST ALASKA CONSERVATION COUNCIL (SEACC) 323
SOUTHFACE ENERGY INSTITUTE 324
STUDENT CONSERVATION ASSOCIATION, INC. 326
THORNE ECOLOGICAL INSTITUTE 329
THRESHOLD, INC. 329
WILDERNESS EDUCATION ASSOCIATION 346

Interpretation

CINCINNATI NATURE CENTER	174
INTERPRETATION CANADA	230
IOWA ASSOCIATION OF NATURALISTS	231
NATIONAL ASSOCIATION FOR INTERPRETATION	256
ORGANIZATION FOR BAT CONSERVATION	291

Interpretive Center

HAWAII NATURE CENTER	214
NORTH AMERICAN BUTTERFLY ASSOCIATION	280

Islands

BARRIER ISLAND TRUST, INC.	160
FRIENDS OF THE SAN JUANS	206
GALIANO CONSERVANCY ASSOCIATION	207
HAWAII AUDUBON SOCIETY	214
HAWAII COOPERATIVE FISHERY RESEARCH UNIT (USDI)	58
HAWAII SOCIETY OF AMERICAN FORESTERS	214
ISLAND CONSERVATION EFFORT	233
ISLAND INSTITUTE, THE	233
ISLAND RESOURCES FOUNDATION	233
MAINE COAST HERITAGE TRUST	245
MICHIGAN NATURAL AREAS COUNCIL	249
PTARMIGANS, THE	300
PUERTO RICO SEA GRANT PROGRAM	103
SAN JUAN PRESERVATION TRUST, THE	308
SANIBEL-CAPTIVA CONSERVATION FOUNDATION, INC.	308
WESTERN PACIFIC REGIONAL FISHERY MANAGEMENT COUNCIL	344

Justice

THREE CIRCLES CENTER FOR MULTICULTURAL ENVIRONMENTAL EDUCATION	329

Lakes

ADIRONDACK PARK AGENCY	88
ADOPT-A-STREAM FOUNDATION, THE	131
AMERICAN SOCIETY OF LIMNOLOGY AND OCEANOGRAPHY	150
ASSOCIATION FOR THE PROTECTION OF THE ADIRONDACKS, THE	155
ATLANTIC STATES LEGAL FOUNDATION	157
CHINA REGION LAKES ALLIANCE	173
COMITE DESPERTAR CIDRENO	102
COOSA RIVER BASIN INITIATIVE	184
FLORIDA AUDUBON SOCIETY	201
FLORIDA FISH AND WILDLIFE CONSERVATION COMMISSION	54
FLORIDA STATE COOPERATIVE EXTENSION SERVICE	54
INDIANA DEPARTMENT OF NATURAL RESOURCES	62
INTERNATIONAL ASSOCIATION OF NATURAL RESOURCE PILOTS	223
IOWA DEPARTMENT OF NATURAL RESOURCES	64
KANSAS DEPARTMENT OF WILDLIFE AND PARKS	65
KANSAS WATER OFFICE	66
LAKE MICHIGAN FEDERATION	240
LAND BETWEEN THE LAKES ASSOCIATION	240
LEAGUE TO SAVE LAKE TAHOE	242
MICHIGAN DEPARTMENT OF ENVIRONMENTAL QUALITY	75
MINNESOTA BOARD OF WATER AND SOIL RESOURCES	75
MINNESOTA SEA GRANT COLLEGE PROGRAM	77
MONITOR INTERNATIONAL	253
MONO LAKE COMMITTEE	254
MUSKIES, INC.	256
NATIONAL BOATING FEDERATION	260
NEBRASKA DEPARTMENT OF WATER RESOURCES	81
NEW HAMPSHIRE LAKES ASSOCIATION	277
NEWFOUNDLAND LABRADOR WILDLIFE FEDERATION	279
NORTH AMERICAN BENTHOLOGICAL SOCIETY	280
NORTH AMERICAN FISHING CLUB	281
NORTH AMERICAN LOON FUND	281
NORTH CASCADES CONSERVATION COUNCIL	283
OHIO ENVIRONMENTAL COUNCIL, INC.	287
OHIO SEA GRANT COLLEGE PROGRAM	95
OKLAHOMA WATER RESOURCES BOARD	97
RESOURCES AGENCY, THE	46
SEAPLANE PILOTS ASSOCIATION	312
SOUTH DAKOTA DEPARTMENT OF ENVIRONMENT AND NATURAL RESOURCES	106
TAHOE REGIONAL PLANNING AGENCY	327
UNIVERSITY OF NEW HAMPSHIRE COOPERATIVE EXTENSION	84
WISCONSIN ASSOCIATION FOR ENVIRONMENTAL EDUCATION, INC.	355
WISCONSIN ASSOCIATION OF LAKES (WAL)	355
WISCONSIN COOPERATIVE FISHERY RESEARCH UNIT (USDI)	120
WISCONSIN SEA GRANT INSTITUTE	121

Land Conservation

ALDO LEOPOLD FOUNDATION, INC.	135
BRANDYWINE CONSERVANCY, INC.	162
COASTAL GEORGIA LAND TRUST, THE	176
GEORGIA ENVIRONMENTAL POLICY INSTITUTE	209
GREAT OUTDOORS CONSERVANCY, THE	212
LAND TRUST ALLIANCE, THE	240
TRUSTEES OF RESERVATIONS, THE	335
VERMONT LAND TRUST	338

Land Management

ALDO LEOPOLD FOUNDATION, INC.	135
CENTER FOR CHESAPEAKE COMMUNITIES	169
COLORADO NATURAL HERITAGE PROGRAM	177
DESERT RESEARCH FOUNDATION OF NAMIBIA, THE	188
GEORGIA ENVIRONMENTAL POLICY INSTITUTE	209
GREAT OUTDOORS CONSERVANCY, THE	212
LAND WATCH MONTEREY COUNTY	241
SANIBEL-CAPTIVA CONSERVATION FOUNDATION, INC.	308
SOUTH CAROLINA COASTAL CONSERVATION LEAGUE	321
TREES FOR TOMORROW, INC., NATURAL RESOURCES EDUCATION CENTER	331
WASHINGTON WILDLIFE HERITAGE FOUNDATION (including Heritage Land Trust)	342
WATERSHED MANAGEMENT COUNCIL	343
WISCONSIN DEPARTMENT OF NATURAL RESOURCES	120
ZERO (REGIONAL ENVIRONMENTAL ORGANIZATION)	361

Land Preservation

ACRES LAND TRUST	130
ADIRONDACK MOUNTAIN CLUB, INC., THE	131
ADIRONDACK NATURE CONSERVANCY/ADIRONDACK LAND TRUST, INC.	131
ARLINGTON OUTDOOR EDUCATION ASSOCIATION, INC.	155
AUDUBON SOCIETY OF RHODE ISLAND	159
BARRIER ISLAND TRUST, INC.	160
CALIFORNIANS FOR POPULATION STABILIZATION (CAPS)	165
COASTAL GEORGIA LAND TRUST, THE	176
COMMUNITY RIGHTS COUNSEL	179
CONSERVANCY OF SOUTHWEST FLORIDA, THE	181
CONSERVATION FEDERATION OF MARYLAND/For A Rural Maryland (F.A.R.M.)	182
DEPARTMENT OF LAND AND NATURAL RESOURCES	58
DESERT TORTOISE COUNCIL	188
EASTERN SHORE LAND CONSERVANCY	193
ECOLOGY CENTER	194
ENVIRONMENTAL AIR FORCE	195
FOREST SOCIETY OF MAINE	204
GALIANO CONSERVANCY ASSOCIATION	207
GEORGIA ENVIRONMENTAL POLICY INSTITUTE	209
GRAND CANYON TRUST (St. George, UT Office)	211
GREAT OUTDOORS CONSERVANCY, THE	212
HOOD CANAL LAND TRUST	216
IDAHO STATE DEPARTMENT OF AGRICULTURE	60
ILLINOIS ASSOCIATION OF CONSERVATION DISTRICTS	218
ILLINOIS AUDUBON SOCIETY	219
ILLINOIS NATURE PRESERVES COMMISSION (INPC)	62

KEYWORD INDEX - Land Protection

INTERTRIBAL BISON COOPERATIVE (ITBC) 231
IOWA NATURAL HERITAGE FOUNDATION 232
IOWA TRAILS COUNCIL 232
IZAAK WALTON LEAGUE OF AMERICA, INC., THE 234
JACKSON HOLE LAND TRUST 236
KANSAS WILDSCAPE FOUNDATION 238
KENTUCKY DEPARTMENT OF PARKS 67
KIDS FOR SAVING EARTH WORLDWIDE 239
LAND WATCH MONTEREY COUNTY 241
LEE COUNTY PARKS AND RECREATION SERVICES 54
MAINE COAST HERITAGE TRUST 245
MASSACHUSETTS AUDUBON SOCIETY, INC. 247
MICHIGAN AUDUBON SOCIETY 249
MICHIGAN NATURE ASSOCIATION 249
MINNESOTA WINGS SOCIETY, INC. 252
MISSOURI PRAIRIE FOUNDATION 253
MONTANA LAND RELIANCE 254
MOUNTAIN LION FOUNDATION 255
NATIONAL PARKS AND CONSERVATION ASSOCIATION
  (NPCA) 263
NATIONAL WILDLIFE FEDERATION 267, 268
NATURAL AREAS ASSOCIATION 270
NATURAL LAND INSTITUTE 270
NATURE CONSERVANCY OF CANADA, THE 272
NATURE SASKATCHEWAN 275
NEW JERSEY AUDUBON SOCIETY 277
NEW JERSEY CONSERVATION FOUNDATION 278
NEW YORK-NEW JERSEY TRAIL CONFERENCE INC. 279
NORTH CASCADES CONSERVATION COUNCIL 283
NORTH DAKOTA PARKS AND RECREATION DEPARTMENT
  93
OUTDOOR CIRCLE, THE 291
PENNSYLVANIA DEPARTMENT OF AGRICULTURE 99
PENNSYLVANIA DEPARTMENT OF CONSERVATION AND
  NATURAL RESOURCES 100
RAILS-TO-TRAILS CONSERVANCY 302
RINCON INSTITUTE, THE 305
SAVE THE DUNES COUNCIL 309
SCENIC AMERICA 310
SCENIC HUDSON, INC. 311
SOUTHERN ENVIRONMENTAL LAW CENTER 324
STATEWIDE PROGRAM OF ACTION TO CONSERVE OUR
  ENVIRONMENT (SPACE) 325
TRUST FOR WILDLIFE, INC. 335
TUG HILL TOMORROW LAND TRUST 335
VERMONT INSTITUTE OF NATURAL SCIENCE 338
VIRGINIA OUTDOORS FOUNDATION 115
WASHINGTON WILDLIFE AND RECREATION COALITION 342
WESTERN PENNSYLVANIA CONSERVANCY 344
WILD ONES - NATURAL LANDSCAPERS, LTD 346
WILDERNESS LAND TRUST, THE 346
WILDLANDS CONSERVANCY 347
WISCONSIN DEPARTMENT OF AGRICULTURE TRADE AND
  CONSUMER PROTECTION 120
WORLD PARKS ENDOWMENT INC. 358
WYOMING DEPARTMENT OF COMMERCE 122
WYOMING STATE BOARD OF LAND COMMISSIONERS ... 123

Land Protection

BARRIER ISLAND TRUST, INC. 160
CATSKILL CENTER FOR CONSERVATION AND
  DEVELOPMENT, INC., THE 168
COASTAL GEORGIA LAND TRUST, THE 176
CONSERVATION TRUST OF PUERTO RICO 183
EASTERN SHORE LAND CONSERVANCY 193
GEORGIA ENVIRONMENTAL POLICY INSTITUTE 209
GREAT OUTDOORS CONSERVANCY, THE 212
LAND TRUST ALLIANCE, THE 240
LAND WATCH MONTEREY COUNTY 241
MOUNTAIN CONSERVATION TRUST OF GEORGIA, INC. . 255
NEW HAMPSHIRE DEPARTMENT OF AGRICULTURE,
  MARKETS, AND FOOD 83
SANIBEL-CAPTIVA CONSERVATION FOUNDATION, INC. 308
SCENIC HUDSON, INC. 311
SHELBURNE FARMS 312

Land Purchase

AMERICAN FARMLAND TRUST 139
AMERICAN LAND CONSERVANCY 146
AMERICAN RESOURCES GROUP 148
ANCIENT FOREST INTERNATIONAL 152
APPALACHIAN TRAIL CONFERENCE 153
ARCHAEOLOGICAL CONSERVANCY 153
COLORADO WILDLIFE HERITAGE FOUNDATION 178
CONSERVATION FUND, THE 182
DELAWARE WILD LANDS, INC. 187
DESERT TORTOISE PRESERVE COMMITTEE, INC. 188
EARTH FOUNDATION 191
FLORIDA PANTHER PROJECT, INC., THE 202
FOREST SOCIETY OF MAINE 204
GALIANO CONSERVANCY ASSOCIATION 207
GEORGIA ENVIRONMENTAL POLICY INSTITUTE 209
GREAT OUTDOORS CONSERVANCY, THE 212
INTERAGENCY COMMITTEE FOR OUTDOOR RECREATION
  (IAC) 116
IOWA DEPARTMENT OF NATURAL RESOURCES 64
IZAAK WALTON LEAGUE OF AMERICA, INC., THE 234
JACKSON HOLE LAND TRUST 236
LAND TRUST ALLIANCE, THE 240
MASSACHUSETTS ASSOCIATION OF CONSERVATION
  COMMISSIONS (MACC) 247
MICHIGAN NATURE ASSOCIATION 249
MINNESOTA PARKS AND TRAILS COUNCIL 251
MISSOURI PRAIRIE FOUNDATION 253
NATIONAL ASSOCIATION OF STATE OUTDOOR
  RECREATION LIAISON OFFICERS 258
NATIONAL ASSOCIATION OF STATE PARK DIRECTORS 258
NATIONAL PARK TRUST 263
NATURAL HERITAGE COMMISSION (ARKANSAS) 44
NATURAL LAND INSTITUTE 270
NATURE CONSERVANCY OF CANADA, THE 272
NATURE CONSERVANCY, THE 272, 273, 274
NEW JERSEY CONSERVATION FOUNDATION 278
OPENLANDS PROJECT 290
PIEDMONT ENVIRONMENTAL COUNCIL 296
PRAIRIE CLUB, THE 298
PUERTO RICO ASSOCIATION OF SOIL AND WATER
  CONSERVATION DISTRICTS 300
PUERTO RICO DEPARTMENT OF NATURAL AND
  ENVIRONMENTAL RESOURCES 103
RIVER NETWORK 306
ROCKY MOUNTAIN ELK FOUNDATION 307
SAVE-THE-REDWOODS LEAGUE 310
SOCIETY FOR THE PROTECTION OF NEW HAMPSHIRE
  FORESTS 319
TRUST FOR PUBLIC LAND, THE 334
TURTLE CREEK WATERSHED ASSOCIATION, INC. 335
WASHINGTON WILDLIFE AND RECREATION COALITION 342
WASHINGTON WILDLIFE FEDERATION 342
WILDERNESS LAND TRUST, THE 346
WILDLIFE FOREVER 348
WORLD PARKS ENDOWMENT INC. 358

Land Use Planning

ADIRONDACK COUNCIL, THE 131
ADIRONDACK PARK AGENCY 88
ADOPT-A-STREAM FOUNDATION, THE 131
ALABAMA NATURAL HERITAGE PROGRAM 132
ALASKA DEPARTMENT OF NATURAL RESOURCES 40
AMERICAN CAVE CONSERVATION ASSOCIATION 138
AMERICAN FARMLAND TRUST 139
AMERICAN GEOGRAPHICAL SOCIETY 145
AMERICAN HIKING SOCIETY 145
AMERICAN HORSE PROTECTION ASSOCIATION 145
AMERICAN PLANNING ASSOCIATION 148
AMERICAN SOCIETY OF LANDSCAPE ARCHITECTS 150
ARIZONA GEOLOGICAL SURVEY 41
ARIZONA LAND DEPARTMENT 41
ASSOCIATION FOR THE PROTECTION OF THE
  ADIRONDACKS, THE 155
ASSOCIATION OF AMERICAN GEOGRAPHERS 155
AUDUBON INTERNATIONAL 158
BRANDYWINE CONSERVANCY, INC. 162

CALIFORNIANS FOR POPULATION STABILIZATION (CAPS) ... 165
CENTER FOR CHESAPEAKE COMMUNITIES ... 169
CENTER FOR WATERSHED PROTECTION ... 171
CHESAPEAKE BAY FOUNDATION, INC. (Maryland Office) . 173
COAST ALLIANCE ... 176
COLORADO NATURAL HERITAGE PROGRAM ... 177
COLORADO STATE FOREST SERVICE ... 49
COLUMBIA RIVER GORGE COMMISSION ... 116
COMMUNITY ENVIRONMENTAL COUNCIL ... 179
COMMUNITY RIGHTS COUNSEL ... 179
CONFEDERATED SALISH AND KOOTENAI TRIBES ... 180
CONNECTICUT COUNCIL ON ENVIRONMENTAL QUALITY 50
CONNECTICUT RIVER WATERSHED COUNCIL INC. ... 181
CONSERVATION FUND, THE ... 182
DELAWARE ASSOCIATION OF CONSERVATION DISTRICTS ... 186
DELAWARE DEPARTMENT OF AGRICULTURE ... 51
DELAWARE STATE EXTENSION SERVICE ... 52
DESERT TORTOISE COUNCIL ... 188
ENVIRONMENTAL DEFENSE CENTER, INC. ... 196
E-P EDUCATION SERVICES, INC. ... 191
FLORIDA AUDUBON SOCIETY ... 201
FLORIDA DEFENDERS OF THE ENVIRONMENT, INC. (Home Office) ... 201
FLORIDA SPORTSMEN'S CONSERVATION ASSOCIATION ... 202
FOREST HISTORY SOCIETY, INC. ... 203
FOREST TRUST ... 204
FOSSIL FUELS POLICY ACTION INSTITUTE/ALLIANCE FOR A PAVING MORATORIUM ... 204
FRIENDS OF THE SAN JUANS ... 206
GALIANO CONSERVANCY ASSOCIATION ... 207
GEORGIA CONSERVANCY, INC., THE ... 209
GLOBAL CITIES PROJECT, THE ... 210
GRAND CANYON TRUST (St. George, UT Office) ... 211
IDAHO STATE DEPARTMENT OF AGRICULTURE ... 60
ILLINOIS DEPARTMENT OF AGRICULTURE ... 61
INTERAGENCY COMMITTEE FOR OUTDOOR RECREATION (IAC) ... 116
INTERNATIONAL ASSOCIATION FOR BEAR RESEARCH AND MANAGEMENT ... 222
INTERNATIONAL ASSOCIATION OF NATURAL RESOURCE PILOTS ... 223
INTERNATIONAL BICYCLE FUND ... 223
IOWA TRAILS COUNCIL ... 232
ISLAND RESOURCES FOUNDATION ... 233
IZAAK WALTON LEAGUE OF AMERICA, INC., THE ... 234
JACKSON HOLE CONSERVATION ALLIANCE ... 236
LAND TRUST ALLIANCE, THE ... 240
LAND WATCH MONTEREY COUNTY ... 241
LEAGUE OF WOMEN VOTERS OF IOWA ... 241
LEAGUE TO SAVE LAKE TAHOE ... 242
LIFE OF THE LAND ... 242
LOWER MISSISSIPPI RIVER CONSERVATION COMMITTEE ... 244
MANOMET CENTER FOR CONSERVATION SCIENCES ... 245
MARIN CONSERVATION LEAGUE ... 246
MAX McGRAW WILDLIFE FOUNDATION ... 248
MICHIGAN ENVIRONMENTAL COUNCIL ... 249
MID-ATLANTIC COUNCIL OF WATERSHED ASSOCIATIONS ... 250
MINNESOTA BOARD OF WATER AND SOIL RESOURCES . 75
MONTANA AUDUBON ... 254
MONTANA ENVIRONMENTAL INFORMATION CENTER ... 254
MONTANA ENVIRONMENTAL QUALITY COUNCIL ... 81
NATIONAL ASSOCIATION OF RECREATION RESOURCE PLANNERS ... 257
NATIONAL ASSOCIATION OF STATE PARK DIRECTORS . 258
NATIONAL GRANGE, THE ... 262
NATIONAL MILITARY FISH AND WILDLIFE ASSOCIATION 263
NATIONAL TRUST FOR HISTORIC PRESERVATION ... 265
NATURAL LAND INSTITUTE ... 270
NEVADA BUREAU OF MINES AND GEOLOGY ... 82
NEW HAMPSHIRE ASSOCIATION OF CONSERVATION COMMISSIONS ... 276
NEW HAMPSHIRE LAKES ASSOCIATION ... 277
NEW JERSEY CONSERVATION FOUNDATION ... 278
NEW JERSEY ENVIRONMENTAL LOBBY ... 278
NEW JERSEY PINELANDS COMMISSION ... 85
NEW YORK GEOLOGICAL SURVEY AND STATE MUSEUM 90
NORTH CAROLINA COASTAL FEDERATION, INC. ... 282
NORTH CASCADES CONSERVATION COUNCIL ... 283
NORTH DAKOTA GEOLOGICAL SURVEY ... 93
OFFICE OF ENERGY EFFICIENCY AND ENVIRONMENT ... 91
OKLAHOMA GEOLOGICAL SURVEY ... 96
OPENLANDS PROJECT ... 290
OREGON B.A.S.S. CHAPTER FEDERATION ... 290
OUTDOOR RECREATION COUNCIL OF BRITISH COLUMBIA ... 292
PRIORITIES INSTITUTE, THE ... 299
PUBLIC LANDS FOUNDATION ... 300
RENEWABLE NATURAL RESOURCES FOUNDATION ... 304
RESOURCES FOR THE FUTURE ... 304
RINCON INSTITUTE, THE ... 305
RIVER FEDERATION ... 306
SCENIC AMERICA ... 310
SIERRA CLUB FOUNDATION, THE ... 317
SOCIETY FOR RANGE MANAGEMENT ... 319
SONORAN INSTITUTE ... 320
SOUTH CAROLINA B.A.S.S. CHAPTER FEDERATION ... 321
SOUTH CAROLINA COASTAL CONSERVATION LEAGUE 321
SOUTHEAST ALASKA CONSERVATION COUNCIL (SEACC) ... 323
STATE WATER RESOURCES BOARD (RHODE ISLAND) .. 104
TAHOE REGIONAL PLANNING AGENCY ... 327
THRESHOLD, INC. ... 329
TROUT UNLIMITED, PENNSYLVANIA COUNCIL ... 333
UNIVERSITY OF NEW HAMPSHIRE COOPERATIVE EXTENSION ... 84
URBAN HABITAT PROGRAM ... 337
VIRGINIA B.A.S.S. CHAPTER FEDERATION ... 339
WEST MICHIGAN ENVIRONMENTAL ACTION COUNCIL ... 343
WISCONSIN ASSOCIATION OF LAKES (WAL) ... 355
WISCONSIN DEPARTMENT OF AGRICULTURE TRADE AND CONSUMER PROTECTION ... 120
WYOMING STATE GEOLOGICAL SURVEY ... 123

Landscape Analysis

UTAH COOPERATIVE FISH AND WILDLIFE RESEARCH UNIT (USDI-USGS-BRD-CRU) ... 110

Landscape Architecture

ADKINS ARBORETUM ... 131
AMERICAN SOCIETY OF LANDSCAPE ARCHITECTS ... 150
COLLEGE OF TROPICAL AGRICULTURE AND HUMAN RESOURCES ... 57
FRIENDS OF DISCOVERY PARK ... 205
LADY BIRD JOHNSON WILDFLOWER CENTER ... 240
MISSISSIPPI NATIVE PLANT SOCIETY ... 252
SCENIC AMERICA ... 310
VIRGINIA NATIVE PLANT SOCIETY ... 340

Landscape Ecology

DEPARTMENT OF INTERIOR, U.S.G.S/B.R.D, SOUTH CAROLINA COOPERATIVE FISH AND WILDLIFE RESEARCH UNIT ... 104

Law Enforcement

ASSOCIATION FOR FISH AND WILDLIFE ENFORCEMENT TRAINING ... 155
FEDERAL WILDLIFE OFFICER'S ASSOCIATION ... 199
NORTHEAST CONSERVATION LAW ENFORCEMENT CHIEFS' ASSOCIATION (CLECA) ... 284
OREGON FISH AND WILDLIFE DIVISION/DEPARTMENT OF STATE POLICE ... 98

Legal Advocacy

CONSERVATION FORCE ... 182
FOREST WATCH ... 204
MINNESOTA CENTER FOR ENVIRONMENTAL ADVOCACY (MCEA) ... 251

SOUTH CAROLINA ENVIRONMENTAL LAW PROJECT 321

Leisure

AMERICAN ASSOCIATION FOR LEISURE AND RECREATION (AALR) 136

Librarians/Information Professionals

CALIFORNIA ACADEMY OF SCIENCES 163
NATURAL RESOURCES INFORMATION COUNCIL 271
NEW MEXICO BUREAU OF MINES AND MINERAL RESOURCES 86

Libraries

CALIFORNIA ACADEMY OF SCIENCES 163
COMMITTEE FOR THE NATIONAL INSTITUTE FOR THE ENVIRONMENT (CNIE) 178
CONSERVATION DISTRICTS FOUNDATION INC. 182
NORTHCOAST ENVIRONMENTAL CENTER 284
WILDLIFE CONSERVATION SOCIETY 348

Litter

PENNSYLVANIA RESOURCES COUNCIL, INC., (formerly PA Roadside Council) 295
SAVE OUR RIVERS, INC. 309

Local Resource Conservation

BAMA BACKPADDLERS ASSOCIATION 159
COMMUNITY CONSERVATION CONSULTANTS/HOWLERS FOREVER, INC. 179
PACIFIC INSTITUTE FOR STUDIES IN DEVELOPMENT, ENVIRONMENT, AND SECURITY 293

Mammals

A. E. HOWELL WILDLIFE CONSERVATION CENTER 130
AMERICAN HORSE PROTECTION ASSOCIATION 145
AMERICAN SOCIETY OF MAMMALOGISTS 150
ANIMAL PROTECTION INSTITUTE 152
ANIMAL WELFARE INSTITUTE 152
AUDUBON SOCIETY OF WESTERN PENNSYLVANIA 159
BAT CONSERVATION INTERNATIONAL 160
BOUNTY INFORMATION SERVICE (WILDLIFE) 162
CANADIAN COOPERATIVE WILDLIFE HEALTH CENTRE .. 166
DEPARTMENT OF PLANNING AND NATURAL RESOURCES 112
ELSA WILD ANIMAL APPEAL 194
FEDERAL WILDLIFE OFFICER'S ASSOCIATION 199
FISH AND WILDLIFE INFORMATION EXCHANGE 201
FOUNDATION FOR NORTH AMERICAN BIG GAME 205
FRIENDS OF THE SEA OTTER 206
INTERNATIONAL MARINE MAMMAL PROJECT, THE 226
INTERNATIONAL PRIMATE PROTECTION LEAGUE 226
INTERNATIONAL WILDLIFE COALITION (IWC) AND THE WHALE ADOPTION PROJECT 230
INTERNATIONAL WOLF CENTER (Educational Services) ... 230
MASSACHUSETTS TRAPPER'S ASSOCIATION, INC. 248
MAX McGRAW WILDLIFE FOUNDATION 248
MICHIGAN NATURE ASSOCIATION 249
MOUNTAIN LION FOUNDATION 255
NATIONAL WILDLIFE REHABILITATORS ASSOCIATION ... 269
NATURAL HISTORY SOCIETY OF MARYLAND, INC., THE 270
NATURE SASKATCHEWAN 275
NEWFOUNDLAND LABRADOR WILDLIFE FEDERATION ... 279
PREDATOR PROJECT 299
SAVE THE MANATEE CLUB 310
SCIENTISTS CENTER FOR ANIMAL WELFARE 311
SMITHSONIAN INSTITUTION 317
SOCIETY FOR ANIMAL PROTECTIVE LEGISLATION 318
SOCIETY FOR INTEGRATIVE AND COMPARTIVE BIOLOGY (formerly AMERICAN SOCIETY OF ZOOLOGISTS) 318
TALLAHASSEE MUSEUM OF HISTORY AND NATURAL SCIENCE 327

TRAFFIC NORTH AMERICA 330
UTAH COOPERATIVE FISH AND WILDLIFE RESEARCH UNIT (USDI-USGS-BRD-CRU) 110
WELDER WILDLIFE FOUNDATION 343
WILD DOG FOUNDATION, THE 345
WILDLIFE CENTER OF VIRGINIA, THE 347
WILDLIFE DAMAGE REVIEW (WDR) 348
WILDLIFE FOREVER 348
WILDLIFE WAYSTATION 355
WORLD SOCIETY FOR THE PROTECTION OF ANIMALS (WSPA) 358
YELLOWSTONE GRIZZLY FOUNDATION (YGF) 360

Management Plans

ENVIRONMENTAL LAW AND POLICY CENTER OF THE MIDWEST 198
WESTERN PACIFIC REGIONAL FISHERY MANAGEMENT COUNCIL 344

Manatees

MOTE MARINE LABORATORY 255

Mangrove Habitats

CARIBBEAN NATURAL RESOURCES INSTITUTE 168
PUERTO RICO SEA GRANT PROGRAM 103
SEACAMP ASSOCIATION, INC. 312

Mapping

OKLAHOMA GEOLOGICAL SURVEY 96

Marine Conservation

COASTAL CONSERVATION ASSOCIATION GEORGIA 176
COUSTEAU SOCIETY, INC., THE 185
GEORGIA ENVIRONMENTAL POLICY INSTITUTE 209
NATIONAL AUDUBON SOCIETY, LIVING OCEANS PROGRAM 259
PEOPLE FOR PUGET SOUND 295
POULSBO MARINE SCIENCE CENTER 298, 391
RESOURCE CENTER FOR ENVIRONMENTAL EDUCATION, THE 304
SEACAMP ASSOCIATION, INC. 312

Marine Fisheries

MID-ATLANTIC FISHERY MANAGEMENT COUNCIL 250
SOUTH ATLANTIC FISHERY MANAGEMENT COUNCIL 321

Marine Mammals

ALASKA SEA GRANT COLLEGE PROGRAM 40
AMERICAN CETACEAN SOCIETY 138
AMERICAN SOCIETY OF MAMMALOGISTS 150
ANIMAL PROTECTION INSTITUTE 152
ANIMAL WELFARE INSTITUTE 152
CANADIAN FEDERATION OF HUMANE SOCIETIES 166
CASCADIA RESEARCH 168
CENTER FOR MARINE CONSERVATION 170
CETACEAN SOCIETY INTERNATIONAL 172
EARTH ISLAND INSTITUTE 191
EARTHTRUST 193
EUROPEAN ASSOCIATION FOR AQUATIC MAMMALS 199
EUROPEAN CETACEAN SOCIETY 199
FEDERAL WILDLIFE OFFICER'S ASSOCIATION 199
FRIENDS OF ANIMALS INC 205
FRIENDS OF THE SAN JUANS 206
FUND FOR ANIMALS INC., THE 207
HUMANE SOCIETY OF THE UNITED STATES, THE 217
INTERNATIONAL ECOLOGY SOCIETY (IES) 224
INTERNATIONAL MARINE MAMMAL PROJECT, THE 226
INTERNATIONAL OCEANOGRAPHIC FOUNDATION 226

INTERNATIONAL WILDLIFE COALITION (IWC) AND THE
  WHALE ADOPTION PROJECT 230
MAINE/NEW HAMPSHIRE SEA GRANT PROGRAM 83
MARINE ENVIRONMENTAL RESEARCH INSTITUTE (MERI)
  246
MARINE MAMMAL CENTER, THE 246
MID-ATLANTIC FISHERY MANAGEMENT COUNCIL 250
PACIFIC WHALE FOUNDATION 293
PUERTO RICO SEA GRANT PROGRAM 103
SAVE THE MANATEE CLUB 310
SCIENTISTS CENTER FOR ANIMAL WELFARE 311
SEA SHEPHERD CONSERVATION SOCIETY 311
SMITHSONIAN INSTITUTION 317
SOCIETY FOR ANIMAL PROTECTIVE LEGISLATION 318
SOCIETY FOR MARINE MAMMALOGY, THE 318
WHALE AND DOLPHIN CONSERVATION SOCIETY 345
WORLD SOCIETY FOR THE PROTECTION OF ANIMALS
  (WSPA) 358

Marine Protected Areas

AMERICAN OCEANS CAMPAIGN 147
MARINE CONSERVATION BIOLOGY INSTITUTE 246
PEOPLE FOR PUGET SOUND 295

Migration

BILLFISH FOUNDATION, THE 160
HAWK MOUNTAIN SANCTUARY ASSOCIATION 215

Mineral Resources

ARIZONA GEOLOGICAL SURVEY 41
INDIANA GEOLOGICAL SURVEY 63
MINERAL POLICY CENTER 250
WYOMING STATE GEOLOGICAL SURVEY 123

Mining

ATLANTIC STATES LEGAL FOUNDATION 157
CENTER FOR BIOLOGICAL DIVERSITY 169
DESERT TORTOISE COUNCIL 188
MICHIGAN DEPARTMENT OF ENVIRONMENTAL QUALITY 75
MINERAL POLICY CENTER 250
MONTANA ENVIRONMENTAL INFORMATION CENTER 254
NORTH CASCADES CONSERVATION COUNCIL 283
NORTHERN PLAINS RESOURCE COUNCIL 285
POWDER RIVER BASIN RESOURCE COUNCIL 298
RESOURCES FOR THE FUTURE 304
SOUTH DAKOTA DEPARTMENT OF ENVIRONMENT AND
  NATURAL RESOURCES 106
SOUTHWEST RESEARCH AND INFORMATION CENTER . 324
WEST VIRGINIA HIGHLANDS CONSERVANCY 343
WESTERN ENVIRONMENTAL LAW CENTER 344

Mountain Ecosystems

GREAT OUTDOORS CONSERVANCY, THE 212
HAWK MOUNTAIN SANCTUARY ASSOCIATION 215

Museums

AMERICAN CAVE CONSERVATION ASSOCIATION 138
CALIFORNIA ACADEMY OF SCIENCES 163
CLEVELAND MUSEUM OF NATURAL HISTORY, THE 175
CONSERVANCY OF SOUTHWEST FLORIDA, THE 181
DELAWARE MUSEUM OF NATURAL HISTORY 187
FOREST FIRE LOOKOUT ASSOCIATION 203
GEORGIA TRUST FOR HISTORIC PRESERVATION 210
NEW YORK GEOLOGICAL SURVEY AND STATE MUSEUM 90
SAFARI CLUB INTERNATIONAL 308
TALLAHASSEE MUSEUM OF HISTORY AND NATURAL
  SCIENCE 327
VIRGINIA MUSEUM OF NATURAL HISTORY 115
WORLD FORESTRY CENTER 358

Mussels

UPPER MISSISSIPPI RIVER CONSERVATION COMMITTEE
  337

NAFTA Superhighway

FOSSIL FUELS POLICY ACTION INSTITUTE/ALLIANCE FOR
  A PAVING MORATORIUM 204

National Forests

FOREST WATCH 204
SAVE AMERICA'S FORESTS 309
SOUTHERN APPALACHIAN BOTANICAL SOCIETY 323

National Parks

BIG BEND NATURAL HISTORY ASSOCIATION 160
CANADIAN PARKS AND WILDERNESS SOCIETY 167
ECODEFENSE 193
GRAND CANYON TRUST 211
GREAT SMOKY MOUNTAINS INSTITUTE AT TREMONT ... 212
HIMALAYAN WILDLIFE FOUNDATION 216
NATIONAL PARK FOUNDATION 263
NATIONAL PARK TRUST 263
NATIONAL PARKS AND CONSERVATION ASSOCIATION
  (NPCA) 263
OLYMPIC PARK ASSOCIATES 289
OLYMPIC PARK INSTITUTE 289
RINCON INSTITUTE, THE 305
YOSEMITE RESTORATION TRUST 361

Native Fish

DESERT FISHES COUNCIL 188
OREGON TROUT, INC. 291
PACIFIC RIVERS COUNCIL 293

Native Plants

ABUNDANT LIFE SEED FOUNDATION 130
ADKINS ARBORETUM 131
ALABAMA WILDFLOWER SOCIETY, THE 133
ALDO LEOPOLD FOUNDATION, INC. 135
CALIFORNIA NATIVE PLANT SOCIETY, THE 164
COASTAL GEORGIA LAND TRUST, THE 176
DESERT RESEARCH FOUNDATION OF NAMIBIA, THE ... 188
FLORIDA NATIVE PLANT SOCIETY 202
GREAT PLAINS NATIVE PLANT SOCIETY 212
ILLINOIS NATIVE PLANT SOCIETY 219
ILLINOIS NATURAL HERITAGE FOUNDATION 219
IOWA NATIVE PLANT SOCIETY 232
KANSAS WILDFLOWER SOCIETY 238
MINNESOTA NATIVE PLANT SOCIETY 251
MISSISSIPPI NATIVE PLANT SOCIETY 252
MISSOURI NATIVE PLANT SOCIETY 253
MISSOURI PRAIRIE FOUNDATION 253
NATIVE PLANT SOCIETY OF NORTHEASTERN OHIO 269
NATIVE PLANT SOCIETY OF OREGON 269
NATIVE PLANT SOCIETY OF TEXAS 270
NEW ENGLAND WILD FLOWER SOCIETY, INC 276
NORTH CAROLINA WILD FLOWER PRESERVATION
  SOCIETY 283
OHIO NATIVE PLANT SOCIETY 288
OKLAHOMA NATIVE PLANT SOCIETY 289
OLYMPIC PARK ASSOCIATES 289
RHODE ISLAND WILD PLANT SOCIETY 305
SOUTH CAROLINA NATIVE PLANT SOCIETY 321
SOUTHERN APPALACHIAN BOTANICAL SOCIETY 323
STATE PLANT BOARD (ARKANSAS) 44
VIRGINIA NATIVE PLANT SOCIETY 340
WASHINGTON NATIVE PLANT SOCIETY 341
WATERLOO-WELLINGTON WILDFLOWER SOCIETY
  (Formerly the Dogtooth Group) 342
WILD ONES - NATURAL LANDSCAPERS, LTD 346
WILDFLOWER ASSOCIATION OF MICHIGAN 347

KEYWORD INDEX - Natural Areas

WYOMING NATIVE PLANT SOCIETY 360

Natural Areas

ADIRONDACK MOUNTAIN CLUB, INC., THE 131
ALABAMA NATURAL HERITAGE PROGRAM 132
ARIZONA STATE PARKS BOARD 42
AUDUBON COUNCIL OF CONNECTICUT 158
BIG BEND NATURAL HISTORY ASSOCIATION 160
COASTAL GEORGIA LAND TRUST, THE 176
COLUMBIA RIVER GORGE COMMISSION 116
CONFERENCE OF NATIONAL PARK COOPERATING
    ASSOCIATIONS 180
DELAWARE NATURE SOCIETY 187
DESERT FISHES COUNCIL 188
EASTERN SHORE LAND CONSERVANCY 193
FAIRFAX AUDUBON SOCIETY 199
FEDERATION OF ONTARIO NATURALISTS 200
FLORIDA EXOTIC PEST PLANT COUNCIL 202
FLORIDA NATIVE PLANT SOCIETY 202
FLORIDA TRAIL ASSOCIATION, INC. 203
FOREST WATCH 204
GALIANO CONSERVANCY ASSOCIATION 207
GEORGIA ENVIRONMENTAL POLICY INSTITUTE 209
HAWAII AUDUBON SOCIETY 214
IDAHO FISH AND WILDLIFE FOUNDATION 60
ILLINOIS NATIVE PLANT SOCIETY 219
INTERNATIONAL ASSOCIATION OF NATURAL RESOURCE
    PILOTS 223
IOWA DEPARTMENT OF NATURAL RESOURCES 64
IOWA NATURAL HERITAGE FOUNDATION 232
IZAAK WALTON LEAGUE OF AMERICA ENDOWMENT 234
IZAAK WALTON LEAGUE OF AMERICA, INC., THE 234
LAND BETWEEN THE LAKES ASSOCIATION 240
MAINE COAST HERITAGE TRUST 245
MANOMET CENTER FOR CONSERVATION SCIENCES ... 245
MAX McGRAW WILDLIFE FOUNDATION 248
MICHIGAN NATURE ASSOCIATION 249
MISSOURI NATIVE PLANT SOCIETY 253
MONTANA LAND RELIANCE 254
NATURAL AREAS ASSOCIATION 270
NATURAL HERITAGE COMMISSION (ARKANSAS) 44
NATURAL LAND INSTITUTE 270
NATURE SASKATCHEWAN 275
NEW JERSEY CONSERVATION FOUNDATION 278
NEW YORK-NEW JERSEY TRAIL CONFERENCE INC. 279
NORTH CASCADES CONSERVATION COUNCIL 283
NORTHERN ALASKA ENVIRONMENTAL CENTER 285
OKLAHOMA NATIVE PLANT SOCIETY 289
OREGON NATURAL RESOURCES COUNCIL 290
OREGON PARKS AND RECREATION DEPARTMENT 98
OUTDOOR CIRCLE, THE 291
OZARK SOCIETY, THE 292
PARTNERS IN PARKS 293
PENNSYLVANIA DEPARTMENT OF CONSERVATION AND
    NATURAL RESOURCES 100
PUERTO RICO SEA GRANT PROGRAM 103
RINCON INSTITUTE, THE 305
SCENIC AMERICA 310
SOUTH CAROLINA DEPARTMENT OF NATURAL
    RESOURCES 105
SOUTHERN ENVIRONMENTAL LAW CENTER 324
TALLAHASSEE MUSEUM OF HISTORY AND NATURAL
    SCIENCE 327
TENNESSEE CITIZENS FOR WILDERNESS PLANNING 328
TUG HILL TOMORROW LAND TRUST 335
UTAH B.A.S.S. CHAPTER FEDERATION 337
VIRGINIA FORESTRY ASSOCIATION 340
VIRGINIA NATIVE PLANT SOCIETY 340
WASHINGTON TRAILS ASSOCIATION 341
WILD ONES - NATURAL LANDSCAPERS, LTD 346
WILDFLOWER ASSOCIATION OF MICHIGAN 347
WYOMING NATIVE PLANT SOCIETY 360

Natural History

ADIRONDACK MOUNTAIN CLUB, INC., THE 131
ALABAMA NATURAL HERITAGE PROGRAM 132
ALASKA NATURAL HISTORY ASSOCIATION 134
ALASKA NATURAL RESOURCE AND OUTDOOR
    EDUCATION ASSOCIATION 134
AMERICAN ASSOCIATION OF ZOO KEEPERS, INC. 137
AMERICAN BASS ASSOCIATION OF WEST VIRGINIA, THE
    138
AMERICAN MUSEUM OF NATURAL HISTORY 147
AMERICAN NATURE STUDY SOCIETY 147
AMERICAN SOCIETY FOR ENVIRONMENTAL HISTORY .. 149
AUDUBON NATURALIST SOCIETY OF THE CENTRAL
    ATLANTIC STATES 158
AUDUBON SOCIETY OF MISSOURI 158
AUDUBON SOCIETY OF PORTLAND 159
AUDUBON SOCIETY OF WESTERN PENNSYLVANIA 159
CALIFORNIA ACADEMY OF SCIENCES 163
CHIHUAHUAN DESERT RESEARCH INSTITUTE 173
CINCINNATI NATURE CENTER 174
COASTAL GEORGIA LAND TRUST, THE 176
CORNELL LAB OF ORNITHOLOGY 184
DELAWARE MUSEUM OF NATURAL HISTORY 187
ENVIRONMENT COUNCIL OF RHODE ISLAND 195
ENVIRONMENTAL RESOURCE CENTER (ERC) 198
ENVIROSOUTH, INC. 199
EUROPEAN CETACEAN SOCIETY 199
FEDERATION OF ALBERTA NATURALISTS 200
FLORIDA ORNITHOLOGICAL SOCIETY 202
GLACIER INSTITUTE, THE 210
GREAT SMOKY MOUNTAINS INSTITUTE AT TREMONT ... 212
GREEN MOUNTAIN CLUB INC., THE 213
HAWAII NATURE CENTER 214
HEADLANDS INSTITUTE 215
HIGH DESERT MUSEUM, THE 216
HOLDEN ARBORETUM, THE 216
HUMBOLT FIELD RESEARCH INSTITUTE 217
INTERNATIONAL WILDLIFE REHABILITATION COUNCIL
    (IWRC) 230
KANSAS ACADEMY OF SCIENCE 237
KANSAS HERPETOLOGICAL SOCIETY 237
MAINE AUDUBON SOCIETY 244
MAINE ENVIRONMENTAL EDUCATION ASSOCIATION, INC.
    245
MANITOBA NATURALISTS SOCIETY 245
MARYLAND ORNITHOLOGICAL SOCIETY, INC. 247
MASSACHUSETTS AUDUBON SOCIETY, INC. 247
MATTS (MID-ATLANTIC TURTLE AND TORTOISE SOCIETY,
    INC.) 248
MICHIGAN NATURE ASSOCIATION 249
MISSISSIPPI NATIVE PLANT SOCIETY 252
MISSOURI NATIVE PLANT SOCIETY 253
NATIONAL ASSOCIATION FOR INTERPRETATION 256
NATIONAL GEOGRAPHIC SOCIETY 262
NATURAL HISTORY SOCIETY OF MARYLAND, INC., THE 270
NATURAL RESOURCES INFORMATION COUNCIL 271
NATURAL SCIENCE FOR YOUTH FOUNDATION 271
NATURE SASKATCHEWAN 275
NEW ENGLAND WILD FLOWER SOCIETY, INC. 276
NEW JERSEY AUDUBON SOCIETY 277
NEW MEXICO BUREAU OF MINES AND MINERAL
    RESOURCES 86
NORTH DAKOTA NATURAL SCIENCE SOCIETY 284
NORTHWEST INTERPRETIVE ASSOCIATION 286
OHIO BIOLOGICAL SURVEY 287
OKLAHOMA ACADEMY OF SCIENCE 288
PENNSYLVANIA AUDUBON SOCIETY 294
PENNSYLVANIA RESOURCES COUNCIL, INC., (formerly PA
    Roadside Council) 295
ROGER TORY PETERSON INSTITUTE 307
SCENIC AMERICA 310
SCENIC HUDSON, INC. 311
SMITHSONIAN INSTITUTION 317
SOCIETY FOR MARINE MAMMALOGY, THE 318
SOUTH DAKOTA B.A.S.S. CHAPTER FEDERATION 322
SOUTHEASTERN FISHES COUNCIL 323
SOUTHERN APPALACHIAN BOTANICAL SOCIETY 323
TALLAHASSEE MUSEUM OF HISTORY AND NATURAL
    SCIENCE 327
TRUST FOR WILDLIFE, INC. 335
VERMONT B.A.S.S. CHAPTER FEDERATION 338
WASHINGTON FARM FORESTRY ASSOCIATION 341
WILSON ORNITHOLOGICAL SOCIETY 355

WISCONSIN GEOLOGICAL AND NATURAL HISTORY
    SURVEY 121
WORLD FORESTRY CENTER 358
WYOMING NATIVE PLANT SOCIETY 360

Natural Resource Conservation

ACADEMY FOR EDUCATIONAL DEVELOPMENT 130
ALASKA CENTER FOR THE ENVIRONMENT 133
ALASKA NATURAL HISTORY ASSOCIATION 134
CATSKILL CENTER FOR CONSERVATION AND
    DEVELOPMENT, INC., THE 168
ENVIRONMENTAL LAW INSTITUTE, THE 198
KEYSTONE CENTER, THE 239
NATIONAL COUNCIL OF STATE GARDEN CLUBS, INC 260
NATIONAL NETWORK OF FOREST PRACTITIONERS 263
NEBRASKA ASSOCIATION OF RESOURCE DISTRICTS 275
REP AMERICA/REPUBLICANS FOR ENVIRONMENTAL
    PROTECTION 304
SOUTH CAROLINA ENVIRONMENTAL LAW PROJECT 321
WEST VIRGINIA HIGHLANDS CONSERVANCY 343
ZUNGAROCOCHA RESEARCH CENTER 361

Natural Science

NATURAL RESOURCES INFORMATION COUNCIL 271
THORNE ECOLOGICAL INSTITUTE 329

Natural Systems

SHELBURNE FARMS 312
SOUTHWEST FLORIDA WATER MANAGEMENT DISTRICT
    (SWFWMD) 55

Nature Centers

CINCINNATI NATURE CENTER 174
CONSERVANCY OF SOUTHWEST FLORIDA, THE 181
GREEN MOUNTAIN AUDUBON SOCIETY 213
HAWAII NATURE CENTER 214
IDAHO FISH AND WILDLIFE FOUNDATION 60
JACK MINER MIGRATORY BIRD FOUNDATION, INC. 236
POULSBO MARINE SCIENCE CENTER 298, 391
WILDLANDS CONSERVANCY 347

Nature Preservation

ADOPT-A-STREAM FOUNDATION, THE 131
ALABAMA NATURAL HERITAGE PROGRAM 132
ALASKA AUDUBON SOCIETY 133
ALBERTA WILDERNESS ASSOCIATION 135
AUDUBON NATURALIST SOCIETY OF THE CENTRAL
    ATLANTIC STATES 158
BIG BEND NATURAL HISTORY ASSOCIATION 160
BIRDLIFE INTERNATIONAL 161
BOTANICAL CLUB OF WISCONSIN 162
BROOKS BIRD CLUB INC., THE 163
CALIFORNIA ACADEMY OF SCIENCES 163
CALIFORNIA WILDLIFE DEFENDERS 164
CHESAPEAKE BAY FOUNDATION, INC. (Virginia Office) 173
COALITION FOR EDUCATION IN THE OUTDOORS 175
COASTAL GEORGIA LAND TRUST, THE 176
CONNECTICUT BOTANICAL SOCIETY 180
DEFENDERS OF WILDLIFE 186
DEPARTMENT OF PARKS AND RECREATION (GUAM) 57
DESERT TORTOISE COUNCIL 188
EASTERN SHORE LAND CONSERVANCY 193
FEDERATION OF ALBERTA NATURALISTS 200
GENERAL FEDERATION OF WOMEN'S CLUBS 208
GEORGE MIKSCH SUTTON AVIAN RESEARCH CENTER
    INC. 208
ILLINOIS NATURE PRESERVES COMMISSION (INPC) 62
INDIANA NATIVE PLANT AND WILDFLOWER SOCIETY 220
INTERNATIONAL MARINE MAMMAL PROJECT, THE 226
IOWA NATURAL HERITAGE FOUNDATION 232
IOWA TRAILS COUNCIL 232
KIDS FOR SAVING EARTH WORLDWIDE 239

LEE COUNTY PARKS AND RECREATION SERVICES 54
MAX McGRAW WILDLIFE FOUNDATION 248
MICHIGAN NATURAL AREAS COUNCIL 249
MICHIGAN NATURE ASSOCIATION 249
MINNESOTA HERPETOLOGICAL SOCIETY (James Ford Bell
    Museum of Natural History) 251
MISSOURI NATIVE PLANT SOCIETY 253
MONTANA LAND RELIANCE 254
MOUNT GRACE LAND CONSERVATION TRUST 255
NATIONAL PARK FOUNDATION 263
NATURAL AREAS ASSOCIATION 270
NEVIS HISTORICAL AND CONSERVATION SOCIETY 276
NEW JERSEY CONSERVATION FOUNDATION 278
NORTH CASCADES CONSERVATION COUNCIL 283
NORTH DAKOTA PARKS AND RECREATION DEPARTMENT
    93
NORTHWEST ECOSYSTEM ALLIANCE 285
OFFICE OF STATE PARKS, DEPARTMENT OF CULTURE,
    RECREATION, AND TOURISM 69
OHIO BIOLOGICAL SURVEY 287
OKLAHOMA TOURISM AND RECREATION DEPARTMENT . 96
PARTNERS IN PARKS 293
RHODE ISLAND STATE ASSOCIATION OF CONSERVATION
    DISTRICTS 305
SIERRA NEVADA FOREST PROTECTION CAMPAIGN 317
STATE PARKS AND RECREATION COMMISSION
    (WASHINGTON) 116
TRUST FOR WILDLIFE, INC. 335
TRUSTEES OF RESERVATIONS, THE 335
UTAH B.A.S.S. CHAPTER FEDERATION 337
WASHINGTON WILDLIFE AND RECREATION COALITION 342
WATERLOO-WELLINGTON WILDFLOWER SOCIETY
    (Formerly the Dogtooth Group) 342
WHITE CLAY WATERSHED ASSOCIATION 345
WILD ONES - NATURAL LANDSCAPERS, LTD 346
WOLF EDUCATION AND RESEARCH CENTER 357
WYOMING DEPARTMENT OF COMMERCE 122
YOSEMITE RESTORATION TRUST 361

Nature Study

DESERT RESEARCH FOUNDATION OF NAMIBIA, THE 188
INDIAN CREEK NATURE CENTER 219
PENNSYLVANIA RESOURCES COUNCIL, INC., (formerly PA
    Roadside Council) 295
ROGER TORY PETERSON INSTITUTE 307
SEACAMP ASSOCIATION, INC. 312
STUDENTS PARTNERSHIP WORLDWIDE 327

Navigation

MISSISSIPPI RIVER BASIN ALLIANCE 252

Networking

ECODEFENSE 193
INSTITUTE FOR CIVIC INITIATIVES SUPPORT 221
LEARNING FOR ENVIRONMENTAL ACTION PROGRAMME
    (LEAP) 242
NEW ENGLAND COALITION FOR SUSTAINABLE
    POPULATION (NECSP) 276
NORTH AMERICAN ASSOCIATION FOR ENVIRONMENTAL
    EDUCATION 280
RESOURCE CENTER FOR ENVIRONMENTAL EDUCATION,
    THE 304

Noise

MASSACHUSETTS HIGHWAY DEPARTMENT 74

Nongame Wildlife

ADIRONDACK MOUNTAIN CLUB, INC., THE 131
ADOPT-A-STREAM FOUNDATION, THE 131
AMERICAN SOCIETY OF MAMMALOGISTS 150
ANIMAL PROTECTION INSTITUTE 152
ARIZONA GAME AND FISH DEPARTMENT 41

ARIZONA STATE PARKS BOARD 42
AUDUBON INTERNATIONAL 158
BAT CONSERVATION INTERNATIONAL 160
BIODIVERSITY LEGAL FOUNDATION 161
CALIFORNIA WILDLIFE DEFENDERS 164
CASCADIA RESEARCH 168
COLORADO COOPERATIVE FISH AND WILDLIFE
    RESEARCH UNIT (USDI) 49
CORNELL LAB OF ORNITHOLOGY 184
DEPARTMENT OF INTERIOR, U.S.G.S/B.R.D, SOUTH
    CAROLINA COOPERATIVE FISH AND WILDLIFE
    RESEARCH UNIT 104
DESERT TORTOISE PRESERVE COMMITTEE, INC. 188
FAIRFAX AUDUBON SOCIETY 199
FEDERAL WILDLIFE OFFICER'S ASSOCIATION 199
FISH AND WILDLIFE INFORMATION EXCHANGE 201
FISH AND WILDLIFE REFERENCE SERVICE 201, 409
FLORIDA ORNITHOLOGICAL SOCIETY 202
FLORIDA PANTHER PROJECT, INC., THE 202
FRIENDS OF DISCOVERY PARK 205
GEORGE MIKSCH SUTTON AVIAN RESEARCH CENTER
    INC. 208
GOPHER TORTOISE COUNCIL 211
HAWAII AUDUBON SOCIETY 214
HAWK MOUNTAIN SANCTUARY ASSOCIATION 215
INTERNATIONAL ASSOCIATION OF NATURAL RESOURCE
    PILOTS 223
INTERNATIONAL OSPREY FOUNDATION INC., THE 226
KANSAS HERPETOLOGICAL SOCIETY 237
LOUISIANA AUDUBON COUNCIL 243
MANOMET CENTER FOR CONSERVATION SCIENCES 245
MAX McGRAW WILDLIFE FOUNDATION 248
MICHIGAN NATURE ASSOCIATION 249
MINNESOTA COOPERATIVE FISH AND WILDLIFE
    RESEARCH UNIT 76
MINNESOTA HERPETOLOGICAL SOCIETY (James Ford Bell
    Museum of Natural History) 251
MINNESOTA ORNITHOLOGISTS' UNION 251
MISSISSIPPI COOPERATIVE FISH AND WILDLIFE
    RESEARCH UNIT (USDI) 77
MONTANA COOPERATIVE WILDLIFE RESEARCH UNIT
    (USGS/BRD) 80
MOUNTAIN LION FOUNDATION 255
NATURAL AREAS ASSOCIATION 270
NEW HAMPSHIRE FISH AND GAME DEPARTMENT 84
NEW YORK TURTLE AND TORTOISE SOCIETY 279
NEWFOUNDLAND LABRADOR WILDLIFE FEDERATION ... 279
NORTH AMERICAN LOON FUND 281
NORTH AMERICAN NATIVE FISHES ASSOCIATION 281
NORTH CAROLINA WILDLIFE RESOURCES COMMISSION 92
NORTH DAKOTA GAME AND FISH DEPARTMENT 93
NORTH DAKOTA NATURAL SCIENCE SOCIETY 284
NORTHEAST WILDLIFE ADMINISTRATORS ASSOCIATION
    284
OKLAHOMA BIOLOGICAL SURVEY 95
OKLAHOMA COOPERATIVE FISH AND WILDLIFE
    RESEARCH UNIT (USDI) 95
OKLAHOMA TOURISM AND RECREATION DEPARTMENT . 96
OREGON COOPERATIVE FISH AND WILDLIFE RESEARCH
    UNIT (USDI) 97
PREDATOR PROJECT 299
PURPLE MARTIN CONSERVATION ASSOCIATION 301
RAPTOR RESEARCH FOUNDATION, INC. 303
SCIENTISTS CENTER FOR ANIMAL WELFARE 311
TALLAHASSEE MUSEUM OF HISTORY AND NATURAL
    SCIENCE 327
TENNESSEE CITIZENS FOR WILDERNESS PLANNING ... 328
TRUMPETER SWAN SOCIETY, THE 334
UTAH B.A.S.S. CHAPTER FEDERATION 337
UTAH COOPERATIVE FISH AND WILDLIFE RESEARCH UNIT
    (USDI-USGS-BRD-CRU) 110
VERMONT AUDUBON COUNCIL 338
WEST VIRGINIA COOPERATIVE FISH AND WILDLIFE
    RESEARCH UNIT 119
WEST VIRGINIA DIVISION OF NATURAL RESOURCES 119
WILD HORSE ORGANIZED ASSISTANCE, INC. (WHOA) ... 346
WILDLIFE CENTER OF VIRGINIA, THE 347
WILDLIFE FOREVER 348
WILDLIFE RESOURCES AGENCY 107
WILDLIFE SOCIETY, THE 350
WOLF EDUCATION AND RESEARCH CENTER 357
WORLD SOCIETY FOR THE PROTECTION OF ANIMALS
    (WSPA) 358
WYOMING COOPERATIVE FISH AND WILDLIFE RESEARCH
    UNIT (USDI) 122
WYOMING GAME AND FISH DEPARTMENT 123

Nonpoint Source Pollution

CENTER FOR CHESAPEAKE COMMUNITIES 169
CLEAN OCEAN ACTION 174
FRIENDS OF THE REEDY RIVER 206
MISSISSIPPI SOIL AND WATER CONSERVATION
    COMMISSION 78
NATIONAL WATER RESOURCES ASSOCIATION 266
OKLAHOMA STATE CONSERVATION COMMISSION 96
SOUTH CAROLINA COASTAL CONSERVATION LEAGUE 321
WATERSHED MANAGEMENT COUNCIL 343

North Atlantic Salmon

NORTH ATLANTIC SALMON CONSERVATION
    ORGANIZATION 282

Nuclear Abolition

PHYSICIANS FOR SOCIAL RESPONSIBILITY 296

Nuclear Energy

ECODEFENSE 193
SAFE ENERGY COMMUNICATION COUNCIL 308
UNION OF CONCERNED SCIENTISTS 336

Nuclear/Radiation

AGENCY OF NATURAL RESOURCES 111
CONSERVATION COUNCIL OF NORTH CAROLINA 181
GREEN PARTY USA 213
GREENPEACE, INC. 213
INDIANA STATE DEPARTMENT OF HEALTH 63
MANASOTA-88 245
PHYSICIANS FOR SOCIAL RESPONSIBILITY 296
SEACOAST ANTI-POLLUTION LEAGUE 312
STUDENT PUGWASH USA 326
TEXAS DEPARTMENT OF HEALTH 108

Ocean Conservation

AMERICAN SOCIETY OF LIMNOLOGY AND
    OCEANOGRAPHY 150
NATIONAL AUDUBON SOCIETY, LIVING OCEANS
    PROGRAM 259
OREGON PARKS AND RECREATION DEPARTMENT 98
SEACAMP ASSOCIATION, INC. 312

Oceanography

ALASKA SEA GRANT COLLEGE PROGRAM 40
FRIENDS OF THE SAN JUANS 206
GEORGIA SEA GRANT COLLEGE PROGRAM 56
HAWAII COOPERATIVE FISHERY RESEARCH UNIT (USDI) 58
HUNTSMAN MARINE SCIENCE CENTRE 217
INTERNATIONAL OCEANOGRAPHIC FOUNDATION 226
MAINE SEA GRANT PROGRAM 71
MAINE/NEW HAMPSHIRE SEA GRANT PROGRAM 83
MARINE LABORATORY (FLORIDA) 55
MARINE TECHNOLOGY SOCIETY 246
MARYLAND SEA GRANT COLLEGE 72
NATIONAL GEOGRAPHIC SOCIETY 262
NORTH CAROLINA SEA GRANT PROGRAM 92
NORTHWEST ATLANTIC FISHERIES ORGANIZATION
    (NAFO) 285
OREGON SEA GRANT PROGRAM 98
POULSBO MARINE SCIENCE CENTER 298, 391
PUERTO RICO SEA GRANT PROGRAM 103

Oil and Gas

MONTANA DEPARTMENT OF NATURAL RESOURCES AND CONSERVATION ... 81

Oil Spill Response

PEOPLE FOR PUGET SOUND ... 295
TRI-STATE BIRD RESCUE AND RESEARCH, INC. ... 331

Open Space

RESOURCES AGENCY, THE ... 46
SOUTH CAROLINA SEA GRANT CONSORTIUM ... 106
WASHINGTON SEA GRANT PROGRAM ... 118
WATER RESOURCES RESEARCH CENTER ... 59
WOODS HOLE OCEANOGRAPHIC INSITITUTION (WHOI) SEA GRANT PROGRAM ... 74

ADIRONDACK COUNCIL, THE ... 131
ADIRONDACK NATURE CONSERVANCY/ADIRONDACK LAND TRUST, INC. ... 131
ADOPT-A-STREAM FOUNDATION, THE ... 131
AMERICAN SOCIETY OF LANDSCAPE ARCHITECTS ... 150
ASSOCIATION OF NEW JERSEY ENVIRONMENTAL COMMISSIONS ... 157
AUDUBON SOCIETY OF RHODE ISLAND ... 159
CALIFORNIANS FOR POPULATION STABILIZATION (CAPS) ... 165
COASTAL GEORGIA LAND TRUST, THE ... 176
COMMUNITY RIGHTS COUNSEL ... 179
CONNECTICUT AUDUBON SOCIETY, INC. ... 180
CONNECTICUT FUND FOR THE ENVIRONMENT ... 180
EASTERN SHORE LAND CONSERVANCY ... 193
FRIENDS OF DISCOVERY PARK ... 205
GEORGIA CONSERVANCY, INC., THE ... 209
GLOBAL CITIES PROJECT, THE ... 210
GREAT OUTDOORS CONSERVANCY, THE ... 212
JACKSON HOLE CONSERVATION ALLIANCE ... 236
JACKSON HOLE LAND TRUST ... 236
MAINE COAST HERITAGE TRUST ... 245
MONTANA LAND RELIANCE ... 254
MOUNT GRACE LAND CONSERVATION TRUST ... 255
NATIONAL ASSOCIATION OF RECREATION RESOURCE PLANNERS ... 257
NEW HAMPSHIRE LAKES ASSOCIATION ... 277
NEW JERSEY CONSERVATION FOUNDATION ... 278
NEW YORK-NEW JERSEY TRAIL CONFERENCE INC. ... 279
NORTH CAROLINA RECREATION AND PARK SOCIETY, INC. ... 283
OUTDOOR CIRCLE, THE ... 291
ROCKY MOUNTAIN ELK FOUNDATION ... 307
SCENIC HUDSON, INC. ... 311
SOUTHERN ENVIRONMENTAL LAW CENTER ... 324
STATE PARKS AND RECREATION COMMISSION (WASHINGTON) ... 116
TRUST FOR PUBLIC LAND, THE ... 334
TRUSTEES OF RESERVATIONS, THE ... 335
TUG HILL TOMORROW LAND TRUST ... 335
URBAN WILDLIFE RESOURCES ... 337
VIRGINIA OUTDOORS FOUNDATION ... 115
WASHINGTON TRAILS ASSOCIATION ... 341

Open Spaces

GEORGIA TRUST FOR HISTORIC PRESERVATION ... 210
UNIVERSITY OF NEW HAMPSHIRE COOPERATIVE EXTENSION ... 84

Otters

FRIENDS OF THE SEA OTTER ... 206
RIVER OTTER ALLIANCE, THE ... 306

Outdoor Education

COALITION FOR EDUCATION IN THE OUTDOORS ... 175
GREAT OUTDOORS CONSERVANCY, THE ... 212
LVIV REGIONAL INSTITUTE OF EDUCATION ... 244
PITTSBURGH HERPETOLOGICAL SOCIETY, THE ... 296
SEACAMP ASSOCIATION, INC. ... 312
STROUD WATER RESEARCH CENTER ... 326
WILDFLOWER ASSOCIATION OF MICHIGAN ... 347

Outdoor Ethics

IZAAK WALTON LEAGUE OF AMERICA, INC., THE ... 234

Outdoor Recreation

ADIRONDACK MOUNTAIN CLUB, INC., THE ... 131
AMERICAN ASSOCIATION FOR LEISURE AND RECREATION (AALR) ... 136
AMERICAN BASS ASSOCIATION OF WEST VIRGINIA, THE ... 138
AMERICAN BIRDING ASSOCIATION ... 138
AMERICAN CAMPING ASSOCIATION, INC. ... 138
AMERICAN CONSERVATION ASSOCIATION, INC. ... 139
AMERICAN FORESTS (formerly American Forestry Association) ... 144
AMERICAN HIKING SOCIETY ... 145
AMERICAN LEAGUE OF ANGLERS AND BOATERS ... 146
AMERICAN NATURE STUDY SOCIETY ... 147
APPALACHIAN MOUNTAIN CLUB ... 153
APPALACHIAN TRAIL CONFERENCE ... 153
ARCHERY MANUFACTURERS AND MERCHANTS ORGANIZATION (AMO) ... 154
ARIZONA STATE PARKS BOARD ... 42
ARKANSAS DEPARTMENT OF PARKS AND TOURISM ... 42
ASSOCIATION OF CONSERVATION ENGINEERS ... 156
ASSOCIATION OF MIDWEST FISH AND GAME LAW ENFORCEMENT OFFICERS ... 156
AUDUBON SOCIETY OF PORTLAND ... 159
BAMA BACKPADDLERS ASSOCIATION ... 159
BOY SCOUTS OF AMERICA ... 162
CALIFORNIA TROUT, INC. ... 164
CAMP FIRE BOYS AND GIRLS ... 165
CANADIAN NATIONAL SPORTSMEN'S SHOWS ... 167
COALITION FOR EDUCATION IN THE OUTDOORS ... 175
COLORADO DEPARTMENT OF NATURAL RESOURCES ... 49
COLORADO STATE UNIVERSITY COOPERATIVE EXTENSION ... 50
COLUMBIA RIVER GORGE COMMISSION ... 116
CONFERENCE OF NATIONAL PARK COOPERATING ASSOCIATIONS ... 180
DEPARTMENT OF PARKS AND RECREATION (GUAM) ... 57
ECOTOURISM SOCIETY, THE ... 194
ENERGY, MINERALS, AND NATURAL RESOURCES DEPARTMENT ... 86
EVERGLADES COORDINATING COUNCIL (ECC) ... 199
FEDERATION OF WESTERN OUTDOOR CLUBS ... 200
FISHAMERICA FOUNDATION ... 201
FLORIDA FISH AND WILDLIFE CONSERVATION COMMISSION ... 54
FLORIDA SPORTSMEN'S CONSERVATION ASSOCIATION ... 202
FLORIDA TRAIL ASSOCIATION, INC. ... 203
FRIENDS OF ACADIA ... 205
FRIENDS OF THE RIVER ... 206
FUTURE FISHERMAN FOUNDATION ... 207
GIRL SCOUTS OF THE UNITED STATES OF AMERICA ... 210
GREEN MOUNTAIN CLUB INC., THE ... 213
IDAHO DEPARTMENT OF PARKS AND RECREATION ... 60
ILLINOIS PRAIRIE PATH ... 219
INDIANA DEPARTMENT OF NATURAL RESOURCES ... 62
INTERAGENCY COMMITTEE FOR OUTDOOR RECREATION (IAC) ... 116
INTERNATIONAL HUNTER EDUCATION ASSOCIATION ... 225
INTERNATIONAL OCEANOGRAPHIC FOUNDATION ... 226
IOWA NATURAL HERITAGE FOUNDATION ... 232
IOWA TRAILS COUNCIL ... 232
IOWA TRAPPERS ASSOCIATION, INC. ... 232
IZAAK WALTON LEAGUE OF AMERICA ENDOWMENT ... 234
KANSAS DEPARTMENT OF WILDLIFE AND PARKS ... 65
KENTUCKY DEPARTMENT OF PARKS ... 67
LEAGUE OF WOMEN VOTERS OF WASHINGTON ... 242

LEE COUNTY PARKS AND RECREATION SERVICES 54
LOUISIANA DEPARTMENT OF AGRICULTURE AND
    FORESTRY 68
MANITOBA NATURALISTS SOCIETY 245
MICHIGAN DEPARTMENT OF NATURAL RESOURCES 75
MINNESOTA PARKS AND TRAILS COUNCIL 251
MISSISSIPPI DEPARTMENT OF WILDLIFE, FISHERIES, AND
    PARKS 78
MISSOURI DEPARTMENT OF NATURAL RESOURCES 79
MONTANA DEPARTMENT OF FISH, WILDLIFE, AND PARKS
    80
MOUNTAINEERS, THE (Conservation Division) 256
MULE DEER FOUNDATION, THE 256
MUSKIES, INC. 256
NATIONAL ASSOCIATION OF RECREATION RESOURCE
    PLANNERS 257
NATIONAL ASSOCIATION OF STATE OUTDOOR
    RECREATION LIAISON OFFICERS 258
NATIONAL ASSOCIATION OF STATE PARK DIRECTORS . 258
NATIONAL BOATING FEDERATION 260
NATIONAL FOREST FOUNDATION 261
NATIONAL PARK FOUNDATION 263
NATIONAL RIFLE ASSOCIATION OF AMERICA 264
NATIONAL SHOOTING SPORTS FOUNDATION, INC. 265
NATURAL SCIENCE FOR YOUTH FOUNDATION 271
NEW HAMPSHIRE LAKES ASSOCIATION 277
NEW YORK STATE FISH AND WILDLIFE MANAGEMENT
    BOARD 90
NEW YORK STATE OFFICE OF PARKS, RECREATION AND
    HISTORIC PRESERVATION 91
NEW YORK-NEW JERSEY TRAIL CONFERENCE INC. 279
NORTH AMERICAN BUTTERFLY ASSOCIATION 280
NORTH CAROLINA BEACH BUGGY ASSOCIATION, INC... 282
NORTH CAROLINA RECREATION AND PARK SOCIETY, INC.
    283
NORTH CASCADES CONSERVATION COUNCIL 283
NORTHERN VIRGINIA REGIONAL PARK AUTHORITY 113
NORTHWEST INTERPRETIVE ASSOCIATION 286
OFFICE OF STATE PARKS, DEPARTMENT OF CULTURE,
    RECREATION, AND TOURISM 69
OHIO DEPARTMENT OF NATURAL RESOURCES 94
OKLAHOMA TOURISM AND RECREATION DEPARTMENT. 96
OREGON PARKS AND RECREATION DEPARTMENT 98
OUTDOOR RECREATION COUNCIL OF BRITISH COLUMBIA
    292
OUTDOOR WRITERS ASSOCIATION OF AMERICA, INC. . 292
PACIFIC NORTHWEST TRAIL ASSOCIATION 293
PAWS/OLYMPIC WILDLIFE RESCUE 294
PENNSYLVANIA AUDUBON SOCIETY 294
PENNSYLVANIA DEPARTMENT OF CONSERVATION AND
    NATURAL RESOURCES 100
PENNSYLVANIA FISH AND BOAT COMMISSION 101
PENNSYLVANIA FORESTRY ASSOCIATION, THE 295
PENNSYLVANIA RESOURCES COUNCIL, INC., (formerly PA
    Roadside Council) 295
PIEDMONT ENVIRONMENTAL COUNCIL 296
POTOMAC APPALACHIAN TRAIL CLUB 298
PRAIRIE CLUB, THE 298
QUEBEC WILDLIFE FEDERATION 301
RAILS-TO-TRAILS CONSERVANCY 302
RESOURCES AGENCY, THE 46
RIVER FEDERATION 306
RIVERS COUNCIL OF WASHINGTON (formerly Northwest
    Rivers Council) 306
SAVE THE DUNES COUNCIL 309
SEACAMP ASSOCIATION, INC. 312
SEAPLANE PILOTS ASSOCIATION 312
SOUND EXPERIENCE 320
SOUTH DAKOTA GAME, FISH, AND PARKS DEPARTMENT
    106
SOUTHEAST ALASKA CONSERVATION COUNCIL (SEACC)
    323
STATE MARINE BOARD (OREGON) 99
STATE PARKS AND RECREATION COMMISSION
    (WASHINGTON) 116
TEXAS ORGANIZATION FOR ENDANGERED SPECIES 329
TREAD LIGHTLY! INC. 330
TRUST FOR PUBLIC LAND, THE 334
TUG HILL COMMISSION 91
UTAH WILDERNESS COALITION 338

WASHINGTON NATIVE PLANT SOCIETY 341
WASHINGTON RECREATION AND PARK ASSOCIATION . 341
WASHINGTON TOXICS COALITION 341
WASHINGTON TRAILS ASSOCIATION 341
WASHINGTON WILDLIFE HERITAGE FOUNDATION
    (including Heritage Land Trust) 342
WILDERNESS EDUCATION ASSOCIATION 346
WILDLIFE ACTION, INC. 347
WILDLIFE FOREVER 348
WISCONSIN CONSERVATION CORPS 120
WISCONSIN DEPARTMENT OF NATURAL RESOURCES . 120
WOLF EDUCATION AND RESEARCH CENTER 357
WYOMING DEPARTMENT OF COMMERCE 122
YOSEMITE RESTORATION TRUST 361
YOUNG ENTOMOLOGISTS' SOCIETY, INC. 361

Overconsumption

LEARNING FOR ENVIRONMENTAL ACTION PROGRAMME
    (LEAP) 242
NEW ENGLAND COALITION FOR SUSTAINABLE
    POPULATION (NECSP) 276
RAINFOREST RELIEF 302

Ozone Depletion

OZONE ACTION 292
PACIFIC INSTITUTE FOR STUDIES IN DEVELOPMENT,
    ENVIRONMENT, AND SECURITY 293

Pedestrian Environment

DEPARTMENT OF PUBLIC WORKS 52
FLORIDA TRAIL ASSOCIATION, INC. 203
GEORGIA TRUST FOR HISTORIC PRESERVATION 210
INTERNATIONAL BICYCLE FUND 223
PACIFIC NORTHWEST TRAIL ASSOCIATION 293
PIEDMONT ENVIRONMENTAL COUNCIL 296
PRIORITIES INSTITUTE, THE 299

People of Color in the Environment

ATLANTIC STATES LEGAL FOUNDATION 157
CENTER FOR HEALTH, ENVIRONMENT, AND JUSTICE ... 170
ECOLOGY CENTER 194
ENVIRONMENTAL CAREER CENTER 195
ENVIRONMENTAL CAREERS ORGANIZATION, INC., THE 195
INTERNATIONAL SONORAN DESERT ALLIANCE 228
MISSISSIPPI RIVER BASIN ALLIANCE 252
NATIONAL ASSOCIATION OF SERVICE AND
    CONSERVATION CORPS (NASCC) 258
STUDENT CONSERVATION ASSOCIATION, INC. 326
URBAN HABITAT PROGRAM 337

Pest Management

MONTANA DEPARTMENT OF AGRICULTURE 80
NORTHWEST COALITION FOR ALTERNATIVES TO
    PESTICIDES 285

Pesticides

AMERICAN PIE (PUBLIC INFORMATION ON THE
    ENVIRONMENT) 148
ARIZONA DEPARTMENT OF AGRICULTURE 41
BEYOND PESTICIDES/NATIONAL COALITION AGAINST THE
    MISUSE OF PESTICIDES 160
BIO-INTEGRAL RESOURCE CENTER 161
CALIFORNIA ENVIRONMENTAL PROTECTION AGENCY ... 44
CENTER FOR SCIENCE IN THE PUBLIC INTEREST 171
COLLEGE OF TROPICAL AGRICULTURE AND HUMAN
    RESOURCES 57
COLORADO DEPARTMENT OF AGRICULTURE 49
COLORADO STATE UNIVERSITY COOPERATIVE
    EXTENSION 50
CONCERN, INC. 179
DELAWARE DEPARTMENT OF AGRICULTURE 51

DELAWARE STATE EXTENSION SERVICE 52
ECOLOGY CENTER 194
E-P EDUCATION SERVICES, INC. 191
FEDERAL WILDLIFE OFFICER'S ASSOCIATION 199
FRIENDS OF THE EARTH 206
GALIANO CONSERVANCY ASSOCIATION 207
GEORGIA DEPARTMENT OF AGRICULTURE 55
HUMAN ECOLOGY ACTION LEAGUE, INC. THE (HEAL) 217
IDAHO STATE DEPARTMENT OF AGRICULTURE 60
ILLINOIS DEPARTMENT OF AGRICULTURE 61
ILLINOIS ENVIRONMENTAL COUNCIL 219
ILLINOIS WALNUT COUNCIL 219
IOWA ENVIRONMENTAL COUNCIL 232
KENTUCKY DEPARTMENT OF AGRICULTURE 66
LAKE SUPERIOR GREENS 240
LEGAL ENVIRONMENTAL ASSISTANCE FOUNDATION INC.
  (LEAF) 242
MANOMET CENTER FOR CONSERVATION SCIENCES 245
MARYLAND DEPARTMENT OF AGRICULTURE 71
MICHIGAN DEPARTMENT OF AGRICULTURE 74
MICHIGAN STATE UNIVERSITY EXTENSION 75
MINNESOTA CENTER FOR ENVIRONMENTAL ADVOCACY
  (MCEA) 251
MINNESOTA DEPARTMENT OF AGRICULTURE 76
MONTANA DEPARTMENT OF AGRICULTURE 80
NATIONAL 4-H COUNCIL 256
NATIONAL ASSOCIATION OF STATE DEPARTMENTS OF
  AGRICULTURE 258
NEW JERSEY STATE EXTENSION SERVICES 86
NEW YORK DEPARTMENT OF AGRICULTURE AND
  MARKETS 88
NEW YORK PUBLIC INTEREST RESEARCH GROUP
  (NYPIRG 279
NORTH CAROLINA DEPARTMENT OF AGRICULTURE 92
NORTH DAKOTA STATE SOIL CONSERVATION COMMITTEE
  93
NORTHWEST COALITION FOR ALTERNATIVES TO
  PESTICIDES 285
OKLAHOMA STATE BOARD OF AGRICULTURE 96
OREGON ENVIRONMENTAL COUNCIL 290
PENNSYLVANIA DEPARTMENT OF AGRICULTURE 99
PENNSYLVANIA RECREATION AND PARK SOCIETY, INC.
  295
PHYSICIANS FOR SOCIAL RESPONSIBILITY 296
RACHEL CARSON COUNCIL, INC. (formerly Rachel Carson
  Trust for the Living Environment Inc.) 301
RHODE ISLAND COOPERATIVE EXTENSION SERVICE ... 104
SOUTH DAKOTA STATE EXTENSION SERVICES 106
VERMONT DEPARTMENT OF HEALTH 112
VIRGINIA DEPARTMENT OF AGRICULTURE AND
  CONSUMER SERVICES 113
WASHINGTON DEPARTMENT OF AGRICULTURE 117
WEST VIRGINIA DEPARTMENT OF AGRICULTURE 119
WEST VIRGINIA STATE EXTENSION SERVICE 120
WESTERN ENVIRONMENTAL LAW CENTER 344
WILDLIFE DAMAGE REVIEW (WDR) 348

Physiology

OREGON COOPERATIVE FISH AND WILDLIFE RESEARCH
  UNIT (USDI) 97

Planning Management

ALABAMA DEPARTMENT OF ECONOMIC AND COMMUNITY
  AFFAIRS, COASTAL PROGRAMS (ADECA) 38
AMERICAN PLANNING ASSOCIATION 148
AMERICAN WATER WORKS ASSOCIATION (AWWA) 151
COMMUNITY RIGHTS COUNSEL 179
COUNCIL FOR PLANNING AND CONSERVATION 185
E-P EDUCATION SERVICES, INC. 191
GLOBAL ENVIRONMENTAL MANAGEMENT INITIATIVE
  (GEMI) 210
GUAM COASTAL MANAGEMENT PROGRAM 57
ISSAQUAH ALPS TRAILS CLUB (I.A.T.C.) 233
KANSAS WATER OFFICE 66
LEGACY INTERNATIONAL 242
NATIONAL ASSOCIATION OF RECREATION RESOURCE
  PLANNERS 257
NATIONAL ASSOCIATION OF STATE OUTDOOR
  RECREATION LIAISON OFFICERS 258
NEBRASKA NATURAL RESOURCES COMMISSION 82
NEW JERSEY PINELANDS COMMISSION 85
NEW YORK STATE COOPERATIVE EXTENSION 90
OREGON WATER RESOURCES DEPARTMENT 99
ORGANIZATION OF WILDLIFE PLANNERS 291
PINCHOT INSTITUTE FOR CONSERVATION 296
RESOURCE RENEWAL INSTITUTE, THE 304
RIVER FEDERATION 306
SOUTHERN ENVIRONMENTAL LAW CENTER 324
SOUTHERN NEW ENGLAND FOREST CONSORTIUM, INC.
  (SNEFCI) 324
STEAMBOATERS, THE 325
TENNESSEE ENVIRONMENTAL COUNCIL 328
TEXAS WATER DEVELOPMENT BOARD 109
TUG HILL COMMISSION 91
UNITED STATES DEPARTMENT OF TRANSPORTATION ... 31
VERMONT AUDUBON COUNCIL 338

Plant Propagation

INTERNATIONAL PLANT PROPAGATION SOCIETY, INC.,
  THE 226
NORTH CAROLINA WILD FLOWER PRESERVATION
  SOCIETY 283
WILDFLOWER ASSOCIATION OF MICHIGAN 347

Plants

FLORIDA EXOTIC PEST PLANT COUNCIL 202
SOUTHERN APPALACHIAN BOTANICAL SOCIETY 323
TREES ATLANTA 330

Politics and Government

GREEN PARTY USA 213
ILLINOIS ENVIRONMENTAL COUNCIL 219
LEAGUE OF CONSERVATION VOTERS 241
LEAGUE OF WOMEN VOTERS OF IOWA 241
REP AMERICA/REPUBLICANS FOR ENVIRONMENTAL
  PROTECTION 304
WYOMING OUTDOOR COUNCIL 360

Pollution Control

ENVIRONMENTAL LAW INSTITUTE, THE 198
UNITED STATES CHAMBER OF COMMERCE 336

Pollution Prevention

ALLIANCE FOR THE CHESAPEAKE BAY 135
AMERICAN COUNCIL FOR AN ENERGY-EFFICIENT
  ECONOMY 139
AMERICAN OCEANS CAMPAIGN 147
AMERICAN WATER WORKS ASSOCIATION (AWWA) 151
ANACOSTIA WATERSHED SOCIETY 152
ARIZONA DEPARTMENT OF ENVIRONMENTAL QUALITY . 41
ASSOCIATION OF NEW JERSEY ENVIRONMENTAL
  COMMISSIONS 157
ATLANTIC STATES LEGAL FOUNDATION 157
BRANDYWINE CONSERVANCY, INC. 162
CENTER FOR MARINE CONSERVATION 170
CENTRO de INFORMACION, INVESTIGACION y EDUCACION
  SOCIAL (CIIES) 172
CHINA REGION LAKES ALLIANCE 173
CHLORINE-FREE PAPER CONSORTIUM (CPC) 173
COALITION FOR CLEAN AIR 175
COLORADO DEPARTMENT OF EDUCATION 49
DEPARTMENT OF THE ENVIRONMENT 71
ENVIRONMENTAL DEFENSE FUND, INC. 196
ENVIRONMENTAL ENTERPRISES ASSISTANCE FUND, INC.
  197
GEORGIA CONSERVANCY, INC., THE 209
GLOBAL CITIES PROJECT, THE 210
GREAT LAKES UNITED 211

KEYWORD INDEX - Population Growth

GREEN (GLOBAL RIVERS ENVIRONMENTAL EDUCATION NETWORK) 212
GROUNDWATER FOUNDATION, THE 213
INSTITUTE FOR CONSERVATION LEADERSHIP 221
INTERNATIONAL ASSOCIATION FOR ENVIRONMENTAL HYDROLOGY (IAEH) 222
KANSAS STATE DEPARTMENT OF HEALTH AND ENVIRONMENT 66
KIDS FOR SAVING EARTH WORLDWIDE 239
LAKE MICHIGAN FEDERATION 240
LEAGUE OF WOMEN VOTERS OF IOWA 241
LEGAL ENVIRONMENTAL ASSISTANCE FOUNDATION INC. (LEAF) 242
MAINE DEPARTMENT OF ENVIRONMENTAL PROTECTION 70
MICHIGAN DEPARTMENT OF ENVIRONMENTAL QUALITY 75
MICHIGAN ENVIRONMENTAL COUNCIL 249
NOVA SCOTIA FORESTRY ASSOCIATION 286
OHIO ENVIRONMENTAL COUNCIL, INC. 287
OKLAHOMA DEPARTMENT OF ENVIRONMENTAL QUALITY 95
OREGON ENVIRONMENTAL COUNCIL 290
PENNSYLVANIA RESOURCES COUNCIL, INC., (formerly PA Roadside Council) 295
REP AMERICA/REPUBLICANS FOR ENVIRONMENTAL PROTECTION 304
STATE OFFICE OF CONSERVATION (LOUISIANA) 69
TENNESSEE DEPARTMENT OF AGRICULTURE 107
U.S. PUBLIC INTEREST RESEARCH GROUP 336
VIRGIN ISLANDS CONSERVATION SOCIETY, INC. 339
WISCONSIN ASSOCIATION OF LAKES (WAL) 355

Population Growth

ALLIANCE FOR THE CHESAPEAKE BAY 135
AMERICAN ASSOCIATION FOR THE ADVANCEMENT OF SCIENCE 136
AVSC INTERNATIONAL 159
CALIFORNIANS FOR POPULATION STABILIZATION (CAPS) 165
CARRYING CAPACITY NETWORK 168
CONSERVATION AND RESEARCH FOUNDATION, INC., THE 181
EARTHSCAN 193
EDUCATIONAL COMMUNICATIONS, INC. 194
FLORIDA AUDUBON SOCIETY 201
FOSSIL FUELS POLICY ACTION INSTITUTE/ALLIANCE FOR A PAVING MORATORIUM 204
NEW ENGLAND COALITION FOR SUSTAINABLE POPULATION (NECSP) 276
NORTHWEST ENVIRONMENT WATCH 285
PANOS INSTITUTE, THE 293
PLANNED PARENTHOOD FEDERATION OF AMERICA, INC. 297
POPULATION ACTION INTERNATIONAL 297
POPULATION COMMUNICATIONS INTERNATIONAL 297
POPULATION INSTITUTE, THE 298
POPULATION REFERENCE BUREAU, INC. 298
POPULATION-ENVIRONMENT BALANCE, INC. 298
WORLD PAL (WORLD POPULATION ALLOCATION LIMITED INC.) 358
WORLDWATCH INSTITUTE 359
ZERO POPULATION GROWTH, INC. 361

Prairies

ALDO LEOPOLD FOUNDATION, INC. 135
AUDUBON OF KANSAS (formerly Kansas Audubon Council) 158
BIODIVERSITY LEGAL FOUNDATION 161
GEORGE MIKSCH SUTTON AVIAN RESEARCH CENTER INC. 208
ILLINOIS NATIVE PLANT SOCIETY 219
INDIANA NATIVE PLANT AND WILDFLOWER SOCIETY 220
INTERTRIBAL BISON COOPERATIVE (ITBC) 231
IOWA NATIVE PLANT SOCIETY 232
IOWA NATURAL HERITAGE FOUNDATION 232
IOWA PRAIRIE NETWORK 232
KANSAS BIOLOGICAL SURVEY 65
KANSAS NATURAL RESOURCE COUNCIL 237
KANSAS WILDFLOWER SOCIETY 238
LAND BETWEEN THE LAKES ASSOCIATION 240
MICHIGAN NATURAL AREAS COUNCIL 249
MICHIGAN NATURE ASSOCIATION 249
MINNESOTA NATIVE PLANT SOCIETY 251
MISSOURI NATIVE PLANT SOCIETY 253
MISSOURI PRAIRIE FOUNDATION 253
NATIVE PLANT SOCIETY OF NORTHEASTERN OHIO 269
NATIVE PRAIRIES ASSOCIATION OF TEXAS 270
NORTH DAKOTA NATURAL SCIENCE SOCIETY 284
OKLAHOMA NATIVE PLANT SOCIETY 289
PRAIRIE GROUSE TECHNICAL COUNCIL 299
PREDATOR PROJECT 299
SOCIETY FOR RANGE MANAGEMENT 319
SOCIETY OF TYMPANUCHUS CUPIDO PINNATUS LTD. 320
SOUTH DAKOTA COOPERATIVE FISH AND WILDLIFE RESEARCH UNIT (USDI) 106
VIRGINIA NATIVE PLANT SOCIETY 340
WILDFLOWER ASSOCIATION OF MICHIGAN 347

Precision Farming

COLORADO STATE UNIVERSITY COOPERATIVE EXTENSION 50
CONSERVATION TECHNOLOGY INFORMATION CENTER 183
DELAWARE STATE EXTENSION SERVICE 52
NATIONAL ASSOCIATION OF STATE DEPARTMENTS OF AGRICULTURE 258

Predators

ALASKA AUDUBON SOCIETY 133
ANIMAL PROTECTION INSTITUTE 152
BIODIVERSITY LEGAL FOUNDATION 161
CALIFORNIA TRAPPERS ASSOCIATION 164
CALIFORNIA WILDLIFE DEFENDERS 164
COLORADO TRAPPERS ASSOCIATION 178
CRAIGHEAD WILDLIFE-WILDLANDS INSTITUTE 185
DEFENDERS OF WILDLIFE 186
FEDERAL WILDLIFE OFFICER'S ASSOCIATION 199
GEORGE MIKSCH SUTTON AVIAN RESEARCH CENTER INC. 208
KANSAS STATE EXTENSION SERVICES 66
MOUNTAIN LION FOUNDATION 255
NORTHWEST ECOSYSTEM ALLIANCE 285
PREDATOR PROJECT 299
SINAPU 317
UTAH COOPERATIVE FISH AND WILDLIFE RESEARCH UNIT (USDI-USGS-BRD-CRU) 110
WILD CANID SURVIVAL AND RESEARCH CENTER 345
WILD DOG FOUNDATION, THE 345
WILDLIFE DAMAGE REVIEW (WDR) 348
WOLF EDUCATION AND RESEARCH CENTER 357

Preservation

EAGLE NATURE FOUNDATION, LTD. 191

Preservation and Protection

COASTAL CONSERVATION ASSOCIATION GEORGIA 176
COOSA RIVER BASIN INITIATIVE 184
DELAWARE AUDUBON SOCIETY 186
FOREST FIRE LOOKOUT ASSOCIATION 203
PRIORITIES INSTITUTE, THE 299
SIERRA NEVADA FOREST PROTECTION CAMPAIGN 317
STUDENTS PARTNERSHIP WORLDWIDE 327
WILD DOG FOUNDATION, THE 345

Private Land Development

GREATER YELLOWSTONE COALITION 212

Professional Development

CINCINNATI NATURE CENTER	174
MASSACHUSETTS ENVIRONMENTAL EDUCATION SOCIETY	248
NORTH AMERICAN ASSOCIATION FOR ENVIRONMENTAL EDUCATION	280

Professional Organization

AMERICAN FISHERIES SOCIETY	140, 141, 142, 143, 144
AMERICAN INSTITUTE OF FISHERY RESEARCH BIOLOGISTS	146
ASSOCIATION OF CONSULTING FORESTERS OF AMERICA	156
CANADIAN INSTITUTE OF FORESTRY/INSTITUT FORESTIER DU CANADA	167
CANADIAN SOCIETY OF ENVIRONMENTAL BIOLOGISTS	167
ECOLOGICAL SOCIETY OF AMERICA, THE	193
FEDERAL WILDLIFE OFFICER'S ASSOCIATION	199
FOREST SERVICE EMPLOYEES FOR ENVIRONMENTAL ETHICS (FSEEE)	204
MASSACHUSETTS ENVIRONMENTAL EDUCATION SOCIETY	248
NATIONAL ASSOCIATION FOR INTERPRETATION	256
NATIONAL ASSOCIATION OF ENVIRONMENTAL PROFESSIONALS, THE (National Office)	257
NATIONAL ASSOCIATION OF STATE FORESTERS	258
NATIONAL ASSOCIATION OF STATE PARK DIRECTORS	258
NATIONAL MILITARY FISH AND WILDLIFE ASSOCIATION	263
NEW ENGLAND ASSOCIATION OF ENVIRONMENTAL BIOLOGISTS (NEAEB)	276
NORTHEAST CONSERVATION LAW ENFORCEMENT CHIEFS' ASSOCIATION (CLECA)	284
NORTHEAST WILDLIFE ADMINISTRATORS ASSOCIATION	284
SOCIETY FOR RANGE MANAGEMENT	319

Protecting Special Places

BAMA BACKPADDLERS ASSOCIATION	159
LAKE MICHIGAN FEDERATION	240
LAND WATCH MONTEREY COUNTY	241

Public Access

GREAT OUTDOORS CONSERVANCY, THE	212

Public Farming

NATIONAL ASSOCIATION OF STATE DEPARTMENTS OF AGRICULTURE	258

Public Health Protection

ALASKA DEPARTMENT OF ENVIRONMENTAL CONSERVATION	39
AMERICAN OCEANS CAMPAIGN	147
AMERICAN WATER WORKS ASSOCIATION (AWWA)	151
ASSOCIATION OF STATE AND TERRITORIAL HEALTH OFFICIALS	157
ATLANTIC STATES LEGAL FOUNDATION	157
CITIZENS ADVISORY COUNCIL TO PENNSYLVANIA DEPARTMENT OF ENVIRONMENTAL PROTECTION	99
COLLEGE OF TROPICAL AGRICULTURE AND HUMAN RESOURCES	57
DELAWARE SOLID WASTE AUTHORITY	52
DELAWARE STATE EXTENSION SERVICE	52
FLORIDA STATE DEPARTMENT OF HEALTH	54
IDAHO STATE DEPARTMENT OF AGRICULTURE	60
INDIANA STATE DEPARTMENT OF HEALTH	63
KANSAS STATE DEPARTMENT OF HEALTH AND ENVIRONMENT	66
MAINE DEPARTMENT OF MARINE RESOURCES	71
MICHIGAN DEPARTMENT OF COMMUNITY HEALTH	74
NORTH DAKOTA DEPARTMENT OF HEALTH	93
PENNSYLVANIA DEPARTMENT OF AGRICULTURE	99
PENNSYLVANIA DEPARTMENT OF ENVIRONMENTAL PROTECTION	101
SCIENTISTS CENTER FOR ANIMAL WELFARE	311
SOUTH CAROLINA DEPARTMENT OF HEALTH AND ENVIRONMENTAL CONTROL	105
STATE WATER RESOURCES BOARD (RHODE ISLAND)	104
TENNESSEE ENVIRONMENTAL COUNCIL	328
UTAH DEPARTMENT OF HEALTH	110
WATER RESOURCES RESEARCH CENTER	59
WEST VIRGINIA DEPARTMENT OF AGRICULTURE	119
ZERO POPULATION GROWTH, INC.	361

Public Information

ARIZONA GEOLOGICAL SURVEY	41

Public Lands

ADIRONDACK MOUNTAIN CLUB, INC., THE	131
ALASKA AUDUBON SOCIETY	133
ALASKA DEPARTMENT OF NATURAL RESOURCES	40
ALBERTA WILDERNESS ASSOCIATION	135
AMERICAN FEDERATION OF MINERALOGICAL SOCIETIES	139
AMERICAN FORESTS (formerly American Forestry Association)	144
AMERICAN HIKING SOCIETY	145
AMERICAN HORSE PROTECTION ASSOCIATION	145
AMERICAN LAND CONSERVANCY	146
AMERICAN LANDS (formerly Western Ancient Forest Campaign)	146
AMERICAN RESOURCES GROUP	148
AMERICAN SOCIETY FOR ENVIRONMENTAL HISTORY	149
AMERICAN SOCIETY OF LANDSCAPE ARCHITECTS	150
AMERICAN WILDLANDS	151
ANIMAL PROTECTION INSTITUTE	152
APPALACHIAN MOUNTAIN CLUB	153
ARIZONA LAND DEPARTMENT	41
ASSOCIATION FOR THE PROTECTION OF THE ADIRONDACKS, THE	155
BIODIVERSITY LEGAL FOUNDATION	161
BOONE AND CROCKETT CLUB	161
CALIFORNIA STATE LANDS COMMISSION	46
CANADA-UNITED STATES ENVIRONMENTAL COUNCIL (United States Office)	166
CAVE RESEARCH FOUNDATION	168
CENTER FOR BIOLOGICAL DIVERSITY	169
COLORADO DEPARTMENT OF AGRICULTURE	49
COLORADO DEPARTMENT OF NATURAL RESOURCES	49
COLORADO ENVIRONMENTAL COALITION	177
CONFERENCE OF NATIONAL PARK COOPERATING ASSOCIATIONS	180
DESERT TORTOISE COUNCIL	188
EARTHJUSTICE LEGAL DEFENSE FUND (formerly Sierra Club Legal Defense Fund, Inc.)	192
ECOLOGY CENTER	194
FEDERATION OF ALBERTA NATURALISTS	200
FLORIDA AUDUBON SOCIETY	201
FLORIDA SPORTSMEN'S CONSERVATION ASSOCIATION	202
FOREST HISTORY SOCIETY, INC.	203
FOREST SERVICE EMPLOYEES FOR ENVIRONMENTAL ETHICS (FSEEE)	204
FOREST WATCH	204
FRIENDS OF ACADIA	205
GRAND CANYON TRUST (St. George, UT Office)	211
GREAT BEAR FOUNDATION	211
GREATER YELLOWSTONE COALITION	212
HAWAII AUDUBON SOCIETY	214
IDAHO CONSERVATION LEAGUE	218
ILLINOIS PRAIRIE PATH	219
INTERAGENCY COMMITTEE FOR OUTDOOR RECREATION (IAC)	116
INTERNATIONAL ASSOCIATION FOR BEAR RESEARCH AND MANAGEMENT	222
IZAAK WALTON LEAGUE OF AMERICA, INC., THE	234
KANSAS DEPARTMENT OF WILDLIFE AND PARKS	65
KEEP AMERICA BEAUTIFUL, INC.	238
KENTUCKY DEPARTMENT OF PARKS	67

KEYWORD INDEX - Public Participation

LAND BETWEEN THE LAKES ASSOCIATION 240
LEAGUE OF WOMEN VOTERS OF WASHINGTON............. 242
LEE COUNTY PARKS AND RECREATION SERVICES 54
MARIN CONSERVATION LEAGUE 246
MARYLAND DEPARTMENT OF NATURAL RESOURCES..... 72
MASSACHUSETTS ASSOCIATION OF CONSERVATION
   COMMISSIONS (MACC) 247
MICHIGAN DEPARTMENT OF NATURAL RESOURCES....... 75
MINERAL POLICY CENTER... 250
MINNESOTA PARKS AND TRAILS COUNCIL 251
MISSISSIPPI FORESTRY COMMISSION 78
MISSOURI DEPARTMENT OF NATURAL RESOURCES....... 79
MISSOURI NATIVE PLANT SOCIETY 253
MONTANA WILDERNESS ASSOCIATION 255
MOUNTAINEERS, THE (Conservation Division)..................... 256
NATIONAL ASSOCIATION OF RECREATION RESOURCE
   PLANNERS 257
NATIONAL ASSOCIATION OF STATE DEPARTMENTS OF
   AGRICULTURE.. 258
NATIONAL ASSOCIATION OF STATE FORESTERS........... 258
NATIONAL ASSOCIATION OF STATE PARK DIRECTORS. 258
NATIONAL FOREST FOUNDATION 261
NATIONAL GEOGRAPHIC SOCIETY 262
NATIONAL MILITARY FISH AND WILDLIFE ASSOCIATION 263
NATIONAL PARK FOUNDATION 263
NATIONAL PARK TRUST 263
NATIONAL PARKS AND CONSERVATION ASSOCIATION
   (NPCA) 263
NATIONAL TREE TRUST 265
NATIONAL WILD TURKEY FEDERATION, INC., THE........... 267
NATIONAL WILDLIFE REFUGE ASSOCIATION 269
NATURAL RESOURCES COUNCIL OF AMERICA............... 271
NEVADA BUREAU OF MINES AND GEOLOGY 82
NEW JERSEY CONSERVATION FOUNDATION 278
NEW YORK STATE FISH AND WILDLIFE MANAGEMENT
   BOARD 90
NORTH DAKOTA STATE FOREST SERVICE 93
NORTHCOAST ENVIRONMENTAL CENTER 284
NORTHERN ALASKA ENVIRONMENTAL CENTER............. 285
OFFICE OF STATE PARKS, DEPARTMENT OF CULTURE,
   RECREATION, AND TOURISM... 69
OKLAHOMA NATIVE PLANT SOCIETY 289
OKLAHOMA TOURISM AND RECREATION DEPARTMENT. 96
OREGON NATURAL RESOURCES COUNCIL 290
OUTDOOR CIRCLE, THE... 291
PACIFIC NORTHWEST TRAIL ASSOCIATION 293
PACIFIC RIVERS COUNCIL 293
PARTNERS IN PARKS 293
PENNSYLVANIA FORESTRY ASSOCIATION, THE 295
PENNSYLVANIA GAME COMMISSION................................. 102
PIEDMONT ENVIRONMENTAL COUNCIL 296
PINCHOT INSTITUTE FOR CONSERVATION 296
PREDATOR PROJECT... 299
PUBLIC EMPLOYEES FOR ENVIRONMENTAL
   RESPONSIBILITY (PEER) 300
PUBLIC LANDS FOUNDATION... 300
QUEBEC WILDLIFE FEDERATION 301
SAVE AMERICA'S FORESTS 309
SAVE THE DUNES COUNCIL 309
SAVE-THE-REDWOODS LEAGUE 310
SIERRA CLUB.. 312, 314, 315, 316, 317
SIERRA CLUB FOUNDATION, THE 317
SINAPU... 317
SOCIETY FOR RANGE MANAGEMENT 319
SOCIETY OF AMERICAN FORESTERS................ 291, 319, 341
SONORAN INSTITUTE 320
SOUTHEAST ALASKA CONSERVATION COUNCIL (SEACC)
   323
SOUTHERN ENVIRONMENTAL LAW CENTER 324
STATE PARKS AND RECREATION COMMISSION
   (WASHINGTON) 116
STUDENT CONSERVATION ASSOCIATION, INC............... 326
TENNESSEE CITIZENS FOR WILDERNESS PLANNING.... 328
TEXAS FOREST SERVICE 108
TEXAS GENERAL LAND OFFICE.. 109
UTAH NATURE STUDY SOCIETY 337
UTAH STATE EXTENSION SERVICES................................. 111
UTAH WILDERNESS COALITION 338
VIRGINIA NATIVE PLANT SOCIETY 340
WASHINGTON NATIVE PLANT SOCIETY 341
WASHINGTON TOXICS COALITION..................................... 341
WASHINGTON WILDLIFE AND RECREATION COALITION 342
WEST VIRGINIA B.A.S.S. CHAPTER FEDERATION............ 343
WILDERNESS SOCIETY, THE 346
WILDLIFE FOREVER 348
WISCONSIN LAND AND WATER CONSERVATION
   ASSOCIATION 356
WYOMING DEPARTMENT OF COMMERCE....................... 122
WYOMING OUTDOOR COUNCIL 360
WYOMING STATE BOARD OF LAND COMMISSIONERS... 123

Public Participation

CITIZENS ADVISORY COUNCIL TO PENNSYLVANIA
   DEPARTMENT OF ENVIRONMENTAL PROTECTION 99
LEARNING FOR ENVIRONMENTAL ACTION PROGRAMME
   (LEAP) 242
PENNSYLVANIA CITIZENS ADVISORY COUNCIL TO
   DEPARTMENT OF ENVIRONMENTAL PROTECTION 294

Rainforests

ALASKA RAINFOREST CAMPAIGN.. 134
EARTH FOUNDATION 191
HAWAII NATURE CENTER 214
RAINFOREST ACTION NETWORK 302
RAINFOREST ALLIANCE 302
RAINFOREST RELIEF.. 302
RAINFOREST TRUST, INC., THE... 302
SIERRA CLUB.. 312, 314, 315, 316, 317
SOUTHEAST ALASKA CONSERVATION COUNCIL (SEACC)
   323
WORLD PARKS ENDOWMENT INC. 358
ZUNGAROCOCHA RESEARCH CENTER 361

Raptors

A. E. HOWELL WILDLIFE CONSERVATION CENTER......... 130
ADOPT-A-STREAM FOUNDATION, THE 131
AUDUBON SOCIETY OF WESTERN PENNSYLVANIA 159
CRAIGHEAD ENVIRONMENTAL RESEARCH INSTITUTE.. 185
FAIRFAX AUDUBON SOCIETY 199
FEDERAL WILDLIFE OFFICER'S ASSOCIATION 199
FLORIDA AUDUBON SOCIETY 201
GEORGE MIKSCH SUTTON AVIAN RESEARCH CENTER
   INC. 208
HAWK AND OWL TRUST, THE 215
HAWK MIGRATION ASSOCIATION OF NORTH AMERICA. 215
HAWK MOUNTAIN SANCTUARY ASSOCIATION 215
HAWKWATCH INTERNATIONAL, INC. 215
INTERNATIONAL OSPREY FOUNDATION INC., THE......... 226
KANSAS ORNITHOLOGICAL SOCIETY 237
MACBRIDE RAPTOR PROJECT 244
NATIONAL AVIARY 259
NORTH AMERICAN FALCONERS ASSOCIATION 281
NORTHWEST ECOSYSTEM ALLIANCE............................... 285
OREGON COOPERATIVE FISH AND WILDLIFE RESEARCH
   UNIT (USDI) 97
ORNITHOLOGICAL COUNCIL.. 291
PEREGRINE FUND, THE 296
RAPTOR CENTER, THE 303
RAPTOR EDUCATION FOUNDATION, INC.......................... 303
RAPTOR RESEARCH FOUNDATION, INC. 303
SOCIETY FOR THE PRESERVATION OF BIRDS OF PREY 319
SOUTH DAKOTA B.A.S.S. CHAPTER FEDERATION 322
VERMONT B.A.S.S. CHAPTER FEDERATION 338
WILDLIFE CENTER OF VIRGINIA, THE................................ 347
WILDLIFE FOREVER 348
WILDLIFE INFORMATION CENTER, INC. 349
WILDLIFE WAYSTATION 355
WORLD BIRD SANCTUARY (formerly Raptor Rehabilitation
   and Propagation Project Inc. The) 357

Recreational Boating

MAINE DEPARTMENT OF INLAND FISHERIES AND
   WILDLIFE... 70
STATE MARINE BOARD (OREGON) 99

Recycling

ACADEMY FOR EDUCATIONAL DEVELOPMENT 130
ALABAMA ENVIRONMENTAL COUNCIL 132
JOHN INSKEEP ENVIRONMENTAL LEARNING CENTER .. 236
PENNSYLVANIA RESOURCES COUNCIL, INC., (formerly PA Roadside Council) 295

Reforestation

FOREST WATCH 204
JANE GOODALL INSTITUTE, THE 236
NATIONAL NETWORK OF FOREST PRACTITIONERS 263
TEXAS FORESTRY ASSOCIATION 329

Rehabilitation

ORGANIZATION FOR BAT CONSERVATION 291

Reintroduction

WILD CANID SURVIVAL AND RESEARCH CENTER 345

Remedial Action Plans

LAKE ERIE CLEAN-UP COMMITTEE, INC. 240

Renewable Resources

A.B. ENVIRONMENTAL EDUCATION CENTER 130
ALABAMA FORESTRY COMMISSION 39
ALASKA DEPARTMENT OF FISH AND GAME 39
ALASKA DEPARTMENT OF NATURAL RESOURCES 40
AMERICAN FISHERIES SOCIETY 140, 141, 142, 143, 144
AMERICAN FOREST FOUNDATION 144
AMERICAN INSTITUTE OF FISHERY RESEARCH BIOLOGISTS 146
AMERICAN RESOURCES GROUP 148
AMERICAN WATER RESOURCES ASSOCIATION 151
ARIZONA LAND DEPARTMENT 41
ARKANSAS STATE EXTENSION SERVICES 43
ASSOCIATION OF CONSULTING FORESTERS OF AMERICA 156
ASSOCIATION OF MIDWEST FISH AND GAME LAW ENFORCEMENT OFFICERS 156
ATLANTIC STATES LEGAL FOUNDATION 157
AUDUBON INTERNATIONAL 158
BOONE AND CROCKETT FOUNDATION 161
CALIFORNIA TRAPPERS ASSOCIATION 164
CANVASBACK SOCIETY 167
CARRYING CAPACITY NETWORK 168
CENTER FOR RESOURCEFUL BUILDING TECHNOLOGY 171
CHESAPEAKE BAY FOUNDATION, INC. (Maryland Office) . 173
COLLEGE OF TROPICAL AGRICULTURE AND HUMAN RESOURCES 57
COLORADO STATE UNIVERSITY COOPERATIVE EXTENSION 50
CONFEDERATED SALISH AND KOOTENAI TRIBES 180
CONSERVATION AND RESEARCH FOUNDATION, INC., THE 181
ECOLOGY CENTER 194
ENERGY, MINERALS, AND NATURAL RESOURCES DEPARTMENT 86
ENVIRONMENT COUNCIL OF RHODE ISLAND 195
ENVIRONMENTAL CONCERN INC. 196
ENVIRONMENTAL ENTERPRISES ASSISTANCE FUND, INC. 197
ENVIRONMENTAL LEAGUE OF MASSACHUSETTS 198
ENVIROSOUTH, INC. 199
FOREST LANDOWNERS ASSOCIATION, INC. 203
GEORGE MIKSCH SUTTON AVIAN RESEARCH CENTER INC. 208
GEORGIA CONSERVANCY, INC., THE 209
GEORGIA SEA GRANT COLLEGE PROGRAM 56
GREEN SEAL 213
IDAHO STATE SOIL CONSERVATION COMMISSION 60
ILLINOIS DEPARTMENT OF AGRICULTURE 61
ILLINOIS WALNUT COUNCIL 219
INTERNATIONAL SOCIETY OF TROPICAL FORESTERS, INC. 228
KANSAS DEPARTMENT OF AGRICULTURE 65
KANSAS FOREST SERVICE 65
KEEP FLORIDA BEAUTIFUL, INC. 238
KENTUCKY-TENNESSEE SOCIETY OF AMERICAN FORESTERS 239
LOUISIANA DEPARTMENT OF AGRICULTURE AND FORESTRY 68
LOUISIANA SEA GRANT COLLEGE PROGRAM 69
MAINE/NEW HAMPSHIRE SEA GRANT PROGRAM 83
MARYLAND FORESTS ASSOCIATION 247
MICHIGAN WILDLIFE HABITAT FOUNDATION 250
MISSISSIPPI FORESTRY COMMISSION 78
NATIONAL 4-H COUNCIL 256
NATIONAL FARMERS UNION 261
NATIONAL FFA ORGANIZATION 261
NATIONAL FORESTRY ASSOCIATION 262
NATIONAL SHOOTING SPORTS FOUNDATION, INC. 265
NATIONAL TRAPPERS ASSOCIATION, INC. 265
NATIONAL TRUST FOR HISTORIC PRESERVATION 265
NEBRASKA STATE EXTENSION SERVICES 82
NEW ENGLAND NATURAL RESOURCES CENTER 276
NEW JERSEY DEPARTMENT OF AGRICULTURE 84
NEW YORK STATE COOPERATIVE EXTENSION 90
NORTH AMERICAN COALITION ON RELIGION AND ECOLOGY (NACRE) 280
NORTH CAROLINA FORESTRY ASSOCIATION 282
NW ENERGY COALITION 286
OFFICE OF ENERGY EFFICIENCY AND ENVIRONMENT 91
OHIO OFFICE OF ENERGY EFFICIENCY 94
OREGON SMALL WOODLANDS ASSOCIATION 290
PACIFIC FISHERY MANAGEMENT COUNCIL 292
PAWS/OLYMPIC WILDLIFE RESCUE 294
POPULATION ACTION INTERNATIONAL 297
PUBLIC LANDS FOUNDATION 300
QUEBEC WILDLIFE FEDERATION 301
RENEWABLE ENERGY POLICY PROJECT (REPP) 303
RENEWABLE NATURAL RESOURCES FOUNDATION 304
RESOURCE RENEWAL INSTITUTE, THE 304
RESOURCES FOR THE FUTURE 304
SAFE ENERGY COMMUNICATION COUNCIL 308
SOCIETY FOR ECOLOGICAL RESTORATION 318
SOCIETY FOR RANGE MANAGEMENT 319
SOCIETY OF AMERICAN FORESTERS 291, 319, 341
SOIL AND WATER CONSERVATION SOCIETY (formerly Soil Conservation Society of America) 320
SOUTH CAROLINA ENERGY OFFICE 105
SOUTH CAROLINA WILDLIFE FEDERATION 321
SOUTH DAKOTA STATE EXTENSION SERVICES 106
SOUTH DAKOTA WILDLIFE FEDERATION 323
STATE FORESTRY DIVISION (WYOMING) 122
STATE WATER RESOURCES BOARD (RHODE ISLAND) .. 104
STUDENT CONSERVATION ASSOCIATION, INC. 326
TEXAS AGRICULTURAL EXTENSION SERVICE 108
TEXAS FOREST SERVICE 108
TEXAS STATE SOIL AND WATER CONSERVATION BOARD 109
TREES FOR THE FUTURE, INC. 330
TROUT UNLIMITED, OKLAHOMA COUNCIL 333
UNION OF CONCERNED SCIENTISTS 336
UNIVERSITY OF MASSACHUSETTS EXTENSION 74
UTAH COOPERATIVE FISH AND WILDLIFE RESEARCH UNIT (USDI-USGS-BRD-CRU) 110
UTAH STATE EXTENSION SERVICES 111
UTAH STATE SOIL CONSERVATION COMMISSION 111
VIRGINIA SEA GRANT PROGRAM 115
WASHINGTON B.A.S.S. CHAPTER FEDERATION 340
WASHINGTON STATE CONSERVATION COMMISSION 118
WASHINGTON STATE EXTENSION SERVICES 118
WEST VIRGINIA STATE EXTENSION SERVICE 120
WILDLIFE SOCIETY, THE 350
WISCONSIN WILDLIFE FEDERATION 356
WORLD FORESTRY CENTER 358
WORLD RESOURCES INSTITUTE 358
WORLDWATCH INSTITUTE 359
WYOMING STATE BOARD OF LAND COMMISSIONERS ... 123
ZERO POPULATION GROWTH, INC. 361

Reproductive Rights

NEW ENGLAND COALITION FOR SUSTAINABLE
  POPULATION (NECSP) 276
PLANNED PARENTHOOD FEDERATION OF AMERICA, INC.
  297

Reptiles and Amphibians

ADOPT-A-STREAM FOUNDATION, THE 131
AMERICAN SOCIETY OF ICHTHYOLOGISTS AND
  HERPETOLOGISTS 149
AUDUBON SOCIETY OF WESTERN PENNSYLVANIA 159
CALIFORNIA ACADEMY OF SCIENCES 163
CANADIAN COOPERATIVE WILDLIFE HEALTH CENTRE .. 166
CHICAGO HERPETOLOGICAL SOCIETY 173
DESERT TORTOISE COUNCIL 188
FISH AND WILDLIFE INFORMATION EXCHANGE 201
FLORIDA COOPERATIVE FISH AND WILDLIFE RESEARCH
  UNIT (USDI) 52
GOPHER TORTOISE COUNCIL 211
KANSAS HERPETOLOGICAL SOCIETY 237
MICHIGAN NATURE ASSOCIATION 249
MINNESOTA HERPETOLOGICAL SOCIETY (James Ford Bell
  Museum of Natural History) 251
NATURAL HISTORY SOCIETY OF MARYLAND, INC., THE 270
NEW YORK TURTLE AND TORTOISE SOCIETY 279
NORTH CAROLINA HERPETOLOGICAL SOCIETY 283
NORTHWEST ECOSYSTEM ALLIANCE 285
PITTSBURGH HERPETOLOGICAL SOCIETY, THE 296
SCIENTISTS CENTER FOR ANIMAL WELFARE 311
SMITHSONIAN INSTITUTION 317
SOCIETY FOR INTEGRATIVE AND COMPARTIVE BIOLOGY
  (formerly AMERICAN SOCIETY OF ZOOLOGISTS) 318

Research

AMERICAN WILDLIFE RESEARCH FOUNDATION, INC. 151
ARCHBOLD BIOLOGICAL STATION 153
ARIZONA GEOLOGICAL SURVEY 41
ARKANSAS COOPERATIVE RESEARCH UNIT 42
ASSOCIATION OF FIELD ORNITHOLOGISTS 156
ATLANTIC SALMON FEDERATION 157
AUDUBON INTERNATIONAL 158
BAT CONSERVATION INTERNATIONAL 160
BILLFISH FOUNDATION, THE 160
CALIFORNIA ACADEMY OF SCIENCES 163
CANADIAN COOPERATIVE WILDLIFE HEALTH CENTRE .. 166
CETACEAN SOCIETY INTERNATIONAL 172
CHLORINE-FREE PAPER CONSORTIUM (CPC) 173
CLEVELAND MUSEUM OF NATURAL HISTORY, THE 175
COLLEGE OF TROPICAL AGRICULTURE AND HUMAN
  RESOURCES 57
CRAIGHEAD WILDLIFE-WILDLANDS INSTITUTE 185
DELAWARE GEOLOGICAL SURVEY 52
DELAWARE MUSEUM OF NATURAL HISTORY 187
DELAWARE SOLID WASTE AUTHORITY 52
DEPARTMENT OF INTERIOR, U.S.G.S/B.R.D, SOUTH
  CAROLINA COOPERATIVE FISH AND WILDLIFE
  RESEARCH UNIT 104
DEPARTMENT OF TRANSPORTATION (OREGON) 97
EARTHWATCH INSTITUTE 193
ENVIRONMENTAL CENTER 58
ENVIRONMENTAL CONCERN INC. 196
H. JOHN HEINZ III CENTER FOR SCIENCE, ECONOMICS,
  AND THE ENVIRONMENT 214
HENRY A. WALLACE INSTITUTE FOR ALTERNATIVE
  AGRICULTURE (HAWIAA) 215
HUMMINGBIRD SOCIETY, THE 217
HUNTSMAN MARINE SCIENCE CENTRE 217
ILLINOIS WALNUT COUNCIL 219
INTERNATIONAL CENTER FOR GIBBON STUDIES 224
IOWA COOPERATIVE FISH AND WILDLIFE RESEARCH UNIT
  64
ISLAND CONSERVATION EFFORT 233
KENTUCKY ACADEMY OF SCIENCE 238
KODIAK BROWN BEAR TRUST 240
LEARNING FOR ENVIRONMENTAL ACTION PROGRAMME
  (LEAP) 242
LOUISIANA FORESTRY ASSOCIATION 243
MAINE/NEW HAMPSHIRE SEA GRANT PROGRAM 83
MANOMET CENTER FOR CONSERVATION SCIENCES 245
MONTANA COOPERATIVE FISHERY RESEARCH UNIT
  (USDI) 80
NATIONAL BIRD-FEEDING SOCIETY 259
NATIONAL NETWORK OF FOREST PRACTITIONERS 263
NEW YORK SEA GRANT 90
OHIO SEA GRANT COLLEGE PROGRAM 95
OKLAHOMA ACADEMY OF SCIENCE 288
OKLAHOMA COOPERATIVE FISH AND WILDLIFE
  RESEARCH UNIT (USDI) 95
OUTDOOR RECREATION COUNCIL OF BRITISH COLUMBIA
  292
PARTNERS IN PARKS 293
PINCHOT INSTITUTE FOR CONSERVATION 296
PINE BLUFF COOPERATIVE FISHERY RESEARCH
  PROJECT 44
PUERTO RICO CONSERVATION FOUNDATION, THE (PRCF
  300
RAILS-TO-TRAILS CONSERVANCY 302
RESPONSIVE MANAGEMENT 305
RINCON INSTITUTE, THE 305
SAVE THE DUNES COUNCIL 309
SCIENTISTS CENTER FOR ANIMAL WELFARE 311
SOIL AND WATER CONSERVATION SOCIETY (formerly Soil
  Conservation Society of America) 320
SOUTHERN APPALACHIAN BOTANICAL SOCIETY 323
STANFORD ENVIRONMENTAL LAW SOCIETY 325
STROUD WATER RESEARCH CENTER 326
UNIVERSITY OF VERMONT EXTENSION 112
UPPER CHATTAHOOCHEE RIVERKEEPER 337
VIRGINIA MUSEUM OF NATURAL HISTORY 115
WILD CANID SURVIVAL AND RESEARCH CENTER 345
WILDFOWL TRUST OF NORTH AMERICA, INC., THE 347
WILSON ORNITHOLOGICAL SOCIETY 355
WOLF EDUCATION AND RESEARCH CENTER 357
ZUNGAROCOCHA RESEARCH CENTER 361

Research Grants

CHARLES A. AND ANNE MORROW LINDBERGH
  FOUNDATION, THE 172
ECODEFENSE 193
LVIV REGIONAL INSTITUTE OF EDUCATION 244
NATIONAL WILD TURKEY FEDERATION, CANADA, INC.,
  THE 266
NATIONAL WILD TURKEY FEDERATION, INC., THE 267
NORTH CAROLINA WILD FLOWER PRESERVATION
  SOCIETY 283
ORNITHOLOGICAL COUNCIL 291
RESOURCE CENTER FOR ENVIRONMENTAL EDUCATION,
  THE 304
WILDLIFE HABITAT CANADA 349

Resource Law Enforcement

ALASKA DEPARTMENT OF PUBLIC SAFETY 40
ASSOCIATION FOR FISH AND WILDLIFE ENFORCEMENT
  TRAINING 155
NORTH CAROLINA COALITION, INC. 282

Restoration

ALDO LEOPOLD FOUNDATION, INC. 135
CHESAPEAKE BAY FOUNDATION, INC. 172, 173
COOSA RIVER BASIN INITIATIVE 184
HUMBOLT FIELD RESEARCH INSTITUTE 217
IOWA AUDUBON 231
NATIVE PRAIRIES ASSOCIATION OF TEXAS 270
SAVE THE SOUND, INC. 310
SOCIETY FOR ECOLOGICAL RESTORATION 318
WILDFLOWER ASSOCIATION OF MICHIGAN 347

Riparian Restoration

AMERICAN RIVERS (formerly American Rivers Conservation
  Council) 149

FRIENDS OF THE REEDY RIVER 206
NATIONAL ASSOCIATION OF SERVICE AND
   CONSERVATION CORPS (NASCC) 258
RINCON INSTITUTE, THE 305
SAVE OUR RIVERS, INC. 309
SIERRA NEVADA FOREST PROTECTION CAMPAIGN 317
SONORAN INSTITUTE 320
STROUD WATER RESEARCH CENTER 326

River Conservation

PRAIRIE RIVERS NETWORK (Formerly Central States
   Education Center) 299

Rivers

ADIRONDACK PARK AGENCY 88
ADOPT-A-STREAM FOUNDATION, THE 131
ALLIANCE FOR THE CHESAPEAKE BAY 135
AMERICAN RIVERS (formerly American Rivers Conservation
   Council) 149
AMERICAN SOCIETY OF LIMNOLOGY AND
   OCEANOGRAPHY 150
AMERICAN WATER RESOURCES ASSOCIATION 151
AMERICAN WHITEWATER   151
ANACOSTIA WATERSHED SOCIETY 152
APPALACHIAN MOUNTAIN CLUB 153
BAMA BACKPADDLERS ASSOCIATION 159
BORDER ECOLOGY PROJECT (BEP) 162
CHRISTINA CONSERVANCY, INC. 174
CONNECTICUT RIVER WATERSHED COUNCIL INC. 181
CONSERVATION COUNCIL OF NORTH CAROLINA 181
CRAIGHEAD ENVIRONMENTAL RESEARCH INSTITUTE .. 185
DRAGONFLY SOCIETY OF THE AMERICAS, THE 188
FLORIDA AUDUBON SOCIETY 201
FLORIDA DEFENDERS OF THE ENVIRONMENT, INC. (Home
   Office) 201
FRIENDS OF THE REEDY RIVER 206
FRIENDS OF THE RIVER 206
GOVERNOR OF SOUTH CAROLINA 104
GREEN (GLOBAL RIVERS ENVIRONMENTAL EDUCATION
   NETWORK) 212
IDAHO DEPARTMENT OF PARKS AND RECREATION 60
INDIANA DEPARTMENT OF NATURAL RESOURCES 62
INTERNATIONAL RIVERS NETWORK (IRN) 226
IOWA NATURAL HERITAGE FOUNDATION 232
IZAAK WALTON LEAGUE OF AMERICA, INC., THE 234
KANSAS NATURAL RESOURCE COUNCIL 237
KANSAS WATER OFFICE 66
LEAGUE OF WOMEN VOTERS OF WASHINGTON 242
LEGAL ENVIRONMENTAL ASSISTANCE FOUNDATION INC.
   (LEAF) 242
LONG LIVE THE KINGS 243
LOWER MISSISSIPPI RIVER CONSERVATION COMMITTEE
   244
MAINE ATLANTIC SALMON COMMISSION (formerly Maine
   Atlantic Salmon Authority) 69
MID-ATLANTIC COUNCIL OF WATERSHED ASSOCIATIONS
   250
MISSISSIPPI COOPERATIVE FISH AND WILDLIFE
   RESEARCH UNIT (USDI) 77
MISSISSIPPI INTERSTATE COOPERATIVE RESOURCE
   ASSOCIATION 252
MISSISSIPPI RIVER BASIN ALLIANCE 252
MISSOURI COOPERATIVE FISH AND WILDLIFE RESEARCH
   UNIT (USDI) 79
MONTANA COOPERATIVE FISHERY RESEARCH UNIT
   (USDI) 80
MONTANA LAND RELIANCE 254
MOUNTAINEERS, THE (Conservation Division) 256
NATIONAL BOATING FEDERATION 260
NATIONAL WATERWAYS CONFERENCE INC. 266
NATURAL AND SCENIC RIVERS COMMISSION (ARKANSAS)
   43
NATURAL HERITAGE COMMISSION (ARKANSAS) 44
NEBRASKA DEPARTMENT OF WATER RESOURCES 81
NEBRASKA NATURAL RESOURCES COMMISSION 82
NORTH CAROLINA COALITION, INC. 282
NORTHERN ALASKA ENVIRONMENTAL CENTER 285
OKLAHOMA NATIVE PLANT SOCIETY 289
OKLAHOMA WATER RESOURCES BOARD 97
OREGON ENVIRONMENTAL COUNCIL 290
OREGON PARKS AND RECREATION DEPARTMENT 98
OREGON WATER RESOURCES DEPARTMENT 99
OUTDOOR RECREATION COUNCIL OF BRITISH COLUMBIA
   292
PACIFIC RIVERS COUNCIL 293
PINE BLUFF COOPERATIVE FISHERY RESEARCH
   PROJECT 44
PRAIRIE RIVERS NETWORK (Formerly Central States
   Education Center) 299
RESOURCES AGENCY, THE 46
RIVER ALLIANCE OF WISCONSIN 305
RIVER FEDERATION 306
RIVER NETWORK 306
RIVER OTTER ALLIANCE, THE 306
RIVERS COUNCIL OF WASHINGTON (formerly Northwest
   Rivers Council) 306
SAVE OUR RIVERS, INC. 309
SCENIC HUDSON, INC. 311
SEAPLANE PILOTS ASSOCIATION 312
SOUTH DAKOTA COOPERATIVE FISH AND WILDLIFE
   RESEARCH UNIT (USDI) 106
SOUTHEAST ALASKA CONSERVATION COUNCIL (SEACC)
   323
SOUTHEASTERN FISHES COUNCIL 323
SOUTHWEST FLORIDA WATER MANAGEMENT DISTRICT
   (SWFWMD) 55
STROUD WATER RESEARCH CENTER 326
TENNESSEE CITIZENS FOR WILDERNESS PLANNING 328
TEXAS B.A.S.S. CHAPTER FEDERATION 329
TEXAS WATER DEVELOPMENT BOARD 109
TROUT UNLIMITED 331, 332, 333, 334
TURTLE CREEK WATERSHED ASSOCIATION, INC. 335
UPPER CHATTAHOOCHEE RIVERKEEPER 337
UPPER MISSISSIPPI RIVER CONSERVATION COMMITTEE
   337
WATER RESOURCES ASSOCIATION OF THE DELAWARE
   RIVER BASIN 342
WATERSHED MANAGEMENT COUNCIL 343
WEST VIRGINIA B.A.S.S. CHAPTER FEDERATION 343
WEST VIRGINIA COOPERATIVE FISH AND WILDLIFE
   RESEARCH UNIT 119
WILDLANDS CONSERVANCY 347
WISCONSIN COOPERATIVE FISHERY RESEARCH UNIT
   (USDI) 120

Road Construction

FOSSIL FUELS POLICY ACTION INSTITUTE/ALLIANCE FOR
   A PAVING MORATORIUM 204

Runoff

COAST ALLIANCE 176
FRIENDS OF THE REEDY RIVER 206
NORTH CAROLINA COALITION, INC. 282
SAVE OUR RIVERS, INC. 309
TERRENE INSTITUTE, THE 328

Rural Development

ASSOCIATION OF NEW JERSEY ENVIRONMENTAL
   COMMISSIONS 157
CARIBBEAN NATURAL RESOURCES INSTITUTE 168
CATSKILL CENTER FOR CONSERVATION AND
   DEVELOPMENT, INC., THE 168
COLORADO STATE UNIVERSITY COOPERATIVE
   EXTENSION 50
FOOD AND AGRICULTURE ORGANIZATION OF THE UNITED
   NATIONS 203
FOREST TRUST 204
FORESTRY COMMISSION (SOUTH CAROLINA) 105
GEORGIA TRUST FOR HISTORIC PRESERVATION 210
NATIONAL ASSOCIATION OF STATE DEPARTMENTS OF
   AGRICULTURE 258
NATIONAL NETWORK OF FOREST PRACTITIONERS 263

NEBRASKA STATE EXTENSION SERVICES 82
NEW HAMPSHIRE DEPARTMENT OF AGRICULTURE,
    MARKETS, AND FOOD 83
OKLAHOMA NATIVE PLANT SOCIETY 289
OZARKS RESOURCE CENTER 292
STUDENTS PARTNERSHIP WORLDWIDE 327
TREES FOR THE FUTURE, INC. 330
TUG HILL COMMISSION 91
WISCONSIN DEPARTMENT OF AGRICULTURE TRADE AND
    CONSUMER PROTECTION 120
YOSEMITE RESTORATION TRUST 361

Salmon Recovery

AMERICAN RIVERS (formerly American Rivers Conservation
    Council) 149
ATLANTIC SALMON FEDERATION 157
NORTH ATLANTIC SALMON CONSERVATION
    ORGANIZATION 282
NW ENERGY COALITION 286
OLYMPIC PARK ASSOCIATES 289
PEOPLE FOR PUGET SOUND 295

Scholarships

ALABAMA WILDFLOWER SOCIETY, THE 133
BAT CONSERVATION INTERNATIONAL 160
OHIO ENERGY PROJECT 287

Scholarships and Grants

AMERICAN GROUND WATER TRUST 145
ATLANTIC CENTER FOR THE ENVIRONMENT 157
BOONE AND CROCKETT CLUB 161
CALIFORNIA DEPARTMENT OF EDUCATION 44
CALIFORNIA TRAPPERS ASSOCIATION 164
CAMP FIRE CONSERVATION FUND 165
CAVE RESEARCH FOUNDATION 168
CENTER FOR HEALTH, ENVIRONMENT, AND JUSTICE ... 170
CHICAGO HERPETOLOGICAL SOCIETY 173
GAME CONSERVANCY U.S.A. (formerly American Friends of
    the Game Conservancy) 207
GARDEN CLUB OF AMERICA, THE 208
INTERNATIONAL WILD WATERFOWL ASSOCIATION 229
LOUISIANA FORESTRY ASSOCIATION 243
LVIV REGIONAL INSTITUTE OF EDUCATION 244
NATIONAL FIELD ARCHERY ASSOCIATION 261
NEW YORK SEA GRANT 90
NORTH AMERICAN LOON FUND 281
TEXAS FORESTRY ASSOCIATION 329
WASHINGTON FARM FORESTRY ASSOCIATION 341
WELDER WILDLIFE FOUNDATION 343
WILDLIFE HABITAT CANADA 349
WISCONSIN ENVIRONMENTAL EDUCATION BOARD (WEEB)
    121

Schoolyard Habitats

COLORADO DEPARTMENT OF EDUCATION 49

Sea Grass

FLORIDA AUDUBON SOCIETY 201
FRIENDS OF THE SAN JUANS 206
MAINE/NEW HAMPSHIRE SEA GRANT PROGRAM 83

Sea Turtles

CONSERVANCY OF SOUTHWEST FLORIDA, THE 181
MOTE MARINE LABORATORY 255

Seabed Disturbance

MARINE CONSERVATION BIOLOGY INSTITUTE 246

Seafood Technology

NORTH CAROLINA SEA GRANT PROGRAM 92

Sensitive Species

NEVADA NATURAL HERITAGE PROGRAM 83

Shorebirds

WESTERN HEMISPHERE SHOREBIRD RESERVE NETWORK
    (WHSRN) 344

Shorelines

FRIENDS OF THE SAN JUANS 206

Smart Growth

GEORGIA CONSERVANCY, INC., THE 209
GEORGIA TRUST FOR HISTORIC PRESERVATION 210
TRUST FOR PUBLIC LAND, THE 334

Snowmobiling

MAINE DEPARTMENT OF INLAND FISHERIES AND
    WILDLIFE 70

Social Justice

STUDENT ENVIRONMENTAL ACTION COALITION (SEAC)
    326

Soil Conservation

BIOMASS USERS NETWORK 161
COMMITTEE ON AGRICULTURAL SUSTAINABILITY FOR
    DEVELOPING COUNTRIES 179
CONSERVATION DISTRICTS FOUNDATION INC. 182
DELAWARE ASSOCIATION OF CONSERVATION DISTRICTS
    186
DELAWARE DEPARTMENT OF NATURAL RESOURCES AND
    ENVIRONMENTAL CONTROL 51
IDAHO STATE DEPARTMENT OF AGRICULTURE 60
IDAHO STATE SOIL CONSERVATION COMMISSION 60
ILLINOIS DEPARTMENT OF AGRICULTURE 61
ILLINOIS WALNUT COUNCIL 219
INDIANA DEPARTMENT OF NATURAL RESOURCES 62
INTERNATIONAL EROSION CONTROL ASSOCIATION (IECA)
    224
KANSAS STATE CONSERVATION COMMISSION 66
KENTUCKY DEPARTMENT OF AGRICULTURE 66
LEAGUE OF WOMEN VOTERS OF IOWA 241
MICHIGAN DEPARTMENT OF AGRICULTURE 74
MINNESOTA BOARD OF WATER AND SOIL RESOURCES . 75
MISSISSIPPI SOIL AND WATER CONSERVATION
    COMMISSION 78
MONTANA DEPARTMENT OF NATURAL RESOURCES AND
    CONSERVATION 81
NATIONAL ARBOR DAY FOUNDATION 256
NATIONAL ASSOCIATION OF CONSERVATION DISTRICTS
    257
NATIONAL ASSOCIATION OF STATE FORESTERS 258
NATIONAL FARMERS UNION 261
NATIONAL GRANGE, THE 262
NEBRASKA NATURAL RESOURCES COMMISSION 82
NEW HAMPSHIRE DEPARTMENT OF AGRICULTURE,
    MARKETS, AND FOOD 83
NEW JERSEY DEPARTMENT OF AGRICULTURE 84
NEW YORK DEPARTMENT OF AGRICULTURE AND
    MARKETS 88
NORTH CAROLINA DEPARTMENT OF AGRICULTURE 92
NORTH DAKOTA STATE SOIL CONSERVATION COMMITTEE
    93
OHIO DEPARTMENT OF NATURAL RESOURCES 94
OKLAHOMA STATE CONSERVATION COMMISSION 96

PENNSYLVANIA DEPARTMENT OF AGRICULTURE............99
PUBLIC LANDS FOUNDATION...300
PUERTO RICO STATE EXTENSION SERVICES..................103
SOIL AND WATER CONSERVATION SOCIETY (formerly Soil Conservation Society of America)..320
STATE SOIL AND WATER CONSERVATION COMMISSION (GEORGIA)..56
TENNESSEE DEPARTMENT OF AGRICULTURE.................107
TEXAS STATE SOIL AND WATER CONSERVATION BOARD 109
UTAH STATE SOIL CONSERVATION COMMISSION..........111
VERMONT DEPARTMENT OF AGRICULTURE, FOOD, AND MARKETS 112
VIRGIN ISLANDS CONSERVATION SOCIETY, INC. 339
WASHINGTON STATE CONSERVATION COMMISSION...118
WEST VIRGINIA DEPARTMENT OF AGRICULTURE..........119
WISCONSIN DEPARTMENT OF AGRICULTURE TRADE AND CONSUMER PROTECTION..120
WISCONSIN GEOLOGICAL AND NATURAL HISTORY SURVEY..121

Solar Energy

ENVIRONMENTAL ENTERPRISES ASSISTANCE FUND, INC. 197
LEGAL ENVIRONMENTAL ASSISTANCE FOUNDATION INC. (LEAF) 242
MERCK FOREST AND FARMLAND CENTER, INC..............248
NORTHEAST SUSTAINABLE ENERGY ASSOCIATION 284
NW ENERGY COALITION...286
OHIO OFFICE OF ENERGY EFFICIENCY 94
SOUTH CAROLINA ENERGY OFFICE 105
UNION OF CONCERNED SCIENTISTS 336

Solid Waste

ALABAMA ENVIRONMENTAL COUNCIL 132
ALASKA HEALTH PROJECT...40
CHESAPEAKE BAY FOUNDATION, INC. (Pennsylvania Office) 173
CONSERVATION COUNCIL OF NORTH CAROLINA...........181
DEPARTMENT OF ENVIRONMENTAL QUALITY (ARKANSAS) 43
DEPARTMENT OF PUBLIC WORKS..52
ILLINOIS ENVIRONMENTAL COUNCIL 219
ISSAQUAH ALPS TRAILS CLUB (I.A.T.C.) 233
KANSAS STATE DEPARTMENT OF HEALTH AND ENVIRONMENT...66
MAINE ASSOCIATION OF CONSERVATION COMMISSIONS (MACC)..244
MASSACHUSETTS HIGHWAY DEPARTMENT 74
MINERAL POLICY CENTER..250
NATIONAL ENVIRONMENTAL HEALTH ASSOCIATION 260
NEW HAMPSHIRE DEPARTMENT OF ENVIRONMENTAL SERVICES...84
OHIO ENVIRONMENTAL PROTECTION AGENCY................94
PENNSYLVANIA RECREATION AND PARK SOCIETY, INC. 295
SOUTH CAROLINA ENERGY OFFICE....................................105
SOUTH DAKOTA DEPARTMENT OF ENVIRONMENT AND NATURAL RESOURCES..106
WASHINGTON B.A.S.S. CHAPTER FEDERATION.............340
WISCONSIN DEPARTMENT OF NATURAL RESOURCES..120
WYOMING OUTDOOR COUNCIL...360

Solid Waste Management

AGENCY OF NATURAL RESOURCES....................................111
AIR AND WASTE MANAGEMENT ASSOCIATION 132
ALABAMA DEPARTMENT OF ENVIRONMENTAL MANAGEMENT..38
ALASKA DEPARTMENT OF ENVIRONMENTAL CONSERVATION..39
ARIZONA DEPARTMENT OF ENVIRONMENTAL QUALITY..41
ATLANTIC STATES LEGAL FOUNDATION 157
BORDER ECOLOGY PROJECT (BEP)....................................162
CALIFORNIA ENVIRONMENTAL PROTECTION AGENCY....44
COLORADO STATE UNIVERSITY COOPERATIVE EXTENSION...50
COMMUNITY ENVIRONMENTAL COUNCIL........................179
CONCERN, INC. 179
CONNECTICUT PUBLIC INTEREST RESEARCH GROUP (Conn PIRG)..181
DELAWARE SOLID WASTE AUTHORITY 52
DEPARTMENT OF THE ENVIRONMENT 71
ENVIRONMENTAL EDUCATION ASSOCIATION OF ILLINOIS 197
ENVIROSOUTH, INC..199
GENERAL FEDERATION OF WOMEN'S CLUBS 208
GLOBAL CITIES PROJECT, THE...210
HOOSIER ENVIRONMENTAL COUNCIL 216
IDAHO STATE DEPARTMENT OF AGRICULTURE...............60
INFORM, INC. 221
IZAAK WALTON LEAGUE OF AMERICA, INC., THE...........234
KEEP AMERICA BEAUTIFUL, INC. 238
KEEP FLORIDA BEAUTIFUL, INC. 238
LEAGUE OF WOMEN VOTERS OF IOWA............................241
MAINE DEPARTMENT OF ENVIRONMENTAL PROTECTION 70
MICHIGAN DEPARTMENT OF ENVIRONMENTAL QUALITY 75
MONTANA ENVIRONMENTAL INFORMATION CENTER....254
NATIONAL ASSOCIATION OF ENVIRONMENTAL PROFESSIONALS, THE (National Office) 257
NEW JERSEY STATE EXTENSION SERVICES 86
NEW YORK PUBLIC INTEREST RESEARCH GROUP (NYPIRG..279
NEW YORK STATE COOPERATIVE EXTENSION................90
NEWFOUNDLAND LABRADOR WILDLIFE FEDERATION ..279
NORTH DAKOTA DEPARTMENT OF HEALTH 93
NORTHERN PLAINS RESOURCE COUNCIL 285
OKLAHOMA DEPARTMENT OF ENVIRONMENTAL QUALITY 95
OREGON DEPARTMENT OF ENVIRONMENTAL QUALITY (DEQ) 98
SOUTH CAROLINA DEPARTMENT OF HEALTH AND ENVIRONMENTAL CONTROL 105
SOUTH DAKOTA DEPARTMENT OF ENVIRONMENT AND NATURAL RESOURCES..106
SOUTH DAKOTA ORNITHOLOGISTS' UNION 322
STOP..13, 326
STUDENT ENVIRONMENTAL ACTION COALITION (SEAC) 326
TENNESSEE ENVIRONMENTAL COUNCIL 328
U.S. PUBLIC INTEREST RESEARCH GROUP.....................336
VIRGINIA DEPARTMENT OF ENVIRONMENTAL QUALITY 114
WASHINGTON STATE OFFICE OF ENVIRONMENTAL EDUCATION 118

Sport Fishing

ALASKA DEPARTMENT OF FISH AND GAME......................39
ALASKA DEPARTMENT OF PUBLIC SAFETY 40
AMERICAN BASS ASSOCIATION OF MARYLAND, THE ...137
AMERICAN BASS ASSOCIATION, INC..................................137
AMERICAN LEAGUE OF ANGLERS AND BOATERS 146
ARIZONA GAME AND FISH DEPARTMENT...........................41
BASS ANGLERS SPORTSMAN SOCIETY (B.A.S.S, INC.)..160
BILLFISH FOUNDATION, THE..160
CALIFORNIA TROUT, INC. 164
CAMP FIRE CLUB OF AMERICA, THE 165
CENTRAL OHIO ANGLERS AND HUNTERS CLUB 172
COASTAL CONSERVATION ASSOCIATION.......................176
DEPARTMENT OF FISH AND WILDLIFE (WASHINGTON) . 116
DEPARTMENT OF INTERIOR, U.S.G.S/B.R.D, SOUTH CAROLINA COOPERATIVE FISH AND WILDLIFE RESEARCH UNIT 104
DEPARTMENT OF WILDLIFE CONSERVATION...................95
FEDERATION OF FLY FISHERS..200
FISH AND WILDLIFE INFORMATION EXCHANGE 201
FISHAMERICA FOUNDATION..201
FLORIDA FISH AND WILDLIFE CONSERVATION COMMISSION..54
FUTURE FISHERMAN FOUNDATION....................................207
GREAT LAKES SPORT FISHING COUNCIL.........................211
IDAHO FISH AND GAME DEPARTMENT 60
INTERNATIONAL GAME FISH ASSOCIATION....................225

KANSAS DEPARTMENT OF WILDLIFE AND PARKS 65
MAINE ATLANTIC SALMON COMMISSION (formerly Maine
 Atlantic Salmon Authority) 69
MAINE DEPARTMENT OF INLAND FISHERIES AND
 WILDLIFE 70
MAINE/NEW HAMPSHIRE SEA GRANT PROGRAM 83
MISSISSIPPI COOPERATIVE FISH AND WILDLIFE
 RESEARCH UNIT (USDI) 77
MISSISSIPPI INTERSTATE COOPERATIVE RESOURCE
 ASSOCIATION 252
MONTANA DEPARTMENT OF FISH, WILDLIFE, AND PARKS
 80
MUSKIES, INC. 256
NATIONAL COALITION FOR MARINE CONSERVATION 260
NATIONAL FIELD ARCHERY ASSOCIATION 261
NEW HAMPSHIRE FISH AND GAME DEPARTMENT 84
NORTH AMERICAN FISHING CLUB 281
NORTH CAROLINA BEACH BUGGY ASSOCIATION, INC ... 282
NORTH DAKOTA GAME AND FISH DEPARTMENT 93
PACIFIC FISHERY MANAGEMENT COUNCIL 292
PENNSYLVANIA FISH AND BOAT COMMISSION 101
QUEBEC WILDLIFE FEDERATION 301
STRIPERS UNLIMITED, INC. 326
UTAH COOPERATIVE FISH AND WILDLIFE RESEARCH UNIT
 (USDI-USGS-BRD-CRU) 110
WEST VIRGINIA DIVISION OF NATURAL RESOURCES 119
WILDLIFE FOREVER 348
WILDLIFE FOUNDATION OF FLORIDA, INC. 349
WILDLIFE LEGISLATIVE FUND OF AMERICA, THE, AND
 WILDLIFE CONSERVATION FUND OF AMERICA, THE .. 349
WILDLIFE RESOURCES AGENCY 107
WISCONSIN COOPERATIVE FISHERY RESEARCH UNIT
 (USDI) 120

Sprawl

NEW ENGLAND COALITION FOR SUSTAINABLE
 POPULATION (NECSP) 276
SCENIC HUDSON, INC. 311
TRUST FOR PUBLIC LAND, THE 334

State Forests

PENNSYLVANIA DEPARTMENT OF CONSERVATION AND
 NATURAL RESOURCES 100

State Parks

PENNSYLVANIA DEPARTMENT OF CONSERVATION AND
 NATURAL RESOURCES 100
SOUTHERN APPALACHIAN BOTANICAL SOCIETY 323

Stewardship

COASTAL GEORGIA LAND TRUST, THE 176
COOSA RIVER BASIN INITIATIVE 184
ENVIRONMENTAL EDUCATION COUNCIL OF OHIO 197
GEORGIA ENVIRONMENTAL POLICY INSTITUTE 209
MOUNT GRACE LAND CONSERVATION TRUST 255
NORTH CAROLINA WILD FLOWER PRESERVATION
 SOCIETY 283
SHELBURNE FARMS 312
SONORAN INSTITUTE 320
TREES ATLANTA 330
WILDLIFE HABITAT CANADA 349

Streams

AMERICAN SOCIETY OF LIMNOLOGY AND
 OCEANOGRAPHY 150
NORTH AMERICAN BENTHOLOGICAL SOCIETY 280
NORTH CAROLINA COALITION, INC. 282
PITTSBURGH HERPETOLOGICAL SOCIETY, THE 296
SAVE OUR RIVERS, INC. 309
SAVE THE DUNES COUNCIL 309
WATERSHED MANAGEMENT COUNCIL 343

Sustainability

CENTER FOR CHESAPEAKE COMMUNITIES 169
CENTER FOR INDEPENDENT SOCIAL RESEARCH 170
CONSERVATION FORCE 182
ENVIRONMENTAL LAW AND POLICY CENTER OF THE
 MIDWEST 198
GEORGIA ENVIRONMENTAL POLICY INSTITUTE 209
IZAAK WALTON LEAGUE OF AMERICA, INC., THE 234
LAKE SUPERIOR GREENS 240
LVIV REGIONAL INSTITUTE OF EDUCATION 244
NATURAL RESOURCES INFORMATION COUNCIL 271
NEW ENGLAND COALITION FOR SUSTAINABLE
 POPULATION (NECSP) 276
RENEW AMERICA 303
SIERRA NEVADA FOREST PROTECTION CAMPAIGN 317
TEXAS FORESTRY ASSOCIATION 329
WEST MICHIGAN ENVIRONMENTAL ACTION COUNCIL ... 343
WINDSTAR FOUNDATION, THE 355

Sustainable Agriculture

ECODEFENSE 193
HENRY A. WALLACE INSTITUTE FOR ALTERNATIVE
 AGRICULTURE (HAWIAA) 215
SHELBURNE FARMS 312

Sustainable Buildings

NORTHEAST SUSTAINABLE ENERGY ASSOCIATION 284

Sustainable Development

ADIRONDACK COUNCIL, THE 131
ADIRONDACK NATURE CONSERVANCY/ADIRONDACK
 LAND TRUST, INC. 131
AFRICAN WILDLIFE FOUNDATION 132
ALABAMA FORESTRY COMMISSION 39
ALASKA CONSERVATION ALLIANCE 133
ALASKA CONSERVATION VOICE 134
ALLIANCE FOR THE CHESAPEAKE BAY 135
AMERICAN GEOGRAPHICAL SOCIETY 145
AMERICAN LIVESTOCK BREEDS CONSERVANCY 147
ARIZONA LAND DEPARTMENT 41
ASSOCIATION FOR THE PROTECTION OF THE
 ADIRONDACKS, THE 155
ASSOCIATION OF NEW JERSEY ENVIRONMENTAL
 COMMISSIONS 157
ATLANTIC CENTER FOR THE ENVIRONMENT 157
ATLANTIC STATES LEGAL FOUNDATION 157
AUDUBON INTERNATIONAL 158
AUDUBON NATURALIST SOCIETY OF THE CENTRAL
 ATLANTIC STATES 158
AUDUBON SOCIETY OF PORTLAND 159
BIOMASS USERS NETWORK 161
BOONE AND CROCKETT FOUNDATION 161
CAMPAIGN FOR A PROSPEROUS GEORGIA 165
CARIBBEAN NATURAL RESOURCES INSTITUTE 168
CARRYING CAPACITY NETWORK 168
CATSKILL CENTER FOR CONSERVATION AND
 DEVELOPMENT, INC., THE 168
CATSKILL FOREST ASSOCIATION 168
CENTER FOR RESOURCE ECONOMICS 171
CENTER FOR RESOURCEFUL BUILDING TECHNOLOGY 171
CHARLES A. AND ANNE MORROW LINDBERGH
 FOUNDATION, THE 172
CIRCUMPOLAR CONSERVATION UNION 174
CLIMATE INSTITUTE 175
COASTAL GEORGIA LAND TRUST, THE 176
COASTAL SOCIETY, THE 177
COLORADO ENVIRONMENTAL COALITION 177
COLORADO STATE UNIVERSITY COOPERATIVE
 EXTENSION 50
COMMITTEE FOR THE NATIONAL INSTITUTE FOR THE
 ENVIRONMENT (CNIE) 178
COMMITTEE ON AGRICULTURAL SUSTAINABILITY FOR
 DEVELOPING COUNTRIES 179
COMMUNITY ENVIRONMENTAL COUNCIL 179

COMMUNITY RIGHTS COUNSEL 179
CONCERN, INC. 179
CONNECTICUT AUDUBON SOCIETY, INC. 180
CONSERVATION FEDERATION OF MARYLAND/For A Rural
  Maryland (F.A.R.M.) 182
DELAWARE GREENWAYS, INC. 187
DESERT FISHES COUNCIL 188
DESERT RESEARCH FOUNDATION OF NAMIBIA, THE 188
EARTH ISLAND INSTITUTE 191
EARTHSCAN 193
EARTHWATCH INSTITUTE 193
ECOTOURISM SOCIETY, THE 194
ENVIRONMENTAL ENTERPRISES ASSISTANCE FUND, INC.
  197
ENVIRONMENTAL LAW INSTITUTE, THE 198
FEDERATION OF ENVIRONMENTAL EDUCATION IN ST.
  PETERSBURG 200
FOREST TRUST 204
FOSSIL FUELS POLICY ACTION INSTITUTE/ALLIANCE FOR
  A PAVING MORATORIUM 204
FRIENDS OF THE SAN JUANS 206
GEORGIA ENVIRONMENTAL ORGANIZATION, INC (GEO) 209
GEORGIA SEA GRANT COLLEGE PROGRAM 56
GLOBAL CITIES PROJECT, THE 210
GLOBAL ENVIRONMENTAL MANAGEMENT INITIATIVE
  (GEMI) 210
GRAND CANYON TRUST (St. George, UT Office) 211
GREEN PARTY USA 213
GREEN SEAL 213
GUAM COASTAL MANAGEMENT PROGRAM 57
HAWAII SOCIETY OF AMERICAN FORESTERS 214
HEADLANDS INSTITUTE 215
ILLINOIS WALNUT COUNCIL 219
INTERFAITH COUNCIL FOR THE PROTECTION OF ANIMALS
  AND NATURE INC. (ICPAN) 222
INTERNATIONAL BICYCLE FUND 223
INTERNATIONAL CENTRE FOR CONSERVATION
  EDUCATION 224
INTERNATIONAL INSTITUTE FOR ENERGY
  CONSERVATION 225
INTERNATIONAL MARITIME ORGANIZATION 226
INTERNATIONAL SOCIETY FOR ECOLOGICAL ECONOMICS
  227
INTERNATIONAL SONORAN DESERT ALLIANCE 228
INTERNATIONAL UNION FOR CONSERVATION OF NATURE
  AND NATURAL RESOURCES (IUCN) THE WORLD
  CONSERVATION UNION 228
INTERTRIBAL BISON COOPERATIVE (ITBC) 231
IOWA NATURAL HERITAGE FOUNDATION 232
ISLAND INSTITUTE, THE 233
KANSAS WATER OFFICE 66
LEGACY INTERNATIONAL 242
LOUISIANA SEA GRANT COLLEGE PROGRAM 69
MAINE/NEW HAMPSHIRE SEA GRANT PROGRAM 83
MINNESOTA DEPARTMENT OF AGRICULTURE 76
MINNESOTA ENVIRONMENTAL QUALITY BOARD 76
MINNESOTA SEA GRANT COLLEGE PROGRAM 77
MONITOR INTERNATIONAL 253
MONO LAKE COMMITTEE 254
NATIONAL 4-H COUNCIL 256
NATIONAL NETWORK OF FOREST PRACTITIONERS 263
NATIONAL TRAPPERS ASSOCIATION, INC. 265
NATIONAL WILDLIFE FEDERATION 267, 268
NEVIS HISTORICAL AND CONSERVATION SOCIETY 276
NEW HAMPSHIRE DEPARTMENT OF AGRICULTURE,
  MARKETS, AND FOOD 83
NEW JERSEY CONSERVATION FOUNDATION 278
NEW JERSEY ENVIRONMENTAL LOBBY 278
NORTHWEST ENVIRONMENT WATCH 285
NORTHWEST RESOURCE INFORMATION CENTER 286
OHIO ENVIRONMENTAL COUNCIL, INC. 287
OREGON WATER RESOURCES DEPARTMENT 99
OZARKS RESOURCE CENTER 292
PACIFIC INSTITUTE FOR STUDIES IN DEVELOPMENT,
  ENVIRONMENT, AND SECURITY 293
PANOS INSTITUTE, THE 293
PENNSYLVANIA ENVIRONMENTAL COUNCIL, INC. (PEC) 294
POPULATION ACTION INTERNATIONAL 297
POPULATION REFERENCE BUREAU, INC. 298
PRIORITIES INSTITUTE, THE 299

QUEBEC WILDLIFE FEDERATION 301
RAINBOW PUSH COALITION 302
RAINFOREST ALLIANCE 302
RESOURCE RENEWAL INSTITUTE, THE 304
RESOURCES FOR THE FUTURE 304
RETURNED PEACE CORPS VOLUNTEER FOR
  ENVIRONMENT AND DEVELOPMENT (RPCV-ED) 305
RINCON INSTITUTE, THE 305
SAVE AMERICA'S FORESTS 309
SOCIETY FOR CONSERVATION BIOLOGY 318
SOIL AND WATER CONSERVATION SOCIETY (formerly Soil
  Conservation Society of America) 320
SONORAN INSTITUTE 320
SOUTH CAROLINA SEA GRANT CONSORTIUM 106
SOUTHEAST ALASKA CONSERVATION COUNCIL (SEACC)
  323
SOUTHFACE ENERGY INSTITUTE 324
STUDENTS PARTNERSHIP WORLDWIDE 327
TENNESSEE ENVIRONMENTAL COUNCIL 328
TEXAS AGRICULTURAL EXTENSION SERVICE 108
TEXAS ORGANIZATION FOR ENDANGERED SPECIES 329
TOGETHER FOUNDATION, THE 330
TREES FOR THE FUTURE, INC. 330
UNION OF CONCERNED SCIENTISTS 336
UNIVERSITY OF VERMONT EXTENSION 112
UPPER MISSISSIPPI RIVER CONSERVATION COMMITTEE
  337
UTAH STATE SOIL CONSERVATION COMMISSION 111
WASHINGTON ENVIRONMENTAL COUNCIL 340
WASHINGTON SEA GRANT PROGRAM 118
WILDLIFE HABITAT COUNCIL 349
WORLD ASSOCIATION OF GIRL GUIDES AND GIRL
  SCOUTS (WAGGGS) 357
WORLD PAL (WORLD POPULATION ALLOCATION LIMITED
  INC.) 358
WORLD RESOURCES INSTITUTE 358
WORLD WOMEN IN THE DEFENSE OF THE ENVIRONMENT
  (WorldWIDE) 359
WORLDWATCH INSTITUTE 359
WYOMING STATE EXTENSION SERVICES 123
ZERO POPULATION GROWTH, INC. 361

Sustainable Ecosystems

ALASKA AUDUBON SOCIETY 133
ALASKA CONSERVATION FOUNDATION 134
AMERICAN INSTITUTE OF BIOLOGICAL SCIENCES 146
ATLANTIC STATES LEGAL FOUNDATION 157
BIODIVERSITY LEGAL FOUNDATION 161
BOONE AND CROCKETT FOUNDATION 161
CATSKILL FOREST ASSOCIATION 168
CENTER FOR MARINE CONSERVATION 170
CENTER FOR RESOURCE ECONOMICS 171
COLORADO STATE FOREST SERVICE 49
COLORADO STATE UNIVERSITY COOPERATIVE
  EXTENSION 50
COLORADO WILDLIFE HERITAGE FOUNDATION 178
COMMITTEE FOR THE NATIONAL INSTITUTE FOR THE
  ENVIRONMENT (CNIE) 178
COUSTEAU SOCIETY, INC., THE 185
CRAIGHEAD WILDLIFE-WILDLANDS INSTITUTE 185
EARTHWATCH INSTITUTE 193
FOREST SOCIETY OF MAINE 204
FOREST WATCH 204
FOSSIL RIM WILDLIFE CENTER 205
FRIENDS OF DISCOVERY PARK 205
GLACIER INSTITUTE, THE 210
GUAM COASTAL MANAGEMENT PROGRAM 57
HAWAII COOPERATIVE FISHERY RESEARCH UNIT (USDI) 58
HUNTSMAN MARINE SCIENCE CENTRE 217
ILLINOIS ASSOCIATION OF CONSERVATION DISTRICTS 218
INDIANA NATIVE PLANT AND WILDFLOWER SOCIETY 220
INTERNATIONAL SNOW LEOPARD TRUST 227
INTERNATIONAL SOCIETY FOR ECOLOGICAL ECONOMICS
  227
INTERNATIONAL SOCIETY OF TROPICAL FORESTERS, INC.
  228
IOWA COOPERATIVE FISH AND WILDLIFE RESEARCH UNIT
  64

KEYWORD INDEX - Sustainable Energy

KANSAS BIOLOGICAL SURVEY 65
LOUISIANA DEPARTMENT OF AGRICULTURE AND
    FORESTRY 68
LOWER MISSISSIPPI RIVER CONSERVATION COMMITTEE
    244
MAGIC 244
MAINE/NEW HAMPSHIRE SEA GRANT PROGRAM 83
MANASOTA-88 245
MARYLAND FORESTS ASSOCIATION 247
MINNESOTA ENVIRONMENTAL QUALITY BOARD 76
MINNESOTA SEA GRANT COLLEGE PROGRAM 77
MONTANA WILDERNESS ASSOCIATION 255
NATURAL HERITAGE COMMISSION (ARKANSAS) 44
NEBRASKA STATE EXTENSION SERVICES 82
NEW JERSEY CONSERVATION FOUNDATION 278
NEW JERSEY PINELANDS COMMISSION 85
NEW YORK STATE COOPERATIVE EXTENSION 90
NORTH CAROLINA WILD FLOWER PRESERVATION
    SOCIETY 283
NORTHERN ALASKA ENVIRONMENTAL CENTER 285
NORTHWEST ECOSYSTEM ALLIANCE 285
NORTHWEST RESOURCE INFORMATION CENTER 286
OHIO ENVIRONMENTAL COUNCIL, INC. 287
OREGON WATER RESOURCES DEPARTMENT 99
PACIFIC INSTITUTE FOR STUDIES IN DEVELOPMENT,
    ENVIRONMENT, AND SECURITY 293
PENNSYLVANIA FOREST STEWARDSHIP PROGRAM 102
PINCHOT INSTITUTE FOR CONSERVATION 296
RAINFOREST TRUST, INC., THE 302
REEF RELIEF 303
RESOURCE RENEWAL INSTITUTE, THE 304
RINCON INSTITUTE, THE 305
RIVERS COUNCIL OF WASHINGTON (formerly Northwest
    Rivers Council) 306
SAVE AMERICA'S FORESTS 309
SOCIETY OF WETLAND SCIENTISTS 320
SOIL AND WATER CONSERVATION SOCIETY (formerly Soil
    Conservation Society of America) 320
SOUTH CAROLINA SEA GRANT CONSORTIUM 106
UNIVERSITY OF MASSACHUSETTS EXTENSION 74
WASHINGTON STATE EXTENSION SERVICES 118
WASHINGTON STATE OFFICE OF ENVIRONMENTAL
    EDUCATION 118
WESTERN HEMISPHERE SHOREBIRD RESERVE NETWORK
    (WHSRN) 344
WESTERN PENNSYLVANIA CONSERVANCY 344
WILDERNESS SOCIETY, THE 346
WISCONSIN ASSOCIATION OF LAKES (WAL) 355

Sustainable Energy

ENVIRONMENTAL LAW AND POLICY CENTER OF THE
    MIDWEST 198
LEAGUE OF ENVIRONMENTAL JOURNALISTS 241
LIFE OF THE LAND 242
NORTHEAST SUSTAINABLE ENERGY ASSOCIATION 284
OHIO OFFICE OF ENERGY EFFICIENCY 94

Sustainable Resources

FOREST SOCIETY OF MAINE 204
MISSOURI FOREST PRODUCTS ASSOCIATION 253
NATIONAL FORESTRY ASSOCIATION 262
NATURAL RESOURCES INFORMATION COUNCIL 271
SOCIETY FOR RANGE MANAGEMENT 319

Taiga

NORTHERN ALASKA ENVIRONMENTAL CENTER 285

Terrestrial Habitats

FISH AND WILDLIFE INFORMATION EXCHANGE 201
HAWAII NATURE CENTER 214
INTERNATIONAL ASSOCIATION OF WILDLAND FIRE
    (formerly Fire Research Institute) 223
MICHIGAN WILDLIFE HABITAT FOUNDATION 250
NEW HAMPSHIRE NATURAL HERITAGE INVENTORY 84

OKLAHOMA NATIVE PLANT SOCIETY 289
RHODE ISLAND STATE ASSOCIATION OF CONSERVATION
    DISTRICTS 305
RINCON INSTITUTE, THE 305
SOUTH DAKOTA GAME, FISH, AND PARKS DEPARTMENT
    106
UTAH COOPERATIVE FISH AND WILDLIFE RESEARCH UNIT
    (USDI-USGS-BRD-CRU) 110

Tortoises

MATTS (MID-ATLANTIC TURTLE AND TORTOISE SOCIETY,
    INC.) 248

Tourism

ECOTOURISM SOCIETY, THE 194

Toxic Reduction

CHLORINE-FREE PAPER CONSORTIUM (CPC) 173
MINNESOTA CENTER FOR ENVIRONMENTAL ADVOCACY
    (MCEA) 251
WASHINGTON TOXICS COALITION 341

Toxic Substances

AGENCY OF NATURAL RESOURCES 111
ALLIANCE FOR THE CHESAPEAKE BAY 135
ARIZONA DEPARTMENT OF ENVIRONMENTAL QUALITY .. 41
BORDER ECOLOGY PROJECT (BEP) 162
CALIFORNIA ENVIRONMENTAL PROTECTION AGENCY 44
CENTER FOR HEALTH, ENVIRONMENT, AND JUSTICE ... 170
CHLORINE-FREE PAPER CONSORTIUM (CPC) 173
COMMUNITY ENVIRONMENTAL COUNCIL 179
CONNECTICUT FUND FOR THE ENVIRONMENT 180
CONNECTICUT PUBLIC INTEREST RESEARCH GROUP
    (Conn PIRG) 181
COOK INLET KEEPER 184
FLORIDA STATE DEPARTMENT OF HEALTH 54
GREAT LAKES UNITED 211
GREENPEACE, INC. 213
HUMAN ECOLOGY ACTION LEAGUE, INC. THE (HEAL) ... 217
IDAHO STATE DEPARTMENT OF AGRICULTURE 60
ILLINOIS ENVIRONMENTAL PROTECTION AGENCY 61
INDIANA STATE DEPARTMENT OF HEALTH 63
INFORM, INC. 221
KENTUCKY RESOURCES COUNCIL 239
LAKE SUPERIOR GREENS 240
MANASOTA-88 245
MICHIGAN DEPARTMENT OF ENVIRONMENTAL QUALITY 75
MINERAL POLICY CENTER 250
MONTANA ENVIRONMENTAL INFORMATION CENTER 254
NATIONAL ENVIRONMENTAL HEALTH ASSOCIATION 260
NEW MEXICO COOPERATIVE FISH AND WILDLIFE
    RESEARCH UNIT 87
NEW YORK PUBLIC INTEREST RESEARCH GROUP
    (NYPIRG 279
OHIO ENVIRONMENTAL COUNCIL, INC. 287
PHYSICIANS FOR SOCIAL RESPONSIBILITY 296
POWDER RIVER BASIN RESOURCE COUNCIL 298
RACHEL CARSON COUNCIL, INC. (formerly Rachel Carson
    Trust for the Living Environment Inc.) 301
RAINBOW PUSH COALITION 302
SIERRA CLUB 312, 314, 315, 316, 317
SOUTH CAROLINA DEPARTMENT OF HEALTH AND
    ENVIRONMENTAL CONTROL 105
SOUTH DAKOTA DEPARTMENT OF ENVIRONMENT AND
    NATURAL RESOURCES 106
STOP 13, 326
STRIPERS UNLIMITED, INC. 326
TENNESSEE ENVIRONMENTAL COUNCIL 328
TEXAS DEPARTMENT OF HEALTH 108
UTAH DEPARTMENT OF HEALTH 110
VERMONT DEPARTMENT OF HEALTH 112
WASHINGTON TOXICS COALITION 341
WATER ENVIRONMENT FEDERATION 342
WESTERN ENVIRONMENTAL LAW CENTER 344

WILDLIFE DAMAGE REVIEW (WDR) 348
WYOMING OUTDOOR COUNCIL 360

Toxicology

BEYOND PESTICIDES/NATIONAL COALITION AGAINST THE
  MISUSE OF PESTICIDES 160
CENTER FOR SCIENCE IN THE PUBLIC INTEREST 171
COLORADO DEPARTMENT OF AGRICULTURE 49
FLORIDA STATE DEPARTMENT OF HEALTH 54
INDIANA STATE DEPARTMENT OF HEALTH 63
MICHIGAN DEPARTMENT OF ENVIRONMENTAL QUALITY 75
MINNESOTA COOPERATIVE FISH AND WILDLIFE
  RESEARCH UNIT 76
NORTHWEST COALITION FOR ALTERNATIVES TO
  PESTICIDES 285
OHIO SEA GRANT COLLEGE PROGRAM 95
TEXAS DEPARTMENT OF HEALTH 108
UTAH DEPARTMENT OF HEALTH 110
VERMONT DEPARTMENT OF HEALTH 112
WASHINGTON COOPERATIVE FISH AND WILDLIFE
  RESEARCH UNIT (USDI) 117
WEST VIRGINIA COOPERATIVE FISH AND WILDLIFE
  RESEARCH UNIT 119

Trade/Business

UNITED STATES CHAMBER OF COMMERCE 336

Trail

ADIRONDACK MOUNTAIN CLUB, INC., THE 131
AMERICAN HIKING SOCIETY 145
APPALACHIAN MOUNTAIN CLUB 153
APPALACHIAN TRAIL CONFERENCE 153
FLORIDA TRAIL ASSOCIATION, INC. 203
FRIENDS OF THE REEDY RIVER 206
GREEN MOUNTAIN CLUB INC., THE 213
ILLINOIS PRAIRIE PATH 219
IOWA NATURAL HERITAGE FOUNDATION 232
IOWA TRAILS COUNCIL 232
MINNESOTA PARKS AND TRAILS COUNCIL 251
NATIONAL ASSOCIATION OF SERVICE AND
  CONSERVATION CORPS (NASCC) 258
NEW YORK-NEW JERSEY TRAIL CONFERENCE INC. 279
POTOMAC APPALACHIAN TRAIL CLUB 298
WASHINGTON TRAILS ASSOCIATION 341

Training

ALASKA HEALTH PROJECT 40
ALASKA NATURAL RESOURCE AND OUTDOOR
  EDUCATION ASSOCIATION 134
ALDO LEOPOLD FOUNDATION, INC. 135
ASSOCIATION OF NEW JERSEY ENVIRONMENTAL
  COMMISSIONS 157
CARIBBEAN NATURAL RESOURCES INSTITUTE 168
CONFERENCE OF NATIONAL PARK COOPERATING
  ASSOCIATIONS 180
CONSERVATION FUND, THE 182
ECODEFENSE 193
ENVIRONMENTAL CAREER CENTER 195
GEORGIA FORESTRY ASSOCIATION, INC. 209
HUNTSMAN MARINE SCIENCE CENTRE 217
INITIATIVE FOR SOCIAL ACTION AND RENEWAL IN
  EURASIA 221
INSTITUTE FOR CIVIC INITIATIVES SUPPORT 221
INSTITUTE FOR CONSERVATION LEADERSHIP 221
INSTITUTO BRASIL DE EDUCACAO AMBIENTAL 222
INTERNATIONAL CENTER FOR GIBBON STUDIES 224
INTERNATIONAL HUNTER EDUCATION ASSOCIATION ...225
INTERPRETATION CANADA 230
IOWA WOMEN IN NATURAL RESOURCES 233
LOUISIANA FORESTRY ASSOCIATION 243
MASSACHUSETTS ENVIRONMENTAL EDUCATION
  SOCIETY 248
MINNESOTA BOARD OF WATER AND SOIL RESOURCES .75
MISSOURI FOREST PRODUCTS ASSOCIATION 253

NATIONAL ASSOCIATION OF SERVICE AND
  CONSERVATION CORPS (NASCC) 258
NATIONAL WHISTLEBLOWER CENTER 266
NORTH AMERICAN ASSOCIATION FOR ENVIRONMENTAL
  EDUCATION 280
OKLAHOMA ACADEMY OF SCIENCE 288
QUEBEC WILDLIFE FEDERATION 301
RESOURCE CENTER FOR ENVIRONMENTAL EDUCATION,
  THE 304
RESPONSIVE MANAGEMENT 305
SAFE ENERGY COMMUNICATION COUNCIL 308
SOIL AND WATER CONSERVATION SOCIETY (formerly Soil
  Conservation Society of America) 320
STUDENTS PARTNERSHIP WORLDWIDE 327
THREE CIRCLES CENTER FOR MULTICULTURAL
  ENVIRONMENTAL EDUCATION 329
WOLF EDUCATION AND RESEARCH CENTER 357
WORLD ASSOCIATION OF GIRL GUIDES AND GIRL
  SCOUTS (WAGGGS) 357

Transportation

AMERICAN COUNCIL FOR AN ENERGY-EFFICIENT
  ECONOMY 139
CHESAPEAKE BAY FOUNDATION, INC. (Pennsylvania Office)
 173
CONSERVATION LAW FOUNDATION, INC. (CLF) 183
COUNCIL FOR PLANNING AND CONSERVATION 185
DELAWARE GREENWAYS, INC. 187
DEPARTMENT OF PUBLIC WORKS 52
DEPARTMENT OF TRANSPORTATION (OREGON) 97
DEPARTMENT OF TRANSPORTATION (RHODE ISLAND) 104
ENVIRONMENTAL AND ENERGY STUDY INSTITUTE (EESI)
 195
ENVIRONMENTAL DEFENSE FUND, INC. 196
ENVIRONMENTAL LAW AND POLICY CENTER OF THE
  MIDWEST 198
FOSSIL FUELS POLICY ACTION INSTITUTE/ALLIANCE FOR
  A PAVING MORATORIUM 204
FRIENDS OF THE EARTH 206
GEORGIA CONSERVANCY, INC., THE 209
GEORGIA FORESTRY ASSOCIATION, INC. 209
GLOBAL CITIES PROJECT, THE 210
ILLINOIS DEPARTMENT OF TRANSPORTATION 61
INFORM, INC. 221
INTERNATIONAL BICYCLE FUND 223
INTERNATIONAL INSTITUTE FOR ENERGY
  CONSERVATION 225
INTERNATIONAL MARITIME ORGANIZATION 226
IOWA TRAILS COUNCIL 232
LAND WATCH MONTEREY COUNTY 241
MASSACHUSETTS HIGHWAY DEPARTMENT 74
NATIONAL 4-H COUNCIL 256
NATIONAL GRANGE, THE 262
NEW JERSEY ENVIRONMENTAL LOBBY 278
NEW YORK PUBLIC INTEREST RESEARCH GROUP
  (NYPIRG) 279
NORTHEAST SUSTAINABLE ENERGY ASSOCIATION 284
NORTHWEST ENVIRONMENT WATCH 285
OHIO OFFICE OF ENERGY EFFICIENCY 94
OREGON B.A.S.S. CHAPTER FEDERATION 290
OREGON ENVIRONMENTAL COUNCIL 290
PRIORITIES INSTITUTE, THE 299
RESOURCES FOR THE FUTURE 304
SCENIC HUDSON, INC. 311
SOUTH CAROLINA B.A.S.S. CHAPTER FEDERATION 321
SOUTH CAROLINA ENERGY OFFICE 105
SOUTHERN ENVIRONMENTAL LAW CENTER 324
STATE OFFICE OF CONSERVATION (LOUISIANA) 69
STOP 13, 326
UNION OF CONCERNED SCIENTISTS 336
UNITED STATES DEPARTMENT OF TRANSPORTATION ...31
URBAN HABITAT PROGRAM 337
WASHINGTON TOXICS COALITION 341
YOSEMITE RESTORATION TRUST 361

Trapping

ALASKA DEPARTMENT OF PUBLIC SAFETY 40

KEYWORD INDEX - Travel

ANIMAL PROTECTION INSTITUTE 152
ANIMAL WELFARE INSTITUTE 152
BOUNTY INFORMATION SERVICE (WILDLIFE) 162
CALIFORNIA TRAPPERS ASSOCIATION 164
CALIFORNIA WILDLIFE DEFENDERS 164
CANADIAN FEDERATION OF HUMANE SOCIETIES 166
COLORADO TRAPPERS ASSOCIATION 178
FRIENDS OF ANIMALS INC. 205
FUND FOR ANIMALS INC., THE 207
HUMANE SOCIETY OF THE UNITED STATES, THE 217
INTERNATIONAL ECOLOGY SOCIETY (IES) 224
IOWA TRAPPERS ASSOCIATION, INC. 232
KANSAS STATE EXTENSION SERVICES 66
MASSACHUSETTS TRAPPER'S ASSOCIATION, INC. 248
NATIONAL HUNTERS ASSOCIATION, INC. 262
NATIONAL TRAPPERS ASSOCIATION, INC. 265
NEW HAMPSHIRE FISH AND GAME DEPARTMENT 84
NEWFOUNDLAND LABRADOR WILDLIFE FEDERATION ... 279
NORTHWEST ECOSYSTEM ALLIANCE 285
PENNSYLVANIA GAME COMMISSION 102
RIVER OTTER ALLIANCE, THE 306
ROCKY MOUNTAIN BIGHORN SOCIETY 306
SOCIETY FOR ANIMAL PROTECTIVE LEGISLATION 318
WILDLIFE DAMAGE REVIEW (WDR) 348
WILDLIFE LEGISLATIVE FUND OF AMERICA, THE, AND
   WILDLIFE CONSERVATION FUND OF AMERICA, THE .. 349

Travel

ECOTOURISM SOCIETY, THE 194

Trees

AMERICAN FORESTS (formerly American Forestry
   Association) 144
COMMITTEE FOR NATIONAL ARBOR DAY 178
FOREST WATCH 204
ILLINOIS WALNUT COUNCIL 219
LADY BIRD JOHNSON WILDFLOWER CENTER 240
MISSOURI FOREST PRODUCTS ASSOCIATION 253
NATIONAL ARBOR DAY FOUNDATION 256
OUTDOOR CIRCLE, THE 291
SOUTHERN APPALACHIAN BOTANICAL SOCIETY 323
TREEPEOPLE 330
TREES ATLANTA 330
TREES FOR TOMORROW, INC., NATURAL RESOURCES
   EDUCATION CENTER 331

Tropical Biodiversity and Conservation

INTERNATIONAL CENTER FOR TROPICAL ECOLOGY 224
RAINFOREST RELIEF 302
WORLD PARKS ENDOWMENT INC. 358
ZUNGAROCOCHA RESEARCH CENTER 361

Trout

CALIFORNIA TROUT, INC. 164

Tundra

NORTHERN ALASKA ENVIRONMENTAL CENTER 285

Turtles

MATTS (MID-ATLANTIC TURTLE AND TORTOISE SOCIETY,
   INC.) 248

Upstream Flood Prevention

NORTH CAROLINA COALITION, INC. 282
OKLAHOMA STATE CONSERVATION COMMISSION 96

Urban and Rural Development

CANADIAN ARCTIC RESOURCES COMMITTEE, INC. 166
COUNCIL FOR PLANNING AND CONSERVATION 185
NORTH CAROLINA COALITION, INC. 282
PRIORITIES INSTITUTE, THE 299
ROGER TORY PETERSON INSTITUTE 307
SOUTH CAROLINA COASTAL CONSERVATION LEAGUE 321
URBAN WILDLIFE RESOURCES 337

Urban Environment

ADOPT-A-STREAM FOUNDATION, THE 131
AMERICAN CONSERVATION ASSOCIATION, INC. 139
AMERICAN GEOGRAPHICAL SOCIETY 145
AMERICAN NATURE STUDY SOCIETY 147
AMERICAN PLANNING ASSOCIATION 148
AMERICAN SOCIETY OF LANDSCAPE ARCHITECTS 150
ASSOCIATION OF AMERICAN GEOGRAPHERS 155
ATLANTIC STATES LEGAL FOUNDATION 157
AUDUBON SOCIETY OF PORTLAND 159
BIO-INTEGRAL RESOURCE CENTER 161
CENTER FOR WATERSHED PROTECTION 171
COLORADO DEPARTMENT OF EDUCATION 49
COLORADO STATE UNIVERSITY COOPERATIVE
   EXTENSION 50
COMITE DESPERTAR CIDRENO 102
COMMUNITY RIGHTS COUNSEL 179
COUNCIL FOR ENVIRONMENTAL EDUCATION 184, 237
DELAWARE ASSOCIATION OF CONSERVATION DISTRICTS
   186
DEPARTMENT OF PUBLIC WORKS 52
EARTH ISLAND INSTITUTE 191
EARTHSCAN 193
ELSA WILD ANIMAL APPEAL 194
FOSSIL FUELS POLICY ACTION INSTITUTE/ALLIANCE FOR
   A PAVING MORATORIUM 204
GEORGIA CONSERVANCY, INC., THE 209
GEORGIA TRUST FOR HISTORIC PRESERVATION 210
GIRL SCOUTS OF THE UNITED STATES OF AMERICA ... 210
HEADLANDS INSTITUTE 215
HUMAN ECOLOGY ACTION LEAGUE, INC. THE (HEAL) ... 217
INTERNATIONAL PLANT PROPAGATION SOCIETY, INC.,
   THE 226
LAND WATCH MONTEREY COUNTY 241
MAGIC 244
MICHIGAN ENVIRONMENTAL COUNCIL 249
NATIONAL ASSOCIATION OF CONSERVATION DISTRICTS
   257
NATIONAL ASSOCIATION OF SERVICE AND
   CONSERVATION CORPS (NASCC) 258
NATIONAL TRUST FOR HISTORIC PRESERVATION 265
NEW JERSEY CONSERVATION FOUNDATION 278
NEW JERSEY DEPARTMENT OF AGRICULTURE 84
NORTH AMERICAN ASSOCIATION FOR ENVIRONMENTAL
   EDUCATION 280
NORTH AMERICAN COALITION ON RELIGION AND
   ECOLOGY (NACRE) 280
OKLAHOMA STATE BOARD OF AGRICULTURE 96
OPENLANDS PROJECT 290
RAINBOW PUSH COALITION 302
RENEWABLE NATURAL RESOURCES FOUNDATION 304
SCENIC AMERICA 310
SIERRA CLUB FOUNDATION, THE 317
STATE SOIL AND WATER CONSERVATION COMMISSION
   (GEORGIA) 56
STOP 13, 326
TREEPEOPLE 330
TREES ATLANTA 330
UNITED NATIONS ENVIRONMENT PROGRAMME 336
URBAN HABITAT PROGRAM 337
URBAN WILDLIFE RESOURCES 337
WESTERN PENNSYLVANIA CONSERVANCY 344
WORLD WILDLIFE FUND 359
YMCA EARTH SERVICE CORPS 360

Urban Forestry

ALABAMA FORESTRY COMMISSION 39
AMERICAN FORESTS (formerly American Forestry
   Association) 144
CLIMATE INSTITUTE 175

COLORADO STATE FOREST SERVICE............................... 49
DELAWARE DEPARTMENT OF AGRICULTURE 51
DIVISION OF FORESTRY AND SOIL RESOURCES OF GUAM
  57
EARTHSTEWARDS NETWORK 193
ELM RESEARCH INSTITUTE 194
FOREST LANDOWNERS ASSOCIATION, INC. 203
FOREST WATCH 204
FORESTRY COMMISSION (SOUTH CAROLINA)................. 105
GLOBAL CITIES PROJECT, THE 210
INTERNATIONAL PLANT PROPAGATION SOCIETY, INC.,
  THE.. 226
INTERNATIONAL SOCIETY OF TROPICAL FORESTERS, INC.
  228
KANSAS FOREST SERVICE.. 65
KENTUCKY-TENNESSEE SOCIETY OF AMERICAN
  FORESTERS.. 239
LOUISIANA DEPARTMENT OF AGRICULTURE AND
  FORESTRY.. 68
MISSISSIPPI FORESTRY COMMISSION................................ 78
MISSOURI FOREST PRODUCTS ASSOCIATION................ 253
NATIONAL ARBOR DAY FOUNDATION 256
NATIONAL ASSOCIATION OF STATE FORESTERS........... 258
NATIONAL TREE TRUST.. 265
NORTH DAKOTA STATE FOREST SERVICE........................ 93
OKLAHOMA STATE EXTENSION SERVICES 96
OREGON DEPARTMENT OF FORESTRY 98
OUTDOOR CIRCLE, THE... 291
SOUTHERN NEW ENGLAND FOREST CONSORTIUM, INC.
  (SNEFCI) 324
STATE FORESTRY DIVISION (WYOMING)......................... 122
TEXAS FOREST SERVICE 108
TREEPEOPLE.. 330
TREES ATLANTA 330
UNIVERSITY OF MASSACHUSETTS EXTENSION............... 74
UNIVERSITY OF NEW HAMPSHIRE COOPERATIVE
  EXTENSION.. 84
URBAN WILDLIFE RESOURCES 337
VIRGINIA NATIVE PLANT SOCIETY 340
WASHINGTON NATIVE PLANT SOCIETY 341
YMCA EARTH SERVICE CORPS 360

Utility Restructuring

AMERICAN COUNCIL FOR AN ENERGY-EFFICIENT
  ECONOMY 139

Vision Quest

THRESHOLD, INC. 329

Volunteering

EARTHWATCH INSTITUTE... 193
PEOPLE FOR PUGET SOUND 295
WASHINGTON TRAILS ASSOCIATION 341

Waste Management

DELAWARE DEPARTMENT OF NATURAL RESOURCES AND
  ENVIRONMENTAL CONTROL.. 51
LEAGUE OF ENVIRONMENTAL JOURNALISTS.................. 241
PENNSYLVANIA RESOURCES COUNCIL, INC., (formerly PA
  Roadside Council) 295
WEST MICHIGAN ENVIRONMENTAL ACTION COUNCIL ... 343

Waste Resources

PENNSYLVANIA CITIZENS ADVISORY COUNCIL TO
  DEPARTMENT OF ENVIRONMENTAL PROTECTION 294

Water and Air Quality

DELAWARE AUDUBON SOCIETY 186
NORTH CAROLINA COALITION, INC................................... 282
WEST VIRGINIA HIGHLANDS CONSERVANCY 343

Water Conservation

CALIFORNIA TROUT, INC. 164
COOSA RIVER BASIN INITIATIVE 184
DESERT RESEARCH FOUNDATION OF NAMIBIA, THE 188
PACIFIC INSTITUTE FOR STUDIES IN DEVELOPMENT,
  ENVIRONMENT, AND SECURITY....................................... 293
SOUTHWEST FLORIDA WATER MANAGEMENT DISTRICT
  (SWFWMD) 55

Water Pollution

ALABAMA ENVIRONMENTAL COUNCIL.............................. 132
ALLIANCE FOR THE CHESAPEAKE BAY 135
AMERICAN FISHERIES SOCIETY 140, 141, 142, 143, 144
AMERICAN GROUND WATER TRUST 145
AMERICAN OCEANS CAMPAIGN 147
ANACOSTIA WATERSHED SOCIETY.................................. 152
ARIZONA DEPARTMENT OF ENVIRONMENTAL QUALITY . 41
BAMA BACKPADDLERS ASSOCIATION 159
BASS ANGLERS SPORTSMAN SOCIETY (B.A.S.S, INC.) .. 160
BROTHERHOOD OF THE JUNGLE COCK, INC., THE 163
CASCADIA RESEARCH 168
CENTER FOR MARINE CONSERVATION 170
CHINA REGION LAKES ALLIANCE 173
CLEAN OCEAN ACTION 174
COAST ALLIANCE 176
COASTAL SOCIETY, THE.. 177
COMMUNITIES FOR A BETTER ENVIRONMENT 179
CONNECTICUT FUND FOR THE ENVIRONMENT 180
CONNECTICUT RIVER WATERSHED COUNCIL INC. 181
CONSERVATION LAW FOUNDATION, INC. (CLF)............. 183
COOSA RIVER BASIN INITIATIVE 184
DEPARTMENT OF ENVIRONMENTAL QUALITY (ARKANSAS)
  43
DEPARTMENT OF PUBLIC WORKS..................................... 52
DEPARTMENT OF THE ENVIRONMENT 71
ENVIRONMENTAL ENTERPRISES ASSISTANCE FUND, INC.
  197
FISHAMERICA FOUNDATION... 201
FRIENDS OF THE SEA OTTER 206
FUTURE FISHERMAN FOUNDATION.................................. 207
GREAT LAKES UNITED 211
GREEN (GLOBAL RIVERS ENVIRONMENTAL EDUCATION
  NETWORK)... 212
IDAHO CONSERVATION LEAGUE 218
IDAHO STATE DEPARTMENT OF AGRICULTURE 60
ILLINOIS ENVIRONMENTAL PROTECTION AGENCY 61
INTERNATIONAL ASSOCIATION FOR ENVIRONMENTAL
  HYDROLOGY (IAEH) 222
INTERNATIONAL EROSION CONTROL ASSOCIATION (IECA)
  224
KANSAS GEOLOGICAL SURVEY 66
KANSAS STATE CONSERVATION COMMISSION 66
LAKE MICHIGAN FEDERATION 240
LEAGUE TO SAVE LAKE TAHOE 242
LEGAL ENVIRONMENTAL ASSISTANCE FOUNDATION INC.
  (LEAF) 242
MAINE/NEW HAMPSHIRE SEA GRANT PROGRAM 83
MICHIGAN DEPARTMENT OF ENVIRONMENTAL QUALITY 75
MID-ATLANTIC COUNCIL OF WATERSHED ASSOCIATIONS
  250
MINERAL POLICY CENTER 250
MINNESOTA DEPARTMENT OF AGRICULTURE 76
MINNESOTA SEA GRANT COLLEGE PROGRAM 77
MISSISSIPPI SOIL AND WATER CONSERVATION
  COMMISSION 78
NATIONAL ASSOCIATION OF CONSERVATION DISTRICTS
  257
NATIONAL ASSOCIATION OF STATE DEPARTMENTS OF
  AGRICULTURE... 258
NATIONAL BOATING FEDERATION.................................... 260
NATIONAL ENVIRONMENTAL HEALTH ASSOCIATION..... 260
NATIONAL GROUND WATER ASSOCIATION, THE 262
NATIONAL WATER RESOURCES ASSOCIATION 266
NEW HAMPSHIRE DEPARTMENT OF ENVIRONMENTAL
  SERVICES 84
NEW JERSEY DEPARTMENT OF AGRICULTURE................ 84
NORTH CAROLINA COALITION, INC. 282

KEYWORD INDEX - Water Pollution Management

NORTH CAROLINA SEA GRANT PROGRAM...............92
NORTH DAKOTA GEOLOGICAL SURVEY 93
OHIO ENVIRONMENTAL COUNCIL, INC.....................287
OHIO ENVIRONMENTAL PROTECTION AGENCY................94
OHIO SEA GRANT COLLEGE PROGRAM...................95
OREGON ENVIRONMENTAL COUNCIL 290
PENNSYLVANIA RECREATION AND PARK SOCIETY, INC.
....295
PRAIRIE RIVERS NETWORK 299
PUGET SOUNDKEEPER ALLIANCE 300
RACHEL CARSON COUNCIL, INC. (formerly Rachel Carson Trust for the Living Environment Inc.) 301
RIVER ALLIANCE OF WISCONSIN 305
SAVE OUR RIVERS, INC. 309
SAVE SAN FRANCISCO BAY ASSOCIATION 309
SAVE THE DUNES COUNCIL 309
SAVE THE HARBOR/SAVE THE BAY 310
SAVE THE SOUND, INC...310
SOUTH DAKOTA DEPARTMENT OF ENVIRONMENT AND NATURAL RESOURCES...106
SOUTHEAST ALASKA CONSERVATION COUNCIL (SEACC)
....323
SOUTHWEST RESEARCH AND INFORMATION CENTER .324
STOP 13, 326
STRIPERS UNLIMITED, INC. 326
STROUD WATER RESEARCH CENTER 326
STUDENTS PARTNERSHIP WORLDWIDE 327
TAHOE REGIONAL PLANNING AGENCY 327
TENNESSEE ENVIRONMENTAL COUNCIL 328
U.S. PUBLIC INTEREST RESEARCH GROUP 336
VERMONT DEPARTMENT OF AGRICULTURE, FOOD, AND MARKETS 112
WATER RESOURCES ASSOCIATION OF THE DELAWARE RIVER BASIN..342
WHALE AND DOLPHIN CONSERVATION SOCIETY 345
WISCONSIN SEA GRANT INSTITUTE 121
WOODS HOLE OCEANOGRAPHIC INSITITUTION (WHOI) SEA GRANT PROGRAM..74

Water Pollution Management

A.B. ENVIRONMENTAL EDUCATION CENTER 130
ALABAMA DEPARTMENT OF ENVIRONMENTAL MANAGEMENT...38
ALASKA DEPARTMENT OF ENVIRONMENTAL CONSERVATION...39
AMERICAN FISHERIES SOCIETY........ 140, 141, 142, 143, 144
BORDER ECOLOGY PROJECT (BEP)................................162
CALIFORNIA ENVIRONMENTAL PROTECTION AGENCY....44
CANVASBACK SOCIETY 167
CENTER FOR WATERSHED PROTECTION 171
CHLORINE-FREE PAPER CONSORTIUM (CPC).................173
CONNECTICUT PUBLIC INTEREST RESEARCH GROUP (Conn PIRG) 181
DELAWARE ASSOCIATION OF CONSERVATION DISTRICTS
....186
DELAWARE DEPARTMENT OF NATURAL RESOURCES AND ENVIRONMENTAL CONTROL 51
ENVIRONMENTAL LEAGUE OF MASSACHUSETTS 198
EUROPEAN ASSOCIATION FOR AQUATIC MAMMALS 199
INTERNATIONAL MARITIME ORGANIZATION 226
KENTUCKY RESOURCES COUNCIL 239
LAKE ERIE CLEAN-UP COMMITTEE, INC................240
LVIV REGIONAL INSTITUTE OF EDUCATION...........244
NATURAL AND SCENIC RIVERS COMMISSION (ARKANSAS)
....43
OREGON DEPARTMENT OF ENVIRONMENTAL QUALITY (DEQ)...98
REEF RELIEF..303
RHODE ISLAND COOPERATIVE EXTENSION SERVICE ...104
SAVE THE BAY, INC. 309
SOUTH CAROLINA WILDLIFE FEDERATION 321
SOUTH DAKOTA WILDLIFE FEDERATION 323
SOUTHERN ENVIRONMENTAL LAW CENTER 324
TROUT UNLIMITED, OKLAHOMA COUNCIL.............333
WASHINGTON STATE OFFICE OF ENVIRONMENTAL EDUCATION 118
WASHINGTON WILDLIFE FEDERATION..................342
WATER ENVIRONMENT FEDERATION.....................342

WATER RESOURCES RESEARCH CENTER 59
WATERSHED MANAGEMENT COUNCIL 343
WEST VIRGINIA B.A.S.S. CHAPTER FEDERATION...........343
WISCONSIN ASSOCIATION FOR ENVIRONMENTAL EDUCATION, INC..355
WISCONSIN WILDLIFE FEDERATION 356

Water Quality

ALASKA DEPARTMENT OF ENVIRONMENTAL CONSERVATION...39
ALLIANCE FOR THE CHESAPEAKE BAY 135
AMERICAN BASS ASSOCIATION, INC......................137
AMERICAN OCEANS CAMPAIGN..............................147
AMERICAN WATER WORKS ASSOCIATION (AWWA)........151
ARIZONA DEPARTMENT OF ENVIRONMENTAL QUALITY .41
ASSOCIATION OF NEW JERSEY ENVIRONMENTAL COMMISSIONS 157
AUDUBON INTERNATIONAL 158
AUDUBON NATURALIST SOCIETY OF THE CENTRAL ATLANTIC STATES 158
BAMA BACKPADDLERS ASSOCIATION 159
CHESAPEAKE BAY FOUNDATION, INC. (Virginia Office) ...173
CHINA REGION LAKES ALLIANCE.............................173
CHLORINE-FREE PAPER CONSORTIUM (CPC).................173
COASTAL CONSERVATION ASSOCIATION 176
COASTAL CONSERVATION ASSOCIATION GEORGIA...... 176
COASTAL GEORGIA CENTER FOR SUSTAINABLE DEVELOPMENT 176
CONNECTICUT RIVER WATERSHED COUNCIL INC. 181
CONSERVATION TECHNOLOGY INFORMATION CENTER
....183
COOK INLET KEEPER 184
COOSA RIVER BASIN INITIATIVE 184
DELAWARE DEPARTMENT OF NATURAL RESOURCES AND ENVIRONMENTAL CONTROL 51
ENVIRONMENTAL CENTER 58
ENVIRONMENTAL DEFENSE FUND, INC. 196
ENVIRONMENTAL EDUCATION ASSOCIATES..................196
FLORIDA DEFENDERS OF THE ENVIRONMENT, INC. (Home Office)..201
FRIENDS OF THE BOUNDARY WATERS WILDERNESS ...206
FRIENDS OF THE EARTH 206
GLOBAL CITIES PROJECT, THE 210
GREAT LAKES UNITED..211
GREEN (GLOBAL RIVERS ENVIRONMENTAL EDUCATION NETWORK)..212
GREEN PARTY USA 213
HOOD CANAL LAND TRUST 216
HOOSIER ENVIRONMENTAL COUNCIL 216
IDAHO STATE DEPARTMENT OF AGRICULTURE 60
INDIANA DEPARTMENT OF NATURAL RESOURCES..........62
IOWA ENVIRONMENTAL COUNCIL 232
IZAAK WALTON LEAGUE OF AMERICA, INC., THE............234
KANSAS FOREST SERVICE 65
KANSAS STATE CONSERVATION COMMISSION 66
KANSAS STATE DEPARTMENT OF HEALTH AND ENVIRONMENT...66
LAKE SUPERIOR GREENS 240
LEAGUE OF WOMEN VOTERS OF IOWA 241
LOWER MISSISSIPPI RIVER CONSERVATION COMMITTEE
....244
MAINE DEPARTMENT OF ENVIRONMENTAL PROTECTION
....70
MASSACHUSETTS HIGHWAY DEPARTMENT.....................74
MINNESOTA CENTER FOR ENVIRONMENTAL ADVOCACY (MCEA)..251
MISSISSIPPI RIVER BASIN ALLIANCE 252
MISSISSIPPI SOIL AND WATER CONSERVATION COMMISSION..78
MISSOURI AUDUBON COUNCIL 253
MONTANA ENVIRONMENTAL INFORMATION CENTER.... 254
MONTANA ENVIRONMENTAL QUALITY COUNCIL 81
NATIONAL ASSOCIATION OF STATE DEPARTMENTS OF AGRICULTURE...258
NATIONAL WILDLIFE FEDERATION 267, 268
NEW HAMPSHIRE LAKES ASSOCIATION 277
NEW JERSEY DEPARTMENT OF AGRICULTURE...............84
NORTH CAROLINA COASTAL FEDERATION, INC. 282

NORTH CAROLINA SEA GRANT PROGRAM..........................92
NORTH DAKOTA DEPARTMENT OF HEALTH.......................93
NORTHERN ALASKA ENVIRONMENTAL CENTER.............285
NORTHERN PLAINS RESOURCE COUNCIL.......................285
OHIO ENVIRONMENTAL COUNCIL, INC................................287
OKLAHOMA DEPARTMENT OF ENVIRONMENTAL QUALITY
....95
OKLAHOMA WATER RESOURCES BOARD 97
OREGON B.A.S.S. CHAPTER FEDERATION..........................290
OREGON ENVIRONMENTAL COUNCIL....................................290
PEOPLE FOR PUGET SOUND...295
PITTSBURGH HERPETOLOGICAL SOCIETY, THE............296
PRAIRIE RIVERS NETWORK 299
PRAIRIE RIVERS NETWORK (Formerly Central States
  Education Center)...299
PUGET SOUNDKEEPER ALLIANCE 300
RIVER OTTER ALLIANCE, THE..306
SAVE THE HARBOR/SAVE THE BAY 310
SOCIETY FOR RANGE MANAGEMENT 319
SOIL AND WATER CONSERVATION SOCIETY (formerly Soil
  Conservation Society of America)...320
SOUTH CAROLINA COASTAL CONSERVATION LEAGUE.321
SOUTH CAROLINA ENVIRONMENTAL LAW PROJECT 321
SOUTH DAKOTA DEPARTMENT OF ENVIRONMENT AND
  NATURAL RESOURCES...106
SOUTHEAST ALASKA CONSERVATION COUNCIL (SEACC)
....323
SOUTHWEST FLORIDA WATER MANAGEMENT DISTRICT
  (SWFWMD) 55
STATE MARINE BOARD (OREGON)..99
STATE OF IDAHO DIVISION OF ENVIRONMENTAL QUALITY
....61
STATE WATER RESOURCES BOARD (RHODE ISLAND) ..104
STROUD WATER RESEARCH CENTER 326
TENNESSEE DEPARTMENT OF AGRICULTURE................107
TEXAS FOREST SERVICE 108
TROUT UNLIMITED, PENNSYLVANIA COUNCIL.................333
TURTLE CREEK WATERSHED ASSOCIATION, INC..........335
UPPER MISSISSIPPI RIVER CONSERVATION COMMITTEE
....337
VIRGINIA B.A.S.S. CHAPTER FEDERATION 339
WESTERN ENVIRONMENTAL LAW CENTER......................344
WHITE CLAY WATERSHED ASSOCIATION..........................345
WISCONSIN DEPARTMENT OF AGRICULTURE TRADE AND
  CONSUMER PROTECTION..120

Water Resources

AGENCY OF NATURAL RESOURCES......................................111
ALASKA CONSERVATION FOUNDATION...............................134
ALLIANCE FOR THE CHESAPEAKE BAY 135
AMERICAN BASS ASSOCIATION OF MARYLAND, THE.....137
AMERICAN CAVE CONSERVATION ASSOCIATION...........138
AMERICAN GROUND WATER TRUST 145
AMERICAN LEAGUE OF ANGLERS AND BOATERS 146
AMERICAN RIVERS (formerly American Rivers Conservation
  Council)...149
AMERICAN SOCIETY FOR ENVIRONMENTAL HISTORY...149
AMERICAN WATER RESOURCES ASSOCIATION...............151
AMERICAN WATER WORKS ASSOCIATION (AWWA)........151
ANGLERS FOR CLEAN WATER...152
ARIZONA GEOLOGICAL SURVEY 41
ARIZONA LAND DEPARTMENT 41
ASSOCIATION OF AMERICAN GEOGRAPHERS 155
ASSOCIATION OF CONSERVATION ENGINEERS 156
ASSOCIATION OF NEW JERSEY ENVIRONMENTAL
  COMMISSIONS..157
BAMA BACKPADDLERS ASSOCIATION 159
BASS ANGLERS SPORTSMAN SOCIETY (B.A.S.S, INC.)..160
BRANDYWINE CONSERVANCY, INC. 162
BUREAU OF ECONOMIC GEOLOGY...108
CALIFORNIA SEA GRANT COLLEGE SYSTEM......................45
CALIFORNIA WATERFOWL ASSOCIATION...........................164
CANVASBACK SOCIETY 167
CHARLES A. AND ANNE MORROW LINDBERGH
  FOUNDATION, THE...172
CHINA REGION LAKES ALLIANCE..173
COASTAL CONSERVATION ASSOCIATION 176
COLORADO DEPARTMENT OF NATURAL RESOURCES....49
CONCERN, INC. 179
CONSERVATION DISTRICTS FOUNDATION INC................182
CONSERVATION FUND, THE 182
COOSA RIVER BASIN INITIATIVE 184
COUSTEAU SOCIETY, INC., THE 185
DEEP-PORTAGE CONSERVATION RESERVE 186
DELAWARE GEOLOGICAL SURVEY 52
DEPARTMENT OF LAND AND NATURAL RESOURCES......58
DESERT FISHES COUNCIL...188
EARTH SHARE..192
ENVIRONMENTAL AND ENERGY STUDY INSTITUTE (EESI)
....195
ENVIRONMENTAL DEFENSE CENTER, INC.........................196
ENVIRONMENTAL DEFENSE FUND, INC..............................196
FISHAMERICA FOUNDATION 201
FLORIDA DEFENDERS OF THE ENVIRONMENT, INC. (Home
  Office)..201
FRIENDS OF THE RIVER 206
FUTURE FISHERMAN FOUNDATION.......................................207
GEORGIA CONSERVANCY, INC., THE 209
GRAND CANYON TRUST (St. George, UT Office) 211
GREAT LAKES UNITED 211
GREEN (GLOBAL RIVERS ENVIRONMENTAL EDUCATION
  NETWORK)..212
GROUNDWATER FOUNDATION, THE 213
IDAHO STATE SOIL CONSERVATION COMMISSION 60
ILLINOIS ENVIRONMENTAL COUNCIL 219
INDIANA DEPARTMENT OF NATURAL RESOURCES.........62
INTERNATIONAL ASSOCIATION FOR ENVIRONMENTAL
  HYDROLOGY (IAEH) 222
ISLAND RESOURCES FOUNDATION.......................................233
IZAAK WALTON LEAGUE OF AMERICA, INC., THE............234
J.N. (DING) DARLING FOUNDATION...235
KANSAS DEPARTMENT OF AGRICULTURE 65
KANSAS FOREST SERVICE 65
KANSAS GEOLOGICAL SURVEY 66
KANSAS NATURAL RESOURCE COUNCIL 237
KANSAS STATE CONSERVATION COMMISSION 66
KANSAS STATE DEPARTMENT OF HEALTH AND
  ENVIRONMENT..66
KANSAS WATER OFFICE..66
LAKE ERIE CLEAN-UP COMMITTEE, INC. 240
LEAGUE OF WOMEN VOTERS OF THE U.S. 241
LONG LIVE THE KINGS 243
LOUISIANA GEOLOGICAL SURVEY..69
MAGIC...244
MAINE ASSOCIATION OF CONSERVATION COMMISSIONS
  (MACC)..244
MARINE TECHNOLOGY SOCIETY 246
MICHIGAN DEPARTMENT OF ENVIRONMENTAL QUALITY75
MICHIGAN STATE UNIVERSITY EXTENSION 75
MID-ATLANTIC COUNCIL OF WATERSHED ASSOCIATIONS
....250
MINNESOTA BOARD OF WATER AND SOIL RESOURCES.75
MINNESOTA ENVIRONMENTAL QUALITY BOARD 76
MINNESOTA GEOLOGICAL SURVEY 76
MINNESOTA SEA GRANT COLLEGE PROGRAM..................77
MISSISSIPPI INTERSTATE COOPERATIVE RESOURCE
  ASSOCIATION..252
MISSISSIPPI SOIL AND WATER CONSERVATION
  COMMISSION..78
MONO LAKE COMMITTEE 254
MONTANA BUREAU OF MINES AND GEOLOGY...................80
MONTANA DEPARTMENT OF NATURAL RESOURCES AND
  CONSERVATION..81
MONTANA ENVIRONMENTAL QUALITY COUNCIL 81
MONTANA LAND RELIANCE...254
MUSKIES, INC. 256
NATIONAL ASSOCIATION OF ENVIRONMENTAL
  PROFESSIONALS, THE (National Office) 257
NATIONAL ASSOCIATION OF STATE DEPARTMENTS OF
  AGRICULTURE...258
NATIONAL ASSOCIATION OF STATE FORESTERS...........258
NATIONAL ENVIRONMENTAL HEALTH ASSOCIATION.....260
NATIONAL GROUND WATER ASSOCIATION, THE............262
NATIONAL WATER RESOURCES ASSOCIATION 266
NATIONAL WATERWAYS CONFERENCE INC.....................266
NATURAL AND SCENIC RIVERS COMMISSION (ARKANSAS)
....43
NATURAL RESOURCES COUNCIL OF AMERICA...............271

KEYWORD INDEX - Waterfowl

NEBRASKA DEPARTMENT OF WATER RESOURCES......... 81
NEBRASKA NATURAL RESOURCES COMMISSION 82
NEVADA BUREAU OF MINES AND GEOLOGY 82
NEW HAMPSHIRE ASSOCIATION OF CONSERVATION COMMISSIONS.. 276
NEW HAMPSHIRE DEPARTMENT OF AGRICULTURE, MARKETS, AND FOOD 83
NEW HAMPSHIRE DEPARTMENT OF ENVIRONMENTAL SERVICES 84
NEW JERSEY DEPARTMENT OF AGRICULTURE 84
NEW JERSEY DEPARTMENT OF ENVIRONMENTAL PROTECTION 85
NEW JERSEY PINELANDS COMMISSION 85
NEW MEXICO BUREAU OF MINES AND MINERAL RESOURCES 86
NEW YORK GEOLOGICAL SURVEY AND STATE MUSEUM 90
NEW YORK SEA GRANT 90
NEW YORK STATE COOPERATIVE EXTENSION 90
NEW YORK STATE FISH AND WILDLIFE MANAGEMENT BOARD 90
OHIO DEPARTMENT OF NATURAL RESOURCES 94
OHIO ENVIRONMENTAL COUNCIL, INC. 287
OKLAHOMA GEOLOGICAL SURVEY 96
OKLAHOMA WATER RESOURCES BOARD 97
OREGON B.A.S.S. CHAPTER FEDERATION 290
OREGON WATER RESOURCES DEPARTMENT 99
PENNSYLVANIA CITIZENS ADVISORY COUNCIL TO DEPARTMENT OF ENVIRONMENTAL PROTECTION 294
PENNSYLVANIA FOREST STEWARDSHIP PROGRAM...... 102
POPULATION INSTITUTE, THE 298
POWDER RIVER BASIN RESOURCE COUNCIL.................. 298
PRAIRIE RIVERS NETWORK (Formerly Central States Education Center).. 299
PUBLIC EMPLOYEES FOR ENVIRONMENTAL RESPONSIBILITY (PEER).. 300
RESOURCES AGENCY, THE 46
RHODE ISLAND COOPERATIVE EXTENSION SERVICE ... 104
RIVER FEDERATION.. 306
RIVERS COUNCIL OF WASHINGTON (formerly Northwest Rivers Council)... 306
SAVE SAN FRANCISCO BAY ASSOCIATION 309
SAVE THE HARBOR/SAVE THE BAY 310
SEAPLANE PILOTS ASSOCIATION 312
SOCIETY FOR RANGE MANAGEMENT 319
SOCIETY OF WETLAND SCIENTISTS.................................. 320
SOUTH CAROLINA DEPARTMENT OF HEALTH AND ENVIRONMENTAL CONTROL 105
SOUTH DAKOTA DEPARTMENT OF ENVIRONMENT AND NATURAL RESOURCES 106
SOUTH DAKOTA ORNITHOLOGISTS' UNION 322
SOUTH DAKOTA STATE EXTENSION SERVICES 106
SOUTHWEST FLORIDA WATER MANAGEMENT DISTRICT (SWFWMD) 55
STATE ENGINEER OFFICE/INTERSTATE STREAM COMMISSION 88
STATE SOIL AND WATER CONSERVATION COMMISSION (GEORGIA) 56
STATE WATER RESOURCES BOARD (RHODE ISLAND) .. 104
STROUD WATER RESEARCH CENTER 326
TENNESSEE CITIZENS FOR WILDERNESS PLANNING.... 328
TERRENE INSTITUTE, THE.. 328
TEXAS B.A.S.S. CHAPTER FEDERATION 329
TEXAS STATE SOIL AND WATER CONSERVATION BOARD 109
TEXAS WATER DEVELOPMENT BOARD 109
UNITED NATIONS ENVIRONMENT PROGRAMME 336
UNIVERSITY OF NEW HAMPSHIRE COOPERATIVE EXTENSION 84
UPPER CHATTAHOOCHEE RIVERKEEPER....................... 337
UPPER MISSISSIPPI RIVER CONSERVATION COMMITTEE 337
UTAH STATE EXTENSION SERVICES 111
VIRGINIA DEPARTMENT OF ENVIRONMENTAL QUALITY 114
WASHINGTON ENVIRONMENTAL COUNCIL 340
WASHINGTON STATE CONSERVATION COMMISSION 118
WATER ENVIRONMENT FEDERATION............................... 342
WATER RESOURCES ASSOCIATION OF THE DELAWARE RIVER BASIN 342
WATER RESOURCES RESEARCH CENTER........................ 59
WEST MICHIGAN ENVIRONMENTAL ACTION COUNCIL... 343
WEST VIRGINIA DEPARTMENT OF AGRICULTURE 119
WEST VIRGINIA HIGHLANDS CONSERVANCY 343
WEST VIRGINIA STATE EXTENSION SERVICE 120
WISCONSIN ASSOCIATION FOR ENVIRONMENTAL EDUCATION, INC... 355
WISCONSIN CONSERVATION CORPS 120
WISCONSIN DEPARTMENT OF AGRICULTURE TRADE AND CONSUMER PROTECTION... 120
WISCONSIN DEPARTMENT OF NATURAL RESOURCES . 120
WISCONSIN GEOLOGICAL AND NATURAL HISTORY SURVEY.. 121
WORLDWATCH INSTITUTE 359
WYOMING STATE EXTENSION SERVICES 123

Waterfowl

ALABAMA WATERFOWL ASSOCIATION, INC. (AWA)........ 133
AUDUBON SOCIETY OF WESTERN PENNSYLVANIA 159
CALIFORNIA WATERFOWL ASSOCIATION 164
CANVASBACK SOCIETY 167
CONNECTICUT WATERFOWL ASSOCIATION, INC. 181
DELTA WATERFOWL FOUNDATION 187
DUCKS UNLIMITED CANADA 188
HOOD CANAL LAND TRUST 216
INDIANA AUDUBON SOCIETY, INC..................................... 220
INTERNATIONAL WILD WATERFOWL ASSOCIATION 229
IOWA DEPARTMENT OF NATURAL RESOURCES............... 64
J.N. (DING) DARLING FOUNDATION................................... 235
JACK MINER MIGRATORY BIRD FOUNDATION, INC......... 236
LAKE ERIE CLEAN-UP COMMITTEE, INC. 240
MINNESOTA ORNITHOLOGISTS' UNION 251
MISSOURI COOPERATIVE FISH AND WILDLIFE RESEARCH UNIT (USDI) 79
MONTANA COOPERATIVE WILDLIFE RESEARCH UNIT (USGS/BRD) 80
NORTH AMERICAN GAMEBIRD ASSOCIATION, INC. 281
ORNITHOLOGICAL COUNCIL 291
QUEBEC WILDLIFE FEDERATION 301
SOUTH DAKOTA B.A.S.S. CHAPTER FEDERATION 322
SUNCOAST SEABIRD SANCTUARY INC. 327
TRUMPETER SWAN SOCIETY, THE 334
WHOOPING CRANE CONSERVATION ASSOCIATION INC. 345
WILDLIFE FOREVER 348
WISCONSIN SOCIETY FOR ORNITHOLOGY, INC., THE.... 356
WISCONSIN WATERFOWL ASSOCIATION, INC................ 356

Watershed Protection

PRAIRIE RIVERS NETWORK 299
UPPER CHATTAHOOCHEE RIVERKEEPER 337

Watersheds

ALLIANCE FOR THE CHESAPEAKE BAY 135
AMERICAN RIVERS (formerly American Rivers Conservation Council) 149
ANACOSTIA WATERSHED SOCIETY.................................. 152
ASSOCIATION OF NEW JERSEY ENVIRONMENTAL COMMISSIONS 157
CADDO LAKE INSTITUTE, INC. 163
CENTER FOR BIOLOGICAL DIVERSITY............................. 169
CENTER FOR ENVIRONMENTAL STUDY 170
CENTER FOR MARINE CONSERVATION 170
CENTER FOR WATERSHED PROTECTION 171
CHESAPEAKE BAY FOUNDATION, INC. 172, 173
CHINA REGION LAKES ALLIANCE 173
CONNECTICUT RIVER WATERSHED COUNCIL INC. 181
CONSERVATION TECHNOLOGY INFORMATION CENTER 183
COOK INLET KEEPER 184
COOSA RIVER BASIN INITIATIVE 184
ENVIRONMENTAL DEFENSE FUND, INC........................... 196
FLORIDA DEFENDERS OF THE ENVIRONMENT, INC. (Home Office) 201
FOSSIL FUELS POLICY ACTION INSTITUTE/ALLIANCE FOR A PAVING MORATORIUM 204
FRIENDS OF THE REEDY RIVER.. 206

FRIENDS OF THE RIVER 206
GEORGIA ENVIRONMENTAL POLICY INSTITUTE 209
GREAT LAKES UNITED 211
GREAT OUTDOORS CONSERVANCY, THE 212
GREEN! (GLOBAL RIVERS ENVIRONMENTAL EDUCATION
  NETWORK) 212
IDAHO STATE DEPARTMENT OF AGRICULTURE 60
ILLINOIS WALNUT COUNCIL 219
IZAAK WALTON LEAGUE OF AMERICA, INC., THE 234
JOHN INSKEEP ENVIRONMENTAL LEARNING CENTER ... 236
KANSAS STATE CONSERVATION COMMISSION 66
LAKE MICHIGAN FEDERATION 240
MARYLAND DEPARTMENT OF NATURAL RESOURCES 72
MINNESOTA BOARD OF WATER AND SOIL RESOURCES .. 75
MONTANA LAND RELIANCE 254
MOUNTAIN CONSERVATION TRUST OF GEORGIA, INC. .. 255
NATURAL LAND INSTITUTE 270
NEW HAMPSHIRE LAKES ASSOCIATION 277
NEW JERSEY CONSERVATION FOUNDATION 278
NEW JERSEY DEPARTMENT OF AGRICULTURE 84
NORTH CAROLINA COALITION, INC 282
NORTHCOAST ENVIRONMENTAL CENTER 284
NORTHWEST RESOURCE INFORMATION CENTER 286
OHIO ENVIRONMENTAL COUNCIL, INC 287
OPENLANDS PROJECT 290
OREGON NATURAL RESOURCES COUNCIL 290
PACIFIC RIVERS COUNCIL 293
PENNSYLVANIA ENVIRONMENTAL COUNCIL, INC. (PEC) 294
PRAIRIE RIVERS NETWORK (Formerly Central States
  Education Center) 299
RESOURCES AGENCY, THE 46
RIVER ALLIANCE OF WISCONSIN 305
RIVER NETWORK 306
RIVERS COUNCIL OF WASHINGTON (formerly Northwest
  Rivers Council) 306
SAVE OUR RIVERS, INC. 309
SAVE THE BAY, INC. 309
SAVE THE DUNES COUNCIL 309
SAVE THE HARBOR/SAVE THE BAY 310
SOCIETY FOR RANGE MANAGEMENT 319
SOIL AND WATER CONSERVATION SOCIETY (formerly Soil
  Conservation Society of America) 320
SOUTH DAKOTA DEPARTMENT OF ENVIRONMENT AND
  NATURAL RESOURCES 106
SOUTHEAST ALASKA CONSERVATION COUNCIL (SEACC)
  323
SOUTHEASTERN FISHES COUNCIL 323
STROUD WATER RESEARCH CENTER 326
TENNESSEE CITIZENS FOR WILDERNESS PLANNING 328
TERRENE INSTITUTE, THE 328
THORNE ECOLOGICAL INSTITUTE 329
TROUT UNLIMITED, PENNSYLVANIA COUNCIL 333
TRUST FOR PUBLIC LAND, THE 334
TURTLE CREEK WATERSHED ASSOCIATION, INC 335
VIRGINIA NATIVE PLANT SOCIETY 340
WATERSHED MANAGEMENT COUNCIL 343
WHITE CLAY WATERSHED ASSOCIATION 345
WILDLANDS CONSERVANCY 347
WISCONSIN ASSOCIATION OF LAKES (WAL) 355
WISCONSIN DEPARTMENT OF AGRICULTURE TRADE AND
  CONSUMER PROTECTION 120

Wetland Habitat

MAINE COOPERATIVE FISH AND WILDLIFE RESEARCH
  UNIT (USDI) 70
WHOOPING CRANE CONSERVATION ASSOCIATION INC.
  345

Wetlands

A. E. HOWELL WILDLIFE CONSERVATION CENTER 130
A.B. ENVIRONMENTAL EDUCATION CENTER 130
ACRES LAND TRUST 130
ADIRONDACK PARK AGENCY 88
ADKINS ARBORETUM 131
ALABAMA DEPARTMENT OF ENVIRONMENTAL
  MANAGEMENT 38
ALABAMA WATERFOWL ASSOCIATION, INC. (AWA) 133

ALASKA AUDUBON SOCIETY 133
ALASKA CONSERVATION ALLIANCE 133
ALASKA CONSERVATION VOICE 134
ALLIANCE FOR THE CHESAPEAKE BAY 135
AMERICAN FARMLAND TRUST 139
AMERICAN FISHERIES SOCIETY 140, 141, 142, 143, 144
AMERICAN LITTORAL SOCIETY 146
AMERICAN RIVERS (formerly American Rivers Conservation
  Council) 149
AMERICAN SOCIETY OF LIMNOLOGY AND
  OCEANOGRAPHY 150
AMERICAN WATER RESOURCES ASSOCIATION 151
AUDUBON COUNCIL OF ILLINOIS 158
AUDUBON SOCIETY OF PORTLAND 159
BRANDYWINE CONSERVANCY, INC 162
CADDO LAKE INSTITUTE, INC. 163
CALIFORNIA NATIVE PLANT SOCIETY, THE 164
CALIFORNIA SEA GRANT COLLEGE SYSTEM 45
CALIFORNIA TRAPPERS ASSOCIATION 164
CALIFORNIA WATERFOWL ASSOCIATION 164
CANVASBACK SOCIETY 167
CENTER FOR RESOURCE ECONOMICS 171
COASTAL CONSERVATION ASSOCIATION 176
COASTAL GEORGIA LAND TRUST, THE 176
COASTAL SOCIETY, THE 177
COMMUNITY RIGHTS COUNSEL 179
CONNECTICUT BOTANICAL SOCIETY 180
CONNECTICUT FUND FOR THE ENVIRONMENT 180
CONNECTICUT RIVER WATERSHED COUNCIL INC. 181
CONNECTICUT WATERFOWL ASSOCIATION, INC. 181
CONSERVATION DISTRICTS FOUNDATION INC. 182
CONSERVATION TREATY SUPPORT FUND 183
COOSA RIVER BASIN INITIATIVE 184
DELAWARE NATURE SOCIETY 187
DELAWARE WILD LANDS, INC. 187
DELTA WATERFOWL FOUNDATION 187
DELTA WILDLIFE, INC 187
DEPARTMENT OF INTERIOR, U.S.G.S/B.R.D, SOUTH
  CAROLINA COOPERATIVE FISH AND WILDLIFE
  RESEARCH UNIT 104
DRAGONFLY SOCIETY OF THE AMERICAS, THE 188
DUCKS UNLIMITED CANADA 188
ENVIRONMENTAL CONCERN INC. 196
ENVIRONMENTAL DEFENSE FUND, INC. 196
ENVIRONMENTAL LAW INSTITUTE, THE 198
ENVIRONMENTAL LEAGUE OF MASSACHUSETTS 198
E-P EDUCATION SERVICES, INC. 191
EVERGLADES COORDINATING COUNCIL (ECC) 199
FLORIDA COOPERATIVE FISH AND WILDLIFE RESEARCH
  UNIT (USDI) 52
FORESTRY COMMISSION (SOUTH CAROLINA) 105
FRIENDS OF DISCOVERY PARK 205
GEORGIA CONSERVANCY, INC., THE 209
GEORGIA ENVIRONMENTAL POLICY INSTITUTE 209
GOVERNOR OF SOUTH CAROLINA 104
GREAT LAKES SPORT FISHING COUNCIL 211
GREAT LAKES UNITED 211
GREEN (GLOBAL RIVERS ENVIRONMENTAL EDUCATION
  NETWORK) 212
HAWAII NATURE CENTER 214
HOOD CANAL LAND TRUST 216
HUMBOLT FIELD RESEARCH INSTITUTE 217
ILLINOIS NATIVE PLANT SOCIETY 219
INSTITUTE FOR ECOLOGICAL STUDIES 92
INTERNATIONAL CRANE FOUNDATION 224
IOWA NATIVE PLANT SOCIETY 232
IOWA NATURAL HERITAGE FOUNDATION 232
ISSAQUAH ALPS TRAILS CLUB (I.A.T.C.) 233
KANSAS DEPARTMENT OF AGRICULTURE 65
KANSAS STATE CONSERVATION COMMISSION 66
KANSAS STATE EXTENSION SERVICES 66
KANSAS WILDSCAPE FOUNDATION 238
KENTUCKY DEPARTMENT OF AGRICULTURE 66
LAKE ERIE CLEAN-UP COMMITTEE, INC. 240
LAKE SUPERIOR GREENS 240
LEE COUNTY PARKS AND RECREATION SERVICES 54
LOUISIANA AUDUBON COUNCIL 243
LOUISIANA GEOLOGICAL SURVEY 69
LOUISIANA SEA GRANT COLLEGE PROGRAM 69
MAINE/NEW HAMPSHIRE SEA GRANT PROGRAM 83

MASSACHUSETTS ASSOCIATION OF CONSERVATION COMMISSIONS (MACC)	247
MASSACHUSETTS HIGHWAY DEPARTMENT	74
MASSACHUSETTS TRAPPER'S ASSOCIATION, INC.	248
MICHIGAN NATURE ASSOCIATION	249
MICHIGAN WILDLIFE HABITAT FOUNDATION	250
MID-ATLANTIC FISHERY MANAGEMENT COUNCIL	250
MINNESOTA BOARD OF WATER AND SOIL RESOURCES	75
MISSISSIPPI DEPARTMENT OF WILDLIFE, FISHERIES, AND PARKS	78
MISSISSIPPI RIVER BASIN ALLIANCE	252
MISSOURI COOPERATIVE FISH AND WILDLIFE RESEARCH UNIT (USDI)	79
MONO LAKE COMMITTEE	254
MONTANA AUDUBON	254
MONTANA COOPERATIVE WILDLIFE RESEARCH UNIT (USGS/BRD)	80
MONTANA LAND RELIANCE	254
NATIONAL ASSOCIATION OF STATE DEPARTMENTS OF AGRICULTURE	258
NATIONAL COALITION FOR MARINE CONSERVATION	260
NATIONAL WATER RESOURCES ASSOCIATION	266
NATIONAL WILDLIFE FEDERATION	267, 268
NATIVE PLANT SOCIETY OF NORTHEASTERN OHIO	269
NEW HAMPSHIRE ASSOCIATION OF CONSERVATION COMMISSIONS	276
NEW HAMPSHIRE DEPARTMENT OF AGRICULTURE, MARKETS, AND FOOD	83
NEW HAMPSHIRE DEPARTMENT OF ENVIRONMENTAL SERVICES	84
NEW YORK STATE COOPERATIVE EXTENSION	90
NORTH AMERICAN CRANE WORKING GROUP	281
NORTH DAKOTA STATE SOIL CONSERVATION COMMITTEE	93
OHIO AUDUBON COUNCIL, INC.	287
OHIO ENVIRONMENTAL PROTECTION AGENCY	94
OKLAHOMA NATIVE PLANT SOCIETY	289
PENNSYLVANIA AUDUBON SOCIETY	294
PUERTO RICO ASSOCIATION OF SOIL AND WATER CONSERVATION DISTRICTS	300
RESOURCES AGENCY, THE	46
RHODE ISLAND COOPERATIVE EXTENSION SERVICE	104
SANIBEL-CAPTIVA CONSERVATION FOUNDATION, INC.	308
SAVE SAN FRANCISCO BAY ASSOCIATION	309
SAVE THE SOUND, INC.	310
SHELBURNE FARMS	312
SOCIETY FOR RANGE MANAGEMENT	319
SOCIETY OF WETLAND SCIENTISTS	320
SOIL AND WATER CONSERVATION SOCIETY (formerly Soil Conservation Society of America)	320
SOUTH CAROLINA B.A.S.S. CHAPTER FEDERATION	321
SOUTH CAROLINA COASTAL CONSERVATION LEAGUE	321
SOUTH CAROLINA DEPARTMENT OF AGRICULTURE	105
SOUTH CAROLINA DEPARTMENT OF HEALTH AND ENVIRONMENTAL CONTROL	105
SOUTH CAROLINA ENVIRONMENTAL LAW PROJECT	321
SOUTH CAROLINA SEA GRANT CONSORTIUM	106
SOUTH CAROLINA WILDLIFE FEDERATION	321
SOUTH DAKOTA COOPERATIVE FISH AND WILDLIFE RESEARCH UNIT (USDI)	106
SOUTH DAKOTA WILDLIFE FEDERATION	323
SOUTHERN ENVIRONMENTAL LAW CENTER	324
SOUTHWEST FLORIDA WATER MANAGEMENT DISTRICT (SWFWMD)	55
STATE SOIL AND WATER CONSERVATION COMMISSION (GEORGIA)	56
TAHOE REGIONAL PLANNING AGENCY	327
TERRENE INSTITUTE, THE	328
THORNE ECOLOGICAL INSTITUTE	329
TROUT UNLIMITED, OKLAHOMA COUNCIL	333
TRUMPETER SWAN SOCIETY, THE	334
U.S. PUBLIC INTEREST RESEARCH GROUP	336
UNITED STATES TOURIST COUNCIL	336
UTAH STATE EXTENSION SERVICES	111
VERMONT AUDUBON COUNCIL	338
VIRGINIA NATIVE PLANT SOCIETY	340
VIRGINIA SEA GRANT PROGRAM	115
WASHINGTON NATIVE PLANT SOCIETY	341
WASHINGTON SEA GRANT PROGRAM	118
WASHINGTON WILDLIFE FEDERATION	342
WATER RESOURCES ASSOCIATION OF THE DELAWARE RIVER BASIN	342
WESTERN HEMISPHERE SHOREBIRD RESERVE NETWORK (WHSRN)	344
WETLAND HABITAT ALLIANCE OF TEXAS	345
WILDFOWL TRUST OF NORTH AMERICA, INC., THE	347
WILDLIFE HABITAT CANADA	349
WISCONSIN ASSOCIATION OF LAKES (WAL)	355
WISCONSIN DEPARTMENT OF AGRICULTURE TRADE AND CONSUMER PROTECTION	120
WISCONSIN SOCIETY FOR ORNITHOLOGY, INC., THE	356
WISCONSIN WATERFOWL ASSOCIATION, INC.	356
WISCONSIN WILDLIFE FEDERATION	356

Whales

EUROPEAN CETACEAN SOCIETY	199
INTERNATIONAL WILDLIFE COALITION (IWC) AND THE WHALE ADOPTION PROJECT	230
PACIFIC WHALE FOUNDATION	293

Whirling Disease

COLORADO COOPERATIVE FISH AND WILDLIFE RESEARCH UNIT (USDI)	49

Wild Cats

INTERNATIONAL SOCIETY FOR ENDANGERED CATS (ISEC)	227

Wild Dogs

WILD DOG FOUNDATION, THE	345

Wilderness

ADIRONDACK MOUNTAIN CLUB, INC., THE	131
ALASKA CONSERVATION ALLIANCE	133
ALASKA CONSERVATION VOICE	134
ALBERTA WILDERNESS ASSOCIATION	135
AMERICAN FEDERATION OF MINERALOGICAL SOCIETIES	139
ANTARCTICA PROJECT	153
BERKSHIRE-LITCHFIELD ENVIRONMENTAL COUNCIL, INC.	160
CALIFORNIA TRAPPERS ASSOCIATION	164
CANADIAN PARKS AND WILDERNESS SOCIETY	167
CARRYING CAPACITY NETWORK	168
CENTER FOR ENVIRONMENTAL PHILOSOPHY	169
COLORADO ENVIRONMENTAL COALITION	177
DEFENDERS OF WILDLIFE	186
FOSSIL FUELS POLICY ACTION INSTITUTE/ALLIANCE FOR A PAVING MORATORIUM	204
FRIENDS OF THE BOUNDARY WATERS WILDERNESS	206
GREAT OUTDOORS CONSERVANCY, THE	212
IDAHO CONSERVATION LEAGUE	218
INTERNATIONAL WILDERNESS LEADERSHIP (WILD) FOUNDATION	230
JACKSON HOLE CONSERVATION ALLIANCE	236
MICHIGAN NATURAL AREAS COUNCIL	249
MONTANA WILDERNESS ASSOCIATION	255
MOUNTAINEERS, THE (Conservation Division)	256
NORTHCOAST ENVIRONMENTAL CENTER	284
NORTHERN ALASKA ENVIRONMENTAL CENTER	285
NORTHWEST INTERPRETIVE ASSOCIATION	286
OKLAHOMA NATIVE PLANT SOCIETY	289
OLYMPIC PARK ASSOCIATES	289
OREGON NATURAL RESOURCES COUNCIL	290
OUTDOOR RECREATION COUNCIL OF BRITISH COLUMBIA	292
OZARK SOCIETY, THE	292
PAWS/OLYMPIC WILDLIFE RESCUE	294
SIERRA NEVADA FOREST PROTECTION CAMPAIGN	317
STUDENT ENVIRONMENTAL ACTION COALITION (SEAC)	326
TENNESSEE CITIZENS FOR WILDERNESS PLANNING	328

Organization	Page
TEXAS B.A.S.S. CHAPTER FEDERATION	329
THRESHOLD, INC.	329
TRUST FOR PUBLIC LAND, THE	334
UTAH NATURE STUDY SOCIETY	337
UTAH WILDERNESS COALITION	338
WASHINGTON WILDERNESS COALITION	342
WEST VIRGINIA B.A.S.S. CHAPTER FEDERATION	343
WEST VIRGINIA HIGHLANDS CONSERVANCY	343
WILDERNESS EDUCATION ASSOCIATION	346
WILDERNESS LAND TRUST, THE	346
WILDERNESS SOCIETY, THE	346
WILDERNESS WATCH	347
WILDLANDS PROJECT, THE	347
YOSEMITE RESTORATION TRUST	361

Wildflowers

Organization	Page
ALABAMA WILDFLOWER SOCIETY, THE	133
GREAT PLAINS NATIVE PLANT SOCIETY	212
LADY BIRD JOHNSON WILDFLOWER CENTER	240
NORTH CAROLINA WILD FLOWER PRESERVATION SOCIETY	283
OHIO NATIVE PLANT SOCIETY	288
RHODE ISLAND WILD PLANT SOCIETY	305
SOUTHERN APPALACHIAN BOTANICAL SOCIETY	323
WILDFLOWER ASSOCIATION OF MICHIGAN	347

Wildlands

Organization	Page
ALASKA AUDUBON SOCIETY	133
ALASKA CENTER FOR THE ENVIRONMENT	133
ALBERTA WILDERNESS ASSOCIATION	135
AMERICAN WILDLANDS	151
CALIFORNIA TRAPPERS ASSOCIATION	164
COALITION FOR EDUCATION IN THE OUTDOORS	175
DELAWARE WILD LANDS, INC.	187
FRIENDS OF THE BOUNDARY WATERS WILDERNESS	206
INTERNATIONAL ASSOCIATION OF WILDLAND FIRE (formerly Fire Research Institute)	223
INTERNATIONAL WILDERNESS LEADERSHIP (WILD) FOUNDATION	230
IOWA NATURAL HERITAGE FOUNDATION	232
MISSOURI NATIVE PLANT SOCIETY	253
NATURAL AREAS ASSOCIATION	270
NORTHERN ALASKA ENVIRONMENTAL CENTER	285
OREGON NATURAL RESOURCES COUNCIL	290
SINAPU	317
WILDLANDS CONSERVANCY	347
WILDLANDS PROJECT, THE	347
WYOMING NATIVE PLANT SOCIETY	360

Wildlands Management

Organization	Page
ADIRONDACK MOUNTAIN CLUB, INC., THE	131
SIERRA NEVADA FOREST PROTECTION CAMPAIGN	317

Wildlife and Wildlife Habitat

Organization	Page
ADIRONDACK COUNCIL, THE	131
ADKINS ARBORETUM	131
AFRICAN WILDLIFE FOUNDATION	132
AFRICAN WILDLIFE NEWS SERVICE	132
ALABAMA COOPERATIVE FISH AND WILDLIFE RESEARCH UNIT (USDI)	38
ALABAMA WATERFOWL ASSOCIATION, INC. (AWA)	133
ALASKA AUDUBON SOCIETY	133
ALASKA CONSERVATION FOUNDATION	134
ALASKA COOPERATIVE FISH AND WILDLIFE RESEARCH UNIT	39
ALASKA DEPARTMENT OF FISH AND GAME	39
ALBERTA WILDERNESS ASSOCIATION	135
AMERICAN BIRDING ASSOCIATION	138
AMERICAN CETACEAN SOCIETY	138
AMERICAN CHESTNUT FOUNDATION, THE	139
AMERICAN WILDLANDS	151
ANIMAL PROTECTION INSTITUTE	152
ARCHERY MANUFACTURERS AND MERCHANTS ORGANIZATION (AMO)	154
ARIZONA GAME AND FISH DEPARTMENT	41
ARKANSAS COOPERATIVE RESEARCH UNIT	42
ARKANSAS STATE EXTENSION SERVICES	43
ASSOCIATION OF CONSERVATION ENGINEERS	156
ASSOCIATION OF CONSULTING FORESTERS OF AMERICA	156
ATLANTIC SALMON FEDERATION	157
AUDUBON COUNCIL OF ILLINOIS	158
AUDUBON INTERNATIONAL	158
AUDUBON OF KANSAS (formerly Kansas Audubon Council)	158
AUDUBON SOCIETY OF MISSOURI	158
AUDUBON SOCIETY OF NEW HAMPSHIRE	159
AUDUBON SOCIETY OF WESTERN PENNSYLVANIA	159
BAT CONSERVATION INTERNATIONAL	160
BIODIVERSITY LEGAL FOUNDATION	161
BIRDLIFE INTERNATIONAL	161
BOONE AND CROCKETT CLUB	161
BOONE AND CROCKETT FOUNDATION	161
BOUNTY INFORMATION SERVICE (WILDLIFE)	162
BROOKS BIRD CLUB INC., THE	163
CADDO LAKE INSTITUTE, INC.	163
CALIFORNIA TRAPPERS ASSOCIATION	164
CALIFORNIA WILDLIFE DEFENDERS	164
CALIFORNIA WILDLIFE FEDERATION	165
CAMP FIRE CLUB OF AMERICA, THE	165
CAMP FIRE CONSERVATION FUND	165
CANADA-UNITED STATES ENVIRONMENTAL COUNCIL (United States Office)	166
CANADIAN FEDERATION OF HUMANE SOCIETIES	166
CENTER FOR ENVIRONMENTAL STUDY	170
CHARLES A. AND ANNE MORROW LINDBERGH FOUNDATION, THE	172
CHESAPEAKE WILDLIFE HERITAGE (CWH)	173
COASTAL GEORGIA LAND TRUST, THE	176
COLORADO DEPARTMENT OF EDUCATION	49
COLORADO ENVIRONMENTAL COALITION	177
COLORADO WILDLIFE HERITAGE FOUNDATION	178
COLUMBIA BASIN FISH AND WILDLIFE AUTHORITY	178
COLUMBIA RIVER GORGE COMMISSION	116
COMMITTEE FOR THE NATIONAL INSTITUTE FOR THE ENVIRONMENT (CNIE)	178
CONNECTICUT AUDUBON SOCIETY, INC.	180
CONNECTICUT WATERFOWL ASSOCIATION, INC.	181
CONSERVATION AND RESEARCH FOUNDATION, INC., THE	181
CONSERVATION FORCE	182
CONSERVATION TREATY SUPPORT FUND	183
CRAIGHEAD ENVIRONMENTAL RESEARCH INSTITUTE	185
DEEP-PORTAGE CONSERVATION RESERVE	186
DEFENDERS OF WILDLIFE	186
DELTA WILDLIFE, INC.	187
DEPARTMENT OF FISH AND WILDLIFE (WASHINGTON)	116
DEPARTMENT OF INTERIOR, U.S.G.S/B.R.D, SOUTH CAROLINA COOPERATIVE FISH AND WILDLIFE RESEARCH UNIT	104
DESERT TORTOISE COUNCIL	188
DESERT TORTOISE PRESERVE COMMITTEE, INC.	188
EARTH SHARE	192
EARTHJUSTICE LEGAL DEFENSE FUND (formerly Sierra Club Legal Defense Fund, Inc.)	192
EARTHTRUST	193
ECOLOGICAL SOCIETY OF AMERICA, THE	193
ECOLOGY CENTER	194
EDUCATIONAL COMMUNICATIONS, INC.	194
ENVIRONMENT COUNCIL OF RHODE ISLAND	195
ENVIRONMENTAL AIR FORCE	195
ENVIRONMENTAL DEFENSE CENTER, INC.	196
ENVIRONMENTAL EDUCATION ASSOCIATION OF ILLINOIS	197
EVERGLADES COORDINATING COUNCIL (ECC)	199
FAIRFAX AUDUBON SOCIETY	199
FEDERATION OF NEW YORK STATE BIRD CLUBS, INC.	200
FEDERATION OF WESTERN OUTDOOR CLUBS	200
FISH AND WILDLIFE INFORMATION EXCHANGE	201
FISH AND WILDLIFE REFERENCE SERVICE	201, 409
FLORIDA AUDUBON SOCIETY	201
FLORIDA DEFENDERS OF THE ENVIRONMENT, INC. (Home Office)	201

KEYWORD INDEX - Wildlife and Wildlife Habitat

FLORIDA FISH AND WILDLIFE CONSERVATION COMMISSION ... 54
FLORIDA PANTHER PROJECT, INC., THE ... 202
FLORIDA SPORTSMEN'S CONSERVATION ASSOCIATION ... 202
FOREST SERVICE EMPLOYEES FOR ENVIRONMENTAL ETHICS (FSEEE) ... 204
FOREST WATCH ... 204
FOUNDATION FOR NORTH AMERICAN BIG GAME ... 205
FOUNDATION FOR NORTH AMERICAN WILD SHEEP ... 205
FRANKFURT ZOOLOGICAL SOCIETY--HELP FOR THREATENED WILDLIFE ... 205
FRIENDS OF ANIMALS INC. ... 205
FUND FOR ANIMALS INC., THE ... 207
GAME CONSERVANCY U.S.A. (formerly American Friends of the Game Conservancy) ... 207
GAME CONSERVATION INTERNATIONAL (GAME COIN) .. 207
GEORGIA COOPERATIVE FISH AND WILDLIFE RESEARCH UNIT (USDI) ... 55
GLACIER INSTITUTE, THE ... 210
GOPHER TORTOISE COUNCIL ... 211
GREAT BEAR FOUNDATION ... 211
GREAT OUTDOORS CONSERVANCY, THE ... 212
GREATER YELLOWSTONE COALITION ... 212
HAWAII AUDUBON SOCIETY ... 214
HAWK AND OWL TRUST, THE ... 215
HAWKWATCH INTERNATIONAL, INC. ... 215
HIGH DESERT MUSEUM, THE ... 216
HOOD CANAL LAND TRUST ... 216
HUMANE SOCIETY OF THE UNITED STATES, THE ... 217
IDAHO COOPERATIVE FISH AND WILDLIFE RESEARCH UNIT (USDI) ... 60
IDAHO FISH AND WILDLIFE FOUNDATION ... 60
ILLINOIS AUDUBON SOCIETY ... 219
ILLINOIS ENVIRONMENTAL COUNCIL ... 219
ILLINOIS PRAIRIE PATH ... 219
ILLINOIS WALNUT COUNCIL ... 219
INSTITUTE FOR ECOLOGICAL STUDIES ... 92
INTERFAITH COUNCIL FOR THE PROTECTION OF ANIMALS AND NATURE INC. (ICPAN) ... 222
INTERNATIONAL ECOLOGY SOCIETY (IES) ... 224
INTERNATIONAL MARINE MAMMAL PROJECT, THE ... 226
INTERNATIONAL SOCIETY FOR ENDANGERED CATS (ISEC) ... 227
INTERNATIONAL WILD WATERFOWL ASSOCIATION ... 229
INTERNATIONAL WILDLIFE COALITION (IWC) AND THE WHALE ADOPTION PROJECT ... 230
INTERNATIONAL WILDLIFE REHABILITATION COUNCIL (IWRC) ... 230
INTERNATIONAL WOLF CENTER (Educational Services) ... 230
INTERTRIBAL BISON COOPERATIVE (ITBC) ... 231
IOWA AUDUBON ... 231
IOWA COOPERATIVE FISH AND WILDLIFE RESEARCH UNIT ... 64
IOWA NATURAL HERITAGE FOUNDATION ... 232
IOWA TRAPPERS ASSOCIATION, INC. ... 232
J.N. (DING) DARLING FOUNDATION ... 235
JACKSON HOLE CONSERVATION ALLIANCE ... 236
JACKSON HOLE LAND TRUST ... 236
JANE GOODALL INSTITUTE, THE ... 236
KANSAS ORNITHOLOGICAL SOCIETY ... 237
KANSAS STATE EXTENSION SERVICES ... 66
KANSAS WILDSCAPE FOUNDATION ... 238
KENTUCKY DEPARTMENT OF FISH AND WILDLIFE RESOURCES ... 66
KODIAK BROWN BEAR TRUST ... 240
LEAGUE OF WOMEN VOTERS OF WASHINGTON ... 242
LEE COUNTY PARKS AND RECREATION SERVICES ... 54
LOUISIANA AUDUBON COUNCIL ... 243
LOUISIANA DEPARTMENT OF WILDLIFE AND FISHERIES . 68
LOUISIANA FORESTRY ASSOCIATION ... 243
MAGIC ... 244
MAINE COOPERATIVE FISH AND WILDLIFE RESEARCH UNIT (USDI) ... 70
MAINE DEPARTMENT OF INLAND FISHERIES AND WILDLIFE ... 70
MANITOBA WILDLIFE FEDERATION ... 245
MARYLAND ORNITHOLOGICAL SOCIETY, INC. ... 247
MASSACHUSETTS AUDUBON SOCIETY, INC. ... 247
MASSACHUSETTS COOPERATIVE FISH AND WILDLIFE RESEARCH UNIT (USDI) ... 74
MASSACHUSETTS TRAPPER'S ASSOCIATION, INC. ... 248
MICHIGAN NATURE ASSOCIATION ... 249
MICHIGAN WILDLIFE HABITAT FOUNDATION ... 250
MINNESOTA COOPERATIVE FISH AND WILDLIFE RESEARCH UNIT ... 76
MINNESOTA WINGS SOCIETY, INC. ... 252
MISSISSIPPI STATE EXTENSION SERVICES ... 79
MISSOURI COOPERATIVE FISH AND WILDLIFE RESEARCH UNIT (USDI) ... 79
MONTANA DEPARTMENT OF FISH, WILDLIFE, AND PARKS ... 80
MONTANA LAND RELIANCE ... 254
MONTANA WILDERNESS ASSOCIATION ... 255
MOUNT GRACE LAND CONSERVATION TRUST ... 255
MOUNTAIN CONSERVATION TRUST OF GEORGIA, INC. .. 255
MOUNTAIN LION FOUNDATION ... 255
MOUNTAINEERS, THE (Conservation Division) ... 256
MULE DEER FOUNDATION, THE ... 256
NATIONAL 4-H COUNCIL ... 256
NATIONAL ASSOCIATION OF UNIVERSITY FISHERIES AND WILDLIFE PROGRAMS ... 259
NATIONAL AVIARY ... 259
NATIONAL FISH AND WILDLIFE FOUNDATION ... 261
NATIONAL FOREST FOUNDATION ... 261
NATIONAL MILITARY FISH AND WILDLIFE ASSOCIATION 263
NATIONAL PARK TRUST ... 263
NATIONAL RIFLE ASSOCIATION OF AMERICA ... 264
NATIONAL SHOOTING SPORTS FOUNDATION, INC. ... 265
NATIONAL TRAPPERS ASSOCIATION, INC. ... 265
NATIONAL WILDLIFE REFUGE ASSOCIATION ... 269
NATIONAL WILDLIFE REHABILITATORS ASSOCIATION .. 269
NATURAL RESOURCES COUNCIL OF AMERICA ... 271
NATURE CONSERVANCY, THE ... 272, 273, 274
NEBRASKA STATE EXTENSION SERVICES ... 82
NEW MEXICO COOPERATIVE FISH AND WILDLIFE RESEARCH UNIT ... 87
NEW YORK STATE FISH AND WILDLIFE MANAGEMENT BOARD ... 90
NEWFOUNDLAND LABRADOR WILDLIFE FEDERATION .. 279
NORTH AMERICAN CRANE WORKING GROUP ... 281
NORTH AMERICAN GAMEBIRD ASSOCIATION, INC. ... 281
NORTH AMERICAN LOON FUND ... 281
NORTH AMERICAN WOLF SOCIETY ... 282
NORTH CAROLINA COALITION, INC. ... 282
NORTH CAROLINA WILDLIFE RESOURCES COMMISSION 92
NORTH DAKOTA NATURAL SCIENCE SOCIETY ... 284
NORTHEAST WILDLIFE ADMINISTRATORS ASSOCIATION ... 284
NORTHWEST ECOSYSTEM ALLIANCE ... 285
OHIO AUDUBON COUNCIL, INC. ... 287
OKLAHOMA ACADEMY OF SCIENCE ... 288
OKLAHOMA BIOLOGICAL SURVEY ... 95
OKLAHOMA COOPERATIVE FISH AND WILDLIFE RESEARCH UNIT (USDI) ... 95
OREGON COOPERATIVE FISH AND WILDLIFE RESEARCH UNIT (USDI) ... 97
OREGON FISH AND WILDLIFE DIVISION/DEPARTMENT OF STATE POLICE ... 98
OREGON TROUT, INC. ... 291
OREGON WILDLIFE HERITAGE FOUNDATION ... 291
OUTDOOR WRITERS ASSOCIATION OF AMERICA, INC. .. 292
PACIFIC SEABIRD GROUP ... 293
PAWS/OLYMPIC WILDLIFE RESCUE ... 294
PENNSYLVANIA AUDUBON SOCIETY ... 294
PENNSYLVANIA FOREST STEWARDSHIP PROGRAM ... 102
PENNSYLVANIA GAME COMMISSION ... 102
PENNSYLVANIA RESOURCES COUNCIL, INC., (formerly PA Roadside Council) ... 295
PHEASANTS FOREVER, INC. ... 296
PRAIRIE CLUB, THE ... 298
PRAIRIE GROUSE TECHNICAL COUNCIL ... 299
PREDATOR PROJECT ... 299
PTARMIGANS, THE ... 300
QUAIL UNLIMITED, INC. ... 301
QUEBEC WILDLIFE FEDERATION ... 301
RAINFOREST TRUST, INC., THE ... 302
RAPTOR RESEARCH FOUNDATION, INC. ... 303
ROCKY MOUNTAIN BIGHORN SOCIETY ... 306

ROCKY MOUNTAIN ELK FOUNDATION 307
RUFFED GROUSE SOCIETY, THE 307
SAFARI CLUB INTERNATIONAL 308
SAN JUAN PRESERVATION TRUST, THE 308
SANIBEL-CAPTIVA CONSERVATION FOUNDATION, INC. 308
SAVE SAN FRANCISCO BAY ASSOCIATION 309
SIERRA NEVADA FOREST PROTECTION CAMPAIGN 317
SINAPU 317
SOCIETY FOR ANIMAL PROTECTIVE LEGISLATION 318
SOCIETY FOR THE PROTECTION OF NEW HAMPSHIRE
  FORESTS 319
SOCIETY OF TYMPANUCHUS CUPIDO PINNATUS LTD. .. 320
SOIL AND WATER CONSERVATION SOCIETY (formerly Soil
  Conservation Society of America) 320
SOUTH CAROLINA B.A.S.S. CHAPTER FEDERATION 321
SOUTH DAKOTA GAME, FISH, AND PARKS DEPARTMENT
  106
SOUTHEASTERN ASSOCIATION OF FISH AND WILDLIFE
  AGENCIES 323
TALL TIMBERS RESEARCH STATION 327
TEXAS ORGANIZATION FOR ENDANGERED SPECIES 329
THORNE ECOLOGICAL INSTITUTE 329
THRESHOLD, INC. 329
TRUMPETER SWAN SOCIETY, THE 334
TRUST FOR WILDLIFE, INC. 335
TURTLE CREEK WATERSHED ASSOCIATION, INC. 335
UNIVERSITY OF NEW HAMPSHIRE COOPERATIVE
  EXTENSION 84
URBAN WILDLIFE RESOURCES 337
UTAH B.A.S.S. CHAPTER FEDERATION 337
UTAH COOPERATIVE FISH AND WILDLIFE RESEARCH UNIT
  (USDI-USGS-BRD-CRU) 110
VERMONT AUDUBON COUNCIL 338
VIRGINIA COOPERATIVE FISH AND WILDLIFE RESEARCH
  UNIT (USDI) 113
WASHINGTON COOPERATIVE FISH AND WILDLIFE
  RESEARCH UNIT (USDI) 117
WASHINGTON FARM FORESTRY ASSOCIATION 341
WASHINGTON STATE OFFICE OF ENVIRONMENTAL
  EDUCATION 118
WASHINGTON TRAILS ASSOCIATION 341
WASHINGTON WILDLIFE AND RECREATION COALITION 342
WASHINGTON WILDLIFE HERITAGE FOUNDATION
  (including Heritage Land Trust 342
WELDER WILDLIFE FOUNDATION 343
WEST VIRGINIA COOPERATIVE FISH AND WILDLIFE
  RESEARCH UNIT 119
WESTERN ENVIRONMENTAL LAW CENTER 344
WHALE AND DOLPHIN CONSERVATION SOCIETY 345
WHITETAILS UNLIMITED, INC. 345
WILDFOWL TRUST OF NORTH AMERICA, INC., THE 347
WILDLIFE CENTER OF VIRGINIA, THE 347
WILDLIFE CONSERVATION SOCIETY 348
WILDLIFE FOUNDATION OF FLORIDA, INC. 349
WILDLIFE HABITAT CANADA 349
WILDLIFE HABITAT COUNCIL 349
WILDLIFE INFORMATION CENTER, INC. 349
WILDLIFE LEGISLATIVE FUND OF AMERICA, THE, AND
  WILDLIFE CONSERVATION FUND OF AMERICA, THE . 349
WILDLIFE PRESERVATION TRUST INTERNATIONAL, INC.
  350
WILDLIFE SOCIETY, THE 350
WILSON ORNITHOLOGICAL SOCIETY 355
WISCONSIN SOCIETY FOR ORNITHOLOGY, INC., THE 356
WOLF FUND, THE 357
WORLD CONSERVATION MONITORING CENTRE 358
WORLD WILDLIFE FUND 359
WYOMING COOPERATIVE FISH AND WILDLIFE RESEARCH
  UNIT (USDI) 122
WYOMING GAME AND FISH DEPARTMENT 123
WYOMING OUTDOOR COUNCIL 360
YELLOWSTONE GRIZZLY FOUNDATION (YGF) 360

Wildlife Disease

CANADIAN COOPERATIVE WILDLIFE HEALTH CENTRE .. 166
FOUNDATION FOR NORTH AMERICAN WILD SHEEP 205
GAME CONSERVANCY U.S.A. (formerly American Friends of
  the Game Conservancy) 207
INTERNATIONAL WILDLIFE REHABILITATION COUNCIL
  (IWRC) 230
MARINE MAMMAL CENTER, THE 246
OREGON COOPERATIVE FISH AND WILDLIFE RESEARCH
  UNIT (USDI) 97
SOUTHEASTERN COOPERATIVE WILDLIFE DISEASE
  STUDY 323
TRI-STATE BIRD RESCUE AND RESEARCH, INC. 331
WILDLIFE CENTER OF VIRGINIA, THE 347
WILDLIFE DISEASE ASSOCIATION 348
WILDLIFE PRESERVATION TRUST INTERNATIONAL, INC.
  350

Wildlife Management

AFRICAN WILDLIFE NEWS SERVICE 132
ALABAMA COOPERATIVE EXTENSION SYSTEM 38
ALABAMA COOPERATIVE FISH AND WILDLIFE RESEARCH
  UNIT (USDI) 38
ALASKA COOPERATIVE FISH AND WILDLIFE RESEARCH
  UNIT 39
ALASKA DEPARTMENT OF PUBLIC SAFETY 40
AMERICAN ASSOCIATION OF ZOO KEEPERS, INC. 137
AMERICAN HORSE PROTECTION ASSOCIATION 145
AMERICAN ZOO AND AQUARIUM ASSOCIATION (AZA) ... 151
ARCHERY MANUFACTURERS AND MERCHANTS
  ORGANIZATION (AMO) 154
ARIZONA GAME AND FISH DEPARTMENT 41
ARKANSAS COOPERATIVE RESEARCH UNIT 42
ASSOCIATION FOR FISH AND WILDLIFE ENFORCEMENT
  TRAINING 155
ASSOCIATION OF CONSULTING FORESTERS OF AMERICA
  156
ASSOCIATION OF MIDWEST FISH AND GAME LAW
  ENFORCEMENT OFFICERS 156
ATLANTIC SALMON FEDERATION 157
AUDUBON SOCIETY OF RHODE ISLAND 159
BOUNTY INFORMATION SERVICE (WILDLIFE) 162
CALIFORNIA WILDLIFE DEFENDERS 164
CAMP FIRE CLUB OF AMERICA, THE 165
CAMP FIRE CONSERVATION FUND 165
CANADA-UNITED STATES ENVIRONMENTAL COUNCIL
  (United States Office) 166
CANADIAN FEDERATION OF HUMANE SOCIETIES 166
CENTER FOR MARINE CONSERVATION 170
COLORADO DEPARTMENT OF NATURAL RESOURCES 49
COLORADO TRAPPERS ASSOCIATION 178
CONFEDERATED SALISH AND KOOTENAI TRIBES 180
CONNECTICUT WATERFOWL ASSOCIATION, INC. 181
CONSERVATION DISTRICTS FOUNDATION INC. 182
CONSERVATION FORCE 182
DELAWARE DEPARTMENT OF NATURAL RESOURCES AND
  ENVIRONMENTAL CONTROL 51
DEPARTMENT OF INTERIOR, U.S.G.S/B.R.D, SOUTH
  CAROLINA COOPERATIVE FISH AND WILDLIFE
  RESEARCH UNIT 104
DEPARTMENT OF LAND AND NATURAL RESOURCES 58
DESERT TORTOISE PRESERVE COMMITTEE, INC. 188
EUROPEAN CETACEAN SOCIETY 199
EVERGLADES COORDINATING COUNCIL (ECC) 199
FEDERAL CARTRIDGE COMPANY 199
FISH AND WILDLIFE INFORMATION EXCHANGE 201
FISH AND WILDLIFE REFERENCE SERVICE 201, 409
FLORIDA FISH AND WILDLIFE CONSERVATION
  COMMISSION 54
FLORIDA STATE COOPERATIVE EXTENSION SERVICE 54
FOUNDATION FOR NORTH AMERICAN BIG GAME 205
FOUNDATION FOR NORTH AMERICAN WILD SHEEP 205
GAME CONSERVANCY U.S.A. (formerly American Friends of
  the Game Conservancy) 207
GAME CONSERVATION INTERNATIONAL (GAME COIN) . 207
GEORGIA COOPERATIVE FISH AND WILDLIFE RESEARCH
  UNIT (USDI) 55
GOPHER TORTOISE COUNCIL 211
GREATER YELLOWSTONE COALITION 212
IDAHO FISH AND GAME DEPARTMENT 60
INDIANA DEPARTMENT OF NATURAL RESOURCES 62
INTERNATIONAL ASSOCIATION FOR BEAR RESEARCH
  AND MANAGEMENT 222

KEYWORD INDEX - Wildlife Protection

INTERNATIONAL CENTER FOR GIBBON STUDIES 224
INTERNATIONAL ECOLOGY SOCIETY (IES) 224
INTERNATIONAL HUNTER EDUCATION ASSOCIATION ... 225
INTERNATIONAL OSPREY FOUNDATION INC., THE 226
INTERNATIONAL WOLF CENTER (Educational Services) ... 230
IOWA DEPARTMENT OF NATURAL RESOURCES 64
IOWA TRAPPERS ASSOCIATION, INC. 232
IZAAK WALTON LEAGUE OF AMERICA, INC., THE 234
JAPAN WILDLIFE RESEARCH CENTER (JWRC) 236
KANSAS STATE EXTENSION SERVICES 66
MAINE COOPERATIVE FISH AND WILDLIFE RESEARCH
   UNIT (USDI) 70
MARYLAND DEPARTMENT OF NATURAL RESOURCES 72
MASSACHUSETTS COOPERATIVE FISH AND WILDLIFE
   RESEARCH UNIT (USDI) 74
MASSACHUSETTS TRAPPER'S ASSOCIATION, INC. 248
MICHIGAN DEPARTMENT OF NATURAL RESOURCES 75
MICHIGAN STATE UNIVERSITY EXTENSION 75
MINNESOTA SEA GRANT COLLEGE PROGRAM 77
MINNESOTA WINGS SOCIETY, INC. 252
MISSISSIPPI DEPARTMENT OF WILDLIFE, FISHERIES, AND
   PARKS 78
MISSISSIPPI STATE EXTENSION SERVICES 79
MOUNTAIN LION FOUNDATION 255
MULE DEER FOUNDATION, THE 256
MUSKIES, INC. 256
NATIONAL TRAPPERS ASSOCIATION, INC. 265
NATIONAL WILD TURKEY FEDERATION, INC., THE 267
NATIVE AMERICAN FISH AND WILDLIFE SOCIETY (NAFWS)
   269
NEW HAMPSHIRE FISH AND GAME DEPARTMENT 84
NEW YORK STATE COOPERATIVE EXTENSION 90
NORTH AMERICAN GAMEBIRD ASSOCIATION, INC. 281
NORTH AMERICAN WOLF SOCIETY 282
NORTH CAROLINA COOPERATIVE EXTENSION SERVICE 91
NORTH CAROLINA WILDLIFE RESOURCES COMMISSION 92
NORTH DAKOTA GAME AND FISH DEPARTMENT 93
NORTHEAST WILDLIFE ADMINISTRATORS ASSOCIATION
   284
OHIO DEPARTMENT OF NATURAL RESOURCES 94
OKLAHOMA STATE EXTENSION SERVICES 96
OREGON COOPERATIVE FISH AND WILDLIFE RESEARCH
   UNIT (USDI) 97
PENNSYLVANIA GAME COMMISSION 102
PEREGRINE FUND, THE 296
PRAIRIE GROUSE TECHNICAL COUNCIL 299
PREDATOR PROJECT 299
PURPLE MARTIN CONSERVATION ASSOCIATION 301
QUEBEC WILDLIFE FEDERATION 301
ROCKY MOUNTAIN BIGHORN SOCIETY 306
RUFFED GROUSE SOCIETY, THE 307
SINAPU 317
SOCIETY FOR ECOLOGICAL RESTORATION 318
SOCIETY FOR MARINE MAMMALOGY, THE 318
SOCIETY FOR THE PROTECTION OF NEW HAMPSHIRE
   FORESTS 319
SOCIETY OF TYMPANUCHUS CUPIDO PINNATUS LTD. .. 320
SOUTH CAROLINA DEPARTMENT OF NATURAL
   RESOURCES 105
SOUTHEASTERN ASSOCIATION OF FISH AND WILDLIFE
   AGENCIES 323
SOUTHEASTERN COOPERATIVE WILDLIFE DISEASE
   STUDY 323
STATE FORESTRY DIVISION (WYOMING) 122
TALL TIMBERS RESEARCH STATION 327
TEXAS ORGANIZATION FOR ENDANGERED SPECIES 329
TEXAS WILDLIFE ASSOCIATION 329
TRAFFIC NORTH AMERICA 330
URBAN WILDLIFE RESOURCES 337
UTAH NATURE STUDY SOCIETY 337
VIRGINIA COOPERATIVE FISH AND WILDLIFE RESEARCH
   UNIT (USDI) 113
WASHINGTON TRAILS ASSOCIATION 341
WELDER WILDLIFE FOUNDATION 343
WEST VIRGINIA DIVISION OF NATURAL RESOURCES 119
WESTERN ASSOCIATION OF FISH AND WILDLIFE
   AGENCIES 344
WESTERN HEMISPHERE SHOREBIRD RESERVE NETWORK
   (WHSRN) 344
WHITETAILS UNLIMITED, INC. 345
WILDLIFE CONSERVATION SOCIETY 348
WILDLIFE DAMAGE REVIEW (WDR) 348
WILDLIFE FOUNDATION OF FLORIDA, INC. 349
WILDLIFE HABITAT COUNCIL 349
WILDLIFE LEGISLATIVE FUND OF AMERICA, THE, AND
   WILDLIFE CONSERVATION FUND OF AMERICA, THE .. 349
WILDLIFE MANAGEMENT INSTITUTE 349
WILDLIFE RESOURCES AGENCY 107
WILDLIFE SOCIETY, THE 350
WOLF FUND, THE 357
WYOMING COOPERATIVE FISH AND WILDLIFE RESEARCH
   UNIT (USDI) 122
WYOMING STATE EXTENSION SERVICES 123
YELLOWSTONE GRIZZLY FOUNDATION (YGF) 360

Wildlife Protection

ALASKA CONSERVATION ALLIANCE 133
ALASKA CONSERVATION VOICE 134
AMERICAN SOCIETY OF INTERNATIONAL LAW/WILDLIFE
   INTEREST GROUP 150
HIMALAYAN WILDLIFE FOUNDATION 216
KODIAK BROWN BEAR TRUST 240

Wildlife Rehabilitation

A. E. HOWELL WILDLIFE CONSERVATION CENTER 130
ASSOCIATION OF AVIAN VETERINARIANS 156
AUDUBON SOCIETY OF PORTLAND 159
CALIFORNIA WILDLIFE DEFENDERS 164
COLUMBIA BASIN FISH AND WILDLIFE AUTHORITY 178
CONSERVANCY OF SOUTHWEST FLORIDA, THE 181
ELSA WILD ANIMAL APPEAL 194
FOUNDATION FOR NORTH AMERICAN WILD SHEEP 205
FUND FOR ANIMALS INC., THE 207
GAME CONSERVANCY U.S.A. (formerly American Friends of
   the Game Conservancy) 207
INTERNATIONAL PRIMATE PROTECTION LEAGUE 226
INTERNATIONAL WILDLIFE REHABILITATION COUNCIL
   (IWRC) 230
IOWA WILDLIFE REHABILITATORS ASSOCIATION 233
MACBRIDE RAPTOR PROJECT 244
MARINE MAMMAL CENTER, THE 246
NATIONAL WILDLIFE REHABILITATORS ASSOCIATION .. 269
NATURAL SCIENCE FOR YOUTH FOUNDATION 271
NEW YORK TURTLE AND TORTOISE SOCIETY 279
PAWS/OLYMPIC WILDLIFE RESCUE 294
RAPTOR CENTER, THE 303
RIVER OTTER ALLIANCE, THE 306
ROCKY MOUNTAIN BIGHORN SOCIETY 306
SUNCOAST SEABIRD SANCTUARY INC. 327
TRI-STATE BIRD RESCUE AND RESEARCH, INC. 331
TROUT UNLIMITED, PENNSYLVANIA COUNCIL 333
TRUST FOR WILDLIFE, INC. 335
WILDLIFE CENTER OF VIRGINIA, THE 347
WILDLIFE WAYSTATION 355
WOLF FUND, THE 357
WORLD BIRD SANCTUARY (formerly Raptor Rehabilitation
   and Propagation Project Inc. The) 357
WORLD SOCIETY FOR THE PROTECTION OF ANIMALS
   (WSPA) 358

Wildlife Research

JANE GOODALL INSTITUTE, THE 236
JAPAN WILDLIFE RESEARCH CENTER (JWRC) 236
MAINE COOPERATIVE FISH AND WILDLIFE RESEARCH
   UNIT (USDI) 70

Wolves

DEFENDERS OF WILDLIFE 186
INTERNATIONAL WOLF CENTER (Educational Services) ... 230
SINAPU 317
WILD CANID SURVIVAL AND RESEARCH CENTER 345
WILD DOG FOUNDATION, THE 345
WOLF EDUCATION AND RESEARCH CENTER 357

Women in the Environment

ACADEMY FOR EDUCATIONAL DEVELOPMENT	130
CENTER FOR HEALTH, ENVIRONMENT, AND JUSTICE	170
ECOLOGY CENTER	194
GIRL SCOUTS OF THE UNITED STATES OF AMERICA	210
INITIATIVE FOR SOCIAL ACTION AND RENEWAL IN EURASIA	221
IOWA WOMEN IN NATURAL RESOURCES	233
LEARNING FOR ENVIRONMENTAL ACTION PROGRAMME (LEAP)	242
NATIONAL WILD TURKEY FEDERATION, INC., THE	267
STUDENTS PARTNERSHIP WORLDWIDE	327
WORLD ASSOCIATION OF GIRL GUIDES AND GIRL SCOUTS (WAGGGS)	357
WORLD WOMEN IN THE DEFENSE OF THE ENVIRONMENT (WorldWIDE)	359

Youth Leadership

OHIO ENERGY PROJECT	287

Youth Organizations

ACTION FOR NATURE, INC.	130
AMERICAN BASS ASSOCIATION OF MARYLAND, THE	137
AMERICAN CAMPING ASSOCIATION, INC.	138
AMERICAN NATURE STUDY SOCIETY	147
ARCHERY MANUFACTURERS AND MERCHANTS ORGANIZATION (AMO)	154
BOY SCOUTS OF AMERICA	162
BROTHERHOOD OF THE JUNGLE COCK, INC., THE	163
CADDO LAKE INSTITUTE, INC.	163
CENTER FOR ENVIRONMENTAL EDUCATION	169
CENTER FOR ENVIRONMENTAL STUDY	170
EARTH FORCE	191
EARTHSTEWARDS NETWORK	193
ENVIRONMENTAL EDUCATION COUNCIL OF OHIO	197
FUTURE FISHERMAN FOUNDATION	207
GIRL SCOUTS OF THE UNITED STATES OF AMERICA	210
KANSAS STATE EXTENSION SERVICES	66
KANSAS WILDSCAPE FOUNDATION	238
KIDS FOR SAVING EARTH WORLDWIDE	239
LEGACY INTERNATIONAL	242
NATIONAL 4-H COUNCIL	256
NATIONAL ASSOCIATION OF SERVICE AND CONSERVATION CORPS (NASCC)	258
NATIONAL FFA ORGANIZATION	261
NATIONAL FIELD ARCHERY ASSOCIATION	261
NATIONAL GARDENING ASSOCIATION	262
NATIONAL HUNTERS ASSOCIATION, INC.	262
NATIONAL RIFLE ASSOCIATION OF AMERICA	264
NATURAL SCIENCE FOR YOUTH FOUNDATION	271
NEW JERSEY STATE EXTENSION SERVICES	86
NORTH CAROLINA COOPERATIVE EXTENSION SERVICE	91
NORTH CAROLINA RECREATION AND PARK SOCIETY, INC.	283
OHIO ACADEMY OF SCIENCE, THE	286
OHIO ENERGY PROJECT	287
PENNSYLVANIA FORESTRY ASSOCIATION, THE	295
PUERTO RICO STATE EXTENSION SERVICES	103
RESOURCE CENTER FOR ENVIRONMENTAL EDUCATION, THE	304
SOUND EXPERIENCE	320
STUDENT CONSERVATION ASSOCIATION, INC.	326
STUDENT ENVIRONMENTAL ACTION COALITION (SEAC)	326
STUDENTS PARTNERSHIP WORLDWIDE	327
TREEPEOPLE	330
TRUST FOR WILDLIFE, INC.	335
UNIVERSITY OF VERMONT EXTENSION	112
WASHINGTON NATIVE PLANT SOCIETY	341
WILDLIFE ACTION, INC.	347
WORLD ASSOCIATION OF GIRL GUIDES AND GIRL SCOUTS (WAGGGS)	357
YMCA EARTH SERVICE CORPS	360
YOUNG ENTOMOLOGISTS' SOCIETY, INC.	361

Zoological Parks

AMERICAN ZOO AND AQUARIUM ASSOCIATION (AZA)	151
EUROPEAN ASSOCIATION FOR AQUATIC MAMMALS	199
FRANKFURT ZOOLOGICAL SOCIETY--HELP FOR THREATENED WILDLIFE	205
ORGANIZATION FOR BAT CONSERVATION	291
TALLAHASSEE MUSEUM OF HISTORY AND NATURAL SCIENCE	327
WILDLIFE CONSERVATION SOCIETY	348

Zoology

AMERICAN ASSOCIATION OF ZOO KEEPERS, INC.	137
AMERICAN INSTITUTE OF BIOLOGICAL SCIENCES	146
AMERICAN MUSEUM OF NATURAL HISTORY	147
AMERICAN SOCIETY OF ICHTHYOLOGISTS AND HERPETOLOGISTS	149
CHICAGO HERPETOLOGICAL SOCIETY	173
DESERT FISHES COUNCIL	188
DESERT RESEARCH FOUNDATION OF NAMIBIA, THE	188
EARTHWATCH INSTITUTE	193
ENTOMOLOGICAL SOCIETY OF AMERICA	195
INTERNATIONAL CENTER FOR GIBBON STUDIES	224
MATTS (MID-ATLANTIC TURTLE AND TORTOISE SOCIETY, INC.)	248
MONTANA NATURAL HERITAGE PROGRAM	81
NATIONAL ASSOCIATION OF BIOLOGY TEACHERS	257
NATIONAL AVIARY	259
NEW YORK TURTLE AND TORTOISE SOCIETY	279
OKLAHOMA BIOLOGICAL SURVEY	95
PACIFIC SEABIRD GROUP	293
SOCIETY FOR INTEGRATIVE AND COMPARATIVE BIOLOGY (formerly AMERICAN SOCIETY OF ZOOLOGISTS)	318
TALLAHASSEE MUSEUM OF HISTORY AND NATURAL SCIENCE	327
WASHINGTON NATURAL HERITAGE PROGRAM	118
WILSON ORNITHOLOGICAL SOCIETY	355
YOUNG ENTOMOLOGISTS' SOCIETY, INC.	361

STAFF NAME INDEX

A

AAGARD, STEVE 123
AASHEIM, RON 80
AASNESS, PERRY 76
ABBEY, JIM 308
ABBEY, ROBERT 28
ABE, ELAINE T. 58
ABEDON, DAVID 104
ABENT, ROB 75
ABER, JOHN 380
ABERLE, ELTON D. 392
ABERNETHY, VIRGINIA 168, 298
ABEYTA, DAN 48
ABLER, RONALD F. 155
ABRAHAM, FRED 189
ABRAHAM, RONALD 94
ABRAMS, SHELDON 147
ABRAMSON, RAYMOND 44
ABRAMSON, SUSAN 165
ABSHER, CURTIS 67
ABZUG, BELLA 357
ACEVEDO, MIGUEL 389
ACFALLE, JOSEPH L.M.. 57
ACHITOFF, PAUL 192
ACHTERMANN, ADRIAN 320
ACK, BRAD 211
ACKELSON, MARK232, 302
ACKELSON, MARK C. ... 232
ACKER, FREDERICK G.248
ACKER, RANDY 117
ACKERMAN, JOY 379
ACORD, BOBBY R. 12
ACOSTA, CARLOS, JR. 361
ADAIR, JANICE 39
ADAIR, SUE 200
ADAMS, AUDREY 33
ADAMS, BETSY 19
ADAMS, BILL 119
ADAMS, CHARLES M. .. 141
ADAMS, CHARLOTTE M. 32
ADAMS, CINDY 134, 294
ADAMS, CLARK 354
ADAMS, DOYLE 234
ADAMS, EDWARD B. 118
ADAMS, GILBERT. 161, 162
ADAMS, JOHN 35
ADAMS, JOHN H. 271
ADAMS, KEVIN 29
ADAMS, LINDA 366
ADAMS, LOWELL 337
ADAMS, PAMELA A. 51
ADAMS, RON 165
ADAMS, STAN 234, 258
ADAMS, STANFORD M. . 91
ADAMS, STEPHEN S. ... 208
ADAMS, STEVE 83
ADAMS, TIM 105
ADAMS, VIVIAN 216
ADAMS, WENDY 135
ADAMSON, LARRY 126
ADAMSON, TERRENCE B. 262
ADCOCK, STEVE 78
ADDIS, JAMES T. 121
ADDISON, PAUL 37
ADELAJA, ADESOJI 380
ADELMAN, IRA R. 377
ADELMANN, GERALD W. 290
ADELMANN, PEGGY 76
ADHIKARI, AMBIKA 229
ADKINS, ANN 63
ADKINS, DALE 136
ADLER, BILL 179
AFTON, ALAN D. 68
AGLE, JIM 91
AGLI, JIM 136
AGRANOFF, ROBERT ..371
AGRISS, TERRY 89
AGUIRRE, A. ALONSO, Ph.D. 350
AHERN, BILL 46
AHERN, CATHERINE A. 148
AHERN, JOHN 289
AHKEAH, ROBERT 154
AHMAD, MUJAHID 216
AHMED, A. KARIM 179
AIKEN, PATRICIA 331
AILES, JOHN 119
AKERS, JOHN 67
AKISHINO, PRINCE 359
ALAIMO, ELLEN 294
ALBERICI, THERESA ... 102
ALBERS, MARK 149
ALBERTS, BRUCE M. ... 264
ALBERTS, JAMES J. 369
ALBO, LIA 207
ALBRECHT, JEAN 377
ALBRIGHT, LARRY 173
ALBRIGHT, MADELEINE.20
ALBRIGHT, MEL 140
ALBRINK, ANNE 325
ALBRO, DEAN 104
ALDERSON, JAMES 270
ALDRICH, ALYSSA 14
ALDRICH, DORRIE Y. 32
ALDRICH, WINTHROP J. 91
ALESCH, RIC 151
ALEXANDER, BEN 320
ALEXANDER, EDWARD J. 178
ALEXANDER, GERALD ..67
ALEXANDER, GLEN 258
ALEXANDER, H. LLOYD, JR. 51
ALEXANDER, LaVERNE210
ALEXANDER, LLOYD 64
ALEXANDER, MAURICE M. 151
ALEXANDER, MIKE 36
ALEXANDER, PETER A.247
ALEXANDER, VERA 362
ALEXEEV, SEZGEI 200
ALEY, TOM 138
ALFEN, NEAL VAN 46
AL-GAIN, ABDULBAR 224
ALIE, RONALD 84, 284
ALIPIO, MEL 225
ALKIRE, BILL 117
ALLAN, J. COLIN 111
ALLAN, J. DAVID 149
ALLARD, G. 36
ALLEE, A. LEE 68
ALLEE, BRIAN J. 178
ALLEN, ALAN 329
ALLEN, ARTHUR S. 373
ALLEN, BETTY 275
ALLEN, BILL 190
ALLEN, BRUCE 86
ALLEN, CHRISTOPHER 101
ALLEN, CRAIG R. 104
ALLEN, DARCY 211
ALLEN, DAVID B. 30
ALLEN, DENNIS M. 387
ALLEN, GARY C. 169
ALLEN, GERALD 364
ALLEN, J. FRED 56
ALLEN, JEFF 290
ALLEN, JERRY W. 301
ALLEN, JOHN 82
ALLEN, JOHN H. 217
ALLEN, MELODY 360
ALLEN, ROBIN L. 8
ALLEN, TIM 379
ALLEN, W. DALE 335
ALLEN, WILLIAM L. 262
ALLER, CHUCK 53
ALLERY, VIRGINIA P. 267
ALLEY, JAMIE 124
ALLGOOD, DAVID 175
ALLHANDS, LAURA 174
ALLINGER, STEVE 195
ALLISON, CHRIS 88
ALLISON, DAVID L. 140
ALLISON, K. L. 98
ALLISON, M. LEE 66
ALLMAN, DENNIS 299
ALLRED, C. STEPHEN 61
ALLSHOUSE, WOODY K.48
ALMOND, LINCOLN 103
ALPAUGH, LES 85
ALSOP, TED J. 390
ALTADONNA, LEIGH 294
ALTER, THEODORE R. ..102
ALTMAN, ELLIE 131
AMACK, REX 82, 398
AMARATUNGA, T. 285
AMATO, GEORGE 348
AMBROSINO, MARGIE..302
Ambs, TODD L. 306
AMENT, DON 49
AMES, OAKES 195
AMIN, ADNAN Z. 336
AMIOTTE, SUE 275
AMON, LAWRENCE J.267, 268, 269
AMONTREE, TOM 12
AMOR, ADLAI 213
AMORELLO, MATTHEW J. 74
AMTMANN, LINDSEY 342
ANABLE, MICHAEL E. 41
ANANA, MIKE 241
ANASTOR, DENNY 308
ANAYA, SCOTT 133
ANDELT, WILLIAM F. 50
ANDERS, KRISTIE 309
ANDERSEN, DAVID E.76, 378
ANDERSON, ALETA 130
ANDERSON, BOB ... 25, 344
ANDERSON, BROOK D. ..18
ANDERSON, BRUCE 281
ANDERSON, D. C. 358
ANDERSON, D. LARRY.110
ANDERSON, DAVID 74, 366
ANDERSON, DAVID R. 49
ANDERSON, DEBORAH ANDRACA 198
ANDERSON, DERS 290
ANDERSON, DONALD K. 101
ANDERSON, DORTHY ..377
ANDERSON, ERIC 393
ANDERSON, FLETCHER 263
ANDERSON, GREG 193
ANDERSON, GREGORY J. 146
ANDERSON, HAROLD 78
ANDERSON, JOHN 341
ANDERSON, JOHN W.225, 289
ANDERSON, JOHN W., II 225
ANDERSON, JON W. 112
ANDERSON, KARL 278
ANDERSON, KEN 106
ANDERSON, MARK 374
ANDERSON, PAUL 230
ANDERSON, PAUL D. ...223
ANDERSON, RENAE 15
ANDERSON, RICHARD 370
ANDERSON, ROBERT.... 24
ANDERSON, ROBERT D.57
ANDERSON, ROLF 213
ANDERSON, SCOTT, Ph.D. 362
ANDERSON, SHARON .. 93
ANDERSON, STANLEY H. 122, 393
ANDERSON, STEVE 203
ANDERSON, SUSAN 136
ANDERSON, THOMAS C. 74
ANDERSON, THOMAS R. 309, 310
ANDERTON, KATE 310
ANDO, RODOLFO L. 57
ANDRADE, WILLIAM ... 248
ANDREA, RICHARD 203
ANDREAS, TERRY L. 375
ANDREN, ANDERS W. ... 121
ANDREW, JON 30
ANDREWS, ADOLPHUS, JR. 242
ANDREWS, BILL44, 185, 399
ANDREWS, DAVID J. ... 298
ANDREWS, EMILIE M. 50
ANDREWS, JOHN 91
ANDREWS, OAKLEY V. 167
ANDREWS, SCOTT 306
ANDRICK, JILL 260
ANDRIGUETTO, JOSE MILTON 395
ANGEL, ELSA M. 207
ANGELL, JOHN M. 18
ANGELL, TONY ... 119, 401
ANGELLE, PEDRO 68
ANGERMEIER, PAUL L. 113
ANGERS, JEFF 176
ANGLE, RICHARD W., JR. 302
ANGVIK, JANE 40
ANNELLI, JOSEPH 13
ANSAH, ELLIOT O. 241
ANTHONY, CARL 337
ANTHONY, MARK 94
ANTHONY, ROBERT G.97, 384
ANTISTA, JAMES V. 54
ANTWI, KWABENA 198
AOKI, LENNA 28
APA, TONY 351
APGAR, BILL 19
APODACA, TED 88
APP, LEON E. 114
APPEL, BRAD VAN 184
APPEL, MADELEINE 310
APPEL, PAT 149
APPLEGATE, LINDA D. 232
APPLE, BOB 155
APPLE, MIKE 107
APPLEGATE, MICHAEL.. 21
APSLEY, BRUCE 331
APSLEY, DAVE 25
ARAMBURU, AL 46
ARB, SANDRA VON 351
ARCHER, HUGH N. 67
ARCHER, WILLIAM R. 108
ARCHIBALD, GEORGE. 224
ARCHULETA, RICHARD231
AREEN, JUDITH C. 368
AREIAS, RUSTY 48
ARENA, CHRISTINE 331
ARENDT, RANDALL G. .. 271
ARGANBRIGHT, DONALD G. 363
ARGO, GENE 238

Staff Name Index

STAFF NAME INDEX - B

ARGOW, KEITH A. 149, 203, 262, 269
ARIAS, SANTIAGO 103
ARMAS, LUPE 31
ARMBRISTER, JENEE ROSS 238
ARMITAGE, BRIAN J. ... 287
ARMOUR, HARRIS A., III 327
ARMOUR, KARYN 129
ARMSTRONG, DONALD R. 392
ARMSTRONG, JAMES 38, 392
ARMSTRONG, JAMES B. 350
ARMSTRONG, MARIA J. 94
ARMY, THOMAS J. 15
ARNETT, ED. 353
ARNETT, STUART 83
ARNEY, KEN 258
ARNOLD, CATHERINE ... 53
ARNOLD, MATTHEW 358
ARNOLDI, JOAN M. 13
ARONICA, LOUIS 247
ARONOFF, MARCIA 196
ARRINGTON, BOB 117
ARRINGTON, NANCY ... 340
ARRIOLA, VINCENT P. .. 57
ARSENAULT, BILL 290
ARSENAULT, GEORGE 128
ART, HENRY W. 376
ARTERO, VICTOR T. 57
ARTHUR, BILL 313
ARTHUR, GREGG 123
ARTHUR, PAUL 245
ARTHUR, SHEILA 300
ARTHUR, STEVE 47
ARTLEY, DON 81
ASBELL, G. FRED 297
ASBURY, DONNA 185
ASBURY, DORIS 343
ASHCROFT, MARY 339
ASHE, DANIEL M. 29
ASHEY, MIKE 54
ASHLEY, KEN 177
ASHLEY, SHARON 35
ASHMEADE-HAWKINS, BRETT EVELYN 302
ASHMEADE-HAWKINS, MARK EVELYN 302
ASKINS, RENEE 357
ASKINS, ROBERT A. 367
ASLIN, RAYMOND G. 66
ASMUSSEN, DENNIS 76
ASNER, EDWARD 227
ASPER, EDWARD 230
ASPERODITES, PHILIP N. 69
ASPRODITES, PHILIP N. 68
ATCHISON, ROBERT L. .. 66
ATEN, CAROL 264
ATERNO, KATHLEEN ... 175
ATKIN, JOHN 310
ATKINSON, NANCY 15
ATKINSON, SAMUEL F. 389
ATKINSON, THOMAS 83
ATWOOD, JOHN 131
ATWOOD, TIM. 261
AUFDERHEIDE, NADIA 216
AUGULIS, RICHARD P. ... 17
AUGUSTINE, ED 225
AUGUSTINE, GENE 22
AULUM, CLAUDIA 357
AUMEN, NICK 312
AUNAN, LAURI 341
AURAND, DARWIN 101
AUSTIN, ALICE 249
AUSTIN, BARBARA 88
AUSTIN, BOB 73
AUSTIN, JANE 284
AUSTIN, JIM 89
AUSTIN, TERRY 261
AUYONG, JAN 99
AVALOS, EDWARD 87
AVARY, KATHERINE LEE 120
AVENI, VIRGINIA 287
AVERY, DAVID L. 63
AVISSAR, RONI 380
AXLINE, MICHAEL. 198, 344
AXLINE, MICHAEL D. ... 385
AXON, JAMES 66
AYER, CLAIRE 338
AYERS, JOSEPH 375
AYERS, KENNETH 103
AYLSWORTH, LINDA ... 230
AYLWARD, KEVIN 125
AYRES, ED 359
AYRES, HENRY F., JR. 165
AYRES, JANET S. 63
AZEEZ, MICHAEL 243

B

BAAS, JOHN M. 354
BABB, JOHN 33
BABBITT, BRUCE 8, 27, 263
BABCOCK, KENNETH... 189
BABCOCK, SUSAN M. .. 303
BABIN, DANIEL J. 69
BABIN, EDWARD 297
BACA, SYLVIA 27
BACCA, DENISE 361
BACH, CATHERINE 376
BACH, MARYANNE 28
BACHERT, RUSSEL E., JR. 312
BACHMAN, PETER H. .. 251
BACINSKI, PETE 278
BACKUS, PETER 305
BACON, BOB 106
BACON, LAWRENCE R. 148
BACONE, JOHN 63
BADGER, RUTHE 121
BADGLEY, ANN 30, 178
BAER, KATHERINE 337
BAER, RICHARD A. 381
BAESLER, LARRY 307
BAETGE, JIM 327
BAGENT, JACK L. 69
BAGGOTT, ERIN E. 121
BAGLEY, CHUCK 118
BAGLEY, LAUREN 200
BAGNALL, CLAIRE 193
BAICICH, PAUL 138
BAILEY, ALAN 177
BAILEY, DICK 99
BAILEY, ED 196
BAILEY, JAMES 25
BAILEY, RICHARD 59
BAILEY, ROBERT 126
BAILEY, VICKY A. 19
BAILIFF, MEGAN 118
BAILIFF, MEGAN D. 177
BAILY, JIM 263
BAIN, MARK B. 88
BAINES, PRESCOTT S. 105
BAIRD, DENNIS 218
BAIRD, ROBERT 343
BAIRD, RONALD C. 18
BAIRD, WARREN .. 220, 269
BAKAMJIAN, LYNN 159
BAKER, BRUCE 323
BAKER, BRUCE J. 121
BAKER, D. JAMES 17
BAKER, DALE 90
BAKER, DAYTON 259
BAKER, ELAINE 224
BAKER, EVERARD 78
BAKER, J. 8
BAKER, JOHN R. 199
BAKER, MICHAEL 94
BAKER, PETER 276
BAKER, ROBERT J. 150
BAKER, TOM. 67
BAKER, VICTOR R. 363
BAKER, WILLIAM C. 172
BAKKER, JOE 54
BAKUNAS, EDWARD J. .. 21
BALAAM, ROBERT J. 84
BALD, GEORGE 83, 84
BALDES, RICHARD J. .. 267
BALDOCK, JAMES 267
BALDWIN, DICK 98
BALDWIN, MARK 307
BALE, CHARLES 67
BALENOVIC, IVAN 166
BALFOUR, DAVID 36, 74
BALFREY, WILLO 255
BALL, ALLAN 70
BALL, I. J. 80
BALL, JIM 137
BALL, LINDSAY A. 98
BALL, LOUISE M. 383
BALLANTYNE, CHRIS .. 313
BALLANTYNE, JOE 129
BALLARD, BILL 254
BALLARD, DENNY 182
BALLARD, JOE N. 26
BALLENTINE, JANE 151
BALLIET, KRIS 170
BALSILLIE, D. 394
BALSILLIE, DAVID 127
BALTON, DAVID A. 20
BAMBERY, CAROL 75
BAMBRICK, DALE 116
BAN, HIDEYUKI 174
BANCROFT, THOMAS .. 347
BANDY, JOHN 61
BANE, SANDRA O. 347
BANGART, RICHARD L. . 34
BANGERT, SUZANNE .. 121
BANK, DEBBIE 348
BANKER, HARRY J. 178
BANKER, MARK E. 308
BANKERS, GARY . 294, 357
BANKS, GEORGE 308
BANNER, DIANA 234
BANNER, ROGER E. 111
BANSLEY, MARCIA 330
BANTA, JOHN 88
BANZHAF, WILLIAM H. 319
BAPST, RICHARD 295
BAQUET, CHARLES, III . 34
BARAJAS, GRACIELA .. 228
BARASH, JEAN 236
BARBARO, HENRY 74
BARBEE, ROBERT 29
BARBER, EDNA 25
BARBER, GERALD 267
BARBER, HARRY A. 354
BARBER, PATRICIA S. .. 52
BARBER, SYD 128
BARCINAS, JEFF 57
BARCLAY, JOHN S. 51
BARD, JOHN F. 238
BARDSLEY, MARC 283
BAREISS, ROBERT 202
BARELS, GAIL 232
BARFIELD, BETSY 327
BARGER, DON 264
BARKER, BOB 137
BARKER, DAVID READ 254
BARKER, I. 166
BARKER, RICHARD F. ... 85
BARKER, ROY 21
BARKLEY, BILL 124
BARKOW, LEE 28
BARLATT, ROGERS 380
BARLOW, MICHELE 360
BARLOW, MIKE 290
BARLOW, RICHARD J. .. 50
BARLOW, ROGER 78
BARLOW, VIRGINIA 339
BARNA, DAVID 29
BARNARD, GEOFFREY S. 211
BARNARD, WILLIAM H. 215
BARNES, A. JAMES 371
BARNES, ALLEN 164
BARNES, DONALD G. 10
BARNES, ELAINE 287
BARNES, JAMES 238
BARNES, JIM 153
BARNES, JUDY 354
BARNES, MISTIANNA H. 66
BARNES, PETRA 14
BARNES, ROY 55
BARNES, SUSAN 238
BARNES, THOMAS G. ... 67
BARNETT, AUDREY 137
BARNETT, CLAIRE L ... 155
BARNETT, EMILY 285
BARNETT, TIMOTHY L. 131
BARNETT, ZRNIE 53
BARNETTE, JAMES 5
BARNEYCASTLE, CHRIS 209
BARNHART, GERRY 89, 398
BARON, DAVID 192
BARON, ROBERT 230
BARONE, GEORGE J., JR. 51
BARR, JOHN 243
BARRAM, DAVID 33
BARRE, DAVID 213
BARRESI, JAMES 85
BARRET, MORLEY 124
BARRETO, JOSÉ L. 184
BARRETT, GARY 146
BARRETT, J. DAVID 116
BARRETT, LONICE C. ... 56
BARRETT, WILLIAM O. 161
BARRICKLOW, DEANNA 220
BARRINGTON, GENE .. 332
BARRITT, DAVID 225
BARRON, EDWIN N. 109
BARROW, WILLIE T. ... 302
BARRY, DONALD J. 27
BARRY, JOHANNAH 152
BARRY, PAMELA 32
BARRY, ROBERT 23
BARRY, WILLIAM N. ... 217
BARSAMILAN, LORETTA 45
BARSCH, RAYMOND E. . 47
BARSHIELD, ROBERT ... 89
BARSTOW, ROBBINS .. 172
BARTH, ELLEN 281
BARTH, ERIK J. 113
BARTHOLOMEW, CHARLES L. 386
BARTLEMAN, LARRY 64
BARTLETT, CHRIS 71
BARTLETT, EDMUND .. 326
BARTLETT, TERRI 297
BARTLETT, TINA L. 351
BARTLEY, JULIE 331
BARTNICKI, PENNY L. . 354
BARTO, JOHN, ESQ 325
BARTON, BOB 167
BARTON, RICK 72
BARTON, SANDY 111
BARTON, STEPHEN 60
BARTON, THOMAS 63
BARUFFE, ROSANE 302
BARZEN, JEB 224

STAFF NAME INDEX - B

BASDEN, THOMAS J. ... 120
BASKANIC, ROBERT J. 101
BASMAN, CEM 257
BASS, EDWARD P. 359
BASS, LEE M. 109
BASSETT, KAREN 240
BASSI, RICHARD J. 130
BASTIAN, BLAIR 125
BATES, BOB 24
BATES, DAVID R. 162
BATES, JENNIFER 161
BATES, MIKE 43
BATES, NORMAN 107
BATES, RICK 128
BATES, ROBERT M. 66
BATES, SYLVIA 159
BATKER, CAROL A. 92
BATORY, JOAN 295
BATT, AL 251
BATT, BRUCE 189
BATTEN, GERALD 201
BATTEY, JAMES F. 390
BATTOCCHI, RON 33
BAUCHMAN, ANN 81
BAUER, JEFFREY 384
BAUER, TOM 30
BAUGH, DONALD R. 172
BAUGHMAN, JOHN 123, 223, 399
BAUGHMAN, MELVIN J. .. 77
BAUM, BOB 28
BAUM, CHARLES 117
BAUM, ELLEN 271
BAUM, KENT 29
BAUMANN, MIKE 205
BAUMGARTNER, DAVID M. 118
BAUST, JOE 239
BAUST, JOHN 54
BAXTER, PATRICIA J. ... 278
BAY, CRANDALL 364
BAY, MICHAEL 289
BAYDACK, RICHARD ... 394
BAYER, ROBERT 71
BAYER, ROBIN 244
BAYES, MARK 137
BAYLES, DAVID 293
BAYLESS, STEVE R. 190
BAYLIFF, WILLIAM H. ... 8
BAYNES, A. SIDNEY 92
BAZZELL, DARRELL L. .. 120
BEACH, ARTHUR B. 34
BEACH, DANA 321
BEACH, GARY 122
BEACH, GARY G. 122
BEACH, JEAN 309
BEACH, PAUL 192
BEACHY, BOB 238
BEAL, CAROL 35
BEAL, KATHERINE F. ... 353
BEAL, KENNETH L. 140
BEALS, ED 373
BEAN, HAROLD 53
BEAN, LARRY 64
BEANE, JEFF 283
BEANE, MARJORIE 358
BEAR, DINAH 10
BEARD, DAN 259
BEARD, DANIEL 259
BEARD, MOLLY 276
BEARD, RON 71
BEARZI, JAMES 87
BEASLEY, R. SCOTT 388
BEASON, ROBERT C. ... 355
BEATTIE, JAMES T. 103
BEATTY, ROBERT 157
BEAUDETTE, PAUL A. ... 195
BEAUMONT, LUCIEN ... 128
BEAUPRE, G. 36
BECH, REBECCA 12

BECHARD, MARC J. 303
BECHTEL, JOHN H., III . 265
BECK, CHRIS 369
BECK, JIM A. 393
BECK, LOUIS A. 48
BECK, MIKE 158
BECK, MILTON 22
BECK, RAY 81
BECK, ROBIN 41
BECK, TREY 177
BECKER, CARL 270
BECKER, CHARLIE 238
BECKER, DALE 352
BECKER, DENNIS 287
BECKER, KENNETH 112
BECKER, LAWRENCE R. 112
BECKER, NANCY 219
BECKER, RONALD E. ... 69
BECKER, S. WILLIAM ... 325
BECKERMAN, ROBERT 382
BECKETT, DAVID 378
BECKMAN, DAVE 129
BECKWITH, ERNEST E. . 50
BECKWITH, JANE 290
BEDFORD, CHARLES 49
BEDNARZ, JIM C. 351
BEDNARZ, ROBERT 260
BEDRIN, MICHAEL 101
BEECHER, BOB 127
BEECHER, WILLIAM M. .. 34
BEEGLE, ROBERT 164
BEELMAN, JOYCE 25
BEEMAN, MICHELLE ... 76
BEEMER, JAMES 27, 263
BEESON, M. GAULT, JR. 347
BEGGS, GAIL 127
BEGIN, PAUL 128
BEHLEN, THOMAS 8
BEHLING, MARY C. 120
BEHRENS, WILMA 135
BEINECKE, JOHN B. 215
BEISSINGER, STEVEN . 148
BELCHER, JENNIFER M. 117
BELEW, JOHNNY 154
BELFIT, SCOTT 25
BELICH, MEL F., Q.C. ... 188
BELISLE, BRAD 180
BELK, PERDITA 14
BELKNAP, DANIEL 374
BELL, BOB 164
BELL, ELIZABETH 251
BELL, HUBERT 34
BELL, LARRY 87
BELL, NANCY 182
BELL, RICHARD C. 359
BELL, WILLIAM 244
BELLAFIORE, VINCENT J. 370
BELLINGER, JOHN 26
BELLIS, EDWARD 333
BELLON, JIM 22
BELOTE, MONTE 152
BELOVSKY, GARY E. 389
BELSON, JERRY 29
BELZ, JOHN 189
BEMELMANS, MADELEINE 318
BEMIS, JILL A. 271
BENDER, BOB 67
BENDER, DAVE 61
BENDER, MARY 100
BENDER, NORMAN 51
BENDLER, THOMAS 263
BENEDICK, ROBERT 272
BENEDICT, LES 325
BENEDICT, MARK A. ... 182

BENEDICT, MICHELLE 298, 391
BENEDICT, PHILIP R. ... 112
BENEFIELD, GARY 133
BENEKE, JOHN 44
BENEKE, PATRICIA 27
BENFORADO, JAY 10
BENGTSON, JOHN 319
BENJAMIN, CHARLES ... 237
BENJAMIN, SHARON K. 250
BENNER, J. MERLIN 353
BENNET, DEBBY 131
BENNETT, BETSY 91
BENNETT, C. THOMAS 223, 397
BENNETT, C. TOM 66
BENNETT, CHUCK 43
BENNETT, COLIN 340
BENNETT, D. W. 147
BENNETT, DAVID 56
BENNETT, DERY .. 174, 176
BENNETT, EARL H. 60
BENNETT, JAMES P. 162
BENNETT, JIM 187
BENNETT, JOEL 186
BENNETT, KAREN 84
BENNETT, ROBERT 4, 73
BENNETT, SHAUN 255
BENNETT, TONY 321
BENNETT, WILLIAM 231
BENNETT, WILLIAM J. .. 48
BENOIT, MARY ANN 351
BENSON, CAMERON 196
BENSON, CARL 154
BENSON, DELWIN E. 50
BENSON, LAURA 151
BENSON, RALPH W. 334
BENSON, ROBERT A. ... 384
BENSON, SERENA 348
BENSON, SUSAN 70
BENSON, THOMAS 75
BENSON, WILLIAM F. ... 19
BENTLEY, WILLIAM R. .. 382
BENTON, DAVID 39
BENTON, JO A. 131
BENTON, MICHELLE 117
BENTZ, EARL 107
BENTZ, JOHN 177
BERENDSEN, PIETER 66, 237
BERG, ADAM 213
BERG, DAVID 306
BERG, DENNIS 364
BERG, JUDITH 306
BERG, NORMAN A. 320
BERG, THOMAS 93, 94
BERGEN, ROGER 193
BERGER, ALAN 152
BERGER, J. 393
BERGER, JOEL 379
BERGERON, ROBERT ... 35
BERGERSEN, ERIC P. ... 49
BERGEY, HANS 324
BERGHAIER, ROBERT .. 346
BERGIN, PATRICK J. 132
BERGMAN, HAROLD ... 221
BERGMAN, JIM 343
BERGSTROM, MARK ... 164
BERINGER, PETER 70
BERKELEY, STEVEN 141
BERKOVITS, ANNETTE 348
BERKOWITZ, ALAN R. .. 222
BERKOWITZ, FRANCINE 318
BERLAT, WILLIAM 41
BERLIN, GARY 155
BERNARD, STEVE 73
BERNASKI, WILLIAM 89
BERNER, ROBERT 246
BERNHEIMER, R. A. 47

BERNHJELM, BILL 76
BERNSTEIN, CAROL 352
BERNSTEIN, JOHN 72
BERRY, BILL 48
BERRY, CHARLES R. ... 387
BERRY, CHARLES R., JR. 106
BERRY, JIM 307
BERRY, JOYCE 366
BERRY, M. JOHN 27
BERRY, RICHARD 97
BERRYHILL, DON 54
BERSTEIN, NEIL 231
BERTHELSEN, PETER S. 296
BERTHIAUME, LUC 128
BERTI, BOB 277
BERTSCH, PAUL 369
BESSE, MARK 218
BEST, CONSTANCE 241
BEST, STEPHEN 230
BEST, TROY L. 150
BETHEA, SALLY 337
BETHELL, HELEN D. 247
BETIT, ROD 110
BETSCHART, A. A. 15
BETTAS, GEORGE 307
BETTAS, GEORGE A. ... 161
BETTINGER, MARK 313
BETTS, LYNN 14
BEVACQUA, FRANK 8
BEVAN, DAVID 35
BEVERLIN, JERRY 61
BEVERLY, JOHN 295
BEYERLE, J. MICHAEL .. 98
BEZANSON, JANICE 329
BHALTA, BISHNU 327
BHUMBLA, D. K. 120
BIAGGI, ALLEN 82
BIAGGI, ROBERTO E. .. 300
BIANCHI, STEPHANIE .. 33
BIBEAULT, LUCIEN 305
BIBLER, BART 54
BICKERTON, DAVID 35
BICKFORD, JAMES 67
BICKNELL, WILLIAM B. 353
BIDDLE, JOEL 303
BIDER, BILL 66
BIDWELL, DENNIS 139
BIECHELE, DOUG 190
BIEKER, CHIRS 15
BIENEMAN, GRETCHEN L. 165
BIENFANG, PAUL K. 142
BIERCE, ROSE 170
BIERMA, THOMAS, PH.D. 370
BIESINGER, ESTHER ... 110
BIESIOT, PATRICIA 378
BIFERA, FRANK 89
BIGGS, JAMES R. 353
BILBERRY, GRADY 13
BILBREY, ELLEN 42
BILDSTEIN, KEITH L. 215, 303
BILES, LARRY 16
BILLIG, PRISCILLA P. ... 59
BILLING, VESTA C. 70
BILODEAU, GILBERT M. 71
BILSKI, NANINE 136
BINGAMAN, BOB 312, 314, 338
BINGAMAN, LARRY 310
BINGHAM, DEREK 358
BINGHAM, W. RICHARD 163
BINNEY, GEORGE A. ... 330
BIRCH, CLARE J. 128
BIRCHFIELD, SUSAN ... 97
BIRD, DARIN 110

STAFF NAME INDEX - B

BIRD, DAVID M. 395
BIRD, MARY LYNNE 145
BIRD, PAUL E. 34
BIRDSALL, JOHN 296
BIRES, FRAN 221
BISBEE, G. DANA 84
BISCHOFF, DONALD C. 32
BISHOP, CHARLES 38
BISHOP, GERALD 267
BISHOP, JOE 332
BISHOP, PARVIN L. 162
BISHOP, RICHARD 64
BISHOP, SARAH G. 294
BISHTON, TIMOTHY 114
BISSELL, JAMES 175
BISSET, DOUGLAS 132
BISSEX, GLYN 394
BISSON, ALAIN 301
BISSON, HENRI 28
BISSONETTE, JOHN A. 110
BITTLE, CINDI 130
BIVANS, WAYNE 307
BIVENS, SANDY 195
BIVINGS, ALBERT E. 27
BIXBY, DONALD 147
BJORNLIE, HARVEY 254
BJORNN, THEODORE C. 60
BLACK, SCOTT HOFFMAN 317
BLACK, SUSAN 73
BLACK, SUSAN C. 121
BLACKBURN, WILBERT 15
BLACKMON, BOB 43, 364
BLACKMORE, E. 125
BLACKMORE, MARY 158
BLACKWELDER, BRENT 206
BLACKWELL, JACK A. 16
BLACKWELL, LINDA 106
BLACKWELL, RAYMOND L. 162
BLADES, MICHAEL 303
BLAHA, KATHY 334
BLAIR, AARON 301
BLAIR, BOWEN 335
BLAIS, CLAUDETTE 128
BLAKE, ED, JR. 185
BLAKE, J. 63, 125
BLAKE, ROBERT O. 179
BLAKE, WILLIAM M. 349
BLAKELY, DON 307
BLAKEMAN, PETER 84
BLAKESLEE, GEORGE M. 369
BLANCHARD, KATHLEEN A. 157
BLANCHARD, MARY JOSIE 29
BLANCHE, CATALINO 16
BLANCHFIELD, JEFFRY 48
BLANCO, FRANCISCO JAVIER 184
BLANDIN, ALICE 318
BLANKENSHIP, TERRY L. 343
BLANTON, NANCY 118
BLAUVELT, MARK 333
BLAUWKAMP, TERRY 308
BLAZER, ARTHUR 269
BLEDSOE, PAUL 28
BLEED, ANN SALOMON 81, 82
BLEIER, W. J. 383
BLEM, CHARLES R. 355
BLESSINGTON, JACQUE 137
BLEVINS, HEATHER 233
BLICK, LARRY 14
BLILEY, THOMAS 5
BLISS, PATTY 133

BLOCH, BARBARA 46
BLOCK, RANCE 307
BLOCKSTEIN, DAVID E. 291
BLOMQUIST, JIM 314
BLOOD, BRAD R. 354
BLOOD, MARCUS 22
BLOOM, ARNOLD J. 365
BLOOM, FLOYD E. 136
BLOOMBERG, AL 117
BLOOME, PETER 99
BLOT, KIM T. 88
BLOUNT, JAMES 55
BLOYD, BARRY 96
BLUE, KAREN 181
BLUEMLE, JOHN P. 93
BLUM, PETE 62
BLUMBERG, FRED 108
BLUME, TED 82
BLUMSTEIN, CARL 139
BLUNDO, JOHN 74
BOATWRIGHT, MIKE 67
BOBARAKIS, STEPHEN 89
BOBZIEN, STEVEN 354
BOCHENEK, ELEANOR A. 86
BODDICKER, MAJ. L. 178
BODE, JEFFREY JON 285
BODIN, MARK 326
BOE, JANET S. 352
BOEHM, DAVID 385
BOEHMER, PEGGY 156
BOEHMKE, JOHN 28
BOER, ARNOLD 223, 399
BOER, ARNOLD H. 125
BOERBOOM, JIM 76
BOERGERS, DAVID P. 19
BOESCH, DONALD F. 375
BOEZI, LOUIS J. 17
BOGAN, SANDRA 201
BOGAR, DEBRA A. 257
BOGARD, CAROL 249
BOGENSCHUTZ, TODD 351
BOGER, BRUCE A. 34
BOGGESS, WILLIAM P., II 208
BOGGS, EVELYN 366
BOGGUS, TOM G. 109
BOGNER, TERRY 218
BOHAM, RUSSEL 364
BOHLEN, E.U. CURTIS 170
BOHLENDER, JERRY, DVM 49
BOHMFALK, ERWIN 348
BOICE, L. PETER 18
BOKMA, ROBERT 12
BOLDUC, HERVE 128
BOLEN, PATRICK 153
BOLENBAUGH, ALAN J. 220
BOLEY, JAMES 284
BOLIVER, BRUCE 385
BOLLINGER, DON 341
BOLLINGER, TRENT 166
BOLTON, BERNIE 231
BOLTON, HANNIBAL 29, 141
BONDRUP-NIELS, SOREN 394
BONER, REX R. 183
BONGOLAN, DIXIE 293
BONILLA, HILDA 300
BONINE, JOHN 198
BONNEY, RICK 184
BONOMO, JACQUELYN 344
BOOHER, SAM 304
BOOKER, DAVID 24
BOOKS, DAVE 80
BOONE, KATHY 309
BOONE, ROBERT E. 152
BOPP, DENNY 80
BORD, ROGER 356

BORDELON, MIKE 98
BORDEN, DAVID V.D. 7
BORDOGNA, JOSEPH 33
BOREN, ANN 311
BOREN, ANN F. 186
BOREN, JON 88
BOREN, MIKE 160
BORGELD, JEFFRY 364
BORJA, MELVIN B. 57
BORN, STEPHEN 331
BORNER, MARKUS 205
BORRE, LISA 254
BORTONE, STEVE 181
BORUFF, CHET 61
BORZEUERI, BOB 45
BOSH, JONI 152
BOSMAN, CORRIE 134
BOSSELMAN, FRED 320
BOSSENMAIER, GRETA 35
BOSTIC, JAMES E., JR. 209
BOSTICK, WILLIAM G., JR. 349
BOSTON, WILLIAM TERRY 35
BOSWELL, TED 272
BOSWORTH, DALE 16
BOSWORTH, ROBERT 39
BOSWORTH, ROBERT W. 320
BOTELER, FRANK 116
BOTH, MEL 211
BOTTMAN, ROBERT P. 118
BOTTOMLEY, TIMOTHY 23
BOTTORFF, JIM 354
BOTTS, DEWEY 91
BOUCHARD, J. ROBERT 191
BOULDEN, R. 36
BOULTON, MARK N. 224
BOURQUE, HERB 14
BOURQUE, PETER M. 70
BOURQUE, WAYNE 292
BOUTIN, TOM 40
BOVWER, EDWARD J. 374
BOWDEN, SHIRLEY 186
BOWEN, JOHN H. 204
BOWER, GWEN 100
BOWERS, JANET L. 151
BOWERS, JEFFREY S. 119
BOWERS, RICHARD 151
BOWIE, D. 36
BOWIE, DAVID 331
BOWLER, TOM 231
BOWLES, JOHN 163
BOWLING, GILBERT O. 71
BOWMAN, MARGARET 149
BOWMAN, MARLENE 70
BOWMAN, PHIL 69
BOWMAN, STEVEN G. 113
BOWYER, JOHN S., JR. 84
BOXRUCKER, JEFF C. 140
BOYCE, MARK S. 355
BOYCE, TIMOTHY C. 39
BOYD, AVIS E. 326
BOYD, HYLAN 340
BOYD, KEN 40
BOYD, KENNETH 25
BOYD, ROBERT 216
BOYD, SUSAN 179
BOYD, TERRY 38
BOYD, TOM 275
BOYDSTUN, L. B. 47
BOYER, JEFF 382
BOYER, TOM 116
BOYKIN, BILL 105
BOYKIN, ESTHER 243
BOYLE, BARBARA 313
BOYLE, E. MICHAEL 344
BOYLE, HARVEY 124
BOYLE, STEWART 226

BOYLESTON, LARRY 105
BOYUM, BILL 117, 118
BOZEK, MICHAEL 393
BOZEK, MICHAEL A. 120
BOZEK, NANCY C. 356
BRABANDER, JERRY 353
BRACE, ROBERT J. 358
BRACK, CARL ELLIOT 208
BRACKETT, DAVID 35, 228
BRACKETT, SUSAN A. 250
BRADBERY, TERRY 114
BRADBURY, BETSY 262
BRADDOCK, JOAN 362
BRADFORD, DEREK 386
BRADLE, TIM 258
BRADLEY, BILL 83
BRADLEY, DARBY 338
BRADLEY, PHIL 251
BRADLEY, RUTH S. 216
BRADSHAW, LINDA 155
BRADSTREET, MICHAEL 161
BRADT-BARNHART, JUDY 269
BRADY, PAM 159
BRAIBANTI, RALPH 21
BRAINERD, LYMAN B., JR. 159
BRAKKE, DENNIS 200
BRAMBLE, BARBARA J. 267
BRAME, DICK 176
BRANAN, JOHNNY 56
BRANCA, BARBARA A. 90
BRANCA, SALLY 210
BRANCEL, BEN 120
BRANCH, CHARLES T. 78
BRANDES, RUSSELL 64
BRANDRUP, MIKE 65
BRANDT, CHUCK 312
BRANDT, MIKE 256
BRANDWEIN, PAUL F. 297
BRANNAN, MARK 31
BRANNON, EDGAR B. 296
BRANTLY, ROBERT M. 323, 349
BRASSARD, BILL 265
BRASWELL, ALLEN 25
BRASWELL, ALVIN 283
BRAUNWORTH, WILLIAM 99
BRAUS, JUDY 280
BRAXTON, LOWELL 110
BRAY, CARLA 105
BRAY, HARVEY 301
BRAY, PAUL M. 155
BRAY, SHIRLEY 135
BRAZELTON, DON 63
BRAZIL, DIRK 116
BRAZIL, J. 125
BRDICKA, BARBARA 94
BREAKELL, JOHN 180
BREATHITT, LINDA K. 19
BREAU, KASHA 180
BREAZEALE, DANIEL P., SR. 105
BRECHER, ALAN M. 195
BRECKENRIDGE, ROY M 60
BREDY, JIM 223
BREEN, BARRY N. 11
BREESE, LYNN 291
BREEZE, ROGER 15
BREITE, DENNIS V. 358
BREITMEYER, RICHARD 46
BREMER, LINDA M. 349
BREMER, WALTER D., ASLA 364
BREMICKER, TIM 76
BRENNAN, LEONARD A. 327

STAFF NAME INDEX - B

BRENNEMAN, CLOYD E. 294
BRENNEMAN, KRISTINE 142
BRENNEMAN, RUSSELL L. 276
BRESSOR, JAMES E. 111
BRESTRUP, CRAIG 205
BREUNIG, ROBERT G., Ph.D. 240
BREZONIK, PATRICK... 378
BRICE, WILLIAM 76
BRICKLEY, DAVID G. ... 114
BRIDGES, ROCK 190
BRIDI, JEFFREY S. 102
BRIENICH, ANNA 294
BRIENZO, GARY 256
BRIGGS, MARK..... 305, 320
BRIGGS, ROGER 45
BRIGGS, XAVIER de-SOUZA........................ 20
BRININSTOOL, BILL 87
BRINKER, RICHARD W. 362
BRINKLEY, JESSIE 264
BRISCOE, ROBBIE B..... 79
BRISKEY, LISA M........ 348
BRISTER, BOB............. 317
BRISTOL, PETER 216
BRISTOW, TAMMY 267
BRITT, BRUCE 203
BRITT, PEGGY 75
BRITTELL, DAVE 116
BRITTINGHAM, MARGARET............... 102
BRO, KENNETH M. 392
BROADWAY, MICHAEL J. 376
BROBRCK, ROD 291
BROCK, GREG 54
BROCK, MIKE............... 331
BROCK, RICHARD E....... 59
BROCK, ROBERT H., JR. 382
BROCK, VIRGINIA 203
BROCKMAN, CONNIE .. 174
BROCKMAN, D. MATT.. 108
BROCKMANN, JANE ... 146
BRODA, HERB 197
BRODDRICK, RYAN 47
BRODERICK, BRIAN....... 74
BRODERICK, STEPHEN. 51
BRODERICK, THOMAS F. 74
BRODIE, W. B............... 285
BRODY, ANNIE 191
BROGIE, MARK 275
BROHMAN, MARK 82
BROKAW, HOWARD P. 138
BROMLEY, PETER T. 92
BRONSTON, DAVID 131
BROOKE, STEVE......... 149
BROOKRESON, BILL... 117
BROOKS, BOB 188
BROOKS, CHRISTOPHER L. 105
BROOKS, CONNIE........ 111
BROOKS, IRENE B. 101
BROOKS, JAMES........... 70
BROOKS, JERRY 53
BROOKS, KEVIN 39
BROOKS, LILA 165
BROOKS, MICHAEL J... 189
BROOKS, WILLIAM 105
BROOKS, WILLIAM S. .. 356
BROOKS, WILLIAM T. ... 29
BROSMAN, KEN 220
BROTHERS, DAN 38
BROUGHTON, WILLIAM C. 118
BROUHA, PAUL 16, 146
BROUSSARD, AMY 109
BROWDER, HAL C. 361
BROWER, DAVID R. 192
BROWN, A. GILSON..... 136
BROWN, ANITA 14
BROWN, ART................ 117
BROWN, ARTHUR R., JR. 85, 277
BROWN, BETH 233
BROWN, BOB 388
BROWN, CARL............. 267
BROWN, CAROL 10, 97, 357
BROWN, DIANE V. 102
BROWN, DON............... 66
BROWN, DONALD........ 308
BROWN, FRANK 67
BROWN, GARY............. 123
BROWN, GREGORY N. 391
BROWN, JAMES E......... 98
BROWN, JEANETTE L. ...10
BROWN, JESSICA........ 157
BROWN, JOHN W. 57
BROWN, JUDY 336
BROWN, JUNE G. 19
BROWN, KAREN 36
BROWN, KARL G. 100
BROWN, KAY......97, 134
BROWN, KEVIN 307
BROWN, KIRK 61
BROWN, LESTER R...... 359
BROWN, LINFIELD C.... 375
BROWN, LISA 44
BROWN, LORI 359
BROWN, MARVIN D. 79
BROWN, MARY 232
BROWN, MICHELE 39
BROWN, OTIS 226
BROWN, OTIS B. 368
BROWN, PATRICK W. ... 370
BROWN, PERRY J.378, 379
BROWN, PETER G........ 190
BROWN, QUINCALEE... 342
BROWN, RANDALL L. 48
BROWN, ROBERT D. ... 350
BROWN, ROGER K. 260
BROWN, RONALD A. 79
BROWN, SCOTT 87, 218
BROWN, STEPHANIE ... 166
BROWN, STEVE............ 90
BROWN, TIM................ 212
BROWN, TOM..........54, 307
BROWN, TOMMY L. 90
BROWN, TORREY C..... 347
BROWN, VALERIE 335
BROWN, WENDY 281
BROWNBACK, SAM 2, 6
BROWNE, BOB............. 240
BROWNE, BROOKS...... 197
BROWNELL, WILLIAM .. 263
BROWNER, CAROL 10
BROWNING, DENNIS J. 352
BROWNING, WILLIAM R., M.D. 158
BROZ, GORDON 74
BRUBAKER, CAROLE CASTO 62
BRUBAKER, DAVID R., Ph.D. 374
BRUBAKER, KEVIN....... 198
BRUCE, ANN 327
BRUCE, GERON............ 40
BRUCE, JAMES R. 320
BRUCKER, THOMAS H. 283
BRUCKNER, CHARLES 100
BRUELL, HARRY 258
BRUENE, DAN 231
BRUFFY, ROBERT 20
BRUMBACH, JOE 98
BRUMM, JERRY 299
BRUMMETT, KEN......... 337
BRUNER, CLARK............ 38
BRUNINGA, KRISTIN RIPPETO 210
BRUNNER, JUDI 117
BRUNNER, THOMAS..... 173
BRUNS, DALE A. 386
BRUS, KEITH 296
BRUSENDORFF, ANNE CHRISTINE 7
BRUSH, GRACE S........ 374
BRUSH, PETER N.......... 18
BRYAN, CHARLES F. 68, 373
BRYAN, RORKE B. 394
BRYAN, SUSAN MILES .255
BRYANT, BUNYAN 377
BRYANT, DANA 54
BRYANT, DAVID 56
BRYANT, DOUGLAS E. .105
BRYANT, FRED C. 389
BRYANT, HAROLD 15
BRYANT, LARRY 173
BRYANT, MAGALEN O..261
BRYANT, SHERMAN 220
BRYCE, PHILIP A........... 83
BRYNE, DONALD H....... 114
BRYNER, GARY........... 367
BRYSON, CAROLYN 220
BRZUSZEK, BOB........... 186
BUCCINI, J. 36
BUCHANAN, GALE A..... 56
BUCHANAN, PATRICIA J. 62
BUCHANAN, STUART 89
BUCHERT, BEVERLY.... 385
BUCHNER, JAY 334
BUCHNER, KATHY 331
BUCK, CAMILLE 206
BUCK, LEANN 250
BUCK, MICHAEL G......... 58
BUCK, PAIGE MITCHELL 14
BUCKELEW, A. R., JR. ..163
BUCKLEY, LAWERNCE J. 387
BUCKLEY, ROBERT G. .109
BUCKLIN, ANN C. 83
BUCKMAN, ARTHUR...... 22
BUDD, BOB 319
BUDD, WILLIAM 391
BUDNEY, GREGORY 184
BUDNIK, STEVE 256
BUDZIK, MICHAEL......... 94
BUECHLER, DENNIS..... 178
BUEHLER, DAVID......... 354
BUFFETT, JIMMY 310
BUFFINGTON, JOHN D...31
BUHLER, ANDY 163
BUHLER, MARILYN 163
BUISCH, WILLIAM W...... 13
BULL, DAVE 205
BULL, JULIANNA F. 94
BULLARD, JAMES 163
BULLINGTON, RANDALL B. 351
BULLOCK, MIKE 54
BULLOCK, STEVE 185
BULLOCK, THOMAS F. .278
BULMAN, JIM 65
BULMAN, LESLEY 357
BUMA, GERRIT 354
BUMP, JEFF 147
BUNDY, SUSAN 104
BUNDY, WILLIAM F. 104
BUNN, RICHARD 263
BUNNING, BONNIE 118
BUNTING, BRUCE W..... 359
BUNTY, ROBERT.......... 100
BUNURI, TARIQ J. 228
BURACK, TOM............. 159
BURBANK, CYNTHIA L...32
BURCH, TOMMY 329
BURCHELL, L. CHARLES 378
BURCHFIELD, JAMES .. 378
BURDETTE, JOHN 343
BURDICK, BARBARA.... 374
BURDICK, LALOR 276
BURDICK, NEAL 131
BUREAU, SANDRA 88
BUREK, TOM 133
BURGDORF, JAYNA 109
BURGER, ALAN 293
BURGER, BILL 351
BURGER, CARL V. 140
BURGER, D. W. 365
BURGESS, DAVID 386
BURGESS, HARRIET.... 146
BURGESS, JIM 355
BURGESS, VAN 110
BURGETT, MEG 133
BURGOYNE, GEORGE E., JR. 75
BURHENNE, W. E. 224
BURKE, ALBERTA 165
BURKE, DAVID 72
BURKE, MARK A. 344
BURKE, PATRICIA M. 77
BURKE, STEVEN F. 281
BURKE, TIMOTHY 131
BURKE, TOM 282
BURKERT, RONALD P. 308
BURKHALTER, PAUL 56
BURKHART, HAROLD E. 391
BURKS, DENNIS 43
BURKS, JEFFREY S. 111
BURKS, JOCKO 341
BURKS, MARGARET 246
BURLEY, JEFFERY 228
BURLINGTON, D. BRUCE 19
BURMAN, HOWARD R. 208
BURNETT, GROVE 344
BURNETT, STEVE 165
BURNEY, DARYL 252
BURNHAM, KENNETH P. 49
BURNHAM, WILLIAM A. 296
BURNLEY, BEN R. 190
BURNS, DENVER P. 17
BURNS, HERBERT 75
BURNS, KATHRYN 266
BURNS, STEPHEN G...... 34
BURNS, VANESSA 52
BURNS, WILLIAM.......... 25
BURNS, WILLIAM C.150, 293
BURPEE, ROBERT 17
BURR, STEPHEN W. 111
BURRESON, E. M. 390
BURT, MICHAEL D.B. ... 217
BURTON, JIM 41
BURTON, JOHN V.......... 43
BURTON, MIKE 189
BURTON, NELSON 234
BURTON, ROBERT 25
BURTT, TONY 225
BURWELL, DAVID 302
BUSBICE, BILL, JR......... 68
BUSCH, RICK 115
BUSCH, STEPHAN D.... 187
BUSE, JOHN 196
BUSH, C. E. 204
BUSH, CHARLES 67
BUSH, DONNA 345
BUSH, GEORGE W. 108
BUSH, JEB 52
BUSHEY, THOMAS 112
BUSHLY, MICHAEL....... 333
BUSHWAY, RODNEY.... 374
BUSHY, TOM 112

Staff Name Index

STAFF NAME INDEX - C

BUSSERT, ELLEN............ 96
BUSTAMANTE, CRUZ M. 46
BUSTY, F. E. 111
BUTAMINA, KABUIKA ... 383
BUTLER, BARBARA...... 200
BUTLER, C. 125
BUTLER, JEROME 30
BUTLER, KEVIN 203
BUTLER, PAUL J. 303
BUTLER, SYDNEY J. 151
BUTLER, VIRGINIA P..... 20
BUTLER, WALTER 107
BUTTERFIELD, BRUCE 262
BUTTFIELD, CAREY 248
BUTTON, KAREN 133
BUTTON, LYLE 307
BUTTS, GREG 42
BUZICKY, GREG 76
BYERS, C. RANDALL.... 161
BYERS, KURT 40
BYFORD, JIM 388
BYFORD, RON 88
BYKER, GAYLEN J. 308
BYMUM, NORA 382
BYNUM, JOSEPH R. 35
BYRNE, CHRIS............. 207
BYRNE, LESLIE.............. 19
BYRNE, ROBERT L....... 350
BYRUM, LARRY 96

C

CABASSO, ISRAEL 382
CABLE, TED T. 372
CABLES, RICK 16, 424
CABOT, CHARLES C., JR.
.... 183
CABUSAO, DOMINGO S. 57
CACCESE, ALBERT E. ... 91
CACKETTE, TOM 44
CADUTO, MARIE
 LEVESQUE.............. 339
CAESER, DELANE........ 108
CAFAZZO, VEDA M. 287
CAFFEY, REX 69
CAHILL, JOHN P. 89
CAHILL, M..................... 125
CAHOON, DONALD 320
CAIN, ALAN G. 40
CAIRNS, JOHN, JR. 391
CAISSIE, BETH 285
CALAMBOKIDIS, JOHN 168
CALDER, JEFFERY 206
CALDWELL, COLLEEN A.
.... 87
CALDWELL, EVELYN ... 283
CALDWELL, JACK 68
CALDWELL, LARRY D. . 352
CALDWELL, MARTYN .. 390
CALFEE, ALAN 248
CALHOUN, CHARLES ... 29
CALHOUN, JEAN A. 41
CALKINS, JOHN 154
CALKINS, WILLIAM 28
CALLAHAN, DEB........... 241
CALLAHAN, JOHN J. 19
CALLAHAN, RAMON..... 253
CALLAN, LEONARD J. .. 34
CALLAWAY, DIANE 137
CALLAWAY, GEORGE E.
.... 105
CALLAWAY, RISA 151
CALLENDER, WILLIAM C.
.... 242
CALLERY, TOM 107
CALLICOTT, J. BAIRD169, 227
CALUMPONG, HILCONIDA
.... 395

CALVERLEY, BRETT 189
CALVERT, WILLIAM 23
CALVO, PATRICK........... 292
CAMENZIND, FRANZ J. 236
CAMERON, BOB 125
CAMERON, DON 260
CAMHI, MERRY 259
CAMP, MEGAN C. 312
CAMP, PAUL J. 29
CAMP, SAMUEL 58
CAMPBELL, BRAD 10
CAMPBELL, CARL 68
CAMPBELL, CECIL....... 105
CAMPBELL, ERICK 184
CAMPBELL, FAITH T.... 183
CAMPBELL, JAMES 250
CAMPBELL, JOHN 292
CAMPBELL, KEVIN 290
CAMPBELL, LEE 177
CAMPBELL, LINDA 329
CAMPBELL, LURLIE 235
CAMPBELL, MARILYN F.
.... 219
CAMPBELL, MARY
 KATHRYN 304
CAMPBELL, TREVOR 55
CAMPEN, DONALD O., JR.
.... 114
CAMPION, DENNIS R. ... 62
CAMPION, TOM 285
CANCILLA, JODEANE.. 244
CANDEE, ROGER 161
CANFIELD, MICHAEL..... 94
CANFIELD, VERONICA. 359
CANHAM, CHARLES D. 222
CANNALEY, PAUL 169
CANNON, ED 282
CANNON, MONA 317
CANNON, SHELTON M.. 19
CANNON, STUART M. ... 27
CANNON, SUE 96
CANNY, M. 8
CANTER, BRAM D.E., ESQ
.... 201
CANTON, STEVE 280
CANTOR, RAY 85
CANTRELL, SHAWN 206
CANTU, NORMA V. 18
CANTU, REYNALDO 228
CANZANO, PASQUALE S.
.... 52
CAPITO, CHARLES P.... 119
CAPLINGER, KEN 119
CAPORALE, WALTER... 225
CAPOTOSTO, PAUL 181
CAPPELLI, MARTIN A.. 103
CAPUTO, GUY P. 34
CARACO, NINA M. 222
CARAVETTA, JOHN 41
CARBONELL,
 MONSERRAT 189
CARBONNEAU, SCOTT 106
CARDAMONE, JEREMIAH
 J., ESQ 342
CARETTE, JACQUES...... 37
CAREY, DAVID 50
CAREY, HENRY H. 204
CAREY, KAREN 114
CAREY, ROBERT L....... 353
CARGILE, R. L. 42
CARL, A.B. 335
CARL, MELINDA 51
CARLES, BOB............... 129
CARLEY, WAYNE W. 257
CARLIN, DAVE................. 12
CARLINE, ROBERT F.99, 140, 385
CARLOUGH, YOLA 205
CARLSON, BETH 134
CARLSON, CHUCK 254

CARLSON, DAVID 49
CARLSON, FRED............ 85
CARLSON, FREDERICK G.
.... 100
CARLSON, HERB 298
CARLSON, MERLYN 81
CARLSON, MIKE 133
CARLSON, STEPHAN 77
CARLSON, STEVEN A. .364
CARLSON, SUSAN 184
CARLSTROM, TERRY 29
CARLTON, GARY 45
CARLTON, JASPER 161
CARLY, KEITH 164
CARMAN, SAM 197
CARMICHAEL, TIM 175
CARMICHAEL, WILLIAM D.
.... 293
CARMON, LEE 209
CARNAHAN, MEL 79
CARNEVALE, ELLEN.... 298
CARNEY, JAMES 82
CARNEY, JAN K. 112
CARNEY, R. SCOTT..... 144
CAROLAN, LEE 66
CARON, DIANE 86
CAROTHERS, LESLIE... 180
CAROTHERS, SARAH... 335
CARPENTER, BETSY...... 85
CARPENTER, JESSE A. 305
CARPENTER, LEN 350
CARPENTER, LEN H. ... 350
CARPENTER, PHIL......... 51
CARPENTER, TAMMY L.
.... 139
CARPER, THOMAS R..... 51
CARR, BRUCE 151
CARR, DAVID........ 168, 256
CARR, TIMOTHY 66
CARRIER, DAVID.......... 256
CARRIER, MIKE.............. 65
CARRIER, NORMAN D. .128
CARRIERRE, MURDOCH
.... 128
CARRIGAN, WADE 282
CARRILLO, PAUL 47
CARROLL, AUSTIN....... 240
CARROLL, JAMES L..... 268
CARROLL, JOHN 340
CARROLL, LESLIE........ 184
CARROLL, ROBERT 288
CARROW, CYNTHIA..... 344
CARSALADE, H. 203
CARSON, C. DEAN....... 105
CARSON, CHARLES G., III
.... 349
CARSON, EVERETT B. .271
CARSON, GENE 154
CARSON, JACK 96
CARSON, PAUL E......... 308
CARTEE, LARRY D. 291
CARTER, ALLEN............. 42
CARTER, ALLEN D. 277
CARTER, BILLY 78
CARTER, COLIN A. 365
CARTER, CURT 197
CARTER, DAVID 261
CARTER, DOUGLAS 306
CARTER, ED 107
CARTER, JAMES A. 75
CARTER, JIMMY 134
CARTER, LARRY 220
CARTER, RONALD R. ... 104
CARTER, THOMAS 234
CARTER, TRACY 107
CARTIN, ANITA 279
CARTLIDGE, ROBERT.. 288
CARTON, PETER D. 188
CARTWRIGHT, ALLEN W., JR. 72

CARUFEL, AMANDA..... 300
CARUSO, MICHAEL...... 236
CASADA, JIM................ 292
CASADEVALL, THOMAS J.
.... 30
CASE, BOYD 37
CASE, DELBERT W. 190
CASE, GLENN 87
CASE, JAMES C. 123
CASE, LARRY D. 261
CASE, MARILYN 347
CASE, MARSHAL T. 335
CASE, RONALD M 379
CASELLA, SAM 148
CASEY, CHARLIE 206
CASEY, SEAN 181
CASHNER, ROBERT C. 150
CASRER, JOHN 85
CASSADA, DAWN L. 50
CASSANI, JOHN R. 141
CASSAT, RICHARD 43
CASSELMAN, TRACY... 353
CASSTEVENS, KAY L... 18
CASTAÑEDA, KENIA 228
CASTLES, TOM 254
CASTLETON, CARL....... 12
CASTRO, BERNADETTE 91
CATANESE, CAROL 345
CATANIA, CHRIS 145
CATE, NANCY 160
CATE, WILLIAM P. 321
CATES, GEORGE L. 265
CATES, ROBERT D. 48
CATLIN, RONALD 106
CATO, JAMES C. 54
CATON, PATTI 386
CATTANY, RONALD W... 49
CATTON, JON 212
CAUTHEN, STEPHEN M. 39
CAVALETTO, CATHERINE
 G. 58
CAVALLO, SHARON 256
CAVANAUGH-GRANT,
 DEBORAH 218
CAVERLY, TIM 70
Caves, H.A. 96
CAWTHON, DON 388
CAYETANO, BENJAMIN. 57
CECCHINI, DAN, JR. 281
CECCHINI, SUE 281
CECERE, AL LOUIS 262
CECIL, JARVIS B. 344
CECIL, MARIA W. 186
CEILLEY, DAVID 309
CELEBREZZE, ANTHONY
 J., III 287
CELLARIUS, RICHARD. 317
CELLUCCI, ARGEO PAUL
.... 73
CENARRUSA, PETE T... 59
CERAMI, EMMA 79
CERTO, RICK 12
CERVOSKI, ANDREA.... 355
CESSNA, STELLA 78
CESTERO, BARB 320
CHABOT, ANGELA........ 325
CHABOT, WARNER 170
CHACKO, A. JIM 373
CHAFEE, JOHN H. 6
CHAFFEE, BILL 156
CHAFFIN, CHRIS .. 155, 265
CHAIKOVSKY, HELEN. 197
CHALLINOR, DAVID...... 132
CHALMERS-WATSON,
 NICOLA 358
CHAMBERLAIN, DENISE K.
.... 101
CHAMBERLAIN, LEE 199
CHAMBERLAIN, WILLIAM
.... 279

STAFF NAME INDEX - C

CHAMBLEE, CARY D.... 105
CHAMPEAU, RANDY 393
CHAMUT, PAT 35
CHAN, STELLA 193
CHAN, SUSAN 137
CHANADY, ATTILA 275
CHANCELLOR, RICHARD 122
CHANDA, DAVID 85
CHANDLER, ALLAN T... 218
CHANDLER, C. RAY 156
CHANDLER, HARRY 339
CHANDLER, JAMES S., JR. 321
CHANDLER, MIKE 43
CHANDLER, RALPH 45
CHANDLER, WILLIAM J. 264
CHANEY, ED 286
CHANG, DAVID 381
CHANG, MINGTEH 388
CHANIPAGNE, ALICE... 337
CHANNEL, DAVID 360
CHANTRY, CHRISTINE 257
CHAPCO, WILLIAM....... 395
CHAPE, STUART 228
CHAPIN, JIM 165
CHAPLIN, MIKE 371
CHAPMAN, BOB C 43
CHAPMAN, BRIAN R. ... 369
CHAPMAN, DANA 320
CHAPMAN, DEB 197
CHAPPELL, JOHN 241
CHAPPELL, WILLIAM D. 144
CHAPPLE, TOM 39
CHARETTE, EMILY 300
CHARLAND, DAVE 199
CHARLES, ... 63
CHARLES, CHERYL 355
CHARLES, LALORA 325
CHASAN, REBECCA..... 146
CHASE, HELEN K. 168
CHASE, JAYNI 169
CHASE, ROBERT F. 260
CHATEAUNEUF, RUSSELL J. 103
CHATWOOD, CAROL ... 294
CHAZIN, DANIEL 279
CHEATER, MARK 272
CHEKAY, D. A. 189
CHENOWETH, RICHARD 300
CHEPEL, LEONARD I. .. 285
CHEREL, DONNA 272
CHERRY, AL 227
CHERRY, FRANCIS R. ... 28
CHERRY, HARVEY 252
CHERRY, JOHN 53
CHERRY, PHIL 327
CHESAK, CHRIS 145
CHESEMORE, RONALD G. 19
CHESKY, DAVID 224
CHESNEY, NORMA 208
CHEZEM, LINDA 63
CHICKERING, PERI 329
CHILD, DENNIS 367
CHILD, WILLIAM 62
CHILDRESS, DON 64, 80
CHILDS, JOHN 94
CHILDS, STARLING W. 160
CHINCHILLI, JOLENE173, 294
CHING, PATRICK 24
CHINN, JIM 299
CHIPLEY, ROBERT 138
CHIPMAN, RICHARD B. 353
CHIPPONERI, L. LUCINDA 48
CHIPPS, STEVEN R. 106

CHISM, JOHN E. 239
CHISOLM, CHARLES H. .. 78
CHOKSI, KASHYAP 256
CHOLVIN, VALERIE 206
CHONGUICA, EBENIZARIO 229
CHREST, HELEN 136
CHRISMAN, MIKE 48
CHRISOTOMO, DAVID P. 57
CHRISTENBURY, EDWARD S. 35
CHRISTENSEN, ALAN .. 307
CHRISTENSEN, BILL 307
CHRISTENSEN, DALE 97
CHRISTENSEN, JAMES110
CHRISTENSEN, MARY . 159
CHRISTENSEN, NORMAN L., JR. 382
CHRISTENSEN, STAN .. 290
CHRISTENSEN, WALTER A. 12
CHRISTENSON, JAMES A. 42
CHRISTIAN, QUENTINE 136
CHRISTIANSEN, JODY ... 14
CHRISTIANSON, JAY.... 110
CHRISTIE, NANCY 277
CHRISTIE, RHIANNON K.E. 352
CHRISTIE, RICHARD W. 144
CHRISTISEN, D. M. 253
CHRISTMAN, RUSSELL F. 383
CHRISTOPHERSON, KRISTEN 22
CHRYSSOSTOMIDIS, CHRYS 74
CHUDLEIGH, TED 127
CHURA, MARK R. 51
CHURCHLAND, LESLIE . 36
CHYTILO, MARC 196
CIELO, ANGEL 12
CILEK, JEFFREY R. 296
CINFIO, RALPH 307
CIRILLO, JULIE A. 31
CIRMO, CHRISTOPHER381
CISAR, ELIZABETH J. .. 182
CISNEROS, ELLA 330
CITSAY, MARK 251
CITTA, JOE, JR. 275
CLAEYS, THOMAS 93
CLAIR, FRANK ST. 80
CLAMEN, MURRAY 8
CLANCY, JOHN 298
CLANTON, PAUL V. 308
CLAPP, EUGENE H. 183
CLARK, BETH 153
CLARK, BRUCE 61
CLARK, CAMERON D. .. 127
CLARK, CHRISTOPHER184
CLARK, EDWARD E., JR. 348
CLARK, JAMES H. 342
CLARK, JAMIE RAPPAPORT 28, 29
CLARK, JERRY 261
CLARK, JOHN 164
CLARK, JON 179
CLARK, MARTHA 246
CLARK, MIKE 212
CLARK, NANCY 42, 200
CLARK, PEGGY 204
CLARK, RENEE 160
CLARK, ROBERT 262
CLARK, ROBERT O. 362
CLARK, ROSS 372
CLARK, SANDY 79
CLARK, SHARON 76
CLARK, SUSAN 339

CLARK, TOM 251
CLARK, WALTER 177
CLARKE, CHARLES C. ... 11
CLARKE, H. A. 36
CLARKE, KATHLEEN 110
CLARKE, LORETTA 124
CLARKE, MARION L. 54
CLARKE, NANCY 200
CLAVELLE, JACQUES..... 35
CLAXTON, APRIL 181
CLAY, BOB 189
CLAY, BRUCE 61
CLAY, L. 168
CLAY, WILLIAM H. 12
CLAYPOOLE, DALE 45
CLAYTON, CHARLES... 235
CLAYTON, CHUCK 323
CLAYTON, PAT 200
CLAYTON, RICHARD A. 171
CLEAR, JAMES J. 20
CLEARY, D. M. 98
CLEARY, FRANCES 279
CLEARY, MICHAEL 189
CLEAVER, JERRY 21
CLEGG, MICHAEL T. 45
CLEM, FIONA 91
CLEM, JOHN C. 223
CLEMENT, KENT 366
CLEMENT, STEPHANIE M. 205
CLEMMER, GLENN82, 83, 416
CLEVELAND, THEODORE G. 389
CLEVER, ROBERT E. ... 330
CLEWELL, RICHARD 25
CLIFFORD, RICHARD K. . 50
CLINCH, BUD 81
CLINE, DAVE 240
CLINE, JOHN R. 253
CLINE, MIKE 244
CLINE, TIM 361
CLOSSON, LARRY 61
CLOTWORTHY, CHRISTOPHER 304
CLOUGH, RICH 80
CLOUTIER, TERRY 307
CLOVER, DARLENE 242
CLUGSTON, RICHARD M. 217
CLUSEN, CHARLES 139
CLUTTER, DAVID 219
COAD, JOSEPHINE B. 57
COAN, GENE 312
COATES, KATHLEEN E. . 55
COATES, PHILIP G. 73
COATS, J. D. 290
COATS, ROBERT 220
COBB, DAVID T. 92
COBB, JAMES C. 67
COBB, JANET S. 361
COBB, JONATHON 171
COBB, THOMAS L. 155
COBOURN, JOHN 83
COBURN, NANCY 265
COCHRAN, DONALD K. .. 73
COCHRAN, LARRY 340
COCHRAN, PHIL 342
COCHRAN, STEVE 196
COCHRANE, CHARLES S. 271
COCHRANE, SUSAN 47
COCKRELL, DAVID 346
CODERRE, SONJA S. 14
COEN, AMY 297
COFFEY, CLARENCE... 107
COFFEY, DAN J. 39
COFFIN, BARBARA 378
COFFMAN, CHARLES C. 119

COFFMAN, DAVE 341
COHEN, BARBARA 147
COHEN, DAVE 154
COHEN, ELANA 242
COHEN, JULES 305
COHEN, MICHELLE SHERBURNE 353
COHEN, NEVIN 221
COHEN, WILLIAM 18
COHEN, WILLIAM M. 20
COILE, NANCY 324
COKER, JOE 307
COLANGELO, PETER A. 101
COLBERT, K. 125
COLBURN, KENNETH A. 84
COLBURN, WILLIAM..... 305
COLBY, RICHARD H. 380
COLE, BRUCE 187
COLE, CATHY 206
COLE, JEANIE 276
COLE, JONATHAN J. ... 222
COLE, LESLIE 68
COLE, MARILYN 137
COLE, MOLLY, ... 377
COLE, PRESTON 256
COLE, ROGER H. 151
COLEMAN, BOB 24
COLEMAN, CATHERINE 27
COLEMAN, ELIZABETH B. 69
COLEMAN, JAMES 73
COLEMAN, JOHN........... 47
COLEMAN, MARK S. 95
COLEMAN, RUTH 193
COLEMAN, STEPHEN A. 67
COLEMAN, STEVE 68
COLEMAN, TOM 25
COLETTE, MARTINE ... 355
COLEY, CAMILLE E. 177
COLEY, R. W. 188
COLGROVE, GARY S. ... 13
COLLIER, CAROL 101
COLLIER, CAROL R. 7
COLLINI, KELLY 221
COLLINS, ALAN 392
COLLINS, EDMOND B. . 120
COLLINS, KEITH 12
COLLINS, LEROY, III..... 160
COLLINS, MARK 358
COLLINS, NANCY 230
COLLINS, PATRICK 12
COLLINS, RALPH 67
COLLINS, RESEE 201
COLLINS, RICHARD W. .. 71
COLLINS, SAMUEL J. 34
COLLISON, DEBBIE 173
COLLOREDO-MANSFELD, FRANZ 335
COLOMA-AGARAN, GILBERT S. 58
COLON, NORBERTO ... 300
COLTON, ELDON L. 232
COLTON, JOHN H. 247
COLVIN, GORDON.......... 89
COLVIN, WILLIAM 190
COLWELL, KEITH 126
COLWELL, MARK 364
COLWELL, RITA 33, 136
COLWELL, STEPHEN... 184
COMBEST, LARRY 4, 5
COMBS, DANIEL L. 388
COMBS, SUSAN 108
COMBS, TERRY 178
COMEAU, ROXANNE M. 167
COMOSS, EUGENE J. .. 100
COMPTON, JIM 306
COMPTON, JOHN 243
COMPTON, STEVEN C. 262

STAFF NAME INDEX - C

COMSTOCK, DON 391
COMUS, STEVE 308
CONDA, JUDY 202
CONDER, GRACE M..... 210
CONDON, BABS 208
CONE, JOSEPH 99
CONGALTON, RUSSELL
.... 380
CONGEL, FRANK........... 34
CONGLETON, JAMES L. 60
CONKEY, ALICE 264
CONKLE, TAMMY 263
CONKLIN, ED 53
CONKLING, PHILIP W. . 233
CONLEY, JAN 240
CONLEY, JERRY M. 79, 398
CONLEY, RON 55
CONNELL, JIM 129
CONNELL, KATHLEEN ... 46
CONNELLY, B. A. 127
CONNELLY, KENNETH L.
.... 162
CONNELLY, PETER 124
CONNER, MARK C. 173
CONNOLLY, JAMES 152
CONNOR, MICHAEL J.,
Ph.D. 188
CONNORS, RHEA 286
CONOVER, MARION 64
CONOVER, MICHAEL... 389
CONRAD, CAROLYN 163
CONROE, DOUGLAS 9
CONROY, DONALD B... 281
CONROY, MICHAEL J. ... 55
CONSOLVO, CHARLES W.
.... 233
CONTI, FRANK 48
CONTRERAS, GLEN K. 141
CONWAY, KEVIN 110
CONWAY, MICHAEL D. 101
CONWAY, MIKE 39
COOCH, EDWARD W., JR.
.... 174
COOGAN, MIKE 287
COOK, ALISON 306
COOK, ANNE 356
COOK, DEAN 131
COOK, DIANE M. 226
COOK, DON 125
COOK, ERNEST 334
COOK, GARY 108
COOK, HARRY N. 266
COOK, JIM D. 344
COOK, JOHN 2, 272
COOK, JOHN E. 29
COOK, JOHN R., JR. 196
COOK, MICHAEL B. 11
COOK, MICHAEL L. 160
COOK, RICHARD 159
COOK, ROBERT..... 78, 348
COOK, ROBERT L. 109
COOK, S. BRADFORD.. 144
COOK, S. KAYE 30
COOK, SUSAN 118
COOK, WAYNE E. 10
COOK, WM. RON 12
COOKE, DAVID D. 18
COOKE, GREGG 11
COOKE, TODD J. 375
COOKE, TREY 188
COOKENDORFER, PAUL
.... 325
COOKSEY, SARAH 51
COOKSIE, CAROLYN 13
COOL, DONALD A. 34
COOL, K. L. 75
COOLEY, DON 38
COOMER, RICHARD 176
COON, JOHN 293
COON, MAGGIE 272

COON, THOMAS 376
COON, THOMAS G. 140
COONROD, BRUCE 106
COOPER, CARDELL 19
COOPER, GEORGE 15
COOPER, GORDON...... 279
COOPER, JACK 216
COOPER, JAMES A. 77
COOPER, JOHN 106, 398
COOPER, KATHY 166
COOPER, KEVIN 351
COOPER, RICK 118
COOPER, RITA............. 116
COOPER, TOBY 256
COOPERMAN, HOWARD 33
COPELAND, TIMOTHY . 144
COPONY, JAMES A. 113
COPPELMAN, PETER D. 20
COPPING, ANDREA...... 118
COPPINGER, PAUL L. ... 19
CORAN, LAURIE 349
CORBIN, JOHN S. 58
CORBIN, LEROY C....... 100
CORDES, JOHN F., JR... 34
CORDIVIOLA, STEVEN J.
.... 67
CORDOVA, ROBERT 177
CORKRAN, DON K. 160
CORLETT, WILLIAM S. . 295
CORLEY, MELLISSA 246
CORNELIUS, MICHAEL .. 21
CORNELIUS, STEVE..... 320
CORNELL, JILL............. 269
CORNETT, BRUCE 287
CORNFORTH, SUSAN .. 322
CORNUS, H. P. 285
CORNWALL, G. 36
CORR, WILLIAM 19
CORRAL, THAIS........... 357
CORRDO, VINCENT...... 344
CORRELL, DAVID L. 317
CORTEZ, BECKY 257
CORVEN, JIM 344
CORWIN, WICKHAM 190
COSSETTE, ALAIN........ 301
COSTA, CHARLES 370
COSTA-PIERCE, BARRY A.
.... 39, 78
COSTELLO, JOHN T. 62
COSTELLO, MICHAEL E.
.... 143
COSTIE, STEVE 256
COSTON, D. C. 96
COTE, DIANA 40
COTE, LAWRENCE S.... 120
COTNOIR, LILIANE 212
COTSWORTH, ELIZABETH
.... 11
COTTER, B. PAUL, JR. .. 34
COTTINGHAM, KALEEN
.... 117
COTTINGHAM, SUSAN... 81
COTTLE, CURT 104
COTTRELL, KIRBY 61
COTTRELL, MARIE 24
COUCH, JOHN 341
COUFAL, JAMES E. 319
COUGHLAN, DAVID J. .. 143
COUGHLIN, PAUL F. 354
COUINS, VANNESSA.... 159
COULOMBE, MARY 296
COULON, CHRISTINA 14
COULSTON, PATRICK J.
.... 142
COULTER, JANE 15
COULTER, L. L. 139
COUMBE, LOUISE 174
COURSON, BUD 68
COURTER, J. CARLTON, III
.... 113

COURTNEY, ELIZABETH
.... 339
COURTNEY, F. G. 179
COURTNEY, WILL 243
COURVILLE, MARY L. ...345
COUSINS, WALTER B. ...321
COUSTEAU, FRANCINE
.... 185
COUSTON, TOM............211
COVELL, DARREL......... 277
COVERDELL, PAUL.....1, 6
COVEY, SUSAN 287
COWAN, JOHN 137, 138
COWAN, MIKE 160
COWART, VICKI 49
COWEN, RAYMOND, III.. 89
COWIN, TIMOTHY H........ 91
COWLING, TERRI L. 104
COWPERTHWAITE,
JAMES 178
COX, CAROLINE............285
COX, CRAIG................... 320
COX, GREGORY............ 248
COX, JIM 202
COX, LINDA J. 114
COX, MICHAEL 269
COZENS, TOBY 140
CRABB, DAN 54
CRABTREE, ELDON......220
CRADDOCK, J. HILL......139
CRADICK, AMY................ 85
CRAFT, JEREMY 53
CRAFT, ROBERT D. 113
CRAGO, TRACEY I. 74
CRAIG, CHARLES 97
CRAIG, CLIFFORD B. 111
CRAIG, JON 96
CRAIG, RAY 98
CRAIGHEAD, CHARLES S.
.... 185
CRAIGHEAD, FRANK C.,
JR. 185
CRAIGHEAD, FRANK L. 185
CRAIGHEAD, JOHN J.... 185
CRAM, ROBERT 325
CRAMER, JOYCE W......298
CRANDALL, DERRICK ..146
CRANDALL, DERRICK A.
.... 148
CRANE, FRED............... 232
CRANE, NEIL 244
CRANER, LORI 279
CRANFORD, GERALD F. 34
CRAPA, JOSEPH R. 10
CRAVEN, BILL 313
CRAVEN, SCOTT 122
CRAVES, JULIE 249
CRAWFORD, BOB 52
CRAWFORD, BRUCE 116
CRAWFORD, LARRY..... 284
CRAWFORD, RICHARD .. 93
CRAWFORD, RICHARD D.
.... 383
CRAWFORD, WALTER C.,
JR. 358
CRAWFORD, WM. H........ 95
CRAWFORTH, TERRY 82
CRAWFORTH, TERRY R.
....................................83, 397
CREECH, DENNIS......... 324
CREEDON, LESLI 304
CRENSHAW, DAVID B. .389
CRENSHAW, TERESA 51
CREWS, TIM 363
CRICK, MERIBETH 133
CRICKENBERGER,
ROGER........................... 91
CRIER, TIMBER 277
CRINER, GEORGE 374
CRISELL, ROB 153

CRISMORE, WILLIAM..... 81
CRISPIN, SUSAN 81
CRIST, LARRY 112
CRISTINI, ANGELA 147
CROKE, L. 125
CRONENBERGER,
VIRGINIA 163
CRONIN, LESLIE 158
CRONK, EDYE 325
CROOKS, JOAN 341
CROONQUIST, DAVE... 156
CROSBY, GREG 16
CROSS, BILLY JOE....... 190
CROSS, BOB 44
CROSS, GERALD H. 116
CROSSMAN, MARIAN159,
294
CROTEAU, ELLEN 269
CROTTY, ERIN 89
CROUCH, BARTH V. 296
CROUCH, ROGER 133
CROUCH, SHERRY 291
CROUSE, DAN 131
CROUSE, RICHARD J.... 145
CROW, RICK 22
CROWELL, CRAVEN 35
CRUDELE, JULIE 213
CRUDEN, JOHN 20
CRUEA, DARRELL......... 106
CRUM, ED....................... 334
CRUMP, JOHN PATRICK
.... 166
CRUZ, ELISABETH T. 57
CRUZ, JOAQUIN Q. 57
CUBBAGE, JAMES........ 168
CUDMORE, PAT 60
CUELLAR, YVONNE 227
CULLEN, J. B. 83
CULLY, JACK F., JR.65,
372
CULP, CARSON 28
CULP, SUSAN 320
CULPEPPER, JAMES L. . 68
CULTER, RAY 272
CUMBERLAND, CAROL 158
CUMBERLIDGE, NEIL .. 376
CUMBIE, RICHARD H. ... 39
CUMMINGS, B. J. 301
CUMMINGS, BOB.......... 244
CUMMINGS, DIANNE.... 153
CUMMINGS, J. GLEN.... 124
CUMMINGS, ROBERT .. 359
CUMMINGS, THERESA.. 61
CUMMINS, DAVID G. 176
CUMMINS, JAMES D. 8
CUMMINS, KENNETH.... 44
CUNNINGHAM, DON 82
CUNNINGHAM, GARY ... 12
CUNNINGHAM, JAMES A.
.... 259
CUNNINGHAM, RICHARD
N. 84
CUNNINGHAM, WILLIAM
.... 151
CUOMO, ANDREW M. 19
CURL, SAM E. 96
CURLAND, JAMES 206
CURLEY, ROSEMARY .. 128
CURNEW, K. 125
CURNOW, RICHARD D. . 12
CURRAN, WILLIAM J. 88
CURRIE, PATRICIA 227
CURRIER, MARY 79
CURRY, GRANT 239
CURTIS, HENRY Q 243
CURTIS, MARC 252
CURTIS, PAUL 90
CURTISS, BILL 192
CURTNER, KATHRYN A.
.... 121

STAFF NAME INDEX - D

CURTNER, TOM R. 43
CUSHMAN, JOHN C. 162
CUSHMAN, ROBERT M. .. 18
CUSTER, ADRIE 13
CUSTODIO, NARCISO G.,
P.E. 57
CUTHBERT, FRANCESCA
.... 377
CUTLER, RUTH 180
CYPHER, BRIAN 354
CYR, KAREN D. 34
CZAPLEWSKI, MARK M.
.... 352
CZINSKI, BEN 376

D

DABBS, KARL 152
DABNEY, WALTER D. 109
DAGGERHART, RENEE 105
DAGGETT, SUSAN 192
DAHL, GEOFFREY 374
DAIGLE, J.J. 188
DAILEY, FRED L. 94
DAKE, RUTH J. 249
DALE, BOB 204
DALE, BOLEYN 340
DALE, CHIP 97
DALEY LAURSEN, STEVEN
B. 77
DALEY, BILL 49
DALEY, JAMES G. 353
DALEY, WAYNE J. 140
DALEY, WILLIAM M. 17
DALEYLAURSEN, STEVEN
B. 378
DALMAS, THELMA 340
DALPRA, CURTIS 8
DALTON, BERNADETTE
.... 224
DALTON, CAROL ANN . 165
DALTON, MORRIS 308
DALTON, PENELOPE 17
DALTON, RICHARD 85
DAMIAN, FRANCIS P. 57
D'AMICO, JOSEPH S. 40
DAMRON, JACK 24
DAMRON, JOHN E. 195
DANDO, MURIEL A. 217
DANELLO, MARY ANN ... 19
D'ANGELO, ROBERT 102
DANIEL, DAVID E. 370
DANIEL, GLENDA 290
DANIEL, W. B. 119
DANIELL, ROBERT 67
DANIELS, HARRY V. 91
DANIELS, JAMES 234
DANIELS, JOYCE 75
DANIELS, KEVIN 176
DANIELS, MICHAEL B. ... 43
DANIELS, SAM 145
DANN, SHARI L. 75
DANSON, TED 148
DANVIR, RICK E. 111
DANZIG, RICHARD 31
DAOUST, PIERRE-YVES
.... 166
DAPHNE WOOD 327
DARROW, ROBERT, M.D.
.... 339
DARTLAND, DIANA 54
DASHER, DOUG 25
DASTRUP, B. CURTIS .. 111
DATRES, DANA A. 100
DATTILIO, MIKE 248
DAUBENDIEK, BERTHA 250
DAUDI, SABIHA 197
DAUGHARTY, DAVID A. 394
DAUGHTRY, DAVE 41

DAUKAS, JIMMY 139
DAVID MCLARN 166
DAVID, KIRK 218
DAVID, ROBERT 260
DAVIDSEN, DONALD R. .. 88
DAVIDSON, AL 178
DAVIDSON, CHARLES .. 182
DAVIDSON, DENNIS 85
DAVIDSON, JASON 83
DAVIDSON, MARILYN ... 298
DAVIDSON, SUSAN 260
DAVIES, BRIAN D. 225
DAVIES, ERIC 382
DAVIES, J. CLARENCE, III
.... 304
DAVIES, KATE 186
DAVIES, PETER 359
DAVIES, RICHARD W. 42
DAVIES, RUSS 267
DAVIES, TUDOR T. 11
DAVILA, RAFAEL F. 103
DAVIS, AL 41
DAVIS, BOB 189
DAVIS, CAMERON 240
DAVIS, CAROLYN D. 72
DAVIS, CHARLES A. 270
DAVIS, CLARK M. 9
DAVIS, DON 354
DAVIS, DONALD R., ... 363
DAVIS, GARY S. 281
DAVIS, GEORGE H. 208
DAVIS, GRAY 44
DAVIS, JERRY D. 133
DAVIS, JOHN 36, 63
DAVIS, JOHN C. 66
DAVIS, JOHN F. 38
DAVIS, KIM 170
DAVIS, LORETTA 298
DAVIS, LORI 330
DAVIS, MARILYN 111
DAVIS, MARILYN A. 121
DAVIS, MIKI 166
DAVIS, PAUL 107, 195
DAVIS, RAYMOND E. 114
DAVIS, ROBERT L., JR. 265
DAVIS, ROD 124
DAVIS, ROGER L. 96
DAVIS, WAYNE 82
DAVIS, WILLIAM E. .67, 355
DAVIS-HAMILTON, S. ... 345
DAVISON, DAVE 130
DAVISON, IAN 71
DAVIT, CAROL 253
DAVY, JOHN R. 114
DAWS, RUSSELL 327
DAY, BETTY 177
DAY, BRIAN A. 130
DAY, GUS 163
DAY, JENNIFER 8
DAY, M. H. 163
DAY, MARK 10
DAY, ROBERT D., JD 304
DE DARDEL, CLAES 228
DE GHETALDI, EVELYN
BALLARD 131
de la ROCHA, ROSAMELIA
.... 19
DE STEIGUER, ED 363
DE XAXAS, MERCEDES
MAS 297
DEACON, JAMES 379
DeALTERIS, JOSEPH ... 104
DEAN, CAROLINE R. 133
DEAN, ED. 129
DEAN, ELLEN A. 365
DEAN, HOWARD 111
DEAN, ROB 125
DEAN, TOMMY 301
DEAN, TONY 290
DEANE, JAMES G. 166, 186

DEARBORN, RONALD K. 40
DEASON, WAYNE O. 28
DEATHERAGE, KAREN. 134
DEATON, LINDA 327
DEATON, ROGER 104
DEBEL, DANA 311
DEBOW, RICHARD 276
DeBRES, KAREN 237
DeBRUIN, RODNEY H. .. 123
DeBRUYCKERE, LISA 97
DeCECCO, STEVE 123
DECKER, BARBARA, Ph.D.
.... 255
DECKER, BOB 25, 255
DECKER, STEVE 80
DECOOK, JOHN 317
DEDRICK, ALLEN 15
DEEB, DAN 267
DEENEY, DAVID 357
DEFOLIART, LINDA 285
DeGARMO, GLEN 24
DEGEN, PAULA 180
DEGENHARDT, ARYA ... 254
DEGOLIER, LAURA 120
DEGRAAF, RICHARD M.
.... 375
deGRAFFENREID, JEFF
.... 132
DEGROSKY, MIKE 223
DEHART, DOUG 97
DeHART, H. GRANT 72
DeHART, MICHELE 178
DEHAVEN, RON 12
DEHAYES, DONALD H. . 390
DEIGER, GARY E. 102
DEISNER, VICKI LEE 287
DeKING, DAVID L. 276
DEKLINSKI, KAREN K. .. 101
DEL GIUDICE, PAULA J.
.... 267, 268
DELANEY, DENISE 240
DELANEY, EDWARD L. . 347
DELANEY, KEVIN 39
DELANEY, RICHARD F. 376
DELANO, EVERETT 179
DELANY, BILLY 373
DeLEERS, JR., LAWRENCE
N. 320
DELFAY, ROBERT T. 265
DELLER, NANCY 47
DELOACH, JAMIE 53
DeMARSH, PETER 269
DEMARTINO, JOSEPH.. 190
DEMASTER, DOUGLAS P.
.... 319
DeMATTEO, JENELL 321
DEMPSEY, BERNARD ... 187
DENKER, TERRY 65
DENKERS, STEPHEN G.
.... 191
DENMAN, SCOTT 308
DENNERLEIN, CATHERINE
.... 133
DENNERLEIN, CHIP 264
DENNIS, JANE 356
DENNIS, MIKE 272
DENNY, ARTHUR, JR. ... 231
deNOYELLES, FRANK 65
DENTE, CHUCK R. 353
DENTINO, DAVID 22
DENTON, DAN 190
DENTON, JOAN E. 45
DEOPSCINE, SARAH 243
DePERRY, GERALD 7
DePINTO, JOHN A. 370
DePOLO, MICHAEL 250
DEPPNER, DAVE 331
DEPPNER, REMEDIOS G.
.... 331
DEPUIT, EDWARD J. 391

DERDERIAN, JAMES 5
DERKSEN, ARTHUR J. . 143
DEROSA, SHERI D. 74
DERR, CHARLES W. 138
DERR, FREDERICK M. . 255
DERR, REX 117
DERRY, JAMES 334
DERTY, CHANTAL 225
DERUITER, DARLA S. .. 346
DES CLERS, BERTRAND
.... 182
DESCHENES, JOE 24, 27
D'ESPOSITO, STEPHEN
.... 250
DESSECKER, DAN 308
DESSUREAULT, MICHEL
.... 395
DeSTEFANO, STEVE 74
DETER, ROSS 47
DETHLEFSEN, BETH 257
DEUSCHL, DENNIS E. 32
DEUTSCHER, ARLENE .. 12
DEUVALL, DALE 333
DEVANE, BEN 32
DEVANEY, EARL 27
DEVANEY, EARL E. 10
DEVANEY, LAUREL 134
DEVAUL, GERALD A. 163
DEVEREAUX, AL 53
DeVERTER, DEBRA 47
DEVICK, WILLIAM 58
DEVILLARS, JOHN P. 11
DEVINE, ALICE 65
DEVINE, JAMES F. 30
DEVINE, RITA 279
DEVINEY, LEE 108
DEVITT, R. J. 210
DEVOE, M. RICHARD ... 106
DEVOIR, LYNN M., CLP 341
DeVRIES, DENNIS 254
DEW, ALOMA 68
DEW, STEPHANIE 238
DEWALD, SANDRA 309
DeWALLE, WENDY VAN
.... 233
DEWEES, CHRISTOPHER
.... 45
DEWELL, DAN 17
DEWEY, ROBERT 186
DEWHURST, DAVID 109
DEWITT, LAURENCE B. . 91
DEXTER, DAVID 176
DEYRUP, NANCY 153
DHALIWAL, HERB 35
DHONDT, ANDRE 184
DI GIULIO, RICHARD T. 382
DI LEVA, CHARLES 228
DIA, LATAWNYA 14
DIAMANTE, JOHN 330
DIANA, JAMES S. 377
DIANICH, MIKE 300
DIAS, NELSON GOMES 228
DIAZ, DONNA 41
DIAZ-SOLTERO, HILDA .. 16
DIBATTISTA, CARMINE N.
.... 50
DIBBLEE, RANDALL 128
DIBLASI, PHILIP 169
DiCAMILLO, JODI 265
DICKENSON, DAN 335
DICKERSON, BILL 92
DICKERSON, DENNIS ... 45
DICKERSON, MARIA 337
DICKERSON, MARK 21
DICKEY, ELBERT C. 82
DICKSON, ANDREW 359
DICKSON, JAMES 373
DICKSON, JAN 169, 389
DICKSON, KENNETH L 389
DICKSON, LANA 87

STAFF NAME INDEX - E

DICTSON, BILLY 88
DIDRICKSON, BETSY... 224
DIEFENBACH, DUANE ... 99
DIERSING, VIC 24
DIETRICK, LARRY 39
DiFAZIO, FAYE E. 113
DIFLEY, JANE A. 319
DILLARD, JIM 107
DILLER, LOWELL 351
DILLER, TOM 301
DILLINGHAM, HUGH J., III
.... 349
DILTZ, DOTTY 53
DIMASE, JOSEPH D. 159
DINGER, JAMES S. 67
DINKINS, GERRY 323
DINTAMAN, RAY C., JR. . 72
DIOUF, JACQUES 203
DIPAOLO, TONLY 247
DIPASQUALE, NICHOLAS
A. 51
DIPESO, JIM 304
DiPIETRO, BARBARA ... 132
DIPOLVERE, EDWARD ... 277
DIPPEL, DONNIE 108
DIPPEL, JOSEPH J. 50
DIRINGER, ELLIOT 10
DIRUS, GRETA J. 34
DISHNER, O. GENE 115
DISILVA, A. J. 277
DITTMAR, ARTHUR 250
DITTMER, BOB 308
DITTO, ROSE M. 208
DIX, DAVID 170, 253
DIXON, BEVERLY A. 140
DIXON, BRIAN 361
DIXON, DAVID 170
DIXON, DORIS 207
DIXON, FREDDIE 368
DIXON, JOHN R. 339
DOAK, GARY 74
DOAN, DOUG 126
DOBBERPUHL, JUNE ... 162
DOCHERTY, MOLLY70,
415
DODD, JAMES F., III 190
DODDS, JANE 15
DODIER, JOSE, JR. 329
DODSON, ERIC 158
DODSON, RONALD G. . 158
DOGGETT, MARJORIE .. 226
DOHERTY, CATE 310
DOHM, SUZANNE 279
DOKKEN, WILLIAM A. ... 60
DOLAN, ALAN 287
DOLAN, JoANN 279
DOLAN, JOHN 254
DOLAN, PETER 160
DOLD, JENNIFER 341
DOLENCE, ROBERT C. 101
DOLINER, J. D. 197
DOLLIVER, SHARON 56
DOLLOFF, C. ANDREW 391
DOMBECK, MIKE 16
DOMBROSKI, MARK..... 203
DOMBROWSKI, DAN ... 283
DOMINGUEZ, ANNETTE
.... 109
DOMINGUEZ, LARRY 87
DOMINITZ, SID 284
DOMURAT, RON 176
DONAHOE, JEFFERY M.8,
29
DONAHUE, JEFF 130
DONALDSON, PETER .. 298
DONALDSON, WALT 111
DONAUER, KATHLEEN 275
DONCASTER, ANNE 230
DONELIN, DAN 371, 372
DONHEFFNER, PAUL E. 99

DONLON, JEANNE 85
DONNA, DAVID 252
DONNAN, EDMUND A., JR.
.... 236
DONNELLY, GERALD T.
.... 136
DONNELLY, KEVIN 52
DONNELLY, LLOYD J. ... 34
DONNELLY, PAULA 158
DONNELLY, T.W. 188
DONNELLY, THOMAS F.
.... 266
DONNELLY, TOM 349
DONOGHUE, LINDA R. .. 16
DONOHUE, GAVIN 89
DONOHUE, TERRY 61
DOODY, ALLAN 32
DOOLEY, MARLEN 85
DOOLITTLE, GUERRY B.
.... 204
DOOLITTLE, WARREN T.
.... 228
DOOM, CHUCK 322
DORAN, JEFF 202
DORAN, TERRY 117
DORFMAN, MARK 200
DORNFELD, SUSAN 159
DOROFF, SUE 306
DORRANCE, MIKE 350
DORRANCE, SAMUEL .. 171
DORRELL, TONY 256
DORSEY, CHRIS 190
DOSCHER, PAUL A. 319
DOSS, JIM 287
DOTT, DON S. 68
DOTT, DONALD S., JR. .. 67
DOUBLEDAY, WILLIAM .. 36
DOUCETTE, BOB 257
DOUGAL, EDWARD 388
DOUGHERTY, CYNTHIA C.
.... 11
DOUGLAS, DONALD J. . 187
DOUGLAS, JAMES 82
DOUGLAS, JEAN
  WALLACE 136
DOUGLAS, LARRY 127
DOUGLAS, MICHAEL E. 150
DOUGLAS, PETER 46
DOUGLAS, TILLMAN.... 324
DOUGLASS, GUS R. 119
DOVEY, LAURIE LEE ... 292
DOW, BOB 23
DOW, JOCELYN 357
DOWD, CHRISTOPHER E.
.... 200
DOWDLE, ELIZABETH B.
.... 183
DOWLER, BERNARD F. 119
DOWLING, DAVID C. 114
DOWLING, EDWARD D. 208
DOWNEY, LAURA 237
DOWNEY, MORTIMER L. 31
DOWNING, DARLENE .. 168
DOWNS, JOAN 348
DOXTATER, GARY .. 63, 397
DOYLE, BECKY 61
DOYLE, BOB 28
DOYLE, BRIAN 83
DOYLE, FRANCES 24
DOYLE, PAT 167
DOYLE, ROBERT 389
DOYLE, WAYNE 65
DOZIER, ALAN 56
DR. JAMES EFLIN, HUGH
  J. BROWN 370
DRAGICEVICH, RODNEY
.... 249
DRAHOVZAL, JAMES 67
DRAKE, CARL 48
DRAKE, DEBBIE 46

DRAPER, WAYNE............ 36
DRAUGHON, DAVID...... 107
DRAWE, D. LYNN 343
DREESEN, ALAN D. 108
DREHER, KARL J. 60
DREIBAND, SUSAN....... 30
DREIMAN, JOHN 220
DRENNAN, KATHLEEN .155
DREW, MIMI 53, 54
DREW, RICHARD 54
DREW, STEVEN J. 234
DREYER, GLENN D. 367
DRICKAMER, LEE C. 362
DRIER, DAVID, (CA) 5
DRISH, MARY ANN 64
DROBNEY, RONALD D. . 79
DROEGE, JIM 220
DRUCKENMILLER, STAN
.... 121
DRUDING, BARBARA.... 331
DRUMMOND, KAREN.... 265
DRURY, RICHARD
  TOSHIYUK 179
DRYDEN, DOUG 124
DRYDEN, RON 204
DUBICK, DENISE 345
DUBOIS, FRANK A. 87
DUBOIS, JACK 245
DUBORD, DANIEL J. 173
DuBROCK, CALVIN W. .. 102
DUDA, MARK DAMIAN .. 305
DUDLEY, NICK 214
DUDLEY, SALLY 157
DUENO, JOSE A. 300
DUERR, NAOMI 82
DUESER, RAYMOND D. 389
DUESTERHAUS, RICHARD
L. 304
DUFAULT, ARTHUR W. . 110
DUFF, DON 331
DUFF, JAMES H. 162
DUFFY, AMY 104
DUFFY, CLARK 66, 237
DUFFY, GREG 323, 398
DUFFY, GREG D. 95
DUFFY, PATRICIA 33
DUFFY, WALTER 364
DUFFY, WALTER G. 44
DUGAN, PATRICK 228
DUGGAN, JOSEPH R. .. 296
DUGUAY, JEFFERY P. .. 388
DUGUAY, LINDA 45
DUINKER, PETER M., Ph.D.
.... 394
DUJACK, STEPHEN R. . 198
DUKEMINIER, CLARICE 285
DULL, JACK 53
DUMELIE, MIKE 128
DUNAGAN, ROB ... 160, 173
DUNBAR, LYNN 153
DUNCAN, B. L., Ph.D. ... 362
DUNCAN, CHARLES D. 156
DUNCAN, JEFFREY 20
DUNCAN, JUDY 96
DUNCAN, PETER 89
DUNCAN, ROBERT W. . 115
DUNKERLEY, MIKE 294
DUNKLE, S.W. 188
DUNKLE, SAMUEL J. ... 102
DUNKS, JIMMY 190
DUNLAP, THOMAS R. .. 203
DUNMYER, JAMES W. .. 72
DUNN, ALLEN 104
DUNN, CHRIS 25
DUNN, CINDY ADAMS .. 294
DUNN, DIANNA K. 361
DUNN, FRANK 126
DUNN, GARY A. 361
DUNN, MIKE 12
DUNN, ROBERT G. 251

DUNNAGAN, ROBERT .. 332
DUNNAM, SYLVIA 203
DUNNE, PETER 278
DUNNIGAN, JOHN H. 7
DUNNING, CHERY L. 23
DUNSTAN, FRANK 89
DUNSTAN, THOMAS C. 370
DUNWELL, FRAN 89
DuPAUL, WILLIAM 115
DUPAUL, WILLIAM D. .. 390
DuPREE, GALE 276
DUPREE, THOMAS 103
DUPUIS, JOSEPH E. 180
DUPUY, CHARLES 243
DURAN, DAVID 87
DURAN, LYDIA 87
DURAND, BOB 73
DURAND, LEILANI 215
DURANT, JOHN 375
DURHAM, DAVID F. 168
DURHAM, FLOYD 43
DURHAM, KAREN 242
DURHAM, MEGAN 30
DURHAM, PATRICK 269
DURKIN, ELIZABETH.... 298
DURNING, ALAN 286
DURNWALD, ESTHER . 347
DUROCHER, PHIL 109
DURST, DOUGLAS 191
DUTTENHEFNER, KATHY
.... 93, 416
DUTTON, MARK 24
DUVALL, FERN P., II 351
DUYVEJONCK, JON 337
DUZAN, STEVE 155
DYE, PAUL 230
DYER, A. ALLEN 366
DYER, POLLY 289
DYKES, JOHN 65
DYKSTRA, BETTY 308
DYKSTRA, DENNIS 358
DZIUBEK, DAN 385
DZUS, ELSTON H. 350

E

EADIE, DIANE 276
EAGAN, LLOYD L. 121
EAGLE, KEMPER E. 198
EAGLE, TIM 107
EAGLETON, MARGARET
.... 285
EAKINS, DOUG 172
EAKLE, WADE 263
EAMES, CLIFF 133
EARLE, PAMELA 264
EARLEY, LARRY S. 92
EASTER, BECKY 164
EASTERLY, RICHARD .. 341
EASTERSON, BRAD 148
EASTERSON, TONI
  BENNETT 148
EASTON, CHUCK 279
EASTON, DAN 39
EATON, AMY 255
EATON, DAN E. 45
EATON, PAM 338
EATON, PAMELA 347
EAV, BOV B 16
EBEID, NADIA M. 37
EBERSBACH, PAUL 22
EBERT, SUSAN 109
EBNETER, STEWART D. 34
ECHEVERRIA, JOHN.... 152
ECHOLS, ALEX 261
ECHOLS, LOUIE S. 118
ECK, EDWIN 379
ECK, ROBERT 80
ECKBERG, CHARLES... 179

STAFF NAME INDEX - F

ECKER, MICHAEL E. 186
ECKERT, AL 43
ECKERT, ROBERT T. ... 380
ECKES, MARTIN 30
EDELBROCK, JERRY ... 246
EDELMAN, JIM 338
EDELSON, NAOMI 223
EDER, TIM 268
EDGAR, CECILIA F. 92
EDGE, W. DANIEL .. 99, 350
EDGERTON, ANNE 227
EDGERTON, WAYNE 76
EDMINSTER, CARL 363
EDMONDS, ROBERT LEE
.... 84
EDSON, DAVID 149
EDSON, DEAN 275
EDSON, JACK D. 356
EDWARD, ROB 317
EDWARDS, ALLEN 165
EDWARDS, CHIQUITA . 221
EDWARDS, GORDON .. 189
EDWARDS, ROBERT L... 54
EDWARDS,, THOMAS C.,
  JR. 110
EFLIN, JAMES 370
EGAR, D. 36
EGBERT, ALLAN L. 54, 223,
  349, 397
EGE, FREDERICK 333
EGELSTON, DAVE 89
EGER, REBECCA 245
EGGERT, PAUL 12
EGOL, LEW 346
EHLERS, ANGELA 322
EHLERT, CHARLES 283
EHM, WILLIAM 64
EHRENREICH, DIXIE L. 369
EHRESMAN, MARLENE 233
EHRET, PAUL 62
EHRHARDT, BARBARA J.
.... 371
EHRLICH, ANNE 312
EHRLICH, PAUL R. 361, 365
EICHBAUM, WILLIAM M.
.... 359
EIDT, DAN 126
EIKEN, DOUGLAS 80
EISELE, TIMOTHY 356
EISENKRAFT, ARTHUR 265
EISNER, THOMAS 360
EITNIEAR, JACK CLINTON
.... 171
EIZENSTAT, STUART E. 32
EK, ALAN 377
EKDAHL, JAMES 75
EKEY, ROBERT 346
ELAM, DAYTON 329
ELAM, ROBERT 20
ELBOW, GARY 260
ELDER, AL 12
ELDER, DON 306
ELDER, JAMES 280
ELDERKIN, SUSAN 342
ELDERS, CONNIE 237
ELDRENKAMP, PAUL ... 284
ELDRIDGE, CHARLES L.
.... 234
ELEKES, JUDITH 287
ELFNER, LYNN EDWARD
.... 286
ELFNER, MARY A. 177
ELLEDGE, SHANNON 24
ELLERBROCK, DOLLY . 297
ELLIKER, ROBERT 235
ELLIOT, HERSCHEL 385
ELLIOT, STATIA 124
ELLIOTT, B. 35
ELLIOTT, CATHERINE 71,
  117

ELLIOTT, CHARLES 372
ELLIOTT, CHARLES L.... 352
ELLIOTT, DANIELLE 165
ELLIOTT, JAMES 74
ELLIOTT, JONI 277
ELLIOTT, MARILYN 38
ELLIOTT, RICH 47
ELLIOTT-FISK, DEBORAH,
  Ph.D. 365
ELLIS, CINDY 163
ELLIS, JANET 254
ELLIS, JONATHON 62
ELLIS, TOM 92
ELOWE, KENNETH D. 70
ELROD, LEWIS 139
ELROD, SCOTT M. 248
ELS, DAVID E. 262
ELSER, ALLEN 111
ELSING, HENRY 322
ELSON, JUDY 312
ELTON, JOSEPH 114
ELWART, DAVID M. 104
ELY, CRAIG 97
ELZERMAN, ALAN W. ... 387
EMBREY, MONTEY S. .. 265
EMERY, MARILYN 182
EMMANUELE, KURT A. 137
EMMETT, KATHRYN 126
EMO, KYRA 300
EMORY, WILLIAM H. 320
EMPSON, G. RAYMOND
.... 238
ENCIC, JOHN 100
ENDTER-WADA, JOANNA
.... 389
ENEVOLDSEN, DOUG ... 96
ENGBERG, KRISTEN ... 213
ENGEL, JAY 331
ENGELMAN, LYNN 21
ENGELMAN, ROBERT .. 297
ENGELMANN, EB 97
ENGELSMA, FRANS J. . 199
ENGESAETER, SIGMUND 9
ENGFELDT, CHRISTINA
.... 203
ENGH, DOUG 154
ENGLE, CAROLE R. 43
ENGLE, DAVID M. 384
ENGLER, JOHN 74
ENGSTROM, CATHY ... 232
ENGSTROM, R. TODD .. 202
ENNS, BOB 125
ENO, AMOS S. 261
ENO, JACKSON F. 296
ENSOR, DALE 388
ENTZ, J. MICHAEL 289
EPIFANIO, JOHN M. 141
EPLIN, JIM 300
EPSTEIN, SARAH G. 298
ERB, JAMES E. 101
ERDMANN, RICHARD L.
.... 182
ERICKSON, DAVID W. 79
ERICKSON, DONNA 377
ERICKSON, GARY 190
ERICKSON, GERRY RING
.... 186
ERICKSON, KIM 95
ERICKSON, RON 128
ERICKSON, TERESA 285
ERNST, GERALD J. 235
ERNST, MARION V. 358
ERNSTER, JOHN 76
ERSKINE, ANDREA L. 70
ERTMER, SUSAN 191
ERTTER, ROBERT S. 267
ERVEY, EARL F. 277
ERVIN, DAVID E. 215
ESCARCEGA, FERNANDO
.... 109

ESCOE, WAYNE 56
ESHBAUGH, DAVE 159
ESPINOSA, JUDITH 267
ESPY, JAMES J. ... 241, 245
ESPY, JAMES J., JR. 245
ESSON, JOHN 24, 195
ESTABROOK, E. PENN...71
ESTABROOK, NORMAN B.
.... 246
ESTACION, JANET 395
ESTES, CHUCK 328
ESTILL, ELIZABETH 17
ETGEN, ROBERT J. 193
ETHELSTON, SALLY 297
ETHRIDGE, TOM 209
ETTEMA, ROBERT 371
EUSTON, SUSANNA
  MACKENZIE 209
EVANICH, DAVID 359
EVANS, BARBARA 376
EVANS, BROCK 195, 200
EVANS, DAVID L. 18
EVANS, GAIL 149
EVANS, JEFF 206
EVANS, JOSEPH R. 301
EVANS, KEVIN 277
EVANS, LEMUEL A. 246
EVANS, MARSHA
  JOHNSON 210
EVANS, PETER 49, 199
EVANS, RHYS 263
EVANS, RICHARD M. ... 388
EVANS, TANIA 236
EVANS, THOMAS W. 198
EVANS, WALLACE 100
EVENSON, KIRK 331
EVERAGE. CYNTHIA ... 191
EVERETT, MELISSA 217
EVERETT, MIKE 60
EVERITT, BOB 116
EVERTS, TODD 81
EWART, JOHN W. 52
EWERT, D. MERRILL 90
EWING, JOHN 112
EWING, PATRICIA 359
EWING, ROBERT 29
EXTER, RANDEE 18

F

FABER, SCOTT 149
FABIAN, NELSON E. 260
FABIAN, TERRY R. 101
FACCIANI, STEVE 123
FAESY, NANCY 181
FAGE, ERNIE 126
FAHEY, JOHN M., JR. ... 262
FAHEY, TIMOTHY J. 381
FAHLUND, ANDREW 149
FAIRBANK, BOB 253
FAIRCHILD, LAURIE 348
FAIRFIELD, CAROL 319
FAIRLEIGH, LARRY 116
FAKIR, SALIEM 229
FAKUNDINY, ROBERT H.
.... 90
FALCO, CARL 92
FALENDER, ANDREW J.
.... 153
FALES, DANFORTH 159
FALK, DONALD A. 318
FALKENHEINER, DORIS
.... 243
FALKNER, BOB 341
FALSTROM, KEN 196
FALTEISEK, JAN 251
FALWELL, JEROME C. .240
FANCY, CLAIR 53
FARBER, LAURIE 221

FARIAS, ENRIQUE G. 44
FARLAND, WILLIAM H. .. 11
FARLEY, DENNIS L. 101
FARLEY, GREG 238
FARLEY, TIM 47
FARMER, BARB 123
FARNSWORTH, LARRY 373
FARR, CLARENCE 60
FARRAR, SALLY 357
FARRELL, DOLORES 47
FARRELL, THOMAS 136
FARREN, RICHARD 203
FARRIS, ALLEN 64
FARRISH, KENNETH 388
FARRO, ANTHONY J. 85
FARWELL, FRANCIS C. 268
FAST, DON 124
FATZ, RAYMOND J. 24
FAULKNER, ANNIE 276
FAUSKE, GLENDA 93
FAUST, RALPH 46
FAUST, RICHARD 205
FAUTH, LAURA 302
FAZIO, JAMES R. 256
FEDEWA, DENNIS 75
FEDORENKO, VLADIMIR . 9
FEDORKO, NICK, III 120
FEDUCCIA, DONALD P. . 68
FEDULLO, CHARLES 39
FEE, EVERETT J. 150
FEE, GARNET 33
FEIERABEND, J. SCOTT
.... 267
FEINBERG, WILLIAM 174
FELDHAMER, GEORGE
.... 351, 370
FELDMAN, JAY 160, 192
FELDMAN, MARCUS W. 365
FELDMAN, RICHARD D. . 63
FELDT, GLORIA 297
FELLOWS, EDRISE 276
FELLOWS, LARRY D. 41
FELSKE, BEVERLY 292
FELT, STEVE 219
FENN, DENNIS B. 30, 31
FENNELL, ROSE 346
FENNELLY, KATHERINE 77
FENNESSY, FRANCIS M.
.... 120
FENSTEMACHER, RON 215
FENTY, GREG 275
FENWICK, GEORGE H. 138
FERAL, PRISCILLA 205
FERENCE, LARRY 265
FERENSTEIN, JENNIFER
.... 312
FERGUSON, BRUCE 167
FERGUSON, JAMES 92
FERGUSON, JOHN L. 42
FERGUSON-SOUTHARD,
  DENISE 51
FERNANDEZ, BOBBY 33
FERNANDEZ, IVAN 374
FERNANDEZ, NOE 110
FERNANDEZ, NURIA 32
FERNANDEZ, PETER 12
FERNHOLM, BO 8
FERRANTE, GRETCHEN
.... 277
FERRE, ANTONIO LUIS 184
FERREIRA, JAMES 89
FERRELL, BLAINE 238
FERRELL, STEVE 41
FERRELL, YVONNE 60, 258
FERRING, REID 389
FERRIS, CRAIG 190
FERRIS, DONALD 234
FERRIS, ROBERT M. 186
FERRIS, SHIRLEY 50
FERRITER, AMY 202

STAFF NAME INDEX - F

FERRULO, MARK 202
FERRY, MILES 110, 111
FERTIG, WALTER 360
FESSENDEN, JOSEPH E.
.... 71
FESTER, JAMES 103
FETTEROLF, CARLOS . 140
FEWIN, ROBERT F. 109
FEWLESS, DENNIS 93
FICKES, ROGER 101
FICKES, TED 177
FICKIES, ROBERT H. 90
FIELD, DAVID B. 153, 374
FIELD, REBECCA 74
FIELDER, JOHN 346
FIELDER, NICK 107
FIELDS, JAMES D. 119
FIELDS, JIM 187
FIELDS, TIMOTHY, JR. ... 11
FIFIELD, SHIRLEY 133
FIGERT, DAN ERIC 352
FIGUEROA, FRANK 33
FIJALKOWSKI, DENNIS 250
FILIATRAULT, PATRICK 301
FILION, BERNARD 189
FINCH, FRANK, P.E. 55
FINCH, JAMIE 33
FINCH, JOHN 282
FINCK, ELMER 284, 352, 371
FINDEN, JEFFERY S. ... 296
FINDLAY, STUART E.G. 222
FINFER, LARRY 28
FINGERHUT, BERT 346
FINLAYSON, ANN 231
FINLEY, CHUCK 280
FINLEY, DAVID A. 122
FINN, SUSAN 224
FINNERTY, MAUREEN ... 29
FINNEY, DANA 24
FINNEY, GEORGE 36
FINSER, JACK 121
FIRKINS, JIM 86
FIRST, JOSH 100
FISCHER, BURNELL 63
FISCHER, DUF 152
FISCHER, EDWARD 335
FISCHER, HANK 186
FISCHER, JOHN 206
FISCHER, R. MONTGOMERY 267
FISCHER, ROBERT U. .. 370
FISCHER, STEVEN A. .. 143
FISH, STEVEN O. 51
FISHER, FRANK M. 388
FISHER, JACK 218
FISHER, JANET L. 119
FISHER, JONATHAN 267
FISHER, LYNDAL 22
FISHER, NICHOLAS S. 382
FISHER, RANDY 10
FISHER, THOMAS W. ... 234
FISHER, W. L. 108
FISHER, WAYNE 124
FISHER, WILLIAM L. 95
FISHMAN, JAMES 259
FISK, ANDREW 70
FISKE, KEN 218
FITCH, LARRY 111
FITCHETT, ROGER 339
FITE, EDWARD D., III ... 306
FITTS, DANIEL T. 88
FITZGERALD, ANNE 51
FITZGERALD, BEN 340
FITZGERALD, BRIAN T. 153
FITZGERALD, MARTHA 172
FITZGERALD, ROBERT 246
FITZGERALD, SUSAN M.
.... 351
FITZGERALD, TOM 239

FITZGIBBON, JOHN E. ... 394
FITZHUGH, E. LEE 46
FITZPATRICK, JIM 303
FITZPATRICK, JOHN 148, 184
FITZPATRICK, NEAL 158
FITZPATRICK, SCOTT .. 159
FITZSIMMONS, KEVIN ... 42
FITZSIMMONS, TOM 117
FITZSIMONS, JOSEPH B.C.
.... 329
FJELD, PAM 387
FLANDERS, P. HOWARD
.... 111
FLANIGAN, FRANCES .. 135
FLATTERY, TOM 61
FLAVIN, CHRISTOPHER
.... 359
FLECKENSTEIN, LEONARD J. 11
FLEMING, EMILY J. 119
FLEMING, GENE 47
FLEMING, HOWARD 182
FLEMING, MARY 292
FLESKES, CAROL 117
FLETCHER, KATHY 255, 295
FLETCHER, MADYLYN . 387
FLETCHER, RODERICK 101
FLICK, GEORGE J., JR. 116
FLICK, PAMELA 317
FLICKER, JOHN 259
FLICZUK, JIM 163
FLINT, JIM 262
FLINT, PETER H. 187
FLINT, ROBERT B., JR. 317
FLOOD, DAVID JAY 215
FLOOD, JAMES 190
FLORA, JOHN J. 221
FLORY, RONALD K. 101
FLOWERS, KEVIN 235
FLOWERS, LISA 162
FLOYD, BARRY 190
FLOYD, KIM 360
FLOYD, THELMA 16
FLOYD, TIMOTHY 360
FLOYD, VERONICA 146
FLUHARTY, MARLENE 317
FOCAZIO, PAUL 90
FOGEL, GARY 173
FOGERTY, DANIEL J. 63
FOLEY, DANA 271
FOLEY, GARY J., Ph.D. .. 11
FOLEY, KATHY 55
FOLKS, JOHN C. 53
FONDREN, WALTER W., III
.... 176
FONG, D. 125
FONTAINE, COLETTE ... 124
FONTANA, LOUIS A. 104
FONTENOT, BENNIE 69
FOOS, ANNABELLE 384
FOOTE, EDWARD T., II 226
FOOTE, FRANK 243
FOOTE, KAREN 69
FOOTE, RAY 310
FOOTE-SMITH, CHRISTY
.... 73
FORAND, LISEANNE 36
FORBES, JOHN RIPLEY
.... 271
FORBES, LOREN 233
FORCE, JO ELLEN 369
FORCIER, LAWRENCE K.
.... 112
FORD, ARTHUR 29
FORD, BILL 176
FORD, BRITT J. 265
FORD, C. FREDERICK.. 235
FORD, CHARLES 24

FORD, CINDY 237
FORD, CYNTHIA 238
FORD, ELLEN 357
FORD, MARLENE 215
FORD, MIKE 307
FORD, PAT 218
FORD, RICHARD 375
FORD, THOMAS P. 101
FORD, TIM 201
FORD, TOM 201
FORDHAM, WAYNE 21
FORDICE, KIRK 77
FOREMAN, DAVE 347
FORER, LYLE 100
FOREST, BEN 174
FORESTELL, PAUL H. . 293
FORGEY, WILLIAM W. . 346
FORKAN, PATRICIA 217
FORNOS, WERNER 298
FORRENOT, WILLIE, S. 252
FORREST, CLAYTON 167
FORREST, ROSEMARY 369
FORSGREN, TED 176
FORSING, JOHN 17
FORTIN, CAROL 367
FORTIN, MARTY 197
FORTUNA, ROGER A. ... 33
FORTUNE, JAMES 349
FOSBRE, MIKE 138
FOSBURGH, WHIT 331
FOSTER, BARBARA 67
FOSTER, BILL 42
FOSTER, BOB 332
FOSTER, DAVID E. 43
FOSTER, DAVID G. 138
FOSTER, HOWARD 104
FOSTER, JEFF 366
FOSTER, KENT 218
FOSTER, M. J., JR. 68
FOSTER, NANCY CARTER
.... 20
FOSTER, NANCY, Ph.D. 17
FOTI, TOM 44, 415
FOUNTAIN, MICHAEL .. 388
FOUST, ALLEN 279
FOUST, BRADY 392
FOUST, CHAD 213
FOUT, EVE D. 296
FOUTS, MARK D. 308
FOWLER, BILL 332
FOWLER, JAMES F. 69
FOWLER, JERRY 12
FOWLER, JOHN 33
FOWLER, ROB B. 189
FOWLER, RON 106
FOWLER, TIM 248
FOX, DOUG 373
FOX, HOWARD 192
FOX, JEANNE M. 11
FOX, JENNIFER 159
FOX, JIM 116
FOX, JOHN C. 226
FOX, JOHN E.D. 228
FOX, JONHATHAN C. 11
FOX, MARVIN 356
FOX, RON 107
FOX, SHERRY 341
FOX, SUSAN 294
FOX, TOM 163
FOY, DOUGLAS 191
FOY, DOUGLAS I. 183
FOY, MIKE 355
FRALEY, GEORGE 288
FRAME, BRUCE C. 32
FRAMPTON, GEORGE T., JR.
.... 10
FRAMSTEAD, PAUL 256
FRANCE, SUSAN A. 82
FRANCE, THOMAS M. .. 268
FRANCIS, MICHAEL 346

FRANCIS, ROBERT T., II 33
FRANCIS, RONALD G.182, 257
FRANCISCO, GENE 121
FRANCK, SCOTT 279
FRANCKO, DAVID A. 384
FRANCO, ROBERTO 229
FRANK, ANNETTE R. 222
FRANK, BARBARA 39
FRANK, BOBBI 359
FRANK, DAVID 18
FRANK, JEFF 239
FRANK, MICHAEL 335
FRANKLIN, THOMAS M. 350
FRANTZ, PETER J. 61
FRANZI, ANITA 246
FRASER, CELESTE 260
FRASIER, GARY 319
FRASIER, JOHN E. 345
FRATE, GINO DEL 350
FRATICELLI, BECKY 14
FRAWLEY, BRIAN 351
FRAYER, W. E. 376
FRAZEE, JOAN 341
FRAZER, GARY 29
FRAZER, SCOTT E. 354
FRAZIER, GERALD W. . 156
FREAKER, GUY 62
FREDERICK, DAVID 39
FREDERICK, ROBERT . 372
FREDERICKS, TODD 73
FREDIN, TRACY 377
FREDRIKSSON, KURT ... 39
FREE, STUART L. 151
FREEDGOOD, JULIA 139
FREEDMAN, DAVID 56
FREEL, MAETON 351
FREELAND, AL 24
FREELAND, KATHY 132
FREEMAN, BRENDA 111
FREEMAN, CHARLES 96
FREEMAN, CRAIG C. ... 238
FREEMAN, GEORGE ... 295
FREEMAN, HELEN 227
FREESE, ED 232
FREGONARA, JIM 354
FREHNER, SYLVIA 37
FREIMUND, WAYNE 379
FRENCH, HILARY 359
FRENCH, JIM 116
FRENCH, MARILYN 360
FRENCH, STEVEN P. ... 360
FRESCO, NANCY 285
FRESH, KURT L. 143
FRETZ, THOMAS 374
FRETZ, THOMAS A. 72
FREWING, JOHN 99
FREY, KEVIN J. 142
FREY, LOIS 112
FREY, PAUL D. 68
FREZIERS, JOHN 177
FRI, ROBERT 214, 317
FRICK, LINDA 89
FRIDAY, KATIE S. 214
FRIDGEN, CYNTHIA 376
FRIDGEN, JOSEPH D. . 376
FRIED, MICHELLE 337
FRIEDE, JOHN 135
FRIEDLAND, KEVIN 375
FRIEDMAN, MITCH 285
FRIEDMAN, ROBERT ... 214
FRINK, JOHN 331
FRISCHKORN, CARL ... 119
FRIST, BILL 6
FRISTOE, BRAD 25
FRITZ, BETSY 140
FRITZ, EDWARD 329
FRITZELL, ERIK 259
FRITZELL, ERIK K. 384
FRIZZELL, BRUCE 31

STAFF NAME INDEX - G

FROCHLICH, DAVID 250
FROHMAN, GARY 201
FROMAN, SANDRA S... 264
FRONT, ALAN 335
FROST, CECIL 92
FROST, DAN 297
FROST, PETER 344
FRUCI, DICK 277
FRUMKIES, JOAN 279
FRY, JOHN 296, 340
FRY, TOM 28
FRYE, CLAYTON W., JR.
.... 236
FRYE, E. O. 233
FRYE, GRANVILLE H. 13
FRYE, JACK E. 114
FRYE, MEL 91
FUENTES, PEDRO J. 300
FUHRMAN, RUSSEL 26
FUJIOKA, ROGER 58
FULBRIGHT, DENNIS ... 139
FULCHER, SANDY 231
FULFORD, LOY 107
FULGENZI, JIM 61
FULGHAM, KEN 364
FULGHAM, TOM 190
FULLER, CHERI 165
FULLER, DAVID P. 353
FULLER, JAMES 82
FULLER, JOSEPH 108
FULLER, KATHRYN S. .. 359
FULLER, MANLEY K. 203
FULLER, MARJI 347
FULLWOOD, CHARLES R.
.... 91, 92
FULLWOOD,, CHARLES R., JR. 91
FULMER, CAROL 105
FULMER, TOM 115
FULTON, DAVID C. 76
FULTON, SCOTT C. 10
FUNCHES, JESSE L. 34
FUNDERBURLS, STEVE .. 9
FURLONG, DANIEL T. .. 250
FURNESS, GEORGE A., JR. 183
FURNISH, JIM 16
FUTRELL, J. WILLIAM .. 198
FUTTER, ELLEN V. 147

G

GABELHOUSE, DON, JR. 82
GABRIEL, NANCY 149, 203, 262
GABRIELE, LARRY 123
GADBERY, EARL 153
GADD, COLLEEN 178
GADDY, JOY 272
GADZIK, CHUCK 70
GAETANO, FIORAVANTE
.... 22
GAFFNEY, SUSAN 20
GAGE, B. TIMOTHY 46
GAGE, LINDA 48
GAGE, ROBERT 43
GAGEN, CHARLIE 363
GAGNER, DAVID 257
GAGNON, ALAIN 301
GAGNON, MANON 301
GAGNON, RONALD 104
GAILOR, ALLEN K. 67
GAINER, CARL E. 119
GAINES, BILL 164
GAINES, GARY 80
GAINES, SALLY 254
GALANTI, GERI-ANN ... 224
GALAT, DAVID L. 79
GALDA, BEATA 80
GALE, JAMES R. 200
GALES, LAWRENCE A. .. 96
GALIZIOLLI, STEVE 154
GALL, BONNIE 289
GALL, LESLIE 43
GALLAGHER, ANDY 119
GALLAGHER, DAWN 70
GALLAGHER, FRANK 85
GALLAGHER, JOHN J., JR.
.... 84
GALLAGHER, TIM 184
GALLAGHER, WILLIAM J.
.... 215
GALLAY, PAUL 89
GALLIK, KENNETH 261
GALLOWAY, BOB 127
GALVIN, DENIS 29
GAMBELL, R. 8
GAMEZ, RODRIGO 37
GAMILL, STEWART, III. 186
GAMMILL, LYNN 185
GAMON, JOHN :.... 118, 417
GANGLOFF, DEBORAH 145
GANN, GEORGE 318
GANOUNG, KAREN 238
GANSAUER, DIANE 178
GANSBERG, BILL 117
GANSELL, STUART I. ... 101
GANSKE, TED 134, 135
GANTZ, RICHARD 63
GANZLIN, BILL K. 378
GARAVELLI, RON 78
GARBER, ALLEN 76
GARBISCH, EDGAR W. 196
GARBISCH, JOANNA L. 196
GARBISCH, JON O. 369
GARCES, GRACE OMEGA
.... 57
GARCIA, BENITO 87
GARCIA, EUGENE 18
GARCIA, JUANITA 103
GARCIA, KWAME N., SR.
.... 113
GARCIA, MARCELO 23
GARCIA, SANTANA 46
GARCIA, TERRY D. 17
GARD, MATT 288
GARDILL, WALTER 162
GARDINER, DAVID M. 11
GARDNER, CHARLES 91
GARDNER, DAN, Ph.D. 189
GARDNER, DENNIS 306
GARDNER, DERRY T. ... 329
GARDNER, JUDY 108
GARDNER, LORI 319
GARDNER, MIKE 392
GARDNER, PAUL 153
GARIBALDI, LOUIS 348
GARLAND, BILL 25
GARLAND, KATHLEEN ... 86
GARLAND, L. BROOKS. 107
GARMAN-SQUIER, CYNTHIA 15
GARNER, CHERYL 184
GARNER, JAMES W. 113
GARNER, JIM 61
GARNER, SUE 328
GARNER, WILLIAM B. 38
GARNHAM, DARLENE .. 245
GARRETT, ELIZABETH A.
.... 253
GARRETT, GARY 188
GARRISON, JOHN R. 147
GARRISON, LYNN 67
GARRISON, SAMUEL 84
GARTSIDE, MICHAEL ... 171
GARVEY, JANE 31
GASKA, JEFF 296
GASKINS, DARIUS W., JR.
.... 304
GASPERI, ENRICO 339
GASTON, JANE W. 132
GATCHELL, JOHN 255
GATES, BILL 25
GATES, BRYAN 163
GATES, JESSICA 165
GATES, KEITH 56
GATES, PHIL 331
GATES, RICK 98
GATEWOOD, STEVE 347
GATJE, PETER 298
GAUBERT, KEVIN 243
GAUDET, DIANE 128
GAUDETTE, ROBERT P. 72
GAULDIN, MICHAEL 28
GAUME, NORMAN 88
GAUNT, CAROL 288
GAUTHIER, CLAUDE 301
GAUVIN, CHARLES F. .. 331
GAVALLA, GEORGE 32
GAW, HERSHEL 25
GAY, CHARLES W. 111
GAY, GEORGE 112
GAYMAN, BEN 319
GEALT, MICHAEL A. 385
GEATZ, RON 272
GEBALLE, GORDON 181
GEBHARDT, ALLEN S. .. 107
GEBHARDT, BRUCE 281
GEER, BILL 307
GEER, WILLIS 298
GEHRING, JANET L. 370
GEHRKE, CRAIG 346
GEIGER, RAYMOND K. .. 53
GEIGER, SHARON 217
GEIGER, TOM 341
GEIWITZ, JOHN 137
GELABERT, PEDRO A. 103, 398
GELFAND, JULIE .. 166, 167
GELL, ROBERT L. 217
GELLER, HOWARD 139
GELLER, MARVIN A. 382
GELLER, MICHAEL D. .. 380
GENETTI, ALBERT J., JR.
.... 26
GENNINGS, MIKE 56
GENNRICH, RUTH 237
GENTER, ROBERT 390
GENTRY, GEORGE D. .. 156
GENTZ, EDWARD J. 348
GEORGE, CLINTON 113
GEORGE, DEBORAH 124
GEORGE, FELICIA 62
GEORGE, JAKE 309
GEORGE, LOUIS S. 308
GEORGE, PAUL 117
GEORGE, SARAH B. 156
GEORGE, SUSAN 186
GERARD, JENNIE 334
GERBER, JOHN E. 173
GERBER, JOHN M. 74
GERBRACHT, JIM 351
GERGELA, JOE 279
GERHARDT, JOHN 49
GERINGER, JIM 122, 123
GERL, JANET 345
GERL, PETER J. 345
GERL, WILLIAM E., JR. . 345
GERMIDA, JIM J. 395
GERREIN, DAVID 67
GERSON, LESLIE 21
GERTEISEN, DON 54
GESKE, JOEL 232
GESKE, NANCY 231
GESNER, SUSAN 166
GHAI, DHARAM 37
GHOLZ, HENRY L. 369
GIBBONS, JERRY 246
GIBBONS, ROBERT M. .. 12
GIBBONS, WHIT 369
GIBBS, LOIS MARIE 170
GIBBS, TREY 209
GIBERSON, DONNA 280
GIBSON, DAVID H. 155
GIBSON, MARGE 230
GIBSON, NANCY 393
GIBSON, RICK 98
GIESECKE, JOHN H. 267
GIESEN, KENNETH 299
GIESFELDT, MARK F. .. 121
GIFFHORN, KENWOOD 101
GIGSTAD, ORUIL 275
GIGUERE, SUZANNE ... 128
GILBERT, ALPHONSE H.
.... 390
GILBERT, BRIAN .. 126, 269
GILBERT, CAROLINE 207
GILBERT, DAVID E. 98
GILBERT, JAMES R. 374
GILCHREST, NORMAN 136
GILDER, GIL 38
GILES, WARREN 235
GILFORD, JAMES 250
GILL, DEBORAH 279
GILL, FRANK 148, 259
GILL, JOSEPH P. 72
GILLAN, KIM 81
GILLEPSIE, JAMES 359
GILLESPIE, BRIAN 125, 399
GILLESPIE, FRANCIS P. 34
GILLESPIE, HOLLIS J. .. 181
GILLESPIE, JAMES 64
GILLESPIE, TERRY 394
GILLET, F. WARRINGTON, JR. 207
GILLETTE, AMY 218
GILLETTE, LARRY 334
GILLEY, SUSAN 304
GILLIGAN, PAT 307
GILLILAND, KIM 39
GILLILAND, MARY 275
GILLILAND, ROBERT L. 111
GILLIS, JIM L., JR. 56
GILLIS, RANNIE 286
GILLS, ROY 327
GILMAN, BENJAMIN A. . 3, 5
GILMORE, BRUCE 72
GILMORE, GEORGE 247
GILMORE, JAMES S., II 113
GILMORE, R. GRANT ... 142
GILMORE, THOMAS J. . 278
GILSDORF, MICHAEL 13
GILSON, JAMES 43
GILWORTH, RON 278
GIMELLO, RICHARD 85
GINGERY, GARY L. 80
GINSBURG, ALAN L. 18
GIOVANNITTI, ERNEST F.
.... 101
GIPSON, CHESTER 13
GIPSON, PHILIP S. . 65, 372
GIRTON, DON 239, 269
GISH, STACEY 66
GLASER, LUIS 226
GLASS, GARY B. 123
GLASS, JOHN D. 40
GLASS, ROBERT H. 281
GLASSBERG, JEFFREY 280
GLASSCOCK, SELMA N.
.... 343
GLASSMAN, HAL 20
GLAZE, WILLIAM H. 383
GLEASON, JIM 189
GLEIBER, JOHN 318
GLEICK, PETER 293
GLENDENING, PARRIS N.
.... 71
GLICKMAN, DAN 12
GLISSMAN, INGE 226

STAFF NAME INDEX - G

GLOCK, JAMES W. 293
GLODEN, TERESA 75
GLOMAN, NANCY 29
GLOUTNEY, MARK 189
GLOVER, EDWARD N. .. 162
GLOVER, RONALD L. 79
GLOWKA, ARTHUR 310
GLUECK, TOM 25
GNAM, ROSEMARIE 233
GOBER, PATRICIA 155
GODBY, DAVID 67
GODDARD, CHRIS 7
GODDARD, KEN 30
GODFREY, TED 332
GODISH, DR. JOHN
  PICHTEL, DR. FRED
  SIEWERT, THAD 370
GODISH, THAD 370
GODWIN, KRISTINA
  CASSCLES 352
GOELZ, PETER 33
GOERGEN, GLENN N. ... 320
GOERL, VINCETTE 16
GOETTEL, ROBIN G. 62
GOETZ, RAY 93
GOFF, BENNY 252
GOFF, DEBORAH L. 79
GOFF, GARY R. 90
GOGGINS, ELIZABETH 339
GOING, TONY 278
GOLD, ART 104
GOLD, LORETTA 249
GOLD, PAULA W. 183
GOLDEN, JENNIFER 327
GOLDEN, OLIVIA 19
GOLDEN, RAYMOND L. 268
GOLDEN, WILLIAM T. ... 136
GOLDENTYER,
  ELIZABETH 12
GOLDMAN, CAROLINE
  TAYLOR 182
GOLDMAN, LYNN R. 11
GOLDMAN, PATTI 192
GOLDSWORTHY, PATRICK
  D. 283
GOLLEDGE, REGINALD G.
  155
GOLLIN, JIM 302
GOLLY, WAYNE 77
GOMES, JAMES 198
GOMES, W. R. 45
GONZALES, GABRIEL 23
GONZALES, TOM 267
GONZALEZ, I. MILEY 15
GONZALEZ, MANUEL ... 228
GONZALEZ, MILEY 12
GONZALEZ-
  JETTINGHOFF, ISABEL
  151
GONZOLEZ, MARIA
  LOURDES 37
GOOD, ALICIA M. 103
GOODE, ANDREW 157
GOODE, ANN E. 10
GOODE, RALPH 180
GOODENOUGH, ERIC .. 190
GOODHEART, JIM 250
GOODLET, KAREN 372
GOODLING, BILL 5
GOODMAN, ALBERT W.
  342
GOODMAN, DAVID 366
GOODMAN, JIM 67
GOODNIGHT, BILL 218
GOODPASTER, GARY . 190
GOODSON, RALPH 209
GOODWIN, ANDREW 43
GOODWIN, DANIEL 318
GOODWIN, GARY 188
GOODWIN, RICHARD H.,
  SR. 181
GOODYEAR, MOLLY 198
GOOHART, JIM 42
GORDON, BRUCE 243
GORDON, CLAY 23
GORDON, GAYLE 28
GORDON, GUY 75
GORDON, KATHY 28
GORDON, KEN 10
GORDON, RUE E. 267
GORDON, THEODORE . 188
GORE, BOB 117
GORE, RON 38
GORMAN, ROBERT F. 40
GOROSPE, KATHY 11
GORSEN, MAUREEN 46
GOSLINER, MICHAEL L. .. 8
GOSSELIN, ANDRE 395
GOSSELIN, LISA 259
GOSSWEILER, WILLIAM 25
GOSTING, DIANE 272
GOSTOMSKI, TED 392
GOSWAMI, D. YOGI 368
GOTHARD, TIM 133
GOTLIEB, ALAN 112
GOTSCH, JERRY 168
GOTT, EDWIN H., JR. .. 308
GOTTFRIED, KURT 336
GOTT-JANZEN,
  GEORGEEN 292
GOUDY, WILLIAM H. 308
GOUGH, MARY 220
GOUGH, STEPHEN 396
GOULARD, CARY 364
GOULD, JOHN E. 145
GOULD, MARK, ... 386
GOULD, RICK 223
GOURLAY, JIM 157
GOVER, CHARLES H. .. 120
GOVER, CHUCK 120
GOVER, KEVIN 27, 28
GOVONI, JEFF 140
GRABB, ROBERT W. 113
GRABER, STEVE 220
GRABOWICZ, GREGORY
  J. 102
GRACE, AMI 175
GRACE, JAMES 102
GRACE, JAMES R. 100
GRACI, JOSEPH P. 101
GRADY, SUE 121
GRAEBNER, JEAN 159
GRAEF, HENRY 298
GRAF, WILLIAM L. 155
GRAFF, DELANO R. 101
GRAFF, WALTER 153
GRAFTON, WILLIAM 120
GRAHAM, BOB 1, 97
GRAHAM, C. 36
GRAHAM, CHRISTOPHER
  L. 249
GRAHAM, DANIEL J. 126
GRAHAM, GARY 109
GRAHAM, JAMES A. 92
GRAHAM, PATRICK 223
GRAHAM, PATRICK J. ... 80
GRAHAM, SHERI 42
GRAMS, DENNIS D. 11
GRAMS, ROD 2, 6
GRAND, JAMES B. 38
GRANDY, JOHN W. 217
GRANN, DOUGLAS H. . 348
GRANOFF, MICHAEL D. 336
GRANQUIST, DEBORAH
  338
GRANSKOU, MARY 167
GRANT, ANDREW H., II 339
GRANT, GARY 200
GRANT, JAMES E., JR. .. 43
GRANT, MALCOLM J. 103
GRANT, R. ALEXANDER . 19
GRANT, WILLIAM 234
GRAVES, BILL 65
GRAVES, DONALD H. .. 372
GRAVES, J. E. 390
GRAVES, LEON C. 112
GRAVES, RANDY L. 189
GRAVES, SAM BRUCE,
  SR. 253
GRAY, BRIAN T. 188
GRAY, DAVID 329
GRAY, DON 195
GRAY, GERALD J. 145
GRAY, JAN 321
GRAY, KATHLEEN 383
GRAY, MARY McPHAIL .. 50
GRAY, PAMELA 182
GRAY, PAUL 83
GRAY, RACHEL 199
GRAY, SHEILA 118
GRAY, STEVEN 364
GRAY, TERRENCE 104
GRAYBEAL, JAMES 51
GRAYBEAL, NANCY 16
GRAYBILL,, J. CARL, JR.
  102
GREATHEAD, R. SCOTT
  139
GREELEY, MAUREEN L.
  357
GREEN, BUTCH 137
GREEN, DANA 22
GREEN, DANIEL 212
GREEN, EMORY 90
GREEN, EVON 122
GREEN, GEORGE 109
GREEN, JAY 250
GREEN, KIRBY 53
GREEN, KIRBY, III 53
GREEN, LANE 327
GREEN, ORVILLE 61
GREEN, PAUL 138
GREEN, TERRY 110
GREENE, BETSY 242
GREENE, BRIAN 278
GREENE, DALE 209
GREENE, JEFF 38
GREENE, JOSEPH A. .. 101
GREENE, JUANITA 234
GREENE, THOMAS 284
GREENE, WADE 241
GREENFIELD, TONY ... 163
GREENHALGH, RANDY 337
GREENLEE, JACK 25
GREENLEE, JASON 223
GREENWOOD, CARY ... 98
GREENWOOD, M. R. 136
GREENWOOD, STEVE .. 98
GREER, JACK 72
GREER, JIM 97, 344, 398
GREEVES, JOHN T. 34
GREGG, FRANK 320
GREGG, GEORGE 100
GREGG, JUGE 325
GREGG, PETE 88
GREGG, WILLIAM 31
GREGORY, ALBERT 54
GREGORY, GARY 47
GREGORY, GARY L. 46
GREGORY, JOHN 107
GREGORY, TOMMY 78
GREIFER, JOHN 12
GRESCZYK, BRUCE H. .. 50
GRESE, ROBERT 249
GREVE, WILLIAM F., JR.
  303
GRIBBLE, ROBERT 342
GRICE, RICK 50
GRIEBLING, RICHARD .. 49
GRIER, NORMA 285
GRIES, DANIEL 356
GRIFFEN, PHILIP 89
GRIFFIN, HOLLIS 112
GRIFFIN, JOHN R. 72
GRIFFIN, JUNE 340
GRIFFIN, STAN 331, 332
GRIFFIN-JONES, MARY
  MURRAY 131
GRIFFITH, BRAD 39
GRIFFITH, GARY A. 217
GRIFFITH, LEON 62
GRIFFITH, ROBERT D. . 295
GRIFFITHS, DON 292
GRIFFITHS, PETER 275
GRIGGS, JAMES H. 38
GRILLEY, DORIAN 252
GRILLOT, CHRIS 232
GRIMES, BRIAN K. 34
GRIMES, ROY 67, 352
GRIMES, SALLY 145
GRIMES, STANELY 277
GRIMM, ERIC 54
GRIMM, NANCY 362
GRIMM, NANCY B. 280
GRIMMETT, HAROLD K. 44
GRINDAL, BRUCE T. ... 368
GRINDSTAFF, GARY 61
GRIP, KJELL 7
GRISHAW, LETITIA J. 20
GRIZZARD, KENT 78
GRIZZLE, JOHN M. 362
GROAT, CHARLES 27
GROAT, CHARLES G. 30
GROFFMAN, PETER M. 222
GRONOWSKI, ROBERT . 82
GROSBOLL, CAROLYN T.
  62
GROSBOLL, CAROLYN
  TAFT 62
GROSS, DAVID W. 90
GROSS, HOWARD 215
GROSS, JOEL 20
GROSS, JOHN 219
GROSS, MICHAEL 393
GROSS, PORTER J., (FL) 5
GROSSI, RALPH E. 139
GROSSWILER, ED 360
GROSVENOR, GILBERT M.
  262
GROTON, JIMMY 328
GROTY, KEITH 250
GROUNDS, JOHN S., III 151
GROVE, THURMAN L. . 383
GROVER, TONY 117
GROVES, PAM 285
GROW, ROBERT J. 295
GRUBER, ALAN 153
GRUBINGER, VERN 112
GRUE, CHRISTIAN E. .. 117
GRUENBERG, PHIL 45
GRUENEBAUM, JANE . 242
GRUMBACH, ANTONIA M.
  236
GRUMBINE, DENNIS ... 100
GRUNDMAN, KELLY ... 139
GRUSPE, OSCAR V. 331
GRUTHOFF, BRUCE ... 190
GRYDER, R. J. 40
GRYNIEWSKI, JAMES ... 76
GUARINO, JENNIFER . 338
GUDAUSKAS, HERTA . 245
GUDES, SCOTT B. 17
GUENSLER, DARRELL . 46
GUENTHER, JOHN 76
GUERTIN, D. PHILLIP . 363
GUEST, DAVID G. 192
GUFFEY, CAROL 43
GUGGENHEIM, DAVID E.
  181

STAFF NAME INDEX - H

GUILFOYLE, JOAN 155
GUILIANO, WILLIAM 385
GUINN, KENNY 82
GUION, ANN F............. 180
GUISE, DENNIS T. 101
GUISINGER, ALLEN W.267, 268
GUITJENS, JOHN C. 379
GULLESTAD, P. 285
GULLIFER, JOANNE M. 350
GULLIFORD, JAMES B... 64
GULLIVER, R. 125
GUNDERSON, JEFFREY 77
GUNN, ROBERTA M. 301
GUNN, SUE 346
GUNTER, LINDA 308
GUNTON, RUSSELL 100
GUPTA, GIAN 375
GURITZ, DAVE 197
GUSTAFSON, COLE 93
GUTHRIE, RANDY 301
GUTIERREZ, CARL T.C.. 57
GUTIERREZ, FRANKLIN J. 57
GUTOWSKI, CAROLYN M. 281
GUTZMER, MICHAEL P.143
GUY, CHRISTOPHER S.65, 372
GUYMON, JIM 111
GUZMAN, LOUANN C..... 57
GUZZO, DOROTHY P..... 85
GWIN, KELLY 117
GWINN, CONSTANCE.. 154
GYN, THOMAS W. 361
GYAN, ISABELLA 241

H

HAAG, KIM H. 280
HAAS, WAYNE T. 60
HABEL, SIMON.............. 330
HABERMAN, BOB 340
HABERMAN, STEVE 312
HACK, DON 25
HACKING, ELISABETH BARRATT 396
HACKLEY, PATRICK D. 277
HADAN, ASHOK C. 34
HADDAD, KEN................ 53
HADDIX, C. BRIAN.......... 44
HADDOCK, JAMES D. .. 130
HADDOW, KIM 312
HADI, DIANE................... 53
HADLEY, KATHY 255
HAECKER, CATHERINE. 44
HAERING, HANS PETER 359
HAFFNER, MARLENE..... 19
HAFNER, CINDY 94
HAGAN, MARK 22, 263
HAGEL, CHUCK 2, 6
HAGELE, F. JOHN 191
HAGEMEYER, RICHARD H. 17
HAGENER, JEFF............. 81
HAGENIERS, MARILYN 236
HAGENSTEIN, PERRY . 276
HAGGIE, MICHAEL ROBIN 173
HAGLEY, CYNTHIA 77
HAHN, LESLIE E. 271
HAHN, MARIANNE 158
HAHN, MARTHA G. 28
HAHN, ROGER 356
HAIR, JAY D. 267
HAIRE, MICHAEL 71
HAKES, JAY E. 18
HALBLOM, DAVID......... 200

HALBLOM, SUSAN........200
HALBRENDT, CATHERINE 112
HALDEMAN, DICK.........301
HALE, BARRY.................87
HALE, MARTY...............141
HALES, DAVID................21
HALEY, WENDELL P.....234
HALFHILL, MICHELE119, 197
HALFPENNY, GEOFF ...187
HALL, BARBARA 215
HALL, CATHY 182
HALL, CHARLENE A. ...353
HALL, GEORGE A. 247
HALL, J. MICHAEL..........18
HALL, JAMES..................33
HALL, JEANNE 55
HALL, JIM 85
HALL, JOHN 111
HALL, KEN 163
HALL, LINNEA...............354
HALL, PATRICIA 303
HALL, PINKY 53
HALL, RICHARD 110
HALL, ROBERT E. 132
HALL, STEVE.......190, 226
HALL, STEVEN 103
HALL, WILLIAM W. 177
HALLAM, ROBERT 224
HALLETT, DIANA 350
HALLETT, JEAN 206
HALLIBURTON, BOBBY J. 262
HALLINAN, JACQUELINE 343
HALLOCK, STEPHANIE ..98
HALLOWELL, SAMUEL H., JR. 159
HALLUM, ALAN...............56
HALLWARD, CLARE 172
HALMAN, EDWARD L. ...34
HALSTEAD, PETE 220
HALTER, CINDY 355
HALVERSON, DIANE 152
HALVERSON, MARK........6
HALVERSON, MARVIN ...93
HALVORSON, CHRISTINE 135
HALVORSON, WILLIAM 318, 363
HAM, MICHAEL L. 57
HAM, SUSAN M. 57
HAMANN, RICHARD, ESQ 201
HAMAS, MICHAEL........376
HAMBLEY, MARK...........21
HAMBURG, MARGARET E. 12
HAMDY, FAROUK 12
HAMILTON, ARTHUR E.. 31
HAMILTON, BRUCE 312
HAMILTON, CHRIS 245
HAMILTON, JOAN 312
HAMILTON, JOHN 252
HAMILTON, JOHN M. 62
HAMILTON, KEVIN 326
HAMILTON, LARRY E.28, 419
HAMILTON, LISA 340
HAMILTON, MILTON H., JR. 107
HAMILTON, RICHARD B. 92
HAMILTON, SAM 30
HAMILTON, STANLEY F. 59
HAMILTON, THOMAS E.. 16
HAMLETT, SHELBY P. ...208
HAMLIN, LINDA 178
HAMLIN, PETE................64
HAMM, RONALD P. 113
HAMM, W. R. 266

HAMMAKER, JOHN L. ...271
HAMMEL, PAT...............287
HAMMER, R. DAVID 378
HAMMERSCHMIDT, PAUL 144
HAMMERSCHMIDT, RON 66
HAMMON, JOSEPH 332
HAMMOND, BRAD..........61
HAMMOND, K. R............168
HAMMOND, STEPHEN ...89
HAMRE, JOHN J. 18
HANCHEY, JAMES 68
HANCOCK, DON............325
HANCOCK, J. 125, 399
HAND, EDWARD F. 304
HANDLEY, BARBARA....215
HANDLEY, JOSEPH 126
HANDLEY, VIRGINIA 207
HANDS, PAUL 23
HANELINE, ELLEN 376
HANES, KIKU A.............182
HANEY, DONALD C. 67
HANKINSON, JOHN H., JR. 11
HANLEY, DONALD P......118
HANNA, CAROLYN 392
HANNA, GLENDA 135
HANNA, ROBERT B.......382
HANNAH, JUDITH..........366
HANNIGAN, THOMAS M. 48
HANNON, BRUCE M......299
HANOUSEK, RICHARD O. 296
HANSBROUGH, MIKE ...301
HANSCH, SUSAN 46
HANSEL, JOHN P. 194
HANSELKA, C. WAYNE.108
HANSELL, TYLER............99
HANSEN, DAVE 126
HANSEN, DAVID............232
HANSEN, DOUG 106
HANSEN, ED 137
HANSEN, FREDERIK C., JR 208
HANSEN, HARLEY 190
HANSEN, KATY 305
HANSEN, KELLY............153
HANSEN, MICHAEL J. ...144
HANSEN, PAUL 234, 379
HANSEN, PEDER 52
HANSEN, SUSAN TAYLOR 135
HANSON, JAMES 72
HANSON, JESSE 93
HANSON, LINDA..............64
HANSON, MARTIN........252
HANSON, MICHAEL T. ...351
HANSON, NELS 269, 341
HANUS, ANN.................98
HAPPE-VONARB, DEB..320
HARASEWYCH, OLEH ..244
HARCHARIK, D. 203
HARDER, LES.................48
HARDIE, DAVID 236
HARDIN, TIMOTHY S. ...143
HARDING, BEN 263
HARDING, DAVID 363
HARDING, ROBIN.........275
HARDING, RUSSELL J...75
HARDISKY, TOM 353
HARDY, FRED................244
HARDY, GEORGE E., JR.,MD,MPH 157
HARDY, GERALD 38
HARDY, JOHN T. 391
HARDY, YVAN 37
HARELSON, THOMAS L. 121
HARGER, CHUCK..........328

HARGETT, DAVE 206
HARGRAVE, NANCY G. 145
HARGRAVES, ED......... 137
HARGROVE, EUGENE . 389
HARGROVE, EUGENE C. 169, 389
HARIZANOFF, LARRY .. 114
HARKIN, TOM 2, 6
HARLAND, JIM 110
HARLOW, HENRY J. 393
HARLOW, TRUDY P. 30
HARLOWE, ANNA 194
HARMON, BOB............ 107
HARMON, DAVID 208
HARMON, LARRY 190
HARNACK, RONALD D... 76
HARNER, GREG 46
HARO, ROGER J........... 392
HARPER, CRAIG 107
HARPER, HERBERT..... 107
HARPER, JAKE 132
HARPER, LARRY 365
HARPER, MAX L............ 49
HARPER, ROBERT D..... 68
HARPER, SALLYANNE... 10
HARRIGAN, JACK 155
HARRIMAN, BETTIE R.. 356
HARRINGTON, H. MICHAEL 59
HARRINGTON, RALPH. 208
HARRINGTON, RICK 79
HARRINGTON, RUBE..... 13
HARRINGTON, SHIRL .. 204
HARRINGTON, STEVEN A. 204
HARRIS, B. L. 108
HARRIS, BETTY H. 185
HARRIS, BILL 307
HARRIS, BOBBY 55
HARRIS, C. COLEMAN . 261
HARRIS, DONNY........... 42
HARRIS, DOUGLAS 262
HARRIS, DUANE 56
HARRIS, EARL 55
HARRIS, ELIZABETH.... 249
HARRIS, ELLEN STERN185
HARRIS, FRED...... 92, 140
HARRIS, HALLETT J..... 392
HARRIS, HERBERT S., JR. 270
HARRIS, JACK H........... 253
HARRIS, JAMES........... 224
HARRIS, JIM 117
HARRIS, MARY C..267, 268
HARRIS, MIKE 56
HARRIS, PAT 253
HARRIS, RAY 280
HARRIS, RAY E. 123
HARRIS, RAYMOND 244
HARRIS, ROD 124
HARRIS, WILL 70
HARRISON, CHARLES W. 104
HARRISON, DAVID B..... 85
HARRISON, JAMES M. 9
HARRISON, JOHN T.58, 214
HARRISON, MARK......... 96
HARRISON, ROBERT ... 328
HARRISON, ROSS 64
HARRISON, TED 335
HARRISON, TOM 129
HARRISON, VERNA E. .. 72
HARRISON, WILLIAM E.. 66
HARRISON, WILLIAM F.. 85
HARRISTON, PEYTON T., JR. 35
HARROD, LEIGH 251
HARSHAW, HOWARD L. 102

HART, DONNA 230
HART, LARRY G. 114
HART, MARJORIE L. 311
HART, ROBERT F.X. 146
HART, T. MIKE 41
HARTE, EDWARD H. 139
HARTER, ROBERT 380
HARTFIELD, LIBBY 78
HARTLE, WILLIAM E. ... 102
HARTLEY, MAURICE 380
HARTLEY, MITSCHKA J.
.... 352
HARTMAN, BRAD 54
HARTMAN, HERB 70
HARTMAN, MARCIA 291
HARTMANN, CINDY A. . 141
HARTNETT, DAVID C. .. 372
HARTWELL, DAVID 241
HARTWIG, WILLIAM F. 30
HARTY, KIMM 110
HARVEY, ALYNN D. 247
HARVEY, DAVE 128
HARVEY, HOLGER H. .. 187
HARVEY, JOHN. 253
HARVEY, M. 8
HARVEY, MARK 149
HARVEY, ROSE 335
HARVEY, TOM 109
HARWOOD, TERRY 135
HASELTINE, SUSAN D. ... 31
HASENYAGER, ROBERT
.... 111
HASHAGEN, KEN . 141, 415
HASHIMOTO, ANDREW. 97
HASLETT, BILLYE 25
HASSANEIN, NEVA, Ph.D.
.... 285
HASSEL, HARRY S. 18
HASSELL, JOHN 183
HASSETT, JOHN 382
HASSLER, CURT 392
HATAKEYAMA, HISAKO 359
HATCH, CHARLES R. ... 369
HATCH, ELLIS 84
HATCH, WHITNEY 149, 335
HATCHER, BOB 107
HATCHER, RICHARD 95
HATHAWAY, MARTA 193
HATT, ROYD 281
HAUB, CARL 298
HAUGE, THOMAS M. ... 121
HAUGH, JOSEPH S. 114
HAUGHIAN, PHIL 225
HAUGHWOUT, MARK... 203
HAUGLAND, GARY 279
HAUN, LES 107
HAUPTMAN, MIKE 255
HAUREZ, CARRIE L. 351
HAUSEL, W. DAN 123
HAUSER, RON 253
HAUSRATH, ALAN 218
HAVERLAND, PAM 141
HAVERMAN, JAMES K., JR.
.... 75
HAVERSTOCK, GREG.. 126
HAVILAND, JIM 254
HAVLIN, JOHN L. 382
HAWES, BILL 238
HAWKES, JANET 147
HAWKEY, DAVID J. 345
HAWKINS, H. ROSS 217
HAWKINS, JOYCE 13
HAWKINS, RICHARD 42
HAWKINS, T. EVELYN .. 302
HAWKS, RICHARD 382
HAWLEY, CLIFF 87
HAWLEY, JOYCE 164
HAWLEY, KYLE 218
HAWLEY, SUSAN 263

HAWTHORNE, JOSETTA
.... 185
HAYAKAWA, MITSUTOSHI
.... 174
HAYASHI, DENNIS W. 19
HAYASHI, STUART 25
HAYDEN, ELIZABETH A. 33
HAYDEN, MIKE 151, 207
HAYDEN, WORTH 125
HAYES, HELEN 240
HAYES, IRENE 248
HAYES, LARK 324
HAYES, RANDY 302
HAYES, ROY 87
HAYES, SAMUEL E., JR.
.... 100
HAYES, TOM 248
HAYES, WILLIAM 56
HAYES, YVONNE 235
HAYNE, JAMES L. 329
HAYNES, JANE 287
HAYNES, JIM 107
HAYNING, JOHN E. 150
HAYWARD, WINCHELL 201
HAYWOOD, CARLTON 8
HAYWOOD, MARY JOY 162
HAZARD, NANCY 284
HAZELWOOD, SUSAN.. 158
HAZEN, DALE 308
HEALEY, BURKE 96
HEALEY, M. 393
HEALY, BRIAN 144
HEALY, JONATHAN 73
HEAPE, TOYE 107
HEAPS, CHIP 190
HEARN, J. L. 71
HEARN, SHELLEY 374
HEARNE, RAETTE 108
HEATH JR., RALPH T. .. 327
HEATH, HELEN B. 327
HEATH, RICHARD 109
HEATON, LOUIS, III. 68
HEATON, RAYMOND V. 111
HEATWOLE, CHARLES A.
.... 381
HEAVEY, GEORGE 33
HEBER, SHARON 54
HEBERT, GEORGES..... 326
HEBERT, MICHELE 40
HEBERT, PAUL D.N. 217
HECHINGER, DEBORAH S.
.... 359
HECKER, VINCE 300
HECKLY, SUSAN 230
HEDDEN, BILL 211
HEDGE, ROGER 220
HEDRICH, ANNE 271
HEEMSTRA, THEODORE
H. 130
HEFFERAN, COLIEN 15
HEFFERNAN, LAUREL . 364
HEGEMAN, INGEBORG 247
HEHR, JOHN 332
HEIDE, CHERYL 76
HEIDER, WILLIAM A. 260
HEIDORN, RANDY 62
HEIDT, GARY A. 363
HEIKEN, DOUG 290
HEIKES, DAVID 43
HEIL, GERALD 76
HEILIG, DAN 360
HEIMERICKS, GARY 80
HEIMERMANN, DALE 76
HEIN, LISA 232
HEINEKAMP, NEIL 155
HEINEMANN, GENE 270
HEINRICH, GEORGE 211
HEINS, DAVID C. 373
HEINZE-LACEY, BEVERLY
.... 269

HEISSEL, DAN 63
HEISTAD, ERLING 181
HEITSERBERG, JON 353
HELD, ANDY 306
HELFMAN, GENE S. 150
HELFRICH, LOUIS A. 116
HELFRICH, PHILIP 59
HELINSKI, RONALD R. . 350
HELL, DAVID 53
HELLEM, STEVEN B. 210
HELLER, VICTOR J. 54
HELLIKER, PAUL 45
HELLMAN, JOHAN 256
HELLMAN, RICHARD A. 336
HELLWIG, RAY 117
HELMER, WILLIAM 88
HELMS, JESSE 3, 6
HELMS, JOHN 321
HELSEL, ZANE R. 86
HELSLEY, CHARLES 59
HEMENWAY, JOHN 339
HEMMER, DENNIS 122
HEMMING, JIM 184
HEMOND, JOHN A. 244
HEMPEL, FRED J. 31
HENDEE, JOHN 230
HENDEE, JOHN C. 370
HENDERSON, BRIAN 23
HENDERSON, CLAY 201
HENDERSON, CLIFF ... 123
HENDERSON, JOAN 97
HENDERSON, K. R. 67
HENDERSON, KARLA .. 283
HENDERSON, PATRICK M.
.... 239
HENDERSON, SCOTT 42
HENDERSON, WILLIAM M.
.... 10
HENDREN, DIANE 61
HENDRICKS, CAROL ... 292
HENDRICKS, DONALD R.
.... 186
HENDRICKS, ELAINE G.
.... 186
HENDRICKS, SCOTT ... 208
HENERT, MARTIN M. ... 121
HENKE, SCOTT E. 354
HENKIN, DAVID 192
HENNE, PAUL W. 29
HENNEY, JANE 19
HENNINGER, A. R. 262
HENNINGS, RONALD ... 121
HENNIS, SUE 197
HENRY, ... 24
HENRY, GENE M. 189
HENRY, MARK 295
HENRY, ROBERT D. 51
HENRY, STEVE 87
HENSCHEL, KIRA 174
HENSEL, DAVE 62
HENSLER, RONALD 393
HENSLEY, DEMPSLY ... 391
HENSLEY, DOUG 67
HENSLEY, JOHN 32
HENTGES, ROBERT 80
HEPHNER, TRACY
    SEIDMAN 88
HERB, WILLIAM 25
HERBERT, CURTIS L., JR.
.... 19
HERBST, DAVID L. 62
HEREFORD, SCOTT 281
HERGLOTZ, KEVIN 46
HERLIHY, THOMAS R. 19
HERMAN, ALEXIS M. 20
HERMAN, KENNETH 267
HERMAN, LYNN 51
HERMAN, STEVEN A. 10
HERMANN, ELIZABETH
    DEAN 386

HERPEL, RACHAEL 213
HERR, CHRISTIAN R. ... 100
HERRERA, MARCAREO
.... 154
HERRGESELL, PERRY .. 47
HERRICK, THERESA A. 363
HERRICKS, ROSETTA M. 9
HERRING, HARTWELL. 212
HERRING, JENNIFER ... 348
HERSCHLER, MICHAEL 286
HERSHEY, DON 101
HERSHEY, ROGER W. . 317
HERTZ, ANNABELL 359
HERTZEL, ANTHONY ... 251
HERWIG, MARK 296
HERZBERG, MARK 278
HESLA, CHRIS 323
HESS, DAVID E. 101
HESS, GENE K. 187
HESS, RICHARD 100
HESS, THOMAS, JR. 352
HESS, TIM 111
HESSELINK, FRITZ 228
HESSION, JACK 312
HESTER, CAROL 94
HESTON, CHARLTON .. 264
HETTINGER, EDWARD 227
HEUMANN, JUDITH 18
HEWLETT, ELIZABETH .. 73
HEYMAN, IRA MICHAEL
.... 317
HHULL-SEIG, CAROLYN
.... 319
HIATT, KEMP 243
HIBBARD, DON 58
HIBBARD, JOHN E. 180
HICKEY, DAN 262
HICKLE, RODNEY 283
HICKOX, WINSTON H. 44
HICKS, ANNA 74
HICKS, BILLY G. 107
HICKS, JOHN 89
HICKS, RONALD J., C.A.
.... 188
HICKSON, JO 177
HIERONYMOUS, ALAN 225
HIGBY, SUE. 204, 339
HIGGINS, KENNETH F. 106
HIGGS, ERIC 318
HIGHSMITH, R. TOD. ... 356
HIGHT, ROBERT C. 46, 47, 397
HILBAID, MARION B. 260
HILDEBRAND, CINDY. . 232
HILDEBRAND, DEAN C. . 93
HILDEBRANDT, DON.... 356
HILDRETH, HORACE A.,
    JR. 233
HILDT, NATALIE 130
HILER, EDWARD A. 108
HILGENDORF, MARAN 181
HILL, AIMEE 155
HILL, BRIAN 294
HILL, CARLTON LEE 114
HILL, ISABEL 104
HILL, JAMES R., III 301
HILL, JOHN R. 63
HILL, LAWRENCE W. ... 319
HILL, MEREDITH L. 101
HILL, MURRAY 126
HILL, TESSA 240
HILL, THOMAS D. 108
HILL, THOMAS K. 107
HILL, WILLIAM 51
HILLARD, ANNE 15
HILLBERRY, GARY 32
HILLMAN, BOB 60
HILLMAN, CONRAD N. . 190
HILLS, DAVIE 312
HILLY, JAMES 325

STAFF NAME INDEX - H

HILTERBRAND, KELLEY 320
HILTON, J. RICHARD... 319
HILTON, JAREL 132
HILTON, KEN 342
HIMLAN, ED 247
HIMMELMAN, JO-ANNE 126
HINCHEY, DON 198
HINES, JAMES 73
HINESLEY, PHILLIP 38
HINEY, JIM 109
HINKLEY, BILL 54
HINMAN, KEN 260
HINSHAW, JEFFREY M.. 92
HINSON, CHARLES O., III 238
HINTON, KAREN 83
HIPPENSTEEL, PETER A. 63
HIRAI, LAWRENCE 25
HIRAIWA, GAISHI 211
HIRREL, SUZANNE SMITH 43, 154
HIRSCH, ROBERT M. 30
HIRSH, HEIDI 22
HIRSHFIELD, MICHAEL 172
HIRST, ERIC 328
HIRTH, DAVID H............ 390
HISEY, GLENN E............ 297
HITCH, KENNETH 96
HITCHCOCK, LOREN 42
HITCHINGHAM, RICHARD 249
HITZ, RUSSELL 356
HJERTAAS, DALE 275
HJERTAAS, PAULE 275
HLUCHY, MICHELE M.. 380
HOACHLANDER, SHAYNE 353
HOAGLAND, BRUCE 95, 416
HOAGLAND, JULIANNE 353
HOAGLAND, ROY . 152, 173
HOARE, JOHN 348
HOBBS, ALMA 15
HOBSON, CYNTHIA......... 47
HOBSON, DAVID C. 113
HOBSTETTER, PETE ... 223
HOCHHALTER, SCOTT.. 93
HOCHMAN, PATRICIA.. 181
HOCHMUTH, JAY C. 120
HOCHSTADT, JOHN W. 272
HOCK, WINAND K........... 102
HOCKER, JEAN W. 241
HOCOG, ESTANISLAO. 292
HOCUTT, CHARLES..... 375
HODANBOSI, ROBERT .. 94
HODDER, JAN................ 293
HODGDON, HARRY E. . 350
HODGE, JANICE D. 112
HODGES, JEFF 301
HODGES, JEFF L. 352
HODGES, JIM 104
HODGES, M. WAYNE 34
HODGES, MIKE 233
HODGES, THERESA 66
HODGSON, CHRIS 127
HODSDON, JOHN 277
HODSON, RONALD G. ... 92
HOECKER, JAMES 19
HOEDT, JEFF 94
HOEFER, PHIL 50
HOERNER, GAIA 174
HOESE, SCOTT 250
HOFER, DOUG 106
HOFF, DARREL.............. 231
HOFF, DENA 285
HOFF, FRED 13
HOFFBUHR, JACK W. .. 151
HOFFMAN, DOUGLAS MICHAEL.................. 351
HOFFMAN, HENRY 335
HOFFMAN, JOSEPH K..... 8
HOFFMAN, JUDIE 241
HOFFMAN, JULIE 342
HOFFMAN, NANCY 208
HOFFMAN, NINA 262
HOFFMAN, ROBERT C. 306
HOFFMAN, STEVEN M. 251
HOFMAN, ROBERT J....... 8
HOGAN, KATHLEEN 222
HOGG, JOHN T. 185
HOHENSEE, JEFF......... 330
HOHMAN, TOM 63
HOHMANN, STEPHEN.... 68
HOKIT, JIM 178
HOLAHAN, GARY M........ 34
HOLBEN, GREG 172
HOLBROOK, TODD 56
HOLDEN, NELDA 322
HOLDER, GLENN 127
HOLDERMAN, REED 335
HOLENSTEIN, JULIAN . 212
HOLFORD, MATT 333
HOLLABAUGH, PAUL ... 220
HOLLAND, BRUCE.......... 22
HOLLAND, CLAIRE 133, 134
HOLLAND, DAVID 29
HOLLAND, MATTHEW.. 296
HOLLAND, MAURICE J. 385
HOLLE, DEBORAH 329
HOLLENHORST, STEVEN 370
HOLLERN, MICHAEL ... 216
HOLLEY, AMY................. 30
HOLLEY, ROBERT D..... 326
HOLLIFIELD, JAMES..... 282
HOLLINGSWORTH, CAROL 14
HOLLIS, SUE 253
HOLLOWAY, THOMAS.. 181
HOLLUMS, DON 49, 399
HOLMAN, BILL 91
HOLMAN, BLAIR............ 344
HOLMER, STEVE 146
HOLMES, CHARLES A. 132
HOLMES, JERRY 243
HOLMES, JOHN R........... 45
HOLMES, MARK 289
HOLMES, MARTY 307
HOLMES, ROBERT 24
HOLMES, ROGER ... 76, 261
HOLMES, ROGER M..... 223
HOLMES, STEPHAN 339
HOLPERIN, JIM 331
HOLSINGER, SHAWN..... 24
HOLST, GLENDA........... 135
HOLSTON, SHARON SMITH 19
HOLT, DENNIS 38
HOLTHUIJZEN, ANTHONIE M.A. 351
HOLZ, BERNIE............... 123
HOMAN, THOMAS R..... 119
HOMANN, RICH.............. 50
HOMER, PEGGY 329
HOMULAS, PETER 35
HONICK, KENNARD...... 153
HONNOLD, DOUGLAS L. 192
HOOD, LAMARTING...... 385
HOOD, LAURA............... 186
HOOD, WAYNE J........... 137
HOOKS, CLEGG 53
HOOPER, BILL.............. 164
HOOPER, IRENE 312
HOOPER, JON................ 364
HOOT, LYNNE 246
HOOTEN, CHARLES R. 119
HOOTMAN, LARRY 122
HOOVEN, LYNN.............. 56
HOOVER, CRAIG.......... 330
HOPKINS, ELIZABETH.. 229
HOPKINS, LORAH 250
HOPKINS, SUZANNE B. 246
HOPPE, RICHARD T..... 352
HOPPER, GEORGE M.. 388
HOPPER, HILARY LAMBERT 145
HOPPER, STEVE 253
HOPPIE, ROBERT W....... 60
HOPPLE, WILLIAM H., III 174
HORAN, JAMES 117
HORIUCHI, CINDY 49
HORN, CHARLES .. 38, 324
HORN, CHARLES E....... 114
HORN, FLOYD P............. 15
HORN, THOMAS F......... 157
HORN, WILLIAM P......... 349
HORNBACK, JOHN E. 67
HORNER, WESLEY R... 162
HORRIGAN, JIM 312
HORRIGAN, LEO, M.H.S. 374
HORTON, ALISON 249
HORTON, DICK 264
HORTON, JESSE............ 25
HORTON, MAURICE........ 16
HORTON, P. M. 104
HORTON, PAUL.............. 82
HORTON, TERRY 154
HORVATH, BILL............. 257
HORWICH, ROB 179
HORZEPA, GEORGE...... 84
HOSENFELD, ROBERT W. 30
HOSHINO, MAKOTO 359
HOSKINS, DONALD M... 101
HOSKINS, SHERM......... 110
HOSKINS, ZACHARY 234
HOSKISSON, WAYNE... 338
HOTALING, A. CAROLINE 162
HOUCK, OLIVER A. 373
HOUGH-GOLDSTEIN, JUDITH A. 368
HOUGHLAND, PAUL, JR. 214
HOUGHTON, JOHN 157
HOUGLUM, LYLA............ 99
HOURCLE, LAURENT R. 368
HOUSER, ANDREW 127, 399
HOUSER, RON 134
HOUSKA, THOMAS E., II. 52
HOUSTON, EDWARD.... 390
HOUSTON, WILLIAM E. 238
HOVENCAMP, MARIAN. 381
HOVER, JEROLD............ 65
HOVORKA, DUANE 275
HOWARD, ALICE 31
HOWARD, BRUCE S. ... 310
HOWARD, CONNIE 146
HOWARD, DENNIS 96
HOWARD, MARILYN 59
HOWARD, PRESTON 91
HOWARD, RICHARD P.. 358
HOWARD, STEVE.......... 347
HOWARD, THEODORE E. 380
HOWARD, WILLIAM W. . 349
HOWE, HENRY F........... 179
HOWE, PAUL 340
HOWE, PAUL R............. 340
HOWE, RICHARD 335
HOWE, ROBERT W. 392
HOWE, SANDY 201
HOWELL, ARTHUR E., JR. 130
HOWELL, CALVIN 276
HOWELL, DAVID 301
HOWELL, DOROTHY 130
HOWELL, LYNN 14
HOWELL, RALPH 78
HOWELL, STEVE 272
HOWERTH, ELIZABETH 348
HOWERTON, LORRAINE 261
HOWEY, GARY 156
HOWMAN, KEITH 358
HOWREY, MYRA 242
HOYLE, JOHN C. 34
HOYLE, JOYCE 107
HOYT, JOHN A. 222
HOYT, ROBERT G. 71
HUBBARD, JAMES E. 50
HUBBARD, RICHARD 73
HUBBELL, STEPHEN P. 179
HUBER, ERIC 192
HUBER, MICHAEL......... 147
HUBER, PHIL 24
HUBERT, CRAIG 218
HUBERT, MARTIN A. ... 108
HUBERT, WAYNE A...... 122
HUCKABEE, MIKE 42
HUDKINS, CORDIE 119
HUDSON, CAMPBELL, III 181
HUDSON, JOYCE 161
HUDSON, LESLIE 204
HUDSON, MIKE 25
HUDSON, STEWART 236
HUEBLE, TOM 321
HUEBNER, E. 394
HUEBNER, ELAYNE 53
HUEBNER, MARTIN 201
HUELMAN, PATRICK 77
HUERTA, SERGIO 52
HUEY, KIM 237
HUFF, JANE 158
HUFFAKER, STEVE 60
HUFFAKER, WELLINGTON 135
HUFFMAN, ALAN 253
HUFFMAN, RANDY 119
HUFFMAN, RICK 321
HUFFORD, RONALD H. 329
HUGES, DANIEL C., JR. 187
HUGHES, CLAUDE 147
HUGHES, DEBBIE 278
HUGHES, GARY R. 75
HUGHES, JOHN A. 51
HUGHES, MARK 193
HUGHES, ROBERT M... 141
HUGHES, WALT 47
HUGO, NANCY 340
HUGOSON, GENE 76
HUISBAND, THOMAS P. 387
HULBERT, JAMES 190
HULL, DONALD A............ 97
HULL, HADLAI A............ 182
HULL, JAMES B............. 109
HULL, JANE DEE 40
HULL, KENT 342
HULSEY, BRETT 313
HULTIN, JERRY MACARTHUR 31
HUMPHREY, GILBERT W. 349
HUMPHREY, STEPHEN R. 318
HUMPHREYS, DAVID J. 148
HUMPHRIES, REBECCA 75
HUMPHRIES, WILLIAM C., JR. 156

HUMRICKHOUSE, SCOTT 121
HUNSAKER, J. E. 98
HUNST, MIKE 76
HUNT, DUTSON 88
HUNT, FRAN 346
HUNT, GARY 91
HUNT, HUGH 128
HUNT, JAMES B., JR. 91
HUNT, JANICE 335
HUNT, JOEL 249
HUNT, JOHN DIXON 385
HUNT, KAYE 322
HUNT, SUZELLE 152
HUNTER, ALEXANDER 166
HUNTER, BRUCE 389
HUNTER, DAVID B. 170
HUNTER, DICK................. 127
HUNTER, JIM.................... 263
HUNTER, LEON 15
HUNTER, NORMAN R. .. 394
HUNTER, RHONDA 124
HUNTER, RICHARD G. ... 54
HUNTER, TIM 23
HUNTER, TOM 7
HUNTINGTON, JENNIFER 153
HUNTINGTON, JIM 238
HUNTSMAN, GENE R. ... 146
HUNTZINGER, TOM 65
HUNYADI, BILL................ 307
HUPPERT, GEORGE 392
HURD, DAVID.................. 232
HURLEY, FREDERICK B., JR. 70
HURST, NATHAN 10
HURWICH, EVELYN M. 174
HURWITZ, JOSEPH 255
HUSE, BRIAN 264
HUSSAIN, MOHAMMED ZAKIR................................. 229
HUSSEY, SHARON WOODS 210
HUSSEY, STEPHANIE L. 352
HUSSMANN, WILLIAM H.73
HUST, GEORGE............... 333
HUTCHENS, THOMAS P. 187
HUTCHEON, RICHARD J. 17
HUTCHESON, DONALD W. 67
HUTCHINGS, JAMES..... 153
HUTCHINS, MICHAEL ... 151
HUTCHINS, SAMUEL ... 112
HUTCHINSON, ALAN.... 204
HUTCHISON, BUCK....... 178
HUTCHISON, FRED....... 152
HUTCHISON, LYNNE 152
HUTT, CARLY.................. 210
HUTTLINGER, RETTA .. 262
HUXMANN, JEFFERY M. 174
HYATT, LEEDRUE 278
HYDE, ARNOUT, JR. 119
HYGNSTROM, SCOTT E.82
HYLAND, JOSEPH M. ... 190

I

IBACH, GREG.................... 81
IFIE, TONY....................... 117
IFJU, GEZA 391
IMBERGAMO, BILL 258
IMBRECHT, CHARLES R. 47
IMLAY, MARC 247
IMLAY, MARK.................... 25
IMMERGUT, MEL M. 161
IMPALLOMENI, VICTORIA 303
INCERPI, ANGELO......... 111
INCH, TONY.................... 180
INGLE, DON.................... 249
INGMAN, DAN................ 117
INGRAHAM, RUTH ANN 220
INGRAM, DEWAYNE L..372
INGRAM, JULIETTE 262
INGRAM, TERRENCE N. 191
INMAN, PAM 107
INMAN, ROGER............... 54
INOUYE, DAVID............. 375
INOUYE, TED.................. 214
INTEMANN, LESLIE 184
INTINO, FRANK A........... 50
IOANNIDES, GERRY...... 94
IONNO, SANDRA 326
IRBY, LYNN R. 378
IRELAND, JOHN 163
IRELAND, KATE ... 327, 349
IRVIN, TOMMY................ 55
IRVIN, WILLIAM ROBERT 170
IRVING, MARTIN 126
IRWIN, ELISE R. 38
IRWIN, FRANCISCA 131
IRWIN, JOE R. 307
IRWIN, MARILYN 232
IRWIN, PAUL................... 223
IRWIN, PAUL G.217, 222, 359
ISAACSON, M. 393
ISELY, J. JEFFERY 104
ISENBERG, HENRY 203
ISLAM, ANWARUL......... 228
ISOM, NOELYN................ 82
ISON, JEANNE JAHNIGEN9
ISRAEL, JANE 321
ISRAEL, NELLIE 285
ISTOMA, ELENA 312
ITCHMONEY, ROBERT...85
ITURREGUI, MIGUEL.... 300
IURI, MARIA GRAZIA 228
IVANKO, JOHN 280
IVERSON, DAVE 204
IVERSON, PAUL J. 82
IVES, SUSAN 335
IVEY, OLIN M.................. 209
IWAMA, GEORGE K. 141
IZARD, JOHN, JR 209
IZMAILOV, V. 9

J

JABLOW, JUDY 10
JACANGELO, DOMINIC..91
JACK, JEFF..................... 373
JACK, MARY L................ 158
JACKSON BIRD, W. L. .. 93
JACKSON, BEN D. 56
JACKSON, CHARLES N. 319
JACKSON, JANET 201
JACKSON, JEFFERY J...56
JACKSON, JEROME A..156
JACKSON, JESSE L..... 302
JACKSON, JOHN J., III.. 182
JACKSON, KATHRYN J. .35
JACKSON, KEN 67
JACKSON, KRISTINA ... 202
JACKSON, LOIS 14
JACKSON, MARION T... 371
JACKSON, PATTI 340
JACKSON, R. MARK 352
JACKSON, SCOTT D......74
JACKSON, SHIRLEY ANN 34
JACKSON, SUSAN M......... 8
JACOBI, JOHN 108
JACOBS, CANDACE...... 117
JACOBS, LYNDA 201
JACOBS, MARK................ 77
JACOBS, ROBERT T. 16
JACOBSEN, DON 181
JACOBSON, JEFFERY S. 378
JACOBSON, K. N. 111
JACOBSON, MICHAEL F. 171
JACOBSON, RONALD D. 283
JACQUEZ, ALBERT S.....32
JACQUOT, RAYMOND G. 235
JAGNANDAN, SALLY 64
JAGNOW, DAVID 265
JAHN, LARRY A 370
JAHNKE, MARLENE 224
JAHNS-SOUTHWICK, BRENDA............................. 48
JAHRAUS, DALE............ 219
JAMES, CAROL 168
JAMES, FRANCES C. ... 146
JAMES, M. R. 297
JAMES-GRIFFIN, BRENDA 55
JAMISON, DAPHNE W. .339
JAMISON, KATHLEEN..... 51
JANECKA, RICK.............. 87
JANES, STEWART......... 385
JANEWAY, KATE 295
JANEWAY, KATHERINE 360
JANIK, PHIL 16
JANKLOW, WILLIAM J...106
JANN, BEATRICE 199
JANOWSKI, JOHN P...... 187
JANSEN, RUUD 228
JANSSEN, LEN 325
JANTUAH, F. A............... 198
JAQUET, NEIL................ 178
JARANOWSKI, MARTIN 156
JARRETT, JEFFREY D..101
JARVI, CHRIS.................. 264
JARVIS, R....................... 125
JAYEWARDENE, HIRAN 230
JAYNE, JERRY 218
JAYROE, JAYNE.............. 97
JEAN, DENYS 128
JEAN, YVES 167
JEANNERET, DOUG...... 349
JEANS, RICK.................. 288
JEFF, GLORIA J.............. 31
JEFFORDS, JAMES.......... 6
JEFFRIES, KEVIN 239
JELINSKI, DAVID 120
JENGO, JUDY.................. 85
JENKINS, CAROLYN JEFFERSON 242
JENKINS, JAMES H., JR. 68
JENKINS, NEAL 345
JENKINS, OLIVIA............ 38
JENKINS, RONALD S. .. 113
JENKINS, STEVE............ 38
JENKS, BRETT 303
JENNE, ALAN E. 353
JENNINGS, CECIL A....... 55
JENNINGS, KENT.......... 200
JENNINGS, TERRY 184
JENNINGS, WILLIAM R. 104
JENNY, J. PETER 296
JENSEN, ALLAN P........... 71
JENSEN, DEBORAH...... 272
JENSEN, DOUG............... 77
JENSEN, JIM.................. 254
JENSEN, JOHN 211
JENSEN, JOHN W.......... 362
JENSEN, MIA................. 236
JENSEN, SHARON......... 46
JEPPSON, PHIL 60
JERNIGAN, ALEX.......... 176
JESERNIG, JIM.............. 117
JESSE, DICK 105
JESSUP, WILLIAM 310
JEWETT, FREEBORN... 152
JEWETT, FREEBORN G., JR. 301
JEWETT, JOAN 30
JEWETT, MIKE 99
JEZOWSKI, TERRENCE W. 159
JOAQUIN, JOSEPH........ 228
JOB, CHRISTINE VAN HORN................................ 354
JOCK, KEN 325
JOHANNES, CLINT 275
JOHANNS, MIKE 81
JOHANSEN, PAUL 343
JOHANSEN, PAUL R. ... 119
JOHANSSON, RUSSELL 270
JOHN, CHACKO J............ 69
JOHNDROWN, WAYNE . 25
JOHNS, CAROLYN E. ... 381
JOHNS, DAVID 6, 347
JOHNS, KEITH 132
JOHNS, PAUL 303, 354, 397
JOHNSEN, ARTHUR M. 291
JOHNSEN, ANDREW W. 294
JOHNSON, BARBARA ... 234
JOHNSON, BERN.......... 198
JOHNSON, BERNARD.. 111
JOHNSON, BOB 28
JOHNSON, BRUCE 221
JOHNSON, BUSTER 328
JOHNSON, CARL 89
JOHNSON, CATHERINE SCALES 268
JOHNSON, CHARLES... 112
JOHNSON, CHARLES R. 391
JOHNSON, CHRISTINE M. 32
JOHNSON, DALE 379
JOHNSON, DAVID..... 6, 390
JOHNSON, DEREK 200
JOHNSON, DONNA....... 267
JOHNSON, EARL 82
JOHNSON, EILEEN MORGAN 267, 268, 269
JOHNSON, ELAINE77, 352, 431
JOHNSON, ERIC 116
JOHNSON, ERIC A.262, 269
JOHNSON, FREEMAN K.82
JOHNSON, GARY 86
JOHNSON, GEORGE E. 224
JOHNSON, GERALD....... 22
JOHNSON, HAROLD L. 199
JOHNSON, HOWARD ... 200
JOHNSON, HUEY D. 304
JOHNSON, JAMES E. ... 116
JOHNSON, JAMES R. ... 106
JOHNSON, JIM 356
JOHNSON, JODIE 210
JOHNSON, JUDITH......... 18
JOHNSON, JUDY 116
JOHNSON, K. ROBERT 331
JOHNSON, KENDALL ... 370
JOHNSON, KENNETH S. 96
JOHNSON, LADY BIRD 240
JOHNSON, LARRY.. 80, 337
JOHNSON, LAURA 247, 272

STAFF NAME INDEX - K

JOHNSON, LAURA ECKERT ... 116
JOHNSON, LEE ... 180
JOHNSON, LEONARD R. ... 369
JOHNSON, LESLIE ... 346
JOHNSON, LLORAN ... 307
JOHNSON, MARK ... 307
JOHNSON, MARSHA 210, 234
JOHNSON, MARTHA R. ... 38
JOHNSON, MICHAEL ... 363
JOHNSON, NOLTON ... 56
JOHNSON, PAM ... 295
JOHNSON, PAT ... 256, 308
JOHNSON, PATRICIA S. ... 107
JOHNSON, PAUL ... 303, 397
JOHNSON, PAUL W. ... 64
JOHNSON, PAULETTE ... 385
JOHNSON, PHYLLIS E. ... 15
JOHNSON, RALPH ... 199
JOHNSON, REX ... 272
JOHNSON, RICHARD ... 198
JOHNSON, RICHARD S. ... 190
JOHNSON, RICK ... 182, 218
JOHNSON, ROBERT J. ... 349
JOHNSON, ROBERT KARL ... 150
JOHNSON, ROGER ... 93
JOHNSON, ROSS ... 48
JOHNSON, RUSSELL ... 346
JOHNSON, SAM ... 3, 98, 272
JOHNSON, SHIRLEY ... 213
JOHNSON, STANLEY ... 225
JOHNSON, STANLEY S. ... 115
JOHNSON, STEVE ... 348
JOHNSON, TOM ... 341
JOHNSON, TRUDYE MORGAN ... 73
JOHNSON, TULLIE HOYLE ... 168
JOHNSON, TWIG ... 359
JOHNSON, VARRI ... 163
JOHNSON, VICTOR ... 242
JOHNSON, WALTER ... 264
JOHNSON, WARREN ... 28
JOHNSON, WENDY ... 214
JOHNSON, WES ... 334
JOHNSTAD, KRISTIN ... 361
JOHNSTON, JOHN ... 119
JOHNSTON, TRACY ... 306
JOHNSTON, WALLACE ... 328
JOLLIFFE, LANE ... 60
JOLLY, BILL ... 116, 341
JOLLY, WILLIAM C. ... 117
JONASSON, HARLEY ... 124
JONES, ALAN ... 328
JONES, ANDREW T. ... 376
JONES, BARRY ... 127
JONES, BOBBY ... 161
JONES, BRAD ... 100
JONES, BRENDA A. ... 261
JONES, CAROL ... 20
JONES, CHRISTA ... 220
JONES, CHRISTOPHER ... 94
JONES, CINDA ... 261
JONES, CLIFFORD L. ... 215
JONES, CLIVE G. ... 222
JONES, DAVID ... 91, 371
JONES, DENA ... 152
JONES, DONNA ... 292
JONES, DOUG ... 54, 190
JONES, GORD ... 124
JONES, GWILYM S. ... 375
JONES, JACK ... 378
JONES, JAMES ... 119
JONES, JANE ... 43
JONES, JEFF ... 195
JONES, JIM ... 84
JONES, JOHN PAUL, III ... 155
JONES, KEN ... 48
JONES, KENT ... 110
JONES, LLOYD ... 4, 126
JONES, LYDIA C. ... 217
JONES, MARSHALL ... 29
JONES, MIKE ... 327
JONES, PEG ... 282, 309
JONES, PETER ... 170
JONES, PHIL ... 241
JONES, PHYLLIS ... 200
JONES, PIERCE H. ... 54
JONES, RICHARD G. ... 237
JONES, RICHARD W. ... 123
JONES, ROBERT ... 24, 27
JONES, ROGER ... 355
JONES, SAMUEL ... 247
JONES, SANDRA ... 237
JONES, SHEILA ... 197
JONES, SHELDON R. ... 41
JONES, SONJA B. ... 18
JONES, STEPHEN B. ... 38
JONES, TODD ... 30
JONES, W. ALLEN ... 187
JONKEL, CHARLES ... 211
JONTZ, JIM ... 146
JOOSS, JUDY ... 355
JORDAN, CARL ... 237
JORDAN, DERRILL ... 27
JORDAN, EDWARD L. ... 34
JORDAN, JUDY ... 289
JORDAN, KEITH C. ... 128
JORDAN, ROBERT R. ... 52
JORDAN, SUSAN ... 243
JORGENSEN, ED ... 276
JORGENSEN, ERIC ... 192
JOSEPH, JIM ... 85
JOSIAH, TIMOTHY W. ... 32
JOSLIN, LOWELL ... 64
JOSLIN, PAUL ... 134
JOST, DANA N. ... 276
JOY, JAMES A., III ... 105
JUDD, H. LEE ... 205
JUDGE, NANCY ... 357
JUDYCKI, DENNIS C. ... 31
JUDZIEWICZ, EMMET J. ... 162
JULIAN, RICHARD ... 180
JULICH, TINA ... 289
JURIS, RONALD ... 118
JURZYKOWSKI, M. CHRISTINE ... 205
JUST, SALLY ... 100

K

KABISH, SALLY ... 312
KABRAJI, ABAN MARKER ... 229
KADERKA, SUSAN ... 268
KADUCK, JENNIFER ... 56
KAHN, BERND ... 369
KAHN, MOHAMED ... 52
KAHRS, ROBERT F. ... 13
KAIA, JOLOYCE ... 214
KAILING, ALEX F. ... 356
KAINER, KAREN ... 385
KAISER, JACK ... 234
KAISER, KIM ... 278
KAKABADSE, SRA YOLANDA N. ... 228
KAKABADSE, YOLANDA N. ... 228
KAKAKHEL, SHAFQAT ... 336
KAKFWI, STEPHEN ... 126
KALES, MATT ... 337
KALINOWSKI, LIZ ... 72
KAM, ALAN ... 59
KAM, WENDELL W.S. ... 58
KAMALPOUR, HAMID ... 22
KAMBESIS, PATRICIA ... 169
KAMENS, RICHARD ... 383
KAMERZEL, THOMAS J. ... 101, 284
KAMIENIECKI, SHELDON ... 366
KAMMEYER, FRANCINE ... 46
KAMP, DICK ... 162
KAMP, MARTY ... 289
KANAREK, HAROLD ... 71
KANDLE, JAY ... 277
KANE, ABDOULAYE ... 229
KANE, ANTHONY R. ... 31
KANE, ELYSE ... 116
KANE, PATRICIA ... 278
KANE, RICHARD ... 278
KANE, WILLIAM F. ... 34
KANIA, GARY ... 261
KAPLAN, LORI ... 62
KAPLAN-HENRY, TERRY ... 343
KAPPE, KARL ... 110
KAPPNER, AGUSTA ... 18
KAPUSCINSKI, ANNE 77, 377
KARAS, CHRISTINE ... 29
KARIAN, MICHAEL ... 377
KARIMI, HAMID ... 52
KARNES, ROSES MARIE ... 154
KARPAN, KATHERINE ... 28
KARPAN, KATHY ... 29
KARPINSKI, GENE ... 336
KARPOWICZ, ZBIGNIEW ... 229
KARR, BOB ... 378
KARR, CRAIG L. ... 120, 258
KARSON, JEFFREY A. ... 382
KARSTEN, ARLIN ... 244
KARWATOWSKI, CHESTER ... 333
KASABACH, HAIG ... 85
KASENOW, MICHAEL ... 376
KASHGARIAN, MICHAEL ... 181
KASHIWADA, STEPHEN L. ... 48
KASPRZAK, RICK A. ... 142
KASSEL, JOHN ... 111
KASTER, GARY ... 288
KASTL, MIKE ... 96
KATERERE, YEMI ... 229, 361
KATONA, STEVEN ... 373
KATSOUROS, MARY HOPE ... 214
KATTELMANN, RICK ... 343
KATULA, RAYMOND S. ... 281
KATZ, DANIEL ... 358
KATZ, DANIEL R. ... 302
KATZ, LAWRENCE S. ... 308
KATZ, STEVE ... 192
KAUFFMAN, JOHN T. ... 135
KAUFFMAN, REAH JANISE ... 359
KAUFMAN, GREGORY D. ... 293
KAUFMAN, IRA ... 242
KAUFMAN, NANCY ... 30
KAUFMANN, MICHAEL ... 146
KAUFMANN, MILTON M. ... 254
KAUL, N. G. ... 89
KAVALOK, TONY ... 307
KAVITS, PHILIP B. ... 267
KAWAMATSU, KIYOSHI ... 211
KAWAMURA, MITSUGU ... 359
KAYA, HARRY ... 365
KAYE, JORDAN ... 57
KAYS, JONATHAN ... 72
KEA, PHIL ... 55
KEANE, KATHLEEN M. ... 354
KEARNEY, STEVE ... 125
KEARSLEY, STEVEN ... 227
KEATHLEY, DANIEL E. ... 376
KEATING, FRANK ... 95
KEATING, JIM ... 218
KEATING, TIM ... 302
KEATON, JACK ... 223
KECK, ROB ... 267
KEEFER, DONALD ... 248
KEEGAN, DAWN R. ... 353
KEEGAN, JOHN ... 137
KEEL, RALPH M. ... 354
KEELS, VALERIE ... 250
KEENE, W. JAMES ... 282
KEENEY, DENNIS ... 232
KEESE, STEPHEN ... 298
KEIR, JAMES R. ... 355
KEIR, TED ... 101
KEIRY, BILL ... 106
KEISER, TERRY D. ... 287
KEITH, ALLAN R. ... 138
KEITH, BILL ... 114
KEITH, EDWARD O. ... 319
KEITH, ROBERT ... 212
KEITHLEY, C. A. ... 371
KELBER, MIM ... 357
KELIHER, PAT ... 176
KELLAR, BRYAN ... 42
KELLEHER, DANIEL L. ... 85
KELLER, BEA ... 149
KELLER, C. LAWRENCE ... 278
KELLER, CHARLES E. ... 220
KELLER, CRAIG ... 33
KELLER, J. TIMOTHY ... 371
KELLER, JANET ... 103
KELLER, JAY ... 361
KELLER, SCOTT ... 279
KELLER, SUE ... 40
KELLEY, CHARLES D. ... 38
KELLEY, ERIC DAMIAN ... 148
KELLEY, MIKE ... 94
KELLEY, PAT ... 92
KELLOGG, BOB ... 96
KELLOGG, CYNTHIA ... 278
KELLSEY, DONNA ... 128
KELLY, ALLAN L. ... 291
KELLY, CHARLES J., JR. ... 172
KELLY, EAMON A. ... 33
KELLY, J. MICHAEL ... 371
KELLY, JACK ... 87, 421
KELLY, JOHN ... 89
KELLY, JOHN J., JR. ... 17
KELLY, KATHERINE ... 61
KELLY, KATHY ... 48, 244
KELLY, KEITH ... 13
KELLY, NATHAN (... 87
KELLY, PADGETT, Ph.D. ... 387
KELLY, RAY ... 184
KELLY, RAYMOND W. ... 32
KELLY, RICHARD ... 340
KELLY, THOMAS E. ... 11
KELSCH, STEVEN ... 383
KELSCH, STEVEN W. ... 142
KELSCH, TOM ... 261
KELSEY, DARWIN ... 147
KELSEY, HARRY ... 279
KELSEY, HARVEY M., JR. ... 155
KEMPER, STEVE ... 82
KEMPTHORNE, DIRK ... 59
KENDALL, KATE ... 222
KENDROT, STEVE ... 186

STAFF NAME INDEX - K

KENISTON-LONGRIE, JOY 118
KENITZ, ALICE 275
KENNAMER, JAMES EARL, Ph.D. 267
KENNAY, JILL 270
KENNEDY, BILL 187
KENNEDY, DAVID K. 353
KENNEDY, DONNA 253
KENNEDY, EILEEN 15
KENNEDY, FRANCES H. 182
KENNEDY, JAMES C. 191
KENNEDY, JAMES H. 389
KENNEDY, JIM 126
KENNEDY, JODY 177
KENNEL, CHARLES F., Ph.D. 366
KENNELLY, JOHN J. 393
KENNINGTON, JOHN 288
KENNY, MICHAEL P. 44
KENRICH, JOHN 127
KENT, AL 278
KENT, FRED 191
KENT, ROBERT 90
KENT, SHERMAN T. 180
KEOUGH, DOROTHY 24
KEOUGH, JANET 320
KEPPY, KAROL 183
KERAMIDA, VASILIKI, JR. 9
KERN, CAROLE 232
KERN, PENNY 130
KERN, WILLIAM H. 54
KERNS, JUNIOR 25
KEROSKY, SUSAN 290
KERR, BOB 56
KERR, DOUG 299
KERR, LORALEE 76
KERR, PATSY 23
KERR, THOMAS J. 347
KERTON, ALLAN 249
KERTULLA, JAY 40
KESSEN, ANN 251
KESSLER, ED. 283
KESSLER, WINIFRED 393
KETCHAM, PAUL 159
KETCHESON, DOUG 37
KETCHUM, JUNE 289
KETTEL, BONNIE 395
KEULARTS, JOZEF 113
KEY, SANDRA 16
KEY, TOMMY 209
KEYSER, EMMETT 106
KHADR, NIRVANA 37
KHANNA, DAVINDER 263
KHARE, PRAD 342
KIBLER, MANDY 104
KIDD, CLAREN 96
KIDD, SUSAN 209, 266
KIDWELL, BIRTRUN, JR. 235
KIEFER, JOHN D. 67
KIERNAN, MICHAEL 7
KIESER, WALTER F. 361
KIKEL, DAVID A. 294
KILBOURNE, JAMES 20
KILEY, MICHAEL 62
KILGUSS, KATE 309
KILLIAN, H. STEVEN 43
KILLISHEK, MARTHA 356
KILPATRICK, BARBARA 172
KILROY, KEN 32
KIMBALL, GORDON 258
KIMBALL, JOHN 110, 344, 398
KIMBALL, KENNETH 153
KIMBLE, CHRISTY 288
KIMBLE, MELINDA L. 20, 21
KIME, P. L. 323
KIMMEL, J. TIMOTHY 281
KIMMEL, WILLIAM 385
KIMMETT, D. 36
KINCAID, DAN 344
KINCANNON, LINN 218
KINDERFATHER, KATHY 136
KINDINGER, PAUL 183
KINDLER, RANDY 329
KINDLER, ROGER A. 217
KINDRACHUK, ROBERT 188
KING, ALBERT D. 125
KING, ANGUS S., JR. 69
KING, BRIAN B. 153
KING, DIANA 214
KING, FREDERICK J. 161
KING, GERALD 44
KING, JAMES 175, 189
KING, JUSTIN W. 352
KING, KENNETH V., JR. 217
KING, MARYDE 155
KING, MATTHEW 36
KING, NICELMA J. 45
KING, PAUL 132
KING, PETER 3, 94
KING, ROBERT 25
KING, WARREN 338
KINGSLEY, ERIC W. 277
KINKAID, BILL 43
KINNEY, STEPHANIE 20
KINSCH, MICHELLE 342
KINSELLA, JOHN S. 13
KINSINGER, ANNE E. 30
KIRBY, SHANNON 81
KIRCHHOFF, RICHARD W. 258
KIRCHOFF, MATT 134
KIRK, JOHN 106
KIRKLAND, GORDON L., JR. 150
KIRKPATRICK, MARTHA 70
KIRN, DON J. 205
KIRSCH, EILEEN 184
KIRSCH, FRED 241
KIRSCH, KATYA 323
KIRSCH, PETER 150
KIRSCHENMANN, THOMAS R. 296
KIRSHNER, LYN 183
KIRTLEY, J. ROSS 97
KISEDA, JOHN 55
KISER, CLARK 306
KISIAH, BUTCH 283
KISNER, BRENDA 299
KISSINGER, WILL 80
KISSNER, ANDREW D. 234
KITCHENS, WILEY M. 52
KITTLE, JAKE 320
KITTS, JAMES R. 77
KITZHABER, JOHN A. 97
KIVIAT, ERIK 217
KIVIRIST, LISA 280
KLAASSEN, HAROLD E. 371
KLABUNDE, CHARLES 328
KLASE, BILL 122
KLATASKE, RON 158
KLEIN, HANK 132
KLEIN, MARY 177, 178, 415
KLEIN, RICK 158
KLEIN, WILLIAM J. 308
KLEINER, DONALD 70
KLEINTJES, PAULA 392
KLEISS, BARBARA 320
KLIMEK, JENNIFER 135
KLINE, LAWRENCE 265
KLING, JEANNE M. 235
KLINGER, PAMELA 25
KLINGHAMMER, ERICH 282
KLINGMAN, BRUCE 345
KLIPPENSTEIN, MURRAY 167
KLOCKE, ROBERT A. 147
KLOPFENSTEIN, NORM 14
KLOSE, ELIZA 221
KLUENDER, RICHARD 43
KNAPP, JILL 231
KNAPP, MALCOLM R. 33
KNAPP, MARY 32
KNAPP, WILLIAM 29
KNATTERUD, NEIL 93
KNECHT, LARRY 278
KNEIPP, SARA 163
KNELL, STEVEN F. 182
KNERR, ANTHONY D. 168
KNICKERBOCKER, DENNIS 250
KNIGHT, DAVID 170
KNIGHT, ELAINE 106
KNIGHT, JIM 81, 92
KNIGHTON, RAYMOND 16
KNIPLING, EDWARD 15
KNOBBE, EDWARD T. 384
KNOBLOCH, KEVIN 153
KNOCHE, LARRY 66
KNOLL, RALPH 70
KNOLL, RICHARD 251
KNOTT, JOHN 48
KNOTTS, DAVID M. 225
KNOTTS, HOWARD 344
KNOUF, KEN 25
KNOWLES, BOBBY 132
KNOWLES, CAROL 61
KNOWLES, TOMMY 109
KNOWLES, TONY 39
KNOX, JOHN A. 192
KNOX, ROBERT J. 10
KNOX, ROBIN F. 140
KNUFFKE, DARRELL 347
KNUTH, BARBARA 141, 381
KNUTSON, OWEN 250
KOBERSTEIN, INGRID 205
KOBRIGER, GERALD D. 350
KOCH, DON 64
KOCH, LOUISA 18
KOCH, MINDY 75
KOCH, STELLA 152
KOCHERT, MICHAEL N. 303
KOCHEVAR, RICHARD 87
KOCH-WESER, MARIETTA R. VON BIBERSTEIN 228
KOCIK, JOHN F. 144
KOCIOLEK, PATRICK 163
KOECHLIN, MANFRED 212
KOEHLER, BART 323
KOEHLER, MICKEY 221
KOEHLER, ROBERT P. 303
KOENEKE, MARY ALICE 200
KOENIG, ROBERT 220
KOENIG, STANLEY W. 248
KOENIG, WALTER 184
KOEPPEL, BONNIE SEVY 348
KOEPSEL, KIRK 313
KOERNER, BETTE 255
KOERTH, RICHARD 65
KOESTER, KEVIN 218
KOFMEL, PHYLLIS 286
KOFORD, ROLF R. 64
KOGON, D. 301
KOHLENBERG, A. MAX 159
KOHLER, CHRISTOPHER 140
KOHLER, CHRISTOPHER C. 370
KOHN, BARBARA 148
KOHN, STEPHEN M. 266
KOHRING, MARGARET A. 182
KOHRING, PEG 270
KOJIS, BARBARA 112, 113
KOK, C. K. 98
KOLB, C. HAVEN 270
KOLB, PETER 254
KOLBASH, RON 94
KOLBENSCHLAG, PETE 177
KOLL, LAURENCE F. 252
KONCELIK, JOSEPH 94
KONDO, ED 37
KONDRASHOVA, LILIA 304
KONIGSMARK, KEN 234
KONOP, DANE 18
KONSIS, KEN 218, 219
KOONTZ, DOROTHY 287
KOONTZ, FRED W., Ph.D. 350
KOOP, WAYNE C. 22
KOOSER, JAIME 46
KOPECKY, MARY JO 121
KOPF, VIRGIL E. 114
KOPP, RICK 372
KORBONITS, ROBERT 100
KORDEK, WALT 119
KORDELL, NORM 76
KORNEGAY, DOCK 283
KOROLERA, ALEXANDRA 193
KOSS, BILL 117
KOSS, CHRISTOPHER D. 235
KOSTAKOW-KAMPE, RITVA 7
KOSTMAYER, PETER H. 361
KOTCHMAN, LARRY 93, 258
KOTEFF, STEVE 184
KOTT, RUSSELL 277
KOUDA, MICHEL 228
KOUKOL, DAVID 275
KOVACS, WILLIAM 336
KOVALICK, WALTER W., JR. 11
KOVEN, ANNE 290
KOVEN, JOAN F. 246
KOWAL, DON 9
KOYL, GREG 124
KRAAIJVANGER, DANIELLE 304
KRAFT, PAUL 126
KRAMER, DAN 221
KRAMER, DONALD E. 40
KRAMER, JERRY 148
KRAMER, JOE 65, 261
KRAMER, JONATHAN 72
KRAMER, LARRY E. 190
KRAMER, R. J. F. 224
KRAMER, STUART 128
KRANTZBERG, JOAN 127
KRAPF, KRISTEN L., MS 304
KRASNY, MARIANNE E. 90
KRAUS, DOUGLAS L. 159
KRAUSE, TOM 265
KRAUTHAMER, JUDITH T. 246
KREAG, GLENN 77
KREAMER, DAVID 379
KREBS, WILLIAM A. 325
KREIDER, KALEE 213
KREIDER, KARIN 302
KREIL, RANDY 93
KREMENTZ, DAVID G. 42
KREMER, JOHN 218, 236
KREMER, ROXANNE 227
KREMSER, ULRICH 7

STAFF NAME INDEX - L

KRESEK, RAY 149
KRESS, EMILY 63
KRESS, STEPHEN 259
KRICHER, JOHN C. 355
KRIEGER, WAYNE 98
KRILL, ROBERT M. 121
KRIPOWITCZ, ROBERT S.
.... 18
KRIS, MARY ELLEN 89
KRISHNA, CHANDRU,
  MBA, CPA 304
KRIV, LAURA 130
KROENIG, NANCY 206
KROENING, NANCY 201
KROHN, WILLIAM B. 70, 374
KROLL, JAMES C. 388
KROLL, WENDI 14
KRONBERG, SCOTT 107
KRONEMAN, LOREN 357
KRONRAD, GARY D. 388
KRONSBERG, JONATHAN
.... 189
KROP, LINDA 196
KROPF, MARTHA 163
KROSHUS, JAMES 309
KRUCKENBERG, LARRY
.... 123, 344
KRUEGER, CHARLES C.
.... 381
KRUEGER, CHUCK 15
KRUEGER, WILLIAM 76, 384
KRUG, KELLY 46
KRUIDENIER, BILL 227
KRULISCH, LEE 311
KRULL, JOHN N. 376
KRUMPERMAN, CHRIS 180
KRUPNICK, ALAN 304
KRUPOVAGE, JOHN 23
KRUPP, FRED 196
KRUSE, KARL 311
KRUSE, KIPP C. 370
KRUZAN, JOHN C. 190
KRUZANSKY, CHARLES
.... 195
KRYZUDA, AURIE 304
KUEHL, S. A. 390
KUEHN, ROBERT R. 373
KUESTER, ED 54
KUHLMANN, MICHAEL W.
.... 57
KUHN, ROGER 82
KUHNS, MIKE 111
KULETZ, KATHY 293
KULHAVY, DAVID 388
KULHAVY, DAVID L. 388
KULIK, BRANDON H. 141
KULLBERG, JOHN F. 318
KUMABE, ELIZABETH 59
KUMMEL, JOHN C. 39
KUNKEL, PETER 180
KUNKEL, TOM 89
KUNKLE, DAN R. 349
KURTH, JIM 29
KURTZ, JAMES A. 121
KURTZ, SANDI 328
KURTZMAN, SCOTT 295
KUSHNERIUK, ROBERT
.... 143
KUTTEL, MIKE 116
KUWABARA, JEFF 59
KUZILA, MARK S. 81
KUZVART, MILOS 37
KWETZ, BARBARA 73
KWON, HYE YEONG 171
KYANKA, GEORGE H. .. 382
KYLER, DAVID 176

L

LA VINE, KRISTEN P. 352
LÄÄNE, AIN 7
LaBARR, MARK 161
LABEDZ, TOM 275
LABIE, SYLVIA 53
LABONDE, JERRY 156
LABORDE, SARA 116
LABOSKY, PETER 385
LABRECQUE, JEAN 200
LACAVE, GERALDINE .. 199
LACK, JOE PAUL, JR. ... 278
LACKEY, JEANINE 352
LACKEY, JOANNA 87
LACROIX, CAROLE ANN
.... 343
LACY, GARY 263
LACY, JAMES 239
LaFAYETTE, RUBY 275
LAFLAMME, BRIAN 22
LAFOLLETE, SHARRON E.,
  PH.D. 370
LAFRAMBOISE, ROY 93
LAFRANCHI, TIM 48
LAFRENIERE, NORMAND
.... 37
LaGRASSA, CARI ANN . 130
LAHMANN, ENRIQUE ... 229
LAHSHER, CARL W. 21
LAI, CHUM 228
LAIRD, JIMMY 78
LAIST, DAVID W. 8
LAITE, MURRAY 294
LAKE, BARRY 107, 328
LALLY, MIKE 145
LALO, JULIE 345
LAM, JULIA 261
LAMAIR, MIKE 232
LAMB, EUGENE 257
LAMB, G. WILLIAM 28
LAMB, GEORGE R. 165, 236
LAMB, ROBERT L. 27
LAMBERSON, TOM 81
LAMBERT, DONALD 247
LAMBERT, WILLIAM 78
LAMBERT, WILLIAM R. .. 56
LAMBERTSON, RONALD E.
.... 30
LaMEE, BILL 212
LAMONT, GIL 152
LAMSON, DOT 245
LAMSON, SUSAN 265
LANCE, ALAN G. 59
LANCE, LINDA 10
LANCERO, ROSALIE A. . 57
LANCTOT, RANDY P. 244
LAND, EDWARD J., JR.. 264
LANDAU, MATTHEW 380
LANDEN, LAURA 195
LANDERS, RICHARD 253
LANDHERR, LARRY 77
LANDIS, WAYNE G. 391
LANDRENEAU, DWIGHT 69
LANDRUM, NEY C. 258
LANE, JOE 41
LANE, MARGARET 277
LANE, PETER 221
LANE, S. R. 98
LANG, CHUCK 290
LANG, MAC 225
LANGE, ROBERT 30
LANGE, TED 285
LANGFORD, DAVID K. .. 329
LANGFORD, LAWTON .. 327
LANGFORD, LYNDA 129
LANGLOIS, C. 36
LANGSTAFF, MAXIM 130
LANING, BRENT 65

LANPHEAR, KATHLEEN
.... 103
LANT, CHRISTOPHER .. 151
LANTAGNE, DOUG 112
LANZA, GUY R. 375
LANZA, LAURA 194
LaPAZ, LOURDES 226
LAPERRIERE,
  JACQUELINE D. 39
LAPHAM, BURKS 179
LAPIERRE, WAYNE R., JR.
.... 265
LAPOINT, TOM 389
LAPOINTE, BRIAN 303
LAPOINTE, GEORGE 69, 71
LAPPIN, BERT 346
LAPPIN, DAWN Y. 346
LAREAU, JANE 321
LARKINS, JOHN T. ... 33, 34
LARMER, JEFF 151
LaROCK, RICHARD 87
LAROSE, LOUIS 231
LARSEN, MIKE 323
LARSON, BRETT 356
LARSON, GARY E. 12
LARSON, L. KEVILLE ... 204
LARSON, LOREN .. 149, 262
LARSON, LYNN 41
LARSON, PETER 77
LARSON, ROBERT P. ... 296
LARSON, STAN 284
LaRUE, ED 188
LASANE, RODOLPHE .. 301
LASH, JONATHAN 358
LASHER, DOUGLAS N. 189
LASKIN, SARAH 10
LASMANIS, RAY 117
LASSILA, KATHRIN 271
LASSOIE, JAMES P. 90, 381
LATTIMER, DICK 154
LATTIS, RICHARD 151, 348
LAUGHLIN, CHARLES W.
.... 15
LAUGHLIN, KEITH 10
LAUGHLIN, SUSAN 45
LAUN, H. CHARLES 162
LAURIN, NICHOLAS 167
LAUSTALOT, TOM 164
LAUTMAN, KAY 136
LAVERTY, KENT 218
LAVERTY, LYLE 17
LAVIN, JOHNNY 154
LAVKULICH, L. M. 393
LAWAETZ, HANS 339
LAWALL, LINA ANN 191
LAWHERN, TIM 225
LAWING, JACQUIE 20
LAWLEY, ROBERT 61
LAWLOR, TIMOTHY 364
LAWRENCE, JEFF 189
LAWRENCE, LOUISE 72
LAWRENCE, ROBERT S.,
  M.D. 374
LAWS, BRENT 190
LAWSON, JAY 123
LAWSON, MARVIN A. ... 113
LAWSON, SHIRLEY 262
LAWTHERS, MARTY 213
LAX-EDISON, DONNA . 191
LAXTON, WILLIAM 10
LAYER, MARILYN W. 339
LAYZER, JAMES B. 107
LAZENBY, WILLIAM R. ... 56
LEA, GEORGE D. 300
LEACH, DAN 220
LEACH, EDWIN F., II 361
LEACH, FRANKLIN R. .. 288
LEACH, JIM 2, 96
LEACH, LARRY 248
LEADER, RICHARD 270

LEAHY, P. PATRICK 30
LEAMAN, BRUCE M. 8
LEAPE, JAMES P. 359
LEAPER, ERIC 263
LEAPHART, MALCOLM 334
LEARNER, HOWARD A. 198
LEARY, BILL 10
LEARY, JOHN 342
LEASTER, EARNEST C.,
  JR. 20
LEAVERS, DOUG 292
LEAVITT, DALE F. 74
LEAVITT, MARCY 87
LEAVITT, MIKE 110
LEAVITT, PETER 395
LEBARRON, SANDY 89
LEBLANC, TIM 165
LeBOUBON, D. 125
LeCAVALIER, JOHN 236
LECHLIDER, GEORGE . 246
LECHNER, LARRY 129
LECKIE, FRED D. 115
LECOUNT, ALBERT 383
LEDBETTER, BROWNIE
.... 357
LEDDY, LINDA E. 246
LEDGERWOD, RAY 257
LEDGERWOOD, RAY 97
LeDOUX, AL 66
LEE, AMY FREEMAN ... 217
LEE, CHARLES 201, 352
LEE, CHARLES D. 66
LEE, DOROTHY 321
LEE, JIM 288
LEE, MERCEDES 259
LEE, NELSON 335
LEECH, MICHAEL 225
LEEK, NANCY McINNIS 126
LEEMAN, WAYNE 125
LEES, MARY ELLEN 248
LEETE, JEANETTE 251
LEFEBVRE, RICHARD ... 88
LEFF, DAVID K. 50
LeGATE, SHARI 357
LEGG, MICHAEL 388
LEGGETT, DONNA 267
LEHMANN, PAM 138
LEHMBERG, VERNE 200
LEHOLM, ARLEN G. 75
LEIB, JONATHAN 260
LEIGHTON, F. A. 166
LEIMAN, SARA 291
LEIN, GREGORY M. 141
LEIN, M. ROSS 148
LEINBACH, PHIL 343
LEINEN, JOHN, JR. 252
LEINER-MALANGA, SALLY
.... 205
LEITHOLF, KURT 100
LEITMAN, STEVE 202
LeJEUNE, CYRIL 68
LEKENS, RICHARD 63
LEKWA, STEVE 63
LeMASTER, DENNIS ... 296
LEMASTER, DENNIS C. 371
LeMAY, BILL 86
LEMCHE, E. 9
LEMKE, DAVID 329
LEMKE, DEAN 64
LEMMERMAN, JAMES . 251
LEMMERT, BRUCE A. .. 354
LEMMON, CAROL 180
LEMON, JOHN R. 30
LEMONS, PEGGY 253
LEMUS, JUDY, Ph.D. 45
LENAHAN, TIM 95
LENHART, CYNTHIA 138
LENHART, CYNTHIA R. 215
LENNON, GEORGE D. ... 16
LENZINI, PAUL A. 223

STAFF NAME INDEX - M

LEONARD, CHRIS 22
LEONARD, DOROTHY L. 72
LEONARD, NANCY 99
LEONARD, STEPHEN... 198
LEONARD, TOM............ 343
LEONI, KIRK 159
LEOPOLD, BRUCE D.... 378
LEOPOLD, ESTELLA B. 135
LEPINE, BEATRICE 126
LEPO, JOE EUGENE, Ph.D. 369
LEPRIEUR, GERRY 126
LeQUIRE, ROGER W. 92
LERNER, JOEL A. 73
LERUP, LARS 388
LESCHNER, BECKY 76
LESESNE, JOAB M. 105
LESINO, ROBERT C. 30
LESLIE, DAVID M., JR.95, 384
LESLIE, GRETCHEN..... 100
LESSER, CHARLES A. .. 51
LETELLIER, SYLVIE ... 37
LEUPOLD, JAMES C. 30
LEUTHOLD, PAUL 356
LeVAKE, BARBARA 48
LeVASSEUR, DOUG 280
LEVIN, ARNOLD E. 34
LEVINE, GREG............. 330
LEVINE, MANNY 200
LEVINE, MEGAN LESSER 91
LEVITT, JOSEPH A. 19
LEVITT, MICHAEL......... 225
LEVKOVITZ, THEA....... 342
LEVY, CHERI................ 171
LEVY, RON 24
LEWIN, JULIE 207
LEWIS, A. 393
LEWIS, ANN 152
LEWIS, CEDRICK.......... 339
LEWIS, CYNDI 342
LEWIS, DARRELL L. 26
LEWIS, DAVID 309
LEWIS, DONALD........... 366
LEWIS, GEORGE W. 56
LEWIS, JAMES 33
LEWIS, JEFF 77, 88
LEWIS, JIM 53
LEWIS, KATE 73
LEWIS, LARRY S. 208
LEWIS, LESLIE 194
LEWIS, PETER G. 145
LEWIS, ROBERT............. 16
LEWIS, STEVE 332
LEWIS, STUART............. 94
LEWIS, SYLVIA 148
LEWIS, W. BRUCE 189
LEWIS, WILLIAM M., JR. 150
LI, HIRAM W. 97
LI, SHIYOU 388
LIBERTY, DAVID 7
LIBONATI, MARGARET, M.D. 349
LIBOUS-BAILEY, LYNN 252
LICHTMAN, PAMELA ... 236
LICK, ROLAND 199
LIDHOLM, ELAINE J. 113
LIEB, MARILYN M. 241
LIEBERMAN, DAVID A. 226
LIEBERMAN, IRENE 14
LIEBERMAN, JAMES 34
LIEBOW, PAUL 271
LIECHTI, PAUL M. 65
LIECHTY, KAREN 254
LIECHTY, THORN 254
LIEDEL, CHRISTOPHER A. 262
LIEDTKE, CLIFF 98

LIEGEL, KONRAD 341
LIEPMANN, SUZANNA.. 338
LIFFMANN, MICHAEL M. 69
LIFT, JIM 193
LIGHTFUSS, DALE........ 356
LIGON, DAVID 96
LIKENS, GENE E. 222
LILES, F. GRAHAM, JR... 56
LILIEN, JACK 377
LILLARD, DAVID 145
LILLEBO, TIM 290
LILLEY, CHARLES......... 291
LIME, DAVE W. 377
LIMING, ROBERT G. 104
LIMTIACO, DAVID T. 57
LINAM, LEE ANN 329
LINAM, LEE ANN JOHNSON 354
LINCICOME, KAY 298
LINCK, MADELEINE 334
LIND, POLLYANNA 285
LINDAHL, DEBORAH ... 178
LINDAHL, LASSE.......... 374
LINDBERGH, KRISTINA 172
LINDBERGH, REEVE 172
LINDBLAD, ERICK 309
LINDEKUGEL, BUCK.... 323
LINDER, DON 288
LINDER, MICHAEL 81
LINDER, SANDRA 163
LINDGREN, CORY J...... 352
LINDGREN, RICHARD .. 166
LINDHEIM, LEONARD C. 32
LINDSEY, S. MARK 32
LINDSEY, SUE 345
LINDSTRAND, LEN, JR. 165
LINDZEY, FRED G......... 122
LINE, LES..................... 335
LINEBAUGH, JIM 319
LINEHAN, JOHN J. 34
LINGLE, GARY R........... 281
LINGLEBACH, JENEPHER 338
LINK, PHILIP S................ 18
LINKHART, DAVID......... 288
LINKOUS, FRANK A. 115
LINTNER, MARLI 159
LINTON, GORDON J. 32
LINZEY, ALICIA V.......... 150
LIPKIS, ANDY 330
LIPPE, PAMELA 191
LIPPHARDT, GEORGIA .. 48
LIPPOLD, BOB.............. 158
LIPTON, DOUG............... 72
LISA, GWEN 22
LISS, CATHY................. 152
LISS, LAUREN A............. 73
LITTLE, DARRYL............ 44
LITTLE, EDWARD T. 163
LITTLE, IRENE 34
LITTLER, CHRIS 389
LIVERETT, JAMES 63
LIVERETT, JIM............... 63
LIVERMORE, MICHAEL 279
LIVESAY, DAKOTA........ 307
LIVINGSTON, GIL 339
LIVINGSTON, WILLIAM. 374
LLEWELLYN, SIMON 36
LLEWELLYZ, JANET....... 53
LLEWELYN, MICHAEL... 98
LLOYD, ALAN C.............. 44
LLOYD, HERB............... 239
LLOYD, JAMES W. 172
LLOYD-JONES, DONALD 145
LLOYD-O'CONNOR, SHARON 242
LOCHMANN, STEVE....... 44
LOCKARD, FRANK R. ... 190
LOCKE, GARY 116

LOCKE, HARVEY........... 347
LOCKE, PAUL 374
LOCKETT, PETER J. 124
LOCKWOOD, DAN......... 283
LOCKWOOD, JEFFREY 302
LOCKWOOD, MAGGIE.. 331
LOCKYER, CHRISTINA .199
LOEB, MICHAEL 317
LOEHR, CHARLES 73
LOEHRLEIN, MYRNA ... 241
LOESCH, MARTIN 342
LOEWEN, JAMES 24
LOFTIN, CYNTHIA S....... 70
LOFTIN, KELLY 43
LOGAN, EDWARD W. 32
LOGAN, ROBERT W....... 67
LOGGINS, TOMMY 56
LOHAUS, PAUL H. 34
LOHNES, ROBIN C. 145
LOHRER, FRED 153
LOISELLE, BETTE 224
LOKEN, STEVE............. 171
LOKKESMOE, KENT....... 76
LOMENZO, SUE............ 347
LONG, EILEEN 392
LONG, FRANKLIN, JR .. 294
LONG, J. ROBERT 255
LONG, JACK................... 93
LONG, JAMES 207
LONG, MICHAEL B. 49
LONG, MIKE C. 53
LONG, NANCY 40
LONG, STEPHEN.......... 339
LONGEST, HENRY L., II..11
LONGINI, ROSE 207
LONGO, LILIANA 36
LONG-THOMPSON, JILL.12
LOOCK, HARRY VAN ... 202
LOPEZ, AURTHER ANDREW..................... 32
LOPEZ, DONALD T......... 88
LOPEZ, GLENN............. 382
LOPEZZO, THOMAS...... 331
LORENZ, JEROME 259
LORENZ, JOYCE 309
LORRAIN, JANICE 292
LOSCUTOFF, WILLIAM V. 45
LOSORDO, THOMAS M. .92
LOTZE, JOERG-HENNER 217
LOUCKS, WILLIAM L. 65
LOUI, RAE M. 58
LOUIS, RACHEL J......... 376
LOUKO, KEN 332
LOUNDS, JOHN 272
LOUYS, ROBERT............ 78
LOVAGLIO, RONALD B...70
LOVE, DAVID W. 86
LOVE, DUNCAN 199
LOVE, JANE 86
LOVE, KATHRYN S......... 79
LOVE, RHODA 270
LOVELADY, GREGORY W. 116
LOVELAND, DAVID....... 226
LOVELESS, DAVID 66
LOVELL, JOHN 244
LOVELL, STEWART........ 52
LOVETT, GARY M......... 222
LOW, ERIC 245
LOWE, WILLIAM R........ 230
LOWENSTEIN, MARCO.392
LOWEY, JACQUELINE... 29
LOWNES, PHIL 114
LOWREY, JEFFIFER 276
LOWREY, KATHY 246
LOWRY, EDWIN.............. 45
LUBER, GAYE 240
LUCAS, CLINTON 343

LUCAS, DON 290
LUCAS, HAROLD 19
LUCAS, STEVEN 62
LUCAS, TERRI 24
LUCCHESI, JOHN C...... 369
LUCE, DAVID................ 137
LUCE, RAY 56
LUCERO, JESSYCA...... 143
LUDDER, DAVID 242
LUDKE, J. LARRY 31
LUDWIG, DAN............... 275
LUDWIG, DANEIL R. 269
LUDWIG, JOHN 190
LUECKENHOFF, WILLIAM F. 79
LUESHEN, WILLETTA... 221
LUFT, LEROY D. 59
LUFTIG, STEPHEN D..... 11
LUGAR, RICHARD 6
LUHIKULA, G. 123
LUKAS, DEBBIE 204
LUKASCYK, JOSEPH... 191
LUKASIK, LYNDA 212
LUKENS, RONALD R. 7
LUKENS, SCOTT........... 159
LUKOWSKI, PAUL 24
LUM, CALVIN W.S. 58
LUND, LANNY 45
LUND, TY 123, 399
LUNDBERG, JAN 204
LUNDIN, CLIFFORD R.. 277
LUNDY, JAMES 251
LUNNEY, ELIZABETH... 342
LUPARDUS, APRIL 133
LUPKES, ALICIA N. 351
LUSE, KEITH 6
LUSK, VIRGINIA 133
LUSTIGMAN, BONNIE K. 380
LUTTRELL, ALLEN......... 68
LUTZ, CHARLES G. 69
LUTZ, JUDY.................. 208
LUVEN, DAVID VAN 84
LYLES, ETTA 71
LYMAN, ROBERT M...... 123
LYMN, NADINE............. 194
LYNCH, GEORGE 241
LYNCH, KATHY 164
LYNCH, KENNETH.......... 89
LYNCH, LARRY 340
LYNCH, LORETTA 46
LYNCH, ROBERT L. 46
LYNCH, SEAN P............ 158
LYNE, RANDY 145
LYNN, FRANCES 383
LYON, DAVID 232
LYON, DR. PAUL CHANDLER, TIMOTHY F. 370
LYON, JONATHAN 179
LYON, TIMOTHY F.370, 371
LYONS, CATHY 156
LYONS, CHARLES 373
LYONS, JAMES 12
LYONS, JOHANNA........ 312
LYONS, MIKE 307
LYTLE, TOM 307

M

MAAS, RICHARD P. 383
MABE, DAVID 61
MacARTOR, JUNE 187
MacAULAY, DON........... 129
MacAULAY, ED............. 126
MACAULAY, STEVE 48
MacCALLUM, WAYNE F. 73
MACCANNELL, DEAN... 365
MacCASKEY, MICHAEL 262

STAFF NAME INDEX - M

MacCOLL, KIM, JR. 291
MACDERMOTT, FRANCES
.... 193
MACDONALD, BILL 233
MacDONALD, CAROL 28
MACDONALD, CHARLES
.... 249
MacDONALD, JIM 365
MacDONALD, JULIE 46
MacDONALD, LARRY ... 244
MacDONALD, LAURIE .. 186
MacDONALD, WILLIAM 139
MacDOUGALL, GERALD
.... 128
MacDUFF, BARBARA ... 299
MACE, ARNETT C., JR. 369
MACFARLANE, DAVID . 125
MACFARLANE, LEWIS . 227
MACGREGOR, BARB .. 232
MACGREGOR, FORREST
.... 139
MacGREGOR, MOLLY .. 306
MACHEK, RICHARD 53
MACHLIS, GARY 369
MACHOL, BEN 57
MacINTYRE, DONALD D. 81
MacINTYRE, JAMES 330
MacIVER, DONALD 247
MACK, WAYNE 105
MacKENZIE, A. 36
MACKLEY, JAMES 13
MacLAUCHLAN, DONALD
E. 223
MACLEAN, DAVID A. ... 394
MacLEAN, JIM 127
MacPHEE, NANCY 55
MacRAVEY, RICHARD D.
.... 178
MACRORY, BOB 38
MACY, JIM 80
MACY, SYDNEY S. 183
MADAN, ARUN 312
MADDEN, ERIN 290
MADDEN, KEVIN P. 19
MADDEN, MARY 19
MADDEN, MURDAUGH 359
MADDEN, ROY 31
MADDEN, WILLIAM B. .. 109
MADDOCK, LEESA 317
MADDOX, F. ALEX, JR . 349
MADDOX, LORI 344
MADDOX, TERRY 212
MADDY, DEBORAH 99
MADDY, JAMES D. 263
MADEWELL, TERRY 23
MADIGAN, PATRICIA 94
MADISON, ELIZABETH M.
.... 182
MADRID, TITO 87
MADRONE, ROSE 152
MADSEN, CARL R. 354
MADY, JAMES 252
MAGGIORE, PETER 87
MAGIN, DEBBIE 108
MAGNUSSEN, STEPHEN 28
MAGUIRE, MEG 310
MAHADEVAN, KUMAR . 255
MAHAYNI, RIAD G. 371
MAHER, CONNIE 152
MAHER, JAMES V. 386
MAHER, RON 189
MAHFOOD, STEPHEN M.
.... 80
MAHLER, ROY 154
MAHON, JIM 212
MAHONEY, RONALD L . 60
MAHONEY, S. 125
MAHOOD, ROBERT K. . 321
MAIER, ANDREW 343

MAINELLA, FRAN 53, 54
MAJERES, JOHN D. 322
MAJKUT, STEPHEN 103
MAJOR, MARLA 205
MAJOT, JULIETTE 227
MAK, KING 23
MAKAREVICH, PAUL, JR.
.... 190
MAKEMSON, JEFF L. .. 350
MAKKONEN, HANNU ... 382
MAKRIS, JAMES L. 11
MALCOLM, ANN 47
MALCOLMSON, PATRICIA
E. 127
MALDONADO, WALTER 337
MALECHEK, JOHN 390
MALECKI, RICHARD A. ... 88
MALER, TRACIE 200
MALHADAS, ZIOLE Z. . 395
MALICK, BUCK 9
MALLECK, KATE 269
MALLET, JERRY 60, 397
MALLETT, ROBERT L. ... 17
MALLEY, ANNE MARIE. 164
MALLISON, PETE 53, 54
MALLON, TIM 202
MALLORY, BILL 157
MALLOW, JAMES 72
MALLOW, JIM 258
MALLOY, KATHLENN ... 158
MALLOY, TIMON 191
MALM, RICHARD L 340
MALMBERG, PAUL 117
MALMQUIST, A. K. 288
MALMSHEIMER, MARY
BETH 279
MALONE, THOMAS C.150,
375
MALONE, WILLIAM 55
MALONEY, PATIE 198
MALONEY, RICK 96
MALOUF, ROBERT E. 99
MALSAWMA, ZUALI 298
MALSCH, MARTIN G. 34
MALTBY, EDWARD 228
MALUIA, PHILO F. 40
MAMANE, M. M. 229
MANACKE, NANCY 94
MANDELL, STACEY 145
MANES, ROB 65
MANFREDO, MICHAEL 367
MANICH, DAVID ROZ 62
MANION, ANDREA 317
MANKIN, CHARLES J. 96
MANLEY, DONALD J. ... 190
MANN MACDONALD, JEAN
.... 206
MANN, DAVE 341
MANN, DEBORA 252
MANNAUSA, LEONARD 240
MANNER, MARK 195
MANNING, AL 233
MANNING, BRENT 61
MANNING, ED. 254
MANNING, G. BRENT 223,
397
MANNING, GLORIA 16
MANNING, HARVEY 234
MANNING, ROBERT E. . 390
MANNO, JACK 212
MANSFIELD, TERRY 47
MANSIUS, DON 70
MANSON, CONNIE 117
MANSPEAKER, BARBARA
.... 137
MANTELL, MICHAEL A.. 46
MANTHEY, REBECCA .. 173
MANTLER, FRAN 260
MANTON, LINDA 45
MANTRAS, CARLOS 300

MANUEL, HILDA 27
MANUEL, HILDA A. 28
MANUS, ANDREW T. 51,
223, 397
MANZ, BILL 95
MARACCHINI, JERRY 87,
344, 398
MARCACCIO, MELANIE 103
MARCOUX, RON 307
MARCUM, LARRY 107
MARCUM, TERRY 307
MARCUS, ANDREW 284
MARCUS, FELICIA A. 11
MARCUS, NANCY H. 55
MARDON, RUSSELL 54
MAREK, KRISTINA S. 97
MARET, JOSEPH 43
MARGOLIS, KEN 306
MARGRAF, F. JOSEPH ... 39
MARHEINE, BRUCE 190
MARINA, MARTY 328
MARINO, JIM 248
MARINO, MICHAEL 135
MARINOSKE, STAN. 129
MARKARIAN, MICHAEL 207
MARKEE, W. D. 98
MARKEN, WILLIAM R. .. 242
MARKER, NANCY 51
MARKHAM, DANIEL 263
MARKS, ELLIOT 272
MARKS, KATHLEEN 97
MARKS, MARTHA A., Ph.D.
.... 304
MARLETT, PATRICIA ... 158
MAROON, JOSEPH 173
MARQUARD, ROBERT.. 216
MARQUEZ, ANGEL B. 57
MARQUIS, MICHAEL 12
MARR, KATHRYN 72
MARRERO, BRENDA
ECHEVARRIA 103
MARROCCO, FREDERICK
A. 101
MARS, ADRIENNE 359
MARS, VICTORIA B. 350
MARS, VIRGINIA C. 350
MARSH, KENNETH B. ... 277
MARSH, LANGDON 98
MARSH, MINA 44
MARSHALL, GREGORY A.
.... 85
MARSHALL, JOHN 327
MARSHALL, KENNETH .325
MARSHALL, MICHAEL .110
MARSHALL, S. A. 394
MARSHALL, TOM 201
MARSTON, RICHARD A.
.... 155
MARTEL, ANDRE 128
MARTEL, GARY F. 114
MARTENS, CHRISTOPHER
.... 383
MARTENS, LAUREN 177
MARTENS, TOM ... 225, 256
MARTI, MONTE 340
MARTIAN, THOMAS T. ... 34
MARTIN, ARTHUR 240
MARTIN, BRUCE 80
MARTIN, CHIP 301
MARTIN, GALE 79, 252
MARTIN, JACK W. 19
MARTIN, JAMES 324
MARTIN, JAMES D. 38
MARTIN, JERRY 45
MARTIN, JOHN 25
MARTIN, JOHN K. 170
MARTIN, JOHN Q. 33
MARTIN, JR, W. TOM 264
MARTIN, KEITH W. 289
MARTIN, RAY 295

MARTIN, ROSS 110
MARTIN, STEPHANIE ... 339
MARTIN, STEVE 231
MARTIN, THOMAS 148, 213
MARTIN, THOMAS D. ... 191
MARTIN, THOMAS E. 80
MARTIN, TOM D. 191
MARTIN, VANCE G. 230
MARTIN, VICKI 382
MARTIN, WILLIAM 372
MARTINEAU, DANIEL .. 166
MARTINELLI, DEBRA K.121
MARTINEZ, ARTHUR C.186
MARTINEZ, CAMERON 269
MARTINEZ, ELUID L. 27, 28
MARTINEZ, FRANK 154
MARTINEZ, NEFTALI
GARCIA 172
MARTINEZ, RICARDO 32
MARTINEZ, TOBY ... 86, 258
MARTINEZ, WILDA 15
MARTINKO, ED 372
MARTINKO, EDWARD 65
MARTINSON, KAHLER .159
MARTOGLIO, MEGAN B.
.... 353
MARVINNEY, ROBERT.. 70
MARXER, DALE 254
MARYNOWSKI, SUSAN 168
MASAKI, CARL T. 58
MASICA, SUE 29
MASON, CHRIS 284
MASON, LAWRENCE N.183
MASON, TIMOTHY A. ... 186
MASONIS, ROB 149
MASSEY, JOSEPH G. .. 377
MASSEY, WILLIAM L. 19
MASSICOT, PAUL 72
MASSMAN, CAROLE 81
MASSO, TOM 76
MASSUCCI, STEFANIE .. 90
MAST, GARY 257
MASTENBROOK, BRIAN G.
.... 352
MASTERS, A. 125
MASTERS, RONALD 96
MASTERS, SANDY 262, 410
MASTERSON, MARK 151
MATA, ERIC 37
MATAAC, CELSO 331
MATEO, NICOLAS 37
MATHENY, CHARLES ... 240
MATHER, CHARLES M. 288
MATHER, JOHN R. 145
MATHER, MARTHA 375
MATHER, MARTHA E. 74
MATHER, RICHARD P... 101
MATHER, SANDRA 260
MATHERNE, CHARLES. 68
MATHESON, MARY PAT
.... 136
MATHEWS, BOB 65
MATHEWS, KATE 186
MATHEWS, LAURIE 49
MATHEWS-AMOS, AMY 246
MATHIAS, WARREN 100
MATHIS, BILL 370
MATHIS, DONALD 368
MATHIS, MAXINE 257
MATHIS, RANDALL 43
MATHIS, SUZANNE 264
MATHUR, BHARAT 61
MATLACK, GLENN 378
MATLOCK, JULIA 143
MATOWANYIKA, JOSEPH
Z. 361
MATSUI, CONNIE L. 210
MATSUO, PAUL T. 58
MATSUURA, RENEE 110
MATTERN, VICKI 136

Staff Name Index

549

STAFF NAME INDEX - M

MATTESON, SUMNER . 356
MATTHEW, EARL B. 267
MATTHEWS, DOUG 126
MATTHEWS, GEORGE C. 225
MATTHEWS, GEORGE G. 349
MATTHEWS, MICHAEL J. 353
MATTHEWS, ROBIN . 391
MATTHEWSON, CHARLES 41
MATTICE, JACK S. 90
MATTISON, ANDREA ... 243
MATTISON, CLYDE 243
MATTISON, JIM 124
MATTSON, LESLIE 236
MATUSZEWSKI, MARK .. 68
MATYAS, JAIME BERMAN 267
MATZ, MIKE 324, 338
MAUERMANN, SUE 117
MAUGHAN, O. EUGENE41, 363
MAUGHAN, RALPH 218
MAULSON, TOM 7
MAURER, GLENN E. 101
MAURER, JAMIE 157
MAURER, RICK 67
MAURO, FLO 147
MAURO, FLORENCE147, 297
MAUTZ, WILLIAM 84
MAVNEY, STEVE 328
MAXFIELD, LONNIE 204
MAXINO, MIKHAIL, ESQ. 395
MAXWELL, BILL 256
MAXWELL, COLIN 167
MAXWELL, FRANK 276
MAY, CAROL ANN 259
MAY, DALE 51
MAY, DALE W. 51
MAY, ELIZABETH 313
MAY, HENRY 76
MAY, JEANINE 14
MAY, JOHN D. 120
MAY, MICHAEL 188
MAYBANK, BLAKE 138
MAYER, ERIC 216
MAYER, MIKE 221
MAYEUX, L. J. 189, 191
MAYFIELD, PAUL 154
MAYNARD, C. CHARLES 53
MAYNARD, CAROLINE P. 168
MAYNES, FRANK E. 10
MAZAMBANI, DAVID 161
MAZGAJ, BOB 190
MAZIK, PATRICIA 119
MAZIK, ROBERT A., SR. 335
MAZMANIAN, DANIEL A. 377
MAZUMDER, ASIT 150
MAZUR, DOUG 129
McADAM, STEVE 48
McAFEE, ROBERT 154
McALLISTER, DON E. ... 286
McATEER, J. DAVITT 20
MCBRIDE, GREGORY B. 32
McBURNEY, MARY 335
MCCABE, GREG 186
MCCABE, JOHN J. 145
MCCABE, RICHARD E. .. 349
McCAIN, JOHN 1, 6
McCALL, JERRY C. 17
McCALL, VIRGINIA 201
McCALLEY, DAVID V. .. 231
McCANDLESS, GARY ... 156
McCARDLE, EUGENE... 165
McCARREN, DAVID 52
McCARTER, KATHERINE S. 194
McCARTHY, JOHN 218
McCARTHY, KELCY 356
McCARTHY, LAURA 204
McCARTHY, PATRICIA 209
McCARTY, COLLEEN.... 210
McCARTY, GENE 109
McCARTY, JEANNE 236
McCASLIN, GARY 88
McCLAIN, RUSS 156
McCLAREN, MITCHEL . 363
McCLELLAN, SARAH 40
McCLELLAND, STEVEN W. 120
McCLELLAND, WILLIAM .92
McCLINTOCK, KENNON 218
McCLOSKEY, J. MICHAEL 250
McCLOY, TOM 85
McCLURE, BETH 104
McCOLLOUGH, MARK .. 352
McCOLLUM, JERRY 210
MCCOMB, WILLIAM C... 375
McCONKEY, PAM 117
MCCONNAUGHAY, KELLY 370
McCONNELL, CORDREE 75
McCORD, M. BRAD 352
MCCORMICK, COURTENAY 201
McCORMICK, DALE 171
McCORMICK, STEVE ... 273
McCOWAN, ROD 18
McCOWN, JOHN 313
MCCOY, SANDY 164
McCRACKEN, JAMES ... 24
McCRAE, JOHN 335
McCRANIE, ANN 300
McCRAY, KEVIN 262
McCREA, EDWARD J. ... 280
McCUE, CATHRYN 324
McCULLOUGH, BRIAN. 189
MCCULLOUGH, F. ALBERT, III 196
MCCULLOUGH, FRED.. 163
MCCULLOUGH, KAREN 154
McCULLY, PATRICK 227
McCURDY, KEVIN 24
McCURDY, MARY 263
McCUTCHEON, GLORIA L. 121
McCYNSKI, PAUL 270
McDANIEL, CARL N. 381
McDANIEL, CAROL 280
McDANNOLD, DORI 133
McDERMOTT, JAMES F. 33
McDEVITT, WAYNE 91
McDONALD, DAVID 276
McDONALD, JOHN 290
McDONALD, JOHN E. .. 353
McDONALD, JULIE 361
McDONALD, MARY V. ... 148
McDONALD, MOIRA 261
McDONALD, NORRIS ... 169
McDONALD, ROBERT B. 53
McDONALD, SANDRA F. 216
McDOUGALL, DANIEL 36
McDOUGLE, JANICE 16
McDOWELL, JUDITH E. .. 74
McDOWELL, ROBERT .. 223
McDOWELL, ROBERT L. 85
MCDOWELL, SUZY 149
McDOWELL, WILLIAM .. 380
McELWAINE, ANDREW S. 294
MCEUEN, ARCHIE......... 209
McEVOY, THOM J 112
McFADDEN, JACK 127
McFALL, DON 62
McFARLAND, ROBERT J. 43
MCFATE, R. BRUCE...... 295
MCGARLAND, ALBERT M. 11
MCGARRAHAN, MARY BETH 317
MCGAUGHEY, JAMES ..370
McGAUGHEY, LARRY ... 310
McGEHEE, ROSS 79
McGEORGE, LESLIE 85
McGHEE, STEVE 301
MCGILL, WILLIAM 64
MCGINN, JOSEPH.......... 74
McGINNES, MARC 196
McGINNIS, JIM 41
MCGLAUFLIN, KATHY... 185
McGLENN, JOHN 342
McGLENN, RONNI 235
McGLYNN, DIANE 293
MCGONIGLE, JAMES V. 326
MCGOVERN, JOE 232
MCGOVERN, MICHAEL... 14
McGOWAN, KEVIN 184
McGOWAN, R. MOKE... 104
McGRADY, CHARLES .. 312
MCGRANE, PAT 14
MCGRATH, CHRIS 353
McGRATH, DAVID B. 301
McGRATH, M. 125
MCGREAL, SHIRLEY 226
McGREGOR, BONNIE A. .31
McGREGOR, GREGOR I. 247
McGUIGAN, DAVE 106
McGUIRE, A. DAVID 39
McGUIRE, ROBERT 24
McGUIRE, STEVE 254
McGUIRE, TERRY W. 45
McGUIRE, WALTER 210
MCGURRIN, JOSEPH ... 331
McHENRY, THOMAS J. P. 350
McHUGH, JOHN......... 3, 127
McHUGH, MARTIN J. 85
McHUGH, MARY-MARGARET 136
MCINERNEY, JAN 254
McINNIS, MARTHA 199
MCINTOSH, ALAN 390
MCINTOSH, ALAN W. ... 390
MCINTOSH, HENRY P., IV 132
MCINTOSH, PATRICIA ..209
McINTOSH, WINSOME 186, 241
McINTYRE, GARY. 219, 270
McINTYRE, JIM 129
McINTYRE, ROBERT W. 334
MCKAY, CATHY 355
MCKAY, KAREN 257
McKAY, TIM 284
McKEAG, MICHAEL 270
McKEATING, GERALD ... 36
McKEE, DES 127
McKEE, KATHLEEN DRISCOLL 207
MCKEE, KATHY 232
McKEE, LARRY 96
McKEEL, DALE 311
McKENNA, MIKE 93
McKENNEY, DENNIS D. 325
McKEON, JOHN 89
McKEOWN, W. B. 348
McKIBBEN, CAREY 220
MCKIM, ROBERT 272
MCKINLEY, BERTHA ... 164
MCKINLEY, CRAIG R. 92
McKINNEY, DAVID 107
McKINNEY, KIM 345
McKINNEY, LARRY 109
McKNELLY, PHIL 91
McKNIGHT, BETTY 147
MCLAMB, SAM 151
MCLANDRESS, ROBERT 164
MCLAREN, BRIAN 248
MCLARN 166
MCLAUD, LARRY 218
McLAUGHLIN, WAYNE. 117
MCLAVEY, ROBERT G. ... 49
MCLEAD, MARY 20
MCLEAN, BOB 64
MCLEAN, J. 393
MCLEAN, ROBERT 348
McLEAN, WALLACE 111
McLELLAN, ANNE 37
MCLELLAN, BRUCE 222
MCLELLAN, JIM 252
McLEMORE, JULIA 78
MCLENAGHAN, THERESA 166
MCLENNAN, DAN 139
MCLEOD, CHARLES..... 242
MCLEOD, DAVID 92
MCLEOD, JAMES 321
McLEOD, RICHARD 83
McLOSKEY, JEAN C. 37
MCMAHON, EDWARD T. 182
MCMAHON, JIM 211
MCMAHON, KIMBERLY A. 207
MCMAHON, THOMAS E. 143
MCMANUS, BRIAN.......... 81
MCMANUS, ROGER E. ... 170
McMULLEN, BRAD 301
McMULLIN, STEVE L. ... 144
McMURRAY, DENNIS 62
MCMURRAY, JOHN 176
MCNAGNY, CAROLYN . 130
MCNAMARA, CAROLE J. 259
McNAMARA, DANIEL G., JR. 182
MCNAMARA, ED 290
MCNAMARA, TIMOTHY... 25
McNANEY, RICK 12
MCNAUGHT, SCOTT 376
MCNAUGHTEN, STEVE 235
MCNEEL, JOSEPH 392
McNEELY, JEFFREY A. 228
MCNEIL, EDWARD 131
MCNEILLY, KATHLEEN 168
McNICHOL, LAURA 257
McNICHOLL, MARTIN K. 163
McNULTY, TIM 289
MCNULTY-HUFFMAN, DAN 351
MCNUSSEN, JOHN 299
MCOUAT, MARC 135
MCPEAKE, REBECCA STOUT 43
McPHERSON, RONALD D. 17
McQUEEN, MIKE 182
McQUILKIN, GEOFFREY 254
MCQUILLAN, RICHARD 225
MCQUINN, MARY ANN ... 14
McSHANE, JOAN 265
MCSHANE, LISA 166

STAFF NAME INDEX - M

McSHARRY, JOSEPH... 270
McSWEENEY, KEVIN..... 392
McTAVISH, BLAIR 124
McTEER, WILLIAM S. ... 105
McVAY, LAURA 232
McVETY, PAM 53
MCWHITE, RICK 22
MCWILLIAMS, RICHARD H. 142
MEACHAM, STEVE 118
MEAD, ROBERT 117
MEADE, GLADYS........... 175
MEADE, MARION 235
MEADOWS, WILLIAM H., III 346
MEARS, DAVID 117
MECH, L. DAVID............ 230
MECHLER, JOHN 307
MECOM, DOUG 39
MEDEMA, DAVID B. 308
MEDFORD, MARK O....... 35
MEDINA, KOL 325
MEDWID, WALTER M. ... 230
MEEHAN, PAT.................. 47
MEEK, LANCE 289
MEEK, ROYCE 289
MEFFE, GARY 318
MEHAN, G. TRACY 75
MEHLHAFF, LARRY...... 313
MEHMEL, GRETCHEN .. 352
MEIER, DAVID J............. 120
MEIKLE, DOUGLAS B... 384
MEIKLEJOHN, DOUGLAS 279
MEIKLEJOHN, JAMES .. 276
MEILLEUR, BRIEN A..... 171
MEINEN, BOB.................. 98
Melcher, Duane.............. 293
MELCHER, STEVE 147
MELDRUM, VINCE 213
MELIUS, THOMAS O. 29
MELLGREN, TIM 171
MELLON, DIANNE 160
MELLON, S. PROSSER 307
MELLOTT, JOHN............. 97
MELSIN, JOHN 319
MELTON, MICHAEL R. ... 97
MELVILLE, W. KENDALL, Ph.D. 366
MENDES, VALERIE 214
MENDEZ, KENNETH..... 331
MENEDEZ, BIANCA 298
MENG, C. H. 394
MENGAK, KATHY 391
MENGAK, MICHAEL 391
MENGEL, DAVID B. 372
MENKE, ROBERT 87
MENSINGER, JOANNE. 233
MENZEL, BRUCE W.259, 371
MERAL, GERALD........... 297
MERCER, DR. LINDA...... 71
MERCER, MALCOLM.... 228
MERCHANT, HENRY 368
MERCHANT, JAMES A. 371
MEREDITH, DENISE 28
MERKER, BJORN 224
MERLINI, LAURAINE 210
MERRELL, WILLIAM J. . 214
MERRIAM, ANNE 247
MERRIAM, DAN............. 237
MERRIMAN, TIM 257
MERRIMIAN, ALEX 305
MERRITT, CLIFTON....... 151
MERRITT, JOYCE S...... 137
MERRITT, REGNA 290
MERSKY, RONALD L.... 386
MERTENS, TOM............. 242
MESCHIEVITZ, JESSIE ... 9
MESLOW, E. CHARLES 350

MESNER, NANCY 111
MESS, WALTER L.......... 113
MESSER, SUSAN 298
MESSERLE, KERRY L. . 102
MESSICS, DAVE 307
MESSINGER, LUKE E. . 186
MESSMER, TERRY A. .. 111
METCALF, MARY 312
METCALFE, ED 335
METHIER, RON 56
METHOD, TIMOTHY 62
METTENBRINK, ROGER 235
METTER, JEFF 247
METZ, LORRAINE 124
METZGER, ED............... 137
METZGER, KATHERINE276
MEYER, BILL 91
MEYER, CATHY 197
MEYER, CHRIS.............. 279
MEYER, FRED 263
MEYER, GEORGE E.120, 223, 399
MEYER, GERALD F......... 19
MEYER, GORDY 251
MEYER, JEFF 145
MEYER, JOSEPH S....... 393
MEYER, STEVEN R....... 118
MEYERS, LEE................. 55
MEYERS, ROGER 25
MEYRELES, KAREN 47
MEZAINIS, VALDIS......... 16
MIANO, MICHAEL P. 119
MICHAEL, ED................ 212
MICHAELS, ARTHUR J. 101
MICHAELS, GAIL........... 324
MICHAELS, KEITH 43
MICHEL, MARK............. 153
MICHEL, SHARON L. ... 121
MICHELI, RON 122
MICHLIN, LEE 45
MICKA, RICHARD G..... 240
MIDDAUGH, DANIEL...... 40
MIDDAUGH, JIM 290
MIDDLETON, FREDERICK S., III 324
MIELKE, ART 284
MIES, ROB 291
MIGET, RUSSELL.......... 109
MIGHETTO, LISA........... 149
MIGLARESE, JOHN V. .. 105
MIHALO, MARK 309
MIKICS, DENISE.............. 85
MIKOL, GERALD 89
MILA, BOGDAN 221
MILANESE, SYLVIA......... 20
MILANO, STEVE 238
MILBURN, CINDY 225
MILBURN, PHILIP 330
MILES, BOB 223
MILES, DENNY 290
MILES, JOHN 87
MILES, JOHN C. 391
MILHOAN, JAMES L. 34
MILIUS, PAULINE H. 20
MILLARD, KEN............... 207
MILLER, A. WILLIAM, II. 262
MILLER, ALLAN 385
MILLER, ALLEN H. 121
MILLER, AMY................. 234
MILLER, BARBARA 180
MILLER, BEN 354
MILLER, BETH............... 355
MILLER, BETHANY 116
MILLER, BILL 209
MILLER, BRIAN.......... 21, 62
MILLER, BRIAN K. 63
MILLER, BRUCE J. 59
MILLER, C.W.................. 177
MILLER, CAROLYN 14

MILLER, CHARLIE 210
MILLER, CHRIS.............. 340
MILLER, CHRISTOPHER G. 296
MILLER, CLAIRE............ 289
MILLER, CRAIG 47, 186
MILLER, DAMIEN........... 307
MILLER, DAVID..... 176, 219
MILLER, DAVID E. 119
MILLER, DAVID R. 51
MILLER, DEBORAH....... 197
MILLER, DENNIS J. 173
MILLER, DORTHY P. 176
MILLER, EDWIN 238
MILLER, EDWIN L. 384
MILLER, ERICA A., DVM 269
MILLER, GERALD 343
MILLER, GLENN ... 103, 379
MILLER, GORDON........... 37
MILLER, HENRY 19
MILLER, HUBERT J......... 34
MILLER, JACQUELIN N... 58
MILLER, JAMES E. . 16, 350
MILLER, JANE................ 220
MILLER, JERRY 62, 220
MILLER, JOHN 25
MILLER, KARIN E. 247
MILLER, KITTY............... 277
MILLER, LUTHER T. 353
MILLER, MARC 299
MILLER, MARION G....... 365
MILLER, MARVIN........... 178
MILLER, MELISSA 164
MILLER, MIKE 65
MILLER, PAMELA K. 184
MILLER, PAUL 335
MILLER, PAUL F., JR..... 359
MILLER, RANDALL.......... 78
MILLER, ROBERT. 227, 393
MILLER, S. FRANCES..... 63
MILLER, SARAH 166
MILLER, STEPHAN 263
MILLER, STEVEN W...... 120
MILLER, TODD...... 176, 282
MILLER, WATKINS W. ... 379
MILLER, WILLIAM R., III 328
MILLING, MARCUS E. ... 145
MILLION, JOHN.............. 131
MILLS, ANN 149
MILLS, BOB 202
MILLS, EDWARD L. 381
MILLS, ROBERT H.......... 69
MILLS, THOMAS J. 16
MILLS, W. L., JR............. 371
MILLS, WAYNE A........... 172
MILMORE, DOLOLRES .182
MILNER, KELSEY 379
MILTON, JOHN P............ 330
MIMS, ROBERT D.......... 189
MIMS, SUSAN 38
MINAYA, THERESA 233
MINCEY, JOHN 212
MINCHAK, MARTHA J. .. 352
MINER, EDNA 236
MINER, KIRK W. 236
MINER, TOM 181
MINGES, DAVID A. 72
MINOR, MARIE F. 340
MINTON, DWIGHT.......... 212
MINTON, R. VERNON...... 38
MIOFF, STEPHANIE 294
MIRAGLIA, FRANK 34
MIRANDA, L. E................. 78
MIRANDE, CLAIRE 224
MIRELSON, ROBERT N. .26
MISHKIN, STEPHEN R. .132
MISSELDINE, CAROL K. 249
MISTER, HAGNER R. 71

MITCHELL, ANDREW ... 193
MITCHELL, ANNE . 167, 226
MITCHELL, BRAD 73
MITCHELL, CHARLES265, 328
MITCHELL, DENNIS...... 132
MITCHELL, DON R........ 154
MITCHELL, FRANK S..... 84
MITCHELL, FRED........... 76
MITCHELL, GARY R...... 66
MITCHELL, JOHN HANSON 247
MITCHELL, KAREN 101
MITCHELL, LARRY .13, 261
MITCHELL, MICHAEL S.. 38
MITCHELL, PETER 124
MITCHELL, RALPH 23
MITCHELL, RICK 53
MITCHELL, ROBERT 211
MITCHELL, ROBERT C. 102
MITCHELL, ROBIN 202
MITCHELL, STACY 14
MITCHELL, VASTINE.... 282
MITCHELSON, WILLIAM D. 260
MITSCH, WILLIAM......... 320
MITTEN, SUE 128
MITTERMEIER, RUSSELL 183
MITTON, LINDA R. 157
MITTON-WALKER, CYNTHIA J.A. 144
MITZEL, DAVID 331
MIX, TERRY 289
MIXSON, ANDREW 92
MIZUNO, FRANCES........ 48
MLECOCH, COLLEEN 76
MOATS, L. R. 189
MOBERLY, STANLEY A. 267
MOBLEY, JULIA PECK ... 43
MOBLEY, MIKE 107
MOCK, GEORGE B. 156
MODEL, ALLEN J. 350
MODISETTE, CHRISTOPHER 324
MOE, RICHARD.............. 266
MOEHL, THOMAS 220
MOEHLE, CARM 332
MOEHLE, MARK 288
MOEN, SHARON 77
MOFFAT, ALLEN 96
MOFFITT, CHRISTINE M. 140
MOFFITT, DONNA........... 91
MOFFITT, PETE 321
MOFFOT, JANE-KERIN 158
MOHLER, LOWELL 190
MOLINARES, ALEXIS ... 184
MOLITORIS, JOLENE M. 32
MOLL, GARY 145
MOLL, RUSSELL 75
MOLL, RUSSELL A......... 150
MOLVRAY, MIA 95
MOMBOURQUETTE, JOHN 126
MONAHAN, EDWARD C. 51
MONCUR, JAMES E. T. .. 59
MONEY, CHARLES........ 134
MONGER, DOUG 80
MONIZ, GARY 58
MONROE, BILL............... 292
MONROE-LORD, LILLIE. 52
MONSON, JOHN 277
MONTAGNE, ROLAND G. 142
MONTAGUE, CHRISTOPHER......... 255
MONTAGUE, DEADERICK C. 324

MONTALBANO, FRANK, III 54
MONTGOMERY, EDWARD B. 20
MONTGOMERY, STEVEN L. 267
MONTOYA, DAVID 28
MOOBERRY, DAVID D. 331
MOODY, BLAIR 291
MOODY, DAVID W. 304
MOODY, HOWARD H. ... 265
MOODY, J. WILLIAM 94
MOODY, JOAN 186
MOODY, JUDY GILSON 308
MOODY, MICHAEL W. 69
MOOERS, STEFFI 242
MOON, MELISSA 299
MOON, THOMAS 385
MOORE, ANDREW 258
MOORE, BARBARA 18
MOORE, BARRY K. 102
MOORE, BOB .. 56, 202, 400
MOORE, BRAD 76
MOORE, CARLTON D. 47
MOORE, CHUCK 155
MOORE, DAVID F. 278
MOORE, DEB 285
MOORE, GEORGE S. 31
MOORE, GREG 263
MOORE, J. 36
MOORE, JENNIFER 35
MOORE, JERRY N. 216
MOORE, JIM 38
MOORE, JOCELYN 210
MOORE, JOHN R. 330
MOORE, JULIA A. 33
MOORE, MONTGOMERY 111
MOORE, PAUL 325
MOORE, PETER B. 278
MOORE, RANDY ... 257, 424
MOORE, RICHARD 159
MOORE, ROBERT 299
MOORE, RONALD 25
MOORE, STEVE 105
MOORE, TERRENCE D. . 85
MOORE, VIRGIL K. 60
MOORING, JEAN 219
MOORING, PAUL 219
MOORMAN, CHRIS 92
MOOTNICK, ALAN 224
MOQUIN, GABRIEL F. 50
MOQUIN, RICHARD 84
MORAN, CHARLES A. .. 221
MORAN, GREG 332
MORAN, MARC 89
MORAN, MARK 22
MORAN, MICHAEL 269
MORAST, DANIEL 230
MORAVCIK, PHILIP S. 59
MORDEN, CLIFFORD ... 215
MORDICA, JAMES 78
MOREHOUSE, DOUG ... 210
MOREHOUSE, W. BRADLEY 180
MORELAND, LUCY 43
MORENO, MARIO 18
MORETTI, MILES 111
MORETZ, CRAIG 283
MOREY, GLENN B. 77
MORGAN, ANN 28
MORGAN, DON R. 205
MORGAN, DONALD ACE 297
MORGAN, ELLEN B. 78
MORGAN, EMILY 170
MORGAN, ERIKA 70
MORGAN, MAX G. 110
MORGAN, RICK 289
MORGAN, ROBERT L. .. 110
MORGAN, ROY 152
MORGAN, WALDO 108
MORGENWECK, RALPH 30
MORGESTER, JAMES J. 44
MORI, ART 243
MORI, BETTY N. 209
MORIARTY, MARVIN E. .. 30
MORIGEAU, SAM 180
MORING, JOHN R. 70
MORKILL, ANNE 350
MORRELL, L. ROSS 54
MORRILL, VALERIE 25
MORRILL, WILLIAM F. .. 160
MORRILL, WILLIAM I., Ph.D. 256
MORRIS, BILL M. 34
MORRIS, CROCKETT ... 340
MORRIS, DAVID 154, 428
MORRIS, DON 22
MORRIS, ED 43
MORRIS, EDWARD W., JR. 31
MORRIS, FREDERICK E. 183
MORRIS, GEORGE F. ... 207
MORRIS, JIM 94
MORRIS, JOHN 91
MORRIS, LARRY 44
MORRIS, LAWRENCE B. 157
MORRIS, LISA 94
MORRIS, MERVIN G. 163
MORRISON, DAVID L. 34
MORRISON, JAMES 163
MORRISON, MERRIE ... 138
MORRISON, RON 126
MORRISON, TOM 70
MORRISON, VENNING . 321
MORRISON, WILLIAM V. 46
MORRISSEY, ROBIN 43
MORRISSEY, WILLIAM ... 76
MORRITT, CLIFTON 151
MORROS, PETER G. 82
MORROW, DAVE 110
MORROW, PATRICK 25
MORSE, CHARLIE 227
MORSE, COY 96
MORSE, DANA 71
MORSE, HERBERT 325
MORSE, STEVE 76
MORTENSEN, CHARLES O. 370
MORTON, DAVID 374
MOSER, CHRISTOPHER 308
MOSER, DON 318
MOSER, LOWELL 379
MOSES, AMOS 97
MOSES, JOHN LEE 265
MOSHER, JIM 234
MOSHER, PETER N. 70
MOSHKALO, VLADIMIR 229
MOSLEY, CAROLYN 10
MOSS, DEWITT 266
MOSS, KAREN 220
MOSTELLER, DALE 283
MOTE, WILLIAM R. 255
MOTT, DAVE 80
MOTTERSHAW, RICHARD 61
MOTYKA, CONNIE 258
MOTYKA, CONRAD 111
MOULTON, NORM 245
MOUNT, DANA K. 93
MOUNT, PAMELA 277
MOUNT, PAUL 46
MOUNTAIN, BRUCE 232
MOURAD, TERESA M. . 197
MOURADJIAN, LARRY .. 103
MOUTON, EDMOND, LDWF 352
MOWRY, KENNETH 100
MOYER, BRUCE 99
MOYER, EDWIN J. 54
MOYER, STEVEN N. 331
MOYER, WILLIAM F. 52
MOYER-ANGUS, MARIA 192
MOYO, SAM 361
MOZER, DAVID 223
MOZLEY, SAMUEL C. ... 382
MTELITS, MICHAEL D. ... 20
MUCKENFUSS, ED 105
MUCKENFUSS, G. EDWARD 204
MUDD, EDWARD W., JR. 161
MUDD, RONALD 299
MUELDENER, KARL 66
MUELLER, MIKE 307
MUESSIG, KARL 85
MUHLSTOCK, BESS 299
MUHWEEZI, ALEX 229
MUISE, LEO 126
MULALA, SALLY LINDA 229
MULDOON, JOE 129
MULDOON, PAUL 166
MULFORD, JON K. 346
MULIERI, BONNIE 72
MULKEY, MARCIA E. 11
MULLANE, NEIL 98
MULLEN, BOB 97
MULLER, CARL 100
MULLIGAN, SHAWN 329
MULLIGAN, TIM 364
MULLIN, TOM 245, 373
MULLINS, ART 343
MULLINS, GARY 95
MULLINS, GARY W. 384
MULLINS, TOM 373
MULRANE, TONI E. 94
MULVIHILL, JOHN 306
MUMMA, JOHN 49, 397
MUMMA, TRACY 171
MUND, NAT 182
MUNDHEIM, MARIE C. ... 14
MUNDY, ROY, JR. 9
MUNGARI, ROBERT 88
MUNN, JOHN H. 118
MUNOZ, MANNY 53
MUNOZ, MIGUEL 103
MUNRO, KAREN 342
MUNSON, RICHARD H. 216
MURARO, JOAN 62
MURCHISON, GARY 394
MURDOCH, TOM 131
MURKOWSKI, FRANK 6
MURPHY, COLLEEN M. .. 82
MURPHY, DOUGLAS 168
MURPHY, ED 293
MURPHY, HOY 119
MURPHY, JAMES 24
MURPHY, KAREN 285
MURPHY, KIRK 307
MURPHY, MIKE 64
MURPHY, MITCH 128
MURPHY, PATRICIA M. .. 42
MURPHY, REG 262
MURRAY, ALAN 43
MURRAY, BENNIE 25
MURRAY, BRUCE 33
MURRAY, J. 35
MURRAY, JOHN A. 345
MURRAY, NANCY A. 145
MURRAY, NORMAN 214
MURRAY, PETER 224
MURRAY, RICHARD 73
MURRAY, WILLIAM 163
MURRAY, WILLIAM E. .. 207
MURRELL, K. DARWIN ... 15
MURRIET, JOAQUIN 320
MURRINER, EDWARD... 344
MURZIN, RICHARD 128
MUSGRAVE, RUTH S. .. 172
MUSIL, ROBERT K. 296
MUTSIGWA, J. K. 361
MYERS, GARY T. .. 107, 398
MYERS, GORDON 92
MYERS, JAN 220
MYERS, LARRY 48
MYERS, MARVIN 24
MYERS, NETTIE H. 106
MYRON, JIM 291
MYTON, DAVID 376

N

NABORS, JOHNSIE 31
NACHTIGALL, PAUL E. . 319
NADARAJAH, RAMANI . 166
NADEL, STEVE 139
NAFTZGER, ROY E. 225
NAGATA, RALSTON H. .. 58
NAGY, LEWIS, JR. 90
NAIL, ANNE 154
NAJJAR, STEPHEN 23
NAKAMOTO, GUY 243
NAKAMURA, CHAROTTE 59
NAKANO, JIM 99
NAKATANI, JAMES 58
NAKAZAWA, ANTHONY T. 40
NANCE, JIM 107
NANCE, TONI T. 104
NANEE, LARRY 43
NANNINI, EDWARD N. . 205
NAPIER, MARSI 193
NAPOLI, PAT 35
NARDOZZI, CHARLIE ... 262
NARVA, JIM 360
NASH, ARTHUR R., JR. .. 75
NASH, CHARLES 261
NASH, CLAUDE 78
NASH, HENRY 53
NASON, ROCHELLE 242
NASSAR, RON 244
NATES, LARRY E. 321
NAUGHTON, NELL 152
NAUMAN, ARLINDA 59
NAVARRE, A. EDWARD . 73
NAVARRO-MONZO, JULIO 330
NAVO, KIRK 351
NAYDOL, ALLAN 24
NAZE, KEVIN 345
NAZIR, MUHAMMAD 125
NDINGA, ASSITOU 229
NEAL, MARY 12
NEAVE, DAVID J. 349
NEBLETT, ANDREW 109
NEELY, DAN 227
NEELY, ROBERT 376
NEENAN, TOM F. 232
NEGRI, SHARON 299
NEHRIG, R. EDWIN 100
NEIGHBOR, BRUCE 192
NELISCHER, MAURICE 394
NELLIS, DAVID 112
NELLIS, LEE 320
NELSON, COURTLAND 110
NELSON, COURTLAND C. 258
NELSON, D. JAMES 296
NELSON, DAVID 322
NELSON, DENNIS 185
NELSON, DONALD E. 16
NELSON, EDWARD N. . 288
NELSON, GARLAND 56

STAFF NAME INDEX - O

NELSON, GAYLORD..... 346
NELSON, HARVEY K.... 334
NELSON, JEFFREY 189
NELSON, JIM.............. 373
NELSON, JOHN I., JR..... 84
NELSON, JON 206
NELSON, KAREN 76
NELSON, KIMBERLY ... 101
NELSON, KIRK 82
NELSON, LARRY 76, 104
NELSON, LORI 264
NELSON, MICHAEL J. 72
NELSON, MIKE........... 158
NELSON, PATT 289
NELSON, ROBERT R.... 255
NELSON, RON 99
NELSON, RUSSELL S. ... 54
NELTNER, THOMAS 62
NEMSICK, KATHY 175
NERRIE, BRIAN L. 116
NERVIG, ROBERT M. 13
NESBITT, STEPHEN A. 281
NESBITT, WILLIAM HAROLD 205
NESBITT, WM. HAROLD 223
NeSMITH, MARTIN 176
NETTLES, VICTOR F. ... 323
NEU, TIM 23
NEUBACHER, DON 246, 428
NEUDORF, JENNIFER.. 275
NEUHAUSER, HANS 209
NEUMAN, JANET 98
NEVENDORF, KLAUS.... 97
NEVES, RICHARD J.113, 391
NEWBOLD, JOHN 282
NEWBOLD, SHARON ... 282
NEWBROUGH, STACEY SNYDER 231
NEWCOMER, RICHARD 298
NEWHOUSE, BRUCE ... 270
NEWHOUSE, DAVID..... 155
NEWLAND, LEO 389
NEWMAN, ARNOLD..... 227
NEWMAN, CHRISTIAN . 211
NEWMAN, CONSTANCE BERRY..................... 317
NEWMAN, DEBBIE SCOTT 219
NEWMAN, MARK 96
NEWMAN, SHAWN 294
NEWMAN, THEODORE 157
NEWTON, CARLTON M.390
NEWTON, STEVE 204
NIBBELINK, NATHAN P.144
NIBLETT, GREGORY ... 130
NICHOLAS, WENDY 266
NICHOLS, DENISE....... 341
NICHOLS, GEORGE D.. 253
NICHOLS, JAMES 32
NICHOLS, LACY 51
NICHOLS, MARVIN 20
NICHOLS, NANCY 257
NICHOLS, RON 15
NICHOLSON, AL 60
NICHOLSON, BETH...... 310
NICHOLSON, RICHARD S. 136
NICKAS, GEORGE 347
NICKENS, EDDIE 283
NICKERSON, DONNIE W. 308
NICKERSON, NORMA .. 379
NICKUM, DAVID........... 331
NICOLESCU, JERRY 61
NICOLICH, JANE 281
NICOLL, JILL 263
NIELAND, JENNIFER.... 356

NIELSEN, CRAIG A. 71
NIELSEN, LARRY A........385
NIERING, WILLIAM........318
NIESWIADOMY, MIKE... 389
NIEUWENHUIS, RICHARD 277
NIEVES, TERESA..........103
NIGHTINGALE, STUART L. 19
NIKIDES, HARRY 63
NIKIDES, HARRY S........63
NILAND, GARY F..........101
NILES, LARRY 85
NIMRY, BASIL................64
NISHI, YUJI 174
NISHIDA, JANE T. 71
NIX, DAN 47
NIX, SHAUNI 287
NIX, T. LARRY 208
NIXON, PHILIP.............281
NIXON, SCOTT W. 104, 387
NOAH, JIM ....'......253
NOCK, LAURIE 7
NOECHEL, PAUL... 137, 138
NOEL, JOAN 239
NOEM, ROLLIE 106
NOERENBERG, CHANDLER................341
NOKA, RANDY.............269
NOLAN, DALE..............307
NOLAN, PAT 208
NOLAN, PATRICIA A., MD, MPH..........................157
NOLAND, STEWART 292
NOLD, CARL R. 75
NOLT, BEN 100
NOLTE, DAVID..............331
NOLTE, RICHARD H. 145
NOMSEN, DAVID E. 296
NOONAN, PATRICK F. ..182
NORBRIGA, DAVID 214
NORDEN, ARNOLD.......270
NORDLIE, FRANK 201
NORDSTROM, CARL R...85
NORGARRD, RICHARD 227
NORLAND, ERIK 95
NORMAN, GAYLE 14
NORMAN, PHILIP C. 352
NORRENA, ED................36
NORRIS, BARRY 99
NORRIS, JENNY 133
NORRIS, LANCE 308
NORRIS, SHARON 14
NORRY, PATRICIA G. 34
NORSE, ELLIOTT A.......246
NORTH, DOUG 306
NORTH, GARY.............236
NORTHCUTT, BEN 225
NORTHCUTT, MARVINA W. 260
NORTHUP, JIM..............204
NORTON, JAMES 333
NORTON, JANE E.........49
NORTON, JEANNE........235
NORTON, W. W. 346
NORWOOD, EARL D., JR. 190
NOSS, REED 318
NOTZ, JANIS 290
NOVAK, CHRISTINA 101
NOVAK, MICHAEL 384
NOVOSAT-GRADERT, LISA, ESQ. 287
NOVOTNY, LAWRENCE 322
NOWAK, MATT 25
NOWASAD, ROBERT....309
NSANJAMA, HENRI 359
NUMATA, MAKOTO.......275
NUNLEY, JOHN F., III....122
NUNNARI, BARBARA....208

NYAHAY, RICHARD..........90
NYE, JOHN C. 52
NYMARK, DENNIS.........203

O

O' TOOLE, A. 35
OAKES, CHERYL............203
OAKES, JOY.......... 152, 313
OATES, FRANCES HAMILTON 217
OATES, WILLIAM E. 109
O'BANNON, FRANK........62
OBARA, LINDA..............281
OBER, RICHARD 319
OBIAS, VIRGILIO L. 57
OBR, JOE 64
O'BRIEN, DONAL C., JR.50, 259
O'BRIEN, DONALD C., JR. 157
O'BRIEN, ERIC..............264
O'BRIEN, G. PATRICK....41
O'BRIEN, PHILIP J..........84
O'BRIEN, RINDY...........347
O'BRIEN, W. JOHN 372
O'CONNOR, CARL 122
O'CONNOR, DAVID J. 10
O'CONNOR, J. DENNIS.317
O'CONNOR, JOE 124
O'CONNOR, MATTHEW B. 296
O'CONNOR, MICHAEL 24
O'CONNOR, ROY..........254
O'CONNOR, TONY 36
ODATO, GENE 102
ODELL, DANIEL K........319
ODOM, BOB 68
ODOM, PERRY 53
O'DONNELL, CATHY 180
O'DOWD, DAVID 330
OELSCHLAEGER, MAX 169
O'FALLON, SHANNON ..134
OFFIELD, PAXSON H. ..296
OFFUTT, SUSAN 13
OFTERDAHL, LENORA 7
O'GARA, ANITA.............232
OGARRIO, RODOLFO...267
OGBURN, STEW............47
OGDEN, KEITH 256
OGDEN, MARK 220
OGE, MARGO T. 10
OGILVIE, KEN 297
OGLE, CHARLIE 312
OGLESBY, GENE 275
OGLESBY, RON 44
O'GORMAN, DENIS 124
O'GRADY, RICHARD 146
OGUNLEYE, BISI 357
O'HARA, FREDERICK M., JR. 169
O'HARA, J. STEPHEN ...267
O'HARA, JAMES A.........19
OHMSTEDE, WILL.........176
OKECHUKWU, ALEXANDER...............188
O'KEEFE, JOYCE............62
OKOH, JOESPH............375
OKUN, MELVA FARGER 383
OKUTOMI, KIYOSHI 275
OLAH, OTTO................126
O'LAUGHLIN, JAY.........369
OLDHAM, CARLA 283
OLDROYD, RICHARD....338
OLDS, JERRY 110
O'LEARY, NORMA 180
OLENA, HELEN.............101
OLIVER, JOHN C. 100

OLIVER, KESHA A. 195
OLIVER, TERRY KRAFT226
OLIVIER, W. S. 323
OLIVIERI, ALISON......... 180
OLIVIERO, MELANIE BETH 293
OLMEDA, RAFAEL 103
OLMES, JAMES E. 195
OLMSTEAD, CHARLES 367
OLMSTEAD, DON 10
OLMSTEAD, FRANCIS H., JR 162
OLMSTEAD, WILLIAM J.. 34
OLMSTED, ED.............. 177
OLNEY, JOHN E., SR. ... 144
OLSEN DE LEON, ROY 395
OLSEN, GEORGE 255
OLSEN, GLENN H. 156
OLSEN, JILL 190
OLSEN, LARRY 75
OLSON, DAN 122
OLSON, GLENN E. 259
OLSON, JEFF 252, 346
OLSON, KIM 107
OLSON, LAYTON 298
OLSON, LEONARD 110
OLSON, ROGER O. 71
OLSON, STEVEN G. 92
OLSON, THERESA........ 353
OLSON, W. KENT 205
OLTMANN, JULIE E. 47
OMANS, JIM 31
O'NEIL, WILLIAM A. 226
O'NEILL, CHARLES 221
O'NEILL, JAMES 51
O'NEILL, MARY 76
O'NEILL, RICHARD P..... 19
O'NEILL, SHEILA 310
O'NEILL, THOMAS, JR.... 82
ONIZUICA, ERIC W. 58
ONSTAD, CHARLES 15
OPLER, PAUL................ 360
OPPELT, TIMOTHY......... 11
OPPEN, BILL 129
OPPENHEIMER, JOHN R. 381
ORAM, JOHN................ 177
ORASIN, CHARLES J.... 186
ORAZE, MICHAEL J. 12
ORBACH, MICHAEL K.177, 382
ORCUTT-BAILEY, ANNE M. 59
O'REGAN, FRED 225
OREN, CARRIE 182
ORENDORFF, BEA 269
ORENSTEIN, RONALD . 230
ORGAN, JOHN F........... 350
O'RIORDAN, JON 124
ORLANDI, ROBIN.......... 303
OROST, BILL 128
OROSZ, SUSAN E. 156
O'ROURKE, JIM............ 319
ORR, DAVID 384
ORT, JON F. 91
ORTH, DONALD J. 391
ORTON, MARY 149
ORVILLIAN, LARAE....... 357
OSBORN, BRENDA K. .. 308
OSBORN, NIC 160
OSBORN, OZZIE........... 218
OSBORN, SCOTT 351
OSBORNE, NA`TAKI..... 165
OSBORNE, PATRICK 224
OSBURN, BENNIE 45
OSBURN, GERALD....... 100
OSBURN, HAL 109
OSETO, CHRISTIAN Y.. 195
OSHIMA, YASUYUKI..... 236
OSKAY, CLARE............. 220

STAFF NAME INDEX - P

OSLEEB, JEFFERY P. ... 381
OSMAN, JOSEPH 102
OSTBY, FREDERICK P. ... 17
OSTER, WALTER G. 167
OSTERBAUER, RON 303
OSTERBY, BRUCE 392
OSTERMANN, THOMAS W. 122
OSTERVICH, JOSEPH A. 161, 162
OSTFELD, RICHARD S. 222
OSTOJSKI, MIECZYSLAW S. 7
O'SULLIVAN, PATRICK 368
OSWALD, BRIAN 388
OTEY, KIRK 331, 333
OTHBERG, KURT L. 60
OTIS, DAVID L. 104
O'TOOLE, MICHAEL 89
OTOS, LARRY 341
OTT, MARTY 110
OTTE, CHUCK 238
OTTE, RONALD L. 40
OTTENBREIT, RODNEY J. 28
OTTER, RICHARD C. ... 310
OTTINGER, RICHARD L. 195
OTTO, BETSY 149
OTTO, LORRIE 174
OTTO, RALPH 15
OTTUM, MARGARET ... 390
OUELLETTE, MARTI ... 215
OUTLAW, BRENDA 282
OVCAMINS, ANNIE 227
OVERCASH, JESSE L. .. 354
OWEN, DANA 323
OWEN, JAMES E. 48
OWEN, JON 342
OWEN, LUTHER 25
OWEN, T. PAGE 367
OWENDOFS, JAMES M. .. 18
OWENS, DAN 283
OWENS, JIM 340
OWENS, STEVE 67
OWINGS, RAYMOND 32
OWNBY, JAMES D. 384
OWUSU, F. A. 198
OWUSU, JOHN KWADWO 198
OXENHANDLER, SALLY 79
OXFORD, RICHARD B. ... 42
OXLEY, FLO 240
OXLEY, MARY J. 94
OZENBERGER, JIM 360

P

PABLO, MICHAEL T. 180
PABST, D. ANN 319
PACE, MICHAEL L. 222
PACHAL, DIANNE 135
PACHECO, PEGGY FANTOZZI 247
PACKER, MARY JEANNE 338
PADALINO, JOHN 297
PADOR, MILA P. 57
PADOVAN, LYNNE 219
PAGAC, GERALD............ 63
PAGANO, PENNY 136
PAGE, LARRY M. 150
PAGE, PETER 85
PAGEL, MARTHA O. 99
PAHL, BARBARA 266
PAIGE, DAN............ 80
PAIGE, STEVE 66
PAINTER, DOUGLAS.... 265

PALAZZO, JOSE TRUDA, JR. 230
PALIN, BRUCE............ 62
PALMASSE, CANUTE ... 111
PALMER, CHARLES...... 110
PALMER, CHRISTOPHER 269
PALMER, JEFFREY......... 322
PALMER, JERRY 31
PALMER, LANGDON 278
PALMER, MOLLIE 53
PALMER, WILLIAM H. ... 342
PALMISANO, A. WILLIAM 31
PALOLA, ERIC 268
PALUMBO, NANCY 91
PAMPUSH, GEOFF 291
PANIO, JOHN, JR. 225
PAPERIELLO, CARL J. ... 34
PAPPAS, PETER 384
PAQUETTE, CHUCK 152, 192
PAQUIN, EMERY 126
PARADIS, BRUNO......... 301
PARADIS, RICHARD 325
PARADIS-BRANT, LAURIE 180
PARDUE, LEN. 168
PARENT, DAVID 251
PARENT, TOM 70
PARENTEAU, AL 128
PARK, JAMES 62
PARKER, BRIAN............ 200
PARKER, BUCK 192
PARKER, DAVID C. 156
PARKER, DIANE............ 41
PARKER, EDWARD......... 284
PARKER, EDWARD C. 50
PARKER, FORD H. 130
PARKER, GRANT 307
PARKER, JOHN 87
PARKER, MARY BETH .. 210
PARKER, MIKE 296
PARKER, NICK C. 108
PARKER, PETER............ 165
PARKER, RANDY 110
PARKER, RON 88
PARKER, WARREN K. 205
PARKER, WILLIAM......... 394
PARKER, ZOANN 100
PARKHURST, JAMES A. 116
PARKS, PETER 380
PARMER, ALYCE 53
PARMER, DELARIE......... 24
PARR, MIKE 138
PARRELLA, MICHAEL P., Ph.D. 365
PARRISH, GREG 100
PARRISH, JAMES D. 58, 369
PARROTT, GARY 216
PARRY, CHRISTIANE 46
PARSONS, GARY 284
PARSONS, GLENN 143
PARSONS, KATHARINE C. 245
PARSONS, M. 125
PARSONS, RICHARD 308
PARTRIDGE, ELLEN 240
PARUPIA, IQBAL 317
PASHLEY, DAVID 138
PASQUARELLO, THOMAS 381
PASQUIER, ROGER...... 358
PASQUIER, ROGER F. . 303
PASSACANTANDO, JOHN 292
PASSI, HENRY 71
PASSMORE, SAM 321
PASTORE, CARLA 136

PATAKI, GEORGE E. 88
PATE, DENNIS 320
PATE, PRESTON 91
PATEL, DHUN B. 84
PATINO, REYNALDO...... 108
PATRICK, LISA P. 209
PATRICK, STEVE 108
PATTEN, DUNCAN 320
PATTERSEN, DANIEL ... 188
PATTERSON, CHARLOTTE 283
PATTERSON, DAVE 164
PATTERSON, GARY...... 380
PATTERSON, GREGG 43
PATTERSON, NANCI 192
PATTERSON, REBECCA 42
PATTERSON, RICH 220
PATTERSON, ROGER K. 81
PATTON, DAN 109
PATTON, DOROTHY E. 11
PATTON, GARY A. 241
PATTON, JAMES L. 69
PATTON, MARK 95
PATTON, PAUL E. 66
PATTON, SARA 286
PAUL, ELLEN 291
PAUL, PAT 15
PAUL, TOM 99
PAULIN, KATHLEEN M. .354
PAULSON, JR, HENRY M. 296
PAVIA, JERRY 218
PAWELL, JUDY 64
PAXSON, DON 237
PAXTON, GREGORY B. 210
PAYER, RON 76
PAYNE, JACK 190
PAYNE, LARRY 16
PAZZISH, DEBBIE 53
PEABODY, TIMOTHY 70
PEACOCK, PATRICIA.... 350
PEAK, WAYNE 367
PEARCE, RON 31
PEARCE, TIM 187
PEARIGEN, MIKE 328
PEARL, MARY C., Ph.D. 350
PEARLMAN, NANCY 194
PEARSALL, SAM 270
PEARSE, JOHN S. 163
PEARSON, JAMES 13
PEARSON, WILLIAM D. .373
PEASE, JAMES L. 65
PECHMANN, JOHN E. 92
PECHURA, CONSTANCE 326
PECK, JAMES W. 143
PECK, W. RALPH............ 80
PEDDICORD, CAROL J. 350
PEDERSEN, AMANDA..... 19
PEDERSEN, CRAIG D. ..109
PEDERSEN, JIM 300
PEDERSEN, JORDAN ... 111
PEDERSON, RONALD...279
PEDROTTI, DANIEL A. 161, 162
PEEBLES, ROBERT K. ..162
PEEBLES, ROGER W. ...222
PEEK, MOTTELL D. 165
PEEL, ELLEN 161
PEELER, MARIA VICTORIA 117
PEET, MAITLAND 289
PEIRNO, THERESA 72
PEISER, BOBBY 270
PEKINS, PETER 380
PELIKAN, MATT 138
PELLEGRINO, ROBERT R. 50
PELLERIN, JOANNA...... 84
PELSUE, NEIL 112

PELZ, JOYCE 287
PELZMAN, RON 47
PENA, MICHELE 175
PENCE, DANIEL B. 348
PENDEXTER, KARLA ... 236
PENN, JULIE............ 323
PENNAZ, STEVE 281
PENNER, FRANK 245
PENNINGTON, STEPHEN 65
PENNY, DALE 326
PEPPER, TERRY 186
PERCIASEPE, ROBERT . 10
PERCIVAL, DEAN 248
PERCIVAL, H. FRANKLIN52
PERCIVAL, ROBERT 198
PEREZ-GIBSON, MICHAEL 117
PERHONIS, JOHN............ 152
PERKEY, ARLYN............ 262
PERKINS, CALVIN J. 277
PERKINS, LOGAN 299
PERKINS, MITCH 105
PERKINS, NATHAN 394
PERKO, DANIEL J. 122
PERKS, ROBERT 300
PERL, DIANE M. 319
PERNAS, ANTONIO J. .. 202
PEROCK, WAYNE............ 82
PERRIN, WILLIAM F. 319
PERRY, EARL 263
PERRY, FRED 180
PERRY, JIM 377
PERRY, LEE 69, 397
PERRY, LEE E. 70
PERRY, RALPH............ 175
PERRY, RANDALL 56
PERRY, STEPHEN G. 84
PERSCHEL, ROBERT... 347
PERSINGER, CHARLES320
PERSSON, CAROL V. 136
PESACHOWITZ, ALVIN M. 10
PESCHKEN, DIETHER .. 275
PETE, MARY............ 39
PETER, MARIA 380
PETERMAN, LARRY 80
PETERSEN, MARK 57
PETERSEN, WAYNE R. 138
PETERSON, ACE 154
PETERSON, ALLEN 143
PETERSON, ANNE 115
PETERSON, ARLENE ...345
PETERSON, BILL 42
PETERSON, CHARLES 351
PETERSON, CURT 367
PETERSON, DOUGLAS 376
PETERSON, GAYLE 251
PETERSON, GORDON .. 235
PETERSON, JACK D. 41
PETERSON, JAMES F. .. 260
PETERSON, JEFF 219
PETERSON, JOHN W. ... 266
PETERSON, JUDY 338
PETERSON, L. EARL...... 53
PETERSON, LESLIE 236
PETERSON, MARK 264
PETERSON, MIKE............ 342
PETERSON, R. MAX 223
PETERSON, ROLF......... 230
PETERSON, SUSAN 329
PETERSON, THOM......... 343
PETERSON, YVONNE .. 339
PETRICHENKO, PAUL ... 14
PETRITZ, DAVID C. 63
PETRON, STEPHEN E. .. 267
PETRONGOLO, TONY.... 85
PETROSKY, BERNARD R. 143
PETRUCCI, BRYAN 139

STAFF NAME INDEX - Q

PETSONK, ANNIE......... 196
PETTERSON, ELIZABETH
.... 246
PETTIT, WALT................ 45
PETTUS, VICKI................ 68
PETZING, KIM................ 197
PEYTON, BERNIE........ 222
PEZOLD, FRANK.......... 323
PFAENDER, FREDERIC 383
PFANNMULLER, LEE 76
PFEIFFER, DAN............ 340
PFEIFFER, DONALD..... 351
PFEIFFER, MICHAEL A. 203
PFEIFFER, PETER W..... 66
PFERRMAN, GARY....... 325
PFISTER, ROBERT........ 379
PFUND, ROSE T. 59
PHARES, DONALD P..... 119
PHELPS, JOHN E........... 370
PHELPS, ROBERT.......... 42
PHENNEGER, SHARON 139
PHILIP, CRAIG E............ 266
PHILLIPS, ABE............. 182
PHILLIPS, ADRIAN........ 228
PHILLIPS, BRAD........... 355
PHILLIPS, DAVE........... 128
PHILLIPS, DAVID .. 192, 226
PHILLIPS, DWAIN.......... 14
PHILLIPS, JOHN............. 73
PHILLIPS, JOHN C........ 160
PHILLIPS, PASCHAL 239
PHILLIPS, PATRICIA A. .. 78
PHILLIPS, PAULA 134
PHILLIPS, RICHARD..... 111
PHILLIPS, VICTOR D. ... 393
PHILLIPS, WILLIAM...... 176
PHILLIPS, WILSON H., JR.
.... 264
PHILP, JAMES F. 71
PHIPPS, TIM T. 392
PIACENTINI, RICHARD V.
.... 136
PIASECKI, BRUCE W. ... 381
PICHLER, SUSAN 297
PICHTEL, JOHN R. 370
PICKERD, HOWARD C. 122
PICKERING, RAY......... 100
PICKETT, FRANK......... 352
PICKETT, STEWARD T.A.
.... 222
PIDGEON, WALTER W., JR
.... 349
PIEGAT, JAMES............ 251
PIERCE, BERT E............ 119
PIERCE, BETH.............. 176
PIERCE, CLAY L. 64
PIERCE, JACQUELYN .. 208
PIERCE, JIM................. 175
PIERCE, PAMELA 234
PIERCE, POLLY............. 276
PIERCE, RICHARD 245
PIERCE, RICHARD B.... 189
PIERCE, ROBERT A., II .. 80
PIERCE, VIRGINIA........ 331
PIERGROSSI, MONICA 177
PIERINI, ELIZABETH ... 242
PIERNO, THERESA 173
PIERSON, AL............28, 421
PIERSON, GEORGE H. 278
PIKE, DOUG................. 176
PIKE, JOHN.................... 84
PIKE, STEPHEN J. 115
PILCHER, THOMAS........ 21
PILKINGTON, ALAN R. 186
PIMLOTT, DOROTHY ... 231
PINCETL, STEPHANIE . 179
PINDAR, GEORGINE.... 271
PINFORD, ROSALAND. 126
PINGREE, SUMNER 303
PINNIX, CLEVE 116, 341

PIOTROW, PHYLLIS T. . 297
PIOTROWSKI, GENE...... 72
PIPER, RUSSELL 289
PIPKEN, JAMES 28
PIRAINO, NANCY 355
PIRET, FERN V................ 73
PIRNER, STEVE............ 106
PISANI, DONALD J. 149
PISTER, EDWIN P. 188
PITELKA, LOUIS F. 374, 375
PITTMAN, JANNIE........ 169
PITTMAN, WILLIAM....... 24
PITTMAN-EVANS, BRAD 12
PITTS, ALEXANDRA 30
PITTS, DON 22, 263
PITTS, GREG................ 200
PIVA, ALFIO................... 37
PIZZUTO, ERNEST 276
PLAGEMAN, TIM 353
PLAGENZ, JOEL........... 196
PLANTE, PATRICK........ 189
PLASKETT, DEAN C., ESQ.
.... 112
PLASTERS, BRET......... 190
PLATT, DAVID 233
PLATT, DOROTHY K..... 337
PLATT, DWIGHT R. 238
PLAYNE, JACK............. 267
PLEMMONS, TIM.......... 187
PLEMONS, J. M............... 56
PLETSCHER, DANIEL H.
.... 379
PLITT, PAT................... 344
PLOCH, MANDY........... 346
PLONSKI, JOHN............ 101
POAGUE, TERRY.......... 132
POCIUS, E. WAYNE...... 205
PODOLSKY, W. J........... 125
PODRABSKY, GAYLE .. 206
POHLAD, BOB R. 390
POINDEXTER, ALFRED, III,
MD................................ 297
POIRIER, LUC............... 128
POKRAS, MARTHA....... 269
POKRYWKA, GREGORY
.... 248
POLAR, TOM................ 351
POLASEK, JOSEPH P... 121
POLIS, GARY................ 365
POLISCHUK,, WASYL J.,
JR.................................. 101
POLITINO, TONY.......... 119
POLK, MARIE................. 83
POLLACK, AMY E......... 159
POLLARD, BEN 96
POLLES, SAM................ 78
POLLI, RUDOLPH......... 112
POLLOCK, GLENN 232
POLLS, IRWIN.............. 348
POLTAK, RONALD F. 9
POMERANCE, RAFE...... 20
POMEROY, PAUL W. 34
POMEROY, TOM........... 218
POMEROY, WALTER L. 135
POMROY, WALTER 213
POND, ROBERT B......... 326
PONGRATZ, EVA.......... 199
PONTIUS, DALE............. 27
PONTTI, MICHAEL R..... 216
POOLE, ANNE.............. 278
POOLE, DANA.............. 337
POOLE, JOHN................ 38
POOLE, KERRY............ 125
POOLE, WILLIAM J., JR.
.... 265
POOR, DEBORAH 305
POPE, CARL................. 312
POPE, DAVID L. 65
POPE, PHILLIP E............ 62
POPHAM, JAMES........... 23

POPKIN, RODGER 138
POPPINO, JOHN............ 291
PORTER, MARY JANE 19
PORTER, MICHAEL D. 140, 353
PORTER, SANDRA......... 54
PORTER, WILLIAM F.... 382
PORTERFIELD, RANDY 307
PORTERFIELD, RICHARD
.... 145
PORTNER, LINDA E........ 34
PORTNEY, PAUL R. 304
POST, DIANA M. 301
POST, JENNIFER............ 89
POST, ROGER A. 350
POTTER, BRUCE G....... 233
POTTER, DAVE 373
POTTER, JERRY........... 312
POTTER, THOMAS D...... 17
POTTER, WILLIAM GRAY
.... 56
POTTIE, JAMES.............. 25
POTTINAER, LORI 227
POTTINGER, LORI 227
POTTS, ROBERT.......... 272
POTUCEK, DOROTHY . 309
POULSEN, DOROTHY.. 254
POWELKA, JOE........... 346
POWELL, ANN 335
POWELL, ANNE............ 150
POWELL, BARBARA JEAN
.... 199
POWELL, BRADLEY E.16, 423
POWELL, DAVE 134
POWELL, DAVID........... 167
POWELL, DON 243
POWELL, JIMMIE............. 6
POWELL, LOUCHES, JR.
.... 157
POWELL, PETER.......... 319
POWELL, ROYDEN .. 71, 72
POWELL, STEVE............ 72
POWELL, SUSAN 128
POWER, DONNA 191
POWERS, BRAD............. 71
POWERS, JOHN............ 177
POWERS, ROY, JR........ 138
POWERS, TOM.............. 47
POYNTER, KEN Q......... 269
POZDENA, RANDY....... 290
PRAKASH, GEORGIA.... 270
PRANIS, EVE 262
PRATT, JAMES R. 385
PRATT, JEROME J. 345
PRCHAL, DOUG............. 93
PREBBLE, DEBBIE 53
PRECARIO, PETE......... 287
PRENDERGAST, GREGORY 74
PRESNAL, DANNY 108
PRESS, DANIEL............ 196
PREUSS, PETER W......... 11
PRICE, ANNE................ 303
PRICE, HARRY F........... 119
PRICE, HUGH C............ 252
PRICE, JIM 156, 313
PRICE, JONATHAN G..... 82
PRICE, SCOTT.............. 302
PRICE, WILLIAM E........ 114
PRICHARD, MICHAEL... 252
PRICHETT, REBECCA .. 133
PRICKETT, TOMMY........ 69
PRIDDLE, HARLAND.... 238
PRIETO, CLAUDIO R...... 18
PRIME, MEREDITH........ 131
PRINCE, BERNADINE.. 139
PRINDLE, BARB 251
PRINGLE, PAT.............. 294
PRITCHARD, CHUCK.... 164

PRITCHARD, MARY LOU
.... 275
PRITCHARD, PAUL C... 263
PRITCHARD, PETER.... 172
PRITCHETT, BRYAN..... 267
PROBASCO, IRENE....... 287
PROBST, MARIAN........ 207
PROCTOR, LEZLIN......... 78
PROESCHOLDT, KEVIN 206
PROPST, LUTHER 305, 320
PROSSER, KATHY 239
PROULX, CARLEEN 326
PROUSE, C. GORDON . 124
PROUTY, JORDAN S..... 281
PROUTY, SALLY 94
PROWSE, HAROLD 249
PRUE, THOMAS D......... 161
PRUIT, PHILIP 23
PRUITT, WILLIAM A...... 113
PRUSS, MICHAEL T..... 351
PRYOR, EMILIE M......... 303
PUCHY, CLAIRE A. 116
PUFFINBERGER, CHARLES W.................. 71
PUGH, ELIZABETH B.... 311
PUGH, LARRY.............. 307
PUGH, MICHELLE 233
PUGLIA, LEZLIE 48
PULINS, BENITA, CPA,MBA
.... 215
PUNTER, DAVID 394
PUPPE, GARY.............. 284
PURCELL, ROBIN 218
PURNELL, TIL 310
PURSER, PAUL, JR....... 289
PURSGLOVE, SAMUEL R.
.... 308
PUTNAM, COURTNEY.. 391
PUTNAM, HUGH, JR..... 248
PUTT, SAMANTHA........ 197
PYLE, LIZBETH A......... 155

Q

QUACKENBUSH, EVERETT...................... 90
QUACKENBUSH, LANNY 98
QUACKENBUSH, MARY 286
QUAKENBUSH, LORI.... 39
QUALLEY, GEORGE....... 48
QUAN, FELIX 292
QUARLES, LYNN 12
QUARLES, WILLIAM 161
QUATRANO, RALPH..... 378
QUAYLE, FREDERICK M.
.... 114
QUAYLE, MOURA 393
QUIGLEY, KRISTEN...... 342
QUIGLEY, MIKE 63
QUILL, STEPHEN F....... 308
QUINK, THOMAS ... 74, 247
QUINN, BUD 116
QUINN, CATHERINE.... 337
QUINN, DAN 304
QUINN, GAIL 241
QUINN, RANDY 25
QUINN, ROBERT............ 91
QUINSENBERRY, SHARRON 195
QUIRK, BILL................... 25
QUIRK, THOMAS F. 165
QUIRKE, KELLY 302
QUIROLO, CRAIG 303
QUIROLO, DEEVON 303
QUISENBERRY, BILL...... 78
QUY, LAURENCE.......... 245
QZBAL, HAFIZ MUHAMMRAD........... 396

R

RABB, HARRIET S. 19
RABBON, PETER D. 48
RABENI, CHARLES....... 378
RABENI, CHARLES F. 79
RACE, SAMUEL R..... 84, 85
RACHLIN, JOSEPH W. .. 146
RACICOT, MARC 80
RADER, JOHN B. 119
RADFORD, GINNY 357
RADOMSKI, PAUL J...... 143
RADOSEVICH, STEVEN R. 384
RAEL, WILFRED............ 325
RAESIDE, ROBERT 394
RAFFAELE, HERBERT A.30
RAFLE, PETER.............. 331
RAGANTESI, DAVE 307
RAGLIN, KENNETH A. 34
RAGOUZINA, GALINA .. 193
RAHDER, BARBARA L. 395
RAHMAN, ANIS UR 216
RAINEY, C. TOM 349
RAINEY, JOHN S. .. 267, 268
RAINFORD, SYLVIA....... 14
RAINS, GLORIA 245
RAINS, MICHAEL T........ 16
RAINWATER, BILL 154
RAIT, KEN 290
RAKESTRAW, DARIEL .186
RAKOCY, JAMES 113
RAKOW, SALLY 47
RALEY, CATHERINE 354
RALSTON, ART............. 231
RALSTON, PATRICK R... 62
RALSTON, PETER 233
RAMAN, N. V. 51
RAMEY, BARBARA 372
RAMIN, ROBERT........... 151
RAMSAY, RICHARD E. . 232
RAMSAY, SCOTT............ 70
RAMSEY, CHARLES 105
RAMSEY, O. J. 217
RANDALL, ROBERT 335
RANDLES, RICHARD K. . 89
RANDOLPH, ANITA 80
RANDOLPH, LANNY 275
RANDS, TIM 192
RANKEL, GARY L. 28
RANKER, KEVIN 206
RANKIN, BOBBY J. 380
RANKIN, STARLENE 213
RANNEY, SALLY A. 151
RANSEL, KATHERINE .. 149
RANSOM, MICHEL D. ... 372
RAO, S. T. 89
RAPIER, KENNY 67
RAPPA, PETER J. 59
RAPPAPORT, BRET 346
RASCHKE, BOB 257
RASH, J. E. 242
RASKER, RAY 320
RASKIN, FRED C. 266
RASMUSSEN, G. ALLEN 111
RASMUSSEN, JAMES L. 18
RASMUSSEN, JAY.......... 99
RASMUSSEN, JERRY L. 252
RASMUSSEN, MATT 204
RASOR, LORI 291, 341
RASOR, LORI D.218, 291, 341
RASSAM, GHASSAN N. 140
RATCLIFF, D. C............. 108
RATCLIFFE, JERE B..... 162
RATHBUN, DENNIS K..... 34
RATZ, MARGARET 345
RAUSCHER, KEN 74
RAUSSER, GORDON C..46
RAWLINS, CHIP 360
RAWLINS, WAYNE 97
RAWSON, MAC, JR......... 56
RAY, ARTHUR W............. 71
RAY, JOHN 254
RAYBURN, RICHARD G..48
RAYMOND, JANIS......... 126
RAYMOND, STEPHANIE 295
READ, CHARLOTTE J... 309
READ, EDITH................ 318
REAGOR, KAREN P...... 239
REAMES, CLARK 25
REAMES, DEBORAH 192
REAMES, SPENCER E. 286
REAN, RUSS................... 23
REARDON, JEFF........... 332
REBACH, STEVE 375
RECHT, PHILIP R. 32
RECK, RUTH A. 365
RECKHOW, KENNETH H. 382
RECORD, RICHARD 70
REDDEN, DAVID N........ 311
REDDING, AL................ 132
REDDING, BILL.....252, 313
REDDING, JOHN H. 208
REDDING, RUSSELL C. 100
REDIG, PATRICK T. 303
REDMAN, CHARLES L.. 362
REDMAN, DONNELL E. 270
REDMAN, DONNER E... 270
REDMOND, DENNIS 220
REEB, MARY LOU 121
REECE, GARY 255
REED, A. SCOTT............ 99
REED, ANDREA 207
REED, BILL 343
REED, CHARLES J......... 51
REED, CYNTHIA............ 212
REED, DANNY 67
REED, DONALD P........... 69
REED, HOLLY 330
REED, JOEL 94
REED, MARCY 328
REED, MARSHALL 338
REED, MARY 279
REED, TIM 299
REED, WENDY G.......... 331
REED-SMITH, JAN 137
REES, SANDY 116
REESE, HUDSON.......... 339
REESE, KERRY PAUL .. 362
REESE, PEG 15
REES-WEBBE, ROBIN. 215
REEVES, BILL........ 107, 252
REEVES, JO LYN 267
REEVES, JOHN B. 105
REEVES, REGGIE......... 107
REEVES, WILLIAM B..... 200
REGAN, RON........ 111, 398
REGELIN, WAYNE 39
REGENSTEIN, LEWIS G. 222
REGER, SCOTT J......... 141
REGISTER, RICHARD.. 204
REGISTER, WAYNE...... 329
REGN, ANN............ 114, 304
REGO, PAUL................. 353
REHARD, JAMES 80
REHEIS, HAROLD 56
REICE, SETH R. 383
REICH, RICHARD 92
REICH, TIM 257
REICHARD, SARAH 318
REICHARDT, WILLIAM A. 216
REICHELT, CYNTHIA.... 204
REICHER, DAN W. 18
REICHERT, BILL 294
REID, ALAN 396
REID, C.P. PATRICK......363
REID, KENNETH D. 151
REID, RON 200
REID, SHARON 154
REID, TIMOTHY W.........234
REIFEL, GEORGE C......188
REIFSNIDER, BETSY ...206
REIFSNYDER, DANIEL A. 20
REIFSTECK, SHAWN 184
REILLY, PATRICK W. 32
REILLY, ROBIN 126
REILLY, SHARON 214
REILLY, WILLIAM K. 139
REINHARDT, VIKTOR, D.M.V., PH.D. 152
REINNGER, THOMAS ...288
REINOSO, JENNIFER...203
REISDORF, THOMAS....334
REISER, HILDY 23
REISING-JONES, CATHERINE 155
REISTLE, WENDY 257
REITER, AL 289
REITER, CHRIS 145
REITER, LAWERNCE W., Ph.D. 11
REITSMA, JAN H. 103
REMMICK, RONALD......142
REMPE............................47
REMUS, JR., KURT W. ..320
REMUS, LAUREL............89
RENARD, YVES 168
RENE, GAURAB 327
RENEAU, JACK.............161
RENJEL, LOUIS 336
RENNER, ROBERT C....151
RENNER, TRACY 359
RENO, JANET 20
RENWICK, RITA 219
RESHETNIAK, PETER...303
RESS, PAULA 292
RESSMEYER, JOHN 97
REUTER, DON 91
REUTTER, JEFFREY M...95
REVIER, PAUL 309
REWERTS, MILAN A. 50
REXROAD, CAIRD..........15
REYES, CARMEN. 139, 236
REYES, LUIS A. 34
REYNOLDS, DEBBIE.....303
REYNOLDS, JAMES B..362
REYNOLDS, JAMES R...12
REYNOLDS, JIM 61
REYNOLDS, JIMMY.......154
REYNOLDS, JOHN 29
REYNOLDS, MARY 230
REYNOLDS, STEPHAN.123
REYNOLDS, STEPHEN.187
REZAC, DON 237
RHOADES, KEVIN 292
RHOADS, JOHN..............72
RHODE, ARLYNE 261
RHODES, ED.................339
RHODES, HOWARD........53
RHODES, LISA................74
RHODES, ROXANNE.....321
RHODES, TOM 243
RHORER, SKIP................68
RHOTON, JOHN S. 293
RICART, JUAN L. 300
RICE, CHUCK................283
RICE, DAVID K. 83, 155
RICE, JAMES A...............92
RICE, JIM.......................249
RICE, JOE DAVID 42
RICE, MARY 324
RICE, MARY E. 318
RICE, RONALD L............. 33
RICE, RUDY................... 257
RICH, JAMES 67
RICH, TOM............... 81, 97
RICHARDS, CARL........... 77
RICHARDS, DOUGLAS P. 378
RICHARDS, HARRY E. . 102
RICHARDS, KARYN B..... 88
RICHARDS, KEITH 339
RICHARDS, LYNDA 253
RICHARDS, LYRA 276
RICHARDS, NORM 127
RICHARDSON, BILL....... 18
RICHARDSON, CHERYL 133
RICHARDSON, DAVID .. 124
RICHARDSON, JEFF 133
RICHARDSON, JOAN ... 277
RICHARDSON, JUDITH 180
RICHARDSON, KERMIT W. 262
RICHARDSON, LINDA R. 216
RICHARDSON, NANCY 158
RICHARDSON, RUSTY.347
RICHARDSON, STEVEN 28
RICHARDSON, TIM....... 240
RICHBOURG, JOE 105
RICHERSON, PAT.......... 21
RICHERSON, ROBIN ... 243
RICHMOND, ALAN 22
RICHMOND, MILO E. 88
RICHMOND, TOM 81
RICHTER, DANIEL D. ... 382
RICKARDS, WILLIAM L. 115
RICKER, KAREN T. 95
RIDDLE, PHIL 360
RIDENHOUR, CORY T.. 253
RIDEOUT, DAVID 36
RIDGE, TOM 99
RIDGEWAY, LORI 36
RIDGLEY, HEIDI 186
RIDINGTON, JILLIAN ... 207
RIDLEY, TAZ 205
RIEFF, SUSAN 267
RIEHM, JOHN P. 369
RIEPE, DONALD 147
RIESENBERG, LOU 60
RIESSEN, JACK 64
RIGBY, WILLIAM 337
RIGSBY, ALEX 290
RIKE, KAY...................... 105
RILEY, BARB 126
RILEY, BECKY 285
RILEY, DAN 256
RILEY, DANNY 53
RILEY, DAVID T. 189
RILEY, MICHAEL E. 232
RILEY, RICHARD W........ 18
RILEY, TERRY Z. 349
RILEY, TOM L., JR. 43
RILEY, VINCE 300
RILEY, WILSON............. 298
RILLERO, ANNE............ 293
RIMMER, CHRISTOPHER 338
RIMMER, DAVID............ 176
RINALDI, THOMAS......... 89
RINEER, ROBERT........ 247
RING, BETTINA K......... 113
RING, GINETTE 261
RING, ROBERT L. 238
RINGENBERG, JAY 81
RINGLER, NEIL H.......... 382
RINGO, JEROME C. 267
RINGUET, ISABELLE..... 36
RINK, THOMAS C.......... 174
RIORDAN, J. 36
RIOTTE, NICOLE R. 194

STAFF NAME INDEX - S

RIPLEY, ARLENE.......... 280
RIPLEY, BARBARA G. ... 111
RIPLEY, BOB................. 108
RIPLEY, J. DOUGLAS..... 21
RIPLEY, J. JOY............. 166
RIS, HOWARD, JR. 336
RISDON, KARLA 278
RISK, PAUL H................ 388
RISKA, MIKE................. 187
RISNES, PHILLIP 322
RISSLER, RICHARD L. ... 13
RISTOW, MARK............. 324
RITCHIE, IAN................. 395
RITCHIE, J. TIMOTHY... 290
RITCHIE, LEAH COX 75
RITTENOUR, CHARLES
  W., JR. 132
RITTER, MARK.............. 160
RIUTOR, RAUL H........... 205
RIVERA, DENNIS 302
RIVERS, CAITLIN........... 256
RIZZIO, TONY 25
ROACH, GREG............... 126
ROBAK, SYD.................. 125
ROBBINS, CHANDLER S.
  247
ROBBINS, CHRIS........... 330
ROBBINS, JENNIE 245
ROBBINS, MICHELLE... 145
ROBBINS, RUSSELL 78
ROBEL, ROBERT J. 372
ROBERG, REX R. 43
ROBERSON, DONNIS 78
ROBERTS, ADAM 153
ROBERTS, CHRISTOPHER
  M. 7
ROBERTS, JACKIE
  PRINCE...................... 196
ROBERTS, JOANNE 342
ROBERTS, KENNETH J.. 69
ROBERTS, KITTY 29
ROBERTS, LUCIA 112
ROBERTS, M. H.............. 390
ROBERTS, ROBY 304
ROBERTS, TERRY 46
ROBERTS, THOMAS M. 368
ROBERTSON,
  CHARLOTTE 216
ROBERTSON, GEORGE,
  JR. 132
ROBERTSON, GORDON C.
  119
ROBERTSON, HOPE E. 278
ROBERTSON, JAMES .. 121
ROBERTSON, JENNIFER
  B. 264
ROBERTSON, JIM 109, 231
ROBERTSON, JOHN M. . 75
ROBERTSON, KEN 335
ROBERTSON, PETER D. 10
ROBERTUS, JOHN 45
ROBICHAUD, JACQUE... 36
ROBINETTE, RANDALL 366
ROBINS, TODD 300
ROBINSON, BILL 42
ROBINSON, BINA 224
ROBINSON, JILL 225
ROBINSON, JOHN 348
ROBINSON, JOHN M. ... 245
ROBINSON, KAYNE B. . 264
ROBINSON, MARY 331
ROBINSON, MICHAEL154,
  317
ROBINSON, MURIEL 158
ROBINSON, NICHOLAS 228
ROBINSON, SCOTT 266
ROBINSON, SCOTT K. . 370
ROBINSON, SHARON 18
ROBINSON, STEVE 288
ROBINSON, TOM .. 118, 211

ROBISON, ROD............. 218
ROBOHM, RICHARD..... 341
ROBSON, DIANA BIZECKI
  275
ROBY, DANIEL D............ 97
ROBY, ROBERT 322
ROBY, TIM....................... 75
ROCK, LESLIE............... 354
ROCK, TIM..................... 286
ROCKEFELLER, DAVID,
  JR. 134
ROCKEFELLER,
  LAURANCE................ 139
ROCKEFELLER,
  LAURANCE S. ... 139, 236
ROCKEFELLER,
  WINTHROP P. 161
ROCKEY, SALLY 15
ROCKWOOD, STEPHEN V.
  351
ROCQUE, ARTHUR J., JR
  50
ROCZICKA, GREG 39
RODD, JUDY................. 343
RODEFELD, NELS 95
RODEMACHER, GUS C. .68
RODEN, ROBERT W. ... 121
RODENBURG, FRANCES
  166
RODERICK, AMY.......... 360
RODGERS, A. J. 286
RODGERS, JOHN 387
RODGERS, KIRK............ 29
RODIN, A....................... 285
RODRIGUES, VERA...... 222
RODRIGUEZ BERRIOS,
  OLGA I....................... 103
RODRIGUEZ, CARLOS
  MARIO 37
RODRIGUEZ, DAN 23
RODRIGUEZ, KATJA..... 286
RODRIGUEZ, MIGDALIA
  300
RODRIGUEZ, PEDRO... 103
ROEHRICH, KENNETH. 277
ROEKEL, DENNIS VAN. 260
ROEMER, ELEANOR 219
ROEMER, PETER 151
ROER, KATHLEEN 75
ROGERS, BILL.............. 178
ROGERS, JOHN G., JR.. 29
ROGERS, KATRINA 211
ROGERS, KENNETH C... 34
ROGERS, MARIHELEN. 261
ROGERS, MITCHELL J. 190
ROGERS, NANCY 181
ROGERS, RAYMOND A.
  395
ROGERS, SAM 87
ROGERS, STAN 21
ROGERS, WILL............. 334
ROHALL, RONALD 294
ROHRBACK, DONALD H.
  352
ROHY, DAVID A.............. 47
ROJAS, ESTHER........... 300
ROJAS, SONIA 37
ROLFE, GARY L. 370
ROLFE, KEVIN............... 134
ROLFSMEYER, CHUCK 356
ROLLINS, HARDOLD B. 386
ROLLS, ALICE............... 197
ROLOSON, RANDY....... 267
ROLSTON, DENNIS E... 365
ROM, BECKY................ 206
ROMANIUK, NESTOR... 167
ROMANO, GREGORY..... 84
ROMANO, JEFFREY 245
ROMANO, KATHIE 349
ROMINE, RICHARD A. ... 73

ROMINGER, RICHARD....12
ROMMEL, FRED 100
ROMO, JOHN................ 297
RON REMPE.................... 47
RONNERUD, JAMES 191
RONNING, KATHLEEN.. 216
ROOSEVELT, THEODORE,
  IV............................... 241
ROSA, KARL DALLA 214
ROSE, BEN................... 213
ROSE, CHRIS................ 335
ROSE, GERALD............. 76
ROSE, KRISTI.................. 9
ROSE, MARCI L. 303
ROSE, PAT..................... 53
ROSEN, RON................ 238
ROSEN, RUDOLPH A... 308
ROSENBERG, DAVID M.
  280
ROSENBUSCH, WALT ...27
ROSENKRANCE, LESTER
  28
ROSENKRANZ, HERBERT
  S................................ 386
ROSENOW, JOHN......... 256
ROSENTHAL, LYNN 390
ROSEVEAR, WILLIAM E.
  295
ROSEWATER, ANN....... 19
ROSS, CARL................. 309
ROSS, DAVID................ 138
ROSS, DENWOOD F. 33
ROSS, GALE 70
ROSS, GEORGE........... 127
ROSS, GERALD E. 79
ROSS, LAWRENCE 198
ROSS, S. P.................... 98
ROSS, STEPHEN T. 323,
  378
ROSS, VERNON R. 102, 398
ROSSELLO, PEDRO J... 102
ROSSI, C. E. 34
ROSSI, JIM.................... 177
ROSSI, PATRIZIA 199
ROSSITER, WILLIAM W.
  172
ROSS-SHANNON, BRUCE
  270
ROSTER, TOM................ 64
ROSTVET, ROGER......... 93
ROSWAL, GLENN 136
ROTENBERRY, JOHN T.
  184
ROTH, FRANK A., II........ 43
ROTH, JON................... 164
ROTH, PETER................. 37
ROTH, RICHARD R........ 351
ROTH, ROBERT.............. 95
ROTH, ROLAND R. 176
ROTHBART, PAUL........ 181
ROTHE, ANN L............. 335
ROTHMAN, HAL........... 203
ROTHMAN, HAL K. 149
ROTMAN, ART.............. 168
ROUDNA, MILENA......... 37
ROUNDS, JOHN 290
ROUSSEL, JOHN........... 69
ROUSSOPOULOS, PETER
  J. 17
ROUTTEN, BARBARA ... 195
ROW, GREG................. 272
ROWAN, FRAN 136
ROWAN, GLORIA J........ 120
ROWAN, JOSEPH F. 190
ROWDABAUGH, KIRK..... 41
ROWE, SEAN 202
ROWELL, CHESTER M., JR
  270
ROWLAND, JOHN G....... 50
ROWLAND, MELANIE.... 341

ROWLAND, NATHAN 23
ROWLEY, JIM................ 131
ROWNTREE, LESTER .. 364
ROYCE, BOB.................. 60
ROZUM, MARY ANN 16
RUBENSTEIN, JAMES M.
  384
RUBENSTEIN, PAUL D.. 26
RUBER, ERNEST.......... 375
RUBIN, PETE................ 275
RUBINGH, JIM................ 49
RUBINOFF, IRA............. 318
RUBINOFF, ROBERTA . 318
RUCH, JEFFREY.......... 300
RUDDELL, JOHN............ 54
RUDDELL, JOHN M........ 53
RUDE, MARY.................. 55
RUDY, CAROL............... 221
RUE, FRANK........... 39, 397
RUECKERT, RON 121
RUEFF, MATHEW........... 62
RUEGER, WALTER...... 261
RUFF, MARGARET....... 289
RUFF, ROBERT L......... 122
RUGG, ROBIN 330
RUGGLES, BOB 129
RUGO, FRED................ 332
RUHL, B. SUZI 242
RUMERY, ALICE 275
RUMP, JACK.................. 46
RUNDQUIST, ERIC 237
RUNGE, RUSSELL....... 253
RUNNELS, BRUCE 272
RUNNING, STEVEN 379
RUNNING-GRASS, ... 329
RUSCH, DONALD H. 120
RUSSELL, CLAYTON... 392
RUSSELL, DIANNE 221
RUSSELL, EARL B......... 82
RUSSELL, JOHN 385
RUSSELL, KEITH C....... 167
RUSSELL, LIANE B....... 328
RUSSELL, ROBERT C. . 234
RUST, MARIE 29
RUTH, TERRY 25
RUTHERFORD, BRENT M.
  395
RUTHERFORD, JAMIE ... 51
RUTHERFORD, JAY 111
RUTHERFORD, NELSON
  291
RUTLEDGE, WALLACE .. 98
RUTTLE, JACK.............. 262
RUVELSON, ALAN, JR. 252
RUYLE, GEORGE ... 42, 363
RUZYCKI, ELAINE.......... 77
RYAN, BARBARA............ 30
RYAN, BARBARA J......... 30
RYAN, GEORGE............. 61
RYAN, J. HUGH............ 105
RYAN, JOHN................ 286
RYAN, W. S.................... 10
RYDELL, MICHELE 145
RYDEN, HOPE 346
RYDER, LONNIE 53
RYEL, KEN..................... 95

S

SAAVEDRA, PAUL........... 88
SABEAN, BARRY C....... 127
SABELLA, SUSAN......... 213
SABINA, JOHN.............. 333
SABLAN, JOSEPH G....... 57
SACKETT, BRUCE.......... 82
SADLER, LYNN 256
SADLER, WILLIAM 345
SADUSKY, NANCY 310
SAER, ANNE 241

STAFF NAME INDEX - S

SAFINA, CARL.............. 259
SAGE, DON 90
SAGE, SAMUEL H.......... 157
SAGOFF, MARK 227
SAGSVEEN, MURRAY.... 93
SAHAJ, JANET L. 32
SAIDI, WENDY 336
SAINSBURY, JACK 97
SAKAGAWA, GARY 146
SAKOFS, MITCHELL 346
SAKUMA, TOMOKO...... 296
SALARI, AHMAD 110
SALAS, JESUS T............. 57
SALAZAR, RODOLFO... 228
SALAZAR-HENRY,
  ROBERTA..................... 87
SALBER, LEE 189
SALDANA, LYDIA 109
SALEH, FARIDA 389
SALISBURY, JENNIFER 86, 87
SALKIN, CHARLES 51
SALKIN, CHARLES A 258
SALLEY, MARK 25
SALMONSON, GENEVIEVE
  59
SALVAGGIO, JAMES M. 101
SALWASSER, HAL 16
SAMA, JEFFREY 89
SAMMON, ROBERT....... 258
SAMPLE, V. ALARIC 296
SAMPLES, ORBIN E., III 325
SAMPLES, PETER O. ... 325
SAMPLINER, TOM 269
SAMPSON, CAROL L. 19
SAMPSON, DON 7
SAMS, M. PAUL.............. 104
SAMSON, ANSLEY 192
SAMUEL, JOSEPH 339
SAMUELS, WILLIAM 202
SAN NICHOLAS,
  CLARISSA D. 57
SANBORN, CLINT 309
SAND, MAURE 93
SANDALOW, DAVID 10
SANDBERG, JULIE 117
SANDERS, DWIGHT E.... 46
SANDERS, GREGORY L.
  113
SANDERS, JOE............. 107
SANDERS, REED............ 67
SANDERS, RODNEY 78
SANDERS, WILLIAM H., III
  11
SANDERSON, H. REED 351
SANDERSON, RICHARD E.
  10
SANDHEINRICH, MARK B.
  392
SANDIFER, PAUL A. 105, 398
SANDLER, CRAIG D. 265
SANDO, ROD 76
SANDOVAL, J. R. 61
SANDS, DAVID 275
SANDT, JOSH 72
SANFORD, CAROLYN .. 159
SANJANWALA, UMESH.. 78
SANSOM, ANDREW 109, 398
SANT, ROGER W. 359
SANTACROCE, LISA 180
SANTANGINI, JOHN 54
SANTASANIA, CARMEN
  294
SANTEL, TIMOTHY J. ... 200
SANTIAGO, VIVIAN
  MORALES.................. 103
SANTUCCI, VICTOR J. . 142
SARABI, BRIGETTE...... 306

SARGENT, LORI G........ 352
SARJEANT, WILLIAM..... 275
SARKO, ANATOLE........ 382
SARRO, JAMES V. 48
SARTAR, MARGARET ... 23
SARTY, JIM 126
SASS, RONALD L. 388
SATERSON, KATHRYN A.
  162
SATHER, DAWN 248
SATO, KEN 35, 36
SATO, MIKE 295
SATRE, SONNY 64
SATTERLEE, FRANCIS. 223
SAUNDERS, DAVID K.... 237
SAUNDERS, JOHN L...... 79
SAUNDERS, LINDA....... 241
SAUNDERS, LLOYD....... 26
SAUNDERS, NORM 247
SAUNDERS, RICHARD . 337
SAUNDERS, STUART T.,
  JR 132
SAUNDRERS, GERRY... 367
SAUNDRY, PETER D. ... 179
SAUSVILLE, LISA P....... 354
SAVAGE, MICHAEL........ 94
SAVARD, MICHEL......... 301
SAVERY, JOE 328
SAVILLE, DAVE 343
SAVIOE, BRANDT 68
SAVITT, CHARLES 171
SAVITZ, JACQUELINE .. 176
SAWHILL, JOHN 214
SAWHILL, JOHN C. 272
SAWICKI, JOAN 124
SAYRE, DAN 171
SAYRE, JOHN A. 243
SAZAKI, MARE 188
SCALET, CHARLES G. 259, 387
SCALF, ANNA MARIE ... 232
SCALICE, JOHN A. 35
SCALPONE, JAN 174
SCAMEHORN, EILEEN . 249
SCANLON, EDWARD H. 178
SCANLON, JOHN 35
SCARBRO, MAXINE S. . 208
SCARDACI, TONY 209
SCARTH, JONATHAN ... 187
SCELZA, BROOKE 75
SCHACHTER, JOSH 305, 320
SCHACKER, B. 36
SCHADEWALD, PAUL 93
SCHAEFER, JOESPH M. 54
SCHAEFER, JOYCE...... 208
SCHAEFER, LARRY...... 191
SCHAEFER, MICHAEL.. 191
SCHAEFER, RICK 357
SCHAFER, EDWARD T.... 92
SCHAFER, JACQUELIN E.
  41
SCHAFFER, CORLISS ... 292
SCHAFFER, ERIC V. 10
SCHAFFER, MARY........ 14
SCHAFFER, REBECCA F.
  19
SCHALCH, NANCY........ 284
SCHALLERT, RUSSELL C.
  320
SCHARBER, WAYNE..... 107
SCHASSER, JAMES..... 262
SCHASSLER, STEVE...... 89
SCHATZ, DANIEL 104
SCHAUER, RON 354
SCHEBERLE, DENISE
  LYNNE....................... 392
SCHECHTER, CLAUDIA 263
SCHEIBELHUT, BECKY 267
SCHEIBLE, MICHAEL..... 44

SCHELBLE, RAY............ 338
SCHELVAN, LANCE 307
SCHEMAN, CAROL 19
SCHENCK, JOHN 25
SCHENDEL, BEVERLY.. 356
SCHENK, WILLIAM 29
SCHERCH, JONATHAN. 391
SCHERER, MATT 65
SCHERKENBACH,
  TIMOTHY K.................. 77
SCHERR, JACOB........... 293
SCHICK, ART 341
SCHICKEDANZ, JERRY G.
  88
SCHIFF, DAVID T........... 348
SCHIFFER, LOIS J.......... 20
SCHILLER, FRED 203
SCHIMMOLER, VINCENT
  F................................... 31
SCHINKTEN, JEFFREY B.
  345
SCHISLER, JOHN 129
SCHISLER, LEE C., JR.. 159
SCHLACHTENHAUFEN,
  AMY 243
SCHLENDER, JAMES H.... 7
SCHLENK, CORNELIA G. 90
SCHLICKEISEN, RODGER
  186
SCHLIMGEN-WILSON,
  MINDY 149
SCHLOSS, ALICE 216
SCHLOSS, JEFFREY....... 84
SCHLUTER, CARRIE 236
SCHMIDLIN, KENT 123
SCHMIDLIN, THOMAS W.
  286
SCHMIDT, BOB............. 156
SCHMIDT, ELLEN 219
SCHMIDT, GENE 220
SCHMIDT, JOHN L......... 190
SCHMIDT, JOHN V. 288
SCHMIDT, LOU 331
SCHMIDT, ROBERT 111
SCHMIDT, ROBERT E... 281
SCHMIDT, W. JOHN....... 48
SCHMIDT, WALTER 54
SCHMIT, LARA............. 320
SCHMIT, MICHAEL W.... 102
SCHMITT, JOHN 61
SCHNAPF, ANN 202
SCHNEIDER, JOAN 64
SCHNEIDER, JOHN 52, 250
SCHNEIDER, KEITH 249
SCHNEIDER, NEAL 121
SCHNEIDER, PAT......... 174
SCHNEIDER, REBECCA L.
  90
SCHNEIDERVIN, ROGER
  W. 142
SCHOCH, DEBORAH 338
SCHOCK, ANDREW 268
SCHOCKLY, TOM 122
SCHOEN, JOHN W. 133
SCHOENFELDER, JACK
  173
SCHOENROCK, LINDA . 189
SCHOLES, PETER........ 342
SCHOLL, RUSS 94
SCHOLL, STEVE............ 46
SCHOLLE, PETER.......... 86
SCHOLLENBERG,
  SHIRLEY 133
SCHOLLEY, SUSAN 327
SCHONING, JIM 45
SCHOOLMASTER, ANDY
  389
SCHOONMAKER, PETER
  R. 345
SCHOONOVER, ROY L. 265

SCHRAM, GUS, III.......... 176
SCHRAMEL, JOHN 164
SCHRAMM, HAROLD L.,
  JR................................. 78
SCHRAUFNAGEL, JOHN
  240
SCHRECK, CARL B. 97, 384
SCHREUDER, JACK 125
SCHROADER, BOBBY.. 234
SCHROEDER, ANNA M. 354
SCHROEDER, DAVID B.
  367
SCHROEDER, LELAND 382
SCHROEDER, RICHARD T.
  248
SCHROM, DAVID 244
SCHUBERT, PAUL 35
SCHUECK, THOMAS 43
SCHUERCH, KATE 181
SCHUERG, ALVIN 108
SCHUKMAN, JOHN 238
SCHUL, LANCE 307
SCHULER, RICHARD.... 203
SCHULLER, REID 270
SCHULTZ, BOB............. 138
SCHULTZ, CAROLINE 161, 167
SCHULTZ, CHARLES.... 332
SCHULTZ, CLIFFORD J.
  189
SCHULTZ, RANDALL D. 142
SCHULTZ, WILLIAM D. . 102
SCHULTZE, GORDON .. 277
SCHULZ, JOHN H. 352
SCHULZ, JOHN W. 353
SCHULZ, WILLIAM 31
SCHULZE, MILES.......... 289
SCHUMACHER, AUGUST
  12
SCHUMACHER, MARTHA
  186
SCHUMACHER, MILTON
  305
SCHUNIESING,
  ELIZABETH................ 206
SCHUSTER, HENRY, JR.
  113
SCHUTTE, TED 205
SCHUURMANS, ROBERT
  106
SCHVARTZ, GARY 235
SCHWAAB, ERIC C......... 72
SCHWALBE, CHARLES.. 12
SCHWARTZ, JIM 122
SCHWARTZ, JOHN D. 75
SCHWARTZ, SAM 130
SCHWARTZ, SUZANNE 109
SCHWARTZMAN,
  ANDREW................... 308
SCHWARZ, FREDERICK
  A., JR......................... 271
SCHWEICH, PAULA J... 132
SCHWEIGART, JOSEPH 55
SCHWEIGER, LARRY J. 344
SCHWEITZER, SARAH . 351
SCHWERD, WILLIAM M.
  151
SCHWETZ, BERNARD A. 19
SCHWINDT, FRANCIS.... 93
SCHWOLERT, PHIL 50
SCIASCA, JAMES C...... 353
SCIUTO, FRANK 159
SCOBEL, MATT............ 306
SCOLES, GRAHAM J.... 395
SCORBY, R. D................ 98
SCOTT, 1, 4, 10, 17, 25, 42,
  70, 74, 82, 87, 93, 94,
  104, 106, 107, 121, 123,
  133, 137, 141, 149, 155,
  159, 165, 184, 208, 210,

STAFF NAME INDEX - S

218, 224, 248, 250, 263, 266, 279, 281, 295, 297, 298, 302, 306, 308, 317, 326, 351, 354, 362, 370, 387, 414, 419, 423, 436
SCOTT, BOB 123
SCOTT, DON 128
SCOTT, DOUG 295
SCOTT, J. MICHAEL 60, 184, 369
SCOTT, LORNE.............128
SCOTT, MIKE 391
SCOTT, ROBERT R. 321
SCOTT, STEVE 105
SCOTT, SUE 157
SCOTT, WILLIAM 396
SCRIBNER, TOM...........286
SCROGGINS, RONALD M. 34
SCUDDAY, JAMES F. ...173
SCULLY, R. TUCKER......20
SEABORN, ERIC 25
SEACREST, SUSAN 213
SEAGER, JOHN 361
SEALE, ROBERT L. 34
SEALES, FRANK, JR. 32
SEAMAN, WILLIAM 54
SEARLE, COLGATE 386
SEAROCK, TERESA 135
SEARS, MARK K. 394
SEASE, DEBBIE 314
SEASE, STEPHEN B. ...111
SEAY-GREENEY, CAROL 41
SEBENS, KENNETH P. ..375
SEBERT, D. 266
SEBERT, DAN A. 96
SEBESTA, DAWN, PHD 215
SEBREN, RAY 42
SECKLER, THOMAS 85
SECRIST, GLEN.............319
SEDGWICK, WALTER C. 327
SEDGWICK-POLING, SUSAN 358
SEDINGER, JAMES S. ..362
SEDIVEC, KEVIN K. 93
SEEDORF, DON 241
SEEGARS, WES 92
SEEKINS, RODDY 109
SEELEY, ROD R., Ph.D. 369
SEELING, MIKE 156
SEELY, CLARK 98
SEELY, MARY 188
SEGELKE, MIKE 154
SEGER, JAMES L. 293
SEGERSON, LUCY 137
SEIBEL, JOHN...............355
SEIF, JAMES M. 101
SEIP, WILLIAM F. 270
SEITH, WILLIAM.............61
SEITZ, JOHN S. 10
SEKERAK, CAROLYN...351
SEKSCIENSKI, STEVE ..25
SEKUL, GEORGE 7
SELBIG, WILLIAM 121
SELIGMANN, PETER 183
SELIN, STEVE 392
SELL, ROBIN 351
SELLARS, RICHARD W. 208
SELLERS, STEPHEN 63
SELLSTROM, GAIL 284
SELVA, STEVEN 373
SELVIDGE, MAGGIE......239
SELZ, KATHLEEN 258
SELZER, LAWRENCE A. 183, 349
SEMENCHUK, GLEN 200
SENN, MIKE 41
SENNER, STANLEY E. ..133

SEPTOFF, ALAN 250
SEPTON, GREGORY 320
SEPULVEDA, JOSE 172
SEPULVEDA, MARIA ...298
SERCHUK, ADAM 304
SEREY, REN 72
SEROLD, BRYAN 108
SERYNEK, THOMAS 309
SETLIFF, ED 394
SETSER, JIM 56
SETTERGREN, CARL ...378
SETTINA, NITA 72
SEVIER, HELEN 152, 160
SEWARD, ROY E. 113
SEXSON, TERRY 30
SEXTON, BARBARA A. .101
SEXTON, KAREN 180
SEXTON, ROBERT T. ...349
SEXTON, TERRY 131
SEYDEL, ERICKA 62
SEYMOUR, CARL 279
SEYMOUR, ROSIE 240
SHACKLETON, D. M. 393
SHADDOX, BILL 29
SHADE, HARMON 267
SHAFER, PHYLLIS 117
SHAFER, THOMAS 24
SHAFFER, DIANA A. 41
SHAFFER, EL 110
SHAFFER, MARK 186
SHAFFER, MARTHA 235
SHAFFER, VERNON K..102
SHAHEEN, JEANNE 83
SHAKELY, WILLIAM W. .101
SHALALA, DONNA 19
SHALLENBERGER, MARY 297
SHAMROCK, CINDY 48
SHAND, VALERIE J. 326
SHANK, CHRIS C. 350
SHANK, FRED R. 19
SHANKLIN, DONNA R....43
SHANKS, BERNARD 116
SHANNON, JOHN T. 43
SHANNON, KATHY 233
SHANTORA, V. 36
SHAO, LAWRENCE C. 34
SHARIK, TERRY L. 389
SHARP, DEBBIE..............97
SHARP, DIANE 13
SHARP, GREGORY 335
SHARP, JANE 182
SHARP, WARREN 298
SHARPE, SEAN 167
SHARPLESS, JANANNE.47
SHARPWOLF, KAREN ..339
SHATTUCK, WILLIAM ...106
SHAVELSON, BOB 184
SHAVER, PAT 319
SHAVER, STEPHEN 388
SHAW, FRANK...............128
SHAW, JAMES H. ..353, 384
SHAW, LARRY 77
SHAW, R. LEWIS 105
SHAW, ROGER H. 365
SHAW, SANDI................165
SHAW, SUSAN D. 246
SHAW, WILLIAM W. 363
SHAWYER, COLIN 215
SHEA, ALLEN K. 121
SHEA, ERNEST 182
SHEA, ERNEST C. 257
SHEA, RUTH 212
SHEA, RUTH E. 334
SHEAFFER, C. BRUCE..29
SHEAVLEY, SEBA 170
SHEAY, RON 278
SHEDLOCK, MARLO.....134
SHEEHAN, FRANCIS 89
SHEERAN, LORI............224

SHEESLEY, DAN 12
SHEFFIELD, JIM 82
SHELBURNE, JENNIFER 130
SHELBY, CLIFF.............292
SHELBY, JAMES 148
SHELBY, LUKE 87
SHELDON, DAVID 73
SHELDON, FRED...........148
SHELDON, KARIN P. 250, 390
SHELL, JIM 43
SHELLEY, JOSEE, CPA 233
SHELLMAN, DWIGHT....163
SHELTON, A. J. 57
SHELTON, DWIGHT 221
SHELTON, JO-ANN 366
SHELTON, L. ROBERT....32
SHEPARD, BILL 247
SHEPARD, JOHN...........320
SHEPHERD, WILLIAM M. 44
SHEPPARD, JACK..........73
SHER, SARAH 330
SHERBURNE, FREDA...300
SHERBY, LOUISE..........381
SHERIDAN, NEIL W. 181
SHERMAN, BRUCE A. 50
SHERMAN, C. WENDY...20
SHERMAN, ROBERT.....210
SHEROAN, DONALD 25
SHERON, BRIAN 34
SHERRATT, DENNIS129, 399
SHERRIN, TISH 130
SHERRINGTON, PETER 135
SHERROD, C. LEE 329
SHERROD, STEVE K. 95, 208
SHERWOOD, MIKE 192
SHETLER, STAN, Ph.D. 158
SHETLER, STANWYN ...340
SHEWMAKER, GLENN E. 60
SHIBLEY, GAIL R...........31
SHICK, J. MALCOLM 374
SHIEK, ABDUL 25
SHIEL, VINCENT W. 349
SHIELDS, ANNE 27
SHIELDS, DAVID D. 162
SHIER, CARL 167
SHIMALLA, THOMAS....297
SHIMBERG, STEVEN 268
SHIMBERG, STEVEN J. 267
SHINGLETON, MICHAEL V. 119, 144
SHINN, ROBERT C., JR..85
SHIPMAN, CLYDE 51
SHIPMAN, SUSAN 7
SHIPP, CAROL 84
SHIRE, MIKE 189, 190
SHIREY, RUTH I. 260
SHIRLEY, KAREN 360
SHIRREFF, S. 35
SHIRRELL, JIM 43
SHISHIDO, DOREEN K..58
SHIVELY, JOHN 40
SHOESMITH, MERLIN...124
SHON, FREDERICK J.....34
SHOR, WILLISTON 281
SHORMA, GARY 123
SHORT, CATHLEEN 29
SHORT, GARY L. 208
SHOSTAL, H. CLAUDE..168
SHOUN, GARY 49
SHRINER, ERNIE...........208
SHROPSHIRE, TOMMY 78, 291
SHROUFE, DUANE L. 41
SHUFFIELD, BOB 25

SHUGART, DENNIS.......278
SHULTS, DAN 98
SHULTZ, MICHAEL 172
SHUPE, TODD F. 69
SHUPP, BRUCE 152, 160
SHUSTER, BUD 3, 5
SHUSTER, GUENTER ..372
SHUSTER, LOIS DUPRE 260
SHUTE, PEGGY 323
SHUTT, BARRY 100
SHY, MARILYN 248
SIAR, CHARLES 234
SIBLEY, JOHN A., III 209
SICKING, JOE 276
SIDDIQUI, ISI 12, 46
SIDELL, BRUCE 374
SIEG, TERENCE Y. 324
SIEGELMAN, DONALD ..38
SIEGENTHALER, KIM ...382
SIEGRIST, GARY 249
SIEMBIEDA, WILLIAM ..364
SIENER, JOSEPH 62
SIEVERS, DONALD 351
SIEVERS, LeROY W. 82
SIEWERT, RACHEL 35
SIGAFUS, PHYLLIS 191
SIGG, JACOB 164
SIGMAN, WILLIAM 220
SIKORSKI, JERRY 285
SILBERHORN, GENE M. 390
SILBERSTEIN, JANE 392
SILKONIS, LINDA 248
SILVA, ERALD 87
SILVA, MARY H. 20
SILVA, RALPH 73
SILVER, CHRISTOPHER 370
SILVER, DAN 117
SILVER, JONATHAN 145
SILVER, ROBIN 169
SILVERBERG, ALAN 41
SILVESTER, ROBERT ..354
SILVEY, PATRICIA 20
SILVY, NOVA J. 350
SIM, LEE H. 110
SIMCOX, DAVID E. 364
SIMINO, LARRY 111
SIMMONDS, MARK.......345
SIMMONS, DON 117
SIMMONS, JOHN F. 101
SIMMONS, RODERICK HOYT 247
SIMMONS, RON 308
SIMMS, HERMAN L. 32
SIMMS, KAREN M. 351
SIMMS, WILLIAM 163
SIMON, DAVID 264
SIMON, JAMES F. 20
SIMON, LAURA 207
SIMONDS, KITTY M. 344
SIMONS, BOB 202
SIMONSEN, CHARLIE ...32
SIMPSON, ANN 211
SIMPSON, BILL 227
SIMPSON, HAROLD 49
SIMPSON, JOHN 63
SIMPSON, LARRY B. 7
SIMPSON, MICHAEL 191, 379
SIMPSON, NANCY 62
SIMPSON, ROBERT......144
SIMPSON, TOMMY 347
SIMS, OLIN 359
SIMS, ROBERT B. 262
SINAY, KEN 255
SINCLAIR, ELLERY W. .160
SINCLAIR, MARK 111
SINGER, HAROLD 45

SINGER, JOHN............374
SINGER, PHILIP C.........383
SINGERMAN, PHILLIP A. 17
SINGH, SUSAN.............305
SINGHAUS, BARBARA. 297
SINGHURST, JASON....329
SINGLETARY, PAT........297
SIRCH, JAMES..............180
SIRY, JOE......................201
SISKA, PETER...............388
SIVER, PETER A............367
SIX, LAWRENCE D........293
SKEELE, TOM...............299
SKEEN, MARIANNE J...153
SKELTON, KAREN E......31
SKIERA, BOB.................145
SKINNER, KATHERINE 272
SKINNER, PETER............88
SKINNER, RICHARD........70
SKINNER, THOMAS V....61
SKINNER, TOM...............73
SKOLFIELD, MELISSA....19
SKOUSEN, JEFFREY G.
.....................................120
SKOVRON, DAVID.........131
SKUMAUTZ, KELLEY....198
SLAFER, ANNA.............303
SLATER, CARL A..........163
SLATER, JOE.................248
SLATER, RODNEY..........31
SLATTERLY, MARK........64
SLAYTON, MICHAEL......55
SLEDD, CHARLES A.....114
SLEDGE, JAMES L., JR. 78
SLETTELAND, TRYG....293
SLIFER, JAMES C............61
SLITER, J. THOMAS.........6
SLIVKEN, SUSAN
GOODYEAR................260
SLOAN, MARY MARGARET
.....................................145
SLOCUM, ROBERT W., JR.
.....................................283
SLOMAN, RICHARD D...168
SLUSHER, JOHN P..........80
SLUTZ, JIM......................63
SMALL, CHRISTINE......186
SMALL, DAVID................51
SMALL, EUGENE L........191
SMALLIDGE, PETER J....90
SMALLWOOD, JOHN A. 355
SMARDON, RICHARD C.
.....................................382
SMART, MILES..............158
SMART, ROBERT..........125
SMELOFF, ED...............284
SMITH, ALISON...............89
SMITH, ALLEN...............346
SMITH, ALSON M..........345
SMITH, ANDREW............14
SMITH, ARTHUR............128
SMITH, B. F....................119
SMITH, BILL...................126
SMITH, BILLY RAY..........66
SMITH, BRADLEY F......391
SMITH, BRUCE..............116
SMITH, C. HOLMES......221
SMITH, CARL J..............120
SMITH, CARRY..............266
SMITH, CHAD................149
SMITH, CHARLES.........340
SMITH, CHARLES R......381
SMITH, CHRISTIAN.........80
SMITH, CHRISTOPHER3,
348
SMITH, CLYDE, JR........168
SMITH, CONNIE G..........96
SMITH, D. V...................263
SMITH, DANIEL B..........104
SMITH, DANIEL C..........145

SMITH, DAVID...............377
SMITH, DAVID A...............9
SMITH, DAVID N..............35
SMITH, DAWN..................94
SMITH, DEB...................286
SMITH, DEEN DAY........260
SMITH, DIANA...............361
SMITH, DONALD...........324
SMITH, DONALD H..........50
SMITH, DOUGLAS W......19
SMITH, DUANE A............97
SMITH, ED......................83
SMITH, EDWARD LEE..353
SMITH, ELAINE.............340
SMITH, ERNEST H........109
SMITH, FAYE M.............263
SMITH, FRANCIS...........334
SMITH, GEORGE A.......325
SMITH, GORDON H.........6
SMITH, GREG..................94
SMITH, GUY, IV.............160
SMITH, H. DUANE.........150
SMITH, J. READ............257
SMITH, JACK.................299
SMITH, JACKIE.............202
SMITH, JANE A...............79
SMITH, JEFF.........158, 215
SMITH, JIM....................256
SMITH, JOAN LOVE........13
SMITH, JOHN64, 92, 108,
334
SMITH, JOHN W..............79
SMITH, JON...........253, 331
SMITH, JOSEPH..............20
SMITH, JULIA DIXON....115
SMITH, KAREN L.............41
SMITH, KATHY..............116
SMITH, KEITH..................95
SMITH, KELLY.........75, 256
SMITH, KEN.....................87
SMITH, KENT...................47
SMITH, KEVIN...............203
SMITH, KITTY..................13
SMITH, LARRY C...234, 343
SMITH, LAWRENCE.....246
SMITH, LAWRENCE R. .114
SMITH, LES....................225
SMITH, LORA.................211
SMITH, MARK..........56, 85
SMITH, MARSHALL........18
SMITH, MARY GRACE....42
SMITH, McCLAIN...........249
SMITH, MICHAEL..........181
SMITH, MICKY.................39
SMITH, MITCHELL........160
SMITH, NANCY.......29, 198
SMITH, NEVIN.................53
SMITH, P. GREGORY....319
SMITH, PEG...................138
SMITH, R. DAVID.............90
SMITH, RAY...................331
SMITH, RIC....................333
SMITH, RICH..................287
SMITH, ROB..................314
SMITH, ROBERT L..........50
SMITH, ROGER...............24
SMITH, SARAH..............277
SMITH, SCOTT......155, 263
SMITH, STACEY............335
SMITH, STEWART J.....165
SMITH, TAT....................388
SMITH, THOMAS L........114
SMITH, TIM....................110
SMITH, TOM...........22, 417
SMITH, WALTER M.......298
SMITH, WAYNE.............288
SMITH, WAYNE H.........369
SMITH, WILLIAM...........130
SMITH, WILLIAM H.......121
SMITH, WINSTON P.....150

SMITH, ZANE G., JR......145
SMITHERMAN, JOHN....334
SMITHERS, F. SYDNEY 335
SMITH-WALTERS, CINDI,
Ph.D...........................387
SMOAK, CAMERON.......55
SMOLKO, JOHN............107
SMULIAN, ROBERT D...209
SMYRL, PETER J..........271
SNAPE, WILLIAM J., III.186
SNEATH, WILLIS A.......102
SNIDER, PAT.................177
SNIFFEN, JAMES..........336
SNODGRASS, JERRY...219
SNOOK, JOHN...............162
SNYDER, ED..................391
SNYDER, ELLEN.............84
SNYDER, JAMES P.......101
SNYDER, KEITH A........102
SNYDER, STEVE...........105
SO, FRANK....................148
SOARES, JOSEPH H....374
SOBECK, EILEEN...........20
SOBEL, DAVID..............169
SOBEL, JACK................170
SOBEL, KELLI..................75
SOCHASKY, LEE.............10
SOCOLOFSKY, KATHLEEN
.....................................136
SOEST, SALLY W..........289
SOHN, ARNIE..................65
SOHN, HOWARD.............98
SOKOLOV, V......................9
SOLANO, PATRICK J....101
SOLBERG, TRYGVE A..121
SOLDWEDEL, ROBERT..85
SOLES, ROGER E...........21
SOLIVA, BELMINA I........57
SOLLMAN, DAVE...........265
SOLOMON, KENNETH E.
.....................................296
SOLOW, STEVEN............20
SOMACH, STUART........206
SOMMARSTROM, SARI 343
SOMMER, GEORGE......337
SOMMERS, LARRY.......262
SOMONOVIC, SLOBODAN
.....................................394
SONDERMEYER, GARY. 85
SONIAT, LYLE M..............69
SONNTAG, DOUG.........307
SOOTS, ROBERT F., JR. 26
SOPER, L........................125
SOPER, NANCY...............85
SORENSEN, ANN..........139
SORENSEN, BOB..........379
SORENSEN, CARL........238
SORENSEN, STEVEN...238
SOSNOWSKI, SUSNA...104
SOTO, TOM....................254
SOUBA, FRED, JR.........331
SOUERS, AMY...............149
SOUKUP, MICHAEL........29
SOUTHWICK, DAVID L...77
SOVAS, GREGORY.........89
SOWERS, RAYMON D.A.
.....................................106
SOWERS, RAYMOND A.
.....................................106
SPAGNOLE, JAMES........44
SPAIDE, ROBERT............12
SPALDING, H. CURTIS..309
SPALINK, DAN...............234
SPALT, ALLEN...............160
SPALTHOFF, YVONNE .194
SPAN, KRISTIN..............360
SPANGENBERG, N. EARL
.....................................151
SPANGLER, CONRAD T.,
III.................................115

SPANGLER, KATHY......264
SPANGLER, SCOTT.....297
SPARKMAN, CHRIS........78
SPARKS, JACK..............146
SPARKS, JAMES...........267
SPARKS, JULIE HOLMES
....64
SPARROWE, ROLLIN D.
.....................................349
SPAULDING, SARA JANE
.....................................187
SPAYD, PHILIP................33
SPEAKER, BOB...............25
SPEAR, BOB..................149
SPEAR, FRANK.............381
SPEAR, MICHAEL J........30
SPEAR, ROBERT W........70
SPEARS, JAMES D.........39
SPECK, SAMUEL W........94
SPECTOR, PAUL...........147
SPECTOR, PAUL C.......216
SPEED, MARLA.............253
SPEEDY, LOREE...........162
SPEICE, ALLEN.............108
SPEICH, STEVEN M......293
SPEIR, JERRY...............373
SPEIS, THEMIS P............33
SPELKE, LEE.................247
SPELL, LESTER, JR........78
SPENCE, BETTY...........152
SPENCE, DON...............202
SPENCER, JIM................42
SPENCER, JOHN W........32
SPENCER, MARCUS R. 352
SPERLING, LARRY.......121
SPERRY, THYRA C.......153
SPICER, BRADLEY E......68
SPICKLEMIER, STEVE. 218
SPICKLER, DONALD....246
SPIGARELLI, STEVEN A.
.....................................377
SPILDE, ERIC................331
SPINOSA, SALVATOR..111
SPITLER, RON...............249
SPITZER, STEVE...........173
SPIVAK, RANDI.............146
SPIVY-WEBER, FRANCIS
.....................................254
SPOCK, NICHOLS.........102
SPONENBERG, PHILLIP
.....................................147
SPONSLER, MIKE...........63
SPOONER, CHARLIE....325
SPRAGUE, ANN............354
SPRANGER, MICHAEL S.
.....................................118
SPRATLING, BOYD.........83
SPRECHER-KEATING,
KAREN..........................27
SPRENKLE, RICHARD G.
.....................................101
SPRING, LYNELLE........124
SPRINGER, GARY.........290
SPRINGER, JIM.............280
SPRINGER, MICHAEL L. 34
SPRUANCE, HALSEY... 162
SPRYNCZYNATYK, DAVID
A....................................94
SPURGER, STEVE........389
SPURLOCK, THAD..........68
SQUIER, ANNE..............116
SRONCE, KEVIN..............61
ST. JOHN, JUDITH...........15
ST.GERMAIN, EILEEN.. 205
STAAKE, JEFF.................80
STABB, JO ANN............365
STABENO, DEBRA........108
STABLES, ANDREW.....396
STACEY, B.......................36
STACEY, PAMELA........246

STAFF NAME INDEX - S

STACY, DONNIE L. 190
STADLER, G. MARK 70
STAEBLER, REBECCA N. 319
STAFFORD, SUSAN 367
STAGGS, MICHAEL D. .. 121
STAHL, ANDY 204
STAHL, JANE 50
STALCUP, STEVE 219
STALEY, DOROTHY 14
STALLING, DICK 373
STALLINGS, E. F. 310
STANFIELD, RICHARD. 247
STANGEL, PETER W. ... 261
STANGELL, JULIE 291
STANKEWICH, HENRY G. 102
STANKEY, GEORGE H. 384
STANKIEWICZ, STEVE... 65
STANLEY, DERREK 167
STANLEY, ELAINE G. 10
STANLEY, PATRICIA M. 238
STANLEY, ROYA 65
STANLEY, SHELLEY 50
STANSELL, KENNETH B. 30
STANT, JEFF 216
STANT, JEFFREY 216
STANTON, NANCY L. ... 393
STANTON, ROBERT G. 28, 29, 263
STAPANIAN, MARTIN ... 384
STAPLES-BORTNER, SANDRA 350
STAPLETON, CARL R. . 363
STAPLETON, JOHN 68
STAPLETON, MICHAEL 385
STAPP, WILLIAM 213
STARK, MARION 207
STARK, ROBERT M. 345
STARKE, BO 133
STARKWEATHER, JEAN 246
STARLING, D. ALLEN ... 190
STARNER, ROSS E. 100
STARR, C. M., III 165
STARR, JAMES D. 113
STARR, PATRICK 294
STARRS, PAUL 145
STARTZELL, DAVID N. .. 153
STAUFFER, JAMES L. .. 232
STAUFFER, JAY R., JR. 385
STAUNTON, NICKY 340
STAUTON, EDWARD P. 180
STEARNS, FRANK 100
STEELE, JIM 47
STEELE, ROBERT L. 185
STEELE, SALLY 282
STEEN, DALE 112
STEENSTRA, NORM 343
STEFFES, LAUREL J. ... 121
STEGALL, RODGER 164
STEGMIER, ROBERT ... 234
STEHSEL, DONALD L. . 164
STEIGER, GRETCHEN . 168
STEIGERWALDT, WILLIAM M. 156
STEIMLE, FRANK 147
STEIN, JEFF 149
STEIN, KALMAN 192
STEIN, ROLAND 65
STEINBACH, DONNY W. 108
STEINBACH, TOM 153
STEINDLER, MARTIN J. .. 34
STEINER, KIM C. 385
STEINER, MARY 292
STEINER, ROLAND C. 8
STEINMAUS, MARY 305
STEINWAND, TERRY 93
STELLING, TOM 254

STENBACK, JANINE 47
STENMETZ, JOHN C. 63
STENSTROM, MICHAEL K. 365
STEPHENS, KYLE 110
STEPHENS, RON 390
STEPHENS, WITT, JR. ... 42
STEPHENSON, CHARLES 169
STEPHENSON, JOHN R. 354
STEPHENSON, ROBERT 13
STERLING, PAMELA P ... 11
STERN, LOREN 117
STERNER, ROBERT W. 377
STESSMAN, NEAL 28
STEUBER, JOHN E. 96
STEVENS, CHRISTINE 152, 318
STEVENS, DAVID .. 111, 338
STEVENS, GRETCHEN 217
STEVENS, MARY P. 78
STEVENS, ROGER L. .. 318
STEVENS, RON 206
STEVENS, TED 1, 6
STEVENS, WILLIAM 199
STEVENSON, BARBARA 167
STEVENSON, FRED 200
STEVENSON, KATE 29
STEVENSON, NANCY ... 117
STEVENSON, STEPHANIE 21
STEVENSON, TOD 87
STEVER, DONALD 198
STEVIS, DIMITRIS 367
STEWART, ALLAN 127
STEWART, CONNIE 284
STEWART, DAVID 333
STEWART, DEAN 79
STEWART, DOUG . 126, 399
STEWART, GARLAND .. 332
STEWART, GARY 189
STEWART, GEORGE 146
STEWART, HARRY T. 84
STEWART, JIM, Ph.D. .. 365
STEWART, JON 237
STEWART, RONALD 16
STEWART-KENT, DEBORAH 203
STEWIG, JOE 141
STICKLES, VAN A. 104
STICKNEY, ROBERT R. 109
STIEGLITZ, RONALD D. 392
STILES, DAVID A. 394
STILES, LYNN 380
STILLER, KATHLEEN 51
STILLINGER, DANIEL ... 301
STILLMAN, NEIL 19
STILSON, TERRI 211
STINE, JEFFREY 149
STIRLING, ED 219
STIRLING, EDWIN W. .. 270
STITH, JOHN 213
STITZHAL, DAVID 341
STOCKDALE, JUDITH M. 196
STOCKLEY, CAROL 131
STOECKEL, JOSEPH ... 363
STOFAN, JAMES L. 267
STOFFLE, CARLA J. 363
STOFLET, ROGER 25
STOGNER, JOSEPH D. 390
STOIBER, CARLTON R. .. 34
STOKES, DONALD 260
STOKES, HANK 95
STOKES, JOHN C. 85
STOKES, JUDY 84, 155
STOKES, JULIA S. 91
STOKES, ROBERT 85

STOKES, RODNEY 75
STOLEN, ERIC 202
STOLGITIS, JOHN 103, 398
STOLTZ, JIM 299
STOLTZ, MICHAEL 99
STONE, ALAN T. 374
STONE, ALEXANDER ... 147
STONE, ANDREW W. ... 145
STONE, CHARLIE 98
STONE, LEE 270
STONE, M. BRIAN 111
STONE, MIKE 123
STONE, NATHAN M. 43
STONE, RENEE 27
STONE, SHERIDAN 25
STONECIPHER, HARLAND 95
STOPLMAN, PAUL M. 10
STOREY, RICHARD D. . 257
STORMO, JACK 31
STORTZ, PETER J. 40
STORY, RICK 349
STOSSEL, ROBERT, JR. 203
STOTT, WILLIAM, JR. ... 347
STOUDER, DEANA 384
STOUT, GENE 24
STOWE, JOE C. 342
STRAHL, STUART 259
STRAILEY, ROBERT 102
STRAIT, DONALD S. 181
STRASSER, VIRGINIA 19
STRATMAN, OMAR 133
STRATTON, JIM 40
STRAUCH, NANCY 309
STRAUGHAN, BAIRD ... 221
STRAUGHAN, THOMAS.. 97
STRAUSE, HOWARD 254
STRAWN, SHEILA 289
STRAYER, DAVID L. 222
STREET, KATHRYN 345
STREETER, TRACY D. .. 66
STREICH, JOHN 95
STREIFEL, DENNIS 124
STREIT, TED 119
STRICKLAND, TIMOTHY .16
STRICKLER, JOHN 237
STRICKLER, RICHARD .101
STRINGER, BILL 321
STROBEL, MARK 252
STROEDER, CELINA ... 126
STROHM, BOB D. 267
STROM, PETER 380
STROMSTAD, RONALD A. 189
STRONG, DAVID 294
STROUD, CHRIS 345
STROUP, EDDIE 282
STRUBLE, DAVE 70
STRUBLE, ROBERT, JR. 250
STUART, DAVID W. 368
STUART, DON 340
STUBBS, MITIZ 78
STUBCHAER, JAMES M. 45
STUCHLIK-EDWARDS, SUSAN 51
STUCKEY, RONALD L. .286
STUCKY, DONALD J. ... 370
STUCKY, NORM 252
STUCKY, NORMAN P. 79
STUDER, MARIE 193
STUDLEY, JANNIENNE S. 18
STUDT, JOHN 26
STULTS, JACK 81
STUMBOUGH, GRANT ..122
STUMVOLL, RANDALL ...90
STUNTZNER, RONALD E. 156

STURDY, JERRY 24
STURGEON, WALTER B., JR. 230
STURGES, WILTON 368
STURGESS, MELINDA ... 95
STURGILL, JAMES 172
STURLA, KIMBERLY 207
STURM, CHARLES 174
STURM, ROBERT 6
STURM, RUSSELL 226
STURMER, JERRY 179
STURTEVANT, BOB 50
STUSHNOFF, BRIAN G. 185
STUTZMAN, ROGER ... 218
STUWE, BRUCE 342
STYMMES, RIC 200
SU, CHIN 22
SUBLETT, ROSS 348
SUBLETTE, DICK 54
SUCKLING, KIERAN 169
SUECK, PATRICIA 294
SULKIN, STEPHEN D. . 391
SULLIVAN, ALFRED D. .. 377
SULLIVAN, BETH 241
SULLIVAN, CHARLES 89
SULLIVAN, DAVE T. 137
SULLIVAN, EDWARD O. .. 70
SULLIVAN, JEREMIAH J. 32
SULLIVAN, JOHN H. 151
SULLIVAN, KATE 306
SULLIVAN, LARRY 42
SULLIVAN, MICHAEL 76
SULLIVAN, MICHELE 50
SULLIVAN, MONICA 242
SULLIVAN, NED 311
SULLIVAN, RICK 170
SULLIVAN, TADE 13
SULLIVAN, TIMOTHY ... 252
SUMMERS, JIM 343
SUMMERS, LAWRENCE H. 32
SUMMERS, WILLIAM J. .. 21
SUNDERLAND, LARRY 159
SUNDQUIST, DON 107
SUNIA, TAUESE P.F. 40
SUNLEY, WILLIAM T. 61
SURBER, LAURA 233
SURKIN, ELLIOT 335
SUTCLIFFE, DAN 353
SUTCLIFFE, SCOTT 184
SUTHERLAND, DAVID M. 182
SUTTLES, RON 95
SUTTON, KEITH 42
SUTTON, MAUREEN ... 182
SUTTON, ROBERT 103
SUTTON, SCOTT T. 165
SUTTON, WALTER L. 31
SVEDARSKY, DANIEL .. 377
SVEDARSKY, W. DANIEL 350
SVEIKAUSKAS, GEDDY 168
SVENSEN, GENE 23
SVETAHOR, EMIL 102
SWACINA, LINDA 12
SWADER, FRED 16
SWAIN, HILARY 153
SWAN, CHRISTOPHER 375
SWANEY, JIM, Ph.D. 287
SWANSON, D. 285
SWANSON, DAVID 322
SWANSON, GERRY 36
SWANSON, MERV 128
SWANSON, PAUL F. 102
SWANSON, ROBERT ... 305
SWANSON, SHERMAN .. 83
SWARTZ, PAUL O. 10
SWARTZ, ROSALEE 379
SWARTZ, STEVEN 319
SWATFIGURE, RON 116

Staff Name Index

STAFF NAME INDEX - T

SWAYNE, CHERYL......... 65
SWEATMAN, MICHAEL 230
SWEDBURG, RANDY .. 136
SWEENEY, BERNARD W.
.... 326
SWEENEY, JOHN R.104, 387
SWEENEY, KEVIN 292
SWEET, DAN................ 172
SWEET, MELINDA M. ... 238
SWEETEN, JERRY 142
SWEETLAND, HELEN ... 312
SWEETMAN, SARAH.... 308
SWEETWOOD, SAGE... 297
SWENARCHUK, MICHELLE
.... 166
SWENGEL, ANN............ 280
SWENGEL, SCOTT........ 224
SWENSON, GUY A. 281
SWENSON, HEATHER . 219
SWENSON, LELAND H. 261
SWENSON, PAUL 76
SWENSON, SMOKEY ... 256
SWIADON, LAURIE 161
SWIFT, BYRON 358
SWIHART, ROBERT K.. 371
SWINGLE, WAYNE E.... 214
SWITKES, GLENN 227
SWOPE, MARJORY 84
SWOPE, MARJORY M.. 276
SYKES, JACK C. 114
SYLVESTER, SUSAN L. 120
SZCZYTKO, STAN 393
SZELC, GARY 157
SZRAMOSKI, MATTHEW
.... 265
SZYMANSKI, EDWARD S.
.... 103

T

TABATA, RAYMOND S. .. 59
TABOR, LANCE............. 119
TABORSKY, THERESEA
.... 386
TAFF, STEVEN................ 77
TAFT, JANE 287
TAFT, JOHN 223
TAFT, LAWRENCE 159
TAFT, ROBERT 94
TAGGART, JUDY 328
TAHTINEN, SHARON...... 64
TAILLON, ANDRE 128
TAIT, LYN 124
TAITANO, CONCHITA S.N.
.... 57
TAK, JETTY 225
TAKASUGI, PATRICK A.. 60
TALBOT, MARTHA H. ... 301
TALBOTT, SCOTT......... 123
TALLEY, JOHN H. 52
TALLMAN, DAN............. 322
TALSMA, ART................ 307
TALUTO, SUSAN 89
TAMARU, CLYDE 59
TAMAYOSE, JOY 351
TAN, BETSY JOY 395
TANAKA, ROBERT T. 13
TANNER, GREGG 83
TAPIA, ALVARO ARAGON
.... 171
TAPPERO, DENICE 340
TARANTINO, HELEN ... 115
TARBURTON, JOHN F., JR. 51
TARKINGTON, KEN 107
TARNOPOL, JOE 25
TARPLIN, RICHARD 19
TATARIAN, TRISH 354

TATE, DAVID 219
TATE, MICHAEL J. 118
TATE, ROBERT 380
TATES, DENNIS 23
TAUBERT, BRUCE 41
TAUER, JONATHON 284
TAVARES, AIMEE 195
TAVER, CHARLES 96
TAYER, JEFF 116
TAYLOR, ALFRED H., JR.
.... 139
TAYLOR, ANNE 91
TAYLOR, BARBARA...... 216
TAYLOR, BARBARA S. . 119
TAYLOR, BILL............... 157
TAYLOR, CHARLES 383
TAYLOR, CONSTANCE E.S. 288
TAYLOR, DAISAN........... 25
TAYLOR, DAVID 332
TAYLOR, G. DONALD 70
TAYLOR, GARY J. 223
TAYLOR, J. BLAKE......... 63
TAYLOR, J. MARVIN 156
TAYLOR, JAMES M. 34
TAYLOR, JANICE 187
TAYLOR, JANICE E....... 264
TAYLOR, JEFFREY H. 83
TAYLOR, JENNIFER 160
TAYLOR, JIMMY D. 352
TAYLOR, KEN 39
TAYLOR, KENT 107
TAYLOR, M. 36
TAYLOR, MICHAEL R. 19
TAYLOR, ROBERT 95
TAYLOR, ROBERT W.... 380
TAYLOR, STEPHEN H.83, 84
TAYLOR, STEVEN........ 239
TAYLOR, SYLVIA M. 249
TAYLOR, THOMAS N. .. 372
TAYLOR, TIM 197
TAYLOR, TOM 212
TAYLOR, WALT 56
TAYLOR, WILLIAM W.... 75
TAYLOR-ROGERS, SARAH J. 72
TAYON, JIM 23
TAZIK, DAVE................. 263
TAZL, B. M. 228
TEAGUE, WADE 301
TEAL, JOHN M. 183
TEBO, PAUL 239
TEDERKO, ZENON 229
TEER, JAMES 182
TEETERS, NELSON 220
TEFFEAU, K. MARC 131
TEIG, DONALD 25
TEILLON, H. BRENTON 111
TEMPERO, JAMES........ 335
TEMPLE, RYAN S.......... 204
TEMPLETON, BILLY R.. 265
TEMPLETON, DAVID 106
TENEYCK, ELIZABETH Q.
.... 34
TENNENBAUM, CELIA.. 259
TENNISON, HARRY 208
TENORE, KENNETH R.. 375
TERRELL, GRETA 210
TERRELL, SANDRA 389
TERRY, GORDON 249
TERRY, LYNN 44
TERWILLIGER, MICHELLE
.... 311
TESITOR, CARLOS 339
TESKE, RICHARD H....... 19
TESSLER, ALLAN......... 236
THACHER, THOMAS D., II
.... 131
THACKER, RANDALL K.354

THACKSTON, EDWARD L.
.... 388
THADANI, ASHOK C........ 34
THADEN, GERALD 322
THAIN, DAVID 82
THAYER, DAN 202
THAYER, PAUL D. 46
THE RIGHT HONORABLE THE EARL OF SHAFTESBURY, ... 215
THEISEN-WATT, LEE.... 230
THELEN, MICHELLE...... 252
THERKELSEN, ROBERT L.
.... 47
THEURER, MIKE............. 65
THIAW, IBRAHIM 229
THIBAULT, ROGER E. .. 383
THIBEAULT, GERALD 45
THIBEDEAU, RICHARD... 73
THIEDE, GERALD 75
THIELE, JOHN, JR. 197
THIELE, TIM 189
THIELGES, BART 384
THIERET, JOHN W. 238
THIERMANN, ALEX B..... 12
THIESSEN, LARRY 245
THOELECKE, TIMOTHY N.
.... 248
THOEMKE, KRIS........... 268
THOM, DERRICK J. 390
THOM, RICHARD H. 79
THOMANN, JUDY DIOUS 62
THOMAS, CHRISTINE ... 393
THOMAS, CRAIG .. 4, 6, 317
THOMAS, DAN 211
THOMAS, DAVE............. 72
THOMAS, DIANE C. 217
THOMAS, DONNA 164
THOMAS, EDWARD L. ... 32
THOMAS, EMY 339
THOMAS, EVAN............ 127
THOMAS, GARY 155
THOMAS, JACK WARD162, 379
THOMAS, JAMES B., JR. 18
THOMAS, JEANETTE.... 370
THOMAS, JIM 218
THOMAS, JOHN............ 252
THOMAS, JUDY ISACOFF
.... 160
THOMAS, LISA.............. 184
THOMAS, MARSHALL ... 209
THOMAS, MATTHEW E. 142
THOMAS, SANDY 284
THOMAS, TIMOTHY P... 355
THOMASHOW, CINDY .. 169
THOMASHOW, MITCHELL
.... 379
THOMASON, BILL........... 78
THOMAS-SLAYTER, BARBARA P. 375
THOMLISON, BRYAN ... 213
THOMPSON, BRUCE C...87
THOMPSON, CHARLES 202
THOMPSON, CHRISTINE P. 321
THOMPSON, CINDY........ 38
THOMPSON, CLYDE....... 16
THOMPSON, CRAIG...... 360
THOMPSON, DEREK..... 124
THOMPSON, DIANNE E. 19
THOMPSON, DONNA ... 136
THOMPSON, DOUG 233
THOMPSON, EDWARD, JR.
.... 139
THOMPSON, ELIZABETH
.... 196
THOMPSON, F. E. 79
THOMPSON, HUGH L., JR.
.... 34

THOMPSON, JOHN....... 219
THOMPSON, JOHN D.248, 351
THOMPSON, LARRY201, 242
THOMPSON, LYNN ALAN
.... 203
THOMPSON, MARK........ 68
THOMPSON, MAX C. 238
THOMPSON, NINA......... 80
THOMPSON, PATRICIA 142
THOMPSON, ROBIN L.... 16
THOMPSON, RUDI......... 389
THOMPSON, STEPHEN E.
.... 334
THOMPSON, STEVE..... 356
THOMPSON, STEVEN A. 96
THOMPSON, TERRIE H.
.... 363
THOMPSON, THOMAS. 284
THOMPSON, TOMMY G.
.... 120
THOMPSON, WARREN S.
.... 378
THOMSON, DAVID........ 167
THONG, NGUYEN MINH
.... 229
THORN, CLANCY, JR. .. 137
THORN, COLIN E. 370
THORNDIKE, DAN 99
THORNE, OAKLEIGH 331
THORNE, OAKLEIGH, II 329
THORNE, TOM 355
THORNTON, BILL 127
THOROUGHGOOD, CAROLYN, ... 52
THORP, LYNN 213
THORP, TOM 283
THORPE, DORIS 159
THORPE, KENNETH..... 300
THORSON, GARY 122
THORVIG, LISA J. 77
THRAILKILL, JIM A........ 353
THRALLS, MIKE.............. 96
THRASHER, BARBARA SUE............................. 340
THRONSON, HOWARD 118
THRUNE, ELAINE M. 269
THURM, KEVIN 19
THURMAN, STEVE 25
THURMOND, JIMMIE V., III
.... 329
THURSTON, ANCYL 245
TIBBETTS, DAVID......... 152
TICE, R. DEAN 264
TICHENOR, CAREY........ 67
TICHY, TED 277
TIDEMANN, LARRY J... 106
TIEFENTHALER, JAMES, JR. 121
TIELL, JENNIFER 94
TIERNAN, JOSEPH A.... 135
TIERNEY, TIMOTHY 131
TIERNEY, VANYLA S. ... 295
TIGHE, DENNIS............. 255
TIGNER, TIMOTHY C.... 113
TILESTON, JULES 40
TILESTON, PEG 134
TILLSON, JOHN 78
TILT, WHITNEY C. 261
TIMKO, JOHN F. 41
TIMMEL, BERTHA M. ... 239
TIMMERMAN, JAMES A., JR. 105
TIMMONS, TOM J. 372
TINDAL, D. LESLIE 105
TINDALL, BARRY 264
TINLIN, DICK 307
TINSLEY, JOHN, III 169
TINSLEY, NIKKI I. 10

STAFF NAME INDEX - U

TINSLEY, RICHARD...... 345
TINTERA, MARCY......... 379
TIPPETT, RUSSELL K. . 383
TIPTON, W. HORD .. 28, 421
TISCHLER, BONNI G. 32
TITUS, ELIZABETH C. .. 326
TIXIER, SUSAN 177
TJADEN, BOB................. 72
TOBIN, DAVID 269
TOBIN, RICHARD........... 254
TOBORG, BARBARA 147
TODD, CLYDE M. 243
TODD, LAURA 353
TOEPFER, KAREN........ 237
TOEPFER, KLAUS 336
TOEWS, DON 129
TOKUE, MICHIAKI......... 280
TOLLIVER, JIM 150
TOM, GARRY 220
TOMAN, MICHAEL 304
TOMASSON, DAVID 124
TOMB, SPENCER 267
TOMERA, PATSY 275
TOMLINSON, DENISE .. 291
TOMLINSON, JEANIE ... 355
TOMPKINS, DAVID L. ... 105
TONNING, STEPHEN 189
TONSO, STEVE 190
TONSOR, STEPHEN J. . 386
TOOHEY, MARY M. 117
TOOHEY, MICHAEL J. .. 266
TOOLE, JOSEPH S. 31
TOOLE, ROBERT........... 257
TOOR, WILL 367
TOOTHAKER, JAMES S.
.... 101
TOPHAM, GORDON 110
TOPLISEK, TIMOTHY R.. 26
TOPPING, JANE............ 200
TOPPING, JOHN C., JR.175
TOPPING, STEVEN 125
TORELL, DAVE 307
TORGERSON, OLIVER A.
.... 79
TORIDIS, THEODORE G.
.... 368
TORLEY, CORAL 235
TOROK, LAURANCE S. 353
TORRENCE, JIM 286
TORRES, ALFONSO....... 13
TORRES, ELEANOR 330
TORRES, RAMON L....... 103
TORSBERG, ROBERT.. 191
TOTMAN, LORI A. 186
TOTTEN, DEBBIE 286
TOUGAARD, O................. 9
TOUT, SUE N. 228
TOW, KENNETH R........... 64
TOWERY, DAN.............. 183
TOWLE, EDWARD L. 233
TOWLE, EVERETT........ 245
TOWLE, JUDITH A. 233
TOWNS, ELEANOR S. ... 17
TOWNSEND, GEORGIA C.
.... 234
TOWNSEND, GEROGIA C.
.... 234
TOWNSEND, LAIRD 194
TOWNSEND, PETER 383
TOWNSEND, TOM 278
TRAINER, DANIEL O. ... 345
TRAISI, CHUCK 207
TRAMMONTANO, RONALD
.... 89
TRANTHAM, KATHI 292
TRAORE, MOCTAR 229
TRASK, R...................... 125
TRAUB, PAT.................. 346
TRAVELSTEAD, JACK G.
.... 113

TRAVER, TIM................ 338
TRAVERS, WILLIAM D....34
TRAVIS, WILL 48
TRAVOUS, KENNETH E.42, 258
TREACY, DENNIS H...... 114
TREANOR, ROBERT R. .. 48
TREFRY, STU 118
TREJO, TAMARA........... 213
TREMBLAY, JEAN-PIERRE
.... 301
TREMBLAY, MARC J..... 305
TREMBLE, ELAINE.......... 14
TRENOWETH, ROY W....83
TRENT, TRACEY............. 60
TREVETT, DAVID H....... 189
TRIESTE, MARION........ 313
TRIFF, MICHAEL 335
TRIMBLE, BOB 219
TRINE, CHERYL 148
TRIPOLI, FRANK 284
TRIPP, JAMES T............ 196
TRIPP, JIM 191
TROTTA, LEE 251
TROXELL, PAM 392
TROY, DICK 48
TROYCHAK, MARY 360
TROYER, THOMAS A.... 250
TRUBY, BILL 55
TRUDEAU, MAURICE ... 104
TRUE, TODD................. 192
TRUEBLOOD, JACK....... 60
TRUESDELL, CHARMANE
.... 247
TRUITT, BRUCE A. 215
TRUJILLO, TOM.............. 86
TRULAND, MARY W...... 172
TRULAND, ROBERT W. 172
TRUPPA, MICHAEL 198
TRUSSO, SAMARA 223
TRYON, CRAIG................ 90
TSCHANZ, ERIC 136
TSOSIE, CARL A. 231
TUBBS, NANCY JO 230
TUCK, AL 78
TUCKER, DANA 270
TUCKER, JUDY 177
TUCKER, KELLEY 138
TUCKER, RICHARD G. . 158
TUCKER, RICHARD THOMPSON................. 248
TUCKER, ROBERT.......... 70
TUCKER, THURMAN..... 252
TUDOR, BOB................... 85
TUFTEY, JAMES 89
TUFTS, ROBERT............. 48
TUGAEFF, BARBARA ... 152
TUGGLE, BENJAMIN 29
TUGNED, TOM................ 94
TUKAHIRWA, ELDAD ... 229
TULANG, MIKE 214
TULL, J F....................... 368
TULLBANE, JOSEPH D. 392
TULLIUS, MARY 110
TULLOCH, DAVE........... 128
TULLOCH, LYNN 128
TULLY, CLARE 259
TUMINSKI, RONALD 85
TUNBERG, GAIL........... 353
TUNGESVICK, KEVIN ... 220
TUOHY, MARY BETH...... 62
TUPPER, DOUG 123
TURK, ERIK, RPF 290
TURLINGTON, JEFF 282
TURNBOW, ROBERT...... 25
TURNBULL, CHARLES W.
.... 112
TURNER, DANIEL C...... 216
TURNER, DEE 237
TURNER, JOHN............ 241

TURNER, JOHN F..........182
TURNER, JOSH 255
TURNER, ROBERT J.....353
TURNER, RONALD 49
TURNER, RONALD J......80
TURNER, TIM................266
TURNER, TOM...............192
TURNER, WAYNE.........328
TURNEY, JOHN 278
TURNEY, THOMAS C.....88
TURNIPSEED, R. MICHAEL
....83
TURNPENNY, COLLIN ..127
TURRINI, TONY 267
TURVILLE, HAL..............201
TUSSENBROOK, LEE VAN
......................................116
TUTEN, JOHN C., JR.....350
TUTTLE, ANDREA E........47
TUTTLE, MERLIN D.......160
TUYN, PETER VAN........335
TWISS, JOHN R., JR.........8
TYER, ED......................225
TYLER, BOB....................78
TYLER, DARRYL..............51
TYLER, DUDE 254
TYLER, HARRY R., JR..270
TYLER, JACK D.............289
TYMCHUK, LEE.............135
TYRL, RONALD J..........288
TYSER, ROB..................392
TYSON, TISH 199
TYZBIR, ROBERT..........112

U

UBOH, CORNELIUS E...100
UCELLI, LORETTA M......10
UCHIDA, DEAN 58
UDALL, STEWART.........256
UDELL, BERT................269
UECKER, CHERYL 345
UERZ, JEFFREY A.........114
UGARENKO, LEN 223
UHAZY, LESLIE 348
UHER, JEROME............264
UHLENDORF, KAREN ...390
UHLENHUTH, KAREN ...253
UHMANN, TANYS 352
UHSIE, LARRY...............249
ULLENSVANG, LEON P.
......................................358
ULMAN, SUZANNE........165
ULMER, F. 9
ULRICH, ANN R. 336
ULRICH, DAVID A...........11
ULTEE, CASPER J.........180
UMANSKY, DAVID..........318
UMBER, HAROLD............93
UMSTEAD, GERALYN...100
UNDERHILL, TODD 201
UNDERWOOD, CECIL7, 119
UNDERWOOD, H. BRIAN
......................................382
UNDERWOOD, JOANNA D.
......................................221
UNDERWOOD, PETER .126
UNGER, DANIEL 388
UNKENHOLZ, DENNIS..106
UNSWORTH, MICHAEL H.
......................................384
UPGREN, TED 93
UPSHAW, GRACE 312
URBAN, DICK................328
URBAN, RIC 137
URQUHART, THOMAS A.
......................................244
URRUTIA, AL...................22

USINGER-LESQUEREUX, JANET............................ 83
UYEHARA, LETITIA N..... 58
UZZELL, JAMES............ 122

V

VAIL, NITA 46
VAIL, VIRGINIA................ 53
VALDE, MICHAEL 64
VALDEZ, ANA GLENA..... 37
VALDEZ, LORI 14
VALDEZ-PIZZINI, MANUEL
.... 103
VALENCIC, CYNTHIA ... 242
VALENTINE, AL............. 221
VALENTINE, BRADLEY E.
.... 350
VALENTINE, GARY 329
VALENTINE, GAYLE 60
VALENTINE, LUISE 135
VALENTINETTI, RICHARD A............................... 111
VALLEE, JUDITH 310
VALLENDER, LEONARD J.
.... 165
VALLET, RUDY................ 90
VAN ABBEMG, JIM........ 279
VAN AKEN, ALAN G........ 57
VAN ATTA, SUSAN 179
VAN DER ZEL, D. W. 323
VAN ES, JOHN C............. 62
VAN GILDER, GAIL L..... 187
VAN HUSEN, CARL....... 245
VAN LOCKWOOD, PETER
.... 175
VAN MATRE, STEVE 221
VAN PUTTEN, MARK267, 269
VAN RAALTE, GERRIT ... 37
VAN ROEKEL, JOEL 231
VAN ROSSUM, MAYA... 147
VANALLER, ROBERT T.. 77
VANBLARICOM, GLENN R.
.... 319
VANBUECKEN, DONNA 346
VANCE, GRACE 272
VANCE, LAWRENCE 94
VANCE, TAMARA 115
VANDEL, GEORGE64, 106, 261
VANDENBERG, THOMAS
.... 160
VANDERMARK, PETER 312
VANDERMEY, SHELLY 129
VANDERSTEEN, CHARLES A. 243
VANG, ALFRED H. 105
VANICEK, C. DAVID...... 364
VANLOPIK, JACK R......... 69
VANNICE, DEREK 227
VanZYLL de JONG, M. .. 125
VARLAMOFF, SUSAN... 209
VARNES, BARBARA 285
VARNEY, ROBERT 84
VARNEY, ROBERT W..... 84
VASILOFF, HEIDI 41
VASUKI, N. C. 52
VATTIMO, BRIAN R......... 91
VAUGHAN, ANGUS M... 251
VAUGHAN, KATHERINE G.
.... 68
VAUGHAN, MICHAEL R.
.... 113
VAUGHN, CARYN C........ 95
VAUGHN, DENISE 292
VAUGHN, JAMES 62
VAUX, HENRY J., JR....... 45
VEEMAN, MICHELE...... 393

VEGA, ROGER R. 60
VEHRS, KRISTIN 151
VEILLON, EDGAR F. 244
VEITH, GILMAN D., Ph.D. 11
VENEMAN, ANN M. 46
VENSKUS, JILL 158
VENTURA, JESSE 75
VENTURINI, PETER D. 45
VERANTH, JOHN 338
VERARDO, DENZIL 48
VERDOLIVA, FRAN. 89
VERGATA, NAPOLEON 228
VERIGIN, STEVE 48
VERPLOEG, ALAN J. ... 123
VESSELL, C. RANDALL 378
VETTER, WAYNE E. 84
VEVERKA, MARY JO 19
VIBERT, JOAN. 237
VICE, DAVID. 63
VICENTE, RALPH 161
VICK, CHRIS. 345
VICKERMAN, SARA 186
VICKERS, KYLE 79
VICORY, ALAN H., JR. 9
VICTOR, PETER, ... 395
VICTOR, ROBERT 172
VIDRINE, WINTON 68
VIETOR, JEAN. 220
VIGIL, ALFREDO, MD ... 297
VIGOTSKY, TIMOTHY G. 27
VIGUE, CHARLES L., Ph.D. 367
VILARDO, FRANK 371
VILCHES, MARIA 172
VILELLA, FRANCISCO J. 78
VILJOEN, C. 323
VILLAFANE, AWILDA. 32
VILSACK, TOM 63
VINCE, SUSAN 202
VINCENT, FREDERICK J. 103
VINCENT, HOWARD K. 296
VINCENT, MATT. 152
VINCENT, RANDALL. 219
VINCENT, RANDALL G. 270
VINCENT, WILLIAM J. ... 136
VINCENTI, FRANK 346
VINES, SUSAN TURNER-LOWE. 264
VINES, TERRY L. 264
VINEY, ANGELA 321
VINING, LEN 308
VINSON, NANCY 321
VINT, MARY. 305
VIRDEN, TERRY 28
VIRGIN, RANDY 133
VIRGINIA, ROSS A. 379
VIRTS, D.V.M., HENRY A. 71
VISSERS, BERT 127
VLADECK, BRUCE C. 19
VLAHOVICH, STJEPAN ... 95
VODAK, MARK C. 86
VODEHNAL, WILLIAM L. 352
VOELTZ, BARBARA 82, 271
VOGEL, DAVID S. 92
VOGEL, HARRY 159
VOGEL, RICHARD M. ... 375
VOGELMANN, H. W. 181
VOGT, ALBERT R. 378
VOIGHTS, BRUCE 231
VOKATY, CHRIS 251
VOLESKY, MIKE 254
VOLK, JOHN 50
VOLK, MICHAEL 312
VOLLBREECHT, MARY ELLEN 337
VOLLERS, JOLI 233
VOLPÉ, JEANNOT 125

VON EHWEGAN, TODD 231
VON FINGER, KEVIN 24
VON RUEDEN, GERALD. 22
VONDRACEK, BRUCE C. 76
VONNAHME, DON 61
VOORHIS, KEN 212
VORAC, TOM 25
VORE, JOHN. 352
VORONKOV, VICTOR ... 170
VORONTSOVA, MASHA 225
VOSS, HANS. 249
VRANCART, RON. 127
VREELAND, JUSTIN 351
VULK, JAN 321
VYSE, ERNEST R. 378

W

WAADE, LINDA 175
WAAK, PATRICIA 259
WADDEL, IAN G. 124
WADDILL, CHRISTINE T. 54
WADE, JAMES. 72
WADE, JEPTHA H. 245
WADE, JERRY & EDGE 159
WADSWORTH, FRANK H. 228
WAGENER, KARL J. 50
WAGGONER, LYNDA ... 345
WAGNER, BARBARA 339
WAGNER, BRAD 356
WAGNER, BRAIN K. 141
WAGNER, CURTIS J., JR. 19
WAGNER, DAWN 22
WAGNER, DON 279
WAGNER, JR., SIDNEY 235
WAGNER, PHILIP. 63
WAGNER, PHILLIP 190
WAGNER, ROBERT 139, 294
WAGNER, STEVE 292
WAGNER, WILLIAM R. .. 169
WAHL, MARY 98
WAINMAN, BARBARA 30
WAINWRIGHT, JANET. 342
WAINWRIGHT, NANCY. 348
WAIT, PAUL 232
WAITE, G. THOMAS, III. 217
WAITO, BARRY 166
WAKIMOTO, ROGER M. 365
WAKOLBINGER, TOM..... 61
WALCHER, GREG 49
WALDMAN, DOUG 197
WALDO, THOMAS S. 192
WALDON, CAROLYN 267
WALDON, JEFFERSON L. 201, 354
WALKE, TED R. 101
WALKER, ALICE 152
WALKER, BILL 7
WALKER, BRUCE 326
WALKER, DON 66
WALKER, DOUGLAS C. 271
WALKER, HIRAM J. 32
WALKER, JAMES B. 153
WALKER, JIM. 78, 124
WALKER, LEE 115
WALKER, MARK 83
WALKER, MARTIN 390
WALKER, MARVIN 33
WALKER, MASON 25
WALKER, NATHALIE. ... 192
WALKER, POLLY, M.D. . 374
WALKER, RANDY .. 165, 245
WALKER, RICHARD E. . 130
WALKER, RICHARD L.H. 189
WALKER, ROGER 379

WALKER, WILLIAM W. 77
WALKER-GAYLE, C. 290
WALKINGSTICK, TAMARA L. 43
WALKOWIAK, JOHN 65
WALL, CAROL 297
WALL, DIANA 194, 367
WALL, JULIUS F. 189
WALLA, WALTER J. 67
WALLACE, ALICE 218
WALLACE, BILL 118
WALLACE, CHARLES R. 374
WALLACE, DON 46
WALLACE, KATHLEEN ... 76
WALLACE, RICHARD K. 39, 78
WALLER, DAVID 56
WALLER, DAVID J. 223, 397
WALLER, STEVE 379
WALLER, WILLIAM T. ... 389
WALLIN, PHIL 306
WALLIS, CLIFF 135, 167
WALLIS, PHILIP S. 271
WALLS, SUSAN 378
WALPER, FRANK 238
WALRATH, GARY 80
WALSBERG, GLENN E. 184
WALSH, BILL 213
WALSH, BOB 28
WALSH, EDWARD J., JR. 207
WALSH, JOHN 359
WALSH, KATHLEEN 45
WALSH, KEVIN 74
WALSH, LINDY 306
WALSH, MADELINE 376
WALSH, PAT 263
WALSH, PATRICK 122
WALSH, WILLIAM 32
WALSH-McGEHEE, MARTHA 233
WALTERS, DAVE 239
WALTERS, DIANE 226
WALTERS, TOM 232
WALTHER, CECILIA 352
WALTMAN, JIM 346
WALTON, ANNE 261
WALTON, BECKY J. 105
WALTON, BRUCE R. 51
WALTON, EMMA 265
WALTON, JOHN 107
WALTON, LYNN 56
WALTY, ALYSON 300
WALTZ, DON 47
WALTZ, ROBERT 63
WALVOORD, THOMAS . 147
WALZ, STEPHEN A. 115
WAMPLER, GLEN 25
WAMPLER, STEVE 25
WANKEL, EDWARD F. ... 91
WAPATO, TIMOTHY 231
WARBURTON, GORDON 222
WARBURTON, GORDON S. 353
WARD, BETTYE 298
WARD, BRUCE R. 140
WARD, BUTCH 247
WARD, C. HERB 388
WARD, HAROLD R. 386
WARD, J. KEVIN 109
WARD, ROBERT L. 277
WARD, SARA 94
WARD, SYLVIA 285
WARD, VIVIAN LEE 257
WARD, WESLEY 335
WARDWELL, BOB 25
WARE, JAMES L. 189
WARE, NINA 345

WARGO, JO 354
WARING, LINDA 117
WARKENTINE, BARBARA E. 146
WARLAND, ROBERT 89
WARMAN, TIM 139
WARNER, BARRY L. 102
WARNER, GLENN 51
WARNER, JAKE 309
WARNER, JAMES 77
WARNER, JOSEPH S. .. 222
WARNER, LAURIE 98
WARNER, LIZ 14
WARNER, RICHARD 62
WARNER, RICHARD D. 387
WARNER, ROBERT 327
WARNER, THOMAS. 372
WARNOCK, ROBERT 275
WARR, JAMES W. 38
WARREN, BOB 31
WARREN, CHARLES L. 178
WARREN, DAVID 95, 155
WARREN, L. J. 188
WARREN, MAGGIE 224
WARREN, MELVIN L., JR. 323
WARREN, PHILIP D. 190
WARREN, ROBERT J. .. 350
WARREN, THOMAS L. .. 267
WARREN, WAYNE 94
WARRENDER, VIRGINIA 305
WARSKOW, BILL 42
WARTENBERG, CHARLES 230
WASCOM, KATHY 244
WASHINGTON, VAL. 195
WASLEY, BILL 16
WASSERMAN, JEANNE 294
WASSERMAN, PAMELA 361
WASSON, THOMAS 291
WASTE, STEPHEN M. .. 140
WATERLAND, LUTHER 254
WATERS, MIKE 283
WATIKER, LORI 94
WATKINS, CAROLYN 94
WATKINS, ERIC 23
WATKINS, JOYCE 14
WATKINS, SHIRLEY 12
WATSON, ALAN 394
WATSON, ALEXANDER 272
WATSON, CAROLYN 72
WATSON, DENNIS 67
WATSON, GARY 227
WATSON, JAY 346
WATSON, JIM 78, 325
WATSON, JOEL 356
WATSON, LEROY 262
WATSON, MICKEY 53
WATSON, PAUL 311
WATSON, RAY ANN 48
WATT, DORIS J. 355
WATTERS, EUGENE 288
WATTON, DAVE 127
WATTS, DAVID L. 78
WATTS, DEBRA 178
WATWOOD, MARY E., Ph.D. 369
WAUGH, GARY W. 32
WAUGH, NATALIE 263
WAYLAND, ROBERT H., III 11
WEATHERS, KATHLEEN C. 222
WEAVER, BURTON D., JR. 68
WEAVER, DENNIS 110
WEAVER, G. H. 373
WEAVER, REG 260
WEAVER, SCOTT C. 326

STAFF NAME INDEX - W

WEBB, ALEXANDER S. 312
WEBB, DONALD W. 280
WEBB, ROBERT. 242
WEBB, ROBERT C. 67
WEBBER, JOE. 33
WEBBER, MATT. 235
WEBBER, PETER. 73
WEBER, ANDY. 15
WEBER, BARBARA. 16
WEBER, GARY. 203
WEBER, JOHN. 360
WEBER, KEN. 159
WEBER, MIKE. 223
WEBER, ROBERT C. 130
WEBER, SEWARD. 338
WEBER, STEVEN J. 84
WEBER, SUSAN N. 48
WEBER, TERRANCE. 251
WEBER, WILLIAM D. 234
WEBSTER, BILLY. 18
WECKER, KENDRA S. 353
WEDDLE, GORDON K. 238
WEDDLE, TOM. 70
WEEDEN, NORMAN. 378
WEEDON, RONALD. 212
WEEKES, DAVID. 272
WEEKS, BILL. 272
WEEKS, HARMON, JR. 351
WEERTS, BURT. 56
WEFER, FRED L. 265
WEGE, PETER M. 170
WEGWART, GORDON. 77
WEHRI, TOM. 164
WEIDENHAFT, RAY A. 122
WEIDLER, MARK E. 87
WEIHING, WAYNE. 323
WEIKERT, BILL. 305
WEIL, MICHAEL. 392
WEILER, BILL. 221
WEILER, JEFF. 180
WEILER, SUSAN C. 150
WEIN, HOWARD. 295
WEINBERG, PEGGY. 346
WEINGARDEN, KAREN 250
WEINSOFF, DAVID. 196
WEINSTEIN, KENNETH. 32
WEINSTEIN, MICHAEL P. 86
WEINSTOCK, LAWRENCE G. 10
WEIR, DAVID. 302
WEISMILLER, RICHARD A. 374
WEISS, ZEZE. 135
WEISSER, PETE. 48
WEISSMAN, ARTHUR. 213
WEISZ, SAM. 185
WELCH, ALISON. 126
WELCH, PATRICIA. 368
WELCH, ROBERT I. 347
WELCH, SUSAN. 86
WELCH, THOMAS. 80
WELD, CHRISTOPHER M. 260
WELDON, DANIEL M. 165
WELDON, I. DEWAYNE 109
WELF, KELLEY. 172
WELLER, CANDACE. 202
WELLER, GENE. 83
WELLFORD, L. CARTER. 366
WELLING, CURTIS. 131
WELLINGS, LINDA. 339
WELLMAN, TRINA. 341
WELLS, J. DENNIS. 41
WELLS, JEAN. 242
WELLS, ROGER. 301
WELLS, SUE. 260
WELLS, THOMAS. 85
WELLS-HARLEY, MARY. 73

WELP, LAURA. 360
WELSCH, DAVID. 108
WELSH, DONALD S. 101
WELSH, JIM. 69
WELSH, LES. 243
WELTER, JOHN. 334
WELTON, RICHARD. 176
WELTY, CLAIRE. 385
WENGER, KARL F. 319
WENTWORTH, RAND. 335
WENTZ, MARILYN. 261
WENTZ, W. ALAN. 190
WENZLICK, JOHN. 333
WERNER, CAROL. 195
WERTHMAN, IONE. 275
WESLEY, CARLOS. 184
WESLEY, DAVID. 307
WESSEL, PAUL C. 347
WESSELS, THOMAS. 379
WESSON, JIM. 113
WEST, B. KENNETH. 263
WEST, BOB. 154
WEST, CHARLES F. 277
WEST, CYNTHIA D. 378
WEST, DAN. 94
WEST, GARY. 87
WEST, JANE NOLL. 334
WEST, MARY BETH. 20
WEST, RICHARD F. 278
WEST, RICHARD L. 202
WEST, ROBERT. 78
WEST, STANFORD. 337
WEST, TIMOTHY J. 30
WEST, W. E., JR. 108
WESTBROOK, CHRISTOPHER. 382
WESTENBERGER, JANE. 145
WESTERHOLT, DUANE. 82
WESTIN, CLARENCE. 186
WESTLUND, MARK. 302
WESTON, JUDY J. 105
WESTRA, LAURA. 227
WESTWORTH, FRANK W. 310
WETHERELL, JODEEN. 310
WETHERELL, VIRGINIA B. 53
WETTER, LES. 189
WETZEL, RICHARD L. 390
WETZEL, WAYNE. 81
WEXLER, MARK. 267
WEYMOUTH, GEORGE A. 162
WEYRICK, RICHARD. 380
WHARTON, TOM. 292
WHATLEY, CAROLYN A. 38
WHEATLEY, CLARA. 67, 68
WHEATLEY, HENRY U. 233
WHEATON, CHRIS. 97
WHEATON, JIM. 206
WHEELER, DAN. 107
WHEELER, DOUGLAS P. 46
WHEELER, GERALD F. 265
WHEELER-BARTOL, ANN. 290
WHELAN, TENSIE. 152
WHIDDEN, ARDEN. 126
WHINNERY, ELLIE. 113
WHIPKEY, BOB. 344
WHIPPEN, WILLIAM. 250
WHIPPLE, CRAIG. 111
WHIPPLE, GLEN. 123
WHITACRE, EDWARD E., JR. 162
WHITAKER, GENE. 257
WHITCOMB, MARYANN. 18
WHITCOMB, ROGER. 111
WHITE, BEATRICE E. 329
WHITE, BEN. 152

WHITE, BILL. 42
WHITE, CAROL. 325
WHITE, CHARLES R. 48
WHITE, DAVID 90, 354, 372
WHITE, DAVID C. 13
WHITE, DAVID J. 202
WHITE, DONALD. 193
WHITE, GWEN. 140
WHITE, HOWARD S. 234
WHITE, J. PHELPS, III. 88
WHITE, JACQUES. 295
WHITE, JEAN. 337
WHITE, JERALD. 152
WHITE, JESSE L., JR. 7
WHITE, JIM. 24, 187
WHITE, JOHN R. 39
WHITE, KATIE. 181
WHITE, MARGY. 29
WHITE, MARLENE. 172
WHITE, NORM. 338
WHITE, RHETT. 91
WHITE, ROBERT G. 80
WHITE, RON. 307
WHITE, RONALD. 147
WHITE, RONALD J. 87
WHITE, STEPHEN B. 372
WHITEHEAD, CLIFTON J. 107
WHITEHEAD, DAVID. 354
WHITEHOUSE, RICHARD A. 180
WHITEHURST, DAVID K. 114
WHITFIELD, BRUCE. 282
WHITING, R. MONTAGUE. 388
WHITMAN, CHRISTINE T. 84
WHITMAN, F. BRUCE. 102
WHITMORE, ROBERT. 392
WHITNEY, JACK. 340
WHITNEY, MARK D. 351
WHITNEY, STEVE 341, 347
WHITSON, BOB. 388
WHITTEKIEND, J. C. 319
WHITTEMORE, DON. 66
WHITTEN, NORMAN. 326
WHITTEN, R. 125
WHITWORTH, MICHAEL. 86
WHORISKEY, FREDERICK. 157
WIANT, HARRY V., JR. 320
WICH, KENNETH. 261
WICHERS, BILL. 123
WICK, FRANK. 289
WICKERSHAM, JAY. 73
WIDEN, JEFF. 177
WIEBERS, DAVID O. 217
WIEDENFELD, DAVID. 148
WIERSMA, BRUCE. 374
WIESE, LYNDA M. 120
WIESSNER, ANDY. 346
WIEST, JENNIFER. 248
WILAND, LAURENCE. 392
WILCOX, BILL. 50
WILCOX, PAMELA B. 82
WILCOX, RICK. 239
WILCOXSON, CATHERINE. 257
WILDEMAN, JOHN. 89
WILDER, GEORGE. 269
WILDES, EMERSON. 305
WILDIE, JOHN. 23
WILDS, JANE. 185
WILDY, WAYNE. 219
WILES, CHARLES. 234
WILES, KIRK. 108
WILGIS, TED. 282
WILHELMI, DEBRA. 116
WILK, PETER. 296

WILKENSON, RIP. 264
WILKES, HOMER. 320
WILKINS, CHRISTINE. 260
WILKINS, JANE. 212
WILKINSON, BOB. 192
WILKINSON, JIM. 159
WILKINSON, JOE. 233
WILKINSON, MINDY. 215
WILKINSON, TERRY. 54
WILKOFF, LESLIE. 258
WILLARD, PATRICK. 328
WILLARD, STEVE. 24
WILLCOCKS, AL. 129
WILLEKE, GENE E. 384
WILLER, CHUCK. 146
WILLIAMS, ANGELA. 319
WILLIAMS, BRUCE. 67, 92
WILLIAMS, BRUCE A. 205
WILLIAMS, CARMEN S. 295
WILLIAMS, CECILIA. 87
WILLIAMS, CHARLES W. 77
WILLIAMS, CHUCK. 270
WILLIAMS, CINDY. 142
WILLIAMS, DARRYL. 131
WILLIAMS, DEBORAH. 134
WILLIAMS, DOUG. 190
WILLIAMS, ERIC. 84
WILLIAMS, EVAN T. 384
WILLIAMS, FRANKLIN. 282
WILLIAMS, GENE S. 322
WILLIAMS, HANS M. 388
WILLIAMS, J. D. 59
WILLIAMS, J. DAVID. 322
WILLIAMS, JAMES H. 80
WILLIAMS, JEAN E. 20
WILLIAMS, JIM. 251, 280
WILLIAMS, JOEL E., JR. 176
WILLIAMS, JOHN. 70
WILLIAMS, JUANITA B. 29
WILLIAMS, KIM. 291
WILLIAMS, MARY. 54
WILLIAMS, MYRA. 53
WILLIAMS, PHIL. 227
WILLIAMS, ROSE. 221
WILLIAMS, ROY L. 162
WILLIAMS, STEVE. 97, 397
WILLIAMS, STEVEN A. 65, 223
WILLIAMS, SYBIL. 247
WILLIAMS, TIM. 295
WILLIAMSON, CAROL. 237
WILLIAMSON, DAVID. 272
WILLIAMSON, DAYLE E. 82
WILLIAMSON, JERRY. 25
WILLIAMSON, JOHN E. 390
WILLIAMSON, LARRY. 101
WILLIAMSON, MARY JANE. 223
WILLIAMSON, MICHELLE. 275
WILLIAMSON, ROBERT L. 12
WILLIAMSON, SCOT J. 350
WILLICH, MIKE. 127
WILLICK, MIKE. 127
WILLIS, ELIZABETH. 266
WILLIS, JACK. 332
WILLMOTT, JOHN. 53
WILLSEY, BILL R. 189, 191
WILMERDING, PETER. 350
WILMORE, SANDRA. 310
WILSHIRE, HOWARD. 300
WILSON, BILLY. 288
WILSON, BRIAN. 36
WILSON, BUD. 330
WILSON, CHARLES L. 137
WILSON, CYNTHIA. 152
WILSON, EDWARD M. 15
WILSON, EVERETT. 29
WILSON, G. RICHARD. 110

WILSON, GEORGE A.... 296
WILSON, J. LARRY 388
WILSON, JACK A. 67
WILSON, JAMES R. 210
WILSON, JOHN CHARLES
.... 327
WILSON, JOHN H. 196
WILSON, JONATHAN
  SINCLAIR.................. 193
WILSON, LARRY 43, 62
WILSON, LARRY J. 64
WILSON, LEONARD 339
WILSON, LYNN C. 156
WILSON, MICHAEL D. 58
WILSON, MICHELLE 134
WILSON, MIKE 193
WILSON, NORMA 292
WILSON, P. G. 203
WILSON, PATRICIA 266
WILSON, PAUL...... 201, 409
WILSON, PAUL L. 235
WILSON, RICHARD D..... 10
WILSON, RUTH 123
WILSON, SALLY 225
WILSON, SCOTT 395
WILSON, STEPHEN R. ... 43
WILSON, STEVE N. 42, 397
WILSON, SUSAN M. 99, 294
WILSON, TED 324
WILTSE, MILTON 40
WILTSHIRE, BOB 200
WILZBACH, MARGARET 44
WINANT, CLINTON 45
WINBERG, CARL 304
WINCHCOMBE, RAYMOND
  J. 222
WINDISH, DOROTHY C.. 52
WINDISH, RICHARD 213
WINDLER, DON 324
WINDLER, PETER 21
WINDSOR, DAVE 155
WINDSOR, M.L. 282
WINDUS, WALTER 312
WINEGRAD, GERALD .. 138
WINGO, W. BRUCE 114
WINKEL, ROB................. 85
WINKEL-LEDIN,
  MARGARET.................. 76
WINKLEMAN, DANA L. ... 95
WINKLER, KARL P.......... 48
WINN, CHESTER M. 48
WINN, RON.................... 200
WINSETT, FLOYD 193
WINSOR, DEANE............ 90
WINSTEAD, JACK 252
WINSTEAD, JOE 324
WINSTEAD, JOE E. 372
WINSTEIN, MARK 309
WINSTON, ELEANOR ... 251
WINSTON, GARY W. 382
WINSTON, JUDY........... 115
WINTER, LINDA 138
WINTER, MICHAEL A. 32
WINTER, WAYNE 106
WINTERON, GUY.......... 127
WINTERS, BARABARA... 56
WINTERS, OWEN D...... 271
WINTERS, S. JEFF 257
WINTHROP, FREDERIC 335
WINWOOD, CHARLES W.
  32
WIRTH, BARRY 29
WISE, JIM 244
WISE, LOIS 371
WISE, W. M. 382
WISEMAN, EARL 35
WISEMAN, LAURENCE D.
  144
WISHART, BRUCE 295
WISHART, RICK............ 189

WISIOL, KLAUS 346
WISNIEWSKI, JOSEPH. 356
WITHEE, GREGORY W... 17
WITMER, PAMELA A..... 101
WITMER, RICHARD E..... 30
WITT, BRAD....,............... 98
WITT, LARRY.................. 82
WITT, PETER A. 388
WITTE, DOUG................ 133
WITTE, JEFF M............... 87
WITTMAN, STEPHEN.... 121
WIYGUL, ROBERT 192
WIZNER, ANDY 181
WOBESER, G. A. 166
WODDER, REBECCA R.
  149
WOEHR, JAMES R. 350
WOGAN, TERRI............. 208
WOHL, JIM 189
WOLCOTT, JAMES E...... 26
WOLF, ANNETT.............. 148
WOLF, CHRISTINE........ 207
WOLF, DAVE 295
WOLF, HAZEL................ 201
WOLF, MICHAEL 101
WOLF, THOMAS............ 333
WOLF-ARMSTRONG,
  MARK........................... 302
WOLFE, GARY J., Ph.D. 307
WOLFE, MATT 205
WOLFE, MYRNA 275
WOLFE, SHELDON 246
WOLGAST, TIMOTHY B.. 32
WOLKONOWSKI, CHRIS
  301
WOLMAN, M. GORDON 374
WOMACK, MONA 30
WONG, ALBERT W.C... 57
WONG, LYLE 58
WOO, ROY...................... 98
WOOD 327
WOOD, BARRY E. 190
WOOD, BOB 168
WOOD, DIANE W. 359
WOOD, DOUGLAS 215
WOOD, GEORGE 133
WOOD, JIM 154, 400
WOOD, JUNE P. 260
WOOD, LARRY F............ 53
WOOD, MARY................ 344
WOOD, MEGAN EPLER 194
WOOD, PETRA BOHALL
  119
WOOD, ROYCE 205
WOOD, WENDELL 290
WOODBURY, PAUL 189
WOODFIELD, GRANT ... 131
WOODFIN, BILL............. 323
WOODFIN, WILLIAM R., JR.
  .... 114, 398
WOODFORD, EILEEN... 264
WOODFORK, LARRY D. 120
WOODLEY, JOHN PAUL,
  JR. 113
WOODRING, STEPHEN 332
WOODRUFF, TOM 233
WOODS, BILL and ERIN 341
WOODS, SUSAN E........ 71
WOODS, SUSANNE 238
WOODS, TERRY K........ 138
WOODSON, BILL............ 24
WOODSUM, HAROLD E.,
  JR. 245
WOODWARD, DAVE..... 107
WOODWARD, JOHN 243
WOODWARD, SUE 288, 361
WOODWELL, DAVITT... 294
WOODWORTH, NEIL.... 131
WOOLAWAY, CHRISTINE
  59

WOOLBRIGHT,
  LAWRENCE 158
WOOLEY, BOB 125
WOOLEY, JAMES B., JR.
  296
WOOLF, ALAN 370
WOOLLEY, TED............. 110
WOOLSEY, SUZANNE H.
  264
WOOTEN, CURTIS 190
WOOTEN, MICHAEL C.. 362
WOOTTON, SUSAN...... 209
WORD, DAVID................. 56
WORDEN, NIK............... 321
WORKMAN, MATTHEW 204
WORLEY, IAN A. 390
WORTHEN, MIKE 12
WORTHINGTON, DAVID
  249
WOTEKI, CATHY 12
WOTKYNS, STEELE...... 211
WOTT, JOHN A. 226
WOUTERS, WAYNE 35
WRANGLER, EVELYNN 167
WRAY, PAT 97
WRAY, PAUL H. 65
WRAZEN, JOHN 390
WRIGHT, ALFRED 28
WRIGHT, ALVIN 105
WRIGHT, ANGUS 364
WRIGHT, BISHOP.......... 203
WRIGHT, BOSLEY......... 163
WRIGHT, CHUCK 24
WRIGHT, G. TOD........... 188
WRIGHT, KATHERINE R.
  114
WRIGHT, L. DONELSON
  390
WRIGHT, LLOYD D. 383
WRIGHT, MARY............... 48
WRIGHT, R. GERALD...... 60
WRIGHT, R. MICHAEL... 132
WRIGHT, SCOTT M. 137
WRONA, NANCY C. 41
WROTH, L. KINVIN, ... 390
WUEBKER, PETE 348
WUERCH, H. VICTOR..... 57
WURSTER, SCOTT C.... 210
WURTZ, DON 18
WYANT, DAN 74
WYATT, ROBERT 354
WYATT, RODNEY............ 52
WYERMAN, JAMES K... 130
WYKLE, KENNETH R. 31
WYKOFF, RANDOLPH ... 19
WYLDE, JOHN 243
WYLIE, THOMAS C....... 102
WYNN, G. 393
WYNN, ROBERT............. 46
WYSE, JAMES P............ 278
WYSOCKI, JOE 16
WYSS, HANSJORG 324
WYSS, JOHN................... 13

Y

YACKULIC, CORRIE..... 344
YAGER, JILL................. 383
YAGER, MARY............. 256
YAICH, SCOTT C. 42
YAMAKAWA, DAVID...... 131
YAMAMURA, TSUNETOSHI
  174
YAMANAKA, MARILOU B.
  57
YAMASE, KAZUHIRO ... 236
YANK, ANDREA J. 271
YANKE, RONALD C. 296
YAPLE, CHARLES H...... 175

YARRIS, GREG 164
YARROW, GREG 104
YASARATNE, SHIRANEE
  229
YASUMOTO, AKINOBU 211
YATES, A. J. 46
YATES, MARYLYNN
  VILLINISKI 366
YATSKIEVYCH, GEORGE
  253
YEADON, GEOFFREY .. 201
YEAGER, PAULA 221
YEATES, J. WILLIAM ... 256
YEE, LANE 46
YEE, PETRA 227
YELLOWTAIL, WILLIAM P.,
  JR. 11
YEN, A. M. 32
YERGER, DALE 186
YETTER, AARON P. 351
YEXLEY, GARY 290
YODER, MELVIN J. 288
YORK, SHERRIE 303
YORKS, J. WAYNE 100
YOSHIDA, TOMIO 359
YOSHINAGA, ALVIN 215
YOUELL, CAROL E. 180
YOUNG, BILL 1, 5, 308
YOUNG, BOBBY R. 109
YOUNG, CHIP 387
YOUNG, COLIN 135
YOUNG, D. A. 189, 191
YOUNG, DEBORAH 42
YOUNG, DON 1, 4
YOUNG, DON A. 188
YOUNG, FRANK 343
YOUNG, H. VANCE 84
YOUNG, JAMES A. 101
YOUNG, JAMES H. 382
YOUNG, JIM 46, 127, 243,
  313
YOUNG, JOHN A. 80
YOUNG, LARRY 338
YOUNG, NINA 170
YOUNG, NORMAN C. 60
YOUNG, THOMAS A. 66
YOUNGBERG, GARTH 215
YOUNGREN, JIM 243
YOUNGSON, JIM 46
YOUNKER, GORDON ... 337
YOUNKIN, DAVE 223
YOUNKMAN, DAVID 148
YOUNT, ROBERT E. 42
YOUSEY, THOMAS J., III
  335
YOWELL, ROBERT C... 101
YUDELMAN, MONTAGUE
  298
YUILL, THOMAS M........ 393
YURKOW, RUSSELL..... 127

Z

ZABEL, RICHARD 344
ZABER, JOHN 390
ZACKHEIM, HUGH 306
ZAELKE, DURWOOD J. 170
ZALE, ALEXANDER 80
ZALESKY, PHIL 283
ZALESKY, PHILIP.......... 289
ZAMORA, NATALIA......... 37
ZARILLO, KIM 202
ZAWADOWSKI, JOE 283
ZAWADZKI, ALICE 283
ZAW-MON, MERRYLIN... 71
ZEGEL, WILLIAM C. 132
ZEHM, POLLY 117
ZEIGER, JEFF 393
ZEITLER, KAREN 187

STAFF NAME INDEX - Z

ZEKOR, DAN 291
ZELAZNY, JOHN 334
ZELAZNY, JULIAN 159
ZEMEK, SUE 117
ZEMEK, SUSAN 116
ZENCEY, MATTHEW 134
ZENICH, HAROLD, Ph.D. 11
ZENN, RICK 358
ZEPATOS, THALIA A. ... 306
ZEPH, PAUL 231
ZEPP, ANDREW 241
ZERINGUE, OSWALD J. . 35
ZEVIN, SUSAN 17
ZEZULAK, DAVE 47
ZIARNO, GERARD 138
ZICHELLA, CARL 313
ZIEHM, ROBERT 246
ZIELINSKI, ELAINE 28
ZIELINSKI, SALLY A. 247
ZIEMER, ROBERT R. 364
ZIERENBERG, NANCY . 348
ZIGROSSI, NORMAN A. . 35
ZILUCA, PAUL G. 115
ZIMMERMAN, ERIC 366
ZIMMERMAN, GERALD R.
.... 47
ZIMMERMAN, H. NEIL .. 279
ZIMMERMAN, HERBERT
M. 121
ZIMMERMAN, JAY 23
ZIMMERMAN, RICHARD
.... 120
ZIMMERMAN, ROY P. 34
ZIMMERMANN, ALBERT W.
.... 282
ZINCK, SUSAN MADER 126
ZINN, JAN 295
ZIPF, CINDY 174
ZIPPERER, WAYNE 382
ZIRKLE, ERNEST 84
ZODER, KATHERINE 188
ZODY, SCOTT 94
ZOELLNER, CRAIG 232
ZOON, KATHRYN C. 19
ZOPF, RICHARD 169
ZUCKERMAN, KAREN .. 197
ZUKOWSKY, RON 129
ZUPP, RICHARD 250
ZURAWSKI, RON 107
ZUURING, HANS R. 379
ZWANK, PHILLIP J. 389
ZWARTS, PATTY 44
ZWETTLER, KATHLEEN
.... 121
ZWICK, DAVID 175
ZWOLINSKI, MALCOM J.
.... 363
ZYGMUT, ED 295

GEOGRAPHIC INDEX

AUSTRALIA
GOVERNMENT ORGANIZATIONS
    DEPARTMENT FOR ENVIRONMENT, HERITAGE AND ABORIGINAL AFFAIRS 35
NON-GOVERNMENTAL ORGANIZATIONS
    SEA SHEPHERD CONSERVATION SOCIETY
        Australia Office 311
NEW SOUTHWALES
NON-GOVERNMENTAL ORGANIZATIONS
    INTERNATIONAL FUND FOR ANIMAL WELFARE
        Austraian Office 225

BANGLADESH
DHAKA
NON-GOVERNMENTAL ORGANIZATIONS
    INTERNATIONAL UNION FOR CONSERVATION OF NATURE AND NATURAL RESOURCES (IUCN) THE WORLD CONSERVATION UNION
        Bangladesh Country Office 228

BELGIUM
BRUSSELS
NON-GOVERNMENTAL ORGANIZATIONS
    INTERNATIONAL FUND FOR ANIMAL WELFARE
        Belgium Office 225

BOTSWANA
GABORONE
NON-GOVERNMENTAL ORGANIZATIONS
    INTERNATIONAL UNION FOR CONSERVATION OF NATURE AND NATURAL RESOURCES (IUCN) THE WORLD CONSERVATION UNION
        Botswana Country Office 228

BRAZIL
NON-GOVERNMENTAL ORGANIZATIONS
    INSTITUTO BRASIL DE EDUCACAO AMBIENTAL 222
    INTERNATIONAL UNION FOR CONSERVATION OF NATURE AND NATURAL RESOURCES (IUCN) THE WORLD CONSERVATION UNION
        Regional Office for Central Africa 229

BURKINA FASSO
NON-GOVERNMENTAL ORGANIZATIONS
    INTERNATIONAL UNION FOR CONSERVATION OF NATURE AND NATURAL RESOURCES (IUCN) THE WORLD CONSERVATION UNION
        Regional Office for West Africa 229
OUAGADOUGOU
NON-GOVERNMENTAL ORGANIZATIONS
    INTERNATIONAL UNION FOR CONSERVATION OF NATURE AND NATURAL RESOURCES (IUCN) THE WORLD CONSERVATION UNION
        Burkina Country Fasso Office 228

CANADA
GOVERNMENT ORGANIZATIONS
    DEPARTMENT OF CANADIAN HERITAGE 35
    DEPARTMENT OF FISHERIES AND OCEANS 35
    ENVIRONMENTAL PROTECTION SERVICE 36
ALBERTA
GOVERNMENT ORGANIZATIONS
    ENVIRONMENTAL CONSERVATION SERVICE 36
NON-GOVERNMENTAL ORGANIZATIONS
    ALBERTA FISH AND GAME ASSOCIATION, THE 134
    ALBERTA TRAPPERS ASSOCIATION 134
    ALBERTA WILDERNESS ASSOCIATION 135
    ARCTIC INSTITUTE OF NORTH AMERICA 154
    ASSOCIATION FOR FISH AND WILDLIFE ENFORCEMENT TRAINING 155
    DUCKS UNLIMITED (Alberta, Canada)............................ 189
    FEDERATION OF ALBERTA NATURALISTS 200
    SIERRA CLUB, PRAIRIE CHAPTER (AB, MB, SK).......... 316
    WILDLIFE SOCIETY, ALBERTA CHAPTER 350
STATE GOVERNMENT ORGANIZATIONS
    ALBERTA DEPARTMENT OF ENVIRONMENTAL PROTECTION 123
        Communications Division..................................... 105, 123
        Corporate Management Service..................................... 123
        Environmental Service 41, 48, 52, 54, 67, 87, 94, 97, 106, 123, 405
        Land and Forest Service.. 123
        Natural Resources Service 124
BRITISH COLUMBIA
GOVERNMENT ORGANIZATIONS
    NORTH PACIFIC ANADROMOUS FISH COMMISSION .. 9
    PACIFIC SALMON COMMISSION.................................... 9
    ENVIRONMENTAL CONSERVATION SERVICE 36
NON-GOVERNMENTAL ORGANIZATIONS
    AMERICAN FISHERIES SOCIETY
        Canadian Aquatic Resources Section 140
        Physiology Section.. 141
    BRITISH COLUMBIA FIELD ORNITHOLOGISTS 163
    BRITISH COLUMBIA WATERFOWL SOCIETY, THE 163
    CRESTON VALLEY WILDLIFE MANAGEMENT AUTHORITY 185
    GALIANO CONSERVANCY ASSOCIATION 207
    OUTDOOR RECREATION COUNCIL OF BRITISH COLUMBIA 292
    SEA SHEPHERD CONSERVATION SOCIETY
        Canada Office 8, 311, 313
    SIERRA CLUB, BRITISH COLUMBIA CHAPTER............. 314
STATE GOVERNMENT ORGANIZATIONS
    MINISTRY OF ENVIRONMENT, LANDS, AND PARKS 124
    MINISTRY OF FISHERIES 124
    MINISTRY OF SMALL BUSINESS TOURISM AND CULTURE 124
MANITOBA
NON-GOVERNMENTAL ORGANIZATIONS
    AMERICAN FISHERIES SOCIETY, MID-CANADA CHAPTER 143
    DELTA WATERFOWL FOUNDATION 187
    DUCKS UNLIMITED CANADA
        Oak Hammock Marsh Conservation Centre................... 188
    MANITOBA NATURALISTS SOCIETY............................... 245
    MANITOBA WILDLIFE FEDERATION 245
    WILDLIFE SOCIETY, MANITOBA CHAPTER 352
STATE GOVERNMENT ORGANIZATIONS
    DEPARTMENT OF INDUSTRY, TRADE AND TOURISM. 124
    MANITOBA DEPARTMENT OF NATURAL RESOURCES 124
        Central Region 12, 13, 17, 30, 31, 82, 99, 102, 111, 117, 118, 121, 125, 267
        Eastern Region 12, 13, 16, 17, 31, 98, 99, 117, 125, 137, 153, 263, 267
        Northeastern Region 12, 125
        Northwestern Region 125
        Western Region 12, 13, 17, 31, 82, 98, 125, 153, 183, 189, 263, 264, 267, 269, 301, 335
NEW BRUNSWICK
GOVERNMENT ORGANIZATIONS
    ENVIRONMENTAL CONSERVATION SERVICE 36
NON-GOVERNMENTAL ORGANIZATIONS
    ATLANTIC SALMON FEDERATION 157
    HUNTSMAN MARINE SCIENCE CENTRE....................... 217
    NEW BRUNSWICK WILDLIFE FEDERATION.................. 276
STATE GOVERNMENT ORGANIZATIONS
    NEW BRUNSWICK DEPARTMENT OF NATURAL RESOURCES AND ENERGY 125
NEWFOUNDLAND
NON-GOVERNMENTAL ORGANIZATIONS
    NEWFOUNDLAND LABRADOR WILDLIFE FEDERATION 279
STATE GOVERNMENT ORGANIZATIONS
    NEWFOUNDLAND DEPARTMENT OF FOREST RESOURCES AND AGRIFOODS.................................. 125
        Ecosystem Health Division 125

GEOGRAPHIC INDEX - CANADA

    Inland Fish and Wildlife Division 125
    Legislation and Compliance Division 125
    Regional Offices 125

NOVA SCOTIA
NON-GOVERNMENTAL ORGANIZATIONS
  DUCKS UNLIMITED (Nova Scotia, Canada) 189
  NORTHWEST ATLANTIC FISHERIES ORGANIZATION
    (NAFO) 285
  NOVA SCOTIA FEDERATION OF ANGLERS AND
    HUNTERS 286
  NOVA SCOTIA FORESTRY ASSOCIATION 286
STATE GOVERNMENT ORGANIZATIONS
  NOVA SCOTIA DEPARTMENT OF FISHERIES AND
    AQUACULTURE 126
  NOVA SCOTIA DEPARTMENT OF NATURAL RESOURCES
    126
    Corporate Service Unit 126
    Land Services Branch 126
    Regional Services Branch 126
    Renewable Resources Branch 126

ONTARIO
GOVERNMENT ORGANIZATIONS
  INTERNATIONAL JOINT COMMISSION 8
  DEPARTMENT OF FISHERIES AND OCEANS 35
  ENVIRONMENTAL CONSERVATION SERVICE 36
  ENVIRONMENTAL PROTECTION SERVICE 36
  NATURAL RESOURCES CANADA, CANADIAN FOREST
    SERVICE 37
NON-GOVERNMENTAL ORGANIZATIONS
  AMERICAN FISHERIES SOCIETY, NORTHWESTERN
    ONTARIO CHAPTER 143
  AMERICAN FISHERIES SOCIETY, SOUTHERN ONTARIO
    CHAPTER 144
  BIRDLIFE INTERNATIONAL 161
  CANADIAN ARCTIC RESOURCES COMMITTEE, INC. ... 166
  CANADIAN ENVIRONMENTAL LAW ASSOCIATION 166
  CANADIAN FEDERATION OF HUMANE SOCIETIES 166
  CANADIAN FORESTRY ASSOCIATION 166
  CANADIAN INSTITUTE FOR ENVIRONMENTAL LAW AND
    POLICY (CIELAP) 166
  CANADIAN INSTITUTE OF FORESTRY/INSTITUT
    FORESTIER DU CANADA 167
  CANADIAN NATIONAL SPORTSMEN'S SHOWS 167
  CANADIAN NATURE FEDERATION 167
  CANADIAN PARKS AND WILDERNESS SOCIETY 167
  CANADIAN SOCIETY OF ENVIRONMENTAL BIOLOGISTS
    167
  CANADIAN WILDLIFE FEDERATION 167
  DUCKS UNLIMITED (Ontario, Canada) 189
  FEDERATION OF ONTARIO NATURALISTS 200
  INTERNATIONAL SOCIETY FOR ENVIRONMENTAL
    ETHICS 227
  INTERPRETATION CANADA 230
  JACK MINER MIGRATORY BIRD FOUNDATION, INC 236
  LEARNING FOR ENVIRONMENTAL ACTION PROGRAMME
    (LEAP) 242
  NATIONAL WILD TURKEY FEDERATION, CANADA, INC.,
    THE 266
  NATURE CONSERVANCY OF CANADA, THE 272
  OCEAN VOICE INTERNATIONAL 286
  ONTARIO FEDERATION OF ANGLERS AND HUNTERS,
    INC., THE 289
  ONTARIO FORESTRY ASSOCIATION 289
  POLLUTION PROBE FOUNDATION 297
  SIERRA CLUB
    Canada Office 8, 311, 313
  SIERRA CLUB, EASTERN CANADA CHAPTER 314
  WATERLOO-WELLINGTON WILDFLOWER SOCIETY
    (Formerly the Dogtooth Group) 342
  WILDLIFE HABITAT CANADA 349
STATE GOVERNMENT ORGANIZATIONS
  MINISTRY OF NATURAL RESOURCES
    Algonquin Forestry Authority 127
    Corporate Services Division 127
    Field Services Division 99, 127
    Fish and Wildlife Branch 127, 129, 399
    Natural Resource Management Division 127
    Northeast Region 29, 30, 80, 102, 111, 118, 121, 127, 137,
      162, 264, 269, 307

    Northwest Region 16, 29, 62, 98, 99, 102, 117, 118, 127,
      149, 206, 307, 335
    Ontario 8, 35, 36, 37, 64, 127, 128, 137, 143, 144, 161,
      166, 167, 188, 189, 200, 212, 217, 227, 230, 231, 236,
      242, 266, 272, 284, 286, 287, 289, 290, 297, 313, 314,
      342, 343, 349, 385, 394, 399, 402, 404, 414
    Science and Information Resources Division 127
    South Central Region 121, 127, 301
  NIAGARA ESCARPMENT COMMISSION 128

PRINCE EDWARD ISLAND
STATE GOVERNMENT ORGANIZATIONS
  PRINCE EDWARD ISLAND DEPARTMENT OF
    TECHNOLOGY AND ENVIRONMENT 128

QUEBEC
GOVERNMENT ORGANIZATIONS
  CANADIAN WILDLIFE SERVICE 35
  ENVIRONMENTAL CONSERVATION SERVICE 36
NON-GOVERNMENTAL ORGANIZATIONS
  ATLANTIC CENTER FOR THE ENVIRONMENT
    QLF Canada Office 157
  DUCKS UNLIMITED (Quebec, Canada) 189
  GREAT LAKES UNITED
    Montreal Office/Canada at-Large 212
  INTERNATIONAL UNION FOR CONSERVATION OF
    NATURE AND NATURAL RESOURCES (IUCN) THE
    WORLD CONSERVATION UNION
    Canada Country Office 228
  PROVINCE OF QUEBEC SOCIETY FOR THE
    PROTECTION OF BIRDS, INC. 299
  QUEBEC WILDLIFE FEDERATION 301
  STOP 13, 326
STATE GOVERNMENT ORGANIZATIONS
  DEPARTMENT OF ENVIRONMENT AND WILDLIFE
    (QUEBEC) 128

SASKATCHEWAN
NON-GOVERNMENTAL ORGANIZATIONS
  CANADIAN COOPERATIVE WILDLIFE HEALTH CENTRE
    166
  DUCKS UNLIMITED (Saskatchewan Operation, Canada) 189
  NATURE SASKATCHEWAN 275
  SASKATCHEWAN WILDLIFE FEDERATION 309
STATE GOVERNMENT ORGANIZATIONS
  SASKATCHEWAN ENVIRONMENT AND RESOURCE
    MANAGEMENT 128
    Corporate Services 35, 124, 127, 128
    East Boreal EcoRegion 128
    Enforcement and Compliance Branch 128
    Fire Management and Forest Protection Branch 128
    Grassland EcoRegion 128
    Operations 5, 6, 12, 13, 16, 17, 19, 21, 28, 29, 30, 32, 34,
      35, 36, 38, 39, 40, 41, 42, 46, 47, 51, 53, 55, 62, 65, 74,
      75, 76, 80, 82, 87, 91, 96, 101, 104, 105, 106, 107, 108,
      111, 116, 117, 124, 128, 157, 159, 186, 189, 190, 196,
      198, 205, 227, 241, 243, 250, 257, 259, 265, 272, 284,
      291, 307, 310, 339, 342, 348, 359, 361, 413, 417
    Parkland EcoRegion 128
    Policy and Assessment 129
    Programs 5, 10, 11, 12, 13, 16, 17, 20, 22, 23, 30, 31, 32,
      33, 34, 37, 38, 39, 41, 42, 45, 46, 47, 50, 53, 54, 57, 75,
      81, 87, 88, 91, 93, 95, 99, 100, 103, 112, 114, 116, 117,
      129, 131, 139, 146, 147, 149, 153, 157, 159, 164, 166,
      167, 170, 171, 174, 175, 179, 182, 183, 189, 190, 191,
      192, 194, 196, 198, 205, 209, 211, 212, 213, 230, 240,
      241, 244, 245, 256, 257, 261, 262, 265, 267, 284, 286,
      289, 290, 304, 306, 307, 312, 319, 325, 326, 330, 331,
      335, 340, 344, 349, 369, 371, 379, 382, 383, 385, 386,
      387, 393, 394, 395, 401, 407, 415
    Shield EcoRegion 129
    West Boreal EcoRegion 129

YUKON TERRITORY
NON-GOVERNMENTAL ORGANIZATIONS
  YUKON FISH AND GAME ASSOCIATION 361
STATE GOVERNMENT ORGANIZATIONS
  DEPARTMENT OF RENEWABLE RESOURCES 129

CARIBBEAN

ST. JOHNS
NON-GOVERNMENTAL ORGANIZATIONS
ISLAND RESOURCES FOUNDATION
Eastern Caribbean Biodiversity Program Office 233

CHINA

KOWLOON
NON-GOVERNMENTAL ORGANIZATIONS
INTERNATIONAL FUND FOR ANIMAL WELFARE
Hong Kong Office 225

COLOMBIA

SANTA FE DE BOGATA
NON-GOVERNMENTAL ORGANIZATIONS
FUNDACION NATURA - COLOMBIA 207

COSTA RICA

GOVERNMENT ORGANIZATIONS
INSTITUTO NACIONAL DE BIODIVERSIDAD (INBIO) ... 37
SAN JOSE
NON-GOVERNMENTAL ORGANIZATIONS
INTERNATIONAL UNION FOR CONSERVATION OF NATURE AND NATURAL RESOURCES (IUCN) THE WORLD CONSERVATION UNION
Regional Office for Meso America 229

CZECH REPUBLIC

GOVERNMENT ORGANIZATIONS
MINISTRY OF THE ENVIRONMENT OF THE CZECH REPUBLIC 37

ECUADOR

QUITO
NON-GOVERNMENTAL ORGANIZATIONS
INTERNATIONAL UNION FOR CONSERVATION OF NATURE AND NATURAL RESOURCES (IUCN) THE WORLD CONSERVATION UNION
Regional Office for South America 229

EGYPT

GOVERNMENT ORGANIZATIONS
EGYPTIAN ENVIRONMENTAL AFFAIRS AGENCY 37

FINLAND

GOVERNMENT ORGANIZATIONS
HELSINKI COMMISSION/ BALTIC MARINE ENVIRONMENT PROTECTION COMMISSION 7

FRANCE

FISMES
NON-GOVERNMENTAL ORGANIZATIONS
INTERNATIONAL FUND FOR ANIMAL WELFARE
French Office 225
PARIS
NON-GOVERNMENTAL ORGANIZATIONS
COUSTEAU SOCIETY, INC., THE (France Office) 185

GERMANY

GOVERNMENT ORGANIZATIONS
UNITED STATES DEPARTMENT OF THE AIR FORCE MAJOR AIR COMMANDS 21
NON-GOVERNMENTAL ORGANIZATIONS
FRANKFURT ZOOLOGICAL SOCIETY--HELP FOR THREATENED WILDLIFE 205
SEA SHEPHERD CONSERVATION SOCIETY
Germany Office/European Community 311
ADENAUERALLE
NON-GOVERNMENTAL ORGANIZATIONS
INTERNATIONAL COUNCIL OF ENVIRONMENTAL LAW 224
BONN
NON-GOVERNMENTAL ORGANIZATIONS
INTERNATIONAL UNION FOR CONSERVATION OF NATURE AND NATURAL RESOURCES (IUCN) THE WORLD CONSERVATION UNION
Environmental Law Centre 228
GRAFENAU
NON-GOVERNMENTAL ORGANIZATIONS
EUROPARC FEDERATION 199
HAMBURG
NON-GOVERNMENTAL ORGANIZATIONS
INTERNATIONAL FUND FOR ANIMAL WELFARE
German Office 225
STRALSUND
NON-GOVERNMENTAL ORGANIZATIONS
EUROPEAN CETACEAN SOCIETY 199

GHANA

NON-GOVERNMENTAL ORGANIZATIONS
LEAGUE OF ENVIRONMENTAL JOURNALISTS 241
ASAWASI-KUMASI
NON-GOVERNMENTAL ORGANIZATIONS
ENVIRONMENTAL PROTECTION ASSOCIATION OF GHANA 198

GUINEA-BISSAU

NON-GOVERNMENTAL ORGANIZATIONS
INTERNATIONAL UNION FOR CONSERVATION OF NATURE AND NATURAL RESOURCES (IUCN) THE WORLD CONSERVATION UNION
Guinea-Bissau Country Office 228

ITALY

ROME
NON-GOVERNMENTAL ORGANIZATIONS
FOOD AND AGRICULTURE ORGANIZATION OF THE UNITED NATIONS 203
INTERNATIONAL FUND FOR ANIMAL WELFARE
Italian Office 225

JAPAN

OSAKA
NON-GOVERNMENTAL ORGANIZATIONS
CITIZENS ALLIANCE FOR SAVING THE ATMOSPHERE AND THE EARTH (CASA) 174
TOKYO
NON-GOVERNMENTAL ORGANIZATIONS
GLOBAL INDUSTRIAL AND SOCIAL PROGRESS RESEARCH INSTITUTE (GISPRI) 211
JAPAN WILDLIFE RESEARCH CENTER (JWRC) 236
NATURE CONSERVATION SOCIETY OF JAPAN, THE (NACS-J) 274
NIPPON ECOLOGY NETWORK 280
WWF JAPAN (WORLD WIDE FUND FOR NATURE JAPAN) 359

KENYA

NAIROBI
NON-GOVERNMENTAL ORGANIZATIONS
INTERNATIONAL UNION FOR CONSERVATION OF NATURE AND NATURAL RESOURCES (IUCN) THE WORLD CONSERVATION UNION
Regional Office for Eastern Africa 229
UNITED NATIONS ENVIRONMENT PROGRAMME 336

LAO

NON-GOVERNMENTAL ORGANIZATIONS
INTERNATIONAL UNION FOR CONSERVATION OF NATURE AND NATURAL RESOURCES (IUCN) THE WORLD CONSERVATION UNION
Lao People's Democratic Republic Country Office.........228

MALI

BAMAKO
NON-GOVERNMENTAL ORGANIZATIONS
INTERNATIONAL UNION FOR CONSERVATION OF NATURE AND NATURAL RESOURCES (IUCN) THE WORLD CONSERVATION UNION
Mali Country Office..229

MEXICO

CIUDAD VICTORIA
NON-GOVERNMENTAL ORGANIZATIONS
CENTER FOR THE STUDY OF TROPICAL BIRDS, INC. (Field Office)..171

MOZAMBIQUE

NON-GOVERNMENTAL ORGANIZATIONS
INTERNATIONAL UNION FOR CONSERVATION OF NATURE AND NATURAL RESOURCES (IUCN) THE WORLD CONSERVATION UNION
Mozambique Country Office..229

NAMIBIA

NON-GOVERNMENTAL ORGANIZATIONS
DESERT RESEARCH FOUNDATION OF NAMIBIA, THE 188

NEPAL

KATHMANDU
NON-GOVERNMENTAL ORGANIZATIONS
INTERNATIONAL UNION FOR CONSERVATION OF NATURE AND NATURAL RESOURCES (IUCN) THE WORLD CONSERVATION UNION
Nepal Country Office..229
STUDENTS PARTNERSHIP WORLDWIDE.......................327

NETHERLANDS

NON-GOVERNMENTAL ORGANIZATIONS
INTERNATIONAL FUND FOR ANIMAL WELFARE
Holland Office.....................................225
SEA SHEPHERD CONSERVATION SOCIETY
Netherlands Office..312
TILBURG
NON-GOVERNMENTAL ORGANIZATIONS
INTERNATIONAL UNION FOR CONSERVATION OF NATURE AND NATURAL RESOURCES (IUCN) THE WORLD CONSERVATION UNION
Regional Office for Europe...229
RHENEN
NON-GOVERNMENTAL ORGANIZATIONS
EUROPEAN ASSOCIATION FOR AQUATIC MAMMALS..199

PAKISTAN

ISLAMABAD
NON-GOVERNMENTAL ORGANIZATIONS
HIMALAYAN WILDLIFE FOUNDATION..............................216
KARACHI
NON-GOVERNMENTAL ORGANIZATIONS
INTERNATIONAL UNION FOR CONSERVATION OF NATURE AND NATURAL RESOURCES (IUCN) THE WORLD CONSERVATION UNION
Pakistan Country Office..229

PERU

NON-GOVERNMENTAL ORGANIZATIONS
ZUNGAROCOCHA RESEARCH CENTER........................361

PHILIPPINES

QUEZON CITY
NON-GOVERNMENTAL ORGANIZATIONS
INTERNATIONAL FUND FOR ANIMAL WELFARE
Philippines Office...225

POLAND

NON-GOVERNMENTAL ORGANIZATIONS
INTERNATIONAL UNION FOR CONSERVATION OF NATURE AND NATURAL RESOURCES (IUCN) THE WORLD CONSERVATION UNION
Subregional Office for Central Europe............................229

RUSSIA

NON-GOVERNMENTAL ORGANIZATIONS
CENTER FOR INDEPENDENT SOCIAL RESEARCH......170
ECODEFENSE...193
FEDERATION OF ENVIRONMENTAL EDUCATION IN ST. PETERSBURG..200
INSTITUTE FOR CIVIC INITIATIVES SUPPORT..............221
RESOURCE CENTER FOR ENVIRONMENTAL EDUCATION, THE..304
MOSCOW
NON-GOVERNMENTAL ORGANIZATIONS
INTERNATIONAL FUND FOR ANIMAL WELFARE
Russian Office..225

SENEGAL

DAKAR
NON-GOVERNMENTAL ORGANIZATIONS
INTERNATIONAL UNION FOR CONSERVATION OF NATURE AND NATURAL RESOURCES (IUCN) THE WORLD CONSERVATION UNION
Senegal Country Office...229

SOUTH AFRICA

NON-GOVERNMENTAL ORGANIZATIONS
SAFARI CLUB INTERNATIONAL
South Africa Office..308
PRETORIA
NON-GOVERNMENTAL ORGANIZATIONS
INTERNATIONAL UNION FOR CONSERVATION OF NATURE AND NATURAL RESOURCES (IUCN) THE WORLD CONSERVATION UNION
P.O. Box 11536..229
SOUTHERN AFRICAN INSTITUTE OF FORESTRY........323
RIVONIA
NON-GOVERNMENTAL ORGANIZATIONS
INTERNATIONAL FUND FOR ANIMAL WELFARE
South African Office..225

SRI LANKA

COLUMBO
NON-GOVERNMENTAL ORGANIZATIONS
INTERNATIONAL UNION FOR CONSERVATION OF NATURE AND NATURAL RESOURCES (IUCN) THE WORLD CONSERVATION UNION
Sri Lanka Country Office...229

ST. KITTS AND NEVIS

CHARLESTOWN
NON-GOVERNMENTAL ORGANIZATIONS
NEVIS HISTORICAL AND CONSERVATION SOCIETY...276

SWITZERLAND

GOVERNMENT ORGANIZATIONS
UNITED NATIONS RESEARCH INSTITUTE FOR SOCIAL DEVELOPMENT (UNRISD).................................37

TANZANIA

STATE GOVERNMENT ORGANIZATIONS
TANZANIA COASTAL MANAGEMENT PARTNERSHIP...123

THAILAND

PATHUMTHANI
NON-GOVERNMENTAL ORGANIZATIONS
INTERNATIONAL UNION FOR CONSERVATION OF NATURE AND NATURAL RESOURCES (IUCN) THE WORLD CONSERVATION UNION
Regional Office of South and Southeast Asia.................229

UGANDA

KAMPALA
NON-GOVERNMENTAL ORGANIZATIONS
INTERNATIONAL UNION FOR CONSERVATION OF NATURE AND NATURAL RESOURCES (IUCN) THE WORLD CONSERVATION UNION
Uganda Country Office.......................................229

UKRAINE

NON-GOVERNMENTAL ORGANIZATIONS
LVIV REGIONAL INSTITUTE OF EDUCATION.................244

UNITED KINGDOM

GOVERNMENT ORGANIZATIONS
INTERNATIONAL WHALING COMMISSION....................8
NORTHEAST ATLANTIC FISHERIES COMMISSION..9
NON-GOVERNMENTAL ORGANIZATIONS
SEA SHEPHERD CONSERVATION SOCIETY
Great Britain Office..311
WORLD ASSOCIATION OF GIRL GUIDES AND GIRL SCOUTS (WAGGGS)...........................357
WORLD CONSERVATION MONITORING CENTRE........358

BATH
NON-GOVERNMENTAL ORGANIZATIONS
WHALE AND DOLPHIN CONSERVATION SOCIETY.......345

BERKS
NON-GOVERNMENTAL ORGANIZATIONS
WORLD PHEASANT ASSOCIATION..............................358

CHELTENHAM
NON-GOVERNMENTAL ORGANIZATIONS
INTERNATIONAL CENTRE FOR CONSERVATION EDUCATION...224

EAST SUSSEX
NON-GOVERNMENTAL ORGANIZATIONS
INTERNATIONAL FUND FOR ANIMAL WELFARE
United Kingdom8, 9, 193, 207, 215, 224, 225, 226, 228, 230, 282, 311, 345, 357, 358, 395, 401

EDINBURGH
NON-GOVERNMENTAL ORGANIZATIONS
NORTH ATLANTIC SALMON CONSERVATION ORGANIZATION...282

LONDON
NON-GOVERNMENTAL ORGANIZATIONS
EARTHSCAN...193
HAWK AND OWL TRUST, THE............................215
INTERNATIONAL MARITIME ORGANIZATION.............226

UNITED STATES

GOVERNMENT ORGANIZATIONS
ENVIRONMENTAL PROTECTION AGENCY..................10
UNITED STATES DEPARTMENT OF AGRICULTURE
ANIMAL AND PLANT HEALTH INSPECTION SERVICE 12
UNITED STATES DEPARTMENT OF THE AIR FORCE
MAJOR AIR COMMANDS.................................21
UNITED STATES DEPARTMENT OF THE AIR FORCE
MAJOR U.S. INSTALLATIONS...........................22
UNITED STATES DEPARTMENT OF THE NAVY
U.S. MARINE CORPS....................................31

ALABAMA
GOVERNMENT ORGANIZATIONS
TENNESSEE VALLEY AUTHORITY.............................35
UNITED STATES DEPARTMENT OF THE ARMY
U.S. ARMY CORPS OF ENGINEERS.........................25
NON-GOVERNMENTAL ORGANIZATIONS
ALABAMA ASSOCIATION OF SOIL AND WATER CONSERVATION DISTRICTS.............................132
ALABAMA B.A.S.S. CHAPTER FEDERATION................132
ALABAMA ENVIRONMENTAL COUNCIL....................132
ALABAMA NATURAL HERITAGE PROGRAM................132
ALABAMA WATERFOWL ASSOCIATION, INC. (AWA)....133
ALABAMA WILDFLOWER SOCIETY, THE....................133
ALABAMA WILDLIFE FEDERATION.........................133
AMERICAN FISHERIES SOCIETY, ALABAMA CHAPTER 141
AMERICAN FISHERIES SOCIETY, AUBURN UNIVERSITY CHAPTER..141
ANGLERS FOR CLEAN WATER.............................152
BAMA BACKPADDLERS ASSOCIATION....................159
BASS ANGLERS SPORTSMAN SOCIETY (B.A.S.S, INC.) 160
ENVIROSOUTH, INC..199
NATIONAL SPELEOLOGICAL SOCIETY, INC................265
NATURE CONSERVANCY, THE, ALABAMA CHAPTER..272
SIERRA CLUB
Southeast Office..313
SIERRA CLUB, ALABAMA CHAPTER........................314
WILDLIFE SOCIETY, ALABAMA CHAPTER..................350
STATE GOVERNMENT ORGANIZATIONS
ALABAMA COOPERATIVE EXTENSION SYSTEM...........38
ALABAMA COOPERATIVE FISH AND WILDLIFE RESEARCH UNIT (USDI)...................................38
ALABAMA DEPARTMENT OF AGRICULTURE AND INDUSTRIES...38
ALABAMA DEPARTMENT OF CONSERVATION AND NATURAL RESOURCES.................................38
ALABAMA DEPARTMENT OF ECONOMIC AND COMMUNITY AFFAIRS, COASTAL PROGRAMS (ADECA)...38
ALABAMA DEPARTMENT OF ENVIRONMENTAL MANAGEMENT..38
ALABAMA FORESTRY COMMISSION.......................39
ALABAMA SEA GRANT PROGRAM.........................39
ALABAMA SOIL AND WATER CONSERVATION COMMITTEE...39
GOVERNOR OF ALABAMA..................................38

ALASKA
GOVERNMENT ORGANIZATIONS
UNITED STATES DEPARTMENT OF AGRICULTURE
UNITED STATES FOREST SERVICE..........................16
UNITED STATES DEPARTMENT OF THE ARMY
U.S. ARMY CORPS OF ENGINEERS.........................25
UNITED STATES DEPARTMENT OF THE INTERIOR
UNITED STATES FISH AND WILDLIFE SERVICE..........29
NON-GOVERNMENTAL ORGANIZATIONS
ALASKA ASSOCIATION OF SOIL AND WATER CONSERVATION DISTRICTS.............................133
ALASKA AUDUBON SOCIETY................................133
ALASKA CENTER FOR THE ENVIRONMENT.................133
ALASKA CONSERVATION ALLIANCE........................133
ALASKA CONSERVATION FOUNDATION....................134
ALASKA CONSERVATION VOICE............................134
ALASKA NATURAL HISTORY ASSOCIATION...............134
ALASKA NATURAL RESOURCE AND OUTDOOR EDUCATION ASSOCIATION............................134
ALASKA RAINFOREST CAMPAIGN..........................134
ALASKA WILDLIFE ALLIANCE, THE..........................134
AMERICAN FISHERIES SOCIETY, ALASKA CHAPTER...141
COOK INLET KEEPER.......................................184
EARTHJUSTICE LEGAL DEFENSE FUND (formerly Sierra Club Legal Defense Fund, Inc.)
Southeast Alaska Office...................................192
IZAAK WALTON LEAGUE OF AMERICA, INC., THE

GEOGRAPHIC INDEX - UNITED STATES

Alaska Division 234
KODIAK BROWN BEAR TRUST 240
NATIONAL PARKS AND CONSERVATION ASSOCIATION (NPCA)
    Alaska Regional Office 30, 264
NATIONAL WILDLIFE FEDERATION
    Alaska Office (AK, HI) 267
NATURE CONSERVANCY, THE, ALASKA CHAPTER 272
NORTHERN ALASKA ENVIRONMENTAL CENTER 285
SIERRA CLUB
    Alaska Office 267, 312
    Alaska Rainforest Campaign Office 312
SIERRA CLUB, ALASKA CHAPTER 314
SOUTHEAST ALASKA CONSERVATION COUNCIL (SEACC) 323
TROUT UNLIMITED, ALASKA COUNCIL 331
TRUSTEES FOR ALASKA 335
WILDLIFE FEDERATION OF ALASKA 348
WILDLIFE SOCIETY, ALASKA CHAPTER 350

STATE GOVERNMENT ORGANIZATIONS
ALASKA COOPERATIVE FISH AND WILDLIFE RESEARCH UNIT 39
ALASKA DEPARTMENT OF ENVIRONMENTAL CONSERVATION 39
ALASKA DEPARTMENT OF FISH AND GAME 39
ALASKA DEPARTMENT OF NATURAL RESOURCES 40
ALASKA DEPARTMENT OF PUBLIC SAFETY 40
    Division of Fish and Wildlife Protection 40
ALASKA HEALTH PROJECT 40
ALASKA SEA GRANT COLLEGE PROGRAM 40
ALASKA STATE EXTENSION SERVICES 40
GOVERNOR OF ALASKA 39

AMERICAN SAMOA
STATE GOVERNMENT ORGANIZATIONS
AMERICAN SAMOA DEPARTMENT OF AGRICULTURE .. 40
GOVERNOR OF AMERICAN SAMOA 40

ARIZONA
NON-GOVERNMENTAL ORGANIZATIONS
AMERICAN FISHERIES SOCIETY, ARIZONA-NEW MEXICO CHAPTER 141
AMERICAN RIVERS (formerly American Rivers Conservation Council)
    Southwest Regional Office 30, 80, 117, 149, 153, 264
ARIZONA ASSOCIATION OF CONSERVATION DISTRICTS 154
ARIZONA B.A.S.S. CHAPTER FEDERATION 154
ARIZONA WILDLIFE FEDERATION 154
BORDER ECOLOGY PROJECT (BEP) 162
CENTER FOR BIOLOGICAL DIVERSITY 169
GRAND CANYON TRUST 211
INTERNATIONAL SONORAN DESERT ALLIANCE 228
NATIONAL ASSOCIATION OF STATE PARK DIRECTORS 258
NATURE CONSERVANCY, THE, ARIZONA CHAPTER ... 272
RINCON INSTITUTE, THE 305
ROCKY MOUNTAIN ELK FOUNDATION
    Pacific Southwest Region Office 307
SAFARI CLUB INTERNATIONAL 308
SIERRA CLUB
    Southwest Office 314
SIERRA CLUB, GRAND CANYON CHAPTER 314
SONORAN INSTITUTE 320
THRESHOLD, INC. 329
TROUT UNLIMITED, ARIZONA COUNCIL 332
WILDLANDS PROJECT, THE 347
WILDLIFE DAMAGE REVIEW (WDR) 348
WILDLIFE SOCIETY, ARIZONA CHAPTER 350

STATE GOVERNMENT ORGANIZATIONS
ARIZONA COOPERATIVE FISH AND WILDLIFE RESEARCH UNIT (USDI) 40
ARIZONA DEPARTMENT OF AGRICULTURE 41
    Animal Services Division 41
    Environmental Services Division 41, 87
    Integrated Pest Management (IPM) 41
    Plant Services Division 41
ARIZONA DEPARTMENT OF ENVIRONMENTAL QUALITY 41
ARIZONA GAME AND FISH DEPARTMENT 41
ARIZONA GEOLOGICAL SURVEY 41
ARIZONA LAND DEPARTMENT 41
ARIZONA STATE EXTENSION SERVICES 42
ARIZONA STATE PARKS BOARD 42
GOVERNOR OF ARIZONA 40

ARKANSAS
GOVERNMENT ORGANIZATIONS
UNITED STATES DEPARTMENT OF THE ARMY
    U.S. ARMY CORPS OF ENGINEERS 25
NON-GOVERNMENTAL ORGANIZATIONS
AMERICAN FISHERIES SOCIETY, ARKANSAS CHAPTER 141
ARKANSAS ASSOCIATION OF CONSERVATION DISTRICTS 154
ARKANSAS B.A.S.S. CHAPTER FEDERATION 154
ARKANSAS ENVIRONMENTAL EDUCATION ASSOCIATION 154
ARKANSAS WILDLIFE FEDERATION 154
NATURE CONSERVANCY, THE, ARKANSAS CHAPTER 273
OZARK SOCIETY, THE 292
SIERRA CLUB, ARKANSAS CHAPTER 314
TROUT UNLIMITED, ARKANSAS COUNCIL 332
WILDLIFE SOCIETY, ARKANSAS CHAPTER 351

STATE GOVERNMENT ORGANIZATIONS
ARKANSAS COOPERATIVE RESEARCH UNIT 42
ARKANSAS DEPARTMENT OF PARKS AND TOURISM ... 42
ARKANSAS GAME AND FISH COMMISSION 42
ARKANSAS STATE EXTENSION SERVICES 43
DEPARTMENT OF ENVIRONMENTAL QUALITY (ARKANSAS) 43
FORESTRY COMMISSION (ARKANSAS) 43
GOVERNOR OF ARKANSAS 42
NATURAL AND SCENIC RIVERS COMMISSION (ARKANSAS) 43
NATURAL HERITAGE COMMISSION (ARKANSAS) ... 44
PINE BLUFF COOPERATIVE FISHERY RESEARCH PROJECT 44
STATE PLANT BOARD (ARKANSAS) 44

CALIFORNIA
GOVERNMENT ORGANIZATIONS
INTER-AMERICAN TROPICAL TUNA COMMISSION 8
ENVIRONMENTAL PROTECTION AGENCY 10
UNITED STATES DEPARTMENT OF AGRICULTURE
    ANIMAL AND PLANT HEALTH INSPECTION SERVICE 12
    RESEARCH EDUCATION AND ECONOMICS 15
    UNITED STATES FOREST SERVICE 16
UNITED STATES DEPARTMENT OF THE ARMY
    U.S. ARMY CORPS OF ENGINEERS 25
UNITED STATES DEPARTMENT OF THE INTERIOR
    BUREAU OF RECLAMATION 28
    UNITED STATES FISH AND WILDLIFE SERVICE 29
UNITED STATES DEPARTMENT OF TREASURY
    U.S. CUSTOMS SERVICE 32
NON-GOVERNMENTAL ORGANIZATIONS
ACTION FOR NATURE, INC. 130
AMERICAN CETACEAN SOCIETY 138
AMERICAN FISHERIES SOCIETY
    Fish Health Section 140
    Western Division 141, 272
AMERICAN FISHERIES SOCIETY, CALIFORNIA-NEVADA CHAPTER 142
AMERICAN FISHERIES SOCIETY, HUMBOLDT CHAPTER 142
AMERICAN INSTITUTE OF FISHERY RESEARCH BIOLOGISTS 146
AMERICAN LAND CONSERVANCY 146
AMERICAN OCEANS CAMPAIGN 147
AMERICAN SOCIETY OF INTERNATIONAL LAW/WILDLIFE INTEREST GROUP 150
ANCIENT FOREST INTERNATIONAL 152
ANIMAL PROTECTION INSTITUTE 152
BIO-INTEGRAL RESOURCE CENTER 161
CALIFORNIA ACADEMY OF SCIENCES 163
    California Academy of Sciences Library 163
CALIFORNIA ASSOCIATION OF RESOURCE CONSERVATION DISTRICTS 164
CALIFORNIA B.A.S.S. CHAPTER FEDERATION 164
CALIFORNIA NATIVE PLANT SOCIETY, THE 164
CALIFORNIA TRAPPERS ASSOCIATION 164
CALIFORNIA TROUT, INC. 164
CALIFORNIA WATERFOWL ASSOCIATION 164
CALIFORNIA WILDLIFE DEFENDERS 164

CALIFORNIA WILDLIFE FEDERATION 165
CALIFORNIA, FOREST LANDOWNERS OF 165
CALIFORNIANS FOR POPULATION STABILIZATION
  (CAPS) 165
COALITION FOR CLEAN AIR 175
COMMUNITIES FOR A BETTER ENVIRONMENT 179
COMMUNITY ENVIRONMENTAL COUNCIL 179
COOPER ORNITHOLOGICAL SOCIETY 184
CORAL REEF ALLIANCE, THE (CORAL) 184
COUNCIL FOR PLANNING AND CONSERVATION 185
DESERT FISHES COUNCIL 188
DESERT TORTOISE COUNCIL 188
DESERT TORTOISE PRESERVE COMMITTEE, INC. 188
EARTH ISLAND INSTITUTE 191
EARTHJUSTICE LEGAL DEFENSE FUND (formerly Sierra
  Club Legal Defense Fund)
  California Office 192, 326
EARTHJUSTICE LEGAL DEFENSE FUND (formerly Sierra
  Club Legal Defense Fund, Inc.) 192
ECOLOGY CENTER 194
EDUCATIONAL COMMUNICATIONS, INC. 194
ENVIRONMENTAL DEFENSE CENTER, INC. 196
ENVIRONMENTAL DEFENSE FUND, INC.
  West Coast Office 196
ENVIRONMENTAL EDUCATION ASSOCIATES 196
ENVIRONMENTAL MEDIA ASSOCIATION 198
FOSSIL FUELS POLICY ACTION INSTITUTE/ALLIANCE
  FOR A PAVING MORATORIUM 204
FRIENDS OF THE RIVER 206
FRIENDS OF THE SEA OTTER 206
GLOBAL CITIES PROJECT, THE 210
HEADLANDS INSTITUTE 215
INTERNATIONAL ASSOCIATION FOR BEAR RESEARCH
  AND MANAGEMENT 222
INTERNATIONAL CENTER FOR EARTH CONCERNS 223
INTERNATIONAL CENTER FOR GIBBON STUDIES 224
INTERNATIONAL MARINE MAMMAL PROJECT, THE 226
INTERNATIONAL RIVERS NETWORK (IRN) 226
INTERNATIONAL SOCIETY FOR THE PRESERVATION OF
  THE TROPICAL RAINFOREST, THE 227
INTERNATIONAL WILDERNESS LEADERSHIP (WILD)
  FOUNDATION 230
INTERNATIONAL WILDLIFE REHABILITATION COUNCIL
  (IWRC) 230
IZAAK WALTON LEAGUE OF AMERICA, INC., THE
  California Division 234
LAND WATCH MONTEREY COUNTY 241
LEAGUE TO SAVE LAKE TAHOE 242
LIGHTHAWK 243
MAGIC 244
MARIN CONSERVATION LEAGUE 246
MARINE MAMMAL CENTER, THE 246
MONO LAKE COMMITTEE 254
MOUNT SHASTA AREA AUDUBON SOCIETY 255
MOUNTAIN LION FOUNDATION 255
NATIONAL FIELD ARCHERY ASSOCIATION 261
NATIONAL PARKS AND CONSERVATION ASSOCIATION
  (NPCA)
  Pacific Regional Office 30, 264
NATIONAL TRUST FOR HISTORIC PRESERVATION
  Western5, 6, 12, 13, 17, 28, 31, 35, 72, 82, 83, 98, 125,
    131, 136, 141, 153, 156, 159, 162, 178, 183, 188, 189,
    203, 216, 238, 258, 263, 264, 266, 267, 268, 269, 272,
    290, 294, 301, 307, 308, 320, 335, 343, 344, 350, 385,
    393, 417, 435
NATURAL RESOURCES DEFENSE COUNCIL, INC.
  Los Angeles, California Office 271
  San Francisco, California Office 271
NATURE CONSERVANCY, THE
  Western Division Office 272
NATURE CONSERVANCY, THE, CALIFORNIA CHAPTER
  273
NORTHCOAST ENVIRONMENTAL CENTER 284
PACIFIC INSTITUTE FOR STUDIES IN DEVELOPMENT,
  ENVIRONMENT, AND SECURITY 293
PLANNING AND CONSERVATION LEAGUE 297
RAINFOREST ACTION NETWORK 302
RESOURCE RENEWAL INSTITUTE, THE 304
SAVE SAN FRANCISCO BAY ASSOCIATION 309
SAVE-THE-REDWOODS LEAGUE 310
SCENIC AMERICA
  Scenic California 311
SEA SHEPHERD CONSERVATION SOCIETY 311
  USA Office 312
SIERRA CLUB 312, 314, 315, 316, 317
  California/Nevada/Hawaii Office and California Legislative
    Office 313
  Oakland/San Francisco Bay Area Field Office 313
  Southern California/Nevada Field Office 313
SIERRA CLUB FOUNDATION, THE 317
SIERRA CLUB, ANGELES CHAPTER 314
SIERRA CLUB, KERN-KAWEAH CHAPTER 315
SIERRA CLUB, LOMA PRIETA CHAPTER 315
SIERRA CLUB, LOS PADRES CHAPTER 315
SIERRA CLUB, MOTHER LODE CHAPTER 315
SIERRA CLUB, REDWOOD CHAPTER (Northern California)
  316
SIERRA CLUB, SAN DIEGO CHAPTER (Sourthern
  California) 316
SIERRA CLUB, SAN FRANCISCO BAY CHAPTER (Northern
  California) 316
SIERRA CLUB, SAN GORGONIO CHAPTER (Southern
  California) 316
SIERRA CLUB, SANTA LUCIA CHAPTER 316
SIERRA CLUB, TEHIPITE CHAPTER (Northern California)
  316
SIERRA CLUB, VENTANA CHAPTER (Northern California)
  316
SIERRA NEVADA FOREST PROTECTION CAMPAIGN .. 317
SOCIETY FOR THE PRESERVATION OF BIRDS OF PREY
  319
STANFORD ENVIRONMENTAL LAW SOCIETY 325
STUDENT CONSERVATION ASSOCIATION, INC.
  California Office 192, 326
THREE CIRCLES CENTER FOR MULTICULTURAL
  ENVIRONMENTAL EDUCATION 329
TREEPEOPLE 330
TROUT UNLIMITED, CALIFORNIA COUNCIL 332
TRUST FOR PUBLIC LAND, THE 334
URBAN HABITAT PROGRAM 337
WATERSHED MANAGEMENT COUNCIL 343
WILDLIFE SOCIETY, CALIFORNIA CENTRAL COAST
  CHAPTER 351
WILDLIFE SOCIETY, CALIFORNIA NORTH COAST
  CHAPTER 351
WILDLIFE SOCIETY, SACRAMENTO-SHASTA CHAPTER
  353
WILDLIFE SOCIETY, SAN FRANCISCO BAY AREA
  CHAPTER 354
WILDLIFE SOCIETY, SAN JOAQUIN VALLEY CHAPTER 354
WILDLIFE SOCIETY, SOUTHERN CALIFORNIA CHAPTER
  354
WILDLIFE WAYSTATION 355
YOSEMITE RESTORATION TRUST 361
STATE GOVERNMENT ORGANIZATIONS
CALIFORNIA COOPERATIVE FISHERY RESEARCH UNIT
  (USGS) 44
CALIFORNIA DEPARTMENT OF EDUCATION
  Office of Environmental Education 44, 91, 94, 400
CALIFORNIA ENVIRONMENTAL PROTECTION AGENCY 44
  California Air Resources Board 44
  Department of Pesticide Regulation 44, 45
  Department of Toxic Substances Control 44, 45
  Office of Environmental Health Hazard Assessment . 44, 45
  Water Resources Control Board 44, 45
CALIFORNIA SEA GRANT COLLEGE SYSTEM 45
CALIFORNIA STATE EXTENSION SERVICES 45
CALIFORNIA STATE LANDS COMMISSION 46
DEPARTMENT OF FOOD AND AGRICULTURE
  (CALIFORNIA) 46
GOVERNOR OF CALIFORNIA 44
RESOURCES AGENCY, THE 46
  California Coastal Commission 46
  California Coastal Conservancy 46
  California Conservation Corps 46
  California Energy Commission 47
  California Water Commission 47
  Colorado River Board of California 47
  Department of Boating and Waterways 47

GEOGRAPHIC INDEX - UNITED STATES

Department of Conservation 38, 47, 75, 76, 79, 155, 291, 398, 415, 416, 417
Department of Fish and Game 39, 47, 48, 60, 155, 397, 415, 421
Department of Forestry and Fire Protection 47
Department of Parks and Recreation 48, 310, 327
Department of Water Resources 48
Fish and Game Commission 47, 48
Native American Heritage Commission 48
San Francisco Bay Conservation and Development Commission 48
State Reclamation Board 48
Wildlife Conservation Board 48

COLORADO
GOVERNMENT ORGANIZATIONS
ENVIRONMENTAL PROTECTION AGENCY 10
UNITED STATES DEPARTMENT OF AGRICULTURE
RESEARCH EDUCATION AND ECONOMICS 15
UNITED STATES FOREST SERVICE 16
UNITED STATES DEPARTMENT OF THE AIR FORCE
MAJOR AIR COMMANDS 21
UNITED STATES DEPARTMENT OF THE INTERIOR
BUREAU OF LAND MANAGEMENT 28, 418
BUREAU OF RECLAMATION 28
UNITED STATES FISH AND WILDLIFE SERVICE 29

NON-GOVERNMENTAL ORGANIZATIONS
AMERICAN BIRDING ASSOCIATION 138
AMERICAN FISHERIES SOCIETY
Fisheries Administrators Section 140
AMERICAN HUMANE ASSOCIATION 145
AMERICAN WATER WORKS ASSOCIATION (AWWA) 151
AMERICAN WILDLANDS 151
ASSOCIATION OF MIDWEST FISH AND GAME LAW ENFORCEMENT OFFICERS 156
BIODIVERSITY LEGAL FOUNDATION 161
CADDO LAKE INSTITUTE, INC. 163
COLORADO ASSOCIATION OF SOIL CONSERVATION DISTRICTS 177
COLORADO B.A.S.S. CHAPTER FEDERATION 177
COLORADO ENVIRONMENTAL COALITION 177
COLORADO FORESTRY ASSOCIATION 177
COLORADO NATURAL HERITAGE PROGRAM 177
COLORADO TRAPPERS ASSOCIATION 178
COLORADO WATER CONGRESS 178
COLORADO WILDLIFE FEDERATION 178
COLORADO WILDLIFE HERITAGE FOUNDATION 178
EARTHJUSTICE LEGAL DEFENSE FUND (formerly Sierra Club Legal Defense Fund, Inc.)
Rocky Mountain Office 192, 196
EARTHLAW 192
ENVIRONMENTAL DEFENSE FUND, INC.
Rocky Mountain Office 192, 196
INTERNATIONAL EROSION CONTROL ASSOCIATION (IECA) 224
INTERNATIONAL HUNTER EDUCATION ASSOCIATION 225
IZAAK WALTON LEAGUE OF AMERICA, INC., THE
Colorado Division 49, 155, 178, 223, 234, 351, 397
KEYSTONE CENTER, THE 239
LIGHTHAWK
Southern Rocky Mountain Field Office 243
NATIONAL ASSOCIATION FOR INTERPRETATION 256
NATIONAL ENVIRONMENTAL HEALTH ASSOCIATION . 260
NATIONAL FARMERS UNION 261
NATIONAL ORGANIZATION FOR RIVERS (NORS) 263
NATIONAL PARKS AND CONSERVATION ASSOCIATION (NPCA)
Rocky Mountain Regional Office 264
NATIONAL TRUST FOR HISTORIC PRESERVATION
Mountains and Plains 266, 268
NATIONAL WILDLIFE FEDERATION
Rocky Mountain Natural Resource Center (AZ, CO, IA, KS, MO, NE, NM, UT) 268
NATIVE AMERICAN FISH AND WILDLIFE SOCIETY (NAFWS) 269
NATURE CONSERVANCY, THE
Rocky Mountain Division Office 272
NATURE CONSERVANCY, THE, COLORADO CHAPTER 273
NORTH AMERICAN WOLF SOCIETY 282
PRIORITIES INSTITUTE, THE 299
RAPTOR EDUCATION FOUNDATION, INC. 303
RIVER OTTER ALLIANCE, THE 306
ROCKY MOUNTAIN BIGHORN SOCIETY 306
ROCKY MOUNTAIN ELK FOUNDATION
Intermountain Region Office 307
SIERRA CLUB
Colorado Field Office 313
SIERRA CLUB, ROCKY MOUNTAIN CHAPTER (Colorado) 316
SINAPU 317
SOCIETY FOR RANGE MANAGEMENT 319
THORNE ECOLOGICAL INSTITUTE 329
TROUT UNLIMITED, COLORADO COUNCIL 332
WILDERNESS EDUCATION ASSOCIATION 346
WILDLIFE SOCIETY, COLORADO CHAPTER 351
WINDSTAR FOUNDATION, THE 355
YELLOWSTONE GRIZZLY FOUNDATION (YGF) 360

STATE GOVERNMENT ORGANIZATIONS
COLORADO COOPERATIVE FISH AND WILDLIFE RESEARCH UNIT (USDI) 49
COLORADO DEPARTMENT OF AGRICULTURE 49
COLORADO DEPARTMENT OF EDUCATION 49
COLORADO DEPARTMENT OF NATURAL RESOURCES 49
Colorado Geologic Survey 49
Division of Minerals and Geology 49
Division of Parks and Outdoor Recreation 40, 49
Division of Water Resources 49, 52, 83, 91, 110
Division of Wildlife 39, 49, 54, 67, 82, 92, 94, 110, 398, 417
Oil and Gas Conservation Commission 41, 49
Soil Conservation Board 49
State Board of Land 49, 59
Water Conservation Board 49, 109
COLORADO DEPARTMENT OF PUBLIC HEALTH AND ENVIRONMENT 49
COLORADO STATE FOREST SERVICE 49
COLORADO STATE UNIVERSITY COOPERATIVE EXTENSION 50
GOVERNOR OF COLORADO 49

CONNECTICUT
NON-GOVERNMENTAL ORGANIZATIONS
AMERICAN BASS ASSOCIATION OF CONNECTICUT, THE 137
AMERICAN PIE (PUBLIC INFORMATION ON THE ENVIRONMENT) 148
AUDUBON COUNCIL OF CONNECTICUT 158
BERKSHIRE-LITCHFIELD ENVIRONMENTAL COUNCIL, INC. 160
CETACEAN SOCIETY INTERNATIONAL 172
CONNECTICUT ASSOCIATION OF SOIL AND WATER CONSERVATION DISTRICTS, INC. 180
CONNECTICUT AUDUBON SOCIETY, INC. 180
CONNECTICUT B.A.S.S. CHAPTER FEDERATION 180
CONNECTICUT BOTANICAL SOCIETY 180
CONNECTICUT FOREST AND PARK ASSOCIATION 180
CONNECTICUT FUND FOR THE ENVIRONMENT 180
CONNECTICUT PUBLIC INTEREST RESEARCH GROUP (Conn PIRG) 181
CONNECTICUT WATERFOWL ASSOCIATION, INC. 181
E-P EDUCATION SERVICES, INC. 191
FRIENDS OF ANIMALS INC. 205
KEEP AMERICA BEAUTIFUL, INC. 238
NATIONAL SHOOTING SPORTS FOUNDATION, INC. ... 265
NATURE CONSERVANCY, THE, CONNECTICUT CHAPTER 273
SAVE THE SOUND, INC. 310
SIERRA CLUB, CONNECTICUT CHAPTER 314
TROUT UNLIMITED, CONNECTICUT COUNCIL 332
WILDLIFE SOCIETY, NEW ENGLAND CHAPTER 353

STATE GOVERNMENT ORGANIZATIONS
CONNECTICUT COUNCIL ON ENVIRONMENTAL QUALITY 50
CONNECTICUT DEPARTMENT OF AGRICULTURE 50
CONNECTICUT DEPARTMENT OF ENVIRONMENTAL PROTECTION 50
CONNECTICUT SEA GRANT 51
GOVERNOR OF CONNECTICUT 50
UNIVERSITY OF CONNECTICUT COOPERATIVE EXTENSION 51

GEOGRAPHIC INDEX - UNITED STATES

DELAWARE

GOVERNMENT ORGANIZATIONS
UNITED STATES DEPARTMENT OF THE INTERIOR
  UNITED STATES FISH AND WILDLIFE SERVICE 29

NON-GOVERNMENTAL ORGANIZATIONS
AMERICAN FISHERIES SOCIETY, MID-ATLANTIC CHAPTER 143
CHRISTINA CONSERVANCY, INC. 174
COALITION FOR NATURAL STREAM VALLEYS, INC. 175
DELAWARE ASSOCIATION OF CONSERVATION DISTRICTS 186
DELAWARE AUDUBON SOCIETY 186
DELAWARE B.A.S.S. CHAPTER FEDERATION 187
DELAWARE FORESTRY ASSOCIATION 187
DELAWARE GREENWAYS, INC. 187
DELAWARE MUSEUM OF NATURAL HISTORY 187
DELAWARE NATURE SOCIETY 187
DELAWARE WILD LANDS, INC. 187
DELMARVA ORNITHOLOGICAL SOCIETY 187
HUMMINGBIRD SOCIETY, THE 217
MID-ATLANTIC FISHERY MANAGEMENT COUNCIL 250
NATURE CONSERVANCY, THE, DELAWARE CHAPTER 273
SAVE WETLANDS AND BAYS 310
SIERRA CLUB
  Atlantic Coast Office 313
SIERRA CLUB, DELAWARE CHAPTER 314
TRI-STATE BIRD RESCUE AND RESEARCH, INC. 331

STATE GOVERNMENT ORGANIZATIONS
DELAWARE DEPARTMENT OF AGRICULTURE 51
DELAWARE DEPARTMENT OF NATURAL RESOURCES AND ENVIRONMENTAL CONTROL 51
  Division of Air and Waste Management 51
  Division of Fish and Wildlife 29, 40, 51, 63, 76, 112, 113, 261, 397
  Division of Parks and Recreation 51, 76, 94, 104, 110, 258, 416
  Division of Water Resources 49, 52, 83, 91, 110
DELAWARE DEPARTMENT OF NATURAL RESOURCES AND ENVIRONMENTAL CONTROL
  Division of Soil and Water Conservation 51, 92, 94, 114
DELAWARE GEOLOGICAL SURVEY 52
DELAWARE SEA GRANT PROGRAM 52
DELAWARE SOLID WASTE AUTHORITY 52
DELAWARE STATE EXTENSION SERVICE 52
GOVERNOR OF DELAWARE 51

DISTRICT OF COLUMBIA

GOVERNMENT ORGANIZATIONS
HOUSE COMMITTEE ON AGRICULTURE 4
HOUSE COMMITTEE ON APPROPRIATIONS 5
HOUSE COMMITTEE ON COMMERCE 5
HOUSE COMMITTEE ON EDUCATION AND THE WORKFORCE 5
HOUSE COMMITTEE ON INTERNATIONAL RELATIONS 5
HOUSE COMMITTEE ON RULES 5
HOUSE COMMITTEE ON TRANSPORTATION AND INFRASTRUCTURE 5
SENATE COMMITTEE ON APPROPRIATIONS 6
SENATE COMMITTEE ON COMMERCE SCIENCE AND TRANSPORTATION 6
SENATE COMMITTEE ON ENERGY AND NATURAL RESOURCES 6
SENATE COMMITTEE ON ENVIRONMENT AND PUBLIC WORKS 6
SENATE COMMITTEE ON FOREIGN RELATIONS 6
APPALACHIAN REGIONAL COMMISSION 7
ATLANTIC STATES MARINE FISHERIES COMMISSION 7
INTERNATIONAL JOINT COMMISSION 8
MIGRATORY BIRD CONSERVATION COMMISSION 8
COUNCIL ON ENVIRONMENTAL QUALITY 10
ENVIRONMENTAL PROTECTION AGENCY 10
ADVISORY COUNCIL ON HISTORIC PRESERVATION 33
GENERAL SERVICES ADMINISTRATION 33
NATIONAL TRANSPORTATION SAFETY BOARD 33
NUCLEAR REGULATORY COMMISSION 33
PEACE CORPS 34
UNITED STATES DEPARTMENT OF AGRICULTURE 11
  ANIMAL AND PLANT HEALTH INSPECTION SERVICE 12
  ECONOMIC RESEARCH SERVICE 13
  NATURAL RESOURCES CONSERVATION SERVICE (formerly Soil Conservation Service) 13
  RESEARCH EDUCATION AND ECONOMICS 15
  UNITED STATES FOREST SERVICE 16
UNITED STATES DEPARTMENT OF COMMERCE 17
  ECONOMIC DEVELOPMENT ADMINISTRATION 17
  NATIONAL OCEANIC AND ATMOSPHERIC ADMINISTRATION 17
UNITED STATES DEPARTMENT OF DEFENSE 18
UNITED STATES DEPARTMENT OF EDUCATION 18
UNITED STATES DEPARTMENT OF ENERGY 18
  FEDERAL ENERGY REGULATORY COMMISSION 18
UNITED STATES DEPARTMENT OF HEALTH AND HUMAN SERVICES 19
UNITED STATES DEPARTMENT OF HOUSING AND URBAN DEVELOPMENT 19
UNITED STATES DEPARTMENT OF JUSTICE 20
UNITED STATES DEPARTMENT OF LABOR 20
  JOB CORPS 20
UNITED STATES DEPARTMENT OF STATE 20
  BUREAU OF OCEANS AND INTERNATIONAL ENVIRONMENTAL AND SCIENTIFIC AFFAIRS 20
  UNITED STATES MAN AND THE BIOSPHERE PROGRAM (U.S. MAB) 21
UNITED STATES DEPARTMENT OF THE AIR FORCE 21
  MAJOR AIR COMMANDS 21
UNITED STATES DEPARTMENT OF THE ARMY 24
  U.S. ARMY CORPS OF ENGINEERS 25
UNITED STATES DEPARTMENT OF THE INTERIOR 27
  BUREAU OF INDIAN AFFAIRS 28
  BUREAU OF LAND MANAGEMENT 28, 418
  BUREAU OF RECLAMATION 28
  NATIONAL PARK SERVICE 29
  OFFICE OF SURFACE MINING RECLAMATION AND ENFORCEMENT 29
  UNITED STATES FISH AND WILDLIFE SERVICE 29
UNITED STATES DEPARTMENT OF THE NAVY 31
  U.S. MARINE CORPS 31
UNITED STATES DEPARTMENT OF TRANSPORTATION 31
  FEDERAL AVIATION ADMINISTRATION 31
  FEDERAL HIGHWAY ADMINISTRATION 31
  FEDERAL RAILROAD ADMINISTRATION 32
  FEDERAL TRANSIT ADMINISTRATION 32
  NATIONAL HIGHWAY TRAFFIC SAFETY ADMINISTRATION 32
  SAINT LAWRENCE SEAWAY DEVELOPMENT CORPORATION 32
  UNITED STATES COAST GUARD 32
UNITED STATES DEPARTMENT OF TREASURY 32
  U.S. CUSTOMS SERVICE 32

NON-GOVERNMENTAL ORGANIZATIONS
20/20 VISION 130
ACADEMY FOR EDUCATIONAL DEVELOPMENT 130
AFRICAN WILDLIFE FOUNDATION 132
AMERICA THE BEAUTIFUL FUND 135
AMERICAN ASSOCIATION FOR THE ADVANCEMENT OF SCIENCE 136
AMERICAN BIRD CONSERVANCY 138
AMERICAN CONSERVATION ASSOCIATION, INC. 139
AMERICAN COUNCIL FOR AN ENERGY-EFFICIENT ECONOMY 139
AMERICAN FARMLAND TRUST 139
AMERICAN FOREST FOUNDATION 144
AMERICAN FORESTS (formerly American Forestry Association) 144
AMERICAN HORSE PROTECTION ASSOCIATION 145
AMERICAN INSTITUTE OF BIOLOGICAL SCIENCES 146
AMERICAN LANDS (formerly Western Ancient Forest Campaign) 146
AMERICAN LEAGUE OF ANGLERS AND BOATERS 146
AMERICAN OCEANS CAMPAIGN
  Washington, DC Office 134, 148, 192, 308, 314, 324
AMERICAN ORNITHOLOGISTS' UNION 148
AMERICAN PLANNING ASSOCIATION 148
AMERICAN RECREATION COALITION 148
AMERICAN RIVERS (formerly American Rivers Conservation Council) 149
AMERICAN SOCIETY OF LANDSCAPE ARCHITECTS ... 150
AMERICANS FOR THE ENVIRONMENT 152
ANIMAL WELFARE INSTITUTE 152

GEOGRAPHIC INDEX - UNITED STATES

ANTARCTICA PROJECT 153
ASSOCIATION OF AMERICAN GEOGRAPHERS 155
ASSOCIATION OF STATE AND TERRITORIAL HEALTH
   OFFICIALS 157
BEYOND PESTICIDES/NATIONAL COALITION AGAINST
   THE MISUSE OF PESTICIDES 160
CANADA-UNITED STATES ENVIRONMENTAL COUNCIL
   (United States Office) 166
CARRYING CAPACITY NETWORK 168
CENTER FOR ENVIRONMENT 169, 170, 375
CENTER FOR INTERNATIONAL ENVIRONMENTAL LAW
   (CIEL) 170
CENTER FOR MARINE CONSERVATION 170
CENTER FOR RESOURCE ECONOMICS 171
CENTER FOR SCIENCE IN THE PUBLIC INTEREST 171
CIRCUMPOLAR CONSERVATION UNION 174
CLEAN WATER ACTION 175
CLEAN WATER FUND 175
CLEAN WATER NETWORK, THE 175
CLIMATE INSTITUTE 175
COAST ALLIANCE 176
COMMITTEE FOR THE NATIONAL INSTITUTE FOR THE
   ENVIRONMENT (CNIE) 178
COMMITTEE ON AGRICULTURAL SUSTAINABILITY FOR
   DEVELOPING COUNTRIES 179
COMMUNITY RIGHTS COUNSEL 179
CONCERN, INC. 179
CONSERVATION INTERNATIONAL 183
DEFENDERS OF WILDLIFE 186
DISTRICT OF COLUMBIA SOIL AND WATER
   CONSERVATION DISTRICT 188
EARTH SHARE 192
EARTHJUSTICE LEGAL DEFENSE FUND (formerly Sierra
   Club Legal Defense Fund, Inc.)
   Washington, DC Office 134, 148, 192, 308, 314, 324
ECOLOGICAL SOCIETY OF AMERICA, THE 193
ENDANGERED SPECIES COALITION 194
ENVIRONMENTAL AND ENERGY STUDY INSTITUTE
   (EESI) 195
ENVIRONMENTAL DEFENSE FUND, INC.
   Capital Office 196, 326
ENVIRONMENTAL LAW INSTITUTE, THE 198
FRIENDS OF THE EARTH 206
GENERAL FEDERATION OF WOMEN'S CLUBS 208
GLOBAL ENVIRONMENTAL MANAGEMENT INITIATIVE
   (GEMI) 210
GREEN SEAL 213
GREENPEACE, INC. 213
H. JOHN HEINZ III CENTER FOR SCIENCE, ECONOMICS,
   AND THE ENVIRONMENT 214
HUMANE SOCIETY OF THE UNITED STATES, THE 217
INITIATIVE FOR SOCIAL ACTION AND RENEWAL IN
   EURASIA 221
INTERNATIONAL ASSOCIATION OF FISH AND WILDLIFE
   AGENCIES 222
INTERNATIONAL INSTITUTE FOR ENERGY
   CONSERVATION 225
INTERNATIONAL UNION FOR CONSERVATION OF
   NATURE AND NATURAL RESOURCES (IUCN) THE
   WORLD CONSERVATION UNION
   U.S. Office, Washington, DC 229
ISLAND RESOURCES FOUNDATION 233
LAND TRUST ALLIANCE, THE 240
LEAGUE OF CONSERVATION VOTERS 241
LEAGUE OF WOMEN VOTERS OF THE U.S. 241
MARINE TECHNOLOGY SOCIETY 246
MINERAL POLICY CENTER 250
NATIONAL ASSOCIATION OF CONSERVATION
   DISTRICTS 257
NATIONAL ASSOCIATION OF SERVICE AND
   CONSERVATION CORPS (NASCC) 258
NATIONAL ASSOCIATION OF STATE DEPARTMENTS OF
   AGRICULTURE 258
NATIONAL ASSOCIATION OF STATE FORESTERS 258
NATIONAL AUDUBON SOCIETY
   Washington, D.C. Office 259, 271
NATIONAL EDUCATION ASSOCIATION 260
NATIONAL FISH AND WILDLIFE FOUNDATION 261
NATIONAL FOREST FOUNDATION 261
NATIONAL GEOGRAPHIC SOCIETY 262
NATIONAL GRANGE, THE 262
NATIONAL PARK FOUNDATION 263
NATIONAL PARK TRUST 263
NATIONAL PARKS AND CONSERVATION ASSOCIATION
   (NPCA) 263
NATIONAL RESEARCH COUNCIL 264
NATIONAL TREE TRUST 265
NATIONAL TRUST FOR HISTORIC PRESERVATION 265
NATIONAL WATERWAYS CONFERENCE INC 266
NATIONAL WHISTLEBLOWER CENTER 266
NATIONAL WILDLIFE FEDERATION
   Office of Federal and International Affairs 268
NATIONAL WILDLIFE REFUGE ASSOCIATION 269
NATURAL RESOURCES COUNCIL OF AMERICA 271
NATURAL RESOURCES DEFENSE COUNCIL, INC.
   Washington, D.C. Office 259, 271
NORTH AMERICAN ASSOCIATION FOR
   ENVIRONMENTAL EDUCATION 280
NORTH AMERICAN COALITION ON RELIGION AND
   ECOLOGY (NACRE) 280
ORNITHOLOGICAL COUNCIL 291
OZONE ACTION 292
PANOS INSTITUTE, THE 293
PARTNERS IN PARKS 293
PHYSICIANS FOR SOCIAL RESPONSIBILITY 296
PINCHOT INSTITUTE FOR CONSERVATION 296
POPULATION ACTION INTERNATIONAL 297
POPULATION INSTITUTE, THE 298
POPULATION REFERENCE BUREAU, INC. 298
POPULATION-ENVIRONMENT BALANCE, INC. 298
PUBLIC EMPLOYEES FOR ENVIRONMENTAL
   RESPONSIBILITY (PEER) 300
RAILS-TO-TRAILS CONSERVANCY 302
RAINBOW PUSH COALITION 302
RENEW AMERICA 303
RENEWABLE ENERGY POLICY PROJECT (REPP) 303
RESOURCES FOR THE FUTURE 304
RIVER NETWORK
   Eastern Office 306
SAFE ENERGY COMMUNICATION COUNCIL 308
SAVE AMERICA'S FORESTS 309
SCENIC AMERICA 310
SIERRA CLUB
   Washington, DC Office 134, 148, 192, 308, 314, 324
SIERRA CLUB, NEW COLUMBIA CHAPTER 315
SMITHSONIAN INSTITUTION 317
   National Museum of Natural History 148, 317
   National Zoological Park 317
   Office of Fellowships and Grants 317
   Office of International Relations 318
   Smithsonian Press/Smithsonian Productions 318
SOCIETY FOR ANIMAL PROTECTIVE LEGISLATION 318
STUDENT PUGWASH USA 326
TRAFFIC NORTH AMERICA 330
TROUT UNLIMITED, NORTH CAROLINA 333
U.S. PUBLIC INTEREST RESEARCH GROUP 336
UNITED STATES CHAMBER OF COMMERCE 336
UNITED STATES COMMITTEE FOR THE UNITED
   NATIONS ENVIRONMENT PROGRAMME THE (U.S. and
   UNEP) 336
UNITED STATES TOURIST COUNCIL 336
WILDERNESS SOCIETY, THE 346
WILDLIFE MANAGEMENT INSTITUTE 349
WILDLIFE SOCIETY, NATIONAL CAPITAL CHAPTER 352
WORLD PARKS ENDOWMENT INC. 358
WORLD RESOURCES INSTITUTE 358
WORLD WILDLIFE FUND 359
WORLD WOMEN IN THE DEFENSE OF THE
   ENVIRONMENT (WorldWIDE) 359
WORLDWATCH INSTITUTE 359
ZERO POPULATION GROWTH, INC. 361

STATE GOVERNMENT ORGANIZATIONS
   DEPARTMENT OF PUBLIC WORKS 52
   DISTRICT OF COLUMBIA DEPARTMENT OF HEALTH
      Environmental Health Administration, Watershed
      Protection Division 52
   DISTRICT OF COLUMBIA STATE EXTENSION SERVICES
   52

FLORIDA

GOVERNMENT ORGANIZATIONS
UNITED STATES DEPARTMENT OF THE AIR FORCE 21
   MAJOR AIR COMMANDS 21
UNITED STATES DEPARTMENT OF THE ARMY
   U.S. ARMY CORPS OF ENGINEERS 25
UNITED STATES TREASURY DEPARTMENT
   U.S. CUSTOMS SERVICE 32

NON-GOVERNMENTAL ORGANIZATIONS
AMERICAN FISHERIES SOCIETY
   Introduced Fish Section 141
   Socioeconomics Section 141
   Southern Division 48, 141
AMERICAN FISHERIES SOCIETY, FLORIDA CHAPTER 142
AMERICAN LITTORAL SOCIETY
   Coral Reef Conservation Center Office 147
ARCHBOLD BIOLOGICAL STATION 153
ARCHERY MANUFACTURERS AND MERCHANTS
   ORGANIZATION (AMO) 154
ASSOCIATION OF AVIAN VETERINARIANS 156
BARRIER ISLAND TRUST, INC. 160
BILLFISH FOUNDATION, THE 160
CARIBBEAN CONSERVATION CORPORATION 168
CONSERVANCY OF SOUTHWEST FLORIDA, THE 181
EARTHJUSTICE LEGAL DEFENSE FUND (formerly Sierra Club Legal Defense Fund, Inc.)
   Florida Office 183, 192
EVERGLADES COORDINATING COUNCIL (ECC) 199
FLORIDA ASSOCIATION OF SOIL AND WATER
   CONSERVATION DISTRICTS 201
FLORIDA AUDUBON SOCIETY 201
FLORIDA B.A.S.S. CHAPTER FEDERATION 201
FLORIDA DEFENDERS OF THE ENVIRONMENT, INC.
   (Home Office) 201
FLORIDA EXOTIC PEST PLANT COUNCIL 202
FLORIDA FORESTRY ASSOCIATION 202
FLORIDA NATIVE PLANT SOCIETY 202
FLORIDA ORNITHOLOGICAL SOCIETY 202
FLORIDA PANTHER PROJECT, INC., THE 202
FLORIDA PUBLIC INTEREST RESEARCH GROUP (Florida
   PIRG) 202
FLORIDA SPORTSMEN'S CONSERVATION ASSOCIATION
   202
FLORIDA TRAIL ASSOCIATION, INC. 203
FLORIDA WILDLIFE FEDERATION 203
GAME CONSERVANCY U.S.A. (formerly American Friends of the Game Conservancy) 207
GOPHER TORTOISE COUNCIL 211
GREAT OUTDOORS CONSERVANCY, THE 212
GULF OF MEXICO FISHERY MANAGEMENT COUNCIL 214
INTERNATIONAL GAME FISH ASSOCIATION 225
INTERNATIONAL OCEANOGRAPHIC FOUNDATION 226
INTERNATIONAL OSPREY FOUNDATION INC., THE 226
ISLAND CONSERVATION EFFORT 233
IZAAK WALTON LEAGUE OF AMERICA, INC., THE
   Florida Division 234
J.N. (DING) DARLING FOUNDATION 235
KEEP FLORIDA BEAUTIFUL, INC. 238
LEGAL ENVIRONMENTAL ASSISTANCE FOUNDATION
   INC. (LEAF) 242
MANASOTA-88 245
MOTE MARINE LABORATORY 255
NATIONAL ASSOCIATION OF ENVIRONMENTAL
   PROFESSIONALS, THE (National Office) 257
NATIONAL AUDUBON SOCIETY
   Everglades Campaign Office 259
   Tavernier Science Center 259
NATIONAL WILDLIFE FEDERATION
   Everglades Project Office 267
NATURE CONSERVANCY, THE
   Southeast Division Office 272
NATURE CONSERVANCY, THE, FLORIDA CHAPTER ... 273
RAINFOREST TRUST, INC., THE 302
REEF RELIEF 303
SANIBEL-CAPTIVA CONSERVATION FOUNDATION, INC.
   308
SAVE THE MANATEE CLUB 310
SCENIC AMERICA
   Citizens for a Scenic Florida 310
SEACAMP ASSOCIATION, INC. 312
SIERRA CLUB
   Florida Field Office 313
   Florida-Miami Field Office 313
SIERRA CLUB, FLORIDA CHAPTER 314
SMITHSONIAN INSTITUTION
   Smithsonian Marine Station at Link Port 318
   Smithsonian Tropical Research Institute 318
SUNCOAST SEABIRD SANCTUARY INC. 327
TALL TIMBERS RESEARCH STATION 327
TALLAHASSEE MUSEUM OF HISTORY AND NATURAL
   SCIENCE 327
WILDLIFE FOUNDATION OF FLORIDA, INC. 349
WILDLIFE SOCIETY, FLORIDA CHAPTER 351

STATE GOVERNMENT ORGANIZATIONS
FLORIDA COOPERATIVE FISH AND WILDLIFE
   RESEARCH UNIT (USDI) 52
FLORIDA DEPARTMENT OF AGRICULTURE AND
   CONSUMER SERVICES 52
   Division of Forestry40, 53, 58, 63, 68, 76, 83, 94, 110, 119, 392
   Office of Agricultural Water Policy 53
   Soil and Water Conservation Council 53
FLORIDA DEPARTMENT OF ENVIRONMENTAL
   PROTECTION 53
   Air Resources Management Division 53
   Beaches and Shores Division 53
   Ecosytem Management Division 53
   Environmental Resource Permitting Division 53
   Law Enforcement Division51, 53, 68, 84, 105, 107, 114, 284
   Legislative and Cabinet Affairs Division 53
   Marine Resource Division 53
   Recreation and Parks division 54
   State Lands Division 54
   Waste Management Division 54, 64, 65, 84, 87
   Water Facilities Division 54
FLORIDA FISH AND WILDLIFE CONSERVATION
   COMMISSION 54
FLORIDA SEA GRANT COLLEGE 54
FLORIDA STATE COOPERATIVE EXTENSION SERVICE 54
FLORIDA STATE DEPARTMENT OF HEALTH 54
GOVERNOR OF FLORIDA 52
LEE COUNTY PARKS AND RECREATION SERVICES 54
MARINE LABORATORY (FLORIDA) 55
SOUTH FLORIDA WATER MANAGEMENT DISTRICT 55
SOUTHWEST FLORIDA WATER MANAGEMENT DISTRICT
   (SWFWMD) 55

GEORGIA

GOVERNMENT ORGANIZATIONS
ENVIRONMENTAL PROTECTION AGENCY 10
UNITED STATES DEPARTMENT OF AGRICULTURE
   RESEARCH EDUCATION AND ECONOMICS 15
   UNITED STATES FOREST SERVICE 16
UNITED STATES DEPARTMENT OF THE AIR FORCE
   MAJOR AIR COMMANDS 21
UNITED STATES DEPARTMENT OF THE ARMY
   U.S. ARMY CORPS OF ENGINEERS 25
   U.S. ARMY FORCES COMMAND 27
UNITED STATES DEPARTMENT OF THE INTERIOR
   UNITED STATES FISH AND WILDLIFE SERVICE 29

NON-GOVERNMENTAL ORGANIZATIONS
AMERICAN FISHERIES SOCIETY, GEORGIA CHAPTER
   142
CAMPAIGN FOR A PROSPEROUS GEORGIA 165
COASTAL CONSERVATION ASSOCIATION GEORGIA .. 176
COASTAL GEORGIA CENTER FOR SUSTAINABLE
   DEVELOPMENT 176
COASTAL GEORGIA LAND TRUST, THE 176
COOSA RIVER BASIN INITIATIVE 184
ENVIRONMENTAL FUND FOR GEORGIA 197
FOREST LANDOWNERS ASSOCIATION, INC. 203
GEORGIA ASSOCIATION OF CONSERVATION DISTRICT
   SUPERVISORS 208
GEORGIA B.A.S.S. CHAPTER FEDERATION 208
GEORGIA CONSERVANCY, INC., THE 209
GEORGIA ENVIRONMENTAL COUNCIL, INC. 209
GEORGIA ENVIRONMENTAL ORGANIZATION, INC (GEO)
   209
GEORGIA ENVIRONMENTAL POLICY INSTITUTE 209
GEORGIA FEDERATION OF FOREST OWNERS 209

GEOGRAPHIC INDEX - UNITED STATES

GEORGIA FORESTRY ASSOCIATION, INC. 209
GEORGIA TRAPPERS ASSOCIATION 209
GEORGIA TRUST FOR HISTORIC PRESERVATION 210
GEORGIA WILDLIFE FEDERATION 210
HUMAN ECOLOGY ACTION LEAGUE, INC. THE (HEAL) 217
INTERFAITH COUNCIL FOR THE PROTECTION OF
  ANIMALS AND NATURE INC. (ICPAN) 222
MOUNTAIN CONSERVATION TRUST OF GEORGIA, INC.
  255
  NATIONAL WILDLIFE FEDERATION
    Southeastern Natural Resource Center (AL, FL, GA, NC,
    SC, TN, VI) 268
  NATURAL SCIENCE FOR YOUTH FOUNDATION 271
  NORTH AMERICAN ASSOCIATION FOR
  ENVIRONMENTAL EDUCATION
    Conference, Publications and Membership Office 280
  SIERRA CLUB
    Georgia Field Office/Louisiana and Alabama Field Office
    313
  SIERRA CLUB, GEORGIA CHAPTER 314
  SOUTHEASTERN COOPERATIVE WILDLIFE DISEASE
    STUDY 323
  SOUTHFACE ENERGY INSTITUTE 324
  TREES ATLANTA 330
  TROUT UNLIMITED, GEORGIA COUNCIL 332
  UPPER CHATTAHOOCHEE RIVERKEEPER 337
  WILDLIFE SOCIETY, GEORGIA CHAPTER 351
STATE GOVERNMENT ORGANIZATIONS
  GEORGIA COOPERATIVE FISH AND WILDLIFE
    RESEARCH UNIT (USDI) 55
  GEORGIA DEPARTMENT OF AGRICULTURE 55
    Consumers Services Library 55
  GEORGIA DEPARTMENT OF EDUCATION 55
  GEORGIA DEPARTMENT OF NATURAL RESOURCES 56
    Coastal Resources Division 56
    Environmental Protection Division 47, 56, 64, 87, 112
    Historic Preservation Division 56
    Parks, Recreation and Historic Sites Division 56
    Pollution Prevention Assistance Division 56
    Program Support Division 56
    Wildlife Resources Division 56, 223, 397, 415
  GEORGIA FORESTRY COMMISSION 56
  GEORGIA SEA GRANT COLLEGE PROGRAM 56
  GEORGIA STATE EXTENSION SERVICE 56
  GOVERNOR OF GEORGIA 55
  STATE SOIL AND WATER CONSERVATION COMMISSION
    (GEORGIA) 56

GUAM
NON-GOVERNMENTAL ORGANIZATIONS
  PACIFIC BASIN ASSOCIATION OF SOIL AND WATER
    CONSERVATION DISTRICTS 292
STATE GOVERNMENT ORGANIZATIONS
  DEPARTMENT OF PARKS AND RECREATION (GUAM) .. 57
  DIVISION OF FORESTRY AND SOIL RESOURCES OF
    GUAM 57
  GOVERNOR OF GUAM 57
  GUAM COASTAL MANAGEMENT PROGRAM 57
  GUAM COOPERATIVE EXTENSION SERVICE 57
  GUAM DEPARTMENT OF AGRICULTURE 57
    Division of Aquatic and Wildlife Resources 57
  GUAM ENVIRONMENTAL PROTECTION AGENCY 57

HAWAII
GOVERNMENT ORGANIZATIONS
  UNITED STATES DEPARTMENT OF THE AIR FORCE
    MAJOR AIR COMMANDS 21
  UNITED STATES DEPARTMENT OF THE ARMY
    U.S. ARMY CORPS OF ENGINEERS 25
NON-GOVERNMENTAL ORGANIZATIONS
  AMERICAN FISHERIES SOCIETY, HAWAII CHAPTER ... 142
  CONSERVATION COUNCIL FOR HAWAII 181
  EARTHJUSTICE LEGAL DEFENSE FUND (formerly Sierra
    Club Legal Defense Fund, Inc.)
    Hawaii Office 192
  EARTHTRUST 193
  HAWAII ASSOCIATION OF CONSERVATION DISTRICTS
    214
  HAWAII AUDUBON SOCIETY 214
  HAWAII NATURE CENTER 214
  HAWAII SOCIETY OF AMERICAN FORESTERS 214
  HAWAIIAN BOTANICAL SOCIETY 214
  LIFE OF THE LAND 242
  NATURE CONSERVANCY, THE, ASIA/PACIFIC PROGRAM
    273
  NATURE CONSERVANCY, THE, HAWAII CHAPTER 273
  OUTDOOR CIRCLE, THE 291
  PACIFIC WHALE FOUNDATION 293
  SIERRA CLUB, HAWAII CHAPTER 314
  WESTERN PACIFIC REGIONAL FISHERY MANAGEMENT
    COUNCIL 344
  WILDLIFE SOCIETY, HAWAII CHAPTER 351
STATE GOVERNMENT ORGANIZATIONS
  COLLEGE OF TROPICAL AGRICULTURE AND HUMAN
    RESOURCES 57
  DEPARTMENT OF LAND AND NATURAL RESOURCES
    Division of Boating and Ocean Recreation (DOBOR) 58
    Division of Water Resource Management, ... 58
  DEPARTMENT OF LAND AND NATURAL RESOURCES
    (HAWAII) 58
    Division of Aquatic Resources 58
    Division of Conservation and Resources Enforcement 58
    Division of Forestry and Wildlife 58
    Division of Historic Preservation 58, 63
    Division of State Parks 38, 58, 63, 80, 82, 114, 122
    Land Division 38, 58, 120
  ENVIRONMENTAL CENTER 58
  GOVERNOR OF HAWAII 57
  HAWAII COOPERATIVE FISHERY RESEARCH UNIT
    (USDI) 58
  HAWAII DEPARTMENT OF AGRICULTURE 58
  HAWAII DEPARTMENT OF HEALTH 58
  HAWAII SEA GRANT PROGRAM 59
  INSTITUTE OF MARINE BIOLOGY 59
  UNIVERSITY OF HAWAII COOPERATIVE EXTENSION
    PROGRAM 59
  WATER RESOURCES RESEARCH CENTER 59

IDAHO
GOVERNMENT ORGANIZATIONS
  UNITED STATES DEPARTMENT OF THE INTERIOR
    BUREAU OF LAND MANAGEMENT 28, 418
    BUREAU OF RECLAMATION 28
NON-GOVERNMENTAL ORGANIZATIONS
  AMERICAN FISHERIES SOCIETY, IDAHO CHAPTER 142
  ENVIRONMENTAL RESOURCE CENTER (ERC) 198
  IDAHO ASSOCIATION OF SOIL CONSERVATION
    DISTRICTS 218
  IDAHO B.A.S.S. CHAPTER FEDERATION 218
  IDAHO CONSERVATION LEAGUE 218
  IDAHO ENVIRONMENTAL COUNCIL 218
  IDAHO FOREST OWNERS ASSOCIATION 218
  IDAHO WILDLIFE FEDERATION 218
  NATURE CONSERVANCY, THE, IDAHO CHAPTER 273
  NORTHWEST RESOURCE INFORMATION CENTER 286
  PEREGRINE FUND, THE 296
  RAPTOR RESEARCH FOUNDATION, INC. 303
  ROCKY MOUNTAIN ELK FOUNDATION
    Northwest Region Office 307
  SIERRA CLUB, NORTHERN ROCKIES CHAPTER
    (Idaho/Washington) 315
  TROUT UNLIMITED, IDAHO COUNCIL 332
  WILDLIFE SOCIETY, IDAHO CHAPTER 351
  WOLF EDUCATION AND RESEARCH CENTER 357
STATE GOVERNMENT ORGANIZATIONS
  DEPARTMENT OF LANDS (IDAHO) 59
  GOVERNOR OF IDAHO 59
  IDAHO COOPERATIVE EXTENSION 59
  IDAHO COOPERATIVE FISH AND WILDLIFE RESEARCH
    UNIT (USDI) 60
  IDAHO DEPARTMENT OF PARKS AND RECREATION 60
  IDAHO DEPARTMENT OF WATER RESOURCES 60
  IDAHO FISH AND GAME DEPARTMENT 60
  IDAHO FISH AND WILDLIFE FOUNDATION 60
  IDAHO GEOLOGICAL SURVEY 60
  IDAHO STATE DEPARTMENT OF AGRICULTURE 60
  IDAHO STATE SOIL CONSERVATION COMMISSION 60
  STATE OF IDAHO DIVISION OF ENVIRONMENTAL
    QUALITY 61

ILLINOIS
GOVERNMENT ORGANIZATIONS
  ENVIRONMENTAL PROTECTION AGENCY 10
  UNITED STATES DEPARTMENT OF AGRICULTURE

GEOGRAPHIC INDEX - UNITED STATES

    RESEARCH EDUCATION AND ECONOMICS 15
UNITED STATES DEPARTMENT OF THE AIR FORCE
    MAJOR AIR COMMANDS 21
UNITED STATES DEPARTMENT OF THE ARMY
    U.S. ARMY CORPS OF ENGINEERS............................. 25
UNITED STATES DEPARTMENT OF TREASURY
    U.S. CUSTOMS SERVICE 32

NON-GOVERNMENTAL ORGANIZATIONS
    AMERICAN FISHERIES SOCIETY
        Fish Culture Section 140
    AMERICAN FISHERIES SOCIETY, ILLINOIS CHAPTER . 142
    ASSOCIATION OF CONSERVATION ENGINEERS 156
    AUDUBON COUNCIL OF ILLINOIS 158
    CHICAGO HERPETOLOGICAL SOCIETY 173
    EAGLE NATURE FOUNDATION, LTD............................ 191
    EAST CENTRAL ILLINOIS FUR TAKERS 193
    ENVIRONMENTAL EDUCATION ASSOCIATION OF
        ILLINOIS.. 197
    ENVIRONMENTAL LAW AND POLICY CENTER OF THE
        MIDWEST.. 198
    GREAT LAKES SPORT FISHING COUNCIL 211
    ILLINOIS ASSOCIATION OF CONSERVATION DISTRICTS
        218
    ILLINOIS ASSOCIATION OF SOIL AND WATER
        CONSERVATION DISTRICTS 218
    ILLINOIS AUDUBON SOCIETY....................................... 219
    ILLINOIS B.A.S.S. CHAPTER FEDERATION 219
    ILLINOIS ENVIRONMENTAL COUNCIL 219
    ILLINOIS NATIVE PLANT SOCIETY 219
    ILLINOIS NATURAL HERITAGE FOUNDATION 219
    ILLINOIS PRAIRIE PATH... 219
    ILLINOIS WALNUT COUNCIL 219
    INTERNATIONAL SOCIETY OF ARBORICULTURE 227
    IZAAK WALTON LEAGUE OF AMERICA, INC., THE
        Illinois Division 234
    LAKE MICHIGAN FEDERATION 240
    MAX McGRAW WILDLIFE FOUNDATION 248
    NATIONAL BIRD-FEEDING SOCIETY............................. 259
    NATIONAL TRAPPERS ASSOCIATION, INC................... 265
    NATIONAL TRUST FOR HISTORIC PRESERVATION
        Midwest Office 15, 182, 234, 252, 266, 313
    NATURAL LAND INSTITUTE 270
    NATURE CONSERVANCY, THE, ILLINOIS CHAPTER 273
    OPENLANDS PROJECT 290
    PRAIRIE CLUB, THE 298
    PRAIRIE RIVERS NETWORK 299
    PRAIRIE RIVERS NETWORK (Formerly Central States
        Education Center) 299
    REP AMERICA/REPUBLICANS FOR ENVIRONMENTAL
        PROTECTION 304
    SIERRA CLUB, ILLINOIS CHAPTER 314
    SOCIETY FOR INTEGRATIVE AND COMPARTIVE
        BIOLOGY (formerly AMERICAN SOCIETY OF
        ZOOLOGISTS)... 318
    TROUT UNLIMITED, ILLINOIS COUNCIL 332
    UPPER MISSISSIPPI RIVER CONSERVATION
        COMMITTEE 337
    WILDLIFE SOCIETY, ILLINOIS CHAPTER...................... 351
    WINCHESTER NILO FARMS 355

STATE GOVERNMENT ORGANIZATIONS
    GOVERNOR OF ILLINOIS... 61
    ILLINOIS DEPARTMENT OF AGRICULTURE................... 61
        Soil and Water Conservation Districts Advisory Board..... 61
    ILLINOIS DEPARTMENT OF NATURAL RESOURCES...... 61
    ILLINOIS DEPARTMENT OF TRANSPORTATION 61
    ILLINOIS ENVIRONMENTAL PROTECTION AGENCY 61
    ILLINOIS NATURE PRESERVES COMMISSION (INPC).... 62
    UNIVERSITY OF ILLNOIS EXTENSION 62

INDIANA
NON-GOVERNMENTAL ORGANIZATIONS
    ACRES LAND TRUST.. 130
    AMERICAN CAMPING ASSOCIATION, INC. 138
    AMERICAN FISHERIES SOCIETY
        Equal Opportunities Section................................ 140
    AMERICAN FISHERIES SOCIETY, INDIANA CHAPTER .142
    CONSERVATION TECHNOLOGY INFORMATION CENTER
        183
    ENVIRONMENTAL EDUCATION ASSOCIATION OF
        INDIANA 197
    HOOSIER ENVIRONMENTAL COUNCIL 216

    INDIANA ASSOCIATION OF SOIL AND WATER
        CONSERVATION DISTRICTS, INC............................. 220
    INDIANA AUDUBON SOCIETY, INC. 220
    INDIANA B.A.S.S. CHAPTER FEDERATION 220
    INDIANA FORESTRY AND WOODLAND OWNERS
        ASSOCIATION... 220
    INDIANA NATIVE PLANT AND WILDFLOWER SOCIETY 220
    INDIANA STATE TRAPPERS ASSOCIATION, INC. 220
    INDIANA WILDLIFE FEDERATION................................. 220
    IZAAK WALTON LEAGUE OF AMERICA, INC., THE
        Indiana Division 234, 397
    NATURE CONSERVANCY, THE, INDIANA CHAPTER.... 273
    NORTH AMERICAN WILDLIFE PARK FOUNDATION, INC.
        281
    SAVE THE DUNES COUNCIL 309
        Save the Dunes Conservation Fund................... 309
    SIERRA CLUB, HOOSIER CHAPTER 314
    WILDLIFE SOCIETY, INDIANA CHAPTER...................... 351

STATE GOVERNMENT ORGANIZATIONS
    GOVERNOR OF INDIANA.. 62
    ILLINOIS-INDIANA SEA GRANT PROGRAM..................... 62
    INDIANA DEPARTMENT OF ENVIRONMENTAL
        MANAGEMENT 62
    INDIANA DEPARTMENT OF NATURAL RESOURCES...... 62
        Division of Soil Conservation 63, 64
    INDIANA GEOLOGICAL SURVEY 63
    INDIANA STATE DEPARTMENT OF HEALTH................... 63
    PURDUE UNIVERSITY EXTENSION SERVICES............... 63

IOWA
NON-GOVERNMENTAL ORGANIZATIONS
    AMERICAN FISHERIES SOCIETY, IOWA CHAPTER 142
    AMERICAN RIVERS (formerly American Rivers Conservation
        Council)
        Quad Cities Field Office 149
    INDIAN CREEK NATURE CENTER................................. 219
    IOWA ACADEMY OF SCIENCE...................................... 231
    IOWA ASSOCIATION OF NATURALISTS........................ 231
    IOWA ASSOCIATION OF SOIL AND WATER
        CONSERVATION DISTRICT COMMISSIONERS 231
    IOWA AUDUBON... 231
    IOWA B.A.S.S. CHAPTER FEDERATION 231
    IOWA CONSERVATION EDUCATION COUNCIL, INC..... 231
    IOWA ENVIRONMENTAL COUNCIL 232
    IOWA NATIVE PLANT SOCIETY 232
    IOWA NATURAL HERITAGE FOUNDATION 232
    IOWA TRAILS COUNCIL... 232
    IOWA TRAPPERS ASSOCIATION, INC. 232
    IOWA WILDLIFE FEDERATION..................................... 233
    IOWA WILDLIFE REHABILITATORS ASSOCIATION....... 233
    IOWA WOMEN IN NATURAL RESOURCES................... 233
    IOWA WOODLAND OWNERS ASSOCIATION 233
    IZAAK WALTON LEAGUE OF AMERICA ENDOWMENT. 234
    IZAAK WALTON LEAGUE OF AMERICA, INC., THE
        Iowa Division 234
    LEAGUE OF WOMEN VOTERS OF IOWA...................... 241
    MACBRIDE RAPTOR PROJECT 244
    MISSISSIPPI INTERSTATE COOPERATIVE RESOURCE
        ASSOCIATION... 252
    NATIONAL ASSOCIATION OF UNIVERSITY FISHERIES
        AND WILDLIFE PROGRAMS................................ 259
    NATURE CONSERVANCY, THE, IOWA CHAPTER 273
    RETURNED PEACE CORPS VOLUNTEER FOR
        ENVIRONMENT AND DEVELOPMENT (RPCV-ED) 305
    SIERRA CLUB, IOWA CHAPTER 315
    SOIL AND WATER CONSERVATION SOCIETY (formerly
        Soil Conservation Society of America) 320
    WILDLIFE SOCIETY, IOWA CHAPTER........................... 351

STATE GOVERNMENT ORGANIZATIONS
    GOVERNOR OF IOWA.. 63
    IOWA ASSOCIATION OF COUNTY CONSERVATION
        BOARDS... 63
    IOWA COOPERATIVE FISH AND WILDLIFE RESEARCH
        UNIT... 64
    IOWA DEPARTMENT OF AGRICULTURE AND LAND
        STEWARDSHIP
        Bureau of Field Services.............................. 64, 76
        Bureau of Financial Incentive Program................ 64
        Bureau of Mines and Minerals 64
        Bureau of Water Resources................................ 64
        Division of Soil Conservation 63, 64

GEOGRAPHIC INDEX - UNITED STATES

IOWA DEPARTMENT OF NATURAL RESOURCES........... 64
   Administrative Services Division44, 46, 47, 64, 65, 66, 79, 86, 87, 99, 105, 107
   Cooperative North American Shotgunning Education Program.................. 64
   Energy and Geological Resources Division............ 64
   Environmental Protection Division 47, 56, 64, 87, 112
   Fish and Wildlife Division 64, 98, 112, 128
   Forests and Prairies Division 65
   Parks27, 29, 42, 51, 53, 56, 58, 64, 65, 67, 69, 70, 73, 75, 77, 80, 82, 83, 91, 97, 101, 103, 106, 107, 109, 111, 113, 114, 117, 119, 121, 124, 126, 127, 128, 129, 133, 137, 142, 144, 152, 160, 167, 169, 188, 193, 199, 205, 211, 212, 216, 223, 228, 238, 257, 258, 261, 263, 264, 283, 289, 291, 295, 305, 310, 324, 327, 346, 348, 351, 352, 354, 358, 361, 364, 372, 378, 388, 392, 394, 397, 398, 399, 402, 414, 416, 417
   Waste Management Division 54, 64, 65, 84, 87
IOWA STATE EXTENSION SERVICES............................. 65

KANSAS
GOVERNMENT ORGANIZATIONS
ENVIRONMENTAL PROTECTION AGENCY 10
NON-GOVERNMENTAL ORGANIZATIONS
AMERICAN ASSOCIATION OF ZOO KEEPERS, INC. 137
AMERICAN FISHERIES SOCIETY, KANSAS CHAPTER . 142
AUDUBON OF KANSAS (formerly Kansas Audubon Council) 158
GRASSLAND HERITAGE FOUNDATION.......................... 211
HOLLY SOCIETY OF AMERICA, INC............................... 216
KANSAS ACADEMY OF SCIENCE 237
KANSAS ADVISORY COUNCIL FOR ENVIRONMENTAL EDUCATION 237
KANSAS ASSOCIATION FOR CONSERVATION AND ENVIRONMENTAL EDUCATION.................. 237
KANSAS ASSOCIATION OF CONSERVATION DISTRICTS 237
KANSAS HERPETOLOGICAL SOCIETY........................... 237
KANSAS NATURAL RESOURCE COUNCIL 237
KANSAS ORNITHOLOGICAL SOCIETY........................... 237
KANSAS WILDFLOWER SOCIETY 238
KANSAS WILDLIFE FEDERATION 238
KANSAS WILDSCAPE FOUNDATION.............................. 238
NATIONAL FLYWAY COUNCIL
   Central Flyway Office 261
NATURE CONSERVANCY, THE, KANSAS CHAPTER 273
NORTH AMERICAN BENTHOLOGICAL SOCIETY........... 280
NORTH AMERICAN FALCONERS ASSOCIATION........... 281
NORTH DAKOTA NATURAL SCIENCE SOCIETY............ 284
SIERRA CLUB, KANSAS CHAPTER 315
SOCIETY OF WETLAND SCIENTISTS............................. 320
WILDLIFE DISEASE ASSOCIATION 348
WILDLIFE SOCIETY, KANSAS CHAPTER 352
STATE GOVERNMENT ORGANIZATIONS
GOVERNOR OF KANSAS 65
KANSAS BIOLOGICAL SURVEY 65
KANSAS COOPERATIVE FISH AND WILDLIFE RESEARCH UNIT 65
KANSAS DEPARTMENT OF AGRICULTURE 65
KANSAS DEPARTMENT OF WILDLIFE AND PARKS........ 65
   Operations Office 12, 30, 65, 272
   Region 1 .... 16, 34, 65, 89, 102, 267, 405, 437
   Region 2 .... 17, 34, 65, 89, 102, 267, 437
   Region 3 .... 17, 34, 65, 89, 90, 102, 155, 267, 437
   Region 4 .... 16, 34, 65, 89, 90, 267, 437
   Region 5 ....65, 89, 90, 267, 438
KANSAS FOREST SERVICE 65
KANSAS GEOLOGICAL SURVEY 66
KANSAS STATE CONSERVATION COMMISSION 66
KANSAS STATE DEPARTMENT OF HEALTH AND ENVIRONMENT 66
KANSAS STATE EXTENSION SERVICES........................ 66
KANSAS WATER OFFICE.. 66

KENTUCKY
GOVERNMENT ORGANIZATIONS
UNITED STATES DEPARTMENT OF THE ARMY
   U.S. ARMY CORPS OF ENGINEERS.............................. 25
NON-GOVERNMENTAL ORGANIZATIONS
AMERICAN BASS ASSOCIATION OF KENTUCKY, THE. 137
AMERICAN CAVE CONSERVATION ASSOCIATION....... 138
AMERICAN FISHERIES SOCIETY, KENTUCKY CHAPTER 142
CAVE RESEARCH FOUNDATION 168
KENTUCKY ACADEMY OF SCIENCE............................. 238
KENTUCKY ASSOCIATION FOR ENVIRONMENTAL EDUCATION (KAEE) 239
KENTUCKY ASSOCIATION OF CONSERVATION DISTRICTS 239
KENTUCKY AUDUBON COUNCIL 239
KENTUCKY B.A.S.S. CHAPTER FEDERATION 239
KENTUCKY RESOURCES COUNCIL 239
KENTUCKY WOODLAND OWNERS ASSOCIATION 239
KENTUCKY-TENNESSEE SOCIETY OF AMERICAN FORESTERS 239
LAND BETWEEN THE LAKES ASSOCIATION 240
LEAGUE OF KENTUCKY SPORTSMEN, INC.................. 241
NATURE CONSERVANCY, THE, KENTUCKY CHAPTER273
SIERRA CLUB, CUMBERLAND CAHPTER 314
SOUTHEASTERN ASSOCIATION OF FISH AND WILDLIFE AGENCIES.................. 323
TROUT UNLIMITED, KENTUCKY COUNCIL 332
WILDLIFE SOCIETY, KENTUCKY CHAPTER.................. 352
STATE GOVERNMENT ORGANIZATIONS
GOVERNOR OF KENTUCKY 66
KENTUCKY DEPARTMENT OF AGRICULTURE............... 66
KENTUCKY DEPARTMENT OF FISH AND WILDLIFE RESOURCES 66
KENTUCKY DEPARTMENT OF PARKS 67
KENTUCKY GEOLOGICAL SURVEY 67
KENTUCKY SOIL AND WATER CONSERVATION COMMISSION 67
KENTUCKY STATE COOPERATIVE EXTENSION SERVICES 67
KENTUCKY STATE NATURE PRESERVES COMMISSION 67
NATURAL RESOURCES AND ENVIRONMENTAL PROTECTION CABINET.................. 67
   Department for Environmental Protection 67
   Department for Natural Resources 67
   Department for Surface Mining Reclamation and Enforcement.................. 68
   Environmental Quality Commission................................. 68
   Nature Preserves Commission 62, 68, 415

LOUISIANA
GOVERNMENT ORGANIZATIONS
UNITED STATES DEPARTMENT OF THE ARMY
   U.S. ARMY CORPS OF ENGINEERS.............................. 25
UNITED STATES DEPARTMENT OF TREASURY
   U.S. CUSTOMS SERVICE 32
NON-GOVERNMENTAL ORGANIZATIONS
AMERICAN FISHERIES SOCIETY, LOUISIANA CHAPTER 142
CONSERVATION FORCE 182
EARTHJUSTICE LEGAL DEFENSE FUND (formerly Sierra Club Legal Defense Fund, Inc.)
   Louisiana Office 192
ELSA WILD ANIMAL APPEAL
   Louisiana Chapter... 194
LOUISIANA ASSOCIATION OF CONSERVATION DISTRICTS 243
LOUISIANA AUDUBON COUNCIL.................................. 243
LOUISIANA B.A.S.S. CHAPTER FEDERATION............... 243
LOUISIANA FORESTRY ASSOCIATION 243
LOUISIANA WILDLIFE FEDERATION, INC..................... 243
NATURE CONSERVANCY, THE, LOUISIANA CHAPTER273
SIERRA CLUB, DELTA CHAPTER 314
WHOOPING CRANE CONSERVATION ASSOCIATION INC. 345
WILDLIFE SOCIETY, LOUISIANA CHAPTER.................. 352
STATE GOVERNMENT ORGANIZATIONS
GOVERNOR OF LOUISIANA.. 68
LOUISIANA COOPERATIVE FISH AND WILDLIFE RESEARCH UNIT (USDI).................. 68
LOUISIANA DEPARTMENT OF AGRICULTURE AND FORESTRY 68
   Office of Forestry.. 68
LOUISIANA DEPARTMENT OF NATURAL RESOURCES. 68
   Office of Coastal Restoration and Management.............. 68
   Office of Conservation 68, 69
   Office of Mineral Resources... 68

LOUISIANA DEPARTMENT OF WILDLIFE AND FISHERIES 68
LOUISIANA GEOLOGICAL SURVEY 69
LOUISIANA SEA GRANT COLLEGE PROGRAM 69
LOUISIANA STATE EXTENSION SERVICES 69
OFFICE OF STATE PARKS, DEPARTMENT OF CULTURE, RECREATION, AND TOURISM 69
STATE OFFICE OF CONSERVATION (LOUISIANA) 69

MAINE
GOVERNMENT ORGANIZATIONS
ST. CROIX INTERNATIONAL WATERWAY COMMISSION 10

NON-GOVERNMENTAL ORGANIZATIONS
A. E. HOWELL WILDLIFE CONSERVATION CENTER 130
AMERICAN BASS ASSOCIATION OF MAINE, THE 137
AMERICAN FISHERIES SOCIETY, ATLANTIC INTERNATIONAL CHAPTER 141
AMERICAN RIVERS (formerly American Rivers Conservation Council)
  Maine Field Office 149
ASSOCIATION OF FIELD ORNITHOLOGISTS 156
CHINA REGION LAKES ALLIANCE 173
CONSERVATION LAW FOUNDATION, INC. (CLF) 183
FOREST SOCIETY OF MAINE 204
FRIENDS OF ACADIA 205
HUMBOLT FIELD RESEARCH INSTITUTE 217
ISLAND INSTITUTE, THE 233
MAINE ASSOCIATION OF CONSERVATION COMMISSIONS (MACC) 244
MAINE ASSOCIATION OF CONSERVATION DISTRICTS 244
MAINE AUDUBON SOCIETY 244
MAINE B.A.S.S. CHAPTER FEDERATION 245
MAINE COAST HERITAGE TRUST 245
MAINE ENVIRONMENTAL EDUCATION ASSOCIATION, INC. 245
MAINE, SMALL WOODLAND OWNERS ASSOCIATION OF, ... 245
NATURAL RESOURCES COUNCIL OF MAINE 271
NATURE CONSERVANCY, THE, MAINE CHAPTER 273
SIERRA CLUB, MAINE CHAPTER 315
TROUT UNLIMITED, MAINE COUNCIL 332
WILDLIFE SOCIETY, MAINE CHAPTER 352

STATE GOVERNMENT ORGANIZATIONS
GOVERNOR OF MAINE 69
MAINE ATLANTIC SALMON COMMISSION (formerly Maine Atlantic Salmon Authority) 69
MAINE COOPERATIVE FISH AND WILDLIFE RESEARCH UNIT (USDI) 70
MAINE DEPARTMENT OF AGRICULTURE, FOOD, AND RURAL RESOURCES 70
MAINE DEPARTMENT OF CONSERVATION 70
  Maine Forest Service 70
  Natural Resource Information & Mapping 70
MAINE DEPARTMENT OF ENVIRONMENTAL PROTECTION 70
MAINE DEPARTMENT OF INLAND FISHERIES AND WILDLIFE 70
MAINE DEPARTMENT OF MARINE RESOURCES 71
MAINE SEA GRANT PROGRAM 71
UNIVERSITY OF MAINE COOPERATIVE EXTENSION 71

MARYLAND
GOVERNMENT ORGANIZATIONS
INTERSTATE COMMISSION ON THE POTOMAC RIVER BASIN 8
MARINE MAMMAL COMMISSION 8
DEPARTMENT OF COMMERCE
  NATIONAL OCEANIC AND ATMOSPHERIC ADMINISTRATION 17
UNITED STATES DEPARTMENT OF AGRICULTURE RESEARCH EDUCATION AND ECONOMICS 15
UNITED STATES DEPARTMENT OF AGRICULTURE ANIMAL AND PLANT HEALTH INSPECTION SERVICE 12
UNITED STATES DEPARTMENT OF COMMERCE
  NATIONAL OCEANIC AND ATMOSPHERIC ADMINISTRATION 17
UNITED STATES DEPARTMENT OF HEALTH AND HUMAN SERVICES
  FOOD AND DRUG ADMINISTRATION 19
UNITED STATES DEPARTMENT OF THE AIR FORCE
  MAJOR AIR COMMANDS 21
UNITED STATES DEPARTMENT OF THE ARMY
  U.S. ARMY CORPS OF ENGINEERS 25

NON-GOVERNMENTAL ORGANIZATIONS
ADKINS ARBORETUM 131
AMERICAN BASS ASSOCIATION OF MARYLAND, THE 137
AMERICAN FISHERIES SOCIETY 140, 141, 142, 143, 144
  Estuaries Section 140
  Genetics Section 140
AMERICAN FISHERIES SOCIETY, POTOMAC CHAPTER 144
AMERICAN HIKING SOCIETY 145
AMERICAN WHITEWATER 151
AMERICAN ZOO AND AQUARIUM ASSOCIATION (AZA) 151
ANACOSTIA WATERSHED SOCIETY 152
AUDUBON NATURALIST SOCIETY OF THE CENTRAL ATLANTIC STATES 158
BROTHERHOOD OF THE JUNGLE COCK, INC., THE 163
CENTER FOR CHESAPEAKE COMMUNITIES 169
CENTER FOR WATERSHED PROTECTION 171
CHESAPEAKE BAY FOUNDATION, INC. 172, 173
CHESAPEAKE BAY FOUNDATION, INC. (Maryland Office) 173
CHESAPEAKE FARMS 173
CHESAPEAKE WILDLIFE HERITAGE (CWH) 173
CONFERENCE OF NATIONAL PARK COOPERATING ASSOCIATIONS 180
CONSERVATION FEDERATION OF MARYLAND/For A Rural Maryland (F.A.R.M.) 182
CONSERVATION TREATY SUPPORT FUND 183
EASTERN SHORE LAND CONSERVANCY 193
ENTOMOLOGICAL SOCIETY OF AMERICA 195
ENVIRONMENTAL CONCERN INC. 196
FISH AND WILDLIFE REFERENCE SERVICE 201, 409
HENRY A. WALLACE INSTITUTE FOR ALTERNATIVE AGRICULTURE (HAWIAA) 215
INSTITUTE FOR CONSERVATION LEADERSHIP 221
INTERNATIONAL SOCIETY OF TROPICAL FORESTERS, INC. 228
IZAAK WALTON LEAGUE OF AMERICA, INC., THE 234
  Maryland Division 234
JANE GOODALL INSTITUTE, THE 236
MARYLAND ASSOCIATION OF CONSERVATION DISTRICTS 246
MARYLAND B.A.S.S. CHAPTER FEDERATION 247
MARYLAND FORESTS ASSOCIATION 247
MARYLAND NATIVE PLANT SOCIETY 247
MARYLAND ORNITHOLOGICAL SOCIETY, INC. 247
MATTS (MID-ATLANTIC TURTLE AND TORTOISE SOCIETY, INC.) 248
MONITOR INTERNATIONAL 253
NATIONAL 4-H COUNCIL 256
NATIONAL BOATING FEDERATION 260
NATIONAL MILITARY FISH AND WILDLIFE ASSOCIATION 263
NATURAL HISTORY SOCIETY OF MARYLAND, INC., THE 270
NATURE CONSERVANCY, THE, MARYLAND/D.C. CHAPTER 273
RACHEL CARSON COUNCIL, INC. (formerly Rachel Carson Trust for the Living Environment Inc.) 301
RENEWABLE NATURAL RESOURCES FOUNDATION ... 304
RIVER FEDERATION 306
SCIENTISTS CENTER FOR ANIMAL WELFARE 311
SEAPLANE PILOTS ASSOCIATION 312
SIERRA CLUB, MARYLAND CHAPTER 315
SOCIETY OF AMERICAN FORESTERS 319
TREES FOR THE FUTURE, INC. 330
TROUT UNLIMITED, MARYLAND COUNCIL (Mid-Atlantic) 332
URBAN WILDLIFE RESOURCES 337
WILDFOWL TRUST OF NORTH AMERICA, INC., THE ... 347
WILDLIFE HABITAT COUNCIL 349
WILDLIFE SOCIETY, MARYLAND-DELAWARE CHAPTER 352
WILDLIFE SOCIETY, THE 350

STATE GOVERNMENT ORGANIZATIONS
DEPARTMENT OF THE ENVIRONMENT 71
GOVERNOR OF MARYLAND 71

GEOGRAPHIC INDEX - UNITED STATES

MARYLAND DEPARTMENT OF AGRICULTURE 71
    Agricultural Commission 71, 72
    State Soil Conservation Committee 71, 107
MARYLAND DEPARTMENT OF NATURAL RESOURCES 72
    Chesapeake Bay and Watershed Programs 72
    Management Services 28, 43, 48, 54, 65, 72, 103, 116, 122, 124, 125
    Public Lands Division 72
    Resource Management Services 72
MARYLAND SEA GRANT COLLEGE 72
MARYLAND STATE COOPERATIVE EXTENSION 72
MARYLAND-NATIONAL CAPITAL PARK AND PLANNING COMMISSION 72

MASSACHUSETTS
GOVERNMENT ORGANIZATIONS
NEW ENGLAND INTERSTATE WATER POLLUTION CONTROL COMMISSION 9
UNITED STATES DEPARTMENT OF THE ARMY
    U.S. ARMY CORPS OF ENGINEERS 25
UNITED STATES DEPARTMENT OF THE INTERIOR
    UNITED STATES FISH AND WILDLIFE SERVICE 29
UNITED STATES DEPARTMENT OF TREASURY
    U.S. CUSTOMS SERVICE 32

NON-GOVERNMENTAL ORGANIZATIONS
AMERICAN BASS ASSOCIATION OF MASSACHUSETTS, THE 137
AMERICAN FISHERIES SOCIETY, SOUTHERN NEW ENGLAND CHAPTER 144
APPALACHIAN MOUNTAIN CLUB 153
ATLANTIC CENTER FOR THE ENVIRONMENT 157
CONNECTICUT RIVER WATERSHED COUNCIL INC. ... 181
CONSERVATION LAW FOUNDATION, INC. (CLF) 183
EARTHWATCH INSTITUTE 193
ENVIRONMENTAL CAREERS ORGANIZATION, INC., THE 195
ENVIRONMENTAL LEAGUE OF MASSACHUSETTS 198
GREEN PARTY USA 213
INTERNATIONAL FUND FOR ANIMAL WELFARE 225
INTERNATIONAL WILDLIFE COALITION (IWC) AND THE WHALE ADOPTION PROJECT 230
MANOMET CENTER FOR CONSERVATION SCIENCES 245
MASSACHUSETTS ASSOCIATION OF CONSERVATION COMMISSIONS (MACC) 247
MASSACHUSETTS ASSOCIATION OF CONSERVATION DISTRICTS 247
MASSACHUSETTS AUDUBON SOCIETY, INC. 247
MASSACHUSETTS B.A.S.S. CHAPTER FEDERATION ... 247
MASSACHUSETTS ENVIRONMENTAL EDUCATION SOCIETY 248
MASSACHUSETTS FORESTRY ASSOCIATION 248
MASSACHUSETTS TRAPPER'S ASSOCIATION, INC. ... 248
MOUNT GRACE LAND CONSERVATION TRUST 255
NATIONAL PARKS AND CONSERVATION ASSOCIATION (NPCA)
    Northeast Regional Office 30, 80, 264
NATIONAL TRUST FOR HISTORIC PRESERVATION
    Northeast Office 266, 313
NATURE CONSERVANCY, THE, MASSACHUSETTS CHAPTER 273
NEW ENGLAND ASSOCIATION OF ENVIRONMENTAL BIOLOGISTS (NEAEB) 276
NEW ENGLAND NATURAL RESOURCES CENTER 276
NEW ENGLAND WILD FLOWER SOCIETY, INC. 276
NORTHEAST SUSTAINABLE ENERGY ASSOCIATION .. 284
SAVE THE HARBOR/SAVE THE BAY 310
SIERRA CLUB, MASSACHUSETTS CHAPTER 315
STRIPERS UNLIMITED, INC. 326
TROUT UNLIMITED, MASSACHUSETTS/RHODE ISLAND COUNCIL 332
TRUSTEES OF RESERVATIONS, THE 335
UNION OF CONCERNED SCIENTISTS 336
WESTERN HEMISPHERE SHOREBIRD RESERVE NETWORK (WHSRN) 344
WILSON ORNITHOLOGICAL SOCIETY 355
WORLD SOCIETY FOR THE PROTECTION OF ANIMALS (WSPA) 358

STATE GOVERNMENT ORGANIZATIONS
EXECUTIVE OFFICE OF ENVIRONMENTAL AFFAIRS
    Division of Fisheries and Wildlife 73, 74
EXECUTIVE OFFICE OF ENVIRONMENTAL AFFAIRS (MASSACHUSETTS) 73
    Animal Health 13, 73, 78, 84, 100, 117, 140
    Bureau of Land Use 73
    Bureau of Markets 73
    Bureau of Pesticides 73
    Department of Environmental Management 62, 73, 103, 416, 421, 422
    Department of Environmental Protection 73, 101, 123, 397, 415, 421
    Department of Fisheries, Wildlife, and Environmental Law Enforcement 73
    Department of Food and Agriculture 73
    Division of Agricultural Development 73
    Division of Regulatory Services 73
    Division of Wetlands and Waterways, ... 73
    Metropolitan District Commission, ... 73
    Watershed Division 74
GOVERNOR OF MASSACHUSETTS 73
MASSACHUSETTS COOPERATIVE FISH AND WILDLIFE RESEARCH UNIT (USDI) 74
MASSACHUSETTS HIGHWAY DEPARTMENT 74
MIT SEA GRANT COLLEGE PROGRAM 74
UNIVERSITY OF MASSACHUSETTS EXTENSION 74
WOODS HOLE OCEANOGRAPHIC INSITITUTION (WHOI) SEA GRANT PROGRAM 74

MICHIGAN
GOVERNMENT ORGANIZATIONS
GREAT LAKES FISHERY COMMISSION 7
UNITED STATES DEPARTMENT OF THE ARMY
    U.S. ARMY CORPS OF ENGINEERS 25

NON-GOVERNMENTAL ORGANIZATIONS
AMERICAN FISHERIES SOCIETY
    Education Section 65, 140
    Fisheries History Section 140
AMERICAN FISHERIES SOCIETY, MICHIGAN CHAPTER 143
CENTER FOR ENVIRONMENTAL STUDY 170
GEORGE WRIGHT SOCIETY, THE 208
IZAAK WALTON LEAGUE OF AMERICA, INC., THE
    Michigan Division 234
LAKE ERIE CLEAN-UP COMMITTEE, INC. 240
MICHIGAN ASSOCIATION OF CONSERVATION DISTRICTS 248
MICHIGAN AUDUBON SOCIETY 249
MICHIGAN B.A.S.S. CHAPTER FEDERATION 249
MICHIGAN ENVIRONMENTAL COUNCIL 249
MICHIGAN FORESTS ASSOCIATION 249
MICHIGAN LAND USE INSTITUTE 249
MICHIGAN NATURAL AREAS COUNCIL 249
MICHIGAN NATURE ASSOCIATION 249
MICHIGAN UNITED CONSERVATION CLUBS, INC. 250
MICHIGAN WILDLIFE HABITAT FOUNDATION 250
NATURE CONSERVANCY, THE, MICHIGAN CHAPTER . 273
ORGANIZATION FOR BAT CONSERVATION 291
SAFARI CLUB INTERNATIONAL
    Michigan Office 308
SCENIC AMERICA
    Scenic Michigan 311
SIERRA CLUB, MACKINAC CHAPTER 315
TROUT UNLIMITED, MICHIGAN COUNCIL 332
WEST MICHIGAN ENVIRONMENTAL ACTION COUNCIL 343
WILDLIFE SOCIETY, MICHIGAN CHAPTER 352
YOUNG ENTOMOLOGISTS' SOCIETY, INC. 361

STATE GOVERNMENT ORGANIZATIONS
GOVERNOR OF MICHIGAN 74
MICHIGAN DEPARTMENT OF AGRICULTURE 74
MICHIGAN DEPARTMENT OF COMMUNITY HEALTH 74
MICHIGAN DEPARTMENT OF ENVIRONMENTAL QUALITY 75
MICHIGAN DEPARTMENT OF NATURAL RESOURCES .. 75
MICHIGAN SEA GRANT COLLEGE PROGRAM 75
MICHIGAN STATE UNIVERSITY EXTENSION 75

MINNESOTA
GOVERNMENT ORGANIZATIONS
UNITED STATES DEPARTMENT OF AGRICULTURE
    UNITED STATES FOREST SERVICE 16
UNITED STATES DEPARTMENT OF THE ARMY
    U.S. ARMY CORPS OF ENGINEERS 25

UNITED STATES DEPARTMENT OF THE INTERIOR
UNITED STATES FISH AND WILDLIFE SERVICE 29
NON-GOVERNMENTAL ORGANIZATIONS
AMERICAN FISHERIES SOCIETY, MINNESOTA CHAPTER 143
CHARLES A. AND ANNE MORROW LINDBERGH FOUNDATION, THE 172
DEEP-PORTAGE CONSERVATION RESERVE 186
FEDERAL CARTRIDGE COMPANY 199
FRIENDS OF THE BOUNDARY WATERS WILDERNESS 206
INTERNATIONAL ECOLOGY SOCIETY (IES) 224
INTERNATIONAL WOLF CENTER (Administrative Offices) 230
INTERNATIONAL WOLF CENTER (Educational Services) 230
IZAAK WALTON LEAGUE OF AMERICA, INC., THE
Minnesota Division 235
KIDS FOR SAVING EARTH WORLDWIDE 239
MINNESOTA ASSOCIATION OF SOIL AND WATER CONSERVATION DISTRICTS 250
MINNESOTA B.A.S.S. CHAPTER FEDERATION.............. 250
MINNESOTA CENTER FOR ENVIRONMENTAL ADVOCACY (MCEA) 251
MINNESOTA CONSERVATION FEDERATION.................. 251
MINNESOTA FORESTRY ASSOCIATION 251
MINNESOTA GROUND WATER ASSOCIATION 251
MINNESOTA HERPETOLOGICAL SOCIETY (James Ford Bell Museum of Natural History) 251
MINNESOTA NATIVE PLANT SOCIETY 251
MINNESOTA ORNITHOLOGISTS' UNION 251
MINNESOTA PARKS AND TRAILS COUNCIL 251
MINNESOTA WILDLIFE HERITAGE FOUNDATION, INC. 252
MINNESOTA WINGS SOCIETY, INC............................... 252
MISSISSIPPI RIVER BASIN ALLIANCE............................ 252
NATIONAL FLYWAY COUNCIL
Mississippi Flyway Office 261
NATIONAL PARKS AND CONSERVATION ASSOCIATION (NPCA)
Heartland Regional Office 264
NATIONAL WILDLIFE REHABILITATORS ASSOCIATION 269
NATURE CONSERVANCY, THE
Great Plains Division 272
NATURE CONSERVANCY, THE, MINNESOTA CHAPTER 273
NORTH AMERICAN FISHING CLUB 281
PHEASANTS FOREVER, INC. 296
POPE AND YOUNG CLUB 297
RAPTOR CENTER, THE 303
SIERRA CLUB, NORTH STAR CHAPTER (Minnesota) 315
TROUT UNLIMITED, MINNESOTA COUNCIL.................. 333
TRUMPETER SWAN SOCIETY, THE 334
WILDLIFE FOREVER.. 348
WILDLIFE SOCIETY, MINNESOTA CHAPTER 352
STATE GOVERNMENT ORGANIZATIONS
GOVERNOR OF MINNESOTA 75
MINNESOTA BOARD OF WATER AND SOIL RESOURCES 75
MINNESOTA COOPERATIVE FISH AND WILDLIFE RESEARCH UNIT 76
MINNESOTA DEPARTMENT OF AGRICULTURE 76
MINNESOTA DEPARTMENT OF NATURAL RESOURCES 76
MINNESOTA ENVIRONMENTAL QUALITY BOARD 76
MINNESOTA GEOLOGICAL SURVEY 76
MINNESOTA POLLUTION CONTROL AGENCY 77
Brainerd, MN 77, 346
Detroit Lakes, MN.. 77, 433
Duluth, MN.. 77, 424
Marshall, MN 77
Rochester, MN 77
MINNESOTA SEA GRANT COLLEGE PROGRAM 77
MINNESOTA STATE EXTENSION SERVICES 77

MISSISSIPPI
GOVERNMENT ORGANIZATIONS
GULF STATES MARINE FISHERIES COMMISSION 7
UNITED STATES DEPARTMENT OF AGRICULTURE
RESEARCH EDUCATION AND ECONOMICS................ 15
UNITED STATES DEPARTMENT OF THE ARMY
U.S. ARMY CORPS OF ENGINEERS............................ 25
NON-GOVERNMENTAL ORGANIZATIONS
AMERICAN FISHERIES SOCIETY
Computer User Section... 140
AMERICAN FISHERIES SOCIETY, MISSISSIPPI CHAPTER 143
CROSBY ABORETUM, THE, Mississippi State University 185
DELTA WILDLIFE, INC. 187
LOWER MISSISSIPPI RIVER CONSERVATION COMMITTEE.. 244
MISSISSIPPI ASSOCIATION OF CONSERVATION DISTRICTS, INC. 252
MISSISSIPPI B.A.S.S. CHAPTER FEDERATION 252
MISSISSIPPI NATIVE PLANT SOCIETY 252
MISSISSIPPI WILDLIFE FEDERATION 253
NATURE CONSERVANCY, THE, MISSISSIPPI CHAPTER 273
SIERRA CLUB, MISSISSIPPI CHAPTER 315
SOUTHEASTERN FISHES COUNCIL 323
WILDLIFE SOCIETY, MISSISSIPPI CHAPTER................ 352
STATE GOVERNMENT ORGANIZATIONS
GOVERNOR OF MISSISSIPPI.. 77
GULF COAST RESEARCH LABORATORY 77
MISSISSIPPI COOPERATIVE FISH AND WILDLIFE RESEARCH UNIT (USDI) 77
MISSISSIPPI DEPARTMENT OF AGRICULTURE AND COMMERCE... 78
MISSISSIPPI DEPARTMENT OF ENVIRONMENTAL QUALITY
Office of Land and Water Resources..................... 78
Office of Pollution Control 78
MISSISSIPPI DEPARTMENT OF WILDLIFE, FISHERIES, AND PARKS 78
MISSISSIPPI FORESTRY COMMISSION 78
MISSISSIPPI SEA GRANT PROGRAM 78
MISSISSIPPI SOIL AND WATER CONSERVATION COMMISSION.. 78
MISSISSIPPI STATE DEPARTMENT OF HEALTH............ 79
MISSISSIPPI STATE EXTENSION SERVICES.................. 79

MISSOURI
GOVERNMENT ORGANIZATIONS
UNITED STATES DEPARTMENT OF THE ARMY
U.S. ARMY CORPS OF ENGINEERS............................ 25
NON-GOVERNMENTAL ORGANIZATIONS
AMERICAN FISHERIES SOCIETY
North Central Division 141
AMERICAN FISHERIES SOCIETY, MISSOURI CHAPTER 143
AUDUBON SOCIETY OF MISSOURI 158
BOUNTY INFORMATION SERVICE (WILDLIFE)............. 162
CAMP FIRE BOYS AND GIRLS...................................... 165
CENTER FOR PLANT CONSERVATION 170
CONSERVATION FEDERATION OF MISSOURI.............. 182
INTERNATIONAL CENTER FOR TROPICAL ECOLOGY. 224
KANSAS B.A.S.S. CHAPTER FEDERATION 237
MISSOURI ASSOCIATION OF SOIL AND WATER CONSERVATION DISTRICTS..................................... 253
MISSOURI AUDUBON COUNCIL 253
MISSOURI B.A.S.S. CHAPTER FEDERATION 253
MISSOURI FOREST PRODUCTS ASSOCIATION 253
MISSOURI NATIVE PLANT SOCIETY 253
MISSOURI PRAIRIE FOUNDATION 253
NATIONAL COUNCIL OF STATE GARDEN CLUBS, INC. 260
NATURE CONSERVANCY, THE, MISSOURI CHAPTER. 273
OZARKS RESOURCE CENTER 292
ROCKY MOUNTAIN ELK FOUNDATION
South-Central Region Office 307
SCENIC AMERICA
Scenic Missouri 311
SIERRA CLUB, OZARK CHAPTER (Missouri) 316
WILD CANID SURVIVAL AND RESEARCH CENTER 345
WILDLIFE SOCIETY, MISSOURI CHAPTER 352
WORLD BIRD SANCTUARY (formerly Raptor Rehabilitation and Propagation Project Inc. The) 357
STATE GOVERNMENT ORGANIZATIONS
GOVERNOR OF MISSOURI 79
MISSOURI COOPERATIVE FISH AND WILDLIFE RESEARCH UNIT (USDI)... 79
MISSOURI DEPARTMENT OF AGRICULTURE 79
MISSOURI DEPARTMENT OF CONSERVATION 79

GEOGRAPHIC INDEX - UNITED STATES

Administrative Services Division 44, 46, 47, 64, 65, 66, 79, 86, 87, 99, 105, 107
Design and Development Division 79
Fisheries Division 47, 50, 69, 79, 84, 105, 114
Forestry Division 41, 50, 64, 79, 81, 107
Human Resources Section 79
Natural History Section 79
Outreach and Education Division 79
Protection Division 79, 117
Wildlife Division 51, 65, 69, 79, 84, 87, 97, 106, 115, 123, 144, 399
MISSOURI DEPARTMENT OF NATURAL RESOURCES ... 79
MISSOURI STATE EXTENSION SERVICES 80

MONTANA
GOVERNMENT ORGANIZATIONS
UNITED STATES DEPARTMENT OF AGRICULTURE
UNITED STATES FOREST SERVICE 16
UNITED STATES DEPARTMENT OF THE INTERIOR
BUREAU OF RECLAMATION 28
NON-GOVERNMENTAL ORGANIZATIONS
AMERICAN FISHERIES SOCIETY, MONTANA CHAPTER 143
AMERICAN RIVERS (formerly American Rivers Conservation Council)
Montana Field Office 149, 313
BOONE AND CROCKETT CLUB 161
BOONE AND CROCKETT FOUNDATION 161
CENTER FOR RESOURCEFUL BUILDING TECHNOLOGY 171
CONFEDERATED SALISH AND KOOTENAI TRIBES 180
CRAIGHEAD WILDLIFE-WILDLANDS INSTITUTE 185
EARTHJUSTICE LEGAL DEFENSE FUND (formerly Sierra Club Legal Defense Fund, Inc.)
Montana Office 182, 192
FEDERATION OF FLY FISHERS 200
GLACIER INSTITUTE, THE 210
GREAT BEAR FOUNDATION 211
GREATER YELLOWSTONE COALITION 212
LIGHTHAWK
Northern Rocky Mountain Field Office 243
MONTANA ASSOCIATION OF CONSERVATION DISTRICTS 254
MONTANA AUDUBON 254
MONTANA B.A.S.S. CHAPTER FEDERATION 254
MONTANA ENVIRONMENTAL INFORMATION CENTER 254
MONTANA FOREST OWNERS ASSOCIATION 254
MONTANA LAND RELIANCE 254
MONTANA WILDERNESS ASSOCIATION 255
MONTANA WILDLIFE FEDERATION 255
NATIONAL WILDLIFE FEDERATION
Northern Rockies Project Office (ID, MT, WY) 268
NATURE CONSERVANCY, THE, MONTANA CHAPTER . 273
NORTHERN PLAINS RESOURCE COUNCIL 285
OUTDOOR WRITERS ASSOCIATION OF AMERICA, INC. 292
PREDATOR PROJECT 299
RIVER NETWORK
Northern Rockies Office
Riverlands Conservancy Field Office 306
ROCKY MOUNTAIN ELK FOUNDATION 307
SIERRA CLUB
Montana Field Office 149, 313
SIERRA CLUB, MONTANA CHAPTER 315
SONORAN INSTITUTE
Northwest Office 313, 320, 326
TROUT UNLIMITED, MONTANA COUNCIL 333
WILDERNESS WATCH 347
WILDLIFE SOCIETY, MONTANA CHAPTER 352
STATE GOVERNMENT ORGANIZATIONS
GOVERNOR OF MONTANA 80
MONTANA BUREAU OF MINES AND GEOLOGY 80
MONTANA COOPERATIVE FISHERY RESEARCH UNIT (USDI) 80
MONTANA COOPERATIVE WILDLIFE RESEARCH UNIT (USGS/BRD) 80
MONTANA DEPARTMENT OF AGRICULTURE 80
MONTANA DEPARTMENT OF FISH, WILDLIFE, AND PARKS 80
MONTANA DEPARTMENT OF NATURAL RESOURCES AND CONSERVATION 81
MONTANA ENVIRONMENTAL QUALITY COUNCIL 81
MONTANA NATURAL HERITAGE PROGRAM 81
MONTANA STATE EXTENSION SERVICES 81

NEBRASKA
GOVERNMENT ORGANIZATIONS
UNITED STATES DEPARTMENT OF THE ARMY
U.S. ARMY CORPS OF ENGINEERS 25
NON-GOVERNMENTAL ORGANIZATIONS
AMERICAN FISHERIES SOCIETY, NEBRASKA CHAPTER 143
AMERICAN RIVERS (formerly American Rivers Conservation Council)
Nebraska Field Office 149
ASSOCIATION OF GREAT LAKES OUTDOOR WRITERS 156
GROUNDWATER FOUNDATION, THE 213
INLAND BIRD BANDING ASSOCIATION 221
IOWA PRAIRIE NETWORK 232
IZAAK WALTON LEAGUE OF AMERICA, INC., THE
Nebraska Division 235
NATIONAL ARBOR DAY FOUNDATION 256
NATURE CONSERVANCY, THE, NEBRASKA CHAPTER 273
NEBRASKA ASSOCIATION OF RESOURCE DISTRICTS 275
NEBRASKA AUDUBON COUNCIL 275
NEBRASKA B.A.S.S. CHAPTER FEDERATION 275
NEBRASKA ORNITHOLOGISTS' UNION, INC. (University of Nebraska State Museum) 275
NEBRASKA WILDLIFE FEDERATION, INC. 275
NORTH AMERICAN CRANE WORKING GROUP 281
SIERRA CLUB, NEBRASKA CHAPTER 315
WILDLIFE SOCIETY, NEBRASKA CHAPTER 352
STATE GOVERNMENT ORGANIZATIONS
CONSERVATION AND SURVEY DIVISION (NEBRASKA). 81
GAME AND PARKS COMMISSION
Game and Parks Commission 81, 398, 416
GAME AND PARKS COMMISSION-NEBRASKA
Ak-Sar-Ben Aquarium 81
GOVERNOR OF NEBRASKA 81
NEBRASKA DEPARTMENT OF AGRICULTURE 81
NEBRASKA DEPARTMENT OF ENVIRONMENTAL QUALITY 81
NEBRASKA DEPARTMENT OF WATER RESOURCES 81
NEBRASKA GAME AND PARKS COMMISSION 82
NEBRASKA NATURAL RESOURCES COMMISSION 82
NEBRASKA STATE EXTENSION SERVICES 82

NEVADA
GOVERNMENT ORGANIZATIONS
UNITED STATES DEPARTMENT OF THE INTERIOR
BUREAU OF RECLAMATION 28
NON-GOVERNMENTAL ORGANIZATIONS
MULE DEER FOUNDATION, THE 256
NATURE CONSERVANCY, THE, NEVADA CHAPTER 273
NEVADA ASSOCIATION OF CONSERVATION DISTRICTS 275
NEVADA WILDLIFE FEDERATION 276
SIERRA CLUB, TOIYABE CHAPTER (Nevada/Eastern California) 316
TAHOE REGIONAL PLANNING AGENCY 327
WILD HORSE ORGANIZED ASSISTANCE, INC. (WHOA) 346
WILDLIFE SOCIETY, NEVADA CHAPTER 353
STATE GOVERNMENT ORGANIZATIONS
GOVERNOR OF NEVADA 82
NEVADA BUREAU OF MINES AND GEOLOGY 82
NEVADA DEPARTMENT OF AGRICULTURE 82
NEVADA DEPARTMENT OF CONSERVATION AND NATURAL RESOURCES 82
NEVADA DIVISION OF WILDLIFE 83
NEVADA NATURAL HERITAGE PROGRAM 83

NEW HAMPSHIRE
GOVERNMENT ORGANIZATIONS
NORTHEASTERN FOREST FIRE PROTECTION COMMISSION 9
UNITED STATES DEPARTMENT OF THE ARMY
U.S. ARMY CORPS OF ENGINEERS 25
NON-GOVERNMENTAL ORGANIZATIONS
AMERICAN BASS ASSOCIATION OF NEW HAMPSHIRE, THE 137
AMERICAN GROUND WATER TRUST 145

ASSOCIATION FOR CONSERVATION INFORMATION, INC. 155
AUDUBON SOCIETY OF NEW HAMPSHIRE 159
ELM RESEARCH INSTITUTE 194
NATURE CONSERVANCY, THE, NEW HAMPSHIRE CHAPTER 273
NEW ENGLAND COALITION FOR SUSTAINABLE POPULATION (NECSP) 276
NEW HAMPSHIRE ASSOCIATION OF CONSERVATION COMMISSIONS 276
NEW HAMPSHIRE ASSOCIATION OF CONSERVATION DISTRICTS 277
NEW HAMPSHIRE B.A.S.S. CHAPTER FEDERATION ... 277
NEW HAMPSHIRE LAKES ASSOCIATION 277
NEW HAMPSHIRE TIMBERLAND OWNERS ASSOCIATION 277
NEW HAMPSHIRE WILDLIFE FEDERATION 277
NORTH AMERICAN LOON FUND 281
SEACOAST ANTI-POLLUTION LEAGUE 312
SIERRA CLUB, NEW HAMPSHIRE CHAPTER 315
SOCIETY FOR THE PROTECTION OF NEW HAMPSHIRE FORESTS 319
STATEWIDE PROGRAM OF ACTION TO CONSERVE OUR ENVIRONMENT (SPACE) 325
STUDENT CONSERVATION ASSOCIATION, INC. 326
TROUT UNLIMITED, NEW HAMPSHIRE COUNCIL 333
STATE GOVERNMENT ORGANIZATIONS
COUNCIL ON RESOURCES AND DEVELOPMENT 83
DEPARTMENT OF RESOURCES AND ECONOMIC DEVELOPMENT 83
GOVERNOR OF NEW HAMPSHIRE 83
MAINE/NEW HAMPSHIRE SEA GRANT PROGRAM 83
NEW HAMPSHIRE DEPARTMENT OF AGRICULTURE, MARKETS, AND FOOD 83
State Conservation Committee 83
NEW HAMPSHIRE DEPARTMENT OF ENVIRONMENTAL SERVICES 84
NEW HAMPSHIRE FISH AND GAME DEPARTMENT 84
NEW HAMPSHIRE NATURAL HERITAGE INVENTORY ... 84
UNIVERSITY OF NEW HAMPSHIRE COOPERATIVE EXTENSION 84

NEW JERSEY
GOVERNMENT ORGANIZATIONS
DELAWARE RIVER BASIN COMMISSION 7
NON-GOVERNMENTAL ORGANIZATIONS
AMERICAN LITTORAL SOCIETY 146
ASSOCIATION OF NEW JERSEY ENVIRONMENTAL COMMISSIONS 157
BIOMASS USERS NETWORK 161
CLEAN OCEAN ACTION
Main Office 174, 183, 279
Mid-Coast Office 175
South Jersey Office 175
COMMITTEE FOR NATIONAL ARBOR DAY 178
NATURE CONSERVANCY, THE, NEW JERSEY CHAPTER 274
NEW JERSEY AGRICULTURAL SOCIETY 277
NEW JERSEY ASSOCIATION OF CONSERVATION DISTRICTS 277
NEW JERSEY AUDUBON SOCIETY 277
NEW JERSEY B.A.S.S. CHAPTER FEDERATION 278
NEW JERSEY CONSERVATION FOUNDATION 278
NEW JERSEY ENVIRONMENTAL LOBBY 278
NEW JERSEY FORESTRY ASSOCIATION 278
NORTH AMERICAN BUTTERFLY ASSOCIATION 280
NORTHEAST ASSOCIATION OF FISH AND WILDLIFE RESOURCE AGENCIES 284
SIERRA CLUB, NEW JERSEY CHAPTER 315
STUDENT CONSERVATION ASSOCIATION, INC.
Newark Office 326
TROUT UNLIMITED, NEW JERSEY COUNCIL 333
WILDLIFE SOCIETY, NEW JERSEY CHAPTER 353
STATE GOVERNMENT ORGANIZATIONS
GOVERNOR OF NEW JERSEY 84
NEW JERSEY DEPARTMENT OF AGRICULTURE 84
State Soil and Conservation Committee 84
NEW JERSEY DEPARTMENT OF ENVIRONMENTAL PROTECTION 85
Division of Fish, Game, and Wildlife 85
Division of Parks and Forestry 85
Division of Publicly Funded Site Remediation 85
Division of Solid and Hazardous Waste 85
Geological Survey 27, 30, 38, 42, 44, 64, 68, 70, 76, 77, 79, 85, 88, 90, 94, 105, 106, 117, 237, 375
Green Acres and Recreation Program 85
NEW JERSEY PINELANDS COMMISSION 85
NEW JERSEY SEA GRANT COLLEGE PROGRAM 86
NEW JERSEY STATE EXTENSION SERVICES 86

NEW MEXICO
GOVERNMENT ORGANIZATIONS
UNITED STATES DEPARTMENT OF AGRICULTURE
UNITED STATES FOREST SERVICE 16
UNITED STATES DEPARTMENT OF THE AIR FORCE 21
UNITED STATES DEPARTMENT OF THE ARMY
U.S. ARMY CORPS OF ENGINEERS 25
UNITED STATES DEPARTMENT OF THE INTERIOR
UNITED STATES FISH AND WILDLIFE SERVICE 29
NON-GOVERNMENTAL ORGANIZATIONS
AMERICAN FISHERIES SOCIETY, NEW MEXICO STATE UNIVERSITY STUDENT CHAPTER 143
ARCHAEOLOGICAL CONSERVANCY 153
CENTER FOR WILDLIFE LAW 171
FOREST TRUST 204
NATIONAL NETWORK OF FOREST PRACTITIONERS .. 263
NATIONAL PARKS AND CONSERVATION ASSOCIATION (NPCA)
Southwest Regional Office 30, 80, 117, 149, 153, 264
NATURE CONSERVANCY, THE, NEW MEXICO CHAPTER 274
NEW MEXICO ASSOCIATION OF CONSERVATION DISTRICTS 278
NEW MEXICO B.A.S.S. CHAPTER FEDERATION 278
NEW MEXICO ENVIRONMENTAL LAW CENTER 278
NEW MEXICO WILDLIFE FEDERATION 279
SIERRA CLUB, RIO GRANDE CHAPTER (New Mexico/West Texas) 316
SOUTHWEST RESEARCH AND INFORMATION CENTER 324
WILDLIFE SOCIETY, NEW MEXICO CHAPTER 353
WILDLIFE SOCIETY, TEXAS CHAPTER 354
STATE GOVERNMENT ORGANIZATIONS
ENERGY, MINERALS, AND NATURAL RESOURCES DEPARTMENT 86
Administrative Services Division 44, 46, 47, 64, 65, 66, 79, 86, 87, 99, 105, 107
Energy Conservation and Management Division 86
Forestry and Resources Conservation Division 86
Mining and Minerals Division 86
Oil Conservation Division 86
State Parks and Recreation Division 86
GOVERNOR OF NEW MEXICO 86
NEW MEXICO BUREAU OF MINES AND MINERAL RESOURCES 86
Geological Information Center Library 87
NEW MEXICO COOPERATIVE FISH AND WILDLIFE RESEARCH UNIT 87
NEW MEXICO DEPARTMENT OF AGRICULTURE 87
NEW MEXICO DEPARTMENT OF GAME AND FISH 87
Albuquerque NM Office 87
Las Cruces NM Office 87
Raton NM Office 87
Roswell NM Office 87
NEW MEXICO ENVIRONMENT DEPARTMENT 87
NEW MEXICO SOIL AND WATER CONSERVATION COMMISSION 88
NEW MEXICO STATE EXTENSION SERVICES 88
STATE ENGINEER OFFICE/INTERSTATE STREAM COMMISSION 88

NEW YORK
GOVERNMENT ORGANIZATIONS
ENVIRONMENTAL PROTECTION AGENCY 10
UNITED STATES DEPARTMENT OF AGRICULTURE
ANIMAL AND PLANT HEALTH INSPECTION SERVICE 12
UNITED STATES DEPARTMENT OF THE ARMY
U.S. ARMY CORPS OF ENGINEERS 25
U.S. MILITARY ACADEMY 27
UNITED STATES DEPARTMENT OF TREASURY
U.S. CUSTOMS SERVICE 32
NON-GOVERNMENTAL ORGANIZATIONS
ADIRONDACK COUNCIL, THE 131

GEOGRAPHIC INDEX - UNITED STATES

ADIRONDACK MOUNTAIN CLUB, INC., THE 131
ADIRONDACK NATURE CONSERVANCY/ADIRONDACK
   LAND TRUST, INC. 131
AMERICAN CONSERVATION ASSOCIATION, INC.
   New York Office 139, 147, 157
AMERICAN FISHERIES SOCIETY
   Northeastern Division 141
AMERICAN FISHERIES SOCIETY, COLLEGE OF
   ENVIRONMENTAL SCIENCE AND FORESTRY
   CHAPTER 142
AMERICAN FISHERIES SOCIETY, NEW YORK CHAPTER
   143
AMERICAN GEOGRAPHICAL SOCIETY 145
AMERICAN LITTORAL SOCIETY
   New York Office 139, 147, 157
AMERICAN LUNG ASSOCIATION 147
AMERICAN MUSEUM OF NATURAL HISTORY 147
AMERICAN WILDLIFE RESEARCH FOUNDATION, INC. 151
ASSOCIATION FOR THE PROTECTION OF THE
   ADIRONDACKS, THE 155
ATLANTIC STATES LEGAL FOUNDATION 157
AUDUBON INTERNATIONAL 158
AVSC INTERNATIONAL 159
CAMP FIRE CLUB OF AMERICA, THE 165
CAMP FIRE CONSERVATION FUND 165
CATSKILL CENTER FOR CONSERVATION AND
   DEVELOPMENT, INC., THE 168
CATSKILL FOREST ASSOCIATION 168
CENTER FOR ENVIRONMENTAL EDUCATION 169
CENTER FOR ENVIRONMENTAL INFORMATION 169
COALITION FOR EDUCATION IN THE OUTDOORS 175
CORNELL LAB OF ORNITHOLOGY 184
DRAGONFLY SOCIETY OF THE AMERICAS, THE 188
EARTH DAY NEW YORK 191
ENVIRONMENTAL ADVOCATES 195
ENVIRONMENTAL DEFENSE FUND, INC. 196
FEDERATION OF NEW YORK STATE BIRD CLUBS, INC.
   200
FUND FOR ANIMALS INC., THE 207
GARDEN CLUB OF AMERICA, THE 208
GIRL SCOUTS OF THE UNITED STATES OF AMERICA 210
GREAT LAKES UNITED 211
HUDSONIA LIMITED 216
INFORM, INC. 221
INSTITUTE OF ECOSYSTEM STUDIES 221
IZAAK WALTON LEAGUE OF AMERICA, INC., THE
   New York Division 235
MARINE ENVIRONMENTAL RESEARCH INSTITUTE
   (MERI) 246
NATIONAL AUDUBON SOCIETY 259
   Project Puffin 259
   Scully Science Center 259
NATIONAL AUDUBON SOCIETY, LIVING OCEANS
   PROGRAM 259
NATIONAL FLYWAY COUNCIL
   Atlantic Flyway Office 261
NATURAL RESOURCES DEFENSE COUNCIL, INC. 271
NATURE CONSERVANCY, THE, EASTERN NEW YORK
   CHAPTER 273
NATURE CONSERVANCY, THE, NEW YORK
   ADIRONDACK CHAPTER 274
NATURE CONSERVANCY, THE, NEW YORK
   CENTRAL/WESTERN CHAPTER 274
NATURE CONSERVANCY, THE, NEW YORK CITY
   CHAPTER 274
NATURE CONSERVANCY, THE, NEW YORK LONG
   ISLAND CHAPTER 274
NATURE CONSERVANCY, THE, NEW YORK LOWER
   HUDSON CHAPTER 274
NATURE CONSERVANCY, THE, NEW YORK SOUTH
   FORK/SHELTER ISLAND CHAPTER 274
NEW YORK ASSOCIATION OF CONSERVATION
   DISTRICTS, INC. 279
NEW YORK B.A.S.S. CHAPTER FEDERATION 279
NEW YORK FOREST OWNERS ASSOCIATION, INC. 279
NEW YORK PUBLIC INTEREST RESEARCH GROUP
   (NYPIRG 279
NEW YORK TURTLE AND TORTOISE SOCIETY 279
NEW YORK-NEW JERSEY TRAIL CONFERENCE INC. ... 279
NORTHEAST WILDLIFE ADMINISTRATORS ASSOCIATION
   284
PLANNED PARENTHOOD FEDERATION OF AMERICA,
   INC. 297
POPULATION COMMUNICATIONS INTERNATIONAL 297
RAINFOREST ALLIANCE 302
RAINFOREST RELIEF 302
ROGER TORY PETERSON INSTITUTE 307
SAVE THE SOUND, INC. At GARVIES POINT MUSEUM 310
SCENIC HUDSON, INC. 311
SIERRA CLUB
   New York City Office 313
   Northeast Office 266, 313
SIERRA CLUB, ATLANTIC CHAPTER 314
ST. REGIS MOHAWK TRIBE 325
TROUT UNLIMITED, NEW YORK COUNCIL 333
TUG HILL TOMORROW LAND TRUST 335
UNITED NATIONS ENVIRONMENT PROGRAMME
   North America Regional Office 336
WILD DOG FOUNDATION, THE 345
WILDLIFE CONSERVATION SOCIETY 348
WILDLIFE SOCIETY, NEW YORK CHAPTER 353
WORLD PAL (WORLD POPULATION ALLOCATION
   LIMITED INC.) 358

STATE GOVERNMENT ORGANIZATIONS
ADIRONDACK PARK AGENCY 88
ENVIRONMENTAL PROTECTION BUREAU 88
GOVERNOR OF NEW YORK 88
NEW YORK COOPERATIVE FISH AND WILDLIFE
   RESEARCH UNIT 88
NEW YORK DEPARTMENT OF AGRICULTURE AND
   MARKETS 88
   State Soil and Water Conservation Committee 68, 89
NEW YORK DEPARTMENT OF ENVIRONMENTAL
   CONSERVATION 89
   Division of Air Resources 89
   Division of Environmental Enforcement 89
   Division of Environmental Permits 89
   Division of Environmental Remediation 89
   Division of Fish, Wildlife and Marine Resources 89, 284
   Division of Forest Protection & Fire Management 89
   Division of Information Services 89
   Division of Lands and Forests 89
   Division of Law Enforcement 29, 53, 54, 63, 66, 89
   Division of Legal Affairs 89
   Division of Management and Budget 89
   Division of Mineral Resources 89, 115
   Division of Operations 89
   Division of Public Affairs and Education 89
   Division of Solid & Hazardous Materials 89
   Division of Water 49, 52, 53, 58, 63, 67, 76, 77, 82, 83, 89,
      91, 93, 94, 110
   Press Office 89, 100
   Regional Directors 89
NEW YORK DEPARTMENT OF HEALTH 89
NEW YORK GEOLOGICAL SURVEY AND STATE MUSEUM
   90
NEW YORK SEA GRANT 90
NEW YORK STATE COOPERATIVE EXTENSION 90
NEW YORK STATE FISH AND WILDLIFE MANAGEMENT
   BOARD 90
   Region 3 .... 17, 34, 65, 89, 90, 102, 155, 267, 437
   Region 4 .... 16, 34, 65, 89, 90, 267, 437
   Region 5 .... 65, 89, 90, 267, 438
   Region 6 .... 89, 90, 267, 438
   Region 7 .... 89, 90, 267, 438
   Region 8 .... 17, 89, 91, 267
   Region 9 .... 89, 91, 267
NEW YORK STATE OFFICE OF PARKS, RECREATION
   AND HISTORIC PRESERVATION 91
OFFICE OF ENERGY EFFICIENCY AND ENVIRONMENT 91
TUG HILL COMMISSION 91

NORTH CAROLINA
GOVERNMENT ORGANIZATIONS
   UNITED STATES DEPARTMENT OF AGRICULTURE
      UNITED STATES FOREST SERVICE 16
   UNITED STATES DEPARTMENT OF THE ARMY
      U.S. ARMY CORPS OF ENGINEERS 25
NON-GOVERNMENTAL ORGANIZATIONS
   AMERICAN FISHERIES SOCIETY

GEOGRAPHIC INDEX - UNITED STATES

Early Life History 140
AMERICAN FISHERIES SOCIETY, NORTH CAROLINA
  CHAPTER 143
AMERICAN LIVESTOCK BREEDS CONSERVANCY 147
AMERICAN SOCIETY FOR ENVIRONMENTAL HISTORY
  149
CAROLINA BIRD CLUB, INC. 168
CONSERVATION COUNCIL OF NORTH CAROLINA 181
ENVIRONMENTAL DEFENSE FUND, INC.
  North Carolina Office 196, 324
ENVIRONMENTAL EDUCATORS OF NORTH CAROLINA
  (EENC) 197
FOREST HISTORY SOCIETY, INC. 203
NATIONAL HUNTERS ASSOCIATION, INC. 262
NATURE CONSERVANCY, THE
  Mid-Atlantic Division Office 272
NATURE CONSERVANCY, THE, NORTH CAROLINA
  CHAPTER 274
NORTH CAROLINA ASSOCIATION OF SOIL AND WATER
  CONSERVATION DISTRICTS 282
NORTH CAROLINA B.A.S.S. CHAPTER FEDERATION... 282
NORTH CAROLINA BEACH BUGGY ASSOCIATION, INC.
  282
NORTH CAROLINA COALITION, INC. 282
NORTH CAROLINA COASTAL FEDERATION, INC. 282
NORTH CAROLINA FORESTRY ASSOCIATION 282
NORTH CAROLINA RECREATION AND PARK SOCIETY,
  INC. 283
NORTH CAROLINA WILD FLOWER PRESERVATION
  SOCIETY 283
NORTH CAROLINA WILDLIFE FEDERATION 283
PROFESSIONAL BOWHUNTERS SOCIETY 299
SAVE OUR RIVERS, INC. 309
SCENIC AMERICA
  Scenic North Carolina 311
SIERRA CLUB, NORTH CAROLINA CHAPTER 315
SOCIETY FOR MARINE MAMMALOGY, THE 318
TROUT UNLIMITED, NORTH CAROLINA COUNCIL 333
WILDLIFE SOCIETY, NORTH CAROLINA CHAPTER 353
STATE GOVERNMENT ORGANIZATIONS
  GOVERNOR OF NORTH CAROLINA 91
  NORTH CAROLINA DEPARTMENT OF ENVIRONMENT
    AND NATURAL RESOURCES 91
  NORTH CAROLINA COOPERATIVE EXTENSION SERVICE
    91
  NORTH CAROLINA COOPERATIVE FISH AND WILDLIFE
    RESEARCH UNIT (USDI) 92
  NORTH CAROLINA DEPARTMENT OF AGRICULTURE ... 92
  NORTH CAROLINA DEPARTMENT OF ENVIRONMENT
    AND NATURAL RESOURCES
    State Soil and Water Conservation Commission ... 92
  NORTH CAROLINA SEA GRANT PROGRAM 92
  NORTH CAROLINA WILDLIFE RESOURCES COMMISSION
    92

NORTH DAKOTA
NON-GOVERNMENTAL ORGANIZATIONS
  AMERICAN FISHERIES SOCIETY, DAKOTA CHAPTER. 142
  MUSKIES, INC. 256
  NATURE CONSERVANCY, THE, NORTH DAKOTA
    CHAPTER 274
  NORTH DAKOTA ASSOCIATION OF SOIL
    CONSERVATION DISTRICTS 283
  NORTH DAKOTA WILDLIFE FEDERATION, INC. 284
  SIERRA CLUB, DACOTAH CHAPTER 314
  WILDLIFE SOCIETY, NORTH DAKOTA CHAPTER 353
STATE GOVERNMENT ORGANIZATIONS
  GOVERNOR OF NORTH DAKOTA 92
  INSTITUTE FOR ECOLOGICAL STUDIES 92
  NORTH DAKOTA DEPARTMENT OF AGRICULTURE 93
  NORTH DAKOTA DEPARTMENT OF HEALTH 93
  NORTH DAKOTA GAME AND FISH DEPARTMENT 93
  NORTH DAKOTA GEOLOGICAL SURVEY 93
  NORTH DAKOTA PARKS AND RECREATION
    DEPARTMENT 93
  NORTH DAKOTA STATE EXTENSION SERVICE 93
  NORTH DAKOTA STATE FOREST SERVICE 93
  NORTH DAKOTA STATE SOIL CONSERVATION
    COMMITTEE 93
  NORTH DAKOTA WATER COMMISSION 93

OHIO
GOVERNMENT ORGANIZATIONS
  OHIO RIVER VALLEY WATER SANITATION
    COMMISSION 9
  UNITED STATES DEPARTMENT OF THE AIR FORCE
    MAJOR AIR COMMANDS 21
  UNITED STATES DEPARTMENT OF THE ARMY
    U.S. ARMY CORPS OF ENGINEERS 25
NON-GOVERNMENTAL ORGANIZATIONS
  AMERICAN FISHERIES SOCIETY, OHIO CHAPTER 143
  CANVASBACK SOCIETY 167
  CENTRAL OHIO ANGLERS AND HUNTERS CLUB 172
  CINCINNATI NATURE CENTER 174
  CLEVELAND MUSEUM OF NATURAL HISTORY, THE ... 175
  DAWES ARBORETUM, THE 186
  ENVIRONMENTAL EDUCATION COUNCIL OF OHIO 197
  HOLDEN ARBORETUM, THE 216
  INTERNATIONAL SOCIETY FOR ENDANGERED CATS
    (ISEC) 227
  INTERNATIONAL WILD WATERFOWL ASSOCIATION ... 229
  IZAAK WALTON LEAGUE OF AMERICA, INC., THE
    Ohio Division 223, 235, 291, 398
  LEAGUE OF OHIO SPORTSMEN 241
  NATIONAL GROUND WATER ASSOCIATION, THE 262
  NATIVE PLANT SOCIETY OF NORTHEASTERN OHIO .. 269
  NATURE CONSERVANCY, THE
    Midwest Division Office 272
  OHIO ACADEMY OF SCIENCE, THE 286
  OHIO ALLIANCE FOR THE ENVIRONMENT 287
  OHIO AUDUBON COUNCIL, INC. 287
  OHIO B.A.S.S. CHAPTER FEDERATION 287
  OHIO BIOLOGICAL SURVEY 287
  OHIO ENERGY PROJECT 287
  OHIO ENVIRONMENTAL COUNCIL, INC. 287
  OHIO FEDERATION OF SOIL AND WATER
    CONSERVATION DISTRICTS 288
  OHIO FORESTRY ASSOCIATION, INC., THE 288
  OHIO NATIVE PLANT SOCIETY 288
  SIERRA CLUB
    Cleveland Office 313
  SIERRA CLUB, OHIO CHAPTER 315
  TROUT UNLIMITED, OHIO COUNCIL 333
  WILDLIFE LEGISLATIVE FUND OF AMERICA, THE, AND
    WILDLIFE CONSERVATION FUND OF AMERICA, THE
    349
  WILDLIFE SOCIETY, OHIO CHAPTER 353
STATE GOVERNMENT ORGANIZATIONS
  ENVIRONMENTAL REVIEW APPEALS COMMISSION 94
  GOVERNOR OF OHIO 94
  OHIO DEPARTMENT OF AGRICULTURE 94
  OHIO DEPARTMENT OF NATURAL RESOURCES 94
  OHIO ENVIRONMENTAL PROTECTION AGENCY 94
  OHIO OFFICE OF ENERGY EFFICIENCY 94
  OHIO SEA GRANT COLLEGE PROGRAM 95
  OHIO STATE EXTENSION SERVICES 95

OKLAHOMA
GOVERNMENT ORGANIZATIONS
  UNITED STATES DEPARTMENT OF THE ARMY
    U.S. ARMY CORPS OF ENGINEERS 25
NON-GOVERNMENTAL ORGANIZATIONS
  AMERICAN FEDERATION OF MINERALOGICAL
    SOCIETIES 139
  AMERICAN FISHERIES SOCIETY
    Fisheries Management Section 140
  AMERICAN FISHERIES SOCIETY, OKLAHOMA CHAPTER
    143
  GEORGE MIKSCH SUTTON AVIAN RESEARCH CENTER
    INC. 208
  NATURE CONSERVANCY, THE, OKLAHOMA CHAPTER
    274
  OKLAHOMA ACADEMY OF SCIENCE 288
  OKLAHOMA ASSOCIATION OF CONSERVATION
    DISTRICTS 288
  OKLAHOMA AUDUBON COUNCIL 288
  OKLAHOMA B.A.S.S. CHAPTER FEDERATION 288
  OKLAHOMA NATIVE PLANT SOCIETY 289
  OKLAHOMA ORNITHOLOGICAL SOCIETY 289
  OKLAHOMA WILDLIFE FEDERATION 289
  OKLAHOMA WOODLAND OWNERS ASSOCIATION 289
  SIERRA CLUB, OKLAHOMA CHAPTER 315

GEOGRAPHIC INDEX - UNITED STATES

TROUT UNLIMITED, OKLAHOMA COUNCIL 333
WILDLIFE SOCIETY, OKLAHOMA CHAPTER   353
STATE GOVERNMENT ORGANIZATIONS
DEPARTMENT OF WILDLIFE CONSERVATION 95
GOVERNOR OF OKLAHOMA 95
OKLAHOMA BIOLOGICAL SURVEY 95
OKLAHOMA COOPERATIVE FISH AND WILDLIFE
  RESEARCH UNIT (USDI) 95
OKLAHOMA DEPARTMENT OF ENVIRONMENTAL
  QUALITY 95
OKLAHOMA GEOLOGICAL SURVEY 96
OKLAHOMA STATE BOARD OF AGRICULTURE 96
OKLAHOMA STATE CONSERVATION COMMISSION 96
OKLAHOMA STATE EXTENSION SERVICES 96
OKLAHOMA TOURISM AND RECREATION DEPARTMENT
  96
OKLAHOMA WATER RESOURCES BOARD 97

OREGON
GOVERNMENT ORGANIZATIONS
COLUMBIA RIVER INTER-TRIBAL FISH COMMISSION . 7
PACIFIC STATES MARINE FISHERIES COMMISSION ... 9
UNITED STATES DEPARTMENT OF AGRICULTURE
  UNITED STATES FOREST SERVICE 16
UNITED STATES DEPARTMENT OF THE ARMY
  U.S. ARMY CORPS OF ENGINEERS 25
UNITED STATES DEPARTMENT OF THE INTERIOR
  UNITED STATES FISH AND WILDLIFE SERVICE 29
NON-GOVERNMENTAL ORGANIZATIONS
AMERICAN FISHERIES SOCIETY
  Marine Fisheries Section 141
  Water Quality Section 141
AMERICAN FISHERIES SOCIETY, GREATER PORTLAND,
  OR CHAPTER 142
AMERICAN FISHERIES SOCIETY, OREGON CHAPTER 143
AUDUBON SOCIETY OF PORTLAND 159
COLUMBIA BASIN FISH AND WILDLIFE AUTHORITY ... 178
ENVIRONMENTAL LAW ALLIANCE WORLDWIDE (E-LAW)
  197
FOREST SERVICE EMPLOYEES FOR ENVIRONMENTAL
  ETHICS (FSEEE) 204
HIGH DESERT MUSEUM, THE 216
JOHN INSKEEP ENVIRONMENTAL LEARNING CENTER
  236
NATIVE PLANT SOCIETY OF OREGON 269
NATURAL AREAS ASSOCIATION 270
NATURE CONSERVANCY, THE, OREGON CHAPTER ... 274
NORTHWEST COALITION FOR ALTERNATIVES TO
  PESTICIDES 285
OREGON ASSOCIATION OF CONSERVATION DISTRICTS
  290
OREGON B.A.S.S. CHAPTER FEDERATION 290
OREGON ENVIRONMENTAL COUNCIL 290
OREGON NATURAL RESOURCES COUNCIL 290
OREGON SMALL WOODLANDS ASSOCIATION 290
OREGON SOCIETY OF AMERICAN FORESTERS 291
OREGON TROUT, INC. 291
OREGON WILDLIFE HERITAGE FOUNDATION 291
PACIFIC FISHERY MANAGEMENT COUNCIL 292
PACIFIC RIVERS COUNCIL 293
PUBLIC EMPLOYEES FOR ENVIRONMENTAL
  RESPONSIBILITY (PEER) (West Coast Office) 300
RIVER NETWORK 306
SIERRA CLUB, OREGON CHAPTER 316
STEAMBOATERS, THE 325
TROUT UNLIMITED, OREGON COUNCIL 333
WASHINGTON SOCIETY OF AMERICAN FORESTERS . 341
WESTERN ENVIRONMENTAL LAW CENTER 344
WESTERN FORESTRY AND CONSERVATION
  ASSOCIATION 344
WILDERNESS LAND TRUST, THE 346
WILDLIFE SOCIETY, OREGON CHAPTER 353
WORLD FORESTRY CENTER 358
XERCES SOCIETY, THE 360
STATE GOVERNMENT ORGANIZATIONS
DEPARTMENT OF FISH AND WILDLIFE (OREGON) 97
DEPARTMENT OF GEOLOGY AND MINERAL INDUSTRIES
  97
DEPARTMENT OF TRANSPORTATION (OREGON) 97
GOVERNOR OF OREGON 97
OREGON COOPERATIVE FISH AND WILDLIFE
  RESEARCH UNIT (USDI) 97
OREGON COOPERATIVE FISH AND WILDLIFE
  RESEARCH UNIT (USDI) 97
OREGON DEPARTMENT OF AGRICULTURE 97
OREGON DEPARTMENT OF ENVIRONMENTAL QUALITY
  (DEQ) 98
OREGON DEPARTMENT OF FORESTRY 98
OREGON FISH AND WILDLIFE DIVISION/DEPARTMENT
  OF STATE POLICE 98
OREGON PARKS AND RECREATION DEPARTMENT 98
OREGON SEA GRANT PROGRAM 98
OREGON STATE EXTENSION SERVICES 99
OREGON WATER RESOURCES DEPARTMENT 99
  Water Resources Commission 99, 105
STATE MARINE BOARD (OREGON) 99

PENNSYLVANIA
GOVERNMENT ORGANIZATIONS
SUSQUEHANNA RIVER BASIN COMMISSION 10
ENVIRONMENTAL PROTECTION AGENCY 10
UNITED STATES DEPARTMENT OF AGRICULTURE
  RESEARCH EDUCATION AND ECONOMICS 15
UNITED STATES FOREST SERVICE 16
UNITED STATES DEPARTMENT OF THE ARMY
  U.S. ARMY CORPS OF ENGINEERS 25
NON-GOVERNMENTAL ORGANIZATIONS
AIR AND WASTE MANAGEMENT ASSOCIATION 132
ALLIANCE FOR THE CHESAPEAKE BAY
  Harrisburg Office 135
AMERICAN ASSOCIATION OF BOTANICAL GARDENS
  AND ARBORETA, INC. 136
AMERICAN BASS ASSOCIATION OF EASTERN
  PENNSYLVANIA/ NEW JERSEY, THE 137
AMERICAN BASS ASSOCIATION OF LAKE ERIE REGION,
  THE (Western PA and Western NY) 137
AMERICAN FISHERIES SOCIETY, PENNSYLVANIA
  CHAPTER 143
AMERICAN LITTORAL SOCIETY
  Delaware Riverkeeper Crossin 147
AMERICAN NATURE STUDY SOCIETY 147
AUDUBON SOCIETY OF WESTERN PENNSYLVANIA ... 159
BOTANICAL SOCIETY OF WESTERN PENNSYLVANIA. 162
BRANDYWINE CONSERVANCY, INC. 162
CHESAPEAKE BAY FOUNDATION, INC. (Pennsylvania
  Office) 173
ENVIRONMENTAL AIR FORCE 195
HAWK MIGRATION ASSOCIATION OF NORTH AMERICA
  215
HAWK MOUNTAIN SANCTUARY ASSOCIATION 215
IZAAK WALTON LEAGUE OF AMERICA, INC., THE
  Pennsylvania Division 235
MID-ATLANTIC COUNCIL OF WATERSHED
  ASSOCIATIONS 250
NATIONAL AVIARY 259
NATIONAL COUNCIL FOR GEOGRAPHIC EDUCATION 260
NATIONAL TRUST FOR HISTORIC PRESERVATION
  Mid Atlantic 266
NATURAL LANDS TRUST, INC. 271
NATURE CONSERVANCY, THE
  Eastern Division Office 272
NATURE CONSERVANCY, THE, PENNSYLVANIA
  CHAPTER 274
NORTH AMERICAN NATIVE FISHES ASSOCIATION 281
NORTHEAST CONSERVATION LAW ENFORCEMENT
  CHIEFS' ASSOCIATION (CLECA) 284
PENNSYLVANIA ASSOCIATION OF CONSERVATION
  DISTRICT DIRECTORS, INC. 294
PENNSYLVANIA AUDUBON SOCIETY 294
PENNSYLVANIA B.A.S.S. CHAPTER FEDERATION, INC.
  294
PENNSYLVANIA CITIZENS ADVISORY COUNCIL TO
  DEPARTMENT OF ENVIRONMENTAL PROTECTION 294
PENNSYLVANIA ENVIRONMENTAL COUNCIL, INC. (PEC)
  294
PENNSYLVANIA FEDERATION OF SPORTSMEN'S CLUBS
  295
PENNSYLVANIA FORESTRY ASSOCIATION, THE 295
PENNSYLVANIA RECREATION AND PARK SOCIETY, INC.
  295

PENNSYLVANIA RESOURCES COUNCIL, INC., (formerly
  PA Roadside Council) 295
PITTSBURGH HERPETOLOGICAL SOCIETY, THE 296
POCONO ENVIRONMENTAL EDUCATION CENTER 297
PURPLE MARTIN CONSERVATION ASSOCIATION 301
RARE CENTER FOR TROPICAL CONSERVATION 303
ROCKY MOUNTAIN ELK FOUNDATION
  Northeast Region Office 307
RUFFED GROUSE SOCIETY, THE 307
SIERRA CLUB, PENNSYLVANIA CHAPTER 316
STROUD WATER RESEARCH CENTER
STUDENT ENVIRONMENTAL ACTION COALITION (SEAC)
  326
TROUT UNLIMITED, PENNSYLVANIA COUNCIL 333
TURTLE CREEK WATERSHED ASSOCIATION, INC. 335
WATER RESOURCES ASSOCIATION OF THE DELAWARE
  RIVER BASIN 342
WESTERN PENNSYLVANIA CONSERVANCY 344
WHITE CLAY WATERSHED ASSOCIATION 345
WILDLANDS CONSERVANCY 347
WILDLIFE INFORMATION CENTER, INC. 349
WILDLIFE PRESERVATION TRUST INTERNATIONAL, INC.
  350
WILDLIFE SOCIETY, PENNSYLVANIA CHAPTER 353
STATE GOVERNMENT ORGANIZATIONS
CITIZENS ADVISORY COUNCIL TO PENNSYLVANIA
  DEPARTMENT OF ENVIRONMENTAL PROTECTION .. 99
GOVERNOR OF PENNSYLVANIA 99
PENNSYLVANIA COOPERATIVE FISH AND WILDLIFE
  RESEARCH UNIT 99
PENNSYLVANIA DEPARTMENT OF AGRICULTURE 99
  Region I 11, 100, 102, 107, 108, 115
  Region II 11, 100, 107, 108, 115
  Region III 11, 100, 107, 115
  Region IV 11, 100, 102, 108, 115
  Region V 11, 100, 102, 115
  Region VI 11, 100, 102
  Region VII 11, 100
  State Conservation Commission 100, 106, 112
PENNSYLVANIA DEPARTMENT OF CONSERVATION AND
  NATURAL RESOURCES 100
PENNSYLVANIA DEPARTMENT OF ENVIRONMENTAL
  PROTECTION 101
PENNSYLVANIA FISH AND BOAT COMMISSION 101
  Region 1 Northwest 102
  Region 2 Southwest 102
  Region 3 Northeast 102
  Region IV Southeast 102
  Region V North Central 102
  Region VI South Central 102
PENNSYLVANIA FOREST STEWARDSHIP PROGRAM .. 102
PENNSYLVANIA GAME COMMISSION 102
PENNSYLVANIA STATE EXTENSION SERVICES 102

PUERTO RICO
NON-GOVERNMENTAL ORGANIZATIONS
CENTRO de INFORMACION, INVESTIGACION y
  EDUCACION SOCIAL (CIIES) 172
CONSERVATION TRUST OF PUERTO RICO 183
PUERTO RICO ASSOCIATION OF SOIL AND WATER
  CONSERVATION DISTRICTS 300
PUERTO RICO CONSERVATION FOUNDATION, THE
  (PRCF) 300
STATE GOVERNMENT ORGANIZATIONS
COMITE DESPERTAR CIDRENO 102
GOVERNOR OF PUERTO RICO 102
PUERTO RICO DEPARTMENT OF AGRICULTURE 103
PUERTO RICO DEPARTMENT OF NATURAL AND
  ENVIRONMENTAL RESOURCES 103
PUERTO RICO SEA GRANT PROGRAM 103
PUERTO RICO STATE EXTENSION SERVICES 103
SOIL CONSERVATION COMMITTEE OF PUERTO RICO 103

RHODE ISLAND
NON-GOVERNMENTAL ORGANIZATIONS
AUDUBON SOCIETY OF RHODE ISLAND 159
ENVIRONMENT COUNCIL OF RHODE ISLAND 195
NATURE CONSERVANCY, THE
  Northeast Division Office 272
NATURE CONSERVANCY, THE, RHODE ISLAND
  CHAPTER 274
RHODE ISLAND B.A.S.S. CHAPTER FEDERATION 305
RHODE ISLAND FOREST CONSERVATORS
  ASSOCIATION 305
RHODE ISLAND STATE ASSOCIATION OF
  CONSERVATION DISTRICTS 305
RHODE ISLAND WILD PLANT SOCIETY 305
SAVE THE BAY, INC. 309
SIERRA CLUB
  Sierra Student Coalition 313
SIERRA CLUB, RHODE ISLAND CHAPTER 316
SOUTHERN NEW ENGLAND FOREST CONSORTIUM, INC.
  (SNEFCI) 324
STATE GOVERNMENT ORGANIZATIONS
DEPARTMENT OF ENVIRONMENTAL MANAGEMENT
  (RHODE ISLAND) 103
DEPARTMENT OF TRANSPORTATION (RHODE ISLAND)
  104
GOVERNOR OF RHODE ISLAND 103
RHODE ISLAND COOPERATIVE EXTENSION SERVICE 104
RHODE ISLAND SEA GRANT 104
RHODE ISLAND STATE CONSERVATION COMMITTEE 104
STATE WATER RESOURCES BOARD (RHODE ISLAND)
  104

SOUTH CAROLINA
GOVERNMENT ORGANIZATIONS
UNITED STATES DEPARTMENT OF THE ARMY
  U.S. ARMY CORPS OF ENGINEERS 25
NON-GOVERNMENTAL ORGANIZATIONS
AMERICAN FISHERIES SOCIETY, SOUTH CAROLINA
  CHAPTER 144
AMERICAN SOCIETY OF ICHTHYOLOGISTS AND
  HERPETOLOGISTS 149
FRIENDS OF THE REEDY RIVER 206
INTERNATIONAL PRIMATE PROTECTION LEAGUE 226
NATIONAL ASSOCIATION OF RECREATION RESOURCE
  PLANNERS 257
NATIONAL TRUST FOR HISTORIC PRESERVATION
  Southern Office 266
NATIONAL WILD TURKEY FEDERATION, INC., THE 267
NATURE CONSERVANCY, THE, SOUTH CAROLINA
  CHAPTER 274
NORTH AMERICAN GAMEBIRD ASSOCIATION, INC. 281
QUAIL UNLIMITED, INC. 301
SIERRA CLUB, SOUTH CAROLINA CHAPTER 316
SOUTH ATLANTIC FISHERY MANAGEMENT COUNCIL 321
SOUTH CAROLINA ASSOCIATION OF CONSERVATION
  DISTRICTS 321
SOUTH CAROLINA B.A.S.S. CHAPTER FEDERATION ... 321
SOUTH CAROLINA COASTAL CONSERVATION LEAGUE
  321
SOUTH CAROLINA ENVIRONMENTAL LAW PROJECT 321
SOUTH CAROLINA FORESTRY ASSOCIATION 321
SOUTH CAROLINA NATIVE PLANT SOCIETY 321
SOUTH CAROLINA WILDLIFE FEDERATION 321
SOUTHERN APPALACHIAN BOTANICAL SOCIETY 323
TROUT UNLIMITED, SOUTH CAROLINA COUNCIL 333
WILDFLOWER ASSOCIATION OF MICHIGAN 347
WILDLIFE ACTION, INC. 347
WILDLIFE SOCIETY, SOUTH CAROLINA CHAPTER 354
STATE GOVERNMENT ORGANIZATIONS
CLEMSON UNIVERSITY EXTENSION SERVICE 104
DEPARTMENT OF PARKS, RECREATION AND TOURISM
  104
FORESTRY COMMISSION (SOUTH CAROLINA) 105
GOVERNOR OF SOUTH CAROLINA 104
SOUTH CAROLINA DEPARTMENT OF AGRICULTURE . 105
SOUTH CAROLINA DEPARTMENT OF HEALTH AND
  ENVIRONMENTAL CONTROL 105
  Office of Ocean and Coastal Resource Management
    (OCRM) 105
SOUTH CAROLINA DEPARTMENT OF NATURAL
  RESOURCES 105
SOUTH CAROLINA ENERGY OFFICE 105
SOUTH CAROLINA SEA GRANT CONSORTIUM 106

SOUTH DAKOTA
NON-GOVERNMENTAL ORGANIZATIONS
GREAT PLAINS NATIVE PLANT SOCIETY 212
INTERTRIBAL BISON COOPERATIVE (ITBC) 231
IZAAK WALTON LEAGUE OF AMERICA, INC., THE
  South Dakota Division 235
NATIONAL FLYWAY COUNCIL 261

GEOGRAPHIC INDEX - UNITED STATES

NATURE CONSERVANCY, THE, SOUTH DAKOTA CHAPTER 274
ROCKY MOUNTAIN ELK FOUNDATION
   North-Central Region Office............................. 307
SIERRA CLUB, SOUTH DAKOTA CHAPTER 316
SOUTH DAKOTA ASSOCIATION OF CONSERVATION DISTRICTS... 322
SOUTH DAKOTA B.A.S.S. CHAPTER FEDERATION 322
SOUTH DAKOTA ORNITHOLOGISTS' UNION 322
SOUTH DAKOTA RESOURCES COALITION 322
SOUTH DAKOTA WILDLIFE FEDERATION 323
WILDLIFE SOCIETY, SOUTH DAKOTA CHAPTER 354
STATE GOVERNMENT ORGANIZATIONS
BOARD OF MINERALS AND ENVIRONMENT............. 106
GOVERNOR OF SOUTH DAKOTA.................................. 106
SOUTH DAKOTA COOPERATIVE FISH AND WILDLIFE RESEARCH UNIT (USDI)............................... 106
SOUTH DAKOTA DEPARTMENT OF AGRICULTURE..... 106
   Division of Resource Conservation and Forestry 106
   State Conservation Commission.................. 100, 106, 112
SOUTH DAKOTA DEPARTMENT OF ENVIRONMENT AND NATURAL RESOURCES............................. 106
SOUTH DAKOTA GAME, FISH, AND PARKS DEPARTMENT.. 106
SOUTH DAKOTA STATE EXTENSION SERVICES.......... 106

TENNESSEE
GOVERNMENT ORGANIZATIONS
TENNESSEE VALLEY AUTHORITY 35
UNITED STATES DEPARTMENT OF ENERGY
   CARBON DIOXIDE INFORMATION ANALYSIS CENTER 18
UNITED STATES DEPARTMENT OF THE ARMY
   U.S. ARMY CORPS OF ENGINEERS............................. 25
NON-GOVERNMENTAL ORGANIZATIONS
AMERICAN ASSOCIATION OF FIELD BOTANISTS......... 136
AMERICAN CANAL SOCIETY, INC................................ 138
AMERICAN FISHERIES SOCIETY, TENNESSEE CHAPTER 144
DUCKS UNLIMITED, INC.................................... 189, 191
ENVIRONMENTAL ACTION FUND (EAF)...................... 195
GREAT SMOKY MOUNTAINS INSTITUTE AT TREMONT 212
HARDWOOD FOREST FOUNDATION 214
NATIONAL FOUNDATION TO PROTECT AMERICA'S EAGLES (Save The Eagle)............................ 262
NATIONAL PARKS AND CONSERVATION ASSOCIATION (NPCA)
   Southeast Regional Office 30, 80, 264
NATURE CONSERVANCY, THE, TENNESSEE CHAPTER 274
ROCKY MOUNTAIN ELK FOUNDATION
   Southeast Region Office................................ 307
SIERRA CLUB, TENNESSEE CHAPTER 316
TENNESSEE ASSOCIATION OF CONSERVATION DISTRICTS.. 327
TENNESSEE B.A.S.S. CHAPTER FEDERATION 328
TENNESSEE CITIZENS FOR WILDERNESS PLANNING 328
TENNESSEE CONSERVATION LEAGUE........................ 328
TENNESSEE ENVIRONMENTAL COUNCIL 328
TENNESSEE FORESTRY ASSOCIATION 328
TENNESSEE WOODLAND OWNERS ASSOCIATION 328
TROUT UNLIMITED, TENNESSEE COUNCIL 334
WILDLIFE SOCIETY, TENNESSEE CHAPTER................ 354
STATE GOVERNMENT ORGANIZATIONS
DEPARTMENT OF ENVIRONMENT AND CONSERVATION (TENNESSEE) 107
GOVERNOR OF TENNESSEE.. 107
TENNESSEE AGRICULTURAL EXTENSION SERVICES 107
TENNESSEE COOPERATIVE FISHERY RESEARCH UNIT (USDI).. 107
TENNESSEE DEPARTMENT OF AGRICULTURE............ 107
   State Soil Conservation Committee.......................71, 107
WILDLIFE RESOURCES AGENCY.................................. 107

TEXAS
GOVERNMENT ORGANIZATIONS
ENVIRONMENTAL PROTECTION AGENCY 10
UNITED STATES DEPARTMENT OF AGRICULTURE
   ANIMAL AND PLANT HEALTH INSPECTION SERVICE 12
   RESEARCH EDUCATION AND ECONOMICS................ 15
UNITED STATES DEPARTMENT OF THE AIR FORCE..... 21

MAJOR AIR COMMANDS.. 21
UNITED STATES DEPARTMENT OF THE ARMY
   U.S. ARMY CORPS OF ENGINEERS............................. 25
UNITED STATES DEPARTMENT OF TREASURY
   U.S. CUSTOMS SERVICE... 32
NON-GOVERNMENTAL ORGANIZATIONS
AMERICAN FISHERIES SOCIETY, TEXAS A&M CHAPTER 144
AMERICAN FISHERIES SOCIETY, TEXAS CHAPTER.... 144
AMERICAN SOCIETY OF LIMNOLOGY AND OCEANOGRAPHY 150
AMERICAN SOCIETY OF MAMMALOGISTS.................. 150
BAT CONSERVATION INTERNATIONAL 160
BIG BEND NATURAL HISTORY ASSOCIATION 160
BOY SCOUTS OF AMERICA 162
CENTER FOR ENVIRONMENTAL PHILOSOPHY........... 169
CHIHUAHUAN DESERT RESEARCH INSTITUTE 173
COASTAL CONSERVATION ASSOCIATION................... 176
CONSERVATION DISTRICTS FOUNDATION INC.......... 182
COUNCIL FOR ENVIRONMENTAL EDUCATION............ 184
EARTH FOUNDATION 191
ENVIRONMENTAL DEFENSE FUND, INC.
   Texas Office 182, 196
FOSSIL RIM WILDLIFE CENTER 205
GAME CONSERVATION INTERNATIONAL (GAME COIN) 207
INTERNATIONAL ASSOCIATION FOR ENVIRONMENTAL HYDROLOGY (IAEH) 222
LADY BIRD JOHNSON WILDFLOWER CENTER............ 240
NATIONAL ASSOCIATION OF CONSERVATION DISTRICTS
   League City Office... 257
NATIONAL TRUST FOR HISTORIC PRESERVATION
   Texas and New Mexico Offices 266
NATIONAL WILDLIFE FEDERATION
   Gulf States Natural Resource Center (AR, LA, MS, TX) 268
NATIVE PLANT SOCIETY OF TEXAS............................. 270
NATIVE PRAIRIES ASSOCIATION OF TEXAS................ 270
NATURE CONSERVANCY, THE
   South Central Division Office............................ 272
NATURE CONSERVANCY, THE, TEXAS CHAPTER....... 274
PRAIRIE GROUSE TECHNICAL COUNCIL 299
SCENIC AMERICA
   Scenic Texas... 311
SIERRA CLUB
   Southeast Texas/Arkansas Field Office......................... 313
SIERRA CLUB, LONE STAR CHAPTER 315
TEXAS ASSOCIATION OF SOIL AND WATER CONSERVATION DISTRICTS 328
TEXAS B.A.S.S. CHAPTER FEDERATION 329
TEXAS COMMITTEE ON NATURAL RESOURCES 329
TEXAS FORESTRY ASSOCIATION 329
TEXAS ORGANIZATION FOR ENDANGERED SPECIES 329
TEXAS WILDLIFE ASSOCIATION 329
WELDER WILDLIFE FOUNDATION 343
WETLAND HABITAT ALLIANCE OF TEXAS.................... 345
STATE GOVERNMENT ORGANIZATIONS
BUREAU OF ECONOMIC GEOLOGY 108
GOVERNOR OF TEXAS 108
GUADALUPE-BLANCO RIVER AUTHORITY................... 108
TEXAS AGRICULTURAL EXTENSION SERVICE 108
TEXAS COOPERATIVE FISH AND WILDLIFE RESEARCH UNIT 108
TEXAS DEPARTMENT OF AGRICULTURE 108
TEXAS DEPARTMENT OF HEALTH 108
TEXAS FOREST SERVICE... 108
TEXAS GENERAL LAND OFFICE 109
TEXAS PARKS AND WILDLIFE DEPARTMENT.............. 109
TEXAS SEA GRANT PROGRAM.................................... 109
TEXAS STATE SOIL AND WATER CONSERVATION BOARD... 109
TEXAS WATER DEVELOPMENT BOARD 109

UTAH
GOVERNMENT ORGANIZATIONS
UPPER COLORADO RIVER COMMISSION................... 10
UNITED STATES DEPARTMENT OF AGRICULTURE
   UNITED STATES FOREST SERVICE 16
UNITED STATES DEPARTMENT OF THE INTERIOR
   BUREAU OF RECLAMATION 28

GEOGRAPHIC INDEX - UNITED STATES

NON-GOVERNMENTAL ORGANIZATIONS
  AMERICAN FISHERIES SOCIETY, BONNEVILLE CHAPTER 141
  GRAND CANYON TRUST (Moab, Utah Office) 211
  GRAND CANYON TRUST (St. George, UT Office) 211
  HAWKWATCH INTERNATIONAL, INC. 215
  JACK H. BERRYMAN INSTITUTE FOR WILDLIFE DAMAGE MANAGEMENT 235
  NATURAL RESOURCES INFORMATION COUNCIL 271
  NATURE CONSERVANCY, THE, UTAH CHAPTER 274
  SIERRA CLUB
    Utah Field Office 314
  SIERRA CLUB, UTAH CHAPTER 316
  SOUTHERN UTAH WILDERNESS ALLIANCE (SUWA) ...324
  TREAD LIGHTLY! INC. 330
  TROUT UNLIMITED, UTAH COUNCIL 334
  UTAH ASSOCIATION OF SOIL CONSERVATION DISTRICTS 337
  UTAH B.A.S.S. CHAPTER FEDERATION 337
  UTAH NATURE STUDY SOCIETY 337
  UTAH WILDERNESS COALITION 338
  UTAH WILDLIFE FEDERATION 338
  UTAH WOODLAND OWNERS COUNCIL 338
  WILDLIFE SOCIETY, UTAH CHAPTER 354
STATE GOVERNMENT ORGANIZATIONS
  GOVERNOR OF UTAH 110
  UTAH COOPERATIVE FISH AND WILDLIFE RESEARCH UNIT (USDI-USGS-BRD-CRU) 110
  UTAH DEPARTMENT OF AGRICULTURE 110
  UTAH DEPARTMENT OF HEALTH 110
  UTAH GEOLOGICAL SURVEY 110
  UTAH STATE DEPARTMENT OF NATURAL RESOURCES 110
    Division of Forestry, Fire and State Lands 110
    Division of Oil, Gas and Mining 110
    Division of Parks and Recreation 51, 76, 94, 104, 110, 258, 416
    Division of Water Resources 49, 52, 83, 91, 110
    Division of Water Rights 110
    Division of Wildlife Resources 110, 398, 417
    Office of Energy and Resource Planning 111
  UTAH STATE EXTENSION SERVICES 111
  UTAH STATE SOIL CONSERVATION COMMISSION 111

VERMONT
NON-GOVERNMENTAL ORGANIZATIONS
  AMERICAN CHESTNUT FOUNDATION, THE 139
  ATLANTIC CENTER FOR THE ENVIRONMENT
    New England Office 157
  BLUEBIRDS ACROSS VERMONT PROJECT 161
  CONSERVATION AND RESEARCH FOUNDATION, INC., THE 181
  CONSERVATION LAW FOUNDATION (CLF) (Vermont Office)
    New England Region 183, 335
  ECOTOURISM SOCIETY, THE 194
  FOREST WATCH 204
  GREEN MOUNTAIN AUDUBON SOCIETY 213
  GREEN MOUNTAIN CLUB INC., THE 213
  MERCK FOREST AND FARMLAND CENTER, INC. 248
  NATIONAL GARDENING ASSOCIATION 262
  NATIONAL WILDLIFE FEDERATION
    Northeast Natural Resource Center (CT, MA, ME, NH, RI, VT) 268
  NATURE CONSERVANCY, THE, VERMONT CHAPTER 274
  SHELBURNE FARMS 312
  SIERRA CLUB, VERMONT CHAPTER 316
  TOGETHER FOUNDATION, THE 330
  TROUT UNLIMITED, VERMONT COUNCIL 334
  TRUST FOR WILDLIFE, INC. 335
  VERMONT ASSOCIATION OF CONSERVATION DISTRICTS 338
  VERMONT AUDUBON COUNCIL 338
  VERMONT B.A.S.S. CHAPTER FEDERATION 338
  VERMONT INSTITUTE OF NATURAL SCIENCE 338
  VERMONT LAND TRUST 338
  VERMONT NATURAL RESOURCES COUNCIL 339
  VERMONT STATE-WIDE ENVIRONMENTAL EDUCATION PROGRAMS (SWEEP) 339
  VERMONT WOODLANDS ASSOCIATION 339

STATE GOVERNMENT ORGANIZATIONS
  AGENCY OF NATURAL RESOURCES 111
    Department of Environmental Conservation 88, 89, 90, 111, 261, 291, 398, 416
    Department of Fish and Wildlife 98, 111, 184, 223, 323, 397, 398
    Department of Forests, Parks, and Recreation 111
    Environmental Board 112
    Vermont Geological Survey 112
  GOVERNOR OF VERMONT 111
  UNIVERSITY OF VERMONT EXTENSION 112
    Publications Office 112, 156
  VERMONT DEPARTMENT OF AGRICULTURE, FOOD, AND MARKETS 112
    Natural Resources Conservation Council 112
    State Conservation Commission 100, 106, 112
  VERMONT DEPARTMENT OF HEALTH 112

VIRGIN ISLANDS
NON-GOVERNMENTAL ORGANIZATIONS
  NATURE CONSERVANCY, THE, VIRGIN ISLANDS CHAPTER 274
  VIRGIN ISLANDS CONSERVATION DISTRICT 339
  VIRGIN ISLANDS CONSERVATION SOCIETY, INC. 339
STATE GOVERNMENT ORGANIZATIONS
  DEPARTMENT OF PLANNING AND NATURAL RESOURCES 112
    Division of Fish and Wildlife 29, 40, 51, 63, 76, 112, 113, 261, 397
  GOVERNOR OF THE VIRGIN ISLANDS 112
  VIRGIN ISLANDS COOPERATIVE EXTENSION SERVICE 113
  VIRGIN ISLANDS SOIL AND WATER CONSERVATION DIVISION 113

VIRGINIA
GOVERNMENT ORGANIZATIONS
  NORTH AMERICAN WETLANDS CONSERVATION COUNCIL 9
  NATIONAL SCIENCE FOUNDATION 33
  UNITED STATES DEPARTMENT OF LABOR
    MINE SAFETY AND HEALTH ADMINISTRATION 20
  UNITED STATES DEPARTMENT OF THE AIR FORCE
    MAJOR AIR COMMANDS 21
  UNITED STATES DEPARTMENT OF THE ARMY
    ARMY TRAINING AND DOCTRINE COMMAND 24
    HEADQUARTERS, U.S. ARMY TRAINING AND DOCTRINE COMMAND 24
    HQ ARMY MATERIAL COMMAND 25
    U.S. ARMY CORPS OF ENGINEERS 25
  UNITED STATES DEPARTMENT OF THE INTERIOR
    UNITED STATES GEOLOGICAL SURVEY 30
NON-GOVERNMENTAL ORGANIZATIONS
  ALLIANCE FOR THE CHESAPEAKE BAY 135
    CRIS Office 135
  AMERICAN ALLIANCE FOR HEALTH PHYSICAL EDUCATION AND RECREATION AND DANCE 136
  AMERICAN ASSOCIATION FOR LEISURE AND RECREATION (AALR) 136
  AMERICAN BASS ASSOCIATION OF VIRGINIA, THE 138
  AMERICAN BASS ASSOCIATION, INC. 137
  AMERICAN FISHERIES SOCIETY
    Fisheries Law Section 140
    International Fisheries Section 141
    Native People Fisheries Section 141
  AMERICAN FISHERIES SOCIETY, TIDEWATER CHAPTER 144
  AMERICAN FISHERIES SOCIETY, VIRGINIA CHAPTER 144
  AMERICAN FISHERIES SOCIETY, VIRGINIA TECH CHAPTER 144
  AMERICAN GEOLOGICAL INSTITUTE 145
  AMERICAN RESOURCES GROUP 148
  AMERICAN SPORTFISHING ASSOCIATION 150
  AMERICAN WATER RESOURCES ASSOCIATION 151
  ARLINGTON OUTDOOR EDUCATION ASSOCIATION, INC. 155
  ASSOCIATION OF CONSULTING FORESTERS OF AMERICA 156
  CENTER FOR HEALTH, ENVIRONMENT, AND JUSTICE 170
  CHELONIA INSTITUTE 172
  CHESAPEAKE BAY FOUNDATION, INC. (Virginia Office) 173

GEOGRAPHIC INDEX - UNITED STATES

COASTAL SOCIETY, THE..177
CONSERVATION FUND, THE..182
COUSTEAU SOCIETY, INC., THE....................................185
EARTH FORCE...191
ENVIRONMENTAL CAREER CENTER............................195
ENVIRONMENTAL ENTERPRISES ASSISTANCE FUND, INC..197
FAIRFAX AUDUBON SOCIETY..199
FISH AND WILDLIFE INFORMATION EXCHANGE..........201
FISHAMERICA FOUNDATION...201
FOREST FIRE LOOKOUT ASSOCIATION.......................203
FOUNDATION FOR NORTH AMERICAN BIG GAME......205
FUTURE FISHERMAN FOUNDATION...............................207
GREEN (GLOBAL RIVERS ENVIRONMENTAL EDUCATION NETWORK)..212
INTERNATIONAL ASSOCIATION OF NATURAL RESOURCE PILOTS...223
INTERNATIONAL SOCIETY FOR ECOLOGICAL ECONOMICS...227
IZAAK WALTON LEAGUE OF AMERICA, INC., THE
   Virginia Division...235, 417
LEGACY INTERNATIONAL...242
NATIONAL ASSOCIATION OF BIOLOGY TEACHERS....257
NATIONAL COALITION FOR MARINE CONSERVATION 260
NATIONAL FFA ORGANIZATION.......................................261
NATIONAL FORESTRY ASSOCIATION............................262
NATIONAL RECREATION AND PARK ASSOCIATION....264
NATIONAL RIFLE ASSOCIATION OF AMERICA.............264
NATIONAL SCIENCE TEACHERS ASSOCIATION..........265
NATIONAL WATER RESOURCES ASSOCIATION..........266
NATIONAL WATERSHED COALITION..............................266
NATIONAL WILDLIFE FEDERATION.......................267, 268
NATIONAL WILDLIFE FEDERATION ENDOWMENT, INC. 268
NATIONAL WILDLIFE PRODUCTIONS, INC....................268
NATIONAL WOODLAND OWNERS ASSOCIATION........269
NATURE CONSERVANCY, THE....................272, 273, 274
NATURE CONSERVANCY, THE, GEORGIA CHAPTER..273
NATURE CONSERVANCY, THE, LATIN AMERICA AND CARRIBBEAN DIVISION..273
NATURE CONSERVANCY, THE, VIRGINIA CHAPTER...274
NORTH CAROLINA HERPETOLOGICAL SOCIETY.........283
PIEDMONT ENVIRONMENTAL COUNCIL.......................296
POTOMAC APPALACHIAN TRAIL CLUB.........................298
PUBLIC LANDS FOUNDATION...300
RESOURCE-USE EDUCATION COUNCIL.......................304
RESPONSIVE MANAGEMENT..305
SAFARI CLUB INTERNATIONAL
   Washington, DC Office............134, 148, 192, 308, 314, 324
SIERRA CLUB
   Appalachian Field Office..312
SIERRA CLUB, VIRGINIA CHAPTER................................316
SOUTHERN ENVIRONMENTAL LAW CENTER...............324
STUDENT CONSERVATION ASSOCIATION, INC.
   Capital Office...196, 326
TERRENE INSTITUTE, THE...328
TROUT UNLIMITED...331, 332, 333, 334
TROUT UNLIMITED, VIRGINIA COUNCIL.......................334
VIRGINIA ASSOCIATION OF CONSERVATION DISTRICTS 339
VIRGINIA B.A.S.S. CHAPTER FEDERATION...................339
VIRGINIA CONSERVATION NETWORK...........................339
VIRGINIA FORESTRY ASSOCIATION..............................340
VIRGINIA NATIVE PLANT SOCIETY.................................340
VIRGINIA SOCIETY OF ORNITHOLOGY.........................340
WATER ENVIRONMENT FEDERATION...........................342
WILDLIFE CENTER OF VIRGINIA, THE..........................347
WILDLIFE SOCIETY, VIRGINIA CHAPTER......................354

STATE GOVERNMENT ORGANIZATIONS
   DEPARTMENT OF FORESTRY....................................113
   GOVERNOR OF VIRGINIA..113
   MARINE RESOURCES COMMISSION (VIRGINIA).....113
   NORTHERN VIRGINIA REGIONAL PARK AUTHORITY..113
   VIRGINIA COOPERATIVE FISH AND WILDLIFE RESEARCH UNIT (USDI)..113
   VIRGINIA DEPARTMENT OF AGRICULTURE AND CONSUMER SERVICES..113
   VIRGINIA DEPARTMENT OF CONSERVATION AND RECREATION..114
      Board of Conservation and Recreation...................114
      Breaks Interstate Park Commission.......................114
      Chippokes Plantation Farm Foundation.................114
      Conservation and Development of Public Beaches Board 114
      Division of Administration.........................39, 84, 97, 114
      Division of Dam Safety..114
      Division of Natural Heritage............................114, 417
      Division of Planning and Recreation Resources...114
      Division of Soil and Water Conservation.......51, 92, 94, 114
      Division of State Parks............38, 58, 63, 80, 82, 114, 122
      Virginia Cave Board...114
      Virginia Soil and Water Conservation Board........114
   VIRGINIA DEPARTMENT OF ENVIRONMENTAL QUALITY 114
   VIRGINIA DEPARTMENT OF GAME AND INLAND FISHERIES..114
      Region I...11, 100, 102, 107, 108, 115
      Region II (Lynchburg)...115
      Region III..11, 100, 107, 115
      Region IV (Staunton)..115
      Region V...11, 100, 102, 115
   VIRGINIA DEPARTMENT OF HEALTH.......................115
   VIRGINIA DEPARTMENT OF MINES, MINERALS AND ENERGY..115
      Division of Energy..68, 80, 115
      Division of Gas and Oil..115
      Division of Mined Land Reclamation....................115
      Division of Mineral Mining.....................................115
      Division of Mineral Resources.........................89, 115
   VIRGINIA DEPARTMENT OF MINES, MINERALS, AND ENERGY
      Division of Mines..94, 115
   VIRGINIA MUSEUM OF NATURAL HISTORY..............115
   VIRGINIA OUTDOORS FOUNDATION........................115
   VIRGINIA SEA GRANT PROGRAM.............................115
   VIRGINIA STATE EXTENSION SERVICES................116

WASHINGTON
GOVERNMENT ORGANIZATIONS
   INTERNATIONAL PACIFIC HALIBUT COMMISSION........8
   ENVIRONMENTAL PROTECTION AGENCY...................10
   UNITED STATES DEPARTMENT OF THE ARMY
      U.S. ARMY CORPS OF ENGINEERS.........................25

NON-GOVERNMENTAL ORGANIZATIONS
   ABUNDANT LIFE SEED FOUNDATION.......................130
   ADOPT-A-STREAM FOUNDATION, THE.....................131
   AFRICAN WILDLIFE NEWS SERVICE.........................132
   AMERICAN FISHERIES SOCIETY
      Bioengineering Section..140
   AMERICAN FISHERIES SOCIETY, NORTH PACIFIC INTERNATIONAL CHAPTER................................143
   AMERICAN RIVERS (formerly American Rivers Conservation Council)
      Northwest Regional Office.....................62, 117, 149, 206
   CASCADIA RESEARCH...168
   EARTHJUSTICE LEGAL DEFENSE FUND (formerly Sierra Club Legal Defense Fund, Inc.)
      Seattle, Washington Office...................................192
   EARTHSTEWARDS NETWORK....................................193
   ENVIRONMENTAL EDUCATION ASSOCIATION OF WASHINGTON..197
   FEDERATION OF WESTERN OUTDOOR CLUBS......200
   FRIENDS OF DISCOVERY PARK.................................205
   FRIENDS OF THE EARTH
      Northwest Regional Office (WA, OR, ID)..............206
   FRIENDS OF THE SAN JUANS....................................206
   HOOD CANAL LAND TRUST...216
   INTERNATIONAL ASSOCIATION OF WILDLAND FIRE (formerly Fire Research Institute).........................223
   INTERNATIONAL BICYCLE FUND.................................223
   INTERNATIONAL PLANT PROPAGATION SOCIETY, INC., THE...226
   INTERNATIONAL SNOW LEOPARD TRUST................227
   ISSAQUAH ALPS TRAILS CLUB (I.A.T.C.)...................233
   IZAAK WALTON LEAGUE OF AMERICA, INC., THE
      Washington Division...235
   LEAGUE OF WOMEN VOTERS OF WASHINGTON....242
   LIGHTHAWK
      Northwest Field Office..243
   LONG LIVE THE KINGS...243
   MARINE CONSERVATION BIOLOGY INSTITUTE.......246

GEOGRAPHIC INDEX - UNITED STATES

MOUNTAINEERS, THE (Conservation Division)............256
NATURE CONSERVANCY, THE
   Northwest & Hawaii Division Office............................272
NATURE CONSERVANCY, THE, WASHINGTON CHAPTER 274
NORTH CASCADES CONSERVATION COUNCIL 283
NORTHWEST ECOSYSTEM ALLIANCE.........................285
NORTHWEST ENVIRONMENT WATCH............................285
NORTHWEST INTERPRETIVE ASSOCIATION................286
NW ENERGY COALITION...286
OLYMPIC PARK ASSOCIATES 289
OLYMPIC PARK INSTITUTE..289
PACIFIC NORTHWEST TRAIL ASSOCIATION................293
PACIFIC SEABIRD GROUP 293
PAWS/OLYMPIC WILDLIFE RESCUE................................294
PEOPLE FOR PUGET SOUND...295
   North Sound Office..295
   South Sound Office...295
POULSBO MARINE SCIENCE CENTER...................298, 391
PTARMIGANS, THE...300
PUGET SOUNDKEEPER ALLIANCE..................................300
RIVERS COUNCIL OF WASHINGTON (formerly Northwest
   Rivers Council)...306
SAN JUAN PRESERVATION TRUST, THE.......................308
SIERRA CLUB
   Columbia Basin Office..313
   Northwest Office...313, 320, 326
SIERRA CLUB, CASCADE CHAPTER................................314
SOCIETY FOR CONSERVATION BIOLOGY.....................318
SOUND EXPERIENCE...320
STUDENT CONSERVATION ASSOCIATION, INC.
   Northwest Office...313, 320, 326
TEENS FOR RECREATION AND ENVIRONMENTAL
   CONSERVATION (TREC)...327
TROUT UNLIMITED, WASHINGTON COUNCIL...............334
WASHINGTON ASSOCIATION OF CONSERVATION
   DISTRICTS...340
WASHINGTON B.A.S.S. CHAPTER FEDERATION 340
WASHINGTON ENVIRONMENTAL COUNCIL 340
WASHINGTON FARM FORESTRY ASSOCIATION..........341
WASHINGTON FOUNDATION FOR THE ENVIRONMENT 341
WASHINGTON NATIVE PLANT SOCIETY........................341
WASHINGTON RECREATION AND PARK ASSOCIATION 341
WASHINGTON TOXICS COALITION..................................341
WASHINGTON TRAILS ASSOCIATION.............................341
WASHINGTON WILDERNESS COALITION......................342
WASHINGTON WILDLIFE AND RECREATION COALITION 342
WASHINGTON WILDLIFE FEDERATION...........................342
WASHINGTON WILDLIFE HERITAGE FOUNDATION
   (including Heritage Land Trust.......................................342
WILDLIFE SOCIETY, WASHINGTON CHAPTER..............354
WOLF HAVEN INTERNATIONAL...357
YMCA EARTH SERVICE CORPS..360
STATE GOVERNMENT ORGANIZATIONS
COLUMBIA RIVER GORGE COMMISSION 116
DEPARTMENT OF FISH AND WILDLIFE (WASHINGTON) 116
GOVERNOR OF WASHINGTON 116
INTERAGENCY COMMITTEE FOR OUTDOOR
   RECREATION (IAC)..116
STATE PARKS AND RECREATION COMMISSION
   (WASHINGTON) 116
   Eastern Region12, 13, 16, 17, 31, 98, 99, 117, 125, 137, 153, 263, 267
   Northwest Region16, 29, 62, 98, 99, 102, 117, 118, 127, 149, 206, 307, 335
   Puget Sound Region 117
   Southwest Region16, 30, 80, 99, 102, 117, 118, 149, 153, 264, 301, 335, 363
WASHINGTON COOPERATIVE FISH AND WILDLIFE
   RESEARCH UNIT (USDI)..117
WASHINGTON DEPARTMENT OF AGRICULTURE 117
WASHINGTON DEPARTMENT OF ECOLOGY.................117
   Central Regional Office...31, 117
   Eastern Regional Office 12, 13, 31, 117
   Northwest Regional Office 62, 117, 149, 206
   Southwest Regional Office........... 30, 80, 117, 149, 153, 264

WASHINGTON DEPARTMENT OF NATURAL RESOURCES 117
   Central Region12, 13, 17, 30, 31, 82, 99, 102, 111, 117, 118, 121, 125, 267
   Northeast Region29, 30, 80, 102, 111, 118, 121, 127, 137, 162, 264, 269, 307
   Northwest Region16, 29, 62, 98, 99, 102, 117, 118, 127, 149, 206, 307, 335
   Olympic Region 118
   South Puget Sound Region 118
   Southeast Region29, 30, 80, 102, 118, 121, 145, 264, 301, 307, 335
   Southwest Region16, 30, 80, 99, 102, 117, 118, 149, 153, 264, 301, 335, 363
WASHINGTON NATURAL HERITAGE PROGRAM 118
WASHINGTON SEA GRANT PROGRAM........................... 118
WASHINGTON STATE CONSERVATION COMMISSION 118
WASHINGTON STATE EXTENSION SERVICES 118
WASHINGTON STATE OFFICE OF ENVIRONMENTAL
   EDUCATION... 118

WEST VIRGINIA
GOVERNMENT ORGANIZATIONS
UNITED STATES DEPARTMENT OF THE ARMY
   U.S. ARMY CORPS OF ENGINEERS 25
UNITED STATES DEPARTMENT OF THE INTERIOR
   UNITED STATES FISH AND WILDLIFE SERVICE......... 29
NON-GOVERNMENTAL ORGANIZATIONS
A.B. ENVIRONMENTAL EDUCATION CENTER.............. 130
AMERICAN BASS ASSOCIATION OF WEST VIRGINIA, THE 138
AMERICAN FISHERIES SOCIETY, WEST VIRGINIA
   CHAPTER 144
APPALACHIAN TRAIL CONFERENCE 153
BROOKS BIRD CLUB INC., THE 163
INSTITUTE FOR EARTH EDUCATION, THE 221
IZAAK WALTON LEAGUE OF AMERICA, INC., THE
   West Virginia Division 119, 235, 399
NATURE CONSERVANCY, THE, WEST VIRGINIA
   CHAPTER 274
ORGANIZATION OF WILDLIFE PLANNERS 291
SIERRA CLUB, WEST VIRGINIA CHAPTER 316
TROUT UNLIMITED, WEST VIRGINIA COUNCIL............. 334
WEST VIRGINIA ASSOCIATION OF CONSERVATION
   DISTRICT SUPERVISORS ASSOCIATION, INC. 343
WEST VIRGINIA B.A.S.S. CHAPTER FEDERATION 343
WEST VIRGINIA HIGHLANDS CONSERVANCY.............. 343
WEST VIRGINIA WILDLIFE FEDERATION, INC. 343
WEST VIRGINIA, WOODLAND OWNERS ASSOCIATION
   OF 344
WILDLIFE SOCIETY, WEST VIRGINIA CHAPTER........... 354
STATE GOVERNMENT ORGANIZATIONS
GOVERNOR OF WEST VIRGINIA....................................... 119
WEST VIRGINIA BUREAU OF ENVIRONMENT................ 119
WEST VIRGINIA COOPERATIVE FISH AND WILDLIFE
   RESEARCH UNIT 119
WEST VIRGINIA DEPARTMENT OF AGRICULTURE...... 119
   West Virginia Soil Conservation Agency 119
WEST VIRGINIA DIVISION OF NATURAL RESOURCES 119
WEST VIRGINIA GEOLOGICAL AND ECONOMIC SURVEY 119
WEST VIRGINIA STATE EXTENSION SERVICE 120

WISCONSIN
GOVERNMENT ORGANIZATIONS
GREAT LAKES INDIAN FISH AND WILDLIFE
   COMMISSION.. 7
MINNESOTA-WISCONSIN BOUNDARY AREA
   COMMISSION.. 9
UNITED STATES DEPARTMENT OF AGRICULTURE
   UNITED STATES FOREST SERVICE 16
NON-GOVERNMENTAL ORGANIZATIONS
ALDO LEOPOLD FOUNDATION, INC. 135
AMERICAN BASS ASSOCIATION OF WISCONSIN, THE 138
AMERICAN FISHERIES SOCIETY, WISCONSIN CHAPTER 144
BOTANICAL CLUB OF WISCONSIN 162
CHLORINE-FREE PAPER CONSORTIUM (CPC) 173
CITIZENS NATURAL RESOURCES ASSOCIATION OF
   WISCONSIN, INC. 174
COMMUNITY CONSERVATION
   CONSULTANTS/HOWLERS FOREVER, INC. 179

FEDERAL WILDLIFE OFFICER'S ASSOCIATION 199
INTERNATIONAL CRANE FOUNDATION 224
IZAAK WALTON LEAGUE OF AMERICA, INC., THE
    Wisconsin Division 235
LAKE SUPERIOR GREENS 240
NATIONAL ASSOCIATION OF STATE OUTDOOR
    RECREATION LIAISON OFFICERS 258
NATURE CONSERVANCY, THE, WISCONSIN CHAPTER
    274
NORTH AMERICAN BLUEBIRD SOCIETY 280
RIVER ALLIANCE OF WISCONSIN 305
SIERRA CLUB
    Midwest Office 15, 182, 234, 252, 266, 313
SIERRA CLUB, JOHN MUIR CHAPTER 315
SOCIETY FOR ECOLOGICAL RESTORATION 318
SOCIETY OF TYMPANUCHUS CUPIDO PINNATUS LTD.
    320
TREES FOR TOMORROW, INC., NATURAL RESOURCES
    EDUCATION CENTER 331
TROUT UNLIMITED, WISCONSIN COUNCIL 334
WHITETAILS UNLIMITED, INC. 345
WILD ONES - NATURAL LANDSCAPERS, LTD 346
WILDLIFE SOCIETY, WISCONSIN CHAPTER 354
WISCONSIN ASSOCIATION FOR ENVIRONMENTAL
    EDUCATION, INC. 355
WISCONSIN ASSOCIATION OF LAKES (WAL) 355
WISCONSIN B.A.S.S. CHAPTER FEDERATION 355
WISCONSIN LAND AND WATER CONSERVATION
    ASSOCIATION 356
WISCONSIN PARK AND RECREATION ASSOCIATION . 356
WISCONSIN SOCIETY FOR ORNITHOLOGY, INC., THE 356
WISCONSIN WATERFOWL ASSOCIATION, INC. 356
WISCONSIN WILDLIFE FEDERATION 356
WISCONSIN WOODLAND OWNERS ASSOCIATION 356
STATE GOVERNMENT ORGANIZATIONS
    GOVERNOR OF WISCONSIN 120
    WISCONSIN CONSERVATION CORPS 120
    WISCONSIN COOPERATIVE FISHERY RESEARCH UNIT
    (USDI) 120
    WISCONSIN COOPERATIVE·WILDLIFE RESEARCH UNIT
    (USDI) 120
    WISCONSIN DEPARTMENT OF AGRICULTURE TRADE
    AND CONSUMER PROTECTION
        Land and Water Resources Bureau 120
    WISCONSIN DEPARTMENT OF NATURAL RESOURCES
    120
    WISCONSIN DEPARTMENT OF PUBLIC INSTRUCTION 121
    WISCONSIN ENVIRONMENTAL EDUCATION BOARD
    (WEEB) 121
    WISCONSIN GEOLOGICAL AND NATURAL HISTORY
    SURVEY 121
    WISCONSIN SEA GRANT INSTITUTE 121
    WISCONSIN STATE EXTENSION SERVICES 122
WYOMING
    NON-GOVERNMENTAL ORGANIZATIONS
        AMERICAN FISHERIES SOCIETY, COLORADO-WYOMING
        CHAPTER 142
        AMERICAN FISHERIES SOCIETY, UNIVERSITY OF
        WYOMING STUDENT CHAPTER 144
        CRAIGHEAD ENVIRONMENTAL RESEARCH INSTITUTE
        185
        FOUNDATION FOR NORTH AMERICAN WILD SHEEP .. 205
        JACKSON HOLE CONSERVATION ALLIANCE 236
        JACKSON HOLE LAND TRUST 236
        NATURE CONSERVANCY, THE, WYOMING CHAPTER . 274
        POWDER RIVER BASIN RESOURCE COUNCIL 298
        SIERRA CLUB
            Northern Plains 15, 313
        SIERRA CLUB, WYOMING CHAPTER 317
        TROUT UNLIMITED, WYOMING COUNCIL 334
        WESTERN ASSOCIATION OF FISH AND WILDLIFE
        AGENCIES 344
        WILDLIFE SOCIETY, WYOMING CHAPTER 355
        WOLF FUND, THE 357
        WYOMING ASSOCIATION OF CONSERVATION
        DISTRICTS 359
        WYOMING B.A.S.S. CHAPTER FEDERATION 359
        WYOMING NATIVE PLANT SOCIETY 360
        WYOMING OUTDOOR COUNCIL 360
        WYOMING WILDLIFE FEDERATION 360

STATE GOVERNMENT ORGANIZATIONS
    DEPARTMENT OF COMMERCE 122
    ENVIRONMENTAL QUALITY DEPARTMENT 122
    GOVERNOR OF WYOMING 122
    INDUSTRIAL SITING DIVISION/DEPARTMENT OF
    ENVIRONMENTAL QUALITY 122
    STATE FORESTRY DIVISION (WYOMING) 122
    WYOMING COOPERATIVE FISH AND WILDLIFE
    RESEARCH UNIT (USDI) 122
    WYOMING DEPARTMENT OF AGRICULTURE 122
    WYOMING DEPARTMENT OF COMMERCE
        Division of State Parks and Historic Sites 122
    WYOMING GAME AND FISH DEPARTMENT 123
    WYOMING STATE BOARD OF LAND COMMISSIONERS
    123
    WYOMING STATE EXTENSION SERVICES 123
    WYOMING STATE GEOLOGICAL SURVEY 123

VIETNAM

NON-GOVERNMENTAL ORGANIZATIONS
    INTERNATIONAL UNION FOR CONSERVATION OF
    NATURE AND NATURAL RESOURCES (IUCN) THE
    WORLD CONSERVATION UNION
        Vietnam Country Office 229

WEST AFRICA

NIGER
    NON-GOVERNMENTAL ORGANIZATIONS
        INTERNATIONAL UNION FOR CONSERVATION OF
        NATURE AND NATURAL RESOURCES (IUCN) THE
        WORLD CONSERVATION UNION
            Niger Country Office 229

WEST INDIES

ST. LUCIA
    NON-GOVERNMENTAL ORGANIZATIONS
        CARIBBEAN NATURAL RESOURCES INSTITUTE 168

ZAMBIA

LUSAKA
    NON-GOVERNMENTAL ORGANIZATIONS
        INTERNATIONAL UNION FOR CONSERVATION OF
        NATURE AND NATURAL RESOURCES (IUCN) THE
        WORLD CONSERVATION UNION
            Zambia Country Office 229

ZIMBABWE

HARARE
    NON-GOVERNMENTAL ORGANIZATIONS
        INTERNATIONAL UNION FOR CONSERVATION OF
        NATURE AND NATURAL RESOURCES (IUCN) THE
        WORLD CONSERVATION UNION
            Regional Office for Southern Africa (ROSA) 229
        ZERO (REGIONAL ENVIRONMENTAL ORGANIZATION) 361

UPDATE YOUR LISTING/CHANGE OF ADDRESS

Please help us keep the information in the directory up to date. Use this form to let us know of changes to your listing such as a new address or a new e-mail.

PLEASE TYPE OR PRINT CLEARLY

ORGANIZATION NAME: _____

ADDRESS: STREET: _____

CITY: _____ STATE: _____ ZIP: _____ - _____

COUNTRY: _____ E-MAIL: _____

WEB SITE: _____

PHONE NUMBER: _____-_____-_____ FAX NUMBER: _____-_____-_____

PAGE NUMBER IN 2000 DIRECTORY _____

CHANGES TO YOUR DESCRIPTION: _____

_____

_____

_____

ADD CONTACT PERSON: _____

REMOVE CONTACT PERSON: _____

PLEASE GIVE US A CONTACT NAME FOR THE PERSON WE CAN OBTAIN UPDATES FROM.

NAME: _____ PHONE: _____-_____

Further updating materials will be sent to all organizations listed in the 2000 *Conservation Directory* when updating begins for the 2001 *Conservation Directory*.

**PLEASE MAIL FORM TO:
NATIONAL WILDLIFE FEDERATION
ATTN: CONSERVATION DIRECTORY
8925 LEESBURG PIKE
VIENNA, VA 22184**

PHONE: 703-790-4000 FAX: 703-790-4468

Information may be submitted on photocopies of this form.

APPLICATION REQUEST

If you would like your organization to be listed in the *Conservation Directory* or you have a suggestion of an organization that should be listed in the directory, please let us know. We will send interested parties an information packet and application in the summer of 2000 when we begin preparations for the 2001 Directory. An electronic version of this form is available at www.nwf.org/pubs/consdir/.

PLEASE TYPE OR PRINT CLEARLY

❏ **Request for Listing**   ❏ **Suggested New Organization**

ORGANIZATION NAME: _____

ADDRESS: STREET: _____

CITY: _____ **STATE:** _____ **ZIP** _____-_____

COUNTRY: _____ **E-MAIL:** _____

WEB SITE: _____

PHONE NUMBER: _____-_____-_____   **FAX NUMBER:** _____-_____-_____

CONTACT PERSON: _____

**PLEASE MAIL FORM TO:
NATIONAL WILDLIFE FEDERATION
ATTN: CONSERVATION DIRECTORY
8925 LEESBURG PIKE
VIENNA, VA 22184**

PHONE: 703-790-4000   FAX: 703-790-4468

Information may be submitted on photocopies of this form.

Join National Wildlife Federation Today!

Since 1936, National Wildlife Federation has been the nation's largest and most effective member supported conservation group. Through our network of regional offices across this great land of ours we actively work to achieve our conservation goals in partnership with a wide range of regional, state, national and international groups. NWF has an effective common-sense conservation agenda and a membership including educators, scientists, gardeners, anglers, birders, hikers, campers, volunteer activists and wildlife enthusiasts who want to secure a lasting place for wildlife in the modern world.

National Wildlife Federation is in your community

An NWF Natural Resource Center or regional office near you is always ready to address local problems that concern you and your neighbors ... and to solve them with the help of NWF's tremendous nationwide resources. NWF educates children, families, community, political and business leaders. National Wildlife Federation equips grassroots activists with scientifically-based common sense solutions. And we reach out to people worldwide, to share information on how we can all work for a brighter tomorrow for wildlife, for nature, and for ourselves.

Your membership supports NWF's six-point action agenda

Together, we can work to strengthen landmark legislation like the Endangered Species Act ... safeguard fragile habitats ... educate and inspire our children ... save endangered species ... preserve waters and wetlands ... and help young and old alike enjoy the natural world through such programs as our *Backyard Wildlife Habitat*™ program.

Exclusive Member Benefits of National Wildlife Federation

A FULL YEAR OF THE "WORLD'S MOST BEAUTIFUL NATURE MAGAZINE"
Witness rare views of animals, visit wild places, discover nature's hidden secrets, and get the latest conservation updates.

A DISTINCTIVE NWF TOTE BAG
Holds your everyday items, conserves natural resources and marks you out as a friend of wildlife.

PLUS a membership card, decal, wildlife stamps, nature travel opportunities, wildlife alerts ... and more!

CALL NOW! 1-800-822-9919
or
visit our website at www.nwf.org
for more information on how you can join the nation's largest conservation organization

(89% of what you give to NWF goes directly to our vital conservation programs)

NATIONAL WILDLIFE FEDERATION®
8925 Leesburg Pike • Vienna, Virginia 22184-0002 • www.nwf.org

YOU CAN MAKE A REAL DIFFERENCE FOR ONLY $15